GOLF DIGEST'S
PLACES *to* PLAY

FOURTH EDITION

Fodor's Travel Publications

New York • Toronto • London • Sydney • Auckland

Fodor's   GolfDigest

While every care has been taken to ensure the accuracy of the information in this guide, time brings change, and consequently the publisher cannot accept responsibility for errors that may occur. Prudent travelers should therefore call ahead to verify prices and other "perishable" information.

SPECIAL SALES

Fodor's Travel Publications are available at special discounts for bulk purchases for sales promotions or premiums. Special editions, including personalized covers, excerpts of existing guides, and corporate imprints, can be created in large quantities for special needs. For more information, contact your local bookseller or write to Special Markets, Fodor's Travel Publications, 201 East 50th Street, New York, NY 10022. Inquiries from Canada should be directed to your local Canadian bookseller or sent to Random House of Canada, Ltd., Marketing Department, 2775 Matheson Boulevard East, Mississauga, Ontario L4W 4P7. Inquiries from the United Kingdom should be sent to Fodor's Travel Publications, 20 Vauxhall Bridge Road, London SW1V 2SA, England.

PRINTED IN THE UNITED STATES OF AMERICA
10 9 8 7 6 5 4 3 2 1

Cover photograph by Stephen Szurlej,
taken at Running Y Ranch in Klamath Falls, Oregon.

Contents

Welcome to Golf Digest's Places to Play

Golf course construction continues, providing golfers with more places to tee up their golf ball. The growth of the game shows no sign of abating. There are new courses on mountain tops, across searing deserts, amid tropical jungles, alongside oceans, and downtown in a city near you. Never has there been such a choice of great places to go and play golf.

Faced with so many options, how do you decide which course deserves your money? There's nothing worse than paying out a hefty green fee only to be confronted by a boring layout in bad condition, where the staff is rude and the sandwiches in the clubhouse are stale.

As with all good decisions, the key is in having the right information, and that's where *Golf Digest's Places to Play* steps in. The goal of *Places to Play* is simple: to provide you with the most comprehensive information on public-access golf courses in North America. No one else has attempted to rate all of the best courses on a national basis. And the courses are not rated by the editors of GOLF DIGEST, nor by a panel of experts, but by the most knowledgeable people in the game: you the golfers.

We began *Places to Play* in 1963. In this edition, some 20,000 GOLF DIGEST readers have filled out course ballots, sharing their opinions and experiences on more than 6,000 courses in the United States, Canada, Mexico and the Caribbean.

The readers were asked to rate each course they had played within the previous year on five criteria: the overall golf experience, the value for the money, the standard of service at the facility, the overall conditioning of the course, and the normal pace of play for an 18-hole round of golf. In addition, readers were invited to write comments on their experiences at each of the courses they rated—both the good and the bad.

All the numbers and comments were fed into our massive database. The top 200 courses in the Value, Service, Conditioning, and Pace of Play categories have received special designations in this book for their outstanding achievement. The top 50 and ties received the highest awards of Great Value, Great Service, Great Conditioning and Great Pace of Play. The next 150 and ties received Good Value, Good Service, Good Conditioning and Good Pace of Play awards.

A team of 11 editors spent countless hours editing the comments for each individual course—great care was taken to use comments that were fair, accurate and representative of the sample. Meanwhile, all the 6,000-plus courses were contacted for their latest, up-to-date information, such as their name, address, green fee and directions. All of the new information was fed into the database. Finally, the whole book was fact-checked and edited.

It was a long but rewarding task, one that has made *Places to Play* the only book you'll need to plan your golf vacation or find a new and interesting course to play.

The Players: Executive Editor: Bob Carney. **Editorial Project Coordinator:** Sue Sawyer. **Editors:** John Barton, Mike Johnson, Mary Jane McGirr, Mike O'Malley, Sue Sawyer, Cliff Schrock, Topsy Siderowf, Kathy Stachura, Mike Stachura, Lisa Sweet, Melissa Yow. **Editorial Assistants and Fact Checking:** Mary Damon, Agnes Farkas, Annie Giuntoli, Phyllis Mast, Kathy Stachura, Joan Sweet. **IT, EPP, and Art:** Nick DiDio, Louisa Grigorian, Gary Holland, Byrute Johnson, Larry Kother, Karen Musmanno, Liz Quinnones, Steve Scipioni, Bill Walsh.

Pretend it's Scotland, and other secrets to a successful golf trip

By Bob Carney and the Editors

One would think that it would be hard to mess up a golf trip, but actually it doesn't take much effort at all. In fact, the less effort you put into a trip, the greater likelihood that it will be botched. "Happiness," said Willa Cather, "is to be dissolved into something complete and great." We suggest you get dissolved into your trip so that it will be great.

As the survivor of an annual eight-man pilgrimage to Amelia Island now in its 16th year, I've been nominated to gather the combined wisdom of the GOLF DIGEST editorial staff.

These 18 tips have been paid for with dozens of ruined weekends, lousy rounds and lost friends. Of course, it was still golf, so we have no regrets. But why not make yours a trip to remember? One round of suggestions:

1. Above all, compatibility. It seems obvious, but you've got to get along. Go with folks you like. The courses, the climate, the new Burner driver won't make up for the wrong companions. We're not suggesting that everyone play to the same level, party to the same level, or tolerate Golf in the Kingdom. But if you don't, it's got to be all right that you don't.

A seemingly compatible foursome of low handicappers we know played 36-a-day at a great complex of courses in Florida. Good golf, strong competition, a great trip—until it came time to split the bill. Our "accountant" had divided it four ways. "Hey," said Tim, a teetotaler, "Take that off my tab. I'm not paying for that beer". It was kind of a principle with Tim and he was kind of gone after that. It wasn't the money. He just didn't get it.

Let's face it, under the unyielding stress of nothing-but-golf, the smallest things about people can drive you batty. Guys saying "nice shot" when they have no clue whether it is or not. Guys pretending they're sorry you missed a putt to lose $20 to them. Guys who, at the poshest resort in North America, are whining about the shuttle service. Guys refusing to go out for dinner. Guys refusing to stay in for dinner. Guys calling you "Pal" for five days. Guys that make their beds. You get the idea. Just because you like A and you like B doesn't mean A will like B. Be ruthless about weeding out, or not inviting, people who don't fit. It's not that they're bad people. They're just part of someone else's trip. By the way, it need not be all guys or all girls. Some mixed groups do fine—if they're compatible.

2. Plan it. "A painting of a rice cake does not satisfy hunger," my acupuncturist is fond of saying. But talking about your trip, and planning it in as much detail as you can, helps a lot. We start each year the day we return home. We didn't always. Our group once bought a four-day golf package to Grenelefe Resort and neglected to make tee times. When we got there, there were none left. Thank God six of us were lobbyists or we wouldn't have played a hole. You don't have to be the planner in the group to make his or her job easier. Agree on place and dates early. Get your deposit in. Don't bitch about your room assignment. Don't moan about the site. Or the tee time. Or the shuttle service.

3. Fill the roles. The booker is just one of the role-players you'll need. The editors suggest these others: an accountant, a tournament director, a shopper, a cook, a designated driver. Let me add one last one: The Conscience. In our group it's Bill. He is the soul of our group. He is the arbiter of disputes. He is the last to gripe, the first to agree to sleep on the couch, the one who competes hardest and takes it the least seriously. "Those who want the fewest things are closest to the gods," somebody like Socrates once said. Find your Bill.

4. Set the rules. Spell out what kind of a trip it's going to be. We once had a member who had urgent work to do whenever it rained or the temperature dropped below 50. "Fifty miles south of here it's 75 and sunny," he said 1500 times if he said it once. He's no longer with us—his choice—after we spelled out the ground rules. *Rule 1*: It's a golf trip, you play at least 18 a day, barring a blizzard. As for the weather, when in doubt, pretend it's Scotland. *Rule 2*: Everyone goes out to dinner together one night. *Rule 3*: Though the trip is five days, four are mandatory. Your rules may differ. In some, cell phones will be fine. In others, working in the afternoon is okay. Some guys gamble big, some don't. Some carouse, some don't. The important thing is, make the ground rules clear to everyone. Confront offenders, gently.

5. Prepare yourself. Don't make the mistake of taking a golf lesson the day before you leave in hopes of improving your play. You'll spend the whole trip struggling with your swing. Take a lesson about a month before and then build up to the trip by hitting balls. Get loose. At a minimum begin exercising, stretching especially, a week before the trip. Your body is your temple. It will have to stand up to rich food, bad wine and cheap cigars. "Live as though your hair is on fire," the philosopher said, but bring a comb.

6. Choose courses carefully. This is big. Watching six hackers and two single-digits lose a gross of balls from the back tees at Old Marsh a few years back convinced me: There are courses for foursomes. Find a track or a group of them that fit your group. The more diverse the group the more diverse the courses, I'd argue. Play the easy one first if you can and build up to the tougher ones. Corollary: Play the right tees. Don't brutalize the high-handicappers with the back tees. Vary it. An interesting second-round format: Play six holes back, six middle and six forward. Great way to find your comfort zone. Whatever you do, take the time to choose really good courses. Call ahead to make sure they're not overseeding that week, or doing construction. This book will help a lot. A Bulgarian proverb goes: "If you wish to drown, do not torture yourself with shallow water." Go deep.

7. Compete. It's fun to compete. Team competitions ala the Ryder Cup are great because they take the pressure off individual games, which are often very rusty. Teams work great for mixed groups, too, and groups with diverse playing levels. (Don't be afraid to adjust handicaps after a couple of rounds; it may salvage the experience for the one getting the extra strokes). I especially like formal competitions—maybe a one-day event—because they spawn silly trophies and a lot of bragging. Some groups make up teams before they go. Some continue the same four-vs.-four, for example, year to year. Gauge your group's appetite for competition and don't overdo it. Make sure there is "down" time when folks can just play their games. Warning sign that you've got too competitive: Teams are eating at different restaurants. But if you have any doubts, ask Bill.

8. Beware the money. It's the root of most resentment on golf trips, especially with players of divergent means. Keep accounting as simple and clear as possible. *Step 1*: When the trip's over, put all the non-personal receipts in a pile. *Step 2*: Add them up and divide by the number of players. *Step 3*: Pay. Do not nit-pick. Do not whimper. To avoid misunderstanding, let everyone know prior to the trip, especially newcomers, what it will cost and what costs are included. (You'll probably handle airfare individually). Agree on betting ground rules and if you can, keep the stakes light. Really heavy betting makes too much of the stroke allocation and really frosts the guys who have a bad week. For the heavier gamblers, create side games. A small sub-committee of big egos in our group play $5 birdies, $10 eagles and $100 for holes-in-one (we've had a couple). Multiply by ten if you're loaded.

9. Watch the drinking. Next to money, nothing can throw the train off the track like drinking. In about the fifth year of our trip, after a particularly rainy and alcoholic four days, we got religion. We knew we had gone over the line when a waitress told us she hadn't had so much fun since Teamster President Jackie Presser visited. So we decided as a group to tone it down. Looking back, it was an incredibly mature act by an incredibly immature bunch of guys, but it saved us from resentments, arguments, missed tee times and a general lack of decorum that would have eventually driven us apart. As time has gone on, the desire to wring every last drop of pleasure out of the trip has decreased, leaving us time to enjoy it.

10. Leave room for après golf. "Après" is French for you don't have to play 27. Find something else to do one afternoon. A walk on the beach, a nap, a swim, March Madness, even shopping. If possible, stay somewhere with a sauna, great for those post-round aches. "How refreshing, the whinny of the packhorse unloaded of everything," goes the zen saying. Ditto for the fat dentist freed from that final nine.

11. Equip yourself. Bring more than one pair of golf shoes. Bring a rainsuit. (For what most resorts charge for them, you can buy a small Korean car). If your destination is subject to cold fronts, bring a pair of silk hiking underwear. It will allow you to play in weather ten degrees colder than you're accustomed to. Bring all-weather gloves, cart mittens, a ski cap.

12. Get directions. Once on site, give yourself plenty of time to get to the course every day, warm up and decide on the format. Don't trust the shuttle; leave extra time. Schedule play so that same-day courses are as close together as possible.

13. Voting rights. Most people are created equal. I'm sure there are groups that work well with benevolent dictators, but I've always preferred the democratic method, within reason. Give everyone a say on formats, tees, dinner. Share the clicker.

14. Eight is great. We know of groups comprised of four, twelve, six-teen and more. But we like eight. It makes for a variety of cart partners, allows for interesting group competition, and means you'll have an afternoon foursome even if half the group heads for the beach. It's also easier to "hide" personality conflicts if they emerge, as in, "If I have to ride with that imbecile again, I'm going home." No problem, pal.

15. It's the golf, stupid. I've known folks who went on golf trips to con-duct affairs, to gamble, to have an excuse to get completely blotto every day. I've known guys who spent the week on their laptops or their cell phones. Not that there is anything wrong with these things. But remember the thing that brought you together: golf. As Yogi Berra said, "You can't think and hit at the same time."

16. Gifts are part of golf. The first CD-Rom version of *Golf Digest's Places to Play* included an interactive ad from DeBeers, the diamond com-pany. And how fitting. It's always a good idea to bring a gift home to your spouse. My wife brings me back expensive golf shirts with exotic crests. Because my trip is longer and my taste in clothing suspect, I tend toward jewelry. Whatever suits, give yourself time to find something nice, figuring the longer the trip the nicer the something. Albert Einstein said, "The true value of a human being can be found in the degree to which he has attained libera-tion from the self." At my house, it is also measured in what one brings home from a golf trip.

17. Call home. Check in at least once a day and more often if one or more of the members of your family are in the hospital.

18. Expect nothing. It will never be as perfect as last year or the year you shot 72 or the time they finally got the greens right. The weather will never be the same, the morning fairway will never glisten as magically, that first martini won't ever quite match That First Martini. "One cannot step twice into the same river," said the Greek philosopher Heraclitus, who I suspect was a golfer and probably liked to carry his own bag.

Expect the worst. One year, on our first night at the resort, the Weather Channel anchor actually said these words: "Those in the northeast corner of Florida can only hope our forecast is wrong." We had record rain, record cold and record wind. We still played every day and 36 a couple of days. It's a legend, that trip. And fifty miles south of there it was 75 and sunny.

★★★★★

The *Five Star* Courses

These are the 16 sublime courses that received the highest *Places to Play* rating from GOLF DIGEST readers: the maximum five stars.

Bay Harbor Golf Club, Bay Harbor, MI

Blackwolf Run Golf Club (Meadows Valley Cse.), Kohler, WI

Blackwolf Run Golf Club (River Cse.), Kohler, WI

Bulle Rock (South Cse.), Havre de Grace, MD

Casa de Campo Resort & Country Club (Teeth of the Dog), Dominican Republic

The Challenge at Manele, Lanai City, HI

Coeur d'Alene Resort Golf Course, Coeur d'Alene, ID

Highlands Links Golf Course, Nova Scotia, Canada

Kiawah Island Resort (Ocean Cse.), Kiawah Island, S.C.

The Links at Crowbush Cove, Prince Edward Island, Canada

Pebble Beach Golf Links, Pebble Beach, CA

Pinehurst Country Club (No. 2 Course), Pinehurst, N.C.

Pinon Hills Golf Course, Farmington, N.M.

St. Ives Golf Club, Stanwood, MI

Spyglass Hill Golf Course, Pebble Beach, CA

World Woods Golf Club (Pine Barrens Course), Brooksville, FL

The *Great Value* Courses

The top-50 golf courses in North America in terms of value for money, as rated by GOLF DIGEST readers.

UNITED STATES
Alabama
Grand National G.C. (Short Cse.)
Magnolia Grove G.C. (Crossings Cse.)
Magnolia Grove G.C. (Short Cse.)
California

Fall River Valley G. & C.C.
The G.C. at Whitehawk Ranch
Colorado
Walking Stick G.Cse.
Connecticut
Crestbrook Park G.C.
Florida
Orange County National G. Ctr. & Lodge (Crooked Cat)
Georgia
Georgia Vetarans Memorial G.Cse.
Idaho
Pinecrest Municipal G.Cse.
Illinois
The Bourne G.C.
Iowa
Muscatine Municipal G.Cse.
Kansas
Buffalo Dunes G.Cse.
Kentucky
Gibson Bay G.Cse.
Michigan
Cascades G.Cse.
George Young Rec. Complex
Grand View G.Cse.
L.E. Kaufman G.C.
Milham Park Municipal G.C.
Pierce Lake G.Cse.
TimberStone G.Cse.
Minnesota
Bellwood Oaks G.Cse.
Montana
Old Works G.Cse.
Nebraska
Woodland Hills G.Cse.
New Hampshire
Bretwood G.Cse. (South Cse.)
New Jersey
Howell Park G.Cse.
New Mexico
Pinon Hills G.Cse.
New York
Bethpage State Park (Black Cse.)
Chenango Valley State Park
Montauk Downs State Park G.Cse.
North Dakota
The Links of North Dakota at Red Mike Resort
Ohio
Mohican Hills G.C.
Oregon
Elkhorn Valley G.Cse.
Meadow Lakes G.Cse.

Pennsylvania
Stoughton Acres G.C.
Tennessee
Graysburg Hills G.Cse.
  (Fodderstack/Chimneytop)
Texas
Painted Dunes Desert G.Cse.
Utah
Birch Creek G.C.
Bountiful Ridge G.Cse.
Hobble Creek G.C.
Moab G.C.
Wasatch State Park G.C. (Lake)
Virginia
Draper Valley G.C.
Wisconsin
Turtleback G. & Conf. Ctr.
Wyoming
Buffalo G.C.
CANADA
Alberta
Kananaskis Country G.C. (Mt.
  Lorette Cse.)
Nova Scotia
Bell Bay G.C.
Highlands Links G.Cse.
Ontario
Upper Canada G.Cse.
Prince Edward Island
The Links at Crowbush Cove

The *Good Value* Courses
**The next 150 Golf Courses
in North America in terms of
value for money, as rated by
GOLF DIGEST readers.**

UNITED STATES
Alabama
Cambrian Ridge G.C.
  (Canyon/Loblolly)
Grand National G.C. (Lake Cse.)
Grand National G.C. (Links Cse.)
Highland Oaks G.Cse.
  (Highlands/Magnolia)
Lake Guntersville G.C.
Magnolia Grove G.C. (Falls Cse.)
Oxmoor Valley G.C. (Short Cse.)
Arizona
Emerald Canyon G.Cse.
California
Bennett Valley G.Cse.
La Purisima G.Cse.

Pacific Grove Municipal Golf Links
Poppy Hills G.Cse.
Poppy Ridge G.Cse.
  (Chardonnay/Zinfandel)
Primm Valley G.C. (Desert Cse.)
Primm Valley G.C. (Lakes Cse.)
The SCGA Members' C. at Rancho
  California
Singing Hills Resort (Willow Glen Cse.)
Stevinson Ranch G.C. (Savannah
  Cse.)
Colorado
Battlement Mesa G.C.
Eisenhower G.C. (Blue Cse.)
Eisenhower G.C. (Silver Cse.)
Riverdale G.C. (Dunes Cse.)
Florida
The C. at Hidden Creek
The Moors G.C.
Orange County National G. Ctr. &
  Lodge (Panther Lake G.Cse.)
PGA G.C. at the Reserve (North Cse.)
PGA G.C. at the Reserve (South Cse.)
St. Johns County G.C.
Sandridge G.C. (Dunes Cse.)
Sandridge G.C. (Lakes Cse.)
Tiger Point G. & C.C. (West Cse.)
World Woods G.C. (Pine Barrens Cse.)
World Woods G.C. (Rolling Oaks Cse.)
Hawaii
Hickam G.Cse. (Mamala Bay
  Championship)
Kaneohe Klipper G.C.
Kiahuna G.C.
Wailua G.Cse.
Illinois
The Den at Fox Creek G.C.
Heritage Bluffs G.C.
Lick Creek G.Cse.
Newman G.Cse.
Orchard Valley G.C.
Prairie Vista G.Cse.
Railside G.C.
Rolling Hills G.Cse.
Indiana
Brookwood G.C.
Rock Hollow G.C.
Kansas
Quail Ridge G.Cse.
Rolling Meadows G.Cse.
Kentucky
Eagle Trace G.Cse.
Kearney Hill Golf Links

Lassing Pointe G.Cse.
The Peninsula Golf Resort
Maryland
Eagle's Landing G.Cse.
Mount Pleasant G.C.
Massachusetts
George Wright G.Cse.
Westover G.Cse.
Michigan
Gaylord C.C.
Gracewil Pines G.C.
Hampshire C.C.
Lakewood Shores Resort (The
   Gailes Cse.)
Oak Crest G.Cse.
St. Ives G.C.
Stonehedge G.Cse. (South Cse.)
Minnesota
Albion Ridges G.Cse.
Giants Ridge Golf & Ski Resort
Hidden Greens G.C.
Mount Frontenac G.Cse.
New Prague G.C.
Purple Hawk C.C.
Tianna C.C.
Whitefish G.C.
Willinger's G.C.
Mississippi
Mallard Pointe G.Cse.
   (Championship Cse.)
Mississippi State University G.Cse.
Timberton G.C.
Missouri
Country Creek G.C.
Eagle Lake G.C.
Schifferdecker G.Cse.
Montana
Buffalo Hill G.Cse. (Championship
   Cse.)
Nebraska
Heritage Hills G.Cse.
Nevada
Boulder City G.C.
New Jersey
Hominy Hill G.Cse.
Sunset Valley G.Cse.
New York
Bethpage State Park (Blue Cse.)
Bethpage State Park (Red Cse.)
Durand Eastman G.Cse.
Mark Twain State Park (Soaring
   Eagles G.C.)
Saratoga Spa G.Cse.

Tioga C.C.
Wayne Hills C.C.
North Carolina
Bald Head Island C.
Bryan Park & G.C. (Champions Cse.)
The Neuse G.C.
Oak Hollow G.Cse.
The Sound Golf Links at Albemarle
   Plantation
Ohio
Carroll Meadows G.Cse.
Hawks Nest G.C.
The Links at Echo Springs
Mill Creek G.C.
Orchard Hills G. & C.C.
River Greens G.Cse.
Salt Fork State Park G.Cse.
Oklahoma
Cedar Creek G.Cse.
Oregon
Indian Creek G.C.
Running Y Ranch Resort
StoneRidge G.Cse.
Tokatee G.C.
Pennsylvania
Chestnut Ridge G.C.
Upper Perk G.Cse.
South Carolina
Hunter's Creek Plantation G.C.
Ocean Point Golf Links
South Carolina National G.C.
Texas
Lady Bird Johnson Municipal
G.Cse.
Mission Del Lago G.Cse.
Sugartree G.C.
Utah
Wolf Creek Golf Resort
Vermont
St. Johnsbury C.C.
Virginia
Ford's Colony C.C. (Marsh Hawk
   Cse.)
Shenandoah Valley G.C. (Blue/Red)
Washington
Gold Mountain Golf Complex
   (Olympic Cse.)
Gold Mountain Golf Complex
   (Cascade Cse.)
Hangman Valley G.Cse.
Indian Canyon G.Cse.
Lake Padden G.Cse.
MeadowWood G.Cse.

West Virginia
Locust Hill G.Cse.
Snowshoe Mountain (Hawthorne
   Valley at Snowshoe)
Wisconsin
Brighton Dale G.C. (Blue Spruce
   Cse.)
Brown County G.Cse.
Clifton Highlands G.Cse.
Eagle River G.Cse.
Hayward Golf & Tennis Center
Lake Breeze G.C.
Naga-Waukee G.Cse.
Nemadji G.Cse. (East/West Cse.)
Northbrook C.C.
St. Germain Municipal G.C.
University Ridge G.Cse.
Washington County G.Cse.
Whispering Springs G.C.
CANADA
Alberta
Jasper Park Lodge G.Cse.
Kananaskis Country G.C. (Mt. Kidd
   Cse.)
British Columbia
Golden G. & C.C.
Manitoba
Teulon G. & C.C.
Prince Edward Island
Brudenell River Resort (Brudenell
   River G.Cse.)
Mill River G.Cse.
MEXICO
Baja Norte
Bajamar Ocean Front Golf Resort
   (Lagos/Vista)
Real Del Mar G.C.
ISLANDS
Dominican Republic
Casa de Campo Resort & C.C.
   (Teeth of The Dog)

The *Great Service* Facilities

**The top-50 golf facilities in North
America in terms of service, as
rated by GOLF DIGEST readers.**
UNITED STATES
Alabama
Cambrian Ridge G.C.
Magnolia Grove G.C.
Arizona

The Boulders C.
Grayhawk G.C.
The Phoenician G.C.
Pointe Hilton South Mountain Resort
The Raven G.C. at Sabino Springs
The Raven G.C. at South Mountain
Troon North G.C.
California
The G.C. at Whitehawk Ranch
Ojai Valley Inn & Spa
Pebble Beach Golf Links
Primm Valley G.C.
Florida
Doral Golf Resort & Spa
Grand Cypress G.C.
The Moors G.C.
PGA G.C. at the Reserve
Saddlebrook Resort
Turnberry Isle Resort & C.
Walt Disney World Resort
Georgia
Sea Island G.C.
Hawaii
The Challenge at Manele
The Experience at Koele
Hualalai G.C.
Mauna Lani Resort
Idaho
Coeur d'Alene Resort G.Cse.
Kentucky
The Peninsula Golf Resort
Maryland
Bulle Rock
Michigan
Bay Harbor G.C.
Crystal Mountain Resort
George Young Rec. Complex
St. Ives G.C.
TimberStone G.Cse.
Minnesota
Grand View Lodge Resort
Mississippi
Dancing Rabbit G.C.
Nevada
Las Vegas Paiute Resort
New Hampshire
The Balsams Grand Resort
North Carolina
The Neuse G.C.
Pinehurst Resort & C.C.
Oregon
The Reserve Vineyards & G.C.
Pennsylvania

Stoughton Acres G.C.
Texas
La Cantera G.C.
Painted Dunes Desert G.Cse.
Virginia
Draper Valley G.C.
Ford's Colony C.C.
West Virginia
The Greenbrier
Wisconsin
Blackwolf Run G.C.
Nemadji G.Cse.
CANADA
British Columbia
Westwood Plateau G. & C.C.
ISLANDS
Nevis
Four Seasons Resort Nevis

The *Good Service*
Facilities

The next 150 (and ties) golf facilities in North America in terms of
service, as rated by GOLF DIGEST
readers.

UNITED STATES
Alabama
Grand National G.C.
Hampton Cove G.C.
Highland Oaks G.Cse.
Oxmoor Valley G.C.
Rock Creek G.C.
Silver Lakes G.C.
Arizona
The ASU Karsten G.Cse.
The G.C. at Vistoso
Las Sendas G.C.
Los Caballeros G.C.
Ventana Canyon Golf & Racquet C.
The Wigwam G. & C.C.
California
Carmel Valley Ranch G.C.
The Cse. at Wente Vineyards
Coyote Hills G.Cse.
Four Seasons Resort Aviara
Golf Resort at Indian Wells
The Links at Spanish Bay
Rancho San Marcos G.C.
Spyglass Hill G.Cse.
Strawberry Farms G.C.
Colorado

The Broadmoor G.C.
Dalton Ranch G.C.
Eisenhower G.C.
Keystone Ranch G.Cse.
The Ridge at Castle Pines North
Florida
Arnold Palmer's Bay Hill C. &
Lodge
Gateway G. & C.C.
Bluewater Bay Resort
The Breakers C.
The C. at Hidden Creek
Emerald Dunes G.Cse.
Lely Resort G. & C.C.
Mission Inn Golf & Tennis Resort
Orange County National G. Ctr. &
Lodge
PGA National G.C.
Regatta Bay G. & C.C.
River Hills C.C.
St. Lucie West C.C.
Sandestin Resort
Tiger Point G. & C.C.
Tournament Players C. at
Sawgrass
World Golf Village
World Woods G.C.
Georgia
Callaway Gardens Resort
Reynolds Plantation
White Columns G.C.
Hawaii
Hapuna G.Cse.
Kapalua G.C.
Kauai Lagoons Resort
Makena Resort G.Cse.
Princeville Resort
Wailea G.C.
Illinois
Cantigny Golf
Eagle Ridge Inn & Resort
WeaverRidge G.C.
Indiana
Pheasant Valley G.C.
Prairie View G.C.
Iowa
Brooks G.C.
Spencer G. & C.C.
Maine
Sugarloaf G.C.
Maryland
Swan Point Golf Yacht & C.C.
Massachusetts

Crumpin-Fox C.
Cyprian Keyes G.C.
Farm Neck G.C.

Michigan
Boyne Highlands Resort
Elk Ridge G.C.
Garland
The G.C. at Thornapple Pointe
Patsy Lou Williamson's Sugarbush
    G.C.
Hawk Hollow G.C.
Lakewood Shores Resort
Little Traverse Bay G.C.
Shanty Creek
Treetops Sylvan Resort
The Wilds G.C.

Minnesota
Giants Ridge Golf & Ski Resort
Madden's on Gull Lake
Rush Creek G.C.
The Wilds G.C.

Missouri
Millwood Golf & Racquet C.
Pevely Farms G.C.

Montana
Old Works G.Cse.

Nebraska
Woodland Hills G.Cse.

Nevada
Edgewood Tahoe G.Cse.
The Legacy G.C.

New York
Greystone G.C.
The Links at Hiawatha Landing
Malone G.C.

North Carolina
Bald Head Island C.
Grandover Resort & Conf. Ctr.
Pine Needles Lodge & G.C.
Salem Glen C.C.
The Sound Golf Links at Albemarle
    Plantation

North Dakota
The Links of North Dakota at Red
    Mike Resort

Ohio
The G.C. at Yankee Trace
Mill Creek G.C.
Shaker Run G.C.
StoneWater G.C.
The Vineyard G.Cse.

Oklahoma
Karsten Creek G.C.

Oregon
Pumpkin Ridge G.C.
Sunriver Lodge & Resort

Pennsylvania
Chestnut Ridge G.C.
Hartefeld National G.C.
Nemacolin Woodland Resort
& Spa

South Carolina
Caledonia Golf & Fish C.
The C. at Seabrook Island
Daufuskie Island C. & Resort
Heritage C.
Hunter's Creek Plantation G.C.
Kiawah Island Resort
The Legends
Ocean Creek G.Cse.
Palmetto Dunes Resort
Pine Lakes International C.C.
Wild Wing Plantation

Tennessee
Egwani Farms G.Cse.

Texas
Barton Creek Resort & C.C.
Canyon Springs G.C.
Four Seasons Resort & C.
Hill Country G.C.

Utah
The G.C. at Thanksgiving Point

Vermont
Basin Harbor C.

Virginia
Golden Horseshoe G.C.
The Homestead Resort
Raspberry Falls Golf & Hunt C.
Stonehouse G.C.

Washington
Desert Canyon Golf Resort
McCormick Woods G.Cse.
Semiahmoo G. & C.C.
Skamania Lodge G.Cse.

West Virginia
Glade Springs Resort

Wisconsin
The Bog
Clifton Highlands G.Cse.
Foxfire G.C.
Geneva National G.C.
Grand Geneva Resort & Spa
University Ridge G.Cse.

Wyoming
Jackson Hole Golf & Tennis C.
Teton Pines Resort & C.C.

CANADA
Alberta
Kananaskis Country Golf
British Columbia
Chateau Whistler G.C.
Harvest G.C.
Manitoba
The Links at Quarry Oaks
Nova Scotia
Bell Bay G.C.
Highlands Links G.Cse.
Ontario
Lionhead G. & C.C.
Loch March G. & C.C.
ISLANDS
Bermuda
The Mid Ocean C.
Dominican Republic
Casa de Campo Resort & C.C.
Grand Bahama Islands
Bahamas Princess Resort & Casino
Jamaica
Sandals G. & C.C.
Puerto Rico
Rio Mar C.C.

The *Great Condition* Courses

The top 50 (and ties) Golf Courses in North America in terms of optimum course conditions, as rated by GOLF DIGEST readers.

UNITED STATES
Arizona
The Boulders C. (South Cse.)
The G.C. at Vistoso
Grayhawk G.C. (Talon Cse.)
Legend Trail G.C.
The Raven G.C. at South Mountain
Troon North G.C. (Monument Cse.)
Troon North G.C. (Pinnacle Cse.)
California
Desert Willow Golf Resort (Firecliff Cse.)
The G.C. at Whitehawk Ranch
Primm Valley G.C. (Lakes Cse.)
Florida
Gateway G. & C.C.
Grand Cypress G.C. (North/South/East)
Orange County National G. Ctr. &
Lodge (Crooked Cat)
Orange County National G. Ctr. & Lodge (Panther Lake G.Cse.)
Tournament Players C. at Sawgrass (Stadium Cse.)
Georgia
Reynolds Plantation (Great Waters Cse.)
Reynolds Plantation (National Cse.)
Reynolds Plantation (Plantation Cse.)
White Columns G.C.
Hawaii
The Challenge at Manele
Hualalai G.C.
Idaho
Coeur d'Alene Resort G.Cse.
Indiana
Brickyard Crossing G.C.
Iowa
Spencer G. & C.C.
Maryland
Bulle Rock (South Cse.)
Michigan
Bay Harbor G.C.
Elk Ridge G.C.
The Fortress
HawksHead G.L.
Lakewood Shores Resort (The Gailes Cse.)
St. Ives G.C.
TimberStone G.Cse.
The Wilds G.C.
Minnesota
The Wilds G.C.
Montana
Old Works G.Cse.
Nevada
Desert Inn G.C.
Las Vegas Paiute Resort (Nu-Wav Kaiv Cse.)
Las Vegas Paiute Resort (Tav-ai Kaiv Cse.)
New Mexico
Pinon Hills G.Cse.
North Carolina
Grandover Resort & Conference Center (West Cse.)
Ohio
Quail Hollow Resort & C.C. (Weiskopf-Morrish Cse.)
StoneWater G.C.
Oklahoma
Forest Ridge G.C.

Karsten Creek G.C.
Oregon
Hartefeld National G.C.
Pennsylvania
Hartefeld National G.C.
South Carolina
Caledonia Golf & Fish C.
Kiawah Island Resort (Ocean Cse.)
Wild Wing Plantation (Wood Stork
   Cse.)
Washington
Desert Canyon Golf Resort
West Virginia
Snowshoe Mountain (Hawthorne
   Valley at Snowshoe)
Wisconsin
Blackwolf Run G.C. (Meadow Valleys
   Cse.)
Blackwolf Run G.C. (River Cse.)
University Ridge G.Cse.
CANADA
Nova Scotia
Bell Bay G.C.
Ontario
Angus Glen G.C.
Peninsula Lakes G.C.
Prince Edward Island
The Links at Crowbush Cove

The *Good Condition* Courses

**The next 150 (and ties) Golf
Courses in North America in
terms of optimum course conditions, as rated by GOLF DIGEST
readers.**

UNITED STATES
Alabama
Grand National G.C. (Short Cse.)
Kiva Dunes G.C.
Magnolia Grove G.C. (Short Cse.)
Oxmoor Valley G.C. (Short Cse.)
Silver Lakes G.C.
   (Heartbreaker/Backbreaker/
Mindbreaker)
Arizona
The Boulders C. (North Cse.)
The G.C. at Eagle Mountain
Grayhawk G.C. (Raptor Cse.)
La Paloma C.C. (Canyon/Hill)
The Phoenician G.C.

(Desert/Canyon/Oasis)
Pointe Hilton South Mountain Resort
   (Phantom Horse G.C.)
The Raven G.C. at Sabino Springs
SunRidge Canyon G.C.
Ventana Canyon Golf & Racquet C.
   (Canyon Cse.)
California
The Cse. at Wente Vineyards
Desert Princess C.C. & Resort
   (Lagos/Cielo/Vista)
Diablo Grande Resort (Ranch Cse.)
Four Seasons Resort Aviara (Aviara
   G.C.)
Half Moon Bay G.C. (Ocean Cse.)
Hunter Ranch G.Cse.
The Links at Spanish Bay
Pebble Beach Golf Links
Poppy Hills G.Cse.
Primm Valley G.C. (Desert Cse.)
Rancho San Marcos G.C.
San Juan Oaks G.C.
Spyglass Hill G.Cse.
Stevinson Ranch G.C. (Savannah
   Cse.)
Colorado
The Ridge at Castle Pines North
River Valley Ranch G.C.
Florida
Amelia Island Plantation (Long Point
   G.C.)
The C. at Eaglebrooke
Emerald Dunes G.Cse.
Grand Cypress G.C. (New Cse.)
LPGA International (Champions)
LPGA International (Legends)
The Moors G.C.
PGA G.C. at the Reserve
   (North Cse.)
PGA G.C. at the Reserve
   (South Cse.)
River Hills C.C.
Riverwood G.C.
Walt Disney World Resort (Osprey
   Ridge G.Cse.)
Walt Disney World Resort (Palm
   G.Cse.)
World Golf Village (The Slammer
   &The Squire)
World Woods G.C. (Pine Barrens Cse.)
World Woods G.C. (Rolling Oaks Cse.)
Hawaii
Kapalua G.C. (The Plantation Cse.)

(Maple/Willow/Oak)
Kiawah Island Resort (Turtle Point)
Tidewater G.C. & Plantation
Wild Wing Plantation (Avocet Cse.)
Wild Wing Plantation (Falcon Cse.)
Wild Wing Plantation (Hummingbird Cse.)

Tennessee
Legends C. of Tennessee (Roper's Knob Cse.)

Texas
Barton Creek Resort & C.C. (Fazio Cse.)
Barton Creek Resort & C.C. (Palmer-Lakeside Cse.)
La Cantera G.C.
Painted Dunes Desert G.Cse.
The Quarry G.C.

Vermont
Rutland C.C.

Virginia
Augustine G.C.
Draper Valley G.C.
Golden Horseshoe G.C. (Gold Cse.)
The Homestead Resort (Cascades Cse.)
Lansdowne G.C.
Stonehouse G.C.

Washington
Gold Mountain Golf Complex (Olympic Cse.)
McCormick Woods G.Cse.

West Virginia
The Greenbrier (Greenbrier Cse.)

Wisconsin
The Bog
Geneva National G.C. (Palmer Cse.)
Geneva National G.C. (Trevino Cse.)
Lake Arrowhead G.Cse. (Pines Cse.)
SentryWorld G.Cse.
Turtleback G. & Conf. Ctr.

CANADA
British Columbia
Harvest G.C.
Westwood Plateau G. & C.C.

Manitoba
Hecla G.Cse. at Gull Harbor Resort

Ontario
Deerhurst Resort (Deerhurst Highlands G.Cse.)
Silver Lakes G. & C.C.

MEXICO
Baja Sur

Cabo Real G.C.
The Ocean Cse. at Cabo del Sol
Palmilla G.C. (Arroyo/Ocean/Mountain)
ISLANDS
Aruba
Tierra Del Sol C.C.

The *Great Pace* Courses

The top 50 Golf Courses in North America in terms of speediest pace of play, as rated by GOLF DIGEST readers.

UNITED STATES
Alabama
Grand National G.C. (Short Cse.)
Magnolia Grove G.C. (Short Cse.)
Arizona
Lake Powell National G.C. (Mesa Cse.)
Oakcreek C.C.
California
Diablo Grande Resort (Ranch Cse. at Diablo)
The G.C. at Whitehawk Ranch
Marriott's Desert Springs Resort & Spa (Valley Cse.)
Primm Valley G.C. (Lakes Cse.)
Colorado
Dalton Ranch G.C.
Eisenhower G.C. (Blue Cse.)
Florida
The C. at Hidden Creek
Gateway G. & C.C.
Orange County National G. Ctr. & Lodge (Crooked Cat)
Orange County National G. Ctr. & Lodge (Panther Lake G.Cse.)
River Hills C.C.
Hawaii
The Challenge at Manele
The Experience at Koele
Grand Waikapu Resort, Golf & Spa
Hualalai G.C.
Kaluakoi Hotel & G.C.
Idaho
Coeur d'Alene Resort G.Cse.
Illinois
El Paso G.C.
Iowa
Spencer G. & C.C.
Kentucky

Lafayette G.Cse.
The Peninsula Golf Resort
Maryland
Bulle Rock (South Cse.)
Michigan
Bay Harbor G.C.
Belvedere G.C.
Chestnut Valley G.Cse.
The Rock at Drummond Island
TimberStone G.Cse.
Mississippi
Kirkwood National G.C.
Nebraska
Heritage Hills G.Cse.
New York
Greystone G.C.
North Carolina
Bald Head Island C.
Grandover Resort & Conf. Ctr. (West Cse.)
St. James Plantation (Players C.)
The Sound Golf Links at Albemarle Plantation
North Dakota
The Links of North Dakota at Red Mike Resort
Oklahoma
Karsten Creek G.C.
South Carolina
Daufuskie Island C. & Resort (Bloody Point)
Daufuskie Island C. & Resort (Melrose Cse.)
Utah
Birch Creek G.C.
Virginia
Draper Valley G.C.
Wyoming
Buffalo G.C.
CANADA
Nova Scotia
Bell Bay G.C.
Highlands Links G.Cse.
ISLANDS
Dominican Republic
Casa de Campo Resort & C.C. (Teeth of The Dog)
Jamaica
Sandals G. & C.C.
Turks & Caicos Island
Provo G.C.

The *Good Pace* Courses
The next 150 (and ties) Golf Courses in North America in terms of quick pace of play, as rated by GOLF DIGEST readers.

UNITED STATES
Alabama
Highland Oaks G.Cse. (Highlands/Magnolia/Marshwood)
Magnolia Grove G.C. (Crossings Cse.)
Oxmoor Valley G.C. (Short Cse.)
Arizona
The G.C. at Eagle Mountain
Grande Valle G.C.
Las Sendas G.C.
Los Caballeros G.C.
The Raven G.C. at South Mountain
Silver Creek G.C.
SunRidge Canyon G.C.
Troon North G.C. (Monument Cse.)
Ventana Canyon Golf & Racquet C. (Canyon Cse.)
California
Fall River Valley G. & C.C.
Hesperia G. & C.C.
Primm Valley G.C. (Desert Cse.)
Rams Hill C.C.
The Sea Ranch Golf Links
The Westin Mission Hills Resort (Mission Hills North)
Colorado
Battlement Mesa G.C.
The Broadmoor G.C. (West Cse.)
Eisenhower G.C. (Silver Cse.)
Grand Lake G.Cse.
Haymaker G.Cse.
Sonnenalp G.C.
Florida
Bluewater Bay Resort (Magnolia/Marsh Cse.)
The C. at Eaglebrooke
The Dunes G.C. at Seville
Grand Cypress G.C. (North/East/South)
Marriott at Sawgrass Resort (Marsh Landing G.C.)
Mission Inn Golf & Tennis Resort (El Campeon Cse.)
The Moors G.C.
PGA G.C. at the Reserve (North Cse.)

PGA G.C. at the Reserve (South Cse.)
World Golf Village (The Slammer & The Squire)
World Woods G.C. (Pine Barrens Cse.)
World Woods G.C. (Rolling Oaks Cse.)

Georgia
Georgia Veterans Memorial G.Cse.
Reynolds Plantation (Great Waters Cse.)
Reynolds Plantation (National Cse.)
Reynolds Plantation (Plantation Cse.)
Sea Island G.C. (Plantation)

Hawaii
Hapuna G.Cse.
Kapalua G.C. (The Village Cse.)
Kauai Lagoons Resort (Kiele Cse.)
Kauai Lagoons Resort (Mokihana Cse.)
Makena Resort G.Cse. (North Cse.)
Poipu Bay Resort G.C.
Princeville Resort (Makai G.C.—Lakes/Woods)
Princeville Resort (Prince Cse.)
Turtle Bay Resort (The Links at Kuilima)
Turtle Bay Resort (The Turtle Bay C.C.)

Idaho
Shadow Valley G.C.

Illinois
Pine Meadow G.C.
Railside G.C.

Kansas
Buffalo Dunes G.Cse.

Kentucky
Eagle Trace G.Cse.
Lassing Pointe G.Cse.

Maine
Sugarloaf G.C.

Maryland
Beechtree G.C.
Worthington Valley C.C.

Massachusetts
Brookside G.C.
Farm Neck G.C.

Michigan
Black Bear Golf Resort
Gaylord C.C.
Lakewood Shores Resort (The Gailes Cse.)
Oak Crest G.Cse.
The Quest G.C.
Stonehedge G.Cse. (North Cse.)
Twin Lakes G.C.

Minnesota
Giants Ridge Golf & Ski Resort
Grand View Lodge Resort (The Preserve G.Cse.)
Mount Frontenac G.Cse.
New Prague G.C.
Purple Hawk C.C.
Wildflower at Fair Hills

Mississippi
Dancing Rabbit G.C. (The Azaleas)
Timberton G.C.

Missouri
Eagle Knoll G.C.

Montana
Mission Mountain C.C.
Northern Pines G.C.

Nebraska
Woodland Hills G.Cse.

Nevada
Desert Inn G.C.
Las Vegas National G.C.
Las Vegas Paiute Resort (Tav-ai Kaiv Cse.—Sun Mountain)
Oasis Resort Hotel Casino (Oasis G.Cse.)

New Hampshire
The Balsams Grand Resort Hotel (Panorama G.C.)

New Mexico
Pinon Hills G.Cse.

New York
Chautauqua G.C. (Hills Cse.)
Chautauqua G.C. (Lake Cse.)
Concord Resort Hotel (International G.Cse.)
Island's End G. & C.C.
Lake Placid Resort (Links Cse.)
Wayne Hills C.C.

North Carolina
Carolina National G.C.
Cypress Lakes G.Cse.
Grandover Resort & Conference Center (East Cse.)
Olde Beau G.C. at Roaring Gap
Pine Needles Lodge & G.C.
Pinehurst Resort & C.C. (Pinehurst No. 7)
Pinehurst Resort & C.C. (Pinehurst No. 8)

River Ridge G.C.
Salem Glen C.C.
Ohio
River Greens G.Cse.
StoneWater G.C.
Oregon
Eagle Point G.Cse.
Meadow Lakes G.Cse.
Pumpkin Ridge G.C. (Ghost Creek Cse.)
Running Y Ranch Resort
Sandpines Golf Links
Sunriver Lodge & Resort (Crosswater C.)
Pennsylvania
Bucknell G.C.
South Carolina
Hunter's Creek G.C. (Maple/Willow/Oak)
Kiawah Island Resort (Ocean Cse.)
Palmetto Dunes Resort (Arthur Hills Cse.)
South Carolina National G.C.
Wild Wing Plantation (Wood Stork Cse.)
Texas
The Bandit G.C.
Barton Creek Resort & C.C. (Palmer-Lakeside Cse.)
The Cliffs Resort
The Falls Resort & C.C.
Painted Dunes Desert G.Cse.
Sweetwater C.C.
White Bluffs G.C. (Old Cse.)
Utah
Entrada at Snow Canyon
Vermont
Sugarbush G.Cse.
Virginia
Ford's Colony C.C. (Marsh Hawk Cse.)
Golden Horseshoe G.C. (Green Cse.)
The Tides Inn (Golden Eagle G.Cse.)
Washington
Apple Tree G.Cse.
Legion Memorial G.Cse.
North Bellingham G.Cse.
Semiahmoo G. & C.C.
West Virginia
Glade Springs Resort
The Woods Resort (Mountain View Back/Stony Lick)

Wisconsin
Blackwolf Run G.C. (Meadow Valleys Cse.)
Blackwolf Run G.C. (River Cse.)
Bristlecone Pines G.C.
The G.Cses of Lawsonia (Links Cse.)
The Springs G.C. Resort (Back/North)
Turtleback G. & Conf. Ctr.
Washington County G.Cse.
Wyoming
Jackson Hole Golf & Tennis C.
Teton Pines Resort & C.C.
CANADA
Alberta
Redwood Meadows G. & C.C.
British Columbia
Golden G. & C.C.
MEXICO
Baja Sur
Cabo San Lucas C.C.
The Ocean Cse. at Cabo del Sol
Palmilla G.C. (Arroyo/Ocean/Mountain)
ISLANDS
Aruba
Tierra Del Sol C.C.
Bermuda
The Mid Ocean C.
Ocean View G.Cse.
Dominican Republic
Casa de Campo Resort & C.C. (Links Cse.)
Jamaica
Half Moon Golf, Tennis & Beach C.
Super Clubs G.C. at Runaway Bay
Nevis
Four Seasons Resort Nevis

Standard Abbreviations:

C. = Club
C.C. = Country Club
Cse. = Course
G. = Golf
G. & C.C. = Golf & Country Club
G. & Conf. Ctr. = Golf & Conference Center
G.C. = Golf Club
G.Cse. = Golf Course
G. Ctr. = Golf Center
G.L. = Golf Links
Plant. = Plantation

How to Use This Guide

Sample Entry

ANYWHERE GOLF RESORT
★★★ **ANYWHERE GOLF COURSE.** *Service+, Condition*
PU-100 Anywhere Drive, Centerville, 10001, Nice County, (212)000-9999,
(888)123-4567, 25 miles S of Nowhere. **E-mail:** good golf@xyz.com **Web:**
www.anywheregolfcourse.com
Holes: 18. **Yards:** 6,500/5,500. **Par:** 70/71. **Course Rating:** 72.5/71.5.
Slope: 145/135. **Green Fee:** $75/$125. **Cart Fee:** Included in Green Fee.
Walking Policy: Walking at certain times. **Walkability**: 4. **Opened:** 1920.
Architect: AW Tillinghast. **Season:** April-Oct. **High:** April-Oct. **To obtain tee
times:** Call golf shop. **Miscellaneous:** Reduced fees (low season), discount
packages, metal spikes, range (grass), caddies, club rentals, lodging (200
rooms), credit cards (MC, V, AE, Diners Club), beginner friendly (Women to
Fore, junior clinics on Fridays).
Notes: Ranked 5th in 1997 Best in State. 1990 Anywhere Golf Classic.
Reader comments: Like St. Andrews and Pebble Beach, play it at least
once in your life...Too expensive...Older course, needs renovating.
Special Notes: Formerly known as Somewhere Golf Club.

Explanation

ANYWHERE GOLF RESORT—The name of the resort or facility.
★★★—The Star Rating; a rating of the golf experience according to
GOLF DIGEST readers. See ratings chart below.
ANYWHERE GOLF COURSE—The name of the course at Anywhere Golf
Resort (generally only appears when there is more than one course at the
facility).
Service+, Condition—Indicators of major award winners. Award
categories include: Great Value (Value+), Great Service (Service+), Great
Conditioning (Condition+), Great Pace of Play (Pace+) to the top 50 (and
ties) vote getters in each category; Good Value (Value), Good Service
(Service), Good Conditioning (Condition), and Good Pace of Play (Pace) to
the next 150 (and ties) winners. *New categories*
PU—Public course. **PM:** Municipal or County owned course. **R:** Resort
course. **SP:** Semi-private course. **M:** Military course. *New categories*
100 Anywhere Drive, Centerville, 10001, Nice County—The address, zip
code and county.
(212)000-9999—The phone number of the facility. Please note that all phone
numbers were accurate at the time of going to press, but numbers and area
codes are subject to change.
(888)123-4567—The toll free number for the course, if available.
25 miles S of Nowhere—Approximate directions as provided by the club..
E-mail—The e-mail address for the course. *New*
Web—The web site address for the course. *New*
Holes—The number of holes. 27-hole facilities will show 27-holes for each
combination of 18 holes.
Yards—The yardage from the back/front tees.
Par—The figures shown represent the par from the back/front tees.
Course Rating—The USGA course rating from the back/front tees.
Slope—The USGA Slope rating from the back/front tees.

Green Fee—Fees listed represent the lowest/highest fee for an 18-hole rounds of golf. Published fees are subject to change.

Golf Carts—Price of renting golf carts at the course either per person or per cart as designated by the club. If the cart fee is included in the green fee, that information will be listed instead. Some facilities allow the player to walk even though the cart fee is included in the green fee. See Walking Policy for further information. Published fees are subject to change.

Walking policy—Unrestricted walking: Walking is allowed at any time. Walking at certain times: Carts may be mandatory at certain (usually busy) times. Mandatory cart: Walking is never an option.

Walkability—On a 1 to 5 scale, with 1 being flat and 5 extremely hilly, courses have rated the terrain of their course. *New*

Opened—The year the course first opened.

Architect—The architect of the golf course.

Season—Months of the year when the course is open for play.

High—When the course is likely to be busiest and the rates typically higher.

To obtain tee times—Procedure established by the course to secure a tee time.

Miscellaneous—This category reflects amenities available and certain policies at the course including reduced fees, discount packages, if metal spikes are allowed, golf range, if caddies are available, if rental clubs are available, lodging and the number of rooms, credit cards, if the facility is beginner friendly including programs for beginners. *New categories*

Notes—Relevant additional information, including GOLF DIGEST rankings, GOLF DIGEST school sites, and major professional tournament sites.

Reader comments—A representative sample of comments made by GOLF DIGEST readers in response to an March, 1999 issue survey and a summer *golfdigest.com* survey. These comments come from readers' impressions of the course based on their playing experiences between February 1, 1998 and February 28, 1999 and may not be indicative of current conditions or changes in course ownership.

Special Notes—Additional information such as the former name of a club or if the club has a 9-hole or par-3 course affiliated with it.

N/A—This means that the information was not supplied by the facility by publication date or the information was not applicable.

Ratings

★ Basic golf.

★★ Good, but not great.

★★★ Very good. Tell a friend it's worth getting off the highway to play.

★★★★ Outstanding. Plan your next vacation around it.

★★★★★ Golf at its absolute best. Pay any price to play at least once in your life.

½ The equivalent of one-half star.

Please note that a number of courses do not have a Star Rating. A course that did not receive a minimum of 10 ballots, either because it is very new or simply was not visited by a sufficient number of GOLF DIGEST subscribers, remains unrated.

America's 100 Greatest Golf Courses, 1999-2000

The following courses, both public and private, are the top 100 in the United States as ranked by GOLF DIGEST in its biennial ranking. Courses marked in red are public-access facilities and are featured in this book.

FIRST 10
1. **Pine Valley G.C.,** Pine Valley, N.J.
2. **Augusta National G.C.,** Augusta, Ga.
3. **Cypress Point Club,** Pebble Beach, Calif.
4. **Pebble Beach G. Links,** Pebble Beach, Calif.
5. **Shinnecock Hills G.C.,** Southampton, N.Y.
6. **Merion G.C. (East),** Ardmore, Pa.
7. **Oakmont C.C.,** Oakmont, Pa.
8. **Winged Foot G.C. (West),** Mamaroneck, N.Y
9. **Pinehurst Resort & C.C. (No. 2),** Pinehurst, N.C.
10. **Oakland Hills C.C. (South),** Bloomfield Hills, Mich.

SECOND 10
11. **The Olympic Club (Lake),** San Francisco
12. **The Country Club (Clyde/Squirrel),** Brookline, Mass.
13. **Prairie Dunes C.C.,** Hutchinson, Kan.
14. **Seminole G.C.,** North Palm Beach, Fla.
15. **Muirfield Village G.C.,** Dublin, Ohio
16. **Crystal Downs C.C.,** Frankfort, Mich.
17. **National Golf Links,** Southampton, N.Y.
18. **San Francisco G.C.,** San Francisco
19. **Medinah C.C. (No. 3),** Medinah, Ill.
20. **Shadow Creek G.C.,** North Las Vegas, Nev.

THIRD 10
21. **Quaker Ridge G.C.,** Scarsdale, N.Y.
22. **Wade Hampton G.C.,** Cashiers, N.C.
23. **The Golf Club,** New Albany, Ohio
24. **Riviera C.C.,** Pacific Palisades, Calif.
25. **Southern Hills C.C.,** Tulsa, Okla.
26. **Oak Hill C.C. (East),** Rochester, N.Y.
27. **Los Angeles C.C. (North),** Los Angeles
28. **Garden City G.C.,** Garden City, N.Y
29. **Inverness Club,** Toledo, Ohio
30. **Spyglass Hill G. Cse.,** Pebble Beach, Calif.

FOURTH 10
31. **Sand Hills G.C.,** Mullen, Nebraska
32. **Peachtree G.C.,** Atlanta, Ga.
33. **Cherry Hills C.C.,** Englewood, Colo.
34. **Baltusrol G.C. (Lower),** Springfield, N.J.
35. **Chicago G.C.,** Wheaton, Ill.
36. **Winged Foot G.C. (East),** Mamaroneck, N.Y.
37. **Scioto C.C.,** Columbus, Ohio
38. **Maidstone Club,** East Hampton, N.Y.
39. **Kittansett Club,** Marion, Mass.
40. **Cog Hill G. & C.C. (No. 4),** Lemont, Ill.

FIFTH 10
41. **Olympia Fields C.C.(North),** Olympia Fields, Ill.
42. **The Honors Course,** Chattanooga, Tenn.
43. **Prince Course,** Princeville Resort, Kauai HI
44. **Plainfield C.C.,** Plainfield, N.J.
45. **Somerset Hills C.C.,** Bernardsville, N.J.
46. **Castle Pines G.C.,** Castle Rock, Colo.
47. **Colonial C.C.,** Fort Worth
48. **Sanctuary G.C.,** Sedalia, Co.

49. **Wannamoisett C.C.,** Rumford, R.I.
50. **Baltimore C.C. (East),** Timonium, Md.

SIXTH 10
51. **Laurel Valley G.C.,** Ligonier, Pa.
52. **TPC At Sawgrass (Stadium),** Ponte Vedra Beach, Fla.
53. **Cascades G. Cse.,** Homestead Resort, Hot Springs, Va.
54. **Interlachen C.C.,** Edina, Minn.
55. **Blackwolf Run (River),** Kohler, Wis.
56. **Long Cove Club,** Hilton Head Island, S.C.
57. **Forest Highlands G.C. (Canyon),** Flagstaff, Ariz.
58. **Black Diamond Ranch G & C.C. (Quarry),** Lecanto, Fla.
59. **Congressional C.C. (Blue),** Bethesda, Md.
60. **Double Eagle Club,** Galena, Oh.

SEVENTH 10
61. **Shoal Creek,** Shoal Creek, Ala.
62. **The Ocean Course,** Kiawah Island, S.C.
63. **Desert Forest G.C.,** Carefree, Ariz.
64. **Canterbury G.C.,** Beachwood, Ohio
65. **The Estancia Club,** Scottsdale, Ariz.
66. **East Lake G.C.,** Atlanta, Ga.
67. **Butler National G.C.,** Oak Brook, Ill.
68. **Valhalla G.C.,** Louisville, Ky.
69. **Mauna Kea G. Cse.,** Kamuela, Hi.
70. **Stanwich Club,** Greenwich, Conn.

EIGHTH 10
71. **Harbour Town G. Links,** Hilton Head Island, S.C.
72. **Milwaukee C.C.,** Milwaukee, Wis.
73. **The Quarry at La Quinta,** La Quinta, Calif.
74. **Hazeltine National G.C.,** Chaska, Minn.
75. **World Woods G.C. (Pine Barrens),** Brooksville, Fla.
76. **Haig Point Club (Calibogue),** Daufuskie Island, S.C.
77. **Bellerive C.C.,** Creve Coeur, Mo.
78. **Salem C.C.,** Peabody, Mass.
79. **Atlantic G.C.,** Bridgehampton, N.Y.
80. **Crosswater,** Sunriver Lodge, Sunriver, Ore.

NINTH 10
81. **Point O'Woods G. & C.C.,** Benton Harbor, Mich.
82. **Camargo Club,** Indian Hill, Ohio
83. **Sycamore Hills G.C.,** Fort Wayne, Ind.
84. **Royal New Kent G.C.,** Providence Forge, Va.
85. **NCR C.C. (South),** Kettering, Ohio
86. **Pumpkin Ridge G.C. (Witch Hollow),** Cornelius, Ore.
87. **Eugene C.C.,** Eugene, Ore.
88. **Valley C. Of Montecito,** Santa Barbara, Calif.
89. **Wilmington C.C. (South),** Greenville, Del.
90. **Crooked Stick G.C.,** Carmel, Ind.

TENTH 10
91. **Ocean Forest G.C.,** Sea Island, Ga.
92. **Oak Tree G.C.,** Edmond, Okla.
93. **Greenville C.C. (Chanticleer),** Greenville, S.C.
94. **Pasatiempo G.C.,** Santa Cruz, Calif.
95. **Jupiter Hills Club (Hills),** Tequesta, Fla.
96. **Saucon Valley C.C. (Grace),** Bethlehem, Pa.
97. **Pete Dye G.C.,** Bridgeport, W.Va.
98. **Sahalee C.C. (South/North),** Redmond, Wash.
99. **Edgewood Tahoe G. Cse.,** Stateline, Nev.
100. **Naples National G.C.,** Naples, Fla.

AMERICA'S BEST NEW COURSES—1999

The Golf Digest annual survey of America's Best New Courses.

BEST NEW UPSCALE COURSES:
Maximum green fee more than $50.
1. **Bandon Dunes G.C.**, Bandon, Ore.
2. **Whistling Straits G.C. (Straits Cse.)**, Haven, Wis.
3. **Bay Harbor G.C. (Links & Quarry 9s)**, Bay Harbor, Mich.
4. **The Trophy Club**, Lebanon, Ind.
5. **Belgrade Lakes G.C.**, Belgrade Lakes, Me.
6. **Reflection Bay G.C.**, Henderson, Nev.
7. **The Golf Club at Cuscowilla**, Eatonton, Ga.
8. **Limestone Springs G.C.**, Oneonta, Ala.
9. **TPC at Myrtle Beach**, Murrells Inlet, S.C.
T10. **Tobacco Road G.C.**, Sanford, N.C.
T10. **Pine Barrens G.C.**, Jackson, N.J.

BEST NEW AFFORDABLE PUBLIC COURSES:
Maximum green fee $50 or less.
1. **El Diablo G. & C.C.**, Citrus Springs, Fla.
2. **Canebrake G.C.**, Hattiesburg, Miss.
3. **Wild Horse G.C.**, Gothenburg, Neb.
4. **Pilgrim's Run G.C.**, Pierson, Mich.
5. **The River G.C.**, North Augusta, S.C.
6. **Cateechee G.C.**, Hartwell, Ga.
7. **Red Hawk Ridge G. Cse.**, Castle Rock, Colo.
8. **Cobblestone G. Cse.**, Kendallville, Ind.
9. **Mystic Hills G.C.**, Culver, Ind.
10. **Vicwood Golf Links**, Lacey, Wash.

BEST NEW CANADIAN
1. **Greywolf G. Cse.**, Panorama, British Columbia
2. **SilverTip G. Cse.**, Canmore, Alberta
3. **The Links of GlenEagles**, Cochrane, Alberta

Part I

The United States

ALABAMA

★★★ ABI SPA GOLF RESORT
PU-7410 Hwy. 231S, Dothan, 36301, Houston County, (334)677-3326, 4 miles S of Dothan.
Holes: 18. **Yards:** 7,242/5,470. **Par:** 72/72. **Course Rating:** 74.5/71.1. **Slope:** 123/113. **Green Fee:** $12/$18. **Cart Fee:** $11/person. **Walking Policy:** Walking at certain times. **Walkability:** N/A. **Opened:** 1968. **Architect:** Bob Simmons. **Season:** Year-round. **High:** March-June. **To obtain tee times:** Call golf shop. **Miscellaneous:** Reduced fees (twilight), discount packages, metal spikes, range (grass), club rentals, lodging, credit cards (MC, V, AE, D, Diners Club).
Reader Comments: With proper maintenance, the US Open could be played here ... 9 and 18 long par 4s ... Long course, no fairway bunkers, few water holes ... Friendly staff ... Best 19th hole in Southeastern Alabama ... Improvements being made.

★★½ ALPINE BAY GOLF & COUNTRY CLUB
R-9855 Renfore Rd., Alpine, 35014, Talladega County, (256)268-2920, 40 miles SE of Birmingham. **E-mail:** bobame76@aol.com.
Holes: 18. **Yards:** 6,518/5,518. **Par:** 72/72. **Course Rating:** 70.9/69.8. **Slope:** 129/120. **Green Fee:** $15/$24. **Cart Fee:** $10/person. **Walking Policy:** Walking at certain times. **Walkability:** 3. **Opened:** 1972. **Architect:** Robert Trent Jones. **Season:** Year-round. **High:** May-Sept. **To obtain tee times:** Call anytime. **Miscellaneous:** Reduced fees (weekdays, resort guests, twilight), range (grass), club rentals, lodging, credit cards (MC, V, AE, D).
Reader Comments: Great new bent-grass greens ... I enjoyed it ... A good place for introducing youth to the game ... A good course to play, not too hard ... Striving to improve ... Very enjoyable ... Nice layout ... Interesting course, hilly, good doglegs.

ANDERSON CREEK GOLF CLUB
PU-Rte. 1, Anderson, 35610, Lauderdale County, (256) 247-5913.
Special Notes: Call club for further information.

★★★½ AUBURN LINKS AT MILL CREEK
PU-826 Shell-Toomer Pkwy., Auburn, 36830, Lee County, (334)887-5151, 4 miles NW of Auburn-Opelika.
Holes: 18. **Yards:** 7,145/5,320. **Par:** 72/72. **Course Rating:** 72.5/68.5. **Slope:** 129/118. **Green Fee:** $32/$39. **Cart Fee:** Included in Green Fee. **Walking Policy:** Walking at certain times. **Walkability:** 3. **Opened:** 1991. **Architect:** Ward Northrup. **Season:** Year-round. **High:** April-Oct. **To obtain tee times:** Call up to 7 days in advance. **Miscellaneous:** Reduced fees (low season, resort guests, seniors, juniors), discount packages, metal spikes, range (grass), club rentals, credit cards (MC, V).
Reader Comments: Beautiful course, difficult but fair layout, good service ... Tricky sloping greens, good par 3s ... Tough and not outrageously expensive ... People are nice, course is fun to play ... Excellent condition ... Great first hole, it sets the mood ... Nice course, bent greens ... Great value—good people.

★★★½ AZALEA CITY GOLF COURSE
PM-1000 Gaillard Dr., Mobile, 36608, Mobile County, (334)342-4221, 10 miles W of Mobile.
Holes: 18. **Yards:** 6,850/5,347. **Par:** 72/72. **Course Rating:** 72.1/70.3. **Slope:** 126/122. **Green Fee:** $10/$15. **Cart Fee:** $10/person. **Walking Policy:** Unrestricted walking. **Walkability:** 2. **Opened:** 1957. **Architect:** R.B Harris. **Season:** Year-round. **High:** March-Oct. **To obtain tee times:** Call golf shop up to 14 days in advance for weekday tee times and the Wednesday prior to the weekend call at 8:00 a.m. **Miscellaneous:** Reduced fees (weekdays, twilight), metal spikes, range (grass), club rentals, credit cards (MC, V, AE).
Reader Comments: New greens which are fast and hard ... Player-friendly course made for amateurs, outstanding course ... Very quiet and in good shape ... New greens will be good when they soften ... Excellent conditions for public course ... Good for long drives off the tee.

★½ BAY OAKS GOLF CLUB
SP-7960 Edgar Roberts Road, Irvington, 36544, Mobile County, (334)824-2429, (800)338-9826, 10 miles S of Mobile.
Holes: 18. **Yards:** 6,623/5,504. **Par:** 72/72. **Course Rating:** 69.3/70.3. **Slope:** 126/114. **Green Fee:** $12/$14. **Cart Fee:** $12/person. **Walking Policy:** Unrestricted walking. **Walkability:** 2. **Opened:** 1963. **Architect:** Boots Lange. **Season:** Year-round. **High:** Nov.-March. **To obtain tee times:** Tee times on weekends and holidays. Call on Thursday a.m. for weekend tee times. **Miscellaneous:** Reduced fees (weekdays), metal spikes, range (grass), credit cards (MC, V, AE, D), beginner friendly (junior golf clinics and lessons available).

BENT BROOK GOLF COURSE
PU-7900 Dickey Springs Rd., Bessemer, 35023, Jefferson County, (205)424-2368, 10 miles S of Birmingham.
Holes: 27. **Green Fee:** $23/$33. **Cart Fee:** $11/person. **Walking Policy:** Walking at certain times. **Opened:** 1988. **Architect:** Ward Northrup. **Season:** Year-round. **To obtain tee times:** Call up to 3 days in advance. **Miscellaneous:** Reduced fees (weekdays), metal spikes, range (grass), club rentals, credit cards (MC, V, AE, D).

ALABAMA

★★★½ BROOK/GRAVEYARD
Yards: 7,053/5,364. **Par:** 71/71. **Course Rating:** 71.7/70.9. **Slope:** 121/124. **Walkability:** 2.
Reader Comments: Great service ... Run like country club ... Fair, impeccable conditions ... Challenging course, but marshalls can be crabby ... Nice clubhouse, has the look and feel of private club ... Wide open ... Bring balls ... Beautiful, Old South farmland scenery ... Exquisite greens.

★★★½ WINDMILL/BROOK
Yards: 6,934/5,333. **Par:** 71/71. **Course Rating:** 69.6/70.3. **Slope:** 117/120. **Walkability:** N/A.
Reader Comments: Great for all levels of golf ... Conditions improving, greens redone ... Fun, long par 4s ... When wind gets up it plays extra, extra long ... Wide open but fairly challenging ... Mixture of tough & easy holes ... Very well maintained. Nice clubhouse. Excellent finishing holes on all nines ... No tricks.

★★★½ WINDMILL/GRAVEYARD
Yards: 6,847/5,321. **Par:** 70/70. **Course Rating:** 69.2/70.6. **Slope:** 116/123. **Walkability:** 2.
High: March-Sept.
Reader Comments: Best of the three; playable by all levels ... Great place ... Bent Brooks facilities are excellent, good for weekend golfers ... Open, not too many hills, super greens...Fun course, not difficult. Quality course.

★★ CAHABA VALLEY GOLF & COUNTRY CLUB
7905 Roper Rd., Trussville, 35173, Jefferson County, (205)655-2095.
Special Notes: Call club for further information.

CAMBRIAN RIDGE GOLF CLUB   *Service+*
PU-101 Sunbelt Pkwy., Greenville, 36037, Butler County, (334)382-9787, (800)949-4444, 40 miles S of Montgomery.
Holes: 27. **Green Fee:** $48/$58. **Cart Fee:** $19/person. **Walking Policy:** Unrestricted walking.
Opened: 1993. **Architect:** Robert Trent Jones. **Season:** Year-round. **High:** March-May; Sept.-Nov. **To obtain tee times:** Call 1-800-949-4444.

★★★★ CANYON/LOBLOLLY   *Value*
Yards: 7,297/4,772. **Par:** 71/71. **Course Rating:** 74.6/67.8. **Slope:** 140/126. **Walkability:** 5.
Miscellaneous: Reduced fees (low season, twilight, juniors), discount packages, metal spikes, range (grass/mats), club rentals, credit cards (MC, V, AE, D).
Reader Comments: Thrilling ... Target golf: Help! ... Some great water holes, No. 9 is a brute! ... Beautiful, excellent staff, fun ... Canyon and Sherling are the best ... Choice of tees makes playable for any golfer ... Beautiful at a bargain price ... Tight fairways, drastic elevation changes, very nice clubhouse ... Bring camera.

★★★★ CANYON/SHERLING
Yards: 7,424/4,857. **Par:** 72/72. **Course Rating:** 75.4/68.1. **Slope:** 142/127. **Walkability:** 5.
Miscellaneous: Reduced fees (weekdays, low season, twilight, seniors, juniors), discount packages, metal spikes, range (grass/mats), club rentals, credit cards (MC, V, AE, D).
Notes: Ranked 6th in 1999 Best in State; 13th in 1996 America's Top 75 Affordable Courses.
Reader Comments: Championship-quality course playable for a 16 handicap ... Typical risk/reward Trail course ... Tough, target golf ... Entire complex is outstanding ... Great vistas, another Trail gem ... Severe greens ... Rolling hills ... Gracious staff.

★★★★ LOBLOLLY/SHERLING
Yards: 7,232/2,435. **Par:** 71/36. **Course Rating:** 73.9/67.0. **Slope:** 133/119. **Walkability:** 4.
Miscellaneous: Reduced fees (low season, twilight, juniors), discount packages, metal spikes, range (grass/mats), club rentals, credit cards (MC, V, AE, D).
Reader Comments: A pleasure to see and play ... Course in great shape ... Excellent—best course played all year ... Trail encourages you to use every club in your bag ... Stern test from any tee ... Huge undulating greens put premium on iron play and putting ... Super golf, great staff; a must play.
Special Notes: Complex also includes Short Course, a 9-hole par-3 layout.

CEDAR CREEK COUNTRY CLUB
SP-900 Green Isle Dr., Bessemer, 35020, Jefferson County, (205)424-8450.
Special Notes: Call club for further information.

CEDAR RIDGE GOLF CLUB
PU-Rte. 5, Decatur, 35603, Morgan County, (256)353-4653.
Special Notes: Call club for further information.

CHEROKEE COUNTRY CLUB
SP-Hwy. 9 S, Centre, 35960, Cherokee County, (256)927-5070.
Special Notes: Call club for further information.

★ CHRISWOOD GOLF COURSE
511 Wellington Rd., Athens, 35611, Limestone County, (256)232-9759.
Special Notes: Call club for further information.

ALABAMA

★★½ CITRONELLE MUNICIPAL GOLF COURSE
PM-18350 Lakeview Dr., Citronelle, 36522, Mobile County, (334)866-7881, 45 miles N of Mobile.
Holes: 18. **Yards:** 5,916/5,201. **Par:** 71/71. **Course Rating:** 70.0/69.4. **Slope:** 126/116. **Green Fee:** $12/$12. **Cart Fee:** $10/person. **Walking Policy:** Walking at certain times. **Walkability:** 4.
Opened: 1975. **Season:** Year-round. **High:** May-Aug. **To obtain tee times:** Call 334-866-7881.
Miscellaneous: Metal spikes, range (grass), club rentals, credit cards (MC, V).
Reader Comments: Nice course for the money ... One of best courses in our area. Great tournament course ... Fast elevated greens. Will test your putting skills ... Course keeps you thinking ... Front nine wide open, back short and tight. Great snack bar, best food in Alabama ... Woodsy, rolling hills, good-value municipal.

★★ COLONIAL GOLF CLUB
PU-400 Colonial Drive, Meridianville, 35759, Madison County, (256)828-0431.
Holes: 18. **Yards:** 65,710/6,153. **Par:** 72/72. **Course Rating:** 69.5/67.6. **Slope:** 114/110. **Green Fee:** $16/$18. **Cart Fee:** $9/person. **Walking Policy:** Unrestricted walking. **Walkability:** N/A.
Opened: 1963. **Season:** Year-round. **High:** March-Sept. **Miscellaneous:** Reduced fees (weekdays), metal spikes, credit cards (MC, V, D).

COUNTRY CLUB OF ALABAMA
SP-Eufaula, 36027, Barbour County, (334)687-2007.
Special Notes: Call club for further information.

CRAFT FARMS
★★★★ COTTON CREEK COURSE
SP-3840 Cotton Creek Blvd., Gulf Shores, 36542, Baldwin County, (334)968-7766, (800)327-2657, 40 miles E of Mobile. **Web:** www.craftfarms.com.
Holes: 18. **Yards:** 7,028/5,175. **Par:** 72/72. **Course Rating:** 74.1/70.9. **Slope:** 136/122. **Green Fee:** $50/$60. **Cart Fee:** Included in Green Fee. **Walking Policy:** Mandatory cart. **Walkability:** 1. **Opened:** 1987. **Architect:** Arnold Palmer/Ed Seay. **Season:** Year-round. **High:** March-Oct. **To obtain tee times:** Call up to 60 days in advance. **Miscellaneous:** Reduced fees (low season, twilight, juniors), discount packages, metal spikes, range (grass/mats), club rentals, lodging (114 rooms), credit cards (MC, V, AE), beginner friendly (clinics).
Reader Comments: Exquisite and much fun for average player ... Old course best ... Nice test, fair... Nice people and good crowds ... Excellent course, great shape ... Long, open-well designed ... Women-friendly & fun ... Liked it so much we retired here! Green year-round. Near beach.

★★★½ CYPRESS BEND COURSE
SP-3840 Cotton Creek Blvd., Gulf Shores, 36542, Baldwin County, (334)968-7766, (800)327-2657, 40 miles E of Mobile. **Web:** www.craftfarms.com.
Holes: 18. **Yards:** 6,848/5,045. **Par:** 72/72. **Course Rating:** 72.4/68.4. **Slope:** 127/112. **Green Fee:** $48/$55. **Cart Fee:** Included in Green Fee. **Walking Policy:** Mandatory cart. **Walkability:** 1. **Opened:** 1987. **Architect:** Arnold Palmer. **Season:** Year-round. **High:** March-Oct. **To obtain tee times:** Call up to 60 days in advance. **Miscellaneous:** Reduced fees (low season, juniors), discount packages, metal spikes, range (grass), club rentals, lodging (114 rooms), credit cards (MC, V, AE), beginner friendly (clinics).
Reader Comments: Great course for the occasional golfer as well as the advanced golfer... Friendly layout—excellent clubhouse ... Good course, watch scores climb as wind blows!.

★★★★ THE WOODLANDS COURSE
SP-19995 Oak Rd. W., Gulf Shores, 36542, Baldwin County, (334)968-4133, (800)327-2657, 30 miles W of Pensacola, FL. **Web:** www.craftfarms.com.
Holes: 18. **Yards:** 6,484/5,145. **Par:** 72/72. **Course Rating:** 70.8/67.9. **Slope:** 123/109. **Green Fee:** $45/$53. **Cart Fee:** Included in Green Fee. **Walking Policy:** Walking at certain times. **Walkability:** 1. **Opened:** 1994. **Architect:** Larry Nelson. **Season:** Year-round. **High:** Feb.-May. **To obtain tee times:** Call up to 60 days in advance. **Miscellaneous:** Reduced fees (weekdays, low season, twilight, juniors), discount packages, metal spikes, range (grass), club rentals, lodging (114 rooms), credit cards (MC, V, AE), beginner friendly (clinics for seniors in the fall. lessons for juniors in the summer).
Reader Comments: Every hole has personality ... Accommodating & great value ... Layout great ... Good shape, fun to play ... Great from all tees, well kept, warm staff ... Challenging, fair, fun course ... Good husband & wife course ... Must use every club in bag ... Water and marsh ... Love the pines!.

★★½ CULLMAN GOLF COURSE
PU-2321 County Rd. 490, Hanceville, 35077, Cullman County, (205)739-2386, 50 miles N of Birmingham. **E-mail:** golf@net-3.net.
Holes: 18. **Yards:** 6,361/4,495. **Par:** 72/72. **Course Rating:** 69.8/67.7. **Slope:** 120/115. **Green Fee:** $16/$18. **Cart Fee:** $11/person. **Walking Policy:** Unrestricted walking. **Walkability:** 3.
Opened: 1950. **Architect:** Curtis Davis. **Season:** Year-round. **High:** May-Aug. **To obtain tee times:** Reservations taken for weekends and holidays only. Call after 7 a.m. on Wednesday.

Miscellaneous: Reduced fees (weekdays, twilight, seniors, juniors), metal spikes, range (grass), club rentals, credit cards (MC, V, D).
Reader Comments: Good greens; not bad for the money ... Best value ... beautiful greens, tight fairways ... Good layout.

★★★ CYPRESS LAKES GOLF & COUNTRY CLUB
R-1311 E. 6th St., Muscle Shoals, 35661, Colbert County, (205)381-1232, 50 miles W of Huntsville.
Holes: 18. **Yards:** 6,562/5,100. **Par:** 71/71. **Course Rating:** 71.8/69.3. **Slope:** 126/128. **Green Fee:** $23/$28. **Cart Fee:** $13/person. **Walking Policy:** Walking at certain times. **Walkability:** 3. **Opened:** 1991. **Architect:** Gary Roger Baird. **Season:** Year-round. **High:** March-Oct. **To obtain tee times:** Call golf shop. **Miscellaneous:** Reduced fees (weekdays, low season, juniors), discount packages, range (grass), club rentals, credit cards (MC, V, AE).
Reader Comments: Challenging, lots of water ... Excellent greens, little sand ... Short but demanding.

★★★ DEER RUN GOLF COURSE
PM-1175 County Rd. 100, Moulton, 35650, Lawrence County, (256)974-7384, 24 miles SW of Decatur.
Holes: 18. **Yards:** 6,745/5,457. **Par:** 72/72. **Course Rating:** 70.9/70.9. **Slope:** 119/111. **Green Fee:** $14/$17. **Cart Fee:** $16/cart. **Walking Policy:** Unrestricted walking. **Walkability:** 3. **Opened:** 1981. **Architect:** Earl Stone. **Season:** Year-round. **High:** April-Oct. **Miscellaneous:** Range (grass), club rentals.
Reader Comments: Good design, well manicured ... Facilities good ... Good bent-grass greens ... Scenic, challenging in places ... Fast greens ... Back nine plays into Bankhead Forest. Excellent test from blues.

DEERFIELD GOLF & COUNTRY CLUB
SP-Hwy. 56 East, Chatom, 36518, Washington County, (205)847-2056.
Special Notes: Call club for further information.

DOGWOOD HILLS GOLF CLUB
PU-26460 AL Hwy. 71, Flat Rock, 35966, Jackson County, (256)632-3634, 30 miles S of Chattanooga. **E-mail:** DCslater@farmerstel.com.
Holes: 18. **Yards:** 6,463/5,029. **Par:** 72/72. **Course Rating:** 69.7/63.7. **Slope:** 115/102. **Green Fee:** $15/$21. **Cart Fee:** $12/person. **Walking Policy:** Walking at certain times. **Walkability:** 2. **Opened:** 1977. **Architect:** Bryce Slater. **Season:** Year-round. **High:** March-Oct. **To obtain tee times:** Call 256-632-3634 on Monday prior to the weekend of desired tee time. Tee times not required for weekdays. **Miscellaneous:** Reduced fees (weekdays, low season, twilight, seniors), range (grass), credit cards (MC, V, D).

★½ DON A. HAWKINS GOLF COURSE
PM-8920 Robuck Rd., Birmingham, 35206, Jefferson County, (205)836-7318.
Special Notes: Call club for further information.

★★★★ EAGLE POINT GOLF CLUB
PU-4500 Eagle Point Dr., Birmingham, 35242, Shelby County, (205)991-9070, 18 miles SE of Birmingham.
Holes: 18. **Yards:** 6,470/4,691. **Par:** 71/70. **Course Rating:** 70.2/61.9. **Slope:** 127/108. **Green Fee:** $27/$37. **Cart Fee:** $12/person. **Walking Policy:** Unrestricted walking. **Walkability:** 3. **Opened:** 1990. **Architect:** Earl Stone. **Season:** Year-round. **High:** April-Sept. **To obtain tee times:** Call up to 5 days in advance. **Miscellaneous:** Reduced fees (seniors), range (grass), club rentals, credit cards (MC, V, AE, D).
Reader Comments: Good course, good service ... Don't sell beer, if you can believe that! ... A pleasure ... My top 10... Tight layout makes you think, very enjoyable to play ... Garden spot, small area, fairways close ... No alcohol, decent greens, can walk but hilly, range fair.

★★ FRANK HOUSE MUNICIPAL GOLF CLUB
PU-801 Golf Course Rd., Bessemer, 35022, Jefferson County, (205)424-9540, 15 miles S of Birmingham.
Holes: 18. **Yards:** 6,320/5,034. **Par:** 72/75. **Course Rating:** 69.0/63.3. **Slope:** 119/107. **Green Fee:** $12/$15. **Cart Fee:** $10/person. **Walking Policy:** Walking at certain times. **Walkability:** 5. **Opened:** 1972. **Architect:** Earl Stone. **Season:** Year-round. **High:** May-Aug. **To obtain tee times:** First come, first served. **Miscellaneous:** Reduced fees (weekdays, low season, resort guests, twilight, seniors), metal spikes, club rentals, credit cards (MC, V, AE, D).

★★★½ GLENLAKES GOLF CLUB
SP-9530 Clubhouse Dr., Foley, 36535, Baldwin County, (334)955-1221, (800)435-5253, 50 miles SE of Mobile. **Web:** www.glenlakesgolf.com.
Holes: 18. **Yards:** 6,938/5,384. **Par:** 72/72. **Course Rating:** 72.2/70.5. **Slope:** 123/115. **Green Fee:** $23/$37. **Cart Fee:** $13/person. **Walking Policy:** Mandatory cart. **Walkability:** 4. **Opened:**

1987. **Architect:** Robert von Hagge/Bruce Devlin. **Season:** Year-round. **High:** Jan.April. **To obtain tee times:** Call up to 6 months in advance. **Miscellaneous:** Reduced fees (weekdays, low season, resort guests, twilight, juniors), discount packages, metal spikes, range (grass), club rentals, credit cards (MC, V, AE, D).
Reader Comments: Interesting back nine ... Front nine quirky; back nine better... Some blind shots ... Need different game and mindset for each nine ... A little bit of Scotland ... Love this course.

★★★★ GOOSE POND COLONY GOLF COURSE
R-417 Ed Hembree Dr., Scottsboro, 35769, Jackson County, (256)574-5353, (800)268-2884, 40 miles E of Huntsville.
Holes: 18. **Yards:** 6,860/5,370. **Par:** 72/72. **Course Rating:** 71.7/70.0. **Slope:** 125/115. **Green Fee:** $14/$21. **Cart Fee:** $9/person. **Walking Policy:** Walking at certain times. **Walkability:** N/A. **Opened:** 1968. **Architect:** George Cobb. **Season:** Year-round. **High:** April-Aug. **To obtain tee times:** Call up to 3 days in advance. Call Monday for upcoming weekend. **Miscellaneous:** Reduced fees (weekdays, resort guests, seniors, juniors), discount packages, metal spikes, range (grass), club rentals, lodging, credit cards (MC, V, D).
Reader Comments: Take name literally: Watch your step! ... Majestic view of Tennessee River ... Nice course really good greens and fairways ... Nice scenery, lots of water. Overall, pleasurable ... My favorite course in Alabama.

GRAND NATIONAL GOLF CLUB *Service*
PU-3000 Sunbelt Pkwy., Opelika, 36801, Lee County, (334)749-9042, (800)949-4444, 55 miles E of Montgomery.
★★★★½ LAKE COURSE *Value*
Holes: 18. **Yards:** 7,149/4,910. **Par:** 72/72. **Course Rating:** 74.9/68.7. **Slope:** 138/117. **Green Fee:** $39/$49. **Cart Fee:** $19/person. **Walking Policy:** Unrestricted walking. **Walkability:** 3. **Opened:** 1992. **Architect:** Robert Trent Jones. **Season:** Year-round. **High:** March-Oct. **To obtain tee times:** Call 334-749-9042 for tee times inside 7 days. Call 800-949-4444 for advance reservations. **Miscellaneous:** Reduced fees (low season, juniors), discount packages, metal spikes, range (grass), club rentals, credit cards (MC, V, AE, D).
Notes: Ranked 5th in 1999 Best in State; 7th in 1996 America's Top 75 Affordable Courses. 1998 LPGA Tournament of Champions site.
Reader Comments: RTJ, what else can I say ... Good people ... What a test, but are greens fair? ... Pleasurable & dreadful ... Play every club in bag ... Tough for average golfer... Crown jewel of trail ... Premium on approach shots to green ... Every par is earned ... Nike Championship conditions a treat! ... LPGA plays here.
★★★★½ LINKS COURSE *Value*
Holes: 18. **Yards:** 7,311/4,843. **Par:** 72/72. **Course Rating:** 74.9/69.6. **Slope:** 141/113. **Green Fee:** $39/$49. **Cart Fee:** $19/person. **Walking Policy:** Unrestricted walking. **Walkability:** 4. **Opened:** 1992. **Architect:** Robert Trent Jones. **Season:** Year-round. **High:** March-Oct. **To obtain tee times:** Call 334-749-9042 for tee times inside 7 days. Call 800-949-4444 for advance reservations. **Miscellaneous:** Reduced fees (low season, juniors), discount packages, metal spikes, range (grass), club rentals, credit cards (MC, V, AE, D).
Notes: Ranked 7th in 1999 Best in State; 9th in 1996 America's Top 75 Affordable Courses.
Reader Comments: Best course I've ever played ... Tough for average players ... Future top 100 ... No. 18 breathtaking ... Every hole a distinct visual masterpiece. Greens very elevated, collarless, fast and undulating. Knowing distance a must ... Have A+ game in bag ... Challenging course cut through the tall pines of Alabama.
★★★★½ SHORT COURSE *Value+, Condition, Pace+*
Holes: 18. **Yards:** 3,328/1,715. **Par:** 54/54. **Course Rating:** N/A. **Slope:** N/A. **Green Fee:** $15/$15. **Cart Fee:** $12/person. **Walking Policy:** Unrestricted walking. **Walkability:** 4. **Opened:** 1992. **Architect:** Robert Trent Jones. **Season:** Year-round. **High:** March-Oct. **To obtain tee times:** Call 334-749-9042 for tee times inside 7 days. Call 800-949-4444 for advance reservations. **Miscellaneous:** Reduced fees (juniors), discount packages, metal spikes, range (grass), club rentals, credit cards (MC, V, AE, D).
Reader Comments: Best short course on the trail ... Best anywhere ... A world-class par 3 course ... Very well run and friendly ... Fun ... Super layout, equal to most long courses. Real challenge.
Special Notes: Part of the Robert Trent Jones Golf Trail.

★★½ GULF SHORES GOLF CLUB
SP-520 Clubhouse Dr., Gulf Shores, 36547, Baldwin County, (334)968-7366, 20 miles W of Pensacola, FL.
Holes: 18. **Yards:** 6,570/5,522. **Par:** 72/72. **Course Rating:** 70.2/70.9. **Slope:** 110/118. **Green Fee:** $32/$40. **Cart Fee:** Included in Green Fee. **Walking Policy:** Mandatory cart. **Walkability:** 1. **Opened:** 1964. **Architect:** Boots Lang. **Season:** Year-round. **High:** Jan.-Aug. **To obtain tee times:** Call golf shop 5 days in advance. **Miscellaneous:** Reduced fees (juniors), range (grass), club rentals, credit cards (MC, V).

ALABAMA

Reader Comments: Use every club, open ... Looks easy, but water on 12 holes ... Tough par 3s ... Nice course, big greens, good shape ... Great pro ... Old, traditional course ... Enjoyable.

★★★ GULF STATE PARK GOLF COURSE

PM-20115 State Hwy. 135, Gulf Shores, 36542, Baldwin County, (334)948-4653, 50 miles W of Mobile.

Holes: 18. **Yards:** 6,563/5,310. **Par:** 72/72. **Course Rating:** 72.5/70.4. **Slope:** N/A. **Green Fee:** $20/$22. **Cart Fee:** $13/person. **Walking Policy:** Unrestricted walking. **Walkability:** 1. **Opened:** 1974. **Architect:** Earl Stone. **Season:** Year-round. **High:** Feb.-April/June-Aug. **To obtain tee times:** Call day before for weekdays, for weekends, call from Wednesday on. **Miscellaneous:** Reduced fees (resort guests, seniors), discount packages, metal spikes, range (grass), club rentals, lodging, credit cards (MC, V, AE).
Reader Comments: Great course for walkers/seniors ... Good condition ... Heavy play ... Very windy ... Greens slow ... One of the better state park courses ... Great morale-builder. Snowbird course ... Flat course with fun, interesting holes.

★★★★ GUNTER'S LANDING GOLF COURSE

SP-1000 Gunter's Landing Rd., Gunterville, 35976, Marshall County, (256)582-3586, (800)833-6663, 35 miles SE of Huntsville.

Holes: 18. **Yards:** 6,863/5,274. **Par:** 72/72. **Course Rating:** 73.3/70.0. **Slope:** 144/113. **Green Fee:** $35/$45. **Cart Fee:** Included in Green Fee. **Walking Policy:** Walking at certain times. **Walkability:** 5. **Opened:** 1992. **Architect:** Jim Kennamer. **Season:** Year-round. **High:** March-Sept. **To obtain tee times:** Call 7 days in advance for weekdays; Thursday prior for weekends. **Miscellaneous:** Reduced fees (weekdays, low season, twilight, seniors, juniors), discount packages, range (grass), credit cards (MC, V, AE, D).
Reader Comments: Good golf, one of my favorites ... Continues to improve ... Take lots of balls ... Spectacular front nine ... Good overall, limited views of lake.

HAMPTON COVE GOLF CLUB *Service*

PU-450 Old Hwy. 431 S., Huntsville, 35763, Madison County, (256)551-1818, (800)949-4444, 5 miles SE of Huntsville.

★★★½ HIGHLANDS COURSE

Holes: 18. **Yards:** 7,262/4,766. **Par:** 72/72. **Course Rating:** 74.1/66.0. **Slope:** 134/118. **Green Fee:** $34/$49. **Cart Fee:** $19/person. **Walking Policy:** Unrestricted walking. **Walkability:** 3. **Opened:** 1992. **Architect:** Robert Trent Jones Sr. **Season:** Year-round. **High:** March-Oct. **To obtain tee times:** Call golf shop or 800 number. **Miscellaneous:** Reduced fees (weekdays, twilight, seniors, juniors), discount packages, metal spikes, range (grass), club rentals, credit cards (MC, V, AE, D).
Reader Comments: Good, not great ... Hard, great course ... Not for the high handicap ... Nice layout. Some holes tough to judge ... Target golf.

★★★½ RIVER COURSE

Holes: 18. **Yards:** 7,507/5,283. **Par:** 72/72. **Course Rating:** 75.6/67.0. **Slope:** 135/118. **Green Fee:** $34/$49. **Cart Fee:** $19/person. **Walking Policy:** Unrestricted walking. **Walkability:** 2. **Opened:** 1993. **Architect:** Robert Trent Jones. **Season:** Year-round. **High:** March-Oct. **To obtain tee times:** Call golf shop or 800 number. **Miscellaneous:** Reduced fees (weekdays, twilight, juniors), discount packages, metal spikes, range (grass), club rentals, credit cards (MC, V, AE, D).
Reader Comments: Outstanding golf ... No sand bunkers, but still tough ... Needs yardage markers in fairway ... Country club atmosphere at a daily fee course. Outstanding service ... A challenging course, good facilities ... Greens are the devil to conquer ... Lots of water.

★★★★ SHORT COURSE

Holes: 18. **Yards:** 3,140/1,829. **Par:** 59/59. **Course Rating:** N/A. **Slope:** N/A. **Green Fee:** $15/$15. **Cart Fee:** $12/person. **Walking Policy:** Unrestricted walking. **Walkability:** 2. **Opened:** 1993. **Architect:** Robert Trent Jones Sr. **Season:** Year Round. **High:** March-Oct. **To obtain tee times:** Call golf shop or 800 number. **Miscellaneous:** Reduced fees (juniors), discount packages, metal spikes, range (grass), club rentals, credit cards (MC, V, AE, D), beginner friendly.
Reader Comments: Great, tough par 3 course ... Positive, could improve on turf and tee boxes ... Fun for golfers of any level ... Great practice for iron play, enjoyable ... Not typical par 3 course—200 yard par 3s over water.
Special Notes: Part of the Robert Trent Jones Golf Trail.

HIDDEN VALLEY GOLF CLUB

PU-Rte. 2, Bryant, 35958, Jackson County, (205)495-9608.
Special Notes: Call club for further information.

HIGH POINT GOLF CLUB

PM-4603 Golf Way Dr., Eight Mile, 36613, Mobile County, 334-452-6531.
Special Notes: Call club for further information.

ALABAMA

HIGHLAND OAKS GOLF COURSE *Service*
PU-904 Royal Pkwy., Dothan, 36305, Houston County, (334)712-2820, (800)949-4444, 100 miles S of Montgomery. **E-mail:** RTJDothan@cyber-south.com. **Web:** golf.jsu.edu.
Holes: 27. **Green Fee:** $29/$39. **Cart Fee:** $15/person. **Walking Policy:** Unrestricted walking. **Walkability:** 2. **Opened:** 1993. **Architect:** Robert Trent Jones. **Season:** Year-round. **High:** March-Oct. **To obtain tee times:** Call up to 7 days in advance. **Miscellaneous:** Reduced fees (low season, twilight, seniors, juniors), discount packages, metal spikes, range (grass), club rentals, credit cards (MC, V, AE, D).
★★★★½ **HIGHLANDS/MAGNOLIA** *Value, Pace*
Yards: 7,591/6,025. **Par:** 72/72. **Course Rating:** 76.0/67.6. **Slope:** 135/118.
Reader Comments: Each hole a new challenge ... Good course, slow play ... Well kept, clean and excellent service ... Play recommended tees ... Outstanding ... Marshwood 9 is superb ... Enjoyable golf experience ... Large bunkers everywhere the ball goes ... Everything 1st class ... Another trail delight, beautiful bermuda greens.
★★★★½ **HIGHLANDS/MARSHWOOD** *Pace*
Yards: 7,704/5,085. **Par:** 72/72. **Course Rating:** 76.9/68.3. **Slope:** 138/120.
Reader Comments: Beautiful ... Best course I have ever played ... Risk/reward is abundant. Elevated greens ... Most playable R.T. Jones course in Alabama.
★★★★½ **MARSHWOOD/MAGNOLIA** *Pace*
Yards: 7,511/6,002. **Par:** 72/72. **Course Rating:** 75.7/67.3. **Slope:** 133/116.
Notes: Ranked 31st in 1996 America's Top 75 Affordable Courses.
Reader Comments: Friendly people ... A gem. Tough challenge ... A must play in southeastern Alabama ... Great condition ... Very long, plush ... Beautiful.
Special Notes: Complex also includes Short Course, a 9-hole par-3 layout.

HIGHLAND PARK GOLF
PU-3300 Highland Ave., Birmingham, 35205, Jefferson County, (205)322-1902.
Holes: 18. **Yards:** 5,801/4,793. **Par:** 70/70. **Course Rating:** 68.1/63.8. **Slope:** 128/114. **Green Fee:** $23/$28. **Cart Fee:** $10/person. **Walking Policy:** Walking at certain times. **Walkability:** 3. **Opened:** 1998. **Architect:** Bob Cupp. **To obtain tee times:** Call up to 3 days in advance. **Miscellaneous:** Reduced fees (twilight, seniors, juniors), range (grass/mats), club rentals, credit cards (MC, V, AE).
Special Notes: Formerly Boswell Highland Golf Club.

★★ **HUNTSVILLE MUNICIPAL GOLF COURSE**
PM-2151 Airport Rd., Huntsville, 35801, Madison County, (256) 880-1151.
Holes: 18. **Yards:** 6,719/4,782. **Par:** 72/72. **Course Rating:** 70.2/63.4. **Slope:** 122/109. **Green Fee:** $14/$15. **Cart Fee:** $8/person. **Walking Policy:** Unrestricted walking. **Walkability:** 2. **Opened:** 1986. **Architect:** Ron Kirby/Denis Griffiths. **Season:** Year-round. **High:** April-Oct. **To obtain tee times:** Call golf shop. **Miscellaneous:** Reduced fees (weekdays, twilight, juniors), metal spikes, club rentals, credit cards (MC, V, AE).

INDIAN OAKS GOLF CLUB
SP-201 Cherokee Trail, Anniston, 36201, Calhoun County, (256)820-4030.
Holes: 18. **Yards:** 6,549/5,177. **Par:** 72/72. **Course Rating:** 71.4/68.0. **Slope:** 125/106. **Green Fee:** $20/$29. **Cart Fee:** $11/person. **Walking Policy:** Unrestricted walking. **Walkability:** 4. **Opened:** 1970. **Season:** Year round. **High:** April-October. **To obtain tee times:** Call up to 2 weeks in advance. **Miscellaneous:** Reduced fees (weekdays, twilight, seniors), range (grass), club rentals, credit cards (MC, V).

★★★ **INDIAN PINES GOLF CLUB**
PU-900 Country Club Lane, Auburn, 36830, Lee County, (334)821-0880, 50 miles W of Montgomery.
Holes: 18. **Yards:** 6,213/4,751. **Par:** 71/71. **Course Rating:** 68.8/62.1. **Slope:** 119/105. **Green Fee:** $11/$16. **Cart Fee:** $9/person. **Walking Policy:** Unrestricted walking. **Walkability:** 2. **Opened:** 1976. **Season:** Year-round. **High:** March-Sept. **To obtain tee times:** Call up to 7 days in advance. **Miscellaneous:** Metal spikes, range (grass/mats), club rentals, credit cards (MC, V), beginner friendly (ladies and junior programs).
Reader Comments: Great public course, great service, nice greens, more than reasonable price ... Slow play, but nice course ... Much improved course—friendly staff ... You can walk for $11 ... Fun.

★★ **ISLE DAUPHINE GOLF CLUB**
PU-100 Orleans Dr., P.O. Box 39, Dauphin Island, 36528, Mobile County, (334)861-2433, 30 miles S of Mobile.
Holes: 18. **Yards:** 6,620/5,619. **Par:** 72/72. **Course Rating:** 70.8/72.6. **Slope:** 123/122. **Green Fee:** $13/$14. **Cart Fee:** $12/person. **Walking Policy:** Unrestricted walking. **Walkability:** 2. **Opened:** 1958. **Architect:** Charles Maddox. **Season:** Year-round. **High:** Jan.-April. **To obtain tee times:** Call up to 3 days in advance. **Miscellaneous:** Reduced fees (weekdays, twilight, juniors), metal spikes, club rentals, credit cards (MC, V).

ALABAMA

★½ JETPORT GOLF COURSE
125 Earl St., Huntsville, 35805, Madison County, (205)772-9872.
Special Notes: Call club for further information.

★★½ JOE WHEELER STATE PARK GOLF COURSE
R-Rte. 4, Box 369A, Rogersville, 35652, Lauderdale County, (256)247-9308, (800)252-7275, 20
miles E of Florence.
Holes: 18. **Yards:** 7,251/6,055. **Par:** 72/72. **Course Rating:** 73.1/67.7. **Slope:** 120/109. **Green
Fee:** $15/$15. **Cart Fee:** $18/cart. **Walking Policy:** Unrestricted walking. **Walkability:** 4.
Opened: 1974. **Architect:** Earl Stone. **Season:** Year-round. **High:** March-Oct. **To obtain tee
times:** March to October tee times required for weekends and holidays taken Monday before
play. **Miscellaneous:** Reduced fees (resort guests, seniors), discount packages, metal spikes,
range (grass), club rentals, lodging (75 rooms), credit cards (MC, V, AE).
Reader Comments: Beautiful course on banks of the Tennessee River ... Fun place. Don't be
short on No. 17, you have to reach green ... Good state park course ... Very good par 3s ... Wide
fairways, challenging par 3s, long.

★★★★ KIVA DUNES GOLF CLUB   *Condition*
PU-815 Plantation Dr., Gulf Shores, 36542, Baldwin County, (334)540-7000, 45 miles W of
Pensacola, FL. **E-mail:** kivadune@gulftel.com. **Web:** kivadunes-golf.com.
Holes: 18. **Yards:** 7,092/4,994. **Par:** 72/72. **Course Rating:** 73.9/68.5. **Slope:** 132/115. **Green
Fee:** $55/$75. **Cart Fee:** Included in Green Fee. **Walking Policy:** Unrestricted walking.
Walkability: 2. **Opened:** 1995. **Architect:** Jerry Pate. **Season:** Year-round. **High:** Feb.-Oct. **To
obtain tee times:** Guests may call up to 60 days in advance. **Miscellaneous:** Reduced fees
(low season), discount packages, range (grass), club rentals, lodging (23 rooms), credit cards
(MC, V, AE, D).
Notes: Ranked 4th in 1999 Best in State; 2nd in 1995 Best New Public Courses.
Reader Comments: Huge everything, fairways, bunkers and greens ... Visually intimidating on
some holes (look harder than they are) ... Watch out for wind! ... Challenge from start to finish ...
Lots of sand and water ... Nice chipping areas around greens.

★★★½ LAGOON PARK GOLF COURSE
PM-2855 Lagoon Park Dr., Montgomery, 36109, Montgomery County, (334)271-7000.
Holes: 18. **Yards:** 6,773/5,342. **Par:** 72/72. **Course Rating:** 71.1/69.6. **Slope:** 124/113. **Green
Fee:** $15/$25. **Cart Fee:** $12/person. **Walking Policy:** Unrestricted walking. **Walkability:** 1.
Opened: 1978. **Architect:** Charles M. Graves. **Season:** Year-round. **High:** April-Oct. **To obtain
tee times:** Call Thursday a.m. for weekend tee times. No reserved times during week.
Miscellaneous: Reduced fees (weekdays, low season), discount packages, range (grass/mats),
club rentals, credit cards (MC, V, D).
Reader Comments: Very crowded, good layout ... Best around ... Outstanding municipal course
... Slow play ... Tough ... Excellent city course.

★★★½ LAKE GUNTERSVILLE GOLF CLUB   *Value*
PU-7966 Alabama Hwy. 227, Guntersville, 35976, Marshall County, (205)582-0379, 40 miles S
of Huntsville.
Holes: 18. **Yards:** 6,785/5,776. **Par:** 72/72. **Course Rating:** 71.2/70.3. **Slope:** 128/124. **Green
Fee:** $16/$16. **Cart Fee:** $20/cart. **Walking Policy:** Unrestricted walking. **Walkability:** 4.
Opened: 1974. **Architect:** Earl Stone. **Season:** Year-round. **High:** July-Aug. **To obtain tee
times:** Call Wednesday prior to weekend. Tee times for weekends and holidays only.
Miscellaneous: Reduced fees (seniors), discount packages, metal spikes, range (grass), club
rentals, lodging (100 rooms), credit cards (MC, V, AE).
Reader Comments: Good course but no water on whole course ... Good fun, great value ...
Good course but needs improvement ... Must try.

★★ LAKEPOINT RESORT GOLF COURSE
R-Hwy. 431, Eufaula, 36027, Barbour County, (334)687-6677, (800)544-5253, 50 miles N of
Columbus, GA.
Holes: 18. **Yards:** 6,752/5,363. **Par:** 72/72. **Course Rating:** 73.6/69.2. **Slope:** 123/N/A. **Green
Fee:** $14/$14. **Cart Fee:** $9/person. **Walking Policy:** Unrestricted walking. **Walkability:** 3.
Opened: 1971. **Architect:** Thomas Nicol. **Season:** Year-round. **High:** March-June. **To obtain tee
times:** Call for weekends tee times only. **Miscellaneous:** Reduced fees (seniors), discount pack-
ages, metal spikes, range (grass), club rentals, lodging (250 rooms), credit cards (MC, V, AE).

LIMESTONE SPRINGS GOLF CLUB
SP-3000 Colonial Dr., Oneonta, 35121, Blount County, (205)274-4653, 31 miles N of
Birmingham. **Web:** limestonesprings.com.
Holes: 18. **Yards:** 6,987/5,042. **Par:** 72/72. **Course Rating:** 74.2/69.6. **Slope:** 139/128. **Green
Fee:** $65/$65. **Cart Fee:** $12/person. **Walking Policy:** Unrestricted walking. **Walkability:** 2.
Opened: 1999. **Architect:** Jerry Pate. **Season:** Year-round. **High:** April-Nov. **To obtain tee

ALABAMA

times: Call (205)274-4653 up to 7 days in advance. **Miscellaneous:** Reduced fees (juniors), range (grass), club rentals, credit cards (MC, V, AE, D).
Notes: Ranked 8th in 1999 Best New Upscale Public.

★★½ THE LINKSMAN GOLF CLUB
PU-3700 St. Andrews Dr., Mobile, 36693, Mobile County, (334)661-0018, 50 miles W of Pensacola.
Holes: 18. **Yards:** 6,275/5,416. **Par:** 72/72. **Course Rating:** 70.1/71.0. **Slope:** 123/121. **Green Fee:** $18/$18. **Cart Fee:** $11/person. **Walking Policy:** Unrestricted walking. **Walkability:** N/A.
Opened: 1987. **Season:** Year-round. **High:** March-June. **To obtain tee times:** Call golf shop.
Miscellaneous: Reduced fees (weekdays, resort guests, twilight, seniors, juniors), discount packages, metal spikes, range (grass), club rentals, credit cards (MC, V, AE, D).
Reader Comments: Bring your flippers for the back 9, water every hole ... Floating balls a must ... Nice staff ... Water, water everywhere.

MAGNOLIA GROVE GOLF CLUB *Service*
PU-7000 Lamplighter Dr., Semmes, 36575, Mobile County, (334)645-0075, (800)949-4444, 16 miles E of Mobile.
★★★★½ CROSSINGS COURSE *Value+, Pace*
Holes: 18. **Yards:** 7,151/5,184. **Par:** 72/72. **Course Rating:** 74.6/70.4. **Slope:** 134/131. **Green Fee:** $34/$49. **Cart Fee:** $15/person. **Walking Policy:** Unrestricted walking. **Walkability:** 3.
Opened: 1992. **Architect:** Robert Trent Jones. **Season:** Year-round. **High:** Feb.-April, October.
To obtain tee times: Call golf shop up to 7 days in advance. Over 7 days call 1-800-949-4444.
Miscellaneous: Reduced fees (weekdays, low season, twilight, seniors, juniors), discount packages, metal spikes, range (grass), club rentals, credit cards (MC, V, AE, D).
Notes: Ranked 50th in 1996 America's Top 75 Affordable Courses.
Reader Comments: Excellent, all kinds of holes, short, long ... Bring balls! ... Excellent southern hospitality ... Very underrated, excellent value ... Beautiful ... Great undulating greens, elevation changes ... More user-friendly than Falls ... Difficult for high handicappers ... Target golf, demanding, super.

★★★★ FALLS COURSE *Value*
Holes: 18. **Yards:** 7,239/5,253. **Par:** 72/72. **Course Rating:** 75.1/71.0. **Slope:** 137/126. **Green Fee:** $34/$49. **Cart Fee:** $15/person. **Walking Policy:** Unrestricted walking. **Walkability:** 4.
Opened: 1992. **Architect:** Robert Trent Jones. **Season:** Year-round. **High:** Feb.-April, October.
To obtain tee times: Call golf shop up to 7 days in advance. Over 7 days call 1-800-949-4444.
Miscellaneous: Reduced fees (weekdays, low season, twilight, seniors, juniors), discount packages, metal spikes, range (grass), club rentals, credit cards (MC, V, AE, D).
Notes: Ranked 10th in 1999 Best in State; 43rd in 1996 America's Top 75 Affordable Courses.
Reader Comments: Bring your 'A' game, no bailout area ... Greens with slopes in every direction ... Tough for average players, fine course ... Great staff ... Not for the faint of heart ... Toughest rough I've ever seen. Greens beautiful, good rangers ... Great course for any golfer.

★★★★½ SHORT COURSE *Value+, Condition, Pace+*
Holes: 18. **Yards:** 3,140/1,829. **Par:** 54/54. **Course Rating:** N/A. **Slope:** N/A. **Green Fee:** $15/$15. **Cart Fee:** $10/person. **Walking Policy:** Unrestricted walking. **Walkability:** 3. **Opened:** 1992. **Architect:** Robert Trent Jones. **Season:** Year-round. **High:** April-Oct. **To obtain tee times:** Call golf shop up to 7 days in advance. Over 7 days call 1-800-949-4444. **Miscellaneous:** Reduced fees (weekdays, juniors), discount packages, metal spikes, range (grass), credit cards (MC, V, AE, D).
Reader Comments: Friendliest people ... Difficult, fair ... If you conquer this baby, pin the par-3 medal on you ... What a blast ... Hills, valleys, marshes and water make this the best 'short' course ever played.
Special Notes: Part of the Robert Trent Jones Golf Trail.

MARCUM COUNTRY CLUB
SP-9621 Bagley Rd., Empire, 35063, Jefferson County, (205)647-3377.
Special Notes: Call club for further information.

MARRIOTT'S LAKEWOOD GOLF CLUB
R-Marriott's Grand Hotel, Scenic Hwy. 98, Point Clear, 36564, Baldwin County, (334)990-6312, (800)544-9933, 30 miles SE of Mobile.
★★★½ AZALEA COURSE
Holes: 18. **Yards:** 6,770/5,307. **Par:** 72/72. **Course Rating:** 72.5/71.3. **Slope:** 128/118. **Green Fee:** $69/$84. **Cart Fee:** Included in Green Fee. **Walking Policy:** Mandatory cart. **Walkability:** 2. **Opened:** 1947. **Architect:** Perry Maxwell/Ron Garl. **Season:** Year-round. **High:** Feb.-May, Oct.-Dec. **To obtain tee times:** Must be a guest of hotel or guest of member to play.
Miscellaneous: Reduced fees (twilight, juniors), discount packages, metal spikes, range (grass), club rentals, lodging (300 rooms), credit cards (MC, V, AE, D).
Reader Comments: Fine golf course ... Typical resort course ... Classic style and kept up well...Fun to play.

10

ALABAMA

★★★ DOGWOOD COURSE
Holes: 18. **Yards:** 6,676/5,532. **Par:** 71/72. **Course Rating:** 72.1/72.6. **Slope:** 124/122. **Green Fee:** $69/$84. **Cart Fee:** Included in Green Fee. **Walking Policy:** Mandatory cart. **Walkability:** 2. **Opened:** 1947. **Architect:** Perry Maxwell/Joe Lee. **Season:** Year-round. **High:** Feb.-May, Oct.-Dec. **To obtain tee times:** Must be a guest of hotel or guest of member to play. **Miscellaneous:** Reduced fees (twilight, juniors), discount packages, metal spikes, range (grass), club rentals, lodging (300 rooms), credit cards (MC, V, AE, D).
Reader Comments: Old-style course ... Hit all clubs ... Fine golf course ... Good old course needs updating to compete in area ... Good basic golf.

★★ MCFARLAND PARK GOLF COURSE
PM-James M. Spain Dr., Florence, 35630, Lauderdale County, (205)760-6428, 120 miles NW of Birmingham. **E-mail:** cparrish@floweb.com.
Holes: 18. **Yards:** 6,660/5,741. **Par:** 72/72. **Course Rating:** 71.9/72.9. **Slope:** 113/106. **Green Fee:** $6/$11. **Cart Fee:** $16/. **Walking Policy:** Unrestricted walking. **Walkability:** 2. **Opened:** 1972. **Architect:** Earl Stone. **Season:** Year-round. **High:** May-Oct. **To obtain tee times:** Call Tuesday before upcoming weekend and holidays. **Miscellaneous:** Reduced fees (low season, seniors, juniors), metal spikes, range (grass), club rentals, credit cards (MC, V).
Special Notes: Course closing end of 1999 for redesign. New municipal golf club opening planned for summer or fall of 2000.

★★★ THE MEADOWS GOLF COURSE
PU-1 Plantation Dr., Harpersville, 35078, Shelby County, (205)672-7529, 20 miles E of Birmingham.
Holes: 18. **Yards:** 6,823/5,275. **Par:** 72/72. **Course Rating:** 71.6/70.1. **Slope:** 122/119. **Green Fee:** $25/$30. **Cart Fee:** Included in Green Fee. **Walking Policy:** Walking at certain times. **Walkability:** 2. **Opened:** 1995. **Architect:** Steve Plumer. **Season:** Year-round. **To obtain tee times:** Call up to 5 days in advance; walk-ons during the week. **Miscellaneous:** Reduced fees (twilight, seniors, juniors), metal spikes, range (grass), club rentals, credit cards (MC, V, AE, D).
Reader Comments: Wide open ... Needs maturity ... Good prices, nice course.

MONTEVALLO GOLF CLUB
1481 Shelby County Hwy. 204, Montevallo, 35115, Shelby County, (205)665-8057, 30 miles S of Birmingham.
Holes: 18. **Yards:** 6,000/4,762. **Par:** 70/70. **Course Rating:** 66.0/70.0. **Slope:** 109/113. **Green Fee:** $12/$16. **Cart Fee:** $9/person. **Walking Policy:** Unrestricted walking. **Walkability:** 3. **Opened:** 1956. **Season:** Year-round. **High:** Feb.-May. **Miscellaneous:** Reduced fees (twilight, seniors, juniors), discount packages, range (grass), club rentals, credit cards (MC, V), beginner friendly.

MOUNTAIN VIEW GOLF CLUB
PU-3200 Mountain View Dr., Graysville, 35073, Jefferson County, (205)674-8362, 17 miles W of Birmingham. **Web:** golf.bizhosting.com.
Holes: 27. **Green Fee:** $25/$30. **Cart Fee:** Included in Green Fee. **Walking Policy:** Mandatory cart. **Walkability:** N/A. **Opened:** 1991. **Architect:** James Thursby. **Season:** Year-round. **High:** March-Oct. **To obtain tee times:** Call up to 3 days in advance for weekends.
★★½ RED/BLUE
Yards: 6,070/4,816. **Par:** 71/71. **Course Rating:** 69.3/69.4. **Slope:** 114/120. **Miscellaneous:** Reduced fees (twilight, seniors), club rentals, credit cards (MC, V, D).
Reader Comments: Short, fun course ... Good for your ego ... My favorite ... Always in good shape ... Never crowded ... Good prices, fun course.
★★½ RED/WHITE
Yards: 5,800/4,702. **Par:** 71/71. **Course Rating:** 67.5/67.5. **Slope:** 111/116. **Miscellaneous:** Reduced fees (twilight, seniors), club rentals, credit cards (MC, V, D).
Reader Comments: Hit fairways or else. Fair for average players. Low numbers for good players ... Good course. Fun to play, many level changes ... Easy on the game and eyes ... Good course, short—target golf ... Very scenic ... Lots of fun for short knockers.
★★½ WHITE/BLUE
Yards: 5,890/4,718. **Par:** 70/70. **Course Rating:** 68.4/68.5. **Slope:** 114/123. **Miscellaneous:** Reduced fees (twilight, seniors), credit cards (MC, V, D).

★★★ OAK MOUNTAIN STATE PARK GOLF COURSE
PU-Findley Dr., Pelham, 35124, Shelby County, (205)620-2522, 15 miles S of Birmingham. **Web:** www.bham.net/oakmtn.
Holes: 18. **Yards:** 6,748/5,615. **Par:** 72/72. **Course Rating:** 71.5/66.5. **Slope:** 127/117. **Green Fee:** $12/$18. **Cart Fee:** $18/person. **Walking Policy:** Unrestricted walking. **Walkability:** 2. **Opened:** 1974. **Architect:** Earl Stone. **Season:** Year-round. **High:** May-Sept. **To obtain tee times:** Call Mondays for upcoming Saturday, Tuesday for Sunday, Wednesday for Monday, etc. **Miscellaneous:** Reduced fees (seniors), discount packages, metal spikes, range (grass), lodging, credit cards (MC, V, AE).

Reader Comments: Great walk ... Hard to get a good tee time in summer months ... Good course to play. It's one of the cheapest courses in Birmingham.

OXMOOR VALLEY GOLF CLUB *Service*
PU-100 Sunbelt Pkwy., Birmingham, 35211, Jefferson County, (205)942-1177, (800)949-4444. **E-mail:** oxmoor@mindspring.com. **Web:** www.rtjgolf.com.

★★★★ **RIDGE COURSE**
Holes: 18. **Yards:** 7,055/4,869. **Par:** 72/72. **Course Rating:** 73.5/69.1. **Slope:** 140/122. **Green Fee:** $39/$49. **Cart Fee:** $15/person. **Walking Policy:** Unrestricted walking. **Walkability:** 4. **Opened:** 1992. **Architect:** Robert Trent Jones. **Season:** Year-round. **High:** April-Nov. **To obtain tee times:** Call course up to 7 days in advance. May reserve tee times up to 120 days in advance by calling toll free reservations number. **Miscellaneous:** Reduced fees (weekdays, low season, juniors), discount packages, metal spikes, range (grass), club rentals, credit cards (MC, V, AE, D).
Reader Comments: Beautiful, just beautiful ... Bring your mountain climbing gear... Severe hills and dales everywhere ... Excellent condition, difficult for a mid to high handicap ... Greens are fast and will make you pay ... Staff makes you feel very welcome ... Tough walk, challenging course, greens are crazy, fairways tight ... Perfection.

★★★★½ **SHORT COURSE** *Value, Condition, Pace*
Holes: 18. **Yards:** 3,154/1,990. **Par:** 54/54. **Course Rating:** N/A. **Slope:** N/A. **Green Fee:** $15/$15. **Walking Policy:** Unrestricted walking. **Walkability:** 4. **Opened:** 1992. **Architect:** Robert Trent Jones Sr. **Season:** Year-round. **High:** April-Nov. **To obtain tee times:** Call course up to 7 days in advance. May reserve tee times up to 120 days in advance by calling toll free reservations number. **Miscellaneous:** Reduced fees (juniors), discount packages, metal spikes, range (grass), club rentals, credit cards (MC, V, AE, D).
Reader Comments: Fantastic par-3 course ... Hilly ... Best deal in the state ... From back tees will use all of your clubs, fun to play.

★★★★ **VALLEY COURSE**
Holes: 18. **Yards:** 7,240/4,866. **Par:** 72/72. **Course Rating:** 73.9/69.4. **Slope:** 135/122. **Green Fee:** $39/$49. **Cart Fee:** $15/person. **Walking Policy:** Unrestricted walking. **Walkability:** 2. **Opened:** 1992. **Architect:** Robert Trent Jones Sr. **Season:** Year-round. **High:** April-Nov. **To obtain tee times:** Call course up to 7 days in advance. May reserve tee times up to 120 days in advance by calling toll free reservations office. **Miscellaneous:** Reduced fees (weekdays, low season, juniors), discount packages, metal spikes, range (grass), club rentals, credit cards (MC, V, AE, D).
Reader Comments: Generous fairways, undulating greens ... Best of the two at Oxmoor... Beautiful setting, relentless from tee to green ... Course management important ... Many elevation changes, good practice ... More forgiving than Ridge course ... Excellent shape, playing time was good.
Special Notes: Part of the Robert Trent Jones Golf Trail.

★★★★ THE PENINSULA GOLF CLUB
PU-20 Peninsula Blvd., Gulf Shores, 36542, Baldwin County, (334)968-8009, 50 miles S of Mobile. **Holes:** 27. **Yards:** 7,026/5,072. **Par:** 72/72. **Course Rating:** 74.7/69.6. **Slope:** 133/121. **Green Fee:** $45/$68. **Cart Fee:** Included in Green Fee. **Walking Policy:** Walking at certain times. **Walkability:** 2. **Opened:** 1995. **Architect:** Earl Stone. **Season:** Year-round. **High:** Feb.-May. **To obtain tee times:** Call up to 30 days in advance. **Miscellaneous:** Reduced fees (twilight, juniors), metal spikes, range (grass), club rentals, credit cards (MC, V, AE, D).
Reader Comments: Outstanding new course ... Greens a tougher read than Tolstoy! ... Super condition ... Lots of water, great layout ... Best overall for this area ... A full day's work from blue ... Plush and playable ... Beautiful clubhouse.

PIN OAKS GOLF CLUB
PU-US 29 South, P.O. Box 1792, Auburn, 36830-1792, Macon County, (334)821-0893, 4 miles S of of I-85 on US 29. **Holes:** 18. **Yards:** 6,208/5,497. **Par:** 72/72. **Course Rating:** N/A. **Slope:** 118/110. **Green Fee:** $12/$14. **Cart Fee:** $10/person. **Walking Policy:** Unrestricted walking. **Walkability:** 1. **Opened:** 1973. **Architect:** Gene Rutherford. **Season:** Year-round. **High:** April-June. **To obtain tee times:** Tee times not required but recommended. **Miscella-neous:** Reduced fees (seniors, juniors), range (grass), club rentals, beginner friendly.

PINE HILL COUNTRY CLUB
SP-175 Pine Hill Dr., Anniston, 36207, Calhoun County, (205)237-2633. **Holes:** 18. **Yards:** 6,191/5,545. **Par:** 72/72. **Course Rating:** 69.8/69.8. **Slope:** 115/115. **Green Fee:** $19/$21. **Cart Fee:** $12/person. **Walking Policy:** Unrestricted walking. **Walkability:** 2. **Season:** Year-round. **High:** April-July. **Miscellaneous:** Reduced fees (weekdays, low season, seniors), metal spikes, range (grass), club rentals, credit cards (MC, V), beginner friendly.

★★★ POINT MALLARD GOLF COURSE
PU-1800 Point Mallard Dr., Decatur, 35601, Morgan County, (256)351-7776, 20 miles SW of Huntsville.

Holes: 18. **Yards:** 7,113/5,437. **Par:** 72/73. **Course Rating:** 73.7/69.9. **Slope:** 125/115. **Green Fee:** $16/$16. **Cart Fee:** $12/person. **Walking Policy:** Unrestricted walking. **Walkability:** 1. **Opened:** 1970. **Architect:** Charles M. Graves. **Season:** Year-round. **High:** April-Sept. **To obtain tee times:** Call Thursday for Saturday tee times. **Miscella-neous:** Reduced fees (weekdays, low season, seniors, juniors), discount packages, metal spikes, range (grass/mats), club rentals, credit cards (MC, V), beginner friendly.

Reader Comments: Great course and layout for the money ... Good value ... Wide open, longer than it looks ... Well conditioned.

★★ QUAIL CREEK GOLF COURSE

PM-19841 Quail Creek Dr., Fairhope, 36532, Baldwin County, (334)990-0240, (888)701-2202, 20 miles SE of Mobile. **Web:** cofairhope.com.
Holes: 18. **Yards:** 6,426/5,305. **Par:** 72/72. **Course Rating:** 70.1/69.6. **Slope:** 112/114. **Green Fee:** $22/$22. **Cart Fee:** $10/person. **Walking Policy:** Walking at certain times. **Walkability:** 1. **Opened:** 1988. **Architect:** City Committee. **Season:** Year-round. **High:** Jan.-April. **To obtain tee times:** Call up to 3 days in advance. **Miscellaneous:** Reduced fees (twilight), discount packages, metal spikes, range (grass), club rentals, credit cards (MC, V, AE, D).

★★½ RIVER RUN GOLF COURSE

PU-P.O. Box 240873, Montgomery, 36124, Montgomery County, (334)271-2811, 3 miles E of Montgomery.
Holes: 18. **Yards:** 6,585/5,079. **Par:** 72/72. **Course Rating:** 69.4/68.6. **Slope:** 114/109. **Green Fee:** $15/$21. **Cart Fee:** $12/person. **Walking Policy:** Unrestricted walking. **Walkability:** 2. **Opened:** 1989. **Architect:** Cam Hardigree. **Season:** Year-round. **High:** March-Oct. **To obtain tee times:** Call 2 days in advance for weekends, 7 days for weekdays. **Miscellaneous:** Reduced fees (weekdays, twilight, juniors), discount packages, range (grass), club rentals, credit cards (MC, V, AE, D).

Reader Comments: Best course in Montgomery area ... Good consistent conditions.

★★★★ ROCK CREEK GOLF CLUB *Service*

SP-140 Clubhouse Dr., Fairhope, 36532, Baldwin County, (334)928-4223, (800)458-8815, 10 miles E of Mobile.
Holes: 18. **Yards:** 6,920/5,135. **Par:** 72/72. **Course Rating:** 72.2/68.4. **Slope:** 129/117. **Green Fee:** $59/$59. **Cart Fee:** Included in Green Fee. **Walking Policy:** Mandatory cart. **Walkability:** N/A. **Opened:** 1993. **Architect:** Earl Stone. **Season:** Year-round. **High:** Spring/Fall. **To obtain tee times:** Call golf shop. **Miscellaneous:** Reduced fees (twilight, juniors), discount packages, metal spikes, range (grass), club rentals, credit cards (MC, V, AE, D).

Reader Comments: Excellent condition ... Nice layout, friendly folks. I will go back ... Real golf ... Housing development course, good condition, worth a visit ... Hilly ... Can score here, some beautiful holes ... Challenging for all levels, great greens ... Love this course, pleeease drop the price ... 11 on a 10 scale.

ROEBUCK MUNICIPAL GOLF CLUB

PU-8920 Roebuck Rd., Birmingham, 35206, Jefferson County, (205)836-7318.
Special Notes: Call club for further information.

SILVER LAKES GOLF CLUB *Service*

PU-1 Sunbelt Pkwy., Glencoe, 35905, Calhoun County, (256)892-3268, (800)949-4444, 15 miles N of Anniston.

★★★★ HEARTBREAKER/BACKBREAKER *Condition*

Holes: 27. **Yards:** 7,674/4,907. **Par:** 72/72. **Course Rating:** 76.7/68.8. **Slope:** 131/120. **Green Fee:** $29/$39. **Cart Fee:** $15/person. **Walking Policy:** Unrestricted walking. **Walkability:** 3. **Opened:** 1993. **Architect:** Robert Trent Jones. **Season:** Year-round. **High:** March-May, Sept.-Nov. **To obtain tee times:** Call golf shop 7 a.m. till dark. **Miscellaneous:** Reduced fees (weekdays, low season, twilight, seniors, juniors), discount packages, metal spikes, range (grass), club rentals, credit cards (MC, V, AE, D).

Reader Comments: Great test for your game ... Elevated greens, lengthy, challenging ... One of the best in Alabama ... Fun, but tough ... Terrific course, outstanding greens ... Needs yardage markers in fairways ... Hard, enjoyable, not crowded ... Tough for high handicaps ... Nice course.

★★★★ MINDBREAKER/BACKBREAKER *Condition*

Holes: 27. **Yards:** 7,425/4,681. **Par:** 72/72. **Course Rating:** 75.2/67.5. **Slope:** 127/119. **Green Fee:** $29/$39. **Cart Fee:** $15/person. **Walking Policy:** Unrestricted walking. **Walkability:** 3. **Opened:** 1993. **Architect:** Robert Trent Jones. **Season:** Year-round. **High:** March-May, Sept.-Nov. **To obtain tee times:** Call golf shop 7 a.m. till dark. **Miscellaneous:** Reduced fees (weekdays, low season, twilight, seniors, juniors), discount packages, metal spikes, range (grass), club rentals, credit cards (MC, V, AE, D).

Reader Comments: Beautiful bent-grass greens, extremely challenging ... Truly outstanding golf, great management and service ... Elevated greens, take one more club ... Tough for beginners, makes you think ... Select tee box that fits your game ... Friendly and hospitable staff everywhere ... Tough but fun.

★★★★ **MINDBREAKER/HEARTBREAKER** *Condition*
Holes: 27. **Yards:** 7,407/4,860. **Par:** 72/72. **Course Rating:** 75.5/68.3. **Slope:** 132/122. **Green Fee:** $29/$39. **Cart Fee:** $15/person. **Walking Policy:** Unrestricted walking. **Walkability:** 3. **Opened:** 1993. **Architect:** Robert Trent Jones. **Season:** Year-round. **High:** March-May, Sept.-Nov. **To obtain tee times:** Call golf shop 7 a.m. till dark. **Miscellaneous:** Reduced fees (weekdays, low season, twilight, seniors, juniors), discount packages, metal spikes, range (grass), club rentals, credit cards (MC, V, AE, D).
Reader Comments: Classic Robert Trent Jones. Great condition ... Scenery is magnificent ... Truly outstanding golf, great management and service ... Hilly layout, tough greens ... Greater diversity of holes make this more interesting but not as hard as other courses here.
Special Notes: Part of the Robert Trent Jones Golf Trail. Complex also includes Short Course, a 9-hole par-3 layout.

STILL WATERS RESORT
R-797 Moonbrook Drive, Dadeville, 36853, Tallapoosa County, (256)825-1353, (888)797-3767, 55 miles NE of Montgomery. **E-mail:** swgolfshop@mindspring.com. **Web:** www.stillwaters.com.
★★★½ **THE LEGEND COURSE**
Holes: 18. **Yards:** 6,407/5,287. **Par:** 72/72. **Course Rating:** 69.9/71.5. **Slope:** 124/125. **Green Fee:** $31/$43. **Cart Fee:** $14/person. **Walking Policy:** Unrestricted walking. **Walkability:** 3. **Opened:** 1972. **Architect:** George Cobb. **Season:** Year-round. **High:** March-Oct. **To obtain tee times:** Call golf shop. **Miscellaneous:** Reduced fees (weekdays, twilight, juniors), discount packages, metal spikes, range (grass), club rentals, lodging (93 rooms), credit cards (MC, V, AE, D).
Reader Comments: How can a new course be called 'The Legend'? Still, a nice layout ... Super ... Very scenic ... Narrow and hilly ... Beautiful course, tight for the most part ... Greens were good.
★★★★ **THE TRADITION COURSE**
Holes: 18. **Yards:** 6,906/5,048. **Par:** 72/72. **Course Rating:** 73.5/69.5. **Slope:** 139/126. **Green Fee:** $31/$43. **Cart Fee:** $14/person. **Walking Policy:** Unrestricted walking. **Walkability:** 5. **Opened:** 1997. **Architect:** Kurt Sandness. **Season:** Year-round. **High:** March-Oct. **To obtain tee times:** Call golf shop. **Miscellaneous:** Reduced fees (weekdays, low season, twilight, juniors), discount packages, metal spikes, range (grass), club rentals, lodging (93 rooms), credit cards (MC, V, AE, D).
Reader Comments: Difficult ... Good course, great location, nice view ... Awesome elevation. Plays across steep gorges. Greens very undulating. Read greens several times, then pray. Great use of land, not contrived. Remote but well worth the trip.

★★ **STONEY MOUNTAIN GOLF COURSE**
PU-5200 Georgia Mtn. Rd., Guntersville, 35976, Marshall County, (205)582-2598, 25 miles S of Huntsville.
Holes: 18. **Yards:** 5,931/4,711. **Par:** 72/72. **Course Rating:** 67.6/66.2. **Slope:** 118/117. **Green Fee:** $17/$23. **Cart Fee:** $15/person. **Walking Policy:** Walking at certain times. **Walkability:** 3. **Season:** Year-round. **High:** April-Dec. **To obtain tee times:** Call golf shop. **Miscellaneous:** Reduced fees (weekdays, seniors), metal spikes, club rentals, credit cards (V).

★★★½ **TANNEHILL NATIONAL GOLF COURSE**
12863 Tannehill Pkwy., McCalla, 35111, Tuscaloosa County, (205)477-4653, (888)218-7888, 15 miles W of Birmingham. **Web:** www.tannehill.com.
Holes: 18. **Yards:** 6,630/5,440. **Par:** 72/72. **Course Rating:** 71.1/70.5. **Slope:** 121/119. **Green Fee:** $21/$31. **Cart Fee:** $14/person. **Walking Policy:** Unrestricted walking. **Walkability:** 2. **Opened:** 1996. **Architect:** Steve Plumer. **Season:** Year-round. **High:** April-July. **To obtain tee times:** Call golf shop. **Miscellaneous:** Reduced fees (weekdays), range (grass), club rentals, credit cards (MC, V, AE, D), beginner friendly.
Reader Comments: Nice course ... Great condition for a new course... Young public course, good potential ... Greens are fast and hard ... Great course for good price ... A most enjoyable course for the average golfer.

★★ **TIMBER RIDGE GOLF CLUB**
PU-101 Ironaton Rd., Talladega, 35160, Talladega County, (256)362-0346, 50 miles E of Birmingham.
Holes: 18. **Yards:** 6,521/5,028. **Par:** 71/71. **Course Rating:** 71.2/70.9. **Slope:** 126/122. **Green Fee:** $14/$30. **Cart Fee:** Included in Green Fee. **Walking Policy:** Unrestricted walking. **Walkability:** 3. **Opened:** 1989. **Architect:** Charlie Carter. **Season:** Year-round. **High:** June-Aug. **To obtain tee times:** Call 2 days in advance. **Miscellaneous:** Reduced fees (weekdays, twilight, seniors, juniors), range (grass), club rentals, credit cards (MC, V, AE).

TIMBERCREEK GOLF CLUB
PU-9650 TimberCreek Blvd., Daphne, 36527, Baldwin County, (334)621-9900, (877)621-9900, 10 miles E of Mobile. **E-mail:** timberck@gulftel.com. **Web:** www.golftimbercreek.com.
★★★★ **DOGWOOD/MAGNOLIA**
Holes: 27. **Yards:** 7,062/4,885. **Par:** 72/72. **Course Rating:** 73.8/66.7. **Slope:** 144/106. **Green Fee:** $29/$34. **Cart Fee:** $15/person. **Walking Policy:** Walking at certain times. **Walkability:** 3.

ALABAMA

Opened: 1993. **Architect:** Earl Stone. **Season:** Year-round. **To obtain tee times:** Call golf shop. **Miscellaneous:** Reduced fees (weekdays, resort guests, twilight, juniors), discount packages, range (grass), club rentals, credit cards (MC, V, AE).
Reader Comments: Great layout ... Dogwood No. 9 tough uphill par-4 finishing hole ... Great place to spend a day ... Three distinctively different nines. Play all 27 holes ... Worth every penny, felt like royalty, course was fit for a king and this was in February ... Very good driving range.

★★★★ **DOGWOOD/PINES**
Holes: 27. **Yards:** 6,928/4,911. **Par:** 72/72. **Course Rating:** 72.9/66.7. **Slope:** 137/105. **Green Fee:** $29/$34. **Cart Fee:** $15/person. **Walking Policy:** Walking at certain times. **Walkability:** 3.
Opened: 1993. **Architect:** Earl Stone. **Season:** Year-round. **To obtain tee times:** Call golf shop. **Miscellaneous:** Reduced fees (weekdays, resort guests, twilight, juniors), discount packages, range (grass), club rentals, credit cards (MC, V, AE).
Reader Comments: Excellent in all respects ... Great fun ... Beautiful layout. Rolling hills ... Excellent 27 holes of golf.

★★★★ **MAGNOLIA/PINES**
Holes: 27. **Yards:** 7,090/4,990. **Par:** 72/72. **Course Rating:** 74.3/67.8. **Slope:** 143/107. **Green Fee:** $29/$34. **Cart Fee:** $15/person. **Walking Policy:** Walking at certain times. **Walkability:** 3.
Opened: 1993. **Architect:** Earl Stone. **Season:** Year-round. **To obtain tee times:** Call golf shop. **Miscellaneous:** Reduced fees (weekdays, resort guests, twilight, juniors), discount packages, range (grass), club rentals, credit cards (MC, V, AE).
Reader Comments: Great course. Fun to play ... Good layout, excellent course ... Good staff/clubhouse/driving range ... Very fair, playable course.

★★ **TWIN LAKES GOLF COURSE**
PU-211 Golfview Dr., Arab, 35016, Marshall County, (205)586-3269, (800)213-3938, 15 miles S of Huntsville.
Holes: 18. **Yards:** 6,711/5,609. **Par:** 72/72. **Course Rating:** 70.9/67.4. **Slope:** 130/114. **Green Fee:** $14/$16. **Cart Fee:** $9/person. **Walking Policy:** Unrestricted walking. **Walkability:** 2.
Opened: 1963. **Season:** Year-round. **To obtain tee times:** Call up to 7 days in advance for weekends. **Miscellaneous:** Reduced fees (weekdays), metal spikes, club rentals, credit cards (MC, V, D).

★★½ **UNIVERSITY OF ALABAMA HARRY PRITCHETT GOLF COURSE**
PU-University of Alabama, Tuscaloosa, 35487, Tuscaloosa County, (205)348-7041.
Holes: 18. **Yards:** 6,180/5,047. **Par:** 71/71. **Course Rating:** 69.7/67.2. **Slope:** 126/121. **Green Fee:** $15/$17. **Cart Fee:** $12/person. **Walking Policy:** Unrestricted walking. **Walkability:** 3.
Architect: Harold Williams/Thomas Nicol. **Season:** Year-round. **High:** May, Aug.-Sept.
Miscellaneous: Reduced fees (weekdays, seniors, juniors), metal spikes, range (grass), club rentals, credit cards (MC, V, D).
Reader Comments: Tight, fast greens. Friendly staff ... Can be crowded.

★★★ **WARRIOR'S POINT GOLF CLUB**
PU-634 River's Edge Trail, Cordova, 35550, Walker County, (205)648-8866, 26 miles W of Birmingham.
Holes: 18. **Yards:** 6,526/6,526. **Par:** 72/72. **Course Rating:** 71.4/71.4. **Slope:** 125/125. **Green Fee:** N/A. **Cart Fee:** Included in Green Fee. **Walking Policy:** Mandatory cart. **Walkability:** 5.
Opened: 1996. **Architect:** Steve Hyche. **Season:** Year-round. **Miscellaneous:** Reduced fees (weekdays, seniors), metal spikes, credit cards (MC, V).
Reader Comments: Be in the fairway or there's trouble, lots of hills and water ... Very challenging and scenic ... Tremendous elevation change ... Can be slow.

★★ **WILLOW OAKS GOLF CLUB**
PU-330 Willow Oaks Dr., Ozark, 36360, Dale County, (334)774-7388.
Holes: 18. **Yards:** 6,001/6,001. **Par:** 72/72. **Course Rating:** 67.0/67.0. **Slope:** 110/110. **Green Fee:** $15/$21. **Cart Fee:** Included in Green Fee. **Walking Policy:** Unrestricted walking. **Walkability:** 4. **Season:** Year-round. **High:** June-Aug. **To obtain tee times:** First come, first served. **Miscellaneous:** Reduced fees (low season), metal spikes, range (grass).

WILLS CREEK COUNTRY CLUB
SP-216 Country Club Dr., Attala, 35954, Etowah County, (256)538-8781.
Holes: 18. **Yards:** 5,830/4,362. **Par:** 70/70. **Course Rating:** 66.6/67.4. **Slope:** 106/104. **Green Fee:** $10/$14. **Cart Fee:** $8/person. **Walking Policy:** Unrestricted walking. **Walkability:** 2.
Opened: 1965. **Season:** Year-round. **High:** March-Sept. **Miscellaneous:** Reduced fees (weekdays, low season), range (grass), club rentals, credit cards (MC, V, AE).
Special Notes: Formerly Attala Country Club.

ALASKA

★★★ ANCHORAGE GOLF COURSE
PU-3651 O'Malley Rd., Anchorage, 99516, Anchorage County, (907)522-3363.
Holes: 18. **Yards:** 6,616/4,848. **Par:** 72/72. **Course Rating:** 72.1/68.2. **Slope:** 130/119. **Green Fee:** $27/$27. **Cart Fee:** $13/person. **Walking Policy:** Walking at certain times. **Walkability:** 4. **Opened:** 1987. **Architect:** Bill Newcomb. **Season:** May-Oct. **High:** June-Aug. **To obtain tee times:** Residents call 5 days in advance, nonresidents 3 days in advance. **Miscellaneous:** Reduced fees (resort guests, seniors, juniors), metal spikes, range (grass), club rentals, credit cards (MC, V, AE, D).
Notes: Ranked 4th in 1999 Best in State.
Reader Comments: Nice greens. A lot of hills ... Short & tight ... A must to tee off after 8:00 pm ... Accuracy more important than length ... Nice views.

BIRCH RIDGE GOLF CLUB
PU-P.O. Box 828, Soldotna, 99669, Kenai County, (907)262-5270, 2 miles NE of Soldotna.
E-mail: birchridge@att.net.
Holes: 9. **Yards:** 5,900/4,873. **Par:** 70/69. **Course Rating:** 68.8/67.8. **Slope:** 120/115. **Green Fee:** $12/$20. **Cart Fee:** $20/cart. **Walking Policy:** Unrestricted walking. **Walkability:** 3. **Opened:** 1973. **Architect:** Thomas R. Smith. **Season:** May-Sept. **High:** June-Aug. **To obtain tee times:** Tee times required on weekends and holidays, call golf shop. **Miscellaneous:** Reduced fees (weekdays, resort guests, seniors, juniors), discount packages, metal spikes, range (grass/mats), club rentals, lodging (8 rooms), credit cards (MC, V, AE).

CHENA BEND GOLF CLUB
PU-Bldg. 2092 Gaffney Rd., Fort Wainwright, 99703, Fairbanks County, (907)353-6223.
Holes: 18. **Yards:** 7,012/5,516. **Par:** 72/72. **Course Rating:** 73.6/71.6. **Slope:** 128/117. **Green Fee:** $11/$30. **Cart Fee:** $21/cart. **Walking Policy:** Unrestricted walking. **Walkability:** 3. **Opened:** 1996. **Architect:** Jerry Matthews. **Season:** May-Sept. **High:** June-July. **To obtain tee times:** Authorized military may call up to 5 days in advance; all others up to 2 days in advance. **Miscellaneous:** Reduced fees (low season, twilight, seniors, juniors), range (grass/mats), club rentals, credit cards (MC, V).
Notes: Ranked 1st in 1999 Best in State.

★★★½ EAGLEGLEN GOLF COURSE
PU-4414 1st Street, Elmendorf AFB, 99506, Anchorage County, (907)552-3821, 2 miles N of Anchorage.
Holes: 18. **Yards:** 6,689/5,457. **Par:** 72/72. **Course Rating:** 71.6/70.4. **Slope:** 128/123. **Green Fee:** $25/$32. **Cart Fee:** $21/cart. **Walking Policy:** Unrestricted walking. **Walkability:** 2. **Opened:** 1973. **Architect:** Robert Trent Jones Jr. **Season:** May-Sept. **High:** June-July. **To obtain tee times:** Call reservation system or call day of play. **Miscellaneous:** Reduced fees (low season, twilight), range (mats), club rentals, credit cards (MC, V), beginner friendly (daily 3 hr. clinics on practice range).
Notes: Ranked 3rd in 1999 Best in State.
Reader Comments: Nice layout ... It's a fun walk ... Lots of birdies out there.

FAIRBANKS GOLF & COUNTRY CLUB
PU-1735 Farmers Loop, Fairbanks, 99709, Fairbanks County, (907)479-6555.
Holes: 9. **Yards:** 6,264/5,186. **Par:** 72/72. **Course Rating:** 69.8/69.9. **Slope:** 120/115. **Green Fee:** $22/$29. **Cart Fee:** $17/cart. **Walking Policy:** Unrestricted walking. **Walkability:** 3. **Opened:** 1946. **Season:** May-Sept. **High:** June-Aug. **To obtain tee times:** Call golf shop. **Miscellaneous:** Reduced fees (seniors, juniors), range (grass), club rentals, credit cards (MC, V).

★★ KENAI GOLF COURSE
PU-1420 Lawton Dr., Kenai, 99611, Kenai County, (907)283-7500, 3 miles E of Airport.
Holes: 18. **Yards:** 6,641/5,644. **Par:** 72/72. **Course Rating:** 73.2/74.4. **Slope:** 135/133. **Green Fee:** $15/$19. **Cart Fee:** $15/cart. **Walking Policy:** Unrestricted walking. **Walkability:** 3. **Opened:** 1986. **Season:** May-Sept. **High:** June-Aug. **To obtain tee times:** Call golf shop. **Miscellaneous:** Reduced fees (seniors, juniors), range (mats), club rentals, credit cards (MC, V).

★★½ MOOSE RUN GOLF COURSE
PU-P.O. Box 5130, Fort Richardson, 99505, Anchorage County, (907)428-0056, 1 miles E of Anchorage.
Holes: 18. **Yards:** 6,499/5,382. **Par:** 72/72. **Course Rating:** 69.8/70.0. **Slope:** 119/120. **Green Fee:** $28/$28. **Cart Fee:** $16/cart. **Walking Policy:** Unrestricted walking. **Walkability:** 2. **Architect:** U.S. Army. **Season:** May-Oct. **High:** July-Aug. **To obtain tee times:** Call golf shop up to 4 days prior to day of play. **Miscellaneous:** Reduced fees (twilight), credit cards (MC, V).
Notes: Ranked 5th in 1999 Best in State.
Reader Comments: Very small greens. Adding new 18 holes for year 2000 ... Beautiful scenery ... Interesting front nine.

NORTH STAR GOLF COURSE
SP-330 Golf Club Dr., Fairbanks, 99712, Fairbanks County, (907)457-4653, 4 miles N of Fairbanks.
Holes: 18. **Yards:** 6,852/5,995. **Par:** 72/72. **Course Rating:** N/A. **Slope:** N/A. **Green Fee:** $20/$24. **Cart Fee:** $14/person. **Walking Policy:** Walking at certain times. **Walkability:** 1. **Opened:** 1993. **Architect:** Jack Stallings. **Season:** May-Oct. **High:** June-Sept. **To obtain tee times:** Call 1 day in advance. **Miscellaneous:** Reduced fees (weekdays, resort guests, juniors), metal spikes, range (grass/mats), club rentals, credit cards (MC, V).

★½ PALMER GOLF COURSE
PU-1000 Lepak Ave., Palmer, 99645, Matanuska County, (907)745-4653, 42 miles N of Anchorage.
Holes: 18. **Yards:** 7,125/5,895. **Par:** 72/73. **Course Rating:** 74.5/74.6. **Slope:** 132/127. **Green Fee:** $20/$22. **Cart Fee:** $18/person. **Walking Policy:** Unrestricted walking. **Walkability:** N/A. **Opened:** 1990. **Architect:** Illiad Group. **Season:** May-Sep. **High:** May-July. **To obtain tee times:** Call golf shop. **Miscellaneous:** Reduced fees (seniors, juniors), discount packages, metal spikes, range (grass), club rentals, credit cards (MC, V).

★★½ SETTLERS BAY GOLF CLUB
PU-Mile 8 Knik Rd., Wasilla, 99687, Matanuska County, (907)376-5466, 50 miles NE of Anchorage.
Holes: 18. **Yards:** 6,596/5,461. **Par:** 72/72. **Course Rating:** 71.4/70.8. **Slope:** 129/123. **Green Fee:** $22/$29. **Cart Fee:** $22/cart. **Walking Policy:** Unrestricted walking. **Walkability:** 3. **Opened:** 1977. **Season:** April-Oct. **High:** June-Aug. **To obtain tee times:** Call golf shop up to 7 days in advance. **Miscellaneous:** Reduced fees (twilight, seniors, juniors), discount packages, metal spikes, range (grass/mats), club rentals, credit cards (MC, V, D).
Notes: Ranked 2nd in 1999 Best in State.
Reader Comments: Best course in Anchorage area ... Front 9 has strange holes ... Outstanding back nine, carved out of forest.

SLEEPY HOLLOW GOLF CLUB
PU-Mile 2 Carney Rd., Wasilla, 99654, Matanuska County, (907)376-5948, 7 miles N of Wasilla.
Holes: 9. **Yards:** 1,304/1,215. **Par:** 27/27. **Course Rating:** N/A. **Slope:** N/A. **Green Fee:** $16/$18. **Cart Fee:** $18/person. **Walking Policy:** Unrestricted walking. **Walkability:** 1. **Opened:** 1989. **Architect:** Carney Bros. **Season:** May-Sept. **High:** June-July. **To obtain tee times:** First come, first served. **Miscellaneous:** Reduced fees (weekdays, juniors), discount packages, metal spikes, range (mats), club rentals.

ARIZONA

★★ AHWATUKEE COUNTRY CLUB
SP-12432 S. 48th St., Phoenix, 85044, Maricopa County, (602)893-1161.
Holes: 18. **Yards:** 6,713/5,506. **Par:** 72/72. **Course Rating:** 71.5/70.3. **Slope:** 124/118. **Green Fee:** $20/$85. **Cart Fee:** Included in Green Fee. **Walking Policy:** Mandatory cart. **Walkability:** 1. **Opened:** 1971. **Architect:** Johnny Bulla. **Season:** Year-round. **High:** Jan.-March. **To obtain tee times:** Call golf shop up to 7 days in advance. **Miscellaneous:** Reduced fees (weekdays, low season, twilight), metal spikes, range (grass), club rentals, credit cards (MC, V).

ANTELOPE HILLS GOLF COURSES
PU-1 Perkins Dr., Prescott, 86301, Yavapai County, (520)776-7888, 90 miles N of Phoenix.
★★★ NORTH COURSE
Holes: 18. **Yards:** 6,829/6,029. **Par:** 72/72. **Course Rating:** 72.1/72.7. **Slope:** 128/127. **Green Fee:** $19/$32. **Cart Fee:** $12/person. **Walking Policy:** Unrestricted walking. **Walkability:** 3. **Opened:** 1956. **Architect:** Lawrence Hughes. **Season:** Year-round. **High:** April-Oct. **To obtain tee times:** Call 7 days in advance. **Miscellaneous:** Reduced fees (twilight, juniors), discount packages, metal spikes, range (grass), club rentals, credit cards (MC, V, AE, D).
Reader Comments: Small traditional greens ... Course is very secluded, peaceful ... Traditional course, some tight fairways; can walk ... Old, tree-lined course, nice clubhouse ... Great deal during summer ... Older of two ... Nice course for the money.
★★★ SOUTH COURSE
Holes: 18. **Yards:** 7,014/5,570. **Par:** 72/72. **Course Rating:** 71.3/69.9. **Slope:** 124/118. **Green Fee:** $19/$32. **Cart Fee:** $12/person. **Walking Policy:** Unrestricted walking. **Walkability:** 4. **Opened:** 1992. **Architect:** Gary Panks. **Season:** Year-round. **High:** April-Oct. **To obtain tee times:** Call 7 days in advance. **Miscellaneous:** Reduced fees (twilight, juniors), discount packages, metal spikes, range (grass), club rentals, credit cards (MC, V, AE, D).
Reader Comments: Wide-open layout; some lengthy holes; can walk ... Average municipal course ... Windswept ... Great potential ... Large greens ... Newer; better.

★★★½ APACHE CREEK GOLF CLUB
PU-3401 S. Ironwood Dr., Apache Junction, 85220, Pinal County, (480)982-2677, 20 miles E of Phoenix.
Holes: 18. **Yards:** 6,591/5,516. **Par:** 72/72. **Course Rating:** 71.6/65.4. **Slope:** 128/110. **Green Fee:** $10/$55. **Cart Fee:** Included in Green Fee. **Walking Policy:** Unrestricted walking. **Walkability:** 1. **Opened:** 1994. **Season:** Year-round. **High:** Oct.-April. **To obtain tee times:** Call 3 days in advance. **Miscellaneous:** Reduced fees (weekdays, low season, twilight, juniors), metal spikes, range (grass), club rentals, credit cards (MC, V).
Reader Comments: Beautiful view of Superstition Mtns. ... Enjoyable, nice layout ... Lots of use ... Best course value in Phoenix area; poor man's Troon ... A good, reasonably priced desert course ... Fun to play ... Short course, flat, great senior track.

ARIZONA BILTMORE COUNTRY CLUB
SP-24th St. and Missouri, Phoenix, 85016, Maricopa County, (602)955-9655.
★★★½ ADOBE COURSE
Holes: 18. **Yards:** 6,800/6,101. **Par:** 72/73. **Course Rating:** 71.5/74.3. **Slope:** 121/123. **Green Fee:** $65/$130. **Cart Fee:** Included in Green Fee. **Walking Policy:** Mandatory cart. **Walkability:** 3. **Opened:** 1928. **Architect:** William P. Bell. **Season:** Year-round. **High:** Jan.-May. **To obtain tee times:** May call 5 days in advance. **Miscellaneous:** Reduced fees (low season), discount packages, metal spikes, range (grass), club rentals, credit cards (MC, V, AE), beginner friendly (practice area available).
Reader Comments: Spectacular fairway condition ... Evergreen trees eat golf balls ... Seems boring, outdated ... Needs some TLC ... Flat ... Old-style course, they don't make them like this any more ... Historic & straightforward. Not too difficult ... Better, tougher than Links.
★★★½ LINKS COURSE
Holes: 18. **Yards:** 6,300/4,747. **Par:** 71/71. **Course Rating:** 69.3/68.0. **Slope:** 122/107. **Green Fee:** $65/$130. **Cart Fee:** Included in Green Fee. **Walking Policy:** Mandatory cart. **Walkability:** 3. **Opened:** 1978. **Architect:** Bill Johnston. **Season:** Year-round. **High:** Jan.-May. **To obtain tee times:** May call 5 days in advance. **Miscellaneous:** Reduced fees (low season), discount packages, metal spikes, range (grass), club rentals, credit cards (MC, V, AE), beginner friendly (practice area available).
Reader Comments: Just ok, overpriced ... You must think ... Some trick holes ... Not cheap, beautiful setting however.... A fun course in an area of stress producers ... Target-style course ... Played in June, had course to myself ... Easier but more fun than Adobe ... Short but tricky.

★★½ THE ARIZONA GOLF RESORT & CONFERENCE CENTER
R-425 S. Power Rd., Mesa, 85206, Maricopa County, (602)832-1661, (800)458-8330, 25 miles SE of Phoenix. **E-mail:** azgolf@earthlink.net. **Web:** www.azgolfresort.com.
Holes: 18. **Yards:** 6,574/6,195. **Par:** 71/71. **Course Rating:** 71.2/68.6. **Slope:** 123/117. **Green Fee:** $25/$75. **Cart Fee:** Included in Green Fee. **Walking Policy:** Mandatory cart. **Walkability:** 2. **Opened:** 1961. **Architect:** Arthur Jack Snyder. **Season:** Year-round. **High:** Jan.-March. **To**

obtain tee times: Call golf shop up to 30 days in advance with credit card. **Miscellaneous:** Reduced fees (weekdays, low season, resort guests, twilight), discount packages, metal spikes, range (grass), club rentals, lodging (187 rooms), credit cards (MC, V, AE, D), beginner friendly (mens and ladies leagues, clinics and golf schools).
Reader Comments: Nice course ... Flat, lots of trees ... Short; well maintained ... Great old course. Requires every shot in bag ... Great par 3s.

★★ ARTHUR PACK DESERT GOLF CLUB
PU-9101 N. Thornydale Rd., Tucson, 85742, Pima County, (520)744-3322.
Holes: 18. **Yards:** 6,900/5,100. **Par:** 72/72. **Course Rating:** 71.8/68.2. **Slope:** 130/117. **Green Fee:** $15/$18. **Cart Fee:** $16/cart. **Walking Policy:** Unrestricted walking. **Walkability:** 2. **Opened:** 1975. **Architect:** Dave Bennet/Lee Trevino. **Season:** Year-round. **High:** Nov.-May. **To obtain tee times:** May call up to 7 days in advance. **Miscellaneous:** Reduced fees (low season, seniors, juniors), metal spikes, range (grass/mats), club rentals, credit cards (MC, V).

★★★½ THE ASU KARSTEN GOLF COURSE *Service*
PU-1125 E. Rio Salado Pkwy., Tempe, 85281, Maricopa County, (602)921-8070, 5 miles SE of Phoenix.
Holes: 18. **Yards:** 7,057/4,765. **Par:** 72/72. **Course Rating:** 74.3/63.4. **Slope:** 133/110. **Green Fee:** $30/$87. **Cart Fee:** Included in Green Fee. **Walking Policy:** Mandatory cart. **Walkability:** 4. **Opened:** 1989. **Architect:** Pete Dye/Perry Dye. **Season:** Year-round. **High:** Jan.-April. **To obtain tee times:** Call golf shop up to 5 days in advance. **Miscellaneous:** Reduced fees (weekdays, low season, juniors), metal spikes, range (grass), club rentals, credit cards (MC, V, AE).
Reader Comments: Great golf shop ... Nice links-style course ... Overpriced, especially in winter ... Average with a lot of Dye moguls ... One of the best deals in AZ. ... Takes forever to play ... Gem in unremarkable setting ... Tough course. Do not play from the back unless you are very long.

THE BOULDERS CLUB *Service+*
R-34631 N. Tom Darlington Dr., Carefree, 85377, Maricopa County, (602)488-9028, 33 miles N of Phoenix.
★★★★½ NORTH COURSE *Condition*
Holes: 18. **Yards:** 6,811/4,900. **Par:** 72/72. **Course Rating:** 72.3/68.2. **Slope:** 135/111. **Green Fee:** $75/$200. **Cart Fee:** Included in Green Fee. **Walking Policy:** Walking at certain times. **Walkability:** 3. **Opened:** 1984. **Architect:** Jay Morrish. **Season:** Year-round. **High:** Feb.-May. **To obtain tee times:** Tee time may be held up to 1 year in advance with confirmed hotel reservation. **Miscellaneous:** Reduced fees (low season), discount packages, range (grass), caddies, club rentals, lodging (200 rooms), credit cards (MC, V, AE, Diners Club), beginner friendly (Women to Fore).
Notes: Ranked 23rd in 1999 Best in State.
Reader Comments: Spectacular. Classic track ... Probably the finest overall experience ... Great challenge from tips; favors long balls ... Everything here is great! ... Overpriced but beautiful ... Course too tough for an 18-handicap ... Great homey feel ... More forgiving than South ... Great service and attitude ... Natural beauty.
★★★★½ SOUTH COURSE *Condition+*
Holes: 18. **Yards:** 6,701/5,141. **Par:** 71/71. **Course Rating:** 72.0/71.8. **Slope:** 140/114. **Green Fee:** $72/$195. **Cart Fee:** Included in Green Fee. **Walking Policy:** Walking at certain times. **Walkability:** 4. **Opened:** 1984. **Architect:** Jay Morrish. **Season:** Year-round. **High:** Feb.-May. **To obtain tee times:** Tee time may be held up to 1 year in advance with confirmed hotel reservation. **Miscellaneous:** Reduced fees (low season), discount packages, range (grass), club rentals, lodging (200 rooms), credit cards (MC, V, AE, Diners Club), beginner friendly (Women to Fore).
Notes: Ranked 22nd in 1999 Best in State.
Reader Comments: Play it once in your life ... Most beautiful course in Arizona ... Best of the best ... What a beauty ... Too tough for the timid ... Best greenside sculpting in the valley ... We love this place ... Weeds are picked before they surface.

★★★½ CANOA HILLS GOLF COURSE
SP-1401 W. Calle Urbano, Green Valley, 85614, Pima County, (520)648-1880, 25 miles S of Tucson.
Holes: 18. **Yards:** 6,610/5,158. **Par:** 72/72. **Course Rating:** 70.8/68.5. **Slope:** 126/116. **Green Fee:** $21/$70. **Cart Fee:** Included in Green Fee. **Walking Policy:** Mandatory cart. **Walkability:** 3. **Opened:** 1984. **Architect:** Dave Bennett. **Season:** Year-round. **High:** Jan.-April. **To obtain tee times:** Call 7 days in advance. **Miscellaneous:** Reduced fees (low season, twilight, juniors), metal spikes, range (grass), club rentals, credit cards (MC, V, AE, D).
Reader Comments: Greens are slick; good putting ... Narrow ... Pleasant, playable ... Enjoyable, player friendly ... Friendly staff, good bargain, beautiful vistas ... Best holding greens in state ... Needs some conditioning help. ... Love the mesquite trees.

★★ CASA GRANDE MUNICIPAL GOLF COURSE
PM-2121 N.Thornton Rd., Casa Grande, 85222, Pinal County, (520)836-9216, 35 miles S of Phoenix.

Holes: 18. **Yards:** 6,396/5,400. **Par:** 72/72. **Course Rating:** 68.6/67.6. **Slope:** 114/110. **Green Fee:** $7/$17. **Cart Fee:** $9/person. **Walking Policy:** Unrestricted walking. **Walkability:** 2. **Opened:** 1981. **Architect:** G. Panks/A. Snyder, F. Richardson. **Season:** Year-round. **High:** Nov.-April. **To obtain tee times:** Nonresidents may call up to 3 days in advance. Residents may call up to 7 days in advance. **Miscellaneous:** Reduced fees (weekdays, low season, twilight, seniors, juniors), metal spikes, range (grass), club rentals, credit cards (MC, V).

★★★ CAVE CREEK GOLF CLUB
PM-15202 N. 19th Ave., Phoenix, 85023, Maricopa County, (602)866-8076.
Holes: 18. **Yards:** 6,876/5,614. **Par:** 72/72. **Course Rating:** 71.1/70.0. **Slope:** 122/112. **Green Fee:** $19/$28. **Cart Fee:** $15/cart. **Walking Policy:** Unrestricted walking. **Walkability:** 3. **Opened:** 1984. **Architect:** Jack Snyder. **Season:** Year-round. **High:** Nov.-April. **To obtain tee times:** Call 2 days in advance. **Miscellaneous:** Reduced fees (low season, twilight, seniors, juniors), metal spikes, range (grass), club rentals, credit cards (MC, V, AE, D).
Reader Comments: Great variety of holes ... Best muny in the valley, hit every club in the bag ... Good condition given the heavy use ... Average muny ... Built on city dump ... Great value. Long, inexpensive, but crowded ... Played once, will not play again ... Great layout, not managed as well.

★★★½ CLUB WEST GOLF CLUB
PU-16400 S. 14th Ave., Phoenix, 85045, Maricopa County, (480)460-4400, 7 miles S of Phoenix airport.
Holes: 18. **Yards:** 7,057/4,985. **Par:** 72/72. **Course Rating:** 73.1/67.0. **Slope:** 129/107. **Green Fee:** $35/$110. **Cart Fee:** Included in Green Fee. **Walking Policy:** Mandatory cart. **Walkability:** 4. **Opened:** 1993. **Architect:** Brian Whitcomb. **Season:** Year-round. **High:** Dec.-April. **To obtain tee times:** Call up to 7 days in advance with credit card. **Miscellaneous:** Reduced fees (low season, twilight, seniors), metal spikes, range (grass), club rentals, credit cards (MC, V, AE, D, Diners Club).
Reader Comments: Nice layout ... Very slow paced ... Price not equal to playing experience ... They make you feel at home ... New management should help ... Nice desert feel ... Nothing special ... Will use every club ... Fun to play, makes you want to come again ... Slow greens, wide fairways, hilly ... Beautiful, challenging, varied terrain.

★★½ CONCHO VALLEY COUNTRY CLUB
SP-HC-30, Box 57, Concho, 85924, Apache County, (520)337-4644, (800)658-8071, 28 miles NE of Show Low.
Holes: 18. **Yards:** 6,656/5,559. **Par:** 72/72. **Course Rating:** 69.1/70.0. **Slope:** 119/128. **Green Fee:** $12/$23. **Cart Fee:** $10/person. **Walking Policy:** Unrestricted walking. **Walkability:** 3. **Opened:** 1975. **Architect:** Arthur Jack Snyder. **Season:** Year-round. **High:** May-Sept. **To obtain tee times:** Call 7 days in advance. **Miscellaneous:** Reduced fees (low season, resort guests, twilight, seniors, juniors), discount packages, metal spikes, range (grass/mats), club rentals, lodging (9 rooms), credit cards (MC, V), beginner friendly (beginners clinics).
Reader Comments: Hidden jewel; fun to play ... Links-style course ... Need to monitor the young kids better ... In the middle of nowhere; few trees; modest golf shop ... Little known; breathtaking.

THE COTTONFIELDS GOLF CLUB
PU-5740 W. Baseline, Laveen, 85339, Maricopa County, (602)237-4567, 5 miles SW of Phoenix.
★★ HARVEST COURSE
Holes: 18. **Yards:** 6,785/5,876. **Par:** 68/73. **Course Rating:** 71.9/72.3. **Slope:** 115/114. **Green Fee:** $8/$30. **Cart Fee:** $8/person. **Walking Policy:** Unrestricted walking. **Walkability:** 1. **Opened:** 1993. **Architect:** Dan Pohl. **Season:** Year-round. **High:** Feb.-March. **Miscellaneous:** Reduced fees (weekdays, low season, twilight, seniors), metal spikes, range (grass), club rentals, credit cards (MC, V).
★★½ MEADOW COURSE
Holes: 18. **Yards:** 6,538/5,754. **Par:** 69/71. **Course Rating:** 71.9/71.6. **Slope:** 115/116. **Green Fee:** $8/$30. **Cart Fee:** $10/person. **Walking Policy:** Unrestricted walking. **Walkability:** 1. **Opened:** 1993. **Architect:** Dan Pohl. **Season:** Year-round. **High:** March-Feb. **Miscellaneous:** Reduced fees (weekdays, low season, twilight, seniors), metal spikes, range (grass), club rentals, credit cards (MC, V).
Reader Comments: Very busy in winter time ... Best of the two ... Good course, good value ... It was like nobody knew about it! ... A very good course to play for the cost.
Special Notes: Formerly Mountain View Golf Club

★★★½ COYOTE LAKES GOLF CLUB
PU-18800 N. Coyote Lakes Pkwy., Surprise, 85374, Maricopa County, (602)566-2323, 4 miles W of Glendale.
Holes: 18. **Yards:** 6,159/4,708. **Par:** 71/71. **Course Rating:** 69.2/65.9. **Slope:** 117/103. **Green Fee:** $16/$63. **Cart Fee:** Included in Green Fee. **Walking Policy:** Mandatory cart. **Walkability:** 2. **Opened:** 1993. **Architect:** Arthur Jack Snyder/Forrest Richardson. **Season:** Year-round. **High:** Jan.-March. **To obtain tee times:** Call 7 days in advance. **Miscellaneous:** Reduced fees (weekdays, low season, twilight, juniors), metal spikes, range (grass), club rentals, credit cards (MC, V).

Reader Comments: Excellent condition, priced right ... You will want to play it more than once ... Really neat facility; great value ... Interesting golf course ... We visit from NY every year. Tricky greens ... Take a good supply of balls—many lakes and sloping fairways will eat up your shots ... Staff creates a pleasurable golf experience.

★★½ DESERT CANYON GOLF CLUB
PU-10440 Indian Wells Dr., Fountain Hills, 85268, Maricopa County, (602)837-1173, 14 miles E of Scottsdale. **E-mail:** fhgolf@primenet.com.
Holes: 18. **Yards:** 6,415/5,352. **Par:** 71/71. **Course Rating:** 69.9/68.9. **Slope:** 123/114. **Green Fee:** $29/$100. **Cart Fee:** Included in Green Fee. **Walking Policy:** Unrestricted walking. **Walkability:** 4. **Opened:** 1971. **Architect:** John Allen. **Season:** Year-round. **High:** Jan.-April. **To obtain tee times:** Call up to 7 days in advance. **Miscellaneous:** Reduced fees (low season, twilight, juniors), range (grass), club rentals, credit cards (MC, V, AE, D), beginner friendly (lessons, clinics).
Reader Comments: High priced and slow, staff needs more training ... My favorite course in Phoenix area ... A gem for all golfers ... Total enjoyment ... Fun, but not difficult. Very hilly in canyon ... Tight little course built among rolling desert hills.

★★★ DESERT HILLS GOLF COURSE
PM-1245 Desert Hills Dr., Yuma, 85364, Yuma County, (520)344-4653, 175 miles SW of Phoenix.
Holes: 18. **Yards:** 6,800/5,726. **Par:** 72/74. **Course Rating:** 71.1/72.4. **Slope:** 117/122. **Green Fee:** $10/$25. **Cart Fee:** $12/person. **Walking Policy:** Unrestricted walking. **Walkability:** N/A. **Opened:** 1973. **Season:** Year-round. **High:** Dec.-April. **To obtain tee times:** Call computerized reservation up to 2 days in advance at 520-341-0644 with a major credit card. **Miscellaneous:** Reduced fees (low season, juniors), metal spikes, range (grass), club rentals, credit cards (MC, V, AE, D).
Reader Comments: Plain Jane, lacks character ... Long and windy; slow ... Great course at an even better price ... Up and down, unusual for Yuma ... Playable; some interesting holes ... Nice muny course ... Hard to get tee times. Seems very busy.

DESERT SPRINGS GOLF CLUB
PU-19900 N Remington Dr, Surprise, 85374, Maricopa County, (623)546-7400, 18 miles NW of Phoenix.
Holes: 18. **Yards:** 7,006/5,250. **Par:** 72/72. **Course Rating:** 73.4/69.6. **Slope:** 131/119. **Green Fee:** $19/$65. **Cart Fee:** Included in Green Fee. **Walking Policy:** Mandatory cart. **Walkability:** 3. **Opened:** 1996. **Architect:** Billy Casper/Greg Nash. **Season:** Year-round. **High:** Nov.-April. **To obtain tee times:** Call 5 days in advance. **Miscellaneous:** Reduced fees (weekdays, low season, twilight, seniors, juniors), range (grass), club rentals, credit cards (MC, V, AE).
Reader Comments: Play it before it goes private ... For Arizona, this is a pretty good deal ... One of the finer courses in the area ... Beautiful desert-type course, scenic; somewhat flat, good test of golf ... Summer bargain ... Nothing tricky, very good.

★★½ DOBSON RANCH GOLF CLUB
PU-2155 S. Dobson Rd., Mesa, 85202, Maricopa County, (602)644-2270, 15 miles SE of Phoenix.
Holes: 18. **Yards:** 6,593/5,598. **Par:** 72/72. **Course Rating:** 71.0/71.3. **Slope:** 117/116. **Green Fee:** $13/$22. **Cart Fee:** $20/cart. **Walking Policy:** Unrestricted walking. **Walkability:** 1. **Opened:** 1973. **Architect:** Red Lawrence. **Season:** Year-round. **High:** Nov.-April. **To obtain tee times:** Call 4 days in advance. **Miscellaneous:** Reduced fees (low season, twilight, juniors), metal spikes, range (grass), club rentals, credit cards (MC, V), beginner friendly (junior and adult clinics and instruction).
Reader Comments: OK public course, old ... Very nice muny ... Needs work to upgrade ... Inexpensive, broke 80 ... More than five-hour rounds. Front 9 too long, back 9 too short ... Houses on both sides. Daunting for most players ... Surprising number of memorable holes ... Nice layout. Good price.

DOVE VALLEY RANCH GOLF CLUB
PU-33244 N. Black Mtn. Pkwy., Cave Creek, 85331, Maricopa County, (480)473-1444, 10 miles N of Phoenix. **Web:** www.dovevalleyranch.com.
Holes: 18. **Yards:** 7,011/5,337. **Par:** 72/72. **Course Rating:** 72.7/70.5. **Slope:** 131/114. **Green Fee:** $55/$125. **Cart Fee:** Included in Green Fee. **Walking Policy:** Unrestricted walking. **Walkability:** 2. **Opened:** 1998. **Architect:** Robert Trent Jones Jr. **Season:** year-round. **High:** Jan.-May. **To obtain tee times:** Call (480)473-1444. **Miscellaneous:** Reduced fees (low season), range (grass), club rentals, credit cards (MC, V, AE, D).

★★★ EAGLE'S NEST COUNTRY CLUB AT PEBBLE CREEK
SP-3645 Clubhouse Dr., Goodyear, 85338, Maricopa County, (602)935-6750, (800)795-4663, 15 miles SW of Phoenix.
Holes: 18. **Yards:** 6,860/5,030. **Par:** 72/72. **Course Rating:** 72.6/68.1. **Slope:** 130/111. **Green Fee:** $21/$51. **Cart Fee:** $9/person. **Walking Policy:** Unrestricted walking. **Walkability:** 2. **Opened:** 1991. **Architect:** Keith Foster. **Season:** Year-round. **High:** Jan.-March. **To obtain tee**

times: Call 2 days in advance. **Miscellaneous:** Reduced fees (low season, twilight), metal spikes, range (grass), club rentals, credit cards (MC, V, AE).
Reader Comments: Nice ... A jewel in the middle of nowhere. Staff very nice. Great shape ... Long, wide open.

★★★ ELEPHANT ROCKS GOLF CLUB
PU-2200 Country Club Rd., Williams, 86046, Coconino County, (520)635-4935, 30 miles W of Flagstaff.
Holes: 18. **Yards:** 5,937/5,309. **Par:** 70/72. **Course Rating:** 67.6/67.3. **Slope:** 123/126. **Green Fee:** $20/$33. **Cart Fee:** $10/person. **Walking Policy:** Walking at certain times. **Walkability:** 5. **Opened:** 1990. **Architect:** Gary Panks. **Season:** April-Oct. **High:** May-Sept. **To obtain tee times:** Call 7 days in advance. **Miscellaneous:** Reduced fees (weekdays, juniors), range (grass), club rentals, credit cards (MC, V).
Reader Comments: It's a beautiful track at the gateway to the Grand Canyon ... My home course, best value in northern Arizona ... Lots of tall ponderosa pines.

★★★★ EMERALD CANYON GOLF COURSE *Value*
PU-72 Emerald Canyon Dr., Parker, 85344, La Paz County, (520)667-3366, 150 miles NW of Phoenix.
Holes: 18. **Yards:** 6,657/4,769. **Par:** 72/71. **Course Rating:** 71.5/67.2. **Slope:** 131/117. **Green Fee:** $18/$42. **Cart Fee:** Included in Green Fee. **Walking Policy:** Mandatory cart. **Walkability:** 4. **Opened:** 1989. **Architect:** William Phillips. **Season:** Year-round. **High:** Nov.-March. **To obtain tee times:** Call up to 7 days in advance. **Miscellaneous:** Reduced fees (weekdays, low season, twilight, juniors), discount packages, metal spikes, range (grass), club rentals, credit cards (MC, V).
Reader Comments: Unique golf experience ... Great natural appeal ... What views! Better than the course ... I loooovve this course ... Long drive from Phoenix but worth it ... Too many blind shots ... Better be on your game ... A must for the desert fan.... Ricochet golf; hit it straight or else.

★★★ ENCANTO GOLF COURSE
PM-2705 N. 15th Ave., Phoenix, 85007, Maricopa County, (602)253-3963.
Holes: 27. **Yards:** 6,386/5,731. **Par:** 70/72. **Course Rating:** 69.0/70.5. **Slope:** 111/111. **Green Fee:** $11/$26. **Cart Fee:** $18/. **Walking Policy:** Unrestricted walking. **Walkability:** N/A. **Opened:** 1937. **Architect:** William P. Bell. **Season:** Year-round. **High:** Feb.-April. **To obtain tee times:** Call 2 days in advance. **Miscellaneous:** Reduced fees (low season, twilight, seniors, juniors), metal spikes, range (grass), club rentals, credit cards (MC, V).
Reader Comments: A real sleeper located downtown ... Not the best muny in Phoenix ... Flat to walk ... Best value in town ... Great to play golf in the middle of the city ... Old muny. Front more exciting than back ... Long holes, elevated greens, very playable ... City course with tons of traffic but very playable.

★★★½ ESTRELLA MOUNTAIN GOLF COURSE
PU-15205 W. Vineyard Dr., Goodyear, 85338, Maricopa County, (623)932-3714, 15 miles SE of Phoenix. **E-mail:** estrella@mciworldcom.net.
Holes: 18. **Yards:** 6,868/5,297. **Par:** 71/72. **Course Rating:** 71.9/68.5. **Slope:** 117/113. **Green Fee:** $10/$27. **Cart Fee:** $10/person. **Walking Policy:** Unrestricted walking. **Walkability:** 2. **Opened:** 1962. **Architect:** Red Lawrence. **Season:** Year-round. **High:** Dec.-April. **To obtain tee times:** Call 7 days in advance. **Miscellaneous:** Reduced fees (low season, twilight, seniors, juniors), metal spikes, range (grass), club rentals, credit cards (MC, V).
Reader Comments: Nice but boring ... Diamond in the rough. Greatest bargain ... Much improved with new management ... Desert, target golf at its best ... Wonderful course that is forgotten about. No crowds.

ESTRELLA MOUNTAIN RANCH GOLF CLUB
PU-11800 S. Golf Club Dr., Goodyear, 85338, Maricopa County, (623)386-2600, 30 miles W of Phoenix. **Web:** www.estrellamtnranch/golf.com.
Holes: 18. **Yards:** 7,102/5,124. **Par:** 72/72. **Course Rating:** 73.8/68.2. **Slope:** 138/115. **Green Fee:** $40/$95. **Cart Fee:** Included in Green Fee. **Walking Policy:** Unrestricted walking. **Walkability:** 3. **Opened:** 1999. **Architect:** Jack Nicklaus II. **Season:** Year-round. **High:** Jan.-May. **To obtain tee times:** Call directly to reservations. Have credit card ready to secure starting time. **Miscellaneous:** Reduced fees (weekdays, low season, twilight, juniors), discount packages, range (grass), club rentals, credit cards (MC, V, AE, D, Diners Club), beginner friendly (golf lessons for residents of Estrella Mountain Ranch).

★★★½ THE 500 CLUB
PU-4707 W. Pinnacle Peak Rd., Glendale, 85310, Maricopa County, (602)492-9500, 20 miles NW of Downtown Phoenix. **E-mail:** the500club@aol.com.
Holes: 18. **Yards:** 6,867/5,601. **Par:** 72/73. **Course Rating:** 71.5/69.8. **Slope:** 121/112. **Green Fee:** $18/$55. **Cart Fee:** $10/person. **Walking Policy:** Unrestricted walking. **Walkability:** 2. **Opened:** 1989. **Architect:** Brian Whitcomb. **Season:** Year-round. **High:** Jan.-March. **To obtain tee times:** Call up to 3 days in advance. **Miscellaneous:** Reduced fees (weekdays, low season,

twilight, juniors), discount packages, metal spikes, range (grass), club rentals, credit cards (MC, V, AE, D, Diners Club).

Reader Comments: Fairly plain but a fun time ... Overplayed, overhyped, overpriced ... Excellent pace of play and priced right ... Good course, challenging layout ... Pleasant, playable, great value ... Greens consistently good, fabulous vistas ... Not overly demanding ... Not a top course ... Congenial staff.

★★★ THE FOOTHILLS GOLF CLUB

SP-2201 E. Clubhouse Dr., Phoenix, 85048, Maricopa County, (480)460-4653, (800)493-1161. **Holes:** 18. **Yards:** 6,968/5,441. **Par:** 72/72. **Course Rating:** 73.2/70.1. **Slope:** 132/114. **Green Fee:** $35/$99. **Cart Fee:** Included in Green Fee. **Walking Policy:** Mandatory cart. **Walkability:** 2. **Opened:** 1987. **Architect:** Tom Weiskopf/Jay Morrish. **Season:** Year-round. **High:** Dec.-March. **To obtain tee times:** Call up to 7 days in advance. Reservations outside 7 days available for higher rate fee. **Miscellaneous:** Reduced fees (weekdays, low season, twilight, juniors), metal spikes, range (grass), club rentals, credit cards (MC, V, AE, Diners Club).

Reader Comments: Good old desert course, but fair ... Staff not the greatest, couldn't find a marshall ... Needs lots of upgrade work ... Pretty, fair, reasonably priced, course condition varies a lot ... Good value for Phoenix area ... Green fee not a good value for course condition and difficulty ... Slow play ... Extremely busy.

★★★½ FRANCISCO GRANDE RESORT & GOLF CLUB

R-26000 Gila Bend Hwy., Casa Grande, 85222, Pinal County, (602)836-6444, (800)237-4238, 45 miles S of Phoenix. **E-mail:** sdes@franciscogrande.com. **Web:** www.franciscogrande.com. **Holes:** 18. **Yards:** 7,594/5,554. **Par:** 72/72. **Course Rating:** 74.9/69.9. **Slope:** 126/112. **Green Fee:** $30/$65. **Cart Fee:** Included in Green Fee. **Walking Policy:** Mandatory cart. **Walkability:** 2. **Opened:** 1961. **Architect:** Ralph Plummer. **Season:** Year-round. **High:** Nov.-April. **To obtain tee times:** Call up to 5 days in advance, or with hotel room reservations. **Miscellaneous:** Reduced fees (low season, twilight, juniors), discount packages, metal spikes, range (grass), club rentals, lodging (110 rooms), credit cards (MC, V, AE, Diners Club).

Reader Comments: Keep ball in fairway, traditional, long ... Great summer rates with hotel package ... Good greens, fairways; much length if you want it ... Old fashioned; one of the longest courses in Arizona from the tips.

★★★½ FRED ENKE GOLF COURSE

PM-8251 E. Irvington Rd., Tucson, 85730, Pima County, (520)296-8607. **Holes:** 18. **Yards:** 6,807/4,700. **Par:** 72/72. **Course Rating:** 73.3/68.8. **Slope:** 137/111. **Green Fee:** $12/$27. **Cart Fee:** $16/cart. **Walking Policy:** Unrestricted walking. **Walkability:** 4. **Opened:** 1982. **Architect:** Brad Benz/Michael Poellot. **Season:** Year-round. **High:** Dec.-April. **To obtain tee times:** Call 6 days in advance. **Miscellaneous:** Reduced fees (weekdays, low season, twilight, seniors, juniors), metal spikes, range (grass), club rentals, credit cards (MC, V, D). **Reader Comments:** Desert target golf with limited turf, great layout ... Narrow; can't daydream ... City owned, target course difficult ... Don't hit it left here ... Challenging; watch for snakes ... Need local knowledge to stay out of desert ... Fine desert course, especially for the price ... A single can get on any time. Avoid winter snowbird season.

GAINEY RANCH GOLF CLUB

R-7600 Gainey Club Dr., Scottsdale, 85258, Maricopa County, (602)483-2582. **Holes:** 27. **Green Fee:** $70/$105. **Cart Fee:** Included in Green Fee. **Walking Policy:** Mandatory cart. **Walkability:** N/A. **Opened:** 1984. **Architect:** Brad Benz/Michael Poellot. **Season:** Year-round. **High:** Jan.-April. **To obtain tee times:** Hotel guests make tee times with hotel golf coordinator. **Miscellaneous:** Reduced fees (low season), metal spikes, range (grass), club rentals, lodging, credit cards (Must charge to hotel room).

★★★½ DUNES/ARROYO

Yards: 6,662/5,151. **Par:** 72/72. **Course Rating:** 70.7/68.5. **Slope:** 124/113. **Reader Comments:** Grass everywhere! Great layout that's not desert style ... Got to make some noise to be serviced ... Good course ... Good mix of holes ... Bermuda greens ... Short but nice in winter.

★★★½ DUNES/LAKES

Yards: 6,614/4,993. **Par:** 72/72. **Course Rating:** 71.1/67.9. **Slope:** 126/115. **Reader Comments:** Fun; good facility ... 9th on Lakes best finishing hole in Arizona ... Challenging.

★★★½ LAKES/ARROYO

Yards: 6,800/5,312. **Par:** 72/72. **Course Rating:** 71.9/70.4. **Slope:** 128/116. **Reader Comments:** Excellent variety, outstanding service ... 9th hole Lakes with waterfall is outstanding ... Expensive, but worth it.

GLEN CANYON COUNTRY CLUB

Bitter Springs Rd., Page, 86040, Coconino County, (520)645-2715. **Holes:** 9. **Yards:** 6,493/5,645. **Par:** 72/72. **Course Rating:** 68.3/71.2. **Slope:** 110/113. **Green Fee:** $14/$18. **Cart Fee:** $10/person. **Walking Policy:** Unrestricted walking. **Walkability:** 2.

Opened: 1959. Season: Year-round. High: May-Oct. Miscellaneous: Reduced fees (juniors), metal spikes, range (grass), club rentals, credit cards (MC, V, AE, D).

GOLD CANYON GOLF RESORT

R-6100 S. Kings Ranch Rd., Gold Canyon, 85219, Pinal County, (480)982-9449, (800)624-6445, 35 miles SE of Phoenix. **Web:** www.gcgr.com.

★★★★ DINOSAUR MOUNTAIN

Holes: 18. **Yards:** 6,584/4,921. **Par:** 70/72. **Course Rating:** 71.1/67.4. **Slope:** 140/115. **Green Fee:** $60/$135. **Cart Fee:** Included in Green Fee. **Walking Policy:** Mandatory cart. **Walkability:** 5. **Opened:** 1997. **Architect:** Ken Kavanaugh. **Season:** Year-round. **High:** Jan.-March. **To obtain tee times:** Call and reserve up to 7 days in advance with a credit card. Call 8-60 days in advance with $5 fee per player. **Miscellaneous:** Reduced fees (weekdays, low season, resort guests, twilight), discount packages, range (grass), club rentals, lodging (101 rooms), credit cards (MC, V, AE, D, Diners Club).
Reader Comments: Spectacular views ... Easy valley gem, fun to play ... Beautiful landscaping ... Great layout ... 10.5 Stimpmeter greens, target golf, huge grass swales, desert adventure. Got my butt kicked and loved every minute of it ... Lots of elevation changes ... Play late afternoon for the colors ... Way out there but well worth the trip.

★★★★ SIDEWINDER

Holes: 18. **Yards:** 6,414/4,529. **Par:** 71/71. **Course Rating:** 71.8/66.5. **Slope:** 133/119. **Green Fee:** $35/$65. **Cart Fee:** Included in Green Fee. **Walking Policy:** Mandatory cart. **Walkability:** 2. **Opened:** 1998. **Architect:** G. Nash/K. Kavanaugh/S. Penge. **Season:** Year-round. **High:** Jan.-March. **To obtain tee times:** Call and reserve up to 7 days in advance with a credit card. Call 8-60 days in advance with $5 fee per player. **Miscellaneous:** Reduced fees (weekdays, low season, resort guests, twilight), discount packages, range (grass/mats), club rentals, lodging (101 rooms), credit cards (MC, V, AE, D, Diners Club), beginner friendly.
Reader Comments: Gorgeous scenery ... Very nice course ... Employees are nice ... Very challenging, scenic ... Too expensive for what you get ... Slow pace, crowded ... Great value, if staying at resort ... Look out for snakes and jumping cactus; stay in the fairway ... Spectacular mountain course ... Wonderful surroundings.

★★★★ THE GOLF CLUB AT EAGLE MOUNTAIN *Condition, Pace*

PU-14915 E. Eagle Mtn. Pkwy., Fountain Hills, 85268, Maricopa County, (602)816-1234, 5 miles E of Scottsdale. **Web:** www.eaglemtn.com.
Holes: 18. **Yards:** 6,755/5,065. **Par:** 71/71. **Course Rating:** 71.7/67.9. **Slope:** 139/118. **Green Fee:** $55/$155. **Cart Fee:** Included in Green Fee. **Walking Policy:** Mandatory cart. **Walkability:** 5. **Opened:** 1996. **Architect:** Scott Miller. **Season:** Year-round. **High:** Jan.-April. **To obtain tee times:** Call golf shop. **Miscellaneous:** Reduced fees (weekdays, low season, twilight, juniors), range (grass), club rentals, lodging (42 rooms), credit cards (MC, V, AE).
Reader Comments: Too many fairways funnel to middle ... Greens fast ... A fun course, perhaps the most interesting desert course I've played ... Pricey in the summer, but worth it ... Breathtaking golf course ... Great elevation changes ... Beautiful, challenging course; watch out for the rattlesnake habitats.

★★★★½ THE GOLF CLUB AT VISTOSO *Service, Condition+*

PU-955 W. Vistoso Highlands Dr., Tucson, 85737, Pima County, (520)797-9900, 12 miles NW of Tucson. **Web:** www.vistosogolf.net.
Holes: 18. **Yards:** 6,905/5,165. **Par:** 72/72. **Course Rating:** 72.1/65.4. **Slope:** 145/111. **Green Fee:** $39/$125. **Cart Fee:** Included in Green Fee. **Walking Policy:** Walking at certain times. **Walkability:** 2. **Opened:** 1995. **Architect:** Tom Weiskopf. **Season:** Year-round. **High:** Jan.-April. **To obtain tee times:** Call up to 7 days in advance. **Miscellaneous:** Reduced fees (weekdays, low season, twilight), metal spikes, range (grass), club rentals, credit cards (MC, V, AE, D).
Notes: Golf Digest School site. Ranked 12th in 1999 Best in State.
Reader Comments: Beautiful topography; great surroundings ... Best course in southern Arizona ... Great service & great course condition ... Every hole is a picture hole ... Cartpath-only rule is a drawback ... Lots of carry off the tee ... Good value in summer ... Second-best course in Tucson ... Like a picture postcard! Expensive but worth it!.

★★★ GRANDE VALLE GOLF CLUB *Pace*

PU-1505 S. Toltec Rd., Eloy, 85231, Pinal County, (520)466-7734, 47 miles SE of Tucson.
Holes: 18. **Yards:** 7,100/5,363. **Par:** 72/72. **Course Rating:** 72.3/69.8. **Slope:** 117/112. **Green Fee:** $24/$24. **Cart Fee:** $16/. **Walking Policy:** Unrestricted walking. **Walkability:** N/A. **Opened:** 1992. **Architect:** Forrest Richardson. **Season:** Year-round. **High:** Oct.-April. **To obtain tee times:** Call 7 days in advance. **Miscellaneous:** Reduced fees (low season, juniors), discount packages, metal spikes, range (grass), club rentals, credit cards (MC, V).
Reader Comments: Greens are better under new ownership ... Fun track, can be windy in p.m. ... This could turn into a great course ... Great course, not-so-great condition.

ARIZONA

GRANITE FALLS GOLF CLUB
SP-15949 W. Clearview Blvd, Surprise, 85374, Maricopa County, (623)546-7575, 18 miles NW of Phoenix.
Holes: 18. **Yards:** 6,840/5,214. **Par:** 72/72. **Course Rating:** 72.1/68.8. **Slope:** 127/114. **Green Fee:** $21/$79. **Cart Fee:** Included in Green Fee. **Walking Policy:** Mandatory cart. **Walkability:** N/A. **Opened:** 1996. **Architect:** Billy Casper/Greg Nash. **Season:** Year-round. **High:** Nov.-April. **To obtain tee times:** Call 5 days in advance. **Miscellaneous:** Reduced fees (weekdays, low season, twilight), range (grass), club rentals, credit cards (MC, V, AE).
Reader Comments: Companion course with Desert Springs, play both in one day if you can go 36 ... Beautiful desert-type course, scenic ... Good deal in the summer heat ... Great test of golf with beauty ... Out of the way, but go play; worth it ... Wide open, new course ... Great to play in summer when snowbirds have left.

GRAYHAWK GOLF CLUB   *Service+*
PU-8620 E Thompson Peak Parkway, Scottsdale, 85255, Maricopa County, (602)502-1800, (800)472-9429, 30 miles N of Scottsdale. **E-mail:** golf@grayhawk.com. **Web:** www.grayhawk.com.
★★★★½ **RAPTOR COURSE**   *Condition*
Holes: 18. **Yards:** 7,135/5,309. **Par:** 72/72. **Course Rating:** 74.0/71.3. **Slope:** 136/127. **Green Fee:** $50/$195. **Cart Fee:** Included in Green Fee. **Walking Policy:** Unrestricted walking. **Walkability:** 2. **Opened:** 1995. **Architect:** Tom Fazio. **Season:** Year-round. **High:** Oct.-May. **To obtain tee times:** Call up to 30 days in advance. 48 hrs. prior to day of play may cancel or make changes. 12 players or more may book up to 6 months in advance. **Miscellaneous:** Reduced fees (low season), metal spikes, range (grass), club rentals, credit cards (MC, V, AE).
Notes: Ranked 18th in 1999 Best in State.
Reader Comments: Very playable ... Crowded, slow pace ... Very, very nice fruit & towels/lotion ... Hit it straight ... Fastest greens I've ever seen ... Great course/must return ... Better layout than Troon North ... Best service in the country; lightning-fast greens ... Great addition to Talon ... Great scenery of AZ desert.
★★★★½ **TALON COURSE**   *Condition+*
Holes: 18. **Yards:** 6,973/5,143. **Par:** 72/72. **Course Rating:** 74.3/70.0. **Slope:** 141/121. **Green Fee:** $50/$195. **Cart Fee:** Included in Green Fee. **Walking Policy:** Unrestricted walking. **Walkability:** 2. **Opened:** 1994. **Architect:** David Graham/Gary Panks. **Season:** Year-round. **High:** Oct.-May. **To obtain tee times:** Call up to 30 days in advance. 48 hrs. prior to day of play may cancel or make changes. 12 players or more may book up to 6 months in advance. **Miscellaneous:** Reduced fees (low season), metal spikes, range (grass), club rentals, credit cards (MC, V, AE).
Notes: Ranked 14th in 1999 Best in State; 56th in 1996 America's Top 75 Upscale Courses.
Reader Comments: Incredible service; Gary McCord hangs out in the restaurant ... Excellent use of flat land ... 'Cartpath only' rule could be deadly in August ... Everyone should try it! ... Excellent clubhouse ... Hard to tell which course is better ... Lightning-fast greens ... Need to visualize the clown's mouth for some of the greens.

★★★½ HAPPY TRAILS RESORT
SP-17200 W. Bell Rd., Surprise, 85374, Maricopa County, (623)584-6000, 20 miles NW of Phoenix.
Holes: 18. **Yards:** 6,646/5,146. **Par:** 72/72. **Course Rating:** 72.1/68.7. **Slope:** 124/113. **Green Fee:** $19/$51. **Cart Fee:** Included in Green Fee. **Walking Policy:** Mandatory cart. **Walkability:** 3. **Opened:** 1983. **Architect:** Greg Nash/Ken Cavanaugh. **Season:** Year-round. **High:** Nov.-April. **To obtain tee times:** Call 3 days in advance during season. Call 7 days in advance during summer. **Miscellaneous:** Reduced fees (weekdays, low season, resort guests, twilight, juniors), range (grass), club rentals, credit cards (MC, V, AE, D).
Reader Comments: Tougher than it looks ... Wow, excellent course and priced right ... Excellent greens ... Great off-season course, good layout ... Love the bent-grass greens ... Challenging opening hole, great par 3s ... Need a cart here; too far between holes, good course ... Friendly staff! Nice place to avoid crowds.

★★½ HAVEN GOLF CLUB
PU-110 N. Abrego, Green Valley, 85614, Pima County, (520)625-4281.
Holes: 18. **Yards:** 6,867/5,588. **Par:** 72/72. **Course Rating:** 72.0/70.6. **Slope:** 123/120. **Green Fee:** $15/$45. **Walking Policy:** Unrestricted walking. **Walkability:** 1. **Opened:** 1966. **Architect:** Arthur Jack Snyder. **Season:** Year-round. **High:** Nov.-March. **Miscellaneous:** Reduced fees (low season), metal spikes, range (grass), club rentals, credit cards (MC, V).
Reader Comments: Good traditional course, lots of old-timers around, retirement community, nice atmosphere ... Flat, basic old track ... New greens are the best in southern Arizona ... Good mountain views ... Mediocre layout.

ARIZONA

★★★★ **HERITAGE HIGHLANDS GOLF & COUNTRY CLUB**
SP-4949 W. Heritage Club Blvd., Marana, 85742, Pima County, (520)579-7000, 10 miles NW of Tucson. **Web:** www.Heritagehighlands.com.
Holes: 18. **Yards:** 6,904/4,901. **Par:** 72/72. **Course Rating:** 72.1/67.7. **Slope:** 134/121. **Green Fee:** $55/$99. **Cart Fee:** Included in Green Fee. **Walking Policy:** Mandatory cart. **Walkability:** 3. **Opened:** 1997. **Architect:** Arthur Hills. **Season:** Year-round. **High:** Dec.-April. **To obtain tee times:** Call up to 7 days in advance. **Miscellaneous:** Reduced fees (weekdays, low season, twilight), range (grass), club rentals, credit cards (MC, V, D).
Reader Comments: Excellent layout, must play before it goes private ... Good desert course; multi-elevations ... Good course for seniors ... Need delicate touch with putter ... Great fast greens ... Practice putting on the hood of your car ... Most beautiful and interesting course I have played ... Course runs near mountainside.

★★★½ **HILLCREST GOLF CLUB**
PU-20002 N. Star Ridge Drive, Sun City West, 85375, Maricopa County, (623)584-1500, 19 miles NW of Phoenix. **E-mail:** Hillcrestaz@westmail.net. **Web:** www.teematic.com/hillcrestaz.
Holes: 18. **Yards:** 7,002/5,489. **Par:** 72/72. **Course Rating:** 72.7/70.7. **Slope:** 126/120. **Green Fee:** $29/$65. **Cart Fee:** Included in Green Fee. **Walking Policy:** Mandatory cart. **Walkability:** 2. **Opened:** 1979. **Architect:** Jeff Hardin/Greg Nash. **Season:** Year-round. **High:** Nov.-April. **To obtain tee times:** Call up to 7 days in advance. **Miscellaneous:** Reduced fees (weekdays, low season, twilight), discount packages, range (grass), club rentals, credit cards (MC, V, AE, D).
Notes: 1983-1988 Senior PGA Tour Arizona Roundup; 1981-1987 LPGA Tour.
Reader Comments: Good price, caters to seniors ... Some greens sloped too severe ... Traditional design, excellent condition ... A real beauty. Solid course ... Flat course with lots of water, great value ... Too much bird droppings ... Wide fairways ... Staff in good humor even though it was 90 degrees by 11 a.m.

★★½ **KEN MCDONALD GOLF COURSE**
PM-800 Divot Dr., Tempe, 85283, Maricopa County, (480)350-5256, 4 miles SE of Phoenix.
Holes: 18. **Yards:** 6,743/5,872. **Par:** 72/73. **Course Rating:** 70.8/70.8. **Slope:** 115/112. **Green Fee:** $13/$21. **Cart Fee:** $8/cart. **Walking Policy:** Unrestricted walking. **Walkability:** 2. **Opened:** 1974. **Architect:** Jack Snyder. **Season:** Year-round. **High:** Nov.-April. **To obtain tee times:** Call up to 2 days in advance. **Miscellaneous:** Reduced fees (low season, twilight, seniors, juniors), discount packages, metal spikes, range (grass), club rentals, credit cards (MC, V).
Reader Comments: Nice public track ... Best-kept muny in the valley ... Too much play; it does well for course conditions ... Good layout.

KIERLAND GOLF CLUB
PU-15636 N. Clubgate Dr., Scottsdale, 85254, Maricopa County, (480)922-9283, 20 miles NE of Phoenix.
Holes: 27. **Cart Fee:** Included in Green Fee. **Walking Policy:** Unrestricted walking. **Walkability:** 3. **Opened:** 1996. **Architect:** Scott Miller. **Season:** Year-round. **High:** Jan.-April. **To obtain tee times:** Guests may call golf shop up to 30 days in advance. **Miscellaneous:** Reduced fees (weekdays, low season, twilight, juniors), metal spikes, range (grass), credit cards (MC, V, AE, D).
★★★★ **IRONWOOD/ACACIA**
Yards: 6,974/4,985. **Par:** 72/72. **Course Rating:** 72.9/69.2. **Slope:** 130/116. **Green Fee:** $40/$140.
★★★★ **IRONWOOD/MESQUITE**
Yards: 7,017/5,017. **Par:** 72/72. **Course Rating:** 73.3/69.4. **Slope:** 133/120. **Green Fee:** $40/$140.
★★★★ **MESQUITE/ACACIA**
Yards: 6,913/4,898. **Par:** 72/72. **Course Rating:** 72.6/69.0. **Slope:** 133/115. **Green Fee:** $40/$125.
Notes: Golf Digest School site.
Reader Comments: Great condition, fairways like tees, excellent greens ... Good 27 holes ... Generous fairways, good greens ... One of best desert courses. A treat to play ... Friendly, great practice area ... Wide open, typical overpriced AZ course ... Great experience; free range balls ... Fast undulating greens ... 27 holes and every one a challenge ... Incredible course, tough but playable, but long rounds are a norm ... Excellent course for women.

★★★ **KOKOPELLI GOLF RESORT**
PU-1800 W. Guadalupe, Gilbert, 85233, Maricopa County, (480)926-3589, (800)468-7918, 10 miles SE of Phoenix.
Holes: 18. **Yards:** 6,716/4,992. **Par:** 72/72. **Course Rating:** 72.2/68.8. **Slope:** 132/120. **Green Fee:** $40/$100. **Cart Fee:** Included in Green Fee. **Walking Policy:** Mandatory cart. **Walkability:** N/A. **Opened:** 1993. **Architect:** William Phillips. **Season:** Year-round. **High:** Jan.-April. **To obtain tee times:** Call up to 60 days in advance. **Miscellaneous:** Reduced fees (weekdays, low season, resort guests, twilight), discount packages, metal spikes, range (grass), club rentals, credit cards (MC, V, AE).
Reader Comments: Great rate, long course, great holes ... Overpriced, especially in winter ... Runs through housing development ... Great staff ... Good design, par 3s same length ... Great layout, not great greens ... Sleeper course.

LA PALOMA COUNTRY CLUB
R-3660 E. Sunrise Dr., Tucson, 85718, Pima County, (602)299-1500, (800)222-1249.
Holes: 27. **Green Fee:** $75/$165. **Cart Fee:** Included in Green Fee. **Walking Policy:** Mandatory cart. **Opened:** 1984. **Architect:** Jack Nicklaus. **Season:** Year-round. **High:** Jan.-May. **To obtain tee times:** Resort guests up to 60 days in advance. **Miscellaneous:** Reduced fees (low season, resort guests), discount packages, metal spikes, range (grass/mats), club rentals, lodging (487 rooms), credit cards (MC, V, AE, D).
★★★★ **CANYON/HILL** *Condition*
Yards: 6,997/5,057. **Par:** 72/72. **Course Rating:** 74.8/67.4. **Slope:** 155/114. **Walkability:** 5.
Reader Comments: Target golf fun ... Majestic ... Class course, tough, bucks ... Early Nicklaus, punishes good shots ... Over priced; sand wasn't good ... Separate dining for nonmembers ... Very expensive, exceptional layout.
★★★★ **RIDGE/CANYON** *Condition*
Yards: 7,088/5,075. **Par:** 72/72. **Course Rating:** 75.2/67.9. **Slope:** 155/121. **Walkability:** N/A.
Notes: Ranked 25th in 1999 Best in State.
Reader Comments: Hard but fair ... Beautiful views ... Tough, difficult to score ... Hit 'em straight.
★★★★ **RIDGE/HILL** *Condition*
Yards: 7,017/4,878. **Par:** 72/72. **Course Rating:** 74.2/66.9. **Slope:** 155/110. **Walkability:** N/A.
Reader Comments: Beautiful, tough.

★★★★ **LAKE POWELL NATIONAL GOLF CLUB** *Pace+*
PU-400 Clubhouse Dr., Page, 86040, Coconino County, (520)645-2023, 270 miles N of Phoenix. **Web:** www.lakepowellgolf.com.
Holes: 18. **Yards:** 7,064/5,097. **Par:** 72/72. **Course Rating:** 73.4/68.0. **Slope:** 139/122. **Green Fee:** $35/$60. **Cart Fee:** Included in Green Fee. **Walking Policy:** Mandatory cart. **Walkability:** 4. **Opened:** 1995. **Architect:** Bill Phillips. **Season:** Year-round. **High:** May-Sept. **To obtain tee times:** Call up to 7 days in advance. **Miscellaneous:** Reduced fees (low season, resort guests, juniors), metal spikes, range (grass), club rentals, lodging (150 rooms), credit cards (MC, V, AE, D).
Reader Comments: Good price, fun to play ... Wind was a little too much, 35-40 mph, but a great course ... Great views of Lake Powell ... Unusual, but fun ... Great layout and scenery ... Staff extremely helpful ... Too many blind shots.

★★★★ **LAS SENDAS GOLF CLUB** *Service, Pace*
PU-7555 E. Eagle Crest Dr., Mesa, 85207, Maricopa County, (480)396-4000, 14 miles E of Phoenix. **Web:** www.lassendas.com.
Holes: 18. **Yards:** 6,836/5,100. **Par:** 71/71. **Course Rating:** 73.8/69.9. **Slope:** 149/126. **Green Fee:** $45/$160. **Cart Fee:** Included in Green Fee. **Walking Policy:** Unrestricted walking. **Walkability:** 4. **Opened:** 1995. **Architect:** Robert Trent Jones Jr. **Season:** Year-round. **High:** Jan.-April. **To obtain tee times:** Call 7 days in advance. Call 8-90 days in advance for $15 fee per player. **Miscellaneous:** Reduced fees (low season, twilight), range (grass), club rentals, credit cards (MC, V, AE).
Notes: Ranked 16th in 1999 Best in State.
Reader Comments: Challenging, great greens ... Great layout ... Best R.T. Jones layout in state ... Stay out of sand ... Bent greens are like glass, very tough! ... Humbling experience ... Toughest opening holes in the desert ... Think you're good, try these par 5s ... Keep times running smoothly ... Scenic, desert golf Friendly staff ... Hilly.

★★★½ **THE LEGEND AT ARROWHEAD GOLF CLUB**
R-21027 N. 67th Ave., Glendale, 85308, Maricopa County, (602)561-1902, (800)468-7918, 15 miles SW of Phoenix.
Holes: 18. **Yards:** 7,005/5,233. **Par:** 72/72. **Course Rating:** 73.0/71.2. **Slope:** 129/119. **Green Fee:** $29/$80. **Cart Fee:** Included in Green Fee. **Walking Policy:** Mandatory cart. **Walkability:** 4. **Opened:** 1989. **Architect:** Arnold Palmer/Ed Seay. **Season:** Year-round. **High:** Jan.-April. **To obtain tee times:** Call 7 days in advance. Call 8-60 days in advance for $7 reservation fee. **Miscellaneous:** Reduced fees (weekdays, low season, twilight, juniors), discount packages, metal spikes, range (grass), club rentals, credit cards (MC, V, AE), beginner friendly (American Golf Learning Center).
Reader Comments: Excellent course in the foothills ... Good views, not a flat putt anywhere ... Fair to all levels. Good summer rates ... An average track among fabulous ones ... Good course over all, but 2 or 3 holes unplayable to mid-handicappers ... Tight course through the houses. Need a real clubhouse.

★★★★ **LEGEND TRAIL GOLF CLUB** *Condition+*
PU-9462 Legendary Trail, Scottsdale, 85262, Maricopa County, (480)488-7434. **Web:** www.troongolf.com.
Holes: 18. **Yards:** 6,845/5,000. **Par:** 72/72. **Course Rating:** 72.3/68.2. **Slope:** 135/122. **Green Fee:** $55/$145. **Cart Fee:** Included in Green Fee. **Walking Policy:** Unrestricted walking. **Walkability:** 2. **Opened:** 1995. **Architect:** Rees Jones. **Season:** Year-round. **High:** Jan.-March.

To obtain tee times: Call golf shop. **Miscellaneous:** Reduced fees (weekdays, low season, twilight, juniors), metal spikes, range (grass), caddies, club rentals, credit cards (MC, V, AE).
Notes: Ranked 19th in 1999 Best in State.
Reader Comments: Memorable golf, great even in summer ... Tough for high handicapper ... A valley favorite, gorgeous, what views! ... Nice people ... Expensive but worth it. Beautiful desert course ... Excellent design ... Great condition ... A parkland design in a desert disguise, good test from the tips ... Up & coming course.

★★★½ **THE LINKS AT CONTINENTAL RANCH**
PU-8480 N. Continental Links Dr., Tucson, 85743, Pima County, (520)744-7443. **E-mail:** linksgolf@fiaaz.net.
Holes: 18. **Yards:** 6,854/5,182. **Par:** 72/72. **Course Rating:** 71.8/69.3. **Slope:** 122/115. **Green Fee:** $29/$59. **Cart Fee:** $15/person. **Walking Policy:** Unrestricted walking. **Walkability:** 2.
Opened: 1997. **Architect:** Brian Huntley. **Season:** Year-round. **High:** Jan.-March.
Miscellaneous: Reduced fees (weekdays, low season, twilight), metal spikes, range (grass), club rentals, credit cards (MC, V, AE, D), beginner friendly (clinics for juniors, lessons for adults).
Reader Comments: Good links course; desert golf, fair, a must play ... Links look-nice change of layout-congenial staff ... Nice change for Tucson courses, different style of layout ... Good course in bad location ... Nothing special ... Fairways close together—stay alert for errant balls ... Great layout allows walkers on resort-style course.

★★½ **THE LINKS AT QUEEN CREEK**
PU-445 E. Ocotillo Rd., Queen Creek, 85242, (480)987-1910, 12 miles E of Mesa.
Holes: 18. **Yards:** 6,100/5,000. **Par:** 70/71. **Course Rating:** N/A. **Slope:** 100/92. **Green Fee:** $18/$38. **Cart Fee:** $10/person. **Cart Fee:** Included in Green Fee. **Walking Policy:** Unrestricted walking. **Walkability:** 2. **Opened:** 1993. **Architect:** Sam West. **Season:** Nov.-May. **High:** Dec.-March. **To obtain tee times:** Call up to 6 days in advance. **Miscellaneous:** Metal spikes, range (grass/mats), club rentals, credit cards (MC, V), beginner friendly.
Reader Comments: Nice, easier than most, fun ... Great short course ... Friendly.

LONDON BRIDGE GOLF CLUB
PU-2400 Clubhouse Dr., Lake Havasu City, 86405, Mohave County, (520)855-2719, 200 miles SE of Las Vegas, NV.
★★ **LONDON BRIDGE COURSE EAST**
Holes: 18. **Yards:** 6,140/5,045. **Par:** 71/71. **Course Rating:** 68.9/68.2. **Slope:** 118/111. **Green Fee:** $30/$45. **Cart Fee:** $15/person. **Walking Policy:** Unrestricted walking. **Walkability:** 4.
Opened: 1979. **Architect:** Arthur Jack Snyder. **Season:** Year-round. **High:** Jan.-April. **To obtain tee times:** Call 520-855-2719. **Miscellaneous:** Reduced fees (weekdays, low season, resort guests, twilight, seniors), discount packages, metal spikes, range (grass/mats), club rentals, credit cards (MC, V, AE).
★★½ **LONDON BRIDGE COURSE WEST**
Holes: 18. **Yards:** 6,678/5,756. **Par:** 71/72. **Course Rating:** 71.7/72.7. **Slope:** 128/123. **Green Fee:** $35/$65. **Cart Fee:** Included in Green Fee. **Walking Policy:** Mandatory cart. **Walkability:** 3. **Opened:** 1969. **Architect:** Jack Snyder. **Season:** Year-round. **High:** Jan.-April. **To obtain tee times:** Call 520-855-2719. **Miscellaneous:** Reduced fees (low season, twilight, seniors, juniors), discount packages, metal spikes, range (grass/mats), club rentals, credit cards (MC, V, AE).
Reader Comments: Fun nine holes ... Too much traffic, but rangers ineffective ... In the summer, have plenty of water ... Nice views of lake.

★★★★ **LONGBOW GOLF CLUB**
PM-5400 E. McDowell Rd., Mesa, 85215, Maricopa County, (480)807-5400. **Web:** www.longbowgolf.com.
Holes: 18. **Yards:** 6,750/4,890. **Par:** 70/70. **Course Rating:** 71.8/67.0. **Slope:** 128/111. **Green Fee:** N/A. **Walking Policy:** Unrestricted walking. **Walkability:** 2. **Opened:** 1997. **Architect:** Ken Kavanaugh. **Season:** Year-Round. **High:** Jan.-April. **Miscellaneous:** Range (grass), club rentals, beginner friendly.
Reader Comments: Some tight fairways, lovely views ... Great value. A real surprise ... Great condition ... Fast greens ... Tough little track ... Great course for the money ... Fun to play, not too demanding ... Young but good ... Gem in the desert, great design ... Hard to find, but worth effort, every hole nice.

★★★★½ **LOS CABALLEROS GOLF CLUB** *Service, Pace*
R-1551 S. Vulture Mine Rd., Wickenburg, 85390, Maricopa County, (520)684-2704, 50 miles NW of Phoenix.
Holes: 18. **Yards:** 6,962/5,690. **Par:** 72/72. **Course Rating:** 73.4/71.2. **Slope:** 136/124. **Green Fee:** $44/$110. **Cart Fee:** Included in Green Fee. **Walking Policy:** Mandatory cart. **Walkability:** 4. **Opened:** 1979. **Architect:** Greg Nash/Jeff Hardin. **Season:** Year-round. **High:** Feb.-April. **To obtain tee times:** Call 2 days in advance. **Miscellaneous:** Reduced fees (low season, resort guests), discount packages, range (grass), club rentals, lodging, credit cards (MC, V).

ARIZONA

Reader Comments: Classic desert course, tough ... Love it ... Very good all around ... Hilly, good condition ... Rustic atmosphere. Nice friendly staff; worth the drive from Phoenix ... Pricey but would play again ... Very challenging ... Always in good shape, great views. Demanding but fair... Beautiful course and nice people.

MARRIOTT'S CAMELBACK GOLF CLUB
R-7847 N. Mockingbird Lane, Scottsdale, 85253, Maricopa County, (602)596-7050, (800)242-2635, 5 miles E of Phoenix.

★★★ INDIAN BEND COURSE
Holes: 18. **Yards:** 7,014/5,917. **Par:** 72/72. **Course Rating:** 72.6/72.0. **Slope:** 122/118. **Green Fee:** $35/$185. **Cart Fee:** Included in Green Fee. **Walking Policy:** Mandatory cart. **Walkability:** 2. **Opened:** 1980. **Architect:** Red Lawrence. **Season:** Year-round. **High:** Jan.-April. **To obtain tee times:** Call up to 30 days in advance. Marriott guests may call up to 45 days in advance.
Miscellaneous: Reduced fees (weekdays, low season, resort guests, twilight), discount packages, metal spikes, range (grass), club rentals, lodging, credit cards (MC, V, AE, D).
Reader Comments: Summer time best play; long; some tough holes ... OK ... The way to enjoy a round of golf ... Short old course; rough around the edges ... Fairly flat ... Beautiful course that wanders along a dry wash ... Pleasant ... Flat, featureless, long links course.

★★ PADRE COURSE
Holes: 18. **Yards:** 6,559/5,626. **Par:** 72/72. **Course Rating:** 71.0/72.0. **Slope:** 125/124. **Green Fee:** $35/$185. **Cart Fee:** Included in Green Fee. **Walking Policy:** Mandatory cart. **Walkability:** 2. **Opened:** 1971. **Architect:** Red Lawrence. **Season:** Year-round. **High:** Jan.-April. **To obtain tee times:** Call up to 30 days in advance. Marriott guests may call up to 45 days in advance.
Miscellaneous: Reduced fees (weekdays, low season, resort guests, twilight, juniors), discount packages, metal spikes, range (grass), club rentals, lodging, credit cards (MC, V, AE, D).

★★★½ MARYVALE GOLF CLUB
PM-5902 W. Indian School Rd., Phoenix, 85033, Maricopa County, (623)846-4022.
Holes: 18. **Yards:** 6,539/5,656. **Par:** 72/72. **Course Rating:** 69.8/70.2. **Slope:** 115/113. **Green Fee:** $8/$28. **Cart Fee:** $18/person. **Walking Policy:** Unrestricted walking. **Walkability:** 1. **Opened:** 1961. **Architect:** William F. Bell. **Season:** Year-round. **High:** Nov.-April. **To obtain tee times:** Call 2 days in advance. Three tee times per hour are reserved for walk-on play.
Miscellaneous: Reduced fees (weekdays, low season, twilight, seniors, juniors), metal spikes, range (grass), club rentals, credit cards (MC, V, AE, D).
Reader Comments: Old, flat, well maintained, lots of trees, fun ... Nice muny in Phoenix ... Best course for its price ... A good municipal course that gets no respect ... Nothing spectacular, but an OK muny ... Lots of water and beautiful homes.

McCORMICK RANCH GOLF CLUB
R-7505 E. McCormick Pkwy., Scottsdale, 85258, Maricopa County, (480)948-0260.

★★★½ PALM COURSE
Holes: 18. **Yards:** 7,044/5,057. **Par:** 72/72. **Course Rating:** 74.4/69.9. **Slope:** 137/117. **Green Fee:** $40/$110. **Cart Fee:** Included in Green Fee. **Walking Policy:** Mandatory cart. **Walkability:** 1. **Opened:** 1972. **Architect:** Desmond Muirhead. **Season:** Year-round. **High:** Jan.-April. **To obtain tee times:** Call 7 days in advance. Call up to 30 days in advance when staying at any Scottsdale or Phoenix hotel. **Miscellaneous:** Reduced fees (low season, twilight, juniors), discount packages, metal spikes, range (grass/mats), club rentals, lodging, credit cards (MC, V, AE), beginner friendly (junior clinics).
Reader Comments: Need a lot of carry on most shots ... OK. Enjoyed Pine more than Palm ... Old-style west Texas course in Arizona ... Flat, well maintained ... Easy resort track ... OK but not worth price at half the cost ... Course was a little soggy, slow greens, nice golf shop.

★★★½ PINE COURSE
Holes: 18. **Yards:** 7,187/5,333. **Par:** 72/72. **Course Rating:** 74.4/69.9. **Slope:** 135/117. **Green Fee:** $40/$110. **Cart Fee:** Included in Green Fee. **Walking Policy:** Mandatory cart. **Walkability:** 1. **Opened:** 1972. **Architect:** Desmond Muirhead. **Season:** Year-round. **High:** Jan.- April. **To obtain tee times:** Call 7 days in advance. Call up to 30 days in advance when staying at any Scottsdale or Phoenix hotel. **Miscellaneous:** Reduced fees (low season, twilight, juniors), discount packages, metal spikes, range (grass/mats), club rentals, lodging, credit cards (MC, V, AE), beginner friendly (junior clinics).
Reader Comments: Expensive for an average course ... Plays long, bring lots of balls! ... Overrated ... Great course, too expensive in-season ... An escape from desert targets ... Slow greens, nice golf shop.

MOUNT GRAHAM MUNICIPAL GOLF COURSE
PM-Golf Course Rd., Safford, 85546, Graham County, (602)348-3140, 120 miles NE of Tucson.
Holes: 18. **Yards:** 6,354/5,691. **Par:** 72/73. **Course Rating:** 69.5/70.6. **Slope:** 116/117. **Green Fee:** $15/$16. **Cart Fee:** $16/cart. **Walking Policy:** Unrestricted walking. **Walkability:** 1. **Season:** Year-round. **To obtain tee times:** Walk on. **Miscellaneous:** Reduced fees (twilight, juniors), metal spikes, range (grass/mats), club rentals.

MOUNTAIN BROOK GOLF CLUB
PU-5783 S. Mountain Brook Dr., Gold Canyon, 85219, Pinal County, (602)671-1000.
Holes: 18. **Yards:** 6,710/5,277. **Par:** 71/71. **Course Rating:** 69.9/66.2. **Slope:** 124/103. **Green Fee:** $20/$65. **Cart Fee:** Included in Green Fee. **Walking Policy:** Mandatory cart. **Walkability:** 2. **Opened:** 1996. **Season:** Year-round. **High:** Nov.-March. **To obtain tee times:** Call golf shop up to 6 days in advance. **Miscellaneous:** Reduced fees (low season, twilight, juniors), metal spikes, range (grass), club rentals, credit cards (MC, V), beginner friendly.

★★★ MOUNTAIN SHADOWS
PU-5641 E Lincoln Dr, Scottsdale, 85253, Maricopa County, (602)951-5427.
Holes: 18. **Yards:** 3,083/2,650. **Par:** 56/56. **Course Rating:** 56.9/55.4. **Slope:** 92/89. **Green Fee:** $30/$70. **Cart Fee:** Included in Green Fee. **Walking Policy:** Mandatory cart. **Walkability:** N/A. **Opened:** 1959. **Architect:** Jack Snyder. **Season:** Year-round. **High:** Jan.-April.
Miscellaneous: Metal spikes, range (grass), club rentals, lodging, credit cards (MC, V, AE, D).
Reader Comments: Not a good choice for serious golfers ... Mature course but not memorable ... Good test of small greens and some tight holes ... Good for short game ... Beautiful; proves length isn't everything.

★★★★ OAKCREEK COUNTRY CLUB *Pace+*
SP-690 Bell Rock Blvd., Sedona, 86351, Yavapai County, (520)284-1660, (888)703-9489, 100 miles N of Phoenix. **E-mail:** OCCC@Sedona.net.
Holes: 18. **Yards:** 6,824/5,579. **Par:** 72/72. **Course Rating:** 72.2/71.0. **Slope:** 132/128. **Green Fee:** $70/$70. **Cart Fee:** Included in Green Fee. **Walking Policy:** Walking at certain times.
Walkability: 2. **Opened:** 1968. **Architect:** Robert Trent Jones. **Season:** Year-round. **High:** March-May, Sept.-Nov. **To obtain tee times:** Call 6 days in advance. **Miscellaneous:** Reduced fees (twilight, juniors), discount packages, range (grass/mats), caddies, club rentals, credit cards (MC, V, AE, D).
Reader Comments: Old original, still great ... Tree-lined course in Arizona; tough, fair, fun ... Beautiful location ... Friendly, scenic ... Breathtaking views. Good test of golf ... Red rocks beautiful ... Great staff.

OCOTILLO GOLF CLUB
R-3751 S. Clubhouse Dr., Chandler, 85248, Maricopa County, (480)917-6660, (888)624-8899, 15 miles SE of Phoenix. **E-mail:** ocotillogolf@email.msn.com. **Web:** ocotillogolf.com.
Holes: 27. **Cart Fee:** Included in Green Fee. **Walking Policy:** Mandatory cart. **Walkability:** 2.
Opened: 1986. **Architect:** Ted Robinson. **Season:** Year-round. **High:** Jan.-April. **Miscellaneous:** Reduced fees (low season, twilight), metal spikes, range (grass/mats), club rentals, credit cards (MC, V, AE, D).
★★★★ BLUE/GOLD
Yards: 6,729/5,128. **Par:** 72/72. **Course Rating:** 71.3/71.3. **Slope:** 131/128. **Green Fee:** $45/$115.
★★★★ BLUE/WHITE
Yards: 6,533/5,134. **Par:** 71/71. **Course Rating:** 70.8/71.0. **Slope:** 128/127. **Green Fee:** $35/$115.
★★★★ WHITE/GOLD
Yards: 6,612/5,124. **Par:** 71/71. **Course Rating:** 71.4/68.4. **Slope:** 128/122. **Green Fee:** $45/$115.
Reader Comments: Water everywhere ... Felt like I was in Seattle; wet fairways ... Snorkel a must if you stray from the fairways ... Very good staff ... Great water hazards, play when tired of desert golf ... One of the better values in Phoenix/Scottsdale ... Clubhouse ranks a 10 ... Beautiful experience, worth the money ... A bargain at twice the price ... A flower garden ... Islands of green in a sea of blue—too cute.... A bit overpriced ... Bring golf balls.

OMNI TUCSON NATIONAL GOLF RESORT & SPA
R-2727 W. Club Dr., Tucson, 85741, Pima County, (520)575-7540, (800)528-4856, 20 miles NW of Tucson.
Holes: 27. **Green Fee:** $55/$135. **Cart Fee:** Included in Green Fee. **Walking Policy:** Mandatory cart. **Opened:** 1962. **Architect:** R.B. Harris/R. von Hagge/B. Devlin. **Season:** Year-round. **High:** Oct.-May. **To obtain tee times:** Call 2 days in advance. Resort guests 30 days in advance.
Miscellaneous: Reduced fees (twilight, juniors), range (grass), club rentals, lodging (169 rooms), credit cards (MC, V, AE, D, Diners Club).
★★★ GOLD/GREEN
Yards: 6,782/5,440. **Par:** 72/72. **Course Rating:** 72.6/71.2. **Slope:** 140/127. **Walkability:** 3.
Reader Comments: Easier than expected, even from tips and even though it's a PGA Tour stop ... Well kept, not difficult, good atmosphere ... Playable rough ... Too many bunkers ... A lot of money; tee times jammed together too close ... The pros play this? ... Strong service even though we weren't staying as guests ... Good value in summer, too pricey in winter.
★★★ ORANGE/GOLD
Yards: 7,103/5,679. **Par:** 73/73. **Course Rating:** 74.6/73.0. **Slope:** 136/127. **Walkability:** 2.
★★★ ORANGE/GREEN
Yards: 6,609/5,375. **Par:** 71/71. **Course Rating:** 72.0/71.2. **Slope:** 135/122. **Walkability:** 2.
Notes: PGA Tour Tucson Chrysler Classic.

ARIZONA

Reader Comments: Highly overrated ... Green 9 totally opposite other 9 ... Very nice course ... Old, tired, boring ... Tough course, excellent condition ... A bit dull ... Nice layout but crowded & expensive.

★★★½ ORANGE TREE GOLF CLUB

R-10601 N. 56th St., Scottsdale, 85254, Maricopa County, (480)948-3730, (800)228-0386.**Web:** www.orangetree.com.

Holes: 18. **Yards:** 6,762/5,632. **Par:** 72/72. **Course Rating:** 71.3/71.8. **Slope:** 122/116. **Green Fee:** $30/$98. **Cart Fee:** Included in Green Fee. **Walking Policy:** Mandatory cart. **Walkability:** 2. **Opened:** 1957. **Architect:** Johnny Bulla. **Season:** Year-round. **High:** Jan.-April. **To obtain tee times:** Call 30 days in advance. **Miscellaneous:** Reduced fees (twilight), discount packages, metal spikes, range (grass), club rentals, lodging (160 rooms), credit cards (MC, V, AE, D, Diners Club).

Reader Comments: Well maintained; flat, old layout, not much imagination ... Overpriced ... Fair, old-fashioned design, long track ... OK, needs course work ... Fairly wide open. Good for high handicapper ... Good greens ... Nice, pleasant tree-lined course ... Old-fashioned jewel, great mix of holes.

★★½ PAINTED MOUNTAIN GOLF CLUB

PU-6210 E. McKellips Rd., Mesa, 85215, Maricopa County, (480)832-0156, 20 miles E of Phoenix.

Holes: 18. **Yards:** 6,021/4,651. **Par:** 70/70. **Course Rating:** 67.2/64.3. **Slope:** 104/97. **Green Fee:** $16/$38. **Cart Fee:** $9/person. **Walking Policy:** Unrestricted walking. **Walkability:** 1. **Architect:** Milt Coggins. **Season:** Year-round. **High:** Jan.-April. **Miscellaneous:** Reduced fees (weekdays, low season, twilight, juniors), range (grass), club rentals, credit cards (MC, V).

Reader Comments: Good mix of holes ... Seemed disorganized ... Overpriced; short course from blue tees.

PALM VALLEY GOLF CLUB

SP-2211 N. Litchfield Rd., Goodyear, 85338, Maricopa County, (623)935-2500, (800)475-2978, 15 miles W of Phoenix. **Web:** www.suncoraz.com.

★★★★ LAKE COURSE

Holes: 18. **Yards:** 4,700/3,200. **Par:** 62/62. **Course Rating:** N/A. **Slope:** N/A. **Green Fee:** $6/$42. **Cart Fee:** Included in Green Fee. **Walking Policy:** Unrestricted walking. **Walkability:** 3. **Opened:** 1999. **Architect:** Hale Irwin. **Season:** Year-round. **High:** Nov.-March. **To obtain tee times:** Call up to 7 days in advance. **Miscellaneous:** Reduced fees (weekdays, low season, twilight, juniors), range (grass), club rentals, lodging (109 rooms), credit cards (MC, V, AE), beginner friendly (junior lessons, group lessons).

Reader Comments: Good track at a fair price ... Best deal in Arizona ... Always first on our list of courses to play in Phoenix area ... Great condition, nice golf shop & staff ... Beautiful clubhouse, excellent service ... Another must play. Must be straight hitter. Fast greens ... Fun course, constantly improving, great practice area.

★★★★ PALM COURSE

Holes: 18. **Yards:** 7,015/5,300. **Par:** 72/72. **Course Rating:** 72.8/68.7. **Slope:** 130/109. **Green Fee:** $19/$64. **Cart Fee:** $12/person. **Walking Policy:** Unrestricted walking. **Walkability:** 4. **Opened:** 1993. **Architect:** Arthur Hills. **Season:** Year-round. **High:** Jan.-March. **To obtain tee times:** Call up to 7 days in advance. **Miscellaneous:** Reduced fees (weekdays, low season, twilight, juniors), range (grass), club rentals, lodging (100 rooms), credit cards (MC, V, AE).

★★★½ PAPAGO GOLF COURSE

PM-5595 E. Moreland St., Phoenix, 85008, Maricopa County, (602)275-8428.

Holes: 18. **Yards:** 7,068/5,937. **Par:** 72/72. **Course Rating:** 73.3/72.4. **Slope:** 132/119. **Green Fee:** $12/$28. **Cart Fee:** $18/cart. **Walking Policy:** Unrestricted walking. **Walkability:** 3. **Opened:** 1963. **Architect:** William F. Bell. **Season:** Year-round. **High:** Jan.-May. **To obtain tee times:** Call 2 days in advance beginning at 6:30 a.m. **Miscellaneous:** Reduced fees (low season, twilight, seniors, juniors), metal spikes, range (grass/mats), club rentals.

Notes: Ranked 51st in 1996 America's Top 75 Affordable Courses.

Reader Comments: Best muny I've ever played ... Good price; good condition ... Pretty track ... Sometimes slow ... Desert view ... Some hills; lots of bunkers ... Staff seemed indifferent to slow play ... Looked nice, but could not get on; had to be there at 6:30 a.m. to get tee times ... Great any time: if you can actually get a tee time!.

★★ PAVILION LAKES GOLF CLUB

PU-8870 E. Indian Bend Rd., Scottsdale, 85250, Maricopa County, (480)948-3370.**Web:** www.pavilolakes.com.

Holes: 18. **Yards:** 6,515/5,135. **Par:** 71/71. **Course Rating:** 70.1/68.2. **Slope:** 120/110. **Green Fee:** $18/$59. **Cart Fee:** Included in Green Fee. **Walking Policy:** Walking at certain times. **Walkability:** 1. **Opened:** 1992. **Season:** Year-round. **High:** Jan.-April. **To obtain tee times:** Call up to 7 days in advance. **Miscellaneous:** Reduced fees (weekdays, low season, twilight, juniors), discount packages, metal spikes, range (grass), club rentals, credit cards (MC, V, AE, Diners Club).

★★ PAYSON GOLF COURSE
PU-1504 W. Country Club Dr., Payson, 85541, Gila County, (520)474-2273, 85 miles NE of Phoenix.
Holes: 18. **Yards:** 5,894/5,094. **Par:** 71/71. **Course Rating:** 66.9/66.7. **Slope:** 114/113. **Green Fee:** $20/$28. **Cart Fee:** $22/cart. **Walking Policy:** Unrestricted walking. **Walkability:** 1.
Opened: 1976. **Architect:** Frank Hughes/Russ Zakarisen. **Season:** Year-round. **High:** April-Oct.
To obtain tee times: Call up to 7 days in advance. **Miscellaneous:** Reduced fees (weekdays, low season, juniors), metal spikes, range (grass/mats), club rentals, credit cards (MC, V, AE).

THE PHOENICIAN GOLF CLUB *Service+*
R-6000 E. Camelback Rd., Scottsdale, 85251, Maricopa County, (602)423-2449, (800)888-8234.
Holes: 27. **Green Fee:** $80/$150. **Cart Fee:** Included in Green Fee. **Walking Policy:** Mandatory cart. **Walkability:** 3. **Opened:** 1988. **Architect:** Homer Flint. **Season:** Year-round. **High:** Oct.-May. **To obtain tee times:** Call up to 30 days in advance. **Miscellaneous:** Reduced fees (low season, resort guests), discount packages, metal spikes, range (grass), club rentals, lodging (654 rooms), credit cards (MC, V, AE, D, TCB)
★★★★ DESERT/CANYON *Condition*
Yards: 6,068/4,777. **Par:** 70/70. **Course Rating:** 69.4/67.7. **Slope:** 131/114. .
★★★★ OASIS/CANYON *Condition*
Yards: 6,258/4,871. **Par:** 70/70. **Course Rating:** 70.1/69.1. **Slope:** 130/111.
★★★★ OASIS/DESERT *Condition*
Yards: 6,310/5,024. **Par:** 70/70. **Course Rating:** 70.3/69.7. **Slope:** 130/113.
Reader Comments: Beautiful but course was a letdown ... Long; great view, wide open, lots of lay-up shots ... Summer rates—outstanding value. Very memorable holes! ... Hard to keep your eye on ball. Course is so beautiful ... Target desert golf ... Great greens ... Pricey for what you get in return ... Fair layout for all levels of player.

★★★★ THE POINTE HILTON RESORT AT TAPATIO CLIFFS
R-11111 N. 7th St., Phoenix, 85020, Maricopa County, (602)866-6356.
Holes: 18. **Yards:** 6,700/5,000. **Par:** 72/72. **Course Rating:** 71.2/68.4. **Slope:** 135/128. **Green Fee:** $45/$145. **Cart Fee:** Included in Green Fee. **Walking Policy:** Mandatory cart. **Walkability:** 4. **Opened:** 1989. **Architect:** Bill Johnston. **Season:** Year-round. **High:** Nov.-May. **To obtain tee times:** Resort guests call 30 days in advance. Golf packages may reserve up to 60 days in advance. Non resort guests, 7 days in advance. **Miscellaneous:** Reduced fees (weekdays, low season, twilight), metal spikes, range (grass), caddies, club rentals, lodging, credit cards (MC, V, AE, D, Diners Club, Carte Blanche).
Notes: 1989 Senior PGA Tour Arizona Classic.
Reader Comments: Wonderful experience, shop staff great ... Beautiful layout, very friendly ... Great undulating fairways ... Front and back are two different 9s ... What desert golf is all about ... Housing has taken away some of its beauty ... Very playable. Excellent greens ... Very scenic, tight, target golf ... Fun course regardless of score.

POINTE HILTON SOUTH MOUNTAIN RESORT
★★★★ PHANTOM HORSE GOLF CLUB *Service+, Condition*
R-7777 S. Pointe Pkwy., Phoenix, 85044, Maricopa County, (602)431-6480, (800)876-4683.
Holes: 18. **Yards:** 6,211/4,550. **Par:** 70/70. **Course Rating:** 69.1/66.2. **Slope:** 124/107. **Green Fee:** $30/$125. **Cart Fee:** Included in Green Fee. **Walking Policy:** Walking at certain times.
Walkability: 3. **Opened:** 1988. **Architect:** Forrest Richardson. **Season:** Year-round. **High:** Jan.-April. **To obtain tee times:** Resort guests call 30 days in advance. Golf packages may reserve up to 60 days in advance. Non resort guests, 7 days in advance. **Miscellaneous:** Reduced fees (weekdays, low season, resort guests, twilight, juniors), discount packages, range (grass), caddies, club rentals, lodging (648 rooms), credit cards (MC, V, AE, D, Diners Club).
Reader Comments: Great shape, great target golf course, makes you earn your score ... Well-kept course, truly great golf, this course does it well ... Duffers shouldn't play from the tips ... Loved every bit of it! ... Nice contrast front to back ... Very scenic ... Not many flat lies, fun course ... Challenging, up and down. Great mix of desert and water.

★★★ PRESCOTT COUNTRY CLUB
SP-1030 Prescott C.C. Blvd., Dewey, 86327, Yavapai County, (520)772-8984.
Holes: 18. **Yards:** 6,783/5,771. **Par:** 72/72. **Course Rating:** 71.2/71.5. **Slope:** 124/126. **Green Fee:** $24/$45. **Cart Fee:** Included in Green Fee. **Walking Policy:** Unrestricted walking.
Walkability: 3. **Opened:** 1970. **Architect:** Milt Coggins. **Season:** Year-round. **High:** May-Sept.
To obtain tee times: Call 7 days in advance. **Miscellaneous:** Reduced fees (weekdays, low season, twilight, juniors), discount packages, metal spikes, range (grass), club rentals, credit cards (MC, V, AE, D).
Reader Comments: A hidden gem ... Beautiful mountain course ... Rolling hills, great par 3s, memorable holes ... Nice layout, fun to play ... Easygoing atmosphere.

ARIZONA

★★½ PUEBLO DEL SOL COUNTRY CLUB

SP-2770 St. Andrews Dr., Sierra Vista, 85650, Cochise County, (520)378-6444, 70 miles SE of Tucson.

Holes: 18. **Yards:** 7,074/5,896. **Par:** 72/74. **Course Rating:** 73.1/73.1. **Slope:** 128/126. **Green Fee:** $15/$35. **Cart Fee:** $20/cart. **Walking Policy:** Unrestricted walking. **Walkability:** 1. **Opened:** 1975. **Architect:** Tenneco Engineers. **Season:** Year-round. **High:** Feb.-March/June-Oct. **To obtain tee times:** Call 7 days in advance. **Miscellaneous:** Reduced fees (weekdays, low season, twilight, seniors, juniors), metal spikes, range (grass/mats), club rentals, credit cards (MC, V, D).

Reader Comments: Nice but doesn't hold a candle to Phoenix courses ... Greens are like iced ski-slopes, cool climate ... Fast greens, old style.

★★ PUEBLO EL MIRAGE RESORT

R-11201 N. El Mirage Rd., El Mirage, 85335, Maricopa County, (602)583-0425, 10 miles W of Phoenix.

Holes: 18. **Yards:** 6,596/5,826. **Par:** 72/72. **Course Rating:** 71.1/71.0. **Slope:** 125/117. **Green Fee:** $12/$39. **Cart Fee:** Included in Green Fee. **Walking Policy:** Walking at certain times. **Walkability:** 2. **Opened:** 1985. **Architect:** Ken Killian/Fuzzy Zoeller. **Season:** Year-round. **High:** Nov.-March. **To obtain tee times:** Call 7 days in advance. **Miscellaneous:** Reduced fees (weekdays, low season, resort guests, twilight, juniors), discount packages, metal spikes, range (grass), club rentals, lodging, credit cards (MC, V), beginner friendly (beginner lessons, private and group).

★★★½ RANCHO MANANA GOLF CLUB

R-5734 E. Rancho Manana Blvd., Cave Creek, 85331, Maricopa County, (602)488-0398, 20 miles N of Phoenix.

Holes: 18. **Yards:** 6,378/5,910. **Par:** 71/71. **Course Rating:** 67.8/68.8. **Slope:** 125/114. **Green Fee:** $30/$115. **Cart Fee:** Included in Green Fee. **Walking Policy:** Mandatory cart. **Walkability:** 5. **Opened:** 1988. **Architect:** Bill Johnston. **Season:** Year-round. **High:** Jan.-April. **To obtain tee times:** Call up to 7 days in advance. **Miscellaneous:** Reduced fees (weekdays, low season, twilight), discount packages, metal spikes, range (grass), club rentals, credit cards (MC, V, AE, D).

Reader Comments: Great risk-reward course ... Nice mountain course, beautiful scenery ... Difficult for average golfer, challenging ... Great service, fun to play ... Tight, hillside course ... Interesting layout ... Short but tough enough ... Priced like a resort, plays like a muny ... Tightest course in Arizona, tremendous views.

RANDOLPH PARK GOLF COURSE

PM-600 S. Alvernon Way, Tucson, 85716, Pima County, (520)325-2811.

★★★½ DELL URICH MUNICIPAL GOLF COURSE

Holes: 18. **Yards:** 6,633/5,270. **Par:** 70/70. **Course Rating:** 70.3/68.8. **Slope:** 119/113. **Green Fee:** $12/$29. **Cart Fee:** $16/cart. **Walking Policy:** Unrestricted walking. **Walkability:** 2. **Opened:** 1996. **Architect:** Ken Kavanaugh. **Season:** Year-round. **High:** Nov.-March. **To obtain tee times:** Computerized system (24Hrs.) 520-791-4336 six days in advance. **Miscellaneous:** Reduced fees (low season, twilight, seniors, juniors), metal spikes, range (grass/mats), club rentals, credit cards (MC, V, D), beginner friendly.

Reader Comments: Good muny, nice layout ... Fun city course, plays more difficult than yardage ... Staff a little stuffy ... Excellent design ... Redesign has added a lot of character ... Very fair for all skill levels. Greens were excellent. A definite play when in the area.

★★★½ NORTH COURSE

Holes: 18. **Yards:** 6,863/5,972. **Par:** 72/73. **Course Rating:** 72.5/73.7. **Slope:** 125/124. **Green Fee:** $14/$29. **Cart Fee:** $16/cart. **Walking Policy:** Unrestricted walking. **Opened:** 1925. **Architect:** William P. Bell. **Season:** Year-round. **High:** Nov.-May. **To obtain tee times:** Call Monday-Friday between 8 a.m. and 4 p.m. **Miscellaneous:** Reduced fees (low season, twilight, seniors, juniors), metal spikes, range (grass), club rentals, credit cards (MC, V, D). **Notes:** LPGA Welch's/Circle K Ch., Major NCAA Event National Qualifiers.

Reader Comments: Best muny in town, traditional, good layout, good par 4s ... Good course, LPGA plays here ... City operated, inexpensive, solid course ... Nice course, although the eating area needs help ... Good layout ... Old-style, good greens, sand tough, rough ... Busy but efficient staff ... Good value for money. Great snack bar.

★★★★½ THE RAVEN GOLF CLUB AT SABINO SPRINGS *Service+, Condition*

PU-9777 E. Sabino Greens Dr., Tucson, 85749, Pima County, (520)749-3636. **E-mail:** ravenss@azstarnet.com.

Holes: 18. **Yards:** 6,776/4,733. **Par:** 71/71. **Course Rating:** 73.2/66.6. **Slope:** 144/112. **Green Fee:** $55/$140. **Cart Fee:** Included in Green Fee. **Walking Policy:** Unrestricted walking. **Walkability:** 5. **Opened:** 1996. **Architect:** Robert Trent Jones Jr. **Season:** Year-round. **High:** Jan.-April. **To obtain tee times:** Call up to 30 days in advance. **Miscellaneous:** Reduced fees (low season, twilight, juniors), metal spikes, range (grass), club rentals, credit cards (MC, V, AE, D, Diners Club).

Notes: Ranked 13th in 1999 Best in State; 7th in 1996 Best New Upscale Courses.
Reader Comments: Phenomenal layout, 18th tee shot is unbelievable ... Excellent desert course, very playable for all ... Felt like everyone knew us personally ... Most fun course in Tucson ... Superb views ... Friendly, unbeatable service ... Expensive, but joy to play ... Hard for high handicapper ... Women-friendly tee boxes.

★★★★½ THE RAVEN GOLF CLUB AT SOUTH MOUNTAIN *Service+, Condition+, Pace*
PU-3636 E. Baseline Rd., Phoenix, 85040, Maricopa County, (602)243-3636.
Holes: 18. **Yards:** 7,078/5,759. **Par:** 72/72. **Course Rating:** 73.9/72.9. **Slope:** 133/124. **Green Fee:** $75/$155. **Cart Fee:** Included in Green Fee. **Walking Policy:** Unrestricted walking. **Walkability:** 2. **Opened:** 1995. **Architect:** David Graham/Gary Panks. **Season:** Year-round. **High:** Oct.-April. **To obtain tee times:** Reservations accepted 10 days in advance with credit card. 48-hour cancellation policy. **Miscellaneous:** Reduced fees (low season, twilight, juniors), metal spikes, range (grass), club rentals, credit cards (MC, V, AE, D, Diners Club).
Notes: Ranked 17th in 1999 Best in State.
Reader Comments: Excellent. Very enjoyable ... California-type course in the desert; lots of sand traps/trees; bring your 'A' game ... Best course in Phoenix ... Service is second to none ... If you can, play at all costs ... Attendants cleaned clubs on driving range and fixed ball marks on par 3s ... Woodland course in desert setting ... Mango-scented iced towels on a hot day ... Best service & staff I've seen.

★★★½ RIO RICO RESORT & COUNTRY CLUB
R-1069 Camino Caralampi, Rio Rico, 85648, Santa Cruz County, (520)281-8567, (800)288-4746, 50 miles S of Tucson. **Web:** www.rioricoresort.com.
Holes: 18. **Yards:** 7,119/5,649. **Par:** 72/72. **Course Rating:** 72.9/70.4. **Slope:** 128/126. **Green Fee:** $25/$75. **Cart Fee:** Included in Green Fee. **Walking Policy:** Mandatory cart. **Walkability:** 2. **Opened:** 1972. **Architect:** Robert Trent Jones. **Season:** Year-round. **High:** Jan.-April. **To obtain tee times:** Call (520)288-4746 for times. 5 Days advance for public—60 days advance w/resort reservation. **Miscellaneous:** Reduced fees (weekdays, low season, resort guests, twilight), range (grass), club rentals, lodging, credit cards (MC, V, AE, D, Diners Club).
Reader Comments: Best course in southern Arizona, great layout ... Well maintained, wide open, with water... Off the beaten path but worth the drive ... Greens not up to speed ... Excellent design & condition. I would return ... Beautiful location & weather... Front 9 toughest ... Friendly staff ... Desert layout, stay on the fairway.

★★★½ SAN IGNACIO GOLF CLUB
PU-4201 S. Camino Del Sol, Green Valley, 85614, Pima County, (520)648-3468, 25 miles S of Tucson.
Holes: 18. **Yards:** 6,704/5,200. **Par:** 71/72. **Course Rating:** 71.4/68.7. **Slope:** 129/116. **Green Fee:** $22/$73. **Cart Fee:** $12/person. **Walking Policy:** Mandatory cart. **Walkability:** N/A. **Opened:** 1989. **Architect:** Arthur Hills. **Season:** Year-round. **High:** Jan.-April. **To obtain tee times:** Call 5 days in advance. **Miscellaneous:** Reduced fees (low season, twilight), range (grass), club rentals, credit cards (MC, V).
Reader Comments: Desert course; narrow; not well maintained ... Variety of holes ... Slow play ... Not improving from year to year ... Excellent value ... Very tight, beautiful, challenging ... Target golf on many holes ... Beautiful view of mountains ... Good layout ... Overpriced for condition of course ... Greens not as good as rest of course ... Windy.

★★★ SANTA RITA GOLF CLUB
PU-16461 Houghton Rd., Corna De Tucson, 85641, Pima County, (520)762-5620, 6 miles SE of Tucson.
Holes: 18. **Yards:** 6,523/5,539. **Par:** 72/72. **Course Rating:** 70.9/69.7. **Slope:** 125/117. **Green Fee:** $15/$49. **Cart Fee:** $8/person. **Walking Policy:** Unrestricted walking. **Walkability:** 3. **Opened:** 1962. **Architect:** Red Lawrence. **Season:** Year-round. **High:** Jan.-April. **To obtain tee times:** Call up to 7 days in advance. **Miscellaneous:** Reduced fees (weekdays, low season, twilight, seniors, juniors), discount packages, metal spikes, range (grass/mats), club rentals, credit cards (MC, V, AE, D), beginner friendly.
Reader Comments: An OK 'out of the way' track ... Difficult; but beautiful scenery ... Don't depend on the par 3s to help your score ... Fast greens—long par 3s ... Often very windy ... Nice, nice course! ... Mountain course, views.

SCOTTSDALE COUNTRY CLUB
SP-7702 E. Shea Blvd., Scottsdale, 85260, Maricopa County, (480)948-6000.
Holes: 27. **Green Fee:** $27/$85. **Cart Fee:** Included in Green Fee. **Walking Policy:** Mandatory cart. **Walkability:** 2. **Architect:** Arnold Palmer/Ed Seay. **Season:** Year-round. **High:** Jan.-March. **To obtain tee times:** Public may call 5 days in advance. 30 days in advance for groups of 8 or more.
★★★ NORTH/EAST
Yards: 6,292/5,339. **Par:** 71/71. **Course Rating:** 69.7/69.4. **Slope:** 119/108. **Opened:** 1986. **Miscellaneous:** Reduced fees (weekdays, low season, twilight), club rentals, credit cards (MC, V, AE).

ARIZONA

Reader Comments: Tight & short, lush grass ... Easy course, nice, good value ... Two very different 9s ... Good value in Scottsdale after 1:30 p.m. ... Mediocre practice area ... Average course wanders through housing developments ... East 9 one of the finest ... A good warm-up course for more challenging ones.

★★★ NORTH/SOUTH
Yards: 6,085/4,800. **Par:** 70/70. **Course Rating:** 68.8/69.0. **Slope:** 118/111. **Opened:** 1954. **Miscellaneous:** Reduced fees (weekdays, low season, twilight), range (grass), club rentals, credit cards (MC, V, AE).
Reader Comments: Fun course ... Tight with lots of trees.

★★★ SOUTH/EAST
Yards: 6,335/5,241. **Par:** 71/71. **Course Rating:** 69.6/68.8. **Slope:** 118/109. **Opened:** 1954. **Miscellaneous:** Reduced fees (weekdays, low season, twilight), range (grass), club rentals, credit cards (MC, V, AE).
Reader Comments: Narrow course, homes ... Good value for area ... Too short ... Very good greens.

★★★★ SEDONA GOLF RESORT
R-35 Ridge Trail Dr., Sedona, 86351, Yavapai County, (520)284-9355, 100 miles N of Phoenix.
Holes: 18. **Yards:** 6,646/5,059. **Par:** 71/71. **Course Rating:** 70.3/67.0. **Slope:** 129/114. **Green Fee:** $79/$95. **Cart Fee:** Included in Green Fee. **Walking Policy:** Unrestricted walking. **Walkability:** 4. **Opened:** 1988. **Architect:** Gary Panks. **Season:** Year-round. **High:** March-Nov. **To obtain tee times:** Call up to 14 days in advance with credit card. **Miscellaneous:** Reduced fees (twilight), discount packages, range (grass), club rentals, lodging (225 rooms), credit cards (MC, V, AE).
Notes: Ranked 15th in 1999 Best in State.
Reader Comments: Good condition and test ... Breathtaking ... Fair course, world's greatest scenery ... First-class resort course, too many tourists ... Nice place to play ... Bring your camera ... Used to be a good value, now too expensive ... Scenic, don't let area construction dissuade you ... Red rock views are God's masterpiece.

SHADOW MOUNTAIN GOLF CLUB
SP-1105 Irene St., Pearce, 85625, Cochise County, (520)826-3412, 70 miles SE of Tucson.
Holes: 18. **Yards:** 6,632/5,876. **Par:** 72/72. **Course Rating:** 71.1/72.3. **Slope:** 126/125. **Green Fee:** $10/$17. **Cart Fee:** $16/cart. **Walking Policy:** Unrestricted walking. **Walkability:** 1. **Opened:** 1960. **Season:** Year-round. **High:** Jan.-May. **To obtain tee times:** Call 30 days in advance. **Miscellaneous:** Reduced fees (low season, twilight, juniors), club rentals, credit cards (MC, V, AE).

SHERATON EL CONQUISTADOR COUNTRY CLUB
R-10555 N. La Canada, Tucson, 85737, Pima County, (520)544-1800.

★★★ SUNRISE COURSE
Holes: 18. **Yards:** 6,819/5,255. **Par:** 72/72. **Course Rating:** 71.7/69.4. **Slope:** 123/116. **Green Fee:** $25/$125. **Cart Fee:** Included in Green Fee. **Walking Policy:** Mandatory cart. **Walkability:** 4. **Opened:** 1984. **Architect:** Greg Nash/Jeff Hardin. **Season:** Year-round. **High:** Feb.-April. **Miscellaneous:** Reduced fees (low season, resort guests), discount packages, range (grass), club rentals, lodging, credit cards (MC, V, AE, D).
Reader Comments: Good value in summer, overpriced in winter ... Cart mandatory ... Should play, good food ... Not a great track ... Easy to hit homes; poorly maintained ... Nice course ... Very tight ... If you aren't a member or in a tournament, forget service ... Terrific practice facilities ... Narrow ... Several good holes.

★★★½ SUNSET COURSE
Holes: 18. **Yards:** 6,763/5,323. **Par:** 71/71. **Course Rating:** 71.2/69.5. **Slope:** 123/114. **Green Fee:** $25/$125. **Cart Fee:** Included in Green Fee. **Walking Policy:** Mandatory cart. **Walkability:** 3. **Opened:** 1984. **Architect:** Greg Nash/Jeff Hardin. **Season:** Year-round. **High:** Jan.-April. **Miscellaneous:** Reduced fees (low season, resort guests), discount packages, range (grass), club rentals, lodging, credit cards (MC, V, AE, D).
Reader Comments: Better of the two courses ... Always good ... Several good holes ... Too costly for caliber of course, no walking allowed ... Miss elevated greens—oops! ... Excellent for members ... In summer bring your own water ... Tight.

★★★ SHERATON SAN MARCOS GOLF CLUB
SP-100 N. Dakota St., Chandler, 85224, Maricopa County, (480)963-3358, 15 miles S of Phoenix.
Holes: 18. **Yards:** 6,551/5,431. **Par:** 72/73. **Course Rating:** 70.0/69.4. **Slope:** 117/112. **Green Fee:** $30/$79. **Cart Fee:** Included in Green Fee. **Walking Policy:** Walking at certain times. **Walkability:** 4. **Opened:** 1923. **Architect:** Watson. **Season:** Year-round. **High:** Jan.-April. **To obtain tee times:** Call 7 days in advance. **Miscellaneous:** Reduced fees (weekdays, low season, twilight, juniors), discount packages, range (grass), club rentals, lodging, credit cards (MC, V, AE, D).
Reader Comments: Traditional versus desert ... Charge too much for this old course ... Very old ... Overpriced, play was so slow you could see the grass grow ... Good peak-season value ... Old course, nostalgic, one of Arizona's oldest, wide open.

★★★★ SILVER CREEK GOLF CLUB *Pace*

PU-2051 Silver Lake Blvd., Show Low, 85901, Navajo County, (520)537-2744, (800)909-5981, 12 miles NE of Show Low.
Holes: 18. **Yards:** 6,813/5,193. **Par:** 71/71. **Course Rating:** 71.5/68.0. **Slope:** 131/120. **Green Fee:** $17/$38. **Cart Fee:** $24/cart. **Walking Policy:** Unrestricted walking. **Walkability:** 3. **Opened:** 1985. **Architect:** Gary Panks. **Season:** Year-round. **High:** June-Sept. **To obtain tee times:** Call 3 days in advance. **Miscellaneous:** Reduced fees (weekdays, low season, twilight, seniors, juniors), discount packages, metal spikes, range (grass), club rentals, credit cards (MC, V, D).
Reader Comments: Great course, great price ... Probably best value in the state. Greens great condition, lightning fast! ... Need ranger to move play along ... A jewel ... Best kept secret in Arizona ... In Boondocks but cool in summer ... Great high-country golf ... Challenge for every level. Often windy, greens dry out & get very fast.

★★★½ SILVERBELL GOLF COURSE

PM-3600 N. Silverbell, Tucson, 85745, Pima County, (520)743-7284.
Holes: 18. **Yards:** 6,824/5,800. **Par:** 72/73. **Course Rating:** 71.2/72.2. **Slope:** 123/125. **Green Fee:** $16/$27. **Cart Fee:** $8/person. **Walking Policy:** Unrestricted walking. **Walkability:** 2. **Opened:** 1978. **Architect:** Jack Snyder. **Season:** Year-round. **High:** Oct.-April. **To obtain tee times:** Call up to 7 days in advance. **Miscellaneous:** Reduced fees (low season, twilight, seniors, juniors), metal spikes, range (grass/mats), club rentals, credit cards (MC, V, AE, D).
Reader Comments: Flat, friendly course; pumps the ego ... City operated, good test for all handicaps ... Good condition ... Great value for the money ... If in Tucson you won't be disappointed ... City should upgrade; spend $$$.

★★★★ STARR PASS GOLF CLUB

SP-3645 W. Starr Pass Blvd., Tucson, 85745, Pima County, (520)670-0400, (800)503-2898, 4 miles W of I10 Starr Pass Blvd Tucson. **Web:** www.starrpasstucson.com.
Holes: 18. **Yards:** 6,910/5,071. **Par:** 71/71. **Course Rating:** 74.6/70.7. **Slope:** 139/121. **Green Fee:** $48/$125. **Cart Fee:** Included in Green Fee. **Walking Policy:** Mandatory cart. **Walkability:** N/A. **Opened:** 1986. **Architect:** Robert Cupp. **Season:** Year-round. **High:** Jan.-May. **To obtain tee times:** Call up to 90 days in advance. **Miscellaneous:** Reduced fees (low season, resort guests, twilight), discount packages, range (grass), club rentals, lodging, credit cards (MC, V, AE, D).
Reader Comments: One of the best, but oh those houses ... Tight, forces good course management ... Target course, expensive, difficult ... Danger lurks ... Nasty, deep bunkers ... Very challenging and gorgeous desert-mountain course ... Fast, small greens ... Very difficult course, good condition ... Service was fine.

★★★½ STONECREEK GOLF CLUB

SP-4435 E. Paradise Village Pkwy. S., Phoenix, 85032, Maricopa County, (602)953-9111.
Holes: 18. **Yards:** 6,839/5,098. **Par:** 71/71. **Course Rating:** 72.6/68.4. **Slope:** 134/118. **Green Fee:** $20/$125. **Cart Fee:** Included in Green Fee. **Walking Policy:** Mandatory cart. **Walkability:** 3. **Opened:** 1989. **Architect:** Arthur Hills. **Season:** Year-round. **High:** Jan.-April. **To obtain tee times:** Call in advance up to a year. Non-refundable reservation fee if applicable.
Miscellaneous: Reduced fees (weekdays, low season, resort guests, twilight, juniors), discount packages, metal spikes, range (grass), club rentals, credit cards (MC, V, AE, Diners Club).
Reader Comments: Some strong holes ... One of the best golf shops in town ... Links-style desert course. Great for ego ... Pleasant play with locals; good golf ... Tough hazards ... Good, interesting, can get slow ... One of the best in Phoenix, but vastly overpriced ... Desert-style links ... Challenging par 3s.

★★★★ SUNRIDGE CANYON GOLF CLUB *Condition, Pace*

PU-13100 N. SunRidge Dr., Fountain Hills, 85268, Maricopa County, (480)837-5100, (800)562-5178, 1 miles E of Scottsdale. **E-mail:** jay.haffner@sunridgecanyongolfaz.com. **Web:** www.sunridgecanyongolfaz.com.
Holes: 18. **Yards:** 6,823/5,141. **Par:** 71/71. **Course Rating:** 73.4/70.1. **Slope:** 140/125. **Green Fee:** $65/$145. **Cart Fee:** Included in Green Fee. **Walking Policy:** Mandatory cart. **Walkability:** 4. **Opened:** 1995. **Architect:** Keith Foster. **Season:** Year-round. **High:** Nov.-April. **To obtain tee times:** Call golf shop up to 30 days in advance. **Miscellaneous:** Reduced fees (low season, juniors), range (grass), club rentals, credit cards (MC, V, AE).
Reader Comments: Best course in Phoenix ... Very good finishing holes ... Picturesque, challenging, enjoyable ... Very tough back nine ... Whew! What views ... Great four-hole finish ... Fastest greens in Phoenix area ... Pro treatment, great staff ... Quick, smooth greens ... What an awesome course in an awesome setting.

★★★½ SUPERSTITION SPRINGS GOLF CLUB

R-6542 E. Baseline Rd., Mesa, 85206, Maricopa County, (480)985-5622, (800)468-7918, 20 miles E of Phoenix.
Holes: 18. **Yards:** 7,005/5,328. **Par:** 72/72. **Course Rating:** 74.1/70.9. **Slope:** 135/120. **Green Fee:** $30/$125. **Cart Fee:** Included in Green Fee. **Walking Policy:** Mandatory cart. **Walkability:**

3. **Opened:** 1986. **Architect:** Greg Nash. **Season:** Year-round. **High:** Oct.-April. **To obtain tee times:** Accepted up to 14 days in advance. Tee time accepted 8-60 days in advance for no surcharge for groups. **Miscellaneous:** Reduced fees (weekdays, low season, resort guests, twilight), discount packages, metal spikes, range (grass/mats), club rentals, credit cards (MC, V, AE, D). **Reader Comments:** Fun; great golf shop ... Busy, but well managed ... Gorgeous layout ... An Arizona must ... Lots of water & sand make or break game ... Spectacular fun layout, large greens ... Always windy ... Tough water holes ... Nothing spectacular, but great golf ... Not a desert-style course, more like resort courses of Florida.

TALKING STICK GOLF CLUB
PU-9998 East Indian Bend Rd., Scottsdale, 85256, Maricopa County, (602)860-2221, 2 miles E of Scottsdale. **Web:** www.troongolf.com.

★★★½   NORTH COURSE
Holes: 18. **Yards:** 7,133/5,532. **Par:** 70/70. **Course Rating:** 73.8/70.0. **Slope:** 125/116. **Green Fee:** $40/$110. **Cart Fee:** Included in Green Fee. **Walking Policy:** Unrestricted walking. **Walkability:** 2. **Opened:** 1998. **Architect:** Ben Crenshaw/Bill Coore. **Season:** Year-round. **High:** Nov.-April. **To obtain tee times:** Call golf shop up to 30 days in advance. Groups of 16 or more may call up to 6 months in advance. **Miscellaneous:** Reduced fees (weekdays, low season, juniors), metal spikes, range (grass), club rentals, credit cards (MC, V, AE).
Notes: Ranked 21st in 1999 Best in State. Golf Digest School site.
Reader Comments: Simple layout ... Needs another year to season ... Personnel helpful ... Tremendous links track ... Wait until it matures ... Awfully good course ... Hit it straight; long tough greens ... A lot of money for courses not yet ready ... Good deal at $100; fun, flat, wide open ... A diamond in the rough, best new valley course in years.

★★★½   SOUTH COURSE
Holes: 18. **Yards:** 6,833/5,428. **Par:** 71/71. **Course Rating:** 72.7/69.1. **Slope:** 129/118. **Green Fee:** $40/$110. **Cart Fee:** Included in Green Fee. **Walking Policy:** Unrestricted walking. **Walkability:** 2. **Opened:** 1998. **Architect:** Ben Crenshaw/Bill Coore. **Season:** Year-round. **High:** Nov.-April. **To obtain tee times:** Call golf shop up to 30 days in advance. Groups of 16 or more may call up to 6 months in advance. **Miscellaneous:** Reduced fees (weekdays, low season, juniors), metal spikes, range (grass), club rentals, credit cards (MC, V, AE).
Reader Comments: Too many holes look and feel the same ... Flat & featureless ... Desert-links course ... Wide open, small greens ... Needs a little maturity but still great ... Play was slow ... Most forgiving course in valley ... Both courses easy to walk & carry ... Too new! Lots of room to improve ... Pedestrian, most holes look alike.

★★★½   TATUM RANCH GOLF CLUB
PU-29888 N. Tatum Ranch Dr., Cave Creek, 85331, Maricopa County, (602)585-2399, (800)468-7918, 25 miles N of Phoenix.
Holes: 18. **Yards:** 6,856/5,081. **Par:** 72/72. **Course Rating:** 71.8/69.3. **Slope:** 127/115. **Green Fee:** $25/$110. **Cart Fee:** Included in Green Fee. **Walking Policy:** Mandatory cart. **Walkability:** 2. **Opened:** 1987. **Architect:** Robert Cupp. **Season:** Year-round. **High:** Nov.-April. **To obtain tee times:** Call 7 days in advance for no charge. Call up to 60 days in advance with a surcharge. **Miscellaneous:** Reduced fees (weekdays, low season, resort guests, twilight, juniors), metal spikes, range (grass), club rentals, credit cards (MC, V, AE).
Reader Comments: Great shape, nice staff, but not cheap ... Boring! ... Mediocre in every way ... Fast rolling greens ... Good desert course ... Super condition ... Helpful employees, fun 19th hole ... Going private, too bad.

TONTO VERDE GOLF CLUB
SP-18401 El Circulo Dr., Rio Verde, 85263, Maricopa County, (602)471-2710, 20 miles NE of Scottsdale.
★★★★   PEAKS COURSE AT TONTO VERDE
Holes: 18. **Yards:** 6,736/5,376. **Par:** 72/72. **Course Rating:** 71.1/70.8. **Slope:** 132/124. **Green Fee:** $40/$125. **Walking Policy:** Walking at certain times. **Walkability:** 2. **Opened:** 1994. **Architect:** David Graham/Gary Panks. **Season:** Year-round. **High:** Dec.-April. **To obtain tee times:** Tee time must be made no sooner than 7 days in advance. Saturday tee time may be booked on Tuesday. **Miscellaneous:** Reduced fees (low season, resort guests), discount packages, range (grass), club rentals, lodging, credit cards (MC, V, AE, D).
Reader Comments: Tight fairways ... Firm course ... Very playable, fun ... Long way from Scottsdale ... Great fairways; ordinary layout ... Excellent service ... Great desert layout & enjoyable ... Nice staff ... Pretty desert course. Too narrow, with fairways sloped toward desert edges. Great place to eat ... Great views.
RANCH COURSE AT TONTO VERDE
Holes: 18. **Yards:** 6,988/5,788. **Par:** 72/72. **Course Rating:** 73.1/72.2. **Slope:** 133/127. **Green Fee:** $40/$125. **Cart Fee:** Included in Green Fee. **Walking Policy:** Walking at certain times. **Walkability:** N/A. **Opened:** 1999. **Season:** Year-round. **High:** Dec.-April. **To obtain tee times:** Tee time must be made no sooner than 7 days in advance. Saturday tee time may be booked on

Tuesday. **Miscellaneous:** Reduced fees (low season, resort guests), discount packages, range (grass), club rentals, lodging, credit cards (MC, V, AE, D).

★★★½ TORRES BLANCAS GOLF CLUB
SP-3233 S. Abrego, Green Valley, 85614, Pima County, (520)625-5200, 20 miles S of Tucson. **Holes:** 18. **Yards:** 6,894/5,077. **Par:** 72/72. **Course Rating:** 71.6/67.8. **Slope:** 125/119. **Green Fee:** $19/$59. **Cart Fee:** Included in Green Fee. **Walking Policy:** Mandatory cart. **Walkability:** 2. **Opened:** 1996. **Architect:** Lee Trevino. **Season:** Year-round. **High:** Jan.-April. **To obtain tee times:** Call golf shop or make reservations through Best Western at (520)625-2250. **Miscellaneous:** Reduced fees (low season, resort guests, twilight, seniors), metal spikes, range (grass), club rentals, credit cards (MC, V).
Reader Comments: Flat, well maintained, good scoring ... Overpriced ... Good conditioning for a young course ... Great shape, great prices for condition of course ... Short, open, should score on this one ... Fun course, hidden obstacles ... Pleasant design. Fast greens. Good kitchen ... A good place to work out the rust.

TOURNAMENT PLAYERS CLUB OF SCOTTSDALE
R-17020 N. Hayden Rd., Scottsdale, 85255, Maricopa County, (480)585-3939. **Web:** www.pgatour.com.
★★★½ DESERT COURSE
Holes: 18. **Yards:** 6,552/4,715. **Par:** 71/71. **Course Rating:** 71.4/66.3. **Slope:** 112/109. **Green Fee:** $31/$41. **Walking Policy:** Unrestricted walking. **Walkability:** 2. **Opened:** 1987. **Architect:** Tom Weiskopf/Jay Morrish. **Season:** Year-round. **High:** Oct.-April. **To obtain tee times:** Call up to 7 days in advance. **Miscellaneous:** Reduced fees (low season, twilight, seniors, juniors), metal spikes, range (grass/mats), club rentals, lodging, credit cards (MC, V, AE).
Reader Comments: Don't miss ... Brown, flat fairways, so-so greens ... More fun than Stadium ... Excellent course ... Links style in the desert, inexpensive & fun to play ... Nice but a factory, you're just a number ... Greens inconsistent, like a rock ... Great value compared with Stadium ... Good winter value.
★★★★ STADIUM COURSE
Holes: 18. **Yards:** 7,509/5,567. **Par:** 71/71. **Course Rating:** 73.9/71.6. **Slope:** 131/122. **Green Fee:** $62/$149. **Cart Fee:** $16/person. **Walking Policy:** Mandatory cart. **Walkability:** 2. **Opened:** 1986. **Architect:** Tom Weiskopf/Jay Morrish. **Season:** Year-round. **High:** Jan.-April. **To obtain tee times:** Call 90 days in advance. **Miscellaneous:** Reduced fees (low season, twilight), metal spikes, range (grass/mats), club rentals, lodging, credit cards (MC, V, AE).
Notes: Phoenix Open site.
Reader Comments: Worth playing, but overpriced ... Looks better on TV. Deepest bunkers I've seen ... Affordable in summer, no rough! ... Nice tough course, totally overpriced ... Way overrated ... Boring, except last four holes ... Good course, ruined by poor service and very slow play ... Too artificial, too contrived.

★★★ TRINI ALVAREZ EL RIO MUNICIPAL GOLF COURSE
PM-1400 W. Speedway Blvd., Tucson, 85745, Pima County, (520)623-6783, (520)791-4336. **Holes:** 18. **Yards:** 6,316/5,697. **Par:** 70/73. **Course Rating:** 69.7/72.3. **Slope:** 121/123. **Green Fee:** $11/$27. **Cart Fee:** $16/cart. **Walking Policy:** Unrestricted walking. **Walkability:** 1. **Season:** Year-round. **High:** Nov.-April. **To obtain tee times:** Call tee time reservation phone (520)791-4336. **Miscellaneous:** Reduced fees (weekdays, low season, twilight, seniors, juniors), discount packages, metal spikes, range (grass), club rentals, credit cards (MC, V, D), beginner friendly.
Reader Comments: Many small greens ... Old, good esthetics, friendly staff, good condition ... Short, city owned, inexpensive ... Very good public course ... Swift, small greens test your patience. Clubby bunch of players.

TROON NORTH GOLF CLUB *Service+*
★★★★½ MONUMENT COURSE *Condition+, Pace*
SP-10320 E. Dynamite Blvd., Scottsdale, 85255, Maricopa County, (602)585-5300. **Holes:** 18. **Yards:** 7,008/5,050. **Par:** 72/72. **Course Rating:** 73.3/68.5. **Slope:** 147/117. **Green Fee:** $75/$240. **Cart Fee:** Included in Green Fee. **Walking Policy:** Unrestricted walking. **Walkability:** 4. **Opened:** 1990. **Architect:** Tom Weiskopf/Jay Morrish. **Season:** Year-round. **High:** Nov.-May. **To obtain tee times:** Call 5 days in advance of play. 6-30 days in advance is subject to $20.00 advanced booking deposit. **Miscellaneous:** Reduced fees (low season, juniors), metal spikes, range (grass), club rentals, credit cards (MC, V, AE).
Notes: Golf Digest School site; ranked 91st in 1997-98 America's 100 Greatest; 4th in 1999 Best in State; 10th in 1996 America's Top 75 Upscale Courses.
Reader Comments: Expensive but forget about the price ... Play only at summer rates ... Heavenly, best greens anywhere ... Each hole looked like a classic painting ... One of the great experiences in golf ... A must play ... When I die bury me on the 3rd green ... Epitomizes quality and excellence, worth every penny ... Great condition, too much hype ... Don't miss this one! ... From the time you enter, first class.
★★★★½ PINNACLE COURSE *Condition+*

PU-10320 E. Dynamite Blvd., Scottsdale, 85255, Maricopa County, (602)585-5300.
Holes: 18. **Yards:** 7,044/4,980. **Par:** 72/72. **Course Rating:** 73.4/68.6. **Slope:** 147/120. **Green Fee:** $75/$240. **Cart Fee:** Included in Green Fee. **Walking Policy:** Unrestricted walking. **Walkability:** 5. **Opened:** 1996. **Architect:** Tom Weiskopf. **Season:** Year-round. **High:** Nov.-May. **To obtain tee times:** Call up to 5 days in advance. 6-30 days in advance is subject to a $20.00 advanced booking deposit. **Miscellaneous:** Reduced fees (low season, juniors), metal spikes, range (grass), credit cards (MC, V, AE).
Notes: Golf Digest School site. Ranked 9th in 1999 Best in State; 2nd in 1996 Best New Upscale Courses.
Reader Comments: Excellent course, lots of fun ... Egos get in the way. The tips weren't designed for the 20-plus handicappers ... Expensive, but a must once a year ... Great condition, but 5½-hour pace is a disgrace ... Wonderful desert course; great compliment to Monument Course ... Nothing but high marks ... Desert golf at its best. Greens to make Augusta turn envious.
Special Notes: Soft spikes encouraged.

★★★ TUBAC GOLF RESORT

R-1 Otera Rd., Tubac, 85646, Santa Cruz County, (520)398-2021, (800)848-7893, 35 miles S of Tucson. **E-mail:** tgr@theriver.com. **Web:** www.arizonaguide.com/tubac.
Holes: 18. **Yards:** 6,839/5,475. **Par:** 71/71. **Course Rating:** 72.4/70.5. **Slope:** 128/120. **Green Fee:** $29/$70. **Cart Fee:** Included in Green Fee. **Walking Policy:** Walking at certain times. **Walkability:** 3. **Opened:** 1960. **Architect:** Red Lawrence. **Season:** Year-round. **High:** Jan.-April. **To obtain tee times:** Call up to 7 days in advance. Resort guests may make tee times with room reservation. **Miscellaneous:** Reduced fees (resort guests, twilight), metal spikes, range (grass), club rentals, lodging (46 rooms), credit cards (MC, V, AE).
Reader Comments: Gets better each year ... Good old course; nice surrounding mountain views ... Overpriced ... Needs some work. Some tight holes ... Quiet resort ... Well maintained, pleasant ... Where Costner filmed 'Tin Cup' ... Remote, but worth it! ... Nice relaxing place to stay ... Great back nine makes up for average front.

★★★ VALLE VISTA COUNTRY CLUB

PU-9686 Concho Dr, Kingman, 86401, Mohave County, (520)757-8744.
Reader Comments: Enjoyable ... Wonderful atmosphere ... Pretty desert setting ... Nondescript, short, windy ... Very good layout ... Greens nicely contoured.
Special Notes: Call club for further information.

VENTANA CANYON GOLF & RACQUET CLUB *Service*

R-6200 N. Clubhouse Lane, Tucson, 85715, Pima County, (520)577-4061, (800)828-5701.
★★★★½ CANYON COURSE *Condition, Pace*
Holes: 18. **Yards:** 6,819/4,919. **Par:** 72/72. **Course Rating:** 72.7/68.3. **Slope:** 141/114. **Green Fee:** $75/$150. **Cart Fee:** Included in Green Fee. **Walking Policy:** Mandatory cart. **Walkability:** N/A. **Opened:** 1987. **Architect:** Tom Fazio. **Season:** Year-round. **High:** Oct.-May. **To obtain tee times:** Call 7 days in advance. **Miscellaneous:** Reduced fees (low season, resort guests, twilight), discount packages, range (grass), club rentals, lodging, credit cards (MC, V, AE, Diners Club).
Reader Comments: Several great holes ... Better than Mountain Course; quiet and secluded ... The epitome of fine golf ... One of my favorites ... Hard course for the average player ... Tough but fun ... Small desert animals often seen ... Breathtaking beauty ... Excellent condition ... Gorgeous! ... Friendly management.
★★★★½ MOUNTAIN COURSE
Holes: 18. **Yards:** 6,926/4,789. **Par:** 72/72. **Course Rating:** 74.2/66.9. **Slope:** 146/112. **Green Fee:** $95/$175. **Cart Fee:** Included in Green Fee. **Walking Policy:** Mandatory cart. **Walkability:** 3. **Opened:** 1984. **Architect:** Tom Fazio. **Season:** Year-round. **High:** Oct.-May. **To obtain tee times:** Call 7 days in advance. **Miscellaneous:** Reduced fees (low season, resort guests, twilight), discount packages, range (grass), club rentals, lodging, credit cards (MC, V, AE, Diners Club).
Notes: Ranked 20th in 1999 Best in State.
Reader Comments: A must stop ... Outstanding values in summertime when rates are affordable ... Could play both forever and never be bored ... Many memorable holes, too many houses ... A worthy match for its sister course ... Nice clubhouse ... Very playable if you stay out of desert scrub ... Unmatched service ... Best of two courses.

WESTBROOK VILLAGE GOLF CLUB
★★★ WESTBROOK VILLAGE GOLF CLUB

SP-19260 N. Westbrook Pkwy., Peoria, 85382, Maricopa County, (602)566-3439.
Yards: 6,412/5,370. **Par:** 71/71. **Course Rating:** 69.9/69.5. **Slope:** 120/111. **Green Fee:** $35/$74. **Cart Fee:** Included in Green Fee. **Walking Policy:** Unrestricted walking. **Walkability:** 2. **Opened:** 1983. **Architect:** Ted Robinson. **Season:** Year-round. **High:** Dec.-April. **Miscellaneous:** Reduced fees (low season), credit cards (MC, V).
Reader Comments: Two of the best finishing holes..
★★★ THE VISTAS
PU-18823 N. Country Club Pkwy., Peoria, 85382, Maricopa County, (602)566-1633, 5 miles W of Phoenix.

Holes: 18. **Yards:** 6,544/5,225. **Par:** 72/73. **Course Rating:** 70.3/68.2. **Slope:** 121/109. **Green Fee:** $35/$74. **Cart Fee:** Included in Green Fee. **Walking Policy:** Unrestricted walking. **Walkability:** 2. **Opened:** 1990. **Season:** Year-round. **High:** Dec.-April. **To obtain tee times:** Call up to 3 days in advance. **Miscellaneous:** Reduced fees (low season), range (grass), club rentals, credit cards (MC, V).
Reader Comments: Well-kept course that gets a lot of play.
Special Notes: Formerly the Vistas Club.

★★½ WESTERN SKIES GOLF CLUB

PU-1245 E. Warner Rd., Gilbert, 85234, Maricopa County, (480)545-8542, 20 miles E of Phoenix.
Holes: 18. **Yards:** 6,673/5,639. **Par:** 72/72. **Course Rating:** 70.0/68.6. **Slope:** 120/116. **Green Fee:** $20/$50. **Cart Fee:** Included in Green Fee. **Walking Policy:** Unrestricted walking.
Walkability: 3. **Opened:** 1992. **Architect:** Brian Whitcomb. **Season:** Year-round. **High:** Jan.-March. **To obtain tee times:** Call up to 7 days in advance. **Miscellaneous:** Reduced fees (twilight), metal spikes, range (grass), club rentals, credit cards (MC, V, AE).
Reader Comments: Easy course, nice driving range, slow play, wide open fairways ... Good for all levels. Basic golf ... A tough but relaxing course.

THE WIGWAM GOLF & COUNTRY CLUB *Service*

R-451 N. Litchfield Rd., Litchfield Park, 85340, Maricopa County, (602)272-4653, (800)909-4224, 20 miles W of Phoenix.

★★★ BLUE COURSE

Holes: 18. **Yards:** 6,130/5,235. **Par:** 70/70. **Course Rating:** 67.9/69.3. **Slope:** 115/115. **Green Fee:** $34/$95. **Cart Fee:** Included in Green Fee. **Walking Policy:** Mandatory cart. **Walkability:** 1. **Opened:** 1961. **Architect:** Robert Trent Jones. **Season:** Year-round. **High:** Jan.-May. **To obtain tee times:** Call 5 days in advance. Hotel guests can book up to 6 months in advance. **Miscellaneous:** Reduced fees (low season, resort guests), discount packages, metal spikes, range (grass), caddies, club rentals, lodging, credit cards (MC, V, AE, D).
Reader Comments: Excellent courses but many high greens ... Excellent value in the summer ... Flat. Short enough to manage ... Courses very well kept ... Highly overrated ... Fine course in legendary desert resort ... Old style, nothing fancy, mature resort course ... Great place to play. Good summertime values.

★★★★ GOLD COURSE

Holes: 18. **Yards:** 7,021/5,737. **Par:** 72/72. **Course Rating:** 74.1/72.8. **Slope:** 133/126. **Green Fee:** $34/$125. **Cart Fee:** Included in Green Fee. **Walking Policy:** Mandatory cart. **Walkability:** 1. **Opened:** 1961. **Architect:** Robert Trent Jones. **Season:** Year-round. **High:** Jan.-May. **To obtain tee times:** Call 5 days in advance. Hotel guests can book up to 6 months in advance. **Miscellaneous:** Reduced fees (low season, resort guests), discount packages, metal spikes, range (grass), caddies, club rentals, lodging (351 rooms), credit cards (MC, V, AE, D).
Reader Comments: Not the best course for the average player ... Pace of play at a snail's pace ... Very flat, featureless course. Some nice doglegs ... Experience this resort at least once ... Was disappointed in everything but staff ... A classic. A treat ... You have to grind ... Can be very tough ... Challenging, but not that interesting.

★★★ RED COURSE

Holes: 18. **Yards:** 6,867/5,821. **Par:** 72/72. **Course Rating:** 72.4/72.4. **Slope:** 126/118. **Green Fee:** $34/$95. **Cart Fee:** Included in Green Fee. **Walking Policy:** Mandatory cart. **Walkability:** 1. **Opened:** 1974. **Architect:** Red Lawrence. **Season:** Year-round. **High:** Jan.-May. **To obtain tee times:** Call 5 days in advance. Hotel guests can book up to 6 months in advance. **Miscellaneous:** Reduced fees (low season, resort guests), discount packages, metal spikes, range (grass/mats), caddies, club rentals, lodging (351 rooms), credit cards (MC, V, AE, D).
Reader Comments: Good resort ... Great finishing hole ... Neat little course for the average player ... My favorite of the three at Wigwam ... Tough greens ... Really fun, forgiving course. Pretty ... Traditional layout ... Most interesting of three at Wigwam.

★★★★ WILDFIRE AT DESERT RIDGE GOLF CLUB

PU-5225 E. Pathfinder Dr, Phoenix, 85024, (602)473-0205, (888)705-7775, 10 miles N of Phoenix.
Holes: 18. **Yards:** 7,170/5,505. **Par:** 72/72. **Course Rating:** 73.3/70.1. **Slope:** 135/116. **Green Fee:** $60/$125. **Cart Fee:** Included in Green Fee. **Walking Policy:** Unrestricted walking.
Walkability: 3. **Opened:** 1997. **Architect:** Arnold Palmer. **Season:** Year-round. **High:** Jan.-April. **To obtain tee times:** 7 days in advance, secure with credit card. **Miscellaneous:** Reduced fees (weekdays, twilight), range (grass), club rentals, credit cards (MC, V, AE, D).
Reader Comments: Challenging, enjoyable layout ... A great value in north Phoenix ... Good, huge greens ... Fair course, pretty, desert style, pricey ... Superb new course, great greens, good sand, fun ... Tough/long and manicured. Great course ... Very good walking ... Scenic design ... Desert without intimidation.

ARKANSAS

BALD KNOB COUNTRY CLUB
SP-Box 789 216 Country Club Drive, Bald Knob, 72010, White County, (501)724-3537, 2 miles W of Searcy.
Holes: 9. **Yards:** 6,217/5,012. **Par:** 72/73. **Course Rating:** 69.2/69.2. **Slope:** 114/114. **Green Fee:** $12/$15. **Cart Fee:** $17/person. **Walking Policy:** Unrestricted walking. **Walkability:** 5. **Opened:** 1969. **Season:** Year-round. **High:** March-Oct. **Miscellaneous:** Range (grass).

★★★½ BELVEDERE COUNTRY CLUB
SP-385 Belvedere Dr., Hot Springs, 71902, Garland County, (501)623-2305.
Holes: 18. **Yards:** 6,800/5,400. **Par:** 72/72. **Course Rating:** 72.8/72.8. **Slope:** 134/132. **Green Fee:** $55/$65. **Cart Fee:** $13/. **Walking Policy:** Unrestricted walking. **Walkability:** 4. **Opened:** 1963. **Architect:** Tom Clark. **Season:** Year-round. **High:** April-Sept. **Miscellaneous:** Range (grass), club rentals, lodging (20 rooms), credit cards (MC, V).
Reader Comments: Everything is first class ... Tough ... A lot of narrow fairways ... Weird, smart course, tons of risk-reward, some gimmicks, some grandeur.

BEN GEREN REGIONAL PARK GOLF COURSE
PU-7200 S. Zero, Fort Smith, 72903, Sebastian County, (501)646-5301.
Holes: 27. **Green Fee:** $13/$16. **Cart Fee:** $23/cart. **Walking Policy:** Unrestricted walking. **Walkability:** 2. **Opened:** 1972. **Architect:** Marvin Ferguson/Jeff Brauer. **Season:** Year-round. **High:** April-Oct. **To obtain tee times:** Call 1 day in advance. **Miscellaneous:** Reduced fees (weekdays, twilight, seniors, juniors), range (grass/mats), club rentals, credit cards (MC, V), beginner friendly (golf clinics).
★★½ MAGNOLIA/WILLOW
Yards: 6,782/5,023. **Par:** 72/73. **Course Rating:** 71.7/67.7. **Slope:** 120/109.
★★½ SILO HILL/MAGNOLIA
Yards: 6,840/5,347. **Par:** 72/74. **Course Rating:** 69.3/68.5. **Slope:** 114/112. .
Reader Comments: Excellent conditions for the price ... Wide open ... Worth playing ... Excellent greens ... Very busy, well maintained ... A swamp in wet weather ... One of the best public courses in Arkansas ... Great greens.
★★½ SILO HILL/WILLOW
Yards: 6,812/5,126. **Par:** 72/73. **Course Rating:** 69.3/68.5. **Slope:** 114/112.

BEVERLY HILLS GOLF COURSE
PU-Dixie Rd & Hwy. 49 North, Brookland, 72417, Craighead County, (870)932-3253, 6 miles N of Jonesboro.
Holes: 9. **Yards:** 2,820/2,730. **Par:** 36/36. **Course Rating:** N/A. **Slope:** N/A. **Green Fee:** $10/$12. **Cart Fee:** $18/cart. **Walking Policy:** Unrestricted walking. **Walkability:** 3. **Opened:** 1969. **Season:** Year Round. **High:** March-Sept. **Miscellaneous:** Reduced fees (weekdays), range (grass), club rentals, credit cards (MC, V, AE), beginner friendly.
Special Notes: Formerly University Heights Golf Club

BURNS PARK GOLF COURSE
PM-30 Championship Dr., North Little Rock, 72115, Pulaski County, (501)758-5800.
★★★ CHAMPIONSHIP COURSE
Holes: 18. **Yards:** 6,350/5,189. **Par:** 71/71. **Course Rating:** 69.5/67.8. **Slope:** 106/97. **Green Fee:** $11/$13. **Cart Fee:** $20/cart. **Walking Policy:** Unrestricted walking. **Walkability:** 2. **Opened:** 1964. **Architect:** Joe Finger/Steve Ralston. **Season:** Year-round. **High:** April-Sept. **To obtain tee times:** Call up to 7 days in advance. **Miscellaneous:** Reduced fees (twilight, seniors, juniors), metal spikes, range (grass/mats), club rentals, credit cards (MC, V, AE), beginner friendly (clinics).
Reader Comments: Very unpredictable ... Greens fast ... Public course gets lots of play ... Very enjoyable course ... Typical overplayed public course ... Good old course ... Good combination of tough and easy holes ... Very clean, good greens, scenic ... Good shape for all of the abuse ... Needs new clubhouse.
★★½ TOURNAMENT COURSE
Holes: 18. **Yards:** 5,725/5,400. **Par:** 70/70. **Course Rating:** 65.1/70.8. **Slope:** 102/104. **Green Fee:** $11/$13. **Cart Fee:** $20/cart. **Walking Policy:** Unrestricted walking. **Walkability:** 2. **Opened:** 1995. **Architect:** Steve Ralston. **Season:** Year-round. **High:** April-Sept. **To obtain tee times:** Call up to 4 days in advance. **Miscellaneous:** Reduced fees (twilight, seniors, juniors), metal spikes, range (grass/mats), club rentals, credit cards (MC, V, AE), beginner friendly (clinics).
Reader Comments: Greens tough to putt ... Fairways dry ... The newer nine has some great shots, but course needs time to mature.

★★★½ CHEROKEE VILLAGE GOLF CLUB
R-Laguna Dr., Cherokee Village, 72529, Sharp County, (870)257-2555, 120 miles N of Little Rock.
Holes: 18. **Yards:** 7,058/5,270. **Par:** 72/72. **Course Rating:** 73.5/70.4. **Slope:** 128/116. **Green Fee:** $16/$27. **Cart Fee:** $11/person. **Walking Policy:** Walking at certain times. **Walkability:** 4. **Opened:** 1972. **Architect:** Edmund Ault. **Season:** Year-round. **High:** May-Sept. **To obtain tee**

times: First come, first served. **Miscellaneous:** Metal spikes, range (grass), club rentals, credit cards (MC, V).

Reader Comments: Nice course ... Worth the trip ... Undervalued as to fees ... Nice course ... The retired folks slow the pace ... Excellent course for the price ... Tees are setup for any skill level ... A gem in the hills.

★★ THE CREEKS GOLF COURSE

PU-1499 S. Main, Cave Springs, 72718, Benton County, (501)248-1000, 1 miles S of Fayetteville. **Web:** realark.com/creeks.
Holes: 18. **Yards:** 6,009/5,031. **Par:** 71/71. **Course Rating:** 67.5/64.2. **Slope:** 111/104. **Green Fee:** $16/$20. **Cart Fee:** $20/cart. **Walking Policy:** Unrestricted walking. **Walkability:** 2.
Opened: 1990. **Architect:** Reed & Hughes. **Season:** Year-round. **High:** March-July. **To obtain tee times:** Call anytime in advance. **Miscellaneous:** Reduced fees (weekdays, twilight, seniors, juniors), discount packages, range (grass), club rentals, credit cards (MC, V, AE).
Special Notes: Formerly The Creeks Public Links.

CYPRESS CREEK COUNTRY CLUB

SP-Hwy. 64, Augusta, 72006, Woodruff County, (870)347-3211.
Special Notes: Call club for further information.

★★½ DAWN HILL GOLF & RACQUET CLUB

R-R.R. No.1 Dawn Hill Rd., Siloam Springs, 72761, Benton County, (501)524-4838, (800)423-3786, 35 miles NW of Fayetteville.
Holes: 18. **Yards:** 6,852/5,330. **Par:** 72/73. **Course Rating:** 71.3/69.1. **Slope:** 114/110. **Green Fee:** $20/$22. **Cart Fee:** $10/person. **Walking Policy:** Walking at certain times. **Walkability:** 2.
Opened: 1966. **Architect:** Ralph Jones. **Season:** Year-round. **High:** May-Oct. **To obtain tee times:** Call anytime in advance. **Miscellaneous:** Reduced fees (twilight), discount packages, metal spikes, range (grass), club rentals, lodging, credit cards (MC, V, AE, D).
Reader Comments: Good facilities ... Great layout ... The local homeowners tend to think they own the course ... Not maintained properly ... Quality course, you'll use every club in bag ... Tough when windy.

DEER RUN GOLF COURSE

1075 Cannon Dr., Little Rock AFB, 72099-4942, Pulaski County, (501)987-6199.
Holes: 18. **Yards:** 6,834/5,727. **Par:** 72/72. **Course Rating:** 72.0/72.0. **Slope:** 123/118. **Green Fee:** $5/$15. **Cart Fee:** $7/person. **Walking Policy:** Unrestricted walking. **Walkability:** 4. **Season:** Year-round. **High:** May-Oct. **Miscellaneous:** Range (grass), club rentals, credit cards (MC, V, Military Club Card), beginner friendly (free golf clinics once a year for military and their families).

★★★ DEGRAY LAKE RESORT STATE PARK GOLF COURSE

PU-2027 State Park Entrance Road, Bismarck, 71929, Hot Spring County, (501)865-2807, (800)737-8355, 25 miles S of Hot Springs.
Holes: 18. **Yards:** 6,930/5,731. **Par:** 72/72. **Course Rating:** 60.7/67.0. **Slope:** 134/123. **Green Fee:** $10/$13. **Cart Fee:** $18/cart. **Walking Policy:** Unrestricted walking. **Walkability:** 3.
Opened: 1977. **Season:** Year-round. **High:** April-Sept. **To obtain tee times:** Call anytime.
Miscellaneous: Reduced fees (weekdays, twilight, seniors), discount packages, range (grass/mats), club rentals, credit cards (MC, V, AE, D).
Reader Comments: A joy to play ... Fairways need improvement ... Disinterested personnel ... Adequate, has potential ... Good for state park course ... Bring your long game or it's a long day ... Well-kept public course ... Front nine open, back nine tight ... Could be a great course with more upkeep and landscaping ... Scenic views.

★★½ DIAMOND HILLS GOLF COURSE

SP-Rte. 7 N. Diamond Blvd., Diamond City, 72630, Boone County, (870)422-7613, 35 miles SE of Branson, MO.
Holes: 18. **Yards:** 6,311/5,491. **Par:** 69/72. **Course Rating:** 69.7/71.1. **Slope:** 125/115. **Green Fee:** $17/$17. **Cart Fee:** $18/cart. **Walking Policy:** Unrestricted walking. **Walkability:** 2.
Opened: 1971. **Architect:** Maury Bell. **Season:** Year-round. **High:** May-Sept. **To obtain tee times:** Tee times not required. **Miscellaneous:** Metal spikes, range (grass), club rentals.
Reader Comments: Good layout ... Course needs work.

EAGLE CREST GOLF COURSE

PU-542 Edwards Rd., Alma, 72921, Crawford County, (501)632-8857, (888)966-4653.
Holes: 18. **Yards:** 6,869/5,254. **Par:** 71/71. **Course Rating:** 73.3/70.4. **Slope:** 125/117. **Green Fee:** $25/$37. **Walkability:** N/A. **Opened:** 1997. **Architect:** Mark Hayes. **Season:** Year-round. **High:** March-Nov. **Miscellaneous:** Reduced fees (weekdays, low season, twilight, seniors, juniors), range (grass), club rentals, credit cards (MC, V, AE).

EL DORADO LIONS CLUB GOLF COURSE

PU-E. 19th & N. Quaker, El Dorado, 71730, Union County, (870)881-4180.

ARKANSAS

Holes: 18. **Yards:** 6,300/6,138. **Par:** 72/72. **Course Rating:** 69.0/68.2. **Slope:** 107/106. **Green Fee:** $10/$12. **Cart Fee:** $16/cart. **Walking Policy:** Unrestricted walking. **Walkability:** 4. **Architect:** Herman Hackbarth. **Season:** Year-round. **High:** June-Aug. **Miscellaneous:** Reduced fees (seniors), range (grass), club rentals, credit cards (MC, V, AE, D), beginner friendly.

ENGLAND COUNTRY CLUB
SP-Clear Lake Rd., England, 72046, Lonoke County, (501)842-2781.
Special Notes: Call club for further information.

★★ FOXWOOD COUNTRY CLUB
701 Foxwood Dr., Jacksonville, 72076, Pulaski County, (501)982-1254, 15 miles N of Little Rock.
Holes: 18. **Yards:** 6,413/5,225. **Par:** 72/72. **Course Rating:** 69.8/69.2. **Slope:** 110/111. **Green Fee:** $10/$17. **Cart Fee:** $16/cart. **Walking Policy:** Walking at certain times. **Walkability:** 1. **Opened:** 1975. **Season:** Year-round. **High:** April-Oct. **To obtain tee times:** Call for weekend times. **Miscellaneous:** Reduced fees (seniors, juniors), discount packages, metal spikes, range (grass), credit cards (MC, V, AE, D).

GALLA CREEK GOLF COURSE
SP-Hwy.. 247, Pottsville, 72858, Pope County, (501)890-6653, 1 miles S of Hwy. 64 in Pottsville.
Holes: 18. **Yards:** 6,140/5,442. **Par:** 71/71. **Course Rating:** 71.0/68.7. **Slope:** 122/115. **Green Fee:** $15/$15. **Cart Fee:** $15/cart. **Walking Policy:** Unrestricted walking. **Walkability:** 3. **Opened:** 1994. **Architect:** James Mackey. **Season:** Year Round. **High:** April-Sept. **Miscellaneous:** Range (grass), club rentals.
Special Notes: Only course in Arkansas with a par 6, (685 yards).

★★★★ GLENWOOD COUNTRY CLUB
PU-Hwy. 70 E, Glenwood, 71943, Pike County, (870)356-4422, (800)833-3110, 32 miles W of Hot Springs.
Holes: 18. **Yards:** 6,550/5,076. **Par:** 72/72. **Course Rating:** 70.8/64.1. **Slope:** 128/114. **Green Fee:** $18/$25. **Cart Fee:** $20/cart. **Walking Policy:** Unrestricted walking. **Walkability:** 4. **Opened:** 1994. **Architect:** Bobby McGee. **Season:** Year-round. **High:** April-Sept. **Miscellaneous:** Reduced fees (weekdays, low season, twilight, seniors), range (grass), club rentals, lodging (12 rooms), credit cards (MC, V, AE, D).
Reader Comments: Wonderful, lush course ... Slow play because of blind shots ... Nice, sporty course ... Impeccable greens ... Outstanding course in the mjddle of nowhere ... Fun to play ... Springtime will remind one of Augusta National ... 4 greens near some water ... Prettiest par 3's I've ever played ... Very 'women-friendly' course.

★★½ HARRISON COUNTRY CLUB
SP-Hwy. 62-65 N., Harrison, 72601, Boone County, (870)741-4947.
Holes: 18. **Yards:** 6,066/5,049. **Par:** 70/72. **Course Rating:** 69.3/69.7. **Slope:** 121/122. **Green Fee:** $23/$27. **Cart Fee:** $19/cart. **Walking Policy:** Unrestricted walking. **Walkability:** 4. **Opened:** 1920. **Season:** Year-round. **High:** March-Oct. **To obtain tee times:** Call golf shop. **Miscellaneous:** Reduced fees (twilight), range (grass/mats), club rentals, credit cards (MC, V).
Reader Comments: Short ... Outstanding bent-grass greens ... Greens severely sloped, a 13 on stimpmeter ... Short course made better with new bunkers ... Worth the trip ... Better than you would think.

★★½ HINDMAN PARK GOLF COURSE
PM-60 Brookview Dr., Little Rock, 72209, Pulaski County, (501)565-6450.
Holes: 18. **Yards:** 6,393/4,349. **Par:** 72/72. **Course Rating:** 68.9/68.6. **Slope:** 109/121. **Green Fee:** $8/$10. **Cart Fee:** $17/cart. **Walking Policy:** Unrestricted walking. **Walkability:** N/A. **Architect:** Dave Bennett/Leon Howard. **Season:** Year-round. **High:** May-Aug. **To obtain tee times:** Call golf shop for reservations 7 days in advance of playing date. Saturday-Tuesday reservations must be made in person at the golf course. **Miscellaneous:** Reduced fees (low season, twilight, seniors, juniors), metal spikes, range (grass), club rentals, credit cards (D).
Reader Comments: Lots of par 3's with many hazards ... Lots of trees, hills, water, not much sand ... With more improvement, it could be best in the city ... Fairways need improvement ... Good layout, hilly, tight fairways, very challenging ... Needs care.

HOLIDAY ISLAND COUNTRY CLUB
R-1 Country Club Dr., Holiday Island, 72631, (501)253-9511.
Special Notes: Call club for further information.

HOT SPRINGS COUNTRY CLUB
R-101 Country Club Dr., Hot Springs, 71901, Garland County, (501)624-2661, 60 miles W of Little Rock.
★★★★ ARLINGTON COURSE
Holes: 18. **Yards:** 6,646/6,206. **Par:** 72/74. **Course Rating:** 73.9/75.6. **Slope:** 127/137. **Green Fee:** $90/$90. **Cart Fee:** Included in Green Fee. **Walking Policy:** Unrestricted walking. **Walkability:** 4. **Opened:** 1932. **Architect:** Bill Diddel. **Season:** Year-round. **High:** March-Nov. **To**

obtain tee times: Call 2 days in advance. **Miscellaneous:** Reduced fees (resort guests), discount packages, range (grass), club rentals, credit cards (MC, V).
Notes: Ranked 4th in 1999 Best in State. Hosted PGA tour event in 1950's and 1960's.
Reader Comments: A good old course ... A nice surprise ... Varied shotmaking needed ... Deep bunkers and fast greens ... Pleasing to the eye ... Beautiful, hilly & quite challenging ... Very nice after redesign ... Beautiful layout, long.

★★★ MAJESTIC COURSE
Holes: 18. **Yards:** 6,715/5,541. **Par:** 72/72. **Course Rating:** 72.7/70.9. **Slope:** 131/121. **Green Fee:** $60/$60. **Cart Fee:** Included in Green Fee. **Walking Policy:** Unrestricted walking.
Walkability: 2. **Opened:** 1908. **Architect:** Willie Park Jr. **Season:** Year-round. **High:** March-Oct.
To obtain tee times: Call 2 days in advance. **Miscellaneous:** Reduced fees (resort guests), discount packages, range (grass/mats), club rentals, credit cards (MC, V).
Reader Comments: Friendly staff; some holes neglected ... Generous fairways ... Plain Jane ... Beautiful restaurant ... A nice challenge with long par 3s ... Beautiful.
Special Notes: Complex also includes 9-hole par-33 Pineview Course.

LAKE VILLAGE COUNTRY CLUB
SP-118 Lakeshore Dr., Lake Village, 71653, Chicot County, (870)265-3146.
Special Notes: Call club for further information.

LIL' BIT A HEAVEN GOLF CLUB
PU-Rte 1, Box 140, Magazine, 72943, Logan County, (501)969-2203, 50 miles E of Ft Smith.
Holes: 18. **Yards:** 6,308/5,836. **Par:** 72/78. **Course Rating:** N/A. **Slope:** N/A. **Green Fee:** $9/$12. **Cart Fee:** $14/cart. **Walking Policy:** Unrestricted walking. **Walkability:** 1. **Opened:** 1992. **Architect:** Jack Fleck. **Season:** Year-round. **High:** April-Nov. **To obtain tee times:** Call 1 day in advance. **Miscellaneous:** Reduced fees (weekdays, seniors, juniors), discount packages, metal spikes, range (grass), club rentals.

LITTLE CREEK RECREATIONAL CLUB
PU-Hwy.. 22 West, Ratcliff, 72951, Logan County, (501)635-5551.
Special Notes: Call club for further information.

★★½ LONGHILLS GOLF CLUB
SP-327 Hwy.. 5 N., Benton, 72018, Saline County, (501)316-3000, 9 miles SW of Little Rock.
E-mail: LHPRO@aol.com.
Holes: 18. **Yards:** 6,539/5,350. **Par:** 72/73. **Course Rating:** 69.9/69.5. **Slope:** 110/110. **Green Fee:** $15/$19. **Cart Fee:** $18/cart. **Walking Policy:** Unrestricted walking. **Walkability:** 3. **Opened:** 1955. **Architect:** William T. Martin. **Season:** Year-round. **High:** April-Sept. **To obtain tee times:** Call anytime for weekdays. For weekends and holidays call Wednesday prior beginning at 8 a.m. **Miscellaneous:** Reduced fees (juniors), range (grass), credit cards (MC, V).
Reader Comments: Not too hard, but challenging ... Nice greens ... No bunkers.

★★★★ MOUNTAIN RANCH GOLF CLUB
R-820 Lost Creek Pkwy., Fairfield Bay, 72088, Van Buren County, (501)884-3400, (800)726-2418, 84 miles N of Little Rock. **E-mail:** RoryBradley@linkscorp.com. **Web:** www.mountainranchgolf.com.
Holes: 18. **Yards:** 6,780/5,325. **Par:** 72/72. **Course Rating:** 71.8/69.8. **Slope:** 129/121. **Green Fee:** $15/$35. **Cart Fee:** $12/person. **Walking Policy:** Walking at certain times. **Walkability:** 4. **Opened:** 1983. **Architect:** Edmund B. Ault. **Season:** Year-round. **High:** May-Oct. **To obtain tee times:** Call up to 14 days in advance. **Miscellaneous:** Reduced fees (weekdays, low season, resort guests, twilight), discount packages, metal spikes, range (grass/mats), club rentals, lodging, credit cards (MC, V, AE, D), beginner friendly (stroke saver golf clinic).
Reader Comments: Super course ... A must play for the money ... Tight back nine ... Well designed, well maintained, wonderful course ... Wide open ... Beautiful setting ... Back nine especially challenging ... Watch for deer crossing ... Better hit it straight ... Very pretty & inviting course.

NATURE VALLEY GOLF
PU-Sunny Gap Rd., Conway, 72173, Faulkner County, (501)327-7627.
Special Notes: Call club for further information.

OUACHITA GOLF COURSE
PU-Hwy.. 88 East, Mena, 71953, Polk County, (501)394-5382.
Special Notes: Call club for further information.

PARAGOULD COUNTRY CLUB
SP-3300 Pruitt Chapel Rd., Paragould, 72450, Greene County, (501)239-2328.
Special Notes: Call club for further information.

★★★½ PRAIRIE CREEK COUNTRY CLUB
PU-Hwy.. 12 E.,1585 Rountree Drive, Rogers, 72757, Benton County, (501)925-2414, 100 miles E of Tulsa, OK.

Holes: 18. **Yards:** 6,707/5,599. **Par:** 72/77. **Course Rating:** 73.1/75.3. **Slope:** 135/127. **Green Fee:** $10/$16. **Cart Fee:** $18/person. **Walking Policy:** Unrestricted walking. **Walkability:** 2. **Opened:** 1968. **Architect:** Joe Sanders. **Season:** Year-round. **High:** April-Sept. **To obtain tee times:** First come, first served. **Miscellaneous:** Reduced fees (weekdays, resort guests, twilight), discount packages, metal spikes, range (grass), club rentals.
Reader Comments: Need to allow carts in fairway on front nine ... Extremely tough, best finishing holes around ... Hit it straight or you will need a lot of balls ... Two different nines, top nine is virtually on top of the hill, bottom nine has spring-fed creek in middle of course ... Back nine is phenomenal.

PRESCOTT COUNTRY CLUB
PU-Hwy.. 67 North, Prescott, 71857, Nevada County, (870)887-5341.
Special Notes: Call club for further information.

★ RAZORBACK PARK GOLF COURSE
PU-2514 W. Lori Dr., Fayetteville, 72704, Washington County, (501)443-5862.
Holes: 18. **Yards:** 6,622/5,620. **Par:** 72/72. **Course Rating:** 66.9/71.5. **Slope:** 108/110. **Green Fee:** $11/$11. **Cart Fee:** $17/cart. **Walking Policy:** Unrestricted walking. **Walkability:** 2.
Opened: 1959. **Architect:** E.H. Sonneman/David Taylor. **Season:** Year-round. **High:** May-Sept.
To obtain tee times: None required. **Miscellaneous:** Club rentals, credit cards (MC, V, D).

★★ REBSAMEN PARK GOLF COURSE
PM-Rebsamen Park Rd., Little Rock, 72202, Pulaski County, (501)666-7965.
Holes: 27. **Yards:** 6,271/5,651. **Par:** 71/71. **Course Rating:** 67.9/68.8. **Slope:** 100/106. **Green Fee:** $9/$11. **Cart Fee:** $16/cart. **Walking Policy:** Unrestricted walking. **Walkability:** 2. **Opened:** 1956. **Architect:** Herman Hackbarth. **Season:** Year-round. **High:** May-Aug. **To obtain tee times:** In person. **Miscellaneous:** Metal spikes.

★★½ THE RED APPLE INN & COUNTRY CLUB
R-325 Club Rd., Heber Springs, 72543, Cleburne County, (501)362-3131, (800)255-8900, 65 miles N of Little Rock. **E-mail:** appleinn&suebell.net. **Web:** www.redappleinn.com.
Holes: 18. **Yards:** 6,402/5,137. **Par:** 71/71. **Course Rating:** 71.5/65.5. **Slope:** 128/117. **Green Fee:** $30/$30. **Cart Fee:** $18/cart. **Walking Policy:** Unrestricted walking. **Walkability:** 3.
Opened: 1984. **Architect:** Gary Panks. **Season:** Year-round. **High:** April-Nov. **To obtain tee times:** Call 1 day in advance. **Miscellaneous:** Reduced fees (juniors), discount packages, metal spikes, range (grass/mats), club rentals, lodging (59 rooms), credit cards (MC, V, AE, D), beginner friendly (golf lessons anytime).
Reader Comments: Great course ... Service outstanding ... Nice course on Greers Ferry Lake ... Like cutting a diamond, due to its tight fairways ... Nice elevation, excellent views ... Fun course for average players.

RED RIVER GOLF CLUB
PU-2 Factory Rd., Clinton, 72031, Van Buren County, (501)745-8774.
Special Notes: Call club for further information.

RIVERCLIFF GOLF CLUB
SP-1 Golf Course Dr., Bull Shoals, 72619, Marion County, (870)445-4800.
Special Notes: Call club for further information.

SAGE MEADOWS GOLF CLUB
PU-4406 Clubhouse Drive, Jonesboro, 72401, Craighead County, (870)932-4420.**E-mail:** Driddle@sagemeadows.com. **Web:** www.sagemeadows.com.
Holes: 18. **Yards:** 6,901/4,947. **Par:** 72/72. **Course Rating:** 72.5/69.2. **Slope:** 129/119. **Green Fee:** $14/$24. **Cart Fee:** $11/person. **Walking Policy:** Unrestricted walking. **Walkability:** 4.
Opened: 1998. **Architect:** Kevin Tucker. **Season:** Year-round. **High:** April-Oct. **To obtain tee times:** Call up to 7 days in advance. **Miscellaneous:** Reduced fees (seniors, juniors), range (grass), club rentals, credit cards (MC, V, AE, D), beginner friendly (beginner clinics monthly April-Oct).

★★½ SOUTH HAVEN GOLF CLUB
PU-Route 10, Box 201, Texarkana, 71854, Miller County, (870)774-5771.
Holes: 18. **Yards:** 6,227/4,951. **Par:** 71/71. **Course Rating:** 69.3/69.8. **Slope:** 123/117. **Green Fee:** $10/$12. **Cart Fee:** $16/cart. **Walking Policy:** Unrestricted walking. **Walkability:** 2.
Opened: 1931. **Architect:** Jeff Miers. **Season:** Year-round. **High:** April-Sept. **To obtain tee times:** Call for weekdays only. **Miscellaneous:** Reduced fees (seniors, juniors), metal spikes, range (grass/mats), club rentals.
Reader Comments: Narrow fairways ... Sand traps need work ... Superior course for the heavy use ... The front and back nines like playing two courses the same day ... Very nice, economical place to play.

STONEBRIDGE MEADOWS GOLF CLUB

PU-3495 E. Goff Farms Rd., Fayetteville, 72701, Washington County, (501)571-3673, 3 miles SE of Fayetteville. **Web:** www.stonebridgemeadows.com.
Holes: 18. **Yards:** 7,150/5,225. **Par:** 72/72. **Course Rating:** 74.8/70.7. **Slope:** 138/128. **Green Fee:** $25/$42. **Cart Fee:** Included in Green Fee. **Walking Policy:** Unrestricted walking.
Walkability: 4. **Opened:** 1997. **Architect:** Randy Heckenkemper. **Season:** Year Round. **High:** April-Oct. **To obtain tee times:** Call up to 4 days in advance. Longer range reservations may be made with credit card. **Miscellaneous:** Reduced fees (weekdays, low season, twilight), range (grass), club rentals, credit cards (MC, V, AE, D).
Notes: Ranked 10th in 1999 Best in State.

★★★ STONELINKS

PU-110 St. Hwy.. 391 N., North Little Rock, 72117, Pulaski County, (501)945-0945.**Web:** www.stonelinks.com.
Holes: 18. **Yards:** 7,050/5,118. **Par:** 72/72. **Course Rating:** 72.8/70.3. **Slope:** 125/120. **Green Fee:** $15/$30. **Cart Fee:** Included in Green Fee. **Walking Policy:** Unrestricted walking.
Walkability: 3. **Opened:** 1993. **Architect:** Tommy Thomason /Tim Deibel/ Steve Holden.
Season: Year-round. **High:** March-Oct. **To obtain tee times:** Call 7 days in advance.
Miscellaneous: Reduced fees (weekdays, low season, twilight, seniors, juniors), discount packages, range (grass/mats), club rentals, credit cards (MC, V), beginner friendly.
Reader Comments: Links-type course with deep rough and no trees ... No diversity in holes ... Will be good with time and care ... Good value ... Forgiving with wide fairways ... Good bentgrass greens ... Lots of water ... Flat and uneventful; needs more trees.

★★★½ TURKEY MOUNTAIN GOLF COURSE

SP-3 Club Rd., Horseshoe Bend, 72512, Izard County, (870)670-5252.
Reader Comments: Scenic mountain course ... Poor design; low maintenance ... Short course, great to work on wedge play ... Great views.
Special Notes: Call club for further information.

★★ TWIN LAKES GOLF CLUB

SP-70 Elkway, Mountain Home, 72653, Baxter County, (870)425-2028, 120 miles SE of Springfield, MO.
Holes: 18. **Yards:** 5,910/5,018. **Par:** 70/70. **Course Rating:** 67.2/69.1. **Slope:** 110/106. **Green Fee:** $15/$20. **Cart Fee:** $20/cart. **Walking Policy:** Unrestricted walking. **Walkability:** 2.
Opened: 1959. **Architect:** Cecil B. Hollingsworth. **Season:** Year-round. **To obtain tee times:** Call for tee times weekends only Memorial Day to Labor Day. **Miscellaneous:** Reduced fees (low season), club rentals, credit cards (V).

★½ VACHE GRASSE COUNTRY CLUB

SP-Country Club Rd., Greenwood, 72936, Sebastian County, (501)996-4191, 15 miles SW of Ft. Smith.
Holes: 18. **Yards:** 6,502/4,966. **Par:** 72/72. **Course Rating:** 70.5/67.4. **Slope:** 114/113. **Green Fee:** $12/$15. **Cart Fee:** $18/cart. **Walking Policy:** Unrestricted walking. **Walkability:** 3.
Opened: 1968. **Architect:** William T. Martin. **Season:** Year-round. **High:** May-Sept. **To obtain tee times:** Tee times taken only in the summer by calling 1 day in advance. **Miscellaneous:** Reduced fees (twilight), range (grass).

★★½ WAR MEMORIAL GOLF COURSE

5511 W Markham, Little Rock, 72205, Pulaski County, (501)663-0854.
Reader Comments: Par 65 course with tricky greens ... Challenging par 3's ... Gets too much play ... Basic golf ... Short, but challenging with good fairways.
Special Notes: Call club for further information.

WESTERN HILLS COUNTRY CLUB

SP-5207 Western Hills Ave., Little Rock, 72204, Pulaski County, (501)565-5830.
Special Notes: Call club for further information.

CALIFORNIA

★★★½ ADOBE CREEK GOLF CLUB
PU-1901 Frates Rd., Petaluma, 94954, Sonoma County, (707)765-3000, 35 miles N of San Francisco.
Holes: 18. **Yards:** 6,886/5,085. **Par:** 72/72. **Course Rating:** 73.8/69.4. **Slope:** 131/120. **Green Fee:** $10/$47. **Cart Fee:** $13/person. **Walking Policy:** Unrestricted walking. **Walkability:** 2. **Opened:** 1990. **Architect:** Robert Trent Jones Jr. **Season:** Year-round. **High:** May-Oct. **To obtain tee times:** Call up to 7 days in advance. **Miscellaneous:** Reduced fees (weekdays, twilight, seniors, juniors), range (grass/mats), club rentals, credit cards (MC, V, AE, D).
Reader Comments: Good winter play; water drains well ... A few great tough holes ... Too many houses! ... Good test for average player ... Tough greens to putt ... Fun course except for wind in the afternoon ... Improving with age ... Challenging. Would like to play it often. Good test.

★★½ ALHAMBRA MUNICIPAL GOLF COURSE
PM-630 S. Almansor St., Alhambra, 91801, Los Angeles County, (818)570-5059, 8 miles E of Los Angeles.
Holes: 18. **Yards:** 5,214/4,501. **Par:** 70/71. **Course Rating:** 64.5/64.7. **Slope:** 107/105. **Green Fee:** $19/$24. **Cart Fee:** $11/person. **Walking Policy:** Unrestricted walking. **Walkability:** 3. **Opened:** 1952. **Architect:** William P. Bell. **Season:** Year-round. **To obtain tee times:** Call up to 7 days in advance at 5:30 a.m. **Miscellaneous:** Reduced fees (weekdays, low season, twilight, seniors, juniors), discount packages, metal spikes, range (mats), club rentals, credit cards (MC, V).
Reader Comments: Sporty course, good short game needed, challenging ... Good public course ... A good chance to break 70 on this short course ... Plenty of water, challenging greens are great. Can shoot low score ... Nice muny, some fun bunkering ... Good for new golfers, juniors and seniors ... Leave driver in bag.

★★★½ THE ALISAL RANCH GOLF COURSE
R-1054 Alisal Rd., Solvang, 93463, Santa Barbara County, (805)688-4215, 40 miles N of Santa Barbara. **Web:** www.alisal.com.
Holes: 18. **Yards:** 6,551/5,752. **Par:** 72/73. **Course Rating:** 72.0/74.5. **Slope:** 133/133. **Green Fee:** $75/$75. **Cart Fee:** $26/cart. **Walking Policy:** Unrestricted walking. **Walkability:** 1. **Opened:** 1955. **Architect:** William F. Bell. **Season:** Year-round. **High:** May-Oct. **To obtain tee times:** Weekdays, 7 days in advance. Weekend, Thursday prior to weekend. **Miscellaneous:** Discount packages, metal spikes, range (grass), club rentals, lodging (75 rooms), credit cards (MC, V), beginner friendly (group and private beginner lessons).
Reader Comments: Nothing special ... Wide open, no trouble ... Great staff, members real friendly ... Challenging but fair test of golf ... Excellent ... Flat but popular. Difficult to get starting time ... Pretty morning course ... Classic golf course.

ALISO VIEJO GOLF CLUB
PU-25002 Golf Club Dr., Aliso Viejo, 92656, Orange County, (949)598-9200, 40 miles S of Los Angeles. **E-mail:** jwhitt@alisogolf.com. **Web:** alisogolf.com.
Holes: 27. **Green Fee:** $60/$125. **Cart Fee:** Included in Green Fee. **Walking Policy:** Mandatory cart. **Walkability:** 4. **Opened:** 1999. **Architect:** Jack Nicklaus/Jack Nicklaus II. **Season:** Year-round. **High:** Sept.-May. **To obtain tee times:** Call. **Miscellaneous:** Reduced fees (weekdays, twilight), range (mats), club rentals, credit cards (MC, V, AE).
CREEK/VALLEY
Yards: 6,435/4,878. **Par:** 71/71. **Course Rating:** 68.9/N/A. **Slope:** 126/N/A.
RIDGE/CREEK
Yards: 6,277/4,736. **Par:** 70/70. **Course Rating:** 68.0/N/A. **Slope:** 125/N/A.
VALLEY/RIDGE
Yards: 6,268/4,740. **Par:** 71/71. **Course Rating:** 67.8/N/A. **Slope:** 123/N/A. .

★★★½ ALTA SIERRA GOLF & COUNTRY CLUB
SP-11897 Tammy Way, Grass Valley, 95949, Nevada County, (530)273-2010, 50 miles NE of Sacramento. **E-mail:** teeoff@altasierragolf.com. **Web:** www.altasierragolf.com.
Holes: 18. **Yards:** 6,537/5,984. **Par:** 72/72. **Course Rating:** 71.2/75.6. **Slope:** 128/134. **Green Fee:** $45/$50. **Cart Fee:** $22/cart. **Walking Policy:** Unrestricted walking. **Walkability:** 3. **Opened:** 1964. **Architect:** Bob Baldock. **Season:** Year-round. **High:** April-June. **To obtain tee times:** Call on first day of the month to book for upcoming month. **Miscellaneous:** Reduced fees (weekdays, juniors), range (grass/mats), club rentals, credit cards (MC, V).
Reader Comments: Great design, no adjacent fairways ... Mountain course, lots of trees ... Too many hackers ... Hill course, challenging, hidden trouble ... Course acceptable ... Relaxed, friendly ... Narrow and fast, but fair with lots of variety.

★★★½ ANAHEIM HILLS GOLF COURSE
PU-6501 Nohl Ranch Rd., Anaheim, 92807, Orange County, (714)998-3041, 25 miles S of Los Angeles.
Holes: 18. **Yards:** 6,245/5,361. **Par:** 71/72. **Course Rating:** 69.6/70.0. **Slope:** 117/115. **Green Fee:** $30/$36. **Cart Fee:** Included in Green Fee. **Walking Policy:** Mandatory cart. **Walkability:**

5. **Opened:** 1972. **Architect:** Richard Bigler. **Season:** Year-round. **To obtain tee times:** Call up to 7 days in advance. **Miscellaneous:** Reduced fees (twilight, seniors, juniors), range (mats), club rentals, credit cards (MC, V).
Reader Comments: Enjoyable round ... Fast greens ... Local knowledge a must for scoring ... Best deal in upscale (overpriced) Orange County ... Helps to be a mountain goat. Fun course ... Can't believe its a public! Spectacular elevation changes ... Fantastic setting ... Interesting, to say the least! ... Lots of trick holes.

★★★ ANCIL HOFFMAN GOLF COURSE
PU-6700 Tarshes Dr., Carmichael, 95608, Sacramento County, (916)482-5660, 12 miles SW of Sacramento.
Holes: 18. **Yards:** 6,794/5,954. **Par:** 72/73. **Course Rating:** 72.5/73.4. **Slope:** 123/123. **Green Fee:** $18/$25. **Cart Fee:** $19/cart. **Walking Policy:** Unrestricted walking. **Walkability:** N/A.
Opened: 1965. **Architect:** William F. Bell. **Season:** Year-round. **To obtain tee times:** Call up to 7 days in advance. Monday morning, tee times taken for the following Saturday, Sunday and Monday. **Miscellaneous:** Reduced fees (weekdays, twilight, seniors, juniors), discount packages, metal spikes, range (grass/mats), club rentals, credit cards (MC, V).
Reader Comments: Mature course, in need of a face lift ... Good public course, good value ... This place is awesome, giant oaks ... Challenging course ... Sacramento area's second best public course.

★★★½ APTOS SEASCAPE GOLF COURSE
PU-610 Clubhouse Dr., Aptos, 95003, Santa Cruz County, (408)688-3213, 20 miles NE of San Jose.
Holes: 18. **Yards:** 6,116/5,576. **Par:** 72/72. **Course Rating:** 69.8/72.6. **Slope:** 126/127. **Green Fee:** $16/$60. **Cart Fee:** $28/cart. **Walking Policy:** Unrestricted walking. **Walkability:** 3.
Opened: 1926. **Season:** Year-round. **High:** April-Oct. **To obtain tee times:** Call up to 7 days in advance for weekdays. Call up to 30 days in advance for an additional $5.00 per player.
Miscellaneous: Reduced fees (weekdays, low season, resort guests, twilight, seniors, juniors), metal spikes, range (mats), club rentals, credit cards (MC, V, AE).
Reader Comments: Must be straight, inventive on some golf shots ... Made major improvements, nice setting ... The right price and a great buffet ... Interesting layout, good value ... Old course, scenic, lots of trees, can get slow ... Poor man's Pasatiempo ... Nice course, doesn't drain well ... Short but challenging.

★★★½ AVILA BEACH RESORT GOLF COURSE
PU-P.O. Box 2140, Avila Beach, 93424, San Luis Obispo County, (805)595-4000, 8 miles S of San Luis Obispo. **Web:** www.avilabeachresort.com.
Holes: 18. **Yards:** 6,443/5,116. **Par:** 71/71. **Course Rating:** 70.9/69.9. **Slope:** 122/126. **Green Fee:** $32/$42. **Cart Fee:** $12/person. **Walking Policy:** Unrestricted walking. **Walkability:** 3.
Opened: 1969. **Architect:** Desmond Muirhead. **Season:** Year-round. **High:** April-Oct. **To obtain tee times:** Call up to 7 days in advance. **Miscellaneous:** Reduced fees (twilight, seniors, juniors), discount packages, metal spikes, range (grass), club rentals, credit cards (MC, V).
Reader Comments: Short shotmakers' course ... Location! Location! Location! ... Quirky front 9, too many blind shots ... Nice track, challenging ... Tight front through canyon, back wide open ... Great value, a lot of good holes, a must play ... Old course, funny layout in parts ... Good course, near ocean.

★★ AZUSA GREENS GOLF COURSE
PU-919 W. Sierra Madre Blvd., Azusa, 91702, Los Angeles County, (626)969-1727, 12 miles E of Pasadena.
Holes: 18. **Yards:** 6,220/5,601. **Par:** 70/72. **Course Rating:** 69.1/70.9. **Slope:** 112/115. **Green Fee:** $14/$33. **Cart Fee:** Included in Green Fee. **Walking Policy:** Mandatory cart. **Walkability:** 1. **Opened:** 1963. **Architect:** Bob Baldock. **Season:** Year-round. **To obtain tee times:** Call up to 7 days in advance. **Miscellaneous:** Reduced fees (weekdays, twilight, seniors, juniors), metal spikes, range (grass/mats), club rentals, credit cards (MC, V, AE).

★★★ BALBOA PARK GOLF CLUB
PU-2600 Golf Course Dr., San Diego, 92102, San Diego County, (619)239-1632.
Holes: 18. **Yards:** 6,267/5,369. **Par:** 72/72. **Course Rating:** 69.8/71.4. **Slope:** 119/119. **Green Fee:** $17/$34. **Cart Fee:** $22/cart. **Walking Policy:** Unrestricted walking. **Walkability:** 4.
Opened: 1915. **Architect:** William P. Bell. **Season:** Year-round. **High:** Summer. **To obtain tee times:** Call or walk on. **Miscellaneous:** Reduced fees (twilight), metal spikes, range (mats), club rentals, credit cards (MC, V).
Reader Comments: Nothing to complain about nor rave about ... OK, fun ... Great layout, take care of it! ... Very busy public course, but ya gotta play it ... Every hole different, hilly but not excessive ... Sliced a tee shot that hit car on highway dead center ... Great staff attitude ... Improvements should make for better play.

★★★ BARTLEY W. CAVANAUGH GOLF COURSE
PU-8301 Freeport Blvd., Sacramento, 95832, Sacramento County, (916)665-2020.

CALIFORNIA

Holes: 18. **Yards:** 6,265/4,723. **Par:** 71/71. **Course Rating:** 69.0/66.3. **Slope:** 114/107. **Green Fee:** $12/$24. **Cart Fee:** $22/cart. **Walking Policy:** Unrestricted walking. **Walkability:** 1. **Opened:** 1995. **Architect:** Perry Dye. **Season:** Year-round. **High:** May-Sept. **To obtain tee times:** Call up to 7 days in advance. **Miscellaneous:** Reduced fees (weekdays, twilight, seniors, juniors), club rentals, credit cards (MC, V).
Reader Comments: Fun little course ... Nothing memorable ... Fairways too close together, short and easy ... Links-type course ... Shorter, fun course. Nice greens ... Always well-maintained, great staff, particularly in the bar!

BAYONET/BLACK HORSE GOLF COURSES
PU-1 McClure Way, Seaside, 93955, Monterey County, (831)899-7271, 8 miles S of Pebble Beach.
★★★★ **BLACK HORSE COURSE**
Holes: 18. **Yards:** 7,009/5,648. **Par:** 72/72. **Course Rating:** 74.4/72.5. **Slope:** 135/129. **Green Fee:** $35/$70. **Cart Fee:** $10/person. **Walking Policy:** Walking at certain times. **Walkability:** 4.
Opened: 1963. **Architect:** General Karnes & General McClure. **Season:** Year-round. **High:** March-Nov. **To obtain tee times:** Call 2 weeks in advance. May call up to 30 days in advance with a $10.00 per person non-refundable deposit. **Miscellaneous:** Reduced fees (weekdays, low season, twilight, seniors, juniors), metal spikes, range (grass/mats), caddies, club rentals, credit cards (MC, V, AE).
Reader Comments: Don't miss, cheaper than Carmel ... The fairways are narrow, must be straight ... 10 strokes easier than Bayonet ... Completely improved ... Greens break toward ocean ... View of Pacific Ocean great ... Good hard, long, windy ... Too many short par 4s ... Fantastic golf, let's keep it undiscovered ... Former military courses.
★★★★ **BAYONET COURSE**
Holes: 18. **Yards:** 7,094/5,763. **Par:** 72/74. **Course Rating:** 75.1/73.7. **Slope:** 139/134. **Green Fee:** $40/$80. **Cart Fee:** $10/person. **Walking Policy:** Walking at certain times. **Walkability:** 3.
Opened: 1954. **Architect:** General Bob McClure. **Season:** Year-round. **High:** March-Nov. **To obtain tee times:** Call 2 weeks in advance. May call up to 30 days in advance with a $10.00 per person non-refundable deposit. **Miscellaneous:** Reduced fees (weekdays, twilight, seniors, juniors), metal spikes, range (grass/mats), club rentals, credit cards (MC, V, AE).
Notes: Ranked 71st in 1996 America's Top 75 Affordable Courses.
Reader Comments: You get all the challenge you want in 'the combat zone,' 3 tough holes in a row ... Trees that eat balls ... 2 or 3 grossly unfair doglegs ... What a test! ... Toughest course on Monterey Peninsula ... As tough as any course in U.S. ... Brutal back 9 ... Felt like falling on a bayonet after playing.

★★ BEAU PRE GOLF CLUB
SP-1777 Norton Rd., McKinleyville, 95519, Humboldt County, (707)839-2342, (800)931-6690, 10 miles N of Eureka.
Holes: 18. **Yards:** 5,910/4,976. **Par:** 71/72. **Course Rating:** 68.1/67.6. **Slope:** 118/112. **Green Fee:** $18/$25. **Cart Fee:** $18/cart. **Walking Policy:** Unrestricted walking. **Walkability:** 4.
Opened: 1967. **Architect:** Don Harling. **Season:** Year-round. **High:** May-Sept. **To obtain tee times:** Call golf shop. **Miscellaneous:** Reduced fees (weekdays, twilight, juniors), discount packages, metal spikes, range (grass/mats), club rentals, credit cards (MC, V, D), beginner friendly.

★★★ BENNETT VALLEY GOLF COURSE *Value*
PM-3330 Yulupa Ave., Santa Rosa, 95405, Sonoma County, (707)528-3673, 50 miles N of San Francisco.
Holes: 18. **Yards:** 6,600/5,958. **Par:** 72/75. **Course Rating:** 70.6/72.5. **Slope:** 112/123. **Green Fee:** $10/$25. **Cart Fee:** $20/cart. **Walking Policy:** Unrestricted walking. **Walkability:** 1.
Opened: 1969. **Architect:** Ben Harmon. **Season:** Year-round. **High:** May-Sept. **To obtain tee times:** Call up to 7 days in advance. **Miscellaneous:** Reduced fees (weekdays, twilight, seniors, juniors), metal spikes, range (grass/mats), club rentals, credit cards (MC, V).
Reader Comments: Great value, easy layout, slow ... Outstanding muny course ... Flat course. Some parallel fairways. Great value ... Fun to play ... OK course.

★★★ BETHEL ISLAND GOLF COURSE
PM-3303 Gateway Rd., Bethel Island, 94511, Contra Costa County, (925)684-2654, 25 miles SE of Stockton.
Holes: 18. **Yards:** 6,632/5,813. **Par:** 72/74. **Course Rating:** 70.8/72.2. **Slope:** 118/117. **Green Fee:** $13/$23. **Cart Fee:** $22/cart. **Walking Policy:** Unrestricted walking. **Walkability:** N/A.
Opened: 1960. **Architect:** Ted Robinson. **Season:** Year-round. **High:** April-Oct. **To obtain tee times:** Call up to 7 days in advance. **Miscellaneous:** Reduced fees (weekdays, low season, twilight, seniors), discount packages, metal spikes, range (grass), club rentals, credit cards (MC, V, AE, D).
Reader Comments: Windy, hard fairways ... Course holds up well after rains ... Flat, no pizzazz ... Good golf, food, awesome scenery ... Great inclement weather course ... Stays dry in winter ... Very friendly.

CALIFORNIA

★★★ BIDWELL PARK GOLF COURSE
PU-3199 Golf Course Rd., Chico, 95973, Butte County, (530)891-8417, 90 miles N of Sacramento.
Holes: 18. **Yards:** 6,363/5,855. **Par:** 72/71. **Course Rating:** 70.2/73.1. **Slope:** 123/123. **Green Fee:** $14/$22. **Cart Fee:** $19/cart. **Walking Policy:** Unrestricted walking. **Walkability:** 2. **Opened:** 1930. **Architect:** City of Chico. **Season:** Year-round. **High:** June-July. **To obtain tee times:** Call 2 days in advance for weekday. Week advance for weekends. **Miscellaneous:** Reduced fees (twilight, seniors, juniors), metal spikes, club rentals, credit cards (MC, V, AE), beginner friendly.
Reader Comments: Challenging layout, tough greens ... Friendly, forgiving, very natural ... An overall nice experience ... Typical country day ... A good walk unspoiled, beautiful course ... Over-rated course ... Gets a lot of play ... #13, drive across big creek to landing area ... OK, flat course.

★★½ BING MALONEY GOLF COURSE
PU-6801 Freeport Blvd., Sacramento, 95822, Sacramento County, (916)428-9401, 40 miles E of Stockton.
Holes: 18. **Yards:** 6,558/5,972. **Par:** 72/73. **Course Rating:** 70.3/72.6. **Slope:** 113/119. **Green Fee:** $18/$20. **Cart Fee:** $23/cart. **Walking Policy:** Unrestricted walking. **Walkability:** 1. **Opened:** 1952. **Architect:** Mike McDonagh. **Season:** Year-round. **High:** March-Aug. **To obtain tee times:** Call up to 7 days in advance. **Miscellaneous:** Reduced fees (weekdays, low season, twilight, seniors, juniors), range (mats), club rentals, credit cards (MC, V), beginner friendly (executive course beginner clinic).
Reader Comments: Your basic public ... Nothing memorable ... Nice mediocre public course ... Nice city course ... Old-style city course, flat greens; trees biggest trouble ... Very playable.

BLACK LAKE GOLF RESORT
R-1490 Golf Course Lane, Nipomo, 93444, San Luis Obispo County, (805)343-1214, (800)423-0981, 10 miles N of Santa Maria.
Holes: 27. **Green Fee:** $19/$47. **Cart Fee:** $17/person. **Walking Policy:** Walking at certain times. **Opened:** 1964. **Architect:** Ted Robinson. **Season:** Year-round. **High:** May-Sept. **To obtain tee times:** Resort guests tee times are set when reservation is made. Nonguests call 7 days in advance. **Miscellaneous:** Reduced fees (weekdays, low season, resort guests, twilight), discount packages, metal spikes, range (grass/mats), club rentals, lodging, credit cards (MC, V, AE).
★★★½ CANYON/OAKS
Yards: 6,034/5,047. **Par:** 71/71. **Course Rating:** 69.3/70.5. **Slope:** 121/120. **Walkability:** 3.
Reader Comments: Best-kept secret ... Oak trees have arms ... Great track, excellent condition ... Tall eucalyptus-lined fairways made for a scenic but challenging day ... Some funky holes ... A few exciting views and carries ... Oaks 9 a great design.
★★★½ LAKES/CANYON
Yards: 6,401/5,628. **Par:** 72/72. **Course Rating:** 70.9/72.9. **Slope:** 123/126. **Walkability:** N/A.
★★★½ LAKES/OAKS
Yards: 6,185/5,161. **Par:** 71/71. **Course Rating:** 69.7/70.8. **Slope:** 121/124. **Walkability:** 3.

★½ BLUE SKIES COUNTRY CLUB
PU-55100 Martinez Trail, Yucca Valley, 92284, San Bernardino County, (760)365-0111, (800)877-1412, 19 miles N of Palm Springs.
Holes: 18. **Yards:** 6,400/5,757. **Par:** 71/73. **Course Rating:** 69.8/71.6. **Slope:** 115/119. **Green Fee:** $6/$19. **Cart Fee:** $12/person. **Walking Policy:** Unrestricted walking. **Walkability:** 1. **Opened:** 1957. **Architect:** William F. Bell. **Season:** Year-round. **High:** Oct. **To obtain tee times:** Call up to 7 days in advance. **Miscellaneous:** Reduced fees (weekdays, low season, resort guests, twilight, seniors, juniors), discount packages, metal spikes, range (grass/mats), club rentals, credit cards (MC, V), beginner friendly (adult and junior clinics).

BLYTHE MUNICIPAL GOLF CLUB
PU-4708 Wells Rd., Blythe, 92225, Riverside County, (760)922-7272, 4 miles N of Blythe.
Holes: 18. **Yards:** 6,866/5,684. **Par:** 72/73. **Course Rating:** 71.3/72.6. **Slope:** 117/117. **Green Fee:** N/A/$20. **Cart Fee:** $20/cart. **Walking Policy:** Unrestricted walking. **Walkability:** 3. **Opened:** 1968. **Architect:** William F. Bell. **Season:** Year-round. **High:** Dec.-April. **To obtain tee times:** Taken Jan.-April 1 day in advance starting at 7 a.m. **Miscellaneous:** Reduced fees (low season), metal spikes, range (grass/mats), club rentals, beginner friendly (beginners welcome May 1-Oct. 15 light play).

★★★½ BODEGA HARBOUR GOLF LINKS
R-21301 Heron Dr., Bodega Bay, 94923, Sonoma County, (707)875-3538, 20 miles W of Santa Rosa.
Holes: 18. **Yards:** 6,267/4,731. **Par:** 70/69. **Course Rating:** 72.4/69.7. **Slope:** 134/120. **Green Fee:** $35/$85. **Cart Fee:** $15/person. **Walking Policy:** Walking at certain times. **Walkability:** 4. **Opened:** 1976. **Architect:** Robert Trent Jones Jr. **Season:** Year-round. **High:** April-Oct. **To obtain tee times:** Call up to 90 days in advance. **Miscellaneous:** Reduced fees (weekdays, low

season, resort guests, twilight, juniors), discount packages, metal spikes, range (mats), caddies, club rentals, lodging, credit cards (MC, V, AE).
Reader Comments: A couple of tricked up holes ... A stunning oceanside course on sunny days ... Beautiful views of harbor ... Beautiful beyond belief ... Fog conditions a big problem ... Two 9s like playing two different courses ... Too many blind shots ... Bizarre housing on front, good solid back, 16, 17, 18 excellent ... Can be cold and windy ... Grueling course, not for the high handicapper.

BORREGO SPRINGS COUNTRY CLUB
PU-1112 Tilting T Dr., Borrego Springs, 92004, (760)767-3330.
Holes: 18. **Yards:** 6,569/4,754. **Par:** 71/71. **Course Rating:** 70.4/66.7. **Slope:** 117/104. **Green Fee:** N/A. **Walking Policy:** Mandatory cart. **Walkability:** 1. **Opened:** 1998. **Architect:** Cary Bickler. **Season:** Year-round. **High:** Nov.-April. **Miscellaneous:** Range (grass), club rentals, lodging (100 rooms).

★★★ BOULDER CREEK GOLF & COUNTRY CLUB
R-16901 Big Basin Hwy., Boulder Creek, 95006, Santa Cruz County, (408)338-2121, 15 miles N of Santa Cruz. **Web:** www.webfairway.com.
Holes: 18. **Yards:** 4,396/4,027. **Par:** 65/67. **Course Rating:** 61.5/63.3. **Slope:** 104/104. **Green Fee:** $14/$40. **Cart Fee:** $18/cart. **Walking Policy:** Unrestricted walking. **Walkability:** 2. **Opened:** 1961. **Architect:** Jack Fleming. **Season:** Year-round. **High:** April-Oct. **To obtain tee times:** Call golf shop up to 7 days in advance. Resort guests can book tee times with reservation.
Miscellaneous: Reduced fees (weekdays, low season, resort guests, twilight, seniors, juniors), discount packages, metal spikes, club rentals, lodging (45 rooms), credit cards (MC, V, AE, D).
Reader Comments: Very pretty, serene, short course ... Long waiting periods on tees ... Short course in redwoods ... Fun course, always tough putts ... The course is a gem ... Very short course ... Towering redwoods.

★★★ BOUNDARY OAK COUNTRY CLUB
PM-3800 Valley Vista Rd., Walnut Creek, 94596, Contra Costa County, (925)934-6212. **Web:** www.boundaryoak.com.
Yards: 7,063/5,699. **Par:** 72/72. **Course Rating:** 73.9/72.0. **Slope:** 130/120. **Green Fee:** $12/$25. **Cart Fee:** $25/cart. **Walking Policy:** Mandatory cart. **Walkability:** 4. **Season:** Year-round. **High:** April-Sept. **Miscellaneous:** Reduced fees (weekdays, twilight, seniors, juniors), metal spikes, range (grass/mats), club rentals, credit cards (MC, V).
Reader Comments: Loved clubhouse ... Challenging, fun, good value ... Best public course in northern California for the dollar ... Long, nice layout, good shape for a lot of rounds ... Tricky, harder than it looks, greens really test you ... Well-run operation ... Great city-run course ... Good variety. Challenging par 3s ... Great muny, good value.

BROOKSIDE GOLF CLUB
PM-1133 N. Rosemont Ave., Pasadena, 91103, Los Angeles County, (626)796-8151, 7 miles NE of Los Angeles.
★★★ C.W. KOINER COURSE
Holes: 18. **Yards:** 7,037/6,104. **Par:** 72/75. **Course Rating:** 73.6/74.7. **Slope:** 128/128. **Green Fee:** $30/$40. **Cart Fee:** $24/cart. **Walking Policy:** Unrestricted walking. **Walkability:** 1. **Opened:** 1928. **Architect:** William P. Bell. **Season:** Year-round. **High:** April-Oct. **To obtain tee times:** Call up to 7 days ahead for weekdays, Mondays after 9:30 a.m. for Saturday and Tuesdays after 9:30 for Sunday. **Miscellaneous:** Reduced fees (weekdays, twilight, seniors, juniors), range (mats), club rentals, credit cards (MC, V, AE, D).
Reader Comments: Rose Bowl nearby ... Sentimental favorite ... A classic true test of golf ... Best municipal in L.A. ... Long and tough, beautiful, crowded ... Great muny course, long par 4s ... Historic 'old style' course, lots of fun.
★★½ E.O. NAY COURSE
Holes: 18. **Yards:** 6,046/5,377. **Par:** 70/71. **Course Rating:** 68.4/70.5. **Slope:** 115/117. **Green Fee:** $30/$40. **Cart Fee:** $24/cart. **Walking Policy:** Unrestricted walking. **Walkability:** 1. **Opened:** 1952. **Architect:** Billy Bell. **Season:** Year-round. **High:** April-Oct. **To obtain tee times:** Call 7 days ahead for weekdays, Mondays after 9:30 a.m. for Saturday and Tuesdays after 9:30 for Sunday. **Miscellaneous:** Reduced fees (weekdays, twilight, seniors, juniors), range (mats), club rentals, credit cards (MC, V, AE, D).
Reader Comments: Not as tough as the 'A' course but beautiful ... Nice scenery ... Crowded ... Short and open.

★★½ CALIMESA COUNTRY CLUB
PU-1300 S3rd St, Calimesa, 92320, Riverside County, (909)795-2488, 8 miles E of Redlands.
Holes: 18. **Yards:** 5,970/5,293. **Par:** 70/72. **Course Rating:** 67.3/69.6. **Slope:** 114/112. **Green Fee:** $9/$22. **Cart Fee:** $10/person. **Walking Policy:** Unrestricted walking. **Walkability:** 1. **Opened:** 1965. **Season:** Year-round. **To obtain tee times:** Call up to 7 days in advance. **Miscellaneous:** Reduced fees (weekdays, twilight), metal spikes, credit cards (MC, V, AE).

Reader Comments: Fun. Blind shots, doglegs ... Great 8th hole ... Dogleg city ... Short and mean ... Helps to know the course.

★★★ CAMARILLO SPRINGS GOLF COURSE
PU-791 Camarillo Springs Rd., Camarillo, 93012, Ventura County, (805)484-1075, 54 miles N of Los Angeles.
Holes: 18. **Yards:** 6,375/5,297. **Par:** 72/72. **Course Rating:** 70.2/70.2. **Slope:** 115/116. **Green Fee:** $22/$45. **Cart Fee:** $12/person. **Walking Policy:** Walking at certain times. **Walkability:** 3. **Opened:** 1972. **Architect:** Ted Robinson. **Season:** Year-round. **High:** May-Aug. **To obtain tee times:** Call 7 days in advance. **Miscellaneous:** Reduced fees (weekdays, resort guests, twilight, seniors, juniors), discount packages, metal spikes, range (mats), club rentals, credit cards (MC, V).
Reader Comments: Neat course nestled in base of Santa Monica mountains ... Interesting holes ... Not much value ... Half the course is fun, back 9 ... Must be straight, plenty of water ... Could be very good ... Beautiful setting ... Always floods after a hard rain, otherwise a good course.

★★★½ CANYON LAKES COUNTRY CLUB
PU-640 Bollinger Canyon Way, San Ramon, 94583, Contra Costa County, (925)735-6511, 30 miles E of San Francisco.
Holes: 18. **Yards:** 6,373/5,191. **Par:** 71/71. **Course Rating:** 71.4/69.9. **Slope:** 129/121. **Green Fee:** $60/$75. **Cart Fee:** Included in Green Fee. **Walking Policy:** Mandatory cart. **Walkability:** 4. **Opened:** 1987. **Architect:** Ted Robinson. **Season:** Year-round. **High:** Feb.-Oct. **To obtain tee times:** Call up to 7 days in advance. **Miscellaneous:** Metal spikes, club rentals, credit cards (MC, V).
Reader Comments: Good views ... Real nice, lots of blind shots ... This baby is plush, a beauty, pricey but fair ... Quirky layout ... Too expensive for what you get, fun track ... Overpriced golf in a wind tunnel.

★★★ CANYON SOUTH GOLF COURSE
PU-1097 Murray Canyon Dr., Palm Springs, 92264, Riverside County, (760)327-2019, 100 miles E of Los Angeles.
Holes: 18. **Yards:** 6,536/5,685. **Par:** 71/71. **Course Rating:** 70.8/72.0. **Slope:** 119/116. **Green Fee:** $25/$65. **Cart Fee:** Included in Green Fee. **Walking Policy:** Mandatory cart. **Walkability:** 1. **Opened:** 1963. **Architect:** William F. Bell. **Season:** Nov.-Sept. **High:** Jan.-March. **To obtain tee times:** Call up to 7 days in advance. **Miscellaneous:** Reduced fees (weekdays, low season, twilight), metal spikes, range (grass), club rentals, credit cards (MC, V, AE), beginner friendly (private and group lessons).
Reader Comments: Good value in Palm Springs ... I saw Bob Hope there ... Good first time course, everything in front of you ... I had a bad day, but I'll play it again ... Good old course, wide fairways ... Fun layout, no frills.

★★★½ CARLTON OAKS COUNTRY CLUB
PU-9200 Inwood Dr., Santee, 92071, San Diego County, (619)448-8500, (800)831-6757, 20 miles NE of San Diego.
Holes: 18. **Yards:** 7,088/4,548. **Par:** 72/72. **Course Rating:** 74.6/62.1. **Slope:** 137/114. **Green Fee:** $55/$75. **Cart Fee:** Included in Green Fee. **Walking Policy:** Walking at certain times. **Walkability:** 3. **Opened:** 1990. **Architect:** Perry Dye. **Season:** Year-round. **To obtain tee times:** Call up to 5 days in advance. **Miscellaneous:** Reduced fees (resort guests, twilight), discount packages, range (grass/mats), club rentals, lodging, credit cards (MC, V, AE).
Reader Comments: Excellent course, great restaurant ... Good condition, most of the time! ... It lulls you asleep then slams the door ... Tough 18 ... Flat course ... Rough is mostly sandy with rocks ... Best course in San Diego ... Great weekend getaway.

★★★½ CARMEL MOUNTAIN RANCH COUNTRY CLUB
PU-14050 Carmel Ridge Rd., San Diego, 92128, San Diego County, (619)487-9224, 15 miles N of San Diego.
Holes: 18. **Yards:** 6,728/5,372. **Par:** 72/72. **Course Rating:** 71.9/71.0. **Slope:** 131/122. **Green Fee:** $50/$85. **Cart Fee:** Included in Green Fee. **Walking Policy:** Mandatory cart. **Walkability:** 4. **Opened:** 1986. **Architect:** Ron Fream. **Season:** Year-round. **To obtain tee times:** Call up to 7 days in advance. **Miscellaneous:** Reduced fees (low season, twilight, seniors, juniors), discount packages, metal spikes, range (mats), club rentals, credit cards (MC, V, AE).
Reader Comments: Tough course, bogeys everywhere ... Somewhat hilly, otherwise good course to play ... More tricks than Houdini! Water, barancas, 40-yard bunkers with boulders in them ... Price a little high, but good course ... Funky layout ... Good, hilly ... A couple of par 3s were extreme ... Good variety of holes.

★★★½ CARMEL VALLEY RANCH GOLF CLUB *Service*
R-1 Old Ranch Rd., Carmel, 93923, Monterey County, (408)626-2510, (800)422-7635, 6 miles E of carmel by the sea.
Holes: 18. **Yards:** 6,515/5,088. **Par:** 70/70. **Course Rating:** 70.1/69.6. **Slope:** 124/135. **Green Fee:** $100/$175. **Cart Fee:** Included in Green Fee. **Walking Policy:** Walking at certain times.

Walkability: 3. **Opened:** 1981. **Architect:** Pete Dye. **Season:** Year-round. **High:** June-Oct. **To obtain tee times:** Resort guests anytime with resort reservation. Outside, call golf shop. **Miscellaneous:** Reduced fees (low season, resort guests, juniors), discount packages, range (grass), club rentals, lodging (144 rooms), credit cards (MC, V, AE, Diners Club), beginner friendly (women to the fore instruction program).

Reader Comments: Plays in valley setting ... Very memorable layout, challenging and scenic ... Holes 10-14 awesome, that's it ... Too expensive ... Deer sleeping in a bunker and wild turkeys abound ... Classic course. Likely to be warm and sunny when coastal courses are fogged.

★★★ CASTLE CREEK COUNTRY CLUB

SP-8797 Circle R Dr., Escondido, 92026, San Diego County, (760)749-2422, (800)619-2465, 30 miles N of San Diego.

Holes: 18. **Yards:** 6,396/4,800. **Par:** 72/72. **Course Rating:** 70.8/67.4. **Slope:** 124/108. **Green Fee:** $22/$40. **Cart Fee:** $10/person. **Walking Policy:** Unrestricted walking. **Walkability:** 5. **Opened:** 1956. **Architect:** Jack Daray Sr. **Season:** Year-round. **High:** Jan.-April. **To obtain tee times:** Call 7 days in advance. **Miscellaneous:** Reduced fees (weekdays, low season, twilight), discount packages, club rentals, credit cards (MC, V, AE).

Reader Comments: Older course, some funky holes ... 10, 11 and 12 a forest, but fun ... Some fairways narrow ... Nice course, interesting holes, narrow ... Fair, river valley course.

★★★★ CASTLE OAKS GOLF CLUB

PU-1000 Castle Oaks Dr., Ione, 95640, Amador County, (209)274-0167, 30 miles SE of Sacramento.

Holes: 18. **Yards:** 6,739/4,953. **Par:** 71/71. **Course Rating:** 72.3/67.3. **Slope:** 129/114. **Green Fee:** $18/$45. **Cart Fee:** $10/person. **Walking Policy:** Included in Green Fee. **Walking Policy:** Walking at certain times. **Walkability:** 3. **Opened:** 1994. **Architect:** Bradford Benz. **Season:** Year-round. **High:** Spring-Fall. **To obtain tee times:** Call up to 7 days in advance. **Miscellaneous:** Reduced fees (weekdays, twilight, seniors, juniors), metal spikes, range (grass), club rentals, credit cards (MC, V), beginner friendly (late 9-hole rates).

Reader Comments: Good test of golf ... Small clubhouse ... Great public, hilly, tight, poor man's Pasatiempo ... One of better courses in Sacramento area... Fun, very different golf course ... The front 9 was outstanding, the back was OK ... A really nice course with lots of variety and challenge ... Scenic, natural setting.

CATHEDRAL CANYON COUNTRY CLUB

SP-68311 Paseo Real, Cathedral City, 92234, Riverside County, (760)328-6571, 10 miles SE of Palm Springs.

Holes: 27. **Cart Fee:** Included in Green Fee. **Walking Policy:** Mandatory cart. **Walkability:** N/A. **Opened:** 1975. **Architect:** David Rainville. **Season:** Year-round. **High:** Jan.-April. **To obtain tee times:** Call up to 4 days in advance. **Miscellaneous:** Reduced fees (weekdays, low season, twilight), discount packages, metal spikes, range (grass), club rentals, credit cards (MC, V, AE, D).

★★★ LAKE VIEW/ARROYO

Yards: 6,366/5,183. **Par:** 72/72. **Course Rating:** 70.9/69.8. **Slope:** 126/124. **Green Fee:** $25/$70.

★★★ LAKE VIEW/MOUNTAIN VIEW

Yards: 6,505/5,423. **Par:** 72/72. **Course Rating:** 71.1/69.5. **Slope:** 130/128. **Green Fee:** $25/$70.

Reader Comments: Older course needs work ... Narrow fairways, lots of trees, interesting course ... Good vacation spot ... Beautiful mature layout.

★★★ MOUNTAIN/VIEW/ARROYO

Yards: 6,477/5,182. **Par:** 72/72. **Course Rating:** 70.9/70.8. **Slope:** 119/124. **Green Fee:** $35/$85.

★★★ CHALK MOUNTAIN GOLF CLUB

PU-10000 El Bordo Ave., Atascadero, 93422, San Luis Obispo County, (805)466-8848.

Holes: 18. **Yards:** 6,299/5,330. **Par:** 72/72. **Course Rating:** 69.2/71.1. **Slope:** 126/125. **Green Fee:** $10/$29. **Walkability:** N/A. **Architect:** Robert Muir Graves. **Season:** Year-round. **To obtain tee times:** Call 7 days in advanced. **Miscellaneous:** Metal spikes, club rentals, credit cards (MC, V, AE).

Reader Comments: Narrow fairways. Hilly, lots of oaks ... Get to know it to play it well, some gimmicky holes ... Friendliest staff ... Liked the course, lots of placement drives ... Quirky and enjoyable ... Great holes, challenging ... Enjoyed the mountain setting ... Good, fun layout ... No. 4: heart attack hill ... A hidden gem.

THE CHARDONNAY GOLF CLUB

SP-2555 Jameson Canyon Rd. Hwy. 12, Napa, 94558, Napa County, (707)257-1900, (800)788-0136, 38 miles NE of San Francisco. **Web:** www.chardonnaygolfclub.com.

★★★★ CLUB SHAKESPEARE

Holes: 18. **Yards:** 7,001/5,448. **Par:** 72/72. **Course Rating:** 74.5/70.9. **Slope:** 137/125. **Green Fee:** $105/$125. **Cart Fee:** Included in Green Fee. **Walking Policy:** Mandatory cart. **Walkability:** 3. **Opened:** 1992. **Architect:** Algie Pulley. **Season:** Year-round. **High:** April-Oct. **To obtain tee times:** Call up to 14 days in advance. **Miscellaneous:** Metal spikes, range (grass), club rentals, credit cards (MC, V, AE, D, JCB).

CALIFORNIA

Reader Comments: Beautiful setting ... Fun course in vineyards ... Greens tough to hit and putt ... Will play again. Lots of fun ... Links style, No. 13 signature hole, stunning ... Unusual setting in the vineyards ... Golf in the wine country ... Easy to get 'high' in this vineyard! ... Vineyards and waterfalls, what could be better? ... Lovely scenery.

★★★½ VINEYARDS COURSE
Holes: 18. **Yards:** 6,811/5,200. **Par:** 71/71. **Course Rating:** 73.7/70.1. **Slope:** 133/126. **Green Fee:** $45/$85. **Cart Fee:** Included in Green Fee. **Walking Policy:** Mandatory cart. **Walkability:** 3. **Opened:** 1987. **Architect:** Algie Pulley. **Season:** Year-round. **High:** April-Oct. **To obtain tee times:** Call up to 14 days in advance. **Miscellaneous:** Reduced fees (weekdays, low season, twilight), discount packages, metal spikes, range (grass), club rentals, credit cards (MC, V, AE, D, JCB).
Reader Comments: Vineyards make course interesting ... No easy lies ... Some great holes ... Cheers to a great course ... Very windy. Hit it low or often ... Wide open, fun ... Not enough variety ... Reasonable price for Napa Valley.

★★★ CHERRY ISLAND GOLF COURSE
PU-2360 Elverta Rd., Elverta, 95626, Sacramento County, (916)991-7293, 10 miles N of Sacramento.
Holes: 18. **Yards:** 6,562/5,163. **Par:** 72/72. **Course Rating:** 71.1/70.0. **Slope:** 124/117. **Green Fee:** $17/$23. **Cart Fee:** $22/cart. **Walking Policy:** Unrestricted walking. **Walkability:** 2. **Opened:** 1990. **Architect:** Robert Muir Graves. **Season:** Year-round. **High:** April-Nov. **To obtain tee times:** Call up to 7 days in advance starting at 6:30 a.m. Call on Monday for weekend times. **Miscellaneous:** Reduced fees (weekdays, low season, twilight, seniors, juniors), metal spikes, range (grass/mats), club rentals.
Reader Comments: The design is a little questionable ... Cheap, kind of quirky layout ... Muny-type course, cheap but nothing special ... Lots of water ... Mickey Mouse layout ... Position play ... Nice layout, friendly management.

★★ CHESTER WASHINGTON GOLF COURSE
PU-1930 W. 120th St., Los Angeles, 90047, Los Angeles County, (323)756-6975, 20 miles of Los Angeles.
Holes: 18. **Yards:** 6,348/5,646. **Par:** 70/70. **Course Rating:** N/A. **Slope:** 107/115. **Green Fee:** $20/$25. **Walking Policy:** Unrestricted walking. **Walkability:** 2. **Season:** Year-round. **High:** June-Aug. **To obtain tee times:** Call (323)756-6975 7 days in advance. **Miscellaneous:** Reduced fees (weekdays, twilight, seniors, juniors), metal spikes, club rentals, credit cards (MC, V, AE), beginner friendly.

★★★ CHIMNEY ROCK GOLF COURSE
PU-5320 Silverado Trail, Napa, 94558, Napa County, (707)255-3363, 62 miles NE of San Francisco.
Holes: 9. **Yards:** 6,824/5,866. **Par:** 72/72. **Course Rating:** 71.5/73.0. **Slope:** 115/122. **Green Fee:** $20/$24. **Cart Fee:** $22/cart. **Walking Policy:** Unrestricted walking. **Walkability:** 1. **Opened:** 1965. **Season:** Year-round. **High:** June-Aug. **To obtain tee times:** Call up to 14 days in advance. **Miscellaneous:** Metal spikes, club rentals, credit cards (MC, V).
Reader Comments: A fun little 9-hole with good scenery ... Above average layout ... Easy course, nice setting ... Playing through and around vineyards ... Not bad.

★★ CHINA LAKE GOLF CLUB
M-411 Midway, China Lake, 93555, Kern County, (760)939-2990.
Holes: 18. **Yards:** 6,850/5,925. **Par:** 72/72. **Course Rating:** 72.5/73.8. **Slope:** 119/123. **Green Fee:** $16/$18. **Cart Fee:** $16/cart. **Walking Policy:** Unrestricted walking. **Walkability:** 1. **Opened:** 1952. **Architect:** William F. Bell. **Season:** Year-round. **High:** April-Oct. **To obtain tee times:** Call Thursday 7 am for Saturday & Sunday tee times. **Miscellaneous:** Reduced fees (twilight, juniors), metal spikes, range (grass/mats), club rentals, credit cards (MC, V, AE).

CHUCK CORICA GOLF COMPLEX
PM-No.1 Clubhouse Memorial Rd., Alameda, 94501, Alameda County, (510)522-4321.
★★★ EARL FRY COURSE
Holes: 18. **Yards:** 6,141/5,560. **Par:** 71/72. **Course Rating:** 69.2/71.0. **Slope:** 119/114. **Green Fee:** $14/$27. **Cart Fee:** $24/cart. **Walking Policy:** Unrestricted walking. **Walkability:** 1. **Opened:** 1927. **Architect:** William Locke/Desmond Muirhead. **Season:** Year-round. **High:** May-Oct. **To obtain tee times:** Call up to 7 days in advance. **Miscellaneous:** Reduced fees (weekdays, twilight, seniors, juniors), metal spikes, range (mats), club rentals, credit cards (MC, V).
Reader Comments: Everyone prefers this to the other course ... One of the neatest public courses, easy + flat = fun ... Basic facilities; lot of hazards ... Short, well designed, flat ... Fun short course, nice greens ... Tight treelined course with lots of water ... Very slow.
★★½ JACK CLARK SOUTH COURSE
Holes: 18. **Yards:** 6,559/5,473. **Par:** 71/71. **Course Rating:** 70.8/70.0. **Slope:** 119/110. **Green Fee:** $14/$27. **Cart Fee:** $24/cart. **Walking Policy:** Unrestricted walking. **Walkability:** 1. **Architect:** William P. Bell/Robert Muir Graves. **Season:** Year-round. **High:** May-Oct. **To obtain**

tee times: Call up to 7 days in advance. **Miscellaneous:** Reduced fees (twilight, seniors, juniors), metal spikes, range (mats), club rentals, credit cards (MC, V).
Reader Comments: Fewer trees ... Flat track, a lot of hackers ... Poor drainage during winter ... Basic facilities; not very scenic ... Hate that kikuyu grass! ... Surprisingly well-maintained muny, but watch out for hidden hazards (including goose poop!).

★★★ CHULA VISTA MUNICIPAL GOLF COURSE
PM-4475 Bonita Rd., Bonita, 91902, San Diego County, (619)479-4141, (800)833-8463, 10 miles S of San Diego.
Holes: 18. **Yards:** 6,759/5,776. **Par:** 73/74. **Course Rating:** 72.3/72.7. **Slope:** 128/124. **Green Fee:** $21/$28. **Cart Fee:** $12/person. **Walking Policy:** Unrestricted walking. **Walkability:** 1. **Opened:** 1963. **Architect:** Harry Rainville. **Season:** Year-round. **High:** July-Sept. **To obtain tee times:** Call 7 days in advance. Call 8-30 days in advance for $1 surcharge Monday-Friday $2.00 surcharge Saturday, Sunday & Holidays. **Miscellaneous:** Reduced fees (weekdays, twilight, seniors, juniors), metal spikes, range (grass/mats), club rentals, credit cards (MC, V, AE).
Reader Comments: Not bad for a public, pace was good ... Short ... Nice little muny ... Challenging, course conditions improving ... Flat; well managed ... Busy.

CINNABAR HILLS GOLF CLUB
PU-23600 McKean Rd., San Jose, 95141, (408)323-7812.
Special Notes: Call club for further information.

★★ CITY OF SAN MATEO GOLF COURSE
PM-1700 Coyote Point Dr., San Mateo, 94401, San Mateo County, (415)347-1461, 18 miles S of San Francisco.
Holes: 18. **Yards:** 5,853/5,451. **Par:** 70/72. **Course Rating:** 67.0/69.8. **Slope:** 104/115. **Green Fee:** $21/$26. **Cart Fee:** $21/cart. **Walking Policy:** Unrestricted walking. **Walkability:** 1. **Opened:** 1933. **Architect:** WPA. **Season:** Year-round. **High:** June-Aug. **To obtain tee times:** Call 7 days in advance. **Miscellaneous:** Reduced fees (weekdays, twilight, juniors), metal spikes, club rentals.

★★ COLTON GOLF CLUB
PU-1901 W. Valley Blvd., Colton, 92324, San Bernardino County, (909)877-1712.
Holes: 18. **Yards:** 310/2,626. **Par:** 57/57. **Course Rating:** 54.2/54.2. **Slope:** 82/82. **Green Fee:** $12/$17. **Cart Fee:** $17/person. **Walking Policy:** Unrestricted walking. **Walkability:** 2. **Opened:** 1961. **Architect:** Robert Trent Jones Sr. **Season:** Year-round. **High:** April-Nov. **To obtain tee times:** Take Reservations 1 week in advance. **Miscellaneous:** Reduced fees (weekdays, twilight, seniors, juniors), discount packages, metal spikes, range (grass/mats), club rentals, credit cards (MC, V), beginner friendly (junior programs).

★½ CORDOVA GOLF COURSE
PM-9425 Jackson Rd, Sacramento, 95826, Sacramento County, (916)362-1196, 9 miles E of Sacramento.
Holes: 18. **Yards:** 4,755/4,728. **Par:** 63/66. **Course Rating:** 61.2/64.9. **Slope:** 90/96. **Green Fee:** $8/$10. **Cart Fee:** $15/cart. **Walking Policy:** Unrestricted walking. **Walkability:** 1. **Opened:** 1960. **Season:** Year-round. **High:** April-Oct. **To obtain tee times:** Call Monday after 10 a.m. for weekend and holiday. Call Friday after 10 a.m. for next weekday. **Miscellaneous:** Reduced fees (weekdays, seniors, juniors), metal spikes, range (grass/mats), club rentals, credit cards (MC, V, ATM), beginner friendly.

★★★½ CORONADO GOLF COURSE
PM-2000 Visalia Row, Coronado, 92118, San Diego County, (619)435-3121, 2 miles S of San Diego.
Holes: 18. **Yards:** 6,590/5,742. **Par:** 72/72. **Course Rating:** 71.5/73.7. **Slope:** 124/126. **Green Fee:** $20/$20. **Cart Fee:** $12/person. **Walking Policy:** Walking at certain times. **Walkability:** 1. **Opened:** 1957. **Architect:** Jack Daray Sr. **Season:** Year-round. **To obtain tee times:** Call 2 days in advance at 7 a.m. Up to 14 days in advance you may buy a time for 11 a.m. or later for $30. Fee must be paid at least 3 days in advance. **Miscellaneous:** Reduced fees (twilight, juniors), metal spikes, range (grass/mats), club rentals, credit cards (MC, V), beginner friendly.
Reader Comments: Best bargain in California, worth hassle of getting in ... Tight muny layout. Over-played and too crowded ... Great location ... Flat walk ... Great deal ... Hard to get on ... One of the prettiest, most walkable, best value courses in the west.

COSTA MESA COUNTRY CLUB
PM-1701 Golf Course Dr., Costa Mesa, 92626, Orange County, (714)540-7500, 25 miles S of Los Angeles.
★★★ LOS LAGOS COURSE
Holes: 18. **Yards:** 6,542/5,925. **Par:** 72/72. **Course Rating:** 70.7/73.3. **Slope:** 116/118. **Green Fee:** $24/$33. **Cart Fee:** $22/cart. **Walking Policy:** Unrestricted walking. **Walkability:** 2. **Architect:** William F. Bell. **Season:** Year-round. **To obtain tee times:** Call up to 7 days in

advance or Monday for Saturday, Sunday, Monday times. **Miscellaneous:** Reduced fees (twilight, seniors, juniors), range (grass/mats), club rentals.
Reader Comments: Can be fun ... Good value for location in Orange County ... Wide open, good variety ... Course is improving, slow play ... Radical improvement in course condition.

★★★ MESA LINDA COURSE

Holes: 18. **Yards:** 5,486/4,591. **Par:** 70/70. **Course Rating:** 66.0/65.6. **Slope:** 104/103. **Green Fee:** $18/$25. **Cart Fee:** $22/cart. **Walking Policy:** Unrestricted walking. **Walkability:** 2. **Architect:** William F. Bell. **Season:** Year-round. **To obtain tee times:** Call up to 7 days in advance or Monday for Saturday, Sunday, Monday. **Miscellaneous:** Reduced fees (twilight, seniors, juniors), range (grass/mats), club rentals.
Reader Comments: Average ... Talk about bang for your buck ... The price is right ... Too crowded ... Short but humbling ... Other, smaller version of above course, but cheaper ... Wide fairways, small greens.

★★★★ THE COURSE AT WENTE VINEYARDS *Service, Condition*

PU-5050 Arroyo Rd., Livermore, 94550, Alameda County, (925)456-2479. **Web:** www.wentegolf.com.
Holes: 18. **Yards:** 6,949/4,975. **Par:** 72/72. **Course Rating:** 74.5/69.4. **Slope:** 142/122. **Green Fee:** $80/$100. **Walking Policy:** Unrestricted walking. **Walkability:** 5. **Opened:** 1998. **Architect:** Greg Norman. **Season:** Year-round. **High:** April-Oct. **Miscellaneous:** Range (grass), club rentals, credit cards (MC, AE).
Reader Comments: Expensive but worth it ... Outside of No. 2 and No. 18, it's good at best ... Attractive, interesting, challenging ... Great course, vineyards in play ... The best course in East Bay region San Francisco ... New, windy, nice use of terrain ... Beautiful views of the Livermore Valley and it's many vineyards ... Lovely setting overall.

★★★½ COYOTE HILLS GOLF COURSE *Service*

PU-1440 E. Bastachury Rd., Fullerton, 92835, Orange County, (714)672-6800, 5 miles N of Anaheim & Disneyland.
Holes: 18. **Yards:** 6,510/4,437. **Par:** 70/70. **Course Rating:** 71.1/64.2. **Slope:** 128/108. **Green Fee:** $50/$95. **Cart Fee:** Included in Green Fee. **Walking Policy:** Walking at certain times. **Walkability:** 4. **Opened:** 1996. **Architect:** Cal Olson/Payne Stewart. **Season:** Year-round. **To obtain tee times:** Call golf shop. **Miscellaneous:** Reduced fees (twilight, juniors), range (grass/mats), club rentals, credit cards (MC, V, AE).
Reader Comments: Soft greens ... Extreme elevation changes, need local knowledge ... Best short course in L.A., but pricey ... Tricked up course ... Interesting, difficult ... Mentally tough from tips ... Country club for a day ... Some great par 3s and 4s ... Fun and challenging ... Some interesting holes ... Cut into hills and canyons.

★★½ CREEKSIDE GOLF COURSE

PM-701 Lincoln Ave., Modesto, 95354, Stanislaus County, (209)571-5123, 25 miles S of Stockton.
Holes: 18. **Yards:** 6,610/5,496. **Par:** 72/72. **Course Rating:** 70.3/69.5. **Slope:** 115/108. **Green Fee:** $8/$20. **Cart Fee:** $20/cart. **Walking Policy:** Unrestricted walking. **Opened:** 1992. **Architect:** Halsey/Durey. **Season:** Year-round. **High:** May-Sept. **To obtain tee times:** Call up to 7 days in advance beginning at 7 a.m. **Miscellaneous:** Reduced fees (weekdays, twilight, seniors, juniors), metal spikes, range (grass), club rentals, credit cards (MC, V).
Reader Comments: Fun to play ... My home course, cheap golf ... Tee areas well situated for ladies.

★★★ CRYSTAL SPRINGS GOLF CLUB

SP-6650 Golf Course Dr., Burlingame, 94010, San Mateo County, (650)342-0603, 20 miles S of San Francisco. **Web:** www.csgolf@pacbell.net.
Holes: 18. **Yards:** 6,683/5,920. **Par:** 72/72. **Course Rating:** 72.1/74.0. **Slope:** 125/130. **Green Fee:** $35/$60. **Cart Fee:** $13/person. **Walking Policy:** Walking at certain times. **Walkability:** 3. **Opened:** 1920. **Architect:** Herbert Fowler. **Season:** Year-round. **High:** April-Oct. **To obtain tee times:** Call up to 7 days in advance for weekdays. For weekends, call Monday before. **Miscellaneous:** Reduced fees (weekdays, twilight, juniors), metal spikes, range (mats), club rentals, credit cards (MC, V, AE).
Reader Comments: One of the prettier courses in Bay Area ... I felt like a billygoat. Rarely a flat, level lie ... New changes, easier course ... Never a problem to get on ... Hills and winds ... Course has nice views ... Pretty location, course ordinary ... A lot of improvements.

★★★½ CYPRESS GOLF CLUB

PU-4921 Katella Ave., Los Alamitos, 90720, Orange County, (714)527-1800, 22 miles S of Los Angeles.
Holes: 18. **Yards:** 6,476/5,188. **Par:** 71/71. **Course Rating:** 71.4/69.0. **Slope:** 129/122. **Green Fee:** $45/$80. **Cart Fee:** Included in Green Fee. **Walking Policy:** Unrestricted walking. **Walkability:** 1. **Opened:** 1992. **Architect:** Perry Dye. **Season:** Year-round. **High:** April-Oct. **To obtain tee times:** Call up to 14 days in advance. **Miscellaneous:** Reduced fees (weekdays, twi-

light, seniors), discount packages, range (grass/mats), club rentals, credit cards (MC, V, AE, D, JCB—Diners).

Reader Comments: Good greens, nice par 3s ... Golf course in confined area ... Course too tight ... Incredible use of limited space ... A thinking course, do not fall asleep ... Target golf ... Tests all of your game ... Mounds everywhere ... Nice layout. Deep bunkers, lots of trees and water, great service in bar.

★★★½ DAD MILLER GOLF COURSE

PM-430 N. Gilbert St., Anaheim, 92801, Orange County, (714)765-3481, 20 miles E of Los Angeles.

Holes: 18. **Yards:** 6,025/5,362. **Par:** 71/71. **Course Rating:** 68.0/70.2. **Slope:** 108/116. **Green Fee:** $20/$26. **Cart Fee:** $24/cart. **Walking Policy:** Unrestricted walking. **Walkability:** 1. **Opened:** 1961. **Architect:** Dick Miller/Wayne Friday. **Season:** Year-round. **To obtain tee times:** Call tee times phone up to 10 p.m., or call golf shop between 6 a.m. and 6 p.m. up to 8 days in advance. **Miscellaneous:** Reduced fees (weekdays, seniors), metal spikes, range (grass/mats), club rentals, credit cards (MC, V, D).

Reader Comments: Short flat course, fast greens ... Good old course ... Not bad for a city course ... Old man's course ... Decent, nothing to write home about ... Few trees.

★★½ DAVIS GOLF COURSE

PU-24439 Fairway Dr., Davis, 95616, Yolo County, (916)756-4010, 12 miles W of Sacramento.

Holes: 18. **Yards:** 4,953/4,428. **Par:** 67/67. **Course Rating:** 62.9/63.9. **Slope:** 102/95. **Green Fee:** $8/$15. **Cart Fee:** $17/cart. **Walking Policy:** Unrestricted walking. **Walkability:** 1. **Opened:** 1964. **Architect:** Bob Baldock. **Season:** Year-round. **To obtain tee times:** Call golf shop up to 7 days in advance. **Miscellaneous:** Reduced fees (weekdays, twilight, seniors, juniors), metal spikes, range (mats), club rentals, credit cards (MC, V), beginner friendly (lessons and clinics for beginners).

Reader Comments: Greens in great shape. Great price on weekends ... Not bad for short course ... Short, fair, can bite back.

★★★ DEBELL GOLF CLUB

PU-1500 Walnut Ave., Burbank, 91504, Los Angeles County, (818)845-0022, 3 miles N of Los Angeles.

Holes: 18. **Yards:** 5,610/5,412. **Par:** 71/73. **Course Rating:** 67.4/72.9. **Slope:** 108/126. **Green Fee:** $15/$19. **Cart Fee:** $20/cart. **Walking Policy:** Unrestricted walking. **Walkability:** 4. **Opened:** 1958. **Architect:** William F. Bell/William H. Johnson. **Season:** Year-round. **To obtain tee times:** Call golf shop up to 5 days in advance. **Miscellaneous:** Reduced fees (weekdays, low season, twilight, seniors, juniors), metal spikes, range (mats), club rentals, credit cards (MC, V).

Reader Comments: Up and down, tight ... Consult your physician before walking this course ... On a rare clear day you can see to the ocean ... Short and hilly but fun ... Short, tight, target, fun ... They call this a thinking man's course.

★★★½ DELAVEAGA GOLF CLUB

PM-401 Upper Park Rd., Santa Cruz, 95065, Santa Cruz County, (831)423-7214, 25 miles S of San Jose. **E-mail:** davel@delaveagagolf.com. **Web:** www.Delaveagagolf.com.

Holes: 18. **Yards:** 6,010/5,331. **Par:** 72/72. **Course Rating:** 70.4/70.6. **Slope:** 133/125. **Green Fee:** $32/$43. **Cart Fee:** $43/person. **Walking Policy:** Unrestricted walking. **Walkability:** 3. **Opened:** 1970. **Architect:** Bert Stamps. **Season:** Year-round. **High:** March-Oct. **To obtain tee times:** Call up to 7 days in advance. **Miscellaneous:** Reduced fees (weekdays, twilight), metal spikes, range (mats), club rentals, credit cards (MC, V, AE, D).

Reader Comments: Tight, challenging, need to be straight off the tee! ... Pretty nice little 'mountain muny' ... Tee shot on 10 is like threading a needle ... Good value, challenging ... Frustratingly narrow, treelined, hilly course. Pretty but muny conditions ... Narrow fairways, small greens ... Beautiful, old, huge oak trees.

★★★★ DESERT DUNES GOLF CLUB

PU-19300 Palm Dr., Desert Hot Springs, 92240, Riverside County, (760)251-5367, (888)423-8637, 5 miles N of Palm Springs. **Web:** www.desertdunes.com.

Holes: 18. **Yards:** 6,876/5,359. **Par:** 72/72. **Course Rating:** 73.8/70.7. **Slope:** 142/122. **Green Fee:** $30/$120. **Cart Fee:** Included in Green Fee. **Walking Policy:** Unrestricted walking. **Walkability:** 2. **Opened:** 1989. **Architect:** Robert Trent Jones Jr. **Season:** Year-round. **High:** Jan.-May. **To obtain tee times:** Call up to 30 days in advance w/credit card. **Miscellaneous:** Reduced fees (weekdays, low season, resort guests, twilight, seniors, juniors), discount packages, range (grass/mats), club rentals, credit cards (MC, V, AE).

Reader Comments: Wind, links-style, fun ... Two different 9s, shotmakers' course, windy ... Best in the desert ... Bring your A-game if windy, and a lot of balls ... Windy as hell ... Great value for Palm Springs area ... Beautiful holes! ... Challenging course ... Unbelievable signature hole.

CALIFORNIA

★★★★ DESERT FALLS COUNTRY CLUB
SP-1111 Desert Falls Pkwy., Palm Desert, 92211, Riverside County, (760)340-4653. **Web:** www.desertfalls.com.
Holes: 18. **Yards:** 7,017/5,313. **Par:** 72/72. **Course Rating:** 75.0/71.7. **Slope:** 145/124. **Green Fee:** $30/$180. **Cart Fee:** Included in Green Fee. **Walking Policy:** Mandatory cart. **Walkability:** 4. **Opened:** 1984. **Architect:** Ron Fream. **Season:** Year-round. **High:** Nov.-April. **To obtain tee times:** Call 3 days in advance with credit card. **Miscellaneous:** Reduced fees (low season, twilight), range (grass), club rentals, lodging, credit cards (MC, V).
Reader Comments: Good layout, challenging greens ... Good desert course ... Nice design, good use of desert plants ... From the back tees one of the best in the desert ... Meticulously kept ... This is a must play when in the Palm Springs Area ... A favorite with the women ... Sunset on 18th hole memorable.

DESERT PRINCESS COUNTRY CLUB & RESORT
R-28-555 Landau Blvd., Cathedral City, 92234, Riverside County, (760)322-2280, (800)637-0577, 2 miles SE of Palm Springs.
Holes: 27. **Green Fee:** $45/$120. **Cart Fee:** Included in Green Fee. **Walking Policy:** Mandatory cart. **Walkability:** 4. **Opened:** 1984. **Architect:** Davis Rainville. **Season:** Year-round. **High:** Nov.-May. **To obtain tee times:** Resort guests call up to 30 days in advance. **Miscellaneous:** Reduced fees (weekdays, low season, resort guests, twilight), discount packages, metal spikes, range (grass), club rentals, lodging, credit cards (MC, V, AE).
★★★★ CIELO/VISTA *Condition*
Yards: 6,764/5,273. **Par:** 72/72. **Course Rating:** 72.5/70.3. **Slope:** 126/118.
★★★★ LAGOS/CIELO *Condition*
Yards: 6,587/5,217. **Par:** 72/72. **Course Rating:** 71.2/69.8. **Slope:** 121/119.
Reader Comments: Enjoyable course ... Beautiful course, mostly flat ... Slow greens ... Short but testy ... Very enjoyable resort-type course ... Great scenery, variety of holes.
★★★★ VISTA/LAGOS *Condition*
Yards: 6,667/5,298. **Par:** 72/72. **Course Rating:** 71.8/69.9. **Slope:** 123/117.

DESERT WILLOW GOLF RESORT
PU-38-995 Desert Willow Drive, Palm Desert, 92260, Riverside County, (760)346-7060, 130 miles E of Los Angeles. **Web:** www.desertwillow.com.
★★★★ FIRECLIFF COURSE *Condition+*
Holes: 18. **Yards:** 7,056/5,079. **Par:** 72/72. **Course Rating:** 74.1/69.0. **Slope:** 138/120. **Green Fee:** $35/$160. **Cart Fee:** Included in Green Fee. **Walking Policy:** Mandatory cart. **Walkability:** 3. **Opened:** 1997. **Architect:** Michael Hurdzan/Dana Fry/John Cook. **Season:** Year-round. **High:** Jan.-April. **To obtain tee times:** Call golf shop up to 30 days in advance. **Miscellaneous:** Reduced fees (weekdays, low season, twilight, juniors), range (grass), club rentals, credit cards (MC, V, AE, D).
Reader Comments: Best public in desert ... Classy, hard course ... Missing the fairway means hitting from rocks ... Sand like the Sahara! ... Flat, uninspiring ... Lots of bunkers ... Nothing stays on the greens ... Well groomed, great desert course ... Monster bunkers ... City-owned golf at its best.
MOUNTAIN VIEW COURSE
Holes: 18. **Yards:** 6,913/4,997. **Par:** 72/72. **Course Rating:** 73.4/69.0. **Slope:** 129/119. **Green Fee:** $35/$160. **Cart Fee:** Included in Green Fee. **Walking Policy:** Mandatory cart. **Walkability:** 3. **Season:** Year-round. **High:** Jan.-April. **To obtain tee times:** Call golf shop up to 30 days in advance. **Miscellaneous:** Reduced fees (weekdays, low season, twilight, juniors), metal spikes, range (grass), club rentals, credit cards (MC, V, AE, D), beginner friendly.

★★★ DIABLO CREEK GOLF COURSE
PU-4050 Port Chicago Hwy., Concord, 94520, Contra Costa County, (925)686-6262, 40 miles NE of San Francisco.
Holes: 18. **Yards:** 6,876/5,484. **Par:** 71/72. **Course Rating:** 72.2/72.5. **Slope:** 122/119. **Green Fee:** $18/$23. **Cart Fee:** $11/person. **Walking Policy:** Unrestricted walking. **Walkability:** 1. **Opened:** 1962. **Architect:** Robert Muir Graves. **Season:** Year-round. **To obtain tee times:** Call Mondays at noon to get available tee times. **Miscellaneous:** Reduced fees (weekdays, twilight, seniors, juniors), discount packages, metal spikes, range (mats), club rentals, credit cards (MC, V, AE).
Reader Comments: Great design and layout ... Fine muny course, need to speed play ... Flat, uninspired, local muny ... Challenging par 5s, long ... New greens, much improved, great muny.

DIABLO GRANDE RESORT
R-10001 Oak Flat Rd., Patterson, 95363, Stanislaus County, (209)892-4653, 75 miles S of Sacramento.
LEGENDS WEST CSE AT DIABLO GRANDE
Holes: 18. **Yards:** 7,112/4,905. **Par:** 72/72. **Course Rating:** 74.3/68.1. **Slope:** 143/120. **Green Fee:** $80/$100. **Cart Fee:** Included in Green Fee. **Walking Policy:** Unrestricted walking. **Walkability:** 4. **Opened:** 1998. **Architect:** Jack Nicklaus/Gene Sarazen. **Season:** Year-round.

CALIFORNIA

High: April-Sept. **To obtain tee times:** Call golf shop up to 7 days in advance. **Miscellaneous:** Reduced fees (resort guests), metal spikes, range (grass/mats), club rentals, credit cards (MC, V, AE, D).

★★★★ **RANCH COURSE AT DIABLO GRANDE** *Condition, Pace+*
Holes: 18. **Yards:** 7,243/5,026. **Par:** 72/71. **Course Rating:** 75.1/69.0. **Slope:** 139/116. **Green Fee:** $40/$80. **Cart Fee:** Included in Green Fee. **Walking Policy:** Unrestricted walking. **Walkability:** 4. **Opened:** 1996. **Architect:** Dennis Griffiths. **Season:** Year-round. **High:** April-Sept. **To obtain tee times:** Call golf shop up to 7 days in advance. **Miscellaneous:** Reduced fees (weekdays, twilight), metal spikes, range (grass/mats), club rentals, credit cards (MC, V, AE, D).
Reader Comments: Long course, fast greens ... Great course; superb service; worth the drive ... Stay and have dinner ... Extremely nice and challenging but pricey ... Rugged course ... Fees a little steep for location ... Beautiful, challenging and good walking course ... Use every club in the bag, maybe every ball, too.

★★½ **DIAMOND BAR GOLF CLUB**
PM-22751 E. Golden Springs Dr., Diamond Bar, 91765, Los Angeles County, (909)861-8282, 25 miles E of Los Angeles. **E-mail:** scott@diamondbargolf.com. **Web:** ww.diamondbargolf.com.
Holes: 18. **Yards:** 6,810/6,009. **Par:** 72/73. **Course Rating:** 72.8/73.9. **Slope:** 125/122. **Green Fee:** $20/$25. **Cart Fee:** $11/person. **Walking Policy:** Unrestricted walking. **Walkability:** 2. **Opened:** 1964. **Architect:** William F. Bell. **Season:** Year-round. **High:** April-Nov. **To obtain tee times:** Call golf shop up to 7 days in advance. **Miscellaneous:** Reduced fees (weekdays, twilight, seniors, juniors), metal spikes, range (mats), club rentals, credit cards (MC, V, AE, D), beginner friendly (group golf classes available).
Reader Comments: Freeway noise! ... Rolling hills. A good local choice ... Mostly flat ... Greens good, all else so-so ... Just a plain ordinary course ... Greens are fast and contoured, best of any L.A. muny course ... Challenging ... Could be great, if not for freeway.

DIAMOND VALLEY GOLF CLUB
PU-31220 Sage Rd., Hemet, 92543, Riverside County, (909)767-0828. **E-mail:** diamondvalleygolf.com. **Web:** www.diamondvalleygolf.com.
Holes: 18. **Yards:** 6,720/5,634. **Par:** 72/72. **Course Rating:** 73.0/72.3. **Slope:** 135/128. **Green Fee:** $30/$51. **Cart Fee:** $11/person. **Walking Policy:** Unrestricted walking. **Walkability:** 3. **Opened:** 1999. **Architect:** Art Magnuson. **Season:** Year-round. **High:** Nov.-May. **To obtain tee times:** Call. **Miscellaneous:** Reduced fees (twilight, seniors, juniors), range (grass), credit cards (MC, V, AE, D).

★★★½ **DOUBLETREE CARMEL HIGHLAND RESORT**
R-14455 Penasquitos Dr., San Diego, 92129, San Diego County, (619)672-9100, 20 miles N of San Diego.
Holes: 18. **Yards:** 6,428/5,361. **Par:** 72/72. **Course Rating:** 70.7/71.9. **Slope:** 123/125. **Green Fee:** $32/$52. **Cart Fee:** Included in Green Fee. **Walking Policy:** Walking at certain times. **Walkability:** 4. **Opened:** 1967. **Architect:** Jack Daray. **Season:** Year-round. **High:** Jan.-April. **To obtain tee times:** Call up to 7 days in advance. Golf packages 30 days in advance. **Miscellaneous:** Reduced fees (weekdays, low season, resort guests, twilight, seniors, juniors), discount packages, metal spikes, range (grass/mats), club rentals, lodging, credit cards (MC, V, AE, D).
Reader Comments: Enjoyable golf ... Challenging course, fun to play ... Greens are tough to read. For the most part, everything breaks down the hill toward the freeway ... Great conditions, great food, bar and service ... Tight layout ... Good scoring course ... Hilly, fairly short resort course.

★★★½ **DRY CREEK RANCH GOLF COURSE**
PU-809 Crystal Way, Galt, 95632, Sacramento County, (209)745-4653, 20 miles S of Sacramento. **E-mail:** drycreek@softcom.net. **Web:** www.drycreekranch.play18.com.
Holes: 18. **Yards:** 6,773/5,952. **Par:** 72/74. **Course Rating:** 72.7/73.9. **Slope:** 129/134. **Green Fee:** $18/$30. **Cart Fee:** $20/cart. **Walking Policy:** Unrestricted walking. **Walkability:** 3. **Opened:** 1962. **Architect:** Jim Fleming. **Season:** Year-round. **High:** April-Sept. **To obtain tee times:** Call up to 14 days in advance. **Miscellaneous:** Reduced fees (weekdays, low season, twilight), metal spikes, range (grass/mats), club rentals, credit cards (MC, V).
Reader Comments: Good value, rustic setting ... Placement golf ... Long, fairly wooded, tight ... Old tough course, condition varies ... Very nice and challenging course! ... All around pleasant day ... Good place to find out how good you are not! ... Nice old style course ... Each hole different, No. 18 is the best finishing hole around.

★★ **DRYDEN PARK GOLF COURSE**
PM-920 Sunset Ave., Modesto, 95351, Stanislaus County, (209)577-5359, 40 miles S of Stockton.
Holes: 18. **Yards:** 6,574/6,048. **Par:** 72/74. **Course Rating:** 69.8/72.5. **Slope:** 119/115. **Green Fee:** $12/$22. **Cart Fee:** $20/cart. **Walking Policy:** Unrestricted walking. **Walkability:** 2. **Opened:** 1953. **Architect:** William F. Bell/William P. Bell. **Season:** Year-round. **High:** May-Sept. **To obtain tee times:** Call tee times phone up to 7 days in advance beginning at 7 a.m. **Miscellaneous:** Reduced fees (weekdays, twilight, seniors, juniors), discount packages, metal

spikes, range (grass), club rentals, credit cards (MC, V), beginner friendly (full range of golf instruction for all skill levels).

★★★½ EAGLE CREST GOLF CLUB

PU-2492 Old Ranch Road, Escondido, 92027, San Diego County, (760)737-9762, 20 miles NE of San Diego.

Holes: 18. **Yards:** 6,417/4,941. **Par:** 72/72. **Course Rating:** 71.6/69.9. **Slope:** 136/123. **Green Fee:** $43/$65. **Cart Fee:** Included in Green Fee. **Walking Policy:** Mandatory cart. **Walkability:** 4. **Opened:** 1993. **Architect:** David Rainville. **Season:** Year-round. **High:** Jan.-April. **To obtain tee times:** Call 7 days in advance. **Miscellaneous:** Reduced fees (twilight, seniors, juniors), range (grass/mats), club rentals, credit cards (MC, V, AE).

Reader Comments: Very good all around ... Target golf ... Tight ... Lost lots of balls, had great time ... Some holes up and down, lots of trees ... Blue tees a masochist's dream! ... Tough short course, true tough greens ... Well maintained, not crowded ... Straight shooting is imperative ... Leave the driver at home.

★★★½ EASTLAKE COUNTRY CLUB

PU-2375 Clubhouse Dr., Chula Vista, 91915, San Diego County, (619)482-5757, 15 miles SE of San Diego.

Holes: 18. **Yards:** 6,606/5,118. **Par:** 72/72. **Course Rating:** 70.7/68.8. **Slope:** 116/114. **Green Fee:** $25/$61. **Cart Fee:** Included in Green Fee. **Walking Policy:** Walking at certain times. **Walkability:** 3. **Opened:** 1991. **Architect:** Ted Robinson. **Season:** Year-round. **High:** Jan.-June. **To obtain tee times:** Call up to 7 days in advance. **Miscellaneous:** Reduced fees (weekdays, twilight, seniors, juniors), range (grass), club rentals, credit cards (MC, V, AE).

Reader Comments: Nice layout ... Pretty darned average ... Target course, very pretty ... Well maintained ... Wide fairways ... Very popular, well-maintained public course ... Slow ... Wide open, grip it and rip it.

★★★ EL DORADO PARK GOLF CLUB

PM-2400 Studebaker Rd., Long Beach, 90815, Los Angeles County, (562)430-5411.

Holes: 18. **Yards:** 6,401/5,918. **Par:** 72/73. **Course Rating:** 70.6/74.3. **Slope:** 121/126. **Green Fee:** $15/$23. **Cart Fee:** $21/cart. **Walking Policy:** Unrestricted walking. **Walkability:** 1. **Opened:** 1960. **Architect:** Ted Robinson. **Season:** Year-round. **To obtain tee times:** Call up to 3 days in advance after 1 p.m. **Miscellaneous:** Metal spikes, range (grass/mats), club rentals, credit cards (MC, V, AE).

Reader Comments: Straightforward, traditional, lots of puddles when it rains ... Tough to get a time, but worth it, lots of trees ... Delightful highs and lows ... Accuracy required ... Old course, price is right ... Back 9 has lots of trees; good value; a sleeper ... Good challenge ... Best public course in Long Beach.

EL PRADO GOLF COURSE

PU-6555 Pine Ave., Chino, 91710, San Bernardino County, (909)597-1751, 30 miles E of Los Angeles.

★★★ BUTTERFIELD STAGE COURSE

Holes: 18. **Yards:** 6,508/5,503. **Par:** 72/73. **Course Rating:** 70.6/72.0. **Slope:** 116/118. **Green Fee:** $10/$28. **Cart Fee:** $23/cart. **Walking Policy:** Unrestricted walking. **Walkability:** 2. **Opened:** 1976. **Architect:** Harry Rainville/David Rainville. **Season:** Year-round. **To obtain tee times:** Weekdays, 7 days in advance. Weekend, the Monday prior. **Miscellaneous:** Reduced fees (weekdays, low season, twilight, seniors, juniors), range (grass), club rentals, credit cards (MC, V).

Reader Comments: Good tune-up course ... Excellent greens and fairways, challenging, make you feel right at home ... Good course for us seniors ... Good greens, layout routine ... Lots of cow smell in summer from dairy farms ... Excellent greens ... No trees, lots of flies.

★★★ CHINO CREEK

Holes: 18. **Yards:** 6,671/5,596. **Par:** 72/73. **Course Rating:** 71.5/72.1. **Slope:** 119/121. **Green Fee:** $10/$28. **Cart Fee:** $23/cart. **Walking Policy:** Unrestricted walking. **Walkability:** 2. **Opened:** 1976. **Architect:** Harry Rainville/David Rainville. **Season:** Year-round. **To obtain tee times:** Weekdays call 7 days in advance. Call Monday for upcoming weekend. **Miscellaneous:** Reduced fees (weekdays, low season, twilight, seniors, juniors), metal spikes, range (grass), club rentals, credit cards (MC, V).

Reader Comments: With two 18s, always able to get on ... Good greens, some tough holes ... Good public ... Great greens, better layout of the two ... Dairy farm odors.

★★½ EL RANCHO VERDE GOLF COURSE

PU-355 E Country Club Drive, Rialto, 92377, San Bernardino County, (909)875-5346, 5 miles W of San Bernardino.

Holes: 18. **Yards:** 6,822/5,563. **Par:** 72/72. **Course Rating:** 72.8/71.9. **Slope:** 126/118. **Green Fee:** $10/$30. **Cart Fee:** $10/person. **Walking Policy:** Unrestricted walking. **Walkability:** 1. **Opened:** 1955. **Architect:** Harry Rainville/David Rainville. **Season:** Year-round. **To obtain tee times:** Call up to 7 days in advance. **Miscellaneous:** Reduced fees (weekdays, low season, twilight, seniors, juniors), metal spikes, range (grass/mats), club rentals, credit cards (MC, V, D).

CALIFORNIA

Reader Comments: Beautiful greens ... Not crowded ... A boring layout ... Long iron course ... Needs work. Very average ... Flat, but a good test.

★★★ EL RIVINO COUNTRY CLUB
PU-5530 El Rivino Rd P.O. Box 3369, Riverside, 92519, Riverside County, (909)684-8905, 3 miles SW of San Bernardino.
Holes: 18. **Yards:** 6,466/5,863. **Par:** 73/73. **Course Rating:** N/A. **Slope:** 111/116. **Green Fee:** $13/$31. **Cart Fee:** $24/cart. **Walkability:** 3. **Opened:** 1956. **Architect:** Joseph Calwell. **Season:** Year-round. **Miscellaneous:** Reduced fees (weekdays, twilight), credit cards (MC, V).
Reader Comments: Reachable par 4s for us seniors ... Fun, wide open course ... Par 6 opening hole, yikes ... Worth going out of way for, very challenging ... Lots of fun, inexpensive.

★★★½ ELKINS RANCH GOLF COURSE
PU-1386 Chambersburg Rd., Fillmore, 93015, Ventura County, (805)524-1440, 20 miles NW of Valencia.
Holes: 18. **Yards:** 6,303/5,700. **Par:** 71/72. **Course Rating:** 69.9/72.7. **Slope:** 117/123. **Green Fee:** $23/$29. **Cart Fee:** $22/person. **Walking Policy:** Unrestricted walking. **Walkability:** 3. **Opened:** 1959. **Architect:** William H. Tucker Jr./Bob Schipper. **Season:** Year-round. **High:** April-Oct. **To obtain tee times:** Call up to 10 days in advance. Include day calling and day tee time is for. **Miscellaneous:** Reduced fees (weekdays, twilight, seniors, juniors), metal spikes, range (grass/mats), club rentals, credit cards (MC, V), beginner friendly (Saturday free junior clinics).
Reader Comments: Burgers are the best around ... Off beaten path, many interesting holes ... Just the view from No.17 makes this a great course ... Lies in the midst of orange groves ... An hour's drive north of Los Angeles, smog-free ... Fun, a few quirky holes ... Back 9 backs up ... Welcoming atmosphere. Beautiful setting and scenery.

EMERALD ISLE
PU-660 S El Camino Real, Oceanside, 92054, San Diego County, (760)721-4700, 25 miles N of San Diego.
Holes: 18. **Yards:** 2,780/2,100. **Par:** 56/56. **Course Rating:** 55.6/56.0. **Slope:** N/A. **Green Fee:** $16/$20. **Cart Fee:** $20/cart. **Walking Policy:** Unrestricted walking. **Walkability:** 4. **Opened:** 1987. **Season:** Year-round. **High:** July-Aug. **To obtain tee times:** Call or walk in for same day tee times. **Miscellaneous:** Reduced fees (twilight, juniors), discount packages, range (grass), club rentals, credit cards (MC, V, AE).

★★★½ EMPIRE LAKES GOLF COURSE
PU-11015 Sixth St., Rancho Cucamonga, 91730, San Bernardino County, (909)481-6663, 1 miles N of Ontario. **E-mail:** empirelakes.com. **Web:** www.empirelakes.com.
Holes: 18. **Yards:** 6,923/5,200. **Par:** 72/72. **Course Rating:** 73.4/70.5. **Slope:** 133/125. **Green Fee:** $55/$80. **Walking Policy:** Unrestricted walking. **Walkability:** 2. **Opened:** 1996. **Architect:** Arnold Palmer/Ed Seay. **Season:** Year-round. **To obtain tee times:** Call up to 7 days in advance. Outside 7 days guaranteed time up to 3 months in advance for $10/player extra. **Miscellaneous:** Reduced fees (twilight, seniors, juniors), range (grass), club rentals, credit cards (MC, V, AE, Diners Club).
Notes: PGA Junior Series.
Reader Comments: Great layout ... Wide open, avoid when windy ... Tricky greens, nice view of mountains ... Nice course, like to play it often, but pricey ... Lots of blind shots ... Great course, tough par 3s ... Looks flat, but it's a real challenge ... Good mix of long/short holes. All the par 3s are outstanding.

★★★½ ENCINITAS RANCH GOLF CLUB
PU-1275 Quail Gardens Dr., Encinitas, 92024, (760)944-1936.
Holes: 18. **Yards:** 6,821/5,285. **Par:** 72/72. **Course Rating:** 72.2/73.7. **Slope:** 127/128. **Green Fee:** $35/$67. **Cart Fee:** $10/person. **Walking Policy:** Unrestricted walking. **Walkability:** 3. **Opened:** 1998. **Architect:** Cary Bickler. **Season:** Year-round. **Miscellaneous:** Reduced fees (twilight, juniors), range (grass/mats), club rentals, credit cards (MC, V, AE, D).
Reader Comments: Great views of Pacific from back 9 ... Great new course, wait until it grows up ... Wide open, lots of low scores there ... Need to speed up play.

★★★★½ FALL RIVER VALLEY GOLF & C. C. *Value+, Pace*
PU-42889 State Hwy., 299 E., Fall River Mills, 96028, Shasta County, (916)336-5555, 70 miles NE of Redding.
Holes: 18. **Yards:** 7,365/6,020. **Par:** 72/72. **Course Rating:** 74.1/74.6. **Slope:** 129/127. **Green Fee:** $14/$27. **Cart Fee:** $22/cart. **Walking Policy:** Unrestricted walking. **Walkability:** 2. **Opened:** 1978. **Architect:** Clark Glasson. **Season:** April-Nov. **High:** May-Sept. **To obtain tee times:** Call up to 14 days in advance. **Miscellaneous:** Reduced fees (weekdays, twilight, seniors, juniors), metal spikes, range (grass/mats), club rentals, credit cards (MC, V), beginner friendly (free junior clinics, afternoon discount rates).
Reader Comments: Great greens ... Super value in a remote area ... Long and beautiful ... Long ways from anywhere but worth it ... A great course in the middle of nowhere ... The unknown

jewel of California ... No one around ... Great hamburgers ... Tough, great wooded area, good lunch.

★★★ FALLBROOK GOLF CLUB
PU-2757 Gird Rd., Fallbrook, 92028, San Diego County, (760)728-8334, 40 miles N of San Diego. **E-mail:** flbkgolf@adnc.com.
Holes: 18. **Yards:** 6,223/5,597. **Par:** 72/72. **Course Rating:** 69.9/73.8. **Slope:** 119/130. **Green Fee:** $13/$35. **Cart Fee:** $22/cart. **Walking Policy:** Unrestricted walking. **Walkability:** N/A. **Opened:** 1961. **Architect:** Harry Rainville. **Season:** Year-round. **To obtain tee times:** Call up to 10 days in advance. **Miscellaneous:** Reduced fees (weekdays, twilight, juniors), discount packages, metal spikes, range (grass/mats), credit cards (MC, V, D).
Reader Comments: Secluded with 2 distinct 9s ... Fun to play, could be in better shape ... Tough track, mature, lots of trees ... Very interesting course, you can walk it ... Tight, like new shoes ... Inexpensive. Huge trees can kill you ... Hilly, moderately difficult.

★★½ FIG GARDEN GOLF CLUB
SP-7700 N. Van Ness Blvd., Fresno, 93711, Fresno County, (209)439-2928. **E-mail:** Affordablegolf@juno.com.
Holes: 18. **Yards:** 6,621/5,605. **Par:** 72/72. **Course Rating:** 70.6/71.9. **Slope:** 113/120. **Green Fee:** $15/$50. **Cart Fee:** $25/cart. **Walking Policy:** Unrestricted walking. **Walkability:** 2. **Opened:** 1958. **Architect:** Nick Lombardo. **Season:** Year-round. **To obtain tee times:** Call golf shop or write. **Miscellaneous:** Reduced fees (weekdays, twilight, juniors), metal spikes, range (mats), club rentals, credit cards (MC, V, AE), beginner friendly.
Reader Comments: Gets a lot of play, in decent shape considering amount of play ... A mid-length, well-maintained course ... Beautiful course but always crowded ... Loved this course! ... Scenic, super hot in summer.

★★★½ FOUNTAINGROVE RESORT & COUNTRY CLUB
SP-1525 Fountaingrove Pkwy., Santa Rosa, 95403, Sonoma County, (707)579-4653, 50 miles N of San Francisco. **Web:** www.fountaingrovegolf.com.
Holes: 18. **Yards:** 6,990/5,424. **Par:** 72/72. **Course Rating:** 73.3/71.0. **Slope:** 135/125. **Green Fee:** $45/$75. **Cart Fee:** Included in Green Fee. **Walking Policy:** Mandatory cart. **Walkability:** N/A. **Opened:** 1985. **Architect:** Ted Robinson. **Season:** Year-round. **High:** May-Oct. **To obtain tee times:** Call up to 7 days in advance. **Miscellaneous:** Reduced fees (weekdays, twilight), discount packages, metal spikes, range (grass), club rentals, credit cards (MC, V, AE).
Reader Comments: Pretty course but play when it's dry ... Very hard from the tips ... Lots of woods! ... Country club atmosphere, felt pampered for a change ... Overall nicest and toughest course in area ... Terrific design ... Cutesy new waterfalls ... Lots of trees, water, long fun course.

★★★★ FOUR SEASONS RESORT AVIARA *Service, Condition*
R-7447 Batiquitos Dr., Carlsbad, 92009, San Diego County, (760)603-6900, 30 miles N of San Diego.
Holes: 18. **Yards:** 7,007/5,007. **Par:** 72/72. **Course Rating:** 74.2/69.1. **Slope:** 137/119. **Green Fee:** $175/$175. **Cart Fee:** Included in Green Fee. **Walking Policy:** Mandatory cart. **Walkability:** 3. **Opened:** 1991. **Architect:** Arnold Palmer/Ed Seay. **Season:** Year-round. **High:** April-Aug. **To obtain tee times:** Call up to 6 days in advance. **Miscellaneous:** Reduced fees (resort guests, juniors), discount packages, range (grass/mats), club rentals, lodging (331 rooms), credit cards (MC, V, AE, Diners Club, JCB).
Reader Comments: Too expensive but gorgeous ... One of the best finishing holes in the state ... Golf for the rich and famous ... Beautiful landscaping ... I want to hire the gardener! ... Demanding, beautiful, long, testing ... Expensive, a wonderful 50th birthday present! ... The beautiful scenery on and around the course was most memorable.

★★★ FRANKLIN CANYON GOLF COURSE
PM-Highway 4, Hercules, 94547, Contra Costa County, (510)799-6191, 22 miles E of San Francisco.
Holes: 18. **Yards:** 6,776/5,516. **Par:** 72/72. **Course Rating:** 70.9/71.2. **Slope:** 118/123. **Green Fee:** $25/$40. **Cart Fee:** $52/person. **Walking Policy:** Unrestricted walking. **Walkability:** 3. **Opened:** 1968. **Architect:** Robert Muir Graves. **Season:** Year-round. **High:** May-Aug. **To obtain tee times:** Call golf shop up to 7 days in advance. **Miscellaneous:** Reduced fees (weekdays, low season, twilight, seniors, juniors), discount packages, metal spikes, range (mats), club rentals, credit cards (MC, V, AE), beginner friendly.
Reader Comments: Excellent public course. Layout interesting, especially the back 9 ... Underrated muny, good mix of holes ... Boring front 9 ... 18 is good par 5 ... Great layout in hills and oaks ... Typical canyon course ... When wet, real sloppy; great greens.

★★ FRESNO WEST GOLF & COUNTRY CLUB
PU-23986 W. Whitesbridge Rd., Kerman, 93630, Fresno County, (559)846-8655, 23 miles W of Fresno.

Holes: 18. **Yards:** 6,959/6,000. **Par:** 72/73. **Course Rating:** 72.6/74.1. **Slope:** 118/118. **Green Fee:** $13/$16. **Cart Fee:** $20/cart. **Walking Policy:** Walking at certain times. **Walkability:** 5. **Opened:** 1966. **Architect:** Bob Baldock. **Season:** Year-round. **High:** March-May/Sept.-Oct. **To obtain tee times:** Call 7 days in advance. **Miscellaneous:** Reduced fees (weekdays, low season, twilight, seniors, juniors), range (grass), club rentals, credit cards (MC, V), beginner friendly.

★½ FURNACE CREEK GOLF COURSE
R-Hwy. 190, Death Valley, 92328, Inyo County, (760)786-2301, 140 miles NW of Las Vegas. **Web:** www.furnacecreekresort.com.
Holes: 18. **Yards:** 6,215/4,724. **Par:** 70/70. **Course Rating:** 69.6/66.0. **Slope:** 114/109. **Green Fee:** $25/$45. **Cart Fee:** $20/cart. **Walking Policy:** Unrestricted walking. **Walkability:** 2. **Opened:** 1937. **Architect:** William P. Bell/Perry Dye. **Season:** Year-round. **High:** Oct.-May. **To obtain tee times:** Call anytime. **Miscellaneous:** Reduced fees (low season, resort guests, twilight, juniors), discount packages, metal spikes, range (grass/mats), club rentals, lodging (224 rooms), credit cards (MC, V, AE, D), beginner friendly.

★★★½ GLEN ANNIE GOLF COURSE
PU-405 Glen Annie Rd., Goleta, 93117, Santa Barbara County, (805)968-6400. **E-mail:** glenannie@aol.com. **Web:** www.glenannie-golf.com.
Holes: 18. **Yards:** 6,420/5,036. **Par:** 71/71. **Course Rating:** 71.1/69.5. **Slope:** 122/118. **Green Fee:** $60/$75. **Cart Fee:** $11/person. **Walking Policy:** Walking at certain times. **Walkability:** 5. **Opened:** 1997. **Architect:** Robert Muir Graves/Damian Pascuzzo/Neal. **Season:** Year-round. **High:** April-Nov. **To obtain tee times:** 7 Day in advance 60 days in advance 5.00 per person fee. **Miscellaneous:** Reduced fees (weekdays, twilight, seniors, juniors), range (grass), club rentals, credit cards (MC, V, AE, D, Diners Club), beginner friendly (junior program).
Reader Comments: Nice but short, 15 excellent holes and 3 fillers ... Country club service ... A little funky ... Lots of elevation changes ... New, but great layout. Fun! ... New course that is great fun to play ... Driveable par 4s ... They wedged some of the holes in ... Fantastic views. Good food ... Mix of great holes and bad holes.

★★½ GOLD HILLS GOLF CLUB
1950 Gold Hill Dr, Redding, 96003, Shasta County, (530)246-7867, 3 miles N of Redding.
Holes: 18. **Yards:** 6,562/4,836. **Par:** 72/72. **Course Rating:** 72.2/68.8. **Slope:** 135/120. **Green Fee:** $25/$30. **Cart Fee:** $10/person. **Walking Policy:** Unrestricted walking. **Walkability:** 4. **Opened:** 1978. **Season:** Year-round. **High:** March-June. **To obtain tee times:** Call up to 7 days in advance. **Miscellaneous:** Reduced fees (seniors, juniors), range (grass/mats), club rentals, lodging, credit cards (MC, V, D).
Reader Comments: Very challenging course ... Not impressive ... A good challenge ... Interesting holes, high enjoyment ... Very challenging; lakes, trees and fast greens ... Traditional layout ... Relatively short course on paper, plays tough.

★★★★½ THE GOLF CLUB AT WHITEHAWK RANCH *Service+, Value+, Condition+, Pace+*
R-1137 Hwy. 89, Clio, 96106, Plumas County, (530)836-0394, (800)332-4295, 60 miles NW of Reno. **E-mail:** whrgolf@psln.com. **Web:** www.graeagle.com/whitehawk.
Holes: 18. **Yards:** 6,928/4,816. **Par:** 71/71. **Course Rating:** 72.4/64.2. **Slope:** 130/115. **Green Fee:** $75/$95. **Cart Fee:** Included in Green Fee. **Walking Policy:** Unrestricted walking. **Walkability:** 3. **Opened:** 1996. **Architect:** Dick Bailey. **Season:** May-Oct. **High:** June-Sept. **To obtain tee times:** Call golf shop. Credit Card required to guarantee time. **Miscellaneous:** Reduced fees (low season, resort guests, twilight, juniors), range (grass), club rentals, lodging, credit cards (MC, V, AE).
Reader Comments: Best practice facilities, excellent staff ... Outstanding, well-run facility ... God landscaped it ... A gem in the Sierras ... Most interesting course in Northern California ... An outstanding golfing experience ... Beautiful mountain setting. In full bloom in spring ... Course layout was friendly to women, as was staff.

GOLF RESORT AT INDIAN WELLS *Service*
R-44-500 Indian Wells Lane, Indian Wells, 92210, Riverside County, (760)346-4653, 19 miles E of Palm Springs.
★★★★ EAST COURSE
Holes: 18. **Yards:** 6,631/5,516. **Par:** 72/72. **Course Rating:** 71.7/70.7. **Slope:** 122/113. **Green Fee:** $40/$120. **Cart Fee:** Included in Green Fee. **Walking Policy:** Mandatory cart. **Walkability:** 3. **Opened:** 1986. **Architect:** Ted Robinson. **Season:** Year-round. **High:** Jan.-May. **To obtain tee times:** Stay at one of 4 participating hotels or call 3 days in advance. **Miscellaneous:** Reduced fees (weekdays, low season, resort guests, twilight), discount packages, metal spikes, range (grass/mats), club rentals, lodging, credit cards (MC, V, AE, Diners Club).
Reader Comments: Setting is nice, pleasant ... Visible and forgiving design ... Nice resort course, joy to play ... Pricey but fun ... Slow play ... Excellent desert conditions, nice ... More interesting than West Course.

CALIFORNIA

★★★★ **WEST COURSE**
Holes: 18. **Yards:** 6,500/5,408. **Par:** 72/72. **Course Rating:** 70.7/70.0. **Slope:** 120/111. **Green Fee:** $40/$120. **Cart Fee:** Included in Green Fee. **Walking Policy:** Mandatory cart. **Walkability:** 3. **Opened:** 1986. **Architect:** Ted Robinson. **Season:** Year-round. **High:** Jan.-May. **To obtain tee times:** Stay at one of 4 participating hotels or phone 3 days in advance. **Miscellaneous:** Reduced fees (weekdays, low season, resort guests, twilight), discount packages, metal spikes, range (grass/mats), club rentals, lodging, credit cards (MC, V, AE, Diners Club).
Reader Comments: Elevated tees and mountainside make tee shots challenging ... Beautiful views. Friendly staff ... Nice views, too slow and too expensive ... Challenging from blues, fun to play ... Nice desert course, challenging ... Don't miss this one ... Really a fun golf course, fairly easy, but very good.

★★★½ **GRAEAGLE MEADOWS GOLF COURSE**
R-Highway 89, Graeagle, 96103, Plumas County, (530)836-2323, 58 miles N of Reno.
Holes: 18. **Yards:** 6,680/5,640. **Par:** 72/72. **Course Rating:** 70.7/71.3. **Slope:** 119/127. **Green Fee:** $25/$40. **Cart Fee:** $30/cart. **Walking Policy:** Unrestricted walking. **Walkability:** 3.
Opened: 1967. **Architect:** Ellis Van Gorder. **Season:** April-Nov. **High:** July-Aug. **To obtain tee times:** Call after Feb. 1 for times during season. **Miscellaneous:** Reduced fees (weekdays, low season, twilight), discount packages, metal spikes, range (grass), club rentals, lodging, credit cards (MC, V).
Reader Comments: Forgiving course ... Challenging, scenic ... Deceivingly long, avoid rough! ... Very nice scenic views of mountains, ball really flew, especially off the elevated tees ... A well laid out, challenging resort course ... Beautiful mountain course (don't tell anyone).

GREEN RIVER GOLF COURSE
PU-5215 Green River Rd., Corona, 91720, Riverside County, (909)737-7393, 25 miles S of San Bernardino.
★★★½ **ORANGE COURSE**
Holes: 36. **Yards:** 6,470/5,725. **Par:** 71/72. **Course Rating:** 71.1/72.8. **Slope:** 126/125. **Green Fee:** $24/$32. **Cart Fee:** $11/person. **Walking Policy:** Unrestricted walking. **Walkability:** 1.
Opened: 1965. **Architect:** Harry Rainville. **Season:** Year-round. **High:** May-Oct. **To obtain tee times:** Call 7 days in advance for weekday tee times. Call Monday for upcoming weekend.
Miscellaneous: Reduced fees (weekdays, twilight, juniors), range (grass), club rentals, credit cards (MC, V, AE, D).
Reader Comments: Staff helpful ... Crowded ... Average layout ... Basic. Some weird holes ... Windy ... Good combination of holes ... Not long, but tests shot creativity ... Small greens, too noisy and windy ... Tough when wind blows through canyon ... Good public course.
★★★½ **RIVERSIDE COURSE**
Holes: 18. **Yards:** 6,275/5,467. **Par:** 72/71. **Course Rating:** 70.6/71.0. **Slope:** 122/115. **Green Fee:** $24/$32. **Cart Fee:** $11/person. **Walking Policy:** Unrestricted walking. **Walkability:** 1.
Opened: 1965. **Architect:** Harry Rainville/Cary Bickler. **Season:** Year-round. **High:** May-Oct. **To obtain tee times:** Call 7 days in advance for weekday tee times. Call Monday for upcoming weekend. **Miscellaneous:** Reduced fees (weekdays, twilight, juniors), range (grass), club rentals, credit cards (MC, V, AE, D).
Reader Comments: Scenic ... Better of the two courses ... Nice country setting, good layout ... Ragged, could be good layout, super clubhouse ... Weekends crowded ... More enjoyable of the two ... Good public course ... Old course, large trees, many leaves.

GREEN TREE GOLF CLUB
PU-999 Leisure Town Rd., Vacaville, 95687, Solano County, (707)448-1420, 30 miles W of Sacramento.
Holes: 18. **Yards:** 6,301/5,261. **Par:** 71/71. **Course Rating:** 70.2/69.9. **Slope:** 119/118. **Green Fee:** $12/$25. **Cart Fee:** $11/person. **Walking Policy:** Unrestricted walking. **Walkability:** 1.
Opened: 1962. **Season:** Year-round. **High:** March-Nov. **To obtain tee times:** Call up to 7 days in advance. **Miscellaneous:** Reduced fees (twilight, seniors, juniors), range (mats), club rentals, credit cards (MC, V).
Reader Comments: Outstanding facilities ... Best bang for the buck! ... You get what you pay for ... Needs some work ... Unusual layout.
EXECUTIVE COURSE
Holes: 9. **Yards:** 3,104. **Par:** 29. **Course Rating:** 28.2. **Slope:** 80. **Green Fee:** $9/$12. **Walking Policy:** Unrestricted walking. **Walkability:** 1. **Opened:** 1962. **Season:** Year-round. **High:** March-Nov. **To obtain tee times:** Call up to 7 days in advance. **Miscellaneous:** Reduced fees (seniors, juniors), range (mats), club rentals, credit cards (MC, V).

★★★ **GREEN TREE GOLF COURSE**
SP-14144 Green Tree Blvd., Victorville, 92392, San Bernardino County, (760)245-4860, 25 miles N of San Bernardio.
Holes: 18. **Yards:** 6,643/5,874. **Par:** 72/72. **Course Rating:** 71.3/72.5. **Slope:** 123/124. **Green Fee:** $19/$23. **Cart Fee:** $23/person. **Walking Policy:** Walking at certain times. **Walkability:**

CALIFORNIA

N/A. **Opened:** 1965. **Architect:** William F. Bell. **Season:** Year-round. **High:** May-Sept. **To obtain tee times:** Call up to 14 days in advance. **Miscellaneous:** Reduced fees (weekdays, low season, resort guests, twilight, seniors, juniors), discount packages, metal spikes, club rentals, lodging, credit cards (MC, V).
Reader Comments: Long walks between holes. Greens are pretty good ... Could be a nice course with work ... Flat, not too interesting.

★★★★ GREENHORN CREEK GOLF CLUB

R-676 McCauley Ranch Rd., Angels Camp, 95222, Calaveras County, (209)736-8111, 50 miles E of Stockton. **E-mail:** request@greenhorncreek.com. **Web:** www.greenhorncreek.com.
Holes: 18. **Yards:** 6,870/5,214. **Par:** 72/72. **Course Rating:** 72.7/70.1. **Slope:** 130/119. **Green Fee:** $30/$53. **Cart Fee:** $18/person. **Walking Policy:** Unrestricted walking. **Walkability:** 3.
Opened: 1996. **Architect:** Donald Boos/Patty Sheehan/Dick Lotz. **Season:** Year-round. **High:** March-Oct. **To obtain tee times:** Call up to 7 days in advance. Automated Tee-Time system. Tournaments (24 players) 1 year in advance. **Miscellaneous:** Reduced fees (weekdays, low season, resort guests, twilight, juniors), range (grass/mats), club rentals, lodging (60 rooms), credit cards (MC, V, AE), beginner friendly (instructional program, forward tee, practice range, club fitting).
Reader Comments: Mountain course, great setting, some interesting and fun holes to play ... Hilly, lots of oak trees, tight, great restaurant ... Lots of variety ... Very playable after first attempt ... Overpriced for location, nice course ... Great views. Good greens. Good wine ... Foothill gem. Underrated ... Staff is outstanding, as are some holes.

GRIFFITH PARK

PM-4730 Crystal Springs Dr., Los Angeles, 90027, Los Angeles County, (323)664-2255.
★★★½ HARDING COURSE
Holes: 18. **Yards:** 6,536/6,028. **Par:** 72/73. **Course Rating:** 70.4/72.5. **Slope:** 115/121. **Green Fee:** $10/$21. **Cart Fee:** $21/cart. **Walking Policy:** Unrestricted walking. **Walkability:** 4.
Opened: 1924. **Architect:** George C. Thomas, Jr. **Season:** Year-round. **High:** March-Sept. **To obtain tee times:** Must have a City of L.A. reservation card to make tee times over the phone. To obtain a card, pick up application at any City course, fill out, pay fee, receive card. Or come to the course and put your name on the waiting list with the starter. **Miscellaneous:** Reduced fees (weekdays, twilight, seniors, juniors), metal spikes, range (mats), club rentals.
Reader Comments: Great layout for a muny ... Great price for a solid course ... Slow, but great value ... Old course, trees galore ... Beautiful old course, gets lots of play, very slow on weekends ... Good condition for some of the most heavily traversed greens in L.A. ... Great old clubhouse.

★★★½ WILSON COURSE
Holes: 18. **Yards:** 6,942/6,330. **Par:** 72/73. **Course Rating:** 72.7/74.6. **Slope:** 117/128. **Green Fee:** $10/$21. **Cart Fee:** $21/cart. **Walking Policy:** Unrestricted walking. **Walkability:** 4.
Opened: 1923. **Architect:** Carl Worthing. **Season:** Year-round. **High:** March-Sept. **To obtain tee times:** Must have a City of L.A. reservation card to make tee times over the phone. To obtain a card, pick up application at any City course, fill out, pay fee, receive card. Or come to the course and put your name on the waiting list with the starter. **Miscellaneous:** Reduced fees (weekdays, twilight, seniors, juniors), metal spikes, range (mats), club rentals.
Reader Comments: Best course in L.A., bar none ... A challenging muny which makes you think, which isn't easy with the freeway nearby ... Great first tee ... Old course, good layout ... L.A. Open used to be here, long and tough. Beautiful old course ... Plenty of resort courses at 4 times the price are not as beautiful as this.

HAGGIN OAKS GOLF COURSE

PU-3645 Fulton Ave., Sacramento, 95821, Sacramento County, (916)575-2526.
★★★ ALISTER MACKENZIE COURSE
Holes: 18. **Yards:** 6,683/5,747. **Par:** 72/72. **Course Rating:** 70.6/72.5. **Slope:** 112/124. **Green Fee:** $5/$23. **Cart Fee:** $10/person. **Walking Policy:** Unrestricted walking. **Walkability:** 1.
Opened: 1932. **Architect:** Alister Mackenzie. **Season:** Year-round. **High:** April-Oct. **To obtain tee times:** Call up to 7 days in advance for weekdays and previous Tuesday after 6:30 a.m. for weekends and holidays. **Miscellaneous:** Reduced fees (weekdays, low season, twilight, seniors, juniors), range (mats), club rentals, beginner friendly.
Reader Comments: Alister Mackenzie had an off day ... They have greens you can actually run the ball up to and on ... Challenges players of all skills ... Overcrowded ... Needs work on some holes ... All around good day ... A links course, tricky ... Okay. Nice wide open (for the most part) course.

★★½ ARCADE CREEK COURSE
Holes: 18. **Yards:** 6,903/5,832. **Par:** 72/72. **Course Rating:** 71.4/71.7. **Slope:** 115/111. **Green Fee:** $5/$23. **Cart Fee:** $10/person. **Walking Policy:** Unrestricted walking. **Walkability:** N/A.
Architect: Michael J. McDonagh. **Season:** Year-round. **High:** April-Sept. **To obtain tee times:** Call up to 7 days in advance for weekdays and previous Tuesday after 6:30 a.m. for weekends and holidays. **Miscellaneous:** Reduced fees (weekdays, low season, twilight, seniors, juniors), range (mats), club rentals, beginner friendly.

Reader Comments: The course is fairly forgiving and wide open ... Gets lots of play, pleasant staff ... Overused course. Predictable layout. No. 18 is great ... Course playable when others in area are not ... No. 18 is the most fun in the area.
Notes: 1992 Women's Amateur.

HALF MOON BAY GOLF CLUB
PU-2000 Fairway Dr., Half Moon Bay, 94019, San Mateo County, (650)726-4438, 20 miles S of San Francisco.

★★★★ **LINKS COURSE**
Holes: 18. **Yards:** 7,131/5,769. **Par:** 72/72. **Course Rating:** 75.0/73.3. **Slope:** 135/128. **Green Fee:** $95/$115. **Cart Fee:** Included in Green Fee. **Walking Policy:** Mandatory cart. **Walkability:** N/A. **Opened:** 1973. **Architect:** Francis Duane/Arnold Palmer. **Season:** Year-round. **To obtain tee times:** Call 21 days in advance. **Miscellaneous:** Reduced fees (weekdays, resort guests, twilight), discount packages, club rentals, lodging (80 rooms), credit cards (MC, V, AE).
Reader Comments: When the weather kicks up, all the challenge you could ever want ... Fun golf, staff always very attentive ... Great views ... Too costly, caters to the wealthy ... Beautiful course ... Not enough ocean views ... Highly overrated ... Player friendly, lovely ocean views ... New facilities, very nice improvement.

★★★★ **OCEAN COURSE** *Condition*
Holes: 18. **Yards:** 6,732/5,109. **Par:** 72/72. **Course Rating:** 71.8/71.6. **Slope:** 125/119. **Green Fee:** $115/$135. **Cart Fee:** Included in Green Fee. **Walking Policy:** Unrestricted walking. **Walkability:** 3. **Opened:** 1997. **Architect:** Arthur Hills. **Season:** Year-round. **High:** April-Sept. **To obtain tee times:** Call 7 days in advance. **Miscellaneous:** Reduced fees (weekdays, resort guests, twilight), discount packages, metal spikes, club rentals, lodging, credit cards (MC, V).
Notes: Ranked 16th in 1999 Best in State.
Reader Comments: A lot of fun and in great condition ... Nice views, you'll want to play No. 16 again ... Pretty good front 9; top-100 quality back 9. Many ocean views ... A reasonable facsimile of Pebble Beach. Cheaper too ... Best new course in California ... Dramatic views, difficult course ... Overpriced and overrated ... An instant classic!

★★★ HANSEN DAM GOLF COURSE
PU-10400 Glen Oaks Blvd., Pacoima, 91331, Los Angeles County, (818)896-0050, 15 miles N of Los Angeles.
Holes: 18. **Yards:** 6,715/6,090. **Par:** 72/75. **Course Rating:** 70.8/73.8. **Slope:** 115/123. **Green Fee:** $17/$23. **Cart Fee:** $21/cart. **Walking Policy:** Unrestricted walking. **Walkability:** 3. **Opened:** 1977. **Architect:** Ray Goates. **Season:** Year-round. **High:** April-Sept. **To obtain tee times:** Advance reservations require an L.A. city reservation card. Daily, first come first serve. **Miscellaneous:** Reduced fees (weekdays, twilight, seniors, juniors), metal spikes, range (mats), club rentals, beginner friendly (lessons available).
Reader Comments: Great greens, No. 9 a real bitch par 4! ... Nice public course ... Three fun holes ... Average local course ... Not too challenging, 18th a par 3 ... Should redesign the 10th hole.

★★½ HARDING PARK GOLF CLUB
PM-Harding Park Rd. at Skyline Blvd., San Francisco, 94132, San Francisco County, (415)664-4690.
Holes: 18. **Yards:** 6,743/6,205. **Par:** 72/73. **Course Rating:** 72.1/74.1. **Slope:** 124/120. **Green Fee:** $26/$31. **Cart Fee:** $22/cart. **Walking Policy:** Unrestricted walking. **Walkability:** N/A. **Opened:** 1925. **Architect:** Willie Watson. **Season:** Year-round. **High:** April-Nov. **To obtain tee times:** Call 6 days in advance. **Miscellaneous:** Reduced fees (weekdays, twilight, seniors, juniors), metal spikes, club rentals, credit cards (MC, V, ATM).
Reader Comments: Great layout ... Beautiful old course, overplayed ... It's a shame that a course like this doesn't get the maintenance it deserves ... Bring wading boots in wet weather ... Could be outstanding ... Great closing holes ... Most-played muny in San Francisco ... Great traditional layout.

★★★★ HERITAGE PALMS GOLF CLUB
SP-44291 Heritage Palms Dr. S., Indio, 92201, (760)772-7334, 15 miles E of Palm Springs.
Holes: 18. **Yards:** 6,727/4,885. **Par:** 72/72. **Course Rating:** 71.9/66.6. **Slope:** 124/107. **Green Fee:** $40/$115. **Walking Policy:** Mandatory cart. **Walkability:** 2. **Opened:** 1996. **Architect:** Arthur Hills. **Season:** Year-round. **High:** Jan.-April. **To obtain tee times:** Call 10 days in advance. Groups of 8 or more may secure tee time with credit card up to 90 days in advance. **Miscellaneous:** Reduced fees (low season, twilight), range (grass), club rentals, credit cards (MC, V, D).
Reader Comments: Can be windy ... Good course, good service ... Nice new course, wide open ... Interesting layout, great condition ... Fast greens, like the course ... Nice layout, still maturing ... Wide open layout, very good greens.

★★★½ HESPERIA GOLF & COUNTRY CLUB *Pace*
PM-17970 Bangor Ave., Hesperia, 92345, San Bernardino County, (760)244-9301, 30 miles N of San Bernardino.
Holes: 18. **Yards:** 6,996/6,136. **Par:** 72/72. **Course Rating:** 74.6/73.9. **Slope:** 133/124. **Green Fee:** $17/$22. **Cart Fee:** $20/cart. **Walking Policy:** Unrestricted walking. **Walkability:** 2.

Opened: 1955. **Architect:** William F. Bell. **Season:** Year-round. **High:** Spring/Fall. **To obtain tee times:** Call up to 14 days ahead. **Miscellaneous:** Reduced fees (weekdays, twilight, seniors, juniors), discount packages, metal spikes, range (mats), club rentals, credit cards (MC, V). **Notes:** Former PGA Stop.
Reader Comments: Stereotypical muny ... Great old course, some very hard holes, one of the greatest values in golf ... Very tough course, very long in wind ... Fast play ... Had a great score through 15; the finish is brutal ... Old-style layout, simple and nice.

★★ HIDDEN HILLS RESORT & GOLF CLUB
SP-7643 Fachada Way , La Grange, 95329, Tuolumne County, (209)852-2242, 38 miles E of Modesto. **E-mail:** hiddenhillresort.com.
Holes: 18. **Yards:** 6,400/5,600. **Par:** 70/70. **Course Rating:** 68.4/71.7. **Slope:** 118/123. **Green Fee:** $10/$25. **Cart Fee:** $10/person. **Walking Policy:** Unrestricted walking. **Walkability:** 4.
Opened: 1973. **Architect:** William F. Bell. **Season:** Year-round. **Miscellaneous:** Reduced fees (weekdays, twilight, juniors), range (mats), club rentals, credit cards (MC, V, AE, D), beginner friendly (educational programs, special tees).

★★★½ HIDDEN VALLEY GOLF CLUB
PU-10 Clubhouse Dr., Norco, 91760, Riverside County, (909)737-1010, 10 miles W of Riverside. **E-mail:** sales@hiddenvalleygolf.com. **Web:** www.hiddenvalleygolf.com.
Holes: 18. **Yards:** 6,721/4,649. **Par:** 72/71. **Course Rating:** 73.3/66.6. **Slope:** 140/116. **Green Fee:** $45/$90. **Walking Policy:** Mandatory cart. **Walkability:** 4. **Opened:** 1997. **Architect:** Casey O'Callaghan. **Season:** Year-round. **High:** Oct.-May. **To obtain tee times:** Call up to 14 days in advance. **Miscellaneous:** Reduced fees (twilight, seniors, juniors), range (grass), club rentals, credit cards (MC, V).
Reader Comments: Beautiful ... Kinda tough for us seniors ... Very challenging course, lots of up and downhill ... Over-priced ... Too many elevation changes ... It's a must play ... Young, great layout, good greens ... Scenery and elevation changes were very interesting and challenging. A thinking golfer's course ... A lot of hills, a lot of blind shots.

★★½ HIDDEN VALLEY LAKE GOLF & COUNTRY CLUB
SP-19210 Hartman Rd., Middletown, 95461, Lake County, (707)987-3035, 40 miles E of Santa Rosa. **Web:** www.hiddenvalleylake.org.
Holes: 18. **Yards:** 6,667/5,546. **Par:** 72/74. **Course Rating:** 72.5/71.5. **Slope:** 124/124. **Green Fee:** $20/$30. **Cart Fee:** $15/person. **Walking Policy:** Walking at certain times. **Walkability:** 5. **Opened:** 1970. **Architect:** William F. Bell. **Season:** Year-round. **To obtain tee times:** Call up to 7 days in advance. **Miscellaneous:** Reduced fees (twilight, seniors, juniors), range (grass), club rentals, credit cards (MC, V, AE, D), beginner friendly (beginner golf classes).
Reader Comments: Superb value and challenge; worth the drive ... Off the beaten path. Long par 4s, short 5s ... Front 9 long, dull. Back 9 tight, canyon, testing shots ... Most fun place ... Back 9 most interesting, good greens ... Good contrast between front and back 9s ... Rough is very tough.

★★★½ HORSE THIEF COUNTRY CLUB
R-28930 Horse Thief Dr., Stallion Spring, Tehachapi, 93561, Kern County, (661)822-5581, 50 miles E of Bakersfield. **Holes:** 18. **Yards:** 6,678/5,677. **Par:** 72/72. **Course Rating:** 72.1/72.1. **Slope:** 124/124. **Green Fee:** $25/$40. **Cart Fee:** $20/person. **Walking Policy:** Unrestricted walking. **Walkability:** 4. **Opened:** 1972. **Architect:** Bob Baldock. **Season:** Year-round. **High:** May-Sept. **To obtain tee times:** Resort guests may make tee time up to 1 year in advance at time of room reservation. Nonguests call up to 10 days in advance. **Miscellaneous:** Reduced fees (weekdays, twilight, seniors, juniors), discount packages, range (mats), club rentals, lodging, credit cards (MC, V, AE, D).
Reader Comments: A gem in the middle of nowhere. Great design in pretty good shape ... A must play ... Nice for an out of the way resort course ... Fun, challenging track, big boulders, old oaks, scenic ... Hard to find, but worth looking for ... Scenic course in mountain setting ... Awkward layout ... A hidden treasure in the mountains.

★★★★½ HUNTER RANCH GOLF COURSE *Condition*
PU-4041 Hwy. 46 E., Paso Robles, 93446, San Luis Obispo County, (805)237-7444, 25 miles NE of San Luis Obispo.
Holes: 18. **Yards:** 6,741/5,639. **Par:** 72/72. **Course Rating:** 72.2/72.8. **Slope:** 136/132. **Green Fee:** $25/$55. **Cart Fee:** $24/cart. **Walking Policy:** Unrestricted walking. **Walkability:** 3.
Opened: 1994. **Architect:** Ken Hunter Jr./Mike McGinnis. **Season:** Year-round. **High:** May-Oct. **To obtain tee times:** Call 7 days in advance. **Miscellaneous:** Reduced fees (twilight, juniors), range (grass), club rentals, credit cards (MC, V).
Reader Comments: Championship course, fast greens, scenic ... Beautiful and tough, wind a factor ... Immaculate greens, not a long course but will definitely test your nerves ... You have to play this course at least once ... Through blue oaks and vineyards on rolling hills ... Lots of elevation changes ... A difficult but memorable course.

★★★ INDIAN HILLS GOLF CLUB
PU-5700 Clubhouse Dr., Riverside, 92509, Riverside County, (909)360-2090, (800)600-2090.
Holes: 18. **Yards:** 6,104/5,562. **Par:** 70/72. **Course Rating:** 70.0/70.7. **Slope:** 126/118. **Green Fee:** $27/$43. **Cart Fee:** Included in Green Fee. **Walking Policy:** Mandatory cart. **Walkability:** 4. **Opened:** 1964. **Architect:** William F. Bell. **Season:** Year-round. **High:** Nov.-June. **To obtain tee times:** Call golf shop. Up to 7 days in advance. **Miscellaneous:** Reduced fees (weekdays, low season, twilight, seniors, juniors), discount packages, metal spikes, range (mats), club rentals, credit cards (MC, V).
Reader Comments: Tight. A challenge ... Well named since there are no level lies. Fun layout ... Mom and Pop course ... A lot of fun in the trees ... Hilly, bring an extra sleeve ... Mandatory carts suck! I want to walk ... Lots of elevation changes, needs work.

★★★ INDIAN SPRINGS COUNTRY CLUB
PU-46-080 Jefferson St., La Quinta, 92253, Riverside County, (760)775-3360, 6 miles S of Palm Desert.
Holes: 18. **Yards:** 6,369/5,717. **Par:** 71/72. **Course Rating:** 69.8/72.4. **Slope:** 112/117. **Green Fee:** $15/$50. **Walking Policy:** Unrestricted walking. **Walkability:** 2. **Opened:** 1960. **Architect:** Doc Gurly/Hogie Carmichael. **Season:** Year-round. **High:** Nov.-May. **To obtain tee times:** Call up to 7 days in advance. **Miscellaneous:** Reduced fees (weekdays, low season, resort guests, twilight), discount packages, metal spikes, range (grass), club rentals, credit cards (MC, V, D).
Reader Comments: You get what you pay for ... Great course and people ... Golf for beginners ... Too slow ... Best value in Palm Springs area ... Long distances between holes ... Old and easy design, in good shape, good value ... Not very interesting.

★★★ INDIAN VALLEY GOLF CLUB
PU-3035 Novato Blvd., Novato, 94948, Marin County, (415)897-1118, 22 miles N of San Francisco. **E-mail:** golf@ivgc.com. **Web:** www.ivgc.com.
Holes: 18. **Yards:** 6,253/5,238. **Par:** 72/72. **Course Rating:** 69.2/70.9. **Slope:** 119/128. **Green Fee:** $14/$45. **Cart Fee:** $22/cart. **Walking Policy:** Walking at certain times. **Walkability:** 4. **Opened:** 1958. **Architect:** Robert Nyberg. **Season:** Year-round. **High:** May-Sept. **To obtain tee times:** Call up to 7 days in advance. **Miscellaneous:** Reduced fees (weekdays, twilight, seniors, juniors), metal spikes, range (mats), club rentals, credit cards (MC, V, AE).
Reader Comments: Great setting, wooded hills ... Course doesn't drain well ... Tram from 13th green to 14th tee ... Very hilly ... Course is beautiful.

INDUSTRY HILLS SHERATON RESORT & CONFERENCE CENTER
R-One Industry Hills Pkwy., City of Industry, 91744, Los Angeles County, (626)810-4653, 25 miles E of Los Angeles.

★★★½ BABE DIDRIKSON ZAHARIAS COURSE
Holes: 18. **Yards:** 6,600/5,363. **Par:** 71/71. **Course Rating:** 72.5/72.4. **Slope:** 134/133. **Green Fee:** $28/$68. **Cart Fee:** Included in Green Fee. **Walking Policy:** Mandatory cart. **Walkability:** 5. **Opened:** 1980. **Architect:** William F. Bell. **Season:** Year-round. **High:** April-July. **To obtain tee times:** Call 3 days in advance. **Miscellaneous:** Reduced fees (weekdays, low season, twilight, seniors), discount packages, metal spikes, range (mats), club rentals, lodging, credit cards (MC, V, AE, D).
Reader Comments: Way too long, too narrow, too tricked up ... Masochist's delight, bring lots of balls ... This course will eat your lunch ... Too difficult for average guy ... Wow. What fun ... . Not much easier than Ike course. Quite a test! ... Only for the very brave ... More playable than the Eisenhower.

★★★★ EISENHOWER COURSE
Holes: 18. **Yards:** 6,735/5,589. **Par:** 72/73. **Course Rating:** 72.9/73.1. **Slope:** 136/135. **Green Fee:** $28/$68. **Cart Fee:** Included in Green Fee. **Walking Policy:** Mandatory cart. **Walkability:** N/A. **Opened:** 1979. **Architect:** William F.Bell. **Season:** Year-round. **High:** April-July. **To obtain tee times:** Call 3 days in advance. **Miscellaneous:** Reduced fees (weekdays, low season, twilight, seniors, juniors), discount packages, range (mats), club rentals, lodging, credit cards (MC, V, AE, D, Diners Club).
Reader Comments: Tiger wouldn't break 80 here ... Superb variety of holes, tough ... Very tight and tough, blind shots ... Add 10 strokes to your handicap ... Great course, too slow ... Great layout, too hard to get a starting time ... OK for a local L.A. course ... Too tough for women ... Fun golf course, wide fairways make it playable.

JACK TONE GOLF
PU-1500 Ruess Rd., Ripon, 95366, San Joaquin County, (209)599-2973, 5 miles N of Modesto. **E-mail:** jtonegolf@aol.com.
Holes: 18. **Yards:** 3,693/3,292. **Par:** 62/62. **Course Rating:** 58.2/57.4. **Slope:** 82/85. **Green Fee:** $13/$17. **Cart Fee:** $18/cart. **Walking Policy:** Unrestricted walking. **Walkability:** 2. **Opened:** 1997. **Architect:** George Buzzini. **Season:** Year-round. **High:** March-Oct. **To obtain tee times:** Call one week in advance. **Miscellaneous:** Reduced fees (weekdays, twilight, seniors, juniors), range (grass), club rentals, credit cards (MC, V, AE), beginner friendly.

CALIFORNIA

★★★ JURUPA HILLS COUNTRY CLUB

PU-6161 Moraga Ave., Riverside, 92509, Riverside County, (909)685-7214, 5 miles W of Riverside.
Holes: 18. **Yards:** 6,022/5,773. **Par:** 70/71. **Course Rating:** 69.5/73.4. **Slope:** 122/123. **Green Fee:** $23/$40. **Cart Fee:** Included in Green Fee. **Walking Policy:** Walking at certain times. **Walkability:** 3. **Opened:** 1960. **Architect:** William F. Bell. **Season:** Year-round. **High:** Year-round. **To obtain tee times:** Call golf club. **Miscellaneous:** Reduced fees (weekdays, low season, twilight, seniors, juniors), discount packages, metal spikes, range (grass/mats), club rentals, credit cards (MC, V).
Reader Comments: Don't let name fool you: this is a walkers' course. Lots of trees ... Short, good greens ... Friendly staff ... Long par 3s ... Lots of doglegs, fun.

★★½ KERN RIVER GOLF COURSE

PU-Rudal Rd., Bakersfield, 93386, Kern County, (805)872-5128.
Holes: 18. **Yards:** 6,458/5,971. **Par:** 70/73. **Course Rating:** 70.5/72.3. **Slope:** 117/116. **Green Fee:** $12/$15. **Cart Fee:** $9/. **Walking Policy:** Unrestricted walking. **Walkability:** 3. **Opened:** 1920. **Architect:** William P. Bell. **Season:** Year-round. **High:** April-Sept. **To obtain tee times:** Call Wednesday at 7 a.m. for weekends. Call 1 day in advance for weekdays. **Miscellaneous:** Reduced fees (weekdays, twilight, seniors, juniors), metal spikes, range (grass), club rentals, credit cards (MC, V, AE, D).

★★★½ LA CONTENTA GOLF CLUB

SP-1653 Hwy. 26, Valley Springs, 95252, Calaveras County, (209)772-1081, (800)446-5321, 30 miles NE of Stockton.
Holes: 18. **Yards:** 6,425/5,120. **Par:** 71/72. **Course Rating:** 70.2/70.8. **Slope:** 125/120. **Green Fee:** $21/$35. **Cart Fee:** $11/person. **Walking Policy:** Unrestricted walking. **Walkability:** 3. **Opened:** 1972. **Architect:** Richard Bigler. **Season:** Year-round. **High:** March-Oct. **To obtain tee times:** Call golf shop up to 14 days in advance. **Miscellaneous:** Reduced fees (weekdays, resort guests, twilight, seniors, juniors), discount packages, metal spikes, club rentals, lodging, credit cards (MC, V, D).
Reader Comments: Some holes unfair ... Course layout great. No two holes alike ... A rollercoaster ... Fun course, but too many quirky holes ... Fun, hilly, blind shots, short ... Best value in the area ... Fun course, always treat you well ... Very hilly and tight.

LA COSTA RESORT & SPA

R-Costa Del Mar Rd., Carlsbad, 92009, San Diego County, (760)438-9111, 30 miles N of San Diego. **E-mail:** info@lacosta.com. **Web:** www.lacosta.com.
★★★½ NORTH COURSE
Holes: 18. **Yards:** 7,021/5,939. **Par:** 72/73. **Course Rating:** 74.8/76.3. **Slope:** 137/137. **Green Fee:** $140/$195. **Cart Fee:** $20/person. **Cart Fee:** Included in Green Fee. **Walking Policy:** Mandatory cart. **Walkability:** 2. **Opened:** 1964. **Architect:** Dick Wilson/Joe Lee. **Season:** Year-round. **To obtain tee times:** Call golf reservations at extension 7608. **Miscellaneous:** Reduced fees (twilight), discount packages, metal spikes, range (grass), caddies, club rentals, lodging (497 rooms), credit cards (MC, V, AE, D, Diners Club, JCB).
Notes: PGA Tour Mercedes Championship; World Golf Championships, Anderson Consulting Match Play Championship.
Reader Comments: Expensive, but great place to be! ... Nice setting ... Great layout when breeze blows ... Golf packages are excellent ... The golf package and weather in late December were both a good memory ... Very overrated and overpriced ... A beautiful, challenging course ... Playable for women, not too many hazards.
★★★½ SOUTH COURSE
Holes: 18. **Yards:** 7,004/5,612. **Par:** 72/74. **Course Rating:** 74.4/74.2. **Slope:** 138/134. **Green Fee:** $140/$195. **Cart Fee:** $20/person. **Cart Fee:** Included in Green Fee. **Walking Policy:** Mandatory cart. **Walkability:** 2. **Opened:** 1964. **Architect:** Dick Wilson. **Season:** Year-round. **To obtain tee times:** Call golf reservations at extension 25. **Miscellaneous:** Reduced fees (twilight), discount packages, metal spikes, range (grass), caddies, club rentals, lodging (497 rooms), credit cards (MC, V, AE, D, Diners Club, JCB).
Notes: PGA Tour Mercedes Championship.
Reader Comments: First-class operation ... Nice course, but not worth the money ... Enjoy the pampered life ... Excellent resort course ... Courses are well maintained and long because one gets absolutely no roll. Tough greens to hit ... Rough too thick, great spa ... Fine, but too expensive, windy at times.

★★★ LA MIRADA GOLF COURSE

PM-15501 E. Alicante Rd., La Mirada, 90638, Los Angeles County, (562)943-7123, 20 miles SE of Los Angeles.
Holes: 18. **Yards:** 6,056/5,652. **Par:** 70/71. **Course Rating:** 68.6/71.6. **Slope:** 114/117. **Green Fee:** $19/$23. **Cart Fee:** $22/cart. **Walking Policy:** Unrestricted walking. **Walkability:** 4. **Opened:** 1962. **Season:** Year-round. **To obtain tee times:** Call 7 days in advance.

Miscellaneous: Reduced fees (weekdays, twilight, seniors, juniors), metal spikes, range (grass/mats), club rentals, credit cards (MC, V, AE).
Reader Comments: Very hilly ... Outstanding for a metropolitan muny. Interesting and pretty ... Short but still challenging ... Good short course ... Slow ... Hilly, but nice layout.

★★★★ LA PURISIMA GOLF COURSE *Value*

PU-3455 State Hwy. 246, Lompoc, 93436, Santa Barbara County, (805)735-8395, 40 miles N of Santa Barbara.
Holes: 18. **Yards:** 7,105/5,762. **Par:** 72/72. **Course Rating:** 74.9/74.3. **Slope:** 143/131. **Green Fee:** $45/$55. **Cart Fee:** $24/cart. **Walking Policy:** Unrestricted walking. **Walkability:** 3.
Opened: 1986. **Architect:** Robert Muir Graves. **Season:** Year-round. **High:** May-Oct. **To obtain tee times:** Call 7 days in advance. **Miscellaneous:** Reduced fees (weekdays, twilight, juniors), metal spikes, range (grass/mats), club rentals, credit cards (MC, V), beginner friendly (clinics, junior golf summer program).
Notes: Ranked 61st in 1996 America's Top 75 Affordable Courses. 1987, 88 LPGA Santa Barbara Open.
Reader Comments: Excellent value, tough, challenging course ... Very demanding course, tough ... . Beautiful and challenging, super condition ... A total hidden gem ... Beautiful setting, hard to find ... Difficult first time out ... Great track, keep it a secret! ... Play in the a.m.; p.m. is windy ... Wind makes this one of the best in California.

LA QUINTA RESORT & CLUB

R-50-200 Vista Bonita, La Quinta, 92253, Riverside County, (760)564-7686, (800)742-9378, 15 miles E of Palm Springs.

★★★½ DUNES COURSE

Holes: 18. **Yards:** 6,747/4,997. **Par:** 72/72. **Course Rating:** 73.1/70.7. **Slope:** 137/125. **Green Fee:** $40/$160. **Cart Fee:** Included in Green Fee. **Walking Policy:** Mandatory cart. **Walkability:** 3. **Opened:** 1981. **Architect:** Pete Dye. **Season:** Year-round. **High:** Nov.-April. **To obtain tee times:** Hotel guests may make tee times up to 1 year in advance. Nonguests call 30 days in advance. **Miscellaneous:** Reduced fees (weekdays, low season, resort guests, twilight), discount packages, range (grass), club rentals, lodging, credit cards (MC, V, AE, JCB, Diners).
Reader Comments: Couple of good holes ... Humbling ... A fine course. Worth playing ... About the best ... Surprisingly good experience ... Overpriced. There are better courses around ... Easiest at La Quinta ... Nice layout, tough, flat, mountain views ... Fun Dye course, won't beat you up.

★★★★ MOUNTAIN COURSE

Holes: 18. **Yards:** 6,758/5,005. **Par:** 72/72. **Course Rating:** 74.1/69.1. **Slope:** 140/123. **Green Fee:** $70/$235. **Cart Fee:** Included in Green Fee. **Walking Policy:** Mandatory cart. **Walkability:** 4. **Opened:** 1981. **Architect:** Pete Dye. **Season:** Year-round. **High:** Nov.-April. **To obtain tee times:** Hotel Guests may make tee times up to 1 year in advance. Others call 3 days in advance. Call (760)564-5729 for all advance tee times. **Miscellaneous:** Reduced fees (weekdays, low season, resort guests, twilight), discount packages, range (grass), club rentals, lodging, credit cards (MC, V, AE, Diners Club).
Notes: 1989 Senior Skins Game.
Reader Comments: Very nice up against the Mountain ... The best experience/challenge in the desert ... Very challenging with elevation changes and very fast greens. Awesome course! ... With fewer condos I'd give it 5 stars ... Easy front 9, killer back side ... A couple holes ate us up and spat us out, what a way to go! Exciting round.

★★★½ LAGUNA SECA GOLF CLUB

PU-10520 York Rd., Monterey, 93940, Monterey County, (831)373-3701. **E-mail:** laguna@golf-monterey.com. **Web:** www.golf-monterey.com.
Holes: 18. **Yards:** 6,157/5,204. **Par:** 71/72. **Course Rating:** 70.7/70.8. **Slope:** 127/121. **Green Fee:** N/A/$60. **Cart Fee:** $32/cart. **Walking Policy:** Unrestricted walking. **Walkability:** 4.
Opened: 1970. **Architect:** Robert Trent Jones. **Season:** Year-round. **High:** April-Oct. **To obtain tee times:** Call 30 days in advance for weekdays and 7 days in advance for weekends. **Miscellaneous:** Reduced fees (twilight), discount packages, club rentals, credit cards (MC, V, AE).
Reader Comments: Sporty track ... Gets a lot of play, nice area ... Native oaks give 'Old California' setting ... The 15th hole goes over the water twice, beautiful scenery ... Nice course, interesting, hilly layout, good value ... Above average ... Plays longer than card ... A fun course.

★★½ LAKE CHABOT GOLF COURSE

PM-11450 Golf Links Rd., Oakland, 94605, Alameda County, (510)351-5812, 10 miles E of Oakland.
Holes: 18. **Yards:** 5,982/5,268. **Par:** 72/71. **Course Rating:** 68.6/68.5. **Slope:** 115/116. **Green Fee:** $10/$23. **Cart Fee:** $22/cart. **Walking Policy:** Unrestricted walking. **Walkability:** 5.
Opened: 1927. **Architect:** William Lock. **Season:** Year-round. **High:** April-Sept. **To obtain tee times:** Call up to 7 days in advance. **Miscellaneous:** Reduced fees (weekdays, twilight, seniors, juniors), metal spikes, range (mats), club rentals, credit cards (MC, V).
Reader Comments: Hilliest course, no flat lies ... Old, very hilly. Tony Lema learned to play here ... Difficult to walk ... No.18 a par 6 ... Etched through peaks and valleys. Nothing bad to say ...

CALIFORNIA

Typical muny facilities; lots of ups and downs ... Good city course, great walk in the hills ... Not many sand traps.

LAKE SHASTINA GOLF RESORT
R-5925 Country Club Dr., Weed, 96094, Siskiyou County, (916)938-3205, (800)358-4653, 7 miles N of Weed.

★★★½ CHAMPIONSHIP COURSE
Holes: 18. **Yards:** 6,969/5,530. **Par:** 72/72. **Course Rating:** 72.6/70.2. **Slope:** 126/114. **Green Fee:** $22/$45. **Cart Fee:** $15/person. **Walking Policy:** Unrestricted walking. **Walkability:** 2. **Opened:** 1973. **Architect:** Robert Trent Jones. **Season:** Year-round. **High:** May-Sept. **To obtain tee times:** Call golf shop up to 30 days in advance. **Miscellaneous:** Reduced fees (low season, resort guests, twilight, seniors, juniors), discount packages, metal spikes, range (mats), club rentals, lodging, credit cards (MC, V, AE).
Reader Comments: Scenic, fun to play ... Mount Shasta dominates the view ... Challenging, long course, windy ... Mosquitos ate me up ... Great course, great value.
Special Notes: Also has 9-hole Scottish Link course.

★★★½ LAKE TAHOE GOLF COURSE
PU-2500 Emerald Bay Rd. Hwy. 50, South Lake Tahoe, 96150, El Dorado County, (530)577-0788, 60 miles SW of Reno.
Holes: 18. **Yards:** 6,685/5,654. **Par:** 71/72. **Course Rating:** 70.9/70.1. **Slope:** 120/115. **Green Fee:** $44/$64. **Cart Fee:** Included in Green Fee. **Walking Policy:** Walking at certain times. **Walkability:** 2. **Opened:** 1960. **Architect:** William F. Bell. **Season:** May-Oct. **High:** June-Sept. **To obtain tee times:** Reservations available 60 days in advance with $7.00 reservation fee. **Miscellaneous:** Reduced fees (low season, twilight, juniors), discount packages, metal spikes, range (grass), club rentals, credit cards (MC, V, AE).
Reader Comments: A perfect mix of Sierra sun, beautiful greens, and blue skies ... Fun course. A good walk in the woods. Not hard ... Breathtaking scenery, hard to concentrate ... Fun layout. Beautiful scenery. Friendly atmosphere ... Everything was awesome! ... Spectacular scenery ... Trees, mountains and meandering streams.

★★★½ LAKEWOOD COUNTRY CLUB
PM-3101 E. Carson St., Lakewood, 90712, Los Angeles County, (562)421-3741.
Holes: 18. **Yards:** 7,045/5,920. **Par:** 72/73. **Course Rating:** 72.9/74.1. **Slope:** 113/121. **Green Fee:** $20/$25. **Cart Fee:** $22/cart. **Walking Policy:** Unrestricted walking. **Walkability:** 1. **Opened:** 1935. **Architect:** William P. Bell. **Season:** Year-round. **High:** April-Oct. **To obtain tee times:** Call or come in 7 days in advance. **Miscellaneous:** Reduced fees (weekdays, twilight, seniors, juniors), metal spikes, range (mats), club rentals, credit cards (MC, V, AE).
Reader Comments: Great greens for a muny ... Crowded on weekends, par 3s are very challenging ... Play your heart out ... Great value and moderately tough ... Prettiest par 3 I've ever seen! (17th hole) ... Plays long from back tees ... Good old parkland style muny. Wide open so you can score.

★★★ LAS POSITAS GOLF COURSE
PM-917 Clubhouse Dr., Livermore, 94550, Alameda County, (925)455-7820, 1 miles W of Livermore.
Holes: 27. **Yards:** 6,725/5,270. **Par:** 72/72. **Course Rating:** 72.1/70.1. **Slope:** 127/120. **Green Fee:** $25/$36. **Cart Fee:** $12/person. **Walking Policy:** Unrestricted walking. **Walkability:** 1. **Opened:** 1966. **Architect:** Robert Muir Graves. **Season:** Year-round. **High:** April-June. **To obtain tee times:** Taken by computer up to 7 days in advance beginning at 5:00 a.m. **Miscellaneous:** Reduced fees (weekdays, low season, twilight, seniors, juniors), metal spikes, range (grass/mats), club rentals, credit cards (MC, V).
Reader Comments: A great value, fits all handicaps ... Heavily played muny, takes a beating but fun course to play ... Noisy place with airport on one side and freeway on other ... Great municipal.

★★ LEMOORE GOLF COURSE
PU-350 Iona Ave., Lemoore, 93245, Kings County, (559)924-9658, 30 miles S of Fresno.
Holes: 18. **Yards:** 6,431/5,126. **Par:** 72/72. **Course Rating:** 70.8/68.8. **Slope:** 121/115. **Green Fee:** $16/$19. **Cart Fee:** $18/cart. **Walking Policy:** Unrestricted walking. **Walkability:** 1. **Opened:** 1930. **Architect:** Bob Baldock/Bill Phillips. **Season:** Year-round. **High:** May-June/Sept.-Oct. **To obtain tee times:** Call Tuesday for weekend times. **Miscellaneous:** Reduced fees (weekdays, twilight, seniors), metal spikes, range (grass/mats), club rentals, credit cards (MC, V).

★★ LINCOLN PARK GOLF COURSE
PU-34th Ave. and Clement St., San Francisco, 94121, San Francisco County, (415)750-4653.
Holes: 18. **Yards:** 5,149/4,984. **Par:** 68/70. **Course Rating:** 64.4/67.4. **Slope:** 106/108. **Green Fee:** $23/$27. **Cart Fee:** $22/cart. **Walking Policy:** Unrestricted walking. **Walkability:** 4. **Opened:** 1916. **Architect:** Jack Fleming. **Season:** Year-round. **High:** April-Nov. **To obtain tee times:** Call 7 days in advance for weekdays; 3 days in advance for weekends. Call 6 days in

advance starting at 7 p.m. (750-golf). **Miscellaneous:** Reduced fees (weekdays, twilight, juniors), metal spikes, club rentals, credit cards (MC, V).

★★★★½ THE LINKS AT SPANISH BAY *Service, Condition*

R-2700 17 Mile Dr., Pebble Beach, 93953, Monterey County, (408)647-7495, (800)654-9300, 2 miles S of Monterey.
Holes: 18. **Yards:** 6,820/5,309. **Par:** 72/72. **Course Rating:** 74.8/70.6. **Slope:** 146/129. **Green Fee:** $165/$185. **Cart Fee:** $25/cart. **Walking Policy:** Unrestricted walking. **Walkability:** 2. **Opened:** 1987. **Architect:** R.T. Jones Jr./Tom Watson/Sandy Tatum. **Season:** Year-round. **High:** Sept.-Nov. **To obtain tee times:** Resort guest call 1 year in advance; outside play may reserve maximum of 60 days in advance. **Miscellaneous:** Reduced fees (resort guests, twilight), discount packages, caddies, club rentals, lodging, credit cards (MC, V, AE, D, JCB). **Notes:** Ranked 99th in 1997-98 America's 100 Greatest; 13th in 1999 Best in State; 48th in 1996 America's Top 75 Upscale Courses.
Reader Comments: Pay a lot, get a lot of challenge, wind ... Great location ... Overpriced, beautiful layout ... Stunningly beautiful ... Very underrated ... Breathtaking views, no bad holes ... Manicured links with an ocean view is hard to beat ... Prettier than Pebble Beach ... Enigmatic greens, challenging approaches ... Very fair to women!.

★★★½ LOCKEFORD SPRINGS GOLF COURSE

PU-16360 N. Hwy. 88, Lodi, 95240, San Joaquin County, (209)333-6275, 35 miles S of Sacramento.
Holes: 18. **Yards:** 6,861/5,951. **Par:** 72/72. **Course Rating:** 72.8/74.0. **Slope:** 121/123. **Green Fee:** $17/$27. **Cart Fee:** $10/person. **Walking Policy:** Unrestricted walking. **Walkability:** 1. **Opened:** 1995. **Architect:** Jim Summers/Sandy Tatum. **Season:** Year-round. **To obtain tee times:** Call 7 days in advance. **Miscellaneous:** Reduced fees (weekdays, twilight), metal spikes, range (grass), club rentals, credit cards (MC, V).
Reader Comments: A little long for an old guy ... Great greens ... Small town, big heart, must play ... Meandering the vineyards of Lodi ... Worth the drive from Bay Area ... Nice clubhouse ... Relatively flat ... Undulating, multi-level greens, long rough. Nice place to hang out. Good food and bar ... Young course, bright future.

LOS ANGELES ROYAL VISTA GOLF COURSE

SP-20055 E. Colima Rd., Walnut, 91789, Los Angeles County, (909)595-7441, 22 miles E of Los Angeles.
Holes: 27. **Green Fee:** $22/$33. **Cart Fee:** $12/person. **Cart Fee:** Included in Green Fee. **Walking Policy:** Walking at certain times. **Walkability:** 4. **Opened:** 1963. **Architect:** William F. Bell. **Season:** Year-round. **High:** April-Sept. **To obtain tee times:** Call 7 days in advance. **Miscellaneous:** Reduced fees (weekdays, low season, resort guests, twilight, seniors, juniors), discount packages, metal spikes, range (mats), club rentals, credit cards (MC, V, D).

★★½ NORTH/EAST
Yards: 6,537/5,545. **Par:** 71/71. **Course Rating:** 70.6/71.3. **Slope:** 121/118.
Reader Comments: Hilly, lots of long drives ... Houses to the left and right ... East 9 is best but tough to walk for an old-timer ... Level terrain ... A pleasant surprise. Improved ... Crowded ... Like 3 different courses, low spots wet in winter.

★★½ NORTH/SOUTH
Yards: 6,243/5,316. **Par:** 71/71. **Course Rating:** 69.3/69.8. **Slope:** 119/117. .

★★½ SOUTH/EAST
Yards: 6,182/5,595. **Par:** 72/72. **Course Rating:** 68.5/71.1. **Slope:** 112/117.

★★½ LOS ROBLES GOLF COURSE

PU-299 S. Moorpark Rd., Thousand Oaks, 91360, Ventura County, (805)495-6421, 30 miles N of Los Angeles.
Holes: 18. **Yards:** 6,134/5,184. **Par:** 69/69. **Course Rating:** 68.7/69.0. **Slope:** 116/115. **Green Fee:** $16/$27. **Cart Fee:** $22/cart. **Walking Policy:** Unrestricted walking. **Walkability:** 2. **Opened:** 1965. **Architect:** William F. Bell. **Season:** Year-round. **To obtain tee times:** Residents call 8 days in advance; all others 7 days. **Miscellaneous:** Reduced fees (weekdays, twilight, seniors, juniors), discount packages, metal spikes, range (grass/mats), club rentals, credit cards (MC, V).
Reader Comments: Very good for a local home course ... Usually windy, 3rd tee always backlogged ... Decent course ... Used to be 'country club' conditions ... Slow play ... Always enjoyable ... Hilly, old oaks ... Good variety of holes.

LOS SERRANOS LAKES GOLF & COUNTRY CLUB

PU-15656 Yorba Ave., Chino Hills, 91709, San Bernardino County, (909)597-1711, 40 miles E of Los Angeles.

★★★½ NORTH COURSE
Holes: 18. **Yards:** 6,440/5,949. **Par:** 72/74. **Course Rating:** 71.3/73.9. **Slope:** 129/125. **Green Fee:** $16/$39. **Cart Fee:** $11/person. **Walking Policy:** Walking at certain times. **Walkability:** 3. **Opened:** 1925. **Architect:** Harry Rainville. **Season:** Year-round. **High:** March-June. **To obtain**

tee times: Call golf shop 7 days in advance. **Miscellaneous:** Reduced fees (weekdays, twilight, seniors), metal spikes, range (grass/mats), club rentals, credit cards (MC, V, AE, D).
Reader Comments: Average layout ... Good layout, variety of holes ... Fantastic for all levels ... Back 9 is boring, long but nothing special ... Treelined fairways, fun course ... Great, challenging ... Beautiful setting and challenging holes ... Great hidden gem.

★★★½ **SOUTH COURSE**
Holes: 18. **Yards:** 7,470/5,957. **Par:** 74/74. **Course Rating:** 76.1/73.9. **Slope:** 135/128. **Green Fee:** $16/$39. **Cart Fee:** $11/person. **Walking Policy:** Walking at certain times. **Walkability:** 4. **Opened:** 1925. **Architect:** Bill Eaton. **Season:** Year-round. **High:** March-Aug. **To obtain tee times:** Call golf shop 7 days in advance. **Miscellaneous:** Reduced fees (weekdays, twilight, seniors), metal spikes, range (grass/mats), club rentals, credit cards (MC, V, AE, D, Optima), beginner friendly (Los Serranos Academy of Great Golf).
Reader Comments: Kinda tough for us seniors ... Challenging and price is right, old but nice ... Try if from the tips, it's brutal ... Want a tough track? This is it ... Long great layout. Stay out of trees ... Worth the drive from L.A. ... Excellent for the money. Dramatic elevations changes ... Bang! 2 par 5s in a row out the gate.

★★★½ **LOS VERDES GOLF COURSE**
PU-7000 W. Los Verdes Dr., Rancho Palos Verdes, 90275, Los Angeles County, (310)377-7888.
Holes: 18. **Yards:** 6,651/5,738. **Par:** 71/72. **Course Rating:** 72.4/71.8. **Slope:** 122/118. **Green Fee:** $17/$21. **Cart Fee:** $10/person. **Walking Policy:** Unrestricted walking. **Walkability:** 3. **Opened:** 1964. **Architect:** William F. Bell. **Season:** Year-round. **High:** June-Sept. **To obtain tee times:** Call 7 days in advance, 6 a.m. on weekdays and 5 a.m. on weekends. **Miscellaneous:** Reduced fees (weekdays, twilight, seniors, juniors), metal spikes, range (grass/mats), club rentals, credit cards (MC, V).
Reader Comments: Great golf. Extremely difficult to get on ... Tricky ocean break on greens ... Great view of Catalina Island ... Slow, slow, slow ... Good layout, great vistas ... Best view in L.A. ... Wide open ... Overlooks Pacific, great value.

★★★½ **MACE MEADOW GOLF & COUNTRY CLUB**
SP-26570 Fairway Dr., Pioneer, 95666, Amador County, (209)295-7020, 19 miles E of Jackson.
Web: www.macemeadow.com.
Holes: 18. **Yards:** 6,285/5,387. **Par:** 72/72. **Course Rating:** 70.0/70.0. **Slope:** 125/118. **Green Fee:** $14/$29. **Cart Fee:** $11/person. **Walking Policy:** Unrestricted walking. **Walkability:** 2. **Opened:** 1973. **Season:** Year-round. **High:** Mar-Oct. **To obtain tee times:** Call golf shop. **Miscellaneous:** Reduced fees (twilight, juniors), metal spikes, range (grass/mats), club rentals, credit cards (MC, V).
Reader Comments: Trees, water and beauty ... Tall pines, rolling hills ... Bargain for the forest setting ... Nice setting in foothills ... Walkable mountain course ... Some tight spots.

★★★½ **MADERA MUNICIPAL GOLF COURSE**
PM-23200 Ave. 17, Madera, 93637, Madera County, (209)675-3504.
Holes: 18. **Yards:** 6,831/5,519. **Par:** 72/72. **Course Rating:** 71.7/70.6. **Slope:** 121/112. **Green Fee:** $12/$17. **Cart Fee:** $19/cart. **Walking Policy:** Unrestricted walking. **Walkability:** 2. **Opened:** 1991. **Architect:** Bob Putman. **Season:** Year-round. **High:** April-Sept. **To obtain tee times:** Call up to 7 days in advance. **Miscellaneous:** Metal spikes, range (grass), club rentals, credit cards (MC, V, D).
Reader Comments: Very nice for a muny, nice greens ... Small trees, yet still challenging ... Not much variety in holes but not bad for a rural muny ... Young course, will be tough ... Best greens in valley, fairways so-so ... Good layout.

★★★½ **MALIBU COUNTRY CLUB**
PU-901 Encinal Canyon Rd., Malibu, 90265, Los Angeles County, (818)889-6680, 30 miles NE of Los Angeles.
Holes: 18. **Yards:** 6,740/5,627. **Par:** 72/72. **Course Rating:** 72.3/71.4. **Slope:** 132/120. **Green Fee:** $52/$77. **Cart Fee:** Included in Green Fee. **Walking Policy:** Mandatory cart. **Walkability:** 4. **Opened:** 1976. **Architect:** William F. Bell. **Season:** Year-round. **To obtain tee times:** Call golf shop. **Miscellaneous:** Reduced fees (seniors, juniors), metal spikes, club rentals, credit cards (MC, V, AE, JCB).
Reader Comments: OK track, overpriced ... Tough course, narrow, unforgiving ... Expensive. But great setting ... Pretty layout ... Pleasant surprise.

MANTECA GOLF COURSE
305 N. Union Rd., Manteca, 95336, (209)825-2500.
Special Notes: Call club for further information.

MARRIOTT'S DESERT SPRINGS RESORT & SPA
R-74-855 Country Club Dr., Palm Desert, 92260, Riverside County, (760)341-1756, (800)331-3112, 85 miles E of Los Angeles.
★★★★ **PALM COURSE**

Holes: 18. **Yards:** 6,761/5,492. **Par:** 72/72. **Course Rating:** 72.1/70.8. **Slope:** 130/116. **Green Fee:** $50/$150. **Cart Fee:** Included in Green Fee. **Walking Policy:** Mandatory cart. **Walkability:** 3. **Opened:** 1987. **Architect:** Ted Robinson. **Season:** Year-round. **High:** Oct.-May. **To obtain tee times:** Hotel guests may call up to 60 days in advance. Nonguests may call 3 days in advance. **Miscellaneous:** Reduced fees (weekdays, low season, resort guests, twilight), discount packages, metal spikes, range (grass), club rentals, lodging (800 rooms), credit cards (MC, V, AE, D, Diners Club), beginner friendly (daily one hour golf clinics).
Reader Comments: Beautiful layout, water, palms, excellent condition ... Pure pleasure, lots of water ... Great resort! ... Early summer it's a bargain ... Excellent resort course ... Better test than the Valley 18 ... Awesome views, great gardens/plantings ... Stay and play: best value in the desert ... Par 3s great.

★★★★ **VALLEY COURSE** *Pace+*
Holes: 18. **Yards:** 6,627/5,262. **Par:** 72/72. **Course Rating:** 71.5/69.6. **Slope:** 127/110. **Green Fee:** $50/$150. **Cart Fee:** Included in Green Fee. **Walking Policy:** Mandatory cart. **Walkability:** 3. **Opened:** 1987. **Architect:** Ted Robinson. **Season:** Year-round. **High:** Oct.-May. **To obtain tee times:** Hotel guests may call up to 60 days in advance. Nonguests may call 3 days in advance. **Miscellaneous:** Reduced fees (weekdays, low season, resort guests, twilight), discount packages, metal spikes, range (grass), club rentals, lodging, credit cards (MC, V, AE, D, Diners Club), beginner friendly (daily golf clinics).
Reader Comments: Better of the 2, uphill and downhill lies ... Great resort! ... It's a must play ... Great course, lots of water, gorgeous views ... Watch for the hummingbirds; no crowds after Memorial Day ... A lot of water for a desert.

MARRIOTT'S RANCHO LAS PALMAS RESORT & COUNTRY CLUB
R-42000 Bob Hope Dr., Rancho Mirage, 92270, Riverside County, (760)862-4551, 5 miles W of Palm Springs.
Holes: 27. **Green Fee:** $59/$129. **Cart Fee:** Included in Green Fee. **Walking Policy:** Mandatory cart. **Walkability:** N/A. **Opened:** 1978. **Architect:** Ted Robinson. **Season:** Year-round. **High:** Jan.-April. **To obtain tee times:** Call up to 7 days in advance. Must be guest at the hotel.
Miscellaneous: Reduced fees (weekdays, low season, resort guests, twilight), discount packages, metal spikes, range (grass), club rentals, lodging (450 rooms), credit cards (MC, V, AE, D)

★★★½ **NORTH/SOUTH**
Yards: 6,019/5,421. **Par:** 71/71. **Course Rating:** 67.2/69.7. **Slope:** 115/113. .
Reader Comments: Like all desert courses; beautiful, fun, challenging ... Some good holes ... Strange layout, all types of terrain ... Tight, target golf ... Well kept, great people ... An oasis of palm trees ... Easy decent course ... Short, fun course for seniors. Very expensive ... A quirky layout; some odd holes.

★★★½ **NORTH/WEST**
Yards: 6,113/5,308. **Par:** 71/71. **Course Rating:** 67.8/66.9. **Slope:** 116/105.

★★★½ **SOUTH/WEST**
Yards: 6,128/5,271. **Par:** 70/70. **Course Rating:** 67.8/66.8. **Slope:** 115/110.

★★★ MATHER GOLF COURSE
PU-4103 Eagles Nest Rd., Mather, 95655, Sacramento County, (916)575-4653, 7 miles E of Sacramento. **E-mail:** mathergc@pacbell.net. **Web:** www.courseco.com.
Holes: 18. **Yards:** 6,721/5,976. **Par:** 72/74. **Course Rating:** 71.3/72.4. **Slope:** 121/119. **Green Fee:** $18/$21. **Cart Fee:** $11/cart. **Walking Policy:** Unrestricted walking. **Walkability:** 2. **Opened:** 1963. **Architect:** Jack Fleming. **Season:** Year-round. **High:** May-Aug. **To obtain tee times:** All reservations taken 7 days in advance. **Miscellaneous:** Reduced fees (weekdays, twilight, seniors, juniors), metal spikes, club rentals, credit cards (MC, V), beginner friendly (instruction groups and planning).
Reader Comments: Standard public course ... Boring ... Many different holes with different challenges ... Former military-only course, underrated ... Long, wide open, hit away ... Continues to improve, good greens ... Older course, drainage problems.

★★★ MEADOW LAKE GOLF COURSE
SP-10333 Meadow Glen Way, Escondido, 92026, San Diego County, (760)749-1620, 30 miles N of San Diego.
Holes: 18. **Yards:** 6,521/5,758. **Par:** 72/74. **Course Rating:** 71.7/75.8. **Slope:** 130/135. **Green Fee:** $26/$38. **Cart Fee:** $12/person. **Walking Policy:** Walking at certain times. **Walkability:** 3. **Opened:** 1965. **Architect:** Tom Sanderson. **Season:** Year-round. **To obtain tee times:** Call up to 7 days in advance. **Miscellaneous:** Reduced fees (weekdays, resort guests, twilight, seniors, juniors), metal spikes, range (grass/mats), club rentals, credit cards (MC, V, AE, Diners Club), beginner friendly (beginner golf clinic).
Reader Comments: Course is a well-kept secret ... Narrow. Stay in fairway ... Mountain course, tough, many huge boulders ... Very tough course ... Tough greens, undulating and fast ... Getting better ... Hilly. Good value ... Great views on higher holes.

CALIFORNIA

★★½ MEADOWOOD NAPA VALLEY GOLF COURSE
SP-900 Meadowood Lane, St. Helena, 94574, Napa County, (707)963-3646, (800)458-8080.
Web: www.meadowood.com.
Holes: 9. **Yards:** 3,869/3,720. **Par:** 31/31. **Course Rating:** 60.1/60.8. **Slope:** 100/97. **Green
Fee:** $35/$35. **Walking Policy:** Unrestricted walking. **Walkability:** 2. **Opened:** 1963. **Architect:**
Jack Fleming. **Season:** Year-round. **High:** April-Oct. **To obtain tee times:** You must be regis-
tered to stay in the hotel or a member of a private golf facility. Call the golf shop to arrange tee
times. **Miscellaneous:** Metal spikes, club rentals, lodging (85 rooms), credit cards (MC, V, AE, D).
Special Notes: Formally Meadowood Resort Golf Course; Pull carts only

MENIFEE LAKES COUNTRY CLUB
SP-29875 Menifee Lakes Dr., Menifee, 92584, Riverside County, (909)672-3090, 20 miles S of
Riverside.
Holes: 27. **Green Fee:** $24/$58. **Cart Fee:** Included in Green Fee. **Walking Policy:** Unrestricted
walking. **Walkability:** 2. **Opened:** 1989. **Architect:** Ted Robinson. **Season:** Year-round. **High:**
Oct.-April. **To obtain tee times:** Call starter 6 days in advance for weekday tee times and
Monday before for weekend. **Miscellaneous:** Reduced fees (weekdays, twilight, juniors), metal
spikes, range (grass), club rentals, credit cards (MC, V).
★★★½ FALLS/LAKES COURSE
Yards: 6,500/5,500. **Par:** 72/72. **Course Rating:** 70.7/72.4. **Slope:** 121/122.
Reader Comments: Thinking man's course ... Three 9s, lots of water, good practice facilities ...
Beware of afternoon wind ... Golf till you drop ... Flat, much water, well kept ... Nice recreational
course ... Plenty of water in play for slicers ... Good test for short hitters ... Can't they slope the
fairways away from the ponds?.
★★★½ LAKES/PALM COURSE
Yards: 6,500/5,500. **Par:** 72/72. **Course Rating:** 70.5/71.5. **Slope:** 120/120.
★★★½ PALMS/FALLS COURSE
Yards: 6,500/5,500. **Par:** 72/72. **Course Rating:** 71.1/70.7. **Slope:** 122/121.
Special Notes: No pullcarts.

★★½ MERCED HILLS GOLF CLUB
PU-5320 North Lake Rd., Merced, 95340, Merced County, (209)383-4943. **E-mail:**
mercedhills.com. **Web:** www.mercedhill.com.
Holes: 18. **Yards:** 6,831/5,397. **Par:** 72/72. **Course Rating:** 72.8/70.6. **Slope:** 128/115. **Green
Fee:** $13/$20. **Cart Fee:** $10/person. **Walking Policy:** Unrestricted walking. **Walkability:** 3.
Opened: 1995. **Season:** Year-round. **High:** April-Oct. **To obtain tee times:** Call golf shop.
Miscellaneous: Reduced fees (weekdays, low season, twilight, seniors, juniors), range (grass),
club rentals, credit cards (MC, V), beginner friendly (junior camps and clinics).
Reader Comments: Lots of character. Better than most comparably-priced courses ... Links-
style, needs a little more work ... Great layout, good and different holes.

★★★½ MESQUITE GOLF & COUNTRY CLUB
PU-2700 E. Mesquite Ave., Palm Springs, 92262, Riverside County, (760)323-1502, 120 miles E
of Los Angeles.
Holes: 18. **Yards:** 6,328/5,244. **Par:** 72/72. **Course Rating:** 69.5/64.7. **Slope:** 117/118. **Green
Fee:** $45/$90. **Cart Fee:** Included in Green Fee. **Walking Policy:** Mandatory cart. **Walkability:**
1. **Opened:** 1984. **Architect:** Bert Stamps. **Season:** Year-round. **High:** Nov.-May. **To obtain tee
times:** (760)323-9377. **Miscellaneous:** Reduced fees (weekdays, low season, twilight), metal
spikes, range (grass/mats), club rentals, credit cards (MC, V, AE).
Reader Comments: Has 6 par 5s, 6 par 4s, 6 par 3s ... Ho-hum ... Not too tough but beautiful ...
A little short and too crowded ... Nice people, nice course ... Flat, nice greens, average design.

★★★½ MICKE GROVE GOLF LINKS
PU-11401 N. Micke Grove Rd., Lodi, 95240, San Joaquin County, (209)369-4410, 5 miles N of
Stockton.
Holes: 18. **Yards:** 6,565/5,286. **Par:** 72/72. **Course Rating:** 71.1/69.7. **Slope:** 118/111. **Green
Fee:** $17/$27. **Cart Fee:** $11/person. **Walking Policy:** Unrestricted walking. **Walkability:** 1.
Opened: 1989. **Architect:** Garrett Gill/George B. Williams. **Season:** Year-round. **High:** March-Nov.
To obtain tee times: Call 7 days in advance. **Miscellaneous:** Reduced fees (weekdays, low sea-
son, twilight, seniors, juniors), metal spikes, range (grass/mats), club rentals, credit cards (MC, V).
Reader Comments: Affordable course in the valley ... Nice people. Fun course ... Has some fun
places to lose your ball ... Good value ... Good links course ... Challenging, fair ... Good condition
... Not much to it.

★★★ MILE SQUARE GOLF COURSE
PM-10401 Warner Ave., Fountain Valley, 92708, Orange County, (714)968-4556, 30 miles S of
Los Angeles.
Holes: 18. **Yards:** 6,629/5,545. **Par:** 72/72. **Course Rating:** 71.0/70.5. **Slope:** 119/109. **Green
Fee:** $26/$35. **Cart Fee:** $22/cart. **Walking Policy:** Unrestricted walking. **Walkability:** 2.

CALIFORNIA

Opened: 1969. Architect: David Rainville. Season: Year-round. High: March-Sept. To obtain tee times: Call 7 days in advance for weekdays; call Monday for Saturday, call Tuesday for Sunday. Miscellaneous: Reduced fees (twilight), range (mats), club rentals, credit cards (MC, V). Reader Comments: Pretty basic ... Good layout, played to death ... Very busy, plain course ... Wind can play havoc. Good par 3s ... A challenging course ... Average muny.

★★★ MISSION LAKES COUNTRY CLUB
SP-8484 Clubhouse Blvd., Desert Hot Springs, 92240, Riverside County, (760)329-8061, 10 miles N of Palm Springs.
Holes: 18. Yards: 6,737/5,390. Par: 71/72. Course Rating: 72.8/71.2. Slope: 131/122. Green Fee: $30/$75. Cart Fee: Included in Green Fee. Walking Policy: Mandatory cart. Walkability: N/A. Opened: 1973. Architect: Ted Robinson. Season: Year-round. High: Jan.-May. To obtain tee times: Call 3 days in advance. Miscellaneous: Reduced fees (weekdays, low season, resort guests, twilight, juniors), metal spikes, range (grass), club rentals, lodging, credit cards (MC, V). Reader Comments: Good golf course, fun to play ... One of my favorites ... Front 9 average, back 9 tremendous elevation changes, can be very windy.

★★★ MONARCH BEACH GOLF LINKS
R-33033 Niguel Rd., Dana Point, 92629, Orange County, (714)240-8247, 60 miles N of San Diego.
Holes: 18. Yards: 6,340/5,046. Par: 70/70. Course Rating: 69.2/68.5. Slope: 128/120. Green Fee: $115/$145. Cart Fee: Included in Green Fee. Walking Policy: Unrestricted walking. Walkability: 3. Opened: 1984. Architect: Robert Trent Jones Jr. Season: Year-round. To obtain tee times: Call 7 days in advance. Or 8 to 30 days in advance with additional $15 per player pre-book fee. Times are held with credit card which will be charged if 24 hour cancellation is not given. Miscellaneous: Reduced fees (twilight, juniors), metal spikes, range (mats), club rentals, credit cards (MC, V, AE, Diners Club).
Reader Comments: Beautiful setting ... Great ... Hills steep ... Slow, fair condition. Average layout ... Tough links course ... Expensive ... Short, but lots of fun ... Good course, overpriced.

★★½ MONTEBELLO COUNTRY CLUB
PM-901 Vía San Clemente, Montebello, 90640, Los Angeles County, (323)725-0892, 9 miles E of Los Angeles.
Holes: 18. Yards: 6,671/5,979. Par: 71/72. Course Rating: 70.4/72.4. Slope: 114/117. Green Fee: $28/$38. Cart Fee: $24/cart. Walking Policy: Unrestricted walking. Walkability: 3. Opened: 1928. Architect: William P. Bell. Season: Year-round. High: April-Oct. To obtain tee times: Call 7 days in advance. Call Monday for weekends. Miscellaneous: Reduced fees (twilight, seniors, juniors), metal spikes, range (mats), credit cards (MC, V).
Special Notes: Formally Montebello Golf Club.

MORENO VALLEY RANCH GOLF CLUB
PU-28095 John F. Kennedy Dr., Moreno Valley, 92555, Riverside County, (909)924-4444, 15 miles E of Riverside.
Holes: 27. Green Fee: $30/$65. Cart Fee: Included in Green Fee. Walking Policy: Mandatory cart. Opened: 1988. Architect: Pete Dye. Season: Year-round. High: Nov.-May. To obtain tee times: Call 7 days in advance.
★★★★ LAKE/VALLEY
Yards: 6,898/5,196. Par: 72/72. Course Rating: 74.1/70.1. Slope: 138/122. Walkability: 3. Miscellaneous: Reduced fees (weekdays, low season, twilight, seniors, juniors), discount packages, metal spikes, range (grass/mats), club rentals, credit cards (MC, V, AE, D, Diners Club).
★★★★ MOUNTAIN/LAKE
Yards: 6,684/5,108. Par: 72/72. Course Rating: 73.1/69.6. Slope: 139/121. Walkability: 4. Miscellaneous: Reduced fees (weekdays, low season, twilight, seniors, juniors), discount packages, metal spikes, range (grass), club rentals, credit cards (MC, V, AE, D, Diners Club).
★★★★ MOUNTAIN/VALLEY
Yards: 6,880/5,196. Par: 72/72. Course Rating: 74.2/70.1. Slope: 140/122. Walkability: N/A. Miscellaneous: Reduced fees (weekdays, low season, twilight, seniors, juniors), discount packages, metal spikes, range (grass), club rentals, credit cards (MC, V, AE, D, Diners Club).
Reader Comments: Great course, a pleasure to play, good greens ... Chip and putt well or shoot large number ... Valley/Mountain best rotation ... Good variety of holes, deceptive greens ... Rugged terrain ... Good test, Mountain 9 a must ... Distinctively different 9s ... Best Bloody Marys ... Tough when windy, excellent layout.

MORGAN RUN RESORT & CLUB
R-5690 Cancha de Golf, Rancho Santa Fe, 92067, San Diego County, (619)756-2471, 20 miles N of San Diego.
Holes: 27. Green Fee: $50/$90. Cart Fee: $20/person. Walking Policy: Mandatory cart. Architect: Harry Rainville. Season: Year-round. To obtain tee times: Call 7 days in advance. Miscellaneous: Reduced fees (twilight), discount packages, club rentals, lodging (89 rooms), credit cards (MC, V, AE).
★★★ EAST/NORTH

CALIFORNIA

Yards: 6,141/5,860. **Par:** 71/71. **Course Rating:** 68.8/70.2. **Slope:** 110/113. **Walkability:** 2.
Reader Comments: Flat layout, not very interesting, a few good holes ... Too short ... Couple of good holes ... Very simple, a beginners' course ... Good framing on each hole ... Too many holes next to main road ... A good layout for confidence building ... Four star accommodations. Challenging course.

★★★ **EAST/SOUTH**
Yards: 6,443/6,136. **Par:** 72/72. **Course Rating:** 70.2/71.3. **Slope:** 112/117. **Walkability:** 1.

★★★ **SOUTH/NORTH**
Yards: 6,346/6,344. **Par:** 71/71. **Course Rating:** 69.7/70.7. **Slope:** 112/115. **Walkability:** 1.

★★★★ **MORRO BAY GOLF COURSE**
PU-201 State Park Rd., Morro Bay, 93442, San Luis Obispo County, (805)772-4341, 15 miles N of San Luis Obispo.
Holes: 18. **Yards:** 6,360/5,055. **Par:** 71/72. **Course Rating:** 70.4/69.5. **Slope:** 118/117. **Green Fee:** $22/$28. **Cart Fee:** $20/cart. **Walking Policy:** Unrestricted walking. **Walkability:** 4.
Opened: 1929. **Architect:** Russell Noyes. **Season:** Year-round. **High:** April-Aug. **To obtain tee times:** N/A **Miscellaneous:** Reduced fees (twilight, seniors, juniors), metal spikes, range (grass/mats), club rentals, credit cards (MC, V, D).
Reader Comments: Ocean views. Double-break greens ... Spectacular. Poor man's Pebble Beach ... Overrated and overcrowded. Almost no bunkers ... Easy to get on, cheap and funky ... Don't get caught in the fog ... Great scenic views ... Beautiful setting; hilly ... Slow play ... Just a great day ... Nice out of the way public course.

★★★★ **MOUNT WOODSON GOLF CLUB**
SP-16422 N. Woodson Dr., Ramona, 92065, San Diego County, (760)788-3555, 25 miles NE of San Diego.
Holes: 18. **Yards:** 6,180/4,441. **Par:** 70/70. **Course Rating:** 68.8/64.7. **Slope:** 130/108. **Green Fee:** $49/$80. **Cart Fee:** Included in Green Fee. **Walking Policy:** Mandatory cart. **Walkability:** 5. **Opened:** 1991. **Architect:** Lee Schmidt/Brian Curley. **Season:** Year-round. **High:** Jan.-April.
To obtain tee times: Call 7 days in advance. **Miscellaneous:** Reduced fees (weekdays, twilight, juniors), club rentals, credit cards (MC, V, AE).
Reader Comments: Fun course, good shape, nice greens ... Bring lots of golf balls, fun ... Hidden treasure! ... Great views ... Most imaginative course I have played ... Course cut into mountains, tough, challenging ... Unique is an understatement ... Loved it. Lots of elevation changes ... Impossible beauty ... Tremendous panoramic views.

★★★½ **MOUNTAIN MEADOWS GOLF CLUB**
PM-1875 N. Fairplex Dr., Pomona, 91768, Los Angeles County, (909)623-3704, 20 miles E of Los Angeles. **E-mail:** vangolf@ibm.net.
Holes: 18. **Yards:** 6,509/5,637. **Par:** 72/72. **Course Rating:** 71.5/71.5. **Slope:** 125/117. **Green Fee:** $14/$25. **Cart Fee:** $10/. **Walking Policy:** Unrestricted walking. **Walkability:** 4. **Opened:** 1977. **Architect:** Ted Robinson. **Season:** Year-round. **High:** May-Aug. **To obtain tee times:** Call 7 days in advance; weekdays at 6:00 a.m.; weekends and holidays at 5:00 a.m. **Miscellaneous:** Reduced fees (weekdays, low season, twilight, seniors, juniors), metal spikes, range (grass), club rentals, credit cards (MC, V, AE, D).
Reader Comments: Tough back 9 ... Good course around hills ... Like playing on the side of a hill ... Great at sunrise, good mountain play ... Best muny in L.A. area ... Good people, great area, views ... Solid course ... Very hilly course, a lot of elevation changes, tough par 3 13th along a canyon. Slow play ... Scenic, good variety of shots.

MOUNTAIN SHADOWS GOLF COURSE
PU-100 Golf Course Dr., Rohnert Park, 94928, Sonoma County, (707)584-7766, 7 miles S of Santa Rosa.
★★★ **NORTH COURSE**
Holes: 18. **Yards:** 7,035/5,503. **Par:** 72/72. **Course Rating:** 72.1/70.5. **Slope:** N/A/117. **Green Fee:** $20/$55. **Cart Fee:** $13/person. **Walking Policy:** Walking at certain times. **Walkability:** 3. **Opened:** 1974. **Architect:** Gary Roger Baird. **Season:** Year-round. **High:** April-Oct. **To obtain tee times:** Call 7 days in advance. **Miscellaneous:** Reduced fees (weekdays, low season, twilight, seniors, juniors), metal spikes, club rentals, credit cards (MC, V, AE).
Reader Comments: Better than South ... Pretty setting ... Wide open course. Long walk from greens to tees ... A feel-good course ... Flat course ... Forgiving on most holes ... Challenging and fun ... Good course for high handicapper.
★★½ **SOUTH COURSE**
Holes: 18. **Yards:** 6,720/5,805. **Par:** 72/72. **Course Rating:** 70.1/71.4. **Slope:** 115/122. **Green Fee:** $15/$40. **Cart Fee:** $13/person. **Walking Policy:** Unrestricted walking. **Walkability:** 2. **Opened:** 1963. **Architect:** Bob Baldock. **Season:** Year-round. **High:** April-Oct. **To obtain tee times:** Call 7 days in advance. **Miscellaneous:** Reduced fees (weekdays, low season, twilight, seniors, juniors), metal spikes, range (mats), club rentals, lodging (500 rooms), credit cards (MC, V, AE), beginner friendly (family tees).

CALIFORNIA

Reader Comments: Ego-booster, easy to score ... Very flat, easy walk ... Flat, boring, little challenge ... Overplayed ... Low green fees.

★★★ MOUNTAIN SPRINGS GOLF CLUB

PU-17566 Lime Kiln Road, Sonora, 95370, Tuolumne County, (209)532-1000, 45 miles E of Stockton. **Web:** www.mountainspringsgolf.com.
Holes: 18. **Yards:** 6,665/5,195. **Par:** 72/72. **Course Rating:** 71.9/68.8. **Slope:** 128/112. **Green Fee:** $21/$32. **Cart Fee:** $12/person. **Walking Policy:** Unrestricted walking. **Walkability:** 4. **Opened:** 1990. **Architect:** Robert Muir Graves. **Season:** Year-round. **High:** April-Sept. **To obtain tee times:** Call up to 14 days in advance. **Miscellaneous:** Reduced fees (twilight, seniors, juniors), discount packages, metal spikes, range (mats), club rentals, credit cards (MC, V) (ladies clinics, beginner lesson program).
Reader Comments: Kind of a 'billygoat' course ... Unusual, hilly course, but fun ... Slow but nice, challenging course ... Some long blind shots, lots of elevation changes; risk and reward.

★★ MOUNTAIN VIEW COUNTRY CLUB

PU-2121 Mountain View Dr., Corona, 91720, Riverside County, (909)737-9798, 10 miles W of Riverside.
Holes: 18. **Yards:** 6,383/5,374. **Par:** 72/73. **Course Rating:** 70.8/71.7. **Slope:** 124/120. **Green Fee:** $29/$39. **Cart Fee:** Included in Green Fee. **Walking Policy:** Walking at certain times. **Walkability:** 3. **Opened:** 1963. **Season:** Year-round. **High:** Oct.-June. **To obtain tee times:** Call 7 days in advance. **Miscellaneous:** Reduced fees (weekdays, low season, resort guests, twilight, seniors, juniors), discount packages, metal spikes, range (grass/mats), club rentals, credit cards (MC, V).

★★★ NAPA MUNICIPAL GOLF CLUB

PM-2295 Streblow Dr., Napa, 94558, Napa County, (707)255-4333, 45 miles NW of San Francisco.
Holes: 18. **Yards:** 6,730/5,956. **Par:** 72/73. **Course Rating:** 71.7/76.8. **Slope:** 127/137. **Green Fee:** $14/$25. **Cart Fee:** $23/cart. **Walking Policy:** Unrestricted walking. **Walkability:** 1. **Opened:** 1967. **Architect:** Jack Fleming. **Season:** Year-round. **High:** April-Nov. **To obtain tee times:** Call 7 days in advance. **Miscellaneous:** Reduced fees (weekdays, low season, twilight, seniors, juniors), metal spikes, range (mats), club rentals, credit cards (MC, V).
Reader Comments: Great layout, water on 14 holes ... Bring your snorkel ... A great value, challenging yet fun ... Lots of water on back 9. Long par 4s ... Very good muny. Lots of water, great design ... Not your typical muny golf course ... Challenging muny, has potential to be great ... Very wet, slow play ... Fun to play ... Great practice green.

★★★ NEEDLES MUNICIPAL GOLF COURSE

PM-144 Marina Dr., Needles, 92363, San Bernardino County, (760)326-3931, 100 miles S of Las Vegas. **E-mail:** ndlsgolf@ctaz.com.
Holes: 18. **Yards:** 6,550/5,850. **Par:** 70/70. **Course Rating:** 71.4/71.1. **Slope:** 117/114. **Green Fee:** $15/$25. **Cart Fee:** $10/person. **Walking Policy:** Unrestricted walking. **Walkability:** 2. **Opened:** 1962. **Season:** Year-round. **High:** Nov.-April. **To obtain tee times:** After 6:00 a.m. call 2 days in advance for weekdays; 1 day in advance for weekends. **Miscellaneous:** Reduced fees (low season, seniors, juniors), metal spikes, range (grass), club rentals, credit cards (MC, V).
Reader Comments: Good value overall ... Inexpensive. Enjoyable flat course ... Great for winter golf ... Interesting ... Windy, but excellent layout and scenic.

★★★½ NORTHSTAR-AT-TAHOE RESORT GOLF COURSE

R-Hwy. 267 and Northstar Dr., Truckee, 96160, Nevada County, (530)562-2490, (800)466-6784, 40 miles W of Reno. **E-mail:** northstar@boothcreek.com. **Web:** www.skinorthstar.com.
Holes: 18. **Yards:** 6,897/5,470. **Par:** 72/72. **Course Rating:** 72.4/71.2. **Slope:** 137/134. **Green Fee:** $45/$75. **Cart Fee:** Included in Green Fee. **Walking Policy:** Unrestricted walking. **Walkability:** 3. **Opened:** 1975. **Architect:** Robert Muir Graves. **Season:** May-Oct. **High:** July-Aug. **To obtain tee times:** Call 21 days in advance, unless hotel guest. **Miscellaneous:** Reduced fees (low season, resort guests, twilight, seniors, juniors), discount packages, metal spikes, club rentals, lodging, credit cards (MC, V, AE, D).
Reader Comments: Great mountain course, must be able to work the ball, must play for sure ... Great course ... Back 9 through tall timber is spectacular ... Mountain 9 extremely tight. Meadow 9 wide open. Interesting change of pace ... Beautiful mountain course with meadow 9 ... 2 courses in one! ... A bit overpriced.

★★★½ OAK CREEK GOLF CLUB

PU-1 Golf Club Dr., Irvine, 92620, Orange County, (714)653-7300, 60 miles S of Los Angeles.
Holes: 18. **Yards:** 6,834/5,605. **Par:** 71/71. **Course Rating:** 71.9/71.2. **Slope:** 127/121. **Green Fee:** $80/$125. **Cart Fee:** Included in Green Fee. **Walking Policy:** Mandatory cart. **Walkability:** 1. **Opened:** 1996. **Architect:** Tom Fazio. **Season:** Year-round. **To obtain tee times:** Call up to 6 days in advance beginning at 6:30 a.m. For additional $15 p/player tee times may be made 7-14 days in advance. **Miscellaneous:** Reduced fees (twilight, seniors, juniors), discount packages, range (grass), club rentals, credit cards (MC, V, AE, Diners Club).

CALIFORNIA

Reader Comments: Worth the price ... Love the set-up of the course ... Will get better with age ... Slow, not too memorable ... Grossly overpriced ... Pretty course, but not much challenge ... Very user friendly course. Fairways are bowled, greens are set in amphitheaters, makes you feel like a pro ... Too many holes look alike.

★★★★ OAK VALLEY GOLF CLUB
PU-1888 Golf Club Drive, Beaumont, 92223, Riverside County, (909)769-7200, 20 miles SE of San Bernadino. **Web:** www.oakvalley.com.
Holes: 18. **Yards:** 7,003/5,494. **Par:** 72/72. **Course Rating:** 73.9/71.1. **Slope:** 136/122. **Green Fee:** $45/$75. **Cart Fee:** Included in Green Fee. **Walking Policy:** Mandatory cart. **Walkability:** 4. **Opened:** 1991. **Architect:** Lee Schmidt/Brian Curley. **Season:** Year-round. **High:** March-June. **To obtain tee times:** Call 7 days in advance. **Miscellaneous:** Reduced fees (weekdays, twilight), discount packages, range (grass), club rentals, credit cards (MC, V, AE).
Reader Comments: Special place, great course, great price ... Links-style, windy, worth it ... Tough finishing holes, a must play in California ... If it had better facilities would be 5 stars ... Tough greens, require local knowledge ... Hidden gem, great value ... Hilly tough course ... Murder for duffers ... Great Links layout in desert.

★★★½ OAKHURST COUNTRY CLUB
SP-1001 Peacock Creek Dr., Clayton, 94517, Contra Costa County, (925)672-9737, (888)455-0300, 2 miles S of Concord.
Holes: 18. **Yards:** 6,739/5,285. **Par:** 72/72. **Course Rating:** 73.1/70.3. **Slope:** 132/123. **Green Fee:** $60/$80. **Cart Fee:** Included in Green Fee. **Walking Policy:** Mandatory cart. **Walkability:** 3. **Opened:** 1990. **Architect:** Ron Fream. **Season:** Year-round. **High:** May-Oct. **To obtain tee times:** Call 3 days in advance for weekends. For members fourteen days, others 7 days in advance. **Miscellaneous:** Reduced fees (twilight, seniors, juniors), metal spikes, range (grass), club rentals, credit cards (MC, V, AE, D).
Reader Comments: 18th a truly great hole ... Good holes/ugly holes ... Absolute beauty, hard as hell but amazing ... Too many houses surrounding ... Killer finishing stretch ... Used to be better ... In the shadow of Mount Diablo ... Tough par 3s.

OAKMONT GOLF CLUB
EAST COURSE
SP-7025 Oakmont Dr., Santa Rosa, 95409, Sonoma County, (707)538-2454, 55 miles N of Santa Rosa.
Holes: 18. **Yards:** 4,293/4,067. **Par:** 63/63. **Course Rating:** 59.8/62.8. **Slope:** 94/102. **Green Fee:** $22/$28. **Cart Fee:** $24/person. **Walking Policy:** Unrestricted walking. **Walkability:** 1. **Opened:** 1976. **Architect:** Ted Robinson. **Season:** Year-round. **To obtain tee times:** Call 7 days in advance for weekends and holidays and 1 day ahead for weekdays. **Miscellaneous:** Reduced fees (twilight), metal spikes, range (grass/mats), club rentals, credit cards (MC, V).

★★★ WEST COURSE
SP-7025 Oakmont Dr., Santa Rosa, 95409, Sonoma County, (707)539-0415, 55 miles N of Santa Rosa.
Holes: 18. **Yards:** 6,379/5,573. **Par:** 72/72. **Course Rating:** 70.5/71.9. **Slope:** 121/128. **Green Fee:** $27/$35. **Cart Fee:** $24/person. **Walking Policy:** Unrestricted walking. **Walkability:** 1. **Opened:** 1963. **Architect:** Ted Robinson. **Season:** Year-round. **High:** June-Oct. **To obtain tee times:** Call 7 days in advance for weekends and holidays and 1 day ahead for weekdays. **Miscellaneous:** Reduced fees (twilight), metal spikes, range (grass/mats), club rentals, credit cards (MC, V).
Reader Comments: One of best values in all of northern California ... Nothing great but solid golf course ... Wide open, a walk in the park ... A few interesting holes with water and oak trees.

THE OAKS GOLF & COUNTRY CLUB
3332 Garden Hwy., Nicolaus, 95659, (916)656-2667.
Special Notes: Call club for further information.

★★½ OCEANSIDE MUNICIPAL GOLF COURSE
PM-825 Douglas Dr., Oceanside, 92054, San Diego County, (760)433-1360, 30 miles N of San Diego.
Holes: 18. **Yards:** 6,450/5,398. **Par:** 72/72. **Course Rating:** 70.8/71.6. **Slope:** 118/121. **Green Fee:** $18/$24. **Cart Fee:** $20/cart. **Walking Policy:** Unrestricted walking. **Walkability:** 2. **Opened:** 1974. **Architect:** Richard Bigler. **Season:** Year-round. **To obtain tee times:** Call 8 days in advance. **Miscellaneous:** Reduced fees (weekdays, twilight, seniors, juniors), metal spikes, range (grass), club rentals, credit cards (MC, V, AE).
Reader Comments: Quaint ... Fun to play, excellent value ... Jammed with too many golfers ... Challenging, tough par 5 into the wind ... Moderately challenging, river bottom muny ... Not great but improving.

★★★★ **OJAI VALLEY INN & SPA** *Service+*
R-Country Club Rd., Ojai, 93023, Ventura County, (805)646-2420, (800)422-6524, 60 miles N of Los Angeles.
Holes: 18. **Yards:** 6,235/5,225. **Par:** 70/71. **Course Rating:** 70.2/70.2. **Slope:** 122/123. **Green Fee:** $86/$105. **Cart Fee:** $15/person. **Walking Policy:** Unrestricted walking. **Walkability:** 4.
Opened: 1923. **Architect:** George Thomas/Jay Morrish. **Season:** Year-round. **High:** March-Oct.
To obtain tee times: Resort guests may make tee times 90 days in advance. All others 7 days in advance. **Miscellaneous:** Reduced fees (resort guests, twilight, juniors), discount packages, metal spikes, range (grass), club rentals, lodging (208 rooms), credit cards (MC, V, AE, D).
Notes: Senior PGA Tour events. 1997 NBC Golf Skills Challenge.
Reader Comments: Great course, great staff, would play over and over ... Great retreat! ... Terrific atmosphere ... Short, very interesting, beautiful ... Back 9 fantastic, bring extra balls ... Best starter in golf! ... A little pricey ... Classic golf experience ... Lush course and a great spa!

★★★½ **OLD DEL MONTE GOLF COURSE**
PU-1300 Sylvan Rd., Monterey, 93940, Monterey County, (831)373-2700, 60 miles S of San Jose.
Holes: 18. **Yards:** 6,339/5,526. **Par:** 72/74. **Course Rating:** 71.3/71.1. **Slope:** 122/118. **Green Fee:** N/A/$80. **Cart Fee:** $18/person. **Walking Policy:** Unrestricted walking. **Walkability:** 2.
Opened: 1897. **Architect:** C. Maud. **Season:** Year-round. **High:** April-Oct. **To obtain tee times:** Call up to 60 days in advance. **Miscellaneous:** Reduced fees (resort guests, twilight, juniors), discount packages, metal spikes, caddies, club rentals, lodging, credit cards (MC, V, AE, D, JCB).
Reader Comments: Least known member of Monterey stable ... Course with great history ... Nothing special ... Can score here ... Nice old course ... Fun course to play ... Enjoyed it ... Underrated ... Price based on history, not quality ... A wonderful golf course! ... Unsung hero in Monterey.

★★★ **OLIVAS PARK GOLF COURSE**
PM-3750 Olivas Park Dr., Ventura, 93001, Ventura County, (805)642-4303, 60 miles NW of Los Angeles.
Holes: 18. **Yards:** 6,760/5,501. **Par:** 72/72. **Course Rating:** 72.6/72.4. **Slope:** 124/119. **Green Fee:** $18/$23. **Cart Fee:** $22/. **Walking Policy:** Unrestricted walking. **Walkability:** 1. **Opened:** 1964. **Architect:** William F. Bell. **Season:** Year-round. **High:** May-Sept. **To obtain tee times:** Call 7 days in advance. **Miscellaneous:** Reduced fees (weekdays, twilight, seniors, juniors), metal spikes, range (grass/mats), caddies, club rentals, credit cards (MC, V, AE).
Reader Comments: Fast fun muny ... Good little course, flat ... Windy ... Open course. Good variety of holes ... Fun. Great course to play with wife ... Good muny course, usually busy ... Not the most interesting course, but well run.

★★★½ **PACIFIC GROVE MUNICIPAL GOLF LINKS** *Value*
PM-77 Asilomar Blvd., Pacific Grove, 93950, Monterey County, (408)648-3175, 17 miles W of Salinas.
Holes: 18. **Yards:** 5,732/5,305. **Par:** 70/72. **Course Rating:** 67.5/70.5. **Slope:** 117/114. **Green Fee:** $30/$35. **Cart Fee:** $26/cart. **Walking Policy:** Unrestricted walking. **Walkability:** 2.
Opened: 1932. **Architect:** Jack Neville/Chandler Egan. **Season:** Year-round. **High:** May-Oct. **To obtain tee times:** Call 7 days in advance (each day for same day next week) beginning 7 a.m.
Miscellaneous: Reduced fees (twilight, juniors), range (grass), club rentals, credit cards (MC, V).
Reader Comments: Great back 9 makes it worthwhile ... A lot of fun, great bargain ... No such thing as a bad course on the Monterey coast ... Great views ... Good course. Good service ... Poor man's Pebble Beach, spectacular ... Rough, but a gem! ... Fun if you like sand and ice plant ... Nice short test ... Great seaside holes!

★★★ **PAJARO VALLEY GOLF CLUB**
PU-967 Salinas Rd., Watsonville, 95076, Santa Cruz County, (408)724-3851, 20 miles SE of Santa Cruz.
Holes: 18. **Yards:** 6,218/5,696. **Par:** 72/72. **Course Rating:** 70.0/72.3. **Slope:** 122/123. **Green Fee:** $27/$55. **Cart Fee:** $28/cart. **Walking Policy:** Unrestricted walking. **Walkability:** 4.
Opened: 1927. **Architect:** Robert Muir Graves. **Season:** Year-round. **High:** April-Oct. **To obtain tee times:** Call golf shop. **Miscellaneous:** Reduced fees (weekdays, twilight), discount packages, metal spikes, range (grass/mats), club rentals, credit cards (MC, V, AE).
Reader Comments: Good old layout. Not long, but challenging ... Course solid, amenities functional ... Good old course ... Easy layout, but tough greens ... Pleasant scenery ... Was wet; long rough.

★★★★ **PALA MESA RESORT**
R-2001 S. Hwy. 395, Fallbrook, 92028, San Diego County, (760)731-6803, (800)722-4700, 40 miles N of San Diego.
Holes: 18. **Yards:** 6,502/5,632. **Par:** 72/72. **Course Rating:** 72.0/74.0. **Slope:** 131/134. **Green Fee:** $39/$80. **Cart Fee:** Included in Green Fee. **Walking Policy:** Mandatory cart. **Walkability:** 2. **Opened:** 1964. **Architect:** Dick Rossen. **Season:** Year-round. **High:** Jan.-May. **To obtain tee times:** Call 7 days in advance. **Miscellaneous:** Reduced fees (weekdays, low season, resort

guests, twilight), discount packages, range (grass/mats), club rentals, lodging, credit cards (MC, V, AE).

Reader Comments: Front 9 in mountains, back 9 in farmland ... Beautiful course and facility ... Quiet resort ... Nice landscaping ... Nice clubhouse and lodging on premises ... Fast greens, tight, wonderfully kept ... Great experience ... Well kept old-style course ... Tight, not too long, good condition.

★★★ PALM DESERT RESORT COUNTRY CLUB
SP-77-333 Country Club Dr., Palm Desert, 92211, Riverside County, (760)345-2791.
Holes: 18. **Yards:** 6,585/5,670. **Par:** 72/72. **Course Rating:** 70.8/71.8. **Slope:** 117/123. **Green Fee:** $25/$70. **Cart Fee:** Included in Green Fee. **Walking Policy:** Mandatory cart. **Walkability:** 3. **Opened:** 1980. **Architect:** Joe Mulleneaux. **Season:** Nov.-Sept. **High:** Nov.-April. **To obtain tee times:** Call 5 days in advance. **Miscellaneous:** Reduced fees (weekdays, low season, twilight), discount packages, metal spikes, range (grass), club rentals, lodging, credit cards (MC, V, D), beginner friendly.
Reader Comments: Average layout, nice greens ... Nice resort course ... One of the better values in the Coachella Valley.

★★★ PALM SPRINGS COUNTRY CLUB
PM-2500 Whitewater Club Dr., Palm Springs, 92262, Riverside County, (760)323-2626.
Holes: 18. **Yards:** 6,396/4,991. **Par:** 72/72. **Course Rating:** 68.9/71.4. **Slope:** 115/113. **Green Fee:** $15/$50. **Cart Fee:** Included in Green Fee. **Walking Policy:** Mandatory cart. **Walkability:** 1. **Season:** Year-round. **High:** Jan.-April. **To obtain tee times:** Call golf shop. **Miscellaneous:** Reduced fees (weekdays, low season, resort guests, twilight, juniors), discount packages, metal spikes, range (grass), club rentals, credit cards (MC, V, D).
Reader Comments: Could be OK. Greens not best shape ... Enjoyed it, so did my 14-year-old ... Good muny golf course.

★★★½ PALOS VERDES GOLF CLUB
SP-3301 Via Campesina, Palos Verdes Estates, 90274, Los Angeles County, (310)375-2759, 20 miles S of Los Angeles.
Holes: 18. **Yards:** 6,116/5,506. **Par:** 71/70. **Course Rating:** 70.4/68.9. **Slope:** 131/126. **Green Fee:** $105/$105. **Cart Fee:** Included in Green Fee. **Walking Policy:** Mandatory cart. **Walkability:** 5. **Opened:** 1924. **Architect:** George C. Thomas, Jr. **Season:** Year-round. **High:** June-Aug. **To obtain tee times:** Call 7 days in advance. **Miscellaneous:** Credit cards (MC, V, AE).
Reader Comments: Great old course, must play ball short on greens ... If you can't play Riviera, play here. No. 7 is a classic ... Some super views ... A great secret.

★★★½ PARADISE VALLEY GOLF COURSE
PM-3950 Paradise Valley Dr., Fairfield, 94533, Solano County, (707)426-1600, 45 miles NE of San Francisco. **E-mail:** pv0492@aol.com.
Holes: 18. **Yards:** 6,993/5,413. **Par:** 72/72. **Course Rating:** 74.1/71.1. **Slope:** 135/119. **Green Fee:** $18/$36. **Cart Fee:** $14/person. **Walking Policy:** Unrestricted walking. **Walkability:** 1. **Opened:** 1993. **Architect:** Robert Muir Graves. **Season:** Year-round. **To obtain tee times:** Call 7 days in advance. **Miscellaneous:** Reduced fees (weekdays, low season, twilight, seniors, juniors), discount packages, metal spikes, range (grass/mats), club rentals, credit cards (MC, V, AE).
Reader Comments: Excellent use of terrain and native oaks ... Top-notch muny ... Great clubhouse; some tough holes ... No. 10 hole very challenging ... Long, wide and lots of room ... Challenging flat course, great value ... Varied and interesting holes ... Wide fairways ... Could be much better ... Enjoyed the course.

★★★★½ PASATIEMPO GOLF CLUB
SP-18 Clubhouse Rd., Santa Cruz, 95060, Santa Cruz County, (831)459-9155, 30 miles S of San Jose. **E-mail:** ray@pasatiempo.com. **Web:** www.pasatiempo.com.
Holes: 18. **Yards:** 6,445/5,629. **Par:** 70/72. **Course Rating:** 72.7/73.6. **Slope:** 141/135. **Green Fee:** $115/$125. **Cart Fee:** $34/cart. **Walking Policy:** Unrestricted walking. **Walkability:** 4. **Opened:** 1929. **Architect:** Alister Mackenzie. **Season:** Year-round. **High:** May-Oct. **To obtain tee times:** Call 7 days in advance for weekdays. Call on Monday after 10 a.m. for upcoming weekend. 90 days in advance with a $20 pp surcharge. **Miscellaneous:** Range (grass/mats), caddies, club rentals, credit cards (MC, V, AE).
Notes: Ranked 94th in 1999-2000 America's 100 Greatest; 10th in 1999 Best in State.
Reader Comments: Don't miss, a jewel ... You'll never forget 11 and 16 ... Beautiful, tough, great greens ... What golf is all about ... Good course except 18th is a par 3 ... Expensive but worth it. A fine old course ... A gem, difficult to get tee time, worth every penny ... 11th hole may be one of the toughest par 4s in the world.

★★★ PEACOCK GAP GOLF & COUNTRY CLUB
SP-333 Biscayne Dr., San Rafael, 94901, Marin County, (415)453-4940, 12 miles N of San Francisco.

Holes: 18. **Yards:** 6,354/5,629. **Par:** 71/73. **Course Rating:** 70.0/71.9. **Slope:** 118/126. **Green Fee:** $30/$52. **Cart Fee:** $24/cart. **Walking Policy:** Walking at certain times. **Walkability:** 2. **Opened:** 1960. **Architect:** William F. Bell. **Season:** Year-round. **High:** March-Oct. **To obtain tee times:** Call 7 days in advance for weekdays. Call Thursday after noon for weekends. **Miscellaneous:** Reduced fees (twilight), discount packages, metal spikes, range (grass/mats), club rentals, credit cards (MC, V, AE).
Reader Comments: Nice course, a little overpriced ... Great course with plenty of challenges.

★★★★★ **PEBBLE BEACH GOLF LINKS** *Service+, Condition*
R-17 Mile Dr., Pebble Beach, 93953, Monterey County, (831)624-3811, (800)654-9300, 115 miles S of San Francisco.
Holes: 18. **Yards:** 6,840/5,197. **Par:** 72/72. **Course Rating:** 74.4/71.9. **Slope:** 142/130. **Green Fee:** $275/$305. **Cart Fee:** $25/person. **Walking Policy:** Unrestricted walking. **Walkability:** 3. **Opened:** 1919. **Architect:** Jack Neville and Douglas Grant. **Season:** Year-round. **High:** March-Nov. **To obtain tee times:** Call 1 day in advance. Stay at the Lodge at Pebble Beach or the Inn at Spanish Bay to guarantee tee times. **Miscellaneous:** Discount packages, metal spikes, range (grass/mats), caddies, club rentals, lodging, credit cards (MC, V, AE, D, Diners Club).
Notes: Ranked 4th in 1999-2000 America's 100 Greatest; 2nd in 1999 Best in State. 1972, 1982, 1992 U.S. Open; AT&T Pebble Beach National Pro Am Annually; 1977 PGA Championship. U.S. Amateur 1929,1947,1961,1997. Host of U.S. Open in 2000.
Reader Comments: It's all that I thought it would be ... One of a kind ... Everyone should play it once ... Slow play, but it is our Sistine Chapel so why rush? ... Breathtaking views ... Sneak preview of heaven ... Too many fat cats who don't understand the game ... First few holes are disappointing ... Felt like I was playing in a dream.

PELICAN HILL GOLF CLUB
R-22651 Pelican Hill Rd., Newport Coast, 92657, Orange County, (949)759-5190, 45 miles S of Los Angeles. **Web:** www.pelicanhill.com.
★★★★ **OCEAN NORTH COURSE**
Holes: 18. **Yards:** 6,856/5,800. **Par:** 71/71. **Course Rating:** 73.6/73.0. **Slope:** 133/125. **Green Fee:** $125/$225. **Cart Fee:** Included in Green Fee. **Walking Policy:** Mandatory cart. **Walkability:** N/A. **Opened:** 1993. **Architect:** Tom Fazio. **Season:** Year-round. **To obtain tee times:** Call 7 days in advance with credit card beginning at 6:30 a.m. Noncancellable reservations may be made 8-60 days in advance. **Miscellaneous:** Reduced fees (resort guests, twilight), discount packages, range (grass), club rentals, credit cards (MC, V, AE, Diners Club, JCB).
Notes: Ranked 29th in 1999 Best in State; 51st in 1996 America's Top 75 Upscale Courses. Diners Club Matches 1999.
Reader Comments: Nice but too expensive ... A little overexposed, but still great ... Very pretty ... Better than Ocean South ... This course is just awesome. If you are in the area, it is definitely a must play ... Gorgeous views ... Great views from every tee ... High price not justified ... Scenic wonder.
★★★★ **OCEAN SOUTH COURSE**
Holes: 18. **Yards:** 6,634/5,366. **Par:** 70/70. **Course Rating:** 72.1/72.5. **Slope:** 130/124. **Green Fee:** $135/$215. **Cart Fee:** Included in Green Fee. **Walking Policy:** Mandatory cart. **Walkability:** 5. **Opened:** 1991. **Architect:** Tom Fazio. **Season:** Year-round. **High:** Year-round. **To obtain tee times:** Call 7 days in advance with credit card beginning at 6:30 a.m. Noncancellable reservations may be made up to 60 days in advance. **Miscellaneous:** Reduced fees (resort guests, twilight), discount packages, metal spikes, range (grass/mats), club rentals, credit cards (MC, V, AE, Diners Club, JCB).
Notes: Ranked 59th in 1996 America's Top 75 Upscale Courses. Diners Club Matches 1999.
Reader Comments: Gorgeous and expensive ... Beautiful but it's 'rich man golf' ... Must try once, great variety ... Some of the best golf holes in California ... More varied and scenic of the two layouts ... Excellent overall ... Back 9 breathtaking ... Very expensive, they think they're Pebble Beach ... Big carries off tee.

PGA WEST RESORT
R-56-150 PGA Blvd., La Quinta, 92253, Riverside County, (760)564-7170, 30 miles SE of Palm Springs.
★★★★ **JACK NICKLAUS TOURNAMENT COURSE**
Holes: 18. **Yards:** 7,204/5,023. **Par:** 72/72. **Course Rating:** 74.7/69.0. **Slope:** 139/116. **Green Fee:** $60/$260. **Cart Fee:** Included in Green Fee. **Walking Policy:** Mandatory cart. **Walkability:** 3. **Opened:** 1987. **Architect:** Jack Nicklaus. **Season:** Year-round. **High:** Jan.-April. **To obtain tee times:** Call golf shop. **Miscellaneous:** Reduced fees (weekdays, low season, resort guests, twilight), discount packages, range (grass/mats), club rentals, lodging, credit cards (MC, V, AE, Diners Club, JCB).
Reader Comments: Very pricey ... Great golf course, very well maintained ... Great layout. Exciting ... You've got to play it once ... First class facility. Terrific layout ... Slow if you are off late ... Classic so-called desert course ... Loved it ... Great course design ... Too many waste areas, not for average golfer.

CALIFORNIA

★★★★ TPC STADIUM COURSE
Holes: 18. **Yards:** 7,266/5,092. **Par:** 72/72. **Course Rating:** 75.9/69.0. **Slope:** 150/124. **Green Fee:** $60/$260. **Cart Fee:** Included in Green Fee. **Walking Policy:** Mandatory cart. **Walkability:** 4. **Opened:** 1986. **Architect:** Pete Dye. **Season:** Year-round. **High:** Jan.-April. **To obtain tee times:** Call golf shop. **Miscellaneous:** Reduced fees (weekdays, low season, resort guests, twilight), range (grass/mats), club rentals, lodging, credit cards (MC, V, AE, Diners Club, JCB). **Notes:** Ranked 27th in 1999 Best in State.
Reader Comments: Very tough, need to play if you're a good golfer ... Exciting and memorable ... Fast greens ... Play it in the summer for best value ... A monster; worth the big bucks ... Overall OK, too many gimmicks ... Way too expensive ... Bring your 64-degree wedge, deep bunkers ... You will love it or hate it; you have to play it.

★★★★ PINE MOUNTAIN LAKE COUNTRY CLUB
SP-19228 Pine Mountain Dr., Groveland, 95321, Tuolumne County, (209)962-8620, 90 miles SE of Sacramento.
Holes: 18. **Yards:** 6,363/5,726. **Par:** 70/72. **Course Rating:** 70.1/73.3. **Slope:** 125/128. **Green Fee:** $18/$40. **Cart Fee:** $26/cart. **Walking Policy:** Walking at certain times. **Walkability:** 3. **Opened:** 1969. **Architect:** William F. Bell. **Season:** Year-round. **High:** May-Sept. **To obtain tee times:** Call up to 10 days in advance. **Miscellaneous:** Reduced fees (twilight), range (grass/mats), club rentals, credit cards (MC, V, AE, D).
Reader Comments: Some great views! ... Fun mountain course ... Scenic mountain views ... Fun, scenic resort layout. Old folks love it.

★★★½ PITTSBURG DELTA VIEW GOLF COURSE
PM-2242 Golf Club Rd., Pittsburg, 94565, Contra Costa County, (925)439-4040, 40 miles NE of San Francisco.
Holes: 18. **Yards:** 6,359/5,405. **Par:** 71/72. **Course Rating:** 71.4/70.0. **Slope:** 130/124. **Green Fee:** $13/$24. **Cart Fee:** $20/cart. **Walking Policy:** Unrestricted walking. **Walkability:** 5. **Opened:** 1947. **Architect:** Robert Muir Graves. **Season:** Year-round. **To obtain tee times:** Call golf shop 7 days in advance. **Miscellaneous:** Reduced fees (twilight, seniors, juniors), metal spikes, range (grass/mats), club rentals, credit cards (MC, V).
Reader Comments: Pretty course; some interesting holes ... Back 9 an excellent, challenging track ... Front 9 open and hilly ... Great layout, not for the weak at heart ... Lots of fun, back 9 is a challenge.

★★★ PLUMAS LAKE GOLF & COUNTRY CLUB
SP-1551 Country Club Ave., Marysville, 95901, Yuba County, (530)742-3201, 6 miles S of Sacramento.
Holes: 18. **Yards:** 6,437/5,759. **Par:** 71/72. **Course Rating:** 70.5/73.2. **Slope:** 122/126. **Green Fee:** $19/$24. **Cart Fee:** $18/cart. **Walking Policy:** Unrestricted walking. **Walkability:** 1. **Opened:** 1926. **Architect:** Jack Bosley/Bob Baldock. **Season:** Year-round. **High:** April-Oct. **To obtain tee times:** Call 7 days in advance. **Miscellaneous:** Reduced fees (weekdays, twilight, seniors, juniors), metal spikes, range (grass/mats), club rentals, credit cards (MC, V).
Reader Comments: Best value for golf, multiple shots required ... Maintained well; good greens ... Very nice course ... Lots of challenge to course, and they're making it better.

★★★ PLUMAS PINES COUNTRY CLUB
PU-402 Poplar Valley Rd., Blairsden, 96103, Plumas County, (530)836-1420, (888)236-8725, 63 miles W of Reno.
Holes: 18. **Yards:** 6,504/5,106. **Par:** 72/72. **Course Rating:** 71.6/68.5. **Slope:** 127/122. **Green Fee:** $50/$55. **Cart Fee:** Included in Green Fee. **Walking Policy:** Walking at certain times. **Walkability:** 5. **Architect:** Homer Flint. **Season:** April-Oct. **High:** June-Sept. **To obtain tee times:** Call golf shop. Or Tee time control (888)236-8725. **Miscellaneous:** Reduced fees (weekdays, low season, twilight), discount packages, metal spikes, range (grass/mats), club rentals, lodging, credit cards (MC, V, AE, D).
Reader Comments: Tight course, fun to play ... Tight, tight fairways. Homes too close ... Slow and crowded, bring lots of balls ... Condos, trees, scenery ... Nice Sierra course.

★★★★½ POPPY HILLS GOLF COURSE   *Value, Condition*
PU-3200 Lopez Rd., Pebble Beach, 93953, Monterey County, (831)625-8239, 60 miles S of San Jose.
Holes: 18. **Yards:** 6,835/5,408. **Par:** 72/72. **Course Rating:** 74.6/72.1. **Slope:** 144/131. **Green Fee:** $115/$130. **Cart Fee:** $30/cart. **Walking Policy:** Unrestricted walking. **Walkability:** 3. **Opened:** 1986. **Architect:** Robert Trent Jones Jr. **Season:** Year-round. **High:** April-Oct. **To obtain tee times:** Call up to 30 days in advance. **Miscellaneous:** Reduced fees (juniors), range (grass), caddies, club rentals, credit cards (MC, V, AE).
Notes: AT&T National Pro Am.
Reader Comments: Great course ... More you play it, the better it gets ... Fairway-sized greens, 3 putts a sure thing ... Always a winner ... Heavy usage all the time ... Good clubhouse ... Tough

course, especially on windy days ... A great course among legends ... Champagne course on a beer budget ... Unbelievable surroundings.

POPPY RIDGE GOLF COURSE
PU-4280 Greenville Rd., Livermore, 94550, Alameda County, (925)456-8202, 10 miles E of Pleasanton. **E-mail:** Pridge@msm.com.
Holes: 27. **Green Fee:** $35/$70. **Cart Fee:** $24/cart. **Walking Policy:** Unrestricted walking. **Opened:** 1996. **Architect:** Rees Jones. **Season:** Year-round. **High:** April-Oct. **To obtain tee times:** Call automated service any time at (510)455-2035.
★★★★ CHARDONNAY/ZINFANDEL *Value*
Yards: 7,048/5,267. **Par:** 72/72. **Course Rating:** 74.6/70.2. **Slope:** 139/120. **Walkability:** 4. **Miscellaneous:** Reduced fees (weekdays, twilight), range (grass), club rentals, credit cards (MC, V, AE), beginner friendly (beginner lessons and learning center).
Reader Comments: Fun to play the afternoon wind, great greens ... 100-plus traps and one tree ... Foggy in the morning ... Good golf, good greens, sparse landscape ... Greens and fairways immaculate ... Innovative. Good test, heavily used ... Only one tree in 27 holes. I hit it ... The toast of the wine country.
★★★★ MERLOT/CHARDONNAY
Yards: 7,106/5,212. **Par:** 72/72. **Course Rating:** 74.6/70.2. **Slope:** 139/120. **Walkability:** 5. **Miscellaneous:** Reduced fees (weekdays, twilight), range (grass), club rentals, credit cards (MC, V, AE), beginner friendly (beginner golf lessons).
Special Notes: Alternate golf shop phone (510)456-8202.
★★★★ ZINFANDEL/MERLOT
Yards: 7,128/5,265. **Par:** 72/72. **Course Rating:** 74.6/70.2. **Slope:** 139/120. **Walkability:** 5. **Miscellaneous:** Reduced fees (weekdays, twilight), range (grass), club rentals, credit cards (MC, V, AE), beginner friendly (beginner golf lessons).

★★★★ PREMIER GOLF & CLUBHOUSE
PU-2708 Overlook Dr., Vallejo, 94591, Solano County, (707)558-1140, (888)773-0330, 40 miles NE of San Francisco.
Holes: 18. **Yards:** 6,638/4,557. **Par:** 72/72. **Course Rating:** 72.8/66.4. **Slope:** 137/117. **Green Fee:** $75/$100. **Cart Fee:** Included in Green Fee. **Walking Policy:** Unrestricted walking. **Walkability:** 4. **Opened:** 1995. **Architect:** Arnold Palmer/Ed Seay. **Season:** Year-round. **To obtain tee times:** Nonmembers call 7 days in advance. **Miscellaneous:** Range (grass/mats), club rentals, credit cards (MC, V, AE, D).
Reader Comments: Nice course; a few funky holes ... Every hole was a postcard picture! ... Arnie does it again! ... Blind shots/trick holes ... Tee shot on No. 1 is a killer ... Challenging, a little expensive ... Great track, target golf, worth the trip ... Nice surprise; very friendly; interesting and fun course ... Terrific variety ... Course very fair to women.

★★ PRESIDENTS CLUB AT INDIAN PALMS
R-48-630 Monroe St., Indio, 92201, Riverside County, (760)347-2326, (800)778-5288, 20 miles E of Palm Springs.
Holes: 27. **Yards:** 6,708/5,849. **Par:** 72/73. **Course Rating:** 72.7/72.1. **Slope:** 131/120. **Green Fee:** $25/$65. **Cart Fee:** Included in Green Fee. **Walking Policy:** Mandatory cart. **Walkability:** 1. **Opened:** 1948. **Architect:** Jackie Cochran/Helen Detweiler. **Season:** Year-round. **High:** Jan.-March. **To obtain tee times:** Call up to 3 days in advance. **Miscellaneous:** Reduced fees (weekdays, low season, resort guests, twilight), discount packages, metal spikes, range (grass), club rentals, lodging, credit cards (MC, V, AE), beginner friendly (morning back-9 discount).

★★★½ PRESIDIO GOLF COURSE
PU-300 Finley Rd at Arguello Gate, San Francisco, 94129, San Francisco County, (415)561-4661, (415)561-4653. **Web:** www.presidiogolf.com.
Holes: 18. **Yards:** 6,477/5,785. **Par:** 72/73. **Course Rating:** 72.2/74.2. **Slope:** 136/131. **Green Fee:** $40/$72. **Cart Fee:** $15/person. **Walking Policy:** Unrestricted walking. **Walkability:** 4. **Opened:** 1895. **Architect:** Robert Johnstone. **Season:** Year-round. **High:** May-Oct. **To obtain tee times:** (415)561-4661 or (415)561-4653 credit card rec'd for tee time. 48 hour cancellation policy. Tee times are taken 30 days in advance. **Miscellaneous:** Reduced fees (weekdays, low season, twilight), metal spikes, club rentals, credit cards (MC, V, AE), beginner friendly (junior camps and clinics, lunch and learn, group and private instruction, corporate clinics).
Reader Comments: The steep hillsides of San Francisco occasionally peeked out of the low clouds. Like playing in heaven ... Hilly, foggy, treelined ... Awesome scenes of San Francisco ... Short, tight and gorgeous ... Super, super experience ... Still needs work, neat old course ... Former military course ... On a sunny day, it's paradise.

PRIMM VALLEY GOLF CLUB *Service+*
R-1 Yates Well Rd., Nipton, 89019, San Bernardino County, (702)679-5510, (800)386-7867, 40 miles S of Las Vegas.
★★★★½ DESERT COURSE *Value, Condition, Pace*

CALIFORNIA

Holes: 18. **Yards:** 7,131/5,397. **Par:** 72/72. **Course Rating:** 74.6/72.1. **Slope:** 138/124. **Green Fee:** $55/$160. **Cart Fee:** Included in Green Fee. **Walking Policy:** Unrestricted walking. **Walkability:** 3. **Opened:** 1998. **Architect:** Tom Fazio with Dennis Wise. **Season:** Year-round. **High:** Jan.-May/Oct.-Dec. **To obtain tee times:** Resort guests may book 60 days in advance. Outside guests 21 days in advance. Advanced tee times with golf packages. **Miscellaneous:** Reduced fees (weekdays, low season, resort guests), discount packages, range (grass), club rentals, credit cards (MC, V, AE, D, Diners Club), beginner friendly (course is very user friendly for beginners). **Notes:** Ranked 25th in 1999 Best in State.

Reader Comments: Very tough ... Had a great time, challenging but fun ... Worth the 40-minute drive from Las Vegas ... Plain vanilla, disappointing, overrated ... Attractive layout near Nevada border ... Outstanding Fazio course ... Best pace to play, period! ... Well done. Fair ... Great round of desert golf ... Too expensive.

★★★★½ **LAKES COURSE** *Value, Condition+, Pace+*

Holes: 18. **Yards:** 6,945/5,019. **Par:** 71/71. **Course Rating:** 74.0/69.1. **Slope:** 134/118. **Green Fee:** $55/$160. **Cart Fee:** Included in Green Fee. **Walking Policy:** Unrestricted walking. **Walkability:** 3. **Opened:** 1997. **Architect:** Tom Fazio. **Season:** Year-round. **High:** Jan.-May/Oct.-Dec. **To obtain tee times:** Resort guests may book 60 days in advance. Outside guests 21 days in advance. Advanced tee times with golf packages. **Miscellaneous:** Reduced fees (weekdays, low season, resort guests), discount packages, range (grass), credit cards (MC, V, AE, D, Diners Club), beginner friendly (course is very user friendly for beginners). **Notes:** Ranked 24th in 1999 Best in State.

Reader Comments: Treated well, good challenge ... Almost Shadow Creek ... Great course ... A little expensive, fun course, fair ... Wonderful practice facility, great Fazio layout, player-friendly ... Great holes Nos. 12, 14, 15, tough back 9 ... Challenging for all grades of golfers. A real surprise ... Excellent condition, layout and service!.

PRO KIDS GOLF ACADEMY & LEARNING CENTER.
PU-4085 52nd St, San Diego, 92105, San Diego County, (619)582-4704.
Holes: 18. **Yards:** 1,525/1,525. **Par:** 54/54. **Course Rating:** N/A. **Slope:** N/A. **Green Fee:** $5/$5. **Walking Policy:** Unrestricted walking. **Walkability:** 3. **Opened:** 1955. **Season:** Year-round. **High:** June-Aug. **To obtain tee times:** Call or walk-ins welcome. **Miscellaneous:** Reduced fees (seniors, juniors), range (mats), club rentals, beginner friendly (junior golf development programs). **Special Notes:** Par 3 course. Formerly Colina Park Golf Course.

★★★ QUAIL RANCH GOLF CLUB
15960 Gilman Springs Rd., Moreno Valley, 92555, Riverside County, (909)654-2727.
Yards: N/A. **Par:** N/A. **Course Rating:** N/A. **Slope:** N/A. **Green Fee:** $29/$45. **Cart Fee:** Included in Green Fee. **Walking Policy:** Unrestricted walking. **Walkability:** 5. **Season:** Year-round. **High:** Nov.-June. **To obtain tee times:** 7 day advance Tee Times. **Miscellaneous:** Reduced fees (weekdays, low season, twilight, seniors, juniors), discount packages, metal spikes, range (grass), club rentals, credit cards (MC, V, AE).

Reader Comments: Could be much better ... Price is right! Interesting layout ... Tough greens, windy ... Tough when it's still; impossible in the wind ... Long and fun ... The best value in Moreno Valley area ... 4-putts possible ... You need local knowledge on greens, or else! ... Shotmaking a premium here.

★★★★ RAMS HILL COUNTRY CLUB *Pace*
R-1881 Rams Hill Rd., Borrego Springs, 92004, San Diego County, (760)767-5124, (800)292-2944, 87 miles E of San Diego. **E-mail:** ramshill@nia.net. **Web:** www.ramshill.com.
Holes: 18. **Yards:** 6,866/5,694. **Par:** 72/72. **Course Rating:** 72.9/73.4. **Slope:** 130/128. **Green Fee:** $40/$105. **Cart Fee:** Included in Green Fee. **Walking Policy:** Mandatory cart. **Walkability:** 3. **Opened:** 1983. **Architect:** Ted Robinson. **Season:** Year-round. **High:** Nov.-April. **To obtain tee times:** Call golf shop up to 14 days in advance. **Miscellaneous:** Reduced fees (low season, resort guests, twilight), discount packages, metal spikes, range (grass/mats), club rentals, lodging (15 rooms), credit cards (MC, V).

Reader Comments: Great course ... Tough going when the wind's up ... A jewel away from Palm Springs, worth the trip ... Has to be one of the best! Expensive ... Watch out for the road runners ... Lovely course ... Gem in the desert ... Beautiful desert course and resort, good food ... 3 putts the norm, ouch.

★★★½ RANCHO BERNARDO INN
R-17550 Bernardo Oaks Dr., San Diego, 92128, San Diego County, (619)675-8470, (800)662-6439.
Holes: 18. **Yards:** 6,458/5,448. **Par:** 72/72. **Course Rating:** 70.6/71.2. **Slope:** 122/119. **Green Fee:** $25/$100. **Cart Fee:** Included in Green Fee. **Walking Policy:** Walking at certain times. **Walkability:** 2. **Opened:** 1962. **Architect:** William F. Bell. **Season:** Year-round. **High:** Dec.-May. **To obtain tee times:** Hotel guests call anytime. Others call 7 days in advance. **Miscellaneous:** Reduced fees (weekdays, resort guests, twilight, juniors), discount packages, metal spikes, range (grass/mats), club rentals, lodging (288 rooms), credit cards (MC, V, AE, D).

Reader Comments: Good quality resort course ... Beautiful resort ... Most enjoyable visit, golf fun ... Very expensive, and hard to play ... Excellent resort course ... Not very challenging.

RANCHO CANADA GOLF CLUB
PU-4860 Carmel Valley Rd., Carmel, 93923, Monterey County, (408)624-0111, (800)536-9459, 8 miles S of Monterey. **E-mail:** rnchglf@carmel-golf.com. **Web:** www.ranchocanada.com.

★★★ EAST COURSE
Holes: 18. **Yards:** 6,109/5,267. **Par:** 71/72. **Course Rating:** 68.7/69.4. **Slope:** 120/114. **Green Fee:** $30/$60. **Cart Fee:** $28/cart. **Walking Policy:** Unrestricted walking. **Walkability:** 2. **Opened:** 1970. **Architect:** Robert Dean Putman. **Season:** Year-round. **High:** April-Oct. **To obtain tee times:** Call golf shop any time. **Miscellaneous:** Reduced fees (twilight), discount packages, range (grass/mats), club rentals, credit cards (MC, V, AE, Diners Club).
Reader Comments: Why the West costs more than the East is a mystery ... Rinky dink layout ... Rebuilt after El Niño, great. No. 12 a winner ... Overrated, OK layout ... Nice ... Not a course to play when it is wet.

★★★ WEST COURSE
Holes: 18. **Yards:** 6,349/5,568. **Par:** 71/72. **Course Rating:** 70.4/71.9. **Slope:** 125/118. **Green Fee:** $40/$75. **Cart Fee:** $28/cart. **Walking Policy:** Unrestricted walking. **Walkability:** 2. **Opened:** 1970. **Architect:** Robert Dean Putman. **Season:** Year-round. **High:** April-Nov. **To obtain tee times:** Call golf shop any time. **Miscellaneous:** Reduced fees (twilight), discount packages, range (grass/mats), club rentals, credit cards (MC, V, AE, Diners Club).
Reader Comments: Nice course, good value, play a little slow ... They go out of their way to make your day ... East Course easier ... Basic golf ... Flat ... In good shape for all the play it gets.

RANCHO CARLSBAD COUNTRY CLUB
PU-5200 El Camino Real, Carlsbad, 92008, San Diego County, (760)438-1772.
Holes: 18. **Yards:** 2,396/1,955. **Par:** 56/56. **Course Rating:** N/A. **Slope:** N/A. **Green Fee:** $12/$15. **Walking Policy:** Unrestricted walking. **Walkability:** 1. **Opened:** 1966. **Season:** Jan.-Dec. **High:** May-Sept. **Miscellaneous:** Reduced fees (twilight, juniors), range (mats), club rentals, credit cards (MC, V).

★★½ RANCHO DEL RAY GOLF CLUB
PU-5250 Green Sands Ave., Atwater, 95301, Merced County, (209)358-7131, 30 miles S of Modesto.
Holes: 18. **Yards:** 6,703/5,987. **Par:** 72/75. **Course Rating:** 72.5/73.6. **Slope:** 124/125. **Green Fee:** $12/$22. **Cart Fee:** $18/cart. **Walking Policy:** Unrestricted walking. **Walkability:** 1. **Season:** Year-round. **High:** Spring-Fall. **To obtain tee times:** Tee times are taken on Monday for Tuesday-Monday. **Miscellaneous:** Reduced fees (weekdays, twilight), range (grass/mats), club rentals, credit cards (MC, V, AE, D, ATM Debit).

★★½ RANCHO MARIA GOLF CLUB
PU-1950 Casmalia Rd., Santa Maria, 93455, Santa Barbara County, (805)937-2019.
Holes: 18. **Yards:** 6,390/5,504. **Par:** 72/73. **Course Rating:** 70.2/71.3. **Slope:** 119/123. **Green Fee:** $17/$28. **Cart Fee:** $18/cart. **Walking Policy:** Unrestricted walking. **Walkability:** 2. **Opened:** 1965. **Architect:** Bob Baldock. **Season:** Year-round. **To obtain tee times:** Call 2 days in advance for weekdays; 7 days in advance for weekends and holidays. **Miscellaneous:** Reduced fees (weekdays, twilight, seniors, juniors), metal spikes, range (grass), club rentals, credit cards (MC, V).
Reader Comments: Mundane course ... Old course, fairly easy, nice greens ... Nothing fancy ... A fun course to play, busy all the time.

RANCHO MURIETA COUNTRY CLUB
SP-7000 Alameda Dr., Rancho Murieta, 95683, Sacramento County, (916)354-3440, 15 miles SE of Sacramento.

★★★½ NORTH COURSE
Holes: 18. **Yards:** 6,839/5,608. **Par:** 72/72. **Course Rating:** 72.6/73.5. **Slope:** 136/135. **Green Fee:** $60/$85. **Cart Fee:** Included in Green Fee. **Walking Policy:** Mandatory cart. **Walkability:** 4. **Opened:** 1971. **Architect:** Bert Stamps/Arnold Palmer/Ed Seay. **Season:** Year-round. **High:** April-Oct. **To obtain tee times:** Call 3 days in advance. **Miscellaneous:** Reduced fees (weekdays, low season, juniors), range (grass/mats), club rentals, credit cards (MC, V, AE).
Reader Comments: Excellent greens ... Very good layout, conditioning average ... No. 3 is an outstanding hole ... Glad to see it open for some public play ... Always hitting down a pipe ... Nice course ... Tough challenging course ... Quaint.

★★★½ SOUTH COURSE
Holes: 18. **Yards:** 6,894/5,583. **Par:** 72/72. **Course Rating:** 72.9/71.8. **Slope:** 129/124. **Green Fee:** $50/$85. **Cart Fee:** Included in Green Fee. **Walking Policy:** Mandatory cart. **Walkability:** 4. **Opened:** 1971. **Architect:** Ted Robinson. **Season:** Year-round. **High:** April-Oct. **To obtain tee times:** Call 3 days in advance. **Miscellaneous:** Reduced fees (weekdays, low season, juniors), range (grass/mats), club rentals, lodging, credit cards (MC, V, AE).

Reader Comments: Almost very good! Fun people! Fun course! ... Like playing here ... Easier than the North ... Wonderful setting, great holes ... Solid.

★★★½ RANCHO PARK GOLF COURSE
PM-10460 W. Pico Blvd., Los Angeles, 90064, Los Angeles County, (310)839-4374.
Holes: 18. **Yards:** 6,585/5,928. **Par:** 71/71. **Course Rating:** N/A. **Slope:** 124/122. **Green Fee:** $17/$23. **Cart Fee:** $20/cart. **Walking Policy:** Unrestricted walking. **Walkability:** 2. **Opened:** 1949. **Architect:** William P. Bell/William H. Johnson. **Season:** Year-round. **High:** April-Oct. **To obtain tee times:** Reservation card issued by city or walk in for waiting list any time. **Miscellaneous:** Reduced fees (weekdays, twilight), metal spikes.
Reader Comments: This place is way too busy ... Impossible to get on ... Still a great play ... More rounds played than any other course in the world ... It's fun to par the hole Arnold Palmer took a 12 on ... Course is great, the pace is awful ... Nice design, based in natural trees ... Beautiful course.

RANCHO SAN DIEGO GOLF CLUB
PU-3121 Willow Glen Dr., El Cajon, 92019, San Diego County, (619)442-9891, 20 miles of San Diego.
★★★½ IVANHOE COURSE
Holes: 18. **Yards:** 6,837/5,686. **Par:** 72/73. **Course Rating:** 72.6/72.4. **Slope:** 126/121. **Green Fee:** $18/$39. **Cart Fee:** $10/person. **Walking Policy:** Unrestricted walking. **Walkability:** 1. **Opened:** 1962. **Architect:** O.W. Moorman/A.C. Sears. **Season:** Year-round. **High:** March-Oct. **To obtain tee times:** Call golf shop up to 14 days in advance. **Miscellaneous:** Reduced fees (weekdays, twilight, seniors), range (grass/mats), club rentals, credit cards (MC, V).
Reader Comments: Clean, neat, well kept ... Tricky, trees get you, a lot of punch shots ... Well worth playing. Super value ... Best greens around, outstanding staff ... Good for beginners ... Good, standard course.
★★½ MONTE VISTA COURSE
Holes: 18. **Yards:** 6,302/5,531. **Par:** 71/72. **Course Rating:** 69.5/75.7. **Slope:** 117/134. **Green Fee:** $16/$36. **Cart Fee:** $10/person. **Walking Policy:** Unrestricted walking. **Walkability:** 1. **Opened:** 1963. **Architect:** O.W. Moorman/A.C. Sears. **Season:** Year-round. **High:** March-Oct. **To obtain tee times:** Call up to 14 days in advance. **Miscellaneous:** Reduced fees (weekdays, twilight, seniors, juniors), metal spikes, range (grass/mats), club rentals, credit cards (MC, V).
Reader Comments: Tough and good ... Long for walking ... Not as good as sister course ... Easy and flat.

★★½ RANCHO SAN JOAQUIN GOLF CLUB
PU-1 Sandburg Way, Irvine, 92612, Orange County, (949)451-0840, 18 miles S of Los Angeles.
Holes: 18. **Yards:** 6,453/5,794. **Par:** 72/72. **Course Rating:** 70.6/73.1. **Slope:** 118/121. **Green Fee:** $13/$60. **Cart Fee:** Included in Green Fee. **Walking Policy:** Unrestricted walking. **Walkability:** 3. **Opened:** 1971. **Architect:** William F. Bell. **Season:** Year-round. **To obtain tee times:** Call golf shop. **Miscellaneous:** Reduced fees (weekdays, twilight, seniors, juniors), metal spikes, range (mats), club rentals, credit cards (MC, V, AE), beginner friendly (junior camps).
Reader Comments: Avoid weekends ... Flat, barren ... New irrigation system being installed ... Constant improvements, bring your putting game ... A public asking upscale green fees.

★★★★½ RANCHO SAN MARCOS GOLF CLUB *Service, Condition*
PU-4600 Hwy. 154, Santa Barbara, 93105, Santa Barbara County, (805)683-6334, (877)776-1804, 12 miles W of Santa Barbara. **Web:** www.rsm/804.com.
Holes: 18. **Yards:** 6,801/5,018. **Par:** 71/71. **Course Rating:** 73.1/69.2. **Slope:** 135/117. **Green Fee:** $49/$101. **Cart Fee:** $17/person. **Walking Policy:** Unrestricted walking. **Walkability:** 4. **Opened:** 1998. **Architect:** Robert Trent Jones Jr. **Season:** Year-round. **High:** May-Oct. **To obtain tee times:** Call 805-683-6334 for computerized tee time menu. Have credit card ready for reservation. **Miscellaneous:** Reduced fees (weekdays, resort guests, twilight, juniors), range (grass), caddies, club rentals, credit cards (MC, V, AE), beginner friendly (lesson programs and 4 to 5 sets of tees).
Notes: Ranked 28th in 1999 Best in State.
Reader Comments: Best new course in Southern California ... Excellent variety of holes ... Back 9 is spectacular ... Love the super fast greens ... Front 9 flat and back is hilly ... Friendly course and people ... A treasure! Best combo of service and golf anywhere ... One unfair hole on back ... Excellent challenge ... Superior setting and views.

★★★½ RANCHO SOLANO GOLF COURSE
PM-3250 Rancho Solano Pkwy., Fairfield, 94533, Solano County, (707)429-4653, 40 miles E of San Francisco.
Holes: 18. **Yards:** 6,705/5,206. **Par:** 72/72. **Course Rating:** 72.1/69.6. **Slope:** 128/117. **Green Fee:** $19/$14. **Cart Fee:** $14/person. **Walking Policy:** Unrestricted walking. **Walkability:** 3. **Opened:** 1990. **Architect:** Gary Roger Baird. **Season:** Year-round. **High:** June-Sept. **To obtain tee times:** Call 7 days in advance after 6 a.m. **Miscellaneous:** Reduced fees (weekdays, twi-

light, seniors, juniors), discount packages, metal spikes, range (mats), club rentals, credit cards (MC, V, AE, D).

Reader Comments: Nice layout ... A great muny course, challenging and fair ... Good variety of holes ... Greens the size of Mars, bring 2 putters ... Nice back 9 ... Has always been great ... Some nice hole layouts. Sometimes pace of play can be slow ... Once you're on the green, the work begins!.

★★★½ RECREATION PARK GOLF COURSE

PM-5001 Deukmejian Dr., Long Beach, 90804, Los Angeles County, (562)494-5000, 15 miles S of Los Angeles.

Holes: 18. **Yards:** 6,405/5,930. **Par:** 72/74. **Course Rating:** 69.9/72.4. **Slope:** 111/119. **Green Fee:** $19/$23. **Cart Fee:** $21/cart. **Walking Policy:** Unrestricted walking. **Walkability:** 2. **Opened:** 1924. **Architect:** William P. Bell. **Season:** Year-round. **To obtain tee times:** Must have reservation card ($10.00/year) to obtain tee times up to 6 days in advance. Without card call 1 day in advance after 12:30 p.m. **Miscellaneous:** Reduced fees (weekdays, twilight, seniors, juniors), metal spikes, range (mats), club rentals, credit cards (MC, V, AE), beginner friendly (group lessons, women in golf day).

Reader Comments: Nice muny course, after first 3 holes ... Classic old course, excellent greens ... Interesting and challenging ... Crowded, but challenging muny track ... A lot of trees, nice layout ... Mixture of good and bad holes ... Fun to play, wide open, watch out for the killer rabbit herd on the 11th tee ... An OK local course.

★★★★ REDHAWK GOLF CLUB

PU-45100 Redhawk Pkwy., Temecula, 92592, Riverside County, (909)602-3850, (800)451-4295, 30 miles S of Riverside.

Holes: 18. **Yards:** 7,139/5,510. **Par:** 72/72. **Course Rating:** 75.7/72.0. **Slope:** 149/124. **Green Fee:** $80/$80. **Cart Fee:** Included in Green Fee. **Walking Policy:** Mandatory cart. **Walkability:** 5. **Opened:** 1991. **Architect:** Ron Fream. **Season:** Year-round. **High:** Nov.-April. **To obtain tee times:** Available 7 days in advance. **Miscellaneous:** Reduced fees (twilight, juniors), range (grass/mats), club rentals, credit cards (MC, V, AE).

Reader Comments: Too far for L.A. golfers ... Great challenge, pace a little slow ... Great course ... A gorgeous and wonderful course ... Tough, upscale course, well maintained ... Some holes blind ... Landscaping on course was exquisite ... Lookout for huge pot bunkers on 14 ... Great par 3s, fast greens ... Too many tricked-up, tiered greens.

THE RESERVE AT SPANOS PARK

PU-6301 West Eight Mile Rd., Stockton, 95219, San Joaquin County, (209)477-4653, 2 miles N of Stockton.

Holes: 18. **Yards:** 7,000/5,490. **Par:** 72/72. **Course Rating:** 74.2/69.9. **Slope:** 133/118. **Green Fee:** $15/$45. **Cart Fee:** $6/$12 per person. **Walking Policy:** Walking at certain times. **Walkability:** 1. **Opened:** 1999. **Architect:** Andy Raugust. **Season:** Year-round. **High:** April-Sept. **To obtain tee times:** Available 14 days in advance. **Miscellaneous:** Reduced fees (low-season, twilight, seniors, juniors), (grass) club rentals, credit cards (MC, V, AE).

★★★½ RESORT AT SQUAW CREEK

R-400 Squaw Creek Rd., Olympic Valley, 96146, Placer County, (530)581-6637, (800)327-3353, 45 miles W of Reno, Nevada.

Holes: 18. **Yards:** 6,931/5,097. **Par:** 71/71. **Course Rating:** 72.9/68.9. **Slope:** 140/127. **Green Fee:** $85/$115. **Cart Fee:** Included in Green Fee. **Walking Policy:** Walking at certain times. **Walkability:** 2. **Opened:** 1992. **Architect:** Robert Trent Jones Jr. **Season:** May-Oct. **High:** June-Sept. **To obtain tee times:** Call golf shop with credit card number to hold a tee time. **Miscellaneous:** Reduced fees (weekdays, low season, twilight, juniors), discount packages, metal spikes, range (mats), club rentals, lodging, credit cards (MC, V, AE).

Reader Comments: Great shotmaking course, great test mentally ... Overpriced and overrated course, but 5-star accommodations ... Way overpriced ... Beautiful preserved wetlands with risky track running through it ... What a pleasant surprise, this was a great course.

THE RIDGE GOLF COURSE

PU-2020 Golf Course Rd., Auburn, 95602, Placer County, (530)888-7888, 25 miles E of Sacramento. **E-mail:** kdickel@ridgegc.com. **Web:** ridgegc.com.

Holes: 18. **Yards:** 6,734/5,855. **Par:** 71/71. **Course Rating:** 72.3/70.7. **Slope:** 137/128. **Green Fee:** $35/$55. **Cart Fee:** $12/person. **Walking Policy:** Unrestricted walking. **Walkability:** 3. **Opened:** 1999. **Architect:** Robert Trent Jones Jr. **Season:** Year-round. **High:** April-Nov. **To obtain tee times:** Call (530)888-7888 Ext. 3. We accept reservations 7 days in advance. If you have a golf package (lodging & 18 holes) you can book up to 4 weeks in advance. **Miscellaneous:** Reduced fees (low season, twilight), discount packages, range (grass/mats), club rentals, credit cards (MC, V, AE), beginner friendly (beginner lesson programs).

RIDGEMARK GOLF & COUNTRY CLUB
R-3800 Airline Hwy., Hollister, 95023, San Benito County, (408)634-2222, (800)637-8151, 40 miles SE of San Jose. **E-mail:** golf@ridgemark.com. **Web:** www.ridgemark.com.

★★★½ **DIABLO COURSE**
Holes: 18. **Yards:** 6,603/5,475. **Par:** 72/72. **Course Rating:** 72.5/71.7. **Slope:** 128/118. **Green Fee:** $52/$62. **Cart Fee:** Included in Green Fee. **Walking Policy:** Mandatory cart. **Walkability:** N/A. **Opened:** 1972. **Architect:** Richard Bigler. **Season:** Year-round. **To obtain tee times:** Call 30 days in advance. **Miscellaneous:** Reduced fees (twilight), discount packages, metal spikes, range (grass/mats), club rentals, lodging, credit cards (MC, V, AE, D, Diners Club).
Reader Comments: Dine and dance on weekends ... Always in great condition ... Nice facilities, friendly staff, good package deals ... Nice layout ... Flat and hot in summer.

★★★½ **GABILAN COURSE**
Holes: 36. **Yards:** 6,781/5,683. **Par:** 72/72. **Course Rating:** 72.9/71.6. **Slope:** 129/118. **Green Fee:** $52/$62. **Cart Fee:** Included in Green Fee. **Walking Policy:** Mandatory cart. **Walkability:** N/A. **Opened:** 1972. **Architect:** Richard Bigler. **Season:** Year-round. **To obtain tee times:** Call 7 days in advance. **Miscellaneous:** Reduced fees (twilight), discount packages, metal spikes, range (grass/mats), club rentals, lodging, credit cards (MC, V, AE, D, Diners Club).
Reader Comments: Challenging course, great greens, windows do come into play ... OK ... Take 2 days and stay and play both ... Fun variety ... Good scenery, good condition ... Not as interesting as Diablo Course.

★★★½ RIO HONDO GOLF CLUB
PU-10627 Old River School Rd., Downey, 90241, Los Angeles County, (562)927-2329, 15 miles E of Los Angeles.
Holes: 18. **Yards:** 6,344/5,080. **Par:** 71/71. **Course Rating:** 70.2/69.4. **Slope:** 119/117. **Green Fee:** $30/$40. **Walking Policy:** Unrestricted walking. **Walkability:** 2. **Opened:** 1921. **Architect:** John Duncan Dunn. **Season:** Year-round. **To obtain tee times:** Call 7 days in advance at 6 a.m. **Miscellaneous:** Reduced fees (twilight, seniors, juniors), range (mats), club rentals, credit cards (MC, V).
Reader Comments: Flat course, tight lies, great greens ... Ho-hum ... Okay, nothing to brag about ... Good layout, wet during winter ... Interesting layout, good maintenance.

★★★★ RIO VISTA GOLF CLUB
PU-1000 Summerset Dr., Rio Vista, 94571, (707)374-2900. **Web:** www.summersetlife.com.
Holes: 18. **Yards:** 6,800/5,330. **Par:** 72/72. **Course Rating:** 73.9/72.4. **Slope:** 131/124. **Green Fee:** $32/$47. **Cart Fee:** $13/. **Walking Policy:** Unrestricted walking. **Walkability:** 2. **Opened:** 1998. **Architect:** Ted Robinson and Ted Robinson Jr. **Season:** Year-round. **High:** March-Nov. **To obtain tee times:** 7 day Advance. **Miscellaneous:** Reduced fees (twilight, juniors), range (grass/mats), club rentals, credit cards (MC, V).
Reader Comments: Good new course but windy ... Attractive water landscaping, play it before more houses built ... Great holes! Water always in play! Don't miss it, it's a memorable course ... Good new course ... Beautiful 9th and 18th holes ... Some holes too tricky, houses too close ... Enjoyable golf. Nice outing ... Maturing well.

★★★½ RIVER COURSE AT THE ALISAL
PU-150 Alisal Rd., Solvang, 93463, Santa Barbara County, (805)688-6042, 35 miles NW of Santa Barbara. **Web:** www.rivercourse.com.
Holes: 18. **Yards:** 6,830/5,815. **Par:** 72/72. **Course Rating:** 73.1/73.4. **Slope:** 126/127. **Green Fee:** $45/$55. **Cart Fee:** $24/cart. **Walking Policy:** Unrestricted walking. **Walkability:** 2. **Opened:** 1992. **Architect:** Halsey/Daray. **Season:** Year-round. **High:** Jan.-March/May/Oct. **To obtain tee times:** Call or come in 7 days in advance. **Miscellaneous:** Reduced fees (weekdays, resort guests, seniors, juniors), discount packages, metal spikes, range (grass/mats), club rentals, credit cards (MC, V, AE).
Reader Comments: Fun course ... You better like to play in the wind ... Player-friendly course, great vacation getaway ... Nice setting ... Easiest course.

★★★½ RIVER RIDGE GOLF CLUB
PM-2401 W. Vineyard Ave., Oxnard, 93030, Ventura County, (805)983-4653, 50 miles N of Los Angeles.
Holes: 18. **Yards:** 6,718/5,351. **Par:** 72/72. **Course Rating:** 72.3/71.3. **Slope:** 121/124. **Green Fee:** $22/$27. **Cart Fee:** $24/cart. **Walking Policy:** Unrestricted walking. **Walkability:** 4. **Opened:** 1986. **Architect:** William F. Bell. **Season:** Year-round. **To obtain tee times:** Call 7 days in advance starting at 6 a.m. (usually sold out by 7 a.m.). **Miscellaneous:** Reduced fees (twilight, seniors, juniors), range (grass), club rentals, lodging (251 rooms), credit cards (MC, V, D).
Reader Comments: Challenging layout in decent shape ... Fun back 9 ... Can be tough in wind ... Open, nice course ... Nice layout, windy in afternoons ... Interesting course, but too many blind holes ... Good test. Lots of wind (close to Pacific) ... Average layout ... Great people ... Nice muny.

★½ RIVER VIEW GOLF COURSE
PU-1800 West Santa Clara, Santa Ana, 92706, Orange County, (714)543-1115.
Holes: 18. **Yards:** 6,100/5,800. **Par:** 70/70. **Course Rating:** 69.0/66.1. **Slope:** 106/103. **Green Fee:** $12/$17. **Cart Fee:** $18/cart. **Walking Policy:** Walking at certain times. **Walkability:** 4.
Opened: 1964. **Architect:** Novel James. **Season:** Year-round. **High:** March-Dec. **To obtain tee times:** Call within 10 days of desired time. **Miscellaneous:** Reduced fees (weekdays, low season, resort guests, twilight, seniors, juniors), discount packages, metal spikes, range (grass/mats), club rentals, credit cards (MC, V).

★★★ RIVERSIDE GOLF COURSE
PU-7672 N. Josephine, Fresno, 93711, Fresno County, (209)275-5900. **E-mail:** rivere@pacbell.net. **Web:** www.courseco.com.
Holes: 18. **Yards:** 6,592/5,979. **Par:** 72/75. **Course Rating:** 71.0/73.8. **Slope:** 122/125. **Green Fee:** $13/$15. **Cart Fee:** $20/cart. **Walking Policy:** Unrestricted walking. **Walkability:** 2.
Opened: 1939. **Architect:** William P. Bell. **Season:** Year-round. **High:** April-Oct. **To obtain tee times:** Call 7 days in advance starting at 6:00 a.m. **Miscellaneous:** Reduced fees (weekdays, twilight, seniors, juniors), metal spikes, range (grass), club rentals, credit cards (MC, V), beginner friendly (junior camps and clinics, adult clinics).
Reader Comments: Inexpensive, but needs work, too much play ... Good course but slow ... Terrific value, good course ... Well maintained greens, lots of trees ... One of my favorites.

RIVERWALK GOLF CLUB
PU-1150 Fashion Valley Rd., San Diego, 92108, San Diego County, (619)296-4653, 7 miles NE of San Diego.
Holes: 27. **Green Fee:** $35/$95. **Cart Fee:** Included in Green Fee. **Walking Policy:** Unrestricted walking. **Opened:** 1998. **Architect:** Ted Robinson/Ted Robinson Jr. **Season:** Year-round. **High:** Nov.-April. **Miscellaneous:** Reduced fees (weekdays, twilight, juniors), range (grass/mats), club rentals, lodging (40 rooms), credit cards (MC, V, AE), beginner friendly (unlimited lessons $95.00 for 1 month).
★★★½ MISSION/FRYERS
Yards: 6,483/5,215. **Par:** 72/72. **Course Rating:** 70.5/69.5. **Slope:** 120/114. **Walkability:** 2.
★★★½ PRESIDIO/FRYERS
Yards: 6,627/5,532. **Par:** 72/72. **Course Rating:** 71.6/70.9. **Slope:** 123/115. **Walkability:** 2.
★★★½ PRESIDIO/MISSIONS
Yards: 6,550/5,427. **Par:** 72/72. **Course Rating:** 71.5/74.3. **Slope:** 120/115. **Walkability:** 4.
Reader Comments: Enjoyable experience, I like what they've done to the place ... Fun to play ... Walk in the park ... Most gorgeous course I have ever played! ... Overpriced tourist trap ... Needs to mature ... Windy, a real challenge ... Getting better.
Special Notes: Formerly Stardust Country Club.

★★★½ ROOSTER RUN GOLF CLUB
PU-2301 East Washington St., Petaluma, 94954, Sonoma County, (707)778-1211.
Holes: 18. **Yards:** 7,001/5,139. **Par:** 72/72. **Course Rating:** 73.9/69.1. **Slope:** 128/117. **Green Fee:** $26/$42. **Cart Fee:** $24/. **Walking Policy:** Unrestricted walking. **Walkability:** 2. **Opened:** 1998. **Architect:** Fred Bliss. **Season:** Year-round. **High:** April-Nov. **Miscellaneous:** Reduced fees (twilight, seniors, juniors), range (grass), club rentals, credit cards (MC, V).
Reader Comments: Good public facility ... Best priced 18 holes in north Bay Area ... Immature ... Impressed with some holes, not all ... Nice layout, local airport is annoying ... Very windy ... Fairly new course, good restaurant, kinda pricey ... No. 16 almost impossible! ... Great location.

★★★ ROSEVILLE DIAMOND OAKS MUNICIPAL GOLF COURSE
PM-349 Diamond Oaks Rd., Roseville, 95678, Placer County, (916)783-4947, 15 miles NE of Sacramento.
Holes: 18. **Yards:** 6,283/5,608. **Par:** 72/73. **Course Rating:** 69.5/70.5. **Slope:** 115/112. **Green Fee:** $10/$19. **Cart Fee:** $19/cart. **Walking Policy:** Unrestricted walking. **Walkability:** 3. **Opened:** 1963. **Architect:** Ted Robinson. **Season:** Year-round. **High:** April-Oct. **To obtain tee times:** Call till midnight 7 days in advance (916)771-4653. **Miscellaneous:** Reduced fees (weekdays, low season, twilight, seniors, juniors), metal spikes, range (mats), club rentals, credit cards (MC, V).
Reader Comments: Much improved ... Too crowded ... Never a dull moment ... Layout fair ... Difficult to find, but when you do it's worth it ... Hard to get on.

★★★★ SADDLE CREEK GOLF CLUB
SP-1001 Saddle Creek Drive, Copperopolis, 95228, Calaveras County, (209)785-3700, (800)852-5787, 35 miles E of Stockton. **E-mail:** proshop@caltel.com. **Web:** www.saddlecreek.com.
Holes: 18. **Yards:** 6,829/4,488. **Par:** 72/72. **Course Rating:** 73.0/65.4. **Slope:** 134/111. **Green Fee:** $35/$62. **Cart Fee:** $13/person. **Walking Policy:** Unrestricted walking. **Walkability:** 3. **Opened:** 1996. **Architect:** Carter Morrish & Associates. **Season:** Year-round. **High:** May-Sept. **To obtain tee times:** Call golf shop up to 14 days in advance. **Miscellaneous:** Reduced fees

CALIFORNIA

(weekdays, low season, twilight, seniors, juniors), discount packages, range (grass), club rentals, credit cards (MC, V, AE), beginner friendly (5 sets of tees).

Reader Comments: Beautiful layout with 3 standout holes ... Beautiful rolling hills, challenging golf ... Fantastic, natural course ... Tough when you play from the tips ... Enjoy before they build houses ... Long drive from civilization ... Greens A+ ... Very, very scenic and interesting holes ... Fun to play, excellent value ... Gold Rush setting.

★★½ SALINAS FAIRWAYS GOLF COURSE
PU-45 Skyway Blvd., Salinas, 93905, Monterey County, (408)758-7300.
Special Notes: Call club for further information.

★★★ SAN BERNARDINO GOLF CLUB
PU-1494 S. Waterman, San Bernardino, 92408, San Bernardino County, (909)885-2414, 45 miles W of Palm Springs.
Holes: 18. **Yards:** 5,779/5,218. **Par:** 70/73. **Course Rating:** 67.5/69.9. **Slope:** 111/114. **Green Fee:** $9/$26. **Cart Fee:** $9/person. **Walking Policy:** Unrestricted walking. **Walkability:** 1. **Opened:** 1967. **Architect:** Dan Brown. **Season:** Year-round. **High:** April-May/Sept.-Oct. **To obtain tee times:** Call up to 7 days in advance. **Miscellaneous:** Reduced fees (weekdays, twilight, seniors, juniors), metal spikes, range (grass/mats), club rentals, credit cards (MC, V, AE, D), beginner friendly.
Reader Comments: Pitch and Putt ... Very nice ... Not long, but sporty layout, never in poor condition ... Greens OK, but short and flat ... Small public course, challenging ... Outstanding public course ... Premium on accuracy.

★★★½ SAN CLEMENTE MUNICIPAL GOLF CLUB
PM-150 E. Magdalena, San Clemente, 92672, Orange County, (949)361-8380, 60 miles N of San Diego.
Holes: 18. **Yards:** 6,447/5,722. **Par:** 72/73. **Course Rating:** 70.6/73.0. **Slope:** 121/120. **Green Fee:** $25/$30. **Cart Fee:** $20/cart. **Walking Policy:** Unrestricted walking. **Walkability:** 3. **Opened:** 1929. **Architect:** William P. Bell. **Season:** Year-round. **High:** June-Aug. **To obtain tee times:** Call 7 days in advance. 3 open times per hour for walk-ons. **Miscellaneous:** Reduced fees (weekdays, twilight), range (mats), club rentals.
Reader Comments: Good course, back 9 hard to walk. Very busy but kept in good condition ... Great layout, reasonable price ... Great value! Get up early ... Best kept secret in Orange County, beautiful ocean views and 15th is awesome ... A muny with an upscale view.

★★★ SAN DIMAS CANYON GOLF CLUB
PM-2100 Terrebonne Ave., San Dimas, 91773, Los Angeles County, (909)599-2313, 25 miles NE of Los Angeles.
Holes: 18. **Yards:** 6,309/5,539. **Par:** 72/74. **Course Rating:** 70.3/73.9. **Slope:** 118/123. **Green Fee:** $20/$39. **Cart Fee:** $12/person. **Walking Policy:** Walking at certain times. **Walkability:** 3. **Opened:** 1962. **Architect:** Jeff Brauer. **Season:** Year-round. **High:** April-Sept. **To obtain tee times:** Call 7 days in advance starting at 6:30 a.m. **Miscellaneous:** Reduced fees (weekdays, low season, twilight, seniors, juniors), discount packages, metal spikes, range (mats), club rentals, credit cards (MC, V, AE, D), beginner friendly (beginner golf league).
Reader Comments: Staff always on top of their game ... Always a challenge, lake, hills, ... A draw is more valuable than a slice at this fun layout ... Fore! ... Nice clubhouse, watch for rattlesnakes, No. 12 great hole ... Great greens, mountain views ... Tough, large undulating greens.

★★★½ SAN GERONIMO GOLF COURSE
PU-5800 Sir Francis Drake Blvd., San Geronimo, 94963, Marin County, (415)488-4030, (888)526-4653, 20 miles NW of San Francisco.
Holes: 18. **Yards:** 6,801/5,140. **Par:** 72/72. **Course Rating:** 73.3/69.9. **Slope:** 130/125. **Green Fee:** $25/$55. **Cart Fee:** $10/person. **Walking Policy:** Unrestricted walking. **Walkability:** 3. **Opened:** 1963. **Architect:** A. Vernon Macan. **Season:** Year-round. **High:** March-Oct. **To obtain tee times:** Call 7 days in advance. **Miscellaneous:** Reduced fees (weekdays, twilight, seniors, juniors), metal spikes, club rentals, credit cards (MC, V, AE).
Reader Comments: A diamond in the rough, good, tough, inexpensive ... Tough scenic track, back nine very isolated ... Boring front 9, back 9 is bizarre ... Pretty and tricky, but mostly pretty ... Back 9 a real challenge; can eat up a lot of balls! Many blind shots ... Putts break uphill.

★★★ SAN JOSE MUNICIPAL GOLF COURSE
PM-1560 Oakland Rd., San Jose, 95131, Santa Clara County, (408)441-4653.
Holes: 18. **Yards:** 6,602/5,594. **Par:** 72/72. **Course Rating:** 70.1/69.7. **Slope:** 108/112. **Green Fee:** $14/$38. **Walking Policy:** Unrestricted walking. **Walkability:** 1. **Opened:** 1968. **Architect:** Robert Muir Graves. **Season:** Year-round. **To obtain tee times:** Call or come in 7 days in advance for weekdays. Call Tuesday before 7 a.m. for weekend, alternating one reservation by phone and one in person. **Miscellaneous:** Reduced fees (weekdays, twilight, seniors, juniors), metal spikes, range (mats), club rentals, credit cards (MC, V, AE, D).

CALIFORNIA

Reader Comments: Ego-builder ... Surprisingly lush for a muny ... Flat, open ... Fun and challenging ... Course is in good condition considering the number of rounds played ... Slow ... You can make a good number.

★★★ SAN JUAN HILLS COUNTRY CLUB
PU-32120 San Juan Creek Rd., San Juan Capistrano, 92675, Orange County, (949)493-1167, 60 miles S of Los Angeles.
Holes: 18. **Yards:** 6,295/5,402. **Par:** 71/71. **Course Rating:** 69.5/71.4. **Slope:** 116/122. **Green Fee:** $22/$35. **Cart Fee:** $10/person. **Walking Policy:** Walking at certain times. **Walkability:** 3. **Opened:** 1966. **Architect:** Harry Rainville. **Season:** Year-round. **High:** May-Sept. **To obtain tee times:** Call up to 10 days in advance. **Miscellaneous:** Reduced fees (weekdays, twilight, seniors, juniors), metal spikes, range (mats), club rentals, credit cards (MC, V).
Reader Comments: Excellent layout ... Nice, but uneven. Some memorable holes ... Nice course. Surprised.

★★★★ SAN JUAN OAKS GOLF CLUB *Condition*
PU-3825 Union Rd., Hollister, 95023, San Benito County, (831)636-6113, (800)453-8337, 45 miles S of San Jose. **E-mail:** sjo@ix.netcom.com. **Web:** www.sanjuanoaks.com.
Holes: 18. **Yards:** 7,133/4,770. **Par:** 72/72. **Course Rating:** 74.8/67.1. **Slope:** 135/116. **Green Fee:** $45/$70. **Cart Fee:** $14/person. **Walking Policy:** Unrestricted walking. **Walkability:** 3. **Opened:** 1996. **Architect:** Fred Couples/Gene Bates. **Season:** Year-round. **High:** April-Oct. **To obtain tee times:** Call golf shop up to 30 days in advance. **Miscellaneous:** Reduced fees (weekdays, twilight, seniors, juniors), range (grass), club rentals, credit cards (MC, V, AE).
Reader Comments: Excellent fairways, fast greens ... A must for the average guy ... A wonderful design in a wind tunnel ... Would like to play it with Freddie ... Way too hard for most people ... Back 9 has some different/great holes ... Great condition and design. Well done Fred! ... Setting makes one reminisce for 'Old California.

★★★½ SAN LUIS REY DOWNS GOLF RESORT
R-31474 Golf Club Dr., Bonsall, 92003, San Diego County, (760)758-9699, (800)783-6967, 40 miles N of San Diego.
Holes: 18. **Yards:** 6,750/5,493. **Par:** 72/72. **Course Rating:** 72.6/71.4. **Slope:** 128/124. **Green Fee:** $25/$55. **Cart Fee:** Included in Green Fee. **Walking Policy:** Walking at certain times. **Walkability:** 1. **Opened:** 1963. **Architect:** William F. Bell. **Season:** Year-round. **High:** March-Sept. **To obtain tee times:** Call 7 days in advance. **Miscellaneous:** Reduced fees (twilight, juniors), discount packages, metal spikes, range (grass), club rentals, lodging, credit cards (MC, V, AE).
Reader Comments: Course condition improved. Good walking course ... Good greens, great layout ... Plays a lot tougher than it looks ... Good place to play and relax ... It's a must play, flat but very tough! ... Flat, well maintained, moderately long ... Watch the trees ... A gem with history ... Great 19th hole.

★★½ SAN RAMON ROYAL VISTA GOLF CLUB
PU-9430 Fircrest Lane, San Ramon, 94583, Contra Costa County, (510)828-6100, 15 miles S of Walnut Creek.
Holes: 18. **Yards:** 6,560/5,770. **Par:** 72/73. **Course Rating:** 70.9/72.7. **Slope:** 115/119. **Green Fee:** $20/$37. **Cart Fee:** $24/cart. **Walking Policy:** Mandatory cart. **Walkability:** 2. **Opened:** 1960. **Architect:** Clark Glasson. **Season:** Year-round. **High:** May-Sept. **To obtain tee times:** Call 7 days in advance. **Miscellaneous:** Reduced fees (twilight, seniors, juniors), metal spikes, range (mats), club rentals, credit cards (MC, V).

★★★ SAN VICENTE INN & GOLF CLUB
SP-24157 San Vicente Rd., Ramona, 92065, San Diego County, (760)789-3477, 25 miles NE of San Diego.
Holes: 18. **Yards:** 6,633/5,543. **Par:** 72/72. **Course Rating:** 71.5/72.8. **Slope:** 123/128. **Green Fee:** $47/$57. **Cart Fee:** Included in Green Fee. **Walking Policy:** Walking at certain times. **Walkability:** 2. **Opened:** 1972. **Architect:** Ted Robinson. **Season:** Year-round. **High:** Dec.-April. **To obtain tee times:** Call up to 5 days in advance. **. Miscellaneous:** Reduced fees (weekdays, resort guests, twilight), discount packages, range (grass/mats), club rentals, lodging (28 rooms), credit cards (MC, V, AE).
Reader Comments: Pretty scenery, average facilities ... Nestled in Ramona valley, lots a trees and playable for all golfers ... Course in good condition when I played ... Hard to get tee times. Most holes are memorable.

★★★★ SANDPIPER GOLF COURSE
PU-7925 Hollister Ave., Goleta, 93117, Santa Barbara County, (805)968-1541, 100 miles N of Los Angeles.
Holes: 18. **Yards:** 7,068/5,725. **Par:** 72/73. **Course Rating:** 74.5/73.3. **Slope:** 134/125. **Green Fee:** $68/$108. **Cart Fee:** $24/cart. **Walking Policy:** Unrestricted walking. **Walkability:** 3. **Opened:** 1972. **Architect:** William F. Bell. **Season:** Year-round. **High:** April-Oct. **To obtain tee**

times: Call 7 days in advance. **Miscellaneous:** Reduced fees (weekdays, low season, twilight, juniors), metal spikes, range (grass), caddies, club rentals, credit cards (MC, V, AE).
Notes: 1997 & 1998 LPGA Tour Santa Barbara Open.
Reader Comments: Some great holes, some ordinary holes, a little pricey ... Pebble Beach of central coast ... Windy, but beautiful. Bring your imagination ... On the ocean; what a layout ... Great back, front boring ... A third the cost of Pebble and just as scenic ... Six great ocean holes ... Best turkeyburgers in California.

★★★ SANTA ANITA GOLF COURSE
PM-405 S. Santa Anita Ave., Arcadia, 91006, Los Angeles County, (626)447-7156, 6 miles SE of Pasadena.
Holes: 18. **Yards:** 6,368/5,908. **Par:** 71/74. **Course Rating:** 70.4/73.1. **Slope:** 122/121. **Green Fee:** $19/$23. **Cart Fee:** $20/. **Walking Policy:** Unrestricted walking. **Walkability:** 3. **Opened:** 1936. **Architect:** L.A. County. **Season:** Year-round. **To obtain tee times:** Call up to 7 days in advance beginning 6 a.m. weekdays, 5 a.m. weekends & holidays. **Miscellaneous:** Reduced fees (twilight, seniors, juniors), metal spikes, range (grass/mats), club rentals, credit cards (MC, V).
Reader Comments: Considering high volume of play this course is in great condition ... Great layout. Fun course. Easy walking ... Nice old-style course, short but challenging ... Decent, but crowded. You can tell you're in the city ... Tough par 3s. Great view of mountains on a clear day.

★★ SANTA BARBARA GOLF CLUB
PM-3500 McCaw Ave., Santa Barbara, 93105, Santa Barbara County, (805)687-7087, 90 miles N of Los Angeles.
Holes: 18. **Yards:** 6,014/5,541. **Par:** 70/72. **Course Rating:** 67.6/71.9. **Slope:** 113/121. **Green Fee:** $18/$35. **Cart Fee:** $24/person. **Walking Policy:** Unrestricted walking. **Walkability:** 4. **Opened:** 1958. **Architect:** Lawrence Hughes. **Season:** Year-round. **High:** May-Sept. **To obtain tee times:** Call Monday for Saturdays and Sunday one week in advance Mon-Fri. **Miscellaneous:** Reduced fees (weekdays, twilight, seniors, juniors), range (mats), club rentals, credit cards (MC, V).

★★★ SANTA CLARA GOLF & TENNIS CLUB
PU-5155 Stars and Stripes Dr., Santa Clara, 95054, Santa Clara County, (408)980-9515, 12 miles W of San Jose.
Holes: 18. **Yards:** 6,822/5,639. **Par:** 72/72. **Course Rating:** 73.0/71.5. **Slope:** 126/115. **Green Fee:** $15/$34. **Cart Fee:** $22/cart. **Walking Policy:** Unrestricted walking. **Walkability:** 2. **Opened:** 1987. **Architect:** Robert Muir Graves. **Season:** Year-round. **High:** April-Sept. **To obtain tee times:** General public 7 days in advance. Santa Clara residents and Westin Hotel guests 8 days in advance. **Miscellaneous:** Reduced fees (weekdays, resort guests, twilight, seniors, juniors), metal spikes, range (mats), club rentals, lodging, credit cards (MC, V, AE).
Reader Comments: Flat, boring ... Good layout, windy area ... Best publinx in Silicon Valley ... Built on an old garbage dump ... Too many people!

★★★½ SANTA TERESA GOLF CLUB
PU-260 Bernal Rd., San Jose, 95119, Santa Clara County, (408)225-2650.
Holes: 18. **Yards:** 6,742/6,032. **Par:** 71/73. **Course Rating:** 71.1/73.5. **Slope:** 121/125. **Green Fee:** $30/$44. **Cart Fee:** $24/cart. **Walking Policy:** Unrestricted walking. **Opened:** 1962. **Architect:** George Santana. **Season:** Year-round. **High:** April-Sept. **To obtain tee times:** Call up to 7 days in advance. **Miscellaneous:** Reduced fees (weekdays, twilight, seniors, juniors), metal spikes, range (mats), club rentals, credit cards (MC, V, D), beginner friendly ("the short course" par 3 program).
Reader Comments: Gets a lot of play ... Back 9 still nice but needs work ... Fun little course; challenging ... A good design ... A tough public course! ... One of the very best munies, a sleeper ... No. 11 and No. 12 is mini Amen Corner ... Pretty good for an overplayed course.

★★★★ THE SCGA MEMBERS' CLUB AT RANCHO CALIFORNIA *Value*
PU-38275 Murrieta Hot Springs Rd., Murrieta, 92563, Riverside County, (909)677-7446, (800)752-9724, 45 miles N of San Diego.
Holes: 18. **Yards:** 7,059/5,355. **Par:** 72/72. **Course Rating:** 73.9/70.5. **Slope:** 132/116. **Green Fee:** $40/$70. **Cart Fee:** Included in Green Fee. **Walking Policy:** Unrestricted walking. **Walkability:** 3. **Opened:** 1972. **Architect:** Robert Trent Jones Sr. **Season:** Year-round. **High:** Jan.-May. **To obtain tee times:** Members call 10 days in advance, nonmembers 7 days. **Miscellaneous:** Reduced fees (weekdays, twilight, juniors), metal spikes, range (grass), club rentals, credit cards (MC, V, AE).
Reader Comments: Classic design. Large greens ... Felt like Pasatiempo only less expensive. Wonderful, a true golf experience ... Course always in good condition ... Friendly staff ... Quiet setting ... Robert Trent Jones Sr. at his best ... Good value, average course ... Slow play, bring your knitting.

★★ SCHOLL CANYON GOLF COURSE
PU-3800 E Glen Oaks Blvd, Glendale, 91206, Los Angeles County, (818)243-4100.

Holes: 18. **Yards:** 3,039/2,400. **Par:** 60/60. **Course Rating:** 56.8. **Slope:** 81. **Green Fee:** $12/ $16. **Cart Fee:** $18/cart. **Walking Policy:** Unrestricted walking. **Walkability:** 3. **Opened:** 1994. **Architect:** George Williams. **Season:** Year-round. **High:** June-Sept. **To obtain tee times:** Call golf shop up to 7 days in advance. **Miscellaneous:** Reduced fees (weekdays, twilight, seniors, juniors), discount packages, metal spikes, range (grass/mats), club rentals, credit cards (MC, V, AE).

★★★½ THE SEA RANCH GOLF LINKS *Pace*
R-4200 Highway 1, The Sea Ranch, 95497, Sonoma County, (707)785-2468, (800)842-3270, 37 miles NW of Santa Rosa. **E-mail:** srgi@mcn.com. **Web:** www.searanchvillage.com.
Holes: 18. **Yards:** 6,598/5,105. **Par:** 72/72. **Course Rating:** 73.2/71.5. **Slope:** 136/123. **Green Fee:** $45/$65. **Cart Fee:** $12/person. **Walking Policy:** Unrestricted walking. **Walkability:** 3. **Opened:** 1996. **Architect:** Robert Muir Graves. **Season:** Year-round. **High:** July-Nov. **To obtain tee times:** Call golf shop up to 6 months in advance. **Miscellaneous:** Reduced fees (weekdays, twilight, juniors), metal spikes, range (grass), club rentals, lodging, credit cards (MC, V, AE).
Reader Comments: Remote area, windy as hell, easy to lose balls ... New back 9 needs tweaking ... A true taste of Scotland, very peaceful place ... A good resort course, extremely difficult new back 9 ... Beautiful ocean scenery.

★★ SELMA VALLEY GOLF COURSE
PU-12389 E. Rose Ave., Selma, 93662, Fresno County, (559)896-2424, 15 miles S of Fresno.
Holes: 18. **Yards:** 5,391/5,170. **Par:** 69/70. **Course Rating:** 64.7/69.6. **Slope:** 107/118. **Green Fee:** $12/$16. **Cart Fee:** $22/cart. **Walking Policy:** Unrestricted walking. **Walkability:** 2. **Opened:** 1963. **Architect:** Bob Baldock. **Season:** Year-round. **To obtain tee times:** Call up to 7 days in advance. **Miscellaneous:** Metal spikes, range (grass/mats), club rentals.

SEPULVEDA GOLF COURSE
PM-16821 Burbank Blvd., Encino, 91436, Los Angeles County, (818)986-4560, 15 miles NW of Los Angeles.
★★½ BALBOA COURSE
Holes: 18. **Yards:** 6,359/5,912. **Par:** 70/72. **Course Rating:** 68.8/70.9. **Slope:** 107/115. **Green Fee:** $18/$23. **Cart Fee:** $21/cart. **Walking Policy:** Unrestricted walking. **Walkability:** 1. **Opened:** 1954. **Architect:** William F. Bell/W.H. Johnson. **Season:** Year-round. **High:** April-Sept. **Miscellaneous:** Reduced fees (weekdays, twilight, seniors, juniors), metal spikes, range (mats), club rentals.
Reader Comments: Lots of play, ragged. Tight course for muny. Flat, good walking course ... An uninteresting muny ... Acceptable ... Pleasant, but dull ... Both courses good value.
★★ ENCINO COURSE
Holes: 18. **Yards:** 6,863/6,133. **Par:** 72/75. **Course Rating:** 71.5/73.4. **Slope:** 116/118. **Green Fee:** $18/$23. **Cart Fee:** $21/person. **Walking Policy:** Unrestricted walking. **Walkability:** 1. **Opened:** 1957. **Architect:** W.F. Bell/W.P. Bell/W.H. Johnson. **Season:** Year-round. **High:** April-Sept. **Miscellaneous:** Reduced fees (weekdays, twilight, seniors, juniors), metal spikes, range (mats), club rentals.

★★★ SEVEN HILLS GOLF CLUB
PM-1537 S. Lyon St., Hemet, 92545, Riverside County, (909)925-4815, 100 miles of Los Angeles.
Holes: 18. **Yards:** 6,557/5,771. **Par:** 72/72. **Course Rating:** 70.2/70.0. **Slope:** 116/109. **Green Fee:** $14/$25. **Cart Fee:** $10/person. **Walking Policy:** Unrestricted walking. **Walkability:** 1. **Opened:** 1970. **Architect:** Harry Rainville/David Rainville. **Season:** Year-round. **High:** Nov.-March. **To obtain tee times:** Call up to 7 days in advance beginning at 6 a.m. **Miscellaneous:** Reduced fees (weekdays, twilight, seniors, juniors), discount packages, range (grass/mats), club rentals, credit cards (MC, V, AE, D).
Reader Comments: Good walkers' course, flat with mature trees and tricky greens ... Good mature course ... Good.challenge.

★★★ SHANDIN HILLS GOLF CLUB
PU-3380 Little Mountain Dr., San Bernardino, 92407, San Bernardino County, (909)886-0669, 60 miles E of Los Angeles.
Holes: 18. **Yards:** 6,517/5,592. **Par:** 72/72. **Course Rating:** 70.3/71.6. **Slope:** 120/122. **Green Fee:** $9/$28. **Cart Fee:** $10/person. **Walking Policy:** Unrestricted walking. **Walkability:** 3. **Opened:** 1980. **Architect:** Cary A. Bickler. **Season:** Year-round. **High:** Oct. **To obtain tee times:** Call 7 days in advance. **Miscellaneous:** Reduced fees (weekdays, twilight, seniors, juniors), discount packages, metal spikes, range (grass/mats), club rentals, credit cards (MC, V, AE, D).
Reader Comments: Plays along freeway ... Good smaller course ... Good layout in the foothills. Wind and slopes are challenging ... Nice public course, hilly, narrow fairways ... Great value ... Try this course, you'll like it ... Up and down ... You'll love #6 ... Occasionally very windy, front 9 good elevation change, back 9 flat.

★★½ SHARP PARK GOLF COURSE
PU-Highway 1, Pacifica, 94044, San Mateo County, (650)359-3380, 15 miles SW of San Francisco.

Holes: 18. **Yards:** 6,273/6,095. **Par:** 72/74. **Course Rating:** 70.6/73.0. **Slope:** 119/120. **Green Fee:** $23/$27. **Cart Fee:** $22/cart. **Walking Policy:** Unrestricted walking. **Walkability:** 2. **Opened:** 1929. **Architect:** Alister McKenzie. **Season:** Year-round. **High:** April-Oct. **To obtain tee times:** Call 6 days in advance for weekdays and 6 days in advance for weekends.
Miscellaneous: Reduced fees (weekdays, twilight, juniors), discount packages, metal spikes, club rentals.
Reader Comments: Good price, that's all ... Only a shadow of what it was ... Slow if you are off late ... Like deceptive bunkers. Dislike course condition.

★★★ SHERWOOD FOREST GOLF CLUB
PU-79 N. Frankwood Ave., Sanger, 93657, Fresno County, (209)787-2611, 18 miles SE of Fresno.
Holes: 18. **Yards:** 6,345/5,597. **Par:** 71/72. **Course Rating:** 69.2/71.4. **Slope:** 118/118. **Green Fee:** $17/$20. **Cart Fee:** $20/cart. **Walking Policy:** Unrestricted walking. **Walkability:** 1.
Opened: 1968. **Architect:** Bob Baldock. **Season:** Year-round. **High:** April-July. **To obtain tee times:** Call up to 7 days in advance. **Miscellaneous:** Reduced fees (twilight, juniors), metal spikes, range (grass), club rentals, credit cards (MC, V, D).
Reader Comments: Nice setting, greens need work, good price ... Nice course ... Short but pretty, 7, 8 and 9 are best challenge, require thought about club selection.

★★½ SHORECLIFFS GOLF CLUB
PU-501 Avenida Vaquero, San Clemente, 92762, Orange County, (949)492-1177. **Web:** www.Suntessa.com.
Holes: 18. **Yards:** 6,228/5,223. **Par:** 72/72. **Course Rating:** 71.3/71.1. **Slope:** 130/123. **Green Fee:** $30/$60. **Cart Fee:** Included in Green Fee. **Walking Policy:** Mandatory cart. **Walkability:** 5. **Opened:** 1965. **Architect:** Joe Williams. **Season:** Year-round. **High:** May-Oct. **To obtain tee times:** Call up to 7 days in advance. Tournaments 1 year in advance. **Miscellaneous:** Reduced fees (weekdays, twilight, seniors), metal spikes, range (mats), club rentals, credit cards (MC, V, AE, D, Diners Club).
Reader Comments: Fun course, typical public course ... Some very interesting holes. Course runs in and out of canyons, up and down hills. Tough for walkers ... Green fee too high for condition.

★★★ SHORELINE GOLF LINKS AT MOUNTAIN VIEW
PM-2940 N. Shoreline Blvd., Mountain View, 94043-1347, Santa Clara County, (650)969-2041, 3 miles NW of San Jose.
Holes: 18. **Yards:** 6,945/5,400. **Par:** 72/72. **Course Rating:** 73.7/66.4. **Slope:** 129/111. **Green Fee:** $30/$42. **Cart Fee:** $22/cart. **Walking Policy:** Unrestricted walking. **Walkability:** 2. **Opened:** 1982. **Architect:** Robert Trent Jones Jr. **Season:** Year-round. **High:** May-Sept. **To obtain tee times:** Call 7 days in advance. **Miscellaneous:** Reduced fees (weekdays, twilight, seniors, juniors), metal spikes, range (grass/mats), club rentals, credit cards (MC, V, AE).
Reader Comments: Has its ups and downs ... Very difficult course, lots of water and fairway bunkers. Acceptable greens ... Wind picks up on the back 9 ... City working to improve condition ... Very long with wind off bay.

SIERRA STAR GOLF CLUB
PU-1 Minaret Rd., Mammoth Lakes, 93546, (760)924-4653.
Holes: 18. **Yards:** 6,708/N/A. **Par:** 70/N/A. **Course Rating:** 71.0/N/A. **Slope:** 133/N/A. **Green Fee:** $85/$115. **Cart Fee:** Included in Green Fee. **Walking Policy:** Walking at certain times. **Walkability:** N/A. **Opened:** 1998. **Architect:** Cal Olson. **Season:** May-Oct. **High:** June-Aug. **To obtain tee times:** You may book tee times 6 months in advance secure with credit card. **Miscellaneous:** Reduced fees (resort guests, twilight), metal spikes, club rentals, credit cards (MC, V, AE).

★★ SIERRA VIEW PUBLIC GOLF COURSE
PU-12608 Ave. 264 at Rd. 124, Visalia, 93277, Tulare County, (209)732-2078, 40 miles S of Fresno.
Holes: 18. **Yards:** 6,388/5,886. **Par:** 72/73. **Course Rating:** 69.7/72.5. **Slope:** 114/118. **Green Fee:** $15/$20. **Cart Fee:** $18/cart. **Walking Policy:** Unrestricted walking. **Walkability:** 1. **Opened:** 1957. **Architect:** Robert Dean Putman. **Season:** Year-round. **To obtain tee times:** Call golf shop. **Miscellaneous:** Reduced fees (seniors, juniors), metal spikes, range (grass/mats), club rentals, credit cards (MC, V).

SILVERADO COUNTRY CLUB & RESORT
R-1600 Atlas Peak Rd., Napa, 94558, Napa County, (707)257-5460, (800)532-0500, 50 miles NE of San Francisco.
★★★½ NORTH COURSE
Holes: 18. **Yards:** 6,900/5,857. **Par:** 72/72. **Course Rating:** 73.4/73.1. **Slope:** 131/128. **Green Fee:** $60/$140. **Cart Fee:** Included in Green Fee. **Walking Policy:** Mandatory cart. **Walkability:** 2. **Opened:** 1955. **Architect:** Robert Trent Jones. **Season:** Year-round. **High:** March-Oct. **To obtain tee times:** May make tee time as far in advance as hotel room reservation.
Miscellaneous: Reduced fees (low season, resort guests, twilight), discount packages, metal spikes, range (grass/mats), club rentals, lodging, credit cards (MC, V, AE, D).

CALIFORNIA

Reader Comments: Less gimmicky than its sister ... Expensive, but great courses ... Excellent country club atmosphere, tough track ... Challenging greens ... Wonderful accommodations ... Old, solid, good test, too many houses ... Beautiful valley layout ... Overpriced, located in a great area.

★★★½ SOUTH COURSE
Holes: 18. **Yards:** 6,685/5,672. **Par:** 72/72. **Course Rating:** 72.4/71.8. **Slope:** 129/123. **Green Fee:** $60/$130. **Cart Fee:** Included in Green Fee. **Walking Policy:** Mandatory cart. **Walkability:** 3. **Opened:** 1955. **Architect:** Robert Trent Jones Jr. **Season:** Year-round. **High:** March-Nov. **To obtain tee times:** May take tee times as far in advance as hotel reservations. **Miscellaneous:** Reduced fees (low season, resort guests, twilight), discount packages, metal spikes, range (grass/mats), club rentals, lodging, credit cards (MC, V, AE, D).
Reader Comments: Overpriced but good course ... More difficult than it looks on TV ... Overplayed ... Fine old course, slow ... Tough, tight course ... Owe it to yourself to feel like the pros do once a year ... Great clubhouse ... Always a treat to play here.

★★★½ SIMI HILLS GOLF CLUB
PM-5031 Alamo, Simi Valley, 93063, Ventura County, (805)522-0803.
Holes: 18. **Yards:** 6,509/5,505. **Par:** 71/71. **Course Rating:** 70.6/65.9. **Slope:** 125/112. **Green Fee:** $22/$32. **Cart Fee:** $12/person. **Walking Policy:** Unrestricted walking. **Walkability:** 2. **Opened:** 1981. **Architect:** Ted Robinson. **Season:** Year-round. **To obtain tee times:** Weekdays 7 days in advance,weekends 5 days. **Miscellaneous:** Reduced fees (weekdays, low season, twilight, seniors, juniors), metal spikes, range (mats), club rentals, credit cards (MC, V, AE, D), beginner friendly (beginner classes).
Reader Comments: Nice track, used every club in the bag ... In and out of canyons. Tough walking. Can be very windy ... Solid course. Easy to get to. Some interesting holes. Crowded ... Very average ... Good muny ... Solid layout ... All the shots needed yet very fair.

SINGING HILLS RESORT
R-3007 Dehesa Rd., El Cajon, 92019, San Diego County, (619)442-3425, (800)457-5568, 17 miles E of El Cajon. **E-mail:** golfshop@singinghills.com. **Web:** www.singinghills.com.
★★★★ OAK GLEN COURSE
Holes: 18. **Yards:** 6,597/5,549. **Par:** 72/72. **Course Rating:** 71.3/71.4. **Slope:** 122/124. **Green Fee:** $30/$40. **Cart Fee:** $20/cart. **Walking Policy:** Unrestricted walking. **Walkability:** 2. **Opened:** 1956. **Architect:** Ted Robinson/Dave Fleming. **Season:** Year-round. **To obtain tee times:** Weekday, 7 days prior; weekends, call prior Monday. **Miscellaneous:** Reduced fees (weekdays, twilight, juniors), discount packages, metal spikes, range (grass/mats), club rentals, lodging, credit cards (MC, V, AE).
Reader Comments: Beautiful course ... Best resort value in California, interesting course, not exceptional ... Out in the country, not too difficult course ... Very crowded course, slow ... Good fair course ... Good shape.

★★★★ WILLOW GLEN COURSE *Value*
Holes: 18. **Yards:** 6,605/5,585. **Par:** 72/72. **Course Rating:** 72.0/72.8. **Slope:** 124/122. **Green Fee:** $37/$45. **Cart Fee:** $22/cart. **Walking Policy:** Unrestricted walking. **Walkability:** 2. **Opened:** 1956. **Architect:** Ted Robinson/Dave Fleming. **Season:** Year-round. **To obtain tee times:** For weekdays call 7 days in advance, for weekends call prior Monday. **Miscellaneous:** Reduced fees (weekdays, low season, twilight, juniors), discount packages, metal spikes, range (grass/mats), club rentals, lodging, credit cards (MC, V, AE, D), beginner friendly.
Reader Comments: Great resort! Courteous people ... Several memorable holes, great resort value ... Nice layout, good condition ... Excellent golf resort, two full 18s, one executive course ... Willow is best course in county.
Special Notes: Formerly Singing Hills Country Club. Also has 18-hole par-54 Pine Glen Course. Non-metal spikes are recommended.

★★★ SKYLINKS GOLF COURSE
PM-4800 E. Wardlow Rd., Long Beach, 90808, Los Angeles County, (562)429-0030.
Holes: 18. **Yards:** 6,372/5,933. **Par:** 72/74. **Course Rating:** 70.5/73.5. **Slope:** 119/119. **Green Fee:** $15/$23. **Cart Fee:** $21/cart. **Walking Policy:** Unrestricted walking. **Walkability:** 1. **Opened:** 1956. **Architect:** William F. Bell. **Season:** Year-round. **To obtain tee times:** Call 3 days in advance. **Miscellaneous:** Reduced fees (twilight, seniors, juniors), metal spikes, range (grass/mats), club rentals, credit cards (MC, V, AE), beginner friendly (Smooth Swing Golf School and Short Game Academy).
Reader Comments: Good value for a city course, slow play ... Muny conditions, greens ... Wide fairways ... Good after-work course ... OK muny, good value.

★★½ SKYWEST GOLF COURSE
PM-1401 Golf Course Rd., Hayward, 94541, Alameda County, (510)278-6188, 22 miles SE of San Francisco.
Holes: 18. **Yards:** 6,930/6,171. **Par:** 72/73. **Course Rating:** 72.9/74.3. **Slope:** 121/123. **Green Fee:** $15/$31. **Cart Fee:** $12/person. **Walking Policy:** Unrestricted walking. **Walkability:** 1. **Opened:** 1965. **Architect:** Bob Baldock. **Season:** Year-round. **To obtain tee times:** Call 8 days

in advance beginning 9 p.m. **Miscellaneous:** Reduced fees (seniors, juniors), metal spikes, range (mats), club rentals, credit cards (MC, V).
Reader Comments: Fun to play ... Pricey for course condition, noisy near airport ... 7,000 yards from the tips makes this a tough course!.

★★★½ SOBOBA SPRINGS ROYAL VISTA GOLF COURSE
SP-1020 Soboba Rd., San Jacinto, 92583, Riverside County, (909)654-9354, 25 miles W of Palm Springs.
Holes: 18. **Yards:** 6,829/5,762. **Par:** 73/74. **Course Rating:** 73.5/73.2. **Slope:** 135/131. **Green Fee:** $25/$50. **Cart Fee:** Included in Green Fee. **Walking Policy:** Mandatory cart. **Walkability:** 1. **Opened:** 1967. **Architect:** Desmond Muirhead. **Season:** Year-round. **High:** Nov.-April. **To obtain tee times:** Call 7 days in advance. **Miscellaneous:** Reduced fees (weekdays, low season, resort guests, twilight, juniors), discount packages, range (grass), club rentals, lodging (15 rooms), credit cards (MC, V), beginner friendly (golf schools, junior programs).
Reader Comments: Trees, trees! ... Good course, large mature trees ... Tremendous course and cheap ... A hidden jewel. Tough back 9 ... Flat track but fun to play. Always a good outing ... Don't tell anyone about it; I keep going back for more ... Narrow, treelined fairways, true test of your skills ... Cottonwoods, sycamores, water. A fair challenge for the average golfer.

★★★★ SONOMA MISSION INN GOLF & COUNTRY CLUB
R-17700 Arnold Dr., Sonoma, 95476, Sonoma County, (707)996-0300, 45 miles N of San Francisco.
Holes: 18. **Yards:** 7,087/5,511. **Par:** 72/72. **Course Rating:** 74.1/71.8. **Slope:** 132/125. **Green Fee:** $40/$100. **Cart Fee:** Included in Green Fee. **Walking Policy:** Unrestricted walking. **Walkability:** 2. **Opened:** 1991. **Architect:** Robert Muir Graves. **Season:** Year-round. **High:** April-Oct. **To obtain tee times:** Call up to 14 days in advance. **Miscellaneous:** Reduced fees (weekdays, low season, twilight), discount packages, range (grass/mats), caddies, club rentals, lodging (250 rooms), credit cards (MC, V, AE).
Reader Comments: A gem, great old-style course ... Great views ... Extremely long for average golfer to the point of being unfair ... As tasteful as Sonoma chardonnay ... Valley oaks 100 years old ... Still a class act. 1930s class and style ... Beautiful hills in the distance ... Fairly flat course, walkable ... Great course if it is dry.

★★★½ SOULE PARK GOLF COURSE
PM-1033 E. Ojai Ave., Ojai, 93024, Ventura County, (805)646-5633, 16 miles NE of Ventura.
Holes: 18. **Yards:** 6,350/5,894. **Par:** 72/72. **Course Rating:** 70.1/73.2. **Slope:** 120/124. **Green Fee:** $22/$28. **Cart Fee:** $24/cart. **Walking Policy:** Unrestricted walking. **Walkability:** 3. **Opened:** 1962. **Architect:** William F. Bell. **Season:** Year-round. **To obtain tee times:** Call 7 days in advance starting at 7 a.m. **Miscellaneous:** Reduced fees (weekdays, twilight, seniors, juniors), metal spikes, range (grass), club rentals.
Reader Comments: Pretty place ... Very nice layout, good condition ... Nice course, well kept. Interesting holes ... 7th hole will kill you. What beauty really is ... Great muny course, great weather, great value ... Fun for all, great treat ... Nothing spectacular, but good ... Almost as beautiful as Ojai Valley Inn but more wide open.

★★★ SOUTHRIDGE GOLF CLUB
SP-9413 S. Butte Rd., Sutter, 95982, Sutter County, (530)755-4653, 8 miles NW of Yuba City.
Web: www.southridge.com.
Holes: 18. **Yards:** 7,047/5,541. **Par:** 72/72. **Course Rating:** 72.7/71.3. **Slope:** 130/122. **Green Fee:** $19/$29. **Cart Fee:** $10/person. **Walking Policy:** Walking at certain times. **Walkability:** 5. **Opened:** 1992. **Architect:** Cal Olson. **Season:** Year-round. **High:** March-June/Sept.-Nov. **To obtain tee times:** Call up to 7 days in advance. **Miscellaneous:** Reduced fees (weekdays, low season, twilight, seniors, juniors), discount packages, range (grass), club rentals, credit cards (MC, V, AE).
Reader Comments: Front 9 nondescript, back 9 wow ... Fun course ... Quirky layout but nice views ... Most improved course in Sacramento Valley ... 5 or 6 superb holes ... Nice layout ... Very challenging. Used all the clubs ... Nice clubhouse! ... Love the back 9, not always 100 percent in condition.

★★★ SPRING VALLEY GOLF CLUB
PM-3441 E. Calaveras Blvd., Milpitas, 95035, Santa Clara County, (408)262-1722.
Holes: 18. **Yards:** 6,100/5,613. **Par:** 70/73. **Course Rating:** 67.7/71.2. **Slope:** 110/120. **Green Fee:** $19/$42. **Cart Fee:** $24/cart. **Walking Policy:** Unrestricted walking. **Walkability:** 2. **Opened:** 1956. **Season:** Year-round. **High:** April-Sept. **Miscellaneous:** Metal spikes, range (mats), club rentals, credit cards (MC, V), beginner friendly.
Reader Comments: Nice course! ... Needs improvement ... Good bargain on greens fees, a fun course, easy to make tee times ... Too many beginners ... Great local course ... Improving ... No. 11 is a par 3 all over water.

CALIFORNIA

★★★★★ **SPYGLASS HILL GOLF COURSE** *Service, Condition*
R-Spyglass Hill Rd. & Stevenson Dr., Pebble Beach, 93953, Monterey County, (408)625-8563, (800)654-9300.
Holes: 18. **Yards:** 6,855/5,642. **Par:** 72/74. **Course Rating:** 75.3/73.7. **Slope:** 148/133. **Green Fee:** $195/$225. **Cart Fee:** $25/person. **Walking Policy:** Unrestricted walking. **Walkability:** 5. **Opened:** 1966. **Architect:** Robert Trent Jones. **Season:** Year-round. **High:** Aug.-Nov. **To obtain tee times:** Call reservations up to 18 months in advance if you're staying at resort or 30 days in advance if you are not. **Miscellaneous:** Reduced fees (resort guests, twilight), discount packages, metal spikes, range (grass/mats), caddies, club rentals, credit cards (MC, V, AE, D, Diners Club, JCB).
Notes: Ranked 30th in 1999-2000 America's 100 Greatest; 7th in 1999 Best in State; 3rd in 1996 America's Top 75 Upscale Courses. Hosts AT&T National Pro-Am.
Reader Comments: A dream course to play, very scenic, don't forget your camera and extra balls ... Great starting hole ... Great test; very, very pricey ... Pebble is heaven. Spyglass is St. Peter's Cathedral ... Tougher than Pebble, ouch ... No. 4 is the toughest approach in golf if pin is back left ... Great layout, pretty views, ocean and woods.

STEELE CANYON GOLF CLUB
SP-3199 Stonefield Dr., Jamul, 91935, San Diego County, (619)441-6900, 20 miles E of San Diego. **E-mail:** steeelecanyon@juno.com. **Web:** www.steeleecanyon.com.
Holes: 27. **Green Fee:** $60/$90. **Cart Fee:** Included in Green Fee. **Walking Policy:** Mandatory cart. **Walkability:** 3. **Opened:** 1991. **Architect:** Gary Player. **Season:** Year-round. **High:** Dec.-May. **To obtain tee times:** Call 7 days in advance.
★★★★ **CANYON/MEADOW**
Yards: 6,672/4,813. **Par:** 71/71. **Course Rating:** 72.2/67.9. **Slope:** 134/118. **Miscellaneous:** Reduced fees (twilight, seniors, juniors), range (grass/mats), club rentals, credit cards (MC, V, AE), beginner friendly (instructional programs).
★★★★ **CANYON/RANCH**
Yards: 6,741/4,655. **Par:** 71/71. **Course Rating:** 72.7/66.6. **Slope:** 135/112. **Miscellaneous:** Reduced fees (twilight, seniors, juniors), discount packages, metal spikes, range (grass/mats), club rentals, credit cards (MC, V, AE, D), beginner friendly (lessons).
★★★★ **RANCH/MEADOW**
Yards: 7,001/5,026. **Par:** 72/72. **Course Rating:** 74.0/69.5. **Slope:** 137/124. **Miscellaneous:** Reduced fees (twilight, seniors, juniors), range (grass/mats), credit cards (MC, V, AE, D), beginner friendly (lessons).
Reader Comments: Beautiful vistas ... Bit pricey, great layout ... Great canyon challenges ... Canyon/Ranch an 'A', Meadow a 'B' ... Canyon 9 outstanding! ... Great variety of terrain, fun to play ... You'll get high from all the elevated tee shots ... Each hole unique ... Best golf in San Diego area ... Women-friendly course.

★★★★½ **STEVINSON RANCH GOLF CLUB** *Value, Condition*
PU-2700 N. Van Clief Rd., Stevinson, 95374, Merced County, (209)668-8200, 9 miles S of Turlock. **E-mail:** www.stevinsonranch.com.
Holes: 18. **Yards:** 7,205/5,461. **Par:** 72/72. **Course Rating:** 74.3/71.9. **Slope:** 140/124. **Green Fee:** $35/$60. **Cart Fee:** $12/person. **Walking Policy:** Unrestricted walking. **Walkability:** 3. **Opened:** 1995. **Architect:** John Harbottle/George Kelley. **Season:** Year-round. **High:** Spring/Fall. **To obtain tee times:** Call 60 days in advance. **Miscellaneous:** Reduced fees (twilight), discount packages, range (grass), caddies, club rentals, lodging (20 rooms), credit cards (MC, V, AE).
Notes: Ranked 8th in 1996 Best New Upscale Courses.
Reader Comments: Great valley golf, exhausting ... Lots of rough, may lose many golf balls ... Great mix of holes ... Not hard from middle of fairway, impossible otherwise ... Remote and very windy ... Great variety in holes. Fun course to play ... Open, flat, marshy. Needs some trees ... Everything was superb ... Links-style, enjoyable.

★★★½ **STRAWBERRY FARMS GOLF CLUB** *Service*
PU-11 Strawberry Farms Rd., Irvine, 92612, (949)551-1811.
Holes: 18. **Yards:** 6,700/4,832. **Par:** 71/72. **Course Rating:** 72.7/68.7. **Slope:** 134/114. **Green Fee:** $85/$125. **Cart Fee:** Included in Green Fee. **Walking Policy:** Mandatory cart. **Walkability:** 2. **Opened:** 1997. **Architect:** Jim Lipe. **Season:** Year-round. **High:** April-Sept. **To obtain tee times:** By phone up to 30 days in advance. Credit card required. **Miscellaneous:** Reduced fees (weekdays, low season, twilight, seniors, juniors), club rentals, credit cards (MC, V, AE).
Reader Comments: Very nice, different holes ... Too much money for what you get! ... Needs maturing ... Lots of challenges, yet fair! Super new course! ... Built around a reservoir ... Narrow course ... Front 9 is plain, but back 9 is fun ... Spectacular and challenging finishing hole ... Another overpriced course in Orange County.

★★★ **SUMMIT POINTE GOLF CLUB**
PU-1500 Country Club Dr., Milpitas, 95035, Santa Clara County, (408)262-8813, (800)422-4653, 5 miles N of San Jose.

Holes: 18. **Yards:** 6,331/5,496. **Par:** 72/72. **Course Rating:** 70.9/70.6. **Slope:** 125/121. **Green Fee:** $10/$68. **Cart Fee:** $15/person. **Walking Policy:** Walking at certain times. **Walkability:** 5. **Opened:** 1968. **Architect:** Marvin Orgill. **Season:** Year-round. **High:** March-Oct. **To obtain tee times:** Call 7 days in advance or 60 days in advance with American Express Golf Card. **Miscellaneous:** Reduced fees (weekdays, twilight, seniors, juniors), discount packages, metal spikes, range (mats), club rentals, credit cards (MC, V, AE).
Reader Comments: Tough course, lots of hills and challenges ... Steep hills, good views of bay. Not demanding ... Difficult course ... Very tough greens ... A couple of holes are unfair.

★★★½ SUN CITY PALM DESERT GOLF CLUB
SP-38-180 Del Webb Blvd., Bermuda Dunes, 92211, Riverside County, (760)772-2200, 10 miles E of Palm Springs.
Holes: 18. **Yards:** 6,720/5,305. **Par:** 72/72. **Course Rating:** 72.3/71.5. **Slope:** 125/116. **Green Fee:** $30/$85. **Cart Fee:** Included in Green Fee. **Walking Policy:** Mandatory cart. **Walkability:** 3. **Opened:** 1992. **Architect:** Billy Casper/Greg Nash. **Season:** Year-round (closed Oct.). **High:** Sept.-May. **To obtain tee times:** Call 2 days in advance for weekdays or 7 days in advance for weekends. **Miscellaneous:** Reduced fees (weekdays, low season, twilight), metal spikes, range (grass), club rentals, lodging, credit cards (MC, V).
Reader Comments: Hot in summer, good course ... Typical desert course ... Can be very windy ... Beautiful scenery, very playable ... One of the best in Palm Springs area ... Wide open, some challenging holes.

★★★½ SUN LAKES COUNTRY CLUB
SP-850 S. Country Club Dr., Banning, 92220, Riverside County, (909)845-2135, 20 miles W of Palm Springs.
Holes: 18. **Yards:** 7,035/5,516. **Par:** 72/72. **Course Rating:** 74.3/72.7. **Slope:** 132/118. **Green Fee:** N/A/$50. **Cart Fee:** Included in Green Fee. **Walking Policy:** Mandatory cart. **Walkability:** 2. **Opened:** 1987. **Architect:** David Rainville. **Season:** Year-round. **High:** April-Oct. **To obtain tee times:** Call up to 4 days in advance. **Miscellaneous:** Reduced fees (twilight, juniors), metal spikes, range (grass/mats), credit cards (MC, V).
Reader Comments: Fairly flat, well maintained, nice course ... A good test, sandy for less than straight shooter ... Tough course, lots of bunkers, some water, nice greens.

★★½ SUNNYVALE GOLF COURSE
PM-605 Macara Lane, Sunnyvale, 94086, Santa Clara County, (408)738-3666, 5 miles N of San Jose.
Holes: 18. **Yards:** 6,249/5,305. **Par:** 70/71. **Course Rating:** 69.7/70.2. **Slope:** 119/120. **Green Fee:** $18/$32. **Cart Fee:** $23/cart. **Walking Policy:** Unrestricted walking. **Walkability:** 1. **Opened:** 1968. **Architect:** David W. Kent. **Season:** Year-round. **High:** March-Sept. **To obtain tee times:** Call 7 days in advance. **Miscellaneous:** Reduced fees (weekdays, twilight, seniors, juniors), metal spikes, club rentals, credit cards (MC, V).
Reader Comments: OK ... Pretty standard course ... Best flat track around, 8th has water everywhere ... Windy location ... A typical muny course ... Overplayed ... On the short side. No.s 7 and 8 is mini Amen Corner ... Noisy. Large planes landing ... Not very challenging.

SUNOL VALLEY GOLF COURSE
PU-6900 Mission Rd., Sunol, 94586, Alameda County, (925)862-2404, 5 miles N of Fremont.
Web: www.sunvalley.com.
★★★ CYPRESS COURSE
Holes: 18. **Yards:** 6,195/5,458. **Par:** 72/72. **Course Rating:** 69.8/70.1. **Slope:** 120/115. **Green Fee:** $14/$48. **Cart Fee:** $24/. **Cart Fee:** Included in Green Fee. **Walking Policy:** Walking at certain times. **Walkability:** 2. **Opened:** 1968. **Architect:** Clark Glasson. **Season:** Year-round. **High:** April-Sept. **To obtain tee times:** Call 7 days in advance. **Miscellaneous:** Reduced fees (twilight, juniors), metal spikes, club rentals, credit cards (MC, V).
Reader Comments: Front 9 is great ... Pretty course ... Difficult for high handicapper ... Poor winter conditions, slow ... Good snack bar ... Super layout ... Nice small greens ... Fun layout, you can spray the ball.
★★½ PALM COURSE
Holes: 18. **Yards:** 6,843/5,997. **Par:** 72/74. **Course Rating:** 72.4/74.4. **Slope:** 126/124. **Green Fee:** $14/$48. **Cart Fee:** $24/. **Cart Fee:** Included in Green Fee. **Walking Policy:** Walking at certain times. **Walkability:** 3. **Opened:** 1968. **Architect:** Clark Glasson. **Season:** Year-round. **High:** April-Sept. **To obtain tee times:** Call 7 days in advance. **Miscellaneous:** Reduced fees (twilight, juniors), metal spikes, range (grass/mats), club rentals, credit cards (MC, V).
Reader Comments: A real challenge on a windy afternoon ... Interesting course ... Easier course ... More interesting than Cypress Course ... Unfair slopes on greens. Overpriced.

★★ SWENSON PARK GOLF CLUB
PM-6803 Alexandria Place, Stockton, 95207, San Joaquin County, (209)937-7360, 6 miles N of Stockton.

Holes: 18. **Yards:** 6,485/6,266. **Par:** 72/74. **Course Rating:** 70.0/73.8. **Slope:** 110/117. **Green Fee:** $7/$16. **Cart Fee:** $20/cart. **Walking Policy:** Unrestricted walking. **Walkability:** 1. **Opened:** 1952. **Architect:** William P. Bell. **Season:** Year-round. **High:** April-Sept. **To obtain tee times:** Call 7 days in advance. **Miscellaneous:** Reduced fees (weekdays, low season, twilight, seniors, juniors), discount packages, metal spikes, range (grass/mats), club rentals, beginner friendly (9-hole par-3 course).
Special Notes: Also 9-hole par- 3 course.

★★½ SYCAMORE CANYON GOLF CLUB
PU-500 Kenmar Lane, Arvin, 93203, Kern County, (661)854-3163, 25 miles SE of Bakersfield.
Holes: 18. **Yards:** 7,100/5,744. **Par:** 72/73. **Course Rating:** 72.8/71.6. **Slope:** 125/120. **Green Fee:** $10/$13. **Cart Fee:** $8/. **Walking Policy:** Unrestricted walking. **Walkability:** N/A. **Opened:** 1989. **Architect:** Bob Putman. **Season:** Year-round. **High:** Feb.-Oct. **To obtain tee times:** Call 7 days in advance. **Miscellaneous:** Reduced fees (weekdays, twilight, seniors, juniors), metal spikes, range (grass), club rentals, credit cards (MC, V).
Reader Comments: Great value and layout, fair condition ... Flat and long. Some tough water holes ... Solid test of golf.

★★½ TABLE MOUNTAIN GOLF COURSE
PU-2700 Oro Dam Blvd. W., Oroville, 95965, Butte County, (916)533-3922, 70 miles N of Sacramento.
Holes: 18. **Yards:** 6,500/5,000. **Par:** 72/68. **Course Rating:** 69.8/66.5. **Slope:** 116/104. **Green Fee:** $16/$20. **Cart Fee:** $18/cart. **Walking Policy:** Unrestricted walking. **Walkability:** 2. **Opened:** 1956. **Architect:** Louis Bertolone. **Season:** Year-round. **High:** May-Sept. **To obtain tee times:** Call 7 days in advance. **Miscellaneous:** Reduced fees (weekdays, twilight, seniors, juniors), discount packages, metal spikes, range (grass/mats), club rentals, credit cards (MC, V), beginner friendly (beginner group lessons, intro to golf course classes).
Reader Comments: Economical ... Good summertime play ... Great people. Good value ... Flat, best greens in my area.

★★★★ TAHOE DONNER GOLF CLUB
SP-12850 Northwoods Blvd., Truckee, 96161, Nevada County, (916)587-9440, 40 miles of Reno.
Holes: 18. **Yards:** 6,952/6,487. **Par:** 72/74. **Course Rating:** 72.4/73.1. **Slope:** 130/138. **Green Fee:** $46/$100. **Cart Fee:** $15/person. **Walking Policy:** Unrestricted walking. **Walkability:** 3. **Opened:** 1975. **Architect:** Joseph B. Williams. **Season:** May-Oct. **High:** July-Aug. **To obtain tee times:** Call 10 days in advance beginning 8:30 a.m. **Miscellaneous:** Reduced fees (low season, twilight), metal spikes, range (grass/mats), club rentals, credit cards (MC, V).
Reader Comments: Best course in Tahoe area (sorry Edgewood) ... Gorgeous! ... A course that you could play every day! ... Mountain course, tough, good test ... Wish it were more affordable ... Great setting ... Typical course in the mountains, trees everywhere ... Narrow treelined course, fall is perfect time to play ... Too slow.

TAHQUITZ CREEK RESORT
PU-1885 Golf Club Dr., Palm Springs, 92264, Riverside County, (760)328-1005, (800)743-2211.
★★★½ LEGEND COURSE
Holes: 18. **Yards:** 6,660/6,077. **Par:** 72/72. **Course Rating:** 71.0/74.0. **Slope:** 117/120. **Green Fee:** $18/$60. **Cart Fee:** $10/person. **Walking Policy:** Walking at certain times. **Walkability:** 2. **Opened:** 1960. **Architect:** William F. Bell. **Season:** Year-round. **High:** Nov.-May. **To obtain tee times:** Call up to 30 days in advance. **Miscellaneous:** Reduced fees (weekdays, low season, resort guests, twilight, seniors, juniors), discount packages, metal spikes, range (grass), club rentals, credit cards (MC, V, AE), beginner friendly (clinics p.m. times).
Reader Comments: Great value in summer ... A fun course to play. Staff were very nice and made me feel welcome ... Neat older course ... Beautiful holes ... My favorite in Palm Springs ... Like a lot of legends it is showing its age ... Great fun for all golfers, good and bad ... Lots of houses but pretty good value for Palm Springs.
★★★★ RESORT COURSE
Holes: 18. **Yards:** 6,705/5,206. **Par:** 72/72. **Course Rating:** 71.4/70.0. **Slope:** 120/119. **Green Fee:** $25/$90. **Cart Fee:** Included in Green Fee. **Walking Policy:** Mandatory cart. **Walkability:** 3. **Opened:** 1995. **Architect:** Ted Robinson. **Season:** Year-round. **High:** Nov.-May. **To obtain tee times:** Call up to 30 days in advance. **Miscellaneous:** Reduced fees (weekdays, low season, resort guests, twilight, seniors, juniors), discount packages, metal spikes, range (grass), club rentals, credit cards (MC, V, AE).
Reader Comments: Excellent, the best in the desert ... Fun course, pretty and long, par-3 No. 8 over water ... One of the best public desert courses ... Bring your camera, water, palms and cactus. Breathtaking ... Island fairway, very enjoyable golf course, great par 3s ... Tough when the wind blows off the desert.

TEMECULA CREEK INN
R-44501 Rainbow Canyon Rd., Temecula, 92592, Riverside County, (909)676-2405, (800)962-7335, 50 miles NE of San Diego.

Holes: 27. **Cart Fee:** Included in Green Fee. **Walking Policy:** Walking at certain times. **Opened:** 1970 **Season:** Year-round. **High:** Nov.-April. **To obtain tee times:** Call up to 7 days in advance. **Miscellaneous:** Reduced fees (weekdays, low season, resort guests, twilight, juniors), discount packages, metal spikes, range (grass/mats), club rentals, lodging (80 rooms), credit cards (MC, V, AE, D).

★★★★   **CREEK/OAKS**
Yards: 6,784/5,737. **Par:** 72/72. **Course Rating:** 72.6/72.8. **Slope:** 126/123. **Green Fee:** $50/$80. **Walkability:** 2. . **Architect:** Dick Rossen.

★★★★   **CREEK/STONEHOUSE**
Yards: 6,605/5,686. **Par:** 72/72. **Course Rating:** 71.4/71.9. **Slope:** 129/120. **Green Fee:** $50/$80. **Walkability:** 3. **Architect:** Dick Rossen/Ted Robinson.

★★★★   **OAKS/STONEHOUSE**
Yards: 6,693/5,683. **Par:** 72/72. **Course Rating:** 72.2/72.4. **Slope:** 128/125. **Green Fee:** $20/$75. **Walkability:** 5. **Architect:** Dick Rossen/Ted Robinson.

Reader Comments: World class, great greens ... Love the big trees, playable ... Resort layout with good setting ... Three great 9s, outstanding food ... Stay and play deal well worth it ... Not very memorable, can score here ... Outstanding 27 holes ... Very nice old course ... OK, not great.

★★★½   **TEMEKU HILLS GOLF & COUNTRY CLUB**
PU-41687 Temeku Dr., Temecula, 92591, Riverside County, (909)693-1440, (800)839-9949, 65 miles N of San Diego.
Holes: 18. **Yards:** 6,522/5,139. **Par:** 72/72. **Course Rating:** 70.3/70.5. **Slope:** 118/123. **Green Fee:** $40/$65. **Cart Fee:** Included in Green Fee. **Walking Policy:** Mandatory cart. **Walkability:** 4. **Opened:** 1995. **Architect:** Ted Robinson. **Season:** Year-round. **High:** Oct.-April. **To obtain tee times:** Call 7 days in advance starting at 6 a.m. **Miscellaneous:** Reduced fees (twilight), range (grass/mats), club rentals, credit cards (MC, V, AE, D).
Reader Comments: Fun course, hit it straight ... Good condition, great clubhouse, a couple of rinky-dink greens ... Love this place ... Great course ... Fun to play ... New course, will be better as it ages ... Fun to play for mid to high handicapper ... Beautiful course ... Great layout. Always well kept.

★★½   **TIERRA DEL SOL GOLF CLUB**
10300 N. Loop Dr., California City, 93505, Kern County, (619)373-2384, (888)465-3837.
Holes: 18. **Yards:** 6,908/5,225. **Par:** 72/72. **Course Rating:** 74.1/68.6. **Slope:** 130/122. **Green Fee:** $14/$18. **Cart Fee:** $20/cart. **Walking Policy:** Unrestricted walking. **Walkability:** 1. **Opened:** 1977. **Architect:** Robert van Hagge/Bruce Devlin. **Season:** Year-round. **To obtain tee times:** You can call up to 2 weeks in advance up until the day you want to play. **Miscellaneous:** Metal spikes, range (grass), club rentals, credit cards (MC, V).
Reader Comments: Inexpensive to play ... Can be windy, great price, good workout ... Considering location, course is on par.

★★★★   **TIJERAS CREEK GOLF CLUB**
PU-29082 Tijeras Creek Rd., Rancho Santa Margarita, 92688, Orange County, (949)589-9793, 50 miles S of Los Angeles. **Web:** www.tijerascreek.com.
Holes: 18. **Yards:** 6,613/5,130. **Par:** 72/72. **Course Rating:** 71.7/69.8. **Slope:** 126/120. **Green Fee:** $75/$110. **Cart Fee:** Included in Green Fee. **Walking Policy:** Mandatory cart. **Walkability:** 5. **Opened:** 1990. **Architect:** Ted Robinson. **Season:** Year-round. **To obtain tee times:** Call 7 days in advance. **Miscellaneous:** Reduced fees (twilight, seniors, juniors), metal spikes, range (grass/mats), club rentals, credit cards (MC, V, AE, Diners Club), beginner friendly (Tijeras Creek Golf School, new golfer group lessons).
Reader Comments: Very challenging ... Enjoyable to play. Nice setting ... Great L.A. golf course ... Back 9 good test from tips ... Great back 9, scenic ... A complete course, it's got it all! ... Superb layout, fun, adventure, highs and lows ... Two completely different 9s: condos on the front, nature walk on the back ... Par 3s are gems.

★★★   **TILDEN PARK GOLF COURSE**
PM-Grizzley Peak and Shasta Rd., Berkeley, 94708, Alameda County, (510)848-7373, 10 miles E of San Francisco.
Holes: 18. **Yards:** 6,300/5,400. **Par:** 70/71. **Course Rating:** 69.9/69.2. **Slope:** 120/116. **Green Fee:** $18/$35. **Cart Fee:** $12/person. **Walking Policy:** Unrestricted walking. **Walkability:** 4. **Opened:** 1936. **Architect:** William P. Bell. **Season:** Year-round. **High:** April-Oct. **To obtain tee times:** Call 7 days in advance. **Miscellaneous:** Reduced fees (weekdays, twilight, seniors, juniors), discount packages, metal spikes, range (mats), club rentals, credit cards (MC, V, AE).
Reader Comments: Nice, but not great ... Classic parkland course, spoiled by overcrowding ... Beautiful treelined layout ... Awesome landscape, hard but worth it ... Toughest starting holes anywhere ... A real good muny ... Hilly course, nice views, small greens ... Hidden gem of Bay Area ... Great closing holes ... Wet in winter.

CALIFORNIA

★★ TONY LEMA GOLF COURSE
PU-13800 Neptune Dr., San Leandro, 94577, Alameda County, (510)895-2162, 5 miles S of Oakland.
Holes: 18. **Yards:** 6,660/5,718. **Par:** 72/72. **Course Rating:** 72.0/67.6. **Slope:** 117/109. **Green Fee:** $12/$20. **Cart Fee:** $24/cart. **Walking Policy:** Unrestricted walking. **Walkability:** 1. **Architect:** William F. Bell. **Season:** Year-round. **High:** May-Nov. **To obtain tee times:** Call up to 7 days in advance starting at 6 a.m. **Miscellaneous:** Reduced fees (twilight, seniors, juniors), metal spikes, range (grass), club rentals, lodging (100 rooms), credit cards (MC, V, AE, D), beginner friendly (american golf learning center).
Special Notes: Course closed until 2001.

TORREY PINES GOLF COURSE
★★★★ NORTH COURSE
PU-11480 N. Torrey Pines Rd., La Jolla, 92037, San Diego County, (619)452-3226, (800)985-4653, 3 miles N of La Jolla.
Holes: 18. **Yards:** 6,647/6,118. **Par:** 72/74. **Course Rating:** 72.1/75.4. **Slope:** 129/134. **Green Fee:** $55/$125. **Cart Fee:** $28/cart. **Walking Policy:** Unrestricted walking. **Walkability:** 2. **Opened:** 1957. **Architect:** William F. Bell. **Season:** Year-round. **To obtain tee times:** You may call 4-8 weeks in advance. **Miscellaneous:** Reduced fees (twilight), metal spikes, range (grass/mats), club rentals, lodging, credit cards (MC, V, AE).
Notes: PGA Tour Buick Invitational (annually); Junior World Championship (annually).
Reader Comments: Nice but be ready for the wind ... Little brother just as good as big brother! ... Outstanding location. Very difficult to get on. Good walking ... A little uninteresting, long, wide open fairways ... Overrated ... Everyone wants to play the South because it's on TV, but the North has more character.

★★★★ SOUTH COURSE
PM-11480 N. Torrey Pines Rd., La Jolla, 92037, San Diego County, (619)452-3226, (800)985-4653, 3 miles N of La Jolla.
Holes: 18. **Yards:** 7,055/6,457. **Par:** 72/76. **Course Rating:** 74.6/77.3. **Slope:** 136/139. **Green Fee:** $55/$125. **Cart Fee:** $28/cart. **Walking Policy:** Unrestricted walking. **Walkability:** 2. **Opened:** 1957. **Architect:** William Bell. **Season:** Year-round. **To obtain tee times:** Call 4-8 weeks in advance. **Miscellaneous:** Reduced fees (twilight), metal spikes, range (grass/mats), club rentals, lodging, credit cards (MC, V, AE).
Notes: Ranked 30th in 1999 Best in State; 58th in 1996 America's Top 75 Upscale Courses. PGA Tour Buick Invitational (annually); Junior World Championship (annually).
Reader Comments: Great old course. Tough but fun ... Hard to get on, but a great course ... Exciting because of the ocean and the history ... Memorable from beginning to end ... Nice scenic layout ... Disappointed ... Playing right off the ocean ... Deep rough ... Fair, no tricks ... Overplayed, too busy.

★★½ TRACY GOLF & COUNTRY CLUB
35200 S. Chrisman Rd., Tracy, 95376, San Joaquin County, (209)835-9463.
Special Notes: Call club foe further information.
Reader Comments: Greens are nice, rest of the course needs work ... Can be very windy in the afternoon ... Tougher than it looks ... Very flat, so fire away.

★★★★ TUSTIN RANCH GOLF CLUB
PU-12442 Tustin Ranch Rd., Tustin, 92780, Orange County, (714)730-1611, 10 miles S of Anaheim. **E-mail:** tustinranch@crowngolf.com. **Web:** www.tustinranchgolf.com.
Holes: 18. **Yards:** 6,803/5,263. **Par:** 72/72. **Course Rating:** 72.4/70.3. **Slope:** 129/118. **Green Fee:** $85/$125. **Cart Fee:** Included in Green Fee. **Walking Policy:** Unrestricted walking. **Walkability:** 2. **Opened:** 1989. **Architect:** Ted Robinson. **Season:** Year-round. **High:** June-Oct. **To obtain tee times:** Call 7 days in advance. **Miscellaneous:** Reduced fees (twilight, seniors, juniors), range (grass/mats), caddies, club rentals, credit cards (MC, V, AE, Diners Club).
Reader Comments: Nice track, overpriced ... Great finishing hole ... Surprisingly interesting ... One of the best in the area ... Picture perfect with water on many holes ... Tough par 3s ... Easy, enjoyable ... Some good holes, too slow ... One of the best in Southern California.

★★★★ TWELVE BRIDGES GOLF CLUB
PU-3070 Twelve Bridges Dr., Lincoln, 95648, Placer County, (916)645-7200, (888)893-5832, 25 miles E of Sacramento. **Web:** www.twelvebridges.com.
Holes: 18. **Yards:** 7,150/5,310. **Par:** 72/72. **Course Rating:** 74.6/71.0. **Slope:** 139/123. **Green Fee:** $30/$60. **Cart Fee:** $15/person. **Walking Policy:** Unrestricted walking. **Walkability:** 4. **Opened:** 1996. **Architect:** Dick Phelps. **Season:** Year-round. **High:** March-Nov. **To obtain tee times:** Call 14 days in advance. 7 days advance w/golf shop 8-59 advance w/tee time central (888)236-8725. **Miscellaneous:** Range (grass), club rentals, credit cards (MC, V, AE), beginner friendly (numerous golf schools workshops and camps).
Notes: Ranked 10th in 1996 Best New Upscale Courses; 1996 Twelve Bridges LPGA Classic; 1996, 1997 AJGA 1998 & 99. 1997, 1998 & 1999 Longs Drugs Challenge.

CALIFORNIA

Reader Comments: Stunning, serene; tough but fair golf ... Best golf course in Sacramento area ... Great variety in beautiful natural setting ... Wonderful escape, tough but fair ... Beautiful clubhouse ... Challenging, lots of 3 putts possible here ... No. 10 is a killer ... Beautiful course, fun holes ... Watch out for well-placed oak trees.

★★★ TWIN OAKS GOLF COURSE
PU-1425 N. Twin Oaks Valley Rd., San Marcos, 92069, San Diego County, (760)591-4653, 3 miles W of Escondido.
Holes: 18. **Yards:** 6,535/5,423. **Par:** 72/72. **Course Rating:** 71.2/71.6. **Slope:** 124/120. **Green Fee:** $29/$67. **Cart Fee:** Included in Green Fee. **Walking Policy:** Mandatory cart. **Walkability:** 3. **Opened:** 1993. **Architect:** Ted Robinson. **Season:** Year-round. **High:** Dec.-April. **To obtain tee times:** Call up to 7 days in advance. **Miscellaneous:** Reduced fees (weekdays, low season, twilight, seniors, juniors), discount packages, range (grass/mats), club rentals, credit cards (MC, V, AE, D, Diners Club).
Reader Comments: Not a course for slicers, excellent greens ... Will be great in 10 years ... Do not allow walkers, the only drawback ... First four holes are tight and tough.

★★½ UPLAND HILLS COUNTRY CLUB
SP-1231 E. 16th St., Upland, 91786, San Bernardino County, (909)946-4711, 20 miles NE of Los Angeles.
Holes: 18. **Yards:** 5,827/4,813. **Par:** 70/70. **Course Rating:** 67.1/66.5. **Slope:** 111/106. **Green Fee:** $17/$31. **Cart Fee:** $11/person. **Walking Policy:** Walking at certain times. **Walkability:** N/A. **Opened:** 1983. **Architect:** Harry Rainville. **Season:** Year-round. **To obtain tee times:** Call 7 days in advance. **Miscellaneous:** Metal spikes, club rentals, credit cards (MC, V, AE, D).

★ VALLE GRANDE GOLF COURSE
PU-1119 Watts Dr., Bakersfield, 93307, Kern County, (661)832-2259, 7 miles E of Bakersfield.
Holes: 18. **Yards:** 6,240/5,531. **Par:** 72/72. **Course Rating:** 69.8/68.9. **Slope:** 116/114. **Green Fee:** $12/$15. **Cart Fee:** $18/cart. **Walking Policy:** Unrestricted walking. **Walkability:** 1. **Opened:** 1952. **Architect:** William P. Bell. **Season:** Year-round. **To obtain tee times:** Call 7 days in advance. **Miscellaneous:** Reduced fees (twilight, seniors, juniors), range (grass/mats), credit cards (MC, V).

VAN BUREN GOLF CENTER
PU-6720 Van Buren Blvd., Riverside, 92503, Riverside County, (909)688-2563. **E-mail:** vbsales@earthlink.net. **Web:** www.vanburengolf.com.
Holes: 18. **Yards:** 2,700/2,109. **Par:** 57/57. **Course Rating:** N/A. **Slope:** N/A. **Green Fee:** $12/$17. **Cart Fee:** $5/person. **Walking Policy:** Unrestricted walking. **Walkability:** 3. **Opened:** 1997. **Architect:** Murray Nonhoff. **Season:** Year-round. **High:** April-July. **To obtain tee times:** Call or e-mail tee times to numbers provided or fax. **Miscellaneous:** Range (grass/mats), club rentals, credit cards (MC, V, AE, D), beginner friendly (beginner group lessons).

★★½ VAN BUSKIRK PARK GOLF COURSE
PU-1740 Houston Ave., Stockton, 95206, San Joaquin County, (209)937-7357, 3 miles S of Stockton.
Holes: 18. **Yards:** 6,928/5,927. **Par:** 72/74. **Course Rating:** 72.2/72.2. **Slope:** 118/113. **Green Fee:** $7/$16. **Cart Fee:** $20/cart. **Walking Policy:** Unrestricted walking. **Walkability:** 1. **Opened:** 1961. **Architect:** Larry Norstrom. **Season:** Year-round. **To obtain tee times:** Call Monday for upcoming weekend. **Miscellaneous:** Reduced fees (twilight, seniors, juniors), metal spikes, range (grass/mats), club rentals.
Reader Comments: Nice clubhouse; course overplayed ... Course is OK ... Best public in Stockton. Easy to get on.

★½ VICTORIA GOLF COURSE
PU-340 E 192nd St., Carson, 90746, Los Angeles County, (310)323-6981, 10 miles S of Los Angeles.
Holes: 18. **Yards:** 6,787/6,098. **Par:** 72/74. **Course Rating:** 70.7/73.0. **Slope:** 109/106. **Green Fee:** $10/$25. **Cart Fee:** $11/person. **Walking Policy:** Unrestricted walking. **Walkability:** 2. **Opened:** 1966. **Season:** Year-round. **High:** May-Sept. **To obtain tee times:** Call up to 7 days in advance. **Miscellaneous:** Reduced fees (weekdays, twilight, seniors, juniors), metal spikes, range (grass/mats), club rentals, credit cards (MC, V, AE).

★★★½ THE VINEYARD AT ESCONDIDO
PM-925 San Pasqual Rd., Escondido, 92025, San Diego County, (760)735-9545, 15 miles N of San Diego.
Holes: 18. **Yards:** 6,531/5,073. **Par:** 70/70. **Course Rating:** 70.3/70.3. **Slope:** 125/117. **Green Fee:** $30/$60. **Cart Fee:** $12/person. **Walking Policy:** Walking at certain times. **Walkability:** 3. **Opened:** 1993. **Architect:** David Rainville. **Season:** Year-round. **To obtain tee times:** Call 7 days in advance. **Miscellaneous:** Reduced fees (weekdays, low season, twilight, seniors, juniors), club rentals, credit cards (MC, V, AE).
Notes: Hosted Senior PGA Q-School last 3 years.

CALIFORNIA

Reader Comments: City course with numerous hackers ... Another pretty place ... A tough course, fun ... Good variety of holes ... Two completely different 9s ... Good greens and lovely views on back 9 ... Tough back 9 especially Nos.10 and 11 ... Smooth, fast greens ... Average.

★★★   WASCO VALLEY ROSE GOLF COURSE
PU-301 N. Leonard Ave., Wasco, 93280, Kern County, (661)758-8301, 19 miles N of Bakersfield. **E-mail:** wbr@aol.com.
Holes: 18. **Yards:** 6,862/5,356. **Par:** 72/72. **Course Rating:** 72.5/70.5. **Slope:** 121/119. **Green Fee:** $8/$14. **Cart Fee:** $18/cart. **Walking Policy:** Unrestricted walking. **Walkability:** 1. **Opened:** 1991. **Architect:** Bob Putman. **Season:** Year-round. **High:** April-June/Oct. **To obtain tee times:** Call 7 days in advance. **Miscellaneous:** Reduced fees (weekdays, low season, twilight, seniors, juniors), range (grass), club rentals, credit cards (MC, V, AE).
Reader Comments: Great greens ... Good challenging course ... Big and open, mostly easy, variety nice ... Great value, best county course.

★★★½   WELK RESORT CENTER
R-8860 Lawrence Welk Dr., Escondido, 92026, San Diego County, (760)749-3225, (800)932-9355, 35 miles N of San Diego.
Holes: 18. **Yards:** 4,002/3,099. **Par:** 62/62. **Course Rating:** 59.1/57.7. **Slope:** 99/90. **Green Fee:** $12/$40. **Cart Fee:** $11/person. **Walking Policy:** Walking at certain times. **Walkability:** 4. **Opened:** 1964. **Architect:** David Rainville. **Season:** Year-round. **High:** Jan.-April. **To obtain tee times:** Call golf shop. Resort guests 2 weeks prior, public one week prior. **Miscellaneous:** Reduced fees (low season, resort guests, twilight, juniors), discount packages, club rentals, lodging (186 rooms), credit cards (MC, V, AE, D), beginner friendly.
Reader Comments: Executive course that you'll play all day and every day ... Best executive course I've seen. Bring every club! ... First class ... Way overpriced for executive course ... Watch out for boulders ... A small gem in the foothills, panoramic, a good couples course.

★★★★½   THE WESTIN MISSION HILLS RESORT
R-70-705 Ramon Rd., Rancho Mirage, 92270, Riverside County, (760)770-9496, (800)358-2211, 5 miles E of Palm Springs. **Web:** www.troongolf.com.
MISSION HILLS NORTH *Pace*
Holes: 18. **Yards:** 7,062/4,907. **Par:** 72/72. **Course Rating:** 73.9/68.0. **Slope:** 134/118. **Green Fee:** $55/$175. **Cart Fee:** Included in Green Fee. **Walking Policy:** Mandatory cart. **Walkability:** 2. **Opened:** 1991. **Architect:** Gary Player. **Season:** Year-round. **High:** Oct.-April. **To obtain tee times:** Public may call within 30 days. If staying at the Westin Mission Hills Resort Hotel, you may book tee times within 90 days. **Miscellaneous:** Reduced fees (weekdays, low season, resort guests, twilight), discount packages, metal spikes, range (grass), club rentals, lodging, credit cards (MC, V, AE, D).
Reader Comments: One of the best in the desert ... Incredible course, fast greens ... Too speedy for me ... Great layout, pace is lightning ... Great course, must play ... Good layout, helpful employees, enjoyed ... OK ... Expensive in winter, good value in summer ... Well worth the visit ... Awesome mountain views ... Very pleasant.

★★★★   PETE DYE GOLF COURSE   *Pace*
R-71-501 Dinah Shore Dr., Rancho Mirage, 92270, Riverside County, (760)328-3198, (800)358-2211, 10 miles E of Palm Springs.
Holes: 18. **Yards:** 6,706/4,841. **Par:** 70/70. **Course Rating:** 73.5/67.4. **Slope:** 137/107. **Green Fee:** $55/$175. **Cart Fee:** Included in Green Fee. **Walking Policy:** Mandatory cart. **Walkability:** N/A. **Opened:** 1987. **Architect:** Pete Dye. **Season:** Year-round. **High:** Oct.-April. **To obtain tee times:** Call 30 days in advance for outside play and 90 days in advance for hotel guests.
Miscellaneous: Reduced fees (low season, resort guests, twilight), discount packages, metal spikes, range (grass), club rentals, lodging (500 rooms), credit cards (MC, V, AE, D).
Reader Comments: Tough course, deep rough ... Very overrated ... Beautiful landscaping ... From the back tees it makes you work ... Diabolical Dr. Dye course! ... Fun challenging, pretty layout ... Play slow, but beautiful course ... Another great course in the desert ... Fun golf course, not severe ... Lots of water lot of fun.

★★   WHISPERING LAKES GOLF COURSE
PM-2525 Riverside Dr, Ontario, 91761, San Bernardino County, (909)923-3673, 15 miles W of San Bernardino.
Holes: 18. **Yards:** 6,700/6,000. **Par:** 72/74. **Course Rating:** 71.4/72.8. **Slope:** 122/117. **Green Fee:** $19/$23. **Cart Fee:** $22/cart. **Walking Policy:** Unrestricted walking. **Walkability:** 2. **Opened:** 1960. **Season:** Year-round. **To obtain tee times:** Call 7 days in advance for weekdays. Call Monday for upcoming weekend. **Miscellaneous:** Reduced fees (twilight, seniors, juniors), metal spikes, range (grass), club rentals, credit cards (MC, V).

★★½   WHITTIER NARROWS GOLF COURSE
PU-8640 E. Rush St., Rosemead, 91770, Los Angeles County, (626)288-1044, 10 miles E of Downtown LA.

Holes: 27. **Yards:** 6,864/5,965. **Par:** 72/74. **Course Rating:** 72.3/73.6. **Slope:** 121/117. **Green Fee:** $20/$25. **Cart Fee:** $22/cart. **Walking Policy:** Unrestricted walking. **Walkability:** 3. **Opened:** 1954. **Architect:** William F. Bell. **Season:** Year-round. **High:** April-Aug. **To obtain tee times:** Call up to 7 days in advance. **Miscellaneous:** Reduced fees (twilight, seniors, juniors), metal spikes, range (grass/mats), club rentals, credit cards (MC, V, AE), beginner friendly (beginner lessons and golf package rental club program).
Reader Comments: Very hilly, good challenge, rough fairways ... Average muny course ... Good layout, hit it long ... Flat ... Inexpensive, crowded.

★★★½ WILDHAWK GOLF CLUB
PM-7713 Vineyard Rd., Sacramento, 95829, (916)688-4653. **Web:** www.woldhawkgolf.com.
Holes: 18. **Yards:** 6,695/4,847. **Par:** 72/72. **Course Rating:** 71.2/67.2. **Slope:** 124/109. **Green Fee:** $30/$43. **Cart Fee:** $6/person. **Walking Policy:** Unrestricted walking. **Walkability:** 3.
Opened: 1997. **Architect:** J. Michael Poellot with Mark Hollinger. **Season:** Year-round. **High:** March-Nov. **To obtain tee times:** 7 days in advance can pre-book for additional $10 Per Player. **Miscellaneous:** Range (grass/mats), club rentals, credit cards (MC, V, AE, Diners).
Notes: Pepsi Tour 1998 & 99.
Reader Comments: Fun, good scoring course ... Let her rip ... Immature, has real potential ... Awesome atmosphere in the woods. Nice layout ... Gem of a course ... Best new course locally. Trees will help.

★★★ WILLOW PARK GOLF CLUB
PU-17007 Redwood Rd., Castro Valley, 94546, Alameda County, (510)537-8989, 20 miles SE of Oakland.
Holes: 18. **Yards:** 5,700/5,193. **Par:** 71/71. **Course Rating:** 67.4/69.2. **Slope:** 110/117. **Green Fee:** $20/$27. **Cart Fee:** $20/person. **Walking Policy:** Unrestricted walking. **Walkability:** 2.
Opened: 1967. **Architect:** Bob Baldock. **Season:** Year-round. **High:** March-Oct. **To obtain tee times:** Call Monday for weekday at 7 a.m. and at 10 a.m. for weekend. **Miscellaneous:** Metal spikes, range (mats), credit cards (MC, V).
Reader Comments: Heavily played public, some very demanding holes ... Needs improvements ... Short, tight course ... Beautiful—deer and rabbits running around, pace is always slow, people are nice ... Great local hideout, picturesque park ... Tight layout ... Fun course, pretty setting.

★★★½ WINDSOR GOLF CLUB
PU-1340 19th Hole Drive, Windsor, 95492, Sonoma County, (707)838-7888, 6 miles N of Santa Rosa.
Holes: 18. **Yards:** 6,650/5,116. **Par:** 72/72. **Course Rating:** 71.7/69.3. **Slope:** 127/125. **Green Fee:** $24/$42. **Cart Fee:** $22/cart. **Walking Policy:** Unrestricted walking. **Walkability:** 2.
Opened: 1989. **Architect:** Fred Bliss. **Season:** Year-round. **To obtain tee times:** Call 7 days in advance at 6:30 a.m. **Miscellaneous:** Reduced fees (weekdays, twilight, seniors, juniors), range (grass), club rentals, credit cards (MC, V), beginner friendly (intro to golf clinics).
Reader Comments: Great public course in great surroundings ... Great value, OK layout ... Nice, challenging course ... Have to think on every hole ... Tiny clubhouse ... A shotmaker's gem ... Course is tougher than it looks! ... Short yardage but lots of trouble. Very pretty course.

★★★½ WOODCREEK GOLF CLUB
PM-5880 Woodcreek Oaks Blvd., Roseville, 95747, Placer County, (916)771-4653, 15 miles E of Sacramento.
Holes: 18. **Yards:** 6,518/4,739. **Par:** 72/70. **Course Rating:** 72.4/66.2. **Slope:** 128/112. **Green Fee:** $25/$31. **Cart Fee:** $12/person. **Walking Policy:** Mandatory cart. **Walkability:** 2. **Opened:** 1995. **Architect:** Robert Muir Graves. **Season:** Year-round. **To obtain tee times:** Call golf shop or automated service. **Miscellaneous:** Reduced fees (weekdays, twilight, seniors, juniors), metal spikes, range (grass/mats), club rentals, credit cards (MC, V, AE, D).
Reader Comments: A muny trying to be a country club ... Very nice ... Nice bar ... Fun course, some real tough holes ... Couple of Mickey Mouse holes ... Gets a lot of play, good layout.

★★★ WOODLEY LAKES GOLF CLUB
PM-6331 Woodley Ave., Van Nuys, 91406, Los Angeles County, (818)787-8163.
Special Notes: Call Club for further information.
Reader Comments: Wide open course ... OK local course ... Very forgiving; a real confidence builder ... Huge, true greens, wind makes course play long ... Great course for beginners ... One of the best for a city course ... . Excellent greens, thereafter it goes downhill fast.

COLORADO

★★★½ ADOBE CREEK NATIONAL GOLF COURSE
PU-876 18 1/2 Rd., Fruita, 81521, Mesa County, (970)858-0521, 9 miles W of Grand Junction. **Holes:** 18. **Yards:** 6,997/4,980. **Par:** 72/72. **Course Rating:** 71.2/55.1. **Slope:** 119/97. **Green Fee:** $16/$22. **Cart Fee:** $16/. **Walking Policy:** Unrestricted walking. **Walkability:** N/A. **Opened:** 1992. **Architect:** Ned Wilson. **Season:** May-Dec. **High:** May-Sep. **To obtain tee times:** Call 2 days in advance. **Miscellaneous:** Reduced fees (weekdays, low season, twilight, seniors, juniors), metal spikes, range (grass), club rentals.
Reader Comments: Nice setting. Very playable ... Good test ... Back tees can make a big difference ... More difficult in wind that often blows ... Great tee boxes ... Great staff Scenic beauty ... No noise, very quiet ... Home course, fun, long and open.

★★★½ APPLETREE GOLF COURSE
PU-10150 Rolling Ridge Rd., Colorado Springs, 80925, El Paso County, (719)382-3649, (800)844-6531, 8 miles S of Denver. **Web:** www.apple-tree.com.
Holes: 18. **Yards:** 6,407/5,003. **Par:** 72/72. **Course Rating:** 68.6/66.9. **Slope:** 122/113. **Green Fee:** $10/$20. **Cart Fee:** $20/cart. **Walking Policy:** Unrestricted walking. **Walkability:** 1. **Opened:** 1972. **Architect:** Lee Trevino/Dave Bennett. **Season:** Year-round. **High:** May-Sept. **To obtain tee times:** Call up to 7 days in advance. **Miscellaneous:** Reduced fees (weekdays, low season, seniors, juniors), range (grass), club rentals, credit cards (MC, V, AE).
Reader Comments: Lots of sand and water... Good mixture of easy playing holes and holes that have to be played smartly and accurately ... Friendly, staff in golf shop.

★★½ APPLEWOOD GOLF COURSE
PU-14001 W. 32nd Ave., Golden, 80401, Jefferson County, (303)279-3003, 13 miles W of Golden.
Holes: 18. **Yards:** 5,992/5,374. **Par:** 71/72. **Course Rating:** 68.2/69.0. **Slope:** 112/118. **Green Fee:** $20/$23. **Cart Fee:** $10/person. **Walking Policy:** Unrestricted walking. **Walkability:** 3. **Opened:** 1954. **Architect:** Press Maxwell. **Season:** Year-round. **High:** April-Oct. **To obtain tee times:** Call 6 days in advance. **Miscellaneous:** Reduced fees (weekdays, twilight, seniors, juniors), discount packages, range (grass/mats), club rentals, credit cards (MC, V, AE).
Reader Comments: Fun...Pretty layout. Next to Coors Beer tours...OK, but not the best in the area...Nos. 14-17 very good holes...Summer length rough can cause tough chips & lost balls...Some testy water hazards.

★★★½ ARROWHEAD GOLF CLUB
PU-10850 W. Sundown Trail, Littleton, 80125, Arapahoe County, (303)973-9614, 25 miles S of Denver.
Holes: 18. **Yards:** 6,682/5,465. **Par:** 70/72. **Course Rating:** 70.9/71.1. **Slope:** 134/127. **Green Fee:** $45/$110. **Cart Fee:** Included in Green Fee. **Walking Policy:** Mandatory cart. **Walkability:** 4. **Opened:** 1972. **Architect:** Robert Trent Jones Jr. **Season:** March-Nov. **High:** June-Sept. **To obtain tee times:** Call 7 days in advance with credit card 30 days for $10/player advanced reservation fee. **Miscellaneous:** Reduced fees (weekdays, low season, twilight, seniors), discount packages, metal spikes, range (grass/mats), club rentals, credit cards (MC, V, AE).
Reader Comments: Incredible golf experience ... Best around Denver... Snaking the course through radiant red rocks makes it memorable ... Facility great ... Rock formations are so spectacular who cares what you shoot ... Excellent course; altitude a factor... Putting greens ... Fun course, must see geography—worth the drive ... Service is very good ... Use all clubs in bag ... Walk on, they worked the two us right on ... Physical beauty, but testy.

★★★½ ASPEN GOLF COURSE
PU-408 E. Cooper, Aspen, 81612, Pitkin County, (970)925-2145.
Holes: 18. **Yards:** 7,165/5,591. **Par:** 71/72. **Course Rating:** 72.2/69.9. **Slope:** 125/116. **Green Fee:** $40/$70. **Cart Fee:** $14. **Walking Policy:** Unrestricted walking. **Walkability:** 2. **Opened:** 1962. **Architect:** Frank Hummel. **Season:** April-Oct. **High:** July-Sept. **To obtain tee times:** Call as far in advance as desired. **Miscellaneous:** Reduced fees (low season, seniors, juniors), metal spikes, range (grass), club rentals, credit cards (MC, V, AE), beginner friendly (clinics, playing lessons).
Reader Comments: Majestic view of Maroon Bell ... Good layout ... Fast greens ... Nice grass in high altitude ... WOW! ... Immaculate course, spectacular views ... Nice course, tough greens, thin air ... Beautiful setting.

★★★ AURORA HILLS GOLF COURSE
PU-50 S. Peoria St., Aurora, 80012, Arapahoe County, (303)364-6111, 10 miles E of Denver. **Web:** www.auroragolf.com.
Holes: 18. **Yards:** 6,735/5,919. **Par:** 72/73. **Course Rating:** 70.0/71.3. **Slope:** 115/109. **Green Fee:** $13/$20. **Cart Fee:** $20/cart. **Walking Policy:** Unrestricted walking. **Walkability:** 2. **Opened:** 1968. **Architect:** Dick Phelps. **Season:** Year-round. **High:** May-Sept. **To obtain tee times:** Call golf shop or tee times phone 4 days in advance. At 303-397-1818. **Miscellaneous:**

COLORADO

Reduced fees (twilight, seniors, juniors), metal spikes, range (grass/mats), club rentals, credit cards (MC, V, D).
Reader Comments: Greens in great shape ... Nice for quick 18! ... Very nice muny ... Fair, flat ... Long rough, plays harder than it looks ... Always in good shape.

★★★★ BATTLEMENT MESA GOLF CLUB *Value, Pace*
PU-3930 N. Battlement Pkwy., Battlement Mesa, 81635, Garfield County, (970)285-7274, (888)285-7274, 42 miles W of Glenwood Springs. **E-mail:** jgbmgc@aol.com.
Holes: 18. **Yards:** 7,309/5,386. **Par:** 72/72. **Course Rating:** 73.7/68.7. **Slope:** 135/116. **Green Fee:** $32/$32. **Cart Fee:** $14/person. **Walking Policy:** Unrestricted walking. **Walkability:** 4. **Opened:** 1987. **Architect:** Finger/Dye/Spann. **Season:** March-Nov. **High:** June-Aug. **To obtain tee times:** Call 3 days in advance or up to 1 year with lodging and golf package.
Miscellaneous: Reduced fees (low season, juniors), discount packages, range (grass), club rentals, lodging (80 rooms), credit cards (MC, V, AE, D).
Reader Comments: Real value .... Worth the drive ... Excellent views, very challenging ... High quality golf ... Play the right tees ... Outstanding value ... Back 9 overlooks Colorado River ... Top of mountain fun—can see for miles ... They treat you as a member ... Fair for ladies ... Wind huge factor .... Wonderful people!! Good golf!

★★★★ BEAVER CREEK GOLF CLUB
R-P.O. Box 915, Avon, 81620, Boulder County, (970)845-5775.
Holes: 18. **Yards:** 6,752/5,200. **Par:** 70/70. **Course Rating:** 69.6/70.3. **Slope:** 140/124. **Green Fee:** $75/$125. **Cart Fee:** Included in Green Fee. **Walking Policy:** Mandatory cart. **Walkability:** 5. **Opened:** 1982. **Architect:** Robert Trent Jones Jr. **Season:** May-Oct. **High:** June-Sept. **To obtain tee times:** Call. **Miscellaneous:** Reduced fees (low season, resort guests), discount packages, metal spikes, range (grass), club rentals, lodging, credit cards (MC, V, AE, D, Diners Club).
Reader Comments: Beauty, with narrow holes ... Gorgeous mountain setting ... First 3 holes great ... Play in fall foliage ... Excellent course to play ... Best of the Rockies courses ... Good combination of woods and opens spaces ... Challenge to stay out of creek ... More private than public.

★★★½ BOOMERANG LINKS
PU-7309 West 4th St., Greeley, 80634, Weld County, (970)351-8934, (970)351-8934, 40 miles N of Denver.
Holes: 18. **Yards:** 7,214/5,285. **Par:** 72/72. **Course Rating:** 72.6/68.5. **Slope:** 131/113. **Green Fee:** $15/$24. **Cart Fee:** $23/cart. **Walking Policy:** Unrestricted walking. **Walkability:** N/A. **Opened:** 1991. **Architect:** William Neff. **Season:** Year-round. **High:** June-Sept. **To obtain tee times:** Call Tuesday for the following 7 days. **Miscellaneous:** Reduced fees (weekdays, low season, twilight, seniors, juniors), range (grass), club rentals, credit cards (MC, V, D).
Reader Comments: Links course ... Hard from back tees ... Good layout ... Don't hit it right. Water on first four holes ... Demanding front 9, challenging back ....Fun course, if you can control your slice ... Tough par 3s .:. Good course, getting better... Fun, challenging, great value ... Plan your shots ... Good greens.

★★★★ BRECKENRIDGE GOLF CLUB
PU-200 Clubhouse Dr., Breckenridge, 80424, Summit County, (970)453-9104, 80 miles W of Denver.
Holes: 18. **Yards:** 7,276/5,063. **Par:** 72/72. **Course Rating:** 73.3/67.6. **Slope:** 149/129. **Green Fee:** $50/$83. **Cart Fee:** $12/person. **Walking Policy:** Walking at certain times. **Walkability:** 3. **Opened:** 1985. **Architect:** Jack Nicklaus. **Season:** May-Oct. **High:** June-Sept. **To obtain tee times:** Call 4 days in advance, or through participating hotels,lodges in Breckenridge.
Miscellaneous: Reduced fees (low season, twilight), discount packages, range (grass), club rentals, credit cards (MC, V, AE).
Notes: Ranked 13th in 1999 Best in State.
Reader Comments: Great course at a great price ... Watch out for the moose ... Best course in Colorado ... Golf at 9,000 feet ... Excellent design ... Great service ... Ball goes farther, but you still must keep it in play ... Maybe the best mountain course in U.S. ... Excellent condition ... Rocky Mountain high.

THE BROADMOOR GOLF CLUB *Service*
R-1 Pourtales Rd., Colorado Springs, 80906, El Paso County, (719)577-5790, (800)634-7711, 60 miles S of Denver. **Web:** www.broadmoor.com.
★★★★ EAST COURSE
Holes: 18. **Yards:** 7,091/5,847. **Par:** 72/72. **Course Rating:** 73.0/72.7. **Slope:** 129/139. **Green Fee:** $140/$140. **Cart Fee:** Included in Green Fee. **Walking Policy:** Walking at certain times. **Walkability:** 3. **Opened:** 1918. **Architect:** Donald Ross/Robert Trent Jones. **Season:** Year-round. **High:** April-Oct. **To obtain tee times:** Confirm reservations in hotel. Call golf shop.
Miscellaneous: Reduced fees (twilight), discount packages, range (grass), caddies, club rentals, lodging (700 rooms), credit cards (MC, V, AE, D, Diners Club).

COLORADO

Notes: Ranked 19th in 1999 Best in State; 1995 U.S. Women's Open. 1955 U.S. Amateur.
Reader Comments: Great golf, well kept ... Loved it! ... Innovative design ... Great mountain views ... Wonderful old course ... Long, wide fairways ... Fast greens ... Hard to beat ... Colorado golf at its best ... Love golf, spa and food! ... Great experience ... Music on green! ... The prettiest course in Colorado.

★★★★ MOUNTAIN COURSE
Holes: 18. **Yards:** 6,781/5,609. **Par:** 72/71. **Course Rating:** 72.1/71.5. **Slope:** 135/126. **Green Fee:** $110/$110. **Cart Fee:** Included in Green Fee. **Walking Policy:** Walking at certain times. **Walkability:** 5. **Opened:** 1976. **Architect:** Arnold Palmer/Ed Seay. **Season:** May-Oct. **High:** May-Oct. **To obtain tee times:** Confirm reservations in hotel. Call golf shop. **Miscellaneous:** Reduced fees (twilight), discount packages, range (grass), caddies, club rentals, lodging (700 rooms), credit cards (MC, V, AE, D, Diners Club).
Notes: 1982 U.S. Womens Amateur.
Reader Comments: Wonderful resort ... Excellent golf ... Splendid way to experience mountain golf... Target, scenic, mountain golf ... Challenging ... Difficult for a flatlander but beautiful ... Best of the Broadmoor.

★★★★ WEST COURSE *Pace*
Holes: 18. **Yards:** 6,937/5,375. **Par:** 72/73. **Course Rating:** 73.0/70.5. **Slope:** 133/127. **Green Fee:** $140/$140. **Cart Fee:** Included in Green Fee. **Walking Policy:** Walking at certain times. **Walkability:** 4. **Opened:** 1918. **Architect:** Donald Ross/Robert Trent Jones. **Season:** Year-round. **High:** April-Oct. **To obtain tee times:** Confirm reservations in hotel. Call golf shop. **Miscellaneous:** Reduced fees (twilight), discount packages, range (grass), caddies, club rentals, lodging (700 rooms), credit cards (MC, V, AE, D, Diners Club).
Notes: 1967 U.S. Amateur.
Reader Comments: Pamper yourself ... This must be heaven! ... Rocky Mountain high ... Great views ... Every golfer's dream ... Hey to be there now ... Great 'target' golf course ... Never the same lie ... Superb facilities, beautiful course.

★★★★ BUFFALO RUN GOLF COURSE
PU-15700 E. 112th Ave., Commerce City, 80022, (303)289-1500, 35 miles NW of Denver.
Holes: 18. **Yards:** 7,411/5,227. **Par:** 72/71. **Course Rating:** 73.5/68.1. **Slope:** 121/119. **Green Fee:** $19/$33. **Cart Fee:** $11/person. **Walking Policy:** Unrestricted walking. **Walkability:** 3. **Opened:** 1996. **Architect:** Keith Foster. **Season:** Year-round. **High:** May-Aug. **To obtain tee times:** Call 3 days in advance. **Miscellaneous:** Reduced fees (seniors, juniors), range (grass), caddies, club rentals, credit cards (MC, V, AE, D).
Notes: Ranked 6th in 1997 Best New Affordable Public Courses.
Reader Comments: Good fair layout ... Good strategic course ... Wide open spaces for full throttle drivers ... Big sky golf ... A nice mix of long and short 4 pars ... Best value ... Staff great ... Wind will blow here ... Will hit every club in bag ... Nice clubhouse and practice range ... Awesome golf course!

★★★½ CANTERBERRY GOLF COURSE
PU-11400 Canterberry Pkwy., Parker, 80134, Douglas County, (303)840-3100.
Holes: 18. **Yards:** 7,180/5,600. **Par:** 72/72. **Course Rating:** 73.0/63.9. **Slope:** 138/104. **Green Fee:** $14/$30. **Cart Fee:** $10/person. **Walking Policy:** Walking at certain times. **Walkability:** 3. **Opened:** 1996. **Architect:** Jeff Brauer. **Season:** Year-round. **High:** March-Oct. **To obtain tee times:** Call up to 3 days in advance after 8 a.m. **Miscellaneous:** Reduced fees (weekdays, low season, twilight, seniors, juniors), discount packages, metal spikes, range (grass), club rentals, credit cards (MC, V, AE).
Reader Comments: Hidden jewel, don't miss ... Good variety of holes ... Terrific layout ... Needs to mature ... Tough course but fair... Delightful layout ... One of Denver's best ... Too many long carries for gals ... Great par 3s.

★★½ CATTAILS GOLF CLUB
PU-6615 North River Rd., Alamosa, 81101, Alamosa County, (719)589-9515, (888)765-4653.
Web: www.alamosacolg.com.
Holes: 18. **Yards:** 6,527/5,107. **Par:** 71/72. **Course Rating:** 69.1/69.0. **Slope:** 123/116. **Green Fee:** $16/$30. **Cart Fee:** $18/cart. **Walking Policy:** Unrestricted walking. **Walkability:** 1. **Architect:** Dick Phelps. **Season:** March-Nov. **High:** June-Aug. **To obtain tee times:** Call golf shop. **Miscellaneous:** Reduced fees (low season, juniors), discount packages, range (grass/mats), club rentals, credit cards (MC, V, D).
Reader Comments: Two completely different 9s ... Leave driver in bag on back ... Lovely course, good greens ... One of the best small town courses ... Excellent condition ... Back 9 challenging and interesting.

★★★ CITY PARK GOLF CLUB
PU-2500 York, Denver, 80218, Denver County, (303)295-2095.
Holes: 18. **Yards:** 6,318/6,181. **Par:** 72/74. **Course Rating:** 68.0/74.1. **Slope:** 111/116. **Green Fee:** $19/$20. **Cart Fee:** $20/cart. **Walking Policy:** Unrestricted walking. **Walkability:** 3. **Opened:** 1913. **Architect:** Tom Bendelow. **Season:** Year-round. **High:** April-Sept. **To obtain tee**

COLORADO

times: Call starter house (303)295-4420. **Miscellaneous:** Range (mats), club rentals, credit cards (MC, V).

Reader Comments: Old course ... Beautiful views of Denver skyline and mountains ... Small greens ... Flat; few hazards; easy to walk ... Urban golf.

THE CLUB AT CORDILLERA
★★★½ **MOUNTAIN COURSE**
SP-655 Club House Dr., Edwards, 81632, Eagle County, (970)926-5100, 100 miles W of Denver.
Holes: 18. **Yards:** 7,444/5,665. **Par:** 72/72. **Course Rating:** 72.0/71.5. **Slope:** 145/138. **Green Fee:** $150/$195. **Cart Fee:** Included in Green Fee. **Walking Policy:** Mandatory cart.
Walkability: N/A. **Opened:** 1994. **Architect:** Hale Irwin/Dick Phelps. **Season:** High: May-Oct. **To obtain tee times:** Call 1 day in advance. **Miscellaneous:** Metal spikes, range (grass/mats), caddies, club rentals, lodging, credit cards (MC, V, AE).
Notes: Ranked 20th in 1999 Best in State.
Reader Comments: If you like views, this is great ... Outstanding scenery ... Beautiful golf holes ... Fast greens ... Bring local knowledge or rabbit's foot ... Always stop and play on the way to Utah.

VALLEY COURSE
SP-101 Legends Dr., Edwards, 81632, Eagle County, (970)926-5950, (800)877-3529, 100 miles W of Denver.
Holes: 18. **Yards:** 7,005/5,087. **Par:** 71/71. **Course Rating:** 71.9/68.1. **Slope:** 125/121. **Green Fee:** N/A. **Cart Fee:** Included in Green Fee. **Walking Policy:** Mandatory cart. **Walkability:** 4.
Opened: 1997. **Architect:** Tom Fazio/Dennis Wise. **Season:** May-Oct. **High:** June-Sept. **To obtain tee times:** Call 1 day in advance. **Miscellaneous:** Metal spikes, range (grass/mats), caddies, club rentals, lodging, credit cards (MC, V, AE).
Notes: Ranked 11th in 1999 Best in State.

★★★½ COAL CREEK GOLF COURSE
PU-585 W. Dillon Rd., Louisville, 80027, Boulder County, (303)666-7888, 4 miles E of Boulder.
Web: www.coalcreekgolf.com.
Holes: 18. **Yards:** 6,957/5,168. **Par:** 72/72. **Course Rating:** 71.1/68.4. **Slope:** 130/114. **Green Fee:** $27/$32. **Cart Fee:** $18. **Walking Policy:** Unrestricted walking. **Walkability:** 3. **Opened:** 1990. **Architect:** Dick Phelps. **Season:** Year-round. **High:** April-Sept. **To obtain tee times:** Call 3 days in advance beginning 8 a.m. **Miscellaneous:** Reduced fees (weekdays, low season, twilight, seniors, juniors), metal spikes, range (grass/mats), club rentals, credit cards (MC, V).
Reader Comments: Big improvement past year, especially greens ... Challenging, picturesque ... Great clubhouse ... Good views of mountains ...18 is great finishing hole, requires two excellent shots ... Hit long drives! ... Good place to practice.

★★★½ COLLINDALE GOLF CLUB
PU-1441 E. Horsetooth Road, Fort Collins, 80525, Larimer County, (970)221-6651, 60 miles N of Denver.
Holes: 18. **Yards:** 7,011/5,472. **Par:** 71/73. **Course Rating:** 71.5/69.9. **Slope:** 126/113. **Green Fee:** $17/$19. **Cart Fee:** $20/cart. **Walking Policy:** Unrestricted walking. **Walkability:** 1.
Opened: 1972. **Architect:** Frank Hummel. **Season:** Year-round. **High:** May-Oct. **To obtain tee times:** Call 3 days in advance. **Miscellaneous:** Reduced fees (weekdays, low season, twilight, seniors, juniors), range (grass/mats), club rentals, credit cards (MC, V).
Reader Comments: Unbelievable greens, fast and true ... Straight forward, flat course ... Best greens in Colorado ... Tough greens ... Quick, fun course ... Best greens in northern Colorado ... Good test of ability.

★★★ CONQUISTADOR GOLF COURSE
2018 N. Delores Rd., Cortez, 81321, Montezuma County, (970)565-9208.
Yards: 6,852/5,576. **Par:** 72/72. **Course Rating:** 69.5/70.2. **Slope:** 113/121. **Green Fee:** $10/$15. **Walkability:** N/A. **Miscellaneous:** Metal spikes.
Reader Comments: Very nice course ... Worth playing if in the area ... Nice, flat, relaxing ... Easy to walk, great layout, good people ... Love this course ... Good price for a fair course.

★★★½ COPPER MOUNTAIN RESORT
R-104 Wheeler Circle, Copper Mountain, 80443, Summit County, (970)968-2882, (800)458-8386, 75 miles W of Denver.
Holes: 18. **Yards:** 6,094/4,374. **Par:** 70/70. **Course Rating:** 67.6/63.8. **Slope:** 124/100. **Green Fee:** $60/$80. **Cart Fee:** Included in Green Fee. **Walking Policy:** Mandatory cart. **Walkability:** 4. **Opened:** 1976. **Architect:** Pete Dye/Perry Dye. **Season:** June-Oct. **High:** July-Aug. **To obtain tee times:** Resort guests up to 60 days in advance, nonguests call 4 days in advance.
Miscellaneous: Reduced fees (low season, resort guests, twilight), discount packages, club rentals, lodging, credit cards (MC, V, AE, D).
Reader Comments: Breathtaking views ... Golf holes are winter ski runs ... Tight and short front 9 ...You need every club and have to place 'em ... Some really great par 3s ... Hills extreme ... Great back 9 cut into mountainside ... High altitude so you get great distance.

★★★ COTTON RANCH CLUB

SP-530 Cotton Ranch Dr., Gypsum, 81637, Eagle County, (970)524-6200, (800)404-3542, 35 miles W of Vail. **Web:** www.cottonranch.com.
Holes: 18. **Yards:** 7,052/5,197. **Par:** 72/72. **Course Rating:** 73.6/70.4. **Slope:** 136/121. **Green Fee:** $45/$100. **Cart Fee:** Included in Green Fee. **Walking Policy:** Walking at certain times. **Walkability:** 4. **Opened:** 1997. **Architect:** Pete Dye. **Season:** March-Nov. **High:** July-Sept. **To obtain tee times:** Tee times may be made 48 hours in advance. **Miscellaneous:** Reduced fees (twilight, juniors), metal spikes, range (grass), club rentals, credit cards (MC, V, AE).
Reader Comments: Two different 9s ... New course going to be great ... Nice place ... Still maturing.

★★★½ COUNTRY CLUB OF COLORADO

R-125 E. Clubhouse Dr., Colorado Springs, 80906, (719)576-5560.
Holes: 18. **Yards:** 7,028/5,357. **Par:** 71/71. **Course Rating:** 72.4/69.3. **Slope:** 138/124. **Green Fee:** N/A. **Walkability:** N/A.
Reader Comments: Great layout, super condition ... Beautiful course with excellent service ... A challenging layout ... Stay out of the rough ... Off we go into the wild blue on 1st tee.

★★★★ CRESTED BUTTE COUNTRY CLUB

SP-385 Country Club Dr., Crested Butte, 81224, Gunnison County, (970)349-6131, (800)628-5496, 28 miles S of Gunnison. **E-mail:** cbcc@crestedbutte.net. **Web:** www.golfcolorado.net.
Holes: 18. **Yards:** 7,208/5,702. **Par:** 72/72. **Course Rating:** 73.0/72.3. **Slope:** 133/128. **Green Fee:** $45/$95. **Cart Fee:** Included in Green Fee. **Walking Policy:** Mandatory cart. **Walkability:** 5. **Opened:** 1983. **Architect:** Robert Trent Jones Jr. **Season:** May-Oct. **High:** June-Sept. **To obtain tee times:** Call in advance deposit required. **Miscellaneous:** Reduced fees (low season, resort guests, twilight), discount packages, range (grass/mats), club rentals, lodging, credit cards (MC, V, AE, D), beginner friendly (golf schools, clinics, twilight play).
Reader Comments: Beautiful, challenging, fun! ... Great shape and condition ... The course grows on you ... Like Scotland at 9,000 feet ... Beautiful views inspire good play ... Views, bunkers, views, bunkers, views ... Good service ... Great views, great course, great carry ... Great place! Great values!.

★★★★ DALTON RANCH GOLF CLUB *Service, Pace+*

SP-589 C.R. 252, Durango, 81301, La Plata County, (970)247-8774, 210 miles NW of Albuquerque. **E-mail:** dalton@frontier.net. **Web:** www.daltonranch.com.
Holes: 18. **Yards:** 6,934/5,539. **Par:** 72/72. **Course Rating:** 72.4/71.7. **Slope:** 135/127. **Green Fee:** $25/$49. **Cart Fee:** $10/person. **Walking Policy:** Unrestricted walking. **Walkability:** 3. **Opened:** 1993. **Architect:** Ken Dye. **Season:** April-Oct. **High:** June-Sept. **To obtain tee times:** Call golf shop. **Miscellaneous:** Reduced fees (low season, resort guests, twilight), discount packages, range (grass), club rentals, credit cards (MC, V, AE).
Reader Comments: 13 of 18 holes could be postcards ... Outstanding round of golf ... Best layout in state ... Difficult, but fair... Awesome scenery ... Take plenty of balls ... Lots of water, but fair... Good service ... Wow! Beautiful, lush course with extraordinary views of river and mountains.

DEER CREEK VILLAGE GOLF CLUB

PM-500 S.E. Jay Ave., Cedaredge, 81413, Delta County, (970)856-7781. **E-mail:** deergolf@itiz.net. **Web:** www.golfcolorado.com/deercreek.
Holes: 18. **Yards:** 6,418/5,077. **Par:** 72/72. **Course Rating:** 70.1/68.4. **Slope:** 128/122. **Green Fee:** $19/$21. **Cart Fee:** $20/cart. **Walking Policy:** Unrestricted walking. **Walkability:** 4. **Opened:** 1992. **Architect:** Byron Coker. **Season:** Feb.-Dec. **High:** May-Oct. **To obtain tee times:** Call up to 7 days in advance. Groups of 20 or more anytime. **Miscellaneous:** Range (grass), club rentals, credit cards (MC, V, D), beginner friendly (several beginner clinics annually).

★★★ DOS RIOS GOLF CLUB

PU-501 Camino Del Rio, Gunnison, 81230, Gunnison County, (970)641-1482.
Yards: 6,566/5,453. **Par:** 71/71. **Course Rating:** 69.4/69.4. **Slope:** 127/125. **Green Fee:** $40. **Walkability:** N/A. **Architect:** John Cochran. **Miscellaneous:** Metal spikes.
Reader Comments: Great mountain course with difficult holes ... Bring your fishing pole ... Nice place to enjoy life ... Lots of water, deep rough ... Bring your 'floaters' for this one ... Fun.

★★★ EAGLE GOLF CLUB

PU-1200 Clubhouse Dr., Broomfield, 80020, Boulder County, (303)466-3322, 15 miles N of Denver.
Holes: 18. **Yards:** 6,609/5,745. **Par:** 71/71. **Course Rating:** 69.7/65.8. **Slope:** 117/111. **Green Fee:** $18/$38. **Cart Fee:** $11/person. **Walking Policy:** Unrestricted walking. **Walkability:** 2. **Opened:** 1968. **Architect:** Dick Phelps. **Season:** Year-round. **High:** May-Sept. **To obtain tee times:** Call up to 7 days in advance. **Miscellaneous:** Reduced fees (weekdays, twilight, seniors,

COLORADO

juniors), range (mats), club rentals, credit cards (MC, V, AE), beginner friendly (junior golf, group clinics, 9-hole specials, Women In Golf Day).
Reader Comments: Easy to get on ... Front 9 good layout ... Flat course ... Beautiful views of mountains ... Everyone walks ... Great bar ... Lots of sand.

★★★★ EAGLE VAIL GOLF CLUB

PU-0431 Eagle Dr., Avon, 81620, Eagle County, (970)949-5267, (800)341-8051, 107 miles W of Denver.
Holes: 18. **Yards:** 6,819/4,856. **Par:** 72/72. **Course Rating:** 71.3/67.4. **Slope:** 131/123. **Green Fee:** $45/$90. **Cart Fee:** Included in Green Fee. **Walking Policy:** Mandatory cart. **Walkability:** 5. **Opened:** 1975. **Architect:** Bruce Devlin/Bob Von Hagge. **Season:** May-Oct. **High:** June-Sept.
To obtain tee times: Call 2 days in advance. **Miscellaneous:** Reduced fees (low season, twilight), range (grass/mats), club rentals, credit cards (MC, V, AE).
Reader Comments: Make you feel at home ... Scenic back 9 ... Don't play here if you have vertigo ... Last 4 holes on mountain side are exciting ... Fun mountain valley golf ... Perfect for playing with your honey.

★★★½ EAGLES NEST GOLF CLUB

PU-305 Golden Eagle Rd., Silverthorne, 80498, Summit County, (970)468-0681, 67 miles W of Denver.
Holes: 18. **Yards:** 7,024/5,556. **Par:** 72/72. **Course Rating:** 72.6/71.9. **Slope:** 141/126. **Green Fee:** $25/$60. **Cart Fee:** Included in Green Fee. **Walking Policy:** Mandatory cart. **Walkability:** N/A. **Opened:** 1985. **Architect:** Richard Phelps. **Season:** May-Oct. **High:** July-Sept. **To obtain tee times:** Call 7 days in advance. **Miscellaneous:** Reduced fees (weekdays, low season, twilight, juniors), discount packages, metal spikes, range (grass/mats), club rentals, credit cards (MC, V).
Reader Comments: Spectacular mountain views ... What's the rule for playing through a herd of elk? ... Club selection critical ... Extreme changes in elevation ... Busy golf ... 14 great holes ... This course is closed 1998 until spring 2000 ... New owners are redoing it entirely.

EISENHOWER GOLF CLUB *Service*

M-USAF Academy, Bldg. 3170, Colorado Springs, 80840, El Paso County, (719)333-4735, 1 miles N of Colorado Springs.
★★★★ BLUE COURSE *Value, Pace+*
Holes: 18. **Yards:** 7,301/5,559. **Par:** 72/72. **Course Rating:** 74.2/65.3. **Slope:** 137/130. **Green Fee:** $10/$50. **Cart Fee:** $18/person. **Walking Policy:** Unrestricted walking. **Walkability:** 4.
Opened: 1963. **Architect:** Robert Trent Jones, Sr. **Season:** Year-round. **High:** May-Oct. **To obtain tee times:** Active duty assigned to the Academy may call in 4 days in advance. All others may call in 3 days in advance. **Miscellaneous:** Reduced fees (twilight, juniors), range (grass/mats), club rentals, credit cards (MC, V), beginner friendly.
Notes: Ranked 7th in 1999 Best in State.
Reader Comments: Well-run and maintained military course, not public ... From the tips, one of the toughest courses in Colorado ... Outstanding views—blue sky and mountains ... Carved it out of dense pine forest ... Rolling, high altitude course ... Excellent shape ... Must be military.
★★★★ SILVER COURSE *Value, Pace*
Holes: 18. **Yards:** 6,519/5,215. **Par:** 72/72. **Course Rating:** 70.5/69.0. **Slope:** 121/119. **Green Fee:** $10/$50. **Cart Fee:** $18/person. **Walking Policy:** Unrestricted walking. **Walkability:** 4.
Opened: 1976. **Architect:** Frank Hummell. **Season:** Year-round. **High:** May-Oct. **To obtain tee times:** Active duty assigned to the academy may call in 4 days in advance. All others may call in 3 days in advance. **Miscellaneous:** Reduced fees (twilight), range (grass/mats), club rentals, credit cards (MC, V), beginner friendly.
Reader Comments: Well-kept course ... Tough greens; don't be above pin ... Uncle Sam takes care of the top dogs ... Better than the Blue Course, shotmaker's delight ... Great layout with breathtaking views.

★★★ ENGLEWOOD GOLF COURSE

PM-2101 W. Oxford Ave., Englewood, 80110, Arapahoe County, (303)762-2670, 5 miles S of Denver.
Holes: 27. **Yards:** 6,836/5,967. **Par:** 72/72. **Course Rating:** 71.0/72.2. **Slope:** 125/128. **Green Fee:** $15/$22. **Cart Fee:** $20/cart. **Walking Policy:** Unrestricted walking. **Walkability:** 3.
Opened: 1977. **Architect:** Dick Phelps. **Season:** Year-round. **High:** May-Oct. **To obtain tee times:** Call up to 4 days in advance. **Miscellaneous:** Reduced fees (seniors, juniors), discount packages, range (grass/mats), club rentals, credit cards (MC, V).
Reader Comments: Interesting ... Nice practice facilities including indoors ... Getting better as front 9 matures ... Good condition and value ... Best deal in town ... Back 9 is beautiful ... Best value in Denver metro area.

★★★½ ESTES PARK GOLF COURSE

PU-1080 South Saint Vrain Ave., Estes Park, 80517, Larimer County, (970)586-8146, 60 miles NW of Denver. **E-mail:** epgolf@oneimage.com. **Web:** www.estesvalleyrecreation.com.

COLORADO

Holes: 18. **Yards:** 6,326/5,250. **Par:** 71/72. **Course Rating:** 68.3/68.2. **Slope:** 118/125. **Green Fee:** $20/$33. **Cart Fee:** $22/cart. **Walking Policy:** Unrestricted walking. **Walkability:** 3. **Opened:** 1917. **Architect:** Henry Hughes/Dick Phelps. **Season:** April-Oct. **High:** June-Sept. **To obtain tee times:** Call 7 days in advance. **Miscellaneous:** Reduced fees (low season, twilight), discount packages, range (grass), club rentals, credit cards (MC, V), beginner friendly (both adult and junior programs).
Reader Comments: An excellent high altitude experience ... Great 19th hole ... Play in fall after tourists go home ... Fun to play with the deer and elk ... Magnificent mountain views ... Fairly short mountain course ... Good practice green ... Beautiful country.

★★½ EVERGREEN FAMILY GOLF CENTER INC.
PU-29614 Upper Bear Creek Rd, Evergreen, 80439, Jefferson County, (303)674-6351, 18 miles W of Denver.
Holes: 18. **Yards:** 4,877/4,494. **Par:** 69/69. **Course Rating:** 62.4/66.7. **Slope:** 111/115. **Green Fee:** N/A. **Walking Policy:** Unrestricted walking. **Walkability:** 5. **Season:** Year-round. **High:** May-Sept. **Miscellaneous:** Club rentals, beginner friendly.
Reader Comments: Mountainside layout makes for tough course ... Mountain course ... Never a flat lie ... Par 3 blind shot over a rock ... Beautiful ... City course ... Too much play.

★★★★ FAIRWAY PINES GOLF CLUB
PU-117 Ponderosa Dr., Ridgway, 81432, Ouray County, (970)626-5284, 25 miles S of Montrose.
Web: www.fairwaypines.com.
Holes: 18. **Yards:** 6,826/5,291. **Par:** 72/72. **Course Rating:** 71.6/72.2. **Slope:** 130/123. **Green Fee:** $38/$42. **Cart Fee:** $11/person. **Walking Policy:** Unrestricted walking. **Walkability:** 3. **Opened:** 1993. **Architect:** Byron Coker. **Season:** April-Oct. **High:** July-Sept. **To obtain tee times:** Call 48 hours in advance. **Miscellaneous:** Reduced fees (twilight, juniors), discount packages, metal spikes, range (grass/mats), club rentals, credit cards (MC, V, D), beginner friendly.
Reader Comments: Narrow, hilly, piney; a shotmaker's dream ... Awesome pro and staff ... Great challenge ... Remote, rustic gem—bring extra film ... Best course I've played on ... Breathtaking views! ... Hard to find, but gorgeous scenery near Telluride.

FITZSIMONS GOLF COURSE
PM-2323 Scranton Street, Aurora, 80045, Adams County, (303)364-8125.
Holes: 18. **Yards:** 6,530/5,914. **Par:** 72/72. **Course Rating:** 69.0/72.9. **Slope:** 115/115. **Green Fee:** $13/$20. **Walking Policy:** Unrestricted walking. **Walkability:** 2. **Opened:** 1941. **Season:** Year-round. **High:** June-July. **Miscellaneous:** Reduced fees (twilight, seniors, juniors), range (grass), club rentals, credit cards (MC, V, D), beginner friendly (clinics, lessons).

★★★ FLATIRONS GOLF COURSE
PU-5706 Araphahoe Rd., Boulder, 80303, Boulder County, (303)442-7851, 15 miles NW of Denver.
Holes: 18. **Yards:** 6,782/5,226. **Par:** 70/70. **Course Rating:** 71.7/68.3. **Slope:** 126/119. **Green Fee:** $19/$26. **Cart Fee:** $20/cart. **Walking Policy:** Unrestricted walking. **Walkability:** 1. **Opened:** 1933. **Architect:** Robert Bruce Harris. **Season:** Year-round. **High:** March-Sept. **To obtain tee times:** Call 1 day in advance for weekdays at 7 a.m. and 3 days in advance for weekends at 7 p.m. **Miscellaneous:** Range (grass/mats), club rentals, credit cards (MC, V), beginner friendly (lessons, Tuesday beginner play period).
Reader Comments: Easiest walking course in Colorado ... Best spring greens ... Doesn't look like much from the road, but will surprise you ... Beginner's course ... Holster your driver and play short and straight ... Tougher than it looks ... Flat ... Old course, narrow fairways.

★★★½ FOOTHILLS GOLF COURSE
PU-3901 South Carr St., Denver, 80235, Denver County, (303)989-3901, 1 miles W of Denver.
Holes: 18. **Yards:** 6,908/6,028. **Par:** 72/74. **Course Rating:** 71.1/72.9. **Slope:** 122/130. **Green Fee:** $13/$24. **Cart Fee:** $10/person. **Walking Policy:** Unrestricted walking. **Walkability:** 3. **Opened:** 1971. **Architect:** Dick Phelps. **Season:** Year-round. **High:** April-Oct. **To obtain tee times:** Nonresidents call 2 days in advance. **Miscellaneous:** Range (grass/mats), club rentals, credit cards (MC, V), beginner friendly (par-3 executive course available).
Reader Comments: Remarkable improvement in past four years ... Fun golf ... The view alone is worth any price ... Challenge is trying to hit over pond on No. 6 ... Nice clubhouse.

FORT CARSON GOLF CLUB
M-Bldg. 7800 Titus Blvd., Fort Carson, 80913, (719)526-4122.
Holes: 18. **Yards:** 6,919/6,599. **Par:** 72/72. **Course Rating:** 71.6/70.2. **Slope:** 126/123. **Green Fee:** $8/$22. **Cart Fee:** $8/person. **Walkability:** 4. **Opened:** 1972. **Season:** Year-round. **High:** May-Oct. **Miscellaneous:** Reduced fees (weekdays, low season, twilight, seniors, juniors), discount packages, range (grass/mats), club rentals, credit cards (MC, V, AE).
Special Notes: Formerly Cheyenne Shadow Golf Course.

COLORADO

★★ FORT MORGAN GOLF CLUB
PU-17586 County Rd. T.5, Fort Morgan, 80701, Morgan County, (970)867-5990, 70 miles NE of Denver.
Holes: 18. **Yards:** 6,575/5,457. **Par:** 72/74. **Course Rating:** 71.0/70.2. **Slope:** 128/118. **Green Fee:** $15/$22. **Cart Fee:** $22/cart. **Walking Policy:** Unrestricted walking. **Walkability:** 4. **Opened:** 1927. **Architect:** Henry B. Hughes. **Season:** Year-round. **High:** April-Oct. **To obtain tee times:** Call 7 days in advance for weekdays and 3 days in advance for weekends and holidays. **Miscellaneous:** Discount packages, range (grass/mats), club rentals, credit cards (MC, V).

FOX HOLLOW AT LAKEWOOD GOLF COURSE
PU-13410 W. Morrison Rd., Lakewood, 80228, Jefferson County, (303)986-7888, 15 miles W of Denver.
Holes: 27. **Green Fee:** N/A/$33. **Cart Fee:** $10/person. **Walking Policy:** Unrestricted walking. **Opened:** 1993. **Architect:** Denis Griffiths. **Season:** Year-round. **High:** April-Oct. **To obtain tee times:** Residents call 7 days in advance after 5 p.m. Nonresidents call 6 days in advance. **Miscellaneous:** Reduced fees (seniors, juniors), range (grass/mats), caddies, club rentals, credit cards (MC, V).

★★★★ CANYON/LINKS
Yards: 7,030/4,802. **Par:** 71/71. **Course Rating:** 72.3/67.5. **Slope:** 134/112. **Walkability:** 5.
Reader Comments: Three great 9s at a great price ... Outstanding variety ... Hard to get on ... Always a great course ... Difficult ... Great mountain views and a full range of elevation and obstacle challenges ... Excellent condition ... Superbly manicured ... Greens putt true ... Best muny course in state ... Nice people ... A+ location; exciting holes on the Canyon Course ... Great staff... Great clubhouse.

★★★★ CANYON/MEADOW
Yards: 6,808/4,439. **Par:** 71/71. **Course Rating:** 71.2/65.3. **Slope:** 138/107. **Walkability:** 2.
Notes: Ranked 24th in 1996 America's Top 75 Affordable Courses.
Reader Comments: Country club feel, challenging from the tips...Lives up to its reputation. Forces good golf shots...Many drives over ravines.

★★★★ MEADOW/LINKS
Yards: 6,888/4,801. **Par:** 72/72. **Course Rating:** 71.1/66.6. **Slope:** 132/107. **Walkability:** 2.
Reader Comments: Meadow flat and easy; Links long climb ... Lots of wind ... Keep it low ... Great challenge; accuracy is a must.

★★★ GLENEAGLE GOLF CLUB
SP-345 Mission Hills Way, Colorado Springs, 80908, El Paso County, (719)488-0900, 5 miles N of Colorado Springs.
Holes: 18. **Yards:** 7,276/5,655. **Par:** 72/72. **Course Rating:** 73.9/73.2. **Slope:** 128/120. **Green Fee:** $14/$29. **Cart Fee:** $22/person. **Walking Policy:** Unrestricted walking. **Walkability:** 4. **Opened:** 1972. **Architect:** Frank Hummel. **Season:** Year-round. **High:** March-Oct. **To obtain tee times:** Call 3 days in advance. Call on Wednesday for weekend. **Miscellaneous:** Reduced fees (low season, twilight, seniors, juniors), range (grass), club rentals, credit cards (MC, V, AE, D).
Reader Comments: Houses on top of fairways, no margin for error... A good workout to walk this course ... Challenging and enjoyable from the tips ... Nice view of Pikes Peak and Air Force Academy ...Hilly, beautiful.

★★★★ GRAND LAKE GOLF COURSE *Pace*
PU-1415 County Rd. 48, Grand Lake, 80447, Grand County, (970)627-8008, 100 miles NW of Denver.
Holes: 18. **Yards:** 6,542/5,685. **Par:** 72/74. **Course Rating:** 70.5/70.9. **Slope:** 131/123. **Green Fee:** $50/$50. **Cart Fee:** $25/cart. **Walking Policy:** Unrestricted walking. **Walkability:** 3. **Opened:** 1964. **Architect:** Dick Phelps. **Season:** May-Oct. **High:** July-Aug. **To obtain tee times:** Call 2 days in advance for weekdays and Thursday 6:30 a.m. prior to weekend. **Miscellaneous:** Metal spikes, range (grass/mats), club rentals, credit cards (MC, V, D).
Reader Comments: Better be straight or you're with the bears! ... Likely to see deer or fox ... One of my favorites ... Narrow landing areas ... Pretty and quiet ... A great mountain course ... Woods, water, worries! ... Nice course in deep woods ... Excellent views ... What a find ... Better than Pole Creek.

★★★★ GRANDOTE PEAKS GOLF CLUB
R-5540 Hwy. 12, La Veta, 81055, Huerfano County, (719)742-3391, (800)457-9986, 45 miles SW of Pueblo.
Holes: 18. **Yards:** 7,085/5,608. **Par:** 72/72. **Course Rating:** 72.8/70.7. **Slope:** 133/117. **Green Fee:** $45/$65. **Cart Fee:** $20/cart. **Walking Policy:** Unrestricted walking. **Walkability:** 3. **Opened:** 1986. **Architect:** Tom Weiskopf/Jay Morrish. **Season:** April-Oct. **High:** July-Sept. **To obtain tee times:** Call anytime. **Miscellaneous:** Reduced fees (weekdays, low season), discount packages, range (grass), club rentals, credit cards (MC, V, AE, D).

Reader Comments: Worth the drive; like having your own course for the day ... Super layout ... Great greens... The best 'unknown' course in Colorado .... Well maintained ... Great holes, beautiful views, nice staff ... Out of the way, but wonderful ... Lots of wildlife and birds.

★★★½ GREAT SAND DUNES GOLF COURSE AT ZAPATA RANCH

R-5303 Hwy. 150, Mosca, 81146, Alamosa County, (719)378-2357, (800)284-9213, 30 miles NE of Alamosa. **E-mail:** zapatainn@sanddunes.com. **Web:** www.greatsanddunes.com.
Holes: 18. **Yards:** 7,006/5,327. **Par:** 72/72. **Course Rating:** 72.2/67.8. **Slope:** 132/118. **Green Fee:** $30/$45. **Cart Fee:** $20/cart. **Walking Policy:** Unrestricted walking. **Walkability:** 3. **Opened:** 1990. **Architect:** John Sanford/R.M. Phelps. **Season:** March-Oct. **High:** July-Sept. **To obtain tee times:** Call golf shop. **Miscellaneous:** Reduced fees (twilight, seniors, juniors), discount packages, metal spikes, range (grass), club rentals, lodging (15 rooms), credit cards (MC, V, AE, D).
Reader Comments: Wind and thin air... Very narrow ... Hard to get to, but worth it ... A surprise! ... A gem in the middle of nowhere ... Fun layout ... Easy walking ... Watch the buffalo ... Another great getaway ... Great mountain scenery.

★★★★ HAYMAKER GOLF COURSE *Pace*

PU-34855 U.S. Hwy. 40 E., Steamboat Springs, 80477, Routi County, (970)870-1846, (888)282-2969.
Holes: 18. **Yards:** 7,308/5,059. **Par:** 72/72. **Course Rating:** 73.4/67.3. **Slope:** 133/119. **Green Fee:** $49/$69. **Cart Fee:** $14/person. **Walking Policy:** Unrestricted walking. **Walkability:** N/A. **Opened:** 1997. **Architect:** Keith Foster. **Season:** May-Oct. **High:** June-Sept. **Miscellaneous:** Reduced fees (low season, twilight), range (grass/mats), club rentals, credit cards (MC, V, AE, D), beginner friendly (forward tee, 5,000 yards).
Reader Comments: Wonderful links-style layout ... A little firm, will be great when it matures ... A nice links in the valley ... Will improve with age ... One of my favorite courses, has British links feel.

★★★½ HIGHLAND HILLS GOLF COURSE

PU-2200 Clubhouse Dr., Greeley, 80634, Weld County, (970)330-7327, 50 miles N of Denver.
Holes: 18. **Yards:** 6,723/6,002. **Par:** 71/75. **Course Rating:** 73.1/73.4. **Slope:** 129/129. **Green Fee:** $19/$24. **Cart Fee:** $23/cart. **Walking Policy:** Unrestricted walking. **Walkability:** 3. **Opened:** 1961. **Architect:** Frank Hummel. **Season:** Feb.-Nov. **High:** May-Sept. **To obtain tee times:** Tuesdays for week through next Tuesday. **Miscellaneous:** Reduced fees (twilight), club rentals, credit cards (MC, V, D), beginner friendly.
Reader Comments: Tight, good shape, makes you think ... Poor man's country club ... Narrow and heavily wooded ... Unbelievable value! ... Must hit straight; lots of trees ... Very well maintained.

HIGHLANDS RANCH GOLF CLUB

PU-9000 Creekside Way, Highlands Ranch, 80126, Douglas County, (303)471-0000, 15 miles S of Denver.
Holes: 18. **Yards:** 7,076/5,405. **Par:** 72/72. **Course Rating:** 71.6/69.9. **Slope:** 123/120. **Green Fee:** $45/$70. **Cart Fee:** Included in Green Fee. **Walking Policy:** Unrestricted walking. **Walkability:** 5. **Opened:** 1998. **Architect:** Hale Irwin. **Season:** Year-round. **High:** June-Sept. **Miscellaneous:** Reduced fees (weekdays, low season, twilight, seniors, juniors), club rentals, credit cards (MC, V, AE, D), beginner friendly (junior,ladies and beginner instructional programs. Dave Pelz & Nicklaus-Flick golf schools).

★★★½ HILLCREST GOLF CLUB

PU-2300 Rim Dr., Durango, 81301, La Plata County, (970)247-1499, 1 miles E of Durango.
Holes: 18. **Yards:** 6,838/5,252. **Par:** 71/71. **Course Rating:** 71.3/68.1. **Slope:** 127/111. **Green Fee:** $17/$17. **Cart Fee:** $17/cart. **Walking Policy:** Unrestricted walking. **Walkability:** 3. **Opened:** 1969. **Architect:** Frank Hummel. **Season:** March-Nov. **High:** June-Aug. **To obtain tee times:** Call 7 days in advance. **Miscellaneous:** Reduced fees (twilight), metal spikes, range (grass/mats), club rentals, credit cards (MC, V, D).
Reader Comments: Sweet little course ... Up and down all day long ... Good public course.... Golf at 6,500 feet ... Enjoyable ... Great view... Fast greens ... Great course and value for a public course ... Fun vacation! ... Durango is great!.

★★★½ HOLLYDOT GOLF COURSE

PU-55 North Parkway, Colorado City, 81019, Pueblo County, (719)676-3341, 20 miles S of Pueblo.
Holes: 27. **Yards:** 7,003/5,224. **Par:** 71/71. **Course Rating:** 71.9/68.3. **Slope:** 126/113. **Green Fee:** $13/$19. **Cart Fee:** $18/cart. **Walking Policy:** Unrestricted walking. **Walkability:** 4. **Opened:** 1989. **Architect:** Frank Hummell. **Season:** Year-round. **High:** April-Oct. **To obtain tee times:** Call on Monday prior to weekend, or 7 days in advance for weekdays. **Miscellaneous:** Reduced fees (weekdays, low season, juniors), range (grass), club rentals, credit cards (AE, D).

COLORADO

Reader Comments: Spectacular scenery ... Best weekend ever ... Nice out of the way course ... Lots of good holes ... One of Colorado's hidden gems ... Huge undulations in greens.

★★★★ HYLAND HILLS GOLF COURSE
PU-9650 N. Sheridan Blvd., Westminster, 80030, Adams County, (303)428-6526, 10 miles N of Denver.
Holes: 18. **Yards:** 7,021/5,654. **Par:** 72/73. **Course Rating:** 71.9/71.9. **Slope:** 132/120. **Green Fee:** $16/$21. **Cart Fee:** $20/cart. **Walking Policy:** Unrestricted walking. **Walkability:** 2. **Opened:** 1964. **Architect:** Henry Hughes. **Season:** Year-round. **High:** June-Aug. **To obtain tee times:** 7 days in advance starting 6:30 p.m. of that day. **Miscellaneous:** Reduced fees (twilight), range (grass/mats), caddies, club rentals, credit cards (MC, V, AE).
Notes: 1990 U.S. Women's Amateur Public Links.
Reader Comments: Classic golf design ... Good facilities and food ... Water comes into play on 10 of 18 holes ...Great value ... Good finishing holes ... Exceptionally well kept ... Country club atmosphere ... Good strong course; several challenging holes ... Nicest in Denver metro ... You get your money's worth.

★★★★ INDIAN PEAKS GOLF CLUB
PU-2300 Indian Peaks Trail, Lafayette, 80026, Boulder County, (303)666-4706, 10 miles SE of Boulder.
Holes: 18. **Yards:** 7,083/5,468. **Par:** 72/72. **Course Rating:** 72.5/69.9. **Slope:** 134/116. **Green Fee:** $30/$34. **Cart Fee:** $22/cart. **Walking Policy:** Unrestricted walking. **Walkability:** N/A. **Opened:** 1993. **Architect:** Hale Irwin/Dick Phelps. **Season:** Year-round. **High:** May-Sept. **To obtain tee times:** Call 2 days in advance for weekdays. Call Monday for Saturday tee time and Tuesday for Sunday tee time. **Miscellaneous:** Metal spikes, range (grass/mats), club rentals, credit cards (MC, V, D).
Reader Comments: 18th hole view WOW! ... Fun course ... Great value ... Hale builds as well as he plays ... Great practice facilities ... Wide fairways, hit away, fun ... Good test, great scenery of mountains ... Excellent rangers ... Public course that is like a country club ... Still young, but coming of age.

★★★ INDIAN TREE GOLF CLUB
PU-7555 Wadsworth Blvd., Arvada, 80003, Jefferson County, (303)403-2541, 10 miles NW of Denver.
Holes: 18. **Yards:** 6,742/5,850. **Par:** 70/75. **Course Rating:** 69.6/71.4. **Slope:** 114/116. **Green Fee:** $24/$24. **Cart Fee:** $22/cart. **Walking Policy:** Unrestricted walking. **Walkability:** 3. **Opened:** 1971. **Architect:** Dick Phelps. **Season:** Year-round. **High:** May-Sept. **To obtain tee times:** Call 1 day in advance. **Miscellaneous:** Reduced fees (juniors), range (grass/mats), club rentals, credit cards (MC, V).
Reader Comments: Great junior golf program, fast greens, little sand. Two water holes—par 3s ... Great place to play with large open fairways ... Some challenging holes ... 12th hole is a very good par 5 ... Beautiful—trees, geese, easy walking ... Par-3 13th makes my best 18 list...Good course to get your game back on track.

★★★½ INVERNESS HOTEL & GOLF CLUB
R-200 Inverness Dr. W., Englewood, 80112, Arapahoe County, (303)397-7878, (800)346-4891, 3 miles S of Denver.
Holes: 18. **Yards:** 6,889/5,681. **Par:** 70/71. **Course Rating:** 71.8/71.7. **Slope:** 131/133. **Green Fee:** $65/$110. **Cart Fee:** Included in Green Fee. **Walking Policy:** Unrestricted walking. **Walkability:** 3. **Opened:** 1974. **Architect:** Press Maxwell. **Season:** Year-round. **High:** June-Aug. **To obtain tee times:** Call golf shop. You must be overnight guest at Inverness Hotel or member to play. **Miscellaneous:** Reduced fees (twilight), discount packages, range (grass), club rentals, lodging, credit cards (MC, V, AE, D).
Reader Comments: Tough from tips ... Some great holes, very challenging ... Classic design, tough greens ... Nice large greens ... Back 9 will surprise you ... Fine layout.

JOHN F. KENNEDY GOLF CLUB
PM-10500 E. Hampden Ave., Aurora, 80014, Arapahoe County, (303)755-0105, (800)661-1419, 8 miles E of Denver.
Holes: 27. **Green Fee:** $17/$21. **Cart Fee:** $24/cart. **Walking Policy:** Unrestricted walking. **Walkability:** 4. **Opened:** 1963. **Architect:** Henry Hughes/Dick Phelps. **Season:** Year-round. **High:** April-Sept. **To obtain tee times:** Central computer for advanced times (303)784-4000. Day of play call starter at (303)751-0311. **Miscellaneous:** Reduced fees (seniors, juniors), range (grass/mats), club rentals, credit cards (MC, V), beginner friendly (9-hole, par 3 beginner lessons).
★★★ EAST/CREEK
Yards: 6,886/5,769. **Par:** 71/71. **Course Rating:** 71.6/N/A. **Slope:** 131/N/A.
Reader Comments: New back 9 along a creek bed is fun ... Big hitters' course ... Nice driving range and pro shop ... Good place to practice fairway irons ... City run course ... Back 9 has great variety ... Great value ... Wide open course ... Easy walking course!

COLORADO

★★★ **WEST/CREEK**
Holes: 27. **Yards:** 6,751/5,729. **Par:** 74/71. **Course Rating:** 70.9/N/A. **Slope:** 124/N/A.
★★★ **WEST/EAST**
Holes: 27. **Yards:** 7,035/6,456. **Par:** 75/73. **Course Rating:** 71.7/N/A. **Slope:** 119/N/A.

★★★★ **KEYSTONE RANCH GOLF COURSE** *Service*
R-P.O. Box 38, Keystone, 80435, Summit County, (970)496-4250, (800)354-4386, 7 miles W of Silverthorne.
Holes: 18. **Yards:** 7,090/5,596. **Par:** 72/72. **Course Rating:** 71.4/70.7. **Slope:** 130/129. **Green Fee:** $105/$125. **Cart Fee:** Included in Green Fee. **Walking Policy:** Walking at certain times. **Walkability:** 3. **Opened:** 1980. **Architect:** Robert T. Jones Jr. **Season:** May-Oct. **High:** June-Sept. **To obtain tee times:** Call 7 days in advance. **Miscellaneous:** Reduced fees (low season, resort guests, twilight, juniors), discount packages, metal spikes, range (grass/mats), club rentals, lodging, credit cards (MC, V, AE, D).
Notes: Ranked 17th in 1999 Best in State.
Reader Comments: Like a country club ... Give your game an extra hour for the views ... Great restaurant ... Great course ... Unbelievable scenery ... Magnificent mountain experience ... Nice friendly people ... Tough ... Nice clubhouse and pitch, chip, putt facilities ... Alpine meadow golf.

★★★ **LAKE ARBOR GOLF COURSE**
PU-8600 Wadsworth Blvd., Arvada, 80003, Jefferson County, (303)423-1650, 15 miles N of Denver.
Holes: 18. **Yards:** 5,865/4,965. **Par:** 70/69. **Course Rating:** 66.7/71.1. **Slope:** 108/113. **Green Fee:** $18/$22. **Cart Fee:** $22/cart. **Walking Policy:** Unrestricted walking. **Walkability:** N/A. **Opened:** 1971. **Architect:** Clark Glasson. **Season:** Year-round. **High:** April-Sept. **To obtain tee times:** Tee times taken. **Miscellaneous:** Range (grass), club rentals, credit cards (MC, V).
Reader Comments: No doubt the best greens ... Condos too close to fairway ... New clubhouse ... Narrow fairways ... You can go low on this course.

★★★½ **LAKE VALLEY GOLF CLUB**
SP-4400 Lake Valley Dr., Niwot, 80503, Boulder County, (303)444-2114, 3 miles N of Boulder.
Holes: 18. **Yards:** 6,725/5,713. **Par:** 70/70. **Course Rating:** 70.8/71.7. **Slope:** 126/126. **Green Fee:** $23/$31. **Cart Fee:** $22/cart. **Walking Policy:** Unrestricted walking. **Walkability:** 2. **Opened:** 1964. **Architect:** Press Maxwell. **Season:** Year-round. **High:** April-Aug. **To obtain tee times:** Non-members 2 days in advance. **Miscellaneous:** Reduced fees (weekdays, twilight, seniors, juniors), discount packages, range (grass), club rentals, credit cards (MC, V).
Reader Comments: A beautiful experience near Denver... Putting is the name of the game here ... Outstanding service ... My 89-year-old mom beat me! ... Great Press Maxwell design in the Rocky Mountain foothills ... You get to use every club in your bag ... Some of the best old-fashioned greens anywhere ... New clubhouse and wonderful restaurant.

★★★★ **LEGACY RIDGE GOLF COURSE**
PM-10801 Legacy Ridge Parkway, Westminster, 80030, Adams County, (303)438-8997, 15 miles NW of Denver. **E-mail:** rfielder@cl.westminster.co.us.
Holes: 18. **Yards:** 7,212/5,383. **Par:** 72/72. **Course Rating:** 74.0/70.6. **Slope:** 144/122. **Green Fee:** $24/$38. **Cart Fee:** $22/cart. **Walking Policy:** Unrestricted walking. **Walkability:** 3. **Opened:** 1994. **Architect:** Arthur Hills. **Season:** Year-round. **High:** April-Oct. **To obtain tee times:** Nonresidents call 2 days in advance starting at 5 p.m. **Miscellaneous:** Reduced fees (weekdays, twilight, seniors, juniors), range (grass/mats), club rentals, credit cards (MC, V, AE, D).
Reader Comments: One of the best in Colorado ... Environmentally friendly ... Clubhouse food is great ... Arthur Hills at his best ... Great view of Rockies ... Too long and narrow for my game ... Superior public course ... New breed of quality munies ... Very good food, dining ... Love the course ... A course you can play every day and not get tired of ... Leave the power carts, walk this one ... Many blind shots to small targets ... Great clubhouse ... Diverse and dastardly.

★★★½ **LONE TREE GOLF CLUB & HOTEL**
PU-9808 Sunningdale Blvd., Littleton, 80124, Arapahoe County, (303)799-9940, 15 miles S of Denver.
Holes: 18. **Yards:** 7,012/5,340. **Par:** 72/72. **Course Rating:** 72.1/70.6. **Slope:** 127/120. **Green Fee:** $32/$42. **Cart Fee:** $11/person. **Walking Policy:** Unrestricted walking. **Walkability:** 3. **Opened:** 1983. **Architect:** Arnold Palmer/Ed Seay. **Season:** Year-round. **High:** April-Oct. **To obtain tee times:** Nonresidents call 3 days in advance after noon. **Miscellaneous:** Reduced fees (resort guests, twilight, seniors), discount packages, range (grass), club rentals, lodging (15 rooms), credit cards (MC, V, AE, D), beginner friendly.
Reader Comments: Good course ... Old country club, now open to public ... Keep the big dog in the bag ... A good course ... Fairly open but trouble lurks ... Hilly too ... Great view of Rocky Mountains ... Narrow fairways and fast greens.

★★ MAD RUSSIAN GOLF COURSE
PU-24361 Highway 257, Milliken, 80543, Weld County, (970)587-5157, 1 miles N of Milliken.
Holes: 18. **Yards:** 5,464/4,250. **Par:** 70/70. **Course Rating:** 65.2/64.1. **Slope:** 117/103. **Green Fee:** $16/$22. **Cart Fee:** $22/cart. **Walking Policy:** Unrestricted walking. **Walkability:** 4. **Opened:** 1987. **Architect:** Robert Ehrlich. **Season:** Year-round. **High:** April-Oct. **To obtain tee times:** Call up to 7 days in advance. **Miscellaneous:** Reduced fees (weekdays, low season, seniors), range (grass), club rentals, credit cards (MC, V).

★★★★ MARIANA BUTTE GOLF COURSE
PM-701 Clubhouse Dr., Loveland, 80537, Larimer County, (970)667-8308, 45 miles N of Denver.
Holes: 18. **Yards:** 6,572/5,420. **Par:** 72/72. **Course Rating:** 71.5/70.2. **Slope:** 132/121. **Green Fee:** $20/$29. **Cart Fee:** $22/cart. **Walking Policy:** Unrestricted walking. **Walkability:** 4. **Opened:** 1992. **Architect:** Dick Phelps. **Season:** Year-round. **High:** April-Oct. **To obtain tee times:** Call automated service @ (970)669-5800 5 days in advance starting @ 7:00 a.m. **Miscellaneous:** Reduced fees (weekdays, low season, twilight), discount packages, range (grass/mats), club rentals, credit cards (MC, V, D).
Reader Comments: Finest muny around ... Awesome views ... Lots of character! ... Always enjoy this track ... Extreme elevation changes ... Beautiful Riverside course ... Little known jewel of the Front Range ... Great routing, really nice around the river ... Remains an inspiring place to play.

★★★½ MEADOW HILLS GOLF COURSE
PU-3609 S. Dawson St., Aurora, 80014, Arapahoe County, (303)690-2500, 6 miles E of Denver.
Holes: 18. **Yards:** 6,492/5,434. **Par:** 70/72. **Course Rating:** 70.5/70.2. **Slope:** 133/120. **Green Fee:** $17/$24. **Cart Fee:** $12/person. **Walking Policy:** Unrestricted walking. **Walkability:** 2. **Opened:** 1957. **Architect:** Henry Hughes. **Season:** Year-round. **High:** May-Sept. **To obtain tee times:** Nonresidents may call 4 days in advance. **Miscellaneous:** Reduced fees (weekdays, twilight, seniors, juniors), range (grass/mats), caddies, club rentals, credit cards (MC, V, D).
Reader Comments: Fine old-style course ... Trees can get you ... Beautiful mature course ... Great finishing hole ... Accuracy off the tee a must ... Narrow fairways on many holes, some tough par 4s ... Great course for price.

★★★½ THE MEADOWS GOLF CLUB
PU-6937 S. Simms, Littleton, 80127, Jefferson County, (303)972-8831, 15 miles SW of Denver.
Holes: 18. **Yards:** 7,011/5,437. **Par:** 72/72. **Course Rating:** 72.2/71.1. **Slope:** 135/124. **Green Fee:** $14/$28. **Cart Fee:** $24/person. **Walking Policy:** Unrestricted walking. **Walkability:** 4. **Opened:** 1984. **Architect:** Dick Phelps. **Season:** Year-round. **High:** May-Sept. **To obtain tee times:** Automated tee time system. Foothills residents call 5 days in advance. Jefferson County residents call 4 days in advance. Non-residents, 3 days. **Miscellaneous:** Reduced fees (seniors, juniors), range (grass), club rentals, credit cards (MC, V).
Reader Comments: Good test of golf ... If accurate on par 5s you have a chance to score well ... No. 18 is the toughest ... Tough to play in the wind ... A very good challenge! ... Unique layout ... Tough course ... Enjoyable golf experience ... Every hole a different challenge ... Underrated muny.

★★½ MIRA VISTA GOLF COURSE
PU-10110 E. Golfer's Way, Aurora, 80010, Arapahoe County, (303)340-1520. **E-mail:** mvgolf@gte.net.
Holes: 18. **Yards:** 6,870/5,919. **Par:** 72/73. **Course Rating:** 71.7/70.5. **Slope:** 130/124. **Green Fee:** $14/$23. **Cart Fee:** $20/cart. **Walking Policy:** Unrestricted walking. **Walkability:** 2. **Opened:** 1992. **Architect:** Robert Baldock. **Season:** Year-round. **High:** May-Aug. **To obtain tee times:** Call 5 days in advance. **Miscellaneous:** Reduced fees (twilight, seniors, juniors), range (grass), club rentals, credit cards (MC, V), beginner friendly (Rocky Mountain Golf Schools).
Reader Comments: Keeps getting better ... Easy to get good tee times ... Former military course ... Good variety of holes ... Improved condition.

MONTROSE GOLF COURSE
SP-1350 Birch St., Montrose, 81401, Montrose County, (970)249-4653. **E-mail:** play@montrosegolf.com. **Web:** www.montrosegolf.com.
Holes: 18. **Yards:** 6,446/5,495. **Par:** 70/72. **Course Rating:** 68.1/68.1. **Slope:** 123/118. **Green Fee:** $20/$24. **Cart Fee:** $11/person. **Walking Policy:** Unrestricted walking. **Walkability:** 2. **Opened:** 1960. **Architect:** Joe Francese. **Season:** Year-round. **High:** March-Oct. **To obtain tee times:** Call 3 days in advance. **Miscellaneous:** Reduced fees (twilight, juniors), discount packages, range (grass/mats), club rentals, credit cards (MC, V, D), beginner friendly ($5 dusk rate).

★★½ OVERLAND PARK GOLF COURSE
PM-1801 S. Huron St., Denver, 80223, Denver County, (303)777-7331, 2 miles S of Denver.
Holes: 18. **Yards:** 6,312/6,126. **Par:** 72/74. **Course Rating:** 69.2/72.7. **Slope:** 114/115. **Green Fee:** $17/$21. **Cart Fee:** $22/cart. **Walking Policy:** Unrestricted walking. **Walkability:** 1.

COLORADO

Opened: 1895. **Season:** Year-round. **High:** April-Nov. **Miscellaneous:** Reduced fees (weekdays, seniors, juniors), range (grass/mats), club rentals, credit cards (MC, V), beginner friendly.
Reader Comments: Nice clubhouse ... Good design ... Easy to walk ... Flat and open ... Good value, nice clubhouse, good practice facilities.

PAGOSA SPRINGS GOLF CLUB
R-One Pines Club Place, Pagosa Springs, 81147, Archuleta County, (970)731-4755, 55 miles E of Durango. **Web:** www.pagosagolf@pagosa.net.
Holes: 27. **Green Fee:** $20/$38. **Cart Fee:** $12/person. **Walking Policy:** Unrestricted walking. **Walkability:** 4. **Opened:** 1972. **Architect:** Johnny Bulla. **Season:** April-Oct. **High:** July-Aug. **To obtain tee times:** Call 14 days in advance. **Miscellaneous:** Reduced fees (low season, twilight, juniors), discount packages, range (grass/mats), rentals, lodging, credit cards (MC, V, AE, D).
★★★½ **PINON/MEADOWS**
Yards: 7,221/5,400. **Par:** 72/72. **Course Rating:** 72.9/68.0. **Slope:** 125/110.
Reader Comments: A good mix of holes ... Stay and play all three ... Facilities as nice as you will find ... Caddies waiting to take your clubs ... Mountain greens were great ... The view .... Fine mountain course.
★★★½ **PINON/PONDEROSA**
Yards: 6,670/5,320. **Par:** 71/71. **Course Rating:** 69.4/67.4. **Slope:** 119/107.
Reader Comments: Play all 3 combos—Pinon/Ponderosa is best ... Good mountain course ... Nice views ... Course nestled in Ponderosa Pines.
★★★½ **PONDEROSA/MEADOWS**
Yards: 6,913/5,074. **Par:** 71/71. **Course Rating:** 70.9/66.2. **Slope:** 123/108.
Reader Comments: Spectacular views ... Makes you work for a good score ... Nice layout ... Bring your best game.

★★★ PARK HILL GOLF CLUB
PU-4141 E. 35th Ave., Denver, 80207, Arapahoe County, (303)333-5411, 1 miles E of downtown Denver.
Holes: 18. **Yards:** 6,585/5,811. **Par:** 71/72. **Course Rating:** 69.4/73.4. **Slope:** 120/124. **Green Fee:** $19/$22. **Cart Fee:** $22/. **Walking Policy:** Unrestricted walking. **Walkability:** N/A. **Opened:** 1931. **Season:** Year-round. **High:** May-Aug. **To obtain tee times:** Call up to 6 days in advance. **Miscellaneous:** Metal spikes, club rentals, credit cards (MC, V).
Reader Comments: A Denver tradition. Play year-round ... Wide open. Slicers paradise! ... Flat and straight away ... Heated practice range open every day ... Fun course ... Easy to get tee times ... Great for beginner ... Great winter course.

★★★½ PATTY JEWETT GOLF COURSE
PU-900 E. Espanola, Colorado Springs, 80907, El Paso County, (719)578-6826.
Holes: 18. **Yards:** 6,811/5,998. **Par:** 72/75. **Course Rating:** 71.5/73.0. **Slope:** 124/124. **Green Fee:** $17/$26. **Cart Fee:** $20/cart. **Walking Policy:** Unrestricted walking. **Walkability:** 1. **Opened:** 1898. **Architect:** Willy Campbell/Mark Mahanna. **Season:** Year-round. **High:** May-Aug. **To obtain tee times:** Call 7 days in advance. **Miscellaneous:** Range (mats), club rentals.
Reader Comments: Crowded, not too difficult ... Wide open, yet good test ... Beautiful setting with views of Pikes Peak ... Rather flat ... Busy, good diversity of holes.

★★★½ PINE CREEK GOLF CLUB
PU-9850 Divot Trail, Colorado Springs, 80920, El Paso County, (719)594-9999, 2 miles N of Colorado Springs. **E-mail:** pinecreek@codenet.net.
Holes: 18. **Yards:** 7,194/5,314. **Par:** 72/72. **Course Rating:** 72.6/70.2. **Slope:** 139/122. **Green Fee:** $32/$32. **Cart Fee:** $12/cart. **Walking Policy:** Unrestricted walking. **Walkability:** 3. **Opened:** 1988. **Architect:** Richard Phelps. **Season:** Year-round. **High:** April-Oct. **To obtain tee times:** Call up to 3 days in advance or 7 days in advance with credit card for foursome using carts; credit card needed for more than 1 tee time. **Miscellaneous:** Range (grass), club rentals, credit cards (MC, V, AE, D).
Reader Comments: Good workout to walk ... Great gambling course on par 5s ... Lots of fun ... Tough back 9 ... Difficult if you play the wrong tees ... Hidden greens leave one guessing ... Another good one ... One of the Phelp's best ... Tight and long! ... You'll use all of your clubs here ...18th is beautiful.

★★★½ PLUM CREEK GOLF & COUNTRY CLUB
SP-331 Players Club Dr., Castle Rock, 80104, Douglas County, (303)688-2611, (800)488-2612.
Holes: 18. **Yards:** 6,700/4,875. **Par:** 72/72. **Course Rating:** 70.1/68.3. **Slope:** 131/118. **Green Fee:** $65/$77. **Cart Fee:** Included in Green Fee. **Walking Policy:** Mandatory cart. **Walkability:** N/A. **Opened:** 1985. **Architect:** Pete Dye. **Season:** Year-round. **High:** June-Sept. **To obtain tee times:** Call up to 3 days in advance. **Miscellaneous:** Reduced fees (weekdays, low season, twilight), metal spikes, range (grass), club rentals, credit cards (MC, V, AE, D).
Reader Comments: Toughest finishing holes ... Beautiful ... Every hole is different ... Worth playing ... Beautiful mountain setting ... Typical Pete Dye, lots of fairway bunkers and railroad ties.

COLORADO

POLE CREEK GOLF CLUB
PU-P.O. Box 3348, Winter Park, 80482, Grand County, (970)726-8847, (800)511-5076, 32 miles NW of Denver. **E-mail:** fvmrd@coweblink.net. **Web:** www.polecreek.org.
Holes: 27. **Green Fee:** $55/$80. **Cart Fee:** $12/person. **Walking Policy:** Unrestricted walking. **Walkability:** 3. **Opened:** 1984. **Architect:** Ron Kirby/Denis Griffiths. **Season:** May-Oct. **High:** June-Sept. **To obtain tee times:** Call up to 7 days in advance. More than 7 days in advance requires credit card and $7.50 per player reservation charge. **Miscellaneous:** Reduced fees (low season, twilight, juniors), range (grass), club rentals, credit cards (MC, V, AE, D).
★★★★ **MEADOW/RANCH**
Yards: 7,106/5,008. **Par:** 72/72. **Course Rating:** 73.7/68.5. **Slope:** 145/130.
Notes: Ranked 18th in 1999 Best in State.
Reader Comments: Great breakfast ... Challenging horseshoe par 5s ... Scenic mountain course ... Watch for moose ... Best mountain course in Colorado ... Good fishing ... Easy walk for mountain course ... Watch out when it gets windy ... Pick your shots— you can't just whale away with your driver ... Fair for women.
★★★★ **RANCH/RIDGE**
Yards: 7,112/5,157. **Par:** 72/72. **Course Rating:** 73.8/N/A. **Slope:** 142/N/A.
★★★★ **RIDGE/MEADOW**
Yards: 7,100/5,101. **Par:** 72/72. **Course Rating:** 73.3/N/A. **Slope:** 139/N/A.

★★½ PUEBLO CITY PARK GOLF COURSE
PU-3900 Thatcher Ave., Pueblo, 81005, Pueblo County, (719)561-4946, 40 miles S of Colorado Springs.
Holes: 18. **Yards:** 6,500/5,974. **Par:** 70/73. **Course Rating:** 68.9/72.5. **Slope:** 111/114. **Green Fee:** $17/$18. **Cart Fee:** $9/person. **Walking Policy:** Unrestricted walking. **Walkability:** 1. **Opened:** 1908. **Architect:** Tom Bendelow. **Season:** Year-round. **High:** May-Sept. **To obtain tee times:** Saturday a.m. for weekdays 7:00 am, Wednesday p.m. for weekends 6:00 pm. **Miscellaneous:** Reduced fees (seniors, juniors), club rentals, credit cards (MC, V).
Reader Comments: Lots of trees ... Flat terrain ... As difficult as you make it ... Nice finishing holes ... Flat course ... Old, tight course ... Play quickly ... Fun, forgiving but still challenging.

★★ PUEBLO WEST GOLF COURSE
PU-251 S. McCulloch Blvd., Pueblo West, 81007, Pueblo County, (719)547-2280, 8 miles W of Pueblo.
Holes: 18. **Yards:** 7,368/5,688. **Par:** 72/72. **Course Rating:** 73.3/71.4. **Slope:** 125/117. **Green Fee:** $13/$16. **Cart Fee:** $8. **Walking Policy:** Unrestricted walking. **Walkability:** N/A. **Opened:** 1972. **Architect:** Clyde B. Young. **Season:** Year-round. **High:** April-Sept. **To obtain tee times:** Call golf shop. **Miscellaneous:** Reduced fees (weekdays, seniors, juniors), metal spikes, range (grass), club rentals, lodging, credit cards (MC, V).

★★★½ RACCOON CREEK GOLF COURSE
PU-7301 W. Bowles Ave., Littleton, 80123, Arapahoe County, (303)973-4653, 3 miles W of downtown Littleton.
Holes: 18. **Yards:** 7,045/5,130. **Par:** 72/72. **Course Rating:** 72.6/68.2. **Slope:** 128/125. **Green Fee:** $32/$40. **Cart Fee:** $12/person. **Walking Policy:** Unrestricted walking. **Walkability:** 4. **Opened:** 1983. **Architect:** Dick Phelps/Brad Benz. **Season:** Year-round. **High:** May-Sept. **To obtain tee times:** Call up to 4 days in advance. **Miscellaneous:** Reduced fees (weekdays, low season, twilight, seniors, juniors), range (grass), club rentals, credit cards (MC, V, D).
Reader Comments: Good driving holes ... Need all your shots on this course ... One of the better Denver area courses ... Excellent course ... Greens to die for ... Good public course ... Gets lots of play ... Excellent practice area ... Very accommodating staff... Good course for iron players.

RED HAWK RIDGE GOLF CLUB
PU-2156 Red Hawk Ridge Dr., Castle Rock, 80104, Douglas County, (303)663-7150, (800)663-7150, 200 miles S of Denver.
Holes: 18. **Yards:** 6,942/4,636. **Par:** 72/72. **Course Rating:** 71.6/67.5. **Slope:** 129/107. **Green Fee:** $40/$50. **Cart Fee:** $12/person. **Walking Policy:** Unrestricted walking. **Walkability:** 4. **Opened:** 1999. **Architect:** Jim Engh. **Season:** Year-round. **High:** May-Oct. **To obtain tee times:** Call 7 days in advance . **Miscellaneous:** Reduced fees (weekdays, low season, twilight, seniors, juniors), range (grass), club rentals, credit cards (MC, V), beginner friendly (clinics in season).
Notes: Ranked 7th in 1999 Best New Affordable Public.

★★★★½ THE RIDGE AT CASTLE PINES NORTH *Service, Condition*
PU-1414 Castle Pines Pkwy., Castle Rock, 80104, (303)688-0100, 6 miles N of Denver.
Holes: 18. **Yards:** 7,013/5,001. **Par:** 71/71. **Course Rating:** 71.8/67.6. **Slope:** 143/123. **Green Fee:** $75/$105. **Cart Fee:** Included in Green Fee. **Walkability:** 4. **Opened:** 1997. **Architect:** Tom Weiskopf. **Season:** April-Nov. **High:** May-Sept. **Miscellaneous:** Reduced fees (twilight), metal spikes, range (grass), club rentals, credit cards (MC, V, AE).
Notes: Ranked 16th in 1999 Best in State.

COLORADO

Reader Comments: Play at any cost ... Sporty course ... Treat you like a king ... Best public course in Colorado ... Beautiful course, but expensive! ... Close to Castle Pines in location, appearance, price ... Beautiful mountain course ... Great design ... Great condition for new course ... I don't know which was better, the view or the greens.

★★★½ RIFLE CREEK GOLF COURSE

SP-3004 State Hwy.325, Rifle, 81650, Garfield County, (970)625-1093, (888)247-0370, 60 miles NE of Grand Junction.
Holes: 18. **Yards:** 6,241/5,131. **Par:** 72/72. **Course Rating:** 69.3/68.5. **Slope:** 123/109. **Green Fee:** $18/$28. **Cart Fee:** $12/person. **Walking Policy:** Unrestricted walking. **Walkability:** 4. **Opened:** 1960. **Architect:** Dick Phelps. **Season:** March-Nov. **High:** June-Sept. **To obtain tee times:** Call up to 7 days in advance. **Miscellaneous:** Reduced fees (low season, twilight, juniors), discount packages, range (grass/mats), club rentals, credit cards (MC, V, D).
Reader Comments: Two completely different 9s, one flat and one in canyons ... Play back 9 twice ... A special layout ... Try it once ... A unique experience ... Scenery, wildlife are all on the Canyon 9 ... Great value.

★★★★ RIVER VALLEY RANCH GOLF CLUB *Condition*

PU-303 River Valley Ranch Dr., Carbondale, 81623, Garfield County, (970)963-3625, 15 miles SE of Glenwood Springs.
Holes: 18. **Yards:** 7,348/5,168. **Par:** 72/72. **Course Rating:** 73.2/68.8. **Slope:** 125/114. **Green Fee:** $45/$90. **Cart Fee:** $15/person. **Walking Policy:** Unrestricted walking. **Walkability:** 2. **Opened:** 1998. **Architect:** Jay Morrish/Carter Morrish. **Season:** April-Nov. **High:** June-Sept. **To obtain tee times:** Call up to 2 weeks in advance. **Miscellaneous:** Reduced fees (low season, twilight), range (grass), club rentals, credit cards (MC, V, AE).
Reader Comments: Best course in the Rockies ... Subtle architecture, natural, not contrived ... Lovely, new track, mountain prices ... Sits in a valley surrounded by mountains ... Each hole has its own character never making you think, didn't I just play this hole? ... The condition of the course is outstanding, and if the green fee is too steep, take advantage of early season or late season rates.

RIVERDALE GOLF CLUB

PU-13300 Riverdale Rd., Brighton, 80601, Adams County, (303)659-6700, 10 miles N of Denver. **E-mail:** Riverdalegolf.com. **Web:** www.riverdalegolf.com.
★★★★½ DUNES COURSE *Value*
Holes: 18. **Yards:** 7,030/4,903. **Par:** 72/72. **Course Rating:** 72.1/67.5. **Slope:** 129/109. **Green Fee:** $24/$29. **Cart Fee:** $21/cart. **Walking Policy:** Unrestricted walking. **Walkability:** 2. **Opened:** 1985. **Architect:** Pete Dye. **Season:** Year-round. **High:** May-Sept. **To obtain tee times:** Call 2 days in advance for weekday. Call Monday at 5:30 p.m. for Saturday and Tuesday at 5:30 p.m. for Sunday. **Miscellaneous:** Range (grass/mats), club rentals, credit cards (MC, V). **Notes:** Ranked 22nd in 1996 America's Top 75 Affordable Courses.
Reader Comments: Fairways as smooth as greens ... Best course in this area ... Nike players said best greens on their tour... Requires good shots to play ... Windy ... Dye design at an affordable price ... Beautiful with great conditions ... Keeps you thinking ... Scotland in the mountains ... Tough greens.
★★★½ KNOLLS COURSE
Holes: 18. **Yards:** 6,756/5,931. **Par:** 71/73. **Course Rating:** 70.2/72.2. **Slope:** 118/117. **Green Fee:** $16/$19. **Cart Fee:** $21/cart. **Walking Policy:** Unrestricted walking. **Walkability:** 2. **Opened:** 1963. **Architect:** Henry B. Hughes. **Season:** Year-round. **High:** May-Sept. **To obtain tee times:** Call 2 days in advance for weekdays. Call Monday at 5:30 p.m. for Saturday and Tuesday at 5:30 p.m. for Sunday. **Miscellaneous:** Metal spikes, range (grass/mats), club rentals, credit cards (MC, V).
Reader Comments: Good course for beginners ... Elevated greens ... Easy to walk, fun to play ...Good greens ... Good value.

★★★★ SADDLE ROCK GOLF COURSE

PM-21705 E. Arapahoe Rd., Aurora, 80016, Arapahoe County, (303)699-3939.
Holes: 18. **Yards:** 7,351/5,407. **Par:** 72/72. **Course Rating:** 73.7/70.9. **Slope:** 136/126. **Green Fee:** $25/$34. **Cart Fee:** $24/cart. **Walking Policy:** Unrestricted walking. **Walkability:** 3. **Opened:** 1997. **Architect:** Dick Phelps. **Season:** Year-round. **High:** April-Oct. **To obtain tee times:** Aurora residents may call 5 days in advance, everyone else may call 4 days in advance 303-397-1818. Same day reservations 303-699-3939. **Miscellaneous:** Reduced fees (weekdays, twilight, seniors, juniors), range (grass), caddies, club rentals, credit cards (MC, V, D), beginner friendly (great practice and learning facility).
Reader Comments: Solid new course in Aurora ... Accuracy trumps length on this layout ... Use all clubs here ... Great new muny ... Great variety of holes ... Great greens, fairways, layout.

★★★★ SHERATON STEAMBOAT RESORT & GOLF CLUB

R-2000 Clubhouse Dr., Steamboat Springs, 80477, Routt County, (970)879-1391, (800)848-8878, 157 miles NW of Denver. **Web:** www.steamboat-sheraton.com.

Holes: 18. **Yards:** 6,902/5,536. **Par:** 72/72. **Course Rating:** 72.0/71.5. **Slope:** 138/127. **Green Fee:** $62/$95. **Cart Fee:** $18/person. **Walking Policy:** Walking at certain times. **Walkability:** 4. **Opened:** 1974. **Architect:** Robert Trent Jones Jr. **Season:** May-Oct. **High:** June-Sept. **To obtain tee times:** Hotel guests up to 1 year in advance. Nonguests call 1 day in advance.
Miscellaneous: Reduced fees (low season, resort guests, twilight, seniors, juniors), discount packages, range (grass/mats), club rentals, lodging (317 rooms), credit cards (MC, V, AE, D, All major).
Reader Comments: Wildlife galore, mountain course ... Fun layout ... Spectacular back 9 ... Lots of interesting doglegs and elevation changes like Vail ... A gem and fun to play ... 66 bunkers ... Mountain beauty.

★★★★ SHERATON TAMARRON RESORT
R-40292 Hwy. 550 N, Durango, 81301, La Plata County, (970)259-2000, (800)678-1000, 280 miles SW of Denver.
Holes: 18. **Yards:** 6,885/5,330. **Par:** 72/72. **Course Rating:** 73.0/70.6. **Slope:** 142/124. **Green Fee:** $69/$129. **Cart Fee:** Included in Green Fee. **Walking Policy:** Mandatory cart. **Walkability:** 5. **Opened:** 1974. **Architect:** Arthur Hills. **Season:** May-Nov. **High:** June-Sept. **To obtain tee times:** Outside play call 7 day before. Resort guests 30 days in advance. Golf package in advance with room reservation. **Miscellaneous:** Reduced fees (low season, resort guests, juniors), discount packages, range (mats), club rentals, lodging (325 rooms), credit cards (MC, V, AE, D).
Notes: Ranked 14th in 1999 Best in State.
Reader Comments: Best mountain course in Colorado ... If you're a golf junkie, overdose here ... Who couldn't fall in love with this setting ... A great place to stay and play ... The most beautiful mountain course anywhere! ... Liked their clinics ... Most enjoyable tough course.

SILVER SPRUCE GOLF COURSE
M-401 Glasgow, Bldg 1054, Colorado Springs, 80914, El Paso County, (719)556-7233, 1 miles E of Colorado Springs on Hwy 24.
Holes: 18. **Yards:** 6,833/6,122. **Par:** 72/73. **Course Rating:** 71.9/73.2. **Slope:** 123/129. **Green Fee:** N/A. **Cart Fee:** $16/cart. **Walking Policy:** Unrestricted walking. **Walkability:** N/A. **Opened:** 1973. **Season:** Year-round. **High:** May-Aug. **Miscellaneous:** Range (grass), club rentals, credit cards (MC, V).

★★★½ SNOWMASS CLUB GOLF COURSE
R-P.O. Box G-2, Snowmass Village, 81615, Pitkin County, (970)923-3148, (800)525-6200, 7 miles W of Aspen.
Holes: 18. **Yards:** 6,662/5,056. **Par:** 71/71. **Course Rating:** 70.1/67.5. **Slope:** 134/127. **Green Fee:** $60/$98. **Cart Fee:** Included in Green Fee. **Walking Policy:** Unrestricted walking. **Walkability:** 4. **Opened:** 1970. **Architect:** Arnold Palmer/Ed Seay. **Season:** May-Oct. **High:** July-Sept. **To obtain tee times:** Nonguests call 1 day in advance. Hotel guests may call up to 14 days in advance. **Miscellaneous:** Reduced fees (low season, resort guests, twilight, juniors), discount packages, range (grass), club rentals, lodging (74 rooms), credit cards (MC, V, AE, D, Diners Club), beginner friendly (schools, first time introduction).
Reader Comments: Best in the valley ... Tough in the wind ... Nice mountain resort course ... Great but expensive ... Early October affords good value and golden aspen ... Mountain views are fantastic!.

★★★★ SONNENALP GOLF CLUB *Pace*
R-1265 Berry Creek Rd., Edwards, 81632, Eagle County, (970)926-3533, (800)-654-8312, 110 miles W of Denver. **Web:** sonnenalp.com.
Holes: 18. **Yards:** 7,059/5,293. **Par:** 71/71. **Course Rating:** 727.3/69.4. **Slope:** 139/12115. **Green Fee:** $50/$150. **Cart Fee:** Included in Green Fee. **Walking Policy:** Unrestricted walking. **Walkability:** 3. **Opened:** 1981. **Architect:** Bob Cupp/Jay Morrish. **Season:** April-Oct. **High:** June-Sept. **To obtain tee times:** Nonresort guests call day of play. Resort guests may reserve tee time upon making reservation. **Miscellaneous:** Reduced fees (weekdays, low season, resort guests, twilight, juniors), discount packages, metal spikes, range (grass), club rentals, credit cards (MC, V, AE).
Reader Comments: My favorite mountain course ... Great course ... Great staff, great holes make a great day ... One of best in Colorado ... Terrific layout ... Well maintained ... Shh! Don't let too many people know.

★★★½ SOUTH SUBURBAN GOLF COURSE
PU-7900 S. Colorado Blvd., Littleton, 80122, Arapahoe County, (303)770-5508, 9 miles S of Denver.
Holes: 18. **Yards:** 6,790/5,274. **Par:** 72/72. **Course Rating:** 70.1/69.3. **Slope:** 122/119. **Green Fee:** $18/$29. **Cart Fee:** $11/person. **Walking Policy:** Unrestricted walking. **Walkability:** 3. **Opened:** 1973. **Architect:** Dick Phelps. **Season:** Year-round. **High:** April-Oct. **To obtain tee times:** Residents call 5 days in advance. Nonresidents call 3 days in advance. **Miscellaneous:**

Reduced fees (seniors), range (grass/mats), club rentals, credit cards (MC, V, D), beginner friendly (9-hole par-3 course).

Reader Comments: Wide open, hard greens ... Good test ... Variety of holes ... Stay below the hole ... Very good for busy muny course ... Walker friendly.

★★★½ SOUTHRIDGE GOLF CLUB

PU-5750 S. Lemay Ave., Fort Collins, 80525, Larimer County, (970)226-2828, 60 miles N of Denver.

Holes: 18. **Yards:** 6,363/5,508. **Par:** 71/71. **Course Rating:** 69.1/69.3. **Slope:** 122/118. **Green Fee:** $15/$18. **Cart Fee:** $18/cart. **Walking Policy:** Unrestricted walking. **Walkability:** 3. **Opened:** 1984. **Architect:** Frank Hummel. **Season:** Year-round. **High:** April-Sept. **To obtain tee times:** Call up to 3 days in advance. **Miscellaneous:** Reduced fees (weekdays, low season, twilight, seniors, juniors), discount packages, range (grass/mats), club rentals, credit cards (MC, V).

Reader Comments: Staff is always helpful and cordial ... Easy when hitting straight ... The back 9 is tough ... Outstanding course with good service ... Fun to walk, great workout ... Some fun holes ... Always well kept ... Lots of elevation change.

SPRING VALLEY GOLF CLUB

PU-42350 Road 21, Elizabeth, 80107, Elbert County, (303)646-4240, 12 miles E of Parker.

Holes: 18. **Yards:** 7,000/5,156. **Par:** 72/72. **Course Rating:** 71.0/68.3. **Slope:** 124/118. **Green Fee:** $20/$25. **Cart Fee:** $20/cart. **Walking Policy:** Unrestricted walking. **Walkability:** 2. **Opened:** 1997. **Architect:** Ross Graves. **Season:** Year-round. **High:** May-Sept. **To obtain tee times:** Call 3 days in advance. **Miscellaneous:** Reduced fees (weekdays, seniors, juniors), range (grass), club rentals, credit cards (MC, V, AE), beginner friendly (golf clinics throughout season).

★★★ SPRINGS RANCH GOLF CLUB

PU-3525 Tutt Blvd., Colorado Springs, 80922, El Paso County, (719)573-4863, (800)485-9771.

Holes: 18. **Yards:** 7,107/5,004. **Par:** 72/72. **Course Rating:** 72.3/67.2. **Slope:** 127/112. **Green Fee:** $18/$22. **Cart Fee:** $28/person. **Walking Policy:** Unrestricted walking. **Walkability:** 3. **Opened:** 1997. **Architect:** Dick Phelps/Rick Phelps. **Season:** Year-round. **High:** May-Sept. **Miscellaneous:** Range (grass), club rentals, credit cards (MC, V), beginner friendly (beginner golf lesson package).

Reader Comments: Nice to have a daily-fee choice ... New course; great staff; fun to play ... Windy ... New course, needs aging ... New course with young greens ... Will be good in the future.

TELLURIDE SKI & GOLF CLUB

R-562 Mountain Village Boulevard, Telluride, 81435, San Miguel County, (970)728-6157, 180 miles S of Grand Junction. **Web:** www.telski.com.

Holes: 18. **Yards:** 6,739/5,724. **Par:** 71/71. **Course Rating:** 71.0/72.4. **Slope:** 130/140. **Green Fee:** $115/$135. **Cart Fee:** Included in Green Fee. **Walking Policy:** Mandatory cart. **Walkability:** 5. **Opened:** 1992. **Season:** May-Sept. **High:** July, Aug. **To obtain tee times:** Members and guests at Peaks Hotel call up to 30 days in advance. Public may call 2 days in advance. **Miscellaneous:** Reduced fees (twilight), discount packages, range (grass), club rentals, lodging (178 rooms), credit cards (MC, V, D).

★★★★ THE OLDE COURSE AT LOVELAND

PU-2115 W. 29th St., Loveland, 80538, Larimer County, (970)667-5256, 45 miles N of Denver.

Holes: 18. **Yards:** 6,827/5,498. **Par:** 72/72. **Course Rating:** 70.9/70.6. **Slope:** 125/124. **Green Fee:** $16/$22. **Cart Fee:** $22/cart. **Walking Policy:** Unrestricted walking. **Walkability:** 2. **Opened:** 1959. **Architect:** Richard Phelps. **Season:** Year-round. **High:** April-Sept. **To obtain tee times:** Call golf shop. **Miscellaneous:** Reduced fees (low season, twilight, juniors), discount packages, range (grass/mats), club rentals, credit cards (MC, V).

Reader Comments: Island green—great hole No. 14 ... Nice muny ... Lots of trees ... Challenging old course ... Best parkland muny I've played ... Excellent practice facilities ... Golf pro fixes sandwiches and stirs your hot chocolate ... Treelined old style, but good value ... Favorite course in northern Colorado.

★★½ THORNCREEK GOLF CLUB

PU-13555 N. Washington St., Thornton, 80241, Adams County, (303)450-7055, 18 miles N of Denver.

Holes: 18. **Yards:** 7,268/5,547. **Par:** 72/72. **Course Rating:** 73.7/70.5. **Slope:** 136/120. **Green Fee:** $28/$28. **Cart Fee:** $12/person. **Walking Policy:** Unrestricted walking. **Walkability:** 4. **Opened:** 1992. **Architect:** Baxter Spann. **Season:** Year-round. **High:** May-Sept. **To obtain tee times:** May call up to 7 days in advance. Reservations may be made for $5 per player for times outside 7-day window. **Miscellaneous:** Reduced fees (weekdays, twilight, seniors, juniors), range (grass), club rentals, credit cards (MC, V, AE).

COLORADO

Reader Comments: Good layout ... Challenging course; fairly good to walk ... Greens could be faster... Decent design but played to death ... Good elevations ... Long from the tips ... Not always in great condition.

★★★½ TIARA RADO GOLF COURSE
PM-2063 S. Broadway, Grand Junction, 81503, Mesa County, (970)245-8085, 4 miles W of Grand Junction.
Holes: 18. **Yards:** 6,289/4,967. **Par:** 71/71. **Course Rating:** 69.0/66.9. **Slope:** 120/113. **Green Fee:** $15/$18. **Cart Fee:** $18/cart. **Walking Policy:** Unrestricted walking. **Walkability:** 3.
Opened: 1972. **Season:** Year-round. **High:** April-Nov. **To obtain tee times:** Call 2 days in advance starting at 7 a.m. **Miscellaneous:** Reduced fees (weekdays, juniors), range (grass), club rentals, credit cards (MC, V).
Reader Comments: Wonderful view of Colorado National monument ... Great layout ... Great value ... Bump and run these greens ... No. 10 magnificent ... Too many homes on fairways ... Beautiful views ... Good food ... Scenic and enjoyable muny course.

★★ TWIN PEAKS GOLF COURSE
PU-1200 Cornell Dr., Longmont, 80503, Boulder County, (303)772-1722, 35 miles N of Denver.
Holes: 18. **Yards:** 6,810/5,398. **Par:** 70/71. **Course Rating:** 71.7/68.8. **Slope:** 123/117. **Green Fee:** N/A$19. **Cart Fee:** $20/cart. **Walking Policy:** Unrestricted walking. **Walkability:** N/A.
Opened: 1977. **Architect:** Frank Hummel. **Season:** Year-round. **High:** May-Sept. **To obtain tee times:** Call or come in 2 days in advance. **Miscellaneous:** Reduced fees (weekdays, seniors, juniors), range (grass), club rentals, credit cards (MC, V).

★★★★ UTE CREEK GOLF COURSE
PU-2000 Ute Creek Dr., Longmont, 80501, (303)776-7662.
Holes: 18. **Yards:** 7,167/5,509. **Par:** 72/72. **Course Rating:** 73.1/69.2. **Slope:** 131/124. **Green Fee:** $15/$30. **Cart Fee:** $22/cart. **Walking Policy:** Unrestricted walking. **Walkability:** 4.
Opened: 1997. **Architect:** Robert Trent Jones Jr./Gary Linn. **Season:** Year-round. **High:** May-Oct. **To obtain tee times:** Call 1 week prior starting at 6:00 pm. **Miscellaneous:** Reduced fees (low season, twilight, seniors, juniors), discount packages, range (grass/mats), caddies, club rentals, credit cards (MC, V).
Reader Comments: Best greens ... A favorite of mine ... If you can't hit these fairways, stick with bowling ... New course, needs maturing ... Playable ...18th hole demands respect.

★★★½ VAIL GOLF CLUB
PU-1778 Vail Valley Dr., Vail, 81657, Eagle County, (970)479-2260, 100 miles W of Denver.
Holes: 18. **Yards:** 7,100/5,291. **Par:** 77/72. **Course Rating:** 70.8/69.5. **Slope:** 121/114. **Green Fee:** $45/$80. **Cart Fee:** $15/person. **Walking Policy:** Walking at certain times. **Walkability:** 3.
Opened: 1966. **Architect:** Press Maxwell. **Season:** May-Oct. **High:** June-Sept. **To obtain tee times:** Call 2 days in advance or outside 2 days by making an advanced reservation of $18.00 per person in addition of green fee & cart. **Miscellaneous:** Reduced fees (low season), metal spikes, range (grass), caddies, club rentals, credit cards (MC, V, AE).
Reader Comments: Mountain scenery and your ball goes farther. What more could you want? ... Good test with great scenery ... Follows along Colorado River ... Tight ... Great layout, a challenge, a little expensive.

★★ VALLEY HI GOLF COURSE
PU-610 S. Chelton Rd., Colorado Springs, 80910, El Paso County, (719)578-6926.
Holes: 18. **Yards:** 6,818/5,388. **Par:** 71/73. **Course Rating:** 70.8/69.3. **Slope:** 114/120. **Green Fee:** $12/$26. **Cart Fee:** $20/cart. **Walking Policy:** Unrestricted walking. **Walkability:** 2.
Opened: 1954. **Architect:** Henry B. Hughes. **Season:** Year-round. **High:** June-Aug. **To obtain tee times:** Call 7 days in advance. **Miscellaneous:** Reduced fees (seniors, juniors), range (grass/mats), club rentals, credit cards (MC, V), beginner friendly (learn to golf program).

★★★★ WALKING STICK GOLF COURSE *Value+*
PM-4301 Walking Stick Blvd., Pueblo, 81001, Pueblo County, (719)584-3400, 40 miles S of Colorado Springs.
Holes: 18. **Yards:** 7,147/5,181. **Par:** 72/72. **Course Rating:** 72.6/69.0. **Slope:** 130/114. **Green Fee:** $22/$24. **Cart Fee:** $18/cart. **Walking Policy:** Unrestricted walking. **Walkability:** 4.
Opened: 1991. **Architect:** Arthur Hills. **Season:** Year-round. **High:** May-Sept. **To obtain tee times:** Call on Wednesday for Saturday or Sunday. Call after Saturday for any day during the week. **Miscellaneous:** Reduced fees (weekdays, twilight, seniors, juniors), range (grass/mats), club rentals, credit cards (MC, V, D).
Reader Comments: Great young course ... Ingenious layout ... Many excellent holes ... Good deal ... Can you keep a secret? ... Bunkers, mounds, gorse, arroyos, cactus ... Too good to be true ... Wow, what an experience ... Outstanding value and course ... For public course, employees think private ... One of the best munies in U.S. ... Best hamburger in the state!

★★★½ WELLSHIRE GOLF COURSE
PU-3333 S. Colorado Blvd., Denver, 80222, Denver County, (303)757-1352.

COLORADO

Holes: 18. **Yards:** 6,608/5,890. **Par:** 71/73. **Course Rating:** 70.1/69.3. **Slope:** 124/121. **Green Fee:** $17/$21. **Cart Fee:** $22/cart. **Walking Policy:** Unrestricted walking. **Walkability:** 3. **Opened:** 1927. **Architect:** Donald Ross. **Season:** Year-round. **High:** April-Sept. **To obtain tee times:** Purchase reservation card $10 for all 5 Denver city courses. Call 5 days in advance at central number (303) 784-4000. **Miscellaneous:** Reduced fees (weekdays), metal spikes, range (mats), club rentals, credit cards (MC, V).
Reader Comments: Old Donald Ross course looking better ... Old course with huge trees ... Good course ... Great setting ... Tight layout rewards accuracy.

WEST WOODS GOLF CLUB
PU-6655 Quaker St., Arvada, 80403, Jefferson County, (303)424-3334, 14 miles NW of Denver.
Holes: 27. **Green Fee:** $25/$30. **Cart Fee:** $22/cart. **Walking Policy:** Unrestricted walking.
Walkability: 3. **Opened:** 1994. **Architect:** Dick Phelps. **Season:** Year-round. **High:** April-Aug. **To obtain tee times:** Call automated tee times (303)424-3334 5 days in advance starting at 8:00 a.m. **Miscellaneous:** Reduced fees (juniors), range (grass/mats), rentals, credit cards (MC, V).
COTTONWOOD/SILO
Yards: 6,761/5,107. **Par:** 72/72. **Course Rating:** 72.7/69.9. **Slope:** 138/119.
★★★½ **SLEEPING INDIAN/COTTONWOOD**
Yards: 7,035/5,197. **Par:** 72/72. **Course Rating:** 73.0/69.3. **Slope:** 136/119.
Reader Comments: If not for the housing development it winds through, it might be the perfect course ... Grounds crew does excellent job ... Hidden gem, try it ... Fairly new suburban course ... Similar to Coal Creek, very playable and in good condition.
★★★½ **SLEEPING INDIAN/SILO**
Yards: 6,722/5,074. **Par:** 72/72. **Course Rating:** 72.3/69.2. **Slope:** 138/121.

★★★ WILLIS CASE GOLF COURSE
PU-4999 Vrain St., Denver, 80212, Denver County, (303)455-9801.
Holes: 18. **Yards:** 6,306/6,122. **Par:** 72/75. **Course Rating:** 68.6/72.0. **Slope:** 119/115. **Green Fee:** $16/$20. **Cart Fee:** $20/cart. **Walking Policy:** Unrestricted walking. **Walkability:** 4.
Opened: 1929. **Season:** Year-round. **High:** June-Aug. **To obtain tee times:** Annual reservation access card or walk on. **Miscellaneous:** Reduced fees (weekdays, seniors, juniors), club rentals, credit cards (MC, V).
Reader Comments: Great city course, excellent mountain views ... Food is outstanding! ... No water but not easy ... Hilly and rolling terrain ... Good service ... Nice course, gets lots of play ... Refreshing break from stuffy courses ... Short ... Fun course to play.

★★★ WOODLAND PARK FUJIKI GOLF & COUNTRY CLUB
SP-100 Lucky Lady Dr., Woodland Park, 80863, Teller County, (719)687-7587, 18 miles NE of Colorado Springs.
Holes: 18. **Yards:** 6,486/5,218. **Par:** 72/72. **Course Rating:** 71.5/69.6. **Slope:** 133/126. **Green Fee:** $29/$39. **Cart Fee:** $22/cart. **Walking Policy:** Unrestricted walking. **Walkability:** 4.
Opened: 1995. **Architect:** John Harbottle. **Season:** Year-round. **High:** May-Sept. **To obtain tee times:** Call 8 days in advance. **Miscellaneous:** Reduced fees (weekdays, low season, seniors, juniors), range (grass/mats), club rentals, credit cards (MC, V, AE, D).
Reader Comments: Narrow fairways, serious rough ... Very challenging ... Beautiful mountain course ... Doesn't appear to be that tough, until you add it up.

★★★ YAMPA VALLEY GOLF CLUB
PU-2194 Hwy. 394, Craig, 81625, Moffat County, (970)824-3673, 200 miles NW of Denver.
Holes: 18. **Yards:** 6,514/5,242. **Par:** 72/72. **Course Rating:** 69.9/67.9. **Slope:** 126/120. **Green Fee:** N/A/$25. **Cart Fee:** $9/person. **Walking Policy:** Unrestricted walking. **Walkability:** 1.
Opened: 1968. **Architect:** William H. Neff. **Season:** April-Oct. **High:** June-Aug. **To obtain tee times:** Call 3 days in advance. **Miscellaneous:** Reduced fees (seniors, juniors), range (grass), club rentals, credit cards (MC, V, AE).
Reader Comments: Don't miss it ... Out of way but worth the trip ... Tight ...Tricky but fun ... My favorite course ... Nesting bald eagles on back 9 ... Pretty course in country.

CONNECTICUT

★★½ **AIRWAYS GOLF CLUB**
PU-1070 S. Grand St., West Suffield, 06093, Hartford County, (860)668-4973, 18 miles N of Hartford.
Holes: 18. **Yards:** 6,000/5,400. **Par:** 71/72. **Course Rating:** 66.7/63.0. **Slope:** 108/105. **Green Fee:** $20/$22. **Cart Fee:** $20/cart. **Walking Policy:** Unrestricted walking. **Walkability:** 1.
Opened: 1976. **Season:** Year-round. **High:** April-Oct. **To obtain tee times:** Call golf shop.
Miscellaneous: Reduced fees (weekdays, low season, seniors), discount packages, metal spikes, club rentals, credit cards (MC, V).
Reader Comments: Trying to improve course ... Great in winter ... Very friendly ... Has potential ... Great course for beginners ... Very flat, very open ... Good course for practicing the short game.

ALLING MEMORIAL GOLF COURSE
PU-35 Eastern St., New Haven, 06513, New Haven County, (203)946-8014.
Special Notes: Call club for further information.

★★½ **BANNER RESORT & COUNTRY CLUB**
PU-10 Banner Rd., Moodus, 06469, Middlesex County, (860)873-9075, 18 miles SE of Hartford.
Holes: 18. **Yards:** 6,100/5,600. **Par:** 72/74. **Course Rating:** 68.9/N/A. **Slope:** 118/N/A. **Green Fee:** $25/$27. **Cart Fee:** $24/cart. **Walking Policy:** Unrestricted walking. **Walkability:** 3.
Opened: 1958. **Architect:** Frank Gamberdella. **Season:** Apr-first snow. **High:** June-Aug. **To obtain tee times:** Call 7 days in advance.
. **Miscellaneous:** Reduced fees (weekdays, low season, seniors, juniors), metal spikes, range (grass), club rentals.
Reader Comments: Not crowded ... Too many tournaments ... Greens were real good ... Back nine is challenging, front nine is ho hum ... Can be wet ... Price is right ... Average course, no frills.

BLACKLEDGE COUNTRY CLUB
PU-180 W. St., Hebron, 06248, Tolland County, (860)228-0250, 15 miles E of Hartford.
Holes: 27. **Green Fee:** $28/$31. **Cart Fee:** $24/cart. **Walking Policy:** Unrestricted walking.
Opened: 1964. **Architect:** Geoffrey Cornish. **Season:** March-Dec. **High:** June-Aug. **To obtain tee times:** Call 7 days in advance for weekday. Call on Monday prior at 8 a.m. for weekend.
★★★ **ANDERSON/GILEAD**
Yards: 6,787/5,458. **Par:** 72/72. **Course Rating:** 72.0/71.7. **Slope:** 128/123. **Walkability:** 2.
Miscellaneous: Reduced fees (weekdays, low season, twilight, seniors, juniors), discount packages, credit cards (MC, V).
Reader Comments: Older 9's best ... New 9 uninteresting ... Slow play, need more marshals ... Greenkeeper does a great job ... Link's course is tough ... Need to define fairways with rough ... Greens have constant five o'clock shadow ... Three nines, three different challenges.
★★★ **GILEAD/LINKS**
Yards: 6,718/5,208. **Par:** 72/72. **Course Rating:** 72.5/70.3. **Slope:** 131/122. **Walkability:** 3.
Miscellaneous: Reduced fees (weekdays, low season, twilight, seniors, juniors), discount packages, credit cards (MC, V).
★★★ **LINKS/ANDERSON**
Yards: 6,701/5,158. **Par:** 72/72. **Course Rating:** 72.3/70.2. **Slope:** 126/117. **Walkability:** 3.
Miscellaneous: Reduced fees (weekdays, low season, twilight, seniors, juniors), discount packages, metal spikes, credit cards (MC, V).

★★★½ **BLUE FOX RUN GOLF CLUB**
PU-65 Nod Rd., Avon, 06001, Hartford County, (860)678-1679, 10 miles NW of Hartford.
Holes: 18. **Yards:** 6,779/5,171. **Par:** 71/72. **Course Rating:** 71.9/69.5. **Slope:** 125/123. **Green Fee:** $24/$33. **Cart Fee:** $14/person. **Walking Policy:** Unrestricted walking. **Walkability:** 1.
Opened: 1974. **Architect:** Joe Brunoli. **Season:** March-Dec. **High:** June-Aug. **To obtain tee times:** Call up to 7 days in advance for weekday. Call at 7:30 a.m. on Tuesday for weekend and holiday. **Miscellaneous:** Reduced fees (weekdays, low season, twilight, seniors, juniors), range (mats), club rentals, credit cards (MC, V, AE).
Reader Comments: Greens a little slow ... River complements the course ... Crowded, even on weekdays ... Very pleasant people ... Must be accurate ... Three par 3s on back 9 ... Need to speed it up ... Public course with a private feel ... Many good changes ... Makes the player hit a variety of shots.

★★★ **BRUCE MEMORIAL GOLF COURSE**
PM-1300 King St., Greenwich, 06831, Fairfield County, (203)531-7261, 20 miles NE of New York City.
Holes: 18. **Yards:** 6,512/5,710. **Par:** 71/73. **Course Rating:** 70.5/73.6. **Slope:** 120/128. **Green Fee:** $11/$15. **Cart Fee:** $22/cart. **Walking Policy:** Unrestricted walking. **Walkability:** 3.
Opened: 1963. **Architect:** Robert Trent Jones. **Season:** April-Nov. **High:** June-Aug. **To obtain tee times:** No reserved tee time for weekdays. For weekends there is a lottery system held on

Wednesday nights, or you can call on Friday after 11 a.m. **Miscellaneous:** Reduced fees (weekdays, seniors, juniors), range (mats), club rentals.

Reader Comments: Better than average municipal ... Yell fore ... Slightly overplayed ... Improving each year.... Heavily used ... A good layout ... For a senior this is a bargain ... Easy front 9 with a challenging back 9.

★★★½ CANDLEWOOD VALLEY COUNTRY CLUB

PU-401 Danbury Rd., New Milford, 06776, Litchfield County, (860)354-9359, (860)354-9359, 8 miles N of Danbury.

Holes: 18. **Yards:** 6,404/5,362. **Par:** 72/72. **Course Rating:** 70.3/70.9. **Slope:** 120/126. **Green Fee:** $27/$33. **Cart Fee:** $24/cart. **Walking Policy:** Unrestricted walking. **Walkability:** 2. **Opened:** 1961. **Architect:** Geoffrey Cornish/Stephen Kay. **Season:** April-Dec. **High:** May-Sept. **To obtain tee times:** Threesomes and Foursomes call up to 4 days in advance beginning at 6:30 am. **Miscellaneous:** Reduced fees (weekdays, twilight, seniors), range (mats), club rentals, credit cards (MC, V).

Reader Comments: Much improved. Back 9 plays tough and very demanding ... Wide open, let it fly ... Worth the hour drive ... Newer holes need seasoning ... Tried to fit too much into little space ... Beautiful course to walk ... Jekyll and Hyde- lullaby front, vicious back.

★★ CANTON PUBLIC GOLF CLUB

PU-110 Rte. 44, Canton, 06019-0305, Hartford County, (860)693-8305, 12 miles W of Hartford.

Holes: 9. **Yards:** 3,068/2,569. **Par:** 36/36. **Course Rating:** 68.2/67.0. **Slope:** 117/123. **Green Fee:** $22/$26. **Cart Fee:** $26/cart. **Walking Policy:** Unrestricted walking. **Walkability:** 3. **Opened:** 1932. **Architect:** Jack Ross. **Season:** March-Dec. **High:** May-Sept. **To obtain tee times:** Call 1 day in advance for weekend and holiday. (860)693-8305. **Miscellaneous:** Reduced fees (seniors, juniors), metal spikes, club rentals, credit cards (MC, V, AE).

★★★ CEDAR KNOB GOLF CLUB

PU-Billings Rd., Somers, 06071, Tolland County, (860)749-3550, 11 miles SE of Springfield, MA.

Holes: 18. **Yards:** 6,734/5,784. **Par:** 72/74. **Course Rating:** 72.3/73.9. **Slope:** 126/129. **Green Fee:** $21/$26. **Cart Fee:** $24/cart. **Walking Policy:** Unrestricted walking. **Walkability:** 3. **Opened:** 1963. **Architect:** Geoffrey Cornish. **Season:** Year-round. **High:** April-Sept. **To obtain tee times:** Call 7 days in advance for weekdays. Call Wednesday after noon for weekend. **Miscellaneous:** Reduced fees (weekdays, low season, seniors, juniors), discount packages, metal spikes, club rentals.

Reader Comments: Variety of long holes and short holes ... Tough little course ... Some memorable holes, conditioning is improving ... Love the layout but needs grooming and rangers ... Greens slow as cold molasses ... Very good drainage system, seldom wet ... Several funky holes ... Need local knowledge ... Two 90-degree par 5s.

★★★★ CRESTBROOK PARK GOLF CLUB *Value+*

PU-834 Northfield Rd., Watertown, 06795, Litchfield County, (860)945-5249, 5 miles N of Waterbury.

Holes: 18. **Yards:** 6,915/5,696. **Par:** 71/75. **Course Rating:** 73.6/73.8. **Slope:** 128/128. **Green Fee:** $12/$22. **Cart Fee:** $24/cart. **Walking Policy:** Unrestricted walking. **Walkability:** 4. **Opened:** 1970. **Architect:** Cornish/Zikoras. **Season:** April-Dec. **High:** June-Aug. **To obtain tee times:** Call 2 days in advance for weekends and holidays. **Miscellaneous:** Reduced fees (weekdays, seniors, juniors), range (grass), club rentals.

Reader Comments: Challenging ... Slick greens ... Tougher than tough ... Pace of play was rather slow ... Very solid course absolutely worth the green fee ... Great layout, a must play ... Tough, especially from tips ... Sloping greens can eat your lunch ... If you have the yips, stay home ... Park-like setting.

D. FAIRCHILD-WHEELER GOLF COURSE

PU-2390 Easton Tpke., Fairfield, 06432, Fairfield County, (203)373-5911.

★★½ BLACK COURSE

Holes: 18. **Yards:** 6,402/5,764. **Par:** 71/73. **Course Rating:** 70.0/71.9. **Slope:** 124/114. **Green Fee:** $16/$20. **Cart Fee:** $20/. **Walking Policy:** Unrestricted walking. **Walkability:** N/A. **Opened:** 1931. **Architect:** Robert White. **Season:** Year-round. **High:** May-Aug. **To obtain tee times:** First come, first serve. **Miscellaneous:** Metal spikes, club rentals.

Reader Comments: Good challenging layout, can be played from many distances ... Sad, once was a real golf course ... What a beautiful layout ... Working to improve, some still to do ... Very hilly.

★½ RED COURSE

Holes: 18. **Yards:** 6,775/6,382. **Par:** 72/79. **Course Rating:** 71.0/78.0. **Slope:** 124/122. **Green Fee:** $16/$20. **Cart Fee:** $20/. **Walking Policy:** Unrestricted walking. **Walkability:** N/A. **Opened:** 1931. **Architect:** Robert White. **Season:** Year-round. **High:** May-Aug. **To obtain tee times:** First come, first serve. **Miscellaneous:** Metal spikes, club rentals.

CONNECTICUT

★★½ E. GAYNOR BRENNAN MUNICIPAL GOLF COURSE
PM-451 Stillwater Rd., Stamford, 06902, Fairfield County, (203)356-0046, 1 miles S of Stamford.
Holes: 18. **Yards:** 6,107/5,736. **Par:** 71/71. **Course Rating:** 69.8/N/A. **Slope:** 122/N/A. **Green Fee:** $13/$34. **Cart Fee:** $22/cart. **Walking Policy:** Unrestricted walking. **Walkability:** 5. **Opened:** 1931. **Architect:** Maurice McCarthy. **Season:** April-Dec. **High:** May-Sept. **To obtain tee times:** Call golf shop. **Miscellaneous:** Reduced fees (twilight, seniors, juniors), metal spikes, club rentals.
Reader Comments: Short but very challenging ... Position course ... Wear a helmet ... Municipal atmosphere ... 5-hour round all summer ... You have to play somewhere ... Actually a great course considering the tiny area it's laid out in.
Special Notes: Also called Hubbard Heights by locals.

★★ EAST HARTFORD GOLF COURSE
PU-130 Long Hill St., East Hartford, 06108, Hartford County, (860)528-5082, 3 miles E of Hartford.
Holes: 18. **Yards:** 6,076/5,072. **Par:** 71/72. **Course Rating:** 68.6/68.1. **Slope:** 114/112. **Green Fee:** $21/$23. **Cart Fee:** $10/person. **Walking Policy:** Unrestricted walking. **Walkability:** 2. **Opened:** 1930. **Architect:** Orrin Smith. **Season:** April-Dec. **High:** May-Aug. **To obtain tee times:** Call or come in 7 days in advance for weekends and holidays. **Miscellaneous:** Reduced fees (seniors, juniors).

★★ EAST MOUNTAIN GOLF CLUB
PM-171 E. Mountain Rd., Waterbury, 06706, New Haven County, (203)756-1676.
Holes: 18. **Yards:** 5,817/5,211. **Par:** 67/67. **Course Rating:** 68.0/67.0. **Slope:** 118/113. **Green Fee:** $13/$21. **Cart Fee:** $20/cart. **Walking Policy:** Unrestricted walking. **Walkability:** 1. **Opened:** 1933. **Architect:** Wayne Stiles. **Season:** April-Dec. **High:** June-Aug. **To obtain tee times:** Call or walk in starting at 6:30 a.m. Call 3 days in advance for weekend. **Miscellaneous:** Reduced fees (low season), metal spikes.

ELMRIDGE GOLF COURSE
SP-Elmridge Rd., Pawcatuck, 06379, New London County, (860)599-2248, 14 miles E of New London.
Holes: 27. **Green Fee:** $24/$28. **Cart Fee:** $11. **Walking Policy:** Unrestricted walking. **Walkability:** N/A. **Opened:** 1968. **Architect:** Joe Rustici/Charlie Rustici. **Season:** March-Dec. **High:** May-Sept. **To obtain tee times:** Call Friday for following Monday through Friday. Call Monday for following weekend or holiday. **Miscellaneous:** Reduced fees (low season, twilight), discount packages, metal spikes, range (grass), club rentals, credit cards (MC, V, AE).
★★★ BLUE/WHITE
Yards: 6,639/N/A. **Par:** 72/N/A. **Course Rating:** N/A. **Slope:** N/A.
Reader Comments: Fairly open layout, true greens ... Another good beginner's course ... All three nines well kept ... Fun layout ... Tests accuracy ... Beautiful scenery ... Recommend playing if in the area ... Play weekend afternoons when it is not as crowded ... Blue and White courses are the most challenging.
★★★ RED/BLUE
Yards: 6,402/N/A. **Par:** 71/N/A. **Course Rating:** N/A. **Slope:** N/A.
★★★ RED/WHITE
Yards: 6,449/N/A. **Par:** 72/N/A. **Course Rating:** N/A. **Slope:** N/A.

GOODWIN PARK GOLF COURSE
PU-25 Stonington St., Hartford, 06106, Hartford County, (860)956-3601.
Reader Comments: Lots of reachable par 4s ... Canadian geese make a mess ... Trying but long way to go ... A get your confidence back course ... Nothing remarkable ... Better than nothing ... Great beginner course.
Special Notes: Call club for further information.

GRASSMERE COUNTRY CLUB
130 Town Farm Rd., Enfield, 06082, (860)749-7740.
Special Notes: Call club for further information.

★★★ GRASSY HILL COUNTRY CLUB
PU-441 Clark Lane, Orange, 06477, New Haven County, (203)795-1422, 8 miles W of New Haven.
Holes: 18. **Yards:** 6,208/5,209. **Par:** 70/71. **Course Rating:** 70.5/71.1. **Slope:** 122/118. **Green Fee:** $20/$42. **Cart Fee:** Included in Green Fee. **Walking Policy:** Walking at certain times. **Walkability:** 2. **Opened:** 1927. **Season:** April-Nov. **High:** April-Oct. **To obtain tee times:** Call golf shop. **Miscellaneous:** Reduced fees (weekdays, seniors), discount packages, metal spikes, range (grass/mats), club rentals, credit cards (MC, V, AE).
Reader Comments: Some of the hardest greens I've played ... You need a hard hat ... Some fun holes, but not enough to make it memorable ... Attitude of country club ... 5-hour plus rounds on

weekends ... Fast greens ... Quiet location with some nice views ... Some difficult undulating greens.

★★★½ H. SMITH RICHARDSON GOLF COURSE

PU-2425 Morehouse Hwy., Fairfield, 06430, Fairfield County, (203)255-7300, (203)255-7300, 50 miles NE of New York.

Holes: 18. **Yards:** 6,700/5,764. **Par:** 72/72. **Course Rating:** 71.0/72.8. **Slope:** 127/129. **Green Fee:** $12/$28. **Cart Fee:** $10/person. **Walking Policy:** Unrestricted walking. **Walkability:** 5. **Opened:** 1972. **Architect:** Hal Purdy. **Season:** March-Dec. **High:** May-Oct. **To obtain tee times:** Call golf shop 6:30 am week in advance for weekday. MC/Visa for lesson & merchandise only. **Miscellaneous:** Reduced fees (weekdays, twilight, seniors, juniors), discount packages, metal spikes, range (grass/mats), club rentals, beginner friendly (golf clinics for beginners).

Reader Comments: Gets lots of play ... During warm months, nearly impossible to get on ... Nice layout, love to play ... Kept in phenomenal shape with intricate and challenging greens ... Not the longest course but bring your A short game.

★★★ HARBOUR RIDGE GOLF CLUB

PU-37 Harrison Rd., Wallingford, 06492, New Haven County, (203)269-6023.

Holes: 18. **Yards:** 6,200/4,900. **Par:** 70/70. **Course Rating:** 70.0/68.0. **Slope:** 125/117. **Green Fee:** $28/$28. **Cart Fee:** $13/person. **Walking Policy:** Walking at certain times. **Walkability:** 5. **Season:** April-Nov. **High:** May-Oct. **Miscellaneous:** Reduced fees (weekdays, twilight, seniors, juniors), metal spikes, range (grass/mats), club rentals, credit cards (MC, V, AE).

Reader Comments: Noisy because near I-91 ... Still the best greens in the state ... A jewel ... T-O-U-G-H ... Nice course if you like playing under power lines.

HOP BROOK GOLF COURSE

PU-615 North Church St., Naugatuck, 06770, (203)729-8013.

Holes: 9. **Yards:** 2,887/2,449. **Par:** 36/36. **Course Rating:** 17.8/67.8. **Slope:** 109/109. **Green Fee:** $26/N/A. **Cart Fee:** $26/cart. **Walking Policy:** Unrestricted walking. **Walkability:** 5. **Opened:** 1906. **Season:** April-Nov. **High:** April-Sept. **To obtain tee times:** Call thurs after 8 for Sat. Fri after 8 for Sunday. **Miscellaneous:** Club rentals.

★★★ HUNTER GOLF CLUB

PM-685 Westfield Rd., Meriden, 06450, New Haven County, (203)634-3366, 12 miles S of Hartford.

Holes: 18. **Yards:** 6,604/5,569. **Par:** 71/72. **Course Rating:** 71.9/72.7. **Slope:** 124/131. **Green Fee:** $20/$27. **Cart Fee:** $23/cart. **Walking Policy:** Unrestricted walking. **Walkability:** 3. **Architect:** Robert Pryde/Al Zikorus. **Season:** March-Dec. **High:** June-Aug. **To obtain tee times:** Lottery system drawn on Wednesday for weekend only. **Miscellaneous:** Reduced fees (weekdays, seniors, juniors), range (grass), club rentals.

Reader Comments: Long and tough ... Very nice muny ... For variety the back nine is more interesting ... Good clubhouse ... Restaurant has great food ... Fairways too close to each other ... Great par 4s.

★★★ KENEY GOLF COURSE

PM-280 Tower Ave., Hartford, 06120, Hartford County, (860)525-3656.

Holes: 18. **Yards:** 5,969/5,005. **Par:** 70/70. **Course Rating:** 68.2/67.2. **Slope:** 118/107. **Green Fee:** $11/$18. **Cart Fee:** $19/. **Walking Policy:** Unrestricted walking. **Walkability:** N/A. **Opened:** 1927. **Architect:** Devereux Emmet/Geoffrey Cornish/William. **Season:** April-Nov. **High:** May-Sept. **To obtain tee times:** Call 7 days in advance. **Miscellaneous:** Reduced fees (weekdays, low season, twilight, seniors, juniors), metal spikes, club rentals, credit cards (MC, V).

Reader Comments: Trying to improve ... Lumpy Sherwood forest, lovely and old fashioned ... Old New England gem, but conditions terrible ... Fun to play ... Very diverse hole to hole, finish by dusk though ... Tee boxes need some TLC ... Tight old layout ... Beautiful old clubhouse.

★★★ LAUREL VIEW GOLF COURSE

PM-310 W. Shepard Ave., Hamden, 06514, New Haven County, (203)287-2656, 15 miles of New Haven.

Holes: 18. **Yards:** 6,899/5,558. **Par:** 72/72. **Course Rating:** 72.7/71.8. **Slope:** 130/130. **Green Fee:** $9/$25. **Cart Fee:** $20/cart. **Walking Policy:** Unrestricted walking. **Walkability:** 3. **Opened:** 1969. **Architect:** Geoffrey S. Cornish/William G. Robinson. **Season:** March-Dec. **High:** May-Aug. **Miscellaneous:** Metal spikes.

Notes: Ben Hogan Qualifying.

Reader Comments: Course has nice layout but needs work ... Tough, tough course ... Par is great here ... Friendly ... Slow greens ... Challenging course ... Back nine is superb ... Very hilly, strongly recommended using a cart ... Great hills ... Long front nine.

★★½ LONGSHORE CLUB PARK

PM-260 Compo Rd. S., Westport, 06880, Fairfield County, (203)222-7535, 13 miles W of Bridgeport.

Holes: 18. **Yards:** 5,845/5,227. **Par:** 69/73. **Course Rating:** 69.3/69.9. **Slope:** 115/113. **Green Fee:** $11/$13. **Cart Fee:** $22/cart. **Walkability:** N/A. **Opened:** 1925. **Architect:** Orrin Smith. **To obtain tee times:** Guests must be accompanied by a resident. **Miscellaneous:** Reduced fees (weekdays, seniors, juniors), metal spikes.

Reader Comments: Toughest par 69 anywhere ... Good greens ... Nice seashore course ... Requires accuracy ... Makes you think, short but tricky.

LYMAN ORCHARDS GOLF CLUB

★★★½ GARY PLAYER COURSE

SP-Rte. 157, Middlefield, 06455, Middlesex County, (860)349-8055, 15 miles N of New Haven. **Holes:** 18. **Yards:** 6,660/4,667. **Par:** 71/71. **Course Rating:** 73.0/67.8. **Slope:** 135/116. **Green Fee:** $31/$47. **Cart Fee:** $12/person. **Walking Policy:** Mandatory cart. **Walkability:** 5. **Opened:** 1994. **Architect:** Gary Player. **Season:** March-Nov. **High:** May-Oct. **To obtain tee times:** Call the automated teletee system 24 hours a day up to 7 days in advance. Times open at 7 p.m. **Miscellaneous:** Reduced fees (weekdays, low season, twilight, seniors, juniors), metal spikes, range (grass/mats), club rentals, credit cards (MC, V, AE).

Reader Comments: Conditions improving ... Use all clubs ... Must ride ... Lost balls end up in orchard, great view, unusual holes ... Gary Player should be shot! ... Definite shotmaker holes ... All irons off tee on front 9 ... Takes back seat to Jones course ... Strange layout.

★★★½ ROBERT TRENT JONES COURSE

SP-Rte. 157, Middlefield, 06455, Middlesex County, (888)995-9626, 20 miles S of Hartford. **Holes:** 18. **Yards:** 7,011/5,812. **Par:** 72/72. **Course Rating:** 73.2/70.0. **Slope:** 129/124. **Green Fee:** $31/$47. **Cart Fee:** $12/person. **Walking Policy:** Unrestricted walking. **Walkability:** 3. **Opened:** 1969. **Architect:** Robert Trent Jones. **Season:** March-Nov. **High:** May-Oct. **To obtain tee times:** Call automated teletee system 24 hours a day 7 days in advance. Times open at 7 p.m. **Miscellaneous:** Reduced fees (weekdays, low season, twilight, seniors, juniors), metal spikes, range (grass/mats), club rentals, credit cards (MC, V, AE), beginner friendly (junior programs, beginner clinics).

Reader Comments: Good test, hard to score ... Too wet at times ... Traditional layouts ... Fair and fun ... Gets a lot of play ... Interesting combination of holes ... Friday is a weekend price ... Better of two layouts ... 6-hour rounds are not fun ... A real test for better players ... That'll be one arm & one leg please ... A must play.

★★★½ MANCHESTER COUNTRY CLUB

SP-305 South Main St., Manchester, 06040, (860)646-0226. **E-mail:** mancc@prodigy.net. **Web:** www.mancc.com. **Holes:** 18. **Yards:** 6,285/5,610. **Par:** 72/72. **Course Rating:** 70.8/72.0. **Slope:** 125/125. **Green Fee:** $28/$34. **Cart Fee:** $12/person. **Walking Policy:** Unrestricted walking. **Walkability:** 3. **Architect:** Tom Bendelow/D. Emmitt. **Season:** March-Dec. **High:** May-Sept. **To obtain tee times:** Call golf shop 36 hours in advance. **Miscellaneous:** Reduced fees (low season, seniors, juniors), range (grass/mats), credit cards (MC, V, AE, D), beginner friendly (lessons through golf shop).

Reader Comments: Very, very fast greens ... Pros are great. 6th hole is one of the best in CT ... 14th a super hole ... Very playable ... Great-old style course ... Great food.

★★★ MILLBROOK GOLF COURSE

PU-147 Pigeon Hill Rd., Windsor, 06095, Hartford County, (860)688-2575, 10 miles N of Hartford. **E-mail:** mbgolf@tiac.net. **Holes:** 18. **Yards:** 6,050/5,184. **Par:** 70/72. **Course Rating:** 69.8/71.5. **Slope:** 119/125. **Green Fee:** $23/$38. **Cart Fee:** $11/person. **Walking Policy:** Unrestricted walking. **Walkability:** 4. **Architect:** Geoffrey S. Cornish. **Season:** April-Nov. **High:** May-Oct. **To obtain tee times:** Call Monday after 8:00 AM for entire week. **Miscellaneous:** Reduced fees (weekdays, low season, seniors, juniors), discount packages, metal spikes, club rentals, credit cards (MC, V, AE).

Reader Comments: Nicely conditioned ... Good test ... Dangerously close fairways ... Wet in spring, summer greens are the best ... Need every club in bag ... Scenic but a little tight ... Tricky 9th and 18th holes ... Need to be a goat to walk ... Tough finish.

★★★½ NORWICH GOLF COURSE

PM-685 New London Tpke., Norwich, 06360, New London County, (860)889-6973. **E-mail:** norwich.golf@snet.net. **Holes:** 18. **Yards:** 6,183/5,104. **Par:** 71/71. **Course Rating:** 69.6/70.2. **Slope:** 123/118. **Green Fee:** $22/$31. **Cart Fee:** $10/person. **Walking Policy:** Unrestricted walking. **Walkability:** 4. **Opened:** 1910. **Architect:** Donald Ross. **Season:** March-Dec. **High:** May-Aug. **To obtain tee times:** Call tee time # (860)892-4529 3 days in advance beginning @ 6:00 pm. **Miscellaneous:** Reduced fees (twilight), metal spikes, range (grass/mats), club rentals, lodging (100 rooms), credit cards (MC, V).

Reader Comments: Good layout, positioning gives reward ... Great beginners course ... Very hard to get a tee time ... Nice old Donald Ross course ... Variety of holes, no flat lies ... Beautiful in autumn.

CONNECTICUT

★★ OAK HILLS GOLF CLUB
PM-165 Fillow St., Norwalk, 06850, Fairfield County, (203)853-8400, 53 miles NE of New York. **Holes:** 18. **Yards:** 6,407/5,221. **Par:** 71/72. **Course Rating:** 70.5/69.2. **Slope:** 125/119. **Green Fee:** $18/$34. **Cart Fee:** $23/cart. **Walking Policy:** Unrestricted walking. **Walkability:** 3. **Opened:** 1969. **Architect:** Alfred H. Tull. **Season:** Year-round. **High:** April-Nov. **To obtain tee times:** Nonresidents must come in to club up to 7 days in advance for weekdays or Wednesday at 6:30 a.m. for weekend. **Miscellaneous:** Reduced fees (twilight), metal spikes, club rentals.

★★★½ ORANGE HILLS COUNTRY CLUB
PU-389 Racebrook Rd., Orange, 06477, New Haven County, (203)795-4161, 7 miles SW of New Haven. **Holes:** 18. **Yards:** 6,389/5,729. **Par:** 71/74. **Course Rating:** 71.2/71.5. **Slope:** 121/120. **Green Fee:** $28/$38. **Cart Fee:** $25/cart. **Walking Policy:** Unrestricted walking. **Walkability:** 2. **Opened:** 1940. **Architect:** Geoffrey Cornish. **Season:** March-Nov. **High:** May-Oct. **To obtain tee times:** Call Wednesday 6 p.m. for weekends. **Miscellaneous:** Credit cards (MC, V). **Reader Comments:** A very good all around course ... Could be private ... Good challenging greens ... Nice in the fall, run like a well-oiled machine, very lush ... Hit the driving range before you arrive, they forgot to build one ... One of my favorites ... Gets better every year, family owned and it shows.

★★ PATTONBROOK COUNTRY CLUB
SP-201 Pattonwood Dr., Southington, 06489, Hartford County, (860)793-6000. **Holes:** 18. **Yards:** 4,433/3,640. **Par:** 61/61. **Course Rating:** 60.6/59.1. **Slope:** 97/92. **Green Fee:** $16/$22. **Cart Fee:** $22/cart. **Walking Policy:** Unrestricted walking. **Walkability:** 3. **Opened:** 1967. **Architect:** Geoff Cornish. **Season:** Mar.-Nov. **High:** May-Aug. **To obtain tee times:** Call Monday for weekend - weekday no tee times reserved. **Miscellaneous:** Reduced fees (weekdays, seniors), club rentals, credit cards (MC, V).

★★★ PEQUABUCK GOLF CLUB
SP-School St., Pequabuck, 06781, Litchfield County, (860)583-7307, 12 miles N of Waterbury. **Holes:** 18. **Yards:** 6,015/5,388. **Par:** 69/72. **Course Rating:** 69.1/71.0. **Slope:** 122/117. **Green Fee:** $40/$40. **Cart Fee:** $14/person. **Walking Policy:** Unrestricted walking. **Walkability:** 4. **Opened:** 1902. **Architect:** Geoffrey S. Cornish/William G. Robinson. **Season:** April-Dec. **High:** May-Sept. **To obtain tee times:** None taken. Course open to public before 2 p.m. on weekdays and after 2 p.m. on weekends and holidays. No public play on Fridays. **Miscellaneous:** Reduced fees (weekdays), range (grass). **Notes:** U.S. Amateur Qualifier. **Reader Comments:** Short but tricky ... 10th hole tricky par 3 ... Outstanding back nine. Front nine easier to score ... 11th hole a classic ... Great greens ... Need accurate iron play ... Very interesting layout.

★★ PEQUOT GOLF CLUB
PU-127 Wheeler Rd., Stonington, 06378, New London County, (860)535-1898, 15 miles N of New London. **Holes:** 18. **Yards:** 5,903/5,246. **Par:** 70/70. **Course Rating:** 68.7/69.4. **Slope:** 108/112. **Green Fee:** $23/$28. **Cart Fee:** $24/cart. **Walking Policy:** Unrestricted walking. **Walkability:** 3. **Opened:** 1959. **Architect:** Wendal Ross. **Season:** Feb.-Dec. **High:** June-Sept. **To obtain tee times:** Call up to 7 days in advance. **Miscellaneous:** Reduced fees (seniors, juniors), discount packages, club rentals, credit cards (MC, V).

★★★★ PINE VALLEY COUNTRY CLUB
PU-300 Welch Rd., Southington, 06489, Hartford County, (860)628-0879, 15 miles SW of Hartford. **Holes:** 18. **Yards:** 6,325/5,482. **Par:** 71/73. **Course Rating:** 70.6/72.0. **Slope:** 123/122. **Green Fee:** $27/$32. **Cart Fee:** $27/cart. **Walking Policy:** Unrestricted walking. **Walkability:** 2. **Opened:** 1960. **Architect:** Orrin Smith. **Season:** March-Dec. **High:** June-Aug. **To obtain tee times:** Call Wednesday 6 p.m. for Saturday or Sunday. For weekdays call 7 days in advance. Must have a foursome to obtain tee time. **Miscellaneous:** Range (grass/mats), club rentals. **Reader Comments:** Friendly service ... Beautiful layout and great views ... A gem in wet conditions, dries out in hours ... Very playable for all levels ... Par-5 holes pretty but tough ... Lots of trees. Stay in the fairway ... 19th hole is great ... Check before you grab driver ... Tight course, but awesome conditions, love it.

★★★½ PORTLAND GOLF COURSE
SP-169 Bartlett St., Portland, 06480, Middlesex County, (860)342-6107, 20 miles S of Hartford. **Holes:** 18. **Yards:** 6,213/5,039. **Par:** 71/71. **Course Rating:** 70.8/68.6. **Slope:** 124/118. **Green Fee:** $26/$31. **Cart Fee:** $12/person. **Walking Policy:** Unrestricted walking. **Walkability:** 3. **Opened:** 1974. **Architect:** Geoffrey Cornish/William Robinson. **Season:** March-Dec. **High:** May-Oct. **To obtain tee times:** Call Monday a.m. for weekend. **Miscellaneous:** Reduced fees (weekdays, seniors, juniors), discount packages, metal spikes, range (grass/mats), club rentals.

Reader Comments: Short par 4s, let it rip! ... Good challenge, particularly front 9 ... Pro shop very friendly to a newcomer ... Tough back nine ... Best from back tees ... Fun layout ... Lots of blind shots, be careful with club selection.

PORTLAND WEST GOLF COURSE
PU-105 Gospel Lane, Portland, 06480, (860)342-6111.
Special Notes: Call club for further information.

★★★½ QUARRY RIDGE GOLF COURSE
PU-9 Rose Hill Rd., Portland, 06480, (860)342-6113
Holes: 18. Yards: 6,369/4,948. Par: 72/72. Course Rating: 70.8/N/A. Slope: 129/N/A. Green Fee: $35/$44. Cart Fee: Included in Green Fee. Walking Policy: Mandatory cart. Walkability: 5. Opened: 1993. Architect: Joe Kelly/Al Zikorus. Season: March-Nov. High: May-Oct. To obtain tee times: Call 1 week in advance for tee times. Miscellaneous: Reduced fees (seniors), metal spikes, rentals, credit cards (MC, V).
Reader Comments: Challenging mountain layout ... Great views, especially in the fall ... Target golf. I love it ... A fine test of golf ... Needs to grow in ... A great 9 holer turned into an average 18 holer ... Very hilly, beautiful views overlooking Connecticut River.

★★ RACEWAY GOLF CLUB
SP-E. Thompson Rd., Thompson, 06277, Windham County, (860)923-9591.
Yards: 6,412/5,437. Par: 71/71. Course Rating: 70.0/71.3. Slope: 111/117. Green Fee: $20/$35. Cart Fee: $22/cart. Walking Policy: Walking at certain times. Walkability: 2. Architect: Donald Hoenig. Season: April-Nov. High: May-Sept. Miscellaneous: Reduced fees (weekdays, low season, twilight, juniors), discount packages, metal spikes, range (grass/mats), credit cards (MC, V).

★★★★ RICHTER PARK GOLF CLUB
PM-100 Aunt Hack Rd., Danbury, 06811, Fairfield County, (203)792-2552, 60 miles NE of New York City.
Holes: 18. Yards: 6,740/5,627. Par: 72/72. Course Rating: 73.0/72.8. Slope: 130/122. Green Fee: $17/$48. Cart Fee: $23/cart. Walking Policy: Unrestricted walking. Walkability: 4. Opened: 1971. Architect: Edward Ryder. Season: April-Nov. High: June-Aug. To obtain tee times: Nonresidents call Thursday 9 a.m. for weekend. Also 3 days in advance for residents & non residents. Miscellaneous: Reduced fees (twilight), club rentals, credit cards (MC, V). Notes: Ranked 4th in 1999 Best in State. New England Public Links, MET Public Links, CT. Public Links.
Reader Comments: The best in CT! ... A steal for residents ... Shotmakers' dream ... New pro brings courtesy back ... Caters to locals ... Scenery is a 5 ... Tough to get on. Worth the effort ... Would play this course every day ... Great par 3s and hot dogs ... Terrible reservation policy ... Lush grass, unbelievable doglegs.

★★★½ RIDGEFIELD GOLF COURSE
PU-545 Ridgebury Rd., Ridgefield, 06877, Fairfield County, (203)748-7008, 1 miles E of Danbury.
Holes: 18. Yards: 6,444/5,295. Par: 71/74. Course Rating: 70.9/70.6. Slope: 123/119. Green Fee: $10/$40. Cart Fee: $24/cart. Walking Policy: Unrestricted walking. Walkability: 3. Opened: 1974. Architect: George Fazio/Tom Fazio. Season: April-Dec. High: June-Aug. To obtain tee times: Lottery for reservations Thursday a.m. Call after 9 a.m. Thursday. Miscellaneous: Reduced fees (twilight, seniors, juniors), range (grass), club rentals, credit cards (MC, V).
Reader Comments: Great back nine ... A notch below Richter ... Challenging hole placements on greens ... Variety ... Reminds me of the Peter Cottontail book series, over the summer you get to know the animals at each hole ... Wide fairways, slow greens ... Great par 3s ... Back 9 very narrow and unforgiving. Must be straight off tee.

★★★★ ROCKLEDGE COUNTRY CLUB
PU-289 S. Main St., West Hartford, 06107, Hartford County, (860)521-3156, 7 miles W of Hartford.
Holes: 18. Yards: 6,366/5,608. Par: 72/74. Course Rating: 71.3/71.5. Slope: 121/118. Green Fee: $16/$27. Cart Fee: $20/cart. Walking Policy: Unrestricted walking. Walkability: 3. Opened: 1949. Architect: Orrin Smith. Season: April-Dec. High: June-July. To obtain tee times: Call 3 days in advance. Miscellaneous: Reduced fees (seniors), range (grass/mats), club rentals, credit cards (MC, V).
Reader Comments: Always lush ... Good food ... Short par 5s make you feel good ... Pro shop personnel wonderful ... Lot of up and down ... Tough putting ... Excellent challenge for senior golfer ... Good pace of play ... I'd eat off of the fairways.

★★★ SHENNECOSSETT MUNICIPAL GOLF COURSE
PM-93 Plant St., Groton, 06340, New London County, (860)445-0262, 2 miles E of New London.

Holes: 18. **Yards:** 6,491/5,796. **Par:** 71/75. **Course Rating:** 71.5/73.2. **Slope:** 122/122. **Green Fee:** $22/$33. **Walking Policy:** Unrestricted walking. **Walkability:** 2. **Opened:** 1898. **Architect:** Donald Ross. **Season:** Year-round. **High:** July-Aug. **To obtain tee times:** Call Tuesday for Saturday tee time and Wednesday for Sunday tee time. Tee times may be made up to 3 days in advance. **Miscellaneous:** Reduced fees (weekdays, juniors), credit cards (MC, V).
Reader Comments: New holes near the water are impressive ... Demanding par 3s ... Great old course ... What golf was meant to be ... Links-type course, wispy grasses ... Ross gem ... Fun to play ... Lots of sand, little water ... Playable most of winter ... New holes are nice fit, wind can play havoc.

★★★½ SIMSBURY FARMS GOLF CLUB

PM-100 Old Farms Rd., West Simsbury, 06092, Hartford County, (860)658-6246, 15 miles NW of Hartford.
Holes: 18. **Yards:** 6,421/5,439. **Par:** 72/72. **Course Rating:** 71.1/70.1. **Slope:** 124/117. **Green Fee:** $14/$26. **Cart Fee:** $22/cart. **Walking Policy:** Unrestricted walking. **Walkability:** 3. **Opened:** 1972. **Architect:** Geoffrey Cornish/William Robinson. **Season:** April-Nov. **High:** May-Sept. **To obtain tee times:** Call 2 days in advance at 10 a.m. **Miscellaneous:** Metal spikes, range (mats), club rentals, credit cards (MC, V).
Reader Comments: Home course, love it! ... A little soggy at times ... Good variety ... All it needs is a 19th hole ... A nice walk in the fall ... Scenery is awesome ... Short but challenging, always great condition ... Fantastic hills and slopes ... Quality golf.

★★½ SKUNGAMAUG RIVER GOLF CLUB

SP-104 Folly Lane, Coventry, 06238, Tolland County, (860)742-9348, 20 miles E of Hartford.
Holes: 18. **Yards:** 5,785/4,838. **Par:** 70/71. **Course Rating:** 69.4/69.3. **Slope:** 120/123. **Green Fee:** $25/$28. **Cart Fee:** $21/cart. **Walking Policy:** Unrestricted walking. **Walkability:** 3. **Opened:** 1963. **Architect:** Joseph Motycka/John Motycka. **Season:** March-Dec. **High:** June-Sept. **To obtain tee times:** Call golf shop up to 7 days in advance for weekday. Call on Monday for upcoming weekend. **Miscellaneous:** Metal spikes, range (grass), club rentals, credit cards (MC, V), beginner friendly (junior programs beginner clinics).
Reader Comments: Interesting front nine, much harder back nine ... Relaxed atmosphere ... Wet in spring ... Very tight, bring plenty of balls ... Leaves are a problem ... Small greens ... Very scenic with lots of potential.

★★★ SOUTHINGTON COUNTRY CLUB

SP-Savage St., Southington, 06489, Hartford County, (860)628-7032, 22 miles SW of Hartford.
Holes: 18. **Yards:** 5,675/5,103. **Par:** 71/73. **Course Rating:** 67.0/69.8. **Slope:** 123/119. **Green Fee:** $26/$30. **Cart Fee:** $27/cart. **Walkability:** 3. **Opened:** 1922. **Season:** April-Nov. **High:** June-Aug. **To obtain tee times:** Call (860)628-7032 after 10:00AM on Tuesdays.
Miscellaneous: Reduced fees (seniors, juniors).
Reader Comments: Very good except after heavy rain ... Great staff ... Good 19th ... Improving each year ... Not crowded, fairly easy and short.

STANLEY GOLF CLUB

PM-245 Hartford Rd., New Britain, 06053, Hartford County, (860)827-8144, 8 miles SW of Hartford.
Holes: 27.**Cart Fee:** $23/cart. **Walking Policy:** Unrestricted walking. **Walkability:** 2. **Opened:** 1930. **Architect:** R.J. Ross/O. Smith/G.S. Cornish. **Season:** April-Dec. **High:** May-Oct. **To obtain tee times:** Call (860)827-1362 or walk in – Wednesday for Saturday;Thursday for Sunday beginning at 6:30 a.m.
★★★½ BLUE/RED
Yards: 6,453/5,681. **Par:** 72/73. **Course Rating:** 71.1/71.6. **Slope:** 115/118. **Green Fee:** $22/$26. **Miscellaneous:** Reduced fees (weekdays), club rentals.
Reader Comments: Good layout, especially for average players ... Nice muny, back 9 gets hilly ... Greens are beautiful ... 9 holes in 3 hours ... A city course that welcomes outsiders ... Beautiful New England course ... Always packed ... Did not like the service ... Imaginative and challenging ... Has improved tremendously.
★★★½ RED/WHITE
Yards: 6,156/5,359. **Par:** 72/72. **Course Rating:** 69.0/69.5. **Slope:** 108/112. **Green Fee:** $16/$26. **Miscellaneous:** Reduced fees (weekdays).
Special Notes: 3 holes will be renovated for 2000 season.
★★★½ WHITE/BLUE COURSE
Yards: 6,329/5,557. **Par:** 72/73. **Course Rating:** 69.8/70.3. **Slope:** 112/118. **Green Fee:** $22/$26. **Miscellaneous:** Reduced fees (weekdays).
Special Notes: 2 holes being renovated for 2000 season.

★★★½ STERLING FARMS GOLF CLUB

PM-1349 Newfield Ave., Stamford, 06905, Fairfield County, (203)329-7888.
Holes: 18. **Yards:** 6,410/5,600. **Par:** 72/73. **Course Rating:** 71.7/72.6. **Slope:** 127/121. **Green Fee:** $14/$40. **Cart Fee:** $20/cart. **Walking Policy:** Unrestricted walking. **Walkability:** 4.

Opened: 1969. **Architect:** Geoffrey Cornish/William Robinson. **Season:** Year-round. **High:** July-Aug. **To obtain tee times:** Call 3 days in advance. **Miscellaneous:** Reduced fees (weekdays, low season, twilight, seniors, juniors), range (mats), club rentals.
Reader Comments: Challenging ... Great range ... Best pro-shop around ... Pace of play is torture ... Hard to get on ... Beautiful greens ... Almost private feeling ... The greenskeeper deserves a medal ... Nice layout, too many outings ... Short from reds.

★★★½ TALLWOOD COUNTRY CLUB

PU-91 N. St., Rte. 85, Hebron, 06248, Tolland County, (860)646-3437, 15 miles SE of Hartford.
Holes: 18. **Yards:** 6,366/5,430. **Par:** 72/72. **Course Rating:** 70.4/70.6. **Slope:** 123/121. **Green Fee:** $22/$30. **Cart Fee:** $20/person. **Walking Policy:** Unrestricted walking. **Walkability:** 3.
Opened: 1970. **Architect:** Mike Ovian. **Season:** March-Dec. **High:** May-Sept. **To obtain tee times:** Call 7 days in advance for weekday and Monday a.m. for upcoming weekend.
Miscellaneous: Reduced fees (low season, twilight, seniors, juniors), discount packages, metal spikes, range (grass/mats), club rentals, credit cards (MC, V).
Reader Comments: Worth the ride ... Slow on weekends ... Back nine more interesting ... Consistent greens ... One of my favorites ... Great spring and fall course ... Tight. Tough greens ... Nice layout ... Speed up play ... Middle of nowhere keeps it quiet ... Wonderful variety of holes ... Lots of water.

★★★ TASHUA KNOLLS GOLF COURSE

PM-40 Tashua Knolls Lane, Trumbull, 06611, Fairfield County, (203)261-5989, 7 miles N of Bridgeport.
Holes: 18. **Yards:** 6,534/5,454. **Par:** 72/72. **Course Rating:** 71.9/71.7. **Slope:** 125/124. **Green Fee:** $15/$30. **Cart Fee:** $23/cart. **Walking Policy:** Unrestricted walking. **Walkability:** 3.
Opened: 1976. **Architect:** Al Zikorus. **Season:** March-Dec. **High:** May-Sept. **To obtain tee times:** Call golf shop. **Miscellaneous:** Reduced fees (seniors, juniors), range (grass/mats), club rentals.
Reader Comments: Good fun... Could lose the surcharge for tee times ... A diverse course ... A few hills ... A little work would really make it ... Back nine has some unusual holes ... Tough to get out, worth the wait ... Very busy on weekends ... Too many geese droppings ... Fantastic scenery in fall ... Huge greens.

★★★½ TIMBERLIN GOLF CLUB

PM-Ken Bates Dr., Kensington, 06037, Hartford County, (860)828-3228, 18 miles S of Hartford.
Holes: 18. **Yards:** 6,733/5,477. **Par:** 72/72. **Course Rating:** 72.2/72.0. **Slope:** 129/125. **Green Fee:** $25/$28. **Cart Fee:** $20/cart. **Walking Policy:** Unrestricted walking. **Walkability:** 2.
Opened: 1970. **Architect:** Al Zikorus. **Season:** April-Nov. **High:** June-Sept. **To obtain tee times:** Call 2 days in advance at 7 a.m. **Miscellaneous:** Range (grass/mats), club rentals, credit cards (MC, V, D).
Reader Comments: Marked improvements, new greenskeeper ... A little hard to get tee time ... The ranger rules ... Thick rough makes it challenging ... Good water holes ... Nice 3 and 5 pars ... Heavy play, best in fall ... Open. Toughened by uphill, elevated greens ... Women-friendly.

TUNXIS PLANTATION COUNTRY CLUB

PU-87 Town Farm Rd., Farmington, 06032, Hartford County, (860)677-1367, 10 miles S of Hartford.

★★★½ GREEN COURSE

Holes: 18. **Yards:** 6,354/4,883. **Par:** 70/70. **Course Rating:** 70.0/71.0. **Slope:** 120/117. **Green Fee:** $24/$32. **Cart Fee:** $25/cart. **Walking Policy:** Unrestricted walking. **Walkability:** 1.
Opened: 1962. **Architect:** Al Zikorus. **Season:** April-Nov. **High:** May-Aug. **To obtain tee times:** Call Tuesday prior to weekend at 7:30 a.m. week in advance for weekday. **Miscellaneous:** Reduced fees (seniors, juniors), metal spikes, range (grass/mats), club rentals, credit cards (MC, V, AE, D).
Reader Comments: Wide open, no real challenge ... Slow play, crowded ... Totally enjoyable ... Flat, good walking course ... Tough 18th ... Far too many tournaments and group functions ... New holes still need to grow in ... Easy to score here.

★★★½ WHITE COURSE

Holes: 18. **Yards:** 6,638/5,744. **Par:** 72/72. **Course Rating:** 72.2/71.5. **Slope:** 121/116. **Green Fee:** $24/$32. **Cart Fee:** $25/cart. **Walking Policy:** Unrestricted walking. **Walkability:** 1.
Opened: 1962. **Architect:** Al Zikorus. **Season:** April-Nov. **High:** May-Aug. **To obtain tee times:** Call Tuesday prior to weekend at 7:30 a.m. One week in advance for weekday. **Miscellaneous:** Reduced fees (seniors, juniors), metal spikes, range (grass/mats), club rentals, credit cards (MC, V, AE, D).
Reader Comments: Several holes seem the same ... Could get crowded ... Modest challenge ... Flat but interesting ... Good to walk ... Great views ... Played here after a torrential storm, the following day conditions were fine ... Water in play on 5 holes.

★★★ TWIN HILLS COUNTRY CLUB

PU-Rte. 31, Coventry, 06238, Tolland County, (860)742-9705, 10 miles E of Hartford.

Holes: 18. **Yards:** 6,257/5,249. **Par:** 71/71. **Course Rating:** 68.7/69.5. **Slope:** 118/116. **Green Fee:** $27/$29. **Cart Fee:** $20/cart. **Walking Policy:** Unrestricted walking. **Walkability:** 3. **Opened:** 1971. **Architect:** Mike McDermott/George McDermott. **Season:** Year-round. **High:** May-Aug. **To obtain tee times:** Call golf shop for weekend play. **Miscellaneous:** Reduced fees (seniors, juniors), metal spikes, club rentals, credit cards (MC, V).
Reader Comments: Back nine my favorite nine ... Nice practice area ... Very slow play ... Buried rocks ... Always being worked on, nice to see your money put into use ... Lots of potential ... A nice course ... Course doesn't take tee times, wait can be very long ... Fun layout.

★★ WESTERN HILLS GOLF CLUB
PM-Park Rd., Waterbury, 06708, New Haven County, (203)755-6828, 60 miles NE of New York.
Holes: 18. **Yards:** 6,427/5,393. **Par:** 72/72. **Course Rating:** 69.6/69.6. **Slope:** 125/122. **Green Fee:** $15/$22. **Cart Fee:** $22/cart. **Walking Policy:** Unrestricted walking. **Walkability:** 3.
Opened: 1961. **Architect:** Al Zikorus. **Season:** April-Dec. **High:** April-Aug. **To obtain tee times:** Call (203)756-1211 Thur. for Sat.; Fri for Sun.; Times start at 7:00 a.m. **Miscellaneous:** Reduced fees (weekdays, low season, seniors, juniors), club rentals.

★★ WESTWOODS GOLF CLUB
Rte. 177, Farmington, 06032, Hartford County, (860)677-9192.
Special Notes: Call club for further information.

★★★ WHITNEY FARMS GOLF COURSE
PU-175 Shelton Rd., Monroe, 06468, Fairfield County, (203)268-0707, 20 miles N of Bridgeport.
Holes: 18. **Yards:** 6,628/5,832. **Par:** 72/73. **Course Rating:** 72.4/72.9. **Slope:** 130/124. **Green Fee:** $37/$42. **Cart Fee:** Included. **Walking Policy:** Mandatory cart. **Walkability:** 1. **Opened:** 1981. **Architect:** Hal Purdy. **Season:** March-Dec. **High:** May-Sept. **To obtain tee times:** Call 7 days in advance for weekday; Thursday after 8:a.m. for weekends. Outing reservations up to 1 year in advance. **Miscellaneous:** Practice range with mats, club rentals, credit cards (MC, V, AE).

★★★★ WILLIMANTIC COUNTRY CLUB
SP-184 Club Rd., Windham, 06280, Windham County, (860)456-1971, 28 miles SE of Hartford.
E-mail: webmaster@wiligolf.com. **Web:** www.wiligolf.com.
Holes: 18. **Yards:** 6,278/5,106. **Par:** 71/71. **Course Rating:** 70.5/68.5. **Slope:** 123/113. **Green Fee:** N/A/$45. **Cart Fee:** $10/person. **Walking Policy:** Walking at certain times. **Walkability:** 3.
Opened: 1922. **Architect:** Designed by members. **Season:** April-Dec. **High:** Summer. **Miscellaneous:** Credit cards (MC, V, AE).
Reader Comments: Fast greens ... Two tee shots across roads, watch for traffic ... Subtle greens, manicured fairways ... Like the course but not real friendly to strangers ... Excellent challenge for a 10-20 handicap ... Greens in great shape ... A lot of play.

★★★ WOODHAVEN COUNTRY CLUB
PU-275 Miller Rd., Bethany, 06524, New Haven County, (203)393-3230, 5 miles N of New Haven. **E-mail:** woodhaven@snet.net.
Holes: 9. **Yards:** 3,387/2,859. **Par:** 36/37. **Course Rating:** 72.7/73.0. **Slope:** 128/125. **Green Fee:** $27/$34. **Cart Fee:** $26/cart. **Walking Policy:** Unrestricted walking. **Walkability:** 2.
Opened: 1968. **Architect:** Al Zikorus. **Season:** Year-round. **High:** April-Nov. **To obtain tee times:** Call up to 7 days in advance. **Miscellaneous:** Reduced fees (weekdays, low season, seniors), range (mats), club rentals, credit cards (MC, V), beginner friendly (lessons).
Reader Comments: Can take a long time to get around ... Good variety of holes ... No. 4 green unfair ... Could use another 9 holes ... Blues and whites keep it interesting if you go around twice ... Large, fast undulating greens.

★★★★ YALE GOLF COURSE
SP-200 Conrad Dr., New Haven, 06515, New Haven County, (203)432-0895.
Holes: 18. **Yards:** 6,749/5,209. **Par:** 70/70. **Course Rating:** 72.9/70.2. **Slope:** 132/123. **Green Fee:** $80/$90. **Cart Fee:** $32/cart. **Walking Policy:** Unrestricted walking. **Walkability:** 5.
Opened: 1926. **Architect:** C.B. Macdonald. **Season:** April-Nov. **High:** Summer. **Miscellaneous:** Metal spikes, range (grass), rentals, credit cards (MC, V).
Notes: Ranked 3rd in 1999 Best in State.
Reader Comments: Historic layout ... 9th is a par 3 over water to a green with a ravine that swallows golfers ... Must make iron shots ... Improves every year ... Super par 3s ... Each hole has its own personality ... Many blind shots, risk reward ... Course management is key ... If you walk bring oxygen ... Very serene ... Picturesque.

★★★½ BACK CREEK GOLF CLUB
PU-101 Back Creek Dr., Middletown, 19709. **E-mail:** backcreekgc@dol.net.
Holes: 18. **Yards:** 7,003/5,014. **Par:** 71/71. **Course Rating:** 74.2/69.3. **Slope:** 134/115. **Green Fee:** $17/$38. **Cart Fee:** $15/person. **Walking Policy:** Unrestricted walking. **Walkability:** 2. **Opened:** 1997. **Architect:** David Horn. **Season:** Year-round. **High:** May-Sept. **Miscellaneous:** Reduced fees (weekdays, low season, twilight, seniors, juniors), range (grass/mats), club rentals, credit cards (MC, V), beginner friendly (weekly clinics).
Reader Comments: Greens were great ... Interesting blend of holes ... A must play.

★★½ DEL CASTLE GOLF CLUB
PU-801 McKennans Church Rd., Wilmington, 19808, New Castle County, (302)995-1990, 20 miles S of Philadelphia.
Holes: 18. **Yards:** 6,628/5,369. **Par:** 72/72. **Course Rating:** 71.0/70.2. **Slope:** 123/118. **Green Fee:** $15/$24. **Cart Fee:** $25/cart. **Walking Policy:** Unrestricted walking. **Walkability:** 3. **Opened:** 1972. **Architect:** Edmund B. Ault. **Season:** Year-round. **High:** March-Nov. **To obtain tee times:** Come in Monday to sign up foursome for upcoming weekend. Tee times are taken for weekends and holidays only. Call (302)995-1990 for information Call in tee times pending. **Miscellaneous:** Reduced fees (low season, twilight, seniors, juniors), metal spikes, range (grass/mats), club rentals, credit cards (MC, V, AE, D).
Reader Comments: Two challenging par 5s (7 & 18) and good par 3s ... Big greens ... Wide open, decent greens, too many geese ... Very crowded ... Hilly ... Grip it and rip it.

EAGLE CREEK GOLF CLUB
M-Building 827, Dover, 19902, Kent County, (302)677-6039.
Holes: 18. **Yards:** 5,904/4,791. **Par:** 69/69. **Course Rating:** 67.8/62.5. **Slope:** 121/103. **Green Fee:** $9/$16. **Cart Fee:** $11/person. **Walking Policy:** Unrestricted walking. **Walkability:** 1. **Season:** Year-round. **High:** April-Sept. **Miscellaneous:** Reduced fees (twilight, juniors), range (grass), club rentals, credit cards (MC, V), beginner friendly.

★★ ED 'PORKY' OLIVER GOLF COURSE
PU-800 N. DuPont Rd., Wilmington, 19807, New Castle County, (302)571-9041, 25 miles S of Philadelphia.
Holes: 18. **Yards:** 6,115/5,674. **Par:** 69/71. **Course Rating:** 69.8/71.8. **Slope:** 118/121. **Green Fee:** $20/$29. **Cart Fee:** $25/cart. **Walking Policy:** Unrestricted walking. **Walkability:** 1. **Opened:** 1901. **Architect:** Wilfrid Reid/Ed Ault. **Season:** Year-round. **High:** May-Sept. **To obtain tee times:** Must be in tee time reservation system. Call 7 days in advance for weekdays. Monday prior to weekends. **Miscellaneous:** Reduced fees (weekdays, low season, twilight, seniors, juniors), metal spikes, range (grass/mats), club rentals, credit cards (MC, V, AE, D), beginner friendly (group and individual lessons, range).

★★ GARRISONS LAKE COUNTRY CLUB
PU-101 Fairways Circle, Smyrna, 19977, Kent County, (302)653-6349, (800)546-5745, 5 miles N of Dover. **Web:** www.garrisonslake.com.
Holes: 18. **Yards:** 7,028/5,460. **Par:** 72/72. **Course Rating:** 73.1/71.6. **Slope:** 125/126. **Green Fee:** $24/$41. **Cart Fee:** Included in Green Fee. **Walking Policy:** Walking at certain times. **Walkability:** 1. **Opened:** 1963. **Architect:** Edmund B. Ault. **Season:** Year-round. **High:** May-Sept. **To obtain tee times:** Call 7 days in advance. **Miscellaneous:** Reduced fees (weekdays, low season, twilight, seniors), discount packages, range (grass/mats), club rentals, credit cards (MC, V, AE, D). **Special Notes:** Formerly Ron Jaworski's Garrisons Lake Club.

★½ OLD LANDING GOLF CLUB
P.O. Box 39, Rehoboth Beach, 19971, Sussex County, (302)227-3616.
Special Notes: Call club for further information.

★★½ ROCK MANOR GOLF COURSE
SP-1319 Caruthers Lane, Wilmington, 19803, (302)658-2412.
Special Notes: Call club for further information.
Reader Comments: Good to work on the game ... Good beginner course ... Heavy play ... Extremely slow pace ... A place to go to get a quick fix ... Short. Beginner's delight.

★★★ THREE LITTLE BAKERS COUNTRY CLUB
SP-3542 Foxcroft Dr., Wilmington, 19808, New Castle County, (302)737-1877, 65 miles S of Philadelphia.
Holes: 18. **Yards:** 6,609/5,209. **Par:** 71/72. **Course Rating:** 71.9/70.5. **Slope:** 130/121. **Green Fee:** $36/$50. **Cart Fee:** Included in Green Fee. **Walking Policy:** Walking at certain times. **Walkability:** 5. **Opened:** 1973. **Architect:** Edmund B. Ault. **Season:** Year-round. **High:** April-Oct. **To obtain tee times:** Call Thursday a.m. for following weekend. **Miscellaneous:** Reduced fees (weekdays, low season, twilight, seniors, juniors), club rentals, credit cards (MC, V, AE, D).
Reader Comments: Extremely hilly, tough walk ... Par-3 first hole backs up play from the start ... Several interesting holes ... Love it ... Best public course in Del.

DISTRICT OF COLUMBIA

★★ **EAST POTOMAC PARK GOLF COURSE**
PU-Ohio Dr., Washington D.C., 20024, District of Columbia County, (202)554-7660.
Holes: 18. **Yards:** 6,303/5,761. **Par:** 72/72. **Course Rating:** 68.5/N/A. **Slope:** 109/N/A. **Green Fee:** $11/$17. **Cart Fee:** $18/cart. **Walking Policy:** Unrestricted walking. **Walkability:** 1. **Opened:** 1920. **Architect:** Robert White/Walter Travis. **Season:** Year-round. **High:** May-Sept. **To obtain tee times:** First come, first served. **Miscellaneous:** Reduced fees (weekdays, seniors), metal spikes, range (mats), club rentals, credit cards (MC, V), beginner friendly.

★★ **LANGSTON GOLF COURSE**
PU-2600 Benning Rd. N.E., Washington D.C., 20001, District of Columbia County, (202)397-8638, 33 miles SW of Baltimore.
Holes: 18. **Yards:** 6,340/N/A. **Par:** 72/N/A. **Course Rating:** 69.6/N/A. **Slope:** 112/N/A. **Green Fee:** $11/$17. **Cart Fee:** $19/cart. **Walking Policy:** Unrestricted walking. **Walkability:** N/A. **Opened:** 1939. **Architect:** William Gordon. **Season:** Year-round. **High:** March-Oct. **To obtain tee times:** First come, first served. **Miscellaneous:** Reduced fees (weekdays), discount packages, metal spikes, range (grass), club rentals.

★½ **ROCK CREEK PARK GOLF COURSE**
PU-16th & Rittenhouse N.W., Washington D.C., 20011, District of Columbia County, (202)882-7332.
Holes: 18. **Yards:** 4,715/4,715. **Par:** 65/65. **Course Rating:** 62.5/65.5. **Slope:** 112/102. **Green Fee:** $11/$19. **Cart Fee:** $18/cart. **Walking Policy:** Unrestricted walking. **Walkability:** 3. **Opened:** 1923. **Architect:** William S. Flynn. **Season:** Year-round. **High:** June-Aug. **To obtain tee times:** First come, first served. **Miscellaneous:** Reduced fees (weekdays, seniors), metal spikes, club rentals, credit cards (MC, V).

FLORIDA

ADMIRAL LEHIGH GOLF RESORT
★★½ NORTH COURSE
R-225 E. Joel Blvd., Lehigh, 33972, Lee County, (941)369-2121x2367, 13 miles E of Fort Myers.
Holes: 18. **Yards:** 5,870/4,703. **Par:** 70/70. **Course Rating:** 70.0/67.3. **Slope:** 119/116. **Green Fee:** $11/$30. **Cart Fee:** $18/person. **Walking Policy:** Walking at certain times. **Walkability:** N/A. **Opened:** 1958. **Architect:** Mark Mahannah. **Season:** Year-round. **High:** Dec.-April. **To obtain tee times:** Call 1 day in advance. **Miscellaneous:** Reduced fees (low season, resort guests, twilight), discount packages, metal spikes, range (mats), club rentals, lodging, credit cards (MC, V, AE, D).
Reader Comments: Very reasonable rates, even during season ... Small greens ... Oldies likely to enjoy it ... Nothing to write home about ... Not too difficult.

★★★ SOUTH COURSE AT MIRROR LAKES
R-670 Milwaukee Ave., Lehigh, 33936, Lee County, (941)369-1322, 12 miles E of Ft. Myers.
Holes: 18. **Yards:** 7,058/5,697. **Par:** 73/73. **Course Rating:** 74.0/72.9. **Slope:** 123/125. **Green Fee:** $11/$30. **Cart Fee:** $18/person. **Walking Policy:** Walking at certain times. **Walkability:** 1. **Opened:** 1973. **Architect:** Mark Mahanna. **Season:** Year-round. **High:** Dec.-April. **To obtain tee times:** Call 1 day in advance. **Miscellaneous:** Reduced fees (low season, resort guests, twilight), discount packages, range (grass/mats), club rentals, credit cards (MC, V, AE, D).
Reader Comments: Tropical Island feel ... Nice course to play ... Great experience ... Basic golf. Enjoyable ... Good test, many improvements.

AMELIA ISLAND PLANTATION
★★★★ LONG POINT GOLF CLUB *Condition*
R-6800 1st Coast Hwy., Amelia Island, 32035, Nassau County, (904)277-5907, (800)874-6878, 35 miles NE of Jacksonville. **Web:** www.aipfl.com.
Holes: 18. **Yards:** 6,775/4,927. **Par:** 72/72. **Course Rating:** 72.9/69.1. **Slope:** 129/121. **Green Fee:** $125/$155. **Cart Fee:** Included in Green Fee. **Walking Policy:** Mandatory cart. **Walkability:** 2. **Opened:** 1987. **Architect:** Tom Fazio. **Season:** Year-round. **High:** Oct.-Nov. **To obtain tee times:** Call 60 day in advance. Resort guests of Amelia Island Plantation only.
Miscellaneous: Reduced fees (low season, resort guests, twilight, juniors), discount packages, range (grass), club rentals, lodging, credit cards (MC, V, AE, D, Resort Charge Card).
Reader Comments: Everything is 1st class ... Great layout; awesome scenery ... We had a blast! ... A real treat! I have to play it again! ... Narrow fairways ... Beautiful setting along the marshes ... Too windy ... Ocean views worth the high cost ... Tricky approach shots.

★★★★ OAK MARSH
R-3000 1st Coast Hwy., Amelia Island, 32035, Nassau County, (904)277-5907, (800)874-6878, 35 miles NE of Jacksonville. **Web:** www.aipfl.com.
Holes: 18. **Yards:** 6,108/4,341. **Par:** 70/70. **Course Rating:** 70.3/66.4. **Slope:** 134/115. **Green Fee:** $115/$145. **Cart Fee:** Included in Green Fee. **Walking Policy:** Mandatory cart. **Walkability:** N/A. **Opened:** 1987. **Architect:** Tom Fazio. **Season:** Year-round. **High:** March-May. **To obtain tee times:** Call 60 day in advance. Resort guests of Amelia Island Plantation only. **Miscellaneous:** Reduced fees (low season, resort guests, twilight, juniors), discount packages, range (grass), club rentals, lodging, credit cards (MC, V, D, Resort Charge Card).
Reader Comments: Immaculate, but nothing really memorable ... Scenic and fun as well as a challenge ... Beautiful course and ocean views ... We return each year.

★★★★ OCEAN LINKS
R-3000 1st Coast Hwy., Amelia Island, 32035, Nassau County, (904)277-5907, (800)874-6878, 35 miles NE of Jacksonville. **Web:** www.aipfl.com.
Holes: 18. **Yards:** 6,592/4,983. **Par:** 72/72. **Course Rating:** 71.7/66.4. **Slope:** 130/115. **Green Fee:** $95/$115. **Cart Fee:** Included in Green Fee. **Walking Policy:** Mandatory cart. **Walkability:** 1. **Opened:** 1987. **Architect:** Tom Fazio. **Season:** Year-round. **High:** Oct-Nov. **To obtain tee times:** Call 60 days in advance. Resort guests of Amelia Island Plantation only. **Miscellaneous:** Reduced fees (low season, resort guests, twilight, juniors), discount packages, range (grass), club rentals, lodging (400 rooms), credit cards (MC, V, AE, D, Resort Charge Card), beginner friendly (golf clinics and golf school).
Reader Comments: Well maintained ... Met expectations ... Beautiful live oaks and marshes ... Short, but fun ... Enjoyed it ... Too much target golf ... Bring all your shots ... Lots of water.

★★ APOLLO BEACH GOLF & SEA CLUB
PU-801 Golf and Sea Blvd., Apollo Beach, 33572, Hillsborough County, (813)645-6212, 15 miles S of Tampa.
Holes: 18. **Yards:** 7,070/4,831. **Par:** 72/72. **Course Rating:** 73.9/69.1. **Slope:** 130/115. **Green Fee:** $22/$40. **Cart Fee:** Included in Green Fee. **Walking Policy:** Mandatory cart. **Walkability:** 1. **Opened:** 1972. **Architect:** Robert Trent Jones. **Season:** Year-round. **High:** Nov.-March. **To obtain tee times:** Call. **Miscellaneous:** Reduced fees (low season, twilight, juniors), discount packages, range (grass), club rentals, credit cards (MC, V, AE, D), beginner friendly (weekly clinics).

★★★★ ARNOLD PALMER'S BAY HILL CLUB & LODGE *Service*
R-9000 Bay Hill Blvd., Orlando, 32819, Orange County, (407)876-2429x630, 15 miles SW of Orlando.
Holes: 27. **Yards:** 7,207/5,235. **Par:** 72/72. **Course Rating:** 75.1/72.7. **Slope:** 139/130. **Green Fee:** $195/$195. **Cart Fee:** Included in Green Fee. **Walking Policy:** Unrestricted walking.
Walkability: 2. **Opened:** 1961. **Architect:** Dick Wilson. **Season:** Year-round. **High:** Jan.-April. **To obtain tee times:** Tee times made through lodge reservation. **Miscellaneous:** Reduced fees (resort guests, juniors), metal spikes, range (grass/mats), caddies, club rentals, lodging (68 rooms), credit cards (MC, V, AE).
Notes: Ranked 97th in 1997-98 America's 100 Greatest; 9th in 1999 Best in State; 25th in 1996 America's Top 75 Upscale Courses. Bay Hill Invitational site.
Reader Comments: Gem of a course ... Way overpriced ... Nice wide fairways ... Crown this one ... Rock solid test of golf ... The king's home is a castle ... My idea of championship golf, tough but fun ... Great finishing holes, 16-18 ... Cozy, private feeling ... Don't be surprised to see Arnie!.

★★½ ARROWHEAD GOLF COURSE
PU-8201 S.W. 24th St., Ft. Lauderdale, 33324, Broward County, (954)475-8200, 5 miles W of Ft. Lauderdale.
Holes: 18. **Yards:** 6,311/4,838. **Par:** 70/70. **Course Rating:** 70.8/68.7. **Slope:** 115/109. **Green Fee:** $18/$49. **Cart Fee:** Included in Green Fee. **Walking Policy:** Mandatory cart. **Walkability:** 2. **Opened:** 1976. **Architect:** Bill Watts. **Season:** Year-round. **High:** Nov.-March. **To obtain tee times:** Call 7 days in advance. **Miscellaneous:** Reduced fees (weekdays, low season, twilight, juniors), discount packages, metal spikes, range (grass/mats), club rentals, credit cards (MC, V, AE).
Reader Comments: New sand in the traps ... A good challenge with lots of water ... Good variety of holes ... Too long of a wait to get on the course ... Narrow ... Reasonably priced.

★★★½ ATLANTIS COUNTRY CLUB & INN
R-190 Atlantis Blvd., Atlantis, 33462, Palm Beach County, (561)968-1300, 7 miles S of West Palm Beach.
Holes: 18. **Yards:** 6,537/5,258. **Par:** 72/72. **Course Rating:** 71.5/70.9. **Slope:** 128/123. **Green Fee:** $20/$60. **Cart Fee:** $15/person. **Walking Policy:** Mandatory cart. **Walkability:** 1. **Opened:** 1972. **Architect:** Robert Simmons. **Season:** Year-round. **High:** Jan.-March. **To obtain tee times:** Public call 2 days in advance. Members and resort guests call 3 days in advance. Groups may book up to 1 year in advance. **Miscellaneous:** Reduced fees (weekdays, low season, resort guests), discount packages, range (grass), club rentals, lodging (24 rooms), credit cards (MC, V, D).
Reader Comments: Fun, very open, good bunkers ... Great restaurant ... Tight course in good condition ... Short driving range ... Short, testy golf ... A pleasure to play ... Great back nine.

★★½ BABE ZAHARIAS GOLF COURSE
PM-11412 Forest Hills Dr., Tampa, 33612, Hillsborough County, (813)631-4374, 20 miles W of St. Petersburg.
Holes: 18. **Yards:** 6,163/5,236. **Par:** 70/71. **Course Rating:** 68.9/68.9. **Slope:** 121/118. **Green Fee:** $16/$35. **Cart Fee:** Included in Green Fee. **Walking Policy:** Unrestricted walking.
Walkability: 1. **Opened:** 1974. **Architect:** Ron Garl. **Season:** Year-round. **High:** Dec.-May. **To obtain tee times:** Call on Thursday for upcoming weekdays. Call on Monday for upcoming weekend. **Miscellaneous:** Reduced fees (weekdays, low season, twilight, seniors, juniors), metal spikes, club rentals, credit cards (MC, V, D).
Reader Comments: Back 9 stronger ... Slow greens ... Very tight fairways ... Improving each visit.

★★★ BARDMOOR NORTH GOLF CLUB
SP-8001 Cumberland Rd., Largo, 33777, Pinellas County, (727)392-1234, 15 miles W of Tampa.
Holes: 18. **Yards:** 7,000/5,550. **Par:** 72/72. **Course Rating:** 74.4/71.8. **Slope:** 129/118. **Green Fee:** $35/$75. **Cart Fee:** Included in Green Fee. **Walking Policy:** Mandatory cart. **Walkability:** 2. **Opened:** 1970. **Architect:** William Diddel. **Season:** Year-round. **High:** Dec.-April. **To obtain tee times:** Call 4 days in advance. **Miscellaneous:** Reduced fees (weekdays, low season, twilight, juniors), discount packages, range (grass/mats), caddies, club rentals, credit cards (MC, V, AE, D).
Notes: 1977-1989 JCPenney Classic.
Reader Comments: Great course, but pricey ... Average service ... Good value ... Good shape for getting lots of play ... Plenty of water ... Pompous attitude ... Very nice and it gets a lot of play ... A few holes standout.

★★½ BAYMEADOWS GOLF CLUB
SP-7981 Baymeadows Circle W., Jacksonville, 32256, Duval County, (904)731-5701.
Holes: 18. **Yards:** 6,939/5,309. **Par:** 72/72. **Course Rating:** 73.7/72.2. **Slope:** 130/130. **Green Fee:** $20/$39. **Cart Fee:** Included in Green Fee. **Walking Policy:** Mandatory cart. **Walkability:** 2. **Opened:** 1969. **Architect:** Desmond Muirhead/Gene Sarazen. **Season:** Year-round. **High:** Dec.-June. **To obtain tee times:** Call 7 days in advance. **Miscellaneous:** Reduced fees (weekdays, low season, resort guests, twilight, seniors, juniors), discount packages, range

(grass/mats), club rentals, lodging (200 rooms), credit cards (MC, V, AE), beginner friendly (beginner summer clinics).
Reader Comments: A good challenge, just enough water ... Not very scenic ... Couple of good holes ... Very good value, easy walking ... Bring in the wrecking ball ... Not much for your buck ... Typical Florida course.

★★ BAYSHORE GOLF COURSE
PU-2301 Alton Rd., Miami Beach, 33140, Dade County, (305)532-3350.
Holes: 18. **Yards:** 6,903/5,538. **Par:** 72/73. **Course Rating:** 73.0/71.6. **Slope:** 127/120. **Green Fee:** $30/$55. **Cart Fee:** Included in Green Fee. **Walking Policy:** Mandatory cart. **Walkability:** 1. **Architect:** Robert von Hagge/Bruce Devlin. **Season:** Year-round. **High:** Dec.-March. **To obtain tee times:** Call 7 days in advance. **Miscellaneous:** Reduced fees (weekdays, low season, twilight, juniors), discount packages, metal spikes, range (mats), club rentals, credit cards (MC, V, AE), beginner friendly (PGA professional instruction).

★★★★ BAYTREE NATIONAL GOLF LINKS
SP-8207 National Dr., Melbourne, 32940, Brevard County, (407)259-9060, (888)955-1234, 50 miles SE of Orlando. **E-mail:** bnglmgr@metrolink.net. **Web:** www.scratch-golf.com.
Holes: 18. **Yards:** 7,043/4,803. **Par:** 72/72. **Course Rating:** 74.4/67.5. **Slope:** 138/118. **Green Fee:** $41/$85. **Cart Fee:** Included in Green Fee. **Walking Policy:** Mandatory cart. **Walkability:** N/A. **Opened:** 1994. **Architect:** Gary Player. **Season:** Year-round. **High:** Jan.-March. **To obtain tee times:** Call 6 days in advance. **Miscellaneous:** Reduced fees (low season, resort guests, twilight), discount packages, metal spikes, range (grass/mats), club rentals, credit cards (MC, V, AE).
Reader Comments: Excellent value! Great condition ... Spectacular vistas, course, service ... Very overrated ... Snobbish ... Not for the fainthearted ... Made me feel at home ... Great challenge from tips with wind ... Didn't live up to expectations ... One of the best on the space coast ... Lots of wildlife ... Great people from arrival to departure.

★★★ BELLA VISTA GOLF & YACHT CLUB
SP-P.O. Box 66, Hwy. 48, Howey-in-the-Hills, 34737, Lake County, (352)324-3233, (800)955-7001, 25 miles W of Orlando.
Holes: 18. **Yards:** 6,321/5,386. **Par:** 71/71. **Course Rating:** 68.4/71.9. **Slope:** 119/123. **Green Fee:** $35/$38. **Cart Fee:** Included in Green Fee. **Walking Policy:** Mandatory cart. **Walkability:** 1. **Opened:** 1990. **Architect:** Lloyd Clifton. **Season:** Year-round. **High:** Sept.-April. **To obtain tee times:** Call 2 days in advance. **Miscellaneous:** Reduced fees (weekdays, low season, resort guests, twilight, seniors, juniors), discount packages, metal spikes, range (grass), club rentals, lodging, credit cards (MC, V).
Reader Comments: Great accommodations ... Play it when it is dry ... Uninteresting architecture .... A challenge, watch out for snakes and gators ... Winter month pace of play is very slow ... Better bring a helmet.

★★ BELLEVIEW BILTMORE RESORT & GOLF CLUB
R-1501 Indian Rocks Rd., Belleair, 34616, Pinellas County, (727)581-5498, 1 miles S of Clearwater. **Web:** www.belleviewbiltmore.com.
Holes: 18. **Yards:** 6,695/5,703. **Par:** 72/74. **Course Rating:** 70.7/72.1. **Slope:** 118/119. **Green Fee:** $35/$75. **Cart Fee:** Included in Green Fee. **Walking Policy:** Mandatory cart. **Walkability:** 2. **Opened:** 1926. **Architect:** Donald Ross. **Season:** Year-round. **High:** Jan.-April. **To obtain tee times:** Hotel guests may make tee times with room reservation. Nonguests call 4 days in advance. **Miscellaneous:** Reduced fees (weekdays, low season, resort guests, twilight, seniors), discount packages, metal spikes, range (grass), club rentals, credit cards (MC, V, AE, D).

BENT OAK GOLF CLUB
PU-4335 Londontown Rd., Titusville, 32796, Brevard County, (407)269-4653, 50 miles E of Orlando.
Holes: 18. **Yards:** 6,433/4,901. **Par:** 70/70. **Course Rating:** 69.9/70.7. **Slope:** 128/125. **Green Fee:** N/A. **Cart Fee:** Included in Green Fee. **Walking Policy:** Unrestricted walking. **Walkability:** 2. **Season:** Year-round. **High:** Nov.-June. **To obtain tee times:** Call Pro Shop. **Miscellaneous:** Reduced fees (weekdays, low season, twilight, juniors), range (grass), club rentals, credit cards (MC, V, AE, D), beginner friendly (clinics).

BIG CYPRESS GOLF & COUNTRY CLUB
SP-10000 N. US Hwy 98, Lakeland, 33809, Polk County, (941)859-6871, 9 miles N of lakeland.
Holes: 36. **Yards:** 6,680/4,803. **Par:** 72/72. **Course Rating:** 72.4/68.1. **Slope:** 134/115. **Green Fee:** $16/$24. **Walking Policy:** Mandatory cart. **Walkability:** 1. **Opened:** 1988. **Architect:** Ron Garl. **Season:** April-Oct. **High:** Oct.-April. **Miscellaneous:** Range (grass), club rentals.

★★★½ THE BILTMORE GOLF COURSE
PU-1210 Anastasia Ave., Coral Gables, 33134, Dade County, (305)460-5364, 3 miles of Miami.
Holes: 18. **Yards:** 6,642/5,237. **Par:** 71/74. **Course Rating:** 71.5/70.1. **Slope:** 119/115. **Green Fee:** $13/$53. **Cart Fee:** $17/person. **Walking Policy:** Walking at certain times. **Walkability:** 1. **Opened:** 1925. **Architect:** Donald Ross. **Season:** Year-round. **High:** Nov.-April. **To obtain tee**

times: Call 48 hours in advance from a touch tone telephone. Same day reservation call starter at (305)460-5365. **Miscellaneous:** Reduced fees (low season, resort guests, twilight, juniors), discount packages, range (grass/mats), club rentals, lodging, credit cards (MC, V, AE).

Reader Comments: Nice clubhouse ... Expensive; but pretty course ... Great old course, 1920's mansions ... Even 20-handicapper should play from the blues ... Needs more TLC ... One of the few 18 hole courses in Miami that lets you walk.

★★★½ BINKS FOREST GOLF COURSE
SP-400 Binks Forest Dr., Wellington, 33414, Palm Beach County, (561)795-0595, 15 miles W of West Palm Beach.
Holes: 18. **Yards:** 7,065/5,599. **Par:** 72/72. **Course Rating:** 75.0/71.9. **Slope:** 138/127. **Green Fee:** $20/$55. **Cart Fee:** Included in Green Fee. **Walking Policy:** Mandatory cart. **Walkability:** 1. **Opened:** 1990. **Architect:** Johnny Miller. **Season:** Year-round. **High:** Nov.-April. **To obtain tee times:** Call 7 days in advance with credit card. **Miscellaneous:** Reduced fees (weekdays, low season, resort guests, twilight), discount packages, metal spikes, range (grass), club rentals, credit cards (MC, V, AE, D), beginner friendly (junior clinics, adult beginner clinics).

Reader Comments: Country club feel ... Tight tree-lined fairways ... Conditioning leaves something to be desired ... More like Carolina ... . Tight, tough and I liked it a lot ... Pro shop staff nice.

★★★½ BLACK BEAR GOLF CLUB
PU-24505 Calusa Blvd., Eustis, 32736, Lake County, (352)357-4732, (800)423-2718, 40 miles N of Orlando.
Holes: 18. **Yards:** 7,002/5,044. **Par:** 72/72. **Course Rating:** 74.7/70.5. **Slope:** 134/121. **Green Fee:** $35/$65. **Cart Fee:** Included in Green Fee. **Walking Policy:** Unrestricted walking. **Walkability:** 3. **Opened:** 1995. **Architect:** P.B. Dye. **Season:** Year-round. **High:** Jan.-March. **To obtain tee times:** Call golf shop. **Miscellaneous:** Reduced fees (weekdays, low season, twilight, juniors), discount packages, metal spikes, range (grass), club rentals, credit cards (MC, V, AE, D). **Notes:** 1999 US Amateur Qualifying Site.

Reader Comments: Lots of blind shots ... Rollercoaster fairways ... Several holes too penal ... Needs more trees ... P.B. Dye strikes again ... Needs to mature ... When wind blows, watch out ... Tough bunkers ... Fun 15th hole, 60-70 yard par 3 ... Terrific greens.

★★★½ BLOOMINGDALE GOLFER'S CLUB
SP-4113 Great Golfers Place, Valrico, 33594, Hillsborough County, (813)685-4105, 15 miles SE of Tampa.
Holes: 18. **Yards:** 7,165/5,506. **Par:** 72/73. **Course Rating:** 74.4/72.1. **Slope:** 131/132. **Green Fee:** $30/$66. **Cart Fee:** Included in Green Fee. **Walking Policy:** Mandatory cart. **Walkability:** 1. **Opened:** 1983. **Architect:** Ron Garl. **Season:** Year-round. **High:** Dec.-April. **To obtain tee times:** Call up to 6 days in advance. **Miscellaneous:** Reduced fees (weekdays, low season, twilight, seniors, juniors), discount packages, range (grass/mats), club rentals, credit cards (MC, V, AE).

Reader Comments: Great local course ... Great practice green ... Check out the alligators ... Great course, out of the way. Greens are not as quick as advertised ... Deserves its high rating. Very difficult course ... The working man's Augusta National.

BLUE CYPRESS GOLF CLUB
4012 University Blvd. N., Jacksonville, 32211, Duval County, (904)744-2124.
Special Notes: Call club for further information.

BLUEWATER BAY RESORT   *Service*
R-1950 Bluewater Blvd., Niceville, 32578, Okaloosa County, (850)897-3241, (800)274-2128, 60 miles E of Pensacola.
★★★½ BAY/LAKE COURSE
Holes: 18. **Yards:** 6,803/5,378. **Par:** 72/72. **Course Rating:** 73.0/70.6. **Slope:** 140/124. **Green Fee:** $35/$45. **Cart Fee:** $15/person. **Walking Policy:** Walking at certain times. **Walkability:** 1. **Opened:** 1981. **Architect:** Tom Fazio/Jerry Pate. **Season:** Year-round. **High:** Feb.-May. **To obtain tee times:** Call anytime. **Miscellaneous:** Reduced fees (low season, resort guests, juniors), discount packages, range (grass), club rentals, lodging, credit cards (MC, V, AE, D).

Reader Comments: A good place to play for the value ... Attractive setting ... Too many condos ... Well maintained ... Tight fairways ... Good layout. Fair.
★★★★ MAGNOLIA/MARSH COURSE   *Pace*
Holes: 18. **Yards:** 6,669/5,048. **Par:** 72/72. **Course Rating:** 72.2/68.4. **Slope:** 132/117. **Green Fee:** $35/$45. **Cart Fee:** $15/person. **Walking Policy:** Walking at certain times. **Walkability:** 1. **Opened:** 1981. **Architect:** Tom Fazio/Jerry Pate. **Season:** Year-round. **High:** Feb.-May. **To obtain tee times:** Call anytime. **Miscellaneous:** Reduced fees (low season, resort guests, juniors), discount packages, range (grass), club rentals, lodging (90 rooms), credit cards (MC, V, AE, D).

Reader Comments: Outstanding! ... Quiet and very nice place ... Out of the way, but worth it ... Very good condition, enjoyable ... Terrific value.

FLORIDA

BOBBY JONES GOLF COMPLEX
PU-1000 Circus Blvd., Sarasota, 34232, Sarasota County, (941)955-8097, (800)955-3529, 60 miles S of Tampa.

★★★ AMERICAN COURSE
Holes: 18. **Yards:** 6,039/4,326. **Par:** 71/71. **Course Rating:** 68.4/64.5. **Slope:** 117/101. **Green Fee:** $9/$24. **Cart Fee:** $12/person. **Walking Policy:** Walking at certain times. **Walkability:** 2. **Opened:** 1957. **Architect:** Ron Garl. **Season:** Year-round. **High:** Dec.-April. **To obtain tee times:** Call automated computer system on touch-tone phone. **Miscellaneous:** Reduced fees (low season, twilight, juniors), range (mats), club rentals, credit cards (MC, V), beginner friendly (lessons available. 9-hole executive course).

Reader Comments: Love the cart computers ... Walking allowed ... Average course ... Good test of golf, crowded ... Improvements would make this a great experience ... Excellent municipal course ... Lots of water.

★★★ BRITISH COURSE
Holes: 18. **Yards:** 6,467/5,670. **Par:** 72/72. **Course Rating:** 70.0/72.3. **Slope:** 111/116. **Green Fee:** $9/$24. **Cart Fee:** $12/person. **Walking Policy:** Walking at certain times. **Walkability:** 1. **Opened:** 1927. **Architect:** Donald Ross. **Season:** Year-round. **High:** Dec.-April. **To obtain tee times:** Call automated system from touch-tone phone. **Miscellaneous:** Reduced fees (low season, twilight, juniors), range (mats), club rentals, credit cards (MC, V), beginner friendly (lessons available. 9 hole executive course).

Reader Comments: Lots of sand ... Fun to play ... Hard fairways ... Great value ... Just plain fun ... Too short ... Government employee attitude.

BOBCAT TRAIL GOLF & COUNTRY CLUB
PU-1350 Bobcat Trail, North Port, 34286, Sarasota County, (941)429-0500, 35 miles S of Sarasota.
Holes: 18. **Yards:** 6,748/4,741. **Par:** 71/71. **Course Rating:** 72.9/68.7. **Slope:** 129/115. **Green Fee:** $14/$50. **Cart Fee:** $15/person. **Walking Policy:** Mandatory cart. **Walkability:** 3. **Opened:** 1998. **Architect:** Lee Singletary/Bob Tway. **Season:** Year-round. **High:** Nov.-April. **To obtain tee times:** Phone up to 7 days in advance. **Miscellaneous:** Reduced fees (low season, twilight), discount packages, range (grass), club rentals, credit cards (MC, V, AE, D).

BOCA RATON RESORT & CLUB
★★★½ COUNTRY CLUB COURSE
R-17751 Boca Club Blvd., Boca Raton, 33487, Palm Beach County, (561)997-8205, (800)327-0101, 17 miles S of West Palm Beach. **E-mail:** rsc@bocaresort.com. **Web:** www.bocaresort.com.
Holes: 18. **Yards:** 6,513/5,365. **Par:** 72/72. **Course Rating:** 71.8/72.1. **Slope:** 131/128. **Green Fee:** $50/$100. **Cart Fee:** $25/person. **Walking Policy:** Mandatory cart. **Walkability:** 2. **Opened:** 1984. **Architect:** Joe Lee. **Season:** Year-round. **High:** Oct.-May. **To obtain tee times:** Call upon registering for resort guest room, a golf starting time may be reserved by providing resort room confirmation number. **Miscellaneous:** Reduced fees (low season, twilight), discount packages, range (grass), club rentals, lodging, credit cards (MC, V, AE, D, Diners Club).

Reader Comments: Old-style course ... Great condition ... Beautiful new course ... Short.

★★★½ RESORT COURSE
R-501 E. Camino Real, Boca Raton, 33432, Palm Beach County, (561)395-3000x3076, (800)327-0101, 22 miles of Palm Beach. **E-mail:** rsc@bocaresort.com. **Web:** www.bocaresort.com.
Holes: 18. **Yards:** 6,253/5,160. **Par:** 71/71. **Course Rating:** 69.3/68.7. **Slope:** 128/122. **Green Fee:** $65/$125. **Cart Fee:** $25/person. **Walking Policy:** Mandatory cart. **Walkability:** 3. **Opened:** 1926. **Architect:** William Flynn. **Season:** Year-round. **High:** Oct.-May. **To obtain tee times:** Call upon registering for a resort guest room, a golf starting time may be reserved by providing resort room confirmation number. **Miscellaneous:** Reduced fees (low season, twilight), discount packages, range (grass), club rentals, lodging (965 rooms), credit cards (MC, V, AE, D, Diners Club).

Reader Comments: Renovated course in very good shape ... Too short ... Beautiful flowers, waterfalls, and some good golf holes ... Fun & challenging ... Very playable if you like wind ... Tight fairways.

BONAVENTURE COUNTRY CLUB
R-200 Bonaventure Blvd., Weston, 33326, Broward County, (954)389-2100, (888)650-4653, 10 miles W of Ft. Lauderdale. **E-mail:** edunes@aol.com.

★★★½ GREEN MONSTER
Holes: 18. **Yards:** 7,011/5,345. **Par:** 72/72. **Course Rating:** 74.2/71.6. **Slope:** 132/122. **Green Fee:** $55/$100. **Cart Fee:** Included in Green Fee. **Walking Policy:** Mandatory cart. **Walkability:** 2. **Opened:** 1971. **Architect:** Joe Lee. **Season:** Year-round. **High:** Nov.-April. **To obtain tee times:** Tee times available up to 30 days in advance. **Miscellaneous:** Reduced fees (low season, resort guests, twilight), metal spikes, range (grass/mats), club rentals, lodging (650 rooms), credit cards (MC, V, AE, D, Diners Club, Carte Blanc).

Reader Comments: Except for waterfall hole this course is typical Florida ... Demanding from tips ... New grass ... Pricey but worth one play ... Long for average player ... Tough when windy ... Good value, fair test.

★★★ RESORT COURSE
Holes: 18. **Yards:** 6,189/4,993. **Par:** 70/70. **Course Rating:** 70.0/69.0. **Slope:** 118/114. **Green Fee:** $45/$70. **Cart Fee:** Included in Green Fee. **Walking Policy:** Mandatory cart. **Walkability:** 1. **Opened:** 1979. **Architect:** Charles Mahannah. **Season:** Year-round. **High:** Dec.-April. **To obtain tee times:** Tee times available up to 30 days in advance. **Miscellaneous:** Reduced fees (low season, resort guests, twilight), range (grass/mats), club rentals, lodging (650 rooms), credit cards (MC, V, AE, D, Diners Club, Carte Blanc).
Reader Comments: Fun course for ladies ... Tough par 5s ... Good alternative to Green Monster ... Overpriced ... Course conditions have really deteriorated.

★★★ BONITA SPRINGS GOLF CLUB
SP-10200 Maddox Lane, Bonita Springs, 34135, Lee County, (941)992-2800, 10 miles N of Naples.
Holes: 18. **Yards:** 6,761/5,306. **Par:** 72/72. **Course Rating:** 71.2/70.1. **Slope:** 129/121. **Green Fee:** $15/$60. **Cart Fee:** Included in Green Fee. **Walking Policy:** Walking at certain times. **Walkability:** 1. **Opened:** 1977. **Architect:** William Maddox. **Season:** Year-round. **High:** Jan.-March. **To obtain tee times:** Call up to 2 days in advance from 7 a.m. to 5 p.m. **Miscellaneous:** Reduced fees (low season, twilight), metal spikes, club rentals, credit cards (MC, V, D).
Reader Comments: Fair test of golf in pleasant surroundings ... Good greens ... Deceptively challenging ... Very narrow, target golf ... Does have some good holes ... Too close to houses.

BOYNTON BEACH MUNICIPAL GOLF COURSE
PM-8020 Jog Rd., Boynton Beach, 33437, Palm Beach County, (561)742-6501, 10 miles S of West Palm Beach.
Holes: 27. **Green Fee:** $13/$24. **Cart Fee:** $12/person. **Walking Policy:** Walking at certain times. **Walkability:** 1. **Opened:** 1984. **Architect:** Von Hagge/Devlin/Ankrom. **Season:** Year-round. **High:** Jan.-March. **To obtain tee times:** Call 1 day in advance for weekdays and 2 days in advance for weekends and holidays. **Miscellaneous:** Reduced fees (low season), metal spikes, range (grass), club rentals, credit cards (MC, V).
★★★ RED/BLUE
Yards: 5,062/4,057. **Par:** 65/65. **Course Rating:** 63.9/63.4. **Slope:** N/A.
Reader Comments: Easy ... Efficiently-run facility ... Nice little course ... Don't stray-you'll pay ... Playable for all levels ... Tight fairways ... Fun course.
★★★ RED/WHITE
Yards: 6,316/4,958. **Par:** 71/71. **Course Rating:** 70.1/67.7. **Slope:** 129/127.
Reader Comments: Great course, facilities, maintenance and service ... Nice course. Fast play. Good complex ... Too hard.
★★★ WHITE/BLUE
Yards: 5,290/4,175. **Par:** 66/66. **Course Rating:** 65.0/63.9. **Slope:** 113/N/A.
Reader Comments: Good maintenance and good service ... Keep the rangers in the clubhouse (very distracting).

BRAMBLE RIDGE GOLF COURSE
PU-2505 Bramble Ridge Drive, Lakeland, 33813, Polk County, (941)667-1988, 2 miles SE of Lakeland.
Holes: 18. **Yards:** 6,000/4,833. **Par:** 72/72. **Course Rating:** 68.1/67.8. **Slope:** 125/119. **Green Fee:** $14/$16. **Walking Policy:** Unrestricted walking. **Walkability:** 2. **Opened:** 1991. **Architect:** Ed Holloway. **Season:** Year-round. **High:** Jan.-March. **To obtain tee times:** Call golf shop. **Miscellaneous:** Reduced fees (low season, resort guests, twilight), metal spikes, range (grass), club rentals, credit cards (MC, V, D).

★★★ THE BREAKERS CLUB *Service*
R-1 S. County Rd., Palm Beach, 33480, Palm Beach County, (561)659-8407, 2 miles E of West Palm Beach. **Web:** www.thebreakers.com.
Holes: 18. **Yards:** 6,139/6,004. **Par:** 70/72. **Course Rating:** 69.3/72.6. **Slope:** 121/122. **Green Fee:** N/A/$85. **Cart Fee:** Included in Green Fee. **Walking Policy:** Walking at certain times. **Walkability:** 1. **Opened:** 1897. **Architect:** Alexander Findlay. **Season:** Year-round. **High:** Dec.-April. **To obtain tee times:** Tee times obtained 30 days in advance. **Miscellaneous:** Reduced fees (juniors), discount packages, metal spikes, range (grass/mats), caddies, club rentals, lodging (572 rooms), credit cards (MC, V, AE, D, All major).
Reader Comments: Like playing in older times ... Great short course with a breeze ... Easy course, great people, feel the tradition ... Short, straight and boring.

BROKEN WOODS COUNTRY CLUB
SP-9001 West Sample Rd., Coral Springs, 33065, Broward County, (954)752-2140.
Holes: 18. **Yards:** 5,904/4,874. **Par:** 70/70. **Course Rating:** 67.3/68.9. **Slope:** 120/119. **Green Fee:** $13/$27. **Cart Fee:** Included in Green Fee. **Walking Policy:** Walking at certain times.

FLORIDA

Walkability: 1. **Season:** Year-round. **High:** Dec.-April. **To obtain tee times:** For non-members 4 days in advance. Members 7 days in advance. **Miscellaneous:** Reduced fees (weekdays, low season, twilight), club rentals, credit cards (MC, V, AE), beginner friendly.

★★★ CALIFORNIA CLUB
SP-20898 San Simeon Way, North Miami, 33179, Dade County, (305)651-3590.
Holes: 18. **Yards:** 6,670/5,675. **Par:** 72/72. **Course Rating:** 70.9/69.7. **Slope:** 125/117. **Green Fee:** $22/$45. **Cart Fee:** Included in Green Fee. **Walking Policy:** Mandatory cart. **Walkability:** 2. **Season:** Year-round. **High:** Dec.-April. **To obtain tee times:** Call golf shop up to 7 days in advance. **Miscellaneous:** Reduced fees (weekdays, low season, twilight), metal spikes, range (grass/mats), club rentals, credit cards (MC, V, AE).
Reader Comments: You have to hit it straight ... Too many homes ... Shh, underplayed ... Narrow fairways ... Layout pinched by condo developments.

★★★½ CALUSA LAKES GOLF COURSE
SP-1995 Calusa Lakes Blvd., Nokomis, 34275, Sarasota County, (941)484-8995, 5 miles S of Sarasota.
Holes: 18. **Yards:** 6,760/5,197. **Par:** 72/72. **Course Rating:** N/A. **Slope:** 124/118. **Green Fee:** $27/$46. **Cart Fee:** Included in Green Fee. **Walking Policy:** Walking at certain times. **Walkability:** 2. **Opened:** 1991. **Architect:** Ted McAnlis. **Season:** Year-round. **High:** Jan.-April. **To obtain tee times:** Call 2 days in advance. **Miscellaneous:** Reduced fees (low season, twilight), metal spikes, range (grass/mats), credit cards (MC, V).
Reader Comments: Hilly layout ... Slow play & expensive ... nice greens ... Good off-season bargain ... Good challenge for all levels.

★★★½ CAPE CORAL GOLF & TENNIS RESORT
R-4003 Palm Tree Blvd., Cape Coral, 33904, Lee County, (941)542-7879, (800)648-1475, 10 miles W of Fort Myers. **E-mail:** info@capecoralgolfresort.com. **Web:** www.capecoralgolfresort.
Holes: 18. **Yards:** 6,707/5,152. **Par:** 72/72. **Course Rating:** 72.0/71.2. **Slope:** 127/119. **Green Fee:** $18/$65. **Cart Fee:** Included in Green Fee. **Walking Policy:** Mandatory cart. **Walkability:** 2. **Opened:** 1963. **Architect:** Dick Wilson. **Season:** Year-round. **High:** Jan.-March. **To obtain tee times:** Call 3 days in advance after 4 p.m. **Miscellaneous:** Reduced fees (low season, resort guests, twilight, juniors), discount packages, range (grass/mats), club rentals, lodging, credit cards (MC, V, AE, D).
Reader Comments: Strict about pace of play ... Hardest 1st hole I ever played ... Better learn how to hit out of sand ... Gets lots of play but not a typical Florida course ... Good vacation golf.

★★★ CAPRI ISLES GOLF CLUB
SP-849 Capri Isles Blvd., Venice, 34292, Sarasota County, (941)485-3371, 60 miles S of Tampa. **E-mail:** caprigolf@aol.com.
Holes: 18. **Yards:** 6,472/5,480. **Par:** 72/72. **Course Rating:** 70.6/70.9. **Slope:** 122/116. **Green Fee:** $29/$48. **Cart Fee:** Included in Green Fee. **Walking Policy:** Walking at certain times. **Walkability:** 2. **Opened:** 1972. **Architect:** Andy Anderson. **Season:** Year-round. **High:** Jan.-April. **To obtain tee times:** Call up to 3 days ahead. **Miscellaneous:** Reduced fees (low season, twilight), metal spikes, range (grass), club rentals, credit cards (MC, V).
Reader Comments: Small greens ... Lots of O.B ... Good place to start a Florida golf vacation ... Tight fairways.

★★★★ CELEBRATION GOLF CLUB
PU-701 Golf Park Dr., Celebration, 34747, Osceola County, (407)566-4653, (888)275-2918, 15 miles S of Orlando. **Web:** www.celebrationgolf.com.
Holes: 18. **Yards:** 6,786/5,724. **Par:** 72/72. **Course Rating:** 73.0/68.1. **Slope:** 135/122. **Green Fee:** $65/$110. **Cart Fee:** Included in Green Fee. **Walking Policy:** Walking at certain times. **Walkability:** 3. **Opened:** 1996. **Architect:** Robert Trent Jones/Robert Trent Jones Jr. **Season:** Year-round. **High:** Jan.-April. **To obtain tee times:** Call up to 30 days in advance. **Miscellaneous:** Reduced fees (low season, twilight, juniors), metal spikes, range (grass), club rentals, credit cards (MC, V, AE), beginner friendly (beginner tees available).
Reader Comments: Beautiful ... Average golf, high price ... Challenging ... Tough carries on many holes ... Nice course but expected more ... A shotmaker's course ... Too expensive.

★★★½ CHAMPIONS CLUB AT JULINGTON CREEK
SP-1111 Durbin Creek Blvd., Jacksonville, 32259, St. Johns County, (904)287-4653, 15 miles S of Jacksonville.
Holes: 18. **Yards:** 6,872/4,994. **Par:** 72/72. **Course Rating:** 72.8/68.6. **Slope:** 126/114. **Green Fee:** $35/$45. **Cart Fee:** Included in Green Fee. **Walking Policy:** Mandatory cart. **Walkability:** 1. **Opened:** 1992. **Architect:** Bob Walker/Steve Melynk. **Season:** Year-round. **High:** March-May/Oct.-Dec. **To obtain tee times:** Call golf shop 5 days in advance for outside guest play. **Miscellaneous:** Reduced fees (weekdays, twilight, seniors, juniors), range (grass), club rentals, credit cards (MC, V, D), beginner friendly (ladies clinics, summer junior clinics).
Notes: 1996-1997,1999 Jacksonville Hooters Tour; 1997 World Jr. Golf Cup U.S. Finals.

FLORIDA

Reader Comments: Good value ... New course with interesting holes ... Fairly open ... Good front nine. Back nine contrived ... Excellent par 3s ... A typical Disney experience.

★★★½ THE CHAMPIONS CLUB AT SUMMERFIELD

PU-3400 S.E. Summerfield Way, Stuart, 34997, Martin County, (561)283-1500, 25 miles N of West Palm Beach. **E-mail:** champllb@gate.net. **Web:** www.thechampionsclub.com.
Holes: 18. **Yards:** 6,809/4,941. **Par:** 72/72. **Course Rating:** 72.8/71.0. **Slope:** 131/120. **Green Fee:** $20/$65. **Cart Fee:** Included in Green Fee. **Walking Policy:** Mandatory cart. **Walkability:** 2. **Opened:** 1994. **Architect:** Tom Fazio. **Season:** Year-round. **High:** Nov.-April. **To obtain tee times:** Call up to 7 days in advance. **Miscellaneous:** Reduced fees (weekdays, low season, resort guests, twilight, juniors), discount packages, metal spikes, range (grass), club rentals, credit cards (MC, V, AE, D).
Reader Comments: Lots of placement shots ... Several signature holes ... Excellent, Excellent ... Gimmicky 18th ... Take plenty of balls ... Scenic and playable ... Very unforgiving ... Good test for all types of shots ... Each hole by itself a wildlife treasure ... Wonderful layout.

★★★½ CHI CHI RODRIGUEZ GOLF CLUB

PU-3030 McMullen Booth Rd., Clearwater, 34621, Pinellas County, (813)726-8829, 15 miles W of Tampa.
Holes: 18. **Yards:** 5,454/3,929. **Par:** 69/71. **Course Rating:** 67.6/64.0. **Slope:** 118/110. **Green Fee:** $22/$25. **Cart Fee:** Included in Green Fee. **Walking Policy:** Walking at certain times. **Walkability:** 3. **Opened:** 1989. **Architect:** Denis Griffiths. **Season:** Year-round. **High:** Feb.-April. **To obtain tee times:** Call 4 days in advance. **Miscellaneous:** Reduced fees (twilight), discount packages, metal spikes, club rentals, credit cards (MC, V, D).
Reader Comments: Tight layout ... Fun ... Not bad for the buck ... Not long-doesn't need to be ... Short, but hilly and tight.

CHIEFLAND GOLF & COUNTRY CLUB

Rte. #2, Chiefland, 32626, Levy County, (352)493-2375.
Special Notes: Call club for further information.

★★★★ CIMARRONE GOLF & COUNTRY CLUB

SP-2690 Cimarrone Blvd., Jacksonville, 32259, Duval County, (904)287-2000, 22 miles S of Jacksonville.
Holes: 18. **Yards:** 6,891/4,707. **Par:** 72/72. **Course Rating:** 72.7/67.8. **Slope:** 132/119. **Green Fee:** $25/$44. **Cart Fee:** Included in Green Fee. **Walking Policy:** Mandatory cart. **Walkability:** 4. **Opened:** 1989. **Architect:** David Postlethwait. **Season:** Year-round. **High:** Spring/Fall. **To obtain tee times:** Call up to 4 days in advance. **Miscellaneous:** Reduced fees (weekdays, low season, twilight, juniors), discount packages, range (grass), club rentals, credit cards (MC, V), beginner friendly (lessons, rentals).
Reader Comments: Great layout. Wish Jacksonville had more like this ... Will eat your lunch!! ... Quick stop off I-95 ... Great value for area ... A real test from back tees ... Large greens ... Too artificial ... Lots of tee options ... More rolling and hilly than most Florida courses ... Bring your ball retriever.

CITRUS HILLS GOLF & COUNTRY CLUB

SP-509 E. Hartford St., Hernando, 34442, Citrus County, (352)746-4425, 90 miles N of Tampa.
★★★ MEADOWS COURSE
Holes: 18. **Yards:** 5,885/4,585. **Par:** 70/70. **Course Rating:** 68.5/66.9. **Slope:** 114/112. **Green Fee:** $14/$35. **Cart Fee:** Included in Green Fee. **Walking Policy:** Walking at certain times. **Walkability:** 2. **Opened:** 1983. **Architect:** Phil Friel. **Season:** Year-round. **High:** Dec.-April. **To obtain tee times:** Call up to 3 days in advance. **Miscellaneous:** Reduced fees (low season, twilight), discount packages, metal spikes, range (grass), lodging, credit cards (MC, V, AE, D).
Reader Comments: Nice greens ... Just too open and easy ... Easy but fun ... Overrated.

★★★½ OAKS COURSE
Holes: 18. **Yards:** 6,323/4,647. **Par:** 70/70. **Course Rating:** 71.0/67.0. **Slope:** 121/114. **Green Fee:** $14/$35. **Cart Fee:** Included in Green Fee. **Walking Policy:** Mandatory cart. **Walkability:** 4. **Opened:** 1985. **Architect:** Phil Friel. **Season:** Year-round. **High:** Dec.-April. **To obtain tee times:** Call 3 days in advance. **Miscellaneous:** Reduced fees (low season, twilight), discount packages, metal spikes, range (grass/mats), lodging, credit cards (MC, V, AE, D).
Reader Comments: Great value ... Challenging ... Tight fairways ... Relatively short ... Great finishing holes.

★★★ CITRUS SPRINGS GOLF & COUNTRY CLUB

SP-8690 Golfview Dr., Citrus Springs, 34434, Citrus County, (352)489-5045, (877)405-GOLF, 4 miles S of Dunellon.
Holes: 18. **Yards:** 6,600/6,242. **Par:** 72/72. **Course Rating:** 72.0/71.0. **Slope:** 126/118. **Green Fee:** $15/$28. **Cart Fee:** Included in Green Fee. **Walking Policy:** Mandatory cart. **Walkability:** 5. **Opened:** 1972. **Season:** Year-round. **High:** Nov.-April. **To obtain tee times:** Call up to 5 days

in advance. **Miscellaneous:** Reduced fees (low season), range (grass), club rentals, credit cards (MC, V).
Reader Comments: 1st hole drops 100 feet! ... A real test ... Could be longer ... A very enjoyable resort course.

★★ CLEARWATER COUNTRY CLUB
SP-525 N. Betty Lane, Clearwater, 33755, Pinellas County, (727)443-5078, 2 miles W of Tampa.
E-mail: eal4ccc@juno.com.
Holes: 18. **Yards:** 6,231/5,202. **Par:** 72/72. **Course Rating:** 69.4/69.7. **Slope:** 123/118. **Green Fee:** $20/$55. **Cart Fee:** Included in Green Fee. **Walking Policy:** Walking at certain times. **Walkability:** 2. **Opened:** 1922. **Season:** Year-round. **High:** Jan.-March. **To obtain tee times:** Call golf shop 3 days in advance. **Miscellaneous:** Reduced fees (weekdays, low season, twilight), range (grass), club rentals, credit cards (MC, V).

CLERBROOK RESORT
R-20005 U.S. Hwy. 27, Clermont, 34711, Lake County, (352)394-6165, 20 miles W of Orlando.
Holes: 18. **Yards:** 5,154/4,140. **Par:** 67/67. **Course Rating:** 64.8/64.8. **Slope:** 108/105. **Green Fee:** $13/$26. **Cart Fee:** $14/cart. **Walking Policy:** Walking at certain times. **Walkability:** 2. **Opened:** 1984. **Architect:** Dean Refram. **Season:** Year-round. **High:** Nov.-March. **To obtain tee times:** Call up to 5 days in advance. **Miscellaneous:** Reduced fees (low season, resort guests, twilight, juniors), range (grass/mats), club rentals, lodging, credit cards (MC, V, D).

CLEVELAND HEIGHTS GOLF COURSE
PM-2900 Buckingham Ave., Lakeland, 33803, Polk County, (863)682-3277, 45 miles E of Tampa.
E-mail: rmccl@city.lakeland.net. **Web:** www.city.lakeland.net.
Holes: 27. **Green Fee:** $18/$29. **Cart Fee:** $10/person. **Walking Policy:** Walking at certain times. **Walkability:** 2. **Opened:** 1925. **Season:** Year-round. **High:** Dec.-March. **To obtain tee times:** Call up to 7 days in advance. **Miscellaneous:** Reduced fees (low season, twilight, juniors), discount packages, range (grass), club rentals, credit cards (MC, V).
★★★ A/B
Yards: 6,378/5,389. **Par:** 72/72. **Course Rating:** 70.3/70.1. **Slope:** 118/116.
Reader Comments: Good city course but often crowded ... Good course for beginners ... Uninteresting ... Would not race back ... Short, easy course ... Fun to play.
★★★ A/C
Yards: 6,517/5,546. **Par:** 72/72. **Course Rating:** 71.0/71.5. **Slope:** 120/115.
★★★ B/C
Yards: 6,459/5,455. **Par:** 72/72. **Course Rating:** 70.3/70.8. **Slope:** 119/116.
Special Notes: Formerly Cleveland Heights Golf & Country Club. Soft spikes only.

CLEWISTON GOLF COURSE
PM-1200 San Luis Rd., Clewiston, 33440, Hendry County, (941)983-1448.
Holes: 18. **Yards:** 6,353/5,052. **Par:** 72/72. **Course Rating:** 70.6/69.5. **Slope:** 120/116. **Green Fee:** $12/$25. **Cart Fee:** $15/cart. **Walking Policy:** Walking at certain times. **Walkability:** 1. **Season:** Year-round. **High:** Oct.-April. **To obtain tee times:** Call up to 3 days in advance. **Miscellaneous:** Metal spikes, range (grass), club rentals, credit cards (MC, V), beginner friendly.

★★★★½ THE CLUB AT EAGLEBROOKE *Condition, Pace*
SP-1300 Eaglebrooke Blvd., Lakeland, 33813, Polk County, (941)701-0101, 30 miles NE of Tampa.
Holes: 18. **Yards:** 7,005/4,981. **Par:** 72/72. **Course Rating:** 74.0/69.0. **Slope:** 136/115. **Green Fee:** $36/$49. **Cart Fee:** $11/person. **Walking Policy:** Walking at certain times. **Walkability:** 3. **Opened:** 1997. **Architect:** Ron Garl. **Season:** Year-round. **High:** Nov.-April. **To obtain tee times:** Call 2 days in advance. **Miscellaneous:** Reduced fees (weekdays, low season, juniors), range (grass), club rentals, credit cards (MC, V, AE, D), beginner friendly.
Reader Comments: Great course! Bring some golf balls ... Good greens ... Absolute joy, fantastic golf ... Carts brought to car ... Awesome, great holes ... Choose the right set of tees!.

★★★★ THE CLUB AT EMERALD HILLS
SP-4100 N. Hills Dr., Hollywood, 33021, Broward County, (954)961-4000, 5 miles S of Ft. Lauderdale. **Web:** www.theclubatemeraldhills.com.
Holes: 18. **Yards:** 7,003/5,032. **Par:** 72/72. **Course Rating:** 74.1/70.1. **Slope:** 133/116. **Green Fee:** $10/$100. **Cart Fee:** $25/person. **Walking Policy:** Mandatory cart. **Walkability:** 3. **Opened:** 1969. **Architect:** B. Devlin/R. von Hagge/C. Ankrom. **Season:** Year-round. **High:** Dec.-April. **To obtain tee times:** Call up to 5 days in advance. Credit Card to secure time in high season. **Miscellaneous:** Reduced fees (weekdays, low season), range (grass), club rentals, credit cards (MC, V, AE).
Reader Comments: Will test anyone's skills ... Too many doglegs ... Good test, good shape, good value ... Nice country club atmosphere ... Great variety of holes ... Lots of sand and water ... Very challenging ... Classy operation.

★★★★½   THE CLUB AT HIDDEN CREEK   *Service, Value, Pace+*
SP-3070 PGA Blvd., Navarre, 32566, Santa Rosa County, (850)939-4604, 20 miles E of Pensacola. **E-mail:** bross@kslf.com. **Web:** www.kslfairways.com.
Holes: 18. **Yards:** 6,862/5,213. **Par:** 72/72. **Course Rating:** 73.2/70.1. **Slope:** 139/124. **Green Fee:** $25/$55. **Cart Fee:** Included in Green Fee. **Walking Policy:** Mandatory cart. **Walkability:** 2. **Opened:** 1988. **Architect:** Ron Garl. **Season:** Year-round. **High:** Jan.-April. **To obtain tee times:** Call up to 7 days in advance. **Miscellaneous:** Reduced fees (weekdays, low season, twilight, juniors), discount packages, range (grass), club rentals, credit cards (MC, V), beginner friendly (summer golf clinics).
Reader Comments: Superb layout at $25.00 ... A hidden jewel ... Several very interesting holes ... Fun course, well kept, good value ... Houses well back from course ... Play beat the pro on par 3 ... An abundance of sandtraps ... Friendly staff.

THE CLUB AT OAK FORD
SP-1552 Palm View Rd., Sarasota, 34240, Sarasota County, (941)371-3680, (888)881-3673, 60 miles S of Tampa.
Holes: 27. **Green Fee:** $15/$45. **Cart Fee:** Included in Green Fee. **Walking Policy:** Mandatory cart. **Walkability:** 2. **Opened:** 1989. **Architect:** Ron Garl. **Season:** Year-round. **High:** Jan.-April. **To obtain tee times:** Call up to 7 days in advance. **Miscellaneous:** Reduced fees (low season), discount packages, metal spikes, range (grass), club rentals, credit cards (MC, V)
★★★   MYRTLE/LIVE OAK
Yards: 6,750/5,085. **Par:** 72/72. **Course Rating:** 72.7/69.0. **Slope:** 131/118. .
Reader Comments: Far off the beaten path ... 27 holes in nature ... Great in season value ... Some hidden shots ... Lots of wildlife ... Worth the drive ... Great target golf for the money.
★★★   MYRTLE/PALMS
Yards: 6,750/5,085. **Par:** 72/72. **Course Rating:** 72.7/69.0. **Slope:** 131/118.
★★★   PALMS/LIVE OAK
Yards: 6,750/5,085. **Par:** 72/72. **Course Rating:** 72.7/69.0. **Slope:** 131/118.

★★★½   THE CLUB AT WINSTON TRAILS
SP-6101 Winston Trails Blvd., Lake Worth, 33463, Palm Beach County, (561)439-3700, 15 miles S of West Palm Beach. **Web:** www.winstontrails.com.
Holes: 18. **Yards:** 6,835/5,405. **Par:** 72/72. **Course Rating:** 73.0/70.0. **Slope:** 130/119. **Green Fee:** $30/$75. **Cart Fee:** Included in Green Fee. **Walking Policy:** Walking at certain times. **Walkability:** 2. **Opened:** 1993. **Architect:** Joe Lee. **Season:** Year-round. **To obtain tee times:** Call 2 days in advance. **Miscellaneous:** Reduced fees (weekdays, low season, twilight), discount packages, range (grass/mats), club rentals, credit cards (MC, V, AE).
Reader Comments: Undulating greens ... Fun from trunk to 19th hole ... Public course with country club atmosphere ... If putt reads straight, read again ... Slicers stay home or bring extra balls ... Big bunkers, big lakes and big challenge.

CLUB MED SANDPIPER
R-3500 S.E. Morningside Blvd., Port St. Lucie, 34952, St. Lucie County, (561)398-5007, 35 miles N of West Palm Beach.
★★   SAINTS COURSE
Holes: 18. **Yards:** 6,478/5,379. **Par:** 72/72. **Course Rating:** 70.7/71.3. **Slope:** 120/119. **Green Fee:** $18/$45. **Cart Fee:** Included in Green Fee. **Walking Policy:** Mandatory cart. **Walkability:** 2. **Opened:** 1961. **Architect:** Mark Mahannah. **Season:** Year-round. **High:** Dec.-April. **To obtain tee times:** Call 1 day in advance. **Miscellaneous:** Reduced fees (low season, juniors), discount packages, metal spikes, club rentals, lodging, credit cards (MC, V, AE), beginner friendly (golf academy, free beginner tips if staying at hotel).
★★   SINNERS COURSE
Holes: 18. **Yards:** 6,888/5,384. **Par:** 72/72. **Course Rating:** 72.3/71.1. **Slope:** 123/116. **Green Fee:** $25/$45. **Cart Fee:** Included in Green Fee. **Walking Policy:** Mandatory cart. **Walkability:** 2. **Opened:** 1961. **Architect:** Mark Mahannah. **Season:** Year-round. **High:** Dec.-April. **To obtain tee times:** Call 1 day in advance. **Miscellaneous:** Reduced fees (low season, juniors), metal spikes, range (grass), club rentals, lodging, credit cards (MC, V, AE), beginner friendly (golf academy, free beginner tips if guest in hotel).

COCOA BEACH GOLF COURSE
PM-5000 Tom Warriner Blvd., Cocoa Beach, 32931, Brevard County, (407)868-3351, 40 miles E of Orlando.
Holes: 27. **Green Fee:** $17/$27. **Cart Fee:** $9/person. **Walking Policy:** Walking at certain times. **Opened:** 1992. **Architect:** Charles Ankrom. **Season:** Year-round. **High:** Dec.-April. **To obtain tee times:** Call 28 days in advance at (407)868-3361. **Miscellaneous:** Reduced fees (weekdays, low season, twilight, juniors), metal spikes, range (grass), club rentals, credit cards (MC, V, AE).
★★★   DOLPHIN/LAKES
Yards: 6,393/4,985. **Par:** 71/71. **Course Rating:** 70.1/68.0. **Slope:** 115/109. **Walkability:** 1.

FLORIDA

Reader Comments: A very good city course ... Add 10 strokes when the wind blows ... Links course, can be tough in wind ... Good, solid golf experience.

★★★ **RIVER/DOLPHIN**
Yards: 6,363/4,903. **Par:** 71/71. **Course Rating:** 69.9/67.5. **Slope:** 116/108. **Walkability:** N/A.

★★★ **RIVER/LAKES**
Yards: 6,714/5,294. **Par:** 72/72. **Course Rating:** 71.7/69.3. **Slope:** 119/113. **Walkability:** 1.

★★★½ **COLONY WEST COUNTRY CLUB**
PU-6800 N.W. 88th Ave., Tamarac, 33321, Broward County, (954)726-8430, 10 miles W of Fort Lauderdale.
Holes: 36. **Yards:** 7,312/5,462. **Par:** 71/71. **Course Rating:** 75.5/71.6. **Slope:** 146/127. **Green Fee:** $35/$70. **Cart Fee:** Included in Green Fee. **Walking Policy:** Mandatory cart. **Walkability:** 1. **Opened:** 1970. **Architect:** Bruce Devlin/Robert von Hagge. **Season:** Year-round. **High:** Dec.-April. **To obtain tee times:** Call golf shop. **Miscellaneous:** Reduced fees (weekdays, low season, twilight), discount packages, metal spikes, club rentals, credit cards (MC, V, AE), beginner friendly (glades course).
Reader Comments: Tough! Tough! ... Practice your long irons ... House-lined fairways feel like you're playing in a bowling alley ... Great layout with lots of water ... Pace of play is major turn-off ... Best group of par 3's I have ever played ... I make sure to always leave time for this one.

★★ **CONTINENTAL COUNTRY CLUB**
SP-50 Continental Blvd., Wildwood, 34785, Sumter County, (352)748-3293, 5 miles W of Leesburg.
Holes: 18. **Yards:** 6,461/5,438. **Par:** 72/73. **Course Rating:** 70.1/71.1. **Slope:** 123/122. **Green Fee:** $20/$35. **Cart Fee:** Included in Green Fee. **Walking Policy:** Mandatory cart. **Walkability:** 1. **Architect:** Ron Garl. **Season:** Year-round. **High:** Nov.-May. **To obtain tee times:** Call up to 2 days in advance. **Miscellaneous:** Reduced fees (low season, twilight), range (grass), club rentals, credit cards (MC, V, D).

★★★½ **CORAL OAKS GOLF COURSE**
PU-1800 N.W. 28th Ave., Cape Coral, 33993, Lee County, (941)573-3100, 12 miles NW of Ft. Myers.
Holes: 18. **Yards:** 6,623/4,803. **Par:** 72/72. **Course Rating:** 71.7/68.9. **Slope:** 123/117. **Green Fee:** $23/$27. **Cart Fee:** $14/person. **Walking Policy:** Walking at certain times. **Walkability:** 2. **Opened:** 1988. **Architect:** Arthur Hills. **Season:** Year-round. **High:** Dec.-April. **To obtain tee times:** Call 2 days in advance. **Miscellaneous:** Reduced fees (low season), discount packages, range (grass), club rentals, credit cards (MC, V, AE, D).
Reader Comments: Very nice, management very friendly ... Unique look for area ... Pool-table flat with plenty of water ... Playable for all levels ... Good for women.

COSTA DEL SOL GOLF & COUNTRY CLUB
SP-100 Costa Del Sol Blvd/102 Ave NW 36 St, Miami, 33178, Dade County, (305)592-9210.
Holes: 18. **Yards:** 6,400/5,487. **Par:** 72/72. **Course Rating:** 70.0/70.2. **Slope:** 118/115. **Green Fee:** $16/$30. **Cart Fee:** Included in Green Fee. **Walking Policy:** Mandatory cart. **Walkability:** 1. **Opened:** 1973. **Architect:** Robert Cupp. **Season:** Year-round. **High:** Nov.-April. **To obtain tee times:** Call up to 2-3 days in advance. **Miscellaneous:** Reduced fees (weekdays, low season, twilight, juniors), metal spikes, range (grass), club rentals, credit cards (MC, V).

★★★½ **THE COUNTRY CLUB AT SILVER SPRINGS SHORES**
SP-565 Silver Rd., Ocala, 34472, Marion County, (904)687-2828, 69 miles NW of Orlando.
Holes: 18. **Yards:** 6,857/5,188. **Par:** 72/72. **Course Rating:** 73.7/70.2. **Slope:** 131/120. **Green Fee:** $16/$39. **Cart Fee:** Included in Green Fee. **Walking Policy:** Mandatory cart. **Walkability:** 3. **Opened:** 1969. **Architect:** Desmond Muirhead. **Season:** Year-round. **High:** Dec.-April. **To obtain tee times:** Call up to 7 days in advance. **Miscellaneous:** Reduced fees (low season, twilight), discount packages, metal spikes, range (grass), club rentals, credit cards (MC, V, AE, D).
Reader Comments: Nice course but needs work ... Nines are different ... Lots of gators ... Stay below the hole ... One of best deals you'll find ... Slow at times ... Very pretty ... Watch for water.

COUNTRY CLUB OF MIAMI
PM-6801 Miami Gardens Dr., Miami, 33015, Dade County, (305)829-4700, 20 miles NW of Miami.

★★★½ **EAST COURSE**
Holes: 18. **Yards:** 6,553/5,025. **Par:** 70/70. **Course Rating:** 70.3/68.8. **Slope:** 124/117. **Green Fee:** $20/$65. **Cart Fee:** Included in Green Fee. **Walking Policy:** Mandatory cart. **Walkability:** 3. **Opened:** 1959. **Architect:** Robert Trent Jones. **Season:** Year-round. **High:** Dec.-April. **To obtain tee times:** Call 3 days in advance. **Miscellaneous:** Reduced fees (weekdays, low season, twilight), discount packages, range (grass/mats), club rentals, credit cards (MC, V, AE, D), beginner friendly (golf clinics, children under 10 play free with adult during summer). **Reader Comments:** Exciting layout for a short course ... Nice, playable ... Nice restaurant ... Expensive without discount ... Need to work on pace of play ... Better than average ... A lot of water.

Holes: 18. **Yards:** 7,017/5,298. **Par:** 72/72. **Course Rating:** 73.5/70.1. **Slope:** 130/123. **Green Fee:** $20/$65. **Cart Fee:** Included in Green Fee. **Walking Policy:** Mandatory cart. **Walkability:** 3. **Opened:** 1940. **Architect:** Robert Trent Jones/Bobby Weed. **Season:** Year-round. **High:** Dec.-April. **To obtain tee times:** Call 3 days in advance. **Miscellaneous:** Reduced fees (weekdays, low season, twilight), discount packages, range (grass), club rentals, credit cards (MC, V, AE, D), beginner friendly (golf clinics, children under 10 play free with adult during summer).
Reader Comments: Tough golf experience from back tees ... Some great holes .:. Well groomed ... Some hidden hazards ... A bit overrated ... Long and difficult, but you can score.
Special Notes: Formerly Golf Club of Miami.

★★★½ COUNTRY CLUB OF MOUNT DORA

SP-1900 Country Club Blvd., Mount Dora, 32757, Lake County, (352)735-2263, 25 miles N of Orlando.
Holes: 18. **Yards:** 6,571/5,002. **Par:** 72/72. **Course Rating:** 72.1/71.0. **Slope:** 125/120. **Green Fee:** $18/$55. **Cart Fee:** Included in Green Fee. **Walking Policy:** Walking at certain times. **Walkability:** 3. **Opened:** 1991. **Architect:** Lloyd Clifton. **Season:** Year-round. **High:** Jan.-March. **To obtain tee times:** Call 5 days in advance. **Miscellaneous:** Reduced fees (weekdays, low season, resort guests, twilight, seniors, juniors), discount packages, range (grass), caddies, club rentals, lodging, credit cards (MC, V).
Reader Comments: Nice course in residential setting ... You'd better be straight ... Hills in Florida ... Nice, challenging course, but too many homes ... Lots of water.

★★★½ COUNTRY CLUB OF SEBRING

SP-4800 Haw Branch Rd., Sebring, 33872, Highlands County, (941)382-3500, 90 miles S of Orlando.
Holes: 18. **Yards:** 6,722/4,938. **Par:** 71/71. **Course Rating:** 72.0/67.7. **Slope:** 124/112. **Green Fee:** $15/$40. **Cart Fee:** Included in Green Fee. **Walking Policy:** Mandatory cart. **Walkability:** 2. **Opened:** 1984. **Architect:** Ron Garl. **Season:** Year-round. **High:** Nov.-April. **To obtain tee times:** Call 2 days in advance Nov.-April. Call up to 7 days in advance May-Oct. **Miscellaneous:** Reduced fees (twilight), range (grass), club rentals, credit cards (MC, V, AE, D).
Reader Comments: Tight course, fun to play 2nd time ... Decent course, not a ripoff ... Good pro shop ... Great course with good people ... Lots of sand ... A great little woodland course ... Good contrast between two nines.

★★½ THE COURSE AT WESTLAND

PU-7502 Plantation Bay Dr., Jacksonville, 32244, Duval County, (904)778-4653, 10 miles S of Jacksonville.
Holes: 18. **Yards:** 6,347/5,380. **Par:** 71/71. **Course Rating:** 70.3/71.2. **Slope:** 121/118. **Green Fee:** $15/$29. **Cart Fee:** Included in Green Fee. **Walking Policy:** Walking at certain times. **Walkability:** 1. **Opened:** 1974. **Architect:** Lloyd Clifton. **Season:** Year-round. **High:** Feb.-May. **To obtain tee times:** Call up to 30 days in advance. **Miscellaneous:** Reduced fees (weekdays, low season, twilight, seniors, juniors), metal spikes, range (grass), club rentals, credit cards (MC, V, AE, D, ATM Debit Cards).
Reader Comments: Nothing to write home about ... Couple of good holes ... Very good value ... Easy walking ... Super staff.

★★★★ CRANDON GOLF AT KEY BISCAYNE

PU-6700 Crandon Blvd., Key Biscayne, 33149, Dade County, (305)361-9120, 7 miles S of Miami.
Holes: 18. **Yards:** 7,180/5,380. **Par:** 72/73. **Course Rating:** 75.4/71.8. **Slope:** 129/125. **Green Fee:** $49/$99. **Cart Fee:** Included in Green Fee. **Walking Policy:** Walking at certain times. **Walkability:** 2. **Opened:** 1972. **Architect:** Robert von Hagge/Bruce Devlin. **Season:** Year-round. **High:** Dec.-May. **To obtain tee times:** Call up to 5 days in advance. **Miscellaneous:** Reduced fees (weekdays, low season, twilight), metal spikes, range (grass), club rentals, credit cards (MC, V, AE).
Notes: Ranked 17th in 1999 Best in State. PGA Senior Tour Royal Caribbean Classic.
Reader Comments: Expensive and difficult to score on ... Beautiful location ... Windy ... Scenes of Miami across water will live forever ... Great challenge ... Pricey course but worth the money ... Great variety ... Front 9 average, back 9 great ... Plays right on the bay with natural mangroves, trees and wildlife making the whole experience a real thrill ... A lot more fun then Doral's Blue Monster ... Outstanding.

CREEKSIDE GOLF CLUB

PU-5555 Esperanto Dr., Pensacola, 32526, Escambia County, (850)944-7969, (877)944-0801, 60 miles E of Mobile.
Holes: 18. **Yards:** 6,107/4,741. **Par:** 72/72. **Course Rating:** 69.6/66.8. **Slope:** 119/113. **Green Fee:** $15/$15. **Cart Fee:** $12/person. **Walking Policy:** Walking at certain times. **Walkability:** 2. **Opened:** 1972. **Season:** Year-round. **To obtain tee times:** Call 2 days in advance.
Miscellaneous: Metal spikes, club rentals, credit cards (MC, V).

CRYSTAL LAKE COUNTRY CLUB
SP-3800 Crystal Lake Dr., Pompano Beach, 33064, Broward County, (954)942-1900, 5 miles N of Fort Lauderdale.

★★½ SOUTH COURSE
Holes: 18. **Yards:** 6,783/5,458. **Par:** 72/72. **Course Rating:** 73.5/71.5. **Slope:** 135/121. **Green Fee:** $28/$55. **Cart Fee:** Included in Green Fee. **Walking Policy:** Mandatory cart. **Walkability:** N/A. **Opened:** 1963. **Architect:** Rees Jones. **Season:** Year-round. **High:** Nov.-April. **To obtain tee times:** Call 2 days in advance. **Miscellaneous:** Reduced fees (low season, twilight), metal spikes, range (mats), club rentals, credit cards (MC, V, AE).
Reader Comments: OK for what it is ... Reachable par 5s ... Pretty course ... Overpriced ... Very narrow fairways.

★★½ TAM O'SHANTER NORTH COURSE
Holes: 18. **Yards:** 6,390/5,205. **Par:** 70/72. **Course Rating:** 71.0/70.0. **Slope:** 122/118. **Green Fee:** $28/$48. **Cart Fee:** Included in Green Fee. **Walking Policy:** Mandatory cart. **Walkability:** 2. **Opened:** 1967. **Architect:** Rees Jones. **Season:** Year-round. **High:** Nov.-April. **To obtain tee times:** Call 2 days in advance. **Miscellaneous:** Reduced fees (low season, twilight), metal spikes, club rentals, credit cards (MC, V, AE).

★★★ CYPRESS CREEK GOLF COURSE
SP-9400 N. Military Trail, Boynton Beach, 33436, Palm Beach County, (561)732-4202, 10 miles S of West Palm Beach.
Holes: 18. **Yards:** 6,808/5,425. **Par:** 72/72. **Course Rating:** 72.0/67.1. **Slope:** 129/109. **Green Fee:** $30/$65. **Cart Fee:** Included in Green Fee. **Walking Policy:** Walking at certain times. **Walkability:** 2. **Opened:** 1964. **Architect:** Robert von Hagge. **Season:** Year-round. **High:** Nov.-April. **To obtain tee times:** Call 30 days in advance. **Miscellaneous:** Reduced fees (weekdays, low season, twilight), metal spikes, range (grass), club rentals, credit cards (MC, V, AE, D).
Reader Comments: Easy course ... Not up to Palm Beach's high standards ... Intelligent design ... Great price.

DAYTONA BEACH GOLF COURSE
PM-600 Wilder Blvd., Daytona Beach, 32114, Volusia County, (904)258-3119.

★★½ NORTH COURSE
Holes: 18. **Yards:** 6,338/4,938. **Par:** 72/72. **Course Rating:** 70.0/68.3. **Slope:** 120/119. **Green Fee:** $10/$15. **Cart Fee:** $16/cart. **Walking Policy:** Unrestricted walking. **Walkability:** 1. **Opened:** 1965. **Architect:** Lloyd Clifton/Slim Deathridge. **Season:** Year-round. **High:** Nov.-May. **To obtain tee times:** Call 3 days in advance (904)239-6630. **Miscellaneous:** Reduced fees (low season, twilight), metal spikes, range (mats), credit cards (MC, V).
Reader Comments: Reasonable green fees ... Good place to practice ... Fun, flat, easy walking.

★★ SOUTH COURSE
Holes: 18. **Yards:** 6,229/5,346. **Par:** 71/71. **Course Rating:** 69.8/70.2. **Slope:** 118/118. **Green Fee:** $10/$15. **Cart Fee:** $16/cart. **Walking Policy:** Unrestricted walking. **Walkability:** 1. **Opened:** 1921. **Architect:** Donald Ross. **Season:** Year-round. **High:** Nov.-May. **To obtain tee times:** Call 3 days in advance (904)239-6630. **Miscellaneous:** Reduced fees (weekdays, low season, twilight), metal spikes, range (mats), credit cards (MC, V).

★★★★ DEBARY GOLF & COUNTRY CLUB
SP-300 Plantation Dr., DeBary, 32713, Volusia County, (407)668-2061, 15 miles N of Orlando.
Holes: 18. **Yards:** 6,776/5,060. **Par:** 72/72. **Course Rating:** 72.3/68.8. **Slope:** 128/122. **Green Fee:** $19/$60. **Cart Fee:** Included in Green Fee. **Walking Policy:** Mandatory cart. **Walkability:** 3. **Opened:** 1990. **Architect:** Lloyd Clifton. **Season:** Year-round. **High:** Feb.-April. **To obtain tee times:** Call up to 7 days in advance. **Miscellaneous:** Reduced fees (low season, twilight, juniors), discount packages, metal spikes, range (grass), club rentals, credit cards (MC, V, AE).
Reader Comments: Best secret in Orlando area ... Great layout, excellent greens ... A good bargain for a good course ... Interesting; worth a visit ... Beautiful ... Nice variety, good red tee placements ... Nice design with plenty of hills.

★★½ DEEP CREEK GOLF CLUB
SP-1260 San Cristobal Ave., Port Charlotte, 33983, Charlotte County, (941)625-6911, 25 miles N of Fort Myers. **E-mail:** pab@deepcreekgc.com. **Web:** www.deepcreekgc.com.
Holes: 18. **Yards:** 6,005/4,860. **Par:** 70/70. **Course Rating:** 67.5/68.0. **Slope:** 112/110. **Green Fee:** $16/$32. **Cart Fee:** $12/person. **Walking Policy:** Walking at certain times. **Walkability:** 1. **Opened:** 1985. **Architect:** Mark McCumber. **Season:** Year-round. **High:** Dec.-April. **To obtain tee times:** Call up to 7 days in advance. **Miscellaneous:** Reduced fees (weekdays, low season, twilight, seniors, juniors), metal spikes, range (grass), club rentals, credit cards (MC, V, D).
Reader Comments: Too expensive for me ... Lots of water ... Wind can make a big difference ... Typical Florida course.

FLORIDA

★★★★ DEER CREEK GOLF CLUB
SP-2801 Country Club Blvd., Deerfield Beach, 33442, Broward County, (954)421-5550, 6 miles N of Fort Lauderdale. **E-mail:** florida-golf.com.
Holes: 18. **Yards:** 7,038/5,319. **Par:** 72/72. **Course Rating:** 74.8/71.6. **Slope:** 133/120. **Green Fee:** $45/$120. **Cart Fee:** Included in Green Fee. **Walking Policy:** Unrestricted walking. **Walkability:** 3. **Opened:** 1971. **Architect:** Bill Watts/Arthur Hills. **Season:** Year-round. **High:** Dec.-April. **To obtain tee times:** Call 3 days in advance. **Miscellaneous:** Reduced fees (weekdays, low season, resort guests, twilight, seniors, juniors), discount packages, metal spikes, range (grass), club rentals, credit cards (MC, V, AE).
Reader Comments: Expensive, but worth one try ... Turbulent greens ... Thinking man's course ... Great rangers ... Love this course ... Always in great shape, a must play ... This place is run by professionals, my most enjoyable golf experience from the moment I walked in and until I left ... Fun layout with hills.

★★★★ DEER ISLAND GOLF AND LAKE CLUB
SP-18000 Eagles Way, Tavares, 32778, Lake County, (352)343-7550, (800)269-0006, 30 miles NW of Orlando. **Web:** www.deerislandgolf.com.
Holes: 18. **Yards:** 6,676/5,139. **Par:** 72/72. **Course Rating:** 73.1/70.4. **Slope:** 137/118. **Green Fee:** $25/$49. **Cart Fee:** Included in Green Fee. **Walking Policy:** Mandatory cart. **Walkability:** 2. **Opened:** 1994. **Architect:** Joe Lee. **Season:** Year-round. **High:** Oct.-March. **To obtain tee times:** Call 7 days in advance. **Miscellaneous:** Reduced fees (weekdays, twilight, seniors), discount packages, metal spikes, range (grass), club rentals, credit cards (MC, V, AE).
Reader Comments: Great layout, fair as well as demanding ... Lots of water, lots of gators, lots of lost balls ... Fun when the wind blows ... Water everywhere ... Great value in the middle of nowhere.

★½ DEERFIELD LAKES GOLF COURSE
PU-3825 Deerfield Country Club Rd., Callahan, 32011, Nassau County, (904)879-1210, 7 miles NW of Jacksonville.
Holes: 18. **Yards:** 6,700/5,266. **Par:** 72/74. **Course Rating:** 70.2/69.0. **Slope:** 114/102. **Green Fee:** $20/$28. **Cart Fee:** Included in Green Fee. **Walking Policy:** Walking at certain times. **Walkability:** 1. **Opened:** 1970. **Season:** Year-round. **High:** Feb.-May. **To obtain tee times:** Call for weekends and holidays. **Miscellaneous:** Reduced fees (weekdays, seniors), metal spikes, range (grass/mats), club rentals, credit cards (MC, V, AE, D).

★★★ DELRAY BEACH GOLF CLUB
PU-2200 Highland Ave., Delray Beach, 33445, Palm Beach County, (561)243-7380, 18 miles S of West Palm Beach.
Holes: 18. **Yards:** 6,907/5,189. **Par:** 72/72. **Course Rating:** 73.0/69.8. **Slope:** 126/117. **Green Fee:** $23/$50. **Cart Fee:** Included in Green Fee. **Walking Policy:** Walking at certain times. **Walkability:** 1. **Opened:** 1923. **Architect:** Donald Ross. **Season:** Year-round. **High:** Dec.-March. **To obtain tee times:** Call 2 days in advance at 6:30 a.m. **Miscellaneous:** Reduced fees (low season, juniors), metal spikes, range (grass/mats), club rentals, credit cards (MC, V), beginner friendly (instructional, individual or group lessons).
Reader Comments: New clubhouse ... Could be better ... Great city course ... Short and easy, a confidence builder ... Fun to play ... A Donald Ross classic! Good test of skills ... Beautifully layout with mature trees.

DELTONA HILLS GOLF & COUNTRY CLUB
SP-1120 Elkcam Blvd., Deltona, 32725, Volusia County, (904)789-4911, 28 miles N of Orlando.
Holes: 18. **Yards:** 6,892/5,668. **Par:** 72/73. **Course Rating:** 72.7/72.5. **Slope:** 125/125. **Green Fee:** $23/$44. **Cart Fee:** Included in Green Fee. **Walking Policy:** Mandatory cart. **Walkability:** 4. **Opened:** 1962. **Architect:** David Wallace. **Season:** Year-round. **High:** Jan.-April. **To obtain tee times:** Call 5 days in advance. **Miscellaneous:** Reduced fees (weekdays, low season, resort guests, twilight, juniors), metal spikes, range (grass/mats), club rentals, credit cards (MC, V). **Special Notes:** Members only may walk course.

★★★ DIAMOND PLAYERS CLUB WEKIVA
PU-200 Hunt Club Blvd., Longwood, 32779, Seminole County, (407)862-5113, (877)372-4653, 10 miles E of Downtown Orlando. **E-mail:** Tamason@IBM.net. **Web:** www.dpcgolf.com.
Holes: 18. **Yards:** 6,640/5,745. **Par:** 72/73. **Course Rating:** 71.9/73.2. **Slope:** 123/126. **Green Fee:** $12/$35. **Cart Fee:** $15/person. **Walking Policy:** Mandatory cart. **Walkability:** 2. **Opened:** 1970. **Architect:** Ward Northrup. **Season:** Year-round. **High:** September-March. **To obtain tee times:** Call golf shop 4 days in advance. **Miscellaneous:** Reduced fees (weekdays, low season, twilight, seniors, juniors), metal spikes, range (grass), club rentals, credit cards (MC, V, AE, D), beginner friendly (PGA instruction).
Reader Comments: Good value ... Good, quality medium length course.

FLORIDA

★★★★ DIAMONDBACK GOLF CLUB
SP-6501 S.R. 544 E., Haines City, 33844, Polk County, (941)421-0437, (800)222-5629, 25 miles SW of Orlando. **E-mail:** dmdbackgc@aol.com. **Web:** www.Diamondbackgc.com.
Holes: 18. **Yards:** 6,805/5,061. **Par:** 72/72. **Course Rating:** 73.3/70.3. **Slope:** 138/122. **Green Fee:** $30/$90. **Cart Fee:** Included in Green Fee. **Walking Policy:** Mandatory cart. **Walkability:** 5. **Opened:** 1995. **Architect:** Joe Lee. **Season:** Year-round. **High:** Nov.-April. **To obtain tee times:** Call 7 days in advance. **Miscellaneous:** Reduced fees (weekdays, twilight, juniors), discount packages, range (grass), club rentals, credit cards (MC, V, AE).
Reader Comments: One of the best experiences I have ever had in golf! ... Great starting hole ... A good deal ... Expected more ... Tight layout ... Must be able to work the ball to score ... Favors left-to-right game ... Very interesting holes carved from wetlands ... Lots of blind shots ... Don't leave the fairways ... A sleeper.

★★½ DODGER PINES COUNTRY CLUB
SP-4600 26th St., Vero Beach, 32966, Indian River County, (561)569-4400, 60 miles N of West Palm Beach.
Holes: 18. **Yards:** 6,692/5,615. **Par:** 73/74. **Course Rating:** 72.3/73.0. **Slope:** 129/123. **Green Fee:** $25/$45. **Cart Fee:** Included in Green Fee. **Walking Policy:** Walking at certain times. **Walkability:** 1. **Opened:** 1971. **Architect:** Marion Luke. **Season:** Year-round. **High:** Jan.-April. **To obtain tee times:** Call 2 days in advance. **Miscellaneous:** Reduced fees (low season, twilight), metal spikes, range (grass), club rentals, credit cards (MC, V, AE).
Reader Comments: Very challenging ... Front and back 9s totally different ... Narrow fairways ... Very playable.

★½ DOG WOOD LAKES GOLF CLUB
SP-State Rd. 177A, Bonifay, 32425, Holmes County, (850)547-4653, (800)832-3064, 40 miles N of Panama City.
Holes: 18. **Yards:** 6,850/5,405. **Par:** 71/71. **Course Rating:** 73.1/68.3. **Slope:** 126/116. **Green Fee:** $20. **Cart Fee:** Included in Green Fee. **Walking Policy:** Unrestricted walking. **Walkability:** 3. **Opened:** 1963. **Season:** Year-round. **High:** Oct.-April. **To obtain tee times:** Call up to 7 days in advance. **Miscellaneous:** Reduced fees (weekdays, low season, twilight, juniors), metal spikes, range (grass), club rentals, credit cards (MC, V, D).
Special Notes: Formerly Bonifay Country Club

★★★½ DON SHULA'S GOLF CLUB
R-7601 Miami Lakes Dr., Miami Lakes, 33014, Dade County, (305)820-8106.
Holes: 18. **Yards:** 7,055/5,287. **Par:** 72/72. **Course Rating:** 72.3/70.1. **Slope:** 121/117. **Green Fee:** $26/$80. **Cart Fee:** $24/person. **Walking Policy:** Mandatory cart. **Walkability:** 2. **Opened:** 1963. **Architect:** Bill Watts. **Season:** Year-round. **High:** Jan.-April. **To obtain tee times:** Call. **Miscellaneous:** Reduced fees (weekdays, low season, resort guests, twilight), discount packages, range (grass/mats), club rentals, lodging (200 rooms), credit cards (MC, V, AE, D).
Reader Comments: Tough greens ... Not worth the money ... A pleasure to play ... Excellent greens ... Interesting and fun ... Tee off early or it's 6 hours.

DORAL GOLF RESORT & SPA   *Service+*
R-4400 N.W. 87th Ave., Miami, 33178, Dade County, (305)592-2000x2105, (800)713-6725.
★★★★ BLUE COURSE
Holes: 18. **Yards:** 7,125/5,392. **Par:** 72/72. **Course Rating:** 74.5/73.0. **Slope:** 130/124. **Green Fee:** $175/$240. **Cart Fee:** Included in Green Fee. **Walking Policy:** Walking at certain times. **Walkability:** 1. **Opened:** 1961. **Architect:** Dick Wilson. **Season:** Year-round. **High:** Oct.-April. **To obtain tee times:** Resort guests may make tee times at time of reservation. Others call 30 days in advance. **Miscellaneous:** Reduced fees (weekdays, low season, resort guests, twilight), discount packages, range (grass/mats), caddies, club rentals, lodging (693 rooms), credit cards (MC, V, AE, D, Diners Club).
Notes: Ranked 23rd in 1999 Best in State; 42nd in 1996 America's Top 75 Upscale Courses. 1962-1999 Doral Ryder Open.
Reader Comments: No. 18 is not as bad as they say ... Doesn't live up to it's reputation ... Lets you use every club ... Too expensive ... Tough, long course ... A duffers dream come true ... Still getting sand out of my shoes! ... Exceptional experience ... Must play at least once.
★★★½ GOLD COURSE
Holes: 18. **Yards:** 6,602/5,179. **Par:** 70/70. **Course Rating:** 73.3/71.4. **Slope:** 129/123. **Green Fee:** $85/$200. **Cart Fee:** Included in Green Fee. **Walking Policy:** Walking at certain times. **Walkability:** 1. **Opened:** 1961. **Architect:** Robert von Hagge. **Season:** Year-round. **High:** Oct.-April. **To obtain tee times:** Guests may make tee times at time of hotel reservation. Others call 30 days in advance. **Miscellaneous:** Reduced fees (weekdays, low season, resort guests, twilight), discount packages, range (grass/mats), caddies, club rentals, lodging, credit cards (MC, V, AE, D, Diners Club).
Reader Comments: Hardest course at Doral ... Tough to stay dry ... Worth playing ... Green fees are bit expensive.

★★★½ RED COURSE

Holes: 18. **Yards:** 6,214/5,216. **Par:** 70/70. **Course Rating:** 69.9/70.6. **Slope:** 118/118. **Green Fee:** $80/$180. **Cart Fee:** Included in Green Fee. **Walking Policy:** Walking at certain times. **Walkability:** 1. **Opened:** 1961. **Architect:** Robert von Hagge. **Season:** Year-round. **High:** Oct.-April. **To obtain tee times:** Guests may make tee times at time of hotel reservation. Others call 30 days in advance. **Miscellaneous:** Reduced fees (weekdays, low season, resort guests, twilight), discount packages, range (grass/mats), caddies, club rentals, lodging (693 rooms), credit cards (MC, V, AE, D, Diners Club).
Reader Comments: Very playable ... Good little course ... Loved it ... Fine practice facilities ... Hard to compare after playing the Blue.

★★★ SILVER COURSE

R-5001 N.W. 104th Ave., Miami, 33178, Dade County, (305)594-0954.
Holes: 18. **Yards:** 6,614/4,661. **Par:** 71/71. **Course Rating:** 72.5/67.1. **Slope:** 131/117. **Green Fee:** $95/$200. **Cart Fee:** Included in Green Fee. **Walking Policy:** Mandatory cart. **Walkability:** 1. **Opened:** 1984. **Architect:** B. Devlin/R. von Hagge/J. Pate. **Season:** Year-round. **High:** Jan.-April. **To obtain tee times:** Guests may make tee times at time of Hotel reservation. Others call 30 days in advance. **Miscellaneous:** Reduced fees (weekdays, low season, resort guests, twilight), discount packages, metal spikes, range (grass/mats), club rentals, credit cards (MC, V, AE).
Reader Comments: Newly renovated ... Elegant, great condition ... Tight in spots ... Water on almost every hole.

★★★½ WHITE COURSE

Holes: 18. **Yards:** 6,208/5,286. **Par:** 72/72. **Course Rating:** 69.7/70.1. **Slope:** 117/116. **Green Fee:** $45/$110. **Cart Fee:** Included in Green Fee. **Walking Policy:** Walking at certain times. **Walkability:** 1. **Opened:** 1961. **Architect:** Robert von Hagge. **Season:** Year-round. **High:** Oct.-April. **To obtain tee times:** Guests may make tee times at time of hotel reservation. Others call 30 days in advance. **Miscellaneous:** Reduced fees (weekdays, low season, resort guests, twilight, seniors, juniors), discount packages, range (grass), caddies, club rentals, lodging, credit cards (MC, V, AE, D, Diners Club).
Reader Comments: Friendly atmosphere ... Great finishing hole ... Easier than the others, but fun to play.
Special Notes: Course redesigned by Greg Norman opening Jan. 2000

★★ DOUG FORD'S LACUNA GOLF CLUB

SP-6400 Grand Lacuna Blvd., Lake Worth, 33467, Palm Beach County, (561)433-3006, 5 miles SW of West Palm Beach.
Holes: 18. **Yards:** 6,700/5,119. **Par:** 71/71. **Course Rating:** N/A. **Slope:** 121/111. **Green Fee:** $17/$37. **Cart Fee:** Included in Green Fee. **Walking Policy:** Mandatory cart. **Walkability:** 1. **Opened:** 1985. **Architect:** Joe Lee. **Season:** Year-round. **High:** Nov.-May. **To obtain tee times:** Call up to 4 days in advance. **Miscellaneous:** Reduced fees (low season), metal spikes, range (grass), club rentals, credit cards (MC, V).

★★★ DUNEDIN COUNTRY CLUB

SP-1050 Palm Blvd., Dunedin, 34698, Pinellas County, (727)733-7836, 20 miles NW of Tampa.
Holes: 18. **Yards:** 6,565/5,726. **Par:** 72/73. **Course Rating:** 71.5/73.1. **Slope:** 125/120. **Green Fee:** $37/$45. **Cart Fee:** Included in Green Fee. **Walking Policy:** Walking at certain times. **Walkability:** 1. **Opened:** 1928. **Architect:** Donald Ross. **Season:** Year-round. **High:** Dec.-April. **To obtain tee times:** Call 2 days in advance. **Miscellaneous:** Reduced fees (low season, twilight), range (grass), club rentals, credit cards (MC, V).
Reader Comments: A great old layout ... No imagination ... Nice clubhouse.

★★★★ THE DUNES GOLF CLUB AT SEVILLE *Pace*

PU-18200 Seville Clubhouse Dr., Brooksville, 34614, Hernando County, (352)596-7888, (800)232-1363, 70 miles N of Tampa.
Holes: 18. **Yards:** 7,140/5,236. **Par:** 72/72. **Course Rating:** 74.9/70.8. **Slope:** 138/126. **Green Fee:** $25/$45. **Cart Fee:** Included in Green Fee. **Walking Policy:** Mandatory cart. **Walkability:** 4. **Opened:** 1988. **Architect:** Arthur Hills. **Season:** Year-round. **High:** Jan.-April. **To obtain tee times:** Call golf shop. **Miscellaneous:** Reduced fees (weekdays, low season, twilight), discount packages, metal spikes, range (grass), club rentals, credit cards (MC, V).
Reader Comments: Hidden gem ... Massive waste bunkers ... Worth the trip ... Fantastic value ... Unbelievable track for serious golfers.

★★★★ EAGLE HARBOR GOLF CLUB

SP-2217 Eagle Harbor Pkwy., Orange Park, 32073, Clay County, (904)269-9300, 5 miles S of Jacksonville. **Web:** www.eagleharborfl.com.
Holes: 18. **Yards:** 6,840/4,980. **Par:** 72/72. **Course Rating:** 72.6/68.2. **Slope:** 133/121. **Green Fee:** $39/$47. **Cart Fee:** Included in Green Fee. **Walking Policy:** Walking at certain times. **Walkability:** 1. **Opened:** 1993. **Architect:** Clyde Johnston. **Season:** Year-round. **High:** April-June. **To obtain tee times:** Call 4 days in advance. **Miscellaneous:** Reduced fees (weekdays, twilight, juniors), discount packages, range (grass), club rentals, credit cards (MC, V).

FLORIDA

Reader Comments: First class all the way ... Beautiful, scenic, challenging ... Houses getting too close to course ... A wonderful place to play ... Excellent condition ... A pleasure to play for all handicaps ... Nice, open course.

EAGLE MARSH GOLF CLUB
SP-3869 N.W. Royal Oak Drive, Jensen Beach, 34957, Martin County, (561)692-3322, 45 miles N of West Palm Beach. **E-mail:** golf@eaglemarsh.com. **Web:** www.eaglemarsh.com.
Holes: 18. **Yards:** 6,904/4,765. **Par:** 72/72. **Course Rating:** 74.0/69.1. **Slope:** 144/113. **Green Fee:** $25/$70. **Cart Fee:** Included in Green Fee. **Walking Policy:** Mandatory cart. **Walkability:** 4. **Opened:** 1998. **Architect:** Tommy Fazio. **Season:** Year-round. **High:** Jan.-April. **To obtain tee times:** Five days advanced tee times. **Miscellaneous:** Reduced fees (low season, juniors), discount packages, range (grass), club rentals, credit cards (MC, V, AE, D).

EAGLE RIDGE GOLF CLUB AT DEL WEBB SPRUCE CREEK
SP-8501 S.E. 140th Lane Rd., Summerfield, 34491, Marion County, (352)307-1668, 3 miles S of Bellview. **Web:** www.delwebb.com.
Holes: 18. **Yards:** 6,840/4,635. **Par:** 72/72. **Course Rating:** 71.8/65.8. **Slope:** 129/104. **Green Fee:** $20/$41. **Cart Fee:** $12/person. **Walking Policy:** Walking at certain times. **Walkability:** 3. **Opened:** 1998. **Architect:** Terry Doss. **Season:** Year round. **High:** Jan.-Feb.-March. **Miscellaneous:** Reduced fees (low season, twilight), discount packages, range (grass), club rentals, credit cards (MC, V).

THE EAGLES GOLF CLUB
SP-16101 Nine Eagles Dr., Odessa, 33556, Hillsborough County, (813)920-6681, 10 miles N of Tampa.
Holes: 27. **Green Fee:** $32/$45. **Cart Fee:** Included in Green Fee. **Walking Policy:** Walking at certain times. **Walkability:** N/A. **Opened:** 1973. **Architect:** Rick Robbins/Gary Koch/Ron Garl. **Season:** Year-round. **High:** Jan.-April. **To obtain tee times:** Call up to 4 days in advance. **Miscellaneous:** Reduced fees (weekdays, low season, twilight), metal spikes, range (grass), club rentals, credit cards (MC, V).
★★★½ **FOREST/LAKES**
Yards: 7,134/5,453. **Par:** 72/73. **Course Rating:** 70.3/70.2. **Slope:** 130/114.
Reader Comments: Very good greens ... Beautiful course ... Very nice wooded layout ... Golf carts feature yardage system ... A great test of golf.
★★★½ **FOREST/OAKS**
Yards: 7,068/5,429. **Par:** 72/72. **Course Rating:** 70.3/70.0. **Slope:** 130/114.
Reader Comments: Plenty of trees ... Challenging ... State-of-the-art technology with carts.
★★★½ **LAKES/OAKS**
Yards: 7,194/5,586. **Par:** 72/73. **Course Rating:** 70.3/70.2. **Slope:** 130/114.
Reader Comments: Narrow ... Nice course, not real difficult ... Fun course for all ability levels.

EAST BAY GOLF CLUB
SP-702 Country Club Dr., Largo, 33771, Pinellas County, (813)581-3333, 5 miles W of St. Petersburg.
Holes: 18. **Yards:** 6,462/5,193. **Par:** 71/71. **Course Rating:** 71.2/70.7. **Slope:** 125/118. **Green Fee:** $20/$38. **Cart Fee:** Included in Green Fee. **Walking Policy:** Walking at certain times. **Walkability:** 2. **Opened:** 1979. **Season:** Year-round. **High:** Nov.-April. **To obtain tee times:** Call up to 3 days in advance. **Miscellaneous:** Reduced fees (low season, twilight), range (grass), credit cards (MC, V).

★★★½ EASTWOOD GOLF CLUB
PU-13950 Golfway Blvd., Orlando, 32828, Orange County, (407)281-4653, 10 miles E of Orlando.
Holes: 18. **Yards:** 7,176/5,393. **Par:** 72/72. **Course Rating:** 73.9/70.5. **Slope:** 124/117. **Green Fee:** $22/$70. **Cart Fee:** Included in Green Fee. **Walking Policy:** Mandatory cart. **Walkability:** 3. **Opened:** 1989. **Architect:** Lloyd Clifton. **Season:** Year-round. **High:** Jan.-April. **To obtain tee times:** Call 7 days in advance. **Miscellaneous:** Reduced fees (weekdays, low season, twilight, seniors, juniors), discount packages, range (grass), club rentals, credit cards (MC, V, AE, D).
Reader Comments: Open, fun to play ... Nice layout, worth money ... Great value and well kept ... Condo golf ... Course is maturing; tough when windy!.

★★★★ EASTWOOD GOLF COURSE
PU-4600 Bruce Herd Lane, Fort Myers, 33994, Lee County, (813)275-4848.
Holes: 18. **Yards:** 6,772/5,116. **Par:** 72/72. **Course Rating:** 73.3/68.9. **Slope:** 130/120. **Green Fee:** $28/$50. **Cart Fee:** Included in Green Fee. **Walking Policy:** Walking at certain times. **Walkability:** N/A. **Opened:** 1977. **Architect:** Robert von Hagge/Bruce Devlin. **Season:** Year-round. **High:** Dec.-March. **To obtain tee times:** Call 1 day in advance at 8 a.m. **Miscellaneous:** Reduced fees (weekdays, low season, twilight), metal spikes, range (grass/mats), club rentals, credit cards (MC, V).

FLORIDA

Reader Comments: What a golf course should be ... Best value in area ... All you see is wilderness ... Must patronize restaurant ... No two holes alike ... Lots of sand ... Excellent course, away from civilization ... Affordable but average golf.

★★★½ EKANA GOLF CLUB

SP-2100 Ekana Dr., Oviedo, 32765, Seminole County, (407)366-1211, 10 miles NE of Orlando. **Holes:** 18. **Yards:** 6,683/5,544. **Par:** 72/72. **Course Rating:** 72.0/72.1. **Slope:** 130/128. **Green Fee:** $22/$60. **Cart Fee:** Included in Green Fee. **Walking Policy:** Mandatory cart. **Walkability:** 3. **Opened:** 1989. **Architect:** Joe Lee. **Season:** Year-round. **High:** Jan.-April. **To obtain tee times:** Call 7 days in advance. **Miscellaneous:** Reduced fees (weekdays, low season, twilight), discount packages, range (grass), club rentals, credit cards (MC, V).

Reader Comments: Lacks polish ... Some memorable holes ... Tight, risk-reward course ... Very playable ... Would play again ... Great greens.

EL DIABLO GOLF & COUNTRY CLUB

PU-10405 N. Sherman Dr., Citrus Springs, 34434, Citrus County, (352)465-0986, (877)ELDIABLO, 20 miles W of Ocala. **E-mail:** robpyle@aol.com. **Web:** el-diablo.net. **Holes:** 18. **Yards:** 7,045/5,144. **Par:** 72/72. **Course Rating:** 75.3/69.8. **Slope:** 147/117. **Green Fee:** $25/$49. **Walking Policy:** Unrestricted walking. **Walkability:** 4. **Opened:** 1998. **Architect:** Jim Fazio. **Season:** Year-round. **High:** Dec.-April. **Miscellaneous:** Reduced fees (low season, twilight), range (grass), club rentals, credit cards (MC, V, AE). **Notes:** Ranked 1st in 1999 Best New Affordable Public. 2000 U.S. Open Qualifier;

★★★½ EMERALD BAY GOLF COURSE

SP-40001 Emerald Coast Pkwy., Destin, 32541, Okaloosa County, (850)837-5197, (888)465-3229, 15 miles E of Fort Walton Beach. **Holes:** 18. **Yards:** 6,802/5,184. **Par:** 72/72. **Course Rating:** 73.1/70.1. **Slope:** 135/122. **Green Fee:** $40/$75. **Cart Fee:** Included in Green Fee. **Walking Policy:** Mandatory cart. **Walkability:** 1. **Opened:** 1991. **Architect:** Robert Cupp. **Season:** Year-round. **High:** March-Nov. **To obtain tee times:** Call two weeks in advance. **Miscellaneous:** Reduced fees (weekdays, low season, resort guests, juniors), range (grass), club rentals, lodging (8 rooms), credit cards (MC, V, AE, D, Diners Club).

Reader Comments: Lots of tough water shots ... Nice course, but short and overpriced ... Some very good holes. A couple of weak ones ... Fun course by beach ... Plenty of water.

★★★★ EMERALD DUNES GOLF COURSE *Service, Condition*

PU-2100 Emerald Dunes Dr., West Palm Beach, 33411, Palm Beach County, (561)684-4653, (888)650-4653, 3 miles W of West Palm Beach. **E-mail:** edunes@aol.com. **Web:** www.emerald-dunes.com. **Holes:** 18. **Yards:** 7,006/4,676. **Par:** 72/72. **Course Rating:** 73.8/67.1. **Slope:** 133/115. **Green Fee:** $80/$160. **Cart Fee:** Included in Green Fee. **Walking Policy:** Unrestricted walking. **Walkability:** 3. **Opened:** 1990. **Architect:** Tom Fazio. **Season:** Year-round. **High:** Dec.-April. **To obtain tee times:** Call and secure with credit card. **Miscellaneous:** Reduced fees (weekdays, low season, twilight, seniors, juniors), metal spikes, range (grass), club rentals, credit cards (MC, V, AE, D, Diners Club), beginner friendly (Executive Womens Golf League, Hook-a-Kid).

Reader Comments: Great course, great shape ... Outstanding ... Expensive but worth it ... Love those mounds ... Neat gators ... Gem of the Palm Beaches ... Tee shot on 18 great ... A pleasurable upper class golfing experience ... It's OK if you refinance your house ... A 'Must.'

★★★ FAIRWINDS GOLF COURSE

PM-4400 Fairwinds Dr., Fort Pierce, 34946, St. Lucie County, (561)462-2722, (800)894-1781, 40 miles N of West Palm Beach. **Holes:** 18. **Yards:** 6,783/5,392. **Par:** 72/72. **Course Rating:** 71.1/68.5. **Slope:** 119/112. **Green Fee:** $20/$40. **Cart Fee:** Included in Green Fee. **Walking Policy:** Walking at certain times. **Walkability:** 1. **Opened:** 1991. **Architect:** Jim Fazio. **Season:** Year-round. **High:** Jan.-April. **To obtain tee times:** Call 2 days in advance. **Miscellaneous:** Reduced fees (low season, twilight, juniors), metal spikes, range (grass), club rentals, credit cards (MC, V), beginner friendly (beginner clinics and leagues).

Reader Comments: Open, wide fairways ... Good public course ... Needs to mature ... Busy muny ... Wide open to lots of wind.

★★★★ FALCON'S FIRE GOLF CLUB

PU-3200 Seralago Blvd., Kissimmee, 34746, Osceola County, (407)239-5445, 3 miles S of Orlando. **E-mail:** proshop@falconsfire.com. **Web:** www.falconsfire.com. **Holes:** 18. **Yards:** 6,901/5,417. **Par:** 72/72. **Course Rating:** 72.5/70.4. **Slope:** 125/118. **Green Fee:** $56/$95. **Cart Fee:** Included in Green Fee. **Walking Policy:** Mandatory cart. **Walkability:** 1. **Opened:** 1993. **Architect:** Rees Jones. **Season:** Year-round. **High:** Jan.-April. **To obtain tee times:** Call 7 days in advance, or 8-30 days in advance with extra fee. Groups may call up to 6 months in advance. **Miscellaneous:** Reduced fees (low season, twilight, juniors), metal spikes, range (grass), club rentals, credit cards (MC, V, AE).

FLORIDA

Reader Comments: Beautiful golf course has it all ... Resort-like experience ... Front 9-sheep; back 9-wolf ... 'Country club for a day' service ... Challenging ... Bowl-like fairways caused by knolls ... Great greens ... Expensive ... A gem just outside Disney ... Well organized staff ... Stay out of sand ... Will visit again ... Too open and easy.

FERNANDINA BEACH MUNICIPAL GOLF COURSE

PM-2800 Bill Melton Rd., Fernandina Beach, 32034, Nassau County, (904)277-7370, (800)646-5997, 35 miles NE of Jacksonville.

Holes: 27. **Green Fee:** $16/$16. **Cart Fee:** $12/person. **Walking Policy:** Walking at certain times. **Walkability:** 1. **Opened:** 1954. **Architect:** Ed Mattson/Tommy Birdsong. **Season:** Year-round. **High:** Jan.-March. **To obtain tee times:** Call 5 days in advance. **Miscellaneous:** Reduced fees (weekdays, twilight, juniors), range (grass), club rentals, credit cards (MC, V).

★★★½ **NORTH/WEST**
Yards: 6,803/5,720. **Par:** 70/72. **Course Rating:** 72.0/71.7. **Slope:** 124/118.

★★★½ **SOUTH/NORTH**
Yards: 6,336/5,156. **Par:** 71/72. **Course Rating:** 70.1/68.7. **Slope:** 124/116.

Reader Comments: Wonderful old course ... Nothing spectacular ... Walked 18 in less than 3 hours.

★★★½ **WEST/SOUTH**
Yards: 7,027/5,308. **Par:** 73/73. **Course Rating:** 73.1/69.4. **Slope:** 128/115.

Reader Comments: Nice to play ... Don't make them like this anymore.

FONTAINEBLEAU GOLF COURSE

PU-9603 Fontainebleau Blvd., Miami, 33172, Dade County, (305)221-5181, 5 miles W of Miami.

★★ **EAST COURSE**
Holes: 18. **Yards:** 7,035/5,586. **Par:** 72/72. **Course Rating:** 73.3/71.5. **Slope:** 122/119. **Green Fee:** $20/$32. **Cart Fee:** Included in Green Fee. **Walking Policy:** Mandatory cart. **Walkability:** 1. **Opened:** 1969. **Architect:** Mark Mahannah. **Season:** Year-round. **High:** Nov.-April. **To obtain tee times:** Call up to 14 days in advance. **Miscellaneous:** Reduced fees (weekdays, low season, resort guests, twilight), discount packages, metal spikes, range (grass), club rentals, credit cards (MC, V, AE, Diners Club).

★ **WEST COURSE**
Holes: 18. **Yards:** 6,944/5,565. **Par:** 72/72. **Course Rating:** 72.5/71.0. **Slope:** 120/118. **Green Fee:** $20/$32. **Cart Fee:** Included in Green Fee. **Walking Policy:** Mandatory cart. **Walkability:** 1. **Opened:** 1976. **Architect:** Mark Mahannah. **Season:** Year-round. **High:** Nov.-April. **To obtain tee times:** Call up to 14 days in advance. **Miscellaneous:** Reduced fees (weekdays, low season, resort guests, twilight), discount packages, metal spikes, range (grass), club rentals, credit cards (MC, V, AE, Diners Club).

★★★★ FOREST LAKE GOLF CLUB OF OCOEE

PU-10521 Clarcona-Ocoee Rd., Ocoee, 34761, Orange County, (407)654-4653, 5 miles W of Orlando.

Holes: 18. **Yards:** 7,113/5,103. **Par:** 72/72. **Course Rating:** 73.6/69.2. **Slope:** 127/113. **Green Fee:** $29/$50. **Cart Fee:** Included in Green Fee. **Walking Policy:** Mandatory cart. **Walkability:** 2. **Opened:** 1994. **Architect:** Clifton/Ezell/Clifton. **Season:** Year-round. **High:** Dec.-March. **To obtain tee times:** Call 5 days in advance. **Miscellaneous:** Reduced fees (weekdays, low season, twilight, juniors), discount packages, range (grass), club rentals, credit cards (MC, V).

Reader Comments: Dogleg par-5 a scary way to start ... Final 5 holes are great ... Very nice ... Narrow fairways are not good for a slice ... Best bang for the buck in Central Florida ... Some nice par 3's.

★★★ FOREST LAKES GOLF CLUB

SP-2401 Beneva Rd., Sarasota, 34232, Sarasota County, (941)922-1312, 40 miles S of Tampa.

Holes: 18. **Yards:** 6,500/5,500. **Par:** 71/71. **Course Rating:** 70.8/71.3. **Slope:** 124/117. **Green Fee:** $16/$42. **Cart Fee:** Included in Green Fee. **Walking Policy:** Walking at certain times. **Walkability:** N/A. **Opened:** 1964. **Architect:** Andy Anderson. **Season:** Year-round. **High:** Jan.-May. **To obtain tee times:** Call golf shop up to 4 days in advance. **Miscellaneous:** Reduced fees (weekdays, low season, resort guests, twilight, juniors), metal spikes, range (grass/mats), club rentals, credit cards (MC, V, AE, D).

Reader Comments: Beautiful greens and fairways ... Wonderful challenge of golf ... Short and tricky ... Potential wasted! ... Lots of wildlife. A real challenge.

★★★½ FORT MYERS COUNTRY CLUB

PU-3591 McGregor Blvd., Fort Myers, 33901, Lee County, (941)936-3126, 120 miles S of Tampa.

Holes: 18. **Yards:** 6,414/5,135. **Par:** 71/71. **Course Rating:** 70.5/70.6. **Slope:** 118/117. **Green Fee:** $13/$32. **Cart Fee:** $15/person. **Walking Policy:** Unrestricted walking. **Walkability:** 1. **Opened:** 1917. **Architect:** Donald Ross. **Season:** Year-round. **High:** Dec.-April. **To obtain tee times:** Call tee times phone 1 day in advance beginning at 8 a.m. **Miscellaneous:** Reduced fees (weekdays, low season, twilight), metal spikes, club rentals, credit cards (MC, V).

Reader Comments: An enjoyable, unaltered Donald Ross design ... Small greens ... No trouble getting tee times ... Walk anytime ... Beautiful ... Good price.

FORT WALTON BEACH GOLF CLUB
★★★ OAKS COURSE
PM-1909 Lewis Turner Blvd., Fort Walton Beach, 32547, Okaloosa County, (904)833-9530, 50 miles E of Pensacola.
Holes: 18. **Yards:** 6,409/5,366. **Par:** 72/72. **Course Rating:** 70.2/67.8. **Slope:** 119/107. **Green Fee:** $15/$15. **Cart Fee:** $8/person. **Walking Policy:** Unrestricted walking. **Walkability:** 1. **Opened:** 1993. **Architect:** David Smith. **Season:** Year-round. **High:** Jan.-Sept. **To obtain tee times:** Outside 400 mile radius may call up to 60 days in advance. **Miscellaneous:** Reduced fees (twilight), discount packages, metal spikes, club rentals, credit cards (MC, V).
Reader Comments: Extremely tight ... Fun to play ... Challenging for a muny.

★★½ PINES COURSE
PM-699 Country Club Dr., Fort Walton Beach, 32547, Okaloosa County, (904)833-9529, 50 miles E of Pensacola.
Holes: 18. **Yards:** 6,802/5,320. **Par:** 72/72. **Course Rating:** 69.9/69.1. **Slope:** 110/107. **Green Fee:** $15/$15. **Cart Fee:** $8/person. **Walking Policy:** Unrestricted walking. **Walkability:** 1. **Opened:** 1961. **Architect:** William Amick. **Season:** Year-round. **High:** Jan.-Sept. **To obtain tee times:** Outside 400 mile radius may call up to 60 days in advance. **Miscellaneous:** Reduced fees (twilight), metal spikes, club rentals, credit cards (MC, V).
Reader Comments: Some fun holes ... More open than Oaks with bunkers.

★★★½ FOX HOLLOW GOLF CLUB
PU-10050 Robert Trent Jones Pkwy., New Port Richey, 34655, Pasco County, (813)376-6333, (800)943-1902, 25 miles NW of Tampa. **Web:** www.sanori.com.
Holes: 18. **Yards:** 7,138/4,454. **Par:** 71/71. **Course Rating:** 75.1/65.7. **Slope:** 137/112. **Green Fee:** $33/$65. **Cart Fee:** Included in Green Fee. **Walking Policy:** Unrestricted walking. **Walkability:** 2. **Opened:** 1994. **Architect:** Robert Trent Jones/Roger Rulewich. **Season:** Year-round. **High:** Jan.-March. **To obtain tee times:** Call up to 4 days in advance. Groups of 8 or more may call up to 1 year in advance. **Miscellaneous:** Reduced fees (weekdays, low season, twilight, juniors), discount packages, metal spikes, range (grass), club rentals, credit cards (MC, V, AE, D, Diners Club).
Reader Comments: Wide open but tricky ... Good greens ... Great course, great price ... Short, but tough ... Better have your sand game up to speed ... Rolling hills. Not flat like Florida ... A beautiful course that gets lot of play.

FOXFIRE GOLF CLUB
PU-7200 Proctor Rd., Sarasota, 34241, Sarasota County, (941)921-7757, 50 miles S of Tampa. **Holes:** 27. **Green Fee:** $16/$49. **Cart Fee:** Included in Green Fee. **Walking Policy:** Unrestricted walking. **Walkability:** 2. **Opened:** 1975. **Architect:** Andy Anderson. **Season:** Year-round. **High:** Jan.-March. **To obtain tee times:** Call up to 7 days in advance. **Miscellaneous:** Reduced fees (weekdays, low season, resort guests, twilight, juniors), discount packages, metal spikes, range (grass), club rentals, credit cards (MC, V, D), beginner friendly (junior and beginner clinics).
★★★½ PALM/OAK
Yards: 6,280/5,024. **Par:** 72/72. **Course Rating:** 70.0/67.7. **Slope:** N/A.
Reader Comments: Great place and nice people ... Would return ... Tees and greens are close ... Short. Easy to score. A good practice course ... Well groomed. Fun course.
★★★½ PINE/OAK
Yards: 6,101/4,941. **Par:** 72/72. **Course Rating:** 69.8/67.6. **Slope:** N/A.
★★★½ PINE/PALM
Yards: 6,213/4,983. **Par:** 72/72. **Course Rating:** 69.8/67.5. **Slope:** 119/115.
Special Notes: Soft spikes preferred.

★★ FOXWOOD COUNTRY CLUB
SP-4927 Antioch Rd., Crestview, 32536, Okaloosa County, (850)682-2012, 40 miles E of Pensacola.
Holes: 18. **Yards:** 6,282/5,016. **Par:** 72/72. **Course Rating:** 69.6/69.7. **Slope:** 127/118. **Green Fee:** $12/$16. **Cart Fee:** $14/person. **Walking Policy:** Walking at certain times. **Walkability:** 2. **Opened:** 1962. **Architect:** Bill Amick/Earl Stone. **Season:** Year-round. **High:** Jan.-March. **To obtain tee times:** Call anytime 7 days in advance. **Miscellaneous:** Reduced fees (weekdays, low season, twilight, seniors, juniors), range (grass), club rentals, credit cards (MC, V, AE, D).

★★★★ GATEWAY GOLF & COUNTRY CLUB   *Service, Condition+, Pace+*
11360 Championship Dr., Fort Myers, 33913, Lee County, (941)561-1010.
Holes: 18. **Yards:** 6,974/5,323. **Par:** 72/72. **Course Rating:** 74.1/70.1. **Slope:** 129/121. **Green Fee:** $35/$115. **Cart Fee:** Included in Green Fee. **Walking Policy:** Mandatory cart. **Walkability:** 1. **Opened:** 1989. **Architect:** Tom Fazio. **Season:** Year-round. **High:** Jan.-March. **To obtain tee times:** Call 2 days in advance. **Miscellaneous:** Reduced fees (low season, twilight), range (grass), club rentals, credit cards (MC, V, AE).

FLORIDA

Reader Comments: Long, flat, windy ... Excellent ... A pleasure to play ... Fast greens ... Love it ... Good variety, good challenge ... Very playable ... Nice layout but a few bad holes.

★★½ GATOR TRACE GOLF & COUNTRY CLUB
SP-4302 Gator Trace Dr., Fort Pierce, 34982, St. Lucie County, (561)464-7442, 40 miles N of West Palm Beach.
Holes: 18. **Yards:** 6,092/4,573. **Par:** 70/70. **Course Rating:** 68.9/67.1. **Slope:** 123/123. **Green Fee:** $18/$40. **Cart Fee:** $15/person. **Walking Policy:** Walking at certain times. **Walkability:** 3. **Opened:** 1986. **Architect:** Arthur Hills. **Season:** Year-round. **High:** Dec.-May. **Miscellaneous:** Reduced fees (weekdays, low season, twilight), discount packages, metal spikes, club rentals, credit cards (MC, V, D).
Reader Comments: When they say water hazard they mean it ... Loved the wildlife ... Very narrow ... Not up to par for area courses ... Overpriced during season ... Not bad after a winter in the North ... Forgiving fairways.

★★★½ GOLDEN BEAR GOLF CLUB AT HAMMOCK CREEK
SP-2400 Golden Bear Way, Palm City, 34990, Martin County, (561)220-2599, (888)841-JACK, 35 miles N of West Beach.
Holes: 18. **Yards:** 7,050/5,130. **Par:** 72/72. **Course Rating:** 73.6/70.0. **Slope:** 134/119. **Green Fee:** $25/$60. **Cart Fee:** Included in Green Fee. **Walking Policy:** Walking at certain times. **Walkability:** 1. **Opened:** 1996. **Architect:** Jack Nicklaus/Jack Nicklaus Jr. **Season:** Year-round. **High:** Jan.-March. **To obtain tee times:** Call golf shop up to 7 days in advance with credit card. **Miscellaneous:** Reduced fees (weekdays, resort guests, twilight, juniors), metal spikes, range (grass), club rentals, credit cards (MC, V, D, Diners Club).
Reader Comments: Good layout but needs to mature ... Greens slicker than the White House lawyers ... Solid design ... Very challenging, beautiful complex ... Tough in the wind ... Huge fast greens.

★★★½ GOLDEN OCALA GOLF & COUNTRY CLUB
PU-8300 N.W. 31st Lane, Ocala, 34482, Marion County, (352)622-2245, (800)251-7674, 85 miles N of Orlando.
Holes: 18. **Yards:** 6,735/5,595. **Par:** 72/72. **Course Rating:** 72.2/72.2. **Slope:** 132/124. **Green Fee:** $30/$59. **Cart Fee:** Included in Green Fee. **Walking Policy:** Mandatory cart. **Walkability:** 3. **Opened:** 1986. **Architect:** Ron Garl. **Season:** Year-round. **High:** Nov.-April. **To obtain tee times:** Call up to 14 days in advance. **Miscellaneous:** Reduced fees (weekdays, low season, twilight), discount packages, range (grass), club rentals, credit cards (MC, V).
Reader Comments: Great replica holes ... Heard great things but didn't see them ... Could play it every day ... Play all the great holes in golf ... Very disappointed, apparent lack of money ... A sleeper ... Memorable experience.

THE GOLF CLUB AT CYPRESS CREEK
SP-880 Cypress Village Blvd., Ruskin, 33573, Hillsborough County, (813)634-8888, 20 miles S of Tampa.
Holes: 18. **Yards:** 6,839/04. **Par:** 72/72. **Course Rating:** 74.0/66.6. **Slope:** 133/114. **Green Fee:** $20/$34. **Cart Fee:** Included in Green Fee. **Walking Policy:** Mandatory cart. **Walkability:** N/A. **Opened:** 1988. **Architect:** Steve Smyers. **Season:** Year-round. **High:** Feb.-April. **To obtain tee times:** Call 7 days in advance. **Miscellaneous:** Reduced fees (weekdays, low season, resort guests, twilight, seniors), discount packages, metal spikes, range (grass), club rentals, credit cards (MC, V).
Special Notes: Also has 18-hole executive Upper Creek Course

★★★ THE GOLF CLUB AT CYPRESS HEAD
PM-6231 Palm Vista St., Port Orange, 32124, Volusia County, (904)756-5449, 5 miles S of Daytona Beach.
Holes: 18. **Yards:** 6,814/4,909. **Par:** 72/72. **Course Rating:** 72.4/68.3. **Slope:** 133/116. **Green Fee:** $30/$48. **Cart Fee:** Included in Green Fee. **Walking Policy:** Walking at certain times. **Walkability:** 3. **Opened:** 1992. **Architect:** Arthur Hills. **Season:** Year-round. **High:** Jan.-April. **To obtain tee times:** Call up to 3 days in advance. **Miscellaneous:** Reduced fees (weekdays, low season, resort guests, twilight, juniors), discount packages, metal spikes, range (grass), club rentals, credit cards (MC, V).
Reader Comments: Good greens ... Very playable ... Best golf for the money ... Great place to raise handicap ... Some weird holes.

★★★★ THE GOLF CLUB AT AMELIA ISLAND
R-4700 Amelia Island Pkwy., Amelia Island, 32034, Nassau County, (904)277-0012, (800)245-4224, 26 miles N of Jacksonville.
Holes: 18. **Yards:** 6,692/5,039. **Par:** 72/72. **Course Rating:** 72.9/70.4. **Slope:** 136/124. **Green Fee:** $120/$120. **Cart Fee:** Included in Green Fee. **Walking Policy:** Mandatory cart. **Walkability:** 3. **Opened:** 1987. **Architect:** Mark McCumber. **Season:** Year-round. **High:** March-Oct. **To obtain tee times:** Guests must stay at Ritz-Carlton, Amelia Island 1-800-241-3333 or

FLORIDA

Summer Beach Resort 1-800-862-9297. **Miscellaneous:** Reduced fees (twilight, juniors), discount packages, range (grass), club rentals, lodging, credit cards (MC, V, AE).
Notes: 1998 Senior PGA Tour Liberty Mutual Legends of Golf.
Reader Comments: A good, tough course ... Great if staying at The Ritz ... Very playable resort course ... Not too tough for average golfer.

★★★★ GOLF CLUB OF JACKSONVILLE

PM-10440 Tournament Lane, Jacksonville, 32222, Duval County, (904)779-0800, 15 miles W of Downtown Jacksonville.
Holes: 18. **Yards:** 6,620/5,021. **Par:** 71/71. **Course Rating:** 70.7/68.0. **Slope:** 120/115. **Green Fee:** $20/$39. **Cart Fee:** Included in Green Fee. **Walking Policy:** Walking at certain times. **Walkability:** 2. **Opened:** 1989. **Architect:** Bobby Weed/Mark McCumber. **Season:** Year-round. **High:** March-June. **To obtain tee times:** Call up to 4 days in advance. For Saturday tee times call on Tuesday. **Miscellaneous:** Reduced fees (weekdays, twilight, seniors, juniors), metal spikes, range (grass), club rentals, credit cards (MC, V, AE).
Reader Comments: Water, mounds, water, mounds ... Good value ... Great practice area ... Wonderful course ... One of the better courses we've played ... Good condition.

★★½ THE GOLF CLUB OF JUPITER

PU-1800 Central Blvd., Jupiter, 33458, Palm Beach County, (561)747-6262.
Holes: 18. **Yards:** 6,265/5,150. **Par:** 70/71. **Course Rating:** 69.9/69.5. **Slope:** 117/118. **Green Fee:** $26/$55. **Cart Fee:** Included in Green Fee. **Walking Policy:** Mandatory cart. **Walkability:** 1. **Opened:** 1982. **Architect:** Lamar Smith. **Season:** Year-round. **High:** Jan.-April. **To obtain tee times:** Call up to 4 days in advance. **Miscellaneous:** Reduced fees (weekdays, low season, twilight), range (grass), club rentals, credit cards (MC, V).
Reader Comments: Boring but affordable ... Tight fairways ... Short course, lots of water ... Too many condos.

GOLF CLUB OF QUINCY

SP-2291 Solomon Dairy Rd., Quincy, 32353, Gadsden County, (850)627-9631, 20 miles NW of Tallahassee. **E-mail:** bd3100308@aol.com.
Holes: 18. **Yards:** 6,742/5,398. **Par:** 72/72. **Course Rating:** 71.2/70.3. **Slope:** 135/117. **Green Fee:** $11/$23. **Cart Fee:** $12/person. **Walking Policy:** Walking at certain times. **Walkability:** 4. **Opened:** 1968. **Architect:** Joe Lee. **Season:** Year-round. **High:** April-May, Sept.-Oct. **To obtain tee times:** Call golf shop. **Miscellaneous:** Reduced fees (weekdays, low season, juniors), range (grass/mats), club rentals, credit cards (MC, V).
Special Notes: Formerly Gadsden G & CC.

★★★ GOLF HAMMOCK COUNTRY CLUB

SP-2222 Golf Hammock Dr., Sebring, 33872, Highlands County, (941)382-2151, 90 miles S of Orlando.
Holes: 18. **Yards:** 6,431/5,352. **Par:** 72/72. **Course Rating:** 71.0/70.2. **Slope:** 127/118. **Green Fee:** $14/$40. **Cart Fee:** Included in Green Fee. **Walking Policy:** Mandatory cart. **Walkability:** 1. **Opened:** 1976. **Architect:** Ron Garl. **Season:** Year-round. **High:** Oct.-April. **To obtain tee times:** Call up to 2 days in advance. **Miscellaneous:** Reduced fees (low season, resort guests, twilight, juniors), range (grass), club rentals, credit cards (MC, V), beginner friendly.
Reader Comments: Tight holes ... Course needs maintenance ... Nice people ... Ordinary ... Open ... Tough par 3s.

GRAND CYPRESS GOLF CLUB *Service+*

R-One N. Jacaranda, Orlando, 32836, Orange County, (407)239-1904, (800)835-7377.
★★★★ NEW COURSE *Condition*
Holes: 18. **Yards:** 6,773/5,314. **Par:** 72/72. **Course Rating:** 72.2/69.8. **Slope:** 122/115. **Green Fee:** $100/$150. **Cart Fee:** Included in Green Fee. **Walking Policy:** Unrestricted walking. **Walkability:** 2. **Opened:** 1988. **Architect:** Jack Nicklaus. **Season:** Year-round. **High:** Oct.-May. **To obtain tee times:** Call starter. You must be a guest at the Villas of Grand Cypress or at the Hyatt Regency Grand Cypress to play golf. You may book up to 4 tee times up to 60 days in advance. **Miscellaneous:** Reduced fees (low season, twilight, juniors), discount packages, metal spikes, range (grass), caddies, club rentals, lodging (896 rooms), credit cards (MC, V, AE, D, Diners Club, Carte Blanche).
Notes: World Cup of Golf.
Reader Comments: Interesting, but not St. Andrews ... A great treat! ... Very windy ... The starter made us feel like it was his honor to meet us ... Double greens are huge! ... Scotland in Florida, and it works ... Felt as if I could speak with a brogue upon finishing the front 9 ... If you can't go to St. Andrews, this is second-best.
Holes: 27. **Green Fee:** $100/$150. **Cart Fee:** Included in Green Fee. **Walking Policy:** Mandatory cart. **Walkability:** 2. **Opened:** 1984. **Architect:** Jack Nicklaus. **Season:** Year-round. **High:** Oct.-May. **To obtain tee times:** Call starter. You must be a guest at the Villas of Grand Cypress or at the Hyatt Regency Grand Cypress to play golf. You may book up to 4 tee times up to 60 days in advance. **Miscellaneous:** Reduced fees (low season, twilight, juniors), discount

packages, range (grass), caddies, club rentals, lodging (896 rooms), credit cards (MC, V, AE, D, Diners Club, Carte Blanche).

★★★★½ **NORTH/EAST** *Condition+, Pace*
Yards: 6,955/5,056. **Par:** 72/72. **Course Rating:** 75.0/69.5. **Slope:** 139/118.
Reader Comments: Gets better with age ... You need every club and every shot ... I wanna go back ... Fairways as nice as they get ... Great length for ladies!.

★★★★½ **NORTH/SOUTH** *Condition+, Pace*
Yards: 6,993/5,328. **Par:** 72/72. **Course Rating:** 75.1/71.6. **Slope:** 137/121.
Notes: LPGA Tournament of Champions; PGA Tour Skills Challenge and Shark Shootout.
Reader Comments: Good quality ... Nice course but not memorable ... Lots of shots over water.

★★★★½ **SOUTH/EAST** *Condition+, Pace*
Yards: 6,906/5,126. **Par:** 72/72. **Course Rating:** 74.7/70.3. **Slope:** 138/121.
Reader Comments: Need to know the course or bring extra golf balls.

GRAND HAVEN GOLF CLUB

SP-2001 Waterside Pkwy., Palm Coast, 32137, Flagler County, (904)445-2327, (888)522-5642, 30 miles N of Daytona Beach. **Web:** www.palmcoastresort.com.
Holes: 18. **Yards:** 7,069/4,985. **Par:** 72/72. **Course Rating:** 74.9/70.4. **Slope:** 135/123. **Green Fee:** $53/$73. **Cart Fee:** Included in Green Fee. **Walking Policy:** Mandatory cart. **Walkability:** 3. **Opened:** 1998. **Architect:** Jack Nicklaus. **Season:** Year-round. **High:** Jan-April. **To obtain tee times:** Call golf shop 7 days in advance for outside play. **Miscellaneous:** Reduced fees (low season, resort guests, juniors), discount packages, range (grass), club rentals, lodging (150 rooms), credit cards (MC, V, AE), beginner friendly (clinics and junior programs).

GRAND PALMS GOLF & COUNTRY CLUB RESORT

R-110 Grand Palms Dr., Pembroke Pines, 33027, Broward County, (954)437-3334, (800)327-9246, 15 miles SW of Ft. Lauderdale.
Holes: 27. **Green Fee:** $35/$75. **Cart Fee:** Included in Green Fee. **Walking Policy:** Mandatory cart. **Walkability:** 1. **Opened:** 1987. **Architect:** Ward Northrup. **Season:** Year-round. **High:** Dec.-April. **To obtain tee times:** Call up to 3 days in advance. **Miscellaneous:** Reduced fees (weekdays, low season, twilight), discount packages, range (grass/mats), club rentals, lodging (140 rooms), credit cards (MC, V, AE).

★★★ **GRAND/ROYAL**
Yards: 6,816/5,245. **Par:** 72/72. **Course Rating:** 71.6/70.8. **Slope:** 127/126.
Reader Comments: Great for the money ... Tight course ... Hilly ... Must play if in area ... Much improved ... Great 3 finishing holes.

★★★ **ROYAL/SABAL**
Yards: 6,736/5,391. **Par:** 73/73. **Course Rating:** 71.9/71.5. **Slope:** 128/122.

★★★ **SABAL/GRAND**
Yards: 6,653/5,198. **Par:** 71/71. **Course Rating:** 71.5/70.7. **Slope:** 124/123.
Reader Comments: Breezes make most shots tricky ... Good greens.

GRENELEFE GOLF & TENNIS RESORT

R-3200 State Rd. 546, Haines City, 33844, Polk County, (941)422-7511, (800)237-9549, 25 miles S of Orlando.

★★★½ **EAST COURSE**
Holes: 18. **Yards:** 6,802/5,114. **Par:** 72/72. **Course Rating:** 72.7/69.5. **Slope:** 131/118. **Green Fee:** $40/$110. **Cart Fee:** Included in Green Fee. **Walking Policy:** Mandatory cart. **Walkability:** 3. **Opened:** 1978. **Architect:** Arnold Palmer/Ed Seay. **Season:** Year-round. **High:** Jan.-April. **To obtain tee times:** Package guests may book starting times 90 days in advance. **Miscellaneous:** Reduced fees (weekdays, low season, resort guests, twilight), discount packages, metal spikes, range (grass), club rentals, lodging (750 rooms), credit cards (MC, V, AE).
Reader Comments: Facilities A-number one ... Tight, tight, tight ... Fun tee off a roof ... Poor greens, good service ... Good track ... Could use a little more maintenance ... For Florida residents the summer deal's a steal.

★★★½ **SOUTH COURSE**
Holes: 18. **Yards:** 6,869/5,174. **Par:** 71/71. **Course Rating:** 72.6/69.5. **Slope:** 124/115. **Green Fee:** $40/$110. **Cart Fee:** Included in Green Fee. **Walking Policy:** Mandatory cart. **Walkability:** 3. **Opened:** 1983. **Architect:** Ron Garl. **Season:** Year-round. **High:** Jan.-April. **To obtain tee times:** Package guests may book starting times 90 days in advance. Non resort guests may book 5 days in advance. **Miscellaneous:** Reduced fees (weekdays, low season, resort guests, twilight), discount packages, metal spikes, range (grass), club rentals, lodging, credit cards (MC, V, AE).
Reader Comments: Long and tough ... Holes 8-12 fun to play ... Stay in fairway! ... Most varied of the Grenelefe three ... Demanding, fair, pleasant ... Sand and water make it a challenge ... Outstanding value ... Average.

★★★½ **WEST COURSE**
Holes: 18. **Yards:** 7,325/5,398. **Par:** 72/72. **Course Rating:** 75.0/71.3. **Slope:** 133/124. **Green Fee:** $32/$120. **Cart Fee:** Included in Green Fee. **Walking Policy:** Mandatory cart. **Walkability:**

3. Opened: 1971. **Architect:** Robert Trent Jones/David Wallace. **Season:** Year-round. **High:** Jan.-April. **To obtain tee times:** Package guests may book starting times 90 days in advance. Non resort guests may book 5 days in advance. **Miscellaneous:** Reduced fees (weekdays, low season, resort guests, twilight), discount packages, metal spikes, range (grass), club rentals, lodging, credit cards (MC, V, AE).

Reader Comments: Don't play championship tees and you'll have a great time ... Just a shell of it's former self ... Strong layout, requires good driving ... Excellent design ... Long, long, long ... Well bunkered ... Expensive for what it is.

★★★½ GULF HARBOUR GOLF & COUNTRY CLUB
SP-14700 Portsmouth Blvd. S.W., Fort Myers, 33908, Lee County, (941)433-4211.
Holes: 18. **Yards:** 6,708/5,248. **Par:** 72/72. **Course Rating:** 72.5/70.1. **Slope:** 130/121. **Green Fee:** $28/$115. **Cart Fee:** Included in Green Fee. **Walking Policy:** Mandatory cart. **Walkability:** 1. **Opened:** 1984. **Architect:** Ron Garl/Chip Powell. **Season:** Year-round. **High:** Jan.-May. **To obtain tee times:** Call up to 2 days in advance. **Miscellaneous:** Reduced fees (low season, twilight), metal spikes, range (grass), club rentals, credit cards (MC, V, AE, D).

Reader Comments: Lots of water, fast greens ... Good course, great amenities ... Treeless, unexciting ... Has potential.

★★★½ HABITAT GOLF COURSE
PU-3591 Fairgreen St., Valkaria, 32905, Brevard County, (407)952-6312, 16 miles S of Melbourne.
Holes: 18. **Yards:** 6,836/4,969. **Par:** 72/72. **Course Rating:** 72.9/68.2. **Slope:** 129/115. **Green Fee:** $13/$25. **Cart Fee:** $9/person. **Walking Policy:** Walking at certain times. **Walkability:** 4. **Opened:** 1991. **Architect:** Charles Ankrom. **Season:** Year-round. **High:** Dec.-April. **To obtain tee times:** Call up to 3 days in advance. **Miscellaneous:** Reduced fees (weekdays, low season, resort guests, juniors), discount packages, range (grass), club rentals, credit cards (MC, V).

Reader Comments: Good price, worth the wait ... Great layout, excellent value ... Like it a lot ... Interesting walk in wildlife ... Bring an extra sleeve of balls for the jungles.

★★★★ HAILE PLANTATION GOLF & COUNTRY CLUB
SP-9905 S.W. 44th Ave., Gainesville, 32608, Alachua County, (352)335-0055, 120 miles N of Tampa.
Holes: 18. **Yards:** 6,526/4,807. **Par:** 72/72. **Course Rating:** 71.5/67.7. **Slope:** 124/109. **Green Fee:** $33/$37. **Cart Fee:** Included in Green Fee. **Walking Policy:** Mandatory cart. **Walkability:** 2. **Opened:** 1993. **Architect:** Gary Player. **Season:** Year-round. **High:** Nov.-April. **To obtain tee times:** Call up to 3 days in advance. **Miscellaneous:** Reduced fees (twilight), range (mats), club rentals, credit cards (MC, V, AE), beginner friendly.

Reader Comments: Short course ... . 6 par 5's, 6 par 4's, 6 par 3's ... A few goofy holes; too many houses ... Unusual routing of holes; can't walk ... Absolutely pretty.

★★★★ HALIFAX PLANTATION GOLF CLUB
SP-3400 Halifax Clubhouse Dr, Ormond Beach, 32174, Volusia County, (904)676-9600, 20 miles N of Daytona Beach. **Web:** www.halifaxplantation.com.
Holes: 18. **Yards:** 7,128/4,971. **Par:** 72/72. **Course Rating:** 74.1/68.3. **Slope:** 128/118. **Green Fee:** $10/$35. **Cart Fee:** $14/person. **Walking Policy:** Walking at certain times. **Walkability:** 1. **Opened:** 1993. **Architect:** Bill Amick. **Season:** Year-round. **High:** Nov.-April. **To obtain tee times:** Call 4 days in advance. **Miscellaneous:** Reduced fees (weekdays, low season, resort guests, twilight), discount packages, metal spikes, range (grass), club rentals, lodging, credit cards (MC, V, AE).

Reader Comments: A beautiful and challenging course ... Compliments to the greenskeeper ... Feel like you can score ... Good layout ... Nice practice facilities ... You won't see any other hole ... A great golf experience.

★½ HALL OF FAME GOLF COURSE
2227 N Westshore Blvd., Tampa, 33607, Hillsborough County, (813)876-4913.
Special Notes: Call club for further information.

★½ HARDER HALL COUNTRY CLUB
PU-3600 Golfview Dr., Sebring, 33872, Highlands County, (941)382-0500, 80 miles S of Orlando.
Holes: 18. **Yards:** 6,300/5,003. **Par:** 72/72. **Course Rating:** 70.5/69.0. **Slope:** 125/108. **Green Fee:** $13/$34. **Cart Fee:** Included in Green Fee. **Walking Policy:** Mandatory cart. **Walkability:** N/A. **Opened:** 1956. **Architect:** Dick Wilson. **Season:** Year-round. **High:** Jan.-April. **To obtain tee times:** Call 2 days in advance in season. **Miscellaneous:** Reduced fees (low season, resort guests, twilight), metal spikes, range (grass), club rentals, credit cards (MC, V, D).

HERITAGE LINKS COUNTRY CLUB AT TURKEY CREEK
SP-11400 Turkey Creek Blvd., Alachua, 32615, Alchua County, (904)462-4655, 5 miles NW of Gainesville.

FLORIDA

Holes: 18. **Yards:** 6,570/5,580. **Par:** 72/72. **Course Rating:** 71.2/71.8. **Slope:** 121/121. **Green Fee:** $19/$28. **Cart Fee:** Included in Green Fee. **Walking Policy:** Walking at certain times. **Walkability:** 3. **Opened:** 1977. **Architect:** Wade Northrup. **Season:** Year-round. **High:** Nov.-March. **To obtain tee times:** Nonmembers call up to 3 days in advance. **Miscellaneous:** Reduced fees (weekdays, low season, resort guests, twilight, juniors), metal spikes, range (grass), caddies, club rentals, lodging, credit cards (MC, V, AE, D).
Special Notes: This course is open only to members on weekends.

HIGHLANDS RESERVE GOLF CLUB
PU-500 Highlands Reserve Blvd., Davenport, 33837, Polk County, (941)420-1724, (877)508-4653, 5 miles W of Orlando. **Web:** www.highlandsreserve.com.
Holes: 18. **Yards:** 6,673/4,875. **Par:** 72/72. **Course Rating:** 72.1/67.4. **Slope:** 118/107. **Green Fee:** $24/$59. **Cart Fee:** $11/person. **Walking Policy:** Unrestricted walking. **Walkability:** 2. **Opened:** 1998. **Architect:** Mike Dasher. **Season:** Year-round. **High:** Nov.-May. **Miscellaneous:** Reduced fees (weekdays, low season, resort guests, twilight, juniors), range (grass), club rentals, credit cards (MC, V, AE).

★½ HILAMAN PARK MUNICIPAL GOLF COURSE
PM-2737 Blairstone Rd., Tallahassee, 32301, Leon County, (904)891-3935.
Holes: 18. **Yards:** 6,364/5,365. **Par:** 72/72. **Course Rating:** 70.1/70.8. **Slope:** 121/116. **Green Fee:** $11/$15. **Cart Fee:** $11/person. **Walking Policy:** Walking at certain times. **Walkability:** 3. **Opened:** 1972. **Architect:** Edward Lawrence Packard. **Season:** Year-round. **High:** March-June. **To obtain tee times:** Call 7 days in advance. **Miscellaneous:** Reduced fees (weekdays, twilight, seniors, juniors), metal spikes, range (grass), club rentals, credit cards (MC, V, D).
Special Notes: Hilaman Park is currently closed for renovations. Re-opening date is scheduled for 9/15/1999.

★★★★ HOMBRE GOLF CLUB
SP-120 Coyote Pass, Panama City Beach, 32407, Bay County, (850)234-3673, 100 miles SE of Pensacola. **E-mail:** hombrebad@aol.com. **Web:** www.hombregolfclub.com.
Holes: 18. **Yards:** 6,820/4,800. **Par:** 72/74. **Course Rating:** 73.4/67.2. **Slope:** 136/118. **Green Fee:** $60/$65. **Cart Fee:** Included in Green Fee. **Walking Policy:** Mandatory cart. **Walkability:** 1. **Opened:** 1990. **Architect:** Wes Burnham. **Season:** Year-round. **High:** March-April/June-July. **To obtain tee times:** Call up to 7 days in advance. Golf package tee times up to 6 months in advance. **Miscellaneous:** Reduced fees (weekdays, low season, resort guests, twilight, juniors), discount packages, range (grass), club rentals, lodging (26 rooms), credit cards (MC, V, D).
Reader Comments: Very comfortable course to play ... Good greens ... High handicap would not enjoy ... Need to hit long and straight to score ... Great design and very challenging ... Lots of water, play your tee ... Greens ultra speedy.

★★★½ HUNTER'S CREEK GOLF CLUB
R-14401 Sports Club Way, Orlando, 32837, Orange County, (407)240-4653, 50 miles NE of Tampa.
Holes: 18. **Yards:** 7,432/5,755. **Par:** 72/72. **Course Rating:** 76.1/72.5. **Slope:** 137/120. **Green Fee:** $35/$80. **Cart Fee:** Included in Green Fee. **Walking Policy:** Mandatory cart. **Walkability:** 1. **Opened:** 1986. **Architect:** Lloyd Clifton. **Season:** Year-round. **High:** Jan.-March. **To obtain tee times:** Call 3 days in advance. **Miscellaneous:** Reduced fees (weekdays, low season, twilight, juniors), discount packages, metal spikes, range (grass), club rentals, credit cards (MC, V, D).
Reader Comments: Play the back tees for a tester ... Good layout, for all golfers ... Has steadily gotten better ... Don't go to the back tees unless your first name is Tiger ... Nice greens ... Good value ... Long but fair ... Fun to play ... Always a challenge.

★★★★ HUNTINGTON HILLS GOLF & COUNTRY CLUB
SP-2626 Duff Rd., Lakeland, 33809, Polk County, (941)859-3689, 33 miles E of Tampa.
Holes: 18. **Yards:** 6,631/5,011. **Par:** 72/72. **Course Rating:** 72.5/68.7. **Slope:** 122/115. **Green Fee:** $25/$45. **Cart Fee:** Included in Green Fee. **Walking Policy:** Mandatory cart. **Walkability:** N/A. **Opened:** 1992. **Architect:** Ron Garl. **Season:** Year-round. **High:** Dec.-March. **To obtain tee times:** Call 3 days in advance. **Miscellaneous:** Reduced fees (weekdays, low season, twilight), discount packages, range (grass), club rentals, credit cards (MC, V, AE, D, Diners Club).
Reader Comments: Well worth the ride ... Interesting layout ... Nice elevations for South Florida ... Greens tough to read ... Imaginative layout ... A challenge.

★★½ HYDE PARK GOLF CLUB
PU-6439 Hyde Grove Ave., Jacksonville, 32210, Duval County, (904)786-5410, 5 miles W of Jacksonville.
Holes: 18. **Yards:** 6,500/5,500. **Par:** 72/73. **Course Rating:** 70.3/71.0. **Slope:** 120/122. **Green Fee:** $15/$18. **Cart Fee:** $14/person. **Walking Policy:** Walking at certain times. **Walkability:** 2. **Opened:** 1925. **Architect:** Donald Ross. **Season:** Year-round. **High:** Nov.-May. **To obtain tee**

times: Week in advance. **Miscellaneous:** Reduced fees (weekdays, twilight, seniors, juniors), range (grass), club rentals, credit cards (MC, V).

Reader Comments: Excellent fairways ... Thinkers course ... Small greens ... Old course with a lot of nostalgia ... Big trees ... A must play for golf history buffs.

★★★½ IMPERIAL LAKEWOODS GOLF CLUB

SP-6807 Buffalo Rd., Palmetto, 34221, Manatee County, (941)747-4653, 20 miles S of Tampa. **E-mail:** imperallakewoods,com. **Web:** www.imperiallakewoods.com .

Holes: 18. **Yards:** 6,658/5,270. **Par:** 72/72. **Course Rating:** 71.5/69.7. **Slope:** 123/117. **Green Fee:** $32/$55. **Cart Fee:** Included in Green Fee. **Walking Policy:** Unrestricted walking. **Walkability:** 3. **Opened:** 1987. **Architect:** Ted McAnlis. **Season:** Year-round. **High:** Nov.-April. **To obtain tee times:** Call or come in 2 days in advance. Up to 2 weeks with credit card deposit. **Miscellaneous:** Reduced fees (weekdays, low season, twilight, juniors), metal spikes, range (grass), club rentals, credit cards (MC, V), beginner friendly (PGA instruction).

Reader Comments: 18th is the closest I'll get to the 18th at Pebble Beach ... Greens need some work ... A beauty ... Open, fair and challenging ... Just average ... Can be very windy.

INDIAN BAYOU GOLF & COUNTRY CLUB

SP-1 Country Club Dr. E., Destin, 32541, Okaloosa County, (850)837-6191, 30 miles W of Pensacola.

Holes: 27. **Green Fee:** $50/$60. **Cart Fee:** Included in Green Fee. **Walking Policy:** Walking at certain times. **Walkability:** 1. **Opened:** 1978. **Architect:** Earl Stone. **Season:** Year-round. **High:** Feb.-Aug. **To obtain tee times:** Call up to 30 days in advance.

★★★½ CHOCTAW/CREEK

Yards: 6,892/5,080. **Par:** 72/71. **Course Rating:** 73.1/69.3. **Slope:** 129/113. **Miscellaneous:** Metal spikes, range (grass), club rentals, credit cards (MC, V, AE).

Reader Comments: Fast greens ... A good value for the area ... Big greens are very easy to three putt ... A little pricey but worth it ... Very enjoyable, lots of fun ... Friendly layout ... Solid course for vacationers.

★★★½ SEMINOLE/CHOCTAW

Yards: 6,958/5,455. **Par:** 72/72. **Course Rating:** 73.3/71.2. **Slope:** 126/116. **Miscellaneous:** Metal spikes, range (grass), club rentals, credit cards (MC, V, AE, D).

★★★½ SEMINOLE/CREEK

Yards: 7,016/5,081. **Par:** 72/71. **Course Rating:** 73.7/69.2. **Slope:** 128/113. **Miscellaneous:** Reduced fees (juniors), metal spikes, range (grass), club rentals, credit cards (MC, V, AE, D).

INDIAN LAKE ESTATES GOLF & COUNTRY CLUB

SP-95 Red Grange Blvd., Indian Lake Estates, 33855, Polk County, (941)692-1514, 17 miles E of Lake Wales.

Holes: 18. **Yards:** 6,485/5,194. **Par:** 72/72. **Course Rating:** 70.7/70.6. **Slope:** 123/116. **Green Fee:** $14/$30. **Cart Fee:** Included in Green Fee. **Walking Policy:** Unrestricted walking. **Walkability:** 1. **Opened:** 1972. **Architect:** George W. Cobb. **Season:** Year-round. **High:** Nov.-April. **To obtain tee times:** Call golf shop between 7 a.m. and 5 p.m. up to 7 days in advance. Groups of 12 or more may call anytime in advance for special rates. **Miscellaneous:** Reduced fees (low season, twilight), metal spikes, range (grass), club rentals, credit cards (MC, V), beginner friendly (par-3 9-hole course available).

★★★½ INDIGO LAKES GOLF CLUB

SP-312 Indigo Dr., Daytona Beach, 32114, Volusia County, (904)254-3607, 1 miles E of Daytona Beach.

Holes: 18. **Yards:** 7,168/5,159. **Par:** 72/72. **Course Rating:** 73.5/69.1. **Slope:** 128/123. **Green Fee:** $30/$55. **Cart Fee:** Included in Green Fee. **Walking Policy:** Mandatory cart. **Walkability:** 1. **Opened:** 1977. **Architect:** Lloyd Clifton. **Season:** Year-round. **High:** Jan.-May. **To obtain tee times:** Call up to 7 days in advance. **Miscellaneous:** Reduced fees (weekdays, low season, twilight), discount packages, metal spikes, range (grass/mats), club rentals, credit cards (MC, V, AE).

Reader Comments: Beautiful layout ... Nice track ... Finally shaping up ... Uninteresting ... Greens are small and fast ... Delightful old-time course.

★★★½ INTERNATIONAL GOLF CLUB

PU-6351 International Golf Club Rd., Orlando, 32821, Orange County, (407)239-6909, (800)371-1165.

Holes: 18. **Yards:** 6,776/5,077. **Par:** 72/72. **Course Rating:** 73.0/69.2. **Slope:** 134/117. **Green Fee:** $55/$95. **Cart Fee:** Included in Green Fee. **Walking Policy:** Mandatory cart. **Walkability:** 1. **Opened:** 1986. **Architect:** Joe Lee. **Season:** Year-round. **High:** Jan.-April. **To obtain tee times:** Call 1 day in advance. **Miscellaneous:** Reduced fees (low season, twilight), metal spikes, range (grass/mats), club rentals, credit cards (MC, V, AE, D).

Reader Comments: Tiny greens ... Overrated and underwatered ... Efficient staff ... Good location in Orlando.

FLORIDA

★★★½ INTERNATIONAL LINKS MIAMI MELREESE GOLF COURSE
PU-1802 N.W. 37th Ave., Miami, 33125, Dade County, (305)633-4583.
Holes: 18. **Yards:** 7,173/5,534. **Par:** 71/71. **Course Rating:** 73.5/71.2. **Slope:** 132/118. **Green Fee:** $45/$90. **Cart Fee:** Included in Green Fee. **Walking Policy:** Walking at certain times. **Walkability:** 2. **Opened:** 1997. **Architect:** Charles Mahannah. **Season:** Year-round. **High:** Dec.-April. **To obtain tee times:** Call 3 days in advance. **Miscellaneous:** Reduced fees (weekdays, low season, twilight, juniors), discount packages, range (grass/mats), club rentals, credit cards (MC, V, AE, D), beginner friendly.
Reader Comments: Renovations make this course the real deal ... Great condition offset by high price ... Airplanes are annoying ... Had a 3-hour layover and got in 18 ... Very playable ... Superb-greens.

★★ IRONWOOD GOLF COURSE
PU-2100 N.E. 39th Ave., Gainesville, 32609, Alachua County, (352)334-3120.
Holes: 18. **Yards:** 6,465/5,234. **Par:** 72/72. **Course Rating:** 71.3/70.2. **Slope:** 122/117. **Green Fee:** $11/$14. **Cart Fee:** $8/person. **Walking Policy:** Unrestricted walking. **Walkability:** 1. **Opened:** 1964. **Architect:** David G. Wallace. **Season:** Year-round. **High:** Feb.-June. **To obtain tee times:** Call 2 days in advance. **Miscellaneous:** Reduced fees (weekdays, low season, twilight, seniors, juniors), metal spikes, range (grass), caddies, club rentals, credit cards (MC, V, D), beginner friendly (beginner clinics, private lessons).
Notes: 1999 Special Olympics Host.

JACARANDA GOLF CLUB
SP-9200 W. Broward Blvd., Plantation, 33324, Broward County, (954)472-5836, (888)955-1234, 12 miles W of Fort Lauderdale. **E-mail:** jacarand@paradise.net. **Web:** www.scratch-golf.com.
★★★½ EAST COURSE
Holes: 18. **Yards:** 7,195/5,638. **Par:** 72/72. **Course Rating:** 74.0/72.3. **Slope:** 130/124. **Green Fee:** $35/$99. **Cart Fee:** Included in Green Fee. **Walking Policy:** Walking at certain times. **Walkability:** 2. **Opened:** 1971. **Architect:** Mark Mahannah. **Season:** Year-round. **High:** Nov.-May. **To obtain tee times:** Call up to 7 days in advance. Anytime in advance with credit card. **Miscellaneous:** Reduced fees (weekdays, low season, twilight), discount packages, metal spikes, range (grass/mats), club rentals, credit cards (MC, V, AE).
Reader Comments: Good course ... Extensive yardage markings are a plus ... Tough rough ... Quality course ... Wide fairways ... Lots of hidden water ... Better than average.
★★★½ WEST COURSE
Holes: 18. **Yards:** 6,729/5,314. **Par:** 72/72. **Course Rating:** 72.5/71.1. **Slope:** 132/118. **Green Fee:** $35/$99. **Cart Fee:** Included in Green Fee. **Walking Policy:** Walking at certain times. **Walkability:** 2. **Opened:** 1972. **Architect:** Mark Mahannah/Charles Mahannah. **Season:** Year-round. **High:** Nov.-May. **To obtain tee times:** Call up to 7 days in advance. Anytime in advance with credit card. **Miscellaneous:** Reduced fees (weekdays, low season, twilight), discount packages, metal spikes, range (grass), club rentals, credit cards (MC, V, AE).
Reader Comments: Very nice ... Good course, great condition ... 18th emulates Doral's Blue Monster ... Tight course.

★★ JACKSONVILLE BEACH GOLF CLUB
PM-605 S. Penman Rd., Jacksonville, 32250, Duval County, (904)247-6184, 10 miles E of Jacksonville.
Holes: 18. **Yards:** 6,510/5,245. **Par:** 72/72. **Course Rating:** 70.5/69.2. **Slope:** 119/114. **Green Fee:** $17/$19. **Walking Policy:** Walking at certain times. **Walkability:** 1. **Opened:** 1959. **Architect:** Robert Walker. **Season:** Year-round. **High:** Spring/Fall. **To obtain tee times:** Call Monday at 7 a.m. for next 7 days only. **Miscellaneous:** Reduced fees (weekdays, low season, twilight, juniors), metal spikes, range (grass/mats), club rentals, credit cards (MC, V).

KELLY PLANTATION GOLF CLUB
SP-307 Kelly Plantation Dr., Destin, 32541, Okaloosa County, (850)650-7600, 3 miles E of Destin. **E-mail:** swright@kellyplantation.com. **Web:** www.kellyplantation.com.
Holes: 18. **Yards:** 7,099/5,170. **Par:** 72/72. **Course Rating:** 74.2/70.9. **Slope:** 146/124. **Green Fee:** $75/$95. **Cart Fee:** Included in Green Fee. **Walking Policy:** Unrestricted walking. **Walkability:** 2. **Opened:** 1998. **Architect:** Fred Couples/Gene Bates. **Season:** Year-round. **High:** March-Oct. **To obtain tee times:** May call up to 60 days in advance. Special events and groups of 16 or more may call with more notice. 48-hour cancellation policy. **Miscellaneous:** Reduced fees (low season, twilight, juniors), range (grass), club rentals, lodging (100 rooms), credit cards (MC, V, AE, D), beginner friendly (player assistants and shorter tees).

★★★½ KEY WEST GOLF CLUB
PU-6450 E. College Rd., Key West, 33040, Monroe County, (305)294-5232.
Holes: 18. **Yards:** 6,526/5,183. **Par:** 70/70. **Course Rating:** 71.2/70.1. **Slope:** 124/118. **Green Fee:** $50/$95. **Cart Fee:** Included in Green Fee. **Walking Policy:** Walking at certain times. **Walkability:** 1. **Architect:** Rees Jones. **Season:** Year-round. **High:** Nov.-April. **To obtain tee**

times: Call up to 14 days in advance. **Miscellaneous:** Reduced fees (low season, twilight, juniors), range (mats), club rentals, credit cards (MC, V, AE).

Reader Comments: Only public course for 100 miles ... Great design, challenging at times but truly enjoyable ... Good for a one time visit.

KILLEARN COUNTRY CLUB & INN
R-100 Tyron Circle, Tallahassee, 32308, Leon County, (850)893-2144, (800)476-4101.
Holes: 27. **Green Fee:** $30/$35. **Cart Fee:** $12/person. **Walking Policy:** Walking at certain times. **Walkability:** 2. **Opened:** 1967. **Architect:** William Amick. **Season:** Year-round. **High:** March-Aug. **To obtain tee times:** Call 7 days in advance. **Miscellaneous:** Reduced fees (low season, resort guests, juniors), discount packages, metal spikes, range (grass/mats), club rentals, lodging, credit cards (MC, V, AE, D).
★★★ **EAST/NORTH**
Yards: 6,760/5,524. **Par:** 72/74. **Course Rating:** 73.1/72.6. **Slope:** 131/120.

Reader Comments: Challenging to hackers and pros alike ... Some water holes ... Average course ... Lakes come into play.
★★★ **SOUTH/EAST**
Yards: 7,025/5,661. **Par:** 72/74. **Course Rating:** 73.9/73.0. **Slope:** 133/123.
★★★ **SOUTH/NORTH**
Yards: 6,899/5,537. **Par:** 72/74. **Course Rating:** 73.3/72.5. **Slope:** 132/121.

Reader Comments: Relies on wind ... 16th, 17th and 18th make a great finish.

KINGS ISLAND GOLF CLUB
SP-175 Kings Highway, Port Charlotte, 33981, Charlotte County, (941)629-7800, 2 miles E of Port Charlotte.
Holes: 18. **Yards:** 4,150/3,005. **Par:** 63/63. **Course Rating:** 61.7/60.0. **Slope:** 108/100. **Green Fee:** $16/$28. **Cart Fee:** Included in Green Fee. **Walking Policy:** Mandatory cart. **Walkability:** 2. **Opened:** 1986. **Architect:** Ted McAnlis. **Season:** Year-round. **High:** Nov.-April. **To obtain tee times:** Call up to 3 days in advance. **Miscellaneous:** Reduced fees (low season, twilight), metal spikes, club rentals, credit cards (MC, V, D).

★★★½ **KISSIMMEE BAY COUNTRY CLUB**
SP-2801 Kissimmee Bay Blvd., Kissimmee, 34744, Osceola County, (407)348-4653, 10 miles S of Orlando.
Holes: 18. **Yards:** 6,846/5,171. **Par:** 71/71. **Course Rating:** 70.1/71.0. **Slope:** 125/122. **Green Fee:** $42/$73. **Cart Fee:** Included in Green Fee. **Walking Policy:** Mandatory cart. **Walkability:** 1. **Opened:** 1990. **Architect:** Lloyd Clifton. **Season:** Year-round. **High:** Jan.-April. **To obtain tee times:** Call 1 day in advance. **Miscellaneous:** Reduced fees (weekdays, low season, twilight), discount packages, range (grass), club rentals, credit cards (MC, V, D).

Reader Comments: Great setting ... Wet & wetter ... Shotmakers' course ... Lots of mounds on sides of fairway ... Nice course, priced right ... Houses too close to course ... Tight.

★★★ **KISSIMMEE GOLF CLUB**
SP-3103 Florida Coach Dr., Kissimmee, 34741, Osceola County, (407)847-2816, 15 miles S of Orlando. **E-mail:** golfkiss@aol.com. **Web:** www.kissgolfclub.com.
Holes: 18. **Yards:** 6,537/5,083. **Par:** 72/72. **Course Rating:** 73.0/68.6. **Slope:** 126/116. **Green Fee:** $30/$48. **Cart Fee:** Included in Green Fee. **Walking Policy:** Walking at certain times. **Walkability:** 1. **Opened:** 1970. **Architect:** Bill Bulmer/Gordon Lewis. **Season:** Year-round. **High:** Dec.-April. **To obtain tee times:** Call up to 4 days in advance. **Miscellaneous:** Reduced fees (low season, resort guests, twilight), discount packages, metal spikes, range (grass), club rentals, credit cards (MC, V), beginner friendly (junior golf camps, golf schools).

Reader Comments: Noisy airport next to it ... Ho hum.

★★ **LAKE ORLANDO GOLF CLUB**
SP-4224 Clubhouse Rd., Orlando, 32808, Orange County, (407)298-4144.
Holes: 18. **Yards:** 6,803/5,488. **Par:** 72/72. **Course Rating:** 72.3/70.3. **Slope:** 130/114. **Green Fee:** $23/$23. **Cart Fee:** Included in Green Fee. **Walking Policy:** Mandatory cart. **Walkability:** 1. **Opened:** 1970. **Architect:** Lloyd Clinton. **Season:** Year-round. **High:** Nov.-March. **To obtain tee times:** Call golf shop. **Miscellaneous:** Reduced fees (weekdays, twilight), metal spikes, range (grass/mats), club rentals, credit cards (MC, V).
Special Notes: Formerly known as Rosemont Golf & Country Club.

★★ **LAKE WORTH GOLF CLUB**
PM-1-7th Ave. N., Lake Worth, 33460, Palm Beach County, (561)582-9713, 7 miles S of Palm Beach.
Holes: 18. **Yards:** 6,113/5,413. **Par:** 70/70. **Course Rating:** 68.6/69.6. **Slope:** 116/113. **Green Fee:** $10/$23. **Cart Fee:** $21/cart. **Walking Policy:** Unrestricted walking. **Walkability:** 1. **Opened:** 1926. **Architect:** William B. Langford/Theodore J. Moreau. **Season:** Year-round. **High:** Jan.-March. **To obtain tee times:** Call 1 day in advance at 9 a.m. **Miscellaneous:** Reduced fees

FLORIDA

(low season, twilight, juniors), discount packages, metal spikes, club rentals, credit cards (MC, V, Debit cards).

★★★½ LANSBROOK GOLF COURSE
SP-4605 Village Center Dr., Palm Harbor, 34685, Pinellas County, (727)784-7333, 20 miles W of Tampa. **E-mail:** lansgolf@aol.com. **Web:** www.lansbrookgolf.com.
Holes: 18. **Yards:** 6,862/5,333. **Par:** 72/72. **Course Rating:** 73.2/70.2. **Slope:** 131/124. **Green Fee:** $27/$59. **Cart Fee:** Included in Green Fee. **Walking Policy:** Mandatory cart. **Walkability:** 1. **Opened:** 1975. **Architect:** Lane Marshall. **Season:** Year-round. **High:** Dec.-April. **To obtain tee times:** Call 4 days in advance. **Miscellaneous:** Reduced fees (weekdays, low season, twilight), metal spikes, range (grass/mats), club rentals, credit cards (MC, V, D).
Reader Comments: Narrow fairways, good greens ... Great for short hitters ... Nice shape for lots of play ... Very fast greens for Florida ... Tight through trees ... Many risk-reward shots.

THE LEGACY CLUB AT ALAQUA LAKES
SP-1700 Alaqua Lakes Blvd., Longwood, 32779, Seminole County, (407)444-9995, 10 miles E of Orlando.
Holes: 18. **Yards:** 7,160/5,383. **Par:** 72/72. **Course Rating:** 74.9/70.7. **Slope:** 140/119. **Green Fee:** $59/$109. **Cart Fee:** $15/person. **Walking Policy:** Walking at certain times. **Walkability:** 3. **Opened:** 1998. **Architect:** Tom Fazio. **Season:** Year-round. **High:** Nov.-April. **To obtain tee times:** Members call one week in advance. Public call 3 days in advance. **Miscellaneous:** Reduced fees (weekdays, low season, resort guests, twilight), discount packages, range (grass), club rentals, credit cards (MC, V), beginner friendly (weekly clinics).

★★★★ THE LEGACY GOLF COURSE AT LAKEWOOD RANCH
PU-8255 Legacy Blvd., Bradenton, 34202, Manatee County, (941)907-7067.
Holes: 18. **Yards:** 7,067/4,886. **Par:** 72/72. **Course Rating:** 73.7/68.2. **Slope:** 143/125. **Green Fee:** $45/$95. **Cart Fee:** Included in Green Fee. **Walking Policy:** Mandatory cart. **Walkability:** 3. **Opened:** 1997. **Architect:** Arnold Palmer/Ed Seay/Vici Martz. **Season:** Year-round. **High:** Jan.-April. **Miscellaneous:** Reduced fees (weekdays, twilight), metal spikes, range (grass), club rentals, credit cards (MC, V, AE).
Reader Comments: A real gem ... Very demanding test of golf ... Feels a little cookie-cutter ... Arnie has his name on it but you can't walk! ... Very open to wind ... Nice layout with water, water, water ... Play twice, once to find trouble, then to keep score ... Large greens.

LELY RESORT GOLF & COUNTRY CLUB   *Service*
PU-8004 Lely Resort Blvd., Naples, 34113, Collier County, (941)793-2223, (800)388-4653, 30 miles S of Ft. Myers.
★★★★ LELY FLAMINGO ISLAND CLUB
Holes: 18. **Yards:** 7,171/5,377. **Par:** 72/72. **Course Rating:** 73.9/70.6. **Slope:** 135/126. **Green Fee:** $35/$135. **Cart Fee:** Included in Green Fee. **Walking Policy:** Mandatory cart. **Walkability:** N/A. **Opened:** 1990. **Architect:** Robert Trent Jones. **Season:** Year-round. **High:** Nov.-April. **To obtain tee times:** Call up to 3 days in advance. Credit card required Nov.-April. **Miscellaneous:** Reduced fees (low season, twilight), metal spikes, range (grass), club rentals, credit cards (MC, V, AE, D).
Reader Comments: Excellent condition, good holes ... A thrilling course from the tips ... Outstanding ... Beautifully laid out course ... Beautiful ... Too much wind, too much sand ... Must play if you come to Southwest Florida.
★★★★ LELY MUSTANG GOLF CLUB
Holes: 18. **Yards:** 7,217/5,197. **Par:** 72/72. **Course Rating:** N/A. **Slope:** N/A. **Green Fee:** $43/$148. **Cart Fee:** Included in Green Fee. **Walking Policy:** Mandatory cart. **Walkability:** N/A. **Opened:** 1997. **Architect:** Charles Mahannah/Lee Trevino. **Season:** Year-round. **High:** Nov.-April. **To obtain tee times:** Call up to 3 days in advance. Credit card required Nov.-April. **Miscellaneous:** Reduced fees (low season, twilight), metal spikes, range (grass), club rentals, credit cards (MC, V, AE, D).
Reader Comments: This is a garden of Eden ... A true test! ... Outstanding ... Excellent challenge ... Tough but fair ... Bring lots of money ... Absolutely fabulous course.

LEMON BAY GOLF CLUB
SP-9600 Eagle Preserve Dr., Englewood, 34224, Charlotte County, (941)697-3729, 4 miles S of Sarasota.
Holes: 18. **Yards:** 6,180/5,081. **Par:** 71/72. **Course Rating:** 69.5/68.2. **Slope:** 126/120. **Green Fee:** $35/$60. **Cart Fee:** Included in Green Fee. **Walking Policy:** Walking at certain times. **Walkability:** 2. **Opened:** 1982. **Architect:** Jim Petrides/Chip Powell. **Season:** Year-round. **High:** Oct.-April. **To obtain tee times:** Call 2 days in advance. **Miscellaneous:** Reduced fees (low season), range (grass), club rentals, credit cards (MC, V).

★★★ THE LINKS OF LAKE BERNADETTE
SP-5430 Links Lane, Zephyrhills, 33541, Pasco County, (813)788-4653, 20 miles N of Tampa.

Holes: 18. **Yards:** 6,392/5,031. **Par:** 71/71. **Course Rating:** 70.0/68.0. **Slope:** 119/118. **Green Fee:** $20/$35. **Cart Fee:** Included in Green Fee. **Walking Policy:** Mandatory cart. **Walkability:** 1. **Opened:** 1985. **Architect:** Dean Refram. **Season:** Year-round. **High:** Jan.-April. **To obtain tee times:** Call 3 days in advance. **Miscellaneous:** Reduced fees (weekdays, low season, twilight), metal spikes, club rentals, credit cards (MC, V, AE).
Reader Comments: Worth the trip ... Tough but fair ... Each hole distinctive ... Real links flavor ... Short but difficult ... Not memorable.

★★★½ LOCHMOOR COUNTRY CLUB
SP-3911 Orange Grove Blvd., North Fort Myers, 33903, Lee County, (941)995-0501, 5 miles N of Fort Myers.
Holes: 18. **Yards:** 6,908/5,152. **Par:** 72/72. **Course Rating:** 73.1/69.1. **Slope:** 128/116. **Green Fee:** $14/$50. **Cart Fee:** Included in Green Fee. **Walking Policy:** Walking at certain times. **Walkability:** 1. **Opened:** 1972. **Architect:** William F. Mitchell. **Season:** Year-round. **High:** Jan.-April. **To obtain tee times:** Call up to 2 days in advance. **Miscellaneous:** Reduced fees (low season, twilight, juniors), range (grass), club rentals, credit cards (MC, V, AE).
Reader Comments: One of the best I've ever played, as far as value and beauty ... Better than before ... Average ... Open, but lots of wind ... Wide fairways.

LONG MARSH GOLF CLUB
SP-20 White Marsh Rd., Rotonda, 33947, Charlotte County, (941)698-0918, 30 miles S of Sarasota.
Holes: 18. **Yards:** 7,120/5,251. **Par:** 72/72. **Course Rating:** 74.2/69.3. **Slope:** 128/112. **Green Fee:** $20/$47. **Cart Fee:** Included in Green Fee. **Walking Policy:** Walking at certain times. **Walkability:** 1. **Opened:** 1999. **Architect:** Ted McAnlis. **Season:** Year-round. **High:** Jan.-April. **To obtain tee times:** Call 3 days in advance. **Miscellaneous:** Range (grass), club rentals, credit cards (MC, V), beginner friendly (group lessons).

★★★ LONGBOAT KEY CLUB
R-361 Gulf of Mexico Dr., Longboat Key, 34228, Sarasota County, (941)387-1632, 3 miles NW of Sarasota.
Holes: 18. **Yards:** 6,792/5,198. **Par:** 72/72. **Course Rating:** N/A. **Slope:** 138/121. **Green Fee:** $65/$129. **Cart Fee:** Included in Green Fee. **Walking Policy:** Mandatory cart. **Walkability:** 1. **Architect:** William F. Mitchell. **Season:** Year-round. **High:** Dec.-May. **To obtain tee times:** Must be a guest at the resort to play. **Miscellaneous:** Reduced fees (low season, twilight), discount packages, metal spikes, range (grass/mats), club rentals, lodging.
Reader Comments: Wind a factor ... Deceptive ... Water hazards difficult ... Blue 9 is beautiful.

LOST KEY PLANTATION
★★★½ LOST KEY GOLF CLUB
PU-625 Lost Key Dr., Perdido Key, 32507, Escambia County, (850)492-1300, (888)256-7853, 5 miles S of Pensacola.
Holes: 18. **Yards:** 6,810/4,825. **Par:** 72/72. **Course Rating:** 74.3/69.6. **Slope:** 144/121. **Green Fee:** $50/$65. **Cart Fee:** Included in Green Fee. **Walking Policy:** Mandatory cart. **Walkability:** 2. **Opened:** 1997. **Architect:** A. Palmer/E. Seay/H. Minchew/E. Wiltse. **Season:** Year-round. **High:** March-Aug. **To obtain tee times:** Call golf shop. **Miscellaneous:** Reduced fees (twilight, juniors), metal spikes, range (grass), club rentals, credit cards (MC, V, AE).
Reader Comments: Target golf at its best ... It's beautiful and humbling ... Too tight for most players ... Only course I've seen where the beverage cart sells balls ... Great greens ... Stray shots are gone forever ... Should be called 'Lost Ball.'

★★★½ LOST LAKE GOLF CLUB
SP-8300 S.E. Fazio Dr., Hobe Sound, 33455, Martin County, (561)220-6666, 25 miles N of West Palm Beach.
Holes: 18. **Yards:** 6,850/5,106. **Par:** 72/72. **Course Rating:** 73.4/69.5. **Slope:** 135/123. **Green Fee:** $22/$33. **Cart Fee:** Included in Green Fee. **Walking Policy:** Mandatory cart. **Walkability:** 3. **Opened:** 1992. **Architect:** Jim Fazio. **Season:** Year-round. **High:** Jan.-April. **To obtain tee times:** Call 3 days in advance. **Miscellaneous:** Reduced fees (low season), metal spikes, range (grass), club rentals, credit cards (MC, V).
Reader Comments: Really nice ... Tough but fair ... Average course ... Tough track ... Extremely challenging but beautiful ... Too windy ... Wow! ... Most enjoyable ... A visual treat.

★★★ LOST OAKS GOLF CLUB
SP-1100 Tarpon Woods Blvd., Palm Harbor, 34685, Pinellas County, (727)784-7606, 20 miles NW of Tampa.
Holes: 18. **Yards:** 6,466/5,205. **Par:** 72/72. **Course Rating:** 71.2/69.5. **Slope:** 128/115. **Green Fee:** $32/$46. **Cart Fee:** Included in Green Fee. **Walking Policy:** Walking at certain times. **Walkability:** N/A. **Opened:** 1975. **Architect:** Lane Marshall. **Season:** Year-round. **High:** Jan.-May. **To obtain tee times:** Call in advance. **Miscellaneous:** Reduced fees (weekdays, low sea-

son, twilight), discount packages, metal spikes, range (grass), club rentals, credit cards (MC, V, AE).

Reader Comments: Challenging course that requires smarts not power ... Nice layout in the woods ... Slowly improving conditions ... Lots of woods and hidden water.

LPGA INTERNATIONAL

PU-300 Champions Dr., Daytona Beach, 32124, Volusia County, (904)274-5742, 40 miles NE of Orlando. **Web:** www.lpga.com.

★★★★ CHAMPIONS *Condition*

Holes: 18. **Yards:** 7,088/5,131. **Par:** 72/72. **Course Rating:** 74.0/68.9. **Slope:** 134/122. **Green Fee:** $30/$78. **Cart Fee:** Included in Green Fee. **Walking Policy:** Walking at certain times. **Walkability:** 3. **Opened:** 1994. **Architect:** Rees Jones. **Season:** Year-round. **High:** Jan.-April. **To obtain tee times:** Call 7 days in advance. **Miscellaneous:** Reduced fees (low season, twilight, juniors), discount packages, metal spikes, range (grass), club rentals, credit cards (MC, V, AE), beginner friendly (new golfer clinics, new golfer play time).
Notes: Home of the LPGA Tour. Site of the LPGA Titleholders Championship **Reader Comments:** Looking forward to playing again. A must if in Daytona area ... Very pretty ... Lots of wildlife ... Challenging but fair & fun.

★★★★ LEGENDS *Condition*

Holes: 18. **Yards:** 6,984/5,131. **Par:** 72/72. **Course Rating:** 74.5/70.2. **Slope:** 138/123. **Green Fee:** $30/$78. **Cart Fee:** Included in Green Fee. **Walking Policy:** Walking at certain times. **Walkability:** 1. **Opened:** 1998. **Architect:** Arthur Hills. **Season:** Year-round. **High:** Jan.-April. **To obtain tee times:** Call 7 days in advance. **Miscellaneous:** Reduced fees (low season, twilight, juniors), discount packages, metal spikes, range (grass), club rentals, credit cards (MC, V, AE), beginner friendly (new golfer clinics, new golfer play time).
Reader Comments: Don't be fooled, difficult from the tips ... Hole for hole truly outstanding ... Windy and open ... Wake up! Market me! ... Great practice facilities ... Straight is a must ... Winds can be tricky ... Blue tees a real golf experience ... Long carries and tough rough ... Female friendly ... Excellent practice facilities.

★★½ MAGNOLIA VALLEY GOLF CLUB

SP-7223 Massachusetts Ave., New Port Richey, 34653, Pasco County, (727)847-2342, 20 miles NW of Tampa.
Holes: 18. **Yards:** 6,106/4,869. **Par:** 71/72. **Course Rating:** 69.1/67.2. **Slope:** 121/112. **Green Fee:** $10/$25. **Cart Fee:** Included in Green Fee. **Walking Policy:** Walking at certain times. **Walkability:** 1. **Opened:** 1965. **Architect:** Phil Leckey. **Season:** Year-round. **High:** Jan.-April. **To obtain tee times:** Call golf shop up to 5 days in advance. **Miscellaneous:** Reduced fees (low season, twilight, seniors), discount packages, metal spikes, range (grass), club rentals, credit cards (MC, V, D).
Reader Comments: Beware the gators ... Must be accurate off tee ... Lots of water and doglegs. **Special Notes:** Also has 9-hole par-3 course.

★★★ MANATEE COUNTY GOLF CLUB

PM-6415 53rd Ave. West, Bradenton, 34210, Manatee County, (941)792-6773, 40 miles S of Tampa.
Holes: 18. **Yards:** 6,747/5,619. **Par:** 72/72. **Course Rating:** 71.6/71.6. **Slope:** 122/119. **Green Fee:** $13/$23. **Walking Policy:** Unrestricted walking. **Walkability:** 2. **Opened:** 1977. **Architect:** Lane Marshall. **Season:** Year-round. **High:** Nov.-April. **To obtain tee times:** Call 2 days in advance. **Miscellaneous:** Reduced fees (weekdays, low season, twilight), metal spikes, range (grass), club rentals, credit cards (MC, V).
Reader Comments: A nice little track ... Better than a day in the office ... Challenging muny ... Walk anytime! ... Beside waste-treatment plant ... Nice variety of holes.

★★★ MANGROVE BAY GOLF COURSE

PM-875 62nd Ave. N.E., St. Petersburg, 33702, Pinellas County, (727)893-7800, 15 miles E of Tampa.
Holes: 18. **Yards:** 6,656/5,176. **Par:** 72/72. **Course Rating:** 71.5/68.5. **Slope:** 120/112. **Green Fee:** $18/$23. **Cart Fee:** $11/person. **Walking Policy:** Unrestricted walking. **Walkability:** 2. **Opened:** 1978. **Architect:** Bill Amick. **Season:** Year-round. **High:** Jan.-April. **To obtain tee times:** Call 7 days in advance. **Miscellaneous:** Reduced fees (low season, twilight), metal spikes, range (grass), club rentals, credit cards (MC, V, D, ATM Debit Card).
Reader Comments: New greens are good ... A super municipal course but busy ... Wide open ... Value for money is good ... Very good muny course.

★★ MARCO SHORES COUNTRY CLUB

PU-1450 Mainsail Dr., Naples, 34114, Collier County, (941)394-2581. **E-mail:** info@marco-shores-golf.com. **Web:** www.marco-shores-golf.com.
Holes: 18. **Yards:** 6,879/5,634. **Par:** 72/72. **Course Rating:** 73.0/72.3. **Slope:** 125/121. **Green Fee:** $24/$87. **Cart Fee:** Included in Green Fee. **Walking Policy:** Mandatory cart. **Walkability:** 1. **Opened:** 1974. **Architect:** Bruce Devlin/Robert von Hagge. **Season:** Year-round. **High:** Jan.-April.

FLORIDA

To obtain tee times: Call or in person 4 days in advance. **Miscellaneous:** Reduced fees (low season, twilight, juniors), metal spikes, range (grass/mats), club rentals, credit cards (MC, V, D).

★★★★ MARCUS POINTE GOLF CLUB
PU-2500 Oak Pointe Dr., Pensacola, 32505, Escambia County, (850)484-9770, (800)362-7287.
Holes: 18. **Yards:** 6,737/5,185. **Par:** 72/72. **Course Rating:** 72.3/69.5. **Slope:** 129/119. **Green Fee:** $27/$36. **Cart Fee:** $13/person. **Walking Policy:** Walking at certain times. **Walkability:** 3. **Opened:** 1990. **Architect:** Earl Stone. **Season:** Year-round. **High:** Feb.-May. **To obtain tee times:** Call up to 3 days in advance. **Miscellaneous:** Reduced fees (weekdays, low season, twilight, juniors), discount packages, metal spikes, range (grass), club rentals, credit cards (MC, V), beginner friendly.

Reader Comments: Some goofy holes, but a good test from the back ... Tight! ... Good course ... Beautiful ... Rolling hills ... Fun. Very playable.

MARRIOTT AT SAWGRASS RESORT
★★★★ MARSH LANDING GOLF CLUB   *Pace*
1000 TPC Blvd., Ponte Vedra Beach, 32082, St. Johns County, (904)273-3720, (800)457-4653, 15 miles E of Jacksonville.
Holes: 18. **Yards:** 6,841/6,001. **Par:** 72/72. **Course Rating:** N/A. **Slope:** 131/120. **Green Fee:** $95/$155. **Walkability:** N/A. **Season:** Year-round. **High:** March-May. **Miscellaneous:** Reduced fees (low season), discount packages, metal spikes, range (grass), lodging, credit cards (MC, V, AE, D).

Reader Comments: Two nines very different ... Worth the price ... Overrated ... Very scenic through the marshes ... Punishes average golfer.
★★½ OAK BRIDGE GOLF CLUB
R-254 Alta Mar Dr., Ponte Vedra Beach, 32082, St. Johns County, (904)285-0204, 12 miles S of Jacksonville.
Holes: 18. **Yards:** 6,383/4,869. **Par:** 70/70. **Course Rating:** 70.3/67.8. **Slope:** 129/116. **Green Fee:** $45/$80. **Cart Fee:** $20/person. **Walking Policy:** Walking at certain times. **Walkability:** 1. **Opened:** 1972. **Architect:** Arnold Palmer. **Season:** Year-round. **High:** Feb.-May. **To obtain tee times:** May book tee times through travel agents when making resort reservations. **Miscellaneous:** Range (grass), club rentals, credit cards (MC, V).

Reader Comments: Six par 3s and lots of water ... Front 9 excellent ... Tough when wind blows.

MARRIOTT'S BAY POINT RESORT
R-P.O. Box 27880, Panama City Beach, 32411, Bay County, (850)235-6950, 90 miles E of Pensacola. **E-mail:** baypoint@panamacity.com. **Web:** www.baypointgolf.com.
★★★½ CLUB MEADOWS COURSE
Holes: 18. **Yards:** 6,913/4,999. **Par:** 72/72. **Course Rating:** 73.3/68.0. **Slope:** 126/118. **Green Fee:** $50/$75. **Cart Fee:** Included in Green Fee. **Walking Policy:** Mandatory cart. **Walkability:** 1. **Opened:** 1973. **Architect:** Willard Byrd. **Season:** Year-round. **High:** Feb.-May. **To obtain tee times:** Call for tee times at (850)235-6909. **Miscellaneous:** Reduced fees (low season, resort guests, twilight, juniors), range (grass), club rentals, lodging, credit cards (MC, V, AE).

Reader Comments: Well kept ... Heavy play by hotel guests ... Very playable for medium handicapper ... Like playing in a photograph ... Enjoyable in spring, fall, summer or winter ... Flat but fun to play ... Tough course but worth the challenge! ... Wind always a hazard.
★★★★ LAGOON LEGEND
Holes: 18. **Yards:** 6,885/4,942. **Par:** 72/72. **Course Rating:** 75.3/69.8. **Slope:** 152/127. **Green Fee:** $50/$85. **Cart Fee:** Included in Green Fee. **Walking Policy:** Mandatory cart. **Walkability:** 2. **Opened:** 1986. **Architect:** Bruce Devlin/Robert von Hagge. **Season:** Year-round. **High:** Feb.-May. **To obtain tee times:** Call for tee times (850)235-6909. **Miscellaneous:** Reduced fees (low season, resort guests, twilight, juniors), discount packages, range (grass), club rentals, lodging (500 rooms), credit cards (MC, V, AE).

Reader Comments: Off the beaten path but wonderful ... Take extra balls ... Great design. Memorable ... Play it every chance I get ... Gorgeous scenery ... Hard as hell but fun to play ... Golf-ball graveyard ... Many forced carries ... Love the challenge of hitting from moonscape mounds ... Waterworld ... First hole is awesome ... No place for ladies.

★★★½ MARRIOTT'S GOLF CLUB AT MARCO
R-3433 Marriott Club Dr., Naples, 34114, Collier County, (941)793-6060.
Holes: 18. **Yards:** 6,898/5,416. **Par:** 72/72. **Course Rating:** 73.1/70.9. **Slope:** 137/122. **Green Fee:** $35/$125. **Cart Fee:** Included in Green Fee. **Walking Policy:** Mandatory cart. **Walkability:** N/A. **Opened:** 1991. **Architect:** Joe Lee. **Season:** Year-round. **High:** Nov.-April. **To obtain tee times:** Call up to 2 days in advance. Confirmed Marriott resort guests may call up to 60 days in advance. **Miscellaneous:** Reduced fees (juniors), metal spikes, range (grass), club rentals, lodging, credit cards (MC, V, AE, D, Diners Club).

Reader Comments: Excellent vacation course ... Overrated ... What a view of the ocean ... Bring the insect repellent.

FLORIDA

MARTIN COUNTY GOLF & COUNTRY CLUB
PU-2000 S.E. Saint Lucie Blvd., Stuart, 34996, Martin County, (561)287-3747, 40 miles N of West Palm Beach.

★★★ BLUE/GOLD COURSE
Holes: 18. **Yards:** 5,900/5,236. **Par:** 72/72. **Course Rating:** 67.5/69.1. **Slope:** 120/120. **Green Fee:** $10/$22. **Cart Fee:** $6/. **Walking Policy:** Mandatory cart. **Walkability:** N/A. **Opened:** 1925. **Architect:** Ron Garl. **Season:** Year-round. **High:** Dec.-April. **To obtain tee times:** Call 5 days in advance. **Miscellaneous:** Reduced fees (low season, juniors), metal spikes, range (grass), club rentals.

Reader Comments: Very good for the cost ... Excellent staff ... Fair challenge, pleasant.

★★½ RED/WHITE COURSE
Holes: 18. **Yards:** 6,200/5,400. **Par:** 72/73. **Course Rating:** 69.1/70.4. **Slope:** 116/120. **Green Fee:** $10/$22. **Walking Policy:** Walking at certain times. **Walkability:** N/A. **Opened:** 1925. **Architect:** Ron Garl. **Season:** Year-round. **High:** Dec.-April. **To obtain tee times:** Call 5 days in advance. **Miscellaneous:** Reduced fees (low season, juniors), metal spikes, range (grass), club rentals.

Reader Comments: Extremely busy ... Challenging.

★★★½ MATANZAS WOODS GOLF CLUB
SP-398 Lakeview Dr., Palm Coast, 32137, Flagler County, (904)446-6330, (800)874-2101, 30 miles N of Daytona Beach.
Holes: 18. **Yards:** 6,985/5,336. **Par:** 72/72. **Course Rating:** 73.3/71.2. **Slope:** 132/126. **Green Fee:** $39/$60. **Cart Fee:** Included in Green Fee. **Walking Policy:** Mandatory cart. **Walkability:** 3. **Opened:** 1985. **Architect:** Arnold Palmer. **Season:** Year-round. **High:** Jan.-April. **To obtain tee times:** Call up to 5 days in advance. **Miscellaneous:** Reduced fees (low season, resort guests, twilight, juniors), discount packages, metal spikes, range (grass), club rentals, credit cards (MC, V, AE, D).

Reader Comments: Trees along fairways suffered from fires ... Challenging layout ... Very enjoyable ... Can use every club in your bag ... Course design excellent ... Expected more.

★★ MAYFAIR COUNTRY CLUB
PU-3536 Country Club Rd., Sanford, 32771, Seminole County, (407)322-2531, (800)279-5098, 15 miles N of Orlando.
Holes: 18. **Yards:** 6,375/5,223. **Par:** 72/72. **Course Rating:** N/A. **Slope:** 119/115. **Green Fee:** $25/$40. **Cart Fee:** Included in Green Fee. **Walking Policy:** Mandatory cart. **Walkability:** 2. **Opened:** 1920. **Season:** Year-round. **High:** Dec.-April. **To obtain tee times:** Call (800)279-5098. **Miscellaneous:** Reduced fees (weekdays, low season), discount packages, metal spikes, range (grass), club rentals, credit cards (MC, V, AE, D).

★★ MEADOWBROOK GOLF CLUB
SP-3200 N.W. 98th St., Gainesville, 32606, Alachua County, (352)332-0577, 60 miles SW of Jacksonville.
Holes: 18. **Yards:** 6,289/4,720. **Par:** 72/72. **Course Rating:** 69.9/66.7. **Slope:** 119/117. **Green Fee:** $7/$24. **Walking Policy:** Walking at certain times. **Walkability:** 3. **Opened:** 1987. **Architect:** Steven R. Smyers. **Season:** Year-round. **High:** Jan.-April. **To obtain tee times:** Call 1 day in advance. **Miscellaneous:** Reduced fees (weekdays, low season, twilight), range (grass), club rentals, credit cards (MC, V, D).

★★★½ METROWEST COUNTRY CLUB
SP-2100 S. Hiawassee Rd., Orlando, 32835, Orange County, (407)299-1099, 10 miles SW of Orlando. **Web:** www.metrowestorlando.com.
Holes: 18. **Yards:** 7,051/5,325. **Par:** 72/72. **Course Rating:** 74.1/70.3. **Slope:** 132/122. **Green Fee:** $40/$80. **Cart Fee:** Included in Green Fee. **Walking Policy:** Mandatory cart. **Walkability:** 4. **Opened:** 1987. **Architect:** Robert Trent Jones. **Season:** Year-round. **High:** Jan.-May. **To obtain tee times:** Call up to 7 days in advance. **Miscellaneous:** Reduced fees (low season, twilight, juniors), discount packages, metal spikes, range (grass), club rentals, credit cards (MC, V, AE).

Reader Comments: Beautiful course that's good for all levels of play ... Wide open ... Not much trouble ... Guts necessary ... How about a smile with that greens fee ... A real pleasure ... Treat you like a member of private club ... The 9th has a plaque for John Daly on an amazing drivelook for it ... Only a couple of memorable holes.

MIAMI NATIONAL GOLF CLUB
SP-6401 Kendale Lakes Dr., Miami, 33183, Dade County, (305)382-3935.
Holes: 27. **Green Fee:** $20/$45. **Cart Fee:** Included in Green Fee. **Walking Policy:** Mandatory cart. **Opened:** 1970. **Architect:** Mark Mahannah. **Season:** Year-round. **High:** Nov.-April. **To obtain tee times:** Call golf shop up to 7 days in advance. May call up to 60 days in advance with credit card and 48-hour cancellation policy.
★★★½ BARRACUDA/MARLIN COURSE

Yards: 6,719/5,445. **Par:** 72/74. **Course Rating:** 73.6/70.1. **Slope:** 132/118. **Walkability:** 3. **Miscellaneous:** Reduced fees (weekdays, low season, twilight, juniors), metal spikes, range (grass/mats), club rentals, credit cards (MC, V, AE).
Reader Comments: Keep pace quick ... Water with a few fairways thrown in ... One of the best value courses in the area ... Nice grass range ... OK course.

★★★½ **DOLPHIN/BARRACUDA COURSE**
Yards: 6,679/5,281. **Par:** 72/73. **Course Rating:** 73.1/69.3. **Slope:** 130/119. **Walkability:** 3. **Miscellaneous:** Reduced fees (weekdays, low season, twilight, juniors), metal spikes, range (grass/mats), club rentals, credit cards (MC, V, AE).

★★★½ **MARLIN/DOLPHIN COURSE**
. **Yards:** 6,678/5,364. **Par:** 72/73. **Course Rating:** 72.9/69.6. **Slope:** 129/119. **Walkability:** 2. **Miscellaneous:** Reduced fees (twilight, juniors), metal spikes, range (grass/mats), credit cards (MC, V, AE).
Reader Comments: Average ... Nice staff, well maintained, some tough holes ... Fun course when we played..
Special Notes: Formerly Kendale Lakes Golf Course.

★★★ **MIAMI SHORES COUNTRY CLUB**
SP-10000 Biscayne Blvd., Miami Shores, 33138, Dade County, (305)795-2366, 15 miles N of Miami.
Holes: 18. **Yards:** 6,400/5,400. **Par:** 71/72. **Course Rating:** 70.6/71.3. **Slope:** 121/126. **Green Fee:** $35/$75. **Cart Fee:** Included in Green Fee. **Walking Policy:** Mandatory cart. **Walkability:** 3. **Opened:** 1938. **Architect:** Red Lawrence. **Season:** Year-round. **High:** Dec.-April. **To obtain tee times:** Call up to 3 days in advance. **Miscellaneous:** Reduced fees (weekdays, low season, twilight), range (grass/mats), club rentals, credit cards (MC, V, AE, Diners Club).
Reader Comments: Perfect for intermediate player ... Tourist Trap ... Small fast greens ... Very good value ... Open but tough!.

★★½ **MILL COVE GOLF CLUB**
PU-1700 Monument Rd., Jacksonville, 32225, Duval County, (904)646-4653.
Holes: 18. **Yards:** 6,671/4,719. **Par:** 71/71. **Course Rating:** 71.7/66.3. **Slope:** 129/112. **Green Fee:** $14/$22. **Cart Fee:** $13/person. **Walking Policy:** Walking at certain times. **Walkability:** N/A. **Opened:** 1990. **Architect:** Arnold Palmer/Ed Seay. **Season:** Year-round. **To obtain tee times:** Call 5 days in advance. **Miscellaneous:** Reduced fees (weekdays, low season, twilight, seniors, juniors), metal spikes, range (grass/mats), club rentals, credit cards (MC, V, AE).
Reader Comments: Fairways and greens very good ... Crowded but pace was good ... Great except for the airplanes ... Short and tight ... Plain ... Hilly, unusual for Florida.

MISSION INN GOLF & TENNIS RESORT *Service,*
★★★★ **EL CAMPEON COURSE** *Pace*
R-10400 County Rd. 48, Howey-in-the-Hills, 34737, Lake County, (352)324-3885, (800)874-9053, 30 miles NW of Orlando. **E-mail:** golf@missioninnresort.com. **Web:** www.missioninnresort.com.
Holes: 18. **Yards:** 6,923/4,811. **Par:** 72/73. **Course Rating:** 73.6/67.3. **Slope:** 133/118. **Green Fee:** $55/$105. **Cart Fee:** Included in Green Fee. **Walking Policy:** Mandatory cart. **Walkability:** 3. **Opened:** 1926. **Architect:** Charles Clark. **Season:** Year-round. **High:** Feb.-April. **To obtain tee times:** Call (352)324-3885. **Miscellaneous:** Reduced fees (weekdays, low season, twilight, seniors, juniors), discount packages, metal spikes, range (grass), club rentals, lodging (187 rooms), credit cards (MC, V, AE, D).
Reader Comments: Dramatic elevation changes ... Fantastic ... Great test off golf ... An old course that stands the test of time ... Layout, good golf, good service equalled a great weekend ... Excellent service ... One of the best-kept surprises in Florida ... Par 3s will get your attention ... Yes, hills in Florida.

★★★½ **LAS COLINAS COURSE**
R-10400 County Rd. 48, Howey-in-the-Hills, 34737, Lake County, (352)324-3885, (800)874-9053, 30 miles NW of Orlando. **E-mail:** golf@missioninnresort.com. **Web:** www.missioninnresort.com.
Holes: 18. **Yards:** 6,879/4,651. **Par:** 72/72. **Course Rating:** 73.2/64.3. **Slope:** 128/103. **Green Fee:** $45/$90. **Cart Fee:** Included in Green Fee. **Walking Policy:** Mandatory cart. **Walkability:** 2. **Opened:** 1992. **Architect:** Gary Koch. **Season:** Year-round. **High:** Feb.-April. **To obtain tee times:** Call (352)324-3885. **Miscellaneous:** Reduced fees (weekdays, low season, twilight), discount packages, metal spikes, range (grass), club rentals, lodging (187 rooms), credit cards (MC, V, AE).
Reader Comments: Lakes, links and parkland all in one ... Fun to play ... Great layout, super greens.

MONARCH GOLF COURSE
SP-5325 St. Andrews Arc, Leesburg, 34748, Lake County, (352)314-9000.
E-mail: monarch@aol.com. **Web:** www.monarchgolf.com.

Holes: 18. **Yards:** 6,084/5,149. **Par:** 72/72. **Course Rating:** 68.8/68.2. **Slope:** 113/106. **Green Fee:** $15/$35. **Cart Fee:** Included in Green Fee. **Walking Policy:** Walking at certain times. **Walkability:** 4. **Opened:** 1997. **Architect:** Len DeBoer. **Season:** Year-round. **High:** Nov.-Dec. **To obtain tee times:** Call 4 days in advance. **Miscellaneous:** Reduced fees (weekdays, low season, twilight, seniors), range (grass), club rentals, credit cards (MC, V, AE, D), beginner friendly.

★★★★½ THE MOORS GOLF CLUB *Service+, Value, Condition, Pace*

PU-3220 Avalon Blvd., Milton, 32583, Santa Rosa County, (850)995-4653, (800)727-1010, 6 miles NE of Pensacola.
Holes: 18. **Yards:** 6,828/5,259. **Par:** 70/70. **Course Rating:** 72.9/70.3. **Slope:** 126/117. **Green Fee:** $25/$33. **Cart Fee:** $12/person. **Walking Policy:** Walking at certain times. **Walkability:** 2. **Opened:** 1993. **Architect:** John B. LaFoy. **Season:** Year-round. **High:** Spring/Fall. **To obtain tee times:** Call 3 days in advance. **Miscellaneous:** Reduced fees (weekdays, resort guests, juniors), metal spikes, range (grass/mats), club rentals, lodging (8 rooms), credit cards (MC, V, AE, D). **Notes:** PGA Senior Tour Emerald Coast Classic site.
Reader Comments: A touch of Scotland ... Great layout ... Windy and hard ... Few trees ... Love at first sight ... Fast, undulating, greens ... Lots of water ... Scotland without the airfare ... Lots of moguls and deep pot bunkers ... Can see entire course from clubhouse ... Some blind shots.

★★★ MOUNT DORA GOLF CLUB

SP-1100 S. Highland, Mount Dora, 32757, Lake County, (352)383-3954, 20 miles N of Orlando.
Holes: 18. **Yards:** 5,719/5,238. **Par:** 70/72. **Course Rating:** 67.9/69.2. **Slope:** 114/113. **Green Fee:** $18/$30. **Cart Fee:** Included in Green Fee. **Walking Policy:** Unrestricted walking. **Walkability:** 3. **Opened:** 1945. **Season:** Year-round. **High:** Jan.-April. **To obtain tee times:** Call up to 3 days in advance. **Miscellaneous:** Reduced fees (low season, twilight), metal spikes, club rentals, credit cards (MC, V, D).
Reader Comments: Twisting fairways and smallish greens ... Loved it ... A good test ... So-so.

MOUNT PLYMOUTH GOLF CLUB

SP-24953 Pine Valley Dr., Mt. Plymouth, 32776, Lake County, (352)383-4821, 20 miles NW of Orlando. **E-mail:** mpgolf@prodigy.net.
Holes: 18. **Yards:** 6,364/5,120. **Par:** 70/70. **Course Rating:** 70.1/70.4. **Slope:** 110/112. **Green Fee:** $4/$18. **Cart Fee:** $11/person. **Walking Policy:** Walking at certain times. **Walkability:** 2. **Opened:** 1926. **Season:** Year-round. **High:** Jan.-April. **To obtain tee times:** Call up to 3 days in advance. **Miscellaneous:** Range (grass), club rentals, credit cards (MC, V, D).

MYAKKA PINES GOLF CLUB

SP-2550 S. River Rd., Englewood, 34223, Sarasota County, (941)474-1745, 11 miles S of Venice.
Holes: 27. **Green Fee:** $15/$30. **Cart Fee:** $28/cart. **Walking Policy:** Walking at certain times. **Walkability:** 1. **Opened:** 1977. **Architect:** Lane Marshall. **Season:** Year-round. **High:** Jan.-April. **To obtain tee times:** Call 2 days in advance beginning at 9 a.m. **Miscellaneous:** Reduced fees (low season, twilight), range (grass), club rentals, credit cards (MC, V, D).
★★½ BLUE/RED
Yards: 6,500/5,208. **Par:** 72/72. **Course Rating:** 71.1/69.7. **Slope:** 118/118.
Reader Comments: Good course for seniors ... Too crowded..No clubhouse.
★★½ RED/WHITE
Yards: 6,137/5,085. **Par:** 72/72. **Course Rating:** 69.2/68.8. **Slope:** 114/116.
★★½ WHITE/BLUE
Yards: 6,046/5,121. **Par:** 72/72. **Course Rating:** 69.0/68.9. **Slope:** 115/115.

★★★½ NAPLES BEACH HOTEL & GOLF CLUB

SP-851 Gulf Shore Blvd. N., Naples, 34102, Collier County, (941)435-2475, (800)237-7600. **E-mail:** www.naplesbeachhotel.com.
Holes: 18. **Yards:** 6,488/5,142. **Par:** 72/72. **Course Rating:** 71.7/70.0. **Slope:** 134/121. **Green Fee:** $40/$120. **Cart Fee:** Included in Green Fee. **Walking Policy:** Mandatory cart. **Walkability:** 1. **Opened:** 1930. **Architect:** Ron Garl. **Season:** Year-round. **High:** Jan.-April. **To obtain tee times:** Hotel guests 90 days in advance, nonguests call 3 days in advance. **Miscellaneous:** Reduced fees (resort guests, twilight, juniors), discount packages, range (grass/mats), club rentals, lodging (315 rooms), credit cards (MC, V, AE, D).
Reader Comments: Redesigned holes are great ... Old-fashioned resort course ... Easy to get a game ... Fun course.

★★ NORMANDY SHORES GOLF COURSE

PU-2401 Biarritz Dr., Miami Beach, 33141, Dade County, (305)868-6502, 1 miles W of collins Ave & 71st Miami Beach.
Holes: 18. **Yards:** 6,402/5,527. **Par:** 71/73. **Course Rating:** 70.5/71.0. **Slope:** 120/119. **Green Fee:** $30/$45. **Cart Fee:** Included in Green Fee. **Walking Policy:** Walking at certain times. **Walkability:** N/A. **Opened:** 1938. **Architect:** William S. Flynn/Howard Toomey. **Season:** Year-round. **High:** Nov.-April. **To obtain tee times:** Call 7 days in advance. **Miscellaneous:** Reduced

fees (weekdays, low season, twilight, juniors), discount packages, range (grass/mats), club rentals, credit cards (MC, V, AE), beginner friendly (clinics every Saturday and Sunday morning).

★★½ NORTH PALM BEACH COUNTRY CLUB
PM-951 U.S. Hwy. 1, North Palm Beach, 33408, Palm Beach County, (561)626-4344, 5 miles N of West Palm Beach.

Holes: 18. **Yards:** 6,281/5,033. **Par:** 72/72. **Course Rating:** 69.9/68.9. **Slope:** 120/114. **Green Fee:** $25/$50. **Cart Fee:** Included in Green Fee. **Walking Policy:** Walking at certain times. **Walkability:** 2. **Opened:** 1963. **Architect:** ZethMark McCumber. **Season:** Year-round. **High:** Nov.-May. **To obtain tee times:** Call 1 day in advance at 8 a.m. **Miscellaneous:** Reduced fees (low season, resort guests, juniors), discount packages, metal spikes, range (grass/mats), club rentals, credit cards (MC, V).

Reader Comments: Nice but could be better ... Decent municipal track.

★★½ NORTHDALE GOLF CLUB
SP-4417 Northdale Blvd., Tampa, 33624, Hillsborough County, (813)962-0428.

Holes: 18. **Yards:** 6,767/5,383. **Par:** 72/72. **Course Rating:** 71.8/71.0. **Slope:** 122/121. **Green Fee:** $40/$0. **Cart Fee:** Included in Green Fee. **Walking Policy:** Mandatory cart. **Walkability:** 2. **Opened:** 1978. **Architect:** Ron Garl. **Season:** Year-round. **High:** Dec.-April. **To obtain tee times:** Call up to 3 days in advance. **Miscellaneous:** Reduced fees (twilight, juniors), metal spikes, club rentals, credit cards (MC, V).

Reader Comments: Bring many balls ... Water, water and then some ... Pleasant surprise in crowded area.

★★½ OAK HILLS GOLF CLUB
PU-10059 Northcliff Blvd., Spring Hill, 34608, Hernando County, (352)683-6830, 37 miles NW of Tampa.

Holes: 18. **Yards:** 6,774/5,468. **Par:** 72/72. **Course Rating:** 72.2/71.1. **Slope:** 123/119. **Green Fee:** $18/$27. **Cart Fee:** Included in Green Fee. **Walking Policy:** Walking at certain times. **Walkability:** 3. **Opened:** 1982. **Architect:** Chuck Almony. **Season:** Year-round. **High:** Dec.-March. **To obtain tee times:** Call(352)683-6830. **Miscellaneous:** Reduced fees (weekdays, low season, twilight, seniors, juniors), discount packages, metal spikes, range (grass), club rentals, credit cards (MC, V, D).

Reader Comments: A good course you can play in winter without taking out a loan ... Lots of trees ... Tricky par 5's; greens spotty in condition.

OKEEHEELEE GOLF COURSE
PM-1200 Country Club Way, West Palm Beach, 33413, Palm Beach County, (561)964-4653, 1 miles W of West Palm Beach.

Holes: 27. **Green Fee:** $22/$49. **Cart Fee:** Included in Green Fee. **Walking Policy:** Walking at certain times. **Walkability:** 1. **Opened:** 1995. **Architect:** Roy Case. **Season:** Year-round. **High:** Dec.-April. **To obtain tee times:** Call. **Miscellaneous:** Metal spikes, range (grass), credit cards (MC, V, AE).

★★★ EAGLE/OSPREY (BLUE/WHITE)
Yards: 6,648/4,591. **Par:** 72/72. **Course Rating:** 71.7/662.7. **Slope:** 130/103.

Reader Comments: Very good for a county course, links design is unique to area ... Lots of doglegs ... Keep it in the fairway ... Water and gators ... 5 sets of tees.

★★★ HERON/EAGLE (RED/BLUE)
Yards: 6,916/4,842. **Par:** 72/72. **Course Rating:** 72.9/63.4. **Slope:** 128/103.

Reader Comments: Water, water everywhere ... Good practice facilities ... Needs another year of growth ... Too many holes are close together.

★★★ OSPREY/HERON (WHITE/RED)
Yards: 6,826/4,731. **Par:** 72/72. **Course Rating:** 72.6/62.9. **Slope:** 130/102.

★★★ OLDE HICKORY GOLF & COUNTRY CLUB
SP-14670 Olde Hickory Blvd., Fort Myers, 33912, Lee County, (941)768-3335, 3 miles S of Fort Meyers.

Holes: 18. **Yards:** 6,601/4,686. **Par:** 72/72. **Course Rating:** 71.9/65.8. **Slope:** 127/113. **Green Fee:** $20/$30. **Cart Fee:** $14/person. **Walking Policy:** Mandatory cart. **Walkability:** N/A. **Opened:** 1992. **Architect:** Ron Garl. **Season:** May 1-Oct. 31 open to public. **To obtain tee times:** Call 2 days in advance. **Miscellaneous:** Reduced fees (low season), range (grass/mats), club rentals, credit cards (MC, V).

Reader Comments: Short, interesting, fun to play ... Drains beautifully, can be played when other are courses closed ... Great value, love it ... Truly enjoyable ... Plenty of water, sand, and trees ... Beautiful Layout.

ORANGE BLOSSOM HILLS GOLF & COUNTRY CLUB
SP-1100 Main St., Lady Lake, 32159, Lake County, (352)753-5200, 60 miles N of Orlando.
Holes: 18. **Yards:** 6,200/5,041. **Par:** 72/72. **Course Rating:** 69.1/68.9. **Slope:** 117/117. **Green Fee:** N/A/$34. **Cart Fee:** $8/person. **Walking Policy:** Unrestricted walking. **Walkability:** 3.

Opened: 1986. **Architect:** Lloyd Clifton. **Season:** Year-round. **High:** Nov.-May. **To obtain tee times:** Call golf shop. **Miscellaneous:** Reduced fees (juniors), discount packages, range (grass), club rentals, lodging (36 rooms), credit cards (MC, V).

ORANGE COUNTY NATIONAL GOLF CENTER & LODGE *Service*
PU-16301 Phil Ritson Way, Winter Garden, 34787, Orange County, (407)656-2626, (888)727-3672, 5 miles W of Disney World. **E-mail:** Info@ocngolf.com. **Web:** www.ocngolf.com.

★★★★½ **CROOKED CAT** *Value+, Condition+, Pace+*
Holes: 18. **Yards:** 7,277/5,262. **Par:** 72/72. **Course Rating:** 75.4/70.3. **Slope:** 140/120. **Green Fee:** $19/$65. **Cart Fee:** Included in Green Fee. **Walking Policy:** Mandatory cart. **Walkability:** 5. **Opened:** 1997. **Architect:** Phil Ritson/David Harman/Isao Aoki. **Season:** Year-round. **High:** Jan.-April. **To obtain tee times:** Reservations can be made 30 days in advance. Tee time must be held by a credit card. **Miscellaneous:** Reduced fees (weekdays, low season, resort guests, twilight, juniors), discount packages, range (grass), club rentals, lodging (50 rooms), credit cards (MC, V, AE, Diners Club), beginner friendly (instructional and range programs).

Reader Comments: Could be a tour course ... Great layout ... Perfection has been found! ... Lots of slopes, x-treme golf ... Exceptional new course ... Many memorable holes.

★★★★½ **PANTHER LAKE GOLF COURSE** *Value, Condition+, Pace+*
Holes: 18. **Yards:** 7,295/5,073. **Par:** 72/72. **Course Rating:** 75.7/71.5. **Slope:** 137/125. **Green Fee:** $19/$75. **Cart Fee:** Included in Green Fee. **Walking Policy:** Mandatory cart. **Walkability:** 5. **Opened:** 1997. **Architect:** Phil Ritson/David Harman/Isao Aoki. **Season:** Year-round. **High:** Jan.-April. **To obtain tee times:** Reservations can be made 30 days in advance. Tee time must be held by a credit card. **Miscellaneous:** Reduced fees (weekdays, low season, resort guests, twilight, juniors), discount packages, range (grass), club rentals, lodging (50 rooms), credit cards (MC, V, AE, Diners Club), beginner friendly (instructional and range programs).
Special Notes: Formerly Panther Lake Golf Club.

ORANGE LAKE COUNTRY CLUB
R-8505 W. Irlo Bronson Mem. Hwy., Kissimmee, 34747, Osceola County, (407)239-1050, 15 miles W of Orlando.
Cart Fee: Included in Green Fee. **Walking Policy:** Mandatory cart. **Walkability:** N/A. **Architect:** Joe Lee. **Season:** Year-round. **High:** Jan.-April. **To obtain tee times:** Call. **Miscellaneous:** Reduced fees (weekdays, low season, resort guests, twilight, juniors), discount packages, range (grass/mats), club rentals, lodging, credit cards (MC, V, AE).

★★★½ **THE LEGENDS AT ORANGE LAKE**
Holes: 18. **Yards:** 7,072/5,188. **Par:** 72/72. **Course Rating:** 74.3/69.6. **Slope:** 132/120. **Green Fee:** $40/$125. **Opened:** 1982.

Reader Comments: Too great to be true ... Nice layout ... It seem like water was everywhere ... A tree, sand and water challenge ... Forced carries over water ... Enjoyable visit.

★★★½ **THE RESORT COURSE AT ORANGE LAKE (CYPRESS/LAKE)**
Holes: 27. **Yards:** 6,571/5,456. **Par:** 72/72. **Course Rating:** 72.3/72.1. **Slope:** 131/128. **Green Fee:** $30/$85. **Opened:** 1998.

★★★½ **THE RESORT COURSE AT ORANGE LAKE (LAKE/ORANGE)**
Holes: 27. **Yards:** 6,531/5,289. **Par:** 72/72. **Course Rating:** 72.2/71.1. **Slope:** 132/126. **Green Fee:** $30/$85. **Opened:** 1998. .

★★★½ **THE RESORT COURSE AT ORANGE LAKE (ORANGE/CYPRESS)**
Holes: 27. **Yards:** 6,670/5,467. **Par:** 72/72. **Course Rating:** 72.6/70.5. **Slope:** 131/128. **Green Fee:** $30/$85. **Opened:** 1998.

Reader Comments: Too great to be true ... Plenty of variety ... 27 holes, 18 assigned by starter ... Forced carries over water ... Well-placed bunkers ... Saw an eagle with fish in talons.
Special Notes: Also has 9-hole par-3 course and a 36-hole mini golf course.

★★½ ORIOLE GOLF & TENNIS CLUB OF MARGATE
PU-8000 W. Margate Blvd., Margate, 33063, Broward County, (954)972-8140, 5 miles N of Fort Lauderdale.
Holes: 27. **Yards:** 6,418/4,875. **Par:** 72/72. **Course Rating:** 70.9/67.7. **Slope:** 120/112. **Green Fee:** $6/$30. **Cart Fee:** $15/person. **Walking Policy:** Mandatory cart. **Walkability:** 2. **Opened:** 1972. **Architect:** Bill Dietsch. **Season:** Year-round. **High:** Jan.-April. **To obtain tee times:** Call 2 days in advance. **Miscellaneous:** Reduced fees (low season, twilight), metal spikes, range (grass/mats), club rentals, credit cards (MC, V), beginner friendly.

Reader Comments: Comfortable ... Good value.

★★★½ ORLANDO WORLD CENTER - MARRIOTT
R-8701 World Center Dr., Orlando, 32821, Orange County, (407)238-8660.
Holes: 18. **Yards:** 6,810/4,890. **Par:** 71/71. **Course Rating:** 69.8/68.5. **Slope:** 121/115. **Green Fee:** $50/$110. **Cart Fee:** Included in Green Fee. **Walking Policy:** Unrestricted walking. **Walkability:** 2. **Opened:** 1986. **Architect:** Robert E. Cupp II 1999. **Season:** Year-round. **High:** Jan.-April. **To obtain tee times:** Call up to 30 days in advance. Hotel guests may call up to 60

days in advance. **Miscellaneous:** Reduced fees (resort guests, twilight, juniors), discount packages, range (grass), club rentals, lodging (2,000 rooms), credit cards (MC, V, AE, D).
Reader Comments: Starting renovations ... Expected more ... Nothing memorable. Nice course with lots of water hazards.

OXBOW GOLF CLUB
R-1 Oxbow Dr., La Belle, 33935, Hendry County, (941)675-4411, (800)282-3375, 30 miles E of Fort Myers.
Holes: 27. **Green Fee:** $10/$49. **Cart Fee:** Included in Green Fee. **Walking Policy:** Walking at certain times. **Walkability:** 4. **Opened:** 1982. **Architect:** LeRoy Phillips/Patrick Grelak. **Season:** Year-round. **High:** Nov.-May. **To obtain tee times:** Call up to 3 days in advance. Resort guests may reserve tee times with confirmed hotel reservations. **Miscellaneous:** Reduced fees (low season), range (grass), club rentals, lodging (50 rooms), credit cards (MC, V, AE).
★★★ **LAKES/WOODS**
Yards: 6,648/4,828. **Par:** 72/72. **Course Rating:** N/A. **Slope:** N/A.
★★★ **RIVER/LAKES**
Yards: 6,885/5,010. **Par:** 72/72. **Course Rating:** N/A. **Slope:** N/A.
★★★ **RIVER/WOODS**
Yards: 6,699/5,038. **Par:** 72/72. **Course Rating:** N/A. **Slope:** N/A.
Reader Comments: Course has been let go ... Challenging tee shots.

OYSTER CREEK GOLF & COUNTRY CLUB
SP-6500 Oriole Blvd., Englewood, 34224, Charlotte County, (941)475-0334, 10 miles S of Venice.
Holes: 18. **Yards:** 4,000/2,600. **Par:** 60/60. **Course Rating:** 59.7/57.3. **Slope:** 100/85. **Green Fee:** $16/$30. **Cart Fee:** Included in Green Fee. **Walking Policy:** Unrestricted walking. **Walkability:** 1. **Opened:** 1993. **Architect:** Ted McAnlis. **Season:** Year-round. **High:** Nov.-April. **Miscellaneous:** Reduced fees (low season, twilight), metal spikes, credit cards (MC, V).

★★★★ PALISADES GOLF COURSE
SP-16510 Palisades Blvd., Clermont, 34711, Lake County, (352)394-0085, 20 miles W of Orlando.
Holes: 18. **Yards:** 6,988/5,528. **Par:** 72/72. **Course Rating:** 73.8/72.1. **Slope:** 127/122. **Green Fee:** $30/$55. **Cart Fee:** Included in Green Fee. **Walking Policy:** Mandatory cart. **Walkability:** 5. **Opened:** 1991. **Architect:** Joe Lee. **Season:** Year-round. **High:** Jan.-April. **To obtain tee times:** Call up to 30 days in advance. **Miscellaneous:** Reduced fees (weekdays, low season, twilight, seniors), discount packages, range (grass), club rentals, credit cards (MC, V).
Reader Comments: Great value. Great challenge ... Gorgeous to the eyes! ... Hilly ... Beautiful views ... Too many hokey holes ... My best golf experience ever ... Worth the 40-minute drive from Orlando ... Tight and tough. Some 'killer' holes.

PALM AIRE SPA RESORT & COUNTRY CLUB
R-3701 Oaks Clubhouse Dr., Pompano Beach, 33069, Broward County, (954)978-1737, 1-888-PALMAIR, 1 miles N of Ft. Lauderdale. **Web:** www.palmairegolf.com.
CYPRESS COURSE
Holes: 18. **Yards:** 6,826/5,307. **Par:** 72/72. **Course Rating:** 74.1/71.8. **Slope:** 143/127. **Green Fee:** $17/$85. **Cart Fee:** Included in Green Fee. **Walking Policy:** Mandatory cart. **Walkability:** 1. **Opened:** 1971. **Architect:** George Fazio/Tom Fazio. **Season:** Year-round. **High:** Nov.-April. **To obtain tee times:** Guests may call one year in advance. **Miscellaneous:** Reduced fees (low season, resort guests, twilight, juniors), discount packages, range (grass), club rentals, lodging, credit cards (MC, V, AE), beginner friendly.
OAKS COURSE
Holes: 18. **Yards:** 6,910/4,860. **Par:** 71/71. **Course Rating:** 73.3/62.9. **Slope:** 131/103. **Green Fee:** $27/$99. **Cart Fee:** Included in Green Fee. **Walking Policy:** Mandatory cart. **Walkability:** 1. **Opened:** 1971. **Architect:** George Fazio/Tom Fazio. **Season:** Year-round. **High:** Nov.-April. **To obtain tee times:** Guests may call one year in advance. **Miscellaneous:** Reduced fees (low season, resort guests, twilight, juniors), discount packages, range (grass), club rentals, lodging, credit cards (MC, V, AE), beginner friendly.

PALM AIRE SPA RESORT & COUNTRY CLUB
R-551 S. Pompano Pkwy., Pompano Beach, 33069, Broward County, (954)974-7699, 1-888-PALMAIR, 1 miles N of Ft. Lauderdale. **E-mail:** www.palmairegolf.com.
★★★ **PALMS COURSE**
Holes: 18. **Yards:** 6,931/5,431. **Par:** 72/72. **Course Rating:** 73.3/71.1. **Slope:** 128/118. **Green Fee:** $17/$85. **Cart Fee:** Included in Green Fee. **Walking Policy:** Mandatory cart. **Walkability:** 1. **Opened:** 1959. **Architect:** William Mitchell. **Season:** Year-round. **High:** Nov.-April. **To obtain tee times:** Members can submit cards 5-7 days in advance. **Miscellaneous:** Discount packages, metal spikes, range (grass), club rentals, lodging, credit cards (MC, V, AE).
Reader Comments: Lots of water ... Just beautiful ... First class and great service ... Fun course.

★★½ PINES COURSE
Holes: 18. **Yards:** 6,610/5,232. **Par:** 72/72. **Course Rating:** 72.5/70.0. **Slope:** 133/116. **Green Fee:** $17/$55. **Cart Fee:** $15. **Cart Fee:** Included in Green Fee. **Walking Policy:** Mandatory cart. **Walkability:** N/A. **Opened:** 1959. **Architect:** Robert von Hagge. **Season:** Year-round. **High:** Nov.-April. **To obtain tee times:** Guests may call one year in advance. **Miscellaneous:** Discount packages, metal spikes, range (grass/mats), club rentals, lodging, credit cards (MC, V, AE). **Special Notes:** Also has 22-hole par-3 Executive Course.

★★★ PALM BEACH GARDENS MUNICIPAL GOLF COURSE
PM-11401 Northlake Blvd., Palm Beach Gardens, 33418, Palm Beach County, (561)775-2556, 8 miles N of West Palm Beach.
Holes: 18. **Yards:** 6,375/4,663. **Par:** 72/72. **Course Rating:** 70.2/66.5. **Slope:** 128/110. **Green Fee:** N/A/$60. **Cart Fee:** Included in Green Fee. **Walking Policy:** Walking at certain times. **Walkability:** 3. **Opened:** 1991. **Architect:** Roy Case. **Season:** Year-round. **High:** Dec.-April. **To obtain tee times:** Call up to 3 days in advance. **Miscellaneous:** Reduced fees (weekdays, low season, twilight, seniors, juniors), discount packages, metal spikes, range (grass), club rentals, credit cards (MC, V).
Reader Comments: Great muny, mild and wild ... Too many blind shots ... Tight, jungle golf ... Water, water everywhere ... Nice ... Marshy ... Great setting. Lots of trouble.

★★★½ PALM COAST RESORT
R-53 Easthampton Blvd., Palm Coast, 32164, Flagler County, (904)437-5807, (800)874-2101, 30 miles N of Daytona Beach. **E-mail:** DJDIIIPRO@aol.com.
Holes: 18. **Yards:** 6,591/5,386. **Par:** 72/72. **Course Rating:** 71.6/69.3. **Slope:** 130/117. **Green Fee:** $18/$70. **Cart Fee:** $18/person. **Walking Policy:** Mandatory cart. **Walkability:** 3. **Opened:** 1990. **Architect:** Gary Player. **Season:** Year-round. **High:** Jan.-April. **To obtain tee times:** Call up to 5 days in advance. **Miscellaneous:** Reduced fees (weekdays, low season, resort guests, twilight, juniors), discount packages, metal spikes, range (grass), club rentals, lodging (154 rooms), credit cards (MC, V, AE, D), beginner friendly.
Reader Comments: Outstanding ... Target golf and great fun ... Great value ... Tight fairways ... Flat greens.

★★★ PALM HARBOR GOLF CLUB
R-Casper Drive Ext., Palm Coast, 32137, Flagler County, (904)445-0845, 30 miles N of Daytona Beach. **Web:** ww.palcoastresort.com.
Holes: 18. **Yards:** 6,572/5,346. **Par:** 72/72. **Course Rating:** 71.8/71.2. **Slope:** 127/128. **Green Fee:** $55/$68. **Cart Fee:** Included in Green Fee. **Walking Policy:** Mandatory cart. **Walkability:** 1. **Opened:** 1973. **Architect:** William W. Amick. **Season:** Year-round. **High:** Jan.-May. **To obtain tee times:** Call up to 5 days in advance. **Miscellaneous:** Reduced fees (low season, resort guests, twilight, juniors), discount packages, metal spikes, range (grass), club rentals, credit cards (MC, V, AE, D).
Reader Comments: Flat layout makes for easy walking ... Friendly but not very challenging ... Large greens ... Boring ... Fun.

★★½ PALM RIVER COUNTRY CLUB
SP-333 Palm River Blvd., Naples, 34110, Collier County, (941)597-6622, 6 miles N of Naples.
Holes: 18. **Yards:** 6,488/5,364. **Par:** 72/72. **Course Rating:** 72.2/70.6. **Slope:** 127/121. **Green Fee:** $30/$70. **Cart Fee:** Included in Green Fee. **Walking Policy:** Mandatory cart. **Walkability:** 1. **Opened:** 1960. **Architect:** Ernie Smith. **Season:** Year-round. **High:** Jan.-March. **To obtain tee times:** Call up to 2 days in advance. **Miscellaneous:** Reduced fees (low season, twilight), metal spikes, range (grass), club rentals, credit cards (MC, V, AE, D).
Reader Comments: Getting better ... Water on many holes ... Slow play ... Wide open ... Range is lacking.

★★½ PALMETTO GOLF COURSE
PM-9300 S.W. 152nd St., Miami, 33157, Dade County, (305)238-2922.
Holes: 18. **Yards:** 6,648/5,710. **Par:** 70/73. **Course Rating:** 72.2/73.4. **Slope:** 128/125. **Green Fee:** $12/$25. **Cart Fee:** $13/. **Walking Policy:** Unrestricted walking. **Walkability:** 1. **Opened:** 1959. **Architect:** Dick Wilson. **Season:** Year-round. **High:** Jan.-March. **To obtain tee times:** Call golf shop up to 7 days in advance. **Miscellaneous:** Reduced fees (weekdays, low season, twilight, juniors), discount packages, metal spikes, range (mats), club rentals, credit cards (MC, V, AE).
Reader Comments: Good par 4's ... Canal in play on several holes ... Too crowded ... Greens great ... Nice layout.

★★★½ PELICAN BAY COUNTRY CLUB
SP-350 Pelican Bay Dr., Daytona Beach, 32119, Volusia County, (904)788-6496, 40 miles NE of Orlando. **E-mail:** pbcchp@aol.com.
Holes: 18. **Yards:** 6,630/5,278. **Par:** 72/72. **Course Rating:** 71.9/70.8. **Slope:** 123/127. **Green Fee:** $25/$50. **Cart Fee:** Included in Green Fee. **Walking Policy:** Mandatory cart. **Walkability:**

2. **Opened:** 1985. **Architect:** Lloyd Clifton. **Season:** Year-round. **High:** Dec.-April. **To obtain tee times:** Call up to 6 days in advance. **Miscellaneous:** Reduced fees (weekdays, low season, twilight), discount packages, metal spikes, club rentals, credit cards (MC, V, D), beginner friendly (reduced rates at non-peak hour).
Reader Comments: Fun, short course ... Bring plenty of balls ... Some very testy water holes.

★★★½ **PELICAN POINTE GOLF & COUNTRY CLUB**
SP-575 Center Rd., Venice, 34292, Sarasota County, (941)496-4653, 15 miles S of Sarasota.
Holes: 18. **Yards:** 7,202/4,939. **Par:** 72/72. **Course Rating:** 74.8/68.2. **Slope:** 145/112. **Green Fee:** $35/$60. **Cart Fee:** Included in Green Fee. **Walking Policy:** Mandatory cart. **Walkability:** 1. **Opened:** 1995. **Architect:** Ted McAnlis. **Season:** Year-round. **High:** Jan.-March. **To obtain tee times:** Call 3 days in advance. **Miscellaneous:** Reduced fees (low season, twilight), range (grass/mats), club rentals, credit cards (MC, V, AE, D).
Reader Comments: Fun with a lot of difficult holes ... Lots of residential construction ... Magnificent golf course ... Interesting ... Tee placement gives advantage for women.

PELICAN SOUND GOLF & RIVER CLUB
SP-4561 Pelican Sound Blvd., Estero, 33928, Lee County, (941)498-9979, 2 miles S of Ft. Myers. **Web:** wci.com.
Holes: 18. **Yards:** 6,781/5,237. **Par:** 71/71. **Course Rating:** 73.0/70.8. **Slope:** 142/123. **Green Fee:** $30/$90. **Cart Fee:** Included in Green Fee. **Walking Policy:** Walking at certain times. **Walkability:** 4. **Opened:** 1998. **Architect:** Chip Powell/Mike Hill. **Season:** Year-round. **High:** Jan.-March. **To obtain tee times:** Call 24 hours a day 7 days a week. Public 3 days advance. **Miscellaneous:** Reduced fees (low season, twilight, juniors), range (grass), club rentals, credit cards (MC, V, AE).

PGA GOLF CLUB   *Service+*
PU-1916 Perfect Dr., Port St. Lucie, 34986, St. Lucie County, (800)800-4653, (800)800-4653, 45 miles N of West Palm Beach. **E-mail:** btaylor@pgahq.com. **Web:** www.pgavillage.com.
★★★★½ fazio's **NORTH COURSE**   *Value, Condition, Pace*
Holes: 18. **Yards:** 7,026/4,993. **Par:** 72/72. **Course Rating:** 73.8/68.8. **Slope:** 133/114. **Green Fee:** $15/$69. **Cart Fee:** Included in Green Fee. **Walking Policy:** Unrestricted walking. **Walkability:** 2. **Opened:** 1996. **Architect:** Tom Fazio. **Season:** Year-round. **High:** Jan.-March. **To obtain tee times:** Call up to 4 days in advance. **Miscellaneous:** Reduced fees (low season, twilight, juniors), discount packages, range (grass), club rentals, lodging (80 rooms), credit cards (MC, V, AE), beginner friendly (tours of facility, clinics for beginners).
Notes: Ranked 7th in 1996 Best New Affordable Courses.
Reader Comments: Outstanding golf ... Too much undulation in greens for public course ... Quite possibly the best value in the country ... Wonderful experience, great staff, 1st class ... Long carries ... Tough to decide which of the two is better ... Summer values are incredible ... A must play ... Incredibly efficient (almost too business like!) ... Golf the way it should be!.
★★★★½ fazio's **SOUTH COURSE**   *Value, Condition, Pace*
Holes: 18. **Yards:** 7,087/4,933. **Par:** 72/72. **Course Rating:** 74.5/68.7. **Slope:** 141/119. **Green Fee:** $15/$69. **Cart Fee:** Included in Green Fee. **Walking Policy:** Unrestricted walking. **Walkability:** 2. **Opened:** 1996. **Architect:** Tom Fazio. **Season:** Year-round. **High:** Jan.-March. **To obtain tee times:** Call up to 3 days in advance. **Miscellaneous:** Reduced fees (low season, twilight, juniors), discount packages, metal spikes, range (grass), club rentals, lodging (80 rooms), credit cards (MC, V, AE), beginner friendly (tours of facility, clinics for beginners).
Notes: Ranked 14th in 1999 Best in State; 1st in 1996 Best New Affordable Courses.
Reader Comments: Outstanding golf, great value ... Great place to play ... The best place to play on East Coast ... Great views ... These courses make you feel important ... I hope people don't discover this place! ... Greens are lightning fast ... Dramatic rises and drops that you don't find in too many Florida courses.

PGA NATIONAL GOLF CLUB   *Service*
R-1000 Ave.of the Champions, Palm Beach Gardens, 33418, Palm Beach County, (561)627-1800, (800)633-9150, 15 miles N of West Palm Beach.
★★★★ **CHAMPION COURSE**
Holes: 18. **Yards:** 7,022/5,377. **Par:** 72/72. **Course Rating:** 74.7/71.1. **Slope:** 142/123. **Green Fee:** N/A/$166. **Cart Fee:** $21/person. **Walking Policy:** Mandatory cart. **Walkability:** N/A. **Opened:** 1981. **Architect:** Tom Fazio/Jack Nicklaus. **Season:** Year-round. **High:** Jan.-April. **To obtain tee times:** Registered resort guests may call up to 1 year in advance. **Miscellaneous:** Reduced fees (low season), discount packages, metal spikes, range (grass), club rentals, lodging, credit cards (MC, V, AE).
Notes: 1987 PGA Championship; 1983 Ryder Cup.
Reader Comments: Bring extra balls ... Great course with marble fast greens ... Course shows a lot of play ... Nice but at a cost ... Long and slow, but enjoyable ... Easy front, tough back ... Great finishing holes ... Expected more.
★★★½ **ESTATE COURSE**

Holes: 18. **Yards:** 6,784/4,903. **Par:** 72/72. **Course Rating:** 73.4/68.4. **Slope:** 131/118. **Green Fee:** N/A/$99. **Cart Fee:** $21/person. **Walking Policy:** Mandatory cart. **Walkability:** N/A. **Opened:** 1984. **Architect:** Karl Litten. **Season:** Year-round. **High:** Jan.-April. **To obtain tee times:** Registered resort guests may call up to 1 year in advance. **Miscellaneous:** Reduced fees (low season), discount packages, metal spikes, range (grass/mats), club rentals, lodging, credit cards (MC, V, AE).
Reader Comments: My favorite at PGA National ... Sometimes late for the spa, because of pace of play ... Everything about this place was top of the shelf ... A very fun course, semi-challenging.

★★★½ GENERAL COURSE

Holes: 18. **Yards:** 6,768/5,324. **Par:** 72/72. **Course Rating:** 73.0/71.0. **Slope:** 130/122. **Green Fee:** N/A/$99. **Cart Fee:** $21/person. **Walking Policy:** Mandatory cart. **Walkability:** N/A. **Opened:** 1984. **Architect:** Arnold Palmer. **Season:** Year-round. **High:** Jan.-April. **To obtain tee times:** Registered resort guests may call up to 1 year in advance. **Miscellaneous:** Reduced fees (low season), discount packages, metal spikes, range (grass/mats), club rentals, lodging, credit cards (MC, V, AE).
Reader Comments: Fun course ... Too flat and too many condos ... Great facilities ... Good hard course ... Pretty.

★★★½ HAIG COURSE

Holes: 18. **Yards:** 6,806/5,645. **Par:** 72/72. **Course Rating:** 73.0/72.5. **Slope:** 130/121. **Green Fee:** N/A/$99. **Cart Fee:** $21/person. **Walking Policy:** Mandatory cart. **Walkability:** 1. **Opened:** 1980. **Architect:** Tom Fazio. **Season:** Year-round. **High:** Jan.-April. **To obtain tee times:** Registered resort guests may call up to 1 year in advance. **Miscellaneous:** Reduced fees (low season), discount packages, metal spikes, range (grass), club rentals, lodging, credit cards (MC, V, AE).
Reader Comments: Too tight for average golfer ... Awesome greens ... For the money it should be way better ... Too many tricks ... Extremely busy.

★★★½ SQUIRE COURSE

Holes: 18. **Yards:** 6,478/4,982. **Par:** 72/72. **Course Rating:** 71.3/69.8. **Slope:** 127/123. **Green Fee:** N/A/$99. **Cart Fee:** $21/person. **Walking Policy:** Mandatory cart. **Walkability:** 1. **Opened:** 1981. **Architect:** Tom Fazio. **Season:** Year-round. **High:** Jan.-April. **To obtain tee times:** Registered resort guests may call up to 1 year in advance. **Miscellaneous:** Reduced fees (low season), discount packages, metal spikes, range (grass), club rentals, lodging, credit cards (MC, V, AE).
Reader Comments: Fun course, challenging, more enjoyable than Champion ... Very similar holes ... So much sand and water.

★★★★ PINE LAKES COUNTRY CLUB

SP-400 Pine Lakes Pkwy., Palm Coast, 32164, Flagler County, (904)445-0852, (800)874-2101, 30 miles N of Daytona Beach.
Holes: 18. **Yards:** 7,074/5,166. **Par:** 72/72. **Course Rating:** 73.5/71.4. **Slope:** 126/124. **Green Fee:** $45/$75. **Cart Fee:** Included in Green Fee. **Walking Policy:** Mandatory cart. **Walkability:** 3. **Opened:** 1980. **Architect:** Arnold Palmer/Ed Seay. **Season:** Year-round. **High:** Jan.-April. **To obtain tee times:** Call up to 5 days in advance. **Miscellaneous:** Reduced fees (low season, resort guests, twilight, juniors), discount packages, metal spikes, range (grass/mats), club rentals, credit cards (MC, V, AE, D).
Reader Comments: Felt like top private C.C ... .Excellent value ... Sand, water, undulating greens. Wide open.

★★ PINE LAKES GOLF CLUB

PU-153 Northside Dr. S., Jacksonville, 32218, Duval County, (904)757-0318, 15 miles N of Jacksonville.
Holes: 18. **Yards:** 6,631/5,192. **Par:** 72/72. **Course Rating:** 71.1/69.8. **Slope:** 127/118. **Green Fee:** $15/$32. **Cart Fee:** Included in Green Fee. **Walking Policy:** Walking at certain times. **Walkability:** 2. **Opened:** 1965. **Season:** Year-round. **High:** Jan.-April. **To obtain tee times:** Call golf shop. **Miscellaneous:** Reduced fees (weekdays, low season, twilight, seniors, juniors), discount packages, metal spikes, range (grass), club rentals, credit cards (MC, V, AE, D).

THE PINES GOLF CLUB

SP-1715 Monastery Road, Orange City, 32763, Volusia County, (904)774-2714, 20 miles of Orlando.
Holes: 18. **Yards:** 6,300/6,000. **Par:** 72/72. **Course Rating:** 71.3/69.1. **Slope:** 121/116. **Green Fee:** $18/$28. **Cart Fee:** Included in Green Fee. **Walking Policy:** Mandatory cart. **Walkability:** 2. **Season:** Year-round. **High:** Nov-April. **Miscellaneous:** Reduced fees (weekdays, low season, twilight, seniors), discount packages, metal spikes, range (grass), club rentals, credit cards (MC, V).
Special Notes: Formerly Monastery Golf & Country Club.

FLORIDA

PLANT CITY GOLF CLUB
SP-3102 Coronet Rd., Plant City, 33566, Hillsborough County, (813)752-1524, 20 miles E of Tampa.
Holes: 18. **Yards:** 6,479/4,929. **Par:** 72/72. **Course Rating:** 70.4/67.3. **Slope:** 118/109. **Green Fee:** $18/$25. **Cart Fee:** Included in Green Fee. **Walking Policy:** Walking at certain times. **Walkability:** N/A. **Opened:** 1932. **Architect:** Built by members. **Season:** Year-round. **High:** Nov.-April. **To obtain tee times:** Call 2 days in advance. **Miscellaneous:** Reduced fees (weekdays, low season, twilight, juniors), metal spikes, range (grass), club rentals, credit cards (MC, V, D).

PLANTATION GOLF & COUNTRY CLUB
SP-500 Rockley Blvd., Venice, 34293, Sarasota County, (941)493-2000, 15 miles S of Sarasota.
★★★½ **BOBCAT COURSE**
Holes: 18. **Yards:** 6,840/5,023. **Par:** 72/72. **Course Rating:** 73.0/70.6. **Slope:** 130/121. **Green Fee:** $31/$60. **Cart Fee:** Included in Green Fee. **Walking Policy:** Mandatory cart. **Walkability:** 3. **Opened:** 1981. **Architect:** Ron Garl. **Season:** May-Oct. **High:** Nov.-April. **To obtain tee times:** Public may call 2 days in advance. Resort guests call 3 days in advance. Open to the public from May 1st - Oct 30th. **Miscellaneous:** Reduced fees (low season, resort guests), range (grass), club rentals, credit cards (MC, V, D).
Reader Comments: Good variety of hole design ... Nice layout, fast play ... Very interesting ... A treat ... Hit every club in your bag ... Tough from the blues ... Great potential.
★★★½ **PANTHER COURSE**
Holes: 18. **Yards:** 6,800/5,000. **Par:** 72/72. **Course Rating:** 70.7/68.0. **Slope:** 124/117. **Green Fee:** $31/$60. **Cart Fee:** Included in Green Fee. **Walking Policy:** Mandatory cart. **Walkability:** 3. **Opened:** 1985. **Architect:** Ron Garl. **Season:** May-Oct. **High:** Nov.-April. **To obtain tee times:** Public may call 2 days in advance. Resort guests call 3 days in advance. Open to the public from May 1st - Oct 30th. **Miscellaneous:** Reduced fees (low season, resort guests), range (grass), club rentals, lodging, credit cards (MC, V, D).
Reader Comments: What a nice experience! ... Very sporty ... Exceptional ... Claws aren't as sharp as sister course ... If the marshalls were any ruder they'd be relatives.

★★★½ PLANTATION INN & GOLF RESORT
R-9301 W. Fort Island Trail, Crystal River, 34429, Citrus County, (352)795-7211, (800)632-6262, 80 miles N of Orlando.
Holes: 18. **Yards:** 6,522/5,205. **Par:** 72/72. **Course Rating:** 72.0/70.7. **Slope:** 128/118. **Green Fee:** $15/$32. **Cart Fee:** Included in Green Fee. **Walking Policy:** Walking at certain times. **Walkability:** 1. **Opened:** 1956. **Architect:** Mark Mahannah. **Season:** Year-round. **High:** Feb.-April. **To obtain tee times:** Call 2 days in advance. **Miscellaneous:** Reduced fees (weekdays, low season, resort guests, twilight, juniors), discount packages, metal spikes, range (grass), club rentals, lodging (150 rooms), credit cards (MC, V, AE, D), beginner friendly (the winter home of the original golf school at mt. snow, vt).
Reader Comments: Very nice ... Lush fairways, perfect greens, great price ... Can't be beat for October off season ... Excellent staff ... Seems better each time ... Water, water everywhere.

★★★ POINCIANA GOLF & RACQUET RESORT
R-500 E. Cypress Pkwy., Kissimmee, 34759, Osceola County, (407)933-5300, (800)331-7743, 14 miles S of Orlando. **E-mail:** golfing@poincianaresort.com. **Web:** www.poincianaresort.com.
Holes: 18. **Yards:** 6,700/4,938. **Par:** 72/72. **Course Rating:** 72.2/68.4. **Slope:** 125/118. **Green Fee:** $35/$65. **Cart Fee:** Included in Green Fee. **Walking Policy:** Mandatory cart. **Walkability:** 1. **Opened:** 1973. **Architect:** Bruce Devlin/Robert von Hagge. **Season:** Year-round. **High:** Jan.-April. **To obtain tee times:** Call 7 days in advance. **Miscellaneous:** Reduced fees (low season, resort guests, twilight, juniors), discount packages, metal spikes, range (grass), club rentals, lodging, credit cards (MC, V, AE), beginner friendly.
Reader Comments: Challenging course, but rewarding! ... Staff extremely friendly, always a smile.

★★★★ POLO TRACE GOLF COURSE
SP-13481 Polo Trace Dr., Delray Beach, 33446, Palm Beach County, (407)495-5300, 30 miles S of West Palm Beach. **E-mail:** emeralddunes@aol.com. **Web:** www.emeralddunes.com.
Holes: 18. **Yards:** 7,096/5,314. **Par:** 72/72. **Course Rating:** 73.4/71.0. **Slope:** 134/124. **Green Fee:** $35/$130. **Cart Fee:** Included in Green Fee. **Walking Policy:** Mandatory cart. **Walkability:** 3. **Opened:** 1989. **Architect:** Karl Litten/Joey Sindelar. **Season:** Year-round. **High:** Dec.-April. **To obtain tee times:** Call golf shop up to 30 days in advance. **Miscellaneous:** Reduced fees (weekdays, low season, resort guests, twilight, seniors, juniors), discount packages, metal spikes, range (grass/mats), club rentals, credit cards (MC, V, AE, D, Diners Club/Carte Blanche), beginner friendly (hock-a-kid, kids golf).
Reader Comments: The Scotland of South Florida ... Mounds galore ... Young but shows great promise ... Good value ... Very tight, rough is thick ... Long, windy and tough ... Going upscale but not worth the premium ... Good greens ... Nice scenery.

FLORIDA

POMPANO BEACH GOLF COURSE
PM-1101 N. Federal Hwy., Pompano Beach, 33062, Broward County, (954)781-0426, 7 miles N of Ft. Lauderdale.

★★★½ PALMS COURSE
Holes: 18. **Yards:** 6,366/5,397. **Par:** 71/72. **Course Rating:** 69.4/70.2. **Slope:** 113/114. **Green Fee:** $20/$39. **Cart Fee:** Included in Green Fee. **Walking Policy:** Unrestricted walking. **Walkability:** 1. **Opened:** 1954. **Architect:** Robert von Hagge/BruceDevlin. **Season:** Year-round. **High:** Jan.-April. **To obtain tee times:** No tee times. First come, first served. **Miscellaneous:** Reduced fees (low season, twilight, juniors), metal spikes, range (grass), club rentals.
Reader Comments: Typical muny ... Slow play ... Wide open, can't lose your ball ... Easy to walk.

★★★ PINES COURSE
Holes: 18. **Yards:** 6,886/5,748. **Par:** 72/74. **Course Rating:** 72.2/72.5. **Slope:** 123/120. **Green Fee:** $20/$39. **Cart Fee:** Included in Green Fee. **Walking Policy:** Unrestricted walking. **Walkability:** 1. **Opened:** 1954. **Architect:** Robert von Hagge/Bruce Devlin. **Season:** Year-round. **High:** Jan.-April. **To obtain tee times:** First come, first served. **Miscellaneous:** Reduced fees (low season, twilight, juniors), metal spikes, range (grass), club rentals.
Reader Comments: Long for a muny ... Let out the shaft!.

PONTE VEDRA INN & CLUB
R-200 Ponte Vedra Blvd., Ponte Vedra Beach, 32082, St. Johns County, (904)285-1111, (800)234-7842, 20 miles SE of Jacksonville.

★★★ LAGOON COURSE
Holes: 18. **Yards:** 5,574/4,641. **Par:** 70/70. **Course Rating:** 66.2/66.9. **Slope:** 110/113. **Green Fee:** N/A/$90. **Cart Fee:** Included in Green Fee. **Walking Policy:** Walking at certain times. **Walkability:** 1. **Opened:** 1962. **Architect:** Robert Trent Jones. **Season:** Year-round. **High:** March-May. **To obtain tee times:** May call as soon as Inn reservations are made. Must be hotel guest to play. **Miscellaneous:** Discount packages, range (grass), club rentals, lodging (202 rooms), credit cards (MC, V, AE, D, Diners Club).
Reader Comments: Scenic and challenging ... Great value ... Very pleasant ... Fewer stressful shots ... Water and sand ... Ocean breeze.

★★★★ OCEAN COURSE
Holes: 18. **Yards:** 6,811/5,237. **Par:** 72/72. **Course Rating:** 73.2/69.6. **Slope:** 138/119. **Green Fee:** N/A$125. **Cart Fee:** Included in Green Fee. **Walking Policy:** Walking at certain times. **Walkability:** 2. **Opened:** 1928. **Architect:** Herbert Strong. **Season:** Year-round. **High:** March-May. **To obtain tee times:** May call as soon as Inn reservation is made. Must be hotel guest to play. **Miscellaneous:** Discount packages, metal spikes, range (grass), club rentals, lodging (202 rooms), credit cards (MC, V, AE, D, Diners Club).
Reader Comments: Greens are tour quality ... Excellent course ... Re-design is a substantial improvement ... New greens are very tough.

QUAIL HEIGHTS COUNTRY CLUB
SP-Route 18, Box 707, Lake City, 32025, Columbia County, (904)752-3339, 45 miles N of Gainesville.
Holes: 27. **Green Fee:** $18/$26. **Walking Policy:** Walking at certain times. **Walkability:** 1. **Opened:** 1972. **Season:** Year-round. **To obtain tee times:** Call in advance. **Miscellaneous:** Reduced fees (weekdays, low season, resort guests, juniors), discount packages, range (grass), club rentals, lodging, credit cards (MC, V).

CREEKS/PONDS COURSE
Yards: 6,672/5,144. **Par:** 72/72. **Course Rating:** 71.6/68.9. **Slope:** 127/113.

DUNES/CREEKS COURSE
Yards: 6,731/5,141. **Par:** 72/72. **Course Rating:** 72.6/69.9. **Slope:** 130/117.

PONDS/DUNES COURSE
Yards: 6,819/5,257. **Par:** 72/72. **Course Rating:** 72.8/70.0. **Slope:** 135/117.

★★½ QUALITY INN & SUITES GOLF RESORT
R-4100 Golden Gate Pkwy., Naples, 34116, Collier County, (941)455-9498, (800)277-0017, 6 miles E of Naples. **E-mail:** golfresort@aol.com.
Holes: 18. **Yards:** 6,570/5,374. **Par:** 72/72. **Course Rating:** 70.8/70.3. **Slope:** 125/123. **Green Fee:** $14/$48. **Cart Fee:** $17/person. **Walking Policy:** Walking at certain times. **Walkability:** 1. **Opened:** 1964. **Architect:** Dick Wilson/Joe Lee. **Season:** Year-round. **High:** Nov.-April. **To obtain tee times:** Public call 7 days in advance. Hotel guests, at time of reservation. **Miscellaneous:** Reduced fees (low season, resort guests, twilight, juniors), discount packages, metal spikes, range (grass), club rentals, lodging, credit cards (MC, V, AE, D).
Reader Comments: Mature Florida course actually has trees ... Enjoyable and challenging ... Middle of road.

FLORIDA

★★★½ RADISSON PONCE DE LEON GOLF & CONFERENCE RESORT

R-4000 U.S. Highway 1 N., St. Augustine, 32095, St. Johns County, (904)829-5314, (888)829-5314, 25 miles S of Jacksonville.
Holes: 18. **Yards:** 6,823/5,308. **Par:** 72/72. **Course Rating:** 72.9/70.7. **Slope:** 131/125. **Green Fee:** $40/$75. **Cart Fee:** Included in Green Fee. **Walking Policy:** Mandatory cart. **Walkability:** 1. **Opened:** 1916. **Architect:** Donald Ross. **Season:** Year-round. **High:** Feb.-May/Oct.-Nov. **To obtain tee times:** Book tee times with hotel reservations up to 1 year in advance. Others call 5 days in advance; with priority card, 2 days in advance. **Miscellaneous:** Reduced fees (weekdays, low season, resort guests, twilight, juniors), discount packages, metal spikes, range (grass), club rentals, lodging (200 rooms), credit cards (MC, V, AE, D, Diners Club).
Reader Comments: Excellent set-up and grooming ... Lots of room to flail away ... Two different nines. Half links, half parkland ... Tough course from back tees ... Nice practice area.

RAINTREE GOLF RESORT

R-1600 S. Hiatus Rd., Pembroke Pines, 33025, Broward County, (954)432-4400, (800)346-5332, 8 miles SW of Ft. Lauderdale.
Holes: 18. **Yards:** 6,456/5,274. **Par:** 72/72. **Course Rating:** 70.8/70.2. **Slope:** 126/122. **Green Fee:** $30/$70. **Cart Fee:** Included in Green Fee. **Walking Policy:** Mandatory cart. **Walkability:** 1. **Opened:** 1985. **Architect:** Charles M. Mahannah. **Season:** Year-round. **High:** Nov.-April. **To obtain tee times:** Call 3 days in advance. **Miscellaneous:** Reduced fees (weekdays, low season, resort guests, twilight), discount packages, range (mats), club rentals, lodging (24 rooms), credit cards (MC, V, AE, D).
Reader Comments: 6 par 3s, 6 par 4s and 6 par 5s ... Lots of water ... Play takes too long ... Water range ... Not a hookers course.

★★★★ RAVINES GOLF & COUNTRY CLUB

SP-2932 Ravines Rd., Middleburg, 32068, Clay County, (904)282-7888, 3 miles SW of Jacksonville. **Web:** www.theravines.com.
Holes: 18. **Yards:** 6,733/4,817. **Par:** 72/70. **Course Rating:** 72.4/67.4. **Slope:** 133/120. **Green Fee:** $25/$50. **Cart Fee:** Included in Green Fee. **Walking Policy:** Mandatory cart. **Walkability:** 4. **Opened:** 1979. **Architect:** Mark McCumber/Ron Garl. **Season:** Year-round. **High:** Jan.-June. **To obtain tee times:** Call 7 days in advance. **Miscellaneous:** Discount packages, range (grass), club rentals, lodging (30 rooms), credit cards (MC, V, AE, D).
Reader Comments: Little part of North Carolina in Florida ... Fast greens ... Very challenging ... A roller coaster in Florida ... Great views ... A great test of golf ... No amenities ... Unforgiving ... . One great hole after another ... A fun course that's hard to find.

REDLAND GOLF & COUNTRY CLUB

SP-24451 S.W. 177th Ave., Homestead, 33030, Dade County, (305)247-8503, 20 miles S of Miami.
Holes: 18. **Yards:** 6,613/5,639. **Par:** 72/72. **Course Rating:** 72.6/72.0. **Slope:** 123/118. **Green Fee:** $20/$37. **Cart Fee:** Included in Green Fee. **Walking Policy:** Mandatory cart. **Walkability:** 1. **Opened:** 1946. **Architect:** Red Lawrence. **Season:** Year-round. **High:** Nov.-April. **To obtain tee times:** Call 7 days in advance. **Miscellaneous:** Reduced fees (weekdays, low season, twilight, juniors), discount packages, range (grass), club rentals, credit cards (MC, V, D), beginner friendly (beginner instructions series lessons).

★★★★½ REGATTA BAY GOLF & COUNTRY CLUB *Service*

SP-465 Regatta Bay Blvd., Destin, 32541, Okaloosa County, (850)650-7800, (800)648-0123.
Web: www.regattabay.com.
Holes: 18. **Yards:** 6,864/5,092. **Par:** 72/72. **Course Rating:** 73.8/70.8. **Slope:** 148/119. **Green Fee:** $35/$70. **Cart Fee:** $15/person. **Walking Policy:** Mandatory cart. **Walkability:** 3. **Opened:** 1998. **Architect:** Bob Walker. **Season:** Year-round. **High:** March-Aug. **To obtain tee times:** Tee times taken up to 3 weeks in advance. Call 850-650-7800 ext 3 Note Range balls included in green fees. **Miscellaneous:** Range (grass), club rentals, credit cards (MC, V, AE), beginner friendly (ladies and juniors beginner programs).
Reader Comments: Excellent new track ... Friendly and accommodating staff ... Wide landing areas ... Plenty of trouble ... Gonna be one of the great ones ... Beautiful! ... Nice experience.

★★★★ REMINGTON GOLF CLUB

PU-2995 Remington Blvd., Kissimmee, 34741, Osceola County, (407)344-4004, 12 miles SE of Orlando.
Holes: 18. **Yards:** 7,111/5,178. **Par:** 72/72. **Course Rating:** 73.9/69.8. **Slope:** 134/118. **Green Fee:** $24/$75. **Cart Fee:** Included in Green Fee. **Walking Policy:** Mandatory cart. **Walkability:** 4. **Opened:** 1996. **Architect:** Lloyd Clifton/George Clifton/Ken Ezell. **Season:** Year-round. **High:** Nov.-March. **Miscellaneous:** Reduced fees (weekdays, low season, resort guests, twilight, seniors, juniors), range (grass), club rentals, credit cards (MC, V, AE).

Reader Comments: Back tees would test all! ... Fast greens ... Tough when windy ... Great practice facility ... Houses growing on course faster than the overseed ... Wide open fairways, excellent greens.

RENAISSANCE VINOY RESORT
R-600 Snell Isle Blvd. N.E., St. Petersburg, 33704, Pinellas County, (727)896-8000.
Holes: 18. **Yards:** 6,267/4,818. **Par:** 70/71. **Course Rating:** 70.2/67.3. **Slope:** 118/111. **Green Fee:** N/A/$105. **Cart Fee:** Included in Green Fee. **Walking Policy:** Walking at certain times. **Walkability:** 3. **Opened:** 1992. **Architect:** Ron Garl. **Season:** Year-round. **High:** Jan.-April. **To obtain tee times:** Unlimited time frame for resort guests. **Miscellaneous:** Reduced fees (twilight), discount packages, metal spikes, range (grass/mats), caddies, club rentals, lodging (360 rooms), credit cards (MC, V, AE, D, Diners Club).

★★★½ RIDGEWOOD LAKES GOLF CLUB
SP-200 Eagle Ridge Dr., Davenport, 33837, Polk County, (941)424-8688, (800)684-8800, 35 miles SW of Orlando. **E-mail:** ridgewoodlakes.com.
Holes: 18. **Yards:** 7,016/5,217. **Par:** 72/72. **Course Rating:** 73.7/69.9. **Slope:** 129/116. **Green Fee:** $20/$70. **Cart Fee:** Included in Green Fee. **Walking Policy:** Mandatory cart. **Walkability:** 1. **Opened:** 1993. **Architect:** Ted McAnlis. **Season:** Year-round. **High:** Nov.-April. **To obtain tee times:** Call up to 7 days in advance. **Miscellaneous:** Reduced fees (low season, resort guests, twilight, seniors), discount packages, range (grass), club rentals, credit cards (MC, V), beginner friendly (range program).
Reader Comments: Another great layout! ... Too much water ... Great course ... Very few trees ... Fastest greens ever, like putting on a dance floor ... Diamond in the rough.

★★★ RIVER BEND GOLF CLUB
SP-730 Airport Rd., Ormond Beach, 32174, Volusia County, (904)673-6000, (800)334-8841, 3 miles N of Daytona Beach. **E-mail:** rbmanatee@aol.com.
Holes: 18. **Yards:** 6,821/5,112. **Par:** 72/72. **Course Rating:** 72.3/69.6. **Slope:** 126/120. **Green Fee:** $28/$40. **Cart Fee:** Included in Green Fee. **Walking Policy:** Mandatory cart. **Walkability:** 5. **Opened:** 1990. **Architect:** Lloyd Clifton. **Season:** Year-round. **High:** Jan.-April. **To obtain tee times:** Call up to 4 days in advance. **Miscellaneous:** Reduced fees (low season, twilight, juniors), discount packages, metal spikes, range (grass), club rentals, credit cards (MC, V, AE).
Reader Comments: Narrow fairways ... Getting better ... OK course ... Greens improving ... Very wooded and scenic ... Lots of wildlife.

★★★★ THE RIVER CLUB
SP-6600 River Club Blvd., Bradenton, 34202, Manatee County, (941)751-4211, 45 miles S of Tampa.
Holes: 18. **Yards:** 7,026/5,252. **Par:** 72/72. **Course Rating:** 74.5/70.4. **Slope:** 135/121. **Green Fee:** $30/$60. **Cart Fee:** Included in Green Fee. **Walking Policy:** Walking at certain times. **Walkability:** 3. **Opened:** 1988. **Architect:** Ron Garl. **Season:** Year-round. **High:** Jan.-April. **To obtain tee times:** Call 2 days in advance. **Miscellaneous:** Reduced fees (weekdays, low season, resort guests, twilight), discount packages, range (grass), club rentals, credit cards (MC, V, AE, D).
Reader Comments: Blue tees are tough ... Just outstanding ... Still an undiscovered pleasure ... Nice ... Bring lots of balls! ... Good greens ... Great use of water ... Hills and mounds a decent challenge for everyone ... Opportunity to use the whole bag.

★★★★ RIVER HILLS COUNTRY CLUB *Service, Condition, Pace+*
SP-3943 New River Hills Pkwy., Valrico, 33594, Hillsborough County, (813)653-3323, 20 miles W of Tampa.
Holes: 18. **Yards:** 7,004/5,236. **Par:** 72/72. **Course Rating:** 74.0/70.4. **Slope:** 132/124. **Green Fee:** $35/$60. **Cart Fee:** $16/person. **Cart Fee:** Included in Green Fee. **Walking Policy:** Mandatory cart. **Walkability:** 2. **Opened:** 1989. **Architect:** Joe Lee. **Season:** Year-round. **High:** Jan.-April. **To obtain tee times:** Call 2 days in advance. **Miscellaneous:** Reduced fees (low season, twilight), discount packages, range (grass), club rentals, credit cards (MC, V, AE).
Reader Comments: Pretty course ... Challenging but fair ... They have their act together here ... A variety of challenges ... Will mature into a true championship course ... Always a good time ... Good rangers.

★★★ RIVER RUN GOLF LINKS
PU-1801 27th St. E., Bradenton, 34208, Manatee County, (941)747-6331, 30 miles S of St. Petersburg. **E-mail:** Riverrun44@aol.com.
Holes: 18. **Yards:** 5,825/4,579. **Par:** 70/70. **Course Rating:** 68.0/67.8. **Slope:** 113/113. **Green Fee:** $9/$18. **Cart Fee:** $10/person. **Walking Policy:** Unrestricted walking. **Walkability:** N/A. **Opened:** 1987. **Architect:** Ward Northrup. **Season:** Year-round. **High:** Jan.-April. **To obtain tee times:** Call 2 days in advance. **Miscellaneous:** Reduced fees (weekdays, low season, twilight), club rentals.

FLORIDA

Reader Comments: Premium is on placement ... Fun layout with good greens ... An enjoyable, fair course ... Not long but very tight.

★★★★ RIVERWOOD GOLF CLUB *Condition*
SP-4100 Riverwood Dr., Port Charlotte, 33953, Charlotte County, (941)764-6661, 45 miles S of Sarasota.
Holes: 18. **Yards:** 6,938/4,695. **Par:** 72/72. **Course Rating:** 73.2/66.8. **Slope:** 131/112. **Green Fee:** $50/$85. **Cart Fee:** Included in Green Fee. **Walking Policy:** Mandatory cart. **Walkability:** 2. **Opened:** 1993. **Architect:** Gene Bates. **Season:** Year-round. **High:** Nov.-April. **To obtain tee times:** Call 3 days in advance. **Miscellaneous:** Reduced fees (low season, resort guests, twilight), discount packages, range (grass), club rentals, lodging, credit cards (MC, V).
Reader Comments: Layout makes you think ... Costly but worth the extra money ... Greens were super ... Tough and tight ... Enjoyable with reasonable challenge ... Loved the environmentally protected areas ... Good pace of play.

★★ RIVIERA COUNTRY CLUB
SP-500 Calle Grande, Ormond Beach, 32174, Volusia County, (904)677-2464, 4 miles N of Daytona Beach.
Holes: 18. **Yards:** 6,302/5,207. **Par:** 71/72. **Course Rating:** 68.0/69.9. **Slope:** 113/122. **Green Fee:** $18/$30. **Cart Fee:** Included in Green Fee. **Walking Policy:** Mandatory cart. **Walkability:** 1. **Opened:** 1935. **Architect:** Dave Wallace. **Season:** Year-round. **High:** Jan.-March. **To obtain tee times:** First come, first served. Call ahead to insure course availability. **Miscellaneous:** Reduced fees (low season, resort guests, twilight), discount packages, metal spikes, range (grass/mats), club rentals, credit cards (MC, V).

★★ ROCKY POINT GOLF COURSE
PM-4151 Dana Shores Dr., Tampa, 33634, Hillsborough County, (813)673-4316.
Holes: 18. **Yards:** 6,398/4,910. **Par:** 71/71. **Course Rating:** 71.1/65.7. **Slope:** 122/111. **Green Fee:** $16/$35. **Cart Fee:** Included in Green Fee. **Walking Policy:** Unrestricted walking. **Walkability:** N/A. **Opened:** 1900. **Architect:** Ron Garl. **Season:** Year-round. **To obtain tee times:** Call Thursday a.m. for the following week. **Miscellaneous:** Reduced fees (low season, juniors), metal spikes, club rentals, credit cards (MC, V, D).

★★½ ROGERS PARK GOLF COURSE
PM-7910 N. 30th St., Tampa, 33610, Hillsborough County, (813)673-4396.
Holes: 18. **Yards:** 6,593/5,922. **Par:** 72/72. **Course Rating:** 71.0/67.3. **Slope:** 120/110. **Green Fee:** $35/$35. **Cart Fee:** Included in Green Fee. **Walking Policy:** Unrestricted walking. **Walkability:** 1. **Opened:** 1950. **Architect:** Ron Garl. **Season:** Year-round. **High:** Jan.-April. **To obtain tee times:** Call 7 days in advance. **Miscellaneous:** Reduced fees (twilight, juniors), discount packages, metal spikes, range (grass), club rentals, credit cards (MC, V, D), beginner friendly.
Reader Comments: City course that could be nice with better conditions ... Fun, easy muny.

★★★ ROLLING GREEN GOLF CLUB
SP-4501 N. Tuttle Ave., Sarasota, 34234, Sarasota County, (941)355-7621.
Holes: 18. **Yards:** 6,343/5,010. **Par:** 72/72. **Course Rating:** 69.7/67.9. **Slope:** 119/110. **Green Fee:** $10/$32. **Cart Fee:** $12/person. **Walking Policy:** Walking at certain times. **Walkability:** 1. **Opened:** 1968. **Architect:** R. Albert Anderson. **Season:** Year-round. **High:** Nov.-April. **To obtain tee times:** Call 3 days in advance. **Miscellaneous:** Reduced fees (low season, seniors), metal spikes, range (grass), club rentals, credit cards (MC, V, AE, D).
Reader Comments: Greens much improved ... Flat and uninteresting ... Too many good courses in area to play this one again ... Easy course ... Fair layout.

★★★ ROSEDALE GOLF & COUNTRY CLUB
SP-5100 87th St. E., Bradenton, 34202, Manatee County, (941)756-0004, 30 miles S of Tampa.
Holes: 18. **Yards:** 6,779/5,169. **Par:** 72/72. **Course Rating:** 72.9/70.4. **Slope:** 134/114. **Green Fee:** $20/$66. **Cart Fee:** Included in Green Fee. **Walking Policy:** Walking at certain times. **Walkability:** 2. **Opened:** 1993. **Architect:** Ted McAnlis. **Season:** Year-round. **High:** Oct.-May. **To obtain tee times:** Call up to 3 days in advance. **Miscellaneous:** Reduced fees (low season, resort guests, twilight), discount packages, range (grass), club rentals, credit cards (MC, V).
Reader Comments: Shotmakers' course ... Tough ... Overrated ... Too many houses ... Target golf ... Very tight ... Great practice facility.

ROTONDA GOLF & COUNTRY CLUB
HILLS COURSE
SP-100 Rotonda Circle, Rotonda, 33947, Charlotte County, (941)697-2414, 10 miles N of Port Charlotte.
Holes: 18. **Yards:** 6,304/5,075. **Par:** 72/72. **Course Rating:** 70.3/69.3. **Slope:** 126/121. **Green Fee:** $20/$40. **Cart Fee:** Included in Green Fee. **Walking Policy:** Walking at certain times. **Walkability:** 2. **Opened:** 1972. **Season:** Year-round. **High:** Nov.-April. **To obtain tee times:** Call

up to 3 days in advance. **Miscellaneous:** Reduced fees (low season, resort guests, twilight), metal spikes, range (grass), credit cards (MC, V).

LINKS COURSE
SP-13 Ann Underwood Dr., Cape Haze, 33947, Charlotte County, (941)697-8877, 10 miles N of Port Charlotte.
Holes: 18. **Yards:** 4,197/3,190. **Par:** 63/63. **Course Rating:** 61.2/59.1. **Slope:** 108/94. **Green Fee:** $20/$30. **Cart Fee:** Included in Green Fee. **Walking Policy:** Walking at certain times. **Walkability:** 2. **Opened:** 1990. **Season:** Year-round. **High:** Nov.-April. **To obtain tee times:** Call up to 3 days in advance. **Miscellaneous:** Reduced fees (low season, resort guests, twilight), metal spikes, credit cards (MC, V).

PALMS COURSE
SP-100 Rotonda Circle, Rotonda, 33947, Charlotte County, (941)697-8118, 10 miles N of Port Charlotte.
Holes: 18. **Yards:** 6,511/4,700. **Par:** 72/72. **Course Rating:** 71.0/67.5. **Slope:** 127/115. **Green Fee:** $32/$49. **Cart Fee:** Included in Green Fee. **Walking Policy:** Walking at certain times. **Walkability:** 2. **Opened:** 1989. **Season:** Year-round. **High:** Nov.-April. **To obtain tee times:** Call up to 3 days in advance. **Miscellaneous:** Reduced fees (low season, resort guests, twilight), discount packages, metal spikes, range (grass), credit cards (MC, V).

★★★★ ROYAL OAK GOLF CLUB
SP-2150 Country Club Dr., Titusville, 32780, Brevard County, (407)268-1550, (800)884-2150, 45 miles E of Orlando.
Holes: 18. **Yards:** 6,709/5,471. **Par:** 71/72. **Course Rating:** 72.3/71.5. **Slope:** 126/128. **Green Fee:** $16/$45. **Cart Fee:** Included in Green Fee. **Walking Policy:** Unrestricted walking. **Walkability:** 3. **Opened:** 1964. **Architect:** Dick Wilson. **Season:** Year-round. **High:** Jan.-April. **To obtain tee times:** Call up to 7 days in advance. **Miscellaneous:** Reduced fees (weekdays, low season, resort guests, twilight, juniors), discount packages, metal spikes, range (grass), club rentals, lodging, credit cards (MC, V, AE, Diners Club).
Reader Comments: Very nice ... Pleasant staff ... Interesting layout ... I could play it everyday ... A good test of all your shots.

ROYAL TEE COUNTRY CLUB
SP-11460 Royal Tee Circle, Cape Coral, 33991, Lee County, (941)283-5522, 15 miles W of Fort Myers.
Holes: 27. **Green Fee:** $15/$49. **Cart Fee:** Included in Green Fee. **Walking Policy:** Walking at certain times. **Walkability:** 1. **Opened:** 1985. **Architect:** Gordon Lewis. **Season:** Year-round. **High:** Jan.-April. **To obtain tee times:** Call up to 3 days in advance. **Miscellaneous:** Reduced fees (low season, twilight, seniors), discount packages, metal spikes, range (grass), club rentals, credit cards (MC, V, D).
★★★½ PRINCE/KING COURSE
Yards: 6,736/4,685. **Par:** 72/72. **Course Rating:** 71.5/67.0. **Slope:** 126/114.
Reader Comments: New 9 is nice ... Water on every hole ... Fun, not too hard, women's tees way up ... Wide open.
★★★½ PRINCE/QUEEN COURSE
Yards: 6,606/4,670. **Par:** 72/72. **Course Rating:** 71.3/66.4. **Slope:** 126/114.
★★★½ QUEEN/KING COURSE
Yards: 6,574/4,631. **Par:** 72/72. **Course Rating:** 71.4/66.2. **Slope:** 128/110.

SADDLEBROOK RESORT *Service+*
R-5700 Saddlebrook Way, Wesley Chapel, 33543, Pasco County, (813)973-1111, (800)729-8383, 30 miles N of Tampa.
★★★★ PALMER COURSE
Holes: 18. **Yards:** 6,469/5,212. **Par:** 71/71. **Course Rating:** 71.0/70.2. **Slope:** 126/121. **Green Fee:** $35/$95. **Cart Fee:** Included in Green Fee. **Walking Policy:** Mandatory cart. **Walkability:** N/A. **Opened:** 1986. **Architect:** Arnold Palmer/Ed Seay. **Season:** Year-round. **High:** Nov.-April. **To obtain tee times:** Call 2 days in advance. Resort guests may reserve tee times 60 days in advance. **Miscellaneous:** Reduced fees (low season), discount packages, metal spikes, range (grass), club rentals, lodging, credit cards (MC, V, AE, D).
Reader Comments: Great resort course ... Biggest gators I ever saw ... Challenging ... Typical Palmer course ... Great landscaping.
★★★★ SADDLEBROOK COURSE
Holes: 18. **Yards:** 6,603/5,183. **Par:** 70/70. **Course Rating:** 72.0/70.8. **Slope:** 124/124. **Green Fee:** $40/$115. **Cart Fee:** Included in Green Fee. **Walking Policy:** Mandatory cart. **Walkability:** N/A. **Opened:** 1976. **Architect:** Dean Refram. **Season:** Year-round. **High:** Nov.-April. **To obtain tee times:** Call 2 days in advance. Resort guests may reserve tee times 60 days in advance. **Miscellaneous:** Reduced fees (low season, resort guests), discount packages, metal spikes, range (grass), club rentals, lodging, credit cards (MC, V, AE, D).

Reader Comments: Very unique layout ... Frequent use of water and sand waste areas ... Great finishing hole ... Perfect greens ... Good challenge for all levels of players.

★½ ST. AUGUSTINE SHORES GOLF CLUB

PU-707 Shores Blvd., St. Augustine, 32086, St. Johns County, (904)794-4653, 50 miles S of Jacksonville.
Holes: 18. **Yards:** 5,719/4,151. **Par:** 71/71. **Course Rating:** 67.5/64.8. **Slope:** 112/106. **Green Fee:** $27/$29. **Cart Fee:** Included in Green Fee. **Walking Policy:** Walking at certain times. **Walkability:** 20. **Opened:** 1974. **Architect:** Chuck Almony. **Season:** Year-round. **High:** Jan.-April. **To obtain tee times:** Call up to 5 days in advance. **Miscellaneous:** Reduced fees (low season, twilight, juniors), range (grass/mats), club rentals, credit cards (MC, V).

★★★★ ST. JOHNS COUNTY GOLF CLUB   *Value*

PU-4900 Cypress Links Blvd., Elkton, 32033, St. Johns County, (904)825-4900, 7 miles W of St Augustine.
Holes: 18. **Yards:** 6,926/5,173. **Par:** 72/72. **Course Rating:** 72.9/68.8. **Slope:** 130/117. **Green Fee:** $17/$20. **Cart Fee:** $10/person. **Walking Policy:** Walking at certain times. **Walkability:** 3. **Opened:** 1989. **Architect:** Robert Walker. **Season:** Year-round. **High:** Jan.-April. **To obtain tee times:** Call up to 7 days in advance. **Miscellaneous:** Reduced fees (low season, twilight), range (grass), club rentals, credit cards (MC, V), beginner friendly (9-hole special).
Reader Comments: Tough public course ... Good challenge ... Well-kept secret, must play ... A real gem for the money ... Perfect for high handicapper ... Love it. Lots of water.

★★★★ ST. LUCIE WEST COUNTRY CLUB   *Service*

SP-951 S.W. Country Club Dr., Port St. Lucie, 34986, St. Lucie County, (561)340-1911, (800)800-4653, 45 miles N of West Palm Beach.
Holes: 18. **Yards:** 6,906/5,035. **Par:** 72/72. **Course Rating:** 74.0/69.8. **Slope:** 134/121. **Green Fee:** $20/$59. **Cart Fee:** Included in Green Fee. **Walking Policy:** Walking at certain times. **Walkability:** 2. **Opened:** 1987. **Architect:** Jim Fazio. **Season:** Year-round. **High:** Jan.-March. **To obtain tee times:** Call 4 days in advance. **Miscellaneous:** Reduced fees (low season, juniors), metal spikes, range (grass), club rentals, credit cards (MC, V, AE).
Reader Comments: Greens smooth as a billiard table ... Lots of water. Bring a dozen balls ... Don't need to be long here ... Tight fairways ... Excellent facilities.

SANDESTIN RESORT   *Service*

R-9300 Hwy. 98 W., Destin, 32541, Okaloosa County, 20 miles E of Fort Walton Beach.
Holes: 27. **Green Fee:** $68/$86. **Cart Fee:** Included in Green Fee. **Walking Policy:** Mandatory cart. **Walkability:** 2. **Opened:** 1985. **Architect:** Tom Jackson. **Season:** Year-round. **High:** Feb.-Oct. **To obtain tee times:** Call 2 days in advance. **Miscellaneous:** Reduced fees (low season, resort guests, twilight, juniors), discount packages, metal spikes, range (grass), club rentals, lodging, credit cards (MC, V, AE, D).

★★★★ BAYTOWNE GOLF COURSE - DUNES/HARBOR

(904)267-8155.
Yards: 6,890/4,862. **Par:** 72/72. **Course Rating:** 73.4/68.5. **Slope:** 127/114.
Reader Comments: Terrific views on Dunes 9 ... Poor pace of play ... Fun, playable resort course ... Take your credit card ... Like the first time every time ... Good test ... Overrated.

★★★★ BAYTOWNE GOLF COURSE - TROON/DUNES

(904)267-8155.
Yards: 7,185/5,158. **Par:** 72/72. **Course Rating:** 74.6/69.1. **Slope:** 128/115.
Reader Comments: Good, but too many holes that look alike ... Fun ... Tight and tough ... Very enjoyable.

★★★★ BAYTOWNE GOLF COURSE - TROON/HARBOR

(904)267-8155.
Yards: 6,891/4,884. **Par:** 72/72. **Course Rating:** 73.9/68.2. **Slope:** 127/113.
Reader Comments: You won't be disappointed ... Lots of water ... Some narrow landing areas.

★★★★ BURNT PINES GOLF COURSE

(904)267-6500.
Holes: 18. **Yards:** 7,046/5,950. **Par:** 72/72. **Course Rating:** 74.1/68.7. **Slope:** 135/124. **Green Fee:** $88/$116. **Cart Fee:** Included in Green Fee. **Walking Policy:** Unrestricted walking. **Walkability:** 2. **Opened:** 1994. **Architect:** Rees Jones. **Season:** Year-round. **High:** Feb.-Oct. **To obtain tee times:** Must be a guest at the resort to play. Call golf shop. **Miscellaneous:** Reduced fees (resort guests, juniors), discount packages, metal spikes, range (grass), club rentals, lodging, credit cards (MC, V, AE, D).
Notes: Ranked 29th in 1999 Best in State; 64th in 1996 America's Top 75 Upscale Courses; 3rd in 1995 Best New Resort Courses.
Reader Comments: Best in the Florida panhandle ... Nice views ... Excellent in all ways ... Great setting and track ... Natural setting makes the course ... Would recommend it to anyone ... Expensive, but don't we all deserve a treat?.

★★★½ LINKS COURSE

(904)267-8144.
Holes: 18. **Yards:** 6,710/4,969. **Par:** 72/72. **Course Rating:** 72.8/69.2. **Slope:** 124/115. **Green Fee:** $68/$86. **Cart Fee:** Included in Green Fee. **Walking Policy:** Unrestricted walking. **Walkability:** 2. **Opened:** 1977. **Architect:** Tom Jackson. **Season:** Year-round. **High:** Feb.-Oct. **To obtain tee times:** Call 2 days in advance. **Miscellaneous:** Reduced fees (low season, resort guests, twilight, juniors), discount packages, metal spikes, range (grass), club rentals, lodging, credit cards (MC, D).
Reader Comments: Short, fun course ... Staff goes beyond call of duty ... Good for all skill levels ... Nice views ... Great value ... Tight, water and wind everywhere.

★★★½ SANDPIPER GOLF CLUB

SP-6001 Sandpipers Dr., Lakeland, 33809, Polk County, (941)859-5461, 30 miles NE of Tampa.
Holes: 18. **Yards:** 6,442/5,024. **Par:** 70/70. **Course Rating:** 70.4/67.7. **Slope:** 120/109. **Green Fee:** $18/$29. **Cart Fee:** Included in Green Fee. **Walking Policy:** Mandatory cart. **Walkability:** 1. **Opened:** 1987. **Architect:** Steve Smyers. **Season:** Year-round. **High:** Jan.-March. **To obtain tee times:** Call a minimum of 2 days in advance and a maximum of 4 days in advance. **Miscellaneous:** Reduced fees (weekdays, low season, twilight), discount packages, metal spikes, club rentals, credit cards (MC, V).
Reader Comments: Great par-4 9th hole ... Practice area is great ... Much improved since last time ... Nice environment.

SANDRIDGE GOLF CLUB

PU-5300 73rd St., Vero Beach, 32967, Indian River County, (561)770-5000, 70 miles N of West Palm Beach.

★★★½ DUNES COURSE *Value*

Holes: 18. **Yards:** 6,900/4,922. **Par:** 72/72. **Course Rating:** 74.0/69.3. **Slope:** 131/120. **Green Fee:** $12/$34. **Cart Fee:** Included in Green Fee. **Walking Policy:** Walking at certain times. **Walkability:** 4. **Opened:** 1987. **Architect:** Ron Garl. **Season:** Year-round. **High:** Jan.-March. **To obtain tee times:** Automated tee time system through telephone. Call (561)770-5000 for automated tee time press 1 and follow directions. **Miscellaneous:** Reduced fees (weekdays, low season, twilight, juniors), discount packages, range (grass), club rentals, credit cards (MC, V, D).
Reader Comments: Tough little course ... Excellent courses, good rates and good service ... Very short. Good for your ego ... A lot of golf course for the money ... Tougher than it looks.

★★★★ LAKES COURSE *Value*

Holes: 18. **Yards:** 6,200/4,625. **Par:** 72/72. **Course Rating:** 70.1/67.1. **Slope:** 128/112. **Green Fee:** $15/$36. **Cart Fee:** Included in Green Fee. **Walking Policy:** Walking at certain times. **Walkability:** 2. **Opened:** 1992. **Architect:** Ron Garl. **Season:** Year-round. **High:** Jan.-April. **To obtain tee times:** Automated tee time system through telephone. Call (561)770-5000 for automated tee time press 1 and follow directions. **Miscellaneous:** Reduced fees (weekdays, low season, twilight, juniors), discount packages, range (grass), club rentals, credit cards (MC, V, D).
Reader Comments: Short course, but challenging ... Beautiful course with lots of water and sand ... Short but interesting ... Tough to get on, but worth the effort.

★★½ SANTA ROSA GOLF & BEACH CLUB

SP-334 Golf Club Dr., Santa Rosa Beach, 32459, Walton County, (850)267-2229, 15 miles E of Destin.
Holes: 18. **Yards:** 6,474/4,988. **Par:** 72/72. **Course Rating:** 71.8/68.8. **Slope:** 128/115. **Green Fee:** $40/$50. **Cart Fee:** $15/person. **Walking Policy:** Walking at certain times. **Walkability:** 2. **Opened:** 1969. **Architect:** Tom Jackson. **Season:** Year-round. **High:** April-Sept. **To obtain tee times:** Call 3 days in advance. **Miscellaneous:** Reduced fees (low season, twilight, juniors), range (grass), club rentals, credit cards (MC, V, AE, Diners Club).
Reader Comments: Off the beaten path ... Tough: tight fairways, trees, water ... Hilly for Florida.

★★½ SARASOTA GOLF CLUB

SP-7280 N. Leewynn Dr., Sarasota, 34240, Sarasota County, (941)371-2431. **E-mail:** ceston99@an.com. **Web:** www.kollstar.com.
Holes: 18. **Yards:** 7,066/5,004. **Par:** 72/72. **Course Rating:** 71.2/67.4. **Slope:** 122/108. **Green Fee:** $22/$40. **Cart Fee:** Included in Green Fee. **Walking Policy:** Walking at certain times. **Walkability:** 1. **Opened:** 1950. **Architect:** Wayne Tredway. **Season:** Year-round. **High:** Jan.-April. **To obtain tee times:** Call 7 days in advance. **Miscellaneous:** Reduced fees (low season, resort guests, twilight, seniors, juniors), discount packages, metal spikes, range (grass), club rentals, credit cards (MC, V, AE, D).
Reader Comments: Plain Jane track ... Old style layout ... Easy if you have a short game.

★★★ SAVANNAHS AT SYKES CREEK GOLF CLUB

PU-3915 Savannahs Trail, Merritt Island, 32953, Brevard County, (407)455-1375, 40 miles E of Orlando. **E-mail:** savannah@digital.net. **Web:** www.golfspacecoast.com.

Holes: 18. **Yards:** 6,636/4,795. **Par:** 72/72. **Course Rating:** 70.6/65.9. **Slope:** 118/108. **Green Fee:** $14/$28. **Cart Fee:** $10/person. **Walking Policy:** Walking at certain times. **Walkability:** 1. **Opened:** 1990. **Architect:** Gordon Lewis. **Season:** Year-round. **High:** Oct.-April. **To obtain tee times:** Call (407)455-1377. **Miscellaneous:** Reduced fees (low season, twilight, juniors), club rentals, credit cards (MC, V).
Reader Comments: Very challenging ... Swamp golf ... Average ... Only time I've hit balls on the practice range and used alligators as the target.

★★★ SCENIC HILLS COUNTRY CLUB
PU-8891 Burning Tree Rd., Pensacola, 32514, Escambia County, (904)476-0611.
Holes: 18. **Yards:** 6,689/5,187. **Par:** 71/71. **Course Rating:** 71.3/70.0. **Slope:** 131/116. **Green Fee:** $25/$45. **Cart Fee:** Included in Green Fee. **Walking Policy:** Mandatory cart. **Walkability:** 4. **Architect:** Chic Adams/Jerry Pate. **Season:** Year-round. **High:** Feb.-April. **To obtain tee times:** Call 48 hours in advance. **Miscellaneous:** Reduced fees (weekdays, low season, resort guests, twilight), discount packages, club rentals, credit cards (MC, V).
Reader Comments: Good value ... Rolling fairways unusual for area ... Nothing special ... A few good holes.

★★½ SCHALAMAR CREEK GOLF & COUNTRY CLUB
SP-4500 U.S. Hwy. 92 E., Lakeland, 33801, Polk County, (941)666-1623, 30 miles E of Tampa.
Holes: 18. **Yards:** 6,399/4,363. **Par:** 72/72. **Course Rating:** 70.9/64.8. **Slope:** 124/106. **Green Fee:** $8/$21. **Cart Fee:** $16. **Walking Policy:** Walking at certain times. **Walkability:** 1. **Opened:** 1987. **Architect:** Ron Garl. **Season:** Year-round. **High:** Jan.-April. **To obtain tee times:** Call 2 days in advance. **Miscellaneous:** Reduced fees (weekdays, low season, twilight), metal spikes, range (grass), club rentals, credit cards (MC, V).
Reader Comments: Narrow and short, but challenging ... Boring ... Tight.

★★★ SEASCAPE RESORT
R-100 Seascape Dr., Destin, 32541, Okaloosa County, (850)654-7888, (800)874-9106, 45 miles E of Pensacola.
Holes: 18. **Yards:** 6,480/5,014. **Par:** 71/71. **Course Rating:** 71.5/70.3. **Slope:** 120/113. **Green Fee:** $37/$45. **Cart Fee:** Included in Green Fee. **Walking Policy:** Walking at certain times. **Walkability:** 1. **Opened:** 1969. **Architect:** Joe Lee. **Season:** Year-round. **High:** March-Oct. **To obtain tee times:** Call up to 2 days in advance. **Miscellaneous:** Reduced fees (low season, resort guests, juniors), discount packages, metal spikes, range (grass), club rentals, lodging, credit cards (MC, V, AE, D).
Reader Comments: Quality greens ... Nice, average vacation course ... Short.

★★ SEBASTIAN MUNICIPAL GOLF COURSE
PM-101 E. Airport Dr., Sebastian, 32958, Indian River County, (561)589-6801, 75 miles SE of Orlando.
Holes: 18. **Yards:** 6,717/5,414. **Par:** 72/72. **Course Rating:** 71.0/71.1. **Slope:** 112/121. **Green Fee:** $14/$31. **Cart Fee:** Included in Green Fee. **Walking Policy:** Walking at certain times. **Walkability:** 1. **Opened:** 1981. **Architect:** Charles Ankrom. **Season:** Year-round. **High:** Nov.-April. **To obtain tee times:** Call (561)589-6800 or (561)589-6801. **Miscellaneous:** Reduced fees (low season, twilight, juniors), discount packages, metal spikes, range (grass), club rentals, credit cards (MC, V), beginner friendly (junior golf).

★★½ SEMINOLE GOLF CLUB
PU-2550 Pottsdamer St., Tallahassee, 32304, Leon County, (850)644-2582.
Holes: 18. **Yards:** 7,033/5,930. **Par:** 72/72. **Course Rating:** 73.4/73.0. **Slope:** 121/111. **Green Fee:** $13/$17. **Cart Fee:** $12/person. **Walking Policy:** Walking at certain times. **Walkability:** 2. **Opened:** 1962. **Architect:** R.A. Anderson. **Season:** Year-round. **High:** Feb.-Nov. **To obtain tee times:** Call on Monday for weekend tee times only. **Miscellaneous:** Reduced fees (weekdays, twilight, juniors), metal spikes, range (grass/mats), club rentals, credit cards (MC, V, D), beginner friendly (clinics).
Reader Comments: Wide open ... FSU college course ... I like the hills and trees.

★★★ SEVEN HILLS GOLFERS CLUB
SP-10599 Fairchild Rd., Spring Hill, 34608, Hernando County, (352)688-8888, 35 miles N of Tampa.
Holes: 18. **Yards:** 6,715/4,902. **Par:** 72/72. **Course Rating:** 70.5/66.5. **Slope:** 126/109. **Green Fee:** $16/$30. **Cart Fee:** Included in Green Fee. **Walking Policy:** Mandatory cart. **Walkability:** 3. **Opened:** 1989. **Architect:** Denis Griffiths. **Season:** Year-round. **High:** Dec.-April. **To obtain tee times:** Call up to 7 days in advance. **Miscellaneous:** Reduced fees (weekdays, low season, twilight), metal spikes, range (grass), club rentals.
Reader Comments: Lots of water ... Wide open ... Heavily played ... Nice clubhouse ... Rolling fairways ... Woods ... Lots of bunkers.

FLORIDA

SEVEN SPRINGS GOLF & COUNTRY CLUB

SP-3535 Trophy Blvd., New Port Richey, 34655, Pasco County, (813)376-0035, 12 miles NW of Tampa.

★★★½ CHAMPIONSHIP COURSE

Holes: 18. **Yards:** 6,566/5,250. **Par:** 72/72. **Course Rating:** N/A. **Slope:** 128/125. **Green Fee:** $31/$45. **Cart Fee:** Included in Green Fee. **Walking Policy:** Mandatory cart. **Walkability:** N/A. **Architect:** Ron Garl. **Season:** Year-round. **High:** Jan.-April. **To obtain tee times:** Call up to 2 days in advance. **Miscellaneous:** Reduced fees (low season, twilight), metal spikes, range (grass), club rentals, credit cards (MC, V).

Reader Comments: Testy Par 5s ... OK ... Not very memorable.

EXECUTIVE COURSE

Holes: 18. **Yards:** 4,310/4,030. **Par:** 64/64. **Course Rating:** N/A. **Slope:** 112/113. **Green Fee:** $18/$25. **Cart Fee:** Included in Green Fee. **Walking Policy:** Mandatory cart. **Walkability:** 1. **Season:** Year-round. **High:** Jan-Apr. **To obtain tee times:** Call up to 2 days in advance. **Miscellaneous:** Reduced fees (low season, twilight), metal spikes, range (grass), credit cards (MC, V), beginner friendly (group and individual lessons).

★★★★ SHALIMAR POINTE GOLF & COUNTRY CLUB

SP-302 Country Club Rd., Shalimar, 32579, Okaloosa County, (904)651-1416, (800)964-2833, 45 miles E of Pensacola.

Holes: 18. **Yards:** 6,765/5,427. **Par:** 72/72. **Course Rating:** 72.9/70.7. **Slope:** 125/115. **Green Fee:** $21/$49. **Cart Fee:** Included in Green Fee. **Walking Policy:** Mandatory cart. **Walkability:** 2. **Opened:** 1968. **Architect:** Joe Finger/Ken Dye. **Season:** Year-round. **High:** Jan.-April. **To obtain tee times:** Call up to 5 days in advance. **Miscellaneous:** Reduced fees (weekdays, low season, resort guests, twilight), discount packages, metal spikes, range (grass), club rentals, credit cards (MC, V, AE).

Reader Comments: Fun course ... Deep bunkers ... Fast and undulating greens ... Many waste areas ... Good course, good value.

★★★½ SHERMAN HILLS GOLF CLUB

PU-31200 Eagle Falls Dr., Brooksville, 34602, Hernando County, (352)544-0990, 45 miles N of Tampa.

Holes: 18. **Yards:** 6,778/4,959. **Par:** 72/72. **Course Rating:** 71.4/68.1. **Slope:** 130/117. **Green Fee:** $15/$30. **Cart Fee:** Included in Green Fee. **Walking Policy:** Mandatory cart. **Walkability:** 3. **Opened:** 1993. **Architect:** Ted McAnlis. **Season:** Year-round. **High:** Oct.-April. **To obtain tee times:** Call up to 7 days in advance. Juniors (under age of 16) play free after 12 with paid adult. **Miscellaneous:** Reduced fees (weekdays, low season, twilight, juniors), discount packages, metal spikes, range (grass/mats), club rentals, credit cards (MC, V), beginner friendly (we have a 3-hole par-3 course for beginners and juniors).

Reader Comments: Scottish flavor and worth the ride ... Wide fairways ... New clubhouse ... Very windy ... Solid if unspectacular ... Every hole has character.

★★★ SHOAL RIVER COUNTRY CLUB

SP-1100 Shoal River Dr., Crestview, 32539, Okaloosa County, (904)689-1010, 25 miles N of Fort Walton Beach.

Holes: 18. **Yards:** 6,782/5,183. **Par:** 72/72. **Course Rating:** 73.5/70.3. **Slope:** 136/124. **Green Fee:** $18/$18. **Cart Fee:** $18/person. **Walking Policy:** Walking at certain times. **Walkability:** 3. **Opened:** 1986. **Architect:** Dave Bennett. **Season:** Year-round. **High:** Feb.-March. **To obtain tee times:** Call up to 3 days in advance. **Miscellaneous:** Reduced fees (weekdays, low season, twilight, juniors), discount packages, metal spikes, range (grass), club rentals, credit cards (MC, V, AE, D), beginner friendly (beginner instructions available).

Reader Comments: Good for duffers and slicers like me ... Average course, some beautiful holes.

★★½ SIGNAL HILL GOLF & COUNTRY CLUB

PU-9615 N. Thomas Dr., Panama City Beach, 32407, Bay County, (904)234-5051, 10 miles W of Panama City.

Holes: 18. **Yards:** 5,617/4,790. **Par:** 71/71. **Course Rating:** 63.6/63.0. **Slope:** 101/103. **Green Fee:** $20/$35. **Walking Policy:** Unrestricted walking. **Walkability:** 2. **Opened:** 1962. **Architect:** John Henry Sherman. **Season:** Year-round. **High:** April-Sept. **To obtain tee times:** Call or come in up to 7 days in advance. **Miscellaneous:** Reduced fees (low season), metal spikes, club rentals, credit cards (MC, V, D).

Reader Comments: Great for walking ... Nice to get away from teenagers at beach ... Short course ... Great value for this area.

★★½ SILVER OAKS GOLF & COUNTRY CLUB

SP-36841 Clubhouse Dr., Zephyrhills, 33541, Pasco County, (813)788-1225, 20 miles NE of Tampa.

Holes: 18. **Yards:** 6,702/5,147. **Par:** 72/72. **Course Rating:** 72.5/68.8. **Slope:** 126/109. **Green Fee:** $10/$35. **Cart Fee:** Included in Green Fee. **Walking Policy:** Mandatory cart. **Walkability:**

2. Opened: 1988. **Architect:** Bobby Simmons. **Season:** Year-round. **High:** Dec-May. **To obtain tee times:** Call, fax or come in person to make tee time. **Miscellaneous:** Reduced fees (weekdays, low season, resort guests, twilight, seniors, juniors), discount packages, metal spikes, range (grass), club rentals, credit cards (MC, V), beginner friendly (terrain distance and largest is friendly).
Reader Comments: Too many trees but a nice course ... Boring design ... Power lines in play.

SILVERTHORN COUNTRY CLUB
SP-4550 Golf Club Lane, Brooksville, 34609, (352)799-2600, 65 miles N of Tampa.
Holes: 18. **Yards:** 6,827/5,259. **Par:** 72/72. **Course Rating:** 72.3/70.4. **Slope:** 131/120. **Green Fee:** $32/$55. **Cart Fee:** Included in Green Fee. **Walking Policy:** Mandatory cart. **Walkability:** 5. **Opened:** 1995. **Architect:** Joe Lee. **Season:** Year-round. **High:** Dec.-April. **To obtain tee times:** Call 7 days in advance. **Miscellaneous:** Reduced fees (weekdays, low season, twilight, juniors), discount packages, range (grass), club rentals, credit cards (MC, V, AE, D), beginner friendly (junior programs, clinics).

★★★★ SOUTHERN DUNES GOLF & COUNTRY CLUB
SP-2888 Southern Dunes Blvd., Haines City, 33844, Polk County, (941)421-4653, (800)632-6400, 20 miles SW of Orlando.
Holes: 18. **Yards:** 7,727/5,200. **Par:** 72/72. **Course Rating:** 74.7/72.4. **Slope:** 135/126. **Green Fee:** $32/$99. **Cart Fee:** Included in Green Fee. **Walking Policy:** Mandatory cart. **Walkability:** 4. **Opened:** 1993. **Architect:** Steve Smyers. **Season:** Year-round. **High:** Oct.-April. **To obtain tee times:** Call up to 7 days in advance April 15-Oct. 15; and 30 days in advance Oct.15-April 15. **Miscellaneous:** Reduced fees (weekdays, low season, resort guests, twilight, juniors), discount packages, metal spikes, range (grass/mats), club rentals, lodging, credit cards (MC, V, D).
Reader Comments: Worth the drive from Orlando ... A hidden gem ... If you like sand, this course if for you ... Awesome course. Great greens ... Very good links-style course ... Nice change from typical Florida swamps ... You'll tell you're friends ... Excellent shape ... Beautiful layout ... An idea carried to an extreme but fun anyway ... Bunker world.

★★½ SOUTHWINDS GOLF COURSE
PM-19557 Lyons Rd., Boca Raton, , Palm Beach County, (561)483-1305, 5 miles W of Boca Raton. **Web:** www.affordablegolf.com.
Holes: 18. **Yards:** 5,559/4,402. **Par:** 70/71. **Course Rating:** 67.7/65.7. **Slope:** 120/112. **Green Fee:** $22/$45. **Cart Fee:** Included in Green Fee. **Walking Policy:** Walking at certain times. **Walkability:** 1. **Opened:** 1955. **Season:** Year-round. **High:** Jan.-April. **To obtain tee times:** Call up to 4 days in advance. **Miscellaneous:** Reduced fees (low season, twilight, juniors), metal spikes, range (grass/mats), club rentals, credit cards (MC, V).
Reader Comments: Good public course ... Short, but challenging ... Lots of water.

★★½ THE SPORTSMAN OF PERDIDO GOLF RESORT
R-One Doug Ford Dr., Pensacola, 32507, Escambia County, (850)492-1223.
Holes: 18. **Yards:** 7,154/5,478. **Par:** 72/72. **Course Rating:** 73.6/71.4. **Slope:** 125/121. **Green Fee:** $20/$35. **Cart Fee:** $15/person. **Cart Fee:** Included in Green Fee. **Walking Policy:** Walking at certain times. **Walkability:** 1. **Opened:** 1963. **Architect:** Bill Amick. **Season:** Year-round. **High:** Jan.-April. **To obtain tee times:** Call. Credit card required if more than 7 days in advance. **Miscellaneous:** Reduced fees (resort guests, twilight, juniors), discount packages, metal spikes, range (grass), club rentals, lodging, credit cards (MC, V, AE, D).
Reader Comments: A challenge for all levels of players ... Tight fairways ... Will be great when renovations are complete.

★★ SPRING HILL GOLF CLUB
SP-12079 Coronado Dr., Spring Hill, 34609, Hernando County, (352)683-2261, 35 miles N of Tampa.
Holes: 18. **Yards:** 6,917/5,588. **Par:** 72/73. **Course Rating:** 73.0/71.8. **Slope:** 133/127. **Green Fee:** $11/$28. **Cart Fee:** Included in Green Fee. **Walking Policy:** Walking at certain times. **Walkability:** 3. **Opened:** 1975. **Architect:** David Wallace. **Season:** Year-round. **High:** Dec.-March. **To obtain tee times:** Call up to 7 days in advance. **Miscellaneous:** Reduced fees (low season, twilight), discount packages, metal spikes, range (grass), club rentals, beginner friendly.

SPRING LAKE GOLF & TENNIS RESORT
R-100 Clubhouse Lane, Sebring, 33870, Highlands County, (941)655-1276, (800)635-7277, 65 miles S of Orlando. **E-mail:** slc@strato.net. **Web:** www.springlakegolf.com.
Holes: 27. **Green Fee:** $17/$36. **Cart Fee:** Included in Green Fee. **Walking Policy:** Mandatory cart. **Walkability:** 1. **Opened:** 1977. **Architect:** Frank Duane. **Season:** Year-round. **High:** Jan.-March. **To obtain tee times:** Call 2 days in advance. **Miscellaneous:** Reduced fees (resort guests, twilight), discount packages, metal spikes, range (grass/mats), club rentals, lodging, credit cards (MC, V, AE, D).
★★★ EAGLE/HAWK
Yards: 6,578/5,000. **Par:** 72/72. **Course Rating:** 71.8/68.8. **Slope:** 126/116.

FLORIDA

Reader Comments: Very well run ... Has potential, but need lots of work.

★★★ **HAWK/OSPREY**
Yards: 6,496/4,939. **Par:** 71/71. **Course Rating:** 71.3/68.4. **Slope:** 122/113.
★★★ **OSPREY/EAGLE**
Yards: 6,272/4,973. **Par:** 71/71. **Course Rating:** 70.1/68.2. **Slope:** 121/113.
Reader Comments: Lots of sand ... Good practice facility.

Special Notes: Also has an executive 9-hole course.

★★★ **SPRUCE CREEK COUNTRY CLUB**
SP-1900 Country Club Dr., Daytona Beach, 32124, Volusia County, (904)756-6114, 45 miles NE of Orlando. **E-mail:** sccc24@bellsouth.net. **Web:** golfdaytonabeach.com.
Holes: 18. **Yards:** 6,751/5,157. **Par:** 72/72. **Course Rating:** 72.2/70.3. **Slope:** 125/121. **Green Fee:** $16/$50. **Cart Fee:** Included in Green Fee. **Walking Policy:** Mandatory cart. **Walkability:** 1. **Opened:** 1971. **Architect:** Bill Amick. **Season:** Year-round. **High:** Jan.-April. **To obtain tee times:** Call 3 days in advance. **Miscellaneous:** Reduced fees (weekdays, low season, resort guests, twilight, juniors), range (grass), club rentals, credit cards (MC, V).
Reader Comments: Nice variety ... Watch for low flying planes ... You will use all your clubs.

★★★★ **STONEYBROOK GOLF & COUNTRY CLUB**
SP-8801 Stoneybrook Blvd., Sarasota, 34238, Sarasota County, (941)966-1800.
Holes: 18. **Yards:** 6,561/4,984. **Par:** 72/72. **Course Rating:** 72.0/68.6. **Slope:** 132/117. **Green Fee:** $35/$70. **Cart Fee:** Included in Green Fee. **Walking Policy:** Mandatory cart. **Walkability:** 2. **Opened:** 1994. **Architect:** Arthur Hills. **Season:** Year-round. **High:** Jan-Mar. **Miscellaneous:** Range (grass), club rentals, credit cards (MC, V).
Reader Comments: Tough from tips ... A great test. Used every club ... I never miss a chance to play it ... No bang for the bucks ... Too many houses ... Great shape all year ... Big, fair greens ... Final four holes a real challenge.

STONEYBROOK GOLF CLUB
PU-21251 Stoneybrook Golf Blvd., Estero, 33928, Lee County, (941)948-3933, 6 miles S of Ft. Myers.
Holes: 18. **Yards:** 7,353/5,644. **Par:** 72/72. **Course Rating:** 75.8/73.1. **Slope:** 141/130. **Green Fee:** $5/$42. **Cart Fee:** $15/person. **Walking Policy:** Walking at certain times. **Walkability:** 2. **Opened:** 1999. **Architect:** Gordon Lewis/Jed Azinger. **Season:** Year-round. **High:** Jan.-April. **To obtain tee times:** Call up to 7 days in advance, or golfgateway.com. **Miscellaneous:** Reduced fees (low season, juniors), range (grass), club rentals, credit cards (MC, V), beginner friendly (hook a kid on golf/sticks for kids).

SUGAR MILL COUNTRY CLUB
SP-100 Clubhouse Circle, New Smyrna Beach, 32168, Volusia County, (904)426-5210, 10 miles S of Daytona Beach.
Holes: 27. **Green Fee:** $42/$82. **Cart Fee:** Included in Green Fee. **Walking Policy:** Mandatory cart. **Walkability:** 2. **Opened:** 1970. **Architect:** Joe Lee. **Season:** Year-round. **High:** Jan.-April. **To obtain tee times:** Call up to 2 days in advance. **Miscellaneous:** Reduced fees (low season), range (grass), club rentals, credit cards (MC, V).
★★★½ **RED/BLUE**
Yards: 6,695/5,404. **Par:** 72/72. **Course Rating:** 72.1/71.7. **Slope:** 126/125.
Reader Comments: Exceptional due to trees and surroundings ... Feels like the Northeast ... Fair ladies tees ... Stuffy atmosphere. Slow pace. Excellent condition.
★★★½ **WHITE/BLUE**
Yards: 6,749/5,478. **Par:** 72/72. **Course Rating:** 72.4/71.8. **Slope:** 127/123.
Reader Comments: Enjoyed ... Treated like a member.
★★★½ **WHITE/RED**
Yards: 6,766/5,428. **Par:** 72/72. **Course Rating:** 72.1/71.5. **Slope:** 125/124.
Reader Comments: OK, but nothing unusual ... Corporate paradise.

★★★ **SUMMERFIELD GOLF CLUB**
SP-13050 Summerfield Blvd., Riverview, 33569, Hillsborough County, (813)671-3311, 15 miles SE of Tampa.
Holes: 18. **Yards:** 6,883/5,139. **Par:** 71/71. **Course Rating:** 73.0/69.6. **Slope:** 125/114. **Green Fee:** $18/$43. **Cart Fee:** Included in Green Fee. **Walking Policy:** Mandatory cart. **Walkability:** 1. **Opened:** 1986. **Architect:** Ron Garl. **Season:** Year-round. **High:** Jan.-April, Nov.-Dec. **To obtain tee times:** Call (813)671-3311 Tee times can be made one week in advance. **Miscellaneous:** Reduced fees (low season, twilight), discount packages, range (grass), club rentals, credit cards (MC, V, AE, D).
Reader Comments: Good course, tough backside ... A bargain ... Tough in the wind.

SUNNYBREEZE GOLF COURSE
SP-8135 S.W. Sunnybreeze Rd., Arcadia, 34266, De Soto County, (941)625-0424, 45 miles N of Fort Myers. **E-mail:** wmbaker@sunline.net.
Holes: 18. **Yards:** 6,261/4,793. **Par:** 70/71. **Course Rating:** 68.7/67.0. **Slope:** 124/117. **Green Fee:** $10/$30. **Cart Fee:** $14/person. **Walking Policy:** Unrestricted walking. **Walkability:** 3. **Opened:** 1971. **Architect:** Andy Anderson/Bill Baker. **Season:** Year-round. **High:** Dec.-April. **To obtain tee times:** Call up to 7 days in advance. **Miscellaneous:** Reduced fees (weekdays, low season), discount packages, metal spikes, range (grass/mats), club rentals, credit cards (MC, V, D), beginner friendly.
Special Notes: Also has a 9-hole par-35 course.

★½ SUNRISE COUNTRY CLUB
SP-7400 N.W. 24th Place, Sunrise, 33313, Broward County, (954)742-4333, 7 miles W of Ft. Lauderdale.
Holes: 18. **Yards:** 6,624/5,317. **Par:** 72/72. **Course Rating:** 71.8/69.8. **Slope:** 126/119. **Green Fee:** $25/$45. **Cart Fee:** Included in Green Fee. **Walking Policy:** Mandatory cart. **Walkability:** 1. **Opened:** 1959. **Architect:** Bill Watts. **Season:** Year-round. **High:** Dec.-April. **To obtain tee times:** Call 7 days in advance. **Miscellaneous:** Reduced fees (twilight), metal spikes, range (grass), club rentals, credit cards (MC, V, AE).

★★★½ SUNRISE GOLF CLUB
SP-5710 Draw Lane, Sarasota, 34238, Sarasota County, (941)924-1402.
Holes: 18. **Yards:** 6,455/5,271. **Par:** 72/72. **Course Rating:** 70.6/69.3. **Slope:** 122/117. **Green Fee:** $19/$47. **Cart Fee:** Included in Green Fee. **Walking Policy:** Walking at certain times. **Walkability:** 2. **Opened:** 1970. **Architect:** Andy Anderson. **Season:** Year-round. **High:** Jan.-April. **To obtain tee times:** Call 7 days in advance. **Miscellaneous:** Reduced fees (low season, twilight, juniors), discount packages, metal spikes, range (grass), club rentals, credit cards (MC, V, AE, D).
Reader Comments: Very nice ... Some of the best greens around ... Nice layout ... Fair, but not very interesting ... Flat.

★★ TANGLEWOOD GOLF & COUNTRY CLUB
PU-5916 Tanglewood Dr., Milton, 32570, Santa Rosa County, (904)623-6176, 10 miles SE of Pensacola.
Holes: 18. **Yards:** 6,455/5,295. **Par:** 72/72. **Course Rating:** 70.0/69.9. **Slope:** 115/118. **Green Fee:** $17/$20. **Cart Fee:** $10. **Walking Policy:** Unrestricted walking. **Walkability:** 1. **Opened:** 1964. **Season:** Year-round. **High:** April-Nov. **To obtain tee times:** Call anytime. **Miscellaneous:** Reduced fees (low season, seniors), metal spikes, range (grass), rentals, credit cards (MC, V).

★★ TARPON SPRINGS GOLF CLUB
PU-1310 Pinellas Ave., S. (Alt. 19), Tarpon Springs, 34689, Pinellas County, (727)937-6906, 25 miles NW of Tampa.
Holes: 18. **Yards:** 6,099/5,338. **Par:** 72/72. **Course Rating:** 68.9/71.5. **Slope:** 112/110. **Green Fee:** $20/$25. **Walking Policy:** Walking at certain times. **Walkability:** N/A. **Opened:** 1927. **Architect:** John Van Kleek/Wayne Stiles. **Season:** Year-round. **High:** Jan.-April. **To obtain tee times:** Call 2 days in advance. **Miscellaneous:** Reduced fees (low season, twilight), metal spikes, range (grass), club rentals.

★★★½ TATUM RIDGE GOLF LINKS
SP-421 N. Tatum Rd., Sarasota, 34240, Sarasota County, (941)378-4211, 55 miles S of Tampa.
Holes: 18. **Yards:** 6,757/5,149. **Par:** 72/72. **Course Rating:** 71.9/68.9. **Slope:** 124/114. **Green Fee:** $17/$46. **Cart Fee:** Included in Green Fee. **Walking Policy:** Mandatory cart. **Walkability:** 1. **Opened:** 1989. **Architect:** Ted McAnlis. **Season:** Year-round. **High:** Nov.-May. **To obtain tee times:** Call 4 days in advance. **Miscellaneous:** Reduced fees (low season, seniors), range (grass), club rentals, credit cards (MC, V).
Reader Comments: Good layout ... Not too long ... Lots of wildlife ... Absence of homes is pleasant.

★★½ THE DUNES GOLF & TENNIS CLUB
R-949 Sandcastle Rd., Sanibel Island, 33957, Lee County, (941)472-2535. **E-mail:** ssrc.com. **Web:** www.ssrc.com.
Holes: 18. **Yards:** 5,578/4,002. **Par:** 70/70. **Course Rating:** 68.0/64.5. **Slope:** 123/111. **Green Fee:** $26/$90. **Cart Fee:** $20/person. **Walking Policy:** Mandatory cart. **Walkability:** 2. **Opened:** 1973. **Architect:** Mark McCumber. **Season:** Year-round. **High:** Jan.-March. **To obtain tee times:** Call the golf shop at (941)472-2535. Public can make tee times up to 4 days in advance. Meristar resort guests are able to make tee times up to 6 days in advance. **Miscellaneous:** Reduced fees (low season, resort guests, twilight, juniors), discount packages, range (grass), club rentals, lodging (400 rooms), credit cards (MC, V, AE, D).
Reader Comments: Short with lots and lots of water ... Water and wildlife everywhere ... Nice.

TIBURON GOLF CLUB

PU-2620 Tiburon Dr., Naples, 34109, Collier County, (941)594-2040, (877)WCI-PLAY, 30 miles S of Ft. Myers.
Holes: 27. **Green Fee:** $55/$200. **Cart Fee:** Included in Green Fee. **Walking Policy:** Mandatory cart. **Walkability:** 2. **Opened:** 1998. **Architect:** Greg Norman. **Season:** Year-round. **High:** Oct.-April. **To obtain tee times:** 60 days in advance, call (877)WCI-PLAY. **Miscellaneous:** Reduced fees (low season, resort guests, twilight), range (grass), club rentals, credit cards (MC, V, AE), beginner friendly (Rick Smith Golf Academy)
NORTH/SOUTH
Yards: 7,170/5,140. **Par:** 72/72. **Course Rating:** 74.5/70.6. **Slope:** 137/124. .
NORTH/WEST
Yards: 7,193/5,148. **Par:** 72/72. **Course Rating:** 74.5/69.6. **Slope:** 135/122.
WEST/SOUTH
Yards: 6,977/4,988. **Par:** 72/72. **Course Rating:** 73.4/70.4. **Slope:** 131/123.

TIERRA DEL SOL GOLF CLUB

SP-1100 Main St., Lady Lake, 32159, Lake County, (352)750-4600, 45 miles N of Orlando. **Web:** www.thevillages.com.
Holes: 18. **Yards:** 6,835/5,486. **Par:** 72/71. **Course Rating:** 72.8/71.7. **Slope:** 124/120. **Green Fee:** $23/$38. **Cart Fee:** Included in Green Fee. **Walking Policy:** Unrestricted walking. **Walkability:** 1. **Opened:** 1996. **Season:** Year-round. **High:** Nov.-April. **To obtain tee times:** Call 2 days in advance. **Miscellaneous:** Reduced fees (low season), range (grass/mats), club rentals, credit cards (MC, V).
Notes: 1998 Samsung LPGA World Championship.

TIGER POINT GOLF & COUNTRY CLUB *Service*

SP-1255 Country Club Rd., Gulf Breeze, 32561, Santa Rosa County, (850)932-1333, (888)218-8463, 15 miles SE of Pensacola.
★★★★ **EAST COURSE**
Holes: 18. **Yards:** 7,033/5,217. **Par:** 72/72. **Course Rating:** 74.2/70.8. **Slope:** 141/125. **Green Fee:** $38/$55. **Cart Fee:** Included in Green Fee. **Walking Policy:** Mandatory cart. **Walkability:** 2. **Opened:** 1979. **Architect:** Bill Amick/Ron Garl/Jerry Pate. **Season:** Year-round. **High:** Feb.-April/Oct.-Nov. **To obtain tee times:** Call up to 7 days in advance between 7 a.m. and 6 p.m. **Miscellaneous:** Reduced fees (weekdays, low season, twilight), discount packages, range (grass), club rentals, credit cards (MC, V, AE, Lung Card & Golf Card).
Reader Comments: Very playable ... Good test, great service ... One green has a bunker in it. One par 3 has a pine tree in center of fairway.
★★★★ **WEST COURSE** *Value*
Holes: 18. **Yards:** 6,737/5,314. **Par:** 71/72. **Course Rating:** 72.9/71.3. **Slope:** 138/123. **Green Fee:** $30/$38. **Cart Fee:** Included in Green Fee. **Walking Policy:** Mandatory cart. **Walkability:** 3. **Opened:** 1965. **Architect:** Bill Amick. **Season:** Year-round. **High:** Feb.-April/Oct.-Nov. **To obtain tee times:** Call up to 7 days in advance. **Miscellaneous:** Reduced fees (weekdays, low season, twilight), discount packages, range (grass), club rentals, credit cards (MC, V, AE, Lung Card & Golf Card), beginner friendly (several clinics offered to all skill levels).
Reader Comments: Easier than East Course ... Lots of wind and water! ... Excellent for the high handicapper.

★★★★ **TIMACUAN GOLF & COUNTRY CLUB**
SP-550 Timacuan Blvd., Lake Mary, 32746, Seminole County, (407)321-0010, (888)955-1234, 15 miles NE of Orlando.
Holes: 18. **Yards:** 6,915/4,576. **Par:** 71/71. **Course Rating:** 73.2/66.8. **Slope:** 133/118. **Green Fee:** $40/$89. **Cart Fee:** Included in Green Fee. **Walking Policy:** Mandatory cart. **Walkability:** N/A. **Opened:** 1987. **Architect:** Ron Garl/Bobby Weed. **Season:** Year-round. **High:** Jan.-April. **To obtain tee times:** Call 5 days in advance. Pre-paid times are available 30 days in advance. **Miscellaneous:** Reduced fees (weekdays, low season, resort guests, twilight), discount packages, metal spikes, range (grass/mats), club rentals, credit cards (MC, V, AE).
Reader Comments: Tough course ... #2 is the toughest hole anywhere ... Front & back nines are very different ... Fast, tricky greens ... Nice course, some elevation changes ... Great variety.

★★★½ **TOMOKA OAKS GOLF & COUNTRY CLUB**
SP-20 Tomoka Oaks Blvd., Ormond Beach, 32174, Volusia County, (904)677-7117, 5 miles N of Daytona Beach.
Holes: 18. **Yards:** 6,745/5,385. **Par:** 72/72. **Course Rating:** 72.0/71.4. **Slope:** 124/121. **Green Fee:** $25/$32. **Cart Fee:** Included in Green Fee. **Walking Policy:** Mandatory cart. **Walkability:** 2. **Opened:** 1962. **Architect:** J. Porter Gibson. **Season:** Year-round. **High:** Jan.-April. **To obtain tee times:** Call golf shop 1 day in advance. **Miscellaneous:** Reduced fees (low season, twilight), discount packages, metal spikes, range (grass), club rentals, credit cards (MC, V, AE, D).
Reader Comments: Fun course to play ... Heavily played, needs some upgrading ... Many trees.

FLORIDA

★★★★ **TOURNAMENT PLAYERS CLUB AT HERON BAY**
PU-11801 Heron Bay Blvd., Coral Springs, 33076, Broward County, (954)796-2000, (800)511-6616, 20 miles NW of Fort Lauderdale. **E-mail:** tpchb@aol.com. **Web:** www.pgatour.com.
Holes: 18. **Yards:** 7,268/4,961. **Par:** 72/72. **Course Rating:** 74.9/68.7. **Slope:** 133/113. **Green Fee:** $59/$110. **Cart Fee:** Included in Green Fee. **Walking Policy:** Unrestricted walking.
Walkability: 3. **Opened:** 1996. **Architect:** Mark McCumber/Mike Beebe. **Season:** Year-round.
High: Dec.-April. **To obtain tee times:** Call golf shop up to 7 days in advance. **Miscellaneous:** Reduced fees (weekdays, low season, twilight, juniors), metal spikes, range (grass), club rentals, credit cards (MC, V, AE, Diners Club).
Notes: PGA Tour Honda Classic since 1997.

Reader Comments: Great course with no trees ... Who put grass on the beach? ... Walks from cart paths longer than some holes ... Flat and boring ... Wind is brutal ... Needs time to mature ... Bring a pail and shovel ... Great course for the money ... Nice course if you have a camel!.

TOURNAMENT PLAYERS CLUB AT SAWGRASS *Service*
R-110 TPC Blvd., Ponte Vedra Beach, 32082, St. Johns County, (904)273-3235, 15 miles SE of Jacksonville. **Web:** www.pgatour.com.

★★★★½ **STADIUM COURSE** *Condition+*
Holes: 18. **Yards:** 6,937/5,000. **Par:** 72/72. **Course Rating:** 73.3/64.9. **Slope:** 138/120. **Green Fee:** $110/$200. **Cart Fee:** $25/person. **Walking Policy:** Unrestricted walking. **Walkability:** 3.
Opened: 1980. **Architect:** Pete Dye. **Season:** Year-round. **High:** Feb.-May. **To obtain tee times:** Guests of Marriott call golf reservations at (800)457-4653. **Miscellaneous:** Reduced fees (low season, juniors), metal spikes, range (grass), club rentals, lodging (515 rooms), credit cards (MC, V, AE, Resort Chg, Diners Club).
Notes: Ranked 52nd in 1999-2000 America's 100 Greatest; 2nd in 1999 Best in State; The Players Championship (annually); U.S. Amateur.

Reader Comments: Everyone should play it at least once ... Expensive but worth every penny ... 4 hours of smiling and swearing ... #17 is an unbelievably fun hole ... Believe the hype! ... Target golf and beautifully maintained ... Carnival golf ... Variety of tees make it fair ... Leave your ego at the bag drop ... Visually intimidating.

★★★★ **VALLEY COURSE**
Holes: 18. **Yards:** 6,864/5,126. **Par:** 72/72. **Course Rating:** 72.6/63.8. **Slope:** 129/117. **Green Fee:** $75/$115. **Cart Fee:** $25/person. **Walking Policy:** Unrestricted walking. **Walkability:** 4.
Opened: 1987. **Architect:** Pete Dye/Bobby Weed. **Season:** Year-round. **High:** Feb.-May. **To obtain tee times:** Guests of Marriott call golf reservations at (800)457-4653. **Miscellaneous:** Reduced fees (low season, juniors), metal spikes, range (grass), club rentals, lodging (515 rooms), credit cards (MC, V, AE, Resort Charge, Diners Club).
Notes: U.S. Amateur; Senior Players Championship.

Reader Comments: Good greens ... Cure for the Stadium Course hangover ... Surprisingly good ... Mounds frame the fairways ... Why does everyone play Stadium only?.

★★★★ **TOURNAMENT PLAYERS CLUB OF TAMPA BAY**
SP-5300 W. Lute Lake Fern Rd, Lutz, 33549, Hillsborough County, (813)949-0091, 15 miles NW of Tampa.
Holes: 18. **Yards:** 6,898/5,036. **Par:** 71/71. **Course Rating:** 73.4/69.1. **Slope:** 130/119. **Green Fee:** $63/$110. **Cart Fee:** Included in Green Fee. **Walking Policy:** Mandatory cart. **Walkability:** 3. **Opened:** 1991. **Architect:** Bobby Weed/Chi Chi Rodriguez. **Season:** Year-round. **High:** Jan.-April. **To obtain tee times:** Call 7 days in advance. **Miscellaneous:** Reduced fees (weekdays, low season, twilight, juniors), metal spikes, range (grass), club rentals, credit cards (MC, V, AE, Diners Club), beginner friendly (juniors $10 after 2 p.m).
Notes: Senior PGA Tour GTE Classic.

Reader Comments: Tough finishing holes ... Nice atmosphere and great pro shop ... Very good practice area ... Just average golf ... You can understand why the senior tour players struggle here ... Hard and fast turf ... Flat, but a good test of golf.

★★★ **THE TROPHY CLUB OF ORLANDO**
SP-2662 Sabal Club Way, Longwood, 32779, Seminole County, (407)869-4622, 5 miles N of Orlando.
Holes: 18. **Yards:** 6,603/5,278. **Par:** 72/72. **Course Rating:** 71.6/70.0. **Slope:** 129/120. **Green Fee:** $25/$55. **Cart Fee:** Included in Green Fee. **Walking Policy:** Mandatory cart. **Walkability:** N/A. **Opened:** 1981. **Architect:** Wade Northrup. **Season:** Year-round. **High:** Jan.-April. **To obtain tee times:** Call 2 days in advance. **Miscellaneous:** Reduced fees (weekdays, low season, twilight, juniors), range (mats), club rentals, credit cards (MC, V, AE).
Reader Comments: Very enjoyable ... Super greens, quick and true ... Typical Florida course.

TURNBERRY ISLE RESORT & CLUB *Service+*
R-19999 W. Country Club Dr., Aventura, 33180, Dade County, (305)933-6929, (800)327-7208, 10 miles S of Fort Lauderdale. **Web:** www.turnberryisle.com.
★★★★ **NORTH COURSE**

Holes: 18. **Yards:** 6,348/4,991. **Par:** 70/70. **Course Rating:** 70.3/67.9. **Slope:** 127/107. **Green Fee:** $55/$100. **Cart Fee:** $19/person. **Walking Policy:** Mandatory cart. **Walkability:** N/A. **Opened:** 1971. **Architect:** Robert Trent Jones Sr. **Season:** Year-round. **High:** Nov.-April. **To obtain tee times:** Reserve tee times when making hotel reservations. **Miscellaneous:** Reduced fees (low season), discount packages, range (grass/mats), club rentals, lodging (395 rooms), credit cards (MC, V, AE).

Reader Comments: Great golf experience ... Great condition ... Expensive but a good course.

★★★★½ **SOUTH COURSE**

Holes: 18. **Yards:** 7,003/5,581. **Par:** 72/72. **Course Rating:** 73.7/71.3. **Slope:** 136/116. **Green Fee:** $55/$100. **Cart Fee:** $19/person. **Walking Policy:** Mandatory cart. **Walkability:** N/A. **Opened:** 1971. **Architect:** Robert Trent Jones Sr. **Season:** Year-round. **High:** Nov.-April. **To obtain tee times:** Reserve tee times when making hotel reservations. **Miscellaneous:** Reduced fees (low season, twilight), discount packages, range (grass/mats), club rentals, lodging, credit cards (MC, V, AE).

Reader Comments: Pro greens. Loved it! ... Excellent resort course ... Not worth a trip.

★★★½ **TURNBULL BAY GOLF COURSE**
SP-2600 Turnbull Estates Dr, New Smyrna Beach, 32168, Volusia County, (904)427-8727.
Holes: 18. **Yards:** 6,400/4,850. **Par:** 72/72. **Course Rating:** 71.6/68.6. **Slope:** 129/119. **Green Fee:** $28/$42. **Cart Fee:** Included in Green Fee. **Walking Policy:** Mandatory cart. **Walkability:** 2. **Opened:** 1995. **Architect:** Gary Wintz. **Season:** Year-round. **High:** Jan.-April. **Miscellaneous:** Reduced fees (low season, twilight), metal spikes, range (grass), club rentals, credit cards (MC, V).

Reader Comments: Scenic and well kept ... Challenging greens ... Saturday morning and no one on it. Our gain, your loss.

★★★ **TURTLE CREEK GOLF CLUB**
PU-1278 Admiralty Blvd., Rockledge, 32955, Brevard County, (407)638-0603, 35 miles SE of Orlando. **E-mail:** info@turtlecreek,com. **Web:** www.turtlecreek.com.
Holes: 18. **Yards:** 6,709/4,880. **Par:** 72/72. **Course Rating:** 70.1/68.8. **Slope:** 129/113. **Green Fee:** $20/$43. **Cart Fee:** Included in Green Fee. **Walking Policy:** Walking at certain times. **Walkability:** 1. **Opened:** 1970. **Architect:** Bob Renaud. **Season:** Year-round. **High:** Jan.-April. **To obtain tee times:** Call up to 7 days in advance. **Miscellaneous:** Reduced fees (weekdays, low season, twilight, juniors), discount packages, range (grass/mats), club rentals, credit cards (MC, V, AE).

Reader Comments: Accuracy is everything ... Tight fairways ... Nice staff ... Very good greens and fairways.

★★★½ **TWISTED OAKS GOLF CLUB**
PU-4545 Forest Ridge Blvd., Beverly Hills, 34465, Citrus County, (352)746-6257, 60 miles N of Tampa.
Holes: 18. **Yards:** 6,876/4,641. **Par:** 72/72. **Course Rating:** 72.9/66.5. **Slope:** 126/114. **Green Fee:** $18/$40. **Cart Fee:** Included in Green Fee. **Walking Policy:** Mandatory cart. **Walkability:** 2. **Opened:** 1990. **Architect:** Karl Litten. **Season:** Year-round. **High:** Nov.-May. **To obtain tee times:** Call 7-days in advance. **Miscellaneous:** Reduced fees (twilight), discount packages, range (grass), club rentals, credit cards (MC, V, D), beginner friendly (twisted oaks golf schools).

Reader Comments: Fun course, all types of shots required ... Really a super value ... Wonderful elevation changes ... I could play this course every day.

★★★ **UNIVERSITY COUNTRY CLUB**
SP-9400 S.W. 130th Ave., Miami, 33186, Dade County, (305)386-5533, 5 miles SW of Miami.
Holes: 18. **Yards:** 7,172/5,476. **Par:** 72/72. **Course Rating:** 74.3/70.9. **Slope:** 123/118. **Green Fee:** $23/$55. **Cart Fee:** Included in Green Fee. **Walking Policy:** Mandatory cart. **Walkability:** 1. **Opened:** 1968. **Architect:** Mark Mahannah. **Season:** Year-round. **High:** Nov.-April. **To obtain tee times:** Call up to 5 days in advance. **Miscellaneous:** Reduced fees (weekdays, low season, resort guests, twilight), range (grass/mats), club rentals, lodging (300 rooms), credit cards (MC, V, AE).

Reader Comments: New owners show promise ... Much improved ... Long, open course.

★★★ **UNIVERSITY OF SOUTH FLORIDA GOLF COURSE**
PU-13801 North 46th Street, Tampa, 33612, Hillsborough County, (813)632-6893.
Holes: 18. **Yards:** 6,876/5,353. **Par:** 71/71. **Course Rating:** 74.2/70.9. **Slope:** 132/115. **Green Fee:** $14/$32. **Cart Fee:** $13/person. **Walking Policy:** Unrestricted walking. **Walkability:** 1. **Opened:** 1967. **Architect:** William Mitchell. **Season:** Year-round. **High:** Nov.-April. **To obtain tee times:** Call golf shop. **Miscellaneous:** Reduced fees (weekdays, low season, twilight, seniors, juniors), metal spikes, range (grass/mats), club rentals, credit cards (MC, V).

Reader Comments: Excellent greens ... Tough from back tees ... Tight fairways ... Tough elevated greens ... Course is awesome, very tight driving holes ... When in good shape it's one of the best courses, but conditions are often iffy at best.

UNIVERSITY PARK COUNTRY CLUB
SP-7671 Park Blvd., University Park, 34201, Manatee County, (941)359-9999, 1 miles N of Sarasota.
Holes: 27.**Green Fee:** $50/$85. **Cart Fee:** Included in Green Fee. **Walking Policy:** Walking at certain times. **Walkability:** 1. **Opened:** 1991. **Architect:** Ron Garl. **Season:** Year-round. **High:** Nov.-April. **To obtain tee times:** Call 3 days in advance. **Miscellaneous:** Reduced fees (week-days, low season, twilight), range (grass/mats), club rentals, credit cards (MC, V, D), beginner friendly (The School of Relaxed Golf).
★★★★　**COURSE 1 & 19**
Yards: 7,247/5,576. **Par:** 72/72. **Course Rating:** 74.4/71.8. **Slope:** 132/122.
Reader Comments: Very fine course ... Solid golf test ... Too expensive ... Play it before it goes private ... Hit and wait, hit and wait ... Disappointing greens.
★★★★　**COURSE 10 & 1**
Yards: 7,001/5,511. **Par:** 72/72. **Course Rating:** 73.6/71.6. **Slope:** 138/126.
★★★★　**COURSE 19 & 10**
Yards: 7,152/5,695. **Par:** 72/72. **Course Rating:** 74.0/72.4. **Slope:** 134/124.

★★★½　**VALENCIA GOLF COURSE AT ORANGETREE**
PU-1725 Double Eagle Trail, Naples, 34120, (941)352-0777, 10 miles E of I-75 Exit 17 Naples.
Holes: 18. **Yards:** 7,145/4,786. **Par:** 72/72. **Course Rating:** 74.3/67.4. **Slope:** 130/113. **Green Fee:** $20/$55. **Cart Fee:** $15/person. **Walking Policy:** Walking at certain times. **Walkability:** 1. **Opened:** 1997. **Architect:** Gordon Lewis. **Season:** Year-round. **High:** Dec.-May. **To obtain tee times:** Please call 3 days in advance. **Miscellaneous:** Reduced fees (low season, juniors), range (grass), club rentals, credit cards (MC, V, D), beginner friendly (free clinics).
Reader Comments: Cheapest on the Gulf coast and nice ... Would play it again ... Great price in a high price area ... Greens need to mature ... A new course but a comer.

VENTURA COUNTRY CLUB
SP-3201 Woodgate Blvd., Orlando, 32822, Orange County, (407)277-2640, 75 miles E of Tampa.
Holes: 18. **Yards:** 5,467/4,392. **Par:** 70/70. **Course Rating:** 66.6/65.1. **Slope:** 113/109. **Green Fee:** $25/$40. **Cart Fee:** Included in Green Fee. **Walking Policy:** Mandatory cart. **Walkability:** 1. **Opened:** 1980. **Architect:** Mark Mahannah. **Season:** Year-round. **High:** Jan.-April. **To obtain tee times:** Call golf shop 2 days in advance. **Miscellaneous:** Reduced fees (low season, resort guests, twilight), metal spikes, range (grass), club rentals, lodging, credit cards (MC, V).

★★★★　**VIERA EAST GOLF CLUB**
PU-2300 Clubhouse Dr., Viera, 32955, Brevard County, (407)639-6500, (888)843-7232, 5 miles N of Melbourne. **E-mail:** Golf@vieragolf.com. **Web:** www.vieragolf.com.
Holes: 18. **Yards:** 6,720/5,428. **Par:** 72/72. **Course Rating:** 72.1/71.0. **Slope:** 129/122. **Green Fee:** $24/$50. **Cart Fee:** $12/person. **Cart Fee:** Included in Green Fee. **Walking Policy:** Walking at certain times. **Walkability:** 1. **Opened:** 1994. **Architect:** Joe Lee. **Season:** Year-round. **High:** Dec.-April. **To obtain tee times:** Call 7 days in advance starting at 7 a.m. **Miscellaneous:** Reduced fees (low season, resort guests, twilight, juniors), metal spikes, range (grass), caddies, club rentals, credit cards (MC, V, AE).
Reader Comments: Not on a windy day ... Practice facility is A-1 ... Wide open.

★★★　**THE VILLAGE GOLF CLUB**
PU-122 Country Club Dr., Royal Palm Beach, 33411, Palm Beach County, (561)793-1400. **E-mail:** villagegolf@aol.com.
Holes: 18. **Yards:** 6,883/5,455. **Par:** 72/72. **Course Rating:** 73.3/71.7. **Slope:** 134/126. **Green Fee:** $24/$50. **Cart Fee:** Included in Green Fee. **Walking Policy:** Mandatory cart. **Walkability:** N/A. **Season:** Year-round. **High:** Nov.-April. **To obtain tee times:** Call golf shop. **Miscellaneous:** Metal spikes, range (grass), club rentals, credit cards (MC, V, AE, D).
Reader Comments: Will only get better ... A little more money invested in this course would go a long way ... Trees, water and trouble ... Not a fun course for the high handicapper.

THE VILLAGES HACIENDA HILLS GOLF & COUNTRY CLUB
SP-1200 Morse Blvd., The Villages, 32159, Sumter County, (352)753-5155, 50 miles NW of Orlando. **E-mail:** greenb@villages.com.
Holes: 27. **Green Fee:** $20/$36. **Cart Fee:** Included in Green Fee. **Walking Policy:** Unrestricted walking. **Walkability:** 3. **Opened:** 1990. **Architect:** Clifton/Ezell/Clifton. **Season:** Year-round. **High:** Nov.-April. **To obtain tee times:** Nonresidents may call starter up to 3 days in advance. **Miscellaneous:** Reduced fees (low season, resort guests, twilight), discount packages, metal spikes, range (grass/mats), club rentals, lodging, credit cards (MC, V, AE).
LAKES/OAKS
Yards: 3,249/2,607. **Par:** 72/72. **Course Rating:** 70.4/69.6. **Slope:** 122/114.
LAKES/PALMS
Yards: 3,168/2,617. **Par:** 72/72. **Course Rating:** 69.7/69.4. **Slope:** 122/116.

PALMS/LAKES
Yards: 3,197/2,613. **Par:** 72/72. **Course Rating:** 69.9/69.6. **Slope:** 121/116.

WALDEN LAKES GOLF & COUNTRY CLUB
SP-2001 Clubhouse Dr., Plant City, 33567, Hillsborough County, (813)754-8575, (888)218-8463, 20 miles E of Tampa.
★★★½ **HILLS COURSE**
Holes: 18. **Yards:** 6,610/4,800. **Par:** 72/72. **Course Rating:** 71.5/68.6. **Slope:** 131/120. **Green Fee:** $25/$50. **Cart Fee:** Included in Green Fee. **Walking Policy:** Mandatory cart. **Walkability:** 2. **Opened:** 1977. **Architect:** Ron Garl/Bob Cupp/Jay Morrish. **Season:** Year-round. **High:** Nov.-April. **To obtain tee times:** Call golf shop anytime. **Miscellaneous:** Reduced fees (weekdays, low season, twilight), range (grass), club rentals, credit cards (MC, V, AE).
Reader Comments: Beautiful course ... Good golf for the average golfer ... Tee times usually available ... Lots of water and challenging greens ... Wooded.
LAKES COURSE
Holes: 18. **Yards:** 6,588/5,016. **Par:** 72/72. **Course Rating:** 71.9/69.0. **Slope:** 131/123. **Green Fee:** $25/$50. **Cart Fee:** Included in Green Fee. **Walking Policy:** Mandatory cart. **Walkability:** 2. **Opened:** 1977. **Architect:** Ron Garl/Jack Nicklaus. **Season:** Year-round. **High:** Nov.-April. **To obtain tee times:** Call golf shop anytime. **Miscellaneous:** Reduced fees (weekdays, low season, twilight), range (grass), club rentals, lodging, credit cards (MC, V, AE).

WALT DISNEY WORLD RESORT   *Service+*
★★★★½ **EAGLE PINES GOLF COURSE**
R-3451 Golf View Dr., Lake Buena Vista, 32830, Orange County, (407)939-4653, 20 miles SW of Orlando Airport. **Web:** www.disney.go.com/disneyworld.
Holes: 18. **Yards:** 6,772/4,838. **Par:** 72/72. **Course Rating:** 72.3/68.0. **Slope:** 131/111. **Green Fee:** $100/$140. **Cart Fee:** Included in Green Fee. **Walking Policy:** Mandatory cart.
Walkability: N/A. **Opened:** 1992. **Architect:** Pete Dye. **Season:** Year-round. **High:** Jan.-April. **To obtain tee times:** Resort guests with confirmed reservation may call 60 days in advance. Nonguests call 30 days in advance with credit card. **Miscellaneous:** Reduced fees (low season, resort guests, twilight), discount packages, metal spikes, range (grass/mats), club rentals, lodging, credit cards (MC, V, AE, The Disney Card).
Notes: PGA Tour Event.
Reader Comments: Beautiful-only golf course ... Great for single walk-on ... Pricey ... Not quite as nice as Osprey Ridge but fair ... Fun to play ... Typical resort course ... Lots of sand.
★★★★ **LAKE BUENA VISTA GOLF COURSE**
R-One Club Lake Dr., Lake Buena Vista, 32830, Orange County, (407)939-4653, 20 miles SW of Orlando Airport. **E-mail:** disney.go.com/disneyworld.
Holes: 18. **Yards:** 6,819/5,194. **Par:** 72/72. **Course Rating:** 72.7/69.4. **Slope:** 128/120. **Green Fee:** $90/$120. **Cart Fee:** Included in Green Fee. **Walking Policy:** Walking at certain times.
Walkability: 1. **Opened:** 1972. **Architect:** Joe Lee. **Season:** Year-round. **High:** Jan.-April. **To obtain tee times:** Resort guests with a confirmed reservation may call 60 days in advance. Nonguests call 30 days in advance with credit card. **Miscellaneous:** Reduced fees (low season, resort guests, twilight), discount packages, metal spikes, range (grass), club rentals, lodging, credit cards (MC, V, AE, The Disney Card).
Notes: PGA Tour Walt Disney World/Oldsmobile Golf Classic; LPGA Tour HealthSouth Inaugural.
Reader Comments: Service to the max ... Tight ... Disappointingly dull ... Thoroughly enjoyed experience. Disney does it right ... Water, water, everywhere ... As cute as Minnie's giggle ... Could play it every day ... Wife appreciated length from forward tees.
★★★★ **MAGNOLIA GOLF COURSE**
R-1950 W. Magnolia Dr., Lake Buena Vista, 32830, Orange County, (407)939-4653, 25 miles SW of Orlando Airport.
Holes: 18. **Yards:** 7,190/5,232. **Par:** 72/72. **Course Rating:** 73.9/70.5. **Slope:** 133/123. **Green Fee:** $90/$120. **Cart Fee:** Included in Green Fee. **Walking Policy:** Mandatory cart. **Walkability:** 1. **Opened:** 1971. **Architect:** Joe Lee. **Season:** Year-round. **High:** Jan.-April. **To obtain tee times:** Resort guests with confirmed reservation may call 60 days in advance. Nonguests call 30 days in advance with credit card. **Miscellaneous:** Reduced fees (low season, resort guests, twilight), discount packages, metal spikes, range (grass/mats), club rentals, lodging, credit cards (MC, V, AE, The Disney Card).
Notes: PGA Tour Walt Disney World/Oldsmobile Classic;.
Reader Comments: Championship quality; great conditioning ... Open and long ... Great service. Pace of play wonderful ... . Par-3 6th has a bunker shaped like Mickey Mouse's head ... Still great ... Tough and long ... Don't play this right off the plane.
★★★½ **OAK TRAIL GOLF COURSE**
R-1950 W. Magnolia Palm Dr., Lake Buena Vista, 32830, Orange County, (407)939-4653, 25 miles SW of Orlando Airport.
Holes: 9. **Yards:** 2,913/2,532. **Par:** 36/36. **Course Rating:** N/A. **Slope:** N/A. **Green Fee:** N/A/$32. **Walking Policy:** Unrestricted walking. **Walkability:** N/A. **Opened:** 1971. **Architect:** Ron Garl/Larry Kanphaus. **Season:** Year-round. **High:** Jan.-April. **To obtain tee times:** Resort

guests with confirmed reservation may call 60 days in advance. Nonguests call 30 days in advance with credit card. **Miscellaneous:** Reduced fees (twilight, juniors), discount packages, metal spikes, range (grass/mats), club rentals, lodging, credit cards (MC, V, AE, The Disney Card).

Reader Comments: Good walking course ... Work your kinks out here ... Other Disney courses are tougher on your wallet and scorecard.
Special Notes: This 9-hole par-36 course is the only course at Walt Disney World that allows walking.

★★★★½ **OSPREY RIDGE GOLF COURSE** *Condition*
R-3451 Golf View Dr., Lake Buena Vista, 32830, Orange County, (407)939-4653, 20 miles SW of Orlando Airport. **Web:** www.disney.go.com/disneyworld.
Holes: 18. **Yards:** 7,101/5,402. **Par:** 72/72. **Course Rating:** 73.9/70.5. **Slope:** 135/122. **Green Fee:** $100/$140. **Cart Fee:** Included in Green Fee. **Walking Policy:** Mandatory cart. **Walkability:** 4. **Opened:** 1992. **Architect:** Tom Fazio. **Season:** Year-round. **High:** Jan.-April. **To obtain tee times:** Resort guests with confirmed reservation call 60 days in advance. Nonguests call 30 days in advance with credit card. **Miscellaneous:** Reduced fees (low season, resort guests, twilight), discount packages, metal spikes, range (grass), club rentals, lodging, credit cards (MC, V, AE, The Disney Card).

Reader Comments: Good track that's tough in the wind ... Plenty of sand..Best Disney has to offer ... Par 3 17th is outstanding ... Best finishing holes I've played ... Bring your camera and 'A' game ... Saw eagles, owls and osprey but no birdies ... Didn't like the alligators.

★★★★ **PALM GOLF COURSE** *Condition*
R-1950 W. Magnolia Dr., Lake Buena Vista, 32830, Orange County, (407)939-4653, 25 miles SW of Orlando Airport. **Web:** www.disney.go.com/disneyworld.
Holes: 18. **Yards:** 6,957/5,311. **Par:** 72/72. **Course Rating:** 73.0/70.4. **Slope:** 133/124. **Green Fee:** $90/$120. **Cart Fee:** Included in Green Fee. **Walking Policy:** Mandatory cart. **Walkability:** N/A. **Opened:** 1971. **Architect:** Joe Lee. **Season:** Year-round. **High:** Jan.-April. **To obtain tee times:** Resort guests with confirmed reservation may call 60 days in advance. Nonguests call 30 days in advance with credit card. **Miscellaneous:** Reduced fees (low season, resort guests, twilight), discount packages, metal spikes, range (grass/mats), club rentals, lodging, credit cards (MC, V, AE, The Disney Card).
Notes: PGA Tour Walt Disney World/Oldsmobile Classic.

Reader Comments: Tons of bunkers ... Most underrated of Disney courses ... Scenic and well kept ... Multiple tees offer a fair test for everyone ... The staff did everything except make my putts ... Lots of water.

WATERFORD GOLF CLUB
SP-1454 Gleneagles Dr., Venice, 34292, Sarasota County, (941)484-6621, 11 miles S of Sarasota.
Holes: 27. **Yards:** 6,498/4,998. **Par:** 72/72. **Course Rating:** 71.4/68.6. **Slope:** 124/115. **Green Fee:** $25/$55. **Cart Fee:** Included in Green Fee. **Walking Policy:** Walking at certain times. **Walkability:** 2. **Opened:** 1989. **Architect:** Ted McAnlis. **Season:** Year-round. **High:** Jan.-April. **To obtain tee times:** Call 2 days in advance. **Miscellaneous:** Reduced fees (low season, twilight), discount packages, metal spikes, range (grass/mats), club rentals, credit cards (MC, V).

★★★ **GLENEAGLES/SAWGRASS COURSE**
Reader Comments: Houses right on fairway ... Challenging 'water world' course.
★★★ **GLENEAGLES/TURNBERRY COURSE**
Yards: 6,504/5,168. **Par:** 72/72. **Course Rating:** 71.5/69.4. **Slope:** 126/115.
★★★ **TURNBERRY/SAWGRASS COURSE**
Yards: 6,670/5,124. **Par:** 72/72. **Course Rating:** 72.3/69.2. **Slope:** 128/115.

WEDGEFIELD GOLF & COUNTRY CLUB
SP-20550 Maxim Pkwy., Orlando, 32833, Orange County, (407)568-2116, (800)573-3118, 15 miles E of Orlando.
Holes: 18. **Yards:** 6,537/5,226. **Par:** 72/72. **Course Rating:** 71.8/70.7. **Slope:** 123/122. **Green Fee:** $15/$38. **Cart Fee:** Included in Green Fee. **Walking Policy:** Mandatory cart. **Walkability:** 1. **Opened:** 1966. **Season:** Year-round. **High:** Nov.-May. **To obtain tee times:** Call up to 7 days in advance. **Miscellaneous:** Reduced fees (weekdays, low season, twilight, seniors, juniors), discount packages, range (grass), club rentals, credit cards (MC, V), beginner friendly.

★★ **WEDGEWOOD GOLF & COUNTRY CLUB**
SP-401 Carpenter's Way, Lakeland, 33809, Polk County, (941)858-4451, 25 miles E of Tampa.
Holes: 18. **Yards:** 6,402/4,885. **Par:** 70/70. **Course Rating:** 69.1/68.1. **Slope:** 115/113. **Green Fee:** $18/$25. **Cart Fee:** Included in Green Fee. **Walking Policy:** Mandatory cart. **Walkability:** N/A. **Opened:** 1984. **Architect:** Ron Garl. **Season:** Year-round. **High:** Nov.-May. **To obtain tee times:** Call 3 days in advance. **Miscellaneous:** Reduced fees (weekdays, low season, twilight), range (grass), club rentals, credit cards (MC, V, AE).
Special Notes: Soft spikes required.

FLORIDA

WEST MEADOWS GOLF CLUB
PU-11400 W. Meadows Dr., Jacksonville, 32221, Duval County, (904)781-4834, 12 miles W of Downtown Jacksonville.
Holes: 18. **Yards:** 6,350/6,000. **Par:** 72/72. **Course Rating:** 70.0/N.A. **Slope:** 108/N.A. **Green Fee:** $15/$23. **Cart Fee:** Included in Green Fee. **Walking Policy:** Walking at certain times. **Walkability:** 1. **Opened:** 1968. **Architect:** Sam Caruso. **Season:** Year-round. **High:** Oct.-May. **To obtain tee times:** Open play. **Miscellaneous:** Reduced fees (weekdays, twilight, seniors), metal spikes, range (grass), club rentals, beginner friendly.

★★★½ WEST PALM BEACH MUNICIPAL COUNTRY CLUB
PM-7001 Parker Ave., West Palm Beach, 33405, Palm Beach County, (561)582-2019. **E-mail:** wpbcl@mindspring.com. **Web:** www.wpalmbeachcountryclub.com.
Holes: 18. **Yards:** 6,800/5,871. **Par:** 72/72. **Course Rating:** 71.0/72.8. **Slope:** 121/121. **Green Fee:** $14/$36. **Cart Fee:** $12/person. **Walking Policy:** Walking at certain times. **Walkability:** 2. **Opened:** 1947. **Architect:** Dick Wilson. **Season:** Year-round. **High:** Dec.-April. **To obtain tee times:** Lottery system. One person per foursome enters names evening before day of play at 7 p.m. As slips are drawn golfer gets choice of available times. Other: call starter after lottery or day of play to secure a time. Saturday and Sunday double crossover lottery. Wednesday evening for Saturday and Thursday for Sunday at 7:30 p.m. **Miscellaneous:** Reduced fees (low season, twilight, juniors), range (grass), club rentals, credit cards (MC, V, D).
Reader Comments: Very large true greens ... All the course any player would want ... Good value, good course to walk ... Nothing tricky ... Great old course.

★★★½ WESTCHASE GOLF CLUB
PU-11602 Westchase Drive, Tampa, 33626, Hillsborough County, (813)854-2331.
Holes: 18. **Yards:** 6,710/5,205. **Par:** 72/72. **Course Rating:** 71.8/69.1. **Slope:** 130/121. **Green Fee:** $29/$69. **Cart Fee:** Included in Green Fee. **Walking Policy:** Mandatory cart. **Walkability:** 2. **Opened:** 1992. **Architect:** Clifton/Ezell/Clifton. **Season:** Year-round. **High:** Jan.-April. **To obtain tee times:** Call up to 3 days in advance. **Miscellaneous:** Reduced fees (weekdays, low season, twilight, juniors), range (grass/mats), club rentals, credit cards (MC, V, AE), beginner friendly (women and children clinics).
Reader Comments: Tough course in very good shape ... Nice stuff ... Bring a dozen to feed the waste areas ... Makes you play all the shots ... Lots of fun ... Tough from tips.

WESTCHESTER GOLF & COUNTRY CLUB
SP-12250 Westchester Club Dr., Boynton Beach, 33437, Palm Beach County, (561)734-6300, 12 miles S of West Palm Beach.
Holes: 27. **Green Fee:** $19/$65. **Cart Fee:** Included in Green Fee. **Walking Policy:** Mandatory cart. **Walkability:** 1. **Opened:** 1988. **Architect:** Karl Litten, Inc. **Season:** Year-round. **High:** Nov.-April. **To obtain tee times:** Call 100 days in advance. **Miscellaneous:** Reduced fees (weekdays, low season, resort guests), discount packages, metal spikes, range (grass), club rentals, credit cards (MC, V, AE).
★★★½ BLUE/GOLD COURSE
Yards: 6,735/4,728. **Par:** 72/72. **Course Rating:** 72.8/69.7. **Slope:** 137/121.
Reader Comments: Good all around course ... Fairly open with lots of water ... No beverage cart ... Lots of wind and water ... Narrow track with water in play.
★★★½ GOLD/RED COURSE
Yards: 6,657/4,808. **Par:** 72/72. **Course Rating:** 72.3/70.0. **Slope:** 134/120.
Reader Comments: Challenging ... Beautiful ... Lots of water ... For first-time player it's difficult to find holes while crossing streets ... Houses get in the way.
★★★½ RED/BLUE COURSE
Yards: 6,772/4,758. **Par:** 72/72. **Course Rating:** 72.9/70.3. **Slope:** 136/119.

THE WESTIN INNISBROOK RESORT
★★★½ EAGLES WATCH COURSE
R-36750 Hwy. 19 N., Palm Harbor, 34684, Pinellas County, (727)942-2000, 25 miles NW of Tampa.
Holes: 18. **Yards:** 6,635/4,975. **Par:** 71/71. **Course Rating:** 72.0/68.4. **Slope:** 127/121. **Green Fee:** $60/$130. **Cart Fee:** Included in Green Fee. **Walking Policy:** Mandatory cart. **Walkability:** N/A. **Opened:** 1971. **Architect:** Lawrence Packard. **Season:** Year-round. **High:** Nov.-April. **To obtain tee times:** Call (727)942-5220. **Miscellaneous:** Reduced fees (low season, resort guests, juniors), discount packages, metal spikes, range (grass), club rentals, lodging, credit cards (MC, V, AE, D).
★★★★ COPPERHEAD COURSE
R-36750 Hwy. 19 N., Palm Harbor, 34684, Pinellas County, (727)942-2000, 25 miles NW of Tampa. **Web:** www.westin-innisbrook.com.
Holes: 18. **Yards:** 7,119/5,537. **Par:** 71/71. **Course Rating:** 74.4/72.0. **Slope:** 140/128. **Green Fee:** $80/$185. **Cart Fee:** Included in Green Fee. **Walking Policy:** Mandatory cart. **Walkability:** N/A. **Opened:** 1972. **Architect:** Lawrence Packard/Roger Packard. **Season:** Year-round. **High:**

Nov.-April. **To obtain tee times:** Call (727)942-5220. **Miscellaneous:** Reduced fees (low season, resort guests, juniors), discount packages, metal spikes, range (grass/mats), club rentals, lodging, credit cards (MC, V, AE, D).

Notes: Ranked 24th in 1999 Best in State. JCPenney Classic.

Reader Comments: 1st tee is super and it gets better ... Every hole is good ... Great greens ... Hilly for this part of Florida ... Calls for good iron play ... Place seemed tired ... Corporate paradise ... Suits all levels of play ... They've read a little too much of their own publicity.

★★★ HAWKS RUN COURSE

R-36750 Hwy. 19 N., Palm Harbor, 34684, Pinellas County, (727)942-2000, 25 miles NW of Tampa. **Web:** www.westin-innisbrook.com.

Holes: 18. **Yards:** 6,405/4,955. **Par:** 71/71. **Course Rating:** 70.5/68.4. **Slope:** 125/118. **Green Fee:** $60/$130. **Cart Fee:** Included in Green Fee. **Walking Policy:** Mandatory cart. **Walkability:** N/A. **Opened:** 1971. **Architect:** Lawrence Packard. **Season:** Year-round. **High:** Nov.-April. **To obtain tee times:** Call (727)942-5550. **Miscellaneous:** Reduced fees (low season, resort guests, juniors), discount packages, metal spikes, range (grass), club rentals, lodging, credit cards (MC, V, AE, D).

Reader Comments: Bring your straight game ... Needs bunker work ... Between a links and traditional course ... Short but sweet ... Good for couples.

★★★★ ISLAND COURSE

R-36750 Hwy. 19 N., Palm Harbor, 34684, Pinellas County, (727)942-2000, 25 miles NW of Tampa. **Web:** www.westin-innisbrook.com.

Holes: 18. **Yards:** 6,999/5,578. **Par:** 72/72. **Course Rating:** 74.1/73.0. **Slope:** 132/129. **Green Fee:** $70/$185. **Cart Fee:** Included in Green Fee. **Walking Policy:** Mandatory cart. **Walkability:** N/A. **Opened:** 1970. **Architect:** Lawrence Packard. **Season:** Year-round. **High:** Nov.-April. **To obtain tee times:** Call (727)942-5220. **Miscellaneous:** Reduced fees (low season, resort guests, juniors), discount packages, metal spikes, range (grass), club rentals, lodging (1,000 rooms), credit cards (MC, V, AE, D).

Reader Comments: Well maintained. Bunkers in good shape ... Gators 'R Us ... Holes 7-14 are great ... Much better than its famous sibling ... Tougher than it looks ... Lots of water.

★★★½ LOST OAKS GOLF CLUB

R-1100 Tarpon Woods Blvd., Palm Harbor, 34684, Pinellas County, (727)784-7606, 25 miles NW of Tampa.

Holes: 18. **Yards:** 6,515/5,245. **Par:** 72/72. **Course Rating:** 72.1/69.5. **Slope:** 128/115. **Green Fee:** $35/$80. **Cart Fee:** Included in Green Fee. **Walking Policy:** Mandatory cart. **Walkability:** N/A. **Opened:** 1970. **Architect:** Lane Marshall. **Season:** Year-round. **High:** Nov.-April. **To obtain tee times:** Call (727)942-5220. **Miscellaneous:** Reduced fees (weekdays, low season, resort guests, twilight, seniors, juniors), discount packages, metal spikes, range (grass), club rentals, lodging, credit cards (MC, V, AE, D).

Reader Comments: Pretty short. Fairly tight ... Great warm-up for the big courses.

Special Notes: Formerly Innisbrook Westin Resort.

WESTMINSTER GOLF CLUB

SP-2199 Berkley Way, Lehigh, 33971, Lee County, (941)368-1110, 3 miles E of Fort Myers. **Web:** www.westminstergolf.com.

Holes: 18. **Yards:** 6,930/5,280. **Par:** 72/72. **Course Rating:** 73.4/70.5. **Slope:** 133/120. **Green Fee:** $25/$60. **Cart Fee:** Included in Green Fee. **Walking Policy:** Mandatory cart. **Walkability:** 3. **Opened:** 1996. **Architect:** Ted McAnlis. **Season:** Year-round. **High:** Dec.-April. **To obtain tee times:** Call 3 days in advance. **Miscellaneous:** Reduced fees (low season), discount packages, range (grass), club rentals, credit cards (MC, V).

WHISPERING OAKS COUNTRY CLUB

SP-34450 Whispering Oaks Blvd., Ridge Manor, 33523, Hernando County, (352)583-4233, 40 miles of Tampa.

Holes: 18. **Yards:** 6,325/5,174. **Par:** 72/72. **Course Rating:** 70.0/69.8. **Slope:** 120/117. **Green Fee:** N/A/$25. **Cart Fee:** Included in Green Fee. **Walking Policy:** Mandatory cart. **Walkability:** 1. **Season:** Year-round. **High:** Nov.-April. **To obtain tee times:** Call up to 7 days in advance. **Miscellaneous:** Reduced fees (weekdays, low season, twilight), discount packages, range (grass), club rentals, credit cards (MC, V).

WILLOW BROOK GOLF COURSE

PU-4200 S.R. 544 E., Winter Haven, 33881, Polk County, (941)291-5899, 3 miles W of Hwy 27 and 544.

Holes: 18. **Yards:** 6,450/5,358. **Par:** 72/72. **Course Rating:** 70.6/70.6. **Slope:** 118/122. **Green Fee:** $20/$30. **Cart Fee:** Included in Green Fee. **Walking Policy:** Walking at certain times. **Walkability:** 3. **Opened:** 1967. **Season:** Year-round. **High:** Jan.-April. **To obtain tee times:** Call(941)291-5898 receive i.d. # then you can use tee time system. **Miscellaneous:** Reduced fees (low season, twilight, juniors), range (grass), club rentals, credit cards (MC, V) (jr golf camp,beginner lessons & clinics).

★★★½ WINDSOR PARKE GOLF CLUB
SP-4747 Hodges Blvd., Jacksonville, 32224, Duval County, (904)223-4653, 12 miles E of Jacksonville.
Holes: 18. **Yards:** 6,740/5,206. **Par:** 72/72. **Course Rating:** 71.9/69.4. **Slope:** 133/123. **Green Fee:** $47/$55. **Cart Fee:** Included in Green Fee. **Walking Policy:** Walking at certain times. **Walkability:** 1. **Opened:** 1991. **Architect:** Arthur Hills. **Season:** Year-round. **High:** March-May. **To obtain tee times:** Call 5 days in advance. **Miscellaneous:** Reduced fees (weekdays, twilight, seniors, juniors), discount packages, range (grass), club rentals, credit cards (MC, V, AE, D).
Reader Comments: Tough track ... Lovely, playable course ... Have to play all clubs ... Challenging ... Demanding par 3s ... Very walkable.

★★★★ WORLD GOLF VILLAGE *Service, Condition, Pace*
PU-2 World Golf Place, St. Augustine, 32095, St Johns County. **E-mail:** ssttime@aug.com. **Web:** www.scratch-golf.com.
the slammer & the squire COURSE
Holes: 18. **Yards:** 6,940/5,001. **Par:** 72/72. **Course Rating:** 73.8/69.1. **Slope:** 135/116. **Green Fee:** $90/$165. **Cart Fee:** Included in Green Fee. **Walking Policy:** Mandatory cart. **Walkability:** 2. **Season:** Year-round. **High:** Oct.-March. **To obtain tee times:** Nonresort guests call within 30 days of play date or call resort hotel or vistana. **Miscellaneous:** Reduced fees (resort guests), range (grass), club rentals, lodging, metal spikes, credit cards (MC, V, AE), beginner friendly (minimal forced carries).
Notes: 1999 Senior PGA Tour Liberty Mutual Legends of Golf.
Reader Comments: What an experience! ... Expensive, but worth it—great condition ... Enjoyed the total experience ... Facilities unmatched. Great front nine ... Outstanding.

WORLD WOODS GOLF CLUB *Service*
R-17590 Ponce De Leon Blvd., Brooksville, 34614, Hernando County, (352)796-5500, 60 miles N of Tampa. **Web:** www.floridagolfing.com.
★★★★★ PINE BARRENS COURSE *Value, Condition, Pace*
Holes: 18. **Yards:** 6,902/5,301. **Par:** 71/71. **Course Rating:** 73.7/70.9. **Slope:** 140/132. **Green Fee:** $50/$85. **Cart Fee:** Included in Green Fee. **Walking Policy:** Unrestricted walking. **Walkability:** 4. **Opened:** 1993. **Architect:** Tom Fazio. **Season:** Year-round. **High:** Jan.-April. **To obtain tee times:** Call up to 30 days in advance with credit card. **Miscellaneous:** Reduced fees (weekdays, low season, twilight), discount packages, range (grass), club rentals, credit cards (MC, V, AE, D, Diners Club).
Notes: Ranked 75th in 1999-2000 America's 100 Greatest; 4th in 1999 Best in State; 9th in 1996 America's Top 75 Upscale Courses.
Reader Comments: Bury me here ... Almost a religious experience and worth every cent ... Could be my favorite, great practice facility ... In the middle of nowhere, but worth the drive ... A real monster from the back tees ... Pine Valley reference is accurate ... Striking views from every tee! ... Good finishing holes.
★★★★½ ROLLING OAKS COURSE *Value, Condition, Pace*
Holes: 18. **Yards:** 6,985/5,245. **Par:** 72/72. **Course Rating:** 73.5/70.7. **Slope:** 136/128. **Green Fee:** $50/$85. **Cart Fee:** Included in Green Fee. **Walking Policy:** Unrestricted walking. **Walkability:** 4. **Opened:** 1993. **Architect:** Tom Fazio. **Season:** Year-round. **High:** Jan.-April. **To obtain tee times:** Call up to 30 days in advance with credit card. **Miscellaneous:** Reduced fees (weekdays, low season), discount packages, range (grass), club rentals, credit cards (MC, V, AE, D, Diners Club).
Notes: Ranked 22nd in 1999 Best in State; 73rd in 1996 America's Top 75 Upscale Courses.
Reader Comments: Scenic beauty ... Lush fairways and greens ... Just a little below its sister course ... Not Augusta National but quite good ... Often overlooked of two courses, but I think the better track ... Wish this was closer to home ... Heaven.

★★½ ZELLWOOD STATION COUNTRY CLUB
SP-2126 Spillman Dr., Zellwood, 32798, Orange County, (407)886-3303, 20 miles N of Orlando.
Holes: 18. **Yards:** 6,400/5,377. **Par:** 72/74. **Course Rating:** 70.5/71.1. **Slope:** 122/122. **Green Fee:** $22/$30. **Cart Fee:** Included in Green Fee. **Walking Policy:** Mandatory cart. **Walkability:** N/A. **Opened:** 1977. **Architect:** William Maddox. **Season:** Year-round. **High:** Nov.-April. **To obtain tee times:** Call 2 days in advance. **Miscellaneous:** Reduced fees (low season, twilight), metal spikes, club rentals.
Reader Comments: A hidden jewel ... Small hills and valleys.

GEORGIA

BACON PARK GOLF COURSE
PU-Shorty Cooper Dr., Savannah, 31406, Chatham County, (912)354-2625, 35 miles S of Hilton Head, SC. **Web:** www.cityofsavannah.com.
Holes: 27. **Green Fee:** $12/$14. **Cart Fee:** $10/person. **Walking Policy:** Walking at certain times. **Opened:** 1927. **Architect:** Donald Ross/Ron Kirby/Denis Griffiths. **Season:** Year-round. **High:** June-Aug. **To obtain tee times:** Call up to 90 days in advance.

★★ **CYPRESS/LIVE OAK**
Yards: 6,679/5,160. **Par:** 72/72. **Course Rating:** 70.5/68.3. **Slope:** 119/116. **Walkability:** 2. **Miscellaneous:** Reduced fees (weekdays, low season, twilight, seniors, juniors), metal spikes, range (grass/mats), club rentals, credit cards (MC, V, AE), beginner friendly (certified pga teaching pro).

★★ **CYPRESS/MAGNOLIA**
Yards: 6,573/4,943. **Par:** 72/72. **Course Rating:** 69.9/66.9. **Slope:** 118/114. **Walkability:** N/A. **Miscellaneous:** Reduced fees (weekdays, low season, twilight, seniors, juniors), metal spikes, range (grass), club rentals, credit cards (MC, V).

★★ **MAGNOLIA/LIVE OAK**
Yards: 6,740/5,309. **Par:** 72/72. **Course Rating:** 70.7/69.4. **Slope:** 120/118. **Walkability:** 2. **Miscellaneous:** Reduced fees (weekdays, low season, twilight, seniors, juniors), metal spikes, range (grass/mats), club rentals, credit cards (MC, V, AE), beginner friendly (certified PGA teaching pro).

★★★ BARRINGTON HALL GOLF CLUB
SP-7100 Zebulon Rd., Macon, 31210, Monroe County, (912)757-8358, 65 miles S of Atlanta. **Holes:** 18. **Yards:** 7,062/5,012. **Par:** 72/72. **Course Rating:** 73.8/69.3. **Slope:** 138/118. **Green Fee:** $19/$29. **Cart Fee:** $10/person. **Walking Policy:** Walking at certain times. **Walkability:** 4. **Opened:** 1992. **Architect:** Tom Clark. **Season:** Year-round. **High:** April-May. **To obtain tee times:** Call golf shop. **Miscellaneous:** Reduced fees (weekdays, twilight, juniors), discount packages, range (grass), club rentals, credit cards (MC, V), beginner friendly.

Reader Comments: Good layout ... Good finishing holes ... Marginal conditioning for semi-private course ... Friendly service ... A good test of golf ... Great layout.

★★ BEAVER KREEK GOLF CLUB
SP-Rte. 4, Box 167, Hwy. 221 N., Douglas, 31533, Coffee County, (912)384-8230, 60 miles NE of Valdosta.
Holes: 18. **Yards:** 6,543/5,424. **Par:** 72/72. **Course Rating:** 71.1/N/A. **Slope:** 119/N/A. **Green Fee:** $24/$24. **Cart Fee:** $16/. **Walking Policy:** Walking at certain times. **Walkability:** N/A. **Opened:** 1988. **Architect:** Kirby Holton. **Season:** Year-round. **High:** April-Oct. **To obtain tee times:** Call golf shop. **Miscellaneous:** Discount packages, metal spikes, range (grass), club rentals, credit cards (MC, V).

★★½ BELLE MEADE COUNTRY CLUB
SP-2660 Twin Pine Rd. N.W., Thomson, 30824, McDuffie County, (706)595-4511, 35 miles W of Augusta.
Holes: 18. **Yards:** 6,403/5,362. **Par:** 72/73. **Course Rating:** 69.9/68.6. **Slope:** 120/113. **Green Fee:** $13/$23. **Cart Fee:** $10/person. **Walking Policy:** Unrestricted walking. **Walkability:** 3. **Opened:** 1968. **Architect:** Boone A. Knox, Pete Knox. **Season:** Year-round. **High:** April-Aug. **To obtain tee times:** Call golf shop. **Miscellaneous:** Reduced fees (weekdays), metal spikes, range (grass), club rentals, credit cards (MC, V).

Reader Comments: A nice, enjoyable golf course ... The 11th is a good, short par 3.

★★★ BLACK CREEK GOLF CLUB
SP-Bill Futch Rd., Ellabell, 31308, Bryan County, (912)858-4653, 30 miles W of Savannah. **Web:** www.blackcreek.com.
Holes: 18. **Yards:** 6,287/4,551. **Par:** 72/72. **Course Rating:** 70.4/66.0. **Slope:** 130/109. **Green Fee:** $27/$34. **Cart Fee:** $8. **Cart Fee:** Included in Green Fee. **Walking Policy:** Mandatory cart. **Walkability:** 1. **Opened:** 1994. **Architect:** Jim Bevins. **Season:** Year-round. **High:** April-Sept. **To obtain tee times:** Call 7 days in advance. **Miscellaneous:** Reduced fees (seniors, juniors), discount packages, range (grass), credit cards (MC, V), beginner friendly.

Reader Comments: Outstanding service ... Every shot requires attention ... Interesting back nine with bridges crossing marsh swamps ... Fairways and greens are nicely maintained ... Knowledgeable pro shop staff ... Short but tight track ... Keep driver in the bag.

★★½ BOBBY JONES GOLF CLUB
PM-384 Woodward Way, Atlanta, 30305, Fulton County, (404)355-1009.
Holes: 18. **Yards:** 6,155/4,661. **Par:** 71/71. **Course Rating:** 69.0/67.6. **Slope:** 119/114. **Green Fee:** $19/$33. **Cart Fee:** $10/. **Walking Policy:** Mandatory cart. **Walkability:** 3. **Opened:** 1932. **Architect:** John Van Kleek/Garrett Gill/George B. Wi. **Season:** Year-round. **High:** May-Sept. **To obtain tee times:** Call. **Miscellaneous:** Reduced fees (weekdays, twilight, seniors, juniors), metal spikes, club rentals, credit cards (MC, V, AE), beginner friendly.

GEORGIA

Reader Comments: An interesting front 9 ... Short course, but good value ... Doesn't quite live up to the name.

★★ BOWDEN GOLF COURSE
SP-3111 Millerfield Rd., Macon, 31201, Bibb County, (912)742-1610.
Holes: 18. **Yards:** 6,570/4,955. **Par:** 72/73. **Course Rating:** 70.7/68.0. **Slope:** 119/106. **Green Fee:** $22/$24. **Cart Fee:** Included in Green Fee. **Walking Policy:** Unrestricted walking. **Walkability:** 3. **Opened:** 1940. **Architect:** Dick Cotton. **Season:** Year-round. **High:** May-Aug. **To obtain tee times:** Call 7 days in advance. **Miscellaneous:** Reduced fees (weekdays, twilight, seniors, juniors), metal spikes, range (grass), club rentals, beginner friendly (junior clinics).

★★★★ BRASSTOWN VALLEY RESORT
R-6321 U.S. Hwy. 76, Young Harris, 30582, Towns County, (706)379-4613, (800)201-3205, 90 miles N of Atlanta. **E-mail:** jjohnson@brasstownvalley.com. **Web:** www.brasstownvalley.com.
Holes: 18. **Yards:** 7,000/5,028. **Par:** 72/72. **Course Rating:** 73.9/69.2. **Slope:** 139/116. **Green Fee:** $55/$65. **Cart Fee:** Included in Green Fee. **Walking Policy:** Walking at certain times. **Walkability:** 3. **Opened:** 1995. **Architect:** Denis Griffiths. **Season:** Year-round. **High:** April-Nov. **To obtain tee times:** Call Pro Shop. **Miscellaneous:** Reduced fees (weekdays, low season, twilight, seniors, juniors), discount packages, metal spikes, range (grass/mats), club rentals, lodging (134 rooms), credit cards (MC, V, AE, D).

Reader Comments: Nice views of mountains ... Rewards good shots, punishes bad ones ... A mountain jewel! ... Beautiful setting ... Exceptional resort facility ... Great course even in the off season ... A golfer's golf course ... Beautiful resort, outstanding course ... Scenic mountain course with beautiful lodge and 72 ft. fireplace ... Beautiful mountain scenery with comfortable rooms, great food.

BRICKYARD PLANTATION GOLF CLUB
SP-1619 U.S. 280 E., Americus, 31709, Sumter County, (912)874-1234, 7 miles E of Americus. **E-mail:** lopgcdeb@sowega.net. **Web:** www.brickyardgolfclub.com.
Holes: 27. **Green Fee:** $16/$16. **Cart Fee:** $12/person. **Walking Policy:** Unrestricted walking. **Walkability:** 1. **Opened:** 1979. **Architect:** W.N. Clark. **Season:** Year-round. **High:** May-Aug. **To obtain tee times:** Call golf shop. **Miscellaneous:** Range (grass), credit cards (MC, V, AE, D).
★★★ DITCHES/MOUNDS
Yards: 6,700/5,300. **Par:** 72/72. **Course Rating:** 70.5/69.9. **Slope:** 129/114.

Reader Comments: Staff is helpful and friendly ... Nice links-style design ... Challenging 27-hole course ... Very reasonable.
★★★ DITCHES/WATERS
Yards: 6,300/5,100. **Par:** 72/72. **Course Rating:** 70.0/70.6. **Slope:** 128/120.
★★★ WATERS/MOUNDS
Yards: 6,400/5,100. **Par:** 72/72. **Course Rating:** 67.7/69.8. **Slope:** 124/116.

BRIDGEMILL ATHLETIC CLUB
SP-1190 BridgeMill Ave., Canton, 30114, Cherokee County, (770)345-5500, 32 miles NW of Atlanta.
Holes: 18. **Yards:** 7,085/4,828. **Par:** 72/72. **Course Rating:** 74.0/69.0. **Slope:** 140/119. **Green Fee:** $39/$59. **Cart Fee:** $16/person. **Walking Policy:** Unrestricted walking. **Walkability:** 4. **Opened:** 1998. **Architect:** Desmond Muirhead, Larry Mize. **Season:** Year-round. **High:** April-Sept. **To obtain tee times:** Calls are permitted up to seven days prior to date of play. **Miscellaneous:** Reduced fees (twilight), range (grass), club rentals, credit cards (MC, V, AE), beginner friendly (beginner clinics).
Special Notes: Formerly the Golf Club at BridgeMill.

★★½ BROWNS MILL GOLF COURSE
PM-480 Cleveland Ave., Atlanta, 30354, Fulton County, (404)366-3573.
Holes: 18. **Yards:** 6,539/5,545. **Par:** 72/72. **Course Rating:** 71.0/71.4. **Slope:** 123/118. **Green Fee:** $17/$22. **Cart Fee:** $10/person. **Walking Policy:** Unrestricted walking. **Walkability:** 2. **Opened:** 1969. **Architect:** George W. Cobb. **Season:** Year-round. **High:** March-Oct. **To obtain tee times:** Call golf shop. **Miscellaneous:** Reduced fees (weekdays, twilight, seniors, juniors), metal spikes, range (grass), club rentals, credit cards (MC, V, AE), beginner friendly (adult and junior classes may-aug).

Reader Comments: Good looking course ... Allows walking, nice design ... Well-designed course ... Wide open fairways good for beginners.

BULL CREEK GOLF COURSE
PU-7333 Lynch Rd., Midland, 31820, Muscogee County, (706)561-1614, 10 miles E of Columbus.
★★★½ EAST COURSE
Holes: 18. **Yards:** 6,705/5,430. **Par:** 72/74. **Course Rating:** 71.2/69.8. **Slope:** 124/114. **Green Fee:** $16/$18. **Cart Fee:** $13/person. **Walking Policy:** Unrestricted walking. **Walkability:** 3. **Opened:** 1972. **Architect:** Joe Lee/Ward Northrup. **Season:** Year-round. **High:** April-Aug. **To**

obtain tee times: Call. **Miscellaneous:** Reduced fees (weekdays, seniors, juniors), discount packages, metal spikes, range (grass), club rentals, credit cards (MC, V).

Reader Comments: Great public course ... Clean and friendly ... Nice challenge ... Hilly layout and heavily wooded ... Conditions are good.

★★★½ **WEST COURSE**

Holes: 18. **Yards:** 6,921/5,385. **Par:** 72/74. **Course Rating:** 72.5/69.9. **Slope:** 130/121. **Green Fee:** $16/$18. **Cart Fee:** $13/person. **Walking Policy:** Unrestricted walking. **Walkability:** 5. **Opened:** 1972. **Architect:** Joe Lee/Ward Northrup. **Season:** Year-round. **High:** April-Aug. **To obtain tee times:** Call. **Miscellaneous:** Reduced fees (weekdays, seniors, juniors), discount packages, metal spikes, range (grass), club rentals, credit cards (MC, V).

Reader Comments: A good course with nice greens ... Great layout, at a great price ... Good course in good condition.

CALLAWAY GARDENS RESORT *Service*

R-U.S. Highway 27, Pine Mountain, 31822, Harris County, (706)663-2281, (800)225-5292, 27 miles N of Columbus. **E-mail:** info@callowaygardens.com. **Web:** www.callowaygardens.com.

★★★½ **GARDENS VIEW COURSE**

Holes: 18. **Yards:** 6,392/5,848. **Par:** 72/72. **Course Rating:** 70.7/72.7. **Slope:** 121/123. **Green Fee:** $55/$75. **Cart Fee:** Included in Green Fee. **Walking Policy:** Walking at certain times. **Walkability:** 1. **Opened:** 1964. **Architect:** Joe Lee. **Season:** Year-round. **High:** March-Nov. **To obtain tee times:** Resort guests can make tee times when room reservations are guaranteed. Nonguests call 800 number 2 days in advance or golf shop day of play. **Miscellaneous:** Reduced fees (low season, twilight), discount packages, range (grass), club rentals, lodging, credit cards (MC, V, AE, D).

Reader Comments: Fun golf setting ... Nice setting ... One of the best resorts ... Beautiful, fun course ... Good food, good golf ... A solid golf course ... Good course for middle handicapper ... Great winter outing.

★★★★ **LAKE VIEW COURSE**

Holes: 18. **Yards:** 6,006/5,452. **Par:** 70/71. **Course Rating:** 69.4/70.3. **Slope:** 115/122. **Green Fee:** $55/$75. **Cart Fee:** Included in Green Fee. **Walking Policy:** Walking at certain times. **Walkability:** N/A. **Opened:** 1952. **Architect:** J.B. McGovern. **Season:** Year-round. **High:** March-Nov. **To obtain tee times:** Resort guests can make tee times when room reservations are guaranteed. Nonguests call 800 number 2 days in advance or golf shop day of play. **Miscellaneous:** Reduced fees (low season, twilight), discount packages, metal spikes, range (grass), club rentals, lodging, credit cards (MC, V, AE, D).

Reader Comments: Great lakeside holes ... Excellent and beautiful course ... Course in great shape ... Best of the Callaways ... Friendly staff ... Nice resort course–great weekend ... Wonderful, great time ... Beautiful scenery along the way! ... Great winter outing.

★★★★ **MOUNTAIN VIEW COURSE**

Holes: 18. **Yards:** 7,057/5,848. **Par:** 72/74. **Course Rating:** 74.1/73.2. **Slope:** 138/122. **Green Fee:** $70/$110. **Cart Fee:** Included in Green Fee. **Walking Policy:** Mandatory cart. **Walkability:** N/A. **Opened:** 1968. **Architect:** Dick Wilson/Joe Lee. **Season:** Year-round. **High:** March-Nov. **To obtain tee times:** Resort guests can make tee times when room reservations are guaranteed. Nonguests call 800 number 2 days in advance or golf shop day of play. **Miscellaneous:** Reduced fees (low season, twilight), discount packages, metal spikes, range (grass), club rentals, lodging, credit cards (MC, V, AE, D).

Reader Comments: A-1 golf, food, service, scenery ... Solid test in beautiful park ... This place is a 10 ... Beautiful course, service excellent ... Excellent ... . A beautiful course-great challenge ... Good course for low-handicapper ... Great fairways and greens, great time ... Bring your big dogs--long shots all the way ... Callaway Gardens in spring is a must ... Tough but beautiful course, worth the trip.

Special Notes: Also 9-hole Sky View Course.

CATEECHEE GOLF CLUB

PU-140 Cateechee Trail, Hartwell, 30643, Hart County, (706)856-4653, 20 miles W of Anderson, S.C. **E-mail:** cateechee@hartcom.net. **Web:** www.cateechee.com.

Holes: 18. **Yards:** 6,611/5,102. **Par:** 71/71. **Course Rating:** 70.8/67.9. **Slope:** 130/118. **Green Fee:** $34/$44. **Walking Policy:** Unrestricted walking. **Walkability:** 3. **Opened:** 1998. **Architect:** Mike Young. **Season:** Year-round. **High:** June-Aug. **Miscellaneous:** Reduced fees (twilight, seniors, juniors), range (grass), club rentals, credit cards (MC, V, AE).

Notes: Ranked 6th in 1999 Best New Affordable Public.

★★★ **CENTENNIAL GOLF CLUB**

PU-5225 Woodstock Rd., Acworth, 30102, Cobb County, (770)975-1000, 15 miles N of Atlanta. **Holes:** 18. **Yards:** 6,850/5,095. **Par:** 72/72. **Course Rating:** 73.1/69.5. **Slope:** 134/122. **Green Fee:** $42/$52. **Cart Fee:** Included in Green Fee. **Walking Policy:** Unrestricted walking. **Walkability:** 3. **Opened:** 1990. **Architect:** Larry Nelson/Jeff Brauer. **Season:** Year-round. **High:** April-Oct. **To obtain tee times:** Call 7 days in advance. **Miscellaneous:** Reduced fees (twilight, seniors), metal spikes, range (grass), club rentals, credit cards (MC, V, AE, D), beginner friendly (Nelson Seagraves Golf Academy).

Reader Comments: Great value ... Challenging but fair ... A few holes with blind shots ... The 18th is a nice finishing hole.

★★★½ THE CHAMPIONS CLUB OF ATLANTA

15135 Hopewell Rd., Alpharetta, 30201, Fulton County, (770)343-9700, 20 miles N of Atlanta.
Holes: 18. **Yards:** 6,725/4,470. **Par:** 72/72. **Course Rating:** 72.9/65.2. **Slope:** 131/108. **Green Fee:** $49/$65. **Cart Fee:** Included in Green Fee. **Walking Policy:** Mandatory cart. **Walkability:** 3. **Opened:** 1991. **Architect:** D.J. DeVictor//Steve Melnyk. **Season:** Year-round. **High:** March-Dec. **To obtain tee times:** Call up to 3 days in advance. **Miscellaneous:** Reduced fees (twilight, seniors, juniors), range (grass), club rentals, credit cards (MC, V, AE).
Reader Comments: Always in good shape, good greens ... Top-notch public course ... Good condition, nice people ... Good layout, good shape ... Good off-season twilight fees.

CHATEAU ELAN RESORT

R-6060 Golf Club Dr., Braselton, 30517, Barrow County, (770)271-6050, (800)233-9463, 45 miles NE of Atlanta. **E-mail:** jross@chateuelan.com. **Web:** wwwchateauelan.com.

★★★★ CHATEAU ELAN COURSE

Holes: 18. **Yards:** 7,030/5,092. **Par:** 71/71. **Course Rating:** 73.5/70.8. **Slope:** 136/124. **Green Fee:** $45/$77. **Cart Fee:** Included in Green Fee. **Walking Policy:** Walking at certain times. **Walkability:** 4. **Opened:** 1989. **Architect:** Denis Griffiths. **Season:** Year-round. **High:** April/Oct. **To obtain tee times:** Call up to 7 days in advance. Weekend tee times guaranteed with credit card. **Miscellaneous:** Reduced fees (weekdays, low season, resort guests, twilight), discount packages, range (grass), club rentals, lodging (300 rooms), credit cards (MC, V, AE, D). **Notes:** Golf Digest School site.
Reader Comments: Great course, nice service, great green ... If wine is as good as the course it must be fantastic ... Great place. Restaurants excellent ... Open fairways, fast greens ... Great resort courses-friendly staff ... Beautiful, fun to play ... Women-friendly–ball washers at women's tee box ... Winery tour after! Added both enjoyment and relaxation ... Wow! What a course!

★★★★ WOODLANDS COURSE

Holes: 18. **Yards:** 6,738/4,850. **Par:** 72/72. **Course Rating:** 72.6/68.5. **Slope:** 131/123. **Green Fee:** $45/$77. **Cart Fee:** Included in Green Fee. **Walking Policy:** Walking at certain times. **Walkability:** 5. **Opened:** 1996. **Architect:** Denis Griffiths. **Season:** Year-round. **High:** April/Oct. **To obtain tee times:** Call up to 7 days in advance. Weekend tee times guaranteed with credit card. **Miscellaneous:** Reduced fees (weekdays, low season, resort guests, twilight), discount packages, metal spikes, range (grass), club rentals, lodging (300 rooms), credit cards (MC, V, AE, D). **Notes:** Golf Digest School site.
Reader Comments: Lovely layout ... Outstanding course with excellent service ... Great place. Restaurants excellent ... Great course to work the ball ... Helpful staff ... A top-notch Georgia course ... Nice layout-hilly, but fair ... Good layout and change of elevation ... Good experience ... Interesting course, good facilities ... One of the best values in state.

★★★½ CHATTAHOOCHEE GOLF CLUB

PU-301 Tommy Aaron Dr., Gainesville, 30506, Hall County, (770)532-0066, 50 miles N of Atlanta.
Holes: 18. **Yards:** 6,700/5,000. **Par:** 72/72. **Course Rating:** 72.6/67.4. **Slope:** 127/113. **Green Fee:** $14/$39. **Cart Fee:** $10/person. **Walking Policy:** Walking at certain times. **Walkability:** 2. **Opened:** 1955. **Architect:** Robert Trent Jones. **Season:** Year-round. **High:** April-Sept. **To obtain tee times:** Call 3 days in advance. **Miscellaneous:** Reduced fees (twilight, juniors), metal spikes, range (grass), club rentals, credit cards (MC, V, AE).
Reader Comments: Good course, very traditional ... Hidden gem in Atlanta ... Walk it ... Very good layout No frills just great golf. Good for all levels ... Good value. A lot of doglegs, especially right to left so if you fade–bring some extra balls ... Wonderful old-style course.

★★★½ CHEROKEE RUN GOLF CLUB

SP-90,000 Centennial Olympic Pkwy., Conyers, 30208, Rockdale County, (770)785-7904, 20 miles E of Atlanta. **Web:** www.cherokeerun.com.
Holes: 18. **Yards:** 7,016/4,948. **Par:** 72/72. **Course Rating:** 74.9/70.0. **Slope:** 142/123. **Green Fee:** $40/$59. **Cart Fee:** Included in Green Fee. **Walking Policy:** Walking at certain times. **Walkability:** 5. **Opened:** 1995. **Architect:** Arnold Palmer/Ed Seay. **Season:** Year-round. **High:** March-Nov. **To obtain tee times:** Call 7 days in advance. **Miscellaneous:** Reduced fees (weekdays, twilight, seniors), discount packages, range (grass), club rentals, credit cards (MC, V, AE, D). **Notes:** Ranked 19th in 1999 Best in State
Reader Comments: Arnie's greens are tough. Good value for Atlanta. Bring you short game ... Very challenging Arnold Palmer course ... Outstanding layout ... One of the top five. Very challenging ... Tough course, great scenic layout ... Worth drive from Atlanta ... Absolutely beautiful & challenging–natural! ... Excellent layout/design ... Arnie made it tough-but fun ... Great greens, fast, very challenging.

GEORGIA

★★★★ CHICOPEE WOODS GOLF COURSE
PU-2515 Atlanta Hwy., Gainesville, 30504, Hall County, (770)534-7322, 30 miles NE of Atlanta.
Holes: 18. **Yards:** 7,040/5,001. **Par:** 72/72. **Course Rating:** 74.0/69.0. **Slope:** 135/117. **Green Fee:** $33/$33. **Cart Fee:** $12/person. **Walking Policy:** Unrestricted walking. **Walkability:** 4. **Opened:** 1991. **Architect:** Denis Griffiths. **Season:** Year-round. **High:** April-Sept. **To obtain tee times:** Call 3 days in advance at 9 a.m. **Miscellaneous:** Reduced fees (twilight), metal spikes, range (grass), club rentals, credit cards (MC, V, AE).

Reader Comments: Best value, always excellent shape ... Very accommodating to senior ... What's fun is playing new course—testing your handicap and your IQ on topography ... Best course for money ... Can be as challenging as you want ... Fun and challenging course ... Great layout. Outstanding bang for the buck. Recommend to anyone.

★★½ CITY CLUB MARIETTA
PU-510 Powder Spring St., Marietta, 30064, Cobb County, (770)528-4653, 15 miles N of Atlanta.
Holes: 18. **Yards:** 5,721/4,715. **Par:** 71/71. **Course Rating:** 67.3/67.5. **Slope:** 118/115. **Green Fee:** $39/$49. **Cart Fee:** Included in Green Fee. **Walking Policy:** Unrestricted walking. **Walkability:** 3. **Opened:** 1991. **Architect:** Mike Young. **Season:** Year-round. **High:** April-Sept. **To obtain tee times:** Call 7 days in advance. **Miscellaneous:** Reduced fees (weekdays, twilight, seniors, juniors), discount packages, range (grass/mats), club rentals, lodging, credit cards (MC, V, AE).

Reader Comments: Short, tight, decent value. 8th hole is best ... Not long, but challenging ... You can score on this course ... Always in good shape ... Short course, but a challenge.

★★★★ THE CLUB AT JONES CREEK
SP-4101 Hammond's Ferry Rd., Evans, 30809, Columbia County, (706)860-4228, 5 miles NW of Augusta.
Holes: 18. **Yards:** 7,008/5,430. **Par:** 72/72. **Course Rating:** 73.8/72.4. **Slope:** 137/130. **Green Fee:** $22/$37. **Cart Fee:** $11/person. **Walking Policy:** Walking at certain times. **Walkability:** 3. **Opened:** 1986. **Architect:** Rees Jones. **Season:** Year-round. **High:** April-Aug. **To obtain tee times:** Call on Friday for following week and weekend. 7 Days in advance. **Miscellaneous:** Reduced fees (seniors, juniors), metal spikes, range (grass), club rentals, credit cards (MC, V, AE).

Reader Comments: Nice layout, good greens ... Expensive, but a nice place to play ... Tight, tough and long ... Beats me every time, but I love it ... Hard on a hacker ... It'll make you sweat ... Errant balls lost easily.

★★★★ COBBLESTONE GOLF COURSE
PU-4200 Nance Rd., Acworth, 30101, Cobb County, (770)917-5151, 20 miles N of Atlanta.
Holes: 18. **Yards:** 6,759/5,400. **Par:** 71/71. **Course Rating:** 73.1/71.5. **Slope:** 140/129. **Green Fee:** $34/$49. **Cart Fee:** $10/person. **Walking Policy:** Walking at certain times. **Walkability:** 3. **Opened:** 1993. **Architect:** Ken Dye. **Season:** Year-round. **High:** March-Oct. **To obtain tee times:** Call 4 days in advance at 7:30 a.m. **Miscellaneous:** Reduced fees (weekdays, low season, twilight, seniors, juniors), metal spikes, range (grass), club rentals, credit cards (MC, V). **Notes:** Ranked 15th in 1999 Best in State.

Reader Comments: Super course, good value ... Very long from back tees, good conditions ... Very unique course, one of a kind ... Busy, busy, busy, course in good condition ... Bring all your clubs ... Beautiful scenery around lake ... Terrific finishing hole ... Good layout, accurate approach shot required. Good test ... Played here many times. Beautiful layout ... Most challenging of all ... Enjoyable course for the high handicapper. Extremely tough. Good! ... Best public daily fee course in Atlanta.

★★★½ COVINGTON PLANTATION GOLF CLUB
SP-10400 Covington Bypass SE, Covington, 30014, Newton County, (770)385-0064, 30 miles E of Atlanta.
Holes: 18. **Yards:** 6,906/4,803. **Par:** 72/72. **Course Rating:** N/A. **Slope:** N/A. **Green Fee:** $39/$49. **Cart Fee:** Included in Green Fee. **Walking Policy:** Walking at certain times. **Walkability:** 3. **Opened:** 1996. **Architect:** Desmond Muirhead. **Season:** Year-round. **High:** March-May; Sept.-Nov. **To obtain tee times:** Call golf shop. **Miscellaneous:** Reduced fees (twilight, seniors), metal spikes, range (grass/mats), club rentals, credit cards (MC, V, AE).

Reader Comments: Greens are outstanding ... Very nice course, good value ... New course, improving with time. Great shape ... Toughest par 3s in Georgia ... Must play at least once ... Nice people, excellent greens, narrow fairway ... I play often. Top 10 course ... Good track, fun, scenic ... Beautiful natural course ... Nice layout, needs maturing ... Tough course, excellent condition. Will be back.

★★★½ CROOKED CREEK GOLF CLUB
SP-3430 Highway 9, Alpharetta, 30004, Fulton County, (770)475-2300, 20 miles N of Atlanta.
Holes: 18. **Yards:** 6,917/4,985. **Par:** 72/72. **Course Rating:** 73.4/70.0. **Slope:** 141/120. **Green Fee:** $62/$85. **Cart Fee:** Included in Green Fee. **Walking Policy:** Mandatory cart. **Walkability:** 3. **Opened:** 1996. **Architect:** Michael Riley. **Season:** Year-round. **High:** May-Sept. **To obtain tee times:** Call 5 days in advance for weekdays and weekends. **Miscellaneous:** Reduced fees (twilight, juniors), range (grass), club rentals, credit cards (MC, V, AE).

GEORGIA

Reader Comments: Good layout, fair, with excellent bunker placement ... Several visually intriguing holes, design values well above average ... Very nice greens ... Great facility.

EAGLE CREEK GOLF CLUB
SP-7436 Georgia Hwy. 46, Statesboro, 30458, Bulloch County, (912)839-3933, 6 miles S of Statesboro.
Holes: 18. Yards: 6,700/5,200. Par: 72/72. Course Rating: 71.6/68.5. Slope: 124/114. Green Fee: $13/$16. Cart Fee: $12/person. Walking Policy: Walking at certain times. Walkability: 2. Opened: 1997. Architect: Paul Massey. Season: Year-round. High: March-May. To obtain tee times: Call 1 week in advance. Miscellaneous: Reduced fees (weekdays, twilight, seniors, juniors), range (grass), club rentals, credit cards (MC, V), beginner friendly (juniors, ladies).

★★★½ EAGLE WATCH GOLF CLUB
SP-3055 Eagle Watch Dr., Woodstock, 30189, Cherokee County, (770)591-1000, 25 miles N of Atlanta.
Holes: 18. Yards: 6,900/5,243. Par: 72/72. Course Rating: 72.6/68.9. Slope: 136/126. Green Fee: $40/$65. Cart Fee: Included in Green Fee. Walking Policy: Mandatory cart. Walkability: N/A. Opened: 1989. Architect: Arnold Palmer/Ed Seay. Season: Year-round. High: June-Aug. To obtain tee times: Call 7 days in advance. Miscellaneous: Reduced fees (weekdays, twilight, seniors, juniors), metal spikes, range (grass), club rentals, credit cards (MC, V, AE).

Reader Comments: Arnie, thanks ... Favorite course ... Excellent course, service ... Lots of doglegs ... The 18th is a great par 5 ... Excellent golf course.

★★★½ EMERALD POINTE GOLF CLUB AT LAKE LANIER ISLANDS
R-7000 Holiday Rd., Buford, 30518, Hall County, (770)945-8787, (800)768-5253, 35 miles NE of Atlanta. Web: www.lakelanierislands.com.
Holes: 18. Yards: 6,341/4,935. Par: 72/72. Course Rating: 70.1/68.3. Slope: 124/117. Green Fee: $27/$56. Cart Fee: $19/person. Walking Policy: Mandatory cart. Walkability: 4. Opened: 1989. Architect: Joe Lee. Season: Year-round. High: April-Oct. To obtain tee times: Call 14 days in advance. Miscellaneous: Reduced fees (weekdays, low season, twilight, seniors), discount packages, range (grass), club rentals, lodging, credit cards (MC, V, AE, D, Diners Club).

Reader Comments: Great course. As hard as you want to make it ... Short yardage but position and accuracy make it fun ... Excellent course in excellent shape. True putting. Beautiful layout ... Excellent course, views outstanding ... Lake views on 13 holes ... Solid par 5s ... Some very interesting holes and great scenery ... Definitely the Pebble Beach of the southeast !

★★★★ FIELDS FERRY GOLF CLUB
PU-581 Fields Ferry Dr., Calhoun, 30701, Gordon County, (706)625-5666, 50 miles N of Atlanta.
Holes: 18. Yards: 6,824/5,355. Par: 72/72. Course Rating: 71.8/70.5. Slope: 123/120. Green Fee: $13/$25. Cart Fee: $10/person. Walking Policy: Unrestricted walking. Walkability: 2. Opened: 1992. Architect: Arthur Davis. Season: Year-round. High: April-Oct. To obtain tee times: Call 3 days in advance. Miscellaneous: Reduced fees (weekdays, low season, twilight, seniors, juniors), metal spikes, range (grass/mats), club rentals, credit cards (MC, V).

Reader Comments: One of the best ... Rangers do an excellent job keeping pace of play ... Friendly and warm reception ... Beautiful links-style design ... The three finishing holes are as good as you'll find ... Great staff, fun ... Playing No. 16 is worth green fee ... Wide open, long, great greens, unique holes ... No matter what the weather, greens are always in great shape, a must play ... One of North Georgia's best secrets.

★★★½ THE FIELDS GOLF CLUB
SP-257 S. Smith Rd., LaGrange, 30240, Troup County, (706)845-7425, 30 miles N of Columbus. E-mail: fgilliii@aol.com. Web: www.teaweb.com/fields.
Holes: 18. Yards: 6,800/5,200. Par: 72/72. Course Rating: 71.4/67.4. Slope: 128/113. Green Fee: $21/$27. Cart Fee: $11/person. Walking Policy: Walking at certain times. Walkability: 4. Opened: 1990. Architect: Butch Gill. Season: Year-round. High: March-Oct. To obtain tee times: Call Monday a.m. prior to weekend. Miscellaneous: Reduced fees (weekdays, low season, twilight, seniors), discount packages, range (grass/mats), club rentals, credit cards (MC, V, AE).

Reader Comments: Good staff, challenging course, good greens ... Good Scottish-style course, not difficult ... Open and good for high handicapper ... Greens are large and fast ... Best winter fairways in Georgia ... You will use all of your clubs ... Great layout, very playable.

★★½ FIELDSTONE COUNTRY CLUB
SP-2720 Salem Rd. SE, Conyers, 30013, Rockdale County, (770)483-4372, 35 miles E of Atlanta.
Holes: 18. Yards: 6,412/5,268. Par: 72/72. Course Rating: 69.2/71.5. Slope: 118/119. Green Fee: $20/$30. Cart Fee: Included in Green Fee. Walking Policy: Walking at certain times. Walkability: 2. Opened: 1969. Architect: Harold Zink. Season: Year-round. High: April-Nov. To obtain tee times: Call in. Miscellaneous: Reduced fees (twilight), metal spikes, range (grass), club rentals, credit cards (MC, V).
Notes: Atlanta Seniors 1999.

GEORGIA

Reader Comments: Nice for the price ... A nice, basic golf course ... Good carts, challenging layout ... A walkable track ... Good greens, comfortable place to play.

FOLKSTON GOLF CLUB
PU-202 Country Club Rd., Folkston, 31537, Charlton County, (912)496-7155, 35 miles N of Jacksonville.
Holes: 18. **Yards:** 6,033/4,776. **Par:** 72/73. **Course Rating:** 67.9/66.4. **Slope:** 116/109. **Green Fee:** $9/$13. **Cart Fee:** $14/person. **Walking Policy:** Walking at certain times. **Walkability:** 2. **Opened:** 1958. **Architect:** Ed Mattson. **Season:** Year-round. **High:** Jan.-April. **Miscellaneous:** Reduced fees (seniors), range (grass), club rentals, credit cards (MC, V, AE).

★★★ FOREST HILLS GOLF CLUB
PM-1500 Comfort Rd., Augusta, 30909, Richmond County, (706)733-0001, 140 miles W of Atlanta.
Holes: 18. **Yards:** 6,875/4,875. **Par:** 72/72. **Course Rating:** 72.2/68.3. **Slope:** 126/116. **Green Fee:** $15/$22. **Cart Fee:** $12/person. **Walking Policy:** Unrestricted walking. **Walkability:** 2. **Opened:** 1926. **Architect:** Donald Ross. **Season:** Year-round. **High:** March-Nov. **To obtain tee times:** Call up to 7 days in advance. **Miscellaneous:** Reduced fees (juniors), metal spikes, range (grass), club rentals, credit cards (MC, V, AE, D).
Reader Comments: Very nice and fun course ... Great old layout ... Challenging, nice staff, excellent greens ... One of the better public courses in area ... Fun, traditional layout ... Good test of golf, tight fairways ... Friendly staff ... Straightforward course, easy to keep ball in play ... Historic Bobby Jones 1st 1930 win here.

FORSYTH COUNTRY CLUB
PU-400 Country Club Dr., Forsyth, 31029, Monroe County, (912)994-5328, 20 miles N of Macon.
Holes: 18. **Yards:** 6,051/4,521. **Par:** 72/72. **Course Rating:** 68.1/65.4. **Slope:** 112/107. **Green Fee:** $10/$12. **Cart Fee:** $20/. **Walking Policy:** Walking at certain times. **Walkability:** N/A. **Opened:** 1936. **Architect:** WPA. **Season:** Year-round. **To obtain tee times:** No tee times. **Miscellaneous:** Metal spikes, range (grass), club rentals.

★★ FOX CREEK GOLF CLUB
PU-1501 Windy Hill Rd, Smyrna, 30080, Cobb County, (770)435-1000, 10 miles N of Atlanta.
Holes: 18. **Yards:** 3,879/2,973. **Par:** 61/61. **Course Rating:** 60.0/57.5. **Slope:** 102/92. **Green Fee:** $23/$36. **Cart Fee:** Included in Green Fee. **Walking Policy:** Unrestricted walking. **Walkability:** 3. **Opened:** 1985. **Architect:** John LaFoy. **Season:** Year-round. **High:** Spring/Fall. **To obtain tee times:** Call up to 7 days in advance. **Miscellaneous:** Reduced fees (twilight, seniors, juniors), metal spikes, range (grass/mats), club rentals, credit cards (MC, V, AE, Diners Club, JCB).
Special Notes: 7 holes are par 4, rest are par 3.

★★½ FOXFIRE GOLF CLUB
SP-1916 Foxfire Dr., Vidalia, 30474, Montgomery County, (912)538-8670, 75 miles W of Savannah.
Holes: 18. **Yards:** 6,118/4,757. **Par:** 72/71. **Course Rating:** 69.3/67.5. **Slope:** 125/116. **Green Fee:** $21/$25. **Cart Fee:** Included in Green Fee. **Walking Policy:** Walking at certain times. **Walkability:** N/A. **Opened:** 1992. **Architect:** Jim Bivins. **Season:** Year-round. **High:** March-Sept. **To obtain tee times:** Call one day in advance. **Miscellaneous:** Reduced fees (weekdays, seniors, juniors), discount packages, metal spikes, range (grass), club rentals, credit cards (MC, V).
Reader Comments: Great course with lots of water.

★★½ FRANCIS LAKE GOLF CLUB
PU-5366 Golf Dr., Lake Park, 31636, Lowndes County, (912)559-7961, 12 miles S of Valdosta.
E-mail: leonard@datasys.net.
Holes: 18. **Yards:** 6,653/5,709. **Par:** 72/72. **Course Rating:** 71.4/70.1. **Slope:** 124/117. **Green Fee:** $22/$30. **Cart Fee:** Included in Green Fee. **Walking Policy:** Walking at certain times. **Walkability:** 1. **Opened:** 1973. **Architect:** Williard C. Byrd. **Season:** Year-round. **High:** Jan.-March. **To obtain tee times:** Call in advance. **Miscellaneous:** Reduced fees (weekdays, low season, resort guests, twilight, seniors, juniors), discount packages, metal spikes, range (mats), club rentals, credit cards (MC, V, AE).
Reader Comments: Beautiful layout with very knowledgeable staff ... The lake view on the 17th was a nice surprise considering the location of the golf course ... Open front nine, tight back nine ... Good location ... A great value!.

★★★½ GEORGIA NATIONAL GOLF CLUB
SP-1715 Lake Dow Rd., McDonough, 30252, Henry County, (770)914-9994, 30 miles S of Atlanta.
Holes: 18. **Yards:** 6,874/5,005. **Par:** 71/71. **Course Rating:** 73.3/68.6. **Slope:** 132/117. **Green Fee:** $31/$55. **Cart Fee:** Included in Green Fee. **Walking Policy:** Walking at certain times. **Walkability:** 5. **Opened:** 1994. **Architect:** Denis Griffiths. **Season:** Year-round. **High:** April-Sept.

GEORGIA

To obtain tee times: Call 5 days in advance. **Miscellaneous:** Reduced fees (weekdays, resort guests, seniors, juniors), range (grass), club rentals, credit cards (MC, V, AE, D).
Reader Comments: Bring A-game. A championship course ... Great variety of holes ... A challenging course, but a lot of fun ... Good design, good condition, nice greens ... A memorable experience ... Great test for all golfers, awesome greens, beautiful course ... Very good practice facilities ... Very enjoyable to play ... Green are quick and true—a great course.

★★★★ GEORGIA VETERANS STATE PARK GOLF CSE. *Value+, Pace*
PM-2315 Hwy. 280 W., Cordele, 31015, Crisp County, (912)276-2377, 45 miles S of Macon.
Holes: 18. **Yards:** 7,088/5,171. **Par:** 72/72. **Course Rating:** 72.1/73.5. **Slope:** 130/124. **Green Fee:** $15/$20. **Cart Fee:** $16/cart. **Walking Policy:** Unrestricted walking. **Walkability:** 1.
Opened: 1990. **Architect:** Denis Griffiths. **Season:** Year-round. **High:** April-Sept. **To obtain tee times:** Tee times accepted daily. **Miscellaneous:** Reduced fees (weekdays, twilight, seniors, juniors), discount packages, metal spikes, range (grass), club rentals, lodging, credit cards (MC, V, AE, D).
Reader Comments: A favorite ... Long and open, lots of fun ... Doesn't get better for the money ... Large greens in good condition ... Rolling, Scottish-like fairways ... Nice clubhouse and staff ... Long and tough ... Well-designed ... Good value ... Great state park golf ... A very friendly, playable course! ... No. 3 is one of my favorite holes around. Excellent course.

★★★★ GOLD CREEK RESORT
PU-1 Gold Creek Dr./P. O. Box 1357, Dawsonville, 30534, Dawson County, (770)844-1327, 45 miles N of Atlanta. **Web:** www.goldcreek.com.
Holes: 27. **Yards:** 6,924/4,760. **Par:** 72/72. **Course Rating:** 73.3/67.2. **Slope:** 130/106. **Green Fee:** $52/$68. **Cart Fee:** Included in Green Fee. **Walking Policy:** Walking at certain times.
Walkability: 3. **Opened:** 1995. **Architect:** Mike Young/D. J. Devictor. **Season:** Year-round. **High:** March-Nov. **To obtain tee times:** 5 days in advance. **Miscellaneous:** Reduced fees (low season, twilight, seniors, juniors), discount packages, range (grass), club rentals, lodging (74 rooms), credit cards (MC, V, AE).
Reader Comments: A true gem in the mountain ... Need every shot in the bag ... Nice course ... Tough track, good test ... Great greens! Scenic ... Par 3s especially good ... Great new course ... Fastest greens this side of Augusta National ... Dramatic elevation changes ... Superb condition ... Good course design ... A fun, pretty mountain course, great value ... Outstanding.

★★★½ THE GOLF CLUB AT BRADSHAW FARM
PU-3030 Bradshaw Club Dr., Woodstock, 30188, Cherokee County, (770)592-2222, 20 miles N of Atlanta.
Holes: 18. **Yards:** 6,838/4,972. **Par:** 72/72. **Course Rating:** 72.7/68.4. **Slope:** 134/116. **Green Fee:** $35/$65. **Cart Fee:** $12/person. **Walking Policy:** Unrestricted walking. **Walkability:** 5.
Opened: 1995. **Architect:** Grant Wencel. **Season:** Year-round. **High:** March-Nov. **To obtain tee times:** Call up to 7 days in advance. **Miscellaneous:** Reduced fees (weekdays, low season, twilight, seniors, juniors), range (grass), club rentals, credit cards (MC, V, AE, D), beginner friendly.
Reader Comments: Beautiful scenery, bring many balls ... They announce you on the first tee, nice ... A fun course ... Challenging layout ... Fun mountain course ... Hilly front nine, flat back ... Spectacular views on front nine ... Great layout, huge greens ... Dramatic opening tee shot.

THE GOLF CLUB AT CUSCOWILLA
SP-354 Cuscowilla Dr., Eatonton, 31024, Putnam County, (706)485-0094, 90 miles E of Atlanta.
Holes: 18. **Yards:** 6,847/5,384. **Par:** 70/72. **Course Rating:** 72.2/69.9. **Slope:** 132/123. **Green Fee:** $75/$90. **Cart Fee:** $15/person. **Walking Policy:** Unrestricted walking. **Walkability:** 1.
Opened: 1998. **Architect:** Bill Coore/Ben Crenshaw. **Season:** year-round. **High:** April-Oct.
Miscellaneous: Reduced fees (resort guests, juniors), range (grass), caddies, club rentals, lodging (30 rooms), credit cards (MC, V, AE, D).
Notes: Ranked 7th in 1999 Best New Upscale Public.

★★★ GOSHEN PLANTATION COUNTRY CLUB
SP-1601 Goshen Clubhouse Dr., Augusta, 30906, Richmond County, (706)793-1168.
Holes: 18. **Yards:** 6,722/5,269. **Par:** 72/72. **Course Rating:** 72.5/70.3. **Slope:** 131/125. **Green Fee:** $24/$37. **Cart Fee:** Included in Green Fee. **Walking Policy:** Walking at certain times.
Walkability: N/A. **Opened:** 1970. **Architect:** Ellis Maples. **Season:** Year-round. **High:** March-Oct. **To obtain tee times:** Call two days in advance. Members, seven days in advance.
Miscellaneous: Reduced fees (weekdays, low season, twilight, seniors, juniors), metal spikes, range (grass), club rentals, credit cards (MC, V).
Reader Comments: Excellent course—not very long, but fun and tough ... Fairways and greens looked great! ... Course well-maintained ... Staff always helpful, great snack bar ... Very large and fast greens ... Designed for a good iron player.

★★★½ HAMILTON MILL GOLF COURSE
PU-1995 Hamilton Mill Pkwy., Dacula, 30211, Gwinnett County, (770)945-4653, 10 miles SE of Buford. **Web:** www.hamiltonmillgolf.com.

GEORGIA

Holes: 18. **Yards:** 6,810/4,744. **Par:** 72/72. **Course Rating:** 73.7/68.4. **Slope:** 137/116. **Green Fee:** $57/$72. **Cart Fee:** Included in Green Fee. **Walking Policy:** Unrestricted walking. **Walkability:** 5. **Opened:** 1995. **Architect:** Gene Bates/Fred Couples. **Season:** Year-round. **High:** May-Sept. **To obtain tee times:** Call up to 5 days in advance. **Miscellaneous:** Reduced fees (weekdays, twilight, juniors), range (grass), club rentals, credit cards (MC, V, AE, D).
Reader Comments: Freddie did a nice job ... Awesome track ... Greens extremely fast and undulating ... Each hole has character. Great use of the terrain ... Couples' best! ... Cross, fairway bunkers keep your attention ... A must play ... Great tough track, good practice area ... Numerous doglegs ... Best 18th hole in the area ... Nice clubhouse amenities ... Very hilly layout, good greens ... Great experience.

★★★★ HAMPTON CLUB
R-100 Tabbystone, St. Simons Island, 31522, Glynn County, (912)634-0255, 70 miles N of Jacksonville, FL. **E-mail:** hampton/@gate.net. **Web:** www.hamptonclub.com.
Holes: 18. **Yards:** 6,400/5,233. **Par:** 72/72. **Course Rating:** 71.4/71.0. **Slope:** 130/123. **Green Fee:** N/A/$58. **Cart Fee:** $18/person. **Walking Policy:** Mandatory cart. **Walkability:** 2. **Opened:** 1989. **Architect:** Joe Lee. **Season:** Year-round. **High:** March-April. **To obtain tee times:** Call 2 days in advance. **Miscellaneous:** Reduced fees (resort guests, juniors), discount packages, range (grass), club rentals, credit cards (MC, V, AE, D).
Reader Comments: Marsh holes very scenic ... Well done ... Classy operation ... The nines are very different ... Gorgeous clubhouse ... An entertaining track ... Watch out for the bugs in May ... Beautiful marsh views with live oaks and Spanish moss ... Accommodating staff ... The golf package is a good deal ... Variety of holes–watch out for gators! ... Great test of golf.

★★★★ HARBOR CLUB
SP-One Club Dr., Greensboro, 30642, Greene County, (706)453-4414, (800)505-4653, 70 miles SE of Atlanta.
Holes: 18. **Yards:** 7,014/5,207. **Par:** 72/72. **Course Rating:** 73.7/70.2. **Slope:** 135/123. **Green Fee:** $29/$57. **Cart Fee:** $12/person. **Walking Policy:** Walking at certain times. **Walkability:** 3. **Opened:** 1991. **Architect:** Tom Weiskopf/Jay Morrish. **Season:** Year-round. **High:** March-Oct. **To obtain tee times:** Call 7 days in advance. **Miscellaneous:** Reduced fees (weekdays, low season, resort guests, seniors, juniors), discount packages, range (grass), club rentals, lodging, credit cards (MC, V, AE).
Reader Comments: Best-kept secret in Georgia ... Beautiful lake views ... Very nice course. Friendly staff ... Mickey Mantle's old hideout ... Will play again ... First-class operation ... An outstanding course in a beautiful setting ... Playable for all skill levels ... Friendly staff ... Fairways and greens are well-maintained ... Fine practice area ... Elevation changes over water are exciting ... Great layout.

★★★½ HARD LABOR CREEK STATE PARK GOLF COURSE
PU-1400 Knox Chapel Road, Rutledge, 30663, Morgan County, (706)557-3006, 45 miles E of Atlanta.
Holes: 18. **Yards:** 6,444/4,854. **Par:** 72/75. **Course Rating:** 71.5/68.6. **Slope:** 129/123. **Green Fee:** $21/$26. **Cart Fee:** $12/person. **Walking Policy:** Unrestricted walking. **Walkability:** N/A. **Opened:** 1967. **Architect:** O.C. Jones. **Season:** Year-round. **High:** April-Oct. **To obtain tee times:** Call up to 14 days in advance. **Miscellaneous:** Reduced fees (seniors, juniors), discount packages, metal spikes, range (grass), club rentals, lodging, credit cards (MC, V, AE, D).
Reader Comments: Excellent state park course ... Glad I played it ... Interesting layout, challenging ... Good value ... Old course, you'll use every club in the bag ... John Daly would love distance ... Great fun for outings, cabins provide a camp-like atmosphere ... Good state park course, variety of looks/elevations ... State park, great layout, stop on your way to Augusta.

★★½ HENDERSON GOLF CLUB
PU-1 A1 Henderson Dr., Savannah, 31419, Chatham County, (912)920-4653, 16 miles S of Savannah.
Holes: 18. **Yards:** 6,650/4,788. **Par:** 71/71. **Course Rating:** 72.4/67.7. **Slope:** 136/115. **Green Fee:** $30/$40. **Cart Fee:** Included in Green Fee. **Walking Policy:** Walking at certain times. **Walkability:** 2. **Opened:** 1995. **Architect:** Mike Young. **Season:** Year-round. **High:** March-Oct. **To obtain tee times:** Call 10 days in advance. **Miscellaneous:** Reduced fees (seniors, juniors), discount packages, metal spikes, range (grass), club rentals, credit cards (MC, V, AE), beginner friendly.
Reader Comments: Gets better, day after day–holes 9 & 18, wow! ... Good layout ... Nicely designed ... Good place to play.

★★★★ THE HERITAGE GOLF CLUB
SP-4445 Britt Rd., Tucker, 30084, Gwinnett County, (770)493-4653, 12 miles N of Downtown Atlanta. **Web:** www.heritagegolfclub.com.
Holes: 27. **Yards:** 6,903/5,153. **Par:** 72/72. **Course Rating:** 73.6/68.8. **Slope:** 145/120. **Green Fee:** $90/$90. **Cart Fee:** Included in Green Fee. **Walking Policy:** Mandatory cart. **Walkability:** 4. **Opened:** 1996. **Architect:** Mike Young. **Season:** Year-round. **High:** March-April June-Nov. **To**

obtain tee times: Tee times are taken 10 days in advance. **Miscellaneous:** Range (grass), club rentals, credit cards (MC, V, AE, D).
Notes: Ranked 20th in 1999 Best in State.
Reader Comments: Wow ... .Hard but fun! ... Great golf course ... Unique and yet simply lovely ... Toughest slope rating around ... Nice new course, fun to play.

★★★½ HIGHLAND GOLF CLUB
SP-2271 Flat Shoals Rd., Conyers, 30208, Rockdale County, (770)483-4235, 12 miles E of Atlanta.
Holes: 18. **Yards:** 6,817/5,383. **Par:** 72/72. **Course Rating:** 72.7/71.0. **Slope:** 128/118. **Green Fee:** $36/$46. **Cart Fee:** Included in Green Fee. **Walking Policy:** Mandatory cart. **Walkability:** 2. **Opened:** 1961. **Architect:** Neil Edwards. **Season:** Year-round. **High:** April-Nov. **To obtain tee times:** Call up to 5 days in advance. **Miscellaneous:** Reduced fees (seniors, juniors), discount packages, range (grass/mats), club rentals, credit cards (MC, V), beginner friendly.
Reader Comments: Nice layout, worth drive from Atlanta ... Great greens ... Not too tough, hard par 3s ... Fun course, 15th is great one-shotter over water ... Nice people ... Picturesque with lots of wildlife ... Wide open, hard to lose a ball course ... Worth playing again ... Not too demanding, but fun and reasonable ... Good overall course.

★★★ HOUSTON LAKE COUNTRY CLUB
SP-2323 Highway 127, Perry, 31069, Houston County, (912)987-3243, 20 miles S of Macon.
Holes: 18. **Yards:** 6,800/5,100. **Par:** 72/72. **Course Rating:** 71.8/70.0. **Slope:** 132/122. **Green Fee:** $30/$37. **Cart Fee:** Included in Green Fee. **Walking Policy:** Unrestricted walking. **Walkability:** 1. **Opened:** 1966. **Architect:** O.C. Jones. **Season:** Year-round. **To obtain tee times:** Call golf shop. **Miscellaneous:** Reduced fees (juniors), discount packages, range (grass/mats), club rentals, credit cards (MC, V, AE).
Reader Comments: Great place to play ... Greens are always nice ... Relatively flat course ... Challenging test ... Good shape, nice people ... Tight shotmaker's course ... Great layout. Great staff. Great finishing hole.

★★★½ INNSBRUCK RESORT & GOLF CLUB
Bahn Innsbruck, Helen, 30545, White County, (706)878-2100, (800)642-2709, 65 miles NE of Atlanta.
Holes: 18. **Yards:** 6,748/5,174. **Par:** 72/72. **Course Rating:** 72.4/N/A. **Slope:** 136/118. **Green Fee:** $30/$40. **Cart Fee:** Included in Green Fee. **Walking Policy:** Mandatory cart. **Walkability:** 5. **Opened:** 1987. **Architect:** Bill Watts. **Season:** Year-round. **High:** April-Oct. **To obtain tee times:** Resort guests may call any time. **Miscellaneous:** Reduced fees (low season, resort guests, twilight, seniors, juniors), discount packages, metal spikes, range (grass), club rentals, lodging, credit cards (MC, V, AE).
Reader Comments: Fastest greens in the South ... Mountain course that is fun! Great views! ... Fun, hilly course ... Nicely designed course ... Tough test, but fair ... Fun and creative holes ... The 15th is a great par 3 ... Deer and wild turkeys roam the fairways ... Tight, scenic ... Great people, fantastic views.

★★ INTERNATIONAL CITY MUNICIPAL GOLF COURSE
PM-100 Sandy Run Lane, Warner Robins, 31088, Houston County, (912)922-3892, 15 miles S of Macon.
Holes: 18. **Yards:** 6,071/4,425. **Par:** 71/71. **Course Rating:** 66.4/66.7. **Slope:** 109/110. **Green Fee:** $10/$14. **Cart Fee:** $10/person. **Walking Policy:** Unrestricted walking. **Walkability:** 2. **Opened:** 1957. **Architect:** Lew Burnette/Arnie Smith. **Season:** Year-round. **High:** Aug.-Dec. **To obtain tee times:** Reservations accepted for holiday and weekends only. Must have 3 or 4 players in group. **Miscellaneous:** Reduced fees (low season, seniors, juniors), discount packages, metal spikes, range (grass), club rentals, credit cards (MC, V), beginner friendly (junior program).

JEKYLL ISLAND GOLF RESORT
★★★½ GREAT DUNES COURSE
R-Beachview Dr., Jekyll Island, 31527, Glynn County, (912)635-2170, (877)4-jekyll, 70 miles N of Jacksonville, FL. **E-mail:** bhendrix@jekyllisland.net. **Web:** www.jekyllisland.com.
Holes: 9. **Yards:** 3,298/2,570. **Par:** 36/36. **Course Rating:** 70.9/N/A. **Slope:** 126/126. **Green Fee:** $12/$29. **Cart Fee:** $14/. **Walking Policy:** Unrestricted walking. **Walkability:** 1. **Opened:** 1898. **Architect:** Dick Wilson/Joe Lee. **Season:** Year-round. **High:** Feb.-April. **To obtain tee times:** May call anytime up to 1 year in advance. **Miscellaneous:** Reduced fees (low season, resort guests, twilight, juniors), discount packages, metal spikes, club rentals, credit cards (MC, V, AE, D).
Reader Comments: An example of how golf used to be! ... Good to play and a great value ... Wind is a factor, 9 holes by the ocean ... Its history earns it a 4-star rating.

★★★ INDIAN MOUND COURSE
R-322 Captain Wylly Rd., Jekyll Island, 31527, Glynn County, (912)635-2368, (877)4-jekyll, 70 miles N of Jacksonville, FL. **E-mail:** bhendrix@jekyllisland.net. **Web:** www.jekyllisland.com.

Holes: 18. **Yards:** 6,596/5,345. **Par:** 72/72. **Course Rating:** 74.3/70.0. **Slope:** 127/122. **Green Fee:** $26/$26. **Cart Fee:** $14/person. **Walking Policy:** Unrestricted walking. **Walkability:** 1. **Opened:** 1975. **Architect:** Dick Wilson/Joe Lee. **Season:** Year-round. **High:** Feb.-April. **To obtain tee times:** May call anytime up to 1 year in advance. **Miscellaneous:** Reduced fees (twilight, juniors), discount packages, metal spikes, range (grass), club rentals, credit cards (MC, V, AE, D).
Reader Comments: Good to play and a great value ... Great place to play 'til you drop ... Open and long ... Well-managed and maintained ... Excellent for golf vacation ... Treated like longtime friends ... Flat, good walking course ... Great vacation getaway.

★★★½ **OLEANDER COURSE**
R-322 Captain Wylly Rd., Jekyll Island, 31527, Glynn County, (912)635-2368, (877)4jekyll, 60 miles N of Jacksonville, FL. **E-mail:** bhendrix@jekyllisland.net. **Web:** www.jekyllisland.com.
Holes: 18. **Yards:** 6,679/5,654. **Par:** 72/72. **Course Rating:** 72.8/72.6. **Slope:** 128/124. **Green Fee:** $26/$26. **Cart Fee:** $14/person. **Walking Policy:** Unrestricted walking. **Walkability:** 1. **Opened:** 1964. **Architect:** Dick Wilson/Joe Lee. **Season:** Year-round. **High:** Feb.-April. **To obtain tee times:** May call anytime up to 1 year in advance. **Miscellaneous:** Reduced fees (low season, resort guests, twilight, juniors), discount packages, metal spikes, range (grass), club rentals, credit cards (MC, V, AE, D).
Reader Comments: Good to play and a great value ... Great vacation getaway ... Friendly service ... Beautiful scenery–challenging ... Great course to walk! ... A bargain in fall/winter ... Good holes, fun and fair test of golf ... Nice public course ... Oldest of Jekyll courses–interesting ... Bermuda greens, nice course, beware the alligators ... We had a great time–we were treated great too.

★★★½ **PINE LAKES COURSE**
R-322 Captain Wylly Rd., Jekyll Island, 31527, Glynn County, (912)635-2368, (877)4jekyll, 70 miles N of Jacksonville, FL. **E-mail:** bhendrix@jekyllisland.net. **Web:** www.jekyllisland.com.
Holes: 18. **Yards:** 6,802/5,742. **Par:** 72/72. **Course Rating:** 72.2/71.9. **Slope:** 130/124. **Green Fee:** $26/$26. **Cart Fee:** $14/person. **Walking Policy:** Walking at certain times. **Walkability:** 1. **Opened:** 1968. **Architect:** Dick Wilson/Joe Lee. **Season:** Year-round. **High:** Feb.-April. **To obtain tee times:** May call anytime up to 1 year in advance. **Miscellaneous:** Reduced fees (low season, resort guests, twilight, juniors), discount packages, metal spikes, range (grass), club rentals, credit cards (MC, V, AE, D).
Reader Comments: Best value in Georgia ... Good to play and a great value ... Friendly pro shop staff ... Interesting wooded course ... . Great vacation getaway ... Play moved very well ... Longest and tightest of Jekyll courses.

★★★ **LAKE ARROWHEAD COUNTRY CLUB**
SP-L.A. Station 20, 598 Country Club Drive, Waleska, 30183, Cherokee County, (770)479-5500, 55 miles NW of Atlanta.
Holes: 18. **Yards:** 6,400/4,468. **Par:** 72/71. **Course Rating:** 71.2/66.3. **Slope:** 140/104. **Green Fee:** $32/$49. **Cart Fee:** Included in Green Fee. **Walking Policy:** Mandatory cart. **Walkability:** 5. **Opened:** 1975. **Season:** Year-round. **High:** May-Aug. **To obtain tee times:** Resort guests may reserve tee times at time of reservation; all others call 2 days in advance. **Miscellaneous:** Reduced fees (weekdays, resort guests, juniors), discount packages, metal spikes, range (grass), club rentals, lodging, credit cards (MC, V, AE, D, Diners Club).
Reader Comments: Excellent layout ... Beautiful setting ... Fine mountain course, good value, friendly staff ... Great fun ... Hilly mountain layout ... Beautiful scenic course ... Challenging ... Great layout ... Pretty lakeside holes ... Getting better in condition ... Most spectacular I ever played!.

★★★½ **LAKE BLACKSHEAR GOLF & COUNTRY CLUB**
PU-2078 Antioch Church Rd., Cordele, 31015, Crisp County, (912)535-4653, 24 miles NE of Albany.
Holes: 18. **Yards:** 6,930/5,372. **Par:** 72/72. **Course Rating:** 71.6/70.0. **Slope:** 129/120. **Green Fee:** $14/$19. **Cart Fee:** $9/person. **Walking Policy:** Walking at certain times. **Walkability:** 3. **Opened:** 1995. **Architect:** Don McMillan/Ray Jensen/Don Marbury. **Season:** Year-round. **High:** Spring/Fall. **To obtain tee times:** Call 24 hours in advance. **Miscellaneous:** Reduced fees (low season), metal spikes, range (grass), club rentals, credit cards (MC, V, AE)
Reader Comments: Good local course. Cheap green fees ... Enjoyable for average golfer ... Nice links-style layout ... Worth playing again ... Long course. Fun and challenging to play. Will visit often.

★★★ **LAKESIDE COUNTRY CLUB**
PU-3600 Old Fairburn Rd., Atlanta, 30331, Fulton County, (404)344-3629, 10 miles W of Atlanta.
Holes: 18. **Yards:** 6,522/5,279. **Par:** 71/71. **Course Rating:** 71.4/70.7. **Slope:** 127/121. **Green Fee:** $20/$45. **Cart Fee:** Included in Green Fee. **Walking Policy:** Mandatory cart. **Walkability:** 3. **Opened:** 1962. **Architect:** George Cobb. **Season:** Year-round. **High:** March-May. **To obtain tee times:** Call up to 14 days in advance. **Miscellaneous:** Reduced fees (weekdays, low sea-

son, twilight, seniors), discount packages, range (grass/mats), club rentals, credit cards (MC, V, AE), beginner friendly (lessons from pro).
Reader Comments: Fun course—a bargain in Atlanta ... Great shape, close to airport ... Excellent value - old-style course ... Nice people ... Surprisingly relaxing for a public course.

LAKEVIEW GOLF CLUB
SP-510 Golf Club Rd., Blackshear, 31516, Pierce County, (912)449-4411, 100 miles NE of Savannah.
Holes: 18. **Yards:** 6,505/4,928. **Par:** 72/72. **Course Rating:** 69.7/69.5. **Slope:** 113/113. **Green Fee:** $15/$15. **Cart Fee:** $8/person. **Walking Policy:** Unrestricted walking. **Walkability:** 2. **Opened:** 1971. **Season:** Year-round. **High:** Year-round. **To obtain tee times:** First come, first served. **Miscellaneous:** Metal spikes, range (grass), club rentals, beginner friendly.

LANDINGS GOLF CLUB
SP-309 Statham's Way, Warner Robins, 31088, Houston County, (912)923-5222, 15 miles SE of Macon.
Holes: 27. **Green Fee:** $16/$23. **Cart Fee:** $10/person. **Walking Policy:** Unrestricted walking. **Walkability:** N/A. **Opened:** 1987. **Architect:** Tom Clark. **Season:** Year-round. **High:** March-Dec. **To obtain tee times:** Members call 9 days in advance. Nonmembers call 5 days in advance. **Miscellaneous:** Reduced fees (weekdays), discount packages, metal spikes, range (grass), club rentals, credit cards (MC, V, AE)
★★★½ **BLUFF/CREEK**
Yards: 6,671/5,157. **Par:** 72/73. **Course Rating:** 71.9/70.6. **Slope:** 130/118..
Reader Comments: Very nice, great time ... Good layout, well-kept greens ... A good test of golf ... Enjoyable course ... A good variety of holes ... Nice layout ... Excellent course.
★★★½ **TRESTLE/BLUFF**
Yards: 6,998/5,481. **Par:** 72/74. **Course Rating:** 73.1/72.0. **Slope:** 133/119.
Reader Comments: A good course ... The 14th is a killer ... A nice pro shop ... Long layout.
★★★½ **TRESTLE/CREEK**
Yards: 6,819/5,174. **Par:** 72/73. **Course Rating:** 72.6/71.8. **Slope:** 131/121.
Reader Comments: All 9s equal in play ... Excellent practice area.

★★★½ LANE CREEK GOLF CLUB
PU-1201 Club Dr., Bishop, 30621, Oconee County, (706)769-6699, (800)842-6699, 8 miles S of Athens.
Holes: 18. **Yards:** 6,752/5,293. **Par:** 72/72. **Course Rating:** 71.9/68.4. **Slope:** 130/115. **Green Fee:** $23/$43. **Cart Fee:** Included in Green Fee. **Walking Policy:** Walking at certain times. **Walkability:** 3. **Opened:** 1992. **Architect:** Mike Young. **Season:** Year-round. **High:** April-June. **To obtain tee times:** Call up to 7 days in advance. **Miscellaneous:** Reduced fees (weekdays, twilight, seniors, juniors), range (grass/mats), club rentals, credit cards (MC, V, D).
Reader Comments: Short but interesting golf course ... Requires some thinking ... Course enjoyable for middle handicap player ... Tough to find but worth the trip ... Outstanding potential.

★★★ LAURA WALKER GOLF COURSE
PU-5500 Laura Walker Rd., Waycross, 31503, Ware County, (912)285-6154, 68 miles N of Jacksonville.
Holes: 18. **Yards:** 6,719/5,536. **Par:** 72/72. **Course Rating:** 71.9/66.6. **Slope:** 122/106. **Green Fee:** $17/$20. **Cart Fee:** $9/person. **Walking Policy:** Unrestricted walking. **Walkability:** 1. **Opened:** 1996. **Architect:** Steve Burns. **Season:** Year-round. **To obtain tee times:** Call (915)285-6155. **Miscellaneous:** Reduced fees (weekdays, seniors, juniors), range (grass), club rentals, credit cards (MC, V, AE, D).
Reader Comments: Really impressed me ... Very good for a public ... Best public course I have ever played ... Very enjoyable new course ... Hidden gem.

LAUREL SPRINGS GOLF CLUB
SP-6400 Golf Club Dr., Suwanee, 30174, Gwinett County, (770)884-0064, 20 miles N of Atlanta.
Holes: 18. **Yards:** 6,804/5,119. **Par:** 71/71. **Course Rating:** 72.3/69.3. **Slope:** 137/125. **Green Fee:** $65/$85. **Cart Fee:** Included in Green Fee. **Walking Policy:** Walking at certain times. **Walkability:** 4. **Opened:** 1998. **Architect:** Jack Nicklaus. **Season:** year-round. **High:** March-Oct. **To obtain tee times:** Call Pro Shop. **Miscellaneous:** Reduced fees (twilight, juniors), range (grass), club rentals, credit cards (MC, V, AE), beginner friendly (full instructional facility).

★★½ THE LINKS GOLF CLUB
PM-340 Hewell Rd., Jonesboro, 30238, Fayette County, (770)461-5100, 3 miles E of Jonesboro.
Holes: 18. **Yards:** 6,376/4,398. **Par:** 70/70. **Course Rating:** 69.4/64.7. **Slope:** 118/111. **Green Fee:** $16/$21. **Cart Fee:** $11/person. **Walking Policy:** Walking at certain times. **Walkability:** 2. **Opened:** 1991. **Season:** Year-round. **High:** June. **To obtain tee times:** Call golf shop. **Miscellaneous:** Reduced fees (twilight, seniors), range (grass), club rentals, credit cards (MC, V), beginner friendly (wee links).

GEORGIA

Reader Comments: Outstanding value ... Very nice course, excellent service ... Fun course to play ... Best course for the price ... Great staff.

★★ LITTLE FISHING CREEK GOLF CLUB

PM-Highway 22 W., Milledgeville, 31061, Baldwin County, (912)445-0796, 35 miles E of Macon.
Holes: 18. **Yards:** 6,718/5,509. **Par:** 72/73. **Course Rating:** 72.4/73.6. **Slope:** 121/121. **Green Fee:** $5/$9. **Cart Fee:** $8/person. **Walking Policy:** Unrestricted walking. **Walkability:** 5. **Opened:** 1981. **Season:** Year-round. **High:** March-June. **To obtain tee times:** Call 9the Tuesday prior to the weekend you wish to play. **Miscellaneous:** Reduced fees (twilight, seniors, juniors), metal spikes, range (grass), club rentals, credit cards (MC, V, AE, D).

★★½ LITTLE MOUNTAIN GOLF COURSE

PU-1850 Little Mountain Rd., Ellenwood, 30294, Henry County, (770)981-7921, 15 miles SE of Atlanta.
Holes: 18. **Yards:** 5,771/4,832. **Par:** 72/72. **Course Rating:** N/A. **Slope:** N/A. **Green Fee:** $14/$21. **Cart Fee:** $22/cart. **Walking Policy:** Unrestricted walking. **Walkability:** 3. **Opened:** 1969. **Season:** Year-round. **High:** April-Sept. **To obtain tee times:** Call golf shop. **Miscellaneous:** Reduced fees (twilight, seniors), range (mats), club rentals, credit cards (MC, V).
Reader Comments: Very enjoyable course, short, friendly, good rates ... Nice layout and friendly staff ... Short track, well-maintained, easy walking ... I hope it stays a secret.

★★½ LOST PLANTATION

1 Clubhouse Dr., Rincon, 31326, Effingham County, (912)826-2092, 20 miles N of Savannah.
Holes: 18. **Yards:** 6,800/5,250. **Par:** 72/72. **Course Rating:** 72.4/69.1. **Slope:** 127/123. **Green Fee:** $18/$32. **Cart Fee:** Included in Green Fee. **Walking Policy:** Walking at certain times. **Walkability:** 2. **Opened:** 1988. **Architect:** Ward Northrup. **Season:** Year-round. **To obtain tee times:** Call up to 7 days in advance. **Miscellaneous:** Reduced fees (weekdays, low season, twilight, seniors, juniors), discount packages, range (grass), club rentals, credit cards (MC, V, D).
Reader Comments: Always enjoyed the course and people ... Good conditions ... Lots of marsh, but well worth it.

MAPLE CREEK GOLF COURSE

PU-1735 Cashtown Rd., Bremen, 30110, Haralson County, (770)537-4172, 40 miles W of Atlanta.
Holes: 18. **Yards:** 5,404/4,454. **Par:** 70/70. **Course Rating:** 65.6/65.3. **Slope:** 114/112. **Green Fee:** $10/$17. **Cart Fee:** $8/. **Walking Policy:** Unrestricted walking. **Walkability:** N/A. **Opened:** 1993. **Season:** Year-round. **High:** March-Oct. **Miscellaneous:** Reduced fees (weekdays, low season, twilight, seniors), metal spikes, club rentals.

★★★ MAPLE RIDGE GOLF CLUB

SP-4700 Maple Ridge Trail, Columbus, 31909, Muscogee County, (706)569-0966.
Holes: 18. **Yards:** 6,652/5,030. **Par:** 71/71. **Course Rating:** 72.2/68.9. **Slope:** 132/127. **Green Fee:** $17/$25. **Cart Fee:** $15/person. **Walking Policy:** Unrestricted walking. **Walkability:** 4. **Opened:** 1993. **Architect:** Mike Young. **Season:** Year-round. **High:** April-July. **To obtain tee times:** Call or come in up to 7 days in advance for weekdays, or 2 days in advance for weekends and holidays. **Miscellaneous:** Reduced fees (weekdays, low season, twilight, seniors, juniors), range (grass), club rentals, credit cards (MC, V, AE).
Reader Comments: Good layout ... Excellent mix of long and short hole ... Fast greens ... A hilly, tight layout ... Tough first hole ... Good staff, nice course.

★★★½ METROPOLITAN GOLF CLUB

SP-300 Fairington Pkwy., Lithonia, 30038, De Kalb County, (770)981-7696, 10 miles SE of Atlanta.
Holes: 18. **Yards:** 6,030/5,966. **Par:** 72/72. **Course Rating:** 74.2/74.8. **Slope:** 138/131. **Green Fee:** $32/$43. **Cart Fee:** Included in Green Fee. **Walking Policy:** Walking at certain times. **Walkability:** N/A. **Opened:** 1967. **Architect:** Robert Trent Jones. **Season:** Year-round. **High:** April-Sept. **To obtain tee times:** Call 5 days in advance. **Miscellaneous:** Reduced fees (weekdays, twilight), metal spikes, range (grass), club rentals, credit cards (MC, V, AE).
Reader Comments: A good hard course ... Fast greens ... Long layout demands smart course management ... No gimmicks ... Interesting layout ... I really enjoyed this course layout ... Tough, long, fair ... Great course!

★★½ MYSTERY VALLEY GOLF COURSE

PU-6094 Shadowrock Dr., Lithonia, 30058, De Kalb County, (770)469-6913, 20 miles S of Atlanta.
Holes: 18. **Yards:** 6,705/5,815. **Par:** 72/75. **Course Rating:** 71.7/73.1. **Slope:** 125/124. **Green Fee:** $15/$25. **Cart Fee:** $11/person. **Walking Policy:** Unrestricted walking. **Walkability:** 3. **Opened:** 1965. **Architect:** Dick Wilson/Joe Lee. **Season:** Year-round. **High:** March-Sept. **To obtain tee times:** Call 1 day in advance for weekdays and 7 days in advance for weekends. **Miscellaneous:** Reduced fees (weekdays, seniors, juniors), range (grass), club rentals, beginner friendly.

Reader Comments: Nice course. Will return ... Tough course ... Good use of sand traps and water ... Hilly ... Nice variety of holes.

★★★★ NOB NORTH GOLF COURSE

PM-298 Nob N. Dr., Cohutta, 30710, Whitfield County, (706)694-8505, 15 miles S of Chattanooga, TN.
Holes: 18. **Yards:** 6,573/5,448. **Par:** 72/72. **Course Rating:** 71.7/71.7. **Slope:** 128/126. **Green Fee:** $20/$24. **Cart Fee:** $10/person. **Walking Policy:** Unrestricted walking. **Walkability:** 3. **Opened:** 1978. **Architect:** Ron Kirby/Player. **Season:** Year-round. **High:** March-Nov. **To obtain tee times:** Call 5 days in advance. **Miscellaneous:** Reduced fees (seniors, juniors), metal spikes, range (grass), club rentals, credit cards (MC, V).
Reader Comments: Neighborhood favorite ... Best public course in north Georgia ... Lot of fun to play ... You get more than you pay for ... Beautiful, tough, great greens ... Test of skills, playable, tough greens ... This course is in great shape and it's a bargain ... Your putter better be hot. Greens are very challenging. Great course ... Well maintained and challenging ... Excellent municipal course.

★★ NORTH FULTON GOLF COURSE

PM-216 W. Wieuca Rd., Atlanta, 30342, Fulton County, (404)255-0723.
Holes: 18. **Yards:** 6,570/5,120. **Par:** 71/71. **Course Rating:** 71.8/69.5. **Slope:** 126/118. **Green Fee:** $14/$16. **Cart Fee:** $10/person. **Walking Policy:** Unrestricted walking. **Walkability:** 2. **Opened:** 1935. **Architect:** H. Chandler Egan. **Season:** Year-round. **High:** July. **To obtain tee times:** Call up to 5 days in advance. **Miscellaneous:** Reduced fees (weekdays, low season, twilight, seniors, juniors), discount packages, metal spikes, club rentals, credit cards (MC, V, AE), beginner friendly (beginner golf lessons).

★★★ OAK GROVE ISLAND GOLF CLUB

SP-100 Clipper Bay, Brunswick, 31523, Glynn County, (912)280-9525, 60 miles S of Savannah.
Holes: 18. **Yards:** 6,910/4,855. **Par:** 72/72. **Course Rating:** 73.2/67.6. **Slope:** 132/116. **Green Fee:** $6/$20. **Cart Fee:** $12/person. **Walking Policy:** Mandatory cart. **Walkability:** 2. **Opened:** 1993. **Architect:** Mike Young. **Season:** Year-round. **High:** March-May. **To obtain tee times:** Public may call up to 21 days in advance. **Miscellaneous:** Reduced fees (weekdays, resort guests, twilight, seniors, juniors), discount packages, metal spikes, range (grass), club rentals, credit cards (MC, V, AE, D), beginner friendly (intermediate tees).
Reader Comments: Good layout ... Good for beginning golfers, also challenging for good golfers ... Nice views ... Great little short course ... Clubhouse staff very friendly.

OAK MOUNTAIN CHAMPIONSHIP GOLF COURSE

SP-960 Oak Mountain Rd., Carrollton, 30116, Carroll County, (770)834-7065.
Holes: 18. **Yards:** 7,056/5,187. **Par:** 72/72. **Course Rating:** 72.8/69.4. **Slope:** 134/127. **Green Fee:** $25/$48. **Cart Fee:** Included in Green Fee. **Walking Policy:** Unrestricted walking. **Walkability:** 4. **Opened:** 1997. **Architect:** Ward Northrup. **Season:** Year-round. **High:** June-Aug. **Miscellaneous:** Reduced fees (weekdays, twilight, seniors, juniors), discount packages, club rentals, credit cards (MC, V, AE, D).

★★★½ THE OAKS GOLF COURSE

SP-11240 Brown Bridge Rd., Covington, 30014, Newton County, (770)786-3801, 30 miles E of Atlanta.
Holes: 18. **Yards:** 6,437/4,600. **Par:** 70/70. **Course Rating:** 70.2/64.5. **Slope:** 121/107. **Green Fee:** $26/$44. **Cart Fee:** Included in Green Fee. **Walking Policy:** Walking at certain times. **Walkability:** 3. **Opened:** 1990. **Architect:** Richard M. Schulz. **Season:** Year-round. **High:** April-Oct. **To obtain tee times:** Call 7 days in advance or visit. **Miscellaneous:** Reduced fees (weekdays, low season, resort guests, twilight, seniors, juniors), discount packages, range (grass), club rentals, credit cards (MC, V, AE, D).
Reader Comments: My wife could challenge me on this course ... Very good mid-handicapper course ... Excellent greens, fair value, friendly staff ... Short but challenging ... . Nice course, great condition ... Good layout–great value–fun to play ... The 11th is a great par 3 ... Fast greens ... Short layout, forces you to think ... A fun course.

OAKVIEW GOLF & COUNTRY CLUB

SP-129 Oakview Club Dr., Macon, 31216, Bibb County, (912)784-8700, 65 miles S of Atlanta. E-mail: oakviewgolf.com. Web: oakviewgolf.com.
Holes: 18. **Yards:** 6,722/4,894. **Par:** 72/72. **Course Rating:** 72.7/68.7. **Slope:** 135/121. **Green Fee:** $12/$24. **Cart Fee:** $12/person. **Walking Policy:** Walking at certain times. **Walkability:** 4. **Opened:** 1999. **Architect:** Barry Edgar. **Season:** year-round. **High:** April-Oct. **To obtain tee times:** You must call the Golf Shop to schedule a tee time. **Miscellaneous:** Reduced fees (weekdays, low season, juniors), range (grass), club rentals, credit cards (V, AE, D), beginner friendly.

GEORGIA

★★★ OLDE ATLANTA GOLF CLUB
SP-5750 Olde Atlanta Pkwy., Suwanee, 30424, Forsyth County, (770)497-0097, 15 miles NE of Atlanta. **E-mail:** oldeatlanta@mindspring.com. **Web:** www.oldeatlanta.com.
Holes: 18. **Yards:** 6,800/5,147. **Par:** 71/71. **Course Rating:** 73.1/69.3. **Slope:** 132/120. **Green Fee:** $61/$93. **Cart Fee:** Included in Green Fee. **Walking Policy:** Walking at certain times. **Walkability:** 3. **Opened:** 1993. **Architect:** Arthur Hills. **Season:** Year-round. **High:** April-Sept. **To obtain tee times:** Call 7 days in advance. **Miscellaneous:** Reduced fees (twilight, seniors), metal spikes, range (grass/mats), club rentals, credit cards (MC, V, AE).
Reader Comments: As good as most private clubs ... Good private atmosphere ... 18th a super finishing ... Play it from the tips ... Friendly service.

ORCHARD HILLS GOLF CLUB
PU-600 E. Hwy. 16, Newnan, 30263, Coweta County, (770)251-5683, 33 miles SW of Atlanta.
Holes: 27. **Green Fee:** $44/$55. **Cart Fee:** Included in Green Fee. **Walking Policy:** Walking at certain times. **Walkability:** 3. **Opened:** 1990. **Architect:** Don Cottle Jr. **Season:** Year-round. **High:** April-May. **To obtain tee times:** Call 7 days in advance.
★★★★ LOGO/ROCK GARDEN
Yards: 7,002/5,052. **Par:** 72/72. **Course Rating:** 73.4/68.4. **Slope:** 134/118. **Miscellaneous:** Reduced fees (weekdays, low season, twilight, seniors, juniors), discount packages, range (grass), club rentals, credit cards (MC, V, AE, D).
Reader Comments: Best links course ... Windy course with links flair ... True diamond in the rough ... Excellent course, true greens ... Great course, beautiful year-round, great staff ... Loved it ... Everything good, worth the drive from Atlanta ... Greens approach Augusta quality ... Fast greens, Scottish links design, a must play in Atlanta ... Make sure to play this one.
★★★★ ORCHARD/LOGO
Yards: 7,012/5,153. **Par:** 72/72. **Course Rating:** 73.4/68.9. **Slope:** 131/116. **Miscellaneous:** Reduced fees (weekdays, low season, twilight, seniors, juniors), discount packages, range (grass), club rentals, credit cards (MC, V, AE, D).
Reader Comments: Good service ... Wide open fun course ... Nice links design, no trees ... Slick greens ... Plays extremely tough when wind blows ... Best deal in town ... Love the par 3s.
★★★★ ROCK GARDEN/ORCHARD
Yards: 7,014/5,245. **Par:** 72/72. **Course Rating:** 72.8/68.4. **Slope:** 132/118. **Miscellaneous:** Reduced fees (weekdays, low season, twilight, seniors, juniors), discount packages, metal spikes, range (grass), club rentals, credit cards (MC, V, AE, D).
Reader Comments: Worth it ... Great course.

★★★★ OSPREY COVE GOLF CLUB
SP-123 Osprey Dr., St. Marys, 31558, Camden County, (912)882-5575, (800)352-5575, 35 miles N of Jacksonville, FL.
Holes: 18. **Yards:** 6,791/5,145. **Par:** 72/72. **Course Rating:** 72.9/69.7. **Slope:** 132/120. **Green Fee:** $47/$69. **Cart Fee:** $16/person. **Walking Policy:** Mandatory cart. **Walkability:** 3. **Opened:** 1990. **Architect:** Mark McCumber. **Season:** Year-round. **High:** Feb.-May. **To obtain tee times:** Call up to 7 days in advance. **Miscellaneous:** Reduced fees (juniors), range (grass), club rentals, credit cards (MC, V, AE), beginner friendly.
Notes: PGA Tour Regional Qualifier.
Reader Comments: Beautiful, challenging but playable ... McCumber, you did good ... Marvelous. Play it twice ... Best public course in Georgia ... Great conditioning and terrific layout ... Well kept secret–great course ... Can't wait to go back ... A must-play gem ... Beautiful links-style course, lots of water fowl and osprey ... Outstanding challenge ... Immaculate conditions.

★★★½ PINE BLUFF GOLF & COUNTRY CLUB
PU-Hwy. 341 S., Eastman, 31023, Dodge County, (912)374-0991, 50 miles S of Macon. **E-mail:** mooret@public.ub.ga.us. **Web:** www.pinebluffcc.com.
Holes: 18. **Yards:** 6,499/5,065. **Par:** 72/72. **Course Rating:** 70.6/69.1. **Slope:** 125/119. **Green Fee:** $8/$12. **Cart Fee:** $8/person. **Walking Policy:** Walking at certain times. **Walkability:** N/A. **Opened:** 1994. **Architect:** Tim Moore. **Season:** Year-round. **High:** March-May. **To obtain tee times:** Call golf shop. **Miscellaneous:** Reduced fees (twilight, seniors, juniors), discount packages, metal spikes, range (grass), club rentals, credit cards (MC, V, D).
Reader Comments: Don't miss it! ... Can't beat the price for golf ... Surprisingly good ... Open front, tight back ... Super-friendly staff ... Best kept secret in area.

★★★★ PORT ARMOR RESORT & COUNTRY CLUB
R-One Port Armor Pkwy., Greensboro, 30642, Greene County, (706)453-4564, (800)804-7678, 50 miles E of Atlanta.
Holes: 18. **Yards:** 6,926/5,177. **Par:** 72/72. **Course Rating:** 74.0/72.8. **Slope:** 140/131. **Green Fee:** $30/$69. **Cart Fee:** Included in Green Fee. **Walking Policy:** Mandatory cart. **Walkability:** 4. **Opened:** 1986. **Architect:** Bob Cupp. **Season:** Year-round. **High:** April-Oct. **To obtain tee times:** Call golf shop. **Miscellaneous:** Reduced fees (low season, resort guests), discount packages, metal spikes, range (grass), club rentals, lodging, credit cards (MC, V, AE).

Reader Comments: Great layout, beautiful course ... Nice resort, course in great shape, good accommodations ... Great course, beautiful view of lake ... One tough customer–bring your best game ... Enjoyable to play ... Challenging, quality layout ... Less crowded than others in Atlanta area ... Memorable holes, good condition ... Tough lakeside track, particularly the 10th hole ... Professional service.

★★★★ RENAISSANCE PINEISLE RESORT

R-9000 Holiday Rd., Lake Lanier Islands, 30518, Hall County, (770)945-8921, (800)468-3571, 45 miles NE of Atlanta.

Holes: 18. **Yards:** 6,527/5,297. **Par:** 72/72. **Course Rating:** 71.6/70.6. **Slope:** 132/127. **Green Fee:** $55/$65. **Cart Fee:** Included in Green Fee. **Walking Policy:** Walking at certain times. **Walkability:** 4. **Opened:** 1973. **Architect:** Arthur Davis/Gary Player/Ron Kirby. **Season:** Year-round. **High:** April-Oct. **To obtain tee times:** Hotel guests may make tee times with confirmed reservation of room. Others call 7 days in advance. **Miscellaneous:** Reduced fees (low season, twilight), discount packages, range (grass/mats), club rentals, lodging (254 rooms), credit cards (MC, V, AE, D).

Reader Comments: Beautiful lake course ... Fun, resort course–relax and enjoy ... Fun back nine ... Beautiful layout, great views of lake ... Recently remodeled ... Hidden gem ... Extremely tight, good test of skills ... Lots of water ... Several interesting holes ... Excellent.

REYNOLDS PLANTATION *Service*

★★★★½ GREAT WATERS COURSE *Condition+, Pace*

R-100 Plantation Drive, Eatonton, 31024, Putnam County, (706)485-0235, (800)852-5885, 70 miles N of Macon.

Holes: 18. **Yards:** 7,058/5,057. **Par:** 72/72. **Course Rating:** 73.8/69.2. **Slope:** 135/114. **Green Fee:** $110/$110. **Cart Fee:** $20/person. **Walking Policy:** Walking at certain times. **Walkability:** 3. **Opened:** 1992. **Architect:** Jack Nicklaus. **Season:** Year-round. **High:** April-Oct. **To obtain tee times:** Overnight guests may obtain tee times through reservations at (800)852-5885. **Miscellaneous:** Reduced fees (weekdays, low season), discount packages, range (grass), club rentals, lodging (99 rooms), credit cards (MC, V, AE, D), beginner friendly (daily clinics). **Notes:** Ranked 7th in 1999 Best in State.

Reader Comments: Worth the price. Great condition. Beautiful views. Great layout ... What can you say about this course that hasn't been said? Great!! Outstanding! ... The greatest resort course I've played ... One of the best I've played ... As good as it gets ... One of Jack's best ... Go for it on 18 ... Beautiful water holes ... A must play ... A miniature Augusta National.

★★★★½ NATIONAL COURSE *Condition+, Pace*

R-100 Linger Longer Rd., Greensboro, 30642, Greene County, (706)467-1142, (800)852-5885, 75 miles E of Atlanta.

Holes: 18. **Yards:** 7,015/5,292. **Par:** 72/72. **Course Rating:** 72.7/69.5. **Slope:** 127/116. **Green Fee:** $110/$110. **Cart Fee:** $20/person. **Walking Policy:** Walking at certain times. **Walkability:** 4. **Opened:** 1997. **Architect:** Tom Fazio. **Season:** Year-round. **High:** April-Aug. **To obtain tee times:** Overnight guests may obtain tee times through reservations at (800)852-5885. **Miscellaneous:** Reduced fees (weekdays, low season), discount packages, range (grass/mats), club rentals, lodging (99 rooms), credit cards (MC, V, AE, D), beginner friendly (daily clinics). **Notes:** Ranked 13th in 1999 Best in State.

Reader Comments: Hard to believe this course is so young. Magnificent, can only get better ... Real challenge ... Terrific layout, every club in use ... Beautiful course.

★★★★½ PLANTATION COURSE *Condition+, Pace*

R-100 Linger Longer Rd., Greensboro, 30642, Greene County, (706)467-3159, (800)852-5885, 75 miles E of Atlanta.

Holes: 18. **Yards:** 6,698/5,121. **Par:** 72/72. **Course Rating:** 71.7/68.9. **Slope:** 128/115. **Green Fee:** $85/$95. **Cart Fee:** $20/person. **Walking Policy:** Walking at certain times. **Walkability:** 3. **Opened:** 1987. **Architect:** Bob Cupp/Fuzzy Zoeller/Hubert Green. **Season:** Year-round. **High:** April-Aug. **To obtain tee times:** Overnight guests may obtain tee times through reservations at 800)852-5885. **Miscellaneous:** Reduced fees (weekdays, juniors), discount packages, range (mats), club rentals, lodging (99 rooms), credit cards (MC, V, AE, D), beginner friendly (daily clinics).

Reader Comments: Play all the courses at Reynolds Plantation, it's worth the stay ... Nice layout in great condition always! ... Beautiful course ... One of 3 great golf courses ... As tough as it gets from the blues ... Nice course.

★★★½ RIVER'S EDGE GOLF COURSE

SP-40 Southern Golf Court, Fayetteville, 30214, Fayette County, (770)460-1098, 19 miles S of Atlanta.

Holes: 18. **Yards:** 6,810/5,641. **Par:** 71/71. **Course Rating:** 72.9/69.9. **Slope:** 135/121. **Green Fee:** $35/$49. **Cart Fee:** Included in Green Fee. **Walking Policy:** Mandatory cart. **Walkability:** 4. **Opened:** 1990. **Architect:** Bobby Weed. **Season:** Year-round. **High:** March-Oct. **To obtain tee times:** Call 7 days in advance. **Miscellaneous:** Reduced fees (weekdays, twilight, seniors, juniors), discount packages, metal spikes, range (grass), club rentals, credit cards (MC, V, AE).

GEORGIA

★★★ RIVERPINES GOLF CLUB
PU-4775 Old Alabama Rd., Alpharetta, 30202, Fulton County, (770)442-5960, 20 miles NE of Atlanta.
Holes: 18. **Yards:** 6,511/4,279. **Par:** 70/70. **Course Rating:** 71.3/65.1. **Slope:** 128/106. **Green Fee:** $53/$60. **Cart Fee:** Included in Green Fee. **Walking Policy:** Walking at certain times. **Walkability:** 3. **Opened:** 1993. **Architect:** Dennis Griffiths. **Season:** Year-round. **High:** April-Sept. **To obtain tee times:** Call on Monday to book for active week. **Miscellaneous:** Reduced fees (twilight, juniors), discount packages, range (grass/mats), club rentals, credit cards (MC, V, AE), beginner friendly (beginner lessons and clinics).
Reader Comments: Some difficult, some easy holes ... Nice fairways and greens ... Friendly staff ... Heavily played ... Good placement of water and bunkers ... Wonderful practice facility ... Tight, short and fun course.

★★★★ ROYAL LAKES GOLF & COUNTRY CLUB
SP-4700 Royal Lakes Dr., Flowery Branch, 30542, Hall County, (770)535-8800, 35 miles NE of Atlanta.
Holes: 18. **Yards:** 6,871/5,325. **Par:** 72/72. **Course Rating:** 72.0/70.4. **Slope:** 131/125. **Green Fee:** $40/$47. **Cart Fee:** Included in Green Fee. **Walking Policy:** Walking at certain times. **Walkability:** N/A. **Opened:** 1989. **Architect:** Arthur Davis. **Season:** Year-round. **High:** March-Sept. **To obtain tee times:** Tee times required. Call 4 days in advance. **Miscellaneous:** Reduced fees (weekdays, twilight, seniors, juniors), metal spikes, range (grass), club rentals, credit cards (MC, V, AE).
Reader Comments: Wonderful scenery ... Nice layout ... Terrific greens, extremely quick ... You must use every shot ... Plenty of trouble ... Rolling terrain, some target golf ... Several memorable holes.

★★ ROYAL OAKS GOLF CLUB
SP-256 Summit Ridge Dr., Cartersville, 30120, Bartow County, (770)382-3999, 40 miles N of Atlanta. **E-mail:** royaloaks@mindsrpring.com. **Web:** www.royaloaksgolf.com.
Holes: 18. **Yards:** 6,409/4,890. **Par:** 71/75. **Course Rating:** 70.0/71.0. **Slope:** 124/121. **Green Fee:** $20/$30. **Cart Fee:** $12/person. **Walking Policy:** Walking at certain times. **Walkability:** 3. **Opened:** 1978. **Architect:** Kirby/Davis/Bingaman. **Season:** Year-round. **High:** April-Oct. **To obtain tee times:** Call 7 days in advance. **Miscellaneous:** Reduced fees (weekdays, low season, twilight, seniors, juniors), discount packages, range (grass/mats), club rentals, credit cards (MC, V).

★★★½ ST. MARLO COUNTRY CLUB
PU-7755 St. Marlo Country Club Pkwy., Duluth, 30097, Forsyth County, (770)495-7725, 25 miles N of Atlanta.
Holes: 18. **Yards:** 6,900/5,300. **Par:** 72/72. **Course Rating:** 73.6/70.3. **Slope:** 137/121. **Green Fee:** $66/$84. **Cart Fee:** Included in Green Fee. **Walking Policy:** Unrestricted walking. **Walkability:** 4. **Opened:** 1995. **Architect:** Denis Griffiths. **Season:** Year-round. **High:** April-Oct. **To obtain tee times:** Call 6 days in advance. **Miscellaneous:** Reduced fees (weekdays, juniors), range (grass/mats), club rentals, credit cards (MC, V, AE, Diners Club).
Notes: Ranked 10th in 1995 Best New Public Courses.
Reader Comments: New, hilly housing development course. Better than most ... Spend the money. It's a treat! Bring balls ... Hilly, good greens, good test ... You must place every shot; perfect condition. I felt like I was at Augusta National ... Big million dollar homes tight to fairways ... Trick holes ... Lots of elevation changes, can be Beauty or Beast.

★★★½ ST. SIMONS ISLAND CLUB
PU-100 Kings Way, St. Simons Island, 31522, Glynn County, (912)638-5130, 4 miles E of Brunswick.
Holes: 18. **Yards:** 6,490/5,361. **Par:** 72/72. **Course Rating:** 71.8/69.8. **Slope:** 133/120. **Green Fee:** N/A/$100. **Cart Fee:** Included in Green Fee. **Walking Policy:** Walking at certain times. **Walkability:** 1. **Opened:** 1974. **Architect:** Joe Lee. **Season:** Year-round. **High:** March-April. **To obtain tee times:** Call starter or golf shop. **Miscellaneous:** Reduced fees (resort guests, juniors), range (grass/mats), caddies, club rentals, credit cards (MC, V).
Reader Comments: Outstanding layout ... Short but narrow ... Enjoyable, plays easier than some courses ... Super course ... Must play.

SCALES CREEK GOLF CLUB
PU-474 Samples-Scales Rd., Homer, 30547, Banks County, (706)677-3333, 65 miles NE of Atlanta. **E-mail:** scalescreek@alltel.net. **Web:** scalescreek.com.
Holes: 18. **Yards:** 6,985/4,778. **Par:** 72/72. **Course Rating:** 73.4/66.5. **Slope:** 132/116. **Green Fee:** $29/$42. **Cart Fee:** Included in Green Fee. **Walking Policy:** Mandatory cart. **Walkability:** 3. **Opened:** 1998. **Architect:** Mark McCumber. **Season:** Year-round. **High:** March-Nov. **To**

obtain tee times: Call golf shop 4 days in advance. **Miscellaneous:** Reduced fees (weekdays, low season, twilight, seniors, juniors), range (grass), club rentals, credit cards (MC, V, D).

SEA ISLAND GOLF CLUB *Service+*

R-100 Retreat Ave., St. Simons Island, 31522, Glynn County, (912)638-5118, (800)732-4752, 50 miles N of Jacksonville, FL.

★★★★ PLANTATION *Pace*

Holes: 18. **Yards:** 7,043/5,223. **Par:** 72/74. **Course Rating:** 73.9/69.8. **Slope:** 135/124. **Green Fee:** $90/$125. **Cart Fee:** Included in Green Fee. **Walking Policy:** Walking at certain times. **Walkability:** 2. **Opened:** 1959. **Architect:** Rees Jones. **Season:** Year-round. **High:** March-Sept. **To obtain tee times:** Call. **Miscellaneous:** Reduced fees (low season, resort guests, twilight, juniors), discount packages, range (grass/mats), caddies, club rentals, lodging (300 rooms), credit cards (MC, V, AE, Sea Island Card).
Reader Comments: Spectacular after Rees Jones redesign ... Great layout, greens, challenging when windy ... Top notch in every way, great service ... Tough! Lots of sand, long course ... 18th just great, go for it if you dare ... Our favorite yearly trip! Easy to get tee times; staff great ... Make sure you hit the driving range for the view.

★★★★ SEASIDE

Holes: 18. **Yards:** 6,900/5,100. **Par:** 70/70. **Course Rating:** N/A. **Slope:** N/A. **Green Fee:** $70/$150. **Cart Fee:** Included in Green Fee. **Walking Policy:** Unrestricted walking. **Walkability:** 1. **Opened:** 1999. **Architect:** Tom Fazio. **Season:** Year-round. **High:** March-April/Oct. **To obtain tee times:** Call. **Miscellaneous:** Reduced fees (resort guests), discount packages, range (grass/mats), caddies, club rentals, lodging (40 rooms), credit cards (MC, V), beginner friendly (clinics, private instruction).
Reader Comments: Outstanding after Fazio redesigned original Seaside and completely redid old Marshside. Perfect ... Might be best 18 holes on East Coast ... Exceptional amenities ... Great caddies.

SEA PALMS RESORT

R-5445 Frederica Rd., St. Simons Island, 31522, Glynn County, (912)638-9041, (800)841-6268, 65 miles N of Jacksonvill, FL.

Holes: 27. **Walking Policy:** Mandatory cart. **Walkability:** 2. **Opened:** 1966. **Season:** Year-round. **High:** Feb.-May. **To obtain tee times:** Call 7 days in advance. Hotel guest may call 30 days in advance.**Miscellaneous:** Reduced fees (weekdays, low season, resort guests, twilight, juniors), discount packages, range (grass/mats), club rentals, lodging, credit cards (MC, V, AE).

★★★ GREAT OAKS/SEA PALMS

Yards: 6,350/5,200. **Par:** 72/72. **Course Rating:** 71.8/69.3. **Slope:** 128/124. **Green Fee:** $35/$45. **Cart Fee:** $16/person. **Architect:** George Cobb/Tom Jackson.
Reader Comments: Marvellous layout ... Hidden jewel, outlying 9 is terrific.

★★★ TALL PINES/GREAT OAKS

Yards: 6,658/5,350. **Par:** 72/72. **Course Rating:** 72.1/70.9. **Slope:** 131/120. **Green Fee:** $35/$50. **Cart Fee:** $17/person. **Architect:** George Cobb.
Reader Comments: Nice resort course ... Friendly staff ... Gets lots of play.

★★★ TALL PINES/SEA PALMS

Yards: 6,198/5,249. **Par:** 72/72. **Course Rating:** 70.6/70.8. **Slope:** 129/127. **Green Fee:** $35/$50. **Cart Fee:** $17. **Architect:** George Cobb.
Reader Comments: Wind and water make it tough.

★★★ SKY VALLEY GOLF & SKI RESORT

R-One Sky Valley, Sky Valley, 30537, Rabun County, (706)746-5303, (800)437-2416, 100 miles N of Atlanta.
Holes: 18. **Yards:** 6,452/5,017. **Par:** 72/72. **Course Rating:** 71.7/69.0. **Slope:** 128/118. **Green Fee:** $25/$40. **Cart Fee:** Included in Green Fee. **Walking Policy:** Walking at certain times. **Walkability:** 3. **Opened:** 1971. **Architect:** Bill Watts. **Season:** Year-round. **High:** April-Oct. **To obtain tee times:** Call up to 20 days in advance. **Miscellaneous:** Reduced fees (weekdays, low season, resort guests, twilight, seniors), metal spikes, range (grass), club rentals, lodging, credit cards (MC, V, AE, D).
Reader Comments: Great mountain course set in a valley ... Best kept secret in Georgia ... Beautiful scenery, better be able to draw it, fade it ... A fun mountain course with challenging greens and unique hole designs. You won't get bored ... Design better than condition.

★★★½ SOUTHBRIDGE GOLF CLUB

SP-415 Southbridge Blvd., Savannah, 31405, Chatham County, (912)651-5455.
Holes: 18. **Yards:** 6,990/5,181. **Par:** 72/72. **Course Rating:** 73.4/69.2. **Slope:** 136/118. **Green Fee:** $35/$41. **Cart Fee:** Included in Green Fee. **Walking Policy:** Mandatory cart. **Walkability:** 1. **Opened:** 1988. **Architect:** Rees Jones. **Season:** Year-round. **High:** April-May. **To obtain tee times:** Call up to 7 days in advance. **Miscellaneous:** Reduced fees (weekdays, low season, twilight, seniors, juniors), metal spikes, range (grass), club rentals, credit cards (MC, V, AE, D).
Reader Comments: Superb track ... Good shape year round ... Very fair, but challenging course. Management and conditioning consistently above par ... Excellent design.

SOUTHERN HILLS GOLF CLUB

SP-Hwy. 247, Hawkinsville, 31036, (912)783-0600, 16 miles E of Perry.
E-mail: southernhill@cstel.net. **Web:** www.southernhillsgolf.com.
Holes: 18. **Yards:** 6,741/5,290. **Par:** 72/72. **Course Rating:** 72.7/70.6. **Slope:** 134/122. **Green Fee:** $21/$32. **Cart Fee:** Included in Green Fee. **Walking Policy:** Unrestricted walking.
Walkability: 4. **Opened:** 1997. **Architect:** Mike Young/Ernest Jones. **Season:** Year-round. **High:** April-Oct. **To obtain tee times:** Call a week in advance. If traveling you can reserve it even earlier.
Miscellaneous: Reduced fees (weekdays, low season, twilight, seniors, juniors), discount packages, range (grass), club rentals, credit cards (MC, V, AE), beginner friendly (beginner clinics).

★★★½ SOUTHERNESS GOLF CLUB

SP-4871 Flat Bridge Rd., Stockbridge, 30281, Rockdale County, (770)808-6000, 20 miles E of Atlanta.
Holes: 18. **Yards:** 6,756/4,916. **Par:** 72/72. **Course Rating:** 73.6/69.0. **Slope:** 136/119. **Green Fee:** $14/$35. **Cart Fee:** $12/person. **Walking Policy:** Mandatory cart. **Walkability:** 3. **Opened:** 1991. **Architect:** Clyde Johnston. **Season:** Year-round. **High:** April-Sept. **To obtain tee times:** Call 5 days in advance. Reduced fees also offered for ladies. **Miscellaneous:** Reduced fees (twilight, seniors), range (grass/mats), club rentals, credit cards (MC, V, AE).
Reader Comments: Excellent links-style layout ... Friendly service ... Nice views, fun place to play ... Drive 'em straight ... The third is a great hole, but the last three are the best ... Challenging. Worth the drive to southeast Atlanta ... Scottish links type, very challenging ... Lots of chances for glory or tragedy ... Fun layout all around, course needs some work ... Great course for women ... They set up a good fun outing for the office gang.

★½ SPRINGBROOK PUBLIC GOLF CLUB

PM-585 Camp Perrin Rd., Lawrenceville, 30243, Gwinnett County, (770)822-5400, 35 miles NE of Atlanta.
Holes: 18. **Yards:** 6,000/4,738. **Par:** 71/72. **Course Rating:** 68.0/67.1. **Slope:** 120/113. **Green Fee:** $34/$38. **Cart Fee:** Included in Green Fee. **Walking Policy:** Walking at certain times.
Walkability: 3. **Opened:** 1963. **Architect:** Perrin Walker. **Season:** Year-round. **High:** April-Nov.
To obtain tee times: Call on Wednesday for weekends. **Miscellaneous:** Reduced fees (weekdays, twilight, seniors, juniors), metal spikes, range (grass), club rentals, credit cards (MC, V).

★★★ STONE CREEK GOLF CLUB

SP-4300 Coleman Rd., Valdosta, 31602, Lowndes County, (912)247-2527.
E-mail: Stnck@datasys.net.
Holes: 18. **Yards:** 6,850/4,750. **Par:** 72/72. **Course Rating:** 71.7/67.5. **Slope:** 121/114. **Green Fee:** $30/$40. **Cart Fee:** Included in Green Fee. **Walking Policy:** Mandatory cart. **Walkability:** 5. **Opened:** 1987. **Architect:** Franzman-Davis. **Season:** Year-round. **High:** April-Oct. **To obtain tee times:** Call **Miscellaneous:** Reduced fees (weekdays), range (grass/mats), club rentals, lodging, credit cards (MC, V, AE, D, Diners Club).
Reader Comments: Good course, good-looking layout.

STONE MOUNTAIN GOLF CLUB

R-1145 Stonewall Jackson Drive, Stone Mountain, 30083, De Kalb County, (770)465-3278, 12 miles E of Atlanta. **Web:** www.stonemountaingolf.com.
★★★½ LAKEMONT COURSE
Holes: 18. **Yards:** 6,444/4,762. **Par:** 71/71. **Course Rating:** 71.3/68.1. **Slope:** 130/117. **Green Fee:** $44/$52. **Cart Fee:** Included in Green Fee. **Walking Policy:** Mandatory cart. **Walkability:** 4. **Opened:** 1987. **Architect:** John LaFoy. **Season:** Year-round. **High:** April-Oct. **To obtain tee times:** Call Tuesday for following weekend and holidays starting at 7:30 a.m. For weekdays call 7 days in advance. **Miscellaneous:** Reduced fees (weekdays, low season, twilight, juniors), discount packages, metal spikes, range (grass/mats), club rentals, lodging (350 rooms), credit cards (MC, V, AE, D, Diners Club), beginner friendly (adult golf schools, junior golf camps and club fitting program).
Reader Comments: Great views, the government does some things right ... Should tell you $6.00 to enter park ... Scenic and fun ... Great design, needs work ... Excellent.
★★★ STONEMONT COURSE
Holes: 18. **Yards:** 6,757/5,492. **Par:** 70/70. **Course Rating:** 73.4/72.2. **Slope:** 131/124. **Green Fee:** $44/$52. **Cart Fee:** Included in Green Fee. **Walking Policy:** Mandatory cart. **Walkability:** 4. **Opened:** 1971. **Architect:** Robert Trent Jones. **Season:** Year-round. **High:** April-Oct. **To obtain tee times:** Call on Tuesday for upcoming weekend or holiday starting at 7:30 a.m. Call 7 days in advance for weekdays. **Miscellaneous:** Reduced fees (weekdays, low season, twilight, juniors), discount packages, metal spikes, range (grass/mats), club rentals, lodging (350 rooms), credit cards (MC, V, AE, D, Diners Club), beginner friendly (adult golf schools, junior golf camps and club fitting program).
Reader Comments: Good views of Stone Mountain ... Good old-fashioned layout ... Mountain course, good layout for state par ... Very tough and long.

★★★½ STONEBRIDGE GOLF CLUB
PM-585 Stonebridge Dr., Rome, 30165, Floyd County, (706)236-5046, (800)336-5046, 50 miles N of Atlanta.
Holes: 18. **Yards:** 6,816/5,130. **Par:** 72/72. **Course Rating:** 72.8/64.6. **Slope:** 123/109. **Green Fee:** $10/$30. **Walking Policy:** Walking at certain times. **Walkability:** 2. **Opened:** 1994.
Architect: Arthur Davis. **Season:** Year-round. **High:** March-Sept. **To obtain tee times:** Call up to 7 days in advance. **Miscellaneous:** Reduced fees (weekdays, twilight, seniors, juniors), discount packages, range (grass/mats), club rentals, credit cards (MC, V, AE).
Notes: Ranked 18th in 1999 Best in State.
Reader Comments: Nice track, getting there tough ... Could be best in N. Georgia ... From the tips, bring all your clubs ... Has a lot of potential. It is a great layout ... Hilly terrain, tough, 9th and 18th ... Took my breath away ... Staff here is always friendly, very nice greens, fun layout.

★★ SUGAR HILL GOLF CLUB
PU-6094 Suwanee Dam Rd., Sugar Hill, 30518, Gwinnett County, (770)271-0519, 35 miles NE of Atlanta.
Holes: 18. **Yards:** 6,423/4,207. **Par:** 72/72. **Course Rating:** 70.7/65.3. **Slope:** 127/112. **Green Fee:** $35/$45. **Cart Fee:** Included in Green Fee. **Walking Policy:** Walking at certain times. **Walkability:** 5. **Opened:** 1992. **Architect:** William Byrd. **Season:** Year-round. **High:** April-Oct. **To obtain tee times:** Tee times taken 2 days in advance. **Miscellaneous:** Reduced fees (low season, twilight, seniors, juniors), metal spikes, range (grass/mats), rentals, credit cards (MC, V).
Special Notes: Spikeless encouraged.

★★★½ TOWNE LAKE HILLS GOLF CLUB
PU-1003 Towne Lake Hills E., Woodstock, 30188, Cherokee County, (770)592-9969, 25 miles N of Atlanta. **Web:** www.townelakehill.com.
Holes: 18. **Yards:** 6,757/4,984. **Par:** 72/72. **Course Rating:** 72.3/69.0. **Slope:** 133/116. **Green Fee:** $50/$69. **Cart Fee:** Included in Green Fee. **Walking Policy:** Unrestricted walking. **Walkability:** N/A. **Opened:** 1994. **Architect:** Arthur Hills. **Season:** Year-round. **High:** May-Oct.
To obtain tee times: Call 7 days in advance. **Miscellaneous:** Reduced fees (weekdays, low season, twilight, seniors), discount packages, metal spikes, range (grass), club rentals, credit cards (MC, V, AE).
Reader Comments: Some good holes, fair test of golf ... Top five public courses in Atlanta. Love it ... Good neighborhood golf, family style ... Expensive on weekends, great layout, best greens ... Very tough, hardly any flat lies in fairways, tricky greens ... Narrow fairways.

★★★½ THE TROPHY CLUB OF APALACHEE
SP-1008 Dacula Rd., Dacula, 30211, Gwinnett County, (770)822-9220.
Holes: 18. **Yards:** 6,620/5,685. **Par:** 72/72. **Course Rating:** 72.5/68.0. **Slope:** 137/116. **Green Fee:** $35/$60. **Cart Fee:** Included in Green Fee. **Walking Policy:** Mandatory cart. **Walkability:** 4. **Opened:** 1994. **Architect:** DJ DeVictor/Steve Melval. **Season:** Year-round. **To obtain tee times:** Call 7 days in advance. **Miscellaneous:** Reduced fees (weekdays, twilight, seniors, juniors), range (grass), club rentals, credit cards (MC, V, AE).
Reader Comments: Nice condition, good design ... Difficult course in good condition. Will return often ... The 8th is a great short hole ... Several interesting holes ... Friendly staff.

★★★ TROPHY CLUB OF GWINNETT
SP-3254 Clubside View Court, Snellville, 30039, Gwinnett County, (770)978-7755, 25 miles E of Atlanta.
Holes: 18. **Yards:** 6,305/4,861. **Par:** 72/72. **Course Rating:** 70.4/68.3. **Slope:** 128/118. **Green Fee:** $47/$60. **Cart Fee:** Included in Green Fee. **Walking Policy:** Walking at certain times. **Walkability:** 3. **Opened:** 1993. **Architect:** Steve Melnyk. **Season:** Year-round. **To obtain tee times:** Call golf shop up to 7 days in advance. **Miscellaneous:** Reduced fees (twilight, seniors, juniors), range (grass/mats), club rentals, credit cards (MC, V, AE).
Reader Comments: Good course ... Excellent course, greens, fairways, bunkers, tees, personnel in pro shop ... Very fast greens ... First hole daunting water carry ... Short target golf, tight ... Course knowledge is important.

★★★½ UNIVERSITY OF GEORGIA GOLF CLUB
PU-2600 Riverbend Rd., Athens, 30605, Clarke County, (706)369-5739, (800)936-4833, 60 miles E of Atlanta.
Holes: 18. **Yards:** 6,890/5,713. **Par:** 72/73. **Course Rating:** 73.4/74.0. **Slope:** 133/128. **Green Fee:** $15/$24. **Cart Fee:** $11/person. **Walking Policy:** Unrestricted walking. **Walkability:** N/A. **Opened:** 1968. **Architect:** Robert Trent Jones/John LaFoy. **Season:** Year-round. **High:** March-June. **To obtain tee times:** Call Wednesdays at 8:00 am for Thursdays-Wednesdays.
Miscellaneous: Reduced fees (weekdays, twilight), metal spikes, range (grass), club rentals, credit cards (MC, V).

Reader Comments: Good condition. Challenging ... Back nine better than front ... Long, big fairways, let it rip ... Nice layout ... The 12th and 13th holes are tough par 5s ... Wait 'til you get to the greens ... Great value ... Long for seniors ... Must hit it straight to score.

★★★ WALLACE ADAMS GOLF COURSE

PM-Hwy. 441 N., McRae, 31055, Telfair County, (912)868-6651, 75 miles SE of Macon. **Holes:** 18. **Yards:** 6,625/5,001. **Par:** 72/72. **Course Rating:** 70.8/69.1. **Slope:** 128/120. **Green Fee:** $17/$22. **Cart Fee:** $16/cart. **Walking Policy:** Unrestricted walking. **Walkability:** 3. **Opened:** 1965. **Architect:** O.C. Jones. **Season:** Year-round. **High:** Spring/Fall. **To obtain tee times:** First come, first served. **Miscellaneous:** Reduced fees (weekdays, resort guests, seniors), discount packages, range (grass), club rentals, lodging (40 rooms), credit cards (MC, V)
Reader Comments: Good conditions, fun golf ... Challenging layout can be fun ... Conditions consistently good, few amenities, but a good value ... Short–tight, great shape, lots of iron shots ... State parks are always in good shape ... Great place for groups, Interesting layout fast greens.

★★★★½ WHITE COLUMNS GOLF CLUB   *Service, Condition+*

SP-300 White Columns Dr., Alpharetta, 30201, Fulton County, (770)343-9025, 25 miles N of Atlanta. **Holes:** 18. **Yards:** 7,053/6,015. **Par:** 72/72. **Course Rating:** 73.6/69.0. **Slope:** 137/116. **Green Fee:** $75/$100. **Cart Fee:** Included in Green Fee. **Walking Policy:** Unrestricted walking. **Walkability:** 3. **Opened:** 1994. **Architect:** Tom Fazio. **Season:** Year-round. **High:** March-Oct. **To obtain tee times:** Call golf shop. **Miscellaneous:** Range (grass), club rentals, credit cards (MC, V, AE).
Notes: Ranked 10th in 1999 Best in State; 6th in 1995 Best New Public Course.
Reader Comments: One of the best in Georgia that you can play ... What a beautiful course! ... Awesome greens, layout ... Always in great shape ... Play the Player tees ... Gigantic Fazio greens ... Course is very playable for all levels of play. Nothing tricked up and you can be comfortable hitting driver all day long ... Staff makes the occasional golfer think he/she is a regular ... Best greens I've ever played.

★★½ WHITEPATH GOLF CLUB

PU-1156 Shenendoah Drive, Ellijay, 30540, Gilmer County, (706)276-3080. **Holes:** 18. **Yards:** 6,511/4,900. **Par:** 72/72. **Course Rating:** 70.0/72.1. **Slope:** 131/128. **Green Fee:** $34/$39. **Cart Fee:** Included in Green Fee. **Walking Policy:** Mandatory cart. **Walkability:** 5. **Opened:** 1984. **Season:** Year-round. **High:** May-Sept. **To obtain tee times:** Call up to 1 week in advance. **Miscellaneous:** Reduced fees (weekdays, resort guests, twilight, seniors, juniors), discount packages, range (grass), club rentals, credit cards (MC, V, AE, D).
Reader Comments: Scenic, great layout, real value.

★★★★ WHITEWATER COUNTRY CLUB

SP-175 Birkdale Dr., Fayetteville, 30214, Fayette County, (770)461-6545, 30 miles S of Atlanta. **Holes:** 18. **Yards:** 6,739/4,909. **Par:** 72/72. **Course Rating:** 72.3/68.2. **Slope:** 133/123. **Green Fee:** $15/$38. **Cart Fee:** $15/person. **Walking Policy:** Mandatory cart. **Walkability:** 3. **Opened:** 1988. **Architect:** Arnold Palmer/Ed Seay. **Season:** Year-round. **High:** March-Oct. **To obtain tee times:** Call 3 days in advance. **Miscellaneous:** Reduced fees (weekdays, low season, twilight, seniors, juniors), discount packages, range (grass), club rentals, credit cards (MC, V, AE).
Reader Comments: Another excellent one ... Overlooked course. Always in great condition. Beautiful clubhouse. Good practice facilities ... Very picturesque. Full of water ... Fun course. Pretty neighborhood ... Tough course.

★★★½ WINDSTONE GOLF CLUB

SP-9230 Windstone Dr., Ringgold, 30736, Catoosa County, (423)894-1231, 6 miles S of Chattanooga. **Holes:** 18. **Yards:** 6,626/4,956. **Par:** 72/72. **Course Rating:** 71.7/66.8. **Slope:** 127/108. **Green Fee:** $16/$23. **Cart Fee:** $11/person. **Walking Policy:** Unrestricted walking. **Walkability:** 4. **Opened:** 1990. **Architect:** Jeff Brauer. **Season:** Year-round. **High:** April-Oct. **To obtain tee times:** Call 2 days in advance. **Miscellaneous:** Reduced fees (low season, seniors), range (grass), club rentals, credit cards (MC, V, AE, D).
Reader Comments: Great challenge, heavy play ... Slick greens. Keep it out of the trees ... Fun course, challenging, great greens ... Slick greens with plenty of breaks.

HAWAII

★★½ ALA WAI GOLF COURSE
PM-404 Kapahulu Ave., Honolulu, 96815, Oahu County, (808)733-7387.
Holes: 18. **Yards:** 6,208/5,095. **Par:** 70/70. **Course Rating:** 67.2/67.2. **Slope:** 116/109. **Green Fee:** $5/$40. **Cart Fee:** $14/cart. **Walking Policy:** Unrestricted walking. **Walkability:** 1. **Opened:** 1931. **Architect:** Donald MacKay/B. Baldock/R. Nelson. **Season:** Year-round. **High:** April-Sept. **To obtain tee times:** Call 7 days in advance at 6:30 a.m. Hawaii residents. Non residents call 3 days in advance at 6:30 am. **Miscellaneous:** Reduced fees (weekdays, seniors, juniors), metal spikes, range (mats), club rentals, credit cards (MC, V).
Reader Comments: World's busiest course ... Any course is great on the island ... Don't waste your time waiting ... City course; heavily played; price is right ... Crowded, great place to meet locals ... Short, wide and cheap ... Cheap to Hawaii residents, but slow as can be ... Straight, easy scoring ... Busiest course, difficult to get tee time.

★★½ BARBERS POINT GOLF COURSE
M-NAS, Barbers Point, 96862, Oahu County, (808)682-1911.
Holes: 18. **Yards:** 6,400/5,522. **Par:** 72/72. **Course Rating:** 69.5/N/A. **Slope:** 120/114. **Green Fee:** $10/$38. **Walking Policy:** Unrestricted walking. **Walkability:** 1. **Opened:** 1968. **Architect:** William Bell. **Season:** Year-round. **High:** June-Aug. **Miscellaneous:** Reduced fees (twilight, juniors), range (grass/mats), club rentals, credit cards (MC, V, AE, D).
Reader Comments: Thin top soil on fairways causing hardpan ... Basic golf ... A below average military course. Have to play ball right to left ... Challenge ... Only fair; nothing special ... Much improved over last two years ... Flat ... Restaurant prices are reasonable ... Give it back to the Navy.

★★★★★ THE CHALLENGE AT MANELE   *Service+, Condition+, Pace+*
R-P.O. Box L, Lanai City, 96763, Lanai County, (808)565-2222.
Holes: 18. **Yards:** 7,039/5,024. **Par:** 72/72. **Course Rating:** N/A. **Slope:** N/A. **Green Fee:** $100/$150. **Cart Fee:** Included in Green Fee. **Walking Policy:** Mandatory cart. **Walkability:** 5. **Opened:** 1993. **Architect:** Jack Nicklaus. **Season:** Year-round. **High:** Nov.-Feb. **To obtain tee times:** Call golf shop. **Miscellaneous:** Reduced fees (resort guests), discount packages, range (grass), club rentals, lodging (250 rooms), credit cards (MC, V, AE).
Notes: Ranked 4th in 1999 Best in State; 55th in 1996 America's Top 75 Upscale Courses.
Reader Comments: Paradise found ... Wonderful! Great course/resort ... 'Scary' signature par 3, tee and green adjacent to cliffs ... Beautiful but expensive ... Worth every penny ... Fairways more generous than they appear ... 'Heaven on earth,' service great ... On the coast, breathtaking views of ocean on every hole. Winds can wreak havoc ... Don't go there. I don't want you there when I go back again and again ... Fairways are like most courses' greens ... Lanai is one of the best places to play on earth.

CORAL CREEK GOLF COURSE
PU-91-1111 Geiger Rd., Ewa Beach, 96706, Oahu County, (808)441-4653, 15 miles W of Honolulu. **E-mail:** ccgc@aloha.net. **Web:** www.coralcreekgolf.com.
Holes: 18. **Yards:** 6,808/4,935. **Par:** 72/72. **Course Rating:** 72.2/68.3. **Slope:** 135/111. **Green Fee:** $45/$125. **Walking Policy:** Unrestricted walking. **Walkability:** 2. **Opened:** 1999. **Architect:** Robin Nelson. **Season:** Year-round. **High:** June-Sept. **To obtain tee times:** Call on the 15th for following months times. **Miscellaneous:** Reduced fees (weekdays, low season, twilight), discount packages, range (grass/mats), club rentals, credit cards (MC, V, AE).

THE DUNES AT MAUI LANI GOLF COURSE
PU-1333 Maui Lani Parkway, Kahului, 96732, Maui County, (808)873-0422. **E-mail:** mauilani@maui.net. **Web:** www.mauilani.com.
Holes: 18. **Yards:** 6,841/4,768. **Par:** 72/72. **Course Rating:** 73.5/67.9. **Slope:** 136/114. **Green Fee:** $35/$70. **Cart Fee:** $20/person. **Walking Policy:** Walking at certain times. **Walkability:** 3. **Opened:** 1999. **Architect:** Robin Nelson. **Season:** Year-round. **High:** April-Dec. **Miscellaneous:** Reduced fees (weekdays, low season, twilight, seniors, juniors), discount packages, range (grass), club rentals, credit cards (MC, V), beginner friendly (informative/helpful staff).

★★★ EWA VILLAGE GOLF COURSE
PM-Mango Tree Rd., Ewa, 96706, Oahu County, (808)682-0033.
Holes: 18. **Yards:** N/A. **Par:** N/A. **Course Rating:** N/A. **Slope:** N/A. **Green Fee:** N/A. **Walkability:** N/A.
Reader Comments: Best muny, windy and narrow ... Too slow; carts can't leave path, No. 9 a dangerous dogleg ... Good-looking course but 5- to 6-hour round ... Challenging ... Windy all the time ... Par 73, tough when windy (almost always) ... Underpriced for challenge and condition it offers ... Good course for long hitters ... Bring a good book, pace slow.

★★★★½ THE EXPERIENCE AT KOELE   *Service+, Pace+*
R-730 Lanai Ave., Lanai City, 96763, Lanai County, (808)565-4653.
Holes: 18. **Yards:** 7,014/5,425. **Par:** 72/72. **Course Rating:** 73.3/66.0. **Slope:** 141/123. **Green Fee:** $100/$175. **Cart Fee:** Included in Green Fee. **Walking Policy:** Mandatory cart. **Walkability:** 3. **Opened:** 1991. **Architect:** Ted Robinson/Greg Norman. **Season:** Year-round. **High:**

Dec.-May. **To obtain tee times:** Call 30 days in advance. **Miscellaneous:** Reduced fees (twilight, juniors), discount packages, range (grass), club rentals, credit cards (MC, V, AE, D, JCB). **Notes:** Ranked 15th in 1997 Best in State.

Reader Comments: Front nine outstanding, No. 8 is greatest signature hole ever ... Awesome in all respects ... Great scenery ... A must play ... Expensive; great experience; windy. Dry, fast greens ... Worth every penny (once) ... Front nine extraordinary, back nine ordinary ... Never a rush; very relaxing ... Lanai is so sparsely populated, it feels like your own personal playground. Course plays through a tropical forest. Very scenic ... Favorite resort course in Hawaii ... Lovely 'aloha friendly' welcome.

★★★★ GRAND WAIKAPU RESORT, GOLF & SPA *Pace+*

R-2500 Honoapiilani Hwy., Wailuku, 96793, Maui County, (808)244-7888, 4 miles S of Wailuku. **Holes:** 18. **Yards:** 7,105/5,425. **Par:** 72/72. **Course Rating:** 74.7/68.6. **Slope:** 139/126. **Green Fee:** $45/$100. **Cart Fee:** Included in Green Fee. **Walking Policy:** Mandatory cart. **Walkability:** 3. **Opened:** 1991. **Architect:** Ted Robinson. **Season:** Year-round. **High:** Jan.-April. **To obtain tee times:** Call up to 1 year in advance. **Miscellaneous:** Reduced fees (resort guests), metal spikes, range (grass), caddies, club rentals, credit cards (MC, V, AE, Diners Club/JCB).

Reader Comments: Service and hospitality were outstanding. Course seemed to be in a little disrepair; overall enjoyable outing ... Pricey; very windy ... Wind makes the course. Some very good holes ... Grand indeed; layout matches clubhouse, great views and uncrowded ... Hillside play ... Playing here brings new meaning to the phrase 'three-club breeze' ... The course was in such good shape I felt bad making divots!.

★★★★ HAPUNA GOLF COURSE *Service, Pace*

R-62-100 Kauna'oa Dr., Kamuela, 96743, Hawaii County, (808)880-3000, 34 miles S of Kailua-Kona. **Holes:** 18. **Yards:** 6,875/5,067. **Par:** 72/72. **Course Rating:** 72.1/63.9. **Slope:** 134/117. **Green Fee:** $85/$135. **Cart Fee:** $20/person. **Walking Policy:** Walking at certain times. **Walkability:** 3. **Opened:** 1992. **Architect:** Arnold Palmer/Ed Seay. **Season:** Year-round. **High:** Nov.-April. **To obtain tee times:** Guests may call 4 days in advance. Off-property guests 2 days in advance. **Miscellaneous:** Reduced fees (resort guests, juniors), discount packages, range (grass), club rentals, lodging, credit cards (MC, V, AE, JCB, Carte Blanche), beginner friendly (free clinic twice a week for hotel guests, special beginner clinics). **Notes:** Ranked 11th in 1997 Best in State.

Reader Comments: A great layout for the average golfer ... Target style, mostly windy ... Excellent condition; windy ... Great views/good test ... Exceptional people in golf shop ... Expensive but good service ... Top-notch facility ... Links style makes you forget you are in Hawaii ... Desert golf in Hawaii ... Treacherous links course in mint condition, but is nearly unplayable in harsh trade winds ... Great course for couples due to the many tee choices.

HAWAII KAI GOLF COURSE

PU-8902 Kalanianaole Hwy., Honolulu, 96825, Oahu County, (808)395-2358, 10 miles E of Waikiki.

★★★ CHAMPIONSHIP COURSE

Holes: 18. **Yards:** 6,614/5,591. **Par:** 72/72. **Course Rating:** 71.4/72.7. **Slope:** 127/124. **Green Fee:** $80/$100. **Cart Fee:** Included in Green Fee. **Walking Policy:** Mandatory cart. **Walkability:** N/A. **Opened:** 1973. **Architect:** William F. Bell. **Season:** Year-round. **High:** Year-round. **To obtain tee times:** Call or fax request. **Miscellaneous:** Reduced fees (weekdays, twilight), metal spikes, range (grass), club rentals, credit cards (MC, V, AE, JCB).

Reader Comments: Tough to get a tee time. Locals have it all tied up ... Ocean views; huge bunkers; quick greens ... Very helpful starters; no waiting ... Great location, needs TLC ... Disappointing; poor fairways; homes too close on some holes ... Too slow but good course ... Very busy, too many tour groups ... Can be very challenging on windy days, bring your complete game.

EXECUTIVE COURSE

Holes: 18. **Yards:** 2,386/2,094. **Par:** 55/55. **Course Rating:** N/A. **Slope:** N/A. **Green Fee:** $29/$34. **Cart Fee:** $8/. **Cart Fee:** Included in Green Fee. **Walking Policy:** Unrestricted walking. **Walkability:** 4. **Opened:** 1950. **Architect:** Robert Trent Jones Sr. **Season:** Year-round. **High:** Year-round. **To obtain tee times:** Call or fax request. **Miscellaneous:** Reduced fees (weekdays, twilight, juniors), metal spikes, range (grass), club rentals, credit cards (MC, V, AE, JCB).

HAWAII PRINCE GOLF CLUB

R-91-1200 Fort Weaver Rd., Ewa Beach, 96706, Oahu County, (808)944-4567, 20 miles W of Honolulu. **Holes:** 27. **Green Fee:** $50/$135. **Cart Fee:** Included in Green Fee. **Walkability:** 3. **Opened:** 1992. **Architect:** Arnold Palmer/Ed Seay. **Season:** Year-round. **High:** Dec.-Feb.

★★★½ A/B

Yards: 7,117/5,275. **Par:** 72/72. **Course Rating:** 74.2/70.4. **Slope:** 131/120. **Walking Policy:** Walking at certain times. **Miscellaneous:** Reduced fees (weekdays, resort guests, twilight, seniors, juniors), discount packages, range (grass), club rentals, credit cards (MC, V, AE, Diners Club, JCB).

★★★½ **A/C**
Yards: 7,166/5,300. **Par:** 72/72. **Course Rating:** 74.4/69.9. **Slope:** 134/118. **Walking Policy:** Mandatory cart. **Walkability:** 3. **Miscellaneous:** Reduced fees (weekdays, resort guests, twilight, seniors, juniors), discount packages, metal spikes, range (grass), club rentals, credit cards (MC, V, AE, Diners Club, JCB).

★★★½ **B/C**
Yards: 7,255/5,205. **Par:** 72/72. **Course Rating:** 75.0/69.5. **Slope:** 132/117. **Walking Policy:** Mandatory cart. **Walkability:** 3. **Miscellaneous:** Reduced fees (weekdays, resort guests, twilight, seniors, juniors), discount packages, metal spikes, range (grass), club rentals, credit cards (MC, V, AE, Diners Club, JCB).

Reader Comments: Fine, fine course ... Nice fun, challenging due to wind conditions ... Superb condition, professional grade ... Course condition & service have improved a lot ... 'B' nine has most character. Great twilight rates ... Excellent course; very windy ... Very good greens ... Long and challenging, wide fairways.

★★★★ **HICKAM GOLF COURSE** *Value*
M-Bldg. 3572, Hickam AFB, Hickam AFB, 96853, Oahu County, (808)449-6490. **E-mail:** thomas.stanfill@hickem.at.mil.
Holes: 18. **Yards:** 6,868/5,675. **Par:** 72/73. **Course Rating:** 71.9/72.9. **Slope:** 129/120. **Green Fee:** $8/$32. **Cart Fee:** $8/person. **Walking Policy:** Unrestricted walking. **Walkability:** 1. **Opened:** 1965. **Season:** Year-round. **High:** April-Sept. **To obtain tee times:** Call 4 days in advance. **Miscellaneous:** Reduced fees (twilight, juniors), range (grass/mats), club rentals, credit cards (MC, V), beginner friendly (golf clinics).

Reader Comments: Great view of ocean and airport ... Best military golf experience in Hawaii! ... Perfect lie every time, great scenery ... Military course—fast greens ... Wide fairways, noisy, next to airport ... Price is very good, but hard to get on ... As an average golfer, course was excellent, a little challenging for me ... Must be accompanied by military member.

HILO MUNICIPAL GOLF COURSE
PM-340 Haihai St., Hilo, 96720, Hawaii County, (808)959-9601.
Holes: 18. **Yards:** 6,325/5,034. **Par:** 71/71. **Course Rating:** 70.4/69.1. **Slope:** 121/114. **Green Fee:** $20/$25. **Cart Fee:** $14/cart. **Walking Policy:** Unrestricted walking. **Walkability:** 3. **Opened:** 1950. **Architect:** Willard Wilkinson. **Season:** Year-round. **To obtain tee times:** Call starter at (808)959-7711. **Miscellaneous:** Reduced fees (weekdays), metal spikes, range (mats).

★★★★ **HUALALAI GOLF CLUB** *Service+, Condition+, Pace+*
R-Mile Marker 87, Queen Kaahumanu Hwy., Kailua Kona, 96745, Hawaii County, (808)325-8480, 15 miles N of Kona.
Holes: 18. **Yards:** 7,117/5,374. **Par:** 72/72. **Course Rating:** 75.7/70.4. **Slope:** 131/118. **Green Fee:** $145/$145. **Cart Fee:** Included in Green Fee. **Walking Policy:** Unrestricted walking. **Walkability:** 2. **Opened:** 1996. **Architect:** Jack Nicklaus. **Season:** Year-round. **High:** Oct.-May. **To obtain tee times:** Play is limited to guests of Four Seasons Hualalai and homeowners. More than 7 days in advance call hotel reservations at (808)325-8108. Within 7 days call golf shop at (808)325-8480. **Miscellaneous:** Reduced fees (juniors), discount packages, range (grass), caddies, club rentals, lodging, credit cards (MC, V, AE, D, JCB).
Notes: Ranked 12th in 1999 Best in State. 1997 Mastercard Championship—Hale Irwin Championship. 1998 Mastercard Championship Gil Morgan. 1999 Mastercard Championship John Jacobs.

Reader Comments: Lots of fun and very fair ... Outstanding practice facility, lodging, food ... Good course, great amenities ... Hard to get on. Outstanding courtesy. Only striking holes are 17 and 18 on ocean ... Flawless condition ... Treat you like a king, great design taking the prevailing wind into account ... So expensive, so worth it ... Not as picturesque as some courses in Hawaii but perhaps the grandest of them all! ... I especially like the cookies at the turn!.

KAANAPALI GOLF COURSES
R-Kaanapali Resort, Lahaina, 96761, Maui County, (808)661-3691, (800)665-4742, 5 miles N of Historic Lahaina Town.
★★★★ **NORTH COURSE**
Holes: 18. **Yards:** 6,994/5,417. **Par:** 71/72. **Course Rating:** 72.8/71.1. **Slope:** 134/123. **Green Fee:** $100/$120. **Cart Fee:** Included in Green Fee. **Walking Policy:** Mandatory cart. **Walkability:** 4. **Opened:** 1963. **Architect:** Robert Trent Jones. **Season:** Year-round. **High:** Dec.-April. **To obtain tee times:** Resort guests call 4 days in advance. Nonguests 2 days in advance. **Miscellaneous:** Reduced fees (low season, resort guests, twilight), discount packages, metal spikes, range (grass/mats), club rentals, lodging, credit cards (MC, V, AE, JCB).
Notes: 1996, 1997 Senior PGA Tour Kaanapali Classic.

Reader Comments: Tradewinds too much! ... Nice open course ... Impeccable ... Typical resort ... Tough rough! ... Very busy, typical resort course ... Scenic and windy ... Worth every lost golf ball ... Best of the Kaanapali courses ... Course conditions could use a makeover ... Best course

I ever played, no comparison ... Great ocean view, overpriced ... Very nice and the big boys play here ... Always a treat to play here ... Pricey, but well worth the experience.

★★★½ SOUTH COURSE
R-Kaanapali Resort, Lahaina, 96761, Maui County, (808)661-3691, (800)665-4742, 5 miles N of Historic Lahaina Town.

Holes: 18. **Yards:** 6,555/5,485. **Par:** 71/71. **Course Rating:** 70.7/69.8. **Slope:** 127/120. **Green Fee:** $100/$120. **Cart Fee:** Included in Green Fee. **Walking Policy:** Mandatory cart. **Walkability:** 3. **Opened:** 1976. **Architect:** Jack Snyder. **Season:** Year-round. **High:** Dec.-April. **To obtain tee times:** Resort guests call 4 days in advance. Nonguests call 2 days in advance. **Miscellaneous:** Reduced fees (low season, resort guests, twilight), discount packages, metal spikes, range (grass/mats), club rentals, lodging, credit cards (MC, V, AE, JCB).

Reader Comments: Another oldie links type ... A real bargain at resident rates ... Beautiful layout ... Greens and tees need a makeover ... Beautiful location ... Nice course, but slow play ... Play before the wind is up ... Not worth $100.

★★★½ KALAKAUA GOLF COURSE
M-Building 1283 schofield Barracks, Wahiawa, 96857, Honolulu County, (808)655-9833, 25 miles N of Honolulu.

Holes: 18. **Yards:** 6,186/5,818. **Par:** 72/73. **Course Rating:** 69.0/75.1. **Slope:** 119/133. **Green Fee:** $9/$55. **Cart Fee:** $8/person. **Walking Policy:** Unrestricted walking. **Walkability:** 1. **Season:** Year-round. **High:** April-Aug. **To obtain tee times:** Various Call Shop @ 808-655-9833. **Miscellaneous:** Range (grass/mats), club rentals, credit cards (MC, V, AE, D).

Reader Comments: Basic golf; very nice ... Expect to play in showers ... Military course missing only a few service items ... Great course when you can get on. Military has preference. Pace is at military pace ... Tight. Need to keep ball in play in correct position ... Wonderful ocean view, fantastic layout ... Not bad for the cost.

★★★★ KALUAKOI HOTEL & GOLF CLUB *Pace+*
R-P.O. Box 26, Maunaloa, 96770, Molokai County, (808)552-2739, (800)435-7208, 20 miles E of Kaunakakai. **E-mail:** Kaluakoi@juno.com.

Holes: 18. **Yards:** 6,600/5,461. **Par:** 72/72. **Course Rating:** 72.3/71.4. **Slope:** 129/119. **Green Fee:** $60/$80. **Cart Fee:** Included in Green Fee. **Walking Policy:** Mandatory cart. **Walkability:** 2. **Opened:** 1977. **Architect:** Ted Robinson. **Season:** Year-round. **High:** Nov.-Feb. **To obtain tee times:** Call 30 days in advance. Groups of 16 or more may call up to 1 year in advance. **Miscellaneous:** Reduced fees (low season, resort guests, twilight, juniors), discount packages, metal spikes, range (grass), club rentals, lodging, credit cards (MC, V, AE, D, JCB, Diners Club).

Reader Comments: Five holes on ocean front ... Course could be excellent if weather cooperates, great staff ... Lack of water, still challenging, will play it again ... Hawaii's best kept secret! ... Felt like we owned the place. Quiet ... My favorite course in the whole world ... Most economical resort course on islands.

★★★½ KANEOHE KLIPPER GOLF CLUB *Value*
M-Kaneohe Marines Corps Air Station, Kanehoe Bay, 96863, Oahu County, (808)254-1745, 15 miles N of Waikiki.

Holes: 18. **Yards:** 6,739/5,575. **Par:** 72/71. **Course Rating:** 71.0/76.3. **Slope:** 130/133. **Green Fee:** $8/$37. **Cart Fee:** $16/cart. **Walking Policy:** Unrestricted walking. **Walk-ability:** N/A. **Opened:** 1948. **Architect:** William P. Bell. **Season:** Year-round. **High:** May-June. **To obtain tee times:** Active duty MCBH may call 6 days in advance. Active duty other may call 4 days in advance. Retired military may call 3 days in advance. **Miscellaneous:** Range (grass/mats), club rentals, credit cards (MC, V, AE, D), beginner friendly.

Reader Comments: Holes 13, 14, 15 run right along the ocean ... Fantastic water holes, play the tips ... Great ocean views, but pretty windy ... Poor man's Pebble Beach! ... Overpriced compared to other courses ... Like many military courses, the pace is too slow ... Flat military course, but good value ... Course is flat on front nine, has two spectacular holes on the back.

KAPALUA GOLF CLUB *Service*
R-300 Kapalua Dr., Kapalua, 96761, Maui County, (877)KAPALUA, 8 miles N of Lahaina. **E-mail:** teetimes@kapaluamaui.com. **Web:** www.kapalamaui.com.

★★★★ THE BAY COURSE
(808)669-8820.

Holes: 18. **Yards:** 6,600/5,124. **Par:** 72/72. **Course Rating:** 71.7/69.6. **Slope:** 138/121. **Green Fee:** $100/$160. **Cart Fee:** Included in Green Fee. **Walking Policy:** Walking at certain times. **Walkability:** 2. **Opened:** 1975. **Architect:** Francis Duane/Arnold Palmer. **Season:** Year-round. **High:** Dec.-March. **To obtain tee times:** Resort guests may reserve tee time 30 days in advance. Nonguests call 4 days in advance. **Miscellaneous:** Reduced fees (resort guests, twilight, juniors), discount packages, metal spikes, range (grass), caddies, club rentals, lodging, credit cards (MC, V, AE, D, Diners Club, JCB).

Notes: Ranked 14th in 1999 Best in State. 1981-1997 PGA Tour Lincoln Mercury Kapalua International.

HAWAII

Reader Comments: Ocean front on several holes ... Expensive but it's Maui ... Design is beautiful ... Have camera ready for Nos. 4 and 5 ... Most beautiful course I have played ... Well maintained ... Hit a ball, watch a whale, hit a ball, watch the sea turtles ... Scenery is everything ... Better (more fun) if play back nine before front ... $140 green fees, breathtaking views, I wanted to play so bad. Money was worth it. Staff went out of its way ... Even more stunning in real life than computer game depicts ... Favorite of the three courses.

★★★★½ **THE PLANTATION COURSE** *Condition*
(808)669-8877.

Holes: 18. **Yards:** 7,263/5,627. **Par:** 73/73. **Course Rating:** 75.2/73.2. **Slope:** 142/129. **Green Fee:** $110/$175. **Cart Fee:** Included in Green Fee. **Walking Policy:** Walking at certain times. **Walkability:** 4. **Opened:** 1991. **Architect:** Bill Coore/Ben Crenshaw. **Season:** Year-round. **High:** Dec.-March. **To obtain tee times:** Resort guests may reserve up to 30 days in advance. Nonguests call 4 days in advance. **Miscellaneous:** Reduced fees (resort guests, twilight, juniors), discount packages, metal spikes, range (grass), caddies, club rentals, lodging, credit cards (MC, V, AE, D, Diners Club, JCB).

Notes: Ranked 5th in 1999 Best in State; 63rd in 1996 America's Top 75 Upscale Courses. 1981-1997 PGA Tour Lincoln Mercury Kapalua International; Mercedes Championships.

Reader Comments: Must play once, when winds are blowing ... Tall rough, easy to lose balls ... Panoramic ocean views with lots of wind ... Unique, incredible golf experience ... Best of Kapalua ... Wow! Very tough but beautiful ... Saw whales from the tees ... Fun to play a tour course ... Over-priced; lot of wind & rain ... Too expensive for the average golfer ... Value a '5' only if you play twilight ... Service & people exceptional ... Too many blind tee shots.

★★★★ **THE VILLAGE COURSE** *Pace*
(808)669-8835.

Holes: 18. **Yards:** 6,632/5,134. **Par:** 71/71. **Course Rating:** 73.3/70.9. **Slope:** 139/122. **Green Fee:** $85/$130. **Cart Fee:** Included in Green Fee. **Walking Policy:** Walking at certain times. **Walkability:** N/A. **Opened:** 1980. **Architect:** Arnold Palmer/Ed Seay. **Season:** Year-round. **High:** Dec.-March. **To obtain tee times:** Resort guests call 7 days in advance. Nonguests call 4 days in advance. **Miscellaneous:** Reduced fees (resort guests, twilight, juniors), discount packages, metal spikes, caddies, club rentals, lodging, credit cards (MC, V, AE, D, Diners Club, JCB).

Reader Comments: Overpriced for quality of course ... Great natural beauty ... Great course but not in top 10% ... Best of Kapalua ... First 5 holes uphill can be tough in wind, but still great ... Play only if you can't get on the Bay or Plantation ... We saw more whales here than on the island tour! ... Can't beat the views, golf it at least once ... Very hilly, very scenic, awesome to play ... Way too expensive ... Least favorite of Kapalua 3, but still nice ... A good warmup for Bay or Plantation ... Tight and challenging layout.

★★★★ **KAPOLEI GOLF COURSE**
91-701 Farrington Hwy., Kapolei, 96707, Oahu County, (808)674-2227. **E-mail:** kapgc@gte.net. **Holes:** 18. **Yards:** N/A. **Par:** N/A. **Course Rating:** N/A. **Slope:** N/A. **Green Fee:** $130/$150. **Cart Fee:** Included in Green Fee. **Walking Policy:** Mandatory cart. **Walkability:** 3. **Season:** Year-round. **Miscellaneous:** Reduced fees (twilight), metal spikes, club rentals, credit cards (MC, V, AE, JCB and Diners Club), beginner friendly.

Reader Comments: Really enjoy playing here ... Well-protected greens, very good test ... From No. 9 on, lots of water. Tricky greens in great shape ... Only played once; course in great condition ... Good layout used by LPGA ... Straightforward Hawaiian golf; tropical, windy, pretty.

KAUAI LAGOONS RESORT *Service*
R-3351 Hoolaulea Way, Lihue, 96766, Kauai County, (808)241-6000, (800)634-6400.

★★★★½ **KIELE COURSE** *Pace*
Holes: 18. **Yards:** 7,070/5,417. **Par:** 72/72. **Course Rating:** 73.7/70.5. **Slope:** 137/123. **Green Fee:** $92/$150. **Cart Fee:** Included in Green Fee. **Walking Policy:** Mandatory cart. **Walkability:** 3. **Opened:** 1988. **Architect:** Jack Nicklaus. **Season:** Year-round. **High:** Jan.-March/Aug. **To obtain tee times:** Call up to 30 days in advance. **Miscellaneous:** Reduced fees (resort guests, juniors), discount packages, metal spikes, range (grass), club rentals, lodging, credit cards (MC, V, AE, Diners Club).

Notes: Ranked 6th in 1999 Best in State; 60th in 1996 America's Top 75 Upscale Courses.

Reader Comments: Expensive but worth it ... Excellent course, a joy to play ... Nicklaus at his best ... One of the best I've played ... Perfection personified! Outstanding views and great holes, need to stay on the fairways ... Not what it used to be ... Service not up to par for money ... Yeah, it was slow, but I am on vacation ... Nice people, better course ... One of Hawaii's underrated jewels ... Price too costly. Staff enjoyable ... Proximity to the airport is the only drawback ... Friendliest staff of any course in Hawaii.

★★★★ **MOKIHANA COURSE** *Pace*
Holes: 18. **Yards:** 6,960/5,607. **Par:** 72/72. **Course Rating:** 73.1/71.8. **Slope:** 127/116. **Green Fee:** $61/$100. **Cart Fee:** Included in Green Fee. **Walking Policy:** Walking at certain times. **Walkability:** 1. **Opened:** 1989. **Architect:** Jack Nicklaus. **Season:** Year-round. **High:** Jan.-March/Aug. **To obtain tee times:** Call up to 30 days in advance. **Miscellaneous:** Reduced fees

(resort guests, twilight, juniors), discount packages, metal spikes, range (grass), club rentals, lodging, credit cards (MC, V, AE, Diners Club).

Reader Comments: Being in Kauai helps the atmosphere. Beautiful ... 1st time in Hawaii, I'll be back ... Long way to go to play golf ... Easy but still a challenge ... Expected more. Only challenge was the wind ... OK only, can't remember holes later. A good warm-up for the Kiele course ... Fair to high handicappers will love it ... Inland not as exciting as Kiele, but well-maintained fun offering ... Nice people. The course is OK ... Very close to noisy airport ... Fun! Got my wife hooked on golf.

★★★★ KIAHUNA GOLF CLUB *Value*

PM-2545 Kiahuna Plantation Dr., Poipu, 96756, Kauai County, (808)742-9595, 15 miles S of Lihue. **Holes:** 18. **Yards:** 6,353/5,631. **Par:** 70/70. **Course Rating:** 69.7/71.4. **Slope:** 128/119. **Green Fee:** $40/$75. **Cart Fee:** Included in Green Fee. **Walking Policy:** Mandatory cart. **Walkability:** 3. **Opened:** 1983. **Architect:** Robert Trent Jones Jr. **Season:** Year-round. **High:** Nov.-March. **To obtain tee times:** Call 1 day in advance. **Miscellaneous:** Reduced fees (weekdays, low season, resort guests, twilight, juniors), metal spikes, range (grass), club rentals, credit cards (MC, V, AE, D, JCB).

Reader Comments: Condition needs work ... Interesting & enjoyable muny ... Target golf, windy, but fun ... Friendly staff ... Good value for money ... Tight fairways! Shotmaker's delight ... Short, tight, easy to get on ... The course is good; keeps you thinking. Facilities are not as good.

★★★★ KO OLINA GOLF CLUB

R-92-1220 Aliinui Dr., Kapolei, 96707, Oahu County, (808)676-5300, 20 miles W of Honolulu. **E-mail:** koolina@aloha.net. **Web:** www.koolinagolf.com.
Holes: 18. **Yards:** 6,867/5,392. **Par:** 72/72. **Course Rating:** 72.3/71.3. **Slope:** 135/126. **Green Fee:** $98/$145. **Walking Policy:** Walking at certain times. **Walkability:** 3. **Opened:** 1990. **Architect:** Ted Robinson. **Season:** Year-round. **High:** Dec.-Feb. **To obtain tee times:** Call up to 7 days in advance. **Miscellaneous:** Reduced fees (resort guests, twilight), discount packages, range (grass/mats), club rentals, lodging, credit cards (MC, V, AE, D, Diners Club, JCB), beginner friendly (early a.m., late p.m. 9-holes).

Reader Comments: Beautiful but costly ... Good course, pretty scenery ... Wide variety of holes, best finishing hole in Hawaii ... Excellent; don't miss ... Typical tropical course ... Great course/top shape ... Best on island ... Windy course ... Very tough.

KONA COUNTRY CLUB

R-78-7000 Alii Dr., Kailua Kona, 96740, Hawaii County, (808)322-2595. **Web:** www.konagolf.com.
★★★★ ALII MOUNTAIN COURSE

Holes: 18. **Yards:** 6,471/4,906. **Par:** 72/72. **Course Rating:** 71.5/69.2. **Slope:** 133/125. **Green Fee:** $95/$150. **Cart Fee:** Included in Green Fee. **Walking Policy:** Mandatory cart. **Walkability:** N/A. **Opened:** 1985. **Architect:** William F. Bell/Robin Nelson/Rodney Wrig. **Season:** Year-round. **High:** Jan.-March. **To obtain tee times:** Call up to 7 days in advance. **Miscellaneous:** Reduced fees (resort guests, twilight, juniors), discount packages, metal spikes, range (grass/mats), club rentals, lodging, credit cards (MC, V, AE, Diners Club, JCB).

Reader Comments: Mountain course to the max ... Popular, gets heavy play ... Just a super place to be! ... Some of the best views of Pacific in Hawaii ... Best Hawaiian golf package on the Big Island! Two good courses. Mtn. Course is tough ... Not a level lie on the course. Tricky greens don't break as much as they look. Cold, wet towels after a round, delightful ... Good service ... Great shape, good value.

★★★★ OCEAN COURSE

Holes: 18. **Yards:** 6,579/5,499. **Par:** 72/73. **Course Rating:** 71.6/71.9. **Slope:** 129/127. **Green Fee:** $95/$150. **Cart Fee:** Included in Green Fee. **Walking Policy:** Mandatory cart. **Walkability:** N/A. **Opened:** 1968. **Architect:** William F. Bell. **Season:** Year-round. **High:** Jan.-March. **To obtain tee times:** Call up to 7 days in advance. **Miscellaneous:** Reduced fees (resort guests, twilight), discount packages, metal spikes, range (grass/mats), club rentals, lodging (500 rooms), credit cards (MC, V, AE, JCB Diners).

Reader Comments: Many different holes ... Great views, great greens, good value ... Beautiful. Good value in Hawaii ... Fun course. Like a good muny course with a view ... Just a super place to be! ... The wind and narrowness make it very interesting ... Nice layout ... Beautiful holes right on the ocean with pounding surf; great rate ... Do yourself a favor, play less popular Mountain course. Bigger challenge and better view.

★★★★ KOOLAU GOLF CLUB

PU-45-550 Kionaole, Kaneohe, 96744, Oahu County, (808)236-4653, 13 miles N of Honolulu. **Holes:** 18. **Yards:** 7,310/5,119. **Par:** 72/72. **Course Rating:** 76.4/72.9. **Slope:** 162/134. **Green Fee:** $50/$100. **Cart Fee:** Included in Green Fee. **Walking Policy:** Unrestricted walking. **Walkability:** 4. **Opened:** 1992. **Architect:** Dick Nugent. **Season:** Year-round. **To obtain tee times:** Call 30 days in advance. **Miscellaneous:** Reduced fees (weekdays, low season, twilight), discount packages, metal spikes, range (grass), club rentals, credit cards (MC, V, AE).
Notes: Ranked 3rd in 1999 Best in State.

Reader Comments: Probably too much 'carry golf' for many ... Toughest in the nation ... Brutal, but fun, 18th hole could take all day ... Would love to see the tour play this one ... I recommend forgetting stroke play, just keep track of lost balls ... Great views! Poor fairways ... One of the most enjoyable places I have played ... First time I shot over 100 in 5 years, and I loved it! ... Pretty layout; pricey ... A masochist's must! More of a survival course than a golf course ... A bit pricey but gotta play it once!.

★★★★ LEILEHUA GOLF COURSE

M-USAG Hawaii Golf , Schofield Barracks, 96857, Oahu County, (808)655-4653.
Holes: 18. **Yards:** N/A. **Par:** N/A. **Course Rating:** N/A. **Slope:** N/A. **Green Fee:** N/A. **Walking Policy:** Unrestricted walking. **Walkability:** 1. **Season:** Year-round. **High:** Jun-Aug.
Miscellaneous: Credit cards (MC, V, AE).
Reader Comments: Well maintained. Probably the most challenging military course in Hawaii ... Although good test, conditions average at best ... Great course but needs some drainage work ... A good value ... Too much military! ... Inexpensive, even for non-military/non-resident ... No attempt to speed up play. A fault of military golf courses ... Wow! Some breathtaking holes.

★★★½ MAKAHA GOLF CLUB

R-84-626 Makaha Valley Rd., Waianae, 96792, Oahu County, (808)695-9544, (800)757-8060, 40 miles W of Honolulu.
Holes: 18. **Yards:** 7,077/5,856. **Par:** 72/72. **Course Rating:** 73.2/73.9. **Slope:** 139/129. **Green Fee:** $90/$160. **Cart Fee:** Included in Green Fee. **Walking Policy:** Mandatory cart. **Walkability:** 4. **Opened:** 1969. **Architect:** William F. Bell. **Season:** Year-round. **High:** Jan.-March. **To obtain tee times:** Call golf shop. **Miscellaneous:** Reduced fees (weekdays, low season, resort guests, twilight, seniors, juniors), metal spikes, range (mats), club rentals, credit cards (MC, V, AE, D, Diners Club, JCB).
Reader Comments: A scenic delight with some of the holes up against the water and others near the mountains ... Not much roll on fairways ... Great value ... A real challenge—worth playing ... Scenic setting, a bit remote ... Very good design, greens now slower, condition down ... Greens hard to read, very grainy ... Needs work, great views ... Fairways wide. Hit long and you're OK.

★★★★ MAKAHA VALLEY COUNTRY CLUB

PU-84-627 Makaha Valley Rd., Waianae, 96792, Oahu County, (808)695-7111, 40 miles NW of Honolulu.
Holes: 18. **Yards:** 6,369/5,720. **Par:** 71/71. **Course Rating:** 69.2/72.7. **Slope:** 133/120. **Green Fee:** $55/$100. **Cart Fee:** Included in Green Fee. **Walking Policy:** Mandatory cart. **Walkability:** 5. **Opened:** 1969. **Architect:** William F. Bell. **Season:** Year-round. **High:** Dec.-March. **To obtain tee times:** Call for tee time. **Miscellaneous:** Metal spikes, range (grass), club rentals, credit cards (MC, V, AE, D, Diners Club).
Reader Comments: Like an old friend ... Too tough for average golfer... Good test but short ... Popular, great views, real challenge ... A bit out of the way, but never crowded ... Ideal location, flowers, water, nice variety of holes, 1st choice for average tourist ... Beautiful facilities.

★★★★ MAKALEI HAWAII COUNTRY CLUB

PU-72-3890 Hawaii Belt Rd., Kailua-Kona, 96740, Hawaii County, (808)325-6625, (800)606-9606, 5 miles N of Kailua-Kona.
Holes: 18. **Yards:** 7,091/5,242. **Par:** 72/72. **Course Rating:** 73.5/64.9. **Slope:** 143/125. **Green Fee:** $110/$110. **Cart Fee:** Included in Green Fee. **Walking Policy:** Mandatory cart.
Walkability: N/A. **Opened:** 1992. **Architect:** Dick Nugent. **Season:** Year-round. **High:** Dec.-March. **To obtain tee times:** Call up to 7 days in advance. **Miscellaneous:** Reduced fees (weekdays, low season, resort guests, twilight, seniors, juniors), discount packages, metal spikes, range (grass), club rentals, credit cards (MC, V, AE, Diners Club, JCB).
Reader Comments: Too radical in course elevations ... 1,000-foot elevation changes ... Flowers, lava rocks, ocean views, a favorite ... Beautiful course and tough holes ... Extremely challenging ... Best value on Big Island ... Inexpensive with coupons easily obtained ... Lots of peacocks, pheasants and turkey get on fairways.

MAKENA RESORT GOLF COURSE   *Service*

R-5415 Makena Alanui, Kihei, 96753, Maui County, (808)879-3344, (800)321-6284, 6 miles S of Kihei.

★★★★ NORTH COURSE   *Pace*

Holes: 18. **Yards:** 6,914/5,303. **Par:** 72/72. **Course Rating:** 72.1/70.9. **Slope:** 139/128. **Green Fee:** $85/$140. **Cart Fee:** Included in Green Fee. **Walking Policy:** Walking at certain times.
Walkability: 5. **Opened:** 1993. **Architect:** Robert Trent Jones Jr. **Season:** Year-round. **High:** Oct.-April/Aug. **To obtain tee times:** Guests of Makena Resort & Maui Prince Hotel may call up to 1 year in advance. Nonguests may call up to 5 days in advance. **Miscellaneous:** Reduced fees (low season, resort guests, twilight, juniors), discount packages, range (grass/mats), caddies, club rentals, lodging, credit cards (MC, V, AE, Diners Club, Carte Blanche).
Notes: Ranked 11th in 1999 Best in State.

Reader Comments: Good course, but pace too slow ... Scenery is so spectacular, you have a hard time keeping your mind on your game ... Best greens in Hawaii... Great course; good value; memorable holes ... Nicer layout than Wailea ... This one is worth it—watch the wind .... Condition not as good as before. Greens are slower ... Not of the quality of nearby courses ... Unbelievable views; both par 3s on the back are downhill toward Molakini ... Nice, quiet getaway.

★★★★ **SOUTH COURSE**

Holes: 18. **Yards:** 7,017/5,529. **Par:** 72/72. **Course Rating:** 72.6/71.1. **Slope:** 138/130. **Green Fee:** $85/$140. **Cart Fee:** Included in Green Fee. **Walking Policy:** Walking at certain times. **Walkability:** 3. **Opened:** 1993. **Architect:** Robert Trent Jones Jr. **Season:** Year-round. **High:** Oct.-April/Aug. **To obtain tee times:** Guests of Makena Resort & Maui Prince Hotel may call up to 1 year in advance. Nonguests may call up to 5 days in advance. **Miscellaneous:** Reduced fees (low season, resort guests, twilight, juniors), discount packages, metal spikes, range (grass), caddies, club rentals, lodging (310 rooms), credit cards (MC, V, AE, Diners Club, Carte Blanche). **Notes:** Ranked 10th in 1999 Best in State.

Reader Comments: Outstanding ... All-world ocean views ... Lot of golf outings, good service ... Excellent test for all abilities ... Excellent condition. A must play! ... Never rains, virtually uninhabited, paradise! ... Need added work ... Expensive, enjoyable to play ... Well-maintained, good par 3s ... Good staff.

★★★★ **MAUNA KEA BEACH GOLF COURSE**

R-62-100 Mauna Kea Beach Dr., Kamuela, 96743, Hawaii County, (808)882-5400, 34 miles S of Kailua-Kona. **E-mail:** maunakeabbeachhotel.com. **Web:** www.maunakeabeachhotel.com. **Holes:** 18. **Yards:** 7,114/5,277. **Par:** 72/72. **Course Rating:** 73.6/70.2. **Slope:** 143/124. **Green Fee:** $90/$150. **Cart Fee:** Included in Green Fee. **Walking Policy:** Walking at certain times. **Walkability:** 5. **Opened:** 1965. **Architect:** Robert Trent Jones. **Season:** Year-round. **High:** Nov.-April. **To obtain tee times:** Guests call up to 4 days in advance. Off-property guests call 2 days in advance. **Miscellaneous:** Reduced fees (resort guests, twilight, juniors), discount packages, metal spikes, range (grass/mats), club rentals, lodging (315 rooms), credit cards (MC, V, AE, JCB, Carte Blanche). **Notes:** Ranked 69th in 1999-2000 America's 100 Greatest; 2nd in 1999 Best in State.

Reader Comments: Some good holes, but overrated ... No. 3 awesome ... Still best in Hawaii. Sadly, homes now invade course ... Beautiful golf for everyone ... An oldie but goodie ... Overrated. Expensive ... My home course is in better shape ... Now a favorite! ... No comments necessary for this course ... Staff a bit bored, living on their laurels ... Wasn't in great condition ... A true gem ... A good course worth the money! ... Staff needs a course at Charm School.

MAUNA LANI RESORT *Service+*

R-68-1310 Mauna Lani Dr., Suite 103, Kohala Coast, 96743, Hawaii County, (808)885-6655, 30 miles N of Kailua-Kona.

★★★★½ **NORTH COURSE** *Condition*

Holes: 18. **Yards:** 6,993/5,474. **Par:** 72/72. **Course Rating:** 73.2/71.4. **Slope:** 136/124. **Green Fee:** $85/$160. **Cart Fee:** Included in Green Fee. **Walking Policy:** Mandatory cart. **Walkability:** 1. **Opened:** 1981. **Architect:** Nelson/Wright/Haworth. **Season:** Year-round. **High:** Nov.-April. **To obtain tee times:** Resort guests call up to 14 days in advance. Off-property guests call up to 3 days in advance. **Miscellaneous:** Reduced fees (low season, twilight), discount packages, metal spikes, range (grass), club rentals, lodging, credit cards (MC, V, AE, Diners Club). **Notes:** Ranked 15th in 1999 Best in State.

Reader Comments: Expensive but very nice ... It's like playing in Colorado surrounded by ocean ... Overrated because of Senior Skins Game ... Very good test with trees coming into play ... Beautiful ... As good as it gets ... Lava bordering both sides of most fairways ... Several unique holes ... Nice layout, not as grand as the South. Both are very playable; wide fairways; nice resort layout ... Enjoyable for all kinds of golfers.

★★★★ **SOUTH COURSE**

Holes: 18. **Yards:** 7,029/5,331. **Par:** 72/72. **Course Rating:** N/A. **Slope:** 133/122. **Green Fee:** $85/$200. **Cart Fee:** Included in Green Fee. **Walking Policy:** Mandatory cart. **Walkability:** 1. **Opened:** 1981. **Architect:** Nelson, Wright/Haworth. **Season:** Year-round. **High:** Dec.-March. **To obtain tee times:** Resort guests may call up to 14 days in advance. Off-property guests may call up to 3 days in advance. **Miscellaneous:** Reduced fees (low season, resort guests, twilight), discount packages, metal spikes, range (grass), club rentals, lodging, credit cards (MC, V, AE, JCB Diners). **Notes:** Ranked 12th in 1997 Best in State.

Reader Comments: Excellent value for twilight time; windy ... Expensive but very nice ... Great scenery ... What a course, what views; great golf shop ... Best I've played ... Unforgettable 15th hole on South Course. A must play! ... Challenging ... Staff is outstanding, bend over backward to please ... Lava is tiresome after a while ... Stunning par 3s ... Sets the standard for Hawaii ... Spotty conditions for the price I paid. Felt ripped off ... Twilight is the best deal.

★★★ MILILANI GOLF CLUB
SP-95-176 Kuahelani Ave., Mililani, 96789, Oahu County, (808)623-2222, 12 miles NW of Honolulu.
Holes: 18. **Yards:** 6,455/5,985. **Par:** 72/72. **Course Rating:** 69.3/73.6. **Slope:** 121/127. **Green Fee:** $89/$95. **Cart Fee:** Included in Green Fee. **Walking Policy:** Mandatory cart. **Walkability:** 1. **Opened:** 1967. **Architect:** Bob Baldock. **Season:** Year-round. **High:** Jan.-Feb./June. **To obtain tee times:** Call up to 30 days in advance. **Miscellaneous:** Reduced fees (weekdays, twilight), discount packages, metal spikes, range (mats), club rentals, credit cards (MC, V, AE, Diners Club).
Reader Comments: Undiscovered gem ... Relatively flat. Fairways could be more defined with a shorter height of cut ... Slowest play in the state.

★★★★ NAVY MARINE GOLF COURSE
M-Bldg. 43, Valkenburgh St., Honolulu, 96818, Oahu County, (808)471-0142.
Special Notes: Call club for further information.

★★★½ NEW EWA BEACH GOLF CLUB
SP-91-050 Fort Weaver Rd., Ewa Beach, 96706, Oahu County, (808)689-8351, 18 miles W of Honolulu.
Holes: 18. **Yards:** 6,541/5,230. **Par:** 72/72. **Course Rating:** 71.3/70.5. **Slope:** 125/121. **Green Fee:** $55/$135. **Cart Fee:** Included in Green Fee. **Walking Policy:** Mandatory cart. **Walkability:** 2. **Opened:** 1992. **Architect:** Robin Nelson/Rodney Wright. **Season:** Year-round. **High:** Aug./Winter. **To obtain tee times:** Call 7 days in advance. Special tournament and club rate available. **Miscellaneous:** Reduced fees (twilight, seniors, juniors), metal spikes, club rentals, credit cards (MC, V, AE, JCB).
Reader Comments: Tough and interesting, especially with the wind ... Nice short course; pleasant ... Nice course but the Keawe trees are not forgiving ... Too pricey for what we get ... Lush, typical for Hawaiian-style course.

★★★ OLOMANA GOLF LINKS
SP-41-1801 Kalanianaole Hwy., Waimanalo, 96795, Oahu County, (808)259-7926.
Holes: 18. **Yards:** 6,326/5,456. **Par:** 72/73. **Course Rating:** 70.3/72.4. **Slope:** 129/128. **Green Fee:** $90/$90. **Cart Fee:** Included in Green Fee. **Walking Policy:** Walking at certain times. **Walkability:** N/A. **Opened:** 1967. **Architect:** Bob Baldock/Robert L. Baldock. **Season:** Year-round. **High:** July-Aug. **To obtain tee times:** Call 30 days in advance. **Miscellaneous:** Reduced fees (weekdays, twilight, seniors), discount packages, metal spikes, range (mats), club rentals, credit cards (MC, V, AE, D, JCB).
Reader Comments: Challenging course, needs maintenance ... OK, not great ... Through-the-green conditions not good due to clay-like soil, but greens are very nice, quick ... My favorite course, play there every Sunday ... Good scoring-course ... Nice atmosphere, nice people ... Pace biggest downer ... Good service and greens ... Narrow fairways.

★★★ PALI MUNICIPAL GOLF COURSE
PM-45-050 Kamehameha Hwy., Kaneohe, 96744, Oahu County, (808)266-7612, 5 miles W of Honolulu.
Holes: 18. **Yards:** 6,500/6,050. **Par:** 72/74. **Course Rating:** 78.8/70.4. **Slope:** 126/127. **Green Fee:** $20/$40. **Cart Fee:** Included in Green Fee. **Walking Policy:** Unrestricted walking. **Walkability:** N/A. **Opened:** 1954. **Architect:** Willard Wilkinson. **Season:** Year-round. **High:** June-Aug. **To obtain tee times:** Call automated tee time system at (808)296-2000 up to 7 days in advance. **Miscellaneous:** Reduced fees (twilight, seniors, juniors), metal spikes, range (grass), credit cards (MC, V).
Reader Comments: Great site ... City course, hilly mountain views, small greens ... Just all right ... Clay, mud ... Public course, hilly, lots a rain ... Good course ... Greens fast ... Excellent service.

★★★½ PEARL COUNTRY CLUB
PU-98-535 Kaonohi St., Aiea, 96701, Oahu County, (808)487-3802, 10 miles W of Honolulu.
E-mail: pearlcc@hi.net.
Holes: 18. **Yards:** 6,787/5,536. **Par:** 72/72. **Course Rating:** 72.0/72.1. **Slope:** 135/130. **Green Fee:** $39/$100. **Cart Fee:** Included in Green Fee. **Walking Policy:** Mandatory cart. **Walkability:** 4. **Opened:** 1967. **Architect:** Akiro Sato. **Season:** Year-round. **High:** Year-round. **To obtain tee times:** Call in advance. **Miscellaneous:** Reduced fees (twilight), metal spikes, range (mats), club rentals, credit cards (MC, V, AE, Diners Club, JCB).
Reader Comments: Very nice condition, with a great view of Pearl Harbor ... Interesting layout ... Liked this course a lot, just pricey ... Well maintained, challenging, hilly, rarely a level lie ... Nice people.

★★★★ POIPU BAY RESORT GOLF CLUB *Condition, Pace*
R-2250 Ainako St., Koloa, 96756, Kauai County, (808)742-8711, (800)858-6300, 16 miles SW of Lihue.

Holes: 18. **Yards:** 6,959/5,241. **Par:** 72/72. **Course Rating:** 73.4/70.9. **Slope:** 132/121. **Green Fee:** $95/$145. **Cart Fee:** Included in Green Fee. **Walking Policy:** Mandatory cart. **Walkability:** N/A. **Opened:** 1990. **Architect:** Robert Trent Jones Jr. **Season:** Year-round. **High:** Jan.-May. **To obtain tee times:** Call up to 30 days in advance. **Miscellaneous:** Reduced fees (resort guests, twilight, juniors), discount packages, metal spikes, range (grass/mats), club rentals, lodging (610 rooms), credit cards (MC, V, AE, Diners Club, JCB), beginner friendly (daily clinics, 3 free clinics weekly).
Notes: Ranked 13th in 1999 Best in State.
Reader Comments: Nice course but too windy ... Staff more interested in giving tips than receiving them ... Big course, beautiful scenery, but left with unsatisfied feeling ... Real pleasure to play ... Every hole special ... A must for Hawaii golf vacationers ... What a view! ... Links-style course. Great finishing holes. Fun ... Fine course, well kept ... Unreal! A pro course ... Felt like I was playing in the Grand Slam! Awesome! ... Can't beat the finishing holes.

PRINCEVILLE RESORT   *Service*

★★★★ **MAKAI GOLF CLUB (LAKES/WOODS)**   *Pace*
R-1 Lei O Papa Rd., Princeville, 96722, Kauai County, (808)826-3580, (800)826-4400, 30 miles N of Lihue.
Holes: 27. **Yards:** 6,901/5,631. **Par:** 72/72. **Course Rating:** 72.9/69.6. **Slope:** 131/115. **Green Fee:** $70/$115. **Cart Fee:** Included in Green Fee. **Walking Policy:** Unrestricted walking. **Walkability:** 2. **Opened:** 1973. **Architect:** Robert Trent Jones Jr. **Season:** Year-round. **High:** Nov.-March. **To obtain tee times:** Call up to 30 days in advance. **Miscellaneous:** Reduced fees (resort guests, twilight, juniors), discount packages, metal spikes, range (grass/mats), club rentals, lodging, credit cards (MC, V, AE, Diners Club).
Reader Comments: Good variety with 3 nines ... Nice but nothing special—good ocean views ... Pricey, but do it at least once in a lifetime; gorgeous, worth it! ... Holes are different, interesting! ... Fairer than Prince Course ... Three 9-hole courses give you more choices ... Not a good course for the money. I can play better courses in Oregon for less money ... Get the multi-play ticket.

★★★★ **MAKAI GOLF CLUB (OCEAN/LAKES)**
R-1 Lei O Papa Rd., Princeville, 96722, Kauai County, (808)826-3580, (800)826-4400, 30 miles N of Lihue. **Web:** www.princeville.com.
Holes: 27. **Yards:** 6,886/5,516. **Par:** 72/72. **Course Rating:** 73.2/69.9. **Slope:** 132/116. **Green Fee:** $70/$115. **Cart Fee:** Included in Green Fee. **Walking Policy:** Unrestricted walking. **Walkability:** 2. **Opened:** 1973. **Architect:** Robert Trent Jones Jr. **Season:** Year-round. **High:** Nov.-March. **To obtain tee times:** Call 30 days in advance. **Miscellaneous:** Reduced fees (weekdays, resort guests, twilight, juniors), discount packages, metal spikes, range (grass/mats), club rentals, lodging, credit cards (MC, V, AE, Diners Club).
Notes: Ranked 7th in 1999 Best in State. 1990.
Reader Comments: Mature, beautiful, user-friendly ... A good challenge. Great for average golfers ... Mix of ordinary and challenging holes.

★★★★ **MAKAI GOLF CLUB (OCEAN/WOODS)**
R-1 Lei O Papa Rd., Princeville, 96722, Kauai County, (808)826-3580, (800)826-4400, 30 miles N of Lihue.
Holes: 27. **Yards:** 6,875/5,631. **Par:** 72/72. **Course Rating:** 72.9/70.4. **Slope:** 131/116. **Green Fee:** $70/$115. **Cart Fee:** Included in Green Fee. **Walking Policy:** Unrestricted walking. **Walkability:** 2. **Opened:** 1973. **Architect:** Robert Trent Jones Jr. **Season:** Year-round. **High:** Nov.-March. **To obtain tee times:** Call 30 days in advance. **Miscellaneous:** Reduced fees (weekdays, resort guests, twilight, juniors), discount packages, metal spikes, range (grass/mats), club rentals, lodging, credit cards (MC, V, AE, D, Diners Club, JCB).
Reader Comments: Every hole unique ... Had fun ... Incredible views.

★★★★½ **PRINCE COURSE**   *Condition, Pace*
R-5-3900 Kuhio Hwy., Princeville, 96722, Kauai County, (808)826-5000, (800)826-4400, 30 miles N of Lihue.
Holes: 18. **Yards:** 7,309/5,338. **Par:** 72/72. **Course Rating:** 75.3/72.0. **Slope:** 145/127. **Green Fee:** $99/$155. **Cart Fee:** Included in Green Fee. **Walking Policy:** Unrestricted walking. **Walkability:** 5. **Opened:** 1991. **Architect:** Robert Trent Jones Jr. **Season:** Year-round. **High:** Nov.-March. **To obtain tee times:** Call 30 days in advance. **Miscellaneous:** Reduced fees (weekdays, resort guests, twilight, juniors), discount packages, metal spikes, range (grass/mats), club rentals, lodging, credit cards (MC, V, AE, D, Diners Club, JCB).
Notes: Ranked 43rd in 1999-2000 America's 100 Greatest; 1st in 1999 Best in State.
Reader Comments: The name 'Prince' describes it all ... Most beautiful course in world ... Stunning views; bring your 7-wood ... Top notch. Great challenging holes ... Best course I've played. Bring plenty of balls ... Slow play because of difficulty ... Worth every penny. A true challenge! ... View of whales off No. 7 tee caused four foursomes to back up. When the whales left, we had to remember who was first off. Beautiful ... A work of art in a tropical jungle ... Fantastic variety of holes ... A 10! Wonderful, but expensive.

HAWAII

★★★ PUKALANI COUNTRY CLUB
PU-360 Pukalani St., Pukalani, 96768, Maui County, (808)572-1314.
Holes: 18. **Yards:** 6,945/5,612. **Par:** 72/74. **Course Rating:** 72.8/71.6. **Slope:** 128/133. **Green Fee:** $35/$55. **Cart Fee:** Included in Green Fee. **Walking Policy:** Mandatory cart. **Walkability:** 3. **Opened:** 1981. **Architect:** Bob Baldock. **Season:** Year-round. **High:** Jan.-March. **To obtain tee times:** Call anytime. **Miscellaneous:** Reduced fees (low season, twilight), metal spikes, range (grass), club rentals, credit cards (MC, V, AE), beginner friendly.
Reader Comments: Very windy, some holes way too easy, others way too hard ... Well maintained, friendly and challenging ... Upland course, good course and clubhouse ... Need friendlier starters. Under-watered course ... Hills, winds and grain of greens make this tough love ... Green fee price outstanding ... Dry, bumpy fairways ... Good views, flat greens.

★★★½ SANDALWOOD GOLF COURSE
PU-2500 Honoapiilani Hwy., Wailuku, 96793, Maui County, (808)242-4653, 4 miles S of Wailuku.
E-mail: gwrgolf@maui.net.
Holes: 18. **Yards:** 6,469/6,011. **Par:** 72/72. **Course Rating:** 70.6/68.3. **Slope:** 129/125. **Green Fee:** $50/$75. **Cart Fee:** Included in Green Fee. **Walking Policy:** Mandatory cart. **Walkability:** 3. **Opened:** 1991. **Architect:** Nelson & Wright. **Season:** Year-round. **High:** Oct.-March. **Miscellaneous:** Reduced fees (low season), metal spikes, range (grass), club rentals, credit cards (MC, V, AE), beginner friendly.
Reader Comments: Very windy ... Best value on Maui, you could pay double for course that's no better ... Wouldn't go back but good value ... Located on side of mountain ... A good course with a great view ... Have let the condition slip ... Worth the money ... Easy in calm conditions ... Hard-to-read greens ... Play early or the wind will get you.

★★½ SEAMOUNTAIN GOLF COURSE
R-Off Hwy. 11, Punaluu, 96777, Hawaii County, (808)928-6222, 56 miles S of Hilo.
Holes: 18. **Yards:** 6,416/5,590. **Par:** 72/72. **Course Rating:** 71.1/70.9. **Slope:** 129/116. **Green Fee:** $25/$40. **Cart Fee:** Included in Green Fee. **Walking Policy:** Mandatory cart. **Walkability:** N/A. **Opened:** 1973. **Architect:** Arthur Jack Snyder. **Season:** Year-round. **High:** Jan.-March. **To obtain tee times:** Call for reservations any time. **Miscellaneous:** Reduced fees (resort guests, juniors), discount packages, metal spikes, range (grass), club rentals, lodging, credit cards (MC, V).
Reader Comments: Very nice views, poor condition, isolated location, very little play ... Cheap ... Lower-priced Hawaiian fun, back 9 tougher ... Beautiful, quiet scenery, old lava fields.

★★★½ SILVERSWORD GOLF CLUB
PU-1345 Piilani Hwy., Kihei, 96753, Maui County, (808)874-0777, 12 miles S of Kahului.
Holes: 18. **Yards:** 6,801/5,265. **Par:** 71/71. **Course Rating:** 72.0/70.0. **Slope:** 124/118. **Green Fee:** $59/$70. **Cart Fee:** Included in Green Fee. **Walking Policy:** Mandatory cart. **Walkability:** 3. **Opened:** 1987. **Architect:** W.J. Newis. **Season:** Year-round. **High:** Jan.-March. **To obtain tee times:** Call up to 30 days in advance. **Miscellaneous:** Reduced fees (low season, twilight), metal spikes, range (grass), club rentals, credit cards (MC, V, AE, JCB).
Reader Comments: Great value & variety ... Good experience to play with locals ... Smart layout, easy to play and and attractive course. Golf in Hawaii is great! ... For the money it is fun and challenging ... 5-hour rounds unacceptable at these prices ... Beautiful views of ocean ... Best value on Maui ... Few amenities, but a very enjoyable track ... Excellent non-resort course.

TED MAKALENA GOLF COURSE
PM-93-059 Waipio Pt. Access Rd., Waipahu, 96797, Oahu County, (808)296-7888.
Special Notes: Call club for further information.

TURTLE BAY RESORT
R-57-049 Kuilima Dr., Kahuku, 96731, Oahu County, (808)293-8574, 35 miles N of Honolulu International Airport. **E-mail:** thelinds@kuilima.com. **Web:** www.kuilima.com.
★★★★ THE LINKS AT KUILIMA *Condition, Pace*
Holes: 18. **Yards:** 7,199/4,851. **Par:** 72/72. **Course Rating:** 75.0/64.3. **Slope:** 141/121. **Green Fee:** $75/$125. **Cart Fee:** Included in Green Fee. **Walking Policy:** Mandatory cart. **Walkability:** 4. **Opened:** 1992. **Architect:** Arnold Palmer/Ed Seay. **Season:** Year-round. **High:** Dec.-March. **To obtain tee times:** Call or fax golf shop or hotel up to 30 days in advance, or up to 6 months in advance if staying at the Hilton Turtle Bay or Hilton Hawaiian Village. Lessons available by PGA certified professionals. **Miscellaneous:** Reduced fees (weekdays, resort guests, twilight), discount packages, metal spikes, range (grass), club rentals, lodging (487 rooms), credit cards (MC, V, AE, D, JCB, Diners card).
Notes: Ranked 9th in 1999 Best in State.
Reader Comments: A long, tough course that tends to humble erstwhile long drivers thanks to the omnipresent winds ... Offers a number of holes that provide optional approaches to the green depending, of course, upon the mental stability and cardiac history of the player ... If I were limited to playing only one course on Oahu, this would be my choice ... Good price for locals on a fantastic course ... Windy ... Worthwhile ... Beautiful course/very tough ... Pricey but worth it ... Bring your A+ game.

HAWAII

★★★★ **THE TURTLE BAY COUNTRY CLUB** *Condition, Pace*
Holes: 9. **Yards:** 3,151/2,771. **Par:** 36/36. **Course Rating:** N/A. **Slope:** N/A. **Green Fee:** $50/$50. **Cart Fee:** Included in Green Fee. **Walking Policy:** Mandatory cart. **Walkability:** 4. **Opened:** 1972. **Architect:** Arnold Palmer/Ed Seay. **Season:** Year-round. **High:** Dec.-March. **To obtain tee times:** Call or fax golf shop or hotel up to 30 days in advance, or up to 6 months in advance if staying at the Hilton Turtle Bay or Hilton Hawaiian Village. **Miscellaneous:** Reduced fees (weekdays, resort guests, twilight), discount packages, metal spikes, range (grass), club rentals, lodging (487 rooms), credit cards (MC, V, AE, D, JCB, Diners card), beginner friendly (lessons available by pga certified professionals).
Reader Comments: Bring your wind game ... Good price for locals on a fantastic course ... Long drive to get there, but worth it ... Fun links course, top shape ... Very slow ... Tough, long, well maintained ... Worthwhile for the course condition and atmosphere ... Beautiful ... A thing of beauty ... Feel like you're alone on every hole ... Even challenging from white tees ... Fair value.

★★½ **VOLCANO GOLF & COUNTRY CLUB**
PU-P.O. Box 46, Volcano Nat'l Park, 96718, Hawaii County, (808)967-7331, 32 miles S of Hilo.
Holes: 18. **Yards:** 6,547/5,567. **Par:** 72/72. **Course Rating:** 70.8/70.7. **Slope:** 128/117. **Green Fee:** $60/$60. **Cart Fee:** Included in Green Fee. **Walking Policy:** Mandatory cart. **Walkability:** 2. **Architect:** Arthur Jack Snyder. **Season:** Year-round. **High:** July-Sept. **Miscellaneous:** Reduced fees (juniors), metal spikes, range (grass), club rentals, credit cards (MC, V, AE, D).
Reader Comments: Only a golf facility; not much else ... 17th hole, one of my favorites on Big Island ... Excellent course ... Next time I'll come during the dry season and not in December ... Coolest course in Hawaii, may need sweater, interesting layout ... Greens in fair shape ... Overpriced, poor conditions and windy.

★★★ **WAIEHU GOLF COURSE**
PU-P.O. Box 507, Wailuku, 96793, Maui County, (808)244-5934, 4 miles N of Waliuku.
Holes: 18. **Yards:** 6,330/5,511. **Par:** 72/71. **Course Rating:** 69.8/70.6. **Slope:** 111/115. **Green Fee:** $25/$30. **Cart Fee:** $16/cart. **Walking Policy:** Unrestricted walking. **Walkability:** 1. **Architect:** Arthur Jack Snyder. **Season:** Year-round. **High:** Nov.-March. **To obtain tee times:** Call 2 days in advance. **Miscellaneous:** Metal spikes, range (grass), club rentals, credit cards (MC, V).
Reader Comments: Beautiful scenic play, enjoyed every hole ... It is fun to not play with rich tourists ... Great ocean front, but windy, very busy ... Very scenic ... Condition a little spotty ... The prettiest, best value, ocean-view public course in all 50 states ... What an experience, golf with the locals ... My must play, love the local flavor.

★★★½ **WAIKELE GOLF CLUB**
SP-94-200 Paioa Place, Waipahu, 96797, Oahu County, (808)676-9000, 15 miles W of Honolulu.
E-mail: wglgolf@ahoha.net.
Holes: 18. **Yards:** 6,663/5,226. **Par:** 72/72. **Course Rating:** 71.7/65.6. **Slope:** 126/113. **Green Fee:** $107/$112. **Cart Fee:** Included in Green Fee. **Walking Policy:** Mandatory cart. **Walkability:** 2. **Opened:** 1993. **Architect:** Ted Robinson. **Season:** Year-round. **High:** Jan.-Feb. **To obtain tee times:** Call golf shop. **Miscellaneous:** Reduced fees (weekdays, twilight), metal spikes, range (grass), club rentals, credit cards (MC, V, AE, D, JCB).
Reader Comments: Lots of water and different types of holes. Tricky greens ... Clean and well kept ... Friendly staff ... Good place to play ... Not too long but compact and challenging course ... Par 5s are short ... Great value. Good greens. Rough too long ... Not a long course, wind plays a factor on some holes. Great driving range with nearby outlet stores.

WAIKOLOA BEACH RESORT

★★★★ **BEACH GOLF COURSE**
R-1020 Keana Place, Waikoloa, 96738, Hawaii County, (808)886-6060, (800)552-1422, 23 miles S of Kailua-Kona.
Holes: 18. **Yards:** 6,566/5,094. **Par:** 72/72. **Course Rating:** 71.5/69.4. **Slope:** 133/119. **Green Fee:** $45/$125. **Cart Fee:** $30/person. **Walking Policy:** Unrestricted walking. **Walkability:** 2. **Opened:** 1981. **Architect:** Robert Trent Jones Jr. **Season:** Year-round. **High:** Dec.-March. **To obtain tee times:** Call or fax 1 year in advance. **Miscellaneous:** Reduced fees (resort guests, twilight, juniors), discount packages, metal spikes, range (grass), club rentals, lodging (2,000 rooms), credit cards (MC, V, AE, D, JCB), beginner friendly (golf clinics 3 days a week for minimal charge).
Reader Comments: Slow play ... Great time here. 'Enjoyed' watching my ball bounce off the lava ... Friendly course ... Service is exceptional ... OK but Kings Course is better ... Beautiful setting; challenging greens ... Beauty does not make up for terrible greens and slow play ... Don't play here, play its sister course, Kings ... Front nine through the lava fun ... Some nice ocean views ... Challenging breezes ... Top-notch restaurant/golf shop ... Par-5 12th is awesome! ... Hawaii at its best.

★★★★ **KINGS GOLF COURSE**
R-600 Waikoloa Beach Dr., Waikoloa, 96738, Hawaii County, (808)886-7888, (800)552-1422, 23 miles S of Kailua-Kona.

Holes: 18. **Yards:** 7,074/5,459. **Par:** 72/72. **Course Rating:** 73.9/71.0. **Slope:** 133/121. **Green Fee:** N/A/$120. **Cart Fee:** Included in Green Fee. **Walking Policy:** Unrestricted walking. **Walkability:** 2. **Opened:** 1990. **Architect:** Tom Weiskopf/Jay Morrish. **Season:** Year-round. **High:** Dec.-March. **To obtain tee times:** Call or fax 1 year in advance. **Miscellaneous:** Reduced fees (resort guests, twilight), discount packages, metal spikes, range (grass), club rentals, lodging, credit cards (MC, V, AE, D, JCB), beginner friendly (golf clinics 3 days a week for minimal charge).
Reader Comments: Flat layout. Forgiving ... Not as scenic as Beach Course. Fairways needed work ... Flat and boring ... A two-sleeve course; stay off the lava ... Beautiful setting; challenging greens ... Great course getting better as plantings mature ... Fair, but challenging ... Tradewinds can make it tough ... Staff sometimes forgets I'm a paying guest. Marshall just rides shotgun. No action on slow play ... Beautiful design. Enjoyable ... Bring some beach toys for all the bunkers!

★★★½ WAIKOLOA VILLAGE GOLF CLUB
R-68-1792 Melia St., Waikoloa, 96738, Hawaii County, (808)883-9621, 18 miles N of Kailua-Kona Airport.
Holes: 18. **Yards:** 6,791/5,479. **Par:** 72/72. **Course Rating:** 71.8/72.1. **Slope:** 130/119. **Green Fee:** $45/$80. **Cart Fee:** Included in Green Fee. **Walking Policy:** Walking at certain times. **Walkability:** 2. **Opened:** 1972. **Architect:** Robert Trent Jones Jr. **Season:** Year-round. **High:** Dec.-Feb. **To obtain tee times:** Call 3 days in advance. Reservations taken 30 days in advance with a 50 percent prepay. Groups of 12 or more call 1 year in advance. **Miscellaneous:** Reduced fees (twilight, juniors), discount packages, metal spikes, range (grass/mats), club rentals, lodging, credit cards (MC, V, AE, JCB), beginner friendly (beginner lessons).
Reader Comments: Good course; away from resort prices ... Good buy for Hawaii, windy ... Fun, fun, fun ... Only for the desperate. Too favorable to condo owners. Course needs essential repairs ... Winds can be vicious in P.M. ... Par 3s are fun ... Like view better than course ... Very friendly staff, all-around enjoyment.

WAILEA GOLF CLUB *Service*
★★★★ BLUE COURSE
R-120 Kaukahi St., Wailea, 96753, Maui County, (808)875-5111, (800)332-1614, 17 miles S of Kahului. **E-mail:** golf@waileagolf.com. **Web:** www.waileagolf.com.
Holes: 18. **Yards:** 6,758/5,291. **Par:** 72/72. **Course Rating:** 71.6/72.0. **Slope:** 130/117. **Green Fee:** $80/$125. **Cart Fee:** Included in Green Fee. **Walking Policy:** Mandatory cart. **Walkability:** N/A. **Opened:** 1972. **Architect:** Arthur Jack Snyder. **Season:** Year-round. **High:** Dec.-April. **To obtain tee times:** Call 30 days in advance. **Miscellaneous:** Reduced fees (low season, resort guests, twilight, juniors), discount packages, metal spikes, range (grass/mats), club rentals, lodging, credit cards (MC, V, AE, D, JCB).
Reader Comments: Overrated & overpriced; very slow play; good practice facilities ... Nice, but not as spectacular as billed ... Good resort course ... Way too crowded but nice course ... Super greens, fairways, views ... Lots of fun ... Good greens, good mix of shots ... Lacks much of the esthetic appeal of other island courses ... Playable for all handicappers, spectacular scenery ... Good service.

★★★★½ EMERALD COURSE *Condition*
R-100 Wailea Golf Club Dr., Wailea, 96753, Maui County, (808)875-7450, (800)332-1614, 17 miles S of Kahului. **E-mail:** golf@waileagolf.com. **Web:** www.waileagolf.com.
Holes: 18. **Yards:** 6,825/5,256. **Par:** 72/72. **Course Rating:** 71.7/69.6. **Slope:** 130/115. **Green Fee:** $80/$125. **Cart Fee:** Included in Green Fee. **Walking Policy:** Mandatory cart. **Walkability:** N/A. **Opened:** 1994. **Architect:** Robert Trent Jones Jr. **Season:** Year-round. **High:** Dec.-April. **To obtain tee times:** Call 30 days in advance. **Miscellaneous:** Reduced fees (low season, resort guests), discount packages, metal spikes, range (grass/mats), club rentals, lodging, credit cards (MC, V, AE, D, JCB).
Notes: Ranked 8th in 1999 Best in State; 2nd in 1995 Best New Resort Courses.
Reader Comments: Fun but slow round ... Way overpriced; challenging layout ... Loved the course for the money ... Overrated and overpriced; very slow play ... Great views, good variety, fun holes ... Good golf shop ... Beautiful course & scenery, lots of bunkers, busy ... Very fair ... Good practice area ... Facilities wonderful; golf shop selection nice ... Great courses; great service ... Courses here are worth the price.

★★★★ GOLD COURSE
R-100 Wailea Golf Club Dr., Wailea, 96753, Maui County, (808)875-7450, (800)332-1614, 17 miles S of Kahului. **E-mail:** golf@waileagolf.com. **Web:** www.waileagolf.com.
Holes: 18. **Yards:** 7,070/5,317. **Par:** 72/72. **Course Rating:** 73.0/70.3. **Slope:** 139/121. **Green Fee:** $85/$130. **Cart Fee:** Included in Green Fee. **Walking Policy:** Mandatory cart. **Walkability:** N/A. **Opened:** 1994. **Architect:** Robert Trent Jones Jr. **Season:** Year-round. **High:** Dec.-April. **To obtain tee times:** Call 30 days in advance. **Miscellaneous:** Reduced fees (low season, resort guests), discount packages, metal spikes, range (grass/mats), club rentals, lodging, credit cards (MC, V, AE, D, JCB).
Reader Comments: Great layout ... Great resort course ... Watch out for lava ... Not difficult ... Overrated; slow play ... Overpriced ... Good practice facilities ... What a way to enjoy a vacation; beautiful in all respects ... Bring straight shots ... Beautiful course, scenery, lots of bunkers, busy

... Best of three great choices. Super service. Love the cold towels ... The best of the three at Wailea, all are a must.

★★★½ WAILUA GOLF COURSE *Value*

PM-3-5350 Kuhio Hwy., Lihue, 96766, Kauai County, (808)245-8092, 3 miles S of Lihue. **Holes:** 18. **Yards:** 6,981/5,974. **Par:** 36/36. **Course Rating:** 73.0/73.1. **Slope:** 136/122. **Green Fee:** $25/$35. **Cart Fee:** $14/cart. **Walking Policy:** Unrestricted walking. **Walkability:** 3. **Opened:** 1963. **Architect:** Toyo Shirai. **Season:** Year-round. **High:** Jan.-April. **To obtain tee times:** Call 7 days in advance, minimum 2 players. **Miscellaneous:** Reduced fees (twilight, seniors), metal spikes, range (grass/mats), club rentals.

Reader Comments: Ocean-front view, local players nice to tourists ... Great value in Kauai and very good course ... Good track, wind, ocean ... Long, dry and windy ... Was an awesome public course, needs better maintenance ... Dry course, long back-ups ... Inexpensive public course; good views ... Hard to get early tee times ... Best muny I've ever played ... Has to be the best value in Hawaii ... Very scenic.

★★★½ WAIMEA COUNTRY CLUB

SP-Mamalohoa Hwy., Kamuela, 96743, Hawaii County, (808)885-8777, 51 miles N of Hilo. **Holes:** 18. **Yards:** 6,661/5,673. **Par:** 72/72. **Course Rating:** 71.1/68.5. **Slope:** 130/126. **Green Fee:** $60/$60. **Cart Fee:** $30/person. **Walking Policy:** Unrestricted walking. **Walkability:** 2. **Opened:** 1994. **Architect:** John Sanford. **Season:** Year-round. **High:** Dec.-March. **To obtain tee times:** Call up to 7 days in advance. **Miscellaneous:** Reduced fees (twilight, seniors, juniors), metal spikes, range (grass/mats), club rentals, credit cards (MC, V, AE, JCB & Diners Club), beginner friendly.

Reader Comments: A very enjoyable experience ... A little known course, but fun to play ... Best buy on the Big Island ... Good value, rolling hills, much like a Wisconsin course. Play in morning, rains almost every afternoon. Cool change of pace from resort courses, good value ... Folksy, cheap, pretty. Can be wet, foggy, cold.

★★½ WEST LOCH GOLF COURSE

PM-91-1126 Okupe St., Ewa Beach, 96706, Oahu County, (808)671-2292, 15 miles W of Honolulu. **Holes:** 18. **Yards:** 6,479/5,296. **Par:** 72/72. **Course Rating:** 70.3/68.6. **Slope:** 123/117. **Green Fee:** $17/$21. **Cart Fee:** Included in Green Fee. **Walking Policy:** Mandatory cart. **Walkability:** 2. **Opened:** 1990. **Architect:** Robin Nelson/Rodney Wright. **Season:** Year-round. **High:** April-Sept. **To obtain tee times:** Call 7 days in advance. **Miscellaneous:** Reduced fees (twilight, seniors, juniors), metal spikes, range (grass/mats), club rentals, credit cards (MC, V).

Reader Comments: Short, wide and cheap ... Play is so slow, you should play cards while you wait ... Good municipal course. Tee-time access acceptable. Would play here regularly if I had the time ... Interesting public course, short but challenging in the wind; can't beat the price.

★★★½ AVONDALE GOLF CLUB

SP-10745 Avondale Loop Rd., Hayden Lake, 83835, Kootenai County, (208)772-5963, 35 miles E of Spokane, WA.
Holes: 18. **Yards:** 6,773/5,180. **Par:** 72/74. **Course Rating:** 71.8/70.9. **Slope:** 124/123. **Green Fee:** $24/$38. **Cart Fee:** $22/cart. **Walking Policy:** Walking at certain times. **Walkability:** 3. **Architect:** Mel "Curley" Hueston. **Season:** March-Oct. **High:** June-Aug. **To obtain tee times:** Call golf shop 7 days in advance. **Miscellaneous:** Reduced fees (low season, twilight, seniors, juniors), range (mats), club rentals, credit cards (MC, V).
Reader Comments: There's a lot of hidden beauty, play it twice ... Best I have played ... Idaho's golf is a good buy and lots of fun ... Excellent golf course with lots of rolling hills and vistas ... Good place to play ... Excellent renovation ... Much improved course ... Enjoyable.

BIGWOOD GOLF COURSE

R-Hwy. 75 North of Ketchum, Ketchum/Sun Valley, 83340, (208)726-4024, 1 miles W of Sun Valley.
Holes: 9. **Yards:** 3,335/2,912. **Par:** 36/37. **Course Rating:** 36.0/37.0. **Slope:** 115/121. **Green Fee:** $40/$40. **Cart Fee:** $16/person. **Walking Policy:** Unrestricted walking. **Walkability:** 2. **Opened:** 1972. **Architect:** Robert Muir Graves. **Season:** March-Oct. **High:** July-Aug. **Miscellaneous:** Range (grass), club rentals, credit cards (MC, V, AE, D).

★★★ BLACKFOOT MUNICIPAL GOLF COURSE

PM-3115 Teeples Dr., Blackfoot, 83221, Bingham County, (208)785-9960, 19 miles N of Pocatello.
Holes: 18. **Yards:** 6,899/6,385. **Par:** 72/78. **Course Rating:** 71.0/75.0. **Slope:** 123/124. **Green Fee:** $16/$16. **Cart Fee:** $16/cart. **Walking Policy:** Unrestricted walking. **Walkability:** 1. **Opened:** 1959. **Architect:** George Von Elm. **Season:** March-Nov. **High:** May-Oct. **To obtain tee times:** Call 2 days in advance. **Miscellaneous:** Reduced fees (weekdays, low season), range (grass), club rentals, credit cards (MC, V).
Reader Comments: Tough front 9 ... Wonderful small-town course, greens and course always in excellent shape, pro and help are all friendly and accommodating ... Excellent greens ... Played late November, a round to remember... Fabulous value.

★★½ BRYDEN CANYON PUBLIC GOLF COURSE

PM-445 O'Connor Rd., Lewiston, 83501, Nez Perce County, (208)746-0863, 100 miles SW of Spokane.
Holes: 18. **Yards:** 6,103/5,380. **Par:** 71/72. **Course Rating:** 67.4/69.9. **Slope:** 106/111. **Green Fee:** $16/$16. **Cart Fee:** $21/cart. **Walking Policy:** Unrestricted walking. **Walkability:** 4. **Opened:** 1975. **Season:** Year-round. **High:** Feb.-Sept. **To obtain tee times:** Call up to 7 days in advance. **Miscellaneous:** Discount packages, metal spikes, range (grass), club rentals, credit cards (MC, V, D), beginner friendly (par strokes).
Reader Comments: Great view... Rolling terrain, busy ... Friendly staff, bring camera for the great view of valley... Nice for a city course, needs more water in the dry season ... Good practice facility.

BURLEY CITY MUNICIPAL

PM-131 East Highway 81, Burley, 83318, Minnadka County, (208)678-9807.
Holes: 18. **Yards:** 6,437/5,565. **Par:** 72/75. **Course Rating:** 69.5/69.7. **Slope:** 115/116. **Green Fee:** $17/$16. **Cart Fee:** $9/person. **Walking Policy:** Unrestricted walking. **Walkability:** 1. **Opened:** 1928. **Season:** Feb.-Nov. **High:** June-Aug. **To obtain tee times:** One day in advance Wednesday for weekend and Holidays Starting at 7:00 am. **Miscellaneous:** Reduced fees (low season, seniors, juniors), range (grass), club rentals, credit cards (MC, V, AE, D).

★★★ CANYON SPRINGS GOLF COURSE

PU-199 Canyon Springs Rd., Twin Falls, 83301, Twin Falls County, (208)734-7609, 110 miles SE of Boise. **E-mail:** csprings@micron.net.
Holes: 18. **Yards:** 6,452/5,190. **Par:** 72/74. **Course Rating:** 68.7/67.1. **Slope:** 116/112. **Green Fee:** $15/$25. **Cart Fee:** $22/cart. **Walking Policy:** Unrestricted walking. **Walkability:** 3. **Opened:** 1975. **Architect:** Max Mueller. **Season:** Feb.-Dec. **High:** May-Sept. **To obtain tee times:** Call up to 3 days in advance. **Miscellaneous:** Reduced fees (weekdays, low season, twilight, juniors), range (grass), club rentals, credit cards (MC, V).
Reader Comments: Nice setting and good variety of holes ... This course gets lots of play, still fun ... Good facilities, course needs a little TLC ... Good variety ... Play inside Snake River Canyon, waterfalls and great views, better when course greens up ... Some very tight, tough, short par 4s ... 'Deals' abound ... Great for public play ... Scenery and wildlife excellent.

★★½ CENTENNIAL GOLF CLUB

PU-Box 52, 2600 Centennial Dr., Nampa, 83653, Canyon County, (208)467-3011.
Web: www.golfcentennial.com.
Green Fee: $14/$17. **Cart Fee:** $16/cart. **Walking Policy:** Unrestricted walking. **Walkability:** 3. **Season:** Year-round. **High:** April-Oct. **To obtain tee times:** Call 2 days in advance.

Miscellaneous: Reduced fees (twilight), range (grass), club rentals, credit cards (MC, V, D), beginner friendly (juniors, ladies, mens).

Reader Comments: Nice place to play ... Wide open ... Nice staff, forgiving course on front, lot of water on back ... The most friendly course in Idaho ... Fast greens, good view ... If in the Boise area a great choice.

★★★ CLEAR LAKE COUNTRY CLUB

SP-403 Clear Lake Lane, Buhl, 83316, Twin Falls County, (208)543-4849, 90 miles E of Boise. **Holes:** 18. **Yards:** 5,905/5,378. **Par:** 72/73. **Course Rating:** 68.2/69.4. **Slope:** 112/113. **Green Fee:** $15/$22. **Walking Policy:** Unrestricted walking. **Walkability:** 5. **Opened:** 1987. **Architect:** Dutch Kuse. **Season:** Year-round. **High:** May-Oct. **To obtain tee times:** Call 4 days in advance. **Miscellaneous:** Reduced fees (weekdays, juniors), range (grass), club rentals, credit cards (MC, V). **Reader Comments:** Everything slopes toward river... Lots of elevation changes ... Course always in good shape ... Right next to Snake River—beautiful ... Great spring golf in Snake River Canyon ... Intriguing. High risk, high rewards. Fun!... Pleasant short course ... Bring your trout rod.

★★★★★ COEUR D'ALENE RESORT GOLF COURSE *Service+, Condition+, Pace+*

R-900 Floating Green Dr., Coeur d'Alene, 83814, Kootenai County, (208)667-4653, (800)688-5253, 32 miles E of Spokane, WA. Web: www.cdaresort.com. **Holes:** 18. **Yards:** 6,309/5,490. **Par:** 71/71. **Course Rating:** 69.9/70.3. **Slope:** 121/118. **Green Fee:** $75/$180. **Cart Fee:** Included in Green Fee. **Walking Policy:** Walking at certain times. **Walkability:** 3. **Opened:** 1991. **Architect:** Scott Miller. **Season:** April-Oct. **High:** June-Sept. **To obtain tee times:** Guests may call up to 1 year in advance. **Miscellaneous:** Reduced fees (low season, resort guests), discount packages, range (grass), caddies, club rentals, lodging, credit cards (MC, V, AE, D). **Notes:** Ranked 2nd in 1999 Best in State. 1992 Merrill Lynch Shootout. **Reader Comments:** Well-manicured. Excellent condition, forecaddies speed play, scenic ... A great experience! They treat you like royalty ... Floating green is exceptional... Service, people, caddies, maintenance outstanding ... Gotta play at least once ... Class all the way ... The Mahogany boat ride from the hotel is a must.

★★★ EAGLE HILLS GOLF COURSE

PU-605 N. Edgewood Lane, Eagle, 83616, Ada County, (208)939-0402, 4 miles NW of Boise. **Holes:** 18. **Yards:** 6,485/5,305. **Par:** 72/72. **Course Rating:** 70.5/70.2. **Slope:** 119/114. **Green Fee:** $20/$27. **Cart Fee:** $10/person. **Walking Policy:** Unrestricted walking. **Walkability:** 3. **Opened:** 1968. **Architect:** C. Edward Trout. **Season:** Year-round. **High:** March-Oct. **To obtain tee times:** Call 7 days in advance. **Miscellaneous:** Reduced fees (weekdays, low season, twilight, seniors, juniors), discount packages, metal spikes, range (grass/mats), club rentals, credit cards (MC, V). **Reader Comments:** A fun little course, well kept ... Wild shots break windows ... Several improvements in last two years ... Back 9 the best, good greens ... A few challenging holes ... A good course lined by a subdivision ... Slicers beware .... Best deal around ... Nice layout, needs attention to detail.

★★★★ ELKHORN RESORT

R-Elkhorn Rd., Sun Valley, 83354, Blaine County, (208)622-6400, (800)355-4676, 150 miles NE of Boise. **Holes:** 18. **Yards:** 7,034/5,414. **Par:** 72/72. **Course Rating:** 72.2/69.3. **Slope:** 127/125. **Green Fee:** N/A/$98. **Cart Fee:** Included in Green Fee. **Walking Policy:** Mandatory cart. **Walkability:** 5. **Opened:** 1974. **Architect:** Robert Trent Jones Sr/R.T. Jones Jr. **Season:** May-Oct. **High:** June-Aug. **To obtain tee times:** Public may call 14 days in advance. Hotel guests call anytime after hotel reservation. **Miscellaneous:** Reduced fees (low season, resort guests, twilight, juniors), discount packages, range (grass/mats), club rentals, lodging, credit cards (MC, V, AE, D). **Notes:** Ranked 5th in 1999 Best in State. Site of 1999 Idaho Open. **Reader Comments:** Great mountain resort ... Course great in summer and fall ... Big course from the 'tips'... Very fair... Every hole has great views ... Fairways lined by condos ... We were treated like royal guests. Our bags were collected from the car and at the end our clubs were cleaned.

EMMETT CITY GOLF COURSE

PU-2102 W. Sales Rd., Emmett, 83617, (208)365-2675, 2 miles SW of Emmett. **Holes:** 9. **Yards:** 2,910/2,737. **Par:** 36/36. **Course Rating:** 67.4/67.7. **Slope:** 111/115. **Green Fee:** $13/N/A. **Walking Policy:** Unrestricted walking. **Walkability:** 1. **Opened:** 1959. **Season:** Year-round. **High:** May-Oct. **Miscellaneous:** Reduced fees (twilight), club rentals, credit cards (V).

GEM COUNTY GOLF COURSE

PU-2102 W. Sales Yard Rd., Emmett, 83617, (208)365-2675. **Special Notes:** Call club for further information.

IDAHO

★★★½ HIDDEN LAKES GOLF RESORT
R-89 Lower Pack River Rd., Sandpoint, 83864, Bonner County, (208)263-1642, (888)806-6673, 86 miles NE of Spokane, WA. **E-mail:** golfidkap@midlink.com. **Web:** www.hiddenlakesgolf.com. **Holes:** 18. **Yards:** 6,655/5,078. **Par:** 71/71. **Course Rating:** 71.5/69.1. **Slope:** 132/119. **Green Fee:** $30/$30. **Cart Fee:** $11/person. **Walking Policy:** Unrestricted walking. **Walkability:** 2. **Opened:** 1986. **Architect:** Jim Krause. **Season:** March-Nov. **High:** May-Sept. **To obtain tee times:** Nonmembers may call 7 days in advance, or any time with credit card. **Miscellaneous:** Reduced fees (low season, resort guests, twilight, seniors, juniors), discount packages, range (grass/mats), club rentals, credit cards (MC, V).
Reader Comments: Excellent target course ... Lots of water and wildlife ... Hidden Lakes Golf Resort is a hidden jewel ... Bring lots of balls ... Lots of water... Helpful staff ... Beautiful course carved out of Idaho wilderness ... Pro shop staff make up for lack of amenities ... Greens good.

★★★ HIGHLAND GOLF COURSE
PU-201 Vonelm Rd., Pocatello, 83201, Bannock County, (208)237-9922.
Holes: 18. **Yards:** 6,512/6,100. **Par:** 72/76. **Course Rating:** 67.5/73.0. **Slope:** 114/117. **Green Fee:** $12/$13. **Cart Fee:** $16/. **Walking Policy:** Unrestricted walking. **Walkability:** N/A. **Opened:** 1963. **Architect:** Babe Hiskey. **Season:** March-Oct. **High:** May-Sept. **To obtain tee times:** Call Thursday for upcoming weekend. **Miscellaneous:** Reduced fees (seniors, juniors), metal spikes, range (grass), club rentals.
Reader Comments: Rolling fairways provide challenge ... A nice course overall ... Good shots required ... Heck, they let me play back 9 for free ... Tough greens to putt .... Hilly course.

★★★ THE HIGHLANDS GOLF & COUNTRY CLUB
PU-N. 701 Inverness Dr., Post Falls, 83854, Kootenai County, (208)773-3673, (800)797-7339, 30 miles E of Spokane.
Holes: 18. **Yards:** 6,369/5,115. **Par:** 72/73. **Course Rating:** 70.7/69.5. **Slope:** 125/121. **Green Fee:** $21/$25. **Cart Fee:** $22/cart. **Walking Policy:** Unrestricted walking. **Walkability:** 4. **Opened:** 1991. **Architect:** Jim Kearns. **Season:** March-Oct. **High:** June-Aug. **To obtain tee times:** Call 7 days in advance. **Miscellaneous:** Reduced fees (weekdays, low season, seniors, juniors), discount packages, range (grass/mats), club rentals, credit cards (MC, V, AE, D), beginner friendly.
Reader Comments: Water holes, surprising layout ... Requires well placed shots ... Great course, nice people ... Several blind shots ... Highlands Golf and Country Club is one of those 'love it or hate it' courses ... The practice range is arguably the best in North Idaho.

★★★ JEROME COUNTRY CLUB
SP-6 mi. S of Town, Jerome, 83338, Jerome County, (208)324-5281, 5 miles NW of Twin Falls.
Holes: 18. **Yards:** 6,429/5,644. **Par:** 72/73. **Course Rating:** 68.8/71.2. **Slope:** 106/114. **Green Fee:** $30/$30. **Cart Fee:** $20/cart. **Walking Policy:** Unrestricted walking. **Walkability:** 3. **Opened:** 1930. **Architect:** Ed Hunnicutt. **Season:** March-Dec. **High:** May-Sept. **To obtain tee times:** Call up to 3 days in advance. **Miscellaneous:** Range (grass), club rentals, credit cards (MC, V).
Reader Comments: Replaced bad front 9 holes to make it better... Windy ... Good track, many tournaments ... Well manicured, relaxed atmo-sphere ... Distinctly different front and back 9s ... Flat front 9, challenging back 9, good layout ... 'Deals' abound.

★★★ MCCALL MUNICIPAL GOLF COURSE
PM-1000 Reedy Lane, McCall, 83638, Valley County, (208)634-7200.
Yards: 6,295/5,552. **Par:** 71/73. **Course Rating:** 67.8/69.9. **Slope:** 119/119. **Green Fee:** $18/$28. **Cart Fee:** $20/cart. **Walking Policy:** Unrestricted walking. **Walkability:** 2. **Season:** May-Nov. **High:** June-Sept. **Miscellaneous:** Club rentals, credit cards (MC, V, D).
Reader Comments: Beautiful mountain setting ... Short but tight. Hit it straight ... Newest 9 is so different from previous 18 ... Potential, never in good shape, still fun ... 27 holes of mountain golf ... Limited good weather ... Enjoyable, lots of trees for Idaho ... Busy place in the summer... Good muny course.

OREGON TRAIL COUNTRY CLUB
PU-2525 Hwy. 30, Soda Springs, 83276, (208)547-2204.
Special Notes: Call club for further information.

★★★★ PINECREST MUNICIPAL GOLF COURSE *Value+*
PM-701 E. Elva St., Idaho Falls, 83401, Bonneville County, (208)529-1485, 180 miles N of Salt Lake City.
Holes: 18. **Yards:** 6,394/6,123. **Par:** 70/75. **Course Rating:** 69.0/73.2. **Slope:** 110/122. **Green Fee:** $16/$17. **Cart Fee:** $15/cart. **Walking Policy:** Unrestricted walking. **Walkability:** 3. **Opened:** 1934. **Architect:** W. H. Tucker. **Season:** March-Nov. **High:** May-Sept. **To obtain tee times:** Call 1 day in advance starting at 6:30 a.m. **Miscellaneous:** Club rentals, credit cards (MC, V, D).

IDAHO

Reader Comments: Best pro shop, service is hard to top ... Great old course ... Huge pine trees ... Best value ever... Best muny I've ever played ... Low price for high quality ... Best muny in Idaho ... No sand traps and luscious fairways ... Great muny... Beautiful course located in the heart of Idaho Falls.

PRESTON GOLF & COUNTRY CLUB
SP-1215 N. 800 E., Preston, 83263, (208)852-2408.
Special Notes: Call club for further information.

★★★ PURPLE SAGE GOLF COURSE
PU-15192 Purple Sage Rd., Caldwell, 83607, Canyon County, (208)459-2223, 25 miles W of Boise.
Holes: 18. Yards: 6,753/5,343. Par: 71/72. Course Rating: 70.8/69.2. Slope: 123/114. Green Fee: $1/$1. Cart Fee: $18/person. Walking Policy: Unrestricted walking. Walkability: 1. Opened: 1963. Architect: A. Vernon Macan. Season: Year-round. High: May-Sept. To obtain tee times: Call 1 day in advance, or on Thursday for coming weekend. Miscellaneous: Reduced fees (weekdays), range (grass), club rentals, credit cards (MC, V).
Reader Comments: Mature course in good shape ... Back tees difficult, small greens, narrow fairways ... Flat course ... A good test ... Lush due to new sprinkler system, plays long ... Great value ... Always windy ... Keep your focus on this course.

★★★½ QUAIL HOLLOW GOLF CLUB
SP-4520 N. 36th St., Boise, 83703, Ada County, (208)344-7807.
Holes: 18. Yards: 6,444/4,530. Par: 70/70. Course Rating: 70.7/68.0. Slope: 128/129. Green Fee: $18/$26. Cart Fee: $9/person. Walking Policy: Unrestricted walking. Walkability: 4. Opened: 1982. Architect: von Hagge & Devlin. Season: Year-round. High: March-Oct. To obtain tee times: Call 5 days in advance. Miscellaneous: Reduced fees (weekdays, low season, seniors, juniors), range (grass), club rentals, credit cards (MC, V).
Reader Comments: Target golf ... Course knowledge needed ... Elevated tees are breathtaking ... Getting better... Unless you're in great shape use a cart ... Challenging course, friendly staff... Unique elevated tees ... Nice greens ... Diverse terrain ... A bit funky, must be creative.

★★★★ RIDGECREST GOLF CLUB
PU-3730 Ridgecrest Dr., Nampa, 83687, Canyon County, (208)468-9073, 15 miles W of Boise.
Web: www.ridgecrestgolf.com.
Holes: 27. Yards: 6,888/5,193. Par: 72/72. Course Rating: 72.0/68.8. Slope: 125/120. Green Fee: $16/$19. Cart Fee: $18/cart. Walking Policy: Unrestricted walking. Walkability: 2. Opened: 1996. Architect: John Harbottle. Season: Year-round. High: April-Sept. To obtain tee times: Call 2 days in advance. Miscellaneous: Reduced fees (weekdays, low season, twilight, juniors), metal spikes, range (grass), club rentals, credit cards (MC, V).
Notes: Ranked 1st in 1999 Best in State. CPC Qualifier; U.S. Am Qualifier; USGA Boys Qualifier.
Reader Comments: Best public course in Idaho! ... Some tough holes ... Great desert course, worth finding ... Outstanding public course ... Hard but fun to play ... Windy and dry... Design is good... 'Computer aided' carts ... Fairly new with promise to be one of the best public courses in Idaho ... A must play. Bring all clubs! .... Popular and crowded public course ... Well run.

★★★ RIVERSIDE GOLF COURSE
PU-3500 S. Bannock Hwy., Pocatello, 83204, Bannock County, (208)232-9515.
Holes: 18. Yards: 6,397/5,710. Par: 72/75. Course Rating: 69.7/72.2. Slope: 114/119. Green Fee: $16/$17. Cart Fee: $19/person. Walking Policy: Unrestricted walking. Walkability: 2. Opened: 1963. Architect: Babe Hiskey. Season: March-Oct. High: May-Aug. To obtain tee times: Call Thursday for upcoming weekend. Miscellaneous: Metal spikes, range (grass), club rentals, credit cards (MC, V).
Reader Comments: Tight course ... Nice old course, laid back play ... Treelined fairways provide shade on hot days ... Course conditions very good ... Love the elevated greens on front nine.

★★★ SAGE LAKES MUNICIPAL GOLF
PU-100 E. 65N, Idaho Falls, 83401, Bonneville County, (208)528-5535.
Holes: 18. Yards: 6,566/4,883. Par: 70/70. Course Rating: 70.4/66.4. Slope: 115/108. Green Fee: $14/$17. Walking Policy: Unrestricted walking. Walkability: 2. Opened: 1993. Season: March-Nov. High: June-Sept. To obtain tee times: Call 1 day in advance. Miscellaneous: Credit cards (MC, V, D).
Reader Comments: Developing into a very good course ... Courteous, friendly staff ... Open, no trees ... A really fun, quiet course ... Watch the water... Beautiful place, 'hooray' Pete Dye.

★★★ SAND CREEK GOLF CLUB
PU-5200 S. Hackman Rd., Idaho Falls, 83403, Bonneville County, (208)529-1115.
Holes: 18. Yards: 6,805/5,770. Par: 72/73. Course Rating: 70.5/72.2. Slope: 115/116. Green Fee: $11/$12. Cart Fee: $14/. Walking Policy: Unrestricted walking. Walkability: N/A. Opened: 1978. Architect: William F. Bell. Season: March-Nov. High: June-Aug. To obtain tee times: Call

1 day in advance. **Miscellaneous:** Reduced fees (seniors, juniors), metal spikes, club rentals, credit cards (MC, V).
Reader Comments: Easy walk ... Friendly, accommodating staff ... Excellent maintenance ... Scenic sand dunes located on course ... A confidence builder, makes me feel like a 6-handicap ... Flat course ... Fun course, well managed ... Play this in a 30 m.p.h. breeze, it is a hoot.

SAND POINT ELKS GOLF COURSE
PU-Highway 200 E, 83864, Bonner County (208)263-4321, 1 miles N of Sandpoint.
Holes: 18. **Yards:** 5,701/5,443. **Par:** 70/70. **Course Rating:** 65.9/71.1. **Slope:** 106/108. **Green Fee:** $18/$18. **Cart Fee:** $20/cart. **Walking Policy:** Unrestricted walking. **Walkability:** 1.
Opened: 1925. **Season:** April-Oct. **High:** July-Aug. **Miscellaneous:** Reduced fees (weekdays, twilight), club rentals, credit cards (MC, V).

★★★½ SCOTCH PINES GOLF COURSE
PU-10610 Scotch Pines Rd., Payette, 83661, Payette County, (208)642-1829, (888)451-0910, 58 miles NW of Boise.
Holes: 18. **Yards:** 6,544/5,586. **Par:** 72/72. **Course Rating:** 69.4/70.3. **Slope:** 111/116. **Green Fee:** $18/$18. **Cart Fee:** $9/person. **Walking Policy:** Unrestricted walking. **Walkability:** 3.
Opened: 1960. **Architect:** Cliff Masingill/Scott Masingill. **Season:** Feb.-Nov. **High:** May-Aug. **To obtain tee times:** Call 2 days in advance. **Miscellaneous:** Reduced fees (weekdays, twilight), range (grass), club rentals, credit cards (MC, V), beginner friendly.
Reader Comments: Best course in the Treasure Valley ... Scotch Pines is one of the true hidden values of the Northwest ... Front 9 narrow, back 9 open ... Rolling terrain ... Great course for such a small community ... Fast play, elevation changes, fun ... Homey, quaint, personable.

★★★½ SHADOW VALLEY GOLF CLUB   *Pace*
PU-15711 Hwy 55, Boise, 83703, Ada County, (208)939-6699, (800)936-7035, 10 miles NW of Boise. **E-mail:** svgolfelesbois.com. **Web:** www.shadowvalley.com.
Holes: 18. **Yards:** 6,433/5,394. **Par:** 72/72. **Course Rating:** 69.2/71.8. **Slope:** 117/117. **Green Fee:** $20/$28. **Cart Fee:** $20/person. **Walking Policy:** Unrestricted walking. **Walkability:** 3.
Opened: 1973. **Architect:** Ed Trout. **Season:** Year-round. **High:** April-Sept. **To obtain tee times:** Call up to 5 days in advance. Credit card is required for Sat., Sun. and holiday tee times before 1 p.m. **Miscellaneous:** Reduced fees (weekdays, seniors, juniors), range (grass), club rentals, credit cards (MC, V, AE, D).
Reader Comments: Several wonderful driving holes, challenging greens ... Every hole is different ... Challenging, awesome course ... 'Keep pace' program very good ... I never get tired of playing this course ... Managed well, plays well ... A good score requires 'A' game.

SHOSHONE GOLF & TENNIS CLUB
PU-Gold Run Mountain, Kellogg, 83837, (208)784-0161.
Holes: 18. **Yards:** N/A. **Par:** N/A. **Course Rating:** N/A. **Slope:** N/A. **Green Fee:** N/A. **Walkability:** N/A. **Architect:** Keith Hellstrum.

★★½ STONERIDGE COUNTRY CLUB
SP-1 Blanchard Rd., Blanchard, 83804, Bonner County, (208)437-4682, 35 miles NE of Spokane. **Web:** www.stoneridgeidaho.com.
Holes: 18. **Yards:** 6,612/5,678. **Par:** 72/72. **Course Rating:** 71.4/72.4. **Slope:** 127/126. **Green Fee:** $15/$20. **Cart Fee:** $23/cart. **Walking Policy:** Unrestricted walking. **Walkability:** 4.
Opened: 1971. **Architect:** Jim Krause. **Season:** April-Oct. **High:** May-Sept. **To obtain tee times:** Call Saturday for next week Mon-Sun. **Miscellaneous:** Reduced fees (resort guests, twilight, seniors, juniors), discount packages, range (grass), club rentals, lodging, credit cards (MC, V).
Reader Comments: Nice course ... Very good price! ... Hard to find, but worth it! ... Good greens, tougher than it looks, fun to play ... Fast greens, good layout ... Back 9 tougher than front, last 3 holes tough ... Beautiful, challenging, fair for all handicaps.

★★★★ SUN VALLEY RESORT GOLF COURSE
R-Sun Valley Rd., Sun Valley, 83353, Blaine County, (208)622-2251, (800)786-8259.
Holes: 18. **Yards:** 6,565/5,241. **Par:** 72/73. **Course Rating:** 71.1/70.4. **Slope:** 128/125. **Green Fee:** $49/$83. **Cart Fee:** Included in Green Fee. **Walking Policy:** Walking at certain times. **Walkability:** N/A. **Opened:** 1938. **Architect:** William P. Bell/Robert Trent Jones Jr. **Season:** April-Oct. **High:** June-Sept. **To obtain tee times:** Hotel guests anytime. Public may call 2 days in advance. All tee times reserved with credit card. **Miscellaneous:** Reduced fees (low season, resort guests), discount packages, metal spikes, range (grass), club rentals, lodging, credit cards (MC, V, AE, D).
Notes: Golf Digest School site. Ranked 3rd in 1999 Best in State.
Reader Comments: Great course in beautiful setting ... Play it straight ... Great resort ... They keep everyone moving so it is the fastest course. You can play 18 holes in 4 hours or under... Views of Bald Mountains are awesome.

IDAHO

★★★ TETON LAKES GOLF COURSE
PM-2000 W. Hibbard Pkwy., Rexburg, 83440, Madison County, (208)359-3036.
Yards: 6,397/5,116. **Par:** 71/73. **Course Rating:** 69.4/66.6. **Slope:** 119/112. **Green Fee:** $14/$14. **Cart Fee:** $16/cart. **Walking Policy:** Unrestricted walking. **Walkability:** N/A. **Opened:** 1979. **Season:** March-Nov. **High:** June-Aug. **To obtain tee times:** Call-in starting at 7 a.m. two days prior. **Miscellaneous:** Club rentals, credit cards (MC, V, AE, D).
Reader Comments: Easy front 9, back 9 is a tester ... Water everywhere ... Nice pro shop, excellent pro ... Lots of new trees ... Great staff... Best it's ever been.

★½ TWIN FALLS MUNICIPAL GOLF COURSE
PU-Grandview Dr., Twin Falls, 83301, Twin Falls County, (208)733-3326
Holes: 18. **Yards:** 5,234/4,961. **Par:** 68/71. **Course Rating:** 64.8/68.0. **Slope:** 106/105. **Green Fee:** $14/$14. **Cart Fee:** $20/person. **Walking Policy:** Unrestricted walking. **Walkability:** 1. **Season:** Year-round. **High:** Feb.-Nov. **To obtain tee times:** Call up to 1 days in advance. **Miscellaneous:** Reduced fees (weekdays, low season, twilight, seniors, juniors), metal spikes, range (grass), club rentals, credit cards (MC, V), beginner friendly.

★★★ TWIN LAKES VILLAGE GOLF COURSE
SP-W. 5500 Village Blvd., Rathdrum, 83858, Kootenai County, (208)687-1311, (888)836-7949, 15 miles N of Coeur d'Alene. **E-mail:** tana@golfnorthidaho.com. **Web:** www.golfnorthidaho.com.
Holes: 18. **Yards:** 6,277/5,363. **Par:** 72/72. **Course Rating:** 70.0/70.5. **Slope:** 121/118. **Green Fee:** $20/$30. **Cart Fee:** $23/cart. **Walking Policy:** Unrestricted walking. **Walkability:** 2. **Opened:** 1975. **Architect:** William Robinson. **Season:** April-Oct. **High:** June-Aug. **To obtain tee times:** Call 7 days in advance. **Miscellaneous:** Reduced fees (weekdays, low season, twilight, seniors, juniors), range (grass), club rentals, lodging, credit cards (MC, V, AE).
Reader Comments: Beautiful location ... Great course, undiscovered ... Front 9 easy, back 9 challenging ... Harder than it looks ... Lots of water, trees and sand ... Beautiful setting ... Houses can keep your ball in play ... Pretty with forest and water hazards.

★★★ UNIVERSITY OF IDAHO GOLF COURSE
PU-1215 Nez Perce, Moscow, 83843, Latah County, (208)885-6171, 85 miles S of Spokane.
Holes: 18. **Yards:** 6,639/5,770. **Par:** 72/72. **Course Rating:** 72.0/73.0. **Slope:** 130/130. **Green Fee:** $14/$22. **Cart Fee:** $20/cart. **Walking Policy:** Unrestricted walking. **Walkability:** 3. **Opened:** 1933. **Architect:** Francis L. James. **Season:** March-Oct. **High:** May-Aug. **To obtain tee times:** Call up to 7 days in advance. **Miscellaneous:** Reduced fees (weekdays, twilight, seniors, juniors), discount packages, metal spikes, range (grass), club rentals, credit cards (MC, V, D).
Reader Comments: A lot of elevated tees and greens with great views of the rolling hills of the Palouse ... Good course for a university ... Tough and quirky ... Many good holes, no flat lies ... Great course design ... Tough course especially in the wind ... Hard course to walk ... Tough par 3s on back 9.

★★ WARM SPRINGS GOLF COURSE
PU-2495 Warm Springs Ave., Boise, 83712, Ada County, (208)343-5661.
Holes: 18. **Yards:** 6,719/5,660. **Par:** 72/72. **Course Rating:** N/A. **Slope:** 113/113. **Green Fee:** $15/$17. **Cart Fee:** $10/person. **Walking Policy:** Unrestricted walking. **Walkability:** 2. **Season:** Year-round. **High:** May-Sept. **To obtain tee times:** Call up to 5 days in advance. **Miscellaneous:** Reduced fees (weekdays, low season, twilight, seniors, juniors), metal spikes, range (grass/mats), credit cards (MC, V, AE, D).

ILLINOIS

THE ACORNS GOLF LINKS
PU-3933 Ahne Rd., Waterloo, 62298, (618)939-7800, (888)922-2676.
Holes: 18. **Yards:** 6,701/4,623. **Par:** 72/72. **Course Rating:** 72.3/67.0. **Slope:** 125/105. **Green Fee:** $28/$48. **Cart Fee:** Included in Green Fee. **Walkability:** N/A. **Opened:** 1997. **Architect:** William Ebeler. **Miscellaneous:** Reduced fees (weekdays, low season, twilight, seniors, juniors), discount packages, credit cards (MC, V, AE, D).
Reader Comments: New course, should get better ... 18th hole will eat your lunch ... Great potential ... Worth the drive ... Wide open ... Interesting ... Friendly staff.

★★★★ ALDEEN GOLF CLUB
PU-1900 Reid Farm Rd., Rockford, 61107, Winnebago County, (815)282-4653, (888)425-3336, 90 miles W of Chicago.
Holes: 18. **Yards:** 7,058/5,038. **Par:** 72/72. **Course Rating:** 73.6/69.1. **Slope:** 126/115. **Green Fee:** $35/$39. **Cart Fee:** $24/cart. **Walking Policy:** Unrestricted walking. **Walkability:** 2. **Opened:** 1991. **Architect:** Dick Nugent. **Season:** April-Oct. **High:** June-Aug. **To obtain tee times:** Call with credit card to reserve up to 7 days in advance. **Miscellaneous:** Reduced fees (weekdays, twilight), metal spikes, range (grass), club rentals, credit cards (MC, V, D).
Reader Comments: Awesome greens ... Nice facilities ... More like a private club ... One of the better public courses I've played ... Excellent practice facility ... Can play long or short ... Wonderful public facility ... Great bargain ... Hit it straight and stay below the hole ... Tough but fun ... Bring your ball retriever.

★★★★½ ANNBRIAR GOLF COURSE *Condition*
PU-1524 Birdie Lane, Waterloo, 62298, Monroe County, (618)939-4653, (888)939-5191, 25 miles SE of St. Louis.
Holes: 18. **Yards:** 6,841/4,792. **Par:** 72/72. **Course Rating:** 72.3/66.4. **Slope:** 141/110. **Green Fee:** $48/$58. **Cart Fee:** Included in Green Fee. **Walking Policy:** Mandatory cart. **Walkability:** 3. **Opened:** 1993. **Architect:** Michael Hurdzan. **Season:** Year-round. **High:** April-Oct. **To obtain tee times:** Call up to 7 days in advance. **Miscellaneous:** Reduced fees (low season), range (grass), club rentals, credit cards (MC, V, AE), beginner friendly.
Reader Comments: Great course is better with age ... Fun to play every hole ... Good variety ... Tough. Very scenic ... Don't miss this gem ... What a back 9 ... Exceptional layout. One of the best ... Great value ... Great greens ... .My favorite ... Hills, hills, hills ... Beautiful.

★★★ ANTIOCH GOLF CLUB
PU-40150 N. Rte. 59, Antioch, 60021, Lake County, (847)395-3004, 60 miles NW of Chicago.
Holes: 18. **Yards:** 6,321/5,556. **Par:** 71/72. **Course Rating:** 68.2/72.4. **Slope:** 114/112. **Green Fee:** $17/$30. **Cart Fee:** $24/cart. **Walking Policy:** Unrestricted walking. **Walkability:** 3. **Opened:** 1925. **Architect:** Mike Hurdzan/Dave Esler. **Season:** Year-round. **High:** May-Sept. **To obtain tee times:** Call up to 7 days in advance (credit card required). **Miscellaneous:** Reduced fees (weekdays, low season, twilight, seniors, juniors), discount packages, metal spikes, club rentals, credit cards (MC, V, AE).
Reader Comments: A few short par 4s squeezed into neighborhood ... Built among homes ... Too many houses near greens ... Some holes like hitting down a residential street.

★★★½ ARBORETUM GOLF CLUB
PU-401 Half Day Rd., Buffalo Grove, 60089, Lake County, (847)913-1112, 15 miles NE of Chicago. **Web:** www.arboretumgolf.com.
Holes: 18. **Yards:** 6,477/5,039. **Par:** 72/72. **Course Rating:** 71.1/68.7. **Slope:** 132/118. **Green Fee:** $25/$47. **Cart Fee:** $26/cart. **Walking Policy:** Walking at certain times. **Walkability:** 2. **Opened:** 1990. **Architect:** Dick Nugent. **Season:** March-Dec. **High:** June-Aug. **To obtain tee times:** Nonresidents call 5 days in advance with credit card. **Miscellaneous:** Reduced fees (weekdays, low season, twilight), discount packages, club rentals, credit cards (MC, V, AE, D).
Reader Comments: Great design ... Nice course ... Great back nine ... Really tough from the tips ... Hard to read undulating greens ... Super value ... Too many water holes ... Poor man's Doral ... Bring plenty of balls ... Challenging.

ARROWHEAD GOLF CLUB
PU-26 W. 151 Butterfield Rd., Wheaton, 60187, Du Page County, (630)653-5800, 35 miles NW of Chicago.
Holes: 27. **Cart Fee:** $25/cart. **Walking Policy:** Unrestricted walking. **Opened:** 1924. **Season:** April-Dec. **High:** May-Oct. **To obtain tee times:** Call up to 7 days in advance for weekdays, Monday before for weekends.
★★★ EAST/SOUTH
Yards: 6,500/5,300. **Par:** 71/71. **Course Rating:** 71.5/70.5. **Slope:** 122/119. **Green Fee:** $20/$37. **Walkability:** N/A. **Architect:** Stan Pelchar/David Gill. **Miscellaneous:** Reduced fees (weekdays, twilight, seniors, juniors), metal spikes, range (mats), rentals, credit cards (MC, V).
Reader Comments: A nice public course ... Typical public course ... Construction on nine of 27 holes slowed play ... Good value.

★★★ **EAST/WEST**
Yards: 6,800/5,400. **Par:** 72/72. **Course Rating:** N/A. **Slope:** N/A. **Green Fee:** $20/$37.
Walkability: N/A. **Architect:** Ralph Weimer. **Miscellaneous:** Reduced fees (weekdays, twilight, seniors, juniors), metal spikes, club rentals, credit cards (MC, V).

★★★ **SOUTH/EAST**
Yards: 6,734/5,033. **Par:** 72/72. **Course Rating:** 72.4/69.1. **Slope:** 131/118. **Green Fee:** $32/$37. **Walkability:** 2. **Architect:** Ralph Weimer, Ken Killian. **Miscellaneous:** Reduced fees (weekdays, twilight, seniors, juniors), range (mats), club rentals, credit cards (MC, V).

ATWOOD HOMESTEAD GOLF COURSE
PM-8890 Old River Road, Rockford, 61103, Winnebago County, (815)623-2411, 5 miles N of Rockford. **Web:** www.wcfpd.org.
Holes: 18. **Yards:** 6,625/5,818. **Par:** 72/72. **Course Rating:** 70.9/72.6. **Slope:** 117/116. **Green Fee:** $14/$25. **Cart Fee:** $24/cart. **Walking Policy:** Unrestricted walking. **Walkability:** 1. **Opened:** 1971. **Architect:** Charles Maddox. **Season:** April-Oct. **High:** May-Aug. **Miscellaneous:** Reduced fees (twilight, seniors, juniors), range (grass).

★★★★ BALMORAL WOODS COUNTRY CLUB
PU-26732 S. Balmoral Woods Dr., Crete, 60417, Will County, (708)672-7448, 40 miles S of Chicago. **Web:** www.balmoralwoods.com.
Holes: 18. **Yards:** 6,683/5,282. **Par:** 72/72. **Course Rating:** 72.6/71.8. **Slope:** 128/117. **Green Fee:** $30/$50. **Cart Fee:** Included in Green Fee. **Walking Policy:** Unrestricted walking. **Walkability:** 4. **Opened:** 1976. **Architect:** Don Mortell. **Season:** March-Nov. **High:** June-Aug. **To obtain tee times:** Call up to 7 days in advance. Credit card required to reserve weekend tee time. **Miscellaneous:** Reduced fees (weekdays, low season, twilight, seniors, juniors), discount packages, range (grass), club rentals, credit cards (MC, V, AE, D) (junior lessons).
Reader Comments: Interesting design ... Good place for outings ... Deceptively tough ... Fast, sloping greens ... Just a fun course ... Nice layout for all players ... Challenging ... Will always be one of my favorites ... Nice course for the money.

★★★½ BARTLETT HILLS GOLF COURSE
PM-800 W. Oneida, Bartlett, 60103, Cook County, (630)837-2741, 25 miles NW of Chicago.
Holes: 18. **Yards:** 6,482/5,488. **Par:** 71/71. **Course Rating:** 71.2/71.8. **Slope:** 124/121. **Green Fee:** $16/$30. **Cart Fee:** $12/person. **Walking Policy:** Unrestricted walking. **Walkability:** 4. **Opened:** 1923. **Architect:** Charles Maddox/Bob Lohmann. **Season:** Year-round. **High:** April-Sept. **To obtain tee times:** Call up to 7 days in advance. **Miscellaneous:** Reduced fees (weekdays, low season, twilight, seniors, juniors), metal spikes, range (grass/mats), club rentals, credit cards (MC, V).
Reader Comments: Good muny ... Hilly, fun course ... Wide fairways, fast greens.... Good and getting better ... Purely local ... New holes are excellent ... New clubhouse, new greens.

★★★½ BELK PARK GOLF COURSE
PU-880 Belk Park Rd., Wood River, 62095, Madison County, (618)251-3115, 10 miles E of St. Louis.
Holes: 18. **Yards:** 6,812/5,726. **Par:** 72/73. **Course Rating:** 71.8/70.8. **Slope:** 121/118. **Green Fee:** $23/$29. **Cart Fee:** $10/person. **Walking Policy:** Walking at certain times. **Walkability:** 2. **Opened:** 1970. **Architect:** E.L. Packard. **Season:** Year-round. **High:** May-Sept. **To obtain tee times:** Call up to 7 days in advance. **Miscellaneous:** Reduced fees (weekdays, low season, twilight, seniors, juniors), range (grass), club rentals, credit cards (MC, V), beginner friendly.
Reader Comments: Good challenge ... Very, very busy ... Good challenge for mid- to high-handicappers ... Very nice over all ... Reasonable money ... Very flat ... Improving ... Variety ... Good public golf for the average player ... Back nine is worth the wait.

★★★½ BIG RUN GOLF CLUB
PU-17211 W. 135th St., Lockport, 60441, Will County, (815)838-1057, 35 miles SW of Chicago.
Holes: 18. **Yards:** 7,025/5,905. **Par:** 72/73. **Course Rating:** 73.9/74.4. **Slope:** 139/131. **Green Fee:** $41/$46. **Cart Fee:** $14/person. **Walking Policy:** Walking at certain times. **Opened:** 1930. **Architect:** Muhlenford/Sneed, Didier, Killian, Nugent. **Season:** April-Nov. **High:** June-Aug. **To obtain tee times:** Call 7 days in advance at 7 a.m. **Miscellaneous:** Reduced fees (low season, twilight, juniors), metal spikes, club rentals, credit cards (MC, V).
Reader Comments: Long & hard ... Very hilly; a lot of fun ... More scenic than Cog Hill ... Great layout through majestic oaks ... Has come a long way in the past 15 years ... Mature, wooded course ... Great experience ... Fun, but humbling ... Watch out for Cardiac Hill.

★★★ BITTERSWEET GOLF CLUB
PU-875 Almond St., Gurnee, 60031, Lake County, (847)855-9031, 40 miles N of Chicago.
Holes: 18. **Yards:** 6,754/5,027. **Par:** 72/72. **Course Rating:** 72.8/69.6. **Slope:** 130/115. **Green Fee:** N/A/$45. **Cart Fee:** $14/person. **Walking Policy:** Walking at certain times. **Walkability:** 2. **Opened:** 1996. **Architect:** Jack Porter/Harry Vignocchi. **Season:** April-Nov. **High:** May-Oct. **To obtain tee times:** Nonresidents may reserve 7 days in advance with credit card. Residents may

reserve 8 days in advance. **Miscellaneous:** Reduced fees (twilight, seniors), metal spikes, range (grass/mats), club rentals, credit cards (MC, V, AE, D).
Reader Comments: Very challenging ... You'll need more golf balls than clubs ... Short holes, long holes, doglegs, lots of water ... Bring a few sleeves ... Too much water ... Hackers don't like it ... Wait until it matures ... Very difficult.

★★★½ BLACKBERRY OAKS GOLF COURSE
PU-2245 Kennedy Rd., Bristol, 60512, Kendall County, (630)553-7170, 40 miles SW of Chicago.
Holes: 18. **Yards:** 6,258/5,230. **Par:** 72/72. **Course Rating:** 69.8/70.1. **Slope:** 121/119. **Green Fee:** $20/$36. **Cart Fee:** $13/person. **Walking Policy:** Unrestricted walking. **Walkability:** 2.
Opened: 1993. **Architect:** David Gill. **Season:** April-Nov. **High:** May-Sept. **To obtain tee times:** Call up to 7 days in advance. **Miscellaneous:** Reduced fees (twilight, seniors, juniors), metal spikes, range (grass), club rentals, credit cards (MC, V, AE, D).
Reader Comments: Nice layout ... Walking OK ... Friendly, fun course ... Great blind holes ... Best score of my life, a 76 ... Give it time ... Great finishing hole ... A joy to play.

★★★½ BLACKHAWK GOLF CLUB
SP-5n748 Burr Rd., St. Charles, 60175, Kane County, (630)443-3500, 40 miles W of Chicago.
Holes: 18. **Yards:** 6,640/5,111. **Par:** 72/72. **Course Rating:** 72.5/70.9. **Slope:** 132/124. **Green Fee:** $26/$42. **Cart Fee:** $14/person. **Walking Policy:** Walking at certain times. **Walkability:** 4.
Opened: 1974. **Architect:** Charles Maddox. **Season:** March-Nov. **High:** May-Aug. **To obtain tee times:** Reservations can be made 7 days in advance by phone or in person. **Miscellaneous:** Reduced fees (low season, twilight, seniors), range (grass), club rentals, credit cards (MC, V, AE, D).
Reader Comments: Challenging front nine ... Some long par 5s ... Has come back under new owner ... Nice ... Chopped up because of housing development ... Surrounding houses are huge ... Makes you think.

★★ BLOOMINGDALE GOLF CLUB
PM-5 N 181 Glen Ellyn Rd., Bloomingdale, 60108, Du Page County, (630)529-6232, 20 miles W of Chicago.
Holes: 18. **Yards:** 6,240/5,871. **Par:** 72/72. **Course Rating:** 69.6/69.6. **Slope:** 108/108. **Green Fee:** $10/$29. **Cart Fee:** $19/cart. **Walking Policy:** Walking at certain times. **Walkability:** 2.
Opened: 1934. **Architect:** Bob Lohmann. **Season:** March-Nov. **High:** June-Aug. **To obtain tee times:** Call up to 7 days in advance. **Miscellaneous:** Reduced fees (weekdays, low season, twilight, seniors, juniors), metal spikes, club rentals, credit cards (MC, V).
Special Notes: Formerly Glendale Country Club.

★★★½ BON VIVANT COUNTRY CLUB
PU-Career Center Rd., Bourbonnais, 60914, Kankakee County, (815)935-0400, (800)248-7775, 2 miles N of Kankakee.
Holes: 18. **Yards:** 7,498/5,979. **Par:** 72/75. **Course Rating:** 75.8/74.8. **Slope:** 130/126. **Green Fee:** $16/$24. **Cart Fee:** $20/cart. **Walking Policy:** Unrestricted walking. **Walkability:** N/A.
Opened: 1980. **Season:** April-Nov. **High:** May-Sept. **To obtain tee times:** Call 7 days in advance. **Miscellaneous:** Metal spikes, range (grass), club rentals, credit cards (MC, V, AE).
Reader Comments: Very long ... A challenge in the wind ... Wide open; huge greens ... Too dry and rock hard ... Deserves more play ... Decently maintained ... Long and tough on a windy day ... Great bang for your buck.

★★★½ BONNIE BROOK GOLF CLUB
PM-2800 N. Lewis Ave., Waukegan, 60087, Lake County, (847)360-4730, 25 miles N of Chicago.
Holes: 18. **Yards:** 6,701/5,559. **Par:** 72/73. **Course Rating:** 72.4/72.2. **Slope:** 126/124. **Green Fee:** $20/$33. **Cart Fee:** $26/cart. **Walking Policy:** Unrestricted walking. **Walkability:** 2.
Opened: 1927. **Architect:** Jim Foulis. **Season:** April-Nov. **High:** May-Sept. **To obtain tee times:** Call 3 days in advance 7 days a week. **Miscellaneous:** Reduced fees (twilight, seniors), range (grass/mats), club rentals, credit cards (MC, V), beginner friendly.
Reader Comments: Great public course ... Always a favorite. Nice variety ... Tough to get a good tee time ... Nice muny ... Challenging, but fair ... Great value ... Salt-of-the-earth clientele.

★★½ BONNIE DUNDEE GOLF CLUB
PU-270 Kennedy Dr., Carpentersville, 60110, Kane County, (847)426-5511, 25 miles NW of Chicago.
Holes: 18. **Yards:** 6,021/5,464. **Par:** 69/75. **Course Rating:** 68.3/71.1. **Slope:** 112/114. **Green Fee:** $15/$26. **Cart Fee:** $13/person. **Walking Policy:** Unrestricted walking. **Walkability:** 1.
Opened: 1924. **Architect:** C. D. Wagstaff. **Season:** April-Nov. **To obtain tee times:** Call 7 days in advance. **Miscellaneous:** Reduced fees (weekdays, seniors, juniors), club rentals, credit cards (MC, V, D).
Reader Comments: Not very challenging ... Has improved ... Would not go out of my way to play it.

ILLINOIS

BOONE CREEK GOLF CLUB
PU-6912 Mason Hill Rd., McHenry, 60050, McHenry County, (815)455-6900.
Holes: 27. **Yards:** 6,524/5,213. **Par:** 71/71. **Course Rating:** 69.5/68.6. **Slope:** 114/110. **Green Fee:** $18/$22. **Cart Fee:** $10/person. **Walking Policy:** Unrestricted walking. **Walkability:** 2. **Opened:** 1997. **Architect:** Gordon Cunningham. **Season:** March-Nov. 30. **High:** June-Aug. **To obtain tee times:** Tee Times are available 7-days in advance by phone or in person.
Miscellaneous: Reduced fees (juniors), range (grass), club rentals, credit cards (MC, V), beginner friendly (both adult and junior programs offered).

★★★★ THE BOURNE GOLF CLUB *Value+*
2359 N. 35th Rd., Marseilles, 61341, La Salle County, (815)496-2301.
Special Notes: Call club for further information.
Reader Comments: Hit it straight ... Bring a lot of balls ... Very challenging ... What a great find, if you can find it ... Eager to play the new nine.

★★★ BRAE LOCH COUNTRY CLUB
PM-33600 N. Route 45, Grayslake, 60030, Lake County, (847)223-5542, 55 miles of Chicago.
Holes: 18. **Yards:** 5,979/5,299. **Par:** 70/70. **Course Rating:** 67.5/69.6. **Slope:** 114/115. **Green Fee:** $21/$25. **Cart Fee:** $25/cart. **Walking Policy:** Unrestricted walking. **Walkability:** 1. **Opened:** 1931. **Season:** Year-round. **High:** June-Aug. **To obtain tee times:** Call on Monday for upcoming weekend. **Miscellaneous:** Reduced fees (twilight), metal spikes, club rentals, credit cards (MC, V).
Reader Comments: Easy ... Good for short game ... Good off-peak rates.

BROKEN ARROW GOLF CLUB
PU-16325 W. Broken Arrow Dr., Lockport, 60441, Will County, (815)836-8858, 30 miles SW of Chicago. **E-mail:** info@brokenarrowgolfclub.com. **Web:** www.brokenarrowgolfclub.com.
Holes: 27. **Green Fee:** $31/$41. **Cart Fee:** $14/person. **Walking Policy:** Unrestricted walking. **Walkability:** 2. **Opened:** 1996. **Architect:** Bob Lohmann. **Season:** Year-round. **High:** May-Aug. **To obtain tee times:** Call up to 14 days in advance.
★★★½ EAST/NORTH COURSE
Yards: 7,034/5,182. **Par:** 72/72. **Course Rating:** 74.1/70.3. **Slope:** 131/121. **Miscellaneous:** Reduced fees (weekdays, low season, twilight, seniors, juniors), discount packages, metal spikes, range (grass/mats), club rentals, credit cards (MC, V).
Reader Comments: Nice addition ... Like the double greens ... Always a good time ... Decent links style ... Great facility. Worth the drive ... Homes will soon encroach on the golf course.
★★★½ NORTH/SOUTH COURSE
Yards: 7,027/5,255. **Par:** 72/72. **Course Rating:** 73.9/70.5. **Slope:** 131/121. **Miscellaneous:** Reduced fees (weekdays, low season, twilight, seniors, juniors), discount packages, range (grass/mats), club rentals, credit cards (MC, V), beginner friendly.
★★★½ SOUTH/EAST
Yards: 6,945/5,211. **Par:** 72/72. **Course Rating:** 73.6/70.4. **Slope:** 129/121. **Miscellaneous:** Reduced fees (weekdays, low season, twilight, seniors, juniors), discount packages, range (grass/mats), club rentals, credit cards (MC, V), beginner friendly (June 2000 par-3 course).
Reader Comments: Outstanding layout in otherwise nothing piece of land ... Challenging ... Great prices for juniors ... Lots of water ... New course trying hard.

★★½ BUFFALO GROVE GOLF CLUB
PM-48 Raupp Blvd., Buffalo Grove, 60089, Lake County, (847)459-5520, 40 miles NW of Chicago.
Holes: 18. **Yards:** 6,892/6,003. **Par:** 72/75. **Course Rating:** 71.5/73.5. **Slope:** 120/122. **Green Fee:** $13/$28. **Cart Fee:** $25/cart. **Walking Policy:** Unrestricted walking. **Walkability:** 1. **Opened:** 1965. **Architect:** Dick Nugent. **Season:** Year-round. **High:** May-Oct. **To obtain tee times:** Call on Monday for upcoming Friday weekend or holiday. First come first served Monday-Thursday. **Miscellaneous:** Reduced fees (low season, twilight, seniors, juniors), discount packages, range (grass), club rentals, credit cards (MC, V, AE, D).
Reader Comments: Open year round ... Condition not always good ... Basic golf ... Good value for a muny.

★★½ BUNKER LINKS MUNICIPAL GOLF COURSE
PU-3500 Lincoln Park Dr., Galesburg, 61401, Knox County, (309)344-1818, 42 miles NW of Peoria.
Holes: 18. **Yards:** 5,934/5,354. **Par:** 71/73. **Course Rating:** 67.4/69.4. **Slope:** 106/108. **Green Fee:** $8/$9. **Cart Fee:** $9/. **Walking Policy:** Unrestricted walking. **Walkability:** N/A. **Opened:** 1922. **Architect:** D.C. Bunker. **Season:** March-Nov. **High:** April-Sept. **To obtain tee times:** Call up to 7 days in advance for weekends only. **Miscellaneous:** Reduced fees (twilight), metal spikes, range (grass).
Reader Comments: Average ... Gets a lot of play ... Tough if you slice it ... Short and tight ... Basic golf.

★★ BUNN GOLF COURSE
PU-2500 S. 11th, Springfield, 62703, Sangamon County, (217)522-2633.
Holes: 18. **Yards:** 6,104/5,355. **Par:** 72/73. **Course Rating:** 68.7/68.4. **Slope:** 118/119. **Green Fee:** $11/$15. **Cart Fee:** $10/person. **Walking Policy:** Unrestricted walking. **Walkability:** 2.
Opened: 1901. **Architect:** Edward Lawrence Packard. **Season:** March-Nov. **High:** June-July. **To obtain tee times:** In person 7 days in advance with nominal fee. **Miscellaneous:** Reduced fees (seniors, juniors), club rentals, credit cards (MC, V), beginner friendly.

BYRON HILLS GOLF COURSE
PU-23316 94th Ave. N., Port Byron, (800)523-9306, (800)523-9306.
Holes: 18. **Yards:** 6,441/5,258. **Par:** 71/71. **Course Rating:** 70.5/69.6. **Slope:** 115/112. **Green Fee:** $16/$18. **Cart Fee:** $10/person. **Walking Policy:** Unrestricted walking. **Walkability:** 3.
Opened: 1967. **Season:** March-Nov. **High:** May-Sept. **Miscellaneous:** Reduced fees (seniors, juniors), club rentals, credit cards (MC, V, D).

CANTIGNY GOLF *Service*
PU-27 W. 270 Mack Rd., Wheaton, 60187, Du Page County, (630)668-3323, 40 miles W of Chicago. **Web:** www.rrmtf.org/cantigny/golf/.
Holes: 27. **Cart Fee:** $15/person. **Walking Policy:** Unrestricted walking. **Walkability:** 3.
Opened: 1989. **Architect:** Roger Packard. **Season:** April-Oct. **High:** June-Aug. **To obtain tee times:** Call up to 7 days in advance. **Miscellaneous:** Reduced fees (seniors, juniors), range (grass/mats), caddies, club rentals, credit cards (MC, V, AE, D).
★★★★½ LAKESIDE/HILLSIDE *Condition*
Yards: 6,793/5,183. **Par:** 72/72. **Course Rating:** 71.8/70.1. **Slope:** 131/119. **Green Fee:** $75/$75.
Reader Comments: Beautiful course with outstanding views ... Great golf, great facility, great service ... Well run ... Pace of play is well monitored ... I would recommend it ... Class act ... Gorgeous ... A must-play ... Great clubhouse ... Fair ... A pleasure ... Perfect for corporate golf ... Top-notch.
★★★★½ WOODSIDE/HILLSIDE *Condition*
Yards: 6,915/5,236. **Par:** 72/72. **Course Rating:** 72.8/70.3. **Slope:** 130/120. **Green Fee:** $75/$75.
Reader Comments: Beautiful ... Excellent conditions ... Fabulous.
★★★★½ WOODSIDE/LAKESIDE *Condition*
Yards: 6,952/5,425. **Par:** 72/72. **Course Rating:** 73.1/71.9. **Slope:** 136/127. **Green Fee:** N/A/$65.
Notes: Ranked 24th in 1999 Best in State; 57th in 1996 America's Top 75 Upscale Courses. Many PGA Tour events.
Reader Comments: Nice 9-hole deal in the P.M. ... Excellent practice facility ... My favorite.

★★½ CARDINAL CREEK GOLF COURSE
PU-615 Dixie Hwy., Beecher, 60401, Will County, (708)946-2800, 30 miles S of Chicago.
Holes: 27. **Yards:** 6,340/5,541. **Par:** 72/72. **Course Rating:** N/A. **Slope:** N/A. **Green Fee:** $14/$26. **Cart Fee:** $12/person. **Walking Policy:** Unrestricted walking. **Walkability:** 3. **Opened:** 1927. **Architect:** R. Albert Anderson. **Season:** Year-round. **High:** June-Sept. **To obtain tee times:** Call anytime. **Miscellaneous:** Reduced fees (weekdays, low season, twilight, seniors, juniors), discount packages, metal spikes, club rentals, credit cards (MC, V).
Reader Comments: Short and forgiving ... Friendly ... Pretty good for the money ... Fair.

★★ CARDINAL GOLF COURSE
PU-Town of Effingham, Effingham, 62401, Effingham County, (217)868-2860.
Holes: 18. **Yards:** 5,980/N/A. **Par:** 72/N/A. **Course Rating:** N/A. **Slope:** N/A. **Green Fee:** N/A/$16. **Cart Fee:** $16/cart. **Walking Policy:** Unrestricted walking. **Walkability:** 1. **Opened:** 1963. **Season:** April-Oct. **To obtain tee times:** First come, first served. **Miscellaneous:** Metal spikes, club rentals.

★★★½ CARILLON GOLF CLUB
PU-21200 S. Carillon, Plainfield, 60544, Will County, (815)886-2132, 30 miles S of Chicago.
Holes: 27. **Yards:** 6,607/5,194. **Par:** 71/71. **Course Rating:** 71.1/68.4. **Slope:** 121/108. **Green Fee:** $33/$44. **Cart Fee:** $14/person. **Walking Policy:** Unrestricted walking. **Walkability:** 1. **Opened:** 1990. **Architect:** Greg Martin. **Season:** March-Nov. **High:** June-Sept. **To obtain tee times:** Call 7 days in advance. **Miscellaneous:** Reduced fees (weekdays, low season, twilight, seniors, juniors), discount packages, metal spikes, range (grass/mats), club rentals, credit cards (MC, V, D).
Reader Comments: Few trees; very windy ... Open .... Scoreable ... Making improvements ... New 9 is great ... Surprisingly good.

★★½ CARRIAGE GREENS COUNTRY CLUB
PU-8700 Carriage Greens Dr., Darien, 60561, Du Page County, (630)985-3730, 25 miles SW of Chicago.

Holes: 18. **Yards:** 6,451/6,009. **Par:** 70/72. **Course Rating:** 70.9/73.5. **Slope:** 121/123. **Green Fee:** $28/$48. **Cart Fee:** Included in Green Fee. **Walking Policy:** Walking at certain times. **Walkability:** 2. **Opened:** 1969. **Season:** March-Nov. **High:** June-Aug. **To obtain tee times:** Call 7 days in advance. **Miscellaneous:** Reduced fees (weekdays, low season, twilight, seniors), discount packages, metal spikes, club rentals, credit cards (MC, V, AE, D).
Reader Comments: Could be good ... Be ready for death march on weekends ... Improved in the past few years ... Nice layout.

★★★½ CARY COUNTRY CLUB
SP-2400 Grove Lane, Cary, 60013, McHenry County, (847)639-3161, 40 miles NW of Chicago. **E-mail:** ilpgawork@aol.com.
Holes: 18. **Yards:** 6,135/5,595. **Par:** 72/77. **Course Rating:** 68.7/70.8. **Slope:** 114/118. **Green Fee:** $23/$27. **Cart Fee:** $28/cart. **Walking Policy:** Unrestricted walking. **Walkability:** 4. **Opened:** 1923. **Season:** April-Oct. **High:** June-Aug. **To obtain tee times:** Call up to 7 days in advance. **Miscellaneous:** Reduced fees (weekdays, seniors), club rentals, credit cards (MC, V, AE, D).
Reader Comments: I wish they'd let the greens get firm and fast ... Sporty, hilly ... Many improvements ... Can never get a tee time ... No driving range.

★★★★ CHALET HILLS GOLF CLUB
PU-943 Rawson Bridge Rd., Cary, 60013, McHenry County, (847)639-0666, 40 miles NW of Chicago. **E-mail:** Chaletgo@mc.net. **Web:** www.chaletgolf.com.
Holes: 18. **Yards:** 6,877/4,934. **Par:** 73/73. **Course Rating:** 73.4/68.1. **Slope:** 131/114. **Green Fee:** $42/$50. **Cart Fee:** $13/person. **Walking Policy:** Walking at certain times. **Walkability:** 4. **Opened:** 1995. **Architect:** Ken Killian. **Season:** April-Oct. **High:** May-Sept. **To obtain tee times:** Call golf shop. Reservations accepted 7 days in advance by phone or e-mail. **Miscellaneous:** Reduced fees (weekdays, low season, twilight, seniors, juniors), range (mats), club rentals, credit cards (MC, V, D).
Reader Comments: Some great holes ... Wonderful terrain ... Must be straight ... Lots of water ... Fantastic ... Eats me alive, but always enjoyable ... Like Kemper Lakes, at a fraction of the cost and a fraction of the attitude ... Memorable ... A course you learn to like ... A real test.

★★½ CHAPEL HILL COUNTRY CLUB
PU-2500 Chapel Hill Rd, McHenry, 60005, McHenry County, (815)385-3337.
Holes: 18. **Yards:** 6,021/5,359. **Par:** 70/72. **Course Rating:** 68.7/70.4. **Slope:** 117/117. **Green Fee:** $20/$27. **Cart Fee:** $12/person. **Walking Policy:** Walking at certain times. **Walkability:** 3. **Opened:** 1928. **Season:** Year-round. **High:** May-Sept. **To obtain tee times:** Call up to 7 days in advance. **Miscellaneous:** Reduced fees (twilight, seniors, juniors), metal spikes, range (grass), club rentals, credit cards (MC, V, AE, D).
Reader Comments: Good practice course ... A good place for 36-handicappers ... Lots of narrow fairways.

★★ CHERRY HILLS GOLF CLUB
191 St & Flossmoor Rd., Flossmoor, 60422, Cook County, (708)799-5600.
Special Notes: Call club for further information.

★★★ CHEVY CHASE GOLF CLUB
PM-1000 N. Milwaukee Ave., Wheeling, 60090, Cook County, (847)537-0082, 30 miles NW of Chicago.
Holes: 18. **Yards:** 6,608/5,215. **Par:** 72/72. **Course Rating:** 71.7/69.3. **Slope:** 126/119. **Green Fee:** $17/$30. **Cart Fee:** $23/cart. **Walking Policy:** Unrestricted walking. **Walkability:** 2. **Opened:** 1923. **Architect:** Tom Bendelow. **Season:** Year-round. **High:** April-Oct. **To obtain tee times:** Call 7 days in advance. **Miscellaneous:** Reduced fees (low season, twilight, seniors, juniors), club rentals, credit cards (MC, V, D).
Reader Comments: Not bad for the cost ... A lot of play ... Standard.

★★ CHICK EVANS GOLF COURSE
PU-6145 Golf Rd., Morton Grove, 60053, Cook County, (847)663-8805.
Holes: 18. **Yards:** 5,680/5,680. **Par:** 73/71. **Course Rating:** 64.7/69.7. **Slope:** 94/105. **Green Fee:** $16/$19. **Cart Fee:** $20/cart. **Walking Policy:** Unrestricted walking. **Walkability:** 2. **Opened:** 1940. **Architect:** N/A. **Season:** March-Dec. **High:** June-Aug. **To obtain tee times:** Call 7 days in advance. **Miscellaneous:** Reduced fees (weekdays, twilight, seniors, juniors), metal spikes, club rentals, credit cards (MC, V, AE, D).

★★★½ CINDER RIDGE GOLF LINKS
PU-24801 Lakepoint Dr., Wilmington, 60481, Will County, (815)476-4000, 55 miles S of Chicago.
Holes: 18. **Yards:** 6,909/4,810. **Par:** 72/72. **Course Rating:** 72.9/N/A. **Slope:** 130/N/A. **Green Fee:** N/A/$33. **Cart Fee:** $11/person. **Cart Fee:** Included in Green Fee. **Walking Policy:** Unrestricted walking. **Walkability:** 3. **Opened:** 1995. **Architect:** George Kappos. **Season:** Year-round. **High:** May-Sept. **To obtain tee times:** Call up to 7 days in advance with a credit card.

ILLINOIS

Yearly times may be purchased with 3 weeks deposit in advance. **Miscellaneous:** Reduced fees (weekdays, twilight, seniors, juniors), range (grass/mats), club rentals, credit cards (MC, V, AE, D).

Reader Comments: Unique; in old strip mine ... Unique; environmentally friendly ... Old coal-dust bunkers ... Better as it matures ... Some excellent holes, some weird.

★★★ CLINTON HILL GOLF COURSE

PU-3700 Old Collinsville Rd., Belleville, 62221, St. Clair County, (618)277-3700, 15 miles W of St. Louis.

Holes: 18. **Yards:** 6,568/5,176. **Par:** 71/71. **Course Rating:** 70.6/68.4. **Slope:** 121/101. **Green Fee:** $14/$24. **Cart Fee:** $12/person. **Walking Policy:** Walking at certain times. **Walkability:** 3. **Opened:** 1969. **Season:** Year-round. **Miscellaneous:** Reduced fees (low season, twilight, seniors, juniors), range (grass/mats), credit cards (MC, V, D).

Reader Comments: Bermuda grass fairways good for summer heat ... Enjoyable ... Heavy play ... Nice turf ... Good place to knock it around.

★★★ CLOVERLEAF GOLF COURSE

PU-3555 Fosterburg Rd, Alton, 62002, Madison County, (618)462-3022.

Holes: 18. **Yards:** 5,671/4,867. **Par:** 70/70. **Course Rating:** 66.8/66.7. **Slope:** 113/103. **Green Fee:** $14/$15. **Cart Fee:** $8/person. **Walking Policy:** Unrestricted walking. **Walkability:** 3. **Opened:** 1931. **Season:** Year-round. **High:** April-Sept. **To obtain tee times:** Tee times can be made 1 week in advance. Group outings can be booked after January 15, 2000. **Miscellaneous:** Reduced fees (low season, seniors, juniors), metal spikes, club rentals.

Reader Comments: Good for beginners; long hitters reach par 4s with drives ... Quaint ... Outdated, but extremely fun ... Good wedge practice.

COG HILL GOLF CLUB

PU-12294 Archer Ave., Lemont, 60439, Cook County, (630)257-5872, 32 miles SW of Chicago. **E-mail:** coghillgolfclub@worldnet.att.net. **Web:** www.coghillgolf.com.

★★★½ COURSE NO. 1

Holes: 18. **Yards:** 6,329/5,594. **Par:** 71/72. **Course Rating:** 69.8/71.4. **Slope:** 118/119. **Green Fee:** $10/$35. **Cart Fee:** $29/cart. **Walking Policy:** Unrestricted walking. **Walkability:** 2. **Opened:** 1928. **Architect:** David McIntosh/Bert Coghill. **Season:** Year-round. **High:** April-Oct. **To obtain tee times:** Call 6 days in advance. **Miscellaneous:** Reduced fees (weekdays, low season, twilight, juniors), range (grass/mats), caddies, club rentals, credit cards (MC, V, D, Diners Club), beginner friendly (no embarrassment golf schools).

Reader Comments: Relaxing 18 ... Played in Feb. and it was great ... Fun ... OK ... Solid ... Too many outings.

★★★½ COURSE NO. 2

Holes: 18. **Yards:** 6,268/5,564. **Par:** 72/72. **Course Rating:** 71.3/72.8. **Slope:** 126/121. **Green Fee:** $24/$45. **Cart Fee:** $29/cart. **Walking Policy:** Unrestricted walking. **Walkability:** 4. **Opened:** 1930. **Architect:** Bert Coghill. **Season:** April-Dec. **High:** April-Oct. **To obtain tee times:** Call 90 days in advance with prepayment or 6 days in advance without. **Miscellaneous:** Reduced fees (weekdays, low season, twilight, juniors), range (grass/mats), caddies, club rentals, credit cards (MC, V, D, Diners Club), beginner friendly (no embarrassment golf schools).

Reader Comments: Well worth the money ... A privilege ... Sporty ... Nice, but crowded ... A great complex ... Short and tight ... Very scenic ... Reasonable ... Good for short hitters to score.

★★★½ COURSE NO. 3

Holes: 18. **Yards:** 6,437/5,321. **Par:** 72/71. **Course Rating:** 69.9/64.8. **Slope:** 116/105. **Green Fee:** $10/$35. **Cart Fee:** $29/cart. **Walking Policy:** Unrestricted walking. **Walkability:** 2. **Opened:** 1964. **Architect:** Dick Wilson. **Season:** Year-round. **High:** April-Oct. **To obtain tee times:** Call 6 days in advance. **Miscellaneous:** Reduced fees (weekdays, low season, twilight, juniors), range (grass/mats), caddies, club rentals, credit cards (MC, V, D, Diners Club), beginner friendly (no embarrassment golf schools).

Reader Comments: Price was right in Feb. ... Another relaxing 18 ... Good layout for average golfer ... Not overly challenging ... Fun.

★★★★½ COURSE NO. 4 DUBSDREAD *Condition*

Holes: 18. **Yards:** 6,930/5,874. **Par:** 72/72. **Course Rating:** 75.4/69.2. **Slope:** 142/131. **Green Fee:** N/A/$110. **Cart Fee:** Included in Green Fee. **Walking Policy:** Unrestricted walking. **Walkability:** 4. **Opened:** 1964. **Architect:** Dick Wilson. **Season:** April-Oct. **High:** April-Oct. **To obtain tee times:** Call up to 90 days in advance with pre-pay on credit card. **Miscellaneous:** Reduced fees (weekdays, twilight, juniors), range (grass/mats), caddies, club rentals, credit cards (MC, V, D, Diners Club), beginner friendly (no embarrassment golf schools).

Notes: Ranked 40th in 1999-2000 America's 100 Greatest; 3rd in 1999 Best in State; 5th in 1996 America's Top 75 Upscale Courses; Motorola Western Open; 1997 U.S. Amateur; 1989, 1970 USGA Amateur Public Links Championship; 1987 USGA Women's Amateur Public Links Championship.

Reader Comments: Best $100 public in America ... One of Dick Wilson's classic designs ... PGA Tour stop ... A must-play ... Difficult ... Always felt rushed by rangers ... Great layout, first-class over all ... One of the great ones ... Beautiful with fall foliage ... Sand, sand and more sand ... Tough but fun to play ... Price keeps going up ... Superb ... Should be a U.S. Open course.

★★ COLONIAL GOLF COURSE
PU-Old Route 51 S., Sandoval, 62882, Marion County, (618)247-3307.
Yards: 5,657/4,739. **Par:** 70/70. **Course Rating:** 65.1/65.1. **Slope:** 102/102. **Green Fee:** $10/$11. **Cart Fee:** $16/. **Walking Policy:** Unrestricted walking. **Walkability:** 2. **Season:** Feb.-Dec. **High:** June-Aug. **Miscellaneous:** Club rentals.

★★½ COLUMBIA GOLF CLUB
PU-125 AA Rd., Columbia, 62236, Monroe County, (618)286-4455, 15 miles N of St. Louis, MO.
Holes: 18. **Yards:** 6,275/5,000. **Par:** 71/72. **Course Rating:** 69.4/68.4. **Slope:** N/A. **Green Fee:** $13/$22. **Cart Fee:** $10/person. **Walking Policy:** Unrestricted walking. **Walkability:** 3. **Opened:** 1972. **Architect:** Al Linkogel. **Season:** Year-round. **High:** April-Oct. **To obtain tee times:** Call golf shop. **Miscellaneous:** Reduced fees (weekdays, low season, seniors), metal spikes, credit cards (MC, V).
Reader Comments: Acceptable ... Playable ... Beware of outings ... Hilly.

★★ COUNTRY LAKES GOLF CLUB
PU-1601 Fairway Dr., Naperville, 60563, Du Page County, (630)420-1060. **E-mail:** gcountry@aol.com.
Holes: 18. **Yards:** 6,850/5,340. **Par:** 73/76. **Course Rating:** 71.5/72.9. **Slope:** 124/124. **Green Fee:** $15/$34. **Cart Fee:** $14/person. **Walking Policy:** Unrestricted walking. **Walkability:** 2. **Opened:** 1970. **Architect:** Rolf Campbell. **Season:** Year-round. **High:** March-Nov. **To obtain tee times:** Call the golf shop 7 days in advance. **Miscellaneous:** Reduced fees (low season, twilight, seniors, juniors), range (grass), club rentals, credit cards (MC, V, AE, D), beginner friendly.

COUNTRYSIDE GOLF COURSE
PU-20800 W. Hawley St., Mundelein, 60060, Lake County, (847)566-5544, 30 miles N of Chicago.
★★★½ PRAIRIE COURSE
Holes: 18. **Yards:** 6,757/5,050. **Par:** 72/72. **Course Rating:** 71.5/68.3. **Slope:** 123/114. **Green Fee:** $15/$31. **Cart Fee:** $25/cart. **Walking Policy:** Unrestricted walking. **Walkability:** 3. **Opened:** 1990. **Architect:** Bob Lohmann. **Season:** March-Dec. **High:** May-Sept. **To obtain tee times:** 5 day advance reservations for residents of Lake County. 3 days for nonresidents. **Miscellaneous:** Reduced fees (weekdays, low season, twilight, seniors, juniors), discount packages, range (grass/mats), club rentals, credit cards (MC, V).
Reader Comments: Above-average course ... Slow play is only negative ... Grip it and rip it ... Not really challenging, but fun to play.
★★★½ TRADITIONAL COURSE
Holes: 18. **Yards:** 6,178/5,111. **Par:** 72/72. **Course Rating:** 69.4/68.8. **Slope:** 114/112. **Green Fee:** $15/$31. **Cart Fee:** $25/cart. **Walking Policy:** Unrestricted walking. **Walkability:** 3. **Opened:** 1927. **Architect:** Bob Lohmann. **Season:** Year-round. **High:** May-Sept. **To obtain tee times:** Call on Monday for upcoming weekend or holiday. 5 day advance reservations for residents of Lake County. 3 days for nonresidents. **Miscellaneous:** Reduced fees (weekdays, low season, twilight, seniors, juniors), discount packages, range (grass/mats), club rentals, credit cards (MC, V).
Reader Comments: Will definitely return ... Older course; many trees ... Not bad ... Some hills.

★★½ CRAB ORCHARD GOLF CLUB
SP-901 W. Grand Ave., Carterville, 62918, Williamson County, (618)985-2321, 100 miles SE of St. Louis.
Holes: 18. **Yards:** 6,448/5,058. **Par:** 70/71. **Course Rating:** 71.0/68.4. **Slope:** 129/114. **Green Fee:** N/A/$20. **Cart Fee:** $10/person. **Walking Policy:** Unrestricted walking. **Walkability:** 3. **Opened:** 1959. **Architect:** Roy Glenn. **Season:** Year-round. **High:** April-Oct. **To obtain tee times:** Call. Must have threesome or foursome to reserve tee time. **Miscellaneous:** Reduced fees (seniors), range (grass), club rentals, credit cards (MC, V, D).
Reader Comments: Looks easier than it is ... Nice, large trees ... Pretty setting.

★★★ CRYSTAL WOODS GOLF CLUB
SP-5915 S. Route 47, Woodstock, 60098, McHenry County, (815)338-3111, 3 miles S of Woodstock. **E-mail:** cwoods@owc.net.
Holes: 18. **Yards:** 6,403/5,488. **Par:** 72/73. **Course Rating:** 70.3/70.5. **Slope:** 117/114. **Green Fee:** $25/$44. **Cart Fee:** Included in Green Fee. **Walking Policy:** Walking at certain times. **Walkability:** 3. **Opened:** 1957. **Architect:** William Langford. **Season:** April-Nov. **High:** June-Sept. **To obtain tee times:** Call up to 7 days in advance. **Miscellaneous:** Reduced fees (low season, twilight, seniors), range (grass), credit cards (MC, V, AE, D).
Reader Comments: Fun ... One of my favorites ... Nice for average golfer ... Fairly challenging ... Easy walking ... Decent.

ILLINOIS

★★★½ DEER CREEK GOLF CLUB
PU-25055 Western Avenue, University Park, 60466, Will County, (708)672-6667, 30 miles S of Chicago.
Holes: 18. **Yards:** 6,755/5,835. **Par:** 72/72. **Course Rating:** 72.4/73.2. **Slope:** 124/120. **Green Fee:** $22/$29. **Cart Fee:** $12/person. **Walking Policy:** Unrestricted walking. **Walkability:** N/A. **Opened:** 1972. **Architect:** Edward Lawrence Packard. **Season:** Year-round. **High:** May-Sept. **To obtain tee times:** Tee times taken 1 week in advance. **Miscellaneous:** Reduced fees (weekdays, twilight, seniors, juniors), metal spikes, range (grass/mats), club rentals, credit cards (MC, V, AE, D).
Reader Comments: Very good three finishing holes ... Pace is too slow for such a wide-open course ... Very good special rates.

★★★ DEERFIELD PARK GOLF CLUB
PU-1201 Saunders Rd., Riverwoods, 60015, Lake County, (847)945-8333, 6 miles W of Highland Park.
Holes: 18. **Yards:** 6,756/5,635. **Par:** 72/74. **Course Rating:** 71.8/71.9. **Slope:** 125/121. **Green Fee:** $26/$32. **Cart Fee:** $24/cart. **Walking Policy:** Unrestricted walking. **Walkability:** N/A. **Architect:** Edward Lawrence Packard. **Season:** April-Dec. **High:** June-Sept. **To obtain tee times:** Call 2 days in advance. **Miscellaneous:** Reduced fees (weekdays, twilight), discount packages, metal spikes, club rentals, credit cards (MC, V, D).
Reader Comments: One of my favorites ... Right along the highway ... Flat course drains really well ... Back nine has some tight holes ... Blocking the highway noise would help.

★★½ DEERPATH PARK GOLF COURSE
PU-500 W. Deerpath, Lake Forest, 60045, Lake County, (847)615-4290, 25 miles N of Chicago.
Holes: 18. **Yards:** 6,105/5,542. **Par:** 70/72. **Course Rating:** 68.7/72.1. **Slope:** 124/122. **Green Fee:** $25/$34. **Cart Fee:** $25/cart. **Walking Policy:** Unrestricted walking. **Walkability:** 2. **Opened:** 1927. **Architect:** Alex Pirie. **Season:** April-Dec. **High:** June-Aug. **To obtain tee times:** Call 1 day in advance. **Miscellaneous:** Reduced fees (seniors, juniors), range (grass/mats), club rentals, credit cards (MC, V).
Reader Comments: OK ... Small greens, tight fairways make up for lack of length.

★★★★ THE DEN AT FOX CREEK GOLF CLUB *Value*
PM-3002 Fox Creek Rd., Bloomington, 61704, (309)434-2300. **E-mail:** jrkenn@aol.com.
Holes: 18. **Yards:** 6,926/5,345. **Par:** 72/72. **Course Rating:** 72.9/70.1. **Slope:** 128/116. **Green Fee:** $28/$34. **Cart Fee:** $10/person. **Walking Policy:** Unrestricted walking. **Walkability:** 3. **Opened:** 1997. **Architect:** Arnold Palmer/Ed Seay. **Season:** March-Oct. **High:** May-Sept. **To obtain tee times:** 7 days in advance via phone or in person. **Miscellaneous:** Reduced fees (twilight, seniors, juniors), range (grass/mats), club rentals, credit cards (MC, V).
Reader Comments: This course has it all ... Too many blind shots ... Magnificent course from a cornfield beginning ... Great for a newer course ... The more you play it, the more you like it ... Always windy; holes 4-6 are a great stretch ... Wind is a major factor at this course.

★★★ DOWNERS GROVE PARK DISTRICT GC
PM-2420 Haddow, Downers Grove, 60515, Du Page County, (630)963-1306, 25 miles W of Chicago.
Holes: 9. **Yards:** 3,230/2,629. **Par:** 38/35. **Course Rating:** 70.5/69.4. **Slope:** 122/115. **Green Fee:** $22/$32. **Cart Fee:** $24/cart. **Walking Policy:** Unrestricted walking. **Walkability:** 4. **Opened:** 1892. **Architect:** C.B. Macdonald/D Gill/S Halberg. **Season:** March-Nov. **High:** June-Aug. **To obtain tee times:** Call 5 days in advance for weekends and holidays. **Miscellaneous:** Reduced fees (weekdays, seniors, juniors), range (grass/mats), rentals, credit cards (MC, V).
Reader Comments: A great old layout ... Great history ... Nice nine-hole layout ... Huge, mature trees ... Old-style fun ... Nice variety.

★★½ DWIGHT COUNTRY CLUB
SP-RR 2, Golf Rd., Dwight, 60420, Livingston County, (815)584-1399.
Holes: 18. **Yards:** 6,269/5,221. **Par:** 71/71. **Course Rating:** 67.3/N/A. **Slope:** 116N/A. **Green Fee:** $12/$12. **Walkability:** N/A. **Miscellaneous:** Metal spikes.
Reader Comments: Fairly easy ... Good beginners' course ... Short.

★★★★ EAGLE CREEK RESORT
R-P.O. Box 230, Findlay, 62534, Shelby County, (217)756-3456, (800)876-3245, 35 miles S of Decatur. **E-mail:** golf@eaglecreekresort.com. **Web:** www.eaglecreekresort.com.
Holes: 18. **Yards:** 6,908/4,978. **Par:** 72/72. **Course Rating:** 73.5/69.1. **Slope:** 132/115. **Green Fee:** $28/$55. **Cart Fee:** Included in Green Fee. **Walking Policy:** Mandatory cart. **Walkability:** 3. **Opened:** 1989. **Architect:** Ken Killian. **Season:** Year-round. **High:** May-Oct. **To obtain tee times:** Call in advance with credit card to guarantee. **Miscellaneous:** Reduced fees (weekdays, low season, resort guests, twilight, seniors, juniors), discount packages, metal spikes, range (grass), club rentals, lodging, credit cards (MC, V, AE, D, Diners Club).

249

ILLINOIS

Reader Comments: Wide open; doglegged to death ... If you use the wrong tees, the course is too hard, leading to slow play ... Winter rates are great ... Very scenic ... Tough from the back tees ... A real sleeper ... Challenging and beautiful. A great golf experience.

EAGLE RIDGE INN & RESORT *Service*
★★★★ NORTH COURSE
R-400 Eagle Ridge Dr., Galena, 61036, Jo Daviess County, (815)777-2500, (800)892-2269, 20 miles SE of Dubuque, IA.
Holes: 18. **Yards:** 6,836/5,578. **Par:** 72/72. **Course Rating:** 73.4/72.3. **Slope:** 134/127. **Green Fee:** $55/$100. **Cart Fee:** Included in Green Fee. **Walking Policy:** Unrestricted walking.
Walkability: 3. **Opened:** 1977. **Architect:** Larry Packard/Roger Packard. **Season:** April-Nov.
High: May-Oct. **To obtain tee times:** Nonguests call up to 7 days in advance. **Miscellaneous:**
Reduced fees (weekdays, low season, resort guests, twilight), discount packages, range (grass), club rentals, lodging, credit cards (MC, V, AE, D, Diners Club).
Reader Comments: Best when you are a guest ... S-L-O-W. Take your CD player with soothing music ... Great scenery ... Memorable ... Expensive, but worth it ... Terrific resort ... Awesome facility ... Many elevation changes ... Women's bathrooms are very disappointing. Obviously an afterthought ... Not a flat lie anywhere, even in the middle of the fairway.

★★★★ SOUTH COURSE
R-10 Clubhouse Dr., Galena, 61036, Jo Daviess County, (815)777-2280, (800)892-2269, 12 miles SE of Dubuque, IA.
Holes: 18. **Yards:** 6,762/5,609. **Par:** 72/72. **Course Rating:** 72.9/72.4. **Slope:** 133/128. **Green Fee:** $55/$100. **Cart Fee:** $28/. **Cart Fee:** Included in Green Fee. **Walking Policy:** Unrestricted walking. **Walkability:** 3. **Opened:** 1984. **Architect:** Roger Packard. **Season:** April-Nov. **High:**
May-Oct. **To obtain tee times:** Nonguests call up to 7 days in advance. **Miscellaneous:**
Reduced fees (weekdays, low season, resort guests, twilight), discount packages, range (grass), club rentals, lodging, credit cards (MC, V, AE, D, Diners Club).
Notes: Ranked 75th in 1996 America's Top 75 Upscale Courses.
Reader Comments: Very picturesque ... Nice in every way ... Good golf ... Great design.
Rewards good shots ... Resort pricing ... Pretty course ... Challenging ... Great par 3s.

★★★★ THE GENERAL COURSE
R-P.O. Box 777, Galena, 61036, Jo Daviess County, (815)777-4525, (800)892-2269, 30 miles SE of Dubuque.
Holes: 18. **Yards:** 6,820/5,335. **Par:** 72/72. **Course Rating:** 73.8/66.7. **Slope:** 137/119. **Green Fee:** $77/$120. **Cart Fee:** Included in Green Fee. **Walking Policy:** Mandatory cart. **Walkability:**
5. **Opened:** 1997. **Architect:** Roger Packard/Andy North. **Season:** May-Oct. **High:** June-Oct. **To obtain tee times:** Nonguests call up to 7 days in advance. **Miscellaneous:** Reduced fees (weekdays, low season, resort guests, twilight), discount packages, range (grass), club rentals, lodging, credit cards (MC, V, AE, D, Diners Club).
Notes: Ranked 18th in 1999 Best in State.
Reader Comments: Very nice addition ... Super layout ... Top-notch ... Carts on path are only bummer ... Doesn't drain well ... Tough walk; great course ... Great place to go on vacation ... 'Cartpath only' leads to some long rounds.
Special Notes: Also has 9-hole, par-34 East Course. Spikeless encouraged.

★★★ EDGEBROOK COUNTRY CLUB
SP-2100 Sudyam Rd., Sandwich, 60548, De Kalb County, (815)786-3058, 35 miles SW of Aurora.
Holes: 18. **Yards:** 6,500/5,134. **Par:** 72/73. **Course Rating:** 69.1/69.5. **Slope:** 123/114. **Green Fee:** $15/$22. **Cart Fee:** $13/person. **Walking Policy:** Unrestricted walking. **Walkability:** 2.
Opened: 1968. **Architect:** Ken Killian/Dick Nugent. **Season:** March-Nov. **High:** April-Sept. **To obtain tee times:** Call at least 5 days in advance. **Miscellaneous:** Reduced fees (low season, twilight, juniors), range (grass/mats), club rentals, credit cards (MC, V, D).
Reader Comments: OK ... Good test for weekend golfers ... Nicely wooded ... Good, average course.

★½ EDGEBROOK GOLF CLUB
6100 North Central Ave., Chicago, 60646, Cook County, (773)775-6947 .
Special Notes: Call club for further information.

EDGEWOOD GOLF COURSE
★★★ GOLD/RED
PU-16497 Kennedy Road, Auburn, 62615, Sangamon County, (217)438-3221, 10 miles S of Springfield.
Holes: 18. **Yards:** 6,400/5,234. **Par:** 71/71. **Course Rating:** 70.5/70.1. **Slope:** 126/121. **Green Fee:** $14/$20. **Cart Fee:** $10/. **Walking Policy:** Unrestricted walking. **Walkability:** 3. **Opened:**
1968. **Season:** Year-round. **High:** April-Oct. **To obtain tee times:** Call 7 days in advance.
Miscellaneous: Reduced fees (twilight, seniors, juniors), club rentals, credit cards (MC, V, AE).
Reader Comments: Good experience ... Some of the green slopes are ridiculous ... Updated and improved.

EDGEWOOD PARK GOLF COURSE
PU-Box 104 Rte 89, Mc Nabb, 61335, Putnam County, (815)882-2317, 40 miles NE of Peoria.
Holes: 18. **Yards:** 6,660/5,780. **Par:** 72/74. **Course Rating:** 70.9/72.0. **Slope:** 117/118. **Green Fee:** $15/$17. **Cart Fee:** $18/cart. **Walking Policy:** Unrestricted walking. **Walkability:** 2.
Opened: 1968. **Architect:** Jim Spean. **Season:** Year-round. **To obtain tee times:** Call golf shop.
Miscellaneous: Reduced fees (weekdays, seniors, juniors), range (grass), club rentals.

★★★★ EL PASO GOLF CLUB *Pace+*
SP-RR 1 Box 63A, El Paso, 61738, Woodford County, (309)527-5225, 10 miles N of Bloomington.
Holes: 18. **Yards:** 6,052/5,064. **Par:** 71/71. **Course Rating:** 70.1/69.9. **Slope:** 122/121. **Green Fee:** N/A/$18. **Cart Fee:** $16/cart. **Walking Policy:** Unrestricted walking. **Walkability:** 4.
Opened: 1924. **Architect:** James Spear. **Season:** March-Nov. **High:** June-Aug. **To obtain tee times:** Call golf shop. Sundays and holidays members only play. Public can call 4 days in advance to make tee times. **Miscellaneous:** Credit cards (MC, V).
Reader Comments: Excellent ... Challenging ... Not long, but has variety ... Quick greens.

★★★ ELLIOTT GOLF COURSE
PU-888 S. Lyford Rd., Rockford, 61108, Winnebago County, (815)987-1687.
Holes: 18. **Yards:** 6,393/6,253. **Par:** 72/69. **Course Rating:** 69.4/70.7. **Slope:** 107/113. **Green Fee:** $16/$21. **Cart Fee:** $22/cart. **Walking Policy:** Unrestricted walking. **Walkability:** 2.
Opened: 1968. **Architect:** Edward Lawrence Packard. **Season:** April-Oct. **High:** May-Aug. **To obtain tee times:** Call or come in 7 days in advance for weekends and holidays.
Miscellaneous: Reduced fees (low season, twilight), range (mats), club rentals, credit cards (MC, V, D).
Reader Comments: Could be above average with more attention ... Conditions have improved ... Lots of traffic.

★★½ EMERALD HILL GOLF & LEARNING CENTER
PU-16802 Prairie Ville Rd., Sterling, 61081, Whiteside County, (815)622-6204.
Holes: 18. **Yards:** 6,244/4,869. **Par:** 71/71. **Course Rating:** 69.5/66.8. **Slope:** 113/108. **Green Fee:** $21/N/A. **Cart Fee:** $21/cart. **Walking Policy:** Unrestricted walking. **Walkability:** 3.
Opened: 1923. **Season:** March-Nov. **High:** June-Aug. **To obtain tee times:** Phone reservations up to 1 week in advance. **Miscellaneous:** Reduced fees (weekdays, seniors, juniors), metal spikes, club rentals, credit cards (MC, V), beginner friendly (beginner lessons available).

★★ EVERGREEN GOLF & COUNTRY CLUB
9140 South Western Ave., Chicago, 60620, Cook County, (773)238-6680.
Special Notes: Call club for further information.

★½ FAIRLAKES GOLF COURSE
PU-RR 1, Box 122, Secor, 61771, Woodford County, (309)744-2222, 10 miles N of Bloomington.
Holes: 18. **Yards:** 5,400/4,274. **Par:** 67/69. **Course Rating:** 64.1/64.8. **Slope:** 102/103. **Green Fee:** $11/$14. **Cart Fee:** $18/cart. **Walking Policy:** Unrestricted walking. **Walkability:** 4.
Opened: 1989. **Architect:** Harold Sparks. **Season:** March-Oct. **High:** June-Aug. **To obtain tee times:** Call up to 7 days in advance, at least 2 days in advance. **Miscellaneous:** Reduced fees (weekdays, seniors), metal spikes, range (grass/mats), club rentals, credit cards (MC, V).

★★★★ FAR OAKS GOLF CLUB *Condition*
PU-419 Old Collinsville Rd., Caseyville, 62232, St. Clair County, (618)628-2900, (314)FUN-GOLF. **E-mail:** farnaks@apci.net.
Holes: 27. **Yards:** 7,016/4,897. **Par:** 72/72. **Course Rating:** 73.3/71.8. **Slope:** 141/114. **Green Fee:** $49/$75. **Walking Policy:** Unrestricted walking. **Walkability:** 4. **Opened:** 1997. **Architect:** Bob Goalby/Kye Goalby. **Season:** Year-round. **High:** April-Nov. **Miscellaneous:** Reduced fees (low season, twilight, juniors), range (grass), club rentals, credit cards (MC, V).
Reader Comments: Excellent new course ... What a clubhouse ... Challenging ... Good mix of links/woods/hills ... Pure nature ... Dramatic layout through 200-year-old trees ... Very nice for a new course ... A little expensive ... Great addition to St. Louis area ... A must-play ... Four sets of tees make the course very playable for all levels.

★★★½ FARIES PARK GOLF COURSE
PU-1 Faries Park, Decatur, 62521, Macon County, (217)422-2211.
Holes: 18. **Yards:** 6,708/5,763. **Par:** 72/75. **Course Rating:** 70.8/73.0. **Slope:** 117/113. **Green Fee:** $12/$17. **Cart Fee:** $16/cart. **Walking Policy:** Unrestricted walking. **Walkability:** 2.
Opened: 1961. **Architect:** Edward Lawrence Packard. **Season:** March-Nov. **High:** June-Aug. **To obtain tee times:** Call on Mondays at 6:30 a.m. for upcoming weekend. Call 7 days in advance for weekdays. **Miscellaneous:** Metal spikes, range (grass/mats), club rentals, credit cards (MC, V).
Reader Comments: Nice course ... Good challenge ... Worth playing ... Good public course for all players ... Good value.

ILLINOIS

★★½ FOSS PARK GOLF CLUB
PM-3124 Argonne Dr., North Chicago, 60064, Lake County, (847)689-7490, 1 miles S of Waukegan.
Holes: 18. **Yards:** 6,914/5,888. **Par:** 72/74. **Course Rating:** 71.9/72.5. **Slope:** 113/117. **Green Fee:** $26/$32. **Walking Policy:** Unrestricted walking. **Walkability:** N/A. **Opened:** 1974. **Season:** April-Nov. **High:** May-Aug. **To obtain tee times:** In person 1 week in advance over the phone Friday before the weekend. Weekdays open play; weekend tee times. **Miscellaneous:** Reduced fees (weekdays, twilight, seniors, juniors), metal spikes, range (grass), club rentals.
Reader Comments: Sneaky tough ... Some very challenging holes, and some very easy ones ... Good value ... Power lines run through middle of course.

★★★ FOUR WINDS GOLF CLUB
PU-Route 176, Mundelein, 60060, Lake County, (847)566-8502, 40 miles N of Chicago.
Holes: 18. **Yards:** 6,501/4,943. **Par:** 71/72. **Course Rating:** 71.5/68.5. **Slope:** 122/114. **Green Fee:** $29/$52. **Cart Fee:** Included in Green Fee. **Walking Policy:** Walking at certain times. **Walkability:** 3. **Opened:** 1963. **Architect:** Herman Schwinge. **Season:** March-Nov. **High:** June-Aug. **To obtain tee times:** Call up to 10 days in advance. Credit card required to guarantee weekend tee times. **Miscellaneous:** Reduced fees (weekdays, low season, twilight, seniors), range (grass), club rentals, credit cards (MC, V, AE, D).
Reader Comments: Nice, simple country course ... Slicer's nightmare ... The money put back into the course shows.

★★★½ FOX BEND GOLF COURSE
PM-Route 34, Oswego, 60543, Kendall County, (630)554-3939, 9 miles W of Route 59.
Holes: 18. **Yards:** 6,800/5,400. **Par:** 72/72. **Course Rating:** 72.1/70.1. **Slope:** 124/116. **Green Fee:** $28/$38. **Cart Fee:** $14/person. **Walking Policy:** Unrestricted walking. **Walkability:** 3. **Opened:** 1967. **Architect:** Brent Wadsworth/Paul Loague. **Season:** March-Dec. **High:** May-Sept. **To obtain tee times:** Call 7 days in advance. **Miscellaneous:** Reduced fees (weekdays, low season, twilight, seniors, juniors), range (grass/mats), club rentals, credit cards (MC, V, AE).
Reader Comments: Better than average muny ... Tough, fair ... Lots of water. I want to fish here, too ... A number of good holes ... Fun, solid course ... Sporty.

★★★★ FOX CREEK GOLF CLUB
PU-6555 Fox Creek Dr., Edwardsville, 62025, Madison County, (618)692-9400, (800)692-9401, 2 miles N of 20 miles NE of St Louis.
Holes: 18. **Yards:** 7,027/5,185. **Par:** 72/72. **Course Rating:** 74.9/72.1. **Slope:** 144/132. **Green Fee:** $25/$45. **Cart Fee:** Included in Green Fee. **Walking Policy:** Mandatory cart. **Walkability:** 5. **Opened:** 1992. **Architect:** Gary Kern. **Season:** Year-round. **High:** May-Sept. **To obtain tee times:** Call 4 days in advance. **Miscellaneous:** Reduced fees (weekdays, low season, twilight, seniors), discount packages, metal spikes, range (grass), club rentals, credit cards (MC, V).
Reader Comments: Toughest course I've ever played ... Outstanding from the back tees ... Not for high-handicapper ... Unforgiving ... Very challenging ... Extremely difficult ... Plenty of bunkers, lakes, creeks and hills ... The back nine is impossible ... Bring lots of balls ... Better be straight.

★★★½ FOX LAKE COUNTRY CLUB
PU-7220 N. State Park Rd., Fox Lake, 60020, Lake County, (847)587-6411, 35 miles N of Chicago.
Holes: 18. **Yards:** 6,347/5,852. **Par:** 72/73. **Course Rating:** 71.7/73.9. **Slope:** 128/125. **Green Fee:** $40/$55. **Cart Fee:** Included in Green Fee. **Walking Policy:** Mandatory cart. **Walkability:** N/A. **Opened:** 1920. **Season:** April-Oct. **To obtain tee times:** Call anytime. **Miscellaneous:** Metal spikes, range (grass), club rentals, credit cards (MC, V).
Reader Comments: Traditional golf ... Lots of hills ... Hitting to blind greens ... Filled with wildlife ... A beauty and a pleasure ... Can't walk this one.

★★★ FOX RUN GOLF LINKS
PM-333 Plum Grove Rd., Elk Grove Village, 60007, Cook County, (847)228-3544, 20 miles NW of Chicago.
Holes: 18. **Yards:** 6,287/5,288. **Par:** 70/70. **Course Rating:** 70.5/70.2. **Slope:** 117/114. **Green Fee:** $12/$30. **Cart Fee:** $13/person. **Walking Policy:** Unrestricted walking. **Walkability:** 2. **Opened:** 1984. **Architect:** William Newcomb. **Season:** April-Nov. **High:** June-Aug. **To obtain tee times:** Call up to 7 days in advance. **Miscellaneous:** Reduced fees (weekdays, twilight, seniors, juniors), discount packages, range (grass/mats), club rentals, credit cards (MC, V, AE).
Reader Comments: Nice little muny ... Bad drainage, even after a light rain ... Wet and squishy ... Very short, even from the tips.

★★★ FOX VALLEY GOLF CLUB
PM-Route 25, N. Aurora, 60542, Kane County, (630)879-1030, 3 miles N of Aurora.
Holes: 18. **Yards:** 5,927/5,279. **Par:** 72/72. **Course Rating:** 68.2/70.4. **Slope:** 118/117. **Green Fee:** $20/$27. **Cart Fee:** $22/cart. **Walking Policy:** Unrestricted walking. **Walkability:** 3.

Opened: 1930. **Season:** March-Nov. **Miscellaneous:** Reduced fees (twilight), credit cards (MC, V).
Reader Comments: Short, sporty ... I love this course and want to keep it a secret ... Good course for average golfer.

★★½ FRESH MEADOWS GOLF COURSE
PU-2144 S. Wolf Rd., Hillside, 60162, Cook County, (708)449-3434, 12 miles W of Chicago. **E-mail:** freshmeadowsgc@aol.com.
Holes: 18. **Yards:** 6,178/5,693. **Par:** 70/70. **Course Rating:** 71.5/69.3. **Slope:** 118/113. **Green Fee:** $30/$35. **Cart Fee:** $13/person. **Walking Policy:** Walking at certain times. **Walkability:** 1.
Opened: 1927. **Season:** Year-round. **High:** May-Sept. **To obtain tee times:** Call up to 8 days in advance. **Miscellaneous:** Reduced fees (weekdays, low season, twilight, seniors, juniors), metal spikes, range (grass/mats), club rentals, credit cards (MC, V, AE), beginner friendly.
Reader Comments: Heavily played ... Only time I've ever walked off ... Open year-round.

GAMBIT GOLF CLUB
PU-1550 St. Rte. 146 E., Vienna, 62995, Johnson County, (618)658-6022, (800)942-6248, 27 miles N of Paducah, KY. **Web:** www.cambitgolf.com.
Holes: 18. **Yards:** 6,546/4,725. **Par:** 71/72. **Course Rating:** 72.4/66.1. **Slope:** 137/102. **Green Fee:** $32/$38. **Cart Fee:** Included in Green Fee. **Walking Policy:** Unrestricted walking.
Walkability: 3. **Opened:** 1996. **Architect:** Richard Osborne. **Season:** Year-round. **High:** March-Sept. **To obtain tee times:** Call up to 7 days in advance. **Miscellaneous:** Reduced fees (twilight, seniors, juniors), metal spikes, range (grass), credit cards (MC, V, AE).

GATEWAY NATIONAL GOLF LINKS
PU-18 Golf Dr., Madison, 62060, Madison County, (614)482-4653, 4 miles E of St. Louis.
Holes: 18. **Yards:** 7,178/5,187. **Par:** 71/71. **Course Rating:** 75.0/69.4. **Slope:** 138/114. **Green Fee:** $28/$59. **Cart Fee:** $6/person. **Walking Policy:** Unrestricted walking. **Walkability:** 1.
Opened: 1998. **Architect:** Keith Foster. **Season:** Year-round. **High:** April-Oct. **To obtain tee times:** Call up to 7 days in advance. Pre-book up to one year in advance $75.00 per player.
Miscellaneous: Reduced fees (weekdays, low season, twilight, seniors, juniors), range (grass), club rentals, credit cards (MC, V, AE).

★★★½ GEORGE W. DUNNE NATIONAL GOLF COURSE
PU-16310 S. Central, Oak Forest, 60452, Cook County, (708)614-2600, 25 miles SW of Chicago.
Holes: 18. **Yards:** 7,170/5,535. **Par:** 72/72. **Course Rating:** 75.1/71.4. **Slope:** 135/121. **Green Fee:** $30/$40. **Cart Fee:** Included in Green Fee. **Walking Policy:** Unrestricted walking.
Walkability: 2. **Opened:** 1982. **Architect:** Killian & Nugent. **Season:** March-Dec. **High:** May-Aug. **To obtain tee times:** Call (708)366-9466 up to 7 days in advance, 24 hours a day. Cook county activity card or major credit card requires for advance tee times. **Miscellaneous:** Reduced fees (weekdays, twilight, seniors, juniors), metal spikes, range (mats), club rentals, credit cards (MC, V, D).
Notes: Ranked 25th in 1996 America's Top 75 Affordable Courses.
Reader Comments: Used to be a great track ... Nice public course ... Excellent variety of holes ... Fabulous layout, but OK greens ... Still a very good value ... A great layout that has been allowed to age ungracefully.

★★★ GIBSON WOODS GOLF COURSE
PU-1321 N. 11th St., Monmouth, 61462, Warren County, (309)734-9968, 16 miles W of Galesburg.
Holes: 18. **Yards:** 6,362/5,885. **Par:** 71/75. **Course Rating:** 70.9/73.9. **Slope:** 119/119. **Green Fee:** $12/$15. **Cart Fee:** $20/cart. **Walking Policy:** Unrestricted walking. **Walkability:** 4.
Opened: 1966. **Architect:** Homer Fieldhouse. **Season:** March-Nov. **High:** June-Aug. **To obtain tee times:** First come, first served. **Miscellaneous:** Reduced fees (weekdays, low season, twilight), metal spikes, range (grass), club rentals.
Reader Comments: Hilly, trees ... Worthy challenge ... Fun ... Worth the drive ... Very tight; not too long ... Hit it straight.

★★★½ GLENCOE GOLF CLUB
PU-621 Westley Rd., Glencoe, 60022, Cook County, (847)835-0981.
Holes: 18. **Yards:** 6,517/5,713. **Par:** 72/73. **Course Rating:** 70.4/71.8. **Slope:** 121/117. **Green Fee:** $19/$37. **Cart Fee:** $28/cart. **Walking Policy:** Unrestricted walking. **Walkability:** 2.
Opened: 1921. **Season:** March-Nov. **High:** May-Sept. **To obtain tee times:** 7 days in person 6 days by phone w/credit card. **Miscellaneous:** Range (grass), club rentals, credit cards (MC, V, AE, D, Diners Club), beginner friendly (group lessons).
Reader Comments: Nice public course near Lake Michigan ... Windy ... Big trees ... Sporty ... Mature course.

ILLINOIS

★★★½ GLENDALE LAKES GOLF COURSE
PU-1550 President St., Glendale Heights, 60139, Du Page County, (630)260-0018, 30 miles E of Chicago.
Holes: 18. **Yards:** 6,143/5,390. **Par:** 71/71. **Course Rating:** 62.1/71.1. **Slope:** 121/124. **Green Fee:** $16/$30. **Cart Fee:** $14/person. **Walking Policy:** Walking at certain times. **Walkability:** 1. **Opened:** 1987. **Architect:** Dick Nugent. **Season:** March-Nov. **High:** June-Aug. **To obtain tee times:** Call 7 days in advance. **Miscellaneous:** Reduced fees (weekdays, low season, twilight, seniors, juniors), discount packages, metal spikes, club rentals, credit cards (MC, V, AE, D, Diners Club).
Reader Comments: If you like water, this is the place for you ... Some homes are too close ... Great course for a once-a-weeker.

GLENEAGLES GOLF CLUB
PU-13070 McNulty Rd., Lemont, 60439, Cook County, (630)257-5466, 25 miles SW of Chicago.
★★★ RED COURSE
Holes: 18. **Yards:** 6,090/6,090. **Par:** 70/74. **Course Rating:** 67.6/71.3. **Slope:** 112/111. **Green Fee:** $23/$30. **Cart Fee:** $13/person. **Walking Policy:** Unrestricted walking. **Walkability:** 3. **Opened:** 1924. **Architect:** Charles Maddox/Frank P. Macdonald. **Season:** March-Dec. **High:** June-Aug. **To obtain tee times:** Call golf shop. **Miscellaneous:** Reduced fees (low season, twilight, seniors), metal spikes, range (grass/mats), club rentals.
Reader Comments: Hilly and fun ... Some good risk/reward holes ... Greens still pretty good.
★★★½ WHITE COURSE
Holes: 18. **Yards:** 6,250/6,080. **Par:** 70/75. **Course Rating:** 70.1/72.3. **Slope:** 120/114. **Green Fee:** $23/$30. **Cart Fee:** $13/person. **Walking Policy:** Unrestricted walking. **Walkability:** 3. **Opened:** 1924. **Architect:** Charles Maddox/Frank P. Macdonald. **Season:** March-Dec. **High:** June-Aug. **To obtain tee times:** Call golf shop. **Miscellaneous:** Reduced fees (low season, twilight, seniors), metal spikes, range (grass/mats), club rentals.
Reader Comments: Not too long, not too hard ... Easy ... Usually crowded ... Some good risk/reward holes.

PU-★★½ GLENVIEW PARK GOLF CLUB
800 Shermer Rd., Glenview, 60025, Cook County, (847)724-0250.
Holes: 18. **Yards:** 6,057/5,734. **Par:** 70/70. **Course Rating:** 68.6/72.5. **Slope:** 121/122. **Green Fee:** $35/$38. **Miscellaneous:** Metal spikes.
Reader Comments: Very pretty ... Nice place.

★★★½ GLENWOODIE GOLF COURSE
PU-193rd and State, Glenwood, 60425, Cook County, (708)758-1212, 25 miles S of Downtown Chicago. **E-mail:** Glenwoodie@crown-golf.com.
Holes: 18. **Yards:** 6,715/5,176. **Par:** 72/72. **Course Rating:** 71.8/68.4. **Slope:** 120/108. **Green Fee:** $19/$33. **Cart Fee:** $12/person. **Walking Policy:** Unrestricted walking. **Walkability:** 2. **Opened:** 1923. **Architect:** Harry Collis. **Season:** Year-round. **High:** April-Sept. **To obtain tee times:** Call up to 7 days in advance. **Miscellaneous:** Reduced fees (weekdays, low season, twilight, seniors, juniors), range (grass), club rentals, credit cards (MC, V).
Reader Comments: Good, fair test of golf ... Very reasonable ... Enjoyable ... Challenging ... A sleeper ... Good opening holes and a great back nine.

★★★½ GOLF CLUB OF ILLINOIS
PU-1575 Edgewood Rd., Algonquin, 60102, McHenry County, (847)658-4400, 35 miles NW of Chicago.
Holes: 18. **Yards:** 7,011/4,896. **Par:** 71/71. **Course Rating:** 74.6/68.6. **Slope:** 133/115. **Green Fee:** $33/$43. **Cart Fee:** $13/person. **Walking Policy:** Walking at certain times. **Walkability:** N/A. **Opened:** 1987. **Architect:** Dick Nugent. **Season:** March-Nov. **High:** May-Sept. **To obtain tee times:** Call 7 days in advance with credit card. **Miscellaneous:** Reduced fees (weekdays, low season, twilight, seniors, juniors), discount packages, metal spikes, range (grass/mats), club rentals, credit cards (MC, V, AE, D).
Reader Comments: The links feel is gone now that they have surrounded the holes with homes ... Smooth fairways ... Wind always blows ... Neat course ... They brag about not one tree on the course ... Fun Scottish layout.

★★★ GOLFMOHR GOLF COURSE
PU-16724 Hubbard Rd., East Moline, 61244, Rock Island County, (309)496-2434. **E-mail:** birdie@revealed.net.
Holes: 18. **Yards:** 6,659/5,402. **Par:** 72/72. **Course Rating:** 71.2/70.0. **Slope:** N/A. **Green Fee:** $9/$17. **Cart Fee:** $18/cart. **Walking Policy:** Unrestricted walking. **Walkability:** 1. **Opened:** 1965. **Architect:** Ted Lockie. **Season:** March-Oct. **High:** June-Aug. **To obtain tee times:** Call up to 7 days in advance. **Miscellaneous:** Reduced fees (weekdays, twilight, seniors, juniors), metal spikes, range (mats), club rentals.
Reader Comments: Nice course ... Reasonably challenging ... Average course, price is right.

★★½ GRAND MARAIS GOLF COURSE

PU-5802 Lake Dr., East St. Louis, 62205, St. Clair County, (618)398-9999, (888)398-9002, 7 miles E of St. Louis, MO.

Holes: 18. **Yards:** 6,600/5,324. **Par:** 72/72. **Course Rating:** 71.7/68.1. **Slope:** 126/120. **Green Fee:** $16/$20. **Cart Fee:** $20/cart. **Walking Policy:** Unrestricted walking. **Walkability:** 1. **Opened:** 1936. **Architect:** Joseph A. Roseman. **Season:** Year-round. **High:** May-Oct. **To obtain tee times:** Call 7 days in advance. **Miscellaneous:** Reduced fees (weekdays, low season, seniors, juniors), metal spikes, range (grass/mats), caddies, club rentals, credit cards (MC, V).

Reader Comments: A really old course making a comeback ... They're trying hard.

★★ GREEN ACRES GOLF COURSE

SP-Route 148 S., Herrin, 62933, Williamson County, (618)942-6816.

Holes: 18. **Yards:** 5,899/4,372. **Par:** 72/72. **Course Rating:** 67.0/66.0. **Slope:** 107/105. **Green Fee:** $14/$16. **Walkability:** N/A. **Miscellaneous:** Metal spikes.

GREEN GARDEN COUNTRY CLUB

PU-9511 W. Monee Manhattan Rd., Frankfort, 60423, Will County, (815)469-3350, 30 miles S of Chicago. **Web:** www.greengardencc.com.

★★★ BLUE COURSE

Holes: 18. **Yards:** 6,665/5,652. **Par:** 72/73. **Course Rating:** 70.1/69.5. **Slope:** 112/110. **Green Fee:** $14/$34. **Cart Fee:** $12/person. **Walking Policy:** Walking at certain times. **Walkability:** 1. **Opened:** 1972. **Architect:** Tom Walsh. **Season:** Year-round. **High:** May-Sept. **To obtain tee times:** Call up to 7 days in advance. **Miscellaneous:** Reduced fees (weekdays, low season, twilight, seniors, juniors), metal spikes, range (grass/mats), rentals, credit cards (MC, V, AE, D).

Reader Comments: Recently redone. Fun ... New holes are well done ... Nice course with some hard holes.

★★★½ GOLD COURSE

Holes: 18. **Yards:** 6,519/5,442. **Par:** 72/72. **Course Rating:** 70.2/70.2. **Slope:** 115/116. **Green Fee:** $14/$34. **Cart Fee:** $12/person. **Walking Policy:** Walking at certain times. **Walkability:** 1. **Opened:** 1992. **Architect:** Buzz Didier. **Season:** Year-round. **High:** May-Sept. **To obtain tee times:** Call up to 7 days in advance. **Miscellaneous:** Reduced fees (weekdays, low season, twilight, seniors, juniors), metal spikes, range (grass/mats), rentals, credit cards (MC, V, AE, D).

Reader Comments: Always seem to play my best here ... Open semi-links ... If you like wind, this is the course for you ... Food in restaurant was very good.

★★★ GREENVIEW COUNTRY CLUB

PU-2801 Putter Lane, Centralia, 62801, Marion County, (618)532-7395.

Holes: 18. **Yards:** 6,600/5,343. **Par:** 72/72. **Course Rating:** 67.0/N/A. **Slope:** 120/N/A. **Green Fee:** $22/$22. **Walkability:** N/A. **Miscellaneous:** Metal spikes.

Reader Comments: A lot better since Tom Wargo took over ... Wargo and his staff are working hard ... Real nice and fun ... Good, but could be a lot better.Real nice and fun ... Worth the drive.

HARBORSIDE INTERNATIONAL GOLF CENTER

PU-11001 S. Doty Ave. E., Chicago, 60628, Cook County, (312)782-7837, 12 miles S of Chicago.

★★★★ PORT COURSE *Condition*

Holes: 18. **Yards:** 7,164/5,164. **Par:** 72/72. **Course Rating:** 75.1/70.8. **Slope:** 136/122. **Green Fee:** $65/$75. **Cart Fee:** Included in Green Fee. **Walking Policy:** Unrestricted walking. **Walkability:** 3. **Opened:** 1995. **Architect:** Tim Nugent. **Season:** April-Nov. **High:** May-Aug. **To obtain tee times:** Foursomes call up to 14 days in advance. Groups of less than four players call up to 2 days in advance. **Miscellaneous:** Reduced fees (twilight), metal spikes, range (grass/mats), club rentals, credit cards (MC, V, AE).

Reader Comments: Great location for city dwellers ... Unique, with industrial views ... Once a landfill; it's perfect now ... From garbage dump to gold mine ... Tough course ... Can't go wrong on either course ... Challenging venue in the wind ... Nice cityscape from the course ... Very well-bunkered ... Don't miss this one ... Every garbage dump should be put to use this way.

★★★★ STARBOARD COURSE

Holes: 18. **Yards:** 7,152/5,106. **Par:** 72/72. **Course Rating:** 75.2/70.4. **Slope:** 137/122. **Green Fee:** $65/$75. **Cart Fee:** Included in Green Fee. **Walking Policy:** Unrestricted walking. **Walkability:** 3. **Opened:** 1995. **Architect:** Dick Nugent/Tim Nugent. **Season:** April-Nov. **High:** May-Aug. **To obtain tee times:** Foursomes call up to 14 days in advance. Groups of less call up to 2 days in advance. **Miscellaneous:** Reduced fees (twilight), metal spikes, range (grass/mats), club rentals, credit cards (MC, V, AE).

Reader Comments: Great concept; great job ... Wonderful ... Too windy ... Good use of land ... Wonderful waterside course that reclaims industrial land ... Beautiful job ... No trees and so hard; it's like the British Open.

Notes: 1997 Golf Digest's Environmental Leaders in Golf Award.

ILLINOIS

★★½ HARRISON PARK GOLF COURSE
PU-W. Voorhees, Danville, 61832, Vermillion County, (217)431-2266.
Holes: 18.**Yards:** 6,330/5,015. **Par:** 71/71. **Course Rating:** 70.3/68.5. **Slope:** 119/110. **Green Fee:** $12/;$14. **Miscellaneous:** Metal spikes.
Reader Comments: A public course that has lots of play and limited budget.

★★★★ HAWTHORN RIDGE GOLF CLUB
PU-621 State Hwy. 94, Aledo, 61231, Mercer County, (309)582-5456. **E-mail:** birdie@revealed.net.
Holes: 18. **Yards:** 6,701/5,674. **Par:** 72/72. **Course Rating:** 71.4/71.6. **Slope:** N/A. **Green Fee:** $9/$18. **Cart Fee:** $19/cart. **Walking Policy:** Unrestricted walking. **Walkability:** 3. **Opened:** 1977. **Architect:** William James Spear. **Season:** March-Oct. **High:** June-Aug. **To obtain tee times:** Call up to 7 days in advance. **Miscellaneous:** Reduced fees (weekdays, twilight, seniors, juniors), metal spikes, range (grass), rentals.
Reader Comments: A must-play ... Lots of sand and water, but fair to play ... Great course for the price ... Really nice ... Best time is after 2 p.m. ... Worth the drive ... Very challenging.

★★★★ HAWTHORN SUITES AT MIDLANE GOLF RESORT
PU-4555 W. Yorkhouse Rd., Wadsworth, 60083, Lake County, (847)623-4653, 50 miles N of Chicago.
Holes: 27. **Yards:** 7,073/5,635. **Par:** 72/73. **Course Rating:** 74.4/72.7. **Slope:** 132/124. **Green Fee:** $37/$65. **Cart Fee:** Included in Green Fee. **Walking Policy:** Walking at certain times. **Walkability:** 3. **Opened:** 1964. **Architect:** Robert Bruce Harris. **Season:** March-Nov. **High:** May-Oct. **To obtain tee times:** Call 7 days in advance. **Miscellaneous:** Reduced fees (weekdays, low season, twilight, seniors), metal spikes, range (grass), club rentals, credit cards (MC, V, AE, D).
Reader Comments: Fair test; good practice facility ... Low-handicappers can enjoy ... Played it once and was impressed ... Getting better ... Nice food and drink in the clubhouse ... Stay below the hole ... Honest layout with huge greens.

★★★★½ HERITAGE BLUFFS GOLF CLUB *Value*
PU-24355 W. Bluff Rd., Channahon, 60410, Will County, (815)467-7888, 45 miles S of Chicago.
Holes: 18. **Yards:** 7,106/4,967. **Par:** 72/72. **Course Rating:** 73.9/68.6. **Slope:** 138/114. **Green Fee:** $30/$40. **Cart Fee:** $13/person. **Walking Policy:** Unrestricted walking. **Walkability:** 4. **Opened:** 1993. **Architect:** Dick Nugent. **Season:** April-Oct. **High:** May-Sept. **To obtain tee times:** Call 7 days in advance with credit card. **Miscellaneous:** Reduced fees (weekdays, twilight, seniors, juniors), range (grass/mats), club rentals, credit cards (MC, V, D).
Reader Comments: Pretty course; very playable ... Another great course from farmland ... Price is reasonable ... Just a lot of fun and a test of golf ... Worth the 45-minute drive from Chicago ... Great mix of holes ... Good condition ... Rolling hills ... Please don't tell anybody about this place ... Bambi followed me for two holes ... Some great scenery.

★★½ HICKORY HILLS COUNTRY CLUB
PU-8201 West 95th St., Hickory Hills, 60457, Cook County, (708)598-6460, 20 miles SW of Chicago.
Holes: 27. **Yards:** 6,018/5,928. **Par:** 71/71. **Course Rating:** 67.9/67.9. **Slope:** 116/116. **Green Fee:** $25/$30. **Cart Fee:** $13/person. **Walking Policy:** Walking at certain times. **Walkability:** 4. **Opened:** 1930. **Season:** Year-round. **High:** May-Sept. **To obtain tee times:** Call up to 7 days in advance. **Miscellaneous:** Reduced fees (weekdays, low season, twilight, seniors), metal spikes, range (mats), club rentals, credit cards (MC, V, AE), beginner friendly.
Reader Comments: Slow play ... Hills, hills and more hills, but fair ... Conditions could be better.

★★★½ HICKORY POINT GOLF CLUB
PM-727 Weaver Road, Forsyth, 62535, Macon County, (217)421-7444,.
Holes: 18. **Yards:** 6,855/5,896. **Par:** 72/73. **Course Rating:** 71.4/N/A. **Slope:** 121/N/A. **Green Fee:** $13/$18. **Walking Policy:** Unrestricted walking. **Walkability:** 1. **Opened:** 1970. **Architect:** Edward L. Packard. **Season:** March-Nov. **High:** June-Aug. **To obtain tee times:** Weekdays, call up to 7 days in advance. Weekend and holidays call the Monday prior to starting at 6:30 a.m. **Miscellaneous:** Reduced fees (twilight, seniors, juniors), metal spikes, range (grass), club rentals, credit cards (MC, V).
Reader Comments: Very nice ... Play needs to be faster ... Challenging ... Great greens ... Very nice municipal course.

★★★★ HICKORY RIDGE GOLF CENTER
PU-2727 West Glenn Rd., Carbondale, 62902, Jackson County, (618)529-4386, 100 miles SE of St. Louis.
Holes: 18. **Yards:** 6,863/5,506. **Par:** 72/72. **Course Rating:** 73.3/71.6. **Slope:** 137/134. **Green Fee:** $15/$18. **Cart Fee:** $9/person. **Walking Policy:** Unrestricted walking. **Walkability:** 4. **Opened:** 1993. **Architect:** William James Spear. **Season:** Year-round. **High:** April-Sept. **To**

obtain tee times: Call 7 days in advance. **Miscellaneous:** Reduced fees (twilight, seniors, juniors), discount packages, range (grass), club rentals, credit cards (MC, V).
Reader Comments: Relatively new course; can only get better ... Tough back nine ... Fabulous layout ... No two holes alike ... Good value.

★★★ HIGHLAND PARK COUNTRY CLUB

PU-1201 Park Ave. West, Highland Park, 60035, Lake County, (847)433-9015, 20 miles N of Chicago.
Holes: 18. **Yards:** 6,522/5,353. **Par:** 70/70. **Course Rating:** 72.1/71.8. **Slope:** 130/122. **Green Fee:** $38/$48. **Cart Fee:** $15. **Walking Policy:** Walking at certain times. **Walkability:** 1. **Opened:** 1966. **Architect:** Ted Lockie. **Season:** April-Nov. **High:** May-Sept. **To obtain tee times:** Call 14 days in advance. **Miscellaneous:** Reduced fees (weekdays, low season, twilight), range (grass), club rentals, credit cards (MC, V).
Reader Comments: Former private club getting too much play ... Fairways too close together ... Not bad ... Great weekday early-bird specials.

★★★ HIGHLAND PARK GOLF COURSE

PU-1613 S. Main, Bloomington, 61701, McLean County, (309)434-2200, 120 miles SW of Chicago.
Holes: 18. **Yards:** 5,725/5,530. **Par:** 70/70. **Course Rating:** 66.9/70.8. **Slope:** 111/115. **Green Fee:** N/A/$14. **Cart Fee:** $16/cart. **Walking Policy:** Unrestricted walking. **Walkability:** 3. **Opened:** 1923. **Season:** Year-round. **High:** April-Oct. **To obtain tee times:** Call golf shop. **Miscellaneous:** Reduced fees (twilight), club rentals, credit cards (MC, V).
Reader Comments: General public course ... Short ... A lot of old trees ... Nice little course ... Average ... Wear a helmet.

★★★ HIGHLAND SPRINGS GOLF CLUB

PM-9500 35th. St. W., Rock Island, 61201, Rock Island County, (309)732-7265, 5 miles S of Davenport. **E-mail:** wcdapro@pga.com.
Holes: 18. **Yards:** 6,800/5,875. **Par:** 72/72. **Course Rating:** 73.1/69.0. **Slope:** 125/122. **Green Fee:** $15/$17. **Cart Fee:** $20/cart. **Walking Policy:** Unrestricted walking. **Walkability:** 3. **Opened:** 1968. **Architect:** William James Spear. **Season:** April-Nov. **High:** May-Aug. **To obtain tee times:** 7 days in advance. **Miscellaneous:** Reduced fees (twilight, seniors, juniors), discount packages, metal spikes, range (grass), club rentals, credit cards (MC, V).
Reader Comments: Good place to build confidence ... Playable ... Too many goose droppings ... Pace a little slow ... Cheap.

★★½ HIGHLAND WOODS GOLF COURSE

PU-2775 N. Ela Rd., Hoffman Estates, 60172, Cook County, (847)358-3727, 20 miles W of Chicago.
Holes: 18. **Yards:** 6,846/5,831. **Par:** 72/72. **Course Rating:** 72.1/72.6. **Slope:** 120/121. **Green Fee:** $21/$25. **Cart Fee:** $20/cart. **Walking Policy:** Unrestricted walking. **Walkability:** N/A. **Opened:** 1975. **Architect:** William James Spear. **Season:** March-Dec. **High:** May-Sept. **To obtain tee times:** Automated call in system. **Miscellaneous:** Reduced fees (weekdays, twilight), metal spikes, credit cards (MC, V).
Reader Comments: With a little work, could be great ... Great value with an activity card ... Cheap.

★★★ HILLDALE GOLF CLUB

PU-1625 Ardwick Dr., Hoffman Estates, 60195, Cook County, (847)310-1100, 40 miles NW of Chicago. **Web:** www.hilldalegolf.com.
Holes: 18. **Yards:** 6,432/5,409. **Par:** 71/72. **Course Rating:** 71.3/72.1. **Slope:** 130/125. **Green Fee:** $40/$39. **Cart Fee:** $13/person. **Walking Policy:** Walking at certain times. **Walkability:** 3. **Opened:** 1971. **Architect:** Robert Trent Jones Sr. **Season:** April-Nov. **High:** June-Aug. **To obtain tee times:** Call up to 7 days in advance. **Miscellaneous:** Reduced fees (weekdays, low season, twilight), discount packages, range (grass), club rentals, credit cards (MC, V, AE, D).
Reader Comments: Overall good experience ... Nice setting and design on back nine ... Some unique holes ... Too many homes ... Improved ... Played well the day after a big rain.

★★★ HOWARD D. KELLOGG GOLF COURSE

7716 North Radnor Rd., Peoria, 61614, Peoria County, (309)691-0293.
Yards: 6,735/5,675. **Par:** 72/72. **Course Rating:** 70.9/71.5. **Slope:** 117/120. **Green Fee:** $10/$14. **Cart Fee:** $15/cart. **Walking Policy:** Unrestricted walking. **Walkability:** 2. **Season:** March-Nov. **To obtain tee times:** Come in up to 7 days in advance. **Miscellaneous:** Reduced fees (twilight, juniors), metal spikes, credit cards (MC, V).
Reader Comments: Average ... Nice greens ... Well-kept.

HUBBARD TRAIL GOLF & COUNTRY CLUB

SP-13937 N. 3680 E. Road, Hoopeston, 60942, Vermillion County, (217)748-6521, 20 miles N of Danville. **E-mail:** grfix@ktb.net.

Holes: 9. **Yards:** 6,107/5,248. **Par:** 72/72. **Course Rating:** 66.6/70.8. **Slope:** 104/112. **Green Fee:** $18/$20. **Cart Fee:** $10/person. **Walking Policy:** Unrestricted walking. **Walkability:** 1. **Season:** Feb.-Dec. **High:** May-Aug. **To obtain tee times:** No tee times required. **Miscellaneous:** Reduced fees (weekdays), club rentals, credit cards (MC, V).

★★★ HUGHES CREEK GOLF CLUB
PU-1749 Spring Valley Dr., Elburn, 60119, Kane County, (630)365-9200, 30 miles SW of Chicago.
Holes: 18. **Yards:** 6,506/5,561. **Par:** 72/72. **Course Rating:** 70.9/71.7. **Slope:** 117/115. **Green Fee:** $14/$22. **Cart Fee:** $12. **Walking Policy:** Unrestricted walking. **Walkability:** N/A. **Opened:** 1993. **Architect:** Gordon Cunningham. **Season:** April-Nov. **High:** June-Aug. **To obtain tee times:** Call 2 days in advance. **Miscellaneous:** Reduced fees (weekdays, low season, twilight, seniors, juniors), metal spikes, club rentals, credit cards (MC, V).
Reader Comments: Condition could be better ... Design beats the condition ... Beautiful site.

★★ HUNTER COUNTRY CLUB
5419 Kenosha St., Richmond, 60071, McHenry County, (815)678-2631.
Special Notes: Call club for further information.

★★★ ILLINOIS STATE UNIVERSITY GOLF COURSE
PU-W. Gregory St., Normal, 61790, McLean County, (309)438-8065, 100 miles SW of Chicago.
E-mail: ljprovo@ilstu.edu. **Web:** www.rec.ilstu.edu.
Holes: 18. **Yards:** 6,533/5,581. **Par:** 71/73. **Course Rating:** 71.1/71.8. **Slope:** 120/119. **Green Fee:** N/A/$15. **Cart Fee:** $17/cart. **Walking Policy:** Unrestricted walking. **Walkability:** 2. **Opened:** 1964. **Architect:** Robert Bruce Harris. **Season:** March-Dec. **High:** May-Aug. **To obtain tee times:** By phone or in person 7 days per week, 7 days in advance. **Miscellaneous:** Reduced fees (twilight, seniors, juniors), club rentals, credit cards (MC, V, D).
Reader Comments: Good layout; they try ... Slicers need not apply ... Great value ... Interesting old-style course ... Fun to play ... Course will be closed next season and redone.

★★★ INDIAN BLUFF GOLF COURSE
PU-6200 78th Ave., Milan, 61264, Rock Island County, (309)799-3868, 185 miles W of Chicago.
Holes: 18. **Yards:** 5,516/4,510. **Par:** 70/71. **Course Rating:** 66.7/67.1. **Slope:** 111/108. **Green Fee:** $13/$14. **Cart Fee:** $10/person. **Walking Policy:** Unrestricted walking. **Walkability:** 4. **Season:** April-Nov. **High:** May-Aug. **To obtain tee times:** Call golf shop. **Miscellaneous:** Reduced fees (twilight, seniors, juniors), metal spikes, club rentals, credit cards (MC, V, D).
Reader Comments: Has a lot of valleys ... Short ... Facilities were OK ... Holes and fairways are too close together.

★½ INDIAN BOUNDARY GOLF COURSE
PM-8600 W. Forest Preserve Dr, Chicago, 60634, Cook County, (773)625-2013.
Holes: 18. **Yards:** 5,838/5,621. **Par:** 70/70. **Course Rating:** 66.3/70.2. **Slope:** 98/107. **Green Fee:** N/A/$19. **Cart Fee:** $20/cart. **Walking Policy:** Unrestricted walking. **Walkability:** 1. **Season:** Year-round. **High:** April-Aug. **To obtain tee times:** Call automated tee times phone (708)366-9466 up to 7 days in advance. **Miscellaneous:** Reduced fees (weekdays, twilight, seniors, juniors), metal spikes, credit cards (MC, V).

★★½ INDIAN HILLS GOLF COURSE
20 Indian Trail Dr., Mt. Vernon, 62864, Jefferson County, (618)244-9697.
Special Notes: Call club for further information.
Reader Comments: Good beginners' course ... Reasonable rates ... No frills ... Love it.

INDIAN LAKES RESORT
R-250 W. Schick Rd., Bloomingdale, 60108, Du Page County, (630)529-0200, (800)334-3417, 30 miles W of Chicago. **Web:** www.indianlakesresort.com.
★★★ EAST COURSE
Holes: 18. **Yards:** 6,890/5,031. **Par:** 72/72. **Course Rating:** 72.4/67.7. **Slope:** 120/106. **Green Fee:** $42/$60. **Cart Fee:** Included in Green Fee. **Walking Policy:** Mandatory cart. **Walkability:** 3. **Opened:** 1965. **Architect:** Robert Bruce Harris. **Season:** March-Dec. **High:** May-Sept. **To obtain tee times:** Call up to 7 days in advance for reservations. Mandatory soft spikes & collared shirts. **Miscellaneous:** Reduced fees (weekdays, low season, twilight), range (mats), club rentals, lodging, credit cards (MC, V, AE, D, Diners Club).
Reader Comments: Pricey, but good resort course ... Visit to the 19th hole was nice ... Need more water fountains.
Special Notes: Formerly Indian Lakes Country Club Iroquois Course.
★★½ WEST COURSE
Holes: 18. **Yards:** 6,901/5,088. **Par:** 72/72. **Course Rating:** 72.1/67.7. **Slope:** 123/106. **Green Fee:** $42/$60. **Cart Fee:** Included in Green Fee. **Walking Policy:** Mandatory cart. **Walkability:** 3. **Opened:** 1965. **Architect:** Robert Bruce Harris. **Season:** March-Dec. **High:** May-Sept. **To obtain tee times:** Call up to 7 days in advance. Mandatory soft spikes & collared shirts.

Miscellaneous: Reduced fees (weekdays, low season, resort guests, twilight), range (mats), club rentals, lodging, credit cards (MC, V, AE, D, Diners Club).
Reader Comments: Much-improved bunkers ... Good resort course ... Pricey.
Special Notes: Formerly Indian Lakes Country Club Sioux Course.

★½ INDIAN VALLEY COUNTRY CLUB
RT 83 & 45, Mundelein, 60060, Lake County, (847)566-1313.
Special Notes: Call club for further information.

★★★ INGERSOLL MEMORIAL GOLF CLUB
PU-101 Daisyfield Rd., Rockford, 61102, Winnebago County, (815)987-8887, 70 miles W of Chicago.
Holes: 18. **Yards:** 6,107/5,820. **Par:** 71/75. **Course Rating:** 68.9/72.6. **Slope:** 111/116. **Green Fee:** $16/$21. **Cart Fee:** $22/cart. **Walking Policy:** Unrestricted walking. **Walkability:** 2.
Opened: 1922. **Architect:** Thomas M. Bendelow. **Season:** April-Oct. **To obtain tee times:** Call 7 days in advance for weekend and Holidays. **Miscellaneous:** Reduced fees (low season, twilight), range (mats), club rentals, credit cards (MC, V, D).
Reader Comments: Treelined fairways require straight hitting ... Short, but challenging ... Small greens ... Tall trees.

★★½ INWOOD GOLF COURSE
PM-3000 W. Jefferson, Joliet, 60435, Will County, (815)741-7265, 40 miles SW of Chicago.
Holes: 18. **Yards:** 6,078/5,559. **Par:** 71/71. **Course Rating:** 69.4/71.4. **Slope:** 117/121. **Green Fee:** $12/$24. **Cart Fee:** $18/. **Walking Policy:** Unrestricted walking. **Walkability:** N/A. **Opened:** 1931. **Architect:** Edward Lawrence Packard. **Season:** April-Oct. **High:** June-Aug. **To obtain tee times:** Call 24 hours in advance for weekday and Monday for upcoming weekend.
Miscellaneous: Reduced fees (weekdays, twilight, seniors, juniors), discount packages, metal spikes, range (grass), club rentals, credit cards (MC, V, D).
Reader Comments: Like the back 9 better ... Typical muny ... You get what you pay for.

★★★★ IRONHORSE GOLF COURSE
PU-2000 N. Prairie, Tuscola, 61953, (217)253-6644.
Holes: 18. **Yards:** 7,046/6,093. **Par:** 72/72. **Course Rating:** 72.7/74.1. **Slope:** 120/118. **Green Fee:** $35/$40. **Cart Fee:** $10/person. **Walking Policy:** Walking at certain times. **Walkability:** 4.
Opened: 1997. **Architect:** Paul Loague. **Season:** March-Dec. **High:** June-Aug. **To obtain tee times:** Call 1 week in advance. **Miscellaneous:** Reduced fees (twilight, seniors), discount packages, range (grass/mats), club rentals, credit cards (MC, V, AE).
Reader Comments: Great course ... Challenging ... Lots of water; no trees ... Front nine is flat and open; back nine is picturesque ... Too far from greens to tees ... Wind can make a difference.

★★★½ IRONWOOD GOLF COURSE
PU-1901 N. Towanda Ave., Normal, 61761, McLean County, (309)454-9620, 100 miles S of Chicago.
Holes: 18. **Yards:** 6,960/5,385. **Par:** 72/72. **Course Rating:** 72.4/69.8. **Slope:** 126/113. **Green Fee:** $11/$18. **Cart Fee:** $10/person. **Walking Policy:** Unrestricted walking. **Walkability:** 2.
Opened: 1990. **Architect:** Roger Packard. **Season:** March-Nov. **High:** May-July. **To obtain tee times:** Call 7 days in advance. **Miscellaneous:** Reduced fees (weekdays, twilight, seniors, juniors), discount packages, metal spikes, range (grass/mats), club rentals, credit cards (MC, V).
Reader Comments: Long, wide-open course needs to mature ... Flat and very windy ... Fun to play ... Big greens ... Will be great in 20 years.

★★ JACKSON PARK GOLF CLUB
6400 S. Richards Dr., Chicago, 60637, Cook County, (312)747-2763.
Holes: 18. **Yards:** 5,538/5,307. **Par:** 70/72. **Course Rating:** N/A. **Slope:** N/A. **Green Fee:** $15/$16. **Walkability:** N/A. **Miscellaneous:** Metal spikes.

JOE LOUIS THE CHAMP GOLF CLUB
131st & Halsted, Riverdale, 60627, Cook County, (708)841-6340.
Special Notes: Call club for further information.

★★★½ KANKAKEE ELKS COUNTRY CLUB
2283 Bittersweet Dr., St. Anne, 60964, Kankakee County, (815)937-9547.
Special Notes: Call club for further information.
Reader Comments: Favorite course ... Old, wooded ... My home course; we need to work on a few areas.

★★★½ KELLOGG GOLF COURSE
PU-7716 N. Radnor Rd., Peoria, 61615, Peoria County, (309)691-0293.
Holes: 18. **Yards:** 6,735/5,675. **Par:** 72/72. **Course Rating:** 70.9/71.5. **Slope:** 117/120. **Green Fee:** $12/$16. **Cart Fee:** $16/cart. **Walking Policy:** Unrestricted walking. **Walkability:** 2.
Opened: 1974. **Architect:** Larry Packard/Roger Packard. **Season:** March-Nov. **High:** June-Aug.

To obtain tee times: 7 days in advance in person. Phone reservations taken only on day of play.
Miscellaneous: Reduced fees (weekdays, twilight, juniors), range (grass/mats), club rentals, credit cards (MC, V, D).

Reader Comments: Always crowded ... Wide open and windy ... Some challenging holes ... Good test.
Special Notes: A 9-hole Executive Course also available.

★★★★ KEMPER LAKES GOLF COURSE *Condition*
PU-Old McHenry Rd., Long Grove, 60049, Lake County, (847)320-3450, 25 miles NW of Chicago.
Holes: 18. **Yards:** 7,217/5,638. **Par:** 72/72. **Course Rating:** 75.7/67.9. **Slope:** 140/125. **Green Fee:** N/A/$125. **Cart Fee:** Included in Green Fee. **Walking Policy:** Unrestricted walking.
Walkability: 2. **Opened:** 1979. **Architect:** Nugent/Killian. **Season:** April-Nov. **High:** June-Aug. **To obtain tee times:** Call 14 days in advance. **Miscellaneous:** Metal spikes, range (grass), club rentals, credit cards (MC, V, AE).
Notes: Ranked 12th in 1999 Best in State. 1989 PGA Championship. 1997-1999 Ameritech Senior Open.

Reader Comments: Great course ... Good course; costs too much ... Well worth playing ... Difficult track ... Classy course with classy green fees ... Beautiful ... Bring extra balls ... Scared of all that water ... My favorite golf outing each year ... Fun; surprisingly forgiving ... Liked the carts with yardages ... Big, classic golf course.

★★★½ KLEIN CREEK GOLF CLUB
PU-1 N. 333 Pleasant Hill Rd., Winfield, 60190, Du Page County, (630)690-0101, 2 miles W of Wheaton.
Holes: 18. **Yards:** 6,701/4,509. **Par:** 72/72. **Course Rating:** 71.9/66.2. **Slope:** 127/110. **Green Fee:** $50/$75. **Cart Fee:** Included in Green Fee. **Walking Policy:** Unrestricted walking.
Walkability: 2. **Opened:** 1994. **Architect:** Dick Nugent. **Season:** April-Nov. **High:** June-Sept. **To obtain tee times:** Call up to 14 days in advance with credit card. **Miscellaneous:** Reduced fees (weekdays, low season, twilight), club rentals, credit cards (MC, V, AE, Diners Club).

Reader Comments: Golf surrounded by developments ... Could you get the homes any closer? ... Narrow fairways ... Too much water ... Great links, target-style play from correct tees ... Very firm greens; bring your balata ... Gladly play this one anytime ... Should be better as it matures ... No practice facility is only minus.

KOKOPELLI GOLF CLUB
SP-1401 Champions Dr., Marion, 62959, Williamson County, (618)997-5656, 100 miles SE of St. Louis.
Holes: 18. **Yards:** 7,150/5,375. **Par:** 72/72. **Course Rating:** 75.2/N/A. **Slope:** 139/N/A. **Green Fee:** $26/$30. **Cart Fee:** $10/person. **Walking Policy:** Walking at certain times. **Walkability:** 3.
Opened: 1997. **Architect:** Steve Smyers. **Season:** Year-round. **High:** April-Nov. **To obtain tee times:** Call up to 5 days in advance. **Miscellaneous:** Range (grass), credit cards (MC, V, D).

LACOMA GOLF COURSE
PU-8080 Timmerman Rd., East Dubuque, 61025, Jo Daviess County, (815)747-3874, 1 miles E of Dubuque.
★★★ BLUE COURSE
Holes: 18. **Yards:** 6,705/5,784. **Par:** 71/71. **Course Rating:** 71.8/70.0. **Slope:** 123/117. **Green Fee:** $12/$16. **Cart Fee:** $20/cart. **Walking Policy:** Unrestricted walking. **Walkability:** 4.
Opened: 1967. **Architect:** Gordon Cunningham. **Season:** March-First snow. **High:** May-Sept. **To obtain tee times:** Call 7 days in advance. **Miscellaneous:** Reduced fees (twilight), range (grass/mats), club rentals, credit cards (MC, V, D).

Reader Comments: Very tight back nine ... Outstanding new holes ... Lots of trees ... New routing is a good addition.
★★½ RED/GOLD COURSE
Holes: 18. **Yards:** 5,552/4,895. **Par:** 69/69. **Course Rating:** 63.5/63.8. **Slope:** 105/102. **Green Fee:** $12/$15. **Cart Fee:** $20/cart. **Walking Policy:** Unrestricted walking. **Walkability:** 2.
Opened: 1967. **Architect:** Gordon Cunningham. **Season:** March-First snow. **High:** May-Sept. **To obtain tee times:** Call 7 days in advance. **Miscellaneous:** Reduced fees (twilight), metal spikes, range (grass), club rentals, credit cards (MC, V, D).
Reader Comments: Don't go the extra mile.
Special Notes: Also 9-hole, par-3 course.

★★★½ LAKE BLUFF GOLF CLUB
PU-Green Bay Rd. & Washington St., Lake Bluff, 60044, Lake County, (847)234-6771, 10 miles of Waukegan.
Holes: 18. **Yards:** 6,537/5,450. **Par:** 72/72. **Course Rating:** N/A. **Slope:** 120/118. **Green Fee:** $17/$35. **Cart Fee:** $26/cart. **Walking Policy:** Unrestricted walking. **Walkability:** 2. **Opened:** 1969. **Season:** April-Nov. **High:** May-Sept. **To obtain tee times:** Call up to 7 days in advance or

come in up to 6 days in advance. **Miscellaneous:** Reduced fees (weekdays, low season, twilight, seniors, juniors), club rentals, credit cards (MC, V).

Reader Comments: A little jewel ... Good course for any level ... Straight and flat ... Improved drainage ... Very windy ... Fun ... Very crowded ... Short and easy.

★★★½ LAKE OF THE WOODS GOLF CLUB

PU-405 N. Lake of the Woods Rd., Mahomet, 61853, Champaign County, (217)586-2183, 8 miles W of Champaign. **Web:** www.mah-online.com/lowgc/.
Holes: 18. **Yards:** 6,520/5,187. **Par:** 72/72. **Course Rating:** 70.6/68.9. **Slope:** 120/115. **Green Fee:** $15/$18. **Cart Fee:** $9/person. **Walking Policy:** Unrestricted walking. **Walkability:** 2.
Opened: 1954. **Architect:** Robert Bruce Harris. **Season:** March-Dec. **High:** June-Aug. **To obtain tee times:** Call 7 days in advance. **Miscellaneous:** Reduced fees (twilight, seniors, juniors), metal spikes, range (grass/mats), club rentals, credit cards (MC, V), beginner friendly (par-3 course).
Reader Comments: Beautiful, scenic ... Good value ... Fun par 5s; must carry water if you go for it ... Lots of improvements ... I forgot how good this course was ... Good challenge from the tips ... Nice, wooded course ... Pleasant setting ... Lots of trees.

★★★½ LAKE SHORE GOLF COURSE

PM-1460 E 1000 North Road, Taylorville, 62568, Christian County, (217)824-5521, 26 miles E of Springfield.
Holes: 18. **Yards:** 6,778/5,581. **Par:** 72/74. **Course Rating:** 72.0/74.0. **Slope:** 117/114. **Green Fee:** N/A/$20. **Cart Fee:** $20/cart. **Walking Policy:** Unrestricted walking. **Walkability:** 4.
Opened: 1969. **Architect:** William James Spear. **Season:** March-Dec. **High:** May-Aug. **To obtain tee times:** Call up to 7 days in advance for weekdays. Call on Monday for upcoming weekend. **Miscellaneous:** Reduced fees (low season, twilight, seniors, juniors), range (grass), club rentals, credit cards (MC, V, D).
Reader Comments: Windy and challenging ... Beautiful views ... Nice place, nice people ... Fun and challenging ... Sporty.

★½ LAKE VIEW COUNTRY CLUB

23319 Hazel Rd., Sterling, 61081, Whiteside County, (815)626-2886.
Special Notes: Call club for further information.

★★½ LAUREL GREENS PUBLIC GOLFERS CLUB

PU-1133 Hwy. 150 E, Knoxville, 61448, Knox County, (309)289-4146, 3 miles E of Peoria - Moline IL.
Holes: 27. **Yards:** 6,703/5,089. **Par:** 72/72. **Course Rating:** N/A. **Slope:** N/A. **Green Fee:** $10/$11. **Cart Fee:** $8/person. **Walking Policy:** Unrestricted walking. **Walkability:** 3. **Opened:** 1971. **Season:** April-Dec. **High:** June-Aug. **To obtain tee times:** Call up to 7 days in advance. **Miscellaneous:** Metal spikes.
Reader Comments: Getting better ... A bit rough in parts ... Lots of character.

LAWRENCE COUNTY COUNTRY CLUB

SP-US #50, Lawrenceville, 62439, Lawrence County, (618)943-2011, 150 miles E of St. Louis.
Holes: 9. **Yards:** 6,252/5,388. **Par:** 72/N/A. **Course Rating:** 68.9/N/A. **Slope:** 113/N/A. **Green Fee:** N/A/$15. **Cart Fee:** $18/cart. **Walking Policy:** Unrestricted walking. **Walkability:** 3.
Opened: 1915. **Architect:** Tom Bendelow. **Season:** March-Nov. **High:** May-Sept. **To obtain tee times:** Call 1 day in advance for weekdays. Members only play weekends. **Miscellaneous:** Metal spikes.

★★★½ THE LEDGES GOLF CLUB

PU-7111 McCurry Rd., Roscoe, 61073, Winnebago County, (815)389-0979, 10 miles N of Rockford. **Web:** www.wcfpd.org.
Holes: 18. **Yards:** 6,417/5,881. **Par:** 72/72. **Course Rating:** 71.1/74.1. **Slope:** 124/129. **Green Fee:** $14/$25. **Cart Fee:** $24/cart. **Walking Policy:** Unrestricted walking. **Walkability:** 3.
Opened: 1965. **Architect:** Edward Lawrence Packard. **Season:** April-Oct. **High:** May-Aug. **To obtain tee times:** Call anytime. **Miscellaneous:** Reduced fees (twilight, seniors, juniors), range (grass).
Reader Comments: A lot of potential ... Challenging ... Scenic ... Wide variety of shots ... Trees, water, elevation changes ... Can be wet after rain ... Water everywhere ... Nice public course.

★★½ LEGACY GOLF CLUB

PU-3500 Cargill Rd., Granite City, 62040, Madison County, (618)931-4653, 12 miles SW of St. Louis.
Holes: 18. **Yards:** 6,300/5,600. **Par:** 71/71. **Course Rating:** 70.4/69.4. **Slope:** 114/110. **Green Fee:** $14/$21. **Cart Fee:** $10/person. **Walking Policy:** Unrestricted walking. **Walkability:** 1. **Opened:** 1990. **Architect:** Jerry Loomis. **Season:** Year-round. **High:** April-Oct. **To obtain tee times:** Call 7 days in advance. **Miscellaneous:** Reduced fees (weekdays, low season, twilight, seniors, juniors), discount packages, metal spikes, range (grass), club rentals, credit cards (MC, V, AE, D).

ILLINOIS

★★½ LEO DONOVAN GOLF COURSE
PU-5805 Knoxville Ave., Peoria, 61614, Peoria County, (309)691-8361.
Holes: 18. **Yards:** 6,735/5,675. **Par:** 72/72. **Course Rating:** 70.9/71.5. **Slope:** 117/120. **Green Fee:** $11/$15. **Walking Policy:** Unrestricted walking. **Walkability:** 2. **Opened:** 1929. **Season:** March-Nov. **High:** April-Aug. **To obtain tee times:** In person up to 7 days in advance. By telephone, day of play. In person 7 days in advance. By telephone up to 6 days in advance.
Miscellaneous: Reduced fees (weekdays, twilight, juniors), club rentals, credit cards (MC, V).
Reader Comments: New irrigation a plus ... Average course; average challenge ... Good course for all skill levels.

★★★★ LICK CREEK GOLF COURSE *Value*
PM-2210 N. Pkwy. Dr., Pekin, 61554, Tazewell County, (309)346-0077, 12 miles S of Peoria.
Holes: 18. **Yards:** 6,909/5,729. **Par:** 72/72. **Course Rating:** 72.8/72.9. **Slope:** 128/125. **Green Fee:** $7/$20. **Cart Fee:** $16/cart. **Walking Policy:** Unrestricted walking. **Walkability:** 4. **Opened:** 1976. **Architect:** Edward Lawrence Packard. **Season:** April-Nov. **High:** June-Sept. **To obtain tee times:** Call 7 days in advance. **Miscellaneous:** Reduced fees (weekdays, twilight, seniors, juniors), range (grass), club rentals, credit cards (MC, V).
Reader Comments: Hilly, treed, tight, challenging. Be patient ... Great value ... Good daily course ... Tough and frustrating ... Can be very difficult ... Very tough from the back tees ... Not for beginners ... Scenic holes ... I enjoyed going there ... Impressed with their junior program.

★★★ LINCOLN GREENS GOLF COURSE
PU-700 E. Lake Dr., Springfield, 62707, Sangamon County, (217)786-4000, 90 miles N of St. Louis.
Holes: 18. **Yards:** 6,582/5,625. **Par:** 72/72. **Course Rating:** 70.3/70.9. **Slope:** 112/114. **Green Fee:** $7/$22. **Cart Fee:** $18/cart. **Walking Policy:** Unrestricted walking. **Walkability:** 1. **Opened:** 1957. **Architect:** Robert Bruce Harris. **Season:** March-Dec. **High:** June-Aug. **To obtain tee times:** Call up to 7 days in advance. $2 charge per tee time—no refund unless it rains or cancel 1 day prior to tee time. **Miscellaneous:** Reduced fees (weekdays, twilight, seniors, juniors), discount packages, metal spikes, range (grass), club rentals, credit cards (MC, V).
Reader Comments: Open, somewhat flat ... Good track ... Fairways made a comeback in the fall ... City needs to take the politics out of how the course is run and maintained ... Good course that could be great ... Used to be excellent ... Heavy play makes for slow rounds.

★★½ LINCOLN OAKS GOLF COURSE
PU-390 Richton Rd., Crete, 60417, Will County, (708)672-9401, 25 miles S of Chicago.
Holes: 18. **Yards:** 6,087/4,699. **Par:** 71/73. **Course Rating:** 68.1/65.8. **Slope:** 112/105. **Green Fee:** $10/$25. **Cart Fee:** $12/person. **Walking Policy:** Unrestricted walking. **Walkability:** 1. **Opened:** 1927. **Architect:** Tom Bendelow. **Season:** Year-round. **High:** June-Aug. **To obtain tee times:** Call up to 7 days in advance. **Miscellaneous:** Reduced fees (weekdays, low season, twilight, seniors, juniors), metal spikes, range (grass), club rentals, credit cards (MC, V).
Reader Comments: Sporty layout ... Short, but nicely kept and has its tough holes ... In a scenic and quiet residential area ... Narrow fairways ... Good value ... Small greens.

★★★½ THE LINKS GOLF COURSE
PM-Nichols Park, Jacksonville, 62650, Morgan County, (217)479-4663, 30 miles W of Springfield.
Holes: 18. **Yards:** 6,836/5,310. **Par:** 72/72. **Course Rating:** 71.3/69.0. **Slope:** 116/108. **Green Fee:** $14/$18. **Cart Fee:** $10/person. **Walking Policy:** Unrestricted walking. **Walkability:** 1. **Opened:** 1979. **Architect:** David Gill. **Season:** Year-round. **High:** May-Sept. **To obtain tee times:** Call 7 days in advance. **Miscellaneous:** Reduced fees (weekdays, seniors, juniors), discount packages, range (grass), club rentals.
Reader Comments: Good layout, great greens, particularly windy ... Fun ... Plays a lot longer than the card reads ... Links-style; wide open ... A windbreaker won't get the job done ... Lots of sand and water.

★½ LOCUST HILLS GOLF CLUB
PU-1015 Belleville St., Lebanon, 62254, St. Clair County, (618)537-4590, 22 miles E of St. Louis, MO.
Holes: 18. **Yards:** 5,662/4,276. **Par:** 71/71. **Course Rating:** 68.2/71.0. **Slope:** 109/113. **Green Fee:** $12/$19. **Cart Fee:** $20/cart. **Walking Policy:** Unrestricted walking. **Walkability:** 2. **Opened:** 1967. **Season:** Feb.-Dec. **High:** April-Sept. **To obtain tee times:** Call up to 7 days in advance. **Miscellaneous:** Reduced fees (weekdays, low season, twilight, seniors, juniors), metal spikes.

★★½ LONGWOOD COUNTRY CLUB
SP-3503 E. Steger Rd., Crete, 60417, Will County, (708)758-1811, 40 miles S of Chicago.
Holes: 18. **Yards:** 3,244/2,785. **Par:** 70/72. **Course Rating:** 70.5/72.1. **Slope:** 121/120. **Green Fee:** $15/$28. **Cart Fee:** $12/person. **Walking Policy:** Unrestricted walking. **Walkability:** 4.

ILLINOIS

Opened: 1957. **Season:** Year-round. **To obtain tee times:** Call up to 7 days in advance.
Miscellaneous: Reduced fees (weekdays, twilight, seniors, juniors), metal spikes, range (grass),
club rentals, credit cards (MC, V, AE).
Reader Comments: Wide open ... Very hilly ... No flat lies ... Good to play in spring for warm-up.

★★★★ LOST NATION GOLF CLUB
PU-6931 S. Lost Nation Rd., Dixon, 61021, Ogle County, (815)652-4212, 90 miles W of Chicago.
Holes: 18. **Yards:** 6,275/5,626. **Par:** 71/72. **Course Rating:** 69.5/72.0. **Slope:** 114/114. **Green
Fee:** $17/$21. **Cart Fee:** $22/cart. **Walking Policy:** Unrestricted walking. **Walkability:** 3.
Opened: 1965. **Season:** March-Dec. **High:** May-Sept. **To obtain tee times:** Call up to 14 days
in advance. **Miscellaneous:** Reduced fees (twilight, seniors), club rentals, credit cards (MC, V).
Reader Comments: Relaxing, but still challenging ... Hard to find, but worth it ... Don't even
think about a sub-five-hour round on Saturday ... Too crowded on weekends.

★★½ MACKTOWN GOLF COURSE
PM-2221 Freeport Rd., Rockton, 61072, Winnebago County, (815)624-7410.
Holes: 18. **Yards:** 5,770/5,403. **Par:** 71/71. **Course Rating:** 67.1/70.3. **Slope:** 109/111. **Green
Fee:** $14/$25. **Cart Fee:** $24/cart. **Walking Policy:** Unrestricted walking. **Walkability:** 3.
Opened: 1931. **Architect:** R. Welsh. **Season:** April-Oct. **High:** May-Aug. **Miscellaneous:**
Reduced fees (weekdays, twilight, seniors, juniors).
Reader Comments: Plain ... Short ... Heavily wooded ... Lots of trees ... Ego-builder ... Not many
obstacles ... Good county course.

★★ MADISON PARK GOLF COURSE
PM-2735 W. Martin Luther King Dr., Peoria, 61604, Peoria County, (309)673-7161.
Holes: 18. **Yards:** 5,476/5,120. **Par:** 69/69. **Course Rating:** 64.5/67.7. **Slope:** 96/100. **Green
Fee:** $12/$13. **Cart Fee:** $16/cart. **Walking Policy:** Unrestricted walking. **Walkability:** 1.
Opened: 1909. **Season:** March-Dec. **High:** June-Sept. **To obtain tee times:** Call up to 6 days in
advance. In person, 7 days in advance. **Miscellaneous:** Reduced fees (weekdays, twilight,
juniors), range (grass), club rentals, credit cards (MC, V, D), beginner friendly.
Notes: First golf course in the Peoria area.

★★½ MANTENO GOLF CLUB
PU-Village Hall 269 N. Main St., Manteno, 60950, Kankakee County, (815)468-8827.
Holes: 18. **Yards:** 6,435/5,145. **Par:** 72/72. **Course Rating:** 70.1/68.5. **Slope:** 118/112. **Green
Fee:** $17/$20. **Cart Fee:** $9/. **Cart Fee:** Included in Green Fee. **Walking Policy:** Unrestricted
walking. **Walkability:** 2. **Opened:** 1974. **Season:** Year-round. **High:** May-Sept. **To obtain tee
times:** May call golf shop up to 2 weeks in advance. **Miscellaneous:** Reduced fees (twilight,
seniors), metal spikes, range (grass), beginner friendly.
Reader Comments: Basic golf ... Flat ... Liked the driving range.

★★★ MAPLE MEADOWS GOLF COURSE
PU-271 South Addison Rd., Wood Dale, 60191, Du Page County, (630)616-8424, 19 miles W of
Chicago.
Holes: 18. **Yards:** 6,438/6,057. **Par:** 70/70. **Course Rating:** 70.1/68.3. **Slope:** 122/118. **Green
Fee:** $27/$45. **Cart Fee:** $14/person. **Walking Policy:** Walking at certain times. **Walkability:** 5.
Opened: 1998. **Season:** April-Dec. **High:** June-Sept. **Miscellaneous:** Reduced fees (weekdays),
club rentals, credit cards (MC, V).
Reader Comments: New back 9 is fun ... New owners ... Much better and much tougher ...
Links-style ... Large trees ... New nine is better ... Fairways and greens need to mature.

★★★½ MARENGO RIDGE GOLF CLUB
PU-9508 Harmony Hill Rd., Marengo, 60152, McHenry County, (815)923-2332, 35 miles NW of
Chicago O'Hare Airport. **E-mail:** rwitek@me.net.
Holes: 18. **Yards:** 6,636/5,659. **Par:** 72/73. **Course Rating:** 71.4/72.2. **Slope:** 122/120. **Green
Fee:** $19/$24. **Walking Policy:** Unrestricted walking. **Walkability:** 3. **Opened:** 1965. **Architect:**
William James Spear. **Season:** March-Dec. **High:** May-Sept. **To obtain tee times:** Call 7 days in
advance. **Miscellaneous:** Reduced fees (weekdays, low season, twilight, seniors, juniors), dis-
count packages, range (grass), club rentals, credit cards (MC, V, D), beginner friendly (hook a
kid on golf, no embarrassment golf lessons).
Reader Comments: Great course, hidden away ... Two different 9s; open vs. woods ... Tough
greens ... Front 9 OK; I enjoyed the back 9.

★★★ MARRIOTT'S LINCOLNSHIRE RESORT
R-Ten Marriott Dr., Lincolnshire, 60069, Lake County, (847)634-5935, 30 miles N of Chicago.
Holes: 18. **Yards:** 6,313/4,892. **Par:** 70/69. **Course Rating:** 71.1/68.9. **Slope:** 129/117. **Green
Fee:** $37/$56. **Cart Fee:** Included in Green Fee. **Walking Policy:** Walking at certain times.
Walkability: 2. **Opened:** 1975. **Architect:** Tom Fazio/George Fazio. **Season:** April-Oct. **High:**
May-Sept. **To obtain tee times:** Call up to 7 days in advance. Resort guests may reserve tee
times with room confirmation up to 90 days in advance. **Miscellaneous:** Reduced fees (week-

days, low season, twilight), discount packages, metal spikes, club rentals, lodging, credit cards (MC, V, AE, D).
Reader Comments: Manicured resort ... Typical resort course ... Some nice holes, but too much money ... Enjoyable ... Back 9 is outstanding.

★½ THE MEADOWS GOLF CLUB OF BLUE ISLAND
PU-2802 W. 123rd St., Blue Island, 60406, Cook County, (708)385-1994,.
Holes: 18. **Yards:** 6,550/4,830. **Par:** 71/71. **Course Rating:** N/A. **Slope:** N/A. **Green Fee:** $12/$11. **Cart Fee:** $10/. **Walking Policy:** Unrestricted walking. **Walkability:** 3. **Opened:** 1994. **Architect:** Porter Gibson. **Season:** March-Dec. **High:** May-Sept. **To obtain tee times:** Call golf shop. **Miscellaneous:** Reduced fees (weekdays, low season, twilight, seniors, juniors), metal spikes, range (grass/mats), credit cards (MC, V).

★★★ MEADOWVIEW GOLF COURSE
PU-6489 Meadowview Lane, Mattoon, 61938, Coles County, (217)258-7888, 50 miles S of Champaign. **Web:** www.meadowviewgolf.com.
Holes: 18. **Yards:** 6,907/5,559. **Par:** 72/72. **Course Rating:** 72.6/71.3. **Slope:** 121/117. **Green Fee:** $18/$20. **Cart Fee:** $10/person. **Walking Policy:** Unrestricted walking. **Walkability:** 2. **Opened:** 1991. **Architect:** William James Spears. **Season:** Feb.-Dec. **High:** June-Aug. **To obtain tee times:** Call up to 7 days in advance. **Miscellaneous:** Reduced fees (weekdays, low season, twilight, seniors, juniors), range (grass), club rentals, credit cards (MC, V, D), beginner friendly (rookie league, junior golf).
Reader Comments: Course condition improves every year ... Much improved over the past two years ... Still maturing ... Good ... Nice place.

★★★★ MILL CREEK GOLF CLUB
PU-39 W. 525 Herrington, Geneva, 60134, Kane County, (630)208-7272, 5 miles W of Geneva.
Holes: 18. **Yards:** 6,724/4,833. **Par:** 73/73. **Course Rating:** 72.1/67.5. **Slope:** 130/118. **Green Fee:** $55/$80. **Cart Fee:** Included in Green Fee. **Walking Policy:** Unrestricted walking. **Walkability:** 3. **Opened:** 1996. **Architect:** Roy Case. **Season:** April-Nov. **High:** May-Oct. **To obtain tee times:** Call up to 7 days in advance. **Miscellaneous:** Reduced fees (weekdays, low season, twilight), metal spikes, range (grass), club rentals, credit cards (MC, V, AE, D, Diners Club), beginner friendly (teaching facility).
Reader Comments: Challenging holes ... Fast greens ... Leave the driver in the bag ... Great par 5s ... Hard, but beautiful ... Great new facility ... Gotta play this one ... Will be great when it matures ... Too many blind holes ... A little pricey.

★★★ MINNE MONESSE GOLF CLUB
SP-15944 E. Six Mi Grove Rd., Grant Park, 60940, Kankakee County, (815)465-6653, (800)339-3126, 20 miles NE of Kankakee.
Holes: 9. **Yards:** 6,500/5,100. **Par:** 72/72. **Course Rating:** 71.1/N/A. **Slope:** 121/N/A. **Green Fee:** $23/$36. **Cart Fee:** Included in Green Fee. **Walking Policy:** Unrestricted walking. **Walkability:** 4. **Opened:** 1926. **Architect:** Ted Lockie, Bob Lohmann. **Season:** March-Dec. **High:** June-Aug. **To obtain tee times:** Call. **Miscellaneous:** Reduced fees (weekdays, low season, twilight, seniors, juniors), discount packages, range (grass), club rentals, credit cards (MC, V, AE, D).
Reader Comments: 3 great new holes ... Cute little tune-up course ... Beautiful old course.

MISTWOOD GOLF COURSE
PU-1700 W. Renwick Rd., Romeoville, 60446, Joliet County, (815)254-3333, 25 miles W of Chicago.
Holes: 18. **Yards:** 6,727/N/A. **Par:** 72/N/A. **Course Rating:** 72.1/N/A. **Slope:** 132/N/A. **Green Fee:** $20/$49. **Cart Fee:** $9/person. **Walking Policy:** Unrestricted walking. **Walkability:** 2. **Opened:** 1998. **Architect:** Ray Hearn. **Season:** March-Nov. **High:** May-Aug. **To obtain tee times:** Call golf shop. **Miscellaneous:** Reduced fees (low season, seniors, juniors), range (grass/mats), club rentals, credit cards (MC, V, AE, D).

★★½ MOUNT CARMEL MUNICIPAL GOLF CLUB
PU-RR #3 Park Rd., Mt. Carmel, 62863, Wabash County, (618)262-5771.
Holes: 18. **Yards:** 6,121/5,504. **Par:** 71/72. **Course Rating:** 69.2/69.6. **Slope:** 123/108. **Green Fee:** $11/$15. **Cart Fee:** $20/cart. **Walking Policy:** Unrestricted walking. **Walkability:** 3. **Opened:** 1928. **Season:** Year-round. **High:** May-Oct. **Miscellaneous:** Club rentals.
Reader Comments: Challenging ... Gaining maturity ... Pace of play good.

★★★½ MOUNT PROSPECT GOLF CLUB
PM-600 See Gwum Ave., Mt. Prospect, 60056, Cook County, (847)259-4200, 6 miles NW of Chicago.
Holes: 18. **Yards:** 6,200/5,355. **Par:** 71/73. **Course Rating:** 70.3/70.8. **Slope:** 128/123. **Green Fee:** $32/$42. **Cart Fee:** $24/cart. **Walking Policy:** Unrestricted walking. **Walkability:** 2. **Opened:** 1927. **Season:** March-Nov. **High:** Summer. **To obtain tee times:** Call up to 5 days in

advance. **Miscellaneous:** Reduced fees (twilight), metal spikes, range (grass/mats), club rentals, credit cards (MC, V, D).

Reader Comments: Nice course ... Rewards accuracy over distance ... Gets a ton of traffic ... Somewhat difficult to get a good tee time.

★★★½ NAPERBROOK GOLF COURSE
PU-22204 111th St., Plainfield, 60544, Will County, (630)378-4215, 24 miles SW of Chicago.
Holes: 18. **Yards:** 6,755/5,381. **Par:** 72/72. **Course Rating:** 72.2/70.5. **Slope:** 125/118. **Green Fee:** $21/$44. **Cart Fee:** $14/person. **Walking Policy:** Unrestricted walking. **Walkability:** 1. **Opened:** 1990. **Architect:** Roger Packard. **Season:** March-Dec. **High:** June-Aug. **To obtain tee times:** Call 7 days in advance starting at 5 p.m. **Miscellaneous:** Reduced fees (weekdays, low season, twilight, seniors, juniors), range (grass), club rentals, credit cards (MC, V), beginner friendly (beginner adult and junior lessons).
Notes: 1995 U.S. Amateur Qualifying.
Reader Comments: Steady course ... Perfect public ... Good overall for any golfer ... Links-type layout ... Every 30-plus-handicapper from 20 miles around plays here ... Had my best round ever ... Good golf at a good price ... Deceivingly tough.

★★ NELSON PARK GOLF COURSE
PU-200 Nelson Blvd, Decatur, 62521, Macon County, (217)422-7241, 45 miles E of Springfield.
Holes: 18. **Yards:** 4,793/4,378. **Par:** 65/65. **Course Rating:** 63.2/63.2. **Slope:** 101/101. **Green Fee:** $9/$15. **Cart Fee:** $18/cart. **Walking Policy:** Unrestricted walking. **Walkability:** 5. **Opened:** 1916. **Season:** Year-round. **High:** May-Sept. **To obtain tee times:** Call on Monday starting at 6:30 a.m. for upcoming weekend. Call up to 7 days in advance for weekdays. **Miscellaneous:** Reduced fees (weekdays, low season, twilight, seniors, juniors), metal spikes, club rentals, credit cards (MC, V).

★★★ NETTLE CREEK COUNTRY CLUB
PU-5355 Saratoga Rd., Morris, 60450, Grundy County, (815)941-4300, 50 miles SW of Chicago.
Web: www.nettlecreek.com.
Holes: 18. **Yards:** 6,489/5,059. **Par:** 71/71. **Course Rating:** 70.4/68.9. **Slope:** 117/114. **Green Fee:** $34/$44. **Cart Fee:** Included in Green Fee. **Walking Policy:** Walking at certain times. **Walkability:** 2. **Opened:** 1993. **Architect:** Buzz Didier. **Season:** March-Nov. **High:** June-Aug. **To obtain tee times:** Call up to 7 days in advance. **Miscellaneous:** Reduced fees (twilight, seniors, juniors), metal spikes, club rentals, credit cards (MC, V).
Reader Comments: Fairly new ... Could be better ... Reasonably priced ... Needs to mature ... Lacks challenge.

★★★★ NEWMAN GOLF COURSE *Value*
PM-2021 W. Nebraska, Peoria, 61604, Peoria County, (309)674-1663.
Holes: 18. **Yards:** 6,838/5,933. **Par:** 71/74. **Course Rating:** 71.8/74.2. **Slope:** 119/120. **Green Fee:** $5/$15. **Cart Fee:** $16/cart. **Walking Policy:** Unrestricted walking. **Walkability:** 3. **Opened:** 1934. **Season:** March-Nov. **High:** April-Aug. **To obtain tee times:** Call 6 days in advance, taken in person 7 days in advance. **Miscellaneous:** Reduced fees (weekdays, twilight, juniors), club rentals, credit cards (MC, V).
Reader Comments: Set back in woods ... I love it, love it, love it ... Tough last 4 holes ... Good challenge ... Nice layout ... Tough from back tees.

★★★ NORDIC HILLS RESORT
R-Nordic Rd., Itasca, 60743, Du Page County, (630)773-3510, 20 miles W of Chicago.
Holes: 18. **Yards:** 5,626/5,035. **Par:** 70/72. **Course Rating:** 67.3/69.6. **Slope:** 108/112. **Green Fee:** $37/$54. **Cart Fee:** Included in Green Fee. **Walking Policy:** Mandatory cart. **Walkability:** 3. **Architect:** Charles Maddox/Frank P. MacDonald. **Season:** April-Nov. **High:** June-Aug. **To obtain tee times:** one week in advance for non-hotel golfers. **Miscellaneous:** Reduced fees (weekdays, low season, twilight), range (mats), club rentals, lodging, credit cards (MC, V, AE, D).
Reader Comments: Short, tight resort course, good for ego ... Good course, nice resort ... Needs some helmets ... Stay alert to avoid getting beaned ... Good for inexperienced players.

OAK BROOK GOLF CLUB
PU-9157 Fruit Rd., Edwardsville, 62025, Madison County, (618)656-5600, 30 miles N of St. Louis.
Holes: 27. **Yards:** 6,250/5,214. **Par:** 71/71. **Course Rating:** 68.2/N/A. **Slope:** 113/N/A. **Green Fee:** $15/$17. **Cart Fee:** $18/cart. **Walking Policy:** Unrestricted walking. **Walkability:** 3. **Opened:** 1972. **Architect:** Larry Suhre. **Season:** Year-round. **High:** April-Sept. **To obtain tee times:** Call up to 7 days in advance. **Miscellaneous:** Reduced fees (seniors, juniors), metal spikes, range (grass).
Reader Comments: Fairly wide open. Expect good scores ... Old-style course ... Too susceptible to weather.

OAK BROOK GOLF COURSE
PU-2606 York Rd., Oak Brook, 60523, Du Page County, (630)990-3032, 15 miles W of Chicago.

Holes: 18. **Yards:** 6,541/5,341. **Par:** 72/72. **Course Rating:** 71.2/70.9. **Slope:** 121/120. **Green Fee:** $32/$36. **Cart Fee:** $12/person. **Walking Policy:** Unrestricted walking. **Walkability:** N/A. **Opened:** 1980. **Architect:** Roger Packard. **Season:** March-Dec. **High:** April-Sept. **To obtain tee times:** Call 7 days in advance. **Miscellaneous:** Reduced fees (twilight), metal spikes, range (grass), club rentals, credit cards (MC, V, AE).
Reader Comments: Interesting back nine ... Second-shot course ... Better putt well if you hope to post a good score ... Too pricey for nonresidents.

★★★ OAK BROOK HILLS HOTEL & RESORT
R-3500 Midwest Rd., Oak Brook, 60522, Du Page County, (630)850-5530, (800)445-3315, 20 miles W of Chicago.
Holes: 18. **Yards:** 6,372/5,152. **Par:** 70/69. **Course Rating:** 70.4/69.2. **Slope:** 122/114. **Green Fee:** $55/$75. **Cart Fee:** Included in Green Fee. **Walking Policy:** Unrestricted walking. **Walkability:** 3. **Opened:** 1987. **Architect:** Dick Nugent. **Season:** March-Nov. **High:** June-Sept. **To obtain tee times:** Hotel guests may reserve up to 45 days in advance. Nonguests may call up to 21 days in advance. **Miscellaneous:** Reduced fees (low season, twilight, seniors, juniors), metal spikes, club rentals, lodging (384 rooms), credit cards (MC, V, AE, D).
Reader Comments: Holes are too close together ... Too crowded ... Very tight ... Good resort experience ... Nice place.

★★★ THE OAK CLUB OF GENOA
PU-11770 Ellwood Greens Rd., Genoa, 60135, De Kalb County, (815)784-5678, 60 miles W of Chicago.
Holes: 18. **Yards:** 7,032/5,556. **Par:** 72/72. **Course Rating:** 74.1/72.5. **Slope:** 135/127. **Green Fee:** $20/$32. **Cart Fee:** Included in Green Fee. **Walking Policy:** Walking at certain times. **Walkability:** 4. **Opened:** 1973. **Architect:** Charles Maddox. **Season:** March-Dec. **High:** May-Sept. **To obtain tee times:** Call 7 days in advance. **Miscellaneous:** Reduced fees (weekdays, low season, twilight, seniors, juniors), range (grass), credit cards (MC, V, AE, D).
Reader Comments: Just started playing more; like it more each time ... Tight fairways ... Worth the drive ... Could be excellent.

OAK GLEN GOLF COURSE
Stoy Rd., Robinson, 62454, Crawford County, (618)592-3030, 50 miles E of Effingham.
Holes: 18. **Yards:** 6,086/5,220. **Par:** 71/71. **Course Rating:** 67.7/67.8. **Slope:** 112/108. **Green Fee:** $10/$15. **Cart Fee:** $15/cart. **Walking Policy:** Unrestricted walking. **Walkability:** 2. **Opened:** 1963. **Season:** March-Nov. **High:** May-Aug. **To obtain tee times:** No tee times reserved. **Miscellaneous:** Reduced fees (weekdays, twilight), metal spikes, range (grass/mats), credit cards (MC, V).

OAK GROVE GOLF COURSE
PU-16914 Oak Grove Rd., Harvard, 60033, McHenry County, (815)648-2550, (877)648-GOLF, 12 miles S of Lake Geneva, Wisc. **E-mail:** rob@oakgrovegolfcourse.com. **Web:** www.oakgrovegolfcourse.com.
Holes: 18. **Yards:** 7,021/5,254. **Par:** 71/71. **Course Rating:** 74.6/70.1. **Slope:** 135/120. **Green Fee:** $65/$75. **Cart Fee:** Included in Green Fee. **Walking Policy:** Mandatory cart. **Walkability:** 5. **Opened:** 1998. **Architect:** Steven Halberg. **Season:** April-Nov. **High:** May-Sept. **Miscellaneous:** Reduced fees (seniors, juniors), range (grass/mats), credit cards (MC, V, D).
Notes: 1999 Illinois P.G.A. and Stroke Play Tournament.
Special Notes: Formerly known as Oak Grove Golf Club.

★★★½ OAK MEADOWS GOLF CLUB
PU-900 N. Wood Dale Rd., Addison, 60101, Du Page County, (630)595-0071, 8 miles NW of Elmhurst.
Holes: 18. **Yards:** 6,718/5,954. **Par:** 71/73. **Course Rating:** 72.1/73.8. **Slope:** 126/128. **Green Fee:** $30/$33. **Cart Fee:** $30/cart. **Walking Policy:** Mandatory cart. **Walkability:** 3. **Opened:** 1925. **Season:** April-Nov. **High:** June-Sept. **To obtain tee times:** Call 1 week in advance. **Miscellaneous:** Reduced fees (twilight), range (grass), club rentals, credit cards (MC, V).
Reader Comments: Former private club ... Challenging ... Hit it straight ... Golf the way it used to be ... Lots of trees ... Good old course ... Long, tough finishing holes ... Great clubhouse ... Worth the effort.

★★½ OAK SPRINGS GOLF COURSE
PU-6740 E.3500 South Rd., St. Anne, 60964, Kankakee County, (815)937-1648, 7 miles E of Kankakee.
Yards: 6,260/N/A. **Par:** 72/N/A. **Course Rating:** 68.6/N/A. **Slope:** 118/N/A. **Green Fee:** $16/$22. **Cart Fee:** $10/person. **Walking Policy:** Unrestricted walking. **Walkability:** 3. **Opened:** 1965. **Season:** March-Nov. **High:** June-Aug. **To obtain tee times:** Call golf shop. **Miscellaneous:** Reduced fees (weekdays, twilight, seniors), club rentals, credit cards (MC, V), beginner friendly.
Reader Comments: Worth the drive ... Good test ... Lots of wedges.

ILLINOIS

★★★½ OAK TERRACE GOLF COURSE
100 Beyers Lake Rd, Pana, 62557, Shelby County, (217)539-4477, 800-577-7598, 30 miles S of Decatur. **Web:** www.oakterrace.com.
Holes: 18. **Yards:** 6,375/4,898. **Par:** 72/72. **Course Rating:** 70.1/67.8. **Slope:** 112/107. **Green Fee:** $15/$23. **Cart Fee:** $12/cart. **Walking Policy:** Unrestricted walking. **Walkability:** 1. **Opened:** 1991. **Season:** March-Nov. **High:** June-Aug. **To obtain tee times:** Call 7 days in advance. **Miscellaneous:** Reduced fees (weekdays, low season, resort guests, twilight, seniors, juniors), discount packages, range (grass), club rentals, lodging (37 rooms), credit cards (MC, V, AE, D), beginner friendly.
Reader Comments: Generic front 9; back 9 cut through woods ... Back 9 is outstanding ... Very scenic ... Some interesting holes.

★★½ THE OAKS GOLF COURSE
PU-851 Dave Stockton Dr., Springfield, 62707-3116, Sangamon County, (217)528-6600.
Holes: 18. **Yards:** 6,054/4,665. **Par:** 70/70. **Course Rating:** 68.4/66.0. **Slope:** 112/112. **Green Fee:** $10/$17. **Cart Fee:** $20/cart. **Walking Policy:** Unrestricted walking. **Walkability:** 4. **Opened:** 1926. **Season:** Year-round. **High:** June-Sept. **To obtain tee times:** Call up to 7 days in advance. **Miscellaneous:** Reduced fees (weekdays, low season, twilight, seniors, juniors), metal spikes, club rentals, credit cards (MC, V), beginner friendly.
Reader Comments: Enjoyable ... Not my first choice to play ... Small, flat greens.

★★★½ ODYSSEY COUNTRY CLUB & GOLF ACADEMY
PU-19110 S. Ridgeland, Tinley Park, 60477, Cook County, (708)429-7400, 20 miles SW of Chicago.
Holes: 18. **Yards:** 7,095/5,564. **Par:** 72/72. **Course Rating:** 73.1/69.3. **Slope:** 131/116. **Green Fee:** $19/$65. **Cart Fee:** Included in Green Fee. **Walking Policy:** Walking at certain times. **Walkability:** 3. **Opened:** 1992. **Architect:** Harry Bowers/Curtis Strange. **Season:** April-Nov. **High:** June-Aug. **To obtain tee times:** Call up to 14 days in advance. **Miscellaneous:** Reduced fees (weekdays, low season, twilight), metal spikes, range (grass/mats), club rentals, credit cards (MC, V, AE).
Reader Comments: Nice place to play ... Always windy ... For a supposedly big-time course, greens were very slow ... Placement golf ... A few holes will jump out and bite you ... Very wet in the spring ... Great clubhouse ... A bit pricey.

★★★ OLD OAK COUNTRY CLUB
PU-14200 S. Parker Rd., Lockport, 60441, Will County, (708)301-3344, 19 miles SW of Chicago.
Holes: 18. **Yards:** 6,535/5,274. **Par:** 71/72. **Course Rating:** 70.1/N/A. **Slope:** 124/N/A. **Green Fee:** $29/$60. **Cart Fee:** $15/person. **Walking Policy:** Walking at certain times. **Walkability:** 2. **Opened:** 1926. **Season:** April-Dec. **High:** June-Sept. **To obtain tee times:** Call up to 7 days in advance. **Miscellaneous:** Reduced fees (weekdays, low season, twilight, seniors, juniors), club rentals, credit cards (MC, V, AE, D).
Reader Comments: Good condition, considering heavy use ... Fast, tough greens ... Wouldn't go back ... Challenging ... Nice old course ... Trees tough ... A lot of leagues.

★★★½ OLD ORCHARD COUNTRY CLUB
PU-700 W. Rand Rd., Mt. Prospect, 60056, Cook County, (847)255-2025.
Holes: 18. **Yards:** 6,119/5,731. **Par:** 70/70. **Course Rating:** 70.1/68.7. **Slope:** 131/127. **Green Fee:** $36/$52. **Cart Fee:** $30/. **Cart Fee:** Included in Green Fee. **Walking Policy:** Walking at certain times. **Walkability:** 2. **Opened:** 1930. **Architect:** Al Wickersham. **Season:** April-Nov. **High:** June-July. **To obtain tee times:** Call up to 7 days in advance. **Miscellaneous:** Reduced fees (weekdays, twilight), metal spikes, club rentals, credit cards (MC, V, AE, D, Diners Club).
Reader Comments: Beautiful course ... Short but enjoyable ... Lots of challenges ... Good greens and fairways ... A hidden treasure ... It gets better every year.

★★½ ORCHARD HILLS GOLF COURSE
PM-38342 N. Green Bay Rd., Waukegan, 60087, Lake County, (847)336-5118, 40 miles N of Chicago.
Holes: 18. **Yards:** 6,458/5,973. **Par:** 71/71. **Course Rating:** 69.7/67.6. **Slope:** 107/101. **Green Fee:** $25/$27. **Cart Fee:** $12/person. **Walking Policy:** Walking at certain times. **Walkability:** 2. **Opened:** 1930. **Architect:** Robert Bruce Harris. **Season:** Year-round. **High:** May-Oct. **To obtain tee times:** Call up to 7 days in advance. **Miscellaneous:** Reduced fees (weekdays, low season, twilight), discount packages, range (grass/mats), club rentals, credit cards (MC, V, D).
Reader Comments: Few hazards; not much of a challenge ... Great special deals ... Wide open ... Cheap; good for practice.

★★★★½ ORCHARD VALLEY GOLF CLUB   *Value, Condition*
PU-2411 W. Illinois Ave., Aurora, 60506, Kane County, (630)907-0500, 35 miles W of Chicago.
Holes: 18. **Yards:** 6,745/5,162. **Par:** 72/72. **Course Rating:** 72.8/70.3. **Slope:** 134/123. **Green Fee:** $43/$50. **Cart Fee:** $13/person. **Walking Policy:** Unrestricted walking. **Walkability:** N/A. **Opened:** 1993. **Architect:** Ken Kavanaugh. **Season:** April-Oct. **High:** June-Sept. **To obtain tee

times: Call 7 days in advance with credit card. Club has a 24-hour cancellation policy.
Miscellaneous: Reduced fees (twilight, seniors, juniors), metal spikes, range (grass/mats), club rentals, credit cards (MC, V, AE).

Reader Comments: Best value in Chicago area ... Beautiful ... Enjoy ... Great course for the money ... Every hole makes you think ... Real golf ... A must-play ... Three par 3s with water carries ... Challenges abound at every hole ... One of my favorite courses ... Wish I could play here every day ... Get rid of the homes ... Nice restaurant and golf shop.

★★★½ THE ORCHARDS GOLF CLUB
PU-1499 Golf Course Dr., Belleville, 62220, St. Clair County, (618)233-8921, (800)452-0358, 20 miles SE of St. Louis.
Holes: 18. **Yards:** 6,405/5,001. **Par:** 71/71. **Course Rating:** 69.0/70.1. **Slope:** 121/120. **Green Fee:** $24/$35. **Cart Fee:** $10. **Walking Policy:** Walking at certain times. **Walkability:** 3. **Opened:** 1991. **Architect:** Bob Goalby. **Season:** Year-round. **High:** April-Oct. **To obtain tee times:** Call up to 7 days. **Miscellaneous:** Reduced fees (weekdays, low season, twilight, seniors, juniors), range (grass), club rentals, credit cards (MC, V, AE).

Reader Comments: Great variety of holes ... Some really challenging holes ... Beautiful layout ... Lots of woods ... A little pricey, but worth it ... Greens are going to be good in a year or 2 ... Some neat holes ... Was in great condition early ... Interesting design.

★★★ PALATINE HILLS GOLF COURSE
PU-512 W. Northwest Hwy., Palatine, 60067, Cook County, (847)359-4020, 25 miles NW of Chicago.
Holes: 18. **Yards:** 6,800/5,975. **Par:** 72/72. **Course Rating:** 71.6/73.2. **Slope:** 120/119. **Green Fee:** $29/$34. **Cart Fee:** $14/person. **Walking Policy:** Unrestricted walking. **Walkability:** 3. **Opened:** 1965. **Architect:** Edward L. Packard. **Season:** April-Nov. **High:** June-Aug. **To obtain tee times:** Call 7 days in advance for tee times. **Miscellaneous:** Reduced fees (weekdays, low season, twilight), discount packages, metal spikes, range (grass/mats), club rentals, credit cards (MC, V).

Reader Comments: Nice local course ... Average layout ... Nothing special .... Improving ... Greens need a little help.

PALOS COUNTRY CLUB
PU-13100 S.W. Hwy., Palos Park, 60464, Cook County, (708)448-6550, 30 miles SW of Chicago.
Holes: 27. **Green Fee:** $25/$30. **Cart Fee:** $26/cart. **Walking Policy:** Walking at certain times. **Walkability:** 3. **Opened:** 1917. **Architect:** Charles Maddox/Frank P. MacDonald. **Season:** Year-round. **High:** March-Oct. **To obtain tee times:** Call up to 7 days in advance. **Miscellaneous:** Reduced fees (weekdays, low season, twilight, seniors), metal spikes, range (grass/mats), club rentals, credit cards (MC, V).
★½ RED/BLUE
Yards: 6,007/5,215. **Par:** 72/72. **Course Rating:** 68.7/69.7. **Slope:** 118/117.
★½ RED/WHITE
Yards: 6,076/5,280. **Par:** 70/70. **Course Rating:** 69.1/70.1. **Slope:** 120/119.
★½ WHITE/BLUE
Yards: 6,378/5,773. **Par:** 72/72. **Course Rating:** 71.3/72.9. **Slope:** 127/124.

PARK HILLS GOLF CLUB
PU-3240 W. Stephenson Road, Freeport, 61032, Stephenson County, (815)235-3611, 100 miles W of Chicago.
★★★½ EAST COURSE
Holes: 18. **Yards:** 6,477/5,401. **Par:** 72/72. **Course Rating:** 69.9/69.8. **Slope:** 116/115. **Green Fee:** $20/$24. **Cart Fee:** $11/person. **Walking Policy:** Unrestricted walking. **Walkability:** 3. **Opened:** 1955. **Architect:** C.D. Wagstaff. **Season:** April-Nov. **High:** June-Aug. **To obtain tee times:** Call 7 days in advance. **Miscellaneous:** Reduced fees (weekdays, juniors), metal spikes, range (grass), club rentals, credit cards (MC, V).

Reader Comments: A well-above-average public course ... I love it and have been playing it for 30 years ... Can't say enough good things about the course and staff ... Fun for the whole family ... Packed on weekends.
★★★½ WEST COURSE
Holes: 18. **Yards:** 6,622/5,940. **Par:** 72/73. **Course Rating:** 71.3/76.2. **Slope:** 121/127. **Green Fee:** $20/$24. **Cart Fee:** $11/person. **Walking Policy:** Unrestricted walking. **Walkability:** 3. **Opened:** 1966. **Architect:** C.D. Wagstaff. **Season:** April-Nov. **High:** June-Aug. **To obtain tee times:** Call 7 days in advance. **Miscellaneous:** Reduced fees (weekdays, juniors), metal spikes, range (grass), club rentals, credit cards (MC, V).

Reader Comments: Pleasure to play ... Fun public course ... Can be tough and long ... A good test ... Good value ... Fun par 5s ... Nice practice range.

★★ PARKVIEW GOLF COURSE
PM-2200 Broadway, Pekin, 61554, Tazewell County, (309)346-8494, 12 miles S of Peoria.

ILLINOIS

Holes: 18. Yards: 6,002/5,376. Par: 70/76. Course Rating: 65.4/63.6. Slope: 102/100. Green Fee: $7/$16. Cart Fee: $16/cart. Walking Policy: Unrestricted walking. Walkability: 3. Season: Year-round. High: May-Sept. Miscellaneous: Reduced fees (weekdays, twilight, seniors, juniors), club rentals, credit cards (MC, V), beginner friendly.
Special Notes: $2 charge for wearing metal spikes.

★★★ PHEASANT RUN RESORT GOLF COURSE
R-4051 East Main St., St. Charles, 60174, Kane County, (630)584-4914, 40 miles of Chicago. E-mail: prrgolf@mail.earthlink.net. Web: www.pheasantrun.com.
Holes: 18. Yards: 6,315/5,452. Par: 71/71. Course Rating: N/A. Slope: 124/121. Green Fee: $28/$58. Cart Fee: Included in Green Fee. Walking Policy: Unrestricted walking. Walkability: 2. Opened: 1963. Architect: Bill Maddox. Season: March-Nov. High: May-Oct. To obtain tee times: Call up to 7 days in advance. Miscellaneous: Reduced fees (weekdays, low season, twilight), discount packages, metal spikes, lodging, credit cards (MC, V, AE, D).
Reader Comments: Plain, flat course, but well-kept ... Good variety ... Nice short course ... Keep it down the middle and you'll score ... Good value before 10:30 a.m. ... Good getaway.

★★ PHILLIPS PARK GOLF COURSE
PU-901 Moses Dr., Aurora, 60507, Kane County, (630)898-7352, 40 miles W of Chicago.
Holes: 18. Yards: 5,634/N/A. Par: 71/N/A. Course Rating: 66.8/N/A. Slope: 109/N/A. Green Fee: $15/$20. Cart Fee: $21/cart. Walking Policy: Unrestricted walking. Walkability: 4. Opened: 1930. Season: March-Nov. High: June-Sept. Miscellaneous: Reduced fees (twilight), metal spikes, credit cards (MC, V).

★★½ PINE LAKES GOLF CLUB
PU-25130 Schuck Rd., Washington, 61571, Tazewell County, (309)745-9344.
Holes: 18. Yards: 6,385/5,187. Par: 71/72. Course Rating: N/A. Slope: 119/117. Green Fee: $15/$19. Cart Fee: $18/cart. Walkability: 3. Opened: 1963. Architect: Day Ault. Season: March-Nov. High: June-Sept. To obtain tee times: Tee times 6 days in advance.
Miscellaneous: Club rentals, credit cards (MC, V).
Reader Comments: Small greens ... Good course for a friendly round ... A little short ... Some good holes.

★★★★ PINE MEADOW GOLF CLUB *Condition, Pace*
PU-1 Pine Meadow Lane, Mundelein, 60060, Lake County, (847)566-4653, 30 miles N of Chicago.
Holes: 18. Yards: 7,141/5,203. Par: 72/71. Course Rating: 74.6/70.9. Slope: 138/125. Green Fee: $68/$68. Cart Fee: $29/cart. Walking Policy: Unrestricted walking. Walkability: 2. Opened: 1985. Architect: Joe Lee/Rocky Roquemore. Season: Year-round. High: April-Nov. To obtain tee times: Call up to 120 days in advance. Green fee must be Guaranteed from May 15th to Oct. 1st. Miscellaneous: Reduced fees (twilight, juniors), metal spikes, range (grass/mats), caddies, club rentals, credit cards (MC, V, D, Diners Club).
Notes: Ranked 11th in 1999 Best in State; 27th in 1996 America's Top 75 Upscale Courses.
Reader Comments: Great course; too bad it's so crowded ... Great range ... Back nine is one of the best in the state; front nine is adequate ... Great challenge ... Gorgeous setting ... A must-play ... Beautiful ... I play here over Kemper Lakes ... Once-a-season treat ... Difficult, but fair ... Firm greens ... Nice training facility.

★★★ PINECREST GOLF & COUNTRY CLUB
PU-11220 Algonquin Rd., Huntley, 60142, McHenry County, (847)669-3111, 50 miles NW of Chicago.
Holes: 18. Yards: 6,636/5,061. Par: 72/72. Course Rating: 71.4/68.9. Slope: 119/112. Green Fee: $26/$46. Cart Fee: $14/person. Walking Policy: Walking at certain times. Walkability: 2. Opened: 1972. Architect: Ted Lockie/Bob Lohmann. Season: March-Dec. High: June-Aug. To obtain tee times: Call 7 days in advance. Miscellaneous: Reduced fees (twilight, seniors, juniors), metal spikes, range (grass), club rentals, credit cards (MC, V, D).
Reader Comments: Open ... Challenging ... Beautiful ... Fun ... Rarely a bad lie ... Affordable ... Walkable ... Good, basic course.

★★★★ PIPER GLEN GOLF CLUB
PU-7112 Piper Glen Dr., Springfield, 62707, Sangamon County, (217)483-6537, 100 miles N of St. Louis. E-mail: proshop@piperglen.com. Web: www.piperglen.com.
Holes: 18. Yards: 6,985/5,138. Par: 72/72. Course Rating: 73.6/70.3. Slope: 133/123. Green Fee: $25/$30. Cart Fee: $12/person. Walking Policy: Unrestricted walking. Walkability: 4. Opened: 1996. Architect: Bob Lohmann. Season: March-Dec. High: May-Sept. To obtain tee times: Call golf shop up to 7 days in advance. Miscellaneous: Reduced fees (seniors, juniors), range (grass), credit cards (MC, V, D).
Reader Comments: New course is really coming along ... Good, tight layout ... Will drive 100 miles twice a month to play ... Small, undulating greens ... Very good, with a lot of variety ...

ILLINOIS

Difficult if windy ... This course has it all ... Nice up-and-comer ... Interesting and fair ... Fair to thinkers and cruel to 'grip-and-rip' players.

★★★½ PLUM TREE NATIONAL GOLF CLUB
PU-19511 Lembcke Rd., Harvard, 60033, McHenry County, (815)943-7474, (800)851-3578, 35 miles NW of Chicago.
Holes: 18. **Yards:** 6,648/5,954. **Par:** 72/72. **Course Rating:** 71.8/74.9. **Slope:** 126/132. **Green Fee:** $44/$65. **Cart Fee:** Included in Green Fee. **Walking Policy:** Walking at certain times. **Walkability:** 3. **Opened:** 1969. **Architect:** Joe Lee. **Season:** April-Dec. **High:** June-Aug. **To obtain tee times:** Call 7 days in advance. **Miscellaneous:** Reduced fees (weekdays, low season, twilight, seniors, juniors), range (grass), club rentals, credit cards (MC, V, AE, D).
Reader Comments: Mature course; nice track ... Great little course ... Classic Joe Lee design ... Very challenging and pretty ... Overall good experience ... Great course in the boonies ... A hidden gem ... Worth the ride ... Has everything ... Not busy during the week.

★★★½ PONTIAC ELKS COUNTRY CLUB
SP-Rte. 116W, Pontiac, 61764, Livingston County, (815)842-1249, 100 miles S of Chicago.
Holes: 18. **Yards:** 6,804/5,507. **Par:** 72/72. **Course Rating:** 72.2/70.6. **Slope:** 122/113. **Green Fee:** $17/$21. **Cart Fee:** $10/person. **Walking Policy:** Unrestricted walking. **Walkability:** 2. **Opened:** 1975. **Season:** March-Nov. **High:** June-Aug. **To obtain tee times:** Call golf shop. **Miscellaneous:** Range (grass), credit cards (MC, V).
Reader Comments: Tough par 3s; reachable par 5s ... Worth playing ... Nice course; 18th hole is beautiful ... Take your camera ... Good greens ... Best tenderloins around.

★★★ POPLAR CREEK COUNTRY CLUB
PU-1400 Poplar Creek Dr., Hoffman Estates, 60194, Cook County, (847)882-2938, 30 miles NW of Chicago.
Holes: 18. **Yards:** 6,311/5,402. **Par:** 70/70. **Course Rating:** 70.2/69.8. **Slope:** 126/122. **Green Fee:** $15/$29. **Walking Policy:** Walking at certain times. **Walkability:** 2. **Opened:** 1971. **Architect:** Dick Nugent/Ken Killian. **Season:** March-Nov. **High:** June-Aug. **To obtain tee times:** Call 7 days in advance. **Miscellaneous:** Reduced fees (weekdays, twilight, seniors, juniors), range (grass/mats), club rentals, credit cards (MC, V, AE, D).
Reader Comments: Short, but fun .., Nice layout ... More difficult than it appears ... Decent ... Above average ... Narrow ... Real nice.

★★★½ POTTAWATOMIE GOLF COURSE
PM-845 N. 2nd Ave., St. Charles, 60174, Kane County, (630)584-8356, 50 miles W of Chicago.
Holes: 9. **Yards:** 3,005/2,546. **Par:** 35/37. **Course Rating:** 68.2/69.2. **Slope:** 116/113. **Green Fee:** $29/$29. **Cart Fee:** $26/cart. **Walking Policy:** Unrestricted walking. **Walkability:** 2. **Opened:** 1939. **Architect:** Robert Trent Jones. **Season:** March-Dec. **High:** June-Aug. **To obtain tee times:** Call 1 day in advance for weekday. Call on Wednesday at noon for weekend. **Miscellaneous:** Club rentals, credit cards (MC, V, D).
Reader Comments: I'll play this Robert Trent Jones course any day ... The best 9-holer around ... Heavy play ... Good value ... Scenic.

PRAIRIE BLUFF GOLF CLUB
PU-19433 Renwick Rd., Lockport, 60441, Will County, (815)836-4653, 30 miles SW of Chicago.
Holes: 18. **Yards:** 6,832/5,314. **Par:** 72/72. **Course Rating:** 72.1/70.1. **Slope:** 122/115. **Green Fee:** $29/$37. **Cart Fee:** $13/person. **Walking Policy:** Unrestricted walking. **Walkability:** 3. **Opened:** 1998. **Architect:** Roger Packard/Andy North. **Season:** April-Nov. **High:** June-Aug. **To obtain tee times:** Call 7 days in advance after 5:00 P.M. **Miscellaneous:** Reduced fees (weekdays, twilight, seniors, juniors), range (grass), club rentals, credit cards (MC, V, AE, D).

★★★★ PRAIRIE ISLE GOLF CLUB
SP-2216 Rte. 176, Prairie Grove, 60012, McHenry County, (815)356-0202, 50 miles NW of Chicago.
Holes: 18. **Yards:** 6,562/5,398. **Par:** 72/73. **Course Rating:** 70.8/71.3. **Slope:** 124/117. **Green Fee:** $25/$48. **Cart Fee:** $12/person. **Walking Policy:** Walking at certain times. **Walkability:** 2. **Opened:** 1994. **Architect:** Gordon Cunningham. **Season:** Year-round. **High:** July-Aug. **To obtain tee times:** Call up to 14 days in advance. **Miscellaneous:** Reduced fees (weekdays, low season, twilight, seniors, juniors), club rentals, credit cards (MC, V, AE, D), beginner friendly (junior program, lessons).
Reader Comments: Excellent ... Every hole is different ... Interesting layout and elevation changes ... Good variety of holes ... Fun course ... Always a pleasant experience ... What a great course ... Never get tired of playing it ... Good mix of holes ... Beautiful back nine ... Breathtaking.

★★★★ PRAIRIE LANDING GOLF CLUB *Condition*
PU-2325 Longest Dr., West Chicago, 60165, Du Page County, (630)208-7600, 30 miles W of Chicago. **Web:** www.prairielanding.com.
Holes: 18. **Yards:** 6,862/4,859. **Par:** 72/72. **Course Rating:** 73.8/69.3. **Slope:** 131/119. **Green Fee:** $55/$87. **Cart Fee:** Included in Green Fee. **Walking Policy:** Unrestricted walking.

Walkability: 3. **Opened:** 1994. **Architect:** Robert Trent Jones, Jr. **Season:** April-Nov. **High:** May-Sept. **To obtain tee times:** Call up to 14 days in advance. **Miscellaneous:** Reduced fees (low season, twilight, juniors), metal spikes, range (grass), club rentals, credit cards (MC, V, AE, D, Diners Club).
Reader Comments: A must-play ... Impossible in the wind ... Beautiful links style ... Private-club feel ... Great practice facility ... Great course ... Extremely well designed and built ... Challenging and fair ... Oh, how the wind can blow ... Worth every penny ... Price could come down some ... Fairways are wide enough to land planes ... Pretty, natural setting.

★★★★ PRAIRIE VISTA GOLF COURSE *Value*

PM-502 Sale Barn Road, Bloomington, 61704, McLean County, (309)434-2217, 140 miles S of Chicago.
Holes: 18. **Yards:** 6,748/5,224. **Par:** 72/71. **Course Rating:** 71.8/68.9. **Slope:** 128/114. **Green Fee:** $23/$23. **Cart Fee:** $10/person. **Walking Policy:** Unrestricted walking. **Walkability:** 3.
Opened: 1991. **Architect:** Roger B. Packard. **Season:** March-Nov. **High:** May-Aug. **To obtain tee times:** Call up to 7 days in advance. **Miscellaneous:** Reduced fees (twilight, seniors, juniors), range (grass/mats), club rentals, credit cards (MC, V).
Reader Comments: Excellent course ... I just wish it were closer to home ... Windy; really fun ... Good design for what they have ... Good value ... Great people ... Wow! What a place! ... A bargain ... Enjoyed it.

★★★★ PRAIRIEVIEW GOLF COURSE

PM-7993 N. River Rd., Byron, 61010, Ogle County, (815)234-4653, 12 miles SW of Rockford. **Web:** www.prairieview.com.
Holes: 18. **Yards:** 7,117/5,269. **Par:** 72/72. **Course Rating:** 72.3/71.6. **Slope:** 123/117. **Green Fee:** $22/$28. **Cart Fee:** $24/cart. **Walking Policy:** Unrestricted walking. **Walkability:** 4.
Opened: 1992. **Architect:** William James Spear. **Season:** March-Nov. **High:** June-Aug. **To obtain tee times:** Call up to 7 days in advance. **Miscellaneous:** Reduced fees (weekdays, low season, twilight, seniors, juniors), range (grass/mats), club rentals, credit cards (MC, V).
Reader Comments: Great greens ... A neat course with several excellent holes ... A sleeper ... Easy to get on ... Fantastic bent-grass fairways ... New clubhouse ... Spending money.

★½ PRESTBURY COUNTRY CLUB

PU-Golfview & Hankes, Sugar Grove, 60554, Kane County, (630)466-4177.
Yards: 5,516/4,651. **Par:** 69/69. **Course Rating:** 65.1/64.9. **Slope:** 106/110. **Green Fee:** $16/$26. **Cart Fee:** $26/cart. **Walking Policy:** Unrestricted walking. **Walkability:** 1. **Season:** March-Sept. **High:** May-Aug. **Miscellaneous:** Reduced fees (weekdays, twilight, seniors, juniors), metal spikes, club rentals, credit cards (MC, V), beginner friendly.

★★★ QUAIL MEADOWS GOLF COURSE

PU-2215 Centennial Dr., Washington, 61571, Tazewell County, (309)694-3139, 5 miles E of washington. **E-mail:** quailtom@worldnet.att.net.
Holes: 18. **Yards:** 6,647/5,492. **Par:** 72/72. **Course Rating:** 71.3/71.6. **Slope:** 121/117. **Green Fee:** N/A/$15. **Cart Fee:** $17/cart. **Walking Policy:** Unrestricted walking. **Walkability:** 2.
Opened: 1972. **Season:** Year-round. **High:** May-Sept. **To obtain tee times:** Call up to 7 days in advance. **Miscellaneous:** Reduced fees (twilight, seniors, juniors), metal spikes, range (grass), club rentals, credit cards (MC, V).
Reader Comments: Much improved the past two years ... Some tough holes ... Would like to see them add a few bunkers ... Shot my best round ever on this course.

★★★★ THE RAIL GOLF CLUB

PU-1400 South Clubhouse Drive, Springfield, 62707, Sangamon County, (217)525-0365, 100 miles N of St. Louis. **Web:** www.fginet/herail/.
Holes: 18. **Yards:** 6,583/5,406. **Par:** 72/72. **Course Rating:** 71.1/70.6. **Slope:** 120/116. **Green Fee:** $30/$38. **Cart Fee:** $12/person. **Walking Policy:** Unrestricted walking. **Walkability:** 2.
Opened: 1968. **Architect:** Robert Trent Jones. **Season:** March-Dec. **High:** May-Sept. **To obtain tee times:** Call up to 10 days in advance. **Miscellaneous:** Reduced fees (weekdays, seniors, juniors), range (grass), club rentals, credit cards (MC, V, AE).
Notes: LPGA State Farm Rail Classic.
Reader Comments: LPGA stop is well-maintained ... Wide open ... Trees are finally maturing ... Nice challenge ... A bit costly ... Flagstick locations can be a little hard to figure ... Nice golf shop ... A relaxing day until one has to putt ... Lots of sand ... Fair test ... Back 9 is like stepping into the wilderness ... Huge driving range.

★★★★ RAILSIDE GOLF CLUB *Value, Pace*

PU-120 W. 19th St., Gibson City, 60936, Ford County, (217)784-5000, 25 miles E of Bloomington. **E-mail:** golf@railside.com. **Web:** www.railside.com.
Holes: 18. **Yards:** 6,801/5,367. **Par:** 72/72. **Course Rating:** 71.8/70.2. **Slope:** 122/115. **Green Fee:** $12/$21. **Cart Fee:** $11/person. **Walking Policy:** Unrestricted walking. **Walkability:** 2.
Opened: 1993. **Architect:** Paul Loague. **Season:** Year-round. **High:** May-Sept. **To obtain tee

times: Call up to 5 days in advance. **Miscellaneous:** Reduced fees (weekdays, low season, twilight, seniors, juniors), discount packages, metal spikes, range (grass), club rentals, credit cards (MC, V, AE, D).
Reader Comments: Very playable links-style course ... Windy ... Course plays long ... Not a flat green on the course ... Tough greens are slick ... Very nice course.

★★★½ RANDALL OAKS GOLF CLUB

PU-37 W. 361 Binnie Rd., Dundee, 60118, Kane County, (847)428-5661, 35 miles NW of Chicago.
Holes: 18. **Yards:** 6,208/5,379. **Par:** 71/71. **Course Rating:** 70.4/71.3. **Slope:** 118/119. **Green Fee:** $17/$29. **Cart Fee:** $14/person. **Walking Policy:** Unrestricted walking. **Walkability:** 3. **Opened:** 1966. **Architect:** William James Spears. **Season:** April-Nov. **High:** June-Aug. **To obtain tee times:** Call 7 days in advance. **Miscellaneous:** Reduced fees (weekdays, twilight, seniors, juniors), range (grass), club rentals, credit cards (MC, V, D).
Reader Comments: Good course ... Lots of dogleg rights; great for the slicer ... Has made improvements ... Fun to play ... Great for the money ... Wonderful place for small learners.

★★ RED HAWK COUNTRY CLUB

SP-Route 154, Tamaroa, 62888, Perry County, (618)357-9704.
Holes: 18. **Yards:** 6,111/4,343. **Par:** 70/71. **Course Rating:** 69.5/68.0. **Slope:** 111/97. **Green Fee:** $15/$20. **Cart Fee:** $10/person. **Walking Policy:** Unrestricted walking. **Walkability:** 3. **Opened:** 1921. **Season:** Year-round. **High:** May-Oct. **To obtain tee times:** Call. **Miscellaneous:** Reduced fees (low season), discount packages, range (grass), caddies, club rentals, credit cards (MC, V), beginner friendly (junior program).
Special Notes: Formerly Perry County Country Club.

★★★★ REDTAIL GOLF CLUB

PU-7900 Redtail Dr., Lakewood, 60014, McHenry County, (815)477-0055, 30 miles NW of Chicago. **Web:** www.redtailgolf.com.
Holes: 18. **Yards:** 6,902/5,455. **Par:** 72/72. **Course Rating:** 72.1/70.3. **Slope:** 123/116. **Green Fee:** $39/$59. **Cart Fee:** Included in Green Fee. **Walking Policy:** Walking at certain times. **Walkability:** 3. **Opened:** 1991. **Season:** March-Nov. **High:** June-Aug. **To obtain tee times:** Call up to 7 days in advance. Must reserve with credit card for weekend. **Miscellaneous:** Reduced fees (weekdays, low season, twilight, seniors, juniors), range (grass), club rentals, credit cards (MC, V, AE).
Reader Comments: Nice course ... Always fun ... Bring your straight game ... Wonderful ... Will get better every year.

REND LAKE GOLF COURSE

PU-12476 Golf Course Dr., Whittington, 62897, Franklin County, (618)629-2353, 90 miles SE of St. Louis. **E-mail:** rlgc@midwest.net.
Holes: 27. **Green Fee:** $22/$26. **Cart Fee:** $10/person. **Walking Policy:** Walking at certain times. **Walkability:** 3. **Opened:** 1975. **Architect:** Edward Lawrence Packard. **Season:** March-Nov. **High:** May-Oct. **To obtain tee times:** Call golf shop. **Miscellaneous:** Reduced fees (weekdays, twilight, seniors), discount packages, range (grass/mats), club rentals, lodging (48 rooms), credit cards (MC, V, AE).
★★★★ EAST/SOUTH
Yards: 6,861/5,830. **Par:** 72/72. **Course Rating:** 72.2/72.5. **Slope:** 130/116.
Reader Comments: I was driving in the middle of nowhere when I saw a water tower designed as a golf ball. Now I make it a point to go whenever I'm within 50 miles ... Great test ... Resort-type setting ... Very wet in the spring.
★★★★ EAST/WEST
Yards: 6,812/5,849. **Par:** 72/72. **Course Rating:** 71.8/72.6. **Slope:** 131/116.
★★★★ WEST/SOUTH
Yards: 6,835/5,861. **Par:** 72/72. **Course Rating:** 73.0/72.6. **Slope:** 133/116.

★★★½ RENWOOD COUNTRY CLUB

PM-1413 Hainesville Rd., Round Lake Beach, 60073, Lake County, (847)546-8242, 50 miles N of Chicago.
Holes: 18. **Yards:** 6,048/5,584. **Par:** 72/72. **Course Rating:** 68.6/71.5. **Slope:** 116/118. **Green Fee:** $10/$28. **Cart Fee:** $12/person. **Walking Policy:** Unrestricted walking. **Walkability:** 1. **Opened:** 1920. **Season:** April-Nov. **High:** May-Sept. **To obtain tee times:** Call up to 5 days in advance with credit card to guarantee. **Miscellaneous:** Reduced fees (weekdays, low season, twilight, seniors, juniors), metal spikes, range (mats), club rentals, credit cards (MC, V, D).
Reader Comments: Narrow and short ... A lot of water ... No frills ... A lot of beginners.

★★★ RIVER OAKS GOLF COURSE

PU-1 Park Ave., Calumet City, 60409, Cook County, (708)366-9466, 3 miles S of Chicago.
Holes: 18. **Yards:** 5,863/5,457. **Par:** 72/72. **Course Rating:** 68.6/73.6. **Slope:** 115/123. **Green Fee:** $6/$19. **Cart Fee:** $20/cart. **Walking Policy:** Unrestricted walking. **Walkability:** 2. **Opened:**

ILLINOIS

1976. **Season:** April-Nov. **High:** June-Aug. **Miscellaneous:** Reduced fees (weekdays, twilight, seniors, juniors), metal spikes, club rentals, credit cards (MC, V, AE, D), beginner friendly.
Reader Comments: Cheap and nice ... Great value.

★★★½ ROLLING HILLS GOLF COURSE *Value*
PU-5801 Pierce Lane, Godfrey, 62035, Madison County, (618)466-8363, 15 miles SE of St. Louis. **E-mail:** rollinhills@piasrnet.com.
Holes: 18. **Yards:** 5,687/4,814. **Par:** 71/71. **Course Rating:** 66.1/66.5. **Slope:** 100/101. **Green Fee:** $16/$18. **Cart Fee:** $10/person. **Walking Policy:** Unrestricted walking. **Walkability:** 3.
Opened: 1964. **Season:** Year-round. **High:** April-Sept. **To obtain tee times:** Call up to 7 days in advance between 6 a.m. and 6 p.m. in season. **Miscellaneous:** Reduced fees (low season, twilight, seniors, juniors), discount packages, range (grass), club rentals, credit cards (MC, V, AE, D, Diners Club).
Reader Comments: Junior rates are fantastic; good course for price ... Nothing special, but always in shape ... Friendly staff ... Scenic and challenging .... Too short.

★★★½ RUFFLED FEATHERS GOLF CLUB
SP-1 Pete Dye Dr., Lemont, 60439, Cook County, (630)257-1000, 20 miles SW of Chicago.
Holes: 18. **Yards:** 6,878/5,273. **Par:** 72/72. **Course Rating:** 73.1/65.7. **Slope:** 134/110. **Green Fee:** $50/$120. **Cart Fee:** Included in Green Fee. **Walking Policy:** Unrestricted walking.
Walkability: N/A. **Opened:** 1992. **Architect:** Pete Dye/P. B. Dye. **Season:** March-Nov. **High:** April-Oct. **To obtain tee times:** Tee times per foursomes only 7 days in advance. Golf events (12 or more players) call any time. **Miscellaneous:** Reduced fees (weekdays, low season, twilight), range (grass/mats), club rentals, credit cards (MC, V, AE).
Notes: Ranked 23rd in 1999 Best in State.
Reader Comments: I'm a true fan ... Too many blind shots ... Tough to read greens ... Beautiful layout ... Bring balls ... Overpriced for what you get ... Slice of heaven ... Too many forced carries ... Good hot dogs ... Course has everything ... Tough but fair ... Never again ... Doesn't get enough recognition ... Personal favorite.

ST. ANDREWS GOLF & COUNTRY CLUB
PU-3N441 Rte. 59, West Chicago, 60185, Du Page County, (630)231-3100, 30 miles W of Chicago.
★★★★ LAKEWOOD COURSE
Holes: 18. **Yards:** 6,666/5,353. **Par:** 72/72. **Course Rating:** 70.9/69.4. **Slope:** 115/112. **Green Fee:** $30/$35. **Cart Fee:** $29/person. **Walking Policy:** Unrestricted walking. **Walkability:** 1.
Opened: 1926. **Architect:** E. D. Dearie Jr. **Season:** Year-round. **High:** May-Sept. **To obtain tee times:** For weekdays call 6 days before day desired; for weekends call on Monday before the weekend. During season players may obtain a guaranteed foursome time for a fee of $140 (on the weekends before 12:00). **Miscellaneous:** Reduced fees (weekdays, low season, twilight, juniors), range (grass/mats), club rentals, credit cards (MC, V, D).
Reader Comments: Course plays welll ... Great practice facility ... Can't beat it ... Great old oak trees ... Great clubhouse with good food ... Painfully slow on weekend afternoons ... High-volume ... Just about only game around during winter.
★★★★ ST. ANDREWS COURSE
Holes: 18. **Yards:** 6,759/5,138. **Par:** 71/71. **Course Rating:** 71.1/67.9. **Slope:** 116/108. **Green Fee:** $30/$35. **Cart Fee:** $29/person. **Walking Policy:** Unrestricted walking. **Walkability:** 1.
Opened: 1926. **Architect:** John McGregor. **Season:** Year-round. **High:** May-Sept. **To obtain tee times:** For weekdays call 6 days before day desired. For the weekend, call on Monday before the weekend. During the season player may obtain a guaranteed 4-some tee time for $140.00 (weekends before 12:00). **Miscellaneous:** Reduced fees (weekdays, low season, twilight, juniors), range (grass/mats), club rentals, credit cards (MC, V, D).
Reader Comments: Solid, well-kept Joe Jemsek course ... Good golf ... Not much to criticize, because I keep coming here to play ... Good place to play ... Great lessons; good instructors ... Greens were immaculate in winter.

SALINE COUNTY GOLF & COUNTRY CLUB
355 Golf Course Rd., Eldorado, 62930, Saline County, (618)273-9002.
Special Notes: Call club for further information.

★★★ THE SANCTUARY GOLF COURSE
PU-485 N. Marley Rd., New Lenox, 60451, Will County, (815)462-4653, 35 miles S of Chicago.
Holes: 18. **Yards:** 6,701/5,120. **Par:** 72/72. **Course Rating:** 72.1/69.1. **Slope:** 122/114. **Green Fee:** $25/$33. **Cart Fee:** $12/person. **Walking Policy:** Unrestricted walking. **Walkability:** 2.
Opened: 1996. **Architect:** Steve Halberg. **Season:** March-Nov. **High:** June-Sept. **To obtain tee times:** Call 7 days in advance. **Miscellaneous:** Reduced fees (weekdays, low season, twilight, seniors, juniors), range (grass/mats), club rentals, credit cards (MC, V, AE, D).
Reader Comments: Up-and-coming new course ... Good contrasts, from very open to very tight ... North Carolina in Illinois ... Dramatic elevation changes ... Round took more than six hours.

★★★½ SANDY HOLLOW GOLF COURSE

PU-2500 Sandy Hollow Rd., Rockford, 61109, Winnebago County, (815)987-8836, 70 miles NW of Chicago.

Holes: 18. **Yards:** 6,228/5,883. **Par:** 71/76. **Course Rating:** 69.4/72.8. **Slope:** 115/120. **Green Fee:** $16/$21. **Cart Fee:** $22/. **Walking Policy:** Unrestricted walking. **Walkability:** 3. **Opened:** 1930. **Architect:** Charles Dudley Wagstaff. **Season:** April-Oct. **High:** June-Aug. **To obtain tee times:** Call 7 days in advance for weekend & holidays. **Miscellaneous:** Reduced fees (low season, twilight), club rentals, credit cards (MC, V, D).

Reader Comments: Great course, but pace is slow ... A lot of fairway and greenside bunkers ... Heavily played ... Requires accurate drives and approach shots.

★★ SAUKIE GOLF CLUB

PM-3101 38th St., Rock Island, 61201, Rock Island County, (309) 732-2278, 2 miles of Rock Island. **E-mail:** wcdapro@pga.com.

Holes: 18. **Yards:** 5,186/4,496. **Par:** 66/66. **Course Rating:** N/A. **Slope:** N/A. **Green Fee:** $14/$16. **Cart Fee:** $20/cart. **Walking Policy:** Unrestricted walking. **Walkability:** 4. **Opened:** 1926. **Season:** Year-round. **High:** May-Aug. **To obtain tee times:** Call 7 days in advance. **Miscellaneous:** Reduced fees (twilight, seniors, juniors), discount packages, metal spikes, club rentals, credit cards (MC, V), beginner friendly.

★★★½ SCHAUMBURG GOLF CLUB

PU-401 N. Roselle Rd., Schaumburg, 60194, Cook County, (847)885-9000, 30 miles W of Chicago.

Holes: 27. **Yards:** 6,542/4,885. **Par:** 72/72. **Course Rating:** 70.7/67.5. **Slope:** 121/114. **Green Fee:** $33/$38. **Cart Fee:** $14/person. **Walking Policy:** Unrestricted walking. **Walkability:** 3. **Opened:** 1926. **Architect:** Robert Lohmann. **Season:** April-Dec. **High:** June-Aug. **To obtain tee times:** Call 7 days in advance. You can call Sunday for the following Sunday. Course Closed on Mondays till 11:00 am. Tuesday Thursday Sunday 6: till dark. **Miscellaneous:** Reduced fees (weekdays, twilight, seniors, juniors), range (grass), club rentals, credit cards (MC, V, AE, D).

NReader Comments: Renovations are filling in nicely ... New 9 is great ... Not a tree anywhere ... A real pleasure ... Hidden gem ... A really good course now ... Good value ... Love the new 9 ... A sleeper.

★★★½ SCOVILL GOLF CLUB

PU-3909 West Main St., Decatur, 62522, Macon County, (217)429-6243, 120 miles N of St. Louis.

Holes: 18. **Yards:** 5,900/4,303. **Par:** 71/71. **Course Rating:** 67.8/64.8. **Slope:** 119/108. **Green Fee:** $12/$15. **Cart Fee:** $16/cart. **Walking Policy:** Unrestricted walking. **Walkability:** 5. **Opened:** 1925. **Architect:** Dick Nugent. **Season:** Year-round. **High:** May-Aug. **To obtain tee times:** Call up to 7 days in advance for weekdays. Call on Monday for upcoming weekend or holiday. **Miscellaneous:** Metal spikes, range (grass/mats), club rentals, credit cards (MC, V).

Reader Comments: Hilly course ... Very hard course to walk ... Short, but you better be straight ... Scenic; plays pretty slow.

★★★½ SENICA OAK RIDGE GOLF CLUB

SP-658 E. Rte. 6, La Salle, 61301, La Salle County, (815)223-7273, 90 miles SW of Chicago.

Holes: 18. **Yards:** 6,900/5,397. **Par:** 72/72. **Course Rating:** 72.6/70.3. **Slope:** 131/120. **Green Fee:** $20/$36. **Cart Fee:** $12/person. **Walking Policy:** Walking at certain times. **Walkability:** 4. **Opened:** 1994. **Architect:** William James Spear. **Season:** Year-round. **High:** June-Sept. **To obtain tee times:** Call anytime. **Miscellaneous:** Reduced fees (weekdays, low season, seniors), metal spikes, range (grass/mats), club rentals, credit cards (MC, V, D).

Reader Comments: New; needs some work ... Needs more trees ... Good test.

★★★ SETTLER'S HILL GOLF COURSE

919 E. Fabyan Pkwy., Batavia, 60510, Kane County, (630)232-1636.

Holes: 18. **Yards:** 6,630/4,945. **Par:** 72/72. **Course Rating:** 72.1/68.9. **Slope:** 130/120. **Green Fee:** $20/$32. **Cart Fee:** $13/person. **Walking Policy:** Unrestricted walking. **Walkability:** 4. **Opened:** 1988. **Architect:** Bob Lohmann. **Season:** March-Dec. **High:** June-Aug. **To obtain tee times:** 7 days in advance. **Miscellaneous:** Reduced fees (twilight, seniors, juniors), range (grass), credit cards (MC, V, AE, D).

Reader Comments: Good challenge built on landfill ... Above average ... Bring lots of balls ... Crowded ... Fair ... Every shot in the bag is needed.

★★★½ SEVEN BRIDGES GOLF CLUB

PU-One Mulligan Dr., Woodridge, 60517, Du Page County, (630)964-7777, 25 miles W of Chicago. **Web:** www.sevenbridges.com.

Holes: 18. **Yards:** 7,118/5,277. **Par:** 72/72. **Course Rating:** 74.6/70.4. **Slope:** 135/121. **Green Fee:** $45/$95. **Cart Fee:** Included in Green Fee. **Walking Policy:** Unrestricted walking. **Walkability:** 3. **Opened:** 1991. **Architect:** Dick Nugent. **Season:** April-Nov. **High:** May-Oct. **To**

obtain tee times: Call 14 days in advance. **Miscellaneous:** Reduced fees (low season, twilight), metal spikes, range (grass/mats), caddies, club rentals, credit cards (MC, V, AE, Diners Club).
Reader Comments: Beautiful front 9; the back should be played with floating balls ... Lot of blind shots ... Beautiful ... Expensive, but I love to play it ... Like playing a country club ... Lovely veranda overlooking the course ... Hit it long and straight.

SILVER LAKE COUNTRY CLUB
PU-147th St. and 82nd Ave., Orland Park, 60462, Cook County, (708)349-6940, (800)525-3465, 22 miles SW of Chicago.

★★★ NORTH COURSE
Holes: 18. **Yards:** 6,826/5,659. **Par:** 72/77. **Course Rating:** 71.9/71.5. **Slope:** 116/116. **Green Fee:** $29/$35. **Cart Fee:** $14/person. **Walking Policy:** Unrestricted walking. **Walkability:** 2.
Opened: 1927. **Architect:** Lenoard Macomber. **Season:** March-Jan. **High:** April-Oct. **To obtain tee times:** Tee time may be made by phone (708-833-8463) up to 14 days in advance.
Miscellaneous: Reduced fees (weekdays, low season, twilight, seniors, juniors), metal spikes, club rentals, credit cards (MC, V, AE, D).
Reader Comments: Nice layout ... Variety of holes ... Nice clubhouse ... Challenging ... Friendly people ... Some interesting par 4s.
Special Notes: Also has 9-hole par-29 course called Rolling Hills.

★★★½ SOUTH COURSE
Holes: 18. **Yards:** 5,948/5,138. **Par:** 70/72. **Course Rating:** 67.9/69.3. **Slope:** 108/109. **Green Fee:** $29/$35. **Cart Fee:** $14/person. **Walking Policy:** Unrestricted walking. **Walkability:** 2.
Opened: 1929. **Architect:** Raymond Didier. **Season:** March-Jan. **High:** April-Oct. **To obtain tee times:** Tee time may be made by phone (708-833-8463) up to 14 days in advance.
Miscellaneous: Reduced fees (weekdays, low season, twilight, seniors, juniors), metal spikes, club rentals, credit cards (MC, V, AE, D).
Reader Comments: More sporty than North Course ... Need to think ... In good shape.

★★★½ SILVER RIDGE GOLF COURSE
SP-3069 N. Hill Rd., Oregon, 61061, Ogle County, (815)734-4440, (800)762-6301, 2 miles N of Oregon.
Holes: 18. **Yards:** 6,614/5,181. **Par:** 72/72. **Course Rating:** 71.2/72.0. **Slope:** 116/106. **Green Fee:** $19/$23. **Cart Fee:** $11/person. **Walking Policy:** Walking at certain times. **Walkability:** 5.
Season: Year-round. **High:** May-Sept. **To obtain tee times:** Call golf shop up to 7 days in advance. **Miscellaneous:** Reduced fees (twilight, seniors, juniors), range (grass), club rentals, credit cards (MC, V, D).
Reader Comments: Older course with beautiful views ... Sporty layout ... Average challenge for average golfers ... Front nine is narrow; back nine is more open ... Peaceful setting ... Panoramic views ... Wildlife abundant.

★★½ SNAG CREEK GOLF COURSE
PU-RR 1, Washburn, 61570, Woodford County, (309)248-7300, (309)248-7300, 25 miles NE of Peoria. **E-mail:** golfsnag@mtco.com.
Holes: 18. **Yards:** 6,300/5,635. **Par:** 72/73. **Course Rating:** 7031.0/70.9. **Slope:** 115/116.
Green Fee: $9/$13. **Cart Fee:** $9/person. **Walking Policy:** Unrestricted walking. **Walkability:** 2.
Opened: 1965. **Season:** March-Oct. **High:** May-Aug. **To obtain tee times:** Call up to 7 days in advance. **Miscellaneous:** Metal spikes, credit cards (MC, V).
Reader Comments: Good test ... No range ... Par 5s are too easy.

★★½ SOUTH SHORE GOLF COURSE
PU-1727 N. River South Rd., Momence, 60954, Kankakee County, (815)472-4407, 7 miles E of Kankakee.
Holes: 18. **Yards:** 6,174/5,439. **Par:** 72/72. **Course Rating:** 68.9/70.2. **Slope:** 122/115. **Green Fee:** $10/$20. **Cart Fee:** $22/person. **Walking Policy:** Unrestricted walking. **Walkability:** 2.
Opened: 1927. **Season:** Year-round. **High:** April-Nov. **To obtain tee times:** Call golf shop.
Miscellaneous: Reduced fees (weekdays, twilight, seniors), metal spikes, range (grass), credit cards (MC, V).
Reader Comments: Fun place to play ... Good management.

★★★½ SPARTAN MEADOWS GOLF CLUB
PU-1969 Spartan, Elgin, 60123, Kane County, (847)931-5950, 40 miles W of Chicago.
Holes: 18. **Yards:** 6,853/5,353. **Par:** 72/72. **Course Rating:** 72.7/70.3. **Slope:** 123/116. **Green Fee:** $19/$29. **Cart Fee:** $24/cart. **Walking Policy:** Unrestricted walking. **Walkability:** 1.
Opened: 1971. **Architect:** Edward Lawrence Packard/Greg Bayor. **Season:** April-Nov. **High:** May-Sept. **To obtain tee times:** Call 7 days in advance. **Miscellaneous:** Reduced fees (weekdays, low season, twilight, seniors, juniors), discount packages, club rentals, credit cards (MC, V, D), beginner friendly (junior golf week, fore ladies only programs).
Reader Comments: Good overall value ... Open, but nice layout ... Some interesting holes.

ILLINOIS

★★★★½ SPENCER T. OLIN COMMUNITY GOLF COURSE *Condition*
PU-4701 College Ave., Alton, 62002, Madison County, (618)465-3111, 25 miles NE of St. Louis.
Holes: 18. **Yards:** 6,941/5,049. **Par:** 72/72. **Course Rating:** 73.8/68.5. **Slope:** 135/117. **Green Fee:** $28/$55. **Cart Fee:** Included in Green Fee. **Walking Policy:** Walking at certain times. **Walkability:** 3. **Opened:** 1989. **Architect:** Arnold Palmer/Ed Seay. **Season:** Year-round. **High:** April-Oct. **To obtain tee times:** Call up to 7 days in advance with credit card to guarantee. Foursomes only accepted for weekends/holidays. **Miscellaneous:** Reduced fees (weekdays, low season, resort guests, twilight, seniors, juniors), discount packages, metal spikes, range (grass), club rentals, credit cards (MC, V, AE), beginner friendly.
Notes: 1996, 1999 USGA Public Links Championship.
Reader Comments: Beautiful ....Has it all: Woods, hills, water ... Very nice facility ... Very well-manicured ... Pleasure to play ... Always a challenge ... My favorite Illinois course ... They make you feel important ... Love this course ... Great variety and staffing ... Playable but challenging.

★★★½ SPORTSMAN'S COUNTRY CLUB
PM-3535 Dundee Rd., Northbrook, 60062, Cook County, (847)291-2351, 2 miles N of Deerfield.
Holes: 27. **Yards:** 6,354/5,470. **Par:** 70/72. **Course Rating:** 70.7/71.9. **Slope:** 124/122. **Green Fee:** $33/$38. **Cart Fee:** $31/cart. **Walking Policy:** Unrestricted walking. **Walkability:** 3. **Opened:** 1931. **Architect:** Edward B. Dearie Jr. **Season:** March-Nov. **High:** June-Aug. **To obtain tee times:** Call 2 days in advance. **Miscellaneous:** Club rentals, credit cards (MC, V, AE), beginner friendly (clinics).
Reader Comments: Nice value if you're a resident ... Ego boost ... Good municipal.

★★½ SPRING CREEK GOLF COURSE
PU-RR 1 Box 386, Spring Valley, 61362, Bureau County, (815)894-2137, 60 miles N of Peoria.
Holes: 18. **Yards:** 6,465/5,196. **Par:** 72/73. **Course Rating:** 71.6/70.9. **Slope:** 125/120. **Green Fee:** $15/$18. **Cart Fee:** $20/cart. **Walking Policy:** Unrestricted walking. **Walkability:** 4. **Opened:** 1964. **Season:** April-Nov. **High:** May-Aug. **To obtain tee times:** Tee times not required. First come, first served. Outings of more than 20 players require reservations. **Miscellaneous:** Reduced fees (weekdays), metal spikes, range (grass), club rentals.
Reader Comments: Excellent conditions and friendly atmosphere ... Workingman's golf.

★★★ SPRINGBROOK GOLF COURSE
PU-2220 83rd St., Naperville, 60564, Du Page County, (630)420-4215, 28 miles SW of Chicago.
Holes: 18. **Yards:** 6,896/5,850. **Par:** 72/73. **Course Rating:** 72.6/72.7. **Slope:** 124/125. **Green Fee:** $24/$33. **Cart Fee:** $12/person. **Walking Policy:** Unrestricted walking. **Walkability:** 3. **Opened:** 1974. **Architect:** Edward Lawrence Packard. **Season:** March-Dec. **High:** May-Aug. **To obtain tee times:** Call up to 7 days in advance after 5 p.m. **Miscellaneous:** Reduced fees (weekdays, low season, twilight, seniors, juniors), metal spikes, range (grass), club rentals, credit cards (MC, V).
Reader Comments: Good for any golfers ... Fun to play; a challenge to all ... Thoughtful design.

★★★★ STEEPLE CHASE GOLF CLUB
PM-200 N. La Vista Dr., Mundelein, 60060, Lake County, (847)949-8900, 35 miles NW of Chicago.
Holes: 18. **Yards:** 6,827/4,831. **Par:** 72/72. **Course Rating:** 73.1/68.1. **Slope:** 129/113. **Green Fee:** $24/$44. **Cart Fee:** $13/person. **Walking Policy:** Walking at certain times. **Walkability:** 3. **Opened:** 1993. **Architect:** Ken Killian. **Season:** April-Nov. **High:** May-Sept. **To obtain tee times:** Call 7 days in advance at 6 a.m.; foursomes only, credit card required. **Miscellaneous:** Reduced fees (weekdays, twilight, seniors, juniors), club rentals, credit cards (MC, V, AE, D).
Reader Comments: Excellent muny ... Closer to private than public ... A great experience ... Very neat course ... Difficult greens ... One of my favorite courses ... Good bargain ... One of my top five in the area ... Very challenging, but playable ... If only I were a resident.

★★★★ STONEWOLF GOLF CLUB
PU-1195 Stonewolf Trail, Fairview Heights, 62208, St. Claire County, (618)624-4653, (888)709-4653, 12 miles E of St. Louis. **Web:** www.fairviewheights.com/stonewolf.htm.
Holes: 18. **Yards:** 6,943/4,849. **Par:** 71/72. **Course Rating:** 74.0/67.2. **Slope:** 141/126. **Green Fee:** $46/$71. **Cart Fee:** Included in Green Fee. **Walking Policy:** Unrestricted walking. **Walkability:** 5. **Opened:** 1996. **Architect:** Jack Nicklaus. **Season:** Year-round. **High:** May-Sept. **To obtain tee times:** Call golf shop. 10 day advance tee times. **Miscellaneous:** Reduced fees (weekdays, twilight, seniors), range (grass), club rentals, credit cards (MC, V, AE).
Notes: Ranked 14th in 1999 Best in State.
Reader Comments: Great design; all Nicklaus ... Very playable; will improve with age ... Still has to mature ... Pricey, so play with discounts ... Excellent conditions and variety ... Jack, I don't get No. 17 ... Elevated greens ... First-class ... Nice once a year.

★★ STORYBROOK COUNTRY CLUB
SP-2124 W Storybrook Rd., Hanover, 61041, Jo Daviess County, (815)591-2210, 40 miles E of Dubuque.

Holes: 9. **Yards:** 6,194/5,501. **Par:** 72/75. **Course Rating:** N/A. **Slope:** N/A. **Green Fee:** $14/$16. **Cart Fee:** $18/cart. **Walking Policy:** Unrestricted walking. **Walkability:** N/A. **Opened:** 1965. **Season:** Year-round. **High:** June-Aug. **To obtain tee times:** Tee times not required. **Miscellaneous:** Metal spikes, range (grass), club rentals, credit cards (MC, V).

★★★ SUNSET VALLEY GOLF CLUB
PM-1390 Sunset Rd., Highland Park, 60035, Lake County, (847)432-7140, 20 miles N of Chicago. **E-mail:** pdhpsunset.com.
Holes: 18. **Yards:** 6,458/5,465. **Par:** 72/72. **Course Rating:** 70.5/71.6. **Slope:** 121/119. **Green Fee:** N/A. **Cart Fee:** $12/. **Walking Policy:** Unrestricted walking. **Walkability:** N/A. **Opened:** 1922. **Architect:** Bob Lohman. **Season:** March-Nov. **High:** March-Aug. **To obtain tee times:** Tee times can be reserved for threesomes or foursomes. Call 30 days in advance with credit card to guarantee. **Miscellaneous:** Reduced fees (weekdays, low season, twilight, seniors, juniors), metal spikes, club rentals, credit cards (MC, V).
Reader Comments: I grew up on this course... Fun ... Busy ... Will go back many more times ... Open all year.

SYCAMORE GOLF CLUB
PM-940 E. State Street, Sycamore, 60178, De Kalb County, (815)895-3884, 50 miles W of Chicago.
Holes: 18. **Yards:** 6,213/5,364. **Par:** 71/72. **Course Rating:** 67.7/69.9. **Slope:** 116/118. **Green Fee:** $24/$28. **Cart Fee:** $12/person. **Walking Policy:** Unrestricted walking. **Walkability:** 1. **Opened:** 1923. **Season:** March-Nov. **High:** May-Aug. **To obtain tee times:** Call up to 7 days in advance. **Miscellaneous:** Reduced fees (low season, twilight), club rentals, credit cards (MC, V), beginner friendly (adult and junior lessons available).
Special Notes: Formerly known as Sycamore Community Golf Course.

★★ SYCAMORE HILLS GOLF CLUB
SP-928 Clinton Rd., Paris, 61944, Edgar County, (217)465-4031, 120 miles W of Indianapolis, IN. **E-mail:** boiler@tigerpaw.com. **Web:** wwwl.tigerpaw/sycamore.
Holes: 18. **Yards:** 6,589/5,222. **Par:** 72/72. **Course Rating:** 72.2/70.6. **Slope:** 124/117. **Green Fee:** $15/$20. **Cart Fee:** $10/person. **Walking Policy:** Unrestricted walking. **Walkability:** 4. **Opened:** 1927. **Season:** Year-round. **High:** May-Aug. **To obtain tee times:** Call anytime for availability. **Miscellaneous:** Reduced fees (weekdays, low season), range (grass), credit cards (MC, V, D).

★★★½ TAMARACK COUNTRY CLUB
PU-800 Tamarack Lane, O'Fallon, 62269, St. Clair County, (618)632-6666, 20 miles E of St. Louis, MO. **E-mail:** tamarackgc@yahoo.com.
Holes: 18. **Yards:** 6,901/5,124. **Par:** 71/74. **Course Rating:** 74.2/67.7. **Slope:** 106/104. **Green Fee:** $19/$22. **Cart Fee:** $10/person. **Walking Policy:** Unrestricted walking. **Walkability:** 1. **Opened:** 1965. **Architect:** Pete Dye. **Season:** Year-round. **High:** April-Sept. **To obtain tee times:** Call 7 days in advance. **Miscellaneous:** Metal spikes, range (grass), club rentals, credit cards (MC, V).
Reader Comments: Easy layout; could play here forever ... Easier and more enjoyable than most courses ... Short ... Pete Dye layout with beautiful greens.

★★★½ TAMARACK GOLF CLUB
SP-24032 Royal Worlington Dr., Naperville, 60564, Will County, (630)904-4000, 20 miles SW of Chicago. **E-mail:** tamarackgc@yahoo.com.
Holes: 18. **Yards:** 6,901/5,016. **Par:** 70/70. **Course Rating:** 74.2/68.8. **Slope:** 131/114. **Green Fee:** $30/$65. **Cart Fee:** Included in Green Fee. **Walking Policy:** Mandatory cart. **Walkability:** 2. **Opened:** 1989. **Architect:** David Gill. **Season:** March-Nov. **High:** June-Sept. **To obtain tee times:** Call 7 days in advance; credit card number needed to reserve tee time. Foursomes only on weekends. **Miscellaneous:** Reduced fees (weekdays, low season, twilight), metal spikes, club rentals, credit cards (MC, V, AE), beginner friendly.
Reader Comments: Water, water everywhere ... Good links ... Lots of wind ... I lost my partner in the rough ... Fun and tough ... Plays fast; I've gotten around in under four hours ... Easy to get on ... Far from me, but worth the trip ... Welcome to water world!

★★ THUNDERBIRD COUNTRY CLUB
SP-1010 E. Northwest Hwy., Barrington, 60010, Cook County, (847)381-6500, 15 miles NW of Chicago.
Holes: 18. **Yards:** 6,169/5,155. **Par:** 71/72. **Course Rating:** 69.6/70.3. **Slope:** 115/117. **Green Fee:** $20/$27. **Cart Fee:** $12. **Walking Policy:** Unrestricted walking. **Walkability:** N/A. **Opened:** 1958. **Season:** Year-round. **High:** May-Sept. **To obtain tee times:** Call Monday at 8:00 a.m. for Tuesday-Sunday play. Call Sunday at 3:00 p.m. for Monday play. **Miscellaneous:** Reduced fees (low season, seniors), metal spikes, range (grass), club rentals, credit cards (MC, V).

ILLINOIS

★★★½ TIMBER TRAILS COUNTRY CLUB
PU-11350 Plainfield Rd., La Grange, 60525, Cook County, (708)246-0275, 20 miles W of Chicago.
Holes: 18. **Yards:** 6,197/5,581. **Par:** 71/73. **Course Rating:** 68.7/71.1. **Slope:** 113/116. **Green Fee:** $33/$44. **Cart Fee:** $30/person. **Walking Policy:** Unrestricted walking. **Walkability:** 3. **Opened:** 1934. **Architect:** Robert Bruce Harris. **Season:** March-Dec. **High:** May-Oct. **To obtain tee times:** Reservations accepted for foursomes, threesomes, twosomes up to 7 days in advance with credit card for guarantee. **Miscellaneous:** Reduced fees (low season, twilight, seniors), metal spikes, club rentals, credit cards (MC, V).
Reader Comments: Pretty old course ... Rolling terrain ... Lots of oak trees ... Trees, trees, everywhere a tree ... Bring a chainsaw ... Active bird wildlife ... Fun place.

★½ TRIPLE LAKES GOLF COURSE
6942 Triple Lakes Rd., Millstadt, 62260, St. Clair County, (618)476-9985.
Yards: N/A. **Par:** N/A. **Course Rating:** N/A. **Slope:** N/A. **Green Fee:** N/A. **Walkability:** N/A. **Miscellaneous:** Metal spikes.

★★½ TUCKAWAY GOLF COURSE
SP-27641 Stony Island, Crete, 60417, Will County, (708)946-2259, 25 miles S of Chicago.
Holes: 18. **Yards:** 6,245/5,581. **Par:** 72/74. **Course Rating:** 68.7/72.4. **Slope:** 110/116. **Green Fee:** $32/$40. **Cart Fee:** Included in Green Fee. **Walking Policy:** Unrestricted walking. **Walkability:** 3. **Opened:** 1961. **Architect:** John Ellis. **Season:** March-Dec. **High:** June-Sept. **To obtain tee times:** Call 7 days in advance. **Miscellaneous:** Reduced fees (low season, twilight, seniors, juniors), range (grass), club rentals, credit cards (MC, V).
Reader Comments: Good ... Small greens make it interesting ... Greens tough to hit from 150 yards ... Greens hard to hold ... Hills and doglegs ... OK for a change of pace.

UNIVERSITY OF ILLINOIS GOLF CLUB
PU-800 Hartwell Dr., Savoy, 61874, Champaign County, (217)359-5613, 120 miles S of Chicago.
★★★½ BLUE COURSE
Holes: 18. **Yards:** 6,579/6,129. **Par:** 73/74. **Course Rating:** 70.4/74.1. **Slope:** 114/118. **Green Fee:** $12/$17. **Cart Fee:** $20/cart. **Walking Policy:** Unrestricted walking. **Walkability:** 1. **Opened:** 1966. **Architect:** C.W. Wagstaff. **Season:** Year-round. **High:** June-Aug. **To obtain tee times:** Call golf shop 7 days in advance. **Miscellaneous:** Reduced fees (low season, twilight, seniors), metal spikes, range (grass), club rentals, credit cards (MC, V, D).
Reader Comments: Good course to learn the game ... Good ... Heavy play ... Nice.
★★★½ ORANGE COURSE
Holes: 18. **Yards:** 6,817/5,721. **Par:** 72/76. **Course Rating:** 72.1/72.2. **Slope:** 120/121. **Green Fee:** $14/$20. **Cart Fee:** $20/. **Walking Policy:** Unrestricted walking. **Walkability:** N/A. **Opened:** 1950. **Architect:** C.W. Wagstaff. **Season:** March-Nov. **High:** June-Aug. **To obtain tee times:** Phone golf shop 7 days in advance. **Miscellaneous:** Reduced fees (low season, twilight, seniors), metal spikes, range (grass), club rentals, credit cards (MC, V, D).
Reader Comments: Good test ... A lot of fun ... Often crowded ... Take dead aim ... Golf on the farm ... Sloping greens .

★★½ URBAN HILLS COUNTRY CLUB
PU-23520 Crawford Ave., Richton Park, 60471, Will County, (708)747-0306, 20 miles S of Chicago.
Holes: 18. **Yards:** 6,650/5,266. **Par:** 71/71. **Course Rating:** 71.1/69.1. **Slope:** 114/110. **Green Fee:** $14/$27. **Cart Fee:** $23/cart. **Walking Policy:** Unrestricted walking. **Walkability:** N/A. **Opened:** 1967. **Architect:** Larry Packard. **Season:** Year-round. **High:** April-Oct. **To obtain tee times:** Call 7 days in advance. **Miscellaneous:** Reduced fees (weekdays, low season, twilight, seniors, juniors), club rentals, credit cards (MC, V).
Reader Comments: Greens were good during the height of summer ... Slower play detracts ... Flat ... Few trees ... Windy ... Relatively easy.

★★★ VILLA OLIVIA COUNTRY CLUB
PU-Rte. 20 and Naperville Rd., Bartlett, 60103, Du Page County, (630)289-1000.
Holes: 18. **Yards:** 6,165/5,546. **Par:** 73/73. **Course Rating:** N/A. **Slope:** 122/122. **Green Fee:** N/A. **Walkability:** N/A. **Architect:** Dick Nugent. **Season:** March-Nov. **High:** May-Oct. **Miscellaneous:** Reduced fees (weekdays, twilight), metal spikes, range (grass), credit cards (MC, V, D).
Reader Comments: Nice, but it needs a couple of new holes ... Worth playing ... OK ... Some challenging holes and some very different ones.

★★½ VILLAGE GREEN COUNTRY CLUB
PU-2501 N. Midlothian Rd., Mundelein, 60060, Lake County, (847)566-7373, 25 miles NW of Chicago.
Holes: 18. **Yards:** 6,235/5,600. **Par:** 70/70. **Course Rating:** 69.2/69.2. **Slope:** 115/118. **Green Fee:** $21/$28. **Cart Fee:** $28/cart. **Walking Policy:** Walking at certain times. **Walkability:** 2.

Opened: 1963. **Architect:** William B. Langford. **Season:** April-Oct. **High:** June-Aug. **To obtain tee times:** Call 7 days in advance. **Miscellaneous:** Reduced fees (weekdays, low season, twilight, seniors, juniors), discount packages, club rentals, credit cards (MC, V).
Reader Comments: A nice after-work course with some interesting holes ... Short; player-friendly ... Great for the ego, but some tough holes ... Bring a hard hat; narrow fairways ... Nice people.

★★★ VILLAGE GREENS OF WOODRIDGE
PU-1575 W. 75th St., Woodridge, 60517, Du Page County, (630)985-3610, 25 miles W of Chicago.
Holes: 18. **Yards:** 6,650/5,847. **Par:** 72/73. **Course Rating:** 71.2/72.2. **Slope:** 121/119. **Green Fee:** $24/$30. **Cart Fee:** $13/person. **Walking Policy:** Unrestricted walking. **Walkability:** 2.
Opened: 1959. **Architect:** Robert Bruce Harris. **Season:** March-Nov. **High:** May-Sept. **To obtain tee times:** Nonresidents call 7 days in advance. Credit card required. **Miscellaneous:** Reduced fees (weekdays, low season, twilight, seniors, juniors), range (grass), club rentals, credit cards (MC, V).
Reader Comments: Much improved ... Shooting gallery; hit by a golf ball 3 times ... Fairly good place in a pinch ... Heavy play.

★★★★ VILLAGE LINKS OF GLEN ELLYN
PM-485 Winchell Way, Glen Ellyn, 60137, Du Page County, (630)469-8180, 20 miles W of Chicago.
Holes: 18. **Yards:** 6,933/5,753. **Par:** 71/73. **Course Rating:** 73.6/73.3. **Slope:** 128/127. **Green Fee:** $44/$48. **Cart Fee:** $28/cart. **Walking Policy:** Unrestricted walking. **Walkability:** 2.
Opened: 1967. **Architect:** David Gill. **Season:** Year-round. **High:** May-Aug. **To obtain tee times:** Call or come in 7 days in advance. **Miscellaneous:** Reduced fees (weekdays, low season), range (grass/mats), caddies, club rentals, credit cards (MC, V, AE, D), beginner friendly (adult group lessons).
Reader Comments: Make sure your driver's working ... Tough ... Good value ... Too slow ... I play it a lot; great course ... Fairly typical muny ... Challenging and fun ... Great golf shop ... My favorite ... Good bargain ... Great deal for residents.

★★★★½ WEAVERRIDGE GOLF CLUB *Service, Condition*
PU-5100 WeaverRidge Blvd., Peoria, 61615, Peoria County, (309)691-3344. **E-mail:** weaverridge.com.
Holes: 18. **Yards:** 7,030/5,046. **Par:** 72/72. **Course Rating:** 73.1/68.9. **Slope:** 136/115. **Green Fee:** $30/$83. **Cart Fee:** $15/person. **Walking Policy:** Unrestricted walking. **Walkability:** 4. **Opened:** 1997. **Architect:** Michael Hurdzan/Dana Fry. **Season:** April-Nov. **High:** June-Sept. **To obtain tee times:** Tee times taken 2 weeks in advance. **Miscellaneous:** Reduced fees (weekdays, low season, twilight, juniors), range (grass/mats), club rentals, credit cards (MC, V).
Notes: Ranked 6th in 1999 Best in State.
Reader Comments: This is what it's all about ... Nice new course ... Very scenic ... Expensive for central Illinois ... Big, undulating greens ... Must-play ... Beautiful ... Great practice area ... Awesome ... Bring a towel, some sunscreen and your imagination for all the bunkers ... Fancy clubhouse ... If you play the correct tee boxes for your playing level, you'll have an incredible day.

★★★★ WEDGEWOOD GOLF COURSE
PU-Rte.59 and Caton Farm Rd., Joliet, 60544, Will County, (815)741-7270, 40 miles SW of Chicago.
Holes: 18. **Yards:** 6,836/5,792. **Par:** 72/72. **Course Rating:** 72.0/72.4. **Slope:** 119/123. **Green Fee:** $13/$26. **Cart Fee:** $20/person. **Walking Policy:** Unrestricted walking. **Walkability:** 3.
Opened: 1970. **Architect:** Edward Lawrence Packard. **Season:** April-Oct. **High:** June-Aug. **To obtain tee times:** Call 1 day in advance for weekday. Call Monday for upcoming weekend. **Miscellaneous:** Reduced fees (weekdays, twilight, seniors, juniors), discount packages, metal spikes, range (grass/mats), club rentals, credit cards (MC, V, D).
Reader Comments: Set in woods with many challenging holes ... A nice course ... A very pleasant surprise ... Nice course ... Greens protected by sand ... Good, sloping greens.

★★★ WESTVIEW GOLF COURSE
PU-S. 36th St., Quincy, 62301, Adams County, (217)223-7499.
Holes: 18. **Yards:** 6,400/5,898. **Par:** 71/71. **Course Rating:** 70.1/70.2. **Slope:** 116/114. **Green Fee:** $14/$24. **Cart Fee:** $10/person. **Walking Policy:** Unrestricted walking. **Walkability:** 3.
Opened: 1946. **Architect:** Scotty Glasgow. **Season:** Jan.-Dec. **High:** May-Aug. **To obtain tee times:** Call 7 days in advance. **Miscellaneous:** Reduced fees (low season, twilight), club rentals, credit cards (MC, V, D).
Reader Comments: A good public course ... Short, but nice ... Outstanding .. Crowded.

WHITE DEER RUN GOLF CLUB
PU-250 W. Gregg's Pkwy., Vernon Hills, 60061, Lake County, (847)680-6100, 25 miles N of Chicago. **Web:** www.whitedeergolf.com.

Holes: 18. **Yards:** 7,101/4,916. **Par:** 72/72. **Course Rating:** 74.6/68.4. **Slope:** 137/116. **Green Fee:** $45/$79. **Cart Fee:** Included in Green Fee. **Walking Policy:** Unrestricted walking. **Walkability:** 3. **Opened:** 1998. **Architect:** Dick Nugent/Tim Nugent. **Season:** April-Nov. **High:** May-Sept. **To obtain tee times:** Call 7 days in advance. **Miscellaneous:** Reduced fees (low season, twilight, seniors, juniors), range (grass/mats), club rentals, credit cards (MC, V, AE), beginner friendly (beginner clinics).

WHITE PINES GOLF CLUB
PM-500 W. Jefferson St., Bensenville, 60106, Du Page County, (630)766-0304 x1, 10 miles W of Chicago. **Web:** www.whitepinesgolf.com.

★★½ **EAST COURSE**
Holes: 18. **Yards:** 6,371/5,331. **Par:** 70/73. **Course Rating:** 70.2/70.3. **Slope:** 122/117. **Green Fee:** $29/$30. **Cart Fee:** $26/cart. **Walking Policy:** Unrestricted walking. **Walkability:** 2. **Opened:** 1930. **Architect:** Jack Daray. **Season:** March-Dec. **High:** May-Oct. **To obtain tee times:** Call 6 days in advance. **Miscellaneous:** Reduced fees (weekdays, low season, twilight), metal spikes, range (grass/mats), club rentals, credit cards (MC, V, AE, D, Debit Cards).
Reader Comments: Heavily played; many outings ... Too many people ... Fair ... Good muny for the money ... Seniors need a break ... Fun.

★★★ **WEST COURSE**
Holes: 18. **Yards:** 6,601/5,998. **Par:** 72/72. **Course Rating:** 71.1/73.2. **Slope:** 118/120. **Green Fee:** $29/$30. **Cart Fee:** $26/cart. **Walking Policy:** Unrestricted walking. **Walkability:** 2. **Opened:** 1930. **Architect:** Jack Daray. **Season:** March-Dec. **High:** May-Oct. **To obtain tee times:** Call 6 days in advance. **Miscellaneous:** Reduced fees (weekdays, low season, twilight), metal spikes, range (grass/mats), club rentals, credit cards (MC, V, AE, D, Debit Cards).
Reader Comments: Don't get into the trees ... Slow play ... Some challenging doglegs.

★★★ **WILLOW POND GOLF COURSE**
PU-1126 Country Club Lane, Rantoul, 61868, Champaign County, (217)893-9000, 15 miles N of Champaign.
Holes: 18. **Yards:** 6,799/6,550. **Par:** 72/72. **Course Rating:** 71.8/71.9. **Slope:** 115/114. **Green Fee:** $14/$18. **Cart Fee:** $18/cart. **Walking Policy:** Unrestricted walking. **Walkability:** 1. **Opened:** 1956. **Architect:** Edward Lawrence Packard. **Season:** March-Nov. **High:** June-Aug. **To obtain tee times:** Reservations taken for weekends only. Call on Tuesday. **Miscellaneous:** Reduced fees (twilight, seniors, juniors), range (grass/mats), rentals, credit cards (MC, V, D).
Reader Comments: Old Air Force base course with a lot of history ... Good ... Windy ... Not too difficult; very open.

★★★ **WILMETTE GOLF COURSE**
PU-3900 Fairway Dr., Wilmette, 60091, Cook County, (847)256-9777, 10 miles N of Chicago.
Holes: 18. **Yards:** 6,093/5,760. **Par:** 70/70. **Course Rating:** 69.5/73.1. **Slope:** 122/127. **Green Fee:** $26/$29. **Cart Fee:** $24. **Walking Policy:** Unrestricted walking. **Walkability:** N/A. **Opened:** 1922. **Architect:** Joseph A. Roseman. **Season:** April-Nov. **High:** June-Sept. **To obtain tee times:** Call 1 day before at 10 a.m. for weekdays and 6 days prior to weekend and holidays. **Miscellaneous:** Reduced fees (weekdays, twilight, juniors), metal spikes, range (grass), club rentals, credit cards (MC, V, D).
Reader Comments: A grand old course ... Staff makes you feel like a long-lost relative who should have stayed lost ... Great shape ... My hometown course; a bargain.

★★★ **WINNETKA GOLF CLUB**
PU-1300 Oak St., Winnetka, 60093, Cook County, (847)501-2050, 12 miles N of Chicago.
Holes: 18. **Yards:** 6,485/5,857. **Par:** 71/72. **Course Rating:** 70.9/73.3. **Slope:** 125/124. **Green Fee:** $24/$40. **Cart Fee:** $28/cart. **Walking Policy:** Unrestricted walking. **Walkability:** 1. **Opened:** 1917. **Architect:** W.H. Langford. **Season:** April-Dec. **High:** May-Aug. **To obtain tee times:** Call 7 days in advance. **Miscellaneous:** Reduced fees (weekdays, low season, twilight), range (mats), club rentals, credit cards (MC, V), beginner friendly (numerous camps & clinics).
Reader Comments: Great value in my hometown ... Gets a lot of play, but the price is right.

★★★ **WOLF CREEK GOLF CLUB**
PU-off Old #66, Pontiac, 61764, Livingston County, (815)842-9008, 35 miles N of Bloomington.
Holes: 18. **Yards:** 6,674/5,470. **Par:** 72/72. **Course Rating:** 70.1/72.8. **Slope:** 119/121. **Green Fee:** N/A/$16. **Cart Fee:** $16/person. **Walking Policy:** Unrestricted walking. **Walkability:** 2. **Opened:** 1973. **Season:** March-Nov. **High:** June-Aug. **To obtain tee times:** Call up to 7 days in advance. **Miscellaneous:** Metal spikes, range (grass), club rentals.
Reader Comments: You get your money's worth, and more ... Greens are the best part ... Very laid-back atmosphere ... Worth getting off the highway.

★★★½ **WOODBINE GOLF COURSE**
PU-14240 W. 151st St., Lockport, 60441, Will County, (708)301-1252, 30 miles SW of Chicago.
Holes: 18. **Yards:** 6,020/5,618. **Par:** 70/70. **Course Rating:** 68.1/71.3. **Slope:** 108/113. **Green Fee:** $26/$35. **Cart Fee:** $13/person. **Walking Policy:** Unrestricted walking. **Walkability:** 2.

ILLINOIS

Opened: 1988. **Architect:** Gordon Cunningham. **Season:** March-Nov. **High:** May-Sept. **To obtain tee times:** Call 7 days in advance. **Miscellaneous:** Reduced fees (weekdays, low season, twilight, seniors, juniors), club rentals, credit cards (MC, V, AE).
Reader Comments: Good place to start the season ... Wide open, but fun (my wife loves it) ... Easy to walk ... Improving each year ... Not Pebble Beach, but a real nice place to play.

★★½ WOODRUFF GOLF COURSE

PU-Gouger Rd., Joliet, 60432, Will County, (815)741-7272, 40 miles SW of Chicago.
Holes: 18. **Yards:** 5,424/5,059. **Par:** 68/68. **Course Rating:** 64.9/67.8. **Slope:** 99/105. **Green Fee:** $14/$28. **Cart Fee:** $22/cart. **Walking Policy:** Unrestricted walking. **Walkability:** 4.
Opened: 1921. **Architect:** Edward Lawrence Packard. **Season:** April-Nov. **High:** June-Aug. **To obtain tee times:** Call 1 day in advance for weekdays and call Monday for upcoming weekend.
Miscellaneous: Reduced fees (weekdays, twilight, seniors, juniors), discount packages, club rentals, credit cards (MC, V, D), beginner friendly.
Reader Comments: Short and tight.

INDIANA

★★½ ARBOR TRACE GOLF CLUB
PU-2500 E. 550 N., Marion, 46952, Grant County, (765)662-8236, 4 miles N of Marion.
Holes: 18. **Yards:** 6,535/5,060. **Par:** 72/72. **Course Rating:** 69.5/67.6. **Slope:** 108/106. **Green Fee:** $16/$18. **Cart Fee:** $10/person. **Walking Policy:** Unrestricted walking. **Walkability:** 1. **Opened:** 1966. **Architect:** H. Lamboley. **Season:** March-Dec. **High:** May-Sept. **To obtain tee times:** Call golf shop. **Miscellaneous:** Reduced fees (seniors), club rentals, credit cards (MC, V, D). **Reader Comments:** Two different courses between whites and blues ... Owner committed to keep making improvements. White tees too easy ,try the blues, great for families.

★★★★ AUTUMN RIDGE GOLF CLUB
SP-11420 Old Auburn Rd., Fort Wayne, 46845, Allen County, (219)637-8727, 2 miles N of Fort Wayne. **Web:** www.golfus.com/autumnridge.
Holes: 18. **Yards:** 7,103/5,273. **Par:** 72/72. **Course Rating:** 73.9/70.1. **Slope:** 134/122. **Green Fee:** $29/$42. **Cart Fee:** Included in Green Fee. **Walking Policy:** Mandatory cart. **Walkability:** 5. **Opened:** 1993. **Architect:** Ernie Schrock. **Season:** March-Dec. **High:** May-Sept. **To obtain tee times:** Call 7 days in advance/out of state 30 days in advance. **Miscellaneous:** Reduced fees (weekdays, low season, twilight, seniors), range (grass), club rentals, credit cards (MC, V, AE). **Reader Comments:** Plenty of water, tough opening hole ... Water on 15 holes ... Good layout, some holes on back close together ... Some great holes, then some back n' forth holes ... Wow! What a course for the price ... Great practice area ... Manicured greens and fairways ... Always in great condition ... Gets tougher each year.

★★★★ BEAR SLIDE GOLF CLUB
PU-6770 E. 231st St., Cicero, 46034, Hamilton County, (317)984-3837, (800)252-8337, 20 miles N of Indianapolis.
Holes: 18. **Yards:** 7,041/4,831. **Par:** 71/71. **Course Rating:** 74.6/69.5. **Slope:** 136/117. **Green Fee:** $35/$45. **Cart Fee:** $13/person. **Walking Policy:** Unrestricted walking. **Walkability:** 4. **Opened:** 1993. **Architect:** Dean Refram. **Season:** March-Dec. **High:** May-Oct. **To obtain tee times:** Call 7 days in advance. **Miscellaneous:** Metal spikes, range (grass), club rentals, credit cards (MC, V, D). **Notes:** Ranked 9th in 1999 Best in State. **Reader Comments:** Two distinct sides, classic finish hole ... Every shot required ... Tough to walk, great variety of holes, tests all clubs ... Not fun for average golfer ... Lots of blind shots ... Huge greens make for long putts ... 1st hole has two bunkers shaped like bear claw's behind green on big mound.

BIRCK BOILERMAKER GOLF COMPLEX
PU-1202 Cherry Lane, West Lafayette, 47907, Tippecanoe County, (765)494-3216, 50 miles NW of Indianapolis. **E-mail:** drhill@purdue.edu. **Web:** www.purdue.edu/athletics/golf.

★★★ ACKERMAN COURSE
Holes: 18. **Yards:** 6,400/5,918. **Par:** 71/71. **Course Rating:** 70.3/68.7. **Slope:** 124/112. **Green Fee:** $20/$26. **Cart Fee:** $13/person. **Walking Policy:** Unrestricted walking. **Walkability:** 3. **Opened:** 1998. **Architect:** Pete Dye. **Season:** March-Dec. **High:** June-Sept. **To obtain tee times:** Tee times may be called in 7 days in advance. **Miscellaneous:** Reduced fees (twilight, seniors, juniors), range (grass/mats), club rentals, credit cards (MC, V, D), beginner friendly. **Reader Comments:** Great price—mature course with a lot of trees ... Rolling hills & blind 2nd shots are great ... With a big enough slice on No. 8 you land in sorority touring area ... Good track, fun, good value.

★★★★ KAMPEN COURSE
Holes: 18. **Yards:** 7,253/5,216. **Par:** 72/72. **Course Rating:** 76.5/65.5. **Slope:** 145/115. **Green Fee:** $48/$55. **Cart Fee:** Included in Green Fee. **Walking Policy:** Mandatory cart. **Walkability:** 4. **Opened:** 1998. **Architect:** Pete Dye. **Season:** March-Dec. **High:** June-Sept. **Miscellaneous:** Reduced fees (twilight, juniors), range (grass), club rentals, credit cards (MC, V, D). **Reader Comments:** A little overpriced, could be great when grown in well ... Great layout, tough links-style course ... Great layout—not a plain hole on this course—soon to be best course in Indiana ... Has a new practice facility ...Opened too soon, rough areas, some good holes.

★★½ BLACK SQUIRREL GOLF CLUB
PU-Hwy. 119 S., Goshen, 46526, Elkhart County, (219)533-1828, 19 miles SE of South Bend. **E-mail:** blacksquirrelgc@juno.com. **Web:** www.golfus.com/blacksquirrel.
Holes: 18. **Yards:** 6,483/5,018. **Par:** 72/72. **Course Rating:** 69.8/67.8. **Slope:** 115/110. **Green Fee:** $15/$22. **Cart Fee:** $10/person. **Walking Policy:** Unrestricted walking. **Walkability:** 2. **Opened:** 1989. **Architect:** Larimer Development. **Season:** March-Nov. **High:** June-Aug. **To obtain tee times:** Call up to 14 days in advance. **Miscellaneous:** Reduced fees (weekdays, low season, juniors), club rentals, credit cards (MC, V). **Reader Comments:** Fast greens, great shape. Great par-5 9th ... Good layout and variety ... Many tight fairways. Best backyard views.

INDIANA

★★★★ BLACKTHORN GOLF CLUB
PU-6100 Nimtz Pkwy., South Bend, 46628, St. Joseph County, (219)232-4653, 90 miles E of Chicago. **Web:** www.blackthorngolf.com.
Holes: 18. **Yards:** 7,106/5,036. **Par:** 72/72. **Course Rating:** 75.2/71.0. **Slope:** 135/120. **Green Fee:** $30/$48. **Cart Fee:** $14/person. **Walking Policy:** Unrestricted walking. **Walkability:** 3. **Opened:** 1994. **Architect:** Michael Hurdzan. **Season:** March-Dec. **High:** May-Sept. **To obtain tee times:** Call up to 14 days in advance. **Miscellaneous:** Reduced fees (weekdays, low season, twilight, juniors), metal spikes, range (grass), club rentals, credit cards (MC, V, AE). **Notes:** Ranked 9th in 1999 Best in State; 4th in 1995 Best New Public Courses.
Reader Comments: Best public course in Indiana ... Nice mix. Challenging holes ... Excellent practice facilities ... Incredible greens ... Great facility, staff outstanding ... Very women friendly, bring your sand wedge ... Like the extra Blarney hole to warm up on.

★★ BRIAR LEAF GOLF CLUB
PU-3233 N. State Rd. 39, La Porte, 46350, La Porte County, (219)326-1992, (877)-briarleaf, 60 miles E of Chicago. **Web:** www.golfus.com/briarleaf.
Holes: 18. **Yards:** 6,681/5,305. **Par:** 72/72. **Course Rating:** 72.1/70.7. **Slope:** 128/121. **Green Fee:** $18/$30. **Cart Fee:** $12/person. **Walking Policy:** Walking at certain times. **Walkability:** 3. **Opened:** 1973. **Season:** Year-round. **High:** April-Oct. **To obtain tee times:** Call golf shop. **Miscellaneous:** Reduced fees (weekdays, low season, twilight, seniors, juniors), metal spikes, range (grass), club rentals, credit cards (MC, V, AE, D), beginner friendly (no fear ladies clinics, junior golf programs).

★★★★½ BRICKYARD CROSSING GOLF CLUB *Condition+*
R-4400 W. 16th St., Indianapolis, 46222, Marion County, (317)484-6572.
Holes: 18. **Yards:** 6,994/5,038. **Par:** 72/72. **Course Rating:** 74.5/68.3. **Slope:** 137/116. **Green Fee:** $90/$90. **Cart Fee:** Included in Green Fee. **Walking Policy:** Walking at certain times. **Walkability:** 3. **Opened:** 1993. **Architect:** Pete Dye. **Season:** April-Oct. **High:** May-Aug. **To obtain tee times:** Call up to 14 days in advance. **Miscellaneous:** Reduced fees (resort guests), range (grass), club rentals, lodging, credit cards (MC, V, AE, D). **Notes:** Ranked 6th in 1999 Best in State. Senior PGA Tour Comfort Classic.
Reader Comments: Too expensive, great layout ... Where else can you hear a race car ... Lots of fun, 15-18 tough holes, inside the track! ... Tough in the wind–can't imagine how seniors scored so well ... Great course/excellent service... Very fair tee to green-very difficult at the greens ... Thinking man's course.

★½ BROADMOOR COUNTRY CLUB
PU-4300 W. 81st St., Merrillville, 46410, Lake County, (219)769-5444.
Yards: 6,021/5,181. **Par:** 71/71. **Course Rating:** 69.8/71.4. **Slope:** 117/110. **Green Fee:** $15/$23. **Walking Policy:** Unrestricted walking. **Walkability:** 3. **Opened:** 1973. **Architect:** R. Albert Anderson. **Season:** year-round. **High:** April-Sept. **To obtain tee times:** call the Monday prior to weekend. **Miscellaneous:** Reduced fees (weekdays, low season, twilight, seniors, juniors), discount packages, range (grass/mats), club rentals, credit cards (MC, V, AE, D).

★★★ BROOK HILL GOLF CLUB
SP-11175 Fairway Lane, Brookville, 47012, Franklin County, (765)647-4522, (800)708-4522, 35 miles NW of Cincinnati.
Holes: 18. **Yards:** 6,361/4,776. **Par:** 71/71. **Course Rating:** 70.2/67.9. **Slope:** 125/125. **Green Fee:** $17/$22. **Cart Fee:** $12/person. **Walking Policy:** Unrestricted walking. **Walkability:** 3. **Opened:** 1975. **Season:** Year-round. **High:** May-Oct. **To obtain tee times:** Call golf shop. **Miscellaneous:** Reduced fees (weekdays, low season, twilight, seniors), metal spikes, range (grass), club rentals, credit cards (MC, V, D).
Reader Comments: Fun to play ... You better have a course map ... Very hilly & scenic course ... Short, but tight, great finishing hole ... Lakes in front of green.

★★½ BROOKSHIRE GOLF CLUB
SP-12120 Brookshire Pkwy., Carmel, 46033, Hamilton County, (317)846-7431, 15 miles N of Indianapolis.
Holes: 18. **Yards:** 6,651/5,635. **Par:** 72/75. **Course Rating:** 71.8/74.4. **Slope:** 123/129. **Green Fee:** $32/$38. **Cart Fee:** Included in Green Fee. **Walking Policy:** Mandatory cart. **Walkability:** N/A. **Opened:** 1971. **Architect:** William H. Diddel. **Season:** Year-round. **High:** May-Oct. **To obtain tee times:** Call up to 3 days in advance. **Miscellaneous:** Reduced fees (weekdays, twilight, juniors), metal spikes, range (grass), club rentals, credit cards (MC, V, AE).
Reader Comments: Good value, good layout, slow play & average condition ... Too many trees for fall season play ... One of the older courses in town, plenty of character.

★★★½ BROOKWOOD GOLF CLUB *Value*
PU-10304 Bluffton Rd., Fort Wayne, 46809, Allen County, (219)747-3136.
Holes: 18. **Yards:** 6,700/6,250. **Par:** 72/73. **Course Rating:** 70.3/67.9. **Slope:** 123/111. **Green Fee:** $18/$20. **Cart Fee:** $20/cart. **Walking Policy:** Unrestricted walking. **Walkability:** 3.

Opened: 1925. **Season:** March-Dec. **High:** April-Sept. **To obtain tee times:** Call ahead. **Miscellaneous:** Range (grass), club rentals, credit cards (MC, V, AE, D).

Reader Comments: Great condition for number of rounds played ... Great people ... Older style layout, through the trees, airplanes bothersome, but keep things interesting ... Best public course in all levels of play. Great value. Great greens ... Play well, score well, (and vice versa).

★★★½ CHESTNUT HILL GOLF CLUB

PU-11502 Illinois Rd., Fort Wayne, 46804, Allen County, (219)625-4146.
Holes: 18. **Yards:** 6,996/5,206. **Par:** 72/72. **Course Rating:** 72.9/68.8. **Slope:** 152/117. **Green Fee:** $30/$30. **Cart Fee:** $12/person. **Walking Policy:** Unrestricted walking. **Walkability:** 3. **Opened:** 1995. **Architect:** Clyde Johnston/Fuzzy Zoeller. **Season:** March-Nov. **High:** May-Sept. **To obtain tee times:** Call up to 7 days in advance for weekdays. Call on Tuesday for upcoming weekend. **Miscellaneous:** Range (grass), club rentals, credit cards (MC, V, AE).

Reader Comments: Fort Wayne's finest ... Course conditions improving quickly, interesting holes ... New course that is excellent value ... Very fair course ... Great variety.

★★★ CHRISTMAS LAKE GOLF COURSE

PU-1 Country Club Dr., Santa Claus, 47579, Spencer County, (800)927-2571, 45 miles E of Evansville. **E-mail:** Tnewport@christmaslake.com. **Web:** www.christmaslake.com.
Holes: 18. **Yards:** 7,191/5,135. **Par:** 72/72. **Course Rating:** 74.4/69.2. **Slope:** 134/117. **Green Fee:** $24/$44. **Cart Fee:** Included in Green Fee. **Walking Policy:** Walking at certain times. **Walkability:** 3. **Opened:** 1968. **Architect:** Edmund Ault. **Season:** Jan.-Dec. **High:** April-Oct. **To obtain tee times:** Call 14 days in advance. **Miscellaneous:** Reduced fees (weekdays, low season, twilight), discount packages, metal spikes, range (grass), club rentals, credit cards (MC, V, D).

Reader Comments: In the country, saw deer last year ... Digital caddy very good ... Course is beautiful ... Course needs some attention ... Rolling, lots of trees. Very long from back tees ... Very challenging ... Very nice for small town.

COBBLESTONE GOLF COURSE

PU-2702 Cobblestone Lane, Kendallville, 46755, Noble County, (219)349-1550, 25 miles N of Ft. Wayne. **E-mail:** pro@kendallville.net. **Web:** www.golfus.com/cobblestone.
Holes: 18. **Yards:** 6,863/4,779. **Par:** 72/72. **Course Rating:** 72.9/67.6. **Slope:** 129/112. **Green Fee:** $24/$29. **Cart Fee:** $11/person. **Walking Policy:** Unrestricted walking. **Walkability:** 3. **Opened:** 1998. **Architect:** Steve Burns. **Season:** April-Nov. **High:** June-Sept. **To obtain tee times:** 1 week in advance. Groups of 16 or more, 30 days in advance. **Miscellaneous:** Reduced fees (twilight, seniors, juniors), range (grass), club rentals, credit cards (MC, V, AE, D).

Notes: Ranked 8th in 1999 Best New Affordable Public.

★★★½ COFFIN GOLF CLUB

PU-2401 Cold Springs Rd., Indianapolis, 46222, Marion County, (317)327-7845, 2 miles NW of Downtown Indianapolis.
Holes: 18. **Yards:** 6,789/5,135. **Par:** 72/72. **Course Rating:** 73.7/70.3. **Slope:** 129/114. **Green Fee:** $20/$22. **Cart Fee:** $15/person. **Walking Policy:** Unrestricted walking. **Walkability:** 3. **Opened:** 1995. **Architect:** Tim Liddy. **Season:** March-Dec. **To obtain tee times:** Call up to 7 days in advance. **Miscellaneous:** Reduced fees (weekdays, low season, twilight, seniors, juniors), metal spikes, club rentals, credit cards (MC, V).

Reader Comments: Course has a lot of potential ... Great layout, good value ... Nos. 10 & 18 not for the faint of heart! ... Good re-vamp job on old course ... Course in good shape ... Nice little course. Tight.... Arrived 45 minutes early, but they let us get right on.

★★½ COOL LAKE GOLF CLUB

PU-520 E. 750 N., Lebanon, 46052, Boone County, (765)325-9271, 35 miles NW of Indianapolis.
Holes: 18. **Yards:** 6,000/4,827. **Par:** 70/72. **Course Rating:** 67.4/67.1. **Slope:** 108/105. **Green Fee:** $14/$18. **Cart Fee:** $12/person. **Walking Policy:** Walking at certain times. **Walkability:** 2. **Opened:** 1962. **Architect:** G&J Design Inc. **Season:** March-Dec. **High:** May-Sept. **To obtain tee times:** Call anytime in advance. **Miscellaneous:** Range (grass), credit cards (MC, V).

Reader Comments: Great little course, nice people ... Back 9 better than front ... Great greens, some good holes.

THE COURSE AT ABERDEEN

PU-245 Tower Rd., Valparaiso, 46385, Porter County, (219)462-5050, 40 miles SE of Chicago. **E-mail:** aberdeen18@aol.com.
Holes: 18. **Yards:** 6,917/4,949. **Par:** 72/72. **Course Rating:** 73.0/68.3. **Slope:** 134/120. **Green Fee:** $49/$59. **Cart Fee:** Included in Green Fee. **Walking Policy:** Unrestricted walking. **Walkability:** 3. **Opened:** 1997. **Architect:** Michael Hurdzan/Dana Fry/Bill Kerman. **Season:** Year-round. **High:** June-August. **To obtain tee times:** Call golf shop 14 days in advance for general public or 30 days for members. **Miscellaneous:** Reduced fees (low season, twilight, juniors), discount packages, range (grass), club rentals, credit cards (MC, V, AE).

INDIANA

★★★★ COVERED BRIDGE GOLF CLUB
SP-12510 Covered Bridge Rd., Sellersburg, 47172, Clark County, (812)246-8880, 12 miles N of Louisville, KY.
Holes: 18. **Yards:** 6,832/5,943. **Par:** 72/72. **Course Rating:** 73.0/74.7. **Slope:** 128/126. **Green Fee:** $50/$60. **Cart Fee:** Included in Green Fee. **Walking Policy:** Mandatory cart. **Walkability:** 1. **Opened:** 1994. **Architect:** Clyde Johnston/Fuzzy Zoeller. **Season:** Year-round. **High:** April-Oct. **To obtain tee times:** Public may call up to 10 days in advance with a credit card to guarantee. **Miscellaneous:** Reduced fees (weekdays, low season), metal spikes, range (grass), club rentals, credit cards (MC, V, AE, D).
Reader Comments: Little overpriced, great course, great layout, great greens ... No outstanding holes ... Great view of course from clubhouse patio ... Interesting course-strong par 3's ... Great greens but fairways are not as good ... Fun to play ... Pleasant atmosphere.

★½ CRESSMOOR COUNTRY CLUB
SP-601 N. Wisconsin St., Hobart, 46342, Lake County, (219)942-9300.
Holes: 18. **Yards:** 6,060/4,914. **Par:** 72/72. **Course Rating:** 68.0/68.0. **Slope:** 108/108. **Green Fee:** N/A. **Walking Policy:** Unrestricted walking. **Walkability:** 1. **Opened:** 1922. **Season:** March-Nov. **High:** July-Aug. **To obtain tee times:** No tee times necessary. **Miscellaneous:** Reduced fees (weekdays, low season, twilight, seniors, juniors), metal spikes, club rentals, beginner friendly.

★★★ CURTIS CREEK COUNTRY CLUB
SP-Rte. 3, Rensselaer, 47978, Jasper County, (219)866-7729, 95 miles S of Chicago.
Holes: 18. **Yards:** 6,118/5,029. **Par:** 72/72. **Course Rating:** 70.6/70.2. **Slope:** 117/106. **Green Fee:** $23. **Cart Fee:** $10/person. **Walking Policy:** Walking at certain times. **Walkability:** 2. **Opened:** 1924. **Architect:** Leonard Macomber. **Season:** March-Nov. **High:** May-Sept. **To obtain tee times:** Public may play on Monday and Friday only. Call golf shop for availability.
Miscellaneous: Range (grass), club rentals, credit cards (MC, V).
Reader Comments: Short but good test ... Nice out of the way course. Good greens.

★★★½ DEER CREEK GOLF CLUB
PU-State Rd. #39, Clayton, 46118, Hendricks County, (317)539-2013, 18 miles W of Indianapolis.
Holes: 18. **Yards:** 6,510/5,033. **Par:** 71/72. **Course Rating:** 71.2/68.8. **Slope:** 128/120. **Green Fee:** $18/$25. **Cart Fee:** $11/person. **Walking Policy:** Walking at certain times. **Walkability:** 3. **Opened:** 1991. **Season:** March-Dec. **High:** May-Oct. **Miscellaneous:** Metal spikes, range (grass/mats), credit cards (MC, V).
Reader Comments: Too many parallel holes ... Good layout ... Great pro & staff plus excellent course ... Too many blind shots! ... Required planned shot placement from tee ... Great layout, slow pace normal for public course.

★★½ DYKEMAN PARK GOLF COURSE
PM-Eberts Rd., Logansport, 46947, Cass County, (219)753-0222.
Holes: 18. **Yards:** 6,185/5,347. **Par:** 70/73. **Course Rating:** 69.4/69.8. **Slope:** 118/102. **Green Fee:** $16/$16. **Cart Fee:** $20/person. **Walking Policy:** Unrestricted walking. **Walkability:** 3. **Architect:** William B. Langford/Theodore J. Moreau. **Season:** March-Nov. **High:** April-Aug. **To obtain tee times:** Call 2 days in advance. **Miscellaneous:** Reduced fees (twilight, seniors, juniors), discount packages, metal spikes, range (grass), club rentals, beginner friendly (junior clinics).
Reader Comments: Very good greens ... Lots of fun–some unique holes.

★★★½ EAGLE CREEK GOLF CLUB
PM-8802 W. 56th St., Indianapolis, 46234, Marion County, (317)297-3366, 12 miles NW of Indianapolis. **Web:** www.eaglecreek.com.
Holes: 18. **Yards:** 7,159/5,800. **Par:** 72/72. **Course Rating:** 74.6/68.2. **Slope:** 139/116. **Green Fee:** $20/$22. **Cart Fee:** $17/person. **Walking Policy:** Unrestricted walking. **Walkability:** 5. **Opened:** 1974. **Architect:** Pete Dye. **Season:** Feb.-Dec. **High:** June-Aug. **To obtain tee times:** Call 7 days in advance for weekdays. Call on Monday for upcoming weekend. **Miscellaneous:** Reduced fees (weekdays, low season, twilight, seniors, juniors), metal spikes, range (grass/mats), club rentals, credit cards (MC, V).
Notes: Hosted 1982 USGA Public Links Championship.
Reader Comments: Beautiful layout, deer, birds & scenery, rangers keep pace going ... Narrow & tricky ... One of the best public courses ... Depending on pin placement, can be tough ... Continues to improve ... Great condition for amount of rounds. Fun course with a great staff ... Fairways very rough, lots of water.

EAGLE PINES GOLF CLUB
SP-1665 Country Club Rd., Mooresville, 46158, Morgan County, (317)831-4774, 1 miles S of Mooresville.
Holes: 18. **Yards:** 6,055/5,032. **Par:** 70/70. **Course Rating:** 67.6/67.3. **Slope:** 113/110. **Green Fee:** $17/$18. **Cart Fee:** $11/person. **Walking Policy:** Unrestricted walking. **Walkability:** 2.

Opened: 1968. **Architect:** Ron Kern. **Season:** Year-round. **High:** May-Oct. **To obtain tee times:** Call course for tee times. **Miscellaneous:** Reduced fees (low season, twilight), metal spikes, beginner friendly.
Special Notes: Formerly Mooresville Golf Club

★★★★ EAGLE POINTE GOLF & TENNIS RESORT
R-2250 E. Pointe Rd., Bloomington, 47401, Monroe County, (812)824-4040, (800)860-8604, 65 miles S of Indianapolis.
Holes: 18. **Yards:** 6,604/5,186. **Par:** 71/71. **Course Rating:** 73.0/71.2. **Slope:** 140/126. **Green Fee:** $31/$49. **Cart Fee:** Included in Green Fee. **Walking Policy:** Mandatory cart. **Walkability:** 3. **Opened:** 1973. **Architect:** Robert Simmons. **Season:** Year-round. **High:** May-Sept. **To obtain tee times:** Call anytime in advance. **Miscellaneous:** Reduced fees (weekdays, low season, twilight), discount packages, metal spikes, range (grass/mats), club rentals, lodging, credit cards (MC, V, AE, D).
Reader Comments: Improved bunkers ... Great resort–good golf ... Two waterfalls on the back 9. Nice course ... Winter price treat for quality course ... Course maintenance, good; play kept at good pace ... Great place to play in the fall, lots of trees ... High cost-classy ... Fun course, great staff and pro shop.

★★★½ ELBEL PARK GOLF COURSE
PM-26595 Auten Rd., South Bend, 46628, St. Joseph County, (219)271-9180.
Holes: 18. **Yards:** 6,700/5,750. **Par:** 72/73. **Course Rating:** 70.7/71.4. **Slope:** 113/114. **Green Fee:** $11/$18. **Cart Fee:** $10/person. **Walking Policy:** Unrestricted walking. **Walkability:** 4. **Opened:** 1963. **Architect:** William J. Spear. **Season:** March-Dec. **High:** June-Aug. **To obtain tee times:** Call up to 7 days in advance. **Miscellaneous:** Reduced fees (weekdays, low season, twilight, seniors, juniors), metal spikes, range (grass/mats), club rentals, credit cards (MC, V).
Reader Comments: A surprise for a muny–great ... Dogleg capital of the world ... Huge greens. Fun layout ... Public course-good condition-good value ... Challenging, entertaining layout ... Great layout. Good test of your skills. Well maintained.

★★★ ERSKINE PARK GOLF CLUB
PU-4200 Miami St., South Bend, 46614, St. Joseph County, (219)291-3216.
Holes: 18. **Yards:** 6,104/5,536. **Par:** 70/74. **Course Rating:** 68.5/70.9. **Slope:** 120/120. **Green Fee:** $11/$21. **Cart Fee:** $10/person. **Walking Policy:** Unrestricted walking. **Walkability:** 3. **Opened:** 1925. **Architect:** William H. Diddel. **Season:** March-Nov. **High:** April-Sept. **To obtain tee times:** Call 7 days in advance. **Miscellaneous:** Reduced fees (twilight, seniors, juniors), discount packages, metal spikes, club rentals, credit cards (MC, V).
Reader Comments: Outstanding treelined course, great variety of holes ... Some interesting holes could be in better condition ... Public course-good condition-good value ... Best value for South Bend area ... Surprisingly difficult.

★★ ETNA ACRES GOLF COURSE
SP-9803 W. 600 S., Andrews, 46702, Huntington County, (219)468-2906, 11 miles N of Marion.
Web: www.golfus.com/etnaacres.
Holes: 18. **Yards:** 6,096/5,142. **Par:** 72/72. **Course Rating:** 68.6/68.9. **Slope:** 109/108. **Green Fee:** $13/$15. **Cart Fee:** $8/person. **Walking Policy:** Unrestricted walking. **Walkability:** 3. **Opened:** 1960. **Architect:** Gene Kaufman. **Season:** March-Nov. **High:** June-Aug. **To obtain tee times:** Call golf shop. **Miscellaneous:** Reduced fees (weekdays, low season, seniors, juniors), discount packages, metal spikes, range (grass/mats), club rentals, beginner friendly (golf lessons and lady friendly).

★★★ FAIRVIEW GOLF COURSE
PU-7102 S. Calhoun St., Fort Wayne, 46807, Allen County, (219)745-7093.
Holes: 18. **Yards:** 6,620/5,125. **Par:** 72/72. **Course Rating:** 70.8/71.1. **Slope:** 119/108. **Green Fee:** $10/$10. **Cart Fee:** $17/. **Walking Policy:** Unrestricted walking. **Walkability:** N/A. **Opened:** 1927. **Architect:** Donald Ross. **Season:** March-Oct. **High:** May-Sept. **To obtain tee times:** Weekend tee times only. Call Tuesday prior. **Miscellaneous:** Metal spikes, range (grass), club rentals, credit cards (MC, V).
Reader Comments: Great value ... Great value ... More difficult than it looks.

★★ FENDRICH GOLF COURSE
PU-1900 Diamond Ave., Evansville, 47711, Vanderburgh County, (812)435-6070.
Holes: 18. **Yards:** 5,791/5,232. **Par:** 70/70. **Course Rating:** 67.1/69.2. **Slope:** 106/109. **Green Fee:** $10/$10. **Cart Fee:** $18. **Walking Policy:** Unrestricted walking. **Walkability:** N/A. **Opened:** 1945. **Architect:** William Diddel. **Season:** Year-round. **High:** April-Sept. **To obtain tee times:** Call 7 days in advance. **Miscellaneous:** Metal spikes, range (grass), club rentals.

FOREST PARK GOLF COURSE
PM-P.O. Box 42, 1018 S.John Stelle Dr., Brazil, 47834, Clay County, (812)442-5681, 15 miles NE of Terre Haute.

Holes: 18. **Yards:** 6,012/5,647. **Par:** 71/73. **Course Rating:** 68.0/69.8. **Slope:** 110/112. **Green Fee:** N/A. **Walking Policy:** Unrestricted walking. **Walkability:** 1. **Opened:** 1935. **Architect:** Pete Dye. **Season:** Year-round. **High:** March-Nov. **To obtain tee times:** Tee times are not taken in advance. **Miscellaneous:** Reduced fees (low season, twilight), discount packages, range (grass), credit cards (MC, V), beginner friendly (lessons).
Reader Comments: Price is high, good condition ... Flat course, great greens! ... Interesting for a flat course.

★★★★ THE FORT GOLF COURSE
PU-6002 N. Post Rd., Indianapolis, 46216, Marion County, (317)543-9597.
Holes: 18. **Yards:** 7,144/5,049. **Par:** 72/71. **Course Rating:** 74.5/69.2. **Slope:** 139/123. **Green Fee:** $28/$43. **Walking Policy:** Unrestricted walking. **Walkability:** 3. **Opened:** 1997. **Architect:** Pete Dye/Tim Liddy. **Season:** March-Nov. **High:** May-Sept. **To obtain tee times:** Call anytime. We take tee times as far in advance as people want to make them. **Miscellaneous:** Reduced fees (twilight, juniors), discount packages, range (grass), club rentals, lodging (25 rooms), credit cards (MC, V, AE, D).
Notes: Ranked 7th in 1999 Best in State.
Reader Comments: Biggest trees this side of the continental divide ... Impossible to walk ... Great public course. Exciting golf course. Well maintained ... Hilly challenge ... Enjoyable time, nice course ... Enjoyable & challenging ... Lots of good holes. Pretty landscape. Good greens.

★★★½ FOX PRAIRIE GOLF CLUB
PM-8465 E. 196th St., Noblesville, 46060, Hamilton County, (317)776-6357, 15 miles N of Indianapolis.
Holes: 18. **Yards:** 6,946/5,533. **Par:** 72/75. **Course Rating:** 72.6/71.4. **Slope:** 118/114. **Green Fee:** $20/$26. **Cart Fee:** $12/person. **Walking Policy:** Unrestricted walking. **Walkability:** 3. **Opened:** 1970. **Architect:** Bill Newcomb. **Season:** March-Nov. **High:** April-Oct. **To obtain tee times:** Call 7 days in advance to reserve for upcoming week and weekend. **Miscellaneous:** Range (grass), club rentals, credit cards (MC, V).
Reader Comments: Still the best greens in Indiana ... Uses a ranger and a big clock each 9 ... Very long from back tees–big greens ... Great city course, recent improvements, new clubhouse ... Best public course around ... Holes too close together ... Good value but crowded.

★★ FOX RIDGE COUNTRY CLUB
PU-1364 N Hillcrest Road, Vincennes, 47591, Knox County, (812)886-5929, 50 miles S of Terre Haute.
Holes: 18. **Yards:** 6,578/5,412. **Par:** 72/72. **Course Rating:** 72.0/71.0. **Slope:** 131/124. **Green Fee:** $25/$30. **Cart Fee:** Included in Green Fee. **Walking Policy:** Walking at certain times. **Walkability:** 5. **Opened:** 1987. **Season:** Year-round. **High:** April-Oct. **To obtain tee times:** Call on Monday for upcoming weekend. First come, first served on weekdays. **Miscellaneous:** Reduced fees (weekdays), range (grass/mats), club rentals, credit cards (MC, V, AE, D).

FRENCH LICK SPRINGS RESORT
R-Hwy. 56., French Lick, 47432, Orange County, (812)936-9300, (800)457-4042, 60 miles NW of Louisville, KY.
★★★★ COUNTRY CLUB COURSE
Holes: 18. **Yards:** 6,650/5,927. **Par:** 70/71. **Course Rating:** 71.6/70.3. **Slope:** 119/116. **Green Fee:** $36/$46. **Cart Fee:** $12. **Walking Policy:** Mandatory cart. **Walkability:** N/A. **Opened:** 1920. **Architect:** Donald Ross. **Season:** March-Nov. **High:** May-Oct. **To obtain tee times:** Call golf shop. Preference given to hotel guests. **Miscellaneous:** Reduced fees (low season, resort guests, twilight), discount packages, metal spikes, club rentals, lodging, credit cards (MC, V, AE, D, Hotel Chg.).
Reader Comments: One of the best 'old courses' ... Greens a bit too fast for this area ... Never a flat lie...Great course/great people ... Beautiful, with some great holes ... Large, tiered greens, some severe ... Interesting, challenging ... Challenging, rewarding, a blast!
★★½ VALLEY COURSE
Holes: 18. **Yards:** 6,001/5,627. **Par:** 70/71. **Course Rating:** 67.6/66.0. **Slope:** 110/106. **Green Fee:** $20/$20. **Cart Fee:** $12. **Walking Policy:** Walking at certain times. **Walkability:** N/A. **Opened:** 1905. **Architect:** Tom Bendelow. **Season:** March-Nov. **High:** May-Oct. **To obtain tee times:** Call golf shop. Preference given to hotel guests. **Miscellaneous:** Reduced fees (low season, resort guests), discount packages, metal spikes, range (grass/mats), club rentals, lodging, credit cards (MC, V, AE, D, Hotel Chg. if guest).
Reader Comments: Average course, loved old hotel ... Nice course, needs some water hazards ... Course very open ... Basic golf. Very flat, nothing fancy.

★★½ GENEVA HILLS GOLF CLUB
PU-13446 S. Geneva Rd., Clinton, 47842, Vermillion County, (765)832-8384, 15 miles N of Terre Haute. **E-mail:** south@abcs.com. **Web:** www.golfer.com/genevahills.
Holes: 18. **Yards:** 6,768/4,785. **Par:** 72/72. **Course Rating:** 70.2/67.3. **Slope:** 118/115. **Green Fee:** $17/$20. **Cart Fee:** $12/person. **Walking Policy:** Unrestricted walking. **Walkability:** 3.

Opened: 1970. **Architect:** R. D. Shaw. **Season:** Year-round. **High:** April-Oct. **To obtain tee times:** Call up to 5 days in advance. **Miscellaneous:** Reduced fees (weekdays, low season, twilight, seniors, juniors), range (grass), club rentals, credit cards (MC, V).

Reader Comments: Nice layout. Greens a little slow ... Improvements constantly being made ... Watch the 12th green—don't think driver all the time.

★★★½ GOLF CLUB OF INDIANA

PU-I 65 at Zionsville Exit 130, Zionsville, 46052, Boone County, (317)769-6388, 16 miles NW of Indianapolis. **E-mail:** jrubenst@pop.iguest.net. **Web:** www.golfindiana.com.
Holes: 18. **Yards:** 7,151/5,156. **Par:** 72/72. **Course Rating:** 73.6/68.9. **Slope:** 132/119. **Green Fee:** $39/$44. **Cart Fee:** $10/person. **Walking Policy:** Unrestricted walking. **Walkability:** 2.
Opened: 1974. **Architect:** Charles Maddox. **Season:** Year-round. **High:** May-Sept. **To obtain tee times:** Call golf shop. **Miscellaneous:** Reduced fees (low season, twilight), range (grass), club rentals, credit cards (MC, V), beginner friendly (golf academy).

Reader Comments: Flat course surrounded by cornfields ... Can play long from the tips ... Tough, but fair ... Best-kept local secret—very difficult course ... Course is always in very good shape ... Better service ... A lot of sand makes you hit good shots on almost every hole.

★★★½ GRAND OAK GOLF CLUB

SP-370 Grand Oak Dr., West Harrison, 47060, Dearborn County, (812)637-3943, 25 miles W of Cincinnati. **E-mail:** golfgogc@aol.com. **Web:** www.grandoakgolfclub.com.
Holes: 18. **Yards:** 6,363/4,842. **Par:** 71/71. **Course Rating:** 70.3/69.4. **Slope:** 127/121. **Green Fee:** $24/$29. **Cart Fee:** $11/person. **Walking Policy:** Unrestricted walking. **Walkability:** 4.
Opened: 1989. **Architect:** Michael Hurdzan. **Season:** Feb.-Dec. **High:** April-Oct. **To obtain tee times:** Call up to 14 days in advance, or schedule through web site. **Miscellaneous:** Reduced fees (weekdays, low season, seniors, juniors), range (grass/mats), club rentals, credit cards (MC, V).

Reader Comments: Very hilly, many blind shots ... Certain holes make me feel like I'm in North Carolina.... No. 11 & No. 12 tee shots awesome ... A hidden gem for Cincinnati golfers ... Outstanding ... Hilly & tricky ... My favorite!.

★★½ GREEN ACRES GOLF CLUB

PU-1300 Green Acres Dr., Kokomo, 40601-9546, Howard County, (765)883-5771, 9 miles W of Kokomo.
Holes: 18. **Yards:** 6,767/5,248. **Par:** 72/72. **Course Rating:** 72.8/72.7. **Slope:** 129/118. **Green Fee:** $18/$21. **Cart Fee:** $11/person. **Walking Policy:** Unrestricted walking. **Walkability:** 3.
Opened: 1968. **Architect:** Bob Simmons. **Season:** March-Dec. **High:** May-Oct. **To obtain tee times:** Call anytime. **Miscellaneous:** Reduced fees (low season, seniors), metal spikes, range (grass), club rentals, credit cards (MC, V, AE, D).

Reader Comments: Interesting layout—beautiful setting ... Variety of holes ... Good layout.

★★★ GREENFIELD COUNTRY CLUB

SP-145 S. Morristown Pike, Greenfield, 46140, Hancock County, (317)462-2706, 15 miles E of Indianapolis.
Holes: 18. **Yards:** 6,773/5,501. **Par:** 72/73. **Course Rating:** 71.2/73.5. **Slope:** 119/120. **Green Fee:** $18/$23. **Cart Fee:** $12/person. **Walking Policy:** Unrestricted walking. **Walkability:** N/A.
Opened: 1927. **Architect:** Gary Kern. **Season:** March-Nov. **High:** May-Sept. **To obtain tee times:** Call 7 days in advance. **Miscellaneous:** Reduced fees (weekdays), metal spikes, range (grass), credit cards (MC, V).

Reader Comments: Use all your clubs.

★★★½ HANGING TREE GOLF CLUB

SP-2302 W. 161st St., Westfield, 46074, Hamilton County, (317)896-2474, 20 miles N of Indianapolis. **Web:** www.golfus.com/hangingtree.
Holes: 18. **Yards:** 6,519/5,151. **Par:** 71/71. **Course Rating:** 72.6/70.6. **Slope:** 130/122. **Green Fee:** $32/$42. **Cart Fee:** Included in Green Fee. **Walking Policy:** Mandatory cart. **Walkability:** 3. **Opened:** 1990. **Architect:** Gary Kern. **Season:** Year-round. **High:** April-Nov. **To obtain tee times:** Call anytime in advance. **Miscellaneous:** Reduced fees (weekdays, low season, twilight), range (grass), club rentals, credit cards (MC, V, D).

Reader Comments: Wide open with thick rough to hard greens ... Tough to walk, good variety of holes, somewhat pricey ... The creek is the thing, it's everywhere ... As good as the wind allows—creek must be considered ... Watch out for the water ... Yardage to hazards crossing fairway (from tees) is great convenience.

HARRISON HILLS GOLF & COUNTRY CLUB

PU-413 E. New St., Attica, 47918, Fountain County, (765)762-1135, 25 miles SW of Lafayette. **E-mail:** hhills@tctc.com. **Web:** www.harrisonhills.com.
Holes: 18. **Yards:** 6,820/5,223. **Par:** 72/72. **Course Rating:** 72.6/69.7. **Slope:** 130/120. **Green Fee:** $21/$26. **Cart Fee:** $12/person. **Walking Policy:** Walking at certain times. **Walkability:** 3.
Opened: 1924. **Architect:** William Langford/Tim Liddy. **Season:** March-Nov. **High:** May-Sept. **To**

obtain tee times: Call up to 7 days in advance. **Miscellaneous:** Reduced fees (weekdays, low season), range (grass), club rentals, credit cards (MC, V, D).

★★½ HELFRICH GOLF COURSE
PM-1550 Mesker Park Dr., Evansville, 47720, Vanderburgh County, (812)435-6075.
Holes: 18. **Yards:** 6,306/5,506. **Par:** 71/74. **Course Rating:** 69.8/71.4. **Slope:** 124/117. **Green Fee:** $12/$12. **Cart Fee:** $20/person. **Walking Policy:** Unrestricted walking. **Walkability:** 5. **Opened:** 1923. **Architect:** Tom Bendelow. **Season:** Year-round. **High:** April-Oct. **To obtain tee times:** Call 7 days in advance. **Miscellaneous:** Metal spikes, club rentals.
Reader Comments: A good muny ... Challenging public course ... Tough backside ... Low cost.

★★★ HIDDEN CREEK GOLF CLUB
PU-4975 Utica Sellersburg Rd., Sellersburg, 47172, Clark County, (812)246-2556, (800)822-2556, 4 miles N of Louisville, KY. **Web:** www.louisville-golfer.com.
Holes: 18. **Yards:** 6,756/5,245. **Par:** 71/71. **Course Rating:** 73.0/70.6. **Slope:** 133/123. **Green Fee:** $19/$22. **Cart Fee:** $10/person. **Walking Policy:** Unrestricted walking. **Walkability:** 2. **Opened:** 1992. **Architect:** David Pfaff. **Season:** Year-round. **High:** March-Oct. **To obtain tee times:** Call 4 days in advance for Monday-Thursday and weekend tee times available after 11 a.m. Call 1 day prior for weekend tee times available before 11 a.m. **Miscellaneous:** Reduced fees (weekdays, low season, twilight, seniors, juniors), discount packages, metal spikes, range (grass/mats), club rentals, credit cards (MC, V, AE, D), beginner friendly (new executive 9 holes, various clinics).
Reader Comments: Some water, lots of trees. 3 holes on the back are tough ... Very short, narrow back 9 ... Some greens slope into water ... 16th hole worth the cost ... Good value.

★★★ HONEYWELL GOLF COURSE
PU-3360 W. Division Rd., Wabash, 46992, Wabash County, (219)563-8663, 45 miles SW of Fort Wayne. **E-mail:** rlundy@ctlnet.com. **Web:** www.golfus/honeywell.com.
Holes: 18. **Yards:** 6,430/5,650. **Par:** 71/71. **Course Rating:** 69.4/70.4. **Slope:** 121/118. **Green Fee:** $21/$21. **Cart Fee:** $11/person. **Walking Policy:** Unrestricted walking. **Walkability:** 2. **Opened:** 1980. **Architect:** Arthur Hills. **Season:** March-Nov. **High:** June-Sept. **To obtain tee times:** Call in advance. **Miscellaneous:** Reduced fees (weekdays, low season, juniors), range (grass), club rentals, credit cards (MC, V).
Reader Comments: Totally different 9, newer holes more interesting than old ... Overall good experience ... Very good greens ... Wonderful old facility, golf course always good ... Front open—back tight—always in good shape (nice pro).

★★★★ HULMAN LINKS GOLF COURSE
PM-990 N. Chamberlain St., Terre Haute, 47803, Vigo County, (812)877-2096, 75 miles SW of Indianapolis.
Holes: 18. **Yards:** 7,225/5,775. **Par:** 72/72. **Course Rating:** 74.9/68.7. **Slope:** 144/127. **Green Fee:** $25/$25. **Cart Fee:** $13/person. **Walking Policy:** Unrestricted walking. **Walkability:** 4. **Opened:** 1978. **Architect:** David Gill. **Season:** March-Dec. **High:** May-Sept. **To obtain tee times:** Call anytime for weekday play. Call on Wednesday for following weekend. **Miscellaneous:** Reduced fees (low season), range (grass), club rentals, credit cards (MC, V, AE, D).
Reader Comments: Outstanding layout ... Could be terrific with more upkeep! ... Nice course. Par 3's were short ... Boy is this course difficult ... No. 11 is unfair.

★★★½ INDIANA UNIVERSITY GOLF CLUB
PU-State Rd. 46 Bypass, Bloomington, 47401, Monroe County, (812)855-7543, 45 miles S of Indianapolis.
Holes: 18. **Yards:** 6,891/5,661. **Par:** 71/72. **Course Rating:** 72.4/73.1. **Slope:** 129/123. **Green Fee:** $19/$21. **Cart Fee:** $11/person. **Walking Policy:** Walking at certain times. **Walkability:** 3. **Opened:** 1959. **Architect:** Jim Soutar. **Season:** March-Dec. **High:** April-Oct. **To obtain tee times:** Call 7 days in advance. **Miscellaneous:** Discount packages, metal spikes, range (grass/mats), club rentals, credit cards (MC, V, D).
Reader Comments: Rock outcroppings, deer crossing the course ... Lots of trees which make for relatively narrow fairways. Very little water, but well-placed sand traps. You pay if you don't hit the ball fairly straight. Course is very well maintained by a friendly staff.

★★ IRONHORSE GOLF CLUB
PU-20 Cedar Island, Logansport, 46947, Cass County, (219)722-1110, 5 miles E of Logansport.
Holes: 18. **Yards:** 6,100/5,400. **Par:** 71/72. **Course Rating:** 67.8/64.8. **Slope:** 109/103. **Green Fee:** $11/$14. **Cart Fee:** $12/person. **Walking Policy:** Unrestricted walking. **Walkability:** 2. **Opened:** 1904. **Architect:** Robert A. Simmons. **Season:** March-Dec. **High:** May-Sept. **To obtain tee times:** Call golf shop. **Miscellaneous:** Reduced fees (weekdays, low season), metal spikes, range (grass), club rentals, credit cards (MC, V), beginner friendly (junior clinics, private lessons).

★★★½ IRONWOOD GOLF CLUB
SP-10955 Fall Rd., Fishers, 46038, Hamilton County, (317)842-0551, 5 miles NE of Indianapolis. **Web:** www.ironwoodgc.com.
Holes: 27. **Yards:** 6,901/5,104. **Par:** 72/72. **Course Rating:** 74.5/70.4. **Slope:** 142/126. **Green Fee:** $25/$30. **Cart Fee:** $12/person. **Walking Policy:** Walking at certain times. **Walkability:** 3. **Architect:** R. N. Thompson/Art Kaser. **Season:** Year-round. **High:** April-Oct. **To obtain tee times:** Call up to 7 days in advance. **Miscellaneous:** Range (grass), club rentals, credit cards (MC, V, D).
Reader Comments: Some great golf holes, still too much play ... Excellent course, don't play after rain ... Good variety of holes ... Great staff, good 27-hole set up ... Long, par 3s hilly. Good work out for walkers. Only one short par 4. A good test ... Very pretty. Challenging.

★★★ JASPER MUNICIPAL GOLF COURSE
PM-17th and Jackson, Jasper, 47546, Dubois County, (812)482-4600, 50 miles NE of Evansville.
Holes: 18. **Yards:** 5,985/5,055. **Par:** 71/71. **Course Rating:** 68.0/68.0. **Slope:** 105/105. **Green Fee:** $14. **Cart Fee:** $9/person. **Walking Policy:** Unrestricted walking. **Walkability:** 4. **Opened:** 1971. **Architect:** William Newcomb. **Season:** Year-round. **High:** June-Aug. **To obtain tee times:** Call golf shop. **Miscellaneous:** Reduced fees (seniors), club rentals, credit cards (MC, V), beginner friendly.
Reader Comments: Neat elevated tees, rolling hills ... Front 9 basic ... Tough, hilly back 9 is a test ... Very friendly staff.

★★★½ JUDAY CREEK GOLF COURSE
SP-14770 Lindy Dr., Granger, 46530, St. Joseph County, (219)277-4653, 5 miles NE of South Bend. **E-mail:** info@judaycreek.com. **Web:** www.judaycreek.com.
Holes: 18. **Yards:** 6,940/5,000. **Par:** 72/72. **Course Rating:** 73.3/67.1. **Slope:** 133/116. **Green Fee:** $23/$28. **Cart Fee:** $12/person. **Walking Policy:** Walking at certain times. **Walkability:** 3. **Opened:** 1989. **Architect:** Ken Killian. **Season:** March-Oct. **High:** June-Aug. **To obtain tee times:** Call anytime. **Miscellaneous:** Reduced fees (twilight, seniors, juniors), metal spikes, range (grass/mats), club rentals, credit cards (MC, V, AE), beginner friendly.
Reader Comments: Wide open course, good facility ... Tough from the tips–best to drive long & straight. Thick rough ... Meticulously maintained, water everywhere ... Good challenge ... Best grass fairways–but watch out for geese.

★★★ LAFAYETTE GOLF CLUB
PM-800 Golf View Dr., Lafayette, 47902, Tippecanoe County, (765)476-4588, 68 miles N of Indianapolis.
Holes: 18. **Yards:** 7,018/5,241. **Par:** 72/75. **Course Rating:** 73.0/71.7. **Slope:** 129/115. **Green Fee:** $13/$15. **Cart Fee:** $10/person. **Walking Policy:** Unrestricted walking. **Walkability:** 2. **Opened:** 1972. **Architect:** Bob Simmons. **Season:** Year-round. **High:** June-Aug. **To obtain tee times:** Call Monday after 8 a.m. for upcoming weekend. Tee available 7 days in advance. **Miscellaneous:** Reduced fees (twilight), range (grass), club rentals, credit cards (MC, V).
Reader Comments: All greens are elevated, always crowded, fun to play ... Nicer in spring and early summer.

LAKE HILLS GOLF CLUB
PU-10001 W. 85th Ave., St. John, 46373, Lake County, (219)365-8601, (888)274-4557, 35 miles SE of Chicago.
★★ CLUB COURSE
Holes: 18. **Yards:** 5,888/4,648. **Par:** 71/72. **Course Rating:** 68.1/66.1. **Slope:** 110/105. **Green Fee:** $18/$40. **Cart Fee:** Included in Green Fee. **Walking Policy:** Unrestricted walking. **Walkability:** 5. **Opened:** 1925. **Architect:** Charles Maddox/Frank P. MacDonald. **Season:** April-Nov. **High:** June-Sept. **To obtain tee times:** Call toll-free number. **Miscellaneous:** Metal spikes, club rentals, credit cards (MC, V, AE, D).
★★ COUNTRY COURSE
Holes: 18. **Yards:** 5,889/4,471. **Par:** 71/72. **Course Rating:** 68.0/65.4. **Slope:** 109/102. **Green Fee:** $18/$40. **Cart Fee:** Included in Green Fee. **Walking Policy:** Unrestricted walking. **Walkability:** 5. **Opened:** 1925. **Architect:** Charles Maddox/Frank P. MacDonald. **Season:** April-Nov. **High:** June-Sept. **To obtain tee times:** Call toll-free number. **Miscellaneous:** Reduced fees (weekdays, low season, twilight, seniors, juniors), club rentals, credit cards (MC, V, AE, D).
★★ PLAYERS COURSE
Holes: 18. **Yards:** 6,194/4,504. **Par:** 70/70. **Course Rating:** 70.1/65.8. **Slope:** 124/111. **Green Fee:** $18/$40. **Cart Fee:** Included in Green Fee. **Walking Policy:** Unrestricted walking. **Walkability:** 5. **Opened:** 1925. **Architect:** Charles Maddox/Frank P. MacDonald. **Season:** April-Nov. **High:** June-Sept. **To obtain tee times:** Call toll-free number. **Miscellaneous:** Metal spikes, club rentals, credit cards (MC, V, AE, D).

★★½ LAKE JAMES GOLF CLUB
PU-1445 W. 275 N., Angola, 46703, Steuben County, (219)833-3967, 45 miles N of Fort Wayne.

Holes: 18. **Yards:** 6,651/5,311. **Par:** 72/73. **Course Rating:** 72.6/69.3. **Slope:** 134/124. **Green Fee:** $20/$25. **Cart Fee:** $12/person. **Walking Policy:** Unrestricted walking. **Walkability:** 4. **Architect:** Robert Beard. **Season:** March-Oct. **High:** June-Aug. **To obtain tee times:** Call golf shop. **Miscellaneous:** Reduced fees (weekdays, seniors, juniors), club rentals, credit cards (MC, V, D).

Reader Comments: New owner has resurrected this course ... Good holes, interesting track ... Great to dump kids/wife at lake and play here ... Tough on your mind.

★★½ LAUREL LAKES GOLF COURSE

PU-2460 E. State Rd. 26 E., Hartford City, 47348, Blackford County, (765)348-4876, 2 miles E of Hartford City.

Holes: 18. **Yards:** 5,962/4,868. **Par:** 70/71. **Course Rating:** 67.8/70.1. **Slope:** 111/115. **Green Fee:** $14/$16. **Cart Fee:** $11/person. **Walking Policy:** Unrestricted walking. **Walkability:** 2. **Opened:** 1971. **Architect:** Mr. Hodges. **Season:** March-Nov. **High:** March-Sept. **Miscellaneous:** Club rentals.

Reader Comments: Basic golf, never crowded ... Excellent service ... Super greens, tons of timber! Perfect pro.

THE LEGENDS OF INDIANA GOLF COURSE

PU-2313 N. Hurricane Rd., Franklin, 46131, Johnson County, (317)736-8186, 12 miles S of Indianapolis. **E-mail:** tblegends@aol.com. **Web:** www.legendsof indiana.com.

Holes: 27. **Green Fee:** $36/$38. **Cart Fee:** $10/person. **Walking Policy:** Walking at certain times. **Walkability:** 2. **Opened:** 1991. **Architect:** Jim Fazio. **Season:** March-Dec. **High:** May-Oct. **To obtain tee times:** Call 14 days in advance. **Miscellaneous:** Reduced fees (twilight), discount packages, range (grass), club rentals, credit cards (MC, V, AE, D).

★★★½ CREEK/MIDDLE

Yards: 7,029/5,287. **Par:** 72/72. **Course Rating:** 74.0/70.3. **Slope:** 132/120.

Reader Comments: Always windy, good test of golf ... Not much elevation change ... Good course for all handicaps; Always in good condition ... Impressive, still young. Will be tough to play in 10 years ... Good practice facility. Great links course—lots of wind!.

★★★½ CREEK/ROAD

Yards: 7,177/5,399. **Par:** 72/72. **Course Rating:** 74.8/71.0. **Slope:** 134/121.

★★★½ MIDDLE/ROAD

Yards: 7,044/5,244. **Par:** 72/72. **Course Rating:** 74.0/71.1. **Slope:** 132/121.

Reader Comments: Challenge when the wind is blowing ... Favorite course, lots of variety ... Rewards accuracy ... Going to be wonderful when it matures ... Tough par 4's...Flat but tough from the blues ... Cut out of cornfield, not many trees ... Fair test for all golfers ... Exceptionally in every way ... Best greens around.

★★½ LIBERTY COUNTRY CLUB

SP-1391 U.S. 27 N., Liberty, 47353, Union County, (765)458-5664, 35 miles N of Cincinnati.

Holes: 18. **Yards:** 6,375/4,544. **Par:** 70/71. **Course Rating:** 70.5/69.3. **Slope:** 120/115. **Green Fee:** $18/$25. **Cart Fee:** $11/person. **Walking Policy:** Unrestricted walking. **Walkability:** 3. **Opened:** 1927. **Architect:** Nipper Campbell/Bob Simmons. **Season:** Year-round. **High:** June-Aug. **To obtain tee times:** Call 3 days in advance. **Miscellaneous:** Reduced fees (weekdays, twilight), discount packages, range (grass), credit cards (MC, V).

Reader Comments: Best-keep secret in midwest ... Great pro. Undiscovered gem.

LIMBERLOST GOLF CLUB

SP-3204 E. Rd 900 N, Rome City, 46784, Noble County, (219)854-4878, 32 miles NW of Fort Wayne.

Holes: 18. **Yards:** 5,770/4,973. **Par:** 70/70. **Course Rating:** 64.9/69.3. **Slope:** 101/109. **Green Fee:** $13/$15. **Cart Fee:** $17/cart. **Walking Policy:** Unrestricted walking. **Walkability:** 3. **Opened:** 1927. **Season:** March-Nov. **High:** May-Sept. **To obtain tee times:** First come, first served. Call golf shop for outings. **Miscellaneous:** Metal spikes, credit cards (MC, V, AE).

THE LINKS AT HEARTLAND CROSSING

PU-6701 S. Heartland Blvd., Camby, 46113, Morgan County, (317)630-1785, 5 miles N of Indianapolis.

Holes: 18. **Yards:** 7,267/5,536. **Par:** 72/72. **Course Rating:** 75.4/69.0. **Slope:** 134/121. **Green Fee:** $23/$43. **Cart Fee:** $6/person. **Walking Policy:** Unrestricted walking. **Walkability:** 2. **Opened:** 1998. **Architect:** Steve Smyers/Nick Price. **Season:** Year-round. **High:** May-Sept. **To obtain tee times:** May call up to 2 weeks in advance. **Miscellaneous:** Reduced fees (weekdays, low season, twilight, juniors), discount packages, range (grass), club rentals, credit cards (MC, V, AE, D).

★★½ THE LINKS GOLF CLUB

PU-11425 N. Shelby 700 W., New Palestine, 46163, Shelby County, (317)861-4466, 15 miles SE of Indianapolis.

Holes: 18. **Yards:** 7,054/5,018. **Par:** 72/72. **Course Rating:** 73.3/68.4. **Slope:** 122/100. **Green Fee:** $32/$43. **Cart Fee:** $5/person. **Walking Policy:** Walking at certain times. **Walkability:** 1. **Opened:** 1972. **Architect:** Charles Maddox. **Season:** Year-round. **High:** May-Sept. **To obtain tee times:** Call 14 days in advance. **Miscellaneous:** Reduced fees (weekdays, low season, twilight, seniors), discount packages, range (grass), club rentals, credit cards (MC, V, D, Novus), beginner friendly.

Reader Comments: Good course. Good service ... Good all-around test ... Huge greens ... Pretty flat but ponds, streams etc ... Great course and fun to play ... Older course has been nicely re-vamped ... Always helpful staff.

★½ MAPLEWOOD GOLF CLUB
SP-4261 E. County Rd. 700 S., Muncie, 47302, Delaware County, (765)284-8007, 7 miles S of Muncie.
Holes: 18. **Yards:** 6,571/5,759. **Par:** 71/76. **Course Rating:** 70.0/68.5. **Slope:** 121/115. **Green Fee:** $15/$19. **Cart Fee:** $11/person. **Walking Policy:** Unrestricted walking. **Walkability:** 2. **Opened:** 1961. **Season:** April-Oct. **High:** June-Sept. **To obtain tee times:** Call after Tuesday for weekend play. **Miscellaneous:** Reduced fees (weekdays, low season), range (grass), club rentals, credit cards (MC, V, D).

★★½ MAXWELTON GOLF CLUB
SP-5721 E. Elkhart County Line Rd., Syracuse, 46567, Kosciusko County, (219)457-3504, 45 miles SE of South Bend.
Holes: 18. **Yards:** 6,490/5,992. **Par:** 72/72. **Course Rating:** 70.1/73.4. **Slope:** 124/128. **Green Fee:** $20/$24. **Cart Fee:** $12/person. **Walking Policy:** Unrestricted walking. **Walkability:** 3. **Opened:** 1930. **Architect:** William B. Langford. **Season:** March-Nov. **High:** May-Sept. **To obtain tee times:** Call anytime. **Miscellaneous:** Club rentals, credit cards (MC, V, AE, D).

Reader Comments: I really appreciate the professional staff ... Great breakfast in summer after 7:00 a.m. Well-stocked golf shop. Has it all ... Great condition for price ...Very hilly, lot of blind shots, hard course to walk ... Best course I have joined.

★★ MICHIGAN CITY MUNICIPAL COURSE
PM-4000 E. Michigan Blvd., Michigan City, 46360, La Porte County, (219)873-1516, 55 miles SE of Chicago.
Holes: 36. **Yards:** 6,169/5,363. **Par:** 72/74. **Course Rating:** 67.6/68.6. **Slope:** 113/113. **Green Fee:** $13/$17. **Cart Fee:** $20/cart. **Walking Policy:** Unrestricted walking. **Walkability:** 2. **Opened:** 1930. **Architect:** Ted Meetz. **Season:** April-Nov. **High:** June-Aug. **To obtain tee times:** Call 7 days in advance. **Miscellaneous:** Reduced fees (low season, twilight, seniors, juniors), metal spikes, club rentals.

MYSTIC HILLS GOLF CLUB
PU-16788 20 B Rd., Culver, 46511, Marshall County, (219)842-2687, 35 miles N of Plymouth.
Web: mystichills.com.
Holes: 18. **Yards:** 6,780/4,958. **Par:** 71/71. **Course Rating:** 72.0/67.5. **Slope:** 132/117. **Green Fee:** $15/$21. **Cart Fee:** $14/person. **Walking Policy:** Walking at certain times. **Walkability:** 4. **Opened:** 1998. **Architect:** Pete Dye/Alice Dye/P.B. Dye. **Season:** March-Oct. **High:** July-Aug. **Miscellaneous:** Reduced fees (weekdays, low season, resort guests, twilight), discount packages, range (grass), club rentals, credit cards (MC, V, AE, D).
Notes: Ranked 9th in 1999 Best New Affordable Public.

OAK GROVE COUNTRY CLUB
PU-State Road 55 South, Oxford, 47971, Benton County, (765)385-2713, 15 miles NW of Lafayette.
Holes: 18. **Yards:** 6,050/5,410. **Par:** 71/73. **Course Rating:** 69.2/68.4. **Slope:** 113/113. **Green Fee:** $12/$14. **Cart Fee:** $9/person. **Walking Policy:** Unrestricted walking. **Walkability:** 1. **Opened:** 1928. **Architect:** William H. Diddel. **Season:** Year-round. **High:** June-Aug. **To obtain tee times:** Call golf shop. **Miscellaneous:** Reduced fees (weekdays, low season, juniors), club rentals, credit cards (MC, V), beginner friendly.
Special Notes: Soft Spikes only.

★½ OAK KNOLL GOLF COURSE
PU-11200 Whitcomb St., Crown Point, 46307, Lake County, (219)663-3349.
Special Notes: Call club for further information.

★★½ OTIS PARK GOLF CLUB
PM-607 Tunnelton Rd., Bedford, 47421, Lawrence County, (812)279-9092, 75 miles S of Indianapolis.
Holes: 18. **Yards:** 6,308/5,184. **Par:** 72/72. **Course Rating:** 70.0/68.1. **Slope:** 128/124. **Green Fee:** $14/$17. **Cart Fee:** $20/cart. **Walking Policy:** Unrestricted walking. **Walkability:** 4. **Opened:** 1920. **Season:** Jan.-Dec. **High:** May-Oct. **To obtain tee times:** Call anytime. **Miscellaneous:** Metal spikes, range (grass/mats), club rentals.
Reader Comments: Front 9 is average, but back 9 is challenging ... Interesting challenge.

OTTER CREEK GOLF CLUB
PU-11522 E. 50 N., Columbus, 47203, Bartholomew County, (812)579-5227, 35 miles S of Indianapolis. **E-mail:** chad@hsonline.net. **Web:** www.ocgc.com.
Holes: 27. **Green Fee:** $40/$70. **Cart Fee:** Included in Green Fee. **Walking Policy:** Unrestricted walking. **Walkability:** 3. **Opened:** 1964. **Architect:** Robert Trent Jones/Rees Jones. **Season:** March-Nov. **High:** May-Sept. **To obtain tee times:** Call anytime in advance with credit card to guarantee reservation. **Miscellaneous:** Reduced fees (weekdays, low season, twilight), discount packages, range (grass/mats), club rentals, credit cards (MC, V, D).
★★★★ **NORTH/EAST**
Yards: 7,224/5,581. **Par:** 72/72. **Course Rating:** 75.6/73.0. **Slope:** 137/125.
★★★★ **NORTH/WEST**
Yards: 7,258/5,690. **Par:** 72/72. **Course Rating:** 75.6/73.5. **Slope:** 138/128.
Notes: Ranked 3rd in 1999 Best in State; 45th in 1996 America's Top 75 Upscale Courses. 1991 USGA Public Links.
★★★★ **WEST/EAST**
Yards: 7,126/5,403. **Par:** 72/72. **Course Rating:** 75.0/71.9. **Slope:** 137/123.
Reader Comments: Superb fairways ... 27 well-designed golf holes ... Long narrow par 4's ... Difficult course ... Highly noted course--just completed major renovation ... Great layout, over-priced, super greens ... Good test of traditional and new designs ... Just straight-up, no-non-sense golf of the classic style.

★★★ **PALMIRA GOLF & COUNTRY CLUB**
SP-12111 W. 109th St., St. John, 46373, Lake County, (219)365-4331, 40 miles SE of Chicago. **E-mail:** nicpon@palmiragolf.com. **Web:** www.palmiragolf.com.
Holes: 18. **Yards:** 6,922/5,725. **Par:** 71/73. **Course Rating:** 72.7/74.6. **Slope:** 128/117. **Green Fee:** $16/$30. **Cart Fee:** $26/cart. **Walking Policy:** Unrestricted walking. **Walkability:** 4. **Opened:** 1972. **Architect:** Bob Lohmann/Rich Nicpon. **Season:** Year-round. **High:** May-Sept. **To obtain tee times:** Call golf shop. **Miscellaneous:** Reduced fees (weekdays, low season, twilight, seniors, juniors), range (grass), club rentals, credit cards (MC, V).
Reader Comments: Many improvements, like a whole new course ... Good course ... One of best in area ... Long with small greens.

PEBBLE BROOK GOLF & COUNTRY CLUB
PU-3110 Westfield Rd., Noblesville, 46060, Hamilton County, (317)896-5596, 30 miles N of Indianapolis.
★★★ **NORTH COURSE**
Holes: 18. **Yards:** 6,392/5,806. **Par:** 70/70. **Course Rating:** 70.5/74.1. **Slope:** 118/115. **Green Fee:** $26/$31. **Cart Fee:** $12/person. **Walking Policy:** Walking at certain times. **Walkability:** 1. **Opened:** 1989. **Architect:** Gary Kern/Ron Kern. **Season:** March-Dec. **High:** May-Sept. **To obtain tee times:** Call on Tuesday for upcoming weekend. Call on Sunday for upcoming week-day. **Miscellaneous:** Reduced fees (weekdays, twilight), range (grass), club rentals, credit cards (MC, V).
Reader Comments: Nice course ... Fairly flat & straight-away ... A very nice outing ... Good value, good holes ... Challenging. Small greens. Tight fairways.
★★★ **SOUTH COURSE**
Holes: 18. **Yards:** 6,557/5,261. **Par:** 72/72. **Course Rating:** 70.5/71.9. **Slope:** 121/115. **Green Fee:** $26/$31. **Cart Fee:** $12/person. **Walking Policy:** Walking at certain times. **Walkability:** 1. **Opened:** 1974. **Architect:** James Dugan. **Season:** March-Dec. **High:** May-Sept. **To obtain tee times:** Call on Tuesday for upcoming weekend. Call on Sunday for following weekday. **Miscellaneous:** Reduced fees (weekdays, twilight), range (grass), club rentals, credit cards (MC, V).
Reader Comments: Good older course, par 5's are reachable, very nice ... Great staff and shop, fun day.

★★★½ **PHEASANT VALLEY GOLF CLUB** *Service*
SP-3838 W. 141st Ave., Crown Point, 46307, Lake County, (219)663-5000, 30 miles SE of Chicago. **Web:** www.pheasantvalley.com.
Holes: 18. **Yards:** 6,869/6,166. **Par:** 72/73. **Course Rating:** 72.3/72.6. **Slope:** 126/N/A. **Green Fee:** $20/$25. **Cart Fee:** $10/person. **Walking Policy:** Unrestricted walking. **Walkability:** 4. **Opened:** 1967. **Architect:** R. Albert Anderson. **Season:** April-Dec. **High:** May-Oct. **To obtain tee times:** Call 7 days in advance. **Miscellaneous:** Reduced fees (weekdays, low season, twilight, seniors, juniors), club rentals, credit cards (MC, V, AE, D).
Reader Comments: Long, tight, very tough and challenging ... Great course—hardest in northern Indiana ... Good hilly/challenging/fast greens–priced right ... Best equipment prices in state.

★★★½ THE PLAYERS CLUB AT WOODLAND TRAILS
PU-6610 W. River Rd., Yorktown, 46224, Delaware County, (765)759-8536, 40 miles NE of Indianapolis. **Web:** www.theplayersclubgolf.com.

Holes: 18. **Yards:** 6,911/5,482. **Par:** 72/72. **Course Rating:** 72.7/71.0. **Slope:** 127/120. **Green Fee:** $15/$23. **Cart Fee:** $12/person. **Walking Policy:** Walking at certain times. **Walkability:** 3. **Opened:** 1991. **Architect:** Gene Bates. **Season:** Year-round. **High:** May-Sept. **To obtain tee times:** Call 7 days in advance. **Miscellaneous:** Reduced fees (weekdays, low season, twilight, seniors, juniors), discount packages, range (grass), club rentals, credit cards (MC, V).
Reader Comments: Excellent course, great service ... Fun and fair ... Super value, great shape, fast greens, friendly ... Nice course, a little tight in the subdivision ... Got nice after 1st hole ... I feel privileged to play it. The best Indiana can offer.

PLUM CREEK COUNTRY CLUB
SP-12401 Lynnwood Blvd., Carmel, 46033, Hamilton County, (317)573-9900, 4 miles N of Indianapolis.
Holes: 18. **Yards:** 6,766/5,209. **Par:** 72/72. **Course Rating:** 72.5/69.6. **Slope:** 127/117. **Green Fee:** $33/$39. **Cart Fee:** $20/person. **Walking Policy:** Walking at certain times. **Walkability:** 1. **Opened:** 1997. **Season:** March-Dec. **High:** May-Sept. **To obtain tee times:** Call up to 7 days in advance. **Miscellaneous:** Range (grass), club rentals, credit cards (MC, V).
Reader Comments: Back 9, fine ... New course with potential. Some fun holes. Greens good.

★★ PLYMOUTH ROCK GOLF COURSE
PU-12641 7B Rd., Plymouth, 46563, Marshall County, (219)936-4405, 20 miles S of South Bend.
Holes: 18. **Yards:** 6,533/5,068. **Par:** 72/74. **Course Rating:** 70.0/68.2. **Slope:** 115/108. **Green Fee:** $11/$15. **Cart Fee:** $10/person. **Walking Policy:** Unrestricted walking. **Walkability:** 2. **Opened:** 1960. **Architect:** Russel Rush. **Season:** Year-round. **High:** May-Sept. **To obtain tee times:** Call in advance in summer. **Miscellaneous:** Reduced fees (weekdays, low season, twilight, seniors, juniors), metal spikes, range (grass/mats), club rentals, credit cards (MC, V), beginner friendly.

★★ POND VIEW GOLF COURSE
PU-850 South 300 E., Star City, 46985, Pulaski County, (219)595-7431, (800)972-9636, 75 miles N of Indianapolis. **E-mail:** Donnell@pwrtc.com. **Web:** www.indianagolfacademy.com.
Holes: 18. **Yards:** 6,270/5,115. **Par:** 70/72. **Course Rating:** 69.7/69.9. **Slope:** 121/121. **Green Fee:** $11/$14. **Cart Fee:** $12/person. **Walking Policy:** Unrestricted walking. **Walkability:** 3. **Architect:** Steve Bonnell. **Season:** March-Nov. **High:** July-Aug. **Miscellaneous:** Metal spikes, range (grass), club rentals, credit cards (MC, V, D).

★★½ POND-A-RIVER GOLF CLUB
PU-26025 River Rd., Woodburn, 46797, Allen County, (219)632-5481, 25 miles E of Fort Wayne.
Holes: 18. **Yards:** 4,694/3,612. **Par:** 69/68. **Course Rating:** 65.0/67.8. **Slope:** 90/90. **Green Fee:** $15/$15. **Cart Fee:** $9/person. **Walking Policy:** Unrestricted walking. **Walkability:** 3. **Season:** April-Nov. **High:** June-Aug. **To obtain tee times:** Call golf shop up to 14 days in advance for weekends. **Miscellaneous:** Reduced fees (low season, seniors, juniors), metal spikes, club rentals.
Reader Comments: Play in early summer ... Back 9 very hilly.

★★½ PORTLAND COUNTRY CLUB
SP-0124 W. 200 S., Portland, 47371, Jay County, (219)726-4646, 2 miles S of Portland.
Holes: 18. **Yards:** 6,505/4,917. **Par:** 70/70. **Course Rating:** 70.7/69.2. **Slope:** 118/89. **Green Fee:** $15/$18. **Cart Fee:** $11/person. **Walking Policy:** Unrestricted walking. **Walkability:** 2. **Opened:** 1922. **Season:** March-Dec. **High:** May-Sept. **To obtain tee times:** Please call in advance. **Miscellaneous:** Reduced fees (weekdays, low season, twilight, juniors), range (grass), club rentals, credit cards (MC, V), beginner friendly (adult and junior clinics, short game area).
Reader Comments: Tough to walk ... Back 9 very rough ... Great shape, uncrowded ... This course is definitely getting better, fun to play. Good people working hard for golfers.

★★★★½ PRAIRIE VIEW GOLF CLUB *Service, Condition*
PU-7000 Longest Dr., Carmel, 46033, Hamilton County, (317)816-3100, (888)646-4653, 10 miles N of Indianapolis. **Web:** www.prairieviewgc.com.
Holes: 18. **Yards:** 7,073/5,203. **Par:** 72/72. **Course Rating:** 74.3/70.5. **Slope:** 138/122. **Green Fee:** $50/$80. **Cart Fee:** Included in Green Fee. **Walking Policy:** Unrestricted walking. **Walkability:** 3. **Opened:** 1997. **Architect:** Robert Trent Jones, Jr. **Season:** March-Dec. **High:** April-Oct. **To obtain tee times:** Call up to 14 days in advance. Groups of 12 or more players must place deposit for one foursome for guarantee. **Miscellaneous:** Reduced fees (weekdays, twilight, juniors), range (grass), club rentals, credit cards (MC, V, AE, D).
Notes: Ranked 4th in 1999 Best in State.
Reader Comments: Play at twilight ... High caliber course ... Great new course, top-notch facility ... Outstanding, will only get better with time, somewhat pricey ... Final 4 holes worth the trip ... Beautiful layout, if you have difficulty hitting out of sand don't play here ... Will hit all the shots.

INDIANA

QUAIL CROSSING GOLF CLUB
PU-5 Quail Crossing Drive, Boonville, 47601, Warrick County, (812)897-1247, 12 miles E of Evansville.
Holes: 18. **Yards:** 6,758/5,081. **Par:** 71/71. **Course Rating:** 72.3/68.8. **Slope:** 126/113. **Green Fee:** $22/$30. **Cart Fee:** $13/person. **Walking Policy:** Unrestricted walking. **Walkability:** 3. **Opened:** 1997. **Architect:** Tom Doak/Bruce Hepner. **Season:** Year-round. **High:** June-Sept. **To obtain tee times:** Call golf shop. **Miscellaneous:** Reduced fees (weekdays, low season, twilight, seniors, juniors), range (grass/mats), club rentals, credit cards (MC, V, AE), beginner friendly (golf clinics).

RABER GOLF COURSE
PU-19396 St. Rd. No.120, Bristol, 46507, Elkhart County, (219)848-4020. **Holes:** 27.
★★ BLUE/RED
Yards: 6,642/5,771. **Par:** 72/74. **Course Rating:** 70.7/N/A. **Slope:** 115/N/A. **Green Fee:** $11/$15. **Walkability:** N/A. **Architect:** Bill Daniel. **Miscellaneous:** Metal spikes.
★★ BLUE/WHITE
Yards: 6,310/5,773. **Par:** 72/73. **Course Rating:** 70.3/N/A. **Slope:** 115/N/A. **Green Fee:** $11/$15. **Walkability:** N/A. **Architect:** Bill Daniel. **Miscellaneous:** Metal spikes.
★★ WHITE/RED
Yards: 6,616/6,191. **Par:** 72/75. **Course Rating:** 71.8/N/A. **Slope:** 119/N/A. **Green Fee:** $11/$15. **Walkability:** N/A. **Architect:** Bill Daniel. **Miscellaneous:** Metal spikes.

★★★ RIVERBEND GOLF COURSE
PU-7207 St. Joe Rd., Fort Wayne, 46835, Allen County, (219)485-2732, 1 miles S of Fort Wayne.
Holes: 18. **Yards:** 6,702/5,633. **Par:** 72/72. **Course Rating:** 72.5/72.5. **Slope:** 127/124. **Green Fee:** $15/$21. **Cart Fee:** $10/person. **Walking Policy:** Unrestricted walking. **Walkability:** 4. **Opened:** 1974. **Architect:** Ernie Schrock. **Season:** March-Nov. **High:** May-Sept. **To obtain tee times:** Call golf shop. **Miscellaneous:** Reduced fees (weekdays, low season, twilight, seniors, juniors), club rentals, credit cards (MC, V).
Reader Comments: Tough layout ... Tight front 9, long back 9. Good greens with tricky pin positions ... Winds along St. Joe River ... Lots of water and trouble.

★★★ RIVERSIDE GOLF COURSE
PU-3502 White River Pkwy., Indianapolis, 46222, Marion County, (317)327-7300.
Holes: 18. **Yards:** 6,260/5,385. **Par:** 70/71. **Course Rating:** 67.9/69.7. **Slope:** 110/104. **Green Fee:** $9/$15. **Cart Fee:** $13/person. **Walking Policy:** Unrestricted walking. **Walkability:** 2. **Opened:** 1901. **Architect:** William H. Diddel. **Season:** Year-round. **High:** May-Sept. **To obtain tee times:** Call 7 days in advance for weekdays. Call Monday at 7 a.m. for upcoming weekend. **Miscellaneous:** Reduced fees (weekdays, low season, twilight, seniors, juniors), metal spikes, range (grass/mats), club rentals, credit cards (MC, V, D).
Reader Comments: Great public course ... Lots of trees, water and sand ... Good confidence builder. Fun!... Flat and long ... Well maintained and run.

★★★★½ ROCK HOLLOW GOLF CLUB *Value, Condition*
PU-County Rd. 250 W., Peru, 46970, Miami County, (765)473-6100, 15 miles N of Kokomo. **E-mail:** rockgolf@netusa1.net. **Web:** golfus.com/rockhollow.
Holes: 18. **Yards:** 6,944/4,967. **Par:** 72/72. **Course Rating:** 74.0/64.8. **Slope:** 132/112. **Green Fee:** $35/$35. **Cart Fee:** $10/person. **Walking Policy:** Unrestricted walking. **Walkability:** 4. **Opened:** 1994. **Architect:** Tim Liddy. **Season:** March-Oct. **High:** June-Sept. **To obtain tee times:** Call up to 14 days (2 weeks) in advance. **Miscellaneous:** Reduced fees (weekdays), range (grass/mats), club rentals, credit cards (MC, V).
Notes: Ranked 8th in 1999 Best in State; 8th in 1995 Best New Public Courses.
Reader Comments: Great variety of golf holes ... Fun layout with plenty of water ... Great newer course, spend lots of time looking for balls ... Rock quarry creates many unique looks ... Tough greens to putt ... A real visual treat and golfing challenge ... Staff will do anything to make your visit more enjoyable.

★★★ ROYAL HYLANDS GOLF CLUB
PU-7629 S. Greensboro Pike, Knightstown, 46148, Henry County, (765)345-2123, 23 miles E of Indianapolis.
Holes: 18. **Yards:** 6,500/5,000. **Par:** 71/71. **Course Rating:** 71.9/68.8. **Slope:** 130/122. **Green Fee:** $22/$27. **Cart Fee:** $12/person. **Walking Policy:** Unrestricted walking. **Walkability:** 3. **Opened:** 1982. **Architect:** Ron Kern. **Season:** March-Dec. **High:** May-Oct. **To obtain tee times:** Call golf shop 1 week in advance. **Miscellaneous:** Reduced fees (weekdays, low season, juniors), discount packages, metal spikes, range (grass), club rentals, lodging (5 rooms), credit cards (MC, V).
Reader Comments: Difficult course. Heather, trouble everywhere ... Best course outside Indy ... Great staff–make you feel welcome ... Very good greens–certain holes don't fit with the rest.

★ **SADDLE BROOK COUNTRY CLUB**
SP-IN 60, Mitchell, 47446, Lawrence County, (812)849-4653.
Special Notes: Formerly The Links Golf Course. Call club for further information.

★★★½ **SADDLEBROOK GOLF CLUB**
PU-5516 Arabian Rd., Indianapolis, 46228, Marion County, (317)290-0539, 7 miles NW of
Indianapolis. **Web:** www.golfus.com/saddlebrook.
Holes: 18. **Yards:** 6,038/4,586. **Par:** 71/71. **Course Rating:** 70.0/68.1. **Slope:** 124/116. **Green
Fee:** $20/$24. **Cart Fee:** $12/person. **Walking Policy:** Walking at certain times. **Walkability:** 2.
Opened: 1994. **Architect:** R.N. Thompson. **Season:** Year-round. **High:** May-Sept. **To obtain tee
times:** Call golf shop 7 days in advance. **Miscellaneous:** Reduced fees (weekdays, low season,
twilight, seniors), range (grass), credit cards (MC, V), beginner friendly.
Reader Comments: Indy's best public course in this price range ... Target golf–think your way
around ... Spacious integration within the subdivision, a little wet even in mid summer.

★★★½ **SALT CREEK GOLF CLUB**
PU-2359 State Road 46 East, Nashville, 47448, Brown County, (812)988-7888, 45 miles S of
Indianapolis. **Web:** www.saltcreek.com.
Holes: 18. **Yards:** 6,407/5,001. **Par:** 72/72. **Course Rating:** 71.2/68.8. **Slope:** 132/122. **Green
Fee:** $33/$39. **Cart Fee:** Included in Green Fee. **Walking Policy:** Mandatory cart. **Walkability:**
5. **Opened:** 1992. **Architect:** Duane Dammeyer. **Season:** March-Nov. **High:** May-Oct. **To obtain
tee times:** Call golf shop. **Miscellaneous:** Reduced fees (weekdays, twilight, juniors), discount
packages, metal spikes, range (grass), club rentals, credit cards (MC, V, D), beginner friendly
(lessons and clinics available).
Reader Comments: Good course–2 different 9s ... Beautiful course, very tight, take extra balls,
a little pricey ... Scenic in resort area ... Very tight course adds to challenge.

★★★ **SANDY PINES GOLF COURSE**
SP-U.S. 231 and County Rd. 1100 N., De Motte, 46310, Jasper County, (219)987-6211, 60 miles
S of Chicago.
Holes: 18. **Yards:** 6,500/4,935. **Par:** 72/72. **Course Rating:** 71.0/71.4. **Slope:** 120/117. **Green
Fee:** $17/$23. **Cart Fee:** $10/person. **Walking Policy:** Unrestricted walking. **Walkability:** 2.
Opened: 1974. **Architect:** William James Spear. **Season:** April-Nov. **High:** June-Aug. **To obtain
tee times:** Call 7 days in advance. **Miscellaneous:** Reduced fees (low season, twilight, seniors,
juniors).
Reader Comments: Nice country setting. Tight fairways... Good, nice terrain, fast greens, trees,
hills, good price ... Off the path ... If you can find it, play it.

★★ **SARAH SHANK GOLF COURSE**
PM-2901 S. Keystone, Indianapolis, 46203, Marion County, (317)784-0631.
Holes: 18. **Yards:** 6,491/5,352. **Par:** 72/72. **Course Rating:** 68.9/70.8. **Slope:** 106/115. **Green
Fee:** $12/$13. **Cart Fee:** $20/. **Walking Policy:** Unrestricted walking. **Walkability:** N/A. **Opened:**
1940. **Architect:** City of Indianapolis. **Season:** Year-round. **High:** March-Sept. **To obtain tee
times:** Call 7 days in advance. **Miscellaneous:** Reduced fees (weekdays, low season, twilight,
seniors, juniors), metal spikes, club rentals, credit cards (MC, V).

★★½ **SCHERWOOD GOLF COURSE**
PU-600 E. Joliet St., Schererville, 46375-0567, Lake County, (219)865-2554, 25 miles S of
Chicago. **Web:** www.scherwood.com.
Holes: 18. **Yards:** 6,900/5,053. **Par:** 71/72. **Course Rating:** 72.0/67.3. **Slope:** 127/108. **Green
Fee:** $18/$25. **Cart Fee:** $23/cart. **Walking Policy:** Unrestricted walking. **Walkability:** 1.
Opened: 1967. **Architect:** Ted Locke. **Season:** April-Dec. **High:** May-Sept. **To obtain tee times:**
Call anytime. **Miscellaneous:** Reduced fees (weekdays, low season, twilight, seniors, juniors),
discount packages, range (grass/mats), club rentals, credit cards (MC, V, AE).
Reader Comments: Nice condition–challenging ... Quality is improving ... The 'feel good' course.
Flat, straight, wide. What's not to like?

★★★ **SHADOWOOD GOLF COURSE**
PU-333 N. Sandy Creek Dr, Seymour, 47274, Jackson County, (812)522-8164, 62 miles S of
Indianapolis.
Holes: 18. **Yards:** 6,713/5,416. **Par:** 72/73. **Course Rating:** 71.8/70.8. **Slope:** 127/118. **Green
Fee:** $16/$28. **Cart Fee:** $12/person. **Walking Policy:** Unrestricted walking. **Walkability:** 2.
Opened: 1994. **Season:** Year-round. **High:** April-Oct. **Miscellaneous:** Reduced fees (week-
days), metal spikes, range (grass/mats), club rentals, credit cards (MC, V).
Reader Comments: Easy course ... Green fees a little high. The course is getting better each
year.

★★½ **SHADY HILLS GOLF COURSE**
PU-1520 W. Chapel Pike, Marion, 46952, Grant County, (765)668-8256, 50 miles N of
Indianapolis.

Holes: 18. **Yards:** 6,513/5,595. **Par:** 71/72. **Course Rating:** 71.6/71.6. **Slope:** 123/110. **Green Fee:** $19/$21. **Cart Fee:** $12/person. **Walking Policy:** Unrestricted walking. **Walkability:** 3. **Opened:** 1957. **Architect:** William H. Diddel. **Season:** March-Nov. **High:** May-July. **To obtain tee times:** Call 14 days in advance. **Miscellaneous:** Reduced fees (weekdays, seniors, juniors), range (grass/mats), club rentals, credit cards (MC, V).

Reader Comments: Good public course layout. Friendly staff ... Good for short hitter.

★★★ SMOCK GOLF COURSE

PU-3910 E. County Line Rd., Indianapolis, 46237, Marion County, (317)888-0036. **Web:** www.smockgolf.com.

Holes: 18. **Yards:** 7,055/5,331. **Par:** 72/72. **Course Rating:** 73.7/69.7. **Slope:** 125/115. **Green Fee:** $15/$16. **Cart Fee:** $13/person. **Walking Policy:** Unrestricted walking. **Walkability:** 2. **Opened:** 1976. **Architect:** Robert Simmons. **Season:** Year-round. **High:** May-Sept. **To obtain tee times:** Call golf shop up to 7 days in advance. **Miscellaneous:** Reduced fees (low season, twilight, seniors, juniors), metal spikes, club rentals, credit cards (MC, V).

Reader Comments: Good public course—good teaching pro ... Long, open, flat basic golf ... Nice because it's long. Wrong fairway is OK ... Usually very crowded ... Very good public course being upgraded. Testy creek challenging.

★★★ SOUTH GROVE GOLF COURSE

PM-1800 W. 18th St., Indianapolis, 46202, Marion County, (317)327-7350.

Holes: 18. **Yards:** 6,259/5,126. **Par:** 70/74. **Course Rating:** 69.3/74.5. **Slope:** 108/108. **Green Fee:** $10/$15. **Cart Fee:** $12/person. **Walking Policy:** Unrestricted walking. **Walkability:** N/A. **Opened:** 1902. **Season:** Year-round. **High:** May-Aug. **To obtain tee times:** Call 7 days in advance for weekdays. Call on Monday at 7 a.m. for upcoming weekend. **Miscellaneous:** Reduced fees (twilight, seniors, juniors), metal spikes, club rentals, credit cards (MC, V), beginner friendly.

Reader Comments: Old style course; lots of trees; a little sand ... Good public course ... Another confidence builder ... Fun course, short, lots of trees. Small greens ... Typical back & forth muny.

★★½ SOUTH SHORE GOLF CLUB

PU-10601 State Rd. 13, Syracuse, 46567, Kosciusko County, (219)457-2832, 2 miles S of Syracuse.

Holes: 18. **Yards:** 6,258/5,245. **Par:** 71/71. **Course Rating:** 68.7/71.1. **Slope:** 120/110. **Green Fee:** $19/$23. **Cart Fee:** $12/person. **Walking Policy:** Walking at certain times. **Walkability:** 2. **Opened:** 1929. **Architect:** William H. Diddel. **Season:** April-Nov. **High:** June-Aug. **To obtain tee times:** 2. **Miscellaneous:** Reduced fees (seniors), range (grass), credit cards (MC, V, D).

Reader Comments: Good beginner's course ... Best shape it's been in years, 37 new trees, best staff found anywhere. Great golf shop. Everyone welcome ... Pretty Indiana country course.

★★★ SUGAR RIDGE GOLF COURSE

PU-21010 Stateline Rd., Lawrenceburg, 47025, Dearborn County, (812)537-0386, 15 miles W of Cincinnati.

Holes: 18. **Yards:** 7,000/4,812. **Par:** 72/72. **Course Rating:** 72.7/66.9. **Slope:** 127/109. **Green Fee:** $25/$40. **Cart Fee:** $12/person. **Walking Policy:** Unrestricted walking. **Walkability:** 3. **Opened:** 1994. **Architect:** Brian Huntley. **Season:** Year-round. **High:** May-Sept. **To obtain tee times:** Must call golf shop 7 days in advance. **Miscellaneous:** Reduced fees (weekdays, low season, twilight, seniors, juniors), range (grass), club rentals, credit cards (MC, V, AE, D).

Reader Comments: Long track, tough to walk ... Don't walk this one—very hilly ... Fun course. Best kept secret in S.E. Indiana ... Up & down, hilly ... Beautiful surroundings. Some memorable holes, some not, good test.

★★★★ SULTAN'S RUN GOLF COURSE

PU-1490 N. Meridian Rd., Jasper, 47546, Dubois County, (812)482-1009, (888)684-3287, 60 miles W of Louisville, KY. **E-mail:** sultan@psci.net. **Web:** www.sultansrun.com.

Holes: 18. **Yards:** 6,859/4,911. **Par:** 72/72. **Course Rating:** 72.9/68.0. **Slope:** 132/118. **Green Fee:** $31/$39. **Cart Fee:** $11/person. **Walking Policy:** Unrestricted walking. **Walkability:** 5. **Opened:** 1992. **Architect:** Tom Jones/Allen Sternberg/Tim Liddy. **Season:** Year-round. **High:** April-Oct. **To obtain tee times:** Call 7 days in advance for groups of 16. For groups of 16 or more call 14 days in advance. **Miscellaneous:** Reduced fees (weekdays, low season, twilight, juniors), discount packages, range (grass), club rentals, credit cards (MC, V, AE, D).

Reader Comments: A little tricky but very enjoyable ... Scenic, challenging course. Excellent design with many elevation changes ... Greens need maturing ... Beautiful 18th hole with waterfall ... Women friendly ... This relatively new course is forgiving, but offers a challenge on some holes. It's long, difficult to walk.

★★½ SUMMERTREE GOLF CLUB

PU-2323 E. 101st St., Crown Point, 46307, Lake County, (219)663-0800, 35 miles SE of Chicago.

Holes: 18. **Yards:** 6,586/5,654. **Par:** 71/72. **Course Rating:** 71.9/72.3. **Slope:** 124/117. **Green Fee:** $15/$21. **Cart Fee:** $21/. **Walking Policy:** Unrestricted walking. **Walkability:** N/A. **Opened:** 1975. **Architect:** Bruce Matthews/Jerry Matthews. **Season:** Year-round. **High:** April-Oct. **To obtain tee times:** Call 7 days in advance. **Miscellaneous:** Reduced fees (low season, seniors), metal spikes, range (grass), club rentals, credit cards (MC, V).
Reader Comments: Long/hilly—some good configuration—not too many trees ... Has potential.

SWAN LAKE GOLF CLUB
R-5203 Plymouth LaPorte Trail, Plymouth, 46563, Marshall County, (219)936-9798, (800)582-7539, 30 miles SW of South Bend. **Web:** www.usgolfacademy.com.
★★★½ **EAST COURSE**
Holes: 18. **Yards:** 6,854/5,289. **Par:** 72/72. **Course Rating:** 72.1/69.4. **Slope:** 121/109. **Green Fee:** $13/$20. **Cart Fee:** $12/person. **Walking Policy:** Unrestricted walking. **Walkability:** 4.
Opened: 1967. **Architect:** Al Humphrey. **Season:** March-Oct. **High:** April-June. **To obtain tee times:** Call golf shop. **Miscellaneous:** Reduced fees (weekdays, twilight, seniors), discount packages, range (grass/mats), club rentals, lodging (93 rooms), credit cards (MC, V, AE, D).
Reader Comments: Shotmaker's course ... Lots of water, bring a net! ... 2 great courses, totally different ... Championship quality and difficulty ... Great course, great value, great service ... Good course-challenging. Rolling terrain-good greens/prices.
★★★½ **WEST COURSE**
Holes: 18. **Yards:** 6,507/5,545. **Par:** 72/72. **Course Rating:** 70.5/71.7. **Slope:** 121/106. **Green Fee:** $13/$20. **Cart Fee:** $12/person. **Walking Policy:** Unrestricted walking. **Walkability:** 4.
Opened: 1967. **Architect:** Al Humphrey. **Season:** March-Oct. **High:** April-June. **To obtain tee times:** Call. **Miscellaneous:** Reduced fees (weekdays, twilight, seniors), discount packages, range (grass/mats), club rentals, lodging (93 rooms), credit cards (MC, V, AE, D).
Reader Comments: Fun to play ... Play them both, friendly folks ... Good course, nice fairways—great price.

★★ TAMEKA WOODS GOLF CLUB
PU-State Rd. 135 and County Rd. 450W, Trafalgar, 46181, Johnson County, (317)878-4331, 22 miles S of Indianapolis. **Web:** www.golfus.com/tamekawoods.
Holes: 18. **Yards:** 6,526/5,341. **Par:** 72/72. **Course Rating:** 70.8/70.0. **Slope:** 123/119. **Green Fee:** $16/$18. **Cart Fee:** $12/person. **Walking Policy:** Unrestricted walking. **Walkability:** 3.
Opened: 1991. **Architect:** James A. Hague III. **Season:** Year-round. **High:** April-Sept. **To obtain tee times:** Call up to 7 days in advance. **Miscellaneous:** Reduced fees (weekdays, low season, twilight, seniors), metal spikes, club rentals, credit cards (MC, V).

★★ TIPTON MUNICIPAL GOLF COURSE
PM-Golf Course Rd., Tipton, 46072, Tipton County, (765)675-6627.
Special Notes: Call club for further information.

★★ TRI COUNTY GOLF CLUB
PU-8170 N. CR 400 W., Middletown, 47356, Henry County, (765)533-4107, 40 miles N of Indianapolis.
Holes: 18. **Yards:** 6,706/5,456. **Par:** 72/73. **Course Rating:** 76.1/70.3. **Slope:** 110/97. **Green Fee:** $14/$17. **Cart Fee:** $12/person. **Walking Policy:** Unrestricted walking. **Walkability:** 1.
Opened: 1964. **Architect:** Robert Solomon. **Season:** Year-round. **High:** May-Sept. **To obtain tee times:** Call or come in. **Miscellaneous:** Reduced fees (seniors), range (grass), club rentals.

★½ TRI-WAY GOLF CLUB
PU-12939-4A Rd., Plymouth, 46563, Marshall County, (219)936-9517, 16 miles S of South Bend. **Web:** www.triwaygolf.com.
Holes: 18. **Yards:** 6,175/5,386. **Par:** 71/71. **Course Rating:** 69.9/68.6. **Slope:** 110/110. **Green Fee:** $10/$13. **Cart Fee:** $16/cart. **Walking Policy:** Unrestricted walking. **Walkability:** 3.
Opened: 1966. **Architect:** Al Humphrey/Don Kinney/Dana Kinney. **Season:** April-Oct. **High:** June-Aug. **To obtain tee times:** Call. **Miscellaneous:** Reduced fees (weekdays, low season), discount packages, club rentals.

THE TROPHY CLUB
PU-3887 N. US Hwy. 52, Lebanon, 46052, Boone County, (765)482-7272, (888)-730-7272, 15 miles N of Indianapolis.
Holes: 18. **Yards:** 7,208/5,050. **Par:** 72/72. **Course Rating:** 74.0/68.5. **Slope:** 131/117. **Green Fee:** $43/$47. **Cart Fee:** $5/person. **Walking Policy:** Unrestricted walking. **Walkability:** 3.
Opened: 1998. **Architect:** Tim Liddy. **Season:** Feb.-Dec. **High:** April-Sept. **To obtain tee times:** Tee times are made available 14 days in advance. **Miscellaneous:** Reduced fees (weekdays, twilight, seniors, juniors), range (grass), club rentals, credit cards (MC, V).
Notes: Ranked 4th in 1999 Best New Upscale Public.

★★ TURKEY CREEK COUNTRY CLUB
SP-6400 Harrison St., Merrillville, 46410, Lake County, (219)980-5170.

INDIANA

Special Notes: Call club for further information.

★★★ TURKEY RUN GOLF COURSE
PU-R.R. 1, Waveland, 47989, Montgomery County, (317)435-2048, 40 miles SE of Indianapolis.
Holes: 18. **Yards:** 6,607/4,834. **Par:** 72/72. **Course Rating:** 71.1/65.1. **Slope:** 120/85. **Green Fee:** $12/$14. **Cart Fee:** $10/person. **Walking Policy:** Walking at certain times. **Walkability:** 5. **Opened:** 1971. **Architect:** Gary Kern. **Season:** Year-round. **High:** April-Sept. **To obtain tee times:** Call golf shop. **Miscellaneous:** Reduced fees (weekdays, low season, twilight, juniors), club rentals, credit cards (MC, V, D), beginner friendly.
Reader Comments: Nice course, small greens ... Fun to play, some tough holes.

★★★★ TWIN BRIDGES GOLF CLUB
PU-1001 Cartersburg Rd., Danville, 46122, Hendricks County, (317)745-9098.
Holes: 18. **Yards:** 7,058/5,470. **Par:** 72/72. **Course Rating:** 74.0/71.6. **Slope:** 130/120. **Green Fee:** $25/$36. **Cart Fee:** $12/person. **Walking Policy:** Unrestricted walking. **Walkability:** 2. **Opened:** 1997. **Architect:** Bob Lohmann/Michael Benkusky. **Season:** March-Oct. **High:** May-Oct. **To obtain tee times:** Call 1 week in advance. **Miscellaneous:** Range (grass), credit cards (MC, V, D).
Reader Comments: Great new club. Great golf pro ... Nice layout. Needs to mature ... Tremendous challenge for all levels of players ... Probably the most pleasant surprise of 1998–not a lot of hype, but a good solid course ... Easy off tees, but bring your best iron game.

★★★ VALLE VISTA GOLF CLUB & CONFERENCE CTR.
PU-755 E. Main St., Greenwood, 46143, Johnson County, (317)888-5313, 10 miles S of Indianapolis. **E-mail:** lew.sharp@vallevista.com. **Web:** www.vallevista.com.
Holes: 18. **Yards:** 6,306/5,680. **Par:** 70/74. **Course Rating:** 70.3/72.4. **Slope:** 127/124. **Green Fee:** $20/$27. **Cart Fee:** $12/person. **Walking Policy:** Unrestricted walking. **Walkability:** 2. **Opened:** 1971. **Architect:** Bob Simmons. **Season:** Year-round. **High:** May-Sept. **To obtain tee times:** Call 7 days in advance. **Miscellaneous:** Reduced fees (weekdays, low season, twilight, seniors, juniors), club rentals, credit cards (MC, V, AE, D), beginner friendly (putt, chip and drive).
Reader Comments: Leave your driver at home. Nice greens ... Tight fairways ... A little short, although a good experience.

★★★½ VALLEY VIEW GOLF CLUB
PU-3748 Lawrence Banet Rd., Floyd Knobs, 47119, Floyd County, (812)923-7291, 5 miles W of Louisville, KY.
Holes: 18. **Yards:** 6,514/5,329. **Par:** 71/75. **Course Rating:** 71.0/71.0. **Slope:** 125/122. **Green Fee:** $21/$24. **Cart Fee:** $10/person. **Walking Policy:** Unrestricted walking. **Walkability:** 3. **Opened:** 1962. **Season:** Year-round. **High:** April-Sept. **To obtain tee times:** Call up to 6 days in advance. **Miscellaneous:** Reduced fees (weekdays, twilight, seniors, juniors), club rentals, credit cards (MC, V).
Reader Comments: Back 9 is the Best ... Good condition for winter play ... Good flat course needs more improvements ... Friendly staff ... Good value but didn't miss the greens.

★★★ VALLEY VIEW GOLF COURSE
SP-6950 W. County Rd. 850 N., Middletown, 47356, Henry County, (765)354-2698, 7 miles E of Anderson.
Holes: 18. **Yards:** 6,421/5,281. **Par:** 72/72. **Course Rating:** 70.3/69.9. **Slope:** 114/109. **Green Fee:** $15/$18. **Cart Fee:** $11/person. **Walking Policy:** Unrestricted walking. **Walkability:** 4. **Opened:** 1964. **Architect:** E.V. Ratliff. **Season:** March-Nov. **High:** May-Sept. **To obtain tee times:** Call for weekends and holidays only. **Miscellaneous:** Reduced fees (seniors).
Reader Comments: Very hilly & scenic, fast greens ... An outstanding golf course. All employees are courteous and polite, they know their jobs well. The course is quite challenging to golfers of all levels. In this rural small town, we are trying to keep it a secret from the big city golfers.

★★★ WABASH VALLEY GOLF CLUB
PU-207 North Dr., Geneva, 46740, Adams County, (219)368-7388, 32 miles S of Fort Wayne. **E-mail:** wvgc@adamswells.com.
Holes: 18. **Yards:** 6,454/5,079. **Par:** 71/71. **Course Rating:** 70.5/68.4. **Slope:** 120/114. **Green Fee:** $14/$18. **Cart Fee:** $12/person. **Walking Policy:** Unrestricted walking. **Walkability:** 1. **Opened:** 1963. **Architect:** Henry Culp/Gary Kern. **Season:** March-Nov. **High:** June-Aug. **To obtain tee times:** Call up to 7 days in advance. **Miscellaneous:** Reduced fees (weekdays, low season), club rentals, credit cards (MC, V), beginner friendly (clinics, lessons).
Reader Comments: Indiana's best value , very scenic, water abounds ... Take plenty of bug spray ... Many difficult holes–tight, accuracy needed.

WALNUT CREEK GOLF COURSE
PU-7453 E. 400 S., Marion, 46953, Grant County, (765)998-7651, (800)998-7651, 4 miles E of Gas City. **E-mail:** randy@walnutcreekgolf.com. **Web:** www.walnutcreekgolf.com.

Holes: 18. **Yards:** 6,880/5,154. **Par:** 72/72. **Course Rating:** 72.1/68.5. **Slope:** 121/109. **Green Fee:** $18/$22. **Cart Fee:** $12/person. **Walking Policy:** Unrestricted walking. **Walkability:** 4. **Opened:** 1970. **Architect:** Randy Ballinger. **Season:** March-Dec. **High:** June-Aug. **To obtain tee times:** Call at least 1 day in advance. Packages may be reserved up to 6 months in advance. **Miscellaneous:** Reduced fees (weekdays, low season, resort guests), discount packages, metal spikes, range (grass/mats), club rentals, credit cards (MC, V).

Reader Comments: Quirky new 18 a lot of fun ... World class service and staff well worth the price ... Interesting track ... Good variety ... Well managed, home-town atmosphere.

★★★½ WESTCHASE GOLF CLUB

SP-4 Hollaway Blvd., Brownsburg, 46112, Hendricks County, (317)892-7888, 10 miles W of Indianapolis. **Web:** www.westchasegolf.com.

Holes: 18. **Yards:** 6,700/4,869. **Par:** 71/71. **Course Rating:** 70.8/68.2. **Slope:** 129/112. **Green Fee:** $30/$35. **Cart Fee:** $10/person. **Walking Policy:** Unrestricted walking. **Walkability:** 3. **Opened:** 1996. **Architect:** Ron Kern. **Season:** Year-round. **High:** May-Oct. **To obtain tee times:** Call. **Miscellaneous:** Reduced fees (weekdays, low season, twilight, juniors), range (grass), club rentals, credit cards (MC, V, AE).

Reader Comments: Backside has a give-me-birdie par 5 475 yards, downhill & downwind ... Great condition, but a couple holes short ... Best kept secret in Indianapolis area ... Nice course, great back 9, hilly ... Great course!! Front 9 is a links style, very wide open. Back 9 is very traditional with trees all around.

WHITE HAWK COUNTRY CLUB

SP-1001 White Hawk Dr., Crown Point, 46307, Lake County, (219)661-2323, 40 miles SE of Chicago. **E-mail:** whitehawkcc@prodigy.net. **Web:** www.whitehawkcc.com.

Holes: 18. **Yards:** 7,025/5,255. **Par:** 72/72. **Course Rating:** 74.0/70.4. **Slope:** 136/118. **Green Fee:** $37/$55. **Walking Policy:** Unrestricted walking. **Walkability:** 3. **Opened:** 1998. **Architect:** Dick Nugent/Tim Nugent. **Season:** March-Nov. **High:** May-Sept. **To obtain tee times:** General public, 14 days in advance. **Miscellaneous:** Reduced fees (low season, twilight), range (grass), club rentals, credit cards (MC, V, AE, D).

★½ WICKER MEMORIAL PARK GOLF COURSE

PU-Indianapolis Blvd. and Ridge Rd., Highland, 46322, Lake County, (219)838-9809, 1 miles N of Hammond.

Holes: 18. **Yards:** 6,515/5,301. **Par:** 72/73. **Course Rating:** 70.8/69.3. **Slope:** 106/107. **Green Fee:** $12/$16. **Cart Fee:** $11/. **Walking Policy:** Unrestricted walking. **Walkability:** 1. **Opened:** 1930. **Architect:** Tom Bendelow. **Season:** Year-round. **High:** May-Sept. **To obtain tee times:** Call in advance. **Miscellaneous:** Reduced fees (weekdays, low season, twilight, seniors, juniors), discount packages, range (grass), club rentals.

★★ WILLIAM S. REA GOLF COURSE

PU-3500 S. 7th St., Terre Haute, 47802, Vigo County, (812)232-0709, 70 miles W of Indianapolis. **E-mail:** Bogeys6263@aol.com.

Holes: 18. **Yards:** 6,482/5,353. **Par:** 72/72. **Course Rating:** 70.2/71.7. **Slope:** 110/110. **Green Fee:** $9/$15. **Cart Fee:** $12/person. **Walking Policy:** Unrestricted walking. **Walkability:** 1. **Opened:** 1900. **Architect:** Rea family. **Season:** March-Dec. **High:** May-Aug. **To obtain tee times:** Call on Wednesday for upcoming weekend. **Miscellaneous:** Reduced fees (low season, juniors), range (grass), club rentals, credit cards (MC, V).

Special Notes: Formerly Rea Park Golf Course.

★★★½ WILLIAM SAHM GOLF COURSE

PU-6800 East 91st. St., Indianapolis, 46250, Marion County, (317)849-0036, 5 miles NE of Indianapolis.

Holes: 18. **Yards:** 6,347/5,459. **Par:** 70/70. **Course Rating:** 69.2/69.2. **Slope:** 105/104. **Green Fee:** $15/$16. **Cart Fee:** $12/person. **Walking Policy:** Unrestricted walking. **Walkability:** 2. **Opened:** 1963. **Architect:** Pete Dye. **Season:** Year-round. **High:** April-Oct. **To obtain tee times:** Call up to 7 days in advance. **Miscellaneous:** Reduced fees (twilight, seniors), metal spikes, range (grass/mats), club rentals, credit cards (MC, V), beginner friendly (teaching pro).

Reader Comments: Simple course. Nice pro. Nice people ... Always crowded ... Good for beginners.

★★★ WINCHESTER GOLF CLUB

PU-Simpson Dr., Winchester, 47394, Randolph County, (765)584-5151, 20 miles E of Muncie. **Holes:** 18. **Yards:** 6,540/5,023. **Par:** 72/74. **Course Rating:** 70.4/67.6. **Slope:** 115/106. **Green Fee:** $10/$20. **Cart Fee:** $14/person. **Walking Policy:** Unrestricted walking. **Walkability:** 1. **Opened:** 1937. **Architect:** William Diddel/Tim Liddy. **Season:** Year-round. **High:** April-Oct. **To obtain tee times:** Call up to 14 days in advance. **Miscellaneous:** Reduced fees (weekdays, low season), range (grass), club rentals, credit cards (MC, V).

Reader Comments: Very good public golf ... Love this course ... Most par 5s very short ... Consistent greens.

INDIANA

★★½ WOODED VIEW GOLF CLUB

PU-2404 Greentree North, Clarksville, 47129, Clark County, (812)283-9274, 5 miles S of Louisville, KY.

Holes: 18. **Yards:** 6,514/5,006. **Par:** 71/73. **Course Rating:** 71.0/67.2. **Slope:** 126/114. **Green Fee:** $12/$17. **Cart Fee:** $10/person. **Walking Policy:** Unrestricted walking. **Walkability:** 2. **Opened:** 1978. **Season:** Year-round. **High:** March-Oct. **To obtain tee times:** Call 3 days in advance. **Miscellaneous:** Reduced fees (seniors, juniors), range (grass), club rentals, beginner friendly (junior clinics).

Reader Comments: A tight course in the woods ... Narrow fairways ... Excellent value, but lots of play slows round.

★★★ ZOLLNER GOLF COURSE AT TRI-STATE UNIVERSITY

PU-300 W. Park St., Angola, 46703, Steuben County, (219)665-4269, 30 miles N of Fort Wayne. **E-mail:** stinson@alpha.trisstate.edu.

Holes: 18. **Yards:** 6,628/5,204. **Par:** 72/73. **Course Rating:** 71.8/70.2. **Slope:** 129/122. **Green Fee:** $15/$18. **Cart Fee:** $11/person. **Walking Policy:** Unrestricted walking. **Walkability:** 4. **Opened:** 1971. **Architect:** Robert Beard. **Season:** March-Dec. **High:** May-Sept. **To obtain tee times:** Call 7 days in advance. **Miscellaneous:** Reduced fees (weekdays, low season, twilight, seniors, juniors), discount packages, range (grass), club rentals, credit cards (MC, V).

Reader Comments: Great layout ... Be sure to take a cart ... Could be an excellent course. Has had its ups and downs ... Hosted NAIA championship. Some holes can play extremely difficult ...Several short par 4s.

IOWA

★★★ A.H. BLANK GOLF COURSE
PM-808 County Line Rd., Des Moines, 50315, Polk County, (515)285-0864, 1 mile N of downtown Des Moines.
Holes: 18. **Yards:** 6,815/5,617. **Par:** 72/72. **Course Rating:** 72.0/70.4. **Slope:** 119/115. **Green Fee:** $16/$20. **Cart Fee:** $22/cart. **Walking Policy:** Unrestricted walking. **Walkability:** 3. **Opened:** 1971. **Architect:** Edward Lawrence Packard. **Season:** March-Oct. **High:** May-Aug. **To obtain tee times:** Call 7 days in advance. **Miscellaneous:** Reduced fees (low season, twilight, seniors, juniors), range (grass/mats), club rentals, credit cards (MC, V).
Reader Comments: Can't get into much trouble ... Zoo next door ... Much better with watered fairways ... Very good muny ... City course, good layout, good value ... Heavily used public course, good for practice ... Best kept muny in Des Moines.

★½ AIRPORT NATIONAL GOLF
PU-3001 Wright Bros. Blvd. E., Cedar Rapids, 52404, Linn County, (319)848-4500, 2 miles E of Cedar Rapids Airport.
Holes: 18. **Yards:** 4,500/3,826. **Par:** 63/64. **Course Rating:** 58.5/N/A. **Slope:** 80/N/A. **Green Fee:** $5/$14. **Cart Fee:** $20/cart. **Walking Policy:** Unrestricted walking. **Walkability:** 4. **Opened:** 1994. **Architect:** T. Lockie, C. Pribble, M. Lemon, G. Mason. **Season:** March-Dec. **High:** May-Aug. **To obtain tee times:** Weekdays first come first serve weekends & Holidays. Tee times taken by previous Tuesday. **Miscellaneous:** Reduced fees (seniors, juniors), metal spikes, range (grass/mats), club rentals, credit cards (MC, V).

★★★★ AMANA COLONIES GOLF COURSE
PU-451 27th Ave., Amana, 52203, Iowa County, (319)622-6222, (800)383-3636, 20 miles SW of Cedar Rapids. **E-mail:** golfacgc@netins.net. **Web:** www.amanagolfcourse.com.
Holes: 18. **Yards:** 6,824/5,228. **Par:** 72/72. **Course Rating:** 73.3/69.7. **Slope:** 136/115. **Green Fee:** $44/$49. **Cart Fee:** Included in Green Fee. **Walking Policy:** Mandatory cart. **Walkability:** 4. **Opened:** 1989. **Architect:** Jim Spear. **Season:** March-Nov. **High:** June-Sept. **To obtain tee times:** Call up to 30 days in advance with credit card for guarantee. **Miscellaneous:** Reduced fees (weekdays, low season, twilight), range (grass), club rentals, lodging, credit cards (MC, V, AE, Diners Club).
Notes: Ranked 8th in 1999 Best in State.
Reader Comments: Scenic holes through wooded hills ... This is Iowa's best ... Breathtaking views, lots of trees ... Tight fairways with doglegs ... A special place in the woods ... Proves Iowa isn't flat ... Bent grass target golf ... Beautiful rolling course ... Good chicken salad sandwich ... Carved out of a forest.

AMERICAN LEGION COUNTRY CLUB
SP-1800 S. Elm St., Shenandoah, 51601, Page County, (712)246-3308, 60 miles SE of Omaha, NE.
Holes: 18. **Yards:** 5,803/5,261. **Par:** 70/72. **Course Rating:** 67.4/69.1. **Slope:** 116/113. **Green Fee:** $17/$20. **Cart Fee:** $20/cart. **Walking Policy:** Unrestricted walking. **Walkability:** 3. **Opened:** 1956. **Architect:** Chic Adams. **Season:** April-Oct. **High:** June-Aug. **To obtain tee times:** Call golf shop. **Miscellaneous:** Discount packages, club rentals, credit cards (MC, V).

AMERICAN LEGION GOLF & COUNTRY CLUB
SP-Rte. 3, Fort Dodge, 50501, Webster County, (515)576-5711, 3 miles N of Fort Dodge.
Holes: 9. **Yards:** 3,161/2,821. **Par:** 37/37. **Course Rating:** N/A. **Slope:** N/A. **Green Fee:** $10/$12. **Cart Fee:** $14/cart. **Walking Policy:** Unrestricted walking. **Walkability:** 3. **Opened:** 1920. **Season:** March-Nov. **High:** June-July-Aug. **To obtain tee times:** Call golf shop. **Miscellaneous:** Reduced fees (twilight), discount packages, club rentals.

AMERICAN LEGION MEMORIAL GOLF COURSE
PU-1301 S. 6th St., Marshalltown, 50158, (515)752-1834.
Special Notes: Call club for further information.

★★★½ BEAVER CREEK GOLF CLUB
PU-11200 N.W. Towner Dr., Grimes, 50111, Polk County, (515)986-3221, 5 miles NW of I-80 in Des Moines.
Holes: 18. **Yards:** 6,685/5,245. **Par:** 72/72. **Course Rating:** 71.8/70.4. **Slope:** 121/122. **Green Fee:** $21/$23. **Cart Fee:** $11/person. **Walking Policy:** Walking at certain times. **Walkability:** 2. **Opened:** 1991. **Architect:** Jerry Raible. **Season:** March-Nov. **High:** May-Aug. **To obtain tee times:** Call or come in 7 days in advance. **Miscellaneous:** Reduced fees (weekdays, seniors, juniors), range (grass), club rentals, credit cards (MC, V, AE).
Reader Comments: One of Iowa's few bent-grass fairways ... Shotmaker's course, narrow fairways ... Well laid out ... Upgrading done each year... Great people ... Good muny... Well kept.

★★★★ BOS LANDEN GOLF RESORT
R-2411 Bos Landen Dr., Pella, 50219, Marion County, (515)628-4625, (800)916-7888, 35 miles SE of Des Moines. **Web:** www.igolf.com/ia/pella.htm.

IOWA

Holes: 18. **Yards:** 6,932/5,155. **Par:** 72/72. **Course Rating:** 73.5/70.9. **Slope:** 136/122. **Green Fee:** $28/$45. **Cart Fee:** Included in Green Fee. **Walking Policy:** Walking at certain times. **Walkability:** 5. **Opened:** 1994. **Architect:** Dick Phelps. **Season:** April-Nov. **High:** April-Oct. **To obtain tee times:** Resort guests may call up to 60 days in advance. Public may call up to 30 days in advance. **Miscellaneous:** Reduced fees (weekdays, low season, resort guests, twilight, seniors, juniors), discount packages, range (grass), club rentals, lodging (87 rooms), credit cards (MC, V, AE).
Notes: Ranked 6th in 1999 Best in State.
Reader Comments: Good facilities, friendly people, great atmosphere ... Recommend it to anyone ... One of the best in the Midwest ... Challenging layout, use every club in your bag ... Greens in poor shape when I played ... Absolutely beautiful ... Requires straight shots, and you must know your yardages.

★★★½ BRIARWOOD GOLF COURSE
PU-3405 N.E. Trilein Dr., Ankeny, 50021, Polk County, (515)964-4653, 15 miles N of Des Moines.
Holes: 18. **Yards:** 7,019/5,250. **Par:** 72/72. **Course Rating:** 74.2/70.4. **Slope:** 128/119. **Green Fee:** $21/$27. **Cart Fee:** $11/person. **Walking Policy:** Walking at certain times. **Walkability:** 3. **Opened:** 1995. **Architect:** Gordon Cunningham. **Season:** March-Nov. **High:** May-Oct. **To obtain tee times:** Call up to 7 days in advance. **Miscellaneous:** Reduced fees (weekdays, twilight), range (grass), club rentals, credit cards (MC, V).
Reader Comments: New course ... Wide open ... Residential course ... Tough in the wind ... Good layout ... Excellent challenge, friendly ... Beautiful course, country club conditions.

★★½ BRIGGS WOODS GOLF COURSE
PU-2501 Briggs Woods Trail, Webster City, 50595, Hamilton County, (515)832-9572, 2 miles S of Fort Dodge.
Holes: 18. **Yards:** 6,502/5,167. **Par:** 72/71. **Course Rating:** 72.0/70.0. **Slope:** 128/118. **Green Fee:** $12/$17. **Cart Fee:** $18/cart. **Walking Policy:** Unrestricted walking. **Walkability:** 5. **Opened:** 1971. **Architect:** Jerry Raible. **Season:** April-Oct. **High:** May-Aug. **To obtain tee times:** Call 7 days in advance. **Miscellaneous:** Reduced fees (weekdays, low season, twilight, juniors), discount packages, range (grass), club rentals, credit cards (MC, V, AE), beginner friendly (new golfer program).
Reader Comments: Tough and tight ... Typical "rural" Iowa course ... Back 9 more fun to play ... Tactically, one of the most challenging courses in Iowa ... A course in a county park ... Lots of wild game to see.

★★★★ BROOKS GOLF CLUB *Service*
R-1201 Brooks Park Lane, Okoboji, 51355, Dickinson County, (712)332-5011, (800)204-0507, 90 miles E of Sioux Falls, SD.
Holes: 18. **Yards:** 6,361/5,109. **Par:** 70/70. **Course Rating:** 69.5/68.5. **Slope:** 117/114. **Green Fee:** $40/$55. **Cart Fee:** Included in Green Fee. **Walking Policy:** Mandatory cart. **Walkability:** 1. **Opened:** 1932. **Architect:** Warren Dickenson. **Season:** May-Oct. **High:** June-Aug. **To obtain tee times:** Call golf shop. Call (800)204-0507 or (712)332-5011. **Miscellaneous:** Reduced fees (low season, twilight, seniors, juniors), discount packages, metal spikes, range (grass), club rentals, lodging, credit cards (MC, V, AE, D).
Reader Comments: Country-club service from start to finish ... Old course ... Big trees ... Playable ... Gorgeous flowers and landscaping ... Open front 9, back has trees and doglegs.

★★½ BROWN DEER GOLF CLUB
SP-1900 Country Club Dr., Coralville, 52241, Johnson County, (319)337-8508, 111 miles E of Des Moines.
Holes: 9. **Yards:** 3,192/2,694. **Par:** 35/36. **Course Rating:** 36.7/35.6. **Slope:** 132/118. **Green Fee:** $14/$18. **Cart Fee:** $10/person. **Walking Policy:** Unrestricted walking. **Walkability:** 5. **Opened:** 1992. **Season:** April-Nov. **To obtain tee times:** Call golf shop. **Miscellaneous:** Reduced fees (resort guests, twilight, seniors, juniors), metal spikes, range (mats), club rentals, credit cards (MC, V).
Reader Comments: Tight, demanding course ... Leave your driver in the bag ... Lots of water... Will eat up your ball supply ... Scenic ... Grass needs help ... Tight fairways ... Tough track.

★★½ BUNKER HILL GOLF COURSE
PM-2200 Bunker Hill Rd., Dubuque, 52001, Dubuque County, (319)589-4261.
Holes: 18. **Yards:** 5,316/4,318. **Par:** 69/69. **Course Rating:** 65.7/64.1. **Slope:** 111/113. **Green Fee:** $12/$14. **Cart Fee:** $9/person. **Walking Policy:** Unrestricted walking. **Walkability:** 5. **Architect:** Gordon Cunningham. **Season:** March-Nov. **High:** May-Sept. **To obtain tee times:** Call 7 days in advance. **Miscellaneous:** Reduced fees (weekdays, low season, twilight, seniors, juniors), metal spikes, club rentals, credit cards (MC, V).
Reader Comments: Short, hilly terrain ... Scenic course in the bluffs along the Mississippi ... Golf amid rock formations ... If you walk, be in shape ... Short course ... I liked the challenge of the hills ... Irrigation has helped ... Interesting muny.

IOWA

CARROLL MUNICIPAL GOLF COURSE
PM-2266 North West St., Carroll, 51401, Carroll County, (712)792-9190.
Holes: 18. **Yards:** 6,160/4,994. **Par:** 71/72. **Course Rating:** 66.0/67.0. **Slope:** 102/102. **Green Fee:** $14/$14. **Cart Fee:** $16/cart. **Walking Policy:** Unrestricted walking. **Walkability:** 2. **Opened:** 1968. **Architect:** Charles Calhoun. **Season:** April -Oct. **High:** May-Sept. **To obtain tee times:** Tee times for weekends and holidays only. Tee time reservations may be made starting at 7:00 A.M. on the Wednesday immediately prior to the weekend. **Miscellaneous:** Club rentals.

CEDAR BEND GOLF
PU-2147 Underwood Ave., Charles City, 50616, Floyd County, (515)228-6465, 1 mile SE of Charles City.
Holes: 18. **Yards:** 6,765/5,337. **Par:** 72/72. **Course Rating:** 71.8/69.7. **Slope:** 118/113. **Green Fee:** $14/$16. **Cart Fee:** $20/cart. **Walking Policy:** Unrestricted walking. **Walkability:** 2. **Opened:** 1964. **Season:** April-Nov. **High:** June-Aug. **To obtain tee times:** Phone to obtain tee times. **Miscellaneous:** Reduced fees (twilight), range (grass), club rentals.
Special Notes: Formerly known as Charles City Country Club

★★½ DODGE PARK GOLF COMPLEX
4041 W. Broadway, Council Bluffs, 51501, Pottawattamie County, (712)322-9970, 4 miles W of downtown Council Bluffs.
Reader Comments: On the river ... Tight fairways ... Fairly short ... Should be great in few years ... Friendly staff ... Fast play ... Easy walking ... Price is right.
Special Notes: Call club for further information.

★★★½ DON GARDNER MEMORIAL GOLF COURSE
PM-5101 Golf Course Rd., Marion, 52302, Linn County, (319)286-5586, (800)373-8433, 2 miles N of Marion.
Holes: 18. **Yards:** 6,629/5,574. **Par:** 72/72. **Course Rating:** N/A. **Slope:** 111/109. **Green Fee:** $9.50/$14.50. **Cart Fee:** $22/cart. **Walking Policy:** Unrestricted walking. **Walkability:** 3. **Architect:** Herman Thompson. **Season:** April-Nov. **High:** June-Sept. **To obtain tee times:** Call up to 10 days. **Miscellaneous:** Reduced fees (twilight, seniors, juniors), no metal spikes, range (grass), club rentals, credit cards (MC, V).
Reader Comments: Good muny ... Easy to walk ... Basic layout ... Pro shop with a golf course ... Just plain my favorite, huge pro shop ... Gets better every year.

★★★ DUCK CREEK GOLF CLUB
PU-Locust and Marlow, Davenport, 52803, Scott County, (319)326-7824.
Holes: 18. **Yards:** 5,900/5,500. **Par:** 70/74. **Course Rating:** 67.9/72.0. **Slope:** 115/120. **Green Fee:** $9/$13. **Cart Fee:** $16/person. **Walking Policy:** Unrestricted walking. **Walkability:** N/A. **Opened:** 1930. **Architect:** William B. Langford. **Season:** April-Nov. **High:** April-Sept. **To obtain tee times:** Call 3 days in advance. **Miscellaneous:** Reduced fees (seniors, juniors), range (grass), club rentals.
Reader Comments: Rolls nicely around Duck Creek ... Many large hardwoods ... Trees line most fairways ... Tough to walk fun to play ... Good course in town ... Nice staff ... No bunkers ... Tough finishing hole ... Nice city course.

★★ EDMUNDSON GOLF COURSE
PU-1608 Edmundson Dr., Oskaloosa, 52577, Mahaska County, (515)673-5120, 60 miles SE of Des Moines.
Holes: 18. **Yards:** 6,031/4,701. **Par:** 70/70. **Course Rating:** 68.6/66.9. **Slope:** 116/112. **Green Fee:** $13/$14. **Cart Fee:** $16/cart. **Walking Policy:** Unrestricted walking. **Walkability:** 4. **Architect:** C.C. (Nick) Carter. **Season:** April-Oct. **High:** May-July. **To obtain tee times:** Call on Thursday for weekend. **Miscellaneous:** Reduced fees (juniors), range (grass), club rentals.

★★★½ ELLIS PARK MUNICIPAL GOLF COURSE
PM-1401 Zika Ave. N.W., Cedar Rapids, 52405, Linn County, (319)286-5589.
Holes: 18. **Yards:** 6,648/5,210. **Par:** 72/72. **Course Rating:** 72.0/70.8. **Slope:** 124/111. **Green Fee:** $13/$14. **Cart Fee:** $20/cart. **Walking Policy:** Unrestricted walking. **Walkability:** 4. **Opened:** 1920. **Architect:** William B. Langford. **Season:** April-Nov. **High:** June-Aug. **To obtain tee times:** Call Monday through Saturday 9 a.m. to 3 p.m. up to 10 days in advance.
Miscellaneous: Reduced fees (weekdays, twilight, seniors, juniors), club rentals, credit cards (MC, V).
Reader Comments: Save your strokes on the front 9 ... You'll need them for the back! ... New watered fairways good ... Great public golf course ... Some tough elevated greens ... Holes 11-14 are neat! ... Nice trees, rolling hills.

★★★½ EMEIS GOLF CLUB
PU-4500 W. Central Park, Davenport, 52804, Scott County, (319)326-7825.
Holes: 18. **Yards:** 6,500/5,549. **Par:** 72/74. **Course Rating:** 71.9/74.0. **Slope:** 120/115. **Green Fee:** $10/$14. **Cart Fee:** $18/person. **Walking Policy:** Unrestricted walking. **Walkability:** 3.

Opened: 1961. **Architect:** C.D. Wagstaff. **Season:** April-Oct. **High:** May-Aug. **To obtain tee times:** Call or come in 3 days in advance. A $2.00 nonrefundable fee required up to 7 days in advance. **Miscellaneous:** Reduced fees (seniors, juniors), range (grass/mats), club rentals.
Reader Comments: Challenging but not brutal ... A good test of your game at a good price ... Good track, fair, easy to walk ... Almost championship course ... Good muny track ... This course is a sleeper... Nice city course ... Outstanding old course.

★★★ EMERALD HILLS GOLF CLUB
SP-808 S. Hwy. 71, Arnolds Park, 51331, Dickinson County, (712)332-7100, 103 miles NE of Sioux City.
Holes: 18. **Yards:** 6,651/5,493. **Par:** 72/72. **Course Rating:** 72.6/72.2. **Slope:** 125/121. **Green Fee:** $23/$38. **Cart Fee:** $10/person. **Walking Policy:** Unrestricted walking. **Walkability:** 3.
Opened: 1972. **Architect:** Leo Johnson. **Season:** April-Oct. **High:** May-Sept. **To obtain tee times:** Call anytime. **Miscellaneous:** Reduced fees (weekdays, low season, twilight, juniors), discount packages, range (grass), club rentals, credit cards (MC, V).
Reader Comments: Fun course ... Good challenge ... Nice vacation golf setting ... Mature course ... Friendly staff... Good condition ... Great atmosphere ... Long and rolling with interesting variety, very enjoyable.

★★★★ FINKBINE GOLF COURSE
PU-1362 W. Melrose Ave., Iowa City, 52246, Johnson County, (319)335-9556, 110 miles E of Des Moines.
Holes: 18. **Yards:** 7,030/5,645. **Par:** 72/72. **Course Rating:** 73.9/73.1. **Slope:** 132/123. **Green Fee:** $25/$30. **Cart Fee:** $22/cart. **Walking Policy:** Unrestricted walking. **Walkability:** 3.
Opened: 1955. **Architect:** Robert Bruce Harris. **Season:** April-Nov. **High:** June-Aug. **To obtain tee times:** Call 7 days in advance. **Miscellaneous:** Reduced fees (twilight), range (grass/mats), club rentals, credit cards (MC, V).
Notes: Ranked 10th in 1999 Best in State. 1991-93 Nike Hawkeye Open.
Reader Comments: Hillside tram from 13th green to 14th tee ... New bunkers make course tougher... Challenging ... Island green #13 will blow your mind ... Better now with renovations ... Won't recognize course now ... University of Iowa course ... Solid parkland course ... Always in good shape ... Interesting layout.

★★ FLINT HILLS MUNICIPAL GOLF CLUB
PM-Highway 61, Burlington, 52601, Des Moines County, (319)752-2018.
Holes: 18. **Yards:** 5,648/4,952. **Par:** 71/71. **Course Rating:** 66.7/N/A. **Slope:** 110/N/A. **Green Fee:** $10/$12. **Cart Fee:** $18/cart. **Walking Policy:** Unrestricted walking. **Walkability:** 2.
Opened: 1943. **Season:** April-Nov. **High:** July-Sept. **To obtain tee times:** Call on Wednesday for upcoming weekend. **Miscellaneous:** Reduced fees (weekdays, twilight, seniors, juniors), club rentals, credit cards (MC, V).

FOX RUN GOLF COURSE
PU-3001 MacIneery Dr., Council Bluffs, 51501, Pottawattamie County, (712)366-4653, 1 miles E of Omaha. **Web:** www.golfllc.com.
Holes: 18. **Yards:** 6,500/4,968. **Par:** 71/71. **Course Rating:** 70.3/69.2. **Slope:** 117/115. **Green Fee:** $15/$18. **Cart Fee:** $10/person. **Walking Policy:** Walking at certain times. **Walkability:** 1.
Opened: 1985. **Season:** Year-round. **High:** April-Sept. **To obtain tee times:** Call up to 7 days in advance. **Miscellaneous:** Reduced fees (weekdays, seniors, juniors), discount packages, range (grass), club rentals, credit cards (MC, V).
Special Notes: Formerly The Links Golf Course.

★★★½ GATES PARK GOLF COURSE
PU-820 E. Donald St., Waterloo, 50701, Black Hawk County, (319)291-4485, 115 miles NE of Des Moines.
Holes: 18. **Yards:** 6,839/5,568. **Par:** 72/72. **Course Rating:** 71.5/69.5. **Slope:** 118/113. **Green Fee:** $12/$12. **Cart Fee:** $20/cart. **Walking Policy:** Unrestricted walking. **Walkability:** 3.
Opened: 1954. **Architect:** Robert Bruce Harris. **Season:** April-Dec. **High:** June-Aug. **To obtain tee times:** Call Tuesday after 8 a.m. for upcoming weekend. **Miscellaneous:** Reduced fees (seniors, juniors), metal spikes, club rentals, credit cards (MC, V).
Reader Comments: Good test for little money ... Adding water to fairways would make this a superb track ... A grand old course ... Good muny ... Easy to walk ... Should be nicknamed 'No Brakes Gates' ... Very flat greens ... Well manicured ... Good value ... A gentle old golf course.

★★★★ GLYNNS CREEK GOLF COURSE
PU-19251 290th St., Long Grove, 52756, Scott County, (319)285-6444, 10 miles N of Davenport.
Holes: 18. **Yards:** 7,036/5,435. **Par:** 72/72. **Course Rating:** 73.5/70.4. **Slope:** 131/124. **Green Fee:** $17/$23. **Cart Fee:** $10/person. **Walking Policy:** Walking at certain times. **Walkability:** 3.
Opened: 1992. **Architect:** Dick Watson. **Season:** April-Oct. **High:** June-Aug. **To obtain tee

times: Call up to 30 days in advance. **Miscellaneous:** Reduced fees (weekdays, low season, twilight, seniors, juniors), range (grass), club rentals, credit cards (MC, V, D).
Notes: N.G.A. Hooter's Tour 1999.
Reader Comments: Native prairie rough ... Environmentally friendly ... Deer, turkeys, birds a plus ... Nice practice facilities ... Must play if in area ... Some tight fairways, but trees in Iowa are rare, enjoy ... Hidden gem ... Pleasant workers ... Just gets better with age ... Always in good condition! ... What a gem ... Great rates.

★★ GRANDVIEW GOLF COURSE
PM-2401 East 29th. St., Des Moines, 50317, Polk County, (515)262-8414.
Holes: 18. **Yards:** 5,422/5,191. **Par:** 70/71. **Course Rating:** 65.5/N/A. **Slope:** 106/N/A. **Green Fee:** $15/$19. **Cart Fee:** $11/person. **Walking Policy:** Unrestricted walking. **Walkability:** 2.
Opened: 1898. **Season:** April-Nov. **High:** June-Aug. **To obtain tee times:** Call on Sunday for Monday tee time and Monday for the rest of that week. **Miscellaneous:** Reduced fees (twilight, seniors, juniors), metal spikes, club rentals, credit cards (MC, V, D).

★★½ GREEN VALLEY GOLF COURSE
4300 Donner Ave., Sioux City, 51106, Woodbury County, (712)252-2025.
Reader Comments: Good course for high handicapper ... Good test for little money ... Tough in the wind ... Nice layout ... Great shape for a muny.
Special Notes: Call club for further information.

★★ HIDDEN HILLS GOLF COURSE
I-80 & Middle Rd., Bettendorf, 52722, Scott County, (319)332-5616.
Special Notes: Call club for further information.

★★½ HIGHLAND PARK GOLF COURSE
PM-944 17th St., N.E., Mason City, 50401, Cerro Gordo County, (515)423-9693, 110 miles N of Des Moines.
Holes: 18. **Yards:** 6,022/5,633. **Par:** 72/74. **Course Rating:** 70.9/70.9. **Slope:** 110/110. **Green Fee:** $10/$17. **Cart Fee:** $18/cart. **Walking Policy:** Unrestricted walking. **Walkability:** 2.
Opened: 1920. **Architect:** David Gill. **Season:** April-Oct. **To obtain tee times:** Call up to 2 days in advance. **Miscellaneous:** Reduced fees (twilight), metal spikes, range (grass), club rentals.
Reader Comments: Good facilities ... Front 9 is a spray hitter's nightmare, back 9 opens up ... Tough the first time you play it ... Good muny course ... Short, fairly easy.

HUNTER'S RIDGE GOLF CLUB
PU-6100 Lucore Rd., Marion, 52302, (319)377-3500.
Special Notes: Call club for further information.
Reader Comments: Getting better as course matures ... Beautiful wildlife habitats ... Great condition ... Lightning fast greens ... Excellent layout ... Well designed ... Best layout between the Missouri and the Mississippi River... Helpful staff.

★★½ IRV WARREN MEMORIAL GOLF COURSE
PM-1000 Fletcher Ave., Waterloo, 50701, Black Hawk County, (319)234-9271, 50 miles NW of Cedar Rapids.
Holes: 18. **Yards:** 6,268/5,325. **Par:** 72/72. **Course Rating:** 68.2/68.6. **Slope:** 113/102. **Green Fee:** $12/$12. **Cart Fee:** $21/cart. **Walking Policy:** Unrestricted walking. **Walkability:** 1.
Opened: 1908. **Season:** April-Nov. **High:** May-Aug. **To obtain tee times:** Tee times on weekends only. Call (319)291-4472 Tuesday after 8:00 a.m. for weekend. **Miscellaneous:** Reduced fees (seniors, juniors), metal spikes, range (grass), club rentals, credit cards (MC, V) (prefer spikeless).
Reader Comments: Hardly any trouble ... Good to play to boost your confidence ... Fairly short ... Decent muny ... Easy walking ... Great greens ... Fun to play ... Beautiful trees, nice green grass, manicured greens.

★★★½ JESTER PARK GOLF COURSE
PU-R.R. No.1, Granger, 50109, Polk County, (515)999-2903, 10 miles NW of Des Moines.
Holes: 18. **Yards:** 6,801/6,062. **Par:** 72/73. **Course Rating:** 72.7/N/A. **Slope:** 125/N/A. **Green Fee:** $16/$19. **Cart Fee:** $21/person. **Walking Policy:** Unrestricted walking. **Walkability:** 3.
Opened: 1970. **Architect:** Richard Phelps. **Season:** March-Oct. **High:** June-Aug. **To obtain tee times:** Call 7 days in advance. **Miscellaneous:** Reduced fees (low season, twilight, seniors, juniors), range (grass/mats), club rentals, credit cards (MC, V).
Reader Comments: Always in great shape ... Great value for the money! ... A long course ... Classic in the cornfields ... The best muny I ever played ... Wide open, lots of play, huge greens ... Lost many trees in tornado... Real treasure for public course.

★★★½ LAKE PANORAMA NATIONAL GOLF COURSE
R-5071 Clover Ridge Rd., Panora, 50216, Guthrie County, (515)755-2024, (800)879-1917, 45 miles W of Des Moines.

Holes: 18. **Yards:** 7,015/5,765. **Par:** 72/72. **Course Rating:** 73.2/73.2. **Slope:** 131/121. **Green Fee:** $25/$40. **Cart Fee:** Included in Green Fee. **Walking Policy:** Walking at certain times. **Walkability:** 4. **Opened:** 1970. **Architect:** Richard Watson. **Season:** April-Nov. **High:** June-Aug. **To obtain tee times:** Call 7 days in advance. Outings with 40+ players may book up to a year in advance. **Miscellaneous:** Reduced fees (weekdays, low season), discount packages, range (grass/mats), club rentals, lodging (39 rooms), credit cards (MC, V, AE, D).
Reader Comments: Long with good greens ... Championship prairie course ... Bring all your woods ... Memorable, beautiful course ... Nice staff ... One of Iowa's best ... Good packages.

★★½ LAKESIDE MUNICIPAL GOLF COURSE
PU-R.R. No.2, Fort Dodge, 50501, Webster County, (515)576-6741.
Holes: 18. **Yards:** 6,436/5,540. **Par:** 72/72. **Course Rating:** 70.1/69.8. **Slope:** 114/109. **Green Fee:** $10/$11. **Cart Fee:** $14/cart. **Walking Policy:** Unrestricted walking. **Walkability:** N/A.
Opened: 1976. **Architect:** City Engineers. **Season:** April-Oct. **High:** June-Aug. **To obtain tee times:** Call 2 days in advance. **Miscellaneous:** Metal spikes, range (grass), club rentals, credit cards (MC, V).
Reader Comments: Good mix of holes ... Tough to read greens ... Too many forced carries on back 9.

LAKEVIEW COUNTRY CLUB
SP-Rte. 2, Box 223, Winterset, 50273, Madison County, (515)462-9962, 40 miles SW of Des Moines.
Holes: 9. **Yards:** 2,880/2,575. **Par:** 35/35. **Course Rating:** 67.0/67.4. **Slope:** N/A/110. **Green Fee:** $16/$18. **Cart Fee:** $16/cart. **Walking Policy:** Unrestricted walking. **Walkability:** 3.
Season: April-Oct. **High:** June-July-Aug. **To obtain tee times:** We do not require tee times but players must come inside club house to sign in and pay fees.

LANDSMEER GOLF CLUB
PU-902 7th St. N.E., Orange City, 51041, Sioux County, (712)737-3429, 40 miles NE of Sioux City.
Holes: 18. **Yards:** 6,370/5,252. **Par:** 71/71. **Course Rating:** 71.1/68.9. **Slope:** 122/107. **Green Fee:** $19/$21. **Cart Fee:** $9/person. **Walking Policy:** Unrestricted walking. **Walkability:** 2.
Opened: 1995. **Architect:** Don Sechrest. **Season:** April-Nov. **High:** May-Aug. **To obtain tee times:** Call up to 5 days in advance. **Miscellaneous:** Discount packages, range (grass/mats), club rentals, credit cards (MC, V, AE).

★★½ LE MARS MUNICIPAL GOLF COURSE
PM-935 Park Lane NE, Le Mars, 51031, Plymouth County, (712)546-6849, 25 miles N of Sioux City.
Holes: 18. **Yards:** 6,232/N/A. **Par:** 71/N/A. **Course Rating:** 68.8/N/A. **Slope:** 124/N/A. **Green Fee:** $15/$17. **Cart Fee:** $16/cart. **Walking Policy:** Unrestricted walking. **Walkability:** 2.
Season: April-Oct. **High:** June-Aug. **To obtain tee times:** Call up to 3 days in advance. **Miscellaneous:** Reduced fees (juniors), range (grass), club rentals.
Reader Comments: Fairways need work ... Good value ... Very challenging ... Good water holes ... Long course for many golfers.

LINCOLN VALLEY GOLF CLUB
SP-1538 235th St., State Center, 50247, (515)483-2054.
Special Notes: Call club for further information.

★★★★ THE MEADOWS GOLF CLUB
PU-15766 Clover Lane, Dubuque, 52001, Dubuque County, (319)583-7385, 5 miles W of Chicago. **E-mail:** DWV3370@aol.com. **Web:** www.meadowgolf.com.
Holes: 18. **Yards:** 6,667/5,199. **Par:** 72/72. **Course Rating:** 72.6/68.7. **Slope:** 132/114. **Green Fee:** $22/$26. **Cart Fee:** $12/person. **Walking Policy:** Unrestricted walking. **Walkability:** 3.
Opened: 1996. **Architect:** Bob Lohmann. **Season:** March-Nov. **High:** June-Aug. **To obtain tee times:** Call up to 7 days in advance. **Miscellaneous:** Reduced fees (weekdays, low season, seniors, juniors), club rentals, credit cards (MC, V, AE).
Reader Comments: New course ... Needs to mature ... Don't miss this test ... Great elevation changes ... Terrific holes .... By far the best fairways (bent-grass) around ... Best thing next to a country club ... Beautiful clubhouse ... Friendly staff.

★★★★ MUSCATINE MUNICIPAL GOLF COURSE *Value+*
PM-1820 Hwy. 38 N., Muscatine, 52761, Muscatine County, (319)263-4735, 1 miles N of Muscatine.
Holes: 18. **Yards:** 6,471/5,471. **Par:** 72/72. **Course Rating:** 69.7/72.5. **Slope:** 117/108. **Green Fee:** $8/$10. **Cart Fee:** $10/person. **Walking Policy:** Unrestricted walking. **Walkability:** 2.
Opened: 1969. **Season:** March-Nov. **High:** May-June. **To obtain tee times:** Call or come in 7 days in advance. **Miscellaneous:** Reduced fees (seniors, juniors), metal spikes, range (grass), club rentals, beginner friendly (golf clinics).

IOWA

Reader Comments: Surprised a municipal course was that nice ... Fun to play for average golfer... Need a lot of different shots ... Tough crowned greens ... Good maintenance ... Great price for quality of course ... Great muny ... Staff helpful ... Best value for the buck anywhere.

★★ OAKLAND ACRES GOLF CLUB
PU-13476 Highway 6, Grinnell, 50112, Poweshiek County, (515)236-7111, 60 miles E of Des Moines.
Holes: 18. **Yards:** 5,878/5,410. **Par:** 69/71. **Course Rating:** 69.0/N/A. **Slope:** 114/N/A. **Green Fee:** $13/$14. **Cart Fee:** $16/cart. **Walking Policy:** Unrestricted walking. **Walkability:** N/A. **Season:** April-Oct. **High:** June-Aug. **To obtain tee times:** First come, first served. **Miscellaneous:** Reduced fees (weekdays, seniors, juniors), range, credit cards (MC, V, D).

★★★ OKOBOJI VIEW GOLF COURSE
PU-1665 Hwy. 86, Spirit Lake, 51360, Dickinson County, (712)337-3372, 74 miles SE of Sioux Falls. **E-mail:** Puttov@rconnect.com. **Web:** www.okoboj.view.play18.com.
Holes: 18. **Yards:** 6,051/5,441. **Par:** 70/73. **Course Rating:** 68.5/70.1. **Slope:** 113/113. **Green Fee:** $28/$35. **Cart Fee:** $11/person. **Walking Policy:** Unrestricted walking. **Walkability:** 2. **Opened:** 1962. **Architect:** E.G. McCoy. **Season:** April-Oct. **High:** June-Aug. **To obtain tee times:** Call 5 day in advance. **Miscellaneous:** Reduced fees (low season, twilight), discount packages, range (grass), club rentals, credit cards (MC, V, AE, D).
Reader Comments: Nice course for big hitters ... Good service and a nice course ... Good twilight rates for a resort area ...Has developed into a dandy ... Great condition.

OLATHEA GOLF COURSE
PU-23200 Great River Rd., Le Claire, 52753, Scott County, (319)289-4653, 15 miles N of Davenport.
Holes: 18. **Yards:** 2,918/2,513. **Par:** 36/36. **Course Rating:** 33.9/33.5. **Slope:** 110/108. **Green Fee:** $8/$13. **Cart Fee:** $16/cart. **Walking Policy:** Unrestricted walking. **Walkability:** 3. **Architect:** Randy Leander. **Season:** April-Oct. **High:** June-Aug. **To obtain tee times:** No tee times accepted. **Miscellaneous:** Reduced fees (low season, seniors, juniors), range (grass/mats), club rentals, credit cards (MC, V), beginner friendly (special youth rates).

ONEOTA GOLF & COUNTRY CLUB
SP-1714 Golf Rd., Decorah, 52101, Winneshiek County, (319)382-9347, 70 miles S of Rochester, Minnesota.
Holes: 18. **Yards:** 6,472/5,656. **Par:** 72/72. **Course Rating:** 70.6/70.4. **Slope:** 122/110. **Green Fee:** $24/$30. **Cart Fee:** $22/person. **Walking Policy:** Unrestricted walking. **Walkability:** 2. **Season:** April-Oct. **High:** May-Aug. **To obtain tee times:** Call golf shop one week in advance. **Miscellaneous:** Range (grass), club rentals.

★★★½ OTTER CREEK GOLF CLUB
PU-1410 N.E. 36th, Ankeny, 50021, Polk County, (515)965-6464, 10 miles N of Des Moines.
Holes: 18. **Yards:** 6,458/5,331. **Par:** 71/74. **Course Rating:** 70.3/N/A. **Slope:** 115/N/A. **Green Fee:** $17/$20. **Cart Fee:** $10/person. **Walking Policy:** Unrestricted walking. **Walkability:** 3. **Opened:** 1981. **Architect:** Don Rippel. **Season:** April-Oct. **High:** April-Oct. **To obtain tee times:** Call up to 7 days in advance. **Miscellaneous:** Reduced fees (weekdays), range (grass), club rentals, credit cards (MC, V).
Reader Comments: A real sleeper, looks easy, but will bite you ... Pretty open ... Good for hacker like me ... Good buy and good golf ... Much improved, but a lot of play ... Best muny in world.

★★★ OTTUMWA MUNICIPAL GOLF COURSE
PM-13120 Angle Rd., Ottumwa, 52501, Wapello County, (515)683-0646, 90 miles SE of Des Moines.
Holes: 18. **Yards:** 6,335/4,954. **Par:** 70/70. **Course Rating:** 70.4/66.7. **Slope:** 118/102. **Green Fee:** $13/$13. **Cart Fee:** $20/cart. **Walking Policy:** Unrestricted walking. **Walkability:** 2. **Opened:** 1931. **Architect:** Tom Bendelow/Chic Adams. **Season:** March-Nov. **High:** June-Aug. **To obtain tee times:** Call up to 7 days in advance. **Miscellaneous:** Range (grass), club rentals, credit cards (MC, V, D).
Reader Comments: A good muny course, wide fairways, not too much trouble but no pushover... Price is very reasonable ... Long ball hitters will like this course ... Good for people just starting to play ... Basic golf ... Good muny.

★★★½ PALMER HILLS MUNICIPAL GOLF COURSE
PM-2999 Middle Rd., Bettendorf, 52722, Scott County, (319)332-8296, 3 miles E of Davenport.
Holes: 18. **Yards:** 6,535/5,923. **Par:** 71/71. **Course Rating:** 71.5/74.0. **Slope:** 124/130. **Green Fee:** $12/$12. **Cart Fee:** $16/cart. **Walking Policy:** Unrestricted walking. **Walkability:** 4. **Opened:** 1975. **Architect:** William James Spear. **Season:** April-Dec. **High:** April-Sept. **To obtain tee times:** Call anytime. **Miscellaneous:** Reduced fees (weekdays, twilight, seniors, juniors), metal spikes, range (mats), club rentals, credit cards (MC, V, D).

IOWA

Reader Comments: A good muny, well kept ... Heavily played, but greens in excellent condition ... Hilly course ... Fun to play ... Great public golf course ... #15 is a killer, #16 will finish you off ... Nice city course ... Excellent fairways ... Unique in design.

★★★½ PHEASANT RIDGE MUNICIPAL GOLF COURSE
PM-3205 W. 12th St., Cedar Falls, 50613, Black Hawk County, (319)266-8266, 5 miles W of Waterloo.
Holes: 27. Yards: 6,730/5,179. Par: 72/70. Course Rating: 72.5/68.4. Slope: 122/101. Green Fee: $12/$12. Cart Fee: $21/person. Walking Policy: Unrestricted walking. Walkability: 1. Opened: 1972. Architect: Donald Brauer. Season: April-Nov. High: April-Sept. To obtain tee times: Call up to 7 days in advance. Miscellaneous: Reduced fees (seniors, juniors), range (grass), club rentals, credit cards (MC, V), beginner friendly (free beginner-only programs).
Reader Comments: Good facilities ... Long ... The wind makes this course a challenge ... Fair but tough test, lots of landing area ... New forward tees improve play for women ... Small greens ... They forgot to raise prices in the '90s.

★★★★ PLEASANT VALLEY GOLF COURSE
PU-4390 S.E. Sand Rd., Iowa City, 52240, Johnson County, (319)337-7209, 100 miles E of Des Moines.
Holes: 18. Yards: 6,472/5,067. Par: 72/72. Course Rating: 71.6/68.4. Slope: 127/111. Green Fee: $15/$25. Cart Fee: $20/cart. Walking Policy: Unrestricted walking. Walkability: 1. Opened: 1987. Architect: William James Spear. Season: April-Oct. High: June-July. To obtain tee times: Call up to 7 days in advance. Miscellaneous: Reduced fees (weekdays, twilight, seniors, juniors), range (grass/mats), club rentals, credit cards (MC, V, AE, D).
Reader Comments: Undulating greens ... Florida-style water and sand ... Outstanding midwest course ... Shotmaker's course ... Easy to walk ... Lots of water... Great condition ... One of the best I have played ... Friendly people.

QUAIL CREEK GOLF COURSE
PU-700 Clubhouse Rd. NE, North Liberty, 52317, Johnson County, (319)626-2281.
Holes: 18. Yards: 7,046/5,492. Par: 72/72. Course Rating: 73.6/74.5. Slope: 124/118. Green Fee: $18/$22. Cart Fee: $21/cart. Walking Policy: Unrestricted walking. Walkability: 2. Opened: 1969. Season: March-Nov. High: June-Aug. To obtain tee times: Tee times may be booked 1 week in advance. Miscellaneous: Range (grass).

★★★ RED CARPET GOLF CLUB
PU-1409 Newell St., Waterloo, 50703, Black Hawk County, (319)235-1242.
Holes: 18. Yards: 6,557/5,754. Par: 72/73. Course Rating: 70.8/72.1. Slope: 119/N/A. Green Fee: $12/$14. Cart Fee: $20/person. Walking Policy: Unrestricted walking. Walkability: 2. Opened: 1920. Season: March-Nov. High: May-Sept. To obtain tee times: Call ahead. May call as early as Tuesday for upcoming weekend. Miscellaneous: Metal spikes, range (grass), club rentals.
Reader Comments: Old country club ... Course in great shape ... Pleasant staff ... Excellent greens ... Fairways are cut short ... Quite open .... Good course to walk.

RICE LAKE GOLF & COUNTRY CLUB
SP-Rte. 2, Lake Mills, 50450, (515)592-8022.
Special Notes: Call club for further information.

★★★ RIVER VALLEY GOLF COURSE
PU-2267 Valley View Trail, Adel, 50003, Dallas County, (515)993-4029, 15 miles W of Des Moines. Web: www.rivervalleygolf.com.
Holes: 18. Yards: 6,635/5,482. Par: 72/72. Course Rating: 71.1/67.4. Slope: 121/114. Green Fee: $13/$22. Cart Fee: $20/cart. Walking Policy: Walking at certain times. Walkability: 4. Opened: 1995. Season: Feb.-Dec. High: April-Oct. To obtain tee times: Call golf shop. Miscellaneous: Reduced fees (weekdays, low season, twilight), range (grass), club rentals, credit cards (MC, V, AE, D).
Reader Comments: Log clubhouse ... A new course that will get better with time ... Three finishing holes are a real challenge ... Wide open ... Good value ... Playable and well kept ... Potential.

★★★ ST. ANDREWS GOLF CLUB
1866 Blairs Ferry Rd. N.E., Cedar Rapids, 52402, Linn County, (319)393-9915.
Reader Comments: Easy to walk ... Front nine is tight ... Back is more open ... Nice for a highly used public course ...Some funky holes on front ... Stiff back 9 ... Doesn't do St. Andrews name justice ... Keep your driver at home! ... Nice course, not too difficult, nice staff.
Special Notes: Call club for further information.

SANBORN GOLF & COUNTRY CLUB
PU-Miller Park Dr., Sanborn, 51248, (712)729-5600.
Special Notes: Call club for further information.

SHADY OAKS GOLF COURSE
PU-1811 Hwy. 92, Ackworth, 50001, Warren County, (515)961-0262, 5 miles E of Indianola.
Holes: 18. **Yards:** 3,101/2,976. **Par:** 35/37. **Course Rating:** 70.0/N/A. **Slope:** 116/N/A. **Green Fee:** $14/$15. **Cart Fee:** $16/cart. **Walking Policy:** Unrestricted walking. **Walkability:** 4. **Opened:** 1972. **Season:** Seasonal. **High:** June-Aug. **To obtain tee times:** No tee times taken. **Miscellaneous:** Reduced fees (weekdays), metal spikes, club rentals.

★★★ SHEAFFER MEMORIAL GOLF PARK
PU-1760 308th Ave., Fort Madison, 52627, Lee County, (319)528-6214, 42 miles N of Burlington.
Holes: 18. **Yards:** 6,303/5,441. **Par:** 72/73. **Course Rating:** 69.9/69.9. **Slope:** 118/113. **Green Fee:** $14/$14. **Cart Fee:** $19/cart. **Walking Policy:** Unrestricted walking. **Walkability:** 1. **Opened:** 1962. **Architect:** C.D. Wagstaff. **Season:** March-Nov. **High:** June-Aug. **To obtain tee times:** Call anytime. Tee times needed on weekends and holidays only. **Miscellaneous:** Reduced fees (weekdays, twilight, seniors, juniors), range (grass/mats), club rentals, credit cards (MC, V, D).
Reader Comments: Challenging front 9, open back ... Somewhat flat ... Fun ... Front and back 9s like night and day.

SHORELINE GOLF COURSE
PU-210 Locust St., Carter Lake, 51510, Douglas County, (712)347-5173, 3 miles W of Omaha, NE. **E-mail:** theshore@radiks.net.
Holes: 18. **Yards:** 6,800/5,439. **Par:** 72/72. **Course Rating:** 71.9/66.0. **Slope:** 124/107. **Green Fee:** $16/$19. **Cart Fee:** $18/cart. **Walking Policy:** Unrestricted walking. **Walkability:** 1. **Opened:** 1991. **Architect:** Pat Wyss. **Season:** Year-round. **High:** April-Oct. **To obtain tee times:** Call 7 days in advance. **Miscellaneous:** Reduced fees (weekdays, low season, seniors, juniors), discount packages, metal spikes, range (grass), club rentals, credit cards (MC, V).

★★★ SOUTH HILLS GOLF COURSE
PU-1830 E. Shaulis Road, Waterloo, 50701, Black Hawk County, (319)291-4268.
Holes: 18. **Yards:** 6,698/5,818. **Par:** 72/72. **Course Rating:** 71.4/N/A. **Slope:** 108/N/A. **Green Fee:** $12/$12. **Cart Fee:** $22/cart. **Walking Policy:** Unrestricted walking. **Walkability:** 4. **Opened:** 1972. **Architect:** City of Waterloo. **Season:** April-Dec. **High:** June-Aug. **To obtain tee times:** Call Tuesday after 8 a.m. for upcoming weekend. **Miscellaneous:** Reduced fees (seniors, juniors), metal spikes, club rentals.
Reader Comments: Fun, hilly course, can be a real challenge in the wind ... Very open course ... The price is right ... Tough for seniors to walk those hills ... Fun to walk ... Will be better when watered ... Lots of wind ... Hard greens, tough from tips.

★★★★½ SPENCER GOLF & COUNTRY CLUB *Service, Condition+, Pace+*
SP-2200 W. 18th St., Spencer, 51301, Clay County, (712)262-2028, 100 miles NE of Sioux City.
Holes: 18. **Yards:** 6,888/5,412. **Par:** 72/72. **Course Rating:** 73.0/70.1. **Slope:** 127/112. **Green Fee:** $31/$38. **Cart Fee:** $11/person. **Walking Policy:** Unrestricted walking. **Walkability:** 2. **Opened:** 1966. **Architect:** David A. Gill. **Season:** March-Nov. **High:** June-Sept. **To obtain tee times:** Call up to 30 days in advance. **Miscellaneous:** Range (grass), club rentals, credit cards (MC, V).
Reader Comments: Really good course ... Tests every club ... One of the best maintained courses in Iowa ... Impeccable ... Best course in NW Iowa ... Greens great ... Good condition ... U.S. Open-type rough.

SPRING VALLEY GOLF COURSE
PU-1101 140th Ave., Livermore, 50558, Kossuth County, (515)379-1259, (515)379-1259, 11 miles N of Humboldt.
Holes: 18. **Yards:** 6,421/5,467. **Par:** 72/72. **Course Rating:** 70.2/69.2. **Slope:** 117/108. **Green Fee:** $13/$16. **Cart Fee:** $16/cart. **Walking Policy:** Unrestricted walking. **Walkability:** 3. **Opened:** 1979. **Season:** March-Oct. **High:** April-Sept.

SUNNY BRAE COUNTRY CLUB
SP-Rte. 5, Osage, 50461, Mitchell County, (515)732-3435, 2 miles S of Osage.
Holes: 9. **Yards:** 2,638/2,474. **Par:** 35/36. **Course Rating:** 65.4/68.6. **Slope:** 115/115. **Green Fee:** $13/N/A. **Cart Fee:** $16/cart. **Walking Policy:** Unrestricted walking. **Walkability:** 4. **Opened:** 1915. **Season:** March-Oct. **High:** July-Aug. **To obtain tee times:** No tee times. **Miscellaneous:** Reduced fees (weekdays, low season), range (grass), club rentals.

★★★ TERRACE HILLS GOLF COURSE
PU-8700 NE 46th. Ave., Altoona, 50009, Polk County, (515)967-2932.
Holes: 18. **Yards:** 6,300/N/A. **Par:** 71/N/A. **Course Rating:** 68.8/N/A. **Slope:** 116/N/A. **Green Fee:** N/A. **Walking Policy:** Unrestricted walking. **Walkability:** 3. **Opened:** 1964. **Season:** March-Nov. **Miscellaneous:** Metal spikes, range (grass), club rentals.

IOWA

Reader Comments: Will always get you out ... Good family course ... One of the few you can play year-round ... Basic golf ... Good layout ... Showing improvements ... Not much variety ... Good public course ... Getting better every year.

★★★ TIMBERLINE GOLF COURSE
PU-19804 E. Pleasant Grove Rd., Peosta, 52068, Dubuque County, (319)876-3422, 20 miles SW of Dubuque.
Holes: 18. **Yards:** 6,545/5,318. **Par:** 72/73. **Course Rating:** 71.4/73.5. **Slope:** 119/113. **Green Fee:** $13/$16. **Cart Fee:** $10/person. **Walking Policy:** Unrestricted walking. **Walkability:** 5.
Opened: 1959. **Season:** April-Oct. **High:** June-Aug. **To obtain tee times:** Call 7 days in advance. **Miscellaneous:** Reduced fees (seniors, juniors), club rentals, credit cards (MC, V).
Reader Comments: As the name implies, lots of timber... Hilly, wooded layout ... Straight driver needed ... Pleasant country setting ... Long course ... The 1st hole and 10th holes challenge you to get across a creek.

★★★ TOAD VALLEY PUBLIC GOLF COURSE & DRIVING RANGE
PU-237 NE 80th St., Runnells, 50237-2028, Polk County, (515)967-9575, 5 miles E of Des Moines.
Holes: 18. **Yards:** 6,170/5,295. **Par:** 71/71. **Course Rating:** 69.1/71.2. **Slope:** 114/114. **Green Fee:** $16/$19. **Cart Fee:** $21/cart. **Walking Policy:** Unrestricted walking. **Walkability:** 4.
Opened: 1973. **Architect:** Tom Brady. **Season:** Year-round. **High:** April-Sept. **To obtain tee times:** Call up to 21 days in advance. **Miscellaneous:** Reduced fees (low season, seniors), range (grass), club rentals, credit cards (MC, V, D).
Reader Comments: Basic golf ... Good value, well kept, nice people ... Short course, small greens ... Good course to learn on ... Fun to play ... Sneaky and tough especially when windy ... Hills, hills, hills.

★★ TWIN PINES GOLF COURSE
3800 42nd St NE, Cedar Rapids, 52402, Linn County, (319)398-5183.
Special Notes: Call club for further information.

★★★½ VALLEY OAKS GOLF CLUB
SP-3330 Harts Mill Rd., Clinton, 52732, Clinton County, (319)242-7221, (800)796-6187, 40 miles NE of Davenport. **E-mail:** huestis@sanasys.com.
Holes: 18. **Yards:** 6,803/5,337. **Par:** 72/73. **Course Rating:** 73.0/70.3. **Slope:** 127/121. **Green Fee:** $16/$19. **Cart Fee:** $10/person. **Walking Policy:** Unrestricted walking. **Walkability:** 3.
Opened: 1966. **Architect:** Robert Bruce Harris. **Season:** April-Oct. **High:** April-Oct. **To obtain tee times:** Call up to 7 days in advance. **Miscellaneous:** Reduced fees (weekdays, juniors), range (grass/mats), club rentals, credit cards (MC, V).
Reader Comments: Nice course ... Has some nice holes ... Course is diverse ... Playable ... Don't let up, will bite you ... It can leave you talking to yourself ... Tough ... Greens are quick; fairways too! ... A value ... Front 9 easy; back hard ... Challenging and hilly ... Beautiful oaks.

★★★★ VEENKER MEMORIAL GOLF COURSE-IOWA STATE UNIVERSITY
PU-Stange Rd., Ames, 50011, Story County, (515)294-6727, 30 miles N of Des Moines. **E-mail:** tbalsley@iastate.edu. **Web:** http://www.fpm.iastate.edu/veenker.
Holes: 18. **Yards:** 6,543/5,357. **Par:** 72/73. **Course Rating:** 71.3/70.6. **Slope:** 124/120. **Green Fee:** $18/$22. **Cart Fee:** $10/person. **Walking Policy:** Unrestricted walking. **Walkability:** 5.
Opened: 1938. **Architect:** Perry Maxwell. **Season:** March-Nov. **High:** June-Aug. **To obtain tee times:** Call up to 7 days in advance. **Miscellaneous:** Reduced fees (weekdays, seniors, juniors), range (grass), club rentals, credit cards (MC, V, D).
Reader Comments: Exciting course ... Wonderful when in good condition ... Tougher than rating would indicate ... Great college course ... Requires long drives ... Nice mature course ... Somewhat hilly ... Nice staff ... A favorite of mine ... Use all 14 here ... Fine public.

★★★½ WAVELAND GOLF COURSE
PU-4908 University Ave., Des Moines, 50311, Polk County, (515)271-8725.
Holes: 18. **Yards:** 6,419/5,295. **Par:** 72/71. **Course Rating:** 71.4/69.4. **Slope:** 126/116. **Green Fee:** $15/$17. **Cart Fee:** $20/cart. **Walking Policy:** Unrestricted walking. **Walkability:** 4.
Opened: 1894. **Architect:** Warren Dickinson. **Season:** March-Nov. **High:** May-Aug. **To obtain tee times:** Call Sunday for Monday tee times and Monday for the rest of the week.
Miscellaneous: Reduced fees (low season, twilight, seniors, juniors), discount packages, metal spikes, club rentals, credit cards (MC, V, D).
Reader Comments: Big trees, hills, small greens, great layout ... One of the oldest publics west of Mississippi ... Great character and maturity with toughest par 5 in town ... Old Des Moines muny with lots of trees ... Tight in spots ... Grand old course ... Good pro ... Hilly 'old type' course, good value.

★★★ WAVERLY GOLF COURSE
PM-Hwy 218S Fairgrounds, Waverly, 50677, Bremer County, (319)352-1530, 15 miles N of Waterloo.

Holes: 18. **Yards:** 5,881/5,440. **Par:** 70/72. **Course Rating:** 69.2/69.5. **Slope:** 115/105. **Green Fee:** $12/$14. **Cart Fee:** $20/cart. **Walking Policy:** Unrestricted walking. **Walkability:** 3. **Season:** April-Nov. **High:** June-Aug. **To obtain tee times:** Call up to 7 days in advance. **Miscellaneous:** Club rentals, credit cards (MC, V, D).
Reader Comments: Nice small-town course ... Not too long ... Short but enjoyable ... Elevation changes ... Small, fast greens ... O.B. everywhere.

★★½ WESTWOOD GOLF CLUB
PU-3387 Hwy. F 48 W., Newton, 50208, Jasper County, (515)792-3087, 25 miles NE of Des Moines.
Holes: 18. **Yards:** 6,321/5,645. **Par:** 71/71. **Course Rating:** 70.5/74.5. **Slope:** 123/N/A. **Green Fee:** $17/$17. **Cart Fee:** $18/cart. **Walking Policy:** Unrestricted walking. **Walkability:** N/A. **Opened:** 1927. **Architect:** Dave Gill. **Season:** April-Oct. **High:** June-Aug. **To obtain tee times:** Call 7 days in advance. **Miscellaneous:** Reduced fees (juniors), range (grass), club rentals.
Reader Comments: Will be better after reconstruction ... Two distinct 9s ... Redesign hurts old course ... May develop.

WILLOW CREEK GOLF COURSE
PU-140 Army Post Rd., West Des Moines, 50265, Polk County, (515)285-4558, 6 miles SW of Des Moines.
★★ BLUE/WHITE COURSE
Holes: 18. **Yards:** 5,385/4,625. **Par:** 68/69. **Course Rating:** 65.4/67.4. **Slope:** N/A. **Green Fee:** $18/$22. **Cart Fee:** $20/cart. **Walking Policy:** Unrestricted walking. **Walkability:** 2. **Opened:** 1961. **Season:** April-Oct. **High:** June-Sept. **To obtain tee times:** Call golf shop. **Miscellaneous:** Metal spikes, range (grass/mats), club rentals, credit cards (MC, V, D).
★★½ RED COURSE
Holes: 18. **Yards:** 6,465/5,758. **Par:** 71/74. **Course Rating:** 70.2/71.4. **Slope:** 116/112. **Green Fee:** $18/$22. **Cart Fee:** $20/cart. **Walking Policy:** Unrestricted walking. **Walkability:** 3. **Opened:** 1961. **Architect:** Dick Phelps. **Season:** April-Oct. **High:** June-Sept. **To obtain tee times:** Call golf shop. **Miscellaneous:** Metal spikes, range (grass/mats), club rentals, credit cards (MC, V, D).
Reader Comments: Nice, but heavily used ... Fun layout for an unplanned day ... Like two different courses with new holes ... Hard fairways and greens ... Lots of play ... Open all year.

WOODLAND HILLS
PU-620 NE 66th Ave., Des Moines, 50313, Polk County, (515)289-1326, 3 miles N of Des Moines.
Holes: 27. **Yards:** 5,550/4,924. **Par:** 70/70. **Course Rating:** 66.1/67.6. **Slope:** 101/103. **Green Fee:** $9/$20. **Cart Fee:** $11/person. **Walking Policy:** Unrestricted walking. **Walkability:** 3. **Opened:** 1928. **Season:** March-Oct. **High:** May-July. **To obtain tee times:** No tee times Monday-Friday. Call (515)289-1326 for Sat. & Sun. times. **Miscellaneous:** Reduced fees (weekdays, seniors), club rentals, credit cards (MC, V, AE, D), beginner friendly.
Special Notes: Also has 9 hole South Course.

KANSAS

★★★★ **ALVAMAR GOLF CLUB**
SP-1800 Crossgate Dr., Lawrence, 66047, Douglas County, (785)842-1907, 25 miles SW of Kansas City. **Web:** www.alvamar.com.
Holes: 18. **Yards:** 7,096/4,892. **Par:** 72/72. **Course Rating:** 75.5/68.1. **Slope:** 141/112. **Green Fee:** $25/$42. **Cart Fee:** $14/person. **Walking Policy:** Unrestricted walking. **Walkability:** 4. **Opened:** 1968. **Architect:** Bob Dunning. **Season:** Year-round. **High:** April-Oct. **To obtain tee times:** Call 14 days in advance. **Miscellaneous:** Reduced fees (weekdays, low season, resort guests, twilight, seniors, juniors), discount packages, range (grass/mats), club rentals, credit cards (MC, V, AE, D).
Notes: Ranked 75th in 1996 America's Top 75 Affordable Courses.
Reader Comments: Well maintained, worth a drive ... Challenging holes, tight ... Really fun to play, can score well ... Tough greens ... Home of superintendents school says it all ... A beaut! Bring your A-game ... Followed a 12-some one day, enough said ... Zoysia fairways!.

★★★ **ARTHUR B. SIM PARK GOLF COURSE**
PM-2020 W. Murdock, Wichita, 67203, Sedgwick County, (316)337-9100.
Holes: 18. **Yards:** 6,330/5,026. **Par:** 71/71. **Course Rating:** 70.2/67.9. **Slope:** 113/103. **Green Fee:** $15/$16. **Cart Fee:** $19/cart. **Walking Policy:** Unrestricted walking. **Walkability:** 1. **Opened:** 1922. **Season:** Year-round. **High:** April-Oct. **To obtain tee times:** Call golf shop (316)337-9100. **Miscellaneous:** Reduced fees (twilight), club rentals.
Reader Comments: Can get dry in summer ... Hell on a windy day ... Recommend for seniors and ladies ... Pins can be put in very tight corners ... Easy walk ... Not much trouble ... A short ego builder ... No water hazards.

BERKSHIRE GOLF CLUB
PU-3720 SW 45th, Topeka, 66610, Shawnee County, (785)267-7888.
Holes: 18. **Yards:** 6,700/5,600. **Par:** 70/70. **Course Rating:** 70.6/69.6. **Slope:** 125/123. **Green Fee:** $10/$15. **Cart Fee:** $10/person. **Walking Policy:** Unrestricted walking. **Walkability:** 2. **Opened:** 1990. **Season:** Year-round. **High:** May-Aug. **To obtain tee times:** Call golf shop at least one week in advance. Tee times available anytime. **Miscellaneous:** Reduced fees (weekdays, seniors, juniors), range (grass), club rentals, credit cards (MC, V), beginner friendly (junior golf, mens, womens, couples clubs).
Special Notes: Formerly Colly Creek Golf Course.

★★½ **BRAEBURN GOLF COURSE AT WICHITA STATE UNIVERSITY**
PU-4201 E. 21st, Wichita, 67208, Sedgwick County, (316)978-4653.
Holes: 18. **Yards:** 6,451/5,257. **Par:** 70/71. **Course Rating:** 71.7/70.5. **Slope:** 128/117. **Green Fee:** $15/$18. **Cart Fee:** $18/cart. **Walking Policy:** Unrestricted walking. **Walkability:** 2. **Opened:** 1924. **Season:** Year-round. **High:** March-Oct. **To obtain tee times:** Call 1 week in advance. **Miscellaneous:** Reduced fees (twilight, seniors, juniors), range (grass), club rentals, credit cards (MC, V), beginner friendly (offer individual & group lessons).
Reader Comments: Conditioning has really improved ... Can hear WSU baseball games anywhere on the course ... Good course for average golfer ... Not a lot of variety ... Has potential ... Old-style design with some real surprises.

★★★★½ **BUFFALO DUNES GOLF COURSE** *Value+, Condition, Pace*
PM-S. Star Rte., Garden City, 67846, Finney County, (316)276-1210, 180 miles NW of Wichita. **E-mail:** buffalodunes@gcnet.com. **Web:** www.garden-city.org.
Holes: 18. **Yards:** 6,767/5,598. **Par:** 72/72. **Course Rating:** 72.5/72.0. **Slope:** 124/114. **Green Fee:** $11/$14. **Cart Fee:** $19/cart. **Walking Policy:** Unrestricted walking. **Walkability:** 3. **Opened:** 1976. **Architect:** Frank Hummel. **Season:** Year-round. **High:** April-Oct. **To obtain tee times:** One week in advance. **Miscellaneous:** Reduced fees (twilight, juniors), range (grass/mats), club rentals, credit cards (MC, V, D).
Notes: Ranked 7th in 1999 Best in State.
Reader Comments: Super tee to green ... Great course for hilly play ... Excellent course in Kansas 'outback' ... Waist-high buffalo grass in rough ... Elevated greens, challenges shotmakers ... Try to play it without the wind, impossible.

★★ **CAREY PARK GOLF CLUB**
PU-15 Emerson Lane, Hutchinson, 67501, Reno County, (316)694-2698, 40 miles W of Wichita.
Holes: 18. **Yards:** 6,410/5,101. **Par:** 71/71. **Course Rating:** 70.4/69.3. **Slope:** 116/114. **Green Fee:** $10/$15. **Cart Fee:** $18/cart. **Walking Policy:** Unrestricted walking. **Walkability:** 1. **Opened:** 1932. **Architect:** Ralph McCarroll. **Season:** Year-round. **High:** June-Aug. **To obtain tee times:** Call up to 7 days in advance. **Miscellaneous:** Reduced fees (weekdays).

CEDARBROOK GOLF COURSE
PU-2700 N. Cottonwood St., Iola, 66749, Allen County, (316)365-2176, 80 miles S of Kansas City.
Holes: 18. **Yards:** 6,363/4,935. **Par:** 72/72. **Course Rating:** 71.2/71.7. **Slope:** 122/114. **Green Fee:** $13/$14. **Cart Fee:** $10/person. **Walking Policy:** Unrestricted walking. **Walkability:** 2.

KANSAS

Architect: Kevin Pargman. **Season:** Year round. **High:** May-Sept. **To obtain tee times:** Call golf shop (316)365-2176. **Miscellaneous:** Reduced fees (weekdays, twilight, seniors, juniors), metal spikes, range (grass), club rentals, credit cards (MC, V), beginner friendly (prefer soft spikes).

CHISHOLM TRAIL GOLF COURSE
PU-645 2400 Ave., Abilene, 67410, Abilene County, (785)263-3377.
Holes: 18. **Yards:** 6,568/4,746. **Par:** 71/72. **Course Rating:** 72.4/71.0. **Slope:** 125/113. **Green Fee:** $12/$15. **Cart Fee:** $9/person. **Walking Policy:** Unrestricted walking. **Walkability:** 3.
Opened: 1999. **Architect:** John Thayer Sr./Bruce Dixon. **Season:** Year-round. **High:** June-Aug.
Miscellaneous: Reduced fees (weekdays, twilight, juniors), range (grass), club rentals, credit cards (MC, V).

★★★½ CUSTER HILL GOLF CLUB
PU-Normandy Dr., Fort Riley, 66442, Geary County, (785)239-5412, 4 miles N of Junction City.
Holes: 18. **Yards:** 7,072/5,323. **Par:** 72/72. **Course Rating:** 74.2/N/A. **Slope:** 127/N/A. **Green Fee:** $13/$15. **Cart Fee:** $18/cart. **Walking Policy:** Unrestricted walking. **Walkability:** 4.
Opened: 1957. **Architect:** Robert Trent Jones. **Season:** Jan.-Dec. **High:** April-June. **To obtain tee times:** Call (913)784-6000 for weekend tee times. **Miscellaneous:** Reduced fees (twilight), range (grass), club rentals, credit cards (MC, V, AE, D).
Reader Comments: Good soft fairways, tough fast greens, nice and long, good pro shop on base, so there is no tax ... Hidden treasure, classic front 9 very hilly ... Needs more care ... Small greens ... Wide fairways ... Greens like tilted dinner plates ... From the tips its a monster.

★★★★ DEER CREEK GOLF CLUB
SP-7000 W. 133rd St., Overland Park, 66209, Johnson County, (913)681-3100, 15 miles S of Kansas City.
Holes: 18. **Yards:** 6,870/5,120. **Par:** 72/72. **Course Rating:** 74.5/68.5. **Slope:** 137/113. **Green Fee:** $65/$75. **Cart Fee:** Included in Green Fee. **Walking Policy:** Unrestricted walking. **Walkability:** 4. **Opened:** 1989. **Architect:** Robert Trent Jones Jr. **Season:** Year-round. **High:** March-Nov. **To obtain tee times:** Call 3 days in advance. **Miscellaneous:** Reduced fees (weekdays, low season, twilight), range (grass/mats), club rentals, credit cards (MC, V).
Reader Comments: Some tough holes, good challenges ... Pricey for area ... If only my game were as beautiful ... Don't pass it by ... Remote practice facility ... Creek in play on most holes ... Fairway wood on many tees ... Brutal wind ... Target markers great idea ... Too many outside tournaments.

DREAD GOLF CLUB
PU-12601 Hollingsworth Rd., Kansas City, 66109. (913)721-1333.
Holes: 18. **Yards:** 6,993/5,474. **Par:** 72/72. **Course Rating:** 73.8/70.4. **Slope:** 133/113. **Green Fee:** $29/$52. **Walking Policy:** Unrestricted walking. **Walkability:** 2. **Architect:** Harold McSpaden. **Season:** Year-round. **High:** April-Oct. **To obtain tee times:** call 5 days in advance/CC reservation Required in Season Fri Sat Sun. **Miscellaneous:** Reduced fees (weekdays, low season, twilight, seniors, juniors), discount packages, range (grass/mats), club rentals, credit cards (MC, V, AE), beginner friendly (lessons with pga pros).

★★★½ DUB'S DREAD GOLF CLUB
PU-12601 Hollingsworth Rd., Kansas City, 66109, Wyandotte County, (913)721-1333.
Holes: 18. **Yards:** 6,987/5,454. **Par:** 72/72. **Course Rating:** 73.6/70.4. **Slope:** 131/121. **Green Fee:** $29/$40. **Cart Fee:** $12/person. **Walking Policy:** Unrestricted walking. **Walkability:** 3.
Opened: 1965. **Architect:** Bob Dunning. **Season:** Year-round. **High:** April-Oct. **To obtain tee times:** Call (913)721-1333 or come in up to 3 days in advance. Credit card required for weekend and holidays. **Miscellaneous:** Reduced fees (low season, twilight, seniors, juniors), discount packages, range (grass/mats), club rentals, credit cards (MC, V, AE, D).
Reader Comments: 35 mph cross-wind ... Needs more time between tee times ... Nice track, narrow fairways ... Very difficult approach to greens ... Mature course, good greens, out in the sticks ... Wicked doglegs, large greens, tough putts ... Requires accuracy.

EAGLE BEND GOLF COURSE
PU-1250 E. 902 Rd., Lawrence, 66047, Douglas County, (785)748-0600, 30 miles W of Kansas City.
Holes: 18. **Yards:** 6,850/6,004. **Par:** 72/72. **Course Rating:** 72.8/70.0. **Slope:** 124/113. **Green Fee:** $15/$18. **Cart Fee:** $11/person. **Walking Policy:** Unrestricted walking. **Walkability:** 2.
Opened: 1998. **Architect:** Jeff Brauer. **Season:** Year-round. **High:** April-Sept. **Miscellaneous:** Reduced fees (twilight, juniors), discount packages, range (grass), rentals, credit cards (MC, V).
Notes: 1999 Lawrence City Amateur.

★★½ ECHO HILLS GOLF COURSE
PU-800 East 53rd North, Wichita, 67219, (316)838-0143, 2 miles N of Wichita. **E-mail:** ehgc@worldnet.att.net. **Web:** www.echohills.com.
Holes: 18. **Yards:** 5,785/5,381. **Par:** 70/71. **Course Rating:** 68.8/70.6. **Slope:** 116/115. **Green Fee:** $10/$15. **Cart Fee:** $19/cart. **Walking Policy:** Unrestricted walking. **Walkability:** 3.

Opened: 1930. **Architect:** Bert Henderson. **Season:** Year-round. **High:** JUne-Aug.
Miscellaneous: Reduced fees (weekdays, twilight, seniors, juniors), club rentals, credit cards (MC, V, D), beginner friendly (summer junior program).
Reader Comments: Hilly and interesting for this part of the country ... Two tough par 3s in a row ... Too short for a challenge ... Should be called Ego Hills ... Improvements being made.

ELK'S COUNTRY CLUB

SP-1800 S. Marymount, Salina, 67401, Saline County, (785)827-8585, 90 miles N of Wichita.
Holes: 18. **Yards:** 6,031/4,979. **Par:** 71/71. **Course Rating:** 69.2/66.8. **Slope:** 120/106. **Green Fee:** $22/$22. **Cart Fee:** $11/person. **Walking Policy:** Unrestricted walking. **Walkability:** 4.
Opened: 1952. **Architect:** James Dalgleish. **Season:** Year round. **High:** April-Aug. **To obtain tee times:** Call golf shop (785)827-8585. **Miscellaneous:** Range (grass), club rentals.

★★½ EMPORIA MUNICIPAL GOLF CLUB

PM-1133 S. Hwy. 99, Emporia, 66801, Lyon County, (316)342-7666, 6 miles S of Emporia.
Holes: 18. **Yards:** 6,500/5,900. **Par:** 71/71. **Course Rating:** 71.4/71.0. **Slope:** 118/114. **Green Fee:** $12/$15. **Cart Fee:** $16/cart. **Walking Policy:** Unrestricted walking. **Walkability:** 3.
Opened: 1971. **Architect:** Bob Dunning. **Season:** Year-round. **High:** May-Sept. **To obtain tee times:** Call on Wednesday for upcoming weekend. **Miscellaneous:** Reduced fees (twilight, seniors, juniors), range (grass), club rentals, credit cards (MC, V).
Reader Comments: New irrigation system, improved condition ... Worth the drive ... Very well run course ... Slow greens, long fairways ... Never crowded, favorite course.

★★★★ FALCON RIDGE GOLF CLUB

PU-20200 Prairie Star Pkwy., Lenexa, 66220, (913)393-4653.
Holes: 18. **Yards:** 6,820/5,160. **Par:** 72/72. **Course Rating:** 72.3/69.6. **Slope:** 127/119. **Green Fee:** $40/$63. **Cart Fee:** Included in Green Fee. **Walking Policy:** Unrestricted walking.
Walkability: 4. **Opened:** 1997. **Architect:** Craig Schreiner. **Season:** Year-round. **High:** April-Sept. **To obtain tee times:** 7 Days in Advance Starting at 9:00 A.M. **Miscellaneous:** Reduced fees (weekdays, low season), range (grass/mats), club rentals, credit cards (MC, V, AE, D).
Notes: Ranked 9th in 1999 Best in State.
Reader Comments: Good variety of challenges ... Overpriced because of area ... Beautiful course ... Play all your clubs ... Needs to mature ... Probably best layout in area ... Elevated tees and greens offer challenge.

★★ GARDNER GOLF COURSE

PU-15810 S. Gardner, Gardner, 66030, Johnson County, (913)856-8858, 5 miles W of Olathe.
Holes: 18. **Yards:** 6,165/5,222. **Par:** 71/71. **Course Rating:** 67.9/68.2. **Slope:** 116/108. **Green Fee:** $14/$15. **Cart Fee:** $10/person. **Walking Policy:** Unrestricted walking. **Walkability:** 3.
Opened: 1987. **Architect:** Kevin Pargman. **Season:** Year round. **High:** June-Aug. **To obtain tee times:** Call golf shop Wed.-Fri for weekend t-times (913)856-8858. **Miscellaneous:** Reduced fees (weekdays, seniors, juniors), range (grass), club rentals, credit cards (MC, V, D).

GIRARD GOLF COURSE

PM-East Hwy. 57, Girard, 66743, Crawford County, (316)724-8855, 45 miles NW of Joplin, MO.
Holes: 9. **Yards:** 5,989/5,654. **Par:** 72/72. **Course Rating:** 69.6/69.2. **Slope:** 116/112. **Green Fee:** $7/$9. **Cart Fee:** $15/cart. **Walking Policy:** Unrestricted walking. **Walkability:** 2. **Opened:** 1950. **Architect:** Vern Grassi. **Season:** Year round. **High:** May-Sept. **To obtain tee times:** Call golf shop. **Miscellaneous:** Reduced fees (weekdays, twilight, juniors), beginner friendly.

GOLDEN BELT COUNTRY CLUB

SP-24th & Frye, Great Bend, 67530, (316)792-4306. **E-mail:** gm@goldenbeltcc.com. **Web:** www.goldenbelt.com.
Holes: 18. **Yards:** 6,383/5,029. **Par:** 71/72. **Course Rating:** 71.6/68.6. **Slope:** 125/112. **Green Fee:** $18/$25. **Cart Fee:** $20/person. **Walking Policy:** Unrestricted walking. **Walkability:** 1.
Season: Jan.-Dec. **High:** April-Oct. **To obtain tee times:** Call the golf shop no more than one week prior to tee time. **Miscellaneous:** Reduced fees (weekdays, twilight), discount packages, credit cards (MC, V, AE), beginner friendly (3 junior golf programs per year).

★★★½ HERITAGE PARK GOLF COURSE

PU-16445 Lackman Rd., Olathe, 66062, Johnson County, (913)829-4653, 12 miles SE of Kansas City.
Holes: 18. **Yards:** 6,876/5,797. **Par:** 71/71. **Course Rating:** 72.6/72.3. **Slope:** 131/121. **Green Fee:** $20/$25. **Cart Fee:** $22/cart. **Walking Policy:** Unrestricted walking. **Walkability:** 3.
Opened: 1990. **Architect:** Don Sechrest. **Season:** Year-round. **High:** March-Oct. **To obtain tee times:** Call 3 days in advance. **Miscellaneous:** Reduced fees (weekdays, low season, twilight, seniors, juniors), range (grass), club rentals, credit cards (MC, V).
Reader Comments: Long tough walk ... Great layout, wide variety of holes, excellent service ... No rescue from the fescue ... Tough Par 3s ... Designed for carts ... Too many forced carries ... Tough back nine ... Plays to 6,800 yards, walks to 10,000 yards ... Water, wind, and sand provide challenge to thinking and shot execution.

KANSAS

★★★½ **HESSTON MUNICIPAL GOLF PARK**
PM-520 Golf Course Dr., Hesston, 67062, Harvey County, (316)327-2331, 35 miles N of Wichita.
Holes: 18. **Yards:** 6,526/5,475. **Par:** 71/71. **Course Rating:** 71.4/66.7. **Slope:** 125/118. **Green Fee:** $12/$16. **Cart Fee:** $9/person. **Walking Policy:** Unrestricted walking. **Walkability:** 2.
Opened: 1976. **Architect:** Frank Hummel. **Season:** Year-round. **High:** May-Sept. **To obtain tee times:** Call golf shop. **Miscellaneous:** Reduced fees (seniors, juniors), range (grass/mats), club rentals, credit cards (MC, V, D).
Reader Comments: Nice people ... Can't buy a beer in the clubhouse ... Very playable ... Helpful staff ... Fun course, good layout ... Tough in windy conditions ... Loved the elevated greens, outstanding clubhouse ... Best small town course you'll find.

★★★ **HIDDEN LAKES GOLF COURSE**
PU-6020 S. Greenwich Rd., Derby, 67037, Sedgwick County, (316)788-2855, 6 miles SE of Wichita.
Holes: 18. **Yards:** 6,523/5,426. **Par:** 72/71. **Course Rating:** 70.9/70.2. **Slope:** 123/120. **Green Fee:** $11/$18. **Cart Fee:** $18/cart. **Walking Policy:** Unrestricted walking. **Walkability:** 2.
Opened: 1960. **Architect:** Floyd Farley. **Season:** Year-round. **High:** March-Oct. **To obtain tee times:** Call 7 days in advance. **Miscellaneous:** Reduced fees (weekdays, twilight, seniors, juniors), metal spikes, range (grass), club rentals, credit cards (MC, V).
Reader Comments: Hidden jewel, greens like concrete ... Long and challenging ... Plenty of water to contend with.

★★★½ **IRONHORSE GOLF CLUB**
PM-15400 Mission Rd., Leawood, 66224, Johnson County, (913)685-4653, 15 miles S of Kansas City. **Web:** www.ironhorse.com.
Holes: 18. **Yards:** 6,889/4,745. **Par:** 72/72. **Course Rating:** 73.8/67.5. **Slope:** 140/119. **Green Fee:** $27/$44. **Cart Fee:** $14/person. **Walking Policy:** Unrestricted walking. **Walkability:** 5.
Opened: 1995. **Architect:** Michael Hurdzan. **Season:** Year-round. **High:** April-Oct. **To obtain tee times:** Call up to 3 days in advance. **Miscellaneous:** Reduced fees (twilight, seniors, juniors), club rentals, credit cards (MC, V, AE), beginner friendly (numerous schools, practice course).
Notes: Ranked 3rd in 1996 Best New Affordable Courses.
Reader Comments: A real challenge from the back ... Unusual par 4s ... Incredible scenery and layout ... Traditional, yet interesting ... Opened too soon. Will be great when mature ... Recovering from green problems ... Super practice facility ... High rough, lost balls ... Visit the grill ... Lots of trickling brooks.

★★★ **L.W. CLAPP GOLF COURSE**
PM-4611 E. Harry, Wichita, 67218, Sedgwick County, (316)688-9341.
Holes: 18. **Yards:** 6,087/4,965. **Par:** 70/70. **Course Rating:** 70.0/69.7. **Slope:** 120/110. **Green Fee:** $15/$16. **Cart Fee:** $9/person. **Walking Policy:** Unrestricted walking. **Walkability:** 3.
Opened: 1923. **Season:** Year-round. **High:** May-Aug. **To obtain tee times:** Call on Sunday at 3 p.m. for following week. **Miscellaneous:** Reduced fees (weekdays, twilight, seniors, juniors), club rentals, credit cards (MC, V, AE).
Reader Comments: Friendly squirrel on #10 tee box takes handouts ... Too busy for a quick round ... Wear a hard hat ... Narrow fairways, small greens ... Blind holes ... Meandering stream keeps me in trouble ... Fun to play.

★★★½ **LAKE SHAWNEE GOLF COURSE**
PU-4141 S.E. East Edge Rd., Topeka, 66609, Shawnee County, (913)267-2295.
Holes: 18. **Yards:** 6,013/5,459. **Par:** 69/69. **Course Rating:** 68.3/70.8. **Slope:** 107/113. **Green Fee:** $10/$19. **Cart Fee:** $11/person. **Walking Policy:** Unrestricted walking. **Walkability:** 3.
Opened: 1970. **Architect:** Larry Flatt. **Season:** Year-round. **High:** May-Sept. **To obtain tee times:** Call 4 days in advance. **Miscellaneous:** Reduced fees (weekdays, seniors, juniors), metal spikes, range (grass/mats), caddies, club rentals.
Reader Comments: Well run, scenic, worth the drive ... Lots of water ... Difficult to walk ... Nice mix of holes ... Beautiful views of Lake Shawnee.

★★½ **LAKESIDE HILLS GOLF COURSE**
PU-2300 Golf Course Rd., Olathe, 66061, Johnson County, (913)782-4192, 2 miles W of Olathe.
Holes: 18. **Yards:** 5,975/5,292. **Par:** 70/71. **Course Rating:** 67.3/69.5. **Slope:** 107/107. **Green Fee:** $16/$18. **Cart Fee:** $22/person. **Walking Policy:** Unrestricted walking. **Walkability:** 3.
Opened: 1963. **Season:** Year-round. **High:** May-Sept. **Miscellaneous:** Reduced fees (twilight, seniors, juniors), range (grass), club rentals, credit cards (MC, V, AE), beginner friendly.
Reader Comments: Small greens, not very challenging ... A few quality holes makes this worth while ... Tight fairways, crowded ... Very hilly.

LAKIN MUNICIPAL GOLF COURSE
PM-West Hwy. 50, Lakin, 67860, Kearny County, (316)355-6946, 25 miles W of Garden City. **E-mail:** iakiac@tld.com.

Holes: 9. **Yards:** 5,930/5,056. **Par:** 70/72. **Course Rating:** N/A. **Slope:** N/A. **Green Fee:** $10/$13. **Cart Fee:** $15/cart. **Walking Policy:** Unrestricted walking. **Walkability:** 2. **Opened:** 1952. **Season:** Year-round. **High:** June-Sept. **To obtain tee times:** No tee times. **Miscellaneous:** Reduced fees (weekdays, twilight, juniors), beginner friendly (youth programs).

LEOTI COUNTRY CLUB
SP-East Hwy. 96, Leoti, 67861, (316)375-2263.
Special Notes: Call club for further information.

★★★ MACDONALD GOLF COURSE
PM-840 N. Yale, Wichita, 67208, Sedgwick County, (316)688-9391.
Holes: 18. **Yards:** 6,911/5,311. **Par:** 71/72. **Course Rating:** 73.9/70.3. **Slope:** 131/116. **Green Fee:** $15/$16. **Cart Fee:** $18/cart. **Walking Policy:** Unrestricted walking. **Walkability:** 3. **Opened:** 1996. **Season:** Year-round. **High:** June-Aug. **To obtain tee times:** Call on Sunday starting at 3 p.m. for following week. **Miscellaneous:** Reduced fees (twilight), metal spikes, club rentals.
Reader Comments: #6 bites me every time ... Recent upgrades improved a lot ... 5-hour round ... Nice variety of holes ... Nice old municipal course, not crowded ... Challenging, especially the back nine ... Lures me back again and again.

★★★ MARIAH HILLS GOLF COURSE
PU-1800 Mattdown Lane, Dodge City, 67801, Ford County, (316)225-8182, 50 miles E of Garden City.
Holes: 18. **Yards:** 6,868/5,458. **Par:** 71/73. **Course Rating:** 72.5/75.3. **Slope:** 112/124. **Green Fee:** $13/$15. **Cart Fee:** $19/cart. **Walking Policy:** Unrestricted walking. **Walkability:** 3. **Opened:** 1975. **Architect:** Frank Hummel. **Season:** Year-round. **High:** April-Sept. **To obtain tee times:** Call golf shop. **Miscellaneous:** Reduced fees (twilight, juniors), range (grass), club rentals, credit cards (MC, V, AE, D, Diners Club, Carte Blanche).
Reader Comments: Long and straight ... Nice new clubhouse ... Fun course ... Fairly flat terrain, good test ... Huge fairways, great greens.

NEWTON PUBLIC GOLF COURSE
PU-329 N.E. 36th Street, Newton, 67114, (316)283-4168.
Holes: 18. **Yards:** 5,744/5,160. **Par:** 70/72. **Course Rating:** 66.9/33.1. **Slope:** 113/99. **Green Fee:** $10/$12. **Cart Fee:** $10/person. **Walking Policy:** Unrestricted walking. **Walkability:** 2. **Opened:** 1960. **Architect:** Ray Schmidt. **Season:** Year-round. **High:** June-Sept. **Miscellaneous:** Reduced fees (weekdays, seniors, juniors), metal spikes, range (grass/mats), club rentals, beginner friendly (group leagues and lessons).

OVERLAND PARK GOLF CLUB
PU-12501 Quivira Rd., Overland Park, 66213, Johnson County, (913)897-3809, 9 miles S of Kansas City.
Holes: 27.**Green Fee:** $18/$18. **Cart Fee:** $11/person. **Walking Policy:** Walking at certain times. **Walkability:** 3. **Opened:** 1970. **Season:** Year-round. **High:** April-Sept. **To obtain tee times:** Call 2 days in advance. **Miscellaneous:** Reduced fees (twilight, seniors, juniors), range (grass/mats), club rentals, credit cards (MC, V, D).
★★★½ NORTH/WEST
Yards: 6,455/5,038. **Par:** 70/70. **Course Rating:** 69.7/67.7. **Slope:** 119/108. **Architect:** Floyd Farley/Craig Schreiner.
Reader Comments: Good city course ... The greens are tough to read but are well maintained ... Busiest course in area, great staff ... Time has made course harder ... They always add a single to your foursome ... 6 hour round! ... Very forgiving.
★★★½ SOUTH/NORTH
Yards: 6,446/5,143. **Par:** 70/71. **Course Rating:** 69.9/68.2. **Slope:** 113/105. **Architect:** Floyd Farley.
★★★½ SOUTH/WEST
Yards: 6,367/5,067. **Par:** 70/71. **Course Rating:** 69.9/67.9. **Slope:** 115/111. **Architect:** Floyd Farley/Craig Schreiner.
Special Notes: Also has 9-hole executive course.

★★★ PAINTED HILLS GOLF COURSE
PU-7101 Parallel Pkwy., Kansas City, 66112, Wyandotte County, (913)334-1111, 6 miles W of Kansas City, MO.
Holes: 18. **Yards:** 5,914/4,698. **Par:** 70/70. **Course Rating:** 67.7/63.5. **Slope:** 119/107. **Green Fee:** $17/$20. **Cart Fee:** $12/cart. **Walking Policy:** Unrestricted walking. **Walkability:** N/A. **Opened:** 1927. **Architect:** James Dalgleish/Jeff Brauer. **Season:** Year-round. **High:** April-Sept. **To obtain tee times:** Call up to 72 Hours in advance. **Miscellaneous:** Reduced fees (weekdays, twilight, seniors, juniors), metal spikes, club rentals, credit cards (MC, V, AE).
Reader Comments: Too many doglegs ... Fun, hilly course ... Tight ... Short and sweet ... An old course being reborn ... Well maintained and designed ... Good for beginners.

KANSAS

★★★ PAWNEE PRAIRIE GOLF COURSE
PU-1931 S. Tyler Rd., Wichita, 67209, Sedgwick County, (316)721-7474.
Holes: 18. **Yards:** 7,361/5,928. **Par:** 72/72. **Course Rating:** 74.8/73.3. **Slope:** 123/119. **Green Fee:** $15/$15. **Cart Fee:** $18/cart. **Walking Policy:** Unrestricted walking. **Walkability:** 3. **Opened:** 1970. **Architect:** Bob Dunning. **Season:** Year-round. **High:** May-Sept. **To obtain tee times:** Call 7 days in advance starting Sunday 3:30 p.m. **Miscellaneous:** Reduced fees (twilight, seniors, juniors), range (grass/mats), club rentals.
Reader Comments: Wide fairways ... Quite a bit of water and sand. Very large greens ... Slowest 18 holes ever ... Keep your eye on the ball, not the airplanes ... Great for errant golfers ... Fun course to play ... Tough playing around all the deer.

PRAIRIE VIEW COUNTRY CLUB
SP-9840 SW 45th, Topeka, 66610, (913)478-9733.
Special Notes: Call club for further information.

★★★★ QUAIL RIDGE GOLF COURSE *Value*
PU-3805 Quail Ridge Dr., Winfield, 67156, Cowley County, (316)221-5645, 35 miles SE of Wichita.
Holes: 18. **Yards:** 6,826/5,328. **Par:** 72/72. **Course Rating:** 73.0/71.5. **Slope:** 125/119. **Green Fee:** $15/$16. **Cart Fee:** $10/person. **Walking Policy:** Unrestricted walking. **Walkability:** 2. **Opened:** 1992. **Architect:** Jerry Slack. **Season:** Year-round. **High:** April-Oct. **To obtain tee times:** Call up to 7 days in advance for weekdays. Call on Monday starting 8 a.m. for following weekend. **Miscellaneous:** Reduced fees (weekdays, resort guests, seniors, juniors), discount packages, range (grass), club rentals, lodging, credit cards (MC, V, AE, D), beginner friendly (introductory classes and clinics).
Reader Comments: Just a delight ... This will be a tough course in 30 years ... Staff great ... Better hope you stay in fairway ... Solid track ... Exceptional new course ... Loved the challenging greens ... Women friendly course.

★★★★ ROLLING MEADOWS GOLF COURSE *Value*
PM-7550 Old Milford Rd., Milford, 66514, Geary County, (913)238-4303, 60 miles W of Topeka.
Web: www.rollingmeadowsgc.com.
Holes: 18. **Yards:** 6,879/5,515. **Par:** 72/72. **Course Rating:** 74.0/70.7. **Slope:** 134/116. **Green Fee:** $10/$17. **Cart Fee:** $9/person. **Walking Policy:** Unrestricted walking. **Walkability:** 1. **Opened:** 1981. **Architect:** Richard Watson. **Season:** Year-round. **High:** April-Oct. **To obtain tee times:** Call Wednesday a.m. for following weekend. **Miscellaneous:** Reduced fees (weekdays, twilight), discount packages, range (grass/mats), club rentals, credit cards (MC, V, AE, D).
Reader Comments: Hidden gem, great holes, great service, highly recommended ... Better play it smart, or bring balls ... Good layout ... A fun course, water, trees, sand ... Tough but fair.

RUSSELL COUNTRY CLUB
PU-2nd & Copeland, Russell, 67665, (785)483-2852. **E-mail:** ithompson@russellks.net.
Holes: 18. **Yards:** 6,282/5,516. **Par:** 72/72. **Course Rating:** 71.0/72.9. **Slope:** 120/120. **Green Fee:** $13/$15. **Cart Fee:** $16/cart. **Walking Policy:** Unrestricted walking. **Walkability:** 1. **Season:** Year-round. **High:** April-Nov. **To obtain tee times:** Call (785)483-2852 48 hours in advance if possible. **Miscellaneous:** Range (grass), club rentals, credit cards (MC, V, AE, D).

★★★ ST. ANDREW'S GOLF COURSE
PU-11099 W. 135th St., Overland Park, 66221, Johnson County, (913)897-3804, 10 miles S of Kansas City. **E-mail:** pgamp165@aol.com.
Holes: 18. **Yards:** 6,205/4,713. **Par:** 70/70. **Course Rating:** 69.5/67.7. **Slope:** 109/108. **Green Fee:** $13/$18. **Cart Fee:** $11/person. **Walking Policy:** Unrestricted walking. **Walkability:** N/A. **Opened:** 1962. **Architect:** Jess Nash/John Nash. **Season:** Year-round. **High:** June-July. **To obtain tee times:** Call 3 days in advance. **Miscellaneous:** Reduced fees (twilight, seniors, juniors), metal spikes, range (grass), club rentals, credit cards (MC, V).
Reader Comments: Some tough holes, good value ... Zoysia fairways being added ... Flat, easy to walk, new clubhouse ... A very open course ... 5½ hr rounds, marriage murder ... Par 4s are long ... Uncreative layout ... Too many easy par 3s ... New clubhouse a great improvement ... Short from the front tees, very long from the back.

★★★ SALINA MUNICIPAL GOLF CLUB
PM-2500 E. Crawford St., Salina, 67401, Saline County, (785)826-7450. **E-mail:** shard@informatics.net.
Holes: 18. **Yards:** 6,500/4,800. **Par:** 70/70. **Course Rating:** 72.1/68.0. **Slope:** 117/110. **Green Fee:** $10/$12. **Cart Fee:** $10/person. **Walking Policy:** Unrestricted walking. **Walkability:** 3. **Opened:** 1969. **Architect:** Floyd Farley. **Season:** Year-round. **High:** April-Oct. **To obtain tee times:** Call up to 5 days in advance. **Miscellaneous:** Reduced fees (twilight, juniors), range (grass), club rentals, credit cards (MC, V), beginner friendly (golf clinics throughout season).
Reader Comments: Very busy course ... Long course, front flat, back hills ... Tough course in usual windy conditions ... Long ball hitters delight.

KANSAS

SENECA GOLF CLUB
PU-1400 Elk Street, Seneca, 66538, Nemoa County County, (785)336-3568.
Holes: 9. **Yards:** 5,897/5,557. **Par:** 72/72. **Course Rating:** 66.9/66.9. **Slope:** 103/103. **Green Fee:** $13/$13. **Cart Fee:** $15/cart. **Walking Policy:** Unrestricted walking. **Walkability:** 2. **Season:** April-Oct. **High:** May-Aug. **Miscellaneous:** Club rentals.

SIM PARK MEN'S CLUB
PU-2020 W. Murdock, Wichita, 67203, (316)267-5383.
Special Notes: Call club for further information.

★★★ STAGG HILL GOLF CLUB
SP-4441 Ft. Riley Blvd., Manhattan, 66502, Riley County, (785)539-1041, 60 miles W of Topeka.
Holes: 18. **Yards:** 6,697/5,524. **Par:** 72/72. **Course Rating:** 73.1/72.8. **Slope:** 131/117. **Green Fee:** $16/$17. **Cart Fee:** $20/cart. **Walking Policy:** Unrestricted walking. **Walkability:** 1. **Opened:** 1968. **Architect:** Richard Morse/Ray Weisenberger. **Season:** Year-round. **High:** April-Oct. **To obtain tee times:** Members call Wednesday for weekend tee times. Nonmembers call on Thursday. **Miscellaneous:** Reduced fees (twilight, juniors), range (mats), club rentals, credit cards (MC, V, AE, D).
Reader Comments: Nice staff, good fairways ... Clubhouse needs help ... Very challenging course ... Unique par 5s ... Much improved from flood years ... Bring extra balls.

★★★½ SUNFLOWER HILLS GOLF CLUB
PU-122 Riverview, Bonner Springs, 66012, Wyandotte County, (913)721-2727, 15 miles W of Kansas City.
Holes: 18. **Yards:** 7,001/5,850. **Par:** 72/73. **Course Rating:** 73.3/72.6. **Slope:** 124/124. **Green Fee:** $12/$23. **Cart Fee:** $24/cart. **Walking Policy:** Unrestricted walking. **Walkability:** 4. **Opened:** 1977. **Architect:** Roger Packard. **Season:** Year-round. **High:** April-Sept. **To obtain tee times:** Call 4 days in advance. **Miscellaneous:** Reduced fees (weekdays, twilight, seniors, juniors), range (grass/mats), club rentals, credit cards (MC, V), beginner friendly (junior golf, beginner lessons).
Reader Comments: Long. Very long ... 5½ hour rounds ... Nice layout ... The greatest bunkers ... No. 15 killer par 4 ... Will test your skills ... Fun, not really hard, but not too easy ... Needs better care ... Can't wait to play again.

SUPPESVILLE GOLF COURSE
PU-Rte. 1, Milton, 67106, (316)478-2626.
Special Notes: Call club for further information.

★★★★ TERRADYNE RESORT HOTEL & COUNTRY CLUB
R-1400 Terradyne, Andover, 67002, Butler County, (316)733-5851, (800)892-4613, 10 miles E of Wichita.
Holes: 18. **Yards:** 6,704/5,048. **Par:** 71/71. **Course Rating:** 74.3/70.2. **Slope:** 139/121. **Green Fee:** $35/$55. **Cart Fee:** $10/person. **Walking Policy:** Unrestricted walking. **Walkability:** 2. **Opened:** 1987. **Architect:** Don Sechrest. **Season:** Year-round. **High:** April-Oct. **To obtain tee times:** Resort guests call 7 days in advance. **Miscellaneous:** Reduced fees (resort guests), discount packages, range (grass), club rentals, lodging (42 rooms), credit cards (MC, V, AE).
Reader Comments: Links-style, huge greens ... Test for better players ... Tough in wind ... Better hit it straight here. If you didn't know better you might think you were in Scotland ... If you're in the area, play it ... Hit the fairways and you'll enjoy the course.

★★★ TOMAHAWK HILLS GOLF CLUB
PU-17501 Midland Dr., Shawnee, 66218, Johnson County, (913)631-8000, 5 miles S of Kansas City.
Holes: 18. **Yards:** 6,003/5,643. **Par:** 70/71. **Course Rating:** 69.1/71.1. **Slope:** 118/117. **Green Fee:** $17/$21. **Cart Fee:** $24/person. **Walking Policy:** Unrestricted walking. **Walkability:** 5. **Opened:** 1911. **Architect:** Bill Leonard. **Season:** Year-round. **High:** April-Oct. **To obtain tee times:** Call 2 days in advance. **Miscellaneous:** Reduced fees (weekdays, low season, twilight, seniors, juniors), range (grass/mats), club rentals, credit cards (MC, V).
Reader Comments: Too hilly, short holes, small greens ... Thin tee boxes, small crowned greens ... Different ... A fun course ... Hills is an understatement ... Nice greens, crowded on weekends ... Interesting 9th and 18th holes from a cliff ... Very steep hills, hard to walk.

★★½ TOPEKA PUBLIC GOLF CLUB
PM-2533 S.W. Urish Rd., Topeka, 66614, Shawnee County, (785)272-0511.
Holes: 18. **Yards:** 6,313/5,445. **Par:** 71/71. **Course Rating:** 70.4/72.6. **Slope:** 117/121. **Green Fee:** $12/$13. **Cart Fee:** $10/person. **Walking Policy:** Unrestricted walking. **Walkability:** 3. **Opened:** 1954. **Architect:** William Leonard/L.J."Dutch" McLellan. **Season:** Year-round. **High:** May-Sept. **To obtain tee times:** Call Tuesday after 7 a.m. for weekends and holidays only. **Miscellaneous:** Reduced fees (seniors, juniors), discount packages, range (grass), club rentals, credit cards (MC, V).

KANSAS

Reader Comments: No yardage markers ... Great greens ... Fairways need some work, hard in summer ... Rather plain, but still a fun round, no surprises ... Wide open course. Crowded.

★★★½ TURKEY CREEK GOLF COURSE
PU-1000 Fox Run, McPherson, 67460, McPherson County, (316)241-8530, 50 miles N of Wichita. E-mail: turkeycreek@mpks.net.
Holes: 18. Yards: 6,241/5,327. Par: 70/70. Course Rating: 71.3/69.6. Slope: 125/116. Green Fee: $14/$16. Cart Fee: $20/cart. Walking Policy: Unrestricted walking. Walkability: 3. Opened: 1991. Architect: Phillip Smith. Season: Year-round. High: April-Oct. To obtain tee times: Call (316)241-8530 7 days in advance for weekdays. Call on Wednesday for upcoming weekend or holiday. Miscellaneous: Reduced fees (twilight), range (grass), club rentals, credit cards (MC, V, AE, D).
Reader Comments: Blind shots ... Very well kept ... You must hit the ball straight, water all over ... From back tees, tough but fun ... Flooding problems are better but you need to call ahead if it rains ... A test of your game ... Love to play this course.

TWIN LAKES GOLF COURSE
M-53469 Mulvane Rd., Bldg. 1336, McConnell AFB, 67221, Sedgwick County, (316)759-4038, 1 miles S of Wichita. Web: www.mcconnell.af.mil.
Holes: 18. Yards: 6,904/5,151. Par: 72/72. Course Rating: 73.1/71.0. Slope: 120/120. Green Fee: $8/$16. Cart Fee: $16/cart. Walking Policy: Unrestricted walking. Walkability: 1. Season: Year-round. High: June-Aug. Miscellaneous: Reduced fees (twilight, juniors), range (grass), club rentals, credit cards (MC, V), beginner friendly (lessons given).

★★★ VILLAGE GREENS GOLF CLUB
PU-5815 Highway 92, Meriden, 66512, Jefferson County, (785)876-2255, 20 miles NE of Topeka.
Holes: 18. Yards: 6,392/5,588. Par: 72/72. Course Rating: 70.2/N/A. Slope: 114/N/A. Green Fee: $12/$13. Cart Fee: $18/cart. Walking Policy: Unrestricted walking. Walkability: 2. Opened: 1970. Architect: Buck Blankenship/L.J. McClellan. Season: Year-round. High: May-Sept. To obtain tee times: No tee times. Miscellaneous: Reduced fees (weekdays, juniors), metal spikes, range (grass/mats) (golf school in summer).
Reader Comments: Fun, out of the way public course... A gem in the country ... Worth the time to drive ... Course getting better every year ... Watch out for the wind!

★★½ WELLINGTON GOLF CLUB
PM-1500 W. Harvey, Wellington, 67152, Sumner County, (316)326-7904, 28 miles S of Wichita.
Holes: 18. Yards: 6,201/5,384. Par: 70/70. Course Rating: 70.5/70.9. Slope: 135/113. Green Fee: $11/$13. Cart Fee: $17/cart. Walking Policy: Unrestricted walking. Walkability: 2. Opened: 1919. Architect: Built by members. Season: Year-round. High: April-Sept. To obtain tee times: Call up to 7 days in advance. Miscellaneous: Reduced fees (weekdays, twilight), range (grass/mats), rentals, credit cards (MC, V).
Reader Comments: Quiet when no trains go through ... Fun course ... Wonderful staff ... Very small, very very fast greens ... Will bring you to your knees.

★★★ WESTERN HILLS GOLF CLUB
SP-8533 S.W. 21st. St., Topeka, 66615, Shawnee County, (785)478-4000.
Holes: 18. Yards: 6,089/4,728. Par: 70/70. Course Rating: 69.2/66.1. Slope: 121/110. Green Fee: $13/$15. Cart Fee: $10/person. Walking Policy: Unrestricted walking. Walkability: 2. Opened: 1967. Architect: Maury Bell. Season: Year-round. High: April-Sept. To obtain tee times: Call (785)478-4000 Wednesday for weekend tee time. Miscellaneous: Reduced fees (weekdays), club rentals, credit cards (MC, V, AE, D).
Reader Comments: Neat rolling terrain ... Wide open fairways ... Good course to walk, getting better every year ... Gets lots of play ... Good water holes ... I can drive some of the par 4s ... Nice clubhouse, nice place for a drink & food.

WILLOW TREE GOLF COURSE
PU-1800 W. 15th St., Liberal, 67901, Seward County, (316)626-0175, 60 miles S of Garden City.
Holes: 18. Yards: 5,900/5,052. Par: 72/72. Course Rating: 70.2/N/A. Slope: 121/N/A. Green Fee: $10/$12. Cart Fee: $17/cart. Walking Policy: Unrestricted walking. Walkability: 1. Season: Year-round. High: May-Sept. To obtain tee times: Call golf shop. Miscellaneous: Reduced fees (weekdays, seniors, juniors), range (grass), caddies, club rentals, credit cards (MC, V).

KENTUCKY

★★★½ A.J. JOLLY GOLF COURSE
PM-5350 South U.S. 27, Alexandria, 41001, Campbell County, (606)635-2106. **Web:** www.net-caddy.com.
Holes: 18. **Yards:** 6,219/5,418. **Par:** 71/75. **Course Rating:** 69.3/70.3. **Slope:** 118/115. **Green Fee:** $18/$19. **Cart Fee:** $11/person. **Walking Policy:** Unrestricted walking. **Walkability:** 2. **Opened:** 1962. **Season:** Feb-Dec. **High:** April-Sept. **To obtain tee times:** Weekends—call 8 days in advance Weekdays—call week in advance. **Miscellaneous:** Club rentals, credit cards (MC, V), beginner friendly.
Reader Comments: Not a long course, but very enjoyable to play ... Great looking course-mid/length-lots of water/woods, No.16 very tough par 4 ... Go for views, service ... Great secret-excellent value, great greens.... Quiet, laid back place to relax ... One of the best in northern Ky.

BALLARD COUNTY COUNTRY CLUB
SP-Rte. 1, La Center, 42056, (502)665-5557.
Special Notes: Call club for further information.

★★½ BARREN RIVER STATE PARK GOLF COURSE
PU-1149 State Park Rd., Lucas, 42156, Barren County, (270)646-4653, (800)295-1876, 30 miles SE of Bowling Green. **E-mail:** golfpro@csip.net.
Holes: 18. **Yards:** 6,440/4,919. **Par:** 72/72. **Course Rating:** 69.1/66.6. **Slope:** 118/106. **Green Fee:** $18/$20. **Cart Fee:** $10/person. **Walking Policy:** Unrestricted walking. **Walkability:** 5. **Opened:** 1967. **Architect:** Fred Rux. **Season:** Year-round. **High:** April-Sept. **To obtain tee times:** Call anytime. **Miscellaneous:** Reduced fees (weekdays, twilight), discount packages, club rentals, lodging, credit cards (MC, V, AE, D).
Reader Comments: Good value for money ... Great state park food & service, very scenic course plays along 10,000 acre lake ... Bring extra balls ... Front side by lake, back through woods, you see deer ... A real pleasure to play, all kinds of holes.

BEAR CREEK COUNTRY CLUB
PU-200 Fairway Dr., Catlettsburg, 41125, (606)928-5335.
Special Notes: Call club for further information.

BEN HAWES STATE PARK GOLF
PU-400 Boothfield Rd., Owensboro, 42302, (502)685-2011.
Special Notes: Call club for further information.

BIG HICKORY GOLF COURSE
SP-Rte. 5, Manchester, 40962, (606)598-8053.
Special Notes: Call club for further information.

★★ BOB-O-LINK GOLF ENTERPRISES
PU-1450 Fox Creek Rd, Lawrenceburg, 40342, Anderson County, (502)839-4029, 2 miles SW of Lawrenceburg.
Holes: 18. **Yards:** 6,650/4,889. **Par:** 71/71. **Course Rating:** 69.7/67.5. **Slope:** 109/105. **Green Fee:** $15/$15. **Cart Fee:** $10/person. **Walking Policy:** Walking at certain times. **Walkability:** 2. **Opened:** 1968. **Architect:** Harold England/Jack Ridge. **Season:** Year-round. **High:** April-Oct. **To obtain tee times:** Call golf shop. **Miscellaneous:** Reduced fees (weekdays, low season, twilight, seniors, juniors), metal spikes, range (grass), caddies, club rentals, credit cards (MC, V).

BOGIE BUSTERS GOLF CLUB
SP-346 Leesburg Rd., Georgetown, 40324, (502)863-0754.
Special Notes: Call club for further information.

BOONE LINKS
PU-19 Clubhouse Dr., Florence, 41042, Boone County, (606)371-7550, 10 miles S of Cincinnati.
★★★½ BROOKVIEW/LAKEVIEW
Holes: 27. **Yards:** 6,634/5,648. **Par:** 72/72. **Course Rating:** 72.1/71.1. **Slope:** 128/123. **Green Fee:** N/A/$21. **Cart Fee:** $11/person. **Walking Policy:** Unrestricted walking. **Walkability:** 4. **Opened:** 1980. **Architect:** Robert von Hagge/Michael Hurdzan. **Season:** Feb-Dec. **High:** May-Aug. **To obtain tee times:** Call 7 days in advance at 7:30 a.m. **Miscellaneous:** Reduced fees (weekdays, seniors, juniors), club rentals, credit cards (MC, V).
Reader Comments: Great staff, excellent shape, interesting layout ... Very good course-variety of challenging holes ... Excellent shape and decent challenge ... Great 1st hole par 5, too nice!! ... With 3 9s, one course is always open ... Tough par 3's ... Outstanding value.
★★★½ BROOKVIEW/RIDGEVIEW
Holes: 27. **Yards:** 5,950/4,725. **Par:** 70/70. **Course Rating:** 68.4/69.2. **Slope:** 118/122. **Green Fee:** N/A/$21. **Cart Fee:** $11/person. **Walking Policy:** Unrestricted walking. **Walkability:** 4. **Opened:** 1980. **Architect:** Robert von Haggee. **Season:** Year-round. **High:** May-Aug. **To obtain tee times:** Call 7 days in advance at 7:30 a.m. **Miscellaneous:** Reduced fees (weekdays, seniors, juniors), club rentals, credit cards (MC, V).

KENTUCKY

★★★½ RIDGEVIEW/LAKEVIEW COURSE
Holes: 27. **Yards:** 6,110/4,749. **Par:** 70/70. **Course Rating:** 69.2/66.8. **Slope:** 122/113. **Green Fee:** N/A/$21. **Cart Fee:** $11/person. **Walking Policy:** Unrestricted walking. **Walkability:** 4. **Opened:** 1980. **Architect:** Robert von Haggee. **Season:** Year-round. **High:** May-Aug. **To obtain tee times:** Call 7 days in advance at 7:30 a.m. **Miscellaneous:** Reduced fees (weekdays, seniors, juniors), club rentals, credit cards (MC, V).

BRECKENRIDGE COUNTY COMMUNITY CENTER
SP-Rte 1, Hardinsburg, 40143, (502)756-2841.
Special Notes: Call club for further information.

★★★ BRIGHT LEAF GOLF RESORT
R-1742 Danville Rd., Harrodsburg, 40330, Mercer County, (606)734-4231, (800)469-6038, 29 miles SW of Lexington.
Holes: 27. **Yards:** 6,474/5,800. **Par:** 72/77. **Course Rating:** 69.8/66.1. **Slope:** 118/109. **Green Fee:** $17/$19. **Cart Fee:** $20/cart. **Walking Policy:** Unrestricted walking. **Walkability:** N/A. **Opened:** 1964. **Architect:** Buck Blankenship. **Season:** March-Oct. **High:** March-Oct. **To obtain tee times:** Call 7 days in advance. Lighted 9-hole par 3 till 11:00 p.m. **Miscellaneous:** Reduced fees (weekdays, low season, twilight), discount packages, metal spikes, club rentals, lodging, credit cards (MC, V, AE, D).
Reader Comments: Lovely people own and run resort, wish I played more ... Place to go if all you want to do is golf ... Very friendly place & good value ... Short, greens slow, good for high handicapper ... Nice lighted par-3 course on premises.

★★ CABIN BROOK GOLF CLUB
PU-2260 Lexington Rd., Versailles, 40383, Woodford County, (606)873-8404, 7 miles W of Lexington.
Holes: 18. **Yards:** 7,017/5,233. **Par:** 72/72. **Course Rating:** 72.4/68.3. **Slope:** 117/108. **Green Fee:** $13/$20. **Cart Fee:** $10/person. **Walking Policy:** Walking at certain times. **Walkability:** 1. **Opened:** 1965. **Architect:** Danny McQueen. **Season:** Year-round. **High:** May-Sept. **To obtain tee times:** Call 7 days in advance. **Miscellaneous:** Reduced fees (weekdays, twilight), metal spikes, range (grass), club rentals, credit cards (MC, V).

CALVERT CITY GOLF & COUNTRY CLUB
SP-Country Club Lane, Calvert City, 42029, (502)395-5831, 20 miles W of Paducah.
Holes: 18. **Yards:** 6,405/5,005. **Par:** 72/72. **Course Rating:** 69.1/67.0. **Slope:** 107/103. **Green Fee:** $20/$25. **Cart Fee:** $20/cart. **Walking Policy:** Unrestricted walking. **Walkability:** 2. **Opened:** 1970. **Season:** Year-round. **High:** May-Sept. **Miscellaneous:** Reduced fees (twilight), range (grass), credit cards (MC, V).

CAMPBELL HOUSE COUNTRY CLUB
SP-427 Parkway Dr., Lexington, 40504, (606)254-3631.
Special Notes: Call club for further information.

CEDAR-FIL GOLF COURSE
PU-2330 New Shepardsville Rd., Bardstown, 40004, (502)348-8981, 2 miles W of Bardstown.
Holes: 18. **Yards:** 5,938/5,233. **Par:** 72/72. **Course Rating:** N/A. **Slope:** N/A. **Green Fee:** $10/$12. **Cart Fee:** $10/person. **Walking Policy:** Unrestricted walking. **Walkability:** 1. **Opened:** 1967. **Architect:** Harold Filiatreau. **Season:** Year-round. **High:** June-Sept.

★★ CHARLIE VETTINER GOLF COURSE
PM-10207 Mary Dell Lane, Jeffersontown, 40299, Jefferson County, (502)267-9958, 25 miles SE of Louisville.
Holes: 18. **Yards:** 6,914/5,388. **Par:** 72/73. **Course Rating:** 72.3/70.0. **Slope:** 123/116. **Green Fee:** $12/$12. **Cart Fee:** $24/cart. **Walking Policy:** Unrestricted walking. **Walkability:** 4. **Opened:** 1967. **Architect:** Jack Kidwell/Michael Hurdzan. **Season:** Year-round. **High:** April-Nov. **To obtain tee times:** Call 2 days in advance. **Miscellaneous:** Reduced fees (twilight, seniors, juniors), club rentals.

★★★ CONNEMARA GOLF LINKS
PU-2327 Lexington Rd., Nicholasville, 40356, Jessamine County, (606)885-4331, 5 miles S of Lexington.
Holes: 18. **Yards:** 6,533/4,956. **Par:** 71/71. **Course Rating:** 71.1/69.5. **Slope:** 115/111. **Green Fee:** $14/$18. **Cart Fee:** Included in Green Fee. **Walking Policy:** Walking at certain times. **Walkability:** 4. **Opened:** 1992. **Architect:** Jack Ridge. **Season:** Year-round. **High:** April-Sept. **To obtain tee times:** Call 5 days in advance. Tee times will be accepted further in advance for long-distance travelers. **Miscellaneous:** Reduced fees (weekdays, low season, twilight, seniors, juniors), range (grass/mats), club rentals, credit cards (MC, V, AE, D).
Reader Comments: Nice greens, fast play, good price ... Overall look is a little rough ... Nice course for the money, beautifully laid out ... Course has yet to mature ... Lots of winding, long up & downhill par 4's ... Very receptive to wayward shots.

COUNTRY CREEK GOLF COURSE
PU-1075 Kenny Perry Dr., Franklin, 42134, (502)586-9373, 3 miles S of Franklin. **E-mail:** kpc-cgc@apex.net. **Web:** www.kpcountrycreek.com.
Holes: 18. **Yards:** 6,545/5,416. **Par:** 72/72. **Course Rating:** 69.5/64.0. **Slope:** 105/93. **Green Fee:** $22/$25. **Walking Policy:** Unrestricted walking. **Walkability:** 3. **Opened:** 1995. **Architect:** Ken Perry. **Season:** year-round. **High:** April-Sept,. **Miscellaneous:** Reduced fees (low season, seniors, juniors), metal spikes, range (grass), club rentals, credit cards (MC, V, AE, D), beginner friendly.

★★★★ CROOKED CREEK GOLF CLUB
SP-781 Crooked Creek Dr., London, 40744, Laurel County, (606)877-1993, 66 miles S of Lexington.
Holes: 18. **Yards:** 7,007/5,087. **Par:** 72/72. **Course Rating:** 73.4/71.3. **Slope:** 134/122. **Green Fee:** $35/$35. **Cart Fee:** Included in Green Fee. **Walking Policy:** Unrestricted walking. **Walkability:** 5. **Opened:** 1993. **Architect:** Brian M. Silva. **Season:** Year-round. **High:** March-Oct. **To obtain tee times:** Call up to 7 days in advance. **Miscellaneous:** Reduced fees (juniors), range (grass), club rentals, credit cards (MC, V, AE, D).
Reader Comments: Long, long, long, great layout, tough, tough, one of best in state ... Tough but fair... Very nice layout with great views ... Really hard ... Beautiful setting.

★★ DEVOU PARK GOLF COURSE
PM-1344 Audubon Rd., Covington, 41011, Kenton County, (606)431-8030, 2 miles S of Cincinnati, OH. **E-mail:** landrumglf@aol.com. **Web:** www.netcaddy.com.
Holes: 18. **Yards:** 6,091/5,065. **Par:** 70/70. **Course Rating:** 65.8/66.7. **Slope:** 112/110. **Green Fee:** $11/$19. **Cart Fee:** $11/person. **Walking Policy:** Unrestricted walking. **Walkability:** 5. **Opened:** 1928. **Architect:** Gene Bates. **Season:** Year-round. **High:** May-Sept. **To obtain tee times:** Call up to 7 days in advance. **Miscellaneous:** Reduced fees (weekdays, low season, seniors), metal spikes, club rentals, credit cards (MC, V), beginner friendly.

★★★ DOE VALLEY GOLF CLUB
SP-1 Doe Valley Pkwy., Brandenburg, 40108, Meade County, (270)422-3397, 30 miles SW of Louisville.
Holes: 18. **Yards:** 6,471/5,409. **Par:** 71/72. **Course Rating:** 69.8/70.3. **Slope:** 119/118. **Green Fee:** $11/$17. **Cart Fee:** $11/person. **Walking Policy:** Walking at certain times. **Walkability:** 4. **Opened:** 1972. **Architect:** Dick Watson. **Season:** Year-round. **High:** April-Sept. **To obtain tee times:** Call 7 days in advance. **Miscellaneous:** Reduced fees (weekdays, low season, twilight), credit cards (MC, V).
Reader Comments: Great layout. Needs conditioning ... Very good course with potential ... Tough back 9 ... Pond on 18th hole ... Narrow fairways.

★★★★ EAGLE TRACE GOLF COURSE *Value, Pace*
SP-1000 Ramey Ridge Rd., Morehead, 40351, Rowan County, (606)783-9973, 60 miles W of Lexington. **Web:** eagletrace.com.
Holes: 18. **Yards:** 6,902/5,247. **Par:** 72/72. **Course Rating:** 73.8/70.8. **Slope:** 139/127. **Green Fee:** $10/$24. **Cart Fee:** $9/person. **Walking Policy:** Unrestricted walking. **Walkability:** 3. **Opened:** 1995. **Architect:** David Pfaff. **Season:** Year-round. **High:** April-Sept. **To obtain tee times:** Call 8 days in advance. **Miscellaneous:** Reduced fees (low season, twilight, seniors, juniors), range (grass/mats), club rentals, credit cards (MC, V, AE, D).
Reader Comments: Tight fairways ... Tough course. Opening 2 holes long and tight. Bring your 'A' game ... Well worth the drive—balanced course ... Wonderful challenge and beautiful ... Fun to play ... Variety of holes in layout keeps players challenged ... A lot of rolling fairways.

★★★ EAGLE'S NEST COUNTRY CLUB
SP-Hwy. 39 N., Somerset, 42501, Pulaski County, (606)679-7754, 70 miles S of Lexington.
Holes: 18. **Yards:** 6,404/5,010. **Par:** 71/72. **Course Rating:** 69.8/67.9. **Slope:** 123/117. **Green Fee:** $36/$45. **Cart Fee:** Included in Green Fee. **Walking Policy:** Unrestricted walking. **Walkability:** 5. **Opened:** 1979. **Architect:** Ben Wihry. **Season:** Feb.-Dec. **High:** May-Oct. **To obtain tee times:** Call in advance. If you live in the county you must be a member of the course to play. **Miscellaneous:** Range (grass), club rentals, credit cards (MC, V).
Reader Comments: Everything good, a must ... Best kept secret–a must play ... Quite beautiful & good hole variety ... Good design, well maintained, excellent staff.

FAIRWAY GOLF COURSE
PU-4940 Hwy. 227 N, Wheatley, 40359, Owen County, (502)463-2338, 50 miles N of Louisville.
Holes: 18. **Yards:** 5,900/5,400. **Par:** 70/70. **Course Rating:** 66.0/68.6. **Slope:** 100/101. **Green Fee:** $22/$25. **Cart Fee:** Included in Green Fee. **Walking Policy:** Walking at certain times. **Walkability:** 3. **Opened:** 1960. **Architect:** Harold England. **Season:** Year-round. **High:** April-Oct. **To obtain tee times:** Call up to 14 days in advance. **Miscellaneous:** Reduced fees (low season, juniors), metal spikes, range (grass), credit cards (MC, V, AE).

★★½ FLAGG SPRINGS GOLF CLUB
PU-46 Smith Rd., California, 41007, Campbell County, (606)635-2170, 10 miles S of Alexandria. **Holes:** 18. **Yards:** 6,137/4,634. **Par:** 71/71. **Course Rating:** 68.3/66.0. **Slope:** 111/104. **Green Fee:** $19/$19. **Cart Fee:** $10/person. **Walking Policy:** Unrestricted walking. **Walkability:** 3. **Opened:** 1997. **Season:** year-round. **High:** April-Nov. **Miscellaneous:** Reduced fees (seniors, juniors), metal spikes, range (grass/mats), club rentals, credit cards (MC, V).

Reader Comments: Several unfair, hilly holes ... Course still has to mature. Has some good holes but also some odd ones ... No. 11 a tough par 3 ... Watch out for flying balls ... Fairly new course, has some potential ... Too many blind tee shots.

FORT KNOX
M-7955 Wilson Rd., Fort Knox, 40121, (502)624-4218, (888)548-5728, 20 miles SW of Louisville, KY.
ANDERSON GOLF COURSE
Holes: 18. **Yards:** 6,509/5,135. **Par:** 72/72. **Course Rating:** 70.2/68.3. **Slope:** 120/114. **Green Fee:** $16/$18. **Cart Fee:** $10/person. **Walking Policy:** Unrestricted walking. **Walkability:** 4. **Season:** Year-round. **High:** April-Oct. **Miscellaneous:** Reduced fees (twilight), discount packages, range (grass/mats), club rentals, credit cards (MC, V, AE).
LINDSEY GOLF COURSE
Holes: 18. **Yards:** 6,668/5,314. **Par:** 72/72. **Course Rating:** 71.4/69.8. **Slope:** 122/110. **Green Fee:** $16/$18. **Cart Fee:** $10/person. **Walking Policy:** Unrestricted walking. **Walkability:** 3. **Season:** Year-round. **High:** April-Oct. **Miscellaneous:** Range (grass), club rentals, credit cards (MC, V, AE).

★★★½ FRANCES E. MILLER GOLF COURSE
PU-2814 Pottertown Rd., Murray, 42071, Calloway County, (270)762-2238, 3 miles E of Murray. **E-mail:** millergc@altavista.com.
Holes: 18. **Yards:** 6,592/5,058. **Par:** 71/71. **Course Rating:** 71.6/68.9. **Slope:** 125/117. **Green Fee:** N/A/$17. **Cart Fee:** $10/person. **Walking Policy:** Walking at certain times. **Walkability:** 3. **Opened:** 1983. **Architect:** Jack Kidwell/Michael Hurdzan. **Season:** Year-round. **High:** March-Oct. **To obtain tee times:** Call golf shop. **Miscellaneous:** Reduced fees (twilight, seniors, juniors), range (grass), club rentals, credit cards (MC, V).

Reader Comments: You know before you go, always good ... Not plush, but a good fun course ... Nice hilly layout, some tight holes ... Challenging course, varied 9s.

★★ GENERAL BURNSIDE STATE PARK GOLF COURSE
PU-8801 S. Highway 27, Burnside, 42519, Pulaski County, (606)561-4104, 71 miles S of Lexington.
Holes: 18. **Yards:** 5,905/5,905. **Par:** 71/71. **Course Rating:** 67.5/71.6. **Slope:** N/A. **Green Fee:** $18/$18. **Cart Fee:** $10/cart. **Walking Policy:** Unrestricted walking. **Walkability:** 4. **Opened:** 1958. **Season:** Year-round. **High:** June-Sept. **To obtain tee times:** Tee times required weekends and holidays. **Miscellaneous:** Reduced fees (weekdays, low season, twilight, juniors), club rentals, credit cards (MC, V, AE, D).

★★★★½ GIBSON BAY GOLF COURSE *Value+*
PM-2000 Gibson Bay Dr., Richmond, 40475, Madison County, (606)623-0225, 20 miles S of Lexington. **Web:** www.gibsonbay.com.
Holes: 18. **Yards:** 7,113/5,069. **Par:** 72/72. **Course Rating:** 74.1/69.1. **Slope:** 128/115. **Green Fee:** $4/$18. **Cart Fee:** $8/person. **Walking Policy:** Unrestricted walking. **Walkability:** 4. **Opened:** 1993. **Architect:** Michael Hurdzan. **Season:** Year-round. **To obtain tee times:** Call 7 days in advance. Group tee times taken up to a year in advance. **Miscellaneous:** Reduced fees (weekdays, twilight, seniors, juniors), metal spikes, range (grass/mats), club rentals, credit cards (MC, V).

Reader Comments: Best-kept secret in Kentucky ... Greens were a little rough the day I played ... One of the best public courses in Kentucky ... Beautiful course & good value before 10 am ... Sharp long course–very picturesque, lots of blind shots ... Challenging, well-kept.

THE GOLF CLUB
SP-286 West, Paducah, 42001, (502)488-3907.
Special Notes: Call club for further information.

THE GOLF COURSES AT KENTON COUNTY
PU-3908 Richardson Rd., Independence, 41051, Kenton County, (606)371-3200, 15 miles S of Cincinnati.
★★★½ FOX RUN COURSE
Holes: 18. **Yards:** 7,055/4,707. **Par:** 72/72. **Course Rating:** 74.8/68.1. **Slope:** 143/123. **Green Fee:** N/A/$42. **Cart Fee:** Included in Green Fee. **Walking Policy:** Mandatory cart. **Walkability:** 4. **Opened:** 1992. **Architect:** Arthur Hills. **Season:** April-Oct. **High:** May-Aug. **To obtain tee times:** Call or come in up to 10 days in advance for weekends and 7 days in advance for weekdays. **Miscellaneous:** Range (grass/mats), club rentals, credit cards (MC, V).

KENTUCKY

Notes: Ranked 9th in 1997 Best in State.
Reader Comments: Need better yardage markings on par 3's ... Solid test of golf, 18th too gimmicky ... Nice Sunday change of pace ... Not for 15+ handicappers ... A great track for the price ... Hilly, difficult course, pace gets slow ... Great condition. Tough par 3's. Great No.18. Always have a sidehill lie.

★★★ PIONEER COURSE
Holes: 18. **Yards:** 6,059/5,336. **Par:** 70/71. **Course Rating:** 67.9/69.5. **Slope:** 114/115. **Green Fee:** $9/$18. **Cart Fee:** $12/person. **Walking Policy:** Unrestricted walking. **Walkability:** 3. **Opened:** 1968. **Architect:** Taylor Boyd. **Season:** Year-round. **High:** May-Aug. **To obtain tee times:** Call or come in up to 10 days in advance for weekends and 7 days in advance for weekdays. **Miscellaneous:** Reduced fees (weekdays, seniors, juniors), range (grass/mats), club rentals, credit cards (MC, V), beginner friendly.
Reader Comments: Warm up for Fox Run ... Flat, no challenge ... Tough par 3's, 180-220 yards uphill ... Nice course for beginners ... No. 16 a great hole.

★★★★ WILLOWS COURSE
Holes: 18. **Yards:** 6,791/5,669. **Par:** 72/72. **Course Rating:** 72.5/74.0. **Slope:** 130/129. **Green Fee:** $18/$21. **Cart Fee:** $12/person. **Walking Policy:** Unrestricted walking. **Walkability:** 3. **Opened:** 1976. **Architect:** Jack Kidwell/Michael Hurzdan. **Season:** March-Nov. **High:** May-Sept. **To obtain tee times:** Call or come in up to 10 days in advance for weekends and 7 days in advance for weekdays. **Miscellaneous:** Reduced fees (seniors, juniors), range (grass/mats), club rentals, credit cards (MC, V).
Reader Comments: Better than Fox Run and half the price ... Beautiful and well managed ... A fair test of golf. Always in good condition ... Very enjoyable to play, a lot of 2-tiered greens ... Very good course. Excellent mixture of par 3's, par 4's and par 5's. No. 10 very tough par 4 ... A very fair & enjoyable course.

★★★ HARTLAND MUNICIPAL GOLF COURSE
PM-1031 Wilkinson Trace, Bowling Green, 42103, Warren County, (270)393-3559, (800)786-7263, 45 miles N of Nashville, TN.
Holes: 18. **Yards:** 6,523/5,016. **Par:** 71/72. **Course Rating:** 70.9/68.3. **Slope:** 123/114. **Green Fee:** $14/$17. **Cart Fee:** $10/person. **Walking Policy:** Walking at certain times. **Walkability:** 3. **Opened:** 1989. **Architect:** Kevin Tucker. **Season:** Year-round. **High:** July-Aug. **To obtain tee times:** Call 7 days in advance. **Miscellaneous:** Reduced fees (weekdays, low season, twilight, seniors, juniors), club rentals, credit cards (MC, V, AE).
Reader Comments: Great greens ... Good course for average golfer ... Excellent greens, interesting dry lakes ... Tight fairways ... 'Coach' is the best marshall in Ky.

HENRY COUNTY COUNTRY CLUB
SP-Hwy. 421, New Castle, 40050, Henry County, (502)845-2375.
Holes: 18. **Yards:** 6,570/4,759. **Par:** 72/70. **Course Rating:** 70.7/67.4. **Slope:** 129/114. **Green Fee:** $11/$16. **Cart Fee:** $9/person. **Walking Policy:** Walking at certain times. **Walkability:** 3. **Architect:** Buck Blankenship. **Season:** Year-round. **High:** May-Oct. **Miscellaneous:** Reduced fees (seniors), range (grass).

HIDDEN VALLEY GOLF COURSE
PU-530 Hidden Valley Rd., Morgantown, 42261, Butler County, (502)526-4643.
Holes: 18. **Yards:** 6,200/58,000. **Par:** 72/72. **Course Rating:** N/A. **Slope:** N/A. **Green Fee:** N/A. **Walking Policy:** Unrestricted walking. **Walkability:** 2. **Opened:** 1984. **Architect:** Gary Robbins. **Season:** Year-round. **High:** April-Oct. **Miscellaneous:** Club rentals.

HIGHPOINT GOLF COURSE
PU-1215 Highpoint Dr., Nicholasville, 40356, (606)887-4614.
Special Notes: Call club for further information.

★★★½ HOUSTON OAKS GOLF COURSE
SP-555 Houston Oaks Drive, Paris, 40361, Bourbon County, (606)987-5600, 12 miles E of Lexington.
Holes: 18. **Yards:** 6,842/5,079. **Par:** 72/73. **Course Rating:** 73.9/69.3. **Slope:** 127/114. **Green Fee:** $18/$21. **Cart Fee:** $9/person. **Walking Policy:** Unrestricted walking. **Walkability:** 3. **Opened:** 1996. **Architect:** Jack Ridge. **Season:** Year-round. **High:** May-Sept. **To obtain tee times:** Call up to 7 days in advance. **Miscellaneous:** Reduced fees (low season, seniors, juniors), range (grass), club rentals, credit cards (MC, V, AE).
Notes: Ranked 10th in 1999 Best in State.
Reader Comments: Magnificent, mature trees on this new course ... Beautiful golf course and challenging.... A hidden gem. Not yet discovered ... With a little work, could be very good ... Great design—no blind shots ... Well worth a drive from just about anywhere in the state. Great course, good greens, bring all your clubs.

KENTUCKY

★★★ INDIAN SPRINGS GOLF CLUB
SP-3408 Indian Lake Dr., Louisville, 40241, Jefferson County, (502)426-7111, 8 miles NE of Downtown Louisville.
Holes: 18. **Yards:** 6,799/5,253. **Par:** 72/72. **Course Rating:** 71.4/68.4. **Slope:** 133/122. **Green Fee:** $20/$25. **Cart Fee:** $10/person. **Walking Policy:** Walking at certain times. **Walkability:** 3. **Opened:** 1994. **Season:** Year-round. **High:** May-Sept. **To obtain tee times:** Call up to 3 days in advance. **Miscellaneous:** Reduced fees (low season, twilight, juniors), range (grass), club rentals, credit cards (MC, V, AE, D).
Reader Comments: Great course for price ... Several very good holes ... Excellent service. Made to feel very welcome ... Difficult back-to-back par 5s (9 and 10).

★★ IROQUOIS GOLF COURSE
PU-1501 Rundill Rd., Louisville, 40214, Jefferson County, (502)363-9520.
Holes: 18. **Yards:** 6,138/5,004. **Par:** 71/73. **Course Rating:** 67.3/70.2. **Slope:** 106/112. **Green Fee:** $6/$12. **Cart Fee:** $10/person. **Walking Policy:** Unrestricted walking. **Walkability:** 4. **Opened:** 1947. **Architect:** Robert Bruce Harris. **Season:** Year-round. **High:** April-Nov. **To obtain tee times:** Call 2 days in advance. **Miscellaneous:** Reduced fees (twilight, seniors, juniors), club rentals, beginner friendly (lessons offered).

★★ JUNIPER HILLS GOLF COURSE
PU-800 Louisville Rd., Frankfort, 40601, Franklin County, (502)875-8559, 35 miles W of Louisville.
Holes: 18. **Yards:** 6,200/5,904. **Par:** 70/74. **Course Rating:** 68.7/67.7. **Slope:** 111/106. **Green Fee:** $12/$15. **Cart Fee:** $10/person. **Walking Policy:** Unrestricted walking. **Walkability:** 3. **Opened:** 1956. **Architect:** Buck Blankenship. **Season:** Year-round. **High:** April-Oct. **To obtain tee times:** Call 7 days in advance. **Miscellaneous:** Reduced fees (twilight), metal spikes, club rentals, beginner friendly.

★★★★ KEARNEY HILL GOLF LINKS *Value*
PM-3403 Kearney Rd., Lexington, 40511, Fayette County, (606)253-1981, 5 miles NW of Lexington.
Holes: 18. **Yards:** 6,987/5,362. **Par:** 72/72. **Course Rating:** 73.5/70.1. **Slope:** 128/118. **Green Fee:** $35/$35. **Cart Fee:** $10/person. **Walking Policy:** Unrestricted walking. **Walkability:** 2. **Opened:** 1989. **Architect:** P.B. Dye & Pete Dye. **Season:** Year-round. **High:** April-Oct. **To obtain tee times:** Call up to 7 days in advance for threesomes or foursomes. **Miscellaneous:** Reduced fees (twilight, seniors, juniors), range (grass), club rentals, credit cards (MC, V, D).
Reader Comments: Scottish links-type course–scenic, a great challenging 18 holes... Good value–nice layout ... Great course/better value ... Always windy. Long to begin with. Very tough layout. Play when you are at the top of your game ... Don't miss this, one of Kentucky's best ... Very friendly staff ... Greens, traps need work.

★★★½ KENTUCKY DAM VILLAGE STATE RESORT PARK GOLF COURSE
R-Highway 641, Gilbertsville, 42044, Marshall County, (502)362-8658, (800)295-1877, 20 miles E of Paducah. **Web:** www.kystateparks.com.
Holes: 18. **Yards:** 6,704/5,094. **Par:** 72/72. **Course Rating:** 73.0/70.0. **Slope:** 135/124. **Green Fee:** $16/$16. **Walking Policy:** Unrestricted walking. **Walkability:** 3. **Opened:** 1952. **Architect:** Perry Maxwell/Press Maxwell. **Season:** Year-round. **High:** March-Oct. **To obtain tee times:** Call golf shop at (800)295-1877 or lodge at (800)325-0146. **Miscellaneous:** Reduced fees (weekdays, low season, twilight, juniors), discount packages, range (grass), club rentals, lodging (74 rooms), credit cards (MC, V, AE, D).
Reader Comments: Tough greens, good layout, worth playing ... Lots of traffic, always good shape ... Picturesque hills ... Challenging state-park course.

★★★ LA GRANGE WOODS COUNTRY CLUB
SP-2820 S. Hwy. 53, La Grange, 40031, Oldham County, (502)222-7927, 25 miles NW of Louisville. **E-mail:** birdcrawford1025@netscape.net.
Holes: 18. **Yards:** 6,104/4,577. **Par:** 71/71. **Course Rating:** 68.9/65.8. **Slope:** 115/106. **Green Fee:** $14/$19. **Cart Fee:** $9/person. **Walking Policy:** Walking at certain times. **Walkability:** 3. **Opened:** 1970. **Architect:** Buck Blankenship/Rick Crawford. **Season:** Year-round. **High:** March-Oct. **To obtain tee times:** Call 7 days in advance. **Miscellaneous:** Reduced fees (weekdays, seniors), discount packages, club rentals, credit cards (MC, V).
Reader Comments: Friendly ... Small greens make challenge ... A perfect course, but don't leave your sand game at home ... Owner works hard to make an outstanding course.

★★★★ LAFAYETTE GOLF COURSE *Pace+*
PU-57 Jennie Green Rd., Falls of Rough, 40119, Grayson County, (502)257-2105, (888)257-2105. **E-mail:** lafayette@bbtel.com. **Web:** lafayettegolfcourse.com.
Holes: 18. **Yards:** 6,888/5,286. **Par:** 72/72. **Course Rating:** 73.9/71.7. **Slope:** 133/124. **Green Fee:** $26/$29. **Cart Fee:** $9/person. **Walking Policy:** Walking at certain times. **Walkability:** 3. **Opened:** 1997. **Architect:** Jodie Kinney. **Season:** Year-round. **High:** May-Oct,. **To obtain tee**

times: Call as far ahead as you like, credit card needed for mor than one 4-some.
Miscellaneous: Reduced fees (weekdays, low season, seniors), range (grass), club rentals, credit cards (MC, V, AE, D), beginner friendly (clinics, schools and private lessons).
Reader Comments: Tough for any skill level ... Course is new, well designed ... Brought out the best of my golf & the worst of my language ... Good fairways, staff and facilities, had to wait on deer on No. 2 ... The holes are worked into the natural flow of the land ... It was very challenging on some holes and forgiving on others.

★★★ LAKE BARKLEY STATE PARK

PU-Hwy. 68 W., Cadiz, 42211, Trigg County, (502)924-9076, (800)295-1878, 8 miles W of Cadiz,KY.
Holes: 18. **Yards:** 6,751/5,191. **Par:** 72/72. **Course Rating:** 72.7/70.2. **Slope:** 131/121. **Green Fee:** $20/$25. **Cart Fee:** $10/person. **Walking Policy:** Unrestricted walking. **Walkability:** 1.
Opened: 1972. **Architect:** Edward Lawrence Packard. **Season:** Year-round. **High:** May-Oct. **To obtain tee times:** Call up to a year in advance. Ph: (800)295-1878. **Miscellaneous:** Reduced fees (weekdays, low season, twilight), discount packages, range (grass/mats), club rentals, lodging (150 rooms), credit cards (MC, V, AE, D), beginner friendly (lessons, slow play times).
Reader Comments: Few tight holes, good course to play ... Pretty country and course ... Very reasonably priced state park–scenic ... Long course with undulating greens.

★★★½ LAKESIDE GOLF CLUB

PU-3725 Richmond Rd., Lexington, 40509, Fayette County, (606)263-5315.
Holes: 18. **Yards:** 6,844/5,269. **Par:** 72/72. **Course Rating:** 72.2/69.6. **Slope:** 123/116. **Green Fee:** $12/$18. **Cart Fee:** $8/person. **Walking Policy:** Unrestricted walking. **Walkability:** 2.
Opened: 1970. **Architect:** Bob Carr. **Season:** Year-round. **High:** April-Sept. **To obtain tee times:** Threesomes and foursomes may call up to 7 days in advance. Groups of more than 16 (outing fee applies 35.00 each person M-F.). **Miscellaneous:** Reduced fees (twilight, seniors, juniors), metal spikes, range (grass), club rentals, credit cards (MC, V, D), beginner friendly (golf schools and clinics).
Reader Comments: Long and open. Inexpensive ... Good course for the money, but very crowded ... well maintained ... Pace of play is usually swift ....Very challenging, tough 615-yard finisher ... Good course to walk.

LARUE COUNTY COUNTRY CLUB

SP-1175 Greensburg Rd., Hodgenville, 42748, (502)358-9727.
Special Notes: Call club for further information.

★★★★½ LASSING POINTE GOLF COURSE *Value, Condition, Pace*

PU-2266 Double Eagle Dr., Union, 41091, Boone County, (606)384-2266, 12 miles S of Cincinnati.
Holes: 18. **Yards:** 6,724/5,153. **Par:** 71/71. **Course Rating:** 72.2/69.5. **Slope:** 132/122. **Green Fee:** N/A/$28. **Cart Fee:** $11/person. **Walking Policy:** Unrestricted walking. **Walkability:** 3.
Opened: 1994. **Architect:** Michael Hurdzan. **Season:** April-Nov. **High:** May-Sept. **To obtain tee times:** Call 7 days in advance for weekdays. **Miscellaneous:** Reduced fees (weekdays, seniors, juniors), metal spikes, range (grass), club rentals, credit cards (MC, V).
Reader Comments: Creative layout ... Perfect golf topography-rolling & nothing is blind ... Challenging, fun golf course ... Tough from the back tees. Lots of water and woods ... Large greens, long par 3's ... Great value! Great walking course ... Easy to walk, have to stay on cart paths ... I love No. 18. 100 yard green!

★★★½ LINCOLN HOMESTEAD STATE PARK

PU-5079 Lincoln Park Rd., Springfield, 40069, Washington County, (606)336-7461, 50 miles SW of Louisville. **Web:** http://www.state.ky.us/agencies/parks/linchome.htm.
Holes: 18. **Yards:** 6,359/5,472. **Par:** 71/73. **Course Rating:** 70.0/71.0. **Slope:** 119/118. **Green Fee:** $15/$20. **Cart Fee:** $10/person. **Walking Policy:** Walking at certain times. **Walkability:** 4.
Opened: 1958. **Architect:** Buck Blankenship. **Season:** Year-round. **High:** April-Oct. **To obtain tee times:** Call or come in person. **Miscellaneous:** Reduced fees (weekdays, low season, twilight, juniors), discount packages, club rentals, credit cards (MC, V, AE, D).
Reader Comments: Wonderful setting, club-like conditions ... Front 9 difficult, hilly & rolling-back 9 flat & easy... Good value in off season ... Hidden jewel off beaten path.

LINCOLN TRAIL COUNTRY CLUB

SP-Country Club Road, Vine Grove, 40175, Hardin County, (502)877-2181, 40 miles S of Louisville.
Holes: 18. **Yards:** 6,529/5,276. **Par:** 72/72. **Course Rating:** 70.6/69.9. **Slope:** 122/117. **Green Fee:** $15/$20. **Cart Fee:** $10/person. **Walking Policy:** Walking at certain times. **Walkability:** 2.
Opened: 1969. **Season:** Year-round. **High:** April-Oct. **Miscellaneous:** Reduced fees (low season), range (grass/mats), club rentals, credit cards (MC, V, AE, D).

KENTUCKY

LINKS AT LILLY CREEK RESORT

PU-500 Lilly Creek Resort Rd., Jamestown, 42629, Russell County, (270)343-4653. **E-mail:** the-links@Duo-county.com.
Holes: 18. **Yards:** 6,105/4,730. **Par:** 72/72. **Course Rating:** 68.7/67.0. **Slope:** 112/106. **Green Fee:** $15/$15. **Cart Fee:** $10/person. **Walking Policy:** Unrestricted walking. **Walkability:** N/A. **Opened:** 1996. **Architect:** Joe David Polston. **Season:** Year-round. **High:** April-Oct.
Miscellaneous: Reduced fees (resort guests, twilight, seniors, juniors), discount packages, metal spikes, range (grass), club rentals, credit cards (MC, V).

★★ LONG RUN GOLF CLUB

PU-1605 Flatrock Rd., Anchorage, 40245, Jefferson County, (502)245-0702.
Holes: 18. **Yards:** 6,839/5,562. **Par:** 72/73. **Course Rating:** 71.5/71.4. **Slope:** 111/111. **Green Fee:** $9/$18. **Cart Fee:** $20/cart. **Walking Policy:** Unrestricted walking. **Walkability:** 2. **Opened:** 1965. **Architect:** Benjamin Wihry. **Season:** Year-round. **High:** May-Aug. **To obtain tee times:** Call up to 2 days in advance. **Miscellaneous:** Reduced fees (weekdays, low season, twilight, seniors, juniors), range (grass), club rentals.

LONGVIEW GOLF COURSE

PU-3243 Frankfort Pike, Georgetown, 40324, Scott County, (502)863-2165, (800)572-0210, 6 miles W of Georgetown.
Holes: 18. **Yards:** 6,600/5,300. **Par:** 72/73. **Course Rating:** 70.7/67.0. **Slope:** 120/114. **Green Fee:** $25/$30. **Cart Fee:** Included in Green Fee. **Walking Policy:** Walking at certain times. **Walkability:** 3. **Opened:** 1967. **Architect:** Buck Blankenship. **Season:** Year round. **High:** Apr.-Sept. **To obtain tee times:** Call (800)572-0210. **Miscellaneous:** Discount packages, range (grass/mats), credit cards (MC, V, AE), beginner friendly.
Special Notes: Formerly known as Longview Country Club.

MAPLEHURST GOLF COURSE

PU-700 Bellsville Rd., Shepherdsville, 40165, (502)957-3370.
Special Notes: Call club for further information.

★★★★ MARRIOTT'S GRIFFIN GATE GOLF CLUB

R-1720 Newtown Pike, Lexington, 40511, Fayette County, (606)231-5100. **E-mail:** kypgapro@aol.com.
Holes: 18. **Yards:** 6,830/4,994. **Par:** 72/72. **Course Rating:** 73.3/69.3. **Slope:** 132/119. **Green Fee:** $42/$52. **Cart Fee:** Included in Green Fee. **Walking Policy:** Mandatory cart. **Walkability:** 1. **Opened:** 1981. **Architect:** Rees Jones. **Season:** Year-round. **High:** March-Oct. **To obtain tee times:** Call (606)288-6193 7 days in advance. **Miscellaneous:** Reduced fees (low season, twilight, seniors), discount packages, club rentals, lodging (400 rooms), credit cards (MC, V, AE, D, Diners Club).
Notes: 1982-89 Bank One Senior Classic.
Reader Comments: Many trees, hills, improving ... Green fees too high for area ... Excellent course. Very tough/fast greens. Front 9 is wide open; back 9 surrounded by condo's ... Great value for in-state players. Great pro shop ... This place has made a great comeback! .... Perfect for outings.

★★★★ MAYWOOD GOLF CLUB

PU-130 Maywood Ave., Bardstown, 40004, Nelson County, (502)348-6600, (800)791-8633, 34 miles S of Louisville.
Holes: 18. **Yards:** 6,965/4,711. **Par:** 72/72. **Course Rating:** 72.2/66.5. **Slope:** 121/107. **Green Fee:** $19/$22. **Cart Fee:** $10/person. **Walking Policy:** Unrestricted walking. **Walkability:** 4. **Opened:** 1995. **Architect:** David Pfaff. **Season:** Year-round. **High:** March-Nov. **To obtain tee times:** Call up to 14 days in advance. **Miscellaneous:** Reduced fees (weekdays, twilight), discount packages, range (grass), club rentals, credit cards (MC, V, AE, D).
Reader Comments: Links course, very finely maintained, fine greens ... Good value-early bird special even better .... Open layout, out-of-bounds markers not friendly to hookers. Mixture of links and traditional style holes.

★★½ MY OLD KENTUCKY HOME STATE PARK GOLF CLUB

PU-668 Loretto Road, Bardstown, 40004, Nelson County, (502)349-6542, (800)323-7803, 30 miles S of Louisville.
Holes: 18. **Yards:** 6,065/5,239. **Par:** 70/71. **Course Rating:** 69.5/70.2. **Slope:** 119/118. **Green Fee:** $18/$20. **Cart Fee:** $10/person. **Walking Policy:** Unrestricted walking. **Walkability:** 3. **Opened:** 1938. **Architect:** H.H. Rudy/David Pfaff. **Season:** Year-round. **High:** April-Sept. **To obtain tee times:** Call up to 7 days in advance. **Miscellaneous:** Reduced fees (weekdays, low season, twilight, juniors), metal spikes, range (grass), club rentals, credit cards (MC, V, AE, D), beginner friendly (First Tee junior program in 2001).
Reader Comments: Good state-park course, love the bells ringing 'My Old Kentucky Home' ... Front side average, backside wooded & interesting ... 2 completely different 9s.

★★★½ NEVEL MEADE GOLF COURSE

SP-3123 Nevel Meade Dr., Prospect, 40059, Oldham County, (502)228-9522, (502)228-2091, 10 miles N of Louisville. **E-mail:** nevelmeade@aol.com.
Holes: 18. **Yards:** 6,956/5,616. **Par:** 72/72. **Course Rating:** 72.2/70.4. **Slope:** 122/117. **Green Fee:** $18/$24. **Cart Fee:** $11/person. **Walking Policy:** Unrestricted walking. **Walkability:** 3. **Opened:** 1991. **Architect:** Steve Smyers. **Season:** Year-round. **High:** March-Nov. **To obtain tee times:** Call 4 days in advance for weekdays and Wednesday morning for weekend tee times. **Miscellaneous:** Reduced fees (twilight, juniors), range (grass), rentals, credit cards (MC, V).

Reader Comments: Challenging–no trees, Scottish links style! ... Scenic–Scottish style course–good service, good condition ... Small greens for a links-style course.

★★ OLD BRIDGE GOLF CLUB

SP-1 Old Bridge Rd., Danville, 40422, Boyle County, (606)236-6051, (800)783-7153, 20 miles SW of Lexington.
Holes: 18. **Yards:** 6,400/4,600. **Par:** 72/72. **Course Rating:** 68.0/64.9. **Slope:** 117/104. **Green Fee:** $14/$20. **Cart Fee:** $20/cart. **Walking Policy:** Walking at certain times. **Walkability:** 3. **Opened:** 1990. **Architect:** Benjamin Wihry. **Season:** Year-round. **High:** May-Aug. **To obtain tee times:** Call in advance anytime. **Miscellaneous:** Reduced fees (low season), discount packages, range (grass/mats), club rentals, credit cards (MC, V).

OLDHAM COUNTY COUNTRY CLUB

SP-2300 N. Hwy. 393, La Grange, 40031, (502)222-9133.
Special Notes: Call club for further information.

PARK MAMMOTH RESORT

★½ NO. 1 COURSE

R-Hwy. U.S. 31W., Park City, 42160, Edmonson County, (270)749-4101, 19 miles E of Bowling Green.
Holes: 18. **Yards:** 6,073/5,299. **Par:** 70/70. **Course Rating:** 68.0/69.0. **Slope:** 114/114. **Green Fee:** $10/$10. **Cart Fee:** $10/person. **Walking Policy:** Unrestricted walking. **Walkability:** 4. **Opened:** 1964. **Architect:** Buck Blankenship. **Season:** Year-round. **High:** Mar.-June,Sept.-Oct. **To obtain tee times:** Tee times required from 7:00-12:00. Open play after 12:00. **Miscellaneous:** Discount packages, lodging (92 rooms), credit cards (MC, V, AE, D).
Special Notes: Formerly known as Best Western Park Monmouth Resort.

NO. 2 COURSE

R-Hwy. U.S. 31W., Park City, 42160, Edmonson County, (270)749-4101, 19 miles E of Bowling Green.
Holes: 18. **Yards:** 6,306/6,047. **Par:** 72/72. **Course Rating:** 69.3/71.5. **Slope:** 109/113. **Green Fee:** $10/$10. **Cart Fee:** $10/person. **Walking Policy:** Unrestricted walking. **Walkability:** 4. **Opened:** 1964. **Architect:** Gary Robbins. **Season:** Year-round. **High:** April-June,Sept-Oct. **To obtain tee times:** Tee times required from 7:00-12:00. Open play after 12:00. **Miscellaneous:** Discount packages, lodging (92 rooms), credit cards (MC, V, AE, D).

★★ PAXTON PARK GOLF CLUB

PM-841 Berger Rd., Paducah, 42002, McCracken County, (270)444-9514, 140 miles W of Nashville, TN.
Holes: 18. **Yards:** 6,581/5,799. **Par:** 71/76. **Course Rating:** 71.1/70.6. **Slope:** 117/116. **Green Fee:** $11/$15. **Cart Fee:** $17/cart. **Walking Policy:** Unrestricted walking. **Walkability:** 3. **Opened:** 1940. **Season:** Year-round. **High:** May-Oct. **To obtain tee times:** Call up to 5 days in advance. **Miscellaneous:** Reduced fees (twilight), range (grass), club rentals, credit cards (MC, V, AE), beginner friendly.

★★★★½ THE PENINSULA GOLF RESORT *Service+, Value, Condition, Pace+*

PU-200 Club House Dr., Lancaster, 40444, (606)548-5055.
Holes: 18. **Yards:** 6,700/5,000. **Par:** 72/72. **Course Rating:** 71.5/68.5. **Slope:** 124/115. **Green Fee:** $25/$38. **Cart Fee:** Included in Green Fee. **Walking Policy:** Walking at certain times. **Walkability:** 3. **Opened:** 1997. **Architect:** Pete Dye/Tom Liddy. **Season:** Year-round. **High:** May-Sept. **To obtain tee times:** Call 2 weeks in advance. **Miscellaneous:** Reduced fees (resort guests, twilight, seniors, juniors), discount packages, range (grass), credit cards (MC, V). **Notes:** Ranked 8th in 1999 Best in State.

Reader Comments: A new, hidden gem–much potential ... Very pleasurable experience! ... Tough course. Really enjoyed. Some holes unforgiving ... Firm, fast greens ... Great course, well maintained. Good staff, good management ... Some of the best greens in the state.

PENN RUN GOLF COURSE

PU-12900 Christman Rd., Louisville, 40229, Bullitt & Jefferson County, (502)957-5940, 12 miles S of Louisville.
Holes: 18. **Yards:** 6,217/5,511. **Par:** 71/73. **Course Rating:** 68.6/70.2. **Slope:** 111/113. **Green Fee:** $10/$12. **Cart Fee:** $18/person. **Walking Policy:** Unrestricted walking. **Walkability:** 3.

KENTUCKY

Opened: 1970. Architect: McCawley & Emberson. Season: Year round. High: April-Aug.
Miscellaneous: Reduced fees (twilight, seniors, juniors), metal spikes, club rentals.

PERRY PARK COUNTRY CLUB
PU-Rte. 355, Perry Park, 40363, Owen County, (502)484-5776, 50 miles S of Cincinnati.
Holes: 18. Yards: 7,240/5,900. Par: 72/72. Course Rating: 73.4/72.3. Slope: 119/116. Green
Fee: $21/$24. Cart Fee: $12/person. Walking Policy: Unrestricted walking. Walkability: 2.
Opened: 1968. Season: Feb.-Dec. High: June-Sept. Miscellaneous: Reduced fees (seniors,
juniors), range (grass), club rentals, credit cards (MC, V).
Special Notes: Formerly Glenwood Hall Country Club.

★★½ PINE VALLEY COUNTRY CLUB & RESORT
R-805 Pine Valley Dr., Elizabethtown, 42701, Hardin County, (270)737-8300, (800)844-1904, 35
miles S of Louisville.
Holes: 18. Yards: 6,648/5,357. Par: 72/73. Course Rating: 71.3/69.6. Slope: 119/114. Green
Fee: $20/$20. Cart Fee: $10/person. Walking Policy: Walking at certain times. Walkability: 3.
Opened: 1968. Architect: Bill Amick/Jack Ridge. Season: Year-round. High: April-Oct. To
obtain tee times: Call (270)737-8300 or (800)844-1904. Miscellaneous: Reduced fees (weekdays, low season, resort guests, twilight, seniors, juniors), discount packages, metal spikes,
range (grass/mats), club rentals, lodging (56 rooms), credit cards (MC, V, D), beginner friendly
(kids course by Jack Ridge).
Reader Comments: Slow greens, a few good holes ... Friendly people in charge ... Looks easy,
play tough ... The first time I ever saw two doglegs on a par 5 ... Tight course, good challenge.

PLAYERS CLUB OF LEXINGTON
SP-4850 Leestown Rd., Lexington, 40511, Fayette County, (606)255-1011, 5 miles W of
Lexington.
★★★½ NEW COURSE
Holes: 18. Yards: 6,804/5,042. Par: 71/71. Course Rating: 70.6/64.6. Slope: 128/116. Green
Fee: $18/$28. Cart Fee: $10/person. Walking Policy: Walking at certain times. Walkability: 3.
Opened: 1991. Architect: Danny McQueen. Season: Year-round. High: April-Oct. To obtain tee
times: Out-of-state guests may call up to 21 days in advance. Local guests may call up to 7
days in advance for weekday play and Monday for upcoming weekend. Miscellaneous:
Reduced fees (weekdays, low season, twilight, seniors), range (grass), club rentals, credit cards
(MC, V).
Reader Comments: Best public course in Kentucky ... Outstanding ... When trees mature, will
be great ... Challenging, good conditions, good clubhouse ... Good variety of holes ... Fun holes,
lots of options ... Truly fine, just enough water hazards ... Very good condition, horse country.
Special Notes: Formerly Island/Lake Course.
★★★★ OLD COURSE
Holes: 18. Yards: 6,818/4,850. Par: 72/72. Course Rating: 72.1/68.1. Slope: 128/116. Green
Fee: $18/$28. Cart Fee: $10/person. Walking Policy: Walking at certain times. Walkability: 3.
Opened: 1991. Architect: Danny McQueen. Season: Year-round. High: April-Oct. To obtain tee
times: Out-of-state guests may call up to 21 days in advance. Local guests may call up to 7
days in advance for weekday play and Monday for upcoming weekend. Miscellaneous:
Reduced fees (weekdays, low season, twilight, seniors), range (grass), club rentals, credit cards
(MC, V).
Reader Comments: Wide fairways, elevated greens, very scenic-course good condition ...
Island green ... Good value ... Excellent facility. Each 9 is different and a challenge. Interesting
golf ... Need to be great wind player to enjoy ... Great course & staff.
Special Notes: Formerly Creek/Island Course.

QUAIL CHASE GOLF CLUB
PU-7000 Cooper Chapel Rd., Louisville, 40229, Jefferson County, (502)239-2110, (877)239-
2110. Web: www.quailchase.com.
★★★★ EAST/SOUTH
Holes: 27. Yards: 6,728/5,361. Par: 72/72. Course Rating: 71.7/77.6. Slope: 127/136. Green
Fee: $18/$25. Cart Fee: $10/person. Walking Policy: Unrestricted walking. Walkability: 3.
Opened: 1988. Architect: David Pfaff. Season: Year-round. High: May-Aug. To obtain tee
times: Call 2 days in advance. Out-of-town players may call up to a year in advance.
Miscellaneous: Reduced fees (weekdays, low season, twilight, seniors, juniors), discount pack-
ages, range (grass/mats), club rentals, credit cards (MC, V, AE), beginner friendly.
Reader Comments: Nice! Tough course ... Well managed ... Good all around course ...
Enjoyable ... Excellent 27 holes of public golf ... Heavy play, but still a fine public course ...
Fairways need seeding ... Challenging.
★★★★ SOUTH/WEST
Holes: 27. Yards: 6,493/5,117. Par: 72/72. Course Rating: 70.5/76.3. Slope: 124/133. Green
Fee: $18/$25. Cart Fee: $10/person. Walking Policy: Unrestricted walking. Walkability: N/A.
Opened: 1988. Architect: David Pfaff. Season: Year-round. High: May-Aug. To obtain tee
times: Call 2 days in advance. Out-of-town players may call up to a year in advance.

Miscellaneous: Reduced fees (weekdays, low season, twilight, seniors, juniors), discount packages, range (grass/mats), club rentals, credit cards (MC, V, AE), beginner friendly.
Reader Comments: Good mix of rolling layouts ... Challenging ... Narrow fairways. Some blind shots from tees.

★★★★ **WEST/EAST**

Holes: 27. **Yards:** 6,715/5,122. **Par:** 72/72. **Course Rating:** 72.0/77.9. **Slope:** 133/141. **Green Fee:** $18/$25. **Cart Fee:** $10/person. **Walking Policy:** Unrestricted walking. **Walkability:** N/A. **Opened:** 1988. **Architect:** David Pfaff. **Season:** Year-round. **High:** May-Aug. **To obtain tee times:** Call 2 days in advance. Out-of-town players may call up to a year in advance.
Miscellaneous: Reduced fees (weekdays, low season, twilight, seniors, juniors), discount packages, range (grass/mats), club rentals, credit cards (MC, V, AE), beginner friendly.
Reader Comments: Louisville's most popular ... The 3 9s make this facility enjoyable, and different every time ... Excellent test of golf, sees a lot of play ... Upscale, excellent condition.

ROLLING HILLS GOLF COURSE

PU-1600 Pine Dr., Russellville, 42276, (502)726-8700.
Holes: 18. **Yards:** 6,379/4,877. **Par:** 71/71. **Course Rating:** 69.4/67.2. **Slope:** 111/106. **Green Fee:** $9/$15. **Cart Fee:** $8/person. **Walking Policy:** Unrestricted walking. **Walkability:** 4. **Season:** Year-round. **High:** July-Aug. **Miscellaneous:** Reduced fees (seniors), range (grass/mats), club rentals, credit cards (MC, V, AE, D).

★★★½ SENECA GOLF COURSE

PM-2300 Seneca Park Rd., Louisville, 40206, Jefferson County, (502)458-9298.
Holes: 18. **Yards:** 7,034/5,469. **Par:** 72/73. **Course Rating:** 73.7/71.5. **Slope:** 130/122. **Green Fee:** $8/$9. **Cart Fee:** $22/cart. **Walking Policy:** Unrestricted walking. **Walkability:** 3. **Opened:** 1935. **Architect:** Michael Hurdzan/Alex McKay. **Season:** Year-round. **High:** April-Sept. **To obtain tee times:** Call 2 days in advance for weekday play. Sign in at golf shop on Tuesday or call in on Thursday for weekends. **Miscellaneous:** Reduced fees (weekdays, twilight, seniors, juniors), metal spikes, range (grass/mats), club rentals.
Reader Comments: Rolling hills with grass mounds around greens, water comes into play on 4 holes ... This is the star of the munys ... Good course to walk, a challenge to play water holes ... Much improved ... Great price ... Best city course.

★★★½ SHAWNEE GOLF COURSE

PU-460 Northwestern Pkwy., Louisville, 40212, Jefferson County, (502)776-9389.
Holes: 18. **Yards:** 6,402/5,476. **Par:** 70/70. **Course Rating:** 66.7/68.9. **Slope:** 100/105. **Green Fee:** $7/$12. **Walking Policy:** Unrestricted walking. **Walkability:** 2. **Opened:** 1933. **Architect:** Alex McKay. **Season:** Year-round. **High:** May-Oct. **To obtain tee times:** Call 2 days in advance. **Miscellaneous:** Reduced fees (twilight, seniors, juniors), metal spikes, range (grass), club rentals, beginner friendly (first tee facility).
Reader Comments: Flat course along Ohio River. Bermuda grass tees & fairways ... Good level course to walk ... Excellent beginner course ... Very friendly, accommodating. Changed my tee time 3 times. No problem! Love it!

SHELBYVILLE COUNTRY CLUB

SP-Smithfield Rd., Shelbyville, 40066, Shelby County, (502)633-0542, 20 miles W of Frankfort.
Holes: 18. **Yards:** 6,331/5,231. **Par:** 72/73. **Course Rating:** 70.2/69.7. **Slope:** 122/118. **Green Fee:** $25/$25. **Cart Fee:** Included in Green Fee. **Walking Policy:** Mandatory cart. **Walkability:** 3. **Season:** Year-round. **High:** July-Aug. **To obtain tee times:** Open play Wednesday, Thursday, Friday before noon. Call the day of for tee times. **Miscellaneous:** Range (grass), club rentals, credit cards (MC, V, D).

THE SILOS GOLF CLUB

SP-270 N. Country Club Lane KY 286, Paducah, 42002, McCrackey County, (270)488-2182.
Holes: 18. **Yards:** 6,780/5,876. **Par:** 72/72. **Course Rating:** 73.3/69.9. **Slope:** 128/117. **Green Fee:** $22/$28. **Cart Fee:** $18/cart. **Walking Policy:** Unrestricted walking. **Walkability:** 3. **Opened:** 1997. **Architect:** Jerry Lemons. **Season:** Year-round. **High:** July-Aug. **To obtain tee times:** Call (270)488-2182 24 hours in advance. **Miscellaneous:** Range (grass).
Special Notes: Formerly Westwood Country Club

★★ SOUTHWIND GOLF COURSE

SP-2480 New Boonesboro Rd., Winchester, 40391, Clark County, (606)744-0375, 15 miles E of Lexington.
Holes: 18. **Yards:** 6,265/4,700. **Par:** 71/71. **Course Rating:** 67.1/70.0. **Slope:** 113/102. **Green Fee:** $11/$13. **Cart Fee:** $8/person. **Walking Policy:** Walking at certain times. **Walkability:** 3. **Opened:** 1992. **Architect:** Dan McQueen/Ken Arnold. **Season:** Feb.-Dec. **High:** May-Sept. **To obtain tee times:** Call for tee times 7 days a week. **Miscellaneous:** Reduced fees (weekdays, low season, seniors), discount packages, range (grass/mats), club rentals.

KENTUCKY

SPORTLAND GOLF COURSE
PU-4199 Lexington Rd., Winchester, 40391, Clark County, (606)744-9959, (800)273-5001, 18 miles E of Lexington.
Holes: 18. **Yards:** 6,714/4,717. **Par:** 72/72. **Course Rating:** 70.0/64.6. **Slope:** 116/104. **Green Fee:** $15/$21. **Cart Fee:** Included in Green Fee. **Walking Policy:** Unrestricted walking. **Walkability:** 5. **Opened:** 1967. **Season:** March-Nov. **High:** July-Aug. **Miscellaneous:** Reduced fees (seniors) (reduced fees for srs. w/card).

SUGAR BAY GOLF COURSE
SP-Rte. 1, Box 276D, Warsaw, 41095, (606)567-2601.
Special Notes: Call club for further information.

★★★½ THE SUMMIT
SP-6501 Summit Dr., Owensboro, 42303, Daviess County, (502)281-4653, 6 miles E of Owensboro. **E-mail:** summit@milesnmore.com. **Web:** www.summitky.com.
Holes: 18. **Yards:** 6,600/4,890. **Par:** 72/72. **Course Rating:** 71.3/67.6. **Slope:** 128/117. **Green Fee:** $29/$55. **Cart Fee:** Included in Green Fee. **Walking Policy:** Mandatory cart. **Walkability:** 4. **Opened:** 1993. **Architect:** Don Charles. **Season:** Year-round. **High:** March-Oct. **To obtain tee times:** Tee times may be made one week in advance. **Miscellaneous:** Reduced fees (twilight, seniors), range (grass), club rentals, credit cards (MC, V).

Reader Comments: Great layout, tough greens especially No. 9 ... Won't disappoint you ... A long water hole fun to drive ... It plays a little long from the back tees but has enough challenge throughout the course to keep you on your toes ...Greens in great shape, very true.

SWEET HOLLOW GOLF COURSE
PU-424 Sweet Hollow Road, Corbin, 40701, Laurel County, (606)523-1241, 3 miles N of Corbin.
Holes: 9. **Yards:** 3,022/2,649. **Par:** 36/36. **Course Rating:** 69.6/69.6. **Slope:** 125/119. **Green Fee:** $21/$23. **Cart Fee:** $10/person. **Cart Fee:** Included in Green Fee. **Walkability:** 3. **Season:** Year-round. **Miscellaneous:** Range (grass), club rentals, credit cards (MC, V).

★★★½ TANGLEWOOD GOLF COURSE
PU-245 Tanglewood Dr., Taylorsville, 40071, Spencer County, (502)477-2468, 25 miles SE of Louisville.
Holes: 18. **Yards:** 6,626/5,275. **Par:** 72/72. **Course Rating:** 70.2/68.8. **Slope:** 121/115. **Green Fee:** $12/$16. **Cart Fee:** $11/person. **Walking Policy:** Walking at certain times. **Walkability:** 4. **Opened:** 1984. **Architect:** Buck Blankenship. **Season:** Year-round. **High:** May-Sept. **To obtain tee times:** Call 3 days in advance. **Miscellaneous:** Reduced fees (weekdays, low season, resort guests, twilight, seniors, juniors), discount packages, range (grass/mats), club rentals, lodging, credit cards (MC, V).

Reader Comments: Good course, enjoyed it ... Reasonable rates ... Many sidehill lies ... The first time I played this course—the golf pro said hit everything to the left—he was right! ... Good course for scramblers.

★★½ TATES CREEK GOLF COURSE
PM-1400 Gainesway Dr., Lexington, 40502, Fayette County, (606)272-3428.
Holes: 18. **Yards:** 6,310/5,260. **Par:** 72/73. **Course Rating:** 69.5/69.3. **Slope:** 120/117. **Green Fee:** $12/$18. **Cart Fee:** $16/person. **Walking Policy:** Unrestricted walking. **Walkability:** 3. **Opened:** 1957. **Architect:** Buck Blankenship. **Season:** Year-round. **High:** April-Oct. **To obtain tee times:** Call 7 days in advance. Must be at least 3 players in group to reserve tee time. Beginning at 7:15 am. **Miscellaneous:** Reduced fees (twilight, seniors, juniors), club rentals, credit cards (MC, V, D).

Reader Comments: Can't beat price ... Short, tight, small greens ... Much-played muny–short & tight ... Hilly, course is always in good shape.

★★★½ TWIN OAKS GOLF COURSE
PU-43rd & Michigan Ave., Covington, 41015, Kenton County, (606)581-2410, 5 miles S of Cincinnati, OH.
Holes: 18. **Yards:** 6,400/5,078. **Par:** 70/70. **Course Rating:** 70.6/68.5. **Slope:** 121/114. **Green Fee:** $19/$19. **Cart Fee:** $12/person. **Walking Policy:** Unrestricted walking. **Walkability:** 1. **Opened:** 1928. **Season:** Year-round. **High:** May-Oct. **To obtain tee times:** Call in advance. **Miscellaneous:** Reduced fees (seniors, juniors), club rentals, credit cards (MC, V, D).

Reader Comments: Great new clubhouse ... A real gem! You tee off and the course takes you around its layout ... Continue to make improvements on course. New clubhouse is a real asset....Front 9 is wide open; back 9 is harder and longer.

★★★½ WEISSINGER HILLS GOLF COURSE
PU-2240 Mt. Eden Rd., Shelbyville, 40065, Shelby County, (502)633-7332, 15 miles E of Louisville.
Holes: 18. **Yards:** 6,534/5,165. **Par:** 72/73. **Course Rating:** 70.8/69.0. **Slope:** 118/112. **Green Fee:** $13/$18. **Cart Fee:** $10/person. **Walking Policy:** Walking at certain times. **Walkability:** 3.

Opened: 1990. **Architect:** Jack Ridge. **Season:** Year-round. **High:** April-Sept. **To obtain tee times:** Call 7 days in advance. **Miscellaneous:** Reduced fees (weekdays, low season, twilight, seniors, juniors), discount packages, range (grass), club rentals, credit cards (MC, V, AE).

Reader Comments: Reasonable rates ... Clubhouse is an old barn ... Easy, but in good shape ... Very accessible, lots of local history, well maintained, good layout, staff, facilities ... Easy to score but small greens!.

★★★½ WESTERN HILLS GOLF COURSE

PU-2160 Russellville Rd., Hopkinsville, 42240, Christian County, (502)885-6023, 60 miles N of Nashville.

Holes: 18. **Yards:** 6,907/3,921. **Par:** 72/72. **Course Rating:** 73.8/64.0. **Slope:** 134/109. **Green Fee:** $14/$16. **Cart Fee:** $16/cart. **Walking Policy:** Walking at certain times. **Walkability:** 4. **Opened:** 1985. **Architect:** Earl Stone. **Season:** Year-round. **High:** May-Sept. **To obtain tee times:** Call up to 7 days in advance. **Miscellaneous:** Reduced fees (weekdays, seniors), metal spikes, range (grass/mats), credit cards (MC, V).

Reader Comments: Great staff & value for your money ... Greens very fast, like putting on highway ... Wide open, good course ... Very nice, especially fairways.

WOODFORD HILLS COUNTRY CLUB

SP-McCowans Ferry Rd., Versailles, 40383, (606)873-8122.
Special Notes: Call club for further information.

WOODLAWN SPRINGS GOLF CLUB

SP-103 Woodhill Rd., Bardstown, 40004, Nelson County, (502)348-2200, (877)748-2200.
Holes: 18. **Yards:** 6,530/5,050. **Par:** 72/72. **Course Rating:** 71.5/69.0. **Slope:** 125/117. **Green Fee:** $13/$18. **Cart Fee:** $11/person. **Walking Policy:** Unrestricted walking. **Walkability:** 4. **Opened:** 1995. **Architect:** George Young. **Season:** Year-round. **High:** April-Oct. **To obtain tee times:** Call golf shop. **Miscellaneous:** Reduced fees (seniors), range (grass), credit cards (MC, V, AE), beginner friendly.

★★★ WOODSON BEND RESORT

R-14 Woodson Bend, Bronston, 42518, Wayne County, (606)561-5316, 60 miles S of Lexington.
Holes: 18. **Yards:** 6,189/5,155. **Par:** 72/75. **Course Rating:** 69.2/72.0. **Slope:** 117/113. **Green Fee:** $18/$23. **Cart Fee:** Included in Green Fee. **Walking Policy:** Mandatory cart. **Walkability:** N/A. **Opened:** 1973. **Architect:** Dave Bennett/Lee Trevino. **Season:** Feb.-Dec. **High:** May-Sept. **To obtain tee times:** Call 7 days in advance. **Miscellaneous:** Reduced fees (low season, juniors), discount packages, metal spikes, range (grass/mats), club rentals, lodging, credit cards (MC, V).

Reader Comments: Scenic course ... Too many blind approach shots to greens ... Trees and condos line most fairways ... Nice course, tight if played from back tees ... Good resort course, well maintained.

LOUISIANA

★★½ ABITA SPRINGS GOLF & COUNTRY CLUB
SP-73433 Oliver St., Abita Springs, 70420, (504)893-2463. **Web:** www.Abitagolf.com.
Holes: 18. **Yards:** 6,384/4,756. **Par:** 72/72. **Course Rating:** 69.9/N/A. **Slope:** N/A. **Green Fee:** $15/$20. **Cart Fee:** $11/person. **Walking Policy:** Unrestricted walking. **Walkability:** 2. **Season:** Year-round. **High:** March-Dec. **To obtain tee times:** 7 days in advance—call 893-2463.
Miscellaneous: Reduced fees (twilight, seniors, juniors), range (grass), club rentals, credit cards (MC, V, AE, D, Diners Club), beginner friendly.
Reader Comments: Very family friendly ... Keep it inbounds and you can score ... Improved lately ... Good day of golf ... Have scrambles every Tuesday and Thursday Fun group of golfers.

ALPINE GOLF & COUNTRY CLUB
PU-8311 Shreveport Hwy., Pineville, 71360, (318)640-4030.
Holes: 9. **Yards:** 6,054/5,087. **Par:** 72/72. **Course Rating:** 71.2/72.1. **Slope:** 127/122. **Green Fee:** $10/$12. **Cart Fee:** $16/cart. **Walking Policy:** Walking at certain times. **Walkability:** 5. **Season:** Year-round. **High:** April-Aug. **Miscellaneous:** Reduced fees (seniors), club rentals, credit cards (MC, V, AE, D).
Special Notes: Hosted 1999 Senior Olympics

★★ ALPINE MEADOWS GOLF CLUB
PU-5730 Meadowlake, Keithville, 71047, Caddo County, (318)925-9547, 5 miles SW of Shreveport.
Holes: 18. **Yards:** 6,473/5,345. **Par:** 72/72. **Course Rating:** 70.5/69.1. **Slope:** 113/108. **Green Fee:** $10/$12. **Cart Fee:** $16/cart. **Walking Policy:** Unrestricted walking. **Walkability:** 1. **Opened:** 1962. **Season:** Jan.-Dec. **High:** May-Aug. **To obtain tee times:** Call anytime between 7 a.m. and 6 p.m. **Miscellaneous:** Reduced fees (twilight, seniors, juniors), metal spikes, club rentals, credit cards (MC, V, AE, D).
Special Notes: Formerly known as Meadowlake Country Club

★★ AUDUBON GOLF CLUB
PU-473 Walnut St., New Orleans, 70118, (504)865-8260.
Holes: 18. **Yards:** 5,739/5,181. **Par:** 62/62. **Course Rating:** 64.4/70.0. **Slope:** 96/115. **Green Fee:** $8/$12. **Cart Fee:** $18/cart. **Walkability:** 1. **Opened:** 1898. **Season:** Year Round. **High:** April-Oct. **Miscellaneous:** Reduced fees (twilight), metal spikes, club rentals, credit cards (MC, V, AE, D), beginner friendly.

BARKSDALE GOLF CLUB
185 Bossier Rd., Barksdale AFB, 71110, (318)456-4767. **E-mail:** Larry.busch@barksdale.af.mil.
Holes: 18. **Yards:** N/A. **Par:** N/A. **Course Rating:** N/A. **Slope:** N/A. **Green Fee:** $6/$18. **Cart Fee:** $13/person. **Walking Policy:** Unrestricted walking. **Walkability:** 1. **Season:** Year-round. **High:** March-Oct. **Miscellaneous:** Reduced fees (twilight), range (grass), club rentals, credit cards (MC, V), beginner friendly (beginner clinics 2 per year).

BAYOU OAKS GOLF COURSES
PM-1040 Filmore, New Orleans, 70124, Orleans County, (504)483-9396.
★★★½ CHAMPIONSHIP COURSE
Holes: 18. **Yards:** 7,061/6,013. **Par:** 72/72. **Course Rating:** 71.5/73.3. **Slope:** 116/118. **Green Fee:** $12/$20. **Cart Fee:** $18/cart. **Walking Policy:** Unrestricted walking. **Walkability:** 1. **Opened:** 1936. **Season:** Year-round. **High:** April-June/Sept.-Oct. **To obtain tee times:** Call 1 day in advance for weekends and holidays. Weekdays, first come, first served. **Miscellaneous:** Reduced fees (twilight, seniors, juniors), metal spikes, range (grass/mats), club rentals, credit cards (ATM debit cards), beginner friendly (clinics and individual instruction).
Reader Comments: Flat but fun ... Good lies where ball flies ... Solid muny ... Friendly staff moves 'em in and moves 'em out ... Easy par-5s ... Be patient if you play on the weekends ... Very long, must pump-up the driver.
★★ LAKESIDE COURSE
Holes: 18. **Yards:** 6,054/5,872. **Par:** 70/70. **Course Rating:** 68.5/70.5. **Slope:** 110/103. **Green Fee:** $9/$14. **Cart Fee:** $18/cart. **Walking Policy:** Unrestricted walking. **Walkability:** 1. **Opened:** 1936. **Season:** Year-round. **High:** April-June/Sept.-Oct. **To obtain tee times:** Call 1 day in advance for weekends and holidays. Weekdays first come, first served. **Miscellaneous:** Reduced fees (twilight, seniors, juniors), metal spikes, range (grass/mats), club rentals, credit cards (ATM debit card), beginner friendly (clinics and individual instruction).
Special Notes: Also has 18-hole par-68 Little Course.
★★ WISNER COURSE
Holes: 18. **Yards:** 6,465/5,707. **Par:** 72/72. **Course Rating:** 70.5/71.8. **Slope:** 111/116. **Green Fee:** $9/$14. **Cart Fee:** $18/cart. **Walking Policy:** Unrestricted walking. **Walkability:** 1. **Opened:** 1936. **Season:** Year-round. **High:** April-June/Sept.-Oct. **To obtain tee times:** Call 1 day in advance for weekends and holidays. Weekdays, first come, first served. **Miscellaneous:** Reduced fees (twilight, seniors, juniors), metal spikes, range (grass/mats), rentals, beginner friendly (clinics, individual instruction).

LOUISIANA

★★★½ BELLE TERRE COUNTRY CLUB
SP-111 Fairway Dr., La Place, 70068, St. John the Baptist Parish County, (504)652-5000, 20 miles W of New Orleans.
Holes: 18. **Yards:** 6,840/5,510. **Par:** 72/72. **Course Rating:** 72.2/71.6. **Slope:** 130/113. **Green Fee:** $35/$45. **Cart Fee:** Included in Green Fee. **Walking Policy:** Mandatory cart. **Walkability:** 1. **Opened:** 1977. **Architect:** Pete Dye. **Season:** Year-round. **High:** April-Oct. **To obtain tee times:** Nonmembers call 4 days in advance. **Miscellaneous:** Reduced fees (weekdays, twilight, juniors), metal spikes, range (grass), club rentals, credit cards (MC, V, AE).
Reader Comments: Good layout ... Very friendly staff ... Uncrowded, good practice range, challenging but fair ... Gators in the hazards. Goose droppings on the greens ... A lot of potential ... Not well marked ... Good test. Great greens ... Retiree dream.

★½ BRECHTEL GOLF COURSE
PM-3700 Behrman Place, New Orleans, 70114, Orleans County, (504)362-4761.
Holes: 18. **Yards:** 6,065/5,556. **Par:** 70/70. **Course Rating:** 66.0/N/A. **Slope:** 97/N/A. **Green Fee:** $8/$10. **Cart Fee:** $14/cart. **Walking Policy:** Unrestricted walking. **Walkability:** 1. **Opened:** 1965. **Architect:** R.W. LaConte/T. McAnlis. **Season:** Year-round. **High:** April-Oct. **To obtain tee times:** First come, first served. **Miscellaneous:** Reduced fees (twilight, seniors, juniors), metal spikes, range (grass/mats), club rentals.

BRIARWOOD GOLF CLUB
PU-13209 Airline Hwy., Baton Rouge, 70817, (225)753-1989.
Special Notes: Call club for further information.

★★½ CHENNAULT PARK GOLF COURSE
PM-8475 Millhaven Rd., Monroe, 71203, Quachita County, (318)329-2454.
Holes: 18. **Yards:** 7,044/5,783. **Par:** 72/72. **Course Rating:** 72.6/71.5. **Slope:** 115/113. **Green Fee:** $15/$16. **Cart Fee:** $16/cart. **Walking Policy:** Unrestricted walking. **Walkability:** 1. **Opened:** 1975. **Architect:** Winnie Cole. **Season:** Year-round. **High:** May-Sept. **To obtain tee times:** Tee times are taken @ 8:00 am the Friday before the weekend. **Miscellaneous:** Reduced fees (seniors, juniors), metal spikes, range (grass), credit cards (MC, V).
Reader Comments: Long course with nice fairways and greens ... Good course to learn on ... In flight pattern of airport ... Lots of trees and water ... Easy to walk ... Really upgraded the course in the last year ... Plays long.

CITY PARK GOLF COURSE
PU-1121 Mudd Ave., Lafayette, 70501, Lafayette County, (318)291-5557. **E-mail:** mikeguidry@worldnet.att.net.
Holes: 18. **Yards:** 6,426/5,447. **Par:** 72/72. **Course Rating:** 70.1/72.0. **Slope:** 117/N/A. **Green Fee:** $11/$11. **Cart Fee:** $17/cart. **Walking Policy:** Unrestricted walking. **Walkability:** 1. **Opened:** 1926. **Season:** Year-round. **High:** April-Dec. **To obtain tee times:** call 48 hours in advance of request. **Miscellaneous:** Credit cards (MC, V, AE)Beginner friendly (weekdays after 4 pm).

★★★★ THE CLUB AND LODGE AT THE BLUFFS ON THOMPSON CREEK
R-Hwy. 965 at Freeland Rd., St. Francisville, 70775, West Feliciana County, (225)634-5551, (888)634-3410, 25 miles NW of Baton Rouge. **E-mail:** info@the bluffs.com. **Web:** www.the-bluffs.com.
Holes: 18. **Yards:** 7,154/4,781. **Par:** 72/72. **Course Rating:** 74.6/69.0. **Slope:** 143/123. **Green Fee:** $40/$70. **Cart Fee:** $12/person. **Walking Policy:** Walking at certain times. **Walkability:** 4. **Opened:** 1989. **Architect:** Arnold Palmer/Ed Seay. **Season:** Year-round. **High:** March-June/Sept.-Nov. **To obtain tee times:** Lodge guests may arrange tee times when room reservations are made. **Miscellaneous:** Reduced fees (weekdays, low season, resort guests), discount packages, metal spikes, range (grass), club rentals, lodging (39 rooms), credit cards (MC, V, AE, D).
Notes: Ranked 2nd in 1999 Best in State.
Reader Comments: Outstanding layout; fine course to play ... Nos.17 and 18 are memorable ... Make sure you play it ... Long, tight but beautiful ... Worth the drive ... Bluff views terrific ... No. 17 excellent par 3 ... Tough course to find ... Enjoyed visit.

EASTOVER COUNTRY CLUB
SP-5889 Eastover Dr., New Orleans, 70128, Orleans County, (504)245-7347, 12 miles E of Downtown New Orleans. **E-mail:** golfinfo@eastovercc.com. **Web:** www.eastovercc.com.
RABBIT'S FOOT
Holes: 18. **Yards:** 6,825/5,470. **Par:** 72/72. **Course Rating:** 72.5/72.2. **Slope:** 129/123. **Green Fee:** $70/$82. **Cart Fee:** $13/person. **Walking Policy:** Unrestricted walking. **Walkability:** 2. **Opened:** 1987. **Architect:** Joe Lee/Rocky Roquemore. **Season:** Year-round. **To obtain tee times:** Call in advance. **Miscellaneous:** Reduced fees (low season), range (grass), credit cards (MC, V, AE, D, Diners Club), beginner friendly (Jimmy Headrick Golf Academy).

LOUISIANA

★★★★ TEETH OF THE GATOR
Holes: 36. **Yards:** 7,025/5,560. **Par:** 72/72. **Course Rating:** 72.7/72.3. **Slope:** 131/124. **Green Fee:** $70/$82. **Cart Fee:** $13/person. **Walking Policy:** Unrestricted walking. **Walkability:** 2. **Opened:** 1987. **Architect:** Joe Lee/Rocky Roquemore. **Season:** Year-round. **High:** Mar.-June, Sept.-Nov. **To obtain tee times:** Call in advance. **Miscellaneous:** Reduced fees (low season), metal spikes, range (grass), credit cards (MC, V, AE, D).
Reader Comments: Short, but testy ... Excellent shape, great food and service, rough is thick ... Too many players ... Nice layout ... The best in New Orleans! ... Very well run course ... Cut down a lot of trees to add new 18 holes ... Interesting but flat ... Difficult par 3s, especially for ladies.

★★½ EMERALD HILLS GOLF RESORT
R-Hwy. 171 South, Florien, 71429, Sabine County, (318)586-4661, (800)533-5031, 75 miles NW of Florien.
Holes: 18. **Yards:** 6,548/5,432. **Par:** 72/72. **Course Rating:** 71.0/69.4. **Slope:** 125/114. **Green Fee:** $25/$35. **Cart Fee:** Included in Green Fee. **Walking Policy:** Mandatory cart. **Walkability:** 5. **Season:** Year-round. **High:** April-Sept. **To obtain tee times:** Call Pro Shop. **Miscellaneous:** Reduced fees (resort guests, twilight), discount packages, metal spikes, range (grass), rentals, lodging (50 rooms), credit cards (MC, V, AE, D).
Reader Comments: Tight, leave driver at home. Great greens ... Lots of trees, tight through woods ... Bring bug spray, gnats are terrible ... Some doglegs, several uphill greens, tough sand ... Tough layout; tired facilities ... Good course in the wilderness.

FORT POLK GOLF COURSE
M-Paterson Dr. Bldg. 323, Fort Polk, 71459, Vernon Parish County, (318)531-4661, 45 miles SW of Alexandria.
Holes: 18. **Yards:** 6,555/5,141. **Par:** 71/69. **Course Rating:** 71.0/68.4. **Slope:** 121/119. **Green Fee:** $10/$14. **Cart Fee:** $8/person. **Walking Policy:** Unrestricted walking. **Walkability:** 5. **Season:** Year-round. **High:** April-Oct. **To obtain tee times:** Tee times required Fri.-Sun. & Holidays. Call golf shop during week before weekend. **Miscellaneous:** Reduced fees (weekdays, twilight, seniors, juniors), range (grass), club rentals, credit cards (MC, V, AE), beginner friendly (offer clinics & lessons april-oct. summer camp for kids).
Special Notes: Reduced greens fees for military personnel.

GEMSTONE GOLF COURSE
SP-101 Gemstone Dr., Franklinton, 70438, Washington County, (504)795-8900.
Special Notes: Call club for further information.

HIDDEN OAKS GOLF COURSE
PU-200 Oak Dr., Braithwaite, 70040, Plaquemines County, (504)682-2685.
Holes: 18. **Yards:** 6,775/5,424. **Par:** 72/72. **Course Rating:** 70.0/71.1. **Slope:** 117/109. **Green Fee:** $20/$26. **Cart Fee:** Included in Green Fee. **Walking Policy:** Walking at certain times. **Walkability:** 1. **Opened:** 1963. **Architect:** John Cottage. **Season:** Year-round. **High:** Year-round. **Miscellaneous:** Club rentals, credit cards (MC, V).
Special Notes: Formerly known as Braithwaite Golf Course.

★½ HOWELL PARK GOLF COURSE
PU-5511 Winbourne Ave., Baton Rouge, 70805, East Baton Rouge County, (225)357-9292.
Holes: 18. **Yards:** 5,779/4,577. **Par:** 70/70. **Course Rating:** 67.6/65.3. **Slope:** 113/109. **Green Fee:** $7/$7. **Cart Fee:** $14/cart. **Walking Policy:** Unrestricted walking. **Walkability:** N/A. **Opened:** 1956. **Season:** Year-round. **High:** March-Sept. **To obtain tee times:** Call in for weekends & Holidays. **Miscellaneous:** Reduced fees (twilight, seniors, juniors), metal spikes, club rentals, credit cards (MC, V).

★★½ HUNTINGTON PARK GOLF COURSE
PU-8300 Pines Rd., Shreveport, 71129, Caddo County, (318)673-7765.
Holes: 18. **Yards:** 7,294/6,171. **Par:** 72/74. **Course Rating:** 73.3/74.7. **Slope:** N/A. **Green Fee:** $10/$13. **Cart Fee:** $8/person. **Walking Policy:** Unrestricted walking. **Walkability:** 5. **Opened:** 1969. **Architect:** Tommy Moore. **Season:** Year-round. **High:** May-Sept. **To obtain tee times:** Call or come in on Thursday at 7 a.m. for upcoming weekend. Weekdays, first come, first served. **Miscellaneous:** Reduced fees (weekdays, twilight, seniors, juniors), metal spikes, range (grass), club rentals, credit cards (MC, V).
Reader Comments: Long and lots of water ... Well designed ... Busy on weekends ... No. 10 is a bear ... No. 18 hardest hole, must carry water on second shot for any chance of par ... Big receptive greens.

JOE BARTHOLOMEW GOLF COURSE
PU-6514 Congress Dr., New Orleans, 70126, Orleans County, (504)288-0928.
Holes: 18. **Yards:** 7,265/5,971. **Par:** 72/72. **Course Rating:** 70.4/N/A. **Slope:** 101/N/A. **Green Fee:** $8/$11. **Cart Fee:** $18/cart. **Walking Policy:** Unrestricted walking. **Walkability:** 2.

Architect: Joe Bartholomew. **Season:** Year round. **High:** March-May, Sept.-Dec.
Miscellaneous: Range (grass), club rentals, beginner friendly (youth golf free lesson).

★★★   **LES VIEUX CHENES GOLF CLUB**
PU-340 Blue Des Vieux Chenes, Youngsville, 70592, Lafayette County, (318)837-1159, 9 miles S
of Lafayette.
Holes: 18. **Yards:** 6,900/5,600. **Par:** 72/74. **Course Rating:** 70.1/69.1. **Slope:** 119/113. **Green
Fee:** $8/$8. **Cart Fee:** $13/person. **Walking Policy:** Unrestricted walking. **Walkability:** N/A.
Opened: 1977. **Architect:** Dr. Marvin Ferguson. **Season:** Year-round. **High:** June-Sept. **To
obtain tee times:** Call 2 days in advance. **Miscellaneous:** Reduced fees (twilight, seniors,
juniors), metal spikes, range (grass), credit cards (MC, V, AE).
Reader Comments: Good course, well taken care of ... Fairways are wide, very little rough ...
Very crowded year-round ... Occasional challenges keep you from relaxing ... 5-6 hours to play
here ... Wonderful course for beginners, wide fairways, generous greens, tough to get times.

LSU GOLF COURSE
PU-Nicholson Dr. & Burbank, Baton Rouge, 70893, East Baton Rouge Parish County, (225)388-
3394. **Web:** www.LSU.edu.
Holes: 18. **Yards:** 6,727/5,086. **Par:** 72/72. **Course Rating:** 72.3/N/A. **Slope:** 131/N/A. **Green
Fee:** $15/$27. **Cart Fee:** $8/person. **Walking Policy:** Unrestricted walking. **Walkability:** 3.
Opened: 1958. **Architect:** Bill Thompson. **Season:** Year-round. **High:** Sept.-June. **To obtain tee
times:** Call (225)388-3394 on Wed. before weekend. **Miscellaneous:** Reduced fees (weekdays,
low season, twilight, seniors, juniors), range (grass), club rentals, credit cards (MC, V), beginner
friendly.
Special Notes: Reduced fees for students.

★★★   **MALLARD COVE GOLF COURSE**
PM-Chennault Air Base, Lake Charles, 70601, Calcasieu County, (318)491-1204, 125 miles W
of Baton Rouge.
Holes: 18. **Yards:** 6,903/5,294. **Par:** 72/72. **Course Rating:** 72.4/70.1. **Slope:** 125/117. **Green
Fee:** $10/$13. **Cart Fee:** $8/person. **Walking Policy:** Unrestricted walking. **Walkability:** 1.
Opened: 1976. **Architect:** A. James Wall. **Season:** Year-round. **High:** April-Oct. **To obtain tee
times:** Call or come in up to 2 days in advance. **Miscellaneous:** Reduced fees (weekdays, twilight, seniors, juniors), range (grass/mats), club rentals, credit cards (MC, V, D).
Reader Comments: The best holes will challenge you ... Very long from back tees ... Excellent
greens, nice fairways ... Good place, large greens ... The course is more challenging than ratings
indicate ... Worth the drive.

MEADOW LAKE GOLF & COUNTRY CLUB
SP-152 Golf Course Rd., Bernice, 71222, Union Parish County, (318)285-7425, 25 miles N of
Ruston.
Holes: 9. **Yards:** 6,342/5,501. **Par:** 72/72. **Course Rating:** N/A. **Slope:** N/A. **Green Fee:** $5/$15.
Cart Fee: $21/cart. **Walking Policy:** Walking at certain times. **Walkability:** 2. **Opened:** 1985.
Season: Year-round. **High:** Apr.-June. **To obtain tee times:** None. **Miscellaneous:** Reduced
fees (weekdays, low season, seniors), range (grass), credit cards (MC, V).

MEADOWLAKE COUNTRY CLUB
SP-5730 Meadowlake Rd., Keithville, 71047, (318)925-9547.
Special Notes: Call club for further information.

NAS GOLF COURSE
M-Morale Welfare & Rec. Bldg. 49 Code 100, New Orleans, 70143, (504)678-3453, 2 miles E of
New Orleans.
Holes: 18. **Yards:** 6,464/5,362. **Par:** 72/72. **Course Rating:** 69.1/69.8. **Slope:** 115/110. **Green
Fee:** $14/$19. **Cart Fee:** Included in Green Fee. **Walking Policy:** Unrestricted walking.
Walkability: 1. **Opened:** 1964. **Season:** Year-round. **High:** May-Oct. **To obtain tee times:** Call
on Wednesdays for upcoming weekend. **Miscellaneous:** Reduced fees (twilight), credit cards
(MC, V, AE, D).

NORTHWOOD GOLF & COUNTRY CLUB
SP-5000 Northwood Hills Dr., Shreveport, 71107, (318)929-2380.
Holes: 18. **Yards:** 6,550/5,165. **Par:** 72/73. **Course Rating:** 69.6/69.4. **Slope:** 116/110. **Green
Fee:** $27/$40. **Cart Fee:** $20/person. **Walking Policy:** Walking at certain times. **Walkability:** 4.
Architect: Golf Scapes. **Season:** Year-round. **High:** May-Sept,. **Miscellaneous:** Reduced fees
(twilight), range (grass), credit cards (MC, V, AE).

★★★★   **OAK HARBOR GOLF CLUB**
SP-201 Oak Harbor Blvd., Slidell, 70458, St. Tammany County, (504)646-0110, 25 miles NE of
New Orleans. **Web:** www.oakharborgolf.com.
Holes: 18. **Yards:** 6,896/5,305. **Par:** 72/72. **Course Rating:** 72.7/70.0. **Slope:** 132/118. **Green
Fee:** $32/$69. **Cart Fee:** Included in Green Fee. **Walking Policy:** Mandatory cart. **Walkability:**

3. **Opened:** 1991. **Architect:** Lee Schmidt. **Season:** Year-round. **High:** Apr.-July/Sept.-Nov. **To obtain tee times:** Call 7 days in advance. **Miscellaneous:** Reduced fees (twilight), discount packages, metal spikes, range (grass), club rentals, credit cards (MC, V, AE, D).
Reader Comments: Tee it low, wind is problem ... Nice course ... Too many holes alike ... Bring lots of balls ... Great staff ... Tight, lots of water ... Par 3s to remember ... Top notch, excellent greens ... Beautiful layout, came a long way from 3 years ago ... Beautiful new clubhouse makes the course complete.

★★ PINE SHADOWS GOLF CENTER
PU-750 Goodman Rd, Lake Charles, 70601, Calcasieu County, (318)433-8681.
Special Notes: Call club for further information.

★★ PINEWOOD COUNTRY CLUB
SP-405 Country Club Blvd, Slidell, 70458, St. Tammany County, (504)643-6893, 20 miles N of New Orleans.
Holes: 18. **Yards:** 6,366/5,077. **Par:** 72/72. **Course Rating:** 68.5/70.2. **Slope:** 121/117. **Green Fee:** $27/$32. **Cart Fee:** Included in Green Fee. **Walking Policy:** Mandatory cart. **Walkability:** 2. **Opened:** 1963. **Architect:** Bill Bergin. **Season:** Year-round. **To obtain tee times:** Call up to 2 days in advance. **Miscellaneous:** Reduced fees (juniors), range (grass), club rentals, credit cards (MC, V, AE, D), beginner friendly (lessons available).

★★ QUERBES PARK GOLF COURSE
PU-3500 Beverly Place, Shreveport, 71104, Caddo County, (318)673-7773.
Holes: 18. **Yards:** 6,207/5,360. **Par:** 71/71. **Course Rating:** 69.0/70.0. **Slope:** 118/110. **Green Fee:** $6/$13. **Cart Fee:** $16/cart. **Walking Policy:** Unrestricted walking. **Walkability:** N/A. **Opened:** 1922. **Season:** Year-round. **High:** May-Oct. **To obtain tee times:** Call golf shop. **Miscellaneous:** Reduced fees (weekdays, twilight, seniors, juniors), metal spikes, range (grass/mats), club rentals, credit cards (MC, V).

★★★ ROYAL GOLF CLUB
PU-201 Royal Dr., Slidell, 70460, St. Tammany Parish County, (504)643-3000, 20 miles N of N. Orleans.
Holes: 18. **Yards:** 6,655/5,544. **Par:** 72/72. **Course Rating:** 73.1/68.0. **Slope:** 111/101. **Green Fee:** $11/$15. **Cart Fee:** $10/person. **Walking Policy:** Unrestricted walking. **Walkability:** 1. **Opened:** 1969. **Architect:** Gerald Gatlin. **Season:** Year-round. **High:** Apr.-Sept. **To obtain tee times:** Call up to 7 days in advance. **Miscellaneous:** Reduced fees (weekdays, juniors), range (grass), club rentals, credit cards (MC, V, D), beginner friendly.
Reader Comments: The 18th hole needs redesign ... Strange layout ... Good staff and service ... Subdivision golf ... Small greens ... Overall a good day of golf ... No. 18 is a silly hole.

★★★½ SANTA MARIA GOLF COURSE
PU-19301 Old Perkins Rd., Baton Rouge, 70810, East Baton Rouge County, (504)752-9667.
Holes: 18. **Yards:** 7,051/5,267. **Par:** 72/72. **Course Rating:** 72.9/69.6. **Slope:** 129/120. **Green Fee:** $18/$22. **Cart Fee:** $8/person. **Walking Policy:** Unrestricted walking. **Walkability:** 3. **Opened:** 1986. **Architect:** Robert Trent Jones. **Season:** Year-round. **High:** April-Oct. **To obtain tee times:** Call up to 6 days in advance. **Miscellaneous:** Reduced fees (twilight, seniors, juniors), metal spikes, range, credit cards (MC, V).
Reader Comments: Great place for the money ... Good layout, conditions could have been better ... Some tee box changes needed ... Good driving range; fun to play ... Great place to play ... Some nice par 4s ... Will be tough when trees grow ... Imaginative layout ... Pretty par 3s ... Nice clubhouse.

SOUTHERN OAKS GOLF CLUB
SP-1000 Bayou Black Drive, Houma, 70360, Terrebonne Parish County, (504)851-6804, 60 miles SW of Downtown New Orleans.
Holes: 9. **Yards:** 6,245/5,518. **Par:** 71/74. **Course Rating:** 68.4/71.0. **Slope:** 116/116. **Green Fee:** $15/$20. **Cart Fee:** $8/person. **Walking Policy:** Unrestricted walking. **Walkability:** 1. **Opened:** 1928. **Season:** Year-round. **High:** Mar.-Dec. **To obtain tee times:** Tee times for members up to 11:00. Open play after 11:00 a.m. **Miscellaneous:** Reduced fees (weekdays), credit cards (MC, V, AE, D) (Bayou Junior Tour in summer).
Special Notes: Carts to become mandatory.

SPANISH TRAIL GOLF CLUB
SP-1655 Old Spanish Trail, Cade, 70519, St Martin County, (318)364-2263, 1 miles S of Hwy 182.
Holes: 18. **Yards:** 6,042/5,120. **Par:** 71/71. **Course Rating:** 69.9/69.1. **Slope:** 118/113. **Green Fee:** $17/$23. **Cart Fee:** $9/person. **Walking Policy:** Unrestricted walking. **Walkability:** 3. **Opened:** 1955. **Season:** Year-round. **High:** April-June. **Miscellaneous:** Reduced fees (weekdays), range (grass), credit cards (MC, V).

LOUISIANA

SUGAR OAKS GOLF & COUNTRY CLUB
SP-4002 Sugar Oaks Road, New Iberia, 70560, (318)364-7611, (318)364-7611.
Holes: 18. **Yards:** 7,002/5,600. **Par:** 72/72. **Course Rating:** 70.0/70.0. **Slope:** N/A. **Green Fee:** $12/$18. **Cart Fee:** $10/person. **Walking Policy:** Unrestricted walking. **Walkability:** 1. **Opened:** 1959. **Architect:** Luca Barbato. **Season:** Year Round. **High:** Spring/Summer. **To obtain tee times:** Call Pro Shop 1 week in advance. **Miscellaneous:** Metal spikes, range (grass), beginner friendly.

★★ WEBB MEMORIAL GOLF COURSE
PU-1352 Country Club Dr., Baton Rouge, 70806, East Baton Rouge County, (225)383-4919.
Holes: 18. **Yards:** 6,412/5,442. **Par:** 72/72. **Course Rating:** 70.1/70.3. **Slope:** 120/N/A. **Green Fee:** $6/$6. **Cart Fee:** $14/cart. **Walking Policy:** Unrestricted walking. **Walkability:** 1. **Opened:** 1932. **Architect:** E.E. Evans/Al Michael. **Season:** Year-round. **High:** May-Aug. **To obtain tee times:** Call up to 2 days in advance. **Miscellaneous:** Reduced fees (twilight, juniors), metal spikes, club rentals, credit cards (MC, V).

WESTSIDE GOLF CLUB
SP-Choctaw Rd., Brusly, 70719, (504)749-8832.
Special Notes: Call club for further information.

WILLOWDALE GOLF CLUB
SP-500 Willowdale Blvd., Luling, 70070, (504)785-2478.
Holes: 18. **Yards:** 6,656/5,528. **Par:** 72/72. **Course Rating:** 70.5/71.0. **Slope:** 118/118. **Green Fee:** $13/$25. **Cart Fee:** $10/person. **Walking Policy:** Unrestricted walking. **Walkability:** 2. **Opened:** 1968. **Season:** Year-round. **High:** April-Oct. **To obtain tee times:** Call golf shop (504)785-2478. **Miscellaneous:** Metal spikes, range (grass), club rentals, credit cards (MC, V, AE).

WOODROW W. DUMAS GOLF COURSE
PU-3400 Lavey Lane, Baker, 70714, East Baton Rouge Parish County, (225)775-9166, 9 miles N of Baton Rouge.
Holes: 18. **Yards:** 6,700/5,208. **Par:** 72/72. **Course Rating:** 71.3/N/A. **Slope:** 119/N/A. **Green Fee:** $8/$8. **Cart Fee:** $14/cart. **Walking Policy:** Unrestricted walking. **Walkability:** 2. **Opened:** 1961. **Season:** Year-round. **High:** March-July. **To obtain tee times:** Call 2 days in advance. **Miscellaneous:** Reduced fees (twilight, seniors, juniors), range (grass), club rentals, credit cards (MC, V).
Special Notes: Formerly Greenwood Park Golf Course

MAINE

★★★½ AROOSTOOK VALLEY COUNTRY CLUB
SP-Russell Rd., Fort Fairfield, 04742, Aroostook County, (207)476-8083, 15 miles NE of Presque Isle.
Holes: 18. **Yards:** 6,304/5,393. **Par:** 72/72. **Course Rating:** 69.8/70.0. **Slope:** 117/108. **Green Fee:** $22/$22. **Cart Fee:** $22/cart. **Walking Policy:** Unrestricted walking. **Walkability:** 4. **Opened:** 1927. **Architect:** Howard Watson. **Season:** May-Oct. **High:** July-Aug. **To obtain tee times:** Call 2 days in advance. **Miscellaneous:** Reduced fees (low season), range (grass/mats), club rentals, credit cards (MC, V).
Reader Comments: Outstanding in every way ... Has everything, elevation changes, woods, nice views ... Scenic course, good mix of holes, 1 double green ... Best underplayed course in state ... Play in two countries (US & Canada).

★★★½ BANGOR MUNICIPAL GOLF COURSE
PM-278 Webster Ave., Bangor, 04401, Penobscot County, (207)941-0232.
Holes: 27. **Yards:** 6,345/5,173. **Par:** 71/71. **Course Rating:** 67.9/69.1. **Slope:** 112/111. **Green Fee:** $19/$22. **Cart Fee:** $20/cart. **Walking Policy:** Unrestricted walking. **Walkability:** 2. **Opened:** 1964. **Architect:** Geoffrey Cornish. **Season:** April-Nov. **High:** June-Aug. **To obtain tee times:** Call up to 7 days in advance on the 9-hole course. No tee times taken on the 18. **Miscellaneous:** Reduced fees (weekdays, twilight), metal spikes, range (grass), club rentals, credit cards (MC, V), beginner friendly (group lessons for beginners).
Reader Comments: Wide landing areas ... Fun for everyone ... Relaxed golf ... Jet flight path to nearby airport a distraction ... Front 9 wide open, back 9 tighter.

★★½ BAR HARBOR GOLF COURSE
PU-Rte. 204 and 3, Trenton, 04605, Hancock County, (207)667-7505, 3 miles SE of Ellsworth.
Holes: 18. **Yards:** 6,680/5,542. **Par:** 71/73. **Course Rating:** 71.1/70.4. **Slope:** 122/119. **Green Fee:** $25/$35. **Cart Fee:** $28/cart. **Walking Policy:** Unrestricted walking. **Walkability:** 2. **Opened:** 1968. **Architect:** Phil Wogan. **Season:** April-Oct. **High:** June-Aug. **Miscellaneous:** Reduced fees (low season), metal spikes, range (grass), club rentals, credit cards (MC, V).
Reader Comments: Wind and length provide the challenge ... Very scenic ... Many blind shots.

★★½ BATH COUNTRY CLUB
SP-387 Wiskeag Road, Bath, 04530, Sagadahoc County, (207)442-8411, 30 miles N of Portland. **Web:** bathcountryclub.com.
Holes: 18. **Yards:** 6,216/4,708. **Par:** 70/70. **Course Rating:** 70.2/67.0. **Slope:** 128/115. **Green Fee:** $18/$25. **Cart Fee:** $12/person. **Walking Policy:** Unrestricted walking. **Walkability:** 3. **Opened:** 1932. **Season:** April-Nov. **High:** June-Aug. **To obtain tee times:** Call up to 7 days in advance. **Miscellaneous:** Reduced fees (low season, twilight), club rentals, credit cards (MC, V, AE, D).
Reader Comments: Would like to play everyday ... Several strangely designed holes ... Long carries over swamps.

BELGRADE LAKES GOLF CLUB
PU-West Rd., Belgrade Lakes, 04918, Kennebec County, (207)495-4653, 13 miles N of Augusta. **E-mail:** blgolfclub@aol.com. **Web:** www.belgradelakesgolf.com.
Holes: 18. **Yards:** 6,653/4,881. **Par:** 71/71. **Course Rating:** 71.6/67.1. **Slope:** 142/117. **Green Fee:** $50/$75. **Cart Fee:** $20/person. **Walking Policy:** Unrestricted walking. **Walkability:** 3. **Opened:** 1998. **Architect:** Clive Clark. **Season:** May-Oct. **High:** July-Sept. **To obtain tee times:** Tee times available up to seven days in advance by phone or e-mail. **Miscellaneous:** Reduced fees (low season, twilight, juniors), caddies, club rentals, credit cards (MC, V, AE).
Notes: Ranked 5th in 1999 Best New Upscale Public.

★★★½ THE BETHEL INN & COUNTRY CLUB
R-Broad St., Bethel, 04217, Oxford County, (207)824-6276, (800)654-0125, 70 miles NW of Portland.
Holes: 18. **Yards:** 6,663/5,280. **Par:** 72/72. **Course Rating:** 72.3/71.4. **Slope:** 133/129. **Green Fee:** $30/$50. **Cart Fee:** $28/cart. **Walking Policy:** Unrestricted walking. **Walkability:** 3. **Opened:** 1913. **Architect:** Geoffrey Cornish. **Season:** May-Oct. **High:** July-Aug. **To obtain tee times:** Call up to 2 days in advance. **Miscellaneous:** Reduced fees (weekdays, low season, resort guests, twilight), discount packages, range (grass/mats), club rentals, lodging (116 rooms), credit cards (MC, V, AE, D).
Reader Comments: Great resort—take a sleeping bag on the weekend ... Good course, great fun, good pros ... The fastest greens in New England! ... Beautiful mountain views, new holes very tight ... Great blend of old and new ... Excellent restaurant for dinner.

★★★★ BIDDEFORD SACO COUNTRY CLUB
SP-101 Old Orchard Rd., Saco, 04072, York County, (207)282-5883, 13 miles S of Portland.
Holes: 18. **Yards:** 6,192/5,053. **Par:** 71/72. **Course Rating:** 69.6/69.2. **Slope:** 123/110. **Green Fee:** $25/$40. **Cart Fee:** $25/cart. **Walking Policy:** Unrestricted walking. **Walkability:** 2. **Opened:** 1921. **Architect:** Donald Ross. **Season:** April-Nov. **High:** June-Aug. **To obtain tee**

times: Call 3 days in advance. **Miscellaneous:** Reduced fees (low season, twilight), range (grass/mats), club rentals, credit cards (MC, V, AE, D, All).
Reader Comments: 2 different 9s ... Leave driver in bag on back ... Thoroughly enjoyed myself the entire round ... Well maintained ... A gem ... Very woody and tough. Great fairways and greens ... Sleepy, small town feel.

BOOTHBAY COUNTRY CLUB
R-Country Club Rd., Boothbay, 04537, Lincoln County, (207)633-6085, **Web:** www.BoothBay.com.
Holes: 18. **Yards:** 2,800/2,500. **Par:** 34/34. **Course Rating:** 66.1/64.7. **Slope:** 116/114. **Green Fee:** $20/$25. **Cart Fee:** $12/person. **Walking Policy:** Mandatory cart. **Walkability:** 3. **Opened:** 1921. **Architect:** Wayne Stiles/Van Kleek. **Season:** April-Nov. **High:** June-Sept. **To obtain tee times:** Call up to 5 days in advance. **Miscellaneous:** Reduced fees (low season), range (mats), club rentals, credit cards (MC, V, AE, D).

BRIDGTON HIGHLANDS COUNTRY CLUB
PU-RR 3, Box 1065 Highland Ridge, Bridgton, 04009, Cumberland County, (207)647-3491, 35 miles W of Portland. **Web:** bridgtonhighlands.com.
Holes: 18. **Yards:** 6,059/2,527. **Par:** 72/74. **Course Rating:** 70.2/70.0. **Slope:** 126/119. **Green Fee:** $24/$32. **Cart Fee:** $12/person. **Walking Policy:** Unrestricted walking. **Walkability:** 3. **Opened:** 1926. **Architect:** Ralph Martin Barton/Fred Ryan. **Season:** April-Nov. **High:** July-Aug. **To obtain tee times:** Call 3 days in advance for tee times for non-members. Call (207)647-3491. **Miscellaneous:** Reduced fees (weekdays, low season, resort guests, juniors), discount packages, club rentals, credit cards (MC, V, D).

★★★ BRUNSWICK GOLF CLUB
SP-River Rd., Brunswick, 04011, Cumberland County, (207)725-8224, 30 miles N of Portland.
Holes: 18. **Yards:** 6,609/5,772. **Par:** 72/74. **Course Rating:** 69.5/72.9. **Slope:** 123/128. **Green Fee:** $30/$38. **Cart Fee:** $24/cart. **Walking Policy:** Unrestricted walking. **Walkability:** 1. **Opened:** 1918. **Architect:** Stiles/Van Kleek/Cornish/Robinson. **Season:** April-Nov. **High:** July-Aug. **To obtain tee times:** Call up to 3 days in advance for weekend tee times. **Miscellaneous:** Range (mats), club rentals, credit cards (MC, V).
Reader Comments: Fun to play ... More deer than birdies ... Great, tight layout. Hard greens ... Well seasoned ... Fair, challenging, friendly ... Good, solid test.

★★★½ CAPE ARUNDEL GOLF CLUB
SP-19 River Rd., Kennebunkport, 04046, York County, (207)967-3494, 20 miles S of Portland.
Holes: 18. **Yards:** 5,869/5,134. **Par:** 69/70. **Course Rating:** 67.0/68.6. **Slope:** 117/106. **Green Fee:** $40/$40. **Cart Fee:** $24/cart. **Walking Policy:** Unrestricted walking. **Walkability:** 2. **Opened:** 1897. **Architect:** Walter Travis. **Season:** April-Oct. **High:** July-Sept. **To obtain tee times:** Call 1 day in advance. **Miscellaneous:** Caddies, club rentals.
Reader Comments: Always enjoy it, other than 'Fore!'... Could run into George Bush anytime ... Fun course in the tidal basin ... Interesting links-type course ... Great layout, water in play on half the holes ... Encouraged walking.

CARIBOU COUNTRY CLUB
PU-Sweeden Rd., Caribou, 04736, Aroostook County, (207)493-3933.
Holes: 9. **Yards:** 6,433/5,631. **Par:** 72/72. **Course Rating:** 69.6/N/A. **Slope:** 116/N/A. **Green Fee:** $18/$18. **Cart Fee:** $15/cart. **Walking Policy:** Unrestricted walking. **Walkability:** 4. **Opened:** 1971. **Architect:** Geoffrey Cornish. **Season:** May-Oct. **High:** May-Oct. **To obtain tee times:** None needed. **Miscellaneous:** Range (grass), club rentals, credit cards (MC, V).

CASTINE GOLF CLUB
PU-Battle Ave., Castine, 04421, (207)326-8844.
Special Notes: Call club for further information.

DUNEGRASS GOLF CLUB
PU-200 Wild Dunes Way, Old Orchard Beach, 04064, York County, (207)934-4513, (800)521-1029, 12 miles S of Portland. **E-mail:** dunegrassgolf@customnet.com. **Web:** www.dunegrass.com.
Holes: 18. **Yards:** 6,515/5,479. **Par:** 71/71. **Course Rating:** 71.1/71.5. **Slope:** 131/127. **Green Fee:** $52/$75. **Cart Fee:** Included in Green Fee. **Walking Policy:** Walking at certain times. **Walkability:** 2. **Opened:** 1998. **Architect:** Dan Maples. **Season:** April-Nov. **High:** June-Sept. **Miscellaneous:** Range (grass), club rentals, credit cards (MC, V, AE).

★★ DUTCH ELM GOLF CLUB
PU-5 Brimstone Rd., Arundel, 04046, York County, (207)282-9850, 20 miles S of Portland. **E-mail:** dutchelm@cybertours.com.
Holes: 18. **Yards:** 6,230/5,384. **Par:** 72/73. **Course Rating:** 71.0/70.1. **Slope:** 125/115. **Green Fee:** $20/$30. **Cart Fee:** $22/cart. **Walking Policy:** Unrestricted walking. **Walkability:** 3. **Opened:** 1965. **Architect:** Lucian Bourque. **Season:** April-Nov. **High:** July-Aug. **To obtain tee**

times: Call 282-9850. **Miscellaneous:** Reduced fees (weekdays, low season, resort guests, twilight, seniors), discount packages, range (grass/mats), club rentals, credit cards (MC, V).
Special Notes: Spikeless shoes encouraged.

★★½ FAIRLAWN GOLF & COUNTRY CLUB
SP-434 Empire Rd., Poland, 04274, Androscoggin County, (207)998-4277, 25 miles N of Portland.
Holes: 18. **Yards:** 6,300/5,379. **Par:** 72/72. **Course Rating:** 69.4/69.9. **Slope:** 118/112. **Green Fee:** $18/$20. **Cart Fee:** $12/cart. **Walking Policy:** Unrestricted walking. **Walkability:** 2. **Opened:** 1963. **Architect:** Chick Adams. **Season:** May-First Snow. **High:** July-Aug. **To obtain tee times:** No tee times taken. First come, first served. **Miscellaneous:** Reduced fees (weekdays, twilight), metal spikes, range (grass), club rentals, credit cards (MC, V).
Reader Comments: Unknown gem, easy par course ... Very fast greens ... Best course for the price in Maine ... Very friendly ... Good walking course ... All types of shots needed.

FORT KENT GOLF CLUB
PU-St. John Rd., Fort Kent, 04743, Aroostook County, (207)834-3149, 3 miles E of Presque Isle.
Holes: 18. **Yards:** 6,367/5,361. **Par:** 71/72. **Course Rating:** 69.0/69.0. **Slope:** 112/112. **Green Fee:** $15/$15. **Cart Fee:** $16/cart. **Walking Policy:** Unrestricted walking. **Walkability:** 3. **Opened:** 1968. **Architect:** Ben Gray. **Season:** Apr.-Oct. **High:** June-Aug. **Miscellaneous:** Reduced fees (low season), range (grass), club rentals, credit cards (MC, V).

FOXCROFT GOLF CLUB
PU-36 Foxcroft Center Rd., Dover-Foxcroft, 04426, Piscataquis County, (207)564-8887, 38 miles NW of Bangor. **Web:** www.dover.foxcroft.org.
Holes: 9. **Yards:** 3,136/2,763. **Par:** 36/38. **Course Rating:** 67.7/67.1. **Slope:** 110/101. **Green Fee:** $18/$18. **Cart Fee:** $18/cart. **Walking Policy:** Unrestricted walking. **Walkability:** 3. **Opened:** 1964. **Architect:** Renaldo Reynolds. **Season:** May-Oct. **High:** July-Aug. **Miscellaneous:** Metal spikes.

GOLF AT PROVINCE LAKE
SP-Rte. 153, Parsonsfield, 04047, York County, (207)793-9577, (800)325-4434, 24 miles S of Conway, N. H. **E-mail:** gpl@golfatprovlake.com.
Holes: 18. **Yards:** 6,232/4,874. **Par:** 71/71. **Course Rating:** 70.1/70.8. **Slope:** 127/120. **Green Fee:** $24/$32. **Cart Fee:** $11/person. **Walking Policy:** Walking at certain times. **Walkability:** 3. **Opened:** 1919. **Architect:** Brian Silva/Lawrence Van Etten. **Season:** April-Oct. **High:** June-Aug. **To obtain tee times:** Call (800)325-4434 up to 7 days in advance. **Miscellaneous:** Reduced fees (weekdays, low season, twilight, juniors), range (grass/mats), club rentals, credit cards (MC, V), beginner friendly (instruction, clinics, schools).
Special Notes: Formerly known as Province Lake Country Club.

★★ GORHAM GOLF CLUB
SP-134 McClellan Rd., Gorham, 04038, Cumberland County, (207)839-3490, 10 miles S of Portland.
Holes: 9. **Yards:** 6,552/5,868. **Par:** 71/73. **Course Rating:** 70.8/71.4. **Slope:** 116/124. **Green Fee:** $24/$26. **Cart Fee:** $20/person. **Walking Policy:** Unrestricted walking. **Walkability:** 3. **Opened:** 1960. **Architect:** Jim McDonald Sr. **Season:** April-Nov. **High:** June-Aug. **To obtain tee times:** Call Thursday a.m. for upcoming weekend. **Miscellaneous:** Metal spikes, range (grass/mats), credit cards (MC, V, AE), beginner friendly.

★★ HERMON MEADOW GOLF CLUB
PU-RR8, Box 6160, Bangor, 04401, Penobscot County, (207)848-3741, 3 miles W of Bangor.
Holes: 18. **Yards:** 6,329/5,395. **Par:** 72/73. **Course Rating:** 69.4/70.9. **Slope:** 117/120. **Green Fee:** $18/$20. **Cart Fee:** $9/person. **Walking Policy:** Unrestricted walking. **Walkability:** N/A. **Opened:** 1964. **Season:** April-Dec. **High:** July-Aug. **To obtain tee times:** First come, first served. **Miscellaneous:** Reduced fees (weekdays), metal spikes, range (grass/mats), club rentals, credit cards (MC, V, AE).

★★★★ KEBO VALLEY GOLF COURSE
PU-Eagle Lake Rd., Bar Harbor, 04609, Hancock County, (207)288-3000, 42 miles SE of Bangor.
Holes: 18. **Yards:** 6,131/5,440. **Par:** 70/72. **Course Rating:** 69.0/68.0. **Slope:** 130/121. **Green Fee:** $30/$63. **Cart Fee:** $32/cart. **Walking Policy:** Unrestricted walking. **Walkability:** 3. **Opened:** 1888. **Architect:** H. Leeds/A.E. Liscombe- D Ross rev. 1926. **Season:** April-Nov. **High:** July-Aug. **To obtain tee times:** Call 3 days in advance. **Miscellaneous:** Reduced fees (low season), metal spikes, club rentals, credit cards (MC, V, AE).
Notes: Ranked 3rd in 1999 Best in State.
Reader Comments: One of the best links courses on east coast ... Some great old holes ... Tradition, tradition, tradition ... Small greens, tough course ... 8th and 9th holes are monsters back to back ... Heaven in eastern Maine ... Some of the biggest and highest bunkers I've seen ... Only choice in the area, fun though.

★★★ KENNEBEC HEIGHTS COUNTRY CLUB
PU-1 Fairway Lane, Farmingdale, 04344, Kennebec County, (207)582-2000, 3 miles S of Augusta.
Holes: 18. **Yards:** 6,003/4,820. **Par:** 70/70. **Course Rating:** 69.0/67.7. **Slope:** 129/119. **Green Fee:** $20/$25. **Cart Fee:** $22/person. **Walking Policy:** Unrestricted walking. **Walkability:** 2. **Opened:** 1964. **Architect:** Brian Silva. **Season:** April-Oct. **High:** June-Aug. **To obtain tee times:** Non-members may call up to 3 days in advance. **Miscellaneous:** Range (mats), club rentals, credit cards (MC, V).
Reader Comments: Back 9 is PGA Tour material.

LAKEWOOD GOLF COURSE
PU-Rte. 201 Lakewood Center, Madison, 04950, Somerset County, (207)474-5955, 5 miles NE of Madison.
Holes: 18. **Yards:** 6,300/5,500. **Par:** 72/72. **Course Rating:** 68.4/121.0. **Slope:** 122/70. **Green Fee:** $20/$22. **Cart Fee:** $22/person. **Walking Policy:** Unrestricted walking. **Walkability:** 4. **Opened:** 1927. **Architect:** C.F. Humphrey, P. Wogan 1994 back 9. **Season:** April-Nov. **High:** June-Aug. **To obtain tee times:** Call 474-5955 Weekends & Holidays only. **Miscellaneous:** Reduced fees (low season, twilight, juniors), discount packages, metal spikes, range (grass), club rentals, lodging (9 rooms), beginner friendly.

THE LEDGES GOLF CLUB
PU-1 Ledges Dr., York, 03909, York County, (207)351-3000, 15 miles NW of Portsmouth, NH.
Holes: 18. **Yards:** 6,981/4,988. **Par:** 72/72. **Course Rating:** 74.3/65.6. **Slope:** 144/129. **Green Fee:** $40/$75. **Cart Fee:** $12/person. **Walking Policy:** Unrestricted walking. **Walkability:** 4. **Opened:** 1998. **Architect:** William Bradley Booth. **Season:** Apr.-Nov. **High:** July-Aug. **To obtain tee times:** Call 4 days in advance (207)351-9999. **Miscellaneous:** Reduced fees (twilight), range (grass), club rentals, credit cards (MC, V).

★★½ MINGO SPRINGS GOLF COURSE
PU-Proctor Rd. and Rte. 4, Rangeley, 04970, Franklin County, (207)864-5021, 120 miles N of Portland.
Holes: 18. **Yards:** 6,014/5,158. **Par:** 70/70. **Course Rating:** 66.3/67.4. **Slope:** 109/110. **Green Fee:** $28/$32. **Cart Fee:** $14/person. **Walking Policy:** Unrestricted walking. **Walkability:** 4. **Opened:** 1925. **Architect:** Skip Wogan. **Season:** May-Oct. **High:** July-Sept. **To obtain tee times:** Call (207)864-5021. **Miscellaneous:** Reduced fees (low season), metal spikes, range (grass), club rentals, credit cards (MC, V), beginner friendly (lessons available).
Reader Comments: You can see forever ... No. 12 prettiest hole in Maine ... Challenging layout ... Confidence builder ... Breathtaking scenery.

NAS BRUNSWICK GOLF COURSE
M-NASB Bldg. 78, Brunswick, 04011, Cumberland County, (207)921-2155. **E-mail:** verhey@nasb.navy.mil. **Web:** www.nfmwr.com/mwrbrunswick.
Holes: 9. **Yards:** 6,284/5,594. **Par:** 72/74. **Course Rating:** 68.9/71.4. **Slope:** 119/119. **Green Fee:** $17/$23. **Cart Fee:** $18/cart. **Walking Policy:** Unrestricted walking. **Walkability:** 3. **Opened:** 1958. **Season:** April-Nov. **High:** July-Aug. **To obtain tee times:** Call 5 days prior to desired date of play. **Miscellaneous:** Range (grass/mats), club rentals, credit cards (MC, V, AE), beginner friendly.

NATANIS GOLF COURSE
PU-Webber Pond Rd., Vassalboro, 04989, Kennebec County, (207)622-3561, 7 miles N of Augusta.
Holes: 27. **Green Fee:** $27/$27. **Cart Fee:** $22/cart. **Walking Policy:** Unrestricted walking. **Walkability:** 3. **Opened:** 1965. **Architect:** Paul Browne/Philip Wogan. **Season:** April-Nov. **High:** July-Aug. **To obtain tee times:** Call 1 week in advance. **Miscellaneous:** Metal spikes, range (grass), club rentals, credit cards (MC, V).
★★★½ ARROWHEAD/INDIAN TERRITORY
Yards: 6,338/5,019. **Par:** 72/73. **Course Rating:** 67.8/68.7. **Slope:** 116/117.
Reader Comments: 3 nines, tourist Mecca, funky holes ... Great in every way ... Best 27 holes in state ... Love it ... Something for everybody.
★★★½ ARROWHEAD/TOMAHAWK
Yards: 6,261/5,263. **Par:** 72/73. **Course Rating:** 67.7/70.7. **Slope:** 112/116.
Reader Comments: 3 nines, tourist Mecca, funky holes ... Great in every way ... Best 27 holes in state ... Love it ... Something for everybody.
★★★½ INDIAN TERRITORY/TOMAHAWK
Yards: 6,677/5,376. **Par:** 72/72. **Course Rating:** 68.5/71.6. **Slope:** 118/122.
Reader Comments: 3 nines, tourist Mecca, funky holes ... Great in every way ... Best 27 holes in state ... Love it ... Something for everybody.

MAINE

PALMYRA GOLF & RV RESORT
PU-147 Lang hill Road, Palmyra, 04965, Somerset County, (207)938-4947, 3 miles W of Newport. **E-mail:** palmyra@www.palmyra-me.com. **Web:** www.palmyra-me.com.
Holes: 18. **Yards:** 6,617/5,464. **Par:** 72/72. **Course Rating:** 70.1/69.9. **Slope:** 120/118. **Green Fee:** $20/N/A. **Cart Fee:** $20/cart. **Walking Policy:** Unrestricted walking. **Walkability:** 3.
Opened: 1965. **Architect:** Dick Cayer. **Season:** April-Nov. **High:** June-Aug. **To obtain tee times:** Call Pro Shop @ 207-938-4947 and ask for tee time. They will walk you through it.
Miscellaneous: Reduced fees (resort guests), range (grass/mats), club rentals, lodging (50 rooms), credit cards (MC, V), beginner friendly.

★★★★ PENOBSCOT VALLEY COUNTRY CLUB
SP-366 Main St., Orono, 04473, Penobscot County, (207)866-2423, 5 miles N of Bangor.
Holes: 18. **Yards:** 6,450/5,856. **Par:** 72/74. **Course Rating:** 70.3/73.2. **Slope:** 123/126. **Green Fee:** $50/$50. **Cart Fee:** $11/person. **Walking Policy:** Unrestricted walking. **Walkability:** 4.
Opened: 1924. **Architect:** Donald Ross. **Season:** April-Oct. **High:** June-Aug. **To obtain tee times:** Call 7 days in advance. **Miscellaneous:** Range (grass), rentals, credit cards (MC, V).
Notes: Ranked 4th in 1997 Best in State.
Reader Comments: Short and sweet, greens will either make you or break you ... Great old course, nice layout ... Always in good shape ... Tiny, well-protected greens.

★★★★ POINT SEBAGO RESORT
R-Rte. 302, Casco, 04015, Cumberland County, (207)655-2747, (800)655-1232. **E-mail:** info@pointsebago.com. **Web:** pointsebago.com.
Holes: 18. **Yards:** 7,002/4,866. **Par:** 72/72. **Course Rating:** 73.7/68.4. **Slope:** 135/117. **Green Fee:** $38/$55. **Cart Fee:** Included in Green Fee. **Walking Policy:** Mandatory cart. **Walkability:** 3. **Opened:** 1996. **Architect:** Phil Wogan/George Sargent. **Season:** May-Oct. **High:** July-Aug. **To obtain tee times:** Call golf shop up to 7 days in advance. **Miscellaneous:** Reduced fees (weekdays, low season, resort guests, twilight), discount packages, range (grass/mats), club rentals, lodging, credit cards (MC, V, D).
Notes: Ranked 5th in 1997 Best in State; 4th in 1996 Best New Affordable Courses.
Reader Comments: True test, great greens, many tourists ... Miles between tees and greens ... Interesting layout. Need to use a cart ... Tight fairways ... Beautiful scenery ... Memorable ... Who'd have thought you could find great golf at an RV Resort? ... Tests your shotmaking skills.

★★★ POLAND SPRING COUNTRY CLUB
R-41 Ricker Rd., Poland Spring, 04274, Androscoggin County, (207)998-6002, 25 miles NW of Portland. **E-mail:** Polandsprg@aol.com. **Web:** www.polandspringinns.com.
Holes: 18. **Yards:** 6,200/5,097. **Par:** 71/74. **Course Rating:** 68.2/68.6. **Slope:** 119/110. **Green Fee:** $21/$21. **Cart Fee:** $21/cart. **Walking Policy:** Unrestricted walking. **Walkability:** 4.
Opened: 1896. **Architect:** A.H. Fenn/Donald Ross. **Season:** May-Oct. **High:** June-Sept. **To obtain tee times:** Call up to a year in advance. **Miscellaneous:** Reduced fees (resort guests), discount packages, club rentals, lodging (210 rooms), credit cards (MC, V, AE, D).
Reader Comments: Outstanding summit golf, watch out for weekend tourists ... Beautiful vistas ... Small greens ... Nos. 11-14 holes are as challenging as they come ... Morale booster.

★★½ PRESQUE ISLE COUNTRY CLUB
SP-35 Parkhurst Siding Rd. (Rte. 205), Presque Isle, 04769, Aroostook County, (207)764-0430, 4 miles NE of Presque Isle.
Holes: 18. **Yards:** 6,730/5,600. **Par:** 72/72. **Course Rating:** 71.4/72.5. **Slope:** 122/119. **Green Fee:** $20/$20. **Cart Fee:** $20/cart. **Walking Policy:** Unrestricted walking. **Walkability:** 3.
Opened: 1958. **Architect:** Ben Gray/Geoffrey Cornish. **Season:** May-Oct. **High:** June-Aug. **To obtain tee times:** First come, first served. **Miscellaneous:** Reduced fees (low season), discount packages, range (grass), club rentals, credit cards (MC, V).
Reader Comments: Must play it ... Best 18 holes in Maine.

★½ PROSPECT HILL GOLF COURSE
SP-694 S. Main St., Auburn, 04210, Androscoggin County, (207)782-9220, 5 miles W of Lewiston.
Holes: 18. **Yards:** 5,846/5,227. **Par:** 71/73. **Course Rating:** 66.9/68.7. **Slope:** 111/119. **Green Fee:** $16/$18. **Cart Fee:** $18/cart. **Walking Policy:** Unrestricted walking. **Walkability:** 3.
Opened: 1957. **Architect:** Arthur David Chapman. **Season:** April-Nov. **High:** April-Nov. **To obtain tee times:** No tee times given. **Miscellaneous:** Reduced fees (weekdays, twilight), club rentals, credit cards (MC, V, D).

RIVER MEADOW GOLF CLUB
PU-216 Lincoln St., Westbook, 04092, Cumberland County, (207)854-1625, 2 miles W of Portland.
Holes: 9. **Yards:** 2,915/2,610. **Par:** 35/36. **Course Rating:** 67.5/69.4. **Slope:** 112/117. **Green Fee:** $17/$20. **Cart Fee:** $16/cart. **Walking Policy:** Unrestricted walking. **Walkability:** 1.
Opened: 1963. **Architect:** Rufus Jordan. **Season:** April-Nov. **High:** June-Aug. **To obtain tee**

times: Weekend tee times available only. Call no more than 48 hours in advance.
Miscellaneous: Reduced fees (weekdays, low season, twilight, seniors), club rentals, beginner friendly (clinics, private lessons).

★★½ RIVERSIDE MUNICIPAL GOLF COURSE
PU-1158 Riverside St., Portland, 04103, Cumberland County, (207)797-3524.
Holes: 18. **Yards:** 6,450/5,640. **Par:** 72/72. **Course Rating:** 69.5/70.7. **Slope:** 115/112. **Green Fee:** $15/$18. **Cart Fee:** $22/cart. **Walking Policy:** Unrestricted walking. **Walkability:** 4.
Opened: 1935. **Architect:** Wayne Stiles. **Season:** April-Nov. **High:** July-Aug. **To obtain tee times:** Call Wednesday prior to weekend of play. **Miscellaneous:** Reduced fees (seniors, juniors), range (grass), club rentals, credit cards (MC, V).
Reader Comments: Excessive play, slow weekends and Fridays ... Many switch backs ... Narrow and rocky ... Vanilla, a Maine classic ... Great layout.

★★★½ ROCKLAND GOLF CLUB
SP-606 Old County Rd., Rockland, 04841, Knox County, (207)594-9322, 45 miles E of Augusta.
Web: RGC@MIDCOAST.COM.
Holes: 18. **Yards:** 6,121/5,583. **Par:** 70/73. **Course Rating:** 67.8/71.8. **Slope:** 115/119. **Green Fee:** $20/$35. **Cart Fee:** $24/cart. **Walking Policy:** Unrestricted walking. **Walkability:** 2.
Opened: 1932. **Architect:** Wayne Stiles/Roger Sorrent. **Season:** April-Oct. **High:** June-Sept. **To obtain tee times:** Call 3 days in advance. **Miscellaneous:** Reduced fees (twilight, juniors), metal spikes, club rentals, credit cards (MC, V).
Reader Comments: Great sea coast golf ... Greens hard and fast ... Always look forward to playing here ... One of the first courses to open in spring ... Lacks interesting holes ... Slicer's delight ... Little advantage for females ... Very friendly.

★★★½ SABLE OAKS GOLF CLUB
PU-505 Country Club Dr., South Portland, 04106, Cumberland County, (207)775-6257.
Holes: 18. **Yards:** 6,359/4,786. **Par:** 70/72. **Course Rating:** 71.8/N/A. **Slope:** 134/121. **Green Fee:** $23/$29. **Cart Fee:** $22/cart. **Walking Policy:** Unrestricted walking. **Walkability:** N/A.
Opened: 1989. **Architect:** Geoffrey Cornish/Brian Silva. **Season:** April-Dec. **High:** April-Sept. **To obtain tee times:** Call 7 days in advance. **Miscellaneous:** Reduced fees (twilight), metal spikes, caddies, credit cards (MC, V).
Reader Comments: Kicks my butt, made me better ... Target golf ... Ravines-R-Us ... Very tight. Keep it straight or you're toast ... Great variety of holes ... A real gem ... Tests all parts of your game ... Fast greens ... Bring plenty of ammo.

SALMON FALLS COUNTRY CLUB
R-Salmon Falls Rd., Hollis, 04042, York County, (207)929-5233, (800)734-1616.
Holes: 18. **Yards:** 5,948/5,298. **Par:** 72/70. **Course Rating:** 67.6/69.5. **Slope:** 121/112. **Green Fee:** $15/$20. **Cart Fee:** $20/cart. **Walking Policy:** Unrestricted walking. **Walkability:** 4.
Opened: 1974. **Architect:** Jim Jones. **Season:** April-Sep. **High:** July-Aug. **Miscellaneous:** Range (grass), club rentals, lodging (7 rooms), credit cards (MC, V, AE, D).

★★★★ SAMOSET RESORT GOLF CLUB
R-220 Warrenton St., Rockport, 04856, Knox County, (207)594-1431, (800)341-1650, 80 miles NE of Portland.
Holes: 18. **Yards:** 6,548/5,360. **Par:** 70/72. **Course Rating:** 70.8/70.1. **Slope:** 129/120. **Green Fee:** $55/$100. **Cart Fee:** Included in Green Fee. **Walking Policy:** Unrestricted walking.
Walkability: 2. **Opened:** 1978. **Architect:** Robert Elder. **Season:** April-Nov. **High:** June-Sept. **To obtain tee times:** Hotel guests may reserve tee times with room confirmation as early as April 1. Members may reserve up to 7 days in advance. Others may reserve up to 2 days in advance.
Miscellaneous: Reduced fees (low season, resort guests), discount packages, range (grass/mats), club rentals, lodging (222 rooms), credit cards (MC, V, AE, D).
Notes: Ranked 2nd in 1999 Best in State.
Reader Comments: Fun but tricky ... Holes on the water unbelievable ... A good walk unspoiled during autumn's colorful backdrop ... Clubhouse is poor for quality of course ... Hard to concentrate. Views incredible ... Big greens ... Sailboats everywhere ... Slowest ever, but so is Maine ... Always score well here, greens are great.

ST. CROIX COUNTRY CLUB
SP-River Rd., Calais, 04619, Washington County, (207)454-8875.
Holes: 9. **Yards:** 2,767/2,567. **Par:** 35/36. **Course Rating:** 64.8/68.6. **Slope:** 102/111. **Green Fee:** $20/$20. **Cart Fee:** $17/cart. **Walking Policy:** Unrestricted walking. **Walkability:** 2.
Opened: 1930. **Architect:** Earl T. Gray. **Season:** May-Oct. **High:** July-Aug. **To obtain tee times:** Call 48 hours ahead. **Miscellaneous:** Reduced fees (low season), club rentals, credit cards (MC, V).

★★★★½ SUGARLOAF GOLF CLUB *Service, Condition, Pace*
R-R.R. No.1, P.O. Box 5000, Carrabassett Valley, 04947, Franklin County, (207)237-2000, (800)843-5623, 100 miles N of Portland.

Holes: 18. **Yards:** 6,910/5,376. **Par:** 72/72. **Course Rating:** 70.8/73.7. **Slope:** 137/136. **Green Fee:** $53/$96. **Cart Fee:** $17/person. **Walking Policy:** Unrestricted walking. **Walkability:** 4. **Opened:** 1986. **Architect:** Robert Trent Jones Jr. **Season:** May-Oct. **High:** Aug.-Sept. **To obtain tee times:** Call 14 days in advance. Guests may make tee times with room reservations at (800)843-5623. **Miscellaneous:** Reduced fees (low season, resort guests, twilight, juniors), discount packages, metal spikes, range (grass/mats), club rentals, lodging (1,000 rooms), credit cards (MC, V, AE, D), beginner friendly (special tees, golf school).
Notes: Ranked 1st in 1999 Best in State.
Reader Comments: Still the best in the state ... Stay in the fairway ... Take lots of balls ... Worth the four hour drive ... Enjoy the views ... Just us and the moose out theyah ... Bring 6 balls, go home with 5—all different! ... Narrow fairways, fast greens and tall mountains ... 10 and 11 are unforgettable ... Superb fall foliage ... Stunning!

★★★ VA JO WA GOLF COURSE
R-142A Walker Rd., Island Falls, 04747, Aroostook County, (207)463-2128, 85 miles NE of Bangor. **E-mail:** vajowa@webtv.net. **Web:** www.vajowa.com.
Holes: 18. **Yards:** 6,223/5,065. **Par:** 72/72. **Course Rating:** 70.4/69.6. **Slope:** 125/119. **Green Fee:** $21/$24. **Cart Fee:** $24/cart. **Walking Policy:** Unrestricted walking. **Walkability:** 5. **Opened:** 1964. **Architect:** Vaughan Walker/Warren Walker. **Season:** May-Oct. **High:** July-Sept. **To obtain tee times:** Call 1 day in advance. **Miscellaneous:** Reduced fees (weekdays, low season, resort guests, twilight, juniors), discount packages, range (grass), club rentals, lodging (35 rooms), credit cards (MC, V, D).
Reader Comments: Good variety of holes ... Front nine in a valley, bordering a lake—back 9 in mountains ... Scenic ... A good test.

★★★½ VAL HALLA GOLF & RECREATION CENTER
PM-1 Val Halla Rd., Cumberland, 04021, Cumberland County, (207)829-2225, 10 miles N of Portland.
Holes: 18. **Yards:** 6,574/5,437. **Par:** 72/72. **Course Rating:** 71.1/70.4. **Slope:** 126/116. **Green Fee:** $22/$30. **Cart Fee:** $30/person. **Walking Policy:** Unrestricted walking. **Walkability:** 3. **Opened:** 1965. **Architect:** Phil Wogan. **Season:** April-Nov. **High:** June-Sept. **To obtain tee times:** Call 7 days in advance. **Miscellaneous:** Reduced fees (weekdays, seniors, juniors), discount packages, range (grass/mats), club rentals, credit cards (MC, V).
Reader Comments: Good par 3s ... Back nine better than front 9 ... Tougher than it appears. Some tricky holes ... Lots of variety and fun to play ... Best finishing holes in the state ... Earn your pars here ... Got to like the 2nd hole ... Very crowded, lots of play ... Vanilla with sprinkles, some great holes.

★★★½ WATERVILLE COUNTRY CLUB
SP-Country Club Rd., Oakland, 04963, Kennebec County, (207)465-9861, 5 miles W of Waterville.
Holes: 18. **Yards:** 6,427/5,466. **Par:** 70/73. **Course Rating:** 69.6/71.3. **Slope:** 124/119. **Green Fee:** $45/$45. **Cart Fee:** $26/cart. **Walking Policy:** Unrestricted walking. **Walkability:** 3. **Opened:** 1916. **Architect:** Orrin Smith/Geoffrey S. Cornish. **Season:** April-Nov. **High:** May-Sept. **To obtain tee times:** Call 3 days in advance. **Miscellaneous:** Range (grass/mats), club rentals.
Reader Comments: Use all clubs, good test, nice layout ... One of the best kept secrets in Maine ... Great old style course ... Requires precise iron play ... Nice mix, good greens ... Staff very friendly.

★★★ WILLOWDALE GOLF CLUB
PU-52 Willowdale Rd., Scarborough, 04074, Cumberland County, (207)883-9351, 9 miles S of Portland.
Holes: 18. **Yards:** 5,980/5,344. **Par:** 70/70. **Course Rating:** 68.7/73.7. **Slope:** 110/112. **Green Fee:** $25/$27. **Cart Fee:** $22/cart. **Walking Policy:** Unrestricted walking. **Walkability:** 2. **Opened:** 1924. **Architect:** Eugene Wogan. **Season:** April-Oct. **High:** July-Aug. **To obtain tee times:** Call Wednesday for following weekend. **Miscellaneous:** Reduced fees (twilight), club rentals, credit cards (MC, V, D).
Reader Comments: Few hazards, back nine more interesting ... Very basic golf, good for beginners ... Biggest mosquitos in New England ... Easy & wide open ... Confidence builder ... Front nine fairways quite close together ... Friendly staff, different front and back.

MARYLAND

ANDREWS AFB GOLF COURSE
M-4442 Perimeter Rd., Andrews AFB, 20762, Prince George's County, (301)981-5010.
Special Notes: Call club for further information.

ANNAPOLIS GOLF CLUB
SP-2638 Carrollton Rd., Annapolis, 21403, Anne Arundel County, (410)263-6771.
Holes: 9. **Yards:** 6,405/5,373. **Par:** 72/74. **Course Rating:** 70.1/75.9. **Slope:** 121/128. **Green Fee:** $18/$18. **Cart Fee:** $20/cart. **Walking Policy:** Unrestricted walking. **Walkability:** 3. **Opened:** 1928. **Architect:** Charles Banks. **Season:** Year-round. **High:** April-Oct. **To obtain tee times:** 1 day in advance weekdays. Nonmembers after noon Wednesday for weekend. **Miscellaneous:** Club rentals.

THE BAY CLUB
R-9122 Libertytown Rd., Berlin, 21811, Worcester County, (800)229-2582, (800)229-2582, 7 miles W of Ocean City. **E-mail:** Bogey@shore.intercom.net. **Web:** www.thebayclub.com.
★★★½   **WEST COURSE**
Holes: 18. **Yards:** 6,958/5,609. **Par:** 72/72. **Course Rating:** 73.1/71.3. **Slope:** 126/118. **Green Fee:** $25/$65. **Cart Fee:** Included in Green Fee. **Walking Policy:** Unrestricted walking. **Walkability:** 1. **Opened:** 1989. **Architect:** Russell Roberts. **Season:** Year-round. **High:** April-Oct. **To obtain tee times:** Call up to a year in advance. **Miscellaneous:** Reduced fees (weekdays, low season, resort guests, twilight, juniors), discount packages, range (grass/mats), club rentals, credit cards (MC, V, AE, D), beginner friendly.
Reader Comments: Fun to play, different holes ... Wind is often a factor ... A lot of water and OB ... Bunkers are a real challenge ... Challenging course, island par three ... Good greens.
EAST COURSE
Holes: 18. **Yards:** 7,004/5,231. **Par:** 72/72. **Course Rating:** 74.6/67.4. **Slope:** 134/115. **Green Fee:** $25/$65. **Cart Fee:** Included in Green Fee. **Walking Policy:** Unrestricted walking. **Walkability:** 1. **Opened:** 1999. **Architect:** Charles Priestley. **Season:** Year-round. **High:** April-Oct. **To obtain tee times:** Call up to a year in advance. **Miscellaneous:** Reduced fees (weekdays, low season, resort guests, twilight, juniors), discount packages, range (grass), club rentals, credit cards (MC, V, AE, D).

★★★   BAY HILLS GOLF CLUB
SP-545 Bay Hills Dr., Arnold, 21012, Anne Arundel County, (410)974-0669, 10 miles E of Annapolis.
Holes: 18. **Yards:** 6,423/5,029. **Par:** 70/70. **Course Rating:** 70.8/69.2. **Slope:** 118/121. **Green Fee:** $36/$44. **Cart Fee:** Included in Green Fee. **Walking Policy:** Mandatory cart. **Walkability:** 3. **Opened:** 1969. **Architect:** Ed Ault. **Season:** Year-round. **High:** April-Oct. **To obtain tee times:** Call up to 3 days in advance. **Miscellaneous:** Reduced fees (twilight), club rentals, credit cards (MC, V, AE), beginner friendly.
Reader Comments: Nice course for the money ... Short, expect to beat your handicap. Greens true ... Some challenging holes, a couple excellent ones ... Walked on and always got to play ... Well-groomed fairways.

THE BEACH CLUB GOLF LINKS
SP-9715 Deer Park Dr., Berlin, 21811, Worcester County, (410)641-4653, (800)435-9223, 7 miles W of Ocean City. **E-mail:** bchclb@dmv.com. **Web:** www.ocean-city.com/beahpsg.htm.
★★★½   **INNER LINKS COURSE**
Holes: 18. **Yards:** 7,020/5,167. **Par:** 72/72. **Course Rating:** 73.0/69.0. **Slope:** 128/117. **Green Fee:** $25/$60. **Cart Fee:** Included in Green Fee. **Walking Policy:** Walking at certain times. **Walkability:** 2. **Opened:** 1991. **Architect:** Brian Ault. **Season:** Year-round. **High:** April-Oct. **To obtain tee times:** Call anytime with credit card to confirm. **Miscellaneous:** Reduced fees (low season, twilight), discount packages, range (mats), club rentals, credit cards (MC, V, AE, D).
Reader Comments: Shotmaker's course ... Nice greens ... Nice layout, well maintained ... Challenging and fun at the same time ... Recommend it when in Ocean City area ... Requires accuracy, picturesque.
★★★½   **OUTER LINKS COURSE**
Holes: 18. **Yards:** 6,548/5,022. **Par:** 72/72. **Course Rating:** 71.7/68.6. **Slope:** 134/119. **Green Fee:** $25/$60. **Cart Fee:** Included in Green Fee. **Walking Policy:** Walking at certain times. **Walkability:** 2. **Opened:** 1991. **Architect:** Brian Ault. **Season:** Year-round. **High:** April-Oct. **To obtain tee times:** Call anytime with credit card to confirm. **Miscellaneous:** Reduced fees (low season, twilight), discount packages, range (mats), club rentals, credit cards (MC, V, AE, D).
Reader Comments: Hard ... Good price, excellent condition ... A tough round in the wind ... Do not bring your draw to this course ... Great condition.

★★★   BEAR CREEK GOLF CLUB
SP-2158 Littlestown Rd., Westminster, 21158, (410)876-4653.
Special Notes: Call club for further information.

★★★ BEAVER CREEK COUNTRY CLUB

SP-9535 Mapleville Rd., Hagerstown, 21740, Washington County, (301)733-5152, 60 miles NW of Baltimore.

Holes: 18. **Yards:** 6,878/5,636. **Par:** 72/73. **Course Rating:** 71.6/71.4. **Slope:** 117/124. **Green Fee:** $30/$35. **Cart Fee:** $10/person. **Walking Policy:** Walking at certain times. **Walkability:** N/A. **Opened:** 1956. **Architect:** Reuben Hines. **Season:** Year-round. **High:** May-Oct. **To obtain tee times:** Call 7 days in advance. **Miscellaneous:** Reduced fees (weekdays, low season, twilight, seniors, juniors), metal spikes, range (grass/mats), club rentals.
Reader Comments: Back 9 very good ... Challenging, many raised tee boxes ... Nice course in a surprising location.

★★★½ BEECHTREE GOLF CLUB *Pace*

PU-811 South Stepney Rd., Aberdeen, 21001, Harford County, (410)297-9700, (877)233-2487. **Web:** www.beechtreegolf.com.

Holes: 18. **Yards:** 7,023/5,363. **Par:** 71/71. **Course Rating:** 74.9/70.4. **Slope:** 142/121. **Green Fee:** $115/$115. **Cart Fee:** Included in Green Fee. **Walking Policy:** Unrestricted walking. **Walkability:** 3. **Opened:** 1998. **Architect:** Tom Doak. **Season:** April-Nov. **High:** May-Oct. **To obtain tee times:** 30 days in advance. **Miscellaneous:** Range (grass), caddies, club rentals, credit cards (MC, V, AE, D).
Reader Comments: First class ... A true gem ... Excellent routing through Maryland countryside ... Fabulous greens ... Very good back nine ... Generous fairways ... Solid track, good greens ... Blind tee shots ... What a treat, an old-style course from a modern architect.

★★★★ BLACK ROCK GOLF COURSE

PM-20025 Mt. Aetna Rd., Hagerstown, 21742, Washington County, (301)791-3040, 70 miles W of Baltimore.

Holes: 18. **Yards:** 6,646/5,179. **Par:** 72/74. **Course Rating:** 70.7/64.7. **Slope:** 124/112. **Green Fee:** $14/$25. **Cart Fee:** $12/person. **Walking Policy:** Walking at certain times. **Walkability:** 3. **Opened:** 1989. **Architect:** Robert L. Elder. **Season:** Year-round. **High:** May-Sept. **To obtain tee times:** Call 7 days in advance for weekday tee times. Call Monday at 7:30 a.m. for upcoming weekend. **Miscellaneous:** Reduced fees (twilight, seniors, juniors), discount packages, metal spikes, range (grass/mats), club rentals, credit cards (MC, V).
Reader Comments: Best muny in area, excellent condition and value ... Excellent layout and hilly ... Good greens, good clubhouse ... Not the toughest, but a good challenge ... One of most scenic courses to play ... Playable, fair ... Worth the 90-minute ride.

BOWIE GOLF & COUNTRY CLUB

SP-7420 Laurel-Bowie Road, Bowie, 20715, Prince George's County, (301)262-8141.

Holes: 18. **Yards:** 6,142/5,106. **Par:** 70/73. **Course Rating:** 69.8/69.6. **Slope:** 114/113. **Green Fee:** $25/$30. **Cart Fee:** $12/person. **Walking Policy:** Walking at certain times. **Walkability:** 3. **Opened:** 1959. **Season:** Year-round. **High:** May-Oct. **Miscellaneous:** Range (mats), club rentals, credit cards (MC, V, AE).

★★ BRANTWOOD GOLF CLUB

SP-1190 Augustine Herman Hwy., Elkton, 21921, Cecil County, (410)398-8849, 15 miles S of Wilmington, DE.

Holes: 18. **Yards:** 6,101/5,237. **Par:** 70/72. **Course Rating:** 67.6/70.5. **Slope:** 118/114. **Green Fee:** $22/$27. **Cart Fee:** $12/person. **Walking Policy:** Walking at certain times. **Walkability:** 2. **Opened:** 1962. **Architect:** Wallace William. **Season:** Year-round. **High:** April-Oct. **To obtain tee times:** First come, first served on weekdays. Call 7 days in advance for weekends and holidays. **Miscellaneous:** Reduced fees (twilight, seniors, juniors), metal spikes, range, club rentals.

★★★ BRETON BAY GOLF & COUNTRY CLUB

SP-21935 Society Hill Rd., Leonardtown, 20650, St. Mary's County, (301)475-2300, 7 miles N of Leonardtown.

Holes: 18. **Yards:** 6,933/5,457. **Par:** 72/73. **Course Rating:** 73.0/70.0. **Slope:** 126/117. **Green Fee:** $25/$25. **Cart Fee:** $13/person. **Walking Policy:** Walking at certain times. **Walkability:** 2. **Opened:** 1974. **Architect:** J. Porter Gibson. **Season:** March-Dec. **High:** May-Aug. **To obtain tee times:** Call on Thursday for weekend play. **Miscellaneous:** Reduced fees (juniors), range (grass/mats), club rentals, credit cards (MC, V).
Reader Comments: Scenic opening holes, views of the Potomac ... Nicely-conditioned course ... Easy start, gets harder ... Water on three of last four holes.

★★★★★ BULLE ROCK *Service+, Condition+, Pace+*

PU-320 Blenheim Lane, Havre de Grace, 21078, Harford County, (410)939-8887, (888)285-5375. **E-mail:** BulleRock@iximd.com. **Web:** www.bullerock.com.

Holes: 18. **Yards:** 7,375/5,426. **Par:** 72/72. **Course Rating:** 76.4/71.1. **Slope:** 147/127. **Green Fee:** $138/$138. **Cart Fee:** Included in Green Fee. **Walking Policy:** Unrestricted walking. **Walkability:** 3. **Opened:** 1998. **Architect:** Pete Dye. **Season:** April-Nov. **High:** April-Nov. **To**

obtain tee times: 30 days in advance or ahead for any weekend in the season. **Miscellaneous:** Range (grass), caddies, club rentals, credit cards (MC, V, AE, D).
Notes: Ranked 3rd in 1999 Best in State.
Reader Comments: One of Dye's best. Each hole individually unique and beautiful. Range is phenomenal. So is service ... Interesting, very difficult, scenic; shrimp salad is the best ever ... A Pete Dye masterpiece ... Super green complexes, very natural; 18 different holes.

★★½ CAMBRIDGE COUNTRY CLUB

SP-Horns Point Rd., Cambridge, 21613, Dorchester County, (410)228-4808, 40 miles NW of Salisbury.
Holes: 18. **Yards:** 6,387/5,416. **Par:** 72/73. **Course Rating:** 69.3/71.0. **Slope:** 113/118. **Green Fee:** $35/$35. **Walking Policy:** Unrestricted walking. **Walkability:** N/A. **Opened:** 1925. **Architect:** Russell Roberts. **Season:** Year-round. **High:** May-Oct. **To obtain tee times:** Only members and guests of members can play on the weekends. No tee time required for weekdays. **Miscellaneous:** Reduced fees (resort guests), discount packages, metal spikes, range (grass), club rentals, credit cards (MC, V).
Reader Comments: Great view from the clubhouse ... Open layout ... The eighth hole plays short but extremely difficult.

★★ CARROLL PARK GOLF COURSE

PU-2100 Washington Blvd., Baltimore, 21230, Baltimore County, (410)685-8344, 3 miles SW of Baltimore.
Holes: 12. **Yards:** 3,214/2,862. **Par:** 44/43. **Course Rating:** N/A. **Slope:** N/A. **Green Fee:** N/A/$8. **Cart Fee:** $15/cart. **Walking Policy:** Unrestricted walking. **Walkability:** 1. **Opened:** 1923. **Season:** Year-round. **High:** March-Oct. **To obtain tee times:** Call golf shop. **Miscellaneous:** Reduced fees (weekdays, twilight, seniors, juniors), metal spikes, range (grass/mats), club rentals, credit cards (MC, V).

CEDAR POINT GOLF CLUB

Bldg. 663—NAWC, Patuxent River, 20670, 301)826-3597.
Special Notes: Call club for further information.

★★★½ CHANTILLY MANOR COUNTRY CLUB

SP-128 Karen Dr., Rising Sun, 21911, Cecil County, (410)658-4343, 18 miles S of Wilmington, DE. **Web:** www.chantillymanorgolf.com.
Holes: 18. **Yards:** 6,593/5,233. **Par:** 71/71. **Course Rating:** 72.3/70.4. **Slope:** 130/119. **Green Fee:** $42/$50. **Cart Fee:** Included in Green Fee. **Walking Policy:** Unrestricted walking. **Walkability:** 2. **Opened:** 1967. **Architect:** Russell Roberts. **Season:** Year-round. **High:** April-Oct. **To obtain tee times:** Call up to 7 days in advance. **Miscellaneous:** Reduced fees (weekdays, low season, twilight, seniors, juniors), discount packages, range (grass), club rentals, credit cards (MC, V), beginner friendly (junior golf program).
Reader Comments: Good condition of greens ... Awesome and big greens, nice layout, challenging ... Good service ... Good course for average golfers ... Great shape ... True, firm, fast greens ... Long par 3s.

★★★ CHESAPEAKE BAY GOLF CLUB

PU-1500 Chesapeake Club Dr, North East, 21901, Cecil County, (410)287-0200, 25 miles S of Baltimore. **E-mail:** cbgc@chessapeakegolf.com. **Web:** http://www.chesapeakegolf.com.
Holes: 18. **Yards:** 6,434/4,811. **Par:** 70/70. **Course Rating:** 71.2/70.1. **Slope:** 132/110. **Green Fee:** $35/$60. **Cart Fee:** Included in Green Fee. **Walking Policy:** Unrestricted walking. **Walkability:** 3. **Opened:** 1994. **Architect:** Andrew Barbin. **Season:** Year-round. **High:** March-Nov. **To obtain tee times:** Call up 14 days in advance. **Miscellaneous:** Reduced fees (weekdays, low season, resort guests, twilight, seniors, juniors), discount packages, range (grass/mats), club rentals, credit cards (MC, V, AE, D), beginner friendly (beginner recommended tees and clinics).
Reader Comments: Tough course, great layout ... Nice place, private feel with woods all around... Early holes are tight ... Long distances between holes ... Target golf, leave driver home ... Some great holes, need to be straight.

CHESAPEAKE HILLS GOLF CLUB

SP-Rte. 765, Lusby, 20657, (410)326-4653.
Special Notes: Call club for further information.

CLIFTON PARK GOLF COURSE

PU-2701 St. Lo Dr., Baltimore, 21213, (410)243-3500.
Holes: 18. **Yards:** 5,954/5,469. **Par:** 71/73. **Course Rating:** 68.0/66.6. **Slope:** 116/104. **Green Fee:** $14/$17. **Cart Fee:** Included in Green Fee. **Walking Policy:** Unrestricted walking. **Walkability:** 3. **Season:** Year-round. **High:** May-Aug. **To obtain tee times:** Call 2 weeks ahead. **Miscellaneous:** Reduced fees (weekdays, twilight, juniors), metal spikes, club rentals, credit cards (MC, V), beginner friendly (new GPS system in golf carts).

MARYLAND

★★★ **CLUSTERED SPIRES GOLF COURSE**
PU-8415 Gas House Pike, Frederick, 21701, Frederick County, (301)624-1295, 45 miles NW of Baltimore.
Holes: 18. **Yards:** 6,769/5,230. **Par:** 72/72. **Course Rating:** 70.5/70.0. **Slope:** 115/124. **Green Fee:** $18/$25. **Cart Fee:** $12/person. **Walking Policy:** Unrestricted walking. **Walkability:** 1. **Opened:** 1991. **Architect:** Brian T. Ault. **Season:** Year-round. **High:** April-Oct. **To obtain tee times:** Call up to 5 days in advance. **Miscellaneous:** Reduced fees (weekdays, low season, twilight, seniors, juniors), range (grass), club rentals, credit cards (MC, V), beginner friendly (clinics, junior camp).
Reader Comments: Open course, nice holes ... Easy, enjoyable, and affordable muny ... Great for beginners/winterized ... At 38 degrees and 10-20 mile-per-hour winds, this open links offered a lot of fun and challenge. It would probably play well even in good weather.

THE COURSES FORT MEADE
Bldg. 6800, Fort Meade, 20755, Anne Arundel County, (301)677-5326. **Web:** www.ftmeadegolf.com.
APPLEWOOD COURSE
Holes: 18. **Yards:** 6,494/5,436. **Par:** 72/74. **Course Rating:** 70.8/70.2. **Slope:** 116/113. **Green Fee:** $14/$26. **Cart Fee:** $17/cart. **Walking Policy:** Unrestricted walking. **Walkability:** 2. **Opened:** 1944. **Season:** Year-round. **High:** April-Oct. **To obtain tee times:** Call 1 day before the day of play. Wednesday's for weekends. **Miscellaneous:** Reduced fees (twilight), range (grass/mats), club rentals, credit cards (MC, V, AE, D), beginner friendly (clinics for beginners).
★★★½ **PARKS COURSE**
Holes: 18. **Yards:** 6,811/5,333. **Par:** 72/73. **Course Rating:** 71.6/69.0. **Slope:** 117/110. **Green Fee:** $14/$26. **Cart Fee:** $17/cart. **Walking Policy:** Unrestricted walking. **Walkability:** 2. **Opened:** 1955. **Season:** Year-round. **High:** April-Oct. **To obtain tee times:** Call 1 day before day of play. Wednesday's for weekends. **Miscellaneous:** Reduced fees (twilight), range (grass/mats), club rentals, credit cards (MC, V, AE, D), beginner friendly (clinics for beginners).
Reader Comments: Traditional, toughest greens in area ... Long holes, great greens, beautiful course ... Wide fairways, good layout ... Shotmaking required.

★★★ **DIAMOND RIDGE GOLF COURSE**
PM-2309 Ridge Rd., Woodlawn, 21244, Baltimore County, (410)887-1349, 10 miles W of Baltimore.
Holes: 18. **Yards:** 6,550/5,833. **Par:** 70/72. **Course Rating:** 71.0/73.2. **Slope:** 120/123. **Green Fee:** $15/$17. **Cart Fee:** $18/cart. **Walking Policy:** Unrestricted walking. **Walkability:** N/A. **Opened:** 1968. **Architect:** Ed Ault. **Season:** Year-round. **High:** April-Oct. **To obtain tee times:** Call anytime. **Miscellaneous:** Reduced fees (twilight, seniors, juniors), metal spikes, range (grass), club rentals.
Reader Comments: Varied layout, mix of easy and difficult holes ... Good public links test ... Could stand some work on course ... Some tight holes.

★★★★ **EAGLE'S LANDING GOLF COURSE** *Value*
PU-12367 Eagle's Nest Rd., Berlin, 21811, Worcester County, (410)213-7277, (800)283-3846, 3 miles S of Ocean City. **Web:** ocean-city.com/eagles-landing.htm.
Holes: 18. **Yards:** 7,003/4,896. **Par:** 72/72. **Course Rating:** 74.3/69.3. **Slope:** 126/115. **Green Fee:** $20/$32. **Cart Fee:** $18/person. **Walking Policy:** Unrestricted walking. **Walkability:** 1. **Opened:** 1991. **Architect:** Michael Hurdzan. **Season:** Year-round. **High:** April-Nov. **To obtain tee times:** Call up to a year in advance. **Miscellaneous:** Reduced fees (weekdays, low season, twilight, juniors), discount packages, caddies, club rentals, credit cards (MC, V, AE, D).
Notes: Ranked 13th in 1999 Best in State; 45th in 1996 America's Top 75 Affordable Courses.
Reader Comments: Affordable, great layout, nice finishing hole ... Spectacular use of wetlands ... A scenic wonder ... Best value in D.C.-Md. area ... Excellent challenge for all levels ... Best views of wildlife of any course ... A great value ... Large undulating greens.

★★★½ **THE EASTON CLUB**
SP-28449 Clubhouse Dr., Easton, 21601, Talbot County, (410)820-9017, (800)277-9800, 60 miles SE of Baltimore. **E-mail:** tec@crosslink.net. **Web:** www.eastonclub.com.
Holes: 18. **Yards:** 6,703/5,230. **Par:** 72/72. **Course Rating:** 72.3/70.2. **Slope:** 129/119. **Green Fee:** $34/$51. **Cart Fee:** $14/person. **Walking Policy:** Walking at certain times. **Walkability:** 2. **Opened:** 1995. **Architect:** Robert Rauch. **Season:** Year-round. **High:** April-Oct. **To obtain tee times:** Call 14 days in advance. **Miscellaneous:** Reduced fees (low season, twilight, juniors), metal spikes, range (grass/mats), club rentals, credit cards (MC, V, D).
Reader Comments: Tough for average player ... Fairways and greens are top notch ... Every hole is different and tough ... No. 3's island green, need I say more?

★★½ **EISENHOWER GOLF COURSE**
PM-1576 General Hwy., Crownsville, 21032, Anne Arundel County, (410)571-0973, 4 miles N of Annapolis.

Holes: 18. **Yards:** 6,659/4,884. **Par:** 71/70. **Course Rating:** 70.8/68.7. **Slope:** 122/115. **Green Fee:** $17/$26. **Cart Fee:** $13/person. **Walking Policy:** Unrestricted walking. **Walkability:** 4. **Opened:** 1970. **Architect:** Eddie Ault. **Season:** Year-round. **High:** May-Oct. **To obtain tee times:** Call 7 days in advance for weekdays/ Tuesday @ 8:00 a.m. for weekends. **Miscellaneous:** Reduced fees (twilight, seniors, juniors), range (mats), club rentals, credit cards (MC, V, AE).
Reader Comments: Improved over the past three years steadily ... Great layout, long, fair.

★★★½ ENTERPRISE GOLF COURSE
PU-2802 Enterprise Rd., Mitchellville, 20721, Prince George's County, (301)249-2040, 2 miles E of Washington DC.
Holes: 18. **Yards:** 6,586/5,157. **Par:** 72/72. **Course Rating:** 71.7/69.6. **Slope:** 128/114. **Green Fee:** $14/$30. **Cart Fee:** $24/cart. **Walking Policy:** Walking at certain times. **Walkability:** 3. **Opened:** 1976. **Architect:** Dunovan & Assoc. **Season:** Year-round. **High:** March-Oct. **To obtain tee times:** Tee times–from Tuesday through Monday of the following week. **Miscellaneous:** Reduced fees (weekdays, low season, twilight, seniors, juniors), metal spikes, range (mats), club rentals, credit cards (MC, V).
Reader Comments: Very playable public course, not a pushover ... Very scenic with mature, towering oaks ... Well-groomed tee boxes and fairways, medium-fast greens. Fairly easy to walk. A good value but the secret's out.

★★½ FALLS ROAD GOLF CLUB
PU-10800 Falls Rd., Potomac, 20854, Montgomery County, (301)299-5156, 20 miles SE of Washington, DC.
Holes: 18. **Yards:** 6,257/5,476. **Par:** 71/75. **Course Rating:** 67.7/59.3. **Slope:** 120/111. **Green Fee:** $15/$24. **Cart Fee:** $20/cart. **Walking Policy:** Unrestricted walking. **Walkability:** N/A. **Opened:** 1955. **Architect:** Edward Ault. **Season:** Year-round. **High:** April-Nov. **To obtain tee times:** Call 7 days in advance for weekends only. **Miscellaneous:** Reduced fees (seniors, juniors), metal spikes, club rentals.
Reader Comments: Fairways, greens are in great shape, course personnel pleasant ... Wide open, good when you haven't played in awhile, no penalties ... Short, busy, public course ... Back nine is good, front nine is easy.

★★½ FOREST PARK GOLF CLUB
PU-2900 Hillsdale Rd., Baltimore, 20331, Baltimore County, (410)448-4653.
Holes: 18. **Yards:** 6,127/4,824. **Par:** 71/71. **Course Rating:** 68.2/66.0. **Slope:** 116/100. **Green Fee:** N/A/$10. **Walking Policy:** Unrestricted walking. **Walkability:** N/A. **Architect:** Alex (Nipper) Campbell. **Season:** Year-round. **High:** April-Oct. **To obtain tee times:** Call golf shop. **Miscellaneous:** Reduced fees (weekdays, twilight, seniors, juniors), metal spikes, club rentals, credit cards (MC, V).
Reader Comments: Short, but fun to play ... Great value.

FREDERICK GOLF CLUB
5519 South Renn Road, Frederick, 21703, (301)846-0694, 4 miles W of Frederick.
Holes: 18. **Yards:** 5,160/3,985. **Par:** 69/69. **Course Rating:** 61.8/55.9. **Slope:** 100/98. **Green Fee:** $8/$12. **Cart Fee:** $19. **Walking Policy:** Unrestricted walking. **Walkability:** 2. **Opened:** 1997. **Architect:** R. Carels Milligan. **Season:** Year-round. **To obtain tee times:** Call golf shop. **Miscellaneous:** Reduced fees (weekdays, low season, twilight, seniors), club rentals, credit cards (MC, V).

GENEVA FARM GOLF CLUB
PU-217 Davis Rd., Street, 21154, Harford County, (410)452-8800.
Holes: 18. **Yards:** 6,450/5,394. **Par:** 72/73. **Course Rating:** 69.5/71.4. **Slope:** 120/116. **Green Fee:** $30/$35. **Cart Fee:** Included in Green Fee. **Walking Policy:** Unrestricted walking. **Walkability:** 3. **Opened:** 1990. **Architect:** Bob Elder. **Season:** Year-round. **High:** April-Sept. **Miscellaneous:** Range (grass), club rentals, credit cards (MC, V), beginner friendly.
Special Notes: Formerly Geneva Golf Course.

★★★★ GLADE VALLEY GOLF CLUB
PU-10502 Glade Rd., Walkersville, 21793, Frederick County, (301)898-5555, 4 miles N of Frederick.
Holes: 18. **Yards:** 6,787/4,953. **Par:** 72/72. **Course Rating:** 72.5/67.4. **Slope:** 123/110. **Green Fee:** $20/$43. **Cart Fee:** Included in Green Fee. **Walking Policy:** Walking at certain times. **Walkability:** 2. **Opened:** 1991. **Architect:** Robert L. Elder. **Season:** Year-round. **High:** April-Nov. **To obtain tee times:** 14 days in advance. **Miscellaneous:** Reduced fees (low season, twilight, seniors, juniors), discount packages, range (grass/mats), club rentals, credit cards (MC, V), beginner friendly (clinics for men, women and youths).
Reader Comments: Above average ... Easy, several interesting holes ... Open course, rarely crowded ... Great course for women, too.

★★★½ GLENN DALE GOLF CLUB

PU-11501 Old Prospect Hill Rd., Glenn Dale, 20769, Prince George's County, (301)262-1166, 15 miles NE of Washington, DC. **Web:** www.commercepage.com/glenndale.
Holes: 18. **Yards:** 6,282/4,809. **Par:** 70/70. **Course Rating:** 70.0/67.2. **Slope:** 115/107. **Green Fee:** $22/$34. **Cart Fee:** $24/cart. **Walking Policy:** Walking at certain times. **Walkability:** 3. **Opened:** 1955. **Architect:** George W. Cobb. **Season:** Year-round. **High:** April-Oct. **To obtain tee times:** Call 1 day in advance for weekday. Call on Monday at 11 a.m. for weekend or holiday. **Miscellaneous:** Reduced fees (low season, twilight, seniors, juniors), metal spikes, range (mats), club rentals, credit cards (MC, V).

Reader Comments: Average layout, short, always in good shape ... Tough, small, crowned greens ... Under new management, nice people! ... Great bartender ... Short, but challenging.

★★★½ THE GOLF CLUB AT WISP

R-296 Marsh Hill Rd., P.O. Box 629, McHenry, 21541, Garrett County, (301)387-4911, 90 miles SE of Pittsburgh, PA. **E-mail:** wispinfo@gcnet. **Web:** www.gcnet.net/wisp.
Holes: 18. **Yards:** 6,911/5,166. **Par:** 72/72. **Course Rating:** 73.7/75.8. **Slope:** 141/131. **Green Fee:** $48/$58. **Cart Fee:** Included in Green Fee. **Walking Policy:** Walking at certain times. **Walkability:** 4. **Opened:** 1979. **Architect:** Dominic Palombo. **Season:** April-Oct. **High:** July-Sept. **To obtain tee times:** Call (301)387-4911. **Miscellaneous:** Reduced fees (low season, resort guests), discount packages, range (grass/mats), club rentals, lodging (73 rooms), credit cards (MC, V, AE, D).

Reader Comments: Vista, views from mountainside tees ... Straightforward, but not easy ... Tough course, need to hit it straight ... Tough for even good golfers ... Hilly, long, tight, long water carries ... A killer course with tons of water! Lots of elevated greens, great finishing hole.

★★★ GREAT HOPE GOLF COURSE

PU-8380 Crisfield Hwy., Westover, 21872, Somerset County, (410)651-5900, (800)537-8009, 10 miles S of Salisbury.
Holes: 18. **Yards:** 7,047/5,204. **Par:** 72/72. **Course Rating:** 72.8/68.5. **Slope:** 125/112. **Green Fee:** $18/$26. **Cart Fee:** $11/person. **Walking Policy:** Unrestricted walking. **Walkability:** 1. **Opened:** 1995. **Architect:** Michael Hurdzan. **Season:** Year-round. **High:** April-Oct. **To obtain tee times:** Call golf shop. **Miscellaneous:** Reduced fees (weekdays, low season, resort guests, twilight, juniors), discount packages, metal spikes, range (grass), club rentals, credit cards (MC, V).

Reader Comments: Hidden gem ... Lots of hazards. Fast greens ... Average rural public course ... Best greens around.

★★★ GREEN HILL YACHT & COUNTRY CLUB

SP-5473 Whitehaven Rd., Quantico, 21856, Wicomico County, (410)749-1605, (888)465-3855, 30 miles W of Ocean City. **Web:** greenhillgolf.com.
Holes: 18. **Yards:** 6,800/5,600. **Par:** 72/72. **Course Rating:** 72.2/72.0. **Slope:** 126/126. **Green Fee:** $30/$69. **Cart Fee:** Included in Green Fee. **Walking Policy:** Mandatory cart. **Walkability:** 2. **Opened:** 1927. **Architect:** Alfred H. Tull. **Season:** Year-round. **High:** Summer. **To obtain tee times:** Call golf shop. Members take priority. **Miscellaneous:** Reduced fees (weekdays, low season), discount packages, range (grass), club rentals, credit cards (MC, V, AE).

Reader Comments: Good greens, great condition. Good test, pretty course.

GREENFIELDS GOLF

PU-8804 Logtown Rd., Berlin, 21811, Worcester County, (410)629-0060, (888)790-4653. **E-mail:** golfpro@greenfieldsgolf.com. **Web:** greenfieldsgolf.com.
Holes: 18. **Yards:** 6,105/4,072. **Par:** 70/70. **Course Rating:** 69.4/68.8. **Slope:** 115/110. **Green Fee:** $30/$30. **Cart Fee:** $12/person. **Walking Policy:** Unrestricted walking. **Walkability:** 1. **Opened:** 1997. **Architect:** Lindsay Ervin. **Season:** Year-round. **High:** April-Oct. **Miscellaneous:** Reduced fees (low season, twilight), range (grass/mats), club rentals, credit cards (MC, V, D), beginner friendly (clinics, mentor).

★★★★ GREYSTONE GOLF COURSE

PU-2115 White Hall Rd., White Hall, 21161, Baltimore County, (410)887-1945, 10 miles N of Hunt Valley. **Web:** Baltimoregolfing.com.
Holes: 18. **Yards:** 6,925/4,800. **Par:** 72/72. **Course Rating:** 73.5/67.5. **Slope:** 139/112. **Green Fee:** $25/$59. **Cart Fee:** Included in Green Fee. **Walking Policy:** Unrestricted walking. **Walkability:** 5. **Opened:** 1997. **Architect:** Joe Lee. **Season:** Year-round. **High:** April-Oct. **To obtain tee times:** Call Golf Shop up to 7 days in advance. **Miscellaneous:** Reduced fees (weekdays, low season, twilight, seniors, juniors), range (grass), club rentals, credit cards (MC, V, AE, D).
Notes: Ranked 15th in 1999 Best in State.

Reader Comments: Very interesting holes for a public course ... Run like a private club ... Scenic views ... Lightning greens, very scenic, difficult ... Beautiful rolling countryside ... Lush fairways ... Blind shots.

MARYLAND

GUNPOWDER GOLF CLUB
SP-14300 Gunpowder Rd., Laurel, 20707, Prince George's and Montgomery County, (301)725-4532, 5 miles N of Washington, D.C.
Holes: 18. **Yards:** 6,061/4,710. **Par:** 70/70. **Course Rating:** 67.3/64.8. **Slope:** 98/105. **Green Fee:** $9/$14. **Cart Fee:** $19/cart. **Walking Policy:** Unrestricted walking. **Walkability:** 5. **Opened:** 1956. **Architect:** R. Carels Milligan. **Season:** Year-round. **High:** May-Nov. **Miscellaneous:** Reduced fees (weekdays, low season, twilight, seniors), credit cards (MC, V).

★★★ HARBOURTOWNE GOLF RESORT & COUNTRY CLUB
R-Rte. 33 at Martingham Dr., St. Michaels, 21663, Talbot County, (410)745-5183, (800)446-9066, 75 miles SE of Baltimore.
Holes: 18. **Yards:** 6,320/5,036. **Par:** 70/71. **Course Rating:** 69.5/68.5. **Slope:** 120/113. **Green Fee:** N/A/$38. **Cart Fee:** $12/person. **Walking Policy:** Mandatory cart. **Walkability:** 3. **Opened:** 1971. **Architect:** Pete Dye/Roy Dye. **Season:** Year-round. **High:** April-Oct. **To obtain tee times:** Call. **Miscellaneous:** Reduced fees (low season, resort guests), discount packages, metal spikes, range (grass), club rentals, lodging (111 rooms), credit cards (MC, V, AE, D).
Reader Comments: Back nine very tight with some length, hit it straight ... Flat.

★★★★ HOG NECK GOLF COURSE
PM-10142 Old Cordova Rd., Easton, 21601, Talbot County, (410)822-6079, (800)200-1790, 50 miles SE of Baltimore.
Holes: 18. **Yards:** 7,000/5,500. **Par:** 72/72. **Course Rating:** 73.8/71.3. **Slope:** 131/125. **Green Fee:** $36/$46. **Cart Fee:** $14/person. **Walking Policy:** Unrestricted walking. **Walkability:** 2. **Opened:** 1976. **Architect:** Lindsay Ervin. **Season:** Feb.-Dec. **High:** April-Oct. **To obtain tee times:** Call for entire season from February 1st on. **Miscellaneous:** Reduced fees (weekdays, low season, twilight, juniors), range (mats), club rentals, credit cards (MC, V), beginner friendly (beginner and junior clinics).
Notes: Ranked 10th in 1999 Best in State.
Reader Comments: Two contrasting nines; open and woods ... Good test of your golf skills ... One of the best in Maryland ... Back nine is a bear, worth the drive ... Changes in elevation ... Something you will not forget ... Tight but beautiful ... Outstanding ... Over 100 sand traps ... A nice surprise, very appealing course ... A favorite.

★★★ LAKE ARBOR COUNTRY CLUB
SP-1401 Golf Course Dr., Mitchellville, 20721, (301)336-7771.
Special Notes: Call club for further information.

★★½ LAYTONSVILLE GOLF COURSE
PU-7130 Dorsey Rd., Laytonsville, 20882, Montgomery County, (301)948-5288, 18 miles N of Washington, DC.
Holes: 18. **Yards:** 6,311/5,439. **Par:** 70/73. **Course Rating:** 69.8/71.4. **Slope:** 117/113. **Green Fee:** $21/$28. **Cart Fee:** $24/cart. **Walking Policy:** Unrestricted walking. **Walkability:** 2. **Opened:** 1973. **Architect:** Roger Peacock. **Season:** Year-round. **High:** April-Sept. **To obtain tee times:** In person 1 week in advance then 7:00 a.m. Monday over the phone. **Miscellaneous:** Reduced fees (seniors, juniors), range (grass/mats), club rentals, credit cards (MC, V), beginner friendly.
Reader Comments: Different fairway width makes play interesting ... Short, want to shoot a good score ... Fairly short but well-kept ... Strong par 4s on the front.

★★★ THE LINKS AT CHALLEDON
PU-6166 Challedon Circle, Mount Airy, 21771, (301)829-3000, 18 miles W of Baltimore.
Holes: 18. **Yards:** 6,730/5,355. **Par:** 72/72. **Course Rating:** 71.3/70.7. **Slope:** 124/122. **Green Fee:** N/A/$55. **Cart Fee:** Included in Green Fee. **Walking Policy:** Walking at certain times. **Walkability:** 3. **Opened:** 1996. **Season:** Year-round. **High:** March-Oct. **To obtain tee times:** Call up to 5 days in advance. **Miscellaneous:** Reduced fees (weekdays, low season, twilight, seniors, juniors), range (grass/mats), club rentals, credit cards (MC, V, AE).
Reader Comments: Course will improve as it matures ... Great service and amenities ... Scenic, links-style layout ... Greens and fairways are well-groomed ... The fourth hole is a terrific par 4 ... Nice Ault-Clark design.... A beautiful place to play. Over water approaches are a challenge to 'Tin Cuppers' ... Everyone scores well.

★★★½ LITTLE BENNETT GOLF COURSE
PM-25900 Prescott Rd., Clarksburg, 20871, Montgomery County, (301)253-1515, (800)366-2012, 15 miles S of Frederick.
Holes: 18. **Yards:** 6,706/4,921. **Par:** 72/72. **Course Rating:** 72.9/68.2. **Slope:** 133/115. **Green Fee:** $25/$30. **Cart Fee:** $12/person. **Walking Policy:** Unrestricted walking. **Walkability:** 5. **Opened:** 1994. **Architect:** Hurdzan Design Group. **Season:** Year-round. **High:** April-Oct. **To obtain tee times:** For advanced reservations call Mon. 7:00 a.m.
for following weekend or next 6 days. Call after 9:00 a.m. for the day of play. **Miscellaneous:**

MARYLAND

Reduced fees (low season, seniors, juniors), discount packages, range (grass), club rentals, credit cards (MC, V).
Reader Comments: Very hilly, a good bargain ... Excellent bent grass greens ... Target golf, beautiful touch course ... Challenging course ... Fun course, six very good holes ... Many hills providing difficult lies ... Some tough holes, need local knowledge ... Tough course, but love to play it ... Plenty of blind shots.

LONGVIEW GOLF CLUB
PU-1 Cardigan Rd., Timonium, 21093, Baltimore County, (410)628-6362, 22 miles N of Baltimore. **Web:** www.baltimoregolfing.com.
Holes: 18. **Yards:** 6,038/5,394. **Par:** 70/71. **Course Rating:** 68.2/66.6. **Slope:** 110/105. **Green Fee:** $15/$17. **Cart Fee:** $11/person. **Walking Policy:** Unrestricted walking. **Walk- ability:** 1. **Opened:** 1964. **Architect:** Ed Ault. **Season:** Year-round. **High:** March-Oct.
To obtain tee times: Call (410) 887-4653. **Miscellaneous:** Reduced fees (weekdays, twilight, seniors, juniors), range (grass/mats), club rentals, credit cards (MC, V, AE, D).

★★½ MAPLE RUN GOLF COURSE
PU-13610-A Moser Rd., Thurmont, 21788, Frederick County, (301)271-7870, 15 miles N of Frederick.
Holes: 18. **Yards:** 6,553/4,822. **Par:** 72/72. **Course Rating:** 71.2/66.1. **Slope:** 128/114. **Green Fee:** $15/$22. **Cart Fee:** $10/person. **Walking Policy:** Unrestricted walking. **Walkability:** 2.
Opened: 1992. **Architect:** Russell/Joe Moser. **Season:** Year-round. **High:** April-Oct. **To obtain tee times:** Call golf shop. **Miscellaneous:** Reduced fees (weekdays, low season, twilight, seniors), discount packages, range (mats), club rentals, credit cards (MC, V, D).
Reader Comments: Family-run golf course ... Fun open front nine, several doglegs on the back...Small greens, narrow fairways and high rough ... Short but challenging ... Pictures of Clinton playing there, Camp David nearby, but didn't see him when I was there ... Needs maintenance, nice place ... Some holes are too difficult.

★★★ MARLBOROUGH COUNTRY CLUB
SP-4750 John Rodgers Blvd., Upper Marlboro, 20772, Prince George's County, (301)952-1350, (888)218-8463, 20 miles E of Washington, DC.
Holes: 18. **Yards:** 6,119/5,130. **Par:** 71/71. **Course Rating:** 69.5/69.5. **Slope:** 124/120. **Green Fee:** $17/$27. **Cart Fee:** $13/person. **Walking Policy:** Walking at certain times. **Walkability:** 1.
Opened: 1974. **Architect:** Algie Pulley. **Season:** Year-round. **High:** April-Oct. **To obtain tee times:** Call 7 days in advance. **Miscellaneous:** Reduced fees (weekdays, low season, twilight), discount packages, metal spikes, range (mats), club rentals, credit cards (MC, V).
Reader Comments: Short, but very tight; leave driver home ... Shotmakers' course, tight! ... Traditional and playable ... Back nine tougher.

★★★½ MOUNT PLEASANT GOLF CLUB   *Value*
PU-6001 Hillen Rd., Baltimore, 21239, Baltimore County, (410)254-5100.
Holes: 18. **Yards:** 6,728/5,294. **Par:** 71/73. **Course Rating:** 71.8/69.4. **Slope:** 119/118. **Green Fee:** $12/$16. **Cart Fee:** $14/cart. **Walking Policy:** Unrestricted walking. **Walkability:** 4.
Opened: 1933. **Architect:** Gus Hook. **Season:** Year-round. **High:** June-Aug. **To obtain tee times:** Lottery times for weekends. Call up to 14 days in advance for weekdays. **Miscellaneous:** Reduced fees (weekdays, twilight, seniors, juniors), metal spikes, club rentals, credit cards (MC, V).
Reader Comments: Great city course ... Toughest greens in the area ... Experience every possible type of lie ... Site of Àrnie's 1st win/classic design/large tricky greens ... The best test of a public course anywhere ... Good layout for old public course ... Beats other courses in town.

THE MOUNTAIN CLUB AT RAWLINGS
PU-16300 Racquet Club Dr., Rawlings, 21557, (301)729-0758.
Special Notes: Call club for further information.

★★½ NASSAWANGO COUNTRY CLUB
SP-3940 Nassawango Rd., Snow Hill, 21863, Worcester County, (410)632-3144, 18 miles SE of Salisbury.
Holes: 18. **Yards:** 6,644/5,760. **Par:** 72/73. **Course Rating:** 70.2/72.1. **Slope:** 125/125. **Green Fee:** N/A/$27. **Cart Fee:** $12/person. **Walking Policy:** Mandatory cart. **Walkability:** 3. **Opened:** 1970. **Architect:** Russell Roberts. **Season:** Year-round. **High:** May-Oct. **To obtain tee times:** Call. **Miscellaneous:** Reduced fees (low season), discount packages, metal spikes, club rentals, credit cards (MC, V).
Reader Comments: Good greens, peaceful, good test ... Course sets up left to right.

★★★ NEEDWOOD GOLF COURSE
PU-6724 Needwood Rd., Derwood, 20855, Montgomery County, (301)948-1075, 22 miles N of Washington, DC.
Holes: 27. **Yards:** 6,254/5,112. **Par:** 70/72. **Course Rating:** 69.1/69.2. **Slope:** 113/105. **Green Fee:** $23/$28. **Cart Fee:** $24/cart. **Walking Policy:** Unrestricted walking. **Walkability:** 3.

MARYLAND

Opened: 1969. **Architect:** Lindsay Ervin. **Season:** Year-round. **High:** May-Sept. **To obtain tee times:** Weekday, first come, first served; weekend, reservations optional. **Miscellaneous:** Reduced fees (weekdays, seniors, juniors), range (mats), club rentals, credit cards (MC, V).
Reader Comments: Great staff; nice basic course ... Best-kept old course ... Greens roll true, fairways very nice, a favorite ... The T.L.C. shows, lots of play ... Pretty course.

★★★ NORTHWEST PARK GOLF COURSE

PU-15701 Layhill Rd., Wheaton, 20906, Montgomery County, (301)598-6100, 15 miles N of Washington, DC.
Holes: 27. **Yards:** 7,376/6,184. **Par:** 72/74. **Course Rating:** 74.0/74.5. **Slope:** 122/126. **Green Fee:** $22/$27. **Cart Fee:** $12/person. **Walking Policy:** Unrestricted walking. **Walkability:** 3.
Opened: 1964. **Architect:** Edmund B. Ault/Russell Roberts. **Season:** Year-round. **High:** June-Aug. **To obtain tee times:** Call up to 6 days in advance for weekdays. Call on Monday a.m. for upcoming weekend. **Miscellaneous:** Reduced fees (weekdays, seniors, juniors), range (mats), club rentals, credit cards (MC, V).
Reader Comments: Long and challenging. A lot of trees ... Too long and difficult for average golfer ... Nice and open, hard to lose balls ... Long, good condition, challenging and fair... Wide open, fairway woods abound ... Needs work ... For long hitters this is a treasure ... Long and wide, beginner friendly.

★★★½ NUTTERS CROSSING GOLF CLUB

SP-30287 S. Hampton Bridge Rd., Salisbury, 21804, Wicomico County, (410)860-4653. **Web:** www.nutterscrossing.com.
Holes: 18. **Yards:** 6,033/4,800. **Par:** 70/70. **Course Rating:** 67.1/66.5. **Slope:** 115/110. **Green Fee:** $18/$42. **Cart Fee:** $12/person. **Walking Policy:** Walking at certain times. **Walkability:** 3.
Opened: 1991. **Architect:** Ault/Clark. **Season:** Year-round. **High:** April-May; Sept.-Oct. **To obtain tee times:** Call anytime during the week. **Miscellaneous:** Reduced fees (low season, twilight), range (grass), club rentals, credit cards (MC, V).
Reader Comments: Not too hard but lots of fun ... Good conditions ... Lots of couples play ... Tricky water hazard holes ... Always in great shape.

OAKLAND GOLF COURSE

SP-Oakland Sang Run Rd., Oakland, 21550, (301)334-3883.
Special Notes: Call club for further information.

★★★½ OAKMONT GREEN GOLF COURSE

SP-2290 Golf View Lane, Hampstead, 21074, Carroll County, (410)374-1500.
Holes: 18. **Yards:** 6,600/5,139. **Par:** 72/72. **Course Rating:** 71.4/69.3. **Slope:** 122/116. **Green Fee:** $16/$26. **Cart Fee:** $10/person. **Walking Policy:** Unrestricted walking. **Walkability:** 3.
Opened: 1991. **Architect:** Leeland Snyder. **Season:** March-Dec. **High:** May-Sept.
Miscellaneous: Reduced fees (weekdays, low season, twilight, seniors, juniors), metal spikes, range (grass/mats), club rentals, credit cards (MC, V), beginner friendly (clinics, junior programs).
Reader Comments: Distance is not as important as accuracy and strategy; wind can wreak havoc on drives on Nos. 3, 4 and 5 ... Some houses.

OCEAN CITY GOLF & YACHT CLUB

R-11401 Country Club Dr., Berlin, 21811, Worcester County, (410)641-1779, (800)442-3570, 5 miles SE of Ocean City.
★★★★ NEWPORT BAY COURSE
Holes: 18. **Yards:** 6,526/5,396. **Par:** 72/72. **Course Rating:** 71.7/71.3. **Slope:** 121/119. **Green Fee:** $13/$49. **Cart Fee:** $21/person. **Walking Policy:** Walking at certain times. **Walkability:** 1.
Opened: 1998. **Architect:** Russell Roberts/Lester George. **Season:** Year-round. **High:** April-Oct.
To obtain tee times: Call. Credit card needed to guarantee tee time. **Miscellaneous:** Reduced fees (weekdays, low season, twilight, juniors), discount packages, range (grass/mats), club rentals, credit cards (MC, V).
Reader Comments: Excellent improvements ... Hard to concentrate on your game here. Beautiful course ... Greens perfect, fast, true. Best conditions in area ... Difficult (especially in wind), but a true golf experience, gorgeous ... Simply outstanding all around ... Redone course, better than old one ... Flat... Hard for the average golfer.
Special Notes: Formerly Bayside Course.
★★★½ SEASIDE COURSE
Holes: 18. **Yards:** 6,520/5,848. **Par:** 73/75. **Course Rating:** 70.9/73.1. **Slope:** 115/119. **Green Fee:** $13/$39. **Cart Fee:** $21/person. **Walking Policy:** Walking at certain times. **Walkability:** 1.
Opened: 1959. **Architect:** William Gordon/David Gordon/Russell Robe. **Season:** Year-round.
High: April-Oct. **To obtain tee times:** Call. Credit card needed to guarantee tee time.
Miscellaneous: Reduced fees (weekdays, low season, twilight, juniors), discount packages, range (grass/mats), club rentals, credit cards (MC, V).

MARYLAND

Reader Comments: Very well maintained, great stuff ... Fairways in great shape. Greens very fast and true. Best conditions in area ... Very few tough holes, easy play ... Good resort course, not too difficult, playable.

P.B. DYE GOLF CLUB
SP-9526 Dr. Perry Rd., Ijamsville, 21754, Frederick County, (301)607-4653, 10 miles S of Frederick. **Web:** www.pbdyegolf.com.
Holes: 18. **Yards:** 7,036/5,391. **Par:** 72/73. **Course Rating:** 74.6/71.5. **Slope:** 141/129. **Green Fee:** $49/$79. **Cart Fee:** Included in Green Fee. **Walking Policy:** Walking at certain times. **Walkability:** 3. **Opened:** 1999. **Architect:** P.B. Dye. **Season:** Year round. **High:** April-Oct. **To obtain tee times:** Call (301)607-GOLF. **Miscellaneous:** Reduced fees (weekdays, low season, twilight), range (grass/mats), club rentals, credit cards (MC, V, AE).
Special Notes: Installing computer/internet tee-time system in 2000.

★★★ PATUXENT GREENS COUNTRY CLUB
SP-14415 Greenview Dr., Laurel, 20708, Prince George's County, (301)776-5533, 15 miles S of Baltimore.
Holes: 18. **Yards:** 6,294/5,279. **Par:** 71/71. **Course Rating:** 71.1/70.1. **Slope:** 131/117. **Green Fee:** $38/$44. **Cart Fee:** Included in Green Fee. **Walking Policy:** Mandatory cart. **Walkability:** 1. **Opened:** 1970. **Architect:** George Cobb/Buddy Loving. **Season:** Year-round. **High:** March-Oct. **To obtain tee times:** Call 4 days in advance. **Miscellaneous:** Reduced fees (weekdays, low season, twilight), club rentals, credit cards (MC, V, AE).

Reader Comments: Good for walking, flat, tight, water on 15 holes ... Better conditioning would make it really nice ... Bring a lot of balls ... Some funky holes ... Flat, narrow, water. A little bit of Florida in Laurel.

★★★½ PINE RIDGE GOLF COURSE
PU-2101 Dulaney Valley Rd., Lutherville, 21093, Baltimore County, (410)252-1408, 15 miles N of Baltimore.
Holes: 18. **Yards:** 6,724/5,679. **Par:** 72/72. **Course Rating:** 71.9/71.3. **Slope:** 123/119. **Green Fee:** $12/$13. **Cart Fee:** $14/cart. **Walking Policy:** Walking at certain times. **Walkability:** 3. **Opened:** 1958. **Architect:** Gus Hook. **Season:** Year-round. **High:** June-Aug. **To obtain tee times:** Call up to 14 days in advance. Weekday tee times cost $2 in person, $5 over the phone with a credit card. Weekend a.m. tee times are sold in a lottery, weekend p.m. times cost $5. **Miscellaneous:** Reduced fees (weekdays, twilight, seniors, juniors), metal spikes, range (mats), club rentals, credit cards (MC, V).

Reader Comments: Great layout, former LPGA stop ... Could be so much better ... Course built around a reservoir ... Busy ... Beautiful layout ... Great views of the water... Beautiful course, great value.

★★½ POOLESVILLE GOLF COURSE
PU-16601 W. Willard Rd, Poolesville, 20837, Montgomery County, (301)428-8143, 25 miles NW of Washington, DC.
Holes: 18. **Yards:** 6,811/5,521. **Par:** 71/73. **Course Rating:** 72.3/71.4. **Slope:** 123/118. **Green Fee:** $22/$27. **Cart Fee:** $25/cart. **Walking Policy:** Unrestricted walking. **Walkability:** 2. **Opened:** 1959. **Architect:** Edmund B. Ault/Al Jamison. **Season:** Year-round. **High:** May-Oct. **To obtain tee times:** Call or come in 7 days in advance for weekends and holidays. **Miscellaneous:** Reduced fees (seniors, juniors), range (grass/mats), club rentals, credit cards (MC, V).

Reader Comments: Fun muny course ... In a neat smalltown USA ... Long and straight with little trouble ... Let it all hang out.

★★½ POTOMAC RIDGE GOLF LINKS
PU-15800 Sharperville Rd., Accokeek, 20601, Prince Georges County, (301)372-1305, (800)791-9078. **E-mail:** prgl@mdgolf.com. **Web:** mdgolf.com.
Holes: 18. **Yards:** N/A. **Par:** N/A. **Course Rating:** N/A. **Slope:** N/A. **Green Fee:** $25/$40. **Walking Policy:** Unrestricted walking. **Walkability:** 3. **Opened:** 1995. **Architect:** Tom Clark. **Season:** Year-round. **High:** April-Oct. **To obtain tee times:** Call or visit 10 days in advance after 9:00 a.m. for tee times. Outings of 13 or more players may call (800)827-5257 up to 1 year in advance. **Miscellaneous:** Reduced fees (weekdays, low season, twilight, seniors, juniors), metal spikes, range (grass/mats), club rentals, credit cards (MC, V, AE).

Reader Comments: New, but improving ... Good mixture of holes ... New management, doing great, course is shaping up ... Terrific greens and tee boxes ... Plenty of water.

QUEENSTOWN HARBOR GOLF LINKS
PU-310 Links Lane, Queenstown, 21658, Queen Anne's County, (410)827-6611, (800)827-5257, 45 miles SE of Baltimore.
★★★★ LAKES COURSE
Holes: 18. **Yards:** 6,537/4,576. **Par:** 71/71. **Course Rating:** 71.0/66.6. **Slope:** 124/111. **Green Fee:** $25/$65. **Cart Fee:** Included in Green Fee. **Walking Policy:** Unrestricted walking.

Walkability: 2. **Opened:** 1991. **Architect:** Lindsay Ervin. **Season:** Year-round. **High:** April-Oct. **To obtain tee times:** Call 10 days in advance after 12 p.m. **Miscellaneous:** Reduced fees (weekdays, twilight, seniors, juniors), metal spikes, range (grass/mats), club rentals, credit cards (MC, V, AE), beginner friendly (clinics). **Notes:** Ranked 11th in 1999 Best in State.

Reader Comments: Outstanding layout, demanding tee shots ... Awesome ... Easier than the River course, but still good ... One of the best I've ever played ... Hold on to your hat. Wind is wicked and wild ... Beautiful place to play ... Challenging courses worth playing again ... Solid ... Great condition.

★★★★ RIVER COURSE

Holes: 18. **Yards:** 7,110/5,026. **Par:** 72/72. **Course Rating:** 74.2/69.0. **Slope:** 138/123. **Green Fee:** $35/$80. **Cart Fee:** Included in Green Fee. **Walking Policy:** Unrestricted walking. **Walkability:** 2. **Opened:** 1991. **Architect:** Lindsay Ervin. **Season:** Year-round. **High:** April-Oct. **To obtain tee times:** Call 7 days in advance after 12 p.m. **Miscellaneous:** Reduced fees (weekdays, twilight, seniors, juniors), metal spikes, range (grass/mats), club rentals, credit cards (MC, V, AE). **Notes:** Ranked 6th in 1999 Best in State.

Reader Comments: Just a great track! ... Can be a bear when the wind is up ... Very challenging. Nice view overlooking the river ... Bring your A game ... Great views of the Chesapeake Bay ... Best in the area ... Tight and challenging, very scenic ...Beautifully sculpted into sensitive environmental area ... Women-friendly ... Top of the heap, requires thoughtful play.

★★★½ REDGATE MUNICIPAL GOLF COURSE

PM-14500 Avery Rd., Rockville, 20853, Montgomery County, (301)309-3055, 10 miles N of Washington, DC.
Holes: 18. **Yards:** 6,432/5,271. **Par:** 71/71. **Course Rating:** 71.7/70.2. **Slope:** 131/121. **Green Fee:** $24/$28. **Cart Fee:** $24/cart. **Walking Policy:** Unrestricted walking. **Walkability:** 4. **Opened:** 1974. **Architect:** Thurman Donovan. **Season:** Year-round. **High:** April-Nov. **To obtain tee times:** Tee times for weekends only. Call Monday 7:30 a.m. for upcoming weekend. **Miscellaneous:** Reduced fees (seniors, juniors), range (grass/mats), club rentals.

Reader Comments: Very good muny ... Nice layout, few holes with water ... Hilly ... Two par fives are challenging ... Exciting, tough layout ... Gorgeous course for long and short hitters ... Great condition for a muny.

★★★½ RIVER DOWNS GOLFERS' CLUB

SP-1900 River Downs Dr., Finksburg, 21048, Carroll County, (410)526-2000, (800)518-7337, 30 miles NW of Baltimore.
Holes: 18. **Yards:** 6,873/5,003. **Par:** 72/72. **Course Rating:** 72.6/70.4. **Slope:** 129/122. **Green Fee:** $21/$58. **Cart Fee:** Included in Green Fee. **Walking Policy:** Mandatory cart. **Walkability:** 4. **Opened:** 1995. **Architect:** Arthur Hills. **Season:** Year-round. **High:** April-Oct. **To obtain tee times:** Call up to 7 days in advance. **Miscellaneous:** Reduced fees (weekdays, low season, twilight), metal spikes, range (grass), club rentals, credit cards (MC, V).

Reader Comments: Great new course ... Some great scenery ... Hilly, blind shots, can't just rip the driver ... Elevation changes require thought, narrow fairways ... Tough but fair layout ... Computers in the carts ... Another course where local knowledge is needed ... Hidden gem. Championship layout.

★★★★ RIVER RUN GOLF CLUB

PU-11605 Masters Lane, Berlin, 21811, Worcester County, (410)641-7200, (800)733-7786, 110 miles SE of Washington, DC.
Holes: 18. **Yards:** 6,705/5,002. **Par:** 71/71. **Course Rating:** 70.4/73.1. **Slope:** 128/117. **Green Fee:** $8/$36. **Cart Fee:** $12/person. **Walking Policy:** Walking at certain times. **Walkability:** N/A. **Opened:** 1991. **Architect:** Gary Player. **Season:** Year-round. **High:** April-Oct. **To obtain tee times:** Call (800)733-7786 with credit card to confirm. **Miscellaneous:** Reduced fees (weekdays, low season, resort guests, twilight, juniors), discount packages, range (grass), club rentals, lodging, credit cards (MC, V, AE, D).

Reader Comments: No two holes alike. Both water and woods ... Scottish links front nine, tree-lined back nine ... From start to finish, outstanding ... Fair for any level, a tee for everyone ... Great fairways and greens ... Picturesque, tight, fast, and fair ... Tremen-dous fun for mid-range player ... Great clubhouse, chicken sandwich ... Beautiful, tough and rewarding.

ROBIN DALE GOLF CLUB

SP-15851 McKendree Rd., Brandywine, 20613, Prince George's County, (301)372-8855, 22 miles SE of Washington D.C. **E-mail:** rdggp@aol.com.
Holes: 18. **Yards:** 6,667/5,888. **Par:** 72/73. **Course Rating:** 71.3/72.3. **Slope:** 123/117. **Green Fee:** $20/$36. **Cart Fee:** Included in Green Fee. **Walking Policy:** Walking at certain times. **Walkability:** 1. **Opened:** 1966. **Season:** Year-round. **High:** May-Sept. **To obtain tee times:** Tee times 7-10 days in advance/outings 90 days. **Miscellaneous:** Reduced fees (weekdays, low season, twilight, seniors, juniors), range (mats), club rentals, credit cards (MC, V, AE), beginner friendly.
Special Notes: Formerly Robin Dale Golf & Country Club.

MARYLAND

ROCKY GAP LODGE & GOLF RESORT
R-P.O. Box 1199, Cumberland, 21501, Cumberland County, (800)724-0828, (800)724-0828. **Web:** www.rockygapresort.com.
Holes: 18. **Yards:** 7,006/5,212. **Par:** 72/72. **Course Rating:** N/A. **Slope:** N/A. **Green Fee:** $46/$67. **Cart Fee:** Included in Green Fee. **Walking Policy:** Mandatory cart. **Walkability:** 5. **Opened:** 1998. **Architect:** Jack Nicklaus. **Season:** Year-round. **High:** June-Sept. **To obtain tee times:** Hotel guests can call anytime. Other tee times 7 days in advance. **Miscellaneous:** Reduced fees (low season, resort guests, twilight, juniors), discount packages, range (grass/mats), club rentals, lodging (220 rooms), credit cards (MC, V, AE, D).

★★★½ ROCKY POINT GOLF COURSE
PU-1935 Back River Neck Rd., Essex, 21221, Baltimore County, (410)391-2906, (888)246-5384, 9 miles E of Baltimore. **Web:** baltimorecountry.com.
Holes: 18. **Yards:** 6,753/5,750. **Par:** 72/74. **Course Rating:** 72.3/73.1. **Slope:** 122/121. **Green Fee:** $15/$17. **Cart Fee:** $22/cart. **Walking Policy:** Unrestricted walking. **Walkability:** 2. **Opened:** 1971. **Architect:** Russell Roberts. **Season:** Year-round. **High:** April-Sept. **To obtain tee times:** Call up to 7 days in advance. **Miscellaneous:** Reduced fees (weekdays, twilight, seniors, juniors), range (grass/mats), club rentals, credit cards (MC, V, AE, D), beginner friendly.
Reader Comments: Great views of bay, great course to walk ... Well laid out holes ... Brewed coffee, good ... A good open course ... Fun course, varied layout.

RUGGLES GOLF COURSE
Bldg. 5600, Aberdeen, 21005, (410)278-4794.
Special Notes: Call club for further information.

★★★★ RUM POINTE SEASIDE GOLF LINKS
R-7000 Rum Pointe Lane, Berlin, 21811, Worcester County, (410)629-1414, (888)809-4653, 7 miles S of Ocean City. **E-mail:** Ruarkgolf@aol.com. **Web:** www.rumpointe.com.
Holes: 18. **Yards:** 7,001/5,276. **Par:** 72/72. **Course Rating:** 72.6/70.3. **Slope:** 122/120. **Green Fee:** $25/$80. **Cart Fee:** $12/person. **Walking Policy:** Unrestricted walking. **Walkability:** 3. **Opened:** 1997. **Architect:** Pete Dye/P.B. Dye. **Season:** Year-round. **High:** April-Oct. **To obtain tee times:** Call up to a year in advance. **Miscellaneous:** Reduced fees (weekdays, low season, resort guests, twilight, juniors), discount packages, range (grass), club rentals, lodging (1 rooms), credit cards (MC, V).
Reader Comments: Makes great use of Sinepuxent Bay ... Great views, very helpful staff, even the rangers are nice ... The best at the beach, end of story ... Good test of golf ... If you can play in the wind, you can score. If not, you can lose your butt ... Greens are 1st rate ... Must play at least once.

★★★★ SOUTH RIVER GOLF LINKS
PU-3451 Solomon's Island Rd., Edgewater, 21037, Anne Arundel County, (410)798-5865, (800)767-4837, 4 miles S of Annapolis. **E-mail:** bedwards@mdgolf.com. **Web:** mdgolf.com.
Holes: 18. **Yards:** 6,723/4,935. **Par:** 72/72. **Course Rating:** 71.8/66.9. **Slope:** 133/115. **Green Fee:** $30/$65. **Cart Fee:** Included in Green Fee. **Walking Policy:** Unrestricted walking. **Walkability:** 4. **Opened:** 1996. **Architect:** Brian Ault. **Season:** Year-round. **High:** May-Sept. **To obtain tee times:** Call up to 10 days in advance after noon. **Miscellaneous:** Reduced fees (twilight, seniors, juniors), metal spikes, range (mats), club rentals, credit cards (MC, V, AE).
Notes: Ranked 8th in 1999 Best in State.
Reader Comments: Many environmental hazards ... Has long difficult fairways ... Good mix of holes. None are alike .... Challenging, favors long hitters ... Some great tee shots ... Great layout. Lots of wetlands. Always in good condition ... Bring lots of balls.

★★★★ SWAN POINT GOLF YACHT & COUNTRY CLUB *Service*
SP-11550 Swan Point Blvd., Issue, 20645, Charles County, (301)259-0047, 50 miles SE of Washington, DC. **E-mail:** deanbvcfan@aol.com. **Web:** swanpointgc.com.
Holes: 18. **Yards:** 6,761/5,009. **Par:** 72/72. **Course Rating:** 72.5/69.3. **Slope:** 126/116. **Green Fee:** $37/$60. **Cart Fee:** Included in Green Fee. **Walking Policy:** Walking at certain times. **Walkability:** 2. **Opened:** 1990. **Architect:** Arthur Davis/Bob Cupp. **Season:** March-Dec. **High:** June-Sept. **To obtain tee times:** Call up to 7 days in advance with credit card. **Miscellaneous:** Reduced fees (weekdays, low season, twilight, seniors, juniors), discount packages, range (grass/mats), club rentals, credit cards (MC, V), beginner friendly.
Reader Comments: Great course in superb condition ... One of the best in Maryland, in the middle of nowhere ... Great challenging course ... Beautiful course on the water ... Target golf ... The first course I've played where there isn't a bad hole ... Beautiful! watch your ball—the Bermuda rough will gobble it up.

★★★½ THE TIMBERS OF TROY
PU-6100 Marshalee Dr., Elkridge, 21227, Howard County, (410)313-4653, 10 miles S of Baltimore.

Holes: 18. **Yards:** 6,652/4,926. **Par:** 72/72. **Course Rating:** 72.1/68.5. **Slope:** 134/115. **Green Fee:** $23/$37. **Cart Fee:** $12/person. **Walking Policy:** Unrestricted walking. **Walkability:** 3. **Opened:** 1996. **Architect:** Brian Ault/Ken Killian. **Season:** Feb.-Dec. **High:** May-Sept. **To obtain tee times:** Call up to 7 days in advance. **Miscellaneous:** Reduced fees (low season, twilight), range (grass/mats), club rentals, credit cards (MC, V, AE).
Reader Comments: Will be great ... Great layout, target golf ... Great finishing hole ... Not so fast with that driver!

★★½ TROTTERS GLEN GOLF COURSE

PU-16501 Batchellors Forest Rd., Olney, 20832, Montgomery County, (301)570-4951, 15 miles NW of Washington, DC.
Holes: 18. **Yards:** 6,220/4,983. **Par:** 72/72. **Course Rating:** 69.3/68.2. **Slope:** 113/111. **Green Fee:** $17/$29. **Cart Fee:** $13/person. **Walking Policy:** Unrestricted walking. **Walkability:** 1. **Opened:** 1993. **Architect:** Ault, Clark and Assoc. **Season:** Year-round. **High:** June-Aug. **To obtain tee times:** Call Monday 8 a.m. for current week and upcoming weekend. **Miscellaneous:** Reduced fees (weekdays, low season, twilight, seniors, juniors), range (grass/mats), club rentals, lodging, credit cards (MC, V, AE), beginner friendly (junior lessons and junior camp).
Reader Comments: Difficult ... Only a couple interesting holes, shaky maintenance ... Greens very challenging.

TURF VALLEY RESORT

R-2700 Turf Valley Rd., Ellicott City, 21042, Howard County, (410)465-1504, (800)666-8873, 20 miles W of Baltimore. **Web:** www.turfvalley.com.

★★★ EAST COURSE

Holes: 18. **Yards:** 6,554/5,389. **Par:** 71/71. **Course Rating:** 71.1/71.6. **Slope:** 132/131. **Green Fee:** $37/$52. **Cart Fee:** $13/person. **Walking Policy:** Walking at certain times. **Walkability:** 3. **Opened:** 1959. **Architect:** Edmund B. Ault/Al Jamison. **Season:** Year-round. **High:** April-Oct. **To obtain tee times:** In person, 7 days in advance. By phone, 6 days in advance. **Miscellaneous:** Reduced fees (weekdays, low season, resort guests, twilight), discount packages, range (grass/mats), club rentals, lodging (220 rooms), credit cards (MC, V, AE, D).
Reader Comments: Excellent for a hotel course. Service was great, too ...Three courses make it easy to play 18 in 2 1/2 hours. Where else can your do that? ... Great layout, wooded, tight.

★★★ NORTH COURSE

Holes: 18. **Yards:** 6,586/5,466. **Par:** 71/71. **Course Rating:** 71.4/71.8. **Slope:** 126/124. **Green Fee:** $37/$52. **Cart Fee:** $13/person. **Walking Policy:** Walking at certain times. **Walkability:** 3. **Opened:** 1959. **Architect:** Edmund B. Ault/Al Jamison. **Season:** Year-round. **High:** April-Oct. **To obtain tee times:** In person, 7 days in advance. By phone, 6 days in advance. **Miscellaneous:** Reduced fees (weekdays, low season, resort guests, twilight), discount packages, range (grass/mats), club rentals, lodging (220 rooms), credit cards (MC, V, AE, D).
Reader Comments: Nice place to spend the weekend ... Scenic course, wildlife abound.

★★½ SOUTH COURSE

Holes: 18. **Yards:** 6,271/5,469. **Par:** 70/71. **Course Rating:** 70.3/72.3. **Slope:** 131/126. **Green Fee:** $37/$52. **Cart Fee:** $13/person. **Walking Policy:** Walking at certain times. **Walkability:** 3. **Opened:** 1963. **Architect:** Edmund B. Ault. **Season:** Year-round. **High:** April-Oct. **To obtain tee times:** In person, 7 days in advance. By phone, 6 days in advance. **Miscellaneous:** Reduced fees (weekdays, low season, resort guests, twilight), discount packages, range (grass/mats), club rentals, lodging (220 rooms), credit cards (MC, V, AE, D).
Reader Comments: Decent tracks ... Easy layout, easy to walk.

★★½ TWIN SHIELDS GOLF CLUB

PU-2425 Roarty Rd., Dunkirk, 20754, Calvert County, (410)257-7800, 15 miles E of Washington, DC.
Holes: 18. **Yards:** 6,527/5,318. **Par:** 70/70. **Course Rating:** 69.4/67.6. **Slope:** 119/113. **Green Fee:** $23/$30. **Cart Fee:** $24/cart. **Walking Policy:** Walking at certain times. **Walkability:** 4. **Opened:** 1969. **Architect:** Roy Shields/Ray Shields. **Season:** Year-round. **High:** April-Oct. **To obtain tee times:** Weekdays—call 7 days in advance. Weekends—call preceding Monday. **Miscellaneous:** Reduced fees (low season, twilight, seniors, juniors), range (grass/mats), club rentals.
Reader Comments: Above average. Very tight in spots ... Always a pleasure to play.

★★★½ UNIVERSITY OF MARYLAND GOLF COURSE

SP-University Blvd., College Park, 20740, Prince George's County, (301)403-4299, 5 miles E of Washington, DC. **E-mail:** jmaynor@union.umd.edu. **Web:** www.inform.umd.edu/golfcourse.
Holes: 18. **Yards:** 6,654/5,563. **Par:** 71/72. **Course Rating:** 71.6/70.6. **Slope:** 125/111. **Green Fee:** $17/$38. **Cart Fee:** $12/person. **Walking Policy:** Walking at certain times. **Walkability:** 3. **Opened:** 1956. **Architect:** George W. Cobb. **Season:** Year-round. **High:** April-Oct. **To obtain tee times:** Call 5 days in advance. **Miscellaneous:** Reduced fees (weekdays, low season, twilight, seniors, juniors), range (grass/mats), club rentals, credit cards (MC, V, D).

MARYLAND

Reader Comments: Putt these greens, if you can ... Great par 3s ... Fred Funk's training ground ... Challenging but fair ... Great college course, practice facilities, well maintained.

★★★½ WAKEFIELD VALLEY GOLF & CONFERENCE CENTER
SP-1000 Fenby Farm Rd., Westminster, 21158, Carroll County, (410)876-6662, 30 miles NW of Baltimore. **Web:** www.wakefieldvalley.com.
Holes: 27. **Yards:** 6,933/5,549. **Par:** 72/73. **Course Rating:** 74.4/73.3. **Slope:** 139/132. **Green Fee:** $35/$42. **Cart Fee:** Included in Green Fee. **Walking Policy:** Walking at certain times. **Walkability:** 4. **Opened:** 1978. **Architect:** Wayne Weller/Russell Roberts. **Season:** Year-round. **High:** May-Oct. **To obtain tee times:** Call or come in up to 14 days in advance. **Miscellaneous:** Reduced fees (low season, twilight), discount packages, range (grass/mats), club rentals, credit cards (MC, V, D).
Reader Comments: 27 holes, nice course for area ... Good design, slick greens ... Gold is probably toughest, distance again not key, be accurate ... Toughest greens in Maryland.

WAVERLY WOODS GOLF CLUB
PU-2100 Warwick Way, Marriottsville, 21104, Howard County, (410)313-9182, 7 miles W of Baltimore. **Web:** www.waverlywoods.com.
Holes: 18. **Yards:** 7,024/4,808. **Par:** 72/72. **Course Rating:** 73.1/67.8. **Slope:** 132/115. **Green Fee:** $25/$50. **Cart Fee:** $10/person. **Walking Policy:** Unrestricted walking. **Walkability:** 4. **Opened:** 1998. **Architect:** Arthur Hills. **Season:** Year-round. **High:** Apr.-Nov. **To obtain tee times:** Call up to 10 days in advance; walk-on based on availability. **Miscellaneous:** Reduced fees (weekdays, low season, twilight, seniors, juniors), range (grass), club rentals, credit cards (MC, V, AE), beginner friendly (junior golf school/family programs).

★★★ WHITE PLAINS REGIONAL PARK GOLF CLUB
St. Charles Pkwy., White Plains, 20695, Charles County, (301)843-2947.
Special Notes: Call club for further information.

★★½ WICOMICO SHORES MUNICIPAL GOLF COURSE
PM-Rte. 234, 20621 Aviation Yacht & CC Rd., Chaptico, 20621, St. Mary's County, (301)934-8191, 45 miles SE of Washington, DC.
Holes: 18. **Yards:** 6,482/5,460. **Par:** 72/72. **Course Rating:** 70.7/68.3. **Slope:** 120/120. **Green Fee:** $16/$20. **Cart Fee:** $12/person. **Walking Policy:** Unrestricted walking. **Walkability:** 3. **Opened:** 1962. **Architect:** Edmund B. Ault. **Season:** Year-round. **High:** May-Sept. **To obtain tee times:** Call Thursday for upcoming weekend or holiday. **Miscellaneous:** Reduced fees (weekdays, twilight, seniors, juniors), discount packages, metal spikes, range (grass/mats), club rentals, credit cards (MC, V, AE), beginner friendly (large junior program, group beginner lessons).
Reader Comments: Spectacular view from clubhouse ... Narrow fairways, small greens.

THE WOODLANDS GOLF COURSE
PU-2309 Ridge Rd., Woodlawn, 21244, Baltimore County, (410)887-1349, (888)246-5384, 18 miles W of Downtown Baltimore. **Web:** www.baltimoregolfing.com.
Holes: 18. **Yards:** 7,014/5,452. **Par:** 72/72. **Course Rating:** 74.4/66.8. **Slope:** 143/122. **Green Fee:** $25/$59. **Cart Fee:** Included in Green Fee. **Walking Policy:** Unrestricted walking. **Walkability:** 4. **Opened:** 1998. **Architect:** Lindsay Ervin. **Season:** Year-round. **High:** April-Oct. **To obtain tee times:** Call (410)887-GOLF. **Miscellaneous:** Reduced fees (weekdays, low season, twilight, seniors, juniors), discount packages, range (mats), club rentals, credit cards (MC, V, AE, D).
Notes: PGA Super Senior event August,1999.

WORTHINGTON MANOR GOLF CLUB
PU-8329 Fingerboard Rd., Urbana, 21704, Frederick County, (301)874-5400, (888)987-2582, 30 miles N of Washington DC. **E-mail:** comments@worthingtonmanor.com. **Web:** www.worthington-manor.com.
Holes: 18. **Yards:** 7,014/5,206. **Par:** 72/72. **Course Rating:** 74.0/70.1. **Slope:** 143/116. **Green Fee:** $29/$64. **Cart Fee:** $11/person. **Walking Policy:** Walking at certain times. **Walkability:** 4. **Opened:** 1998. **Architect:** Brian Ault/Eric Ault. **Season:** Year-round. **High:** March-Oct. **To obtain tee times:** Tee times accepted two weeks in advance. **Miscellaneous:** Reduced fees (weekdays, low season, twilight, seniors, juniors), range (grass/mats), rentals, credit cards (MC, V, AE).

★★★½ WORTHINGTON VALLEY COUNTRY CLUB *Pace*
SP-12425 Greenspring Ave., Owings Mills, 21117, Baltimore County, (410)356-8355, 12 miles N of Baltimore.
Holes: 18. **Yards:** N/A. **Par:** N/A. **Course Rating:** N/A. **Slope:** N/A. **Green Fee:** $15/$20. **Cart Fee:** $20/cart. **Walking Policy:** Unrestricted walking. **Walkability:** 3. **Opened:** 1954. **Season:** March-Dec. **High:** April-Oct. **To obtain tee times:** Call anytime. **Miscellaneous:** Metal spikes.
Reader Comments: Challenging layout ... Trying hard to rehab it, so far so good. A fun place to play ... Great tight track ... A good mix of short and long par 4s, some beautiful views, and a great finishing hole ... Course is in great shape.

MASSACHUSETTS

ACUSHNET RIVER VALLEY GOLF COURSE
PU-685 Main St., Acushnet, 02743, Bristol County, (508)998-7777, 4 miles E of New Bedford.
Holes: 18. **Yards:** 6,807/5,099. **Par:** 72/72. **Course Rating:** 72.5/68.4. **Slope:** 124/115. **Green Fee:** $28/$35. **Cart Fee:** $14/person. **Walking Policy:** Unrestricted walking. **Walkability:** 2. **Opened:** 1998. **Architect:** Brian Silva. **Season:** April-Nov. **High:** June-Sept. **To obtain tee times:** 7 days in advance. **Miscellaneous:** Reduced fees (weekdays, twilight, juniors), range (mats), club rentals, credit cards (MC, V, AE, D).

★★★ AGAWAM MUNICIPAL GOLF COURSE
PM-128 Southwick, Feeding Hills, 01030, Hamden County, (413)786-2194, 7 miles SW of Springfield.
Holes: 18. **Yards:** 6,119/5,370. **Par:** 71/71. **Course Rating:** 67.0/70.2. **Slope:** 110/110. **Green Fee:** $14/$17. **Cart Fee:** $10/person. **Walking Policy:** Unrestricted walking. **Walkability:** 4. **Opened:** 1927. **Season:** March-Dec. **High:** May-Oct. **To obtain tee times:** Call 3 days in advance. **Miscellaneous:** Reduced fees (twilight, seniors, juniors), beginner friendly
Reader Comments: Big improvements ... A course that improved when purchased by the city ... Good challenge ... Long par 4s ... The greens are small, and the bunkers are everywhere.

AMESBURY GOLF & COUNTRY CLUB
SP-50 Monroe St., Amesbury, 01913, Essex County, (978)388-5153.
Holes: 9. **Yards:** 6,312/5,381. **Par:** 70/70. **Course Rating:** 70.5/71.9. **Slope:** 125/126. **Green Fee:** $25/$27. **Cart Fee:** $24/person. **Walking Policy:** Unrestricted walking. **Walkability:** 3. **Opened:** 1923. **Architect:** Wayne Stiles. **Season:** April-Nov. **High:** June-Aug. **To obtain tee times:** Call up to 5 days in advance. **Miscellaneous:** Club rentals.

★★½ AMHERST GOLF CLUB
SP-365 South Pleasant St., Amherst, 01002, Hampshire County, (413)256-6894, 25 miles N of Springfield.
Holes: 9. **Yards:** 6,083/5,608. **Par:** 70/72. **Course Rating:** 68.6/71.6. **Slope:** 117/122. **Green Fee:** N/A/$25. **Cart Fee:** $20/cart. **Walking Policy:** Unrestricted walking. **Walkability:** 3. **Opened:** 1900. **Architect:** Walter Hatch. **Season:** April-Nov. **High:** May-Sept. **Miscellaneous:** Club rentals, credit cards (MC, V), beginner friendly (lessons by PGA pro).
Reader Comments: Pretty course ... Wear a baseball helmet, great greens ... Challenging 9-holer.

★★★½ ATLANTIC COUNTRY CLUB
PU-450 Little Sandy Pond Rd., Plymouth, 02360, Plymouth County, (508)888-6644, 50 miles S of Boston.
Holes: 18. **Yards:** 6,728/4,918. **Par:** 72/72. **Course Rating:** 71.5/67.4. **Slope:** 130/113. **Green Fee:** $37/$42. **Cart Fee:** $13/person. **Walking Policy:** Unrestricted walking. **Walkability:** 3. **Opened:** 1994. **Architect:** Geoffrey Cornish/Brian Silva/Mark Mungea. **Season:** March-Dec. **High:** June-Aug. **To obtain tee times:** Call 2 days in advance. **Miscellaneous:** Reduced fees (weekdays, low season, twilight), metal spikes, range (grass/mats), club rentals, credit cards (MC, V).
Reader Comments: Long par 3s ... No easy lies ... Good test with irons.... Must keep up ... Best 19th hole grilled chicken sandwich anywhere ... Yardage markers everywhere ... Starts groups on 1 and 10 ... Solid golf experience ... Never too slow, but never rushed ... Forward tees set up well for women.

★★★½ BALLYMEADE COUNTRY CLUB
SP-125 Falmouth Woods Rd., North Falmouth, 02556, Barnstable County, (508)540-4005, 58 miles S of Boston. **E-mail:** jbshaw@aol.com. **Web:** www.ballymeade.com.
Holes: 18. **Yards:** 6,928/5,001. **Par:** 72/72. **Course Rating:** 74.3/68.9. **Slope:** 139/119. **Green Fee:** $40/$75. **Cart Fee:** Included in Green Fee. **Walking Policy:** Mandatory cart. **Walkability:** 5. **Opened:** 1988. **Architect:** Jim Fazio. **Season:** Year-round. **High:** June-Aug. **To obtain tee times:** Call 7 days in advance. **Miscellaneous:** Reduced fees (weekdays, low season, twilight), range (grass), club rentals, credit cards (MC, V, AE, D).
Reader Comments: Beautiful course, conditions and surroundings ... Some tough shots and carries ... First class all the way ... Windy, gimmick holes, leg stretcher ... Course hard for over 15 handicap ... Nice practice area, beautiful clubhouse ... Great views, tight fairways ... Very difficult for average golfer ... Too many blind shots.

★★★½ BASS RIVER GOLF COURSE
PU-Highbank Rd., South Yarmouth, 02664, Barnstable County, (508)398-9079, 90 miles S of Boston.
Holes: 18. **Yards:** 6,129/5,343. **Par:** 72/72. **Course Rating:** 68.5/69.9. **Slope:** 115/115. **Green Fee:** $30/$45. **Cart Fee:** $25/cart. **Walking Policy:** Unrestricted walking. **Walkability:** 1. **Opened:** 1900. **Architect:** P. Sheppard/Donald Ross. **Season:** Year-round. **High:** May-Sept. **To obtain tee times:** Call 4 days in advance. **Miscellaneous:** Reduced fees (low season, twilight), club rentals, credit cards (MC, V).

MASSACHUSETTS

Reader Comments: Nice but short ... Old classic ... Completely different 9s ... A lot of fun to play. Nice views. Links feel on back 9 ... Good confidence booster ... Small greens test shot skills ... Good course for beginners ... Leave driver at home.

★★★½ BAY POINTE COUNTRY CLUB
SP-Onset Ave., Onset Beach, 02558, Plymouth County, (508)759-8802, 30 miles S of Boston.
Holes: 18. **Yards:** 6,301/N/A. **Par:** 70/N/A. **Course Rating:** 69.1/N/A. **Slope:** 118/N/A. **Green Fee:** $19/$40. **Cart Fee:** $15/person. **Walking Policy:** Unrestricted walking. **Walkability:** 3. **Architect:** Geoffrey Cornish. **Season:** Year-round. **To obtain tee times:** Call 4 days in advance. **Miscellaneous:** Club rentals, credit cards (MC, V, AE.D).

★★★½ BAYBERRY HILLS GOLF COURSE
PM-W. Yarmouth Rd., West Yarmouth, 02673, Barnstable County, (508)394-5597, 75 miles S of Boston.
Holes: 18. **Yards:** 7,172/5,323. **Par:** 72/72. **Course Rating:** 74.3/69.7. **Slope:** 127/119. **Green Fee:** $25/$45. **Cart Fee:** $25/cart. **Walking Policy:** Unrestricted walking. **Walkability:** 2. **Opened:** 1987. **Architect:** Brian Silva/Geoffrey S. Cornish. **Season:** April-Nov. **High:** May-Oct. **To obtain tee times:** Call 4 days in advance; earlier reservations require prepayment. **Miscellaneous:** Reduced fees (low season, twilight), range (grass), club rentals, credit cards (MC, V).
Reader Comments: Terrific design ... Good for all skill levels ... Too busy in summer... Tight in spots ... Interesting track; makes you play different shots ... My favorite on the Cape.

BEVERLY GOLF & TENNIS CLUB
SP-134 McKay St., Beverly, 01915, Essex County, (978922-9072. **E-mail:** frielgolf@aol.com. **Web:** NorthofBoston.com.
Holes: 18. **Yards:** 6,237/5,429. **Par:** 70/73. **Course Rating:** 70.6/70.3. **Slope:** 123/113. **Green Fee:** $31/$37. **Cart Fee:** $24/cart. **Walking Policy:** Unrestricted walking. **Walkability:** 3. **Opened:** 1910. **Season:** March-Dec. **High:** May-Sept. **To obtain tee times:** May call 7 days in advance, max 2 times per call. **Miscellaneous:** Reduced fees (twilight), metal spikes, range (grass), club rentals, beginner friendly (beginner recreation clinics and private lessons).

★★★½ BLISSFUL MEADOWS GOLF CLUB
SP-801 Chockalog Rd., Uxbridge, 01569, Worcester County, (508)278-6113, 20 miles SE of Worcester.
Holes: 18. **Yards:** 6,656/5,072. **Par:** 72/72. **Course Rating:** 71.3/69.1. **Slope:** 128/122. **Green Fee:** $28/$38. **Cart Fee:** $12/person. **Walking Policy:** Unrestricted walking. **Walkability:** 3. **Opened:** 1992. **Architect:** Geoffrey Cornish/Brian Silva. **Season:** Year-round. **High:** May-Oct. **To obtain tee times:** Call up to 2 days in advance. **Miscellaneous:** Reduced fees (low season, twilight, seniors), range (grass), club rentals, credit cards (MC, V, AE), beginner friendly (beginner clinics, junior clinics).
Reader Comments: Remote location makes it easier to get times ... Greens are fast ... Backside better layout ... Good par 3s ... Worth the drive ... Front 9 narrow must keep in play, back 9 let it rip ... Hit ball 12 inches off fairway, couldn't find it. Need I say more.

★★★★½ BLUE ROCK GOLF COURSE
PU-48 Todd Rd., South Yarmouth, 02664, Barnstable County, (508)398-9295, (800)237-8887, 70 miles SE of Boston.
Holes: 18. **Yards:** 3,000/2,200. **Par:** 54/54. **Course Rating:** 56.4/55.8. **Slope:** 83/80. **Green Fee:** $29/$33. **Cart Fee:** $4/cart. **Walking Policy:** Unrestricted walking. **Walkability:** 2. **Opened:** 1962. **Architect:** Geoffrey Cornish. **Season:** Year-round. **High:** June-Sept. **To obtain tee times:** Call 7 days in advance with credit card confirmation or 150 days with premium payment. **Miscellaneous:** Reduced fees (twilight), discount packages, metal spikes, range (grass), club rentals, lodging, credit cards (MC, V).
Reader Comments: A perfect 10—service, conditions, atmosphere ... Elevation changes are challenging ... Trust yardage, huge greens, don't 4-putt ... Great beginner's course.

★★★ BRADFORD COUNTRY CLUB
PU-201 Chadwick Rd., Bradford, 01835, Essex County, (978)372-8587, 25 miles N of Boston.
Holes: 18. **Yards:** 6,511/4,939. **Par:** 70/70. **Course Rating:** 72.8/67.8. **Slope:** 141/129. **Green Fee:** $23/$31. **Cart Fee:** $13/person. **Walking Policy:** Unrestricted walking. **Walkability:** 4. **Opened:** 1990. **Architect:** Geoffrey Cornish/Brian Silva. **Season:** April-Dec. **High:** May-Sept. **To obtain tee times:** Call up to 5 days in advance. **Miscellaneous:** Reduced fees (weekdays, low season, twilight, seniors, juniors), discount packages, metal spikes, club rentals, credit cards (MC, V, AE).
Reader Comments: Ball placement important ... Target golf at its best. Back 9 a killer to walk ... Unusual layout. Tricky greens. Great challenge.

★★★½ BRAINTREE MUNICIPAL GOLF COURSE
PU-101 Jefferson St., Braintree, 02184, (781)843-9781.
Special Notes: Call club for further information.

★★½ **BROOKMEADOW COUNTRY CLUB**
PU-100 Everendon Rd., Canton, 02021, Norfolk County, (718)828-4444, 20 miles SW of Boston.
Holes: 18. **Yards:** 6,660/5,690. **Par:** 72/72. **Course Rating:** 71.6/71.2. **Slope:** 123/114. **Green Fee:** $27/$32. **Cart Fee:** $28/cart. **Walking Policy:** Unrestricted walking. **Walkability:** 1.
Opened: 1967. **Architect:** Samuel Mitchell. **Season:** Year-round. **High:** April-Oct. **To obtain tee times:** For weekdays call 5 days in advance. For weekends call 5 days in advance.
Miscellaneous: Reduced fees (low season, twilight, seniors, juniors), metal spikes, range (grass/mats), club rentals, credit cards (MC, V, D).
Reader Comments: Great for practicing ... Very flat ... Lots of play ... Every hole looks the same ... Great for seniors.

BROOKSHIRE INN & GOLF CLUB
PU-205 W. Church, Williamstown, 48895, Berkshire County, (517)655-4694.
Special Notes: Call club for further information.

★★★½ **BROOKSIDE GOLF CLUB** *Pace*
PU-1 Brigadoon St., Bourne, 02532, Plymouth County, (508)743-4653. **Web:** www.golfcapecod.com/brookside.htm.
Holes: 18. **Yards:** 6,300/5,130. **Par:** 70/70. **Course Rating:** 71.1/69.6. **Slope:** 126/118. **Green Fee:** $40/$50. **Cart Fee:** Included in Green Fee. **Walking Policy:** Walking at certain times. **Walkability:** 5. **Opened:** 1997. **Architect:** Michael Hurdzan. **Season:** Year-round. **High:** May-Oct. **To obtain tee times:** Tee times taken 7 days in advance. **Miscellaneous:** Reduced fees (weekdays, low season, twilight, seniors, juniors), range (grass/mats), club rentals, credit cards (MC, V, AE, D).
Reader Comments: Nice views of bay ... Lots of hills, excellent greens ... Lots of blind drives ... Good, friendly course ... New course, rough around edges, but looks promising.

★★★½ **BUTTERNUT FARM GOLF CLUB**
PU-115 Wheeler Rd., Stow, 01775, Middlesex County, (978)897-3400, 22 miles NW of Boston.
E-mail: bfgcgolf@aol.com. **Web:** www.butternutfarm.com.
Holes: 18. **Yards:** 6,205/4,778. **Par:** 70/70. **Course Rating:** 69.9/67.7. **Slope:** 125/117. **Green Fee:** $29/$38. **Cart Fee:** $24/cart. **Walking Policy:** Unrestricted walking. **Walkability:** 1.
Opened: 1993. **Architect:** Robert Page III. **Season:** April-Nov. **High:** May-Oct. **To obtain tee times:** Call (978)897-3400 in advance to schedule tee time. **Miscellaneous:** Reduced fees (seniors), club rentals.
Reader Comments: Keep driver in the bag ... Easy to get on, fun to play ... Great for walking ... Might want to invest in a hard hat ... Elevated greens ... Some gimmicky holes ... Not long, but narrow and testing woods ... Excellent shotmakers course.

★★★½ **CAPE COD COUNTRY CLUB**
PU-Theater Rd., North Falmouth, 02556, Barnstable County, (508)563-9842, 50 miles S of Boston.
Holes: 18. **Yards:** 6,404/5,348. **Par:** 71/72. **Course Rating:** 71.0/70.6. **Slope:** 122/119. **Green Fee:** $35/$42. **Cart Fee:** $24/cart. **Walking Policy:** Unrestricted walking. **Walkability:** 4.
Opened: 1929. **Architect:** Devereux Emmett/Alfred H. Tull. **Season:** Year-round. **High:** March-Oct. **To obtain tee times:** Call Friday for following Friday, Saturday and Sunday. Call 7 days in advance for weekdays. **Miscellaneous:** Reduced fees (weekdays, low season, twilight), metal spikes, club rentals, credit cards (MC, V).
Reader Comments: Cape Cod is flat, but this course isn't ... Gets a lot of use... Much tougher course from back tees ... No. 13 is a delight ... Challenging layout ... Hills, hills, hills.

★★★½ **CAPTAINS GOLF COURSE**
PM-1000 Freeman's Way, Brewster, 02631, Barnstable County, (508)896-1716, 100 miles SE of Boston.
Holes: 36. **Yards:** 6,794/5,388. **Par:** 72/72. **Course Rating:** 72.7/70.5. **Slope:** 130/117. **Green Fee:** $30/$50. **Cart Fee:** $24/cart. **Walking Policy:** Unrestricted walking. **Walkability:** 3.
Opened: 1985. **Architect:** G. Cornish/Brian Silva. **Season:** Year-round. **High:** May-Oct. **To obtain tee times:** Call 2 days prior at 6 p.m. on automated system or prepaid by calling through-out the year with payment by check at least 14 days prior to play date. **Miscellaneous:** Reduced fees (low season, twilight), range (grass), club rentals, credit cards (MC, V).
Notes: Ranked 70th in 1996 America's Top 75 Affordable Courses.
Reader Comments: Always in great condition ... Very busy in season, great layout ... Tee time system makes it very difficult ... Lots of trees ... Just a neat place to play ... Getting on as a single is easy ... No gimmicks ... A Cape Cod favorite ... Nos 12-14 great stretch of holes ... All holes named for sea captains.

★★★ **CHEQUESSETT YACHT & COUNTRY CLUB**
Chequessett Neck Rd., Wellfleet, 02667, Barnstable County, (508)349-3704.
Special Notes: Call club for further information.

MASSACHUSETTS

★★★½ CHICOPEE GOLF CLUB
PU-1290 Burnett Rd., Chicopee, 01020, Hampden County, (413)594-9295, 15 miles W of Springfield.
Holes: 18. **Yards:** 6,742/5,123. **Par:** 71/71. **Course Rating:** 73.0/72.5. **Slope:** 126/115. **Green Fee:** $16/$20. **Cart Fee:** $22/person. **Walking Policy:** Unrestricted walking. **Walkability:** 1. **Opened:** 1964. **Architect:** Geoffrey S. Cornish. **Season:** April-Nov. **High:** May-Aug. **To obtain tee times:** Call golf shop. **Miscellaneous:** Club rentals, credit cards (MC, V, AE).
Reader Comments: Does not over-challenge ... Too many blind shots ... Cargo planes from Airforce base distracting ... Good course, lots of improvement.

COUNTRY CLUB OF GREENFIELD
SP-244 Country Club Rd., Greenfield, 01301, Franklin County, (413)773-7530.
Holes: 18. **Yards:** 6,287/5,444. **Par:** 72/73. **Course Rating:** 69.2/70.6. **Slope:** 117/119. **Green Fee:** $25/$40. **Cart Fee:** $21/cart. **Walking Policy:** Unrestricted walking. **Walkability:** 3. **Opened:** 1896. **Architect:** George Barton. **Season:** April-Nov. **High:** June-Aug. **Miscellaneous:** Reduced fees (weekdays), range (grass), club rentals, credit cards (MC, V).

★★★½ CRANBERRY VALLEY GOLF COURSE
PU-183 Oak St., Harwich, 02645, Barnstable County, (508)430-7560, 85 miles S of Boston.
Holes: 18. **Yards:** 6,745/5,518. **Par:** 72/72. **Course Rating:** 71.9/71.3. **Slope:** 129/115. **Green Fee:** $40/$50. **Cart Fee:** $24/cart. **Walking Policy:** Unrestricted walking. **Walkability:** 2. **Opened:** 1974. **Architect:** Cornish/Robinson. **Season:** Year-round. **High:** March-Nov. **To obtain tee times:** Prepayment by check or cash starting March 1st or 2 days in advance with no prepayment, starting at 8 a.m. **Miscellaneous:** Reduced fees (weekdays, low season, twilight), range (grass/mats), club rentals.
Reader Comments: Walk it and soak it up ... Played in fall, beautiful setting ... A nice workout ... Heavy and slow play ... Tough par fives... Cranberry bogs-love it! ... Too crowded ... I love No. 18.

★★★½ CRANWELL RESORT & GOLF CLUB
R-55 Lee Rd, Lenox, 01240, Berkshire County, (413)637-1364, (800)272-6935. **Web:** www.cranwell.com.
Holes: 18. **Yards:** 6,204/5,271. **Par:** 70/71. **Course Rating:** 70.0/72.4. **Slope:** 125/129. **Green Fee:** $42/$85. **Cart Fee:** Included in Green Fee. **Walking Policy:** Walking at certain times. **Walkability:** 5. **Opened:** 1926. **Architect:** Stiles/Van Kleek. **Season:** April-Nov. **High:** June-Sept. **To obtain tee times:** Call golf shop. **Miscellaneous:** Reduced fees (weekdays, low season, resort guests, twilight), discount packages, range (grass), club rentals, lodging, credit cards (MC, V, AE, D, Diners Club).
Reader Comments: Long walk from greens to tees ... Sweet layout ... Old course, great holes.

★★★★ CRUMPIN-FOX CLUB   *Service*
SP-Parmenter Rd., Bernardston, 01337, Franklin County, (413)648-9101, 30 miles N of Springfield.
Holes: 18. **Yards:** 7,007/5,432. **Par:** 72/72. **Course Rating:** 73.8/71.5. **Slope:** 141/131. **Green Fee:** $59/$59. **Cart Fee:** $14/person. **Walking Policy:** Unrestricted walking. **Walkability:** 4. **Opened:** 1978. **Architect:** Roger Rulewich. **Season:** April-Nov. **High:** June-Oct. **To obtain tee times:** Public call 3 days in advance. Members or golf and dinner packages may book as far in advance as desired. **Miscellaneous:** Reduced fees (resort guests, juniors), discount packages, range (grass), caddies, club rentals, lodging, credit cards (MC, V, AE, D).
Notes: Ranked 12th in 1999 Best in State.
Reader Comments: One of the best layouts anywhere ... Tight fairways, small greens ... Lost a few balls ... Every hole is a challenge ... Go for the dinner package ... No. 8 is one of the best par 5's you will ever play ... Very demanding but fair ... Golf heaven in Autumn ... Par 3s are killers ... Worth finding!.

★★★ CRYSTAL SPRINGS GOLF CLUB
PU-940 N. Broadway, Haverhill, 01830, Essex County, (978)374-9621, 35 miles NE of Boston. **E-mail:** csbigpro@aol.
Holes: 18. **Yards:** 6,706/5,596. **Par:** 72/73. **Course Rating:** 72.0/71.1. **Slope:** 116/112. **Green Fee:** $18/$25. **Cart Fee:** $20/cart. **Walking Policy:** Unrestricted walking. **Walkability:** 3. **Opened:** 1961. **Architect:** Geoffrey S. Cornish. **Season:** March-Nov. **High:** May-Aug. **To obtain tee times:** Call one week in advance—weekends only. **Miscellaneous:** Metal spikes, range (grass/mats).
Reader Comments: Front nine is wet in spring ... Strong par 4's ... Working man's golf course ... Confidence builder.

★★★★ CYPRIAN KEYES GOLF CLUB   *Service*
PU-284 East Temple St., Boylston, 01505, Worcester County, (508)869-9900, 5 miles W of Worcester.
Holes: 18. **Yards:** 6,844/5,079. **Par:** 72/72. **Course Rating:** 72.7/69.2. **Slope:** 132/119. **Green Fee:** $42/$52. **Cart Fee:** $14/person. **Walking Policy:** Unrestricted walking. **Walkability:** 4.

Opened: 1997. **Architect:** Mark Mungeam. **Season:** April-Nov. **High:** May-Sept. **To obtain tee times:** Call 3 days in advance. **Miscellaneous:** Reduced fees (weekdays, twilight, juniors), range (grass/mats), club rentals, credit cards (MC, V, AE, D), beginner friendly (multiple tee area, 9-hole par-3 course, golf school).
Notes: Ranked 10th in 1999 Best in State.
Reader Comments: Target golf at its best ... Outstanding new course ... Tight track ... A thinker's course ... Will be great with time ... What a joy! Shotmaker's paradise ... Country club quality ... Unbelievable hole variations ... Course knowledge helps.
Special Notes: Also has 9-hole par-3 course.

★★ D.W. FIELD GOLF CLUB
PM-331 Oak St., Brockton, 02401, Plymouth County, (508)580-7855.
Holes: 18. **Yards:** 5,972/5,415. **Par:** 70/70. **Course Rating:** 68.4/70.1. **Slope:** 127/111. **Green Fee:** $17/$21. **Cart Fee:** $22/cart. **Walking Policy:** Unrestricted walking. **Walkability:** N/A.
Opened: 1926. **Architect:** Wayne Stiles/John Van Kleek. **Season:** Year-round. **High:** June-Aug.
To obtain tee times: First come, first serve. **Miscellaneous:** Reduced fees (low season, twilight, juniors), metal spikes, club rentals.

★★★½ DENNIS HIGHLANDS GOLF COURSE
PM-825 Old Bass River Rd., Dennis, 02638, Barnstable County, (508)385-9826, 80 miles S of Boston.
Holes: 18. **Yards:** 6,464/4,927. **Par:** 71/71. **Course Rating:** 70.9/67.8. **Slope:** 120/112. **Green Fee:** $35/$45. **Cart Fee:** $24/cart. **Walking Policy:** Unrestricted walking. **Walkability:** 4.
Opened: 1984. **Architect:** Jack Kidwell/Michael Hurdzan. **Season:** Year-round. **High:** April-Nov.
To obtain tee times: Call 4 days in advance or guarantee with prepayment (no refunds) anytime in advance. **Miscellaneous:** Reduced fees (weekdays, low season, twilight), metal spikes, range (grass), club rentals, credit cards (MC, V).
Reader Comments: Toughest greens on cape ... Play it out of season and you will have nice relaxing round ... Easy to 3-putt ... Beautiful rolling hills ... Links feel ... Very accommodating.

★★★½ DENNIS PINES GOLF COURSE
PM-Golf Course Rd., East Dennis, 02641, Barnstable County, (508)385-9826, 80 miles S of Boston.
Holes: 18. **Yards:** 7,029/5,798. **Par:** 72/73. **Course Rating:** 74.2/73.6. **Slope:** 133/126. **Green Fee:** $35/$45. **Cart Fee:** $24/cart. **Walking Policy:** Unrestricted walking. **Walkability:** 2.
Opened: 1964. **Architect:** Henry Mitchell. **Season:** Year-round. **High:** April-Nov. **To obtain tee times:** Call 4 days in advance or guarantee with prepayment (no refund) anytime in advance.
Miscellaneous: Reduced fees (weekdays, low season, twilight), metal spikes, range (mats), club rentals, credit cards (MC, V).
Reader Comments: Great greens ... Tough to get a tee time ... Long, tight, tough, but in good condition ... Tests your skills.

★★½ EAST MOUNTAIN COUNTRY CLUB
PU-1458 E. Mountain Rd., Westfield, 01085, (413)568-1539.
Reader Comments: Too easy, no challenge ... Fun and friendly course ... Fast playing.
Special Notes: Call club for further information.

EASTON COUNTRY CLUB
SP-265 Purchase St., South Easton, 02375, Bristol County, (508)238-2500, 25 miles S of Boston.
Holes: 18. **Yards:** 6,328/5,271. **Par:** 71/72. **Course Rating:** 68.8/70.2. **Slope:** 119/112. **Green Fee:** $23/$35. **Cart Fee:** $22/person. **Walking Policy:** Unrestricted walking. **Walkability:** 4.
Opened: 1961. **Architect:** Sam Mitchell. **Season:** Year-round. **High:** May-Sept. **To obtain tee times:** Call 2 days in advance. **Miscellaneous:** Reduced fees (weekdays, twilight, juniors), range (grass), club rentals, credit cards (MC, V, D).

★★½ EDGEWOOD GOLF COURSE OF SOUTHWICK
SP-161 Sheep Pasture Rd., Southwick, 01077, Hampshire County, (413)569-6826, 15 miles W of Springfield.
Holes: 18. **Yards:** 6,510/5,580. **Par:** 71/71. **Course Rating:** 69.1/71.8. **Slope:** 115/109. **Green Fee:** $16/$20. **Cart Fee:** $22/person. **Walking Policy:** Unrestricted walking. **Walkability:** 3.
Opened: 1963. **Architect:** Geoffrey Cornish. **Season:** March-Nov. **High:** June-Aug.
Miscellaneous: Reduced fees (seniors, juniors), discount packages, metal spikes, range (grass), credit cards (MC, V, AE, D), beginner friendly (women's and junior clinics).
Reader Comments: Short, beats not playing. Great restaurant ... Poor greenskeeping, good lay-out ... Great course for working people who love to play.

ELINWOOD COUNTRY CLUB
SP-1928 Pleasant St., Athol, 01331, Worcester County, (978)249-7460, 37 miles NW of Worcester.

Holes: 18. **Yards:** 6,207/5,737. **Par:** 71/71. **Course Rating:** 70.1/68.8. **Slope:** 123/117. **Green Fee:** $22/$27. **Cart Fee:** $24/cart. **Walking Policy:** Unrestricted walking. **Walkability:** 4. **Opened:** 1929. **Architect:** Donald Ross. **Season:** April-Oct. **High:** June-Aug. **Miscellaneous:** Reduced fees (weekdays), credit cards (MC, V).

★★★ FALMOUTH COUNTRY CLUB

PU-630 Carriage Shop Rd., East Falmouth, 02536, Barnstable County, (508)548-3211, 70 miles S of Boston.
Holes: 27. **Yards:** 6,665/5,551. **Par:** 72/72. **Course Rating:** 70.0/74.0. **Slope:** 118/125. **Green Fee:** $27/$50. **Cart Fee:** $24/person. **Walking Policy:** Unrestricted walking. **Walkability:** 2. **Opened:** 1969. **Architect:** Vinnie Bartlet. **Season:** Year-round. **High:** May-Oct. **Miscellaneous:** Reduced fees (twilight), range (grass/mats), club rentals, credit cards (MC, V, AE), beginner friendly.
Reader Comments: Great walking course, fun to play ... Wide fairways, great greens ... Nothing to write home about ... Flat course ... Needs some challenge to make it interesting.

★★★½ FAR CORNER GOLF CLUB

PU-Main St. and Barker Rd., West Boxford, 01885, Essex County, (978)352-8300.
Holes: 27. **Yards:** N/A. **Par:** N/A. **Course Rating:** N/A. **Slope:** N/A. **Green Fee:** N/A. **Walkability:** N/A. **Opened:** 1995. **Architect:** Geoffrey S. Cornish/William G. Robinson.
Reader Comments: Nice layout, but overplayed ... Tough walk, hilly ... Back 9 very challenging ... Watch out for clubhouse on 15th tee shot.

★★★★½ FARM NECK GOLF CLUB *Service, Condition, Pace*

SP-Farm Neck Way, Oak Bluffs, 02557, Dukes County, (508)693-3057, 90 miles S of Boston.
Holes: 18. **Yards:** 6,807/5,004. **Par:** 72/72. **Course Rating:** 72.1/68.3. **Slope:** 129/120. **Green Fee:** $36/$80. **Cart Fee:** $25/cart. **Walking Policy:** Walking at certain times. **Walkability:** 2. **Opened:** 1979. **Architect:** Cornish/Robinson. **Season:** April-Dec. **High:** July-Aug. **To obtain tee times:** Call 2 days in advance. **Miscellaneous:** Reduced fees (low season, twilight), range (grass/mats), club rentals, credit cards (MC, V, AE), beginner friendly (clinics, junior programs).
Reader Comments: Tough to get on in summer ... WOW! No wonder the president loves this course ... Great ocean views ... Awesome ... Heavy summer play impacts conditions ... Don't miss playing here ... Close to nature–osprey nests, ocean breezes ... Go off season ... Pace is better without secret service ... Clone the management.

★★★½ FERNCROFT COUNTRY CLUB

R-50 Ferncroft Rd., Danvers, 01923, Essex County, (978)777-5614, 15 miles N of Boston.
Holes: 18. **Yards:** 6,601/5,543. **Par:** 72/73. **Course Rating:** 73.2/72.5. **Slope:** 132/128. **Green Fee:** $75/$75. **Cart Fee:** Included in Green Fee. **Walking Policy:** Mandatory cart. **Walkability:** 3. **Opened:** 1970. **Architect:** Robert Trent Jones. **Season:** April-Dec. **High:** May-Oct. **To obtain tee times:** Hotel guests call 2 days prior to play. **Miscellaneous:** Reduced fees (low season), discount packages, range (grass), club rentals, lodging (365 rooms), credit cards (MC, V, AE, D), beginner friendly (9-hole par-3 executive course).
Reader Comments: Too many outings, cart path only ... Tough to get on if you're not a member... You will cry less if you play from the white tees ... Lovely lounge area to relax after... Always a favorite for local players ... Challenging, shotmaker's delight.

★★★★ FOXBOROUGH COUNTRY CLUB

SP-33 Walnut St., Foxboro, 02035, Norfolk County, (508)543-4661, 12 miles NE of Providence, RI.
Holes: 18. **Yards:** 6,725/5,832. **Par:** 72/73. **Course Rating:** 72.2/73.4. **Slope:** 126/122. **Green Fee:** $40/$65. **Cart Fee:** $23/cart. **Walking Policy:** Walking at certain times. **Walkability:** 3. **Opened:** 1955. **Architect:** Geoffrey Cornish. **Season:** May-Nov. **High:** May-Nov. **To obtain tee times:** Call for available public times. **Miscellaneous:** Reduced fees (weekdays), range (grass), club rentals, credit cards (MC, V, AE, D).
Notes: Nike Tour Qualifier, 2000 US Senior Open qualifying site.
Reader Comments: Private club feel, good pace of play, a challenge ... Nice layout ... Scenic woodlands. Great par 3s ... Limited tee times for non-members ... More difficult than rating.

★★ FRANCONIA GOLF COURSE

PM-619 Dwight Rd., Springfield, 01108, Hampden County, (413)734-9334.
Holes: 18. **Yards:** 6,250/5,250. **Par:** 71/71. **Course Rating:** 68.5/68.5. **Slope:** 117/117. **Green Fee:** $15/$17. **Cart Fee:** $21/cart. **Walking Policy:** Mandatory cart. **Walkability:** 3. **Opened:** 1929. **Architect:** Wayne Stiles/John Van Kleek. **Season:** April-Nov. **High:** July-Sept. **Miscellaneous:** Reduced fees (weekdays, twilight, seniors, juniors), discount packages.

★★★½ GARDNER MUNICIPAL GOLF COURSE

PM-152 Eaton St., Gardner, 01440, Worcester County, (978)632-9703, 20 miles N of Worcester.
Holes: 18. **Yards:** 6,106/5,653. **Par:** 71/75. **Course Rating:** 68.9/72.2. **Slope:** 124/123. **Green Fee:** $15/$30. **Cart Fee:** $22/cart. **Walking Policy:** Unrestricted walking. **Walkability:** 3.

MASSACHUSETTS

Opened: 1936. **Architect:** Samuel Mitchell. **Season:** April-First snow. **High:** June-Sept. **To obtain tee times:** Call 2 days in advance. Thursday for Saturday and Friday for Sunday. **Miscellaneous:** Reduced fees (weekdays, twilight, juniors), range (grass/mats), club rentals, beginner friendly (clinics and programs for beginners).
Reader Comments: Pleasant scenic walk ... Easy front nine, tough back nine ... Nice but busy.

★★★★ GEORGE WRIGHT GOLF COURSE *Value*
PU-420 W. St., Hyde Park, 02136, Suffolk County, (617)361-8313, 5 miles S of Boston.
Holes: 18. **Yards:** 6,400/5,500. **Par:** 70/70. **Course Rating:** 69.5/70.3. **Slope:** 126/115. **Green Fee:** $21/$27. **Cart Fee:** $24/person. **Walking Policy:** Unrestricted walking. **Walkability:** 3.
Opened: 1938. **Architect:** Donald Ross. **Season:** Year-round. **High:** June-Aug. **To obtain tee times:** Call on Thursday after 11:00 a.m.for upcoming weekend. **Miscellaneous:** Reduced fees (juniors), metal spikes, club rentals, credit cards (MC, V).
Reader Comments: A classic course ... Great design, lots of elevation changes and blind shots. Check it out ... Lots of fun. Long and challenging ... Every tee shot makes you think ... Very tough to score here.

★★½ GLEN ELLEN COUNTRY CLUB
PU-84 Orchard St., Millis, 02054, Norfolk County, (508)376-2775, 25 miles SW of Boston. **E-mail:** www.cjhgolf.com. **Web:** www.cjhgolf.com.
Holes: 18. **Yards:** 6,592/5,123. **Par:** 72/72. **Course Rating:** 71.8/69.2. **Slope:** 123/121. **Green Fee:** $23/$34. **Cart Fee:** $26/cart. **Walking Policy:** Walking at certain times. **Walkability:** 2.
Opened: 1962. **Season:** Feb.-Dec. **High:** June-Aug. **To obtain tee times:** Tee times can be made 7 days in advance for 2 or more players by calling the Pro-Shop at (508)376-2775 x8.
Miscellaneous: Reduced fees (twilight, seniors), range (grass), rentals, credit cards (MC, V, AE).
Reader Comments: Great greens, wide open ... Too many geese ... Good course layout.

GRANDVIEW COUNTRY CLUB
SP-454 Wachusett St., Leominster, 01453, Worcester County, (978)537-0614.
Holes: 18. **Yards:** 6,746/6,264. **Par:** 72/74. **Course Rating:** 68.8/68.8. **Slope:** 113/113. **Green Fee:** $21/$24. **Cart Fee:** $23/cart. **Walking Policy:** Unrestricted walking. **Walkability:** 3.
Opened: 1961. **Architect:** Eddie Vachon. **Season:** April-Nov. **High:** June-Aug. **To obtain tee times:** Call 5 days ahead. **Miscellaneous:** Reduced fees (twilight), club rentals.

★★★ GREEN HARBOR GOLF CLUB
PU-624 Webster St., Marshfield, 02050, Plymouth County, (781)834-7303, 30 miles S of Boston.
Holes: 18. **Yards:** 6,211/5,355. **Par:** 71/71. **Course Rating:** 69.1/69.3. **Slope:** 115/109. **Green Fee:** $27/$30. **Walking Policy:** Unrestricted walking. **Walkability:** 1. **Opened:** 1971. **Architect:** Manuel Francis. **Season:** March-Dec. **High:** March-Dec. **To obtain tee times:** Call 2 days prior at 6 a.m. for 18 holes; day of play at 6 a.m. for 9 holes. **Miscellaneous:** Reduced fees (twilight), metal spikes, club rentals.
Reader Comments: This course has really improved in last 3 years ... No motorized carts ... Challenging ... Wide open all around ... Very forgiving ... Easy from front tees, good test from back. Flat and fun to walk ... Nice rangers and starters.

GREEN HILL GOLF CLUB
PU-1 Marsh Ave., Worcester, 01605, Worcester County, (508)799-1359.
Holes: 18. **Yards:** 6,487/5,547. **Par:** 72/71. **Course Rating:** 70.4/69.9. **Slope:** 122/116. **Green Fee:** $20/$25. **Cart Fee:** $24/cart. **Walking Policy:** Unrestricted walking. **Walkability:** 4.
Opened: 1929. **Season:** April-Dec. **High:** April-Dec. **Miscellaneous:** Reduced fees (twilight, juniors), discount packages, club rentals, credit cards (MC, V), beginner friendly (free junior golf programs).

★★★½ HAMPDEN COUNTRY CLUB
PU-128 Wilbraham Rd., Hampden, 01036, Hampden County, (413)566-8010.
Holes: 18. **Yards:** 6,833/5,283. **Par:** 72/72. **Course Rating:** 72.5/72.3. **Slope:** 129/113. **Green Fee:** $25/$34. **Cart Fee:** $12/person. **Walking Policy:** Unrestricted walking. **Walkability:** 5.
Opened: 1975. **Season:** March-Dec. **High:** June-Sept. **To obtain tee times:** Call 7 days in advance. **Miscellaneous:** Reduced fees (weekdays, twilight), metal spikes, range (grass), club rentals, credit cards (MC, V).
Reader Comments: Good bailout areas ... Hilly start, hilly finish, forgiving in middle ... Very scenic during the fall ... Can't wait to play it again.

★★ HEATHER HILL COUNTRY CLUB
PU-149 W. Bacon St., Plainville, 02762, Norfolk County, (508)695-0309.
Special Notes: Call club for further information.

★★★ HERITAGE COUNTRY CLUB
SP-Sampson Rd., Charlton, 01507, (508)248-3591.
Special Notes: Call club for further information.

★★★½ HICKORY HILLS GOLF CLUB
PU-200 North Lowell, Methuen, 01844, Essex County, (978)686-0822, 4 miles W of Lawrence.
Holes: 18. **Yards:** 6,276/5,397. **Par:** 71/73. **Course Rating:** 69.2/73.2. **Slope:** 122/127. **Green Fee:** $34/$38. **Cart Fee:** $24/cart. **Walking Policy:** Unrestricted walking. **Walkability:** 3.
Opened: 1968. **Architect:** Manuel Francis. **Season:** April-Nov. **High:** June-Aug. **To obtain tee times:** Call Tuesday morning for Thursday, Friday, Saturday and Sunday times. **Miscellaneous:** Reduced fees (weekdays, twilight), range (grass), credit cards (MC, V).
Reader Comments: Nice clubhouse ... Family feel ... Interesting variety of holes ... Tight, tough back 9 ... Friendly club, great bar ... 9s like 2 different courses.

★★★★ HICKORY RIDGE COUNTRY CLUB
SP-191 W. Pomeroy Lane, Amherst, 01002, Hampshire County, (413)253-9320.
Holes: 18. **Yards:** 6,794/5,340. **Par:** 72/72. **Course Rating:** 72.5/70.3. **Slope:** 129/114. **Green Fee:** $40/$50. **Cart Fee:** $25/cart. **Walking Policy:** Unrestricted walking. **Walkability:** 2.
Opened: 1970. **Architect:** Geoffrey Cornish/William Robinson. **Season:** April-Nov. **High:** May-Sept. **To obtain tee times:** Outside play call 1 day in advance. **Miscellaneous:** Reduced fees (weekdays, juniors), range (grass/mats), club rentals, credit cards (MC, V, AE).
Reader Comments: 18th hole is a beauty ... Very good layout ... Great finishing hole ... Water on 7 holes, but still forgiving ...Draws you back ... Sometimes very wet ... Keep tee shot below hole on No. 8 ... Good food.

★★★½ HIGHLAND GOLF LINKS
PU-Lighthouse Road, P.O. Box 162, North Truro, 02652, Barnstable County, (508)487-9201, 45 miles N of Hyannis.
Holes: 9. **Yards:** 5,299/4,782. **Par:** 70/74. **Course Rating:** 65.0/67.4. **Slope:** 103/107. **Green Fee:** N/A/$30. **Cart Fee:** $21/cart. **Walking Policy:** Unrestricted walking. **Walkability:** 3.
Opened: 1892. **Architect:** Isiah Small. **Season:** April-Oct. **High:** June-Sept. **To obtain tee times:** Call 2 days in advance.
. **Miscellaneous:** Reduced fees (low season), metal spikes, club rentals, credit cards (MC, V).
Reader Comments: 150-foot cliff to Atlantic ocean ... Most beautiful views on Cape Cod ... Fun on windy days ... Historic old course ... Like being in Scotland ... A real natural old style links ... Yes, there is a Scotland without the airfare ... The lighthouse and the scenery only improve the ambiance ... Like a trip back in time.

HILLCREST COUNTRY CLUB
SP-325 Pleasant St., Leicester, 01524, (508)892-9822.
Special Notes: Call club for further information.

HILLSIDE COUNTRY CLUB
SP-82 Hillside Ave., Rehoboth, 02769, Bristol County, (508)252-9761, 8 miles E of Providence.
Holes: 18. **Yards:** 5,820/4,860. **Par:** 71/72. **Course Rating:** 69.5/72.8. **Slope:** 126/124. **Green Fee:** $20/$25. **Cart Fee:** $11/person. **Walking Policy:** Unrestricted walking. **Walkability:** 4.
Opened: 1999. **Architect:** George Cardono. **Season:** Year-round. **High:** April-Oct. **To obtain tee times:** Call up to 7 days in advance. **Miscellaneous:** Reduced fees (weekdays, seniors, juniors), discount packages, metal spikes, club rentals, credit cards (MC, V, D).

HOLDEN HILLS COUNTRY CLUB
PU-1800 Main St., Jefferson, 01522, Worcester County, (508)829-3129, 10 miles N of Worcester.
Holes: 18. **Yards:** 6,022/5,241. **Par:** 71/74. **Course Rating:** 71.9/70.0. **Slope:** 125/115. **Green Fee:** $22/$27. **Cart Fee:** $13/person. **Walking Policy:** Unrestricted walking. **Walkability:** 4.
Opened: 1957. **Season:** April-Dec. **High:** June-Sept. **To obtain tee times:** Call 1 day in advance for weekdays. Call 5 days in advance for weekend. **Miscellaneous:** Reduced fees (weekdays, twilight, seniors, juniors), club rentals, credit cards (MC, V).

★★★½ HOLLY RIDGE GOLF CLUB
PU-Country Club Rd., South Sandwich, 02563, Barnstable County, (508)428-5577. **Web:** www.hollyridgegolf.com.
Holes: 18. **Yards:** 2,952/2,194. **Par:** 54/54. **Course Rating:** N/A. **Slope:** N/A. **Green Fee:** $16/$25. **Cart Fee:** $8/person. **Walking Policy:** Unrestricted walking. **Walkability:** 2. **Opened:** 1966. **Architect:** Geoffrey Cornish. **Season:** Year-round. **High:** June-Aug. **To obtain tee times:** Call up to 7 days in advance. **Miscellaneous:** Reduced fees (weekdays, low season, twilight, seniors, juniors), metal spikes, range (mats), club rentals, credit cards (MC, V, AE), beginner friendly (free saturday clinics and new golfer program).
Reader Comments: Family golf at it's best ... Ideal par 3's ... Beautiful greens, awesome scenery ... Excellent short course through forest ... A fun course ... Great beginner track.

HOLYOKE COUNTRY CLUB
SP-Smiths Ferry Rd., Holyoke, 01040, Hampden County, (413)534-1933.

MASSACHUSETTS

Holes: 9. **Yards:** 6,309/5,411. **Par:** 72/74. **Course Rating:** 69.0/69.6. **Slope:** 118/120. **Green Fee:** $20/$20. **Cart Fee:** $12/person. **Walking Policy:** Unrestricted walking. **Walkability:** 4. **Opened:** 1906. **Season:** April-Nov. **High:** June-Aug. **To obtain tee times:** Call the golf shop. **Miscellaneous:** Club rentals, credit cards (MC, V, D).

HOPE DALE COUNTRY CLUB
SP-Mill St., Hopedale, 01747, (508)473-9876.
Special Notes: Call club for further information.

★★★½ HYANNIS GOLF CLUB AT IYANOUGH HILLS
PU-Rte. 132, Hyannis, 02601, Barnstable County, (508)362-2606, 1 miles N of Hyannis. **Web:** golfcapecod.com.
Holes: 18. **Yards:** 6,711/5,149. **Par:** 71/72. **Course Rating:** 69.4/69.0. **Slope:** 121/125. **Green Fee:** $35/$55. **Cart Fee:** $15/person. **Walking Policy:** Unrestricted walking. **Walkability:** 3. **Opened:** 1976. **Architect:** Geoffrey Cornish/William Robinson. **Season:** Year-round. **High:** May-Sept. **To obtain tee times:** Call golf shop. Call up to 1 year in advance. **Miscellaneous:** Reduced fees (weekdays, low season, twilight, seniors), discount packages, range (grass/mats), club rentals, credit cards (MC, V, AE, D), beginner friendly (player development tees, short course).
Reader Comments: Too much play! ... Greens are fast and undulating, probably the toughest on the Cape ... Better than it used to be ... Many sidehill lies ... Much improved ... Back nine harder than front ... Fine old course, good variety ... Fun course especially in the winter.

JUNIPER HILL GOLF COURSE
PU-202 Brigham St., Northborough, 01532, Worcester County, (508)393-2444, 15 miles E of Worcester. **E-mail:** juniper@MA.ultranet.com.
★★★½ LAKESIDE COURSE
Holes: 18. **Yards:** 6,140/4,707. **Par:** 71/71. **Course Rating:** 69.9/65.3. **Slope:** 127/102. **Green Fee:** $30/$35. **Cart Fee:** $24/cart. **Walking Policy:** Walking at certain times. **Walkability:** 3. **Opened:** 1991. **Architect:** Homer Darling/Philip Wogan. **Season:** April-Dec. **High:** May-Sept. **To obtain tee times:** Call 7 days in advance. **Miscellaneous:** Reduced fees (seniors, juniors), range (grass), club rentals, credit cards (MC, V).
Reader Comments: Uses natural terrain effectively ... Narrow fairways & tough shots ... A challenging course, with friendly people ... Target golf ... Delightful, good walking course ... Require carts on paths.
★★★½ RIVERSIDE COURSE
Holes: 18. **Yards:** 6,306/5,373. **Par:** 71/71. **Course Rating:** 70.4/70.2. **Slope:** 123/117. **Green Fee:** $30/$35. **Cart Fee:** $24/cart. **Walking Policy:** Walking at certain times. **Walkability:** 3. **Opened:** 1931. **Architect:** Homer Darling/Geoff Cornish. **Season:** April-Dec. **High:** May-Sept. **To obtain tee times:** Call 7 days in advance. **Miscellaneous:** Reduced fees (seniors, juniors), range (grass), club rentals, credit cards (MC, V).
Reader Comments: Very forgiving golf course ... Fun test, used every club in bag ... Best par 3's in central Mass. ... Greens too small ... Wide open fairways ... 8 to10 strokes easier than Lakeside ... Clubhouse very old. Parking is tough ... Too many frost delays in fall.

★★★½ KINGS WAY GOLF CLUB
SP-Rte. 6-A, Yarmouth Port, 02675, Barnstable County, (508)362-8870.
Holes: 18. **Yards:** 3,953/2,937. **Par:** 59/59. **Course Rating:** 60.5/55.8. **Slope:** 95/85. **Green Fee:** $35/$34. **Cart Fee:** Included in Green Fee. **Walking Policy:** Mandatory cart. **Walkability:** 3. **Opened:** 1988. **Season:** April-Nov. **High:** July-Sept. **Miscellaneous:** Reduced fees (low season, twilight), club rentals, credit cards (MC, V), beginner friendly.
Reader Comments: Executive course very tough ... My wife likes the 'nine & dine' ... Nice course but too much bucks for the hype ... Not an easy par 3 ... What a gem ... Good to tune the irons ... Exceeds expectations for an exec. course ... Beautiful scenery.

★★★ LAKEVILLE COUNTRY CLUB
PU-44 Clear Pond Rd., Lakeville, 02347, Plymouth County, (508)947-6630, 50 miles S of Boston.
Holes: 18. **Yards:** 6,274/5,297. **Par:** 72/72. **Course Rating:** 70.1/68.5. **Slope:** 123/118. **Green Fee:** $25/$30. **Cart Fee:** $20/cart. **Walking Policy:** Unrestricted walking. **Walkability:** 2. **Opened:** 1970. **Season:** Year-round. **High:** May-Sept. **To obtain tee times:** Call 7 days ahead with a major credit card. Foursomes only on weekends and holidays during the morning. **Miscellaneous:** Credit cards (MC, V, D).
Reader Comments: Huge greens ... Can get very wet ... Winter play makes it tough for spring ... 16th and 17th island greens make the course, nice river views ... Great beginners course ... Nice variety, some narrow fairways ... Fun course, few holes close together ... Pleasant surprise.

★★★½ LARRY GANNON GOLF CLUB
PM-60 Great Woods Rd., Lynn, 01904, Essex County, (781)592-8238, 15 miles N of Boston.

Holes: 18. **Yards:** 6,106/5,215. **Par:** 70/71. **Course Rating:** 69.9/68.8. **Slope:** 118/115. **Green Fee:** $22/$30. **Cart Fee:** $24/cart. **Walking Policy:** Unrestricted walking. **Walkability:** 5. **Opened:** 1932. **Architect:** Wayne Stiles. **Season:** March-Dec. **High:** June-Aug. **To obtain tee times:** First come, first serve except for weekends. **Miscellaneous:** Reduced fees (low season, seniors), club rentals (pro runs jr. programs).
Reader Comments: Excellent test of golf ... Course rating is too low ... Great vistas. Hard to believe severity of slope on many greens! ... Many blind shots and some pin positions are almost unfair ... A total surprise 10 miles from Boston ... Small fast greens ... Hard to get tee time.

★★ LEO J. MARTIN MEMORIAL GOLF COURSE
PU-190 Park Rd., Weston, 02193, (781)894-4903.
Special Notes: Call club for further information.

★★★ LITTLE HARBOR COUNTRY CLUB
PU-Little Harbor Rd., Wareham, 02571, Plymouth County, (508)295-2617, (800)649-2617, 15 miles NE of New Bedford.
Holes: 18. **Yards:** 3,038/2,692. **Par:** 56/56. **Course Rating:** 54.4/51.9. **Slope:** 79/72. **Green Fee:** $15/$20. **Cart Fee:** $18/cart. **Walking Policy:** Unrestricted walking. **Walkability:** 2. **Opened:** 1963. **Season:** Year-round. **High:** July-Aug. **To obtain tee times:** Call up to 3 days in advance. **Miscellaneous:** Reduced fees (weekdays, low season, twilight, seniors, juniors), metal spikes, credit cards (MC, V).
Reader Comments: Hit it straight or don't go here ... Great course to tune up short game ... Limited food ... Best par 3 exec. I have ever played, matched with service.

★★★ MAPLEGATE COUNTRY CLUB
PU-160 Maple St., Bellingham, 02019, Norfolk County, (508)966-4040, 25 miles SW of Boston. **E-mail:** maplegate@ncounty.net. **Web:** www.maplegate.com.
Holes: 18. **Yards:** 6,815/4,852. **Par:** 72/72. **Course Rating:** 74.2/70.2. **Slope:** 133/124. **Green Fee:** $26/$46. **Cart Fee:** $14/person. **Walking Policy:** Walking at certain times. **Walkability:** 2. **Opened:** 1990. **Architect:** Phil Wogan. **Season:** March-Dec. **High:** June-Aug. **To obtain tee times:** Call 6 days in advance, reserve w/credit card. **Miscellaneous:** Reduced fees (weekdays, low season, twilight, juniors), range (grass/mats), club rentals, credit cards (MC, V), beginner friendly (various clinics; dave pelz golf school).
Reader Comments: Difficult & long, fast greens, blind shots ... Scenic; forced to lay up too often ... Tough to get a tee time ... Target course ... Rangers tough ... Tough front 9 with long par 4s ... No clubhouse but nice design.

★★ MERRIMACK GOLF CLUB
SP-210 Howe St., Methuen, 01844, Essex County, (508)683-7771.
Holes: 18. **Yards:** 6,220/5,151. **Par:** 71/72. **Course Rating:** 69.3/72.3. **Slope:** 120/116. **Green Fee:** $18/$28. **Cart Fee:** $24/cart. **Walking Policy:** Unrestricted walking. **Walkability:** 3. **Opened:** 1910. **Architect:** Donald Ross. **Season:** Year-round. **High:** April-Oct. **To obtain tee times:** Call 5 days in advance. **Miscellaneous:** Reduced fees (low season, seniors, juniors).

★½ MIACOMET GOLF CLUB
PU-12 Miacomet Rd., Nantucket, 01908, Nantucket County, (508)325-0333, 25 miles SE of Hyannis.
Holes: 9. **Yards:** 3,337/3,002. **Par:** 37/38. **Course Rating:** 71.2/76.2. **Slope:** 118/118. **Green Fee:** $45/$45. **Cart Fee:** $30/cart. **Walking Policy:** Unrestricted walking. **Walkability:** 2. **Opened:** 1988. **Architect:** Ralph Marble. **Season:** Year-round. **High:** July-Aug. **To obtain tee times:** Call up to 4 days in advance. **Miscellaneous:** Range (mats), club rentals, credit cards (MC, V, AE, D).

★★ MINK MEADOWS GOLF CLUB
SP-320 Golf Club Rd., Vineyard Haven, 02658, Dukes County, (508)693-0600, 80 miles S of Boston.
Holes: 9. **Yards:** 6,091/5,569. **Par:** 71/71. **Course Rating:** 69.6/71.7. **Slope:** 125/123. **Green Fee:** $26/$55. **Cart Fee:** $26/cart. **Walking Policy:** Unrestricted walking. **Walkability:** 2. **Opened:** 1936. **Architect:** Wayne Stiles/Ron Prichard. **Season:** Year-round. **High:** May-Sept. **To obtain tee times:** Call up to 2 days in advance. **Miscellaneous:** Range (grass), club rentals, credit cards (MC, V).

MONOOSOCK COUNTRY CLUB
SP-Monoosock Ave., Leominster, 01453, Worcester County, (978)534-9738, 15 miles N of Worcester. **E-mail:** mcc@bicnet.net.
Holes: 9. **Yards:** N/A. **Par:** N/A. **Course Rating:** N/A. **Slope:** N/A. **Green Fee:** $18/$20. **Cart Fee:** $11/person. **Walking Policy:** Unrestricted walking. **Walkability:** 2. **Opened:** 1949. **Season:** April-Nov. **High:** May-Aug. **To obtain tee times:** Call golf shop or come in. **Miscellaneous:** Reduced fees (low season), range (grass).

NEW BEDFORD MUNICIPAL GOLF COURSE
PM-581 Hathaway Rd., New Bedford, 02740, (508)996-9393.
Special Notes: Call club for further information.

★★★★ **NEW ENGLAND COUNTRY CLUB**
PU-180 Paine St., Bellingham, 02019, Norfolk County, (508)883-2300, 35 miles S of Boston.
Holes: 18. **Yards:** 6,430/4,908. **Par:** 71/71. **Course Rating:** 70.8/68.7. **Slope:** 130/121. **Green Fee:** $42/$63. **Cart Fee:** Included in Green Fee. **Walking Policy:** Walking at certain times. **Walkability:** 4. **Opened:** 1990. **Architect:** Hale Irwin. **Season:** April-Nov. **High:** June-Sept. **To obtain tee times:** Call golf shop up to 5 days in advance. **Miscellaneous:** Reduced fees (weekdays, low season, twilight), discount packages, range (grass), club rentals, credit cards (MC, V). **Reader Comments:** Tough course, target golf, leave the driver at home ... They really keep you moving ... Course is a tough one ... Fast greens ... Blind shots to greens ... Very narrow ... GPS system a great help ... Potential for greatness.

NEW SEABURY COUNTRY CLUB
SP-Shore Drive West, Mashpee, 02649, Barnstable County, (508)477-9110, 15 miles W of Hyannis. **Web:** www.newseabury.com.
★★★★ **BLUE COURSE**
Holes: 18. **Yards:** 7,200/5,764. **Par:** 72/72. **Course Rating:** 75.3/73.8. **Slope:** 130/128. **Green Fee:** $56/$150. **Cart Fee:** Included in Green Fee. **Walking Policy:** Mandatory cart. **Walkability:** 4. **Opened:** 1962. **Architect:** William Mitchell. **Season:** Year-round. **High:** June-Sept. **To obtain tee times:** Members 7 days in advance; resort guests 4 days in advance; public 3 days in advance w/credit card. **Miscellaneous:** Reduced fees (low season), range (grass/mats), club rentals, lodging (100 rooms), credit cards (MC, V, AE).
Notes: Ranked 5th in 1999 Best in State.
Reader Comments: Excellent ... Nantucket Sound views super ... Beautiful holes along water, pray the wind doesn't blow! ... Best on Cape Cod ... Better than expected, beautiful setting ... Tough walking ... Wildlife galore ... Friendliest starter in the world ... Front and back like two different courses ... Nightlife great for stay and play.
★★★½ **GREEN COURSE**
Holes: 18. **Yards:** 6,035/4,827. **Par:** 70/70. **Course Rating:** 69.0/67.6. **Slope:** 120/112. **Green Fee:** $46/$90. **Cart Fee:** Included in Green Fee. **Walking Policy:** Mandatory cart. **Walkability:** 3. **Opened:** 1962. **Architect:** William Mitchell. **Season:** Year-round. **High:** June-Sept. **To obtain tee times:** Members 7 days in advance; resort guests 4 days in advance; public 3 days in advance w/credit card. **Miscellaneous:** Reduced fees (low season), range (grass/mats), club rentals, lodging (100 rooms), credit cards (MC, V, AE).
Reader Comments: Easier of the two courses ... Winds through forest, beautiful ... Good scoring course ... Very good for ladies and seniors ... Nice complement to Blue ... Short course, accuracy counts.

★★ **NEWTON COMMONWEALTH GOLF COURSE**
PU-212 Kenrick St, Newton, 02158, Middlesex County, (617)630-1971, 5 miles W of Boston.
Holes: 18. **Yards:** 5,313/4,466. **Par:** 70/70. **Course Rating:** 67.0/69.4. **Slope:** 125/118. **Green Fee:** $21/$28. **Cart Fee:** $23/cart. **Walking Policy:** Unrestricted walking. **Walkability:** 4. **Opened:** 1897. **Architect:** Donald Ross. **Season:** Year-round. **High:** May-Sept. **To obtain tee times:** Call up to 4 days in advance. **Miscellaneous:** Reduced fees (weekdays, twilight, seniors, juniors), club rentals, credit cards (MC, V, AE), beginner friendly (group lessons, league).

NICHOLS COLLEGE GOLF COURSE
SP-80 Airport Rd., Dudley, 01571, Worcester County, (508)943-4538, 20 miles S of Worcester.
Holes: 9. **Yards:** 3,241/2,848. **Par:** 36/36. **Course Rating:** 71.4/71.3. **Slope:** 123/115. **Green Fee:** $23/$23. **Cart Fee:** $15/cart. **Walking Policy:** Unrestricted walking. **Walkability:** 2. **Opened:** 1926. **Season:** April-Dec. **High:** June-Aug. **To obtain tee times:** Call Thursday @ I:00 p.m. for Saturday. Call Friday @ 1:00 p.m. for Sunday. **Miscellaneous:** Reduced fees (juniors), credit cards (MC, V).

NORTH HILL COUNTRY CLUB
PU-Merry Ave., Duxbury, 02332, (617)934-5800.
Special Notes: Call club for further information.

★★★½ **NORTON COUNTRY CLUB**
SP-188 Oak St., Norton, 02766, (508)285-2400.
Special Notes: Call club for further information.

★½ **NORWOOD COUNTRY CLUB**
PU-400 Providence Hwy., Norwood, 02062, Norfolk County, (781)769-5880, 15 miles SW of Boston. **E-mail:** info@norwoodgolf.com. **Web:** www.norwoodgolf.com.
Holes: 18. **Yards:** 6,009/4,997. **Par:** 71/71. **Course Rating:** 67.1/68.7. **Slope:** 112/108. **Green Fee:** $20/$25. **Cart Fee:** $24/cart. **Walking Policy:** Unrestricted walking. **Walkability:** 1.

MASSACHUSETTS

Opened: 1974. **Architect:** Samuel Mitchell. **Season:** Year-round. **High:** Apr.-Oct. **To obtain tee times:** Call up to 7 days in advance. **Miscellaneous:** Reduced fees (weekdays, twilight, seniors), metal spikes, range (mats), club rentals, credit cards (MC, V, AE, D), beginner friendly (prefer soft spikes).
Special Notes: No 9-hole play on weekends (Fri.-Sun.) or holidays.

★★★★ OAK RIDGE GOLF CLUB
PU-850 S. Westfield St., Feeding Hills, 01030, Hampden County, (413)789-7307, 10 miles NW of Springfield.
Holes: 18. **Yards:** 6,819/5,307. **Par:** 70/70. **Course Rating:** 71.2/70.0. **Slope:** 124/124. **Green Fee:** $22/$33. **Cart Fee:** $14/person. **Walking Policy:** Unrestricted walking. **Walkability:** 2. **Opened:** 1974. **Architect:** George Fazio/Tom Fazio. **Season:** March-Dec. **High:** April-Oct. **To obtain tee times:** Call 7 days in advance for weekday and Wednesdays for weekend play. **Miscellaneous:** Reduced fees (weekdays, low season, seniors, juniors), metal spikes, club rentals.
Reader Comments: One of the best public courses in MA ... Nice course, good finishing holes, enjoyable ... Tough course ... Staff tries hard to please ... Fun course ... Good water holes. I always enjoy this course ... Hosts too many tournaments ... Good test from back tees.

★★★½ OCEAN EDGE GOLF CLUB
R-832 Villages Dr., Brewster, 02631, Barnstable County, (508)896-5911, (800)343-6074, 90 miles S of Boston. **E-mail:** oceanedge@oceanedge.
Holes: 18. **Yards:** 6,665/5,098. **Par:** 72/72. **Course Rating:** 71.9/70.6. **Slope:** 129/123. **Green Fee:** $44/$64. **Cart Fee:** $15/person. **Walking Policy:** Walking at certain times. **Walkability:** 5. **Opened:** 1986. **Architect:** Geoffrey S. Cornish/Brian M. Silva. **Season:** Year-round. **High:** June-Sept. **To obtain tee times:** Hotel guests may make tee times at time of room reservation. Public may make tee times 1 week in advance for Monday-Thursday and 48 hours in advance for Friday, Saturday, Sunday and holidays. **Miscellaneous:** Reduced fees (weekdays, low season, resort guests, juniors), discount packages, range (grass), club rentals, lodging (320 rooms), credit cards (MC, V, AE).
Reader Comments: Par 5's will eat you alive ... Busy in summer ... Small landing areas ... Punishes poor play ... Challenging but fair ... 8th hole a great uphill par 5, 18 a tricked-up downhill par 5 ... Great pin placements...Some interesting holes.

OLD SALEM GREENS GOLF COURSE
PU-Willson St., Salem, 01970, Essex County, (978)744-2149.
Holes: 9. **Yards:** 3,046/2,483. **Par:** 35/35. **Course Rating:** 68.4/70.7. **Slope:** 116/112. **Green Fee:** $22/$28. **Walking Policy:** Unrestricted walking. **Walkability:** 4. **Opened:** 1933. **Season:** April-Nov. **High:** May-Aug. **To obtain tee times:** Call (978)744-2124 24 hours in advance Monday-Friday between 10:00 a.m. and 1:00 p.m. for tee times. **Miscellaneous:** Reduced fees (weekdays, twilight, seniors, juniors).

★★★½ OLDE BARNSTABLE FAIRGROUNDS GOLF COURSE
PU-Rte. 149, Marstons Mills, 02648, Barnstable County, (508)420-1141, 5 miles N of Hyannis.
Holes: 18. **Yards:** 6,503/5,162. **Par:** 71/71. **Course Rating:** 70.7/69.2. **Slope:** 123/118. **Green Fee:** $25/$55. **Cart Fee:** $26/cart. **Walking Policy:** Unrestricted walking. **Walkability:** 2. **Opened:** 1992. **Architect:** Geoffrey Cornish/Brian Silva/Mark Mungea. **Season:** Year-round. **High:** April-Nov. **To obtain tee times:** Call 2 days in advance at 10 a.m. Prepaid reservations by mail with no restrictions. **Miscellaneous:** Reduced fees (weekdays, twilight), range (mats), club rentals, credit cards (MC, V).
Reader Comments: Soft spikes have improved greens greatly ... Not too tough ... Fun new track, challenging ... Have to keep your eye on the ball, not the gliders ... Good driving range ... 5-3-5-3 start is unique ... Some very interesting holes.

★★★★ OLDE SCOTLAND LINKS AT BRIDGEWATER
PU-690 Pine St., Bridgewater, 02324, Plymouth County, (508)279-3344, 25 miles S of Boston.
Holes: 18. **Yards:** 6,790/4,949. **Par:** 72/72. **Course Rating:** 72.0/67.5. **Slope:** 117/107. **Green Fee:** $26/$35. **Cart Fee:** $12/person. **Walking Policy:** Unrestricted walking. **Walkability:** 1. **Opened:** 1997. **Architect:** Brian Silva/Mark Mungeam. **Season:** March-Dec. **High:** May-Sept. **To obtain tee times:** Call for tee times 7 days in advance beginning at 6:00 a.m. Credit card guarantee. **Miscellaneous:** Reduced fees (weekdays, seniors, juniors), range (grass/mats), club rentals, credit cards (MC, V, AE).
Reader Comments: A neat little course, but no trees doesn't mean LINKS ... Underrated. USGA slope out of whack. Much more difficult ... Nice-links-style layout.

THE ORCHARDS GOLF COURSE
SP-Silverwood Terrace, South Hadley, 01075, Hampshire County, (413)534-3806.
Holes: 18. **Yards:** 6,424/5,359. **Par:** 71/72. **Course Rating:** 71.3/71.3. **Slope:** 127/124. **Green Fee:** N/A/$100. **Cart Fee:** Included in Green Fee. **Walking Policy:** Unrestricted walking. **Walkability:** 3. **Opened:** 1922. **Architect:** Donald Ross. **Season:** April-Dec. **High:** July-Aug. **To**

obtain tee times: For tee times, call golf shop as early as possible. **Miscellaneous:** Range (grass), club rentals, credit cards (MC, V).

OULD NEWBURY GOLF CLUB
SP-Rte. 1, Newburyport, 01950, Essex County, (978)465-9888, 35 miles N of Boston.
Holes: 18. **Yards:** 3,092/2,767. **Par:** 35/38. **Course Rating:** 69.6/71.5. **Slope:** 120/115. **Green Fee:** $28/$28. **Cart Fee:** $22/cart. **Walking Policy:** Unrestricted walking. **Walkability:** 4.
Opened: 1916. **Architect:** Jim Lowe. **Season:** April-Nov. **High:** June-Aug. **To obtain tee times:** First come, first served, should call. **Miscellaneous:** Metal spikes, club rentals, credit cards (MC, V, D).

★★½ PAUL HARNEY GOLF COURSE
74 Club Valley Dr., East Falmouth, 02536, Barnstable County, (508)563-3454, 70 miles S of Boston.
Holes: 18. **Yards:** 4,000/N/A. **Par:** 59/N/A. **Course Rating:** N/A. **Slope:** N/A. **Green Fee:** N/A.
Walking Policy: Unrestricted walking. **Walkability:** 3. **Season:** Year-round. **High:** June-Sept.
Miscellaneous: Metal spikes.
Reader Comments: Tough par 3 course, not a chip and putt! Play it ... Good iron practice round ... Great executive course.

★★★ PEMBROKE COUNTRY CLUB
PU-W. Elm St., Pembroke, 02359, Plymouth County, (781)826-5191, 25 miles S of Boston. **Web:** www.pembrokecc.com.
Holes: 18. **Yards:** 6,532/5,887. **Par:** 71/75. **Course Rating:** 71.1/73.4. **Slope:** 124/120. **Green Fee:** $15/$40. **Cart Fee:** $12/person. **Walking Policy:** Unrestricted walking. **Walkability:** 2.
Opened: 1972. **Architect:** Phil Wogan. **Season:** Year-round. **High:** June-Sept. **To obtain tee times:** Call Wednesday morning for weekend play; anytime for weekdays. **Miscellaneous:** Reduced fees (weekdays, low season, twilight), metal spikes, range (grass/mats), club rentals, credit cards (MC, V), beginner friendly.
Reader Comments: With some work it could be very nice ... Favors long hitters. Narrow track with water on 7 holes ... Good layout ... Tough doglegs with well-placed hazards, fast greens ... Hard to get tee times due to events ... It's an experience ... Good clubhouse and restaurant ... Great course, too bad everybody knows it.

PETERSHAM COUNTRY CLUB
PU-N. Main St., Petersham, 01366, Worcester County, (978)724-3388, 4 miles N of Petersham.
Holes: 9. **Yards:** 6,007/5,053. **Par:** 70/72. **Course Rating:** 68.4/64.4. **Slope:** 118/112. **Green Fee:** $20/$22. **Cart Fee:** $12/person. **Walking Policy:** Unrestricted walking. **Walkability:** 3.
Opened: 1924. **Architect:** Donald Ross. **Season:** April-Nov. **High:** May-Sept. **To obtain tee times:** Members-Call 7 days in advance. Non-members-Call 3 days in advance. **Miscellaneous:** Reduced fees (weekdays, twilight, juniors), club rentals, beginner friendly (junior program).

PINE GROVE GOLF COURSE
PU-254 Wilson Rd., Northampton, 01062, Hampshire County, (413)584-4570, 15 miles N of Springfield.
Holes: 18. **Yards:** 6,115/4,890. **Par:** 72/72. **Course Rating:** 68.8/67.3. **Slope:** 121/114. **Green Fee:** $13/$19. **Cart Fee:** $20/cart. **Walking Policy:** Unrestricted walking. **Walkability:** 3.
Architect: Gill Verillo. **Season:** April-Dec. **High:** April-Oct. **To obtain tee times:** Call up to one week ahead for weekend tee times. **Miscellaneous:** Reduced fees (weekdays, seniors), metal spikes, beginner friendly (mon. night women's league).

PLYMOUTH COUNTRY CLUB
SP-Warren Ave., Plymouth, 02361, (508)746-0476.
Special Notes: Call club for further information.

★★★ PONKAPOAG GOLF CLUB
PU-2167 Washington St., Canton, 02021, Norfolk County, (781)575-1001, 10 miles S of Boston.
Holes: 36. **Yards:** 6,728/5,523. **Par:** 72/74. **Course Rating:** 72.0/70.8. **Slope:** 126/115. **Green Fee:** $12/$20. **Cart Fee:** $19/cart. **Walking Policy:** Unrestricted walking. **Walkability:** 2.
Opened: 1933. **Architect:** Donald Ross. **Season:** April-Dec. **High:** May-Aug. **To obtain tee times:** First come, first serve. **Miscellaneous:** Reduced fees (weekdays, seniors, juniors), range (grass/mats), club rentals, credit cards (MC, V), beginner friendly (junior golf camp).
Reader Comments: Always improving, but very slow ... Nice scenery ... Too crowded to enjoy ... Classic layout ... Greens like pool tables.

PONTOOSUC LAKE COUNTRY CLUB
PU-Kirkwood Dr., Pittsfield, 01201, Berkshire County, (413)445-4217.
Holes: 18. **Yards:** 6,207/5,240. **Par:** 70/70. **Course Rating:** 68.1/68.2. **Slope:** 114/115. **Green Fee:** $8/$20. **Cart Fee:** $20/cart. **Walking Policy:** Unrestricted walking. **Walkability:** 3. **Opened:** 1920. **Architect:** Wayne Stiles. **Season:** April-Nov. **High:** May-Sept. **To obtain tee times:** Call

(413)445-4543 for weekend and holiday play only. **Miscellaneous:** Reduced fees (weekdays, seniors), beginner friendly.

★★★★ POQUOY BROOK GOLF CLUB

PU-20 Leonard St., Lakeville, 02347, Plymouth County, (508)947-5261, 45 miles SE of Boston.
Holes: 18. **Yards:** 6,762/5,415. **Par:** 72/73. **Course Rating:** 72.4/71.0. **Slope:** 128/114. **Green Fee:** $34/$37. **Cart Fee:** $14/person. **Walking Policy:** Unrestricted walking. **Walkability:** 2. **Opened:** 1962. **Architect:** Geoffrey S. Cornish. **Season:** Year-round. **High:** May-Oct. **To obtain tee times:** Call up to 7 days in advance for weekdays; 2 days in advance for weekends. **Miscellaneous:** Reduced fees (weekdays, low season, twilight, juniors), range (grass), club rentals, credit cards (MC, V, AE, D, Debit Card).
Reader Comments: Awesome ... Solid course, good par 4 selection ... Hard to get a tee time ... Beautiful landscape ... Great facility & layout ... Nos. 16-18 are as challenging a finish as anywhere ... Scenic tree-lined course ... Excellent clubhouse ... Looks easy plays hard ... Too many mosquitoes ... Bar has deck overlooking 18th green.

PUTTERHAM GOLF CLUB

PU-1281 W. Roxbury Pkwy., Brookline, 02467, Suffolk County, (617)730-2078, 5 miles W of Boston.
Holes: 18. **Yards:** 6,307/5,680. **Par:** 71/72. **Course Rating:** 70.2/72.1. **Slope:** 123/121. **Green Fee:** $22/$32. **Cart Fee:** $26/cart. **Walking Policy:** Unrestricted walking. **Walkability:** 2. **Opened:** 1931. **Architect:** Wayne Stiles/Van Kleek. **Season:** Year-round. **High:** April-Nov. **Miscellaneous:** Reduced fees (twilight, seniors, juniors), club rentals, credit cards (MC, V, AE), beginner friendly (clinics).

★★★½ QUASHNET VALLEY COUNTRY CLUB

PU-309 Old Barnstable Rd., Mashpee, 02649, Barnstable County, (508)477-4412, (800)433-8633, 55 miles S of Boston.
Holes: 18. **Yards:** 6,602/5,094. **Par:** 72/72. **Course Rating:** 71.7/70.3. **Slope:** 132/119. **Green Fee:** $25/$52. **Cart Fee:** $13/person. **Walking Policy:** Walking at certain times. **Walkability:** 3. **Opened:** 1974. **Architect:** Geoffrey Cornish/William Robinson. **Season:** Year-round. **High:** April-Oct. **To obtain tee times:** Call 7 days in advance or up to 6 months in advance for prepaid. **Miscellaneous:** Reduced fees (weekdays, low season, twilight), metal spikes, range (grass), club rentals, credit cards (MC, V).
Reader Comments: Bring at least 2 dozen balls–H2O ... A lot of memorable holes ... Watch out for marshes ... Tough in the wind ... Only if you like target golf ... Bring the OFF ... Challenging course ... Keep it in the fairway ... Great scenery through the wetlands ... Interesting second shots; suckers beware.

★★★ REHOBOTH COUNTRY CLUB

PU-155 Perryville Rd., Rehoboth, 02769, Bristol County, (508)252-6259, 15 miles E of Providence.
Holes: 18. **Yards:** 6,950/5,450. **Par:** 72/75. **Course Rating:** 72.5/70.4. **Slope:** 125/115. **Green Fee:** $22/$27. **Cart Fee:** $12/person. **Walking Policy:** Unrestricted walking. **Walkability:** 1. **Opened:** 1966. **Architect:** Geoffrey Cornish/William Robinson. **Season:** Year-round. **High:** May-Sept. **To obtain tee times:** Tee times taken 3 days in advance for weekends only. **Miscellaneous:** Reduced fees (twilight, seniors, juniors), credit cards (MC, V).
Reader Comments: Always improving the course ... Interesting course with water and well-placed trees ... A hidden gem awaiting to be polished. Clubhouse needs work ... Awesome greens, slick putts ... Heavily played and good test ... Beautiful country setting. Don't miss!

★★½ RIDDER GOLF CLUB

PU-300 Oak St., Rte. 14, Whitman, 02382, Plymouth County, (781)447-9003, 25 miles S of Boston.
Holes: 18. **Yards:** 5,909/4,862. **Par:** 70/70. **Course Rating:** 68.1/67.1. **Slope:** 113/107. **Green Fee:** $29/$32. **Cart Fee:** $12/cart. **Walking Policy:** Unrestricted walking. **Walkability:** 2. **Opened:** 1961. **Architect:** Henry Hohman/Geoffrey S. Cornish. **Season:** Year-round. **High:** May-Nov. **To obtain tee times:** Call up to 2 days in advance. **Miscellaneous:** Reduced fees (weekdays, low season, juniors), range (grass), club rentals, beginner friendly (have junior programs and learning center).
Reader Comments: Good course for beginners ... Wide open, flat, very few trees on course ... Fun course, easy ... Hard to lose a ball ... A good confidence builder.

★★★ ROUND HILL COUNTRY CLUB

SP-Round Hill Rd., East Sandwich, 02537, Barnstable County, (508)888-3384, 60 miles S of Boston.
Holes: 18. **Yards:** 6,220/4,894. **Par:** 71/70. **Course Rating:** 70.4/68.1. **Slope:** 124/115. **Green Fee:** $17/$45. **Cart Fee:** $28/cart. **Walking Policy:** Walking at certain times. **Walkability:** 3. **Opened:** 1972. **Architect:** Richard Cross. **Season:** Year-round. **High:** June-Sept. **To obtain tee**

times: Call up to 7 days in advance. **Miscellaneous:** Reduced fees (weekdays, low season, twilight), metal spikes, range (grass), club rentals, credit cards (MC, V).
Reader Comments: Back 9 very hilly & unfair... View from lounge with telescope is outstanding .... Nice hilly heaven. Very woody. Good greens ... Hadn't played it for 10 years. Glad I went back! ... Interesting elevation changes ... Great 19th hole views ... Lots of blind shots ... I thought the Cape was flat.

ROWLEY COUNTRY CLUB
PU-Dodge Rd., Rowley, 01969, Essex County, (978)948-2731, 33 miles N of Boston.
Holes: 9. **Yards:** 3,325/2,470. **Par:** 36/35. **Course Rating:** 70.7/67.5. **Slope:** 127/109. **Green Fee:** $28/$32. **Cart Fee:** $24/cart. **Walking Policy:** Unrestricted walking. **Walkability:** 3. **Season:** Year-round. **High:** April-Sept. **Miscellaneous:** Reduced fees (twilight, seniors), discount packages, range (grass/mats), club rentals, credit cards (MC, V), beginner friendly (2-day schools for adults and juniors, summer camps and nike golf camps).

★★★ SADDLE HILL COUNTRY CLUB
PU-204 Saddle Hill Rd., Hopkinton, 01748, Middlesex County, (508)435-4630, 26 miles W of Boston.
Holes: 18. **Yards:** 6,900/5,619. **Par:** 72/72. **Course Rating:** 72.8/70.3. **Slope:** 124/108. **Green Fee:** $22/$28. **Cart Fee:** $12/person. **Walking Policy:** Walking at certain times. **Walkability:** 4. **Opened:** 1963. **Architect:** William F. Mitchell. **Season:** March-Dec. **High:** June-Sept. **To obtain tee times:** Call up to 7 days in advance for weekdays; Wednesday prior for weekends.
Miscellaneous: Reduced fees (seniors), metal spikes, range (mats), club rentals, credit cards (MC, V).
Reader Comments: One of my favorites ... Hilly with great golf holes, risk-reward par 5s ... Felt like I was playing on a PGA Tour course ... Pretty and playable ... Very little water ... Tough from the tips.

★★★ SAGAMORE SPRING GOLF CLUB
PU-1287 Main St., Lynnfield, 01940, Essex County, (781)334-3151, 15 miles N of Boston.
Holes: 18. **Yards:** 5,936/4,784. **Par:** 70/70. **Course Rating:** 68.6/66.5. **Slope:** 119/112. **Green Fee:** $30/$38. **Cart Fee:** $24/cart. **Walking Policy:** Unrestricted walking. **Walkability:** 2. **Opened:** 1929. **Architect:** Richard Luff. **Season:** March-Dec. **High:** June-Sept. **To obtain tee times:** Call 4 days in advance between 9 a.m. and 5 p.m. **Miscellaneous:** Reduced fees (weekdays, low season, seniors), metal spikes, range (mats), club rentals, credit cards (MC, V, D).
Reader Comments: Lots of play ... Not that difficult ... Staff friendliness much improved ... Rolling hills, but wide fairways, fair test ... Forget a weekend tee time ... Ends with back-to-back par 3s ... Always a favorite.

★★ ST. ANNE COUNTRY CLUB
PU-781 Shoemaker Lane, Feeding Hills, 01030, Hampden County, (413)786-2088, 6 miles W of Springfield.
Special Notes: Call club for further information.

★★½ SANDY BURR COUNTRY CLUB
SP-103 Cochituate Rd., Wayland, 01778, Middlesex County, (508)358-7211, 16 miles W of Boston.
Holes: 18. **Yards:** 6,412/4,561. **Par:** 72/69. **Course Rating:** 70.8/66.2. **Slope:** 125/110. **Green Fee:** $35/$40. **Cart Fee:** $30/cart. **Walking Policy:** Unrestricted walking. **Walkability:** 3. **Opened:** 1922. **Architect:** Donald Ross. **Season:** April-Dec. **High:** June-Sept. **Miscellaneous:** Reduced fees (twilight, seniors, juniors), club rentals, credit cards (MC, V).
Reader Comments: Wear a hard hat on many holes ... Spectacular in fall, very crowded, fun course ... Nice Par 5s ... Ego builder ... Too slow ... Jam golfers on course ... Back nine more challenging than front.

★★★★ SHAKER HILLS GOLF CLUB
PU-146 Shaker Rd., Harvard, 01451, Middlesex County, (978)772-2227, 35 miles NW of Boston.
Web: www.shakerhills.com.
Holes: 18. **Yards:** 6,850/5,001. **Par:** 71/71. **Course Rating:** 72.3/67.9. **Slope:** 135/116. **Green Fee:** $55/$60. **Cart Fee:** Included in Green Fee. **Walking Policy:** Unrestricted walking. **Walkability:** 4. **Opened:** 1991. **Architect:** Brian M. Silva. **Season:** April-Nov. **High:** June-Sept. **To obtain tee times:** Call automated 24-hour tee time Call 4 days in advance for the general public. **Miscellaneous:** Reduced fees (twilight), range (grass/mats), club rentals, credit cards (MC, V).
Reader Comments: Dramatic, challenging ... Flawless ... Difficult to score well ... Stay in fairway ... Public golf with a private club experience ... Hilly with elevated tees ... You must walk to enjoy it ... Par 3s are excellent ... Too bad the secret's out ... Down hill cart rides scary!

★★★ SHERATON COLONIAL GOLF CLUB
PU-427 Walnut St., Lynnfield, 01940, Middlesex County, (781)245-9300, 12 miles N of Boston.

Holes: 18. **Yards:** 6,565/5,280. **Par:** 70/72. **Course Rating:** 72.8/69.5. **Slope:** 130/109. **Green Fee:** $46/$59. **Cart Fee:** Included in Green Fee. **Walking Policy:** Mandatory cart. **Walkability:** 2. **Opened:** 1929. **Architect:** Bill Mitchell. **Season:** March-Dec. **High:** May-Oct. **To obtain tee times:** Hotel guests 21 days in advance. Public call 3 days in advance. **Miscellaneous:** Reduced fees (low season, twilight, seniors, juniors), discount packages, metal spikes, range (grass/mats), club rentals, lodging (280 rooms), credit cards (MC, V, AE, D, Diners Club).
Reader Comments: Some challenging holes ... 6-hour rounds common ... Assembly line golf ... Fair challenge ... Very windy, located in a marsh, can be frustrating ... Back nine is work.

★★★ SHERATON TWIN BROOKS GOLF COURSE
R-W. End Circle, Hyannis, 02601, Barnstable County, (508)775-7775, 75 miles S of Boston.
Holes: 18. **Yards:** 2,621/2,239. **Par:** 54/54. **Course Rating:** N/A. **Slope:** N/A. **Green Fee:** $18/$33. **Cart Fee:** $22/cart. **Walking Policy:** Unrestricted walking. **Walkability:** 1. **Opened:** 1965. **Architect:** Geoffrey Cornish/William Robinson. **Season:** Year-round. **High:** June-Sept. **To obtain tee times:** Call golf shop. **Miscellaneous:** Reduced fees (weekdays, low season, twilight, seniors, juniors), metal spikes, range (grass), club rentals, lodging (243 rooms), credit cards (MC, V, AE, D).
Reader Comments: Must be accurate with irons ... Most holes are very secluded ... Challenge with winds. Front 9 very short ... Good restaurant ... Use all your clubs on this par 3, interesting greens ... Lack of room makes for out of bounds on several holes ... Joy to play.

★★★★ SOUTH HAMPTON COUNTRY CLUB
PU-329 College Hwy., Southampton, 01073, (413)527-9815.
Reader Comments: Improves every year ... Worlds best kept secret ... As nice as any private course ... Very a few bunkers, keeps pace of play faster ... Easy to get tee time.
Special Notes: Call club for further information.

★★★ SOUTH SHORE COUNTRY CLUB
SP-274 South St., Hingham, 02043, Plymouth County, (781)749-8479, 19 miles SE of Boston.
E-mail: jkgolfpro@aol.com. **Web:** www.jkgolfpro.com.
Holes: 18. **Yards:** 6,444/5,064. **Par:** 72/72. **Course Rating:** 71.0/69.3. **Slope:** 128/116. **Green Fee:** $25/$36. **Cart Fee:** $25/cart. **Walking Policy:** Unrestricted walking. **Walkability:** 4. **Opened:** 1925. **Architect:** Wayne Stiles. **Season:** April-Dec. **High:** June-Sept. **To obtain tee times:** Call up to 4 days in advance. **Miscellaneous:** Reduced fees (twilight, seniors, juniors), range (mats), club rentals, credit cards (MC, V).
Reader Comments: Good solid track ... Improving each year ... Slow, but worth it ... Hilly New England layout. Plenty of wind near the ocean ... Good food ... Best challenge in the area ... Not too many flat lies.

SOUTHWICK COUNTRY CLUB
PU-739 College Hwy., Southwick, 01077, Hampden County, (413)569-0136.
Holes: 18. **Yards:** 6,100/5,900. **Par:** 71/71. **Course Rating:** 106.0/N/A. **Slope:** N/A. **Green Fee:** $14/$22. **Cart Fee:** $22/cart. **Walking Policy:** Unrestricted walking. **Walkability:** 1. **Opened:** 1928. **Season:** March-Dec. **High:** May-Sept. **To obtain tee times:** Call 24 hours in advance. **Miscellaneous:** Reduced fees (weekdays, low season, twilight, seniors), club rentals, beginner friendly (junior clinic).

★★★ SQUIRREL RUN GOLF & COUNTRY CLUB
PU-Rte. 44, Carver Rd., Plymouth, 02360, Plymouth County, (508)746-5001, 40 miles S of Boston.
Holes: 18. **Yards:** 2,859/1,990. **Par:** 57/57. **Course Rating:** 85.0/82.0. **Slope:** 55/54. **Green Fee:** $15/$25. **Cart Fee:** $10/person. **Walking Policy:** Unrestricted walking. **Walkability:** 1. **Opened:** 1991. **Architect:** Ray Richard. **Season:** Year-round. **High:** July-Aug. **To obtain tee times:** Call 7 days in advance. **Miscellaneous:** Reduced fees (twilight, seniors, juniors), range (grass/mats), club rentals, credit cards (MC, V), beginner friendly (beginner clinics, junior clinics).
Reader Comments: Nice greens for an executive course ... Fun exec. course. Nice staff ... Strictly a short-iron 18 holer ... A beginner's paradise ... Treacherous greens and traps, what fun! You can't wait to play it again.

STONE LEA GOLF COURSE
PU-1411 County St., Attleboro, 02703, Bristol County, (508)222-9735.
Holes: 18. **Yards:** 6,042/5,150. **Par:** 70/70. **Course Rating:** 69.5/67.8. **Slope:** 116/112. **Green Fee:** $17/$24. **Cart Fee:** $20/cart. **Walking Policy:** Unrestricted walking. **Walkability:** 2. **Opened:** 1958. **Architect:** Ed Lapierre, Sr. **Season:** Year-round. **High:** May-Oct. **To obtain tee times:** First come, first serve. **Miscellaneous:** Reduced fees (seniors), beginner friendly.

STOW ACRES COUNTRY CLUB
PU-58 Randall Rd., Stow, 01775, Middlesex County, (978)568-1100, 25 miles NW of Boston. **E-mail:** mgiles@shore.net. **Web:** www.stowacres.com.

★★★½ NORTH COURSE
Holes: 18. **Yards:** 6,950/6,011. **Par:** 72/72. **Course Rating:** 72.8/70.6. **Slope:** 130/120. **Green Fee:** $36/$45. **Cart Fee:** $27/cart. **Walking Policy:** Unrestricted walking. **Walkability:** 2. **Opened:** 1965. **Architect:** Geoffrey S. Cornish. **Season:** March-Dec. **High:** April-Nov. **To obtain tee times:** Call 6 days in advance. **Miscellaneous:** Reduced fees (weekdays, low season, twilight, seniors, juniors), range (mats), club rentals, credit cards (MC, V, AE), beginner friendly (golf school).
Notes: Ranked 28th in 1996 America's Top 75 Affordable Courses.
Reader Comments: Too many dogleg lefts; slicers nightmare hookers paradise ... Enjoyable ... Excellent conditions for public courses ... Brutally slow ... Great clubhouse, deck and food ... Everyone in Massachusetts seems to be here ... Plan a day around it ... Excellent golf shop ... Play it in the off season.

★★★ SOUTH COURSE
Holes: 18. **Yards:** 6,520/5,642. **Par:** 72/72. **Course Rating:** 71.8/69.7. **Slope:** 120/116. **Green Fee:** $36/$45. **Cart Fee:** $27/cart. **Walking Policy:** Unrestricted walking. **Walkability:** 4. **Opened:** 1922. **Architect:** Geoffrey S. Cornish. **Season:** March-Dec. **High:** April-Nov. **To obtain tee times:** Call 6 days in advance. **Miscellaneous:** Reduced fees (weekdays, low season, twilight, seniors, juniors), range (mats), club rentals, credit cards (MC, V, AE), beginner friendly (golf school).
Reader Comments: Wide landing areas ... Great back nine with constant elevation changes ... Slow play ... Front nine lulls you to sleep, back nine ouch ... Easier of the two courses ... 6 hours! 6 hours! 6 hours! ... Great design, very hilly ... Tall trees abound ... South more forgiving.

SUN VALLEY GOLF COURSE
PU-329 Summer St., Rehoboth, 02769, (508)336-8686.
Special Notes: Call club for special information.

★★★★ SWANSEA COUNTRY CLUB
PU-299 Market St., Swansea, 02777, Bristol County, (508)379-9886, 10 miles E of Providence, RI.
Holes: 18. **Yards:** 6,840/5,239. **Par:** 72/72. **Course Rating:** 72.7/69.9. **Slope:** 124/109. **Green Fee:** $22/$32. **Cart Fee:** $24/cart. **Walking Policy:** Unrestricted walking. **Walkability:** 2. **Opened:** 1963. **Architect:** Geoffrey S. Cornish. **Season:** Year-round. **High:** April-Sept. **To obtain tee times:** Call 5 days in advance. Tee sheets posted: Tuesday 12:00 noon for weekend and Thursday 12:00 noon for up-coming Monday-Friday. **Miscellaneous:** Reduced fees (weekdays, low season, twilight, seniors, juniors), range (grass), club rentals, credit cards (MC, V, AE, D).
Reader Comments: New watered fairways, but rocks in traps ... Improving daily ... Very fast greens ... Very tight, championship layout, stay below the hole ... Investing in many improvements ... Flat and straight, great for average player ... A bit damp in low places./

★★★★½ TACONIC GOLF CLUB *Condition*
SP-Meacham St., Williamstown, 01267, Berkshire County, (413)458-3997, 35 miles E of Albany, NY.
Holes: 18. **Yards:** 6,614/5,202. **Par:** 71/71. **Course Rating:** 70.5/69.9. **Slope:** 127/123. **Green Fee:** $80/$80. **Cart Fee:** Included in Green Fee. **Walking Policy:** Mandatory cart. **Walkability:** N/A. **Opened:** 1896. **Architect:** Wayne E. Stiles/John R. Van Kleek. **Season:** April-Nov. **High:** July-Sept. **To obtain tee times:** Call up to 7 days in advance. **Miscellaneous:** Metal spikes, range (grass), club rentals, credit cards (MC, V).
Reader Comments: Great layout and scenery ... Beautiful New England mountain golf ... Old design, don't leave your ball above the cup ... Excellent test from back tees ... Super fast greens ... A great tournament course ... Great sense of tradition both on and off the course ... A treasure in the Berkshires.

★★★½ TEKOA COUNTRY CLUB
SP-459 Russell Rd., Westfield, 01085, Hampden County, (413)568-1064, 10 miles W of Springfield.
Holes: 18. **Yards:** 6,002/5,115. **Par:** 70/74. **Course Rating:** 69.6/71.0. **Slope:** 118/116. **Green Fee:** $15/$25. **Cart Fee:** $23/cart. **Walking Policy:** Unrestricted walking. **Walkability:** 1. **Opened:** 1929. **Architect:** Geoffrey Cornish/Donald Ross. **Season:** March-Nov. **High:** May-Aug. **To obtain tee times:** Call for tee reservations 5 days in advance. **Miscellaneous:** Reduced fees (low season, seniors, juniors), discount packages, club rentals.
Reader Comments: Short but fair, position golf ... Tight little course ... Easy walking.

TOUISSET COUNTRY CLUB
PU-221 Pearse Rd., Swansea, 02777, Bristol County, (508)679-9577, 15 miles E of Providence, R.I.
Holes: 9. **Yards:** 6,211/5,565. **Par:** 71/73. **Course Rating:** 69.1/71.0. **Slope:** 111/114. **Green Fee:** $15/$19. **Cart Fee:** $24/cart. **Walking Policy:** Unrestricted walking. **Walkability:** 1. **Opened:** 1962. **Architect:** Ray Brigham. **Season:** Year-round. **High:** April-Sept. **Miscellaneous:**

MASSACHUSETTS

Reduced fees (weekdays, twilight, seniors, juniors), club rentals, credit cards (MC, V), beginner friendly (lessons, clinics, junior school).

★★★★½ TRULL BROOK GOLF COURSE *Condition*
PU-170 River Rd., Tewksbury, 01876, Middlesex County, (978)851-6731, 28 miles NW of Boston. **Web:** www.trullbrookgolf.com.
Holes: 18. **Yards:** 6,350/5,193. **Par:** 72/72. **Course Rating:** 69.8/69.6. **Slope:** 123/118. **Green Fee:** $35/$39. **Cart Fee:** $27/cart. **Walking Policy:** Unrestricted walking. **Walkability:** 4.
Opened: 1963. **Architect:** Geoffrey S. Cornish. **Season:** March-Nov. **High:** June-Aug. **To obtain tee times:** Call up to 7 days in advance. **Miscellaneous:** Reduced fees (weekdays, low season, twilight, seniors, juniors), metal spikes, club rentals, credit cards (MC, V).
Reader Comments: Super track, super condition ... A gem! Terrific greens, varied holes ... Runs along Merrimack River ... A pure joy to play ... Must score well on short par 5s ... Very scenic, beautiful older course.

VETERANS GOLF COURSE
PU-1059 S. Branch Pkwy., Springfield, 01118, (413)783-9611.
Special Notes: Call club for further information.

★★★½ WACHUSETT COUNTRY CLUB
SP-187 Prospect St., West Boylston, 01583, Worcester County, (508)835-2264, 7 miles N of Worcester. **Web:** www.wachusettcountryclub.com.
Holes: 18. **Yards:** 6,608/6,216. **Par:** 72/72. **Course Rating:** 71.7/70.0. **Slope:** 124/120. **Green Fee:** $15/$40. **Cart Fee:** $28/cart. **Walking Policy:** Unrestricted walking. **Walkability:** 2.
Opened: 1928. **Architect:** Donald Ross. **Season:** April-Nov. **High:** May-Oct. **To obtain tee times:** Call (508)835-4453 for groups of 3 or more. **Miscellaneous:** Reduced fees (low season, twilight), range (grass/mats), club rentals, credit cards (MC, V, AE, D), beginner friendly (clinics, junior program).
Reader Comments: Plays much tougher then it looks ... Nice assortment of holes ... Fun to play ... Old hilly course, don't walk ... Mr Donald Ross at his best!.

★★★★ WAHCONAH COUNTRY CLUB
SP-15 Orchard Rd., Dalton, 01226, Berkshire County, (413)684-1333, 4 miles N of Pittsfield.
Holes: 18. **Yards:** 6,567/5,567. **Par:** 71/73. **Course Rating:** 71.9/72.5. **Slope:** 126/123. **Green Fee:** $50/$60. **Cart Fee:** $24/cart. **Walking Policy:** Unrestricted walking. **Walkability:** 3.
Opened: 1930. **Architect:** W. Stiles/G.S. Cornish/R. Armacost. **Season:** April-Nov. **High:** April-Nov. **To obtain tee times:** Call 8 days in advance. **Miscellaneous:** Metal spikes, range (grass), credit cards (MC, V).
Reader Comments: Everyone has fun here ... Beautiful Berkshires ... Layout is challenging, greens tough ... Terrific views.

★★★½ WAUBEEKA GOLF LINKS
PU-137 New Ashford Rd., Williamstown, 01267, Berkshire County, (413)458-8355, 12 miles N of Pittsfield.
Holes: 18. **Yards:** 6,394/5,023. **Par:** 72/72. **Course Rating:** 70.6/69.6. **Slope:** 126/119. **Green Fee:** $30/$35. **Cart Fee:** $25/cart. **Walking Policy:** Unrestricted walking. **Walkability:** 3.
Opened: 1966. **Architect:** Rowland Armacost. **Season:** April-Nov. **High:** July-Aug. **To obtain tee times:** Call in advance. **Miscellaneous:** Reduced fees (juniors), range (grass), club rentals, credit cards (MC, V, AE, D).
Reader Comments: Good mix of holes ... Front 9 hilly, back 9 flat ... Nice views ... Excellent greens, always improving ... Interesting course, beautiful setting.

WAVERLY OAKS GOLF CLUB
R-444 Long Pond Rd., Plymouth, 02360, Plymouth County, (508)224-6016, 40 miles S of Boston.
Holes: 18. **Yards:** 7,114/5,587. **Par:** 72/72. **Course Rating:** 73.5/71.4. **Slope:** 130/127. **Green Fee:** $63/$75. **Cart Fee:** Included in Green Fee. **Walking Policy:** Unrestricted walking. **Walkability:** 4. **Opened:** 1998. **Architect:** Brian Silva. **Season:** March-Nov. **High:** June-Sept. **To obtain tee times:** Can be made up to 7 days in advance. **Miscellaneous:** Range (grass/mats), club rentals, credit cards (MC, V, AE), beginner friendly (executive nine).
Special Notes: Also have a 9-hole, par 33 Executive course.

★★½ WESTMINSTER COUNTRY CLUB
SP-51 Ellis Rd., Westminster, 01473, Worcester County, (978)874-5938, 22 miles N of Worcester.
Holes: 18. **Yards:** 6,491/5,453. **Par:** 71/71. **Course Rating:** 71.2/71.3. **Slope:** 124/117. **Green Fee:** $25/$30. **Cart Fee:** $22/cart. **Walking Policy:** Unrestricted walking. **Walkability:** 3.
Opened: 1957. **Architect:** Manny Francis. **Season:** April-Nov. **High:** May-Sept. **To obtain tee times:** Call 1 day in advance for weekdays and on Friday for weekend times. **Miscellaneous:** Reduced fees (weekdays, twilight), club rentals, credit cards (MC, V, AE, D).

MASSACHUSETTS

Reader Comments: Terrific course. Very challenging, fast greens ... Tough shots if you miss greens ... Firm fairways ... Hilly backside, flat front...Course seems to improve each year.

★★★½ **WESTOVER GOLF COURSE** *Value*
PU-South St., Granby, 01033, Hampshire County, (413)547-8610, 10 miles NE of Springfield.
Holes: 18. **Yards:** 7,025/5,980. **Par:** 72/72. **Course Rating:** 73.9/72.0. **Slope:** 131/118. **Green Fee:** $14/$19. **Cart Fee:** $17/cart. **Walking Policy:** Unrestricted walking. **Walkability:** 2.
Opened: 1957. **Architect:** Al Zikorus. **Season:** April-Dec. **High:** May-Sept. **To obtain tee times:** Call or come in 2 days in advance. **Miscellaneous:** Reduced fees (twilight, seniors, juniors), range (grass), club rentals, credit cards (MC, V, AE, D).
Reader Comments: Long, long, long ... Lots of play, but in good shape ... Tough course ... Plays longer than card ... Bring plenty of balls ... Noisy, right next to Air Force base.

★★★½ **WIDOW'S WALK GOLF COURSE**
PU-250 The Driftway, Scituate, 02066, Plymouth County, (781)544-7777.
Holes: 18. **Yards:** 6,403/4,562. **Par:** 72/72. **Course Rating:** 69.8/65.9. **Slope:** 123/109. **Green Fee:** $22/$38. **Cart Fee:** $12/person. **Walking Policy:** Unrestricted walking. **Walkability:** 4.
Opened: 1997. **Architect:** Michael Hurdzan/Bill Kerman. **Season:** April-Nov. **High:** June-Aug. **To obtain tee times:** Reservations are accepted up to 4 days in advance. **Miscellaneous:** Reduced fees (weekdays, low season, seniors, juniors), range (grass), club rentals, credit cards (MC, V, AE), beginner friendly (adult and junior introduction classes).
Reader Comments: Hardest par 3s in New England ... Needs time to mature ... A jungle nightmare off the fairways, stock up on balls ... Beautiful course, if you have all day ... Lost too many balls, but a fine experience ... Brutal if you don't keep it straight ... A number of forced carries ... Fascinating design.

WILLIAM J. DEVINE GOLF COURSE
PU-1 Circuit Dr., Dorchester, 02121, (617)265-4084.
Special Notes: Call club for further information.

WINCHENDON COUNTRY CLUB
PU-172 Ash St., Winchendon, 01475, Worcester County, (978)297-9897.
Holes: 18. **Yards:** 5,427/5,030. **Par:** 70/72. **Course Rating:** 65.7/68.5. **Slope:** 114/116. **Green Fee:** $17/$21. **Cart Fee:** $11/person. **Walking Policy:** Unrestricted walking. **Walkability:** 2.
Opened: 1920. **Architect:** Donald Ross. **Season:** April-Nov. **High:** June-Aug. **To obtain tee times:** Call golf shop. **Miscellaneous:** Reduced fees (weekdays, twilight), club rentals, credit cards (MC, V, D), beginner friendly (beginner clinics).

WYCKOFF COUNTRY CLUB
SP-233 Easthampton Rd., Holyoke, 01040, (413)536-3602.
Special Notes: Call club for further information.

MICHIGAN

★★★★ A-GA-MING GOLF CLUB
PU-McLachlan Rd., Kewadin, 49648, Antrim County, (616)264-5081, (800)678-0122, 9 miles N of Elk Rapids. **E-mail:** agamingc@aol. **Web:** www.a-ga-ming.com.
Holes: 18. **Yards:** 6,663/5,125. **Par:** 72/72. **Course Rating:** 73.2/69.2. **Slope:** 133/124. **Green Fee:** $25/$55. **Cart Fee:** Included in Green Fee. **Walking Policy:** Walking at certain times.
Walkability: 5. **Opened:** 1986. **Architect:** "Chick" Harbert. **Season:** April-Oct. **High:** July-Sept.
To obtain tee times: Call in advance. **Miscellaneous:** Reduced fees (weekdays, low season, resort guests, twilight, juniors), discount packages, range (grass), club rentals, lodging (23 rooms), credit cards (MC, V, AE, D).
Reader Comments: Breathtaking views ... Decent course and value ... Good variety of holes, a solid test of golf ... Beautiful scenery, especially in fall ... Aggressive play rewarded ... Friendly staff ... Hills, hills, hills ... Nice greens, outstanding scenery ... Beautiful setting, tough greens.

★★★ ALPENA GOLF CLUB
PU-1135 Golf Course Rd., Alpena, 49707, Alpena County, (517)354-5052. **E-mail:** agci@alpanagolf.com. **Web:** wwwalpenagolf.com.
Holes: 18. **Yards:** 6,459/5,100. **Par:** 72/72. **Course Rating:** 70.5/69.0. **Slope:** 120/113. **Green Fee:** $22/$24. **Cart Fee:** $20/cart. **Walking Policy:** Unrestricted walking. **Walkability:** 1.
Opened: 1934. **Architect:** Warner Bowen. **Season:** April-Oct. **High:** July-Aug. **To obtain tee times:** Call. **Miscellaneous:** Reduced fees (seniors, juniors), discount packages, range (grass), club rentals, credit cards (MC, V).
Reader Comments: Short but nice ... Facilities were outstanding, course was in great shape and greens were as fast as ever.

★★★ ANTRIM DELLS GOLF CLUB
PU-12352 Antrim Drive, Atwood, 49729, Antrim County, (616)599-2679, (800)872-8561, 35 miles N of Traverse City.
Holes: 18. **Yards:** 6,606/5,493. **Par:** 72/72. **Course Rating:** N/A. **Slope:** 125/121. **Green Fee:** $30/$49. **Cart Fee:** Included in Green Fee. **Walking Policy:** Mandatory cart. **Walkability:** 4.
Opened: 1973. **Architect:** Bruce Matthews/Jerry Matthews. **Season:** April-Oct. **High:** July-Aug.
To obtain tee times: Call in advance. **Miscellaneous:** Reduced fees (weekdays, low season, twilight, juniors), metal spikes, range (grass), club rentals, credit cards (MC, V).
Reader Comments: Wide open fairways. Minimal bunkering.

★★½ BALD MOUNTAIN GOLF COURSE
PU-3350 Kern Rd., Lake Orion, 48360, Oakland County, (248)373-1110, 30 miles N of Detroit.
Holes: 18. **Yards:** 6,624/5,775. **Par:** 71/72. **Course Rating:** 71.2/72.9. **Slope:** 120/120. **Green Fee:** $24/$29. **Cart Fee:** $22/cart. **Walking Policy:** Unrestricted walking. **Walkability:** 4.
Opened: 1929. **Architect:** Wilfrid Reid. **Season:** April-Nov. **High:** May-Sept. **To obtain tee times:** Call 3 days in advance for weekdays and 7 days in advance for weekends and holidays.
Miscellaneous: Reduced fees (low season, twilight), metal spikes, range (grass), credit cards (MC, V, AE, D).
Reader Comments: A cheap thrill! ... Decent layout ... A nice place to play ... Hilly blind shots.

★★★ BAY COUNTY GOLF COURSE
PU-584 Hampton Rd., Essexville, 48732, Bay County, (517)892-2161, 6 miles NE of Bay City.
Holes: 18. **Yards:** 6,557/5,706. **Par:** 72/74. **Course Rating:** 71.3/72.4. **Slope:** 113/114. **Green Fee:** $14/$20. **Cart Fee:** $20/cart. **Walking Policy:** Unrestricted walking. **Walkability:** 1.
Opened: 1966. **Architect:** Moranci. **Season:** March-Dec. **High:** May-Aug. **To obtain tee times:** Call up to 7 days in advance. **Miscellaneous:** Reduced fees (weekdays, seniors, juniors), metal spikes, range (grass), club rentals, credit cards (MC, V), beginner friendly (junior program, clinics for women and beginners).
Reader Comments: Nice, clean, well kept ... Very young course, will be nice ... Very open course ... Beautiful scenery ... Fun course, well managed ... Flat but long, well maintained, velvet greens ... Course condition is exceptional!.

★★★★★ BAY HARBOR GOLF CLUB   *Service+, Condition+, Pace+*
SP-5800 Coastal Ridge, Bay Harbor, 49770, Emmet County, (231)439-4028, (800)462-6963, 5 miles S of Petoskey.
Holes: 18. **Yards:** 6,800/4,151. **Par:** 72/72. **Course Rating:** 72.2/69.3. **Slope:** N/A. **Green Fee:** $68/$240. **Cart Fee:** Included in Green Fee. **Walking Policy:** Mandatory cart. **Walkability:** 4.
Opened: 1996. **Architect:** Arthur Hills. **Season:** May-Oct. **High:** July-Aug. **To obtain tee times:** For general public, 48 hours in advance. Resort guests can book at the beginning of the season.
Miscellaneous: Reduced fees (low season, resort guests, twilight), discount packages, range (grass), club rentals, lodging (735 rooms), credit cards (MC, V, AE, D, Diners Club).
Reader Comments: Outstanding ... Breathtaking views ... Pebble Beach of the Midwest ... Expensive, but worth every penny. Rarely saw other players, some of the most scenic holes in golf ... Spectacular views of Lake Michigan and quarry, very playable ... Stunning! ... Links course lives up to hype ... Truly awesome.

MICHIGAN

★★★½ BAY VALLEY GOLF CLUB
R-2470 Old Bridge Rd., Bay City, 48706, Bay County, (517)686-5400, (800)292-5028, 5 miles S of Bay City.
Holes: 18. **Yards:** 6,610/5,151. **Par:** 71/71. **Course Rating:** 71.3/68.5. **Slope:** 125/114. **Green Fee:** $46/$54. **Cart Fee:** Included in Green Fee. **Walking Policy:** Mandatory cart. **Walkability:** N/A. **Opened:** 1973. **Architect:** Desmond Muirhead. **Season:** April-Oct. **High:** June-Sept. **To obtain tee times:** Call in advance. **Miscellaneous:** Reduced fees (weekdays, low season), metal spikes, range (grass), club rentals, lodging, credit cards (MC, V, AE, D).
Reader Comments: Lots of water in play ... Nice course... So much water... Speedy greens, hit it long and straight ... New owners making improvements ... A delight to play, pure.

★★½ BEAVER CREEK GOLF LINKS
SP-850 Stoney Creek Rd., Oakland Township, 48363, Oakland County, (248)693-7170, 5 miles N of Rochester.
Holes: 27. **Yards:** 6,415/5,047. **Par:** 72/72. **Course Rating:** 69.5/67.8. **Slope:** 129/116. **Green Fee:** $33/$43. **Cart Fee:** Included in Green Fee. **Walking Policy:** Mandatory cart. **Walkability:** 5. **Opened:** 1991. **Season:** Year-round weather permitting. **High:** May-Oct. **To obtain tee times:** Call up to 7 days in advance in peak season. **Miscellaneous:** Metal spikes, club rentals.
Reader Comments: Good price, boardwalk throughout course ... Lots of water. Bring plenty of balls ... Tough tee boxes ... Too many hazards make very slow play ... Like miniature golf on a larger scale.

★★★ BEDFORD HILLS GOLF CLUB
PU-6400 Jackman Rd., Temperance, 48182, Monroe County, (734)854-4653, 1 miles N of Toledo, OH.
Holes: 27. **Yards:** 6,231/4,876. **Par:** 72/72. **Course Rating:** 68.1/65.1. **Slope:** 113/107. **Green Fee:** $21/$27. **Cart Fee:** $11/person. **Walking Policy:** Unrestricted walking. **Walkability:** 2. **Opened:** 1993. **Season:** April-Oct. **High:** June-Sept. **To obtain tee times:** Call up to 7 days in advance. **Miscellaneous:** Reduced fees (low season, twilight, seniors, juniors), range (mats), credit cards (MC, V).
Reader Comments: Nice condition ... Mix of short and long, great place for average golfer ... Challenging, shotmaker's course ... Nice clubhouse, 3 unique 9s.

★★★½ BEDFORD VALLEY GOLF COURSE
PU-23161 Waubascon Rd., Battle Creek, 49017, Calhoun County, (616)965-3384, 10 miles N of Battle Creek.
Holes: 18. **Yards:** 6,876/5,104. **Par:** 71/72. **Course Rating:** 73.8/70.0. **Slope:** 135/119. **Green Fee:** $31/$33. **Cart Fee:** $12/person. **Walking Policy:** Walking at certain times. **Walkability:** 2. **Opened:** 1966. **Architect:** Bill Mitchell. **Season:** April-Nov. **High:** May-Aug. **To obtain tee times:** Call. **Miscellaneous:** Reduced fees (weekdays, low season, resort guests, twilight, juniors), discount packages, metal spikes, range (grass), club rentals, credit cards (MC, V, D), beginner friendly (ngcoa get linked).
Reader Comments: Open front, tight back. Excellent ... Challenging and playable ... Long course. Looks easy, very challenging ... Front 9 and back 9 are very different courses ... Good long, hard par 3s ... Older, traditional, no surprises ... Big trees, big traps, big greens, big fun! ... Classic American golf.

★★ BEECH HOLLOW GOLF COURSE
PU-7494 Hospital Rd., Freeland, 48623, Freeland County, (517)695-5427, 5 miles NW of Saginaw.
Holes: 18. **Yards:** 5,700/N/A. **Par:** 72/N/A. **Course Rating:** 66.0/N/A. **Slope:** 112/N/A. **Green Fee:** $14/$20. **Cart Fee:** $20/cart. **Walking Policy:** Unrestricted walking. **Walkability:** 1. **Opened:** 1969. **Season:** March-Nov. **High:** May-Aug. **To obtain tee times:** Call. **Miscellaneous:** Reduced fees (weekdays, low season, seniors), metal spikes, club rentals, credit cards (MC,   V,   D).

★★★ BELLE RIVER GOLF & COUNTRY CLUB
PU-12564 Belle River Rd., Memphis, 48041, St. Clair County, (810)392-2121, 20 miles W of Port Huron.
Holes: 18. **Yards:** 6,556/5,159. **Par:** 72/72. **Course Rating:** 71.4/67.7. **Slope:** 118/111. **Green Fee:** $18/$22. **Cart Fee:** $20/cart. **Walking Policy:** Unrestricted walking. **Walkability:** 4. **Opened:** 1981. **Season:** April-Nov. **High:** June-Sept. **To obtain tee times:** Call golf shop. **Miscellaneous:** Reduced fees (seniors, juniors), range (grass), club rentals, credit cards (MC, V), beginner friendly.
Reader Comments: Great greens, fantastic value ... Open course, limited sand traps... Great terrain, virtually unknown.

BELLO WOODS GOLF CLUB
PU-23650-23 Mile Rd., Macomb, 48042, Macomb County, (810)949-1200, 36 miles N of Detroit.

Holes: 27. **Green Fee:** $18/$22. **Cart Fee:** $20/cart. **Walking Policy:** Unrestricted walking. **Walkability:** 3. **Opened:** 1969. **Season:** April-Nov. **High:** July-Sept. **To obtain tee times:** Call up to 30 days in advance for weekends. Call up to 7 days in advance for weekdays. **Miscellaneous:** Reduced fees (weekdays, low season, seniors, juniors), club rentals, credit cards (MC, V).

★★½ **RED/GOLD**
Yards: 6,093/5,242. **Par:** 72/72. **Course Rating:** N/A. **Slope:** N/A.
Reader Comments: Easy ... Good course for seniors and beginners ... Family owned and run, good league course ... Nice course ... It's golf, but nothing spectacular... Short, crowded ... Not bad for quick round on short notice.

★★½ **RED/WHITE**
Yards: 6,201/5,528. **Par:** 72/72. **Course Rating:** N/A. **Slope:** N/A.

★★½ **WHITE/GOLD**
Yards: 6,020/5,062. **Par:** 72/72. **Course Rating:** N/A. **Slope:** N/A.

★★★★ **BELVEDERE GOLF CLUB** *Pace+*
SP-P.O. Box 218, Charlevoix, 49720, Charlevoix County, (231)547-2611, 40 miles NE of Traverse City.
Holes: 18. **Yards:** 6,715/5,489. **Par:** 72/72. **Course Rating:** 72.9/72.0. **Slope:** 129/123. **Green Fee:** $33/$77. **Cart Fee:** $13/person. **Walking Policy:** Walking at certain times. **Walkability:** 2. **Opened:** 1927. **Architect:** William Watson. **Season:** April-Oct. **High:** July-Aug. **To obtain tee times:** Call. **Miscellaneous:** Reduced fees (low season, resort guests, twilight), discount packages, range (grass), caddies, credit cards (MC, V).
Reader Comments: A little-known gem in northern Michigan ... Classic, old-style greens.... One of my top 25, and I've played more than 300 ... Favorite course in U.S. ... Traditional ... Shotmaking at a premium ... Wonderful ... Great track ... Short, but outstanding layout ... A must if in the area.

★★ **BENT PINE GOLF CLUB**
PU-2480 Duck Lake Rd., Whitehall, 49461, Muskegon County, (231)766-2045, 8 miles NW of Muskegon.
Holes: 18. **Yards:** 6,007/5,429. **Par:** 71/72. **Course Rating:** N/A. **Slope:** N/A. **Green Fee:** $10/$17. **Cart Fee:** $9/person. **Walking Policy:** Unrestricted walking. **Walkability:** 1. **Architect:** Oiler Family. **Season:** March-Nov. **High:** May-Sept. **To obtain tee times:** Call. **Miscellaneous:** Reduced fees (weekdays, low season, seniors, juniors), metal spikes, range (grass), club rentals, credit cards (MC, V, AE).

★★★½ **BINDER PARK GOLF COURSE**
PM-6723 B Dr. S., Battle Creek, 49014, Calhoun County, (616)966-3459, 5 miles S of Battle Creek.
Holes: 18. **Yards:** 6,328/4,965. **Par:** 72/75. **Course Rating:** 69.9/68.4. **Slope:** 114/109. **Green Fee:** $16/$17. **Cart Fee:** $22/cart. **Walking Policy:** Unrestricted walking. **Walk-ability:** 3. **Opened:** 1962. **Season:** April-Oct. **High:** June-Aug. **To obtain tee times:** Call. **Miscellaneous:** Reduced fees (weekdays, seniors, juniors), discount packages, range (grass/mats), club rentals, credit cards (MC, V, AE, D), beginner friendly (classes and lessons).
Reader Comments: Very challenging pin positions, tight fairways ... Slow play overshadows fine track ... Great muny, gets a lot of play ... Price is unbeatable for the quality ... Outstanding, don't let length fool you ... No. 12 toughest par 4 in the state ... Great condition ... Decent course, turtle pace.

★★★★ **BLACK BEAR GOLF RESORT** *Pace*
R-1500 W. Alexander Rd., Vanderbilt, 49795, Ostego County, (517)983-4505, (800)923-2711, 8 miles N of Gaylord. **Web:** webgolfer.com/blackbear/index.html.
Holes: 18. **Yards:** 6,500/4,400. **Par:** 72/72. **Course Rating:** 136.0/124.0. **Slope:** 70/67. **Green Fee:** $25/$59. **Cart Fee:** Included in Green Fee. **Walking Policy:** Mandatory cart. **Walkability:** 4. **Opened:** 1996. **Season:** May-Oct. **High:** June-Aug. **To obtain tee times:** Call anytime. **Miscellaneous:** Reduced fees (weekdays, low season, resort guests, twilight), discount packages, range (grass), club rentals, lodging (3 rooms), credit cards (MC, V, AE).
Reader Comments: Seeing wild elk was a thrill ... Very new, very challenging ... Nice vistas, needs to mature ... Know your club distances ... Excellent shape ... Northern Michigan at its best ... Open fairways, fast greens ... Will improve with age ... Treats women fairly ... Tough greens ... Hilly terrain, blind shots ... Not very well marked ... Gorgeous in the fall.

BLACK FOREST & WILDERNESS VALLEY GOLF RESORT
R-7519 Mancelona Rd., Gaylord, 49735, Otsego County, (616)585-7090, 15 miles SW of Gaylord.
★★★½ **VALLEY COURSE**
Holes: 18. **Yards:** 6,485/4,889. **Par:** 71/71. **Course Rating:** 70.6/67.8. **Slope:** 126/115. **Green Fee:** $15/$23. **Cart Fee:** $18/cart. **Walking Policy:** Unrestricted walking. **Walkability:** 2. **Opened:** 1971. **Architect:** Al Watrous. **Season:** April-Oct. **High:** July-Aug. **To obtain tee times:** Call golf shop. **Miscellaneous:** Reduced fees (weekdays, low season, resort guests, twilight,

seniors, juniors), discount packages, metal spikes, range (grass/mats), club rentals, lodging, credit cards (MC, V, AE, D), beginner friendly (practice course).
Reader Comments: Splendor on the grass! ... Too tough ... Fee too high ... Need to work the ball, great layout ... Friendly service ... Needs time ... Love this layout, beautiful ... In good shape ... Use all clubs, great wildlife.

★★★★ BLACK FOREST COURSE
Holes: 18. **Yards:** 7,044/5,282. **Par:** 73/74. **Course Rating:** 75.3/71.8. **Slope:** 145/131. **Green Fee:** $20/$40. **Cart Fee:** $25/cart. **Walking Policy:** Unrestricted walking. **Walkability:** 5. **Opened:** 1992. **Architect:** Tom Doak. **Season:** April-Oct. **High:** July-Aug. **To obtain tee times:** Call golf shop. **Miscellaneous:** Reduced fees (weekdays, low season, resort guests, twilight, seniors, juniors), discount packages, metal spikes, range (grass/mats), club rentals, lodging, credit cards (MC, V, AE, D), beginner friendly (forward tees, practice course).
Notes: Ranked 23rd in 1999 Best in State.
Reader Comments: Hard for novices ... Tons of fun ... Don't miss, great value, keep the ball below the pin or else ... Great stay and play ... Unbelievable greens ... Affordable and challenging ... Long, tough par 3s.... Secluded gem ... Breathtaking ... Excellent condition ... Bunkers would scare Stephen King ... Awesome test ... More hills than a roller coaster ... Best in Michigan.

BLACKBERRY PATCH GOLF COURSE
PU-130 One Straight Dr., Coldwater, 49036, Branch County, (517)238-8686, 6 miles SE of Coldwater. **E-mail:** blackberg@cbpo.com.
Holes: 18. **Yards:** 7,133/5,173. **Par:** 72/72. **Course Rating:** 73.8/70.8. **Slope:** 141/118. **Green Fee:** $25/$39. **Cart Fee:** Included in Green Fee. **Walking Policy:** Walking at certain times. **Walkability:** 4. **Opened:** 1998. **Architect:** Ernie Schrock. **Season:** March-Dec. **High:** June-Aug. **To obtain tee times:** Call up to 7 days in advance. **Miscellaneous:** Reduced fees (weekdays, low season, twilight, seniors, juniors), range (grass), credit cards (MC, V, AE).

BLACKHEATH GOLF CLUB
PU-3311 North Rochester Rd., Rochester Hills, 48309, Oakland County, (248)601-8000, 4 miles N of Rochester.
Holes: 18. **Yards:** 6,768/5,354. **Par:** 71/71. **Course Rating:** 73.0/70.8. **Slope:** 137/124. **Green Fee:** $35/$60. **Cart Fee:** Included in Green Fee. **Walking Policy:** Walking at certain times. **Walkability:** 2. **Opened:** 1998. **Architect:** Kevin Aldridge. **Season:** March-Dec. **High:** May-Aug. **Miscellaneous:** Reduced fees (low season, twilight, seniors, juniors), club rentals, credit cards (MC, V, AE).
Reader Comments: Outstanding greens for a new course ... Great golf! ... Tough links style ... Heather makes it slow! ... Interesting Scottish layout ... Needs to mature ... Overrated ... You'll forget you're in Michigan ... Greens superb! Could play every day! ... No trees ... Good finishing holes ... Pricey ... Classic links.

★½ BLOSSOM TRAILS GOLF COURSE
SP-1565 E. Britain Ave., Benton Harbor, 49022, Berrien County, (616)925-4951, 90 miles E of Chicago.
Holes: 18. **Yards:** 5,980/4,957. **Par:** 70/70. **Course Rating:** 68.3/N/A. **Slope:** 121/118. **Green Fee:** $16/$18. **Cart Fee:** $9/. **Walking Policy:** Unrestricted walking. **Walkability:** N/A. **Opened:** 1959. **Architect:** Bruce Mathews. **Season:** March-Nov. **High:** May-Aug. **To obtain tee times:** Call. **Miscellaneous:** Reduced fees (weekdays, low season), metal spikes, range (grass), club rentals, credit cards (MC, V, D).
Special Notes: Also has a 9-hole par 3 course.

★★★ BOGIE LAKE GOLF CLUB
PU-11231 Bogie Lake Rd., White Lake, 48386, Oakland County, (248)363-4449, 10 miles W of Pontiac.
Holes: 18. **Yards:** 6,120/N/A. **Par:** 71/N/A. **Course Rating:** 68.9/N/A. **Slope:** 122/N/A. **Green Fee:** $20/$24. **Cart Fee:** $22/cart. **Walking Policy:** Unrestricted walking. **Walkability:** 5. **Opened:** 1963. **Season:** Year-round. **High:** June-Aug. **To obtain tee times:** Call (248)363-4449 or (248)363-4416 any day 7:00 a.m.-11:00 p.m. **Miscellaneous:** Reduced fees (weekdays, low season, twilight, seniors, juniors), discount packages, metal spikes, range (grass/mats), club rentals.
Reader Comments: A 'billygoat' course—tons of hills and trees ... Needs some work ... Decent layout, 230-yard par 3, elevated tee ... Average ... Always enjoyable, out in the country ... A little of everything. Should be called Bogie Hills ... Holds rain well, challenging ... Hard to Bogie any of these holes.

BOULDER CREEK GOLF CLUB
PU-5750 Brewer Ave., Belmont, 49306, Kent County, (616)363-1330, 6 miles NE of Grand Rapids.
Holes: 18. **Yards:** 6,975/4,996. **Par:** 72/72. **Course Rating:** 73.0/67.4. **Slope:** 122/109. **Green Fee:** $25/$49. **Cart Fee:** Included in Green Fee. **Walking Policy:** Mandatory cart. **Walkability:** 4. **Opened:** 1998. **Architect:** Mark DeVries. **Season:** March-Nov. **High:** April-Sept.

MICHIGAN

Miscellaneous: Reduced fees (weekdays, low season, twilight, seniors, juniors), range (grass), club rentals, credit cards (MC, V, AE, D).

BOYNE HIGHLANDS RESORT   *Service*
R-600 Highland Dr., Harbor Springs, 49740, Emmet County, (231)526-3028, (800)462-6963, 6 miles NW of Petoskey.

★★★★   DONALD ROSS MEMORIAL COURSE
Holes: 18. **Yards:** 6,814/4,929. **Par:** 72/72. **Course Rating:** 73.4/68.5. **Slope:** 132/119. **Green Fee:** $45/$99. **Cart Fee:** Included in Green Fee. **Walking Policy:** Mandatory cart. **Walkability:** 3. **Opened:** 1985. **Architect:** Newcomb/E. Kircher/Flick/S. Kircher. **Season:** May-Oct. **High:** June-Aug. **To obtain tee times:** Call anytime. **Miscellaneous:** Reduced fees (low season, resort guests, twilight), discount packages, metal spikes, range (grass), club rentals, lodging, credit cards (MC, V, AE, D).
Reader Comments: Great food, ambience, golf—never had a better time ... Spectacu-lar late fall ... Beautiful scenery ... Overrated ... Not too challenging ... Never get tired of this one ... Interesting fun test ... One of the toughest I've played ... Still young. High-lands and mountains are golfer's paradise ... Bring your sand game. Bunkers galore ... Great variety.

★★★★½   HEATHER COURSE   *Condition*
Holes: 18. **Yards:** 7,210/5,245. **Par:** 72/72. **Course Rating:** 74.0/67.8. **Slope:** 131/111. **Green Fee:** $51/$110. **Cart Fee:** Included in Green Fee. **Walking Policy:** Walking at certain times. **Walkability:** 3. **Opened:** 1968. **Architect:** Robert Trent Jones. **Season:** May-Oct. **High:** June-Aug. **To obtain tee times:** Call anytime. **Miscellaneous:** Reduced fees (low season, resort guests, twilight), discount packages, range (grass), club rentals, lodging, credit cards (MC, V, AE, D).
Notes: Ranked 21st in 1999 Best in State.
Reader Comments: One of the best I've ever played ... Nice but expensive ... Monster sand traps ... Electronic yardage on some carts ... Great traditional golf ... Weather dominates play ... Not sure it's worth the cost, but awful nice ... Awesome finishing hole ... Scenic ... Best greens in Michigan ... Worth every dollar ... Splendid.

★★★★   MOOR COURSE
Holes: 18. **Yards:** 7,127/5,459. **Par:** 72/72. **Course Rating:** 74.0/70.0. **Slope:** 131/118. **Green Fee:** $36/$70. **Cart Fee:** Included in Green Fee. **Walking Policy:** Mandatory cart. **Walkability:** 3. **Opened:** 1972. **Architect:** William Newcomb. **Season:** May-Dec. **High:** June-Aug. **To obtain tee times:** Call anytime. **Miscellaneous:** Reduced fees (low season, resort guests, twilight), dis-count packages, metal spikes, range (grass), club rentals, lodging, credit cards (MC, V, AE, D).
Reader Comments: Long, traditional, tree-lined fairways ... Fair, enjoyable ... Lots of deer ... Never had a wait ... Outstanding course and service ... Too costly ... Tough course, lots of water, beautiful views ... Gets boring if played too much ... Variety of beautiful holes ... Woods, mead-ows and marsh ... Great greens and scenery.

BOYNE MOUNTAIN RESORT
R-Deer Lake Rd., Boyne Falls, 49713, Charlevoix County, (231)549-6029, (800)462-6963, 18 miles S of Petoskey.

★★★★   ALPINE COURSE
Holes: 18. **Yards:** 7,017/4,986. **Par:** 72/72. **Course Rating:** 73.6/68.4. **Slope:** 129/114. **Green Fee:** $21/$80. **Cart Fee:** Included in Green Fee. **Walking Policy:** Mandatory cart. **Walkability:** 4. **Architect:** Bill Newcombe. **Season:** April-Oct. **High:** June-Aug. **To obtain tee times:** Call 800 number up to 30 days in advance. **Miscellaneous:** Reduced fees (low season, resort guests, twilight), discount packages, metal spikes, range (grass/mats), club rentals, lodging, credit cards (MC, V, AE, D, Diners Club).
Reader Comments: Still one of the best up north ... Too pricey ... Deer, turkey, wildlife ... Fair and fun ... Wide landing areas, low stress ... Great scenery ... Nice ladies layout ... Picturesque ... Hilly ... Underrated ... Rolling layout, lots of elevation and woods ... MUST.

★★★★   MONUMENT COURSE
Holes: 18. **Yards:** 7,086/4,909. **Par:** 72/72. **Course Rating:** 75.0/68.9. **Slope:** 139/122. **Green Fee:** $21/$80. **Cart Fee:** Included in Green Fee. **Walking Policy:** Mandatory cart. **Walkability:** 4. **Opened:** 1986. **Architect:** Bill Newcomb. **Season:** April-Oct. **High:** June-Aug. **To obtain tee times:** Call 800 number up to 30 days in advance. **Miscellaneous:** Reduced fees (low season, resort guests, twilight), discount packages, metal spikes, range (grass/mats), club rentals, lodg-ing, credit cards (MC, V, AE, D, Diners Club).
Reader Comments: Island green is menacing ... Nice elevations ... Like teeing off a cliff ... Deer, turkey, wildlife ... Lost lots of balls ... Uphill climbs ... Time will help this beauty mature ... Great finish ... Nos. 1, 4, and 5 will make grown men cry ... Needs better maintenance ... Fast greens, natural terrain.

★★½   BRAE BURN GOLF COURSE
PU-10860 W 5 Mile Rd., Plymouth, 48170, Wayne County, (734)453-1900, (800)714-6700, 20 miles W of Detroit.

Holes: 18. **Yards:** 6,320/5,072. **Par:** 70/71. **Course Rating:** 70.0/70.6. **Slope:** 120/119. **Green Fee:** $19/$42. **Cart Fee:** Included in Green Fee. **Walking Policy:** Walking at certain times. **Walkability:** 4. **Opened:** 1923. **Architect:** Wilford Reed. **Season:** April-Nov. **High:** April-Sept. **To obtain tee times:** Call up to 7 days in advance. Outings may be booked a year in advance. **Miscellaneous:** Reduced fees (weekdays, low season, twilight, seniors, juniors), range (grass/mats), club rentals, credit cards (MC, V, AE).
Reader Comments: One of the toughest par 5s ever ... Average ... Over-watered ... Greens are too fast ... Fun, challenging ... There's no cutting corners on the double dogleg ... Pack a lunch, slow play ... Empty, inexpensive in spring.

★★★ BRAESIDE GOLF COURSE
PU-5460 Eleven Mile Rd., Rockford, 49341, Kent County, (616)866-1402, 12 miles NE of Grand Rapids.
Holes: 18. **Yards:** 6,810/5,440. **Par:** 71/72. **Course Rating:** 72.8/71.5. **Slope:** 136/131. **Green Fee:** $22/$24. **Cart Fee:** $24/cart. **Walking Policy:** Unrestricted walking. **Walkability:** 3. **Opened:** 1979. **Season:** April-Oct. **High:** June-Sept. **To obtain tee times:** Call in on a daily basis or one week ahead of time. **Miscellaneous:** Reduced fees (weekdays, seniors, juniors), metal spikes, club rentals, credit cards (MC, V).
Reader Comments: Fun course if you're in the area ... Tough course ... Very nice, hilly, tight ... Fast greens ... Play is slow ... Good test.

★★½ BRAMBLEWOOD GOLF COURSE
PU-2154 Bramblewood Rd., Holly, 48442, Oakland County, (248)634-3481, 20 miles W of Pontiac.
Holes: 18. **Yards:** 6,005/5,052. **Par:** 70/72. **Course Rating:** 70.0/74.0. **Slope:** 113/113. **Green Fee:** $15/$21. **Cart Fee:** $10/person. **Walking Policy:** Walking at certain times. **Walkability:** 4. **Opened:** 1965. **Season:** April-Oct. **High:** June-Aug. **To obtain tee times:** Call golf shop. **Miscellaneous:** Reduced fees (weekdays, low season, seniors, juniors), metal spikes, club rentals, credit cards (MC, V).
Reader Comments: Small, family owned, challenging back 9 ... Nice, quiet, tight ... OK ... Some unique holes ... Average, but price is good.

★★½ BRANSON BAY GOLF COURSE
PU-215 Branson Bay Dr., Mason, 48854, Ingham County, (517)663-4144, 8 miles S of Lansing.
Holes: 18. **Yards:** 6,497/5,145. **Par:** 72/73. **Course Rating:** 71.5/69.5. **Slope:** 124/116. **Green Fee:** $12/$19. **Cart Fee:** $20/cart. **Walking Policy:** Unrestricted walking. **Walkability:** 3. **Opened:** 1968. **Season:** March-Nov. **High:** June-Aug. **To obtain tee times:** Call in advance. **Miscellaneous:** Reduced fees (low season, twilight), range (grass), club rentals, credit cards (MC, V).
Reader Comments: Good course ... Good league course—open and long ... A lot of blind green shots.

★★★ BRIAR DOWNS GOLF COURSE
PU-5441 E. M-115, Mesick, 49668, Wexford County, (616)885-1220, 26 miles S of Traverse City.
Holes: 18. **Yards:** 5,876/4,549. **Par:** 71/71. **Course Rating:** 69.4/67.3. **Slope:** 116/104. **Green Fee:** $16/$25. **Cart Fee:** $10/person. **Walking Policy:** Unrestricted walking. **Walkability:** 3. **Opened:** 1989. **Architect:** Orman Bishop. **Season:** April-Oct. **High:** June-Aug. **To obtain tee times:** Call. Reservations not necessary. **Miscellaneous:** Reduced fees (weekdays, low season, twilight, seniors, juniors), discount packages, metal spikes, club rentals, credit cards (MC, V).
Reader Comments: Great for the price ... Needs to mature some ... Just average, but price is good ... Very scenic ... Nice course.

BRIAR HILL GOLF COURSE
PU-950 W. 40th St., Fremont, 49412, Newaygo County, (616)924-2070, 40 miles NW of Grand Rapids.
Holes: 18. **Yards:** 6,134/4,624. **Par:** 72/71. **Course Rating:** 67.5/65.8. **Slope:** 113/104. **Green Fee:** $17/$20. **Cart Fee:** $10/person. **Walking Policy:** Unrestricted walking. **Walkability:** 2. **Opened:** 1928. **Architect:** William Wuthenow/Forrest Lewis. **Season:** March-Dec. **High:** June-Aug. **To obtain tee times:** Call. No restrictions. **Miscellane-ous:** Reduced fees (weekdays, low season, resort guests, twilight, seniors, juniors), metal spikes, range (grass/mats), club rentals, credit cards (MC, V, D).

BRIARWOOD
PU-2900 92nd St., Caledonia, 49316, Kent County, (616)698-8720, 10 miles S of Grand Rapids.
Holes: 27. **Green Fee:** $13/$22. **Cart Fee:** $23/cart. **Walking Policy:** Unrestricted walking. **Walkability:** 2. **Opened:** 1963. **Season:** March-Nov. **High:** April-Sept. **To obtain tee times:** Call anytime. **Miscellaneous:** Reduced fees (weekdays, low season, seniors, juniors), range (grass), club rentals, credit cards (MC, V, AE, D)
★★★½ **EAST/BACK**
Yards: 6,571/5,681. **Par:** 72/78. **Course Rating:** N/A. **Slope:** N/A. .

Reader Comments: Keep it straight ... Nice clubhouse ... Hilly, but fair... Great practice course ... Has character, water, no houses ... Play extremely slow, some holes very short ... Fair greens.

★★★½ FRONT/BACK
Yards: 6,285/5,244. Par: 72/76. Course Rating: N/A. Slope: N/A.
Reader Comments: Nice layout challenging for average golfer ... In nice shape.

★★★½ FRONT/EAST
Yards: 6,364/5,503. Par: 72/78. Course Rating: N/A. Slope: N/A.

★★½ BRIGADOON GOLF CLUB
PU-12559 Bagley Ave., Grant, 49327, Newaygo County, (231)834-8200, (800)839-8206, 30 miles N of Grand Rapids. Web: www.brigadoongolf.com.
Holes: 27. Yards: 6,115/4,825. Par: 72/72. Course Rating: 70.9/68.6. Slope: 135/124. Green Fee: $25/$31. Cart Fee: Included in Green Fee. Walking Policy: Walking at certain times. Walkability: 5. Opened: 1989. Architect: Grant McKinley. Season: April-Nov. High: May-Aug. To obtain tee times: Call. Miscellaneous: Reduced fees (weekdays, low season, seniors), discount packages, metal spikes, range (grass/mats), club rentals, credit cards (MC, V).
Reader Comments: Scenic and challenging ... Nicknamed 'bring-a-dozen' ... Unique layout ... Amateur design job ... Pretty course, short and tight ... Very difficult.

★★ BROADMOOR COUNTRY CLUB
PU-7725 Kraft Ave. SE, Caledonia, 49316, Kent County, (616)891-8000, 8 miles SE of Grand Rapids.
Holes: 18. Yards: 6,400/5,800. Par: 72/74. Course Rating: N/A. Slope: N/A. Green Fee: $13/$22. Cart Fee: $23/cart. Walking Policy: Unrestricted walking. Walkability: 2. Opened: 1964. Season: March-Nov. High: April-Sept. Miscellaneous: Reduced fees (weekdays, low season, seniors, juniors), range (grass), club rentals, credit cards (MC, V, AE), beginner friendly (junior programs).

★★★ BROOKWOOD GOLF COURSE
SP-6045 Davison Rd, Burton, 48509, Genesee County, (810)742-4930, 5 miles E of Flint.
Holes: 18. Yards: 6,972/5,977. Par: 72/72. Course Rating: 72.9/78.7. Slope: 123/122. Green Fee: $16/$26. Cart Fee: $23/cart. Walking Policy: Unrestricted walking. Walkability: 3. Opened: 1938. Season: April-Nov. High: June-Aug. To obtain tee times: Call up to 7 days in advance. Miscellaneous: Metal spikes, range (grass), club rentals, credit cards (MC, V).
Reader Comments: Great layout ... Lots of play ... Nice ... Even with all the rain, course was well kept up ... Challenging, water in play on 12 holes, greens hard but smooth ... Woods, back-to-nature course, made players welcome.

★★½ BURR OAK GOLF CLUB
PU-3491 N. Parma Rd., Parma, 49269, Jackson County, (517)531-4741, 5 miles W of Jackson.
Holes: 18. Yards: 6,329/5,011. Par: 72/72. Course Rating: 69.7/N/A. Slope: N/A. Green Fee: $14/$16. Cart Fee: $9/person. Walking Policy: Unrestricted walking. Walkability: 3. Opened: 1965. Season: April-Oct. High: May-Aug. To obtain tee times: Call anytime. Miscellaneous: Reduced fees (twilight, seniors, juniors), discount packages, metal spikes, range (grass).
Reader Comments: Nice pair of par 3s on back 9 ... Fairly flat and open, good for the ego, can score ... Nice course.

★★★ BYRON HILLS GOLF CLUB
PU-7330 Burlingame Rd., Byron Center, 49315, Kent County, (616)878-1522, 10 miles S of Grand Rapids.
Holes: 18. Yards: 5,622/5,041. Par: 71/75. Course Rating: 67.3/70.1. Slope: 110/112. Green Fee: $13/$20. Cart Fee: $20/cart. Walking Policy: Unrestricted walking. Walkability: 2. Opened: 1963. Architect: Fred Ellis. Season: March-Dec. High: May-Sept. To obtain tee times: Call up to 30 days in advance for weekends and holidays. Miscellaneous: Reduced fees (weekdays, low season, seniors, juniors), metal spikes, club rentals, credit cards (MC, V).
Reader Comments: Very busy ... Nice, short course ... Mostly open, can shoot scores low ... Ego trip ... Hidden dangers ... The 'Feel Good' course of western Michigan.

★★★ CABERFAE PEAKS SKI & GOLF RESORT
R-Caberfae Rd., Cadillac, 49601, Wexford County, (616)862-3000, 12 miles W of Cadillac.
E-mail: caberfae@michweb.net. Web: www.michiweb.com/cabpeaks.
Holes: 9. Yards: 3,341/2,186. Par: 36/36. Course Rating: N/A. Slope: N/A. Green Fee: $18/$24. Cart Fee: $14/person. Walking Policy: Unrestricted walking. Walkability: 2. Opened: 1995. Architect: Harry Bowers. Season: May-Nov. High: July-Aug. To obtain tee times: Call or walk-in. Miscellaneous: Reduced fees (weekdays, low season, resort guests, twilight), discount packages, metal spikes, range (grass), club rentals, lodging (36 rooms), credit cards (MC, V, D).
Reader Comments: Deer and wild turkey on the course ... We were treated like they wanted us there.

MICHIGAN

★★ CAIN'S BURNING OAK COUNTRY CLUB
PU-4345 Redwood Dr., Roscommon, 48653, Roscommon County, (517)821-9821, 62 miles SE of Traverse City.
Holes: 18. **Yards:** 6,240/5,256. **Par:** 72/72. **Course Rating:** 69.7/70.0. **Slope:** 117/115. **Green Fee:** $20/$20. **Cart Fee:** $9/person. **Walking Policy:** Unrestricted walking. **Walkability:** 1. **Opened:** 1962. **Season:** April-Oct. **High:** June-Aug. **To obtain tee times:** Call. **Miscellaneous:** Reduced fees (juniors), range (grass/mats), club rentals, credit cards (MC, V, D).

★★★★ CANDLESTONE GOLF CLUB
R-8100 N. Storey, Belding, 48809, Ionia County, (616)794-1580, 20 miles NE of Grand Rapids.
Holes: 18. **Yards:** 6,692/5,547. **Par:** 72/74. **Course Rating:** 72.8/73.1. **Slope:** 129/126. **Green Fee:** $23/$27. **Cart Fee:** $12/person. **Walking Policy:** Unrestricted walking. **Walkability:** 3. **Opened:** 1975. **Architect:** Bruce Matthews/Jerry Matthews. **Season:** March-Oct. **High:** May-Sept. **To obtain tee times:** Call 7 days in advance. **Miscellaneous:** Reduced fees (weekdays, low season, resort guests, twilight, seniors), discount packages, metal spikes, range (grass/mats), club rentals, lodging (24 rooms), credit cards (MC, V, AE, D).
Reader Comments: Fun course, small, but well-conditioned greens ... Last 4 holes are exceptional ... Nice and tough ... Open, but tight ... Well maintained ... Demanding ... Older course ... Variety ... Good test ... Challenging, great value ... Best played weekday mornings—no crowds.

★★½ CARLETON GLEN GOLF CLUB
SP-13470 Grafton Rd., Carleton, 48117, Monroe County, (734)654-6201, 19 miles SW of Detroit.
Holes: 18. **Yards:** 6,496/5,602. **Par:** 71/71. **Course Rating:** 70.0/73.0. **Slope:** 114/112. **Green Fee:** $20/$25. **Cart Fee:** $12/person. **Walking Policy:** Unrestricted walking. **Walkability:** 3. **Opened:** 1960. **Architect:** Robert G. Milosch. **Season:** April-Nov. **High:** May-Sept. **To obtain tee times:** Call 7 days in advance. Send money for earlier times. **Miscellaneous:** Reduced fees (weekdays, low season, twilight, seniors, juniors), metal spikes, range (grass), credit cards (MC, V, D).

★★★½ CASCADES GOLF COURSE *Value+*
PM-1992 Warren Ave., Jackson, 49203, Jackson County, (517)788-4323, 37 miles E of Battle Creek.
Holes: 18. **Yards:** 6,614/5,282. **Par:** 72/73. **Course Rating:** 71.8/70.5. **Slope:** 122/117. **Green Fee:** $13/$17. **Cart Fee:** $10/person. **Walking Policy:** Unrestricted walking. **Walkability:** 2. **Opened:** 1929. **Architect:** Tom Bendelow. **Season:** March-Oct. **High:** July-Sept. **To obtain tee times:** Call 7 days in advance. **Miscellaneous:** Reduced fees (weekdays, low season, twilight, seniors, juniors), range (grass), club rentals, credit cards (MC, V).
Reader Comments: Great old-country course, a classic ... Old gem ... Pleasant surprise ... Nice front nine, so-so back nine ... Superb value, excellent condition, challenging ... Excellent for the price ... Nice traditional layout through the woods ... Tremendous muny ... Beautiful.

★★★½ CATTAILS GOLF CLUB
PU-57737 W. 9 Mile Rd., South Lyon, 48178, Oakland County, (248)486-8777, 25 miles W of Detroit. **E-mail:** cattailsgc@aol.com. **Web:** www.cattails.simplenet.com.
Holes: 18. **Yards:** 6,436/4,974. **Par:** 72/72. **Course Rating:** 72.1/70.2. **Slope:** 131/118. **Green Fee:** $28/$40. **Cart Fee:** $14/person. **Walking Policy:** Walking at certain times. **Walkability:** 3. **Opened:** 1991. **Architect:** Doug Palm. **Season:** April-Nov. **High:** June-Aug. **To obtain tee times:** Call 7 days in advance. **Miscellaneous:** Reduced fees (weekdays, low season, twilight, seniors, juniors), discount packages, range (grass/mats), club rentals, credit cards (MC, V, AE).
Reader Comments: Course is pretty, but too 'junked up' ... Lots of crazy, fun hazards, but slope of the greens is ridiculous ... Full length miniature golf! ... Well conditioned, somewhat short but challenging ... Overrated course ... Well-kept secret ... Good southern Michigan course ... Cattails all over the course ... Use your mind not muscles ... Target golf.

★★★½ CEDAR CHASE GOLF CLUB
PU-7551 17 Mile Rd. N.E., Cedar Springs, 49319, Kent County, (616)696-2308, 20 miles N of Grand Rapids.
Holes: 18. **Yards:** 7,115/5,115. **Par:** 72/72. **Course Rating:** 74.6/69.7. **Slope:** 132/122. **Green Fee:** $25/$33. **Cart Fee:** $12/person. **Walking Policy:** Unrestricted walking. **Walkability:** 3. **Opened:** 1993. **Architect:** Bruce Matthews III. **Season:** April-Nov. **High:** June-Aug. **To obtain tee times:** Call up to 14 days in advance. **Miscellaneous:** Reduced fees (weekdays, low season, seniors, juniors), range (grass), club rentals, credit cards (MC, V, AE, D).
Reader Comments: Immature, but developing ... Improving ... Central course with Northern feel—hills, trees, sand ... Very nice day of golf ... Difficult, but fair ... Solid ... Needs maturing and price cut ... Worth the drive ... Tough finishing holes ... Well-balanced design ... Fast greens, tightness causes slow play, excellent value.

MICHIGAN

★★½ CEDAR CREEK GOLF COURSE
PU-14000 Renton Rd., Battle Creek, 49017, Calhoun County, (616)965-6423, 10 miles E of Kalamazoo.
Holes: 18. **Yards:** 6,422/4,914. **Par:** 72/72. **Course Rating:** 70.9/68.8. **Slope:** 124/115. **Green Fee:** $12/$19. **Cart Fee:** $10/person. **Walking Policy:** Unrestricted walking. **Walkability:** 3.
Opened: 1974. **Architect:** Robert Beard. **Season:** Year round. **High:** May-Aug. **Miscellaneous:** Reduced fees (low season, seniors, juniors), range (grass), club rentals, credit cards (MC, V), beginner friendly (junior and adult beginner programs).
Reader Comments: Very forgiving fairways, fast greens, lots of water ... Great course to get your swing back after winter... OK course at OK price.

★★ CEDAR GLEN GOLF CLUB
SP-36860 25 Mile Rd., New Baltimore, 48047, Macomb County, (810)725-8156, 16 miles NE of Mount Clemens.
Holes: 18. **Yards:** 6,140/5,052. **Par:** 71/71. **Course Rating:** 69.5/69.9. **Slope:** 118/119. **Green Fee:** $20/$26. **Cart Fee:** $20/cart. **Walking Policy:** Unrestricted walking. **Walkability:** 1.
Opened: 1968. **Architect:** Jerry Matthews. **Season:** April-Nov. **High:** May-Sept. **To obtain tee times:** Call. **Miscellaneous:** Reduced fees (weekdays, low season, twilight, seniors, juniors), metal spikes, club rentals, credit cards (MC, V), beginner friendly (junior clinic).

★★★ CENTENNIAL ACRES GOLF COURSE
PU-12485 Dow Rd., Sunfield, 48890, Eaton County, (517)566-8055, 15 miles W of Lansing.
Holes: 27. **Yards:** 6,581/4,932. **Par:** 72/72. **Course Rating:** 72.8/69.0. **Slope:** 126/113. **Green Fee:** $13/$21. **Cart Fee:** $10/person. **Walking Policy:** Unrestricted walking. **Walkability:** 3.
Opened: 1979. **Architect:** Warner Bowen. **Season:** April-Nov. **High:** June-Aug. **To obtain tee times:** Call. **Miscellaneous:** Reduced fees (low season, seniors, juniors), discount packages, club rentals, credit cards (MC, V, D).
Reader Comments: Secluded and peaceful ... Out in nowhere land, but a good course ... Variety.

★½ CENTER VIEW GOLF COURSE
564 N. Adrian Hwy., Adrian, 49221, Lenawee County, (517)263-8081.
Special Notes: Call club for further information.

★★★½ CHARLEVOIX COUNTRY CLUB
SP-9600 Clubhouse Dr, Charlevoix, 49720, Charlevoix County, (616)547-1922, (800)618-9796, 40 miles N of Traverse City.
Holes: 18. **Yards:** 6,520/5,084. **Par:** 72/72. **Course Rating:** 70.6/68.4. **Slope:** 127/115. **Green Fee:** $39/$60. **Cart Fee:** Included in Green Fee. **Walking Policy:** Mandatory cart. **Walkability:** 3. **Opened:** 1994. **Architect:** Jerry Matthews. **Season:** May-Oct. **High:** June-Aug. **To obtain tee times:** Call. **Miscellaneous:** Reduced fees (weekdays, low season, resort guests, twilight), discount packages, metal spikes, range (grass), club rentals, credit cards (MC, V, AE).
Reader Comments: Short but fun ... Lots of water on front and trees on back ... Very nice layout ... Plays long, tight fairways ... I love this course ... Score on the front course, back is brutal.

★★½ CHASE HAMMOND GOLF COURSE
PU-2454 N. Putnam Rd., Muskegon, 49445, Muskegon County, (231)766-3035, 40 miles NW of Grand Rapids.
Holes: 18. **Yards:** 6,307/5,135. **Par:** 72/72. **Course Rating:** 71.2/71.1. **Slope:** 133/123. **Green Fee:** $13/$22. **Cart Fee:** $10/person. **Walking Policy:** Unrestricted walking. **Walkability:** 2.
Opened: 1970. **Architect:** Mark DeVries. **Season:** March-Nov. **High:** June-Aug. **To obtain tee times:** Call up to 7 days in advance. **Miscellaneous:** Reduced fees (weekdays, low season, twilight, seniors, juniors), range (grass), club rentals, credit cards (MC, V, AE, D).
Reader Comments: Woody and hilly, but not too challenging ... One of Michigan's finest public courses ... Rough shape ... New family owners are making positive changes ... Good for beginners and old ladies—short ... Nice course, excellent value ... Shooting gallery ... Fun.

★★½ CHEBOYGAN GOLF & COUNTRY CLUB
SP-1431 Old Mackinaw Rd., Cheboygan, 49721, Cheboygan County, (616)627-4264, 12 miles SE of Mackinaw City.
Holes: 18. **Yards:** 6,003/4,653. **Par:** 70/71. **Course Rating:** 67.4/67.7. **Slope:** 120/113. **Green Fee:** $16/$23. **Cart Fee:** $12/person. **Walking Policy:** Unrestricted walking. **Walkability:** 3.
Opened: 1922. **Architect:** Bill Newcomb. **Season:** April-Oct. **High:** June-Aug. **To obtain tee times:** We welcome reservations at anytime. **Miscellaneous:** Reduced fees (low season, twilight, seniors, juniors), metal spikes, range (grass), club rentals, credit cards (MC, V, AE, D).
Reader Comments: I love the short par 5s ... Old but not forgotten!

★★★½ CHERRY CREEK GOLF CLUB
PU-52000 Cherry Creek Dr., Shelby Township, 48316, Macomb County, (810)254-7700, 16 miles NW of Detroit.

Holes: 18. **Yards:** 6,784/5,012. **Par:** 72/72. **Course Rating:** 72.7/67.1. **Slope:** 139/114. **Green Fee:** $35/$55. **Cart Fee:** Included in Green Fee. **Walking Policy:** Walking at certain times. **Walkability:** 3. **Opened:** 1995. **Architect:** Lanny Wadkins/Mike Bylen. **Season:** April-Dec. **High:** All. **To obtain tee times:** Call up to 7 days in advance. **Miscellaneous:** Reduced fees (low season, seniors, juniors), metal spikes, range (grass/mats), club rentals, credit cards (MC, V). **Reader Comments:** Public that seems private ... Outstanding, picturesque ... Ridicu-lously slow play ... Good test without overwhelming you ... Terrific new course ... Beauti-ful clubhouse ... If the golf course was as good as their clubhouse and service, it would be better to play ... Overrated ... Walk it early in the morning! ... Easy and enjoyable.

CHESHIRE HILLS GOLF COURSE
PU-3829 102nd Ave., Allegan, 49010, Allegan County, (616)673-2882, 10 miles S of Allegan.
Holes: 27. **Green Fee:** $17/$19. **Cart Fee:** $9/person. **Walking Policy:** Unrestricted walking. **Walkability:** 3. **Opened:** 1972. **Architect:** Herb Johnson. **Season:** April-Oct. **High:** June-Aug. **To obtain tee times:** Call ahead. **Miscellaneous:** Reduced fees (seniors, juniors), range (grass/mats), club rentals, credit cards (MC, V, D).
★★★ **BLUE BIRD/RED FOX**
Yards: 6,112/4,564. **Par:** 70/70. **Course Rating:** 68.8/64.7. **Slope:** 114/103.
Reader Comments: Country course, deer, foxes, great treat ... 27 holes of excellent golf.
★★★ **BLUE BIRD/WHITETAIL**
Yards: 5,904/4,482. **Par:** 70/70. **Course Rating:** 68.8/64.7. **Slope:** 114/103.
★★★ **RED FOX/WHITETAIL**
Yards: 6,026/4,490. **Par:** 70/70. **Course Rating:** 68.8/64.7. **Slope:** 114/103.

★★★★ CHESTNUT VALLEY GOLF COURSE *Pace+*
SP-1875 Clubhouse Dr, Harbor Springs, 49740, Emmet County, (616)526-9100, (877)284-3688, 10 miles N of Petoskey.
Holes: 18. **Yards:** 6,406/5,166. **Par:** 72/72. **Course Rating:** 71.8/72.1. **Slope:** 125/116. **Green Fee:** $40/$70. **Cart Fee:** Included in Green Fee. **Walking Policy:** Walking at certain times. **Walkability:** 4. **Opened:** 1994. **Architect:** Larry Mancour. **Season:** May-Nov. **High:** June-Sept. **To obtain tee times:** Call golf shop. **Miscellaneous:** Reduced fees (weekdays, low season, resort guests, twilight), discount packages, range (grass), club rentals, credit cards (MC, V, D). **Reader Comments:** Quiet setting ... Well kept, rather short ... Nice northern course ... Women friendly ... Beautiful course in the woods ... Love this course.

★½ CHISHOLM HILLS COUNTRY CLUB
2395 S. Washington Rd., Lansing, 48911, Ingham County, (517)694-0169.
Special Notes: Call club for further information.

★★½ CHOCOLAY DOWNS GOLF COURSE
PU-125 Chocolay Downs Golf Dr., Marquette, 49855, Marquette County, (906)249-3683, 7 miles E of Marquette.
Holes: 18. **Yards:** 6,375/4,878. **Par:** 72/72. **Course Rating:** N/A. **Slope:** N/A. **Green Fee:** $20/$20. **Cart Fee:** $18/cart. **Walking Policy:** Unrestricted walking. **Walkability:** 2. **Opened:** 1992. **Architect:** Jerry Matthews. **Season:** April-Nov. **High:** June-Aug. **To obtain tee times:** Call golf shop. **Miscellaneous:** Reduced fees (low season, seniors), discount packages, range (grass/mats), club rentals, credit cards (MC, V).
Reader Comments: World's largest putting green ... Breathtaking views of Lake Superior ... Excellent golf experience, trees and flowers ... Laid back, relaxing ... Mediocre design.

★★ CLARK LAKE GOLF CLUB
PU-5535 Wesch Rd. P.O. Box 519, Brooklyn, 49230, Jackson County, (517)592-6259, 17 miles S of Jackson.
Holes: 18. **Yards:** 6,632/5,511. **Par:** 73/73. **Course Rating:** N/A. **Slope:** N/A. **Green Fee:** $9/$14. **Cart Fee:** $24/cart. **Walking Policy:** Unrestricted walking. **Walkability:** 2. **Opened:** 1919. **Season:** Year-round. **High:** May-Oct. **To obtain tee times:** First come, first served. **Miscellaneous:** Reduced fees (weekdays, seniors), metal spikes, range (grass), club rentals.
Special Notes: Also has a 9-hole par-35 course.

★★ CLARKSTON CREEK GOLF CLUB
SP-6060 Maybee Rd., Clarkston, 48346, Oakland County, (248)625-3731, 35 miles N of Detroit.
Holes: 18. **Yards:** 6,300/5,300. **Par:** 71/74. **Course Rating:** 69.5/70.6. **Slope:** 126/120. **Green Fee:** $19/$30. **Cart Fee:** $22/cart. **Walking Policy:** Unrestricted walking. **Walkability:** 3. **Opened:** 1969. **Architect:** William Newcombe. **Season:** March-Nov. **High:** May-Sept. **To obtain tee times:** Call up to 7 days in advance. **Miscellaneous:** Reduced fees (weekdays, low season, twilight, seniors, juniors), metal spikes, range (grass/mats), club rentals, credit cards (MC, V, AE). **Special Notes:** Formerly Spring Lake Country Club.

MICHIGAN

★★★ CLEARBROOK GOLF CLUB
PU-6494 Clearbrook Dr., Saugatuck, 49453, Allegan County, (616)857-2000, 25 miles SW of Grand Rapids. **Web:** www.webgolfer.comlakeshoregolf.
Holes: 18. **Yards:** 6,453/5,153. **Par:** 72/74. **Course Rating:** 72.8/70.0. **Slope:** 132/127. **Green Fee:** $27/$32. **Cart Fee:** $12/person. **Walking Policy:** Unrestricted walking. **Walkability:** 2.
Opened: 1920. **Architect:** Charles Darl Scott. **Season:** April-Oct. **High:** June-Aug. **To obtain tee times:** Call up to 6 days in advance. **Miscellaneous:** Reduced fees (low season, juniors), discount packages, range (grass/mats), club rentals, credit cards (MC, V, AE, D), beginner friendly (clinics and professional instruction available).
Reader Comments: Nice people and course ... Too many blind shots ... Overpriced, nice but not great ... Dandy ... Need local knowledge ... Clubhouse much better than course.

★★★½ CONCORD HILLS GOLF COURSE
PU-7331 Pulaski Rd., Concord, 49237, Jackson County, (517)524-8337, 12 miles SW of Jackson.
Holes: 18. **Yards:** 6,422/5,104. **Par:** 72/72. **Course Rating:** 71.5/71.0. **Slope:** 125/125. **Green Fee:** $16/$19. **Cart Fee:** $9/person. **Walking Policy:** Unrestricted walking. **Walkability:** 3.
Opened: 1976. **Architect:** William Newcomb. **Season:** April-Nov. **High:** June-Sept. **To obtain tee times:** Call up to 7 days in advance. Groups or hotel guests may call up to 1 year in advance with deposit or credit card. **Miscellaneous:** Reduced fees (weekdays, low season, resort guests, twilight, seniors, juniors), discount packages, metal spikes, range (grass), club rentals, credit cards (MC, V).
Reader Comments: Well-kept fairways and greens, very scenic ... Feels like northern resort course ... Lots of elevation ... Super staff, worth the money, fairly short, but a good test of golf, fits in well with terrain ... Beautiful, quick place to play on weekend afternoons ... Marvelous.

COPPER HILL GOLF & COUNTRY CLUB
SP-2125 Lakeville Rd., Oxford, 48370, Oakland County, (248)969-9808. **E-mail:** junglegolf@aol. **Web:** www.copperhills.com.
Holes: 27. **Cart Fee:** Included in Green Fee. **Walking Policy:** Mandatory cart. **Walkability:** 5.
Opened: 1997. **Architect:** Curtis Wright. **Season:** April-Dec. **High:** April-Oct. **To obtain tee times:** May call 2 weeks in advance, must guarantee weekends with a credit card.
Miscellaneous: Reduced fees (weekdays, low season, twilight, seniors), club rentals, credit cards (MC, V, AE), beginner friendly (5 sets of tees).
★★★½ HILL/JUNGLE
Yards: 6,539/4,673. **Par:** 72/72. **Course Rating:** N/A. **Slope:** N/A. **Green Fee:** $40/$60.
★★★½ MARSH/HILL
Yards: 6,714/4,714. **Par:** 72/72. **Course Rating:** 73.1/68.3. **Slope:** 145/120. **Green Fee:** $40/$55.
Notes: Ranked 16th in 1999 Best in State.
Reader Comments: Wonderful topography! ... Way over priced! ... New course, interesting layout ... They justly brag of toughness ... Enjoyable to play ... Some holes tricked up ... Very tough, bring balls, uncrowded, play once... Like being up north ... Temporary clubhouse ... Secluded, wide fairways with beautiful vistas.
★★★½ MARSH/JUNGLE
Yards: 6,493/4,771. **Par:** 72/72. **Course Rating:** N/A. **Slope:** N/A. **Green Fee:** $40/$60.

★★★½ COUNTY HIGHLANDS GOLF CLUB
SP-Hwy. 31S., Bear Lake, 49614, Manistee County, (616)864-3817, 40 miles S of Traverse city.
Holes: 18. **Yards:** 6,527/5,188. **Par:** 72/72. **Course Rating:** 71.0/70.1. **Slope:** 121/121. **Green Fee:** $22/$26. **Cart Fee:** $10/person. **Walking Policy:** Unrestricted walking. **Walkability:** 3.
Opened: 1966. **Season:** April-Oct. **High:** June-Aug. **To obtain tee times:** Call. **Miscellaneous:** Reduced fees (low season, twilight, juniors), discount packages, club rentals, credit cards (MC, V, D).
Reader Comments: Good condition ... Excellent ... A good course getting better ... Challenging but playable.

★★★ COYOTE GOLF CLUB
PU-28700 Milford Rd., New Hudson, 48165, Oakland County, (248)486-1228, 30 miles NW of Detroit.
Holes: 18. **Yards:** 7,201/4,923. **Par:** 72/72. **Course Rating:** 73.8/68.4. **Slope:** 130/114. **Green Fee:** $18/$42. **Cart Fee:** $13/person. **Walking Policy:** Walking at certain times. **Walkability:** 3.
Opened: 1996. **Architect:** Scott Thacker. **Season:** March-Nov. **High:** June-Sept. **To obtain tee times:** Call up to 14 days in advance. 24 hours cancellation policy. **Miscellaneous:** Reduced fees (weekdays, low season, twilight, seniors, juniors), range (grass/mats), club rentals, credit cards (MC, V).
Reader Comments: Enjoyable layout, wide open at times ... Fairways end, rough starts in strange places ... A tough target course ... New course ... Top course for seniors ... Long. Fairly new, decent, fun to play, has potential ... Not worth price ... Needs maturing.

MICHIGAN

★★★ CRACKLEWOOD GOLF CLUB
PU-18215 24 Mile Macomb Township, Mt. Clemens, 48858, Macomb County, (810)781-0808, 4 miles N of Mt. Clemens.
Holes: 18. **Yards:** 6,538/4,764. **Par:** 72/72. **Course Rating:** 70.4/67.3. **Slope:** 122/112. **Green Fee:** $23/$27. **Cart Fee:** $23/person. **Walking Policy:** Walking at certain times. **Walkability:** 2. **Opened:** 1989. **Architect:** Jerry Matthews. **Season:** Year-round. **High:** May-Sept. **To obtain tee times:** Call up to 1 week in advance. **Miscellaneous:** Reduced fees (low season, twilight, seniors, juniors), metal spikes, range (grass), club rentals, credit cards (MC, V, AE, Diners Club), beginner friendly (ladies and junior clinics).
Reader Comments: Lots of trees, must keep drive in play ... Needs better yard markers ... Decent course ... Good course for seniors ... Will become better with age ... Flat back 9 ... Not bad, but short ... Ho-Hum suburban golf ... Tight front-open back.

★½ CROOKED CREEK GOLF CLUB
PU-9387 Gratiot Rd., Saginaw, 48609, Saginaw County, (517)781-0050.
Holes: 18. **Yards:** 5,600/4,883. **Par:** 72/78. **Course Rating:** 66.5/67.4. **Slope:** 110/114. **Green Fee:** $19/$20. **Cart Fee:** $22/cart. **Walking Policy:** Unrestricted walking. **Walkability:** 2. **Opened:** 1959. **Season:** April-Dec. **High:** May-Sept. **To obtain tee times:** Call (517)781-0050. **Miscellaneous:** Reduced fees (low season, seniors, juniors), discount packages, range (grass/mats), club rentals, credit cards (MC, V, D), beginner friendly (junior & adult golf lessons).

★★★★ CROOKED TREE GOLF CLUB
PU-600 Crooked Tree Dr., Petoskey, 49770, Emmet County, (616)439-4030, 100 miles NE of Grand Rapids.
Holes: 18. **Yards:** 6,671/4,631. **Par:** 71/71. **Course Rating:** 72.8/68.0. **Slope:** 140/121. **Green Fee:** $42/$90. **Cart Fee:** Included in Green Fee. **Walking Policy:** Walking at certain times. **Walkability:** 4. **Opened:** 1995. **Architect:** Harry Bowers. **Season:** April-Nov. **High:** June-Aug. **To obtain tee times:** Call with credit card to reserve. **Miscellaneous:** Reduced fees (weekdays, low season, resort guests, twilight), range (grass/mats), club rentals, credit cards (MC, V, AE, D).
Reader Comments: Everything you could want and more ... Beautiful scenery ... Pretentious ... Too many blind shots ... Super track, super views, a favorite ... Entertaining once a year ... Wide landing areas ... Table top greens ... Gimmicky, but fun ... Several silly holes. Good value for the money.

★★ CRYSTAL LAKE GOLF CLUB
R-Hwy. 31, Beulah, 49617, Benzie County, (616)882-4061, 30 miles W of Traverse City.
Holes: 18. **Yards:** 6,400/5,500. **Par:** 70/72. **Course Rating:** 70.4/69.6. **Slope:** 118/113. **Green Fee:** $18/$25. **Walkability:** 2. **Opened:** 1970. **Architect:** Bruce Matthews/Jerry Matthews. **Season:** May-Oct. **High:** July-Aug. **To obtain tee times:** Call golf shop. **Miscellaneous:** Reduced fees (low season, twilight, seniors, juniors), metal spikes, range (grass), credit cards (MC, V).
Special Notes: Spikeless shoes encouraged.

CRYSTAL MOUNTAIN RESORT *Service+*
R-12500 Crystal Mountain Dr., Thompsonville, 49683, Benzie County, (616)378-2000, (800)968-7686, 30 miles S of Traverse City. **E-mail:** info@crystalmtn.com. **Web:** www.crystalmtn.com.
★★★★ BETSIE VALLEY GOLF COURSE
Holes: 18. **Yards:** 6,357/4,902. **Par:** 71/71. **Course Rating:** 70.2/68.5. **Slope:** 127/121. **Green Fee:** $40/$40. **Cart Fee:** $13/person. **Walking Policy:** Unrestricted walking. **Walkability:** 2. **Opened:** 1977. **Architect:** William Newcomb. **Season:** April-Oct. **High:** June-Aug. **To obtain tee times:** Call 800 number. **Miscellaneous:** Reduced fees (weekdays, low season, resort guests, twilight, juniors), discount packages, range (grass/mats), club rentals, lodging (220 rooms), credit cards (MC, V, AE, D).
Reader Comments: Top shelf ... Super place to play ... Beautiful ... Tough Nos. 15, 16 and 17 ... Luxury resort ... very hilly ... Good golf, good food, and a good time ... Course is often wet, need to improve drainage ... Real value for the money ... Friendly staff ... Fun.
★★★★ MOUNTAIN RIDGE GOLF COURSE
Holes: 18. **Yards:** 7,007/4,956. **Par:** 72/72. **Course Rating:** 73.3/68.2. **Slope:** 132/119. **Green Fee:** $48/$70. **Cart Fee:** Included in Green Fee. **Walking Policy:** Mandatory cart. **Walkability:** 4. **Opened:** 1992. **Architect:** William Newcomb. **Season:** April-Oct. **High:** June-Aug. **To obtain tee times:** Call 800 number. **Miscellaneous:** Reduced fees (weekdays, low season, resort guests, twilight, juniors), discount packages, range (grass/mats), club rentals, lodging (220 rooms), credit cards (MC, V, AE, D).
Reader Comments: Good golf, nice, well maintained ... Doubles as ski resort; golf cart needs good brakes! ... Typical resort course with wide fairways, slow greens, slow play ... Breathtaking views, challenging golf, women friendly ... Blind green shots, ... Beautiful terrain ... Very picturesque

MICHIGAN

★★ CURRIE MUNICIPAL GOLF COURSE
PM-1006 Currie Pkwy., Midland, 48640, Midland County, (517)839-9600.
Holes: 18. **Yards:** 6,523/5,244. **Par:** 72/72. **Course Rating:** 71.0/69.2. **Slope:** 118/109. **Green Fee:** $17/$17. **Cart Fee:** $12/person. **Walking Policy:** Unrestricted walking. **Walkability:** 1.
Opened: 1954. **Architect:** Gill Currie. **Season:** April-Oct. **High:** May-Sept. **To obtain tee times:** Call 3 days in advance. **Miscellaneous:** Reduced fees (twilight, seniors, juniors), range (grass/mats), club rentals.
Special Notes: Also has 9-hole West Course.

★★½ DAMA GOLF COURSE
PU-410 E. Marr Rd., Howell, 48843, Livingston County, (517)546-4635, 45 miles W of Detroit.
Holes: 18. **Yards:** 6,500/5,700. **Par:** 72/72. **Course Rating:** 69.6/66.1. **Slope:** 119/109. **Green Fee:** $19/$23. **Cart Fee:** $11/person. **Walking Policy:** Walking at certain times. **Walkability:** 3.
Opened: 1969. **Season:** March-Nov. **High:** May-Oct. **To obtain tee times:** Call golf shop.
Miscellaneous: Reduced fees (weekdays, low season, twilight, seniors, juniors), range (grass), club rentals, credit cards (MC, V).
Reader Comments: Multiple risks ... Course got better every year I played it ... Just average, but price is good.

★★½ DE MOR HILLS GOLF COURSE
10275 Ranger Hwy., Morenci, 49256, Lenawee County, (517)458-6679, 15 miles SW of Adnan.
Yards: 6,340/6,130. **Par:** 72/72. **Course Rating:** N/A. **Slope:** N/A. **Green Fee:** $17/$18.
Walkability: N/A. **Miscellaneous:** Metal spikes.
Reader Comments: Good course ... Not much rough.

★★★½ DEARBORN HILLS GOLF CLUB
PU-1300 S. Telegraph Rd., Dearborn, 48124, Wayne County, (313)563-4653.
Holes: 18. **Yards:** 4,495/3,217. **Par:** 60/60. **Course Rating:** 61.2/57.7. **Slope:** 100/92. **Green Fee:** $13/$24. **Cart Fee:** $20/cart. **Walking Policy:** Unrestricted walking. **Walkability:** 3.
Opened: 1992. **Architect:** Warner Bowen. **Season:** March-Nov. **High:** May-Oct. **To obtain tee times:** Call golf shop. **Miscellaneous:** Reduced fees (twilight, seniors, juniors), club rentals, credit cards (MC, V, D), beginner friendly (junior clinics).
Reader Comments: Good executive course ... Nice for couples ... Tough from the black tees ... Good for beginners ... Challenging for a short course.

★★★½ DEER RUN GOLF CLUB
13955 Cascade Rd., Lowell, 49331, Kent County, (616)897-8481.
Yards: 6,964/5,327. **Par:** 72/72. **Course Rating:** 126/70.7. **Slope:** 118/73.4. **Green Fee:** $20/$22. **Walkability:** N/A. **Miscellaneous:** Metal spikes.
Reader Comments: Long and challenging ... Long walk in the park ... Good greens ... Tough back nine ... Good value.

DEER RUN GOLF COURSE
PU-Pineview Dr., Mancelona, 49659, Antrim County, (616)585-6800, (800)851-4653, 18 miles SW of Gaylord.
Holes: 18. **Yards:** 6,996/5,465. **Par:** 72/74. **Course Rating:** 73.3/71.3. **Slope:** 130/123. **Green Fee:** $25/$40. **Cart Fee:** Included in Green Fee. **Walking Policy:** Unrestricted walking.
Walkability: 4. **Opened:** 1974. **Architect:** William Newcombe. **Season:** April-Oct. **High:** July-Aug. **To obtain tee times:** Call. **Miscellaneous:** Reduced fees (weekdays, low season, twilight, juniors), discounts, metal spikes, range (grass), club rentals, lodging, credit cards (MC, V, D).

DEME ACRES GOLF COURSE
PU-17655 Albain Rd., Petersburg, 49270, Monroe County, (734)279-1151, 15 miles N of Sylvania, OH.
Holes: 18. **Yards:** 5,735/5,200. **Par:** 70/70. **Course Rating:** N/A. **Slope:** N/A. **Green Fee:** $13/$18. **Cart Fee:** $9/person. **Walking Policy:** Unrestricted walking. **Walkability:** 1. **Opened:** 1962. **Season:** April-Oct. **High:** June-Aug. **To obtain tee times:** Tee times not required.
Miscellaneous: Reduced fees (weekdays, seniors, juniors), club rentals.

★★★½ DEVIL'S RIDGE GOLF CLUB
PU-3700 Metamora Rd., Oxford, 48371, Oakland County, (248)969-0100, 11 miles N of Pontiac.
Holes: 18. **Yards:** 6,722/4,130. **Par:** 72/72. **Course Rating:** 72.2/64.4. **Slope:** 123/100. **Green Fee:** $43/$55. **Cart Fee:** Included in Green Fee. **Walking Policy:** Mandatory cart. **Walkability:** 4. **Opened:** 1995. **Architect:** Patrick Conroy. **Season:** April-Nov. **High:** May-Sept. **To obtain tee times:** Call 7 days in advance. **Miscellaneous:** Reduced fees (weekdays, low season, twilight, seniors), range (grass/mats), club rentals, credit cards (MC, V, AE, D).
Reader Comments: Short, tight, challenging ... Slow play ... Many blind shots ... Lots of trick holes ... Great course, too much to play ... Very enjoyable ... Good course ... Odd design.

MICHIGAN

★★★★ THE DREAM
PU-5166 Old Hwy. 76, West Branch, 48661, Ogemaw County, (517)345-6300, (888)833-7326, 3 miles W of West Branch.
Holes: 18. **Yards:** 7,000/5,118. **Par:** 72/72. **Course Rating:** 73.7/68.6. **Slope:** 135/117. **Green Fee:** $44/$62. **Cart Fee:** Included in Green Fee. **Walking Policy:** Mandatory cart. **Walkability:** 5. **Opened:** 1997. **Architect:** Jeff Gorney. **Season:** April-Oct. **High:** May-Sept. **Miscellaneous:** Reduced fees (weekdays, low season, twilight), range (grass), club rentals, credit cards (MC, V).
Reader Comments: Going to be very popular ... Excellent new course ... Elevation changes ... Everthing you can dream of ... Good layout, very fair ... Huge fairways ... It's in the name ... I want to go back again ... Nice place ... Beautiful.... Bring your sand wedge!.

★★ THE DUNES GOLF CLUB
PU-6489 W. Empire Hwy., Empire, 49630, Leelanau County, (616)326-5390, 18 miles W of Traverse City.
Holes: 18. **Yards:** 5,868/5,041. **Par:** 72/72. **Course Rating:** 67.3/68.1. **Slope:** 112/114. **Green Fee:** $16/$16. **Cart Fee:** $18/cart. **Walking Policy:** Walking at certain times. **Walkability:** 2. **Opened:** 1984. **Season:** April-Oct. **High:** July-Aug. **To obtain tee times:** Call golf shop. **Miscellaneous:** Reduced fees (low season, twilight), club rentals, credit cards (MC, V).

★★★½ DUNHAM HILLS GOLF & COUNTRY CLUB
PU-13561 Dunham Rd., Hartland, 48353, Livingston County, (248)887-9170, 23 miles W of Pontiac.
Holes: 18. **Yards:** 6,820/5,310. **Par:** 71/74. **Course Rating:** 72.5/71.1. **Slope:** 133/123. **Green Fee:** $45/$55. **Cart Fee:** Included in Green Fee. **Walking Policy:** Walking at certain times. **Walkability:** 5. **Opened:** 1968. **Architect:** Built by owners. **Season:** March-Nov. **High:** May-Sept. **To obtain tee times:** Call. **Miscellaneous:** Reduced fees (weekdays, twilight, seniors, juniors), range (grass), credit cards (MC, V).
Reader Comments: Difficult, but fun ... Lots of elevation ... Enjoyable, challenging track ... Overpriced ... Tight fairways ... Too busy on weekends ... Tough from the back tees ... Solid, traditional ... Not a level spot on whole course ... Slick greens ... Lots of variety, interesting ... Too tight, lots of trees.

★★★½ DUNMAGLAS GOLF CLUB
PU-09031 Boyne City Rd., Charlevoix, 49720, Charlevoix County, (616)547-1022, (888)847-0909, 50 miles NE of Traverse City.
Holes: 18. **Yards:** 6,897/5,259. **Par:** 72/73. **Course Rating:** 73.5/69.8. **Slope:** 139/123. **Green Fee:** $50/$85. **Cart Fee:** Included in Green Fee. **Walking Policy:** Mandatory cart. **Walkability:** 5. **Opened:** 1992. **Architect:** Larry Mancour. **Season:** May-Oct. **High:** July-Aug. **To obtain tee times:** Call anytime in advance with credit card to confirm. **Miscellaneous:** Reduced fees (low season, twilight), discount packages, range (grass), club rentals, credit cards (MC, V, AE).
Notes: Ranked 22nd in 1999 Best in State.
Reader Comments: Tough--good luck breaking 90 ... Extremely tricky ... Great views and elevation changes ... Overpriced ... Overrated ... Another excellent links ... Extremely tight ... Only mountain goats can walk here ... Could be in better shape ... Best be straight ... Wow! Many memorable holes ... Gets better every year... Gorgeous ... Too difficult to enjoy.

★★ DUTCH HOLLOW GOLF CLUB
8500 E. Lansing Rd., Durand, 48429, Shiawassee County, (517)288-3960.
Holes: 18., **Yards:** 5,688/5,128. **Par:** 70/74. **Course Rating:** N/A. **Slope:** N/A. **Green Fee:** $12. **Walkability:** N/A. **Miscellaneous:** Metal spikes.

★★★½ EAGLE CREST GOLF CLUB
R-1275 Huron St., Ypsilanti, 48197, Washtenaw County, (734)487-2441, 30 miles SW of Detroit.
Holes: 18. **Yards:** 6,750/5,185. **Par:** 72/72. **Course Rating:** 73.6/69.7. **Slope:** 138/124. **Green Fee:** $40/$58. **Cart Fee:** Included in Green Fee. **Walking Policy:** Walking at certain times. **Walkability:** 2. **Opened:** 1989. **Architect:** Karl V. Litten. **Season:** March-Nov. **High:** June-Aug. **To obtain tee times:** Call up to 14 days in advance. **Miscellaneous:** Reduced fees (weekdays, low season, twilight, seniors, juniors), discount packages, range (grass/mats), club rentals, lodging (240 rooms), credit cards (MC, V, AE).
Reader Comments: Water, water everywhere .... slow play weekends ... Fun ... Many interesting holes on back 9 ... One of my favorites in the state! ... Worth the money and more ... Good variety ... University course, treat you well ... Will play again ... Narrow fairways, good test, not too long ... Waterfowl ... Awesome views!

★★★★ EAGLE GLEN GOLF COURSE
PU-1251 Club House Dr., Farwell, 48622, Clare County, (517)588-4653.
Holes: 18. **Yards:** 6,602/5,119. **Par:** 72/72. **Course Rating:** 71.1/69.2. **Slope:** 123/116. **Green Fee:** $21/$28. **Cart Fee:** $12/person. **Walking Policy:** Walking at certain times. **Walkability:** 3. **Opened:** 1992. **Architect:** Jerry Matthews. **Season:** April-Oct. **High:** May-Sept. **To obtain tee**

times: Call anytime. **Miscellaneous:** Reduced fees (weekdays, low season, resort guests, seniors, juniors), discount packages, range (grass), club rentals, credit cards (MC, V, D).

Reader Comments: The wind, the wind, my gosh, the wind ... Hit and run Scottish course ... Great links ... Challenging layout ... Great wildlife–fox checked out my ball ... Short, but not easy ... Beautiful ... Best bang for buck in Mid-Michigan.

★★½ EASTERN HILLS GOLF CLUB
PM-6075 East G Ave., Kalamazoo, 49004, Kalamazoo County, (616)385-8175, 2 miles E of Kalamazoo. **E-mail:** shecky4@aol.com. **Web:** www.kalamazoogolf.org.
Holes: 27. **Yards:** 6,626/5,516. **Par:** 72/72. **Course Rating:** 70.5/70.4. **Slope:** 118/113. **Green Fee:** $18/$20. **Cart Fee:** $12/person. **Walking Policy:** Unrestricted walking. **Walkability:** 2.
Opened: 1957. **Season:** March-Nov. **High:** June-Aug. **To obtain tee times:** Call 3 days in advance for weekends and holidays only. **Miscellaneous:** Reduced fees (seniors, juniors), range (grass), club rentals, credit cards (MC, V, AE, D).

Reader Comments: Great greens, lots of slopes, bunkers, trees ... Improvements have done this course proud ... Short, nice to walk.

★★ EL DORADO COUNTRY CLUB
PU-2869 Pontiac Trail, Walled Lake, 48390, Oakland County, (248)624-1736, 40 miles NW of Detroit.
Holes: 18. **Yards:** 5,753/4,846. **Par:** 70/74. **Course Rating:** 68.3/68.0. **Slope:** 122/116. **Green Fee:** $25/$33. **Cart Fee:** $12/person. **Walking Policy:** Walking at certain times. **Walkability:** 2.
Opened: 1967. **Architect:** Walter R. Lorang, Sr. **Season:** April-Oct. **High:** June-Aug. **To obtain tee times:** Call golf shop. **Miscellaneous:** Reduced fees (weekdays, low season, twilight, seniors, juniors), range (grass), club rentals, credit cards (MC, V, AE).

EL DORADO GOLF COURSE
PU-3750 Howell Rd., Mason, 48854, Ingham County, (517)676-2854, 7 miles S of Lansing.
Holes: 27. **Green Fee:** $23/$26. **Cart Fee:** $11/person. **Walking Policy:** Unrestricted walking.
Walkability: 2. **Opened:** 1968. **Season:** March-Nov. **High:** April-Oct. **To obtain tee times:** Call up to 7 days in advance. **Miscellaneous:** Reduced fees (weekdays, low season, twilight, seniors, juniors), range (grass), club rentals, credit cards (MC, V, D).

Reader Comments: Outstanding scenery, large beautiful greens, plays very long ... Very nice ... Average layout ... New holes are good ... Nice variety ... No trees, very narrow fairways ... Nothing exciting.
★★★½ **BLUE/WHITE COURSE**
Yards: 6,536/6,536. **Par:** 71/71. **Course Rating:** N/A. **Slope:** N/A.
★★★½ **RED/BLUE COURSE**
Yards: 6,712/5,498. **Par:** 72/72. **Course Rating:** N/A. **Slope:** N/A.
★★★½ **RED/WHITE COURSE**
Yards: 6,400/5,393. **Par:** 71/71. **Course Rating:** N/A. **Slope:** N/A.

★★★½ ELDORADO
PU-1 Automotive Ave., Cadillac, 49601, Wexford County, (616)779-9977, (888)374-8318, 75 miles N of Grand Rapids. **E-mail:** golfeldorado.com. **Web:** golfeldorado.com.
Holes: 18. **Yards:** 7,070/5,050. **Par:** 72/72. **Course Rating:** 73.0/68.2. **Slope:** 132/125. **Green Fee:** $30/$35. **Cart Fee:** $10/person. **Walking Policy:** Unrestricted walking. **Walkability:** 1.
Opened: 1996. **Architect:** Bob Meyer. **Season:** April-Oct. **High:** June-Aug. **To obtain tee times:** Call golf shop. **Miscellaneous:** Reduced fees (weekdays), metal spikes, range (grass), club rentals, credit cards (MC, V).

Reader Comments: Fore! ... Greens were great, some holes too close together ... A real gem ... Very classy down to the tee markers ... Huge greens, challenging swamps! ... Many forced carries ... Friendliest staff we've ever met! ... Very challenging and very pretty.

★★★★½ ELK RIDGE GOLF CLUB *Service, Condition+*
PU-9400 Rouse Rd., Atlanta, 49709, Montmorency County, (517)785-2275, (800)626-4355, 30 miles E of Gaylord. **E-mail:** elkridgegc@aol.com. **Web:** www.elkridgegolf.com.
Holes: 18. **Yards:** 7,072/5,261. **Par:** 72/72. **Course Rating:** 74.7/72.3. **Slope:** 143/130. **Green Fee:** $50/$70. **Cart Fee:** Included in Green Fee. **Walking Policy:** Walking at certain times.
Walkability: 4. **Opened:** 1991. **Architect:** Jerry Matthews. **Season:** May-Oct. **High:** June-Aug.
To obtain tee times: Call golf shop anytime with credit card. **Miscellaneous:** Reduced fees (weekdays, low season, seniors, juniors), discount packages, range (grass), club rentals, credit cards (MC, V, AE, D).
Notes: Ranked 10th in 1999 Best in State.

Reader Comments: Excellent ... It doesn't get much better than this ... Beautiful, not to difficult from white tees, enjoyable ... Best of the Best! ... Great ham sandwich ... Most beautiful course I've played ... 300-foot drop on No. 10 tee to green ... Pristine, animals, great clubhouse ... Doglegs ... Beautiful, tough layout ... Well run ... Great track, end of discussion.

MICHIGAN

★★★ ELLA SHARP PARK GOLF COURSE
PM-2800 4th St., Jackson, 49203, Jackson County, (517)788-4066, 35 miles S of Lansing.
Holes: 18. **Yards:** 5,751/5,168. **Par:** 71/71. **Course Rating:** 67.4/69.1. **Slope:** 113/114. **Green Fee:** $15/$16. **Cart Fee:** $14/cart. **Walking Policy:** Unrestricted walking. **Walkability:** 2.
Opened: 1923. **Architect:** Tom Bendelow. **Season:** March-Dec. **High:** June-Aug. **To obtain tee times:** Call golf shop. **Miscellaneous:** Reduced fees (weekdays, low season, twilight, seniors, juniors), discount packages, metal spikes, range (mats), club rentals.
Reader Comments: Good muny ... Tight, fairly cramped, but fantastic value ... Great people and price.

★★★ ELMBROOK GOLF COURSE
PU-420 Hammond Rd., Traverse City, 49684, Grand Traverse County, (616)946-9180.
Holes: 18. **Yards:** 6,131/5,194. **Par:** 72/72. **Course Rating:** 68.4/68.5. **Slope:** 114/112. **Green Fee:** $22/$31. **Cart Fee:** $14/person. **Walking Policy:** Unrestricted walking. **Walkability:** 3.
Opened: 1966. **Architect:** Jerry Matthews. **Season:** April-Nov. **High:** June-Aug. **To obtain tee times:** Call golf shop in advance. **Miscellaneous:** Reduced fees (low season, resort guests), discount packages, range (grass/mats), club rentals, credit cards (MC, V, D).
Reader Comments: Excellent local course, incredible value ... Fun.

★★★½ THE EMERALD AT MAPLE CREEK GOLF COURSE
PU-8103 N. U.S. 27, St. Johns, 48879, Clinton County, (517)224-6287, (800)924-5993, 25 miles N of Lansing. **Web:** www.michigangolfer.com/emerald.
Holes: 18. **Yards:** 6,644/5,166. **Par:** 72/72. **Course Rating:** 70.9/68.2. **Slope:** 123/113. **Green Fee:** $33/$37. **Cart Fee:** $24/cart. **Walking Policy:** Unrestricted walking. **Walkability:** 3.
Opened: 1996. **Architect:** Jerry Matthews. **Season:** April-Oct. **High:** May-Sept. **To obtain tee times:** Call golf shop. **Miscellaneous:** Reduced fees (weekdays, low season, twilight, seniors, juniors), discount packages, range (grass), club rentals, credit cards (MC, V).
Reader Comments: Beautiful long holes, powder sand ... Tough walker... Fun to play ... Nice course but too many short par 4's ... Easy on the ego and wallet ... Great design, hill after hill ... Nothing more than a 9 iron needed ... Decent.

EMERALD VALE GOLF CLUB
PU-6867 E. Michigan Hwy. 42, Manton, 49663, Wexford County, (616)824-3631, (800)890-3407, 12 miles N of Cadillac. **Web:** www.emeraldvale.com.
Holes: 18. **Yards:** 6,785/5,247. **Par:** 72/72. **Course Rating:** 72.6/70.0. **Slope:** 130/122. **Green Fee:** $28/$28. **Cart Fee:** $11/person. **Walking Policy:** Unrestricted walking. **Walkability:** 4.
Opened: 1998. **Architect:** Bruce Matthews III. **Season:** April-Oct. **High:** June-Aug. **To obtain tee times:** Call ahead. **Miscellaneous:** Reduced fees (twilight, seniors), discount packages, range (grass), club rentals, credit cards (MC, V), beginner friendly (junior program).

★★ ENGLISH HILLS GOLF COURSE
1200 Four Mile Rd., Grand Rapids, 49504, Kent County, (616)784-3420.
Holes: 18. **Yards:** 5.575/4,915. **Par:** 69/69. **Course Rating:** N/A. **Slope:** 117/117. **Green Fee:** $17.50/$20. **Walkability:** N/A. **Architect:** Mark DeVries. **Miscellaneous:** Metal spikes.

★★½ FALCON HEAD GOLF CLUB
PU-13120 Northland Dr., Big Rapids, 49307, Mecosta County, (616)796-2613, (888)264-0407, 50 miles N of Grand Rapids.
Holes: 18. **Yards:** 6,166/4,799. **Par:** 72/72. **Course Rating:** 71.8/68.8. **Slope:** 133/120. **Green Fee:** $13/$22. **Cart Fee:** $13/person. **Walking Policy:** Walking at certain times. **Walkability:** 3.
Season: Year-round. **High:** May-Sept. **To obtain tee times:** Call up to 2 weeks advance. Groups and outings call further in advance. **Miscellaneous:** Reduced fees (weekdays, low season, resort guests, twilight, seniors, juniors), discount packages, range (grass), club rentals, credit cards (MC, V, AE, D).

★★★½ FAULKWOOD SHORES GOLF CLUB
PM-300 S. Hughes Rd., Howell, 48843, Livingston County, (517)546-4180, 20 miles W of Detroit.
Holes: 18. **Yards:** 6,828/5,341. **Par:** 72/72. **Course Rating:** 74.3/71.8. **Slope:** 140/128. **Green Fee:** $24/$37. **Cart Fee:** Included in Green Fee. **Walking Policy:** Walking at certain times. **Walkability:** 2. **Opened:** 1967. **Architect:** Ralph Banfield. **Season:** April-Nov. **High:** June-Sept. **To obtain tee times:** Call 7 days in advance for weekdays and weekend. **Miscellaneous:** Reduced fees (weekdays, low season, twilight, seniors, juniors), metal spikes, range (grass/mats), club rentals, credit cards (MC, V).
Reader Comments: Extremely demanding ... Bring big stick and straight arrows ... Great! ... Unrelenting, like a visit to the dentist ... Slow ... Could use some work ... Challenging, but fair... Some scary putts ... This course is a beast ... Good, tough course that won't assault the wallet.

FELLOWS CREEK GOLF CLUB
PU-2936 Lotz Rd., Canton, 48188, Washtenaw County, (734)728-1300, 20 miles W of Detroit.

Holes: 27. **Green Fee:** $19/$22. **Cart Fee:** $11/. **Walking Policy:** Unrestricted walking. **Walkability:** N/A. **Opened:** 1961. **Architect:** Bruce Matthews/Jerry Matthews. **Season:** April-Dec. **High:** June-Aug. **To obtain tee times:** Call during the week for a weekend time. **Miscellaneous:** Reduced fees (weekdays, low season, twilight, seniors, juniors), metal spikes, credit cards (MC, V).

★★★ **EAST/SOUTH**
Yards: 6,489/5,276. **Par:** 72/72. **Course Rating:** 71.0/70.0. **Slope:** 118/N/A.
Reader Comments: Short and flat ... Nice ... Typical muny ... Improving.

★★★ **EAST/WEST**
Yards: 6,399/5,290. **Par:** 72/72. **Course Rating:** 70.9/69.9. **Slope:** N/A.

★★★ **SOUTH/WEST**
Yards: 6,430/5,346. **Par:** 72/72. **Course Rating:** 70.9/69.9. **Slope:** N/A.

★★½ **FENTON FARMS GOLF CLUB**
PU-12312 Torrey Rd., Fenton, 48430, Genesee County, (810)629-1212, 10 miles S of Flint. **Holes:** 18. **Yards:** 6,596/5,196. **Par:** 72/70. **Course Rating:** 71.7/69.8. **Slope:** 125/117. **Green Fee:** $18/$23. **Cart Fee:** $12/person. **Walking Policy:** Unrestricted walking. **Walkability:** 3. **Opened:** 1920. **Season:** April-Nov. **High:** May-Sept. **To obtain tee times:** Call up to 7 days in advance. **Miscellaneous:** Reduced fees (weekdays, low season, twilight, seniors, juniors), metal spikes, range (grass), club rentals, credit cards (MC, V).

Reader Comments: Improved, with 2 new holes, pretty good ... Love back nine ... Front nine still too back and forth ... People outstanding ... Too much money for an average course ... A nice place, but hard to score.

★★ **FERN HILL GOLF & COUNTRY CLUB**
PU-17600 Clinton River Rd., Clinton Township, 48044, Macomb County, (810)286-4700, 20 miles SW of Detroit. **Holes:** 18. **Yards:** 6,018/4,962. **Par:** 70/73. **Course Rating:** 67.6/65.7. **Slope:** 115/108. **Green Fee:** $10/$17. **Cart Fee:** $18/cart. **Walking Policy:** Unrestricted walking. **Walkability:** 2. **Opened:** 1972. **Architect:** Fred Severini III. **Season:** April-Nov. **High:** June-Sept. **To obtain tee times:** Call golf shop. **Miscellaneous:** Reduced fees (low season, twilight, seniors), discount packages, metal spikes, credit cards (MC, V).

★★★ **FERRIS STATE UNIVERSITY/KATKE GOLF COURSE**
PU-1003 Perry St., Big Rapids, 49307, Mecosta County, (231)591-3765, 50 miles N of Grand Rapids. **Holes:** 18. **Yards:** 6,729/5,344. **Par:** 72/72. **Course Rating:** 72.5/70.8. **Slope:** 124/119. **Green Fee:** $20/$22. **Cart Fee:** $13/person. **Walking Policy:** Unrestricted walking. **Walkability:** 3. **Opened:** 1974. **Architect:** Robert Beard. **Season:** April-Nov. **High:** May-Sept. **To obtain tee times:** Call up to 14 days in advance. **Miscellaneous:** Reduced fees (weekdays, seniors, juniors), discount packages, range (grass/mats), club rentals, lodging (118 rooms), credit cards (MC, V, D), beginner friendly (women's and junior programs). **Notes:** Home of the Ferris State University/Professional Golf Management Program.

Reader Comments: A killer! ... Very nice course ... What can I say, I am an alumni ... It has come a long way ... Hope to play here again.

★★½ **FIREFLY GOLF LINKS**
PU-7795 S. Clare Ave., Clare, 48617, Clare County, (517)386-3510, 45 miles NW of Saginaw. **E-mail:** bogey@voyager.net. **Holes:** 18. **Yards:** 5,929/4,515. **Par:** 72/72. **Course Rating:** 67.9/65.6. **Slope:** 124/113. **Green Fee:** $21/$27. **Cart Fee:** $12/person. **Walking Policy:** Unrestricted walking. **Walkability:** 3. **Opened:** 1932. **Architect:** Darell & Fran Loar. **Season:** April-Oct. **High:** June-Aug. **To obtain tee times:** Call golf shop. **Miscellaneous:** Reduced fees (weekdays, low season, seniors), discount packages, club rentals, credit cards (MC, V, AE, D).

Reader Comments: Visit it yearly ... Seasoned course ... A pasture, but a nice one.

FOREST AKERS GOLF COURSE AT MSU
PU-Mich. St. Univ. Harrison Rd., East Lansing, 48823, Ingham County, (517)355-1635, 3 miles E of Lansing. **Web:** golfmsu.msu.edu.

★★★½ **EAST COURSE**
Holes: 18. **Yards:** 6,510/5,380. **Par:** 72/73. **Course Rating:** 71.4/70.4. **Slope:** 118/115. **Green Fee:** $18/$20. **Cart Fee:** $24/cart. **Walking Policy:** Unrestricted walking. **Walkability:** 2. **Opened:** 1972. **Architect:** M.S.U. Campus Planning. **Season:** March-Oct. **High:** May-Sept. **To obtain tee times:** Call up to 7 days in advance. **Miscellaneous:** Discount packages, metal spikes, range (grass/mats), club rentals, credit cards (MC, V).

Reader Comments: For an AG school, course in poor condition ... Easy to score on ... Slow.... Wide open ... Long holes ... Good, clean golf ... Great deal for the dough ... Not as tough as west but worth a go ... I enjoyed it ... Better since redesign at some holes.

★★★★ **WEST COURSE**
Holes: 18. **Yards:** 7,003/5,251. **Par:** 72/72. **Course Rating:** 74.4/70.0. **Slope:** 139/119. **Green Fee:** $30/$34. **Cart Fee:** $24/cart. **Walking Policy:** Unrestricted walking. **Walkability:** 4. **Opened:** 1958. **Architect:** Bruce Matthews/Arthur Hills. **Season:** March-Oct. **High:** May-Sept. **To obtain tee times:** Call up to 7 days in advance. **Miscellaneous:** Discount packages, metal spikes, range (grass/mats), club rentals, credit cards (MC, V).

Reader Comments: Great views, perfect greens, challenging on every hole ... Classic test ... Excellent ... Thought course would be more plush with agricultural tech program ... Big 10 golf with no tricks .... Beautiful ... Gets a ton of play ... Best value in Lansing area ... Will never get sick of this course ... Course looks easier than it plays ... Perfect autumn colors.

★★★★ **THE FORTRESS** *Condition+*
R-950 Flint St., Box 304, Frankenmuth, 48734, Saginaw County, (517)652-0400, (800)863-7999, 15 miles SE of Saginaw. **Web:** www.zehnders.com.
Holes: 18. **Yards:** 6,813/4,837. **Par:** 72/72. **Course Rating:** 73.6/68.8. **Slope:** 138/124. **Green Fee:** $39/$65. **Cart Fee:** Included in Green Fee. **Walking Policy:** Walking at certain times. **Walkability:** 3. **Opened:** 1992. **Architect:** Dick Nugent. **Season:** April-Oct. **High:** June-Sept. **To obtain tee times:** Call with credit card to reserve. 48-hour cancellation policy. **Miscellaneous:** Reduced fees (weekdays, low season, resort guests, twilight, seniors, juniors), discount packages, range (grass), club rentals, credit cards (MC, V, D).

Reader Comments: Sand & water, the fortress lives up to its name ... Fabulous condition even better layout ... Exceptional ... The staff make this place a must play ... Terminator rangers ... Play it at least once ... Improved condition ... Holes packed like sardines ... Fun ... Want a challenge? ... Price a bit high.

★★½ **FOX CREEK GOLF COURSE**
PU-36000 Seven Mile, Livonia, 48152, Wayne County, (248)471-3400, 15 miles NW of Detroit.
Holes: 18. **Yards:** 6,612/5,231. **Par:** 71/71. **Course Rating:** 71.4/69.8. **Slope:** 123/117. **Green Fee:** $17/$25. **Cart Fee:** $24/cart. **Walking Policy:** Unrestricted walking. **Walkability:** 3. **Opened:** 1988. **Architect:** Mike DeVries. **Season:** Year-round weather permitting. **High:** April-Nov. **To obtain tee times:** Call up to 2 days in advance. **Miscellaneous:** Reduced fees (twilight, seniors, juniors), club rentals, credit cards (MC, V).

Reader Comments: Nice layout ... Slow play ... Fair.

FOX HILLS GOLF & CONFERENCE CENTER
PU-8768 N. Territorial Rd., Plymouth, 48170, Wayne County, (734)453-7272, 25 miles W of Detroit. **E-mail:** foxhillsinfo@msn.com. **Web:** www.foxhills.com.
★★★½ **GOLDEN FOX COURSE**
Holes: 18. **Yards:** 6,783/5,040. **Par:** 72/72. **Course Rating:** 73.0/69.7. **Slope:** 136/122. **Green Fee:** $55/$60. **Cart Fee:** Included in Green Fee. **Walking Policy:** Mandatory cart. **Walkability:** 3. **Opened:** 1989. **Architect:** Arthur Hills. **Season:** April-Nov. **High:** May-Sept. **To obtain tee times:** Call. **Miscellaneous:** Reduced fees (weekdays, low season, twilight, seniors), discount packages, range (grass), club rentals, credit cards (MC, V, AE, D).

Reader Comments: Flat but challenging ... A joy ... Upscale city course ... Tough from back tees ... Fairways are lush ... Nice test with a variety of holes.... Slightly over priced, great on weekdays ... Well maintained ... Pride in operation, treated very good ... Great greens, nice layout.
Holes: 27. **Walking Policy:** Unrestricted walking. **Walkability:** 3. **Opened:** 1921. **Architect:** Jim Lipe. **Season:** Year-round weather permitting. **High:** April-Oct. **To obtain tee times:** Call.
★★★½ **HILLS/WOODLANDS**
Yards: 6,398/5,588. **Par:** 70/73. **Course Rating:** 67.4/70.0. **Slope:** 104/100. **Green Fee:** $25/$28. **Cart Fee:** $26/cart. **Miscellaneous:** Reduced fees (weekdays, low season, twilight, seniors, juniors), discount packages, range (grass), club rentals, credit cards (MC, V, AE, D).

Reader Comments: Challenging and fun ... Great fish fry! ... 27 very different holes ... Some areas are congested with holes tightly packed ... Good game with wife! ... Plenty of holes–spend the day ... Love the course.
★★★½ **LAKES/HILLS**
Yards: 6,784/6,028. **Par:** 71/75. **Course Rating:** 69.4/72.6. **Slope:** 112/108. **Green Fee:** $22/$26. **Cart Fee:** $25/cart. **Miscellaneous:** Reduced fees (weekdays, low season, twilight, seniors, juniors), discount packages, metal spikes, range (grass), club rentals, credit cards (MC, V, AE, D).
★★★½ **WOODLANDS/LAKES**
Yards: 6,514/5,548. **Par:** 71/72. **Course Rating:** 67.8/69.9. **Slope:** 112/107. **Green Fee:** $25/$28. **Cart Fee:** $26/cart. **Miscellaneous:** Reduced fees (weekdays, low season, twilight, seniors, juniors), discount packages, range (grass), club rentals, credit cards (MC, V, AE, D).

★★★★ **FOX RUN COUNTRY CLUB**
PU-5825 W. Four Mile Rd., Grayling, 49738, Crawford County, (517)348-4343, (800)436-9786, 40 miles E of Traverse City. **Web:** www.foxruncc.com.

Holes: 18. **Yards:** 6,362/4,829. **Par:** 72/72. **Course Rating:** 71.0/69.7. **Slope:** 128/119. **Green Fee:** $29/$29. **Cart Fee:** $16/person. **Walking Policy:** Walking at certain times. **Walkability:** 3. **Opened:** 1990. **Architect:** J. John Gorney. **Season:** April-Oct. **High:** June-Sept. **To obtain tee times:** Call. Credit card required to reserve more than 1 tee time. **Miscellaneous:** Reduced fees (low season, twilight), metal spikes, range (grass), club rentals, credit cards (MC, V, AE).

Reader Comments: Played weekend in under 4 hours, great shape, great staff ... Tight, wooded fairways ... Green slopes severe ... Lots of tricky holes ... Challenging for all levels ... Great course to walk, not too tough or too easy ... Real nice layout, well groomed ... Fair value ... Outstanding value after Labor Day ... Worth the trip ... Beauty.

★★ FRUITPORT GOLF CLUB
PU-6330 S. Harvey, Muskegon, 49444, Muskegon County, (616)798-3355, 4 miles N of Grand Haven.
Holes: 18. **Yards:** 5,725. **Par:** 71. **Course Rating:** 68.9. **Slope:** N/A. **Green Fee:** $17/$19. **Cart Fee:** $19/cart. **Walking Policy:** Unrestricted walking. **Walkability:** 1. **Opened:** 1971. **Architect:** Dennis Snider. **Season:** March-Nov. **To obtain tee times:** Call. **Miscellaneous:** Reduced fees (weekdays, low season, seniors), metal spikes, range (grass), club rentals.

GARLAND   *Service*
★★★½ FOUNTAINS COURSE
R-HCR-1 Box 364M, Lewiston, 49756, Oscoda County, (517)786-2211, (800)968-0042, 30 miles E of Gaylord. **Web:** www.garlandusa.com.
Holes: 18. **Yards:** 6,760/4,617. **Par:** 72/72. **Course Rating:** 73.0/74.1. **Slope:** 130/128. **Green Fee:** $95/$100. **Cart Fee:** Included in Green Fee. **Walking Policy:** Mandatory cart. **Walkability:** 2. **Opened:** 1995. **Architect:** Ron Otto. **Season:** April-Oct. **High:** June-Aug. **To obtain tee times:** Call anytime in advance. Reservations Ext. 1789. **Miscellaneous:** Reduced fees (weekdays, low season, resort guests, twilight, juniors), range (grass/mats), club rentals, lodging (186 rooms), credit cards (MC, V, AE, D, Diners Club).

Reader Comments: Best of the Garland tracks ... Very accommodating, well manicured ... Still a young course ... Beautiful resort ... Needs refinement ... Nothing special ... Flora and fauna ... Beautiful and good conditions ... Lots of water and trouble ... Picturesque!
★★★★ MONARCH COURSE
Holes: 18. **Yards:** 7,188/4,904. **Par:** 72/72. **Course Rating:** 75.6/69.5. **Slope:** 140/123. **Green Fee:** $80/$85. **Cart Fee:** Included in Green Fee. **Walking Policy:** Mandatory cart. **Walkability:** 2. **Architect:** Ron Otto. **Season:** April-Oct. **High:** June-Aug. **To obtain tee times:** Call anytime in advance. Reservations Ext. 1789. **Miscellaneous:** Reduced fees (weekdays, low season, resort guests, twilight, juniors), discount packages, range (grass/mats), club rentals, lodging (186 rooms), credit cards (MC, V, AE, D, Diners Club).

Reader Comments: Worth playing ... Monarch her majesty ... Legendary in Mid-Michigan ... A true enjoyment ... Good golf, great food and lodging ... All four courses very similar, all fun ... Flat, Costly ... Don't play from the blues unless you're a low handicapper... Excellent! ... Course is challenging but not in good condition ... Wildlife adds to scenery.
★★★½ REFLECTIONS COURSE
Holes: 18. **Yards:** 6,407/4,778. **Par:** 72/72. **Course Rating:** 70.4/66.9. **Slope:** 120/110. **Green Fee:** $60/$80. **Cart Fee:** Included in Green Fee. **Walking Policy:** Mandatory cart. **Walkability:** 2. **Opened:** 1990. **Architect:** Ron Otto. **Season:** April-Oct. **High:** June-Aug. **To obtain tee times:** Call anytime in advance. Reservations Ext. 1789. **Miscellaneous:** Reduced fees (weekdays, low season, resort guests, twilight, juniors), discount packages, range (grass/mats), club rentals, lodging (186 rooms), credit cards (MC, V, AE, D, Diners Club).

Reader Comments: Don't overlook this course ... Flat ... Great course ... Nice blend of holes, very playable ... Had a great time with 5 other couples for 4 days ... Staff was excellent ... Some challenges.
★★★★ SWAMPFIRE COURSE
Holes: 18. **Yards:** 6,854/4,791. **Par:** 72/72. **Course Rating:** 73.9/68.4. **Slope:** 138/121. **Green Fee:** $80/$85. **Cart Fee:** Included in Green Fee. **Walking Policy:** Mandatory cart. **Walkability:** 2. **Architect:** Ron Otto. **Season:** April-Oct. **High:** June-Aug. **To obtain tee times:** Call anytime in advance. Reservations Ext. 1789. **Miscellaneous:** Reduced fees (weekdays, low season, resort guests, twilight, juniors), discount packages, range (grass/mats), club rentals, lodging (186 rooms), credit cards (MC, V, AE, D, Diners Club).

Reader Comments: Take a camera–beautiful ... Without holes 14-18, this is a 5-star course ... Strategy course ... Course condition is exceptional! ... Great complex ... Worth a trip north to play ... Bring your wet suit ... Played several times and will again.

★★★★ GAYLORD COUNTRY CLUB   *Value, Pace*
SP-P.O. Box 207, Gaylord, 49735, Otsego County, (616)546-3376, 5 miles W of Gaylord.
Holes: 18. **Yards:** 6,452/5,490. **Par:** 72/72. **Course Rating:** 70.9/71.4. **Slope:** 123/122. **Green Fee:** $30/$35. **Cart Fee:** $15/person. **Walking Policy:** Unrestricted walking. **Walkability:** 3. **Opened:** 1924. **Architect:** Wilfried Reid. **Season:** April-Oct. **High:** June-Aug. **Miscellaneous:** Reduced fees (twilight), range (grass), credit cards (MC, V).

MICHIGAN

★★★ GENESEE VALLEY MEADOWS

PM-5499 Miller Rd., Swartz Creek, 48473, Genesee County, (810)732-1401, 5 miles W of Flint.
Holes: 18. **Yards:** 6,867/6,490. **Par:** 72/72. **Course Rating:** 72.3/72.3. **Slope:** 133/122. **Green Fee:** $19/$23. **Cart Fee:** $24/cart. **Walking Policy:** Walking at certain times. **Walkability:** 2.
Opened: 1965. **Architect:** D. Sincerbaugh. **Season:** April-Nov. **High:** June-Aug. **To obtain tee times:** Call golf shop. **Miscellaneous:** Reduced fees (weekdays, low season, twilight, seniors, juniors), metal spikes, club rentals.
Reader Comments: Not too exciting, reasonable value ... Great condition considering amount of play ... Winds can be a factor ... Nice greens, poor rough ... Beautiful.... Enjoyable.

★★★★ GEORGE YOUNG RECREATIONAL COMPLEX *Service+, Value+*

PU-Hwy. 424 159 Youngs Lane, Gaastra, 49927, Iron County, (906)265-3401, 125 miles N of Green Bay, WI.
Holes: 18. **Yards:** 6,076/5,338. **Par:** 72/72. **Course Rating:** 74.3/71.2. **Slope:** 130/120. **Green Fee:** N/A/$22. **Cart Fee:** $20/cart. **Walking Policy:** Unrestricted walking. **Walkability:** 5.
Opened: 1993. **Season:** May-Oct. **High:** July-Aug. **To obtain tee times:** Call golf shop 7 days in advance.
Reader Comments: Best value and great people ... Lots of white-tail deer ... Excellent course, well worth it! ... Great course in the middle of nowhere ... A great deal for a championship course ... Nice view, sparse grass in fairways ... A quiet gem ... Carved in the woods, bent grass greens, very pretty country.

★★★ GIANT OAK GOLF CLUB

PU-1024 Valetta Dr., Temperance, 48182, Monroe County, (734)847-6733, 5 miles N of Toledo.
Holes: 27. **Yards:** 6,415/4,994. **Par:** 72/72. **Course Rating:** 71.1/68.0. **Slope:** 124/111. **Green Fee:** $21/$24. **Cart Fee:** $12/person. **Walking Policy:** Unrestricted walking. **Walkability:** 2.
Opened: 1969. **Architect:** Arthur Hills. **Season:** March-Dec. weather permitting. **High:** June-Aug. **To obtain tee times:** Call up to 14 days in advance. **Miscellaneous:** Reduced fees (seniors), metal spikes, credit cards (MC, V).
Reader Comments: Nicely laid out ... Good condition ... Not hard but decently maintained.

★★★★ GLACIER CLUB

SP-8000 Glacier Club Dr., Washington, 48094, Macomb County, (810)786-0800, 27 miles N of Detroit.
Holes: 18. **Yards:** 7,018/4,937. **Par:** 72/72. **Course Rating:** 74.1/68.5. **Slope:** 134/116. **Green Fee:** $35/$60. **Cart Fee:** Included in Green Fee. **Walking Policy:** Mandatory cart. **Walkability:** 3. **Opened:** 1994. **Architect:** William Newcomb. **Season:** April-Dec. **High:** May-Sept. **To obtain tee times:** Call 7 days in advance. **Miscellaneous:** Reduced fees (weekdays, twilight, seniors, juniors), range (grass/mats), club rentals, credit cards (MC, V, AE).
Reader Comments: Well kept, long, challenging ... Very good course and staff ... Always enjoyable ... Expensive.... Pretty flat, condos being built on course ... Great fairway roll ... Tough–very tough ... OB everywhere ... Ladies made to feel real welcome.

★★★ GLADSTONE GOLF COURSE

PU-6514 Days River 24-1/2 Rd., Gladstone, 49837, Delta County, (906)428-9646, 10 miles N of Escanaba.
Holes: 18. **Yards:** 6,504/5,427. **Par:** 72/74. **Course Rating:** N/A. **Slope:** N/A. **Green Fee:** $20/$20. **Cart Fee:** $25/cart. **Walking Policy:** Unrestricted walking. **Walkability:** 1. **Opened:** 1936. **Architect:** A. J. Holly. **Season:** April-Sept. **High:** June-Aug. **To obtain tee times:** Call one day in advance. **Miscellaneous:** Range (grass), club rentals, credit cards (MC, V, AE, D).
Reader Comments: Just neat layout ... Some challenging holes ... Lots of blind shots.

★★ GLADWIN HEIGHTS GOLF COURSE

PU-3551 W. M-61, Gladwin, 48624, Gladwin County, (517)426-9941, 30 miles NE of Midland.
Holes: 18. **Yards:** 6,007/5,226. **Par:** 71/72. **Course Rating:** 68.7/69.7. **Slope:** 110/112. **Green Fee:** $15/$16. **Cart Fee:** $18/cart. **Walking Policy:** Unrestricted walking. **Walkability:** 2.
Opened: 1959. **Season:** April-Oct. **High:** July-Aug. **To obtain tee times:** First come, first served. Call ahead to see if course is available due to league play. **Miscellaneous:** Reduced fees (twilight, seniors), metal spikes, range (grass), club rentals, beginner friendly (junior program).

★★★ GLEN OAKS GOLF & COUNTRY CLUB

PM-30500 W-13 Mile Rd., Farmington Hills, 48024, Oakland County, (248)851-8356, 20 miles N of Detroit. **Web:** www.co.oakland.mi.us.
Holes: 18. **Yards:** 6,090/5,088. **Par:** 70/70. **Course Rating:** 67.6/66.5. **Slope:** 114/110. **Green Fee:** $25/$29. **Cart Fee:** $11/person. **Walking Policy:** Unrestricted walking. **Walkability:** 2.
Season: April-Nov. **High:** May-Aug. **To obtain tee times:** Call golf shop. **Miscellaneous:** Reduced fees (weekdays, twilight, seniors, juniors), credit cards (MC, V).

MICHIGAN

Reader Comments: Fun ... Good muny, slow play and crowded ... My home course, it's ok ... Low rates, lots of beginners ... Good shape for heavy amount of play ... Still needs improvement.

★★ GLENBRIER GOLF COURSE
PU-Box 500, 4178 W. Locke Rd., Perry, 48872, Shiawassee County, (517)625-3800, 15 miles NE of Lansing.
Holes: 18. **Yards:** 6,310/5,245. **Par:** 72/72. **Course Rating:** 68.4/69.4. **Slope:** 120/115. **Green Fee:** $17/$19. **Cart Fee:** $20/cart. **Walking Policy:** Unrestricted walking. **Walkability:** 2. **Opened:** 1972. **Architect:** Bob Fink. **Season:** April-Nov. **High:** May-Aug. **To obtain tee times:** Call golf shop. **Miscellaneous:** Reduced fees (weekdays, low season, twilight, seniors, juniors), discount packages, range (grass/mats), club rentals, credit cards (MC, V).

★★★ GLENEAGLE GOLF CLUB
PU-6150 14th Ave., Hudsonville, 49426, Ottawa County, (616)457-3680, (877)832-4537, 8 miles SW of Grand Rapids.
Holes: 18. **Yards:** 6,705/5,215. **Par:** 72/72. **Course Rating:** 73.1/70.8. **Slope:** 143/128. **Green Fee:** $15/$31. **Cart Fee:** $12/person. **Walking Policy:** Walking at certain times. **Walkability:** 4. **Opened:** 1960. **Architect:** Michael Shields. **Season:** April-Nov. **High:** June-Aug. **To obtain tee times:** Call 7 days in advance. **Miscellaneous:** Reduced fees (weekdays, low season, twilight, seniors, juniors), range (grass), club rentals, credit cards (MC, V).
Reader Comments: Overpriced, so-so golf holes ... Tricky greens ... A challenge to be remembered ... Great greens.

★★ GLENHURST GOLF COURSE
PU-25345 W. 6 Mile Rd., Redford, 48240, Wayne County, (313)592-8758, 18 miles W of Detroit.
Holes: 18. **Yards:** 5,502/4,962. **Par:** 70/72. **Course Rating:** 66.1/68.1. **Slope:** 112/111. **Green Fee:** $11/$23. **Cart Fee:** $22/cart. **Walking Policy:** Unrestricted walking. **Walkability:** 2. **Opened:** 1932. **Architect:** Mr. McClane. **Season:** March-Jan. **High:** June-Aug. **To obtain tee times:** Tee times for weekends and holidays only. Reservations taken 7 days in advance. **Miscellaneous:** Reduced fees (weekdays, low season, twilight, seniors, juniors), club rentals.

GOGEBIC COUNTRY CLUB
PU-Country Club Rd., Ironwood, 49938, Gogebic County, (906)932-2515, 20 miles W of Wakefield.
Holes: 18. **Yards:** 5,752/5,132. **Par:** 71/71. **Course Rating:** 66.5/68.5. **Slope:** 109/111. **Green Fee:** $17/$17. **Cart Fee:** $18/cart. **Walking Policy:** Unrestricted walking. **Walkability:** 3. **Opened:** 1922. **Season:** May-Oct. **High:** June-Aug. **To obtain tee times:** Call up to 14 days in advance. **Miscellaneous:** Reduced fees (twilight, juniors), rentals, credit cards (MC, V, AE, D).

THE GOLF CLUB AT APPLE MOUNTAIN
PU-4519 N. River Rd., Freeland, 48623, Saginaw County, (517)781-6789, (888)781-6789, 9 miles W of Saginaw. **E-mail:** bredman@applemountain.com. **Web:** applemountain.com.
Holes: 18. **Yards:** 6,962/4,978. **Par:** 72/72. **Course Rating:** 74.2/69.6. **Slope:** 145/127. **Green Fee:** $45/$65. **Cart Fee:** Included in Green Fee. **Walking Policy:** Mandatory cart. **Walkability:** N/A. **Opened:** 1998. **Architect:** John Sanford. **Season:** April-Nov. **High:** June-Sept. **To obtain tee times:** Tee times made throughout the summer/season. **Miscellaneous:** Reduced fees (low season, twilight, seniors, juniors), discount packages, range (grass), club rentals, credit cards (MC, V, AE), beginner friendly (junior, ladies' & clinics held throughout season).

THE GOLF CLUB AT THORNAPPLE POINTE
PU-4747 Champions Circle S.E., Grand Rapids, 49512, Kent County, (616)554-4747, 15 miles SE of Grand Rapids.
Holes: 18. **Yards:** 6,821/4,878. **Par:** 72/72. **Course Rating:** 73.2/64.3. **Slope:** 133/107. **Green Fee:** $55/$60. **Cart Fee:** Included in Green Fee. **Walking Policy:** Unrestricted walking. **Walkability:** 4. **Opened:** 1997. **Architect:** William Newcomb. **Season:** April-Nov. **High:** June-Sept. **To obtain tee times:** Call 14 days in advance. **Miscellaneous:** Reduced fees (weekdays, low season, twilight, seniors, juniors), range (grass/mats), club rentals, credit cards (MC, V, AE, D).
Reader Comments: Well kept, great views ... Needs to mature ... Expensive, but outstanding layout ... Noisy ... Planes, trains and automobiles ... Good use of available land ... Great course for being so young ... Loved the GPS ... Beautiful and enjoyable.

★★½ GOODRICH COUNTRY CLUB
PU-10080 Hegel Rd., Goodrich, 48438, Genesee County, (810)636-2493, 7 miles S of Davison.
Holes: 18. **Yards:** 5,497/4,365. **Par:** 70/71. **Course Rating:** 66.4/65.0. **Slope:** 104/100. **Green Fee:** $18/$22. **Cart Fee:** $24/cart. **Walking Policy:** Walking at certain times. **Walkability:** 4. **Opened:** 1970. **Season:** April-Oct. **High:** June-Aug. **To obtain tee times:** Call in advance for weekends and holidays. **Miscellaneous:** Reduced fees (weekdays, low season, seniors, juniors), club rentals, credit cards (MC, V).
Reader Comments: Nothing exciting ... Unimaginative greens.

GRACEWIL COUNTRY CLUB
PU-2597 Four Mile Rd. N.W., Grand Rapids, 49504, Kent County, (616)784-2455.
★★ **EAST COURSE**
Holes: 18. **Yards:** 6,155/4,995. **Par:** 72/72. **Course Rating:** 69.9/71.3. **Slope:** N/A. **Green Fee:** $14/$17. **Cart Fee:** $18/. **Walking Policy:** Unrestricted walking. **Walkability:** N/A. **Opened:** 1929. **Architect:** J. Morris Wilson. **Season:** March-Nov. **High:** June-Aug. **To obtain tee times:** Call up to 10 days in advance. Tee times taken on weekends only until 4 p.m. **Miscellaneous:** Reduced fees (weekdays, low season, twilight, seniors, juniors), metal spikes, club rentals, credit cards (MC, V).
★½ **WEST COURSE**
Holes: 18. **Yards:** 6,055/4,817. **Par:** 72/72. **Course Rating:** 69.7/71.0. **Slope:** N/A. **Green Fee:** $14/$17. **Cart Fee:** $18/. **Walking Policy:** Unrestricted walking. **Walkability:** N/A. **Opened:** 1929. **Architect:** J. Morris Wilson. **Season:** March-Nov. **High:** June-Aug. **To obtain tee times:** Call up to 10 days in advance. Tee times taken on weekends only until 4 p.m. **Miscellaneous:** Reduced fees (weekdays, low season, twilight, seniors, juniors), metal spikes, club rentals, credit cards (MC, V).

★★★ GRACEWIL PINES GOLF CLUB *Value*
PU-5400 Trailer Park Dr., Jackson, 49201, Jackson County, (517)764-4200, 20 miles N of Lansing.
Holes: 18. **Yards:** 6,170/4,405. **Par:** 72/72. **Course Rating:** N/A. **Slope:** N/A. **Green Fee:** $10/$13. **Cart Fee:** $18/. **Walking Policy:** Unrestricted walking. **Walkability:** N/A. **Opened:** 1984. **Architect:** Morris Wilson. **Season:** March-Nov. **High:** May-Aug. **To obtain tee times:** Call golf shop. **Miscellaneous:** Reduced fees (weekdays, low season, twilight, seniors, juniors), discount packages, metal spikes, club rentals, credit cards (V).
Reader Comments: Narrow, treelined fairways ... Nice people and surprising quality for the price! ... Pretty little course, can score well, great value ... Tight ... Very nice front, very bad back ... Leave your drivers at home ... Nice for the money ... Rough condition, super value.

GRAND BLANC GOLF & COUNTRY CLUB
PU-5270 Perry Rd., Grand Blanc, 48439, Genesee County, (810)694-5960, 7 miles S of Flint.
★★★½ **NORTH COURSE**
Holes: 18. **Yards:** 7,023/5,471. **Par:** 72/72. **Course Rating:** 73.5/71.0. **Slope:** 122/118. **Green Fee:** $20/$23. **Cart Fee:** $22/cart. **Walking Policy:** Walking at certain times. **Walkability:** 4. **Opened:** 1997. **Architect:** Ron Lenard/Joe Roeski. **Season:** Year-round weather permitting. **High:** May-Sept. **To obtain tee times:** Call up to 7 days in advance. **Miscellaneous:** Reduced fees (low season, twilight, seniors, juniors), range (grass), credit cards (MC, V).
Reader Comments: 9 new holes ... Much redone and layout is really nice ... Greens in great shape and fast ... Wide-open, much nicer than South course, confidence builder ... Player friendly, great hot dogs ... Courses were soggy, but it was Feb. in Michigan, and it was open!
★★ **SOUTH COURSE**
Holes: 18. **Yards:** 6,545/5,774. **Par:** 72/74. **Course Rating:** 71.0/72.8. **Slope:** 122/120. **Green Fee:** $20/$23. **Cart Fee:** $22/cart. **Walking Policy:** Walking at certain times. **Walkability:** 3. **Opened:** 1970. **Architect:** Bruce & Jerry Matthews. **Season:** Year-round weather permitting. **High:** May-Sept. **To obtain tee times:** Call up to 7 days in advance. **Miscellaneous:** Reduced fees (low season, twilight, seniors, juniors), range (grass), credit cards (MC, V).

★★★½ GRAND HAVEN GOLF CLUB
SP-17000 Lincoln St., Grand Haven, 49417, Ottawa County, (616)842-4040, (888)657-8821, 28 miles E of Grand Rapids. **E-mail:** golf@grandhavengolfclub.com. **Web:** www.grandhavengolfclub.com.
Holes: 18. **Yards:** 6,725/5,256. **Par:** 72/72. **Course Rating:** 73.3/70.6. **Slope:** 134/122. **Green Fee:** $24/$37. **Cart Fee:** $13/person. **Walking Policy:** Walking at certain times. **Walkability:** 3. **Opened:** 1965. **Architect:** W. Bruce Matthews/Jerry Matthews. **Season:** March-Nov. **High:** June-Aug. **To obtain tee times:** Call 7 days in advance for weekday or weekend. **Miscellaneous:** Reduced fees (weekdays, low season, twilight, seniors, juniors), range (grass), club rentals, credit cards (MC, V).
Reader Comments: Good way to enjoy the outdoors ... Money well spent ... Tough course and long from back tees ... What happened to this old gem?... Every hole cut out of woods–beautiful ... Rustic! Trees in the Lake Michigan dunes ... Coming back to top form ... Tough putts ... Still one of the best values in state!

★★½ GRAND HOTEL GOLF CLUB
R-Mackinac Island, Mackinac Island, 49757, Mackinac County, (906)847-3331, 250 miles N of Detroit.
Holes: 18. **Yards:** 5,415/4,212. **Par:** 67/67. **Course Rating:** 65.7/N/A. **Slope:** 110/106. **Green Fee:** $75/$75. **Cart Fee:** Included in Green Fee. **Walking Policy:** Unrestricted walking. **Walkability:** 2. **Opened:** 1911. **Architect:** Jerry Matthews. **Season:** May-Oct. **High:** June-Aug.

To obtain tee times: Call. **Miscellaneous:** Metal spikes, lodging (340 rooms), credit cards (MC, V, AE).
Reader Comments: Many spectacular views, relaxing ... The ride from No. 9 to No. 10 has to be the most unique in golf! ... Long way between nines ... 1st 9 short and easy, 2nd 9 scenic and difficult ... A vacation–beautiful ... Play more than once ... Best putting greens.

★½ GRAND ISLAND GOLF RANCH

PU-6266 W. River Dr., Belmont, 49306, Kent County, (616)363-1262, 8 miles NW of Grand Rapids. **E-mail:** tallen@netonecom.net.
Holes: 18. **Yards:** 6,266/5,522. **Par:** 72/73. **Course Rating:** 68.7/69.1. **Slope:** 109/110. **Green Fee:** $18/$19. **Cart Fee:** $20/cart. **Walking Policy:** Unrestricted walking. **Walkability:** 2.
Opened: 1965. **Architect:** Jake Brunsink/Ade VanLiere. **Season:** March-Dec. **High:** May-Sept.
To obtain tee times: Call 7 days in advance. **Miscellaneous:** Reduced fees (low season, seniors, juniors), range (grass/mats), club rentals, credit cards (MC, V), beginner friendly (junior program and league).

★★ GRAND LEDGE COUNTRY CLUB

PU-5811 St Joe Highway, Grand Ledge, 48837, Eaton County, (517)627-2495, 10 miles W of Lansing.
Holes: 18. **Yards:** 6,347/4,714. **Par:** 72/72. **Course Rating:** 70.2/66.5. **Slope:** 116/111. **Green Fee:** $19/$21. **Cart Fee:** $20/cart. **Walking Policy:** Unrestricted walking. **Walkability:** 3.
Opened: 1958. **Architect:** Steve Lipkowitz. **Season:** April-Nov. **High:** June-Aug. **To obtain tee times:** Call up to 3 days in advance. **Miscellaneous:** Reduced fees (low season), metal spikes, range (grass), club rentals, credit cards (MC, V).

GRAND PRAIRIE GOLF COURSE

PU-3620 Grand Prairie Rd., Kalamazoo, 49006, Kalamazoo County, (616)388-4447, 2 miles NW of Kalamazoo. **E-mail:** shecky4@aol.com. **Web:** www.kalamazoogolf.org.
Holes: 9. **Yards:** 1,710/1,589. **Par:** 30/30. **Course Rating:** N/A. **Slope:** N/A. **Green Fee:** $11/$11. **Cart Fee:** $16/cart. **Walking Policy:** Unrestricted walking. **Walkability:** 2. **Opened:** 1961. **Season:** March-Nov. **High:** June-Aug. **Miscellaneous:** Reduced fees (seniors, juniors), metal spikes, club rentals, credit cards (MC, V, AE, D), beginner friendly (junior and adult clinics).

GRAND RAPIDS GOLF CLUB

PU-4300 Leonard N.E., Grand Rapids, 49525, Kent County, (616)949-2820, (800)709-1100, 5 miles NE of Grand Rapids.
Holes: 27. **Green Fee:** $20/$22. **Cart Fee:** $22/cart. **Walking Policy:** Unrestricted walking. **Walkability:** 4. **Opened:** 1969. **Season:** March-Nov. **High:** May-Aug. **To obtain tee times:** Call golf shop up to 7 days in advance. Groups 12 to 200 call up to 1 year in advance.
Miscellaneous: Reduced fees (weekdays, low season, twilight, seniors, juniors), range (grass/mats), club rentals, credit cards (MC, V), beginner friendly (summer junior program, golf lessons).
★★ BLUE/RED
Yards: 5,887/4,582. **Par:** 70/70. **Course Rating:** 68.5/66.2. **Slope:** 107/103.
★★ RED/WHITE
Yards: 6,127/4,926. **Par:** 72/72. **Course Rating:** 70.3/68.9. **Slope:** 116/113.
★★ WHITE/BLUE
Yards: 6,194/4,854. **Par:** 72/72. **Course Rating:** 69.8/67.9. **Slope:** 115/110.

GRAND TRAVERSE RESORT AND SPA

R-6300 U.S. 31 N., Acme, 49610, Grand Traverse County, (231)938-1620, (800)748-0303, 6 miles NE of Traverse City. **Web:** www.grandtraverseresort.com.
★★★★ SPRUCE RUN
Holes: 18. **Yards:** 6,304/4,726. **Par:** 70/70. **Course Rating:** 70.8/68.2. **Slope:** 130/125. **Green Fee:** $50/$90. **Cart Fee:** Included in Green Fee. **Walking Policy:** Mandatory cart. **Walkability:** 2. **Opened:** 1979. **Architect:** William Newcomb. **Season:** April-Oct. **High:** June-Aug. **To obtain tee times:** Hotel guests may reserve tee times with room confirmation. Public may call 7 days in advance. **Miscellaneous:** Reduced fees (weekdays, low season, resort guests, twilight), discount packages, range (grass), club rentals, lodging, credit cards (MC, V, AE, D, Diners Club, JCB).
Reader Comments: Enjoyable, resort fun ... Hidden, overshadowed by 'Bear', a great course, tough, challenging in its own way ... Well manicured ... Traditional ... Picturesque.
★★★★ THE BEAR *Condition*
Holes: 18. **Yards:** 7,083/5,424. **Par:** 72/72. **Course Rating:** 76.8/73.1. **Slope:** 146/137. **Green Fee:** $50/$130. **Cart Fee:** Included in Green Fee. **Walking Policy:** Mandatory cart. **Walkability:** 4. **Opened:** 1985. **Architect:** Jack Nicklaus. **Season:** April-Oct. **High:** June-Aug. **To obtain tee times:** Hotel guests may reserve tee times with room reservation. Public may call 7 days in advance. **Miscellaneous:** Reduced fees (weekdays, low season, resort guests, twilight), discount packages, range (grass), club rentals, lodging, credit cards (MC, V, AE, D, Diners Club, JCB).

MICHIGAN

Notes: Ranked 20th in 1999 Best in State. Host of 1990 Ameritech Senior Open.
Reader Comments: My favorite in Michigan ... A bear ... GPS is nice ... Overpriced, but a yearly must play ... Hard! ... I wish Jack was a hooker ... Lots of sand around greens ... Unforgiving ... Beautiful course, excellent layout, play it more than once ... Too hard for the average golfer to have any fun for the price ... Course beat me up ... Great shape.

THE WOLVERINE

Holes: 18. **Yards:** 7,038/5,029. **Par:** 72/72. **Course Rating:** 73.9/68.1. **Slope:** 144/121. **Green Fee:** $50/$130. **Cart Fee:** Included in Green Fee. **Walking Policy:** Mandatory cart. **Walkability:** 2. **Opened:** 1999. **Architect:** Gary Player. **Season:** April-Oct. **High:** June-Aug. **To obtain tee times:** Hotel guests may reserve tee times with room confirmation. Public may call 7 days in advance. **Miscellaneous:** Reduced fees (weekdays, low season, resort guests, twilight), discount packages, range (grass), club rentals, lodging, credit cards (MC, V, AE, D, Diners Club, JCB).

★★★★½ GRAND VIEW GOLF COURSE *Value+*

PU-5464 S. 68th Ave., New Era, 49446, Oceana County, (616)861-6616, 20 miles N of Muskegon.
Holes: 18. **Yards:** 6,258/4,737. **Par:** 71/71. **Course Rating:** 69.5/66.7. **Slope:** 120/113. **Green Fee:** $17/$19. **Cart Fee:** $20/cart. **Walking Policy:** Unrestricted walking. **Walkability:** 3. **Opened:** 1993. **Architect:** David Goerbig. **Season:** April-Oct. **High:** June-Aug. **To obtain tee times:** Call ahead. Tee times recommended. **Miscellaneous:** Reduced fees (weekdays, seniors), metal spikes, range (grass), club rentals, credit cards (MC, V, D).
Reader Comments: Beautiful layout and the price is right ... Good warmup course for Thoroughbred or rebuild your ego after Thoroughbred ... Play in the orchards, well taken care of ... Excellent ... Fair course, a best buy ... Aptly named.

★★★½ GRANDVIEW GOLF CLUB

PU-3003 Hagni Rd., Kalkaska, 49646, Kalkaska County, (616)258-3244, 30 miles E of Traverse City.
Holes: 18. **Yards:** 6,620/4,964. **Par:** 72/72. **Course Rating:** 72.2/68.4. **Slope:** 133/122. **Green Fee:** $20/$32. **Cart Fee:** $14/person. **Walking Policy:** Walking at certain times. **Walkability:** 5. **Opened:** 1993. **Season:** April-Oct. **High:** June-Aug. **To obtain tee times:** Call. **Miscellaneous:** Reduced fees (weekdays, low season), range (grass/mats), club rentals, credit cards (MC, V).
Reader Comments: Excellent value and service ... A throwback to what golf used to be ... Very hilly, 1 fantastic par 3 ... Great views, greens might fool you ... Nice and fun.

★★½ GRAYLING COUNTRY CLUB

SP-Business I-75 S., Grayling, 49738, Crawford County, (517)348-5618, 25 miles S of Gaylord.
Holes: 18. **Yards:** 5,800/4,609. **Par:** 70/70. **Course Rating:** 67.0/66.0. **Slope:** 115/110. **Green Fee:** $10/$20. **Cart Fee:** $12/person. **Walking Policy:** Unrestricted walking. **Walkability:** 2. **Opened:** 1923. **Season:** April-Oct. **High:** June-Aug. **To obtain tee times:** Call in advance. **Miscellaneous:** Reduced fees (low season, seniors, juniors), metal spikes, range (grass), club rentals, credit cards (MC, V, AE, D).

★★ GREEN ACRES GOLF COURSE

PU-7323 Dixie Hwy, Bridgeport, 48722, Saginaw County, (517)777-3510, 6 miles S of Saginaw.
Holes: 18. **Yards:** 6,400/6,100. **Par:** 72/72. **Course Rating:** 72.0/69.1. **Slope:** 119/115. **Green Fee:** N/A. **Cart Fee:** $20/cart. **Walking Policy:** Unrestricted walking. **Walkability:** 1. **Opened:** 1957. **Season:** April-Nov. **High:** June-Aug. **To obtain tee times:** Call. **Miscellaneous:** Reduced fees (twilight, seniors), metal spikes, range (grass), club rentals, credit cards (MC, V).

★★½ GREEN HILLS GOLF CLUB

PU-1699 N M-13, Pinconning, 48650, Bay County, (517)697-3011, 10 miles N of Bay City.
Holes: 18. **Yards:** 6,000/N/A. **Par:** 71/N/A. **Course Rating:** 67.1/N/A. **Slope:** 112/N/A. **Green Fee:** $18/$20. **Cart Fee:** $20/cart. **Walking Policy:** Unrestricted walking. **Walkability:** 1. **Opened:** 1971. **Architect:** William Newcomb. **Season:** March-Nov. **High:** June-Sept. **To obtain tee times:** Call up to 4 days in advance for weekends during summer. **Miscellaneous:** Reduced fees (seniors), metal spikes, club rentals, credit cards (MC, V, D).

★★ GREEN MEADOWS GOLF COURSE

PU-1555 Strasburg Rd., Monroe, 48161, Monroe County, (734)242-5566, 35 miles S of Detroit.
Holes: 18. **Yards:** 6,391/4,965. **Par:** 70/70. **Course Rating:** 68.6/67.6. **Slope:** 116/108. **Green Fee:** $20/$24. **Cart Fee:** $11/person. **Walking Policy:** Unrestricted walking. **Walkability:** 1. **Opened:** 1973. **Season:** Year-round. **High:** June-Sept. **To obtain tee times:** Call up to 7 days in advance for weekends and holidays. **Miscellaneous:** Reduced fees (seniors, juniors), club rentals, credit cards (MC, V, D).

★★½ GREEN OAKS GOLF COURSE

PM-1775 Clark Rd., Ypsilanti, 48241, Washtenaw County, (313)485-0881, 8 miles E of Ann Arbor.

Holes: 18. **Yards:** 6,500/6,000. **Par:** 71/71. **Course Rating:** 69.5/70.1. **Slope:** 121/123. **Green Fee:** $10/$21. **Cart Fee:** $20/cart. **Walking Policy:** Unrestricted walking. **Walkability:** 2. **Opened:** 1970. **Season:** March-Dec. **High:** July. **To obtain tee times:** Call up to 7 days in advance. **Miscellaneous:** Reduced fees (weekdays, resort guests), metal spikes, credit cards (MC, V).
Reader Comments: Tricky greens make for a lot of 3 putts ... Average ... Good course ... Best and fastest greens for a public course ... Fairways too thin, needs heavier turf.

GREEN VALLEY GOLF CLUB
PU-25379 W. Fawn River Rd. , Rte. 4, Sturgis, 49091, St. Joseph County, (616)651-6331.
Holes: 9. **Yards:** 5,355/5,053. **Par:** 68/71. **Course Rating:** 66.5/67.5. **Slope:** N/A. **Green Fee:** N/A. **Cart Fee:** $18/cart. **Walking Policy:** Unrestricted walking. **Walkability:** 3. **Opened:** 1970. **Season:** March-Oct. **High:** June-Aug. **To obtain tee times:** Call. **Miscellaneous:** Metal spikes.

★★★ GREEN VALLEY GOLF COURSE
PU-5751 Brooklyn Rd., Jackson, 49201, Jackson County, (517)764-0270, 10 miles E of Jackson.
Holes: 18. **Yards:** 6,035/5,000. **Par:** 70/70. **Course Rating:** 70.3/N/A. **Slope:** N/A. **Green Fee:** $14/$16. **Cart Fee:** $20/cart. **Walking Policy:** Unrestricted walking. **Walkability:** 3. **Opened:** 1959. **Season:** April-Oct. **High:** June-Aug. **To obtain tee times:** Call golf shop. **Miscellaneous:** Reduced fees (low season, seniors, juniors), metal spikes, range (grass/mats), club rentals, credit cards (MC, V, D).
Reader Comments: Good value ... Nice public course ... Not impressed.

★★ GREENBRIAR GOLF CLUB
PU-9350 N Lapeer Rd., Mayville, 48744, Tuscola County, (517)843-6575, 17 miles N of Lapeer.
Holes: 18. **Yards:** 5,827/4,970. **Par:** 71/71. **Course Rating:** N/A. **Slope:** N/A. **Green Fee:** $18/$20. **Cart Fee:** $28/person. **Walking Policy:** Unrestricted walking. **Walkability:** 1. **Opened:** 1971. **Season:** April-Oct. **High:** June-Aug. **To obtain tee times:** No tee times needed.
Miscellaneous: Reduced fees (weekdays, seniors, juniors), discount packages, metal spikes, club rentals, beginner friendly (junior golf program).

★★ GREENBRIER GOLF COURSE
14820 Wellwood Rd., Brooklyn, 49230, Jackson County, (517)646-6657.
Specal Notes: Call club for further information.

★★★½ GREYSTONE GOLF CLUB
PU-67500 Mound Rd., Romeo, 48065, Macomb County, (810)752-7030, (888)418-3386, 15 miles NE of Detroit. **Web:** www.golfgreystone.com.
Holes: 18. **Yards:** 6,861/4,816. **Par:** 72/71. **Course Rating:** 73.6/68.5. **Slope:** 132/113. **Green Fee:** $45/$60. **Cart Fee:** Included in Green Fee. **Walking Policy:** Mandatory cart. **Walkability:** 3. **Opened:** 1992. **Architect:** Jerry Matthews. **Season:** March-Nov. **High:** June-Sept. **To obtain tee times:** Call for tee times 30 days in advance. **Miscellaneous:** Reduced fees (low season, twilight, seniors, juniors), range (grass/mats), club rentals, credit cards (MC, V, AE).
Reader Comments: Last 3 holes make the course ... Last 3 holes overrated ... Very nicely maintained course, some tricky holes ... Excellent course, the best finishing hole in southern Michigan ... Tough course, a bit expensive ... Very interesting ... Needs conditioning ... Nice layout ... Demanding finish.

★★★ GROESBECK MUNICIPAL GOLF COURSE
PM-1600 Ormond Ave., Lansing, 48906, Ingham County, (517)483-4232.
Holes: 18. **Yards:** 6,166/4,814. **Par:** 71/73. **Course Rating:** 68.2/67.0. **Slope:** 126/116. **Green Fee:** $18/$22. **Cart Fee:** $22/cart. **Walking Policy:** Unrestricted walking. **Walkability:** 2. **Opened:** 1927. **Architect:** Jack Daray/Jerry Matthews. **Season:** April-Nov. **High:** April-Sept. **To obtain tee times:** Call up to 7 days in advance. **Miscellaneous:** Reduced fees (weekdays, low season, twilight, seniors, juniors), metal spikes, club rentals, credit cards (MC, V, D).
Reader Comments: Beautiful for a muny ... Basic inner-city type course ... Nothing great ... An asset to the community ... Great 9-hole expansion, takes you away.

GULL LAKE VIEW GOLF CLUB
★★★★ EAST COURSE
PU-7417 N. 38th St., Augusta, 49012, Kalamazoo County, (616)731-4148, (800)432-7971, 15 miles NE of Kalamazoo.
Holes: 18. **Yards:** 6,002/4,918. **Par:** 70/70. **Course Rating:** 69.4/68.5. **Slope:** 124/118. **Green Fee:** $31/$33. **Cart Fee:** $25/cart. **Walking Policy:** Walking at certain times. **Walkability:** 4. **Opened:** 1963. **Architect:** Darl Scott. **Season:** April-Nov. **High:** May-Aug. **To obtain tee times:** Call golf shop. **Miscellaneous:** Reduced fees (weekdays, low season, resort guests, twilight, juniors), discount packages, metal spikes, club rentals, lodging (128 rooms), credit cards (MC, V, D), beginner friendly (ngcoa get linked).

MICHIGAN

Reader Comments: Great condition and elevation changes ... Excellent ... A hidden gem that will challenge your game ... Lots of water, beautiful layout ... Very scenic ... Needs better maintenance ... Must be accurate, better than West course ... Short, bring iron game ... Good variety.

★★★½ WEST COURSE

Holes: 18. **Yards:** 6,300/5,218. **Par:** 71/72. **Course Rating:** 70.6/69.0. **Slope:** 123/114. **Green Fee:** $31/$33. **Cart Fee:** $25/cart. **Walking Policy:** Walking at certain times. **Walkability:** 3. **Opened:** 1963. **Architect:** Darl Scott. **Season:** April-Nov. **High:** May-Aug. **To obtain tee times:** Call golf shop. **Miscellaneous:** Reduced fees (weekdays, low season, resort guests, twilight, juniors), discount packages, metal spikes, club rentals, lodging (128 rooms), credit cards (MC, V, D), beginner friendly (ngcoa get linked).
Reader Comments: Another good course at Gull Lake ... Excellent greens ... Not long, but tough ... Well cared for... Scenic course... Good test ... Mature gem at a low price ... Interesting back 9.

HAMPSHIRE COUNTRY CLUB

SP-29592 Pokagon Hwy., Dowagiac, 49047, Cass County, (616)782-7476, 18 miles N of South Bend, IN.

★★★★ hampshire country club

Holes: 18. **Yards:** 7,030/6,185. **Par:** 72/75. **Course Rating:** 72.6/73.0. **Slope:** 125/119. **Green Fee:** $16/$20. **Cart Fee:** $20/cart. **Walking Policy:** Unrestricted walking. **Walkability:** 1. **Opened:** 1962. **Architect:** Edward Packard. **Season:** April-Nov. **High:** June-Aug. **To obtain tee times:** Call up to 7 days in advance. **Miscellaneous:** Reduced fees (weekdays, twilight, juniors), discount packages, credit cards (MC, V).
Reader Comments: Original 18 great ... Good facilities, good condition ... Nice challenging course ... Exceptional value ... Some very scenic holes ... One of the best in Southwest Michigan.

DOGWOOD TRAIL

Holes: 18. **Yards:** 6,795/4,968. **Par:** 72/72. **Course Rating:** 71.8/66.7. **Slope:** 126/111. **Green Fee:** $16/$20. **Cart Fee:** $20/cart. **Walking Policy:** Unrestricted walking. **Walkability:** 3. **Opened:** 1995. **Architect:** Edward Packard. **Season:** April-Nov. **High:** June-Aug. **To obtain tee times:** Call up to 7 days in advance. **Miscellaneous:** Reduced fees (weekdays, twilight, juniors), discount packages, credit cards (MC, V).

★★★ HARBOR POINT GOLF COURSE

SP-8362 South Lake Shore Drive, Harbor Springs, 49740, Emmet County, (231)526-2951, 1 miles N of Harbor Springs.
Holes: 180. **Yards:** 6,003/5,034. **Par:** 71/73. **Course Rating:** 68.7/68.8. **Slope:** 121/122. **Green Fee:** $14/$40. **Cart Fee:** $16/person. **Walking Policy:** Walking at certain times. **Walkability:** 2. **Opened:** 1896. **Architect:** David Gill. **Season:** May-Oct. **High:** July-Aug. **To obtain tee times:** Call the golf shop. **Miscellaneous:** Reduced fees (low season), metal spikes, range (grass), club rentals, credit cards (MC, V).
Reader Comments: Fun, walkable old-style layout ... Great for couples ... Spectacular views.

HARTLAND GLEN GOLF & COUNTRY CLUB

PU-12400 Highland Rd., Hartland, 48353, Livingston County, (248)887-3777, 25 miles N of Ann Arbor.

★★ NORTH COURSE

Holes: 18. **Yards:** 6,280/5,109. **Par:** 72/72. **Course Rating:** 67.6/67.8. **Slope:** 107/105. **Green Fee:** $16/$25. **Cart Fee:** $10/person. **Walking Policy:** Unrestricted walking. **Walkability:** 2. **Opened:** 1972. **Architect:** K. Sustic/J. Neagles. **Season:** April-Nov. **High:** June-Aug. **To obtain tee times:** Call 7 days in advance. **Miscellaneous:** Reduced fees (weekdays, low season, twilight, seniors, juniors), metal spikes, range (grass/mats), club rentals, credit cards (MC, V, AE).

★★ SOUTH COURSE

Holes: 18. **Yards:** 6,175/4,661. **Par:** 71/71. **Course Rating:** 67.0/65.1. **Slope:** 112/107. **Green Fee:** $16/$25. **Cart Fee:** $10/person. **Walking Policy:** Unrestricted walking. **Walkability:** 1. **Opened:** 1992. **Architect:** G. Duke/K. Sustic/R. Boyt. **Season:** April-Nov. **High:** June-Aug. **To obtain tee times:** Call 7 days in advance. **Miscellaneous:** Reduced fees (weekdays, low season, twilight, seniors, juniors), metal spikes, range (grass), club rentals, credit cards (MC, V, AE).

★★★ HASTINGS COUNTRY CLUB

SP-1550 N Broadway, Hastings, 49058, Barry County, (616)945-2756, 20 miles N of Battle Creek.
Holes: 18. **Yards:** 6,331/6,201. **Par:** 72/73. **Course Rating:** 70.9/71.7. **Slope:** 126/119. **Green Fee:** $25/$25. **Cart Fee:** $25/cart. **Walking Policy:** Unrestricted walking. **Walkability:** 5. **Opened:** 1921. **Season:** April-Oct. **High:** May-Aug. **To obtain tee times:** Call golf shop. **Miscellaneous:** Range (grass), credit cards (MC, V).
Reader Comments: Old course ... Very hilly.

HAWK HOLLOW GOLF COURSE *Service*
PU-1501 Chandler Rd., Bath, 48808, Clinton County, (517)641-4295, (888)411-4295, 2 miles N of East Lansing.
Holes: 27. **Green Fee:** $40/$62. **Cart Fee:** Included in Green Fee. **Walking Policy:** Mandatory cart. **Walkability:** N/A. **Opened:** 1996. **Architect:** Jerry Matthews. **Season:** March-Oct. **High:** June-Sept. **To obtain tee times:** Call (517)641-4295 2 weeks in advance. **Miscellaneous:** Range (grass), club rentals, credit cards (MC, V, AE), beginner friendly (many junior programs run by golf pro).

★★★★½ EAST/NORTH *Condition*
Yards: 6,693/N/A. **Par:** 72/N/A. **Course Rating:** 72.8/N/A. **Slope:** 134/N/A.
Reader Comments: This hawk will eat any doves ... Needs to mature ... Holes 1-18 are the best ... Awesome final 3 holes ... Nice course, too much bucks ... As good as it gets ... Wow! ... Best public design in the state ... Beautiful and difficult course. Tough!.

★★★★½ EAST/WEST *Condition*
Yards: 6,487/N/A. **Par:** 72/N/A. **Course Rating:** 71.7/N/A. **Slope:** 129/N/A.
Reader Comments: One of the finest new courses in Michigan ... Gorgeous ... Tight, but not long.

★★★★½ NORTH/WEST *Condition*
Yards: 6,974/5,078. **Par:** 72/72. **Course Rating:** 73.7/69.7. **Slope:** 136/120.

★★★★½ HAWKSHEAD GOLF LINKS *Condition+*
PU-6959 105th Ave., South Haven, 49090, Allegan County, (616)639-2121, 25 miles S of Holland. **Web:** hawksheadlinks.com.
Holes: 18. **Yards:** 6,984/4,960. **Par:** 72/72. **Course Rating:** 73.5/66.9. **Slope:** 131/109. **Green Fee:** $28/$48. **Cart Fee:** $12/person. **Walking Policy:** Unrestricted walking. **Walkability:** 2. **Opened:** 1997. **Architect:** Arthur Hills. **Season:** April-Oct. **High:** June-Sept. **To obtain tee times:** Call up to 6 days in advance. **Miscellaneous:** Reduced fees (weekdays, low season, resort guests, twilight), discount packages, range (grass), club rentals, lodging (9 rooms), credit cards (MC, V, AE, D).
Notes: Ranked 24th in 1999 Best in State.
Reader Comments: Good links course ... Fabulous rugged layout with Pine Valley flavor but with miles of empty land. Why next to a major highway? ... Fun for all skill levels ... Great stuff ... A sleeper... A must play ... Future gem ... Welcomes women ... Windy, but room to hit it off the tee ... Hell if you don't have a sand wedge ... Variety ... Very challenging, but fair.

★★★½ HEATHER HIGHLANDS GOLF CLUB
PU-11450 E. Holly Rd., Holly, 48442, Oakland County, (248)634-6800, 50 miles NW of Detroit.
Holes: 18. **Yards:** 6,879/5,752. **Par:** 72/72. **Course Rating:** 72.6/73.4. **Slope:** 124/122. **Green Fee:** $23/$31. **Cart Fee:** $24/cart. **Walking Policy:** Walking at certain times. **Walkability:** 1. **Opened:** 1966. **Architect:** Robert Bruce Harris. **Season:** April-Nov. **High:** May-Sept. **To obtain tee times:** Call 6 days in advance. **Miscellaneous:** Reduced fees (low season), discount packages, range (grass/mats), club rentals, credit cards (MC, V).
Reader Comments: Outstanding greens ... Fun course, plenty of variety ... Value ... Good, straightforward golf ... Wide open, big tough greens ... All around nice course.

★★★ HEATHER HILLS GOLF COURSE
PU-3100 McKail Rd., Romeo, 48065, Macomb County, (810)798-3971, 17 miles N of Rochester.
Holes: 18. **Yards:** 6,282/5,029. **Par:** 71/71. **Course Rating:** 69.7/68.5. **Slope:** 118/114. **Green Fee:** $18/$27. **Cart Fee:** $20/cart. **Walking Policy:** Unrestricted walking. **Walkability:** 4. **Opened:** 1980. **Season:** April-Oct. **High:** June-Sept. **To obtain tee times:** Call golf shop up to 7 days in advance. **Miscellaneous:** Reduced fees (low season, seniors, juniors), discount packages, metal spikes, range (grass), credit cards (MC, V, D).
Reader Comments: Interesting and playable ... Women-friendly ... Good value ... When they say 'hills,' they are not kidding! ... Great value.

THE HEATHLANDS OF ONEKAMA
PU-6444 Farr Rd., Onekama, 49675, Manistee County, (616)889-5644, 50 miles S of Traverse City. **E-mail:** jread@heathlands.come. **Web:** www.heathlands.com.
Holes: 18. **Yards:** 6,569/4,437. **Par:** 72/72. **Course Rating:** 72.3/66.4. **Slope:** 139/112. **Green Fee:** $20/$35. **Cart Fee:** $10/person. **Walking Policy:** Walking at certain times. **Walkability:** 4. **Opened:** 1997. **Architect:** Jeff Gorney. **Season:** April-Oct. **High:** June-Sept. **To obtain tee times:** Call in advance or email. **Miscellaneous:** Reduced fees (weekdays, low season, twilight, seniors), range (grass), club rentals, credit cards (MC, V, D).

★★★★ HERITAGE GLEN GOLF CLUB
PU-29795 Heritage Lane, Paw Paw, 49079, Van Buren County, (616)657-2552, 10 miles SW of Kalamazoo. **Web:** www.heritageglengolf.com.
Holes: 18. **Yards:** 6,640/4,946. **Par:** 72/72. **Course Rating:** 70.1/68.4. **Slope:** 134/130. **Green Fee:** $28/$32. **Cart Fee:** $14/person. **Walking Policy:** Unrestricted walking. **Walkability:** 3.

Opened: 1994. Architect: Jerry Matthews. Season: April-Nov. High: May-Sept. To obtain tee times: Call anytime. Miscellaneous: Reduced fees (weekdays, low season, twilight, seniors, juniors), discount packages, range (grass), club rentals, credit cards (MC, V, AE).
Reader Comments: Tremendous double dogleg par 5 ... Hit in straight or else ... Upscale hilly course ... Very high on my top 10 in Michigan ... Cut out of the woods-nice track ... First 3 holes let you score, then the monster is unleashed ... Bring balls! ... Beautiful ... Not too long, but still very challenging.

HESSEL RIDGE GOLF COURSE
PU-125 Three Mile Rd., Hessel, 49745, Mackinac County, (906)484-3494, (888)660-9166, 35 miles S of Sault Ste. Marie. E-mail: hrgolf@northernway.net. Web: www.hesselridge.com.
Holes: 18. Yards: 6,415/4,905. Par: 70/70. Course Rating: N/A. Slope: N/A. Green Fee: $9/$30. Cart Fee: $12/person. Walking Policy: Unrestricted walking. Walkability: 2. Opened: 1997. Architect: Jeff Gorney. Season: May-Oct. High: June-Sept. Miscellaneous: Reduced fees (weekdays, low season, twilight, juniors), club rentals, credit cards (MC, V, D).

HICKORY HILLS GOLF CLUB
★★★½ GREEN/WHITE
PU-2540 Parview Dr., Jackson, 49201, Jackson County, (517)750-3636, 35 miles W of Ann Arbor.
Holes: 18. Yards: 6,723/5,377. Par: 72/72. Course Rating: 71.5/68.3. Slope: 126/116. Green Fee: $15/$18. Cart Fee: $18/cart. Walking Policy: Unrestricted walking. Walkability: 4. Opened: 1969. Architect: Bruce Matthews. Season: April-Oct. High: June-Sept. Miscellaneous: Reduced fees (twilight, seniors, juniors), metal spikes, range (grass), club rentals.
Reader Comments: Lots of wildlife, secluded, nice layout ... Super-nice ... Good value, challenging.

★★★ MAIZE/BLUE
PU-2540 Parview Dr., Jackson, 49201, Jackson County, (517)750-3636, 35 miles W of Ann Arbor.
Holes: 18. Yards: 6,715/5,445. Par: 72/72. Course Rating: 72.0/68.7. Slope: 128/118. Green Fee: $15/$18. Cart Fee: $18/cart. Walking Policy: Unrestricted walking. Walkability: 4. Opened: 1974. Architect: Bill Newcomb. Season: April-Oct. High: June-Sept. Miscellaneous: Reduced fees (twilight, seniors, juniors), metal spikes, range (grass), club rentals.

★½ HICKORY HOLLOW GOLF COURSE
PU-49001 North Ave., Macomb, 48042, Macomb County, (810)949-9033, 22 miles N of Detroit.
Holes: 18. Yards: 6,384/5,220. Par: 73/73. Course Rating: 70.1/68.9. Slope: 116/116. Green Fee: $20/$23. Cart Fee: $12/person. Walking Policy: Unrestricted walking. Walkability: 3. Opened: 1963. Season: March-Nov. High: June-Aug. To obtain tee times: Call up to 7 days in advance. Miscellaneous: Reduced fees (seniors), metal spikes, club rentals, credit cards (MC, V).

★★ HICKORY KNOLL GOLF COURSE
7945 Old Channel Trail, Montague, 48042, Muskegon County, (231)894-5535.
Special Notes: Call club for further information.

HIDDEN RIVER GOLF & CASTING CLUB
PU-7688 Maple River Rd., Brutus, 49716, Emmet County, (231)529-4653, (800)325-GOLF, 13 miles N of Petoskey. E-mail: info@hiddenriver.com. Web: www.hiddenriver.com.
Holes: 18. Yards: 7,101/4,787. Par: 72/72. Course Rating: 74.3/67.4. Slope: 140/117. Green Fee: $45/$85. Cart Fee: $15/person. Walking Policy: Walking at certain times. Walkability: 4. Opened: 1998. Architect: Bruce Matthews III. Season: April-Oct. High: June-Aug. To obtain tee times: Call (800)325-GOLF or online: www.hiddenriver.com. Miscellaneous: Reduced fees (weekdays, low season, twilight, juniors), discount packages, range (grass), club rentals, lodging (16 rooms), credit cards (MC, V, D).
Special Notes: Lodging available 2001.

HIDDEN VALLEY COLLECTION OF GREAT GOLF
★★★½ THE CLASSIC
R-696 M-32 East Gaylord, Gaylord, 49735, Otsego County, (517)732-5181, (877)465-3475, 60 miles NE of Traverse City.
Holes: 18. Yards: 6,305/5,591. Par: 72/71. Course Rating: N/A. Slope: 121/113. Green Fee: $30/$62. Cart Fee: Included in Green Fee. Walking Policy: Walking at certain times. Walkability: 2. Opened: 1958. Architect: William H. Diddel. Season: April-Oct. High: June-Sept. To obtain tee times: Call up to 7 days in advance. Miscellaneous: Reduced fees (weekdays, low season, resort guests, twilight), discount packages, range (grass), club rentals, lodging (100 rooms), credit cards (MC, V, AE, D).
Reader Comments: We enjoyed a 3-day, 54-hole blowout! ... OK ... Unchallenging ... Resort course, no trouble ... Rolling hills, nice greens, views ... Totally different front 9 to back 9.
★★★★ THE LAKE

R-1535 Opal Lake Rd., Gaylord, 49375, Otsego County, (517)732-5181, (877)465-3475, 45 miles NE of Traverse City. **Web:** www.otsegoclub.com.
Holes: 18. **Yards:** 6,310/4,952. **Par:** 71/71. **Course Rating:** 71.0/68.5. **Slope:** 136/122. **Green Fee:** $30/$62. **Cart Fee:** Included in Green Fee. **Walking Policy:** Walking at certain times. **Walkability:** 3. **Opened:** 1988. **Architect:** Jerry Matthews. **Season:** April-Oct. **High:** June-Aug. **To obtain tee times:** Call up to 7 days in advance. **Miscellaneous:** Reduced fees (weekdays, low season, resort guests, twilight), discount packages, club rentals, credit cards (MC, V, AE, D).
Reader Comments: Another beautiful course ... Costly ... Creative greens ... Pleasant golf ... Unique blend of holes, best value of Hidden Valley courses ... Once conditions improve this is a winner ... Great layout–hard sidehill lies make good shots go bad ... I should have gotten a refund after losing $30 worth of balls in its lakes!.
Special Notes: Formerly Michaywe Hills Golf Club.

★★★½ THE LOON
R-4400 Championship Dr., Gaylord, 49735, Otsego County, (517)732-5181, (877)465-3475, 55 miles NE of Traverse City.
Holes: 18. **Yards:** 6,701/5,123. **Par:** 71/71. **Course Rating:** 72.7/71.1. **Slope:** 128/121. **Green Fee:** $40/$78. **Cart Fee:** Included in Green Fee. **Walking Policy:** Walking at certain times. **Walkability:** 2. **Opened:** 1994. **Architect:** Mike Husby. **Season:** April-Sept. **High:** June-Sept. **To obtain tee times:** Call 7 days in advance. **Miscellaneous:** Reduced fees (low season, resort guests, twilight), discount packages, range (grass), club rentals, credit cards (MC, V, AE, D).
Reader Comments: Would like to do it again ... Best new course in area ... Nice trek ... Best clubhouse view and finishing hole in Michigan ... Picturesque, wide fairways with many carry shots ... Back 9 needs to mature ... Best of Hidden Valley ... Excellent resort golf ... Close to freeway ... Nice course.

★★★ HIGH POINTE GOLF CLUB
PU-5555 Arnold Rd., Williamsburg, 49690, Grand Traverse County, (231)267-9900, (800)753-7888, 10 miles NE of Traverse City. **Web:** www.highpointegolf.com.
Holes: 18. **Yards:** 6,849/5,101. **Par:** 71/72. **Course Rating:** 72.9/69.6. **Slope:** 135/121. **Green Fee:** $30/$80. **Cart Fee:** $15/person. **Walking Policy:** Walking at certain times. **Walkability:** 4. **Opened:** 1989. **Architect:** Tom Doak. **Season:** April-Oct. **High:** June-Aug. **To obtain tee times:** Call. Credit card may be required for advanced tee times and groups. **Miscellaneous:** Reduced fees (weekdays, low season, twilight, juniors), discount packages, range (grass/mats), club rentals, credit cards (MC, V, AE, D).
Reader Comments: In highlands, mountains, beautiful scenery, tough course ... Favorite course in Michigan ... Overpriced, overrated ... Awesome potential, needs conditioning ... Stark contrast between 9s ... Beautiful, challenging ... On the verge of perfection ... Design pales by comparison to most Michigan resort courses ... Great design, poor maintenance ... Interesting layout.

★★ HIGHLAND GOLF CLUB
SP-3011 U.S. 2-41, Escanaba, 49829, Delta County, (906)466-7457, 90 miles N of Green Bay.
Holes: 18. **Yards:** 6,237/5,499. **Par:** 71/72. **Course Rating:** 69.3/71.0. **Slope:** 117/115. **Green Fee:** $24/N/A. **Cart Fee:** $22/cart. **Walking Policy:** Unrestricted walking. **Walkability:** 1. **Opened:** 1930. **Architect:** Merrill Maissack, Reinhold Bittnor. **Season:** April-Oct. **High:** June-Aug. **To obtain tee times:** Call 7 days in advance. **Miscellaneous:** Club rentals, credit cards (MC, V).

HIGHLAND HILLS GOLF COURSE
1050 E Alward Rd., De Witt, 48820, Clinton County, (517)669-9873.
Yards: 6,621/5,030. **Par:** 72/72. **Course Rating:** 70.2/674. **Slope:** 118/107. **Green Fee:** $10/$23. **Walkability:** N/A. **Miscellaneous:** Metal spikes.

★★★ HILLS HEART OF THE LAKES GOLF CLUB
PU-500 Case Rd., Brooklyn, 49230, Jackson County, (517)592-2110, 20 miles S of Jackson.
Holes: 18. **Yards:** 5,517/4,445. **Par:** 69/69. **Course Rating:** N/A. **Slope:** N/A. **Green Fee:** $13/$17. **Cart Fee:** $20/cart. **Walking Policy:** Unrestricted walking. **Walkability:** 4. **Opened:** 1965. **Season:** March-Oct. **High:** May-Sept. **To obtain tee times:** Weekend tee times only. **Miscellaneous:** Reduced fees (seniors, juniors), metal spikes.
Reader Comments: Always kept up beautifully ... Short course, but tough ... Nice relaxing course.

★★½ HILLTOP GOLF COURSE
PM-47000 Powell Rd., Plymouth, 48170, Wayne County, (734)453-9800, 15 miles W of Detroit.
Holes: 18. **Yards:** 6,100/4,761. **Par:** 70/75. **Course Rating:** 69.7/73.0. **Slope:** 120/115. **Green Fee:** $25/$29. **Cart Fee:** $25/cart. **Walking Policy:** Unrestricted walking. **Walkability:** 4. **Season:** Year-round weather permitting. **High:** April-Sept. **To obtain tee times:** Call up to 7 days in advance. **Miscellaneous:** Reduced fees (weekdays, low season, twilight, seniors, juniors), discount packages, metal spikes, club rentals, credit cards (MC, V, AE).

Reader Comments: Tough greens, hilly but nice ... Small sloping greens ... Ordinary ... Some good holes and worth a play or two ... Low spots very wet ... Surprisingly good layout, very natural terrain ... Narrow fairways with tight lies.

★★★ HUDSON MILLS METRO PARK GOLF COURSE

PU-4800 Dexter-Pickney Rd., Dexter, 48130, Washtenaw County, (734)426-0466, (800)477-3191, 12 miles N of Ann Arbor.

Holes: 18. **Yards:** 6,560/5,411. **Par:** 71/71. **Course Rating:** 70.6/70.2. **Slope:** 118/115. **Green Fee:** $19/$23. **Cart Fee:** $21/person. **Walking Policy:** Unrestricted walking. **Walkability:** 3. **Opened:** 1990. **Architect:** Sue Nyquist. **Season:** March-Nov. **High:** May-Sept. **To obtain tee times:** Call 7 days in advance. **Miscellaneous:** Reduced fees (weekdays, low season, seniors, juniors), club rentals, credit cards (MC, V).

Reader Comments: Very good metro park course ... Flat ... OK ... Good condition, challenging, great price ... 2 great par 5's on back ... Some tough par 4s ... Slow on weekends ... Fun, friendly ... Interesting back 9 ... Decent test.

★★★★ HUNTER'S RIDGE GOLF CLUB

PU-8101 Byron Rd., Howell, 48843, Livingston County, (517)545-4653, 35 miles E of Lansing.

Holes: 18. **Yards:** 6,530/4,624. **Par:** 71/71. **Course Rating:** 71.9/66.6. **Slope:** 134/112. **Green Fee:** $25/$35. **Cart Fee:** $10/person. **Walking Policy:** Walking at certain times. **Walkability:** 3. **Opened:** 1996. **Architect:** Jerry Matthews. **Season:** April-Oct. **High:** June-Aug. **To obtain tee times:** Call. **Miscellaneous:** Reduced fees (weekdays, low season, twilight, seniors, juniors), discount packages, range (grass), club rentals, credit cards (MC, V, D), beginner friendly (Ladies Learning League and family golf night).

Reader Comments: Great layout and price ... Off the beaten path ... Michigan's best greens ... Best-kept secret ... Has 4 of the best par 3s on one golf course ... Hard to find, but worth the effort ... Nice for a fairly new course ... Difficult ... Best ever course carved out of farm land.

★★★½ HURON BREEZE GOLF & COUNTRY CLUB

PU-5200 Huron Breeze Dr., Au Gres, 48703, Arenac County, (517)876-6868, 50 miles N of Bay City.

Holes: 18. **Yards:** 6,806/5,075. **Par:** 72/72. **Course Rating:** 73.1/69.4. **Slope:** 133/123. **Green Fee:** $18/$27. **Cart Fee:** $10/person. **Walking Policy:** Unrestricted walking. **Walkability:** 2. **Opened:** 1991. **Architect:** William Newcomb. **Season:** April-Oct. **High:** June-Sept. **To obtain tee times:** Call in advance, no restrictions. **Miscellaneous:** Reduced fees (weekdays, low season, twilight, seniors, juniors), discount packages, metal spikes, range (grass), club rentals, credit cards (MC, V, D).

Reader Comments: Good golf, good value ... Well managed ... Woods and water make it tough ... Best bargain in Northern Michigan ... Tight, treelined, short ... Fun to play and fast ... Beautiful scenery, cut through the woods ... Saw a Bald Eagle! ... Quiet getaway ... Excellent greens.

★½ HURON HILLS GOLF COURSE

3465 E. Huron River Dr., Ann Arbor, 48104, Washtenaw County, (734)971-6840. **Web:** ci.ann-arbor.mi.us.

Holes: 18. **Yards:** 5,071/4,237. **Par:** 67/67. **Course Rating:** 64.0/67.1. **Slope:** 107/108. **Green Fee:** $16/$17. **Walking Policy:** Unrestricted walking. **Walkability:** 3. **Opened:** 1922. **Architect:** Tom Bendelow. **Season:** March-Nov. **High:** May-Sept. **Miscellaneous:** Reduced fees (weekdays, low season, twilight, seniors, juniors), metal spikes, club rentals, credit cards (MC, V), beginner friendly (instruction).

★★★ HURON MEADOWS GOLF COURSE

PM-8765 Hammel Rd., Brighton, 48116, Livingston County, (810)231-4084, (800)477-3193, 4 miles S of Brighton.

Holes: 18. **Yards:** 6,663/5,344. **Par:** 72/71. **Course Rating:** 71.2/69.9. **Slope:** 122/116. **Green Fee:** $19/$19. **Cart Fee:** $21/cart. **Walking Policy:** Unrestricted walking. **Walkability:** 2. **Opened:** 1982. **Season:** March-Nov. **High:** June-Aug. **To obtain tee times:** Call up to 7 days in advance. **Miscellaneous:** Reduced fees (seniors, juniors), range (mats), club rentals, credit cards (MC, V).

Reader Comments: Beautiful course, very good condition, challenging, great price ... Great staff ... Everyone's a regular ... Part of park system ... Good course for muny.

★★ IDLE WYLD GOLF CLUB

PM-35780 Five Mile Rd., Livonia, 48154, Wayne County, (734)464-6325, 10 miles NW of Detroit.

Holes: 18. **Yards:** 5,817/5,022. **Par:** 70/71. **Course Rating:** 67.3/66.3. **Slope:** 118/111. **Green Fee:** $17/$25. **Cart Fee:** $24/cart. **Walking Policy:** Unrestricted walking. **Walkability:** 2. **Season:** April-Nov. **High:** June-Aug. **To obtain tee times:** Tee times required for weekends only. Residents may call on Wednesday after 9 a.m. Nonresidents may call Thursday after 9 a.m. **Miscellaneous:** Reduced fees (weekdays, twilight), club rentals, credit cards (MC, V). **Special Notes:** Spikeless shoes encouraged.

MICHIGAN

INDIAN LAKE HILLS GOLF COURSE

PU-55321 Brush Lake Rd., Eau Claire, 49111, Cass County, (616)782-2540, (888)398-7897, 12 miles E of St. Joseph. **E-mail:** ilhge@mich.com. **Web:** www.indianlakehills.com.
Holes: 27. **Green Fee:** $15/$22. **Cart Fee:** $22/cart. **Walking Policy:** Walking at certain times. **Walkability:** 3. **Opened:** 1924. **Season:** March-Oct. **High:** June-Aug. **To obtain tee times:** Call up to 7 days in advance or further in advance for large group. **Miscellaneous:** Reduced fees (weekdays, low season, twilight), discount packages, range (grass), club rentals, credit cards (MC, V).

★★★ **WEST/EAST**
Yards: 6,043/5,170. **Par:** 71/73. **Course Rating:** 67.0/68.5. **Slope:** 111/111.
★★★ **EAST/NORTH**
Yards: 6,201/5,156. **Par:** 71/71. **Course Rating:** 67.5/69.8. **Slope:** 112/113.
Reader Comments: Old 9 and new 9 a great combination ... Friendly, treated well ... Fun for the family.

★★★ **WEST/NORTH**
Yards: 6,532/5,450. **Par:** 72/73. **Course Rating:** 68.5/71.3. **Slope:** 113/114.
Reader Comments: Very good ... Not hard ... Some very pretty holes.

★★★ INDIAN RIVER GOLF CLUB

SP-3301Chippewa Beach Rd., Indian River, 49749, Cheboygan County, 231)238-7011, (800)305-4742, 12 miles NE of Petoskey.
Holes: 18. **Yards:** 6,687/5,175. **Par:** 72/72. **Course Rating:** 73.4/70.8. **Slope:** 125/119. **Green Fee:** $27/$45. **Cart Fee:** $14/person. **Walking Policy:** Unrestricted walking. **Walkability:** 3. **Opened:** 1921. **Architect:** Warner Bowen & Sons. **Season:** April-Oct. **High:** July-Aug. **To obtain tee times:** Call anytime. **Miscellaneous:** Reduced fees (weekdays, low season, twilight, juniors), discount packages, range (grass), club rentals, credit cards (MC, V, D).
Reader Comments: Relatively unknown ... Interesting and challenging ... Nice for the money ... Each hole a different challenge ... Want to play here again.

★★½ INDIAN RUN GOLF CLUB

SP-6359 E. RS Ave., Scotts, 49088, Kalamazoo County, (616)327-1327, 6 miles SE of Kalamazoo.
Holes: 18. **Yards:** 6,808/5,028. **Par:** 72/72. **Course Rating:** 72.1/68.8. **Slope:** 126/115. **Green Fee:** $17/$20. **Cart Fee:** $12/person. **Walking Policy:** Unrestricted walking. **Walkability:** N/A. **Opened:** 1966. **Architect:** Charles Darl Scott. **Season:** April-Oct. **High:** May-Sept. **To obtain tee times:** Call. **Miscellaneous:** Reduced fees (weekdays, low season, seniors, juniors), discount packages, metal spikes, range (grass), club rentals, credit cards (MC, V, D).
Reader Comments: Tough fairways, lots of water, forgiving greens ... Course has potential ... Long but fun ... Sloping greens ... Long and flat.

★★★ INDIAN SPRINGS METRO PARK GOLF COURSE

PU-5200 Indian Trail, White Lake, 48386, Oakland County, (248)625-7870, (800)477-3192, 8 miles W of Pontiac.
Holes: 18. **Yards:** 6,688/6,474. **Par:** 71/71. **Course Rating:** 71.0/70.1. **Slope:** 120/114. **Green Fee:** $17/$19. **Cart Fee:** $10/person. **Walking Policy:** Unrestricted walking. **Walkability:** 2. **Opened:** 1989. **Architect:** Sue Nyquist. **Season:** March-Nov. **To obtain tee times:** Call up to 7 days in advance. **Miscellaneous:** Reduced fees (seniors, juniors), range (grass), club rentals, credit cards (MC, V).
Reader Comments: Small greens, no hidden trouble ... Great sport at nice Metro Park ... Good county course ... My league course—not the best ... Decent layout ... Needs conditioning.

★½ INDIAN TRAILS GOLF COURSE

PU-2776 Kalamazoo Ave. S.E., Grand Rapids, 49507, Kent County, (616)245-2021.
Holes: 18. **Yards:** 5,100/4,785. **Par:** 68/72. **Course Rating:** 66.8/71.6. **Slope:** N/A. **Green Fee:** N/A/$14. **Cart Fee:** $17/cart. **Walking Policy:** Unrestricted walking. **Walkability:** 3. **Opened:** 1921. **Architect:** Jeffrey John Gorney. **Season:** April-Oct. **High:** June-Aug. **To obtain tee times:** No tee times required. **Miscellaneous:** Reduced fees (weekdays, low season, seniors, juniors), discount packages, metal spikes, club rentals.

INKSTER VALLEY GOLF COURSE

PU-2150 Middlebelt Rd., Inkster, 48141, Wayne County, (734)722-8020, 10 miles W of Detroit. **Web:** www.waynecountyparks.com.
Holes: 18. **Yards:** 6,709/4,500. **Par:** 72/72. **Course Rating:** 72.0/66.3. **Slope:** 133/109. **Green Fee:** $26/$40. **Cart Fee:** Included in Green Fee. **Walking Policy:** Walking at certain times. **Walkability:** 2. **Opened:** 1998. **Architect:** Harry Bowers. **Season:** March-Nov. **High:** April-Sept. **To obtain tee times:** Up to one week in advance. Credit card required for Saturday & Sunday reservation. **Miscellaneous:** Reduced fees (weekdays, low season, twilight, seniors, juniors), credit cards (MC, V).

MICHIGAN

★★½ INTERLOCHEN GOLF & COUNTRY CLUB
PU-P.O. Box 155, Interlochen, 49643, Grand Traverse County, (616)275-7311, 13 miles SW of Traverse City.
Holes: 18. **Yards:** 6,435/5,136. **Par:** 71/72. **Course Rating:** 70.2/69.2. **Slope:** 130/117. **Green Fee:** $15/$25. **Cart Fee:** $20/cart. **Walking Policy:** Unrestricted walking. **Walkability:** 3.
Opened: 1965. **Season:** April-Oct. **High:** July-Aug. **To obtain tee times:** Call up to 30 days in advance. **Miscellaneous:** Reduced fees (weekdays, low season, twilight, seniors, juniors), discount packages, metal spikes, range (grass), club rentals, credit cards (MC, V).
Reader Comments: Fun ... Lots of play ...Tight ... Good value ... Scenic short course ... Variety ... Busy.

IRONWOOD GOLF CLUB
PU-6902 (M-59) Highland Rd., Howell, 48843, Livingston County, (517)546-3211, 31 miles SE of Lansing.
Holes: 18. **Yards:** 6,083/5,172. **Par:** 72/72. **Course Rating:** 68.3/67.7. **Slope:** 116/117. **Green Fee:** $15/$28. **Cart Fee:** $20/cart. **Walking Policy:** Unrestricted walking. **Walkability:** 2.
Opened: 1972. **Architect:** David Pardun. **Season:** March-Nov. **High:** June-Sept. **To obtain tee times:** Call golf shop. **Miscellaneous:** Reduced fees (weekdays, low season, twilight, seniors, juniors), credit cards (MC, V, AE, D).
Reader Comments: Friendly, well kept ... Inexpensive, challenging ... Entertaining ... Good test for all levels ... Bring your buddies, it's fun.

IRONWOOD GOLF COURSE
PU-3750 64th St. S.W., Byron Center, 49315, Kent County, (616)538-4000, 10 miles S of Grand Rapids.
Holes: 19. **Yards:** 5,405/4,870. **Par:** 71/71. **Course Rating:** N/A. **Slope:** N/A. **Green Fee:** $11/$20. **Cart Fee:** $20/cart. **Walking Policy:** Unrestricted walking. **Walkability:** 1. **Opened:** 1976. **Architect:** George Woolferd. **Season:** March-Nov. **High:** May-Aug. **To obtain tee times:** Call. **Miscellaneous:** Reduced fees (weekdays, low season, seniors, juniors), metal spikes, club rentals.

★★½ KEARSLEY LAKE GOLF COURSE
PM-4266 E Pierson Rd., Flint, 48506, Genesee County, (810)736-0930.
Holes: 18. **Yards:** 6,594/5,766. **Par:** 72/72. **Course Rating:** 70.6/70.1. **Slope:** 113/112. **Green Fee:** $18/$20. **Cart Fee:** $20/cart. **Walking Policy:** Unrestricted walking. **Walkability:** 2.
Season: April-Oct. **High:** May-Aug. **To obtain tee times:** Call on Monday for upcoming weekend or 5 days in advance for weekdays. **Miscellaneous:** Reduced fees (low season, twilight, seniors, juniors), club rentals, credit cards (MC, V).
Reader Comments: Best city course I've ever played ... Well kept ... Course layout counterclockwise ... Nice for us left handers ... Great water holes ... Hard to get on ... Nice muny.

★★★½ KENSINGTON METRO PARK GOLF COURSE
PU-2240 W. Buno Rd., Milford, 48380, Oakland County, (248)685-9332, (800)234-6534, 25 miles NW of Detroit.
Holes: 18. **Yards:** 6,378/5,206. **Par:** 71/71. **Course Rating:** 70.8/69.8. **Slope:** 115/112. **Green Fee:** $18/$22. **Cart Fee:** $10/person. **Walking Policy:** Unrestricted walking. **Walkability:** 3.
Opened: 1961. **Architect:** H.A. Lemley. **Season:** March-Nov. **High:** May-Sept. **To obtain tee times:** Call up to 7 days in advance. **Miscellaneous:** Reduced fees (weekdays, low season, seniors, juniors), credit cards (MC, V).
Reader Comments: Friendly course ... Very reasonable, wide fairways, well kept ... Lots of trees and rolling hills. Deer in fairway ... Overplay has taken toll ... Good condition ... Great metro course ... Always a pleasure to play ... Jam packed ... Pace on weekends is excellent ... Good price, average layout.

★★★½ KIMBERLEY OAKS GOLF CLUB
SP-1100 W Walnut St., St. Charles, 48655, Saginaw County, (517)865-8261, 10 miles SW of Saginaw.
Holes: 18. **Yards:** 6,663/5,156. **Par:** 72/74. **Course Rating:** 72.7/69.9. **Slope:** 134/117. **Green Fee:** $18/$26. **Cart Fee:** $22/cart. **Walking Policy:** Unrestricted walking. **Walkability:** 4.
Opened: 1967. **Season:** April-Oct. **High:** June-Sept. **To obtain tee times:** Call up to 14 days in advance. **Miscellaneous:** Reduced fees (weekdays, low season, twilight, seniors, juniors), range (grass), credit cards (MC, V).
Reader Comments: Good challenge ... Good value ... Worth the drive ... Lots and lots of oaks! ... Very interesting and challenging, some blind shots ... Very challenging ... Long hitter test ... Many new improvements make it a challenging ... Hope you like water! ... Slow play.

★★★ KINCHELOE MEMORIAL GOLF COURSE
PM-50 Woodside Rd., Kincheloe, 49788, Chippewa County, (906)495-5706, 24 miles S of Sault Ste. Marie.

Holes: 18. **Yards:** 6,939/5,016. **Par:** 72/72. **Course Rating:** 73.6/69.2. **Slope:** 127/115. **Green Fee:** $24/$26. **Cart Fee:** $10/person. **Walking Policy:** Unrestricted walking. **Walkability:** 3. **Opened:** 1966. **Architect:** Baldock. **Season:** April-Sept. **High:** June-Aug. **To obtain tee times:** Call ahead for scheduling or walk-ins welcome. **Miscellaneous:** Reduced fees (weekdays, low season, twilight, juniors), range (grass), club rentals, credit cards (MC, V, D), beginner friendly (junior league, beginner league).
Reader Comments: Renovated military course–Good job! ... Enjoyable challenging track, great value ... Wide fairways, lots of trees ... Nice layout and decent condition for summer.

KING'S CHALLENGE GOLF COURSES
PU-4555 East Lime Lake Road , Cedar, 49621, Leelanau County, (231)228-7400, (888)228-0121, 18 miles NW of Traverse City. **Web:** kingschallenge.com.
★★½ **NORTH RESORT COURSE**
Holes: 18. **Yards:** 6,813/5,134. **Par:** 72/74. **Course Rating:** 73.3/70.5. **Slope:** 125/117. **Green Fee:** $35/$45. **Cart Fee:** Included in Green Fee. **Walking Policy:** Walking at certain times. **Walkability:** 4. **Opened:** 1966. **Architect:** C.D. Wagstaff. **Season:** May-Oct. **High:** July-Aug. **To obtain tee times:** Call golf shop. **Miscellaneous:** Reduced fees (weekdays, twilight), discount packages, range (grass/mats), club rentals, lodging, credit cards (MC, V).
Reader Comments: No. 14 will make you wish for a straight ball! ... Classy and challenging ... Costly ... Could be better ... Nice layout ... Blind shots will fool you.
★★½ **SOUTH PALMER COURSE**
Holes: 18. **Yards:** 6,593/4,764. **Par:** 71/71. **Course Rating:** 73.3/68.6. **Slope:** 145/123. **Green Fee:** $35/$45. **Cart Fee:** Included in Green Fee. **Walking Policy:** Walking at certain times. **Walkability:** 5. **Opened:** 1997. **Architect:** C.D. Wagstaff. **Season:** May-Oct. **High:** July-Aug. **To obtain tee times:** Call golf shop. **Miscellaneous:** Reduced fees (weekdays, twilight), discount packages, range (grass/mats), club rentals, lodging, credit cards (MC, V).
Reader Comments: Challenging.

★★★★½ **L.E. KAUFMAN GOLF CLUB** *Value+*
PM-4807 Clyde Park S.W., Wyoming, 49509, Kent County, (616)538-5050, 8 miles S of Grand Rapids.
Holes: 18. **Yards:** 6,812/5,202. **Par:** 72/72. **Course Rating:** 72.0/69.7. **Slope:** 130/117. **Green Fee:** $21/$23. **Cart Fee:** $24/cart. **Walking Policy:** Unrestricted walking. **Walkability:** 3. **Opened:** 1965. **Architect:** Bruce Matthews. **Season:** March-Nov. **High:** June-Aug. **To obtain tee times:** Call up to 7 days in advance. **Miscellaneous:** Reduced fees (seniors, juniors), metal spikes, range (grass/mats), club rentals, credit cards (MC, V).
Reader Comments: Best value for area, private or public ... A muny doesn't get any better ... A must play ... Public golf course with country club conditions ... Fast greens ... Good test of golf ... Excellent course for the low green fees ... Well maintained ... Hard enough to keep away the high handicap ... My Michigan favorite–great shape, great shots, great golf!.

★★ **LAKE CORA HILLS GOLF COURSE**
PU-Red Arrow Hwy., Paw Paw, 49079, Van Buren County, (616)657-4074.
Holes: 18. **Yards:** 6,300/5,702. **Par:** 72/72. **Course Rating:** 69.9/70.9. **Slope:** 121/120. **Green Fee:** $14/$14. **Cart Fee:** $20/person. **Walking Policy:** Unrestricted walking. **Walkability:** 3. **Architect:** Al Humphrey. **Season:** Year-round. **To obtain tee times:** Call ahead for weekends. **Miscellaneous:** Metal spikes, club rentals, credit cards (MC, V).

★★★★ **LAKE DOSTER GOLF CLUB**
SP-136 Country Club Blvd., Plainwell, 49080, Allegan County, (616)685-5308, 10 miles N of Kalamazoo. **E-mail:** parfiveinc@aol.com.
Holes: 18. **Yards:** 6,570/5,330. **Par:** 72/72. **Course Rating:** 72.7/72.8. **Slope:** 134/128. **Green Fee:** $24/$27. **Cart Fee:** $10/person. **Walking Policy:** Walking at certain times. **Walkability:** 3. **Opened:** 1969. **Architect:** Charles Darl Scott. **Season:** April-Oct. **High:** June-Aug. **To obtain tee times:** Call anytime. **Miscellaneous:** Discount packages, metal spikes, range (grass), club rentals, credit cards (MC, V, D).
Reader Comments: Excellent design ... Tough course, tight, some very nice holes ... Little monster par 3 ... Only played the front 9, liked what I saw ... Great challenge for the good golfer ... Offers a variety of shots and terrain ... Best kept secret in Michigan.

★★★½ **LAKE MICHIGAN HILLS GOLF CLUB**
SP-2520 Kerlikowske Rd., Benton Harbor, 49022, Berrien County, (616)849-2722, (800)247-3437, 90 miles N of Chicago.
Holes: 18. **Yards:** 6,911/5,250. **Par:** 72/72. **Course Rating:** 73.9/70.8. **Slope:** 135/124. **Green Fee:** $20/$35. **Cart Fee:** $24/cart. **Walking Policy:** Walking at certain times. **Walkability:** 4. **Opened:** 1969. **Architect:** Charles Maddox Sr. **Season:** April-Nov. **High:** June-Aug. **To obtain tee times:** Call up to 7 days in advance. **Miscellaneous:** Reduced fees (weekdays, low season, twilight, seniors, juniors), discount packages, range (grass), credit cards (MC, V, AE).
Reader Comments: Fun course, changes in elevations ... Great layout ... Service might seem better at a lower price ... A real sleeper! ... Hilly and long, large greens and sand traps ... Tough

MICHIGAN

when wind blows off Lake Michigan ... A Southeast Michigan must play ... Outstanding ... No. 10 tee spectacular ... Some of the fairways too close together.

★★½ LAKELAND HILLS GOLF COURSE
PU-5119 Page Ave., Jackson, 49201, Jackson County, (517)764-5292, 50 miles W of Detroit. **Web:** www.lakelandhills.com.
Holes: 18. **Yards:** 6,199/5,090. **Par:** 72/72. **Course Rating:** 68.9/68.4. **Slope:** 110/109. **Green Fee:** $13/$18. **Cart Fee:** $20/cart. **Walking Policy:** Unrestricted walking. **Walkability:** 3. **Opened:** 1969. **Season:** March-Dec. **High:** April-Sept. **To obtain tee times:** Call 7 days in advance. **Miscellaneous:** Reduced fees (twilight, seniors, juniors), club rentals, credit cards (MC, V, D).
Reader Comments: Watch for errant golf balls ... Wide open, flat ... Not bad.

★★★½ LAKES OF TAYLOR GOLF CLUB
PM-25505 Northline Rd., Taylor, 48180, Wayne County, (313)295-7790, 10 miles SW of Detroit. **Holes:** 18. **Yards:** 7,028/5,119. **Par:** 72/72. **Course Rating:** 73.4/69.4. **Slope:** 136/121. **Green Fee:** $27/$39. **Cart Fee:** $24/cart. **Walking Policy:** Unrestricted walking. **Walkability:** 5. **Opened:** 1996. **Architect:** Arthur Hills/Steve Forrest. **Season:** March-Nov. **High:** June-Sept. **To obtain tee times:** Call golf shop. **Miscellaneous:** Reduced fees (low season, twilight, seniors, juniors), range (grass/mats), club rentals, credit cards (MC, V, AE), beginner friendly (beginner tees).
Reader Comments: Excellent ... Lots of length ... Nice course but too much $ to play ... Very challenging ... Condition declining ... Layout exceptional ... City maintains ... Creative accommodation to environmentally sensitive areas ... Seemed overwhelmed on a Sunday.

★★★½ LAKES OF THE NORTH DEER RUN
PU-8151 Pineview, Mancelona, 49659, Antrim County, (231)585-6800, (800)851-4653, 15 miles W of Gaylord.
Holes: 18. **Yards:** 6,996/5,465. **Par:** 72/74. **Course Rating:** 73.0/N/A. **Slope:** 130/N/A. **Green Fee:** $25/$25. **Cart Fee:** $15/person. **Walking Policy:** Unrestricted walking. **Walkability:** 3. **Opened:** 1989. **Architect:** Jerry Matthews/William Newcomb. **Season:** May-Oct. **High:** June-Aug. **To obtain tee times:** Call golf shop. **Miscellaneous:** Reduced fees (low season, resort guests, twilight, juniors), discount packages, metal spikes, range (grass), club rentals, lodging, credit cards (MC, V).
Reader Comments: Have played a number of times over a decade–nice but never memorable ... Front 9 OK, but back 9 is boring ... Great price and pace ... No problem ... Good course.

LAKESIDE LINKS
PU-5369 W. Chauves Rd., Ludington, 49431, Mason County, (231)843-3660.
★★½ EAST/SOUTH COURSE
Yards: 6,468/5,041. **Par:** 72/72. **Course Rating:** N/A. **Slope:** 122/113. **Green Fee:** $18/$20.
★★½ EAST/WEST COURSE
Yards: 5,766/4,736. **Par:** 69/69. **Course Rating:** N/A. **Slope:** 121/111. **Green Fee:** $20.
★★½ WEST/SOUTH COURSE
Yards: 6,466/4,853. **Par:** 71/71. **Course Rating:** N/A. **Slope:** 126/112. **Green Fee:** $18/$20.
Reader Comments: Not high class, but very nice ... Hilly, small greens ... OK.

LAKEVIEW HILLS COUNTRY CLUB & RESORT
R-6560 Peck Rd. (M-90), Lexington, 48450, Sanilac County, (810)359-8901, 20 miles N of Port Huron. **E-mail:** lakeview@greatlakes.net. **Web:** www.lakeviewhills.com.
★★★ NORTH COURSE
Holes: 18. **Yards:** 6,852/4,995. **Par:** 72/74. **Course Rating:** 73.5/71.8. **Slope:** 139/131. **Green Fee:** $44/$50. **Cart Fee:** Included in Green Fee. **Walking Policy:** Mandatory cart. **Walkability:** 3. **Opened:** 1991. **Architect:** Jeffery John Gorney. **Season:** April-Oct. **High:** July-Sept. **To obtain tee times:** Call. **Miscellaneous:** Reduced fees (weekdays, low season, seniors), discount packages, range (grass/mats), club rentals, lodging (34 rooms), credit cards (MC, V, AE).
Reader Comments: Decent layout–several challenging holes ... Fun and challenging course from the back tees ... Overrated ... Challenging ... Great course, but bring a saw ... Nice views, not too pricey.

★★★ SOUTH COURSE
Holes: 18. **Yards:** 6,290/4,707. **Par:** 72/74. **Course Rating:** 70.1/67.6. **Slope:** 119/116. **Green Fee:** $27/$31. **Cart Fee:** $14/person. **Walking Policy:** Unrestricted walking. **Walkability:** 3. **Opened:** 1928. **Architect:** Walter Hagen. **Season:** April-Oct. **High:** July-Sept. **To obtain tee times:** Call. **Miscellaneous:** Reduced fees (weekdays, low season, twilight, seniors, juniors), discount packages, range (grass), club rentals, lodging (34 rooms), credit cards (MC, V, AE).
Reader Comments: Nice, challenging greens, worth the ride ... Traditional ... Variety and challenge ... Open, rolling terrain ... Excellent changes in elevation ... Mountain hiking gear necessary.

MICHIGAN

LAKEWOOD SHORES RESORT *Service*
R-7751 Cedar Lake Rd., Oscoda, 48750, Iosco County, (517)739-2073, (800)882-2493, 80 miles NE of Saginaw. **E-mail:** lakewoodresort@voyger.net. **Web:** lakewoodshores.com .

★★★★ SERRADELLA COURSE
Holes: 18. **Yards:** 6,806/5,295. **Par:** 72/74. **Course Rating:** 72.9/70.9. **Slope:** 124/116. **Green Fee:** $23/$32. **Cart Fee:** $12/person. **Walking Policy:** Unrestricted walking. **Walkability:** 1. **Opened:** 1969. **Architect:** Bruce Matthews/Jerry Matthews. **Season:** April-Oct. **High:** June-Sept. **To obtain tee times:** Call anytime in advance. **Miscellaneous:** Reduced fees (weekdays, low season, resort guests, twilight, juniors), discount packages, range (grass), club rentals, lodging (64 rooms), credit cards (MC, V), beginner friendly (junior golf camp, youth lessons).
Reader Comments: Very nice, great floral displays ... Much improved in last 3 years ... Well conditioned ... Excellent ... Beautiful ... Best value ... Fair layout, greens good! ... No surprises ... Flat, long, small greens ... Gorgeous flowers!.

★★★★½ THE GAILES COURSE *Value, Condition+, Pace*
Holes: 18. **Yards:** 6,954/5,246. **Par:** 72/73. **Course Rating:** 75.0/72.2. **Slope:** 138/122. **Green Fee:** $30/$50. **Cart Fee:** $12/person. **Walking Policy:** Unrestricted walking. **Walkability:** 1. **Opened:** 1992. **Architect:** Kevin Aldridge. **Season:** April-Oct. **High:** June-Sept. **To obtain tee times:** Call anytime in advance. **Miscellaneous:** Reduced fees (weekdays, low season, resort guests, twilight, juniors), discount packages, range (grass), club rentals, lodging (64 rooms), credit cards (MC, V).
Notes: Ranked 7th in 1999 Best in State.
Reader Comments: Loved it! ... Felt like I was in the British Open ... Bunkers in the middle of the fairways ... Bury me here ... What an experience ... Nice links design ... Authentic Scottish course is demanding, tough and lots of fun ... Great ... Fabulous at sunrise or sunset ... One of the best in Michigan ... Think you're a player, try this one from the tips ... Brutal ... Michigan's Scotland!

★★★½ LAPEER COUNTRY CLUB
PU-3786 Hunt Rd., Lapeer, 48446, Lapeer County, (810)664-2442, 2 miles W of Lapeer.
Holes: 18. **Yards:** 6,109/5,057. **Par:** 72/73. **Course Rating:** N/A. **Slope:** 122/120. **Green Fee:** $18/$20. **Cart Fee:** $23/cart. **Walking Policy:** Unrestricted walking. **Walkability:** 4. **Opened:** 1927. **Season:** March-Nov. **High:** April-Sept. **To obtain tee times:** Call in advance. **Miscellaneous:** Reduced fees (weekdays, seniors, juniors), club rentals, credit cards (MC, V), beginner friendly (weekdays only).
Reader Comments: Country atmosphere ...Wide open with some tight fairways ... Should have taken boat with me on back 9 ... A few tough holes, crowned greens, slow play ... Hilly ... Very reasonable price with cart. Friendly ... Fine test ... Unfair greens ... Another hidden treasure.

★½ LEDGE MEADOWS GOLF COURSE
PU-1801 Grand Ledge Hwy, Grand Ledge, 48837, Eaton County, (517)627-7492, (800)727-8465, 7 miles W of Lansing. **Web:** www.ia4u.net/~ledgegolf/.
Holes: 18. **Yards:** 6,444/4,852. **Par:** 72/72. **Course Rating:** 70.6/67.2. **Slope:** 118/111. **Green Fee:** $15/$19. **Cart Fee:** $11/person. **Walking Policy:** Unrestricted walking. **Walkability:** 3. **Opened:** 1971. **Architect:** Scott Kelly/Harold Weeks. **Season:** March-Nov. **High:** May-Aug. **To obtain tee times:** Call anytime. **Miscellaneous:** Reduced fees (low season, twilight, seniors, juniors), credit cards (MC, V, D), beginner friendly.

★★★★ THE LEGACY GOLF CLUB
PU-7677 U.S. Hwy. 223, Ottawa Lake, 49267, Monroe County, (734)854-1101, (877)854-5100, 5 miles N of Toledo, OH.
Holes: 18. **Yards:** 6,840/4,961. **Par:** 72/72. **Course Rating:** 72.7/68.3. **Slope:** 134/115. **Green Fee:** $29/$48. **Cart Fee:** $16/person. **Walking Policy:** Unrestricted walking. **Walkability:** 3. **Opened:** 1997. **Architect:** Arthur Hills. **Season:** Feb.-Nov. **High:** May-Sept. **To obtain tee times:** Call as much as 30 days in advance. **Miscellaneous:** Reduced fees (weekdays, low season, twilight, seniors), range (grass), club rentals, credit cards (MC, V, D).
Reader Comments: Priced itself out of play ... Beautiful course, very playable for all levels ... Tough with water and sand ... Great bar, excellent food, fun course ... Excellent new course ... A beautiful place to play ...Young course, will get even better... Great layout, challenging, variety.

★★★½ LESLIE PARK GOLF COURSE
PU-2120 Traver Rd., Ann Arbor, 48105, Washtenaw County, (313)994-1163.
Holes: 18. **Yards:** 6,591/4,985. **Par:** 72/72. **Course Rating:** 71.9/68.6. **Slope:** 127/115. **Green Fee:** $22/$25. **Cart Fee:** $24/cart. **Walking Policy:** Unrestricted walking. **Walkability:** 3. **Opened:** 1968. **Architect:** Edward Lawrence Packard. **Season:** March-Nov. **High:** June-Aug. **To obtain tee times:** Call golf shop. **Miscellaneous:** Reduced fees (weekdays, twilight, seniors, juniors), club rentals, credit cards (MC, V).
Reader Comments: Nice old course ... Outstanding public test ... Large, rolling terrain ... Hilly ... Classic layout ... Toughest greens ... Challenging and exciting ... Not bad for money ... Some

good holes and some bad ... If you walk this course, check with cardiologist ... Good solid track ... For a public course, this is up there with the best.

★½ LILAC GOLF CLUB
PU-5090 Armstrong Rd., Newport, 48166, Monroe County, (313)586-9902, 20 miles S of Detroit.
Holes: 18. **Yards:** 7,050/5,900. **Par:** 72/72. **Course Rating:** 72.4/69.9. **Slope:** 125/118. **Green Fee:** $17/$20. **Cart Fee:** $20/cart. **Walking Policy:** Unrestricted walking. **Walkability:** 1.
Opened: 1959. **Architect:** Al Lilac/Sam Lilac. **Season:** March-Nov. **High:** June-Aug. **To obtain tee times:** Call. **Miscellaneous:** Reduced fees (weekdays, twilight, seniors, juniors), metal spikes, range (grass).

★ LINCOLN COUNTRY CLUB
3485 Lake Michigan Dr., Grand Rapids, 49504, Kent County, (616)453-6348.
Special Notes: Call club for further information.

★★½ LINCOLN GOLF CLUB
SP-4907 N Whitehall Rd., Muskegon, 49445, Muskegon County, (231)766-3636, 9 miles N of Muskegon.
Yards: 6,100/5,500. **Par:** 72/76. **Course Rating:** N/A. **Slope:** 116/N/A. **Green Fee:** $12/$22.
Cart Fee: $18/cart. **Walkability:** 3. **Architect:** Jerry Matthews. **Season:** April-Oct. **To obtain tee times:** Call golf shop. **Miscellaneous:** Reduced fees (seniors), range, credit cards (MC, V).

Reader Comments: Good semi-private course ... Well kept, but a marginal layout ... Great greens.

★★★ LINCOLN HILLS GOLF CLUB
SP-1527 N. Lakeshore Dr., Ludington, 49431, Mason County, (231)843-4666, 100 miles NW of Grand Rapids.
Holes: 18. **Yards:** 6,100/N/A. **Par:** 70/N/A. **Course Rating:** 68.7/N/A. **Slope:** 117/N/A. **Green Fee:** $30/$40. **Cart Fee:** $16/person. **Walking Policy:** Unrestricted walking. **Walkability:** 3.
Opened: 1921. **Architect:** Mark Mitchell. **Season:** April-Nov. **High:** June-Aug. **To obtain tee times:** No tee times for nonmembers. Call for walk-on availability. **Miscellaneous:** Range (grass), credit cards (MC, V).

Reader Comments: Semi-private where members are very friendly ... It's been discovered, limited public availability.

THE LINKS AT BOWEN LAKE
PU-12990 Bradshaw NE, Gowen, 49326, Kent County, (616)984-9916, (888)715-4657, 30 miles NE of Grand Rapids.
Holes: 18. **Yards:** 6,900/5,379. **Par:** 71/72. **Course Rating:** N/A. **Slope:** N/A. **Green Fee:** $20/$45. **Cart Fee:** Included in Green Fee. **Walking Policy:** Mandatory cart. **Walkability:** 4.
Opened: 1999. **Architect:** Bill Newcombe. **Season:** April-Oct. **High:** June-Aug. **To obtain tee times:** Call 1 week in advance, unless a group of 12 or more then call anytime. **Miscellaneous:** Reduced fees (weekdays, low season, twilight, seniors, juniors), discount packages, credit cards (MC, V).

★★★½ THE LINKS AT PINEWOOD
PU-8600 P.G.A. Dr., Walled Lake, 48390, Oakland County, (248)669-9802, 30 miles NW of Detroit.
Holes: 18. **Yards:** 6,676/5,300. **Par:** 72/72. **Course Rating:** 72.0/72.3. **Slope:** 125/124. **Green Fee:** $40/$45. **Cart Fee:** Included in Green Fee. **Walking Policy:** Walking at certain times.
Walkability: 1. **Opened:** 1985. **Architect:** Ernest Fuller. **Season:** March-Dec. **High:** May-Sept.
To obtain tee times: Call up to 6 days in advance. **Miscellaneous:** Reduced fees (weekdays, low season, twilight, seniors, juniors), range (grass/mats), club rentals, credit cards (MC, V, AE).

Reader Comments: Challenging ... Outing course that grows on you ... Very crowded ... Back 9 much better than front ... Hosts many outings–and conditions show it ... Has potential ... Friendly staff ... Recent renovation improved greens.

THE LINKS OF NOVI
PU-50395 Ten Mile Rd., Novi, 48374, Oakland County, (248)380-9595, 15 miles NW of Detroit.
Holes: 27. **Green Fee:** $33/$38. **Cart Fee:** $12/person. **Walking Policy:** Walking at certain times. **Walkability:** 3. **Opened:** 1991. **Architect:** Jerry Matthews. **Season:** April-Dec. **High:** June-Aug. **To obtain tee times:** Call 6 days in advance for weekdays. Call Monday for the upcoming weekend. **Miscellaneous:** Reduced fees (twilight, seniors, juniors), range (grass/mats), club rentals, credit cards (MC, V).
★★★½ EAST/SOUTH
Yards: 6,014/4,646. **Par:** 69/72. **Course Rating:** 67.9/66.8. **Slope:** 118/115.

Reader Comments: Overrated ... Pricey, lots of short holes ... Still needs work ... East & West the best ... Fairways beautiful, layout challenging ... Overall just a great course, great greens and condition ... Very good course ... Some tough holes ... Good course for the price ... Fun.

MICHIGAN

★★★½ **EAST/WEST**
Yards: 6,497/5,122. **Par:** 71/74. **Course Rating:** 71.2/70.4. **Slope:** 127/126.
Reader Comments: Nice Scottish layout.

★★★½ **SOUTH/WEST**
Yards: 6,093/4,862. **Par:** 70/74. **Course Rating:** 68.3/68.0. **Slope:** 119/121.
Reader Comments: Country club atmosphere for a public course.

★★★★½ **LITTLE TRAVERSE BAY GOLF CLUB** *Service*
PU-995 Hideaway Valley Rd., Harbor Springs, 49740, Emmet County, (616)526-6200, (888)995-6262, 80 miles NE of Traverse City. **Web:** www.ltbaygolf.com.
Holes: 18. **Yards:** 6,895/5,061. **Par:** 72/72. **Course Rating:** 73.9/69.3. **Slope:** 136/119. **Green Fee:** $55/$80. **Cart Fee:** Included in Green Fee. **Walking Policy:** Mandatory cart. **Walkability:** 5. **Opened:** 1992. **Architect:** Jeff Gorney. **Season:** May-Oct. **High:** June-Sept. **To obtain tee times:** Call golf shop with credit card. Cancellations can be made 2 days prior to play.
Miscellaneous: Reduced fees (weekdays, low season, juniors), metal spikes, range (grass/mats), club rentals, credit cards (MC, V).
Reader Comments: A beauty in the eyes of all beholders ... Million dollar views ... Well kept ... Can see for several miles from 1st tee ... Terrific layout ... Most confusing greens in the world! ... Breathtaking ... Best I've played in Michigan ... Private club feel ... A must play up north ... Tough greens ... Don't miss this one.

LUM INTERNATIONAL GOLF CLUB
PU-5191 Lum Rd., Lum, 48412, Lapeer County, (810)724-0851, 30 miles E of Flint.
Holes: 27. **Green Fee:** $17/$20. **Cart Fee:** $21/cart. **Walking Policy:** Unrestricted walking.
Walkability: 2. **Opened:** 1979. **Season:** March-Nov. **High:** May-Sept. **To obtain tee times:** Call golf shop (810)724-0851. **Miscellaneous:** Reduced fees (weekdays, low season, twilight, seniors, juniors), metal spikes, range (grass), club rentals, credit cards (MC, V, D), beginner friendly (junior league and junior lessons).

★★ **RED/GOLD**
Yards: 6,695/5,239. **Par:** 71/71. **Course Rating:** N/A. **Slope:** N/A.

★★ **RED/WHITE**
Yards: 6,629/5,201. **Par:** 72/72. **Course Rating:** N/A. **Slope:** N/A.

★★ **WHITE/GOLD**
Yards: 6,274/5,082. **Par:** 71/71. **Course Rating:** N/A. **Slope:** N/A.

THE MAJESTIC AT LAKE WALDEN
PU-9600 Crouse Rd., Hartland, 48353, Livingston County, (810)632-5235, (800)762-3280, 45 miles W of Detroit. **E-mail:** majestic @ismi.net. **Web:** www.waldenwoods.com.
Holes: 27. **Green Fee:** $45/$65. **Cart Fee:** Included in Green Fee. **Walking Policy:** Mandatory cart. **Walkability:** 5. **Opened:** 1994. **Architect:** Jerry Matthews. **Season:** March-Nov. **High:** June-Aug. **To obtain tee times:** Call up to 7 days in advance. **Miscellaneous:** Reduced fees (weekdays, low season, twilight, juniors), range (grass), club rentals, credit cards (MC, V, AE, D).

★★★★ **FIRST/SECOND**
Yards: 7,035/5,045. **Par:** 72/72. **Course Rating:** 73.8/68.7. **Slope:** 136/111.
Reader Comments: Best layout in Southeast Michigan ... Fine course ... Hills, trees, lakes, wildlife and a boat ... Slow on a Sunday ... Wow! play this course–bring ammo ... My favorite ... Beauty, challenging ... Needs maturing and price cut ... Best in Southern Michigan ... Up north course in Detroit suburbs ... Name says it all! ... Play so slow you can send out for pizza.

★★★★ **FIRST/THIRD**
Yards: 6,914/5,001. **Par:** 72/72. **Course Rating:** 71.4/67.9. **Slope:** 134/111.
Reader Comments: Gorgeous ... Scenic ... Varied layout ... Target golf.

★★★★ **SECOND/THIRD**
Yards: 6,930/4,916. **Par:** 72/72. **Course Rating:** 72.0/67.6. **Slope:** 137/111.
Reader Comments: Short, tight test.

MANISTEE GOLF & COUNTRY CLUB
SP-500 Cherry St., Manistee, 49660, Manistee County, (231)723-2509, 60 miles S of Traverse City.
Holes: 18. **Yards:** 5,614/5,094. **Par:** 70/71. **Course Rating:** 67.9/70.9. **Slope:** 115/118. **Green Fee:** $40/$40. **Cart Fee:** $12/person. **Cart Fee:** Included in Green Fee. **Walking Policy:** Unrestricted walking. **Walkability:** 2. **Opened:** 1901. **Architect:** Thomas Bendelow/H.B. Matthews. **Season:** April-Oct. **High:** June-Sept. **To obtain tee times:** Call up to 2 days in advance. **Miscellaneous:** Reduced fees (weekdays, low season, resort guests, seniors, juniors), discount packages, range (grass), club rentals, credit cards (MC, V).

MAPLE GROVE GOLF COURSE
PU-6360 Secor Rd., Lambertville, 48144, Monroe County, (734)854-6777, 1 miles N of Toledo.
Holes: 18. **Yards:** 5,403/4,850. **Par:** 69/71. **Course Rating:** N/A. **Slope:** N/A. **Green Fee:** $16/$16. **Cart Fee:** $18/cart. **Walking Policy:** Unrestricted walking. **Walkability:** 2. **Opened:**

1980. **Season:** Year-round. **High:** May-Sept. **To obtain tee times:** First come, first served. **Miscellaneous:** Reduced fees (low season), range (grass/mats), club rentals, credit cards (MC, V, D). **Special Notes:** Also a 9 hole, par 3 course.

★★ MAPLE HILL GOLF COURSE

PU-5555 Ivanrest Ave., Grandville, 49418, Kent County, (616)538-0290, (800)219-1113, 3 miles SW of Grand Rapids. **E-mail:** golf@maplehillgc.com. **Web:** www.maplehillgc.com. **Holes:** 18. **Yards:** 4,724/3,760. **Par:** 68/70. **Course Rating:** N/A. **Slope:** N/A. **Green Fee:** $20/$21. **Cart Fee:** $20/cart. **Walking Policy:** Unrestricted walking. **Walkability:** 2. **Opened:** 1967. **Season:** Year-round. **High:** May-Sept. **To obtain tee times:** Call in advance. **Miscellaneous:** Reduced fees (weekdays, seniors, juniors), metal spikes, range (grass), club rentals, credit cards (MC, V, D), beginner friendly (monday junior program).

MAPLE LANE GOLF COURSE

33203 Maple Lane Dr., Sterling Heights, 48312, Macomb County, (810)754-3020.
★½ **EAST COURSE**
★★ **NORTH COURSE**
★½ **WEST COURSE**
Special Notes: Call club for further information.

MAPLE LEAF GOLF COURSE

PU-158 N. Mackinaw Rd., Linwood, 48634, Bay County, (517)697-3370, 10 miles N of Bay City. **E-mail:** jezowski@toast.net. **Web:** golfmapleleaf.com. **Holes:** 27. **Green Fee:** $18/$20. **Cart Fee:** $18/cart. **Walking Policy:** Unrestricted walking. **Walkability:** 2. **Opened:** 1963. **Architect:** Robert W. Bills/Donald L. Childs. **Season:** April-Nov. **High:** June-Aug. **To obtain tee times:** Call up to 7 days in advance. **Miscellaneous:** Reduced fees (weekdays, low season, seniors, juniors), range (grass/mats), club rentals, credit cards (MC, V, D, Diners Club).
★★★½ **EAST/NORTH**
Yards: 5,762/4,466. **Par:** 71/73. **Course Rating:** 67.6/66.2. **Slope:** 116/113.
Reader Comments: Good value ... Easy course if you stay in the fairway ... Tight ... Smack it straight ... Love island hole ... Beautiful layout and landscaping ... 3 separate 9s—one very nice, other two acceptable
★★★½ **EAST/WEST**
Yards: 5,697/4,752. **Par:** 70/72. **Course Rating:** 66.4/66.7. **Slope:** 109/109.
Reader Comments: A good little course.
★★★½ **NORTH/WEST**
Yards: 5,997/4,794. **Par:** 71/73. **Course Rating:** 68.3/67.5. **Slope:** 114/114.
Reader Comments: Great course ... Reasonably priced.

★★★ MAPLE RIVER CLUB

SP-3459 U.S. 31 N., Brutus, 49716, Emmet County, (616)529-6574, 12 miles N of Petoskey. **Web:** maplerivergolf.com. **Holes:** 18. **Yards:** 6,257/5,059. **Par:** 70/72. **Course Rating:** 71.0/72.0. **Slope:** 113/113. **Green Fee:** $25/$45. **Cart Fee:** $20/cart. **Walking Policy:** Walking at certain times. **Walkability:** 3. **Opened:** 1991. **Architect:** ABK Inc. **Season:** April-Oct. **High:** June-Aug. **To obtain tee times:** Not required. **Miscellaneous:** Reduced fees (low season, twilight), discount packages, metal spikes, range (grass), club rentals, credit cards (MC, V, AE). **Reader Comments:** Narrow course is a ball eater! ... Got what I expected.

★★½ MARION OAKS GOLF CLUB

PU-2255 Pinckney Rd., Howell, 48843, Livingston County, (517)548-0050, 30 miles E of Lansing. **Holes:** 18. **Yards:** 6,706/4,851. **Par:** 70/70. **Course Rating:** 71.3/67.1. **Slope:** 128/110. **Green Fee:** $27/$38. **Cart Fee:** Included in Green Fee. **Walking Policy:** Unrestricted walking. **Walkability:** 3. **Opened:** 1990. **Architect:** Frank Godwin. **Season:** April-Nov. **High:** June-Sept. **To obtain tee times:** Call up to 7 days in advance. **Miscellaneous:** Reduced fees (weekdays, twilight, seniors, juniors), discount packages, range (grass), club rentals, credit cards (MC, V, AE). **Reader Comments:** Good layout ... Could use more H2O ... Hilly, rolling ... Plays longer than card ... Anyone would like this one ... Nice wild flowers ... Great value.

★★★ MARQUETTE GOLF & COUNTRY CLUB

SP-1075 Grove St., Marquette, 49855, Marquette County, (906)225-0721. **Holes:** 18. **Yards:** 6,260/5,161. **Par:** 71/73. **Course Rating:** 70.0/69.7. **Slope:** 124/118. **Green Fee:** $27/$42. **Cart Fee:** $22/cart. **Walking Policy:** Unrestricted walking. **Walkability:** 3. **Opened:** 1926. **Architect:** David Gill. **Season:** April-Oct. **High:** June-Aug. **Miscellaneous:** Range (grass), club rentals, credit cards (MC, V). **Reader Comments:** Trying to be too exclusive for Michigan's short season ... Hard to get on.

★★½ MARQUETTE TRAILS COUNTRY CLUB
PU-R #1, Box 3041 76th St., Baldwin, 49304, Lake County, (231)898-2450. **E-mail:** golfatcarr.inter.net. **Web:** marquettetrailsgolf.com.
Holes: 18. **Yards:** 5,847/4,490. **Par:** 70/70. **Course Rating:** N/A. **Slope:** 113/111. **Green Fee:** $18/$25. **Cart Fee:** $12/person. **Walkability:** 3. **Opened:** 1964. **Season:** April-Nov. **High:** July-Aug. **Miscellaneous:** Reduced fees (seniors, juniors), discount packages, range (grass), club rentals, credit cards (MC, V).
Reader Comments: Nice ... A bit pricey for the area.

★★★★ MARSH RIDGE RESORT
R-4815 Old 27 S., Gaylord, 49735, Otsego County, (517)731-1563, (800)968-2633, 55 miles NE of Traverse City. **E-mail:** teetimes@marshridge.com. **Web:** www.marshridge.com.
Holes: 18. **Yards:** 6,127/4,452. **Par:** 71/71. **Course Rating:** 70.8/66.8. **Slope:** 130/119. **Green Fee:** $37/$60. **Cart Fee:** Included in Green Fee. **Walking Policy:** Mandatory cart. **Walkability:** 5. **Opened:** 1992. **Architect:** Mike Husby. **Season:** April-Oct. **High:** June-Sept. **To obtain tee times:** Call anytime in advance. **Miscellaneous:** Reduced fees (weekdays, low season, resort guests, twilight, seniors, juniors), discount packages, range (grass), club rentals, lodging (59 rooms), credit cards (MC, V, AE, D).
Reader Comments: A great time ... Unusual layout ... Very short but well worth playing ... Tight fairways, great views ... Nice place to stay with family ... Signature hole demands accuracy ... Played in fall, absolutely beautiful ... Food super, course fantastic ... Scenery outstanding ... My wife and I had 5 wonderful days of golf ... Excellent golf packages.

★★★½ MARYSVILLE GOLF COURSE
PM-2080 River Rd., Marysville, 48040, St. Clair County, (810)364-4653, 55 miles N of Detroit.
Holes: 18. **Yards:** 6,542/5,311. **Par:** 72/72. **Course Rating:** 71.4/70.5. **Slope:** 119/115. **Green Fee:** $13/$22. **Cart Fee:** $20/cart. **Walking Policy:** Unrestricted walking. **Walkability:** 2. **Opened:** 1954. **Season:** March-Nov. **High:** June-Sept. **To obtain tee times:** Call at noon on Tuesdays for the next 7 days. **Miscellaneous:** Reduced fees (weekdays, low season, seniors, juniors), metal spikes, range (grass), club rentals, credit cards (MC, V, AE, D).
Reader Comments: Usually a nice course, but greens get burned ... It's worth the drive ... Great course for seniors ... Challenging muny ... A very nice course as far as public courses go ... Mix of long and short holes ... Greens are kept up nicely.

★★★ MARYWOOD GOLF CLUB
PU-21310 N. Ave., Battle Creek, 49017, Calhoun County, (616)968-1168, 3 miles N of Battle Creek.
Holes: 18. **Yards:** 6,631/5,233. **Par:** 72/72. **Course Rating:** 73.0/71.6. **Slope:** 132/126. **Green Fee:** $18/$33. **Cart Fee:** $12/person. **Walking Policy:** Walking at certain times. **Walkability:** 4. **Opened:** 1926. **Architect:** Maurice McCarthy. **Season:** April-Nov. **High:** June-Sept. **To obtain tee times:** Call anytime. **Miscellaneous:** Reduced fees (weekdays, low season, twilight, seniors, juniors), discount packages, range (grass/mats), club rentals, credit cards (MC, V, AE, D).
Reader Comments: Great old-fashioned golf course ... Long par 5s to start the day ... Greens are very quick ... Take advantage of specials ... Could be above average with some TLC ... Very good layout ... Course condition slipped ... Elaborate landscaping ... Busy.

★½ MASON HILLS GOLF COURSE
SP-2602 Tomlinson Rd., Mason, 48854, Eaton County, (517)676-5366, 10 miles SE of Lansing.
Holes: 18. **Yards:** 6,348/5,550. **Par:** 72/72. **Course Rating:** N/A. **Slope:** N/A. **Green Fee:** $15/$15. **Cart Fee:** $22/cart. **Walking Policy:** Unrestricted walking. **Walkability:** 3. **Opened:** 1926. **Architect:** Henry Chisholm. **Season:** March-Oct. **High:** May-Aug. **To obtain tee times:** Call. **Miscellaneous:** Reduced fees (weekdays, low season, twilight, seniors, juniors), discount packages, metal spikes, range (grass), club rentals, credit cards (MC, V, AE, D), beginner friendly.

★★★★ MATHESON GREENS GOLF COURSE
PU-6701 N. Matheson Rd. , Northport, 49670, Leelanau County, (616)386-5171, (800)443-6883, 25 miles N of Traverse City. **E-mail:** golf@mathesongreens. **Web:** www.mathesongreens.com.
Holes: 18. **Yards:** 6,609/4,716. **Par:** 72/72. **Course Rating:** 72.1/67.2. **Slope:** 132/116. **Green Fee:** $25/$38. **Cart Fee:** $10/person. **Walking Policy:** Walking at certain times. **Walkability:** 3. **Opened:** 1991. **Architect:** Steve White/Gary Pulsipher. **Season:** April-Oct. **High:** July-Aug. **To obtain tee times:** Call anytime in advance. **Miscellaneous:** Reduced fees (low season, twilight, juniors), discount packages, range (mats), club rentals, credit cards (MC, V, AE, D), beginner friendly (lessons for beginner golfers).
Reader Comments: Great scenery, hard greens and pin placements ... Ho hum course–nothing outstanding ... Beautiful course ... Greens are so undulating they're impossible to read! ... Nice, fairly easy ... Some of the most challenging par 3s ever! ... Scenic and remote.

MICHIGAN

★★★ MCGUIRE'S RESORT
R-7880 Mackinaw Trail, Cadillac, 49601, Wexford County, (616)775-9947, (800)632-7302, 90 miles N of Grand Rapids. **E-mail:** info@mcguiresresort.com.
Holes: 18. **Yards:** 6,443/5,107. **Par:** 71/71. **Course Rating:** 71.3/69.6. **Slope:** 124/118. **Green Fee:** $35/$60. **Cart Fee:** Included in Green Fee. **Walking Policy:** Mandatory cart. **Walkability:** 3. **Opened:** 1959. **Architect:** Bruce Matthews. **Season:** April-Oct. **High:** May-Sept. **To obtain tee times:** Call in advance. **Miscellaneous:** Reduced fees (resort guests, twilight), discount packages, metal spikes, range (grass), lodging (123 rooms), credit cards (MC, V, AE, D).
Reader Comments: Wonderful golf resort ... A good value all around ... Enjoyable ... Nice place for couples.

MEADOW LANE GOLF COURSE
PU-3356 44th St., S.E., Grand Rapids, 49508, Kent County, (616)698-8034, 2 miles W of Grand Rapids.
Holes: 18. **Yards:** 2,800/2,800. **Par:** 72/72. **Course Rating:** N/A. **Slope:** N/A. **Green Fee:** $15/$18. **Cart Fee:** $16/cart. **Walking Policy:** Unrestricted walking. **Walkability:** 2. **Opened:** 1968. **Season:** April-Nov. **High:** May-Aug. **Miscellaneous:** Reduced fees (weekdays), metal spikes, club rentals, credit cards (V).

★★★★ THE MEADOWS GOLF CLUB
PU-4645 W. Campus Dr., Allendale, 49401, Ottawa County, (616)895-1000, 15 miles W of Grand Rapids.
Holes: 18. **Yards:** 7,034/4,777. **Par:** 71/72. **Course Rating:** 74.5/67.4. **Slope:** 133/117. **Green Fee:** $27/$41. **Cart Fee:** $13/person. **Walking Policy:** Unrestricted walking. **Walkability:** 2. **Opened:** 1994. **Architect:** Michael Hurdzan. **Season:** April-Oct. **High:** June-Sept. **To obtain tee times:** Call up to 10 days in advance. Multiple tee times require credit card guarantee. **Miscellaneous:** Reduced fees (weekdays, low season, juniors), range (grass/mats), club rentals, credit cards (MC, V, AE, D).
Reader Comments: Best in area for public ... Great facilities ... Many holes with marshes, fun, worth it ... College course, true test for golfers of all styles .... Mature, good golf holes ... Proof that a flat piece of land can be transformed into a great golf course ... Pretty good overall.

MECEOLA COUNTRY CLUB
SP-218 N Warren, Big Rapids, 49307, Mecosta County, (616)796-9004, 50 miles N of Grand Rapid.
Holes: 18. **Yards:** 6,504/5,890. **Par:** 72/74. **Course Rating:** 70.7/69.9. **Slope:** 117/121. **Green Fee:** $12/$20. **Cart Fee:** $24/cart. **Walking Policy:** Unrestricted walking. **Walkability:** 1. **Opened:** 1919. **Architect:** Jeff Gorney. **Season:** April-Oct. **High:** May-Aug. **To obtain tee times:** Call in advance. **Miscellaneous:** Reduced fees (weekdays, seniors), metal spikes, range (grass), credit cards (MC, V).

THE MEDALIST GOLF CLUB
R-15701 N. Drive North, Marshall, 49068, Calhoun County, (616)789-4653, 10 miles E of Battle Creek.
Holes: 18. **Yards:** 6,969/5,240. **Par:** 72/72. **Course Rating:** 71.7/N/A. **Slope:** 138/129. **Green Fee:** $30/$40. **Cart Fee:** $15/person. **Walking Policy:** Walking at certain times. **Walkability:** 4. **Opened:** 1996. **Architect:** William Newcomb. **Season:** Year-round. **High:** May-Sept. **To obtain tee times:** Call golf shop. **Miscellaneous:** Reduced fees (weekdays, low season, resort guests, twilight, seniors, juniors), discount packages, range (grass), club rentals, credit cards (MC, V, AE).
Special Notes: Formerly known as Wishbone Glen Golf Club.

★★★½ MICHAYWE HILLS RESORT
R-1535 Opal Lake Rd., Gaylord, 49735, Otsego County, (517)939-8911, (800)322-6636, 5 miles NE of Traverse City.
Holes: 18. **Yards:** 6,835/5,901. **Par:** 72/73. **Course Rating:** 73.5/75.0. **Slope:** 133/130. **Green Fee:** $18/$33. **Cart Fee:** $12/person. **Walking Policy:** Walking at certain times. **Walkability:** 2. **Opened:** 1972. **Architect:** Robert W. Bills/Donald L. Childs. **Season:** April-Oct. **High:** June-Aug. **To obtain tee times:** Call anytime. Credit card necessary to hold tee times for groups of 12 or more. **Miscellaneous:** Reduced fees (weekdays, low season, resort guests, twilight, juniors), discount packages, range (grass), club rentals, lodging, credit cards (MC, V).
Reader Comments: Nice course, but none of the holes linger in my memory ... Classic course that challenges ... Great place to play... Needs more conditioning ... Great greens ... A great traditional course at great price ... Friendly staff ... Grade 'A.'

★½ MIDDLE CHANNEL GOLF & COUNTRY CLUB
PU-2306 Golf Course Rd., Harsens Island, 48028, St. Clair County, (810)748-9922, 25 miles NE of Mt. Clemens.
Holes: 18. **Yards:** 6,140/6,140. **Par:** 70/70. **Course Rating:** N/A. **Slope:** N/A. **Green Fee:** $16/$22. **Cart Fee:** $20/cart. **Walking Policy:** Unrestricted walking. **Walkability:** 1. **Opened:**

MICHIGAN

1923. **Season:** April-Oct. **High:** June-Aug. **To obtain tee times:** Call anytime. **Miscellaneous:** Reduced fees (weekdays, low season, twilight, seniors, juniors), metal spikes, club rentals, credit cards (MC, V).

★★★½ **MILHAM PARK MUNICIPAL GOLF CLUB** *Value+*
PM-4200 Lovers Lane, Kalamazoo, 49001, Kalamazoo County, (616)344-7639. **E-mail:** shecky4@aol.com. **Web:** www.kalamazoogolf.org.
Holes: 18. **Yards:** 6,578/5,582. **Par:** 72/72. **Course Rating:** 71.6/71.6. **Slope:** 130/119. **Green Fee:** $20/$22. **Cart Fee:** $12/person. **Walking Policy:** Unrestricted walking. **Walkability:** 2. **Opened:** 1931. **Architect:** David Millar. **Season:** March-Dec. **High:** June-Aug. **To obtain tee times:** Call 3 days in advance for weekends and holidays only. **Miscellaneous:** Reduced fees (seniors, juniors), range (grass/mats), club rentals, credit cards (MC, V, AE, D).
Reader Comments: Lots of sand, fast greens, forgiving fairways ... Good variety ... Best value in South Michigan ... Heavy play public course; play weekdays ... Great city course ... Busy place, bunkers need work ... Beautiful ... Very friendly ... Reasonable rates ... Nothing fancy ... Well maintained, super value.

★★½ **MISSAUKEE GOLF CLUB**
SP-5300 S Morey Rd, Lake City, 49651, Missaukee County, (231)825-2756, 11 miles E of Cadillac. **E-mail:** goldclub18@hotmail.com. **Web:** www.golfmichigan.net/missaukeegolf.
Holes: 18. **Yards:** 5,952/4,968. **Par:** 71/71. **Course Rating:** 67.0/68.0. **Slope:** 110/110. **Green Fee:** $20/$25. **Cart Fee:** $8/person. **Walking Policy:** Unrestricted walking. **Walkability:** 2. **Opened:** 1970. **Season:** April-Oct. **High:** July-Aug. **To obtain tee times:** Call in advance. **Miscellaneous:** Reduced fees (twilight), range (grass/mats), club rentals, credit cards (MC, V, AE).
Reader Comments: Playable for all ... Fun ... Challenging ... Good for average player ... Wide fairways ... Nice fun, fair, great value.

MISTWOOD GOLF COURSE
PU-7568 Sweet Lake Rd., Lake Ann, 49650, Benzie County, (231)275-5500, 18 miles SW of Traverse City.
Holes: 27. **Green Fee:** $30/$36. **Cart Fee:** $12/person. **Walking Policy:** Unrestricted walking. **Walkability:** 3. **Opened:** 1993. **Architect:** Jerry Matthews. **Season:** April-Nov. **High:** June-Aug. **To obtain tee times:** Call anytime. **Miscellaneous:** Reduced fees (weekdays, low season, resort guests, twilight, seniors, juniors), metal spikes, range (grass), club rentals, credit cards (MC, V, AE, D).
★★★★ **RED/BLUE**
Yards: 6,669/5,032. **Par:** 71/71. **Course Rating:** 72.9/70.2. **Slope:** 143/120.
★★★★ **RED/WHITE**
Yards: 6,460/4,874. **Par:** 70/70. **Course Rating:** 71.6/69.2. **Slope:** 140/117.
★★★★ **WHITE/BLUE**
Yards: 6,695/5,070. **Par:** 71/71. **Course Rating:** 72.9/70.2. **Slope:** 142/123.
Reader Comments: Some unusual holes makes for a fun experience ... Excellent greens ... It keeps improving every year ... Fun and challenging ... Nice design, good variety ... Loved it, even though I was in most traps ... Patchy greens ... Great views! ... Best to play in Fall-spectacular colors, better deal ... Needs maturing, but has possibilities.

★★½ **MORRISON LAKE COUNTRY CLUB**
PU-6425 West Portland Rd., Saranac, 48881, Ionia County, (616)642-9528, 28 miles E of Grand Rapids.
Holes: 18. **Yards:** 5,368/5,100. **Par:** 70/72. **Course Rating:** 65.7/66.4. **Slope:** 102/103. **Green Fee:** $10/$. **Cart Fee:** $18/. **Walking Policy:** Unrestricted walking. **Walkability:** N/A. **Opened:** 1927. **Season:** March-Oct. **High:** April-Sept. **To obtain tee times:** Call anytime. **Miscellaneous:** Reduced fees (weekdays, twilight, seniors, juniors), metal spikes, club rentals.
Reader Comments: Nice and fun ... Good value–short, hilly, no trees.

★★ **MULBERRY FORE GOLF COURSE**
PU-955 N Main St. (M-66), Nashville, 49073, Barry County, (517)852-0760, (800)450-0760, 20 miles N of Battle Creek.
Holes: 18. **Yards:** 6,000/5,460. **Par:** 72/75. **Course Rating:** N/A. **Slope:** N/A. **Green Fee:** $15/$15. **Cart Fee:** $19/person. **Walking Policy:** Unrestricted walking. **Walkability:** 4. **Opened:** 1979. **Season:** March-Nov. **High:** May-Sept. **To obtain tee times:** Call 800 number anytime. **Miscellaneous:** Reduced fees (weekdays, low season, twilight, seniors, juniors), discount packages, club rentals, credit cards (MC, V).

★ **MULBERRY HILLS GOLF CLUB**
PU-3530 Noble Rd., Oxford, 48370, Oakland County, (248)628-2808, 40 miles N of Detroit. **Web:** golf@mulberryhills.com.
Holes: 18. **Yards:** 6,508/4,713. **Par:** 71/71. **Course Rating:** 70.2/67.1. **Slope:** 118/109. **Green Fee:** $17/$22. **Cart Fee:** $22/cart. **Walking Policy:** Unrestricted walking. **Walkability:** 3.

MICHIGAN

Opened: 1962. Architect: Franklin D. Clayton. Season: April-Nov. High: May-Sept. To obtain tee times: Call (248)628-2808 or (248)975-6408. Miscellaneous: Reduced fees (weekdays, low season, twilight, seniors, juniors), metal spikes, range (grass/mats), credit cards (MC, V, AE).

★★½ MULLENHURST GOLF COURSE
9810 Mullen Rd., Delton, 49046, Barry County, (616)623-8383.
Yards: 5,625/5,300. Par: 71/71. Course Rating: N/A. Slope: N/A. Green Fee: $13.Walkability: N/A. Miscellaneous: Metal spikes.
Reader Comments: Short but interesting ... Best public course in the area ... Good value.

MYSTIC CREEK GOLF CLUB
PU-1 Champions Circle, Milford, 48380, Oakland County, (248)684-3333, 45 miles NW of Detroit.
Holes: 27. Green Fee: $35/$48. Cart Fee: Included in Green Fee. Walking Policy: Walking at certain times. Walkability: 4. Opened: 1996. Architect: Pat Conroy/Jim Dewling. Season: March-Nov. High: May-Oct. To obtain tee times: Call golf shop. Miscellaneous: Reduced fees (twilight), range (mats), club rentals, credit cards (MC, V, AE, D).
★★★½ LAKES/WOODS
Yards: 6,802/5,000. Par: 72/72. Course Rating: 72.2/66.7. Slope: 130/114.
Reader Comments: Great layout, but very young course ... Elevation, water ... Great value, great staff ... Lakes Course is too gimmicky ... Heavy traffic was tough on conditions ... Crowded ... Needs better conditioning ... Greens were perfect–ike putting on carpet ... Well maintained ... A real beauty and beast ... Variety ... Tough ... Woods is cut through the woods ... Lakes has many holes on or over water.
★★★½ MEADOWS/LAKES
Yards: 6,700/5,000. Par: 72/72. Course Rating: 71.1/65.4. Slope: 131/109.
Reader Comments: Good golf, good test, fair price, lots of fun ... Lakes is gimmicky ... Great layout ... Well maintained ... Variety ... Lakes circles a lake and has many holes on or over water.
★★★½ MEADOWS/WOODS
Yards: 6,700/5,000. Par: 72/72. Course Rating: 71.5/66.3. Slope: 130/116.
Reader Comments: Great layout ... Well maintained ... Variety ... Meadows is open with numerous bunkers ... Woods has drastic elevation changes.

★★★★ THE NATURAL AT BEAVER CREEK RESORT
R-5004 W. Otsego Lake Dr., Gaylord, 49735, Otsego County, (517)732-1785, 75 miles E of Traverse City. E-mail: bcr@voyager.net. Web: www.beavercreekresort.org.
Holes: 18. Yards: 6,350/4,830. Par: 71/71. Course Rating: 69.3/67.8. Slope: 129/118. Green Fee: $30/$55. Cart Fee: $15/person. Walking Policy: Walking at certain times. Walkability: 4. Opened: 1993. Architect: Jerry Matthews. Season: April-Oct. High: June-Aug. To obtain tee times: Call or use internet. Miscellaneous: Reduced fees (weekdays, low season, resort guests, twilight, seniors, juniors), discount packages, range (grass), club rentals, lodging (21 rooms), credit cards (MC, V, D).
Reader Comments: Best value in Michigan ... Carved out of great terrain! ... A shrine to Mother Nature ... Fall colors outstanding ... Under-appreciated ... Superb layout ... Beautiful without the price tag! ... Deceivingly difficult ... Excellent condition except too many pebbles in sand traps ... Our group goes out of our way to play it ... So many trees! No wonder it's by Beaver Creek.

★★★ NORTH KENT GOLF COURSE
PU-11029 Stout Ave. N.E., Rockford, 49341, Kent County, (616)866-2659.
Yards: 6,326/5,002. Par: 70/70. Course Rating: 71.1/68.1. Slope: 127/117. Green Fee: $19/$20. Walkability: N/A. Miscellaneous: Metal spikes.
Reader Comments: Very well-maintained course ... Very busy ... Fun ... Naturally tough ... Fast greens, polite clubhouse staff ... Home course–great place for everyday play.

NORTH SHORE GOLF CLUB
SP-N 2315 Hwy. M-35, Menominee, 49858, Menominee County, (906)863-8421, 6 miles N of Menominee.
Holes: 18. Yards: 6,428/5,367. Par: 72/72. Course Rating: 69.9/72.3. Slope: 120/122. Green Fee: $25/$30. Cart Fee: $25/cart. Walking Policy: Unrestricted walking. Walkability: 1. Opened: 1928. Season: April-Oct. High: June-Aug. Miscellaneous: Reduced fees (weekdays), range (grass), caddies, credit cards (MC, V, D).

★★ NORTH STAR GOLF & COUNTRY CLUB
4550 South Bagley Rd., Ithaca, 48847, Gratiot County, (517)875-3841.
Special Notes: Call club for further information.

★★ NORTHBROOK GOLF CLUB
PU-21690 27 Mile Rd., Ray Township, 48096, Macomb County, (810)749-3415, (800)477-7756, 6 miles N of Sterling Heights.

421

MICHIGAN

Holes: 18. **Yards:** 6,352/4,949. **Par:** 72/72. **Course Rating:** 70.3/68.5. **Slope:** 121/114. **Green Fee:** $13/$23. **Cart Fee:** $24/cart. **Walking Policy:** Unrestricted walking. **Walkability:** 2. **Opened:** 1965. **Season:** April-Nov. **High:** May-Sept. **To obtain tee times:** Call up to 7 days in advance. **Miscellaneous:** Reduced fees (seniors, juniors), credit cards (MC, V), beginner friendly.

★★ NORTHWOOD GOLF COURSE
PU-2888 Comstock Ave., Fremont, 49412, Newaygo County, (616)924-3380, 40 miles NW of Grand Rapids.
Holes: 18. **Yards:** 6,313/5,608. **Par:** 71/71. **Course Rating:** 69.7/66.1. **Slope:** 115/111. **Green Fee:** $17/$19. **Cart Fee:** $18/cart. **Walking Policy:** Unrestricted walking. **Walkability:** 2. **Opened:** 1968. **Season:** April-Oct. **High:** July-Aug. **To obtain tee times:** Call anytime. **Miscella-neous:** Reduced fees (seniors), metal spikes, range (mats), club rentals, credit cards (MC, V).

★★★★ OAK CREST GOLF COURSE *Value, Pace*
PM-Highway US 8, Norway, 49870, Dickinson County, (906)563-5891.
Holes: 18. **Yards:** 6,158/5,430. **Par:** 72/74. **Course Rating:** 69.2/71.0. **Slope:** 120/121. **Green Fee:** $22/$22. **Cart Fee:** $22/cart. **Walking Policy:** Unrestricted walking. **Walkability:** 2. **Opened:** 1929. **Season:** April-Oct. **High:** June-Aug. **To obtain tee times:** Call up to 7 days in advance. **Miscellaneous:** Range (grass), club rentals.
Reader Comments: Course is rough in some spots ... Great value for average golfer... A good course for a great price ... Great muny ... Tight fairways, small greens, lots of oaks ... Pretty ... Treelined fairways, require good shot making ... A hidden gem of the far north.

★★★ OAK LANE GOLF COURSE
PU-800 North Main St., Webberville, 48892, Ingham County, (517)521-3900, 20 miles E of Lansing.
Holes: 18. **Yards:** 5,714/5,115. **Par:** 70/71. **Course Rating:** 67.3/69.1. **Slope:** 107/115. **Green Fee:** $17/$22. **Cart Fee:** $10/person. **Walking Policy:** Unrestricted walking. **Walkability:** 3. **Opened:** 1967. **Architect:** Harley Hodges. **Season:** April-Oct. **High:** June-Aug. **To obtain tee times:** Call or come in up to 14 days in advance. **Miscellaneous:** Reduced fees (twilight, seniors, juniors), club rentals, credit cards (MC, V).
Reader Comments: Fun course ... Pretty, great price ... Good course to shoot par and lose lots of balls ... Very enjoyable, interesting for a public course ... Could be so much more ... Needs new life ... Average small course ... Very nice, well run and well kept.

★★★½ OAK POINTE
5341 Brighton Rd., Brighton, 48116, Livingston County, (810)227-1381.
Yards: 6,157/5,367. **Par:** 71/71. **Course Rating:** 68.5/69.4. **Slope:** 108/110. **Green Fee:** $25/$30. **Walkability:** N/A. **Miscellaneous:** Metal spikes.
Reader Comments: Beautiful layout ... Greens were picture-perfect as well were the fairways and tee boxes ... Layout remarkable, service great ... Rolling, pretty, narrow ... Nice track.

★★ OAK RIDGE GOLF CLUB
PU-513 W. Pontaluna Rd., Muskegon, 49444, Muskegon County, (231)798-3660, 4 miles S of Muskegon.
Holes: 18. **Yards:** 6,010/5,166. **Par:** 72/73. **Course Rating:** N/A. **Slope:** N/A. **Green Fee:** $21/$23. **Cart Fee:** $22/cart. **Walking Policy:** Unrestricted walking. **Walkability:** 3. **Season:** April-Nov. **High:** May-Aug. **To obtain tee times:** Call (231)798-3660. **Miscellaneous:** Reduced fees (low season, juniors), metal spikes, range (grass), club rentals, credit cards (MC, V, AE, D).

OAK RIDGE GOLF CLUB
PU-35035 26 Mile Rd., New Haven, 48048, Macomb County, (810)749-5151, 20 miles N of Detroit. **E-mail:** clubhouse@oakridgegolf.com. **Web:** www.oakridgegolf.com.
MARSH OAKS AT OAK RIDGE
Holes: 18. **Yards:** 6,706/4,916. **Par:** 72/72. **Course Rating:** 72.4/68.7. **Slope:** 131/112. **Green Fee:** $45/$55. **Cart Fee:** Included in Green Fee. **Walking Policy:** Mandatory cart. **Walkability:** 3. **Opened:** 1996. **Architect:** Bruce Matthews. **Season:** April-Nov. **High:** April-Sept. **To obtain tee times:** Call up to 14 days in advance. **Miscellaneous:** Reduced fees (weekdays, low season, twilight, seniors, juniors), discount packages, range (grass), club rentals, credit cards (MC, V, AE, D).
★★★ OLD OAKS AT OAK RIDGE
Holes: 18. **Yards:** 6,563/5,427. **Par:** 71/71. **Course Rating:** 71.0/72.6. **Slope:** 119/119. **Green Fee:** $24/$28. **Cart Fee:** $12/person. **Walking Policy:** Unrestricted walking. **Walkability:** 1. **Opened:** 1966. **Architect:** Bruce Matthews. **Season:** April-Nov. **High:** April-Sept. **To obtain tee times:** Call up to 14 days in advance. **Miscellaneous:** Reduced fees (weekdays, low season, twilight, seniors, juniors), discount packages, metal spikes, range (grass/mats), club rentals, credit cards (MC, V, AE, D).

Reader Comments: Nice course, good value ... Seniors love it ... Very nice course, not real challenging but very fun.

★★½ OAKLAND HILLS GOLF CLUB
PU-11619 H Dr. North, Battle Creek, 49014, Calhoun County, (616)965-0809, 6 miles E of Battle Creek.
Holes: 18. **Yards:** 6,327/5,517. **Par:** 72/72. **Course Rating:** 71.5/73.3. **Slope:** N/A. **Green Fee:** $16/$17. **Cart Fee:** $20/cart. **Walking Policy:** Unrestricted walking. **Walkability:** 3. **Opened:** 1973. **Architect:** George V. Nickolaou. **Season:** March-Nov. **High:** May-Aug. **To obtain tee times:** Call golf shop. **Miscellaneous:** Reduced fees (weekdays, seniors).
Reader Comments: Worth an afternoon stop ... Very well-groomed greens ... Excellent value ... Good course ... Greens will hold anything you throw at them.

★★½ THE OAKS GOLF CLUB
PU-3711 Niles Rd., St. Joseph, 49085, Berrien County, (616)429-8411, 5 miles S of St. Joseph.
Holes: 18. **Yards:** 6,776/5,860. **Par:** 72/74. **Course Rating:** 71.0/74.4. **Slope:** 126/130. **Green Fee:** $21/$29. **Cart Fee:** $13/person. **Walking Policy:** Walking at certain times. **Walkability:** 2. **Opened:** 1986. **Season:** April-Oct. **High:** June-Aug. **Miscellaneous:** Reduced fees (twilight, seniors), range (grass), club rentals, credit cards (MC, V, AE).
Reader Comments: Nice challenge, straightforward test of golf ... Great back 9.

★★★½ OCEANA GOLF CLUB
PU-3333 W. Weaver Rd., Shelby, 49455, Oceana County, (616)861-4211, 25 miles N of Muskegon. **E-mail:** mringlis@voyager.net. **Web:** westmichgolf.com.
Holes: 18. **Yards:** 6,288/5,103. **Par:** 73/73. **Course Rating:** 71.0/71.8. **Slope:** 121/123. **Green Fee:** $18/$18. **Cart Fee:** $10/person. **Walking Policy:** Unrestricted walking. **Walkability:** 3. **Opened:** 1962. **Architect:** Designed by members. **Season:** April-Oct. **High:** June-Aug. **To obtain tee times:** Call anytime. **Miscellaneous:** Reduced fees (weekdays, low season, juniors), discount packages, range (grass/mats), club rentals, credit cards (MC, V), beginner friendly (junior clinic).
Reader Comments: An enjoyable experience ... Nice, short course to tune up your game ... Very nice for the novice ... Friendly people ... Quite challenging ... Fantastic condition ... Great value ... Nice shape.

★★★½ OLD CHANNEL TRAIL GOLF CLUB
PU-8325 N. Old Channel Trail, Montague, 49437, Muskegon County, (231)894-5076, 20 miles NW of Muskegon.
Holes: 27. **Yards:** 6,605/5,115. **Par:** 72/74. **Course Rating:** 69.5/71.2. **Slope:** 123/118. **Green Fee:** $18/$23. **Cart Fee:** $22/cart. **Walking Policy:** Walking at certain times. **Walkability:** 4. **Opened:** 1927. **Architect:** R.B. Harris/Bruce Matthews/Jerry Matthew. **Season:** April-Oct. **High:** July-Aug. **To obtain tee times:** Call (231)894-5076. **Miscellaneous:** Reduced fees (weekdays, low season, twilight, seniors, juniors), discount packages, range (grass), club rentals, credit cards (MC, V).
Reader Comments: Play the Valley and Woods ... Absolute treasure, owned by former Curtis Cup member, historic ... 9 across road a must ... Great variety.

★★ OLDE MILL GOLF CLUB
SP-6101 West XY Ave., Schoolcraft, 49087, Kalamazoo County, (616)679-5625, 13 miles S of Kalamazoo.
Holes: 18. **Yards:** 6,195/5,139. **Par:** 72/72. **Course Rating:** 69.2/68.4. **Slope:** 117/114. **Green Fee:** $18/$30. **Cart Fee:** $20/cart. **Walking Policy:** Unrestricted walking. **Walkability:** 3. **Opened:** 1968. **Season:** March-Nov. **High:** June-Sept. **To obtain tee times:** Call up to 7 days in advance. **Miscellaneous:** Reduced fees (weekdays, low season, twilight, seniors, juniors), range (grass), club rentals, credit cards (MC, V, D).

★★★ ORCHARD HILLS GOLF COURSE
PU-714 125th Ave., Shelbyville, 49344, Allegan County, (616)672-7096, 20 miles S of Grand Rapids.
Holes: 18. **Yards:** 6,000/5,200. **Par:** 72/74. **Course Rating:** 68.6/68.3. **Slope:** 116/116. **Green Fee:** $15/$21. **Cart Fee:** $24/cart. **Walking Policy:** Unrestricted walking. **Walkability:** 3. **Opened:** 1955. **Architect:** Art Young. **Season:** April-Oct. **High:** May-Aug. **To obtain tee times:** Call in advance. **Miscellaneous:** Reduced fees (weekdays, low season, seniors, juniors), metal spikes, range (grass), club rentals, credit cards (MC, V, AE, D), beginner friendly.
Reader Comments: Long beautiful fairways ... Difficult ... Fun ... Not too hard ... Best public course in the area ... Mountain goats only on 9th green ... Slippery greens.

★★★★ THE ORCHARDS GOLF CLUB *Condition*
PU-62900 Campground Rd., Washington, 48094, Macomb County, (810)786-7200, 30 miles N of Detroit. **E-mail:** jdstalcup@orchards.com.
Holes: 18. **Yards:** 7,036/5,158. **Par:** 72/72. **Course Rating:** 74.5/70.3. **Slope:** 136/123. **Green Fee:** $35/$65. **Cart Fee:** Included in Green Fee. **Walking Policy:** Unrestricted walking.

Walkability: 3. **Opened:** 1993. **Architect:** Robert Trent Jones Jr. **Season:** April-Oct. **High:** May-Sept. **To obtain tee times:** Call 30 days in advance. **Miscellaneous:** Reduced fees (weekdays, low season, twilight), metal spikes, range (grass), club rentals, credit cards (MC, V, AE, D). **Reader Comments:** Beautiful ... Nicely-run facility ... Well marked, for serious players ... Excellent ... What all courses should be ... Country club atmosphere ... Often crowded ... Forces you to use all your clubs ... One of my favorites, spectacular scenery ... Best public golf in state ... Variety ... Great design ... Worth the price ... Good walk ... Top notch.

★★½ OXFORD HILLS GOLF CLUB

PU-300 E. Drahner Rd., Oxford, 48371, Oakland County, (248)628-2518, 8 miles N of Pontiac. **Holes:** 18. **Yards:** 6,522/5,312. **Par:** 72/72. **Course Rating:** 71.4/70.5. **Slope:** 120/116. **Green Fee:** $22/$26. **Cart Fee:** $11/person. **Walking Policy:** Unrestricted walking. **Walkability:** 2. **Opened:** 1964. **Architect:** John Hubbard. **Season:** April-Nov. **High:** June-Aug. **To obtain tee times:** Call in advance. **Miscellaneous:** Reduced fees (weekdays, low season, seniors), metal spikes, club rentals, credit cards (MC, V, AE). **Reader Comments:** Better than average ... Short front, long back ... Fun, good mix of holes ... Gets lots of play ... Very enjoyable.

★★ PALMER PARK GOLF COURSE

Woodward At 7 Mile Rd., Detroit, 48203, Wayne County, (313)883-2525. **Holes:** 18. **Yards:** N/A. **Par:** N/A. **Course Rating:** N/A. **Slope:** N/A. **Green Fee:** $17.50/$19.50. **Walkability:** N/A. **Miscellaneous:** Metal spikes.

PARK SHORE GOLF COURSE

PU-610 Park Shore Dr., Cassopolis, 49031, Cass County, (616)445-2834, 25 miles N of South Bend, IN. **Holes:** 18. **Yards:** 4,981/4,981. **Par:** 68/70. **Course Rating:** 62.8/63.4. **Slope:** 97/90. **Green Fee:** $13/$17. **Cart Fee:** $19/cart. **Walking Policy:** Unrestricted walking. **Walkability:** 2. **Opened:** 1928. **Season:** April-Oct. **High:** June-Aug. **To obtain tee times:** Call. **Miscellaneous:** Reduced fees (twilight, seniors), club rentals.

PARTRIDGE CREEK GOLF COURSE

PU-43843 Romeo Plank Rd., Clinton Township, 48038, Macomb County, (810)228-3030, 29 miles N of Detroit. **Holes:** 27. **Green Fee:** $17/$19. **Cart Fee:** $22/cart. **Walking Policy:** Unrestricted walking. **Walkability:** 2. **Opened:** 1960. **Architect:** Kenny Nieman. **High:** May-Aug. **To obtain tee times:** Call up to 7 days in advance.

★★★ NORTH/SOUTH COURSE

Yards: 6,455/5,165. **Par:** 72/72. **Course Rating:** 70.0/69.0. **Slope:** 114/114. **Season:** March-Nov. **Miscellaneous:** Reduced fees (twilight, seniors, juniors), metal spikes, range (grass), club rentals, credit cards (MC, V, AE).

★★★ NORTH/WEST COURSE

Yards: 6,439/5,220. **Par:** 72/72. **Course Rating:** 70.0/69.0. **Slope:** 114/114. **Season:** March-Nov. **Miscellaneous:** Reduced fees (twilight, seniors, juniors), metal spikes, range (grass), club rentals, credit cards (MC, V, AE). **Reader Comments:** Average condition ... Easy-does-it, relaxing ... Bad condition ... Average, fairly flat course ... Nice, challenging layout ... Designed for league play.

★★★ SOUTH/WEST COURSE

Yards: 6,706/5,225. **Par:** 72/72. **Course Rating:** 70.0/69.0. **Slope:** 114/114. **Season:** April-Nov. **Miscellaneous:** Reduced fees (weekdays, low season, twilight, seniors, juniors), metal spikes, range (grass), club rentals, credit cards (MC, V, AE).

★★★½ THE HAWK

Holes: 18. **Yards:** 7,024/5,366. **Par:** 72/72. **Course Rating:** 73.6/70.6. **Slope:** 132/126. **Green Fee:** $45/$50. **Cart Fee:** Included in Green Fee. **Walking Policy:** Unrestricted walking. **Walkability:** 3. **Opened:** 1996. **Architect:** Jerry Matthews. **Season:** March-Nov. **To obtain tee times:** Call up to 7 days in advance. **Miscellaneous:** Reduced fees (low season, twilight, seniors, juniors), range (grass), club rentals, credit cards (MC, V, AE). **Reader Comments:** A nice course but priced a little high ... Spring and fall values ... Highly overrated ... Great practice facilities! ... Tight fairways, but playable challenge ... Poor shape for cost ... Tough ... Good condition ... Needs to mature ... Lots of sand and water ... Nothing spectacular ... Don't need the big stick to often ... I can't believe it's new, great terrain.

★★★★ PATSY LOU WILLIAMSONS SUGARBUSH GOLF CLUB *Service*

PU-1 Sugarbush Dr., Davison, 48423, Genesee County, (810)653-3326, 8 miles E of Flint. **Holes:** 18. **Yards:** 7,285/5,035. **Par:** 72/72. **Course Rating:** 75.6/70.3. **Slope:** 146/127. **Green Fee:** $39/$49. **Cart Fee:** Included in Green Fee. **Walking Policy:** Unrestricted walking. **Walkability:** 2. **Opened:** 1995. **Architect:** Larry Mancour. **Season:** April-Nov. **High:** June-Aug. **To obtain tee times:** Call 14 days in advance. **Miscellaneous:** Reduced fees (weekdays, low season, twilight, seniors, juniors), discount packages, range (grass/mats), club rentals, credit cards (MC, V, AE).

MICHIGAN

Reader Comments: Stay away if you can't play! ... Want a challenge? ... Beautiful layout and clubhouse. Greens are well thought out ... Need more room for my slice ... Could be a great course ... Well maintained, greens large ... Excellent public course!! ... Fun and challenging to play ... Wetlands areas are something else.

★★½ PAW PAW LAKE GOLF COURSE

PU-4548 Forest Beach Rd., Watervliet, 49098, Berrien County, (616)463-3831, 10 miles NE of Benton Harbor.
Holes: 18. **Yards:** 6,055/4,811. **Par:** 70/73. **Course Rating:** 68.5. **Slope:** N/A. **Green Fee:** $18/$22. **Cart Fee:** $10/person. **Walking Policy:** Unrestricted walking. **Walkability:** 3. **Opened:** 1928. **Season:** April-Nov. **High:** June-Aug. **To obtain tee times:** Call golf shop. **Miscellaneous:** Reduced fees (weekdays, low season, twilight), range (grass), club rentals, lodging (1 rooms).
Reader Comments: Short, scenic course on lake ... Average ... Gets lots of play ... Good to tune up the irons ... Hilly–tough walk ... Owner trying hard to improve yearly, and succeeding ... Always nice!.

★★ PEBBLE CREEK GOLF COURSE

24095 Currie Rd., South Lyon, 48178, Oakland County, (248)437-5411
Yards: 6,110/4,749. **Par:** 72/72. **Course Rating:** 68.7/N/A. **Slope:** 107/N/A. **Green Fee:** $23/$27. **Walkability:** N/A. **Architect:** Don Herford. **Miscellaneous:** Metal spikes.

★★ PEBBLEWOOD COUNTRY CLUB

PU-9794 Jericho Rd., Bridgman, 49106, Berrien County, (616)465-5611, 35 miles NW of South Bend, IN.
Holes: 18. **Yards:** 5,421/4,636. **Par:** 68/70. **Course Rating:** 65.6/65.6. **Slope:** 106/106. **Green Fee:** $18/$20. **Cart Fee:** $18/cart. **Walking Policy:** Unrestricted walking. **Walkability:** 1. **Opened:** 1923. **Season:** March-Nov. **High:** June-Aug. **To obtain tee times:** Call golf shop. **Miscellaneous:** Club rentals, credit cards (MC, V, AE, D).

★★★½ PHEASANT RUN GOLF CLUB

PU-46500 Summit Pkwy., Canton, 48188, Wayne County, 734)397-6460, 15 miles W of Detroit.
Holes: 18. **Yards:** 7,001/5,143. **Par:** 72/72. **Course Rating:** 73.3/69.1. **Slope:** 142/117. **Green Fee:** $37/$60. **Cart Fee:** Included in Green Fee. **Walking Policy:** Mandatory cart. **Walkability:** 3. **Opened:** 1995. **Architect:** Arthur Hills/Steve Forrest. **Season:** April-Nov. **High:** May-Sept. **To obtain tee times:** Call up to 14 days in advance. **Miscellaneous:** Reduced fees (low season, twilight), range (grass/mats), club rentals, credit cards (MC, V, AE), beginner friendly (weekly beginner golf clinics).
Reader Comments: Nice track ... Cost too high for this course ... Great place, each hole makes you think ... Lovely houses and hours to stand around and admire them ... A lot of challenging holes ... Houses way too close to course ... Layout is OK ... Subdivision golf, but nicely done.

★★★★ PIERCE LAKE GOLF COURSE *Value+*

PM-1175 South Main St., Chelsea, 48118, Washtenaw County, (734)475-5858, 15 miles W of Ann Arbor.
Holes: 18. **Yards:** 6,874/4,772. **Par:** 72/72. **Course Rating:** 72.5/67.4. **Slope:** 135/109. **Green Fee:** $20/$24. **Cart Fee:** $10/person. **Walking Policy:** Unrestricted walking. **Walkability:** 4. **Opened:** 1996. **Architect:** Harry Bowers. **Season:** March-Nov. **High:** April-Sept. **To obtain tee times:** Call up to 7 days in advance. **Miscellaneous:** Reduced fees (weekdays, low season, twilight, seniors, juniors), club rentals, credit cards (MC, V).
Reader Comments: Challenging and scenic, only drawback is the highway ... Beautiful, some great holes ... Nice and reasonable ... Best muny in Michigan. Hills, heather, water, has it all ... Good test–can't beat the price ... A very tight, tough back 9 ... Excellent course for all ... Who thought of this variety? ... Front 9 open—good warmup for a tight back ... Best value course I play! ... Nothing fancy.

★½ PIERCE MUNICIPAL PARK GOLF COURSE

2302 Brookside, Flint, 48502, Genesee County, (810)766-7297.
Special Notes: Call club for further information.

PILGRIM'S RUN GOLF CLUB

PU-11401 Newcosta Ave., Pierson, 49339, Newaygo County, (888)533-7742, 22 miles N of Grand Rapids. **E-mail:** JOMalley@pilgrimsrun.com. **Web:** www.pilgrimsrun.com.
Holes: 18. **Yards:** 7,078/4,771. **Par:** 73/73. **Course Rating:** 74.1/67.7. **Slope:** 137/116. **Green Fee:** $35/$45. **Cart Fee:** $10/person. **Walking Policy:** Unrestricted walking. **Walkability:** 3. **Opened:** 1998. **Architect:** Kris Shumaker/Mike DeVries. **Season:** April-Oct. **High:** June-Aug. **To obtain tee times:** Tee times made up to 7 days in advance. **Miscellaneous:** Reduced fees (weekdays, low season, twilight, seniors), metal spikes, range (grass/mats), club rentals, credit cards (MC, V, AE) (metal spikes not allowed in clubhouse).
Notes: Ranked 4th in 1999 Best New Affordable Public.

PINE KNOB GOLF CLUB
PU-5580 Waldon Rd., Clarkston, 48348, Oakland County, (248)625-4430, 9 miles NW of Pontiac.
Holes: 27. **Green Fee:** $45/$58. **Cart Fee:** Included in Green Fee. **Walking Policy:** Mandatory cart. **Walkability:** 5. **Opened:** 1972. **Architect:** Leo Bishop/Lori Viola. **Season:** April-Oct. **High:** June-Sept. **To obtain tee times:** Call 7 days in advance. **Miscellaneous:** Reduced fees (seniors), range (grass/mats), club rentals, credit cards (MC, V, AE, D).
★★★★**FALCON/EAGLE**
Yards: 6,471/4,941. **Par:** 70/69. **Course Rating:** 71.3/67.8. **Slope:** 130/114.
★★★★**HAWK/EAGLE**
Yards: 6,421/4,798. **Par:** 71/70. **Course Rating:** 70.9/69.3. **Slope:** 131/116.
★★★★ **HAWK/FALCON**
Yards: 6,662/4,969. **Par:** 71/71. **Course Rating:** 72.2/69.1. **Slope:** 126/115.
Reader Comments: Many spectacular holes ... No. 10 is very scenic ... Continues to improve year to year ... Too crowded and overpriced ... Some elevated tees ... Fun course ... Very enjoyable ... Close to 'up north' resort golf ... Great views in Fall ... High priced but worth it ... Love to play several times each year.

★★ PINE LAKE GOLF COURSE
PU-1018 Haslett Rd., Haslett, 48840, Ingham County, (517)339-8281, 10 miles E of Lansing.
Holes: 18. **Yards:** 6,155/4,677. **Par:** 71/71. **Course Rating:** 69.9/67.0. **Slope:** 122/113. **Green Fee:** $16/$18. **Cart Fee:** $11/person. **Walking Policy:** Unrestricted walking. **Walkability:** 3. **Opened:** 1954. **Season:** March-Dec. **High:** June-Aug. **To obtain tee times:** Call golf shop. **Miscellaneous:** Reduced fees (weekdays, low season, twilight, seniors, juniors), discount packages, metal spikes, club rentals, credit cards (MC, V).

★★★ PINE RIVER GOLF CLUB
PU-2244 Pine River Rd., Standish, 48658, Arenac County, (517)846-6819, (877)474-6374, 30 miles N of Bay City.
Holes: 18. **Yards:** 6,250/5,156. **Par:** 71/74. **Course Rating:** 70.8/70.7. **Slope:** 126/126. **Green Fee:** $18/$22. **Cart Fee:** $11/person. **Walking Policy:** Unrestricted walking. **Walkability:** 3. **Opened:** 1966. **Architect:** Bruce Matthews/Jerry Matthews. **Season:** April-Oct. **High:** June-Aug. **To obtain tee times:** Call golf shop. **Miscellaneous:** Reduced fees (weekdays, seniors, juniors), metal spikes, range (grass), credit cards (MC, V).
Reader Comments: Tough, tight back nine ... Excellent challenge ... Great for average golfer ... Still a great value ... Challenging ... Two totally different 9's ... Fun course ... Good condition ... Woodsy course ... One of the best ever.

★★★½ PINE TRACE GOLF CLUB
PU-3600 Pine Trace Blvd., Rochester Hills, 48309, Oakland County, (248)852-7100, 30 miles N of Detroit.
Holes: 18. **Yards:** 6,610/4,974. **Par:** 72/72. **Course Rating:** 72.8/69.9. **Slope:** 139/125. **Green Fee:** $45/$55. **Cart Fee:** Included in Green Fee. **Walking Policy:** Walking at certain times. **Walkability:** 5. **Opened:** 1989. **Architect:** Arthur Hills. **Season:** March-Nov. **High:** May-Sept. **To obtain tee times:** Tee times can be reserved up to 7 days in advance. **Miscellaneous:** Reduced fees (low season, seniors, juniors), metal spikes, credit cards (MC, V).
Reader Comments: I always play when in Detroit area ... Weird layout, good condition ... Nice place ... For the price they could at least clean-up after the geese! ... Difficult test ... For better players ... Greens are getting better ... Badgered about place of play while pressing the group in front—marshalls rude ... Rangers not worth it ... Wonderful golf.

PINE VALLEY GOLF CLUB
PU-16801 31 Mile Rd., Ray, 48096, Macomb County, (810)752-9633, 12 miles NW of Mt. Clemens.
Holes: 27. **Green Fee:** $18/$23. **Cart Fee:** $20/cart. **Walking Policy:** Walking at certain times. **Walkability:** N/A. **Opened:** 1968. **Architect:** Otis McKinley. **Season:** March-Nov. **High:** May-Sept. **To obtain tee times:** Call 7 days in advance. **Miscellaneous:** Reduced fees (weekdays, low season, twilight, seniors), metal spikes, range (grass/mats), club rentals, credit cards (MC, V).
★★★ **BLUE/GOLD**
Yards: 6,373/4,971. **Par:** 72/70. **Course Rating:** 68.3/64.5. **Slope:** 114/100.
Reader Comments: A hidden secret ... Beautiful, scenic ... Pure muny ... Basic golf ... Blue is average, improvements to Gold make it a challenge ... Not crowded, can usually play without tee time.
★★★ **RED/BLUE**
Yards: 6,259/5,417. **Par:** 72/72. **Course Rating:** 69.5/65.6. **Slope:** 118/106.
Reader Comments: Good suburban course ... A well kept value ... Good for a challenge ... Pretty course and forgiving confidence booster.

MICHIGAN

★★★ RED/GOLD
Holes: 27. **Yards:** 6,490/5,208. **Par:** 72/70. **Course Rating:** 69.0/64.7. **Slope:** 110/103.
Reader Comments: Average ... Not overplayed ... Fair.

★★★ PINE VIEW GOLF CLUB
PU-5820 Stoney Creek Rd., Ypsilanti, 48197, Washtenaw County, (734)481-0500, (800)214-5963, 3 miles S of Ypsilanti.
Holes: 18. **Yards:** 6,533/5,267. **Par:** 72/72. **Course Rating:** 71.3/70.7. **Slope:** 124/119. **Green Fee:** $13/$32. **Cart Fee:** $13/person. **Walking Policy:** Unrestricted walking. **Walkability:** 3.
Opened: 1990. **Architect:** Harley Hodges/Greg Hodges. **Season:** March-Dec. **High:** April-Sept.
To obtain tee times: Call 14 days in advance. Groups of 20 or more tee times can be made 1 year in advance. **Miscellaneous:** Reduced fees (weekdays, low season, twilight, seniors, juniors), discount packages, metal spikes, range (grass/mats), club rentals, credit cards (MC, V).
Reader Comments: Hard to hold greens, tough driving holes ... They have very cool fast, fast carts ... Tight ... A little rough around the edges ... Unforgettable 3-tier green on No. 4 ... Challenging for every level of play ... Wide fairways and doglegs ... Long and flat ... Conditions can get ugly but layout is challenging ... Nice design, can be slow on weekends.

★★★½ PINECROFT PLANTATION
PU-8260 Henry Rd., Benzonia, 49617, Benzie County, (231)882-9100, 30 miles SW of Traverse City.
Holes: 18. **Yards:** 6,447/4,975. **Par:** 72/72. **Course Rating:** 70.9/68.5. **Slope:** 124/118. **Green Fee:** $15/$29. **Cart Fee:** $10/person. **Walking Policy:** Unrestricted walking. **Walkability:** 4.
Opened: 1992. **Architect:** L. Stone/A. Normal/J. Cole/C. Carlson. **Season:** April-Oct. **High:** June-Aug. **To obtain tee times:** Call golf shop. **Miscellaneous:** Reduced fees (low season, twilight), range (grass), club rentals, credit cards (MC, V).
Reader Comments: Great views ... Fun course ... One of the best values in Michigan ... Deathly fast greens, tight fairways, long Par 3s ... Excellent greens, water is drawn ... Superb course, very challenging greens ... The view of Crystal lake is great.

THE PINES GOLF COURSE
PU-5050 Byron Center Ave., Wyoming, 49509, Kent County, (616)538-8380, 12 miles S of Grand Rapid.
Holes: 18. **Yards:** 5,542/5,124. **Par:** 70/72. **Course Rating:** 67.3/N/A. **Slope:** N/A. **Green Fee:** $12/$18. **Cart Fee:** $20/cart. **Walking Policy:** Mandatory cart. **Walkability:** 2. **Opened:** 1968.
Season: March-Nov. **High:** May-Aug. **To obtain tee times:** Call up to 7 days in advance.
Miscellaneous: Reduced fees (weekdays, low season, seniors, juniors), discount packages, metal spikes, range (grass), club rentals, credit cards (MC, V, D).

★½ PIPESTONE CREEK GOLF COURSE
PU-6768 Naomi Rd., Eau Claire, 49111, Berrien County, (616)944-1611, 10 miles E of Benton Harbor.
Holes: 18. **Yards:** 4,402/4,188. **Par:** 67/68. **Course Rating:** N/A. **Slope:** N/A. **Green Fee:** $16/$19. **Cart Fee:** $20/cart. **Walking Policy:** Unrestricted walking. **Walkability:** 2. **Opened:** 1957. **Season:** March-Oct. **High:** June-Sept. **To obtain tee times:** Call golf shop.
Miscellaneous: Reduced fees (low season), club rentals, credit cards (MC, V).

★★ PLEASANT HILLS GOLF CLUB
PU-4452 E. Millbrook Rd., Mt. Pleasant, 48858, Isabella County, (517)772-0487, 50 miles NW of Saginaw.
Holes: 18. **Yards:** 6,012/4,607. **Par:** 72/72. **Course Rating:** 68.2/65.9. **Slope:** 110/107. **Green Fee:** $18/$20. **Cart Fee:** $20/cart. **Walking Policy:** Unrestricted walking. **Walkability:** 3.
Opened: 1964. **Architect:** Richard Krauss. **Season:** March-Dec. **High:** June-Aug. **To obtain tee times:** Call 1 day in advance. **Miscellaneous:** Reduced fees (weekdays, low season, twilight, seniors, juniors), club rentals, credit cards (MC, V, D).

★★★ PLUM BROOK GOLF CLUB
PU-13390 Plum Brook Dr., Sterling Heights, 48312, Macomb County, (810)264-9411, 10 miles N of Detroit.
Holes: 18. **Yards:** 6,300/5,500. **Par:** 71/71. **Course Rating:** 68.5/68.5. **Slope:** 115/117. **Green Fee:** $21/$25. **Cart Fee:** $20/cart. **Walking Policy:** Unrestricted walking. **Walkability:** 2.
Opened: 1927. **Season:** March-Dec. **High:** May-Sept. **To obtain tee times:** Call.
Miscellaneous: Reduced fees (weekdays, low season, twilight, juniors), club rentals, credit cards (MC, V), beginner friendly (junior rates).
Reader Comments: Has great greens ... Layout is basic, but enjoyable to play due to good conditions ... Excellent public course ... Good price, good product (open late in year) ... Only once ... Suburban gem ... Old course, but well kept ... Easy, but always crowded ... Very good short course.

MICHIGAN

★★★★   POHLCAT GOLF COURSE
R-6595 E. Airport Rd., Mt. Pleasant, 48858, Isabella County, (517)773-4221, (800)292-8891, 60 miles N of Lansing. **Web:** www.pohlcat.net.
Holes: 18. **Yards:** 6,810/5,140. **Par:** 72/72. **Course Rating:** 74.2/70.8. **Slope:** 139/124. **Green Fee:** $29/$69. **Cart Fee:** Included in Green Fee. **Walking Policy:** Walking at certain times. **Walkability:** 3. **Opened:** 1991. **Architect:** Dan Pohl. **Season:** April-Nov. **High:** July-Sept. **To obtain tee times:** Call 800 number after Feb. 1 for anytime. **Miscellaneous:** Reduced fees (weekdays, low season, resort guests, twilight, seniors, juniors), discount packages, range (grass/mats), club rentals, lodging, credit cards (MC, V, AE, D).
Reader Comments: Excellent course ... Played last fall–leaves in glory ... Tough from tips ... My personal favorite ... Some interesting holes ... Par-3 No. 17 just as pretty as Augusta's No. 12, and just as dangerous ... Near casino, high price, busy ... Very scenic ... Well kept ... Nice people ... Overpriced ... Nice layout, nice people, never overcrowded ... Take bug spray!

★★½   PONTIAC COUNTRY CLUB
SP-4335 Elizabeth Lake Rd, Waterford, 48328, Oakland County, (248)682-6333, 3 miles W of Pontiac.
Holes: 18. **Yards:** 6,366/5,552. **Par:** 72/74. **Course Rating:** 70.4/71.6. **Slope:** 125/N/A. **Green Fee:** $25/$34. **Cart Fee:** $22/cart. **Walking Policy:** Unrestricted walking. **Walkability:** 3. **Opened:** 1914. **Season:** April-Nov. **High:** May-Sept. **To obtain tee times:** Call up to 7 days in advance. **Miscellaneous:** Metal spikes, range (grass), club rentals, credit cards (MC, V, AE, D).
Reader Comments: Great old course! ... Not very long but challenging ... Always improving condition and course! ... Great staff, excellent greens and lots of play!.

★★½   PONTIAC MUNICIPAL GOLF COURSE
PM-800 Golf Dr., Pontiac, 48341, Oakland County, (248)858-8990, 30 miles N of Detroit.
Holes: 18. **Yards:** 5,571/4,320. **Par:** 70/70. **Course Rating:** 65.1/63.5. **Slope:** 107/103. **Green Fee:** $19/$24. **Cart Fee:** $24/cart. **Walking Policy:** Walking at certain times. **Walkability:** 3. **Opened:** 1995. **Architect:** Michael Hurdzan. **Season:** April-Nov. **High:** May-Aug. **To obtain tee times:** Call Wednesday of each week. **Miscellaneous:** Reduced fees (weekdays, low season, twilight, seniors, juniors), discount packages, club rentals, credit cards (MC, V).
Reader Comments: Fine municipal course, completely redone ... A redesign that was done very well.

★★½   PORTAGE LAKE GOLF COURSE
PU-Michigan Tech. Univ., US 41, Houghton, 49931, Houghton County, (906)487-2641.
Holes: 18. **Yards:** 6,266/5,297. **Par:** 72/72. **Course Rating:** 69.2/69.8. **Slope:** 115/113. **Green Fee:** $26/$26. **Cart Fee:** $20/cart. **Walking Policy:** Unrestricted walking. **Walkability:** 3. **Opened:** 1902. **Season:** May-Oct. **High:** July-Aug. **To obtain tee times:** Call up to 2 days in advance. **Miscellaneous:** Club rentals, credit cards (MC, V, D).
Reader Comments: Old 9 back and forth, side by side ... Course is owned by Michigan Tech ... Longest and best in area ... Breathtaking views.

PORTLAND COUNTRY CLUB
PU-Divine Hwy, Portland, 48875, Ionia County, (517)647-4521, 20 miles W of Lansing.
Holes: 18. **Yards:** 5,568/4,542. **Par:** 70/70. **Course Rating:** 67.1/70.0. **Slope:** 115/118. **Green Fee:** $15/$15. **Cart Fee:** $18/cart. **Walking Policy:** Unrestricted walking. **Walkability:** 3. **Opened:** 1927. **Architect:** Charles Lockwood/Bob Waara. **Season:** March-Nov. **High:** May-Sept. **To obtain tee times:** Call up to 7 days in advance. **Miscellaneous:** Reduced fees (seniors), club rentals.

★★   PRAIRIE CREEK GOLF COURSE
PU-800 E. Webb Dr., De Witt, 48820, Clinton County, (517)669-1958, 8 miles N of Lansing.
Holes: 18. **Yards:** 6,165/5,171. **Par:** 72/72. **Course Rating:** N/A. **Slope:** N/A. **Green Fee:** $10/$16. **Cart Fee:** $10/person. **Walking Policy:** Unrestricted walking. **Walkability:** 3. **Opened:** 1979. **Season:** March-Oct. **High:** June-Aug. **To obtain tee times:** Call golf shop for weekends. **Miscellaneous:** Reduced fees (weekdays, low season, twilight, seniors, juniors), discount packages, club rentals.

★★   PRAIRIEWOOD GOLF COURSE
PU-315 Prairiewood Dr., Otsego, 49078, Allegan County, (616)694-6633, 14 miles N of Kalamazoo.
Holes: 18. **Yards:** 6,519/4,705. **Par:** 72/72. **Course Rating:** 70.4/66.2. **Slope:** 114/106. **Green Fee:** $16/$20. **Cart Fee:** $10/person. **Walking Policy:** Unrestricted walking. **Walkability:** 1. **Opened:** 1990. **Architect:** Warner Bowen. **Season:** April-Nov. **High:** June-Aug. **To obtain tee times:** Call anytime. **Miscellaneous:** Reduced fees (weekdays, low season, seniors, juniors), range (grass/mats), club rentals, credit cards (MC, V, D).

MICHIGAN

★★★★ **THE QUEST GOLF CLUB** *Pace*
PU-116 Questview Dr., Houghton Lake, 48629, Roscommon County, (517)422-4516, 115 miles N of Lansing.
Holes: 18. **Yards:** 6,773/5,027. **Par:** 72/72. **Course Rating:** 72.0/73.0. **Slope:** 130/118. **Green Fee:** $48/$58. **Cart Fee:** Included in Green Fee. **Walking Policy:** Walking at certain times.
Walkability: N/A. **Opened:** 1994. **Architect:** Ken Green/John Sanford. **Season:** April-Oct. **High:** May-Oct. **To obtain tee times:** Call golf shop. Groups of 9 or more are required to send a deposit or provide a credit card number. **Miscellaneous:** Reduced fees (weekdays, low season), discount packages, metal spikes, range (grass), club rentals, credit cards (MC, V).
Reader Comments: Always enjoy the course, despite its rough edges and price ... This course gets lost among its neighbors but it is every bit equal ... Excellent shape ... Beautiful ... Wildlife and Canadian geese all over. Excellent course ... Good potential ... Outstanding ... Nice design, challenging.

★★★ **RACKHAM GOLF CLUB**
PU-10100 W. Ten Mile Rd., Huntington Woods, 48070, Oakland County, (248)543-4040, 15 miles N of Detroit.
Holes: 18. **Yards:** 6,555/5,413. **Par:** 71/72. **Course Rating:** 71.1/70.7. **Slope:** 118/115. **Green Fee:** $20/$26. **Cart Fee:** $20/cart. **Walking Policy:** Unrestricted walking. **Walkability:** 2.
Opened: 1924. **Architect:** Donald Ross. **Season:** Year-round. **High:** May-Sept. **To obtain tee times:** Call with credit card to guarantee. **Miscellaneous:** Reduced fees (weekdays, low season, twilight, seniors, juniors), discount packages, club rentals, credit cards (MC, V, AE).
Reader Comments: Expensive for what it has to offer ... Great layout ... Crowded ... Has improved greatly ... For all the play it's cut finely ... Nice layout, but pace of play terrible ... Holes 10 and 11 always in the wind ... Surprisingly challenging, would play again ... Still needs more refinement.

RAISIN RIVER COUNTRY CLUB
★★★ **EAST COURSE**
PU-1500 N. Dixie Hwy., Monroe, 48162, Monroe County, (734)289-3700, (800)321-9564, 25 miles S of Detroit.
Holes: 18. **Yards:** 6,930/5,606. **Par:** 71/71. **Course Rating:** 72.9/70.1. **Slope:** 122/111. **Green Fee:** $21/$24. **Cart Fee:** $11/person. **Walking Policy:** Unrestricted walking. **Walkability:** 2.
Opened: 1974. **Architect:** Charles Maddox. **Season:** March-Nov. **High:** May-Sept. **To obtain tee times:** Call 8 days in advance for weekend and holidays only. Tee times not required for weekdays. **Miscellaneous:** Reduced fees (low season, resort guests, seniors, juniors), discount packages, range (grass/mats), club rentals, credit cards (MC, V), beginner friendly (beginner lessons).
Reader Comments: Very large greens, best greens played ... More difficult than West Course but kept better ... Nice enough staff ... No imagination ... Best and Biggest greens of S.E. Michigan's public courses ... Good and fair.
★★½ **WEST COURSE**
Holes: 18. **Yards:** 6,106/5,749. **Par:** 70/74. **Course Rating:** 66.9/70.6. **Slope:** 114/120. **Green Fee:** $19/$24. **Cart Fee:** $11/person. **Walking Policy:** Unrestricted walking. **Walkability:** 1.
Opened: 1964. **Architect:** Charles Maddox. **Season:** March-Nov. **High:** May-Sept. **To obtain tee times:** Call 8 days in advance for weekends and holidays only. Tee times not required for weekday play. **Miscellaneous:** Reduced fees (low season, resort guests, seniors, juniors), discount packages, metal spikes, range (grass/mats), club rentals, credit cards (MC, V), beginner friendly (beginner lessons).
Reader Comments: Well-conditioned course ... Usually busy ... Trying to make too much of something that is not there ... Nicely manicured, easy to walk, fun.

★★½ **RAISIN VALLEY GOLF CLUB**
PU-4057 Comfort Rd., Tecumseh, 49286, Lenawee County, (517)423-2050, 35 miles N of Toledo, OH.
Holes: 18. **Yards:** 5,650/4,630. **Par:** 71/71. **Course Rating:** 67.5/69.0. **Slope:** N/A. **Green Fee:** $14/$18. **Cart Fee:** $19/cart. **Walking Policy:** Unrestricted walking. **Walkability:** 4. **Opened:** 1969. **Architect:** William Porter. **Season:** March-Dec. **High:** April-Oct. **To obtain tee times:** Call 7 days in advance. **Miscellaneous:** Reduced fees (weekdays, low season, seniors, juniors), club rentals, credit cards (MC, V).
Reader Comments: Short on length, but tough to play ... True, fast greens ... Great little course for the money ... Fun course, some reachable holes.

★★½ **RAMMLER GOLF CLUB**
PU-38180 Utica Rd., Sterling Heights, 48312, Macomb County, (810)978-1411, 8 miles N of Detroit.
Holes: 27. **Yards:** 6,305/4,951. **Par:** 71/71. **Course Rating:** 69.5/73.1. **Slope:** 113/119. **Green Fee:** $21/$24. **Cart Fee:** $22/cart. **Walking Policy:** Unrestricted walking. **Walkability:** 1.
Opened: 1922. **Season:** April-Nov. **High:** June-Aug. **To obtain tee times:** Call. **Miscellaneous:**

Reduced fees (seniors), metal spikes, club rentals, credit cards (MC, V) (ladies beginner leagues).

Reader Comments: Good tune-up course, some risks ... Basic ... Too many corporate leagues ... Tough public ... No. 17 a great hole.

★★★½ RATTLE RUN GOLF COURSE

PU-7163 St. Clair Highway, St. Clair, 48054, St. Clair County, (810)329-2070, 23 miles N of Detroit.

Holes: 18. **Yards:** 6,891/5,085. **Par:** 72/75. **Course Rating:** 73.6/70.4. **Slope:** 140/124. **Green Fee:** $35/$49. **Cart Fee:** Included in Green Fee. **Walking Policy:** Walking at certain times. **Walk-ability:** 3. **Opened:** 1977. **Architect:** Lou Powers. **Season:** April-Nov. **High:** May-Sept. **To obtain tee times:** Call up to 14 days in advance. **Miscellaneous:** Reduced fees (low season, twilight, seniors, juniors), discount packages, range (grass), club rentals, credit cards (MC, V, AE, D).

Reader Comments: Beautiful woods, deer, fox abound! ... Was premier, now slipping ... Pretty challenging, some tough doglegs ... Small greens ... Fairways in great shape ... An 'up-north' track ... The best in S.E. Michigan ... Makes the most of existing terrain ... Exciting course ... Humbling from back tees ... Fun course, excellent service.

RAVENNA GOLF COURSE

PU-11566 Hts Ravenna Rd., Ravenna, 49451, Muskegon County, (616)853-6736, 10 miles E of Muskegon.

Holes: 18. **Yards:** 3,181/2,956. **Par:** 37/35. **Course Rating:** N/A. **Slope:** N/A. **Green Fee:** $15/$15. **Cart Fee:** Included in Green Fee. **Walking Policy:** Unrestricted walking. **Walkability:** 2. **Opened:** 1981. **Season:** March-Oct. **High:** May-Aug. **To obtain tee times:** Call anytime. **Miscellaneous:** Reduced fees (weekdays, seniors), metal spikes.

RED ARROW GOLF CLUB

PM-Kings Highway, Kalamazoo, 49001, Kalamazoo County, (616)345-8329. **E-mail:** shecky4@aol.com. **Web:** www.kalamazoogolf.org.

Holes: 9. **Yards:** 1,412/N/A. **Par:** 34/N/A. **Course Rating:** N/A. **Slope:** N/A. **Green Fee:** $10/$12. **Walking Policy:** Unrestricted walking. **Walkability:** 1. **Season:** April-Oct. **High:** June-Aug. **Miscellaneous:** Reduced fees (seniors, juniors), club rentals, beginner friendly.

★★★½ REDDEMAN FARMS GOLF CLUB

PU-555 S. Dancer Rd., Chelsea, 48118, Washtenaw County, (734)475-3020, 8 miles W of Ann Arbor. **E-mail:** reddemangc@aol.com. **Web:** www.annarbor.org.

Holes: 18. **Yards:** 6,525/5,034. **Par:** 72/72. **Course Rating:** 71.6/68.9. **Slope:** 122/120. **Green Fee:** $24/$29. **Cart Fee:** $10/person. **Walking Policy:** Unrestricted walking. **Walkability:** 2. **Opened:** 1991. **Architect:** Bob Louhouse/Howard Smith. **Season:** April-Nov. **High:** June-Sept. **To obtain tee times:** Call anytime. **Miscellaneous:** Reduced fees (weekdays, low season, twilight, seniors, juniors), range (grass), club rentals, credit cards (MC, V, D), beginner friendly (evenings only).

Reader Comments: Challenging, but not overpowering ... Always good conditions, can be slow ... Long for ladies ... Crowned greens ... Long and wide open but no gimme, let 'er rip ... Too expensive ... Looks like an easy track but the small, sloping greens make it challenging to score.

★★★ RICHMOND FOREST GOLF CLUB

PU-33300 32 Mile Rd., Lenox, 48050, Macomb County, (810)727-4742, 30 miles N of Detroit.

Holes: 18. **Yards:** 6,631/5,301. **Par:** 72/72. **Course Rating:** 72.3/70.8. **Slope:** 124/117. **Green Fee:** $23/$30. **Cart Fee:** $10/person. **Walking Policy:** Unrestricted walking. **Walkability:** 1. **Opened:** 1994. **Architect:** W. Bruce Matthews III. **Season:** March-Nov. **High:** June-Aug. **To obtain tee times:** Call or come in up to 7 days in advance. **Miscellaneous:** Reduced fees (weekdays, low season, twilight, seniors, juniors), range (grass), club rentals, credit cards (MC, V).

Reader Comments: Needs cart paths ... Very enjoyable course ... Great course, great price ... Very friendly ... Hidden jewel... Nice course, well kept bunkers ... New ... Can be fun, but needs work, rough cart paths slow play mornings ... Great potential.

★★ RIDGEVIEW GOLF COURSE

10360 W. Main, Kalamazoo, 49009, Kalamazoo County, (616)375-8821.

Holes: 18. **Yards:** 6,980/5,800. **Par:** 72/72. **Course Rating:** N/A. **Slope:** N/A. **Green Fee:** $10/$16. **Walkability:** N/A. **Miscellaneous:** Metal spikes.

RIVER BEND GOLF COURSE

PU-1370 W. State Rd., Hastings, 49058, Barry County, (616)945-3238, 18 miles S of Grand Rapids.

Holes: 27. **Green Fee:** $15/$15. **Cart Fee:** $25/cart. **Walking Policy:** Unrestricted walking. **Walkability:** 2. **Opened:** 1962. **Architect:** Don Haywood, Sr. **Season:** April-Oct. **High:** June-Aug. **To obtain tee times:** Call golf shop. **Miscellaneous:** Metal spikes.

RED/BLUE
Yards: 5,912/5,457. **Par:** 72/72. **Course Rating:** N/A. **Slope:** N/A.
RED/WHITE
Yards: 6,075/5,755. **Par:** 72/72. **Course Rating:** N/A. **Slope:** N/A.
WHITE/BLUE
Yards: 5,947/5,472. **Par:** 72/72. **Course Rating:** N/A. **Slope:** N/A.

RIVERVIEW HIGHLANDS GOLF CLUB
PM-15015 Sibley Rd., Riverview, 48192, Wayne County, (734)479-2266, 20 miles S of Detroit.
Holes: 27. **Green Fee:** $16/$21. **Cart Fee:** $22/cart. **Walking Policy:** Unrestricted walking.
Walkability: 3. **Opened:** 1973. **Architect:** W.K. Newcomb/Arthur Hills. **Season:** March-Dec.
High: May-Sept. **To obtain tee times:** Call. **Miscellaneous:** Reduced fees (weekdays, low season, twilight, seniors, juniors), discount packages, club rentals, credit cards (MC, V, AE, D), beginner friendly (golf practice facility opens August 2000).
★★½ **BLUE/GOLD**
Yards: 6,667/5,293. **Par:** 72/72. **Course Rating:** 71.4/70.1. **Slope:** 119/118.
Reader Comments: Fairly flat, kind of dull ... City course ... Good ... 3 hearty 9-hole courses to choose from ... Challenging and fun ... Blue course is pretty good, others alright ... Blue 9 most challenging ... Nicely manicured, fast greens.
★★½ **GOLD/RED**
Yards: 6,732/5,173. **Par:** 72/70. **Course Rating:** 69.2/69.0. **Slope:** 115/112.
Reader Comments: A little bit of everything, it will test your skills ... Red is tight, Gold is open ... Good basic golf.
★★½ **RED/BLUE**
Yards: 6,485/5,224. **Par:** 72/72. **Course Rating:** 70.8/70.1. **Slope:** 119/118.
Reader Comments: Good golf course ... Red nine in interesting, Blue 9 is a test ... Red has treelined holes.

RIVERWOOD RESORT
R-1313 E. Broomfield Rd., Mt. Pleasant, 48858, Isabella County, (517)772-5726, (800)882-5211, 45 miles N of Lansing.
Holes: 27. **Green Fee:** $22/$28. **Cart Fee:** $12/person. **Walking Policy:** Walking at certain times. **Walkability:** 2. **Opened:** 1932. **Architect:** Jerry Matthews/Richard Figg. **Season:** March-Oct. **High:** June-Aug. **To obtain tee times:** Call 60 days in advance. **Miscellaneous:** Reduced fees (low season, resort guests, twilight, seniors), discount packages, metal spikes, range (grass), club rentals, lodging (8 rooms), credit cards (MC, V, D).
★★★½ **RED/BLUE**
Yards: 6,182/4,462. **Par:** 72/72. **Course Rating:** 70.3/66.6. **Slope:** 121/106.
Reader Comments: A pleasure to play ... Good rates, good value ... Bring mosquito spray ... New holes are great ... Great resort golf ... Secluded play, roomy fairways ... Too many people ... Best greens in Michigan ... Wildlife is abundant.
★★★½ **RED/WHITE**
Yards: 6,600/4,952. **Par:** 72/72. **Course Rating:** 72.0/69.4. **Slope:** 125/116.
Reader Comments: Great fun, a challenge, well kept ... Good value ... Tight and long.
★★★½ **WHITE/BLUE**
Yards: 6,100/4,667. **Par:** 72/72. **Course Rating:** 70.3/66.4. **Slope:** 116/109.
Reader Comments: Pretty course, fair condition, excellent deals ... Fine course for golfers of any skill.

★★★ ROCHESTER HILLS GOLF & COUNTRY CLUB
PU-655 Michelson Rd., Rochester, 48073, Oakland County, (248)852-4800, 30 miles N of Detroit.
Holes: 18. **Yards:** 6,800/5,747. **Par:** 72/72. **Course Rating:** 70.8/72.5. **Slope:** 121/123. **Green Fee:** $23/$28. **Cart Fee:** $11/person. **Walking Policy:** Walking at certain times. **Walkability:** 3. **Opened:** 1905. **Architect:** Thomas Bendelow. **Season:** March-Dec. **High:** May-Sept. **To obtain tee times:** Call up to 5 days in advance. **Miscellaneous:** Metal spikes, credit cards (MC, V, AE, D).
Reader Comments: Course in very poor shape ... Too costly ... Variety, challenge and great panoramic view ... Beautiful layout ... Fun but difficult ... Going downhill fast ... Great course to start year on ... New cart path through entire course.

★★★★ THE ROCK AT DRUMMOND ISLAND *Pace+*
R-26 Maxton Rd.d, Drummond Island, 49726, Chippewa County, (906)493-1006, (800)999-6343, 60 miles SE of Sault Ste. Marie. **Web:** www.drummondisland.com.
Holes: 18. **Yards:** 6,837/4,992. **Par:** 71/71. **Course Rating:** 74.9/70.9. **Slope:** 142/130. **Green Fee:** $30/$65. **Cart Fee:** Included in Green Fee. **Walking Policy:** Mandatory cart. **Walkability:** N/A. **Opened:** 1989. **Architect:** Harry Bowers. **Season:** May-Oct. **High:** June-Aug. **To obtain tee times:** Call golf shop between 9 a.m. and 5 p.m. **Miscellaneous:** Reduced fees (weekdays, low season, resort guests, twilight, juniors), discount packages, metal spikes, range (grass/mats), club rentals, lodging (40 rooms), credit cards (MC, V, AE, D).

MICHIGAN

Reader Comments: Nice course, but not worth the long drive ... Enjoyable to play ... Personal favorite, great golf, lots of wildlife ... Incredibly scenic ... Long, scenic and very quiet ... Long way from anywhere, but beautiful ... Overrated, needs a clubhouse ... Peaceful golf ... Deer on many holes ... Playable for most golfers ... Unique ... Heaven on earth ... Deteriorating conditions.

★★½ ROGELL GOLF COURSE
PM-18601 Berg Rd., Detroit, 48219, Wayne County, (313)578-8007.
Holes: 18. **Yards:** 6,075/4,985. **Par:** 70/70. **Course Rating:** 70.2/68.3. **Slope:** 129/117. **Green Fee:** $23/$23. **Cart Fee:** $24/cart. **Walking Policy:** Unrestricted walking. **Walkability:** 5. **Opened:** 1905. **Architect:** Donald Ross. **Season:** March-Dec. **High:** May-Oct. **To obtain tee times:** Call up to 7 days in advance. **Miscellaneous:** Reduced fees (weekdays, seniors, juniors), metal spikes, club rentals.
Reader Comments: Good layout ... Crowded in summer ... Sand everywhere, well maintained ... Flat, few features to enhance playability ... Beautiful city course, poorly kept ... Could be city champion course ... Needs TLC.

★★½ ROGUE RIVER GOLF COURSE
PU-12994 Paine Ave. N.W., Sparta, 49345, Kent County, (616)887-7182, (888)779-4653, 15 miles N of Grand Rapids. **Web:** www.westmichgolf.com\courses\rogueriver.htm.
Holes: 18. **Yards:** 5,344/4,300. **Par:** 70/70. **Course Rating:** N/A. **Slope:** N/A. **Green Fee:** $14/$20. **Cart Fee:** $10/person. **Walking Policy:** Unrestricted walking. **Walkability:** 2. **Opened:** 1962. **Architect:** Warner Bowen. **Season:** April-Nov. **High:** May-Sept. **To obtain tee times:** Call. **Miscellaneous:** Reduced fees (seniors, juniors), metal spikes, club rentals, credit cards (MC, V, D), beginner friendly.
Reader Comments: Good-but drive and wedge ... Could be a great city course ... Has improved some ... Greens and fairways need improving.

★★ ROLLING HILLS GOLF CLUB
PU-3274 Davison Rd., Lapeer, 48446, Lapeer County, (810)664-2281, 20 miles E of Flint.
Holes: 18. **Yards:** 6,060/5,184. **Par:** 71/72. **Course Rating:** 69.3/69.8. **Slope:** 113/112. **Green Fee:** $12/$18. **Cart Fee:** $24/cart. **Walking Policy:** Unrestricted walking. **Walkability:** 2. **Opened:** 1968. **Architect:** Reitz & Turdales. **Season:** April-Oct. **High:** June-Aug. **To obtain tee times:** Call. Tee times not always required. **Miscellaneous:** Reduced fees (weekdays, low season, twilight, seniors, juniors), range (grass), club rentals, credit cards (MC, V), beginner friendly (junior golf clinic and adult beginners clinic).

★★ ROLLING HILLS GOLF COURSE
PU-3100 Baldwin Dr., Hudsonville, 49426, Ottawa County, (616)669-9768, 15 miles SW of Grand Rapids.
Holes: 18. **Yards:** 5,832/4,693. **Par:** 70/71. **Course Rating:** 67.0/65.7. **Slope:** 106/102. **Green Fee:** $17/$18. **Cart Fee:** $20/cart. **Walking Policy:** Unrestricted walking. **Walkability:** 3. **Season:** April-Nov. **High:** June-Aug. **To obtain tee times:** Call. **Miscellaneous:** Metal spikes, range (grass), club rentals, credit cards (MC, V).

★★ ROLLING MEADOWS GOLF COURSE
PU-6484 Sutton Rd., Whitmore Lake, 48189, Washtenaw County, (734)662-5144, 5 miles N of Ann Arbor.
Holes: 18. **Yards:** 6,474/4,908. **Par:** 70/72. **Course Rating:** 69.9/67.0. **Slope:** 119/110. **Green Fee:** $14/$22. **Cart Fee:** $20/cart. **Walking Policy:** Unrestricted walking. **Walkability:** 2. **Opened:** 1978. **Season:** April-Oct. **High:** June-Aug. **To obtain tee times:** Call ahead or walk in. **Miscellaneous:** Reduced fees (seniors, juniors), range (grass).

★★★ ROMEO GOLF & COUNTRY CLUB
14600-32 Mile Rd., Washington, 48095, Macomb County, (810)752-9673.
Yards: N/A. **Par:** N/A. **Course Rating:** N/A. **Slope:** N/A. **Green Fee:** N/A. **Walkability:** N/A. **Miscellaneous:** Metal spikes.
Reader Comments: Leave the driver in the trunk ... A good course for locals, South Course is very nice ... Caters to seniors ... My personal Juliet ... Like playing on asphalt ... Making great strides ... Just don't raise the price.
Special Notes: Call club for further information.

★★★ ROUGE PARK GOLF CLUB
PU-11701 Burt Rd., Detroit, 48228, Wayne County, (313)837-5900.
Holes: 18. **Yards:** 6,262/4,868. **Par:** 72/72. **Course Rating:** 70.1/69.2. **Slope:** 121/108. **Green Fee:** $10/$29. **Cart Fee:** $12/person. **Walking Policy:** Unrestricted walking. **Walkability:** 3. **Opened:** 1923. **Season:** March-Nov. **High:** May-Aug. **To obtain tee times:** Call in for reservations. **Miscellaneous:** Reduced fees (weekdays, low season, twilight, seniors, juniors), discount packages, metal spikes, range (grass/mats), club rentals, credit cards (MC, V, AE), beginner friendly (junior golf, Women in Golf day).
Reader Comments: Tough but fair, improvements made ... Didn't get what I paid for ... Improved a lot ... Some unique holes.

★★★½ ROYAL SCOT GOLF COURSE
PU-4722 W. Grand River, Lansing, 48906, Clinton County, (517)321-4653.
Holes: 18. **Yards:** 6,568/4,700. **Par:** 71/71. **Course Rating:** 71.7/66.8. **Slope:** 123/117. **Green Fee:** $19/$30. **Cart Fee:** $23/cart. **Walking Policy:** Unrestricted walking. **Walkability:** 3. **Opened:** 1962. **Architect:** Jim Holmes. **Season:** Year-round. **High:** May-Aug. **To obtain tee times:** Call. **Miscellaneous:** Reduced fees (weekdays, low season, resort guests, twilight, seniors, juniors), discount packages, metal spikes, range (grass/mats), club rentals, credit cards (MC, V, AE, D, Diners Club).
Reader Comments: Nice course ... Crowded ... Improvements have helped ... Popular course, pace can be a royal pain ... Great blend of holes, long, short, tight, open ... Very forgiving course, need to space out tee times longer ... Well run ... Best greens in area ... Undulating greens with speed, stay below the hole.

★★½ RUSH LAKE HILLS GOLF CLUB
PU-3199 Rush Lake Rd., Pinckney, 48169, Livingston County, 734)878-9790, 20 miles N of Ann Arbor.
Holes: 18. **Yards:** 6,237/4,964. **Par:** 73/73. **Course Rating:** 69.9/67.3. **Slope:** 120/114. **Green Fee:** $10/$21. **Cart Fee:** $22/cart. **Walking Policy:** Unrestricted walking. **Walkability:** 3. **Opened:** 1960. **Season:** April-Oct. **High:** May-Aug. **To obtain tee times:** Call up to 7 days in advance. **Miscellaneous:** Reduced fees (low season, twilight, seniors, juniors), metal spikes, club rentals, credit cards (MC, V, D).
Reader Comments: Basic golf not bad for the price ... A course that doesn't take itself too seriously ... Proceeds go to charity but course is boring.

★★★ ST. CLAIR SHORES COUNTRY CLUB
PM-22185 Masonic Boulevard, St. Clair Shores, 48082, Macomb County, (810)294-2000.
Yards: 6,040/4,820. **Par:** 70/70. **Course Rating:** N/A. **Slope:** N/A. **Green Fee:** $13/$21. **Walkability:** N/A. **Miscellaneous:** Metal spikes.
Reader Comments: Many seniors ... Very well kept up ... Very busy ... Great course for the price ... Recent redesign adds challenge ... You could use an entire roll of film on every hole.

★★★★★ ST. IVES GOLF CLUB *Service+, Value, Condition+*
PU-9900 St. Ives Dr., Stanwood, 49346, Mecosta County, (231)972-8410, (800)972-4837, 60 miles N of Grand Rapids. **Web:** www.stivesgolf.com.
Holes: 18. **Yards:** 6,702/4,821. **Par:** 72/72. **Course Rating:** 73.3/68.7. **Slope:** 140/120. **Green Fee:** $29/$66. **Cart Fee:** $14/person. **Walking Policy:** Unrestricted walking. **Walkability:** 5. **Opened:** 1996. **Architect:** Jerry Matthews. **Season:** April-Nov. **High:** June-Sept. **To obtain tee times:** Call. **Miscellaneous:** Reduced fees (weekdays, low season, twilight, juniors), discount packages, range (grass), club rentals, credit cards (MC, V, AE, D).
Notes: Ranked 13th in 1999 Best in State.
Reader Comments: Wish I lived closer... Up, down, all around ... Good condition ... If you like your drives, you won't like the course ... Liked it better than Spyglass ... Beautiful vistas, excellent golf ... Very challenging for all levels ... If you hit a ball in the wetlands use your towel to wipe your tears, take your penalty and move on ... Incredibly nice ... Superb layout.

★★½ SAINT JOE VALLEY GOLF CLUB
PU-24953 M 86, Sturgis, 49091, St. Joseph County, (616)467-6275, 10 miles N of Sturgis.
Holes: 18. **Yards:** 5,225/4,616. **Par:** 68/71. **Course Rating:** 64.6/65.7. **Slope:** 109/108. **Green Fee:** $14/$18. **Cart Fee:** $10/person. **Walking Policy:** Unrestricted walking. **Walkability:** 1. **Opened:** 1962. **Season:** April-Oct. **High:** June-Aug. **To obtain tee times:** Call. **Miscellaneous:** Reduced fees (seniors, juniors), club rentals, credit cards (MC, V), beginner friendly (beginner lessons).
Reader Comments: Great little course ... Easy walking, good greens, few hills.

★★½ ST. JOHN'S GOLF CLUB
PU-44115 Five Mile Rd., Plymouth, 48170, Wayne County, (734)453-1047, (877)453-1047, 10 miles W of Detroit. **E-mail:** www.stjohnsgolfcenter.com.
Holes: 27. **Yards:** N/A. **Par:** N/A. **Course Rating:** N/A. **Slope:** N/A. **Green Fee:** $30/$33. **Cart Fee:** $12/person. **Walkability:** 4. **Architect:** Grelac. **Season:** March-Nov. **High:** June-Aug. **To obtain tee times:** Call up to 7 days in advance. **Miscellaneous:** Reduced fees (weekdays, low season, resort guests, twilight, seniors, juniors), metal spikes, range (grass/mats), club rentals, credit cards (MC, V, AE).
Reader Comments: Beautiful course ... Very fun ... Lots of hills ... Good shape ... Play moves ... Tight wooded back 9 ... On the comeback trail.

★★★½ SALEM HILLS GOLF CLUB
PU-8810 W. Six Mile Rd., Northville, 48167, Washentaw County, (248)437-2152, 25 miles NW of Detroit.
Holes: 18. **Yards:** 6,966/5,874. **Par:** 72/76. **Course Rating:** 72.9/73.4. **Slope:** 121/119. **Green Fee:** $27/$27. **Cart Fee:** $11/person. **Walking Policy:** Walking at certain times. **Walkability:** 2.

Opened: 1963. **Architect:** Bruce Matthews/Jerry Matthews. **Season:** April-Nov. **High:** May-Sept. **To obtain tee times:** Call 7 days in advance with credit card to guarantee. **Miscellaneous:** Reduced fees (twilight, seniors, juniors), range (grass), club rentals, credit cards (MC, V). **Reader Comments:** Front 9 so-so, the game starts on back ... No. 11, No. 12 and No. 13 have broken many hearts ... Enjoyed very much ... Big greens with large bunkers ... Fun course ... Long! ... No shade! ... Playable yet challenging, quick greens.

★★ SALT RIVER COUNTRY CLUB
PU-33633 23 Mile Rd., New Baltimore, 48047, Macomb County, (810)725-0311. **Holes:** 18. **Yards:** 6,107/5,196. **Par:** 71/72. **Course Rating:** 69.0/69.6. **Slope:** 115/113. **Green Fee:** $16/$26. **Cart Fee:** $11/person. **Walking Policy:** Unrestricted walking. **Walkability:** 1. **Season:** April until snow. **High:** May-Sept. **To obtain tee times:** Call. **Miscellaneous:** Reduced fees (twilight, seniors), discount packages, metal spikes, credit cards (MC, V, AE, D).

★★½ SANDY RIDGE GOLF COURSE
PU-2750 W. Lauria Rd., Midland, 48642, Bay County County, (517)631-6010, 100 miles NW of Detroit. **Holes:** 18. **Yards:** 6,409/5,304. **Par:** 72/72. **Course Rating:** 70.9/70.5. **Slope:** 132/124. **Green Fee:** $19/$22. **Cart Fee:** $12/person. **Walking Policy:** Unrestricted walking. **Walkability:** 1. **Opened:** 1966. **Architect:** Bruce Matthews. **Season:** April-Oct. **High:** June-Aug. **To obtain tee times:** Call up to 7 days in advance. **Miscellaneous:** Reduced fees (seniors, juniors), discount packages, range (grass/mats), club rentals, credit cards (MC, V, D). **Reader Comments:** Friendly, fun golf course ... Needs work ... Basic golf, lack of water hurts condition ... Decent course, but fairways tend to burn out in summer ... Average design ... Mediocre.

SASKATOON GOLF CLUB
PU-9038 92nd St., Alto, 49302, Kent County, (616)891-9229, 12 miles SE of Grand Rapids.
★★★½ BLUE/WHITE
Holes: 18. **Yards:** 6,750/6,125. **Par:** 73/73. **Course Rating:** 70.7/71.7. **Slope:** 123/122. **Green Fee:** $20/$22. **Cart Fee:** $10/person. **Walking Policy:** Unrestricted walking. **Walkability:** 2. **Opened:** 1963. **Architect:** Mark DeVries. **Season:** March-Dec. **High:** May-July. **To obtain tee times:** Call 14 days in advance for weekdays and 7 days in advance for weekends. **Miscellaneous:** Reduced fees (seniors), range (grass/mats), club rentals, credit cards (MC, V, AE, D). **Reader Comments:** This course is a good combo ... Friendly staff, nice clubhouse a lot of room to roam, never in another player's way ... Greens need work ... Beautiful scenery ... Geese alert ... White much better 9 ... Some tight holes, greens rough ... Use extra club from rough ... Very playable.
★★★½ RED/GOLD
Holes: 18. **Yards:** 6,254/5,300. **Par:** 71/70. **Course Rating:** 69.1/68.0. **Slope:** 123/114. **Green Fee:** $20/$22. **Cart Fee:** $10/person. **Walking Policy:** Unrestricted walking. **Walkability:** 2. **Opened:** 1970. **Architect:** Mark DeVries. **Season:** March-Dec. **High:** May-July. **To obtain tee times:** Call 14 days in advance for weekdays and 7 days in advance for weekends. **Miscellaneous:** Reduced fees (seniors), range (grass/mats), club rentals, credit cards (MC, V, AE, D). **Reader Comments:** Red is short, Gold is near links ... A lot of play–needs help ... Gold is excellent ... Very slow, too many leagues ... Gold side is very challenging ... Tricky links, especially when windy ... Red nine through trees is short; Gold is link-style course and more challenging ... Greens rough.

SAUGANASH COUNTRY CLUB
SP-61270 Lutz Rd., Three Rivers, 49093, St. Jospeh County, (616)278-7825, 3 miles S of Three Rivers. **Holes:** 18. **Yards:** 5,921/4,802. **Par:** 72/72. **Course Rating:** 68.5/68.0. **Slope:** 128/116. **Green Fee:** $20/$25. **Cart Fee:** Included in Green Fee. **Walking Policy:** Unrestricted walking. **Walkability:** 2. **Opened:** 1924. **Season:** March-Nov. **High:** June-Aug. **Miscellaneous:** Reduced fees (weekdays, juniors), discount packages, credit cards (MC, V).

★★ SAULT STE. MARIE COUNTRY CLUB
SP-1520 Riverside Dr., Sault Ste. Marie, 49783, Chippewa County, (906)632-7812. **Holes:** 18. **Yards:** 6,295/5,100. **Par:** 71/72. **Course Rating:** 70.6/70.0. **Slope:** 125/119. **Green Fee:** $18/$22. **Cart Fee:** $16/. **Walking Policy:** Unrestricted walking. **Walkability:** N/A. **Opened:** 1903. **Architect:** Jerry Matthews. **Season:** April-Oct. **High:** June-Aug. **To obtain tee times:** Call up to 3 days in advance. **Miscellaneous:** Reduced fees (low season), metal spikes, range (grass), club rentals, credit cards (MC, V).

THE SAWMILL GOLF CLUB
PU-19 Sawmill Blvd., Saginaw, 48603, (517)793-2692.

Holes: 18. Yards: 6,757/5,140. Par: 72/82. Course Rating: 72.7/70.4. Slope: 139/125. Green Fee: $28/$34. Cart Fee: $14/person. Walking Policy: Walking at certain times. Walkability: 1. Opened: 1997. Architect: John Sanford. Season: April.-Nov. High: May-Sept. To obtain tee times: Phone calls preferred. Miscellaneous: Reduced fees (low season, twilight, seniors), range (grass), club rentals, credit cards (MC, V, AE, D).

★★★ SCENIC COUNTRY CLUB
8364 Filion Rd., Pigeon, 48755, Huron County, (517)453-3350.
Reader Comments: Second year after rebuilding ... Well designed.
Special Notes: Call club for further information.

★★½ SCOTT LAKE COUNTRY CLUB
PU-911 Hayes Rd. N.E., Comstock Park, 49321, Kent County, (616)784-1355, 10 miles N of Grand Rapids.
Holes: 27. Yards: 6,333/4,794. Par: 72/72. Course Rating: 70.8/67.6. Slope: 122/110. Green Fee: $18/$23. Cart Fee: $10/person. Walking Policy: Unrestricted walking. Walkability: 4. Opened: 1962. Architect: Bruce Matthews/Jeff Gorney. Season: April-Nov. High: May-Sept. To obtain tee times: Call 7 days in advance. Miscellaneous: Reduced fees (weekdays, low season, seniors, juniors), metal spikes, range (grass/mats), club rentals, credit cards (MC, V, AE, D).
Reader Comments: Exciting golf, hilly and trees ... Too challenging for most women ... New south 9 is a joy to play ... Lots of up and downs ... Always fun ... Few holes can be very wet ... Super course run by friendly people ... Great new 9.

★★★ SHADOW RIDGE GOLF CLUB
PU-1191 Kelsey Hwy., Ionia, 48846, Ionia County, (616)527-1180, 1 miles S of Ionia.
Holes: 9. Yards: 2,989/2,350. Par: 35/35. Course Rating: 70.3/70.8. Slope: 123/122. Green Fee: $11/$13. Cart Fee: $18/cart. Walking Policy: Unrestricted walking. Walkability: 4. Opened: 1916. Architect: Donald Ross. Season: April-Oct. High: June-Aug. To obtain tee times: Call golf shop. Miscellaneous: Reduced fees (low season, twilight, seniors, juniors), metal spikes, club rentals, credit cards (MC, V).
Reader Comments: Built on top of a mountain, beautiful ... Great par 3's.

★ SHADY HOLLOW GOLF COURSE
PU-34777 Smith Rd. At Wayne, Romulus, 48174, Wayne County, (734)721-0430, 15 miles SW of Detroit.
Holes: 18. Yards: 5,933/5,140. Par: 71/72. Course Rating: N/A. Slope: N/A. Green Fee: $12/$22. Cart Fee: $10/person. Walking Policy: Unrestricted walking. Walkability: 1. Opened: 1972. Season: March-Dec. High: June-Aug. To obtain tee times: Call to book reservation. Miscellaneous: Reduced fees (low season, twilight, seniors, juniors), club rentals, credit cards (MC, V), beginner friendly.

SHAGBARK GOLF CLUB
PU-80 106th Ave., Plainwell, 49080, Allegan County, (616)664-4653, 16 miles N of Kalamazoo.
Holes: 18. Yards: 6,364/4,454. Par: 72/72. Course Rating: 69.9/67.6. Slope: 134/117. Green Fee: $30/$35. Cart Fee: $10/person. Walking Policy: Unrestricted walking. Walkability: 5. Opened: 1997. Architect: Steve DeLoof. Season: April-Oct. High: June-Aug. To obtain tee times: Call (616)664-4653. Miscellaneous: Reduced fees (weekdays, low season, twilight, seniors, juniors), discount packages, range (grass), club rentals, credit cards (MC, V, AE).

SHANTY CREEK   *Service*
R-One Shanty Creek Rd., Bellaire, 49615, Antrim County, (231)533-8621, (800)678-4111, 35 miles NE of Traverse City. E-mail: info@shantycreek.com. Web: www.shantycreek.com.
CEDAR RIVER GOLF CLUB
Holes: 18. Yards: 6,989/5,315. Par: 72/72. Course Rating: N/A. Slope: N/A. Green Fee: $65/$140. Cart Fee: Included in Green Fee. Walking Policy: Unrestricted walking. Walkability: 5. Opened: 1999. Architect: Tom Weiskopf. Season: April-Oct. High: June-Aug. To obtain tee times: Hotel guests may reserve tee time with room reservations. Nonguests may call up to 30 days in advance for weekdays and 14 days in advance for weekends. Miscellaneous: Reduced fees (low season, resort guests, twilight, seniors), discount packages, club rentals, lodging (600 rooms), credit cards (MC, V, AE, D), beginner friendly (Jack Seltzer Golf Academy).
★★★★ SCHUSS MOUNTAIN Golf Club
Holes: 18. Yards: 6,922/5,383. Par: 72/72. Course Rating: 73.4/71.2. Slope: 127/126. Green Fee: $45/$85. Cart Fee: Included in Green Fee. Walking Policy: Unrestricted walking. Walkability: 3. Opened: 1972. Architect: Warner Bowen/Bill Newcomb. Season: April-Oct. High: June-Aug. To obtain tee times: Hotel guests may reserve tee time with room reservations. Nonguests may call up to 30 days in advance for weekdays and 14 days in advance for weekends. Miscellaneous: Reduced fees (low season, resort guests, twilight, seniors), discount packages, range (grass/mats), club rentals, lodging (600 rooms), credit cards (MC, V, AE, D), beginner friendly (junior clinic).

MICHIGAN

Reader Comments: Best at Shanty Creek ... Condition improving ... Good test ... Front 9 a little flat, back 9 makes up for it ... Enjoyable ... Looks easy, plays hard! ... Needs length and variety ... Fairly easy ... Straightforward, great greens ... Stick to The Legend for a real challenge ... Excellent for all levels ... Ponds, wetlands and wild game ... Wonderfully isolated ... Beautiful in October.... Love this course!.

★★★½ SUMMIT GOLF CLUB

Holes: 18. **Yards:** 6,260/4,679. **Par:** 72/72. **Course Rating:** 71.7/70.7. **Slope:** 120/113. **Green Fee:** $35/$60. **Cart Fee:** Included in Green Fee. **Walking Policy:** Unrestricted walking. **Walkability:** 2. **Opened:** 1965. **Architect:** Bill Diddel. **Season:** April-Oct. **High:** June-Aug. **To obtain tee times:** Hotel guests may reserve tee time with room reservations. Nonguests may call up to 30 days in advance for weekdays and 14 days in advance for weekends. **Miscellaneous:** Reduced fees (low season, resort guests, twilight, seniors), discount packages, range (grass), club rentals, lodging (600 rooms), credit cards (MC, V, AE, D), beginner friendly (junior clinic).

Reader Comments: Nice ... Always in great shape ... Above-average enjoyment ... Excellent fairways and greens. Outstanding scenery in a resort area.

★★★★½ THE LEGEND GOLF CLUB *Condition*

Holes: 18. **Yards:** 6,764/4,953. **Par:** 72/72. **Course Rating:** 73.6/69.6. **Slope:** 137/124. **Green Fee:** $75/$140. **Cart Fee:** Included in Green Fee. **Walking Policy:** Unrestricted walking. **Walkability:** 5. **Opened:** 1985. **Architect:** Arnold Palmer/Ed Seay. **Season:** April-Oct. **High:** June-Aug. **To obtain tee times:** Hotel guests may reserve tee time with room reservations. Nonguests may call up to 30 days in advance for weekdays and 14 days in advance for weekends. **Miscellaneous:** Reduced fees (low season, resort guests, twilight, seniors), discount packages, range (grass/mats), club rentals, lodging (600 rooms), credit cards (MC, V, AE, D), beginner friendly (junior clinic).

Notes: Ranked 12th in 1999 Best in State.

Reader Comments: A masterpiece by The King! ... Fantastic scenery, great greens, overall solid course ... Arnie's name guarantees success at an exorbitant cost ... Just perfect ... Great views–rest of course overrated ... If I had to choose 1 to play this is it ... My all-time favorite ... A thrill to play ... Top notch ... Total hole seclusion ... Challenging, but rewarding ... Bring a camera.

★★★ SHENANDOAH GOLF & COUNTRY CLUB

PU-5600 Walnut Lake Rd., West Bloomfield, 48323, Oakland County, (248)682-4300, 15 miles NW of Detroit.

Holes: 18. **Yards:** 6,620/6,409. **Par:** 72/72. **Course Rating:** 72.9/70.8. **Slope:** 129/124. **Green Fee:** $48/$55. **Cart Fee:** Included in Green Fee. **Walking Policy:** Mandatory cart. **Walkability:** 4. **Opened:** 1967. **Architect:** Bruce Matthews/Jerry Matthews. **Season:** March-Dec. **High:** June-Aug. **To obtain tee times:** Call. **Miscellaneous:** Reduced fees (twilight, seniors, juniors), range (grass/mats), club rentals, credit cards (MC, V), beginner friendly (junior, intermediate, advanced programs).

Reader Comments: Houses too close ... Disappointing course–needs work! ... Blind shots ... Front plays long.

SINGING BRIDGE GOLF

PU-1920 Noble Rd, Tawas City, 48763, Iosco County, (517)362-2828, 10 miles S of Tawas City.

Holes: 18. **Yards:** 5,986/4,788. **Par:** 71/71. **Course Rating:** N/A. **Slope:** N/A. **Green Fee:** $12/$18. **Cart Fee:** $10/person. **Walking Policy:** Unrestricted walking. **Walkability:** 2. **Opened:** 1992. **Season:** April-Nov. **High:** June-Aug. **To obtain tee times:** Call golf shop. **Miscellaneous:** Reduced fees (weekdays, seniors), range (grass), club rentals, credit cards (MC, V, D), beginner friendly.

★★★★ SNOW SNAKE SKI & GOLF

PU-3407 E. Mannsiding Rd., Harrison, 48625, Clare County, (517)539-6583, 25 miles N of Mt. Pleasant.

Holes: 18. **Yards:** 6,021/4,447. **Par:** 71/71. **Course Rating:** 69.8/66.3. **Slope:** 133/117. **Green Fee:** $25/$42. **Cart Fee:** Included in Green Fee. **Walking Policy:** Unrestricted walking. **Walkability:** 5. **Opened:** 1994. **Architect:** Jeff Gorney. **Season:** May-Oct. **High:** June-Aug. **To obtain tee times:** Call. **Miscellaneous:** Reduced fees (low season, twilight, seniors), discount packages, range (grass/mats), club rentals, credit cards (MC, V, D).

Reader Comments: A hidden jewel ... Tight, lots of lay-ups ... Challenging terrain ... Good course ... Very tight must be in fairway ... Pretty course ... Some nice holes, some quirky designs ... Sand, hills, water, more hills–a fun place to play! ... Unique, some tricky holes.

★★ SOUTH HAVEN COUNTRY CLUB

Blue Star Hwy., South Haven, 49090, Allegan County, (616)637-3896.
Special Notes: Call club for further information.

★½ SOUTHMOOR COUNTRY CLUB

PU-G-4312 S. Dort Highway, Burton, 48529, Genesee County, (810)743-4080, 5 miles S of Flint.

Holes: 18. **Yards:** 5,205/4,810. **Par:** 69/69. **Course Rating:** 67.0/67.0. **Slope:** 109/109. **Green Fee:** $18/$20. **Cart Fee:** $21/cart. **Walking Policy:** Unrestricted walking. **Walkability:** 2. **Opened:** 1963. **Season:** April-Dec. **High:** May-Aug. **To obtain tee times:** First come, first served. **Miscellaneous:** Reduced fees (weekdays, low season, twilight, seniors, juniors), metal spikes, range (grass/mats), caddies, credit cards (MC, V, AE).

★★★ SPRING VALLEY GOLF COURSE
PU-18396 W. U.S. 10, Hersey, 49639, Osceola County, (616)832-5041, 70 miles N of Grand Rapids.
Holes: 18. **Yards:** 6,439/5,273. **Par:** 72/74. **Course Rating:** 71.5/73.3. **Slope:** 112/113. **Green Fee:** $12/$26. **Cart Fee:** $12/person. **Walking Policy:** Unrestricted walking. **Walkability:** 3. **Opened:** 1962. **Architect:** Donald Semeyn. **Season:** April-Oct. **High:** June-Aug. **To obtain tee times:** Call golf shop. **Miscellaneous:** Reduced fees (weekdays, low season, seniors), metal spikes, range (grass), club rentals, credit cards (MC, V), beginner friendly (beginner lessons). **Reader Comments:** Golfer friendly ... No sand ... Homey clubhouse.

SPRINGBROOK GOLF COURSE
PU-Springvale Rd., Walloon Lake, 49796, Charlevoix County, (616)535-2413, 13 miles SE of Petoskey.
Holes: 18. **Yards:** 6,260/5,980. **Par:** 72/72. **Course Rating:** 67.3/69.5. **Slope:** 113/114. **Green Fee:** $10/$25. **Cart Fee:** $12/person. **Walking Policy:** Unrestricted walking. **Walkability:** 2. **Opened:** 1970. **Season:** April-Oct. **High:** June-Aug. **To obtain tee times:** Call golf shop. **Miscellaneous:** Reduced fees (weekdays, low season, twilight, seniors, juniors), discount packages, metal spikes, club rentals, credit cards (MC, V, AE, D), beginner friendly.

★★★ SPRINGFIELD OAKS GOLF COURSE
PM-12450 Andersonville Rd., Davisburg, 48350, Oakland County, (248)625-2540, 15 miles NW of Pontiac.
Holes: 18. **Yards:** 6,033/4,911. **Par:** 71/71. **Course Rating:** 68.4/68.1. **Slope:** 118/114. **Green Fee:** $14/$23. **Cart Fee:** $10/person. **Walking Policy:** Unrestricted walking. **Walkability:** 4. **Architect:** Mark DeVries. **Season:** March-Nov. **High:** June-Aug. **To obtain tee times:** Call 7 days in advance for weekdays. Call on Wednesday evening starting at 6:00 p.m. in person or 6:15 p.m. by phone for upcoming weekend. **Miscellaneous:** Reduced fees (weekdays, low season, twilight, seniors, juniors), metal spikes, club rentals, credit cards (MC, V). **Reader Comments:** Kept in great shape ... Fantastic facilities ... Such a deal ... Private club quality, beautiful ... Delightful to play, when you can get a tee time.

★★★ STATES GOLF COURSE
PU-20 East West Ave., Vicksburg, 49097, Kalamazoo County, (616)649-1931.
Holes: 18. **Yards:** 6,248/5,605. **Par:** 72/74. **Course Rating:** N/A. **Slope:** N/A. **Green Fee:** $13/N/A. **Walkability:** N/A. **Miscellaneous:** Metal spikes. **Reader Comments:** Excellent, large greens ... Very enjoyable experience ... Very flat-walk.

★★★½ STONEBRIDGE GOLF CLUB
PU-5315 Stonebridge Dr. S., Ann Arbor, 48108, Washtenaw County, (734)429-8383, (888)473-2818, 30 miles W of Detroit. **E-mail:** aasbridge@aol.com. **Web:** www.stonebridge-annarbor.com. **Holes:** 18. **Yards:** 6,932/5,075. **Par:** 72/72. **Course Rating:** 73.6/68.6. **Slope:** 136/122. **Green Fee:** $33/$43. **Cart Fee:** $12/person. **Walking Policy:** Walking at certain times. **Walkability:** 4. **Opened:** 1991. **Architect:** Arthur Hills. **Season:** March-Dec. **High:** June-Aug. **To obtain tee times:** Call up to 5 days in advance. **Miscellaneous:** Reduced fees (low season, twilight, seniors), range (grass), club rentals, credit cards (MC, V, AE). **Reader Comments:** Very challenging ... Friendly and wonderful ... A shotmaker's course ... A bit expensive ... Houses too close at times ... Love the course ... Short, classy ... Worth playing ... Pricey, better than average ... Should've built a few less homes to make room for course ... Too many blind shots ... Nice layout.

STONEHEDGE GOLF COURSE
PU-15503 E. M-89, Augusta, 49012, Kalamazoo County, (616)731-2300, 20 miles NE of Kalamazoo.
★★★★ NORTH COURSE *Pace*
Holes: 18. **Yards:** 6,673/5,785. **Par:** 72/72. **Course Rating:** 72.2/72.1. **Slope:** 127/114. **Green Fee:** $31/$33. **Cart Fee:** $12/person. **Walking Policy:** Walking at certain times. **Walkability:** 5. **Opened:** 1988. **Architect:** Charles Scott. **Season:** April-Nov. **High:** May-Aug. **To obtain tee times:** Call golf shop. **Miscellaneous:** Reduced fees (weekdays, low season, resort guests, juniors), discount packages, metal spikes, range (grass), club rentals, credit cards (MC, V). **Reader Comments:** A beauty ... Better hit it straight and long ... Beautiful ... Another jewel ... Not as good as South Course yet ... As good or better than the South Course ... Excellent ... Tough course ... Great variety ... Super golf! ... Aptly named ... Good course to score on, room to let 'er rip.
★★★★ SOUTH COURSE *Value*

Holes: 18. **Yards:** 6,656/5,191. **Par:** 72/72. **Course Rating:** 72.4/70.3. **Slope:** 133/120. **Green Fee:** $31/$33. **Cart Fee:** $12/person. **Walking Policy:** Walking at certain times. **Walkability:** 5. **Opened:** 1988. **Architect:** Charles Scott. **Season:** April-Nov. **High:** May-Aug. **To obtain tee times:** Call golf shop. **Miscellaneous:** Reduced fees (weekdays, low season, resort guests, juniors), discount packages, metal spikes, range (grass), club rentals, credit cards (MC, V).

Reader Comments: Fast greens, great fairways ... Tough course, reasonable cost ... One of my favorites anywhere ... Plays like a traditional country club course ... Name fits ... Starts easy ... Beautiful, tough finishing holes ... Must play ... Hilly ... Tough to get on but worth the effort ... Northern course in Southern Michigan ... Great variety.

★★★½ STONY CREEK GOLF COURSE
PU-5140 Main Pkwy., Shelby Township, 48316, Macomb County, (810)781-9166, 5 miles NE of Rochester.
Holes: 18. **Yards:** 6,900/5,023. **Par:** 72/72. **Course Rating:** 73.1/74.1. **Slope:** 124/124. **Green Fee:** $20/$27. **Cart Fee:** $23/cart. **Walking Policy:** Unrestricted walking. **Walkability:** 3. **Opened:** 1979. **Season:** April-Nov. **High:** June-Aug. **To obtain tee times:** Call up to 3 days in advance. **Miscellaneous:** Reduced fees (weekdays, seniors, juniors), metal spikes, range (grass), credit cards (MC, V, D).

Reader Comments: Difficult muny, good value ... Typical Metropark course with minimal mainte-nance ... You would never know it's a metro park ... Heavy traffic and hot summers are tough on course ... Can never get on ... Decent course ... Interesting fairways ... If they fix the greens and stop the slow play, it would be a great golf course ... Wide fairways.

★★★½ SUGAR SPRINGS COUNTRY CLUB
SP-1930 Sugar River Blvd., Gladwin, 48624, Gladwin County, (517)426-4111, 11 miles N of Gladwin.
Holes: 18. **Yards:** 6,737/5,636. **Par:** 72/72. **Course Rating:** 72.6/72.5. **Slope:** 124/121. **Green Fee:** $32/$32. **Cart Fee:** $14/person. **Walking Policy:** Unrestricted walking. **Walkability:** 2. **Opened:** 1972. **Season:** April-Oct. **High:** June-Aug. **To obtain tee times:** Call. **Miscellaneous:** Range (grass), credit cards (MC, V).

Reader Comments: Good course, a little of everything ... We were asked to speed up play after completing 1st 9 holes in 2 hours ... Good value ... Fun, wooded holes, wide open, some holes deceiving with wind ... A real nice course and improving all the time.

★ SUNNYBROOK GOLF CLUB
PU-7191 17 Mile Rd., Sterling Heights, 48078, Macomb County, (810)264-2700, 150 miles N of Detroit.
Holes: 27. **Yards:** 6,310/5,730. **Par:** 70/70. **Course Rating:** 69.0/N/A. **Slope:** 121/N/A. **Green Fee:** $21/$24. **Cart Fee:** $20/cart. **Walking Policy:** Unrestricted walking. **Walkability:** 2. **Opened:** 1951. **Architect:** Donald Ross. **Season:** March-Nov. **High:** April-Sept. **Miscellaneous:** Reduced fees (weekdays, low season, twilight, seniors, juniors), discount packages, range (grass), club rentals, lodging (90 rooms).

★★ SWAN VALLEY GOLF COURSE
PU-9499 Geddes Rd., Saginaw, 48603, Saginaw County, (517)781-4653.
Holes: 18. **Yards:** 5,985/4,693. **Par:** 70/72. **Course Rating:** 68.9/66.9. **Slope:** 119/112. **Green Fee:** $20/$21. **Cart Fee:** $22/cart. **Walking Policy:** Unrestricted walking. **Walkability:** 4. **Opened:** 1960. **Season:** April-Dec. **High:** May-Sept. **To obtain tee times:** Call (517)781-4945 or (517)SV1-GOLF. **Miscellaneous:** Reduced fees (low season, seniors, juniors), discount pack-ages, range (grass/mats), club rentals, credit cards (MC, V, D).

★★½ SWARTZ CREEK GOLF COURSE
PM-1902 Hammerberg Rd., Flint, 48503, Genesee County, (810)766-7043, 45 miles N of Detroit.
Holes: 27. **Yards:** 6,662/5,798. **Par:** 72/72. **Course Rating:** 72.1/73.0. **Slope:** 121/123. **Green Fee:** $19/$23. **Cart Fee:** $22/cart. **Walking Policy:** Unrestricted walking. **Walkability:** 3. **Opened:** 1926. **Architect:** Frederick A. Ellis. **Season:** Year-round. **High:** April-Oct. **To obtain tee times:** Call on Monday for upcoming weekend. **Miscellaneous:** Reduced fees (low season, twi-light, seniors, juniors), metal spikes, club rentals, credit cards (MC, V).

Reader Comments: Crowded and slow at times ... River cuts through too many holes ... Back par-3 course real nice ... Open year round, played in Feb.-who cares about conditions! ... Boring ... Good greens ... Great city course, nice layout.

SYCAMORE HILLS GOLF CLUB
PU-48787 North Ave., Macomb, 48042, Macomb County, (810)598-9500, 20 miles N of Detroit.
E-mail: webmaster@sycamorehills. com. **Web:** www.sycamorehills.com.
Holes: 27. **Green Fee:** $22/$38. **Cart Fee:** $12/person. **Walking Policy:** Walking at certain times. **Walkability:** 2. **Opened:** 1990. **Architect:** Jerry Matthews. **Season:** March-Dec. **High:** May-Sept. **To obtain tee times:** Call up to 21 days in advance. **Miscellaneous:** Reduced fees

(weekdays, low season, twilight, seniors, juniors), discount packages, range (grass/mats), club rentals, credit cards (MC, V, AE, D).

★★★ NORTH/WEST
Yards: 6,305/5,070. **Par:** 72/72. **Course Rating:** 70.3/68.3. **Slope:** 123/119. **Reader Comments:** South is tough, West is average, North is easy ... We were lined up 30 minutes at the tee ... Slow play ... Fine golf course ... Lose balls here ... Not user-friendly for women ... Played 20 rounds here! ... Little expensive, but worth it ... Buddy Hackett–short but entertaining ... Straightforward ... Great fairways.

★★★ SOUTH/NORTH
Yards: 6,267/4,934. **Par:** 72/72. **Course Rating:** 70.2/67.2. **Slope:** 132/121.
Reader Comments: South is the toughest of the three 9s ... Short ... Great condition ... Some challenge ...Lots of water holes for a Michigan course.

★★★ SOUTH/WEST
Yards: 6,336/5,119. **Par:** 72/72. **Course Rating:** 70.7/68.5. **Slope:** 130/120.
Reader Comments: South is tough, West is average ... Fine golf.

★★ SYLVAN GLEN GOLF COURSE
PM-5725 Rochester Rd., Troy, 48084, Oakland County, (248)879-0040.
Yards: 6,566/5,295. **Par:** 70/70. **Course Rating:** 71.3/70.0. **Slope:** 115/113. **Green Fee:** $17/$29. **Walkability:** N/A. **Miscellaneous:** Metal spikes.

★★★ THE TAMARACKS
PU-8900 N. Clare Ave., Harrison, 48625, Clare County, (517)539-5441, (888)838-1162, 30 miles N of Mt. Pleasant.
Holes: 18. **Yards:** 5,760/4,370. **Par:** 70/70. **Course Rating:** N/A. **Slope:** N/A. **Green Fee:** $15/$25. **Cart Fee:** $12/person. **Walking Policy:** Unrestricted walking. **Walkability:** 3. **Opened:** 1984. **Architect:** Stephen Hawkins. **Season:** April-Nov. **High:** June-Aug. **To obtain tee times:** Call or stop in. **Miscellaneous:** Reduced fees (weekdays, low season, resort guests, twilight, seniors, juniors), discount packages, metal spikes, range (grass), club rentals, lodging, credit cards (MC, V, AE, D).
Reader Comments: Lots of blind shots ... Fun course with good variety ... Front 9 lots of water–challenging and fun, short ... Best-kept secret in Mid-Michigan ... Bargain, never crowded ... Could be good course, but is poorly maintained.

TANGLEWOOD GOLF CLUB
PU-53503 W. Ten Mile Rd., South Lyon, 48178, Oakland County, (248)486-3355, 25 miles NW of Detroit.
Holes: 27. **Green Fee:** $40/$45. **Cart Fee:** $10/person. **Walking Policy:** Walking at certain times. **Walkability:** 2. **Opened:** 1991. **Architect:** Bill Newcomb. **Season:** March-Nov. **High:** May-Aug. **To obtain tee times:** Call golf shop (248)486-3355 Ext. 2. **Miscellaneous:** Reduced fees (low season, twilight, seniors, juniors), discount packages, range (grass/mats), club rentals, credit cards (MC, V, AE).

★★★½ NORTH/SOUTH
Yards: 7,077/5,011. **Par:** 72/72. **Course Rating:** 73.6/72.9. **Slope:** 129/119.
Reader Comments: Good course ... Solid value and a very nice course ... It is a nice layout, but I had higher expectations due to hype and price ... Good facilities ... Long and pretty open, lots of water ... Fun course ... Beautiful ... Enjoyable! ... Some blind shots ... Average course ... Great layout ... Challenging courses ... Too many outings ... Course was in great shape.

★★★½ NORTH/WEST
Yards: 6,922/4,896. **Par:** 72/72. **Course Rating:** 73.0/72.1. **Slope:** 128/118.
Reader Comments: Very nice ... Variety ... Overrated ... Great layout ... Good facilities ... West is best ... Beautiful challenge ... Average ... Enjoyable.

★★★½ SOUTH/WEST
Yards: 7,117/5,031. **Par:** 72/72. **Course Rating:** 76.4/75.6. **Slope:** 138/128.
Reader Comments: South to West is the best ... Nice course ... Great layout ... Beautiful ... Challenging.

★★ TAWAS CREEK GOLF CLUB
PU-1022 Monument Rd., Tawas City, 48763, Iosco County, (517)362-6262, (888)829-2727, 80 miles NE of Saginaw.
Holes: 18. **Yards:** 6,527/5,006. **Par:** 72/73. **Course Rating:** 71.9/69.3. **Slope:** 126/123. **Green Fee:** $15/$22. **Cart Fee:** $10/person. **Walking Policy:** Unrestricted walking. **Walkability:** 2. **Season:** April-Oct. **High:** July-Aug. **To obtain tee times:** Call up to 7 days in advance. **Miscellaneous:** Reduced fees (twilight), metal spikes, club rentals, credit cards (MC, V).

★★★½ TAYLOR MEADOWS GOLF CLUB
PM-25360 Ecorse Rd., Taylor, 48180, Wayne County, (313)295-0506, 15 miles SW of Detroit.
Web: www.taylorgolf.com.
Holes: 18. **Yards:** 6,049/5,160. **Par:** 71/71. **Course Rating:** 67.7/70.0. **Slope:** 115/115. **Green Fee:** $22/$29. **Cart Fee:** $24/cart. **Walking Policy:** Unrestricted walking. **Walkability:** 3.

MICHIGAN

Opened: 1989. **Architect:** Arthur Hills. **Season:** March-Dec. **High:** May-Oct. **To obtain tee times:** Call 7days in advance for weekdays. **Miscellaneous:** Reduced fees (weekdays, low season, twilight, seniors, juniors), range (mats), club rentals, credit cards (MC, V).
Reader Comments: Fairly good muny ... Good fall rate made for pleasurable day ... Nice, short course ... Excellent ... Slow play.

★★★ TERRACE BLUFF GOLF COURSE
SP-7527 Lake Bluff 19.4 Rd., Gladstone, 49837, Delta County, (906)428-2343, 4 miles N of Escanaba.
Holes: 18. **Yards:** 7,001/5,900. **Par:** 72/72. **Course Rating:** 69.5/71.5. **Slope:** 119/117. **Green Fee:** $24/$24. **Cart Fee:** $20/cart. **Walking Policy:** Unrestricted walking. **Walkability:** 1.
Opened: 1972. **Season:** April-Oct. **High:** June-Aug. **To obtain tee times:** Call up to 15 days in advance. **Miscellaneous:** Range (grass), club rentals, lodging (71 rooms), credit cards (MC, V).
Reader Comments: Scenic ... A nice layout ... Overrated ... A good bargain ... Target golf, short and easy to score.

THE PINES GOLF COURSE
PU-7231 Clubhouse Dr., Weidman, 48893, Isabella County, (517)644-2300, (800)741-3435, 10 miles W of Mt. Pleasant.
Holes: 18. **Yards:** 6,856/5,092. **Par:** 72/72. **Course Rating:** 72.5/70.1. **Slope:** 128/120. **Green Fee:** $22/$28. **Cart Fee:** $12/person. **Walking Policy:** Unrestricted walking. **Walkability:** 2.
Opened: 1969. **Architect:** Bruce Mathews. **Season:** April-Oct. **High:** June-Aug. **To obtain tee times:** Call anytime. **Miscellaneous:** Reduced fees (weekdays, low season, seniors), discount packages, metal spikes, range (grass), club rentals, credit cards (MC, V, D).
Reader Comments: Nice course, some holes not made for left handers on front nine ... Someone needs to invent a ball that will go through pine trees ... Enjoyed round ... Some very challenging holes, some very basic ... One of the best values, in Mid-Michigan.

★★★½ THORNAPPLE CREEK GOLF CLUB
PU-6415 W. F Ave., Kalamazoo, 49009, Kalamazoo County, (616)344-0040, 5 miles N of Kalamazoo.
Holes: 18. **Yards:** 6,595/4,948. **Par:** 72/72. **Course Rating:** 72.3/68.9. **Slope:** 133/121. **Green Fee:** $18/$33. **Cart Fee:** $12/person. **Walking Policy:** Walking at certain times. **Walkability:** 4.
Opened: 1979. **Architect:** Mike Shields. **Season:** April-Nov. **High:** June-Aug. **To obtain tee times:** Call in advance 7 days. Groups of 12 or larger can book anytime with deposit.
Miscellaneous: Reduced fees (weekdays, low season), discount packages, range (grass), club rentals, credit cards (MC, V, AE).
Reader Comments: Lots of water and sand ... Don't miss this one if you want value ... One of the best Western Michigan courses ... Greens are tough ... One of the best par 5's in Michigan ... Need course knowledge ... Challenging ... Scenic river holes ... Beautiful, tricky greens ... Needs drainage on front nine ... Much improved overall in 1998 under new owners ... Gorgeous in autumn.

★ THORNE HILLS GOLF COURSE
PU-12915 Sumpter Rd., Carleton, 48117, Monroe County, (734)587-2332, 9 miles S of Belleville.
Holes: 18. **Yards:** 5,827/5,205. **Par:** 72/72. **Course Rating:** N/A. **Slope:** N/A. **Green Fee:** $14/$16. **Cart Fee:** $14/cart. **Walking Policy:** Unrestricted walking. **Walkability:** 2. **Opened:** 1981. **Architect:** Daniel G. Thorne. **Season:** April-Oct. **High:** July-Aug. **To obtain tee times:** Call golf shop. **Miscellaneous:** Reduced fees (weekdays, low season, seniors).

★★★★½ THOROUGHBRED GOLF CLUB AT DOUBLE JJ RESORT
R-6886 Water Rd., Rothbury, 49452, Oceana County, (231)893-4653, (800)368-2535, 20 miles N of Muskegon. **Web:** www.doublejj.com.
Holes: 18. **Yards:** 6,900/4,851. **Par:** 72/72. **Course Rating:** 74.4/69.5. **Slope:** 147/126. **Green Fee:** $45/$72. **Cart Fee:** Included in Green Fee. **Walking Policy:** Unrestricted walking.
Walkability: 5. **Opened:** 1993. **Architect:** Arthur Hills. **Season:** April-Nov. **High:** June-Sept. **To obtain tee times:** Call up to 7 days in advance. Tee times may be made for entire year with deposit. **Miscellaneous:** Reduced fees (weekdays, low season, resort guests, twilight), discount packages, metal spikes, range (grass), club rentals, lodging (200 rooms), credit cards (MC, V, AE, D).
Notes: Ranked 8th in 1999 Best in State.
Reader Comments: I can't wait to play it again ... What a course! ... One of top 10 courses in U.S. ... Jammed with turkeys, foxes, and horses ... Very tough ... Amid bogs and horse trails ... Awesome beauty ... Incredible layout ... Each hole more exciting then the one before it ... Slow! Disappointed ... What happened to the course condition? ... Hardest ever! ... No. 2 will kick your butt and take your lunch money ... Make the effort to get there, and bring a shepherd ... Beelzebub resides on No. 2.

MICHIGAN

★★★ THUNDER BAY GOLF RESORT
R-27800 M-32 E., Hillman, 49746, Montmorency County, (517)742-4875, (800)729-9375, 22 miles W of Alpena.
Holes: 18. **Yards:** 6,466/5,584. **Par:** 73/75. **Course Rating:** 72.1/72.1. **Slope:** 129/124. **Green Fee:** $19/$26. **Cart Fee:** $12/person. **Walking Policy:** Walking at certain times. **Walkability:** 3. **Opened:** 1971. **Architect:** Jack Matthias. **Season:** April-Nov. **High:** June-Sept. **To obtain tee times:** Call. **Miscellaneous:** Reduced fees (weekdays, low season, resort guests, twilight, seniors, juniors), discount packages, range (grass), club rentals, lodging (40 rooms), credit cards (MC, V, AE, D, Diners Club).
Reader Comments: Very wooded, challenging, beautiful ... Nice accommodations and pleasant hosts ... A nice weekend outing ... Below average course ... Low cost ... Nice in fall.

★★★★ TIMBER RIDGE GOLF COURSE
PU-16339 Park Lake Rd., East Lansing, 48823, Ingham County, (517)339-8000, (800)874-3432, 5 miles E of Lansing.
Holes: 18. **Yards:** 6,497/5,048. **Par:** 72/72. **Course Rating:** 72.4/70.9. **Slope:** 140/129. **Green Fee:** N/A/$40. **Cart Fee:** $12/person. **Walking Policy:** Unrestricted walking. **Walkability:** 4. **Opened:** 1989. **Architect:** Jerry Matthews. **Season:** March-Nov. **High:** May-Sept. **To obtain tee times:** Call 7 days prior for a foursome. Groups of 8 or more may book further in advance. **Miscellaneous:** Reduced fees (weekdays, low season, twilight, seniors), discount packages, range (grass/mats), club rentals, credit cards (MC, V, AE, D), beginner friendly (lessons from pga professional).
Reader Comments: Excellent experience ... Always fun course and friendly staff ... Very tight treelined fairways ... You'll either love or hate your score, but it's hard to knock the layout ... 'Up north' course down south ... Beautifully maintained ... Favorite! Majestic, colorful, challenging ... Outstanding service.

TIMBER TRACE GOLF CLUB
PU-1 Champions Circle, Pinckney, 48169, Livingston County, (734)878-1800, 2 miles W of Downtown Pinckney.
Holes: 18. **Yards:** 7,020/5,100. **Par:** 72/72. **Course Rating:** 72.5/68.9. **Slope:** 129/120. **Green Fee:** $40/$60. **Cart Fee:** Included in Green Fee. **Walking Policy:** Mandatory cart. **Walkability:** 5. **Opened:** 1998. **Architect:** Pat Conroy/James Dewling. **Season:** March-Nov. **High:** May-Aug. **To obtain tee times:** Call up to 1 week in advance w/credit card; weekends mandatory foursomes. **Miscellaneous:** Reduced fees (weekdays, twilight, seniors, juniors), range (grass/mats), club rentals, credit cards (MC, V, AE, D), beginner friendly (group lessons, lesson series, playing lessons).

★★★½ THE TIMBERS GOLF CLUB
R-900 Timbers Trail, Tuscola, 48769, Tuscola County, (517)871-4884, (888)617-1479, 4 miles E of Frankenmuth.
Holes: 18. **Yards:** 6,674/4,886. **Par:** 18/18. **Course Rating:** 72.7/69.1. **Slope:** 133/113. **Green Fee:** $45/$55. **Cart Fee:** Included in Green Fee. **Walking Policy:** Walking at certain times. **Walkability:** 4. **Opened:** 1996. **Architect:** Lorrie Viola. **Season:** March-Nov. **High:** June-Aug. **To obtain tee times:** Call. **Miscellaneous:** Range (grass/mats), club rentals, credit cards (MC, V).
Reader Comments: Good challenging course ... Back 9 a welcome breather, after 1st 9 ... Don't bring your driver! ... Better scorecard needed ... Specials ... Great value! Well-done layout ... You will come back.

★★★★½ TIMBERSTONE GOLF COURSE *Service+, Value+, Condition+, Pace+*
PU-1 TimberStone Dr., Iron Mountain, 49801, Dickinson County, (906)776-0111. **E-mail:** tsgolf@up.net. **Web:** timberstonegolf.com.
Holes: 18. **Yards:** 6,937/5,060. **Par:** 72/72. **Course Rating:** 75.2/72.0. **Slope:** 144/131. **Green Fee:** $35/$58. **Cart Fee:** Included in Green Fee. **Walking Policy:** Unrestricted walking. **Walkability:** 4. **Opened:** 1997. **Architect:** Jerry Matthews/Paul Albanese. **Season:** May-Oct. **High:** June-Aug. **To obtain tee times:** Reservations accepted up to 12 days in advance for general public. Outings (16 or more players), Stay & Play packages, Preferred Players may book earlier. **Miscellaneous:** Reduced fees (weekdays, low season, juniors), discount packages, range (grass), club rentals, lodging (60 rooms), credit cards (MC, V, AE, D), beginner friendly (junior and adult 8-lesson beginner series).
Reader Comments: Real gem ... Some fantastic views ... Best value and best course in midwest ... Outstanding ... Premier course in the middle of nowhere, rates with Blackwolf ... Have to play it ... Fantastic course and staff ... Immaculate ... Views are tremendous ... Amazing vistas ... Challenge—pick the right tees ... More deer than players ... Great elevation changes ... It's heaven!

★★★ TOMAC WOODS GOLF COURSE
PU-14827 26 1/2 Mile Rd., Albion, 49224, Calhoun County, (517)629-8241, 20 miles E of Battle Creek.

Holes: 18. **Yards:** 6,290/5,800. **Par:** 72/72. **Course Rating:** 69.8/76.0. **Slope:** N/A. **Green Fee:** $13/$15. **Cart Fee:** $9/person. **Walking Policy:** Unrestricted walking. **Walkability:** 2. **Opened:** 1964. **Architect:** Robert Beard. **Season:** April-Oct. **High:** June-Aug. **To obtain tee times:** Call anytime. **Miscellaneous:** Reduced fees (weekdays, low season, twilight, seniors, juniors), discount packages, metal spikes, range (grass/mats), club rentals, credit cards (MC, V, D).
Reader Comments: An ego booster ... Good, not super ... Resort style, lots of challenge, but not tricked up ... Great staff ... Nice little place, pretty easy, some woods, lots of open ... Overpriced at $15.

TREETOPS SYLVAN RESORT *Service*
R-3962 Wilkinson Rd., Gaylord, 49735, Otsego County, (517)732-6711, (888)873-3867, 50 miles NW of Traverse City.

★★★★ RICK SMITH SIGNATURE
Holes: 18. **Yards:** 6,653/4,604. **Par:** 70/70. **Course Rating:** 72.8/67.0. **Slope:** 140/123. **Green Fee:** $48/$80. **Cart Fee:** Included in Green Fee. **Walking Policy:** Mandatory cart. **Walkability:** 5. **Opened:** 1993. **Architect:** Rick Smith. **Season:** April-Oct. **High:** June-Sept. **To obtain tee times:** Call with credit card to guarantee 1 year in advance. **Miscellaneous:** Reduced fees (low season, resort guests, twilight, juniors), discount packages, range (grass), club rentals, lodging (250 rooms), credit cards (MC, V, AE).
Reader Comments: Defines golf in Northern Michigan ... Fair, challenging ... Elevated tees everywhere ... Fee high ... Wild grass at edge of bunkers ... Fantasy course ... Picturesque .. Great changes in elevations ... OK but inflated ... Aging well ... Needs a clubhouse ... Best of the bunch ... Many two level greens ... Not easy, but compared to Jones' it's a breath of fresh air... Breathtaking in the fall.

★★★★ ROBERT TRENT JONES MASTERPIECE
Holes: 18. **Yards:** 7,060/4,972. **Par:** 71/71. **Course Rating:** 75.8/70.2. **Slope:** 146/124. **Green Fee:** $48/$80. **Cart Fee:** Included in Green Fee. **Walking Policy:** Mandatory cart. **Walkability:** 5. **Opened:** 1987. **Architect:** Robert Trent Jones/Roger Rulewich. **Season:** April-Oct. **High:** June-Sept. **To obtain tee times:** Call 1 year in advance, hold with a credit card. **Miscellaneous:** Reduced fees (low season, resort guests, twilight, juniors), discount packages, metal spikes, range (grass), club rentals, lodging (250 rooms), credit cards (MC, V, AE).
Notes: Ranked 15th in 1999 Best in State; 46th in 1996 America's Top 75 Upscale Courses.
Reader Comments: First class resort ... Must play ... Georgeous scenery, fast greens, bunkers, tight fairways ... A Masterpiece ... Truly playing in the clouds ... Tough, play the tees that suit your ability ... Stunning, spectacular, won't forget it ... Expensive, but great ... Course slope 146–must play! ... Too hard ... Well worth playing anytime ... Name says it all ... Awesome ... No flat lies.

★★★★½ TOM FAZIO PREMIER *Condition*
Holes: 18. **Yards:** 6,832/5,039. **Par:** 72/72. **Course Rating:** 73.2/70.1. **Slope:** 135/123. **Green Fee:** $48/$80. **Cart Fee:** Included in Green Fee. **Walking Policy:** Mandatory cart. **Walkability:** 5. **Opened:** 1992. **Architect:** Tom Fazio. **Season:** April-Oct. **High:** June-Sept. **To obtain tee times:** Call with credit card to guarantee 1 year in advance. **Miscellaneous:** Reduced fees (low season, resort guests, twilight, juniors), discount packages, metal spikes, range (grass), club rentals, lodging (250 rooms), credit cards (MC, V, AE).
Notes: Ranked 25th in 1999 Best in State.
Reader Comments: First-class resort ... Some of the best golf I've played ... The most fun I've ever had ... Great layout, fair for all levels of players ... Excellent, challenging ... Worth every penny ... AWESOME .... Picturesque–fall is heaven ... Spectacular views! ... Expensive ... Variety of holes ... Elevation changes keep you on your toes ... Best of Treetops ... Will be back!.

★★★★ TRADITION COURSE
R-3962 Wilkinson Rd., Gaylord, 49735, Otsego County, (517)732-6711, (888)873-3867, 50 miles SW of Traverse City.
Holes: 18. **Yards:** 6,467/4,907. **Par:** 72/72. **Course Rating:** N/A. **Slope:** N/A. **Green Fee:** $32/$52. **Cart Fee:** $15/person. **Walking Policy:** Unrestricted walking. **Walkability:** 3. **Opened:** 1997. **Architect:** Rick Smith. **Season:** April-Oct. **High:** June-Sept. **To obtain tee times:** Call with credit card to guarantee. **Miscellaneous:** Reduced fees (low season, resort guests, twilight, juniors), discount packages, metal spikes, range (grass), caddies, club rentals, lodging (250 rooms), credit cards (MC, V, AE).
Reader Comments: Tight sloping fairways; long, fast, beautiful greens ... Too new to be fair ... The heart of golf country ... Superb ... Best buy of Treetops ... Advertised as walkers only, but carts everywhere ... Needs to mature ... Worst of Treetops ... Beautiful in the fall! ... They ruined the walking course by allowing power carts ... Get rid of the golf carts ... Awesome, fair, challenging.

TURTLE CREEK GOLF CLUB
PU-9044 R Drive S., Burlington, 49029, Calhoun County, (517)765-2232, 10 miles SE of Battle Creek.
Holes: 27. **Yards:** 5,905/4,972. **Par:** 72/72. **Course Rating:** 69.0/68.0. **Slope:** 109/109. **Green Fee:** $9/$12. **Cart Fee:** $16/cart. **Walking Policy:** Unrestricted walking. **Walkability:** 2. **Opened:** 1970. **Season:** March-Nov. **High:** June-Aug. **To obtain tee times:** Call for weekends and holi-

days. **Miscellaneous:** Reduced fees (weekdays, low season, twilight, seniors), metal spikes, club rentals, credit cards (MC, V).

★★★ TWIN BIRCH GOLF COURSE
PU-1030 Highway 612 N.E., Kalkaska, 49646, Kalkaska County, (231)258-9691, (800)968-9699, 17 miles E of Traverse City.
Holes: 18. **Yards:** 6,133/4,969. **Par:** 72/70. **Course Rating:** 69.5/68.6. **Slope:** 115/111. **Green Fee:** $27/$27. **Cart Fee:** $24/cart. **Walking Policy:** Unrestricted walking. **Walkability:** 2.
Season: April-Oct. **High:** June-Aug. **To obtain tee times:** Call. **Miscellaneous:** Reduced fees (twilight, seniors, juniors), metal spikes, range (grass), club rentals, credit cards (MC, V).
Reader Comments: Played 'golf nut' package–54 holes with breakfast and lunch! ... Fun course ... Course was in bad shape ... Nice country course ... Pretty! ... Nice folks!.

TWIN BROOK GOLF COURSE
PU-2200 Island Hwy., Charlotte, 48813, Eaton County, (517)543-0570, 12 miles SW of Lansing.
E-mail: tbgc1@ia4u.net.
Holes: 18. **Yards:** 6,668/4,768. **Par:** 72/72. **Course Rating:** 73.1/68.3. **Slope:** 127/113. **Green Fee:** $15/$17. **Cart Fee:** $20/cart. **Walking Policy:** Unrestricted walking. **Walkability:** 2.
Opened: 1970. **Architect:** Delbert Palmer. **Season:** April-Oct. **High:** May-Aug. **To obtain tee times:** First come, first served. **Miscellaneous:** Reduced fees (weekdays, low season, twilight, seniors, juniors), range (grass), club rentals, credit cards (MC, V, AE), beginner friendly (clinics available).
Special Notes: Formerly Butternut Brook Golf Club.

★★ TWIN BROOKS GOLF CLUB
PU-1005 McKeighan Rd., Chesaning, 48616, Saginaw County, (517)845-6403, 20 miles S of Saginaw.
Holes: 18. **Yards:** 6,406/5,361. **Par:** 72/72. **Course Rating:** 71.1/71.4. **Slope:** 121/120. **Green Fee:** $18/$18. **Cart Fee:** $20/cart. **Walking Policy:** Unrestricted walking. **Walkability:** 2.
Opened: 1960. **Season:** April-Oct. **High:** June-Sept. **To obtain tee times:** Call and make tee times in advance. **Miscellaneous:** Reduced fees (seniors, juniors), metal spikes, range (grass), club rentals, credit cards (MC, V), beginner friendly (junior program, group lessons).

★★★★ TWIN LAKES GOLF CLUB *Pace*
SP-455 Twin Lakes Dr., Oakland, 48363, Oakland County, (248)650-4960, 35 miles N of Detroit.
Holes: 18. **Yards:** 6,745/4,701. **Par:** 71/71. **Course Rating:** 71.0/65.9. **Slope:** 122/109. **Green Fee:** $60/$70. **Cart Fee:** Included in Green Fee. **Walking Policy:** Unrestricted walking.
Walkability: 3. **Opened:** 1996. **Architect:** Roy Hearn/Jerry Matthews. **Season:** April-Nov. **High:** June-Aug. **To obtain tee times:** Call up to 14 days in advance. **Miscellaneous:** Reduced fees (low season, twilight, seniors, juniors), range (grass), club rentals, credit cards (MC, V, AE, D).
Reader Comments: Fun to play, one of my favorites ... Very playable, nice design, excellent greens, wide fairways, friendly staff and rangers ... This is a real good golf course ... Outstanding track ... Links-style course that makes you think ... Has potential.

★½ TWIN OAKS GOLF COURSE
PU-6710 W Freeland, Freeland, 48623, Bay County, (517)695-9746, 4 miles NW of Saginaw.
Holes: 18. **Yards:** 5,762/4,490. **Par:** 71/72. **Course Rating:** N/A. **Slope:** N/A. **Green Fee:** $18/$20. **Cart Fee:** $20/cart. **Walking Policy:** Unrestricted walking. **Walkability:** 1. **Opened:** 1965. **Season:** March-Nov. **High:** May-July. **To obtain tee times:** Phone and book 1 week in advance. **Miscellaneous:** Reduced fees (weekdays, seniors, juniors), metal spikes, club rentals, credit cards (MC, V), beginner friendly.
Special Notes: There is also a 9 hole East Course.

★★½ TYLER CREEK RECREATION AREA
PU-13495 92nd St., Alto, 49302, Kent County, (616)868-6751, 25 miles SE of Grand Rapids.
Holes: 18. **Yards:** 6,200/N/A. **Par:** 70/N/A. **Course Rating:** 69.5/N/A. **Slope:** 117/N/A. **Green Fee:** $10/$18. **Cart Fee:** $10/person. **Walking Policy:** Unrestricted walking. **Walkability:** 4.
Season: March-Nov. **High:** June-Aug. **To obtain tee times:** Call or come in up to 7 days in advance. **Miscellaneous:** Reduced fees (weekdays, low season, resort guests, seniors, juniors), discount packages, metal spikes, club rentals, lodging, credit cards (MC, V).
Reader Comments: Fun ... Tiny greens ... Needs sand traps ... First open in W. Michigan each season ... Good place for beginners ... Getting better but not great ... Rough and ragged, but friendly.

★★★ TYRONE HILLS GOLF COURSE
PU-8449 US Highway 23, Fenton, 48430, Livingston County, (810)629-5011, 20 miles S of Flint.
Holes: 18. **Yards:** 6,400/5,200. **Par:** 72/72. **Course Rating:** 70.3/69.1. **Slope:** 123/118. **Green Fee:** $19/$25. **Cart Fee:** $12/person. **Walking Policy:** Unrestricted walking. **Walkability:** 3.
Opened: 1960. **Architect:** Bruce Matthews. **Season:** April-Nov. **High:** June-Aug. **To obtain tee times:** Call up to 7 days in advance. **Miscellaneous:** Reduced fees (low season, twilight, seniors, juniors), metal spikes, credit cards (MC, V).

MICHIGAN

Reader Comments: A little bit of everything ... Outstanding staff ... Basic golf course ... Not bad ... Real nice fun.

★★★★½ UNIVERSITY OF MICHIGAN GOLF COURSE
SP-500 E. Stadium Blvd., Ann Arbor, 48104, Washtenaw County, (734)615-4653. **E-mail:** cegreen@umich.edu. **Web:** www.mgoblue.com.
Holes: 18. **Yards:** 6,687/5,331. **Par:** 71/75. **Course Rating:** 72.5/71.0. **Slope:** 135/125. **Green Fee:** $40/$50. **Cart Fee:** $24/cart. **Walking Policy:** Unrestricted walking. **Walkability:** 5.
Opened: 1931. **Architect:** Alister MacKenzie. **Season:** April-Oct. **High:** May-Sept. **To obtain tee times:** Call 7 days in advance. Call Mondays for weekends. **Miscellaneous:** Reduced fees (twilight), range (grass), club rentals, credit cards (MC, V, AE).
Notes: Ranked 11th in 1999 Best in State. 1948 USGA Junior. 1956, 1970,1994 Western Junior. 1979, 1980 Michigan Open. 1996 NCAA Regional. 1996 Michigan Amateur. Numerous Big 10 Championships.
Reader Comments: Classic ... Traditional, I'll be back ... One of the better university courses ... Great finishing hole ... True test ... Best value for a Mackenzie course anywhere ... Great design ... Hard to get on ... Great value especially for alumni ... Deep traps! ... Please mow the rough ... Practice putting before taking on these greens ... Superb layout, outstanding condition ... Wonderful!

★★★ VALLEY VIEW FARM GOLF COURSE
PU-1435 So Thomas Rd., Saginaw, 48609, Saginaw County, (517)781-1248, 4 miles W of Saginaw.
Holes: 18. **Yards:** 6,228/4,547. **Par:** 71/72. **Course Rating:** 70.1/65.8. **Slope:** 119/111. **Green Fee:** $13/$18. **Cart Fee:** $20/cart. **Walking Policy:** Unrestricted walking. **Walkability:** 1.
Opened: 1975. **Season:** April-Oct. **High:** June-Aug. **To obtain tee times:** First come, first out. Number assigned on weekends. **Miscellaneous:** Reduced fees (low season, seniors), metal spikes, credit cards (MC, V) (walking encouraged).
Reader Comments: Good course ... Fun course ... Excellent older public course ... Very competitive for all handicaps.

★★★ VASSAR GOLF & COUNTRY CLUB
SP-3509 Kirk Rd., Vassar, 48768, Tuscola County, (517)823-7221, 17 miles E of Saginaw.
Holes: 18. **Yards:** 6,439/5,482. **Par:** 72/72. **Course Rating:** 71.1/72.1. **Slope:** 126/125. **Green Fee:** $18/$29. **Cart Fee:** $11/person. **Walking Policy:** Unrestricted walking. **Walkability:** 2.
Opened: 1963. **Architect:** William Newcomb. **Season:** April-Oct. **High:** June-Sept. **To obtain tee times:** Call golf shop. **Miscellaneous:** Reduced fees (low season), range (grass), credit cards (MC, V).
Reader Comments: Hidden gem in the boondocks ... A pleasant experience ...Easy course to walk ... OK course ... Bring the big sticks–it's long ... Overpriced.

★★★ VERONA HILLS GOLF CLUB.
SP-3175 Sand Beach Rd., Bad Axe, 48413, Huron County, (517)269-8132, 7 miles E of Bad Axe.
Holes: 18. **Yards:** 6,497/5,144. **Par:** 71/72. **Course Rating:** 72.6/72.6. **Slope:** 127/127. **Green Fee:** N/A/$35. **Cart Fee:** $15/person. **Walking Policy:** Unrestricted walking. **Walkability:** 4.
Opened: 1924. **Season:** April-Nov. **High:** June-Aug. **To obtain tee times:** Call (517)269-8132. **Miscellaneous:** Range (grass), credit cards (MC, V, D).
Reader Comments: Michigan's thumb area's finest ... Catered to members ... Old layout, lots of doglegs.

★★½ VIENNA GREENS GOLF COURSE
PU-1184 E. Tobias, Clio, 48420, Genesee County, (810)686-1443, 5 miles E of Clio.
Holes: 18. **Yards:** 6,245/4,908. **Par:** 70/70. **Course Rating:** 69.8/67.4. **Slope:** 112/106. **Green Fee:** $16/$16. **Cart Fee:** $17/cart. **Walking Policy:** Unrestricted walking. **Walkability:** 1.
Opened: 1969. **Season:** April-Oct. **Miscellaneous:** Reduced fees (seniors), metal spikes, club rentals, beginner friendly.
Reader Comments: Nice course, low price.

★★★ WALLINWOOD SPRINGS GOLF CLUB
SP-8152 Weatherwax, Jenison, 49428, Ottawa County, (616)457-9920, 15 miles SW of Grand Rapids.
Holes: 18. **Yards:** 6,751/5,067. **Par:** 72/72. **Course Rating:** 72.4/69.1. **Slope:** 128/115. **Green Fee:** $20/$35. **Cart Fee:** $11/person. **Walking Policy:** Walking at certain times. **Walkability:** 3.
Opened: 1992. **Architect:** Jerry Matthews. **Season:** April-Nov. **High:** June-Aug. **To obtain tee times:** Call. **Miscellaneous:** Reduced fees (weekdays, low season, twilight, seniors), discount packages, metal spikes, club rentals, credit cards (MC, V, D).
Reader Comments: Very average ... Lots of water on the back ... Always in great condition ... Huge mosquitoes! ... Strong back 9 ... Played around trees after a big windstorm, but still a nice course.

MICHIGAN

WARREN VALLEY GOLF COURSE
PU-26116 W. Warren, Dearborn Heights, 48127, Wayne County, (313)561-1040, 10 miles SW of Detroit.

★★½ EAST COURSE
Holes: 18. **Yards:** 6,189/5,328. **Par:** 72/72. **Course Rating:** 69.1/70.0. **Slope:** 114/113. **Green Fee:** $15/$24. **Cart Fee:** $22/cart. **Walking Policy:** Unrestricted walking. **Walkability:** 4. **Opened:** 1927. **Architect:** Donald Ross. **Season:** March-Oct. **High:** May-Oct. **To obtain tee times:** Call 7 days in advance. **Miscellaneous:** Reduced fees (weekdays, low season, twilight, seniors, juniors), credit cards (MC, V).
Reader Comments: 36 holes on some great land ... Needs work! ... Used to be better ... Course is a great layout and clubhouse is new.

★★ WEST COURSE
Holes: 18. **Yards:** 6,066/5,150. **Par:** 71/71. **Course Rating:** 68.5/69.2. **Slope:** 115/114. **Green Fee:** $15/$24. **Cart Fee:** $22/cart. **Walking Policy:** Unrestricted walking. **Walkability:** 4. **Opened:** 1927. **Architect:** Donald Ross. **Season:** March-Nov. **High:** May-Oct. **To obtain tee times:** Call 7 days in advance. **Miscellaneous:** Reduced fees (weekdays, low season, twilight, seniors, juniors), credit cards (MC, V).

★★★ WASHAKIE GOLF AND RV RESORT
PU-3461 Burnside Rd., North Branch, 48461, Lapeer County, (810)688-3235, 30 miles NE of Flint.
Holes: 18. **Yards:** 5,805/5,152. **Par:** 72/72. **Course Rating:** N/A. **Slope:** N/A. **Green Fee:** $18/$20. **Cart Fee:** $21/cart. **Walking Policy:** Unrestricted walking. **Walkability:** 3. **Opened:** 1986. **Architect:** Lyle Ferrier. **Season:** April-Nov. **High:** May-Aug. **To obtain tee times:** First come, first served. **Miscellaneous:** Reduced fees (seniors), club rentals, lodging (100 rooms).
Reader Comments: Good mix of water, woods and hills ... Short, well maintained ... High traffic, good novice course ... Ego builder... Good course to warm up on.

★★★½ WAWASHKAMO GOLF CLUB
SP-British Landing Rd., Mackinac Island, 49757, Mackinac County, (906)847-3871. **Web:** www.wawashkamo.com.
Holes: 9. **Yards:** 2,999/2,380. **Par:** 36/36. **Course Rating:** 68.0/N/A. **Slope:** 115/N/A. **Green Fee:** $44/$44. **Cart Fee:** $25/cart. **Walking Policy:** Unrestricted walking. **Walkability:** 2. **Opened:** 1898. **Architect:** Alex Smith. **Season:** May-Sept. **High:** July-Aug. **Miscellaneous:** Reduced fees (twilight), club rentals, credit cards (MC, V).
Reader Comments: A bit of history: It's the oldest continually-played course in Michigan ... Golf as it should be, many turn-of-century design features ... Scottish style rough, arrive by horse drawn taxi and step back in time ... Neat 100-year-old course.

★★★ WAWONOWIN COUNTRY CLUB
SP-3432 County Rd. #478, Champion, 49814, Marquette County, (906)485-1435, 18 miles W of Marquette.
Holes: 18. **Yards:** 6,487/5,379. **Par:** 72/72. **Course Rating:** 71.1/70.8. **Slope:** 124/119. **Green Fee:** $17/$33. **Cart Fee:** $12/person. **Walking Policy:** Unrestricted walking. **Walkability:** 3. **Season:** April-Oct. **High:** June-Aug. **To obtain tee times:** Call golf shop: Members may call 7 days in advance, nonmembers 3 days in advance. **Miscellaneous:** Reduced fees (low season), range (grass), club rentals, credit cards (MC, V).
Reader Comments: Worth the drive ... Everything you want in the middle of nowhere ... Fun course, even if you can't pronounce the name ... Best you've never heard of.

WESBURN GOLF COURSE
PU-5617 S. Huron River Dr., South Rockwood, 48179, Monroe County, (734)379-3555, (888)427-3555.
Holes: 18. **Yards:** 5,981/4,816. **Par:** 72/71. **Course Rating:** N/A. **Slope:** N/A. **Green Fee:** $13/$21. **Cart Fee:** $10/person. **Walking Policy:** Unrestricted walking. **Walkability:** 2. **Opened:** 1910. **Architect:** Dodge Family. **Season:** Year-round. **High:** April-Sept. **Miscellaneous:** Reduced fees (weekdays, low season, twilight, seniors, juniors), range (grass), club rentals, credit cards (MC, V).

★★★★ WEST BRANCH COUNTRY CLUB
SP-198 Fairview, West Branch, 48661, Ogemaw County, (517)345-2501, 60 miles N of Saginaw.
Holes: 18. **Yards:** 6,402/5,436. **Par:** 72/73. **Course Rating:** 70.5/71.4. **Slope:** 122/119. **Green Fee:** $17/$33. **Cart Fee:** $15/person. **Walking Policy:** Unrestricted walking. **Walkability:** 2. **Opened:** 1928. **Architect:** William Newcomb. **Season:** April-Oct. **High:** May-Sept. **To obtain tee times:** Call golf shop up to 14 days in advance. **Miscellaneous:** Reduced fees (low season, twilight, seniors), discount packages, range (grass/mats), club rentals, credit cards (MC, V, D).
Reader Comments: Great course ... Friendly, good food ... Excellent value for golf and dining ... Lots of bunkers and trees in fairways ... Great course ... Attractive flora ... One of the best public in North Michigan ... Fairways well watered, good greens ... Very good staff.

MICHIGAN

★★ WEST OTTAWA GOLF CLUB
PU-6045 136th Ave., Holland, 49424, Ottawa County, (616)399-1678, 7 miles N of Holland.
Holes: 27. **Yards:** 6,250/5,700. **Par:** 70/67. **Course Rating:** 68.5/66.0. **Slope:** N/A. **Green Fee:** $20/$22. **Cart Fee:** $19/cart. **Walking Policy:** Unrestricted walking. **Walkability:** 1. **Opened:** 1965. **Architect:** Bruce Matthews. **Season:** March-Nov. **High:** July-Aug. **To obtain tee times:** Call golf shop (616)399-1678. **Miscellaneous:** Reduced fees (weekdays, low season, seniors, juniors), metal spikes, range (grass/mats), club rentals, credit cards (MC, V).
Special Notes: Also has additional 9 holes.

★½ WESTBROOKE GOLF COURSE
PU-26817 Beck Rd., Novi, 48734, Oakland County, (248)349-2723.
Holes: 18. **Yards:** 5,582/4,943. **Par:** 70/70. **Course Rating:** 68.5/64.9. **Slope:** 107/106. **Green Fee:** $24/$26. **Cart Fee:** $20/cart. **Walking Policy:** Unrestricted walking. **Walkability:** 1. **Season:** April-Oct. **High:** June-Sept. **To obtain tee times:** Call/walk in. **Miscellaneous:** Reduced fees (low season, twilight, seniors), metal spikes.

★★½ WESTERN GREENS GOLF COURSE
PU-2475 Johnson Rd., Marne, 49435, Ottawa County, (616)677-3677, 12 miles W of Grand Rapids.
Holes: 18. **Yards:** 6,460/5,552. **Par:** 71/73. **Course Rating:** N/A. **Slope:** N/A. **Green Fee:** $19/$20. **Cart Fee:** $20/cart. **Walking Policy:** Unrestricted walking. **Walkability:** 3. **Opened:** 1966. **Architect:** Mark DeVries. **Season:** April-Nov. **High:** June-Aug. **To obtain tee times:** Call. **Miscellaneous:** Range (grass), club rentals, credit cards (MC, V).
Reader Comments: A little rough ... Good driving range ... Well laid out ... Lost it's flair–was a nice course ... Friendly staff.

★★½ WHIFFLE TREE HILL GOLF COURSE
PU-15730 Homer Rd., Concord, 49237, Jackson County, (517)524-6655, 15 miles W of Jackson.
Holes: 18. **Yards:** 6,370/4,990. **Par:** 72/72. **Course Rating:** N/A. **Slope:** N/A. **Green Fee:** $8/$16. **Cart Fee:** $8/person. **Walking Policy:** Unrestricted walking. **Walkability:** 3. **Opened:** 1969. **Architect:** Arthur Young. **Season:** April-Oct. **High:** May-Sept. **To obtain tee times:** Call golf shop. **Miscellaneous:** Reduced fees (weekdays, low season, twilight, seniors, juniors), discount packages, metal spikes, range (grass), club rentals, credit cards (MC, V).
Reader Comments: Pretty easy, an ego booster ... Good, yet not super nice ... Course kind of resort style–lots of challenge, but not tricked up ... Great staff, nice little place, some woods, lots of open, can go low, friendly staff ... Small greens ... Fun little course.

★★★½ WHISPERING PINES GOLF CLUB
PU-2500 Whispering Pines Dr., Pinckney, 48169, Livingston County, (734)878-0009, 10 miles N of Ann Arbor.
Holes: 18. **Yards:** 6,440/4,813. **Par:** 71/73. **Course Rating:** 69.8/67.3. **Slope:** 126/117. **Green Fee:** $25/$45. **Cart Fee:** Included in Green Fee. **Walking Policy:** Walking at certain times. **Walkability:** 4. **Opened:** 1992. **Architect:** Donald Moon. **Season:** April-Oct. **High:** May-Sept. **To obtain tee times:** Call up to 7 days in advance. **Miscellaneous:** Reduced fees (weekdays, low season, twilight, seniors), credit cards (MC, V).
Reader Comments: Challenging, scenic, houses don't come into play too much ... Many blind shots make for slow play ... Hard greens ... Sloping, tight fairways ... Remains too hard for mid-handicappers ... Recent improvements make it more playable for weekend golfers ... Trees, trees, trees ... Beautiful.

★★½ WHISPERING WILLOWS GOLF COURSE
PM-20500 Newburg Rd., Livonia, 48152, Wayne County, (248)476-4493, 24 miles NW of Detroit.
Holes: 18. **Yards:** 6,056/5,424. **Par:** 70/72. **Course Rating:** 69.3/71.1. **Slope:** 114/117. **Green Fee:** $17/$25. **Cart Fee:** $24/cart. **Walking Policy:** Unrestricted walking. **Walkability:** 1. **Opened:** 1968. **Architect:** Mark DeVries. **Season:** April-Nov. **High:** June-Aug. **To obtain tee times:** Call up to 3 days in advance from noon to 7 p.m. for weekdays. Nonresidents call on Thursday after 9 a.m. for weekend. **Miscellaneous:** Reduced fees (weekdays, twilight, seniors, juniors), range (grass), club rentals, credit cards (MC, V).
Reader Comments: Good city course.

★½ WHITE BIRCH HILLS GOLF COURSE
PU-360 Ott Rd., Bay City, 48706, Bay County, (517)662-6523.
Holes: 18. **Yards:** 5,600/5,300. **Par:** 70/70. **Course Rating:** N/A. **Slope:** N/A. **Green Fee:** $15/$15. **Cart Fee:** $20/cart. **Walking Policy:** Unrestricted walking. **Walkability:** 1. **Opened:** 1949. **Season:** April-Oct. **High:** June-Aug. **To obtain tee times:** Call. **Miscellaneous:** Reduced fees (seniors, juniors), range (grass), caddies, lodging, credit cards (MC, V, D).

★★½ WHITE DEER COUNTRY CLUB
PU-1309 Bright Angel Dr., Prudenville, 48651, Roscommon County, (517)366-5812, 70 miles N of Saginaw.

Holes: 18. **Yards:** 6,311/5,290. **Par:** 72/72. **Course Rating:** 68.8/69.9. **Slope:** 115/116. **Green Fee:** $17/$18. **Cart Fee:** $9/person. **Walking Policy:** Unrestricted walking. **Walkability:** 1. **Opened:** 1965. **Architect:** Glenn Gulder. **Season:** April-Oct. **High:** July-Aug. **To obtain tee times:** Call golf shop. **Miscellaneous:** Reduced fees (low season, twilight, juniors), discount packages, metal spikes, club rentals, credit cards (MC, V, D), beginner friendly (adult education beginner lessons, junior league).
Reader Comments: Best owners I've ever met ... Nice for family golf ... Lots of play ... Flat and wide open ... Greens large and smooth ... Friendly help ... Very good course, back 9 needs some improvement.

★★½ WHITE LAKE OAKS GOLF COURSE
PM-991 Williams Lake Rd., White Lake, 48386, Oakland County, (248)698-2700, 5 miles W of Pontiac.
Holes: 18. **Yards:** 5,738/4,900. **Par:** 70/71. **Course Rating:** 67.1/67.9. **Slope:** 111/114. **Green Fee:** $12/$20. **Cart Fee:** $20/cart. **Walking Policy:** Unrestricted walking. **Walkability:** 2. **Opened:** 1940. **Season:** April-Nov. **High:** June-Aug. **To obtain tee times:** Call on Wednesday at 6:15 p.m. for upcoming weekend. **Miscellaneous:** Reduced fees (weekdays, low season, twilight, seniors, juniors), club rentals, credit cards (MC, V).
Reader Comments: Great for a fast round ... Nicely-conditioned-shorter muny with lots of play ... Good greens!.

★★★½ WHITE PINE NATIONAL GOLF CLUB
PU-3450 N. Hubbard Lake Rd., P.O. Box 130, Hubbard Lake, 49747, Alcona County, (517)736-3279, 30 miles S of Alpena.
Holes: 18. **Yards:** 6,883/5,268. **Par:** 72/72. **Course Rating:** 72.7/70.5. **Slope:** 127/124. **Green Fee:** $38/$48. **Cart Fee:** Included in Green Fee. **Walking Policy:** Walking at certain times. **Walkability:** 4. **Opened:** 1992. **Architect:** Bruce Wolfrom/Clem Wolfrom. **Season:** April-Nov. **High:** May-Sept. **To obtain tee times:** Call golf shop. **Miscellaneous:** Reduced fees (weekdays, low season, twilight, seniors, juniors), discount packages, range (grass), club rentals, credit cards (MC, V, D).
Reader Comments: A trip through nature, I loved it ... Put on your list of places to play ... Little Augusta-gives you a Georgia feel ... Good layout! ... Playable ... Lot of different holes ... Do play ... It was lots of fun ... Still too new—a good layout with better days ahead.

WHITEFORD VALLEY GOLF CLUB
PU-7980 Beck Rd, Ottawa Lake, 49267, Monroe County, 734)856-4545, 3 miles N of Toledo, OH.
★ EAST COURSE
Holes: 18. **Yards:** 6,631/5,176. **Par:** 72/71. **Course Rating:** 70.8/68.2. **Slope:** 116/108. **Green Fee:** $13/$24. **Cart Fee:** $24/cart. **Walking Policy:** Unrestricted walking. **Walkability:** 2. **Opened:** 1995. **Architect:** Harley Hodges. **Season:** Year-round. **High:** April-Oct. **To obtain tee times:** Call up to 14 days in advance. **Miscellaneous:** Reduced fees (low season, twilight, seniors, juniors), metal spikes, range (grass), club rentals, credit cards (MC, V, D).
★★ NORTH COURSE
Holes: 18. **Yards:** 6,808/5,677. **Par:** 72/73. **Course Rating:** 71.8/71.4. **Slope:** 123/119. **Green Fee:** $13/$24. **Cart Fee:** $22/cart. **Walking Policy:** Unrestricted walking. **Walkability:** 2. **Opened:** 1995. **Architect:** Harley Hodges. **Season:** Year-round. **High:** April-Oct. **To obtain tee times:** Call up to 14 days in advance. **Miscellaneous:** Reduced fees (low season, twilight, seniors, juniors), discount packages, metal spikes, range (grass), club rentals, credit cards (MC, V, D).
★★ SOUTH COURSE
Holes: 18. **Yards:** 6,659/5,195. **Par:** 72/72. **Course Rating:** 70.4/68.7. **Slope:** 116/109. **Green Fee:** $13/$24. **Cart Fee:** $22/cart. **Walking Policy:** Unrestricted walking. **Walkability:** 2. **Opened:** 1995. **Architect:** Harley Hodges. **Season:** Year-round. **High:** April-Oct. **To obtain tee times:** Call up to 14 days in advance. **Miscellaneous:** Metal spikes, range (grass), club rentals, credit cards (MC, V, D).
WEST COURSE
Holes: 18. **Yards:** 7,004/5,318. **Par:** 72/71. **Course Rating:** 72.6/69.8. **Slope:** 122/109. **Green Fee:** $13/$24. **Cart Fee:** $22/cart. **Walking Policy:** Unrestricted walking. **Walkability:** 2. **Opened:** 1995. **Architect:** Harley Hodges. **Season:** Year-round. **High:** April-Oct. **To obtain tee times:** Call up to 14 days in advance. **Miscellaneous:** Reduced fees (low season, twilight, seniors, juniors), metal spikes, range (grass), club rentals, credit cards (MC, V, D).

★★★★ WHITTAKER WOODS GOLF CLUB
PU-12578 Wilson Rd., New Buffalo, 49117, Berrien County, (616)469-3400, 70 miles E of Chicago.
Holes: 18. **Yards:** 7,011/4,912. **Par:** 72/72. **Course Rating:** 74.3/68.6. **Slope:** 144/121. **Green Fee:** $55/$75. **Cart Fee:** Included in Green Fee. **Walking Policy:** Mandatory cart. **Walkability:** 5. **Opened:** 1996. **Architect:** Ken Killian. **Season:** Year-round. **High:** June-Aug. **To obtain tee**

times: Call 7 days in advance. **Miscellaneous:** Reduced fees (weekdays, twilight, seniors), range (grass), club rentals, credit cards (MC, V, AE, D).

Reader Comments: Challenging ... Like a private course during the week ... Excellent layout offers great shot values ... Overrated, overpriced ... Nice layout, but in mediocre condition ... Tough ... Beautiful, wooded with carries over marsh ... Will be great, hit it straight ... Much too difficult for average golfer... No 2 holes alike, nice scenery, lots of trees.

★★½ WILLOW BROOK PUBLIC GOLF CLUB
PU-311 W. Maple, Byron, 48418, Shiawassee County, (810)266-4660.
Yards: 6,077/4,578. **Par:** 72/72. **Course Rating:** 70.6/67.3. **Slope:** 122/111. **Green Fee:** $15/$20. **Walkability:** N/A. **Miscellaneous:** Metal spikes.
Reader Comments: Hard to find, worth the effort ... Charming little 18-hole course in a quaint town ... Some scenic and interesting holes with quirky doglegs ... Good course ... Aeration marks on greens ... Very nice.

★★★½ WILLOW METROPARK GOLF COURSE
PU-22900 Huron River Dr., New Boston, 48164, Wayne County, (734)753-4040, (800)234-6534, 4 miles S of Romulus.
Holes: 18. **Yards:** 6,378/5,278. **Par:** 71/72. **Course Rating:** 71.0/70.9. **Slope:** 126/122. **Green Fee:** $19/$23. **Cart Fee:** $10/person. **Walking Policy:** Unrestricted walking. **Walkability:** 3. **Opened:** 1979. **Architect:** William Newcomb. **Season:** April-Nov. **High:** May-Aug. **To obtain tee times:** Call up to 7 days in advance. **Miscellaneous:** Reduced fees (weekdays, seniors, juniors), range (grass), credit cards (MC, V).
Reader Comments: Dogleg city here–wise use of irons off tee mandatory ... Priced great, very playable, slow play ... Water, trees ... Needs better maintenance ... Good layout and conditions.

★★½ WINDING BROOK GOLF CLUB
PU-8240 S. Genuine, Shepherd, 48883, Isabella County, (517)828-5688, 6 miles S of Mt. Pleasant.
Holes: 18. **Yards:** 6,614/5,015. **Par:** 72/72. **Course Rating:** 72.6/69.2. **Slope:** 127/115. **Green Fee:** $17/$22. **Cart Fee:** $10/person. **Walking Policy:** Unrestricted walking. **Walkability:** 3. **Opened:** 1970. **Season:** March-Nov. **High:** June-Aug. **To obtain tee times:** Call. **Miscellaneous:** Reduced fees (weekdays, low season, twilight, seniors, juniors), discount packages, metal spikes, range (grass), club rentals, credit cards (MC, V, D).
Reader Comments: Good value, lots of tough holes ... Wide open ... Beautiful course, short ... Has potential, needs some work.

★★½ WINDING CREEK GOLF COURSE
PU-4514 Ottogan St., Holland, 49423, Allegan County, (616)396-4516, 20 miles SW of Grand Rapids.
Holes: 27. **Yards:** 6,665/5,027. **Par:** 72/72. **Course Rating:** 71.5/68.6. **Slope:** 128/112. **Green Fee:** $23/$23. **Cart Fee:** $23/person. **Walking Policy:** Unrestricted walking. **Walkability:** 1. **Opened:** 1968. **Architect:** Bruce Matthews/Jerry Matthews. **Season:** April-Oct. **High:** May-Aug. **To obtain tee times:** Call or come in 2 days in advance. Tee times are taken 1 week in advance. **Miscellaneous:** Reduced fees (weekdays, low season, twilight, seniors, juniors), range (grass), club rentals, credit cards (MC, V).
Reader Comments: Friendliest staff I've encountered ... Only game in town–very crowded! ... Nothing exciting ... I'll play it once a year ... Great course.

WOLVERINE GOLF CLUB
PU-17201 25 Mile Rd., Macomb, 48042, Macomb County, (810)781-5544, (800)783-4653, 30 miles N of Detroit.
★★★ BLUE/GREEN
Holes: 18. **Yards:** 6,455/4,967. **Par:** 72/72. **Course Rating:** 70.3/69.6. **Slope:** 120/116. **Green Fee:** $16/$31. **Cart Fee:** $14/person. **Walking Policy:** Walking at certain times. **Walkability:** 1. **Opened:** 1965. **Architect:** Jerry Matthews. **Season:** Year-round weather permitting. **High:** May-Sept. **To obtain tee times:** Call up to 14 days in advance. **Miscellaneous:** Reduced fees (weekdays, low season, twilight, seniors, juniors), range (grass/mats), club rentals, credit cards (MC, V, AE, D), beginner friendly (beginner ladies leagues with clinics).
Reader Comments: Course is always in good shape ... Ho-hum layout ... Overrated course ... Flat practice course ... A shooting gallery ... Nice new range! ... Flat, basic golf for too much money ... Treadmill, but a lot of fun ... Easy to get on, easy to play ... Lot of holes in bad shape.
★★½ RED/GOLD
Holes: 18. **Yards:** 6,443/4,825. **Par:** 72/72. **Course Rating:** 70.7/69.5. **Slope:** 122/119. **Green Fee:** $16/$31. **Cart Fee:** $14/person. **Walking Policy:** Mandatory cart. **Walkability:** 2. **Opened:** 1965. **Architect:** Jerry Matthews. **Season:** Year-round. **High:** May-Sept. **To obtain tee times:** Call up to 14 days in advance. **Miscellaneous:** Reduced fees (low season, twilight, seniors, juniors), range (grass/mats), club rentals, credit cards (MC, V, AE, D), beginner friendly (clinics, leagues).
Reader Comments: Not much challenge ... Nice layout, good condition.

★★½ WHITE
Holes: 9. **Yards:** 3,281/2,539. **Par:** 36/36. **Course Rating:** 35.5/34.5. **Slope:** 117/114. **Green Fee:** $16/$31. **Cart Fee:** $14/person. **Walking Policy:** Unrestricted walking. **Walkability:** 2. **Opened:** 1965. **Architect:** Jerry Matthews. **Season:** Year-round. **High:** May-Sept. **Miscellaneous:** Reduced fees (weekdays, low season, twilight, seniors, juniors), range (grass/mats), club rentals, credit cards (MC, V, AE, D), beginner friendly (clinics and leagues). **Reader Comments:** Good value.

★★★ WOODFIELD GOLF & COUNTRY CLUB
PU-1 Golfside Dr., Grand Blanc, 48439, Genesee County, (810)695-4653, 30 miles NW of Detroit.
Holes: 18. **Yards:** 6,780/5,071. **Par:** 72/72. **Course Rating:** 73.3/68.3. **Slope:** 133/121. **Green Fee:** $30/$40. **Cart Fee:** Included in Green Fee. **Walking Policy:** Unrestricted walking. **Walkability:** N/A. **Opened:** 1994. **Architect:** Raymond Floyd/Harry F. Bowers. **Season:** April-Oct. **High:** June-Aug. **To obtain tee times:** Call up to 30 days in advance. **Miscellaneous:** Reduced fees (weekdays, low season, twilight, seniors, juniors), discount packages, metal spikes, range (grass/mats), club rentals, credit cards (MC, V, AE). **Reader Comments:** Very enjoyable–secluded ... Some good holes ... Great course, great clubhouse ... Very nice clubhouse, nice course too! ... Well spaced, tough greens.

WOODLAND HILLS GOLF CLUB
PU-320 N. Gates Rd., Sandusky, 48471, Sanilac County, (810)648-2400, (800)648-2400, 65 miles E of Saginaw.
Holes: 18. **Yards:** 6,606/5,441. **Par:** 71/71. **Course Rating:** 70.7/71.0. **Slope:** 121/117. **Green Fee:** $13/$17. **Cart Fee:** $10/person. **Walking Policy:** Walking at certain times. **Walkability:** 3. **Opened:** 1980. **Architect:** Dick Blank. **Season:** April-Oct. **High:** May-Aug. **To obtain tee times:** Call. **Miscellaneous:** Reduced fees (twilight, seniors), discount packages, metal spikes, range (grass), club rentals, credit cards (MC, V), beginner friendly (lessons, start-up products).

★★★ WOODLAWN GOLF CLUB
PU-4634 Treat Highway, Adrian, 49221, Lenawee County, (517)263-3288, 25 miles NW of Toledo, OH.
Holes: 18. **Yards:** 6,080/4,686. **Par:** 71/71. **Course Rating:** 69.0/66.0. **Slope:** 116/112. **Green Fee:** $14/$20. **Cart Fee:** $10/person. **Walking Policy:** Unrestricted walking. **Walkability:** 1. **Opened:** 1954. **Season:** April-Oct. **High:** May-Sept. **To obtain tee times:** Call golf shop. **Miscellaneous:** Reduced fees (low season, twilight, seniors, juniors), metal spikes, club rentals. **Reader Comments:** Nice mature course ... Nice course ... Crowded ... Nasty mosquitoes ... Home course for league play ... Fun to play.

★½ AFTON ALPS GOLF COURSE
PU-6600 Peller Ave. S., Hastings, 55033, Washington County, (651)436-1320, (800)328-1328, 20 miles E of St. Paul.
Holes: 18. **Yards:** 5,528/4,866. **Par:** 72/72. **Course Rating:** 67.0/68.4. **Slope:** 108/114. **Green Fee:** $16/$20. **Cart Fee:** $18/cart. **Walking Policy:** Unrestricted walking. **Walkability:** 3.
Opened: 1989. **Architect:** Paul Augustine. **Season:** April-Oct. **High:** June-Aug. **To obtain tee times:** Call golf shop. **Miscellaneous:** Reduced fees (weekdays, seniors), metal spikes, club rentals, credit cards (MC, V).

★★½ ALBANY GOLF COURSE
PM-500 Church Ave., Albany, 56307, Stearns County, (320)845-2505, 15 miles W of St. Cloud.
Holes: 18. **Yards:** 6,415/5,268. **Par:** 72/74. **Course Rating:** 70.7/69.0. **Slope:** 122/113. **Green Fee:** $20/$23. **Cart Fee:** $22/cart. **Walking Policy:** Unrestricted walking. **Walkability:** 2.
Opened: 1960. **Architect:** Willie Kidd, Sr. **Season:** April-Oct. **High:** May-Aug. **To obtain tee times:** Call up to 3 days in advance. **Miscellaneous:** Reduced fees (seniors, juniors), metal spikes, range (grass/mats), club rentals, credit cards (MC, V).
Reader Comments: Nice, rural course ... Very good value, wide-open course ... Decent course, good clubhouse ... Tougher than it looks ... Next to the Interstate ... Small, hard greens.

★★★★ ALBION RIDGES GOLF COURSE *Value*
PU-7771 20th St. NW, Annadale, 55302, Wright County, (320)963-5500, (800)430-7888, 40 miles W of Minneapolis. **E-mail:** albion@teemaster.com. **Web:** teemaster.com.
Holes: 18. **Yards:** 6,555/4,728. **Par:** 72/72. **Course Rating:** 71.1/67.7. **Slope:** 129/115. **Green Fee:** $20/$26. **Cart Fee:** $20/cart. **Walking Policy:** Unrestricted walking. **Walkability:** 3.
Opened: 1991. **Architect:** Todd Severud. **Season:** April-Nov. **High:** May-Sept. **Miscellaneous:** Reduced fees (weekdays, seniors, juniors), range (grass), club rentals, credit cards (MC, V, D).
Reader Comments: Great greens, fast and rolling ... Fun course. Links type ... New, clean, well-kept ... Friendly family operation ... A nice course hidden in the country ... Wide open ... Country club condition public course ... Hilly ... Best greens I played this year ... A gem ... Outstanding fairways.

★★★★ ALEXANDRIA GOLF CLUB
C.R. 42, Alexandria, 56308, Douglas County, (320)763-3605.
Yards: 6,344/5,205. **Par:** 72/73. **Course Rating:** 70.5/70.1. **Slope:** 128/124. **Green Fee:** $38/$38. **Walkability:** N/A. **Architect:** Gerry Pirkl/Donald Brauer. **Miscellaneous:** Metal spikes.
Reader Comments: Good, classic track ... Small but fair greens. Back nine is tight ... Well-maintained ... Beautiful, mature trees, fairways are gorgeous ... Nice par 5s ... Tom Lehman's high school course ... Traditional lake views ... One green shaped like state of Minnesota, one like Oklahoma, one like Texas.

★★★½ BAKER NATIONAL GOLF COURSE
PM-2935 Parkview Dr., Medina, 55340, Hennepin County, (612)473-0800, 20 miles W of Minneapolis.
Holes: 18. **Yards:** 6,762/5,395. **Par:** 72/72. **Course Rating:** 73.9/72.5. **Slope:** 135/128. **Green Fee:** $29/$29. **Cart Fee:** $24/cart. **Walking Policy:** Unrestricted walking. **Walkability:** 4.
Opened: 1990. **Architect:** Michael Hurdzan. **Season:** April-Oct. **High:** June-Aug. **To obtain tee times:** Call 3 days in advance. **Miscellaneous:** Reduced fees (seniors, juniors), range (grass), club rentals, credit cards (MC, V, D).
Reader Comments: Beautiful setting ... Mammoth driving range ... Environmentally sound ... Some outstanding holes, but a grueling walk ... Great public track ... Can be difficult ... Almost every hole a 'signature' ... Keep your slice in the bag ... If you stray of fairways, we'll see you later ... Nature lovers' delight.

★★★ BALMORAL GOLF COURSE
PU-Rte.3 Box 119, Battle Lake, 56515, Otter Tail County, (218)864-5414, 9 miles N of Battle Lake.
Holes: 18. **Yards:** 6,144/5,397. **Par:** 72/72. **Course Rating:** 69.3/71.2. **Slope:** 120/120. **Green Fee:** $16/$27. **Cart Fee:** $20/cart. **Walking Policy:** Unrestricted walking. **Walkability:** 3.
Opened: 1961. **Architect:** Arnold Hemquist. **Season:** April-Oct. **High:** June-Aug. **To obtain tee times:** Call golf shop (or in person) to make tee times. Tee times taken 1 week in advance.
Miscellaneous: Reduced fees (weekdays, twilight), club rentals, credit cards (MC, V, D), beginner friendly.
Reader Comments: Northern Minnesota course, carved out of the woods ... Kept in excellent condition ... Challenging design makes you think ... Very tight course, many trees ... Pretty ... Relaxed ma-and-pa atmosphere.

★★★½ BELLWOOD OAKS GOLF COURSE *Value+*
PU-13239 210th St., Hastings, 55033, Dakota County, (651)437-4141, 25 miles SE of St. Paul.
Holes: 18. **Yards:** 6,775/5,707. **Par:** 73/74. **Course Rating:** 72.5/72.3. **Slope:** 123/126. **Green Fee:** $19/$23. **Cart Fee:** $24/cart. **Walking Policy:** Unrestricted walking. **Walkability:** 3.
Opened: 1972. **Architect:** Don Raskob. **Season:** April-Nov. **High:** May-Sept. **To obtain tee**

times: Call 5 days in advance. **Miscellaneous:** Reduced fees (weekdays, seniors), discount packages, range (grass), club rentals, credit cards (MC, V).
Reader Comments: Gets better every year ... Well maintained. Friendly service ... Easy to get tee times ... Can't beat the value. Pretty course with huge oak trees ... A hidden gem ... Rural setting ... Tough finishing holes ... Nice, quiet and not crowded ... Deceptively long ... Tough last four holes ... Fun ... Hilly ... Only complaint: flat greens.

★★★★ BEMIDJI TOWN & COUNTRY CLUB
R-Birchmont Dr. N.E., Bemidji, 56601, Beltrami County, (218)586-2590, 220 miles NW of Minneapolis/St. Paul.
Holes: 18. **Yards:** 6,535/5,058. **Par:** 72/72. **Course Rating:** 71.8/69.1. **Slope:** 127/120. **Green Fee:** $20/$30. **Cart Fee:** $23/cart. **Walking Policy:** Unrestricted walking. **Walkability:** 3.
Opened: 1920. **Architect:** Joel Goldstrand. **Season:** April-Oct. **High:** June-Aug. **To obtain tee times:** Call golf shop. **Miscellaneous:** Reduced fees (low season, resort guests, twilight), metal spikes, range (grass), club rentals, credit cards (MC, V, AE, D).
Reader Comments: Picturesque setting ... Beautiful in fall ... Wonderful pine-lined fairways ... Fair test for all abilities ... Have to play once ... Variety of holes ... Very hilly ... Scenic holes overlook area lakes ... Charming resort course ... Heavy play, but handled well.

★★★★ BLUEBERRY PINES GOLF CLUB
SP-N. Highway 71, Menahga, 56464, Wadena County, (218)564-4653, (800)652-4940, 115 miles NE of Fargo, ND.
Holes: 18. **Yards:** 6,663/5,024. **Par:** 72/72. **Course Rating:** 72.6/69.3. **Slope:** 132/123. **Green Fee:** $25/$28. **Cart Fee:** $24/cart. **Walking Policy:** Walking at certain times. **Walkability:** 3.
Opened: 1991. **Architect:** Joel Goldstrand. **Season:** April-Oct. **High:** June-Aug. **To obtain tee times:** Call up to 7 days in advance. **Miscellaneous:** Reduced fees (low season, twilight, seniors, juniors), range (grass), club rentals, credit cards (MC, V, AE, D).
Reader Comments: Huge log-cabin clubhouse ... Great course, nice facilities ... Very tight fairways ... Golf and nature in perfect harmony ... Scenic ... Tight and long layout ... Testy greens, lots of breaks ... Difficult to walk ... Ya gotta love the covered bridge ... Northwoods gem.

★★½ BLUFF CREEK GOLF COURSE
PU-1025 Creekwood, Chaska, 55318, Carver County, (612)445-5685, 20 miles SW of Minneapolis. **E-mail:** readygolfres.com.
Holes: 18. **Yards:** 6,234/5,785. **Par:** 70/76. **Course Rating:** 69.8/73.2. **Slope:** 118/125. **Green Fee:** $15/$29. **Cart Fee:** $28/cart. **Walking Policy:** Unrestricted walking. **Walkability:** 4.
Opened: 1972. **Architect:** Gerry Pirkl/Donald G. Brauer. **Season:** April-Nov. **High:** June-Aug. **To obtain tee times:** Weekdays call up to 7 days in advance. Weekends or Holidays call the previous Wednesday. **Miscellaneous:** Reduced fees (weekdays, twilight, seniors, juniors), metal spikes, range (mats), club rentals, credit cards (MC, V), beginner friendly (starter tee boxes).
Reader Comments: Could be a great value if it were better maintained ... Long, but fairly easy ... No memorable features ... Slow greens ... Clubhouse needs improvement ... Could be great layout with some work ... Needs character.

BRAEMAR GOLF COURSE
PU-6364 John Harris Dr., Edina, 55439, Hennepin County, (612)826-6799, 8 miles SW of Minneapolis.
Holes: 27. **Green Fee:** $26/$26. **Cart Fee:** $24/cart. **Walking Policy:** Unrestricted walking. **Walkability:** 3. **Opened:** 1964. **Architect:** Don Brauer. **Season:** April-Oct. **High:** May-Sept. **To obtain tee times:** First come, first served. **Miscellaneous:** Reduced fees (low season, juniors), range (grass/mats), caddies, club rentals, credit cards (MC, V, AE, D), beginner friendly (basic golf classes, large junior program)

★★★½ CASTLE/HAYS
Yards: 6,739/5,702. **Par:** 71/73. **Course Rating:** 71.9/72.7. **Slope:** 125/126. .
Reader Comments: Traditional ... Three very different, very enjoyable nines. Difficult to get tee time unless you're an Edina resident ... Great service ... Good layout and in good shape ... New nine has some holes that need developing ... Very well kept ... Too busy for walk-on play ... Lots of water.

★★★½ CLUNIE/CASTLE
Yards: 6,660/5,579. **Par:** 72/73. **Course Rating:** 72.2/72.5. **Slope:** 129/125.
Reader Comments: Excellent variety of shots, scenic ... New nine is challenging ... Good ranger system ... Old 18 long; new nine short and tight ... Traditional city course ... Gets lots of play ... All 27 holes are an outstanding value.

★★★½ HAYS/CLUNIE
Yards: 6,330/5,361. **Par:** 71/72. **Course Rating:** 70.5/71.0. **Slope:** 126/120.
Reader Comments: Overcrowded, underwatered ... Outstanding value ... New nine OK; old nines great ... Nice public course.
Special Notes: There is also a 9-hole Executive Golf Course.

MINNESOTA

BREEZY POINT RESORT
★★½ TRADITIONAL COURSE
R-HCR 2 Box 70, Breezy Point, 56472, Crow Wing County, (218)562-7166, (800)950-4961, 20 miles N of Brainerd.
Holes: 18. **Yards:** 5,192/5,127. **Par:** 68/72. **Course Rating:** 62.9/65.5. **Slope:** 114/111. **Green Fee:** $27/$30. **Cart Fee:** $14/person. **Walking Policy:** Unrestricted walking. **Walkability:** 3. **Opened:** 1930. **Architect:** Bill Fawcett. **Season:** April-Oct. **High:** June-Sept. **To obtain tee times:** Call 800 number 2 days in advance. **Miscellaneous:** Reduced fees (weekdays, low season, twilight, juniors), discount packages, metal spikes, club rentals, lodging, credit cards (MC, V, AE, D, Diners Club).
Reader Comments: Typical resort course ... Short but very challenging ... Well-used resort course ... Front nine open, back nine will get ya ... Narrow fairways ... Bring a chain saw.
★★★½ WHITEBIRCH GOLF COURSE
R-HCR 2 Box 70 County Rd. 11, Breezy Point, 56472, Crow Wing County, (218)562-7177, (800)950-4960, 20 miles N of Brainerd.
Holes: 18. **Yards:** 6,704/4,711. **Par:** 72/72. **Course Rating:** 71.8/72.8. **Slope:** 124/123. **Green Fee:** $32/$37. **Cart Fee:** $14/person. **Walking Policy:** Unrestricted walking. **Walkability:** 5. **Opened:** 1981. **Architect:** Landecker/Hubbard. **Season:** April-Oct. **High:** June-Sept. **To obtain tee times:** Call up to 2 days in advance. **Miscellaneous:** Reduced fees (weekdays, low season, twilight, juniors), discount packages, range (grass), club rentals, lodging, credit cards (MC, V, AE, D, Diners Club).
Reader Comments: Wide fairways ... Another picturesque northern Minnesota course ... Last four holes are as good as any ... Fun to play. Some very interesting holes ... Course is very fair ... Spectacular clubhouse ... Will be a great course when it matures ... A challenge to walk. Keep an eye out for deer ... Hilly.

★★★ BROOKTREE MUNICIPAL GOLF COURSE
PM-1369 Cherry St., Owatonna, 55060, Steele County, (507)444-2467, 40 miles S of Minneapolis/St. Paul.
Holes: 18. **Yards:** 6,648/5,534. **Par:** 71/72. **Course Rating:** 71.9/71.3. **Slope:** 121/121. **Green Fee:** $14/$16. **Cart Fee:** $17. **Walking Policy:** Unrestricted walking. **Walkability:** N/A. **Opened:** 1957. **Architect:** Gerry Pirkl/Donald G. Brauer. **Season:** April-Oct. **High:** June-Aug. **To obtain tee times:** Call 3 days in advance. **Miscellaneous:** Reduced fees (weekdays), metal spikes, club rentals.
Reader Comments: Fast greens. Beautiful and challenging. We'll go back ... Two nines totally opposite. Front is flat, open; back is tight, hilly ... Fun course ... Nice trees, rolling fairways.

★★★ BROOKVIEW GOLF COURSE
PM-200 Brookview Pkwy., Golden Valley, 55426, Hennepin County, (612)512-2300, 5 miles W of Minneapolis.
Holes: 18. **Yards:** 6,369/5,463. **Par:** 72/72. **Course Rating:** 70.3/71.4. **Slope:** 127/124. **Green Fee:** $20/$26. **Cart Fee:** $22/cart. **Walking Policy:** Unrestricted walking. **Walkability:** 3. **Opened:** 1969. **Architect:** Garrett Gill. **Season:** April-Oct. **High:** June-Sept. **To obtain tee times:** Call 2 days in advance. Patron card holders may call from 3 to 7 days in advance. **Miscellaneous:** Reduced fees (twilight), range (grass/mats), club rentals, credit cards (MC, V).
Reader Comments: Very busy ... By the freeway ... Greens OK ... A challenge ... Goose problem ... Old city course ... Recovering from flooding ... Easy walking ... Crowded, but fun... Great value for popular course ... Will improve.

BUNKER HILLS GOLF COURSE
PU-Highway 242 and Foley Blvd., Coon Rapids, 55448, Anoka County, (612)755-4141, 15 miles N of Minneapolis.
Holes: 27. **Green Fee:** $26/$30. **Cart Fee:** $24/cart. **Walking Policy:** Unrestricted walking. **Walkability:** 2. **Opened:** 1968. **Architect:** David Gill. **Season:** April-Nov. **High:** June-Aug. **To obtain tee times:** Call 3 days in advance after 9 a.m. **Miscellaneous:** Reduced fees (seniors, juniors), metal spikes, range (grass/mats), club rentals, credit cards (MC, V, AE), beginner friendly (beginner golf clinics).
★★★★ EAST/WEST
Yards: 6,901/5,809. **Par:** 72/73. **Course Rating:** 73.4/74.2. **Slope:** 133/128.
Notes: Ranked 35th in 1996 America's Top 75 Affordable Courses.
Reader Comments: One of best public experiences I've had ... Recommend all three 9s ... I know why the senior tour is here ... Great condition ... Challenging holes ... Busy ... Didn't meet expectations ... Meat-and-potatoes golf ... Newest Executive 9 weak; original 18 outstanding ... For above-average golfers ...Three distinctly different nines.
★★★★ NORTH/EAST
Yards: 6,799/5,618. **Par:** 72/72. **Course Rating:** 72.7/72.6. **Slope:** 130/126.
Reader Comments: East.course enjoyable ... Hilly ... North is tough, tight 9 ... Can be long.
★★★★ NORTH/WEST
Yards: 6,938/5,779. **Par:** 72/73. **Course Rating:** 73.1/73.6. **Slope:** 135/130.

MINNESOTA

Reader Comments: The best of the combos. Pine to Parkland ... Nothing tricky; just solid golf.
Special Notes: Also has a 9-hole executive course. Discount for softspikes.

★★★½ CANNON GOLF CLUB
SP-8606 295th St. E., Cannon Falls, 55009, Dakota County, (507)263-3126, 25 miles SE of St. Paul.
Holes: 18. Yards: 6,157/4,988. Par: 71/71. Course Rating: 69.5/70.1. Slope: 127/125. Green Fee: $23/$28. Cart Fee: $27/cart. Walking Policy: Unrestricted walking. Walkability: 3.
Opened: 1927. Architect: Joel Goldstrand. Season: April-Oct. To obtain tee times: Call up to 7 days in advance. Miscellaneous: Reduced fees (weekdays, twilight, seniors, juniors), metal spikes, range (grass), caddies, club rentals, credit cards (MC, V).
Reader Comments: Short course, but not easy ... Fast greens ... Hidden gem ... Very tight fairways ... Lots of water ... Challenging but very enjoyable ... Greens small but fair... Neat little course ... Hilly.

★½ CARRIAGE HILLS COUNTRY CLUB
PU-3535 Wescott Woodlands Dr., Eagan, 55123, Dakota County, (651)452-7211.
Holes: 18. Yards: 5,800/4,920. Par: 71/72. Course Rating: 67.5/68.4. Slope: 119/111. Green Fee: $19/$25. Cart Fee: $19/cart. Walking Policy: Unrestricted walking. Walkability: 4.
Opened: 1965. Season: April-Oct. High: June-Aug. To obtain tee times: Call up to 7 days in advance. Miscellaneous: Reduced fees (weekdays, twilight, seniors, juniors), club rentals, credit cards (MC, V).

★★½ CASTLE HIGHLANDS GOLF COURSE
SP-City Road 23, Highway 71, Bemidji, 56601, Beltrami County, (218)586-2681, 230 miles N of Minneapolis.
Holes: 18. Yards: 5,246/4,448. Par: 70/70. Course Rating: 65.8/65.5. Slope: 111/112. Green Fee: N/A/$26. Cart Fee: $20/cart. Walking Policy: Unrestricted walking. Walkability: 3.
Opened: 1970. Architect: Ray Castle. Season: April-Oct. High: May-Sept. To obtain tee times: Call golf shop. Miscellaneous: Range (grass/mats), club rentals, credit cards (MC, V, D).
Reader Comments: Beautiful course in the woods. Fairly easy ... Peaceful... Short, wooded ... Hit it straight ... Slow greens.

★★★ CEDAR RIVER COUNTRY CLUB
PU-Hwy. 56 W., Adams, 55909, Mower County, (507)582-3595, 16 miles SE of Austin.
Holes: 18. Yards: 6,298/5,553. Par: 72/74. Course Rating: 69.3/71.3. Slope: 117/119. Green Fee: $20/$20. Cart Fee: $20/cart. Walking Policy: Unrestricted walking. Walkability: 2.
Opened: 1969. Architect: Bob Carlson. Season: March-Nov. High: June-Aug. To obtain tee times: Call golf shop. Miscellaneous: Range (grass), club rentals, credit cards (MC, V).
Reader Comments: Lots of pines ... Rewarding ... Rural setting ... You wouldn't expect to find a course like this here.

★★★ CEDAR VALLEY GOLF COURSE
SP-County Rd. 9, Winona, 55987, Winona County, (507)457-3129, 100 miles S of Minneapolis.
Holes: 27. Yards: 6,218/5,560. Par: 72/72. Course Rating: 69.5/71.7. Slope: 119/122. Green Fee: $24/$26. Cart Fee: $20/cart. Walking Policy: Unrestricted walking. Walkability: 3.
Opened: 1992. Season: April-Nov. High: June-Aug. To obtain tee times: Call up to 1 week in advance. Miscellaneous: Range (grass), club rentals, credit cards (MC, V), beginner friendly.
Reader Comments: Friendly little place. Hate to share this hidden gem! ... Beautiful setting. Very good greens ... Valley golf, well-routed ... Will become more challenging as it matures ... Open front nine; tight back nine.

★★★★½ CHASKA TOWN COURSE
PM-3000 Town Course Dr., Chaska, 55318, Carver County, (612)443-3748, 25 miles W of Minneapolis.
Holes: 18. Yards: 6,817/4,853. Par: 72/72. Course Rating: 73.4/69.0. Slope: 125/112. Green Fee: $25/$45. Cart Fee: $26/cart. Walking Policy: Unrestricted walking. Walkability: 3.
Opened: 1997. Architect: Arthur Hills/Brian Yoder. Season: April-Oct. High: June-Aug. Miscellaneous: Credit cards (MC, V).
Notes: Ranked 10th in 1999 Best in State.
Reader Comments: Fantastic layout ... Arthur Hills track ... Almost feels like a country club ... Demanding ... Too pricey for nonresidents ... Lots of forced carries ... Very strict pace. Rangers really keep you moving ... No longer an unknown gem ... Upscale ... It will improve each year.

★★★ CHISAGO LAKES GOLF COURSE
SP-292nd St., Lindstrom, 55045, Chisago County, (612)257-1484, 35 miles NE of St. Paul.
Holes: 18. Yards: 6,529/5,714. Par: 72/72. Course Rating: 71.2/72.7. Slope: 119/124. Green Fee: $21/$24. Cart Fee: $22/cart. Walking Policy: Unrestricted walking. Walkability: 3.
Opened: 1972. Architect: Donald Brauer/Joel Goldstrand. Season: April-Oct. High: June-Aug. To obtain tee times: Call up to 7 days in advance for weekdays; Thursday for weekends.

453

Miscellaneous: Reduced fees (low season, seniors, juniors), range (grass), club rentals, credit cards (MC, V, D).
Reader Comments: Tough starting holes ... Needs new clubhouse, but otherwise a good rural course. Big greens ... Good practice facility ... Nice course, not too busy ... Easy to get on ... Beautiful course to walk. Front nine good warmup for tougher back nine ... Great small-town track ... Fun.

★★½ CHOMONIX GOLF COURSE
PU-646 Sandpiper Dr., Lino Lakes, 55014, Anoka County, (651)482-8484, 22 miles N of Minneapolis.
Holes: 18. **Yards:** 6,596/5,455. **Par:** 72/72. **Course Rating:** 72.2/72.3. **Slope:** 121/123. **Green Fee:** $18/$24. **Cart Fee:** $22/cart. **Walking Policy:** Unrestricted walking. **Walkability:** 2.
Opened: 1970. **Architect:** Don Herfort/Gerry Pirkl. **Season:** April-Nov. **High:** June-Aug. **To obtain tee times:** Call 4 days in advance starting at 6 a.m. **Miscellaneous:** Reduced fees (seniors, juniors), range (grass), club rentals, credit cards (MC, V, D).
Reader Comments: Narrow fairways. Nice layout ... Lots of trees and water. Recent work should decrease wetness ... Bring your mosquito repellent ... Reworked low lying holes. Greatly improved ... Diamond in the rough ... Challenging with water and woods ... Very tight ... I'll go back.

★★★ COLUMBIA GOLF COURSE
PU-3300 Central Ave., Minneapolis, 55418, Hennepin County, (612)789-2627, 3 miles N of Minneapolis (downtown).
Holes: 18. **Yards:** 6,371/5,191. **Par:** 71/71. **Course Rating:** 70.0/69.3. **Slope:** 122/117. **Green Fee:** $23/$25. **Cart Fee:** $23/cart. **Walking Policy:** Unrestricted walking. **Walkability:** 3.
Opened: 1919. **Architect:** Edward Lawrence Packard. **Season:** April-Nov. **High:** May-Sept. **To obtain tee times:** Call up to 4 days in advance. **Miscellaneous:** Reduced fees (weekdays, twilight, seniors, juniors), metal spikes, range (grass/mats), club rentals, credit cards (MC, V).
Reader Comments: Getting better every year ... Hilly front nine ... Basic muny. Some interesting holes ... Re-routed holes a good idea ... Tough walk ... For mountain goats only.

★★★ COMO GOLF COURSE
PU-1431 N. Lexington Pkwy., St. Paul, 55103, Ramsey County, (651)488-9673. **Web:** www.stpaul.gov/parks.
Holes: 18. **Yards:** 5,814/5,068. **Par:** 70/70. **Course Rating:** 67.6/69.0. **Slope:** 117/115. **Green Fee:** $23/$23. **Cart Fee:** $23/cart. **Walking Policy:** Unrestricted walking. **Walkability:** 3.
Opened: 1988. **Architect:** Don Herfort. **Season:** April-Oct. **High:** June-Aug. **To obtain tee times:** Call 1 week in advance for weekdays. For weekends sign up in person on Thursday prior. For holidays call on Thursday prior at 7 a.m. **Miscellaneous:** Reduced fees (low season, twilight, seniors, juniors), metal spikes, club rentals, credit cards (MC, V).
Reader Comments: Short but tricky ... Next to zoo ... Scenic ... Very busy ... Hilly ... Design crammed into too little of an area ... A workout for the walker.

CROSSWOODS GOLF COURSE
PU-35878 County Road #3, Crosslake, 56442, Crow Wing County, (218)692-4653, 23 miles N of Brainerd. **E-mail:** crosgolf@crosslake.net.
Holes: 18. **Yards:** 5,236/4,445. **Par:** 68/68. **Course Rating:** 66.5/67.0. **Slope:** 116/118. **Green Fee:** $16/$22. **Cart Fee:** $20/cart. **Walking Policy:** Unrestricted walking. **Walk-ability:** 3.
Opened: 1997. **Architect:** Michael Stone. **Season:** May-Oct. **High:** June-Aug. **To obtain tee times:** Call golf shop. **Miscellaneous:** Reduced fees (weekdays, low season, twilight, seniors, juniors), discount packages, range (grass/mats), club rentals, credit cards (MC, V, D), beginner friendly (junior program, beginner lessons).
Special Notes: Back 9 is an executive-length course.

★★★ CUYUNA COUNTRY CLUB
SP-20 Golf Country Club Road, Box 40, Deerwood, 56444, Crow Wing County, (218)534-3489, 90 miles NW of Minneapolis.
Holes: 18. **Yards:** 6,407/5,749. **Par:** 72/74. **Course Rating:** 71.9/74.2. **Slope:** 132/138. **Green Fee:** $28/$39. **Cart Fee:** $26/cart. **Walking Policy:** Unrestricted walking. **Walkability:** 3.
Opened: 1923. **Architect:** Don Herfort. **Season:** April-Oct. **High:** July-Aug. **To obtain tee times:** Call or come in 3 days in advance. **Miscellaneous:** Reduced fees (weekdays, low season, resort guests, seniors, juniors), discount packages, range (grass), club rentals, credit cards (MC, V, D).
Reader Comments: Hidden gem ... Could play back nine every day ... Front side has small greens; back side bigger, a lot of woods. A sleeper ... A great golfer's course.

★★★ DAHLGREEN GOLF CLUB
PU-6940 Dahlgreen Rd., Chaska, 55318, Carver County, (612)448-7463, 20 miles SW of Minneapolis.
Holes: 18. **Yards:** 6,761/5,346. **Par:** 72/72. **Course Rating:** 72.4/70.4. **Slope:** 132/124. **Green Fee:** $25/$30. **Cart Fee:** $24/cart. **Walking Policy:** Unrestricted walking. **Walkability:** 3.

MINNESOTA

Opened: 1971. Architect: Gerry Pirkl/Donald Brauer. Season: March-Nov. High: June-Aug. To obtain tee times: Call 5 days in advance for weekdays; Wednesday morning for weekends. Miscellaneous: Reduced fees (weekdays, low season, seniors, juniors), discount packages, range (grass), club rentals, credit cards (MC, V, AE, D).

Reader Comments: Flat greens ... Busy course ... Needs some money pumped into it ... Packed on weekends, but kept in nice shape, will get better ... Poor man's country club. ... Fun, enjoyable.

★★ DAYTONA COUNTRY CLUB

PU-14730 Lawndale Lane, Dayton, 55327, Hennepin County, (612)427-6110, 20 miles NW of Minneapolis.

Holes: 18. Yards: 6,352/5,420. Par: 72/73. Course Rating: 69.8/71.0. Slope: 121/117. Green Fee: $22/$27. Cart Fee: $25/cart. Walking Policy: Unrestricted walking. Walkability: 3. Opened: 1964. Architect: Jerry McCann. Season: Year-round. High: April-Nov. To obtain tee times: Call or come in up to 7 days in advance. Miscellaneous: Reduced fees (weekdays, low season, seniors, juniors), range (grass), club rentals, credit cards (MC, V, AE, D).

★★★ DEER RUN GOLF CLUB

PU-8661 Deer Run Dr., Victoria, 55386, Carver County, (612)443-2351, 20 miles SW of Minneapolis.

Holes: 18. Yards: 6,265/5,541. Par: 71/71. Course Rating: 70.5/72.1. Slope: 122/121. Green Fee: $27/$32. Cart Fee: $26/cart. Walking Policy: Unrestricted walking. Walkability: 4. Opened: 1989. Season: March-Nov. High: June-Aug. To obtain tee times: Call 5 days in advance. Miscellaneous: Reduced fees (twilight, seniors, juniors), range (grass), credit cards (MC, V).

Reader Comments: Nice up-and-down terrain; picturesque ... Hilly ... Poor driving range ... Not long, but tight and challenging ... Accuracy needed ... Surrounded by many homes ... Fun ... More length would have made this layout better.

★★★ DETROIT COUNTRY CLUB

R-Rte. 5, Detroit Lakes, 56501, Becker County, (218)847-5790, 47 miles E of Fargo, ND. Web: www.detroitlakes.com/entertainment/countryclub/dlcc.html.

Holes: 36. Yards: 5,941/5,508. Par: 71/71. Course Rating: 69.2/72.3. Slope: 122/129. Green Fee: $28/$30. Cart Fee: $22/cart. Walking Policy: Unrestricted walking. Walkability: 3. Opened: 1916. Architect: Tom Bendelow/Don Herfort. Season: May-Oct. High: June-Aug. To obtain tee times: Call 7 days in advance. Miscellaneous: Metal spikes, range (grass), caddies, club rentals, credit cards (MC, V, Fall rates.).

Reader Comments: My ball found all the pines ... Short, but very challenging.... Too short and too crowded ... Challenging, a lot of uneven lies ... A gem, but too busy ... Great for match play ... Solid course.

DOUBLE EAGLE GOLF CLUB

PU-R.R.1 County Box 117 Road #3, Eagle Bend, 56446, Todd County, (218)738-5155, 30 miles NE of Alexandria.

★★★ GOLD COURSE

Holes: 9. Yards: 3,556/2,920. Par: 37/37. Course Rating: 37.4/36.8. Slope: 134/128. Green Fee: $21/$21. Cart Fee: $19/cart. Walking Policy: Unrestricted walking. Walkability: 2. Opened: 1982. Architect: Joel Goldstrand. Season: April-Oct. High: July-Aug. To obtain tee times: Call golf shop, (218)738-5155. Miscellaneous: Club rentals, credit cards (MC, V).

Reader Comments: Challenging ... Service was very good.

★★★ GREEN COURSE

Holes: 9. Yards: 3,337/2,790. Par: 36/36. Course Rating: 36.0/36.0. Slope: 127/124. Green Fee: $21/$21. Cart Fee: $19/cart. Walking Policy: Unrestricted walking. Walkability: 2. Opened: 1982. Architect: Joel Goldstrand. Season: April-Oct. High: July-Aug. To obtain tee times: Call golf shop, 218-738-5155. Miscellaneous: Club rentals, credit cards (MC, V).

Reader Comments: Well-maintained, reversible 9-hole course.

Special Notes: First reversible course built in the USA. Play Gold course in one direction, then play Green course in reverse direction to make 18 holes.

★★★ EAGLE CREEK

SP-1000 26th. Ave. N.E., Willmar, 56201, Kandiyohi County, (320)235-1166, 80 miles W of Minneapolis.

Holes: 18. Yards: 6,342/5,271. Par: 72/73. Course Rating: 70.8/70.9. Slope: 129/127. Green Fee: $26/$29. Cart Fee: $22/cart. Walking Policy: Unrestricted walking. Walkability: 2. Opened: 1930. Architect: Albert Anderson. Season: April-Oct. High: May-Aug. To obtain tee times: Call up to 4 days in advance. Miscellaneous: Reduced fees (weekdays, low season), discount packages, range (grass), club rentals, credit cards (MC, V).

Reader Comments: True test of golf ... Great terrain ... Challenging ... Fun back nine; front nine coming along.

★★★½ EAGLE RIDGE GOLF COURSE
PU-1 Green Way, Coleraine, 55722, Itasca County, (218)245-2217, 5 miles E of Grand Rapids.
Holes: 18. **Yards:** 6,772/5,220. **Par:** 72/72. **Course Rating:** 71.8/69.2. **Slope:** 126/114. **Green Fee:** $21/$25. **Cart Fee:** $20/cart. **Walking Policy:** Unrestricted walking. **Walkability:** 3.
Opened: 1996. **Architect:** Garrett Gill. **Season:** March-Oct. **High:** June-Aug. **To obtain tee times:** Call up to 7 days in advance. **Miscellaneous:** Reduced fees (weekdays, low season, resort guests, juniors), metal spikes, range (grass/mats), club rentals, credit cards (MC, V, D).
Reader Comments: Great views ... Carved through woods ... Challenging ... Rocks in fairway ... A few great holes.

★★½ EASTWOOD GOLF CLUB
PM-3505 Eastwood Rd. S.E., Rochester, 55904, Olmsted County, (507)281-6173.
Holes: 18. **Yards:** 6,178/5,289. **Par:** 70/70. **Course Rating:** 69.4/70.3. **Slope:** 119/116. **Green Fee:** $20/$20. **Cart Fee:** $19/cart. **Walking Policy:** Unrestricted walking. **Walkability:** 4.
Opened: 1968. **Architect:** Ray Keller. **Season:** April-Nov. **High:** May-Aug. **To obtain tee times:** Call 2 days in advance. **Miscellaneous:** Metal spikes, range (grass), club rentals, credit cards (MC, V).
Reader Comments: Very hilly. Walking it is a good workout ... Typical muny ... Plays long. Uneven lies.

★★★★ EDINBURGH USA GOLF CLUB
PU-8700 Edinbrook Crossing, Brooklyn Park, 55443, Hennepin County, (612)315-8550, 12 miles N of Minneapolis.
Holes: 18. **Yards:** 6,701/5,255. **Par:** 72/72. **Course Rating:** 73.0/71.4. **Slope:** 133/128. **Green Fee:** $37/$37. **Cart Fee:** $26/cart. **Walking Policy:** Unrestricted walking. **Walkability:** 2.
Opened: 1987. **Architect:** Robert Trent Jones Jr. **Season:** April-Oct. **High:** June-Aug. **To obtain tee times:** Call 4 days in advance of play at 2 p.m. **Miscellaneous:** Reduced fees (twilight, seniors, juniors), metal spikes, range (grass), caddies, club rentals, credit cards (MC, V, AE).
Notes: Ranked 14th in 1999 Best in State; 23rd in 1996 America's Top 75 Affordable Courses. 1992 USGA Public Links Championship; 1990-96 LPGA Tour event.
Reader Comments: Good design, good shape, tough greens ... Tough but fair ... Former LPGA site ... Great practice range ... Busy, but nice when you can get on ... Loaded with sand ... Fun course ... Great condition ... Great clubhouse ... Very humbling course ... Lots of water ... Too tough for me, but beautiful.

★★½ ELK RIVER COUNTRY CLUB
SP-20015 Elk Lake Rd., Elk River, 55330, Sherburne County, (612)441-4111, 45 miles N of Minneapolis.
Holes: 18. **Yards:** 6,480/5,610. **Par:** 72/75. **Course Rating:** 71.1/72.3. **Slope:** 121/122. **Green Fee:** $27/$31. **Cart Fee:** $26/cart. **Walking Policy:** Unrestricted walking. **Walkability:** 3.
Architect: Willie Kidd. **Season:** March-Nov. **High:** June-Aug. **To obtain tee times:** Call golf shop up to 1 week in advance. **Miscellaneous:** Reduced fees (seniors, juniors), range (grass), club rentals, credit cards (MC, V).
Reader Comments: Very testy if wind blows ... Nice, mature course ... Wooded ... Small greens.

★★½ ELM CREEK GOLF LINKS OF PLYMOUTH
PU-18940 Highway 55, Plymouth, 55446, Hennepin County, (612)478-6716, 10 miles W of Minneapolis.
Holes: 18. **Yards:** 6,215/4,839. **Par:** 70/71. **Course Rating:** 70.4/68.0. **Slope:** 132/117. **Green Fee:** $23/$27. **Cart Fee:** $24/cart. **Walking Policy:** Unrestricted walking. **Walkability:** 4.
Opened: 1960. **Architect:** Michael Klatte/Mark Klatte. **Season:** April-Oct. **High:** June-Aug. **To obtain tee times:** Reservation system with credit card. **Miscellaneous:** Reduced fees (weekdays, twilight, seniors, juniors), metal spikes, club rentals, credit cards (MC, V, AE).
Reader Comments: Very hilly, tough to walk ... Challenging back 9 ... Some fairways too close together ... New back 9 is a big improvement ... Drains well in wet weather ... Don't try to walk it unless you're in good shape.

★★½ ENGER PARK GOLF CLUB
PU-1801 W. Skyline Blvd., Duluth, 55806, St. Louis County, (218)723-3451, 149 miles N of Minneapolis.
Holes: 27. **Yards:** 6,434/5,247. **Par:** 72/72. **Course Rating:** 70.9/65.3. **Slope:** 126/115. **Green Fee:** $20/$20. **Cart Fee:** $20/cart. **Walking Policy:** Unrestricted walking. **Walkability:** 3.
Opened: 1927. **Architect:** Dick Phelps. **Season:** April-Nov. **High:** June-Aug. **To obtain tee times:** Call up to 7 days in advance. **Miscellaneous:** Reduced fees (low season, twilight, seniors, juniors), range (grass), club rentals, credit cards (MC, V).
Reader Comments: Great view of Lake Superior and Duluth ... Decent place to play ... Rolling hills; very challenging in wind ... Nice city course.

★★ FALCON RIDGE GOLF COURSE
PU-33942 Falcon Ave., Stacy, 55079, Chisago County, (651)462-5797, 3 miles N of Stacy.

MINNESOTA

Holes: 27. **Yards:** 5,787/5,070. **Par:** 72/72. **Course Rating:** 67.7/69.6. **Slope:** 106/117. **Green Fee:** $18/$25. **Cart Fee:** $24/cart. **Walking Policy:** Unrestricted walking. **Walkability:** 1. **Opened:** 1993. **Architect:** Lyle Kleven/Martin Johnson/Doug Lien. **Season:** April-Oct. **High:** June-Aug. **To obtain tee times:** Call golf shop. **Miscellaneous:** Reduced fees (weekdays, seniors, juniors), range (grass), club rentals, credit cards (MC, V, D), beginner friendly (adult programs, junior camp).
Special Notes: Also has a 9-hole executive course.

★★½ FOUNTAIN VALLEY GOLF CLUB
PU-2830 220th St. W., Farmington, 55024, Dakota County, (651)463-2121, 30 miles S of Minneapolis. **E-mail:** fvgctman@excelonline.com.
Holes: 18. **Yards:** 6,540/5,980. **Par:** 72/72. **Course Rating:** 71.5/73.4. **Slope:** 119/122. **Green Fee:** $19/$24. **Cart Fee:** $12/person. **Walking Policy:** Unrestricted walking. **Walkability:** 2. **Opened:** 1977. **Architect:** Ray Rahn. **Season:** April-Oct. **High:** June-Aug. **To obtain tee times:** Call 7 days in advance. **Miscellaneous:** Reduced fees (weekdays, seniors), range (grass), club rentals, credit cards (MC, V).
Reader Comments: Good small-town course ... Flat ... Wide open; no trouble ... Good mom-and-pop course.

★★★★ FOX HOLLOW GOLF CLUB
SP-4780 Palmgren Lane N.E., Rogers, 55374, Wright County, (612)428-4468, 30 miles NW of Minneapolis. **E-mail:** foxhollow@teemaster.com. **Web:** teemaster.com.
Holes: 18. **Yards:** 6,726/5,161. **Par:** 72/72. **Course Rating:** 72.5/70.7. **Slope:** 135/124. **Green Fee:** $28/$36. **Cart Fee:** $12/person. **Walking Policy:** Unrestricted walking. **Walkability:** 3. **Opened:** 1989. **Architect:** Joel Goldstrand. **Season:** April-Nov. **High:** June-Aug. **To obtain tee times:** Call 3 days in advance at 9 a.m. **Miscellaneous:** Reduced fees (weekdays, seniors, juniors), range (grass), club rentals, credit cards (MC, V, AE, D, Diners Club).
Reader Comments: One of my favorite courses ... Easy to walk ... 3rd hole, with island green, is awesome ... Beautiful, challenging course ... Good shots rewarded ... Well-kept.

★★★ FRANCIS A. GROSS GOLF COURSE
PU-2201 St. Anthony Blvd., Minneapolis, 55418, Hennepin County, (612)789-2542.
Holes: 18. **Yards:** 6,575/5,400. **Par:** 71/71. **Course Rating:** 70.8/73.2. **Slope:** 120/121. **Green Fee:** $23/$25. **Cart Fee:** $23/cart. **Walking Policy:** Unrestricted walking. **Walkability:** 3. **Opened:** 1925. **Architect:** W.C. Clark. **Season:** April-Nov. **High:** June-Aug. **To obtain tee times:** Call up to 4 days in advance. **Miscellaneous:** Reduced fees (weekdays, twilight, seniors, juniors), discount packages, metal spikes, range (grass), club rentals, credit cards (MC, V). **Notes:** 1964 USGA National Public Links Championship.
Reader Comments: Good city course ... Old but good ... Big trees, small greens ... Very playable ... Good walk.

★★★★½ GIANTS RIDGE GOLF & SKI RESORT *Service, Value, Condition, Pace*
R-P.O. Box 190, Biwabik, 55708, (218)865-4143, (800)688-7669, 4 miles NE of Biwabik. **E-mail:** troy@giantsridge.com. **Web:** www.giantsridge.com.
Holes: 18. **Yards:** 6,930/5,084. **Par:** 72/72. **Course Rating:** 73.7/70.3. **Slope:** 133/126. **Green Fee:** $45/$60. **Cart Fee:** Included in Green Fee. **Walking Policy:** Mandatory cart. **Walkability:** 2. **Opened:** 1997. **Architect:** Jeffrey Brauer/Lanny Wadkins. **Season:** May-Oct. **High:** June-Sept. **To obtain tee times:** Can be made 30 days in advance through Giants Ridge, or 60 days in advance through one of the lodging facilities doing packages with us. **Miscellaneous:** Range (grass), lodging (93 rooms), credit cards (MC, V, AE), beginner friendly. **Notes:** Ranked 3rd in 1999 Best in State.
Reader Comments: Best I've ever played on ... Beautiful, rugged landscape ... Minnesota's most scenic course ... Breakthrough course for the area ... No tricks ... Everyone should come to play ... Bring balls ... A must-play ... Exceptional ... Engineering masterpiece ... Every hole is a beauty ... Maturing well.

★★★ GLENCOE COUNTRY CLUB
SP-1325 E 1st. St., Glencoe, 55336, McLeod County, (320)864-3023, 54 miles W of Minneapolis.
Holes: 18. **Yards:** 6,074/4,940. **Par:** 71/71. **Course Rating:** 69.7/69.7. **Slope:** 117/117. **Green Fee:** $20/$25. **Cart Fee:** $20/cart. **Walking Policy:** Unrestricted walking. **Walkability:** 2. **Opened:** 1958. **Season:** April-Oct. **High:** May-Aug. **Miscellaneous:** Reduced fees (seniors, juniors), range (grass), club rentals, credit cards (MC, V, AE, D).
Reader Comments: Long walks between holes ... Some dangerous holes–fore! ... Usually in good condition.

GOLF AT THE LEGACY
PU-1515 Shumway Ave., Faribault, 55021, Rice County, (507)332-7177, 40 miles S of Minneapolis. **Web:** www.legacygolfandhomes.com.

MINNESOTA

Holes: 18. **Yards:** 6,416/5,031. **Par:** 72/72. **Course Rating:** 71.1/69.2. **Slope:** 127/118. **Green Fee:** $22/$27. **Cart Fee:** $22/cart. **Walking Policy:** Unrestricted walking. **Walkability:** 3. **Opened:** 1998. **Architect:** Garrett Gill/George Williams. **Season:** April-Oct. **High:** June-Sept. **To obtain tee times:** Call 5 days in advance. **Miscellaneous:** Reduced fees (weekdays, seniors, juniors), range (grass/mats), club rentals, credit cards (MC, V).

★★ GOODRICH GOLF COURSE
PU-1820 N. Van Dyke, Maplewood, 55109, Ramsey County, (651)777-7355, 3 miles NE of St. Paul.
Holes: 18. **Yards:** 6,174/5,296. **Par:** 70/70. **Course Rating:** 68.6/69.3. **Slope:** 110/113. **Green Fee:** $18/$22. **Cart Fee:** $22/cart. **Walking Policy:** Unrestricted walking. **Walkability:** 2. **Opened:** 1959. **Architect:** Paul Coates. **Season:** April-Nov. **High:** June-Aug. **To obtain tee times:** Call 4 days in advance. **Miscellaneous:** Reduced fees (weekdays, twilight, seniors, juniors), metal spikes, range (mats), club rentals, credit cards (MC, V).

★★★½ GRAND NATIONAL GOLF CLUB
PU-300 Lady Luck Dr., Hinckley, 55037, Pine County, (320)384-7427, 60 miles N of Minneapolis/St. Paul.
Holes: 18. **Yards:** 6,894/5,100. **Par:** 72/72. **Course Rating:** 73.6/69.6. **Slope:** 137/122. **Green Fee:** $27/$30. **Cart Fee:** $26/cart. **Walking Policy:** Unrestricted walking. **Walkability:** 3. **Opened:** 1995. **Architect:** Joel Goldstrand. **Season:** April-Oct. **High:** May-Aug. **To obtain tee times:** Call 7 days in advance. **Miscellaneous:** Reduced fees (resort guests, twilight, seniors), discount packages, metal spikes, range (grass), club rentals, lodging (500 rooms), credit cards (MC, V).
Reader Comments: Flat, but testy ... Casino course. Too many gamblers, not enough golfers ... Too open and flat ... After an all-night rain, course drained well ... Good challenge ... A lot of water ... Good resort course ... Tough when wind blows.

GRAND VIEW LODGE RESORT *Service+*
DEACON'S LODGE
R-Weaver Point Road, Breeze Point Township, 56472, Crow Wing County, (218)562-6262, 88THEPINES, 30 miles N of Brainerd. **E-mail:** deacon'slodge.com. **Web:** www.grandviewlodge.com.
Holes: 18. **Yards:** 6,964/4,766. **Par:** 72/72. **Course Rating:** 73.8/67.6. **Slope:** 128/114. **Green Fee:** $90/$90. **Cart Fee:** Included in Green Fee. **Walking Policy:** Unrestricted walking. **Walkability:** 4. **Opened:** 1999. **Architect:** Arnold Palmer. **Season:** April-Oct. **High:** June-Sept. **To obtain tee times:** Call the tee time number. No restrictions on advanced tee times. **Miscellaneous:** Reduced fees (twilight), discount packages, range (grass), club rentals, lodging (250 rooms), credit cards (MC, V, AE, D).
THE PINES
R-S. 134 Nokomis, Nisswa, 56468, Crow Wing County, (218)963-0001, (888)437-4637, 120 miles NW of Minneapolis. **E-mail:** thepines.com . **Web:** www.grandviewlodge.com.
Holes: 27. **Green Fee:** $54/$64. **Cart Fee:** $16/person. **Walking Policy:** Unrestricted walking. **Walkability:** 2. **Opened:** 1990. **Architect:** Joel Goldstrand. **Season:** April-Oct. **High:** June-Sept. **To obtain tee times:** Lodge guests call up to a year in advance with confirmed reservation. No advance restrictions with credit card.
★★★★ (LAKES/WOODS)
Yards: 6,874/5,134. **Par:** 72/72. **Course Rating:** 74.2/70.6. **Slope:** 137/128. **Miscellaneous:** Reduced fees (weekdays, low season, resort guests, twilight), discount packages, metal spikes, range (grass), club rentals, lodging (250 rooms), credit cards (MC, V, AE, D).
Notes: Ranked 68th in 1996 America's Top 75 Upscale Courses.
Reader Comments: Difficult but fair. Great fun at a great price ... A Midwestern Spyglass Hill ... Good value ... Great layout; natural ... Every hole different.
★★★★ (MARSH/LAKES)
Yards: 6,837/5,112. **Par:** 72/72. **Course Rating:** 73.7/70.0. **Slope:** 134/128. **Miscellaneous:** Reduced fees (weekdays, low season, resort guests, twilight), discount packages, range (grass), club rentals, lodging (250 rooms), credit cards (MC, V, AE, D).
Reader Comments: Started the golf rush to this resort area ...Spectacular course ... Cut out of the woods ... Bring your 'A' game ... Long and tight ... Excellent condition ... Scenic, fun, tough ... Beautiful clubhouse ... Gorgeous track ... We were treated like we were top pros ... Prices keep going up.
★★★★ (WOODS/MARSH)
Yards: 6,883/5,210. **Par:** 72/72. **Course Rating:** 73.3/70.6. **Slope:** 132/125. **Miscellaneous:** Reduced fees (weekdays, low season, resort guests, twilight), discount packages, range (grass), club rentals, lodging (250 rooms), credit cards (MC, V, AE, D).
Reader Comments: Need to bring your 'A' game (or a lot of balls) ... Worth the trip ... Carved through the trees, a great test of golf ... Must plan your shots carefully. Narrow fairways.

★★½ GREEN LEA GOLF COURSE
PU-101 Richway Dr., Albert Lea, 56007, Freeborn County, (507)373-1061, 90 miles S of Minneapolis/St. Paul.
Holes: 18. **Yards:** 6,166/5,404. **Par:** 72/72. **Course Rating:** 70.2/71.4. **Slope:** 122/126. **Green Fee:** $19/$21. **Cart Fee:** $10/person. **Walking Policy:** Unrestricted walking. **Walkability:** 3. **Opened:** 1947. **Architect:** B. L. Greengo. **Season:** April-Oct. **High:** June-Aug. **To obtain tee times:** Call 3 days in advance for weekends and holidays. **Miscellaneous:** Reduced fees (weekdays, low season, twilight, seniors, juniors), discount packages, club rentals, credit cards (MC, V, D), beginner friendly.
Reader Comments: Short par 4s emphasize club selection ... Good public course.

★★★ GREENHAVEN COUNTRY CLUB
PU-2800 Greenhaven Rd., Anoka, 55303, Anoka County, (612)427-3180.
Holes: 18. **Yards:** 6,287/5,418. **Par:** 71/73. **Course Rating:** 69.1/71.5. **Slope:** 121/110. **Green Fee:** $24/$27. **Walkability:** N/A. **Miscellaneous:** Metal spikes.
Reader Comments: OK course ... Tee boxes need some work ... Nice clubhouse ... Good test for the average golfer ... Comfortable ... Large trees ... Not long, but still challenging.

★★½ GREENWOOD GOLF LINKS
PU-4520 E. Viking Blvd., Wyoming, 55092, Chisago County, (651)462-4653, 30 miles N of St. Paul/Minneapolis.
Holes: 18. **Yards:** 5,518/4,791. **Par:** 72/72. **Course Rating:** 67.2/67.3. **Slope:** 105/112. **Green Fee:** $18/$22. **Cart Fee:** $20/cart. **Walking Policy:** Unrestricted walking. **Walkability:** 2. **Opened:** 1986. **Architect:** C.M. Johnson. **Season:** April-Oct. **High:** May-Aug. **To obtain tee times:** Call up to 2 days in advance. **Miscellaneous:** Reduced fees (seniors, juniors), discount packages, metal spikes, club rentals.
Reader Comments: Very inexpensive ... Dangerous in fairways.

★½ HAMPTON HILLS GOLF COURSE
PU-5313 Juneau Lane, Plymouth, 55446, Hennepin County, (612)559-9800, 12 miles NW of Minneapolis. **Web:** www.tc.umn.edu/~hampt007.
Holes: 18. **Yards:** 6,135/5,321. **Par:** 73/73. **Course Rating:** 69.9/70.2. **Slope:** 111/122. **Green Fee:** $19/$22. **Cart Fee:** $20/cart. **Walking Policy:** Unrestricted walking. **Walkability:** 3. **Opened:** 1966. **Season:** April-Oct. **High:** April-Sept. **To obtain tee times:** Call on Monday for reservations for the week. **Miscellaneous:** Reduced fees (low season, twilight, seniors, juniors), discount packages, metal spikes, range (grass), club rentals.

★★½ HAWLEY GOLF & COUNTRY CLUB
PU-Highway 10, Hawley, 56549, Clay County, (218)483-4808, 22 miles E of Fargo, ND.
Holes: 18. **Yards:** 6,106/5,082. **Par:** 71/72. **Course Rating:** 68.6/68.6. **Slope:** 119/113. **Green Fee:** $18/$20. **Cart Fee:** $20/cart. **Walking Policy:** Unrestricted walking. **Walkability:** 3. **Opened:** 1923. **Season:** April-Oct. **High:** June-Aug. **To obtain tee times:** Call up to 7 days in advance for weekdays; Thursday for weekends and holidays. **Miscellaneous:** Reduced fees (weekdays, low season), club rentals, credit cards (MC, V).
Reader Comments: A little rough, but fun and reasonable ... A shorter course; the type I need.

★★★ HEADWATERS COUNTRY CLUB
SP-P.O. Box 9, Park Rapids, 56470, Hubbard County, (218)732-4832, 112 miles NW of St. Cloud.
Holes: 18. **Yards:** 6,506/5,382. **Par:** 72/72. **Course Rating:** 70.7/71.7. **Slope:** 130/123. **Green Fee:** $20/$28. **Cart Fee:** $23/cart. **Walking Policy:** Unrestricted walking. **Walkability:** 3. **Opened:** 1969. **Season:** March-Nov. **High:** June-Aug. **To obtain tee times:** Local call 2 days in advance. Out of town, call anytime. **Miscellaneous:** Reduced fees (low season, twilight, juniors), metal spikes, range (grass), club rentals, credit cards (MC, V).
Reader Comments: Beautiful layout, great day ... Terrific front 9; back 9 is too back and forth ... Very challenging ... Take the family ... Above expectations ... Beautiful setting in lake country ... Loons fly over.

★★★ HIAWATHA GOLF COURSE
PU-4553 Longfellow Ave. S., Minneapolis, 55407, Hennepin County, (612)724-7715.
Holes: 18. **Yards:** 6,645/5,796. **Par:** 73/74. **Course Rating:** 70.6/71.7. **Slope:** 114/123. **Green Fee:** $23/$25. **Cart Fee:** $23/cart. **Walking Policy:** Unrestricted walking. **Walkability:** 1. **Opened:** 1934. **Season:** April-Nov. **High:** June-Aug. **To obtain tee times:** Call up to 4 days in advance. **Miscellaneous:** Reduced fees (weekdays, low season, twilight, seniors, juniors), discount packages, metal spikes, range (grass/mats), club rentals, credit cards (MC, V).
Reader Comments: Old city course; many rounds ... Good city course, but suffers from poor condition ... Not kept up very well ... Rough fairways ... Good value ... Going through repairs ... No etiquette.

MINNESOTA

★★★★ **HIDDEN GREENS GOLF CLUB** *Value*
PU-12977 200th St. E., Hastings, 55033, Dakota County, (651)437-3085, 24 miles SE of Minneapolis.
Holes: 18. **Yards:** 5,954/5,559. **Par:** 72/72. **Course Rating:** 68.8/72.2. **Slope:** 118/127. **Green Fee:** $18/$22. **Cart Fee:** $22/cart. **Walking Policy:** Unrestricted walking. **Walkability:** 2.
Opened: 1976. **Architect:** Joel Goldstrand. **Season:** April-Nov. **High:** July-Aug. **To obtain tee times:** Call after 9 a.m. on Tuesday. **Miscellaneous:** Reduced fees (weekdays, seniors), range (grass), club rentals, credit cards (MC, V).
Reader Comments: Not just a clever name! ... Not very long but very tight. Leave driver at home ... Very clean, no clutter ... Lots of trees.

★★ **HIGHLAND PARK GOLF COURSE**
PU-1403 Montreal Ave., St. Paul, 55116, Ramsey County, (612)699-5825.
Holes: 18. **Yards:** 6,265/5,600. **Par:** 72/73. **Course Rating:** 69.0/71.1. **Slope:** 111/118. **Green Fee:** $19/N/A. **Cart Fee:** $20. **Walking Policy:** Unrestricted walking. **Walkability:** N/A. **Opened:** 1929. **Architect:** G. Pirkl/D. Brauer/E. Perret. **Season:** April-Nov. **High:** May-Sept. **To obtain tee times:** For weekdays call 8 a.m. 1 day in advance. For weekends come in Wednesday in person 6 a.m. to 7 a.m. or call on Thursday after 7 a.m. **Miscellaneous:** Reduced fees (low season, twilight, seniors, juniors), metal spikes, range (grass), club rentals, credit cards (MC, V).

★★★ **HOLLYDALE GOLF COURSE**
PU-4710 Holly Lane N., Plymouth, 55446, Hennepin County, (612)559-9847, 10 miles W of Minneapolis.
Holes: 18. **Yards:** 6,160/5,128. **Par:** 71/73. **Course Rating:** 70.1/69.9. **Slope:** 121/120. **Green Fee:** $21/$24. **Cart Fee:** $23/cart. **Walking Policy:** Unrestricted walking. **Walkability:** 2.
Opened: 1965. **Season:** April-Nov. **High:** June-Aug. **To obtain tee times:** Call Tuesday after 7:30 a.m. for weekends and holidays. **Miscellaneous:** Reduced fees (weekdays, seniors, juniors), range (grass), club rentals.
Reader Comments: Course improving with age. Some poorly-designed holes ... Maturing nicely ... Fun course ... Good public course ... Needs a little work.

★★★½ **INVER WOOD GOLF COURSE**
PU-1850 70th St. E., Inver Grove Heights, 55077, Dakota County, (651)457-3667, 8 miles S of St. Paul.
Holes: 18. **Yards:** 6,724/5,175. **Par:** 72/72. **Course Rating:** 72.0/70.7. **Slope:** 140/128. **Green Fee:** $26/$26. **Cart Fee:** $24/cart. **Walking Policy:** Unrestricted walking. **Walkability:** 5.
Opened: 1992. **Architect:** Garrett Gill/George B. Williams. **Season:** April-Oct. **High:** May-Aug. **To obtain tee times:** Call 3 days in advance. **Miscellane-ous:** Reduced fees (juniors), range (grass/mats), club rentals, credit cards (MC, V).
Reader Comments: A real challenge ... Gets easier the second or third time ... Hilly. Up and down ... Walks are long and hilly ... You'll use all the clubs in your bag ... A great deal ... Heavy play ... Fun to play.

★★★½ **ISLAND VIEW GOLF COURSE**
PU-9150 Island View Rd., Waconia, 55387, Carver County, (612)442-6116, 20 miles W of Minneapolis.
Holes: 18. **Yards:** 6,552/5,382. **Par:** 72/72. **Course Rating:** 70.5/70.0. **Slope:** 129/124. **Green Fee:** $35/$39. **Cart Fee:** $24/cart. **Walking Policy:** Unrestricted walking. **Walkability:** 3.
Opened: 1957. **Architect:** Willie Kidd. **Season:** April-Oct. **High:** June-Aug. **To obtain tee times:** Call up to 2 days in advance. **Miscellaneous:** Range (grass), club rentals, credit cards (MC, V, D).
Reader Comments: Worth the money ... Country-club like course ... Peaceful ... Beautiful ... Hilly.

IZATYS GOLF & YACHT CLUB
R-40005 85th Ave., Onamia, 56359, Mille Lacs County, (612)532-3101, (800)533-1728, 90 miles N of Minneapolis. **E-mail:** izatys@teemaster.com. **Web:** www.izatys.com.
BLACK BROOK
Holes: 18. **Yards:** 6,867/5,119. **Par:** 72/72. **Course Rating:** 74.2/71.1. **Slope:** 140/122. **Green Fee:** $60/$85. **Cart Fee:** $28/person. **Walking Policy:** Unrestricted walking. **Walkability:** 3.
Opened: 1999. **Architect:** John Harbottle III. **Season:** April-Oct. **High:** June-Sept. **To obtain tee times:** Anytime for resort guests or members. Nonguests call 14 days in advance.
Miscellaneous: Reduced fees (weekdays, resort guests), discount packages, metal spikes, range (grass/mats), club rentals, lodging (100 rooms), credit cards (MC, V, AE, D, Diner's Club).
★★★ **THE SANCTUARY**
Holes: 18. **Yards:** 6,646/5,075. **Par:** 72/72. **Course Rating:** 72.6/70.3. **Slope:** 134/125. **Green Fee:** $35/$45. **Cart Fee:** $28/person. **Walking Policy:** Unrestricted walking. **Walkability:** 3.
Opened: 1998. **Architect:** John Harbottle III. **Season:** April-Oct. **High:** June-Sept. **To obtain tee times:** Anytime for resort guests or members. Nonguests call 14 days in advance.
Miscellaneous: Reduced fees (weekdays, resort guests, twilight), discount packages, metal

spikes, range (grass/mats), club rentals, lodging (100 rooms), credit cards (MC, V, AE, D, Diner's Club).

Reader Comments: Great course by the lake ... Bring lots of balls ... Not as spectacular as advertised ... Fun resort course ... First-timers need a lot of balls ... Leave your woods in the trunk.

★★★½ KELLER GOLF COURSE

PU-2166 Maplewood Dr., St. Paul, 55109-2599, Ramsey County, (651)484-3011, 10 miles N of Minneapolis/St. Paul.
Holes: 18. **Yards:** 6,566/5,373. **Par:** 72/73. **Course Rating:** 71.7/71.3. **Slope:** 128/125. **Green Fee:** $25/$25. **Cart Fee:** $22/cart. **Walking Policy:** Unrestricted walking. **Walkability:** 3. **Opened:** 1929. **Architect:** Paul N. Coates. **Season:** March-Nov. **High:** May-Sept. **To obtain tee times:** Call 4 days in advance starting at 7 a.m. **Miscellaneous:** Reduced fees (low season, twilight, seniors, juniors), metal spikes, range (grass), club rentals, credit cards (MC, V).
Notes: 1931 Public Links; 1932 and 1954 PGA Championship ; 1949 Western Open.
Reader Comments: Very challenging ... Well-placed hazards ... Some scary slanted greens ... Former site of the PGA Championship and a former tour stop ... Neat to see wall of champions ... Classic older course ... Busy ... Slow play ... A fun course to play.

★★★ LAKESIDE GOLF CLUB

RR#3, Waseca, 56093, Waseca County, (507)835-2574.
Yards: 6,025/N.A. **Par:** 71/71. **Course Rating:** 68.6/70.5. **Slope:** 116/115. **Green Fee:** $13/$24. **Walkability:** N/A. **Miscellaneous:** Metal spikes.
Reader Comments: Best golf value in southern Minnesota ... Nice course ... Getting better ... Not too many big challenges.

★★ LAKEVIEW GOLF OF ORONO

PU-710 North Shore Drive, W., Mound, 55364, Hennepin County, (612)472-3459, 25 miles W of Minneapolis. **Web:** www.teemaster.com.
Holes: 18. **Yards:** 5,424/4,894. **Par:** 70/70. **Course Rating:** 65.8/67.1. **Slope:** 108/109. **Green Fee:** $16/$24. **Cart Fee:** $24/cart. **Walking Policy:** Unrestricted walking. **Walkability:** 3. **Opened:** 1956. **Architect:** Russ Wenkstern. **Season:** April-Oct. **High:** June-Aug. **To obtain tee times:** Call golf shop. **Miscellaneous:** Reduced fees (twilight, seniors, juniors), metal spikes, club rentals, credit cards (MC, V, AE).

LAKEVIEW NATIONAL GOLF COURSE

PM-1349 Highway 61, Two Harbors, 55616, Lake County, (218)834-2664, 20 miles N of Duluth.
Holes: 18. **Yards:** 6,773/5,364. **Par:** 72/72. **Course Rating:** 72.2/70.7. **Slope:** 126/123. **Green Fee:** $16/$22. **Cart Fee:** $24/cart. **Walking Policy:** Unrestricted walking. **Walkability:** 5. **Opened:** 1997. **Architect:** Garrett Gill/William Fitzpatrick. **Season:** April-Oct. **High:** June-Aug. **To obtain tee times:** Call 30 days in advance. **Miscellaneous:** Reduced fees (weekdays, low season, twilight, juniors), range (grass), club rentals, credit cards (MC, V, AE).

THE LEGACY COURSES AT CRAGUN'S

PU-11000 Craguns Drive, Brainerd, 56401, Cass County, (218)825-2800, (800)272-4867, 8 miles NW of Brainerd. **E-mail:** info@craguns.com. **Web:** www.craguns.com.
Holes: 18. **Yards:** 6,897/5,250. **Par:** 72/72. **Course Rating:** 73.7/71.2. **Slope:** 145/131. **Green Fee:** $35/$105. **Cart Fee:** Included in Green Fee. **Walking Policy:** Unrestricted walking. **Walkability:** 2. **Opened:** 1999. **Architect:** Robert Trent Jones Jr. **Season:** April-Oct. **High:** June-Sept. **To obtain tee times:** Call golf shop, reserve with credit card. **Miscellaneous:** Reduced fees (weekdays, low season, resort guests, twilight), discount packages, range (grass), club rentals, lodging (300 rooms), credit cards (MC, V, AE, D).
Special Notes: 2001 US Amateur Sectional qualifying.

★★★ LES BOLSTAD UNIV. OF MINNESOTA GOLF CLUB

SP-2275 W. Larpenteur Ave., St. Paul, 55113, Ramsey County, (612)627-4000, 5 miles E of Minneapolis/St. Paul.
Holes: 18. **Yards:** 6,123/5,684. **Par:** 71/75. **Course Rating:** 69.2/75.2. **Slope:** 117/132. **Green Fee:** $15/$25. **Cart Fee:** $18/cart. **Walking Policy:** Unrestricted walking. **Walkability:** 3. **Opened:** 1922. **Architect:** Seth Raynor. **Season:** April-Oct. **High:** June-Aug. **To obtain tee times:** Call up to 5 days in advance. **Miscellaneous:** Reduced fees (weekdays, low season, twilight), range (grass), club rentals, credit cards (MC, V, D).
Reader Comments: Great old course ... New bunkers and tees are real improvement ... Narrow, challenging. Good flow ... Great student rates ... Traditional ... Small greens ... Somewhat hilly ... Control course, for thinkers ... Interesting. Never get tired of playing it ... Lots of big old trees ... Too much play.

LESTER PARK GOLF CLUB

PU-1860 Lester River Rd., Duluth, 55804, St. Louis County, (218)525-0828, 3 miles E of Duluth. **E-mail:** lpgcduluth.
Holes: 27. **Green Fee:** $20/$20. **Cart Fee:** $20/cart. **Walking Policy:** Unrestricted walking. **Opened:** 1931. **Architect:** Dick Phelps. **Season:** April-Nov. **High:** June-July. **To obtain tee**

times: Call 7 days in advance. **Miscellaneous:** Reduced fees (low season, twilight, seniors, juniors), range (grass), club rentals, credit cards (MC, V).

★★★ BACK/LAKE
Yards: 6,606/5,486. **Par:** 72/73. **Course Rating:** 71.7/72.1. **Slope:** 126/125. **Walkability:** 4.
Reader Comments: Sporty ... Great value for a public course ... Great views of Lake Superior ... Difficult greens to read ... Does not drain well.

★★★ FRONT/BACK
Yards: 6,371/5,604. **Par:** 72/74. **Course Rating:** 70.8/72.6. **Slope:** 118/122. **Walkability:** 2.
Reader Comments: Pretty wide open ... Scenic.

★★★ FRONT/LAKE
Yards: 6,599/5,504. **Par:** 72/73. **Course Rating:** 71.7/72.7. **Slope:** 125/126. **Walkability:** 4.
Reader Comments: Tough ... Challenging ... Tough bunker placements.

★★★½ THE LINKS AT NORTHFORK
PU-9333 153rd Ave., Ramsey, 55303, Anoka County, (612)241-0506, 20 miles SW of Minneapolis. **E-mail:** linksatnorthfork@prodigy.net.
Holes: 18. **Yards:** 6,989/5,242. **Par:** 72/72. **Course Rating:** 73.7/70.5. **Slope:** 127/117. **Green Fee:** $33/$42. **Cart Fee:** $24/cart. **Walking Policy:** Unrestricted walking. **Walkability:** 3.
Opened: 1992. **Architect:** Joel Goldstrand. **Season:** April-Oct. **High:** June-Aug. **To obtain tee times:** Call 7 days in advance for tee times. **Miscellaneous:** Reduced fees (weekdays, low season, twilight, seniors, juniors), discount packages, metal spikes, range (grass), club rentals, credit cards (MC, V, AE, D).
Reader Comments: Very nice links-style ... Hard to walk ... Wind can have big effect ... Bring a lot of balls ... It looks wide open, but guess again ... Fun ... Solid layout ... Practice holes help ... Noisy. Counted 27 trains going by.

★★½ LITCHFIELD GOLF COURSE
PM-405 W. Pleasure Dr., Litchfield, 55355, Meeker County, (320)693-6059, 70 miles W of Minneapolis.
Holes: 18. **Yards:** 6,350/5,011. **Par:** 70/70. **Course Rating:** 69.8/69.4. **Slope:** 123/121. **Green Fee:** $16/$22. **Cart Fee:** $18/cart. **Walking Policy:** Unrestricted walking. **Walkability:** 2.
Opened: 1974. **Season:** April-Oct. **High:** June-Aug. **To obtain tee times:** Call up to 3 days in advance. **Miscellaneous:** Reduced fees (weekdays), metal spikes, club rentals, credit cards (MC, V).
Reader Comments: Super layout; seldom busy ... Good value, developing layout, although no elevation changes.

★★★ LITTLE CROW COUNTRY CLUB
SP-Highway 23, Spicer, 56288, Kandiyohi County, (320)354-2296, 47 miles SW of St. Cloud.
Holes: 27. **Yards:** 6,765/5,757. **Par:** 72/72. **Course Rating:** 72.3/73.1. **Slope:** 123/125. **Green Fee:** $25/$30. **Cart Fee:** $24/cart. **Walking Policy:** Unrestricted walking. **Walkability:** 2.
Opened: 1969. **Architect:** Don Herfort. **Season:** April-Nov. **High:** June-Aug. **To obtain tee times:** Call 1 day in advance. **Miscellaneous:** Reduced fees (low season), range (grass), club rentals, credit cards (MC, V).
Reader Comments: Step above the average rural course ... Good layout ... Excellent value ... Short but challenging ... Too crowded.

★★½ LITTLE FALLS COUNTRY CLUB
PU-1 Edgewater Dr., Little Falls, 56345, Morrison County, (320)632-3584, 30 miles N of St. Cloud.
Holes: 18. **Yards:** 6,051/5,713. **Par:** 72/72. **Course Rating:** 69.0/72.0. **Slope:** 121/125. **Green Fee:** $18/$20. **Cart Fee:** $18/cart. **Walking Policy:** Unrestricted walking. **Walk-ability:** 1.
Opened: 1982. **Season:** April-Oct. **High:** June-Aug. **To obtain tee times:** Call up to 7 days in advance. **Miscellaneous:** Reduced fees (weekdays, low season, juniors), discount packages, range (grass), club rentals, credit cards (MC, V, AE, D).
Reader Comments: Beautiful old course ... All right, but not great ... Challenging ... Tight, heavily pined course with numerous doglegs ... Fairways look like alleys of pine trees.

★★ LONE PINES COUNTRY CLUB
15451 Howard Lake Rd., Shakopee, 55379, Scott County, (612)445-3575.
Special Notes: Call club for further information.

MADDEN'S ON GULL LAKE *Service*
R-11266 Pine Beach Peninsula, Brainerd, 56401, Cass County, (218)829-2811, (800)642-5363, 120 miles N of Minneapolis. **E-mail:** golf@maddens.com. **Web:** www.maddens.com.
★★★½ PINE BEACH EAST COURSE
Holes: 18. **Yards:** 5,956/5,352. **Par:** 72/72. **Course Rating:** 67.9/70.9. **Slope:** 119/116. **Green Fee:** $18/$35. **Cart Fee:** $30/cart. **Walking Policy:** Unrestricted walking. **Walkability:** 3.
Opened: 1926. **Architect:** James Dalgleish. **Season:** April-Oct. **High:** July-Aug. **To obtain tee times:** Call up to 30 days in advance. **Miscellaneous:** Reduced fees (weekdays, resort guests,

twilight), discount packages, range (grass), club rentals, lodging (400 rooms), credit cards (MC, V), beginner friendly (clinics, golf school).
Reader Comments: Why a par 6? ... Slow play allows mosquitoes to keep pace, especially in the evening ... Cut in the pines ... Great greens.

★★★ PINE BEACH WEST COURSE
Holes: 18. **Yards:** 5,049/4,662. **Par:** 67/67. **Course Rating:** 64.0/66.7. **Slope:** 103/107. **Green Fee:** $18/$35. **Cart Fee:** $30/cart. **Walking Policy:** Unrestricted walking. **Walkability:** 3. **Opened:** 1950. **Architect:** Paul Coates/Jim Madden. **Season:** April-Oct. **High:** July-Aug. **To obtain tee times:** Call up to 30 days in advance. **Miscellaneous:** Reduced fees (weekdays, low season, resort guests, twilight), discount packages, range (grass), club rentals, lodging (400 rooms), credit cards (MC, V), beginner friendly (clinics, golf school).
Reader Comments: Short course etched in the woods. Challenging par 3s ... Some strange holes ... A little too short.

★★★★½ THE CLASSIC AT MADDEN'S RESORT *Condition*
Holes: 18. **Yards:** 7,100/4,883. **Par:** 72/72. **Course Rating:** 74.9/68.6. **Slope:** 139/119. **Green Fee:** $60/$100. **Cart Fee:** Included in Green Fee. **Walking Policy:** Unrestricted walking. **Walkability:** 3. **Opened:** 1997. **Architect:** Scott Hoffman. **Season:** April-Oct. **High:** June-Aug. **To obtain tee times:** Call up to 30 days in advance. **Miscellaneous:** Reduced fees (resort guests), range (grass), caddies, club rentals, lodging (400 rooms), credit cards (MC, V).
Notes: Ranked 7th in 1999 Best New Upscale Public Courses.
Reader Comments: One of the best tracks in Minnesota ... Gorgeous wooded terrain ... Could become a gem ... Outstanding. Could remember the layout a month later ... A must if you're in the area ... Terrorizing water holes ... Too tough for the average player ... No gimmicks ... Truly a great golf course ... Too sterile. Groomed the personality out of the course ... Forget the back tees ... Great facilities.

MAJESTIC OAKS GOLF CLUB
PU-701 Bunker Lake Blvd., Ham Lake, 55304, Anoka County, (612)755-2142, 20 miles N of Minneapolis.

★★★½ GOLD COURSE
Holes: 18. **Yards:** 6,396/4,848. **Par:** 72/72. **Course Rating:** 71.2/68.4. **Slope:** 123/120. **Green Fee:** $22/$26. **Cart Fee:** $24/cart. **Walking Policy:** Unrestricted walking. **Walkability:** 2. **Opened:** 1991. **Architect:** Garrett Gill. **Season:** April-Oct. **High:** June-Aug. **To obtain tee times:** Call 4 days in advance for nonpatrons and 7 days in advance for patrons. **Miscellaneous:** Reduced fees (weekdays, low season, twilight, seniors, juniors), metal spikes, range (grass), club rentals, credit cards (MC, V, AE).
Reader Comments: Not long. Pretty easy if you hit short irons close ... Small greens and big trees ... Renovated clubhouse. Getting better ... Too many slow players.
Special Notes: Also has 9-hole executive course.

★★★ PLATINUM COURSE
Holes: 18. **Yards:** 7,013/5,268. **Par:** 72/72. **Course Rating:** 73.9/71.6. **Slope:** 129/126. **Green Fee:** $24/$29. **Cart Fee:** $24/cart. **Walking Policy:** Unrestricted walking. **Walk-ability:** 3. **Opened:** 1972. **Architect:** Charles Maddox. **Season:** April-Oct. **High:** May-Sept. **To obtain tee times:** Call up to 4 days in advance for nonpatrons and 7 days in advance for patrons. **Miscellaneous:** Reduced fees (weekdays, low season, twilight, seniors, juniors), metal spikes, range (grass), club rentals, credit cards (MC, V, AE).
Reader Comments: Dogleg heaven ... OK course ... Good luck getting a tee time ... Never tire of variety.

★★★½ MANITOU RIDGE GOLF COURSE
PU-3200 N. McKnight Rd., White Bear Lake, 55110, Ramsey County, (651)777-2987, 15 miles N of St. Paul.
Holes: 18. **Yards:** 6,422/5,556. **Par:** 71/71. **Course Rating:** 70.5/71.5. **Slope:** 120/119. **Green Fee:** $23/$23. **Cart Fee:** $22/cart. **Walking Policy:** Unrestricted walking. **Walkability:** 4. **Opened:** 1930. **Architect:** Don Herfort. **Season:** April-Oct. **To obtain tee times:** Call 4 days in advance. **Miscellaneous:** Reduced fees (low season, twilight, seniors, juniors), metal spikes, range (grass), club rentals, credit cards (MC, V).
Reader Comments: Getting better ... Narrow fairways ... Short, with some testing holes ... My favorite day-to-day course ... Heavy play ... Some fun holes.

★★★ MAPLE VALLEY GOLF & COUNTRY CLUB
SP-8600 Maple Valley Rd. S.E., Rochester, 55904, Olmsted County, (507)285-9100, 8 miles S of Rochester.
Holes: 18. **Yards:** 6,270/5,330. **Par:** 71/71. **Course Rating:** 68.9/68.5. **Slope:** 108/108. **Green Fee:** $24/$24. **Cart Fee:** $24/cart. **Walking Policy:** Unrestricted walking. **Walkability:** 4. **Opened:** 1964. **Architect:** Wayne Idso. **Season:** March-Nov. **High:** July-Aug. **To obtain tee times:** Call 5 days in advance. **Miscellaneous:** Club rentals, credit cards (MC, V).

Reader Comments: Some nice holes ... Scenic bluffs, lush valley ... Fun ... Tough par 4s, good greens ... Challenging layout could be outstanding with a little work ... In the fall the scenery is breathtaking ... Water, trees, hills, sand.

★★★½ MARSHALL GOLF CLUB
SP-800 Country Club Dr., Marshall, 56258, Lyon County, (507)537-1622, 90 miles NE of Sioux Falls, SD. **E-mail:** mgcatstar.dotnet.
Holes: 18. **Yards:** 6,601/5,136. **Par:** 71/72. **Course Rating:** 71.6/70.2. **Slope:** 130/124. **Green Fee:** $20/$35. **Cart Fee:** $24/cart. **Walking Policy:** Unrestricted walking. **Walkability:** 2.
Architect: J.W. Whitney. **Season:** April-Oct. **High:** May-Sept. **To obtain tee times:** Call 7 days in advance. **Miscellaneous:** Reduced fees (twilight), discount packages, range (grass), club rentals, credit cards (MC, V).
Reader Comments: Nice layout ... Very enjoyable ... Challenging ... Slick greens and tighter fairways make you think your way around the course ... Ponds and stream.

★★½ MEADOWBROOK GOLF COURSE
PU-201 Meadowbrook Rd., Hopkins, 55343, Hennepin County, (612)929-2077, 3 miles W of Minneapolis.
Holes: 18. **Yards:** 6,593/5,610. **Par:** 72/72. **Course Rating:** 72.1/72.7. **Slope:** 130/129. **Green Fee:** $17/$17. **Cart Fee:** $23/cart. **Walking Policy:** Unrestricted walking. **Walk-ability:** 3.
Opened: 1926. **Architect:** J. Foulis/K. Killian/D.Nugent/D Kirscht. **Season:** April-Nov. **High:** May-Aug. **To obtain tee times:** For weekdays come in 3 days in ad-vance. For weekends come in person the Tuesday before. **Miscellaneous:** Reduced fees (low season, twilight, seniors, juniors), metal spikes, club rentals, credit cards (MC, V).
Reader Comments: Why have rangers? Too many people playing too slowly ... Good test ... Old course ... Fun, with lots of elevation changes ... Blind shots ... Really hilly.

★★★½ THE MEADOWS GOLF COURSE
PU-401 34th St. S., Moorhead, 56560, Clay County, (218)299-5244, 2 miles E of Fargo.
Holes: 18. **Yards:** 6,862/5,150. **Par:** 72/72. **Course Rating:** 72.2/69.3. **Slope:** 125/114. **Green Fee:** $17/$20. **Cart Fee:** $20/cart. **Walking Policy:** Unrestricted walking. **Walkability:** 2.
Opened: 1994. **Architect:** Joel Goldstrand. **Season:** May-Oct. **High:** June-Aug. **To obtain tee times:** Call golf shop 2 days in advance. **Miscellaneous:** Reduced fees (seniors, juniors), range (grass), club rentals, credit cards (MC, V, AE, D).
Reader Comments: Fun and reasonable ... Great links-style track, tough if the wind is blowing ... Windy, very open ... Treated well by staff.

★★★ MESABA COUNTRY CLUB
SP-415 E. 51st St., Hibbing, 55746, St. Louis County, (218)263-4826, 70 miles NW of Duluth.
Holes: 18. **Yards:** 6,792/5,747. **Par:** 72/74. **Course Rating:** 71.7/73.0. **Slope:** 131/129. **Green Fee:** $25/$30. **Cart Fee:** $19/cart. **Walking Policy:** Unrestricted walking. **Walkability:** N/A.
Opened: 1923. **Architect:** Charles Erickson. **Season:** April-Oct. **High:** June-Aug. **To obtain tee times:** Call golf shop. **Miscellaneous:** Reduced fees (weekdays), metal spikes, range (grass/mats), club rentals, credit cards (MC, V).
Reader Comments: Reasonable value ... Nos. 2 and 3 are beautiful, challenging holes.

★★½ MILLE LACS GOLF RESORT
R-18517 Captive Lake Rd., Garrison, 56450, Mille Lacs County, (320)692-4325, (800)435-8720, 95 miles N of Minneapolis. **E-mail:** mlgr@millelacsgolf.com. **Web:** millelacsgolf.com.
Holes: 18. **Yards:** 6,290/5,106. **Par:** 71/72. **Course Rating:** 69.7/68.7. **Slope:** 119/113. **Green Fee:** $23/$35. **Cart Fee:** $13/person. **Walking Policy:** Unrestricted walking. **Walkability:** 3.
Opened: 1964. **Architect:** Robert Murphy. **Season:** April-Oct. **High:** June-Sept. **To obtain tee times:** Call golf shop. Credit card needed to reserve tee time. **Miscellaneous:** Reduced fees (weekdays, low season, resort guests, twilight, juniors), discount packages, range (grass), club rentals, lodging, credit cards (MC, V, D).
Reader Comments: Fun ... Good value ... Some nice holes ... Little trouble ... Be ready for blind tee shots and approaches.

★★★ MINNEWASKA GOLF CLUB
PU-Golf Course Rd., Glenwood, 56334, Pope County, (320)634-3680, 120 miles NW of Minneapolis.
Holes: 18. **Yards:** 6,457/5,398. **Par:** 72/73. **Course Rating:** 70.7/71.7. **Slope:** 122/123. **Green Fee:** $17/$22. **Cart Fee:** $22/cart. **Walking Policy:** Unrestricted walking. **Walkability:** 3.
Opened: 1923. **Architect:** Joel Goldstrand. **Season:** April-Oct. **High:** June-Sept. **To obtain tee times:** Call golf shop 1 week in advance. **Miscellaneous:** Reduced fees (weekdays, low season, resort guests, juniors), discount packages, range (grass/mats), club rentals, credit cards (MC, V).
Reader Comments: New holes are great condition ... Good location, very challenging ... Solid course, usually uncrowded ... Clubhouse and first few holes overlook Lake Minnewaska from a high hill. Beautiful ... OK.

MINNESOTA

★★★ MISSISSIPPI DUNES GOLF LINKS
SP-10351 Grey Cloud Trail, Cottage Grove, 55016, Washington County, (651)768-7611, 15 miles SE of Minneapolis/St. Paul.
Holes: 18. **Yards:** 6,694/4,954. **Par:** 72/72. **Course Rating:** 73.1/69.4. **Slope:** 135/115. **Green Fee:** $30/$35. **Cart Fee:** $14/person. **Walking Policy:** Unrestricted walking. **Walkability:** 3. **Opened:** 1995. **Season:** April-Nov. **High:** May-Sept. **To obtain tee times:** Teemaster.com Internet or phone. **Miscellaneous:** Reduced fees (weekdays, low season, twilight, seniors, juniors), range (grass), club rentals, credit cards (MC, V, AE, D).
Reader Comments: Too many blind shots ... Need to know the course ... Love it or hate it ... Tees too close to greens ... Great piece of land ... Drainage problems, unique holes ... Still a new course ... Still not mature.

MISSISSIPPI NATIONAL GOLF LINKS
PU-409 Golf Links Dr., Red Wing, 55066, Goodhue County, (612)388-1874, 50 miles SE of Minneapolis/St. Paul.
★★★½ HIGHLANDS
Holes: 18. **Yards:** 6,282/5,002. **Par:** 71/71. **Course Rating:** 70.5/69.3. **Slope:** 121/115. **Green Fee:** $26/$28. **Cart Fee:** $27/cart. **Walking Policy:** Mandatory cart. **Walkability:** 5. **Opened:** 1987. **Architect:** Gordon Cunningham. **Season:** April-Oct. **High:** June-Aug. **To obtain tee times:** Call up to 7 days in advance. **Miscellaneous:** Reduced fees (weekdays), range (grass), club rentals, credit cards (MC, V, D).
Reader Comments: Small greens, nice layout ... Clubhouse area is wonderful ... Challenging ... This is a real treat! ... Great scenery, short and tricky.
★★★★ LOWLANDS
Holes: 18. **Yards:** 6,484/5,450. **Par:** 71/72. **Course Rating:** 71.0/71.0. **Slope:** 126/121. **Green Fee:** $26/$28. **Cart Fee:** $27/cart. **Walking Policy:** Walking at certain times. **Walkability:** 5. **Opened:** 1987. **Architect:** Gordon Cunningham. **Season:** April-Oct. **High:** June-Aug. **To obtain tee times:** Call up to 7 days in advance. **Miscellaneous:** Reduced fees (weekdays), range (grass), club rentals, credit cards (MC, V, D).
Reader Comments: Very scenic ... Lots of elevation changes ... Charming town; interesting layout ... Tough sidehill lies ... Hilly, but great ... I prefer to walk, but hills require carts ... Awesome scenery of river bluffs ... I want a longer course ... A must-play course.

★★★½ MONTICELLO COUNTRY CLUB
PU-1201 Golf Course Rd., Monticello, 55362, Wright County, (612)295-4653, 30 miles NW of Minneapolis.
Holes: 18. **Yards:** 6,390/5,298. **Par:** 71/72. **Course Rating:** 70.4/70.8. **Slope:** 118/119. **Green Fee:** $16/$22. **Cart Fee:** $22/. **Walking Policy:** Unrestricted walking. **Walkability:** N/A. **Opened:** 1969. **Architect:** Tim Murphy/Joel Goldstrand. **Season:** April-Oct. **High:** June-Aug. **To obtain tee times:** Call 5 days in advance. **Miscellaneous:** Reduced fees (weekdays, low season, seniors), metal spikes, range (grass), club rentals, credit cards (MC, V).
Reader Comments: OK course ... Very busy ... Fair test.

★★★★ MOUNT FRONTENAC GOLF COURSE *Value, Pace*
PU-Hwy. 61, Frontenac, 55026, Goodhue County, (651)388-5826, (800)488-5826, 9 miles SE of Red Wing. **Web:** www.ski-frontenac.com.
Holes: 18. **Yards:** 6,050/4,832. **Par:** 70/70. **Course Rating:** 69.2/67.7. **Slope:** 119/117. **Green Fee:** $14/$18. **Cart Fee:** $20/cart. **Walking Policy:** Unrestricted walking. **Walkability:** 3. **Opened:** 1985. **Architect:** Gordon Emerson. **Season:** April-Oct. **High:** June-Aug. **To obtain tee times:** Call 10 days in advance. **Miscellaneous:** Reduced fees (weekdays, twilight, seniors), discount packages, range (mats), club rentals, credit cards (MC, V, AE, D), beginner friendly.
Reader Comments: Great views for autumn golf ... Beautiful views of surrounding valley ... Par 3 over gorge is a lot of fun ... Wondrous views of Mississippi River... Nice, open course; great for couples.

★★★★ NEW PRAGUE GOLF CLUB *Value, Pace*
PU-400 Lexington Ave.S., New Prague, 56071, Le Sueur County, (612)758-3126, 40 miles SW of Minneapolis.
Holes: 18. **Yards:** 6,335/5,032. **Par:** 72/72. **Course Rating:** 69.5/68.3. **Slope:** 121/116. **Green Fee:** $25/$30. **Cart Fee:** $25/cart. **Walking Policy:** Unrestricted walking. **Walk-ability:** 3. **Opened:** 1929. **Architect:** Don Herfort/Bob Pomije. **Season:** April-Oct. **High:** May-Aug. **To obtain tee times:** Call 7 days in advance. **Miscellaneous:** Reduced fees (weekdays, low season, seniors, juniors), range (grass/mats), credit cards (MC, V).
Reader Comments: Good, simple golf ... Very well kept ... Old, traditional course.

★★½ NORTH LINKS GOLF COURSE
PU-Nicollet County Rd. 66, North Mankato, 56003, Nicollet County, (507)947-3355, 80 miles SW of Minneapolis.

MINNESOTA

Holes: 18. Yards: 6,073/4,659. Par: 72/72. Course Rating: 69.5/66.9. Slope: 117/114. Green Fee: $18/$20. Cart Fee: $18/cart. Walking Policy: Unrestricted walking. Walkability: N/A. Opened: 1993. Architect: Pat Wyss. Season: April-Nov. High: June-Aug. To obtain tee times: Call up to 7 days in advance. Miscellaneous: Reduced fees (twilight, seniors, juniors), metal spikes, range (grass/mats), club rentals, credit cards (MC, V).
Reader Comments: Very nice newer course ... Grip it and rip it ... Many risk-reward situations ... Much too short ... Good for seniors.

★★★ NORTHERN HILLS GOLF COURSE
PU-4805 41st Ave. N.W., Rochester, 59901, Olmsted County, (507)281-6170, 65 miles S of Minneapolis.
Holes: 18. Yards: 6,315/5,456. Par: 72/72. Course Rating: 70.4/71.6. Slope: 123/123. Green Fee: $20/$20. Cart Fee: $20/cart. Walking Policy: Unrestricted walking. Walkability: 2. Opened: 1976. Architect: Clayton Westrum. Season: April-Oct. High: May-Sept. To obtain tee times: Call 2 days in advance. Miscellaneous: Metal spikes, range (grass), club rentals, credit cards (MC, V).
Reader Comments: Good for average golfer ... Good scoring course ... Fairly short ... Could play it every day.

★★★½ NORTHFIELD GOLF CLUB
SP-707 Prairie St., Northfield, 55057, Dakota County, (507)645-4026, 25 miles S of Minneapolis. Holes: 18. Yards: 5,856/5,103. Par: 69/71. Course Rating: 68.7/70.4. Slope: 128/126. Green Fee: $25/$35. Cart Fee: $20. Walking Policy: Unrestricted walking. Walkability: N/A. Opened: 1926. Architect: Don Herfort. Season: April-Oct. High: April-Sept. To obtain tee times: Call or come in 2 days in advance. Miscellaneous: Metal spikes, caddies, club rentals, credit cards (MC, V).
Reader Comments: Shotmaker's dream ... Well-defined, fun layout ... Changes will change character of course ... Short, treelined challenge.

★★★½ OAK GLEN GOLF CLUB
PU-1599 McKusick Rd., Stillwater, 55082, Washington County, (651)439-6963, 20 miles NE of St. Paul.
Holes: 18. Yards: 6,550/5,626. Par: 72/72. Course Rating: 72.4/73.4. Slope: 131/130. Green Fee: $22/$28. Cart Fee: $11/person. Walking Policy: Unrestricted walking. Walkability: 2. Opened: 1982. Architect: Don Herfort. Season: April-Nov. High: June-Aug. To obtain tee times: Call 3 days in advance. Miscellaneous: Reduced fees (weekdays, twilight), metal spikes, range (grass), club rentals, credit cards (MC, V).
Reader Comments: I could really get addicted to this one ... Fast greens ... Back 9 doesn't fit in ... Nothing special ... Very fair and fun to play.

★★ OAK SUMMIT GOLF COURSE
PU-2751 County Rd. 16 S.W., Rochester, 55902, Olmstead County, (507)252-1808.
Holes: 18. Yards: 6,518/5,159. Par: 71/71. Course Rating: 71.3/69.1. Slope: 121/115. Green Fee: $12/$18. Cart Fee: $18/cart. Walking Policy: Unrestricted walking. Walkability: 3. Opened: 1992. Architect: Leon DeCook. Season: April-Nov. High: June-Aug. To obtain tee times: Call up to 3 days in advance. Miscellaneous: Reduced fees (weekdays, twilight, seniors), metal spikes, range (grass/mats), club rentals, credit cards (MC, V).

★★★ OAKS COUNTRY CLUB
SP-Country Club Rd., Hayfield, 55940, Dodge County, (507)477-3233, 20 miles W of Rochester.
Holes: 18. Yards: 6,404/5,663. Par: 72/72. Course Rating: 69.7/73. Slope: 114/118. Green Fee: $16/$17. Cart Fee: $10/person. Walking Policy: Unrestricted walking. Walkability: 1. Opened: 1977. Architect: John Queenland. Season: April-Oct. High: June-Aug. To obtain tee times: Nonmembers contact golf shop 5 days in advance. Miscellaneous: Reduced fees (low season), discount packages, range (grass), club rentals, credit cards (MC, V).
Reader Comments: Wide open; could use more hazards ... A jewel hidden in the corn.

★★★ ONEKA RIDGE GOLF COURSE
PU-5610 120th St. N., White Bear Lake, 55110, Ramsey County, (651)429-2390, 15 miles N of St. Paul.
Holes: 18. Yards: 6,351/5,166. Par: 72/72. Course Rating: 70.8/69.7. Slope: 118/115. Green Fee: N/A/$24. Cart Fee: $24/cart. Walking Policy: Unrestricted walking. Walkability: 3. Opened: 1996. Season: April-Nov. High: June-July. To obtain tee times: Call 4 days in advance. Miscellaneous: Reduced fees (twilight, seniors, juniors), range (grass), club rentals, credit cards (MC, V), beginner friendly.
Reader Comments: New, but potential ... Easy, relaxing course ... Short and playable ... Needs maturing ... Several short par 4s.

★★★½ ORTONVILLE MUNICIPAL GOLF COURSE
PM-R.R. 1, Ortonville, 56278, Big Stone County, (320)839-3606, 150 miles W of Minneapolis.

Holes: 18. **Yards:** 6,001/5,419. **Par:** 72/72. **Course Rating:** 68.1/70.6. **Slope:** 111/115. **Green Fee:** $17/$20. **Cart Fee:** $20/cart. **Walking Policy:** Unrestricted walking. **Walkability:** 1. **Architect:** Joel Goldstrand. **Season:** April-Oct. **High:** July-Aug. **To obtain tee times:** Call golf shop. **Miscellaneous:** Reduced fees (weekdays), range (grass), club rentals.
Reader Comments: Nice, affordable course ... Hidden treasure.

★★★★ PEBBLE CREEK GOLF CLUB *Condition*
PU-14000 Club House Lane, Becker, 55308, Sherburne County, (612)261-4653, 17 miles NW of St. Cloud.
Holes: 27. **Yards:** 6,820/5,633. **Par:** 72/72. **Course Rating:** 73.2/72.9. **Slope:** 129/127. **Green Fee:** $26/$32. **Cart Fee:** $12/person. **Walking Policy:** Unrestricted walking. **Walkability:** 1. **Opened:** 1987. **Architect:** Don Herfort/Garrett Gill. **Season:** April-Nov. **High:** June-Sept. **To obtain tee times:** Call 7 days in advance. Up to 30 days available with $2.00 advance reservation fee. **Miscellaneous:** Reduced fees (low season, twilight, seniors, juniors), range (grass), club rentals, credit cards (MC, V, AE).
Reader Comments: Original front & back 9 are best; third 9 is fair ... New 9 a little short ... Great course ... Many good holes ... Nicer than many private clubs.

★★★ PEBBLE LAKE GOLF CLUB
PU-County 82 S., Fergus Falls, 56537, Otter Tail County, (218)736-7404, 175 miles NW of Minneapolis.
Holes: 18. **Yards:** 6,711/5,531. **Par:** 72/74. **Course Rating:** 72.3/72.1. **Slope:** 128/126. **Green Fee:** $22/$25. **Cart Fee:** $19/cart. **Walking Policy:** Unrestricted walking. **Walkability:** 3. **Opened:** 1941. **Architect:** Paul Coates. **Season:** April-Oct. **High:** June-Aug. **To obtain tee times:** Call up to 7 days in advance. **Miscellaneous:** Reduced fees (low season, twilight, juniors), metal spikes, range (grass), club rentals, credit cards (MC, V), beginner friendly (junior and adult group lessons).
Reader Comments: Can be a test on occasion ... Too many leaves ... Good walk.

★★★½ PERHAM LAKESIDE COUNTRY CLUB
PU-P.O. Box 313, Perham, 56573, Otter Tail County, (218)346-6070, 20 miles SE of Detroit Lakes. **E-mail:** lakeside@djam.com. **Web:** Plcc@edt.com.
Holes: 18. **Yards:** 6,575/5,312. **Par:** 72/72. **Course Rating:** 72.5/71.1. **Slope:** 128/122. **Green Fee:** $25/$30. **Cart Fee:** $23/cart. **Walking Policy:** Unrestricted walking. **Walk-ability:** 3. **Opened:** 1938. **Architect:** Joel Goldstrand. **Season:** April-Nov. **High:** June-Aug. **To obtain tee times:** Call up to 7 days in advance. **Miscellaneous:** Reduced fees (weekdays, low season, twilight), range (grass), club rentals, credit cards (MC, V, D).
Reader Comments: Very nice course and people ... Good shape for late-season play ... No. 11 is an outstanding par 3 over water; say your prayers.

★★★ PEZHEKEE GOLF CLUB
R-2000 South Lakeshore Dr., Glenwood, 56334, Pope County, (320)634-4501, (800)356-8654, 120 miles NW of Minneapolis/St. Paul. **E-mail:** jim@petersresort.com. **Web:** www.petersresort.com.
Holes: 18. **Yards:** 6,454/5,465. **Par:** 72/75. **Course Rating:** 70.8/71.5. **Slope:** 119/122. **Green Fee:** $27/$32. **Cart Fee:** $25/cart. **Walking Policy:** Unrestricted walking. **Walkability:** 4. **Opened:** 1967. **Architect:** Tim Murphy/Bill Peters. **Season:** May-Oct. **High:** June-Sept. **To obtain tee times:** Call in advance or walk on. **Miscellaneous:** Reduced fees (weekdays, low season, resort guests, twilight, juniors), discount packages, metal spikes, club rentals, lodging (52 rooms), credit cards (MC, V).
Reader Comments: Good mix of old and new holes ... Super views ... Hilly son of a gun ... A few tough holes.

★★½ PHALEN PARK GOLF COURSE
PU-1615 Phalen Dr., St. Paul, 55106, Ramsey County, (651)778-0413.
Holes: 18. **Yards:** 6,101/5,439. **Par:** 70/71. **Course Rating:** 68.7/70.7. **Slope:** 121/121. **Green Fee:** $23/N/A. **Cart Fee:** $23/cart. **Walking Policy:** Unrestricted walking. **Walkability:** 2. **Opened:** 1920. **Architect:** Don Herfort. **Season:** March-Nov. **High:** June-Aug. **To obtain tee times:** Call 7 days in advance for weekdays; Thursday at 6 a.m. for weekends. **Miscellaneous:** Reduced fees (twilight, seniors, juniors), range (grass), club rentals, credit cards (MC, V).
Reader Comments: Very good shorter course ... Heavily played ... Good buy for average golfer ... Tight layout ... Nice trees.

★★★½ PHEASANT ACRES GOLF CLUB
PU-10705 County Rd. 116, Rogers, 55374, Hennepin County, (612)428-8244, 20 miles NW of Minneapolis.
Holes: 18. **Yards:** 6,400/5,200. **Par:** 71/72. **Course Rating:** 69.9/68.7. **Slope:** 117/115. **Green Fee:** $14/$25. **Cart Fee:** $20/cart. **Walking Policy:** Unrestricted walking. **Walkability:** 1. **Opened:** 1988. **Architect:** Lyle Johansen. **Season:** April-Nov. **High:** June-Sept. **To obtain tee times:** Call Tuesday for weekend times; Saturday for weekdays. **Miscellaneous:** Reduced fees

(weekdays, low season, twilight, seniors, juniors), metal spikes, range (grass/mats), club rentals, credit cards (MC, V), beginner friendly (lessons available).
Reader Comments: Improving yearly ... Fun ... Pretty easy; not hard without wind ... Slow ... Open course ... Very playable.

★★½ PINE MEADOWS GOLF COURSE
SP-500 Golf Course Dr., Baxter, 56425, Crow Wing County, (218)829-5733, (800)368-2048, 120 miles NW of Minneapolis/St. Paul.
Holes: 18. **Yards:** 6,372/5,145. **Par:** 72/72. **Course Rating:** 71.5/70.5. **Slope:** 130/129. **Green Fee:** $27/$32. **Cart Fee:** $25/cart. **Walking Policy:** Unrestricted walking. **Walkability:** 2.
Season: April-Oct. **High:** June-Aug. **To obtain tee times:** Call golf shop up to 7 days in advance. Members call 30 days in advance. **Miscellaneous:** Reduced fees (weekdays, low season, resort guests, twilight, seniors, juniors), discount packages, range (grass), club rentals, credit cards (MC, V), beginner friendly (PGA junior program).
Reader Comments: A great mixture of holes. A pleasant public course ... Scenic on back 9 ... Too many fivesomes allowed.

★★★½ POKEGAMA GOLF CLUB
PU-3910 Golf Course Rd., Grand Rapids, 55744, Itasca County, (218)326-3444, (888)307-3444, 4 miles W of Grand Rapids.
Holes: 18. **Yards:** 6,481/5,046. **Par:** 71/72. **Course Rating:** 70.3/67.7. **Slope:** 121/116. **Green Fee:** $24/$28. **Cart Fee:** $22/cart. **Walking Policy:** Unrestricted walking. **Walkability:** 2.
Opened: 1926. **Architect:** Donald Brauer. **Season:** April-Oct. **High:** June-Aug. **To obtain tee times:** Call 7 days in advance. **Miscellaneous:** Reduced fees (weekdays, resort guests, twilight), discount packages, range (grass), club rentals, credit cards (MC, V).
Reader Comments: Beautiful walking course, packages, lake views, woods ... Greens have recovered ... Good resort course.

★★½ PRAIRIE VIEW GOLF LINKS
PU-Hwy. 266 N., Worthington, 56187, Nobles County, (507)372-8670, 50 miles E of Sioux Falls.
Holes: 18. **Yards:** 6,366/5,103. **Par:** 71/71. **Course Rating:** 69.9/68.3. **Slope:** 112/113. **Green Fee:** $18/$20. **Cart Fee:** $9/person. **Walking Policy:** Unrestricted walking. **Walkability:** N/A.
Opened: 1983. **Architect:** Joel Goldstrand. **Season:** April-Oct. **High:** June-Aug. **To obtain tee times:** Call Thursday for weekend times. **Miscellaneous:** Reduced fees (weekdays, twilight), range (grass), club rentals, credit cards (MC, V).
Reader Comments: Good layout ... Links style ... The wind really comes into play.

★★★★½ THE PRESERVE GOLF COURSE *SERVICE+, PACE*
R-C.R. 107, Pequot Lakes, 56472, Crow Wing County, (218)568-4944, (888)437-4637, 20 miles N of Brainerd. **E-mail:** thepines.com. **Web:** www.grandviewlodge.com.
Holes: 18. **Yards:** 6,601/4,816. **Par:** 72/72. **Course Rating:** 71.6/68.8. **Slope:** 135/119. **Green Fee:** $46/$54. **Cart Fee:** $16/person. **Walking Policy:** Unrestricted walking. **Walkability:** 4.
Opened: 1996. **Architect:** Dan Helbling/Mike Morley. **Season:** April-Oct. **High:** June-Sept. **To obtain tee times:** Call the tee time number above. No restrictions on advanced reservations.
Miscellaneous: Reduced fees (weekdays, resort guests, twilight), discount packages, range (grass), club rentals, lodging (250 rooms), credit cards (MC, V, AE, D).
Reader Comments: Awesome views, great course ... Even us duffers had fun ... Has to be among top five in Minnesota ... Very challenging ... Well-manicured ... Will improve with time ... Great staff ... Great setting ... Northern Minnesota perfect.
Special Notes: Formerly The Preserve Golf Club at Grand View Lodge.

★★★½ PRESTWICK GOLF CLUB AT WEDGEWOOD
SP-9555 Wedgewood Dr., Woodbury, 55125, Washington County, (651)731-4779, 10 miles E of St. Paul. **E-mail:** infoatprestwick.com. **Web:** www.prestwick.com.
Holes: 18. **Yards:** 6,699/5,252. **Par:** 72/72. **Course Rating:** 72.5/71.0. **Slope:** 127/121. **Green Fee:** $38/$43. **Cart Fee:** $15/person. **Walking Policy:** Unrestricted walking. **Walkability:** 3.
Opened: 1985. **Architect:** Norb Anderson. **Season:** March-Nov. **High:** April-Sept. **To obtain tee times:** Credit card guarantee required with 24-hour cancellation policy. **Miscellaneous:** Reduced fees (weekdays, twilight, juniors), range (grass), club rentals, credit cards (MC, V, AE, D).
Reader Comments: Traditional design; country-club atmosphere ... Nice, but slow ... Great neighborhood ... Getting too expensive ... A little stuffy ... Homes close.

★★½ PRINCETON GOLF CLUB
SP-Golf Club Rd., Princeton, 55371, Mille Lacs County, (612)389-5109, (800)882-0698, 45 miles N of Minneapolis/St. Paul. **E-mail:** princeton@teemaster .
Holes: 18. **Yards:** 6,271/4,849. **Par:** 71/71. **Course Rating:** 70.8/68.9. **Slope:** 126/115. **Green Fee:** $22/$26. **Cart Fee:** $22/cart. **Walking Policy:** Unrestricted walking. **Walkability:** 3.
Opened: 1951. **Architect:** Joe Goldstrand. **Season:** April-Oct. **High:** June-Aug. **To obtain tee**

times: Call 5 days in advance. **Miscellaneous:** Reduced fees (weekdays, low season, twilight, seniors, juniors), discount packages, range (grass), club rentals, credit cards (MC, V, AE, D).
Reader Comments: Many doglegs; accuracy a must ... Too many trick holes.

★★★★½ PURPLE HAWK COUNTRY CLUB *Value, Pace*
SP-N. Hwy. 65, P. O. Box 528, Cambridge, 55008, Isanti County, (612)689-3800, 60 miles N of Minneapolis/St. Paul. **E-mail:** phcc72@ecenet.com. **Web:** www.purplehawk.com.
Holes: 18. **Yards:** 6,679/5,748. **Par:** 72/74. **Course Rating:** 72.3/73.5. **Slope:** 132/131. **Green Fee:** $21/$27. **Cart Fee:** $24/cart. **Walking Policy:** Unrestricted walking. **Walkability:** 2.
Opened: 1970. **Architect:** Don Herfort. **Season:** April-Oct. **High:** June-Aug. **To obtain tee times:** Call up to 5 days in advance. **Miscellaneous:** Reduced fees (twilight, seniors, juniors), range (grass), club rentals, credit cards (MC, V, D).
Reader Comments: One of my favorites ... Nice course ... Fun ... Great track for the money ... Good small-town course.

★½ RAMSEY GOLF CLUB
PU-R.R. 1, Box 83, Austin, 55912, Mower County, (507)433-9098, 95 miles S of Minneapolis/St. Paul.
Holes: 18. **Yards:** 5,987/5,426. **Par:** 71/72. **Course Rating:** 67.6/70.1. **Slope:** 118/118. **Green Fee:** $18/$18. **Cart Fee:** $19/cart. **Walking Policy:** Unrestricted walking. **Walkability:** 1.
Opened: 1940. **Architect:** Jim Vacura. **Season:** April-Nov. **High:** May-Sept. **To obtain tee times:** First come, first served. Cart reservations are available. **Miscellaneous:** Reduced fees (low season), discount packages, metal spikes, range (grass), club rentals, credit cards (MC, V, AE, D, All).

★★ RICH ACRES GOLF COURSE
PU-2201 E. 66th St., Richfield, 55423, Hennepin County, (612)861-9341, 10 miles SW of Minneapolis.
Holes: 18. **Yards:** 6,606/5,746. **Par:** 71/73. **Course Rating:** 69.8/72.3. **Slope:** 115/121. **Green Fee:** $21/$23. **Cart Fee:** $21/cart. **Walking Policy:** Unrestricted walking. **Walkability:** 2.
Opened: 1980. **Architect:** Jerry Perkl. **Season:** April-Nov. **To obtain tee times:** Call (612)861-9345 or (612)949-4949. **Miscellaneous:** Reduced fees (weekdays, low season, twilight, seniors, juniors), metal spikes, range (grass), club rentals, credit cards (MC, V, D).

★★½ RICH SPRING GOLF CLUB
SP-17467 Fairway Circle, Cold Spring, 56320, Stearns County, (320)685-8810, 20 miles SW of St. Cloud.
Holes: 18. **Yards:** 6,517/5,336. **Par:** 72/72. **Course Rating:** 71.1/70.4. **Slope:** 129/118. **Green Fee:** $20/$23. **Cart Fee:** $22/cart. **Walking Policy:** Unrestricted walking. **Walkability:** 3.
Opened: 1962. **Season:** April-Oct. **High:** May-Sept. **To obtain tee times:** Call up to 3 days in advance. **Miscellaneous:** Reduced fees (seniors), range (grass), club rentals, credit cards (MC, V, D).
Reader Comments: Never that crowded ... Interesting combination of terrain, rock, trees and water ... Country setting ... Small greens.

RICH VALLEY GOLF CLUB
PU-3855 145th St. E., Rosemount, 55068, Dakota County, (651)437-4653, 4 miles E of Rosemount.
Holes: 27. **Green Fee:** $19/$19. **Cart Fee:** $19/cart. **Walking Policy:** Unrestricted walking. **Walkability:** 2. **Opened:** 1988. **Architect:** Ray Rahn. **Season:** April-Oct. **High:** June-Aug. **Miscellaneous:** Reduced fees (seniors, juniors), range (grass), club rentals, credit cards (MC, V), beginner friendly.
RED/BLUE
Yards: 5,286/4,539. **Par:** 69/70. **Course Rating:** 64.1/64.4. **Slope:** 100/101.
RED/WHITE
Yards: 5,289/4,680. **Par:** 67/69. **Course Rating:** 63.7/65.1. **Slope:** 95/99.
WHITE/BLUE
Yards: 5,079/4,397. **Par:** 68/69. **Course Rating:** 63.0/63.7. **Slope:** 98/98.

★★★½ RIDGEWOOD GOLF COURSE
PU-County Rd. 7, Longville, 56655, Cass County, (218)363-2444.
Yards: 6,564/5,669. **Par:** 72/72. **Course Rating:** 72.0/72.9. **Slope:** 129/127. **Green Fee:** $23/$25. **Walkability:** N/A. **Miscellaneous:** Metal spikes.
Reader Comments: Front 9 more mature than back.

★★★½ RIVER OAKS MUNICIPAL GOLF CLUB
PM-11099 S. Highway 61, Cottage Grove, 55016, Washington County, (612)438-2121, 15 miles S of St. Paul.
Holes: 18. **Yards:** 6,433/5,224. **Par:** 71/71. **Course Rating:** 71.4/74.9. **Slope:** 131/137. **Green Fee:** $20/$23. **Cart Fee:** $21/cart. **Walking Policy:** Unrestricted walking. **Walkability:** 1.

Opened: 1991. **Season:** April-Nov. **High:** May-Sept. **To obtain tee times:** Call Monday for weekends, Sunday for weekdays. **Miscellaneous:** Reduced fees (seniors, juniors), metal spikes, range (grass), club rentals, credit cards (MC, V).
Reader Comments: Great views from on top ... Good value ... Pretty nice and straightforward ... Good course for middle-handicappers ... Nice views of the Mississippi River ... Hilly ... Difficult for high-handicappers ... Good test.

★★½ ROSE LAKE GOLF COURSE
PU-2456 104th Street, Fairmont, 56031, Martin County, (507)235-5274, 3 miles E of Fairmont.
Holes: 18. **Yards:** 6,196/5,276. **Par:** 71/71. **Course Rating:** 69.6/70.3. **Slope:** 121/120. **Green Fee:** $17/$20. **Cart Fee:** $18/cart. **Walking Policy:** Unrestricted walking. **Walkability:** 3.
Opened: 1957. **Architect:** Joel Goldstrand. **Season:** April-Nov. **High:** June-Aug. **To obtain tee times:** Call up to 7 days in advance. **Miscellaneous:** Range (grass), club rentals, credit cards (MC, V).
Reader Comments: Have improved condition ... Lots of water ... Good course ... Designed around lake.

★★★½ RUM RIVER HILLS GOLF CLUB
PU-16659 St. Francis Blvd., Anoka, 55303, Anoka County, (612)753-3339, 15 miles N of Minneapolis.
Holes: 18. **Yards:** 6,338/5,095. **Par:** 71/71. **Course Rating:** 70.0/69.6. **Slope:** 117/120. **Green Fee:** $18/$25. **Cart Fee:** $22/cart. **Walking Policy:** Unrestricted walking. **Walkability:** 2.
Opened: 1986. **Architect:** Joel Goldstrand. **Season:** March-Nov. **High:** June-Aug. **To obtain tee times:** Call 3 days in advance. **Miscellaneous:** Reduced fees (twilight, seniors, juniors), discount packages, metal spikes, range (grass), club rentals, credit cards (MC, V, D, Diners Club).
Reader Comments: Nice ... Shot my personal best here ... Too many water holes.

★★★★ RUSH CREEK GOLF CLUB *Service*
PU-7801 C.R. 101, Maple Grove, 55311, Hennepin County, (612)494-8844, 20 miles NW of Minneapolis.
Holes: 18. **Yards:** 7,020/5,317. **Par:** 72/72. **Course Rating:** 74.2/71.1. **Slope:** 137/127. **Green Fee:** $50/$100. **Cart Fee:** $10/person. **Walking Policy:** Unrestricted walking. **Walkability:** 2.
Opened: 1996. **Architect:** Bob Cupp/John Fought. **Season:** April-Oct. **High:** June-Aug. **To obtain tee times:** Call up to 14 days in advance. **Miscellaneous:** Reduced fees (twilight, juniors), range (grass/mats), caddies, club rentals, credit cards (MC, V, AE, Diners Club).
Notes: Ranked 19th in 1999 Best in State. 1997 Edina Realty LPGA Classic; 1998 Rainbow Foods LPGA Classic.
Reader Comments: Great shape ... Pricey ... Nice condition ... A little stuffy ... Great practice green ... 18th is a great finishing hole ... Typical modern design ... Good course for thinking golfer ... Greens can be tricky ... Bent-grass fairways.

★★★★ RUTTGER'S BAY LAKE LODGE
R-Rte. 2, Deerwood, 56401, Crow Wing County, (218)678-2885, (800)450-4545, 15 miles NE of Brainerd.
Holes: 18. **Yards:** 6,750/510. **Par:** 72/72. **Course Rating:** 72.5/69.3. **Slope:** 132/125. **Green Fee:** $24/$40. **Cart Fee:** $14. **Walking Policy:** Unrestricted walking. **Walkability:** N/A. **Opened:** 1992. **Architect:** Joel Goldstrand. **Season:** April-Oct. **High:** May-Sept. **To obtain tee times:** Call 800 number anytime. **Miscellaneous:** Reduced fees (low season, resort guests, twilight), discount packages, metal spikes, range (grass), caddies, club rentals, lodging, credit cards (MC, V, AE, D).
Reader Comments: Nice layout; pretty surroundings ... Fun resort course ... Nice stroll in the woods ... Hit it straight or be dead in the trees ... A little pricey ... Great vistas ... I love it; play it every year ... Always a challenge, especially 17 and 18 ... Too many blind shots ... Everything first-class.

★★ ST. CHARLES GOLF CLUB
SP-1920 Park Rd., St. Charles, 55972, Winona County, (507)932-5444, 20 miles E of Rochester.
Holes: 18. **Yards:** 6,439/N/A. **Par:** 72/72. **Course Rating:** 69.8/69.7. **Slope:** 118/111. **Green Fee:** $20/$20. **Cart Fee:** $20/cart. **Walking Policy:** Unrestricted walking. **Walk-ability:** 3.
Opened: 1991. **Architect:** Wayne Idso. **Season:** March-Nov. **High:** July-Aug. **To obtain tee times:** Tee times taken 7 days in advance. **Miscellaneous:** Range (grass), club rentals, credit cards (MC, V), beginner friendly (beginner and junior classes).

SARTELL GOLF CLUB
PU-801 Pinecone Rd. Box 363, Sartell, 56377, Stearns County, (320)259-0551, 10 miles N of St. Cloud.
Holes: 18. **Yards:** 6,363/5,321. **Par:** 72/72. **Course Rating:** 68.3/69.9. **Slope:** 113/115. **Green Fee:** $18/$21. **Cart Fee:** $20/cart. **Walking Policy:** Unrestricted walking. **Walkability:** 1.
Opened: 1983. **Season:** March-Nov. **High:** May-July. **To obtain tee times:** Call golf shop.

Miscellaneous: Reduced fees (seniors, juniors), range (grass/mats), club rentals, credit cards (MC, V).

★★★½ SAWMILL GOLF CLUB

SP-11177 McKusick Rd., Grant, 55082, Washington County, (651)439-7862, 15 miles NE of St. Paul.
Holes: 18. **Yards:** 6,300/5,300. **Par:** 70/71. **Course Rating:** 70.2/69.5. **Slope:** 125/122. **Green Fee:** $22/$35. **Cart Fee:** $26/cart. **Walking Policy:** Unrestricted walking. **Walkability:** 3.
Opened: 1983. **Architect:** Dan Pohl/John McCarthy/Pat Rooney. **Season:** April-Nov. **High:** May-Sept. **To obtain tee times:** Call 4 days in advance. **Miscellaneous:** Reduced fees (twilight, seniors, juniors), range (grass), club rentals, credit cards (MC, V, AE).
Reader Comments: Getting better ... Fun ... Classy ... Every hole interesting.

★★ SHAMROCK GOLF COURSE

PU-19625 Larkin Rd., Corcoran, 55340, Hennepin County, (612)478-9977, 15 miles NW of Minneapolis. **E-mail:** keeper29@idt.net.
Holes: 18. **Yards:** 6,423/5,793. **Par:** 72/74. **Course Rating:** 69.8/72.1. **Slope:** 111/115. **Green Fee:** $21/$24. **Cart Fee:** $23/cart. **Walking Policy:** Unrestricted walking. **Walkability:** 2.
Opened: 1974. **Season:** April-Oct. **High:** May-Aug. **To obtain tee times:** Call Tuesday morning at 7 a.m. **Miscellaneous:** Reduced fees (weekdays, low season, seniors, juniors).

★★ SHORELAND COUNTRY CLUB

SP-Lake Emily/County 21, St. Peter, 56082, Nicollet County, (507)931-3470.
Holes: 18. **Yards:** 5,592/4,965. **Par:** 69/71. **Course Rating:** 66.6/68.9. **Slope:** 112/117. **Green Fee:** $25/$27. **Cart Fee:** $24/cart. **Walking Policy:** Unrestricted walking. **Walkability:** 4.
Opened: 1929. **Season:** April-Oct. **High:** June-Aug. **To obtain tee times:** Call (507)931-3470. Non-members call call 2 days in advance. **Miscellaneous:** Reduced fees (juniors), club rentals, credit cards (MC, V).

SILVER SPRINGS GOLF COURSE

PU-Cty Rd. 39W, Monticello, 55362, Wright County, (612)295-2951, 30 miles W of Minneapolis. **E-mail:** thecak@uswest.net. **Web:** www.silverspringsgolf.com.

★★½ GOLD COURSE

Holes: 18. **Yards:** 6,458/5,959. **Par:** 72/72. **Course Rating:** 69.8/72.6. **Slope:** 115/121. **Green Fee:** $22/$27. **Cart Fee:** $26/cart. **Walking Policy:** Unrestricted walking. **Walkability:** 1.
Opened: 1984. **Architect:** Al Joyner. **Season:** April-Oct. **High:** May-Sept. **To obtain tee times:** Call up to 7 days in advance. **Miscellaneous:** Reduced fees (weekdays, twilight, seniors, juniors), metal spikes, range (grass), club rentals, credit cards (MC, V, AE, D).
Reader Comments: Huge greens ... Easy to get tee times ... Not too cramped.

★★ SILVER COURSE

Holes: 18. **Yards:** 6,622/6,176. **Par:** 72/74. **Course Rating:** 70.5/73.9. **Slope:** 115/126. **Green Fee:** $22/$27. **Cart Fee:** $26/cart. **Walking Policy:** Unrestricted walking. **Walkability:** 1.
Opened: 1974. **Architect:** Al Joyner. **Season:** March-Oct. **High:** May-Sept. **To obtain tee times:** Call up to 7 days in advance. **Miscellaneous:** Reduced fees (weekdays, twilight, seniors, juniors), metal spikes, range (grass), club rentals, credit cards (MC, V, AE, D).

★★★½ SOUTHERN HILLS GOLF CLUB

PU-18950 Chippendale Ave., Farmington, 55024, Dakota County, (612)463-4653, 20 miles S of Minneapolis.
Holes: 18. **Yards:** 6,314/4,970. **Par:** 71/71. **Course Rating:** 70.4/68.3. **Slope:** 123/116. **Green Fee:** $18/$30. **Cart Fee:** $13/person. **Walking Policy:** Unrestricted walking. **Walkability:** 2.
Opened: 1989. **Architect:** Joel Goldstrand. **Season:** April-Oct. **High:** June-Aug. **To obtain tee times:** Public may call 7 days in advance. **Miscellaneous:** Reduced fees (weekdays, low season, twilight, seniors, juniors), metal spikes, range (grass), club rentals, credit cards (MC, V).
Reader Comments: Great links style ... Easy to get on ... Open. Don't plant any more trees ... Rolling terrain.

★★★★ STONEBROOKE GOLF CLUB

SP-2693 County Rd. 79, Shakopee, 55379, Scott County, (612)496-3171, (800)263-3189, 20 miles SW of Minneapolis. **Web:** http://www.stonebrooke.com.
Holes: 18. **Yards:** 6,614/5,033. **Par:** 71/71. **Course Rating:** 71.7/69.3. **Slope:** 133/118. **Green Fee:** $34/$41. **Cart Fee:** $24/cart. **Walking Policy:** Unrestricted walking. **Walkability:** 3.
Opened: 1989. **Architect:** T.L. Haugen. **Season:** April-Oct. **High:** June-July. **To obtain tee times:** Call 3 days in advance. Play can be set up anytime by non-residents by calling. **Miscellaneous:** Reduced fees (twilight), metal spikes, range (grass/mats), club rentals, credit cards (MC, V).
Reader Comments: Very neat course ... A little pricey ... Challenging ... A real jewel ... Pro helped me on practice green for no money ... Fast pace! No wait! Yeah, baby! ... A little expensive for the working stiff, but worth it ... Give it a whirl ... Power lines a negative ... Take a ferry from 8th tee to fairway.

MINNESOTA

★★½ SUGARBROOKE GOLF CLUB
R-P.O. Box 847, Grand Rapids, 55744, Itasca County, (218)327-1462, (800)450-4555, 12 miles SW of Grand Rapids. **E-mail:** sugarglf@uslink.net. **Web:** www.ruttgerssl.com.
Holes: 18. **Yards:** 6,545/5,032. **Par:** 71/71. **Course Rating:** 71.6/69.3. **Slope:** 124/119. **Green Fee:** $30/$30. **Cart Fee:** $25/cart. **Walking Policy:** Unrestricted walking. **Walkability:** 2. **Opened:** 1994. **Architect:** Joel Goldstrand. **Season:** April-Oct. **To obtain tee times:** Call 7 days (maximum) in advance. **Miscellaneous:** Reduced fees (resort guests, twilight), discount packages, range (grass), club rentals, lodging (120 rooms), credit cards (MC, V, AE, D).
Reader Comments: Potential, but some very rough holes ... Needs work ... I left a club there and they sent it back to me, no charge ... Worth a visit.

★★★ SUNDANCE GOLF CLUB
PU-15240 113th Ave. N., Maple Grove, 55369, Hennepin County, (612)420-4700, 15 miles NW of Minneapolis.
Holes: 18. **Yards:** 6,446/5,548. **Par:** 72/72. **Course Rating:** 70.7/71.6. **Slope:** 127/126. **Green Fee:** $14/$27. **Cart Fee:** $24/cart. **Walking Policy:** Unrestricted walking. **Walkability:** 3. **Opened:** 1970. **Architect:** Ade Simonsen. **Season:** April-Nov. **High:** May-July. **To obtain tee times:** Call up to 7 days in advance for weekdays, Tuesday for weekends. **Miscellaneous:** Reduced fees (weekdays, seniors, juniors), range (grass), club rentals, credit cards (MC, V, AE, D).
Reader Comments: Making improvements ... OK ... Needs attention ... Rocks in bunkers.

SUPERIOR NATIONAL GOLF COURSE
PU-P.O. Box 177, Lutsen, 55612, Cook County, (218)663-7195, 90 miles NE of Duluth.
Holes: 27. **Green Fee:** $34/$43. **Cart Fee:** $30/cart. **Walking Policy:** Unrestricted walking. **Walkability:** 4. **Opened:** 1992. **Architect:** Don Herfort. **Season:** May-Oct. **High:** June-Sept. **To obtain tee times:** Call golf shop. Must guarantee with credit card. **Miscellaneous:** Reduced fees (weekdays, low season, resort guests, twilight, juniors), discount packages, range (grass), club rentals, credit cards (MC, V, AE).
★★★★ CANYON/RIVER
Yards: 6,369/4,969. **Par:** 72/72. **Course Rating:** 71.1/69.4. **Slope:** 127/119.
Reader Comments: If you like views, this is your course ... Very scenic river through course ... Outstanding scenery ... More than breathtaking views ... Never very busy; makes pace of play not a problem with lots of time for lunch between nines ... Very hilly ... Even a beginner can enjoy.
★★★★ MOUNTAIN/CANYON
Yards: 6,768/5,166. **Par:** 72/72. **Course Rating:** 73.0/70.5. **Slope:** 133/119.
Reader Comments: Spectacular views of Lake Superior.
★★★★ RIVER/MOUNTAIN
Yards: 6,575/5,197. **Par:** 72/72. **Course Rating:** 72.1/70.3. **Slope:** 128/120.
Reader Comments: Saw a bear!

★★★ THEODORE WIRTH GOLF COURSE
PU-1300 Theodore Wirth Pkwy., Golden Valley, 55422, Hennepin County, (612)522-4584, 3 miles W of Minneapolis.
Holes: 18. **Yards:** 6,585/5,552. **Par:** 72/72. **Course Rating:** 72.7/72.6. **Slope:** 132/124. **Green Fee:** $20/$25. **Cart Fee:** $23/cart. **Walking Policy:** Unrestricted walking. **Walk-ability:** 5. **Opened:** 1916. **Architect:** Garrett Gill. **Season:** April-Nov. **High:** June-Aug. **To obtain tee times:** Call 4 days in advance. **Miscellaneous:** Reduced fees (weekdays, low season, twilight, seniors, juniors), metal spikes, club rentals, credit cards (MC, V).
Reader Comments: Some beautiful views of downtown Minneapolis ... You better be in good shape to walk the back 9 ... Beautiful setting.

★★★★ TIANNA COUNTRY CLUB   *Value*
SP-7470 State 34 N.W., Walker, 56484, Cass County, (218)547-1712, 60 miles N of Brainerd.
E-mail: tianna@tianna.com. **Web:** www.tianna.com.
Holes: 18. **Yards:** 6,550/5,681. **Par:** 72/74. **Course Rating:** 70.7/73.5. **Slope:** 127/127. **Green Fee:** N/A/$30. **Cart Fee:** $20/cart. **Walking Policy:** Unrestricted walking. **Walkability:** 5. **Opened:** 1925. **Architect:** Ernie Tardiff. **Season:** April-Oct. **High:** June-Aug. **To obtain tee times:** Call. A group of 8 or more, a credit card is required. 24-hour advanced cancellation policy. **Miscellaneous:** Reduced fees (twilight), range (grass), club rentals, credit cards (MC, V, AE, D).
Reader Comments: Woodsy, hilly and pretty ... Nice break from fishing ... Beautiful in the pines.

★★★ TIMBER CREEK GOLF COURSE
SP-9750 County Rd. #24, Watertown, 55388, Carver County, (612)955-3490, 20 miles W of Minneapolis.
Holes: 18. **Yards:** 6,500/5,100. **Par:** 72/72. **Course Rating:** 71.7/72.0. **Slope:** 130/127. **Green Fee:** $20/$27. **Cart Fee:** $22/cart. **Walking Policy:** Unrestricted walking. **Walkability:** 3. **Opened:** 1986. **Architect:** Tim O'Connor. **Season:** April-Nov. **High:** May-Sept. **Miscellaneous:** Reduced fees (twilight, seniors), range (grass), club rentals, credit cards (MC, V).
Reader Comments: Holes too close. Duck! ... Cheap.

TIPSINAH MOUNDS GOLF COURSE
SP-County Rd. #24 to 118 Golf Course Road, Elbow Lake, 56531, Grant County, (218)685-4271, (800)660-8642, 75 miles SE of Fargo, N.D.
Holes: 18. **Yards:** 6,219/4,909. **Par:** 70/34. **Course Rating:** 69.7/68.0. **Slope:** 116/109. **Green Fee:** $19/$20. **Cart Fee:** $19/cart. **Walking Policy:** Unrestricted walking. **Walkability:** 2. **Opened:** 1982. **Architect:** Joel Goldstrand. **Season:** April-Oct. **High:** June-Aug. **To obtain tee times:** Call golf shop. **Miscellaneous:** Reduced fees (weekdays, juniors), discount packages, range (grass), club rentals, credit cards (MC, V).
Special Notes: Spikeless encouraged.

★★★ VALLEY GOLF ASSOCIATION
SP-1800 21st St. N.W., East Grand Forks, 56721, Polk County, (218)773-1207, 5 miles NE of Grand Forks, ND.
Holes: 18. **Yards:** 6,210/5,261. **Par:** 72/72. **Course Rating:** 69.6/69.2. **Slope:** 118/112. **Green Fee:** $13/$13. **Cart Fee:** $16/cart. **Walking Policy:** Unrestricted walking. **Walkability:** 2. **Opened:** 1971. **Season:** April-Oct. **High:** May-Aug. **To obtain tee times:** First come, first served. Tee times for members only. **Miscellaneous:** Reduced fees (twilight, seniors, juniors), metal spikes, club rentals, credit cards (MC, V).
Reader Comments: Heavily wooded ... Don't miss the greens.

★★ VALLEY HIGH GOLF CLUB
PU-Rte 2, Box 234, Houston, 55943, Houston County, (507)896-3239, 15 miles E of La Crosse, WI.
Holes: 18. **Yards:** 6,168/5,319. **Par:** 71/75. **Course Rating:** 68.3/69.2. **Slope:** 113/109. **Green Fee:** $20/$20. **Cart Fee:** $20/cart. **Walking Policy:** Unrestricted walking. **Walkability:** 4. **Opened:** 1970. **Architect:** Homer Fieldhouse. **Season:** April-Oct. **High:** June-Aug. **To obtain tee times:** Call golf shop. **Miscellaneous:** Reduced fees (weekdays, low season, seniors, juniors), discount packages, metal spikes, range (grass), club rentals, credit cards (MC, V), beginner friendly (junior program).
Special Notes: Formerly known as Valley High Country Club.

★★½ VALLEY VIEW GOLF CLUB
PU-23795 Laredo Ave., Belle Plane, 56011, Scott County, (612)873-4653, 30 miles SW of Minneapolis.
Holes: 18. **Yards:** 6,309/4,921. **Par:** 70/71. **Course Rating:** 70.1/68.4. **Slope:** 121/113. **Green Fee:** $22/$25. **Cart Fee:** $22/cart. **Walking Policy:** Unrestricted walking. **Walkability:** 4. **Opened:** 1992. **Architect:** S & H Golf, Inc. **Season:** April-Oct. **High:** June-Aug. **To obtain tee times:** Call up to 3 days in advance with credit card guarantee. **Miscellaneous:** Reduced fees (weekdays, low season, twilight, seniors, juniors), discount packages, metal spikes, range (grass/mats), club rentals, credit cards (MC, V).
Reader Comments: Open, hilly change of pace ... Some good holes.

★★★½ VALLEYWOOD GOLF COURSE
PM-4851 West 125th St., Apple Valley, 55124, Dakota County, (612)953-2323, 10 miles S of Minneapolis.
Holes: 18. **Yards:** 6,421/5,144. **Par:** 71/72. **Course Rating:** 70.6/71.5. **Slope:** 123/122. **Green Fee:** $25/$23. **Cart Fee:** $26/cart. **Walking Policy:** Unrestricted walking. **Walkability:** 3. **Opened:** 1976. **Architect:** Don Ripple. **Season:** April-Nov. **High:** June-Sept. **To obtain tee times:** Call up to 5 days in advance. **Miscellaneous:** Reduced fees (seniors, juniors), range (mats), club rentals, credit cards (MC, V, D).
Reader Comments: Good public venue ... Short but tight ... Challenging for all levels ... Nice setting.

★½ VIKING MEADOWS GOLF COURSE
PU-1788 Viking Blvd., Cedar, 55011, Anoka County, (612)434-4205, 20 miles N of Minneapolis.
Holes: 18. **Yards:** 6,364/5,534. **Par:** 72/73. **Course Rating:** 70.6/71.4. **Slope:** 124/121. **Green Fee:** $18/$23. **Cart Fee:** $21/cart. **Walking Policy:** Unrestricted walking. **Walk-ability:** 2. **Opened:** 1989. **Season:** April-Nov. **High:** July-Aug. **To obtain tee times:** Call up to 7 days in advance for weekdays; Tuesday for weekends. **Miscellaneous:** Reduced fees (weekdays, seniors, juniors), range (grass), club rentals, credit cards (MC, V).

★★★ VIRGINIA GOLF COURSE
PU-1308 18th St. North, Virginia, 55792, St. Louis County, (218)748-7530, 59 miles N of Duluth.
Holes: 18. **Yards:** 6,226/5,460. **Par:** 71/74. **Course Rating:** 69.5/70.9. **Slope:** 118/129. **Green Fee:** $21/$21. **Cart Fee:** $21/cart. **Walking Policy:** Unrestricted walking. **Walkability:** 2. **Opened:** 1932. **Architect:** Hugh Vincent Feehan. **Season:** May-Oct. **High:** July-Aug. **To obtain tee times:** Call up to 2 days in advance. **Miscellaneous:** Reduced fees (low season, twilight), range (grass), club rentals, credit cards (MC, V).
Reader Comments: Easy to score well ... Wide open ... Nice muny.

★★★ WAPICADA GOLF CLUB
SP-4498 15th St. NE, Sauk Rapids, 56379, Stearns County, (320)251-7804, 4 miles E of St. Cloud.
Holes: 18. **Yards:** 6,610/5,491. **Par:** 72/73. **Course Rating:** 70.1/71.5. **Slope:** 124/126. **Green Fee:** $23/$25. **Cart Fee:** $23/cart. **Walking Policy:** Unrestricted walking. **Walkability:** 2.
Opened: 1957. **Season:** April-Oct. **High:** June-Aug. **To obtain tee times:** Call up to 2 days in advance. **Miscellaneous:** Reduced fees (twilight, seniors), range (grass), credit cards (MC, V).
Reader Comments: Good challenge, fair price ... Busy ... Nice holes.

WARROAD ESTATES GOLF COURSE
PU-201 Birch Dr. N., Warroad, 56763, Roseau County, (218)386-2025, 126 miles E of Grand Forks, ND.
Holes: 9. **Yards:** 6,942/5,455. **Par:** 72/73. **Course Rating:** 74.3/72.0. **Slope:** 128/121. **Green Fee:** $13/$17. **Cart Fee:** $18/cart. **Walking Policy:** Unrestricted walking. **Walkability:** 1.
Opened: 1976. **Season:** April-Oct. **High:** June-Aug. **To obtain tee times:** Call golf shop.
Miscellaneous: Reduced fees (weekdays, twilight, seniors, juniors), metal spikes, club rentals, credit cards (MC, V).

★★★½ WENDIGO GOLF COURSE
PU-20108 Golf Crest Dr., Grand Rapids, 55744, Itasca County, (218)327-2211, 180 miles N of Minneapolis.
Holes: 18. **Yards:** 6,756/5,151. **Par:** 72/72. **Course Rating:** 72.0/70.0. **Slope:** 132/127. **Green Fee:** $25/$30. **Cart Fee:** $24/cart. **Walking Policy:** Unrestricted walking. **Walkability:** 4.
Opened: 1995. **Architect:** Joel Goldstrand. **Season:** April-Oct. **High:** June-Aug. **To obtain tee times:** Call up to 7 days in advance. **Miscellaneous:** Reduced fees (twilight), discount packages, metal spikes, range (grass/mats), club rentals, credit cards (MC, V).
Reader Comments: Good scenery ... Has some great holes. Long par 3s over gorges or water ... Lots of trees, hills ... Wish I didn't have to drive an hour and a half to get there.

★★★★½ WHITEFISH GOLF CLUB *Value*
SP-Rte. 1, Pequot Lakes, 56472, Crow Wing County, (218)543-4900, 36 miles N of Brainerd.
E-mail: wfgolf@uslink.net. **Web:** whitefishgolf.com.
Holes: 18. **Yards:** 6,407/5,682. **Par:** 72/72. **Course Rating:** 70.7/72.6. **Slope:** 128/124. **Green Fee:** $28/$35. **Cart Fee:** $24/cart. **Walking Policy:** Unrestricted walking. **Walkability:** 2.
Opened: 1966. **Architect:** Don Herfort. **Season:** April-Oct. **High:** June-Aug. **To obtain tee times:** Call golf shop. **Miscellaneous:** Reduced fees (weekdays, low season, resort guests, twilight), metal spikes, range (grass), club rentals, credit cards (MC, V, AE).
Reader Comments: Definitely will come back this year ... Carved out of pines ... A forest, but nice ... Tight fairways ... Some tough blind shots ... Great course for the money ... Reminds me of a walk in the woods.

★★★★½ WILDFLOWER AT FAIR HILLS *Pace*
PU-19790 County, Hwy 20, Detroit Lakes, 56501, Becker County, (218)439-3357, (888)752-9945, 45 miles E of Fargo, ND. **E-mail:** golf@fairhillsresort.com. **Web:** www.fairhillsresort.com.
Holes: 18. **Yards:** 7,000/5,250. **Par:** 72/72. **Course Rating:** 74.2/71.6. **Slope:** 139/121. **Green Fee:** $21/$39. **Cart Fee:** $14/person. **Walking Policy:** Unrestricted walking. **Walkability:** 4.
Opened: 1993. **Architect:** Joel Goldstrand. **Season:** April-First Snow. **High:** June-Aug. **To obtain tee times:** Call 7 days in advance. Tee times may also be made at www.teemaster.com.
Miscellaneous: Reduced fees (weekdays, low season, resort guests, twilight, seniors, juniors), discount packages, range (grass), club rentals, lodging, credit cards (MC, V, AE, D).
Reader Comments: Sixteen good holes ... I didn't realize a course could cover so many acres ... Lots of sand ... Never crowded ... Tough ... Difficult to walk ... Natural prairie-grass hazards.

★★★★ THE WILDS GOLF CLUB *Service, Condition+*
PU-14819 Wilds Pkwy. N.W., Prior Lake, 55372, Scott County, (612)445-4455, 30 miles SW of Minneapolis.
Holes: 18. **Yards:** 7,025/5,095. **Par:** 72/72. **Course Rating:** 74.7/70.2. **Slope:** 140/126. **Green Fee:** $50/$89. **Cart Fee:** Included in Green Fee. **Walking Policy:** Unrestricted walking.
Walkability: 4. **Opened:** 1995. **Architect:** Tom Weiskopf/Jay Morrish. **Season:** April-Oct. **High:** June-Aug. **To obtain tee times:** Foursomes may call up to 14 days in advance; twosomes and threesomes 5 days in advance. **Miscellaneous:** Reduced fees (weekdays, resort guests, seniors, juniors), caddies, club rentals.
Notes: Ranked 8th in 1999 Best in State; 4th in 1996 Best New Upscale Courses.
Reader Comments: Expensive, but worth it occasionally ... Awesome views ... Has grown up nicely ... Too bad they can't keep cost down ... Excellent condition ... Bring your brain: Lots of shot choices ... A real test from Weiskopf and Morrish ... Fair to all handicaps.

★★★★½ WILLINGER'S GOLF CLUB *Value, Condition*
PU-6900 Canby Trail, Northfield, 55057, Rice County, (612)440-7000, 40 miles S of Minneapolis.

Holes: 18. **Yards:** 6,711/5,166. **Par:** 72/72. **Course Rating:** 73.3/71.6. **Slope:** 140/130. **Green Fee:** $35/$40. **Cart Fee:** $26/cart. **Walking Policy:** Unrestricted walking. **Walkability:** 4. **Opened:** 1992. **Architect:** Garrett Gill. **Season:** April-Oct. **High:** June-Aug. **To obtain tee times:** Call 4 days in advance for weekend times; 7 days in advance for weekday times. **Miscellaneous:** Reduced fees (twilight, seniors, juniors), metal spikes, range (grass), club rentals, credit cards (MC, V). **Notes:** Ranked 16th in 1999 Best in State. **Reader Comments:** Very nice course in good condition ... A little pricey ... Have to hit the ball straight ... Gets better every year ... Diverse 9s; back very narrow ... Nice layout in woods and water ... Gorgeous ... If you enjoy the outdoors, it's tough to beat ... I never miss a chance to go ... With a 36-handicap I can get pretty frustrated, but I just stop and look around.

★★½ WILLOW CREEK GOLF CLUB

SP-1700 S.W. 48th St., Rochester, 55902, Olmstead County, (507)285-0305, 65 miles S of Minneapolis.
Holes: 18. **Yards:** 6,053/5,293. **Par:** 70/70. **Course Rating:** 69.1/70.5. **Slope:** 117/121. **Green Fee:** $19/$19. **Cart Fee:** $20/cart. **Walking Policy:** Unrestricted walking. **Walkability:** 2. **Opened:** 1974. **Architect:** William James Spear. **Season:** March-Nov. **High:** June-Aug. **To obtain tee times:** Call 7 days in advance. **Miscellaneous:** Metal spikes, range (grass), club rentals, credit cards (MC, V).
Reader Comments: Lots of events ... Fun day.

BAY BREEZE GOLF COURSE
M-81st St., Keesler AFB, 39534, (228)377-3832.
Holes: 18. **Yards:** 6,047/5,110. **Par:** 70/70. **Course Rating:** 69.5/70/0. **Slope:** 121/117. **Green Fee:** $14/$16. **Walkability:** N/A.

★★½ BAY POINTE RESORT & GOLF CLUB
SP-800 Bay Pointe Dr., Brandon, 39042, Rankin County, (601)829-1862, 7 miles NE of Jackson.
Holes: 18. **Yards:** 6,600/4,668. **Par:** 72/72. **Course Rating:** 70.6/66.3. **Slope:** 123/108. **Green Fee:** $15/$20. **Cart Fee:** $10/person. **Walking Policy:** Walking at certain times. **Walkability:** 2. **Opened:** 1987. **Architect:** Marvin Ferguson. **Season:** Year-round. **High:** March-Oct. **To obtain tee times:** Call for weekends. **Miscellaneous:** Reduced fees (twilight), metal spikes, range (grass), lodging.
Reader Comments: Narrow, tall pines, water, leave driver at home ... Course is set up for faders & slicers; hookers put driver away ...Tight course...Lots of pine trees. Nice scenery. Houses close to course ... Fun course to play.

BEAR CREEK GOLF CLUB
PU-Hwy. 84 West, Laurel, 39440, Jones County, (601)425-5670.
Holes: 18. **Yards:** 6,482/4,820. **Par:** 72/72. **Course Rating:** 70.3/67.9. **Slope:** 118/110. **Green Fee:** $10/$15. **Cart Fee:** $8/person. **Walking Policy:** Unrestricted walking. **Walkability:** 3. **Opened:** 1985. **Season:** Year-round. **High:** March-June. **Miscellaneous:** Reduced fees (twilight, seniors, juniors), range (grass), beginner friendly (beginner lessons).

★★★½ BIG OAKS COUNTRY CLUB
SP-3481 Big Oaks Blvd., Saltillo, 38866, Lee County, (601)844-8002, 2 miles NE of Tupelo.
Holes: 18. **Yards:** 6,784/5,098. **Par:** 72/72. **Course Rating:** 73.1/69.1. **Slope:** 124/114. **Green Fee:** $36/$36. **Cart Fee:** Included in Green Fee. **Walking Policy:** Unrestricted walking. **Walkability:** 1. **Opened:** 1996. **Architect:** Tracy May. **Season:** Year-round. **High:** April-Oct. **To obtain tee times:** Call up to 14 days in advance. **Miscellaneous:** Reduced fees (low season, twilight, juniors), discount packages, metal spikes, range (grass), credit cards (MC, V, AE, D), beginner friendly (beginner and junior lessons, junior camp).
Reader Comments: No crowds, great price, very fair but long from back tees ... Incredible greens. The course can play easy or hard depending on tees ... Wetlands course-enjoyed the round ... Greens are nicer than carpet.

★½ BLACKJACK BAY GOLF LINKS
PU-15312 Dismuke Dr., Biloxi, 39532, Jackson County, (228)392-0400, 50 miles W of Mobile.
Holes: 18. **Yards:** 6,020/5,000. **Par:** 71/71. **Course Rating:** 69.4/68.0. **Slope:** 118/112. **Green Fee:** $28/$35. **Cart Fee:** Included in Green Fee. **Walking Policy:** Mandatory cart. **Walkability:** 3. **Opened:** 1992. **Architect:** Chuck Gregory. **Season:** Year-round. **High:** Feb.-April. **To obtain tee times:** Call 2 days in advance. **Miscellaneous:** Discount packages, metal spikes, club rentals, credit cards (MC, V).
Special Notes: Formerly Southwind Country Club.

BOONEVILLE COUNTRY CLUB
SP-Rte. 2 Gadston, Booneville, 38829, (601)728-6812.
Holes: 18. **Yards:** 6,403/6,403. **Par:** 72/72. **Course Rating:** 70.9/N/A. **Slope:** 131/N/A. **Green Fee:** $15/$15. **Walkability:** 3.

★★★★ THE BRIDGES GOLF RESORT AT CASINO MAGIC
R-711 Casino Magic Dr., Bay St. Louis, 39520, Hancock County, (800)562-4425, (800)562-4425, 45 miles E of New Orleans, LA. **Web:** http://www.casinomagic.com.
Holes: 18. **Yards:** 6,841/5,108. **Par:** 72/72. **Course Rating:** 73.5/70.1. **Slope:** 138/126. **Green Fee:** $75/$75. **Cart Fee:** Included in Green Fee. **Walking Policy:** Mandatory cart. **Walkability:** 3. **Opened:** 1997. **Architect:** Arnold Palmer/Ed Seay. **Season:** Year-round. **High:** Feb.-April. **To obtain tee times:** Call, reservations can be made up to 1 year in advance. **Miscellaneous:** Reduced fees (resort guests, twilight), discount packages, range (grass), lodging (203 rooms), credit cards (MC, V, AE).
Notes: Ranked 8th in 1999 Best in State.
Reader Comments: Extremely tough and challenging, haven't seen this much water since going deep-sea fishing ... Wow! ... Best course in 3-state area for slicers ... Target golf ... Best course I played all year ... Nice par-5 1st hole ... Arnie, thank you for the pleasure.

CANEBRAKE GOLF CLUB
PU-1 Cane Dr., Hattiesburg, 39402, Lamar County, (601)271-2010, (888)875-5595, 7 miles W of Hattiesburg. **Web:** canebrakegolf.com.
Holes: 18. **Yards:** 7,003/5,129. **Par:** 71/71. **Course Rating:** 73.3/69.5. **Slope:** 130/117. **Green Fee:** $38/$48. **Cart Fee:** $12/person. **Walking Policy:** Unrestricted walking. **Walkability:** 3. **Opened:** 1998. **Architect:** Jerry Pate. **Season:** Year-round. **High:** March-Oct. **Miscellaneous:**

MISSISSIPPI

Reduced fees (weekdays, twilight), discount packages, range (grass), club rentals, credit cards (MC, V, AE), beginner friendly (clinics).
Notes: Ranked 2nd in 1999 Best New Affordable Public.

CAPITOL CITY GOLF CLUB
PM-3200 Woodrow Wilson Dr., Jackson, 39209, (601)960-1905.
Holes: 18. **Yards:** 7,200/6,400. **Par:** 72/72. **Course Rating:** N/A. **Slope:** N/A. **Green Fee:** $12/$15. **Walkability:** 1.

CAROLINE GOLF CLUB
PU-118 Caroline Club Circle, Madison, 39130, (601)853-4554
Holes: 18. **Yards:** 6,845/5,127. **Par:** 72/72. **Course Rating:** 73.3/69.7. **Slope:** 125/119. **Green Fee:** $36/$46. **Walkability:** 2.

★★★★ CHEROKEE VALLEY GOLF CLUB
PU-6635 Crumpler Blvd., Olive Branch, 38654, De Soto County, (601)893-4444, 7 miles S of Memphis, TN. **E-mail:** cv6635@aol.com.
Holes: 18. **Yards:** 6,751/4,422. **Par:** 72/72. **Course Rating:** 72.2/65.4. **Slope:** 128/116. **Green Fee:** $22/$37. **Cart Fee:** $11/person. **Walking Policy:** Walking at certain times. **Walkability:** 3. **Opened:** 1996. **Architect:** Don Cottle, Jr. **Season:** Year-round. **High:** April-Oct. **To obtain tee times:** Call up to 5 days in advance at (601)893-4444 or (901)525-4653. **Miscellaneous:** Reduced fees (weekdays, low season, twilight, seniors, juniors), range (grass/mats), club rentals, credit cards (MC, V, AE).
Reader Comments: Course new, future is good ... One of the best public course values I have ever found ... WOW! A real test ... Great shape ... Great fairways ... Fine course, long distance between green and tee box if walking.

CLEAR CREEK GOLF CLUB
PU-1566 Tiffentown Rd., Vicksburg, 39180, Warren County, (601)638-9395, 7 miles E of Vicksburg.
Holes: 18. **Yards:** 6,661/5,182. **Par:** 72/72. **Course Rating:** 71.8/68.7. **Slope:** 118/109. **Green Fee:** $13/$13. **Cart Fee:** $16/cart. **Walking Policy:** Unrestricted walking. **Walkability:** 2. **Opened:** 1920. **Season:** Year-round. **High:** May-Sept. **Miscellaneous:** Reduced fees (juniors), range (grass), club rentals, credit cards (MC, V), beginner friendly (the Randy Tupper Academy of Golf).

THE CLUB AT NORTH CREEK
SP-8770 North Creek Blvd., Southaven, 38671, Desoto County, (601)280-4653, (877)465-3647, 1 miles S of Memphis. **E-mail:** mm2ncreek@aol.com. **Web:** www.golfmississippi.com.
Holes: 18. **Yards:** 6,433/4,418. **Par:** 72/72. **Course Rating:** 71.2/73.0. **Slope:** 125/113. **Green Fee:** $20/$35. **Cart Fee:** $15/person. **Walking Policy:** Walking at certain times. **Walkability:** 4. **Opened:** 1999. **Architect:** Tracy May. **Season:** Year-round. **High:** May-Oct. **To obtain tee times:** Call (877)465-3647 or (662)280-GOLF 7 days in advace. **Miscellaneous:** Reduced fees (weekdays, low season, resort guests, twilight), discount packages, range (grass/mats), club rentals, credit cards (MC, V, AE).

COAHOMA COUNTRY CLUB
SP-Davenport Rd., Clarksdale, 38614, (601)624-9484.
Holes: 18. **Yards:** 6,126/6,126. **Par:** 72/72. **Course Rating:** N/A. **Slope:** N/A. **Green Fee:** $10/$10. **Walkability:** 1.

COTTONWOODS AT GRAND CASINO TUNICA
R-13615 Old Highway 61 North, Robinsonville, 38664, Tunicz County, (601)357-6079, (800)946-4946, 15 miles S of Memphis, TN. **Web:** www.grandcasinos.com.
Holes: 18. **Yards:** 7,000/5,250. **Par:** 72/72. **Course Rating:** 72.3/69.8. **Slope:** 119/116. **Green Fee:** $69/$150. **Cart Fee:** Included in Green Fee. **Walking Policy:** Mandatory cart. **Walkability:** 2. **Opened:** 1998. **Architect:** Hale Irwin. **Season:** Year-round. **High:** May-Sept. **To obtain tee times:** Call (800)946-4946 Ext. 6079. **Miscellaneous:** Reduced fees (resort guests, twilight), discount packages, range (grass), club rentals, lodging (1,300 rooms), credit cards (MC, V, AE, D).
Special Notes: Formerly known as The Cottonwoods Golf Club.

DANCING RABBIT GOLF CLUB   *Service+*
R-One Choctaw Trail, Philadelphia, 39350, Neshoba County, (601)663-0011.
★★★★ THE AZALEAS   *Pace*
Holes: 18. **Yards:** 7,128/4,909. **Par:** 72/72. **Course Rating:** 74.4/68.6. **Slope:** 135/115. **Green Fee:** $75/$135. **Cart Fee:** $14/person. **Walking Policy:** Unrestricted walking. **Walkability:** 5. **Opened:** 1997. **Architect:** Tom Fazio/Jerry Pate. **Season:** Jan.- Dec. **High:** March-Oct. **To obtain tee times:** Call Golf Shop at (601)663-0011. **Miscellaneous:** Reduced fees (weekdays, low season, resort guests, twilight), discount packages, range (grass), club rentals, lodging (500 rooms), credit cards (MC, V, AE, D), beginner friendly (beginner, junior and resort clinics).
Notes: Ranked 2nd in 1999 Best in State.

MISSISSIPPI

Reader Comments: Great course ... Great layout, will play again ... They have it right ... Very special.

THE OAKS
Holes: 18. **Yards:** 7,076/5,097. **Par:** 72/72. **Course Rating:** 74.6/69.0. **Slope:** 139/123. **Green Fee:** $75/$135. **Cart Fee:** $14/person. **Walking Policy:** Unrestricted walking. **Walkability:** 5. **Opened:** 1997. **Architect:** Tom Fazio/Jerry Pate. **Season:** Jan.- Dec. **High:** March-Oct. **To obtain tee times:** Call Golf Shop at (601)663-0011. **Miscellaneous:** Reduced fees (weekdays, low season, resort guests, twilight), discount packages, range (grass), club rentals, lodging (500 rooms), credit cards (MC, V, AE, D), beginner friendly (beginner, junior and resort clinics).

DIAMONDHEAD COUNTRY CLUB
R-7600 Country Club Circle, Diamondhead, 39525, Hancock County, (601)255-3910, (800)346-8741, 20 miles W of Gulfport.
★★★½ **CARDINAL COURSE**
Holes: 18. **Yards:** 6,831/5,065. **Par:** 72/72. **Course Rating:** 72.7/68.9. **Slope:** 132/117. **Green Fee:** $45/$45. **Cart Fee:** $15/person. **Walking Policy:** Mandatory cart. **Walkability:** 3. **Opened:** 1972. **Architect:** Bill Atkins. **Season:** Year-round. **High:** Feb.-May. **To obtain tee times:** Advanced tee times only available through package deals. Call (800)221-2423 or (800)345-7915 for package information. Packages also available through hotels and motels along the coast. **Miscellaneous:** Reduced fees (low season, resort guests, juniors), discount packages, metal spikes, range (grass/mats), club rentals, lodging, credit cards (MC, V, AE, D).
Reader Comments: Good all-around value ... Loved the course ... Fun ... Tight, good test.
★★★ **PINE COURSE**
Holes: 18. **Yards:** 6,817/5,313. **Par:** 72/72. **Course Rating:** 73.6/71.1. **Slope:** 133/118. **Green Fee:** $28/$45. **Cart Fee:** $15/person. **Walking Policy:** Mandatory cart. **Walkability:** 3. **Opened:** 1977. **Architect:** Earl Stone. **Season:** Year-round. **High:** Feb.-May. **To obtain tee times:** Advanced tee times only available through package deals. Call (800)221-2423 or (800)345-7915 for package information. Packages also available through hotels and motels along the coast. **Miscellaneous:** Reduced fees (low season, resort guests, juniors), discount packages, metal spikes, range (grass/mats), club rentals, lodging, credit cards (MC, V, D).
Reader Comments: Enjoyable ... Old classic, wide fairways, doglegs ... Accuracy, not length is important.

★★½ **DOGWOOD HILLS GOLF CLUB**
SP-17476 Dogwood Hills Dr., Biloxi, 39532, Harrison County, (601)392-9805, 12 miles N of Biloxi. **Web:** www.dogwoodhills.com.
Holes: 18. **Yards:** 6,076/4,687. **Par:** 72/72. **Course Rating:** 69.0/68.7. **Slope:** 118/115. **Green Fee:** $22/$33. **Cart Fee:** Included in Green Fee. **Walking Policy:** Walking at certain times. **Walkability:** 4. **Opened:** 1993. **Architect:** Brent Williams. **Season:** Year-round. **High:** Oct.-April. **To obtain tee times:** Call golf shop. **Miscellaneous:** Reduced fees (low season, juniors), discount packages, metal spikes, range (grass), club rentals, credit cards (MC, V), beginner friendly (golf clinics and lessons).
Reader Comments: Beautiful. Tight layout. Comfortable ... Interesting.

DUNCAN PARK GOLF COURSE
PM-57 Duncan Park Road, Natchez, 39120, Adams County, (601)442-5955.
Holes: 18. **Yards:** 6,017/4,766. **Par:** 71/71. **Course Rating:** 69.4/70.4. **Slope:** 117/119. **Green Fee:** $12/$15. **Cart Fee:** $9/person. **Walking Policy:** Unrestricted walking. **Walkability:** 3. **Opened:** 1928. **Season:** Year-round. **High:** June-Aug. **To obtain tee times:** Call (601)442-5955. **Miscellaneous:** Reduced fees (twilight, seniors, juniors), metal spikes, range (grass/mats), club rentals, credit cards (MC, V), beginner friendly (various programs for all).
Special Notes: Formerly known as Duncan Park Golf Club.

★★½ **EAGLE RIDGE GOLF COURSE**
PU-Hwy. 18 S., Raymond, 39154, Hinds County, (601)857-5993, 10 miles SW of Jackson.
Holes: 18. **Yards:** 6,500/5,135. **Par:** 72/72. **Course Rating:** 68.5/N/A. **Slope:** 113/N/A. **Green Fee:** $10/$13. **Cart Fee:** $18/cart. **Walking Policy:** Unrestricted walking. **Walkability:** 2. **Opened:** 1955. **Architect:** Hinds Community College. **Season:** Year-round. **High:** March-Aug. **To obtain tee times:** Call Thursday for upcoming weekend. **Miscellaneous:** Reduced fees (weekdays, twilight, seniors), metal spikes, range (grass), club rentals, lodging (40 rooms), credit cards (MC, V).
Reader Comments: Great course. You don't always pull your driver out the bag, sometimes you'll hit a 2- or 4 iron. Diverse course ... Not bad for money ... No bunkers on course.

★★½ **EDGEWATER BAY GOLF COURSE**
SP-2674 Pass Rd., Biloxi, 39531, Harrison County, (228)388-9670, 75 miles E of New Orleans.
Holes: 18. **Yards:** 6,200/5,114. **Par:** 71/71. **Course Rating:** 70.0/69.8. **Slope:** 125/121. **Green Fee:** $15/$25. **Cart Fee:** $12/person. **Walking Policy:** Walking at certain times. **Walkability:** 2. **Opened:** 1927. **Season:** Year-round. **High:** Jan.-March. **To obtain tee times:** Call golf shop.

MISSISSIPPI

Miscellaneous: Reduced fees (weekdays, low season, twilight), discount packages, metal spikes, club rentals, lodging, credit cards (MC, V).
Reader Comments: Good course, very popular with locals.

FOREST COUNTRY CLUB
SP-Hwy. 35 South, Forest, 39074, (601)469-9137.
Holes: 18. **Yards:** 6,500/5,128. **Par:** 72/72. **Course Rating:** 69.3/N/A. **Slope:** 122/N/A. **Green Fee:** $23/$26. **Walkability:** 3.

★★ GRAND OAKS RESORT
PU-Corner of Lyles Dr. and Hwy. 7, Oxford, 38655, Lafayette County, (601)236-3008, (800)541-3881, 60 miles S of Memphis.
Holes: 18. **Yards:** 6,355/5,090. **Par:** 70/70. **Course Rating:** 69.7/69.7. **Slope:** 121/121. **Green Fee:** $29/$35. **Cart Fee:** Included in Green Fee. **Walking Policy:** Walking at certain times. **Walkability:** 4. **Opened:** 1994. **Architect:** Greg Clark. **Season:** Year-round. **High:** March-Oct. **To obtain tee times:** Call up to 30 days in advance. **Miscellaneous:** Reduced fees (weekdays, low season, twilight, seniors, juniors), discount packages, metal spikes, range (grass), club rentals, lodging, credit cards (MC, V, AE, D).

★★ THE GREAT SOUTHERN GOLF CLUB
SP-2000 Beach Dr., Gulfport, 39532, Harrison County, (601)896-3536, 69 miles E of New Orleans.
Holes: 18. **Yards:** 6,200/4,881. **Par:** 71/71. **Course Rating:** 69.7/67.5. **Slope:** 117/114. **Green Fee:** $30/$50. **Cart Fee:** Included in Green Fee. **Walking Policy:** Walking at certain times. **Walkability:** 1. **Opened:** 1908. **Architect:** N/A. **Season:** Year-round. **High:** Feb.-May. **To obtain tee times:** Call golf shop. **Miscellaneous:** Reduced fees (twilight, juniors), discount packages, metal spikes, club rentals, credit cards (MC, V, AE, D).
Special Notes: Formerly Broadwater Resort.

GREENVILLE PUBLIC GOLF COURSE
PU-465 Base Golf Road, Greenville, 38703, Washington County, (601)332-4079, 7 miles N of Greenville.
Holes: 18. **Yards:** 6,430/5,650. **Par:** 72/73. **Course Rating:** 70.8/N/A. **Slope:** 114/N/A. **Green Fee:** $3/$10. **Cart Fee:** $14/cart. **Walking Policy:** Unrestricted walking. **Walkability:** 1. **Opened:** 1956. **Season:** Year-round. **High:** April-Sept. **Miscellaneous:** Reduced fees (weekdays, seniors, juniors), range (grass), club rentals, credit cards (MC, V), beginner friendly.

GULF HILLS GOLF CLUB
SP-13701 Paso Rd., Ocean Springs, 39564, Jackson County, (228)872-9663, 4 miles E of Biloxi.
Holes: 18. **Yards:** 6,376/5,438. **Par:** 71/72. **Course Rating:** 70.4/71.7. **Slope:** 126/124. **Green Fee:** $30/$45. **Cart Fee:** Included in Green Fee. **Walking Policy:** Mandatory cart. **Walkability:** 4. **Opened:** 1927. **Architect:** Jack Daray. **Season:** Year-round. **High:** Feb.-Oct. **To obtain tee times:** 72 hour cancellation, weekends and holidays. Groups of 8 or more, credit card guarantee. **Miscellaneous:** Metal spikes, credit cards (MC, V, AE).

HILLANDALE COUNTRY CLUB
SP-Rte. 8, Corinth, 38834, (601)286-8020.
Holes: 18. **Yards:** 6.232/4,842. **Par:** 71/71. **Course Rating:** 70.1/67.5. **Slope:** 120/107. **Green Fee:** $8/$15. **Walkability:** 4.

★★★★ KIRKWOOD NATIONAL GOLF CLUB *Pace+*
SP-785 Hwy. 4 West, Holly Springs, 38635, Marshall County, (662)252-4888, (800)461-4653, 40 miles SE of Memphis. **Web:** www.kirkwoodgolf.com.
Holes: 18. **Yards:** 7,129/4,898. **Par:** 72/72. **Course Rating:** 73.6/68.2. **Slope:** 135/116. **Green Fee:** $35/$55. **Cart Fee:** Included in Green Fee. **Walking Policy:** Walking at certain times. **Walkability:** 5. **Opened:** 1994. **Season:** Year-round. **High:** April-Oct. **To obtain tee times:** Call up to 7 days in advance. **Miscellaneous:** Reduced fees (weekdays, low season, twilight, seniors, juniors), discount packages, range (grass), club rentals, credit cards (MC, V, AE).
Notes: Ranked 7th in 1999 Best in State; 42nd in 1996 America's Top 75 Affordable Courses; 5th in 1995 Best New Public Courses.
Reader Comments: A secret ... Great course, meant for pros, each tee box at different level ... Great shape, a good test ... Outstanding, challenging ... Bring your 'A' game and hit it long ... Beautiful, even in December ... Choice of 5 tees ... Only see the hole you are playing at the time. You can't see other holes so you don't see other people.

★★ LINKS OF WHISPERING WOODS
SP-11300 Goodman Rd., Olive Branch, 38654, De Soto County, (901)525-2402, 2 miles S of Memphis, TN. **E-mail:** links of ww@aol.com.
Holes: 18. **Yards:** 6,905/5,200. **Par:** 72/72. **Course Rating:** N/A. **Slope:** N/A. **Green Fee:** $22/$28. **Cart Fee:** $10/person. **Walking Policy:** Walking at certain times. **Walkability:** 3. **Opened:** 1975. **Architect:** D. A. Weibring. **Season:** Year-round. **High:** May-Sept. **To obtain tee

MISSISSIPPI

times: Call 5 days in advance. **Miscellaneous:** Reduced fees (low season, seniors, juniors), discount packages, range (grass), club rentals, lodging (181 rooms), credit cards (MC, V, AE, D, Diners Club).
Special Notes: Formerly known as Holiday Golf Club

LUCEDALE GOLF & RECREATION
SP-9177 Hwy 63S, Lucedale, 39452, (601)947-2798.
Holes: 18. **Yards:** 5,845/4,820. **Par:** 71/71. **Course Rating:** N/A. **Slope:** N/A. **Green Fee:** $9/$9.
Cart Fee: $6/person. **Walking Policy:** Walking at certain times. **Walkability:** 3. **Opened:** 1979.
Season: Year-round. **To obtain tee times:** Call. **Miscellaneous:** Metal spikes, range (grass).

MALLARD POINTE GOLF COURSE
★★★★ CHAMPIONSHIP COURSE *Value*
PU-John Kyle State Park, Sardis, 39236, Panola County, (601)487-2400, (888)833-6477, 6 miles E of Sardis.
Holes: 18. **Yards:** 7,005/5,300. **Par:** 72/72. **Course Rating:** 73.8/71.5. **Slope:** 131/122. **Green Fee:** $36/$36. **Cart Fee:** Included in Green Fee. **Walking Policy:** Unrestricted walking.
Walkability: 5. **Opened:** 1997. **Architect:** Bob Cupp. **Season:** Year-round. **High:** April-Oct.
Miscellaneous: Range (grass), club rentals, lodging (35 rooms), credit cards (MC, V, AE).
Reader Comments: Beautiful layout, many carryovers, variety of holes, inside State Park with all kinds of facilities ... Very nice design and panorama ... Better stay in fairway ... Personnel fantastic.

MILLBROOK COUNTRY CLUB
SP-Highway 11 North, Picayune, 39466, Pearl River County, (601)798-8711.
Holes: 18. **Yards:** 6,477/4,917. **Par:** 72/72. **Course Rating:** 71.0/68.7. **Slope:** 130/115. **Green Fee:** $20/$25. **Cart Fee:** $11/person. **Walking Policy:** Walking at certain times. **Walkability:** 3.
Opened: 1953. **Season:** Year-round. **High:** March-May. **To obtain tee times:** Must call 24 hours in advance. **Miscellaneous:** Reduced fees (twilight), range (grass), credit cards (MC, V).

★★★½ MISSISSIPPI NATIONAL GOLF CLUB
SP-900 Hickory Hill Dr., Gautier, 39553, Jackson County, (228)497-2372, (800)477-4044, 15 miles E of Biloxi. **Web:** www.linkscorp.com.
Holes: 18. **Yards:** 6,983/5,229. **Par:** 72/72. **Course Rating:** 73.1/69.6. **Slope:** 128/113. **Green Fee:** $20/$60. **Cart Fee:** $12/person. **Walking Policy:** Walking at certain times. **Walkability:** 1.
Opened: 1965. **Architect:** Earl Stone. **Season:** Year-round. **High:** Feb.-April. **To obtain tee times:** Just call. **Miscellaneous:** Reduced fees (weekdays, low season, resort guests, twilight), metal spikes, range (grass/mats), club rentals, credit cards (MC, V).
Notes: Mississippi Coast Classic (Nike Tour)-1997.
Reader Comments: Great condition. Wide open. Well maintained ... Grand old, old, old course ... Good price, hard to get a tee time ... Big, old live oaks, moss, water. Bury me there! ... Only decent course in county ... Course in nice shape.

★★★★ MISSISSIPPI STATE UNIVERSITY GOLF COURSE *Value*
PU-1520 Old Hwy. 82E., Starkville, 39759, Oktibbeha County, (601)325-3028, 120 miles NE of Jackson. **E-mail:** hbm@ra.msstate.edu.
Holes: 18. **Yards:** 6,926/5,443. **Par:** 72/72. **Course Rating:** 73.5/71.8. **Slope:** 130/121. **Green Fee:** $12/$17. **Cart Fee:** $10/person. **Walking Policy:** Unrestricted walking. **Walkability:** 3.
Opened: 1989. **Architect:** Brian Ault. **Season:** Year-round. **High:** March-Sept. **To obtain tee times:** Call on Wednesday for following week. **Miscellaneous:** Reduced fees (weekdays, juniors), metal spikes, range (grass/mats), club rentals, credit cards (MC, V, AE, D).
Reader Comments: Lots of fun ... Great shape, good shots rewarded ... Challenging variety of holes ... Bulldog of a course ... Tops for a college course ... Great condition ... Gorgeous, vicious, open course.

★★½ NATCHEZ TRACE GOLF CLUB
SP-Beech Springs Rd., Saltillo, 38866, Lee County, (601)869-2166, 5 miles N of Tupelo.
Holes: 18. **Yards:** 6,669/4,731. **Par:** 72/72. **Course Rating:** 72.6/67.6. **Slope:** 128/107. **Green Fee:** $15/$24. **Cart Fee:** $18/person. **Walking Policy:** Unrestricted walking. **Walkability:** 5.
Opened: 1964. **Architect:** John Frazier. **Season:** Year-round. **High:** April-Sept. **To obtain tee times:** First come, first served on weekdays. Members only on weekends. **Miscellaneous:** Reduced fees (weekdays, twilight), range (grass), credit cards (MC, V).
Reader Comments: Hard to stay out of trouble.

THE OAKS GOLF CLUB
PU-24384 Clubhouse Drive, Pass Christian, 39571, Harrison County, (228)452-0909, 10 miles W of Gulfport. **E-mail:** theoaksgc@msn.com. **Web:** www.gcww.com/theoaks.
Holes: 18. **Yards:** 6,900/4,700. **Par:** 72/72. **Course Rating:** 72.5/66.4. **Slope:** 131/107. **Green Fee:** $28/$71. **Cart Fee:** $13/person. **Walking Policy:** Walking at certain times. **Walkability:** 3.
Opened: 1998. **Architect:** Chris Cole/Steve Caplinger. **Season:** Year round. **High:** Feb.-April. **To**

obtain tee times: Call or e-mail. **Miscellaneous:** Reduced fees (low season, twilight, juniors), range (grass), club rentals, credit cards (MC, V).
Special Notes: Home of the 1998-2000 Nike Tour.

OKATOMA GOLF COURSE
SP-Hwy. 49 North, Collins, 39428, (601)765-1841.
Holes: 18. **Yards:** 6,440/4,645. **Par:** 72/72. **Course Rating:** 68.9/66.5. **Slope:** 114/111. **Green Fee:** $25/$30. **Walkability:** N/A. **Architect:** Milton/Schell.

OKOLONA COUNTRY CLUB
SP-Hwy. 41 West, Okolona, 38860, (601)447-2033.
Special Notes: Call club for further information.

★★½ OLE MISS GOLF CLUB
PU-U of MS, College Hill Rd. #147 CR 1056, Oxford, 38655, Lafayette County, (662)234-4816, 70 miles S of Memphis.
Holes: 18. **Yards:** 6,563/5,306. **Par:** 72/72. **Course Rating:** 72.8/70.9. **Slope:** 129/120. **Green Fee:** $12/$15. **Cart Fee:** $18/cart. **Walking Policy:** Unrestricted walking. **Walkability:** 3.
Opened: 1965. **Architect:** Sonny Guy. **Season:** Year-round. **High:** May-Aug. **To obtain tee times:** Call in advance. **Miscellaneous:** Reduced fees (seniors, juniors), metal spikes, range (grass/mats), club rentals, credit cards (MC, V).
Reader Comments: Exceptional for amount of play ... Hilly ... Course improving year to year. Greens usually need a little work ... Beautiful course, deer on fairways, lots of fun! ... Shallow sand in bunkers ... Good college course, needs watering in summer.

★★ PASS CHRISTIAN ISLES GOLF CLUB
SP-150 Country Club Dr., Pass Christian, 39571, Harrison County, (228)452-3830, 16 miles W of Gulfport.
Holes: 18. **Yards:** 6,438/5,428. **Par:** 72/72. **Course Rating:** 69.7/71.6. **Slope:** 124/120. **Green Fee:** $24/$24. **Cart Fee:** $12/person. **Walking Policy:** Walking at certain times. **Walkability:** 1.
Opened: 1951. **Architect:** Tom Bendelow. **Season:** Year-round. **High:** Feb.-April. **To obtain tee times:** Call in advance. **Miscellaneous:** Discount packages, metal spikes, club rentals, credit cards (MC, V, AE).

PEARL RIVER GOLF CLUB
PU-Rte. 3, Poplarville, 39470 (601)795-8887.
Holes: 18. **Yards:** 6,366/4,973. **Par:** 72/72. **Course Rating:** 68.5/68.7. **Slope:** 107/113. **Green Fee:** $6/$13. **Walkability:** 2.

★★★ PINE BURR COUNTRY CLUB
800 Pine Burr Dr, Wiggins, 39577, Stone County, (601)928-4911, 32 miles N of Gulfport.
Holes: 18. **Yards:** 6,501/4,854. **Par:** 72/72. **Course Rating:** 71.3/68.5. **Slope:** 131/114. **Green Fee:** $15/$15. **Cart Fee:** $10/person. **Walking Policy:** Unrestricted walking. **Walkability:** 5.
Opened: 1972. **Season:** Year-round. **High:** April-Aug. **To obtain tee times:** Call up to 1 year in advance. **Miscellaneous:** Range (grass), club rentals, credit cards (MC, V, AE, D).
Reader Comments: Very pretty, needs TLC ... Uphills, downhills, tight, open. A definite must ...Tight course, sand, water, hilly, good layout.

PINE CREEK GOLF CLUB
PU-61 Clubhouse Dr., Purvis, 39475, Lamar County, (601)794-6427, (877)234-0385, 12 miles S of Hattiesburg. **Web:** www.play18.com/pinecreek.
Holes: 18. **Yards:** 6,152/4,661. **Par:** 71/72. **Course Rating:** 68.8/67.0. **Slope:** 112/110. **Green Fee:** $7/$11. **Cart Fee:** $9/cart. **Walking Policy:** Unrestricted walking. **Walkability:** 5. **Opened:** 1965. **Season:** Year-round. **High:** March-Nov. **To obtain tee times:** Tee times accepted 6 months in advance. **Miscellaneous:** Reduced fees (seniors, juniors), discount packages, range (grass), club rentals, beginner friendly.

★★ PINE ISLAND GOLF CLUB
SP-2021 Beachview Dr., Ocean Springs, 39564, Jackson County, (228)875-1674, 4 miles E of Biloxi.
Holes: 18. **Yards:** 6,369/4,915. **Par:** 71/71. **Course Rating:** 70.9/67.8. **Slope:** 129/109. **Green Fee:** $14/$30. **Cart Fee:** $12/. **Walking Policy:** Walking at certain times. **Walkability:** 2.
Opened: 1973. **Architect:** Pete Dye. **Season:** Year-round. **High:** Feb.-April. **To obtain tee times:** Call. **Miscellaneous:** Reduced fees (weekdays, low season, resort guests, twilight), discount packages, metal spikes, range (grass), club rentals, credit cards (MC, V, AE).
Special Notes: Currently closed for renovations. Re-opening planned for 2000 with a possible name change.

★★★½ PLANTATION GOLF CLUB
PU-9425 Plantation Rd., Olive Branch, 38654, De Soto County, (601)895-3530, 5 miles S of Memphis, TN. **E-mail:** cv6635@aol.com.

Holes: 18. **Yards:** 6,773/5,055. **Par:** 72/72. **Course Rating:** 72.0/64.4. **Slope:** 122/109. **Green Fee:** $32/$47. **Cart Fee:** $11/person. **Cart Fee:** Included in Green Fee. **Walking Policy:** Walking at certain times. **Walkability:** 2. **Opened:** 1990. **Architect:** William Leathers. **Season:** Year-round. **High:** April-Oct. **To obtain tee times:** Call 5 days in advance. **Miscellaneous:** Reduced fees (weekdays, low season, twilight, seniors, juniors), range (grass/mats), club rentals, credit cards (MC, V, AE).

Reader Comments: Duffers will enjoy ... No. 18 is prettiest par 4 around ... Great Zoysia fairways ... One of the best public course values I have ever found ... Typical easy resort layout ... A fun course to play!

PONTOTOC COUNTRY CLUB
SP-Hwy. 6 East, Pontotoc, 38863, Pontotoc County, (662)489-1962, 5 miles S of Pontotoc.
Holes: 18. **Yards:** 6,377/4,683. **Par:** 72/72. **Course Rating:** 70.9/67.6. **Slope:** 130/128. **Green Fee:** $30/$40. **Cart Fee:** Included in Green Fee. **Walking Policy:** Mandatory cart. **Walkability:** 3. **Opened:** 1964. **Season:** Year-round. **High:** April-June. **Miscellaneous:** Reduced fees (juniors), metal spikes, range (grass), credit cards (MC, V, D).

★★½ THE PRESIDENT BROADWATER GOLF COURSE
R-200 Beauvoir Rd., Biloxi, 39531, Harrison County, (601)385-4081, (800)647-3964, 3 miles E of Gulfport.
Holes: 18. **Yards:** 7,140/5,398. **Par:** 72/72. **Course Rating:** 74.1/70.4. **Slope:** 134/120. **Green Fee:** $44/$44. **Cart Fee:** Included in Green Fee. **Walking Policy:** Mandatory cart. **Walkability:** 1. **Opened:** 1968. **Architect:** Earl Stone. **Season:** Year-round. **High:** Feb.-May. **To obtain tee times:** Call golf shop. **Miscellaneous:** Reduced fees (resort guests, twilight), discount packages, metal spikes, range (grass), club rentals, lodging, credit cards (MC, V, AE, D).
Reader Comments: Average ... Fast greens, water hazard not up to par. Friendly ... Greens are shot.
Special Notes: Formerly Broadwater Resort.

★★★★ QUAIL HOLLOW GOLF COURSE
PU-1102 Percy Quin Dr., McComb, 39648, Pike County, (601)684-2903, (888)465-3647, 90 miles N of Baton Rouge, LA.
Holes: 18. **Yards:** 6,754/N/A. **Par:** 72/N/A. **Course Rating:** 71.9/N/A. **Slope:** 118/N/A. **Green Fee:** $35/$35. **Cart Fee:** Included in Green Fee. **Walking Policy:** Unrestricted walking. **Walkability:** 3. **Opened:** 1997. **Architect:** Arthur Hills. **Season:** Year-round. **High:** April-Sept. **To obtain tee times:** Call golf shop. **Miscellaneous:** Metal spikes, range (grass), club rentals, lodging (30 rooms), credit cards (MC, V, AE).
Notes: Ranked 5th in 1999 Best New Affordable Public Courses.
Reader Comments: Lots of trees, low lying ... Good price. Nice course ... Outstanding layout ... Great overall experience ... Worth the 2-hour ride from New Orleans ... Needs maturing ... Pretty course with lots of hills.

★★ ST. ANDREWS GOLF CLUB
SP-2 Golfing Green Dr., Ocean Springs, 39564, Jackson County, (228)875-7730, (888)875-7730, 10 miles E of Biloxi. **E-mail:** sagc@bellsouth.net.
Holes: 18. **Yards:** 6,540/4,960. **Par:** 72/72. **Course Rating:** 69.7/67.8. **Slope:** 119/111. **Green Fee:** $17/$30. **Cart Fee:** $12/person. **Walking Policy:** Walking at certain times. **Walkability:** 1. **Opened:** 1968. **Season:** Year-round. **High:** Feb.-March. **To obtain tee times:** Call golf shop. **Miscellaneous:** Reduced fees (weekdays, low season, resort guests), discount packages, metal spikes, range (grass), club rentals, lodging (20 rooms), credit cards (MC, V, AE).

SHADY OAKS COUNTRY CLUB
SP-4840 Clinton Blvd, Jackson, 39209, (601)922-2331.
EAST COURSE
Holes: 18. **Yards:** 6,443/5,026. **Par:** 72/72. **Course Rating:** N/A. **Slope:** N/A. **Green Fee:** $15/$20. **Walkability:** N/A.
WEST COURSE
Holes: 18. **Yards:** 6,573/5,014. **Par:** 72/72. **Course Rating:** N/A. **Slope:** N/A. **Green Fee:** $15/$20. **Walkability:** N/A.

SHILOH RIDGE GOLF & RACQUET CLUB
PU-3303 Shiloh Ridge Rd., Corinth, 38834, Alcorn County, (662)286-8000, 85 miles E of Memphis.
Holes: 18. **Yards:** 6,525/5,072. **Par:** 72/72. **Course Rating:** 73.3/N/A. **Slope:** 123/N/A. **Green Fee:** $10/$20. **Cart Fee:** $10/person. **Walking Policy:** Walking at certain times. **Walkability:** 3. **Opened:** 1989. **Architect:** Archie Anderson. **Season:** Year-round. **High:** April-Oct. **To obtain tee times:** Call (662)286-8000 no more than 1 week in advance. **Miscellaneous:** Reduced fees (low season, seniors), club rentals, credit cards (MC, V, AE, D).
Special Notes: Formerly Shiloh Ridge Country Club

MISSISSIPPI

★½ SONNY GUY MUNICIPAL GOLF COURSE
PM-3200 Woodrow Wilson Dr., Jackson, 39209, Hinds County, (601)960-1905.
Holes: 18. **Yards:** 7,200/5,200. **Par:** 72/72. **Course Rating:** N/A. **Slope:** N/A. **Green Fee:** $9/$12. **Cart Fee:** $14/cart. **Walking Policy:** Unrestricted walking. **Walkability:** 1. **Opened:** 1949. **Architect:** Sonny Guy. **Season:** Year-round. **High:** June-July. **To obtain tee times:** Call 1 day in advance. **Miscellaneous:** Reduced fees (weekdays, twilight, seniors, juniors), discount packages, metal spikes, club rentals, credit cards (MC, V).

★★★ SUNKIST COUNTRY CLUB
SP-2381 Sunkist Country Club Rd., Biloxi, 39532, Harrison County, (601)388-3961.
Holes: 18. **Yards:** 6,300/5,300. **Par:** 72/72. **Course Rating:** 69.0/71.0. **Slope:** 117/121. **Green Fee:** $20/$37. **Cart Fee:** Included in Green Fee. **Walking Policy:** Mandatory cart. **Walkability:** 2. **Opened:** 1954. **Architect:** Roland "Robby" Robertson. **Season:** Year-round. **High:** Feb.-April. **To obtain tee times:** Call anytime in advance. **Miscellaneous:** Reduced fees (weekdays, low season, resort guests, twilight), metal spikes, range (grass/mats), club rentals, credit cards (MC, V, D).
Reader Comments: Very short, good greens ... Lots of traffic ... Average ... Nice course—water, sand, small greens, good layout ... Very nice course to play, fun ... Well laid out, best of all in area ... Tree-lined course, fair; nice people ... Fun to play ... Fast greens, tight fairways, fun.

★★★★½ TIMBERTON GOLF CLUB *Value, Condition, Pace*
PU-22 Clubhouse Dr., Hattiesburg, 39401, Forest County, (601)584-4653, (800)848-3222, 90 miles N of New Orleans, LA. **E-mail:** rlhpga@netdoor.com. **Web:** timberton-golf.com.
Holes: 27. **Yards:** 7,028/5,439. **Par:** 72/72. **Course Rating:** 73.4/71.4. **Slope:** 135/132. **Green Fee:** $36/$47. **Cart Fee:** Included in Green Fee. **Walking Policy:** Walking at certain times. **Walkability:** 5. **Opened:** 1991. **Architect:** Mark McCumber/J.R. Carpenter/Ron Hickman. **Season:** Year-round. **High:** March-April. **To obtain tee times:** Call up to 60 days in advance with credit card to guarantee. **Miscellaneous:** Reduced fees (twilight), discount packages, range (grass/mats), club rentals, lodging (15 rooms), credit cards (MC, V).
Notes: Ranked 5th in 1997 Best in State.
Reader Comments: Holes memorable and varied. High marks for challenge, beauty and fun ... Difficult, but fair ... One of the prettiest in the South, great value ... Play from back tees and let rip ... Pro is terrific ... Beautiful, each fairway isolated from others ... Back 9 as good as any.

★★ TRAMARK GOLF COURSE
PU-Washington Avenue, Gulfport, 39503, Harrison County, (228)863-7808, 65 miles E of New Orleans.
Holes: 18. **Yards:** 6,350/5,800. **Par:** 72/72. **Course Rating:** 68.5/69.5. **Slope:** 116/109. **Green Fee:** $14/$14. **Cart Fee:** $20/person. **Walking Policy:** Unrestricted walking. **Walkability:** 1. **Opened:** 1967. **Architect:** Floyd Trehern. **Season:** Year-round. **High:** Feb.-April. **To obtain tee times:** Call anytime. **Miscellaneous:** Reduced fees (juniors), discount packages, metal spikes, range (grass), club rentals, credit cards (MC, V), beginner friendly.

TWIN PINES COUNTRY CLUB
SP-1 Tee Time Dr., Petal, 39465, Forrest County, (601)544-8318, 10 miles E of Hattiesburg.
Holes: 9. **Yards:** 6,690/4,772. **Par:** 72/72. **Course Rating:** 68.5/64.6. **Slope:** 117/106. **Green Fee:** $10/$16. **Cart Fee:** $9/person. **Walking Policy:** Walking at certain times. **Walkability:** 4. **Opened:** 1986. **Season:** Year round. **High:** April-July. **Miscellaneous:** Credit cards (MC, V).

★★½ USM'S VAN HOOK GOLF COURSE
PU-One Golf Course Rd., Hattiesburg, 39402, Forest County, (601)264-1872, 60 miles N of Biloxi.
Holes: 18. **Yards:** 6,429/4,903. **Par:** 72/73. **Course Rating:** 72.2/67.8. **Slope:** 117/110. **Green Fee:** $10/$15. **Cart Fee:** $20/cart. **Walking Policy:** Unrestricted walking. **Walkability:** 3. **Opened:** 1957. **Architect:** Sonny Guy. **Season:** Year-round. **High:** May-Dec. **To obtain tee times:** Call 1 day in advance. **Miscellaneous:** Reduced fees (weekdays, low season, twilight, seniors, juniors), discount packages, club rentals, , credit cards (MC, V), beginner friendly.
Reader Comments: Good track, lots of play ... Getting better. Still a practice course ... Older layout, well developed ... Hilly, very little sand, some water ... Good course for the amount of play it gets.

★★★ WEDGEWOOD GOLF COURSE
SP-5206 Tournament Dr., Olive Branch, 38654, De Soto County, (901)521-8275, 5 miles S of Memphis. **E-mail:** www.golfsolf.com.
Holes: 18. **Yards:** 6,863/5,627. **Par:** 72/72. **Course Rating:** 72.8/69.1. **Slope:** 127/118. **Green Fee:** $29/$45. **Cart Fee:** Included in Green Fee. **Walking Policy:** Walking at certain times. **Walkability:** 2. **Opened:** 1990. **Architect:** John Floyd. **Season:** Year-round. **High:** May-Sept. **To obtain tee times:** Call 7 days in advance. **Miscellaneous:** Reduced fees (weekdays, low season, resort guests, twilight, seniors, juniors), discount packages, range (grass), club rentals, credit cards (MC, V).

MISSISSIPPI

Reader Comments: Nice course for amateurs, very playable ... Fine layout, close to city, busy, enjoyable water ... Good shape, interesting layout ... Deep rough.

WHISPERING PINES GOLF CLUB
Columbus AFB Bldg. 501, Columbus, 39701, (662)434-7932.
Holes: 18. **Yards:** 5,195/4,650. **Par:** 70/72. **Course Rating:** 66.7/67.7. **Slope:** 128/120. **Green Fee:** $8/$15. **Walkability:** 1.

WILLOW CREEK GOLF CLUB
PU-1300 Willowcreek Lane, Brandon, 39042, (601)825-8343.
Holes: 18. **Yards:** 6,424/4,864. **Par:** 72/72. **Course Rating:** 70.1/73.1. **Slope:** 113/117. **Green Fee:** $12/$15. **Walkability:** N/A.

★★★½ WINDANCE COUNTRY CLUB
SP-19385 Champion Circle, Gulfport, 39505, Harrison County, (228)832-4871, 60 miles E of New Orleans, LA.
Holes: 18. **Yards:** 6,678/5,179. **Par:** 72/72. **Course Rating:** 73.1/70.1. **Slope:** 129/120. **Green Fee:** N/A/$60. **Cart Fee:** $15/person. **Walking Policy:** Mandatory cart. **Walkability:** 2. **Opened:** 1986. **Architect:** Mark McCumber. **Season:** Year-round. **High:** Feb.-April. **To obtain tee times:** Call with a credit card to guarantee. There is a 24-hour cancellation policy. Packages are available through most hotels in the area. **Miscellaneous:** Reduced fees (low season), discount packages, range (grass), club rentals, credit cards (MC, V, AE).
Reader Comments: Better than average ... Nice golf, classy place ... Best course in Mississippi, superb challenge ... Almost can't be beat ... Could be good with better maintenance.

WINONA COUNTRY CLUB
SP-Hwy. 407, Winona, 38967, (601)283-4211.
Holes: 18. **Yards:** 6,045/5.146. **Par:** 72/74. **Course Rating:** N/A. **Slope:** N/A. **Green Fee:** $7/$12. **Walkability:** 4.

MISSOURI

ADAMS POINTE GOLF CLUB
PU-1601 R.D. Mize Rd., Blue Springs, 64014, Jackson County, (816)220-3673, 15 miles E of Kansas City. **E-mail:** apgolf@gte.net. **Web:** www/eagl.com.
Holes: 18. **Yards:** 6,938/5,060. **Par:** 72/72. **Course Rating:** 73.8/68.1. **Slope:** 131/114. **Green Fee:** $18/$32. **Cart Fee:** $12/person. **Walking Policy:** Unrestricted walking. **Walkability:** 3. **Opened:** 1998. **Architect:** Don Sechrest. **Season:** Year-round. **High:** May-Sept. **To obtain tee times:** Accepted 5 days in advance. **Miscellaneous:** Reduced fees (low season, twilight, seniors, juniors), range (grass/mats), club rentals, lodging (100 rooms), credit cards (MC, V, AE).

ARTHUR HILLS GOLF CLUB
PU-Rte. 2, Mexico, 65265, (573)581-1330.
Special Notes: Call club for further information.

★★★★ BENT CREEK GOLF COURSE
PU-1 Bent Creek Dr., Jackson, 63755, Cape Girardeau County, (573)243-6060, 90 miles S of St. Louis.
Holes: 18. **Yards:** 6,958/5,148. **Par:** 72/72. **Course Rating:** 72.5/69.8. **Slope:** 136/112. **Green Fee:** $16/$25. **Cart Fee:** $12/person. **Walking Policy:** Walking at certain times. **Walkability:** 3. **Opened:** 1990. **Architect:** Gary Kern. **Season:** Year-round. **High:** May-Sept. **To obtain tee times:** Call up to 7 days in advance. **Miscellaneous:** Reduced fees (weekdays, low season, twilight, seniors, juniors), discount packages, metal spikes, range (grass/mats), club rentals, credit cards (MC, V, AE, D).
Reader Comments: Great fun, beautiful course ... Long par 3 over water is a great hole ... Good variety, convenient to St. Louis ... Always worth the trip, zoysia fairways ... Very hilly, but fun ... Very nice course ... Challenging but not intimidating ... Worth the drive from St. Louis! ... Good layout. Inexpensive.

★★★ BENT OAK GOLF CLUB
PU-1300 S.E. 30th, Oak Grove, 64075, Jackson County, (816)690-3028, 20 miles E of Kansas City.
Holes: 18. **Yards:** 6,855/5,500. **Par:** 72/73. **Course Rating:** 73.1/71.0. **Slope:** 134/119. **Green Fee:** $18/$21. **Cart Fee:** $26/cart. **Walking Policy:** Unrestricted walking. **Walkability:** 3. **Opened:** 1980. **Architect:** Bob Simmons. **Season:** Year-round. **High:** May-Sept. **To obtain tee times:** Call up to 7 days in advance. **Miscellaneous:** Reduced fees (weekdays, low season, twilight, seniors, juniors), discount packages, metal spikes, range (grass), club rentals, credit cards (MC, V, AE, D).
Reader Comments: No two 3s, 4s or 5s alike. Great design ... Long par 4, hilly, nice greens ... Tough course ... Really enjoyed the layout ... Improving every year... One of the best values in western Missouri ... Excellent, good people ... Great course, very difficult, also crowded ...Grand old course, good value.

★★★ BILL & PAYNE STEWART GOLF COURSE
PM-1825 E. Norton, Springfield, 65803, Greene County, (417)833-9962.
Holes: 18. **Yards:** 6,162/5,360. **Par:** 70/71. **Course Rating:** 68.4/70.6. **Slope:** 113/113. **Green Fee:** $12/$17. **Cart Fee:** $20/cart. **Walking Policy:** Unrestricted walking. **Walkability:** 2. **Opened:** 1947. **Architect:** Perry Maxwell. **Season:** Year-round. **High:** March-Oct. **To obtain tee times:** Call golf shop. **Miscellaneous:** Reduced fees (weekdays, seniors, juniors), range (grass), club rentals, credit cards (MC, V).
Reader Comments: Course gets heavy play, but in good shape ... Condition is good for the amount of play ... Nice course, easy to play ... Fun course.

BOOTHEEL GOLF CLUB
PU-1218 N. Ingram, Sikeston, 63801, Scott County, (573)472-6111, (888)472-6111, 150 miles S of St. Louis.
Holes: 18. **Yards:** 6,880/5,825. **Par:** 72/72. **Course Rating:** 73.0/N/A. **Slope:** 123/N/A. **Green Fee:** $17/$20. **Cart Fee:** $10/person. **Walking Policy:** Unrestricted walking. **Walkability:** 1. **Opened:** 1996. **Architect:** David Pfaff. **Season:** Year-round. **High:** April-Nov. **To obtain tee times:** Call up to 14 days in advance. Out-of-town guests may call up to 30 days in advance. **Miscellaneous:** Reduced fees (weekdays, low season, seniors), metal spikes, range (grass/mats), club rentals, credit cards (MC, V, AE).

BRIARBROOK COUNTRY CLUB
SP-502 Briarbrook Dr., Carl Junction, 64834, Jasper County, (417)649-7284, 5 miles N of Joplin. **Web:** briarbrookgolf.com.
Holes: 27. **Yards:** 6,663/5,925. **Par:** 72/76. **Course Rating:** 71.2/74.0. **Slope:** 127/133. **Green Fee:** $16/$16. **Cart Fee:** $9/person. **Walking Policy:** Unrestricted walking. **Walkability:** 4. **Opened:** 1962. **Season:** Year-round. **High:** April-Oct. **Miscellaneous:** Range (grass), club rentals, credit cards (MC, V).

CAPE JAYCEE MUNICIPAL GOLF COURSE
PM-Perryville Rd., Cape Girardeau, 63701, Cape Girardeua County, (573)334-2031.
Holes: 18. **Yards:** 5,616/4,492. **Par:** 70/70. **Course Rating:** 65.2/64.7. **Slope:** 106/101. **Green Fee:** $9/$11. **Cart Fee:** $17/cart. **Walking Policy:** Unrestricted walking. **Walkability:** 3. **Season:** Year-round. **High:** April-Oct. **To obtain tee times:** Call 7 days in advance up to that day.
Miscellaneous: Reduced fees (juniors), club rentals, credit cards (MC, V).
Special Notes: Formerly known as Cape Girardeau Municipal Golf Course.

★★½ CARTHAGE MUNICIPAL GOLF COURSE
PM-2000 Richard Webster Drive, Carthage, 64836, Jasper County, (417)237-7030, 10 miles NE of Joplin.
Holes: 18. **Yards:** 6,402/5,469. **Par:** 71/73. **Course Rating:** 69.4/70.5. **Slope:** 124/115. **Green Fee:** $9/$11. **Cart Fee:** $18/cart. **Walking Policy:** Unrestricted walking. **Walkability:** 3. **Opened:** 1937. **Architect:** Tom Bendelow/Don Sechrest. **Season:** Year-round. **High:** April-Aug. **To obtain tee times:** Call or come in 7 days in advance. **Miscellaneous:** Reduced fees (weekdays, twilight, juniors), range (grass/mats), club rentals, credit cards (MC, V).
Reader Comments: Pretty, tight course. Fun design .:. Nice, open front 9, big greens. ... Price is right ... A hidden gem ... The front nine has a great layout, back nine goes up and back on a hill.

★★★ CASSVILLE GOLF CLUB
SP-Hwy. 112 S., Cassville, 65625, Barry County, (417)847-2399, 55 miles SW of Springfield.
Holes: 18. **Yards:** 6,620/5,802. **Par:** 72/72. **Course Rating:** 71.3/79.9. **Slope:** 118/117. **Green Fee:** $17/$20. **Cart Fee:** $20/cart. **Walking Policy:** Unrestricted walking. **Walkability:** 2. **Opened:** 1966. **Architect:** Ken Sisney. **Season:** Year-round. **High:** April-Oct. **To obtain tee times:** Call up to 14 days in advance. **Miscellaneous:** Range (grass/mats), club rentals, credit cards (MC, V).
Reader Comments: Fun place to be ... Out of the way gem ... Excellent greens ... Superior undulating greens ... Nice water holes.

★★★½ CHERRY HILLS GOLF CLUB
PU-16700 Manchester Rd., St. Louis, 63040, St. Louis County, (314)458-4113, 12 miles W of St. Louis.
Holes: 18. **Yards:** 6,450/5,491. **Par:** 71/72. **Course Rating:** 71.1/72.6. **Slope:** 132/120. **Green Fee:** $30/$50. **Cart Fee:** Included in Green Fee. **Walking Policy:** Unrestricted walking. **Walkability:** 4. **Opened:** 1964. **Architect:** Art Linkogel/Gary Kern. **Season:** Year-round. **High:** May-Aug. **To obtain tee times:** Call up to 7 days in advance. Weekend tee times require a credit card to reserve. **Miscellaneous:** Reduced fees (low season, twilight, seniors), metal spikes, range (grass/mats), club rentals, credit cards (MC, V, AE).
Reader Comments: Beautiful old style. Well kept ... Easy to get on. Pace is good ... Lots of improvements ... One of the best buys in the St Louis area, exciting, challenging and excellent service ... Country club feel ... Nice par 3s, fairly tight ... Price a little high ... Solid test of golf with plush zoysia fairways.

★★★ CLAYCREST GOLF CLUB
SP-925 N. Lightburne, Liberty, 64068, Clay County, (816)781-6522, 15 miles NE of Kansas City.
Holes: 18. **Yards:** 6,457/5,375. **Par:** 72/72. **Course Rating:** 69.5/68.2. **Slope:** 115/109. **Green Fee:** $14/$16. **Cart Fee:** $24/cart. **Walking Policy:** Unrestricted walking. **Walkability:** N/A. **Opened:** 1967. **Architect:** Chet Mendenhall. **Season:** Year-round. **High:** April-Nov. **To obtain tee times:** Call 7 a.m. Wednesday prior to weekend. **Miscel-laneous:** Reduced fees (seniors), metal spikes, club rentals, credit cards (MC, V).
Reader Comments: Good greens, 7 blind tee shots ... Plain course, too much play, seniors love it ... New irrigation system helps ... College course. Long ... Uphill, downhill ... Nice folks, neat pro, average play ... Hard to get a tee time, but worth it when you do.

CLINTON COUNTRY CLUB
SP-225 NE 100, Clinton, 64735, Henry County, (816)885-2521.
Special Notes: Call club for further information.

★★★★ COUNTRY CREEK GOLF CLUB *Value*
PU-21601 E. State Rte. P, Pleasant Hill, 64080, (816)540-5225.
Special Notes: Call club for further information.

★★½ CRACKERNECK GOLF COURSE
PU-18800 E. 40 Hwy., Independence, 64055, Jackson County, (816)795-7771, 13 miles E of Kansas City.
Holes: 18. **Yards:** 6,246/5,175. **Par:** 72/74. **Course Rating:** 69.1/68.8. **Slope:** 115/108. **Green Fee:** $15/$18. **Cart Fee:** $22/cart. **Walking Policy:** Unrestricted walking. **Walkability:** 2. **Opened:** 1964. **Architect:** Charles Maddox/William Maddox. **Season:** Year-round. **High:** June-Aug. **To obtain tee times:** Tee times are not required. **Miscellaneous:** Reduced fees (weekdays, low season, twilight, seniors), range (mats), club rentals, credit cards (MC, V).

MISSOURI

Reader Comments: Short easy walk. Making a lot of improvements ... Best grill in town! Easy course, good for beginners ... Heavy play moves reasonably well.

★★★½ CRYSTAL HIGHLANDS GOLF CLUB

PU-3030 U.S. Highway 61, Crystal City, 63028, Jefferson County, (314)931-3880, 30 miles S of St. Louis.
Holes: 18. **Yards:** 6,480/4,946. **Par:** 72/72. **Course Rating:** 71.6/68.0. **Slope:** 135/109. **Green Fee:** $20/$30. **Cart Fee:** $10/person. **Walking Policy:** Walking at certain times. **Walkability:** N/A. **Opened:** 1988. **Architect:** Michael Hurdzan. **Season:** Year-round. **High:** April-Oct. **To obtain tee times:** Call 5 days in advance. **Miscellaneous:** Reduced fees (weekdays, low season, twilight, seniors, juniors), metal spikes, range (grass), club rentals, credit cards (MC, V, D).
Reader Comments: Challenging, hilly, good price, severe contour greens ... Good variety/grade changes ... Best greens in the area ... Beautiful, tough, long and outstanding ... Picturesque ... Well worth the drive ... Watch out! Elephants buried in greens.

★★★ DOGWOOD HILLS GOLF CLUB & RESORT INN

R-1252 State Hwy. KK, Osage Beach, 65065, Camden County, (573)348-3153, 160 miles SW of St. Louis.
Holes: 18. **Yards:** 6,073/4,641. **Par:** 70/71. **Course Rating:** 68.5/65.2. **Slope:** 116/95. **Green Fee:** $28/$47. **Cart Fee:** Included in Green Fee. **Walking Policy:** Walking at certain times. **Walkability:** 2. **Opened:** 1962. **Architect:** Herman Hackbarth. **Season:** Year-round. **High:** March-Oct. **To obtain tee times:** Call 14 days in advance. **Miscella-neous:** Reduced fees (weekdays, low season, resort guests, twilight), discount pack-
ages, metal spikes, range (grass/mats), club rentals, lodging, credit cards (MC, V, AE, D).
Reader Comments: Excellent layout ... Basic golf, hospitality ... Wide open ... Low cost, easy to get on ... Excellent value, many challenging holes ... Fun vacation course ... A good course for beginners ... Nice course.

EAGLE CREST GOLF & COUNTRY CLUB

PU-Rte. 4, Republic, 65738, (417)732-8487.
Special Notes: Call club for further information.

★★★★ EAGLE KNOLL GOLF CLUB *Pace*

PU-5757 E. Eagle Knoll Dr., Hartsburg, 65039, Boone County, (573)761-4653, (800)909-0564, 18 miles S of Columbia. **E-mail:** eagleknoll@aol.com. **Web:** www.showmegreens.com.
Holes: 18. **Yards:** 6,920/5,323. **Par:** 72/72. **Course Rating:** 73.8/69.1. **Slope:** 141/113. **Green Fee:** $32/$39. **Cart Fee:** Included in Green Fee. **Walking Policy:** Unrestricted walking. **Walkability:** 5. **Opened:** 1996. **Architect:** Gary Kern. **Season:** Year-round. **High:** April-Sept. **To obtain tee times:** Call up to 7 days in advance. **Miscellaneous:** Reduced fees (low season, twilight, seniors, juniors), range (grass/mats), club rentals, credit cards (MC, V, AE, D).
Notes: Ranked tied for 8th in 1996 Best New Affordable Courses.
Reader Comments: Hit it straight, pal; affordable ... Pretty tough course but I like it ... Bring your A game. This baby's tight ... Great course! ... Great layout, very difficult from back tees ... New course, fun, challenging, big greens ... Very tough course, nice views, lots of hills ... Scenic. Reasonable rates.

★★★★ EAGLE LAKE GOLF CLUB *Value*

SP-4215 Hunt Rd., Farmington, 63640, St. Francois County, (573)756-6660, 55 miles S of St. Louis.
Holes: 18. **Yards:** 7,093/5,648. **Par:** 72/72. **Course Rating:** 73.9/71.0. **Slope:** 130/113. **Green Fee:** $25/$35. **Cart Fee:** $10/person. **Walking Policy:** Walking at certain times. **Walkability:** 2. **Opened:** 1993. **Architect:** Gary Kern. **Season:** Year-round. **High:** April-Oct. **To obtain tee times:** Call 7 days in advance. **Miscellaneous:** Reduced fees (low season, twilight, seniors), discount packages, range (grass/mats), club rentals, credit cards (MC, V, AE, D).
Reader Comments: Superb condition ... Excellent ... Always in great shape, people-friendly, good price ... Best overall course I have played ... Long/open/no two holes alike/great shape ... Biggest, great, greens anywhere! ... Interesting layout ... One of the best in Midwest ... Best kept secret, beautiful course, muny prices, a gem.

★★★ EAGLE SPRINGS GOLF COURSE

PU-2575 Redman Rd., St. Louis, 63136, St. Louis County, (314)355-7277.
Holes: 18. **Yards:** 6,563/5,533. **Par:** 72/72. **Course Rating:** 71.4/72.3. **Slope:** 122/121. **Green Fee:** $18/$29. **Cart Fee:** $10/person. **Walking Policy:** Unrestricted walking. **Walkability:** 3. **Opened:** 1989. **Architect:** David Gill. **Season:** Year-round. **High:** May-Sept. **To obtain tee times:** Call golf shop. **Miscellaneous:** Reduced fees (weekdays, low season, seniors, juniors), range (grass), club rentals, credit cards (MC, V).
Reader Comments: Really excellent course, little known ... Short course, confidence builder ... Fun, short and interesting, pace needs to quicken ... Excellent value ... Very accepting of junior play ... Beautiful course ... Greens are very good, fairway needs work ... Unexpected challenging layout, need all your clubs.

★★ EAGLE'S LANDING GOLF COURSE
PU-4200 Bong Ave., Belton, 64012, Cass County, (816)318-0004, 25 miles S of Kansas City. **E-mail:** eglslndg@swbell.net.
Holes: 18. **Yards:** 6,855/5,500. **Par:** 72/73. **Course Rating:** N/A. **Slope:** N/A. **Green Fee:** $12/$27. **Cart Fee:** $24/cart. **Walking Policy:** Unrestricted walking. **Walkability:** 3. **Opened:** 1965. **Architect:** Jeff Klaiber. **Season:** Year-round. **High:** May-Sept. **To obtain tee times:** Call 3 days in advance. **Miscellaneous:** Reduced fees (twilight, seniors, juniors), discount packages, club rentals, credit cards (MC, V).

ELDON GOLF CLUB
SP-35 Golf Club Road, Eldon, 65026, Miller County, (573)392-4172.
Holes: 18. **Yards:** 6,373/4,754. **Par:** 71/73. **Course Rating:** 70.0/66.6. **Slope:** 124/110. **Green Fee:** $35/$40. **Cart Fee:** $10/person. **Walking Policy:** Mandatory cart. **Walkability:** 3. **Season:** Year-round. **High:** May-Oct. **To obtain tee times:** Call 7 days in advance. **Miscellaneous:** Reduced fees (juniors), range (grass), club rentals, credit cards (MC, V), beginner friendly.

★★★½ EXCELSIOR SPRINGS GOLF CLUB
PU-1201 E. Golf Hill Dr., Excelsior Springs, 64024, Ray County, (816)630-3731, 28 miles NE of Kansas City.
Holes: 18. **Yards:** 6,700/5,200. **Par:** 72/72. **Course Rating:** 72.0/65.8. **Slope:** 120/107. **Green Fee:** $18/$22. **Cart Fee:** $12/person. **Walking Policy:** Unrestricted walking. **Walkability:** 4. **Opened:** 1915. **Architect:** Tom Bendelow. **Season:** Feb.-Dec. **High:** May-Sept. **To obtain tee times:** Call on Monday for upcoming weekend or holiday. **Miscellaneous:** Reduced fees (weekdays, twilight), range (grass).
Reader Comments: Great greens, challenging ... Easy to play ... A nice place to play ...Very good greens year-round ... Diamond in the rough. Fast greens, with lots of slopes, great value! Fun ... Great greens ... Best value, in all areas of golf ... Great course, back 9 requires good iron game.

★★½ FAIRVIEW GOLF COURSE
PM-33rd and Pacific Sts., St. Joseph, 64507, Buchanan County, (816)271-5350, 40 miles N of Kansas City.
Holes: 18. **Yards:** 6,312/5,490. **Par:** 72/73. **Course Rating:** 69.5/72.0. **Slope:** 116/120. **Green Fee:** N/A/$14. **Cart Fee:** $20/cart. **Walking Policy:** Unrestricted walking. **Walkability:** 3. **Season:** Year-round. **High:** April-Oct. **To obtain tee times:** Call 1 day in advance for weekdays. Call on Thursday for upcoming weekend. **Miscellaneous:** Re-duced fees (twilight, seniors, juniors), range (mats), club rentals, credit cards (MC, V).
Reader Comments: Lots of play ... Easy, pace of play is good, OK condition ... Fair public course, not worth many repeats.

★★★½ THE FALLS GOLF CLUB
PU-1170 Turtle Creek Dr., O'Fallon, 63366, St. Charles County, (314)240-4653, 17 miles W of St. Louis. **E-mail:** fallgolfnothnbut.net.
Holes: 18. **Yards:** 6,394/4,933. **Par:** 71/71. **Course Rating:** 70.6/67.2. **Slope:** 126/107. **Green Fee:** $25/$33. **Cart Fee:** $11/person. **Walking Policy:** Walking at certain times. **Walkability:** 2. **Opened:** 1995. **Architect:** John Allen. **Season:** Year-round. **High:** May-Oct. **To obtain tee times:** Call up to 7 days in advance. **Miscellaneous:** Reduced fees (twilight), range (grass/mats), club rentals, credit cards (MC, V).
Reader Comments: Greens are in great shape! ... Still maturing, but nice ... Tough greens, best value ... Short, straight, good course ... Easy track, not much trouble short ... Good new course ... A real placement course ... Sprawling, suburban layout, a solid test; staff goes out of their way to be friendly ... Super greens!.

★★★ FOREST PARK GOLF COURSE
PM-5591 Grand Dr., St. Louis, 63112, St. Louis County, (314)367-1337.
Holes: 18. **Yards:** 6,024/5,528. **Par:** 71/74. **Course Rating:** 67.8/67.8. **Slope:** 113/113. **Green Fee:** $13/$31. **Cart Fee:** Included in Green Fee. **Walking Policy:** Unrestricted walking. **Walkability:** 4. **Opened:** 1912. **Architect:** Robert Foulis. **Season:** Year-round. **High:** May-Sept. **To obtain tee times:** Call anytime in advance with credit card to confirm. **Miscellaneous:** Reduced fees (low season, twilight, seniors), metal spikes, club rentals, credit cards (MC, V, AE).
Reader Comments: Fun to play, short but tricky ... A lovely layout ... A St. Louis tradition ... Lots of golf tradition, oldest course around ... Easy access for St. Louis hackers.

★★½ FRANK E. PETERS MUNICIPAL GOLF COURSE
PU-Rte. 3, Box 261-A, Nevada, 64772, Vernon County, (417)448-2750, 100 miles S of Kansas City.
Holes: 18. **Yards:** 6,512/5,159. **Par:** 72/72. **Course Rating:** 70.1/68.2. **Slope:** 109/110. **Green Fee:** $7/$11. **Walking Policy:** Unrestricted walking. **Walkability:** N/A. **Opened:** 1978. **Architect:** Jim Lewis. **Season:** Year-round. **High:** April-Sept. **To obtain tee times:** First come, first served.

Miscellaneous: Reduced fees (weekdays, twilight), metal spikes, range (grass/mats), club rentals, credit cards (MC, V).
Reader Comments: Good, fun, open muny track.

★★½ GUSTIN GOLF CLUB
PU-Stadium Blvd., Columbia, 65211, Boone County, (573)882-6016.
Holes: 18. **Yards:** 6,400/5,565. **Par:** 70/70. **Course Rating:** 69.7/71.3. **Slope:** 123/116. **Green Fee:** $12/$15. **Cart Fee:** $22/cart. **Walking Policy:** Unrestricted walking. **Walkability:** 5. **Architect:** Floyd Farley. **Season:** Year-round. **High:** March-Oct. **To obtain tee times:** Call up to 7 days in advance. **Miscellaneous:** Reduced fees (low season, twilight, juniors), metal spikes, range (grass/mats), club rentals, credit cards (MC, V, D, ATM Debit Cards).
Reader Comments: Very hilly and affordable course.

★★★ HAWK RIDGE GOLF CLUB
PU-18 Hawk Ridge Dr., Lake St. Louis, 63366, St. Charles County, (314)561-2828, 40 miles W of St. Louis.
Holes: 18. **Yards:** 6,619/4,890. **Par:** 72/72. **Course Rating:** 70.8/67.2. **Slope:** 127/105. **Green Fee:** $21/$30. **Cart Fee:** $15/person. **Walking Policy:** Walking at certain times. **Walkability:** 3. **Opened:** 1995. **Architect:** Larry Flatt. **Season:** Year-round. **High:** April-Oct. **To obtain tee times:** Call 7 days in advance. **Miscellaneous:** Reduced fees (weekdays, low season, twilight, seniors, juniors), discount packages, metal spikes, range (grass), club rentals, credit cards (MC, V).
Reader Comments: Good design, new and growing, windy hilly, good price ... Fun short course/good layout ... Holes 4, 5 & 6 are a great combo of challenge and finesse ... New and tough but good ... Expensive ... Hilly, interesting.

HIDDEN TRAILS COUNTRY CLUB
SP-11601 Hidden Trails Drive, Dexter, 63841, Stoddard County, (573)624-3638, 3 miles W of Dexter.
Holes: 18. **Yards:** 6,688/5,506. **Par:** 72/72. **Course Rating:** 70.2/70.0. **Slope:** 122/115. **Green Fee:** $18/$24. **Cart Fee:** $9/person. **Walking Policy:** Walking at certain times. **Walkability:** 3. **Opened:** 1975. **Season:** April-Oct. **High:** May-Sept. **Miscellaneous:** Reduced fees (low season, juniors), discount packages, metal spikes, range (grass), club rentals.

HIDDEN VALLEY GOLF COURSE
PU-800 W. 184th St., Lawson, 64062, Clay County, (816)580-3444.
Holes: 18. **Yards:** 6,707/5,489. **Par:** 72/72. **Course Rating:** 70.9/N/A. **Slope:** 115/N/A. **Green Fee:** $14/$17. **Cart Fee:** $10/person. **Walking Policy:** Unrestricted walking. **Walkability:** 2. **Opened:** 1995. **Architect:** Leo Johnson. **Season:** Year-round. **High:** May-Oct. **Miscellaneous:** Reduced fees (weekdays, seniors, juniors), range (grass), club rentals, credit cards (MC, V).

★★ HIDDEN VALLEY GOLF LINKS
PU-Rte. 1, Clever, 65631, Stone County, (417)743-2860, 18 miles SW of Springfield.
Holes: 18. **Yards:** 6,611/5,237. **Par:** 73/73. **Course Rating:** 71.9/N/A. **Slope:** 118/N/A. **Green Fee:** $14/$18. **Cart Fee:** $20/cart. **Walking Policy:** Unrestricted walking. **Walkability:** N/A. **Opened:** 1975. **Architect:** Mario Alfonzo. **Season:** Year-round. **High:** May-Sept. **To obtain tee times:** Call Monday for upcoming weekend. **Miscellaneous:** Reduced fees (seniors), club rentals, credit cards (MC, V, D).

★★★ HODGE PARK GOLF COURSE
PM-7000 N.E. Barry Rd., Kansas City, 64156, Clay County, (816)781-4152, 10 miles NE of Kansas City.
Holes: 18. **Yards:** 6,223/5,293. **Par:** 71/71. **Course Rating:** 69.5/69.4. **Slope:** 117/115. **Green Fee:** $17/$19. **Cart Fee:** $12/person. **Walking Policy:** Unrestricted walking. **Walkability:** 3. **Opened:** 1975. **Architect:** Larry Runyon/Michael H. Malyn. **Season:** Year-round. **High:** April-Oct. **To obtain tee times:** Call 3 days in advance. Automated system at (816)474-1300. **Miscellaneous:** Reduced fees (twilight, seniors, juniors), range (mats), club rentals, credit cards (MC, V).
Reader Comments: Interesting public course, lots of play. Needs more maintenance. Fun to play ... Good city course, nice folks in charge ... Short, wide open city course ... Easy to score, good ego builder ... Slow play ... Short par 4s ... Good for average golfer.

HOLIDAY HILLS GOLF COURSE
R-630 East Rockford Drive, Branson, 65616, (417)334-4838.
Special Notes: Call club for further information.

★★½ HONEY CREEK GOLF CLUB
PU-R.R. 1, Aurora, 65605, Lawrence County, (417)678-3353, 28 miles SW of Springfield.
Holes: 18. **Yards:** 6,732/5,972. **Par:** 71/79. **Course Rating:** 71.9/N/A. **Slope:** 118/N/A. **Green Fee:** $14/$18. **Cart Fee:** $18/person. **Walking Policy:** Unrestricted walking. **Walkability:** 3. **Opened:** 1932. **Architect:** Horton Smith/Mark , Bill, Scott Welch. **Season:** Year-round. **High:**

April-Oct. **To obtain tee times:** Call Wednesday for weekends. **Miscellaneous:** Reduced fees (weekdays, twilight, seniors, juniors), range (grass), club rentals, credit cards (MC, V, D). **Reader Comments:** Local gem ... Best greens in southwest Missouri ... Great greens ... Local owners take pride in their course.

★★★ HORTON SMITH GOLF COURSE

PM-2409 S. Scenic, Springfield, 65807, Greene County, (417)891-1639.
Holes: 18. **Yards:** 6,317/5,199. **Par:** 70/71. **Course Rating:** 69.5/68.5. **Slope:** 103/101. **Green Fee:** $8/$17. **Cart Fee:** $10/person. **Walking Policy:** Unrestricted walking. **Walkability:** 1. **Opened:** 1962. **Architect:** Tom Talbot. **Season:** Year-round. **High:** May-Sept. **To obtain tee times:** Call golf shop 1 week in advance. Call starter the day of play. **Miscellaneous:** Reduced fees (weekdays, seniors, juniors), discount packages, range (grass), club rentals, credit cards (MC, V), beginner friendly (junior clinics and nike junior camps).
Reader Comments: Excellent short course ... Crowded but nice municipal course ... Easy to walk ... Crowded course, easy to play ... A lot of potential.

★★★½ INNSBROOK RESORT & CONFERENCE CENTER

R-1 Aspen Circle, Innsbrook, 63390, Warren County, (636)928-6886, 20 miles W of St. Charles.
E-mail: innsbrook@mocty.com. **Web:** www.innsbrook-resort.com.
Holes: 18. **Yards:** 6,465/5,035. **Par:** 70/70. **Course Rating:** 72.3/67.7. **Slope:** 133/120. **Green Fee:** $21/$35. **Cart Fee:** $6/person. **Walking Policy:** Walking at certain times. **Walkability:** 3. **Opened:** 1982. **Architect:** Jay Randolph/Mark Waltman. **Season:** Year-round weather permitting. **High:** April-Oct. **To obtain tee times:** Call golf shop. **Miscellaneous:** Reduced fees (weekdays, low season, resort guests, twilight), discount packages, range (grass), club rentals, lodging (100 rooms), credit cards (MC, V).
Reader Comments: One of the best ... Very nice, good challenge, reasonable ... Tight/grade changes/good par 3s ... Great experience ... Out of the way, but unique, enjoyable ... Beautiful, great holes, tough course from back tees.

KENNETT COUNTRY CLUB

SP-Hwy. 412 East, Kennett, 63857, Dunklin County, (573)888-9945, 100 miles N of Memphis, TN.
Holes: 18. **Yards:** 6,389/4,890. **Par:** 72/72. **Course Rating:** 70.5/67.6. **Slope:** 112/106. **Green Fee:** $15/$20. **Cart Fee:** $18/cart. **Walking Policy:** Unrestricted walking. **Walkability:** 1. **Season:** Year-round. **High:** June-Sept. **Miscellaneous:** Range (grass).

KETH MEMORIAL GOLF COURSE

PU-S. Holden St., Warrensburg, 64093, (816)543-4182.
Special Notes: Call club for further information.

★★½ KIRKSVILLE COUNTRY CLUB

SP-S. Hwy. 63, Kirksville, 63501, Adair County, (660)665-5335, 85 miles N of Columbia.
Holes: 18. **Yards:** 6,418/5,802. **Par:** 71/71. **Course Rating:** 70.9/71.6. **Slope:** 118/114. **Green Fee:** $20/$25. **Cart Fee:** $20/cart. **Walking Policy:** Unrestricted walking. **Walkability:** 3. **Opened:** 1921. **Season:** March-Dec. **High:** June-Aug. **To obtain tee times:** Non-members first come, first served. **Miscellaneous:** Range (grass/mats), club rentals, credit cards (MC, V, D).
Reader Comments: Best part is the fast greens ... Short finishing hole ... If you like blind shots, this is the course for you ... Good length, average difficulty.

★★ L.A. NICKELL GOLF COURSE

PM-1800 Parkside Dr., Columbia, 65202, Boone County, (573)445-4213, 110 miles E of Kansas City.
Holes: 18. **Yards:** 6,007/4,869. **Par:** 70/70. **Course Rating:** 65.1/67.7. **Slope:** 100/103. **Green Fee:** $12/$15. **Cart Fee:** $10/person. **Walking Policy:** Unrestricted walking. **Walkability:** 1. **Opened:** 1952. **Season:** Year-round. **High:** April-Sept. **To obtain tee times:** Tee times required for weekends & holidays. **Miscellaneous:** Reduced fees (twilight), metal spikes, range (mats), club rentals, credit cards (MC, V, D).

LAKE OF THE WOODS GOLF COURSE

PU-6700 St. Charles Rd., Columbia, 65202, Boone County, (573)474-7011, 90 miles W of St. Louis. **Web:** www.ci.columbia.mo.us.
Holes: 18. **Yards:** 6,149/4,901. **Par:** 71/71. **Course Rating:** 68.4/68.7. **Slope:** 119/120. **Green Fee:** $12/$15. **Cart Fee:** $10/person. **Walking Policy:** Unrestricted walking. **Walkability:** 2. **Season:** Year-round. **High:** April-Sept. **To obtain tee times:** Call Wednesday for Saturday. Call Thursday for Sunday. **Miscellaneous:** Reduced fees (weekdays, twilight), club rentals, credit cards (MC, V, D).

★★★½ LAKE VALLEY GOLF & COUNTRY CLUB

SP-Lake Rd. 54-79, Camdenton, 65020, Camden County, (573)346-7213, 90 miles NE of Springfield.

Holes: 18. **Yards:** 6,430/5,320. **Par:** 72/74. **Course Rating:** 71.1/70.5. **Slope:** 121/118. **Green Fee:** $34/$60. **Cart Fee:** Included in Green Fee. **Walking Policy:** Walking at certain times. **Walkability:** 3. **Opened:** 1967. **Architect:** Floyd Farley. **Season:** Year-round. **High:** April-Oct. **To obtain tee times:** Call in advance for tee times. **Miscellaneous:** Reduced fees (low season, resort guests, twilight, juniors), discount packages, metal spikes, range (grass/mats), club rentals, credit cards (MC, V).

Reader Comments: Nice course, nice people, nice scenery ... Very nice for the money ... Fun course, fair for all handicaps. Great service ... Very sporty layout, bring a driver ... A real gem ... Great course, love to play.

LEBANON COUNTRY CLUB

SP-W. Hwy. 64, Lebanon, 65536, Laclede County, (417)532-2901, 3 miles W of Lebanon.
Holes: 18. **Yards:** 6,435/5,174. **Par:** 72/72. **Course Rating:** 70.4/69.7. **Slope:** 119/111. **Green Fee:** $36/$38. **Cart Fee:** Included in Green Fee. **Walking Policy:** Mandatory cart. **Walkability:** 3. **Opened:** 1950. **Season:** Year-round. **High:** April-Sept. **To obtain tee times:** Call within 2 weeks. **Miscellaneous:** Reduced fees (low season), range (grass), club rentals, credit cards (MC, V).

THE LODGE OF FOUR SEASONS

R-State Rd. HH at HK's Restaurant, Lake Ozark, 65049, Camden County, (573)365-8532, (800)843-5253, 150 miles SW of St. Louis.
★★★★ ROBERT TRENT JONES COURSE
Holes: 18. **Yards:** 6,557/5,238. **Par:** 71/71. **Course Rating:** 71.4/70.8. **Slope:** 136/124. **Green Fee:** $65/$75. **Cart Fee:** Included in Green Fee. **Walking Policy:** Mandatory cart. **Walkability:** 4. **Opened:** 1969. **Architect:** Robert Trent Jones Sr. **Season:** April-Oct. **High:** May-Sept. **To obtain tee times:** Call central reservations. **Miscellaneous:** Reduced fees (weekdays, twilight), discount packages, range (grass/mats), club rentals, lodging, credit cards (MC, V, AE, D). **Notes:** 1994 National Club Pro Championship.

Reader Comments: Tough and fair... Well kept, excellent tees ... Awesome course ... Best course in area, many blind shots ... Great views ... Each hole is a different experience ... First-class resort golf ... Excellent but pricey for area ... Great service, challenging layout, good greens ... Great views, bring extra balls.

★★★★ SEASONS RIDGE COURSE
R-State Rd. HH and Duckhead Rd., Lake Ozark, 65049, Camden County, (573)365-8544, (800)843-5253, 150 miles SW of St. Louis.
Holes: 18. **Yards:** 6,447/4,617. **Par:** 72/72. **Course Rating:** 71.4/71.0. **Slope:** 130/118. **Green Fee:** $51/$68. **Cart Fee:** Included in Green Fee. **Walking Policy:** Mandatory cart. **Walkability:** 4. **Opened:** 1991. **Architect:** Ken Kavanaugh. **Season:** Year-round. **High:** May-Oct. **To obtain tee times:** Call. **Miscellaneous:** Reduced fees (weekdays, low season, resort guests, twilight), discount packages, range (grass), club rentals, lodging, credit cards (MC, V, AE, D).

Reader Comments: Tough, fair, play this one first ... Scenic & one of the best par 3s in the country ... Hills, hills, hills ... Excellent condition ... Golf at its best ... Services outstanding ... Some beautiful holes–narrow fairways ... Priced high, fun course ... Challenging, a joy to play, one of the best in area.

LOMA LINDA COUNTRY CLUB

R-2407 Douglas Fir Road, Joplin, 64804, Newton County, (417)623-2901, (800)633-3542, 5 miles SE of Joplin. **E-mail:** lomalinda@4state.com. **Web:** www.lomalindagolf.com.
★★★ NORTH COURSE
Holes: 18. **Yards:** 6,628/5,333. **Par:** 72/73. **Course Rating:** 71.8/70.8. **Slope:** 123/125. **Green Fee:** $27/$27. **Cart Fee:** $10/person. **Walking Policy:** Unrestricted walking. **Walkability:** 5. **Opened:** 1984. **Architect:** Don Sechrest. **Season:** Year-round. **High:** April-Sept. **To obtain tee times:** Must be guest of resort to play this course. **Miscellaneous:** Discount packages, range (grass), club rentals, lodging (115 rooms), credit cards (MC, V, AE, D, Diners Club, Carte Blanc).
Reader Comments: Fun course to play ... Loved greens, some real good holes ... Challenging holes, par-3 hole 12 depending on wind can go from 6 iron to driver.

★½ SOUTH COURSE
Holes: 18. **Yards:** 6,397/4,663. **Par:** 71/71. **Course Rating:** 69.2/68.2. **Slope:** 118/120. **Green Fee:** $9/$11. **Cart Fee:** $9/person. **Walking Policy:** Unrestricted walking. **Walkability:** 4. **Architect:** Scott Brown. **Season:** Year-round. **High:** April-Sept. **Miscellaneous:** Reduced fees (weekdays, seniors), discount packages, range (grass), club rentals, lodging (115 rooms), credit cards (MC, V, AE, D, Diners Club/Carte Blanc).

★★★½ LONGVIEW LAKE GOLF COURSE

PU-11100 View High Dr., Kansas City, 64134, Jackson County, (816)761-9445.
Holes: 18. **Yards:** 6,835/5,534. **Par:** 72/72. **Course Rating:** 71.9/70.8. **Slope:** 121/113. **Green Fee:** $12/$16. **Cart Fee:** $22/cart. **Walking Policy:** Unrestricted walking. **Walkability:** N/A. **Opened:** 1986. **Architect:** Benz & Poellet. **Season:** Year-round. **High:** May-

Aug. **To obtain tee times:** Call 7 days in advance. **Miscellaneous:** Reduced fees (weekdays, seniors, juniors), metal spikes, range (grass), club rentals, credit cards (MC, V).

Reader Comments: Good track, nice views of lake, plays longer when wind blows ... Nice, tough, need local knowledge ... Needs clubhouse, fun course, big greens ... Outstanding variety of holes ... Best public fairways, good layout ... Real challenge, par 3 course also, hills and sand ... Nice course, good shape.

★★★½ MARRIOTT'S TAN-TAR-A RESORT

R-State Rd. KK, Osage Beach, 65065, Camden County, (573)348-8521, (800)826-8272, 45 miles SW of Jefferson City.
Holes: 18. **Yards:** 6,442/3,943. **Par:** 71/70. **Course Rating:** 72.1/62.5. **Slope:** 134/103. **Green Fee:** $35/$75. **Cart Fee:** Included in Green Fee. **Walking Policy:** Mandatory cart. **Walkability:** 4. **Opened:** 1980. **Architect:** Bruce Devlin/Robert Von Hagge. **Season:** Year-round. **High:** May-Oct. **To obtain tee times:** Members and hotel guests call up to 45 days in advance. Public call 30 days in advance. **Miscellaneous:** Reduced fees (weekdays, low season, twilight), discount packages, metal spikes, range (grass/mats), club rentals, lodging, credit cards (MC, V, AE, D, Diners Club).

Reader Comments: Expensive, but good value ... Super challenge, very hilly, very expensive ... One of the best ... Lots of elevated tee shots ... Very good short resort course ... Great course, No.18, is the hardest hole in golf ... Stay a week and enjoy the area. Good golf requiring great accuracy. The best during the fall.

MEADOW LAKE COUNTRY CLUB

SP-1000 Watson Parkway, Clinton, 64735, (660)885-5124, 60 miles S of Kansas City.
Holes: 18. **Yards:** 6,172/5,915. **Par:** 71/71. **Course Rating:** 69.1/71.6. **Slope:** 113/113. **Green Fee:** $24/$24. **Cart Fee:** $13/person. **Walking Policy:** Mandatory cart. **Walkability:** 1. **Opened:** 1963. **Architect:** Jim Lewis. **Season:** Year-round. **High:** April-Oct. **To obtain tee times:** None required. **Miscellaneous:** Reduced fees (low season, twilight), metal spikes, range (grass), credit cards (MC, V).

MERAMEC LAKES GOLF CLUB

PU-2164 Gravois, St. Clair, 63077, Franklin County, (636)451-5183, 40 miles W of St. Louis.
Holes: 18. **Yards:** 6,134/5,029. **Par:** 71/71. **Course Rating:** N/A. **Slope:** N/A. **Green Fee:** $11/$18. **Cart Fee:** $10/person. **Walking Policy:** Unrestricted walking. **Walkability:** 3. **Opened:** 1995. **Architect:** Jerry Raible. **Season:** Year-round. **High:** May-Aug. **Miscellaneous:** Reduced fees (weekdays, low season, seniors, juniors), discount packages, range (grass/mats), club rentals, credit cards (MC, V, AE), beginner friendly (junior clinics).

★★½ MID-RIVERS GOLF COURSE

PU-4100 Mid-Rivers Mall Dr., St. Peters, 63376, (314)939-3663.
Special Notes: Call club for further information.

★★★★½ MILLWOOD GOLF & RACQUET CLUB *Service, Condition*

SP-3700 E. Millwood Dr., Springfield, 65809, Greene County, (417)889-2889, 2 miles S of Springfield. **Web:** www.millwoodgolf.com.
Holes: 18. **Yards:** 6,700/4,815. **Par:** 71/72. **Course Rating:** 72.4/68.6. **Slope:** 134/116. **Green Fee:** $50/$50. **Cart Fee:** Included in Green Fee. **Walking Policy:** Mandatory cart. **Walkability:** 4. **Opened:** 1996. **Architect:** Greg Martin. **Season:** Year-round. **High:** May-Oct. **To obtain tee times:** Call 24 hours in advance or have your club Pro call 7 days in advance. **Miscellaneous:** Range (grass/mats), club rentals, credit cards (MC, V, AE), beginner friendly.

Reader Comments: Beautiful course ... Gorgeous course, wonderful staff ... An oasis in the desert ... Great golf for the money ... Excellent condition, difficult but fair, super value ... Beautiful layout/Great service.

★½ MINOR PARK GOLF CLUB

11215 Holmes Rd., Kansas City, 64131, Jackson County, (816)942-4033.
Special Notes: Call club for further information.

★★★★ MISSOURI BLUFFS GOLF CLUB

PU-18 Research Park Circle, St. Charles, 63304, St. Charles County, (314)939-6494, 20 miles W of St. Louis.
Holes: 18. **Yards:** 7,047/5,197. **Par:** 71/71. **Course Rating:** 74.4/69.2. **Slope:** 140/115. **Green Fee:** $95/$115. **Cart Fee:** Included in Green Fee. **Walking Policy:** Unrestricted walking. **Walkability:** 5. **Opened:** 1994. **Architect:** Tom Fazio. **Season:** March-Nov. **High:** May-Oct. **To obtain tee times:** Call 4 days in advance. **Miscellaneous:** Reduced fees (twilight, seniors), range (grass), club rentals, credit cards (MC, V, AE).

Notes: Ranked 9th in 1999 Best in State; 43rd in 1996 America's Top 75 Upscale Courses; 3rd in 1995 Best New Public Courses.

Reader Comments: Super, signature hole tops ... Challenging & hilly fast greens ... Pretty course/can be long from the back/hilly ... Excellent layout, costly ... Not hard from middle tees, beautiful course ... They treat you like royalty ... Beautiful in the fall ... Fantastic scenery and shape ... Overpriced, but nice layout.

MOUNTAIN VIEW GOLF COURSE
PU-115 S. Jackson St., Mountain View, 65548, (417)934-6959.
Special Notes: Call club for further information.

★★★½ MOZINGO LAKE GOLF COURSE
PU-25055 Liberty Road, Maryville, 64468, Nodaway County, (816)562-3864, (888)562-3864, 4 miles E of Maryville. **E-mail:** Mozingolf@msc.net. **Web:** www.mozingo.com.
Holes: 18. **Yards:** 7,072/5,583. **Par:** 72/72. **Course Rating:** 73.5/71.3. **Slope:** 134/124. **Green Fee:** $16/$19. **Cart Fee:** $10/person. **Walking Policy:** Unrestricted walking. **Walkability:** 3. **Opened:** 1996. **Architect:** Don Sechrest. **Season:** Year-round. **High:** May-Sept. **To obtain tee times:** Call. **Miscellaneous:** Reduced fees (weekdays, twilight, juniors), range (grass), club rentals, credit cards (MC, V, D).
Reader Comments: Nice layout, pins tucked, good challenge ... Tough course, pretty windy ... Worth a 100-mile drive, fair test, and value price ... Great for new course ... Good value.

NEOSHO MUNICIPAL GOLF COURSE
PU-1850 Clubhouse Road, Neosho, 64850, Newton County, (417)451-1543.
Holes: 18. **Yards:** 6,312/5,399. **Par:** 71/73. **Course Rating:** 67.7/69.7. **Slope:** 113/115. **Green Fee:** $12/$13. **Cart Fee:** $8/person. **Walking Policy:** Unrestricted walking. **Walkability:** 3. **Season:** Year-round. **High:** March-Oct. **To obtain tee times:** Call the week of. **Miscellaneous:** Range (grass), club rentals.

★★★½ NEW MELLE LAKES GOLF CLUB
PU-404 Foristel Rd., New Melle, 63365, St. Charles County, (314)398-4653, 30 miles W of St. Louis.
Holes: 18. **Yards:** 6,348/4,905. **Par:** 71/71. **Course Rating:** 69.8/68.6. **Slope:** 126/120. **Green Fee:** $30/$40. **Cart Fee:** Included in Green Fee. **Walking Policy:** Walking at certain times. **Walkability:** 4. **Opened:** 1993. **Architect:** Theodore Christener & Assoc. **Season:** Year-round. **High:** April-Oct. **To obtain tee times:** Call or come in 7 days in advance. **Miscellaneous:** Reduced fees (twilight, seniors, juniors), metal spikes, range (grass/mats), club rentals, credit cards (MC, V, AE, D).
Reader Comments: Tight, great greens and staff ... Lots of blind shots, good greens ... Lots of hills & valleys ... Nice, hilly ... Good course, very interesting track, good value ... Nice country setting ... Quite scenic, beautiful in autumn.

★★★ NORMANDIE GOLF CLUB
PU-7605 St. Charles Rock Rd., St. Louis, 63133, St. Louis County, (314)862-4884.
Holes: 18. **Yards:** 6,534/5,943. **Par:** 71/77. **Course Rating:** 71.1/73.1. **Slope:** 120/133. **Green Fee:** $19/$28. **Cart Fee:** $10/person. **Walking Policy:** Unrestricted walking. **Walkability:** 4. **Opened:** 1901. **Architect:** Robert Foulis. **Season:** Year-round. **High:** April-Oct. **To obtain tee times:** Call anytime. **Miscellaneous:** Reduced fees (weekdays, low season, twilight, seniors, juniors), metal spikes, range (grass), club rentals, credit cards (MC, V, AE).
Reader Comments: Great potential, oldest course west of Mississippi River ... Enjoy-able ... An old course with character.... Old-style course design. Large trees. Challenge ... Good layout ... Tremendous potential, but run down ... Great classic layout ... Old beauty.

OAKWOOD GOLF COURSE
PU-Oakwood Estates, Houston, 65483, (417)967-3968.
Special Notes: Call club for further information.

★★★ OLD FLEURISSANT GOLF CLUB
PU-50 Country Club Lane, Florissant, 63033, St. Louis County, (314)741-7444, 15 miles N of St. Louis.
Holes: 18. **Yards:** 6,493/5,593. **Par:** 72/73. **Course Rating:** 69.9/71.0. **Slope:** 120/114. **Green Fee:** $16/$26. **Cart Fee:** $10/person. **Walking Policy:** Unrestricted walking. **Walkability:** 4. **Opened:** 1964. **Architect:** Homer Herpel. **Season:** Year-round weather permitting. **High:** April-Oct. **To obtain tee times:** Call 7 days in advance. **Miscellaneous:** Reduced fees (weekdays, twilight, seniors, juniors), metal spikes, range (grass), club rentals, credit cards (MC, V, D).
Reader Comments: Amazing what care did for this course ... Good public course.

★★★★ OSAGE NATIONAL GOLF CLUB
R-Osage Hills Rd., Lake Ozark, 65049, Miller County, (573)365-1100, 150 miles SW of St. Louis.
Holes: 27. **Yards:** 7,150/5,252. **Par:** 72/72. **Course Rating:** 75.6/70.5. **Slope:** 145/122. **Green Fee:** $69/$85. **Cart Fee:** Included in Green Fee. **Walking Policy:** Mandatory cart. **Walkability:** 3. **Opened:** 1992. **Architect:** Arnold Palmer/Ed Seay. **Season:** Year-round. **High:** April-Oct. **To obtain tee times:** Call up to 30 days in advance. **Miscellaneous:** Reduced fees (weekdays, low season, resort guests, twilight), discount packages, range (grass), club rentals, lodging, credit cards (MC, V, AE, D).

MISSOURI

Reader Comments: Best course I have ever played ... Excellent greens, great challenge ... Phenomenal golf course ... Great overall design with two distinct nines ... Great facilities/service. Lots of elevations, very challenging ... Excellent fairways & greens ... Best in the Ozarks ... Some of the most majestic holes I ever played.

PARADISE POINTE GOLF CLUB
PU-18212 Golf Course Rd., Smithville, 64089, Clay County, (816)532-4100, 25 miles N of Kansas City.

★★★½ OUTLAW COURSE
Holes: 18. **Yards:** 6,988/5,322. **Par:** 72/72. **Course Rating:** 73.8/67.0. **Slope:** 138/118. **Green Fee:** $21/$22. **Cart Fee:** $26/cart. **Walking Policy:** Unrestricted walking. **Walkability:** 3. **Opened:** 1994. **Architect:** Craig Schreiner. **Season:** Year-round. **High:** May-Oct. **To obtain tee times:** Tee times required 7 days per week. **Miscellaneous:** Reduced fees (weekdays, low season, seniors), range (grass), club rentals, credit cards (MC, V, AE, D).
Reader Comments: Great layout ... Fun course, hilly, good layout, greens need help ... Fun layout, tough wind, No. 10 killer par 3 ... Lots of fun ... Great views of lake, fun to play, great service, geese are a problem ... Challenging! Toughest par 3 I've ever played ... Links style surrounded by lake.

★★★ POSSE COURSE
Holes: 18. **Yards:** 6,663/5,600. **Par:** 72/73. **Course Rating:** 71.8/70.0. **Slope:** 125/115. **Green Fee:** $19/$20. **Cart Fee:** $26/cart. **Walking Policy:** Unrestricted walking. **Walkability:** 1. **Opened:** 1982. **Architect:** Tom Clark/Brian Ault. **Season:** Year-round. **High:** May-Oct. **To obtain tee times:** Tee times required 7 days per week. **Miscellaneous:** Reduced fees (weekdays, low season, seniors), range (grass), club rentals, credit cards (MC, V, AE, D), beginner friendly.
Reader Comments: Scenic lakeside holes ... Very demanding courses. Fairly well maintained. Lots of play ... Scenic, challenging holes overlooking Smithville Lake.

★★½ PARADISE VALLEY GOLF & COUNTRY CLUB
PU-Old Hillsboro Rd., Valley Park, 63088, St. Louis County, (314)225-5157, 19 miles W of St. Louis. **E-mail:** parvalgolf@aol.com. **Web:** www.paradisevalleygolf.com.
Holes: 18. **Yards:** 6,097/4,769. **Par:** 70/72. **Course Rating:** 68.6/66.4. **Slope:** 116/109. **Green Fee:** $31/$35. **Cart Fee:** Included in Green Fee. **Walking Policy:** Walking at certain times. **Walkability:** 3. **Opened:** 1965. **Architect:** James Cochran. **Season:** Year-round. **High:** May-Sept. **To obtain tee times:** Call golf shop. **Miscellaneous:** Reduced fees (weekdays, low season, juniors), range (grass/mats), club rentals, credit cards (MC, V, AE), beginner friendly (extensive junior programs).
Reader Comments: Good for a beginner ... Some interesting holes ... A good Sunday course.

★★★★ PEVELY FARMS GOLF CLUB *Service*
PU-400 Lewis Road, St. Louis, 63025, St. Louis County, (636)938-7000, **E-mail:** pevelygc@gte.net. **Web:** eaglgolf.com.
Holes: 18. **Yards:** 7,115/5,250. **Par:** 72/72. **Course Rating:** 74.6/70.7. **Slope:** 138/115. **Green Fee:** $59/$69. **Cart Fee:** Included in Green Fee. **Walking Policy:** Mandatory cart. **Walkability:** 5. **Opened:** 1998. **Architect:** Arthur Hills. **Season:** Year-round. **High:** April-Oct. **To obtain tee times:** 7 days in advance booking. Must reserve with a credit card. **Miscellaneous:** Reduced fees (weekdays, low season, twilight, seniors, juniors), range (grass), club rentals, credit cards (MC, V, AE, Diners Club), beginner friendly (new player clinics).
Reader Comments: Exceptional new course, awesome greens! ... Beautiful views ... Varied terrain. Each hole a new challenge ... Good variety of holes, many elevation changes ... New course, quite challenging & scenic ... Challenging, beautiful layout, utilizes the natural layout of the Ozark terrain, first-class service.

PINEY VALLEY GOLF COURSE
M-Bldg. 10221 Waterintake Road, Fort Leonard Wood, 65473, Pulaski County, (573)329-4770, 88 miles E of Springfield.
Holes: 18. **Yards:** 7,014/5,067. **Par:** 72/72. **Course Rating:** 72.8/68.2. **Slope:** 121/104. **Green Fee:** $18/$20. **Cart Fee:** $15/cart. **Walking Policy:** Unrestricted walking. **Walkability:** 3. **Architect:** U. S. Army Engineers. **Season:** Year-round. **High:** June-Aug. **To obtain tee times:** Call golf shop 573-329-4770. **Miscellaneous:** Reduced fees (weekdays, twilight, juniors), discount packages, credit cards (MC, V, AE), beginner friendly (junior, ladies and seniors).

★★★ POINTE ROYALE GOLF CLUB
R-1000 Pointe Royale Dr., Branson, 65616, Taney County, (417)334-4477, 40 miles S of Springfield. **E-mail:** ptrogolf@aol.com.
Holes: 18. **Yards:** 6,200/4,390. **Par:** 70/70. **Course Rating:** 70.3/64.4. **Slope:** 126/112. **Green Fee:** $40/$65. **Cart Fee:** Included in Green Fee. **Walking Policy:** Mandatory cart. **Walkability:** 4. **Opened:** 1987. **Architect:** Ault & Clark. **Season:** Year-round. **High:** April-Oct. **Miscellaneous:** Reduced fees (low season, resort guests, juniors), discount packages, club rentals, lodging (200 rooms), credit cards (MC, V, AE, D).
Reader Comments: Very hilly ... Lots of fun. You see Andy Williams almost every time you play.

MISSOURI

★★★½ QUAIL CREEK GOLF CLUB
PU-6022 Wells Rd., St. Louis, 63128, St. Louis County, (314)487-1988, 15 miles S of Downtown St. Louis.
Holes: 18. **Yards:** 6,984/5,244. **Par:** 72/72. **Course Rating:** 73.8/70.0. **Slope:** 141/118. **Green Fee:** $32/$52. **Cart Fee:** $11/person. **Walking Policy:** Walking at certain times. **Walkability:** 2. **Opened:** 1988. **Architect:** Gary Kern/Hale Irwin. **Season:** Year-round.
High: April-Oct. **To obtain tee times:** Reservations preferred. **Miscellaneous:** Reduced fees (weekdays, low season, twilight, seniors, juniors), discount packages, metal spikes, range (grass/mats), club rentals, credit cards (MC, V, AE, D) (soft spike discount).
Reader Comments: Great value for a tough golf course ... Most played course in Missouri. Great shape ... Tough course, No. 15 a thriller ... Good test of golf; great finishing holes 14 to 18 ... Hard golf course! Great value ... Excellent layout.

★★ RAINTREE COUNTRY CLUB
SP-5925 Plantation Dr., Hillsboro, 63050, Jefferson County, (636)797-4020, 45 miles S of St. Louis.
Holes: 18. **Yards:** 6,125/4,959. **Par:** 72/71. **Course Rating:** 70.0/68.2. **Slope:** 124/112. **Green Fee:** $10/$18. **Cart Fee:** $10/person. **Walking Policy:** Walking at certain times. **Walkability:** 4. **Opened:** 1980. **Season:** Year-round. **High:** May-Sept. **To obtain tee times:** Call or come in up to 7 days in advance. **Miscellaneous:** Reduced fees (weekdays, low season, seniors, juniors), discount packages, metal spikes, range (grass), club rentals, credit cards (MC, V, D).

★★½ RIVER OAKS GOLF CLUB
PU-14204 St. Andrews Dr., Grandview, 64030, Jackson County, (816)966-8111, 20 miles SE of Kansas City.
Holes: 18. **Yards:** 6,354/5,036. **Par:** 71/73. **Course Rating:** 70.2/69.9. **Slope:** 119/114. **Green Fee:** $16/$19. **Cart Fee:** $24/cart. **Walking Policy:** Unrestricted walking. **Walkability:** 3. **Opened:** 1973. **Architect:** Larry Runyon/Michael H. Malyn. **Season:** Year-round weather permitting. **To obtain tee times:** Call up to 7 days in advance. **Miscellaneous:** Reduced fees (weekdays, twilight, seniors, juniors), metal spikes, club rentals, credit cards (MC, V, D).
Reader Comments: Hilly, good holes, nice layout ... A short course ... Lots of hills.

★★ RIVER PARK GOLF CLUB
SP-10306 N.W. 45 Hwy., Parkville, 64152, Platte County, (816)741-9520, 10 miles NW of Kansas City.
Holes: 18. **Yards:** 6,253/4,939. **Par:** 71/70. **Course Rating:** 69.8/67.4. **Slope:** 119/112. **Green Fee:** $30/$35. **Cart Fee:** Included in Green Fee. **Walking Policy:** Mandatory cart. **Walkability:** 5. **Opened:** 1955. **Architect:** Robert Steigler. **Season:** Year-round. **High:** May-Sept. **To obtain tee times:** Call Friday for upcoming weekend and holidays. Members have preference for tee times. **Miscellaneous:** Reduced fees (juniors), metal spikes, range (grass/mats), club rentals, credit cards (MC, V).

RIVERCUT GOLF COURSE
PU-2350 W. Farm Rd. 190, Springfield, 65810, Greene County, (417)891-1645, 3 miles SW of Springfield, MO. **E-mail:** Rivercutgolfcourse@mailcity.com.
Holes: 18. **Yards:** 7,066/5,483. **Par:** 72/72. **Course Rating:** 74.2/71.3. **Slope:** 134/118. **Green Fee:** $30/$35. **Cart Fee:** Included in Green Fee. **Walking Policy:** Mandatory cart. **Walkability:** 4. **Opened:** 1998. **Architect:** Ken Dye. **Season:** Year round. **High:** April-Sept. **Miscellaneous:** Reduced fees (low season), range (grass), club rentals, credit cards (MC, V).

★★½ RIVERSIDE GOLF COURSE
PU-1210 Larkin Williams Road, Fenton, 63026, St. Louis County, (314)343-6333, 10 miles SW of St. Louis.
Holes: 18. **Yards:** 5,500/5,400. **Par:** 69/70. **Course Rating:** 67.5/67.5. **Slope:** 99/99. **Green Fee:** $19/$22. **Cart Fee:** $20/cart. **Walking Policy:** Unrestricted walking. **Walkability:** 1. **Opened:** 1964. **Architect:** Walter Wolfner/Jack Wolfner. **Season:** Year-round. **High:** April-Oct. **To obtain tee times:** First come, first served. **Miscellaneous:** Reduced fees (weekdays, low season, twilight, seniors, juniors), metal spikes, club rentals, credit cards (MC, V, AE).
Reader Comments: Good service and price ... Low cost, flat track ... Good for neophyte golfers.

★★½ ROCKWOOD GOLF CLUB
PU-2400 Maywood, Independence, 64052, Jackson County, (816)252-2002, 2 miles NE of Kansas City.
Holes: 18. **Yards:** 6,009/5,465. **Par:** 70/71. **Course Rating:** 67.0/69.0. **Slope:** 113/105. **Green Fee:** $15/$17. **Cart Fee:** $11/person. **Walking Policy:** Unrestricted walking. **Walkability:** 2. **Opened:** 1946. **Season:** Year-round. **High:** April-Oct. **To obtain tee times:** Call 5 days in advance. **Miscellaneous:** Reduced fees (seniors), metal spikes, club rentals, credit cards (MC, V, D).
Reader Comments: Needs fairway grass, good test, tight little course ... Very old course, trees.

ROLLING HILLS COUNTRY CLUB
SP-Hwy. 5 North, Versailles, 65084, (573)378-5109.
Special Notes: Call club for further information.

ROYAL MEADOWS GOLF COURSE
PU-10501 E. 47th, Kansas City, 64133, Jackson County, (816)353-1323, 10 miles E of Kansas City.
Holes: 27. **Green Fee:** $17/$20. **Cart Fee:** $6/person. **Walking Policy:** Unrestricted walking. **Walkability:** 3. **Opened:** 1930. **Architect:** Charles Stayton. **Season:** Year-round. **High:** March-Oct. **To obtain tee times:** Public may call 7 days in advance. **Miscellaneous:** Reduced fees (weekdays, low season, twilight, seniors, juniors), club rentals, credit cards (MC, V, AE, D), beginner friendly.
★★　EAST/NORTH
Yards: 5,991/4,860. **Par:** 71/71. **Course Rating:** 67.4/67.4. **Slope:** 109/109.
★★　WEST/EAST
Yards: 6,220/5,211. **Par:** 73/73. **Course Rating:** 68.3/68.8. **Slope:** 110/113.
★★　WEST/NORTH
Yards: 6,143/4,945. **Par:** 72/72. **Course Rating:** 68.0/68.0. **Slope:** 111/111.

★★★½　ROYAL OAKS GOLF CLUB
PU-533 N. Lincoln Dr., Troy, 63379, Lincoln County, (314)462-8633, 55 miles NW of St. Louis.
Holes: 18. **Yards:** 6,256/4,830. **Par:** 72/72. **Course Rating:** 68.7/66.3. **Slope:** 112/100. **Green Fee:** $16/$22. **Cart Fee:** $10/person. **Walking Policy:** Unrestricted walking. **Walkability:** 3. **Opened:** 1993. **Architect:** Lee Redman. **Season:** Year-round. **High:** April-Oct. **To obtain tee times:** Call 1 week in advance. **Miscellaneous:** Reduced fees (seniors), metal spikes, range (grass), club rentals, credit cards (MC, V, AE, D, Debit cards), beginner friendly (lessons available).
Reader Comments: Outstanding value, staff is superb ... Very hilly ... Needs a few more years seasoning ... Short course, a few interesting holes, good for morale ... Great course for seniors.

ROYAL OAKS GOLF COURSE
PU-Bldg 3076, Whiteman AFB, 65305, (816)687-5572.
Special Notes: Call club for further information.

★★★½　ST. ANDREWS GOLF COURSE
PU-2121 St. Andrews Lane, St. Charles, 63301, (636)946-7777.
Holes: 18. **Yards:** 6,003/5,094. **Par:** 68/72. **Course Rating:** 68.3/68.7. **Slope:** 116/113. **Green Fee:** $22/$32. **Cart Fee:** $10/person. **Walking Policy:** Unrestricted walking. **Walkability:** 3. **Opened:** 1967. **Architect:** Stewart Mertz. **Season:** Year-round. **High:** April-Oct. **To obtain tee times:** Call up to 5 days in advance for tee time. Walk-ons welcome. **Miscellaneous:** Reduced fees (weekdays, low season, twilight, seniors, juniors), club rentals, credit cards (MC, V, D), beginner friendly (lessons, leagues, club fitting, forward tees).
Reader Comments: Fine fairways & greens ... The best course for the money ... Nothing spectacular ... Enjoyable ... A old course with narrow fairways ... Short but challenging, great to walk.

★★★½　SCHIFFERDECKER GOLF COURSE　*Value*
PU-506 Schifferdecker, Joplin, 64801, Jasper County, (417)624-3533.
Holes: 18. **Yards:** 6,123/5,251. **Par:** 71/72. **Course Rating:** 68.7/69.7. **Slope:** 108/117. **Green Fee:** $8/$9. **Cart Fee:** $14/cart. **Walking Policy:** Unrestricted walking. **Walkability:** 3. **Opened:** 1920. **Architect:** Perk Latimere. **Season:** Year-round. **High:** April-Sept. **To obtain tee times:** Call on Tuesday prior to weekend. **Miscellaneous:**
Reduced fees (twilight, seniors, juniors), metal spikes, club rentals, credit cards (MC, V).
Reader Comments: Best value in Southwest MO, and fun to play ... Wide open ... Best greens I have ever played. Lots of play. True roll ... Straightforward layout with no water, greens in nice condition ... For a public course, it is in great shape.

SHAMROCK HILLS GOLF COURSE
PU-3161 S. M. 291, Lees Summit, 64082, (816)537-6556†.
Holes: 18. **Yards:** 6,332/5,188. **Par:** 71/73. **Course Rating:** 69.8/68.8. **Slope:** 108/106. **Green Fee:** $15/$17. **Cart Fee:** $11/person. **Walking Policy:** Unrestricted walking. **Walkability:** 2. **Opened:** 1961. **Architect:** Jim Weaver. **Season:** Year-round. **High:** Mar.-Oct. **To obtain tee times:** First come, first served. **Miscellaneous:** Reduced fees (twilight, seniors, juniors), club rentals, credit cards (MC, V, D).

★★★　SHILOH SPRINGS GOLF COURSE
SP-Bethel Rd., Platte City, 64079, Platte County, (816)270-4653, 40 miles N of Kansas City.
Holes: 18. **Yards:** 6,470/5,178. **Par:** 71/71. **Course Rating:** 71.2/70.1. **Slope:** 125/113. **Green Fee:** $23/$28. **Cart Fee:** $28/cart. **Walking Policy:** Unrestricted walking. **Walkability:** 4. **Opened:** 1995. **Architect:** Gary Martin. **Season:** Year-round. **High:** April-June. **Miscellaneous:**

Reduced fees (low season, twilight, seniors, juniors), range (mats), club rentals, credit cards (MC, V, AE, D).

Reader Comments: New and good ... Nice course but green fee a little high ... Fun, interesting holes but many parallel fairways with blind shots ... New course. Fair conditions. Fair to play and fun but tough on beginners ... Excellent fairways and greens, tough layout.

★★★★ SHIRKEY GOLF CLUB

SP-901 Wollard Blvd., Richmond, 64085, Ray County, (816)470-2582, 32 miles NE of Kansas City. **E-mail:** nbnet@hotmail.com. **Web:** www.richmondmissouri.com/shirkey.htm.
Holes: 18. **Yards:** 6,907/5,516. **Par:** 71/74. **Course Rating:** 71.3/73.1. **Slope:** 139/129. **Green Fee:** $22/$27. **Cart Fee:** $13/person. **Walking Policy:** Unrestricted walking. **Walkability:** 2.
Opened: 1969. **Architect:** Chet Mendenhall. **Season:** Year-round. **High:** May-Oct. **To obtain tee times:** Call 2 days in advance for weekends. **Miscellaneous:** Range (grass/mats), club rentals, credit cards (MC, V, AE), beginner friendly (junior golf).
Reader Comments: Best kept secret in Missouri ... Good test of golf for anyone ... Best greens in Missouri ... Zoysia fairways great, slick greens, real polite ... Outstanding greens. A diamond in a small town ... A real challenge! ... Tremendous value ... Great shape & reasonable ... Staff super, course awesome, greens best in state.

SIKESTON COUNTRY CLUB

SP-Country Club Rd., Sikeston, 63801, Scott County, (573)472-4225.
Holes: 18. **Yards:** 6,385/5,090. **Par:** 71/72. **Course Rating:** 71.5/68.5. **Slope:** 109/112. **Green Fee:** $18/$28. **Cart Fee:** $16/cart. **Walking Policy:** Unrestricted walking. **Walkability:** 1.
Season: Year-round. **High:** May-Sept. **To obtain tee times:** Call 7 days in advance.
Miscellaneous: Range (grass), credit cards (MC, V).

★★½ SOUTHVIEW GOLF CLUB

PU-16001 S. 71 Hwy., Belton, 64012, Cass County, (816)331-4042, 5 miles S of Kansas City.
Holes: 18. **Yards:** 6,594/5,805. **Par:** 72/73. **Course Rating:** 70.6/73.0. **Slope:** 115/113. **Green Fee:** $16/$19. **Cart Fee:** $24/cart. **Walking Policy:** Unrestricted walking. **Walk-ability:** 1.
Opened: 1955. **Architect:** Jess Nash. **Season:** Year-round. **High:** May-Aug.
To obtain tee times: First come, first served. **Miscellaneous:** Reduced fees (weekdays, seniors, juniors), metal spikes, range (grass/mats), club rentals, credit cards (MC, V).
Reader Comments: Short & stout ... Small greens, fun to play ... Fun course, easy to play ... Older course, fair, fun easy golf ... Very average, reasonably priced.

★★½ SUGAR CREEK GOLF CLUB

PU-5224 Country Club Dr., High Ridge, 63049, Jefferson County, (314)677-4070, 3 miles W of Fenton.
Holes: 18. **Yards:** 6,316/4,713. **Par:** 70/70. **Course Rating:** 71.3/65.5. **Slope:** 127/112. **Green Fee:** $9/$30. **Cart Fee:** $12/person. **Walking Policy:** Walking at certain times. **Walkability:** 4.
Opened: 1989. **Architect:** Gary Kern. **Season:** Year-round. **High:** April-Oct. **To obtain tee times:** Please call. **Miscellaneous:** Reduced fees (weekdays, low season, resort guests, twilight, seniors, juniors), discount packages, range (grass/ mats), club rentals, credit cards (MC, V), beginner friendly (many clinics).
Reader Comments: Strange layout, up and down ... Rolling hills with very level lies ... Nice layout ... Tight and tough ... Short course but is a fun place to play ... Great during the week.

★★★½ SUN VALLEY GOLF COURSE

PU-Rte. 2, Elsberry, 63343, Lincoln County, (573)898-2613, (800)737-4653, 55 miles N of St. Louis.
Holes: 18. **Yards:** 6,395/5,036. **Par:** 70/70. **Course Rating:** 70.5/69.3. **Slope:** 134/109. **Green Fee:** $16/$21. **Cart Fee:** $9/person. **Walking Policy:** Unrestricted walking. **Walkability:** 4.
Opened: 1988. **Architect:** Gary Kern. **Season:** Year-round. **High:** June-Sept. **To obtain tee times:** Call or come in up to 7 days in advance. **Miscellaneous:** Reduced fees (weekdays, low season, seniors, juniors), metal spikes, range (grass/ mats), club rentals, credit cards (MC, V).
Reader Comments: Nice staff and service ... Good course out in the country, worth the drive ... Fun hilly course/good short par 4s ... A good walking course ... Helps to be long off the tees ... Love it, hilly, good workout ... Nice little country course. Two totally different 9s ... Inexpensive. Scenic. Fun to play.

★★½ SUNSET LAKES GOLF CLUB

PU-13366 W. Watson Rd., St. Louis, 63127, (314)843-3000.
Special Notes: Call club for further information.

★★★½ SWOPE MEMORIAL GOLF COURSE

PM-6900 Swope Memorial Dr., Kansas City, 64132, Jackson County, (816)523-9081.
Holes: 18. **Yards:** 6,274/4,517. **Par:** 72/72. **Course Rating:** 70.9/65.9. **Slope:** 128/107. **Green Fee:** $15/$17. **Cart Fee:** $10/person. **Walking Policy:** Unrestricted walking. **Walkability:** 3.
Opened: 1934. **Architect:** A.W. Tillinghast. **Season:** Year-round. **High:** April-Oct. **To obtain tee

times: Call 1 day in advance. **Miscellaneous:** Reduced fees (twilight, seniors, juniors), club rentals, credit cards (MC, V).
Reader Comments: Short but tough, high rough, hilly ... If you think you can play, try this baby ... Old but good ... Good old muny ... Historic course ... Area's best golf ... Simple yet challenging to all, masterfully designed.

★★★★ TAPAWINGO NATIONAL GOLF CLUB
PU-13001 Gary Player Dr., St. Louis, 63127, St. Louis County, (314)349-3100, 10 miles SW of St. Louis.
Holes: 27. **Yards:** 7,151/5,566. **Par:** 72/72. **Course Rating:** 75.1/72.2. **Slope:** 144/121. **Green Fee:** $50/$60. **Cart Fee:** Included in Green Fee. **Walking Policy:** Walking at certain times. **Walkability:** 4. **Opened:** 1994. **Architect:** Gary Player. **Season:** Year-round. **High:** April-Oct. **To obtain tee times:** Call up to 7 days in advance with a credit card to guarantee. **Miscellaneous:** Reduced fees (weekdays, low season, twilight, seniors, juniors), range (grass), club rentals, credit cards (MC, V, AE).
Notes: Ranked 10th in 1997 Best in State.
Reader Comments: Worth every penny, great staff, greens fair ... Quirky track, great greens ... A little pricey ... Very nice, scenic, pricey ... Stern test ... Great layout, good conditions, nice facilities ... Beautifully designed and maintained ... Demanding and in wonderful shape.

THAYER COUNTRY CLUB
SP-N. Hwy. 63, Thayer, 65791, (417)264-7854.
Special Notes: Call club for further information.

★★★½ THOUSAND HILLS GOLF CLUB
PU-245 S Wildwood Dr, Branson, 65616, Taney County, (417)334-4553, (800)864-4145. **Web:** www.thousandhills.com.
Holes: 18. **Yards:** 5,111/3,616. **Par:** 64/64. **Course Rating:** 66.5/64.1. **Slope:** 125/113. **Green Fee:** $19/$54. **Cart Fee:** Included in Green Fee. **Walking Policy:** Mandatory cart. **Walkability:** 5. **Opened:** 1995. **Architect:** Mike Riley. **Season:** Year-round. **High:** May-Sept. **To obtain tee times:** Tee times may be made up to 30 days in advance by calling (800)864-4145.
Miscellaneous: Reduced fees (low season, resort guests, juniors), discount packages, metal spikes, club rentals, lodging (82 rooms), credit cards (MC, V, AE, D).
Reader Comments: Fair course, elevation changes ... Very difficult ... Well marshalled, beautiful scenery ... Expensive ... Resort price but fun, imaginative track ... Very enjoyable layout.

TIFFANY GREENS GOLF CLUB
PU-6100 N.W. Tiffany Springs Parkway, Kansas City, 64154, Platte County, (816)880-9600, 15 miles N of Downtown Kansas City. **E-mail:** From web site. **Web:** www.tiffanygreensgolf.com.
Holes: 18. **Yards:** 6,977/5,391. **Par:** 72/72. **Course Rating:** 73.5/70.6. **Slope:** 133/121. **Green Fee:** $70/$80. **Cart Fee:** Included in Green Fee. **Walking Policy:** Unrestricted walking. **Walkability:** 3. **Opened:** 1999. **Architect:** Robert Trent Jones Jr. **Season:** Year-round. **High:** April-Oct. **To obtain tee times:** Call (816)880-9600, Ext. 207. **Miscellaneous:** Reduced fees (twilight), range (grass), club rentals, credit cards (MC, V, AE, D) (same fee for walking).

TIMBER LAKE GOLF COURSE
PU-Rte. 3, Moberly, 65270, (816)263-8542.
Special Notes: Call club for further information.

★½ VALLEY HILLS GOLF CLUB
1600 R.D. Mize Rd., Grain Valley, 64029, Jackson County, (816)229-3032.
Special Notes: Call club for further information.

VANDALIA COUNTRY CLUB
PU-Hwy. 54, Vandalia, 63382, (573)594-6666.
Special Notes: Call club for further information.

WEST PLAINS COUNTRY CLUB
SP-1402 Country Club Dr., West Plains, 65775, Howell County, (417)257-2726.
Holes: 18. **Yards:** 6,048/4,807. **Par:** 70/70. **Course Rating:** 68.5/68.0. **Slope:** 113/114. **Green Fee:** N/A/$25. **Cart Fee:** $20/cart. **Walking Policy:** Unrestricted walking. **Walkability:** 1. **Season:** Year-round. **High:** May-Aug. **To obtain tee times:** Call the golf shop. **Miscellaneous:** Range (grass/mats), club rentals, beginner friendly (clinics, lessons, schools).

WINDBROOK COUNTRY CLUB
SP-10306 NW 45 Hwy., Parkville, 64152, (816)741-9520.
Special Notes: Call club for further information.

★★★ WOODS FORT COUNTRY CLUB
SP-1 Country Club Dr., Troy, 63379, (314)462-6600.
Special Notes: Call club for further information.

MONTANA

AIRPORT GOLF CLUB
PU-Hwy. 13 East, Wolf Point, 59201, (406)653-2161.
Special Notes: Call club for further information.

★★ BIG SKY GOLF CLUB
R-2160 Black Otter Rd., Meadow Village, Big Sky, 59716, Gallatin County, (406)995-5780, 45 miles S of Bozeman.
Holes: 18. **Yards:** 6,748/5,374. **Par:** 72/72. **Course Rating:** 69.0/67.4. **Slope:** 111/104. **Green Fee:** $40/$52. **Cart Fee:** Included in Green Fee. **Walking Policy:** Mandatory cart. **Walkability:** 3. **Opened:** 1973. **Architect:** Arnold Palmer. **Season:** May-Oct. **High:** June-Sept. **To obtain tee times:** Call 7 days in advance. **Miscellaneous:** Reduced fees (low season, resort guests, twilight, juniors), discount packages, range (grass), club rentals, lodging (500 rooms), credit cards (MC, V, AE, D).

★★½ BILL ROBERTS MUNICIPAL GOLF COURSE
PU-220 Cole Ave., Helena, 59601, Lewis and Clark County, (406)442-2191.
Holes: 18. **Yards:** 6,782/5,612. **Par:** 72/72. **Course Rating:** 71.2/71.2. **Slope:** 117/120. **Green Fee:** $17/$21. **Cart Fee:** $22/cart. **Walking Policy:** Unrestricted walking. **Walkability:** 2. **Opened:** 1950. **Architect:** Robert Muir Graves. **Season:** March-Nov. **High:** April-Sept. **To obtain tee times:** Call one day in advance for weekdays, call Thursday for weekends (Fri.,Sat.,Sun). **Miscellaneous:** Reduced fees (low season, twilight, seniors, juniors), discount packages, range (grass/mats), club rentals, credit cards (MC, V, D).
Reader Comments: Great course ... Fast play ... Great golf at a reasonable price in the middle of town ... Close to the best beer in Montana at the brewhouse ... Typical city course ... Nice greens ... Worth a visit ... Beautiful view of Helena Valley.

★★★★ THE BRIARWOOD
SP-3429 Briarwood Blvd., Billings, 59101, (406)248-2702.
Reader Comments: Local knowledge important ... Very challenging ... The back 9 is fantastic ... Tough course, windy with trees ... 18 signature holes; nice track ... Tough back—uphill on 7 holes ... Makes most other courses seem easy ... Two different 9s.
Special Notes: Call club for further information.

★★ BRIDGER CREEK GOLF COURSE
PU-2710 McIlahattan Rd., Bozeman, 59715, Gallatin County, (406)586-2333.
Holes: 18. **Yards:** 6,511/4,902. **Par:** 71/71. **Course Rating:** 69.9/66.2. **Slope:** 119/112. **Green Fee:** $22/$24. **Cart Fee:** $20/cart. **Walking Policy:** Unrestricted walking. **Walkability:** 3. **Opened:** 1996. **Architect:** Mac Hunter/Mark Holiday/Dane Gamble. **Season:** April-Oct. **High:** June-Aug. **To obtain tee times:** Call up to 7 days in advance. **Miscellaneous:** Reduced fees (weekdays, juniors), range (grass), credit cards (MC, V), beginner friendly (group lessons for adults and juniors).

★★★★ BUFFALO HILL GOLF COURSE   *Value*
PU-1176 N. Main St., Kalispell, 59901, Flathead County, (406)756-4547, 200 miles E of Spokane.
Holes: 27. **Yards:** 6,525/5,258. **Par:** 72/74. **Course Rating:** 71.4/70.3. **Slope:** 131/125. **Green Fee:** $22/$33. **Cart Fee:** $22/cart. **Walking Policy:** Unrestricted walking. **Walkability:** 4. **Opened:** 1933. **Architect:** Robert Muir Graves. **Season:** April-Oct. **High:** May-Sept. **To obtain tee times:** Call anytime. **Miscellaneous:** Reduced fees (low season), metal spikes, range (mats), club rentals, credit cards (MC, V).
Notes: Ranked 3rd in 1999 Best in State.
Reader Comments: Tough hills ... Marginal shape, great price, decent layout ... A gem! ... Shotmaker's paradise, rewarding experience ... Fun, hilly, windy holes ... Montana's best ... One of the most memorable courses I've ever played ... Top condition ... Thick trees, challenging holes ... Friendly ... Fairly short play, but slow, Wonderful people.

COTTONWOOD COUNTRY CLUB
PU-Sidney Hwy., Glendive, 59330, (406)365-8797.
Special Notes: Call club for further information.

COTTONWOOD HILLS GOLF COURSE
PU-8955 River Rd., Bozeman, 59718, Gallatin County, (406)587-1118, 7 miles W of Bozeman.
Web: avicom.net/cottonwoodgolf.
Holes: 18. **Yards:** 6,753/5,186. **Par:** 70/71. **Course Rating:** 70.8/67.9. **Slope:** 121/110. **Green Fee:** N/A/$25. **Cart Fee:** $20/cart. **Walking Policy:** Unrestricted walking. **Walkability:** 2. **Opened:** 1986. **Architect:** Robert Quick. **Season:** Mar.-Nov. **High:** June-Aug. **To obtain tee times:** Call the golf shop (406)587-1118. **Miscellaneous:** Reduced fees (seniors, juniors), discount packages, range (grass), club rentals, credit cards (MC, V), beginner friendly (lessons and a par-3 course).
Special Notes: Also has a 9 hole Executive Par 3 Course

★★★★ EAGLE BEND GOLF CLUB
SP-279 Eagle Bend Dr., Bigfork, 59911, Flathead County, (406)837-7312, (800)255-5641, 15 miles SE of Kalispell. **E-mail:** golfmt@digisys.net. **Web:** www.golfmt.com.
Holes: 27. **Yards:** 6,802/5,398. **Par:** 72/72. **Course Rating:** 71.7/69.9. **Slope:** 124/122. **Green Fee:** $32/$50. **Cart Fee:** $14/person. **Walking Policy:** Unrestricted walking. **Walkability:** 3. **Opened:** 1988. **Architect:** William Hull/Jack Nicklaus Jr. **Season:** April-Oct. **High:** June-Aug. **To obtain tee times:** Call (800)255-5641 or (406)837-7312. **Miscellaneous:** Reduced fees (low season, twilight, juniors), discount packages, range (grass/mats), club rentals, lodging, credit cards (MC, V, AE, D), beginner friendly.
Reader Comments: Nice layout, good range, friendly staff ... Overrated ... Great shape ... Beautiful views, well maintained, great facilities, interesting layout, a real natural wonder ... Don't miss this one ... Off season, it's like having your own playground ... Expensive for Montana ... Slow, bumpy greens ... Best course in Flathead Valley!.

★★½ FAIRMONT HOT SPRINGS RESORT
R-1500 Fairmont Rd., Anaconda, 59711, Deer Lodge County, (406)797-3241, (800)332-3272, 20 miles NW of Butte.
Holes: 18. **Yards:** 6,741/5,921. **Par:** 72/72. **Course Rating:** 68.5/70.7. **Slope:** 107/109. **Green Fee:** $27/$33. **Cart Fee:** $24/cart. **Walking Policy:** Unrestricted walking. **Walkability:** 3. **Opened:** 1974. **Architect:** Lloyd Wilder. **Season:** April-Oct. **High:** June-Aug. **To obtain tee times:** Call golf shop. **Miscellaneous:** Reduced fees (resort guests), range (grass), club rentals, lodging, credit cards (MC, V, AE, D).
Reader Comments: A very relaxed course ... High and dry ... Overpriced ... Better than expected, fun to play ... Nice views ... Home of the 'Mile Long, Mile High' Par 5.

FORT CUSTER GOLF CLUB
PU-P.O. Box 344, Hardin, 59034, (406)665-2597.
Special Notes: Call club for further information.

★★ GLACIER VIEW GOLF COURSE
PU-River Bend Rd., West Glacier, 59936, Flathead County, (406)888-5471, 15 miles E of Columbia Falls.
Holes: 18. **Yards:** 5,116/4,432. **Par:** 69/69. **Course Rating:** 62.3/63.0. **Slope:** 96/102. **Green Fee:** $20/$20. **Cart Fee:** $18/cart. **Walking Policy:** Unrestricted walking. **Walkability:** 1. **Opened:** 1969. **Architect:** Bob Baldock. **Season:** April-Oct. **High:** June-Aug. **To obtain tee times:** Call up to 7 days in advance or further with credit card to guarantee. **Miscellaneous:** Club rentals, credit cards (MC, V), beginner friendly.

★★½ HAMILTON GOLF CLUB
PU-570 Country Club Lane, Hamilton, 59840, Ravalli County, (406)363-4251.
Reader Comments: Best value in Western Montana ... Good course ... Great mountain views on back nine.
Special Notes: Call club for further information.

HIGHLANDS GOLF CLUB
PU-102 Ben Hogan Dr., Missoula, 59803, Missoula County, (406)728-7360.
Holes: 18. **Yards:** 6,100/5,500. **Par:** 69/72. **Course Rating:** 68.4/70.6. **Slope:** 116/114. **Green Fee:** $20/$25. **Cart Fee:** $12/cart. **Walking Policy:** Unrestricted walking. **Walkability:** 4. **Season:** April-Oct. **High:** May-Sept. **Miscellaneous:** Reduced fees (weekdays, low season, juniors), club rentals.

★★ LAKE HILLS GOLF COURSE
SP-1930 Clubhouse Way, Billings, 59105, Yellowstone County, (406)252-9244.
Holes: 18. **Yards:** 6,802/5,126. **Par:** 72/74. **Course Rating:** 70.1/67.0. **Slope:** 112/104. **Green Fee:** $19/$19. **Cart Fee:** $18/cart. **Walking Policy:** Unrestricted walking. **Walkability:** 3. **Opened:** 1956. **Architect:** George Schneiter Sr. **Season:** Year-round. **High:** May-Sept. **To obtain tee times:** Call 2 days in advance. For weekend tee times call Thursday a.m. **Miscellaneous:** Reduced fees (low season, seniors), metal spikes, range (grass/mats), club rentals, credit cards (MC, V, AE, D).

★★★★ LARCHMONT GOLF COURSE
PU-3200 Old Fort Rd., Missoula, 59801, Missoula County, (406)721-4416.
Holes: 18. **Yards:** 7,114/5,936. **Par:** 72/72. **Course Rating:** 72.7/72.9. **Slope:** 118/118. **Green Fee:** $16/$18. **Cart Fee:** $20/cart. **Walking Policy:** Unrestricted walking. **Walkability:** N/A. **Opened:** 1982. **Architect:** Randy Lilje. **Season:** March-Oct. **High:** May-Aug. **To obtain tee times:** Call 1 day in advance. **Miscellaneous:** Reduced fees (weekdays, seniors, juniors), metal spikes, range (grass), club rentals, credit cards (MC, V, AE, D).
Reader Comments: The whole course in great shape, enjoyable ... Nice, fast greens ... Pretty open ... Good course, greens slow ... Nice, fairly simple course ... Wide open, flat and long ... Huge greens ... Watch out for lightning.

MADISON MEADOWS GOLF CLUB
PU-Golf Course Rd., Ennis, 59729, (406)682-7468
Special Notes: Call club for further information.

MARIAS VALLEY GOLF & COUNTRY CLUB
PU-P.O. Box 784, Shelby, 59474, Toole County, (406)434-5940, 5 miles S of Shelby. **Web:** www.mvgcc.com.
Holes: 18. **Yards:** 6,779/5,042. **Par:** 72/72. **Course Rating:** 71.5/67.7. **Slope:** 122/115. **Green Fee:** $22/$22. **Cart Fee:** $22/cart. **Walking Policy:** Unrestricted walking. **Walkability:** 2.
Opened: 1969. **Architect:** Carl Theusen. **Season:** March-Oct. **High:** June-Aug. **Miscellaneous:** Discount packages, club rentals, credit cards (MC, V), beginner friendly (free beginner lesson program every spring).

★★★½ MEADOW LAKE GOLF RESORT
R-490 St. Andrews Dr., Columbia Falls, 59912, Flathead County, (406)892-2111, (800)321-4653, 12 miles N of Kalispell.
Holes: 18. **Yards:** 6,714/5,344. **Par:** 72/73. **Course Rating:** 70.9/69.8. **Slope:** 124/121. **Green Fee:** $25/$42. **Cart Fee:** $13/person. **Walking Policy:** Unrestricted walking. **Walkability:** 2.
Opened: 1984. **Architect:** Richard Phelps. **Season:** April-Nov. **High:** June-Sept. **To obtain tee times:** Call with credit card to guarantee. **Miscellaneous:** Reduced fees (low season, resort guests, twilight), discount packages, metal spikes, range (grass/mats), club rentals, lodging, credit cards (MC, V, AE, D).
Reader Comments: Short, tight, pretty all around ... Oregon in Montana ... Beautiful course ... Scenic ... Greens hard and fast ... Good course ... Slow play, too much water... Great clubhouse ... Great course with water and trees ... Many interesting holes, magnificent setting ... In the trees ... Very unique, beautiful.

★★★½ MISSION MOUNTAIN COUNTRY CLUB *Pace*
SP-640 Stagecoach Trail, Ronan, 59864, Lake County, (406)676-4653, 60 miles N of Missoula.
Holes: 18. **Yards:** 6,528/5,125. **Par:** 72/73. **Course Rating:** 70.1/69.1. **Slope:** 115/115. **Green Fee:** $24/$24. **Cart Fee:** $22/cart. **Walking Policy:** Unrestricted walking. **Walkability:** 2.
Opened: 1988. **Architect:** Gary Roger Baird. **Season:** March-Oct. **High:** June-Aug. **To obtain tee times:** Call 2 days in advance. **Miscellaneous:** Range (grass), club rentals, credit cards (MC, V).
Reader Comments: A course to score on ... A field with greens, tees and nice views of mountains ... Great views and course ... Beautiful course with some real challenges ... Forgiving, wide fairways ... I give up, how do you play No. 15? ... Very fair, windy, couple of tricky holes ... Best greens in Montana ... Off main strip, not crowded.

★★★★ NORTHERN PINES GOLF CLUB *Pace*
PU-3230 Hwy. 93 North, Kalispell, 59901, Flathead County, (406)751-1950, (800)255-5641, 2 miles N of Kalispell. **E-mail:** golfmt@digisys.net. **Web:** www.golfmt.com.
Holes: 18. **Yards:** 7,015/5,421. **Par:** 72/72. **Course Rating:** 72.5/69.9. **Slope:** 121/118. **Green Fee:** $29/$39. **Cart Fee:** $14/person. **Walking Policy:** Unrestricted walking. **Walkability:** 3.
Opened: 1996. **Architect:** Andy North/Roger Packard. **Season:** April-Oct. **High:** June-Aug. **To obtain tee times:** Call golf shop or 800 number. **Miscellaneous:** Reduced fees (low season, twilight, juniors), discount packages, range (grass), club rentals, credit cards (MC, V, AE), beginner friendly (lessons).
Notes: Ranked 2nd in 1999 Best in State.
Reader Comments: Ball-eating rough ... New course, good range, greens rolled well, great price ... Interesting layout ... In it's infancy—will be better ... Needs maturing ... Would recommend to anyone ... Better hit it straight! ... Had a great time.

★★★★½ OLD WORKS GOLF COURSE *Service, Value+, Condition+*
PM-1205 Pizzini Way, Anaconda, 59711, Deer Lodge County, (406)563-5989, (888)229-4833, 26 miles W of Butte. **E-mail:** oldworks@in.tch.com. **Web:** www.oldworks.org.
Holes: 18. **Yards:** 7,705/5,348. **Par:** 72/72. **Course Rating:** 76.6/70.3. **Slope:** 138/124. **Green Fee:** $29/$36. **Cart Fee:** $12/person. **Walking Policy:** Unrestricted walking. **Walkability:** 3.
Opened: 1997. **Architect:** Jack Nicklaus. **Season:** April-Oct. **High:** June-Sept. **To obtain tee times:** General-Tee times can be made up to 3 days in advance. Advanced reservations may be made up to 30 days in advance for a $10.00 fee per tee time. **Miscellaneous:** Reduced fees (low season, twilight), range (grass), club rentals, credit cards (MC, V, D).
Notes: Ranked 1st in 1999 Best in State.
Reader Comments: Best value, great course ... A real challenge ... Terrific layout on awful site, nice range ... Unique layout, excellent service in a relaxed atmosphere ... Best new course in Montana must play place! ... I remember this course and round as well as any high price course ... Could play have every day ... Wow! Way to go Jack!.

★★ PETER YEGEN JR. GOLF CLUB
PU-3400 Grand Ave., Billings, 59102, Yellowstone County, (406)656-8099.

Holes: 18. **Yards:** 6,617/4,994. **Par:** 71/71. **Course Rating:** 69.7/67.0. **Slope:** 112/109. **Green Fee:** $15/$16. **Cart Fee:** $15/cart. **Walking Policy:** Unrestricted walking. **Walkability:** 1. **Opened:** 1993. **Architect:** Carl Thuesen. **Season:** Year-round. **High:** April-Oct. **To obtain tee times:** Call 3 days in advance. **Miscellaneous:** Discount packages, metal spikes, range (grass/mats), club rentals, credit cards (MC, V, AE).

PINE MEADOWS GOLF COURSE

SP-Country Club Rd., Lewistown, 59457, Fergus County, (406)538-7075, 110 miles SE of Great Falls.
Holes: 9. **Yards:** 6,605/5,853. **Par:** 72/74. **Course Rating:** 69.4/71.1. **Slope:** 109/111. **Green Fee:** $20/$22. **Cart Fee:** $18/cart. **Walking Policy:** Unrestricted walking. **Walkability:** 3. **Opened:** 1947. **Season:** April-Oct. **High:** June-Sept. **To obtain tee times:** Call the Pro Shop. **Miscellaneous:** Reduced fees (weekdays), range (grass), club rentals, credit cards (MC, V, D).

★★★★ POLSON COUNTRY CLUB

PM-111 Bayview Dr., Polson, 59860, Lake County, (406)883-8230, 60 miles N of Missoula. **E-mail:** polsoncc@digisys.net.
Holes: 27. **Yards:** 6,964/5,431. **Par:** 72/72. **Course Rating:** N/A. **Slope:** N/A. **Green Fee:** $24/$24. **Cart Fee:** $22/cart. **Walking Policy:** Unrestricted walking. **Walkability:** 3. **Opened:** 1936. **Architect:** Frank Hummel/John Steidel. **Season:** March-Nov. **High:** June-Aug. **To obtain tee times:** Call up to 2 days in advance. **Miscellaneous:** Reduced fees (low season), discount packages, range (grass/mats), club rentals, credit cards (MC, V).
Reader Comments: Open front, tree-lined back, nice setting ... Great views, hospitality, great shape ... Front 9 open, back 9 narrow ... Best value in Flathead Valley ... Oldest original 9 in Montana ... Scenic ... One old- style 9, one new-style 9 ... RV park next door ... Great views.

PONDEROSA BUTTE GOLF COURSE

PU-1 Long Dr., Colstrip, 59323, (406)748-2700.
Special Notes: Call club for further information.

★★ R.O. SPECK MUNICIPAL GOLF COURSE

PM-29th and River Drive N., Great Falls, 59401, Cascade County, (406)761-1078.
Holes: 18. **Yards:** 6,830/5,817. **Par:** 72/73. **Course Rating:** 69.6/71.4. **Slope:** 111/115. **Green Fee:** $16/$16. **Cart Fee:** $15/. **Walking Policy:** Unrestricted walking. **Walkability:** N/A. **Season:** March-Oct. **High:** April-Oct. **To obtain tee times:** Call 2 days in advance. **Miscellaneous:** Reduced fees (twilight, juniors), metal spikes, range (grass), club rentals.

★★★★ RED LODGE MOUNTAIN RESORT GOLF COURSE

PU-828 Upper Continental Dr., Red Lodge, 59068, Carbon County, (406)446-3344, (800)514-3088, 60 miles SW of Billings.
Holes: 18. **Yards:** 6,863/5,678. **Par:** 72/72. **Course Rating:** 69.3/70.4. **Slope:** 115/115. **Green Fee:** $20/$23. **Cart Fee:** $18/cart. **Walking Policy:** Unrestricted walking. **Walkability:** 3. **Opened:** 1983. **Architect:** Bob Baldock. **Season:** May-Oct. **High:** July-Aug. **To obtain tee times:** Call golf shop. **Miscellaneous:** Reduced fees (weekdays, low season, twilight, juniors), metal spikes, range (grass), club rentals, credit cards (MC, V).
Reader Comments: Very attractive, not forgiving ... Greens small and hard, scenic ... Nice course, could use some trees ... Lots of water, great view of mountains ... Fun course with lots of little streams ... Beautiful ... Lose balls easily ... Elevated boxes ... Nice course in mountains.

★★★ VILLAGE GREENS GOLF CLUB

PU-500 Palmer Dr., Kalispell, 59901, Flathead County, (406)752-4666, 230 miles NE of Spokane, WA. **E-mail:** tee@montanagolf.com. **Web:** www.montanagolf.com.
Holes: 18. **Yards:** 6,401/5,208. **Par:** 70/70. **Course Rating:** 69.8/68.3. **Slope:** 114/114. **Green Fee:** $27/$27. **Cart Fee:** $20/cart. **Walking Policy:** Unrestricted walking. **Walkability:** 1. **Opened:** 1992. **Architect:** William Robinson. **Season:** April-Oct. **High:** June-Aug. **To obtain tee times:** Call up to 3 days in advance. **Miscellaneous:** Reduced fees (twilight, juniors), range (grass), club rentals, credit cards (MC, V, D), beginner friendly.
Reader Comments: Flat course, great shape ... Beautiful greens and scenery ... Wide fairways, few trees, well manicured greens ... Short, easy walking ... Snow on the mountain ... Fairly flat ... Lots of fun.

WHITEFISH LAKE GOLF CLUB

PU-Hwy. 93 N., Whitefish, 59937, Flathead County, (406)862-5960, 130 miles N of Missoula. **E-mail:** wlgc@cyberport.net. **Web:** www.golfwhitefish.com.
★★★½ NORTH COURSE
Holes: 18. **Yards:** 6,556/5,556. **Par:** 72/72. **Course Rating:** 69.8/70.1. **Slope:** 118/115. **Green Fee:** $32/$32. **Cart Fee:** $24/cart. **Walking Policy:** Unrestricted walking. **Walkability:** 2. **Opened:** 1936. **Architect:** John Steidel. **Season:** April-Oct. **High:** June-Sept. **To obtain tee times:** Call 2 days in advance starting at 7 a.m. **Miscellaneous:** Reduced fees (twilight), range (grass/mats), club rentals, credit cards (MC, V).

MONTANA

Notes: Ranked 2nd in 1997 Best in State.

Reader Comments: Pretty layout, good price ... Never get tired of playing this course ... Wide open course to relax and let loose ... Excellent scenery ... Good condition, poor greens ... Bring own food and drink in fall ... Nice views, not difficult ... Busy! Prefer North Course with views of Whitefish Lake.

★★★★ **SOUTH COURSE**

Holes: 18. **Yards:** 6,551/5,361. **Par:** 71/72. **Course Rating:** 70.5/70.3. **Slope:** 122/120. **Green Fee:** $32/$32. **Cart Fee:** $24/cart. **Walking Policy:** Unrestricted walking. **Walkability:** 2. **Opened:** 1980. **Architect:** John Steidel. **Season:** April-Oct. **High:** June-Sept. **To obtain tee times:** Call 2 days in advance starting at 7 a.m. **Miscellaneous:** Reduced fees (twilight), range (grass/mats), club rentals, credit cards (MC, V).

Reader Comments: Good accommodations ... Busy ... New 18 opened in 1994 ... Well laid out, beautiful greens ... Great views and facilities ... Nice setting, challenging ... Great food ... Scenic ... In great shape ... Very professional staff.

★★★ APPLEWOOD GOLF COURSE
PU-6111 S. 99th St., Omaha, 68127, Douglas County, (402)444-4656.
Holes: 18. **Yards:** 6,928/6,026. **Par:** 72/76. **Course Rating:** 73.7/75.3. **Slope:** 124/126. **Green Fee:** $15/$18. **Cart Fee:** $9/person. **Walking Policy:** Unrestricted walking. **Walkability:** 3. **Opened:** 1971. **Architect:** Dave Bennett/Leon Howard. **Season:** Year-round. **High:** May-Sept. **To obtain tee times:** Call 7 days in advance. **Miscellaneous:** Reduced fees (weekdays, seniors, juniors), range (grass).
Reader Comments: Great city course ... A nice valley course ... Challenging yet fair ... Wide open, can be tough or easy ... Priced right ... Good, cheap golf. What this country needs more of! ... Excellent design ... Gets lots of play.

★★★ ASHLAND COUNTRY CLUB
SP-R2, Ashland, 68003, Saunders County, (402)944-3388, 25 miles W of Omaha.
Holes: 18. **Yards:** 6,337/5,606. **Par:** 70/74. **Course Rating:** 70.0/69.8. **Slope:** 112/112. **Green Fee:** $18/$20. **Cart Fee:** $18/. **Walking Policy:** Unrestricted walking. **Walkability:** N/A. **Opened:** 1967. **Architect:** Dick Watson. **Season:** March-Oct. **High:** June-Sept. **To obtain tee times:** Call 7 days in advance. **Miscellaneous:** Metal spikes, club rentals.
Reader Comments: Easy to play ... Tough and fun ... Nice short course, fair price.

★★ BAY HILLS GOLF COURSE
SP-3200 Buccaneer Blvd., Plattsmouth, 68048, Cass County, (402)298-8191, 15 miles S of Omaha. **E-mail:** bayhills@navix.net. **Web:** www.bayhills.com.
Holes: 18. **Yards:** 6,348/4,923. **Par:** 72/74. **Course Rating:** 72.5/76.5. **Slope:** 135/137. **Green Fee:** $15/$20. **Cart Fee:** $10/cart. **Walking Policy:** Unrestricted walking. **Walkability:** 5. **Opened:** 1994. **Season:** March-Dec. **High:** April-Oct. **To obtain tee times:** Call 7 days in advance. **Miscellaneous:** Reduced fees (weekdays, low season, twilight, seniors, juniors), discount packages, range (grass/mats), club rentals, credit cards (MC, V, AE, D).

★★★ BENSON PARK GOLF COURSE
PU-5333 N. 72nd St., Omaha, 68134, Douglas County, (402)444-4626.
Holes: 18. **Yards:** 6,814/6,085. **Par:** 72/78. **Course Rating:** 72.1/73.4. **Slope:** 120/121. **Green Fee:** $12/$13. **Cart Fee:** $16/. **Walking Policy:** Unrestricted walking. **Walkability:** N/A. **Opened:** 1964. **Architect:** Edward Lawrence Packard. **Season:** March-Dec. **High:** May-Sept. **To obtain tee times:** Call 7 days in advance. **Miscellaneous:** Reduced fees (seniors, juniors), discount packages, metal spikes, club rentals.
Reader Comments: Nice layout ... Nice course for as much play as it gets .... Good use of landscape ... Up and down hills ... Popular ... Basic golf ... Excellent price.

CEDAR VIEW COUNTRY CLUB
PU-Calcavecchia Dr., Laurel, 68745, Cedar County, (402)256-3184.
Holes: 9. **Yards:** 3,015/2,491. **Par:** 36/36. **Course Rating:** 34.0/34.0. **Slope:** 112/112. **Green Fee:** $16/$20. **Cart Fee:** $14/cart. **Walking Policy:** Unrestricted walking. **Walkability:** 4. **Opened:** 1965. **Season:** April-Oct. **High:** July-Aug. **To obtain tee times:** Call the golf shop. **Miscellaneous:** Reduced fees (weekdays), beginner friendly (lessons).

COVINGTON LINKS GOLF COURSE
PU-497 Golf Rd., South Sioux City, 68776, Dakota County, (402)494-9841, 1 miles W of South Sioux City, NE.
Holes: 18. **Yards:** 5,977/5,263. **Par:** 71/71. **Course Rating:** N/A. **Slope:** N/A. **Green Fee:** $14/$14. **Cart Fee:** $16/cart. **Walking Policy:** Unrestricted walking. **Walkability:** 2. **Opened:** 1977. **Architect:** Marty Johnson. **Season:** March-Nov. **High:** June-Aug. **To obtain tee times:** Tee times required. Call Thursday after 8 a.m. for upcoming weekend. **Miscellaneous:** Metal spikes, credit cards (MC, V).

★★½ CROOKED CREEK GOLF CLUB
PU-134th & O St., Lincoln, 68520, Lancaster County, (402)489-7899, 3 miles E of Lincoln.
Holes: 18. **Yards:** 6,720/5,024. **Par:** 72/72. **Course Rating:** 70.8/68.2. **Slope:** 113/109. **Green Fee:** $16/$20. **Cart Fee:** $11/person. **Walking Policy:** Unrestricted walking. **Walkability:** 3. **Opened:** 1995. **Architect:** Pat Wyss. **Season:** Year-round. **High:** April-Oct. **To obtain tee times:** Call. **Miscellaneous:** Reduced fees (low season, seniors, juniors), range (grass/mats), club rentals, credit cards (MC, V), beginner friendly.
Reader Comments: A bargain ... Only a few years old, will get better ... Great clubhouse ... Diverse layout ... Fun ... Will be a great course once the trees fill in ... Two of the best finishing holes.

ELDORADO HILLS GOLF CLUB
SP-1227 Eldorado Rd., Norfolk, 68701, Madison County, (402)371-1453, 45 miles N of Columbus. **E-mail:** eldorado@ncfcomn.com.
Holes: 18. **Yards:** 6,700/5,566. **Par:** 72/72. **Course Rating:** 71.8/72.6. **Slope:** 116/115. **Green Fee:** $18/$18. **Cart Fee:** $10/person. **Walking Policy:** Unrestricted walking. **Walkability:** 4. **Opened:** 1987. **Architect:** Bob Cupp. **Season:** March-Oct. **High:** June-Aug. **To obtain tee**

times: Call the Pro Shop. **Miscellaneous:** Reduced fees (weekdays, low season), club rentals, credit cards (MC, V).

ELK'S COUNTRY CLUB
SP-5113 63rd St., Columbus, 68601, (402)564-4930.
Special Notes: Call club for further information.

ELKHORN ACRES GOLF COURSE
PU-Rte. 1, Stanton, 68779, (402)439-2191.
Holes: 18. **Yards:** N/A. **Par:** N/A. **Course Rating:** N/A. **Slope:** N/A. **Green Fee:** N/A. **Walkability:** N/A.

ELMWOOD PARK GOLF COURSE
PU-6232 Pacific St., Omaha, 68106, Douglas County, (402)444-4683.
Holes: 18. **Yards:** 5,000/4,300. **Par:** 68/68. **Course Rating:** 64.0/64.0. **Slope:** 101/101. **Green Fee:** $14/$17. **Cart Fee:** $9/person. **Walking Policy:** Unrestricted walking. **Walkability:** 3. **Opened:** 1934. **Season:** March-Dec. **High:** May-Sept. **To obtain tee times:** Call up to 7 days in advance. **Miscellaneous:** Reduced fees (seniors, juniors), club rentals.

FAIRPLAY GOLF CLUB
SP-55427 837 Road, Norfolk, 68701, Madison County, (402)371-9877.
Holes: 18. **Yards:** 6,444/2,717. **Par:** 72/72. **Course Rating:** 68.1/70.4. **Slope:** 107/108. **Green Fee:** $17/$17. **Cart Fee:** $17/cart. **Walking Policy:** Unrestricted walking. **Walkability:** 1. **Architect:** Martin Johnson. **Season:** March-Nov. **High:** May-July. **Miscellaneous:** Club rentals, beginner friendly.

FALLS CITY COUNTRY CLUB
SP-West Hwy. 8, Falls City, 68355, (402)245-3624.
Holes: 18. **Yards:** N/A. **Par:** N/A. **Course Rating:** N/A. **Slope:** N/A. **Green Fee:** N/A. **Walkability:** N/A.
Special Notes: Call club for further information.

GORDON GOLF & COUNTRY CLUB
SP-West 2nd St., Gordon, 69343, Sheridan County, (308)282-1146.
Holes: 9. **Yards:** 3,209/2,906. **Par:** 36/37. **Course Rating:** 71.8/75.8. **Slope:** 119/127. **Green Fee:** $12/$17. **Cart Fee:** $15/cart. **Walking Policy:** Unrestricted walking. **Walkability:** 2. **Opened:** 1969. **Architect:** Jack Korita. **Season:** April-Oct. **High:** June-July. **To obtain tee times:** Call (308)282-1146. **Miscellaneous:** Reduced fees (weekdays), range (grass).

★★★ GRAND ISLAND MUNICIPAL GOLF COURSE
PM-2800 Shady Bend Rd., Grand Island, 68801, Hall County, (308)385-5340, 90 miles W of Lincoln.
Holes: 18. **Yards:** 6,752/5,487. **Par:** 72/72. **Course Rating:** 71.3/70.8. **Slope:** 118/112. **Green Fee:** $9/$11. **Cart Fee:** $17/cart. **Walking Policy:** Unrestricted walking. **Walkability:** 1. **Opened:** 1977. **Architect:** Frank Hummel. **Season:** Year-round. **High:** April-Sept. **To obtain tee times:** Call 7 days in advance. **Miscellaneous:** Reduced fees (seniors, juniors), range (grass), club rentals, credit cards (MC, V), beginner friendly (junior golf program, beginner clinics).
Reader Comments: Course in good shape ... Thick rough ... One of the best muny courses in Nebraska, great value ... Getting better as it matures ... Short ... A pearl in Nebraska.

★★★★ HERITAGE HILLS GOLF COURSE   *Value, Pace+*
PU-6000 Clubhouse Dr., McCook, 69001, Red Willow County, (308)345-5032, 240 miles SW of Lincoln.
Holes: 18. **Yards:** 6,715/5,475. **Par:** 72/72. **Course Rating:** 72.7/74.8. **Slope:** 130/130. **Green Fee:** $22/$22. **Cart Fee:** $20/cart. **Walking Policy:** Unrestricted walking. **Walkability:** 5. **Opened:** 1981. **Architect:** Phelps/Benz. **Season:** Year-round. **High:** May-Sept. **To obtain tee times:** Call 7 days in advance. **Miscellaneous:** Reduced fees (juniors), metal spikes, range (grass), club rentals, credit cards (MC, V).
Notes: Ranked 10th in 1999 Best in State.
Reader Comments: What a jewel in the middle of nowhere ... Best course in Nebraska for the price ... Challenging ... Great course ... Great fun! Inexpensive ... Very difficult, with blind shots ... Could play everyday—women friendly ... The hills are alive! ... Excellent shape.

★★ HIDDEN VALLEY GOLF COURSE
PU-10501 Pine Lake Rd., Lincoln, 68526, Lancaster County, (402)483-2532.
Holes: 18. **Yards:** 6,080/5,411. **Par:** 71/75. **Course Rating:** 68.3/71.6. **Slope:** 110/114. **Green Fee:** $13/$16. **Cart Fee:** $10/person. **Walking Policy:** Unrestricted walking. **Walkability:** 3. **Opened:** 1962. **Architect:** C.J. Dietrich. **Season:** March-Dec. **High:** June-Aug. **To obtain tee times:** Call 7 days in advance. **Miscellaneous:** Reduced fees (weekdays, low season, seniors, juniors), discount packages, range (grass/mats), club rentals, credit cards (MC, V).
Special Notes: Also has 9-hole par-35 West Course.

★★★½ HIGHLANDS GOLF COURSE

PU-5501 N.W. 12th St., Lincoln, 68521, Lancaster County, (402)441-6081. **E-mail:** hgcpro@aol.com.

Holes: 18. **Yards:** 7,021/5,280. **Par:** 72/72. **Course Rating:** 72.5/69.4. **Slope:** 119/111. **Green Fee:** $14/$18. **Cart Fee:** $11/person. **Walking Policy:** Unrestricted walking. **Walkability:** 4. **Opened:** 1993. **Architect:** Jeff Brauer. **Season:** Year-round. **High:** April-Oct. **To obtain tee times:** Call 7 days in advance. **Miscellaneous:** Reduced fees (twilight, seniors, juniors), range (grass/mats), club rentals, credit cards (MC, V).

Reader Comments: Fun to play ... Challenging links ... Like the real highlands, no trees, lots of sand ... Lincoln's best public course! ... Beautiful with tough greens; neat atmosphere ... Very open, plays tough in wind ... Reasonable fees ... Wide open fun course.

HILLSIDE GOLF COURSE

PM-2616 Hillside Dr., Sidney, 69162, Cheyenne County, (308)254-2311, 170 miles NE of Denver, CO. **E-mail:** sidgolf@wheatbelt.com.

Holes: 18. **Yards:** 6,924/5,308. **Par:** 72/73. **Course Rating:** 72.5/70.0. **Slope:** 121/110. **Green Fee:** $15/$15. **Cart Fee:** $16/cart. **Walking Policy:** Unrestricted walking. **Walkability:** 4. **Season:** March-Dec. **High:** May-Aug. **To obtain tee times:** Call up to 7 days in advance. **Miscellaneous:** Reduced fees (seniors, juniors), range (grass), club rentals, credit cards (MC, V, AE, D).

★★½ HIMARK GOLF COURSE

PU-90th and Augusta Drive, Lincoln, 68520, Lancaster County, (402)488-7888.

Holes: 18. **Yards:** 6,615/4,885. **Par:** 71/70. **Course Rating:** 72.6/68.8. **Slope:** 122/111. **Green Fee:** $8/$22. **Cart Fee:** $12/person. **Walking Policy:** Unrestricted walking. **Walkability:** 3. **Opened:** 1993. **Architect:** Larry Glatt/Lammle Brothers. **Season:** Year-round. **High:** April-Sept. **To obtain tee times:** Call 7 days in advance. **Miscellaneous:** Reduced fees (twilight, seniors, juniors), range (grass/mats), club rentals, credit cards (MC, V).

Reader Comments: Best maintained course in town ... Wind can blow like hell ... Best public greens in town ... Friendly staff ... Great greens and fairways ... Par 4 eagle opportunity.

★★★ HOLMES PARK GOLF COURSE

PU-3701 S. 70th St., Lincoln, 68506, Lancaster County, (402)441-8960.

Holes: 18. **Yards:** 6,805/6,054. **Par:** 72/74. **Course Rating:** 72.2/73.8. **Slope:** 120/126. **Green Fee:** $11/$16. **Cart Fee:** $20/cart. **Walking Policy:** Unrestricted walking. **Walkability:** 3. **Opened:** 1964. **Architect:** Floyd Farley. **Season:** Year-round. **High:** May-June. **To obtain tee times:** Call 7 days in advance. **Miscellaneous:** Reduced fees (weekdays, seniors, juniors), discount packages, range (grass/mats), club rentals, credit cards (MC, V).

Reader Comments: Very playable ... The best in Lincoln, not for the beginner ... Great group running this course ... Pro may join you for a few holes ... Nice course, good value ... High-traffic course ... Great pro shop!

INDIAN CREEK GOLF COURSE

PU-20100 W. Maple Rd., Elkhorn, 68022, Douglas County, (402)289-0900, 5 miles W of Omaha.

★★★½ BLACKBIRD/GRAYHAWK

Holes: 27. **Yards:** 7,154/5,282. **Par:** 72/72. **Course Rating:** 74.1/68.5. **Slope:** 128/113. **Green Fee:** $22/$38. **Cart Fee:** $10/person. **Walking Policy:** Unrestricted walking. **Walkability:** 4. **Opened:** 1992. **Architect:** Frank Hummel/Mark Rathert. **Season:** Year-round. **High:** June-July. **To obtain tee times:** Call 7 days in advance. **Miscellaneous:** Reduced fees (twilight, seniors), range (grass/mats), club rentals, credit cards (MC, V).

Reader Comments: Nice layout ... One of Nebraska's finest ... Fun course ... Bring every club, will need them all... A good course, conveniently located ... Great 27-hole layout; great price ... Top-notch public ... Long from back.

★★★½ RED FEATHER/BLACKBIRD

Holes: 27. **Yards:** 7,157/5,040. **Par:** 72/72. **Course Rating:** 75.0/68.1. **Slope:** 131/112. **Green Fee:** $22/$38. **Cart Fee:** $10/person. **Walking Policy:** Unrestricted walking. **Walkability:** 4. **Opened:** 1992. **Architect:** Frank Hummel/Mark Rathert. **Season:** Year-round. **High:** June-July. **To obtain tee times:** Call 7 days in advance. **Miscellaneous:** Reduced fees (twilight, seniors), range (grass/mats), club rentals, credit cards (MC, V).

Reader Comments: Good challenge, fun course ... New 9 very challenging ... Strong, hilly course ... Long with heavy winds, great shape.

★★★½ RED FEATHER/GRAYHAWK

Holes: 27. **Yards:** 7,041/5,120. **Par:** 72/72. **Course Rating:** 73.9/69.4. **Slope:** 131/115. **Green Fee:** $22/$38. **Cart Fee:** $10/person. **Walking Policy:** Unrestricted walking. **Walkability:** 4. **Opened:** 1992. **Architect:** Frank Hummel/Mark Rathert. **Season:** Year-round. **High:** June-July. **To obtain tee times:** Call 7 days in advance. **Miscellaneous:** Reduced fees (twilight, seniors), range (grass/mats), club rentals, credit cards (MC, V).

INDIAN MEADOWS GOLF COURSE

PU-Rte. 2, North Platte, 69101, Lincoln County, (308)532-6955.

Holes: 9. **Yards:** 3,250/2,784. **Par:** 36/36. **Course Rating:** 70.1/71.0. **Slope:** 111/117. **Green Fee:** $11/$12. **Cart Fee:** $16/cart. **Walking Policy:** Unrestricted walking. **Walkability:** 1. **Opened:** 1970. **Season:** Year-round. **High:** May-Sept. **Miscellaneous:** Range (grass/mats), caddies, club rentals, credit cards (MC, V, AE), beginner friendly (lessons).

★★★ INDIAN TRAILS COUNTRY CLUB
SP-Highway 275, Beemer, 68716, Cuming County, (402)528-3404, 30 miles S of Norfolk.
Holes: 18. **Yards:** 6,302/5,692. **Par:** 71/73. **Course Rating:** 68.8/74.2. **Slope:** 115/120. **Green Fee:** $12/$16. **Cart Fee:** $14/cart. **Walkability:** 3. **Opened:** 1960. **Season:** March-Nov. **High:** May-Aug. **To obtain tee times:** Call up to 7 days in advance. **Miscellaneous:** Metal spikes, range (grass), credit cards (MC, V).
Reader Comments: Great course, river views great ... Windy ... Every one must play at least once ... Big secret.

INDIANHEAD GOLF CLUB
PU-4100 W. Husker Hwy., Grand Island, 68803, Hall County, (308)381-4653, 90 miles W of Lincoln.
Holes: 18. **Yards:** 6,597/5,664. **Par:** 72/72. **Course Rating:** 70.9/71.9. **Slope:** 122/117. **Green Fee:** $10/$12. **Cart Fee:** $9/person. **Walking Policy:** Unrestricted walking. **Walkability:** 1. **Opened:** 1990. **Season:** Year-round. **High:** May-Sept. **To obtain tee times:** Call 7 days in advance. **Miscellaneous:** Reduced fees (low season), metal spikes, range (grass/mats), club rentals, credit cards (MC, V).

IRON EAGLE MUNICIPAL GOLF COURSE
PM-2401 Halligan Dr, North Platte, 69101, Lincoln County, (308)535-6730.
Holes: 18. **Yards:** 6,401/4,459. **Par:** 72/72. **Course Rating:** 70.8/66.3. **Slope:** 120/114. **Green Fee:** $14/$17. **Cart Fee:** $9/person. **Walking Policy:** Unrestricted walking. **Walkability:** 1. **Opened:** 1994. **Architect:** Pat Wyss. **Season:** Year-round weather permitting. **High:** April-Sept. **To obtain tee times:** Call 7 days in advance. **Miscellaneous:** Reduced fees (seniors, juniors), range (grass/mats), club rentals, credit cards (MC, V).

★★★ THE KNOLLS GOLF COURSE
PU-11630 Sahler St., Omaha, 68164, Douglas County, (402)493-1740.
Holes: 18. **Yards:** 6,300/5,111. **Par:** 71/71. **Course Rating:** 69.8/69.8. **Slope:** 123/115. **Green Fee:** $17/$24. **Cart Fee:** $10/person. **Walking Policy:** Unrestricted walking. **Walkability:** 3. **Opened:** 1976. **Season:** Year-round. **High:** April-Oct. **To obtain tee times:** Call or come in. Accepted 7 days in advance. **Miscellaneous:** Reduced fees (weekdays, twilight, seniors, juniors), discount packages, club rentals, credit cards (MC, V, AE).
Reader Comments: Great staff ... Fun course ... Good public course ... Hard, long, narrow ... Good variety on the back.

LAKE MALONEY GOLF COURSE
SP-608 Birdie Lane, North Platte, 69101, Lincoln County, (308)532-9998.
Holes: 18. **Yards:** 6,550/5,050. **Par:** 72/72. **Course Rating:** 72.6/70.1. **Slope:** 124/115. **Green Fee:** $9/$14. **Cart Fee:** $15/cart. **Walking Policy:** Unrestricted walking. **Walkability:** 3. **Opened:** 1990. **Architect:** Bill Burns. **Season:** March-Nov. **High:** May-Aug. **To obtain tee times:** Call golf shop. Tee times required for weekends. **Miscellaneous:** Reduced fees (weekdays), range (grass/mats), club rentals.

LAKESIDE COUNTRY CLUB
PU-RR 2 Box 36A, Elwood, 68937, Gosper County, (308)785-2818, 40 miles W of Kearney.
Holes: 18. **Yards:** 6,200/5,200. **Par:** 72/72. **Course Rating:** 70.0/67.2. **Slope:** 128/128. **Green Fee:** $10/$20. **Cart Fee:** $20/cart. **Walking Policy:** Unrestricted walking. **Walkability:** 4. **Opened:** 1961. **Architect:** Marty Johnson. **Season:** Year-round weather permitting. **High:** May-Sept. **To obtain tee times:** Call up to 14 days in advance. **Miscellaneous:** Reduced fees (juniors), range (grass), club rentals, credit cards (MC, V).

LEGENDS BUTTE GOLF CLUB
PU-W. Highway 20, Crawford, 69339, Dawes County, (308)665-2431.
Holes: 9. **Yards:** 3,178/2,461. **Par:** 36/36. **Course Rating:** 70.4/67.4. **Slope:** 125/110. **Green Fee:** $16/$17. **Cart Fee:** $15/cart. **Walking Policy:** Unrestricted walking. **Walkability:** 3. **Opened:** 1992. **Season:** March-Nov. **High:** June-Aug. **To obtain tee times:** Call the golf shop at (308)665-2431. **Miscellaneous:** Discount packages, metal spikes, range (grass), club rentals, credit cards (MC, V, D, Novus).

LOGAN VALLEY GOLF COURSE
SP-Rte. 1, Wakefield, 68784, (402)287-2343.
Special Notes: Call club for further information.

★★ MAHONEY GOLF COURSE
PM-7900 Adams St., Lincoln, 68507, Lancaster County, (402)441-8969, 40 miles SW of Omaha.

Holes: 18. **Yards:** 6,459/5,582. **Par:** 70/72. **Course Rating:** 69.9/72.6. **Slope:** 113/120. **Green Fee:** $14/$18. **Cart Fee:** $12/person. **Walking Policy:** Unrestricted walking. **Walkability:** 3. **Opened:** 1975. **Architect:** Floyd Farley. **Season:** Year-round weather permitting. **High:** June-Aug. **To obtain tee times:** Call 7 days in advance. **Miscellaneous:** Reduced fees (twilight, seniors, juniors), metal spikes, range (grass/mats), club rentals, credit cards (MC, V, AE, D).

★★★½ MEADOWLARK HILLS GOLF COURSE
PM-3300 30th Ave., Kearney, 68848, Buffalo County, (308)233-3265, 120 miles W of Lincoln. **E-mail:** mhills@nebi.com. **Web:** meadowlark.nebi.com.
Holes: 18. **Yards:** 6,485/4,967. **Par:** 71/72. **Course Rating:** 70.4/68.2. **Slope:** 119/112. **Green Fee:** $17/$19. **Cart Fee:** $10/person. **Walking Policy:** Unrestricted walking. **Walkability:** 5. **Opened:** 1994. **Architect:** David Gill/Steven Halberg. **Season:** Year-round. **High:** May-Aug. **To obtain tee times:** Call 6 days in advance. **Miscellaneous:** Reduced fees (weekdays, low season, seniors, juniors), range (grass/mats), club rentals, credit cards (MC, V).
Reader Comments: Used every club in my bag ... Good mix of open and tight holes ... One of the best public courses in the area ... Risk and reward course ... Getting better every year... View of Platte Valley ... Great muny in good condition.

★★★ MIRACLE HILL GOLF & TENNIS CENTER
PU-1401 N.120th St., Omaha, 68154, Douglas County, (402)498-0220.
Holes: 18. **Yards:** 6,412/5,069. **Par:** 70/70. **Course Rating:** 71.0/69.0. **Slope:** 129/117. **Green Fee:** $16/$24. **Cart Fee:** $19/cart. **Walking Policy:** Unrestricted walking. **Walkability:** 3. **Opened:** 1960. **Architect:** Floyd Farley. **Season:** Year-round. **High:** May-Aug. **To obtain tee times:** Call 7 days in advance. **Miscellaneous:** Reduced fees (twilight, seniors), metal spikes, range (grass/mats), club rentals, credit cards (MC, V).
Reader Comments: Friendly course for a high-handicap golfer... Good service ... Very playable older course ... Course in good shape ... Nice greens ... Long and wide open.

NORFOLK COUNTRY CLUB
SP-North 1700 Riverside Blvd., Norfolk, 68701, (402)379-1188.
Special Notes: Call club for further information.

NORTH PLATTE COUNTRY CLUB
SP-1008 W. 18th St., North Platte, 69101, Lincoln County, (308)532-7550.
Holes: 18. **Yards:** 6,392/5,260. **Par:** 70/72. **Course Rating:** 70.0/70.5. **Slope:** 117/118. **Green Fee:** $20/$35. **Cart Fee:** $8/person. **Walking Policy:** Unrestricted walking. **Walkability:** 1. **Opened:** 1916. **Season:** March-Dec. **High:** May-Aug. **To obtain tee times:** Call up to 7 days in advance. **Miscellaneous:** Range (grass), club rentals.

OAKLAND GOLF CLUB
SP-100 Parsons St., Oakland, 68045, (402)685-5339.
Special Notes: Call club for further information.

★★★ THE PINES COUNTRY CLUB
SP-7516 N. 286th St., Valley, 68064, Douglas County, (402)359-4311, 30 miles W of Omaha.
Holes: 18. **Yards:** 6,629/5,190. **Par:** 72/72. **Course Rating:** 72.1/70.2. **Slope:** 121/116. **Green Fee:** $16/$28. **Cart Fee:** $10/person. **Walking Policy:** Unrestricted walking. **Walkability:** 1. **Opened:** 1979. **Architect:** Bill Kubly. **Season:** March-Oct. **High:** May-Aug. **To obtain tee times:** Call 7 days in advance for weekday. Must be accompanied by a member on weekends. **Miscellaneous:** Reduced fees (weekdays, seniors, juniors), range (grass/mats), club rentals, credit cards (MC, V).
Reader Comments: Great greens ... Flat layout ... Hardly any trouble ... Flat and challenging ... Reasonable prices.

★★★½ PIONEERS GOLF COURSE
PU-3403 W. Van Dorn, Lincoln, 68522, Lancaster County, (402)441-8966, 2 miles W of Lincoln.
Holes: 18. **Yards:** 6,478/5,771. **Par:** 71/74. **Course Rating:** 69.2/73.2. **Slope:** 110/114. **Green Fee:** $13/$16. **Cart Fee:** $20/cart. **Walking Policy:** Unrestricted walking. **Walkability:** 3. **Opened:** 1930. **Architect:** W. H. Tucker. **Season:** Year-round. **High:** June-Aug. **To obtain tee times:** Call up to 7 days in advance. **Miscellaneous:** Reduced fees (weekdays, twilight, seniors, juniors), range (grass), club rentals, credit cards (MC, V).
Reader Comments: One of Nebraska's oldest and most scenic courses ... No bunkers, none needed ... Old course with lots of play ... Nice for beginners ... Challenging holes on back 9 ... Fun fairways thick rough.

★★★ QUAIL RUN GOLF COURSE
PU-327 S. 5th St., Columbus, 68601, Platte County, (402)564-1313, 80 miles NW of Omaha. **E-mail:** jdgolf@quailrungolf.com. **Web:** www.quailrungolf.com.
Holes: 18. **Yards:** 7,024/5,147. **Par:** 72/72. **Course Rating:** 75.1/70.7. **Slope:** 140/125. **Green Fee:** $9/$18. **Cart Fee:** $20/cart. **Walking Policy:** Unrestricted walking. **Walkability:** 1. **Opened:** 1991. **Architect:** Frank Hummel. **Season:** April-Oct. **High:** June-Aug. **To obtain tee times:** Call

3 days in advance. **Miscellaneous:** Reduced fees (weekdays, twilight, seniors, juniors), range (grass/mats), club rentals, credit cards (MC, V), beginner friendly (excellent teaching program). **Reader Comments:** Good golf course ... Excellent course near the river... Half course open, other half tight ... Good value ... Well laid out ... Nice transition from open to wooded.

★★★★ QUARRY OAKS GOLF CLUB

PU-16600 Quarry Oaks Dr., Ashland, 68003-3820, Cass County, (402)944-6000, (888)944-6001, 25 miles W of Omaha. **Web:** www.quarryoaks.com.
Holes: 18. **Yards:** 7,077/5,378. **Par:** 72/72. **Course Rating:** 73.2/70.0. **Slope:** 135/131. **Green Fee:** $35/$45. **Cart Fee:** $12/person. **Walking Policy:** Unrestricted walking. **Walkability:** 5. **Opened:** 1997. **Architect:** John LaFoy. **Season:** March-Nov. **High:** May-Sept. **To obtain tee times:** Call up to 7 days in advance. **Miscellaneous:** Reduced fees (twilight, seniors), range (grass), club rentals, credit cards (MC, V, AE, D).
Notes: Ranked 3rd in 1999 Best in State; 1st Best New Affordable Public Course of 1997.
Reader Comments: Hard to believe this is Nebraska ... Peaceful setting cut into the woods ... Awesome elevated tee shots ... Best public course in the state by far... Too tough ... Outstanding layout in former quarry.

★★★ RIVERVIEW GOLF & COUNTRY CLUB

PU-100928 County Rd. 19, Scottsbluff, 69361, Scotts Bluff County, (308)635-1555, 200 miles NE of Denver, CO.
Holes: 18. **Yards:** 6,024/5,598. **Par:** 70/74. **Course Rating:** 68.1/70.7. **Slope:** 116/120. **Green Fee:** $12/$12. **Cart Fee:** $13/cart. **Walking Policy:** Unrestricted walking. **Walkability:** 1. **Opened:** 1941. **Season:** Year-round. **High:** May-Oct. **To obtain tee times:** Call to be guaranteed a tee time. **Miscellaneous:** Range (grass), club rentals, credit cards (MC, V, D).
Reader Comments: Course in excellent shape ... Fun ...Trees make course challenging ... Lake driving range ... Tough course ... Lots of water and trees ... Good value.

ROLLING GREEN GOLF CLUB

PU-400 South Walsh St., Morrill, 69358, Scotts Bluff County, (308)247-2817, 180 miles S of Denver, C. O.
Holes: 9. **Yards:** 3,186/2,767. **Par:** 36/38. **Course Rating:** 69.0/68.7. **Slope:** 106/111. **Green Fee:** $9/$10. **Cart Fee:** $14/cart. **Walking Policy:** Unrestricted walking. **Walkability:** 3. **Season:** Year-round. **High:** June-Aug. **To obtain tee times:** No tee times needed. **Miscellaneous:** Reduced fees (weekdays), range (grass), club rentals.

SKYVIEW GOLF COURSE

PU-1326 C R 57, Alliance, 69301, Box Butte County, (308)762-1446, 45 miles NE of Scottsbluff.
Holes: 18. **Yards:** 6,501/5,364. **Par:** 70/72. **Course Rating:** 70.0/70.6. **Slope:** 112/115. **Green Fee:** $15/$17. **Cart Fee:** $6/person. **Walking Policy:** Unrestricted walking. **Walkability:** 2. **Opened:** 1953. **Architect:** Henry B. Hughes. **Season:** March-Nov. **High:** June-Aug. **To obtain tee times:** Not necessary. **Miscellaneous:** Reduced fees (juniors), range (grass), club rentals.

SOUTHERN HILLS GOLF COURSE

SP-3005 S. Southern Hills Dr., Hastings, 68901, Adams County, (402)463-8006, 150 miles W of Omaha.
Holes: 18. **Yards:** 6,351/5,195. **Par:** 72/72. **Course Rating:** 70.7/69.6. **Slope:** 127/116. **Green Fee:** N/A/$14. **Cart Fee:** $17/person. **Walking Policy:** Unrestricted walking. **Walkability:** 4. **Season:** Year-round weather permitting. **To obtain tee times:** Call 1 day in advance. **Miscellaneous:** Range (grass).

TARA HILLS GOLF COURSE

PU-1001 Limerick Rd., Papillion, 68046, (402)592-7550.
Special Notes: Call club for further information.

★★★½ TIBURON GOLF CLUB

SP-10302 S. 168th St., Omaha, 68136, Sarpy County, (402)895-2688.
Holes: 27. **Yards:** 6,887/5,335. **Par:** 72/72. **Course Rating:** 73.4/71.0. **Slope:** 131/126. **Green Fee:** $22/$29. **Cart Fee:** $12/person. **Walking Policy:** Unrestricted walking. **Walkability:** 3. **Opened:** 1989. **Architect:** Dave Bennett. **Season:** March-Nov. **High:** June-Sept. **To obtain tee times:** Call 7 days in advance for weekdays, and 7 days in advance for weekends. **Miscellaneous:** Reduced fees (weekdays, seniors, juniors), range (grass/mats), club rentals, credit cards (MC, V, AE, D).
Reader Comments: Gets better every year... Need every club in your bag ... Excellent course ... Front and back 9s quite different ... Amazing greens and fairways ... Really nice course that is worth playing ... Wide open ... Nice greens ... Good service.

★★★½ TREGARON GOLF COURSE

PU-13909 Glen Garry Circle, Bellevue, 68123, Sarpy County, (402)292-9300, 3 miles S of Omaha.

Holes: 18. **Yards:** 6,508/4,417. **Par:** 71/71. **Course Rating:** 70.9/65.1. **Slope:** 122/104. **Green Fee:** $18/$23. **Cart Fee:** $10/person. **Walking Policy:** Unrestricted walking. **Walkability:** 5. **Opened:** 1997. **Architect:** Craig Schreiner. **Season:** Year-round. **High:** April-Oct. **To obtain tee times:** Call 1 week in advance. **Miscellaneous:** Reduced fees (weekdays, low season, twilight, seniors, juniors), club rentals, credit cards (MC, V, AE).
Reader Comments: Challenging, excellent condition ... Water in play on some holes ... Lots of sand and wind on this links course ... A young course with potential ... Great links design ... Favorite new course.

VALLEY VIEW GOLF COURSE
PU-Route 2, Box 44, Fremont, 68025, Saunders County, (402)721-7772.
Holes: 18. **Yards:** 5,295/4,982. **Par:** 71/71. **Course Rating:** 64.6/67.9. **Slope:** 108/116. **Green Fee:** $14/$15. **Cart Fee:** $16/cart. **Walkability:** 4. **Opened:** 1960. **Season:** April-Oct. **To obtain tee times:** Call. **Miscellaneous:** Metal spikes, range (grass/mats), club rentals.

VAN BERG PARK & GOLF CLUB
PU-Pawnee Park, Columbus, 68601, (402)564-0761.
Special Notes: Call club for further information.

WAYNE COUNTRY CLUB
PU-RR#2, Wayne, 68787, Wayne County, (402)375-1152, 100 miles N of Omaha.
Holes: 18. **Yards:** 6,315/5,500. **Par:** 72/72. **Course Rating:** 70.1/71.7. **Slope:** 113/117. **Green Fee:** $18/$21. **Cart Fee:** $15/cart. **Walking Policy:** Unrestricted walking. **Walkability:** 3. **Season:** April-Oct. **High:** June-July. **Miscellaneous:** Range (grass), club rentals, beginner friendly.

WILD HORSE GOLF CLUB
SP-41150 Road 768, Gothenburg, 69138, Dawson County, (308)537-7700, 45 miles E of North Platte.
Holes: 18. **Yards:** 6,805/4,688. **Par:** 72/72. **Course Rating:** 73.0/71.7. **Slope:** 125/123. **Green Fee:** $25/$25. **Cart Fee:** $10/person. **Walking Policy:** Unrestricted walking. **Walkability:** 3. **Opened:** 1999. **Architect:** Dan Proctor/Dave Axland. **Season:** March-Nov. **High:** June-Aug. **To obtain tee times:** Call Pro Shop (308)537-7700. **Miscellaneous:** Reduced fees (juniors), range (grass), caddies, club rentals, credit cards (MC, V, D), beginner friendly (u.s.g.a. grant and youth program).
Notes: Ranked 3rd in 1999 Best New Affordable Public.

WILDWOOD GOLF COURSE
PU-2330 Park Lane, Nebraska City, 68410, (402)873-3661.
Holes: 18. **Special Notes:** Call club for further information.

WILLOW LAKES GOLF COURSE
PU-Bldg. 9950 Offutt AFB, 25th St., Bellevue, 68113, Sarpy County, (402)292-1680, 10 miles S of Omaha.
Holes: 18. **Yards:** 6,850/5,504. **Par:** 72/72. **Course Rating:** 72.8/71.5. **Slope:** 128/125. **Green Fee:** $14/$22. **Cart Fee:** $8/person. **Walking Policy:** Unrestricted walking. **Walkability:** 2. **Opened:** 1962. **Architect:** Robert Trent Jones. **Season:** March-Nov. **High:** May-Aug. **To obtain tee times:** Call on Tuesday for Saturday play. Call on Wednesday for Sunday play.
Miscellaneous: Reduced fees (twilight, seniors), metal spikes, range (mats), club rentals, credit cards (MC, V).

★★★★½ WOODLAND HILLS GOLF COURSE   *Service, Value+, Pace*
PU-6000 Woodland Hills Dr., Eagle, 68347, Otoe County, (402)475-4653, 12 miles E of Lincoln.
E-mail: woodland@direcpc.com. **Web:** www.woodlandhillsgolf.com.
Holes: 18. **Yards:** 6,592/4,945. **Par:** 71/71. **Course Rating:** 72.6/70.3. **Slope:** 132/122. **Green Fee:** $10/$35. **Cart Fee:** $10/person. **Walking Policy:** Unrestricted walking. **Walkability:** 3. **Opened:** 1991. **Architect:** Jeffrey D. Brauer. **Season:** Year-round. **High:** July-Aug. **To obtain tee times:** Call up to 30 days in advance. **Miscellaneous:** Reduced fees (weekdays, low season, resort guests, twilight, seniors, juniors), discount packages, metal spikes, range (grass/mats), caddies, club rentals, credit cards (MC, V, AE, D).
Notes: Ranked 6th in 1999 Best in State. 1995-97 Midwest (Prairie Golf) Pro Tour. 1999 Nebraska State Amateur.
Reader Comments: Nebraska's best kept secret ... Take the time to find and play this championship course ... Excellent condition ... Old tree farm ... Bent grass ... Nice greens ... The best overall experience I've played ... Great design ... Well managed ... Middle of nowhere but worth the trip ... Great layout and holes ... Lots of character ... Private club quality ... Beautiful in fall.

YORK COUNTRY CLUB
SP-West Elm St., York, 68467, (402)362-3721.
Special Notes: Call club for further information.

NEVADA

ANGEL PARK GOLF CLUB
PU-100 S. Rampart Blvd., Las Vegas, 89128, Clark County, (702)254-4653,
(888)446-5358.
★★★½ **MOUNTAIN COURSE**
Holes: 18. **Yards:** 6,722/5,164. **Par:** 71/72. **Course Rating:** 72.4/69.9. **Slope:** 128/119. **Green Fee:** $50/$90. **Cart Fee:** Included in Green Fee. **Walking Policy:** Mandatory cart. **Walkability:** 3. **Opened:** 1989. **Architect:** Arnold Palmer/Ed Seay/Bob Cupp. **Season:** Year-round. **High:** Feb.-June/Sept.-Nov. **To obtain tee times:** Call 60 days in advance. **Miscellaneous:** Reduced fees (low season, twilight, juniors), metal spikes, range (grass/mats), club rentals, credit cards (MC, V, AE).
Reader Comments: Rather golf than gamble ... The par-5 17th is a beauty and a challenge ... Old style, wide fairways, good test ... Great course if not windy ... Wide open and forgiving ... Greens in great shape ... Starters are great! ... Great, fun layout ... Best golf value in Las Vegas.
★★★ **PALM COURSE**
Holes: 18. **Yards:** 6,530/4,570. **Par:** 70/70. **Course Rating:** 72.6/67.6. **Slope:** 130/110. **Green Fee:** $50/$90. **Cart Fee:** Included in Green Fee. **Walking Policy:** Mandatory cart. **Walkability:** 3. **Opened:** 1989. **Architect:** Arnold Palmer/Ed Seay/Bob Cupp. **Season:** Year-round. **High:** Feb.-June/Sept.-Nov. **To obtain tee times:** Call 60 days in advance. **Miscellaneous:** Reduced fees (low season, twilight, juniors), metal spikes, range (grass/mats), club rentals, credit cards (MC, V, AE).
Reader Comments: Pleasant surprise. Enjoyed this course very much. A little bit of everything ... Tighter than Mountain Course, a fair test of golf ... Nice desert course ... Long, open & wide, fun to play.
Special Notes: Also an 18-hole putting course and Cloud 9, a 12-hole par-3 course made up of famous par 3s from around the world.

ARROWCREEK GOLF CLUB
PU-2905 ArrowCreek Pkwy., Reno, 89511, Sparks County, (775)850-4653, 10 miles SW of Downtown Reno.
Holes: 18. **Yards:** 7,310/5,135. **Par:** 72/72. **Course Rating:** 75.0/69.7. **Slope:** 137/130. **Green Fee:** $30/$90. **Cart Fee:** Included in Green Fee. **Walking Policy:** Mandatory cart. **Walkability:** 4. **Opened:** 1999. **Architect:** Arnold Palmer/Ed Seay. **Season:** Year-round. **High:** June-Oct. **Miscellaneous:** Reduced fees (weekdays, low season, twilight), discount packages, range (grass/mats), club rentals, credit cards (MC, V, AE).

★★★½ **THE BADLANDS GOLF CLUB**
R-9115 Alta Dr., Las Vegas, 89128, Clark County, (702)242-4653, 10 miles NW of Las Vegas.
Holes: 27. **Yards:** 6,900/5,875. **Par:** 72/72. **Course Rating:** 73.8/71.0. **Slope:** 134/132. **Green Fee:** $60/$225. **Cart Fee:** Included in Green Fee. **Walking Policy:** Mandatory cart. **Walkability:** 5. **Opened:** 1995. **Architect:** Johnny Miller/Fred Bliss. **Season:** Year-round. **High:** March-Oct. **To obtain tee times:** Credit card guarantee. 48 hour cancellation policy. $25.00 no show fees. **Miscellaneous:** Reduced fees (weekdays, low season, twilight), range (grass/mats), club rentals, credit cards (MC, V, AE).
Reader Comments: Good combination of holes ... Great staff! ... Target-style, very difficult when windy ... Toughest course in town, more fun after a few rounds ... Tough, up & down, real challenge ... Accuracy a must, from tee to green ... Satellite tracking on carts.

★★½ **BLACK MOUNTAIN GOLF & COUNTRY CLUB**
SP-500 E. Greenway Rd., Henderson, 89015, Clark County, (702)565-7933, 15 miles SE of Las Vegas. **E-mail:** golfbmtn@aol.com. **Web:** www.vegasgolfer.com/blackmountain.
Holes: 18. **Yards:** 6,541/5,478. **Par:** 72/72. **Course Rating:** 71.2/71.6. **Slope:** 123/120. **Green Fee:** $35/$70. **Cart Fee:** Included in Green Fee. **Walking Policy:** Walking at certain times. **Walkability:** 2. **Opened:** 1959. **Architect:** Bob Baldock. **Season:** Year-round. **High:** Oct.-May. **To obtain tee times:** Call 4 days in advance. **Miscellaneous:** Reduced fees (low season, twilight, seniors, juniors), discount packages, range (grass), club rentals, credit cards (MC, V).
Reader Comments: Green fees very reasonable ... Nice course for being in Vegas! ... Very playable, easy to score ... A few challenging holes ... Unpredictable winds may blow.

★★★½ **BOULDER CITY GOLF CLUB** *Value*
PM-1 Clubhouse Dr., Boulder City, 89005, Clark County, (702)293-9236, 20 miles S of Las Vegas.
Holes: 18. **Yards:** 6,561/5,566. **Par:** 72/72. **Course Rating:** 70.2/70.7. **Slope:** 110/113. **Green Fee:** $23/$27. **Cart Fee:** $9/person. **Walking Policy:** Unrestricted walking. **Walkability:** 2. **Opened:** 1972. **Architect:** David Rainville/Billy Casper. **Season:** Year-round. **High:** Spring/Fall. **To obtain tee times:** Call 7 days in advance for weekdays. Call up to 9 days in advance for weekends. Call Friday for upcoming Friday, Saturday and Sunday. **Miscellaneous:** Reduced fees (low season, twilight, juniors), range (grass/mats), club rentals, credit cards (MC, V).

NEVADA

Reader Comments: Best city course in Las Vegas area ... Best value in Vegas area ... Excellent municipal ... Back 9 really nice ... Tight, tough, short, laid-back trees ... What a pleasant surprise, tough on a windy day.

★★★ CALVADA VALLEY GOLF & COUNTRY CLUB
SP-Red Butte and Mt. Charleston Rd., Pahrump, 89048, Nye County, (775)727-4653, (877)779-4653, 63 miles NW of Las Vegas.
Holes: 18. **Yards:** 7,025/5,948. **Par:** 71/73. **Course Rating:** 73.2/74.3. **Slope:** 124/123. **Green Fee:** $25/$50. **Cart Fee:** Included in Green Fee. **Walking Policy:** Mandatory cart. **Walkability:** N/A. **Opened:** 1978. **Architect:** William F. Bell. **Season:** Year-round. **High:** Oct.-April. **To obtain tee times:** Call 7 days in advance starting at 7 a.m. **Miscellaneous:** Reduced fees (weekdays, low season), discount packages, range (grass/mats), club rentals, credit cards (MC, V, AE, D).
Reader Comments: A true value, worth the drive ... Long, grass bunkers are tough to get out ... A lot of nice green grass for being just over the hill from 'Death Valley'.

CHIMNEY ROCK MUNICIPAL GOLF COURSE
PU-144 Ventosa Ave., Wells, 89835, Elko County, (775)752-3928. **E-mail:** golf@rabbitbrush.com.
Holes: 9. **Yards:** 6,118/5,510. **Par:** 70/74. **Course Rating:** 67.0/70.8. **Slope:** 109/115. **Green Fee:** $14/N/A. **Cart Fee:** $18/cart. **Walking Policy:** Unrestricted walking. **Walkability:** 2. **Opened:** 1978. **Season:** March-Nov. **High:** June-Aug. **To obtain tee times:** Please call. **Miscellaneous:** Reduced fees (juniors), range (grass), club rentals, credit cards (MC, V). **Special Notes:** Two sets of tees for 18 holes.

★★ CRAIG RANCH GOLF COURSE
PU-628 W. Craig Rd., North Las Vegas, 89030, Clark County, (702)642-9700.
Holes: 18. **Yards:** 6,001/5,221. **Par:** 70/70. **Course Rating:** 66.8/67.4. **Slope:** 105/101. **Green Fee:** $17/$17. **Cart Fee:** $8/person. **Walking Policy:** Unrestricted walking. **Walkability:** 1. **Opened:** 1962. **Architect:** John F. Stimson/John C. Stimson. **Season:** Year-round. **High:** March-May/Oct.-Nov. **To obtain tee times:** Call up to 7 days in advance. **Miscellaneous:** Metal spikes, range (grass), club rentals.

★★★★ DAYTON VALLEY GOLF CLUB
SP-51 Palmer Dr., Dayton, 89403, Lyon County, (775)246-7888, 35 miles SE of Reno.
Holes: 18. **Yards:** 7,218/5,161. **Par:** 72/72. **Course Rating:** 74.2/68.4. **Slope:** 143/121. **Green Fee:** $25/$75. **Cart Fee:** Included in Green Fee. **Walking Policy:** Unrestricted walking. **Walkability:** 2. **Opened:** 1991. **Architect:** Arnold Palmer/Ed Seay. **Season:** Year-round. **High:** May-Oct. **To obtain tee times:** Call 14 days in advance. **Miscellaneous:** Reduced fees (weekdays, low season, twilight, juniors), range (grass), club rentals, credit cards (MC, V).
Reader Comments: Lots of water, windy, tough, good layout ... Always an excellent golfing experience ... A must play! ... Always great condition–can be very windy ... Great risk/reward course ... Long and tricky in the wind ... Fun, different course when wind blows!

★★★★½ DESERT INN GOLF CLUB *Condition+, Pace*
R-3145 Las Vegas Blvd. S., Las Vegas, 89109, Clark County, (702)733-4290, (800)634-6909. **Web:** www.thedesertinn.com.
Holes: 18. **Yards:** 7,066/5,791. **Par:** 72/72. **Course Rating:** 73.9/72.7. **Slope:** 124/121. **Green Fee:** $160/$225. **Cart Fee:** Included in Green Fee. **Walking Policy:** Mandatory cart. **Walkability:** N/A. **Opened:** 1952. **Architect:** Lawrence Hughes. **Season:** Year-round. **High:** Feb.-May. **To obtain tee times:** Call. **Miscellaneous:** Reduced fees (low season, resort guests), metal spikes, range (grass), club rentals, lodging (715 rooms), credit cards (MC, V, AE, D).
Reader Comments: Well worth the cost ... Excellent course, facility & great staff! ... A classic, timeless test ... Enjoyed the rolling hills ... Beautifully maintained, great greens, scenic ... The playing conditions were good ... One of my favorites. Flat course, very female friendly.

DESERT LAKES GOLF COURSE
PU-4000 Farm District Rd., Fernley, 89408, Lyon County, (775)575-4653, 35 miles E of Reno.
Holes: 18. **Yards:** 6,507/5,197. **Par:** 71/71. **Course Rating:** 69.9/68.3. **Slope:** 124/N/A. **Green Fee:** $20/$35. **Cart Fee:** Included in Green Fee. **Walking Policy:** Unrestricted walking. **Walkability:** 2. **Opened:** 1996. **Architect:** Bob Bingham. **Season:** Year-round. **High:** March-Oct. **To obtain tee times:** Call 7 days in advance. **Miscellaneous:** Reduced fees (weekdays, low season, twilight, seniors, juniors), metal spikes, range (grass), club rentals, credit cards (MC, V).

★★★½ DESERT PINES GOLF CLUB
PU-3415 E. Bonanza, Las Vegas, 89101, Clark County, (702)388-4400.
Web: waltersgolf.com.
Holes: 18. **Yards:** 6,810/5,873. **Par:** 71/71. **Course Rating:** 70.4/69.4. **Slope:** 122/116. **Green Fee:** $70/$129. **Cart Fee:** Included in Green Fee. **Walking Policy:** Mandatory cart. **Walkability:** N/A. **Opened:** 1996. **Architect:** Perry Dye. **Season:** Year-round. **High:** Sept.-May. **To obtain tee times:** Call golf shop. **Miscellaneous:** Reduced fees (weekdays, low season, twilight, juniors), range (mats), club rentals, credit cards (MC, V, AE).

NEVADA

Reader Comments: Nice! ... May not be long, but it sure is skinny. Lots of tricks around greens, good track ... Short, narrow, irons get lots of use ... Nice outing in heart of Las Vegas, more pine needles than Pinehurst ... Great course ... Nice, but at a price.

★★ DESERT ROSE GOLF COURSE

PU-5483 Clubhouse Dr., Las Vegas, 89142, Clark County, (702)431-4653, 6 miles E of Las Vegas.
Holes: 18. **Yards:** 6,511/5,458. **Par:** 71/71. **Course Rating:** 70.7/69.6. **Slope:** 112/107. **Green Fee:** $51/$75. **Cart Fee:** Included in Green Fee. **Walking Policy:** Unrestricted walking. **Walkability:** 3. **Opened:** 1962. **Architect:** Dick Wilson/Jeff Brauer. **Season:** Year-round. **High:** Sept.-June. **To obtain tee times:** Call 7 days in advance for weekdays, and 3 days in advance for weekend play. **Miscellaneous:** Reduced fees (low season, twilight, seniors, juniors), metal spikes, range (grass/mats), club rentals, credit cards (MC, V, AE, D).

EAGLE VALLEY GOLF CLUB

PU-3999 Centennial Park Dr., Carson City, 89706, Carson County, (775)887-2380, 30 miles S of Reno.

★★★½ EAST COURSE

Holes: 18. **Yards:** 6,658/5,980. **Par:** 72/72. **Course Rating:** 68.7/72.8. **Slope:** 117/123. **Green Fee:** $18/$18. **Cart Fee:** $17. **Walking Policy:** Walking at certain times. **Walkability:** 2. **Opened:** 1977. **Architect:** Homer Flint. **Season:** Year-round. **High:** May-Sept. **To obtain tee times:** Call Friday at 3 p.m. for the following Monday through Sunday. **Miscellaneous:** Reduced fees (twilight), metal spikes, range (grass), club rentals, credit cards (MC, V).
Reader Comments: Very challenging & look out for the snakes ... Few trees, some water ... Great public course ... Course always in good shape when we go in June. Great price.

★★★½ WEST COURSE

Holes: 18. **Yards:** 6,851/5,293. **Par:** 72/72. **Course Rating:** 73.5/68.8. **Slope:** 131/117. **Green Fee:** $27/$38. **Cart Fee:** $18/cart. **Walking Policy:** Mandatory cart. **Walkability:** 5. **Opened:** 1987. **Architect:** Homer Flint. **Season:** Year-round. **High:** May-Sept. **To obtain tee times:** Call Friday at 3 p.m. for the following Monday through Sunday. **Miscellaneous:** Reduced fees (twilight), metal spikes, range (grass/mats), club rentals.
Reader Comments: Wide fairways and deep rough ... Requires strong course management ... Very challenging public course ... Fun course, best value in Nevada.

★★★★½ EDGEWOOD TAHOE GOLF COURSE *Service, Condition*

PU-180 Lake Parkway, Stateline, 89449, Douglas County, (775)588-3566, 50 miles SW of Reno.
E-mail: edgewood@edgewood-tahoe.com. **Web:** www.edgewood-tahoe.com.
Holes: 18. **Yards:** 7,470/5,547. **Par:** 72/72. **Course Rating:** 75.7/71.3. **Slope:** 139/136. **Green Fee:** $150/$175. **Cart Fee:** Included in Green Fee. **Walking Policy:** Unrestricted walking. **Walkability:** 3. **Opened:** 1968. **Architect:** George Fazio/Tom Fazio. **Season:** May-Oct. **High:** July-Sept. **To obtain tee times:** Call 90 days in advance. There is a $25 booking fee per player. **Miscellaneous:** Metal spikes, range (grass/mats), caddies, rentals, credit cards (MC, V, AE).
Reader Comments: Must do at least once ... Elevation lets you play like Tiger Woods ... Great course, very tough from tips ... Good layout but expensive ... Challenging, gorgeous–water everywhere ... Crowded ... Great atmosphere, nice facilities.... Beautiful lake holes! ... Fabulous views. Wind is tough along the water.

★★★ EMERALD RIVER GOLF COURSE

PU-1155 W. Casino Dr., Laughlin, 89029, Clark County, (702)298-0061, 90 miles S of Las Vegas.
Holes: 18. **Yards:** 6,572/5,230. **Par:** 72/72. **Course Rating:** 73.6/71.3. **Slope:** 144/129. **Green Fee:** $40/$75. **Cart Fee:** Included in Green Fee. **Walking Policy:** Mandatory cart. **Walkability:** 4. **Opened:** 1990. **Architect:** Tom Clark. **Season:** Year-round. **High:** Jan.-May/Oct.-Nov. **To obtain tee times:** Call up to 30 days in advance. **Miscellaneous:** Reduced fees (weekdays, low season, resort guests, twilight, seniors), discount packages, metal spikes, range (grass), club rentals, credit cards (MC, V, AE, D).
Reader Comments: Needs clubhouse & wider fairways ... Great reason to get away from the tables in Laughlin ... Waste area rocks hard on clubs ... Hardest course ever played ... Target your shot or play with the rattlesnakes ... Always enjoy this 'target golf' course ... Very nice, surprising challenge; enjoyed it.

EMPIRE RANCH GOLF COURSE

PU-1875 Fair Way, Carson City, 89701, Carson County, (775)885-2100, 3 miles E of Carson City.
Holes: 27. **Green Fee:** $20/$25. **Cart Fee:** $10/person. **Walking Policy:** Walking at certain times. **Walkability:** 3. **Opened:** 1997. **Architect:** Cary Bickler. **Season:** Year-round. **High:** May-Oct. **To obtain tee times:** Call up to 7 days in advance. **Miscellaneous:** Reduced fees (weekdays, low season, twilight, seniors, juniors), range (grass), club rentals, credit cards (MC, V), beginner friendly (clinics and lessons).
★★★ BLUE/RED

Yards: 6,603/4,719. **Par:** 72/72. **Course Rating:** 70.5/67.4. **Slope:** 127/118.
Reader Comments: Wonderful staff ... Great muny courses-greens roll true ... Relatively new and course conditions will improve ... Lots of look-a-like holes, good greens ... Relatively immature, but playable and enjoyable ... Good basic course.
★★★ **BLUE/YELLOW**
Yards: 6,763/4,883. **Par:** 72/72. **Course Rating:** 71.6/68.1. **Slope:** 129/119.
★★★ **RED/YELLOW**
Yards: 6,840/4,854. **Par:** 72/72. **Course Rating:** 71.3/68.3. **Slope:** 128/123.

FALLON GOLF COURSE
PU-2655 Country Club Dr., Fallon, 89406, (702)423-4616.
Special Notes: Call club for further information.

★★★★ THE GOLF CLUB AT GENOA LAKES
PU-1 Genoa Lakes Dr., Genoa, 89411, Douglas County, (775)782-4653, 15 miles E of So. Lake Tahoe. **E-mail:** genoalks@sierra.net. **Web:** genoalakes.com.
Holes: 18. **Yards:** 7,263/5,008. **Par:** 72/72. **Course Rating:** 73.5/67.6. **Slope:** 134/117. **Green Fee:** $40/$95. **Cart Fee:** Included in Green Fee. **Walking Policy:** Unrestricted walking.
Walkability: 2. **Opened:** 1993. **Architect:** John Harbottle/Peter Jacobsen. **Season:** Year-round.
High: July-Sept. **To obtain tee times:** Call up to 30 days in advance. **Miscellaneous:** Reduced fees (weekdays, low season, twilight, juniors), discount packages, range (grass), club rentals, credit cards (MC, V, AE, D).
Reader Comments: Allows you to use all your clubs, tough course ... Great setting ... A test for all grades of golfers ... Need to space people out more ... Good course, lots of water, windy in afternoon ... Abundance of wildlife ... Very helpful staff. Descriptive play book ... Play conservative to score—let out on par 5's.

HIGHLAND FALLS GOLF CLUB
9201-B Del Webb Blvd., Las Vegas, 89134, Clark County, (702)363-4373.
Special Notes: Call club for further information.

HIGHLAND FALLS GOLF COURSE-PALM VALLEY
SP-9201-B Del Webb Blvd., Las Vegas, 89134, (702)363-4373.
Special Notes: Call club for further information.

INCLINE VILLAGE GOLF RESORT
★★★★ **CHAMPIONSHIP COURSE**
R-955 Fairway Blvd., Incline Village, 89451-9006, Washoe County, (775)832-1146, (888)236-8725, 30 miles SW of Reno. **Web:** www.golfincline.com.
Holes: 18. **Yards:** 6,931/5,245. **Par:** 72/72. **Course Rating:** 72.2/70.1. **Slope:** 133/131. **Green Fee:** N/A/$115. **Cart Fee:** Included in Green Fee. **Walking Policy:** Unrestricted walking.
Walkability: 5. **Opened:** 1964. **Architect:** Robert Trent Jones. **Season:** May-Oct. **High:** June-Sept. **To obtain tee times:** Call 14 days in advance. **Miscellaneous:** Reduced fees (twilight), metal spikes, range (mats), club rentals, credit cards (MC, V).
Notes: Ranked 8th in 1999 Best in State.
Reader Comments: Beautiful, but a little too tough ... Best course in the west over 6000 feet elevation ... Very long and humbling, nice scenery ... Best course I've played—challenging, water! ... A must play, top 5 in Nevada ... Blind shots–narrow–beautiful scenery ... Best Lake Tahoe course; bar none! ... Tight fairways.

MOUNTAIN COURSE
R-690 Wilson Way, Incline Village, 89451, Washoe County, (775)832-1150, 30 miles SW of Reno. **Web:** www.golfincline.com.
Holes: 18. **Yards:** 3,513/3,002. **Par:** 58/58. **Course Rating:** 56.6/57.3. **Slope:** 94/85. **Green Fee:** N/A/$50. **Cart Fee:** Included in Green Fee. **Walking Policy:** Unrestricted walking.
Walkability: 5. **Opened:** 1969. **Architect:** Robert Trent Jones, Jr. **Season:** May-Oct. **High:** May-Oct. **To obtain tee times:** Call 14 days in advance. **Miscellaneous:** Reduced fees (twilight), metal spikes, range (mats), club rentals, credit cards (MC, V).

★★½ JACKPOT GOLF CLUB
R-P.O. Box 370, Jackpot, 89825, Elko County, (775)755-2260, 165 miles SE of Boise, ID.
Holes: 18. **Yards:** 6,934/5,590. **Par:** 72/72. **Course Rating:** 69.4/69.3. **Slope:** 111/108. **Green Fee:** $15/$18. **Cart Fee:** $10/person. **Walking Policy:** Walking at certain times. **Walkability:** 4.
Opened: 1970. **Architect:** Robert Muir Graves. **Season:** March-Nov. **High:** May-Sept. **To obtain tee times:** Call anytime in advance. **Miscellaneous:** Reduced fees (weekdays, juniors), discount packages, metal spikes, range (grass), club rentals, credit cards (MC, V).
Reader Comments: Very fun and playable course ... The good holes make up for the bad ones ... Hilly; lots of blind shots, doglegs, sand.

NEVADA

LAKE LAS VEGAS RESORT

R-75 Montelago Blvd., Henderson, 89011, Clark County, (702)740-4653, (877)698-4653, 17 miles E of Las Vegas. **Web:** www.lakelasvegas.com.
Holes: 18. **Yards:** 7,261/5,166. **Par:** 72/72. **Course Rating:** 74.8/70.0. **Slope:** 138/127. **Green Fee:** $175/$175. **Walking Policy:** Unrestricted walking. **Walkability:** 4. **Opened:** 1998. **Architect:** Jack Nicklaus. **Season:** Year-round. **High:** Oct.-May. **To obtain tee times:** May call within 60 days in advance to secure time. **Miscellaneous:** Range (grass), club rentals, lodging (496 rooms), credit cards (MC, V, AE).

★★★½ LAKE RIDGE GOLF COURSE

PU-1200 Razorback Rd., Reno, 89509, Washoe County, (775)825-2200.
Holes: 18. **Yards:** 6,703/5,159. **Par:** 71/71. **Course Rating:** 70.8/68.5. **Slope:** 127/117. **Green Fee:** $44/$80. **Cart Fee:** Included in Green Fee. **Walking Policy:** Walking at certain times. **Walkability:** 4. **Opened:** 1969. **Architect:** Robert Trent Jones. **Season:** March-Dec. **High:** April-Oct. **To obtain tee times:** Call 7 days in advance through the golf shop via phone or in person; or up to 60 days in advance through Tee Time Central @ (888)236-8725. A surcharge and pre-payment are required through Tee Time Central. **Miscellaneous:** Reduced fees (low season, twilight), metal spikes, range (mats), club rentals, credit cards (MC, V).
Reader Comments: Very hilly, especially back 9 ... Don't hit the Canadian geese ... Played in the sun, wind, rain, hail, snow. All in a day ... Established course with great variety ... 15th hole not to be missed ... Great island green; don't believe yardage ... Highest par 3 in Nevada.

★★★ LAS VEGAS GOLF CLUB

PU-4300 W. Washington, Las Vegas, 89107, Clark County, (702)646-3003.
Holes: 18. **Yards:** 6,631/5,715. **Par:** 72/72. **Course Rating:** 71.8/71.2. **Slope:** 117/113. **Green Fee:** $28/$109. **Cart Fee:** $18/cart. **Walking Policy:** Unrestricted walking. **Walkability:** 2. **Opened:** 1947. **Architect:** William P. Bell. **Season:** Year-round. **High:** Feb.-May. **To obtain tee times:** Call up to 7 days in advance. **Miscellaneous:** Reduced fees (twilight, seniors, juniors), metal spikes, range (grass/mats), club rentals, credit cards (MC, V, AE).
Reader Comments: Best value in Vegas—bar none ... Hit the target ... Good public course.

★★★★ LAS VEGAS NATIONAL GOLF CLUB *Pace*

R-1911 E. Desert Inn Rd., Las Vegas, 89109, Clark County, (702)734-1796, (800)468-7918.
Holes: 18. **Yards:** 6,815/5,741. **Par:** 71/71. **Course Rating:** 72.1/69.5. **Slope:** 130/103. **Green Fee:** $50/$225. **Cart Fee:** Included in Green Fee. **Walking Policy:** Mandatory cart. **Walkability:** 1. **Opened:** 1961. **Architect:** Bert Stamps. **Season:** Year-round. **High:** Feb.-April/Sept.-Nov. **To obtain tee times:** Call American Golf Corporations Resort time office up to 60 days in advance with credit card to guarantee. **Miscellaneous:** Reduced fees (weekdays, low season, resort guests, twilight, juniors), discount packages, range (grass/mats), club rentals, credit cards (MC, V, AE, D).
Reader Comments: Nothing too memorable, but a nice day. They pushed the 'first tee' photos too much ... Great course—high in price ... Bring your 'A' game ... Computerized cart is a plus.

LAS VEGAS PAIUTE RESORT *Service+*

PU-10325 Nu-Wav Kaiv Blvd., Las Vegas, 89124, Clark County, (702)658-1400, (800)711-2833. **E-mail:** teeup@lvpaiutegolf.com. **Web:** lvpaiutegolf.com.
★★★★½ NU-WAV KAIV COURSE (SNOW MOUNTAIN) *Condition+*
Holes: 18. **Yards:** 7,158/5,341. **Par:** 72/72. **Course Rating:** 73.9/70.4. **Slope:** 125/117. **Green Fee:** $60/$135. **Cart Fee:** Included in Green Fee. **Walking Policy:** Mandatory cart. **Walkability:** 3. **Opened:** 1995. **Architect:** Pete Dye/Brian Curley. **Season:** Year-round. **High:** Spring/Fall. **To obtain tee times:** Call up to 60 days in advance with credit card to guarantee. **Miscellaneous:** Reduced fees (weekdays, low season, twilight), range (grass), club rentals, credit cards (MC, V, AE, D).
Reader Comments: Great facility—watch out for wind ... Plays hard and fast ... Great desert golf, truly tests all your skills ... The best golf shop/clubhouse on earth ... Great condition ... Excellent greens. Tough in the wind ... A precious gem. Bravo ... Perfect for women.
Special Notes: Spikeless shoes preferred.
★★★★½ TAV-AI KAIV COURSE (SUN MOUNTAIN) *Condition+, Pace*
Holes: 18. **Yards:** 7,112/5,465. **Par:** 72/72. **Course Rating:** 73.3/71.0. **Slope:** 130/123. **Green Fee:** $60/$135. **Cart Fee:** Included in Green Fee. **Walking Policy:** Mandatory cart. **Walkability:** 3. **Opened:** 1997. **Architect:** Pete Dye/Brian Curley. **Season:** Year-round. **High:** Spring/Fall. **To obtain tee times:** Call up to 60 days in advance with credit card to guarantee. **Miscellaneous:** Reduced fees (weekdays, low season, twilight), range (grass), club rentals, credit cards (MC, V, AE, D).
Reader Comments: The best course I've played in Vegas-outstanding! ... Perfect day, staff excellent, an oasis in the desert ... Great course-high in price ... Beautiful courses. Friendly service ... Wind always blows.
Special Notes: Spikeless shoes preferred.

★★★½ THE LEGACY GOLF CLUB *Service*
PU-130 Par Excellence Dr., Henderson, 89014, Clark County, (702)897-2187, (888)446-5358, 10 miles SE of Las Vegas. **E-mail:** info@thelegacygolf.com. **Web:** www.thelegacygolf.com. **Holes:** 18. **Yards:** 7,233/5,340. **Par:** 72/72. **Course Rating:** 74.9/71.0. **Slope:** 136/120. **Green Fee:** N/A/$135. **Cart Fee:** Included in Green Fee. **Walking Policy:** Mandatory cart. **Walkability:** N/A. **Opened:** 1989. **Architect:** Arthur Hills. **Season:** Year-round. **High:** Sept.-June. **To obtain tee times:** Tee times can be made with a credit card to guarantee. **Miscellaneous:** Reduced fees (weekdays, low season, twilight, juniors), discount packages, metal spikes, range (grass/mats), club rentals, credit cards (MC, V, AE, Diners Club, JCB).
Reader Comments: Green's bumpy, everything else great ... Great course, high in price ... Front 9 long, back 9 short, quite strange ... Great course but too many houses ... Long, tough course ... Serves as U.S. Open qualifier.

MASON VALLEY COUNTRY CLUB
SP-111 Hwy. 208, Yerington, 89447, (702)463-3300.
Special Notes: Call club for further information.

THE MIRAGE GOLF CLUB
R-3650 Las Vegas Blvd. S., Las Vegas, 89177, Clark County, (702)369-7111, (800)217-4653. **Holes:** 18. **Yards:** 7,300/6,163. **Par:** 72/72. **Course Rating:** 73.7/74.5. **Slope:** 132/119. **Green Fee:** $60/$150. **Cart Fee:** Included in Green Fee. **Walking Policy:** Mandatory cart. **Walkability:** N/A. **Opened:** 1964. **Season:** Year-round. **High:** Sep-Nov/Mar-Jun. **To obtain tee times:** Call. **Miscellaneous:** Reduced fees (weekdays, low season, resort guests, twilight), metal spikes, club rentals, credit cards (MC, V, AE, D, Diners Club).

★★★★ MOJAVE RESORT GOLF CLUB
PU-9905 Aha Macav Pkwy., Laughlin, 89029, Clark County, (702)535-4653. **Web:** www.mojaveresort.com.
Holes: 18. **Yards:** 6,939/5,520. **Par:** 72/72. **Course Rating:** 73.2/72.3. **Slope:** 126/124. **Green Fee:** $45/$75. **Cart Fee:** Included in Green Fee. **Walking Policy:** Mandatory cart. **Walkability:** 2. **Opened:** 1997. **Architect:** Landmark Golf Company. **Season:** Year-round. **High:** Jan. **Miscellaneous:** Reduced fees (low season, twilight, seniors), discount packages, range (grass), club rentals, credit cards (MC, V, AE, D).
Reader Comments: Great reason to get away from the tables in Laughlin ... Brutal when the wind blows ... Enjoyable service you ... Beautiful course, great service, lots of sand ... Fun.

NELLIS AFB GOLF COURSE
2841 Kinley Dr., Nellis AFB, 89191, (702)652-2602.
Special Notes: Call club for further information.

★★★ NORTHGATE GOLF COURSE
PU-1111 Clubhouse Dr., Reno, 89523, Washoe County, (702)747-7577, 5 miles NW of Reno. **Holes:** 18. **Yards:** 6,966/5,521. **Par:** 72/72. **Course Rating:** 72.3/70.2. **Slope:** 131/127. **Green Fee:** $29/$46. **Cart Fee:** Included in Green Fee. **Walking Policy:** Unrestricted walking. **Walkability:** 5. **Opened:** 1988. **Architect:** Benz Poellot. **Season:** Year-round. **High:** June-Sept. **To obtain tee times:** Call 7 days in advance. **Miscellaneous:** Reduced fees (weekdays, low season, resort guests, twilight), metal spikes, range (grass/mats), rentals, credit cards (MC, V). **Reader Comments:** Many blind landing areas ... Must keep ball in play to score well ... Keep close eye for rattlesnakes ... True links, windy & firm, need your bump & run ... Trouble abounds ... Excellent layout.

OASIS RESORT HOTEL CASINO
★★★★½ OASIS GOLF COURSE *Condition, Pace*
R-851 Oasis Blvd., Mesquite, 89024, Clark County, (702)346-7820, (800)621-0187, 85 miles N of Las Vegas.
Holes: 27. **Yards:** 6,982/4,627. **Par:** 71/71. **Course Rating:** 73.2/65.7. **Slope:** 141/110. **Green Fee:** $60/$135. **Cart Fee:** Included in Green Fee. **Walking Policy:** Mandatory cart. **Walkability:** 5. **Opened:** 1995. **Architect:** Arnold Palmer/Ed Seay. **Season:** Year-round. **High:** Jan.-May/Oct.-Nov. **To obtain tee times:** Call up to 60 days in advance. **Miscellaneous:** Reduced fees (low season, resort guests, twilight), discount packages, range (grass), club rentals, lodging (1,000 rooms), credit cards (MC, V, AE, D).
Reader Comments: Very challenging ... Canyon holes–awesome! ... Great course, wonderful vistas, a must play ... Great mountains vistas. Wind and elevation changes can make club selection difficult ... Absolutely beautiful! ... Rough not bad and wildflowers were in bloom ... Way too difficult for a high handicapper like me!
★★★½ PALMS GOLF COURSE
R-711 Palms Blvd., Mesquite, 89024, Clark County, (702)346-5232, (800)621-0187, 77 miles NE of Las Vegas.
Holes: 18. **Yards:** 7,008/6,284. **Par:** 72/72. **Course Rating:** 74.9/70.4. **Slope:** 137/122. **Green Fee:** $65/$110. **Cart Fee:** Included in Green Fee. **Walking Policy:** Mandatory cart. **Walkability:**

4. Opened: 1989. **Architect:** William Hull. **Season:** Year-round. **High:** Jan.-May/Oct.-Nov. **To obtain tee times:** Call up to 60 days in advance-guest, 14 days in advance-nonguest. **Miscellaneous:** Reduced fees (weekdays, low season, resort guests, twilight), discount packages, range (grass/mats), club rentals, lodging (1,000 rooms), credit cards (MC, V, AE, D). **Reader Comments:** Great course, good condition, very enjoyable ... Interesting holes & vistas ... Oasis, excellent course, expensive ... Serene front 9, followed by rugged, mountainous back 9. A must play if in the area. **Special Notes:** Formerly Peppermill Palms Golf Club.

★★★★ PAINTED DESERT GOLF CLUB

R-5555 Painted Mirage Way, Las Vegas, 89129, Clark County, (702)645-2570. **Holes:** 18. **Yards:** 6,840/5,711. **Par:** 72/72. **Course Rating:** 73.7/72.7. **Slope:** 136/127. **Green Fee:** $45/$140. **Cart Fee:** Included in Green Fee. **Walking Policy:** Mandatory cart. **Walkability:** N/A. **Opened:** 1987. **Architect:** Jay Morrish. **Season:** Year-round. **High:** Sept.-June. **To obtain tee times:** Call 7 days in advance. **Miscellaneous:** Reduced fees (weekdays, low season, resort guests, twilight, juniors), metal spikes, range (grass/mats), club rentals, credit cards (MC, V, AE). **Reader Comments:** Excellent target course ... Good service. Good holes ... Too expensive ... Worth the drive from the Strip ... Take an old beat up seven iron to get out of desert with ... No. 4 is a signature hole ... Clubhouse and food could improve ... Challenging, creative & witty.

PALM VALLEY GOLF COURSE

SP-9201 Del Webb Blvd., Las Vegas, 89134, Clark County, (702)363-4373. **Holes:** 18. **Yards:** 6,849/5,502. **Par:** 72/72. **Course Rating:** 72.3/70.7. **Slope:** 127/119. **Green Fee:** $42/$101. **Cart Fee:** Included in Green Fee. **Walking Policy:** Mandatory cart. **Walkability:** 3. **Architect:** Greg Nash/Billy Casper. **Season:** Oct.-Sept. **High:** Oct.-May. **To obtain tee times:** We take tee times 7 days in advance after 3:00 p.m. We are semi-private golf course that members do have preference tee times. **Miscellaneous:** Reduced fees (low season), range (grass/mats), club rentals, credit cards (MC, V, AE, D).

PEPPERMILL PALMS GOLF COURSE

R-1137 Mesquite Blvd., Mesquite, 89024, (800)621-0187. **Special Notes:** Call club for further information.

★★★★ REDHAWK GOLF CLUB

PU-7755 Spanish Springs Rd., Sparks, 89436, Washoe County, (775)626-6000, 12 miles NE of Reno. **E-mail:** lanef@concentric.com. **Web:** www.wingfieldsprings.com. **Holes:** 18. **Yards:** 7,127/5,115. **Par:** 72/72. **Course Rating:** 72.9/69.2. **Slope:** 137/125. **Green Fee:** $40/$80. **Cart Fee:** Included in Green Fee. **Walking Policy:** Unrestricted walking. **Walkability:** 3. **Opened:** 1997. **Architect:** Robert Trent Jones Jr. **Season:** Year-round. **High:** May-Sept. **To obtain tee times:** Public call 6 days in advance. **Miscellaneous:** Reduced fees (twilight, juniors), discount packages, range (grass), club rentals, credit cards (MC, V, AE), beginner friendly (golf schools). **Reader Comments:** Quality course but somewhat pricey ... Practice your bunker play before you play here ... Will be excellent, new course ... Flat wetlands ... Groomed to perfection. Well designed and par-3 17th requires mammoth shot with prevailing wind from blue tees.

REFLECTION BAY GOLF CLUB

R-75 MonteLago Blvd., Henderson, 89011, Clark County, (702)740-4653, (877)698-4653, 17 miles SE of Las Vegas Strip. **Web:** www.reflectionbaygolfclub.com. **Holes:** 18. **Yards:** 7,261/5,166. **Par:** 72/72. **Course Rating:** 74.8/70.0. **Slope:** 138/127. **Green Fee:** $200/$200. **Cart Fee:** Included in Green Fee. **Walking Policy:** Mandatory cart. **Walkability:** 5. **Opened:** 1998. **Architect:** Jack Nicklaus. **Season:** Year round. **High:** Jan.-June/Oct.-Nov. **To obtain tee times:** Hyatt Resort guests can call 90 days in advance; public 3 days. **Miscellaneous:** Range (grass), club rentals, lodging (496 rooms), credit cards (MC, V, AE) (Nicklaus/Flick Golf School). **Special Notes:** Host Wendy's 3 Tour Challenge/December.

THE REVERE AT ANTHEM

PU-2600 Evergreen Oaks, Henderson, 89012, Clark County, (702)259-4653, (877)273-8373, 15 miles SE of Las Vegas. **Holes:** 18. **Yards:** 7,143/5,305. **Par:** 72/72. **Course Rating:** 73.6/73.5. **Slope:** 139/122. **Green Fee:** $100/$175. **Cart Fee:** Included in Green Fee. **Walking Policy:** Walking at certain times. **Walkability:** 4. **Opened:** 1999. **Architect:** Billy Casper/Greg Nash. **Season:** Year-round. **High:** Sept.-May. **To obtain tee times:** 60 days in advance. **Miscellaneous:** Reduced fees (twilight), range (grass), club rentals, credit cards (MC, V, AE).

RHODES RANCH COUNTRY CLUB

PU-20 Rhodes Ranch Pkwy., Las Vegas, 89113, Clark County, (702)740-4114, (888)311-8337. **Web:** www.rhodesranch.com. **Holes:** 18. **Yards:** 6,909/5,238. **Par:** 72/72. **Course Rating:** 73.0/64.8. **Slope:** 122/110. **Green Fee:** N/A. **Cart Fee:** Included in Green Fee. **Walking Policy:** Unrestricted walking. **Walkability:**

2. **Opened:** 1997. **Architect:** Ted Robinson/Ted Robinson Jr. **Season:** Jan.-Dec. **High:** March-May/Oct.-Nov. **Miscellaneous:** Reduced fees (weekdays, low season, twilight), range (grass/mats), club rentals, credit cards (MC, V, D).

RIO SECCO GOLF CLUB
PU-2851 Grand Hills Dr., Henderson, 89012, (702)897-9300, (888)867-3226.
Special Notes: Call club for further information.

★★★½ ROSEWOOD LAKES GOLF COURSE
PU-6800 Pembroke Dr., Reno, 89502, Washoe County, (775)857-2892, (888)236-8725.
Holes: 18. **Yards:** 6,693/5,082. **Par:** 72/72. **Course Rating:** 71.1/68.2. **Slope:** 127/117. **Green Fee:** $15/$33. **Cart Fee:** $22/cart. **Walking Policy:** Unrestricted walking. **Walkability:** 2.
Opened: 1991. **Architect:** Bradford Benz. **Season:** Year-round. **High:** April-Nov. **To obtain tee times:** Call 7 days in advance for weekdays and Monday prior for weekends. **Miscellaneous:** Reduced fees (low season, twilight, juniors), metal spikes, range (grass), club rentals, credit cards (MC, V).
Reader Comments: Use every club in bag. Wildlife is great ... Best condition of public courses, target golf ... Gets crowded, little TLC would go a long way ... Lots of natural wetlands with natural growth creating `blind' shots ... Requires accurate shot selection ... Know your hitting distance.

ROYAL LINKS GOLF CLUB
PU-5995 E. Vegas Valley Rd., Las Vegas, 89122, Clark County, (702)450-8123, (888)427-6682, 5 miles E of Las Vegas. **Web:** www.waltersgolf.com.
Holes: 18. **Yards:** 7,029/5,142. **Par:** 72/72. **Course Rating:** 73.7/69.8. **Slope:** 135/115. **Green Fee:** $195/$250. **Cart Fee:** Included in Green Fee. **Walking Policy:** Unrestricted walking.
Walkability: 2. **Opened:** 1999. **Architect:** Perry Dye. **Season:** Year-round. **High:** Oct.-June. **To obtain tee times:** Call reservations line at (888)427-6682. **Miscellaneous:** Reduced fees (weekdays, low season), discount packages, range (grass), caddies, club rentals, credit cards (MC, V, AE, D) (caddy mandatory).

★★★ RUBY VIEW GOLF COURSE
PM-2100 Ruby View Dr., Elko, 89801, Elko County, (775)777-7277. **Web:** golfelko.com.
Holes: 18. **Yards:** 6,945/5,332. **Par:** 71/72. **Course Rating:** 69.5/67.5. **Slope:** 118/117. **Green Fee:** $19/$22. **Cart Fee:** $22/cart. **Walking Policy:** Unrestricted walking. **Walkability:** 2.
Opened: 1967. **Architect:** Jack Snyder. **Season:** March-Nov. **High:** June-Aug. **To obtain tee times:** Call 7 days in advance. **Miscellaneous:** Reduced fees (weekdays, seniors, juniors), range (grass), club rentals, credit cards (MC, V).
Reader Comments: Good course, lush fairways ... Outstanding for this country desert.

SHADOW CREEK GOLF CLUB
R-5400 Losee Rd., North Las Vegas, 89030, (702)399-7111.
Special Notes: Call club for further information.

SIERRA NEVADA GOLF RANCH
PU-2901 Jacks Valley Rd., Genoa, 89411, Douglas County, (775)782-7700, (888)452-4653, 6 miles S of Carson City.
Holes: 18. **Yards:** 7,358/5,129. **Par:** 72/72. **Course Rating:** 75.3/69.5. **Slope:** 137/119. **Green Fee:** $25/$100. **Cart Fee:** Included in Green Fee. **Walking Policy:** Walking at certain times.
Walkability: 5. **Opened:** 1998. **Architect:** Johnny Miller/John Harbottle. **Season:** Year-round.
High: June-Sept. **To obtain tee times:** Call the golf shop. Tee times can be made up to 60 days in advance. Groups 1 year in advance (775)954-4011 (Brooke Collins). **Miscellaneous:** Reduced fees (weekdays, low season, twilight, juniors), discount packages, range (grass), club rentals, credit cards (MC, V, AE), beginner friendly (junior programs/professional instructions).

★★ SIERRA SAGE GOLF COURSE
PM-6355 Silverlake Rd., Reno, 89506, Washoe County, (775)972-1564, 120 miles N of Reno.
Holes: 18. **Yards:** 6,650/5,573. **Par:** 71/72. **Course Rating:** 69.3/69.6. **Slope:** 120/113. **Green Fee:** $18/$24. **Cart Fee:** $10/person. **Walking Policy:** Unrestricted walking. **Walkability:** 3.
Opened: 1963. **Season:** Year-round. **High:** May-Oct. **To obtain tee times:** Call on Monday for upcoming weekend. Call on Tuesday at 7 a.m. for holidays. Call 7 days in advance.
Miscellaneous: Reduced fees (weekdays, low season, twilight, seniors, juniors), metal spikes, range (grass/mats), club rentals, credit cards (MC, V).

SPRING CREEK GOLF COURSE
PU-431 E. Spring Creek Pkwy., Elko, 89801, Elko County, (702)753-6331.
Holes: 18. **Yards:** 6,258/5,658. **Par:** 71/71. **Course Rating:** N/A. **Slope:** 125/119. **Green Fee:** $14/$16. **Walkability:** 5. **Season:** March-Nov. **High:** June-Aug. **To obtain tee times:** Call.
Miscellaneous: Discount packages, range (grass/mats), credit cards (MC, V).

NEVADA

SUN CITY LAS VEGAS GOLF CLUB

SP-10201 Sun City Blvd., Las Vegas, 89134, Clark County, (702)254-7010. **Web:** www.suncity-golf.com.

HIGHLAND FALLS COURSE

Holes: 18. **Yards:** 6,512/5,099. **Par:** 72/72. **Course Rating:** 71.2/68.8. **Slope:** 126/110. **Green Fee:** $59/$101. **Cart Fee:** Included in Green Fee. **Walking Policy:** Mandatory cart. **Walkability:** 3. **Opened:** 1993. **Architect:** Billy Casper/Greg Nash. **Season:** Year-round. **High:** Oct.-May. **To obtain tee times:** Call 7 days in advance for weekends. Call up to 3 days in advance after 3 p.m. for weekdays. **Miscellaneous:** Reduced fees (low season, twilight), metal spikes, range (grass/mats), club rentals, credit cards (MC, V, AE, D).

PALM VALLEY COURSE

SP-9201-B Del Webb Blvd., Las Vegas, 89134, Clark County, (702)254-7010. **Web:** www.suncitygolf.com.

Holes: 18. **Yards:** 6,849/5,502. **Par:** 72/72. **Course Rating:** 72.3/71.5. **Slope:** 127/124. **Green Fee:** $59/$101. **Cart Fee:** Included in Green Fee. **Walking Policy:** Mandatory cart. **Walkability:** 2. **Opened:** 1989. **Architect:** Billy Casper/Greg Nash. **Season:** Year-round. **High:** Oct.-May. **To obtain tee times:** Call 7 days in advance for weekends and 3 days for weekdays after 3 p.m. **Miscellaneous:** Reduced fees (low season, twilight), metal spikes, range (grass/mats), club rentals, credit cards (MC, V, AE, D).

SUNRISE VISTA GOLF CLUB

M-2841 Kinley Dr., Nellis AFB, 89191, Clark County, (702)652-2602, 12 miles N of Las Vegas. **Holes:** 27. **Green Fee:** $35/$35. **Cart Fee:** $9/person. **Walking Policy:** Unrestricted walking. **Walkability:** 2. **Opened:** 1962. **Architect:** Ted Robinson. **Season:** Year-round. **High:** Sept.-April. **To obtain tee times:** Public call day of play. Military call up to 3 days in advance. **Miscellaneous:** Range (grass/mats), club rentals, credit cards (MC, V).

★★★½ **EAGLE/FALCON**
Yards: 7,200/5,380. **Par:** 72/72. **Course Rating:** 73.8/N/A. **Slope:** 127/N/A.
Reader Comments: Very good condition for military course ... New 9, needs to mature.

★★★½ **PHANTOM/EAGLE**
Yards: 7,102/5,460. **Par:** 72/72. **Course Rating:** 72.3/69.1. **Slope:** 119/109.
Reader Comments: Who said the military couldn't get it right! They did! ... New 9 adds a lot, easy walk.

★★★½ **PHANTOM/FALCON**
Yards: 6,950/5,370. **Par:** 72/72. **Course Rating:** 71.8/N/A. **Slope:** 119/N/A.
Reader Comments: Who said the military couldn't get it right! They did! ... New 9 adds a lot, easy walk.

★★★½ **TOANA VISTA GOLF COURSE**

PU-2319 Pueblo Blvd. P. O. Box 2290, Wendover, 89883, Elko County, (775)664-4300, (800)352-4330, 110 miles W of Salt Lake City.

Holes: 18. **Yards:** 6,911/5,220. **Par:** 72/72. **Course Rating:** 72.6/71.0. **Slope:** 124/124. **Green Fee:** $40/$40. **Cart Fee:** Included in Green Fee. **Walking Policy:** Mandatory cart. **Walkability:** 3. **Opened:** 1986. **Architect:** Homer Flint. **Season:** Feb.-Nov. **High:** April-Sept. **To obtain tee times:** Call 14 days in advance. **Miscellaneous:** Reduced fees (resort guests, juniors), discount packages, metal spikes, range (grass/mats), club rentals, credit cards (MC, V). **Reader Comments:** A jewel in the desert. Watch out for snakes and lizards! ... Narrow and tough putting ... Stop here! Play this one.

★★★★ **TOURNAMENT PLAYERS CLUB AT THE CANYONS**

R-9851 Canyon Run Dr., Las Vegas, 89144, Clark County, (702)256-2000, 8 miles NW of Las Vegas. **E-mail:** tplcanyons@isat.com. **Web:** pgatour.com.

Holes: 18. **Yards:** 7,063/5,039. **Par:** 71/71. **Course Rating:** 73.0/67.0. **Slope:** 131/109. **Green Fee:** $35/$145. **Cart Fee:** Included in Green Fee. **Walking Policy:** Walking at certain times. **Walkability:** 5. **Opened:** 1996. **Architect:** Bobby Weed/Raymond Floyd. **Season:** Year-round. **High:** Jan.-May/Oct.-Dec. **To obtain tee times:** Must guarantee tee time reservation with major credit card unless within 48 hours. Reservations can be made up to 1 year in advance and guaranteed with a major credit card. **Miscellaneous:** Reduced fees (low season, juniors), metal spikes, range (grass), club rentals, credit cards (MC, V, AE, Diners Club). **Reader Comments:** Great finishing holes ... Intimidating from the back tees ... Friendly staff, pot bunkers abound ... TPC says it all, great ... Expensive but good experience ... The fairways were in excellent condition ... Great condition, typical Southwest windy condition ... Some spectacular holes, great challenge.

★★★ **WASHOE COUNTY GOLF CLUB**

PM-2601 S. Arlington, Reno, 89509, Washoe County, (775)828-6640, 3 miles S of Reno (downtown). **Web:** www.washoegolf.com.

Holes: 18. **Yards:** 6,695/5,863. **Par:** 72/74. **Course Rating:** 70.0/72.9. **Slope:** 119/122. **Green Fee:** $19/$25. **Cart Fee:** $21/person. **Walking Policy:** Unrestricted walking. **Walkability:** 3.

NEVADA

Opened: 1936. **Architect:** WPA. **Season:** Year-round. **High:** April-Oct. **To obtain tee times:** Call 7 days in advance. **Miscellaneous:** Reduced fees (low season, twilight, seniors, juniors), range (mats), club rentals, credit cards (MC, V).
Reader Comments: Public golf course with lots of play ... Old mature course, small elevated greens ... Good muny course ... Crowded but fun ... Best value in Reno.

★★½ WILD HORSE GOLF CLUB
R-2100 Warm Springs Rd., Henderson, 89014, Clark County, (702)434-9000, (800)468-7918, 8 miles SE of Las Vegas.
Holes: 18. **Yards:** 7,053/5,372. **Par:** 72/72. **Course Rating:** 75.2/71.3. **Slope:** 135/125. **Green Fee:** $50/$140. **Cart Fee:** Included in Green Fee. **Walking Policy:** Mandatory cart. **Walkability:** 3. **Opened:** 1959. **Architect:** Robert Cupp/Hubert Green. **Season:** Year-round. **High:** Sept.-June. **To obtain tee times:** Call 800 for 60 days in advance. Golf shop will book 7 days in advance. **Miscellaneous:** Reduced fees (weekdays, low season, resort guests, twilight, juniors), discount packages, range (grass/mats), club rentals, credit cards (MC, V, AE).
Reader Comments: Well maintained, very professional staff ... Too expensive ... Pretty slow play. Pretty fast greens ... A yardage book would really have helped ... Provides some great blind tee shots and approach shots.

★★★ WILDCREEK GOLF COURSE
PU-3500 Sullivan Lane, Sparks, 89431, Washoe County, (775)673-3100, 1 miles NE of Reno. **E-mail:** wcnggolf@rscva.com.
Holes: 27. **Yards:** 6,932/5,472. **Par:** 72/72. **Course Rating:** 72.5/69.9. **Slope:** 133/127. **Green Fee:** $37/$50. **Cart Fee:** Included in Green Fee. **Walking Policy:** Mandatory cart. **Walkability:** 5. **Opened:** 1978. **Architect:** Benz-Phelps. **Season:** Year-round. **High:** April-Oct. **To obtain tee times:** Call 7 days in advance. **Miscellaneous:** Reduced fees (low season, twilight), metal spikes, range (grass), credit cards (MC, V).
Reader Comments: Hilly golf course ... Very good value & a fun course to play ... Challenging public course recently improved ... Greens hard to read ... Good condition, even in winter ... Greens like rolling glass ... Get done before the winds comes.

WOLF RUN GOLF CLUB
PU-1400 Wolf Run Rd., Reno, 89511, Washoe County, (775)851-3301, 10 miles S of Reno.
Holes: 18. **Yards:** 6,936/5,294. **Par:** 71/71. **Course Rating:** 72.1/69.7. **Slope:** 130/128. **Green Fee:** $20/$50. **Cart Fee:** $10/person. **Walking Policy:** Unrestricted walking. **Walkability:** 3. **Opened:** 1998. **Architect:** John Fleming/Steve van Meter/Lou Eiguren. **Season:** Year round. **High:** May-Sept. **To obtain tee times:** Call golf shop or tee time central (888)CENTRAL. **Miscellaneous:** Reduced fees (weekdays, low season, twilight, seniors, juniors), range (grass/mats), club rentals, credit cards (MC, V, AE), beginner friendly (private/group lessons).

NEW HAMPSHIRE

★★★ AMHERST COUNTRY CLUB
PU-72Ponemah Rd., Amherst, 03031, Hillsborough County, (603)673-9908, 10 miles W of Nashua.
Holes: 18. **Yards:** 6,520/5,532. **Par:** 72/74. **Course Rating:** 71.0/74.2. **Slope:** 123/129. **Green Fee:** $15/$42. **Cart Fee:** $140/person. **Walking Policy:** Unrestricted walking. **Walkability:** 2. **Opened:** 1965. **Architect:** William F. Mitchell. **Season:** March-Dec. **High:** May-Oct. **To obtain tee times:** Call 5 days in advance. **Miscellaneous:** Reduced fees (weekdays, low season, twilight, seniors), club rentals, credit cards (MC, V).
Reader Comments: The best two greens are near the clubhouse ... Well laid out course, lots of dog legs ... Very challenging, my driveway is wider than some of the fairways

ANDROSCOGGIN VALLEY COUNTRY CLUB
SP-2 Main Street, Gorham, 03581, Coos County, (603)466-9468.
Holes: 18. **Yards:** 5,764/4,808. **Par:** 70/70. **Course Rating:** 67.0/70.1. **Slope:** 114/118. **Green Fee:** $20/$24. **Cart Fee:** $25/cart. **Walking Policy:** Unrestricted walking. **Walkability:** 1. **Opened:** 1922. **Season:** May-Oct. **High:** June-Aug. **To obtain tee times:** Call 24 hours in advance. **Miscellaneous:** Reduced fees (weekdays, juniors), discount packages, range (grass), club rentals, lodging (150 rooms), credit cards (MC, V), beginner friendly (junior clinics and ladies clinics).

★★★★½ THE BALSAMS GRAND RESORT HOTEL   *Service+, Pace*
R-Rte. 26, Dixville Notch, 03576, Coos County, (603)255-4961, 110 miles NE of Manchester. E-mail: thebalsams@aol.com . **Web:** www.thebalsams.com.
Holes: 18. **Yards:** 6,804/5,069. **Par:** 72/72. **Course Rating:** 73.9/67.8. **Slope:** 136/115. **Green Fee:** $50/$60. **Cart Fee:** $18/person. **Walking Policy:** Unrestricted walking. **Walkability:** 4. **Opened:** 1912. **Architect:** Donald Ross. **Season:** May-Oct. **High:** July-Aug. **To obtain tee times:** Hotel guests call up to 7 days in advance all others up to 3 days. **Miscellaneous:** Reduced fees (resort guests), discount packages, metal spikes, range (grass/mats), club rentals, lodging (204 rooms), credit cards (MC, V, AE, D).
Notes: Ranked 1st in 1999 Best in State.
Reader Comments: Bring a camera and play at peak foliage ... Save some energy for the 18th hole! ... Great fun. Long holes. Difficult greens ... Donald Ross mountain masterpiece ... Food and service are amazing ... Outstanding panoramic views ... Lots of sidehill lies ... Must be in good shape to walk ... Very good 19th hole.

★★★½ BEAVER MEADOW GOLF CLUB
PU-1 Beaver Meadow Dr., Concord, 03301, Merrimack County, (603)228-8954.
Holes: 18. **Yards:** 6,356/5,519. **Par:** 72/72. **Course Rating:** 70.0/71.8. **Slope:** 121/123. **Green Fee:** $15/$29. **Cart Fee:** $24/cart. **Walking Policy:** Unrestricted walking. **Walkability:** 1. **Opened:** 1896. **Architect:** Geoffrey Cornish. **Season:** April-Nov. **High:** May-Sept. **To obtain tee times:** First come, first served on weekdays. Call Wednesdays at 7:00 a.m. for weekend tee times. **Miscellaneous:** Reduced fees (weekdays, low season, twilight, seniors, juniors), metal spikes, range (grass/mats), club rentals, credit cards (MC, V), beginner friendly.
Reader Comments: Easy front nine, tougher back ... Great views ... Narrow, sound of balls hitting pine trees ... Most picturesque in all New England ... I loved it ... Very tough. Pretty in the fall.

★★ BETHLEHEM COUNTRY CLUB
PM-1901 Main St., Rte. 302, Bethlehem, 03574, Grafton County, (603)869-5745, 80 miles N of Concord.
Holes: 18. **Yards:** 5,808/5,008. **Par:** 70/70. **Course Rating:** 68.2/67.8. **Slope:** 114/109. **Green Fee:** $25/$28. **Cart Fee:** $12/person. **Walking Policy:** Unrestricted walking. **Walkability:** 1. **Opened:** 1898. **Architect:** Donald Ross. **Season:** May-Oct. **High:** July-Aug. **To obtain tee times:** Call the golf shop (603)869-5745 between 7:00 a.m. and 7:00 p.m. **Miscellaneous:** Reduced fees (weekdays, resort guests, twilight, juniors), discount packages, club rentals, credit cards (MC, V), beginner friendly.

BRETWOOD GOLF COURSE
PU-East Surry Rd., Keene, 03431, Cheshire County, (603)352-7626.
★★★★ NORTH COURSE
Holes: 18. **Yards:** 6,974/5,140. **Par:** 72/72. **Course Rating:** 73.3/70.0. **Slope:** 139/121. **Green Fee:** $28/$35. **Cart Fee:** $20/cart. **Walking Policy:** Unrestricted walking. **Walkability:** 3. **Opened:** 1968. **Architect:** Geoffrey Cornish/Hugh Barrett. **Season:** April-Nov. **High:** June-Oct. **To obtain tee times:** Call Wednesday for upcoming weekend. **Miscellaneous:** Reduced fees (twilight), metal spikes, range (grass), club rentals, credit cards (MC, V, D).
Notes: Ranked 6th in 1999 Best in State.
Reader Comments: Well treated ... Scenic, course in great shape ... Best value of any New England course by far ... A treat to play ... Greatest deck for a cold beer ... Sometimes deceiving, unforgiving ... Covered bridges were memorable ... Worth the ride from Boston ... Nice variety.
★★★★ SOUTH COURSE   *Value+*

Holes: 18. **Yards:** 6,952/4,990. **Par:** 72/71. **Course Rating:** 73.7/70.1. **Slope:** 136/120. **Green Fee:** $28/$35. **Cart Fee:** $20/cart. **Walking Policy:** Unrestricted walking. **Walkability:** 3. **Opened:** 1968. **Architect:** Geoffrey Cornish/Hugh Barrett. **Season:** April-Nov. **High:** June-Oct. **To obtain tee times:** Call Wednesday for upcoming weekend. **Miscellaneous:** Reduced fees (twilight), metal spikes, range (grass), club rentals, credit cards (MC, V, D).
Reader Comments: Excellent greens ... Toughest 6 finishing holes one can imagine ... Take a picture of the 16th ... Gives shotmakers a nice challenge ... First hole lulls you into complacency. Then the water comes to drown you ... Starting to outshine the North course.

★★★★ CAMPBELL'S SCOTTISH HIGHLANDS GOLF COURSE
PU-79 Brady Ave., Salem, 03079, Rockingham County, (603)894-4653, 30 miles N of Boston.
Holes: 18. **Yards:** 6,249/5,056. **Par:** 71/71. **Course Rating:** 68.9/68.4. **Slope:** 124/114. **Green Fee:** $28/$35. **Cart Fee:** $12/person. **Walking Policy:** Unrestricted walking. **Walkability:** 3.
Opened: 1994. **Architect:** George F. Sargent & MHF Design. **Season:** April-Nov. **High:** June-Sept. **To obtain tee times:** Call 5 days in advance. **Miscellaneous:** Reduced fees (weekdays, low season, twilight, seniors), range (grass/mats), club rentals, credit cards (MC, V).
Reader Comments: Course for all levels of play... Uniquely Scottish ... Don't play in dry conditions ... Always good ... Front 9 wide open ... Short but greens make it a challenge ... An old farm once stood, now a challenging experience ... Not too difficult ... Good test, some easy holes.

★★★ CANDIA WOODS GOLF LINKS
PU-313 S. Rd., Candia, 03034, Rockingham County, (603)483-2307, (800)564-4344, 10 miles NE of Manchester. **E-mail:** candiawds@aol.com. **Web:** www.candiawoods.com.
Holes: 18. **Yards:** 6,558/5,582. **Par:** 71/73. **Course Rating:** 70.9/71.7. **Slope:** 121/127. **Green Fee:** $29/$39. **Cart Fee:** $12/person. **Walking Policy:** Unrestricted walking. **Walkability:** 3.
Opened: 1964. **Architect:** Phil Wogan. **Season:** March-Dec. **High:** June-Sept. **To obtain tee times:** Call 5 days in advance. **Miscellaneous:** Reduced fees (weekdays, low season, twilight, seniors, juniors), range (grass/mats), club rentals, credit cards (MC, V, D), beginner friendly.
Reader Comments: Tricky greens to read ... Challenging par 3s ... Too many doglegs ... Very busy course, some nice holes ... Very easy, good for beginners.

★★★★ COUNTRY CLUB OF NEW HAMPSHIRE
PU-Kearsarge Valley Rd., North Sutton, 03260, Merrimack County, (603)927-4246, 30 miles NW of Concord. **E-mail:** ccnh@conknet.com.
Holes: 18. **Yards:** 6,727/5,446. **Par:** 72/72. **Course Rating:** 72.5/71.7. **Slope:** 134/127. **Green Fee:** $25/$34. **Cart Fee:** $12/person. **Walking Policy:** Unrestricted walking. **Walkability:** 3.
Opened: 1957. **Architect:** William Mitchell. **Season:** April-Nov. **High:** July-Sept. **To obtain tee times:** Call up to 7 days in advance. Motel guests and outings can book anytime.
Miscellaneous: Reduced fees (weekdays, twilight), discount packages, range (grass), club rentals, lodging (28 rooms), credit cards (MC, V, D), beginner friendly (group lessons).
Notes: Ranked 7th in 1999 Best in State.
Reader Comments: Don't forget your sand wedge ... I'd play here everyday if I could ... Excellent greens, great views ... Good variety of holes ... The views will make you forget those 3 putts ... A must-play New Hampshire course ... Good challenge.

DEN BRAE GOLF COURSE
PU-80 Prescott Rd., Sanborton, 03269, Belknap County, (603)934-9818, 18 miles N of Concord. **Web:** www.denbrae.com.
Holes: 9. **Yards:** 6,040/5,326. **Par:** 72/72. **Course Rating:** 67.0/70.0. **Slope:** 112/123. **Green Fee:** $22/$24. **Cart Fee:** $20/cart. **Walking Policy:** Unrestricted walking. **Walkability:** 3.
Opened: 1958. **Season:** April-Nov. **High:** June-Aug. **To obtain tee times:** Call (603)934-9818. **Miscellaneous:** Reduced fees (low season, twilight, juniors), range (grass), club rentals, credit cards (MC, V, AE).

★★ DERRYFIELD COUNTRY CLUB
PU-625 Mammoth Rd., Manchester, 03104, Hillsborough County, (603)669-0235. **E-mail:** derryfieldgolf@juno.com. **Web:** www.derryfieldgolf.com.
Holes: 18. **Yards:** 6,100/5,535. **Par:** 70/74. **Course Rating:** 68.7/71.0. **Slope:** 113/125. **Green Fee:** $26/$26. **Cart Fee:** $22/cart. **Walking Policy:** Unrestricted walking. **Walkability:** 4.
Opened: 1932. **Architect:** Wayne Stiles/John Van Kleek. **Season:** April-Dec. **High:** June-Sept. **To obtain tee times:** Call on Thursday for upcoming weekend and holiday. First come, first served on weekdays. **Miscellaneous:** Club rentals, credit cards (MC, V).

★★★★ EASTMAN GOLF LINKS
SP-Clubhouse Lane, Grantham, 03753, Sullivan County, (603)863-4500, 43 miles NW of Concord.
Holes: 18. **Yards:** 6,731/5,369. **Par:** 71/73. **Course Rating:** 73.5/71.9. **Slope:** 136/128. **Green Fee:** $40/$40. **Cart Fee:** $16/person. **Walking Policy:** Walking at certain times. **Walkability:** 3.
Opened: 1973. **Architect:** Geoffrey Cornish. **Season:** May-Nov. **High:** July-Sept. **To obtain tee**

times: Call 2 days in advance. **Miscellaneous:** Reduced fees (juniors), range (grass/mats), club rentals, credit cards (MC, V, AE).
Notes: Ranked 9th in 1999 Best in State.
Reader Comments: Beautiful layout and views ... Clubhouse and pro shop is top notch ... Tough course, few flat lies ... Breathtaking in fall ... Blind shots, no room for error ... Accuracy is premium. Course knowledge is important.

GREEN MEADOW GOLF CLUB
PU-59 Steele Rd., Hudson, 03051, Hillsborough County, (603)889-1555, 11 miles S of Manchester.
★★★½ **JUNGLE COURSE**
Holes: 18. **Yards:** 6,495/5,102. **Par:** 72/72. **Course Rating:** 67.6/68.3. **Slope:** 109/113. **Green Fee:** $24/$30. **Cart Fee:** $22/cart. **Walking Policy:** Unrestricted walking. **Walkability:** 2.
Opened: 1959. **Architect:** Philip Friel/David Friel. **Season:** March-Dec. **High:** April-Aug. **To obtain tee times:** Come in 7 days in advance, or call on Monday for upcoming weekend.
Miscellaneous: Reduced fees (weekdays, low season, twilight, seniors, juniors), metal spikes, range (grass), caddies, club rentals, credit cards (MC, V, D).
Reader Comments: Very nice public course ... Flat course, lot of bunkers ... Wide open, great chance to score ... Huge facility. Huge crowds ... New holes add challenge.
★★★ **PRAIRIE COURSE**
Holes: 18. **Yards:** 6,598/5,173. **Par:** 72/72. **Course Rating:** 70.0/71.2. **Slope:** 114/120. **Green Fee:** $24/$30. **Cart Fee:** $22/cart. **Walking Policy:** Unrestricted walking. **Walkability:** 2.
Opened: 1959. **Architect:** Philip Friel/David Friel. **Season:** March-Dec. **High:** April-Aug. **To obtain tee times:** Come in 7 days in advance, or call on Monday for upcoming weekend.
Miscellaneous: Reduced fees (weekdays, low season, twilight, seniors, juniors), metal spikes, range (grass/mats), caddies, club rentals, credit cards (MC, V, D).
Reader Comments: Great new holes ... Gets too much play ... More challenging than North ... Nice wide open course ... Wide open and forgiving holes.

★★★ HANOVER COUNTRY CLUB
SP-Rope Ferry Rd., Hanover, 03755, Grafton County, (603)646-2000, 10 miles N of Lebanon. **E-mail:** www.dartmouth.edu-~/hccweb/.
Holes: 18. **Yards:** 5,876/5,468. **Par:** 69/73. **Course Rating:** 68.7/72.7. **Slope:** 118/127. **Green Fee:** $31/$31. **Cart Fee:** $14/person. **Walking Policy:** Unrestricted walking. **Walkability:** 3.
Opened: 1899. **Architect:** Barton/Smith/Cornish/Robinson. **Season:** April-Nov. **High:** June-Sept. **To obtain tee times:** Call 5 days in advance. **Miscellaneous:** Reduced fees (twilight, juniors), discount packages, metal spikes, range (grass), caddies, club rentals, credit cards (MC, V, AE).
Reader Comments: Beautiful setting ... Sometimes you feel you're in the Alps ... Postage stamp greens, bring your short game ... Needs some work ... If you don't take a cart, may the Lord be with you ... Challenging mountain course.

★★½ HOOPER GOLF CLUB
SP-Prospect Hill, Walpole, 03608, Cheshire County, (603)756-4080, 16 miles N of Keene.
Holes: 9. **Yards:** 3,019/2,748. **Par:** 71/72. **Course Rating:** 69.3/73.5. **Slope:** 122/132. **Green Fee:** N/A/$24. **Cart Fee:** $24/cart. **Walking Policy:** Unrestricted walking. **Walkability:** 3.
Opened: 1927. **Architect:** Wayne Stiles/John Van Kleek. **Season:** April-Oct. **High:** July-Aug. **To obtain tee times:** Tee times not required. Course is closed to public Thursday at 5 p.m. and Saturday and Sunday mornings until 10:30 a.m. **Miscellaneous:** Club rentals, lodging (3 rooms), credit cards (MC, V).
Reader Comments: Beautifully kept, good pace of play ... High and dry in spring ... Great greens, not too hard, not too easy ... Excellent food ... Best golf in fall, scenic ... A great challenge ... WOW.

INDIAN MOUND GOLF CLUB
PU-Old Rte. 16, Center Ossipee, 03814, Carroll County, (603)539-7733.
Holes: 18. **Yards:** 5,700/4,800. **Par:** 70/70. **Course Rating:** 68.5/67.5. **Slope:** 118/117. **Green Fee:** $25/$35. **Cart Fee:** $24/cart. **Walking Policy:** Unrestricted walking. **Walkability:** 3.
Opened: 1972. **Architect:** Phil Wogan. **Season:** April-Nov. **High:** June-Sept. **To obtain tee times:** Call (603)539-7733 for 7 day advance tee times reservations. **Miscellaneous:** Reduced fees (low season, twilight), discount packages, club rentals, credit cards (MC, V).

★★½ JACK O'LANTERN RESORT
R-Rte. 3, Box A, Woodstock, 03292, Grafton County, (603)745-3636, 60 miles N of Manchester.
Holes: 18. **Yards:** 6,003/4,917. **Par:** 70/71. **Course Rating:** 68.6/67.5. **Slope:** 117/113. **Green Fee:** $35/$38. **Cart Fee:** $26/cart. **Walking Policy:** Walking at certain times. **Walkability:** 1.
Opened: 1947. **Architect:** Robert Keating. **Season:** May-Oct. **High:** June-Sept. **To obtain tee times:** Call 1 day in advance. **Miscellaneous:** Reduced fees (weekdays, resort guests, twilight), discount packages, club rentals, lodging (96 rooms), credit cards (MC, V, AE, D).
Reader Comments: Resort course, many dog-legs ... Flat winding layout along river ... Slow play ... Very quiet and scenic ... Nice for a weekend ... Easy track.

★★★ JOHN H. CAIN GOLF CLUB
SP-Unity Rd., Newport, 03773, Sullivan County, (603)863-7787, 35 miles NW of Concord. **Web:** www.johncain.com.
Holes: 18. **Yards:** 6,415/4,738. **Par:** 71/71. **Course Rating:** 72.4/63.8. **Slope:** 134/112. **Green Fee:** $20/$34. **Cart Fee:** $24/cart. **Walking Policy:** Unrestricted walking. **Walkability:** 2. **Opened:** 1920. **Architect:** Phillip Wogan. **Season:** April-Nov. **High:** June-Sept. **To obtain tee times:** Call 7 days in advance. **Miscellaneous:** Reduced fees (weekdays, low season, twilight, seniors, juniors), discount packages, range (grass/mats), club rentals, credit cards (MC, V).
Reader Comments: Nice course some challenging holes ... Hometown favorite ... Last 3 holes are a true test ... In the middle of nowhere ... A superb manicured course ... Lots of water and wildlife ... Dry in summer ... Great challenge especially with 'sucker' holes like 3 and 13, bring plenty of balls.

★★★½ KEENE COUNTRY CLUB
SP-755 W. Hill Rd., Keene, 03431, Cheshire County, (603)352-9722, 60 miles W of Manchester.
Holes: 18. **Yards:** 6,200/5,900. **Par:** 72/75. **Course Rating:** 69.0/72.2. **Slope:** 124/130. **Green Fee:** N/A/$75. **Cart Fee:** Included in Green Fee. **Walking Policy:** Unrestricted walking. **Walkability:** 3. **Opened:** 1900. **Architect:** Wayne Stiles. **Season:** April-Nov. **High:** May-Sept. **To obtain tee times:** Call ahead. **Miscellaneous:** Range (grass), rentals, credit cards (MC, V, AE).
Reader Comments: Great greens. Fairways wet ... Must keep ball below hole ... Fun to play in very good condition ... Nice tight course ... Wonderful classic layout ...Two totally different nines, course can come up and bite you ... A diamond in the rough! ... Nice par 4s.

KINGSTON FAIRWAYS GOLF CLUB
PU-65 Depot Road, Rte. 107, Kingston, 03848, Rockingham County, (603)642-7722, 8 miles S of Exeter.
Holes: 9. **Yards:** 2,864/2,669. **Par:** 35/36. **Course Rating:** 35.5/N/A. **Slope:** 113/N/A. **Green Fee:** $24/$29. **Cart Fee:** $22/cart. **Walking Policy:** Unrestricted walking. **Walkability:** 2. **Opened:** 1994. **Architect:** Colanton. **Season:** April-Oct. **High:** July-Aug. **Miscellaneous:** Reduced fees (weekdays, seniors, juniors), club rentals, credit cards (, Personal Checks). **Special Notes:** Formerly part of East Kingston Golf Club.

KINGSWOOD COUNTRY CLUB
SP-Rte. 28 South Main, Wolfeboro, 03894, Carroll County, (603)569-3569.
Holes: 18. **Yards:** 6,360/5,860. **Par:** 72/72. **Course Rating:** 70.9/68.6. **Slope:** 125/122. **Green Fee:** $20/$40. **Cart Fee:** $26/cart. **Walking Policy:** Walking at certain times. **Walkability:** 3. **Architect:** Donald Ross. **Season:** April-Oct. **High:** June-Sept. **To obtain tee times:** Phone request. **Miscellaneous:** Reduced fees (low season, twilight, juniors), range (grass), club rentals, credit cards (MC, V, D), beginner friendly (youth group lessons and adult group lessons).

★★★½ LACONIA COUNTRY CLUB
SP-607 Elm St., Laconia, 03246, Belknap County, (603)524-1273.
Holes: 18. **Yards:** 6,483/5,552. **Par:** 72/72. **Course Rating:** 71.7/72.1. **Slope:** 128/125. **Green Fee:** $60/$60. **Cart Fee:** Included in Green Fee. **Walking Policy:** Mandatory cart. **Walkability:** N/A. **Opened:** 1926. **Architect:** Wayne Stiles. **Season:** April-Nov. **High:** June-Sept. **To obtain tee times:** Call Thursday for upcoming weekend. **Miscellaneous:** Reduced fees (low season, resort guests, juniors), metal spikes, range (grass), caddies, club rentals, credit cards (MC, V).
Reader Comments: Enjoyable for seniors to play ... Course in midst of 3-year renovation project ... Nice old course, some very nice holes ... 3 long par 3s ... Lots of holes on a hillside.

★★½ MAPLEWOOD COUNTRY CLUB
PU-Rte. 302, Bethlehem, 03574, Grafton County, (603)869-3335, (877)869-3335, 80 miles N of Concord.
Holes: 18. **Yards:** 6,100/5,200. **Par:** 72/72. **Course Rating:** 67.5/68.4. **Slope:** 113/114. **Green Fee:** $27/$32. **Cart Fee:** $12/person. **Walking Policy:** Mandatory cart. **Walkability:** 3. **Opened:** 1907. **Architect:** Donald Ross. **Season:** May-Oct. **High:** May-Sept. **To obtain tee times:** Call anytime. **Miscellaneous:** Reduced fees (weekdays, low season, twilight), discount packages, metal spikes, range (grass), club rentals, credit cards (MC, V, AE, D).
Reader Comments: Par 6 was memorable! ... Improving ... A nice, old course ... Historic ... The front 9 and back 9 are very different. It's like playing two different courses ... Interesting clubhouse design ... Greens can be fastest around.

MOUNT WASHINGTON HOTEL & RESORT
R-Rte. 302, Bretton Woods, 03575, Carroll County, (603)278-4653, (800)258-1330, 90 miles N of Concord.
MOUNT PLEASANT GOLF COURSE
Holes: 9. **Yards:** 3,215/2,475. **Par:** 35/35. **Course Rating:** 71.0/N/A. **Slope:** 122/N/A. **Green Fee:** $35/$40. **Cart Fee:** $25/cart. **Walking Policy:** Walking at certain times. **Walkability:** 2. **Opened:** 1895. **Architect:** Alex Finley/Cornish & Silva. **Season:** May-Oct. **High:** July-Sept. **To obtain tee times:** Call anytime in advance. **Miscellaneous:** Reduced fees (resort guests, twi-

light), discount packages, range (grass), club rentals, lodging (284 rooms), credit cards (MC, V, AE, D).

★★★½ **MOUNT WASHINGTON GOLF COURSE**
Holes: 18. **Yards:** 6,638/5,336. **Par:** 71/71. **Course Rating:** 70.1/70.1. **Slope:** 123/118. **Green Fee:** $35/$40. **Cart Fee:** $25/cart. **Walking Policy:** Walking at certain times. **Walkability:** 3. **Opened:** 1915. **Architect:** Donald Ross. **Season:** May-Oct. **High:** July-Sept. **To obtain tee times:** Call anytime in advance—3days public, 7 days member. With confirmation of booking, advance for guests. **Miscellaneous:** Reduced fees (resort guests, twilight), discount packages, range (grass), club rentals, lodging (284 rooms), credit cards (MC, V, AE, D).
Reader Comments: Always great, especially on clear day ... Awesome scenery! ... Great hotel ... Very impressive ... What views ... Classic design.

MOUNTAIN VIEW GOLF COURSE
PU-Mountain View Rd., Whitefield, 03598 (603)837-3885.
Special Notes: Call club for further information.

★★★½ **NORTH CONWAY COUNTRY CLUB**
SP-Norcross Circle, North Conway, 03860, Carroll County, (603)356-9391.
Holes: 18. **Yards:** 6,522/5,394. **Par:** 71/71. **Course Rating:** 71.9/70.1. **Slope:** 126/118. **Green Fee:** $35/$55. **Cart Fee:** $24/cart. **Walking Policy:** Walking at certain times. **Walkability:** 2. **Opened:** 1895. **Architect:** Alex Findlay/Phil Wogan. **Season:** May-Oct. **High:** June-Oct. **To obtain tee times:** Call 3 days in advance. **Miscellaneous:** Reduced fees (low season, twilight, seniors, juniors), range (grass), club rentals, credit cards (MC, V, AE).
Reader Comments: Easy to play, hard to score. Spectacular views ... Deep rough, well maintained, good stuff ... Lovely setting ... Can be busy in summer ... Tougher than first appears ... Older course with character.

★★★½ **OVERLOOK COUNTRY CLUB**
PU-5 Overlook Dr., Hollis, 03049, Hillsborough County, (603)465-2909, 10 miles W of Nashua.
Holes: 18. **Yards:** 6,290/5,230. **Par:** 71/72. **Course Rating:** 70.2/70.4. **Slope:** 127/121. **Green Fee:** $30/$40. **Cart Fee:** $24/person. **Walking Policy:** Unrestricted walking. **Walkability:** 4. **Opened:** 1989. **Architect:** David E. Friel. **Season:** April-Dec. **High:** June-Aug. **To obtain tee times:** Call 7 days in advance. **Miscellaneous:** Reduced fees (weekdays, twilight, juniors), metal spikes, club rentals, credit cards (MC, V, D).
Reader Comments: Pleasant little track ... Downhill par-3 8th is great ... Beauty, but a little pricey! ... Long from green to tee ... Too slow ... Challenging greens ... Runs along Nashua River ... Wild life all over ... Enjoyable for average golfer ... Many holes are alike ... Great for long hitter.

OWL'S NEST GOLF CLUB
PU-1 Club House Lane, Campton, 03223, Grafton County, (603)726-3076, (888)695-6378, 60 miles N of Concord. **E-mail:** golf@owlsnest.com. **Web:** www.owlsnestgolf.com.
Holes: 18. **Yards:** 6,818/5,296. **Par:** 72/72. **Course Rating:** 74.0/69.8. **Slope:** 133/115. **Green Fee:** $13/$46. **Cart Fee:** $13/person. **Walking Policy:** Walking at certain times. **Walkability:** 4. **Opened:** 1998. **Architect:** Cornish/Silva/Mungeam. **Season:** May-Nov. **High:** May-Oct. **To obtain tee times:** Call (603)726-3076 7 days in advance. The Golf Shop staff answers the phone. **Miscellaneous:** Reduced fees (weekdays, low season, twilight, seniors, juniors), discount packages, range (grass), club rentals, credit cards (MC, V, AE), beginner friendly (novice nesters).

★★★★ **PASSACONAWAY COUNTRY CLUB**
PU-12 Midway Ave., Litchfield, 03052, Hillsborough County, (603)424-4653, 5 miles S of Manchester.
Holes: 18. **Yards:** 6,855/5,369. **Par:** 71/72. **Course Rating:** 72.2/70.3. **Slope:** 126/118. **Green Fee:** $22/$39. **Cart Fee:** $12/person. **Walking Policy:** Unrestricted walking. **Walkability:** 2. **Opened:** 1989. **Architect:** Cornish/Silva. **Season:** April-Dec. **High:** May-Sept. **To obtain tee times:** Call 7 days in advance for weekdays and 5 days in advance for weekends. **Miscellaneous:** Reduced fees (weekdays, low season, twilight, seniors, juniors), club rentals, credit cards (MC, V).
Reader Comments: Large greens ... Always good ... Lots of hackers ... Oh soooo long ... Might rate higher if it weren't for power lines ... Long, windy, tricky greens ... Wear your hard hat ... Good test from blue tees, always windy ... Long hitters dream ... Carts stay on paths ... No need for a 3-wood, except on your 2nd shot.

★★★½ **PEASE GOLF COURSE**
PU-2 Country Club Rd., Portsmouth, 03801, Rockingham County, (603)433-1331.
Holes: 18. **Yards:** 6,328/5,324. **Par:** 71/71. **Course Rating:** 70.8/69.9. **Slope:** 128/120. **Green Fee:** $32/N/A. **Cart Fee:** $12/person. **Walking Policy:** Unrestricted walking. **Walkability:** 2. **Opened:** 1960. **Architect:** Al Zikorus. **Season:** April-Nov. **High:** June-Aug. **To obtain tee times:** Call 3 days in advance. **Miscellaneous:** Range (grass), club rentals, credit cards (MC, V, AE).

Reader Comments: Small greens ... 2 very different 9s; front links, back tree lined and tough ... This former military course is in fantastic condition ... Enjoyable... Crowded ... Aircraft continual.

★★★ PERRY HOLLOW GOLF & COUNTRY CLUB
PU-250 Perry Hollow Rd., Wolfeboro, 03894, Carroll County, (603)569-3055, 3 miles S of Wolfeboro.
Holes: 18. Yards: 6,338/4,788. Par: 71/71. Course Rating: 71.0/67.0. Slope: 132/115. Green Fee: $28/$28. Cart Fee: $24/cart. Walking Policy: Unrestricted walking. Walkability: 4. Architect: Geoffrey S. Cornish/Brian Silva. Season: April-Nov. High: June-Oct. To obtain tee times: Call up to 7 days in advance. Miscellaneous: Reduced fees (low season, juniors), range (grass), club rentals, credit cards (MC, V, AE, D), beginner friendly (school).
Reader Comments: Fancy clubhouse ... Putting green unbelievable ... Spectacular views ... Tight front 9, back 9 needs work ... Good hilly track ... Best layout in state ... Travel to Europe would have been faster ... Some great holes. Good food.

★★★ PLAUSAWA VALLEY COUNTRY CLUB
SP-42 Whittemore Rd., Pembroke, 03275, Merrimack County, (603)224-6267, 3 miles S of Concord.
Holes: 18. Yards: 6,545/5,391. Par: 72/73. Course Rating: 72.6/71.5. Slope: 131/128. Green Fee: $26/$35. Cart Fee: $26/cart. Walking Policy: Unrestricted walking. Walkability: 3. Opened: 1963. Architect: Geoffrey Cornish/Brian Silva/W.Mitchell. Season: April-Nov. High: June-Aug. To obtain tee times: Call 7 days in advance. Miscellaneous: Reduced fees (weekdays, low season, resort guests, twilight, seniors, juniors), discount packages, range (grass), club rentals, credit cards (MC, V).
Reader Comments: Back nine more beautiful & challenging ... Night and day nines. Hard to imagine it is the same course ... Front wide open, back cut through a hilly forest ... Back 9 unique ... Somewhat lengthy with wind.

PONEMAH GREEN FAMILY GOLF CENTER
SP-55 Ponemah Road, Amherst, 03031, Hillsboro County, (603)672-4732, 8 miles W of Nashua. Web: ponemahgreen.com.
Holes: 9. Yards: 4,420/3,608. Par: 68/68. Course Rating: 61.9/62.5. Slope: 114/109. Green Fee: $25/$27. Cart Fee: $24/cart. Walking Policy: Unrestricted walking. Walkability: 2. Opened: 1989. Architect: Geoffrey Cornish. Season: March until snow. High: June-Sept. To obtain tee times: Call 3 days in advance. Miscellaneous: Reduced fees (weekdays, seniors, juniors), range (grass/mats), club rentals, credit cards (MC, V), beginner friendly (adult beginner clinics, golf school).

★★★★ PORTSMOUTH COUNTRY CLUB
SP-80 Country Club Lane, Greenland, 03840, Rockingham County, (603)436-9719, 3 miles W of Portsmouth.
Holes: 18. Yards: 7,050/5,511. Par: 72/76. Course Rating: 74.1/72.6. Slope: 127/126. Green Fee: $70/$70. Cart Fee: $26/cart. Walking Policy: Unrestricted walking. Walkability: 2. Opened: 1957. Architect: Robert Trent Jones. Season: April-Nov. High: June-Sept. To obtain tee times: Call 1 day in advance. Miscellaneous: Reduced fees (twilight), range (grass), club rentals, credit cards (MC, V, D).
Notes: Ranked 5th in 1999 Best in State.
Reader Comments: Staff and facilities excellent ... Long, long, long—driver, 3 wood and a wedge ... Well laid out ... Great ocean views, good greens ... Grip it and rip it ... Long for women ... Tough ... Want to play again.

RIDGEWOOD COUNTRY CLUB
SP-Rte. 109 S., Moultonborough, 03254, Carroll County, (603)476-5930. E-mail: ridgewood-cc@hotmail.com.
Holes: 9. Yards: 3,275/2,355. Par: 36/36. Course Rating: 35.9/34.0. Slope: 127/110. Green Fee: $28/$28. Cart Fee: $11/person. Walking Policy: Unrestricted walking. Walkability: 3. Opened: 1998. Architect: Wogan and Sargeant. Season: May-Nov. High: June-Aug. To obtain tee times: Call up to 3 days in advance. Miscellaneous: Reduced fees (low season, twilight, seniors, juniors), range (mats), club rentals, credit cards (MC, V), beginner friendly (lessons, clinics for adults and juniors).

★★★ ROCHESTER COUNTRY CLUB
SP-Church St., Gonic, 03839, Strafford County, (603)332-9892, 2 miles S of Rochester.
Holes: 18. Yards: 6,596/5,414. Par: 72/73. Course Rating: 72.7/70.4. Slope: 125/123. Green Fee: $45/$45. Cart Fee: Included in Green Fee. Walking Policy: Mandatory cart. Walkability: N/A. Opened: 1916. Architect: Phil Wogan. Season: April-Nov. High: June-Aug. To obtain tee times: First come, first served. Nonmembers must play before 3 p.m. on weekdays, and after 2 p.m. on weekends. Miscellaneous: Metal spikes, club rentals, credit cards (MC, V, AE).

Reader Comments: Outstanding New England style course ...Tricky par 3s, other funny holes, improving conditions ... Nice day of golf ... A good golf course but not difficult, holes are wide open, not much water or sand hazards to challenge shotmaking.

ROCKINGHAM COUNTRY CLUB

PU-Rte. 108 (200 Exeter Road), Newmarket, 03857, Rockingham County, (603)659-9956.
Holes: 9. **Yards:** 2,875/2,622. **Par:** 35/37. **Course Rating:** 65.3/650.0. **Slope:** 104/104. **Green Fee:** $21/$22. **Cart Fee:** $22/cart. **Walking Policy:** Unrestricted walking. **Walkability:** 2.
Opened: 1933. **Season:** April-Dec. **High:** June-Sept. **To obtain tee times:** Non-members may book 5 days in advance and those wishing to book tournaments or leagues, anytime. But, the earlier the better to get time desired. **Miscellaneous:** Reduced fees (weekdays, seniors, juniors), club rentals, credit cards (MC, V, D).

★★½ SAGAMORE-HAMPTON GOLF CLUB

PU-101 North Rd., North Hampton, 03862, Rockingham County, (603)964-5341, 50 miles N of Boston.
Holes: 18. **Yards:** 6,014/5,647. **Par:** 71/71. **Course Rating:** 67.4/71.5. **Slope:** 110/111. **Green Fee:** $25/$29. **Cart Fee:** $22/cart. **Walking Policy:** Unrestricted walking. **Walkability:** 3.
Opened: 1962. **Architect:** C.S. Luff. **Season:** April-Dec. **High:** May-Sept. **To obtain tee times:** Call 7 days in advance for weekends and holidays and 2 days in advance for weekdays.
Miscellaneous: Reduced fees (low season, seniors, juniors), club rentals, credit cards (MC, V, AE), beginner friendly.
Reader Comments: Tough greens to putt, decent test ... Short but enjoyable to play ... Mostly flat and wide open, good for confidence ... Nice variety of holes ... Walking it!

★★★★ SHATTUCK GOLF COURSE

PU-28 Dublin Rd., Jaffrey, 03452, Cheshire County, (603)532-4300, 20 miles E of Keene.
Holes: 18. **Yards:** 6,764/4,632. **Par:** 71/71. **Course Rating:** 74.1/73.1. **Slope:** 145/139. **Green Fee:** $35/$35. **Cart Fee:** $12/person. **Walking Policy:** Unrestricted walking. **Walkability:** 4.
Opened: 1991. **Architect:** Brian Silva. **Season:** May-Oct. **High:** June-Sept. **To obtain tee times:** Call 30 days in advance for weekdays. Call on Tuesday at 7 a.m. for upcoming weekend.
Miscellaneous: Reduced fees (weekdays, low season, twilight), discount packages, metal spikes, range (grass/mats), credit cards (MC, V, D).
Notes: Ranked 4th in 1999 Best in State. New England PGA Senior Championship.
Reader Comments: Gets better every year, treat you like kings ... A must play ... Worth the trip ... Putter's nightmare ... Bring a lot of balls and patience ... Scenery is so nice you don't mind losing 8-10 balls ... Forces creative play ... Two 4 handicaps couldn't break 90 ... Torture is addictive ... The beast in the northeast.

★★★½ SOUHEGAN WOODS GOLF CLUB

PU-65 Thorton Ferry Rd., Amherst, 03031, Hillsborough County, (603)673-0200, 10 miles NW of Nashua.
Holes: 18. **Yards:** 6,497/5,423. **Par:** 72/71. **Course Rating:** 70.4/65.6. **Slope:** 122/111. **Green Fee:** $30/$40. **Cart Fee:** $24/cart. **Walking Policy:** Unrestricted walking. **Walkability:** 1.
Opened: 1992. **Architect:** Phil Friel. **Season:** April-Nov. **High:** May-Aug. **To obtain tee times:** Call up to 5 days before. **Miscellaneous:** Reduced fees (weekdays, twilight), metal spikes, range (grass), club rentals, credit cards (MC, V, D).
Notes: North Atlantic Tour.
Reader Comments: Generous fairways ... Course needs work, but good value ... Lots of sand ... No variety ... Fairway traps in every landing area ... A nice walk in the woods ... More sand than the Sahara!

STONEBRIDGE COUNTRY CLUB

PU-161 Gorham Pond Rd., Goffstown, 03045, Hillsboro County, (603)497-8633, 7 miles W of Manchester. **Web:** www.golfstonebridge.com.
Holes: 18. **Yards:** 6,808/4,747. **Par:** 72/72. **Course Rating:** 73.0/67.6. **Slope:** 138/116. **Green Fee:** $29/$41. **Cart Fee:** $14/person. **Walking Policy:** Unrestricted walking. **Walkability:** 3.
Opened: 1998. **Architect:** Phil Wogan/George Sargent. **Season:** April-Nov. **High:** June-Aug. **To obtain tee times:** Call golf shop three days in advance. **Miscellaneous:** Reduced fees (weekdays, twilight, juniors), range (grass), club rentals, credit cards (MC, V, AE, D).

TORY PINES GOLF CLUB

R-Rte. 47 740 2nd NH Tpke. North, Francestown, 03043, Hillsborough County, (603)588-2923, (800)227-8679
Holes: 18. **Yards:** 6,111/4,604. **Par:** 71/71. **Course Rating:** 70.7/68.4. **Slope:** 138/121. **Green Fee:** $26/$33. **Cart Fee:** $14/person. **Walking Policy:** Unrestricted walking. **Walkability:** 5.
Architect: Donald Ross. **Season:** April-Nov. **High:** July-Sept. **To obtain tee times:** Members call 7 days in advance. Non-members call 5 days in advance. **Miscellaneous:** Reduced fees (twilight), discount packages, range (grass), club rentals, lodging (36 rooms), credit cards (MC, V, AE).

★★★½ WAUKEWAN GOLF CLUB
PU-Waukewan Rd., Center Harbor, 03226, Belknap County, (603)279-6661, 50 miles N of Concord.
Holes: 18. **Yards:** 5,828/5,020. **Par:** 72/72. **Course Rating:** 67.4/67.7. **Slope:** 117/112. **Green Fee:** $22/$28. **Cart Fee:** $24/cart. **Walking Policy:** Unrestricted walking. **Walkability:** 3.
Opened: 1961. **Architect:** Melvyn D. Hale. **Season:** May-Oct. **High:** June-Sept. **To obtain tee times:** Call up to 2 days in advance. **Miscellaneous:** Reduced fees (low season), range (grass), club rentals, credit cards (MC, V).
Reader Comments: Great views ... A fun course, good pin placements ... Mountain views on front 9 ... Not a very exciting course, plain holes.

★½ WAUMBEK GOLF CLUB
PU-Rte. 2, Jefferson, 03583, Coos County, (603)586-7777, 115 miles N of Manchester.
Holes: 18. **Yards:** 6,128/4,772. **Par:** 71/71. **Course Rating:** 69.9/69.9. **Slope:** 107/107. **Green Fee:** $20/$25. **Cart Fee:** $20/cart. **Walking Policy:** Unrestricted walking. **Walkability:** 2.
Opened: 1895. **Architect:** Willie Norton. **Season:** April-Nov. **High:** July-Sept. **To obtain tee times:** Call anytime in advance. **Miscellaneous:** Reduced fees (weekdays, low season, resort guests, twilight, seniors, juniors), discount packages, metal spikes, club rentals, credit cards (MC, V, D).

★★½ WENTWORTH RESORT GOLF COURSE
SP-Rte. 16a, Jackson, 03846, Carroll County, (603)383-9641.
Holes: 18. **Yards:** 5,581/5,087. **Par:** 70/70. **Course Rating:** 66.0/66.7. **Slope:** 115/114. **Green Fee:** $28/$38. **Cart Fee:** $12/person. **Walking Policy:** Walking at certain times. **Walkability:** 4.
Opened: 1895. **Season:** May-Oct. **High:** July-Sept. **To obtain tee times:** Call the Pro Shop up to 5 days in advance. **Miscellaneous:** Reduced fees (weekdays, twilight, juniors), metal spikes, club rentals, credit cards (MC, V, AE).
Reader Comments: Beautiful mountain views ... Short can be difficult ... Sporty, good for the ego ... Great set of par 3s ... Great course to cross country ski on ... Easy but can challenge.

★★★ WHITE MOUNTAIN COUNTRY CLUB
PU-North Ashland Road, Ashland, 03217, Grafton County, (603)536-2227, 25 miles N of Concord.
Holes: 18. **Yards:** 6,464/5,963. **Par:** 71/72. **Course Rating:** 70.4/67.9. **Slope:** 122/119. **Green Fee:** $27/$34. **Cart Fee:** $24/cart. **Walking Policy:** Unrestricted walking. **Walkability:** 1.
Opened: 1974. **Architect:** Cornish. **Season:** May-Oct. **High:** July-Sept. **To obtain tee times:** Call up to 7 days in advance. **Miscellaneous:** Reduced fees (weekdays, resort guests, twilight), metal spikes, range (grass), club rentals, lodging (4 rooms), credit cards (MC, V, D).
Notes: New England PGA Senior Championship 1994, 1996, 1997.
Reader Comments: Nice setting. Gorgeous in the fall ... Fun place ... Ego builder ... Too, too many people ... Easy to walk, most holes wide open ... Improvements are evident ... Flat mountain course.

★★★½ WINDHAM GOLF & COUNTRY CLUB
PU-One Country Club Rd., Windham, 03087, Rockingham County, (603)434-2093, 20 miles N of Boston, MA. **E-mail:** joanne@windhamcc.com. **Web:** www.windhamcc.com.
Holes: 18. **Yards:** 6,442/5,127. **Par:** 72/72. **Course Rating:** 71.3/69.1. **Slope:** 137/123. **Green Fee:** $32/$37. **Cart Fee:** $12/person. **Walking Policy:** Unrestricted walking. **Walkability:** 3.
Opened: 1995. **Architect:** Dean Bowen. **Season:** Year-round. **High:** May-Oct. **To obtain tee times:** Call up to 5 days in advance. **Miscellaneous:** Reduced fees (juniors), metal spikes, range (grass/mats), club rentals, credit cards (MC, V), beginner friendly (golf schools and leagues).
Notes: Ranked 10th in 1999 Best in State.
Reader Comments: Must stay in fairways, very unfair if you don't ... Narrow and hilly ... Bring lots of balls for back nine ... Very tight. Patience on the tees a must ... Tough walking course ... Good variation of holes ... Great first 3 holes ... It has a lot of promise.

★★½ APPLE MOUNTAIN GOLF CLUB

PU-369 Hazen Oxford Rd., Rte. 624, Belvidere, 07823, Warren County, (908)453-3023, (800)752-9465, 80 miles W of New York City. **E-mail:** applemt@nac.net.
Holes: 18. **Yards:** 6,593/5,214. **Par:** 71/71. **Course Rating:** 71.8/69.8. **Slope:** 122/123. **Green Fee:** $22/$49. **Cart Fee:** Included in Green Fee. **Walking Policy:** Walking at certain times.
Walkability: 4. **Opened:** 1973. **Architect:** Andrew Kiszonak. **Season:** Year-round. **High:** June-Aug. **To obtain tee times:** Call up to 2 weeks in advance. **Miscellaneous:** Reduced fees (weekdays, low season, twilight, seniors, juniors), discount packages, metal spikes, club rentals, credit cards (MC, V, AE).
Reader Comments: Very picturesque ... Very accessible, can always get a tee time ... Hills and more hills, but nice views ... Some nice long par fives in woods ... Wide open, easy if you are playing well, interesting par-6 17th.

★★★ ASH BROOK GOLF COURSE

PU-1210 Raritan Rd., Scotch Plains, 07076, Union County, (908)668-8503, 15 miles SW of Newark, N.J.
Holes: 18. **Yards:** 6,962/5,661. **Par:** 72/72. **Course Rating:** 72.1/71.8. **Slope:** 117/119. **Green Fee:** $8/$50. **Cart Fee:** $22/cart. **Walking Policy:** Unrestricted walking. **Walkability:** N/A.
Opened: 1958. **Architect:** Alfred H. Tull. **Season:** Year-round. **High:** March-Oct. **To obtain tee times:** Call golf shop. **Miscellaneous:** Reduced fees (weekdays, seniors, juniors).
Reader Comments: Long course, some nice holes ... Great golf for a municipal course ... Good open/wide course ... Hidden gem ... Great value ... Nice track ... Rather long, if unspectacular, layout, solid muny golf ... Lots of unusual water ... Has potential ... Fair muny course, must play blue tees for challenge.

★★★ AVALON GOLF CLUB

SP-1510 Rte. 9 N., Cape May Court House, 08210, Cape May County, (609)465-4653, (800)643-4766, 30 miles S of Atlantic City.
Holes: 18. **Yards:** 6,325/4,924. **Par:** 71/72. **Course Rating:** 70.3/70.7. **Slope:** 122/122. **Green Fee:** $29/$77. **Cart Fee:** Included in Green Fee. **Walking Policy:** Walking at certain times.
Walkability: 2. **Opened:** 1971. **Architect:** Bob Hendricks. **Season:** Year-round. **High:** May-Sept.
To obtain tee times: Call 14 days in advance. **Miscellaneous:** Reduced fees (weekdays, low season, twilight, juniors), discount packages, metal spikes, range (mats), club rentals, credit cards (MC, V, AE, D).
Reader Comments: Underrated, great views ... Tight, great course ... A nice course with a fine staff ... Nice shore golf ... Average, busy on weekends ... Beautiful course, nicely wooded ... Relative bargain on Jersey Shore ... Fine greens. No two holes alike.

BALLYOWEN GOLF CLUB

PU-105 Wheatsworth Rd., Hamburg, 07419, Sussex County, (973)827-5996, 56 miles NW of New York City. **Web:** www.greatgorgegolf.com.
Holes: 18. **Yards:** 7,032/4,903. **Par:** 72/72. **Course Rating:** 73.1/66.4. **Slope:** 127/103. **Green Fee:** $100/$125. **Cart Fee:** Included in Green Fee. **Walking Policy:** Walking at certain times.
Walkability: 3. **Opened:** 1998. **Architect:** Roger Rulewich. **Season:** March-Nov. **High:** April-Oct.
To obtain tee times: Call (973)827-5996 or Internet up to 10 days in advance. All times secured w/Credit card. **Miscellaneous:** Reduced fees (weekdays, twilight), range (grass), caddies, club rentals, credit cards (MC, V, AE).
Notes: Toyota Golf Skills Challenge 1998.
Special Notes: Walking w/caddies ($30.00 + tip) allowed.

★★★½ BEAVER BROOK COUNTRY CLUB

SP-Rte. #31 S. Country Club Rd., Clinton, 08809, Hunterdon County, (908)735-4022, (800)433-8567, 45 miles W of New York City.
Holes: 18. **Yards:** 6,546/5,283. **Par:** 72/72. **Course Rating:** 71.7/71.7. **Slope:** 125/122. **Green Fee:** $55/$74. **Cart Fee:** Included in Green Fee. **Walking Policy:** Walking at certain times.
Walkability: 4. **Opened:** 1964. **Architect:** Alec Ternyei. **Season:** Year-round. **High:** June-Aug. **To obtain tee times:** Call 7 days in advance. **Miscellaneous:** Reduced fees (twilight), metal spikes, club rentals, credit cards (MC, V, AE).
Reader Comments: Good solid public track ... Be prepared to fade tee shots ... Reachable par four ... tough, fun ... Beautiful course, keep it straight. Hilly ... Beautiful vista views and good scoring course.

★★½ BECKETT GOLF CLUB

RD #2, P.O. Box 76A, Swedesboro, 08085, Gloucester County, (856)467-4700, 5 miles S of Philadelphia.
Special Notes: Call club for further information.

★★★ BEY LEA GOLF CLUB

PU-1536 N. Bay Ave., Toms River, 08753, Ocean County, (732)349-0566.

Holes: 18. **Yards:** 6,677/5,793. **Par:** 72/72. **Course Rating:** 71.3/72.2. **Slope:** 122/117. **Green Fee:** $7/$32. **Cart Fee:** $26/cart. **Walking Policy:** Unrestricted walking. **Walkability:** 1. **Opened:** 1969. **Architect:** Hal Purdy. **Season:** Year-round. **High:** July-Aug. **To obtain tee times:** Saturday and Sunday only. Call 9:00 a.m. Monday for Saturday time and 9:00 a.m. Tuesday for Sunday time. **Miscellaneous:** Reduced fees (twilight, seniors, juniors), metal spikes, club rentals, credit cards (MC, V).

Reader Comments: Easy front nine, hard back ... Wide fairways. Greens good ... Flat, open course ... Another great course to play during the winter. All greens stay open! ... You can land a plane on any of the huge greens.

★★★½ BLACK BEAR GOLF & COUNTRY CLUB

PU-Hwy. 23, Franklin, 07416, Sussex County, (973)209-2226, 50 miles N of New York. **Web:** greatgorgegolf.com.

Holes: 18. **Yards:** 6,673/4,756. **Par:** 72/72. **Course Rating:** 72.2/67.7. **Slope:** 130/116. **Green Fee:** $55/$70. **Cart Fee:** Included in Green Fee. **Walking Policy:** Mandatory cart. **Walkability:** 3. **Opened:** 1996. **Architect:** Jack Kurlander. **Season:** March-Nov. **High:** May-Oct. **To obtain tee times:** Call golf shop. **Miscellaneous:** Reduced fees (weekdays, low season, twilight), range (mats), club rentals, lodging, credit cards (MC, V, AE).

Reader Comments: Very enjoyable course. Smart layout ... Many tight and blind shots, good greens ... They treat you like gold ... Nice design, lots of hills ... Great scenery, difficult course.

BLUE HERON PINES GOLF CLUB

PU-550 W. Country Club Dr., Cologne, Galloway Twsp., 08213, Atlantic County, (609)965-4653, (888)478-2746, 16 miles W of Atlantic City. **E-mail:** info@blueheronpines.com. **Web:** www.blue-heronpines.com.

EAST COURSE

Holes: 18. **Yards:** 7,300/5,500. **Par:** 71/71. **Course Rating:** N/A. **Slope:** N/A. **Green Fee:** $51/$125. **Cart Fee:** Included in Green Fee. **Walking Policy:** Unrestricted walking. **Walkability:** 1. **Opened:** 2000. **Architect:** Steve Smyers. **Season:** Year-round. **High:** May-Oct. **To obtain tee times:** Call up to 5 days in advance. **Miscellaneous:** Reduced fees (weekdays, low season, twilight, juniors), range (grass/mats), club rentals, credit cards (MC, V, AE, D, Diners Club), beginner friendly (golf learning center programs).

Notes: Golf Digest School site.

★★★★ WEST COURSE

Holes: 18. **Yards:** 6,777/5,053. **Par:** 72/72. **Course Rating:** 72.9/69.2. **Slope:** 132/119. **Green Fee:** $51/$125. **Cart Fee:** Included in Green Fee. **Walking Policy:** Unrestricted walking. **Walkability:** 1. **Opened:** 1993. **Architect:** Stephen Kay. **Season:** Year-round. **High:** May-Oct. **To obtain tee times:** Call up to 5 days in advance. **Miscellaneous:** Reduced fees (weekdays, low season, twilight, juniors), range (grass/mats), club rentals, credit cards (MC, V, AE, D, Diners Club), beginner friendly (golf learning center programs).

Notes: Golf Digest School site.

Reader Comments: Hell's Half-Acre, whole course a great tribute to Pine Valley ... No.14 and No. 15 are great par five-par four test ... Good design, condition, no weak holes ... Very tight fairways and very long ... Plenty of bunkers ... Great variety of holes ... Some holes on back 9 are tough without yardage book ... Like putting on ice.

★★★½ BOWLING GREEN GOLF CLUB

SP-Schoolhouse Rd., Milton, 07438, Morris County, (973)697-8688, 45 miles NW of New York City.

Holes: 18. **Yards:** 6,689/4,966. **Par:** 72/72. **Course Rating:** 72.9/69.4. **Slope:** 131/122. **Green Fee:** $33/$52. **Cart Fee:** $18/person. **Walking Policy:** Unrestricted walking. **Walkability:** 3. **Opened:** 1966. **Architect:** Geoffrey Cornish. **Season:** March-Dec. **High:** April-Sept. **To obtain tee times:** Call 5 days in advance after 8 a.m. **Miscellaneous:** Reduced fees (weekdays, twilight), range (mats), credit cards (MC, V, AE).

Reader Comments: Bring your 'A' game ... Woody Woodpecker haven ... Great course, treelined and water ... Leave driver in the trunk ... Straight shots a must ... Solid, challenging course with great greens ... Tight layout is a real challenge, especially form the blue tees. Fourth hole is textbook target golf.

★★★½ BRIGANTINE GOLF LINKS

PU-Roosevelt Blvd. and N. Shore, Brigantine, 08203, Atlantic County, (609)266-1388, (800)698-1388, 5 miles N of Atlantic City. **Web:** agpa.com.

Holes: 18. **Yards:** 6,570/5,460. **Par:** 72/72. **Course Rating:** 70.1/66.9. **Slope:** 121/113. **Green Fee:** $30/$60. **Cart Fee:** Included in Green Fee. **Walking Policy:** Walking at certain times. **Walkability:** 1. **Opened:** 1926. **Architect:** Stiles/Van Kleek/Gill/Williams. **Season:** Year-round. **High:** May-Sept. **To obtain tee times:** Call up to 5 days in advance. **Miscellaneous:** Reduced fees (weekdays, low season, resort guests, twilight), discount packages, metal spikes, caddies, credit cards (MC, V, AE).

Reader Comments: Sort of a links; if wind blows it becomes very tough. Some holes I have never seen anywhere else ... Very underrated, links, with bay ... Watch the tradewinds ... Houses feel close ... When wind is up, a great challenge, when down, it's easy ... Most unique golf experience in N.J.

★★★½ BUENA VISTA COUNTRY CLUB
PU-Box 307, Rte. 40 & Country Club Lane, Buena, 08310, Atlantic County, (609)697-3733, 30 miles SE of Philadelphia, PA. **E-mail:** bvc.allfore.com. **Web:** www.allfore.com.
Holes: 18. **Yards:** 6,869/5,651. **Par:** 72/72. **Course Rating:** 73.5/72.6. **Slope:** 131/124. **Green Fee:** $27/$35. **Cart Fee:** $28/cart. **Walking Policy:** Walking at certain times. **Walkability:** 1. **Opened:** 1957. **Architect:** William Gordon & Son. **Season:** Year-round. **High:** April-Oct. **To obtain tee times:** Call 5 days in advance. **Miscellaneous:** Reduced fees (weekdays, low season, twilight), range (grass), club rentals, credit cards (MC, V).
Reader Comments: Fun course, flat track ... Par five 10th is a real tough test ... Lots of fairway woods ... Nice layout, lots of sand. One of the values in South Jersey ... Tough test hidden in the pinelands ... Pinehurst in New Jersey.

★★★ BUNKER HILL GOLF COURSE
PU-220 Bunker Hill Rd, Princeton, 08540, Somerset County, (908)359-6335, 8 miles S of New Brunswick. **E-mail:** dwasnick@aol.com. **Web:** www.distinctgolf.com.
Holes: 18. **Yards:** 6,200/5,766. **Par:** 72/72. **Course Rating:** 67.9/72.6. **Slope:** 111/113. **Green Fee:** $12/$20. **Cart Fee:** $26/cart. **Walking Policy:** Walking at certain times. **Walkability:** 3. **Opened:** 1972. **Season:** Year-round. **High:** April-Sept. **To obtain tee times:** Call up to 7 days in advance. **Miscellaneous:** Reduced fees (weekdays, low season, twilight, seniors, juniors), metal spikes, club rentals, credit cards (MC, V).
Reader Comments: Private club quality at daily fee price ... Wide open ... A tough course ... Easy to get on ... Excellent finishing holes on both sides ... Nice layout–well kept.

★★★½ CAPE MAY NATIONAL GOLF CLUB
SP-Rte. 9 & Florence Ave., Cape May, 08204, Cape May County, (609)884-1563, (800)227-3874, 35 miles S of Atlantic City. **E-mail:** cmngc@bellatlantic.net. **Web:** www.cmngc.com.
Holes: 18. **Yards:** 6,905/4,711. **Par:** 71/71. **Course Rating:** 72.9/68.8. **Slope:** 136/115. **Green Fee:** $35/$71. **Cart Fee:** Included in Green Fee. **Walking Policy:** Unrestricted walking. **Walkability:** 3. **Opened:** 1991. **Architect:** Karl Litten/Robert Mullock. **Season:** Year-round. **High:** May-Oct. **To obtain tee times:** Call 7 days in advance. **Miscellaneous:** Reduced fees (weekdays, low season, resort guests, twilight, juniors), discount packages, range (grass/mats), club rentals, credit cards (MC, V).
Reader Comments: Delight to play, pay attention to wind ... Always windy ... Challenging, lots of water and wind ... Great layout, no houses, like playing in National Park ... 18th is a masterpiece ... Plays like a Myrtle Beach course... Long par fours. Great holes No.3 and No.14.

★★★ CEDAR CREEK GOLF COURSE
PU-Tilton Blvd., Bayville, 08721, Ocean County, (732)269-4460, 50 miles N of Atlantic City.
Holes: 18. **Yards:** 6,325/5,154. **Par:** 72/72. **Course Rating:** 70.5/69.5. **Slope:** 120/118. **Green Fee:** $8/$26. **Cart Fee:** $26/person. **Walking Policy:** Unrestricted walking. **Walkability:** 1. **Opened:** 1981. **Architect:** Nicholas T. Psiahas. **Season:** Year-round. **High:** May-Sept. **To obtain tee times:** No tee times for Saturday-Sunday-Holidays. Tee times May-September call golf shop one week in advance. **Miscellaneous:** Reduced fees (weekdays, low season, twilight, seniors, juniors), club rentals, credit cards (MC, V, AE).
Reader Comments: Fun course, tough back nine ... Great muny! 230-yard par-three uphill ... Great course for the price... The back nine is outstanding.

★★★ CENTERTON GOLF CLUB
PU-Rte. #540-Almond Rd., Elmer, 08318, Salem County, (609)358-2220, 10 miles W of Vineland.
Holes: 18. **Yards:** 6,725/5,525. **Par:** 71/71. **Course Rating:** 69.2/71.5. **Slope:** 120/120. **Green Fee:** $15/$28. **Cart Fee:** $26/cart. **Walking Policy:** Walking at certain times. **Walkability:** 2. **Opened:** 1962. **Architect:** Ed Carmen. **Season:** Year-round. **High:** May-Aug. **To obtain tee times:** Call 7 days in advance. **Miscellaneous:** Reduced fees (weekdays, low season, twilight), discount packages, metal spikes, range (grass/mats), club rentals, credit cards (MC, V).
Reader Comments: Flat, typical South Jersey course, a nice walk ... Course condition was much better than expected based on green fee ... Sentimental favorite ... Course seems to be coming back ... Great greens.

CHARLESTON SPRINGS GOLF COURSE
PM-207 Sweetman's Lane, Englishtown, 07726, (732)409-7227.
Special Notes: Call club for further information.

★★ COHANZICK COUNTRY CLUB
PU-Bridgeton-Fairton Rd., Fairton, 08320, Cumberland County, (856)455-2127.

Holes: 18. **Yards:** 6,285/5,470. **Par:** 71/71. **Course Rating:** 70.2/70.5. **Slope:** 123/120. **Green Fee:** $13/$17. **Cart Fee:** $22/cart. **Walking Policy:** Walking at certain times. **Walkability:** 5. **Architect:** Alex Findlay. **Season:** Year-round. **High:** May-Oct. **To obtain tee times:** Call 5 days in advance. Tee times are required. **Miscellaneous:** Reduced fees (weekdays, low season, twilight), metal spikes, club rentals, credit cards (MC, V).

★★★ CRANBURY GOLF CLUB
SP-49 Southfield Rd., West Windsor, 08550, Mercer County, (609)799-0341, 6 miles SE of Princeton. **E-mail:** mike@cranburygolf.com. **Web:** www.cranburygolf.com.
Holes: 18. **Yards:** 6,495/5,010. **Par:** 70/71. **Course Rating:** 69.5/69.1. **Slope:** 122/123. **Green Fee:** $22/$40. **Cart Fee:** $15/person. **Walking Policy:** Walking at certain times. **Walkability:** 2. **Opened:** 1963. **Architect:** Garrett Renn. **Season:** Year-round. **High:** May-Sept. **To obtain tee times:** Call 7 days in advance. **Miscellaneous:** Reduced fees (weekdays, low season, twilight, seniors, juniors), range (grass/mats), club rentals, credit cards (MC, V, AE), beginner friendly (clinics, golf schools, afternoon discounts).
Reader Comments: Good course, not overly challenging ... Solid course and fun to play ... Poor man's country club ... Tune up your putter for these greens ... Fun course.

★★★ CREAM RIDGE GOLF CLUB
SP-181 Rte. 539, Cream Ridge, 08514, Monmouth County, (609)259-2849, (800)345-4957, 12 miles SE of Trenton.
Holes: 18. **Yards:** 6,491/5,150. **Par:** 71/70. **Course Rating:** 71.8/69.6. **Slope:** 124/119. **Green Fee:** $18/$37. **Cart Fee:** $15/person. **Walking Policy:** Walking at certain times. **Walkability:** 1. **Opened:** 1958. **Architect:** Frank Miscoski. **Season:** Year-round. **High:** May-Sept. **To obtain tee times:** Call 7 days in advance for weekends. **Miscellaneous:** Reduced fees (weekdays, low season, twilight, seniors, juniors), range (mats), credit cards (MC, V, AE).
Reader Comments: Nice course. An easy round ... Nice old trees ... Fast, tricky greens ... Some very challenging holes ... Lots of water, bring balls ... Back nine much harder than front ... Challenging greens ... Many water holes, great condition.

★★★½ CRYSTAL SPRINGS GOLF CLUB
SP-123 Crystal Springs Rd., Hamburg, 07419, Sussex County, (973)827-1444, 56 miles NW of New York City. **Web:** greatgorgegolf.com .
Holes: 18. **Yards:** 6,857/5,131. **Par:** 72/72. **Course Rating:** 74.1/70.5. **Slope:** 137/123. **Green Fee:** $29/$80. **Cart Fee:** Included in Green Fee. **Walking Policy:** Mandatory cart. **Walkability:** 5. **Opened:** 1991. **Architect:** Robert von Hagge. **Season:** March-Nov. **High:** May-Oct. **To obtain tee times:** Call 10 days in advance. **Miscellaneous:** Reduced fees (weekdays, low season, resort guests, twilight), discount packages, range (grass), club rentals, lodging (50 rooms), credit cards (MC, V, AE).
Reader Comments: Front nine and back nine are two different courses ... Very narrow, challenging course ... Scenic holes. Target golf ... No. 10 is an unforgettable par three ... Several great holes, some are gimmicky ... Bring lots of balls or don't go ... Tough course, links style.

★★★ DARLINGTON COUNTY GOLF COURSE
PM-2777 Campgaw Rd., Mahwah, 07430, Bergen County, (201)327-8770, 8 miles N of Paramas.
Holes: 18. **Yards:** 6,457/5,300. **Par:** 71/72. **Course Rating:** 70.6/69.9. **Slope:** 122/117. **Green Fee:** $13/$45. **Cart Fee:** $20/cart. **Walking Policy:** Unrestricted walking. **Walkability:** 5. **Architect:** Nicholas Psiahas. **Season:** March-Dec. **High:** July-Sept. **To obtain tee times:** Tee times to registered residents only. Walk on spots every 1½ hours. **Miscellaneous:** Reduced fees (weekdays, twilight, seniors, juniors), range (mats), credit cards (MC, V).
Reader Comments: Best of county. Hills and tough rough ... Largest greens, great views ... Par three 12th a beauty ... Short par fives ... Great course. Has improved in the last few years.

★★★½ DEERWOOD GOLF CLUB
SP-Woodland Rd., Westhampton, 08060, Burlington County, (609)265-1800.
Holes: 18. **Yards:** 6,231/4,807. **Par:** 70/70. **Course Rating:** 69.4/67.2. **Slope:** 126/111. **Green Fee:** $63/$73. **Cart Fee:** Included in Green Fee. **Walkability:** N/A. **Opened:** 1993. **Architect:** Jim Blaukovitch. **Season:** Year-round. **Miscellaneous:** Metal spikes.
Reader Comments: Great condition. Fifth hole is a nightmare from the tips ... Great secret, word should get out ... Worth the extra fare. Treat yourself ... Good mix of holes. Some open, some tree lined ... Wide open, brutal rough, big greens, lots of water.

★★ EAST ORANGE GOLF COURSE
SP-440 Parsonage Hill Rd., Short Hills, 07078, Essex County, (973)379-7190, 10 miles W of Newark.
Holes: 18. **Yards:** 6,120/5,640. **Par:** 72/73. **Course Rating:** 67.6/69.8. **Slope:** 100/105. **Green Fee:** $30/$35. **Cart Fee:** $20/cart. **Walking Policy:** Unrestricted walking. **Walkability:** 1. **Opened:** 1920. **Architect:** Tom Bendelow. **Season:** Year-round. **High:** May-Sept. **To obtain tee

times: First come, first served after 11 a.m. weekends only. **Miscellaneous:** Reduced fees (weekdays, twilight, juniors), range (mats), club rentals.

★★★ EMERSON GOLF CLUB

PU-99 Palisade Ave., Emerson, 07630, Bergen County, (201)261-1100, 15 miles NE of New York City.

Holes: 18. **Yards:** 6,702/5,625. **Par:** 71/71. **Course Rating:** 71.1/70.8. **Slope:** 118/117. **Green Fee:** N/A/$69. **Cart Fee:** Included in Green Fee. **Walking Policy:** Walking at certain times. **Walkability:** 1. **Opened:** 1963. **Season:** April-Jan. **High:** May-Sept. **To obtain tee times:** Call up to 5 days in advance. **Miscellaneous:** Reduced fees (weekdays, low season, twilight, juniors), metal spikes, range (grass), club rentals, credit cards (MC, V, AE).

Reader Comments: Long par fours ... Flat, wide open ... Good par threes ... Front nine is long ... Have to place most shots ... Great finishing holes.

FARMSTEAD GOLF & COUNTRY CLUB

PU-88 Lawrence Rd., Lafayette, 07848, Sussex County, (973)383-1666, 5 miles N of Sparta.
Holes: 27. **Green Fee:** $25/$42. **Cart Fee:** $26/cart. **Walkability:** 3. **Opened:** 1963. **Architect:** Byron Phoebus. **Season:** March-Dec. **High:** May-Oct. **To obtain tee times:** Call 7 days in advance. For weekends call after 10 a.m. **Miscellaneous:** Reduced fees (weekdays, low season, twilight, seniors), club rentals, credit cards (MC, V, AE).

★★★½ CLUBVIEW/LAKEVIEW

Yards: 6,680/4,910. **Par:** 71/71. **Course Rating:** 71.1/68.1. **Slope:** 127/116. **Walking Policy:** Walking at certain times.

Reader Comments: Great condition. Lots of water... Grounds kept immaculate, play lake and club nines ... Short, target golf, great condition ... Lakeview 18 has fantastic water holes ... Doglegs keep it interesting ... Good overall. Some goofy greens ... Very enjoyable.

★★★½ CLUBVIEW/VALLEYVIEW

Yards: 6,221/4,822. **Par:** 69/70. **Course Rating:** 68.4/68.1. **Slope:** 119/117. **Walking Policy:** Mandatory cart.

Reader Comments: Very challenging and beautiful ... Front nine great, back nine too much for high handicapper ... Good course, some water comes into play ... Must use every club in bag ... Valleyview from the blues is a tough par-33.

★★★½ LAKEVIEW/VALLEYVIEW

Yards: 6,161/4,636. **Par:** 68/69. **Course Rating:** 69.3/67.1. **Slope:** 118/116. **Walking Policy:** Walking at certain times.

Reader Comments: Farmstead is a true test of will for those nervous on water-lined holes ... Good layout; nice views; reasonable challenges ... Good-sized landing areas. Good par threes ... Good mix of nines ... Easy to get tee time ... Par threes great over water.

FLANDERS VALLEY GOLF COURSE

PU-Pleasant Hill Rd., Flanders, 07836, Morris County, (973)584-5382, 50 miles W of New York City.

★★★★ RED/GOLD COURSE

Holes: 18. **Yards:** 6,770/5,540. **Par:** 72/73. **Course Rating:** 72.6/72.0. **Slope:** 126/123. **Green Fee:** $16/$60. **Cart Fee:** $26/cart. **Walking Policy:** Unrestricted walking. **Walkability:** 4. **Opened:** 1963. **Architect:** Hal Purdy/Rees Jones. **Season:** April-Nov. **High:** May-Aug. **To obtain tee times:** Call golf shop. Must be registered resident of Morris County or New Jersey to use automated telephone system. Walk-on tee times available. **Miscellaneous:** Reduced fees (weekdays, twilight, seniors), club rentals.

Reader Comments: An amazingly good course ... Only bad part is getting a tee time ... Hills and sloping greens ... Back nine holes spectacular ... Tough holes erase 'easy' pars and birdies ... Great layout in the mountains of North Jersey. One of the most picturesque ... A true test. Tight with tough greens.

★★★★ WHITE/BLUE COURSE

Holes: 18. **Yards:** 6,765/5,534. **Par:** 72/72. **Course Rating:** 72.7/71.6. **Slope:** 126/122. **Green Fee:** $16/$60. **Cart Fee:** $26/cart. **Walking Policy:** Unrestricted walking. **Walkability:** 2. **Opened:** 1963. **Architect:** Hal Purdy/Rees Jones. **Season:** April-Nov. **High:** May-Aug. **To obtain tee times:** Call golf shop. Must be registered resident of Morris County or New Jersey to use automated telephone system. Walk-on tee times available. **Miscellaneous:** Reduced fees (weekdays, twilight, seniors), club rentals.

Reader Comments: Level, some sloping greens ... Nos. 12, 13 and 14 usually make or break your round ... Pretty layout, interesting holes ... Solid Northeastern-type course. Keep it straight ... Challenging but almost impossible to get tee time ... Challenging doglegs and placement slots.

★★★ FRANCIS A. BYRNE GOLF CLUB

PU-1100 Pleasant Valley Way, West Orange, 07052, Essex County, (973)736-2306, 25 miles W of New York.
Holes: 18. **Yards:** 6,653/5,384. **Par:** 70/72. **Course Rating:** 70.2/73.0. **Slope:** 128/125. **Green Fee:** $22/$75. **Cart Fee:** $12/person. **Walking Policy:** Walking at certain times. **Walkability:** 3. **Opened:** 1920. **Architect:** Charles H. Banks. **Season:** April-Dec. **High:** June-Aug. **To obtain tee**

times: First come, first served. **Miscellaneous:** Reduced fees (seniors, juniors), metal spikes, club rentals.

Reader Comments: Could be a great course ... Very hilly ... Difficult greens. Challenging ... Challenging, hilly, sharp doglegs ... Beautiful, woodsy, great back nine from the blues ... Nos. 4, 9 and 10 are interesting ... Only one short par five, so it's tough to score.

★★ FREEWAY GOLF COURSE
PU-1858 Sicklerville Rd., Sicklerville, 08081, Camden County, (856)227-1115, 16 miles SE of Philadelphia, PA.
Holes: 18. **Yards:** 6,536/5,395. **Par:** 72/72. **Course Rating:** 73.6/73.4. **Slope:** 111/115. **Green Fee:** $10/$18. **Cart Fee:** Included in Green Fee. **Walking Policy:** Walking at certain times. **Walkability:** 3. **Opened:** 1968. **Architect:** Horace Smith. **Season:** Year-round. **High:** April-June. **To obtain tee times:** Call or come in. **Miscellaneous:** Reduced fees (weekdays, low season, twilight, seniors, juniors), metal spikes, range (grass/mats), rentals, credit cards (MC, V, AE).

★★★ GALLOPING HILL GOLF COURSE
PU-P.O. Box 988, Union, 07083, Union County, (908)686-1556.
Holes: 18. **Yards:** 6,690/5,514. **Par:** 73/76. **Course Rating:** 71.3/N/A. **Slope:** 122/N/A. **Green Fee:** $23/$27. **Cart Fee:** $22/cart. **Walking Policy:** Unrestricted walking. **Walkability:** N/A. **Opened:** 1920. **Architect:** Willard Wilkinson. **Season:** Year-round. **High:** April-Oct. **To obtain tee times:** First come, first served. **Miscellaneous:** Reduced fees (weekdays, twilight, seniors, juniors), metal spikes, club rentals.
Reader Comments: Pretty county course, newly renovated, great exercise for walkers ... Hill and dale. High roughs ... Aptly named, don't plan to walk if not in good shape ... Just redone, real potential ... Good condition and fun to play.

★★½ GAMBLER RIDGE GOLF CLUB
121 Burlington Path , Cream Ridge, 08514, Monmouth County, (609)758-3588, (800)427-8463, 10 miles E of Trenton. **E-mail:** gmblrrdg@aol.com. **Web:** gogolfnj.com/gambler.
Holes: 18. **Yards:** 6,370/5,140. **Par:** 71/71. **Course Rating:** 70.2/69.3. **Slope:** 119/115. **Green Fee:** $9/$35. **Cart Fee:** $7/person. **Walking Policy:** Walking at certain times. **Walkability:** 2. **Opened:** 1983. **Season:** Year-round. **High:** May-June-Sept.-Oct. **To obtain tee times:** Call up to one week in advance. **Miscellaneous:** Reduced fees (weekdays, low season, twilight, seniors), range (mats), credit cards (MC, V, AE, ATM)
Reader Comments: Good place to come out and let it rip, wide open ... Long, long, long, very rough off the fairways ... Good greens ... Great par 3s.

★★★ GOLDEN PHEASANT GOLF CLUB
SP-141 Country Club Dr. & Eayrestown Rd., Medford, 08055, Burlington County, (609)267-4276, 20 miles SE of Philadelphia, PA.
Holes: 18. **Yards:** 6,273/5,105. **Par:** 72/72. **Course Rating:** 68.1/68.4. **Slope:** 119/114. **Green Fee:** $14/$32. **Cart Fee:** $12/person. **Walking Policy:** Walking at certain times. **Walkability:** 3. **Opened:** 1963. **Architect:** Richard Kidder/Carmen N. Capri. **Season:** Year-round. **High:** April-Oct. **To obtain tee times:** Call Monday before weekend and holiday. **Miscellaneous:** Reduced fees (weekdays, twilight, seniors), metal spikes, range (grass/mats), club rentals, credit cards (MC, V).
Reader Comments: Nice place, good food, gets a lot of play ... Short, lots of trees, no blind shots ... Great par 3s ... Fun course ... Imaginative ups and downs. Pineland feel ... Hole No. 4 is difficult ... First four holes close together.

GREAT GORGE COUNTRY CLUB
PU-Rte. 517, McAfee, 07428, Sussex County, (973)827-5757, 50 miles NW of New York City.
Holes: 27. **Green Fee:** $49/$75. **Cart Fee:** Included in Green Fee. **Walking Policy:** Mandatory cart. **Walkability:** 4. **Opened:** 1971. **Architect:** George Fazio. **Season:** March-Nov. **High:** May-Oct. **To obtain tee times:** Call up to 30 days in advance. **Miscellaneous:** Reduced fees (weekdays, low season, twilight, seniors), metal spikes, range (grass/mats), club rentals, lodging, credit cards (MC, V, AE).
★★★★ LAKE/QUARRY
Yards: 6,819/5,390. **Par:** 71/71. **Course Rating:** 73.4/71.4. **Slope:** 132/126.
Reader Comments: A most interesting, well groomed course ... Great views ... Quarry side great nine ... Will use all clubs ... Elevation changes ... Pro tour quality ... Greens good ... Beautiful views, great golf ... Long and tough No. 18.
★★★★ LAKE/RAIL
Yards: 6,921/5,555. **Par:** 72/72. **Course Rating:** 73.5/71.9. **Slope:** 129/125.
Reader Comments: Great greens, excellent par 3s ... Close to a private club in terms of layout, service and facilities ... First tee at Lake has great view of area.
★★★★ QUARRY/RAIL
Yards: 6,826/5,539. **Par:** 71/71. **Course Rating:** 72.8/71.7. **Slope:** 128/122.
Reader Comments: Rail has a few interesting holes, especially No. 3 ... A tough,challenging but beautiful course...Variety of holes ... Great views ... Far away from civilization ... Gorgeous,

demanding ... Nice change from front to back nines ... Quarry course is especially pleasant during fall foliage.

★★★½ GREATE BAY GOLF CLUB
SP-901 Mays Landing Rd., Somers Point, 08244, Atlantic County, (609)927-0066, 8 miles S of Atlantic City.
Holes: 18. **Yards:** 6,705/5,349. **Par:** 70/70. **Course Rating:** 72.0/71.9. **Slope:** 127/122. **Green Fee:** $35/$95. **Cart Fee:** Included in Green Fee. **Walking Policy:** Mandatory cart. **Walkability:** 2. **Opened:** 1923. **Architect:** Willie Park Jr./Ron Garl/George Fazio. **Season:** Year-round. **High:** May-Sept. **To obtain tee times:** Call 5 days in advance. **Miscellaneous:** Reduced fees (weekdays, low season, resort guests, twilight), discount packages, metal spikes, range (grass/mats), club rentals, credit cards (MC, V, AE, D).
Reader Comments: Great clubhouse/19th hole ... Former LPGA site ... Another good South Jersey track, tough to get on in summer weekends.

★★★ GREEN KNOLL GOLF COURSE
PU-587 Garretson Rd., Bridgewater, 08807, Somerset County, (908)722-1301, 30 miles W of New York City.
Holes: 18. **Yards:** 6,443/5,324. **Par:** 71/72. **Course Rating:** 70.5/71.1. **Slope:** 120/124. **Green Fee:** $13/$41. **Cart Fee:** $24/cart. **Walking Policy:** Unrestricted walking. **Walkability:** 3. **Opened:** 1960. **Architect:** William F. Gordon. **Season:** Year-round. **High:** May-Sept. **To obtain tee times:** Call for 24-hour access, for a per reservation fee of $10.00. Annual fee for residents is $30.00, nonresidents $60.00. **Miscellaneous:** Reduced fees (twilight, seniors, juniors), club rentals, credit cards (MC, V, AE).
Reader Comments: Nice wide-open course ... County course with lots of play. Always in good shape. Beautiful scenery ... Pleasant semi-links setup ... Many great challenging holes ... Forgiving course, challenging, nice to walk ... Open course w/small hills.

★★½ HANOVER COUNTRY CLUB
Larrison Rd., Wrightstown, 08562, Burlington County, (609)758-8301.
Special Notes: Call club for further information.

★★★★ HARBOR PINES GOLF CLUB *Condition*
PU-500 St. Andrews Dr., Egg Harbor Township, 08234, Atlantic County, (609)927-0006, 1 miles W of Somers Point. **Web:** www.golflink.net/harborpines.
Holes: 18. **Yards:** 6,827/5,099. **Par:** 72/72. **Course Rating:** 72.3/68.8. **Slope:** 129/118. **Green Fee:** $55/$115. **Cart Fee:** Included in Green Fee. **Walking Policy:** Mandatory cart. **Walkability:** 1. **Opened:** 1996. **Architect:** Stephen Kay. **Season:** Year-round. **High:** May-Sept. **To obtain tee times:** Call up to 7 days in advance with credit card to guarantee. **Miscellaneous:** Reduced fees (weekdays, low season, twilight, juniors), range (grass/mats), club rentals, credit cards (MC, V, AE, D), beginner friendly (beginners, ladies and junior clinics).
Reader Comments: Overall fabulous course, great design ... You can land a C5-A on the fairways ... Huge greens ... Great shape, nice greens ... Could be the best in N.J. for public access ... Similar to Blue Heron, but carts are allowed on course ... Extremely playable ... No. 9 brutal ... Feels like Pinehurst ... Hazards are straightforward ... Great front nine ... Some of the best-putting greens.

HAWORTH GOLF CLUB
SP-5 Lakeshore Dr., Haworth, 07641, (201)384-7300.
Special Notes: Call club for further information.

★½ HENDRICKS FIELD GOLF COURSE
Franklin Ave., Belleville, 07109, Essex County, (973)751-0178.
Special Notes: Call club for further information.

★★½ HIGH MOUNTAIN GOLF CLUB
SP-845 Ewing Ave., Franklin Lakes, 07417, Bergen County, (201)891-4653, 15 miles W of New York.
Holes: 18. **Yards:** 6,347/5,426. **Par:** 71/71. **Course Rating:** 69.5/70.0. **Slope:** 118/117. **Green Fee:** $27/$34. **Cart Fee:** Included in Green Fee. **Walking Policy:** Walking at certain times. **Walkability:** N/A. **Opened:** 1967. **Architect:** Alec Ternyei. **Season:** April-Nov. **High:** May-Oct. **To obtain tee times:** Call Monday of the week of play. **Miscellaneous:** Reduced fees (weekdays, twilight), metal spikes, range (grass), club rentals.
Reader Comments: One short nine, one long nine ... Intimidating 1st hole. Good test ... Great thinking man's 18th hole ... A short course with some interesting holes. Tight layout in spots.

★★★ HIGH POINT COUNTRY CLUB
SP-P.O. Box 1154, Montague, 07827, Sussex County, (973)293-3282, 2 miles E of Milford, P.A. **Web:** www.hpccnj.com.
Holes: 18. **Yards:** 6,783/5,355. **Par:** 73/73. **Course Rating:** 73.3/70.0. **Slope:** 128/120. **Green Fee:** $37/$59. **Cart Fee:** Included in Green Fee. **Walking Policy:** Mandatory cart. **Walkability:**

5. Opened: 1964. **Architect:** Gerald Roby. **Season:** April-Nov. **High:** June-Aug. **To obtain tee times:** Call up to 2 weeks in advance. **Miscellaneous:** Metal spikes, range (grass), club rentals, credit cards (MC, V, AE).
Reader Comments: This is a fun place. Bring lots of golf balls, bring all clubs, bring brain ... Good solid course, 13 water holes.... Long and lots of water... Excellent greens ... Very long, blind shots.

★★½ HILLSBOROUGH COUNTRY CLUB

SP-146 Wertsville Rd., PO Box 365, Neshanic, 08853, Somerset County, (908)369-3322, 7 miles S of Flemington. **E-mail:** hccgolf@eclipse.net. **Web:** www.hillsboroughgolf.com.
Holes: 18. **Yards:** 5,840/5,445. **Par:** 70/73. **Course Rating:** 68.2/74.1. **Slope:** 114/119. **Green Fee:** $15/$38. **Cart Fee:** $14/person. **Walking Policy:** Walking at certain times. **Walkability:** 4.
Season: Year-round weather permitting. **High:** June-Sept. **To obtain tee times:** Call in advance. Call on Monday for upcoming weekend. **Miscellaneous:** Reduced fees (weekdays, twilight, seniors, juniors), range (grass), club rentals, beginner friendly.
Reader Comments: Beautiful hilly scenery, short course, not busy ... Even on a bad day, the 11th tee is worth the trip ... Greens are great.

★★★½ HOLLY HILLS GOLF CLUB

PU-374 Freisburg Rd., Alloway, 08001, Salem County, (856)455-5115, 25 miles E of Wilmington, DE.
Holes: 18. **Yards:** 6,376/5,056. **Par:** 72/72. **Course Rating:** 71.4/68.0. **Slope:** 124/114. **Green Fee:** $30/$40. **Cart Fee:** Included in Green Fee. **Walking Policy:** Walking at certain times.
Walkability: 5. **Opened:** 1970. **Architect:** Horace Smith. **Season:** Year-round. **High:** April-Oct.
To obtain tee times: Call 7 days in advance for weekend tee times only. **Miscellaneous:** Reduced fees (low season, twilight, juniors), metal spikes, range (grass/mats), club rentals, credit cards (MC, V, AE).
Reader Comments: Well-kept secret, worth the drive ... New owners have made vast improvements in conditioning and toughened it with bunkers ... Use every club in bag, challenge ... Nice hilly course in flat South Jersey.

★★★★½ HOMINY HILL GOLF COURSE *Value*

PU-92 Mercer Rd., Colts Neck, 07722, Monmouth County, (732)462-9222, 50 miles S of New York city.
Holes: 18. **Yards:** 7,056/5,794. **Par:** 72/72. **Course Rating:** 74.4/73.9. **Slope:** 132/128. **Green Fee:** $20/$50. **Cart Fee:** $28/cart. **Walking Policy:** Unrestricted walking. **Walkability:** 3.
Opened: 1964. **Architect:** Robert Trent Jones. **Season:** March-Dec. **High:** May-Oct. **To obtain tee times:** Call 7 days in advance. **Miscellaneous:** Reduced fees (weekdays, twilight, seniors, juniors), range (grass/mats), club rentals.
Notes: Ranked 12th in 1999 Best in State; 3rd in 1996 America's Top 75 Affordable Courses.
Reader Comments: Plenty of play, brutal but fair test ... Great golf holes ... Great course if you can get on it, tough to get tee times ... No. 12's a beautiful par three over water ... Super greens ... Better than most country clubs ... Eighth hole is great par four ... The best public course in New Jersey ... Can be U.S. Open tough if they let the rough grow and greens firm up.

★★★★½ HOWELL PARK GOLF COURSE *Value+, Condition*

PU-Yellow Brook and Preventorium Rd., Farmingdale, 07727, Monmouth County, (732)938-4771, 40 miles N of Philadelphia, PA.
Holes: 18. **Yards:** 6,916/5,725. **Par:** 72/72. **Course Rating:** 73.0/72.5. **Slope:** 126/125. **Green Fee:** $20/$41. **Cart Fee:** $30/cart. **Walking Policy:** Unrestricted walking. **Walkability:** 3.
Opened: 1972. **Architect:** Frank Duane. **Season:** March-Dec. **High:** April-Oct. **To obtain tee times:** Call golf shop. **Miscellaneous:** Reduced fees (weekdays, twilight, seniors, juniors), range (mats), club rentals.
Reader Comments: Hidden gem, good shape year-round ... Good test from blue tees; pleasant to play ... Great back 9 challenge ... Beautiful course, one of the best in N.J. ... Private club quality ... A golfer's course! ... Every hole is a new experience ... Always in great shape ... Fairways are like a carpet. Can be a very difficult course.

★★★ JUMPING BROOK COUNTRY CLUB

SP-210 Jumping Brook Rd., Neptune, 07753, Monmouth County, (732)922-6140, 50 miles S of New York City.
Holes: 18. **Yards:** 6,591/5,316. **Par:** 72/72. **Course Rating:** 71.4/71.2. **Slope:** 132/124. **Green Fee:** $33/$51. **Cart Fee:** $17/person. **Walking Policy:** Walking at certain times. **Walkability:** 3.
Opened: 1925. **Architect:** Willard Wilkinson. **Season:** Year-round. **High:** May-Sept. **To obtain tee times:** Call 3 days in advance. **Miscellaneous:** Reduced fees (weekdays, low season, twilight, seniors, juniors), range (grass), club rentals, credit cards (MC, V, AE).
Reader Comments: Getting better all the time ... Many elevated greens ... Pretty, pretty, pretty ... Beautiful vistas ... Some tough holes ... A truly fun and demanding course.

KNOB HILL GOLF CLUB
SP-360 Rte. 33 West, Manalapan, 07726, Monmouth County, (732)792-8118, 4 miles W of Freehold.
Holes: 18. **Yards:** 6,513/4,917. **Par:** 70/70. **Course Rating:** 72.0/69.4. **Slope:** 126/124. **Green Fee:** $25/$60. **Cart Fee:** $18/person. **Walking Policy:** Walking at certain times. **Walkability:** 4. **Opened:** 1998. **Architect:** Mark McCumber. **Season:** Feb.-Dec. **High:** April-Sept. **To obtain tee times:** Call golf shop (732)792-7722. **Miscellaneous:** Reduced fees (weekdays, twilight), club rentals, credit cards (MC, V, AE, D).

KNOLL COUNTRY CLUB
1001 Parsippany Blvd., Parsippany, 07054, Morris County, (973)263-7110.
★★½ **EAST COURSE**
Reader Comments: Fun course, great 18th, N.J.'s best cheeseburgers ... Tees protected by screens ... Great shape. Large greens ... Greens are lightning.
★★★★ **WEST COURSE**
Knoll & Green Bank Rds., Parsippany, 07054, Morris County, (973)263-7110.
Reader Comments: One of the best layouts in the state. It just gets too much play ... Beautiful old trees, good length, attractive course ... Long, but wide open. Good track, great finishing hole ... Good par threes ... Beautiful in the fall.
Special Notes: Call club for further information.

★★½ LAKEWOOD COUNTRY CLUB
PU-145 Country Club Dr., Lakewood, 08701, Ocean County, (732)364-8899, 40 miles S of New York City.
Holes: 18. **Yards:** 6,200/5,800. **Par:** 72/74. **Course Rating:** 71.0/70.7. **Slope:** 117/116. **Green Fee:** $18/$24. **Cart Fee:** $24/cart. **Walking Policy:** Unrestricted walking. **Walkability:** 2. **Opened:** 1902. **Architect:** Willie Dunn Jr. **Season:** Year-round. **High:** June-Aug. **To obtain tee times:** Call 1 day in advance for weekdays. Call 5 days in advance for weekends.
Miscellaneous: Reduced fees (weekdays, twilight), metal spikes, range (mats), club rentals, credit cards (MC, V, AE).
Reader Comments: Continues to improve ... Good variety of holes, can score well here ... Better suited for beginners ... 220-yard 15th is a nail-biter ... Old style course, fun look.

★★½ MAPLE RIDGE GOLF CLUB
SP-Woodbury-Glassboro Rd., Sewell, 08080, Gloucester County, (856)468-3542, 12 miles S of Camden.
Holes: 18. **Yards:** 6,376/5,210. **Par:** 71/71. **Course Rating:** 71.3/71.2. **Slope:** 130/125. **Green Fee:** $18/$25. **Cart Fee:** $10/person. **Walking Policy:** Walking at certain times. **Walkability:** N/A. **Architect:** Wm. F. Gordon/David Gordon. **Season:** Year-round. **High:** April-Oct. **To obtain tee times:** Call anytime. **Miscellaneous:** Reduced fees (weekdays, low season, twilight, seniors), metal spikes, credit cards (MC, V, AE).
Reader Comments: New owners improving everything, testy little course with Carolina feel ... Some real interesting holes ... Long par fives ... Especially challenging layout from 6th through 16th holes ... Fairways getting better, greens tough.

MARRIOTT'S SEAVIEW RESORT
R-401 S. New York Rd., Absecon, 08201, Atlantic County, (609)748-7680, 10 miles NW of Atlantic City. **E-mail:** seaviewpro@aol.com. **Web:** marriott.com.
★★★★ **BAY COURSE**
Holes: 18. **Yards:** 6,247/5,017. **Par:** 71/71. **Course Rating:** 70.7/68.4. **Slope:** 122/114. **Green Fee:** $49/$135. **Cart Fee:** Included in Green Fee. **Walking Policy:** Walking at certain times. **Walkability:** 2. **Opened:** 1914. **Architect:** Donald Ross/AW Tillinghast. **Season:** Year-round. **High:** May-Oct. **To obtain tee times:** Call in advance for tee times. **Miscellaneous:** Reduced fees (weekdays, low season, twilight, juniors), discount packages, range (grass), caddies, club rentals, lodging, credit cards (MC, V, AE, D, Diners Club), beginner friendly.
Reader Comments: Lots of variety with great views ... Links style ... Nice views of Atlantic City ... Fun course to play ... Classic old-style course ... Scenic, good wedge game needed ... Pray for no wind ... Old track that challenges all level of golfer ... Two fine old (and different) courses ... Always fun.
★★★★ **PINES COURSE**
Holes: 18. **Yards:** 6,371/5,276. **Par:** 71/71. **Course Rating:** 71.7/69.8. **Slope:** 128/119. **Green Fee:** $49/$135. **Cart Fee:** Included in Green Fee. **Walking Policy:** Walking at certain times. **Walkability:** 3. **Opened:** 1929. **Architect:** Toomey/Flynn/Gordon. **Season:** Year-round. **High:** May-Oct. **To obtain tee times:** Call in advance for starting times. **Miscellaneous:** Reduced fees (weekdays, low season, twilight, juniors), discount packages, range (grass), caddies, club rentals, lodging, credit cards (MC, V, AE, D, Diners Club), beginner friendly (professional instruction).
Reader Comments: Super-tight, super-tough, super course ... Great place, great golf, 1st class all the way ... Some really long par threes in the wind ... Great course, better hit it straight.

Unique old resort ... These two are a Jersey Shore landmark, very challenging to all levels ... Top-notch, fast greens ... Fantastic practice facility! Course was fun too! ... Long and tight. Exacting shots.

MATTAWANG GOLF CLUB

SP-P.O. Box 577, Belle Mead, 08502, Somerset County, (908)281-0778, 8 miles N of Princeton.
Holes: 18. **Yards:** 6,800/5,469. **Par:** 72/75. **Course Rating:** 73.1/71.8. **Slope:** 130/123. **Green Fee:** $17/$42. **Cart Fee:** $16/person. **Walking Policy:** Walking at certain times. **Walkability:** 2. **Opened:** 1962. **Architect:** Mike Myles. **Season:** March-Jan. **High:** May-Sept. **To obtain tee times:** Available 5 days in advance. **Miscellaneous:** Reduced fees (low season, twilight, seniors, juniors), range (mats), club rentals, credit cards (MC, V, AE, D), beginner friendly (clinics, junior camps).

★★★ MAYS LANDING COUNTRY CLUB

PU-1855 Cates Rd., Mays Landing, 08330, Atlantic County, (609)641-4411, 10 miles W of Atlantic City.
Holes: 18. **Yards:** 6,662/5,432. **Par:** 72/71. **Course Rating:** 72.5/70.7. **Slope:** 124/116. **Green Fee:** $20/$50. **Cart Fee:** $14/person. **Walking Policy:** Walking at certain times. **Walkability:** 2. **Opened:** 1962. **Architect:** Hal Purdy. **Season:** Year-round. **High:** April-Oct. **To obtain tee times:** Call up to 7 days in advance. **Miscellaneous:** Reduced fees (weekdays, low season, resort guests, twilight), discount packages, range (grass), club rentals, credit cards (MC, V, AE), beginner friendly (ladies clinic thursdays).
Reader Comments: Course with potential ... Mature course, fair to all levels. No hidden trouble ... Good test, use every club ... Some nice holes ... Recently reworked with good results.

THE MEADOWS AT MIDDLESEX

PU-70 Hunters Glen Drive, Plainsboro, 08536, Middlesex County, (609)799-4000, 5 miles N of Princeton.
Holes: 18. **Yards:** 6,277/4,762. **Par:** 70/70. **Course Rating:** 70.3/71.5. **Slope:** 121/122. **Green Fee:** $16/$60. **Cart Fee:** $26/cart. **Walking Policy:** Unrestricted walking. **Walkability:** 1. **Opened:** 1972. **Architect:** Joe Finger/Tom Fazio. **Season:** Year-round. **High:** March-Oct. **To obtain tee times:** Call. **Miscellaneous:** Reduced fees (weekdays, resort guests, seniors, juniors), club rentals.

★★½ MEADOWS GOLF CLUB

SP-79 Two Bridges Rd., Lincoln Park, 07035, Morris County, (973)696-7212, 22 miles W of New York City.
Holes: 18. **Yards:** 6,193/4,600. **Par:** 68/70. **Course Rating:** N/A. **Slope:** N/A. **Green Fee:** $27/$47. **Cart Fee:** $30/cart. **Walking Policy:** Walking at certain times. **Walkability:** 2. **Opened:** 1963. **Season:** Year-round. **High:** April-Oct. **To obtain tee times:** Call for weekend tee times only. **Miscellaneous:** Reduced fees (weekdays, twilight, seniors), club rentals.
Reader Comments: Short course with lots of water ... Small, tight ... Short, wide open course.

★★★½ MERCER OAKS GOLF CLUB

PM-County Parks Commission, 640 S. Broad St, Trenton, 08650, Mercer County, (609)936-9603, 5 miles S of Princeton.
Holes: 18. **Yards:** 7,012/6,330. **Par:** 72/72. **Course Rating:** 73.5/70.3. **Slope:** 126/120. **Green Fee:** $9/$34. **Cart Fee:** $23/cart. **Walking Policy:** Unrestricted walking. **Walkability:** 3. **Opened:** 1993. **Architect:** Bill Love/Brian Ault. **Season:** April-Dec. **To obtain tee times:** Call. **Miscellaneous:** Reduced fees (weekdays, twilight, seniors, juniors), metal spikes, range (grass).
Reader Comments: Enjoy blue tees. Good for young guns .... Challenging back nine, especially 15-18, great! ... Myrtle Beach style ... Nice fast greens. State of the art course.

★★ MINEBROOK GOLF CLUB

PU-500 Schooley's Mt. Rd., Hackettstown, 07840, Morris County, (908)979-0366, 45 miles W of Newark.
Holes: 18. **Yards:** 6,349/5,505. **Par:** 70/72. **Course Rating:** 70.9/73.0. **Slope:** 128/122. **Green Fee:** $20/$41. **Cart Fee:** $14/person. **Walking Policy:** Walking at certain times. **Walkability:** 4. **Opened:** 1919. **Architect:** M. Coopman/J. Rocco. **Season:** Year-round. **High:** May-Sept. **To obtain tee times:** Call up to 7 days in advance. **Miscellaneous:** Reduced fees (low season, twilight, seniors, juniors), club rentals, credit cards (MC, V, AE).
Special Notes: Formerly Hidden Hills Golf Club.

★★★ MIRY RUN COUNTRY CLUB

SP-106 B. Sharon Rd., Robbinsville, 08691, Mercer County, (609)259-1010, 8 miles E of Trenton. **Web:** www.snjgolf.com.
Holes: 18. **Yards:** 6,893/5,562. **Par:** 72/72. **Course Rating:** 71.7/70.7. **Slope:** 119/113. **Green Fee:** $15/$25. **Cart Fee:** $15/person. **Walking Policy:** Walking at certain times. **Walkability:** 2. **Opened:** 1961. **Architect:** Fred Lambert. **Season:** Year-round. **High:** May-Sept. **To obtain tee times:** Call up to 4 days in advance. **Miscellaneous:** Reduced fees (low season, twilight), discount packages, metal spikes, range (grass).

NEW JERSEY

Reader Comments: Pretty flat, couple of tough holes ... Landing strip nearby ... High handicappers: If you have three balls left after the fifth you should be OK ... Watch out for the planes landing next to No. 16 ... Long par fours.

★★★½ MOUNTAIN VIEW GOLF COURSE
PM-Bear Tavern Rd., West Trenton, 08650, Mercer County, (609)882-4093.
Holes: 18. **Yards:** 6,775/5,500. **Par:** 72/73. **Course Rating:** 72.0/70.8. **Slope:** 124/118. **Green Fee:** $11/$26. **Walking Policy:** Unrestricted walking. **Walkability:** 5. **Opened:** 1952. **Season:** Year-round weather permitting. **High:** April-Aug. **To obtain tee times:** First come, first served.
Miscellaneous: Reduced fees (twilight, seniors, juniors), metal spikes, range (grass).
Reader Comments: Wide fairways, long ... Great challenge. Blind shots ... Better back nine ... Try to score on first three holes, after that it gets tough ... New watering system adds to quality.

★★★½ NEW JERSEY NATIONAL GOLF CLUB
SP-579 Allen Rd., Basking Ridge, 07920, Somerset County, (908)781-9400, 6 miles SW of Basking Ridge. **Web:** www.njngolfclub.com.
Holes: 18. **Yards:** 7,056/5,019. **Par:** 72/72. **Course Rating:** 73.7/68.8. **Slope:** 137/121. **Green Fee:** $70/$90. **Cart Fee:** Included in Green Fee. **Walking Policy:** Unrestricted walking.
Walkability: 5. **Opened:** 1997. **Architect:** Roy Case. **Season:** Year-round. **High:** May-Sept. **To obtain tee times:** General public may call 6 days in advance (908)781-2575. Members may call 14 days in advance. **Miscellaneous:** Reduced fees (weekdays, low season, twilight), range (grass/mats), club rentals, credit cards (MC, V, AE), beginner friendly (beginner clinics).
Reader Comments: New but neat ... Great greens ... 18th a killer finishing hole ... Terrific design, hills, hills, hills ... First-rate, nice experience ... Lots of trees and water, bring balls ... Super fast greens ... Stupendous scenery. Challenging, yet fair for the average 15-handicapper.

★★½ OAK RIDGE GOLF COURSE
PU-136 Oak Ridge Rd., Clark, 07066, Union County, (732)574-0139.
Holes: 18. **Yards:** 6,388/5,275. **Par:** 70/72. **Course Rating:** 70.0/69.7. **Slope:** 110/106. **Green Fee:** $8/$28. **Cart Fee:** $22/cart. **Walking Policy:** Unrestricted walking. **Walkability:** 1. **Season:** Year-round. **High:** April-Oct. **To obtain tee times:** Call. **Miscellaneous:** Reduced fees (seniors, juniors), club rentals.
Reader Comments: Basic, confidence-building municipal course ... Good county course. Easy ... Good condition. Good pace of play ... Nice greens, enjoyable round.

★★½ OCEAN ACRES COUNTRY CLUB
SP-925 Buccaneer Lane, Manahawkin, 08050, Ocean County, (609)597-9393, 12 miles W of Long Beach Island.
Holes: 18. **Yards:** 6,548/5,412. **Par:** 72/72. **Course Rating:** 70.5/70.7. **Slope:** 120/118. **Green Fee:** $15/$22. **Cart Fee:** $20/cart. **Walking Policy:** Walking at certain times. **Walkability:** N/A.
Opened: 1967. **Architect:** Hal Purdy/John Davies. **Season:** Year-round. **High:** June-Aug. **To obtain tee times:** Call 5 days in advance for weekends and holidays only. **Miscellaneous:** Reduced fees (low season, twilight), metal spikes, club rentals, credit cards (MC, V, AE).
Reader Comments: Back nine worth the trip ... I liked the par threes ... Pine trees and sand galore. Better be able to hit it off of pine needles. Some nice water holes. Great for walking, flat ... Great 10th hole, island par three.

★★★½ OCEAN COUNTY GOLF COURSE AT ATLANTIS
PU-Country Club Blvd., Tuckerton, 08087, Ocean County, (609)296-2444, 30 miles N of Atlantic City.
Holes: 18. **Yards:** 6,848/5,579. **Par:** 72/72. **Course Rating:** 73.6/71.8. **Slope:** 134/124. **Green Fee:** $14/$40. **Cart Fee:** $24/cart. **Walking Policy:** Walking at certain times. **Walkability:** 1.
Opened: 1961. **Architect:** George Fazio. **Season:** Year-round. **High:** May-Sept. **To obtain tee times:** Call 8 days in advance at 6 p.m. I.D. card required. **Miscellaneous:** Reduced fees (twilight, seniors, juniors), metal spikes, club rentals, beginner friendly (golf lessons).
Reader Comments: Tough course, you need your 'A'-game ... Golf and gamble; Atlantic City is close ... Friendly personnel, great No. 17 ... Tour length, wonderful old course ... Tight with small greens ... Best value on Jersey Shore ... Lots of accuracy needed ... Strong par threes, treelined fairways, doglegs ... Long, difficult, slick greens, taxing rough; water in play on four holes.

★★½ OLD ORCHARD COUNTRY CLUB
SP-54 Monmouth Rd., Eatontown, 07724, Monmouth County, (732)542-7666, 40 miles S of New York City.
Holes: 18. **Yards:** 6,588/5,575. **Par:** 72/72. **Course Rating:** 70.5/70.8. **Slope:** 116/115. **Green Fee:** $25/$40. **Cart Fee:** $32/cart. **Walking Policy:** Unrestricted walking. **Walkability:** 2.
Opened: 1929. **Season:** Year-round. **High:** May-Sept. **To obtain tee times:** Call for current month. **Miscellaneous:** Reduced fees (weekdays, low season, twilight, seniors), range (grass), club rentals, credit cards (MC, V, AE).

Reader Comments: Easy course, fun to play ... Flat but fun ... Wide open, some challenging holes ... No. 7: island par five ... Greens are in good shape ... Just off Garden State Parkway on your way to Atlantic City ... Race track nearby makes for a great day.

★★ OVERPECK COUNTY GOLF COURSE

PM-E Cedar Lane, Teaneck, 07666, Bergen County, (201)837-8395, 10 miles W of New York.
Holes: 18. **Yards:** 6,559/5,557. **Par:** 72/72. **Course Rating:** 72.6/73.7. **Slope:** 124/127. **Green Fee:** $45/$45. **Cart Fee:** $20/cart. **Walking Policy:** Unrestricted walking. **Walkability:** N/A.
Opened: 1968. **Architect:** Nicholas Psiahas. **Season:** March-Dec. **High:** June-Sept. **To obtain tee times:** Call golf shop. **Miscellaneous:** Reduced fees (weekdays, twilight, seniors, juniors), metal spikes, range (grass), club rentals.

★★½ PARAMUS GOLF CLUB

PU-314 Paramus Rd., Paramus, 07652, Bergen County, (201)447-6067, 15 miles W of New York City.
Holes: 18. **Yards:** 6,212/5,241. **Par:** 71/70. **Course Rating:** 69.1/72.0. **Slope:** 118/117. **Green Fee:** $14/$32. **Cart Fee:** $23/cart. **Walking Policy:** Unrestricted walking. **Walkability:** 2.
Opened: 1976. **Architect:** Stephen Kay. **Season:** Year-round. **High:** April-Nov. **To obtain tee times:** Reserve in person. **Miscellaneous:** Reduced fees (weekdays, seniors), metal spikes, club rentals.
Reader Comments: Postage stamp greens ... Service not good... Great for retirees ... Need good course management to score well.

★★½ PASCACK BROOK GOLF & COUNTRY CLUB

PU-15 Rivervale Rd., River Vale, 07675, Bergen County, (201)664-5886, 15 miles NW of New York City.
Holes: 18. **Yards:** 5,991/5,117. **Par:** 71/71. **Course Rating:** 69.0/69.3. **Slope:** 119/117. **Green Fee:** N/A/$60. **Cart Fee:** Included in Green Fee. **Walking Policy:** Walking at certain times.
Walkability: 2. **Opened:** 1962. **Architect:** John Handwerg Jr. **Season:** Year-round weather permitting. **High:** May-Sept. **To obtain tee times:** Call up to 5 days in advance. **Miscellaneous:** Reduced fees (weekdays, low season, twilight, seniors, juniors), metal spikes, credit cards (MC, V, AE).
Reader Comments: Easy, short, little trouble, you won't lose a lot of balls ... No. 10 can be driven ... Small greens, gets a lot of play, nice people ... Has potential ... Back nine tricky.

PASSAIC COUNTY GOLF COURSE

209 Totowa Rd., Wayne, 07470, Passaic County, (973)696-8185.
★½ BLUE COURSE
★½ RED COURSE
Special Notes: Call club for further information.

★★★½ PENNSAUKEN COUNTRY CLUB

SP-3800 Haddonfield Rd., Pennsauken, 08109, Camden County, (856)662-4961, 5 miles N of Philadelphia, PA.
Holes: 18. **Yards:** 5,959/4,926. **Par:** 70/70. **Course Rating:** 68.1/67.9. **Slope:** 119/111. **Green Fee:** $24/$30. **Cart Fee:** $14/person. **Walking Policy:** Walking at certain times. **Walkability:** 2.
Opened: 1930. **Season:** Year-round. **High:** May-Sept. **To obtain tee times:** Reserve for weekend or holiday beginning at daylight on Monday prior. Reserve weekdays beginning at daylight on Wednesday prior. **Miscellaneous:** Reduced fees (twilight), metal spikes, club rentals, credit cards (MC, V).
Reader Comments: Very well-kept course ... Great short course ... Great back nine, great price ... Better from the blues ... No. 7 is tough ... Good public course, very walkable ... Greens always in excellent condition, short but nice course ... First-class course, enjoyable wildlife.

★★★★ PINE BROOK GOLF COURSE

PM-1 Covered Bridge Blvd., Englishtown, 07726, Monmouth County, (732)536-7272, 70 miles S of New York City.
Holes: 18. **Yards:** 4,168/3,441. **Par:** 61/61. **Course Rating:** 61.0/61.0. **Slope:** 90/90. **Green Fee:** $10/$32. **Cart Fee:** $22/cart. **Walking Policy:** Unrestricted walking. **Walkability:** 2.
Architect: Hal Purdy. **Season:** March-Dec. **High:** June-Aug. **To obtain tee times:** Call golf shop for credit card reservation. Walk-ons available. **Miscellaneous:** Reduced fees (weekdays, twilight, seniors, juniors), club rentals, beginner friendly.
Reader Comments: Good for beginner or to practice short irons ... Good greens ... Short nine hole course, great for short game practice ... Small but tough, you'll use every club ... Beautiful short course.

★★★ PINELANDS GOLF CLUB

PU-887 S. Mays Landing Rd., Winslow, 08037, Camden County, (609)561-8900, 25 miles NW of Atlantic City.

Holes: 18. **Yards:** 6,224/5,375. **Par:** 71/71. **Course Rating:** 69.7/70.4. **Slope:** 114/119. **Green Fee:** $12/$24. **Cart Fee:** $24/cart. **Walking Policy:** Walking at certain times. **Walkability:** 2. **Opened:** 1963. **Season:** Year-round. **High:** May-Nov. **To obtain tee times:** Call 5 days in advance for minimum of 3 players. **Miscellaneous:** Reduced fees (weekdays, low season, twilight), metal spikes, range (grass/mats), club rentals, credit cards (MC, V).
Reader Comments: A little short but nice ... Much improved! ... Some memorable holes ... Fairways are tight ... Course is so narrow you might not touch your driver.

★★½ PRINCETON GOLF CLUB
PM-Wheeler Way, Princeton, 08611, Mercer County, (609)452-9382, 2 miles S of Princeton.
Holes: 18. **Yards:** 5,845/5,005. **Par:** 70/71. **Course Rating:** 68.6/69.9. **Slope:** 113/113. **Green Fee:** $11/$26. **Cart Fee:** $23/cart. **Walking Policy:** Unrestricted walking. **Walkability:** 1. **Architect:** William Gordon/David Gordon. **Season:** Year-round. **High:** April-Aug. **To obtain tee times:** First come, first served. **Miscellaneous:** Reduced fees (twilight, seniors, juniors), metal spikes, range (grass), club rentals.
Reader Comments: Great layout, enjoyable day ... Good practice field. Don't bring driver. Small greens ... Very tight, but very reachable par fives.

★★★ QUAIL BROOK GOLF COURSE
PU-625 New Brunswick Rd., Somerset, 08873, Somerset County, (732)560-9528, 30 miles W of New York City.
Holes: 18. **Yards:** 6,617/5,385. **Par:** 71/72. **Course Rating:** 71.4/70.9. **Slope:** 123/119. **Green Fee:** $13/$41. **Cart Fee:** $24/cart. **Walking Policy:** Unrestricted walking. **Walkability:** 4. **Opened:** 1982. **Architect:** Edmund Ault. **Season:** Year-round. **High:** May-Sept. **To obtain tee times:** 24-hour access for tee time for a per reservation fee. **Miscellaneous:** Reduced fees (weekdays, low season, twilight, seniors, juniors), range (mats), club rentals, credit cards (MC, V, AE).
Reader Comments: Looks easy, but it's hard to shoot a great score... Nos. 17 and 18 are two toughest in area ... Flat front nine, hilly back nine, No. 14 very tough ... Back nine long walk. Nice layout of holes. Small greens ... Great challenge from the tips.

RAMBLEWOOD COUNTRY CLUB
PU-200 Country Club Pkwy., Mt. Laurel, 08054, Burlington County, (856)235-2118, 8 miles E of Philadelphia.
Holes: 27. **Green Fee:** $31/$43. **Cart Fee:** $16/person. **Walking Policy:** Walking at certain times. **Walkability:** 1. **Opened:** 1962. **Architect:** Edmund Ault. **Season:** Year-round. **High:** April-Oct. **To obtain tee times:** Call 7 days in advance.
★★★ RED/BLUE
Yards: 6,723/5,499. **Par:** 72/73. **Course Rating:** 72.1/71.4. **Slope:** 130/126. **Miscellaneous:** Reduced fees (weekdays, low season, twilight, seniors), discount packages, club rentals, credit cards (MC, V).
Reader Comments: Blue nine the best ... Course long and hard ... Nice course with large flat greens ... Challenging course. Tough holes ... Course well maintained.
★★★ RED/WHITE
Yards: 6,883/5,741. **Par:** 72/74. **Course Rating:** 72.9/72.7. **Slope:** 130/128. **Miscellaneous:** Reduced fees (weekdays, low season, twilight, seniors), discount packages, metal spikes, club rentals, credit cards (MC, V).
Reader Comments: Big greens, good condition ... White has second hardest par four in South Jersey ... Long.
★★★ WHITE/BLUE
Yards: 6,624/5,308. **Par:** 72/73. **Course Rating:** 71.1/70.1. **Slope:** 129/123. **Miscellaneous:** Reduced fees (weekdays, low season, twilight, seniors), discount packages, metal spikes, club rentals, credit cards (MC, V).
Reader Comments: Blue is more difficult ... Wide open fairways fool big hitters ... Blue makes this 18 hard...Very well kept and friendly, great greens.

★★★ RANCOCAS GOLF CLUB
PU-12 Club Ridge Lane, Willingboro, 08046, Burlington County, (609)877-5344, 10 miles N of Philadelphia, PA. **Web:** agpa.com.
Holes: 18. **Yards:** 6,634/5,284. **Par:** 71/72. **Course Rating:** 73.0/70.0. **Slope:** 130/120. **Green Fee:** $42/$42. **Cart Fee:** Included in Green Fee. **Walking Policy:** Unrestricted walking. **Walkability:** 2. **Opened:** 1968. **Architect:** Robert Trent Jones, Sr. **Season:** Year-round. **High:** April-Nov. **To obtain tee times:** Call up to 7 days in advance. **Miscellaneous:** Reduced fees (weekdays, low season, twilight, seniors, juniors), discount packages, metal spikes, range (mats), club rentals, credit cards (MC, V, AE), beginner friendly (junior, women and adult clinics).
Reader Comments: No weak holes ... Front 9 wide open. Back 9 tight ... Check for coupon discounts ... Lots of doglegs... Great, deceptive distances ... An RTJ gem, needs more conditioning.

★★★ RIVER VALE COUNTRY CLUB

PU-660 Rivervale Rd., River Vale, 07675, Bergen County, (201)391-2300, 20 miles N of New York City.

Holes: 18. **Yards:** 6,470/5,293. **Par:** 72/74. **Course Rating:** 71.4/70.7. **Slope:** 128/123. **Green Fee:** $63/$89. **Cart Fee:** Included in Green Fee. **Walking Policy:** Mandatory cart. **Walkability:** 3. **Opened:** 1928. **Architect:** Orrin Smith. **Season:** March-Nov. **High:** June-Sept. **To obtain tee times:** Call up to 14 days in advance. **Miscellaneous:** Reduced fees (low season, twilight), discount packages, range (mats), club rentals, credit cards (MC, V, AE, JCB).

Reader Comments: Pricey but good track, tough greens ... First-rate, great layout and well-maintained ... Enjoyable but not exciting ... A tough little layout ... Beautiful golf course, especially 18th hole, plush fairways and excellent greens. Service excellent.

★★ ROCKLEIGH GOLF COURSE

15 Paris Ave., Rockleigh, 07647, Bergen County, (201)768-6353.
Special Notes: Call club for further information.

★½ ROLLING GREENS GOLF CLUB

PU-214 Newton-Sparta Rd, Newton, 07860, Sussex County, (973)383-3082, 60 miles NW of New York City. **Web:** www.rollinggreensgolf.com.

Holes: 18. **Yards:** 5,189/4,679. **Par:** 65/67. **Course Rating:** 64.8/62.1. **Slope:** 116/98. **Green Fee:** $17/$23. **Cart Fee:** $12/person. **Walking Policy:** Unrestricted walking. **Walkability:** 1. **Opened:** 1969. **Architect:** Nicholas Psiahas. **Season:** Feb.-Dec. **High:** July-Sept. **To obtain tee times:** Call up to 7 days in advance. **Miscellaneous:** Reduced fees (weekdays, low season, twilight, seniors), range (grass), club rentals, credit cards (MC, V, AE).

RON JAWORSKI'S STONY BROOK COUNTRY CLUB

SP-Stony Brook Rd., Hopewell, 08525, (609)466-2215, 12 miles N of Trenton.
Special Notes: Call club for further information.

ROYCE BROOK GOLF CLUB

SP-201 Hamilton Rd., Somerville, 08876, Somerset County, (888)434-3673, (888)434-3673, 10 miles of NW of New Brunswick.

★★★½ EAST COURSE

Holes: 18. **Yards:** 6,983/5,014. **Par:** 72/72. **Course Rating:** 73.6/69.4. **Slope:** 132/114. **Green Fee:** $55/$70. **Cart Fee:** $15/person. **Walking Policy:** Walking at certain times. **Walkability:** 2. **Opened:** 1998. **Architect:** Steve Smyers. **Season:** Year-round. **High:** April-Oct. **Miscellaneous:** Reduced fees (weekdays), range (grass), club rentals, credit cards (MC, V, AE, D).

Reader Comments: Best newcomer in N.J. in '98 ... Good course ... Very nice, could play here 3 days a week, and never get tired of the course ... A ton of sand, looks like a beach. Great design course. A challenge.... ... Bring your A game... Typical new course drawbacks, but will be a really great course in 2-3 years.... Course condition was poor, but given enough time it should improve.

★★★★ WEST COURSE

SP-201 Hamilton Rd., Somerville, 08876, (888)434-3673, (888)434-3673, 10 miles NW of New Brunswick.

Holes: 18. **Yards:** 7,158/5,366. **Par:** 72/72. **Course Rating:** 74.2/70.6. **Slope:** 134/119. **Green Fee:** $55/$80. **Cart Fee:** $15/person. **Walking Policy:** Walking at certain times. **Walkability:** 2. **Opened:** 1998. **Architect:** Steve Smyers. **Season:** March-Nov. **High:** April-Oct. **To obtain tee times:** Call up to 7 days in advance. **Miscellaneous:** Reduced fees (weekdays), range (grass), caddies, club rentals, credit cards (MC, V, AE, D).

Reader Comments: Championship calibre ... Would play every week ... Young course, challenging and interesting ... Best 'new' in New Jersey ... 'Sand Traps-R-Us', masochists delight ... Two words: Desert Storm ... Scottish links-like design with deep bunkers and very long rough (knee high at least) that is beautiful to see and death to play from.

★★★½ RUTGERS UNIVERSITY GOLF COURSE

PU-777 Hoes Lane, Piscataway, 08854, Middlesex County, (732)445-2631, 3 miles N of New Brunswick.

Holes: 18. **Yards:** 6,337/5,359. **Par:** 71/72. **Course Rating:** 70.6/71.3. **Slope:** 123/121. **Green Fee:** $22/$31. **Cart Fee:** $28/cart. **Walking Policy:** Unrestricted walking. **Walkability:** 2. **Opened:** 1963. **Architect:** Hal Purdy. **Season:** March-Dec. **High:** April-Oct. **To obtain tee times:** Call Thursday at noon for following Monday-Friday. Come in up to 7 days in advance for weekend. **Miscellaneous:** Reduced fees (weekdays, twilight, seniors, juniors), cards (MC, V).

Reader Comments: Tough and cheap ... Very good course, great value ... Flat, but a few surprises ... Fun and great conditions, forgiving ... Nice scenery ... New irrigation system has brought the course to a new level ... Nice track, fair ... A sleeper.

SAND BARRENS GOLF CLUB

SP-1765 Rte. 9 North, Swainton, 08210, Cape May County, (609)465-3555, (800)465-3122, 70 miles S of Philadelphia, PA.

Holes: 27. **Green Fee:** $39/$98. **Cart Fee:** Included in Green Fee. **Walking Policy:** Unrestricted walking. **Walkability:** 2. **Opened:** 1997. **Architect:** Michael Hurdzan/Dana Fry. **Season:** Year-round. **High:** May-Sept. **To obtain tee times:** Call up to 7 days in advance. **Miscellaneous:** Reduced fees (weekdays, low season, twilight), range (grass), club rentals, credit cards (MC, V, AE, D).

★★★★ **NORTH/WEST** *Condition*
Yards: 7,092/4,951. **Par:** 72/72. **Course Rating:** 73.2/67.9. **Slope:** 135/119.
★★★★ **SOUTH/NORTH** *Condition*
Yards: 6,969/4,946. **Par:** 72/72. **Course Rating:** 72.7/68.0. **Slope:** 133/120. .
Notes: Ranked 14th in 1999 Best in State.
Reader Comments: Hard but fun, sand lines every fairway, every green ... Huge greens, lots of shot options ... Great sand traps ... Nice scenery, fun ... Always well kept ... Must place all shots ... New nine looks great, too ... One of the best anywhere along the shore ... Pine Valley-like look, sand wedge on all holes ... Outstanding, visually intimidating as hell.

★★★★ **SOUTH/WEST** *Condition*
Yards: 6,895/4,971. **Par:** 72/72. **Course Rating:** 71.7/68.3. **Slope:** 130/119.

★★★½ **SHARK RIVER GOLF COURSE**
PU-320 Old Corlies Ave., Neptune, 07753, Monmouth County, (732)922-4141, 50 miles S of Newark.
Holes: 18. **Yards:** 6,176/5,532. **Par:** 71/71. **Course Rating:** 68.7/70.8. **Slope:** 112/116. **Green Fee:** $18/$42. **Cart Fee:** $28/cart. **Walking Policy:** Unrestricted walking. **Walkability:** 2. **Opened:** 1973. **Architect:** Joseph "Scotty" Anson. **Season:** March-Dec. **High:** June-Sept. **To obtain tee times:** Nonresidents are on first come, first served, for open times. Reservations are booked through our automated system. **Miscellaneous:** Reduced fees (weekdays, twilight, seniors, juniors), club rentals.
Reader Comments: Tight, shotmaking required ... Good mix of holes ... Narrow, no water, lots of traps ... Nasty bunkers ... Best group of par threes (5) in Monmouth County system ... Long hitters can play most holes with irons ... Tough ninth hole.

★★★ **SPOOKY BROOK GOLF COURSE**
PU-582 Elizabeth Ave., Somerset, 08873, Somerset County, (732)231-1122, 30 miles W of New York City.
Holes: 18. **Yards:** 6,612/5,376. **Par:** 71/72. **Course Rating:** 71.0/70.8. **Slope:** 121/122. **Green Fee:** $13/$41. **Cart Fee:** $24/cart. **Walking Policy:** Unrestricted walking. **Walkability:** 1. **Opened:** 1970. **Architect:** Edmund Ault. **Season:** Year-round. **High:** May-Sept. **To obtain tee times:** 24-hour access number for a per reservation fee. **Miscellaneous:** Reduced fees (twilight, seniors, juniors), range (grass/mats), club rentals, credit cards (MC, V, AE).
Reader Comments: Midsize course, three scenic holes ... Bombs away, a lot of drivers ... Hit balls before you start. No. 1 is 430 into wind ... Wide open; great tune-up course ... Another good day-in, day-out public course ... Another fine county course.

★★★½ **SPRING MEADOW GOLF COURSE**
PU-4181 Atlantic Ave., Farmingdale, 07727, Monmouth County, (732)449-0806, 40 miles E of Trenton. **E-mail:** smgc@superlink.net. **Web:** www.smgc@superlink.net.
Holes: 18. **Yards:** 6,224/5,074. **Par:** 72/76. **Course Rating:** 70.4/70.6. **Slope:** 125/121. **Green Fee:** $19/$23. **Cart Fee:** $26/cart. **Walking Policy:** Unrestricted walking. **Walkability:** 3. **Opened:** 1920. **Architect:** Ron Faulseit. **Season:** Year-round. **High:** April-Oct. **To obtain tee times:** First come, first served. **Miscellaneous:** Reduced fees (weekdays, twilight, seniors), metal spikes, range (grass/mats), club rentals, credit cards (MC, V).
Reader Comments: Fun to play–some quirky holes can kill you ... Lay up at the fairway markers or you'll wind up in trouble! Great restaurant ... Great condition for a public course ... Every hole is different ... Short, but challenging, like playing in New England with the hills ...Nos. 10 and 11 are excellent.

★★★★ **SUNSET VALLEY GOLF COURSE** *Value*
PU-W. Sunset Rd., Pompton Plains, 07444, Morris County, (973)835-1515, 18 miles N of Morristown.
Holes: 18. **Yards:** 6,483/5,274. **Par:** 70/70. **Course Rating:** 71.4/70.2. **Slope:** 129/122. **Green Fee:** $13/$60. **Cart Fee:** $26/cart. **Walking Policy:** Unrestricted walking. **Walkability:** 4. **Opened:** 1974. **Architect:** Hal Purdy. **Season:** April-Nov. **High:** May-Sept. **To obtain tee times:** Call or come in person. **Miscellaneous:** Reduced fees (twilight, seniors), club rentals.
Reader Comments: Amazing views of mountains. No. 16 is a brute ... Conditions noticeably better ... Greens extremely tough ... Very challenging target golf with lightning greens ... Huge greens. Nos.16-17-18 are great finishing holes.

TAMARACK GOLF COURSE
PU-97 Hardenburg Lane, East Brunswick, 08816, Middlesex County, (732)821-8881, 6 miles E of New Brunswick.

★★½ EAST COURSE
Holes: 18. **Yards:** 6,226/5,346. **Par:** 71/71. **Course Rating:** 68.7/69.7. **Slope:** 111/113. **Green Fee:** $9/$60. **Cart Fee:** $26/cart. **Walking Policy:** Unrestricted walking. **Walkability:** 1. **Opened:** 1970. **Architect:** Hal Purdy. **Season:** Year-round. **High:** March-Oct. **To obtain tee times:** Call. **Miscellaneous:** Reduced fees (weekdays, seniors, juniors), range (mats), club rentals.

Reader Comments: Could be private club ... One of the best 'second shot' courses around ... Flat and short.

★★½ WEST COURSE
Holes: 18. **Yards:** 7,025/5,810. **Par:** 72/72. **Course Rating:** 72.9/72.5. **Slope:** 124/122. **Green Fee:** $9/$60. **Cart Fee:** $26/cart. **Walking Policy:** Unrestricted walking. **Walkability:** 1. **Opened:** 1970. **Architect:** Hal Purdy. **Season:** Year-round. **High:** March-Oct. **To obtain tee times:** Call. **Miscellaneous:** Reduced fees (weekdays, seniors, juniors), range (mats), club rentals.

Reader Comments: Love this layout, water, good par fives ... Very challenging: long and narrow ... New pace built into course with short par four and par three to start.

★★★ VALLEYBROOK GOLF CLUB
PU-200 Golfview, Blackwood, 08012, Camden County, (856)227-3171, 10 miles SE of Philadelphia, PA.

Holes: 18. **Yards:** 6,123/5,319. **Par:** 72/72. **Course Rating:** 70.6/69.1. **Slope:** 125/120. **Green Fee:** $18/$31. **Cart Fee:** $12/person. **Walking Policy:** Walking at certain times. **Walkability:** 3. **Opened:** 1990. **Season:** Year-round. **High:** April-Oct. **To obtain tee times:** Call 7 days in advance. **Miscellaneous:** Reduced fees (twilight), metal spikes, range (grass/mats), club rentals, credit cards (MC, V, AE, D).

Reader Comments: Nice little course ... Much improved and getting better ... Some memorable holes ... Pleasant surprise ... Challenging back nine ... Blind shots ... Some real hilly holes.

★★★ WARRENBROOK GOLF COURSE
PU-500 Warrenville Rd., Warren, 07059, Somerset County, (908)754-8402, 30 miles W of New York City.

Holes: 18. **Yards:** 6,372/5,095. **Par:** 71/70. **Course Rating:** 70.8/69.2. **Slope:** 124/117. **Green Fee:** $13/$41. **Cart Fee:** $24/cart. **Walking Policy:** Unrestricted walking. **Walkability:** 5. **Opened:** 1978. **Architect:** Hal Purdy. **Season:** April-Nov. **High:** May-Sept. **To obtain tee times:** 24-hour access number; per reservation fee (908)231-1122. **Miscellaneous:** Reduced fees (twilight, seniors, juniors), club rentals, credit cards (MC, V, AE).

Reader Comments: Very narrow fairways, fun to play, with challenging holes ... Hills galore.... Blind shots ... Trees, mountains, trees, a little water, and more trees ... Rocky, hilly, tight, not for spraying ... Deer crossing a challenge, too.

★★ WEDGEWOOD COUNTRY CLUB
PU-200 Hurffville Rd., Turnersville, 08012, Camden County, (856)401-9088, 10 miles E of Philadelphia.

Holes: 18. **Yards:** 7,074/6,356. **Par:** 72/72. **Course Rating:** 73.7/70.6. **Slope:** 133/129. **Green Fee:** $35/$45. **Cart Fee:** $15/person. **Walking Policy:** Walking at certain times. **Walkability:** 3. **Architect:** Gary Wrenn. **Season:** Year-round. **High:** May-Oct. **To obtain tee times:** Five days for members. Seven days for non-members. **Miscellaneous:** Reduced fees (twilight), club rentals, credit cards (MC, V).

★★★½ WESTWOOD GOLF CLUB
PU-850 Kings Hwy., Woodbury, 08096, Gloucester County, (856)845-2000, 10 miles S of Philadelphia, PA.

Holes: 18. **Yards:** 5,968/5,182. **Par:** 71/72. **Course Rating:** 68.2/69.2. **Slope:** 120/116. **Green Fee:** $20/$28. **Cart Fee:** $26/cart. **Walking Policy:** Mandatory cart. **Walkability:** 3. **Opened:** 1961. **Architect:** Horace W. Smith. **Season:** Year-round. **High:** April-Oct. **To obtain tee times:** Call on Monday for upcoming weekend. **Miscellaneous:** Reduced fees (twilight), metal spikes.

Reader Comments: Nice course, good value ... Always in outstanding condition, great greens, fast, multi-levels and good pin placement. The sleeper course in South Jersey ... Nice course for mid-handicappers ... Some tight holes ... Great back nine.

WILD OAKS GOLF CLUB
PU-75 Wild Oaks Dr., Salem, 08079, Salem County, (856)935-0705, 45 miles S of Philadelphia.

Holes: 27. **Green Fee:** $20/$30. **Cart Fee:** Included in Green Fee. **Walking Policy:** Walking at certain times. **Walkability:** 1. **Opened:** 1968. **Season:** Year-round. **High:** May-Sept. **To obtain tee times:** Call for weekends. **Miscellaneous:** Reduced fees (weekdays, low season, twilight), club rentals, credit cards (MC, V).

★★★ PIN OAKS/WHITE CEDAR
Yards: 6,505/5,336. **Par:** 72/72. **Course Rating:** 71.4/71.0. **Slope:** 125/119.

Reader Comments: Greens very fast ... Nice looking course, some tougher holes ... Out of the way, but charming ... Good layout, fair condition, staff is well trained and friendly ... Best buy for the price.

544

★★★ **WHITE CEDAR/WILLOW OAKS**
Yards: 6,726/5,322. **Par:** 72/72. **Course Rating:** 72.1/71.4. **Slope:** 126/118.
★★★ **WILLOW OAKS/PIN OAKS**
Yards: 6,633/5,360. **Par:** 72/72. **Course Rating:** 71.8/71.1. **Slope:** 122/119.

★★½ **WILLOW BROOK COUNTRY CLUB**
SP-4310 Bridgeboro Rd., Moorestown, 08057, Burlington County, (609)461-0131, 10 miles SE of Cherry Hills.
Holes: 18. **Yards:** 6,457/5,028. **Par:** 72/72. **Course Rating:** 71.2/68.3. **Slope:** 125/110. **Green Fee:** $18/$35. **Cart Fee:** $28/cart. **Walking Policy:** Walking at certain times. **Walkability:** 2. **Opened:** 1967. **Architect:** William Gordon. **Season:** Year-round. **High:** May-Sept. **To obtain tee times:** Call Monday to Friday for weekend tee time, call anytime for weekday. **Miscellaneous:** Reduced fees (weekdays, low season, twilight, seniors, juniors), discount packages, range (grass), club rentals, credit cards (MC, V, AE, D), beginner friendly (reduced fees for juniors. walking after 1:00 p.m).
Reader Comments: Good basic golf. 18th a nice finish ... Super value ... No. 14 from blues memorable ... No. 3 a good one ... Best finishing hole in area ... Bring your driver.

★★★½ **WOODLAKE COUNTRY CLUB**
SP-25 New Hampshire Ave., Lakewood, 08701, Ocean County, (732)370-1002, 50 miles S of New York.
Holes: 18. **Yards:** 6,766/5,491. **Par:** 72/74. **Course Rating:** 72.6/72.3. **Slope:** 131/123. **Green Fee:** $25/$65. **Cart Fee:** $18/person. **Walking Policy:** Walking at certain times. **Walkability:** 1. **Opened:** 1972. **Architect:** Edward L. Packard. **Season:** Year-round. **High:** May-Sept. **To obtain tee times:** Nonmembers call 3 days in advance. **Miscellaneous:** Reduced fees (weekdays, low season, twilight, juniors), discount packages, range (grass/mats), credit cards (MC, V, AE).
Reader Comments: Nice design, particularly back nine ... A pleasant place to play ... Tight fairways, well manicured ... Some tough water holes ... Solid choice, usually in good condition ... Course was challenging. Great track ... Super-fast greens.

★★½ ANGEL FIRE COUNTRY CLUB
Drawer B, Angel Fire, 87710, Taos County, (505)377-3055, 150 miles NW of Albuquerque.
Holes: 18. **Yards:** 6,624/5,328. **Par:** 72/72. **Course Rating:** N/A. **Slope:** 128/118. **Green Fee:** N/A. **Cart Fee:** $20/cart. **Walkability:** N/A. **Season:** May-Oct. **High:** June-Sept. **Miscellaneous:** Reduced fees (low season, resort guests), discount packages, metal spikes, lodging, credit cards (MC, V, AE, D).
Reader Comments: Outstanding mountain layout ... Greens need a lot of work.

ANTHONY COUNTRY CLUB
SP-Anthony Gap Hwy. 460, Anthony, 88021 (505)882-272.
Special Notes: Call club for further information.

★★★½ ARROYO DEL OSO MUNICIPAL GOLF COURSE
PM-7001 Osuna Rd. N.E., Albuquerque, 87109, Bernalillo County, (505)884-7505.
Holes: 18. **Yards:** 6,892/5,998. **Par:** 72/73. **Course Rating:** 72.3/72.3. **Slope:** 125/120. **Green Fee:** $15/$20. **Cart Fee:** $10/person. **Walking Policy:** Unrestricted walking. **Walkability:** 3. **Opened:** 1966. **Architect:** Arthur Jack Snyder. **Season:** Year-round. **High:** April-Nov. **To obtain tee times:** Call in advance on Wednesday prior to weekend or holiday. **Miscellaneous:** Reduced fees (twilight, seniors, juniors), range (grass/mats), club rentals, credit cards (MC, V, AE, D).
Reader Comments: Beautiful layout & friendly people ... Best mu. / in Albuquerque but heavily played ... Rates were acceptable ... Interesting ... Great to walk.

CANNON AFB GOLF COURSE-WHISPERING WINDS
M-105 Forrest Dr., Clovis, 88103, Curry County, (505)784-2800, 90 miles W of Lubbock, TX.
Holes: 18. **Yards:** 6,032/4,954. **Par:** 70/70. **Course Rating:** 67.6/64.8. **Slope:** 104/99. **Green Fee:** N/A/$12. **Cart Fee:** $15/cart. **Walking Policy:** Unrestricted walking. **Walkability:** 1. **Opened:** 1994. **Season:** Year-round. **High:** Mar.-Sept. **To obtain tee times:** Call (505)784-2800. **Miscellaneous:** Reduced fees (twilight, seniors, juniors), range (grass), club rentals, credit cards (MC, V).

CLAYTON GOLF COURSE
PU-P.O. Box 4, Clayton, 88415, Union County, (505)374-9957.
Holes: 9. **Yards:** 6,536/5,422. **Par:** 72/72. **Course Rating:** 68.2/68.2. **Slope:** 105/104. **Green Fee:** $8/$10. **Walkability:** 1. **Opened:** 1953. **Season:** Year-round. **High:** April-Oct.
Miscellaneous: Reduced fees (weekdays), metal spikes, range (grass), beginner friendly.

COLONIAL PARK COUNTRY CLUB
SP-1300 Colonial Pkwy., Clovis, 88101, (505)762-4775.
Holes: 27. **Yards:** 6,532/6,064. **Par:** 72/75. **Course Rating:** 69.7/71.9. **Slope:** 111/116. **Green Fee:** $9/$14. **Cart Fee:** $9/person. **Walking Policy:** Unrestricted walking. **Walkability:** 1. **Opened:** 1964. **Season:** Year-round. **High:** May- Sept. **To obtain tee times:** Call the golf shop (505)762-4775. **Miscellaneous:** Metal spikes, range (grass), club rentals, beginner friendly (range, par-3 9-hole course).

CONCHAS DAM GOLF COURSE
PU-Conchas Dam State Park, Conchas Dam, 88416 (505)461-1849.
Special Notes: Call club for further information.

COYOTE DE MALPAIS
PU-2001 Golf Course Road, Grants, 87020, Cibola County, (505)285-5544, (800)748-2142, 79 miles W of Albuquerque. **E-mail:** coyote@7cities.net.
Holes: 18. **Yards:** 7,087/5,138. **Par:** 71/71. **Course Rating:** 71.8/67.2. **Slope:** 120/117. **Green Fee:** $14/$16. **Cart Fee:** $8/person. **Walking Policy:** Unrestricted walking. **Walkability:** 2. **Opened:** 1994. **Season:** Year-round. **High:** June-Aug. **To obtain tee times:** Telephone anytime. **Miscellaneous:** Reduced fees (weekdays, low season, twilight, juniors), range (grass), club rentals, credit cards (MC, V).

CREE MEADOWS COUNTRY CLUB
PU-301 Country Club Dr., Ruidoso, 88345 (505)257-5815.
Special Notes: Call club for further information.

DESERT LAKES GOLF COURSE
PU-2351 Hamilton Rd., Alamogordo, 88310, Otero County, (505)437-0290, 86 miles NE of Ell Paso, TX.
Holes: 18. **Yards:** 6,671/5,724. **Par:** 72/72. **Course Rating:** 70.5/64.8. **Slope:** 122/108. **Green Fee:** $13/$15. **Cart Fee:** $16/cart. **Walking Policy:** Unrestricted walking. **Walkability:** 2. **Opened:** 1950. **Season:** Year-round. **High:** June-Aug. **To obtain tee times:** First come, first served. Tee times suggested for weekends and holidays only. **Miscellaneous:** Reduced fees (twilight, juniors), discount packages, range (grass), club rentals, credit cards (MC, V), beginner friendly.

DOS LAGOS GOLF CLUB
PU-232 Duffer Lane, Anthony, 88021, Dona Ana County, (505)882-2830, 20 miles N of El Paso.

Holes: 18. **Yards:** 6,424/5,658. **Par:** 72/72. **Course Rating:** 70.4/70.6. **Slope:** 120/111. **Green Fee:** $11/$15. **Cart Fee:** $16/person. **Walking Policy:** Unrestricted walking. **Walkability:** 1. **Opened:** 1963. **Architect:** Sam Gillett. **Season:** Year-round. **High:** May-Aug. **To obtain tee times:** Weekends and holidays call up to 7 days in advance. Weekdays, call prior day. **Miscellaneous:** Reduced fees (twilight, juniors), metal spikes, range (grass), club rentals.

EUNICE MUNICIPAL GOLF COURSE
PM-Carlsbad Hwy, Eunice, 88231 (505)394-2881.
Special Notes: Call club for further information.

GALLUP MUNICIPAL GOLF COURSE
PM-1109 Susan St., Gallup, 87301 (505)863-9224.
Special Notes: Call club for further information.

HIDDEN VALLEY COUNTRY CLUB
PU-29 County Rd. 3025, Aztec, 87410, San Juan County, (505)334-3248, 2 miles SW of Aztec.
Holes: 18. **Yards:** 6,850/5,710. **Par:** 72/72. **Course Rating:** N/A. **Slope:** N/A. **Green Fee:** $15/$20. **Walkability:** 2. **Architect:** Ken Lacy. **Season:** Year-round. **High:** April-Sept.
Miscellaneous: Reduced fees (resort guests), discount packages, range (grass), club rentals, credit cards (MC, V, D), beginner friendly.
Special Notes: Course re-opening in July 2000, after renovations.

★★★★ INN OF THE MOUNTAIN GODS GOLF COURSE
R-P.O. Box 269, Rte. 4, Mescalero, 88340, Otero County, (505)257-5141, (800)446-2963, 80 miles NE of Las Cruces.
Holes: 18. **Yards:** 6,834/5,478. **Par:** 72/72. **Course Rating:** 72.1/70.2. **Slope:** 132/128. **Green Fee:** $40/$60. **Cart Fee:** $20/cart. **Walking Policy:** Mandatory cart. **Walkability:** 5. **Opened:** 1975. **Architect:** Theodore G. Robinson. **Season:** March-Dec. **High:** May-Oct. **To obtain tee times:** Resort guests may call anytime. Nonguests call 14 days in advance. **Miscellaneous:** Reduced fees (low season), range (grass/mats), club rentals, lodging (250 rooms), credit cards (MC, V, AE, D).
Notes: Ranked 7th in 1999 Best in State.
Reader Comments: Stunning mountain, lake, forest course ... Beautiful course ... Too far off the beaten path ... Tough mountain course ... Obsessed with pace of play ... Greens like glass ... Worth the money ... People a little rude... When kept in good condition, one of the best ... Great par-3 finishing hole ... Awesome mountain course ... Everybody should play this once in their life!

ISLETA EAGLE GOLF COURSE
PU-4001 Hwy. 47 SE, Albuquerque, 87105, Bernalillo County, (505)869-0950.
Holes: 27. **Green Fee:** $30/$36. **Cart Fee:** Included in Green Fee. **Walking Policy:** Mandatory cart. **Walkability:** N/A. **Opened:** 1996. **Architect:** Bill Phillips. **To obtain tee times:** Call golf shop up to 5 days in advance. **Miscellaneous:** Reduced fees (twilight, seniors, juniors), range (grass), club rentals, credit cards (MC, V, AE, D).
LAKES/ARROYO
Yards: 7,090/5,237. **Par:** 72/72. **Course Rating:** 72.9/68.1. **Slope:** 128/119.
LAKES/MESA
Yards: 7,538/5,620. **Par:** 72/72. **Course Rating:** 75.1/71.3. **Slope:** 131/125.
Notes: Ranked 8th in 1999 Best in State.
MESA/ARROYO
Yards: 7,138/5,235. **Par:** 72/72. **Course Rating:** 73.2/68.9. **Slope:** 127/119.

★★★ LADERA GOLF COURSE
PM-3401 Ladera Dr. N.W., Albuquerque, 87120, Bernalillo County, (505)836-4449.
Holes: 18. **Yards:** 7,307/5,966. **Par:** 72/72. **Course Rating:** 73.0/72.8. **Slope:** 130/116. **Green Fee:** $8/$15. **Cart Fee:** $21/cart. **Walking Policy:** Unrestricted walking. **Walkability:** 2. **Opened:** 1980. **Architect:** Dick Phelps. **Season:** Year-round. **High:** April-Sept. **To obtain tee times:** Call or come in Wednesday at 7 a.m. for upcoming weekend or holiday. Foursomes may call up to 7 days in advance for weekdays. **Miscellaneous:** Reduced fees (twilight, seniors, juniors), discount packages, metal spikes, range (grass/mats), club rentals, credit cards (MC, V, AE, D).
Reader Comments: A very good small course ... Not too many trees ... Basic, flat golf.

LAKE CARLSBAD GOLF COURSE
PU-901 North Muscatel, Carlsbad, 88220 (505)885-5444.
Special Notes: Call club for further information.

LAS CRUCES COUNTRY CLUB
P.O. Box 876, Las Cruces, 88004, Dona Ana County, (505)526-8731.
Special Notes: Call club for further information.

★★★★ THE LINKS AT SIERRA BLANCA
PU-105 Sierra Blanca Dr., Ruidoso, 88345, Lincoln County, (505)258-5330, (800)854-6571, 135 miles NE of El Paso. **E-mail:** links@ruidoso.org. **Web:** www.trekwest.com.

Holes: 18. **Yards:** 6,793/5,071. **Par:** 72/72. **Course Rating:** 71.9/62.7. **Slope:** 127/104. **Green Fee:** $26/$65. **Cart Fee:** $12/person. **Walking Policy:** Walking at certain times. **Walkability:** 3. **Opened:** 1990. **Architect:** Jeff Brauer/Jim Colbert. **Season:** Year-round. **High:** June-Sept. **To obtain tee times:** Call 14 days in advance. **Miscellaneous:** Reduced fees (weekdays, low season, twilight, seniors, juniors), range (grass), club rentals, credit cards (MC, V, AE, D), beginner friendly.
Notes: Ranked 9th in 1999 Best in State.
Reader Comments: Links style on front 9, mountain on back ... Well maintained and fun to play ... Walkable ... A bit expensive ... Excellent course with good service ... Worth playing ... Lots of mounds.

THE LODGE GOLF CLUB
R-1 Corona Place, Cloudcroft, 88317, Otero County, (505)682-2098, (800)395-6343, 100 miles NE of El Paso.
Holes: 9. **Yards:** 2,471/2,036. **Par:** 34/34. **Course Rating:** 63.0/65.0. **Slope:** 97/103. **Green Fee:** $18/$26. **Cart Fee:** $10/person. **Walking Policy:** Unrestricted walking. **Walkability:** 5.
Opened: 1899. **Season:** April-Nov. **High:** June-Aug. **To obtain tee times:** Call with credit card to guarantee. **Miscellaneous:** Reduced fees (weekdays, resort guests, twilight), discount packages, metal spikes, range (grass/mats), club rentals, lodging, credit cards (MC, V, AE, D).

★★★½ LOS ALAMOS GOLF CLUB
PU-4250 Diamond Dr., Los Alamos, 87544, Los Alamos County, (505)662-8139, 35 miles N of Santa Fe. **E-mail:** torresd@lac.losalamos.nm.us..
Holes: 18. **Yards:** 6,496/5,301. **Par:** 72/72. **Course Rating:** 70.2/69.3. **Slope:** 124/120. **Green Fee:** $20/$24. **Cart Fee:** $20/cart. **Walking Policy:** Unrestricted walking. **Walkability:** 4.
Opened: 1947. **Architect:** Bill Keith/William Tucker. **Season:** March-Nov. **High:** June-Sept. **To obtain tee times:** Call 1 day in advance for weekdays. Call on Tuesday evening, phone (505)661-4560 for upcoming weekend or holidays. **Miscellaneous:** Reduced fees (weekdays), discount packages, range (mats), club rentals, credit cards (MC, V).
Reader Comments: Tiny greens ... Back nine is better ... Because of surrounding mountains, greens very difficult to read ... Great, short mountain course off the beaten track ... Condition very dependent on winter weather conditions.

★★½ LOS ALTOS GOLF COURSE
PM-9717 Copper N.E. St., Albuquerque, 87123, Bernalillo County, (505)298-1897. **E-mail:** cemoya@aol.com. **Web:** golfatlosaltos.com.
Holes: 27. **Yards:** 6,459/5,895. **Par:** 71/74. **Course Rating:** 69.9/71.9. **Slope:** 110/113. **Green Fee:** $15/$15. **Cart Fee:** $13/person. **Walking Policy:** Unrestricted walking. **Walkability:** 2.
Opened: 1960. **Architect:** Bob Baldock. **Season:** Year-round. **High:** May-Aug. **To obtain tee times:** Call Tuesday before the upcoming weekend. **Miscellaneous:** Reduced fees (weekdays, low season, twilight, seniors, juniors), range (grass/mats), club rentals, credit cards (MC, V, D).
Reader Comments: Good muny course for the money ... Good layout in good condition ... Good value ... Easy, basic, golf ... Fun to play, very fair, nice greens.

MARTY SANCHEZ LINKS DE SANTA FE
PU-205 Caja del Rio, Santa Fe, 87501, Santa Fe County, (505)438-5200, 6 miles W of Santa Fe. **Web:** www.newmexicogolfcourses.com.
Holes: 18. **Yards:** 7,415/5,045. **Par:** 72/72. **Course Rating:** 72.7/67.8. **Slope:** 124/126. **Green Fee:** $29/$49. **Cart Fee:** $11/person. **Walking Policy:** Unrestricted walking. **Walkability:** 2.
Opened: 1998. **Architect:** Baxter Spann. **Season:** Year-round. **High:** May-Oct. **To obtain tee times:** Call up to 7 days in advance. **Miscellaneous:** Reduced fees (twilight), range (grass/mats), club rentals, credit cards (MC, V, AE, D), beginner friendly (beginner & intermediate group lessons).
Special Notes: Reduced fees for NM residents.

★★★ NEW MEXICO INSTITUTE OF MINING GOLF COURSE
PU-1 Canyon Rd., Socorro, 87801, Socorro County, (505)835-5335, 75 miles S of Albuquerque.
Holes: 18. **Yards:** 6,688/5,887. **Par:** 72/73. **Course Rating:** 71.2/72.8. **Slope:** 126/122. **Green Fee:** $15/$20. **Cart Fee:** $20/cart. **Walking Policy:** Unrestricted walking. **Walkability:** 4.
Opened: 1953. **Architect:** James Voss. **Season:** Year-round. **High:** April-Oct. **To obtain tee times:** Call 7 days in advance. **Miscellaneous:** Reduced fees (twilight, seniors, juniors), discount packages, range (grass/mats), club rentals, credit cards (MC, V, AE, D).
Reader Comments: Tough course ... Low prices ... A fun old course ... Need your whole game, hilly ... Explosions by EMRTC can be heard & felt.

NEW MEXICO MILITARY INSTITUTE GOLF COURSE
PU-201 West Nineteenth St., Roswell, 88201, Chaves County, (505)622-6033, 200 miles S of Albuquerque.
Holes: 18. **Yards:** 6,639/5,275. **Par:** 72/72. **Course Rating:** 70.1/68.2. **Slope:** 116/113. **Green Fee:** $15/N/A. **Cart Fee:** $9/person. **Walking Policy:** Unrestricted walking. **Walkability:** 2.

NEW MEXICO

Season: Year-round. **High:** June-Aug. **Miscellaneous:** Reduced fees (seniors, juniors), range (grass), club rentals, lodging (80 rooms), credit cards (MC, V, AE, D), beginner friendly (lessons).

★★★½ NEW MEXICO STATE UNIVERSITY GOLF COURSE

PU-P.O. Box 30001, Dept. 3595, Las Cruces, 88003, Dona Ana County, (505)646-3219, 45 miles N of El Paso, TX.

Holes: 18. **Yards:** 7,040/5,858. **Par:** 72/74. **Course Rating:** 74.1/70.7. **Slope:** 133/120. **Green Fee:** $20/$25. **Cart Fee:** $8/person. **Walking Policy:** Unrestricted walking. **Walkability:** 3. **Opened:** 1962. **Architect:** Floyd Farley. **Season:** Year-round. **High:** April-May/Sept.-Oct. **To obtain tee times:** Call Thursdays for upcoming weekdays. Call Wednesday for upcoming weekend. **Miscellaneous:** Reduced fees (weekdays, twilight), range (grass/mats), club rentals, credit cards (MC, V, D).

Reader Comments: Everything was lush, greens you dream about! ... Very accommodating ... Long hilly ... Green fees a little high for the area ... Good price, crowded ... Tight landing areas, difficult greens ... Wind-wind-wind.

★★½ OCOTILLO PARK GOLF COURSE

PU-5001 Jack Gomez Blvd., Hobbs, 88240, Lea County, (505)397-9297, 130 miles W of Lubbock, TX.

Holes: 18. **Yards:** 6,716/5,245. **Par:** 72/72. **Course Rating:** 70.5/69.0. **Slope:** 121/108. **Green Fee:** $7/$9. **Cart Fee:** $9/person. **Walking Policy:** Unrestricted walking. **Walkability:** 1. **Opened:** 1955. **Architect:** Warren Cantrell/M. Ferguson. **Season:** Year-round. **High:** April-Aug. **To obtain tee times:** Call Wednesday 8 a.m. **Miscellaneous:** Reduced fees (weekdays, twilight, seniors, juniors), metal spikes, range (grass), club rentals, credit cards (MC, V, AE, D).

★★★ PARADISE HILLS GOLF CLUB

PU-10035 Country Club Lane, Albuquerque, 87114, Bernalillo County, (505)898-7001.

Holes: 18. **Yards:** 6,801/6,090. **Par:** 72/74. **Course Rating:** 71.7/73.5. **Slope:** 125/118. **Green Fee:** $22/$31. **Cart Fee:** $7/person. **Walking Policy:** Mandatory cart. **Walkability:** 2. **Opened:** 1963. **Architect:** Red Lawrence. **Season:** Year-round. **High:** March-Oct. **To obtain tee times:** Call 7 days in advance with credit card to guarantee. **Miscellaneous:** Reduced fees (weekdays, low season, twilight, seniors, juniors), discount packages, range (grass), club rentals, lodging, credit cards (MC, V, AE, D).

Reader Comments: Enjoyable golf ... Love the player's club member benefits ... Boo! ... Nice pro shop ... A good test, a pleasant surprise ... Very nice course with open fairways ... Good course to score on ... Pretty course.

PENDARIES VILLAGE GOLF & COUNTRY CLUB

R-P.O. Box 847, Rociada, 87742 (505)425-6018
Special Notes Call club for further information.

PICACHO HILLS COUNTRY CLUB

SP-6861 Via Campestre, Las Cruces, 88005, Dona Ana County, (505)523-8641, 30 miles N of El Paso, TX.

Holes: 18. **Yards:** 6,880/5,214. **Par:** 72/72. **Course Rating:** 72.9/70.0. **Slope:** 134/118. **Green Fee:** $25/$30. **Cart Fee:** $10/person. **Walking Policy:** Unrestricted walking. **Walkability:** 3. **Opened:** 1978. **Architect:** Joe Finger. **Season:** Year-round. **High:** Aug.-Nov. **To obtain tee times:** Call up to 7 days in advance. Members only play until 11 a.m. daily. **Miscellaneous:** Range (grass), club rentals, credit cards (MC, V).

★★★★★ PINON HILLS GOLF COURSE   *Value+, Condition+, Pace*

PM-2101 Sunrise Pkwy., Farmington, 87402, San Juan County, (505)326-6066, 180 miles N of Albuquerque, NM.

Holes: 18. **Yards:** 7,249/5,522. **Par:** 72/72. **Course Rating:** 73.3/71.1. **Slope:** 130/126. **Green Fee:** $13/$15. **Cart Fee:** $15/cart. **Walking Policy:** Unrestricted walking. **Walkability:** 5. **Opened:** 1989. **Architect:** Ken Dye. **Season:** Year-round. **High:** May-Oct. **To obtain tee times:** Call 3 days in advance. Out-of-town players may call up to 60 days in advance for $5 reservation fee. **Miscellaneous:** Reduced fees (weekdays), range (grass/mats), club rentals, credit cards (MC, V).

Notes: Ranked 2nd in 1999 Best in State; 1st in 1996 America's Top 75 Affordable Courses.

Reader Comments: Best course for the money in USA ... Killer rough, diabolical greens ... Drove 6 hrs. to play and stayed for 2nd day ... Memorable ... Outstanding value, great staff & fine layout ... Lived up to its reputation ... Great hole variety and a great bargain! ... Multi-tiered greens are tough ... Bring your best short game ... Lots of wildlife ... Use every club in bag ... Worth the trip from anywhere.

★★★★ PUEBLO DE COCHITI GOLF COURSE

PU-5200 Cochiti Hwy., Cochiti Lake, 87083, Sandoval County, (505)465-2239, 35 miles SW of Santa Fe.

Holes: 18. **Yards:** 6,451/5,292. **Par:** 72/72. **Course Rating:** 71.2/70.6. **Slope:** 131/121. **Green Fee:** $18/$32. **Cart Fee:** $11/person. **Walking Policy:** Unrestricted walking. **Walkability:** 5.

Opened: 1981. **Architect:** Robert Trent Jones Jr. **Season:** Year-round weather permitting. **High:** March-Sept. **To obtain tee times:** Call up to 7 days in advance. **Miscellaneous:** Reduced fees (weekdays, low season, twilight, juniors), range (grass), club rentals, credit cards (MC, V, D). **Notes:** Ranked 5th in 1999 Best in State; 47th in 1996 America's Top 75 Affordable Courses. **Reader Comments:** Signature arroyo washes, beautiful and tricky ... A shotmaker's course that plays differently every round ... Worth seeking out ... Work on your tee shots or bring extra balls ... Local knowledge helps, worth trip ... Too many goofy holes ... Very hilly, small greens.

RIO MIMBRES COUNTRY CLUB

SP-Motel Drive East, Deming, 88030, Luna County, (505)546-9481, 100 miles NW of El Paso. **Holes:** 18. **Yards:** 3,701/5,454. **Par:** 72/72. **Course Rating:** 72.0/69.0. **Slope:** 125/111. **Green Fee:** $14/$16. **Cart Fee:** $7/. **Walking Policy:** Unrestricted walking. **Walkability:** N/A. **Opened:** 1950. **Architect:** Keith Foster. **Season:** Year-round. **High:** June-Aug. **To obtain tee times:** Tee times for weekends only. Members have priority until Friday morning. **Miscellaneous:** Reduced fees (juniors), discount packages, metal spikes, range (grass), club rentals.

RIVER VIEW GOLF COURSE

PU-4146 U. S. Hwy. 64, Farmington, 87417, San Juan County, (505)598-0140, 7 miles W of Farmington. **E-mail:** reid.desjc.cc.nm.us. **Holes:** 18. **Yards:** 6,853/5,239. **Par:** 72/72. **Course Rating:** 70.5/70.4. **Slope:** 121/118. **Green Fee:** $13/$14. **Cart Fee:** $8/person. **Walking Policy:** Unrestricted walking. **Walkability:** 4. **Opened:** 1978. **Architect:** Baxder Spann. **Season:** Year-round. **High:** May-Oct. **To obtain tee times:** Call 1 week in advance. **Miscellaneous:** Reduced fees (weekdays), range (grass/mats), credit cards (MC, V, D), beginner friendly.

SANTA ANA GOLF CLUB

PU-288 Prairie Star Rd., Bernalillo, 87004, Sandoval County, (505)867-9464, 15 miles N of Albuquerque. **Web:** www.santaanagolf.com. **Holes:** 27.**Green Fee:** $29/$35. **Cart Fee:** $11/person. **Walking Policy:** Unrestricted walking. **Walkability:** 3. **Opened:** 1991. **Architect:** Ken Killian. **Season:** Year-round. **High:** March-Oct. **To obtain tee times:** Call 7 days in advance for weekdays and 3 days in advance for weekends, beginning at 7:30 a. m. **Miscellaneous:** Reduced fees (weekdays, twilight, seniors, juniors), range (grass), club rentals, credit cards (MC, V, AE, D).

★★★½ **CHEENA/STAR**
Yards: 7,152/5,058. **Par:** 71/71. **Course Rating:** 72.9/67.3. **Slope:** 134/121.
Notes: 1999 Women's Amateur Public Links Championship.
Reader Comments: Excellent variety, good services and beautiful new clubhouse ... Thought I was in Scotland ... 27 holes of spectacular views ... Can be very windy ... Nasty rough ... Flat and windy ... Greens are brutal ... Fun

★★★½ **TAMAYA/CHEENA**
Yards: 7,258/5,044. **Par:** 71/71. **Course Rating:** 74.1/68.2. **Slope:** 132/122.
Notes: Ranked 6th in 1999 Best in State. 1999 Women's Amateur Public Links Championship.
Reader Comments: Nice use of natural setting ... Can be very windy.

★★★½ **TAMAYA/STAR**
Notes: 1999 Women's Amateur Public Links Championship.
Reader Comments: Another beauty and challenging ... Tough par 3s. Desert course, greens great but slopes severe.
Special Notes: Formerly Valle Grande Golf Club.

SANTA FE COUNTRY CLUB

SP-Airport Rd., Santa Fe, 87592, Santa Fe County, (505)471-0601, 50 miles N of Albuquerque. **Holes:** 18. **Yards:** 7,098/5,862. **Par:** 72/74. **Course Rating:** 71.7/72.1. **Slope:** 125/129. **Green Fee:** $55/$55. **Cart Fee:** $22/person. **Walking Policy:** Unrestricted walking. **Walkability:** 1. **Opened:** 1941. **Season:** Year-round. **High:** May-Oct. **Miscellaneous:** Reduced fees (juniors), range (grass), club rentals, credit cards (MC, V).

SILVER CITY GOLF CLUB

PU-Fairway Dr., Silver City, 88062 (505)538-5041.
Special Notes: Call club for further information.

SPRING RIVER GOLF COURSE

PU-1612 W. 8th St., Roswell, 88201 (505)622-9506.
Special Notes: Call club for further information.

★★★★ **TAOS COUNTRY CLUB**
SP-54 Golf Course Drive, Rancho de Taos, 87557, Taos County, (505)758-7300, (800)758-7375, 58 miles N of Santa Fe. **Holes:** 18. **Yards:** 7,302/5,343. **Par:** 72/72. **Course Rating:** 72.8/68.7. **Slope:** 124/121. **Green Fee:** $35/$45. **Cart Fee:** $12/person. **Walking Policy:** Unrestricted walking. **Walkability:** 3. **Opened:** 1992. **Architect:** Jep Wille. **Season:** March-Nov. **High:** June-Sept. **To obtain tee times:**

Call 7 days in advance. **Miscellaneous:** Reduced fees (weekdays, low season, twilight, juniors), discount packages, range (grass/mats), caddies, club rentals, credit cards (MC, V, AE, D). **Notes:** Ranked 4th in 1999 Best in State; 15th in 1996 America's Top 75 Affordable Courses. **Reader Comments:** Links style, beautiful rolling valley ... Mounds require creative chipping ... Unbelievable condition, even late in season ... Wonderful greens ... Tends to be windy ... Ball goes a long way at 7000 ft. elevation ... A jewel in the desert ... Go there!

★★★½ TIERRA DEL SOL GOLF COURSE
SP-1000 Golf Course Rd., Belen, 87002, Valencia County, (505)865-5056, 34 miles S of Albuquerque.
Holes: 18. **Yards:** 6,703/5,512. **Par:** 72/72. **Course Rating:** 71.0/71.2. **Slope:** 117/114. **Green Fee:** $15/$19. **Cart Fee:** $9/. **Walking Policy:** Walking at certain times. **Walkability:** N/A.
Opened: 1971. **Season:** Year-round. **High:** April-Oct. **To obtain tee times:** Call up to 7 days in advance. **Miscellaneous:** Reduced fees (weekdays, twilight, juniors), metal spikes, range (grass), club rentals, credit cards (MC, V).
Reader Comments: Very good course ... Condition up & down ... This was so much fun lets do it again ... Too many 90-degree doglegs ... OB on both sides of several holes ... Bent over backwards to be helpful.

TIJERAS ARROYO GOLF COURSE
M-Kirtland AFB, Albuquerque, 87117, Bernalillo County, (505)846-1169.
Holes: 18. **Yards:** 6,970/6,445. **Par:** 72/72. **Course Rating:** 71.9/69.8. **Slope:** 126/121. **Green Fee:** $12/$20. **Cart Fee:** $16/cart. **Walking Policy:** Unrestricted walking. **Walkability:** 2.
Opened: 1971. **Season:** Year-round. **High:** April-Nov. **To obtain tee times:** Call 8 days in advance. **Miscellaneous:** Reduced fees (twilight, seniors, juniors), discount packages, range (grass/mats), club rentals, credit cards (MC, V), beginner friendly (clinics).

TIMBERON GOLF CLUB
PU-Pleasant Valley Rd., Timberon, 88350, Otero County, (505)987-2260, (877)550-9714, 50 miles SE of Alamogordo.
Holes: 18. **Yards:** 6,772/4,648. **Par:** 72/72. **Course Rating:** 71.4/65.0. **Slope:** 126/114. **Green Fee:** $14/$18. **Cart Fee:** $16/person. **Walking Policy:** Walking at certain times. **Walkability:** 5.
Opened: 1978. **Architect:** Basil Smith. **Season:** April-Oct. **High:** May-Sept. **Miscellaneous:** Range (grass), club rentals, credit cards (MC, V, AE, D, Diners Club).

TRUTH OR CONSEQUENCES MUNICIPAL GOLF COURSE
PM-685 Marie St., Truth or Consequences, 87901 (505)894-2603.
Special Notes: Call club for further information.

TUCUMCARI MUNICIPAL GOLF COURSE
PU-4465 C. Rte. 66, Tucumcari, 88401, Quay County, (505)461-1849, 5 miles W of Tucumcari on historical #66. **E-mail:** jcgolf@sr66.com.
Holes: 9. **Yards:** 6,643/5,702. **Par:** 72/74. **Course Rating:** 70.6/71.0. **Slope:** 113/118. **Green Fee:** $7/$11. **Cart Fee:** $18/cart. **Walking Policy:** Unrestricted walking. **Walkability:** 3. **Opened:** 1946. **Season:** Year round. **High:** April-Oct. **To obtain tee times:** Call prior to arrival.
Miscellaneous: Reduced fees (juniors), range (grass), club rentals, beginner friendly (laid-back pace of play).

★★★★ UNIVERSITY OF NEW MEXICO GOLF COURSE   *Condition*
PU-3601 University Blvd., S.E., Albuquerque, 87106, Bernalillo County, (505)277-4546. **Web:** http://www.unm.edu/~golf.
Holes: 18. **Yards:** 7,248/6,031. **Par:** 72/73. **Course Rating:** 74.3/75.1. **Slope:** 134/131. **Green Fee:** $23/$67. **Cart Fee:** $11/person. **Walking Policy:** Unrestricted walking. **Walkability:** 4. **Opened:** 1966. **Architect:** Robert "Red" Lawrence. **Season:** Year-round. **High:** May-Sept. **To obtain tee times:** Call Thursday at 7:30 a.m. for Saturday-Friday tee time. Earlier reservations accepted with a credit card number. **Miscellaneous:** Reduced fees (weekdays, twilight, seniors, juniors), range (grass), club rentals, credit cards (MC, V), beginner friendly (3-hole beginners course).
Notes: Ranked 3rd in 1999 Best in State; 27th in 1996 America's Top 75 Affordable Courses. **Reader Comments:** Great course, great views ... Don't play it all the way back ... Indifferent pro shop staff ... Beautiful hill course, the long ball is a must! ... Monster greens ... Bargain rates ... Need all your clubs ... If the wind is up it plays very long ... Holes 5-10 are nasty ... A wail away with driver kind of place ... Pretty darn long for women with high handicap ... Play more than once ... Not for the weak of heart.

ZUNI MOUNTAIN GOLF COURSE
PU-1523 Horizon Ave., Milan, 87021, Cibola County, (505)287-9239, 80 miles W of Albuquerque.
Holes: 9. **Yards:** 6,556/5,880. **Par:** 72/74. **Course Rating:** 69.8/71.2. **Slope:** 113/123. **Green Fee:** $9/$9. **Cart Fee:** $14/cart. **Walking Policy:** Unrestricted walking. **Walkability:** N/A.
Opened: 1957. **Season:** Year-round. **High:** June-Aug. **Miscellaneous:** Discount packages, metal spikes, range (grass).

NEW YORK

★★★ ADIRONDACK GOLF & COUNTRY CLUB
PU-88 Golf Rd., Peru, 12972, Clinton County, (518)643-8403, (800)346-1761, 70 miles S of Montreal, Quebec, Canada. **E-mail:** support@adirondackgolfclub.com. **Web:** www.adirondack-golfclub.com.
Holes: 18. **Yards:** 6,851/5,069. **Par:** 72/72. **Course Rating:** 71.9/67.9. **Slope:** 123/115. **Green Fee:** $18/$30. **Cart Fee:** $14/person. **Walking Policy:** Unrestricted walking. **Walkability:** 2. **Opened:** 1990. **Architect:** Geoffrey Cornish/Brian Silva. **Season:** March-Dec. **High:** July-Aug. **To obtain tee times:** Call Wednesday for upcoming Saturday, Sunday and Monday. Call Sunday for Tuesday through Friday. **Miscellaneous:** Reduced fees (weekdays, low season, twilight, seniors, juniors), metal spikes, range (grass), club rentals, credit cards (MC, V, D).
Reader Comments: Plush in fall & spring, soft greens ... Nice layout, some beautiful holes through woods ... Challenging and tight fairways ... Challenging and fair... Underrated ... Very tight, treelined, no adjoining fairways, good test ... Nice layout.

★★ AFTON GOLF CLUB
PU-Afton Lake Rd., Afton, 13730, Chenango County, (607)639-2454, (800)238-6618, 23 miles E of Binghamton.
Holes: 18. **Yards:** 6,268/4,835. **Par:** 72/72. **Course Rating:** 69.0/65.6. **Slope:** 113/110. **Green Fee:** $14/$18. **Cart Fee:** $18/cart. **Walking Policy:** Unrestricted walking. **Walkability:** 3. **Architect:** Graden Decker. **Season:** March-Nov. **High:** Summer. **To obtain tee times:** Call 800 number. **Miscellaneous:** Reduced fees (weekdays, seniors, juniors), discount packages, metal spikes, club rentals.

★★½ ALBAN HILLS COUNTRY CLUB
PU-129 Alban Hills Dr., Johnstown, 12095, Fulton County, (518)762-3717, 40 miles W of Albany.
Holes: 18. **Yards:** 6,005/5,094. **Par:** 70/70. **Course Rating:** 66.3/67.6. **Slope:** 103/105. **Green Fee:** $12/$18. **Cart Fee:** $20/cart. **Walking Policy:** Walking at certain times. **Walkability:** 1. **Opened:** 1980. **Architect:** Attillio Albanese. **Season:** April-Nov. **High:** June-Aug. **To obtain tee times:** Call 7 days in advance for weekends. **Miscellaneous:** Reduced fees (weekdays, low season, twilight, seniors, juniors), metal spikes, club rentals, credit cards (MC, V).
Reader Comments: Short, working to improve, smooth greens, back 9 much tougher than front ... Purely average ... Great course.

★★ AMHERST AUDUBON GOLF COURSE
PU-500 Maple Rd., Williamsville, 14221, Erie County, (716)631-7139.
Holes: 18. **Yards:** 6,635/5,963. **Par:** 71/72. **Course Rating:** 69.5/74.2. **Slope:** 112/105. **Green Fee:** $16/$20. **Cart Fee:** $20/cart. **Walking Policy:** Unrestricted walking. **Walkability:** 1. **Opened:** 1928. **Architect:** William Harries. **Season:** April-Nov. **High:** June-Aug. **Miscellaneous:** Reduced fees (weekdays, twilight), club rentals, beginner friendly (lessons and youth programs).

★★ APALACHIN GOLF COURSE
PU-607 S Apalachin Rd, Apalachin, 13732, Tioga County, (607)625-2682, 20 miles W of Binghamton.
Holes: 18. **Yards:** 5,727/5,000. **Par:** 71/73. **Course Rating:** N/A. **Slope:** N/A. **Green Fee:** $8/$15. **Cart Fee:** $18/cart. **Walking Policy:** Unrestricted walking. **Walkability:** 2. **Opened:** 1964. **Architect:** John Martin, Tim Shearer. **Season:** April-First snow. **High:** May-Aug. **To obtain tee times:** Call. **Miscellaneous:** Reduced fees (weekdays, low season, seniors, juniors), discount packages, metal spikes, club rentals.

★★★½ APPLE GREEN GOLF COURSE
PU-161 S. St., Highland, 12528, Ulster County, (914)883-5500, 6 miles W of Poughkeepsie. **E-mail:** applegreen@golflink.net. **Web:** www.applegreen.com.
Holes: 18. **Yards:** 6,576/4,959. **Par:** 71/71. **Course Rating:** 70.4/67.6. **Slope:** 124/122. **Green Fee:** $22/$32. **Cart Fee:** $26/cart. **Walking Policy:** Walking at certain times. **Walkability:** 3. **Opened:** 1995. **Architect:** John Magaletta. **Season:** April-Dec. **High:** June-Aug. **Miscellaneous:** Reduced fees (twilight, seniors, juniors), range (grass/mats), club rentals, credit cards (MC, V, AE, D).
Reader Comments: In and out of apple trees ... Fairways as lush as the greens ... Short from whites, apples good in fall ... Challenging ... Beautiful course, excellent help, great vistas in the fall ... Hidden gem, playing through the orchard is fun, can eat you up, if you don't concentrate. Great value ... Good layout! Nice design.

★★★½ ARROWHEAD GOLF COURSE
PU-7185 E. Taft Rd., East Syracuse, 13057, Onondaga County, (315)656-7563.
Holes: 18. **Yards:** 6,700/5,156. **Par:** 72/73. **Course Rating:** 70.9/68.5. **Slope:** 113/109. **Green Fee:** $18/$18. **Cart Fee:** $20/cart. **Walking Policy:** Unrestricted walking. **Walkability:** 1. **Opened:** 1968. **Architect:** Dick Snyder. **Season:** April-Nov. **High:** May-Sept. **To obtain tee times:** First come, first served. **Miscellaneous:** Reduced fees (seniors, juniors), metal spikes, club rentals.
Reader Comments: Family owned and operated, 27 holes, always thinking about how to improve course ... Always in great shape ... Nice course ... Long but playable ... Owner always

working to make course better ... Walkable ... No sand but plenty of water, greens in great condition ... Good course for all players.
Special Notes: Also has a 9-hole course.

★★½ AUBURN GOLF & COUNTRY CLUB
SP-East Lake Rd., Auburn, 13021, Cayuga County, (315)253-3152, 3 miles S of Auburn. **Web:** auburn golf.com.
Holes: 18. **Yards:** 6,434/5,777. **Par:** 70/72. **Course Rating:** 70.4/73.1. **Slope:** 118/121. **Green Fee:** $14/$20. **Cart Fee:** $22/cart. **Walking Policy:** Unrestricted walking. **Walkability:** 1.
Opened: 1915. **Architect:** Tom Bendelow. **Season:** April-Oct. **High:** June-Aug. **To obtain tee times:** Call the golf shop. **Miscellaneous:** Reduced fees (weekdays), range (grass), club rentals, credit cards (MC, V, AE).
Reader Comments: I'm coming back! ... Front 9 very playable, back 9 more challenging.

★★★½ BALLSTON SPA COUNTRY CLUB
SP-Rte. 67, Ballston Spa, 12020, Saratoga County, (518)885-7935, 20 miles N of Albany. **E-mail:** jchefti@aol.com.
Holes: 18. **Yards:** 6,215/5,757. **Par:** 71/74. **Course Rating:** 69.3/69.4. **Slope:** 124/122. **Green Fee:** $45/$55. **Cart Fee:** Included in Green Fee. **Walking Policy:** Mandatory cart. **Walkability:** 4. **Opened:** 1926. **Architect:** Pete Craig. **Season:** April-Nov. **High:** June-Sept. **To obtain tee times:** Call 7 days in advance. Members only on weekends. **Miscellaneous:** Range (grass/mats), club rentals, credit cards (MC, V), beginner friendly (lessons, short course).
Reader Comments: Nice layout ... Small greens, well kept ... Back nine very narrow ... Food was great! ... Short, nice layout ... Tee-shot placement crucial. Many doglegs. Great value ... A very good semi-private ... Short course, well maintained.

★★★ BARKER BROOK GOLF CLUB
PU-6080 Rogers Rd., Oriskany Falls, 13425, Oneida County, (315)821-6438, 13 miles S of Utica.
Holes: 18. **Yards:** 6,402/5,501. **Par:** 72/72. **Course Rating:** 70.6/71.8. **Slope:** 120/118. **Green Fee:** $15/$18. **Cart Fee:** $20/cart. **Walking Policy:** Unrestricted walking. **Walkability:** 3.
Opened: 1965. **Architect:** David Keshler/C. Miner. **Season:** April-Nov. **High:** June-Aug. **To obtain tee times:** Call up to 3 days in advance. **Miscellaneous:** Reduced fees (weekdays, low season, twilight), metal spikes, range (grass/mats), club rentals, credit cards (MC, V).
Reader Comments: Interesting ... Very generous staff ... Outstanding golf experience .... Thrills in the hills and bunkers that kill!.

★★★ BATAVIA COUNTRY CLUB
SP-7909 Batavia-Byron Rd., Batavia, 14020, Genesee County, (716)343-7600, (800)343-7660, 4 miles NE of Batavia. **Web:** www.bataviacc.com.
Holes: 18. **Yards:** 6,533/5,372. **Par:** 72/72. **Course Rating:** 70.6/71.1. **Slope:** 119/117. **Green Fee:** $13/$19. **Cart Fee:** $20/cart. **Walking Policy:** Walking at certain times. **Walkability:** 3.
Opened: 1964. **Architect:** Tyron & Schwartz. **Season:** April-Oct. **High:** July-Aug. **To obtain tee times:** Call anytime, no more than 2 weeks in advance. **Miscellaneous:** Reduced fees (weekdays, low season, twilight, seniors), discount packages, metal spikes, range (grass), club rentals, credit cards (MC, V, D).
Reader Comments: Long, fairly challenging course ... Nice layout, good value, could use a little better care ... Could be real nice ... Easy public course ... Average layout.

★★½ BATTLE ISLAND STATE PARK
PU-2150 Rte. 48, Battle Island State Park, Fulton, 13069, Oswego County, (315)592-3361, 21 miles N of Syracuse.
Holes: 18. **Yards:** 5,973/5,561. **Par:** 72/72. **Course Rating:** 67.9/68.7. **Slope:** 109/N/A. **Green Fee:** $9/$17. **Cart Fee:** $20/cart. **Walking Policy:** Unrestricted walking. **Walkability:** 3. **Opened:** 1932. **Season:** April-Nov. **High:** Aug.-Sept. **To obtain tee times:** First come, first served. **Miscellaneous:** Reduced fees (seniors, juniors), club rentals, credit cards (MC, V, AE, D).
Reader Comments: Typical muny with historical significance ... Nice public course, lots of walkers ... Short but tricky ... Stay in the fairway ... Hilly.

★★★ BEAVER ISLAND STATE PARK GOLF COURSE
PU-Beaver Island State Park, Grand Island, 14072, Erie County, (716)773-7143, 8 miles N of Buffalo.
Holes: 18. **Yards:** 6,697/6,178. **Par:** 72/74. **Course Rating:** 69.8/70.0. **Slope:** 108/110. **Green Fee:** $17/$21. **Cart Fee:** $20/cart. **Walking Policy:** Unrestricted walking. **Walkability:** 1.
Opened: 1937. **Architect:** William Harries/A. Russell Tryon. **Season:** April-Nov. **High:** July-Aug. **To obtain tee times:** Call up to 4 days in advance between 9 a.m. and 2 p.m. Monday-Friday. **Miscellaneous:** Reduced fees (weekdays, twilight, seniors, juniors), metal spikes, range (grass/mats), club rentals, credit cards (MC, V).

Reader Comments: Some long holes, but very fair & playable ... Reasonable cost, well kept, lots of geese ... Inexpensive flat course ... Good for a state park ... Good value, busy on weekends ... Flat, but challenging.

BEEKMAN COUNTRY CLUB

PU-11 Country Club Rd., Hopewell Junction, 12533, Dutchess County, (914)226-7700, 40 miles N of White Plains.

Holes: 27. **Green Fee:** $18/$40. **Cart Fee:** $13/person. **Walking Policy:** Walking at certain times. **Walkability:** 3. **Opened:** 1963. **Architect:** Phil Shatz. **Season:** April-Nov. **High:** June-Sept. **To obtain tee times:** Call. **Miscellaneous:** Reduced fees (weekdays, twilight, seniors, juniors), discount packages, range (grass/mats), club rentals, credit cards (MC, V, AE), beginner friendly (clinics and lessons).

★★★ HIGHLAND/VALLEY
Yards: 6,094/5,058. **Par:** 71/71. **Course Rating:** 70.3/71.2. **Slope:** 125/123.
Reader Comments: Nice course, spending money to improve ... Nice variety of holes ... Old standby ... Quick movement of play and very good service ... Diverse layout, good price ... A fine course, good test, great greens ... For the price, you cannot go wrong ... Always working to improve ... Improved course condition.

★★★ TACONIC/HIGHLAND
Yards: 6,267/5,275. **Par:** 72/72. **Course Rating:** 71.6/72.6. **Slope:** 128/128.
Reader Comments: Highland perfect, Taconic can use a little work on tall grass and bushes ... Taconic nine is the best with blind finish ... Best combo of two courses.

★★★ TACONIC/VALLEY
Yards: 6,077/5,149. **Par:** 71/71. **Course Rating:** 70.4/70.8. **Slope:** 121/121.
Reader Comments: Nice layout ... Needs some trees ... Typical NY ... Clean, open setting for golf... Valley nine is very plain.

★★★ BELLPORT COUNTRY CLUB

S. Country Rd., Bellport, 11713, Suffolk County, (516)286-7206.
Special Notes: Call club for further information.
Reader Comments: Pretty flat ... Good fairways ... Nice views, flat tract ... Easy ... Short par 4s ... Nice course. Heavy play.

★★½ BERGEN POINT COUNTRY CLUB

PU-69 Bergen Ave., West Babylon, 11704, Suffolk County, (516)661-8282, 30 miles E of New York City.
Holes: 18. **Yards:** 6,637/5,707. **Par:** 71/71. **Course Rating:** 71.3/71.8. **Slope:** 124/123. **Green Fee:** $22/$35. **Cart Fee:** $27/cart. **Walking Policy:** Unrestricted walking. **Walkability:** 3. **Opened:** 1972. **Architect:** William F. Mitchell. **Season:** March-Dec. **High:** June-Oct. **To obtain tee times:** Same day, call in for reservations or advance reservations, call through automated county system. **Miscellaneous:** Reduced fees (weekdays, low season, twilight, seniors, juniors), discount packages, range (mats), club rentals.
Reader Comments: Wind always in play, lots of water hazards ... Much water, flat ... This course has come a long way in recent years ... Wind can make course play very tough ... Holes along Great South Bay are dramatic ... Great course, trees, water ... Greens in great shape, 10th & 18th holes toughest.

BETHPAGE STATE PARK GOLF COURSES

PU-99 Quaker Meetinghouse Road, Farmingdale, 11735, Nassau County, (516)249-4040, 38 miles E of Manhattan. **Web:** nysparks.state.ny.us.

★★★★½ BLACK COURSE *Value+*
Holes: 18. **Yards:** 7,295/6,281. **Par:** 71/71. **Course Rating:** 76.6/71.4. **Slope:** 148/134. **Green Fee:** $11/$39. **Walking Policy:** Unrestricted walking. **Walkability:** 5. **Opened:** 1936. **Architect:** A.W. Tillinghast. **Season:** Year-round. **High:** May-Sept. **To obtain tee times:** Call 7 days in advance for reservations. No carts available on Black and Green Courses. **Miscellaneous:** Reduced fees (weekdays, twilight, seniors), range (mats), club rentals, credit cards (MC, V, AE, D).
Notes: Ranked 14th in 1999 Best in State; 4th in 1996 America's Top 75 Affordable Courses. Site of the 2002 United States Open.
Reader Comments: Lots of trees, soft greens ... Best golf (public) in New York ... Best buy in the state ... Best course for the money anywhere ... A dream come true ... Good course, but poor, poor availability ... Tough, tougher, toughest ... Spectacular tee-to-green ... Incredible bunkers ... One of finest tracks you'll ever play.

★★★½ BLUE COURSE *Value*
Holes: 18. **Yards:** 6,684/6,213. **Par:** 72/72. **Course Rating:** 71.7/75.0. **Slope:** 124/129. **Green Fee:** $9/$29. **Cart Fee:** $27/cart. **Walking Policy:** Unrestricted walking. **Walkability:** 4. **Opened:** 1935. **Architect:** A.W. Tillinghast. **Season:** Year-round. **High:** May-Sept. **To obtain tee times:** Call 7 days in advance. **Miscellaneous:** Reduced fees (weekdays, twilight, seniors), metal spikes, range (mats), club rentals, credit cards (MC, V, AE, D).

Reader Comments: Just a step or two behind the Black ... Good layout. Good value ... Outstanding layout. Must have adequate sand game ... Tough front nine ... Tough, lush, long difficult greens ... Difficult, but fair ... Slow if not out early ... Tough and hilly ... Great price ... Underrated ... Beautiful layout.

★★★½ GREEN COURSE

Holes: 18. **Yards:** 6,267/5,903. **Par:** 71/71. **Course Rating:** 69.5/73.0. **Slope:** 121/126. **Green Fee:** $9/$29. **Walking Policy:** Unrestricted walking. **Walkability:** 4. **Opened:** 1935. **Architect:** A.W. Tillinghast. **Season:** Year-round. **High:** May-Sept. **To obtain tee times:** Call 7 days in advance. No carts available on Green and Black Courses. **Miscellaneous:** Reduced fees (weekdays, twilight, seniors), metal spikes, range (mats), club rentals, credit cards (MC, V, AE, D).

Reader Comments: Tight and demanding layout ... Arrive early, long wait ... The best $20 you can spend ... Very playable with challenging greens ... For walkers only, hope it stays that way ... Good condition because you have to walk ... Good test, deep rough ... A good walk, nice layout ... Fun course. User friendly ... Best greens.

★★★½ RED COURSE *Value*

Holes: 18. **Yards:** 6,756/6,198. **Par:** 70/70. **Course Rating:** 72.2/75.1. **Slope:** 127/130. **Green Fee:** $9/$29. **Cart Fee:** $27/cart. **Walking Policy:** Unrestricted walking. **Walkability:** 3. **Opened:** 1935. **Architect:** A.W. Tillinghast. **Season:** Year-round. **High:** May-Sept. **To obtain tee times:** Call 7 days in advance for reservations. **Miscellaneous:** Reduced fees (weekdays, low season, twilight, seniors), metal spikes, range (mats), club rentals, credit cards (MC, V, AE, D).

Reader Comments: Outstanding ... Prettiest at Bethpage, long but open ... Good test of golf ... Best next to the Black ... Bring A game ... Long course, hardest 1st hole around ... Crowed, slow play, beautiful holes ... My favorite at Bethpage, long & wide ... Dogleg City ... Excellent test for mid-handicappers ... Awesome 1st hole.

★★★½ YELLOW COURSE

Holes: 18. **Yards:** 6,339/5,966. **Par:** 71/71. **Course Rating:** 70.1/72.2. **Slope:** 121/123. **Green Fee:** $9/$29. **Cart Fee:** $27/cart. **Walking Policy:** Unrestricted walking. **Walkability:** 2. **Opened:** 1958. **Architect:** A.W. Tillinghast. **Season:** Year-round. **High:** May-Sept. **To obtain tee times:** Call 7 days in advance. **Miscellaneous:** Reduced fees (weekdays, twilight, seniors), metal spikes, range (mats), club rentals, credit cards (MC, V, AE, D).

Reader Comments: Good greens ... Nice little course in a great complex ... Forgiving, fun course ... Great $24 round of golf ... Harder than it looks ... Easy & plays fast ... Good course, but gets a lot of play ... Not bad for the money.

★★★½ BLUE HILL GOLF CLUB

SP-285 Blue Hill Rd., Pearl River, 10965, Rockland County, (914)735-2094, 20 miles N of New York.

Holes: 27. **Yards:** 6,471/5,651. **Par:** 72/72. **Course Rating:** 70.6/69.8. **Slope:** 124/119. **Green Fee:** $31/$36. **Cart Fee:** $28/cart. **Walking Policy:** Unrestricted walking. **Walkability:** 3. **Opened:** 1924. **Architect:** Stephen Kay. **Season:** March-Dec. **High:** May-Sept. **To obtain tee times:** Call 2 days in advance for nonresidents. **Miscellaneous:** Reduced fees (weekdays, low season, twilight, seniors, juniors).

Reader Comments: Excellent public course ... Great value ... Nice little course ... Nice conditions, 27 holes, nice mix of holes ... Nice course, good play ... Nice open course, great for high handicappers too ... Wide open fairways, easy course ... Good shape, some good holes, good value ... Several great views & holes.

★½ BLUE STONE GOLF CLUB

PU-44 Scott St., Oxford, 13830, Chenango County, (607)843-8352, 28 miles N of Binghamton.

Holes: 18. **Yards:** 6,068/4,290. **Par:** 70/72. **Course Rating:** 66.1/65.2. **Slope:** 121/100. **Green Fee:** $11/$16. **Cart Fee:** $18/cart. **Walking Policy:** Unrestricted walking. **Walkability:** 3. **Opened:** 1930. **Architect:** Bradley/Race. **Season:** March-Nov. **High:** June-Aug. **To obtain tee times:** Call 1 day in advance. **Miscellaneous:** Reduced fees (weekdays, low season, juniors), discount packages, club rentals.

Special Notes: Spikeless shoes encouraged.

★★½ BLUFF POINT GOLF & COUNTRY CLUB

SP-75 Bluff Point Dr., Plattsburgh, 12901, Clinton County, (518)563-3420, (800)438-0985, 60 miles S of Montreal. **Web:** www.bluffpoint.com.

Holes: 18. **Yards:** 6,309/5,295. **Par:** 72/74. **Course Rating:** 70.6/71.0. **Slope:** 122/121. **Green Fee:** $20/$35. **Cart Fee:** $12/person. **Walking Policy:** Unrestricted walking. **Walkability:** 2. **Opened:** 1890. **Architect:** A.W. Tillinghast. **Season:** April-Nov. **High:** June-Sept. **To obtain tee times:** Guests may call 5 days in advance. **Miscellaneous:** Reduced fees (weekdays, low season, resort guests, twilight), discount packages, metal spikes, range (grass), club rentals, lodging (12 rooms), credit cards (MC, V).

Reader Comments: On Lake Champlain, very scenic, good variety of holes ... Third oldest resort course in U.S. on gorgeous Lake Champlain ... Wide open, putts break toward lake ... Good seniors' course ... Delightful course ... Every hole different ... Beautiful, tricky winds.

★★½ BRAEMAR COUNTRY CLUB
SP-4704 Ridge Rd. W., Spencerport, 14559, Monroe County, (716)352-1535.
Special Notes: Call club for further information.

Reader Comments: A lot of fun ... Nice layout ... Small greens, slow play ... Decent layout ... Needs cart paths ... Layout is interesting ... Nice layout.

★★½ BRANTINGHAM GOLF CLUB
PU-P.O. Box 151, Brantingham, 13312, Lewis County, (315)348-8861, 55 miles N of Utica.
Holes: 18. **Yards:** 5,268/4,886. **Par:** 71/74. **Course Rating:** 64.5/N/A. **Slope:** 97/N/A. **Green Fee:** $16/$16. **Cart Fee:** $18/cart. **Walking Policy:** Unrestricted walking. **Walkability:** 1. **Architect:** Fred Rhone. **Season:** April-Oct. **High:** July-Aug. **To obtain tee times:** First come, first served. **Miscellaneous:** Reduced fees (twilight), metal spikes, club rentals.

Reader Comments: Just a place to play when you need to ... Challenging holes and greens ... Nice course ... Very picturesque.

★★½ BRENTWOOD COUNTRY CLUB
PU-100 Pennsylvania Ave., Brentwood, 11717, Suffolk County, (516)436-6060, 45 miles E of New York City.
Holes: 18. **Yards:** 6,173/5,835. **Par:** 72/72. **Course Rating:** 69.3/68.4. **Slope:** 121/111. **Green Fee:** $18/$28. **Cart Fee:** $26/cart. **Walking Policy:** Unrestricted walking. **Walkability:** 1. **Opened:** 1920. **Architect:** Devereux Emmet. **Season:** March-Dec. **High:** May-July. **To obtain tee times:** Call 3 days in advance for weekends only for a $2 fee per person. **Miscellaneous:** Reduced fees (weekdays, low season, twilight, seniors, juniors), metal spikes, club rentals.

Reader Comments: Nice little course ... Good walking course, easy to get out ... Made to feel like a friend by pro & starter ... 17th hole is beautiful 'in the pines' par 5 ... No water, but bunkers provide a challenge.

★★½ BRIAR CREEK GOLF COURSE
PU-2347 Pangburn Rd., Princetown, 12056, Schenectady County, (518)355-6145, 10 miles W of Albany.
Holes: 18. **Yards:** 5,667/5,187. **Par:** 70/71. **Course Rating:** N/A. **Slope:** N/A. **Green Fee:** $17/$20. **Cart Fee:** $22/cart. **Walking Policy:** Unrestricted walking. **Walkability:** 2. **Opened:** 1963. **Architect:** Bob Smith. **Season:** April-Nov. **High:** May-Sept. **To obtain tee times:** Call. **Miscellaneous:** Reduced fees (seniors), club rentals.

Reader Comments: Great place for a beginner, short & open course ... Uphill, downhill mountain-goat country! Fun ... An interesting course, just needs a bit of work.

★★½ BRIGHTON PARK GOLF COURSE
PU-Brompton Rd., Town of Tonawanda, 14150, Erie County, (716)695-2580, 5 miles N of Buffalo.
Holes: 18. **Yards:** 6,535/5,852. **Par:** 72/73. **Course Rating:** 70.7/73.5. **Slope:** 108/109. **Green Fee:** $16/$19. **Cart Fee:** $18/cart. **Walking Policy:** Unrestricted walking. **Walkability:** 1. **Opened:** 1963. **Architect:** William Harries/A. Russell Tyron. **Season:** April-Nov. **High:** June-Aug. **To obtain tee times:** Phone in system 7 days in advance. **Miscellaneous:** Reduced fees (weekdays, low season, twilight, seniors), range (grass), club rentals.

Reader Comments: Wide open, little trouble ... Challenging public course.

★★★★ BRISTOL HARBOUR GOLF & RESORT
R-5400 Seneca Point Rd., Canandaigua, 14424, Ontario County, (716)396-2460, (800)288-8248, 30 miles S of Rochester.
Holes: 18. **Yards:** 6,700/5,500. **Par:** 72/72. **Course Rating:** 72.6/73.0. **Slope:** 126/126. **Green Fee:** $30/$49. **Cart Fee:** Included in Green Fee. **Walking Policy:** Mandatory cart. **Walkability:** 4. **Opened:** 1972. **Architect:** Robert Trent Jones. **Season:** April-Nov. **High:** June-Sept. **To obtain tee times:** General public may call up to 7 days in advance. **Miscellaneous:** Reduced fees (weekdays, low season, resort guests, twilight, seniors, juniors), discount packages, range (grass/mats), club rentals, lodging, credit cards (MC, V, AE).

Reader Comments: Beautiful views of lake country ... Outstanding golf in Finger Lake region. Course has lots of character, service and accommodations outstanding ... Beautiful views, good test ... Two distinct nines ... Gorgeous lake views, front open, nice ravine holes on back.

★★★ BROCKPORT COUNTRY CLUB
SP-3739 County Line Rd., Brockport, 14420, Monroe County, (716)638-6486, 20 miles W of Rochester. **E-mail:** burklew@ibm.net. **Web:** brockportcc.com.
Holes: 18. **Yards:** 6,600/5,000. **Par:** 72/72. **Course Rating:** 70.1/68.0. **Slope:** 130/112. **Green Fee:** $17/$22. **Cart Fee:** $10/person. **Walking Policy:** Unrestricted walking. **Walkability:** 4. **Opened:** 1975. **Architect:** Joe Basso. **Season:** Year-round. **High:** June-Aug. **To obtain tee times:** Call (716)638-6486 to reserve a tee time. **Miscellaneous:** Reduced fees (low season, twilight, seniors, juniors), discount packages, range (grass/mats), club rentals, credit cards (MC, V, AE, D).

Reader Comments: Very nice course, very fairly priced ... Short course, back 9 harder, nice ... New owners are upgrading.

BROOKLAWN GOLF COURSE
PU-Old Thompson Rd., Mattydale, 13211, Onondaga County, (315)463-1831, 2 miles SE of Syracuse.
Holes: 18. **Yards:** 5,014/4,465. **Par:** 64/66. **Course Rating:** N/A. **Slope:** N/A. **Green Fee:** $12/$14. **Cart Fee:** $18/cart. **Walking Policy:** Unrestricted walking. **Walkability:** 1. **Opened:** 1920. **Season:** March-Nov. **High:** April-Sept. **To obtain tee times:** Tee times not taken.
Miscellaneous: Reduced fees (low season, seniors, juniors), discount packages, credit cards (MC, V, AE), beginner friendly (saturday and sunday after 2:00 p.m. juniors under 16 play free with paying adult).

★★★½ BYRNCLIFF GOLF CLUB
R-Rte. 20A, Varysburg, 14167, Wyoming County, (716)535-7300, 35 miles SE of Buffalo. **Web:** www.byrncliff.com.
Holes: 18. **Yards:** 6,783/5,545. **Par:** 72/73. **Course Rating:** 73.1/75.1. **Slope:** 115/119. **Green Fee:** $30/$34. **Cart Fee:** Included in Green Fee. **Walking Policy:** Unrestricted walking. **Walkability:** 3. **Opened:** 1965. **Architect:** Russ Tryon. **Season:** April-Nov. **High:** June-Aug. **To obtain tee times:** Call. **Miscellaneous:** Reduced fees (weekdays, low season, resort guests, twilight, seniors), discount packages, metal spikes, range (grass/mats), club rentals, lodging, credit cards (MC, V, AE, D).
Reader Comments: Hills ... Many difficult holes, great condition ... Long, hilly, challenging ... Up & down, a great mix ... Hilly interesting, they are working hard to improve ... First-class service ... Excellent resort course ... New trees & bunkers are good. Hole No. 5 redesign is superb!

★½ C-WAY GOLF CLUB
PU-37093 NYS Rte 12, Clayton, 13624, Jefferson County, (315)686-4562, 72 miles N of Syracuse. **E-mail:** cwny@gisco.net. **Web:** www.thousandislands.com/cway.
Holes: 18. **Yards:** 6,120/5,780. **Par:** 71/71. **Course Rating:** 68.0/68.0. **Slope:** N/A. **Green Fee:** N/A/$17. **Cart Fee:** $16/cart. **Walking Policy:** Unrestricted walking. **Walkability:** 2. **Opened:** 1964. **Season:** May-Nov. **High:** Summer. **To obtain tee times:** Call up to 3 days in advance. **Miscellaneous:** Reduced fees (low season), discount packages, metal spikes, range (grass/mats), club rentals, lodging (50 rooms), credit cards (MC, V).

★★½ CAMILLUS COUNTRY CLUB
SP-5690 Bennetts Corners Rd., Camillus, 13031, Onondaga County, (315)672-3770, 20 miles W of Syracuse.
Holes: 18. **Yards:** 6,368/5,573. **Par:** 73/73. **Course Rating:** 70.1/71.4. **Slope:** 115/110. **Green Fee:** $15/$18. **Cart Fee:** $20/cart. **Walking Policy:** Unrestricted walking. **Walkability:** 5. **Opened:** 1962. **Season:** April-Nov. **High:** June-Aug. **To obtain tee times:** Call up to 7 days in advance. **Miscellaneous:** Reduced fees (weekdays, low season, seniors, juniors), discount packages, metal spikes, range (grass), club rentals, credit cards (MC, V).
Reader Comments: Fun, but a little hilly to walk ... Play in about 3 1/2 hours.

★½ CANAJOHARIE COUNTRY CLUB
SP-Rte. 163, Canajoharie, 13317, Montgomery County, (518)673-8183, 37 miles SE of Utica.
Holes: 18. **Yards:** 5,854/5,144. **Par:** 71/72. **Course Rating:** 67.9/68.5. **Slope:** 115/115. **Green Fee:** $14/$18. **Cart Fee:** $19/. **Walking Policy:** Unrestricted walking. **Walkability:** 3. **Opened:** 1940. **Architect:** Scott & John North. **Season:** April-Oct. **High:** June-Aug. **To obtain tee times:** Call golf shop for weekend starting times. **Miscellaneous:** Reduced fees (juniors), range (grass), rentals, credit cards (MC, V).

★★★½ CANASAWACTA COUNTRY CLUB
SP-Country Club Rd., Norwich, 13815, Chenango County, (607)336-2685, 37 miles NE of Binghamton.
Holes: 18. **Yards:** 6,271/5,166. **Par:** 70/71. **Course Rating:** 69.9/68.8. **Slope:** 120/114. **Green Fee:** $18/$22. **Cart Fee:** $22/cart. **Walking Policy:** Unrestricted walking. **Walkability:** 3. **Opened:** 1920. **Architect:** Russell Bailey. **Season:** April-Oct. **High:** June-Aug. **To obtain tee times:** Call up to 3 days in advance. **Miscellaneous:** Reduced fees (low season, twilight, juniors), range (grass), club rentals, credit cards (MC, V).
Reader Comments: Beautiful hilly course. Front nine very challenging ... Super clubhouse, very good service ... Old course, fairways tight, greens small, hit ball straight ... This course has 3 of the most challenging holes in New York ... Tough course to walk, long par 4s, challenging.

★½ CARDINAL HILLS GOLF COURSE
PU-Conewango Rd., Randolph, 14772, Chattaraugus County, (716)358-5409, 20 miles E of Jamestown.
Holes: 18. **Yards:** 6,058/5,753. **Par:** 72/73. **Course Rating:** N/A. **Slope:** N/A. **Green Fee:** $18/$20. **Cart Fee:** $18/cart. **Walking Policy:** Unrestricted walking. **Walkability:** 3. **Season:** April-Nov. **High:** July-Aug. **To obtain tee times:** Call 24 hours in advance. **Miscellaneous:**

NEW YORK

Reduced fees (weekdays, low season, twilight), club rentals, credit cards (MC, V), beginner friendly.

★½ CASOLWOOD GOLF COURSE
PU-New Boston Rd., Box 163, Canastota, 13032, Madison County, (315)697-9164, 15 miles E of Syracuse.
Holes: 18. **Yards:** 6,100/5,700. **Par:** 71/71. **Course Rating:** N/A. **Slope:** N/A. **Green Fee:** N/A/$14. **Cart Fee:** $18/cart. **Walking Policy:** Unrestricted walking. **Walkability:** 2. **Opened:** 1969. **Architect:** Richard L. Quick/Richard A. Quick. **Season:** March-Dec. **High:** June-Sept. **To obtain tee times:** Call on Wednesday for upcoming weekend. **Miscellaneous:** Reduced fees (weekdays, seniors), metal spikes, club rentals, credit cards (MC, V).
Special Notes: Spikeless shoes encouraged.

★★★½ CASPERKILL COUNTRY CLUB
SP-575 South Rd., Poughkeepsie, 12601, Dutchess County, (914)433-2222, 70 miles N of New York City. **Web:** www.casperkill.com.
Holes: 18. **Yards:** 6,691/4,868. **Par:** 72/72. **Course Rating:** 72.4/67.9. **Slope:** 130/117. **Green Fee:** $40/$46. **Cart Fee:** $24/cart. **Walking Policy:** Unrestricted walking. **Walkability:** 2. **Opened:** 1944. **Architect:** Robert Trent Jones. **Season:** March-Dec. **High:** April-Oct;. **To obtain tee times:** Call 1 day in advance at 6:45 a.m. for weekdays. Call Thursday at 6:45 a.m. for following weekend. **Miscellaneous:** Reduced fees (weekdays, twilight, juniors), range (mats), club rentals, credit cards (MC, V, AE, D).
Reader Comments: Hidden gem, beautiful in autumn ... Great layout ... Pricey but a really nice course ... Good course ... Fast, true greens ... Steady across the board, great layout ... Always in excellent condition ... Good practice area. Nice layout, No. 9 green too severe ... Lovely, challenging; well-kept, elevated greens.

CEDAR VIEW GOLF COURSE
PU-Rte. 37C, Rooseveltown, 13683, St. Lawrence County, (315)764-9104, 70 miles N of Syracuse.
Holes: 18. **Yards:** 6,027/5,175. **Par:** 72/72. **Course Rating:** 68.8/69.6. **Slope:** 119/121. **Green Fee:** $13/$16. **Cart Fee:** $18/cart. **Walking Policy:** Unrestricted walking. **Walkability:** 1. **Opened:** 1986. **Season:** May-Oct. **High:** July-Aug. **To obtain tee times:** Call. **Miscellaneous:** Reduced fees (twilight, juniors), metal spikes, club rentals, credit cards (MC, V).

CENTENNIAL GOLF CLUB
PU-Simpson Rd., Carmel, 10512, Putnam County, (914)225-5700, 55 miles N of New York City. **Web:** centennialgolf.com.
Holes: 27. **Green Fee:** $75/$105. **Cart Fee:** Included in Green Fee. **Walking Policy:** Mandatory cart. **Walkability:** 5. **Opened:** 1998. **Architect:** Larry Nelson. **Season:** April-Nov. **High:** April-Oct. **To obtain tee times:** Call 6 days in advance on a 24 hour automated reservation system. **Miscellaneous:** Reduced fees (twilight), range (grass/mats), club rentals, credit cards (MC, V, AE).
★★★★ LAKES/FAIRWAYS
Yards: 7,133/5,208. **Par:** 72/72. **Course Rating:** 71.4/73.9. **Slope:** 134/138.
★★★★ MEADOW/FAIRWAYS
Yards: 7,050/5,208. **Par:** 72/72. **Course Rating:** 71.3/73.5. **Slope:** 129/136.
★★★★ MEADOW/LAKES
Yards: 7,115/5,208. **Par:** 72/72. **Course Rating:** 73.8/70.5. **Slope:** 135/126. **Reader Comments:** Outstanding view ... Excellent course ... Great layout, needs time to mature ... Worth the trip, bring your clients ... Not a bad hole ... Expensive but worth it ... Fantastic layout ... Pricey but worth it ... Not yet fully mature. Breathtaking views. Will be a top track in 5 years ... Tops all around.

★★★½ CENTERPOINTE COUNTRY CLUB
SP-2231 Brickyard Rd., Canandaigua, 14424, Ontario County, (716)924-5346, 25 miles SE of Rochester.
Holes: 18. **Yards:** 6,787/5,171. **Par:** 71/71. **Course Rating:** 72.2/69.3. **Slope:** 119/112. **Green Fee:** $15/$22. **Cart Fee:** $20/person. **Walking Policy:** Unrestricted walking. **Walkability:** 3. **Opened:** 1963. **Architect:** John Thornton/Elmer Michaels. **Season:** April-Nov. **High:** June-Aug. **To obtain tee times:** Public may call up to 3 days in advance. **Miscellaneous:** Reduced fees (weekdays, low season, twilight, seniors, juniors), discount packages, metal spikes, range (grass), club rentals, credit cards (MC, V).
Reader Comments: Good course for average golfer. Not much sand or water ... 3 1/2-hour round is possible during the week ... A fun course ... Long, well maintained, a bargain ... Tees & fairways excellent ... Best course for the money! ... Good, solid, golf ... Bunkers not in play ... Underrated ... Interesting course, always windy.

★★★ CENTRAL VALLEY GOLF CLUB
PU-206 Smith Clove Rd., Central Valley, 10917, Orange County, (914)928-6924, 50 miles N of New York City.
Holes: 18. **Yards:** 5,644/5,317. **Par:** 70/73. **Course Rating:** 67.7/70.9. **Slope:** 116/120. **Green Fee:** $23/$33. **Cart Fee:** $24/cart. **Walking Policy:** Unrestricted walking. **Walkability:** 5. **Opened:** 1922. **Architect:** Hal Purdy. **Season:** April-Nov. **High:** May-Aug. **To obtain tee times:** Call up to 7 days in advance. **Miscellaneous:** Reduced fees (weekdays, low season, seniors, juniors), discount packages, metal spikes, club rentals, credit cards (MC, V, AE).
Reader Comments: Hilly ... I like it, interesting holes ... Wide open, let 'er rip! ... Steep hills, use cart, tougher than it looks ... If walking, bring ski poles to climb No. 3 ... Long, elevated greens.

CHAUTAUQUA GOLF CLUB
R-Rte. 394, Chautauqua, 14722, Chautauqua County, (716)357-6211, 70 miles SW of Buffalo.
★★★★ HILLS COURSE *Pace*
Holes: 18. **Yards:** 6,412/5,076. **Par:** 72/72. **Course Rating:** 72.1/72.7. **Slope:** 118/110. **Green Fee:** $19/$34. **Cart Fee:** $11/person. **Walking Policy:** Unrestricted walking. **Walkability:** 5. **Opened:** 1994. **Architect:** Xen Hassenplug. **Season:** April-Nov. **High:** June-Aug. **To obtain tee times:** Please call up to 7 days in advance. Large groups may call further in advance. **Miscellaneous:** Reduced fees (weekdays, low season, twilight), discount packages, metal spikes, range (grass/mats), club rentals, credit cards (MC, V).
Reader Comments: Great course, great service, great price ... Many challenging holes, fun to play ... Hidden gem, great course ... Hills and woods, tight and challenging ... Well kept. Nice scenery ... Tough lakeside course, especially in wind ... Close to heaven.
★★★★ LAKE COURSE *Pace*
Holes: 18. **Yards:** 6,462/5,423. **Par:** 72/74. **Course Rating:** 71.1/71.7. **Slope:** 115/108. **Green Fee:** $19/$34. **Cart Fee:** $11/person. **Walking Policy:** Unrestricted walking. **Walkability:** 2. **Opened:** 1913. **Architect:** Donald Ross. **Season:** April-Nov. **High:** June-Aug. **To obtain tee times:** Call up to 7 days in advance. Large groups may call further in advance. **Miscellaneous:** Reduced fees (weekdays, low season, twilight), discount packages, metal spikes, range (grass/mats), club rentals, credit cards (MC, V).
Reader Comments: Great track–some open, some wooded undulating terrain ... Rangers really work, but very nice about it ... Basically a back and forth layout, staff very friendly and helpful ... Feel-good course, wide open ... Original, still great, need every shot ... Very nice greens.

★★★★ CHENANGO VALLEY STATE PARK *Value+*
PU-153 State Park Rd., Chenango Forks, 13746, Broome County, (607)648-9804, 10 miles E of Binghamton. **E-mail:** cvsp214@juno.com.
Holes: 18. **Yards:** 6,271/5,246. **Par:** 72/72. **Course Rating:** 70.6/69.5. **Slope:** 124/116. **Green Fee:** $17/$21. **Cart Fee:** $20/cart. **Walking Policy:** Unrestricted walking. **Walkability:** 5. **Opened:** 1932. **Architect:** Hal Purdy. **Season:** April-Nov. **High:** June-Aug. **To obtain tee times:** Call (607)648-9700 6 days ahead. **Miscellaneous:** Reduced fees (weekdays, seniors, juniors), metal spikes, club rentals, lodging, credit cards (MC, V, AE).
Reader Comments: Amazing views, roaming wildlife, premium fairways & greens ... Typical state course ...Beautiful course ... Great country setting, good greens ... Good play for all skill levels ... Very nice park ... State park, very scenic, no adjoining fairways, much wildlife ... The State Park system's best-kept secret.

★★★ CHESTNUT HILL COUNTRY CLUB
PU-1330 Broadway, Darien Center, 14040, Genesee County, (716)547-9699, 30 miles E of Buffalo.
Holes: 18. **Yards:** 6,653/5,466. **Par:** 72/72. **Course Rating:** 72.0/70.6. **Slope:** 119/115. **Green Fee:** $19/$32. **Cart Fee:** Included in Green Fee. **Walking Policy:** Mandatory cart. **Walkability:** 4. **Season:** April-Nov. **High:** June-Aug. **To obtain tee times:** Call up to 7 days in advance. **Miscellaneous:** Reduced fees (weekdays), metal spikes, range (grass), club rentals, credit cards (MC, V, D).
Reader Comments: Nice to play here ... Tough to get on, starting to show wear and tear ... Cheap fees, very playable ... Do a great job on outings.

★½ CHILI COUNTRY CLUB
SP-760 Scottsville-Chili Rd., Scottsville, 14546, Monroe County, (716)889-9325, 10 miles S of Rochester. **Web:** www.chiligolf.com.
Holes: 18. **Yards:** 6,618/5,488. **Par:** 72/72. **Course Rating:** 71.3/72.4. **Slope:** 124/117. **Green Fee:** $10/$18. **Cart Fee:** $20/cart. **Walking Policy:** Unrestricted walking. **Walkability:** 2. **Opened:** 1959. **Architect:** Joe DeMino. **Season:** Year-round. **High:** July-Aug. **To obtain tee times:** Call (716)889-9325 Ext. 1. **Miscellaneous:** Reduced fees (weekdays, low season, twilight, seniors, juniors), discount packages, metal spikes, range (grass), club rentals, credit cards (MC, V, D), beginner friendly.

★★★ CITY OF AMSTERDAM MUNICIPAL GOLF COURSE

PM-155 Van Dyke Ave., Amsterdam, 12010, Montgomery County, (518)842-4265, 15 miles NE of Schenectady.

Holes: 18. **Yards:** 6,370/5,352. **Par:** 71/74. **Course Rating:** 70.2/70.2. **Slope:** 120/110. **Green Fee:** $19/$21. **Cart Fee:** $20/cart. **Walking Policy:** Unrestricted walking. **Walkability:** 5. **Opened:** 1938. **Architect:** Robert Trent Jones. **Season:** April-Nov. **High:** July-Aug. **To obtain tee times:** Call 3 days in advance for weekends only. **Miscellaneous:** Reduced fees (weekdays, twilight, seniors, juniors), range (grass/mats), club rentals.
Reader Comments: Top-notch course design, needs better grooming and drainage, very hilly ... Hidden jewel ... Lots of elevation changes ... Fairways and greens in excellent condition.

★★★ CLEARVIEW GOLF CLUB

PM-202-12 Willets Point Blvd., Bayside, 11360, Queens County, (718)229-2570, 8 miles NE of New York City.

Holes: 18. **Yards:** 6,473/5,721. **Par:** 70/70. **Course Rating:** 70.1/70.4. **Slope:** 119/115. **Green Fee:** $19/$22. **Cart Fee:** $25/cart. **Walking Policy:** Unrestricted walking. **Walkability:** 2. **Opened:** 1929. **Architect:** William H. Tucker. **Season:** Year-round. **High:** May-Sept. **To obtain tee times:** Call golf shop reservation office April-Nov. 8:30-2:30 Monday-Friday. **Miscellaneous:** Reduced fees (twilight, seniors, juniors), metal spikes, club rentals, credit cards (MC, V, AE), beginner friendly (teacher/pro on course).
Reader Comments: Nice wide fairways ... Good layout, some six-hour rounds ... Very flat & open course ... Great for beginners, not intimidating ... Nice views ... Challenging ... Crowded muny but a challenge ... A good course ... A little crowded but great game, lots of trees.

★★★★½ COLGATE UNIVERSITY SEVEN OAKS GOLF CLUB

SP-E. Lake and Payne Sts., Hamilton, 13346, Madison County, (315)824-1432, 41 miles E of Syracuse.

Holes: 18. **Yards:** 6,915/5,315. **Par:** 72/72. **Course Rating:** 72.3/71.0. **Slope:** 127/128. **Green Fee:** $25/$52. **Cart Fee:** $23/cart. **Walking Policy:** Unrestricted walking. **Walkability:** 1. **Opened:** 1956. **Architect:** Robert Trent Jones. **Season:** April-Oct. **High:** June-Aug. **To obtain tee times:** Call up to 14 days in advance. **Miscellaneous:** Reduced fees (low season, resort guests, juniors), discount packages, metal spikes, range (grass), caddies, club rentals, credit cards (MC, V).
Reader Comments: Big fast greens ... Great course, very smart ... A must-play in central New York ... Nice finishing holes ... Difficult, fast greens, bring your A game ... Expensive, excellent layout, very enjoyable ... Subtle greatness ... Tough from the get go ... Challenging from tips, well-manicured greens and bunkers.

★★★½ COLONIAL SPRINGS GOLF COURSE

PU-1 Long Island Ave., East Farmingdale, 11735, Suffolk County, (516)643-1056, (800)643-0051, 33 miles E of New York City.

Holes: 27. **Yards:** 6,811/5,485. **Par:** 72/72. **Course Rating:** 71.8/70.5. **Slope:** 126/119. **Green Fee:** $59/$85. **Cart Fee:** Included in Green Fee. **Walking Policy:** Mandatory cart. **Walkability:** 3. **Opened:** 1995. **Architect:** Arthur Hills. **Season:** March-Dec. **High:** April-Oct. **To obtain tee times:** Private on weekends. Public call 1 week in advance for Tuesday-Thursday, 1 day in advance for Friday. **Miscellaneous:** Reduced fees (weekdays, low season, twilight), range (grass/mats), club rentals, credit cards (MC, V, AE).
Reader Comments: South Carolina golf on Long Island ... Don't change a thing ... Gracious, helpful starter. From back tees, a test for accuracy and distance ... Nice course, not cheap ... Beautiful! Top-notch service, outstanding golf, a must play ... Great service, great course, great facility, great time.

CONCORD RESORT HOTEL

R-Kiamesha Lake, Kiamesha Lake, 12751, Sullivan County, (914)794-4000, 90 miles NW of New York. **Web:** www.concordresort.com.

★★★½ INTERNATIONAL GOLF COURSE *Pace*

Holes: 18. **Yards:** 6,619/5,564. **Par:** 71/71. **Course Rating:** 72.2/73.6. **Slope:** 127/125. **Green Fee:** $45/$55. **Cart Fee:** Included in Green Fee. **Walking Policy:** Unrestricted walking. **Walkability:** 3. **Opened:** 1950. **Architect:** A.H. Tull. **Season:** April-Nov. **High:** June-Aug. **To obtain tee times:** Call anytime in advance with credit card. 72-hour cancellation policy. **Miscellaneous:** Reduced fees (weekdays, resort guests, twilight), discount packages, range (grass/mats), club rentals, lodging (42 rooms), credit cards (MC, V, AE, D, Diners Club).
Reader Comments: Good challenge, interesting holes ... Picturesque in fall ... Never a bad moment ... Beautiful, expensive and tough ... Worth the trip from NYC, a gem.

★★★½ MONSTER GOLF COURSE

Holes: 18. **Yards:** 7,966/5,201. **Par:** 72/72. **Course Rating:** 76.4/70.6. **Slope:** 142/121. **Green Fee:** $60/$90. **Cart Fee:** Included in Green Fee. **Walking Policy:** Mandatory cart. **Walkability:** 3. **Opened:** 1963. **Architect:** Joseph Finger. **Season:** April-Nov. **High:** June-Aug. **To obtain tee times:** Call anytime in advance with credit card number. 72-hour cancellation policy.

Miscellaneous: Reduced fees (weekdays, resort guests, twilight), discount packages, range (grass), caddies, club rentals, lodging (42 rooms), credit cards (MC, V, AE, D, Diners Club).
Notes: Ranked 72nd in 1996 America's Top 75 Upscale Courses.
Reader Comments: Premium fairways & greens ... Very long, a real 'monster' ... Course in excellent condition, beautiful layout, service very good ... A true test, long, long & longer ... The greatest, hardest course most of us can play ... Best course in Catskills ... Wonderful course ... Well worth the money.

★★★★½ CONKLIN PLAYERS CLUB

PU-1520 Conklin Rd., Conklin, 13748, Broome County, (607)775-3042, 70 miles S of Syracuse.
Holes: 18. **Yards:** 6,772/4,699. **Par:** 72/72. **Course Rating:** 72.5/67.8. **Slope:** 127/116. **Green Fee:** $26/$34. **Cart Fee:** $10/person. **Walking Policy:** Walking at certain times. **Walkability:** 5.
Opened: 1991. **Architect:** R. Rickard/R. Brown/M. Brown. **Season:** April-Nov. **High:** May-Oct. **To obtain tee times:** Call. **Miscellaneous:** Reduced fees (weekdays, low season, seniors), range (grass), rentals, credit cards (MC, V, AE, D).
Reader Comments: Great, strategic course, challenges the mind as well as body. Gets better every time ... One of the best public courses ever played ... Beautiful, scenic, challenging ... Up, up & away 16,17,18 ... Excellent course, beautiful views, very good service ... Best conditioning, public or private, in region.

★★★ COPAKE COUNTRY CLUB

PU-Lake Copake, Craryville, 12521, Columbia County, (518)325-4338, 15 miles E of Hudson.
Holes: 18. **Yards:** 6,129/5,329. **Par:** 72/72. **Course Rating:** 68.8/69.6. **Slope:** 113/113. **Green Fee:** $11/$25. **Cart Fee:** $12/person. **Walking Policy:** Unrestricted walking. **Walkability:** 3.
Season: April-Nov. **High:** June-Aug. **To obtain tee times:** Call anytime in advance.
Miscellaneous: Reduced fees (weekdays, seniors, juniors), club rentals, credit cards (MC, V).
Reader Comments: Nice people, nice course ... Good greens, nice people, good value ... Wide open, little trouble ... One of the best values in New York, wide-open, fun course ... Great course, tough par 3s ... Cart a must, hilly conditions.

★★½ CRAB MEADOW GOLF CLUB

PU-220 Waterside Rd., Northport, 11768, Suffolk County, (516)757-8800, 28 miles E of New York City.
Holes: 18. **Yards:** 6,575/5,807. **Par:** 72/72. **Course Rating:** 70.2/72.6. **Slope:** 116/116. **Green Fee:** $35/$35. **Cart Fee:** $27/cart. **Walking Policy:** Unrestricted walking. **Walkability:** 3.
Opened: 1960. **Architect:** William F. Mitchell. **Season:** March-Dec. **High:** April-Sept. **To obtain tee times:** Call up to 7 days in advance. **Miscellaneous:** Reduced fees (twilight, seniors, juniors), range (mats), club rentals.
Reader Comments: Nice views of Long Island Sound ... Near water, can be windy ... Good layout, greens need some work, play slow at times ... Good all-around course ... Scenic course, a lot of wind on the back nine.

★★ CRAGIE BRAE GOLF CLUB

PU-4391 Union St., Scottsville, 14546, Monroe County, (716)889-1440, 10 miles SW of Rochester.
Holes: 18. **Yards:** 6,400/5,900. **Par:** 72/72. **Course Rating:** 68.5/68.5. **Slope:** 115/115. **Green Fee:** $13/$15. **Cart Fee:** $20/cart. **Walking Policy:** Walking at certain times. **Walkability:** 3.
Opened: 1963. **Architect:** James G. Harrison. **Season:** April-Nov. **High:** May-July. **To obtain tee times:** Call 2 days before. **Miscellaneous:** Reduced fees (low season, seniors, juniors), metal spikes, range (grass), club rentals.

★★★½ CRAIG WOOD GOLF COURSE

PU-Cascade Rd. Rte. 73, Lake Placid, 12946, Essex County, (518)523-9811, (877)999-9473, 135 miles N of Albany.
Holes: 18. **Yards:** 6,554/5,500. **Par:** 72/72. **Course Rating:** 70.6/70.2. **Slope:** 114/118. **Green Fee:** $15/$25. **Cart Fee:** $12/cart. **Walking Policy:** Unrestricted walking. **Walkability:** 3.
Opened: 1920. **Architect:** Seymour Dunn. **Season:** May-Oct. **High:** July-Aug. **To obtain tee times:** Call. **Miscellaneous:** Reduced fees (resort guests, twilight), discount packages, range (grass/mats), club rentals, credit cards (MC, V).
Reader Comments: Decent course, pretty area ... Nice course, scenery is beautiful ... Great old golf course. Severe terrain changes ... Some beautiful scenic holes ... Nice Adirondack course. Very interesting, back 9 fun ... Friendly people. Nice mountain views ... Nice variety of holes in a mountain setting.

★★½ CRONINS GOLF RESORT

PU-Golf Course Rd., Box 40, Warrensburg, 12885, Warren County, (518)623-9336, 7 miles N of Lake George.
Holes: 18. **Yards:** 6,121/5,757. **Par:** 70/71. **Course Rating:** 68.6/68.3. **Slope:** 119/117. **Green Fee:** $16/$18. **Walking Policy:** Unrestricted walking. **Walkability:** N/A. **Opened:** 1930.

Architect: Patrick Cronin. **Season:** April-Nov. **High:** July-Aug. **To obtain tee times:** Call up to 3 days in advance. **Miscellaneous:** Metal spikes.
Reader Comments: Beautiful views, some really interesting holes, should be played at least once ... Friendly and you won't lose many balls ... Short, tricky back 9.

★★★½ DANDE FARMS COUNTRY CLUB
SP-13278 Carney Rd., Akron, 14001, Erie County, (716)542-2027.
Holes: 18. **Yards:** 6,622/6,017. **Par:** 71/72. **Course Rating:** 70.5/72.1. **Slope:** 113/110. **Green Fee:** $20/$23. **Walkability:** N/A. **Miscellaneous:** Metal spikes.
Reader Comments: No sand, but must hit them good to score ... Not bad, average-type course ... No traps, fast play ... Good course to play ... Wide-open farmland ... Best tee areas I've ever seen, great snack shack ... Fairly easy. No sand.

★★★½ DEERFIELD COUNTRY CLUB
SP-100 Craig Hill Dr., Brockport, 14420, Monroe County, (716)392-8080, 20 miles W of Rochester.
Holes: 18. **Yards:** 7,083/5,623. **Par:** 72/72. **Course Rating:** 73.9/72.4. **Slope:** 138/123. **Green Fee:** $15/$33. **Cart Fee:** Included in Green Fee. **Walking Policy:** Unrestricted walking. **Walkability:** 3. **Opened:** 1963. **Architect:** Peter Craig. **Season:** April-Dec. **High:** June-Aug. **To obtain tee times:** Call up to 7 days in advance. **Miscellaneous:** Reduced fees (weekdays, low season, twilight, seniors, juniors), metal spikes, range (grass), club rentals, credit cards (MC, V, AE, D).
Reader Comments: A good course for mid-handicappers. Plays long. Well kept ... Long hitters have advantage ... Long, good variety of holes ... Great layout, inexpensive ... Good condition, long ... Good length ... Nice people and service.

★★★ DEERWOOD GOLF COURSE
PM-1818 Sweeney St., North Tonawanda, 14120, Niagara County, (716)695-8525, 12 miles N of Buffalo.
Holes: 18. **Yards:** 6,948/6,150. **Par:** 72/73. **Course Rating:** 73.0/75.0. **Slope:** 117/123. **Green Fee:** $9/$21. **Cart Fee:** $19/cart. **Walking Policy:** Unrestricted walking. **Walkability:** 1. **Opened:** 1975. **Architect:** Tryon & Schwartz. **Season:** April-Dec. **High:** June-Aug. **To obtain tee times:** First come, first served. **Miscellaneous:** Reduced fees (weekdays, twilight, seniors, juniors), club rentals.
Reader Comments: Long course, large greens ... Very enjoyable ... Very long and soft ... Flat but tough, gets lots of play ... Layout offers good test ... Good layout, good condition, slow play ... Monster wind, monster par 5s.

DELPHI FALLS GOLF COURSE
PU-2127 Oran-Delphi Rd., Delphi Falls, 13051, Ononadoga County, (315)662-3611, 15 miles SE of Syracuse.
Holes: 18. **Yards:** 4,540/4,540. **Par:** 18/18. **Course Rating:** N/A. **Slope:** N/A. **Green Fee:** $12/$15. **Cart Fee:** $18/cart. **Walking Policy:** Unrestricted walking. **Walkability:** N/A. **Opened:** 1967. **High:** June-Aug. **To obtain tee times:** No tee times needed. **Miscellaneous:** Reduced fees (weekdays), club rentals, beginner friendly (junior programs).

★★½ DOMENICO'S GOLF COURSE
PU-13 Church Rd., Whitesboro, 13492, Oneida County, (315)736-9812, 4 miles W of Utica.
Holes: 18. **Yards:** 6,715/5,458. **Par:** 72/75. **Course Rating:** 70.5/71.5. **Slope:** 118/115. **Green Fee:** $12/$16. **Cart Fee:** $10/person. **Walking Policy:** Unrestricted walking. **Walkability:** 2. **Opened:** 1982. **Architect:** Joseph Spinella. **Season:** March-Nov. **High:** May-Aug. **To obtain tee times:** Call. **Miscellaneous:** Reduced fees (weekdays, twilight), metal spikes, club rentals.
Reader Comments: Good value ... Good course, challenge for local players ... Great walking course.

★★½ DOUGLASTON GOLF CLUB
PU-63-20 Marathon Pkwy., Douglaston, 11363, Queens County, (718)428-1617, 15 miles E of Manhattan.
Holes: 18. **Yards:** 5,585/4,602. **Par:** 67/67. **Course Rating:** 66.2/65.6. **Slope:** 111/107. **Green Fee:** $18/$28. **Cart Fee:** $25/cart. **Walking Policy:** Unrestricted walking. **Walkability:** 4. **Opened:** 1927. **Architect:** William H. Tucker. **Season:** Year-round. **High:** May-Sept. **To obtain tee times:** Call 7 days in advance for weekdays, $2.00 per player. Call 2 Thursdays before a weekend for weekend times. Call Thursday at 4:00 p.m. **Miscellaneous:** Reduced fees (seniors, juniors), metal spikes, club rentals, credit cards (MC, V, AE, D).
Reader Comments: Many par 3s good for ego ... Hilly, not too long, blind shots, nice greens ... Views are nice ... Long, hilly and many geese ... City course, well worn ... Short course ... Lots of hills to test yourself.

★★ DRUMLINS WEST GOLF CLUB
PU-800 Nottingham Rd., Syracuse, 13224, Onondaga County, (315)446-5580, 5 miles E of Syracuse.

Holes: 18. Yards: 6,030/4,790. Par: 70/70. Course Rating: 68.2/71.0. Slope: N/A. Green Fee: $10/$14. Cart Fee: $23/cart. Walking Policy: Unrestricted walking. Walkability: N/A. Opened: 1935. Architect: Leonard MacComber. Season: April-Nov. High: May-Aug. To obtain tee times: Call. Miscellaneous: Reduced fees (twilight, seniors, juniors), discount packages, metal spikes, range (grass/mats), club rentals, credit cards (MC, V, D).

★★★ DUNWOODIE GOLF CLUB
PU-Wasylenko Lane, Yonkers, 10701, Westchester County, (914)968-2771.
Holes: 18. Yards: 5,815/4,511. Par: 70/72. Course Rating: 68.3/67.8. Slope: 117/117. Green Fee: $37/$42. Cart Fee: $22. Walking Policy: Unrestricted walking. Walkability: N/A. Season: April-Dec. High: April-Nov. To obtain tee times: Call (914)593-4653. Miscellaneous: Reduced fees (twilight, seniors, juniors), metal spikes, range (grass), club rentals, credit cards (MC, V, AE).
Reader Comments: Very hilly ... Fun to play, short ... Good public course. Front 9 short & hilly ... Front 9 tough, back 9 easier, course in very good shape ... Best conditioned Westchester County course ... Very well kept, good iron course ... Best of Westchester County public offerings.

★★★½ DURAND EASTMAN GOLF COURSE *Value*
PU-1200 Kings Hwy. N., Rochester, 14617, Monroe County, (716)342-9810.
Holes: 18. Yards: 6,089/5,727. Par: 70/72. Course Rating: 68.8/71.7. Slope: 112/113. Green Fee: $12/$13. Cart Fee: $16/. Walking Policy: Unrestricted walking. Walkability: N/A. Opened: 1935. Architect: Robert Trent Jones. Season: April-Nov. High: June-Aug. To obtain tee times: First come, first served. Miscellaneous: Reduced fees (weekdays, low season, seniors, juniors), discount packages, metal spikes, range (grass), club rentals.
Reader Comments: Hilly, scenic, great shotmaking course ... A beautiful experience ... Some very nice holes ... Scenic, usually crowded ... Outstanding layout, potential to be a championship course ... A small course, but interesting ... Awesome views, lake, must play ... Great layout, fun to play.

★★★½ DUTCH HOLLOW COUNTRY CLUB
SP-Benson Rd., Owasco, 13130, Cayuga County, (315)784-5052, 19 miles SW of Syracuse.
Holes: 18. Yards: 6,460/5,045. Par: 71/72. Course Rating: 68.5/69.0. Slope: 116/117. Green Fee: $17/$20. Cart Fee: $11/person. Walking Policy: Unrestricted walking. Walkability: 3. Opened: 1965. Architect: Willard S. Hall. Season: April-Nov. High: May-Sept. To obtain tee times: Call. Miscellaneous: Reduced fees (weekdays, low season, twilight, seniors, juniors), discount packages, metal spikes, range (grass), club rentals, credit cards (MC, V).
Reader Comments: Lots of water, club selection important ... Course has everything ... Play it again Sam! Great value ... Tricky! ... Bring your long game here ... Nice course, challenging and rewarding to risk takers ... Great fairways. Fast greens. Great steak ... An old favorite, high risk, high reward.

★★½ DYKER BEACH GOLF COURSE
PU-86th St. and 7th Ave., Brooklyn, 11228, Kings County, (718)836-9722, 8 miles E of New York City.
Holes: 18. Yards: 6,548/5,696. Par: 71/72. Course Rating: 68.8/N/A. Slope: 113/N/A. Green Fee: $18/$22. Cart Fee: $25/cart. Walking Policy: Unrestricted walking. Walkability: 2. Opened: 1928. Architect: John Van Kleek. Season: Year-round. High: May-Oct. To obtain tee times: Call (718)225-4653 up to 11 days in advance. Miscellaneous: Reduced fees (weekdays, twilight, seniors, juniors), metal spikes, club rentals, credit cards (MC, V, AE, D), beginner friendly.
Reader Comments: A good find if you can get on ... Best-kept & maintained course in NYC ... Nice for NYC ... Some interesting holes ... Tees & greens always in good shape ... Metropolitan course, nice people ... Always a wait to get on the course.

★★★ EAGLE CREST GOLF CLUB
PU-1004 Ballston Lake Rd., Rte. 146A, Clifton Park, 12065, Saratoga County, (518)877-7082, 12 miles S of Saratoga. Web: www.eaglecrestgolf.com.
Holes: 18. Yards: 6,814/5,082. Par: 72/72. Course Rating: 72.4/68.6. Slope: 126/117. Green Fee: $20/$24. Cart Fee: $22/person. Walking Policy: Unrestricted walking. Walkability: 2. Opened: 1962. Season: March-Nov. High: May-Sept. To obtain tee times: Foursomes may call up to 3 days in advance. All others call up to 2 days in advance. Miscellaneous: Reduced fees (weekdays, seniors), range (grass), club rentals, credit cards (MC, V), beginner friendly (multiple ladies and junior clinics).
Reader Comments: Challenging with sloped, fast greens ... Basic golf ... Good course that will test your skills ... Good conditions ... Course improving rapidly ... Nice course, fair test ... Very nice layout, improving ... Small undulating greens make up for shortness ... In very good condition ... Family-operated course.

★★★ EAGLE VALE GOLF COURSE
PU-4344 Nine Mile Point Rd., Fairport, 14450, Monroe County, (716)377-5200, 15 miles SE of Rochester.

Holes: 18. **Yards:** 6,584/5,801. **Par:** 71/72. **Course Rating:** 71.0/73.0. **Slope:** 121/121. **Green Fee:** $23/$36. **Cart Fee:** Included in Green Fee. **Walking Policy:** Walking at certain times. **Walkability:** 2. **Opened:** 1987. **Architect:** Bill Brown/Neil Hirsch. **Season:** April-Dec. **High:** June-Aug. **To obtain tee times:** Call 1 day in advance for weekdays and 3 days in advance for weekends and holidays. **Miscellaneous:** Reduced fees (weekdays, low season, seniors, juniors), discount packages, range (mats), club rentals, credit cards (MC, V, AE, D), beginner friendly (instruction and clinics).
Reader Comments: Nice course ... Nice greens, front 9 cramped, back more open ... Great course, staff could be friendlier ... Doglegs!

EISENHOWER PARK GOLF
PU-Eisenhower Park, East Meadow, 11554, Nassau County, (516)542-0015, 20 miles E of New York City.

★★★ BLUE COURSE
Holes: 18. **Yards:** 6,026/5,800. **Par:** 72/72. **Course Rating:** 68.7/74.1. **Slope:** 112/122. **Green Fee:** $7/$28. **Cart Fee:** $22/cart. **Walking Policy:** Unrestricted walking. **Walkability:** 1. **Opened:** 1947. **Architect:** Robert Trent Jones. **Season:** Year-round. **High:** May-Oct. **To obtain tee times:** Call (516)542-4653. **Miscellaneous:** Reduced fees (weekdays, low season, seniors), range (mats), club rentals.
Reader Comments: Feel like a tiger, reaching par 5s in two! ... Inexpensive and in good condition ... A great course for a friendly match ... Easy course.

★★★½ RED COURSE
Holes: 18. **Yards:** 6,756/5,449. **Par:** 72/72. **Course Rating:** 71.5/69.8. **Slope:** 119/115. **Green Fee:** $7/$28. **Cart Fee:** $22/cart. **Walking Policy:** Unrestricted walking. **Walkability:** 1. **Opened:** 1914. **Architect:** Robert Trent Jones. **Season:** Year-round. **High:** May-Oct. **To obtain tee times:** Call (516)542-4653. **Miscellaneous:** Reduced fees (weekdays, low season, seniors), range (mats), club rentals.
Notes: 1926 PGA Championship.
Reader Comments: Good condition, nice layout ... Getting better every year ... Tremendous number of rounds per year, but you'd never know it ... Great condition, good value ... Great value, tee times can be hard to secure ... Restored to finest glory! ... Plays tougher than it looks ... Course was long but easy.

★★ WHITE COURSE
Holes: 18. **Yards:** 6,269/5,920. **Par:** 72/72. **Course Rating:** 69.5/71.4. **Slope:** 115/117. **Green Fee:** $7/$28. **Cart Fee:** $22/cart. **Walking Policy:** Unrestricted walking. **Walkability:** 1. **Opened:** 1947. **Architect:** Robert Trent Jones. **Season:** Year-round. **High:** May-Oct. **To obtain tee times:** Call (516)542-4653. **Miscellaneous:** Reduced fees (weekdays, low season, seniors), range (mats), club rentals.

★★ ELM TREE GOLF COURSE
PU-283 St. Rte. No.13, Cortland, 13045, Cortland County, (607)753-1341, 30 miles S of Syracuse.
Holes: 18. **Yards:** 6,251/5,520. **Par:** 70/74. **Course Rating:** 66.4/66.3. **Slope:** 100/99. **Green Fee:** $9/$13. **Cart Fee:** $20/cart. **Walking Policy:** Unrestricted walking. **Walkability:** 3. **Opened:** 1966. **Architect:** Alder Jones. **Season:** April-Nov. **High:** June-Aug. **To obtain tee times:** Call 1 day in advance. **Miscellaneous:** Reduced fees (weekdays, low season, resort guests, twilight, seniors, juniors), discount packages, metal spikes, range (grass/mats), credit cards (MC, V).

★★½ ELMA MEADOWS GOLF CLUB
PU-1711 Girdle Rd., Elma, 14059, Erie County, (716)655-3037, 10 miles E of Buffalo.
Holes: 18. **Yards:** 6,316/6,000. **Par:** 70/75. **Course Rating:** 70.0/74.0. **Slope:** 110/106. **Green Fee:** $11/$13. **Cart Fee:** $19/cart. **Walking Policy:** Unrestricted walking. **Walkability:** 3. **Opened:** 1959. **Architect:** William Harries/A. Russell Tryon. **Season:** Year-round weather permitting. **High:** June-Aug. **To obtain tee times:** First come, first served. **Miscellaneous:** Reduced fees (weekdays, seniors, juniors), range (grass), club rentals.
Reader Comments: Get there early ... Nice layout ... Fun to play, best local county run course ... Good public very busy, greens sometimes bad ... Good public course to play ... Very good for the play it gets ... Nice county course.

★★ ELY PARK MUNICIPAL GOLF COURSE
PM-67 Ridge Road, Binghamton, 13905, Broome County, (607)772-7231.
Holes: 18. **Yards:** 6,410/N/A. **Par:** 70/N/A. **Course Rating:** 69.4/N/A. **Slope:** 115/N/A. **Green Fee:** $12/$13. **Cart Fee:** $18/cart. **Walking Policy:** Unrestricted walking. **Walkability:** 4. **Opened:** 1932. **Architect:** Ernest E. Smith. **Season:** April-Nov. **High:** Summer. **To obtain tee times:** Call for weekends and holidays. **Miscellaneous:** Reduced fees (seniors, juniors), metal spikes, range (grass/mats), club rentals.

★★★★ EN-JOIE GOLF CLUB
PU-722 W. Main St., Endicott, 13760, Broome County, (607)785-1661, (888)436-5643, 9 miles W of Binghamton. **E-mail:** golf@enjoiegolf.com. **Web:** www.enjoiegolf.com.

Holes: 18. **Yards:** 7,016/5,205. **Par:** 72/74. **Course Rating:** 73.0/69.8. **Slope:** 125/118. **Green Fee:** $32/$40. **Cart Fee:** $24/cart. **Walking Policy:** Unrestricted walking. **Walkability:** 2. **Opened:** 1927. **Architect:** Dr. Michael Hurdzan. **Season:** March-Dec. **High:** May-Oct. **To obtain tee times:** Call 7 days in advance. **Miscellaneous:** Reduced fees (weekdays, seniors, juniors), range (grass/mats), club rentals, credit cards (MC, V).
Notes: Home of the PGA Tour's B. C. Open.
Reader Comments: Excellent course, greens, layout ... Nice fairways ... Excellent value, beautiful course ... Good chance to play a tour stop, very reasonably priced ... Many good holes ... Tremendous value. Some good holes to boot ... Impeccable conditions, superior customer service and a fantastic design ... A MUST Place to Play.

★★★ ENDWELL GREENS GOLF CLUB
PU-3675 Sally Piper Rd., Endwell, 13760, Broome County, (607)785-4653, (877)281-6863, 5 miles W of Binghamton. **E-mail:** pga4653@aol.com.
Holes: 18. **Yards:** 7,104/5,382. **Par:** 72/76. **Course Rating:** 73.5/69.0. **Slope:** 129/113. **Green Fee:** $20/$27. **Cart Fee:** $12/person. **Walking Policy:** Walking at certain times. **Walkability:** 4. **Opened:** 1968. **Architect:** Geoffrey Cornish. **Season:** Year-round. **High:** June-Aug. **To obtain tee times:** Public may call 2 days in advance. Members may call up to 14 days in advance. **Miscellaneous:** Reduced fees (weekdays, low season, seniors, juniors), discount packages, metal spikes, range (grass/mats), club rentals, lodging (10 rooms), credit cards (MC, V, D), beginner friendly (six hole executive course).
Reader Comments: Mountain-goat country ... Good, challenging course ... Hilly ... Nice course, condition was fair ... Can't make mistakes, woods, water, narrow and hilly ... Try it, you'll like it! ... Very good clubhouse ... Hilly, scenic, a little pricey ... Short and simple.

★★ FILLMORE GOLF CLUB
SP-Tollgate Hill Road, Locke, 13092, Cayuga County, (315)497-3145, 19 miles S of Auburn.
Holes: 18. **Yards:** 5,523/4,374. **Par:** 71/71. **Course Rating:** 67.1/66.1. **Slope:** 115/115. **Green Fee:** $11/$13. **Cart Fee:** $20/cart. **Walking Policy:** Unrestricted walking. **Walkability:** 3. **Opened:** 1965. **Architect:** Alder Jones. **Season:** April-Oct. **High:** June-Aug. **To obtain tee times:** Phone (315)497-3145 for weekends. **Miscellaneous:** Reduced fees (weekdays, low season, seniors, juniors), discount packages, range (grass), club rentals, credit cards (MC, V), beginner friendly.

FORD HILL COUNTRY CLUB
PU-Rte. 26, Ford Hill Rd., Whitney Point, 13862, Broome County, (607)692-8938, 19 miles N of Binghamton.
Holes: 36. **Green Fee:** $14/$17. **Cart Fee:** $17/person. **Walking Policy:** Unrestricted walking. **Walkability:** 2. **Opened:** 1988. **Architect:** Richard L. Driscoll. **Season:** April-Nov. **High:** July-Aug. **To obtain tee times:** Call (607)692-8938.
★¹⁄₂ BLUE/ORANGE
Yards: 5,436/N/A. **Par:** 70/N/A. **Course Rating:** 68.0/N/A. **Slope:** N/A. **Miscellaneous:** Reduced fees (weekdays), discount packages, club rentals, credit cards (MC, V, AE, D).
★¹⁄₂ RED/BLUE
Yards: 5,254/N/A. **Par:** 70/N/A. **Course Rating:** 68.0/N/A. **Slope:** N/A. **Miscellaneous:** Reduced fees (weekdays, seniors, juniors), discount packages, club rentals, credit cards (MC, V, AE, D).
★¹⁄₂ RED/ORANGE
Yards: 5,218/N/A. **Par:** 70/N/A. **Course Rating:** 68.0/N/A. **Slope:** N/A. **Miscellaneous:** Reduced fees (weekdays, seniors, juniors), discount packages, club rentals, credit cards (MC, V, AE, D).
★¹⁄₂ RED/WHITE
Yards: 5,299/N/A. **Par:** 69/N/A. **Course Rating:** 68.0/N/A. **Slope:** N/A. **Miscellaneous:** Reduced fees (weekdays, seniors, juniors), discount packages, club rentals, credit cards (MC, V, AE, D).

★★★ FOREST PARK GOLF COURSE
PU-Forest Park Dr., Woodhaven, 11421, Queens County, (718)296-0999.
Holes: 18. **Yards:** 5,820/5,431. **Par:** 67/67. **Course Rating:** 67.5/69.5. **Slope:** 111/116. **Green Fee:** $7/$17. **Cart Fee:** $23/. **Walking Policy:** Unrestricted walking. **Walkability:** N/A. **Opened:** 1901. **Architect:** Mr. Elliot. **Season:** Year-round. **High:** April-Sept. **To obtain tee times:** Call in advance up to 7 days. **Miscellaneous:** Reduced fees (weekdays, low season, twilight, seniors, juniors), metal spikes, club rentals, credit cards (MC, V).
Reader Comments: A hidden treasure in Queens ... Upgraded & still improving ... Good layout ... So much potential. Is getting better... Great for all levels ... Best to play in fall... Great improvement. Narrow & terrifically challenging.

★★★¹⁄₂ FOXFIRE AT VILLAGE GREEN
PU-One Village Blvd., Baldwinsville, 13027, Onondaga County, (315)638-2930, 9 miles NW of Syracuse. **E-mail:** foxfire@twcny.rr.com.
Holes: 18. **Yards:** 6,856/5,401. **Par:** 72/74. **Course Rating:** 72.8/71.5. **Slope:** 127/115. **Green Fee:** $20/$22. **Cart Fee:** $11/person. **Walking Policy:** Walking at certain times. **Walkability:** 2. **Opened:** 1974. **Architect:** Hal Purdy. **Season:** March-Nov. **High:** June-Sept. **To obtain tee

times: Call up to 5 days in advance. Call 14 days in advance for Tee-Time Club Members. **Miscellaneous:** Reduced fees (weekdays, seniors, juniors), metal spikes, range (grass/mats), club rentals, credit cards (MC, V). **Reader Comments:** Fun to play ... Tough and tight ... Very nice layout, challenging ... Good upstate golf ... Can be crowded, challenging ... Tough from the tips; some tough driving holes, friendly staff ... Great practice green ... Great layout ... Well-designed course ... Challenging, in good condition ... Nice layout, quick greens.

★★★ GARRISON GOLF CLUB
PU-2015 Rte. 9, Garrison, 10524, Putnam County, (914)424-4747, 50 miles N of New York City. **Holes:** 18. **Yards:** 6,470/5,041. **Par:** 72/70. **Course Rating:** 72.1/69.9. **Slope:** 134/124. **Green Fee:** $40/$75. **Cart Fee:** Included in Green Fee. **Walking Policy:** Walking at certain times. **Walkability:** 5. **Opened:** 1962. **Architect:** Dick Wilson. **Season:** April-Nov. **High:** June-Aug. **To obtain tee times:** Call up to 7 days in advance. **Miscellaneous:** Reduced fees (weekdays, twilight, seniors), range (grass), club rentals, credit cards (MC, V, AE). **Reader Comments:** A hidden gem with spectacular views ... Great track for masochists like me! ... One of the holes fascinated me because it went straight down a steep hill ... Makes everyone humble. Back to the range! ... Scenic, challenging, a total experience ... Beautiful, very tough ... Great layout ... Scenic views of West Point.

GENESEE VALLEY GOLF COURSE
PU-1000 E. River Rd., Rochester, 14623, Monroe County, (716)424-2920.
★★ NEW COURSE
Holes: 18. **Yards:** 5,270/5,270. **Par:** 67/69. **Course Rating:** N/A/67.4. **Slope:** 93/100. **Green Fee:** $12/$13. **Cart Fee:** $9/person. **Walking Policy:** Unrestricted walking. **Walkability:** N/A. **Opened:** 1927. **Architect:** Frances Baker. **Season:** April-Nov. **High:** June-July. **To obtain tee times:** Call for weekends. **Miscellaneous:** Reduced fees (low season, twilight, seniors, juniors), discount packages, metal spikes, club rentals.
★★ OLD COURSE
Holes: 18. **Yards:** 6,374/6,007. **Par:** 71/77. **Course Rating:** 69.3/73.2. **Slope:** 104/112. **Green Fee:** $12/$13. **Cart Fee:** $9/person. **Walking Policy:** Unrestricted walking. **Walkability:** N/A. **Opened:** 1900. **Architect:** Frances Baker. **Season:** April-Nov. **High:** June-July. **To obtain tee times:** Call for weekends. **Miscellaneous:** Reduced fees (low season, twilight, seniors, juniors), discount packages, metal spikes, club rentals.

★★★½ GLEN OAK GOLF COURSE
PU-711 Smith Rd., East Amherst, 14051, Erie County, (716)688-5454, 50 miles N of Buffalo. **Holes:** 18. **Yards:** 6,730/5,561. **Par:** 72/72. **Course Rating:** 72.4/71.9. **Slope:** 129/118. **Green Fee:** $25/$47. **Cart Fee:** Included in Green Fee. **Walking Policy:** Mandatory cart. **Walkability:** N/A. **Opened:** 1969. **Architect:** Robert Trent Jones. **Season:** April-Nov. **High:** June-Aug. **To obtain tee times:** Call up to 5 days in advance, except for outings. **Miscellaneous:** Reduced fees (weekdays, low season, twilight, seniors), range (grass/mats), club rentals, credit cards (MC, V). **Reader Comments:** Tight fairways ... Course management required ... A little more expensive, but, worth it ... Challenging, large greens, lots water ... Fine practice facility ... Best Buffalo-area public course. A bit pricey, quality of greens are worth it. Pace of play can be slow ... Good layout, but play can be slow ... Great track.

★★½ GOLDEN OAK GOLF CLUB
PU-679 NY, Rte. 79 South , Windsor, 13865, Broome County, (607)655-3217, 12 miles SE of Binghamton. **Holes:** 18. **Yards:** 5,500/4,500. **Par:** 69/69. **Course Rating:** 70.8/65.0. **Slope:** 117/112. **Green Fee:** $13/$16. **Cart Fee:** $18/cart. **Walking Policy:** Unrestricted walking. **Walkability:** 3. **Opened:** 1972. **Architect:** Paul Kern. **Season:** April-Nov. **High:** June-Aug. **To obtain tee times:** Call 2 days in advance. **Miscellaneous:** Reduced fees (weekdays), discount packages, club rentals, credit cards (MC, V). **Reader Comments:** Lovely scenery, good price, basic golf ... Front nine, side mountain; back nine flat, woods,water and a river ... Flat, but interesting ... Solid golf ... Best in western NY ... Tough but fair.

★★★½ GREEN LAKES STATE PARK GOLF CLUB
PU-7900 Green Lakes Rd., Fayetteville, 13066, Onondaga County, (315)637-0258, 7 miles S of Syracuse. **Holes:** 18. **Yards:** 6,212/5,481. **Par:** 71/74. **Course Rating:** 68.4/70.6. **Slope:** 113/120. **Green Fee:** $20/$24. **Cart Fee:** $20/person. **Walking Policy:** Unrestricted walking. **Walkability:** 4. **Opened:** 1936. **Architect:** Robert Trent Jones. **Season:** April-Nov. **High:** May-Sept. **To obtain tee times:** Call 4 days in advance. $2.00 fee if tee time reservation is made. **Miscellaneous:** Reduced fees (weekdays, seniors, juniors), metal spikes, rentals, lodging, credit cards (MC, V). **Reader Comments:** A true gem, one of New York's best ... Fun course. Great place to have a beer and watch the 18th hole ... Great course, lots of play, great shape ... As good as golf gets

... Lots of elevation changes; no flat lies or putts on this state course ... Outstanding layout ... Real taxpayer dollars at work.

GREENVIEW COUNTRY CLUB
PU-Whig Hill Rd., West Monroe, 13167, Oswego County, (315)668-2244.

GREEN VALLEY COURSE
Holes: 18. **Yards:** 5,877/5,265. **Par:** 71/72. **Course Rating:** N/A. **Slope:** N/A. **Green Fee:** $14/$18. **Cart Fee:** 16/cart. **Walking Policy:** Walking at certain times. **Walkability:** 2. **Season:** April-Nov. **High:** June-Aug. **To obtain tee times:** Call golf shop. **Miscellaneous:** Reduced fees (weekdays, twilight, junior), metal spikes, club rentals, credit cards (MC, V, AE).

GREENVILLE COURSE
Holes: 18. **Yards:** 6,324/5,832. **Par:** 71/73. **Course Rating:** N/A. **Slope:** N/A. **Green Fee:** $14/$18. **Cart Fee:** 16/cart. **Walking Policy:** Walking at certain times. **Walkability:** 2. **Season:** April-Nov. **High:** June-Aug. **To obtain tee times:** Call golf shop. **Miscellaneous:** Reduced fees (weekdays, twilight, junior), metal spikes, club rentals, credit cards (MC, V, AE).

★★★★½ GREYSTONE GOLF CLUB *Service, Condition, Pace+*
PU-1400 Atlantic Ave., Walworth, 14568, Wayne County, (315)524-0022, (800)810-2325, 12 miles E of Rochester.
Holes: 18. **Yards:** 6,500/5,300. **Par:** 72/72. **Course Rating:** 70.2/70.7. **Slope:** 121/122. **Green Fee:** $28/$38. **Cart Fee:** $12/person. **Walking Policy:** Walking at certain times. **Walkability:** 4. **Opened:** 1996. **Architect:** Craig Schreiner. **Season:** April-Nov. **High:** Summer. **To obtain tee times:** Call up to 7 days in advance. **Miscellaneous:** Reduced fees (weekdays, low season, twilight, seniors), metal spikes, range (grass), club rentals, credit cards (MC, V, AE).
Reader Comments: Outstanding, nicely run! ... Young course, challenging greens ... Great value, fast pace ... Beautiful, different, Scotland in Upstate NY ... Superb condition. Breathtaking tee boxes ... Best public course in Rochester area ... One of the best-conditioned courses ever ... Enormous greens, finely manicured.

GROSSINGER COUNTRY CLUB
PU-26 Rte. 52 E., Liberty, 12754, Sullivan County, (914)292-9000, 98 miles NW of New York City. **E-mail:** tbarker@catskill.net. **Web:** www.grossingergolf.com.

★★★★ THE BIG G
Holes: 18. **Yards:** 6,839/5,875. **Par:** 71/75. **Course Rating:** 72.9/73.2. **Slope:** 134/137. **Green Fee:** $60/$75. **Cart Fee:** Included in Green Fee. **Walking Policy:** Mandatory cart. **Walkability:** 3. **Opened:** 1965. **Architect:** Joe Finger. **Season:** April-Nov. **High:** May-Sept. **To obtain tee times:** Call up to 14 days in advance. **Miscellaneous:** Reduced fees (weekdays, low season, twilight), discount packages, range (grass), club rentals, credit cards (MC, V, AE).
Reader Comments: A hidden gem, great golf ... Best course around! Great greens. Plays very tough, nice people ... Score on front, the back takes it away ... Best course for the buck in NY, big tough greens ... Not a weak hole ... Great course, condition, greens ... Great value, beautiful layout, a challenge.

★★★½ THE LITTLE G
Holes: 9. **Yards:** 3,268/3,024. **Par:** 36/36. **Course Rating:** 35.9/36.6. **Slope:** 126/130. **Green Fee:** $20/$20. **Cart Fee:** $15/person. **Walking Policy:** Mandatory cart. **Walkability:** 4. **Opened:** 1925. **Architect:** Andrew Salerno. **Season:** April-Nov. **High:** May-Sept. **To obtain tee times:** Call up to 14 days in advance. **Miscellaneous:** Reduced fees (seniors), range (grass/mats), club rentals, credit cards (MC, V, AE).
Reader Comments: Back nine takes your breath away ... A must play although out of way ... One of the best, spectacular views! ... Great, tough course.

★½ GROVER CLEVELAND GOLF COURSE
PU-3781 Main St., Amherst, 14226, Erie County, (716)862-9470, 3 miles N of Buffalo.
Holes: 18. **Yards:** 5,584/N/A. **Par:** 69/N/A. **Course Rating:** 65.5/N/A. **Slope:** 101/N/A. **Green Fee:** $9/$10. **Cart Fee:** $18/cart. **Walking Policy:** Unrestricted walking. **Walkability:** 2. **Opened:** 1912. **Season:** April-Nov. **High:** June-Aug. **To obtain tee times:** First come, first served. **Miscellaneous:** Reduced fees (weekdays, seniors, juniors), range (mats), club rentals, credit cards (MC, V).

★★★ HAMLET WIND WATCH GOLF CLUB
PU-1715 Vanderbuilt Motor Pkwy., Hauppauge, 11788, Suffolk County, (631)232-9850, 45 miles E of New York City.
Holes: 18. **Yards:** 6,613/5,188. **Par:** 71/71. **Course Rating:** 71.5/69.9. **Slope:** 130/121. **Green Fee:** $25/$90. **Cart Fee:** Included in Green Fee. **Walking Policy:** Mandatory cart. **Walkability:** 2. **Opened:** 1990. **Architect:** Joe Lee. **Season:** Year-round. **High:** April-Oct. **To obtain tee times:** Hotel guests may call 60 days in advance. Nonguests call 3 days in advance. **Miscellaneous:** Reduced fees (low season, resort guests, twilight, juniors), discount packages, range (grass/mats), club rentals, lodging (360 rooms), credit cards (MC, V, AE, D).

Reader Comments: Well-maintained. Good greens, improving layout ... Short but demanding, windy usually. Attentive staff. Greens challenging, undulations ... Expensive but beautiful, lots of water, narrow ... Real nice, great service, golf shop stocked.

★★★½ HANAH COUNTRY INN & GOLF RESORT

R-Rte. 30, Margaretville, 12455, Deleware County, (914)586-4849, (800)752-6494, 42 miles W of Kingston.
Holes: 18. **Yards:** 7,033/5,294. **Par:** 72/72. **Course Rating:** 73.5/69.7. **Slope:** 133/123. **Green Fee:** $40/$55. **Cart Fee:** Included in Green Fee. **Walking Policy:** Mandatory cart. **Walkability:** N/A. **Opened:** 1992. **Architect:** Koji Nagasaka. **Season:** April-Oct. **High:** June-July. **To obtain tee times:** Call. **Miscellaneous:** Reduced fees (weekdays, low season, resort guests, twilight, seniors), discount packages, range (grass/mats), club rentals, lodging, credit cards (MC, V, D).
Reader Comments: Smooth & relaxing play on nice fairways & greens ... Fun course, good day, lots of water and woods ... 17th super difficult; The Terminator name fits ... I'll be back ... Great value for a fun and demanding course ... Tough test for higher handicaps ... Great layout, fair condition ... Good resort course in Catskills.

HARBOR LINKS GOLF COURSE

PU-1 Fairway Dr., Port Washington, 11050, Nassau County, (516)767-4818, (877)342-7267, 25 miles E of New York City. **Web:** www.harborlinks.com.
Holes: 18. **Yards:** 6,927/5,465. **Par:** 72/72. **Course Rating:** 73.2/71.5. **Slope:** 128/119. **Green Fee:** $40/$90. **Cart Fee:** Included in Green Fee. **Walking Policy:** Walking at certain times. **Walkability:** 4. **Opened:** 1998. **Architect:** Michael Hurdzan/Dana Fry. **Season:** April-Nov. **High:** May-Sept. **To obtain tee times:** Call 1-877-342-7267. Resident tee time card holders can call 30 days in advance. **Miscellaneous:** Reduced fees (twilight, seniors, juniors), range (grass/mats), club rentals, credit cards (MC, V, AE).

HARBOUR POINTE COUNTRY CLUB

PU-Rte. 18 and 98, Waterport, 14571, Orleans County, (716)798-3010.
Special Notes: Call club for further information.

★★★★ HILAND GOLF CLUB

SP-195 Haviland Rd., Queensbury, 12804, Warren County, (518)761-4653, 45 miles N of Albany. **Web:** highlandgolf.com.
Holes: 18. **Yards:** 6,632/5,677. **Par:** 72/72. **Course Rating:** 72.8/72.5. **Slope:** 130/124. **Green Fee:** N/A/$38. **Cart Fee:** $13/person. **Walking Policy:** Walking at certain times. **Walkability:** 2. **Opened:** 1988. **Architect:** Steven Kay. **Season:** April-Nov. **High:** June-Sept. **To obtain tee times:** Call. Tee times required. (518)793-2000 Ext. 228. **Miscellaneous:** Reduced fees (weekdays, low season, resort guests, twilight), range (grass/mats), club rentals, credit cards (MC, V, AE, Diners Club).
Reader Comments: Nice layout and well manicured ... Best course in upstate New York ... Challenging long course but fair ... Excellent conditioning ... Course always in excellent shape ... Looks easy, but it's not ... Sneaky good! Solid course ... One of the finest new courses in the area.

★★ HILLENDALE GOLF COURSE

SP-218 Applegate Rd. N., Ithaca, 14850, Tompkins County, (607)273-2363, 50 miles S of Syracuse. **E-mail:** dargolfer@aol.com. **Web:** http://www.hillendale.com.
Holes: 18. **Yards:** 6,002/5,705. **Par:** 71/73. **Course Rating:** 68.8/69.3. **Slope:** 115/116. **Green Fee:** $16/$18. **Cart Fee:** $20/cart. **Walking Policy:** Unrestricted walking. **Walkability:** 3. **Opened:** 1912. **Architect:** Novickas/Sommer. **Season:** April-Oct. **High:** June-Aug. **To obtain tee times:** Call golf shop up to 7 days in advance. **Miscellaneous:** Reduced fees (weekdays, low season, twilight, seniors, juniors), discount packages, metal spikes, range (grass), club rentals, credit cards (MC, V), beginner friendly ('Dollar a Hole' program for beginners to get introduced to the game).

★★★½ HOLIDAY VALLEY RESORT

R-Rte. 219, Ellicottville, 14731, Cattaraugus County, (716)699-2346, 48 miles S of Buffalo.
Holes: 18. **Yards:** 6,555/5,381. **Par:** 72/73. **Course Rating:** 71.3/74.0. **Slope:** 125/115. **Green Fee:** $15/$34. **Cart Fee:** $11/person. **Walking Policy:** Walking at certain times. **Walkability:** 5. **Opened:** 1961. **Architect:** Russ Tryon. **Season:** April-Oct. **High:** June-Sept. **To obtain tee times:** Call up to 3 days in advance. **Miscellaneous:** Reduced fees (weekdays, low season, resort guests, twilight), discount packages, metal spikes, range (grass/mats), club rentals, lodging, credit cards (MC, V, AE, D).
Reader Comments: Good mountain course ... Built on ski slopes, memorable experience ... Very nice people ... Expensive, challenging ... Narrow & very tight ... Nice course.

HUDSON VALLEY RESORT & SPA

R-400 Lower Granite Rd., Kerhonkson, 12446, Ulster County, (914)626-2972, (888)684-7264, 20 miles S of Kingston. **E-mail:** golf@hudsonvalleyresort.com. **Web:** hudsonvalleyresort.com.

Holes: 18. **Yards:** 6,351/5,300. **Par:** 70/70. **Course Rating:** 69.6/69.3. **Slope:** 119/110. **Green Fee:** $35/$50. **Cart Fee:** Included in Green Fee. **Walking Policy:** Walking at certain times. **Walkability:** 3. **Opened:** 1998. **Architect:** Lee Chen. **Season:** April-Nov. **High:** June-Aug. **To obtain tee time:** Two week advance tee time recommended. **Miscellaneous:** Reduced fees (weekdays, low season, resort guests, seniors, juniors), discount packages, range (grass/mats), club rentals, lodging (306 rooms), credit cards (MC, V, AE, D), beginner friendly (weekly clinics and discounts).

HYDE PARK GOLF COURSE
PU-4343 Porter Rd., Niagara Falls, 14305, Niagara County, (716)297-2067, 20 miles NW of Buffalo.
★½ **NORTH COURSE**
Holes: 18. **Yards:** 6,400/5,700. **Par:** 70/70. **Course Rating:** 70.0/72.0. **Slope:** 110/110. **Green Fee:** $15/$20. **Cart Fee:** $20/cart. **Walking Policy:** Unrestricted walking. **Walkability:** 1. **Opened:** 1920. **Architect:** William Harries. **Season:** April-Nov. **High:** June-Sept. **To obtain tee times:** First come, first served. **Miscellaneous:** Reduced fees (seniors, juniors), metal spikes, range (grass), club rentals.
★½ **RED/WHITE COURSE**
Holes: 18. **Yards:** 6,850/6,500. **Par:** 71/71. **Course Rating:** N/A. **Slope:** N/A. **Green Fee:** $15/$20. **Cart Fee:** $20/cart. **Walking Policy:** Unrestricted walking. **Walkability:** N/A. **Opened:** 1920. **Architect:** William Harries. **Season:** April-Nov. **High:** June-Sept. **To obtain tee times:** First come, first served. **Miscellaneous:** Reduced fees (seniors, juniors), metal spikes, range (grass), club rentals.

★★★ INDIAN ISLAND COUNTRY CLUB
PM-Riverside Dr., Riverhead, 11901, Suffolk County, (516)727-7776, 70 miles E of New York City.
Holes: 18. **Yards:** 6,374/5,545. **Par:** 72/72. **Course Rating:** 70.3/71.3. **Slope:** 122/122. **Green Fee:** $9/$20. **Cart Fee:** $27/cart. **Walking Policy:** Unrestricted walking. **Walkability:** 1. **Opened:** 1972. **Architect:** William Mitchell. **Season:** March-Dec. **High:** May-Sept. **To obtain tee times:** Available only to Suffolk County green key card holders. **Miscellaneous:** Reduced fees (low season, twilight, seniors, juniors), discount packages, range (mats), club rentals.
Reader Comments: Great track ... Beautiful holes along river ... Condition of course improving. Spectacular views on 3rd hole ... Two very different nines, fair amount of water ... Easy scenic walk ... Nice views of bay along course, short par 5s ... Nice views along Peconic River inlet, tough when wind is up.

★★★½ ISLAND GREEN COUNTRY CLUB
PU-P.O. Box 86, Amenia, 12501, Dutchess County, (914)373-9200, 25 miles E of Poughkeepsie.
Holes: 18. **Yards:** 6,617/5,601. **Par:** 72/72. **Course Rating:** 71.8/72.1. **Slope:** 135/131. **Green Fee:** $20/$40. **Cart Fee:** $26/cart. **Walking Policy:** Walking at certain times. **Walkability:** 3. **Opened:** 1992. **Architect:** Albert Zikorus. **Season:** April-Nov. **High:** May-Sept. **To obtain tee times:** Call 6 days in advance starting at 6:30 a.m. **Miscellaneous:** Reduced fees (weekdays, low season, seniors, juniors), range (mats), club rentals, credit cards (MC, V, AE).
Reader Comments: Good layout ... Great back 9 ... Great course ... A corner ... Classy but reasonable! ... Superb setting & conditions ... Course in good condition. Service is very good. Facilities excellent, pace of play excellent ... From the tips, as tough as it gets ... Back 9 more challenging ... Great mountain golf challenge.

ISLAND OAKS GOLF CLUB
SP-7470 Chase Rd., Lima, 14485, Lima County, (716)624-5490, 20 miles S of Rochester.
Holes: 18. **Yards:** 6,059/5,228. **Par:** 71/71. **Course Rating:** N/A. **Slope:** 120/117. **Green Fee:** $17/$22. **Cart Fee:** $10/person. **Walking Policy:** Walking at certain times. **Walkability:** 3. **Opened:** 1994. **Season:** April-Oct. **High:** June-Sept. **To obtain tee times:** Call golf shop up to 7 days in advance. **Miscellaneous:** Reduced fees (weekdays, low season, seniors), range (grass), club rentals, credit cards (MC, V).

★★★★ ISLAND'S END GOLF & COUNTRY CLUB *Pace*
SP-Rte. 25 Box 2066, Greenport, 11944, Suffolk County, (516)477-0777, 2 miles E of Greenport.
Holes: 18. **Yards:** 6,639/5,039. **Par:** 72/72. **Course Rating:** 71.4/68.4. **Slope:** 123/116. **Green Fee:** $31/$35. **Cart Fee:** $15/person. **Walking Policy:** Walking at certain times. **Walkability:** 1. **Opened:** 1961. **Architect:** Herbert Strong. **Season:** Year-round. **High:** May-Oct. **To obtain tee times:** Call at 12 noon the day prior. **Miscellaneous:** Reduced fees (low season), metal spikes, range (grass), club rentals, credit cards (MC, V).
Reader Comments: Greens in great shape ... Greens exceptional. Par 3s exceptional ... Great views. Good condition. A pleasure to play ... Very friendly ... A hidden gem on the North Fork ... Pretty course in good shape, slick greens, focus on wind off water & sloped green on 15 before dramatic view of Long Island Sound on 16.

★★★ JAMES BAIRD STATE PARK GOLF CLUB
PU-122C Freedom Plains Rd., Pleasant Valley, 12569, Dutchess County, (914)473-6200, 5 miles E of Poughkeepsie. **Web:** nysparks.com.
Holes: 18. **Yards:** 6,616/5,541. **Par:** 71/74. **Course Rating:** 71.3/70.9. **Slope:** 124/122. **Green Fee:** $14/$17. **Cart Fee:** $26/cart. **Walking Policy:** Unrestricted walking. **Walkability:** 2. **Opened:** 1947. **Architect:** Robert Trent Jones. **Season:** April-Nov. **High:** May-Aug. **To obtain tee times:** Call 2 days in advance. **Miscellaneous:** Reduced fees (weekdays, low season, twilight, seniors, juniors), metal spikes, range (grass/mats), club rentals, credit cards (MC, V, AE, D), beginner friendly (beginner golf schools and clinics).
Reader Comments: Nice variety of challenges ... Underrated, awesome when windy, 3 great holes ... Big bang for your buck! ... Improving ... Play early in season and then again in fall when the scenery is breathtaking. Excellent service, great value ... Great course ... A gem.

★★½ KISSENA PARK GOLF COURSE
PU-164-15 Booth Memorial Ave., Flushing, 11365, Queens County, (718)939-4594, 15 miles E of New York City.
Holes: 18. **Yards:** 4,727/4,425. **Par:** 64/64. **Course Rating:** 61.8/65.6. **Slope:** 101/106. **Green Fee:** $16/$18. **Cart Fee:** $13/person. **Walking Policy:** Unrestricted walking. **Walkability:** 5. **Opened:** 1937. **Architect:** John Van Kleek. **Season:** Year-round. **High:** June-Sept. **To obtain tee times:** Call 7 days in advance. **Miscellaneous:** Reduced fees (weekdays, twilight, seniors, juniors), metal spikes, range (mats), club rentals.
Reader Comments: Short but fun & challenging ... A great day of golf ... A bit crowded.

★★★ KUTSHER'S COUNTRY CLUB
R-Kutsher Rd., Monticello, 12701, Sullivan County, (914)794-6000, 80 miles N of New York City.
Holes: 18. **Yards:** 7,001/5,676. **Par:** 71/71. **Course Rating:** 74.3/73.3. **Slope:** 126/124. **Green Fee:** $42/$55. **Cart Fee:** Included in Green Fee. **Walking Policy:** Mandatory cart. **Walkability:** 4. **Opened:** 1962. **Architect:** William F. Mitchell. **Season:** April-Nov. **High:** July-Aug. **To obtain tee times:** Call 3 days in advance. Hotel guests may call up to 30 days in advance.
Miscellaneous: Reduced fees (weekdays, resort guests, twilight), discount packages, range (grass/mats), club rentals, lodging.
Reader Comments: Nice layout ... Very hilly front nine ... Good resort course ... Tough, a good test ... Very narrow ... Great layout ... Good test of golf ... Has potential.

★★★ LA TOURETTE GOLF CLUB
PU-1001 Richmond Hill Rd., Staten Island, 10306, Richmond County, (718)351-1889.
Holes: 18. **Yards:** 6,692/5,493. **Par:** 72/72. **Course Rating:** 70.7/70.9. **Slope:** 119/115. **Green Fee:** $20/$22. **Cart Fee:** $25/cart. **Walking Policy:** Unrestricted walking. **Walkability:** 3. **Opened:** 1930. **Architect:** John Van Kleek. **Season:** Year-round. **High:** May-Sept. **To obtain tee times:** Call 7 days in advance. **Miscellaneous:** Reduced fees (twilight, seniors, juniors), metal spikes, range (mats), club rentals, credit cards (MC, V), beginner friendly (beginner lessons).
Reader Comments: Beautiful layout ... Holes 5, 15 and 16 really challenging ... City course, hilly ... A top-notch course, play it again & again ... Wide open ... Best public I've ever played ... Nice public, fairly well maintained ... Nice course layout.

LAKE PLACID RESORT
R-Mirror Lake Dr., Lake Placid, 12946, Essex County, (518)523-4460, (800)874-1980, 20 miles W of Plattsburgh. **E-mail:** golf@lpresort.com. **Web:** www.lpresort.com.

★★★½ LINKS COURSE *Pace*
Holes: 18. **Yards:** 6,759/5,107. **Par:** 71/71. **Course Rating:** 72.5/N/A. **Slope:** 120/N/A. **Green Fee:** $27/$39. **Cart Fee:** $28/cart. **Walking Policy:** Walking at certain times. **Walkability:** 2. **Opened:** 1909. **Architect:** Seymour Dunn. **Season:** April-Oct. **High:** July-Aug. **To obtain tee times:** Call or come in. **Miscellaneous:** Reduced fees (weekdays, low season, resort guests, twilight), discount packages, range (grass), club rentals, credit cards (MC, V, AE, D).
Reader Comments: Need solid iron play to score well ... Great setting ... Better of the two courses. True links ... Good test ... Great old-style course, fun, good, value ... Beautiful condition ... Great way to spend a couple of hours ... Very open ... Nice links design, great value.

★★★½ MOUNTAIN COURSE
Holes: 18. **Yards:** 6,216/4,784. **Par:** 70/70. **Course Rating:** 70.8/N/A. **Slope:** 126/N/A. **Green Fee:** $20/$29. **Cart Fee:** $28/cart. **Walking Policy:** Unrestricted walking. **Walkability:** 4. **Opened:** 1910. **Architect:** Alex Findley/Alister MacKenzie. **Season:** April-Oct. **High:** July-Aug. **To obtain tee times:** Call or come in. **Miscellaneous:** Reduced fees (weekdays, low season, resort guests, twilight), discount packages, metal spikes, range (grass), club rentals, credit cards (MC, V, AE, D).
Reader Comments: Beautiful views ... Pleasant scenery, challenging ... Beautiful scenery ... Relatively short, but plays longer ... Beautiful mountain course, long walk ... Enjoyable layout and fun to play ... Nice layout, challenging. Some blind shots.
Special Notes: Also has 9-hole executive course.

★★★ LAKE SHORE COUNTRY CLUB
SP-1165 Greenleaf Rd., Rochester, 14612, Monroe County, (716)663-0300, 5 miles N of Rochester.
Holes: 18. **Yards:** 6,343/5,561. **Par:** 70/73. **Course Rating:** 67.2/72.0. **Slope:** 116/117. **Green Fee:** $24/$24. **Cart Fee:** $11/person. **Walking Policy:** Unrestricted walking. **Walkability:** 2.
Opened: 1932. **Architect:** Calvin Black. **Season:** April-Nov. **High:** June-Aug. **To obtain tee times:** Call same day for weekdays. Call Thursday for upcoming weekend. **Miscellaneous:** Discount packages, range (grass/mats), credit cards (MC, V, D).
Reader Comments: You can play many different shots, very fair ... Fun, forgiving, great shape ... Play the back tees.

★★ LE ROY COUNTRY CLUB
SP-7759 E. Main Rd., Le Roy, 14482, Genesee County, (716)768-7330, 20 miles W of Rochester.
Holes: 18. **Yards:** 6,422/5,589. **Par:** 71/74. **Course Rating:** 69.8/71.0. **Slope:** 116/117. **Green Fee:** $14/$18. **Cart Fee:** $20/cart. **Walking Policy:** Unrestricted walking. **Walkability:** 2.
Opened: 1930. **Architect:** Don Woodward. **Season:** April-Oct. **High:** June-Aug. **To obtain tee times:** Call. **Miscellaneous:** Reduced fees (weekdays, low season, twilight, seniors, juniors), discount packages, range (grass), caddies, club rentals, credit cards (MC, V).

★★★★ LEATHERSTOCKING GOLF COURSE
R-Lake Street, Cooperstown, 13326, Otsego County, (607)547-5275, 50 miles NW of Albany.
Holes: 18. **Yards:** 6,324/5,254. **Par:** 72/72. **Course Rating:** 70.8/69.2. **Slope:** 132/116. **Green Fee:** $70/$80. **Cart Fee:** $16/person. **Walking Policy:** Walking at certain times. **Walkability:** 4.
Opened: 1909. **Architect:** Devereux Emmet. **Season:** April-Oct. **High:** June-Sept. **To obtain tee times:** Call 6 days in advance. **Miscellaneous:** Reduced fees (resort guests, twilight), range (grass), club rentals, lodging, credit cards (MC, V, AE).
Reader Comments: Cool course, awesome finish, good greens ... Beautiful design, must be played over & over ... Great final three holes, good resort course, scenic ... Simply a great course in a beautiful setting ... Top-notch last 3 holes ... Holes 16, 17, 18 are to die for! ... A beauty but a bit pricey ... Solid, plus great finish.

LIMA GOLF & COUNTRY CLUB
SP-2681 Plank Rd., Lima, 14485, Livingston County, (716)624-1490, 20 miles S of Rochester.
Holes: 18. **Yards:** 6,768/5,624. **Par:** 72/74. **Course Rating:** 72.3/74.0. **Slope:** N/A/117. **Green Fee:** $17/$22. **Cart Fee:** $10/person. **Walking Policy:** Unrestricted walking. **Walkability:** 1.
Opened: 1963. **Season:** April-Oct. **High:** June-Sept. **To obtain tee times:** Call golf shop up to 7 days in advance. **Miscellaneous:** Reduced fees (weekdays, low season, seniors), range (grass), club rentals, credit cards (MC, V).
Reader Comments: Beautiful course ... Long, tough, fair ... Very well kept. Good clubhouse & bar. Very friendly owners, a pleasure to play ... Good layout, interesting ... Best greens in area, fast & true ... Fastest greens in area ... Flat, narrow, windy, woods, water, outstanding layout.

★★★★ THE LINKS AT HIAWATHA LANDING   *Service, Condition*
PU-2350 Marshland Rd., Apalachin, 13732, Tioga County, (607)687-6952, (800)304-6533, 10 miles W of Binghamton. **E-mail:** info@hiawathalinks.com. **Web:** www.hiawathalinks.com.
Holes: 18. **Yards:** 7,104/5,101. **Par:** 72/72. **Course Rating:** 73.5/68.4. **Slope:** 131/113. **Green Fee:** $29/$45. **Cart Fee:** $10/person. **Walking Policy:** Unrestricted walking. **Walkability:** 2.
Opened: 1994. **Architect:** Brian Silva/Mark Mungeam. **Season:** April-Nov. **High:** June-Sept. **To obtain tee times:** Call 7 days in advance. **Miscellaneous:** Reduced fees (weekdays, low season, twilight, juniors), discounts, range (grass), club rentals, credit cards (MC, V, AE, D).
Reader Comments: Top-notch service ... Great risk/reward ratio ... As good as it gets, well worth any price ... Wonderful links-style layout, everything flows nicely ... Superb links course ... Beautiful course in excellent shape ... Link style with a bang; beautifully manicured; strong shot values ... Top-shelf, stunning 14th hole.

★★★ LIVERPOOL GOLF & COUNTRY CLUB
PU-7209 Morgan Rd., Liverpool, 13090, Onondaga County, (315)457-7170, 5 miles N of Syracuse.
Holes: 18. **Yards:** 6,473/5,487. **Par:** 71/73. **Course Rating:** 70.7/69.3. **Slope:** 120/115. **Green Fee:** $18/$20. **Cart Fee:** $20/cart. **Walking Policy:** Unrestricted walking. **Walkability:** 1.
Opened: 1949. **Architect:** Archie S. Ajemian and Sons. **Season:** Year-round. **High:** April-Nov. **To obtain tee times:** Call golf shop. **Miscellaneous:** Reduced fees (weekdays, low season, twilight, seniors, juniors), metal spikes, range (grass), club rentals, credit cards (MC, V), beginner friendly (junior program).
Reader Comments: Always open, even with snow on the carts ... Some interesting holes ... Stays open all year, good greens, No. 2, par 3 over water is good test from tips ... Very busy course but in good shape ... Close to the city ... Nice par 3s.

★★★½ LOCHMOR GOLF COURSE

PM-CR 104, Loch Sheldrake, 12759, Sullivan County, (914)434-9079, 8 miles W of Monticello.
Holes: 18. **Yards:** 6,426/5,129. **Par:** 71/71. **Course Rating:** 69.6/69.4. **Slope:** 117/116. **Green Fee:** $19/$25. **Cart Fee:** $13/person. **Walking Policy:** Walking at certain times. **Walkability:** 4.
Season: April-Oct. **High:** July-Aug. **To obtain tee times:** Call on Wednesday for upcoming Saturday; call on Thursday for upcoming Sunday. **Miscellaneous:** Reduced fees (weekdays, resort guests, twilight, juniors), range (grass/mats), club rentals, credit cards (MC, V).
Reader Comments: Good layout & grooming ... Good public courses ... Good municipal course, front nine wide open ... Great town course ... Good value. Some nice views.

LYNDON GOLF CLUB

PU-7054 East Genesee, Rte. #5, Fayetteville, 13066, Onondaga County, (315)446-1885.
Holes: 18. **Yards:** 4,900/4,900. **Par:** 65/69. **Course Rating:** N/A. **Slope:** N/A. **Green Fee:** $8/$13. **Walking Policy:** Unrestricted walking. **Walkability:** 1. **Season:** March-Nov. **High:** June-Aug. **Miscellaneous:** Metal spikes.

MALONE GOLF CLUB *Service*

SP-Country Club Rd., Malone, 12953, Franklin County, (518)483-2926, 70 miles S of Montreal.
E-mail: mgc@slic.com. **Web:** www.malonegolfclub.com.

★★★★ EAST COURSE

Holes: 18. **Yards:** 6,545/5,224. **Par:** 72/73. **Course Rating:** 71.5/69.9. **Slope:** 123/117. **Green Fee:** $28/$33. **Cart Fee:** $12/person. **Walking Policy:** Unrestricted walking. **Walkability:** 5.
Opened: 1939. **Architect:** Robert T. Jones/W.Wilkinson/A. Murray. **Season:** April-Oct. **High:** June-Aug. **To obtain tee times:** Call up to 7 days in advance. **Miscellaneous:** Reduced fees (weekdays, twilight), discount packages, club rentals, credit cards (MC, V, AE).
Reader Comments: Have 36 very nice holes, East little tougher than West ... I love this course. Marshals push, but that's okay with me ... Golf shop staff makes you feel like a regular ... Good course design/layout; very fair, challenging ... Play it as often as possible.

★★★★ WEST COURSE

Holes: 18. **Yards:** 6,592/5,272. **Par:** 71/72. **Course Rating:** 71.4/70.1. **Slope:** 124/119. **Green Fee:** $28/$33. **Cart Fee:** $12/person. **Walking Policy:** Unrestricted walking. **Walkability:** N/A.
Opened: 1987. **Architect:** Robert T. Jones/W.Wilkinson/A. Murray. **Season:** April-Oct. **High:** June-Aug. **To obtain tee times:** Call 7 days in advance. **Miscellaneous:** Reduced fees (twilight), discount packages, metal spikes, club rentals, credit cards (MC, V, AE).
Reader Comments: Great complex course ... Good test, love the old rambling clubhouse, beer just tastes good here ... Nice course ... Friendly staff ... Good course, a little pricey for area.

★★½ MAPLE MOOR GOLF COURSE

PU-1128 N. St., White Plains, 10605, Westchester County, (914)946-1830, 20 miles N of New York City.
Holes: 18. **Yards:** 6,226/5,812. **Par:** 71/74. **Course Rating:** 68.8/71.9. **Slope:** 110/119. **Green Fee:** $17/$45. **Cart Fee:** $24/cart. **Walking Policy:** Unrestricted walking. **Walkability:** 2.
Opened: 1923. **Architect:** Archie Capper. **Season:** April-Dec. **High:** May-Aug. **To obtain tee times:** Call 7 days in advance. **Miscellaneous:** Reduced fees (twilight, seniors, juniors), metal spikes, club rentals, credit cards (MC, V), beginner friendly.
Reader Comments: Nice bargain ... Nice course layout, but needs work. Slow play. Service good ... Has undergone significant improvements in 1999 ... Nice course ... Flat, wide open ... Tricky approach shots.

★★★ MARINE PARK GOLF CLUB

PU-2880 Flatbush Ave., Brooklyn, 11234, Kings County, (718)338-7113.
Holes: 18. **Yards:** 6,866/5,323. **Par:** 72/72. **Course Rating:** 70.5/N/A. **Slope:** 118/N/A. **Green Fee:** $9/$26. **Cart Fee:** $24/cart. **Walking Policy:** Unrestricted walking. **Walkability:** 1. **Opened:** 1964. **Architect:** Robert Trent Jones. **Season:** Year-round. **High:** May-Aug. **To obtain tee times:** Call 7 days in advance. **Miscellaneous:** Reduced fees (weekdays, low season, twilight, seniors, juniors), metal spikes, club rentals, credit cards (MC, V, AE, D).
Reader Comments: Best greens in NYC ... Pretty long with strong winds ... Great greens ... Course is in surprisingly great shape. Very challenging putting, some tough approach shots ... Good track ... Scratch player's paradise, flat and no trees ... Long, windy but fun to play, nice people.

★★★½ MARK TWAIN GOLF CLUB

PU-2275 Corning Rd., Elmira, 14903, Chemung County, (607)737-5770, 50 miles W of Binghamton.
Holes: 18. **Yards:** 6,829/5,571. **Par:** 72/76. **Course Rating:** 73.6/72.3. **Slope:** 123/121. **Green Fee:** $16/$18. **Cart Fee:** $21/cart. **Walking Policy:** Unrestricted walking. **Walkability:** 4.
Opened: 1939. **Architect:** Donald Ross. **Season:** April-Oct. **High:** June-Aug. **To obtain tee times:** Call. **Miscellaneous:** Reduced fees (weekdays, twilight, seniors, juniors), range (grass), club rentals, credit cards (MC, V, D).

Reader Comments: A well-kept secret in New York's southern tier ... Not too tough ... Interesting course, enjoyable to play ... Good test for all ... Excellent challenge ... Big greens with a lot of break on putts ... All par 3s to blind mostly uphill greens ... Deep bunkers ... Super layout!

★★★★ **MARK TWAIN STATE PARK** *Value*
PU-201 Middle Rd., Horseheads, 14845, Chemung County, (607)796-5059, 10 miles N of Elmira.
Holes: 18. **Yards:** 6,625/4,930. **Par:** 72/72. **Course Rating:** 71.6/67.5. **Slope:** 117/108. **Green Fee:** $9/$21. **Cart Fee:** $22/cart. **Walking Policy:** Unrestricted walking. **Walkability:** 3. **Opened:** 1940. **Architect:** Archibald Craig. **Season:** April-Nov. **High:** June-Sept. **To obtain tee times:** Call 4 days in advance. **Miscellaneous:** Reduced fees (twilight, seniors, juniors), metal spikes, range (grass), club rentals, credit cards (MC, V, AE).
Reader Comments: Enjoyable state park course ... Tough greens ... Excellent value ... Good golf overall ... Nice vistas, good course for all levels ... Some of the most challenging greens I have played. You must play this jewel of a course ... State park, excellent shape, long, good test ... Great course, money well-spent.

★★ **MASSENA COUNTRY CLUB**
PU-Rte. 131, Massena, 13662, St. Lawrence County, (315)769-2293, 160 miles N of Syracuse.
Holes: 18. **Yards:** 6,602/5,361. **Par:** 71/75. **Course Rating:** 70.1/70.0. **Slope:** 110/111. **Green Fee:** N/A/$22. **Cart Fee:** $20/cart. **Walking Policy:** Unrestricted walking. **Walkability:** 2. **Opened:** 1958. **Architect:** Albert Murray. **Season:** May-Oct. **High:** June-Aug. **To obtain tee times:** Call up to 2 days in advance. **Miscellaneous:** Reduced fees (low season, twilight), range (grass/mats), caddies, club rentals, credit cards (MC, V).

★★★½ **MCCANN MEMORIAL GOLF CLUB**
PU-155 Wilbur Blvd., Poughkeepsie, 12603, Dutchess County, (914)471-3917, 65 miles N of New York City.
Holes: 18. **Yards:** 6,524/5,354. **Par:** 72/72. **Course Rating:** 71.5/71.1. **Slope:** 122/114. **Green Fee:** $30/$35. **Cart Fee:** $24/cart. **Walking Policy:** Unrestricted walking. **Walkability:** 2. **Opened:** 1972. **Architect:** William F. Mitchell. **Season:** March-Dec. **High:** April-Oct. **To obtain tee times:** Call. **Miscellaneous:** Reduced fees (seniors, juniors), range (grass), club rentals.
Reader Comments: Big greens, good layout ... Best public course around ... Great value but slow play sometimes ... Won't find a course in the state that's better for the money ... Worth the drive, always in good shape ... Very nice course, well kept ... Great greens, best pro in area ... Wonderful public course.

MIDDLE ISLAND COUNTRY CLUB
PU-Yapank Rd., Middle Island, 11953, Suffolk County, (516)924-5100, 75 miles E of New York City.
Holes: 27. **Green Fee:** $30/$35. **Cart Fee:** $14/person. **Walking Policy:** Walking at certain times. **Walkability:** 3. **Opened:** 1964. **Architect:** Baier Lustgarten. **Season:** Year-round. **High:** April-Oct. **To obtain tee times:** Call 7 days in advance. **Miscellaneous:** Reduced fees (weekdays, low season), metal spikes, range (mats), club rentals.
★★★ **DOGWOOD/OAKTREE**
Yards: 6,934/5,809. **Par:** 72/74. **Course Rating:** 73.2/73.2. **Slope:** 130/127.
Reader Comments: Play all 27 for nice day ... 3 nines, very tough ... Condition is improving ... Some really good holes ... Long from back tees, good value ... Good public course ... Thousands of trees ... Greatly improved conditions ... Woodsy, narrow, bring balls ... Good variety, many trees ... Excellent greens, good value, narrow.
★★★ **DOGWOOD/SPRUCE**
Yards: 7,015/5,909. **Par:** 72/74. **Course Rating:** 73.2/73.2. **Slope:** 130/127. .
Reader Comments: Wooded, great greens, narrow ... Good layout, challenging ... Very interesting course ... Spruce longer but wide open ... Two different 9-hole layouts ... Must stay on fairways to score ... Dogwood is a fun nine.
★★★ **OAKTREE/SPRUCE**
Yards: 7,027/5,906. **Par:** 72/72. **Course Rating:** 73.2/73.2. **Slope:** 130/127.
Reader Comments: Best at Middle Island, keep 'em straight ... Nicely laid out ... Old-style course, great bunkers, narrow in spots ... Stay in the fairway ... Long from the tips ... Oaktree demands an accurate driver, lots of tree-lined holes, pretty parkland course.

★★★ **MOHANSIC GOLF CLUB**
PM-Baldwin Rd., Yorktown Heights, 10598, Westchester County, (914)962-4049, 37 miles N of New York City.
Holes: 18. **Yards:** 6,500/5,594. **Par:** 70/75. **Course Rating:** 69.9/75.2. **Slope:** 120/127. **Green Fee:** $17/$40. **Cart Fee:** $24/cart. **Walking Policy:** Unrestricted walking. **Walkability:** 3. **Opened:** 1925. **Architect:** Tom Winton. **Season:** April-Dec. **High:** June-Aug. **To obtain tee times:** Call computerized tee times (914)242-4653. Call 1 week in advance. **Miscellaneous:** Reduced fees (weekdays, twilight, seniors, juniors), metal spikes, range (mats), club rentals.

Reader Comments: The best public course in Westchester ... Tough, pretty & hard to get tee times ... Fair course ... Very tough course, nice layout, pace of play fair, service is good ... The best of Westchester's muny courses and the toughest. Great value ... A good test ... Challenging; good condition; slow play; hilly.

★★★★½ MONTAUK DOWNS STATE PARK GOLF COURSE *Value+*

PU-S. Fairview Ave., Montauk, 11954, Suffolk County, (516)668-1100, 110 miles E of New York City.
Holes: 18. **Yards:** 6,762/5,797. **Par:** 72/72. **Course Rating:** 73.3/75.9. **Slope:** 133/135. **Green Fee:** $30/$36. **Cart Fee:** $12/person. **Walking Policy:** Unrestricted walking. **Walkability:** 3.
Opened: 1968. **Architect:** Robert Trent Jones. **Season:** Year-round. **High:** July-Sept. **To obtain tee times:** Call up to 7 days in advance with reservation card. Call up to 2 days in advance without card. **Miscellaneous:** Reduced fees (twilight, seniors), metal spikes, range (mats), club rentals, credit cards (MC, V, AE, D).
Notes: Ranked 18th in 1999 Best in State.
Reader Comments: Best public golf on east end ... Worth the trip to Montauk; great golf value ... A must-play on the island ... Super golf course, windy ... A nature lover's course; deer & fox abound ... Fine test of golf ... Challenge, wind is key ... A real challenge & you can walk! ... Difficult, fast greens.

★½ MOSHOLU GOLF COURSE

PU-3700 Jerome Ave., Bronx, 10467, Bronx County, (718)655-9164.
Special Notes: Call club for further information.

NEVELE GRAND RESORT AND COUNTRY CLUB

R-Rte. 209-Nevele Road, Ellenville, 12428, Ulster County, (914)647-6000, (800)647-6000, 90 miles N of New York. **Web:** www.nevele.com.
Holes: 27. **Green Fee:** $42/$60. **Cart Fee:** Included in Green Fee. **Walking Policy:** Walking at certain times. **Walkability:** 2. **Opened:** 1955. **Architect:** Tom Fazio/Robert Trent Jones. **Season:** April-Dec. **High:** May-Oct. **To obtain tee times:** Hotel guests call 30 days in advance. Nonguests call 14 days in advance. **Miscellaneous:** Reduced fees (weekdays, low season, resort guests, twilight, juniors), discount packages, range (grass/mats), club rentals, lodging (700 rooms), credit cards (MC, V, AE, Diners Club), beginner friendly (6 on-site instructors, Ken Venturi Golf Academy).
★★★★ BLUE/RED
Yards: 6,823/5,145. **Par:** 70/70. **Course Rating:** 72.7/72.8. **Slope:** 130/129.
★★★★ RED/WHITE
Yards: 6,532/4,600. **Par:** 70/70. **Course Rating:** 71.4/71.1. **Slope:** 128/126.
★★★★ WHITE/BLUE
Yards: 6,573/4,600. **Par:** 70/70. **Course Rating:** 71.8/71.1. **Slope:** 126/126.
Reader Comments: Beautiful grooming, layout & all around ... Surprisingly good layout and condition ... Good all-around golf course/has all shots ... Nice resort course ... Beautiful course ... Excellent greens & fairways ... Fair test of golf. Fun to play ... Slopes, best in Catskills ... Short, great scenery.
Special Notes: Formerly Nevele Country Club.

★★★ THE NEW COURSE AT ALBANY

PU-65 O'Neil Rd., Albany, 12208, Albany County, (518)489-3526, 3 miles W of Albany.
Holes: 18. **Yards:** 6,300/4,990. **Par:** 71/71. **Course Rating:** 69.4/72.0. **Slope:** 117/113. **Green Fee:** $25/$27. **Cart Fee:** $10/person. **Walking Policy:** Unrestricted walking. **Walkability:** 4.
Opened: 1991. **Architect:** Bob Smith/Ed Bosse. **Season:** April-Nov. **High:** June-Aug. **To obtain tee times:** Call 1 day in advance (518)438-2208. **Miscellaneous:** Reduced fees (twilight), metal spikes, range (grass/mats), club rentals.
Reader Comments: Friendly atmosphere, mountain-goat country! Fun ... Speed up play & you have a great course ... Very hilly, tough to walk ... Elevated greens. Treated like a pro ... Nice municipal course ... Can't beat it ... Nice user-friendly muny.

NEW YORK COUNTRY CLUB

SP-103 Brick Church Rd., New Hempstead, 10977, Rockland County, (914)362-5800, 22 miles N of New York City. **E-mail:** nycountryclub@excite.com. **Web:** nycountryclub.com.
Holes: 18. **Yards:** 6,673/5,671. **Par:** 72/72. **Course Rating:** 71.5/72.2. **Slope:** 129/126. **Green Fee:** $75/$115. **Cart Fee:** Included in Green Fee. **Walking Policy:** Walking at certain times. **Walkability:** 5. **Opened:** 1998. **Architect:** Stephen Kay. **Season:** Year-round. **High:** April-Nov. **To obtain tee times:** Call. **Miscellaneous:** Reduced fees (weekdays, low season, twilight), range (grass), caddies, club rentals, credit cards (MC, V, AE, D).

★★ NIAGARA COUNTY GOLF COURSE

PM-314 Davison Rd., Lockport, 14094, Niagara County, (716)439-7954.
Holes: 18. **Yards:** 6,464/5,182. **Par:** 72/73. **Course Rating:** 69.3/74.1. **Slope:** 108/N/A. **Green Fee:** $10/$18. **Cart Fee:** $18/cart. **Walking Policy:** Unrestricted walking. **Walkability:** 1.

Opened: 1964. **Season:** April-Nov. **High:** July-Aug. **Miscellaneous:** Reduced fees (twilight, seniors, juniors), metal spikes, range (grass), club rentals.
Special Notes: Spikeless shoes encouraged.

★★ NIAGARA ORLEANS COUNTRY CLUB

PU-Telegraph Rd, Middleport, 14105, Niagara County, (716)735-9000, 7 miles E of Lockport.
Holes: 18. **Yards:** 6,018/5,109. **Par:** 71/71. **Course Rating:** 65.0/65.0. **Slope:** 106/106. **Green Fee:** $14/$17. **Cart Fee:** $20/cart. **Walking Policy:** Unrestricted walking. **Walkability:** 3.
Opened: 1931. **Season:** April-Nov. **High:** June-Aug. **To obtain tee times:** Call. **Miscellaneous:** Reduced fees (weekdays, low season, twilight, seniors, juniors), metal spikes, club rentals.

★★½ OLD HICKORY GOLF CLUB

SP-6653 Big Tree Rd., Livonia, 14487, Livingston County, (716)346-2450, 20 miles S of Rochester.
Holes: 18. **Yards:** 6,650/5,450. **Par:** 72/72. **Course Rating:** 70.2/70.7. **Slope:** 109/111. **Green Fee:** $15/$18. **Cart Fee:** $11/person. **Walking Policy:** Unrestricted walking. **Walkability:** 3.
Opened: 1990. **Architect:** Pete Craig. **Season:** April-Oct. **High:** May-Sept. **To obtain tee times:** Call 7 days in advance. **Miscellaneous:** Reduced fees (low season, seniors, juniors), range (grass), club rentals.
Reader Comments: It's wide open, well maintained and long ... Some holes need work ... It has come a long way! ... Nice greens.

ORCHARD VALLEY GOLF CLUB

PU-4693 Cherry Valley Tpke., LaFayette, 13084, (315)677-5180, 10 miles S of Syracuse.
Special Notes: Call club for further information.

★★★½ OYSTER BAY TOWN GOLF COURSE

PU-Southwood Rd., Woodbury, 11797, Nassau County, (516)364-1180, 35 miles E of New York.
Holes: 18. **Yards:** 6,351/5,109. **Par:** 70/70. **Course Rating:** 71.5/70.4. **Slope:** 131/126. **Green Fee:** $40/$50. **Walking Policy:** Unrestricted walking. **Walkability:** 4. **Opened:** 1989. **Architect:** Tom Fazio. **Season:** Year-round. **High:** April-Oct. **To obtain tee times:** First come, first served.
Miscellaneous: Reduced fees (weekdays, low season, twilight, seniors, juniors), range (mats), club rentals.
Reader Comments: Best-conditioned public course on Long Island ... Slow, but good narrow course ... Tight layout, back nine more difficult ... Best finishing holes anywhere ... Fair/short ... Superb greens, strategic course, scenic ... Outstanding and almost as good as Bethpage Black ... Don't miss this one, 17 exceptional holes.

PEEK'N PEAK RESORT

R-1405 Olde Rd., Clymer, 14724, Chautauqua County, (716)355-4141, 20 miles SE of Erie, PA.
E-mail: pk-n-pk@travelbase.com. **Web:** http://www.pknpk.com.
★★★½ LOWER COURSE
Holes: 18. **Yards:** 6,260/5,328. **Par:** 72/72. **Course Rating:** 69.0/69.5. **Slope:** 115/112. **Green Fee:** $25/$34. **Cart Fee:** $11/person. **Walking Policy:** Unrestricted walking. **Walkability:** 1.
Opened: 1974. **Architect:** Fred Garbin. **Season:** April-Nov. **High:** June-Sept. **To obtain tee times:** Call golf shop. **Miscellaneous:** Reduced fees (weekdays, twilight, seniors), discount packages, metal spikes, range (grass), club rentals, lodging (200 rooms), credit cards (MC, V, AE, D).
Reader Comments: Narrow, traps, streams, a real test ... Flat, interesting, great greens, lots of trees ... Beautiful. Needs some work. Will be nice test ... Nice valley course, excellent greens ... Lower in name only ... Flat and friendly ... A little slow, nice clubhouse and staff.
★★★★ UPPER COURSE
Holes: 18. **Yards:** 6,888/4,835. **Par:** 72/72. **Course Rating:** 72.5/67.5. **Slope:** 131/116. **Green Fee:** $48/$58. **Cart Fee:** $11/person. **Cart Fee:** Included in Green Fee. **Walking Policy:** Mandatory cart. **Walkability:** 5. **Opened:** 1991. **Architect:** John Exley. **Season:** April-Nov. **High:** June-Sept. **To obtain tee times:** Call golf shop. **Miscellaneous:** Reduced fees (weekdays, twilight, seniors), discount packages, metal spikes, club rentals, lodging (200 rooms), credit cards (MC, V, AE, D).
Reader Comments: Great course, great place! ... Play on top of ski slopes, great holes & views ... Excellent shape, well laid out ... Back 9 awesome ... Super! Super! Beautiful views, excellent shape, tough course ... All the holes are different ... Challenging and scenic ... Incredibly gorgeous, views are spectacular.

PELHAM-SPLIT ROCK GOLF COURSE

PU-870 Shore Rd., Bronx, 10464, Bronx County, (718)885-1258, 8 miles N of NYC.
★★½ PELHAM COURSE
Holes: 18. **Yards:** 6,601/5,554. **Par:** 71/73. **Course Rating:** 70.9/70.4. **Slope:** 116/113. **Green Fee:** $10/$28. **Cart Fee:** $18/cart. **Walking Policy:** Unrestricted walking. **Walkability:** 2.
Opened: 1901. **Architect:** Lawrence Van Etten. **Season:** Year-round. **High:** May-Sept. **To obtain tee times:** Call up to 12 days in advance for weekends and up to 7 days on weekdays. Credit

card is needed to hold reservation for weekend. **Miscellaneous:** Reduced fees (weekdays, twilight, seniors, juniors), metal spikes, club rentals, credit cards (MC, V, AE), beginner friendly (junior golf and high school programs).

Reader Comments: Longest and tightest public layout in NYC ... Good place to practice ... The best rangers ... Pace of play not bad, conditions fair to good. Service fair.

★★★ **SPLIT ROCK COURSE**
Holes: 18. **Yards:** 6,714/5,509. **Par:** 71/71. **Course Rating:** 72.0/71.7. **Slope:** 129/122. **Green Fee:** $10/$28. **Cart Fee:** $18/cart. **Walking Policy:** Unrestricted walking. **Walkability:** 3. **Opened:** 1934. **Architect:** John Van Kleek. **Season:** Year-round. **High:** May-Sept. **To obtain tee times:** Call up to 12 days in advance for weekends and up to 7 days in advance for weekdays. Credit card needed for weekend reservations. **Miscellaneous:** Reduced fees (weekdays, twilight, seniors, juniors), metal spikes, club rentals, credit cards (MC, V, AE), beginner friendly (junior golf and high school programs).

Reader Comments: Varied topography ... Most difficult fairways in NYC ... A great layout ... If only they put some money into this neglected beauty. It must have been something ... Typical close-to-city public course.

★★½ **PHILIP J. ROTELLA GOLF COURSE**
PM-Thiells and Mt. Ivy Road, Thiells, 10984, Rockland County, (914)354-1616, 20 miles N of New York City.
Holes: 18. **Yards:** 6,502/4,856. **Par:** 72/72. **Course Rating:** 71.4/68.1. **Slope:** 128/117. **Green Fee:** $12/$34. **Cart Fee:** $24/cart. **Walking Policy:** Walking at certain times. **Walkability:** 4. **Opened:** 1985. **Architect:** Hal Purdy. **Season:** March-Dec. **High:** May-Aug. **To obtain tee times:** Call Sunday starting at 6:00 p.m. for upcoming week. **Miscellaneous:** Reduced fees (twilight, seniors, juniors), range (mats), club rentals.

Reader Comments: Nice course, can be tough ... Good value ... Some great views ... Nicely laid-out holes ... Use all the clubs ... Town course, slow play ... Has improved in recent years, especially greens.

★½ **PINE GROVE COUNTRY CLUB**
SP-3185 Milton Ave, Camillus, 13031, Onondaga County, (315)672-9272, 4 miles W of Syracuse.
Holes: 18. **Yards:** 5,326/N/A. **Par:** 71/N/A. **Course Rating:** N/A. **Slope:** N/A. **Green Fee:** $12/$14. **Cart Fee:** $17/cart. **Walking Policy:** Unrestricted walking. **Walkability:** 1. **Opened:** 1960. **Architect:** Barry Jordan. **Season:** Mar-Dec. **High:** May-Aug. **To obtain tee times:** No tee times. **Miscellaneous:** Reduced fees (weekdays, low season, twilight, seniors), metal spikes, range (grass/mats), club rentals, credit cards (MC, V, AE, D).

★★★½ **PINE HILLS COUNTRY CLUB**
SP-1 Country Club Drive, Manorville, 11949, Suffolk County, (516)878-7103, 15 miles W of The Hamptons.
Holes: 18. **Yards:** 72/5,300. **Par:** 73/73. **Course Rating:** 74.0/70.3. **Slope:** 129/119. **Green Fee:** $35/$40. **Cart Fee:** $30/cart. **Walking Policy:** Walking at certain times. **Walkability:** 3. **Opened:** 1972. **Architect:** Roger Tooker. **Season:** Year-round. **High:** April-Oct. **To obtain tee times:** Call reservation system (516)878-4343 2 weeks in advance. **Miscellaneous:** Reduced fees (low season, twilight, seniors), range (grass/mats), credit cards (MC, V).

Reader Comments: Nice course, two very different 9s ... Lots of challenges ... Great course ... Enjoyable ... Challenging course, great value :.. Nice course, always in good condition, back nine has character ... Nice public course, always in good shape ... Smallest,. best-kept greens on Long Island.

★★★ **PUTNAM COUNTRY CLUB**
PU-187 Hill St., Mahopac, 10541, Putnam County, (914)628-4200, 50 miles N of New York City.
Holes: 18. **Yards:** 6,774/5,799. **Par:** 71/73. **Course Rating:** 72.4/73.7. **Slope:** 129/132. **Green Fee:** $26/$48. **Cart Fee:** $12/person. **Walking Policy:** Walking at certain times. **Walkability:** 3. **Opened:** 1955. **Architect:** William F. Mitchell. **Season:** March-Dec. **High:** June-Sept. **To obtain tee times:** Call 7 days in advance. **Miscellaneous:** Reduced fees (weekdays, low season, twilight, seniors, juniors), discount packages, range (grass), club rentals, credit cards (MC, V, AE), beginner friendly (junior clinic).

Reader Comments: Nice town track ... Play is fair to normal. Service is very good ... Best in county ... Enjoyable ... Good overall ... Very fine facility. Tougher than it looks.

★★★★ **RADISSON GREENS GOLF CLUB**
SP-8055 Potter Rd., Baldwinsville, 13027, Onondaga County, (315)638-0092, 15 miles NW of Syracuse. **E-mail:** radgreens@aol.com.
Holes: 18. **Yards:** 7,010/5,543. **Par:** 72/73. **Course Rating:** 73.3/70.0. **Slope:** 135/124. **Green Fee:** $25/$29. **Cart Fee:** $24/person. **Walking Policy:** Walking at certain times. **Walkability:** 3. **Opened:** 1977. **Architect:** Robert Trent Jones. **Season:** April-Nov. **High:** May-Sept. **To obtain tee times:** Call Monday for upcoming weekend or 24 hours in advance for weekday.

Miscellaneous: Reduced fees (low season, seniors), range (grass), club rentals, credit cards (MC, V).

Reader Comments: Great fairways, plenty of bunkers, greens are good ... Takes course management! ... Long, great shape ... Lush ... Great layout, especially tough from tips ... Sheer joy ... Outstanding for the money, great challenges ... Best value in public golf anywhere in U.S. ... A Myrtle Beach type course in central New York!

RICCI MEADOWS GOLF COURSE
PU-1939 Oak Orchard Rd. (Rte. 98), Albion, 14411, Orleans County, (716)682-3280, 30 miles W of Rochester.
Holes: 18. **Yards:** 5,268/4,597. **Par:** 71/72. **Course Rating:** 63.0/63.4. **Slope:** 102/100. **Green Fee:** $11/$11. **Cart Fee:** $10/person. **Walking Policy:** Unrestricted walking. **Walkability:** 1.
Opened: 1957. **Season:** April-Nov. **High:** June-Aug. **To obtain tee times:** Tee times not taken.
Miscellaneous: Reduced fees (weekdays, seniors), metal spikes, range (grass/mats), club rentals.

★★½ RIVERVIEW COUNTRY CLUB
PU-847 Riverview Rd, Rexford, 12148, Saratoga County, (518)399-2345, 15 miles N of Albany.
Holes: 18. **Yards:** 7,095/5,815. **Par:** 73/74. **Course Rating:** 73.7/73.4. **Slope:** 128/124. **Green Fee:** $19/$24. **Cart Fee:** $22/cart. **Walking Policy:** Unrestricted walking. **Walkability:** 3.
Opened: 1964. **Season:** April-Nov. **High:** June-Aug. **To obtain tee times:** Call on Wednesday for upcoming weekend. **Miscellaneous:** Reduced fees (weekdays, low season, twilight, seniors, juniors), discount packages, metal spikes, range (grass), club rentals, credit cards (MC, V, AE).
Reader Comments: Rolling hills, lot of nature, quiet and picturesque ... Nice layout, if improved could be top-notch course ... Typical municipal course. A place to play golf.

★★★★ ROCK HILL COUNTRY CLUB
PU-105 Clancy Rd., Manorville, 11949, Suffolk County, (516)878-2250, 60 miles E of New York City.
Holes: 18. **Yards:** 7,050/5,390. **Par:** 71/72. **Course Rating:** 73.7/71.4. **Slope:** 128/121. **Green Fee:** $15/$35. **Cart Fee:** $30/cart. **Walking Policy:** Walking at certain times. **Walkability:** 4.
Opened: 1965. **Architect:** Frank Duane. **Season:** Year-round. **High:** May-Sept. **To obtain tee times:** Call 7 days in advance. **Miscellaneous:** Reduced fees (weekdays, low season, twilight, seniors, juniors), range (grass), club rentals.
Reader Comments: Challenging, aptly named course in greatly improved shape; front 9 bumpy, back 9 longer & flatter ... Great golf course ... Improved tremendously in last several years, good test when wind blows ... Hilly and interesting to play ... Very nice, worth the price.

★★★ ROCKLAND LAKE STATE PARK GOLF CLUB
PU-100 Rte. 9 W, Congers, 10920, Rockland County, (914)268-6250, 20 miles N of New York City
Holes: 18. **Yards:** 6,864/5,663. **Par:** 72/72. **Course Rating:** 72.3/71.1. **Slope:** 126/122. **Green Fee:** $24/$29. **Cart Fee:** $26/cart. **Walking Policy:** Unrestricted walking. **Walkability:** 3.
Opened: 1969. **Season:** March-Dec. **High:** April-Oct. **To obtain tee times:** Must obtain reservation card for $20.00. With the card tee time reservations can be made 1 week prior. Without card, only 1 day. **Miscellaneous:** Reduced fees (twilight, seniors, juniors), range (mats), club rentals, credit cards (MC, V, AE, D), beginner friendly.
Reader Comments: Very reasonable, nice layout, long round ... Sporty, hilly fun fest ... Good public course ... Course will add ten strokes to anyone ... Very nice par 3s, almost never a flat lie ... Great views, elevated mountain tees ... Real challenge, enjoy playing ... Good New York State course.

ROGUE'S ROOST GOLF CLUB
PU-Rte. 31, Bridgeport, 13030, Madison County, (315)633-9406, 12 miles NE of Syracuse.
★★★ EAST COURSE
Holes: 18. **Yards:** 6,700/5,670. **Par:** 71/74. **Course Rating:** 70.9/69.7. **Slope:** 118/113. **Green Fee:** $18/$20. **Cart Fee:** $20/cart. **Walking Policy:** Walking at certain times. **Walkability:** 2.
Opened: 1966. **Architect:** Bill Galloway. **Season:** March-Nov. **High:** May-Sept. **To obtain tee times:** Call. **Miscellaneous:** Reduced fees (weekdays, low season), discount packages, range (grass), club rentals, credit cards (MC, V, AE, D).
Reader Comments: Two courses, both have own flavor ... Fun to play ... Nice little golf course, good value ... Grade is rising. Someone is doing their homework ... Standard public golf ... Solid course, great value.
WEST COURSE
Holes: 18. **Yards:** 6,400/5,480. **Par:** 71/74. **Course Rating:** 68.6/68.5. **Slope:** 114/108. **Green Fee:** $18/$20. **Cart Fee:** $20/cart. **Walking Policy:** Walking at certain times. **Walkability:** 2.
Opened: 1966. **Architect:** Bill Galloway. **Season:** March-Nov. **High:** May-Sept. **To obtain tee times:** Call. **Miscellaneous:** Reduced fees (weekdays, low season), discount packages, range (grass), club rentals, credit cards (MC, V, AE, D), beginner friendly.

NEW YORK

★★★★ ROME COUNTRY CLUB
SP-5342 Rte. 69, Rome, 13440, Oneida County, (315)336-6464, 25 miles E of Syracuse. **E-mail:** romecc@email.msn.com. **Web:** www.romecountryclub.com.
Holes: 18. **Yards:** 6,775/5,505. **Par:** 72/75. **Course Rating:** 73.6/71.3. **Slope:** 123/118. **Green Fee:** $24/$27. **Cart Fee:** $20/cart. **Walking Policy:** Unrestricted walking. **Walkability:** 3.
Opened: 1929. **Season:** Year-round. **High:** May-Sept. **To obtain tee times:** Call.
Miscellaneous: Reduced fees (weekdays, twilight), discount packages, range (grass/mats), club rentals, credit cards (MC, V, D).
Reader Comments: Well kept ... Good experience ... Good upstate value ... Beautiful course ... Interesting layout with neat elevation changes, soft fairways ... Will hit every club in bag ... A nice course ... Great conditions, great value.

★★★ RONDOUT COUNTRY CLUB
PU-Box 194 Whitfield Rd, Accord, 12404, Ulster County, (914)626-2513, (888)894-9455, 15 miles S of Kingston.
Holes: 18. **Yards:** 6,468/4,822. **Par:** 72/72. **Course Rating:** 72.7/68.4. **Slope:** 128/116. **Green Fee:** $18/$28. **Cart Fee:** $14/person. **Walking Policy:** Walking at certain times. **Walkability:** 2.
Opened: 1970. **Architect:** Perdy. **Season:** March-Oct. **High:** May-Sept. **To obtain tee times:** Call on Monday for upcoming weekend. **Miscellaneous:** Reduced fees (weekdays, juniors), discount packages, metal spikes, range (grass/mats), club rentals, credit cards (MC, V, D).
Reader Comments: Some neat holes ... Nice variety ... Tight par 5s ... Watch this one, good change in ownership ... Well-rounded golf course ... No.13 tough but exciting.

ROTHLAND GOLF COURSE
PU-12089 Clarence Center Rd., Akron, 14001, Erie County, (716)542-4325, 15 miles NE of Buffalo. **E-mail:** play@rothland.com. **Web:** www.rothlandgolf.com.
Holes: 27. **Green Fee:** $19/$24. **Cart Fee:** $20/cart. **Walking Policy:** Unrestricted walking.
Walkability: 2. **Opened:** 1976. **Architect:** Bill Roth. **Season:** April-Nov. **High:** June-Sept. **To obtain tee times:** Call 7 days in advance. **Miscellaneous:** Reduced fees (weekdays, low season, twilight, seniors), range (grass), club rentals, credit cards (MC, V, D), beginner friendly (lesson packages).

★★★ GOLD/WHITE
Yards: 6,176/5,519. **Par:** 72/72. **Course Rating:** 68.1/68.0. **Slope:** 112/112.
Reader Comments: Flat but makes use of woodland and water. A few good, very tight and difficult holes with lots of birdie holes ... Routine golf, solid but layout ... Good course, 27 holes ... Great value.

★★★ RED/GOLD
Yards: 6,486/5,843. **Par:** 72/72. **Course Rating:** 70.2/71.3. **Slope:** 113/112.
Reader Comments: A great pair of nines ... Lots of water, lots of challenge ... Red features long par 4s ... Red/Gold combo can be fun ... All three fairly well maintained.

★★★ RED/WHITE
Yards: 6,348/5,878. **Par:** 72/72. **Course Rating:** 68.7/69.5. **Slope:** 110/110.
Reader Comments: A great experience ... Holes fun to play ... Red and White both pretty wide open ... Start on Red (easy), move to White (challenging) ... Great greens.

★★★★ THE SAGAMORE GOLF CLUB
R-110 Sagamore Rd., Bolton Landing, 12814, Warren County, (518)644-9400, 60 miles N of Albany.
Holes: 18. **Yards:** 6,890/5,261. **Par:** 70/71. **Course Rating:** 72.9/73.0. **Slope:** 130/122. **Green Fee:** $70/$70. **Cart Fee:** Included in Green Fee. **Walking Policy:** Mandatory cart. **Walkability:** 5. **Opened:** 1928. **Architect:** Donald Ross. **Season:** April-Nov. **High:** May-Oct. **To obtain tee times:** You can make tee times when you book your reservations with the resort.
Miscellaneous: Discount packages, metal spikes, range (grass), club rentals, lodging, credit cards (MC, V, AE, D).
Reader Comments: Nothing sagging here! Breathtaking country ... Worth it for the fall views alone ... A super spot! ... Very well taken care of, they treat you great, course is excellent challenge ... A gem ... Back 9 very tight; hit it straight ... Challenging fairways, beautiful greens, scenic area. A beautiful Adirondack course.

★★★ ST. LAWRENCE UNIVERSITY GOLF & COUNTRY CLUB
PU-Rte. 11, Canton, 13617, St. Lawrence County, (315)386-4600, 68 miles S of Ottawa, Canada.
Holes: 18. **Yards:** 6,694/5,430. **Par:** 72/73. **Course Rating:** 72.1/73.1. **Slope:** 122/120. **Green Fee:** $20/$24. **Cart Fee:** $24/cart. **Walking Policy:** Unrestricted walking. **Walkability:** 2.
Opened: 1936. **Architect:** Devereux Emmet. **Season:** April-Oct. **High:** June-Aug. **To obtain tee times:** Call up to 8 days in advance. **Miscellaneous:** Reduced fees (weekdays, low season, resort guests, twilight, juniors), discount packages, metal spikes, range (grass/mats), club rentals, lodging (96 rooms), credit cards (MC, V), beginner friendly (beginner groups).

Reader Comments: Some tight driving holes ... A real gem, great value ... Great layout ... Great greens, flat tree-lined layout, playable from whites ... Fun.

★★ SALMON CREEK COUNTRY CLUB
SP-355 Washington St., Spencerport, 14559, Monroe County, (716)352-4300, 6 miles W of Rochester.
Holes: 18. **Yards:** 6,400/5,525. **Par:** 72/73. **Course Rating:** 69.5/71.4. **Slope:** 121/114. **Green Fee:** $18/$22. **Cart Fee:** $22/cart. **Walking Policy:** Unrestricted walking. **Walkability:** 3. **Opened:** 1963. **Architect:** Pete Craig. **Season:** March-Dec. **High:** May-Sept. **To obtain tee times:** Public may call up to 7 days in advance. **Miscellaneous:** Reduced fees (seniors), discount packages, range (grass/mats), club rentals, credit cards (MC, V).

★ SANCTUARY COUNTRY CLUB
PU-Rte. 118, Yorktown Heights, 10598, Westchester County, (914) 962-8050, 2 miles S of Yorktown Heights.
Holes: 18. **Yards:** 6,277/N/A. **Par:** 72/N/A. **Course Rating:** N/A. **Slope:** N/A. **Green Fee:** N/A/$37. **Cart Fee:** $24/cart. **Walking Policy:** Walking at certain times. **Walkability:** 3. **Architect:** Richard Mandell. **Season:** March-Nov. **High:** May-August. **To obtain tee times:** Call golf shop at (914)962-8050 or (212)964-8366. **Miscellaneous:** Reduced fees (weekdays, seniors), discount packages, metal spikes, club rentals, credit cards (MC, V). **Special Notes:** Formerly Loch Ledge Golf Club. Course is under renovation.

★★★★ SARATOGA SPA GOLF COURSE   *Value*
PU-Saratoga Spa State Park,60 Roosevelt Dr, Saratoga Springs, 12866, Saratoga County, (518)584-2006, 24 miles N of Albany.
Holes: 18. **Yards:** 7,149/5,649. **Par:** 72/72. **Course Rating:** 73.7/72.5. **Slope:** 130/122. **Green Fee:** $22/$25. **Cart Fee:** $24/cart. **Walking Policy:** Unrestricted walking. **Walkability:** 2. **Opened:** 1962. **Architect:** Bill Mitchell. **Season:** April-Nov. **High:** June-Aug. **To obtain tee times:** Call up to 7 days in advance between 2 P.M. and 7 P.M. **Miscellaneous:** Reduced fees (seniors, juniors), range (grass), club rentals, lodging, credit cards (MC, V, D).
Reader Comments: Exceptionally beautiful scenery, well groomed & enjoyable ... Best course for $ ... Great value, very scenic, good greens ... Super value, park setting, fun to play ... First-rate public course ... Great design ... Gorgeous pines ... A must ... Awesome.

★★½ SAXON WOODS GOLF COURSE
PU-315 Old Mamaroneck Rd., Scarsdale, 10583, Westchester County, (914)725-3814, 5 miles N of White Plains.
Holes: 18. **Yards:** 6,240/5,617. **Par:** 71/73. **Course Rating:** 70.4/71.9. **Slope:** 124/124. **Green Fee:** $10/$45. **Cart Fee:** $24. **Walking Policy:** Unrestricted walking. **Walkability:** 2. **Opened:** 1931. **Architect:** Tom Winton. **Season:** April-Dec. **High:** June-Aug. **To obtain tee times:** Call. First 2 hours made in person at office. Total computer reservation system 1-914-242-GOLF. **Miscellaneous:** Reduced fees (weekdays, twilight, seniors, juniors), metal spikes, club rentals, beginner friendly.
Reader Comments: Nice layout ... Try it, you'll like it ... Service is good ... Very surprised at how enjoyable the round was, many improvements ... Great layout ... Long and public. Great combo ... Improvements have been great.

★★★ SCHENECTADY GOLF COURSE
PM-400 Oregon Ave., Schenectady, 12309, Schenectady County, (518)382-5155, 18 miles E of Albany.
Holes: 18. **Yards:** 6,570/5,275. **Par:** 72/72. **Course Rating:** 71.1/68.1. **Slope:** 123/115. **Green Fee:** $19/$21. **Cart Fee:** $21/cart. **Walking Policy:** Unrestricted walking. **Walkability:** 2. **Opened:** 1935. **Architect:** Jim Thomson. **Season:** April-Nov. **High:** May-Aug. **To obtain tee times:** Call 2 days in advance. **Miscellaneous:** Reduced fees (weekdays, seniors, juniors), range (grass), club rentals.
Reader Comments: Great value, slow play. The city put some money into it and its a top-notch course, greens are superb, firm and slick ... Neat and tidy ... A lot of fun, in good condition ... Typical municipal course.

SENECA GOLF CLUB
PU-State Fair Blvd., Baldwinsville, 13027, Onondaga County, (315)635-5695, 6 miles W of Syracuse.
Holes: 9. **Yards:** 5,758/5,030. **Par:** 70/70. **Course Rating:** 68.0/67.0. **Slope:** N/A. **Green Fee:** $11/$15. **Cart Fee:** $20/cart. **Walking Policy:** Unrestricted walking. **Walkability:** 2. **Opened:** 1928. **Season:** April-Nov. **High:** June-Sept. **To obtain tee times:** Call the golf shop anytime. **Miscellaneous:** Range (grass), club rentals, credit cards (MC, V), beginner friendly (beginner clinics).

SENECA LAKE COUNTRY CLUB
PU-Turk Rd., Geneva, (315)789-6737 .

Special Notes: Call club for further information.

★★★½ SHADOW LAKE GOLF & RAQUET CLUB

PU-1850 Five Mile Line Rd., Penfield, 14526, Monroe County, (716)385-2010, 10 miles SE of Rochester.

Holes: 18. **Yards:** 6,164/5,498. **Par:** 71/72. **Course Rating:** 68.5/70.5. **Slope:** 111/112. **Green Fee:** $10/$22. **Cart Fee:** $11. **Walking Policy:** Walking at certain times. **Walkability:** N/A. **Opened:** 1977. **Architect:** Pete Craig. **Season:** March-Dec. **High:** June-Aug. **To obtain tee times:** Call 7 days in advance. **Miscellaneous:** Reduced fees (weekdays, low season, twilight, seniors), metal spikes, club rentals, credit cards (MC, V, AE).

Reader Comments: Excellent conditions for amount of play, short layout ... Fun to play here. Pretty layout ... Great staff , very enjoyable course ... Comfortable course ... A real good league-type course ... Well maintained, good for all levels ... Pretty.

★★★★ SHADOW PINES GOLF CLUB

PU-600 Whalen Rd., Penfield, 14526, Monroe County, (716)385-8550, 10 miles E of Rochester. **Web:** www.234golf.com.

Holes: 18. **Yards:** 6,763/5,292. **Par:** 72/72. **Course Rating:** 72.4/70.4. **Slope:** 124/123. **Green Fee:** $16/$23. **Cart Fee:** $12/person. **Walking Policy:** Mandatory cart. **Walkability:** 4. **Opened:** 1985. **Architect:** Pete Craig/Gardner Odenbach. **Season:** April-Nov. **High:** June-Aug. **To obtain tee times:** Call 7 days in advance. **Miscellaneous:** Reduced fees (weekdays, low season, twilight, seniors), discount packages, range (grass/mats), club rentals, credit cards (MC, V, AE).

Reader Comments: Beautiful layout, picturesque fairways & greens ... Great layout ... You like it or hate it. Some tight holes and blind shots ... A challenge to humble you when you are on your game ... Very challenging, very enjoyable ... Trouble every hole, watch out ... Great back 9 ... Nice layout, fast greens ... Well conditioned.

★★★½ SHERIDAN PARK GOLF CLUB

PM-Center Park Dr., Tonawanda, 14150, Erie County, (716)875-1811, 3 miles N of Buffalo.

Holes: 18. **Yards:** 6,534/5,656. **Par:** 71/74. **Course Rating:** 71.3/74.0. **Slope:** 116/116. **Green Fee:** $16/$19. **Cart Fee:** $18/cart. **Walking Policy:** Unrestricted walking. **Walkability:** 2. **Opened:** 1933. **Architect:** William Harries. **Season:** April-Nov. **High:** June-Aug. **To obtain tee times:** Call 7 days in advance. **Miscellaneous:** Reduced fees (weekdays, twilight), range (mats), club rentals.

Notes: 1962 U.S. Public Links.

Reader Comments: Great variety. Condition improving ... Great short course ... Hilly, tough back nine, price is right ... Long course and challenging. Lots of water, 13 out of 18 holes water in play ... Several zany, but great holes ... A must-play ... Back 9 is a wild ride. Designer went nuts, throw out the textbook. No ordinary muny.

★★★ SILVER LAKE GOLF COURSE

PU-915 Victory Blvd., Staten Island, 10301, Richmond County, (718)447-5686.

Holes: 18. **Yards:** 6,138/5,202. **Par:** 69/69. **Course Rating:** 68.8/71.2. **Slope:** 119/119. **Green Fee:** $19/$22. **Cart Fee:** $25/cart. **Walking Policy:** Unrestricted walking. **Walkability:** 5. **Opened:** 1929. **Architect:** John Van Kleek. **Season:** Year-round. **High:** May-Sept. **To obtain tee times:** Call Central Reservation for 7 N.Y.C. Courses (718)225-4653. **Miscellaneous:** Reduced fees (weekdays, twilight, seniors, juniors), metal spikes, club rentals, credit cards (MC, V, AE).

Reader Comments: Some nice holes, I like this course! ... Kept in excellent shape; very nice staff ... Public beauty. Kudos to grounds crew ... Very narrow fairways ... Greens very good ... Good price ... Current best NYC course.

★★ SIX-S GOLF COURSE

PU-Transit Bridge Rd. 5920 Co. Rte. 16, Belfast, 14711, Allegany County, (716)365-2201, 65 miles SE of Buffalo.

Holes: 18. **Yards:** 6,210/4,826. **Par:** 72/72. **Course Rating:** 69.5/69.7. **Slope:** 120/115. **Green Fee:** $11/$12. **Cart Fee:** $10/person. **Walking Policy:** Unrestricted walking. **Walkability:** 2. **Opened:** 1965. **Architect:** William F. Short. **Season:** March-Nov. **High:** July-Aug. **To obtain tee times:** Tee times not required. **Miscellaneous:** Reduced fees (weekdays, twilight, seniors, juniors), metal spikes, range (grass), credit cards (MC, V, D), beginner friendly (3 school programs).

SKANEATELES GREENS COUNTRY CLUB

PU-Westlake Rd., Skaneateles, 13152, (315)673-4916.
Special Notes: Call club for further information.

★★★½ SMITHTOWN LANDING GOLF CLUB

PU-495 Landing Ave., Smithtown, 11787, Suffolk County, (631)979-6534, 35 miles E of New York.

Holes: 18. **Yards:** 6,114/5,263. **Par:** 72/72. **Course Rating:** 70.9/69.8. **Slope:** 125/122. **Green Fee:** $21/$29. **Cart Fee:** $25/cart. **Walking Policy:** Unrestricted walking. **Walkability:** 3.

Architect: Stephen Kay. **Season:** Year-round. **High:** May-Sept. **To obtain tee times:** Tee times taken weekdays, weekends and holidays for residents only. **Miscellaneous:** Reduced fees (weekdays, low season), metal spikes, range (mats), beginner friendly (group and private lessons for ladies and juniors).

Reader Comments: Nice layout ... Excellent course, constantly improving ... Challenging, inexpensive golf ... Good town course ... Overall a short course, extremely hilly ... Very nice, good lessons ... One of the best of public courses.

★★½ SOUTH SHORE GOLF COURSE

PU-200 Huguenot Ave., Staten Island, 10312, Richmond County, (718)984-0101, 18 miles S of Manhattan.
Holes: 18. **Yards:** 6,366/5,435. **Par:** 72/72. **Course Rating:** 69.9/69.8. **Slope:** 113/114. **Green Fee:** $16/$18. **Cart Fee:** $24/cart. **Walking Policy:** Unrestricted walking. **Walkability:** 1.
Opened: 1927. **Architect:** Devereux Emmet/Alfred Tull. **Season:** Year-round **High:** May-Sept. **To obtain tee times:** Call 10 days in advance. **Miscellaneous:** Reduced fees (twilight, seniors, juniors), metal spikes, club rentals, credit cards (MC, V).

Reader Comments: You'll forget you're in New York City ... Very hilly, greens OK ... City course, open all year, crowded, great for a beginner.

★★★★ SPOOK ROCK GOLF COURSE

PU-233 Spook Rock Rd., Suffern, 10901, Rockland County, (914)357-3085, 30 miles NW of New York City.
Holes: 18. **Yards:** 6,894/4,953. **Par:** 72/72. **Course Rating:** 73.1/68.1. **Slope:** 127/120. **Green Fee:** $45/$45. **Cart Fee:** $27/cart. **Walking Policy:** Unrestricted walking. **Walkability:** 2.
Opened: 1970. **Architect:** Frank Duane. **Season:** April-Nov. **High:** May-Sept. **To obtain tee times:** Call Saturday after 5 p.m. for weekdays and Tuesday after 7 a.m. for weekend play.
Miscellaneous: Reduced fees (twilight, seniors), range (mats), club rentals, beginner friendly (adult beginner clinics, junior clinics).

Reader Comments: Very true, fast, well-maintained ... Great value. Well designed. Friendly starter ... One of the best publics & getting better ... Hidden gem. Excellent condition ... Entire course beautiful, great in the fall ... Nothing spooky about the course! Outstanding test, superb condition.

★★★ SPRAIN LAKE GOLF CLUB

PU-290 Grassy Sprain Rd., Yonkers, 10710, Westchester County, (914)779-9827, 10 miles N of New York City.
Holes: 18. **Yards:** 6,010/5,500. **Par:** 70/71. **Course Rating:** 68.6/70.2. **Slope:** 114/115. **Green Fee:** $35/$45. **Cart Fee:** $23/cart. **Walking Policy:** Unrestricted walking. **Walkability:** 3.
Opened: 1940. **Architect:** Tom Winton. **Season:** April-Dec. **High:** June-Aug. **To obtain tee times:** Walk on time first 2 hours. After 1st 2 hours, call computer (914)242-4653.
Miscellaneous: Reduced fees (weekdays, twilight, seniors, juniors), metal spikes, club rentals.

Reader Comments: Good place to learn ... Well-maintained, fun, challenging course ... OK beginner course ... Quirky 11th hole, fun to play ... Fun course, varied layout ... Flat, water, woods, can't make mistakes ... Several difficult holes.

★★★½ SPRING LAKE GOLF CLUB

PU-30 East Bartlett Rd., Middle Island, 11953, Suffolk County, (516)924-5115, 45 miles E of New York City.
Holes: 18. **Yards:** 7,048/5,732. **Par:** 72/72. **Course Rating:** 73.2/70.0. **Slope:** 128/120. **Green Fee:** $25/$36. **Cart Fee:** $29/cart. **Walking Policy:** Walking at certain times. **Walkability:** 3.
Opened: 1967. **Architect:** Jurgens & Company. **Season:** Year-round. **High:** April-Oct. **To obtain tee times:** Call golf shop. **Miscellaneous:** Reduced fees (weekdays, twilight), metal spikes, range (grass/mats), club rentals, beginner friendly.

Reader Comments: Exceptional condition. Pace OK ... Challenging, an enjoyable day ... Course always in great shape ... Expensive ... Good layout. Fairways easy to hit. 2nd shot critical to large undulating greens ... Staff could be friendlier ... Beautiful course. Greens huge ... Beautiful layout, great pro shop.

★★★ STONEBRIDGE GOLF LINKS & COUNTRY CLUB

SP-Veterans Memorial Hwy., Hauppauge, 11788, Suffolk County, (516)724-7500, 30 miles E of New York City.
Holes: 18. **Yards:** 6,200/4,490. **Par:** 70/N/A. **Course Rating:** N/A. **Slope:** N/A. **Green Fee:** $70/$90. **Cart Fee:** Included in Green Fee. **Walking Policy:** Mandatory cart. **Walkability:** 3.
Opened: 2000. **Architect:** Gil Hanse/George Bahto. **Season:** March-Dec. **High:** May-Oct. **To obtain tee times:** Call up to 7 days in advance Monday-Friday. **Miscellaneous:** Reduced fees (low season), range (mats), club rentals, credit cards (MC, V, AE).

Reader Comments: Good condition, two interesting water holes ... Beautiful course. Great place to take clients ... Short but challenging.

★★★½ STONY FORD GOLF COURSE
PM-211 Rte. 416, Montgomery, 12549, Orange County, (914)457-1532, 60 miles N of New York City.
Holes: 18. **Yards:** 6,551/5,856. **Par:** 72/73. **Course Rating:** 72.4/74.0. **Slope:** 129/129. **Green Fee:** $14/$32. **Cart Fee:** $11/person. **Walking Policy:** Unrestricted walking. **Walkability:** 3. **Opened:** 1968. **Architect:** Hal Purdy. **Season:** April-Nov. **High:** May-Sept. **To obtain tee times:** In person–1 week in advance. By Phone–5 days in advance. **Miscellaneous:** Reduced fees (weekdays, low season, twilight, seniors, juniors), range (grass), club rentals.
Reader Comments: One of 2 very good munies in area ... Great county course ... Lake holes tough; long par 3s ... Very enjoyable, great variety of holes ... Excellent views, interesting shots from elevation changes ... Good course playable for all handicaps. Very forgiving ... Plenty of water and sand ... Staff and facilities great.

SUNKEN MEADOW STATE PARK GOLF CLUB
PU-Sunken Meadow State Park, Rte. 25A, Kings Park, 11754, Suffolk County, (516)544-0036, 40 miles E of New York City.
Holes: 27. **Green Fee:** $22/$27. **Cart Fee:** $12/person. **Walking Policy:** Unrestricted walking. **Opened:** 1964. **Architect:** Alfred Tull. **Season:** Year-round. **High:** April-Sept. **To obtain tee times:** First come, first served same day. Reservations 2 days in advance (516)269-0707. **Miscellaneous:** Reduced fees (seniors), metal spikes, range (mats), club rentals, credit cards (MC, V, AE, D).

★★★ BLUE/GREEN
Yards: 6,185/5,638. **Par:** 71/71. **Course Rating:** 68.7/70.4. **Slope:** 111/112. **Walkability:** 2.
Reader Comments: Good price, basic golf ... Great layout, needs better upkeep ... Nice course ... Fun course. Play can be slow ... 3 interesting 9s will find your strengths & weaknesses.

★★★ BLUE/RED
Yards: 6,100/5,627. **Par:** 71/71. **Course Rating:** 68.2/70.0. **Slope:** 112/112. **Walkability:** 3.
Reader Comments: Good for warm-up ... Fun for quick 9 holes.

★★★ RED/GREEN
Yards: 6,165/5,567. **Par:** 72/72. **Course Rating:** 68.5/70.3. **Slope:** 112/113. **Walkability:** 3.
Reader Comments: Good greens for public course ... Only time I ever putted for an eagle ... Very flat.

★★★½ SWAN LAKE GOLF CLUB
PU-373 River Rd., Manorville, 11949, Suffolk County, (516)369-1818, 10 miles W of Riverhead.
Holes: 18. **Yards:** 7,011/5,245. **Par:** 72/72. **Course Rating:** 72.5/69.0. **Slope:** 121/112. **Green Fee:** $30/$34. **Cart Fee:** $30/cart. **Walking Policy:** Walking at certain times. **Walkability:** 1. **Opened:** 1979. **Architect:** Don Jurgens. **Season:** Year-round. **High:** April-Oct. **To obtain tee times:** Call up to 7 days in advance. **Miscellaneous:** Reduced fees (twilight), metal spikes, club rentals, credit cards (MC, V, AE).
Reader Comments: Huge greens! Need extra club for back pin placement ... Very enjoyable course ... Not too difficult, can be crowded, good value ... Pleasant staff, always in great condition, fun to play, easy to score, good for average golfer... Nice course ... Plush course, friendly people, a pleasure to play ... Large rolling greens.

★★★½ TARRY BRAE GOLF CLUB
PM-Pleasant Valley Rd., South Fallsburg, 12779, Sullivan County, (914)434-2620, 10 miles NE of Monticello.
Holes: 18. **Yards:** 6,888/5,610. **Par:** 72/76. **Course Rating:** 73.4/72.2. **Slope:** 129/126. **Green Fee:** $20/$27. **Cart Fee:** $13/person. **Walking Policy:** Walking at certain times. **Walkability:** 4. **Opened:** 1962. **Architect:** William Mitchell. **Season:** April-Nov. **High:** June-Sept. **To obtain tee times:** Call Wednesday for upcoming Saturday. Call on Thursday for upcoming Sunday. **Miscellaneous:** Reduced fees (weekdays, low season, twilight, juniors), range (grass/mats), club rentals, credit cards (MC, V).
Reader Comments: Nice course, good value, good greens ... Sneaky tough course ... Very good condition, fun, challenging ... Enjoyable, but a workout ... Good test. Use all your clubs ... Great layout ... Course condition excellent, service very good ... Best buy in state, course in good shape ... Super public course.

★★★½ TENNANAH LAKE GOLF & TENNIS CLUB
SP-100 Belle Rd., Suite 2, Roscoe, 12776, Sullivan County, (607)498-5502, (888)561-3935, 60 miles N of Middletown. **E-mail:** tlgtgolf@aol.com. **Web:** www.tennanah.com.
Holes: 18. **Yards:** 6,769/5,797. **Par:** 72/72. **Course Rating:** 73.7/74.7. **Slope:** 132/131. **Green Fee:** $32/$36. **Cart Fee:** $28/cart. **Walking Policy:** Walking at certain times. **Walkability:** 4. **Opened:** 1911. **Architect:** Alfred H. Tull. **Season:** May-Oct. **High:** June-Aug. **To obtain tee times:** Call up to 21 days in advance. **Miscellaneous:** Reduced fees (weekdays, low season, resort guests, twilight, seniors, juniors), discount packages, range (grass/mats), club rentals, lodging (24 rooms), credit cards (MC, V, AE).

NEW YORK

Reader Comments: A hidden gem ... Expensive for location & layout ... Challenging back nine ... Hilly, pretty, good test ... Enjoyable, back nine better ... Every hole is different ... Magnificent scenery ... A little difficult to find ... Small greens and high hills.

TERRY HILLS GOLF COURSE
PU-5122 Clinton St. Rd., Batavia, 14020, Genesee County, (716)343-0860, (800)825-8633, 30 miles E of Buffalo. **E-mail:** terryhills@aol.com. **Web:** www.terryhills.com.
Holes: 27. **Green Fee:** $19/$24. **Cart Fee:** $11/person. **Walking Policy:** Walking at certain times. **Walkability:** 3. **Season:** March-Nov. **High:** June-Aug. **To obtain tee times:** Call up to 7 days in advance.
★★★★ **EAST/SOUTH**
Yards: 6,124/5,180. **Par:** 72/72. **Course Rating:** 68.0/68.3. **Slope:** 120/111. **Opened:** 1930.
Architect: Parker Terry/Mark Mungeam. **Miscellaneous:** Reduced fees (weekdays, low season, twilight, seniors, juniors), club rentals, credit cards (MC, V, AE, D).
Reader Comments: Pleasure to play ... Very challenging, fairly short layout, every club in your bag will be used ... Short, hilly ... None better in area ... Hidden gem, fun course ... Hilly, some blind shots, don't walk it ... Best public course in area, just beautiful ... Staff outstanding!.
★★★★ **NORTH/EAST**
Yards: 6,296/5,229. **Par:** 72/72. **Course Rating:** 68.5/68.3. **Slope:** 118/111. **Opened:** 1930.
Architect: Mark Mungeam/Parker Terry. **Miscellaneous:** Reduced fees (weekdays, low season, twilight, seniors, juniors), discount packages, club rentals, credit cards (MC, V, AE, D).
★★★★ **SOUTH/NORTH**
Yards: 6,358/5,177. **Par:** 72/72. **Course Rating:** 68.9/67.4. **Slope:** 114/107. **Opened:** 1986.
Architect: Ed Ault/Mark Mungeam. **Miscellaneous:** Reduced fees (low season, twilight, seniors, juniors), discount packages, club rentals, credit cards (MC, V, AE, D).

THENDARA GOLF CLUB
SP-Fifth Street, Thendara, 13472, Herkimer County, (315)369-3136, 55 miles N of Utica.
Holes: 18. **Yards:** 6,435/5,757. **Par:** 72/73. **Course Rating:** 70.2/72.8. **Slope:** 124/121. **Green Fee:** $25/$25. **Cart Fee:** $20/cart. **Walking Policy:** Walking at certain times. **Walkability:** 3.
Opened: 1921. **Architect:** Donald Ross. **Season:** May-Oct. **High:** July-Sept. **To obtain tee times:** Non-members may call 2 days in advance. Some tee times are reserved for members on weekends. **Miscellaneous:** Reduced fees (twilight), metal spikes, range (grass/mats), club rentals, credit cards (MC, V).
Reader Comments: Well-kept mountain course ... Two distinct 9s ... Short, great course ... Great to play ... Wide-open front, very tight back, very scenic, beautiful in fall ... Great course, hills, valleys, wildlife, beautiful, backside tight ... Challenging.

THOMAS CARVEL COUNTRY CLUB
PU-Ferris Rd., Pine Plains, 12567, Dutchess County, (518)398-7101, 30 miles NE of Poughkeepsie.
Holes: 18. **Yards:** 7,080/5,066. **Par:** 73/75. **Course Rating:** 73.5/69.0. **Slope:** 127/115. **Green Fee:** $20/$40. **Cart Fee:** Included in Green Fee. **Walking Policy:** Mandatory cart. **Walkability:** 5. **Opened:** 1962. **Architect:** William Mitchell. **Season:** April-Nov. **High:** May-Sept. **To obtain tee times:** Call up to 7 days in advance. **Miscellaneous:** Reduced fees (weekdays, low season, twilight, seniors), discount packages, range (grass), club rentals, credit cards (MC, V, AE).
Reader Comments: Hilly course ... Good greens ... Very tough from blue tees ... Great bargain. Very challenging ... Good variety of holes ... Pretty tough, first hole a bear, strange mix and wind a killer ... Back 9 is awesome ... Beautiful and extremely wellcared for ... Spectacular in autumn ... Big greens, long from the blue tees.

THOUSAND ISLANDS GOLF CLUB
PU-County Rd. 100 Wellesley Island E., Wellesley Island, 13640, Jefferson County, (315)482-9454, 35 miles N of Watertown. **E-mail:** tigolf@thousandislands.com. **Web:** thousandislands.com/tigolfclub.
LAKE COURSE
Holes: 18. **Yards:** 5,005/4,425. **Par:** 70/70. **Course Rating:** N/A. **Slope:** N/A. **Green Fee:** $23/$23. **Cart Fee:** $24/cart. **Walking Policy:** Walking at certain times. **Walkability:** 4. **Opened:** 1988. **Season:** April-Nov. **High:** June-Sept. **To obtain tee times:** Call. **Miscellaneous:** Reduced fees (weekdays, low season, resort guests, twilight, juniors), discount packages, range (grass), club rentals, lodging (20 rooms), credit cards (MC, V, AE), beginner friendly (beginner programs available).
★★★ **OLD COURSE**
Holes: 18. **Yards:** 6,302/5,240. **Par:** 72/74. **Course Rating:** 69.2/68.5. **Slope:** 118/114. **Green Fee:** $23/$33. **Cart Fee:** $24/cart. **Walking Policy:** Walking at certain times. **Walkability:** 4. **Opened:** 1894. **Architect:** Seth Raynor. **Season:** April-Nov. **High:** June-Sept. **To obtain tee times:** Call. **Miscellaneous:** Reduced fees (weekdays, low season, resort guests, twilight, juniors), discount packages, range (grass), club rentals, lodging (20 rooms), credit cards (MC, V, AE).
Reader Comments: New irrigation has made fairways much better... Great views ... Friendly links ... Difficult on windy days ... Heavenly views.

TIMBER POINT GOLF COURSE
PM-Great River Rd., Great River, 11739, Suffolk County, (516)581-2401, 50 miles E of New York City.
Holes: 27. **Green Fee:** $9/$35. **Cart Fee:** $27/cart. **Walking Policy:** Unrestricted walking.
Walkability: 1. **Opened:** 1927. **Architect:** H.S. Colt and C.H. Alison/William Mitche. **Season:** Year-round. **High:** June-Aug. **To obtain tee times:** Nonresidents may call golf shop for same day reservations. Residents may call 7 days in advance.

★★½ **RED/BLUE**
Yards: 6,642/5,455. **Par:** 72/72. **Course Rating:** 72.3/71.7. **Slope:** 123/119. **Miscellaneous:** Reduced fees (weekdays, low season, twilight, seniors, juniors), club rentals.
Reader Comments: Tough par 3s. Great views. Excellent facilities ... Back nine on water is worth it all ... Million dollar views on back, water ... Varied and challenging holes, the Blue course (along the bay) is a stiff challenge when wind blows ... Pretty course, nice views ... Terrific county course. Par 3 over inlet great hole.

★★½ **RED/WHITE**
Yards: 6,441/5,358. **Par:** 72/72. **Course Rating:** 70.8/70.5. **Slope:** 119/117. **Miscellaneous:** Reduced fees (weekdays, low season, twilight, seniors, juniors), range (mats), club rentals.

★★½ **WHITE/BLUE**
Yards: 6,525/5,367. **Par:** 72/72. **Course Rating:** 71.7/71.2. **Slope:** 122/119. **Miscellaneous:** Reduced fees (weekdays, low season, twilight, seniors, juniors), range (mats), club rentals.

★★★½ **TIOGA COUNTRY CLUB** *Value*
PU-151 Ro-Ki Blvd, Nichols, 13812, Tioga County, (607)699-3881, 25 miles W of Binghamton.
Holes: 18. **Yards:** 5,848/5,193. **Par:** 71/72. **Course Rating:** 69.3/70.8. **Slope:** 119/115. **Green Fee:** $16/$20. **Cart Fee:** $24/cart. **Walking Policy:** Unrestricted walking. **Walkability:** 5.
Opened: 1967. **Architect:** Hal Purdy. **Season:** April-Nov. **High:** June-Aug. **To obtain tee times:** Call 1 day in advance. **Miscellaneous:** Reduced fees (twilight), metal spikes, club rentals, credit cards (MC, V).
Reader Comments: Nice course but slow ... Very hilly ... Good test, hilly, variety of holes, use all clubs ... Tough walk, nice greens ... A real treat.

★★½ **TOMASSO'S CHEMUNG GOLF COURSE**
PU-5799 Country Rd. #60, Waverly, 14892, Chemung County, (607)565-2323, 12 miles SE of Elmira.
Holes: 18. **Yards:** 6,000/5,525. **Par:** 69/69. **Course Rating:** 66.3/66.0. **Slope:** N/A. **Green Fee:** $13/$15. **Cart Fee:** $18. **Walking Policy:** Unrestricted walking. **Walkability:** 1. **Opened:** 1962.
Architect: Lou Tomasso. **Season:** Year-round. **High:** May-Sept. **To obtain tee times:** First come, first served. **Miscellaneous:** Reduced fees (weekdays, low season, twilight, seniors), discount packages, metal spikes.
Reader Comments: Basic golf, open all year, great dining, ... Bunkers would make it more interesting ... Gets better each year ... No sand or rough ... Short, sporty course with small greens.

★★★★ **TOWN OF WALLKILL GOLF CLUB**
PU-40 Sands Rd., Middletown, 10940, Orange County, (914)361-1022, 55 miles NW of New York City. **Web:** willycarter.com.
Holes: 18. **Yards:** 6,437/5,171. **Par:** 72/72. **Course Rating:** 70.6/69.7. **Slope:** 128/122. **Green Fee:** $12/$40. **Cart Fee:** $26/cart. **Walking Policy:** Unrestricted walking. **Walkability:** 4.
Opened: 1991. **Architect:** Steve Esposito. **Season:** April-Nov. **High:** June-Aug. **To obtain tee times:** Call Saturday for following week. **Miscellaneous:** Reduced fees (weekdays, low season, twilight, seniors, juniors), discount packages, range (grass/mats), club rentals.
Reader Comments: Young course, great shape ... Sometimes play is slow ... Neat, hilly, pretty, mountain resort feel ... Great layout and conditions ... Great value ... Nos. 2, 9 and18 terrific. Expensive ... Short but interesting ... Wonderful value, distinct layout ... Great little course ... Laudable, lovable, testing and unforgiving.

★★★½ **TRI COUNTY COUNTRY CLUB**
SP-Rte. 39, Forestville, 14062, Chautauqua County, (716)965-9723, 50 miles S of Buffalo.
Holes: 18. **Yards:** 6,639/5,574. **Par:** 71/72. **Course Rating:** 70.9/71.0. **Slope:** 118/113. **Green Fee:** $24/$27. **Cart Fee:** $11/person. **Walking Policy:** Unrestricted walking. **Walkability:** 4.
Opened: 1924. **Architect:** Al Shart. **Season:** April-Oct. **High:** July-Aug. **To obtain tee times:** Call golf shop. **Miscellaneous:** Reduced fees (weekdays), discount packages, metal spikes, range (grass), credit cards (MC, V).
Reader Comments: Long from the blue, great pace to play. Nice grillroom ... Fun course! ... Not your average flat course with wide fairways and a lack of trees, this course has hills and trees. Fairways, tee boxes and greens well maintained ... Tight short front, long open back. Good layout and friendly service.

★★½ **VALLEY VIEW GOLF CLUB**
PU-620 Memorial Pkwy., Utica, 13501, Oneida County, (315)732-8755.

Holes: 18. **Yards:** 6,583/5,942. **Par:** 71/73. **Course Rating:** 69.2/72.6. **Slope:** 118/116. **Green Fee:** $12/$15. **Cart Fee:** $11/person. **Walking Policy:** Unrestricted walking. **Walkability:** 4. **Opened:** 1936. **Architect:** Robert Trent Jones. **Season:** April-Nov. **High:** April-Aug. **To obtain tee times:** First come, first served. **Miscellaneous:** Reduced fees (twilight), range (grass), club rentals.
Reader Comments: Keep ball straight ... Nice course, great greens ... Good layout ... Tough rolling greens ... Very good layout.

★★ VAN CORTLANDT PARK GOLF CLUB
PU-Van Cortlandt Park S. and Bailey Ave., Bronx, 10471, Bronx County, (718)543-4595, 5 miles N of New York. **Web:** www.americangolf.com.
Holes: 18. **Yards:** 6,122/5,421. **Par:** 70/70. **Course Rating:** 68.9/73.0. **Slope:** 112/120. **Green Fee:** $9/$28. **Cart Fee:** $26/cart. **Walking Policy:** Unrestricted walking. **Walkability:** 4. **Opened:** 1895. **Architect:** T. McClure Peters. **Season:** Year-round. **High:** April-Oct. **To obtain tee times:** Call 10 days in advance with credit card to guarantee. **Miscellaneous:** Reduced fees (twilight, seniors, juniors), discount packages, metal spikes, club rentals, credit cards (MC, V, AE, D).

VICTOR HILLS GOLF CLUB
PU-1460 Brace Rd., Victor, 14564, Ontario County, (716)924-3480, 18 miles E of Rochester.
★★★★ NORTH COURSE
Holes: 18. **Yards:** 6,440/6,454. **Par:** 72/72. **Course Rating:** 71.3/72.6. **Slope:** 119/117. **Green Fee:** $21/$21. **Cart Fee:** $20/cart. **Walking Policy:** Unrestricted walking. **Walkability:** 3. **Opened:** 1973. **Architect:** Pete Craig. **Season:** Year-round weather permitting. **High:** May-Sept. **To obtain tee times:** Call up to 7 days in advance. **Miscellaneous:** Reduced fees (twilight), metal spikes, rentals, credit cards (MC, V).
Reader Comments: Holes & layout change almost yearly, fun to play just to see how things change ... A lot of woods & water ... Pretty narrow, you gotta be straight here ... Short, tough, great value ... Well-run and well-cared for course ... Large greens & fairways ... Best public course in upstate N.Y., always in great shape.
★★★★ SOUTH COURSE
Holes: 18. **Yards:** 6,663/5,670. **Par:** 72/72. **Course Rating:** 71.5/72.9. **Slope:** 121/119. **Green Fee:** $21/$21. **Cart Fee:** $20/cart. **Walking Policy:** Unrestricted walking. **Walkability:** 2. **Opened:** 1973. **Architect:** Pete Craig. **Season:** Year-round weather permitting. **High:** May-Sept. **To obtain tee times:** Call up to 7 days in advance. **Miscellaneous:** Reduced fees (twilight), metal spikes, rentals, credit cards (MC, V).
Reader Comments: Fun, but tight on front. Not for slicer/hooker ... Beech trees are a challenge ... More challenging than North course ... Some back & forth, shooting gallery holes.
Special Notes: Also has a 9-hole executive course.

★★★½ VILLA ROMA COUNTRY CLUB
R-Villa Roma Rd., Callicoon, 12723, Sullivan County, (914)887-5097, (800)727-8455, 100 miles N of New York City.
Holes: 18. **Yards:** 6,499/5,329. **Par:** 72/72. **Course Rating:** 70.9/70.3. **Slope:** 124/119. **Green Fee:** $44/$58. **Cart Fee:** Included in Green Fee. **Walking Policy:** Mandatory cart. **Walkability:** 4. **Opened:** 1987. **Architect:** David Postelwaite. **Season:** April-Nov. **High:** May-Sept. **To obtain tee times:** Call golf shop. **Miscellaneous:** Reduced fees (weekdays, resort guests, twilight, seniors), discount packages, metal spikes, range (grass), club rentals, lodging, credit cards (MC, V, AE, D).
Reader Comments: Best fairways, great greens, can play tough ... Bring camera, short but nice ... Women friendly, views ... Everyone was pleasant and capable ... Excellent resort course ... Great track, huge greens.

★★½ WATERTOWN GOLF CLUB
SP-P.O. Box 927, Watertown, 13601, Jefferson County, (315)782-4040, 70 miles N of Syracuse.
Holes: 18. **Yards:** 6,309/5,492. **Par:** 72/73. **Course Rating:** 69.4/67.9. **Slope:** 113/114. **Green Fee:** $20/$20. **Cart Fee:** $9/cart. **Walking Policy:** Unrestricted walking. **Walkability:** 1. **Opened:** 1926. **Architect:** Geoffrey S. Cornish/James Huber. **Season:** April-Oct. **High:** June-Aug. **To obtain tee times:** Call Wednesday for upcoming weekend and call Friday for next Tuesday and Wednesday. **Miscellaneous:** Reduced fees (twilight), discount packages, metal spikes, range (grass), club rentals, credit cards (MC, V, AE).
Reader Comments: Great 3 finishing holes ... Short course, good conditions ... Somewhat short, but very interesting and fun ... Tough 3 holes to finish on ... Course knowledge helpful ... Challenging course, skill needed ... Depends on weather.

★★★★ WAYNE HILLS COUNTRY CLUB *Value, Pace*
SP-2250 Gannett Rd., Lyons, 14489, Wayne County, (315)946-6944, 30 miles E of Rochester.
Holes: 18. **Yards:** 6,854/5,556. **Par:** 72/73. **Course Rating:** 72.8/72.0. **Slope:** 125/116. **Green Fee:** $33/$45. **Cart Fee:** Included in Green Fee. **Walking Policy:** Mandatory cart. **Walkability:** 3. **Opened:** 1959. **Architect:** Lawrence Packard. **Season:** April-Nov. **High:** May-Sept. **To obtain**

tee times: Call 3 days in advance after 3 p.m. **Miscellaneous:** Reduced fees (weekdays, twilight, juniors), range (grass), credit cards (MC, V).
Reader Comments: Outstanding! ... One of the better courses in city ... Exceptional layout challenging, fair, scenic ... Great traditional layout ... No gimmicks ... A masterpiece ... Wide, sloping fairways, contoured greens and multiple options. Augusta-like design and views. Staff rolls out red carpet.

WEBSTER GOLF CLUB
440 Salt Rd., Webster, 14580, Monroe County, , 10 miles E of Rochester.
★★★½ EAST COURSE
SP-(716)265-1920.
Holes: 18. **Yards:** 6,916/5,710. **Par:** 71/73. **Course Rating:** 73.2/73.0. **Slope:** 128/121. **Green Fee:** $21/$24. **Cart Fee:** $22/person. **Walking Policy:** Walking at certain times. **Walkability:** 2. **Opened:** 1957. **Architect:** James G. Harrison. **Season:** April-Nov. **High:** June-Aug. **To obtain tee times:** Call. **Miscellaneous:** Reduced fees (weekdays), metal spikes, range (grass), credit cards (MC, V).
Reader Comments: Good value ... Much potential ... A good test of golf ... Tougher of the two ... Very nice golf course, very tough ... Excellent condition ... Tight course, well-protected greens ... Great greens ... Good mix of long and short holes, must be accurate to score.
★★★ WEST COURSE
PU- (716)265-1307.
Holes: 18. **Yards:** 6,003/5,400. **Par:** 70/70. **Course Rating:** 66.6/68.5. **Slope:** 106/108. **Green Fee:** $15/$18. **Cart Fee:** $15/person. **Walking Policy:** Unrestricted walking. **Walkability:** 1. **Opened:** 1974. **Architect:** Tom Murphy/Eddie Rieflin. **Season:** April-Nov. **High:** June-Sept. **To obtain tee times:** Call. **Miscellaneous:** Reduced fees (seniors, juniors), metal spikes, credit cards (MC, V).
Reader Comments: Short & good fun ... Not really demanding ... Lacks the attention the East course gets ... Small greens ... Short but fun ... Not as tough as its sister.

★★★½ WELLSVILLE COUNTRY CLUB
SP-Riverside Dr, Wellsville, 14895, Allegany County, (716)593-6337, 30 miles E of Orlean.
Holes: 18. **Yards:** 6,253/5,527. **Par:** 71/72. **Course Rating:** 71.5/70.4. **Slope:** 121/120. **Green Fee:** $30/$30. **Cart Fee:** $13/person. **Walking Policy:** Unrestricted walking. **Walkability:** 1. **Opened:** 1911. **Season:** April-Nov. **High:** June-Aug. **To obtain tee times:** Public may call 1-7 days in advance for availability. **Miscellaneous:** Metal spikes, range (grass), credit cards (MC, V, AE).
Reader Comments: Excellent challenge ... Fun on the right day ... Excellent course with fast & small greens ... Short and simple, nice finisher, small greens and flat ... Tough, tight course ... Good variety of holes ... Accuracy is key, greens are fast and a delight.

★★★½ WEST SAYVILLE GOLF CLUB
PU-Montauk Hwy., West Sayville, 11796, Suffolk County, (516)567-1704, 45 miles E of New York.
Holes: 18. **Yards:** 6,715/5,387. **Par:** 72/72. **Course Rating:** 72.5/71.2. **Slope:** 124/119. **Green Fee:** $22/$35. **Cart Fee:** $14/person. **Walking Policy:** Unrestricted walking. **Walkability:** 1. **Opened:** 1968. **Architect:** William Mitchell. **Season:** March-Dec. **High:** May-Sept. **To obtain tee times:** Nonresidents may call same day for tee times. **Miscellaneous:** Reduced fees (weekdays, low season, twilight, seniors, juniors), range (grass/mats), club rentals, credit cards (MC, V, D).
Reader Comments: Excellent staff. Tricky holes. Open fairways ... Reasonable price ... Fun, windy, links style ... Good layout, challenging in wind ... Good test, wind makes it difficult ... Many golfers ... Short course. Very hard, fast greens ... Above average ... Course, flat, wide fairways, forgiving round.

★★★½ WESTPORT COUNTRY CLUB
PU-Liberty St., Westport, 12993, Essex County, (518)962-4470, (800)600-6655, 90 miles S of Montreal, Canada.
Holes: 18. **Yards:** 6,544/5,256. **Par:** 72/72. **Course Rating:** 71.5/70.5. **Slope:** 120/112. **Green Fee:** $10/$25. **Cart Fee:** $10/cart. **Walking Policy:** Walking at certain times. **Walkability:** 3. **Opened:** 1898. **Architect:** Tom Winton. **Season:** April-Oct. **High:** June-Aug. **To obtain tee times:** Call. **Miscellaneous:** Reduced fees (weekdays, low season, resort guests, twilight, juniors), discount packages, metal spikes, range (grass/mats), club rentals, lodging, credit cards (MC, V, D).
Reader Comments: Wonderful surprise and pleasure to play ... Great course, great service, great price ... Always in excellent shape ... A bit deceiving ... Best greens in area ... Wonderful views. Fair to play. Tough greens ... Layout and scenery best ... Challenging from tips, good test from regular tees.

★★★★ WHITEFACE CLUB ON LAKE PLACID
R-P.O. Box 231, Lake Placid, 12946, Essex County, (518)523-2551, 150 miles N of Albany.
Holes: 18. **Yards:** 6,490/5,635. **Par:** 72/74. **Course Rating:** 70.6/73.9. **Slope:** 123/125. **Green Fee:** $20/$30. **Cart Fee:** $28/cart. **Walking Policy:** Unrestricted walking. **Walkability:** 3. **Opened:** 1898. **Architect:** John Van Kleek. **Season:** May-Oct. **High:** July-Aug. **To obtain tee times:** Call anytime.

Miscellaneous: Reduced fees (weekdays, low season, resort guests, twilight, juniors), discount packages, range (grass), club rentals, lodging, credit cards (MC, V, AE, D).
Reader Comments: Nice atmosphere, friendly people, good course ... Beautiful course, narrow & challenging ... Nice mountain course. Good shape. Foxes steal balls ... Old-time wooded mountain course, great views ... Hilly and narrow.

★★★ WILD WOOD COUNTRY CLUB

SP-1201 W. Rush Rd., Rush, 14543, Monroe County, (716)334-5860, 15 miles S of Rochester.
Holes: 18. **Yards:** 6,431/5,368. **Par:** 71/72. **Course Rating:** 71.0/75.9. **Slope:** 127/129. **Green Fee:** $22/$24. **Cart Fee:** $11/person. **Walking Policy:** Unrestricted walking. **Walkability:** 4.
Opened: 1968. **Architect:** Pete Craig. **Season:** April-Oct. **High:** July-Aug. **To obtain tee times:** Call golf shop. **Miscellaneous:** Reduced fees (low season, seniors), discount packages, range (grass), club rentals, credit cards (MC, V).
Reader Comments: Good layout ... Need to be a mountain goat to walk ... Excellent course, the type you could play regularly ... Shotmaker's delight, conditions improving ... Super resort-type back 9, great value, hard ... Well-manicured greens.

WILLOWBROOK COUNTRY CLUB

SP-4200 Lake Ave., Lockport, 14094, Niagara County, (716)434-0111, 15 miles N of Buffalo.
Holes: 27. **Green Fee:** $14/$21. **Cart Fee:** $12/person. **Walking Policy:** Walking at certain times. **Walkability:** 3. **Opened:** 1956. **Architect:** George Graff/Jim Charbonneau. **Season:** April-Nov. **High:** June-Aug. **To obtain tee times:** Call 7 days in advance.

★★★½ NORTH/SOUTH

Yards: 6,329/4,979. **Par:** 72/72. **Course Rating:** 70.0/67.8. **Slope:** 114/118. **Miscellaneous:** Reduced fees (weekdays, low season, twilight, seniors), discount packages, metal spikes, range (grass), club rentals, credit cards (MC, V).
Reader Comments: Leave driver in bag and place shots ... Challenging course ... Real challenge woods, water, hills, small greens ... Lots of fun golf, makes you think before, during, and after... Good mix of long and really short holes, fun test ... Good value public.

★★★½ NORTH/WEST

Yards: 6,399/5,006. **Par:** 71/71. **Course Rating:** 70.3/68.3. **Slope:** 115/116. **Miscellaneous:** Reduced fees (weekdays, low season, twilight, seniors), discount packages, metal spikes, range (grass), club rentals, credit cards (MC, V), beginner friendly.

★★★½ SOUTH/WEST

Yards: 6,100/4,713. **Par:** 71/71. **Course Rating:** 68.9/66.3. **Slope:** 112/112. **Miscellaneous:** Reduced fees (weekdays, low season, twilight, seniors), discount packages, metal spikes, range (grass), club rentals, credit cards (MC, V), beginner friendly.
Reader Comments: Leave driver in bag and place shots ... Challenging course ... Real challenge woods, water, hills, small greens ... Good mix of long and really short holes, fun test ... Good value public ... Very well maintained, back nine has some very tight holes.

★★★½ WINDHAM COUNTRY CLUB

PU-36 South Street, Windham, 12496, Greene County, (518)734-9910, 45 miles SW of Albany.
E-mail: www.drarich299@aol.com. **Web:** www.windhamcountryclub.com.
Holes: 18. **Yards:** 6,088/4,876. **Par:** 71/72. **Course Rating:** 69.9/68.4. **Slope:** 127/114. **Green Fee:** $11/$30. **Cart Fee:** $26/person. **Walking Policy:** Walking at certain times. **Walkability:** 4.
Opened: 1927. **Architect:** Seth Raynor. **Season:** April-Oct. **High:** June-Sept. **To obtain tee times:** Call 1 day in advance for weekdays. Call on Monday after 3:00 p.m. for weekend.
Miscellaneous: Reduced fees (weekdays, low season, resort guests, twilight, seniors, juniors), discount packages, metal spikes, club rentals, credit cards (MC, V).
Reader Comments: Back 9 is harder than front ... Great views during fall ... Bring extra irons; tough, good grub ... Short ... Small mountain course ... Scenery is great and course plays great

★★½ WINGED PHEASANT GOLF LINKS

SP-1475 Sand Hill Rd., Shortsville, 14548, Ontario County, (716)289-8846, 20 miles SE of Rochester.
Holes: 18. **Yards:** 6,400/5,835. **Par:** 70/72. **Course Rating:** 69.0/72.0. **Slope:** 118/119. **Green Fee:** $21/$23. **Cart Fee:** $24/cart. **Walking Policy:** Walking at certain times. **Walkability:** 3.
Opened: 1963. **Architect:** Pete Craig. **Season:** March-Nov. **High:** June-Aug. **To obtain tee times:** Call 7 days in advance. **Miscellaneous:** Reduced fees (weekdays, low season, twilight, seniors, juniors), range (grass/mats), club rentals, credit cards (MC, V, AE, D).
Reader Comments: Nice people, new 9 holes under way ... Some tough holes, not long but not easy ... Improving conditions, but still needs work ... Small greens ... Several tough par-3 holes ... Small greens ... A good practice course.

NORTH CAROLINA

ANGEL'S TRACE GOLF LINKS
PU-1215 Angel's Club Dr. S.W., Sunset Beach, 28468, Brunswick County, (910)579-2277, (800)718-5733, 18 miles N of N.Myrtle Beach, SC. **E-mail:** angeltrace@nccoast.net. **Web:** www.golfnccoast.com/angels.htm.
★★★½ **NORTH COURSE**
Holes: 18. **Yards:** 6,640/4,524. **Par:** 72/72. **Course Rating:** 73.6/68.2. **Slope:** 139/118. **Green Fee:** $10/$55. **Cart Fee:** $18/person. **Walking Policy:** Mandatory cart. **Walkability:** 3. **Opened:** 1995. **Architect:** Clyde Johnston. **Season:** Year-round. **High:** March-May, Oct.-Nov. **To obtain tee times:** Call golf shop up to 365 days in advance. **Miscellaneous:** Reduced fees (low season, juniors), range (grass), club rentals, credit cards (MC, V, AE).
Reader Comments: Plays longer than it looks ... Rough is murder ... Very narrow fairways ... Excellent track and greens ... Loved it! ... Spacious greens ... Not too tough, just right.
SOUTH COURSE
Holes: 18. **Yards:** 6,866/4,811. **Par:** 72/72. **Course Rating:** 74.1/67.7. **Slope:** 139/121. **Green Fee:** $10/$55. **Cart Fee:** $18/person. **Walking Policy:** Mandatory cart. **Walkability:** 3. **Opened:** 1995. **Architect:** Clyde Johnston. **Season:** Year-round. **High:** March-May/Oct.-Nov. **To obtain tee times:** Call golf shop up to 365 days in advance. **Miscellaneous:** Reduced fees (low season, juniors), range (grass), club rentals, credit cards (MC, V, AE).

★★★★½ BALD HEAD ISLAND CLUB *Service, Value, Pace+*
R-P.O. Box 3070, Bald Head Island, 28461, Brunswick County, (910)457-7310, (800)234-1666, 30 miles S of Wilmington.
Holes: 18. **Yards:** 6,855/4,810. **Par:** 72/72. **Course Rating:** 74.3/70.1. **Slope:** 139/117. **Green Fee:** $44/$78. **Cart Fee:** $17/person. **Walking Policy:** Walking at certain times. **Walkability:** 2. **Opened:** 1975. **Architect:** George Cobb. **Season:** Year-round. **High:** May-Sept. **To obtain tee times:** Call pro shop seven days in advance. **Miscellaneous:** Reduced fees (low season, resort guests, juniors), discount packages, range (grass), club rentals, lodging, credit cards (MC, V, AE, D).
Reader Comments: Good place to walk in the late afternoon ... An adventure arriving by ferry! ... Really good layout ... Hope nobody else finds it ... Water comes into play on many holes and factoring in gusting winds makes for an unforgettable experience ... Heavenly. Spectacular scenery ... View from 17 is first rate.

★★★½ BAYONET AT PUPPY CREEK
PU-349 S. Parker Church Rd., Raeford, 28736, Hoke County, (910)904-1500, (888)229-6638, 8 miles W of Fayetteville. **E-mail:** bayonetpc@aol.com. **Web:** www.bayonetgolf.com.
Holes: 18. **Yards:** 7,036/4,453. **Par:** 72/72. **Course Rating:** 74.0/67.5. **Slope:** 134/115. **Green Fee:** $20/$32. **Cart Fee:** $12/person. **Walking Policy:** Walking at certain times. **Walkability:** 3. **Opened:** 1995. **Architect:** Willard Byrd. **Season:** Year-round. **High:** March-May; Sept-Oct. **To obtain tee times:** Call. **Miscellaneous:** Reduced fees (weekdays, low season, resort guests, twilight, seniors, juniors), discount packages, range (grass), club rentals, credit cards (MC, V, AE).
Reader Comments: A good test ... Fun course, not too hard ... Almost empty when I played ... Seek and you will be well pleased ... Sleeper, well worth trip ... A little hard to find ... Used every club ... Tough greens, very demanding.

★★★★ BEACON RIDGE GOLF & COUNTRY CLUB
R-6000 Longleaf Dr., West End, 27376, Moore County, (910)673-2950, (800)416-5204, 10 miles W of Pinehurst.
Holes: 18. **Yards:** 6,414/4,730. **Par:** 72/72. **Course Rating:** 70.7/67.1. **Slope:** 125/115. **Green Fee:** $20/$36. **Cart Fee:** $16/person. **Walking Policy:** Walking at certain times. **Walkability:** N/A. **Opened:** 1988. **Architect:** Gene Hamm. **Season:** Year-round. **High:** Spring/Fall. **To obtain tee times:** Call anytime. **Miscellaneous:** Reduced fees (weekdays, low season, resort guests, twilight, seniors, juniors), discount packages, metal spikes, range (grass), club rentals, lodging, credit cards (MC, V, D).
Reader Comments: Small, fast, undulating greens ... Bring your 'A' short game ... Tees and fairways excellent, greens to fast ... Nice layout ... A bit out of the way, but worth the trip ... Most greens elevated.

★★★ BEAU RIVAGE RESORT & GOLF CLUB
R-649 Rivage Promenade, Wilmington, 28412, New Hanover County, (910)392-9022, (800)628-7080, 7 miles S of Wilmington.
Holes: 18. **Yards:** 6,709/4,612. **Par:** 72/72. **Course Rating:** 72.5/67.1. **Slope:** 136/114. **Green Fee:** $20/$40. **Cart Fee:** Included in Green Fee. **Walking Policy:** Mandatory cart. **Walkability:** 5. **Opened:** 1988. **Architect:** Joe Gestner/Eddie Lewis. **Season:** Year-round. **High:** March-Sept. **To obtain tee times:** Call golf shop. **Miscellaneous:** Reduced fees (weekdays, low season, resort guests, twilight), discount packages, range (grass), club rentals, lodging (30 rooms), credit cards (MC, V, AE, D).
Reader Comments: Dry course when others are wet ... A lot of blind shots ... Too many layup holes, great par 3s ... Good bent greens in the hot summer ... Fun little beach course ... A great day of golf, a test for all skill levels.

★½   BEL AIRE GOLF CLUB
1517 Pleasant Ridge Rd., Greensboro, 27409, Guilford County, (919)668-2413.
Special Notes: Call club for further information.

★★★   BELVEDERE PLANTATION GOLF & COUNTRY CLUB
SP-2368 Country Club Dr., Hampstead, 28443, Pender County, (910)270-2703, 15 miles NE of Wilmington.
Holes: 18. **Yards:** 6,401/4,992. **Par:** 71/72. **Course Rating:** 72.3/69.8. **Slope:** 132/117. **Green Fee:** $20/$45. **Cart Fee:** Included in Green Fee. **Walking Policy:** Mandatory cart. **Walkability:** 2. **Opened:** 1970. **Architect:** Russell Burney. **Season:** Year-round. **High:** March-May. **To obtain tee times:** Call one week in advance. **Miscellaneous:** Reduced fees (low season, resort guests, twilight, juniors), discount packages, range (grass), club rentals, lodging, credit cards (MC, V).
Reader Comments: Nice short course with lots of O.B. ... Fast, elevated greens ... Great layout ... Tougher than it looks.

★★★★   BIRKDALE GOLF CLUB
PU-16500 Birkdale Commons Pkwy., Huntersville, 28078, Mecklenburg County, (704)895-8038, 15 miles N of Charlotte. **Web:** www.birkdale.com.
Holes: 18. **Yards:** 7,013/5,175. **Par:** 72/72. **Course Rating:** 74.1/69.7. **Slope:** 138/123. **Green Fee:** $44/$64. **Cart Fee:** Included in Green Fee. **Walking Policy:** Unrestricted walking. **Walkability:** 3. **Opened:** 1997. **Architect:** Arnold Palmer/Ed Seay. **Season:** Year-round. **High:** April-June; Sept.-Oct. **To obtain tee times:** Call up to 8 days in advance. **Miscellaneous:** Reduced fees (low season, twilight, juniors), range (grass/mats), caddies, club rentals, credit cards (MC, V, AE).
Reader Comments: Needs maturity, staff is friendly, course isn't ... New course on it's way to excellent. Fine layout ... Another winner from Arnie, fantastic finish ... Too many powerlines ... Greens are very fast.

★★★½   BLACK MOUNTAIN GOLF COURSE
PU-106 Montreat Rd., Black Mountain, 28711, Buncombe County, (828)669-2710, 15 miles E of Asheville.
Holes: 18. **Yards:** 6,181/5,780. **Par:** 71/71. **Course Rating:** 69.5/68.1. **Slope:** 129/113. **Green Fee:** N/A. **Walkability:** N/A. **Opened:** 1928. **Architect:** Ross Taylor. **Season:** Year-round. **High:** May-Oct. **Miscellaneous:** Metal spikes, credit cards (MC, V).
Reader Comments: Wonderful view of Intercoastal. ... Tight, tough ... 747-yard par 6 on the side of a hill! ... Course condition improves annually ... Great greens ... Scenery is unbelievable.

★★   BLAIR PARK GOLF CLUB
PM-1901 S. Main St., High Point, 27260, Guilford County, (336)883-3497, 18 miles SW of Greensboro.
Holes: 18. **Yards:** 6,449/5,171. **Par:** 72/72. **Course Rating:** 70.8/69.5. **Slope:** 122/113. **Green Fee:** $11/$13. **Cart Fee:** $11/person. **Walking Policy:** Walking at certain times. **Walkability:** 3. **Opened:** 1936. **Architect:** Rick Briley. **Season:** Year-round. **High:** June-Aug. **To obtain tee times:** Call 2 days in advance. **Miscellaneous:** Reduced fees (twilight, seniors, juniors), metal spikes, club rentals.

★★★★   BLUE RIDGE COUNTRY CLUB
R-Hwy. 221, Linville Falls, 28647, Avery County, (828)756-4013, (800)845-8430, 10 miles N of Marion. **Web:** www.blueridgecc.com.
Holes: 18. **Yards:** 6,862/5,203. **Par:** 72/72. **Course Rating:** 72.9/70.4. **Slope:** 128/116. **Green Fee:** $25/$48. **Cart Fee:** Included in Green Fee. **Walking Policy:** Unrestricted walking. **Walkability:** 3. **Opened:** 1995. **Architect:** Clifton/Ezell/Clifton. **Season:** Year-round. **High:** June-Oct. **To obtain tee times:** Call golf shop. **Miscellaneous:** Reduced fees (weekdays, low season, resort guests, twilight, seniors, juniors), discount packages, range (grass), club rentals, lodging (13 rooms), credit cards (MC, V, AE, D).
Reader Comments: Tight, nice big greens ... Lots of love grass ... No. 3 is not drivable, believe me ... A favorite ... Solid golf in mountains, must be precise ... A hidden gem nestled at the base of the Blue Ridge Mountains. A river runs through most of the course ... Wonderful natural setting ... Rough is unplayable ... Very enjoyable.

★★★½   BOGUE BANKS COUNTRY CLUB
SP-152 Oak Leaf Dr., Pine Knoll Shores, 28512, Carteret County, (252)726-1034, 5 miles S of Morehead City.
Holes: 18. **Yards:** 6,047/5,079. **Par:** 71/73. **Course Rating:** 68.6/68.8. **Slope:** 116/116. **Green Fee:** $17/$33. **Cart Fee:** $12/person. **Walking Policy:** Unrestricted walking. **Walkability:** 1. **Opened:** 1971. **Architect:** Maurice Brackett. **Season:** Year-round. **High:** May-Aug. **To obtain tee times:** Call Pro Shop. **Miscellaneous:** Reduced fees (weekdays, low season, twilight), discount packages, club rentals, credit cards (MC, V), beginner friendly (beginner tees, clinics).

Reader Comments: Nos. 10, 11 and 12 just beautiful ... Strong wind off waterway ... Fun course, pretty holes ... Keep It straight off tee ... Tight, windy and a challenge ... Wonderful views ... Short, good layout.

★★★½ BOONE GOLF CLUB

PU-433 Fairway Drive , Boone, 28607, Watauga County, (828)264-8760, 90 miles N of Charlotte. **E-mail:** info@boonegolfclub.com. **Web:** www.boonegolfclub.com/northcarolina. **Holes:** 18. **Yards:** 6,401/5,199. **Par:** 71/71. **Course Rating:** 70.1/69.1. **Slope:** 120/113. **Green Fee:** $26/$37. **Cart Fee:** $11/person. **Walking Policy:** Unrestricted walking. **Walkability:** 3. **Opened:** 1959. **Architect:** Ellis Maples. **Season:** April-Nov. **High:** June-Aug. **To obtain tee times:** Call up to 7 days in advance. **Miscellaneous:** Reduced fees (weekdays, low season, twilight), discount packages, metal spikes, club rentals, credit cards (MC, V).
Reader Comments: Good food and people ... Hilly ... The scenery in autumn is great ... Very fast undulating greens, quite pretty ... Beautiful & green and a lot of fun ... Very friendly ... A real gem with the Appalachian Mountains as a back drop ... Worth playing again.

★★★½ BRANDYWINE BAY GOLF & COUNTRY CLUB

PU-224 Brandywine Blvd., Morehead City, 28557, Carteret County, (252)247-2541, 40 miles E of New Bern.
Holes: 18. **Yards:** 6,609/5,191. **Par:** 71/71. **Course Rating:** 72.0/68.6. **Slope:** 121/113. **Green Fee:** $18/$23. **Cart Fee:** $15/person. **Walking Policy:** Walking at certain times. **Walkability:** 1. **Opened:** 1980. **Architect:** Bruce Devlin. **Season:** Year-round. **High:** April-Oct. **To obtain tee times:** Call anytime. **Miscellaneous:** Reduced fees (low season, twilight), discount packages, club rentals, credit cards (MC, V).
Reader Comments: Great fairways, fast greens ... Not long, but challenging ... Full of doglegs ... Must drive the ball well ... Nice layout ... Lots of hazards, woods & water ... Need all shots.

★½ BRIARCREEK GOLF CLUB

P.O. Box 440, High Shoals, 28077, Gaston County, (704)922-4208.
Special Notes: Call club for further information.

★★★ BRICK LANDING PLANTATION GOLF & COUNTRY CLUB

R-1900 Goose Creek Rd., Ocean Isle Beach, 28469, Brunswick County, (910)754-5545, (800)438-3006, 15 miles N of N. Myrtle Beach, SC.
Holes: 18. **Yards:** 6,752/4,707. **Par:** 72/71. **Course Rating:** 72.1/67.0. **Slope:** 141/116. **Green Fee:** $31/$61. **Cart Fee:** $20/person. **Walking Policy:** Mandatory cart. **Walkability:** 2. **Opened:** 1988. **Architect:** H.M. Brazeal. **Season:** Year-round. **High:** March-April/Oct. **To obtain tee times:** Call pro shop. **Miscellaneous:** Reduced fees (twilight, juniors), discount packages, range (grass), club rentals, lodging (38 rooms), credit cards (MC, V).
Reader Comments: Target golf ... Buy the yardage book and believe it! ... Water on 16 holes ... Bold and beautiful course.... 18 holes in a 15-hole envelope ... Challenging, can't wait to go back ... Tight and windy ... Several beautiful waterway holes, but design uneven and quirky ... Loved it.

★★½ BRIERWOOD GOLF CLUB

SP-Hwy. 179, Shallotte, 28459, Brunswick County, (910)754-4660, (888)274-3796, 35 miles S of Wilmington.
Holes: 18. **Yards:** 6,607/4,812. **Par:** 72/72. **Course Rating:** 71.0/67.0. **Slope:** 129/114. **Green Fee:** $20/$50. **Cart Fee:** Included in Green Fee. **Walking Policy:** Mandatory cart. **Walkability:** 1. **Opened:** 1966. **Architect:** Ben Ward. **Season:** Year-round. **High:** April-Oct. **To obtain tee times:** Call golf shop. **Miscellaneous:** Reduced fees (weekdays, low season, twilight, seniors), discount packages, club rentals, credit cards (MC, V), beginner friendly.
Reader Comments: Too many golfers on 'packages'–unlimited play ... Older, but well kept ... Good value for couples ... Pleasure to play ... Really enjoyed the course.

★★ BROADMOOR GOLF LINKS

PU-101 French Broad Lane, Fletcher, 28732, Henderson County, (828)687-1500, 7 miles S of Asheville. **E-mail:** par@brinet.com.
Holes: 18. **Yards:** 6,921/5,082. **Par:** 72/72. **Course Rating:** 73.3/69.7. **Slope:** 132/117. **Green Fee:** $28/$34. **Walking Policy:** Mandatory cart. **Walkability:** 1. **Opened:** 1992. **Architect:** Karl Litten. **Season:** Year-round. **High:** April-Oct. **To obtain tee times:** Call up to two weeks in advance. **Miscellaneous:** Reduced fees (low season, seniors), metal spikes, range (grass), club rentals, credit cards (MC, V).
Special Notes: Formerly French Broad Golf Center.

★★★½ BROKEN ARROW GOLF LINKS

SP-1000 Broken Arrow Dr., Statesville, 28677, Iredell County, (704)873-4653, 10 miles W of Charlotte.
Holes: 18. **Yards:** 7,086/4,548. **Par:** 72/72. **Course Rating:** 73.8/66.6. **Slope:** 133/113. **Green Fee:** $28/$38. **Cart Fee:** Included in Green Fee. **Walking Policy:** Walking at certain times. **Walkability:** 5. **Opened:** 1998. **Architect:** Lennie Younce. **Season:** Year-round. **High:** May-

August. **To obtain tee times:** Nonmembers can call 7 days in advance. **Miscellaneous:** Range (grass), club rentals, credit cards (MC, V).
Reader Comments: Tough course ... Mountain course, narrow and challenging ... Great layout, needs maturing ... Very scenic ... Must drive in fairway.

BRUNSWICK PLANTATION GOLF RESORT
R-Hwy. 17 N., Calabash, 28467, Brunswick County, (910)287-7888, (800)848-0290, 25 miles N of Myrtle Beach, SC. **Web:** www.brunswickplantation.com.
Holes: 27.**Green Fee:** $35/$80. **Cart Fee:** Included in Green Fee. **Walking Policy:** Mandatory cart. **Walkability:** 1. **Opened:** 1992. **Architect:** Willard Byrd, Clyde Johnston. **Season:** Year-round. **High:** March-April/Oct. **To obtain tee times:** Obtain tee times through Myrtle Beach packages or call direct. **Miscellaneous:** Reduced fees (weekdays, low season, resort guests, twilight, juniors), discount packages, range (grass), rentals, lodging (150 rooms), credit cards (MC, V, AE, D), beginner friendly.
★★★½ **DOGWOOD/AZALEA**
Yards: 6,772/5,087. **Par:** 72/72. **Course Rating:** 72.7/70.4. **Slope:** 131/125.
★★★½ **MAGNOLIA/AZALEA**
Yards: 6,717/5,140. **Par:** 72/72. **Course Rating:** 72.7/70.4. **Slope:** 131/125.
★★★½ **MAGNOLIA/DOGWOOD**
Yards: 6,845/5,099. **Par:** 72/72. **Course Rating:** 72.8/70.4. **Slope:** 132/126.
Reader Comments: Great pro shop ... A challenge for all levels ... Good restaurant ... Deal for junior golfers ... I'd do it again! ... Lightning greens ... Became one of my favorites ... Crowded on weekends ... Lovely setting.

★★½ BRUSHY MOUNTAIN GOLF CLUB
P.O. Box 457, Taylorsville, 28681, Alexander County, (704)632-4804.
Special Notes: Call club for further information.

BRYAN PARK & GOLF CLUB
PM-6275 Bryan Park Rd., Brown Summit, 27214, Guilford County, (910)375-2200, 10 miles NE of Greensboro.
★★★★ **CHAMPIONS COURSE** *Value*
Holes: 18. **Yards:** 7,135/5,395. **Par:** 72/72. **Course Rating:** 74.4/71.0. **Slope:** 130/122. **Green Fee:** $22/$26. **Cart Fee:** $12/person. **Walking Policy:** Walking at certain times. **Walkability:** 4. **Opened:** 1990. **Architect:** Rees Jones. **Season:** Year-round. **High:** April-Sept. **To obtain tee times:** Call up to 30 days in advance for weekdays; 7 days for weekend and holidays.
Miscellaneous: Reduced fees (weekdays, low season, twilight, seniors, juniors), discount packages, range (grass), club rentals, credit cards (MC, V, AE).
Notes: Ranked 9th in 1999 Best in State; 12th in 1996 America's Top 75 Affordable Courses.
Reader Comments: Very demanding. Public jewel ... Worth every penny ... Outstanding championship layout ... Plays better in summer and fall months ... Bring your camera ... Do not under-club the back nine ... Back nine peaceful as heaven ... Lots of sand & water.
★★★½ **PLAYERS COURSE**
Holes: 18. **Yards:** 7,076/5,260. **Par:** 72/72. **Course Rating:** 73.0/70.5. **Slope:** 128/120. **Green Fee:** $13/$30. **Cart Fee:** $10/person. **Walking Policy:** Unrestricted walking. **Walkability:** 3. **Opened:** 1974. **Architect:** George Cobb/Rees Jones. **Season:** Year-round. **High:** April-Sept. **To obtain tee times:** Call up to one month in advance for weekdays. Call Wednesday at 8 a.m. for weekend and holidays. **Miscellaneous:** Reduced fees (weekdays, low season, twilight, seniors, juniors), discount packages, range (grass), club rentals, credit cards (MC, V, AE), beginner friendly.
Reader Comments: Not too demanding, but still enjoyable ... Nice layout, varied terrain ... Not as tough as Champions ... Killer 1st hole ... Bring your best game, A and B players only ... Quick greens, lots of play ... Long walk between holes ... Bear from the blues.

★★ BUNCOMBE COUNTY MUNICIPAL GOLF CLUB
PM-226 Fairway Dr., Asheville, 28805, Buncombe County, (828)298-1867.
Holes: 18. **Yards:** 6,814/4,744. **Par:** 72/72. **Course Rating:** 71.1/67.2. **Slope:** 122/115. **Green Fee:** $15/$20. **Cart Fee:** $12/person. **Walking Policy:** Unrestricted walking. **Walkability:** 2. **Opened:** 1927. **Architect:** Donald Ross. **Season:** Year-round. **High:** April-Oct. **To obtain tee times:** Call golf shop for weekends only. **Miscellaneous:** Re-duced fees (weekdays, twilight, juniors), metal spikes, club rentals, credit cards (MC, V).

★★★★ CALABASH GOLF LINKS
PU-820 Thomasboro Rd., Calabash, 28467, Brunswick County, (910)575-5000, (800)841-5971, 10 miles N of Myrtle Beach, SC. **E-mail:** info@calabashgolf.com. **Web:** www.calabashgolf.com.
Holes: 18. **Yards:** 6,641/4,907. **Par:** 72/72. **Course Rating:** 72.0/68.4. **Slope:** 128/108. **Green Fee:** $33/$62. **Cart Fee:** Included in Green Fee. **Walking Policy:** Mandatory cart. **Walkability:** 1. **Opened:** 1997. **Architect:** Willard Byrd. **Season:** Year-round. **High:** Sept.-Nov.; March-May. **To obtain tee times:** Call golf shop. **Miscellaneous:** Reduced fees (low season, resort guests, twilight, juniors), discount packages, range (grass), club rentals, credit cards (MC, V, AE, D).

Reader Comments: If you like golf you will love this one ... Nice layout in great shape, fairways and greens like carpet ... Where are the marshals?... Excellent in every respect, but overbooked and slow pace ... Good course for youngsters and oldsters ... Loved it.

★★★½ CAPE GOLF & RACQUET CLUB

SP-535 The Cape Blvd., Wilmington, 28412, New Hanover County, (910)799-3110, (800)291-9847, 55 miles N of Myrtle Beach, SC.
Holes: 18. **Yards:** 6,790/4,948. **Par:** 72/72. **Course Rating:** 73.1/69.3. **Slope:** 133/118. **Green Fee:** $25/$45. **Cart Fee:** Included in Green Fee. **Walking Policy:** Mandatory cart. **Walkability:** 3. **Opened:** 1985. **Architect:** Gene Hamn. **Season:** Year-round. **High:** March-July; Sept. **To obtain tee times:** Call golf shop. **Miscellaneous:** Reduced fees (weekdays, low season, resort guests, twilight, seniors), discount packages, metal spikes, range (grass), club rentals, lodging, credit cards (MC, V, AE, D).
Reader Comments: Consistent Bermuda greens ... Tough at times ... Good variety of holes ... Fun to play ... A little bit of links style.

★★★★ THE CAROLINA

PU-277 Avenue of the Carolina, Whispering Pines, 28327, Moore County, (910)949-2811, (888)725-6372, 45 miles S of Raleigh.
Holes: 18. **Yards:** 6,928/4,828. **Par:** 72/72. **Course Rating:** 73.2/68.6. **Slope:** 142/117. **Green Fee:** $49/$85. **Cart Fee:** Included in Green Fee. **Walking Policy:** Unrestricted walking. **Walkability:** 4. **Opened:** 1997. **Architect:** Arnold Palmer/Ed Seay. **Season:** Year-round. **High:** March-Oct. **To obtain tee times:** Credit card required if reserving a tee time longer than 30 days. **Miscellaneous:** Reduced fees (weekdays, low season, twilight, juniors), discount packages, range (grass), club rentals, credit cards (MC, V, AE, D).
Reader Comments: Fun layout, fast greens, great staff ... Don't miss this new course ... Tough, sloped greens ... Every hole is different ... Will play again ... Palmer has outdone himself ... Summer coupons ... Feels like it has been around a long time ... Bring lots of golf balls ... Good greens, true and all the same speed.

★★★ CAROLINA LAKES GOLF CLUB

PU-53 Carolina Lakes Rd., Sanford, 27330, Harnett County, (919)499-5421, (800)942-8633, 18 miles S of Sanford. **E-mail:** clakes@alltel.net. **Web:** www.fayettevillenc.com/carolina-lakes.
Holes: 18. **Yards:** 6,400/5,010. **Par:** 70/70. **Course Rating:** 70.7/67.0. **Slope:** 117/110. **Green Fee:** $10/$18. **Cart Fee:** $12/person. **Walking Policy:** Walking at certain times. **Walkability:** 3. **Opened:** 1981. **Architect:** Roger Rulewich/Jim Hickey. **Season:** Year-round. **High:** March-May. **To obtain tee times:** Call up to one week in advance. **Miscellaneous:** Reduced fees (weekdays, low season, resort guests, twilight, seniors, juniors), discount packages, range (grass/mats), club rentals, credit cards (MC, V).
Reader Comments: Short, fun course for all skill levels ... Off the beaten path, excellent greens ... Difficult greens will make you cry ... Good test of skill ... Rolling terrain; big greens.

CAROLINA NATIONAL GOLF CLUB

SP-1643 Goley Hewett Rd., S.E., Bolivia, 28422, Brunswick County, (910)755-5200, (888)200-6455. **E-mail:** rslone6590@aol.com. **Web:** www.carolinanatl.com.
Holes: 27.**Green Fee:** $35/$80. **Cart Fee:** Included in Green Fee. **Walking Policy:** Mandatory cart. **Walkability:** 2. **Opened:** 1998. **Architect:** Fred Couples. **Season:** Year-round. **High:** Feb.-April. **To obtain tee times:** Call, through internet or Myrtle Beach Golf Holiday. **Miscellaneous:** Reduced fees (weekdays, low season, juniors), discount packages, range (grass), club rentals, credit cards (MC, V, AE, D), beginner friendly (clinics).
★★★★½ EGRET/HERON *Pace*
Yards: 7,017/4,759. **Par:** 72/72. **Course Rating:** 73.4/63.5. **Slope:** 136/116.
★★★★½ EGRET/IBIS *Pace*
Yards: 6,944/4,631. **Par:** 72/72. **Course Rating:** 74.0/67.1. **Slope:** 147/111.
★★★★½ HERON/IBIS *Pace*
Yards: 6,961/4,548. **Par:** 72/72. **Course Rating:** 74.2/66.6. **Slope:** 145/114.

★★★ CAROLINA PINES GOLF & COUNTRY CLUB

SP-390 Carolina Pines Blvd., New Bern, 28560, Craven County, (252)444-1000, (800)465-3718, 15 miles E of New Bern.
Holes: 18. **Yards:** 6,280/4,766. **Par:** 72/72. **Course Rating:** 70.1/67.8. **Slope:** 124/116. **Green Fee:** N/A/$18. **Cart Fee:** $10/person. **Walking Policy:** Walking at certain times. **Walkability:** 2. **Opened:** 1968. **Architect:** Ron Borsset. **Season:** Year round. **High:** April-Nov. **To obtain tee times:** Call golf shop for tee time info. **Miscellaneous:** Reduced fees (low season), discount packages, range (grass), club rentals, lodging, credit cards (MC, V).
Reader Comments: Fun layout, great folks ... Short, placement type course ... 15th hole one of best in NC ... Many houses along fairways. Slice one, you've bought window.

★★★ CAROLINA SHORES GOLF & COUNTRY CLUB
PU-99 Carolina Shores Dr., Calabash, 28467, Brunswick County, (910)579-2181, (800)579-8292, 7 miles N of Myrtle Beach.
Holes: 18. **Yards:** 6,783/6,231. **Par:** 72/72. **Course Rating:** 72.4/73.0. **Slope:** 128/122. **Green Fee:** $16/$44. **Cart Fee:** $20/person. **Walking Policy:** Mandatory cart. **Walkability:** 2. **Opened:** 1974. **Architect:** Tom Jackson. **Season:** Year-round. **High:** March-April; Oct.-Nov. **To obtain tee times:** Call golf shop. **Miscellaneous:** Reduced fees (low season), metal spikes, range (grass), club rentals, credit cards (MC, V, AE).
Reader Comments: You like sand, we got sand ... Bring a beach towel, you'll spend your day in the sand ... Challenges your driver, wide open in summer ... Don't forget your sand wedge ... I like this one ... They scattered some fairways amongst the sand ... Good test from back tees.

★★★½ CHARLOTTE GOLF LINKS
PU-11500 Providence Rd., Charlotte, 28277, Mecklenburg County, (704)846-7990. **Web:** www.charlottegolf.com.
Holes: 18. **Yards:** 6,700/5,279. **Par:** 71/72. **Course Rating:** 71.5/70.3. **Slope:** 121/117. **Green Fee:** $16/$33. **Cart Fee:** $13/person. **Walking Policy:** Walking at certain times. **Walkability:** 2. **Opened:** 1993. **Architect:** Tom Doak. **Season:** Year-round. **High:** April-Nov. **To obtain tee times:** Call one week in advance (704)358-GOLF. **Miscellaneous:** Reduced fees (weekdays, low season, twilight, seniors, juniors), metal spikes, range (grass), club rentals, credit cards (MC, V, AE).
Reader Comments: Tough par 3s ... Very friendly ... Too difficult for high handicappers ... Not too fond of links style, but course is challenging ... Great design, needs time to grow ... Tough from the tips ... Easy if you stay out of the tall grass ... Target golf ... Great practice facility.

★★½ CHARLOTTE NATIONAL GOLF CLUB
SP-6920 Howey Bottoms Rd., Indian Trail, 28079, Union County, (704)882-8282, 15 miles E of Charlotte.
Holes: 18. **Yards:** 7,227/5,423. **Par:** 72/72. **Course Rating:** 74.9/71.3. **Slope:** 129/127. **Green Fee:** $22/$45. **Cart Fee:** Included in Green Fee. **Walking Policy:** Walking at certain times. **Walkability:** 3. **Opened:** 1996. **Architect:** Russell Breeden. **Season:** Year-round. **High:** March-Oct. **To obtain tee times:** Call golf shop. **Miscellaneous:** Reduced fees (weekdays, low season, seniors), range (grass/mats), club rentals, credit cards (MC, V, AE).
Reader Comments: Great greens, tough from back tees ... Spacious, forgiving, needs a decent clubhouse ... Course generous to stray hitter ... Play from back tees ... Will get better with age.

★★★ CHATUGE SHORES GOLF COURSE
PU-260 Golf Course Rd., Hayesville, 28904, Clay County, (704)389-8940, 110 miles SW of Asheville.
Holes: 18. **Yards:** 6,687/4,950. **Par:** 72/72. **Course Rating:** 71.8/68.8. **Slope:** 126/118. **Green Fee:** $18/$20. **Cart Fee:** $8/person. **Walking Policy:** Unrestricted walking. **Walkability:** 3. **Opened:** 1971. **Architect:** John V. Townsend. **Season:** Year-round. **High:** June-Aug. **To obtain tee times:** Call up to 3 days in advance. **Miscellaneous:** Metal spikes, range (grass/mats), club rentals, credit cards (MC, V).
Reader Comments: Well laid out, mountain course, greens always good ... Good course but weird layout ... Simply a good test of golf ... Beautiful setting ... Tough greens, great character.

★★ CHEROKEE HILLS GOLF & COUNTRY CLUB
R-Harshaw Rd., Murphy, 28906, Cherokee County, (704)837-5853, (800)334-3905, 90 miles N of Atlanta.
Holes: 18. **Yards:** 6,724/5,172. **Par:** 72/72. **Course Rating:** 70.0/68.0. **Slope:** 113/117. **Green Fee:** N/A/$15. **Cart Fee:** $11/person. **Walking Policy:** Walking at certain times. **Walkability:** 4. **Opened:** 1969. **Architect:** Wells and West Inc. **Season:** Year-round. **High:** May-Nov. **To obtain tee times:** Call 48 hours in advance. Tee times can also be made at the same time as reservation of golf package. **Miscellaneous:** Reduced fees (resort guests, juniors), discount packages, metal spikes, range (grass), club rentals, lodging, credit cards (MC, V, AE).

★★★½ CHEVIOT HILLS GOLF CLUB
PU-7301 Capital Blvd., Raleigh, 27616, Wake County, (919)876-9920.
Holes: 18. **Yards:** 6,485/4,965. **Par:** 71/71. **Course Rating:** 70.3/66.5. **Slope:** 116/114. **Green Fee:** $16/$25. **Cart Fee:** $11/person. **Walking Policy:** Walking at certain times. **Walkability:** 3. **Opened:** 1930. **Architect:** Gene Hamm. **Season:** Year-round. **High:** Spring-Fall. **To obtain tee times:** Call up to 7 days in advance for weekdays; Tuesday prior for weekends. **Miscellaneous:** Metal spikes, range (mats), club rentals, credit cards (MC, V).
Reader Comments: Don't be fooled by the short yardage, still fairly tough ... Good variety and par 3s ... Saturdays are off limits here ... Use all of your clubs ... Great layout, nice greens ... Nice course, but it's closed 'til noon on Sundays ... A hike from 17th to 18th.

★★★½ CLEGHORN PLANTATION GOLF & COUNTRY CLUB
PU-200 Golf Circle, Rutherfordton, 28139, Rutherford County, (704)286-9117, 70 miles W of Charlotte. **E-mail:** cleghorngolf@blueridge.net.

Holes: 18. Yards: 6,903/4,751. Par: 72/73. Course Rating: 74.6/68.1. Slope: 134/111. Green Fee: $24/$32. Cart Fee: Included in Green Fee. Walking Policy: Mandatory cart. Walkability: 3. Opened: 1969. Architect: George Cobb. Season: Year-round. High: April-Sept. To obtain tee times: Call in advance. Miscellaneous: Reduced fees (weekdays, seniors), discount packages, range (grass), club rentals, credit cards (MC, V).

Reader Comments: Brutal from tips ... Excellent layout, beautiful setting ... Tough mountain layout ... Requires total concentration ... Hilly, difficult, worth playing ... Must hit long irons ... Stay out of rough ... No room for error here.

★★★½ THE CLUB AT LONGLEAF

SP-2001 Midland Rd., Southern Pines, 28387, Moore County, (910)692-6100, (800)889-5323, 60 miles S of Raleigh. E-mail: longleaf@pinehurst.net. Web: www.danmaples.com/longleaf.

Holes: 18. Yards: 6,600/4,719. Par: 71/71. Course Rating: 69.7/65.7. Slope: 117/108. Green Fee: $48/$98. Cart Fee: Included in Green Fee. Walking Policy: Mandatory cart. Walkability: 3. Opened: 1988. Architect: Dan Maples. Season: Year-round. High: March-May/Sept.-Oct. To obtain tee times: Call the above 800 number. Miscellaneous: Reduced fees (weekdays, low season, resort guests, twilight, juniors), discount packages, range (grass), club rentals, lodging, credit cards (MC, V).

Reader Comments: Course has 2 different and diverse nines ... Easy, fun course.... Plain Jane course, good for practice ... Will come back when I retire ... Back 9 much nicer than front ... Pinehurst style at a bargain ... Tricky greens make play unfair ... Come here for a nice break from tougher Pinehurst courses.

COUNTRY CLUB OF WHISPERING PINES

SP-2 Clubhouse Blvd., Whispering Pines, 28327, Moore County, (910)949-3000, 55 miles S of Raleigh. Web: www.whisperingpinesnc.com.

★★★ EAST COURSE

Holes: 18. Yards: 7,138/5,542. Par: 72/72. Course Rating: 73.9/72.0. Slope: 125/123. Green Fee: $30/$60. Cart Fee: $16/person. Walking Policy: Mandatory cart. Walkability: 2. Opened: 1959. Architect: Ellis Maples. Season: Year-round. High: March-Oct. To obtain tee times: Call in advance. Miscellaneous: Reduced fees (low season, resort guests, juniors), range (grass), club rentals, lodging (40 rooms), credit cards (MC, V).

Reader Comments: Good condition ... Bring driver ... Just plain nice folks ... Enjoyable ... Fair course over sand hills and pine trees ... Greens small and fast.

★★★ WEST COURSE

Holes: 18. Yards: 6,363/5,135. Par: 71/71. Course Rating: 70.3/69.8. Slope: 128/121. Green Fee: $30/$60. Cart Fee: $15/person. Walking Policy: Mandatory cart. Walkability: 2. Opened: 1959. Architect: Ellis Maples. Season: Year-round. High: March-Oct. To obtain tee times: Call two days in advance. Miscellaneous: Reduced fees (low season, resort guests, juniors), range (grass), club rentals, lodging (40 rooms), credit cards (MC, V).

Reader Comments: Fun ... 9 holes hilly; 9 holes level; greens mixed size ... Lots of water for the Pinehurst area.

★★★★ CROOKED CREEK GOLF CLUB

SP-4621 Shady Greens Dr., Fuquay-Varina, 27526, Wake County, (919)557-7529, 12 miles S of Raleigh. E-mail: jhillccgc@aol.com. Web: www.playcrookedcreek.com.

Holes: 18. Yards: 6,271/4,635. Par: 71/71. Course Rating: 70.6/68.0. Slope: 137/116. Green Fee: $23/$34. Cart Fee: $13/person. Walking Policy: Walking at certain times. Walkability: 4. Opened: 1994. Architect: Chuck Smith. Season: Year-round. High: April-July; Sept.-Nov. To obtain tee times: Call golf shop. Miscellaneous: Reduced fees (weekdays, low season, twilight, seniors, juniors), range (grass), club rentals, credit cards (MC, V).

Reader Comments: Hilly, lots of blind shots ... Tough finishing holes, very challenging ... Back 9 beautiful, wooded ... Odd layout, eats balls ... Know the yardage on holes requiring lay up or pay the price ... Good family course ... Open front nine, target golf on back.

★★★½ THE CROSSINGS AT GROVE PARK

PU-4023 Old Wake Forest Rd., Durham, 27703, Durham County, (919)598-8686. E-mail: golfatgp. Web: www.crossingsgolf.com.

Holes: 18. Yards: 6,700/5,008. Par: 72/72. Course Rating: 72.1/69.1. Slope: 138/120. Green Fee: $20/$36. Cart Fee: $13/person. Walking Policy: Walking at certain times. Walkability: 5. Opened: 1997. Architect: Ron Garl. Season: Year-round. High: April-Oct. To obtain tee times: Phone 1(919)598-8686 three days in advance. Miscellaneous: Reduced fees (weekdays, low season, twilight, seniors), club rentals, credit cards (MC, V, AE).

Reader Comments: Best deal ever for seniors ... Tiger would enjoy this one! ... Difficult layout, excellent greens ... Tricked up course ... Nice new course, every club will get a workout.

★½ CRYSTAL SPRINGS GOLF CLUB

P.O. Box 9, Pineville, 28134, Mecklenburg County, (704)588-2640. Special Notes: Call club for further information.

NORTH CAROLINA

★★★★ THE CURRITUCK CLUB
SP-1 Clubhouse Dr. Hwy. 12, Corolla, 27927, Currituck County, (252)453-9400, (888)453-9400, 60 miles S of Virginia Beach, VA.
Holes: 18. **Yards:** 6,885/4,766. **Par:** 72/72. **Course Rating:** 74.0/68.5. **Slope:** 136/120. **Green Fee:** $45/$105. **Cart Fee:** Included in Green Fee. **Walking Policy:** Unrestricted walking. **Walkability:** 1. **Opened:** 1996. **Architect:** Rees Jones. **Season:** Year-round. **High:** June-Aug. **To obtain tee times:** Up to 1 year in advance for members and their guest for peak season (June-August). Up to 14 days in advance. **Miscellaneous:** Reduced fees (low season, resort guests, twilight, juniors), discount packages, range (grass/mats), club rentals, lodging, credit cards (MC, V, AE), beginner friendly (golf schools June-Aug. every Tuesday, Wednesday, Thursday).
Reader Comments: Has its moments ... Great new outer banks course ... Some fairways slope to the water... No crowds in October ... Extremely windy, blowing sand. Temporary clubhouse ... True seaside links ... The back nine is a brilliant links layout. A must! ... Elevation changes around the greens ... Could play every day.

★★★½ CYPRESS LAKES GOLF COURSE   *Pace*
PU-2126 Cypress Lakes Road, Hope Mills, 28348, Cumberland County, (910)483-0359, 10 miles S of Fayetteville.
Holes: 18. **Yards:** 6,943/5,272. **Par:** 72/74. **Course Rating:** 73.2/69.7. **Slope:** 133/118. **Green Fee:** $16/$22. **Cart Fee:** $14/person. **Walking Policy:** Walking at certain times. **Walkability:** 2. **Opened:** 1968. **Architect:** L.B. Floyd. **Season:** Year-round. **High:** Spring/Fall. **To obtain tee times:** Call anytime. **Miscellaneous:** Reduced fees (weekdays, seniors, juniors), discount packages, metal spikes, range (grass), club rentals, credit cards (MC, V).
Reader Comments: Solid course ... Limited trouble ... Great greens ... Fast undulating greens ... Every hole different ... Super people ... Par 3s tough.

★★★★ CYPRESS LANDING GOLF CLUB
SP-600 Clubhouse Dr., Chocowinity, 27817, Pitt County, (252)946-7788, 19 miles E of Greenville.
Holes: 18. **Yards:** 6,850/4,989. **Par:** 72/72. **Course Rating:** 72.8/68.8. **Slope:** 130/118. **Green Fee:** $30/$36. **Cart Fee:** Included in Green Fee. **Walking Policy:** Mandatory cart. **Walkability:** 3. **Opened:** 1996. **Architect:** Bill Love. **Season:** Year-round. **High:** April-May; Sept.-Oct. **To obtain tee times:** Call up to 2 days in advance. **Miscellaneous:** Reduced fees (weekdays), discount packages, range (grass), club rentals, credit cards (MC, V).
Reader Comments: Good course, not too crowded ... Great sleeper, out of the way ... Tough 18th hole ... I want to play this course again ... Lots of water holes ... Course drains well ... Good greens, Pamlico River is great back drop ... A gem!

★★★½ DEERCROFT GOLF CLUB
SP-30000 Deercroft Dr., Wagram, 28396, Scotland County, (910)369-3107, (800)787-7323, 19 miles S of Pinehurst.
Holes: 18. **Yards:** 6,745/5,443. **Par:** 72/72. **Course Rating:** 72.6/67.0. **Slope:** 125/113. **Green Fee:** $15/$40. **Cart Fee:** $17/person. **Walking Policy:** Walking at certain times. **Walkability:** 3. **Opened:** 1984. **Architect:** Gardner Gildey. **Season:** Year-round. **High:** Spring/Fall. **To obtain tee times:** Call golf shop. Tee times also available through most hotels in the area. **Miscellaneous:** Reduced fees (weekdays, low season, twilight, seniors, juniors), discount packages, metal spikes, range (grass), club rentals, credit cards (MC, V, AE).
Reader Comments: Underrated gem in Pinehurst area ... Always great shape ... Great test of abilities ... Nice fairways and good greens ... Beautiful, tough, hilly, must have accurate iron game ... Difficult starting hole ... Rolling terrain, large greens, interesting layout.

★★★★ DEVIL'S RIDGE GOLF CLUB
SP-5107 Linksland Dr., Holly Springs, 27540, Wake County, (919)557-6100, 10 miles SW of Raleigh.
Holes: 18. **Yards:** 7,002/5,244. **Par:** 72/72. **Course Rating:** 73.7/69.8. **Slope:** 138/121. **Green Fee:** $23/$36. **Cart Fee:** $13/person. **Walking Policy:** Walking at certain times. **Walkability:** 3. **Opened:** 1991. **Architect:** John LaFoy. **Season:** Year-round. **High:** April-June. **To obtain tee times:** Call one week in advance. **Miscellaneous:** Reduced fees (weekdays, low season, twilight, seniors, juniors), discount packages, metal spikes, range (grass), club rentals, credit cards (MC, V).
Reader Comments: Love the layout but too many blind shots ... Great course ... Some great holes ... Lots of play, can be slow ... Best public course in Raleigh area ... Getting better ... Fast greens, leave driver at home.

★★★½ THE DIVIDE
PU-6803 Stevens Mill Rd., Matthews, 28105, Mecklenburg/Union County, (704)882-8088, 20 miles SE of Charlotte. **Web:** www.charlottegolf.com.
Holes: 18. **Yards:** 6,973/5,213. **Par:** 72/73. **Course Rating:** 74.4/70.3. **Slope:** 137/N/A. **Green Fee:** $32/$44. **Cart Fee:** Included in Green Fee. **Walking Policy:** Mandatory cart. **Walkability:** 5. **Opened:** 1995. **Architect:** John Cassell. **Season:** Year-round. **High:** April-June; Sept.-Oct. **To**

obtain tee times: Call golf shop at (704)358-GOLF. **Miscellaneous:** Reduced fees (low season, seniors, juniors), range (grass), club rentals, credit cards (MC, V, AE).

Reader Comments: Good layout, suffers from lots of play and occasional neglect ... Very friendly ... Home construction distracting ... Pace of play not enforced, excellent greens ... Nice finishing hole ... Good challenge, good finishing hole.

★½ DUCK HAVEN GOLF CLUB

PU-1202 Eastwood Rd., Wilmington, 28403, New Hanover County, (910)791-7983.
Holes: 18. **Yards:** 6,453/5,361. **Par:** 71/72. **Course Rating:** 71.6/71.8. **Slope:** 125/121. **Green Fee:** $15/$20. **Cart Fee:** Included in Green Fee. **Walking Policy:** Unrestricted walking. **Walkability:** 1. **Opened:** 1961. **Architect:** Raiford Trask Sr. **Season:** Year-round. **High:** March-Oct. **To obtain tee times:** Tee times not required. **Miscellaneous:** Reduced fees (weekdays, twilight, seniors, juniors), discount packages, metal spikes, club rentals.

★★★ DUCK WOODS COUNTRY CLUB

SP-50 S. Dogwood Trail, Kitty Hawk, 27949, Dare County, (252)261-2744, 70 miles S of Norfolk, VA.
Holes: 18. **Yards:** 6,589/5,182. **Par:** 72/72. **Course Rating:** 72.3/70.8. **Slope:** 128/120. **Green Fee:** $50/$90. **Cart Fee:** Included in Green Fee. **Walking Policy:** Mandatory cart. **Walkability:** 1. **Opened:** 1968. **Architect:** Ellis Maples. **Season:** Year-round. **High:** May-Sept. **To obtain tee times:** Call 6 days in advance. **Miscellaneous:** Reduced fees (juniors), range (grass), club rentals, credit cards (MC, V).

Reader Comments: Lots of water holes ... A North Carolina challenge ... Check wind speed before the round ... More water than golf course ... Pleasant course. Friendly staff ... Too many ditches cross fairways ... Keep your ball in play or be a great sand player.

★★★★ DUKE UNIVERSITY GOLF CLUB

PU-Rte. 751 and Science Dr., Durham, 27708, Durham County, (919)681-2288.
Holes: 18. **Yards:** 7,045/5,505. **Par:** 72/73. **Course Rating:** 73.9/71.2. **Slope:** 137/124. **Green Fee:** $38/$53. **Cart Fee:** $17/cart. **Walking Policy:** Unrestricted walking. **Walkability:** N/A. **Opened:** 1957. **Architect:** Robert Trent Jones/Rees Jones. **Season:** Year-round. **High:** March-Sept. **To obtain tee times:** Call up to 7 days in advance. **Miscellaneous:** Reduced fees (weekdays, twilight, seniors, juniors), discount packages, metal spikes, range (grass), club rentals, lodging, credit cards (MC, V).

Notes: Ranked 15th in 1999 Best in State; 17th in 1996 America's Top 75 Affordable Courses.

Reader Comments: Good test, need to drive long and straight ... Great practice facilities ... Need to push golfers to play faster ... Tough second shots ... Decent layout ... Not 'teebox' friendly for women ... Expensive but worth it ... Most cordial welcome ... Very hilly. Had to keep carts on path ... A true test from the tips.

★★★½ EAGLE CHASE GOLF CLUB

3215 Brantley Rd., Marshville, 28103, Union County, (704)385-9000, 30 miles N of Charlotte.
Yards: 6,723/5,139. **Par:** 72/72. **Course Rating:** 72.6/69.6. **Slope:** 128/121. **Green Fee:** $15/$26. **Cart Fee:** $13/person. **Walking Policy:** Unrestricted walking. **Walkabil-ity:** 4. **Opened:** 1994. **Architect:** Tom Jackson. **Season:** Year-round. **High:** April-June; Sept.-Nov. **To obtain tee times:** Call (704)385-9000. **Miscellaneous:** Reduced fees (twilight, seniors, juniors), range (grass), club rentals, credit cards (MC, V, AE).

Reader Comments: Good track ... Very challenging ... A hilly course, but always in good shape ... Awesome tee shot on No. 2 ... Fun to play ... Great par 3s ... Don't tell anyone where it is!

★★ EAGLE CREST GOLF COURSE

PU-4400 Auburn Church Rd., Garner, 27529, Wake County, (919)772-6104, 5 miles S of Raleigh. **E-mail:** eaglecrest@mindspring.com.
Holes: 18. **Yards:** 6,514/4,875. **Par:** 71/71. **Course Rating:** 70.5/67.3. **Slope:** 118/113. **Green Fee:** $15/$23. **Cart Fee:** $11/person. **Walking Policy:** Unrestricted walking. **Walkability:** 2. **Opened:** 1968. **Architect:** Baucom & Assoc. **Season:** Year-round. **High:** April-Sept. **To obtain tee times:** Call one week in advance. **Miscellaneous:** Reduced fees (weekdays, twilight, seniors, juniors), metal spikes, range (grass), club rentals, credit cards (MC, V, AE).

★★★½ ECHO FARMS GOLF & COUNTRY CLUB

SP-4114 Echo Farms Blvd., Wilmington, 28412, New Hanover County, (910)791-9318.
Holes: 18. **Yards:** 7,004/5,232. **Par:** 72/72. **Course Rating:** 74.6/72.3. **Slope:** 129/122. **Green Fee:** $25/$50. **Cart Fee:** Included in Green Fee. **Walking Policy:** Mandatory cart. **Walkability:** 2. **Opened:** 1974. **Architect:** Gene Hamm. **Season:** Year-round. **High:** April-Oct. **To obtain tee times:** Call ahead. **Miscellaneous:** Reduced fees (weekdays, low season, resort guests, twilight, juniors), discount packages, range (grass), club rentals, credit cards (MC, V, AE, D).

Reader Comments: This is my favorite place to play ... Greens by Sherwin Williams ... Take two sand irons, you'll wear one out ... Recent improvements are great ... Some-times good shape, sometimes wet ... Bring your long irons.

★★★½ THE EMERALD GOLF CLUB
SP-5000 Clubhouse Dr., New Bern, 28562, Craven County, 252)633-4440.
Holes: 18. **Yards:** 6,924/5,287. **Par:** 72/72. **Course Rating:** 73.8/68.2. **Slope:** 129/114. **Green Fee:** $24/$42. **Cart Fee:** Included in Green Fee. **Walking Policy:** Mandatory cart. **Walkability:** 3. **Opened:** 1988. **Architect:** Rees Jones. **Season:** Year-round. **High:** March-May/Oct. **To obtain tee times:** Call two days in advance. **Miscellaneous:** Reduced fees (low season, twilight, juniors), discount packages, range (grass), club rentals, credit cards (MC, V).
Reader Comments: Super greens, tight fairways ... Real challenge ... Good coastal course ... Short hitters can score ... Best of everything ... Good test of golf ... Long, tough layout. Plenty of marsh, H2O ... No. 18 great finishing hole.

ETOWAH VALLEY COUNTRY CLUB
R-450 Brickyard Rd., Etowah, 28729, Henderson County, (828)891-7141, (800)451-8174, 18 miles SE of Asheville.
Holes: 27. **Green Fee:** $31/$31. **Cart Fee:** $15/person. **Walking Policy:** Walking at certain times. **Opened:** 1967. **Architect:** Edmund Ault. **Season:** Year-round. **High:** April-Oct. **To obtain tee times:** Call 2 days in advance. **Miscellaneous:** Reduced fees (low season), discount packages, metal spikes, range (grass/mats), club rentals, lodging, credit cards (MC, V, AE, D), beginner friendly (private instruction, group clinics).
★★★½ SOUTH/NORTH
Yards: 6,911/5,391. **Par:** 73/73. **Course Rating:** 72.4/69.9. **Slope:** 125/117. **Walkability:** 3.
Reader Comments: Large greens ... Hidden jewel ... Original 18 very solid ... Very enjoyable, get a group and play till you drop! ... Welcomes singles ... Very lush and scenic ... Lots of hills ... Busy on weekends ... West nine toughest ... You can't tell the quality by the sign ... Scenic.
★★★½ SOUTH/WEST
Yards: 7,108/5,524. **Par:** 72/72. **Course Rating:** 73.3/71.3. **Slope:** 125/119. **Walkability:** 1.
★★★½ WEST/NORTH
Yards: 7,005/5,363. **Par:** 73/73. **Course Rating:** 73.1/70.2. **Slope:** 125/117. **Walkability:** 2.

FAIRFIELD HARBOUR COUNTRY CLUB
SP-1100 Pelican Dr., New Bern, 28560, Craven County, 6 miles SE of New Bern. **Web:** www.harbourgolf.org.
★★★ HARBOUR POINTE COURSE
(252)638-5338.
Holes: 18. **Yards:** 6,650/5,100. **Par:** 72/72. **Course Rating:** 71.8/68.6. **Slope:** 125/111. **Green Fee:** N/A/$29. **Cart Fee:** $12/person. **Walking Policy:** Walking at certain times. **Walkability:** 3. **Opened:** 1989. **Architect:** Dominic Palumbo. **Season:** Year-round. **High:** Spring/Fall. **To obtain tee times:** Call in advance. **Miscellaneous:** Reduced fees (low season, twilight, juniors), discount packages, range (grass), club rentals, lodging, credit cards (MC, V), beginner friendly (clinics, lessons).
Reader Comments: Great vacation spot ... Highly recommend it ... Fair layout ... Blends in with nature ... Loved it ... Interesting and pleasant ... Great golf.
★★★ SHORELINE COURSE
(252)514-0050, (800)706-2999.
Holes: 18. **Yards:** 6,802/5,200. **Par:** 72/72. **Course Rating:** 72.1/70.0. **Slope:** 128/118. **Green Fee:** $25/$29. **Cart Fee:** $12/person. **Walking Policy:** Walking at certain times. **Walkability:** 3. **Opened:** 1972. **Architect:** Dominic Palumbo. **Season:** Year-round. **High:** Spring/Fall. **To obtain tee times:** Call in advance. **Miscellaneous:** Reduced fees (low season, twilight), discount packages, range (grass), club rentals, lodging, credit cards (MC, V).
Reader Comments: Tight layout, very nice ... Missed fairway means water.

★★ FINLEY GOLF CLUB AT UNC
PU-Finley Golf Club Rd., Chapel Hill, 27515, Orange County, (919)962-2349.
Holes: 18. **Yards:** 7,119/4,954. **Par:** 72/72. **Course Rating:** N/A. **Slope:** N/A. **Green Fee:** N/A. **Walking Policy:** Unrestricted walking. **Walkability:** 3. **Opened:** 1999. **Architect:** Tom Fazio. **Season:** Year-round. **High:** April-Oct. **To obtain tee times:** Call Monday prior to weekend or University holiday. Call no earlier than two days in advance for weekdays. **Miscellaneous:** Range (grass), club rentals, credit cards (MC, V).

★★ FOX SQUIRREL COUNTRY CLUB
SP-591 S. Shore Dr., Boiling Spring Lakes, 28461, Brunswick County, (910)845-2625, 25 miles S of Wilmington.
Holes: 18. **Yards:** 6,762/5,349. **Par:** 72/72. **Course Rating:** 72.5/70.7. **Slope:** 125/117. **Green Fee:** $15/$20. **Cart Fee:** $12/person. **Walking Policy:** Unrestricted walking. **Walkability:** 1. **Opened:** 1962. **Architect:** Ed Ricobboni. **Season:** Year-round. **High:** June-Sept. **To obtain tee times:** Call 24 hours in advance. **Miscellaneous:** Discount packages, metal spikes, club rentals, credit cards (MC, V).

FOXFIRE RESORT & COUNTRY CLUB

R-9 Foxfire Blvd., Jackson Springs, 27281, Moore County, (910)295-4563, 60 miles S of Raleigh.

★★★½ EAST COURSE

Holes: 18. **Yards:** 6,851/5,256. **Par:** 72/72. **Course Rating:** 73.5/70.5. **Slope:** 131/119. **Green Fee:** $35/$64. **Cart Fee:** Included in Green Fee. **Walking Policy:** Mandatory cart. **Walkability:** N/A. **Opened:** 1968. **Architect:** Gene Hamm. **Season:** Year-round. **High:** March-May/Sept.-Oct. **To obtain tee times:** Call anytime. **Miscellaneous:** Reduced fees (low season, resort guests, juniors), discount packages, metal spikes, range (grass), club rentals, lodging, credit cards (MC, V, AE, D).

Reader Comments: Changes are very good ... Middle of nowhere ... Both courses present a fair test ... Nice course. New clubhouse will improve layout ... Much improved ... Average for the sand hills ... Overprotective on frost delays ... Good variety of holes.

★★★½ WEST COURSE

Holes: 18. **Yards:** 6,742/5,273. **Par:** 72/72. **Course Rating:** 72.4/70.3. **Slope:** 129/115. **Green Fee:** $35/$64. **Cart Fee:** Included in Green Fee. **Walking Policy:** Mandatory cart. **Walkability:** N/A. **Opened:** 1968. **Architect:** Gene Hamm. **Season:** Year-round. **High:** March-May/Sept.-Oct. **To obtain tee times:** Call anytime. **Miscellaneous:** Reduced fees (low season, resort guests, juniors), discount packages, metal spikes, range (grass), club rentals, lodging, credit cards (MC, V, AE, D).

Reader Comments: Potential. Needs to be toughened up ... Tough number two hole ... Elevation changes ... A good day's entertainment ... Challenging in the wind ... Nice staff.

★½ GASTONIA MUNICIPAL GOLF CLUB

PM-530 Niblick Dr., Gastonia, 28052, Gaston County, (704)866-6945, 20 miles S of Charlotte. **Holes:** 9. **Yards:** 6,474/4,341. **Par:** 71/71. **Course Rating:** 71.3/66.1. **Slope:** 128/110. **Green Fee:** $9/$14. **Cart Fee:** $9/person. **Walking Policy:** Unrestricted walking. **Walk-ability:** 3. **Opened:** 1931. **Architect:** J. Porter Gibson. **Season:** Year-round. **High:** April-Sept. **To obtain tee times:** Call Monday morning for weekends and holidays; no times for weekdays. **Miscellaneous:** Reduced fees (twilight), metal spikes, credit cards (MC, V).

★★★ GATES FOUR COUNTRY CLUB

SP-6775 Irongate Dr., Fayetteville, 28306, Cumberland County, (910)425-2176. **Holes:** 18. **Yards:** 6,865/5,368. **Par:** 72/72. **Course Rating:** 73.9/72.2. **Slope:** 137/127. **Green Fee:** $15/$32. **Cart Fee:** $11/person. **Walking Policy:** Walking at certain times. **Walkability:** 2. **Opened:** 1971. **Architect:** Willard Byrd. **Season:** Year-round. **High:** Spring/Fall. **To obtain tee times:** Call one week in advance. **Miscellaneous:** Reduced fees (weekdays, low season, resort guests, twilight, seniors, juniors), discount packages, range (grass), credit cards (MC, V).

Reader Comments: Hard, hard and hard ... Fun course but still a challenge ... Good design ... Tee times hard to come by on weekend ... Tight fairways ... Enjoyable round ... Nice challenge for all handicaps ... Rather wide fairways.

★★★½ GLEN CANNON COUNTRY CLUB

SP-Wilson Rd., Brevard, 28712, Transylvania County, (828)884-9160, 25 miles S of Asheville. **Holes:** 18. **Yards:** 6,548/5,172. **Par:** 72/72. **Course Rating:** 71.7/69.1. **Slope:** 124/117. **Green Fee:** $25/$50. **Cart Fee:** Included in Green Fee. **Walking Policy:** Mandatory cart. **Walkability:** 2. **Opened:** 1967. **Architect:** Willie B. Lewis. **Season:** Year-round. **High:** April-Oct. **To obtain tee times:** Call one day in advance. **Miscellaneous:** Reduced fees (twilight), metal spikes, range (grass), club rentals, credit cards (MC, V).

Reader Comments: Great mountain course ... Water on 16 holes! ... Playable, pretty course ... Lots of ladies play ... Waterfall hole outstanding ... Take a camera for a picture of No. 2.

GRANDOVER RESORT & CONFERENCE CENTER *Service*

R-1000 Club Rd., Greensboro, 27407, Guilford County, (336)294-1800, (800)472-6301. **Web:** www.grandover.com.

★★★★½ EAST COURSE *Condition, Pace*

Holes: 18. **Yards:** 7,100/5,500. **Par:** 72/72. **Course Rating:** 74.3/71.7. **Slope:** 140/121. **Green Fee:** $70/$70. **Cart Fee:** Included in Green Fee. **Walking Policy:** Walking at certain times. **Walkability:** 4. **Opened:** 1996. **Architect:** David Graham/Gary Panks. **Season:** Year-round. **High:** March-Nov. **To obtain tee times:** Call up to 7 days in advance. **Miscellaneous:** Range (grass), club rentals, lodging (247 rooms), credit cards (MC, V, AE, D, Diners Club).

Reader Comments: A must play ... A little pricey, but a great layout ... Some greens must have small cars buried in them ... This place is nice. Take me back ... Keep it below the hole ... One of the great ones ... Beautiful stone work ... Great clubhouse ... Will not be unknown for long ... Outstanding facilities.

★★★★½ WEST COURSE *Condition+, Pace+*

Holes: 18. **Yards:** 6,800/5,050. **Par:** 72/72. **Course Rating:** 72.5/69.2. **Slope:** 136/116. **Green Fee:** $70/$70. **Cart Fee:** Included in Green Fee. **Walking Policy:** Walking at certain times. **Walkability:** 4. **Opened:** 1997. **Architect:** David Graham/Gary Panks. **Season:** Year-round.

High: March-Nov. **To obtain tee times:** Call up to 7 days in advance. **Miscellaneous:** Range (grass), club rentals, lodging (247 rooms), credit cards (MC, V, AE, D, Diners Club).
Notes: Ranked 23rd in 1999 Best in State.

Reader Comments: Staff was overly nice ... Choose the right tees and you can have a career round ... Good test ... East course is better the West.

★½ GREAT SMOKIES RESORT GOLF CLUB
R-One Holiday Inn Drive, Asheville, 28806, Buncombe County, (704)253-5874, (800)733-3211.
Holes: 18. **Yards:** 5,900/4,600. **Par:** 70/70. **Course Rating:** 69.5/67.0. **Slope:** 118/113. **Green Fee:** $25/$30. **Cart Fee:** $15/person. **Walking Policy:** Unrestricted walking. **Walkability:** 3.
Opened: 1974. **Architect:** William B. Lewis. **Season:** Year-round. **High:** April-Oct. **To obtain tee times:** Hotel guests may call one year in advance; outside play two days in advance.
Miscellaneous: Reduced fees (weekdays, low season, resort guests, twilight), discount packages, metal spikes, club rentals, lodging (275 rooms), credit cards (MC, V, AE, D, Diners Club).

★★★★ GREENSBORO NATIONAL GOLF CLUB
PU-330 Niblick Dr., Summerfield, 27358, Rockingham County, (910)342-1113, 8 miles NW of Greensboro.
Holes: 18. **Yards:** 6,922/4,911. **Par:** 72/72. **Course Rating:** 72.6/67.1. **Slope:** 125/108. **Green Fee:** $35/$40. **Cart Fee:** Included in Green Fee. **Walking Policy:** Walking at certain times.
Walkability: 3. **Opened:** 1995. **Season:** Year-round. **High:** March-Oct. **To obtain tee times:** Call up to 7 days in advance. **Miscellaneous:** Reduced fees (seniors, juniors), range (grass/mats), club rentals, credit cards (MC, V, AE, D).
Reader Comments: Fast greens, attention to detail ... The best hot dogs in the land ... Great layout ... What a pleasure ... Prepare to three-putt! ... Must be able to draw ball ... Excellent par 5s ... Has 'old' look ... Super collection of par 3s.

★★★ THE GROVE PARK INN RESORT
R-290 Macon Ave., Asheville, 28804, Buncombe County, (828)252-2711, (800)438-5800.
Holes: 18. **Yards:** 6,501/4,644. **Par:** 70/70. **Course Rating:** 71.7/68.6. **Slope:** 126/111. **Green Fee:** $50/$80. **Cart Fee:** Included in Green Fee. **Walking Policy:** Walking at certain times.
Walkability: 3. **Opened:** 1894. **Architect:** Willie Park/Donald Ross. **Season:** Year-round. **High:** April-Nov. **To obtain tee times:** Call anytime. **Miscellaneous:** Reduced fees (low season), discount packages, club rentals, lodging, credit cards (MC, V, AE, D, Diners Club), beginner friendly (golf instruction).
Reader Comments: Fun course, excellent views ... Very hilly ... U.S. Open rough, narrow, tree lined and sneaky long ... Rather short but challenging ... Don't expect to score well ... Can only afford to play it once, but worth it once ... Great course for the traditionalists.

★★★ HAWKSNEST GOLF & SKI RESORT
PU-2058 Skyland Dr., Banner Elk, 28607, Watauga County, (828)963-6561, (800)822-4295, 70 miles W of Winston-Salem.
Holes: 18. **Yards:** 6,244/4,799. **Par:** 72/72. **Course Rating:** 68.6/69.4. **Slope:** 113/110. **Green Fee:** $22/$38. **Cart Fee:** Included in Green Fee. **Walking Policy:** Mandatory cart. **Walkability:** 5. **Opened:** 1969. **Architect:** Property owners. **Season:** April-Nov. **High:** July-Aug. **To obtain tee times:** Call. **Miscellaneous:** Reduced fees (weekdays, low season, twilight), discount packages, metal spikes, credit cards (MC, V, D), beginner friendly.
Reader Comments: Somewhat slow play ... Very long rough ... Great greens ... Best views anywhere ... Slick greens ... Couldn't play for looking ... Loved it!

★★½ HEDINGHAM GOLF CLUB
SP-4801 Harbour Towne Dr., Raleigh, 27604, Wake County, (919)250-3030.
Holes: 18. **Yards:** 6,604/4,828. **Par:** 72/72. **Course Rating:** 72.1/66.8. **Slope:** 124/107. **Green Fee:** $20/$31. **Cart Fee:** $14/person. **Walking Policy:** Walking at certain times. **Walkability:** 4.
Opened: 1992. **Architect:** Dave Postlethwait. **Season:** Year-round. **High:** April-May; Sept.-Oct. **To obtain tee times:** Call up to 7 days in advance. **Miscellaneous:** Reduced fees (weekdays, twilight, seniors, juniors), range (grass/mats), club rentals, credit cards (MC, V, AE, D).
Reader Comments: Neighborhood course, worth the effort ... Too many blind shots ... Houses crowd the course ... Tabletop greens ... For all levels of play ... Good for the ego.

★★★ HIGH HAMPTON INN & COUNTRY CLUB
R-Hwy. 107 S., Box 338, Cashiers, 28717, Jackson County, (828)743-2450, (800)334-2551, 65 miles SW of Asheville.
Holes: 18. **Yards:** 6,012/3,748. **Par:** 71/71. **Course Rating:** 68.5/N/A. **Slope:** 120/N/A. **Green Fee:** $18/$28. **Cart Fee:** $11/person. **Walking Policy:** Unrestricted walking. **Walkability:** 3.
Opened: 1923. **Architect:** George Cobb. **Season:** April-Nov. **High:** June-Aug. **To obtain tee times:** Call golf shop. **Miscellaneous:** Reduced fees (low season, resort guests, twilight), discount packages, metal spikes, range (grass), club rentals, lodging, credit cards (MC, V, AE, D), beginner friendly (junior clinics).

Reader Comments: Pretty mountain course ... No distance on par 3s for women ... Interesting older course. Fairly short ... Wet blanket greens ... Great scenery and fun to play ... Excellent lunch buffet ... Good for women and super seniors ... Charming accommodations, good food.

★★★½ HIGHLAND CREEK GOLF CLUB
PU-7001 Highland Creek Pkwy., Charlotte, 28269, Mecklenburg County, (704)875-9000, 10 miles N of Charlotte.
Holes: 18. **Yards:** 7,008/5,005. **Par:** 72/72. **Course Rating:** 73.3/70.1. **Slope:** 133/128. **Green Fee:** $44/$50. **Cart Fee:** Included in Green Fee. **Walking Policy:** Mandatory cart. **Walkability:** 5. **Opened:** 1993. **Architect:** Clifton/Ezell/Clifton. **Season:** Year-round. **High:** April-Sept. **To obtain tee times:** Call 3 days in advance. **Miscellaneous:** Reduced fees (weekdays, low season), metal spikes, range (grass), club rentals, credit cards (MC, V, AE).
Reader Comments: Good course, great finishing hole ... Too tough to take a client for first round ... Great to play during the week, tough weekends ... Good greens ... Accuracy off tee a must ... Lots of water ... Creative layout. Fun holes to play.

HILLCREST GOLF CLUB
PU-2450 S. Stratford Rd., Winston-Salem, 27103, Forsyth County, (336)765-5269.
Holes: 27. **Green Fee:** $14/$18. **Cart Fee:** $12/person. **Walking Policy:** Unrestricted walking.
Walkability: 1. **Opened:** 1931. **Architect:** J. T. Jones. **Season:** Year-round. **High:** March-Sept.
To obtain tee times: Call Thursday 8 a.m. for upcoming weekend. **Miscellaneous:** Reduced fees (weekdays, low season, twilight, seniors, juniors), metal spikes, club rentals, credit cards (MC, V, D), beginner friendly.
★★ CEDARSIDE/HILLSIDE
Yards: 5,839/5,531. **Par:** 72/74. **Course Rating:** 66.5/68.5. **Slope:** 104/107.
★★ CEDARSIDE/LAKESIDE
Yards: 5,848/5,484. **Par:** 72/73. **Course Rating:** 66.5/70.0. **Slope:** 104/111.
★★ HILLSIDE/LAKESIDE
Yards: 5,869/5,485. **Par:** 72/73. **Course Rating:** 66.5/70.0. **Slope:** 104/111.

★★★½ HOUND EARS CLUB
SP-P.O. Box 188, Blowing Rock, 28604, Watauga County, (828)963-4321, 90 miles W of Asheville.
Holes: 18. **Yards:** 6,395/4,959. **Par:** 72/73. **Course Rating:** 70.1/68.5. **Slope:** 127/119. **Green Fee:** $38/$75. **Cart Fee:** $15/person. **Walking Policy:** Walking at certain times. **Walkability:** 3. **Opened:** 1963. **Architect:** George Cobb. **Season:** April-Nov. **High:** June-Sept. **To obtain tee times:** Must stay in Lodge to play. **Miscellaneous:** Reduced fees (juniors), discount packages, metal spikes, range (grass), club rentals, lodging, credit cards (MC, V, AE).
Reader Comments: Great course. Good food ... A fun golf course ... Greens make it a test ... Beautiful and challenging mountain course ... Partly valley, partly mountains, joy to play.

★★★★ HYLAND HILLS GOLF CLUB
PU-4100 U.S. No.1 N., Southern Pines, 28387, Moore County, (910)692-3752, (888)315-2296, 5 miles E of Pinehurst.
Holes: 18. **Yards:** 6,726/4,677. **Par:** 72/72. **Course Rating:** 70.4/66.8. **Slope:** 124/109. **Green Fee:** $20/$55. **Cart Fee:** $18/person. **Walking Policy:** Walking at certain times. **Walkability:** 3. **Opened:** 1974. **Architect:** Tom Jackson. **Season:** Year-round. **High:** March-May/Oct. **To obtain tee times:** Call in advance. **Miscellaneous:** Reduced fees (low season, juniors), discount packages, metal spikes, range (grass), club rentals, lodging, credit cards (MC, V), beginner friendly.
Reader Comments: Best public course in Pinehurst ... Good restaurant ... Short, fun layout ... Hilly terrain ... Local legend ... I love this course ... Good staff.

★★ INDIAN VALLEY GOLF COURSE
PU-1005 Indian Valley Dr., Burlington, 27217, Alamance County, (336)584-7871, 20 miles E of Greensboro.
Holes: 18. **Yards:** 6,610/5,606. **Par:** 70/70. **Course Rating:** 71.3/68.4. **Slope:** 115/113. **Green Fee:** $9/$14. **Cart Fee:** $9/person. **Walking Policy:** Unrestricted walking. **Walkability:** N/A. **Opened:** 1967. **Architect:** Ellis Maples. **Season:** Year-round. **High:** April-Oct. **To obtain tee times:** Call Monday for weekend tee times at 8 a.m. **Miscellaneous:** Reduced fees (weekdays, low season, resort guests, twilight, seniors, juniors), discount packages, metal spikes, range (grass), credit cards (MC, V).

★★★½ JAMESTOWN PARK GOLF CLUB
PM-7014 E. Fork Rd., Jamestown, 27282, Guilford County, (336)454-4912, 3 miles SW of Greensboro.
Holes: 18. **Yards:** 6,665/5,298. **Par:** 72/72. **Course Rating:** 72.6/70.7. **Slope:** 126/118. **Green Fee:** $15/$18. **Cart Fee:** $9/person. **Walking Policy:** Walking at certain times. **Walkability:** 3. **Opened:** 1972. **Architect:** John Townsend. **Season:** Year-round. **High:** May-Sept. **To obtain tee times:** Call one week in advance for weekdays. Call Thursday prior to weekend of play.

Miscellaneous: Reduced fees (weekdays, seniors, juniors), range (grass), club rentals, credit cards (MC, V, D).
Reader Comments: Bargain ... Excellent staff ... Usually in better shape ... Tough par 5s ... Fair test from blues ... A lot of holes uphill to the green ... Same club to all 3 pars ... Lots of character.

★★★★ JEFFERSON LANDING CLUB

Box 110, Jefferson, 28640, Ashe County, (910)246-5555, 80 miles of Winston Salem.
Holes: 18. **Yards:** 7,111/4,960. **Par:** 72/72. **Course Rating:** N/A. **Slope:** 121/103. **Green Fee:** N/A. **Cart Fee:** Included in Green Fee. **Walking Policy:** Mandatory cart. **Walkability:** N/A.
Architect: Larry Nelson/Dennis Lehmann. **Season:** March-Nov. **High:** June-Sept.
Miscellaneous: Reduced fees (weekdays, low season, resort guests, twilight), discount packages, metal spikes, range (grass/mats), lodging, credit cards (MC, V, AE, D).
Reader Comments: Needs seasoning ... Good design, slow play ... Friendly personnel ... Good shot variety ... Needs better signing to tee boxes ... Nice open fairway .... Greens are best I have played ... Beautiful setting ... Very flat for a mountain course ... Worth finding.

★★★½ KEITH HILLS COUNTRY CLUB

SP-Country Club Dr., Buies Creek, 27506, Harnett County, (910)893-5051, (800)334-4111, 30 miles S of Raleigh. **E-mail:** khcc@mailcenter.com. **Web:** www.campbell.edu/keith hills.
Holes: 18. **Yards:** 6,703/5,225. **Par:** 72/72. **Course Rating:** 71.6/69.6. **Slope:** 129/120. **Green Fee:** $18/$26. **Cart Fee:** $14/person. **Walking Policy:** Walking at certain times. **Walkability:** 4.
Opened: 1975. **Architect:** Ellis Maples. **Season:** Year-round. **High:** March-June. **To obtain tee times:** Call golf shop. **Miscellaneous:** Reduced fees (low season, juniors), discount packages, range (grass), club rentals, credit cards (MC, V).
Reader Comments: Best kept secret in Raleigh area. For now ... Well worth the detour from I-95 ... Always excellent condition ... If only the greens met standard of rest of course ... A real jewel, made us forget the pace of play ... Crowned greens ... Best lemonade.

★★★★ KENMURE GOLF CLUB

100 Clubhouse Dr., Flat Rock, 28731, Henderson County, (828-693-8506).
Special Notes: Call club for further information.

LAKE LURE GOLF AND BEACH RESORT
★★★½ APPLE VALLEY GOLF CLUB

R-309 Winesap Road, Lake Lure, 28746, Rutherford County, (828)625-2888, (800)260-1040, 9 miles SE of Lake Lure. **Web:** www.lakeluregolf.com.
Holes: 18. **Yards:** 6,756/4,661. **Par:** 72/72. **Course Rating:** 72.8/66.3. **Slope:** 139/114. **Green Fee:** $28/$46. **Cart Fee:** Included in Green Fee. **Walking Policy:** Mandatory cart. **Walkability:** 3. **Opened:** 1986. **Architect:** Dan Maples. **Season:** Year-round. **High:** April-Oct. **To obtain tee times:** Call golf shop up to.14 days in advance. **Miscellaneous:** Reduced fees (low season, resort guests, twilight, juniors), discount packages, range (grass), club rentals, lodging (50 rooms), credit cards (MC, V, D).
Reader Comments: A favorite foothill course ... Excellent place to stay and play ... More gimmicky than expected ... Nice layout, pretty setting ... Lots of fun. A fair challenge ... Mountains, creeks, its all here ... Dog stole my ball ... No blind shots ... Course knowledge is priceless.

★★★ BALD MOUNTAIN GOLF CLUB

R-112 Mountains Boulevard, Lake Lure, 28746, Rutherford County, (828)625-2626, (800)260-1040, 9 miles SE of Lake Lure. **Web:** www.lakeluregolf.com.
Holes: 18. **Yards:** 6,575/4,808. **Par:** 72/72. **Course Rating:** 72.8/67.9. **Slope:** 137/118. **Green Fee:** $28/$46. **Cart Fee:** Included in Green Fee. **Walking Policy:** Walking at certain times. **Walkability:** 4. **Opened:** 1968. **Architect:** W.B. Lewis. **Season:** Year-round. **High:** April-Oct. **To obtain tee times:** Call golf shop 14 days in advance. **Miscellaneous:** Reduced fees (low season, resort guests, twilight, juniors), discount packages, range (grass), club rentals, lodging (50 rooms), credit cards (MC, V, D).
Reader Comments: Some fun holes, short par 5s ... Real mountain course ... A lot of sidehill lies ... Very narrow fairways, a lot of water ... Course has everything ... Unforgettable golf experience ... Bring your iron game, stay out of creek ... Hard to choose between the two.
Special Notes: Formerly Fairfield Mountains

★★★½ LANE TREE GOLF CLUB

SP-2317 Salem Church Rd., Goldsboro, 27530, Wayne County, (919)734-1245, 43 miles SE of Raleigh. **E-mail:** lanetree@esn.net. **Web:** lanetree.com.
Holes: 18. **Yards:** 7,016/5,217. **Par:** 72/72. **Course Rating:** 72.4/68.9. **Slope:** 131/120. **Green Fee:** $10/$25. **Cart Fee:** $14/person. **Walking Policy:** Walking at certain times. **Walkability:** 3. **Opened:** 1992. **Architect:** John Lafoy. **Season:** Year-round. **High:** April-Sept. **To obtain tee times:** Call 3 days in advance. **Miscellaneous:** Reduced fees (weekdays, low season, twilight, seniors), range (grass), club rentals, credit cards (MC, V, AE).
Reader Comments: Great clubhouse ... Golfers sometimes start on 10th ... Championship caliber from the tips ... Nice place to play ... Good variety of 4s & 3s ... Use all clubs in bag.

★★★★ LEGACY GOLF LINKS
PU-U.S. Hwy. 15-501 S., Aberdeen, 28315, Moore County, (910)944-8825, (800)344-8825, 70 miles SW of Raleigh. **E-mail:** mriddle@legacygolfmgmt.com. **Web:** www.legacypinehurst.com.
Holes: 18. **Yards:** 7,014/4,948. **Par:** 72/72. **Course Rating:** 73.2/68.3. **Slope:** 132/120. **Green Fee:** $39/$85. **Cart Fee:** Included in Green Fee. **Walking Policy:** Mandatory cart. **Walkability:** 3. **Opened:** 1991. **Architect:** Jack Nicklaus II. **Season:** Year-round. **High:** Spring/Fall. **To obtain tee times:** Call in advance. **Miscellaneous:** Reduced fees (low season, resort guests, juniors), discount packages, range (grass), club rentals, credit cards (MC, V, AE), beginner friendly (on-site instruction).
Reader Comments: Very good design with variety of tees ... Great staff ... 18th is a great way to finish a round ... Little Jack did good ... Must play ... Where II is better than I ... Fabulous finishing holes. Very memorable ... Great course for women ... The trees are great in late October ... Hard par 3s.

★★½ LINCOLN COUNTRY CLUB
SP-2108 Country Club Rd., Lincolnton, 28092, Lincoln County, (704)735-1382, 20 miles NW of Charlotte.
Holes: 18. **Yards:** 6,467/5,011. **Par:** 72/72. **Course Rating:** 70.4/69.0. **Slope:** 125/118. **Green Fee:** $22/$28. **Cart Fee:** Included in Green Fee. **Walking Policy:** Unrestricted walking. **Walkability:** N/A. **Opened:** 1991. **Architect:** Peter Tufts. **Season:** Year-round. **High:** April-Oct. **To obtain tee times:** Call 3 days in advance. **Miscellaneous:** Reduced fees (weekdays, seniors, juniors), metal spikes, range (grass), credit cards (MC, V).
Reader Comments: Great front nine, very nice people ... Front nine very tough ... Nice layout ... Short frontside, long backside, not much room for error ... Challenging ... Top of the line.

★★★½ LINVILLE GOLF COURSE
R-Linville Ave., Linville, 28646, Avery County, (828)733-4363, 60 miles NE of Asheville.
Holes: 18. **Yards:** 6,780/5,086. **Par:** 72/72. **Course Rating:** 72.5/69.3. **Slope:** 134/121. **Green Fee:** $70/$70. **Cart Fee:** Included in Green Fee. **Walking Policy:** Mandatory cart. **Walkability:** N/A. **Opened:** 1924. **Architect:** Donald Ross. **Season:** May-Oct. **High:** May-Oct. **To obtain tee times:** Must be a guest at Eseeola Lodge. **Miscellaneous:** Metal spikes, range (grass), club rentals, lodging.
Notes: Ranked 25th in 1999 Best in State; 19th in 1996 America's Top 75 Affordable Courses.
Reader Comments: Like putting on glass ... Great scenery, trout in streams ... Classic short course, tough greens ... Fabulous condition, worth it ... A special time, pampered to the nines ... Simply the best.

★★★½ LITTLE RIVER FARM GOLF LINKS
PU-500 Little River Farm Rd., Carthage, 28374, Moore County, (910)949-4600, (888)766-6538, 5 miles N of Pinehurst. **Web:** www.littleriver.com.
Holes: 18. **Yards:** 6,909/5,092. **Par:** 72/72. **Course Rating:** 73.6/69.4. **Slope:** 132/118. **Green Fee:** $40/$70. **Cart Fee:** $18/person. **Walking Policy:** Mandatory cart. **Walkability:** 5. **Opened:** 1996. **Architect:** Dan Maples. **Season:** Year-round. **High:** April-May; Oct. **To obtain tee times:** Call golf shop. **Miscellaneous:** Discount packages, range (grass), club rentals, credit cards (MC, V).
Reader Comments: Great layout, great clubhouse, great experience ... Very challenging test ... Long and demanding ... Nice par 5s ... Front much longer than back ... Tour stop in April ... Links in the sand hills ... Great greens ... Beautiful view coming up 18.

★★ LOCHMERE GOLF CLUB
SP-2511 Kildare Farm Rd., Cary, 27511, Wake County, (919)851-0611, 5 miles W of Raleigh.
Holes: 18. **Yards:** 6,627/4,904. **Par:** 71/73. **Course Rating:** 71.7/68.4. **Slope:** 129/123. **Green Fee:** $24/$34. **Cart Fee:** $14/person. **Walking Policy:** Walking at certain times. **Walkability:** 1. **Opened:** 1986. **Architect:** Gene Hamm. **Season:** Year-round. **High:** N/A. **To obtain tee times:** Call one week in advance. **Miscellaneous:** Reduced fees (twilight, seniors, juniors), range (grass), club rentals, credit cards (MC, V, AE), beginner friendly.

★★★★ LOCKWOOD FOLLY COUNTRY CLUB
SP-19 Clubhouse Dr. S.W., Holden Beach, 28462, Brunswick County, (910)842-5666, (877)562-9663, 40 miles N of Myrtle Beach, SC. **E-mail:** golfshop@nccoast.net. **Web:** www.lockwoodfolly.com.
Holes: 18. **Yards:** 6,836/5,524. **Par:** 72/72. **Course Rating:** 73.8/70.9. **Slope:** 139/122. **Green Fee:** $25/$62. **Cart Fee:** $19/person. **Walking Policy:** Mandatory cart. **Walkability:** 2. **Opened:** 1988. **Architect:** Willard C. Byrd. **Season:** Year-round. **High:** March-May, Sept-Oct. **To obtain tee times:** Call up to a year in advance between 7 a.m. and 5 p.m. **Miscellaneous:** Reduced fees (low season, resort guests, twilight), discount packages, range (grass), club rentals, lodging, credit cards (MC, V).

Reader Comments: Friendly staff ... Tightest fairways in Myrtle Beach area ... Great 18th hole, excellent greens ... A good beach course ... Take lots of golf balls ... Difficult, but fair ... Good hospitality ... Played it twice, loved it twice, hit it straight ... Watch out for the foxes.

★★ THE LODGE GOLF COURSE
PU-Rte. 3, Hwy. 74 E., Laurinburg, 28352, Scotland County, (910)277-0311, 50 miles S of Fayetteville. **Holes:** 18. **Yards:** 6,570/4,830. **Par:** 72/72. **Course Rating:** 69.4/65.5. **Slope:** 112/102. **Green Fee:** $17/$23. **Walking Policy:** Unrestricted walking. **Walkability:** 1. **Opened:** 1982. **Architect:** Tom Jackson. **Season:** Year-round. **High:** April-Sept. **To obtain tee times:** First come, first served. **Miscellaneous:** Reduced fees (twilight, seniors), discount packages, metal spikes, range (grass), club rentals.

★★★½ MAGGIE VALLEY RESORT & COUNTRY CLUB
R-1819 Country Club Rd., Maggie Valley, 28751, Haywood County, (828)926-6013, (800)438-3861, 40 miles W of Asheville. **E-mail:** golf@maggievalleyresort.com. **Web:** www.maggievalleyresort.com. **Holes:** 18. **Yards:** 6,336/4,645. **Par:** 72/72. **Course Rating:** 69.9/65.9. **Slope:** 121/105. **Green Fee:** $15/$36. **Cart Fee:** $15/person. **Walking Policy:** Walking at certain times. **Walkability:** 3. **Opened:** 1963. **Architect:** Bill Prevost. **Season:** Year-round. **High:** March-Nov. **To obtain tee times:** Call one day in advance. **Miscellaneous:** Reduced fees (weekdays, low season, twilight, juniors), discount packages, range (grass/mats), club rentals, lodging (75 rooms), credit cards (MC, V, AE, D).
Reader Comments: Excellent layout ... Very pleasant mountain course ... Undulating greens ... For golfing couples ... Nicely landscaped ... A tad neglected but nice ... Like to play this one again ... I love it! ... Scenery outstanding ... Front and back nines very different.

★★ MAGNOLIA COUNTRY CLUB
SP-171 Magnolia Country Club Lane, Magnolia, 28453, Duplin County, (910)289-2126, 40 miles N of Wilmington. **Holes:** 18. **Yards:** 6,400/4,600. **Par:** 71/71. **Course Rating:** 69.8/68.3. **Slope:** 120/109. **Green Fee:** $10/$18. **Cart Fee:** $11/person. **Walking Policy:** Unrestricted walking. **Walkability:** 2. **Opened:** 1974. **Architect:** J.P. Smith/Doug Smith. **Season:** Year-round. **High:** June-Aug. **To obtain tee times:** Call for weekend tee times only. **Miscellaneous:** Reduced fees (weekdays, low season, resort guests, twilight, seniors, juniors), range (grass), club rentals, beginner friendly (group instruction for beginners).

★★★★ MAGNOLIA GREENS GOLF PLANTATION
PU-1800 Linkwood Circle, Leland, 28451, Brunswick County, (910)383-0999, (800)677-7534, 5 miles S of Wilmington. **E-mail:** magnoliagolf@navi-gator.com. **Web:** www.magnolia-greens.com. **Holes:** 18. **Yards:** 7,156/5,173. **Par:** 72/72. **Course Rating:** 75.3/70.3. **Slope:** 138/120. **Green Fee:** $25/$45. **Cart Fee:** $15/person. **Walking Policy:** Mandatory cart. **Walkability:** 2. **Opened:** 1998. **Architect:** Tom Jackson. **Season:** Year-round. **High:** March-May-Oct.-Nov. **To obtain tee times:** Call (800)677-7534 or visit website. **Miscellaneous:** Reduced fees (weekdays, low season, resort guests, twilight, seniors, juniors), discount packages, range (grass), club rentals, lodging (12 rooms), credit cards (MC, V, AE, D), beginner friendly.
Reader Comments: Nice course but not very demanding ... Stop by on your way to Myrtle Beach ... Gets plenty of play ... Great greens ... Will be great in time.

★★½ MALLARD HEAD COUNTRY CLUB
SP-185 Mallard Way, Mooresville, 28117, Iredell County, (704)664-7031, 25 miles N of Charlotte. **Holes:** 18. **Yards:** 6,904/5,469. **Par:** 72/72. **Course Rating:** 72.8/70.5. **Slope:** 121/121. **Green Fee:** $16/$21. **Cart Fee:** $10/person. **Walking Policy:** Walking at certain times. **Walkability:** 3. **Opened:** 1979. **Architect:** George Cobb. **Season:** Year-round. **High:** April-Oct. **To obtain tee times:** Call Thursday morning for weekends and holidays; anytime for weekdays. **Miscellaneous:** Reduced fees (weekdays, seniors), metal spikes, range (grass), club rentals, credit cards (MC, V).
Reader Comments: Excellent local course ... Fun for all ... Tight pin placements.

★★★★ MARSH HARBOUR GOLF LINKS
PU-Hwy. 179, Calabash, 28467, Brunswick County, (910)579-3161, (800)377-2315, 15 miles N of Myrtle Beach, SC. **Holes:** 18. **Yards:** 6,690/4,795. **Par:** 71/71. **Course Rating:** 72.4/67.7. **Slope:** 134/115. **Green Fee:** $19/$80. **Cart Fee:** $20/person. **Walking Policy:** Mandatory cart. **Walkability:** 3. **Opened:** 1980. **Architect:** Dan Maples. **Season:** Year-round. **High:** March-April, Oct. **To obtain tee times:** Call up to nine months in advance. Deposit required during high season. **Miscellaneous:** Reduced fees (low season, resort guests), discount packages, range (grass), club rentals, credit cards (MC, V, AE).
Reader Comments: Wind blows a lot ... Pay any price, take camera! ... Overpriced if not on a package ... 17 is a bear ... Use all clubs ... Natural low country setting ... Always want to return ...

Sneaky hard ... 9 holes in the marsh, 9 in the pines. Good diversity ... Wow, must play ... You never know what to expect.

MEADOWLANDS GOLF CLUB
R-P.O. Box 4159, Calabash Rd. NW, Calabash, 28467, Brunswick County, (910)287-7529, (888)287-7529, 2 miles W of Calabash. **E-mail:** meadowlands@nccoast.net. **Web:** www.meadowlandsgolf.com.
Holes: 18. **Yards:** 7,054/5,041. **Par:** 72/72. **Course Rating:** 74.8/70.2. **Slope:** 136/119. **Green Fee:** $20/$60. **Cart Fee:** $19/person. **Walking Policy:** Walking at certain times. **Walkability:** 2. **Opened:** 1997. **Architect:** Willard Byrd. **Season:** Year-round. **High:** March-April; Oct. **To obtain tee times:** Call golf shop. **Miscellaneous:** Reduced fees (weekdays, low season, resort guests, twilight, seniors, juniors), discount packages, range (grass), club rentals, credit cards (MC, V).

★★★★ MEADOWLANDS GOLF COURSE
PU-582 Motsinger Rd., Winston-Salem, 27107, Davidson County, (910)769-1011, 6 miles SE of Winston-Salem.
Holes: 18. **Yards:** 6,706/4,745. **Par:** 72/72. **Course Rating:** 72.7/67.4. **Slope:** 135/117. **Green Fee:** $38/$44. **Cart Fee:** Included in Green Fee. **Walking Policy:** Walking at certain times. **Walkability:** 5. **Opened:** 1995. **Architect:** Hale Irwin/Stan Gentry. **Season:** Year-round. **High:** April-Oct. **To obtain tee times:** Call golf shop. **Miscellaneous:** Reduced fees (weekdays, seniors, juniors), metal spikes, range (grass), club rentals, credit cards (MC, V, AE).
Reader Comments: Nice layout ... Really enjoyed ... Each hole a picture ... Feels like the mountains ... Bring your long iron game ... Narrow fairways.

★★★★ MID PINES INN & GOLF CLUB
R-1010 Midland Rd., Southern Pines, 28387, Moore County, (910)692-9362, (800)323-2114, 70 miles S of Raleigh. **E-mail:** midpines@golfnc.com. **Web:** www.golfnc.com.
Holes: 18. **Yards:** 6,515/4,907. **Par:** 72/72. **Course Rating:** 71.4/68.2. **Slope:** 127/120. **Green Fee:** $59/$135. **Cart Fee:** Included in Green Fee. **Walking Policy:** Unrestricted walking. **Walkability:** 2. **Opened:** 1921. **Architect:** Donald Ross. **Season:** Year-round. **High:** March-May; Sept.-Oct. **To obtain tee times:** Call in advance. **Miscellaneous:** Reduced fees (weekdays, low season, resort guests, twilight, juniors), discount packages, range (grass), club rentals, lodging, credit cards (MC, V, AE).
Reader Comments: Tradition reigns ... Women's Open should be here ... Donald Ross at his best! ... A step back in time ... Beautiful, well-maintained course ... My Pinehurst favorite ... Great staff ... Gorgeous finishing holes ... Very playable for women ... Straight & narrow.

★★★½ MILL CREEK GOLF CLUB
PU-1700 St. Andrews Dr., Mebane, 27302, Alamance County, (919)563-4653, 20 miles W of Durham.
Holes: 18. **Yards:** 7,004/4,884. **Par:** 72/72. **Course Rating:** 73.7/67.5. **Slope:** 141/113. **Green Fee:** $23/$34. **Cart Fee:** $12/person. **Walking Policy:** Walking at certain times. **Walkability:** 4. **Opened:** 1995. **Architect:** Rick Robbins/Gary Koch. **Season:** Year-round. **High:** April-Oct. **To obtain tee times:** Call up to 7 days in advance. **Miscellaneous:** Reduced fees (weekdays, low season, twilight, seniors, juniors), range (grass), club rentals, credit cards (MC, V, AE, D).
Notes: Ranked 6th in 1996 Best New Affordable Courses.
Reader Comments: Worth the trip ... Hard to find, but well worth effort, a real gem ... Tough around greens ... Will get better with age ... Need your long game ... Great cheeseburgers.

★★½ MONROE COUNTRY CLUB
PM-Hwy. 601-S., Monroe, 28110, Union County, (704)282-4661, 20 miles SE of Charlotte.
Holes: 18. **Yards:** 6,759/4,964. **Par:** 72/73. **Course Rating:** 71.8/68.6. **Slope:** 118/117. **Green Fee:** $14/$19. **Cart Fee:** $11/person. **Walking Policy:** Walking at certain times. **Walkability:** 3. **Opened:** 1936. **Architect:** Donald Ross/Tom Jackson. **Season:** Year-round. **High:** May-Aug. **To obtain tee times:** Call up to 5 days in advance. **Miscellaneous:** Reduced fees (weekdays, low season, seniors, juniors), range (grass/mats), credit cards (MC, V).
Reader Comments: Good value, old style ... Fairways are spotty, excellent greens ... Enjoyable track, great finishing holes ... Nice course needs some work ... Views unbelievable.

★★½ MOREHEAD CITY COUNTRY CLUB
Country Club Rd., Morehead City, 28557, Carteret County, (919)726-4917 .
Special Notes: Call club for further information.

★★★★½ MOUNT MITCHELL GOLF CLUB *Condition*
PU-7590 Hwy. 80 S., Burnsville, 28714, Yancey County, (828)675-5454, 55 miles NE of Asheville.
Holes: 18. **Yards:** 6,495/5,455. **Par:** 72/72. **Course Rating:** 71.3/70.9. **Slope:** 141/131. **Green Fee:** $35/$59. **Cart Fee:** Included in Green Fee. **Walking Policy:** Walking at certain times. **Walkability:** 2. **Opened:** 1975. **Architect:** Fred Hawtree. **Season:** April-Nov. **High:** May-Oct. **To obtain tee times:** Call two weeks in advance. You must guarantee with credit card during times

of heavy play. **Miscellaneous:** Reduced fees (weekdays, low season, resort guests), discount packages, club rentals, lodging (40 rooms), credit cards (MC, V, AE).
Reader Comments: Must play ... Not usually crowed ... Beautiful in the fall ... A golfing jewel ... Wonderful mountain course ... Our favorite ... Look forward to going back ... Tough greens ... Super views ... Golf at it's best! ... Bit of a ride, but worth every mile.

★★★ MOUNTAIN AIRE GOLF CLUB
PU-1104 Golf Course Rd., West Jefferson, 28694, Ashe County, (910)877-4716, 80 miles NW of Winston-Salem. **E-mail:** mountainaire@skybest.com. **Web:** www.mountainaire.com.
Holes: 18. **Yards:** 6,404/4,265. **Par:** 72/72. **Course Rating:** 69.8/63.9. **Slope:** 122/108. **Green Fee:** $14/$25. **Cart Fee:** $12/person. **Walking Policy:** Unrestricted walking. **Walkability:** 5. **Opened:** 1950. **Season:** March-Nov. **High:** June-Aug. **To obtain tee times:** Call golf shop. **Miscellaneous:** Reduced fees (weekdays, low season, twilight, juniors), discount packages, metal spikes, range (grass), club rentals, lodging, credit cards (MC, V), beginner friendly (ladies and junior programs).
Reader Comments: Slow greens but great golf holes ... Nose bleed paradise, breathtaking views ... Great layout ... Don't play it on a windy day ... Most beautiful course I've played.

★★★★ MOUNTAIN GLEN GOLF CLUB
Box 326, Newland, 28657, Avery County, (704)733-5804.
Special Notes: Call club for further information.

★★★★ NAGS HEAD GOLF LINKS   *Condition*
SP-5615 S. Seachase Dr., Nags Head, 27959, Dare County, (252)441-8073, (800)851-9404, 75 miles S of Virginia Beach.
Holes: 18. **Yards:** 6,126/4,415. **Par:** 71/71. **Course Rating:** 68.8/64.7. **Slope:** 130/117. **Green Fee:** $40/$85. **Cart Fee:** Included in Green Fee. **Walking Policy:** Mandatory cart. **Walkability:** 1. **Opened:** 1987. **Architect:** Bob Moore. **Season:** Year-round. **High:** June-Aug. **To obtain tee times:** Call golf shop up to one year in advance. **Miscellaneous:** Reduced fees (low season, resort guests, twilight, juniors), discount packages, range (grass/mats), club rentals, lodging, credit cards (MC, V, AE).
Reader Comments: Great links course on the water ... Renovations have really improved the course conditions ... A seaside masterpiece ... Challenging and lots of fun ... Kind to first timers ... Target golf at its best ... A mini Pebble Beach ... The high winds will drive your scores out of sight ... Has a good senior rate.

NATIONAL GOLF CLUB
SP-1 Royal Troon Dr., Pinehurst, 28374, Moore County, (910)295-5340, (800)471-4339. **E-mail:** proshop@nationalgolfclub.com. **Web:** www.nationalgolfclub.com.
Holes: 18. **Yards:** 7,122/5,378. **Par:** 72/72. **Course Rating:** 75.3/72.1. **Slope:** 137/125. **Green Fee:** $95/$210. **Cart Fee:** $20/person. **Walking Policy:** Walking at certain times. **Walkability:** 1. **Opened:** 1988. **Architect:** Jack Nicklaus. **Season:** Year-round. **High:** March-May/Sept.-Oct. **To obtain tee times:** Call golf shop. **Miscellaneous:** Reduced fees (weekdays, low season), range (grass), club rentals, lodging (20 rooms), credit cards (MC, V, AE).

★★★★½ THE NEUSE GOLF CLUB   *Service+, Value, Condition*
SP-918 Birkdale Dr., Clayton, 27520, Johnston County, (919)550-0550, 15 miles S of Raleigh.
Holes: 18. **Yards:** 7,010/5,478. **Par:** 72/72. **Course Rating:** 73.5/72.2. **Slope:** 136/126. **Green Fee:** $22/$33. **Cart Fee:** $14/person. **Walking Policy:** Walking at certain times. **Walkability:** 4. **Opened:** 1993. **Architect:** John LaFoy. **Season:** Year-round. **High:** April-Oct. **To obtain tee times:** Call golf shop. **Miscellaneous:** Reduced fees (weekdays, low season, twilight, seniors, juniors), range (grass), club rentals, credit cards (MC, V, AE).
Notes: Ranked 32nd in 1996 America's Top 75 Affordable Courses.
Reader Comments: Excellent challenge ... Well maintained, target golf ... Deceptively longer than it looks ... No. 14 prettiest hole of memory ... Friendliest rangers.

★★★★ NORTH SHORE COUNTRY CLUB
SP-101 N. Shore Dr., Sneads Ferry, 28460, Onslow County, (910)327-2410, (800)828-5035, 25 miles N of Wilmington.
Holes: 18. **Yards:** 6,866/5,039. **Par:** 72/72. **Course Rating:** 72.8/68.7. **Slope:** 134/122. **Green Fee:** $30/$50. **Cart Fee:** Included in Green Fee. **Walking Policy:** Mandatory cart. **Walkability:** 3. **Opened:** 1988. **Architect:** Bob Moore. **Season:** Year-round. **High:** March-Nov. **To obtain tee times:** Call up to one year in advance. **Miscellaneous:** Reduced fees (weekdays, twilight, juniors), discount packages, range (grass), club rentals, credit cards (MC, V).
Reader Comments: Tough, demanding course ... One of my favorites ... Great bar ... Last 2 holes are stern ... Challenging but fair ... Polite service, fast greens, very windy ... Always fun ... Good variety of holes ... Tough for a short hitter ... Alligator sighting was exciting.

★★★½ OAK HOLLOW GOLF COURSE   *Value*
PM-3400 N. Centennial St., High Point, 27265, Guilford County, (910)883-3260, 8 miles S of Greensboro.

Holes: 18. **Yards:** 6,483/4,796. **Par:** 72/72. **Course Rating:** 71.6/67.4. **Slope:** 124/114. **Green Fee:** $14/$17. **Cart Fee:** $11/person. **Walking Policy:** Walking at certain times. **Walkability:** 3. **Opened:** 1972. **Architect:** Pete Dye. **Season:** Year-round. **High:** April-Aug. **To obtain tee times:** Call 48 hours in advance for weekdays. Call Thursday for upcoming weekend. **Miscellaneous:** Reduced fees (seniors, juniors), metal spikes, range (grass/mats), club rentals.
Reader Comments: Best value for your dollar ... Squeezed me in ... Gets a lot of play ... Dye knows golf ... Too many blind spots but interesting course ... Lots of water, small greens.

★★½ OAK ISLAND GOLF & COUNTRY CLUB
PU-928 Caswell Beach Rd., Oak Island, 28465, Brunswick County, (910)278-5275, 23 miles of Wilmington.
Holes: 18. **Yards:** 6,608/5,437. **Par:** 72/72. **Course Rating:** N/A. **Slope:** 128/121. **Green Fee:** N/A. **Walkability:** N/A. **Architect:** George Cobb. **Season:** Year-round. **High:** June-Oct. **Miscellaneous:** Reduced fees (weekdays, low season), discount packages, metal spikes, range (grass), credit cards (MC, V).
Reader Comments: I learned how to play in a wind tunnel ... Off ocean, always windy ... Good course, greens are slow ... You get your money's worth ... Fairly short, sneaky tough.

★★★★ OAK VALLEY GOLF CLUB
SP-261 Oak Valley Blvd., Advance, 27006, Davie County, (336)940-2000, 10 miles W of Winston-Salem.
Holes: 18. **Yards:** 7,058/5,197. **Par:** 72/72. **Course Rating:** 74.0/68.0. **Slope:** 144/125. **Green Fee:** $28/$47. **Cart Fee:** $14/person. **Walking Policy:** Walking at certain times. **Walkability:** 3. **Opened:** 1995. **Architect:** Arnold Palmer/Ed Seay. **Season:** Year-round. **High:** Summer months. **To obtain tee times:** Call. **Miscellaneous:** Reduced fees (weekdays, twilight, seniors, juniors), discount packages, range (grass), club rentals, credit cards (MC, V, AE).
Reader Comments: Getting better each year ... Modern golf ... Very popular course ... Hard to get tee times ...Excellent layout ... A course for the better player ... Huge, deceptive greens.

★★★½ OCEAN HARBOUR GOLF LINKS
PU-9686 Scenic Drive, Calabash, 28467, Brunswick County, (910)579-3588, (877)592-4653, 2 miles N of Calabash. **Web:** www.oceanharbour.com.
Holes: 18. **Yards:** 6,859/5,056. **Par:** 72/72. **Course Rating:** 75.6/72.4. **Slope:** 142/126. **Green Fee:** $20/$61. **Cart Fee:** $20/person. **Walking Policy:** Walking at certain times. **Walkability:** 3. **Opened:** 1989. **Architect:** Clyde Johnston. **Season:** Year-round. **High:** March-April-Oct. **To obtain tee times:** Call. **Miscellaneous:** Reduced fees (resort guests, juniors), discount packages, range (grass), club rentals, credit cards (MC, V, AE).
Reader Comments: Some oceanside holes ... Love the challenge ... Always play on my trips to Myrtle ... Doesn't get the play it deserves ... Great track ... Too many forced carries ... Beautiful views along intercostal waterway ... Needs attention ... Keep it straight or else ... Greens below average ... Six of the best marsh holes.

★★½ OCEAN ISLE BEACH GOLF COURSE
SP-6000 Pro Shop Dr., S.W., Ocean Isle Beach, 28470, Brunswick County, (910)579-2610, 30 miles N of Myrtle Beach.
Holes: 18. **Yards:** 6,626/5,075. **Par:** 72/72. **Course Rating:** 71.8/69.5. **Slope:** 132/111. **Green Fee:** $10/$30. **Cart Fee:** $18/person. **Walking Policy:** Walking at certain times. **Walkability:** 2. **Opened:** 1977. **Architect:** Russell Breeden/Dan Breeden. **Season:** Year-round. **High:** March/May-Sept./Nov. **To obtain tee times:** Call golf shop. **Miscella-neous:** Reduced fees (weekdays, low season, twilight, juniors), discount packages, metal spikes, range (grass), club rentals, credit cards (MC, V, AE, D), beginner friendly.
Reader Comments: Hidden gem ... Fast play .... Take 2 more clubs, wind is a factor ... Treat us like locals ... A great secret, not flashy, solid value ... Good course for higher handicappers.

OCEAN RIDGE PLANTATION
PU-351 Ocean Ridge Pkwy., Sunset Beach, 28469, Brunswick County, (910)287-1717, (800)233-1801, 9 miles N of North Myrtle Beach, SC.
★★★★ LION'S PAW GOLF LINKS
Holes: 18. **Yards:** 7,003/5,363. **Par:** 72/72. **Course Rating:** 74.6/69.1. **Slope:** 138/118. **Green Fee:** $20/$50. **Cart Fee:** $20/person. **Walking Policy:** Mandatory cart. **Walkability:** 3. **Opened:** 1991. **Architect:** Willard Byrd. **Season:** Year-round. **High:** Spring/Fall. **To obtain tee times:** Golf packages or call golf shop. **Miscellaneous:** Reduced fees (weekdays, low season, resort guests, juniors), discount packages, range (grass), club rentals, credit cards (MC, V, AE, D).
Reader Comments: Very nice ... Play in July, you're asking for slow greens ... Can't wait to go back! Great clubhouse ... Greens could be faster... Tough layout, challenging par 3s ... Very friendly staff ... Well run ... Some great holes and water views ... Let the BIG DOG eat ... Good for women ... Fairways open, no trick holes.
★★★½ PANTHER'S RUN GOLF CLUB
PU-351 Ocean Ridge Pkwy. S.W., Sunset Beach, 28469, Brunswick County, (910)287-1703, (800)233-1801, 9 miles N of North Myrtle Beach, SC.

Holes: 18. **Yards:** 7,086/5,023. **Par:** 72/73. **Course Rating:** 74.8/68.8. **Slope:** 140/116. **Green Fee:** $28/$63. **Cart Fee:** $20/person. **Walking Policy:** Mandatory cart. **Walkability:** 3. **Opened:** 1995. **Architect:** Tim Cate. **Season:** Year-round. **High:** Spring/Fall. **To obtain tee times:** Golf packages or call pro shop. **Miscellaneous:** Reduced fees (weekdays, low season, resort guests, juniors), discount packages, range (grass), club rentals, credit cards (MC, V, AE, D), beginner friendly.
Reader Comments: Comfortable place to play ... Like putting through Panther fur ... Too resorty. A bit of a golf machine ... Great track ... Very quiet round as we wound through the layout ... No trees ... Beautiful course from tee to green ... Too short ... Watch out if it's windy.

★★★★½ OLDE BEAU GOLF CLUB AT ROARING GAP *Condition, Pace*
SP-Hwy. 21, Roaring Gap, 28668, Alleghany County, (910)363-3044, (800)752-1634, 60 miles NW of Winston-Salem.
Holes: 18. **Yards:** 6,705/4,912. **Par:** 72/75. **Course Rating:** 71.2/67.5. **Slope:** 131/118. **Green Fee:** $50/$65. **Cart Fee:** $13/person. **Walking Policy:** Mandatory cart. **Walkability:** 5. **Opened:** 1991. **Architect:** Billy Satterfield. **Season:** March-Dec. **High:** July; Oct. **To obtain tee times:** Call up to 14 days in advance. **Miscellaneous:** Metal spikes, range (grass), club rentals, credit cards (MC, V, AE).
Reader Comments: Most scenic I've played ... My favorite mountain course, fantastic ... Pack your parachute for No. 17 ... Hard mountain course, but it is breathtaking! ... Hilly terrain makes for interesting shotmaking.

OLDE FORT GOLF CLUB
PU-3189 River Rd. SE, Winnabow, 28479, Brunswick County, (910)371-9940, 12 miles S of Wilmington.
Holes: 18. **Yards:** 6,311/4,580. **Par:** 72/72. **Course Rating:** N/A. **Slope:** N/A. **Green Fee:** $13/$20. **Cart Fee:** Included in Green Fee. **Walking Policy:** Unrestricted walking. **Walkability:** N/A. **Opened:** 1985. **Season:** Year-round. **High:** Mar.-Nov. **To obtain tee times:** First come, first served. **Miscellaneous:** Reduced fees (weekdays, low season, resort guests, twilight, seniors, juniors).

★★★ OLDE POINT COUNTRY CLUB
SP-Country Club Dr. & Hwy. 17, N., Hampstead, 28443, Pender County, (910)270-2403, 18 miles N of Wilmington. **Web:** oldep.
Holes: 18. **Yards:** 6,913/5,133. **Par:** 72/72. **Course Rating:** 72.5/69.0. **Slope:** 136/115. **Green Fee:** $25/$45. **Cart Fee:** Included in Green Fee. **Walking Policy:** Mandatory cart. **Walkability:** 4. **Opened:** 1974. **Architect:** Jerry Turner. **Season:** Year-round. **High:** March-May. **To obtain tee times:** Call golf shop in advance. **Miscellaneous:** Reduced fees (weekdays, low season), discount packages, range (grass), club rentals, lodging, credit cards (MC, V, AE).
Reader Comments: Fun to play ... Some great holes ... Course does not drain ... Wet! Wet! Wet! ... Play it just for No. 11. ... Back 9 scenic and challenging ... Still the No. 1 hotdogs in the country ... Members make you feel like one of them.

★★★★ OYSTER BAY GOLF LINKS
PU-Hwy. 179, Sunset Beach, 28468, Brunswick County, (800)697-8372, (800)377-2315, 18 miles N of Myrtle Beach, SC.
Holes: 18. **Yards:** 6,785/4,825. **Par:** 71/71. **Course Rating:** 74.1/67.7. **Slope:** 137/117. **Green Fee:** $30/$105. **Cart Fee:** $18/person. **Walking Policy:** Mandatory cart. **Walkability:** 2. **Opened:** 1983. **Architect:** Dan Maples. **Season:** Year-round. **High:** March/April/Oct. **To obtain tee times:** Call up to nine months in advance. Deposit required during high season. Reservations available for all six Legends Group courses and Legends Resorts. **Miscellaneous:** Reduced fees (low season, resort guests), discount packages, metal spikes, range (grass), club rentals, credit cards (MC, V, AE).
Reader Comments: At least 7 signature holes ... Stunning views ... Interesting approach shots ... Wildlife sanctuary with golf ... Fantastic pro shop, first class service.

★★ PAWTUCKET GOLF CLUB
1 Pawtucket Rd., Charlotte, 28214, Mecklenburg County, (704)394-5909.
Special Notes: Call club for further information.

PEARL GOLF LINKS
PU-1300 Pearl Blvd. SW, Sunset Beach, 28468, Brunswick County, (910)579-8132, (888)947-3275, 10 miles N of Myrtle Beach, S.C.
★★★★ EAST COURSE
Holes: 18. **Yards:** 6,749/5,125. **Par:** 72/72. **Course Rating:** 73.1/73.9. **Slope:** 135/129. **Green Fee:** $35/$69. **Cart Fee:** Included in Green Fee. **Walking Policy:** Mandatory cart. **Walkability:** 3. **Opened:** 1987. **Architect:** Dan Maples. **Season:** Year-round. **High:** Spring/Fall. **To obtain tee times:** Call golf shop. **Miscellaneous:** Reduced fees (twilight, juniors), range (grass), club rentals, credit cards (MC, V, AE, D).

Reader Comments: Good test, excellent shape, scenic ... Great track ... Always worth playing ... Greens take a beating from heavy play ... From the tips real tough ... Good blend of golf and nature ... Food was good and fast ... I'll be back ... Nos. 16 and 17 have spectacular views.

★★★★ WEST COURSE
Holes: 18. Yards: 7,000/5,188. Par: 72/72. Course Rating: 73.2/73.4. Slope: 132/127. Green Fee: $31/$69. Cart Fee: Included in Green Fee. Walking Policy: Mandatory cart. Walkability: 3. Opened: 1987. Architect: Dan Maples. Season: Year-round. High: Spring/Fall. To obtain tee times: Call golf shop. Miscellaneous: Reduced fees (twilight, juniors), range (grass), club rentals, credit cards (MC, V, AE, D).
Reader Comments: Good course, lush fairways ... Greens too firm ... Good pro shop ... Very friendly ... Take extra ammo ... Like putting on cement ... Tough par 5s ... Both Pearl's are just that. Some truly great holes.

★½ PINE GROVE GOLF CLUB
PU-1108 Costner Rd., Shelby, 28150, Cleveland County, (704)487-0455, 45 miles W of Charlotte.
Holes: 18. Yards: 6,238/4,774. Par: 70/70. Course Rating: 67.1/65.1. Slope: 106/103. Green Fee: $12/$14. Cart Fee: $12/person. Walking Policy: Walking at certain times. Walkability: 4. Opened: 1960. Architect: Namon Hamrick. Season: Year-round. High: June-Aug. To obtain tee times: Call for weekends and holidays. Miscellaneous: Reduced fees (weekdays, seniors), discount packages, metal spikes.

★★½ PINE KNOLLS GOLF CLUB
PU-1100 Quail Hollow Rd., Kernersville, 27284, Forsyth County, (910)993-8300, 9 miles NE of Winston Salem.
Holes: 18. Yards: 6,287/4,480. Par: 72/72. Course Rating: 70.0/65.0. Slope: 121/92. Green Fee: $15/$19. Cart Fee: $12/person. Walking Policy: Walking at certain times. Walkability: 3. Opened: 1969. Architect: Clyde Holder. Season: Year-round. High: May-Oct. To obtain tee times: Call up to 7 days in advance. Miscellaneous: Reduced fees (weekdays, low season, twilight, seniors, juniors), discount packages, metal spikes, range (grass/mats), club rentals, credit cards (MC, V).
Reader Comments: Wide open, flat greens ... Large greens.

★★★★½ PINE NEEDLES LODGE & GOLF CLUB *Service, Pace*
R-1005 Midland Rd, Southern Pines, 28387, Moore County, (910)692-8611, (800)747-7272, 70 miles S of Raleigh. E-mail: pineneedles@golfnc.com. Web: www.golfnc.com.
Holes: 18. Yards: 6,708/5,039. Par: 71/71. Course Rating: 72.2/68.4. Slope: 131/118. Green Fee: $75/$135. Cart Fee: Included in Green Fee. Walking Policy: Unrestricted walking. Walkability: 2. Opened: 1927. Architect: Donald Ross. Season: Year-round. High: Spring/Fall. To obtain tee times: Call golf shop once a room reservation is made. Outside play is taken on a space-available basis up to 30 days in advance. Miscellaneous: Reduced fees (low season, resort guests, juniors), discount packages, range (grass), caddies, club rentals, lodging (75 rooms), credit cards (MC, V, AE), beginner friendly (beginner golf school, shortened tees). Notes: Ranked 18th in 1999 Best in State. 1996 U.S. Women's Open Championship.
Reader Comments: Incredible experience ... Tough to get in unless on golf package ... A Ross masterpiece ... A great course from the tips ... Really caters to women ... People in pro shop were great ... Most enjoyable day of golf ever ... Greenkeeper de-serves a bonus ... No wonder the USGA stops here ... Great test.

★★ PINE TREE GOLF CLUB
PU-1680 Pine Tree Lane, Kernersville, 27284, Forsyth County, (910)993-5598, 10 miles W of Greensboro. E-mail: twpga@aol.com.
Holes: 18. Yards: 6,682/4,954. Par: 71/72. Course Rating: 71.0/67.0. Slope: 120/112. Green Fee: $15/$19. Cart Fee: $11/person. Walking Policy: Walking at certain times. Walkability: 3. Opened: 1970. Architect: Gene Hamm. Season: Year-round. High: April-Oct. To obtain tee times: Call up to 10 days in advance. Miscellaneous: Reduced fees (seniors), metal spikes, range (grass), club rentals, credit cards (MC, V).

★★ PINEBLUFF GOLF CLUB
PU-U.S. Hwy. #1 S., Pinebluff, 28373, Moore County, (910)281-3169, (888)281-3169, 12 miles S of Pinehurst.
Holes: 18. Yards: 6,583/4,677. Par: 72/72. Course Rating: 71.8/66.0. Slope: 127/103. Green Fee: $15/$15. Cart Fee: $20/person. Walking Policy: Walking at certain times. Walkability: 2. Opened: 1972. Architect: Frank Hicks. Season: Year-round. High: March-May, Oct.-Dec. To obtain tee times: Call golf shop up to 5 months in advance. Miscellaneous: Reduced fees (low season, resort guests), discount packages, metal spikes, range (grass), club rentals, lodging (40 rooms), credit cards (MC, V), beginner friendly.

NORTH CAROLINA

PINEHURST RESORT & COUNTRY CLUB *Service+*

R-Carolina Vista St., Pinehurst, 28374, Moore County, (910)295-8141, (800)795-4653, 70 miles SW of Raleigh.

★★★½ **PINEHURST NO. 1**

Holes: 18. **Yards:** 6,102/5,307. **Par:** 70/73. **Course Rating:** 68.3/70.1. **Slope:** 117/117. **Green Fee:** $78/$123. **Cart Fee:** Included in Green Fee. **Walking Policy:** Unrestricted walking. **Walkability:** 2. **Opened:** 1898. **Architect:** Donald Ross. **Season:** Year-round. **High:** Spring/Fall. **To obtain tee times:** Call 1-800-ITS-GOLF. You must be a resort guest to play. **Miscellaneous:** Reduced fees (low season, twilight), discount packages, range (grass), caddies, club rentals, lodging (250 rooms), credit cards (MC, V, AE, D, Carte Blanche,Diners Club).

Reader Comments: Excellent greens ... Good contrast to No. 2 ... Tough start but fun.

★★★★★ **PINEHURST NO. 2** *Condition*

Holes: 18. **Yards:** 7,175/5,863. **Par:** 72/74. **Course Rating:** 74.1/74.2. **Slope:** 131/135. **Green Fee:** $178/$223. **Cart Fee:** Included in Green Fee. **Walking Policy:** Unrestricted walking. **Walkability:** 2. **Opened:** 1901. **Architect:** Donald Ross. **Season:** Year-round. **High:** Spring/Fall. **To obtain tee times:** Call 1-800-ITS-GOLF. You must be a guest of the resort to play. **Miscellaneous:** Discount packages, range (grass), caddies, club rentals, lodging, credit cards (MC, V, AE, D, Carte Blanche,Diners Club).

Notes: Ranked 9th in 1999-2000 America's 100 Greatest; 1st in 1999 Best in State.

Reader Comments: Crowded, but I thought it was great! ... Take a caddie ... Still the best in the Southeast ... Simply the best, could play every day ... Sculpture in dirt ... Awesome! Those are greens? ... From 100 yards, unbelievably hard ... Walk through history ... You can feel the ghosts. **Special Notes:** Walking allowed only with a caddy.

★★★ **PINEHURST NO. 3**

Holes: 18. **Yards:** 5,662/5,199. **Par:** 70/72. **Course Rating:** 67.2/70.1. **Slope:** 112/114. **Green Fee:** $78/$123. **Cart Fee:** Included in Green Fee. **Walking Policy:** Unrestricted walking. **Walkability:** 2. **Opened:** 1907. **Architect:** Donald Ross. **Season:** Year-round. **High:** Spring/Fall. **To obtain tee times:** Call 1-800-ITS-GOLF. You must be a resort guest to play. **Miscellaneous:** Reduced fees (low season, twilight), discount packages, range (grass), caddies, club rentals, lodging, credit cards (MC, V, AE, D, Carte Blanche,Diners Club).

Reader Comments: Tough greens, tight ... Really fun ... Small greens ... No. 3 is a great warmup for No. 2 ... Crowned greens will get you ... How do you describe a masterpiece?.

★★★★ **PINEHURST NO. 4**

Holes: 18. **Yards:** 7,046/5,774. **Par:** 72/72. **Course Rating:** N/A. **Slope:** N/A. **Green Fee:** $78/$123. **Cart Fee:** Included in Green Fee. **Walking Policy:** Unrestricted walking. **Walkability:** 3. **Opened:** 1914. **Architect:** Tom Fazio. **Season:** Year-round. **High:** Spring/Fall. **To obtain tee times:** Call 1-800-ITS-GOLF. You must be a resort guest to play. **Miscellaneous:** Reduced fees (low season, twilight), discount packages, range (grass), caddies, club rentals, lodging, credit cards (MC, V, AE, D, Carte Blanche,Diners Club).

Reader Comments: As good as No. 2 in playability ... Great traditional course to walk ... Exceptionally tricky, never a dull shot ... Elegant ... Tougher than it looks ... Stepchild course.

★★★½ **PINEHURST NO. 5**

Holes: 18. **Yards:** 6,848/5,248. **Par:** 72/72. **Course Rating:** 73.4/70.1. **Slope:** 137/119. **Green Fee:** $78/$123. **Cart Fee:** Included in Green Fee. **Walking Policy:** Unrestricted walking. **Walkability:** 2. **Opened:** 1961. **Architect:** Ellis Maples. **Season:** Year-round. **High:** Spring/Fall. **To obtain tee times:** Call 1-800-ITS-TIME. You must be a resort guest to play. **Miscellaneous:** Reduced fees (low season, twilight), discount packages, metal spikes, range (grass), caddies, club rentals, lodging, credit cards (MC, V, AE, D, Carte Blanche,Diners Club).

Reader Comments: Pretty ... Least challenging of Pinehurst Courses.

★★★★ **PINEHURST NO. 6**

R-U.S. 15-501, Pinehurst, 28374, Moore County, (910)295-8145, (800)795-4653, 70 miles SW of Raleigh.

Holes: 18. **Yards:** 7,092/5,436. **Par:** 72/72. **Course Rating:** 75.6/71.2. **Slope:** 139/125. **Green Fee:** $78/$123. **Cart Fee:** Included in Green Fee. **Walking Policy:** Mandatory cart. **Walkability:** 3. **Opened:** 1979. **Architect:** Tom Fazio/George Fazio. **Season:** Year-round. **High:** Spring/Fall. **To obtain tee times:** Call 1-800-ITS-GOLF. You must be a resort guest to play. **Miscellaneous:** Reduced fees (low season, twilight), discount packages, range (grass), club rentals, lodging, credit cards (MC, V, AE, D, Carte Blanche,Diners Club).

Reader Comments: My favorite Pinehurst course ... Least interesting Pinehurst layout ... Feel like you're out in the woods ... Scenic course with some challenging water holes ... Traditional Fazio course ... This will challenge you every time ... Lots of woods, hit it straight.

★★★★ **PINEHURST NO. 7** *Pace*

R-U.S. 15-501, Pinehurst, 28374, Moore County, (910)295-8540, (800)795-4653, 70 miles SW of Raleigh.

Holes: 18. **Yards:** 7,125/4,996. **Par:** 72/72. **Course Rating:** 75.6/69.4. **Slope:** 145/124. **Green Fee:** $138/$183. **Cart Fee:** Included in Green Fee. **Walking Policy:** Unrestricted walking. **Walkability:** 5. **Opened:** 1986. **Architect:** Rees Jones. **Season:** Year-round. **High:** Spring/Fall. **To obtain tee times:** Call 1-800-ITS-GOLF. You must be a resort guest to play. **Miscellaneous:**

Reduced fees (low season, twilight), discount packages, range (grass), club rentals, lodging, credit cards (MC, V, AE, D, Carte Blanche, Diners Club).
Notes: Ranked 14th in 1999 Best in State.
Reader Comments: Top caliber ... Best one at Pinehurst ... Back nine looks like Pine Valley ... Very different from other courses ... Harder than No. 2 or No. 8 ... A great layout for mortals ... Very difficult tee to green, but greens are not as tough ... Fair to women ... Most like a 'northern' course ... The cream of Pinehurst.

★★★★½ **PINEHURST NO. 8** *Condition, Pace*
R-Murdocksville Rd., Pinehurst, 28374, Moore County, (910)295-8760, (800)795-4653, 70 miles SW of Raleigh.
Holes: 18. **Yards:** 7,092/5,177. **Par:** 72/72. **Course Rating:** 74.0/68.9. **Slope:** 135/112. **Green Fee:** $148/$193. **Cart Fee:** Included in Green Fee. **Walking Policy:** Unrestricted walking. **Walkability:** 5. **Opened:** 1996. **Architect:** Tom Fazio. **Season:** Year-round. **High:** Spring/Fall. **To obtain tee times:** Call 1-800-ITS-GOLF. You must be a resort guest to play. **Miscellaneous:** Reduced fees (low season, twilight), range (grass), caddies, club rentals, lodging, credit cards (MC, V, AE, D, Carte Blanche, Diners Club).
Notes: Ranked 6th in 1999 Best in State; 3rd in 1996 Best New Upscale Courses.
Reader Comments: Unbelievable ... Great centennial course ... Could host a major ... Second only to No. 2 ... Most difficult of the four courses we played at Pinehurst ... A modern departure from the old course tradition ... Wow! ... Outstanding water views and lots of sand! ... Eight is great.
Special Notes: Spikeless encouraged.

PINEWILD COUNTRY CLUB OF PINEHURST
SP-Hwy. 211, Pinehurst, 28374, Moore County, (910)295-5145, (800)826-7624. **E-mail:** pinewild@pinewild.com. **Web:** www.pinewildcc.com.
HOLLY COURSE
Holes: 18. **Yards:** 7,024/5,475. **Par:** 72/72. **Course Rating:** 73.4/71.4. **Slope:** 131/126. **Green Fee:** $40/$80. **Cart Fee:** $18/person. **Walking Policy:** Walking at certain times. **Walkability:** 3. **Opened:** 1996. **Architect:** Gary Player. **Season:** Year-round. **High:** April-May-Oct. **To obtain tee times:** Call. **Miscellaneous:** Reduced fees (low season, resort guests, juniors), discount packages, range (grass), club rentals, credit cards (MC, V), beginner friendly (ball drops).
MAGNOLIA COURSE
Holes: 18. **Yards:** 7,276/5,362. **Par:** 72/72. **Course Rating:** 75.0/71.1. **Slope:** 135/121. **Green Fee:** $40/$90. **Cart Fee:** $18/person. **Walking Policy:** Walking at certain times. **Walkability:** 2. **Opened:** 1988. **Architect:** Gene Hamm. **Season:** Year-round. **High:** April-May-Oct.
Miscellaneous: Reduced fees (low season, resort guests, juniors), discount packages, range (grass), club rentals, credit cards (MC, V), beginner friendly.

★★★½ **THE PIT GOLF LINKS**
PU-Highway 5 (between Pinehurst & Aberdeen), Pinehurst, 28374, Moore County, (910)944-1600, (800)574-4653, 35 miles W of Fayetteville. **Web:** www.donmaples.com/pit.
Holes: 18. **Yards:** 6,600/4,759. **Par:** 71/72. **Course Rating:** 72.3/68.4. **Slope:** 139/121. **Green Fee:** $30/$80. **Cart Fee:** $18/person. **Walking Policy:** Mandatory cart. **Walkability:** 3. **Opened:** 1985. **Architect:** Dan Maples. **Season:** Year-round. **High:** March/May-Oct. **To obtain tee times:** Call 800-574-4653. **Miscellaneous:** Reduced fees (low season, twilight, juniors), discount packages, metal spikes, range (grass), club rentals, credit cards (MC, V).
Reader Comments: Very tight! Miss a fairway and the ball is a goner ... Too many blind shots ... A unique and enjoyable design ... You either love it or you hate it ... Too tricked up ... Demanding iron shots ... Don't let the name fool you ... It's fun, but crazy ... Target golf—challenging.

★★★★ **THE PLANTATION GOLF CLUB**
SP-Midland Rd., Pinehurst, 28374, Moore County, (910)695-3193, (800)633-2685, 50 miles SW of Raleigh.
Holes: 18. **Yards:** 7,123/4,845. **Par:** 72/73. **Course Rating:** 74.0/68.9. **Slope:** 140/123. **Green Fee:** $60/$115. **Cart Fee:** Included in Green Fee. **Walking Policy:** Mandatory cart. **Walkability:** 4. **Opened:** 1993. **Architect:** Arnold Palmer/Ed Seay. **Season:** Year-round. **High:** April-May/Oct. **To obtain tee times:** Have head pro set up a tee time. Call golf shop out of season.
Miscellaneous: Reduced fees (resort guests), range (grass), club rentals, credit cards (MC, V).
Notes: Ranked 20th in 1999 Best in State.
Reader Comments: Great variety in sets of tees ... Need to play a few times to know strategy ... Watch out. More difficult than it looks ... Excellent greens and layout ... Arnie did a great job here ... You will be tested ... Very tricky greens.

★★★★ **PORTERS NECK PLANTATION & COUNTRY CLUB**
SP-8403 Vintage Club Dr., Wilmington, 28411, New Hanover County, (910)686-1177, (800)947-8177, 3 miles N of Wilmington.
Holes: 18. **Yards:** 7,209/5,268. **Par:** 72/72. **Course Rating:** 75.6/71.2. **Slope:** 140/124. **Green Fee:** $50/$80. **Cart Fee:** Included in Green Fee. **Walking Policy:** Mandatory cart. **Walkability:** 3. **Opened:** 1991. **Architect:** Tom Fazio. **Season:** Year-round. **High:** Feb.-May; Aug.-Oct. **To**

obtain tee times: Call golf shop in advance. **Miscellaneous:** Reduced fees (weekdays, low season, resort guests, twilight), discounts, range (grass), club rentals, credit cards (MC, V, AE).
Notes: Ranked 19th in 1999 Best in State.
Reader Comments: Clubhouse is great but noisy ... Great par 5s ... Test all your skills ... A real treat ... Very women-friendly course ... Not much water ... Playable for all levels ... Worth the trip, I'll be back.

★★½ QUAIL RIDGE GOLF COURSE
SP-5634 Quail Ridge Dr., Sanford, 27330, Lee County, (919)776-6623, (800)344-6276, 30 miles S of Raleigh. **E-mail:** quailridge@cybernet2k.com. **Web:** www.golfersresource.com.
Holes: 18. **Yards:** 6,875/5,280. **Par:** 72/73. **Course Rating:** 73.2/70.8. **Slope:** 125/117. **Green Fee:** $25/$35. **Cart Fee:** Included in Green Fee. **Walking Policy:** Walking at certain times.
Walkability: 3. **Opened:** 1965. **Architect:** Gene Hamm. **Season:** Year-round. **High:** Spring/Fall.
To obtain tee times: Call golf shop up to one week in ad-vance. **Miscellaneous:** Reduced fees (weekdays, low season, twilight, seniors, juniors), discount packages, range (grass/mats), club rentals, lodging, credit cards (MC, V).
Reader Comments: A nice, nothing fancy, 'let's go play' course ... Can get crowded ... Friendly owners and staff ... A great working man's course.

★½ QUAKER MEADOWS GOLF CLUB
PM-826 N. Green St., Morganton, 28655, Burke County, (704)437-2677.
Yards: 6,410/5,002. **Par:** 71/71. **Course Rating:** 70.0/68.2. **Slope:** 117/110. **Green Fee:** $10/$14. **Cart Fee:** $10/person. **Walking Policy:** Walking at certain times. **Walkability:** N/A.
Architect: Russell Breeden. **Season:** Year-round. **To obtain tee times:** Call up to 7 days in advance for weekends and holidays. **Miscellaneous:** Metal spikes, range (grass).

★★½ QUAKER NECK COUNTRY CLUB
SP-299 Country Club Rd., Trenton, 28585, Jones County, (919)224-5736, (800)657-5156, 10 miles S of New Bern. **E-mail:** quakerneck@cconnect.net.
Holes: 18. **Yards:** 6,575/4,953. **Par:** 72/72. **Course Rating:** 71.7/68.5. **Slope:** 126/115. **Green Fee:** $12/$16. **Cart Fee:** $12/person. **Walking Policy:** Unrestricted walking. **Walkability:** 3.
Opened: 1966. **Architect:** Russell T. Burney. **Season:** Year-round. **High:** April-Sept. **To obtain tee times:** Call golf shop. **Miscellaneous:** Reduced fees (weekdays, low season), discounts, metal spikes, range (grass), club rentals, credit cards (MC, V, AE, D), beginner friendly.
Reader Comments: It's come a long way baby ... Tight fairways ... Must stay on fairway.

★★★ QUARRY HILLS COUNTRY CLUB
George Bason Rd., Graham, 27253, Alamance County, (336)578-2602, 20 miles W of Chapel Hill. **Web:** www.quarryhillscc.com.
Holes: 18. **Yards:** 6,617/4,905. **Par:** 70/70. **Course Rating:** 71.9/68.0. **Slope:** 130/116. **Green Fee:** $25/$25. **Cart Fee:** $11/cart. **Walking Policy:** Unrestricted walking. **Walkability:** 4.
Opened: 1970. **Architect:** Ellis Maples/Ed Seay. **Season:** Year-round. **High:** March-Nov. **To obtain tee times:** Call golf shop. **Miscellaneous:** Reduced fees (weekdays), range (grass/mats), club rentals, credit cards (MC, V, AE, D).
Reader Comments: Great par 3s ... Hit it straight at the quarry hole ... Layout is great ... 13th hole over quarry is fun ... Very nice, very challenging.

★★★½ REEDY CREEK GOLF COURSE
PU-585 Reedy Creek Rd., Four Oaks, 27524, Johnston County, (919)934-7502, (800)331-2572, 20 miles E of Raleigh.
Holes: 18. **Yards:** 6,426/4,632. **Par:** 72/72. **Course Rating:** 70.2/67.5. **Slope:** 126/116. **Green Fee:** $10/$25. **Cart Fee:** $10/person. **Walking Policy:** Walking at certain times. **Walkability:** 3.
Opened: 1988. **Architect:** Gene Hamm. **Season:** Year-round. **High:** April-Sept. **To obtain tee times:** Tee times can be reserved 7 days in advance. Groups requiring 3 or more tee times can schedule in advance of 7 days. **Miscellaneous:** Reduced fees (weekdays, resort guests, twilight, seniors, juniors), discounts, metal spikes, range (grass), club rentals, credit cards (MC, V).
Reader Comments: Fun course, nice people ... Has improved in recent years ... Designed for all players ... Great for walking and working on swing ... Exceptionally friendly staff ... Good food in clubhouse ... Unpretentious, off beaten track.

★★★★ REEMS CREEK GOLF CLUB
SP-Pink Fox Cove Rd., Weaverville, 28787, Buncombe County, (828)645-4393, (800)762-8379, 12 miles N of Asheville. **Web:** www.reemscreekgolf.com.
Holes: 18. **Yards:** 6,492/4,605. **Par:** 72/72. **Course Rating:** 70.5/66.9. **Slope:** 130/114. **Green Fee:** $42/$49. **Cart Fee:** Included in Green Fee. **Walking Policy:** Mandatory cart. **Walkability:** 3. **Opened:** 1989. **Architect:** Martin Hawtree/Fred Hawtree. **Season:** Year-round. **High:** March-Oct. **To obtain tee times:** Call up to 30 days in advance. Groups larger than 24 players call six months in advance. **Miscellaneous:** Reduced fees (weekdays, low season, resort guests, juniors), discount packages, metal spikes, range (grass), club rentals, credit cards (MC, V, AE).

NORTH CAROLINA

Reader Comments: Too many blind shots ... The view overpowers the course ... Excit-ing lay-out, beautiful setting ... Carts on path insures slow pace ... Always mushy ... Even during drought, drives plug in fairway ... First class ... Wonderful layout. Fun to play.

★★★ REYNOLDS PARK GOLF CLUB
PM-2391 Reynolds Park Rd., Winston-Salem, 27107, Forsyth County, (336)650-7660. **Holes:** 18. **Yards:** 6,534/5,446. **Par:** 71/73. **Course Rating:** 69.3/70.2. **Slope:** 118/111. **Green Fee:** $15/$19. **Cart Fee:** $11/person. **Walking Policy:** Walking at certain times. **Walkability:** 3. **Opened:** 1939. **Architect:** Ellis Maples. **Season:** Year-round. **High:** April-Sept. **To obtain tee times:** Call seven days in advance. **Miscellaneous:** Reduced fees (weekdays, low season, twi-light, seniors, juniors), metal spikes, range (grass/mats), rentals, credit cards (MC, V, AE, D). **Reader Comments:** A fun course to play ... Always friendly ... Course is overbooked, very slow ... Some good holes and nice greens ... A great test from the back tees ... Nice practice range.

★★ RICHMOND PINES COUNTRY CLUB
SP-145 Richmond Pines Dr., Rockingham, 28379, Richmond County, (910)895-3279, 50 miles E of Charlotte. **Holes:** 18. **Yards:** 6,267/5,051. **Par:** 72/72. **Course Rating:** 69.9/65.0. **Slope:** 127/113. **Green Fee:** $7/$17. **Cart Fee:** $12/person. **Walking Policy:** Unrestricted walking. **Walkability:** 3. **Opened:** 1926. **Architect:** Donald Ross. **Season:** Year-round. **High:** April-May; Aug-Oct. **To obtain tee times:** Call up to 7 days in advance. **Miscellaneous:** Reduced fees (seniors), range (grass), club rentals, credit cards (MC, V), beginner friendly (beginner lessons).

★★★½ RIVER BEND GOLF CLUB
PU-3005 Longwood Dr., Shelby, 28150, Cleveland County, (704)482-4286, 45 miles W of Charlotte. **Holes:** 18. **Yards:** 6,770/5,225. **Par:** 72/72. **Course Rating:** 72.4/69.5. **Slope:** 134/119. **Green Fee:** $21/$37. **Cart Fee:** Included in Green Fee. **Walking Policy:** Walking at certain times. **Walkability:** 3. **Opened:** 1965. **Architect:** Russell Breeden. **Season:** Year-round. **High:** May-Oct. **To obtain tee times:** Call golf shop one day to one week in advance. **Miscellaneous:** Reduced fees (weekdays, seniors, juniors), discount packages, metal spikes, range (grass), club rentals, credit cards (MC, V, D). **Reader Comments:** In-the-country hospitality, glad to see ya ... Tough greens ... Enjoyable course to play ... Made for walking ... Good tournament course ... A lot of fun ... Snack bar staff gives refills with a smile.

★★★★½ RIVER RIDGE GOLF CLUB *Pace*
PU-3224 Auburn-Knightdale Rd., Raleigh, 27610, (919)661-8374. **Holes:** 18. **Yards:** 6,651/5,769. **Par:** 72/71. **Course Rating:** 72.3/70.3. **Slope:** 135/125. **Green Fee:** $23/$33. **Cart Fee:** $12/person. **Walking Policy:** Walking at certain times. **Walkability:** 3. **Opened:** 1997. **Architect:** Chuck Smith. **Season:** Year-round. **High:** April-Oct. **To obtain tee times:** Call up to 1 week in advance. **Miscellaneous:** Reduced fees (weekdays, low season, twi-light, seniors, juniors), range (grass), club rentals, credit cards (MC, V). **Reader Comments:** Tough greens, No. 6 is fantastic! ... Nice straightforward layout, not tricked up ... Wish I could walk on the weekends ... A shotmaker's course.

RIVERWOOD GOLF CLUB
PU-400 Riverwood Dr., Clayton, 27520, Johnston County, (919)550-1919, 20 miles S of Raleigh. **E-mail:** sunbeltgolfgroup.com. **Holes:** 18. **Yards:** 7,012/4,970. **Par:** 72/72. **Course Rating:** 73.8/68.8. **Slope:** 130/115. **Green Fee:** $20/$31. **Cart Fee:** $13/person. **Walking Policy:** Walking at certain times. **Walkability:** 4. **Opened:** 1997. **Architect:** David Postlethwait. **Season:** Year-round. **High:** April-Sept. **To obtain tee times:** Call golf shop. **Miscellaneous:** Reduced fees (weekdays, low season, twilight, seniors, juniors), range (grass/mats), club rentals, credit cards (MC, V, AE, D).

★★★★ ROCK BARN CLUB OF GOLF
SP-3791 Golf Dr., Conover, 28613, Catawba County, (828)459-9279, (888)725-2276, 60 miles NW of Charlotte. **Holes:** 27. **Yards:** 6,778/4,812. **Par:** 72/72. **Course Rating:** 72.2/67.7. **Slope:** 132/117. **Green Fee:** $31/$38. **Cart Fee:** $12/person. **Walking Policy:** Walking at certain times. **Walkability:** 3. **Opened:** 1969. **Architect:** Tom Jackson/Russell Breeden. **Season:** Year-round. **High:** April-Oct. **To obtain tee times:** Call three days in advance. **Miscellaneous:** Reduced fees (weekdays, seniors), range (grass), club rentals, credit cards (MC, V, AE, D). **Reader Comments:** 3 good 9s, well maintained, fair challenge ... New 9 on back is great ... Small town, big course feel ... Like it very much ... Big greens.

★★★★ ROCKY RIVER GOLF CLUB AT CONCORD
PU-6900 Speedway Blvd., Harrisburg, 28075, Cabarrus County, (704)455-1200, 9 miles N of Charlotte. **E-mail:** RRgolf@ctc.net. **Web:** www.rockyrivergolf.com.

Holes: 18. **Yards:** 6,970/4,754. **Par:** 72/72. **Course Rating:** 73.7/68.7. **Slope:** 141/120. **Green Fee:** $24/$44. **Cart Fee:** $12/person. **Walking Policy:** Walking at certain times. **Walkability:** 3. **Opened:** 1997. **Architect:** Dan Maples. **Season:** Year-round. **High:** March-June. **To obtain tee times:** Up to 6 days in advance, in person or by phone. **Miscellaneous:** Reduced fees (weekdays, low season, twilight, seniors, juniors), range (grass), club rentals, credit cards (MC, V, AE). **Reader Comments:** New course, great shape ... Wide open front 9, tree-lined back ... The natural areas are lovely ... Must play ... Good beginners course.

ST. JAMES PLANTATION
★★★½ GAUNTLET
SP-Hwy. 211., Southport, 28461, Brunswick County, (910)253-3008, (800)247-4806, 28 miles S of Wilmington.
Holes: 18. **Yards:** 7,050/5,048. **Par:** 72/72. **Course Rating:** 75.0/69.7. **Slope:** 142/119. **Green Fee:** $11/$74. **Cart Fee:** $19/person. **Walking Policy:** Mandatory cart. **Walkability:** 2. **Opened:** 1990. **Architect:** P.B. Dye. **Season:** Year-round. **High:** March-May. **To obtain tee times:** Call golf shop. **Miscellaneous:** Reduced fees (low season, seniors), discount packages, range (grass), club rentals, credit cards (MC, V).
Reader Comments: Typical Pete Dye course ... Blind shots. Trick holes and greens ... You like marsh, we got marsh! ... Great challenge if greens are fast ... There is more to golf than a low score ... A real brain beater ... Ocean breeze to keep you cool ... What a gem ... Last 4 holes are outstanding.

★★★★ MEMBERS CLUB
SP-3779 Members Club Blvd. #160, Southport, 28461, Brunswick County, (910)253-9500, (800)474-9277, 28 miles SE of Wilmington.
Holes: 18. **Yards:** 6,887/5,113. **Par:** 72/72. **Course Rating:** 73.9/71.0. **Slope:** 135/123. **Green Fee:** $43/$93. **Cart Fee:** Included in Green Fee. **Walking Policy:** Mandatory cart. **Walkability:** 2. **Opened:** 1996. **Architect:** Hale Irwin. **Season:** Year-round. **High:** Feb.-May. **To obtain tee times:** Call golf shop. **Miscellaneous:** Reduced fees (low season, twilight, juniors), discount packages, range (grass), club rentals, credit cards (MC, V).
Reader Comments: Great beverage cart attendants ... Good track ... This course makes you believe ... Very golfer friendly, wide fairways ...Fast greens ... Outstanding ... Plan your shots.

★★★★ PLAYERS CLUB *Pace+*
SP-3640 Players Club Dr., Southport, 28461, (910)457-0049, (910)457-0460.
Holes: 18. **Yards:** 7,062/4,470. **Par:** 72/70. **Course Rating:** 75.1/66.6. **Slope:** 149/113. **Green Fee:** $48/$98. **Cart Fee:** Included in Green Fee. **Walking Policy:** Mandatory cart. **Walkability:** 2. **Opened:** 1997. **Season:** Year-round. **High:** March-May. **To obtain tee times:** Call golf shop. **Miscellaneous:** Reduced fees (weekdays, low season, twilight, seniors, juniors), discount packages, range (grass), club rentals, credit cards (MC, V).

★★★★ **SALEM GLEN COUNTRY CLUB** *Service, Condition, Pace*
SP-1000 Glen Day Dr., Clemmons, 27012, (336)712-1010, 15 miles W of Winston-Salem.
Holes: 18. **Yards:** 7,012/5,054. **Par:** 71/71. **Course Rating:** 74.2/68.9. **Slope:** 136/116. **Green Fee:** $23/$33. **Cart Fee:** $12/person. **Walking Policy:** Walking at certain times. **Walkability:** 4. **Opened:** 1997. **Architect:** Bruce Borland/Glen Day. **Season:** Year-round. **High:** April-Aug. **To obtain tee times:** Call golf shop. **Miscellaneous:** Reduced fees (weekdays, twilight, seniors, juniors), range (grass), club rentals, credit cards (MC, V, AE, D), beginner friendly.
Reader Comments: Service top quality ... Front 9 like links, back 9 hilly ... The greens are true and fast ... Oh, baby, the best greens I've played on ... Good layout, needs maturity.

★★★★ **SANDPIPER BAY GOLF & COUNTRY CLUB**
PU-800 Sandpiper Bay Dr., Sunset Beach, 28468, Brunswick County, (910)579-9120, (800)356-5827, 25 miles N of Myrtle Beach.
Holes: 18. **Yards:** 6,503/4,869. **Par:** 71/71. **Course Rating:** 71.6/68.3. **Slope:** 119/113. **Green Fee:** $14/$52. **Cart Fee:** $18/person. **Walking Policy:** Mandatory cart. **Walkability:** N/A. **Opened:** 1987. **Architect:** Dan Maples. **Season:** Year-round. **High:** Spring/Fall. **To obtain tee times:** Call golf shop. **Miscellaneous:** Reduced fees (weekdays, low season), discount packages, metal spikes, range (grass), club rentals, credit cards (MC, D).
Reader Comments: Course has come back in last few years ... Would send anyone in Calabash here. Do not miss this one ... Good ego boost and easy ... Hazards not well marked, surprise ... Par 3s make this my wife's favorite ... Very pretty with variety of holes ... Great fun for all levels.

★★ **SANDY RIDGE GOLF COURSE**
PU-2025 Sandy Ridge Rd., Colfax, 27235, Guilford County, (910)668-0408, 5 miles W of Greensboro.
Holes: 18. **Yards:** 6,025/5,600. **Par:** 72/72. **Course Rating:** N/A. **Slope:** N/A. **Green Fee:** $12/$15. **Cart Fee:** $8/person. **Walking Policy:** Walking at certain times. **Walkability:** 2. **Opened:** 1970. **Architect:** Gene Hamm. **Season:** Year-round. **High:** June-Sept. **To obtain tee times:** Call Monday before weekend wanting to play. **Miscellaneous:** Reduced fees (seniors), metal spikes, credit cards (MC, V, D).

★★★½ SAPPHIRE MOUNTAIN GOLF CLUB

R-50 Slicer's Ave., Sapphire, 28774, Jackson County, (828)743-1174, 60 miles SW of Asheville. **E-mail:** smggp@aol.com.
Holes: 18. **Yards:** 6,185/4,547. **Par:** 70/70. **Course Rating:** 69.3/65.9. **Slope:** 127/114. **Green Fee:** $30/$62. **Cart Fee:** Included in Green Fee. **Walking Policy:** Mandatory cart. **Walkability:** 5. **Opened:** 1981. **Architect:** Ron Garl. **Season:** Jan.-Dec. **High:** May-Oct. **To obtain tee times:** Call up to 1 month in advance. **Miscellaneous:** Reduced fees (low season, resort guests, twilight, juniors), discount packages, metal spikes, club rentals, lodging, credit cards (MC, V, AE), beginner friendly (lessons).
Reader Comments: Beautiful design, thoroughly enjoyable ... Fun to play ... Nice course, but it doesn't drain well ... Bring your camera! Lakes, streams, wildlife ... Mountain beauty ... Awesome views, good condition ... Some great holes.

★★½ SCOTHURST GOLF COURSE

SP-Hwy. 20 E. P.O. Box 88, Lumber Bridge, 28357, Robeson County, (910)843-5357, 20 miles S of Fayetteville.
Holes: 18. **Yards:** 7,000/5,150. **Par:** 72/72. **Course Rating:** 72.9/70.0. **Slope:** 118/111. **Green Fee:** $25/$28. **Cart Fee:** Included in Green Fee. **Walking Policy:** Walking at certain times. **Walkability:** N/A. **Opened:** 1965. **Architect:** Everett Nash. **Season:** Year-round. **High:** March-Sept. **To obtain tee times:** Call golf shop. **Miscellaneous:** Reduced fees (weekdays, low season), discount packages, metal spikes, range (grass), club rentals.
Reader Comments: Tight fairways, nice layout, some tough holes ... Very good greens ... Great course with very friendly people ... Plays long, fairly flat.

★★★½ SEA SCAPE GOLF LINKS

R-300 Eckner St., Kitty Hawk, 27949, Dare County, (252)261-2158, 70 miles SE of Norfolk, VA. **E-mail:** info@seascapegolf.com. **Web:** www.seascapegolf.com.
Holes: 18. **Yards:** 6,409/5,536. **Par:** 72/73. **Course Rating:** 70.4/70.9. **Slope:** 123/117. **Green Fee:** $39/$78. **Cart Fee:** Included in Green Fee. **Walking Policy:** Mandatory cart. **Walkability:** 2. **Opened:** 1968. **Architect:** Art Wall. **Season:** Year-round. **High:** May-Oct. **To obtain tee times:** Call anytime between 7 a.m. and 7 p.m. Reservations can be made up to one year in advance. **Miscellaneous:** Reduced fees (low season, resort guests, twilight, juniors), range (grass), club rentals, credit cards (MC, V).
Reader Comments: Excellent elevation changes for seaside course ... Too much sand ... Fun but tough! ... Front 9 windy. Back in forest ... Enjoyable ... Bring lots of balls ... One big sand trap ... Fun for average golfer, forgiving on most holes.

SEA TRAIL PLANTATION

R-211 Clubhouse Rd., Sunset Beach, 28468, Brunswick County, (910)287-1125, (800)546-5748, 5 miles N of Sunset Beach. **E-mail:** seatrail@infoave.net. **Web:** www.sea-trail.com.

★★★★ DAN MAPLES COURSE

Holes: 18. **Yards:** 6,751/5,090. **Par:** 72/72. **Course Rating:** 72.4/69.0. **Slope:** 129/115. **Green Fee:** $18/$62. **Cart Fee:** $20/person. **Walking Policy:** Mandatory cart. **Walkability:** 1. **Opened:** 1985. **Architect:** Dan Maples. **Season:** Year-round. **High:** March-April/Oct. **To obtain tee times:** Call anytime. **Miscellaneous:** Reduced fees (low season, resort guests, twilight, juniors), discount packages, range (grass), club rentals, lodging, credit cards (MC, V, AE, D).
Reader Comments: Great track, excellent people ... Picturesque ... Requires position play ... Great hospitality ... Fast greens ... A great place for groups ... One of my favorite beach courses, well maintained, but play is usually slow ... Can't beat summer package ... Easiest of the three courses.

★★★★ REES JONES COURSE

Holes: 18. **Yards:** 6,761/4,912. **Par:** 72/72. **Course Rating:** 72.4/68.5. **Slope:** 132/115. **Green Fee:** $29/$72. **Cart Fee:** $20/person. **Walking Policy:** Mandatory cart. **Walkability:** 1. **Opened:** 1989. **Architect:** Rees Jones. **Season:** Year-round. **High:** March-April/Oct. **To obtain tee times:** Call anytime. **Miscellaneous:** Reduced fees (low season, resort guests, juniors), discount packages, range (grass), club rentals, lodging, credit cards (MC, V, AE, D).
Reader Comments: Best of the 3 ... Great par 3s ... Love the practice area ... Friendly to women ... Too many holes alike ... Big fairways and mounds ... Just tee it up and let it rip.

★★★★ WILLARD BYRD COURSE

Holes: 18. **Yards:** 6,750/4,697. **Par:** 72/72. **Course Rating:** 72.1/67.9. **Slope:** 128/111. **Green Fee:** $19/$62. **Cart Fee:** $20/person. **Walking Policy:** Mandatory cart. **Walkability:** 1. **Opened:** 1990. **Architect:** Willard Byrd. **Season:** Year-round. **High:** March-April/Oct. **To obtain tee times:** Call anytime. **Miscellaneous:** Reduced fees (low season, resort guests, twilight, juniors), discount packages, range (grass), club rentals, lodging, credit cards (MC, V, AE, D).
Reader Comments: Nice layout, beautiful scenery, lots of wildlife ... Rolling course, some challenge ... Interesting par 5s that give you some eagle possibilities ... Pleasant layout for all skill levels.

★★★★ SEVEN LAKES COUNTRY CLUB

SP-P.O. Box 686, West End, 27376, Moore County, (910)673-1092, (888)47LAKES, 10 miles W of Pinehurst. **E-mail:** slcc@ac.net. **Web:** www.sevenlakes.com.
Holes: 18. **Yards:** 6,927/5,192. **Par:** 72/73. **Course Rating:** 74.0/71.0. **Slope:** 139/124. **Green Fee:** $30/$45. **Cart Fee:** $15/person. **Walking Policy:** Mandatory cart. **Walkability:** 3. **Opened:** 1976. **Architect:** Peter Tufts. **Season:** Year-round. **High:** Spring/Fall. **To obtain tee times:** Call golf shop. **Miscellaneous:** Reduced fees (low season, juniors), discount packages, metal spikes, range (grass), club rentals, lodging, credit cards (MC, V).
Reader Comments: Great greens, fine layout, extremely fair golf course, variety in sets of tees ... Underrated, good design, makes you use every club ... Not as easy as you think ... Seems like every approach is uphill ... Excellent blend of holes ... Left, right, short, long.

★½ SHAMROCK GOLF CLUB

PU-1722 Shamrock Dr., Burlington, 27215, Alamance County, (336)227-8566, 35 miles W of Raleigh.
Holes: 18. **Yards:** 6,416/5,017. **Par:** 72/72. **Course Rating:** 70.5/68.5. **Slope:** 125/114. **Green Fee:** $10/$15. **Cart Fee:** Included in Green Fee. **Walking Policy:** Walking at certain times. **Walkability:** 3. **Opened:** 1952. **Architect:** Calvin Walker. **Season:** Year-round. **High:** March-Oct. **To obtain tee times:** Call up to two weeks in advance. **Miscellaneous:** Reduced fees (weekdays, low season, twilight, seniors, juniors), discount packages, metal spikes, range (grass), club rentals, credit cards (MC, V), beginner friendly.

★★★ SILVER CREEK GOLF CLUB

PU-601 Pelletier Loop Rd., Swansboro, 28584, Carteret County, (252)393-8058, (800)393-6605, 3 miles N of Emerald Isle Bridge. **E-mail:** silvercreek@tcpi.com. **Web:** www.emeraldislegolf.com.
Holes: 18. **Yards:** 6,526/5,412. **Par:** 72/72. **Course Rating:** 71.5/69.2. **Slope:** 128/123. **Green Fee:** $27/$45. **Cart Fee:** Included in Green Fee. **Walking Policy:** Walking at certain times. **Walkability:** 3. **Opened:** 1986. **Architect:** Gene Hamm. **Season:** Year-round. **High:** May-Oct. **To obtain tee times:** Call in advance. For groups of 18 or more please call one week in advance. **Miscellaneous:** Reduced fees (low season, resort guests, twilight, juniors), discount packages, range (grass/mats), club rentals, credit cards (MC, V).
Reader Comments: Didn't do much with flat terrain ... Water, water everywhere ... Old style, with elevated greens ... Good drives a must.

★★★★½ THE SOUND GOLF LINKS AT ALBEMARLE PLANTATION
Service, Value, Pace+

SP-101 Clubhouse Dr., Hertford, 27944, Perquimans County, (252)426-5555, (800)535-0704, 80 miles NE of Norfolk.
Holes: 18. **Yards:** 6,500/4,665. **Par:** 72/72. **Course Rating:** 70.1/66.3. **Slope:** 125/113. **Green Fee:** $30/$49. **Cart Fee:** Included in Green Fee. **Walking Policy:** Mandatory cart. **Walkability:** 1. **Opened:** 1990. **Architect:** Dan Maples. **Season:** Year-round. **High:** April-Sept. **To obtain tee times:** Call four months in advance. **Miscellaneous:** Reduced fees (low season, juniors), discount packages, range (grass), club rentals, lodging (10 rooms), credit cards (MC, V).
Reader Comments: It will eat you ... A guaranteed pleasure ... When you think you have mastered every club try this course ... Southern hospitality abounds ... One-of-a-kind layout ... Hidden Dan Maples victory ... Tight. Two sleeves the norm ... Great finishing holes on the sound ... Don't look for balls in rough–snakes eat em!.

★★½ SOURWOOD FOREST GOLF COURSE

PU-8055 Pleasanthill Church Rd., Snow Camp, 27349, Alamance County, (336)376-8166, 15 miles S of Burlington.
Holes: 18. **Yards:** 6,862/5,022. **Par:** 72/72. **Course Rating:** 72.1/68.0. **Slope:** 117/106. **Green Fee:** $11/$16. **Cart Fee:** $10/person. **Walking Policy:** Walking at certain times. **Walkability:** 3. **Opened:** 1990. **Architect:** Elmo Cobb. **Season:** Year-round. **High:** Spring/Fall. **To obtain tee times:** Call golf shop. **Miscellaneous:** Reduced fees (weekdays, twilight, seniors), metal spikes. **Reader Comments:** Hidden gem ... Best par 3s and 5s in area ... Needs better clubhouse ... Premium on driving the ball ... If you can find it, you'll enjoy it ... Lots of trees, hit it straight, fast greens.

★★★½ SPRINGDALE COUNTRY CLUB

R-200 Golfwatch Rd., Canton, 28716, Haywood County, (828)235-8451, (800)553-3027, 11 miles S of Waynesville. **E-mail:** steven@springdalegolf.com. **Web:** www.springdalegolf.com.
Holes: 18. **Yards:** 6,812/5,421. **Par:** 72/72. **Course Rating:** 72.5/72.4. **Slope:** 130/121. **Green Fee:** $40/$45. **Cart Fee:** Included in Green Fee. **Walking Policy:** Walking at certain times. **Walkability:** 5. **Opened:** 1968. **Architect:** Joseph Holmes. **Season:** Year-round. **High:** April-May/Sept.-Oct. **To obtain tee times:** Call up to 3 days in advance for outside play. **Miscellaneous:** Discount packages, metal spikes, range (grass), club rentals, lodging (108 rooms), credit cards (MC, V, AE), beginner friendly (individual or group lessons, practice facility).

Reader Comments: Beautiful setting ... Ultra-friendly staff ... A favorite ... Back 9 holes not very challenging ... Small mountain resort with sloping front and flat back nines ... Many blind shots ... Excellent food.

STAR HILL GOLF & COUNTRY CLUB
SP-202 Clubhouse Dr., Cape Carteret, 28584, Carteret County, (252)393-8111, 1 miles W of Cape Carteret. **E-mail:** starhill@mail.clis.com.
Holes: 27.**Green Fee:** $25/$40. **Cart Fee:** $10/person. **Walking Policy:** Walking at certain times. **Walkability:** 1. **Opened:** 1967. **Architect:** Russell T. Burney. **Season:** Year-round. **High:** April-Oct. **To obtain tee times:** Call to reserve time for any month of current year.
Miscellaneous: Reduced fees (low season, resort guests, twilight, juniors), discount packages, range (grass), club rentals, credit cards (MC, V).
★★★½ **PINES/LAKES**
Yards: 6,548/4,871. **Par:** 72/72. **Course Rating:** 70.4/67.5. **Slope:** 115/108.
Reader Comments: Wife and I love this little gem ... Excellent, better every year ... Fun layout, great for everyone.
★★★½ **SANDS/LAKES**
Yards: 6,575/4,740. **Par:** 72/72. **Course Rating:** 70.9/73.2. **Slope:** 119/109.
★★★½ **SANDS/PINES**
Yards: 6,361/4,649. **Par:** 72/72. **Course Rating:** 70.5/73.6. **Slope:** 115/107.

STONEBRIDGE GOLF CLUB
SP-2721 Swilcan Burn, Monroe, 28112, Union County, (704)283-8998, (888)337-2582, 10 miles S of Charlotte.
Holes: 18. **Yards:** 6,923/5,145. **Par:** 72/72. **Course Rating:** 73.6/69.6. **Slope:** 132/120. **Green Fee:** $17/$35. **Cart Fee:** $14/person. **Walking Policy:** Walking at certain times. **Walkability:** 1. **Opened:** 1997. **Architect:** Richard B. Osborne. **Season:** Year-round. **High:** April-May/October. **To obtain tee times:** Call up to 4 days in advance. **Miscellaneous:** Reduced fees (weekdays, twilight, seniors, juniors), range (grass), club rentals, credit cards (MC, V, AE), beginner friendly (clinics).

★★★★ STONEY CREEK GOLF CLUB
PU-911 Golf House Rd. E., Stoney Creek, 27377, Guilford County, (336)449-5688, 12 miles E of Greensboro.
Holes: 18. **Yards:** 7,101/4,737. **Par:** 72/72. **Course Rating:** 74.5/69.8. **Slope:** 144/123. **Green Fee:** $25/$35. **Cart Fee:** $14/person. **Walking Policy:** Walking at certain times. **Walkability:** 4. **Opened:** 1992. **Architect:** Tom Jackson. **Season:** Year-round. **High:** Spring/Fall. **To obtain tee times:** Call up to 7 days in advance. **Miscellaneous:** Reduced fees (weekdays, low season, twilight, seniors, juniors), discount packages, range (grass), club rentals, credit cards (MC, V, AE).
Reader Comments: Wow! Love the course, even if it did severely humble me ... Pace of play sometimes slow ... Very tough course ... Killer from tips ... 1st hole strong test ... Good course. Fun to play. Tough for high handicaps ... Excellent. It will be tough to get a tee time in the future ... Greens were great ... Wore me out!

★★★★ TALAMORE RESORT
PU-48 Talamore Drive, Southern Pines, 28387, Moore County, (910)692-5884, 2 miles E of Pinehurst.
Holes: 18. **Yards:** 7,020/4,945. **Par:** 71/72. **Course Rating:** 72.9/69.0. **Slope:** 142/125. **Green Fee:** $39/$95. **Cart Fee:** Included in Green Fee. **Walking Policy:** Walking at certain times. **Walkability:** 4. **Opened:** 1992. **Architect:** Rees Jones. **Season:** Year-round. **High:** Spring/Fall. **To obtain tee times:** Call golf shop. **Miscellaneous:** Reduced fees (low season, resort guests, twilight, juniors), discount packages, range (grass), club rentals, lodging, credit cards (MC, V). **Notes:** Ranked 18th in 1997 Best in State.
Reader Comments: Not heavily played, but one of the best courses in Pinehurst area ... Pick cart or llama ... More sand than most beaches ... Forget the llamas, bring your short game ... Demanding tee shots ... Great par 3s ... Massive fairway bunkers ... Everything very good, but snack bar ... Country club quality for public golfers.

TANGLEWOOD PARK
PU-Hwy. 158 W., Clemmons, 27012, Forsyth County, (336)778-6320, 5 miles W of Winston-Salem. **Web:** www.tanglewoodpark.org.com.
★★★★ **CHAMPIONSHIP COURSE**
Holes: 18. **Yards:** 7,018/5,119. **Par:** 70/74. **Course Rating:** 74.5/70.9. **Slope:** 140/130. **Green Fee:** $16/$50. **Cart Fee:** $14/person. **Walking Policy:** Walking at certain times. **Walkability:** 3. **Opened:** 1957. **Architect:** Robert Trent Jones. **Season:** Year-round. **High:** Spring/Fall. **To obtain tee times:** Call 7 days in advance. Lodge guests may make tee times when booking reservations. **Miscellaneous:** Reduced fees (weekdays, low season, resort guests, twilight, seniors, juniors), discount packages, range (grass), club rentals, lodging, credit cards (MC, V, AE), beginner friendly.
Notes: Ranked 7th in 1999 Best in State.

Reader Comments: Long and difficult ... Lots of tough bunkers ... Fine test of golf ... Bunkers ... A must play ... It's fun playing where the pros play ... Very, very, very good ... Play where the senior pros play ... Greens roll true ... Loved it, what a challenge ... Red sand ... Just goes to show you how good the seniors are.

★★★½ REYNOLDS COURSE

Holes: 18. **Yards:** 6,537/5,308. **Par:** 72/72. **Course Rating:** 71.8/71.5. **Slope:** 135/122. **Green Fee:** $16/$30. **Cart Fee:** $14/person. **Walking Policy:** Walking at certain times. **Walkability:** 4. **Opened:** 1959. **Architect:** Robert Trent Jones. **Season:** Year-round. **High:** Spring/Fall. **To obtain tee times:** Call 7 days in advance. Lodge guests may make tee times when making lodge reservations. **Miscellaneous:** Reduced fees (weekdays, low season, resort guests, twilight, seniors, juniors), discount packages, range (grass), club rentals, lodging, credit cards (MC, V, AE), beginner friendly (junior camps).

Reader Comments: Excellent value for seniors ... Poor sister to Championship course, not comparable ... Long and difficult ... Great layout, only hurt by condition ... Bring a good short game .... Very enjoyable ... Tighter, prettier than Championship course.

THISTLE GOLF CLUB

PU-8840 Old Georgetown Rd., Sunset Beach, 28470, Brunswick County, (910)575-8700, (800)571-6710, 25 miles NE of Myrtle Beach, SC. **Web:** www.thistlegolf.com.
Holes: 18. **Yards:** 6,997/4,612. **Par:** 72/72. **Course Rating:** 74.9/67.2. **Slope:** 136/112. **Green Fee:** $39/$90. **Cart Fee:** $20/person. **Walking Policy:** Walking at certain times. **Walkability:** 2. **Opened:** 1999. **Architect:** Tim Cate. **Season:** Year-round. **High:** March-May, Sept.-Nov. **To obtain tee times:** Call, or e-mail through web site. **Miscellaneous:**
Reduced fees (low season, juniors), range (grass), club rentals, credit cards (MC, V, AE).

TOBACCO ROAD GOLF CLUB

PU-442 Tobacco Rd., Sanford, 27330, Lee County, (919)775-1940, (877)284-3762, 20 miles N of Pinehurst. **Web:** www.tobaccoroadgolf.com.
Holes: 18. **Yards:** 6,554/5,094. **Par:** 71/71. **Course Rating:** 73.2/70.4. **Slope:** 150/128. **Green Fee:** $48/$85. **Cart Fee:** $18/person. **Walking Policy:** Unrestricted walking. **Walkability:** 4. **Opened:** 1999. **Architect:** Mike Strantz. **Season:** Year-round. **High:** March-May; Sept.-Nov. **To obtain tee times:** By phone or in person, w/credit card; 48 hr. cancellation policy. **Miscellaneous:** Reduced fees (weekdays, low season, juniors), discount packages, range (grass), club rentals, credit cards (MC, V). **Notes:** Ranked tied for 10th in 1999 Best New Upscale Public.

★★ TOWN OF MOORESVILLE GOLF COURSE

PM-W. Wilson Rd. P. O. Box 878, Mooresville, 28115, Iredell County, (704)663-2539, 25 miles N of Charlotte. **E-mail:** cbrgolf@ci.mooresville.nc.us. **Web:** http://ci.mooresville.nc.us/.
Holes: 18. **Yards:** 6,603/4,917. **Par:** 72/72. **Course Rating:** 72.4/68.5. **Slope:** 126/113. **Green Fee:** $11/$14. **Cart Fee:** $11/person. **Walking Policy:** Unrestricted walking. **Walkability:** 3. **Opened:** 1940. **Architect:** Donald Ross/J. Porter Gibson. **Season:** Year-round. **High:** March-Sept. **To obtain tee times:** Call 3 days in advance for weekdays and one week in advance for Fridays, Saturdays, Sundays and holidays. **Miscellaneous:** Reduced fees (seniors, juniors), range (grass), club rentals, credit cards (MC, V).

THE TRADITION

PU-3800 Prosperity Church Rd., Charlotte, 28269, Mecklenberg County, (704)549-9400. **Web:** www.charlottegolf.com.
Holes: 18. **Yards:** 6,978/5,422. **Par:** 72/72. **Course Rating:** 72.9/69.4. **Slope:** 140/126. **Green Fee:** $17/$44. **Cart Fee:** $13/person. **Walking Policy:** Walking at certain times. **Walkability:** 3. **Opened:** 1996. **Architect:** John Cassell. **Season:** Year-round. **High:** May-June,Sept.-Nov. **To obtain tee times:** 7 days in advance (704)358-GOLF. **Miscellaneous:** Reduced fees (weekdays, low season, twilight, seniors, juniors), range (grass), club rentals, credit cards (MC, V, AE).

TRILLIUM LINKS

PU-245 Links Dr., Cashiers, 28717, Jackson County, (828)743-4251, (888)909-7171, 70 miles SW of Asheville. **E-mail:** links@dnet.net. **Web:** www.trilliumnc.com.
Holes: 18. **Yards:** 6,505/4,340. **Par:** 71/71. **Course Rating:** 72.4/66.0. **Slope:** 134/120. **Green Fee:** N/A. **Cart Fee:** Included in Green Fee. **Walking Policy:** Mandatory cart. **Walkability:** 5. **Opened:** 1998. **Architect:** Morris Hatalsky. **Season:** April-Nov. **High:** June-Oct. **To obtain tee times:** Call up to 45 days in advance. **Miscellaneous:** Reduced fees (weekdays, low season, twilight), metal spikes, range (grass/mats), club rentals, lodging, credit cards (MC, V, AE).

★★ TWIN OAKS GOLF COURSE

PU-320 Twin Oaks Rd., Statesville, 28625, Iredell County, (704)872-3979, 50 miles N of Charlotte.
Holes: 18. **Yards:** 6,094/4,729. **Par:** 72/72. **Course Rating:** 68.0/65.9. **Slope:** 111/104. **Green Fee:** $12/$22. **Cart Fee:** Included in Green Fee. **Walking Policy:** Walking at certain times. **Walkability:** 1. **Opened:** 1960. **Season:** Year-round. **High:** April-Aug. **To obtain tee times:** Call

anytime. **Miscellaneous:** Reduced fees (weekdays, seniors), metal spikes, range (grass), club rentals, credit cards (MC, V, AE).

★★½ WAKE FOREST GOLF CLUB
SP-13239 Capital Blvd., Wake Forest, 27587, Wake County, (919)556-3416, 12 miles N of Raleigh.
Holes: 18. **Yards:** 6,952/5,124. **Par:** 72/72. **Course Rating:** 74.4/70.0. **Slope:** 135/122. **Green Fee:** $20/$45. **Cart Fee:** Included in Green Fee. **Walking Policy:** Walking at certain times. **Walkability:** 3. **Opened:** 1967. **Architect:** Gene Hamm. **Season:** Year-round. **High:** April-June. **To obtain tee times:** Tee times can be made 7 days in advance. A credit card is required for weekend tee times. **Miscellaneous:** Reduced fees (twilight, seniors, juniors), range (grass), club rentals, credit cards (MC, V, AE).
Reader Comments: Layout good. Greens in poor shape ... Need good iron play.

★★½ WALNUT WOOD GOLF COURSE
PU-3172 Alamance Church Rd., Julian, 27283, Guilford County, (910)697-8140, 15 miles SE of Greensboro.
Holes: 18. **Yards:** 6,409/4,962. **Par:** 73/73. **Course Rating:** 70.1/68.1. **Slope:** 126/114. **Green Fee:** $18/$23. **Cart Fee:** Included in Green Fee. **Walking Policy:** Walking at certain times. **Walkability:** 3. **Opened:** 1978. **Architect:** Ralph Clendenin. **Season:** Year-round. **High:** May-Sept. **To obtain tee times:** First come, first served. **Miscellane-ous:** Reduced fees (seniors), range (grass/mats), club rentals, credit cards (MC, V).
Reader Comments: Easy course ... Unique holes ... Hump-backed greens ... Ego builder ... Tight fairways.

WAYNESVILLE COUNTRY CLUB INN
R-Ninevah Rd., Waynesville, 28786, Haywood County, (704)452-4617, 25 miles W of Asheville.
★★★½ CAROLINA/BLUE RIDGE
Holes: 27. **Yards:** 5,943/5,002. **Par:** 70/70. **Course Rating:** 66.8/67.0. **Slope:** 104/104. **Green Fee:** $13/$28. **Cart Fee:** $15/person. **Walking Policy:** Walking at certain times. **Walkability:** 4. **Opened:** 1926. **Architect:** Tom Jackson. **Season:** Year-round. **High:** March-Oct. **To obtain tee times:** Call one day in advance. Guests at the hotel may make tee times at time of reservation. **Miscellaneous:** Reduced fees (low season, resort guests, twilight, juniors), discount packages, metal spikes, club rentals, lodging, credit cards (MC, V).
Reader Comments: Very relaxing ... Good old folks course ... Pitch & Putt ... A practice course ... Wonderful setup for the everyday player ... Interesting three nines ... 3 very different 9s ... Friendly staff ... The inn is great ... Great food.
★★★½ CAROLINA/DOGWOOD
Holes: 27. **Yards:** 5,798/4,927. **Par:** 70/70. **Course Rating:** 66.4/66.6. **Slope:** 103/103. **Green Fee:** $13/$28. **Cart Fee:** $15/person. **Walking Policy:** Walking at certain times. **Walkability:** 4. **Opened:** 1926. **Architect:** Tom Jackson. **Season:** Year-round. **High:** March-Oct. **To obtain tee times:** Call one day in advance. Guests at the hotel may make tee times at time of reservation. **Miscellaneous:** Reduced fees (low season, resort guests, twilight, juniors), discount packages, metal spikes, club rentals, lodging, credit cards (MC, V).
★★★½ DOGWOOD/BLUE RIDGE
Holes: 27. **Yards:** 5,803/4,565. **Par:** 70/70. **Course Rating:** 66.4/65.0. **Slope:** 105/100. **Green Fee:** $13/$28. **Cart Fee:** $15/person. **Walking Policy:** Walking at certain times. **Walkability:** 4. **Opened:** 1926. **Architect:** Tom Jackson. **Season:** Year-round. **High:** March-Oct. **To obtain tee times:** Call one day in advance. Guests at the hotel may make tee times at time of reservation. **Miscellaneous:** Reduced fees (low season, resort guests, twilight, juniors), discount packages, metal spikes, club rentals, lodging, credit cards (MC, V).

★★ WENDELL COUNTRY CLUB
SP-180 Jake May Dr., Wendell, 27591, Wake County, (919)365-7337, 15 miles E of Raleigh.
Holes: 18. **Yards:** 6,358/4,891. **Par:** 71/71. **Course Rating:** 69.5/68.0. **Slope:** 116/113. **Green Fee:** $10/$19. **Cart Fee:** $10/person. **Walking Policy:** Walking at certain times. **Walkability:** 2. **Architect:** Ken Dye. **Season:** Year-round. **To obtain tee times:** Call golf shop. **Miscellaneous:** Reduced fees (seniors), metal spikes, credit cards (MC, V).

★★ WESTPORT GOLF COURSE
PU-7494 Golf Course Dr. S., Denver, 28037, Lincoln County, (704)483-5604, 25 miles N of Charlotte.
Holes: 18. **Yards:** 6,805/5,600. **Par:** 72/72. **Course Rating:** 72.3/69.5. **Slope:** 123/118. **Green Fee:** $20/$28. **Cart Fee:** $12/person. **Walking Policy:** Walking at certain times. **Walkability:** 3. **Opened:** 1968. **Architect:** Porter Gibson. **Season:** Year-round. **High:** April-Oct. **To obtain tee times:** Call up to 7 days in advance. **Miscellaneous:** Reduced fees (weekdays, low season, twilight, seniors), range (grass), club rentals, credit cards (MC, V, D).

★★½ WHISPERING WOODS GOLF CLUB

SP-26 Sandpiper Dr., Whispering Pines, 28327, Moore County, (910)949-4653, (800)224-5061, 6 miles NE of Pinehurst. **E-mail:** thewoods@psinet.com.
Holes: 18. **Yards:** 6,334/4,924. **Par:** 70/71. **Course Rating:** 70.5/68.7. **Slope:** 122/122. **Green Fee:** $25/$50. **Cart Fee:** Included in Green Fee. **Walking Policy:** Unrestricted walking.
Walkability: 4. **Opened:** 1975. **Architect:** Ellis Maples. **Season:** Year-round. **High:** Spring/Fall.
To obtain tee times: Call up to one year in advance up to day of play. Credit card required for out of town reservation. **Miscellaneous:** Reduced fees (low season, twilight, juniors), discount packages, credit cards (MC, V).
Reader Comments: Some interesting holes and greens ... A relatively short course that can keep you in trouble ... Short hilly course, greens excellent, fairways thin and rough ... Friendly people.

★★★½ WOODBRIDGE GOLF LINKS

PU-1007 New Camp Creek Church Rd., Kings Mountain, 28086, Cleveland County, (704)482-0353, 30 miles W of Charlotte.
Holes: 18. **Yards:** 6,743/5,151. **Par:** 72/73. **Course Rating:** 72.3/70.4. **Slope:** 131/127. **Green Fee:** $28/$38. **Cart Fee:** Included in Green Fee. **Walking Policy:** Walking at certain times.
Walkability: 4. **Opened:** 1976. **Architect:** Bob Toski/Porter Gibson. **Season:** Year-round. **High:** April-Oct. **To obtain tee times:** Call up to one week in advance. **Miscellaneous:** Reduced fees (twilight), range (grass), club rentals, credit cards (MC, V).
Reader Comments: Diamond in the rough, great layout ... Good older course ... No. 12 is a journey ... The back nine is great ... Rangers actually do their job! ... Very nice, somewhat challenging, nice greens ... Nice setting with views ... Always fun, back nine harder than front.

WOODLAKE COUNTRY CLUB

★★★½ MAPLES

R-150 Woodlake Blvd., Vass, 28394, Moore County, (910)245-7137, (888)THE-LAKE, 6 miles N of Pinehurst. **Web:** www.woodlakecc.com.
Holes: 18. **Yards:** 7,043/5,303. **Par:** 72/72. **Course Rating:** 73.2/71.6. **Slope:** 134/130. **Green Fee:** $30/$70. **Cart Fee:** Included in Green Fee. **Walking Policy:** Mandatory cart. **Walkability:** 4. **Opened:** 1973. **Architect:** Ellis Maples/Dan Maples. **Season:** Year- round. **High:** March-May.
To obtain tee times: Call up to a year in advance. **Miscella-neous:** Reduced fees (weekdays, low season, resort guests, twilight, juniors), discount packages, range (grass), club rentals, lodging (70 rooms), credit cards (MC, V, AE).
Reader Comments: Maple course is solid ... Fun to play ... Beautiful lake holes ... Great par 3s ... Greens varying speeds ... A fair course with a great finishing hole ... Double bets on 18 ... Very scenic ... Course very wet in winter and spring ... Nice staff ... Challenging, not overwhelming ... Both courses fun but different.

★★★½ PALMER

R-150 Woodlake Blvd., Vass, 28394, Moore County, (910)245-7137, (800)THE-LAKE, 6 miles N of Pinehurst.
Holes: 18. **Yards:** 6,962/5,223. **Par:** 72/72. **Course Rating:** 73.5/69.6. **Slope:** 133/118. **Green Fee:** $30/$70. **Cart Fee:** Included in Green Fee. **Walking Policy:** Mandatory cart. **Walkability:** 3. **Opened:** 1996. **Architect:** Arnold Palmer. **Season:** Year-round. **High:** March-May. **To obtain tee times:** Call up to a year in advance. **Miscellaneous:** Reduced fees (weekdays, low season, resort guests, twilight), discount packages, range (grass), lodging (70 rooms), credit cards (MC, V, AE), beginner friendly.
Reader Comments: Concentrate on keeping ball dry ... Love the course ... Excellent strategy and fair course ... Great sandhills course.
Special Notes: Formerly Lake Shore/Cranes Cove

NORTH DAKOTA

BEULAH MUNICIPAL GOLF COURSE
PU-Hwy. 49, Beulah, 58523, Mercer County, (701)873-2929, 80 miles NW of Bismarck.
Holes: 9. **Yards:** 3,121/2,613. **Par:** 35/36. **Course Rating:** N/A/67.9. **Slope:** N/A/109. **Green Fee:** $13/$15. **Cart Fee:** $15/cart. **Walking Policy:** Unrestricted walking. **Walkability:** 3. **Season:** April-Oct. **To obtain tee times:** Call Pro Shop. **Miscellaneous:** Range (grass), club rentals.

★★½ BOIS DE SIOUX GOLF CLUB
PU-N. 4th St. and 13th Ave., Wahpeton, 58075, Richland County, (701)642-3673, 45 miles S of Fargo.
Holes: 18. **Yards:** 6,648/5,500. **Par:** 72/72. **Course Rating:** 71.7/71.3. **Slope:** 122/115. **Green Fee:** $19/$21. **Cart Fee:** $20/cart. **Walking Policy:** Unrestricted walking. **Walkability:** 1. **Opened:** 1924. **Architect:** Robert Bruce Harris. **Season:** April-Nov. **High:** April-Sept. **To obtain tee times:** Call 7 days in advance. **Miscellaneous:** Reduced fees (weekdays, juniors), range (grass/mats), club rentals, credit cards (MC, V), beginner friendly (beginner adult and junior classes, beginner friendly adult league).
Reader Comments: Greens especially interesting, plays long ... Courteous staff ... Front 9 is wide open. Back 9 is tight and a good test of skill ... Challenging layout ... Pick the right season to play here, late summer.

CARRINGTON GOLF CLUB
SP-P.O. Box 176, Carrington, 58421, Foster County, (701)652-2601.
Holes: 9. **Yards:** 2,890/2,600. **Par:** 36/36. **Course Rating:** 65.8/69.5. **Slope:** 106/111. **Green Fee:** $14/$14. **Cart Fee:** $14/cart. **Walking Policy:** Unrestricted walking. **Walkability:** 1. **Season:** April-Oct. **High:** May-Sept. **To obtain tee times:** No tee times. **Miscellaneous:** Reduced fees (juniors), range (grass), club rentals.

EDGEWATER MUNICIPAL GOLF COURSE
PU-Hwy. 23, New Town, 58763, Mountrail County, (701)627-9407.
Holes: 9. **Yards:** 3,278/2,758. **Par:** 36/36. **Course Rating:** 70.4/71.4. **Slope:** 113/111. **Green Fee:** $14/$16. **Cart Fee:** $13/cart. **Walking Policy:** Unrestricted walking. **Walkability:** 3. **Season:** April-Oct. **High:** July-Aug. **Miscellaneous:** Discount packages, range (grass), club rentals, credit cards (MC, V), beginner friendly (high school golf program).

★★★½ EDGEWOOD GOLF COURSE
PU-19 Golf Avenue, Fargo, 58102, Cass County, (701)232-2824.
Holes: 18. **Yards:** 6,369/5,176. **Par:** 71/71. **Course Rating:** 68.4/68.9. **Slope:** 122/115. **Green Fee:** $17/$20. **Cart Fee:** $20/cart. **Walking Policy:** Unrestricted walking. **Walkability:** 2. **Opened:** 1951. **Architect:** Robert Bruce Harris. **Season:** April-Nov. **High:** July-Aug. **To obtain tee times:** Call 3 days in advance. **Miscellaneous:** Reduced fees (twilight, seniors, juniors), discount packages, range (grass/mats), club rentals, credit cards (MC, V), beginner friendly (private or group lessons).
Notes: Ranked 5th in 1999 Best in State.
Reader Comments: Mature course ... Old-fashion design ... Fair test ... Fun course, old trees, great value for money ... Wooded, short, very interesting ... Well maintained, lots of trees ... Great golf course ... Must-play in Fargo ... Best course in North Dakota ... Enjoy a 'cold one' in the 19th hole ... Tight course.

★★★½ HEART RIVER MUNICIPAL GOLF COURSE
PM-8th St. S.W., Dickinson, 58601, Stark County, (701)225-9412, 2 miles SW of Dickinson.
Holes: 18. **Yards:** 6,734/4,738. **Par:** 72/72. **Course Rating:** 70.8/71.0. **Slope:** 125/116. **Green Fee:** $10/$14. **Cart Fee:** $15/cart. **Walking Policy:** Unrestricted walking. **Walkability:** 3. **Opened:** 1983. **Architect:** Abe Epinosa/Dick Phelps, Brad Benz and Mike Poellot. **Season:** March-Oct. **High:** June-Aug. **To obtain tee times:** Call 3 days in advance. **Miscellaneous:** Reduced fees (juniors), range (grass), club rentals, credit cards (MC, V), beginner friendly.
Reader Comments: Fun and challenging ... Great course. Lots of water in back 9 ... The course was nice from tee to green.

★★★½ JAMESTOWN COUNTRY CLUB
SP-RR1 SE of City, Jamestown, 58401, Stutsman County, (701)252-5522, 3 miles SE of Jamestown.
Holes: 18. **Yards:** 6,567/5,252. **Par:** 72/72. **Course Rating:** 70.9/69.7. **Slope:** 122/114. **Green Fee:** $25/$30. **Cart Fee:** $24/cart. **Walking Policy:** Unrestricted walking. **Walkability:** 1. **Opened:** 1963. **Season:** April-Oct. **High:** June-Aug. **To obtain tee times:** Call up to 7 days in advance. **Miscellaneous:** Reduced fees (juniors), range (grass), club rentals, credit cards (MC, V).
Reader Comments: Beautiful James River Valley ... Nice track ... Newly revitalized, tree planting ... A little out of shape, partly because of flooding ... Challenging course ... Traditional layout with good shot values.

LANSFORD COUNTRY CLUB
PU-Box 66, Lansford, 58750, (701)784-5585.
Special Notes: Call club for further information.

★★½ LINCOLN PARK GOLF COURSE
PU-P.O. Box 12429, Grand Forks, 58208, Grand Forks County, (701)746-2788.
Holes: 18. **Yards:** 6,006/5,382. **Par:** 71/71. **Course Rating:** 67.0/69.7. **Slope:** 108/112. **Green Fee:** $13/$15. **Cart Fee:** $15/cart. **Walking Policy:** Unrestricted walking. **Walkability:** 2.
Opened: 1929. **Season:** April-Oct. **High:** May-July. **To obtain tee times:** Call up to 7 days in advance. **Miscellaneous:** Reduced fees (twilight), club rentals, credit cards (MC, V).
Reader Comments: Very busy. Very basic ... Easy course but excellent value and service ... Short, crowded ... Short course made interesting with trees ... Nice flat municipal course along the Red River... Nice way to spend a morning.

★★★★½ THE LINKS OF NORTH DAKOTA AT RED MIKE RESORT
Service, Value+, Condition, Pace+
PU-Hwy. 1804, Ray, 58849, Williams County, (701)568-2600, 27 miles E of Williston.
Holes: 18. **Yards:** 7,092/5,249. **Par:** 72/72. **Course Rating:** 73.5/69.5. **Slope:** 126/114. **Green Fee:** $30/$35. **Cart Fee:** $18/cart. **Walking Policy:** Unrestricted walking. **Walkability:** 3.
Opened: 1995. **Architect:** Stephen Kay. **Season:** April-Oct. **High:** July-Sept. **To obtain tee times:** Call golf shop. **Miscellaneous:** Reduced fees (twilight), range (grass), credit cards (MC, V), beginner friendly (teaching pro, driving range, putting green).
Notes: Ranked 1st in 1999 Best in State; 2nd in 1996 Best New Affordable Courses.
Reader Comments: Best value ever... 'Sandhills' for the common man ... Red Mike is very scenic ... Spectacular views of Lake Sakakawea ... Good condition ... Plays tough due to winds off the lake ... Excellent grounds crew... A gem in the middle of nowhere ... Great course in the country ... No homes are by it ... Best course in N.D. ... True links golf with native shrubs and grasses.

MANUEL GOLF COURSE
PU-839 S. 23rd. St., Grand Forks, 58201, (701)696-8268.
Special Notes: Call club for further information

★★★ MAPLE RIVER GOLF CLUB
SP-I-94 Exit 338, Mapleton, 58059, Cass County, (701)282-5415, 12 miles W of Fargo.
Holes: 9. **Yards:** 3,329/2,822. **Par:** 36/37. **Course Rating:** 71.1/71.1. **Slope:** 123/120. **Green Fee:** $17/$19. **Cart Fee:** $20/cart. **Walking Policy:** Unrestricted walking. **Walkability:** 2.
Opened: 1966. **Season:** April-Oct. **High:** June-July-Aug. **To obtain tee times:** Tee times for members only. Walk-ons welcome—first come first served. **Miscellaneous:** Reduced fees (weekdays, seniors, juniors), range (grass), club rentals, credit cards (MC, V).
Reader Comments: Greens excellent, fast, some holes very long ... Excellent greens ... Fun nine holes, can be windy ... Nice challenge ... Fall is beautiful, maple trees ... Best greens in N.D. ... Great secret ... Nice variety in 9 holes.

★★★½ MINOT COUNTRY CLUB
SP-Country Rd. 15 W., Minot, 58701, Ward County, (701)839-6169, 4 miles W of Minot.
Holes: 18. **Yards:** 6,565/5,270. **Par:** 72/72. **Course Rating:** 72.1/70.8. **Slope:** 131/123. **Green Fee:** $32/$32. **Cart Fee:** $19/person. **Walking Policy:** Unrestricted walking. **Walkability:** 2.
Opened: 1929. **Architect:** Tom Vardon/Robert Bruce Harris. **Season:** April-Nov. **High:** June-Aug. **To obtain tee times:** Call one day in advance. **Miscellaneous:** Reduced fees (juniors), range (grass), club rentals, credit cards (MC, V).
Notes: Ranked 4th in 1999 Best in State.
Reader Comments: Best course in N.D. ... Excellent staff ... Compares with the North Country's best ... Well manicured, great staff ... Always in nice shape ... Locals are very friendly ... Trees, water, sand and hills ... Top 5 of more than 200 courses I've played ... Best course in North Dakota ... Nice course, excellent value ... Great pro shop and clubhouse ... Old style course ... Distinctive, memorable.

MOTT COUNTRY CLUB
PU-P.O. Box 232, Mott, 58646, Hettinger County, (701)824-2825, 1 miles E of Mott.
Holes: 9. **Yards:** 3,011/2,811. **Par:** 36/38. **Course Rating:** 69.3/66.6. **Slope:** 109/105. **Green Fee:** $12/$12. **Cart Fee:** $10/cart. **Walking Policy:** Unrestricted walking. **Walkability:** 3.
Season: April-Oct. **High:** June-Aug. **Miscellaneous:** Range (grass), club rentals.

OAKES GOLF CLUB
PU-Rte. 1, Oakes, 58474 (701)742-2405.
Special Notes: Call club for further information.

PAINTED WOODS GOLF COURSE
PU-Hwy. 83 South, Washburn, 58577, McClean County, (701)462-8480, 5 miles S of Bismarck.

Holes: 9. **Yards:** 2,819/2,619. **Par:** 36/37. **Course Rating:** 67.0/67.9. **Slope:** 106/112. **Green Fee:** N/A/$13. **Cart Fee:** $16/cart. **Walking Policy:** Unrestricted walking. **Walkability:** 2. **Opened:** 1979. **Season:** April-Oct. **High:** June-July-Aug. **To obtain tee times:** No tee times. **Miscellaneous:** Range (grass), beginner friendly.

★★½ PLAINSVIEW GOLF COURSE AT GRAND FORKS A.F.B.
M-641 Alert Ave.,Bldg.811, Grand Forks AFB, Grand Forks, 58205, Grand Forks County, (701)747-4279, 15 miles W of Grand Forks. **E-mail:** malcolm.rodacker@grandforks.af.mil.com. **Holes:** 18. **Yards:** 6,685/5,360. **Par:** 72/72. **Course Rating:** 69.9/65.9. **Slope:** 102/100. **Green Fee:** $8/$12. **Cart Fee:** $14/cart. **Walking Policy:** Unrestricted walking. **Walkability:** 1. **Opened:** 1971. **Season:** April-Nov. **High:** June-July. **To obtain tee times:** Call anytime. **Miscellaneous:** Reduced fees (juniors), range (grass/mats), club rentals, credit cards (MC, V).
Reader Comments: Wide open with few trees and out-of-bounds...Hacker's paradise. If you like to spray it, you can.

★★★ PRAIRIE WEST GOLF COURSE
PU-2709 Long Spur Trail, Mandan, 58554, Morton County, (701)667-3222, 2 miles SW of Bismarck.
Holes: 18. **Yards:** 6,681/5,452. **Par:** 72/72. **Course Rating:** 71.6/70.1. **Slope:** 127/118. **Green Fee:** N/A/$17. **Cart Fee:** $17/cart. **Walking Policy:** Unrestricted walking. **Walkability:** 2. **Opened:** 1992. **Architect:** Don Herfort. **Season:** April-Oct. **High:** July-Aug. **To obtain tee times:** Call 1 day in advance. **Miscellaneous:** Reduced fees (seniors, juniors), range (grass), club rentals, credit cards (MC, V).
Reader Comments: Challenging greens and excellent mix of handicap holes ... New course, nice layout ... Thick with trees ... Little room for hooks or slices ... Emerging as second best course in N.D. ... Need to complete bunker project ... Good mix of fade and draw holes.

★★★½ RIVERWOOD GOLF CLUB
PU-725 Riverwood Dr., Bismarck, 58504, Burleigh County, (701)222-6462. **E-mail:** sraulsty@bti-gate.com.
Holes: 18. **Yards:** 6,941/5,196. **Par:** 72/72. **Course Rating:** 70.0/68.6. **Slope:** 130/112. **Green Fee:** $18/$18. **Cart Fee:** $18/cart. **Walking Policy:** Unrestricted walking. **Walkability:** 1. **Opened:** 1969. **Season:** April-Oct. **High:** June-Sept. **To obtain tee times:** Call 1 day in advance. **Miscellaneous:** Reduced fees (seniors, juniors), range (grass), club rentals, credit cards (MC, V, AE, D), beginner friendly.
Reader Comments: Need to know all the shots ... Busy ... Good staff ... Trees are biggest hazard ... Best course I have played in the state ... Play at dusk and enjoy the wildlife ... Still the best in Bismarck/Mandan ... Double-dogleg, par-5 15th a shotmaker's hole ... Tight course ... Whoever would have thought you'd find a gem like this in the middle of N.D.?

★★★ ROSE CREEK GOLF COURSE
PU-1500 Rose Creek Pkwy., Fargo, 58107, Cass County, (701)235-5100.
Holes: 18. **Yards:** 6,616/5,062. **Par:** 72/72. **Course Rating:** 71.4/68.8. **Slope:** 123/114. **Green Fee:** $17/$20. **Cart Fee:** $20/cart. **Walking Policy:** Unrestricted walking. **Walkability:** 1. **Opened:** 1993. **Architect:** Dick Phelps. **Season:** April-Oct. **High:** May-Aug. **To obtain tee times:** Call 3 days in advance. **Miscellaneous:** Reduced fees (twilight, seniors, juniors), discount packages, range (grass), club rentals, credit cards (MC, V).
Reader Comments: Dinner here is a must ... Links-type course ... Difficult when windy... Great restaurant ... Watch the wind ... Constant flooding creates problems every year... The course challenges you, but not at the expense of having a good time.

RUGBY COUNTRY CLUB
PU-P.O. Box 292, Rugby, 58368, Pierce County, (701)776-6917.
Holes: 9. **Yards:** 6,264/5,254. **Par:** 36/36. **Course Rating:** 69.4/70.0. **Slope:** 114/113. **Green Fee:** $15/$18. **Cart Fee:** $17/cart. **Walking Policy:** Unrestricted walking. **Walkability:** 2. **Opened:** 1975. **Season:** April-Oct. **High:** June-Aug. **Miscellaneous:** Reduced fees (weekdays), discount packages, range (grass), club rentals.

★★★½ SOURIS VALLEY GOLF CLUB
PU-2400 14th Ave. S.W., Minot, 58701, Ward County, (701)838-4112.
Holes: 18. **Yards:** 6,815/5,474. **Par:** 72/72. **Course Rating:** 72.5/71.2. **Slope:** 126/118. **Green Fee:** $13/$13. **Cart Fee:** $15/cart. **Walking Policy:** Unrestricted walking. **Walkability:** N/A. **Opened:** 1967. **Architect:** William James Spear. **Season:** April-Oct. **High:** June-Aug. **To obtain tee times:** Call golf shop 24 hours in advance. **Miscellaneous:** Reduced fees (twilight, seniors, juniors), metal spikes, club rentals.
Reader Comments: Busy ... Great course in excellent shape ... Nice course for the money ... Good, tough public ... Tough course, water, sand, trees make for a challenge ... Nice public course ... One of my favorite courses in the USA.

NORTH DAKOTA

★★½ TOM O'LEARY GOLF COURSE
PU-1200 N. Washington St., Bismarck, 58501, Burleigh County, (701)222-6531.
Holes: 18. **Yards:** 5,800/4,026. **Par:** 68/68. **Course Rating:** 65.0/62.3. **Slope:** 110/97. **Green Fee:** $16/$16. **Cart Fee:** $18/cart. **Walking Policy:** Unrestricted walking. **Walkability:** 4.
Opened: 1987. **Architect:** David Gill/Garrett Gill. **Season:** April-Oct. **High:** June-Sept. **To obtain tee times:** Call 1 day in advance. **Miscellaneous:** Reduced fees (seniors, juniors), range (grass/mats), club rentals, credit cards (MC, V, AE, D), beginner friendly.
Reader Comments: Short, but challenging and well maintained ... Fun course ... Hilly, short course, par 68 ... A great aerobic walk and spectacular view of Bismarck.

WESTRIDGE GOLF COURSE
PU-Hwy. 14 West, Underwood, 58576 (701)442-5555, 50 miles N of Bismarck.
Holes: 18. **Yards:** 6,390/5,616. **Par:** 72/72. **Course Rating:** 69.3/70.7. **Slope:** 116/112. **Green Fee:** $12/$12. **Cart Fee:** $16/cart. **Walking Policy:** Unrestricted walking. **Walkability:** 3.
Season: April-Nov. **High:** June-Aug. **Miscellaneous:** Range (grass), club rentals, beginner friendly.

WILLISTON MUNICIPAL GOLF COURSE
PU-, Williston, 58801, Williams County, (701)774-1321, 3 miles NW of Williston.
Holes: 9. **Yards:** 3,107/2,532. **Par:** 36/36. **Course Rating:** 66.8/67.4. **Slope:** 104/105. **Green Fee:** $13/$15. **Cart Fee:** $13/cart. **Walking Policy:** Unrestricted walking. **Walkability:** 4.
Season: April-Sept. **High:** June-Aug. **Miscellaneous:** Reduced fees (seniors, juniors), range (grass), club rentals, credit cards (MC, V, AE, D), beginner friendly (youth programs).

OHIO

★★★ AIRPORT GOLF COURSE
PM-900 N. Hamilton Rd., Columbus, 43219, Franklin County, (614)645-3127.
Holes: 18. **Yards:** 6,383/5,504. **Par:** 70/72. **Course Rating:** 68.1/68.8. **Slope:** 107/110. **Green Fee:** $14/$17. **Cart Fee:** $20/cart. **Walking Policy:** Unrestricted walking. **Walkability:** 2. **Opened:** 1965. **Architect:** Jack Kidwell. **Season:** Year-round. **High:** May-Sept. **To obtain tee times:** Call. **Miscellaneous:** Reduced fees (low season, twilight, seniors, juniors), metal spikes, club rentals, credit cards (MC, V).
Reader Comments: Open course ... Not long, but some cute, scenic holes ... Duck airplanes.

★★★½ APPLE VALLEY GOLF CLUB
PU-433 Clubhouse Dr., Howard, 43028, Knox County, (740)397-7664, (800)359-7664, 6 miles E of Mt. Vernon. **Web:** www.applevalleygolfcourse.com.
Holes: 18. **Yards:** 6,946/6,116. **Par:** 72/75. **Course Rating:** 72.4/72.9. **Slope:** 116/113. **Green Fee:** $19/$24. **Cart Fee:** $11/person. **Walking Policy:** Walking at certain times. **Walkability:** 3. **Opened:** 1971. **Architect:** William Newcomb. **Season:** March-Oct. **High:** June-Aug. **To obtain tee times:** Call as far in advance as possible. **Miscellaneous:** Reduced fees (weekdays, twilight, seniors), range (grass), credit cards (MC, V, D).
Reader Comments: Made you use all your shots, facilities excellent ... Rolling hills, great fast, true greens ... Long par 4s on back nine ... Ton of elevated tee boxes, very scenic ... Excellent layout and conditions, make the trip ... Mature trees, rolling hills.

★★½ ATWOOD RESORT GOLF COURSE
R-2650 Lodge Rd., Dellroy, 44620, Carroll County, (330)735-2211, (800)362-6406, 25 miles NE of Canton.
Holes: 18. **Yards:** 6,152/4,188. **Par:** 70/70. **Course Rating:** 65.7/62.0. **Slope:** 102/91. **Green Fee:** $10/$18. **Cart Fee:** $10/. **Walking Policy:** Unrestricted walking. **Walkability:** N/A. **Opened:** 1951. **Season:** Year-round. **High:** June-Sept. **To obtain tee times:** Call golf shop.
Miscellaneous: Reduced fees (weekdays, low season, resort guests, seniors, juniors), discount packages, metal spikes, club rentals, lodging, credit cards (MC, V, AE, D).
Reader Comments: Great lodge and very tough 600-yard par five ... View from No. 3 green is spectacular ... Very hilly ... Good test of short irons ... Short, rolling hills.

★★★★ AVALON LAKES GOLF COURSE *Condition*
R-One American Way, Warren, 44484, Trumbull County, (330)856-8898, 40 miles SE of Cleveland.
Holes: 18. **Yards:** 7,001/5,324. **Par:** 71/71. **Course Rating:** 74.3/70.1. **Slope:** 127/116. **Green Fee:** N/A/$55. **Cart Fee:** Included in Green Fee. **Walking Policy:** Mandatory cart. **Walkability:** 1. **Opened:** 1968. **Architect:** Pete Dye. **Season:** April-Oct. **High:** June-Aug. **To obtain tee times:** Call. **Miscellaneous:** Reduced fees (weekdays, low season, twilight), metal spikes, range (grass/mats), club rentals, lodging, credit cards (MC, V, AE).
Notes: 1993-present, Giant Eagle LPGA Classic.
Reader Comments: Excellent operation ... Great finishing par 4s ... Always in great shape ... Super condition ... A very good course, could be friendlier ... Lot of water, narrow course ... Good layout. Resort flavor. Slow play ... Condition, challenge and a choice facility ... Flat but still interesting (pretty face).

★★ AVON FIELD GOLF COURSE
PU-4081 Reading Rd., Cincinnati, 45229, Hamilton County, (513)281-0322, 5 miles N of Cincinnati. **Web:** www.cincygolf.com.
Holes: 18. **Yards:** 5,325/4,618. **Par:** 66/66. **Course Rating:** 63.9/63.5. **Slope:** 99/98. **Green Fee:** $14/$18. **Cart Fee:** $11/person. **Walking Policy:** Unrestricted walking. **Walkability:** 4. **Opened:** 1914. **Architect:** William Langford. **Season:** Year-round. **High:** May-Aug. **To obtain tee times:** Call (513)651-GOLF. **Miscellaneous:** Reduced fees (low season, seniors, juniors), discount packages, metal spikes, range (grass/mats), club rentals, credit cards (MC, V).

★★★ BARBERTON BROOKSIDE COUNTRY CLUB
PU-3727 Golf Course Dr., Barberton, 44203, Summit County, (330)825-4539, 5 miles W of Akron.
Yards: 6,448/5,098. **Par:** 72/72. **Course Rating:** 72.0/71.8. **Slope:** 104/104. **Green Fee:** $11/$23. **Cart Fee:** $17/cart. **Walking Policy:** Walking at certain times. **Walkability:** 3. **Season:** Year-round weather permitting. **High:** April-Sept. **To obtain tee times:** Call golf shop.
Miscellaneous: Reduced fees (weekdays, low season, seniors, juniors), credit cards (MC, V).
Reader Comments: Greatly improving each year. Very nice course ... Course keeps getting better and better ... Good layout.

★★★½ BEAVER CREEK MEADOWS GOLF COURSE
PU-12774 St. Rte. 7, Lisbon, 44432, Columbiana County, (330)385-3020, 30 miles S of Youngstown.
Holes: 18. **Yards:** 6,500/5,500. **Par:** 71/72. **Course Rating:** 68.7/65.5. **Slope:** 116/113. **Green Fee:** $12/$16. **Cart Fee:** $18/cart. **Walking Policy:** Unrestricted walking. **Walkability:** 3. **Opened:** 1984. **Architect:** Bruce Weber. **Season:** March-Dec. **High:** June-Aug. **To obtain tee times:** Call. **Miscellaneous:** Reduced fees (weekdays, low season), metal spikes, range (grass).

Reader Comments: Treat golfers real nice ... Great for senior citizens ... Excellent fairways, greens need improvement ... Nice layout ... A high-handicapper's dream ... Target golf ... Nice, flat and well-kept course.

★½ BEDFORD TRAILS GOLF COURSE

PU-713 Bedford Rd., Coitsville, 44436-9504, Mahoning County, (330)536-2234, 1 miles E of Youngstown.
Holes: 18. **Yards:** 6,160/5,170. **Par:** 70/70. **Course Rating:** N/A. **Slope:** N/A. **Green Fee:** $11/$18. **Cart Fee:** $10/person. **Walking Policy:** Unrestricted walking. **Walkability:** 1. **Opened:** 1962. **Architect:** Tom Grischow. **Season:** Year-round. **High:** May-Sept. **To obtain tee times:** Call golf shop. **Miscellaneous:** Reduced fees (weekdays, low season, seniors, juniors), metal spikes, range (grass/mats), credit cards (MC, V).

★★★★ BENT TREE GOLF CLUB

PU-350 Bent Tree Rd., Sunbury, 43074, Delaware County, (614)965-5140, 10 miles N of Columbus.
Holes: 18. **Yards:** 6,805/5,280. **Par:** 72/72. **Course Rating:** 72.1/69.2. **Slope:** 122/113. **Green Fee:** $47/$58. **Cart Fee:** Included in Green Fee. **Walking Policy:** Walking at certain times. **Walkability:** 3. **Opened:** 1988. **Architect:** Dennis Griffiths & Assoc. **Season:** Jan.-Dec. **High:** May-Oct. **To obtain tee times:** Call up to 7 days in advance with credit card to reserve. **Miscellaneous:** Reduced fees (weekdays, low season, twilight, seniors, juniors), discount packages, range (grass), club rentals, credit cards (MC, V, AE, D).
Reader Comments: Short, well groomed ... Great course! A bit pricey ... Challenging, lots of sand ... Short, beautifully kept ... A South Carolina course in Ohio ... Each round is a quality experience throughout the changing seasons ... Pricey, good shape. You can score ... Great course, test, lots of bunkers.

★★ BIG BEAVER CREEK GOLF COURSE

PU-1762 Zahn's Corner Rd., Piketon, 45661, Pike County, (614)289-3643, (800)554-6534, 59 miles S of Columbus.
Holes: 18. **Yards:** N/A. **Par:** N/A. **Course Rating:** N/A. **Slope:** N/A. **Green Fee:** $17/$20. **Cart Fee:** $10/person. **Walking Policy:** Unrestricted walking. **Walkability:** 4. **Opened:** 1996. **Architect:** D.W. Bloomfield. **Season:** March-Nov. **High:** July-Sept. **To obtain tee times:** Call up to 14 days in advance. **Miscellaneous:** Discount packages, metal spikes, range (grass), club rentals, credit cards (MC, V, AE, D).

★★★½ BIG MET GOLF CLUB

PU-4811 Valley Pkwy., Fairview Park, 44126, Cuyahoga County, (216)331-1070, 2 miles W of Cleveland.
Holes: 18. **Yards:** 6,125/5,870. **Par:** 72/74. **Course Rating:** 68.0/72.0. **Slope:** 108/113. **Green Fee:** $11/$15. **Cart Fee:** $18/. **Walking Policy:** Unrestricted walking. **Walkability:** N/A. **Opened:** 1926. **Architect:** Stanley Thompson. **Season:** March-Dec. **High:** May-Aug. **To obtain tee times:** Call 5 days in advance. **Miscellaneous:** Reduced fees (low season, seniors, juniors), discount packages, metal spikes, credit cards (MC, V).
Reader Comments: Rebuilt back 9 ... The most popular public golf course in Ohio. Excellent parkland course, jammed on nice days from 6 a.m. to 9 p.m. ... Better than you'd expect, considering heavy play ... Many improvements, going to be very nice.

★★★½ BLACKHAWK GOLF CLUB

PU-8830 Dustin Rd., Galena, 43021, Delaware County, (740)965-1042, 20 miles NE of Columbus.
Holes: 18. **Yards:** 6,550/4,726. **Par:** 71/71. **Course Rating:** 70.6/66.0. **Slope:** 115/106. **Green Fee:** N/A/$25. **Cart Fee:** $10/person. **Walking Policy:** Unrestricted walking. **Walkability:** 3. **Opened:** 1964. **Architect:** Jack Kidwell. **Season:** March-Dec. **High:** May-Oct. **To obtain tee times:** Call 7 days in advance for weekends. **Miscellaneous:** Reduced fees (low season, twilight, seniors, juniors), metal spikes, range (grass), club rentals, credit cards (MC, V, D).
Reader Comments: Mature course, great service ... Tight on some holes, but nice ... Consistent quality ... Always in great shape ... Great older course, love the treelined fairways ... One of the best in central Ohio ... Hard, fast, true-rolling greens ... Deep rough, lots of elevation change ... Good variety of holes, enjoyable.

★★★ BLACKLICK WOODS GOLF COURSE

PU-7309 E. Livingston Ave., Reynoldsburg, 43068, Franklin County, (614)861-3193, 12 miles E of Columbus.
Holes: 18. **Yards:** 6,819/5,018. **Par:** 72/75. **Course Rating:** 71.9/68.0. **Slope:** 124/116. **Green Fee:** $16/$16. **Cart Fee:** $10/person. **Walking Policy:** Unrestricted walking. **Walkability:** 3. **Opened:** 1965. **Architect:** Jack Kidwell/Jodie Kinney. **Season:** Year-round. **High:** May-Aug. **To obtain tee times:** Call on Monday for upcoming weekend. **Miscellaneous:** Reduced fees (low season, twilight), metal spikes, range (grass/mats), club rentals, credit cards (MC, V).

OHIO

Reader Comments: Excellent value! ... Outstanding ... Difficult to secure tee times ... Scenic course cut through Blacklick Woods ... Great county/city course, great value ... Reconditioned and improving.

★★★½ BLACKMOOR GOLF CLUB
SP-1220 Kragel Rd., Richmond, 43944, Jefferson County, (740)765-5502, 50 miles W of Pittsburgh, PA.
Holes: 18. Yards: 6,500/4,963. Par: 72/72. Course Rating: 71.2/72.0. Slope: 136/124. Green Fee: $26/$35. Cart Fee: Included in Green Fee. Walking Policy: Walking at certain times. Walkability: 4. Opened: 1995. Architect: John Robinson. Season: Year-round. High: May-Sept. To obtain tee times: Call golf shop. Miscellaneous: Reduced fees (weekdays, low season, seniors), range (grass), credit cards (MC, V, AE, D).
Reader Comments: Great definitions and challenge ... Tight, long and tough. Excellent track ... Wonderful par 3s ... Best course in area. Beautiful. Lightning greens ... Some holes have blind shots. Very scenic course.

★★★★ BLUE ASH GOLF COURSE
PU-4040 Cooper Rd., Cincinnati, 45241, Hamilton County, (513)745-8577, 15 miles N of Cincinnati.
Holes: 18. Yards: 6,643/5,125. Par: 72/72. Course Rating: 72.7/70.4. Slope: 135/125. Green Fee: N/A/$25. Cart Fee: $24/person. Walking Policy: Unrestricted walking. Walkability: 3. Opened: 1979. Architect: Kidwell/Hurdzan. Season: Year-round. High: May-Sept. To obtain tee times: Nonresidents call 5 days in advance. Miscellaneous: Reduced fees (low season, seniors, juniors), club rentals, credit cards (MC, V).
Notes: Ranked 67th in 1996 America's Top 75 Affordable Courses.
Reader Comments: Good challenge, well maintained ... Great course, must play, plan ahead, always packed ... Great condition.... Excellent public course, but crowded ... Hilly, don't walk back 9, good course ... Great layout with tough rough ... Course condition excellent ... First three holes are hardest ... Exceptional layout.

★½ BLUFFTON GOLF CLUB
PU-8575 N. Dixie Hwy., Bluffton, 45817, Allen County, (419)358-6230, 15 miles N of Lima.
Holes: 18. Yards: 6,633/5,822. Par: 72/72. Course Rating: 69.2/69.8. Slope: 103/95. Green Fee: N/A/$12. Cart Fee: $9/person. Walking Policy: Unrestricted walking. Walkability: N/A. Opened: 1941. Architect: Ken Mast. Season: March-Nov. High: June-Aug. To obtain tee times: Call 7 days in advance. Miscellaneous: Reduced fees (weekdays, low season, seniors, juniors), metal spikes, range (grass/mats), club rentals.

BOB O'LINK GOLF COURSE
PU-2400 Applegrove St. NW, North Canton, 44720, Stark County, (330)499-7710, (800)203-0331, 1 miles E of North Canton. E-mail: golf2400@aol.com. Web: www.bobolink.com.
BOB-O-LINK NORTH COURSE
Holes: 18. Yards: 5,507/5,073. Par: 70/72. Course Rating: 65.3/68.6. Slope: 97/105. Green Fee: $14/$15. Cart Fee: $10/person. Walking Policy: Unrestricted walking. Walkability: 1. Opened: 1963. Architect: Paul Weber. Season: Year-round. High: April-Oct. To obtain tee times: Call golf shop up to 1 year in advance. Miscellaneous: Reduced fees (weekdays, low season, seniors, juniors), discount packages, range (grass), club rentals, credit cards (MC, V), beginner friendly (beginner clinics; beginner leagues; junior golfer camps; women's clinics).
★★½ BOB-O-LINK SOUTH COURSE
Holes: 18. Yards: 5,700/5,289. Par: 70/75. Course Rating: 66.2/69.5. Slope: 101/111. Green Fee: $14/$15. Cart Fee: $10/person. Walking Policy: Unrestricted walking. Walkability: 2. Opened: 1963. Architect: Paul Weber. Season: Year-round. High: April-Oct. To obtain tee times: Call golf shop up to 1 year in advance. Miscellaneous: Reduced fees (weekdays, low season, seniors, juniors), discount packages, range (grass), club rentals, credit cards (MC, V), beginner friendly (beginner clinics, beginner leagues, junior golfer camps, women's clinics).
Reader Comments: Good greens ... Very good for outings ... Fair price. Okay layout.

BOB-O-LINK GOLF COURSE
PU-4141 Center Rd., Avon, 44011, Lorain County, (216)934-6217, 20 miles W of Cleveland.
Holes: 27. Green Fee: $12/$14. Cart Fee: $20/person. Walking Policy: Unrestricted walking. Walkability: 2. Opened: 1969. Season: Year-round. High: May-Sept. To obtain tee times: Call 7 days in advance.
★★★½ RED/BLUE
Yards: 6,052/4,808. Par: 71/71. Course Rating: 66.6/62.6. Slope: 115/112.
Miscellaneous: Reduced fees (weekdays, seniors, juniors), metal spikes, range (grass), club rentals, credit cards (MC, V), beginner friendly
Reader Comments: Upgrading course everyday, challenging ... A cut above the rest, beautiful and relaxing ... The owner greets everyone and walks the course ... Nice course, go back anytime, reasonable rate ... Great price, nice people, lots of outings.

★★★½ RED/WHITE
Yards: 6,263/5,050. **Par:** 71/71. **Course Rating:** 66.6/62.6. **Slope:** 108/107.
Miscellaneous: Reduced fees (weekdays, seniors, juniors), metal spikes, range (grass), club rentals, credit cards (MC, V), beginner friendly
★★★½ WHITE/BLUE
Yards: 6,383/5,103. **Par:** 72/72. **Course Rating:** 68.4/64.8. **Slope:** 115/115
Miscellaneous: Reduced fees (weekdays, seniors, juniors), metal spikes, range (grass/mats), club rentals, credit cards (MC, V), beginner friendly.

★★ BOLTON FIELD GOLF COURSE
PU-6005 Alkire Rd., Columbus, 43119, Franklin County, (614)645-3050, 81 miles SW of Columbus.
Holes: 18. **Yards:** 7,034/5,204. **Par:** 72/72. **Course Rating:** 71.9/68.6. **Slope:** 118/113. **Green Fee:** $14/$17. **Cart Fee:** $21/cart. **Walking Policy:** Unrestricted walking. **Walkability:** 2. **Opened:** 1971. **Architect:** Jack Kidwell. **Season:** Year-round. **High:** May-Sept. **To obtain tee times:** Call 7 days in advance. **Miscellaneous:** Reduced fees (weekdays, low season, twilight, seniors, juniors), discount packages, metal spikes, range (grass), club rentals, credit cards (MC, V).

★★ BOSTON HILLS COUNTRY CLUB
PU-105/124 E. Hines Hill Rd., Boston Heights, 44236, Summit County, (330)656-2438, 30 miles S of Cleveland. **E-mail:** bhcc@mainet.net.
Holes: 18. **Yards:** 6,117/4,987. **Par:** 71/71. **Course Rating:** 68.2/67.4. **Slope:** 110/105. **Green Fee:** $15/$25. **Cart Fee:** $22/cart. **Walking Policy:** Unrestricted walking. **Walkability:** 2. **Opened:** 1923. **Architect:** Wink Chadwick. **Season:** Year-round. **High:** June-Aug. **To obtain tee times:** Call 7 days in advance. **Miscellaneous:** Reduced fees (weekdays, low season, twilight, seniors, juniors), metal spikes, range (grass/mats), club rentals, lodging, credit cards (MC, V, D), beginner friendly (junior and women's).

★★★½ BRANDYWINE COUNTRY CLUB
PU-5555 Akron Peninsula Rd., Peninsula, 44264, Summit County, (330)657-2525, 10 miles NW of Akron.
Holes: 18. **Yards:** 6,481/5,625. **Par:** 72/75. **Course Rating:** 70.2/70.5. **Slope:** 113/113. **Green Fee:** $20/$26. **Cart Fee:** $24/cart. **Walking Policy:** Unrestricted walking. **Walkability:** 3. **Opened:** 1962. **Architect:** Earl Yesberger. **Season:** Year-round. **High:** May-Sept. **To obtain tee times:** Call 7 days in advance. **Miscellaneous:** Reduced fees (weekdays, twilight, seniors), discount packages, metal spikes, club rentals, beginner friendly.
Reader Comments: Open front 9, very tight back ... The back nine is one of a kind ... Several unusual holes, scenic ... Front nine very fair. Back nine, welcome to my nightmare.

★★ BRIARDALE GREENS GOLF COURSE
PM-24131 Briardale Ave., Euclid, 44123, Cuyahoga County, (216)289-8574, 8 miles E of Cleveland.
Holes: 18. **Yards:** 6,127/4,977. **Par:** 70/70. **Course Rating:** 69.1/70.5. **Slope:** 116/118. **Green Fee:** $18/$20. **Cart Fee:** $10/person. **Walking Policy:** Unrestricted walking. **Walkability:** 1. **Opened:** 1977. **Architect:** Dick LaConte. **Season:** March-Nov. **High:** May-Sept. **To obtain tee times:** Call 7 days in advance. **Miscellaneous:** Reduced fees (seniors, juniors), range (mats), club rentals, credit cards (MC, V).

BRIARWOOD GOLF COURSE
PU-2737 Edgerton Rd., Broadview Heights, 44147, Cuyahoga County, (440)237-5271, 22 miles S of Cleveland.
Holes: 27. **Green Fee:** $22/$26. **Cart Fee:** $12/person. **Walking Policy:** Unrestricted walking. **Walkability:** 3. **Opened:** 1965. **Architect:** Ted McAnlis. **Season:** April-Dec. **High:** May-Sept. **To obtain tee times:** Call Saturday a.m. for following weekend. **Miscellaneous:** Reduced fees (weekdays, low season, twilight, seniors, juniors), range (grass/mats), club rentals, credit cards (MC, V).
★★★ BLUE/RED
Yards: 6,405/5,355. **Par:** 71/71. **Course Rating:** 70.2/69.9. **Slope:** 117/110.
Reader Comments: Just so-so ... Plenty of holes, good variety ... From tips can be a challenge ... Fairways and greens beautiful condition ... Strong par 5s.
★★★ BLUE/WHITE
Yards: 6,500/5,295. **Par:** 71/71. **Course Rating:** 70.8/68.9. **Slope:** 117/108.
★★★ RED/WHITE
Yards: 6,985/5,860. **Par:** 72/72. **Course Rating:** 72.8/71.6. **Slope:** 125/115.
Reader Comments: Nice assortment of holes ... Wide open, minimal hazards ... Challenging.

★★½ BUCKEYE HILLS COUNTRY CLUB
SP-13226 Miami Trace Rd., Greenfield, 45123, Highland County, (937)981-4136, 6 miles W of Greenfield. **E-mail:** wet@bright.net.
Holes: 18. **Yards:** 6,393/4,907. **Par:** 71/72. **Course Rating:** 70.4/67.4. **Slope:** 121/113. **Green Fee:** $15/$20. **Cart Fee:** $11/person. **Walking Policy:** Unrestricted walking. **Walkability:** 4.

Opened: 1970. **Architect:** X. G. Hassenplug. **Season:** March-Nov. **To obtain tee times:** Call up to 7 days in advance. **Miscellaneous:** Reduced fees (low season, seniors), credit cards (MC, V). **Reader Comments:** Nice layout, great greens, a bit far ... Excellent greens, good fairways, excellent service.

★★★½ BUNKER HILL GOLF COURSE

PU-3060 Pearl Rd., Medina, 44256, Medina County, (330)722-4174, (888)749-5827, 20 miles S of Cleveland.
Holes: 18. **Yards:** 6,643/5,074. **Par:** 72/72. **Course Rating:** 70.9/68.2. **Slope:** 117/110. **Green Fee:** $21/$27. **Cart Fee:** $22/cart. **Walking Policy:** Walking at certain times. **Walkability:** 3.
Opened: 1927. **Architect:** Mateo and Sons. **Season:** March-Dec. **High:** May-Sept. **To obtain tee times:** Call anytime for tee times. **Miscellaneous:** Reduced fees (weekdays, low season, seniors, juniors), credit cards (MC, V).
Reader Comments: Very hilly course, striving to better speed play ... Renovations are great ... Challenging layout ... Fair, good fairways ... New holes add length to short course.

★★★ CALIFORNIA GOLF COURSE

PU-5920 Kellogg Ave., Cincinnati, 45228, Hamilton County, (513)231-6513.
Holes: 18. **Yards:** 6,216/5,626. **Par:** 70/71. **Course Rating:** 70.0/71.4. **Slope:** 116/113. **Green Fee:** $16/$17. **Cart Fee:** $19/. **Walking Policy:** Unrestricted walking. **Walkability:** N/A. **Opened:** 1936. **Architect:** Wm. H. Diddel. **Season:** Year-round. **High:** April-Sept. **To obtain tee times:** Call one day in advance. **Miscellaneous:** Reduced fees (low season, seniors, juniors), metal spikes, club rentals.
Reader Comments: Great value, but crowded ... Unremarkable but playable ... No. 16 green to No. 17 tee is a hike ... Old-time city course making improvements ... Tees too close to greens, overplayed ... Interesting layout, too long to walk 18 ... Front side different from back ... Great municipal course, not too difficult.

★★★½ CARROLL MEADOWS GOLF COURSE *Value*

PU-1130 Meadowbrook, Carrollton, 44615, Carroll County, (330)627-2663, (888)519-0576, 1 mile N of Carrollton.
Holes: 18. **Yards:** 6,366/4,899. **Par:** 71/71. **Course Rating:** 69.4/67.4. **Slope:** 114/109. **Green Fee:** $14/$16. **Cart Fee:** $10/person. **Walking Policy:** Unrestricted walking. **Walkability:** 3.
Opened: 1989. **Architect:** John F. Robinson. **Season:** March-Dec. **To obtain tee times:** Call for tee times. **Miscellaneous:** Reduced fees (weekdays, low season, seniors, juniors), discount packages, range (grass), club rentals, credit cards (MC, V, AE).
Reader Comments: Excellent management ... Nice greens, interesting layout, very good price ... Get breakfast, play 18 with cart, enjoy a great course, for reasonable amount ... Price is right ... Great course, good people. Even better as trees mature.

★★★½ CASSEL HILLS GOLF COURSE

PU-201 Clubhouse Way, Vandalia, 45377, Montgomery County, (937)890-1300, 5 miles N of Dayton.
Holes: 18. **Yards:** 6,617/5,600. **Par:** 71/71. **Course Rating:** 72.6/69.6. **Slope:** 131/127. **Green Fee:** $16/$26. **Cart Fee:** $21/cart. **Walking Policy:** Unrestricted walking. **Walkability:** 5.
Opened: 1974. **Architect:** Bruce von Roxburg. **Season:** Feb.-Dec. **High:** April-Oct. **To obtain tee times:** Call up to 7 days in advance. **Miscellaneous:** Reduced fees (weekdays, low season), club rentals, credit cards (MC, V).
Reader Comments: A very challenging course, a lot of fun ... Recent upgrades improved course looks and playability ... Great public course ... Well managed ... Nice course, back 9 scenic ... Back 9 is very hilly, lots of trees.

CASTLE SHANNON GOLF COURSE

PU-105 Castle Shannon Blvd., Hopedale, 43976, Jefferson County, (740)937-2373, (888)937-3311, 58 miles W of Pittsburgh, PA. **Web:** www.pittsburghgolf.com.
Holes: 18. **Yards:** 6,896/4,752. **Par:** 71/71. **Course Rating:** 73.0/65.4. **Slope:** 132/110. **Green Fee:** $25/$35. **Cart Fee:** Included in Green Fee. **Walking Policy:** Unrestricted walking.
Walkability: 5. **Opened:** 1996. **Architect:** Gary Grandstaff. **Season:** Year-round weather permitting. **High:** April-Sept. **To obtain tee times:** Call. **Miscellaneous:** Reduced fees (low season, seniors), range (grass), club rentals, credit cards (MC, V, AE, D).
Reader Comments: Wonderful course, wonderful staff ... Seniors should use senior tees and ride. An unforgettable layout ... What a challenge. Need every club in bag.

★★½ CATAWBA WILLOWS GOLF & COUNTRY CLUB

PU-2590 Sand Rd., Port Clinton, 43452, Ottawa County, 419-734-2524.
Reader Comments: Tourist favorite on Lake Erie, bring a lot of balls ... Over designed, but good condition and a fun challenge ... Water, bring five balls and one spare.
Special Notes: Call club for further information.

OHIO

★★★½ CHAMPIONS GOLF COURSE
PU-3900 Westerville Rd., Columbus, 43224, Franklin County, (614)645-7111, 10 miles NE of Columbus.
Holes: 18. **Yards:** 6,555/5,427. **Par:** 70/72. **Course Rating:** 71.2/71.2. **Slope:** 127/127. **Green Fee:** $21/$31. **Cart Fee:** $22/cart. **Walking Policy:** Walking at certain times. **Walkability:** 3. **Opened:** 1948. **Architect:** Robert Trent Jones. **Season:** Year-round. **High:** May-Oct. **To obtain tee times:** Call 1 week in advance. **Miscellaneous:** Reduced fees (weekdays, low season, twilight, seniors, juniors), discount packages, metal spikes, range (grass/mats), club rentals, credit cards (MC, V).
Reader Comments: Superb layout but city can't keep up with high traffic ... Very nice layout... Gorgeous, mature course, tough ... Pricey ... A beautiful old course with character maintained by the city parks dept.

★★★★ CHAPEL HILL GOLF COURSE
PU-7516 Johnstown Rd., Mount Vernon, 43050, Knox County, (740)393-3999, (800)393-3499, 28 miles NE of Columbus. **E-mail:** chapelhill@axom.com. **Web:** www.chapelhillgolfcourse.com.
Holes: 18. **Yards:** 6,900/4,600. **Par:** 72/72. **Course Rating:** 72.2/69.4. **Slope:** 128/119. **Green Fee:** $19/$25. **Cart Fee:** $11/person. **Walking Policy:** Unrestricted walking. **Walkability:** 4. **Opened:** 1996. **Architect:** Barry Serafin. **Season:** Year-round. **High:** April-Oct. **To obtain tee times:** Call anytime for weekday. Call up to 7 days in advance for weekend. **Miscellaneous:** Reduced fees (weekdays, low season), range (grass), club rentals, credit cards (MC, V).
Reader Comments: Beautiful ... Always a fun course to play, hilly ... Relatively new course, well designed and staff works to please ... Beautiful layout, lot of elevation changes, tough course to walk, most unique clubhouse of any course I've seen. Allow time for 19th hole on patio overlooking 18th green.

★★ CHAPEL HILLS GOLF COURSE
PU-3381 Austinburg Rd., Ashtabula, 44004, Ashtabula County, (440)997-3791, (800)354-9608, 45 miles E of Cleveland. **E-mail:** chgolf@knownet.net. **Web:** www.knownet.net/users/chgolf.
Holes: 18. **Yards:** 5,971/4,507. **Par:** 72/72. **Course Rating:** 68.6/65.7. **Slope:** 112/104. **Green Fee:** $14/$19. **Cart Fee:** $10/person. **Walking Policy:** Unrestricted walking. **Walkability:** 2. **Opened:** 1957. **Architect:** Bill Franklin. **Season:** April-Nov. **High:** June-Sept. **To obtain tee times:** Call Pro Shop. **Miscellaneous:** Reduced fees (weekdays, seniors, juniors), range (grass), club rentals, credit cards (MC, V).

★★★½ CHARDON LAKES GOLF COURSE
PU-470 S. St., Chardon, 44024, Geauga County, (440)285-4653, 35 miles NE of Cleveland.
Holes: 18. **Yards:** 6,789/5,077. **Par:** 71/73. **Course Rating:** 73.1/66.6. **Slope:** 135/111. **Green Fee:** $21/$31. **Cart Fee:** $10/person. **Walking Policy:** Unrestricted walking. **Walkability:** 3. **Opened:** 1931. **Architect:** Birdie Way/Don Tincher. **Season:** April-Nov. **High:** June-Sept. **To obtain tee times:** Call up to 14 days in advance for weekdays. Call Monday after 8 a.m. for upcoming weekend or holiday. **Miscellaneous:** Reduced fees (low season, seniors, juniors), range (grass), club rentals, lodging, credit cards (MC, V, AE, D).
Reader Comments: Heavily wooded, very scenic, tight with fast greens ... Very nice course, well kept ... Superlative! Challenging but fair... Back tees are tough ... Snow golf allowed ... Average course, play it from the tips ... Good honest test.

★★★ CHEROKEE HILLS GOLF CLUB
PU-5740 Center Rd., Valley City, 44280, Medina County, (330)225-6122, 31 miles NW of Akron.
Holes: 18. **Yards:** 6,210/5,880. **Par:** 70/70. **Course Rating:** 68.3/70.3. **Slope:** 109/116. **Green Fee:** $17/$25. **Cart Fee:** $30/cart. **Walking Policy:** Unrestricted walking. **Walkability:** 4. **Opened:** 1981. **Architect:** Brian Huntley. **Season:** Year-round. **High:** April-Oct. **To obtain tee times:** Call in advance. **Miscellaneous:** Reduced fees (weekdays, low season, twilight, seniors, juniors), discount packages, club rentals, credit cards (MC, V).
Reader Comments: Upgrading every year, challenging course ... Challenging and scenic ... Tight! Wide fairways, great greens, and a nice topography ... Overall improvements: par 5s are good ... Good layout.

★★★½ CHEROKEE HILLS GOLF COURSE
SP-4622 County Rd. 49 N., Bellefontaine, 43311, Logan County, (937)599-3221, 45 miles NW of Columbus.
Holes: 18. **Yards:** 6,448/5,327. **Par:** 71/74. **Course Rating:** 70.8/70.3. **Slope:** 115/108. **Green Fee:** $14/$20. **Cart Fee:** $10/person. **Walking Policy:** Unrestricted walking. **Walkability:** 4. **Opened:** 1970. **Architect:** Cherster Kurtz. **Season:** March-Dec. **High:** May-Sept. **To obtain tee times:** Call 7 days in advance. **Miscellaneous:** Reduced fees (weekdays, low season, juniors), discount packages, club rentals, credit cards (MC, V, D).
Reader Comments: Low rolling hills, good family course ... Perfect land for golf course ... Very hilly ... Good layout, fast greens ... Good test of golf, fun course ... Small country club type course with muny prices.

★★★ CHIPPEWA GOLF CLUB
PU-12147 Shank Rd., Doylestown, 44230, Wayne County, (330)658-6126, (800)321-1701, 5 miles S of Akron. **E-mail:** cgc@concentric.net.com. **Web:** www.chipgolf.com.
Holes: 18. **Yards:** 6,273/4,877. **Par:** 71/72. **Course Rating:** 69.1/67.0. **Slope:** 109/103. **Green Fee:** $11/$18. **Cart Fee:** $19/person. **Walking Policy:** Unrestricted walking. **Walkability:** 2. **Opened:** 1962. **Architect:** Harrison/Garbin. **Season:** Year-round. **High:** April-Oct. **To obtain tee times:** Call Pro Shop. **Miscellaneous:** Reduced fees (weekdays, low season, seniors, juniors), range (grass/mats), club rentals, credit cards (MC, V, AE, D).
Reader Comments: A couple of interesting holes ... Challenging back 9 ... Take a cart ... Great service, good course, you feel welcome ... Nice course, could use some work on tees and fairways ... Back 9 is challenge, score on front 9.

CLEARVIEW PAR & BIRDIE GOLF CLUB
SP-8410 Lincoln St., East Canton, 44730, (330)488-0404.
Special Notes: Call club for further information.

★★ CLIFFSIDE GOLF COURSE
PU-100 Cliffside Dr., Gallipolis, 45631, Gallia County, (614)446-4653, 30 miles NE of Huntington.
Holes: 18. **Yards:** 6,598/5,268. **Par:** 72/72. **Course Rating:** 70.5/66.8. **Slope:** 115/109. **Green Fee:** $15/$16. **Cart Fee:** $10/person. **Walking Policy:** Unrestricted walking. **Walkability:** 4. **Opened:** 1988. **Architect:** Jack Kidwell. **Season:** Year-round. **High:** April-Oct. **To obtain tee times:** Call 7 days in advance. **Miscellaneous:** Reduced fees (weekdays, low season), club rentals, credit cards (MC, V).

★★★½ COLONIAL GOLFERS CLUB
PU-10985 Harding Hwy., Harrod, 45850, Allen County, (419)649-3350, (800)234-7468, 10 miles E of Lima.
Holes: 18. **Yards:** 7,000/5,000. **Par:** 72/74. **Course Rating:** 72.2/68.7. **Slope:** 139/111. **Green Fee:** $17/$21. **Cart Fee:** $10/person. **Walking Policy:** Unrestricted walking. **Walkability:** 4. **Opened:** 1973. **Architect:** Bob Holtosberry/Tom Holtosberry. **Season:** March-Dec. **High:** June-Aug. **To obtain tee times:** Call golf shop. **Miscellaneous:** Reduced fees (weekdays, low season, twilight, seniors, juniors), metal spikes, range (grass), club rentals, credit cards (MC, V).
Reader Comments: Fairways always nice! ... Always in good shape ... Clean, good service.

★★★★ COOKS CREEK GOLF CLUB
PU-16405 U.S. Hwy. 23 S., Ashville, 43103, Pickaway County, (740)983-3636, (800)430-4653, 15 miles S of Columbus. **E-mail:** cookscrk@bright.net.com.
Holes: 18. **Yards:** 7,071/4,995. **Par:** 72/72. **Course Rating:** 73.7/68.2. **Slope:** 131/120. **Green Fee:** $38/$60. **Cart Fee:** Included in Green Fee. **Walking Policy:** Walking at certain times. **Walkability:** 4. **Opened:** 1993. **Architect:** Michael Hurdzan/John Cook. **Season:** Year-round. **High:** April-Oct. **To obtain tee times:** Call up to 7 days in advance. **Miscellaneous:** Reduced fees (low season, twilight), range (grass), club rentals, credit cards (MC, V, AE).
Notes: Ranked 18th in 1999 Best New Public Courses.
Reader Comments: Very expensive but worth it ... A bit pricey but, overall, worth it ... Gorgeous, wide fairways, interesting holes, expensive ... Potential to be great.

★★★½ COPELAND HILLS GOLF CLUB
PU-41703 Metz Rd., Columbiana, 44408, Columbiana County, (330)482-3221, 20 miles S of Youngstown.
Holes: 18. **Yards:** 6,859/5,763. **Par:** 72/74. **Course Rating:** 72.7/72.7. **Slope:** 121/120. **Green Fee:** $27/$30. **Cart Fee:** Included in Green Fee. **Walking Policy:** Unrestricted walking. **Walkability:** 2. **Opened:** 1960. **Architect:** R. Albert Anderson. **Season:** April-Dec. **High:** July-Sept. **To obtain tee times:** Call up to 1 year in advance. **Miscellaneous:** Reduced fees (weekdays, low season, seniors, juniors), metal spikes, range (grass), club rentals, beginner friendly (group lessons and junior golf program).
Reader Comments: Excellent condition ... Long and challenging ... Long course, big greens, nice fairways ... Must play if in area ... Not only is it the longest course in the area at 7100 yards, but it is a very challenging course.

★★★ COUNTRY ACRES GOLF CLUB
PU-17374 St. Rte. 694, Ottawa, 45875, Putnam County, (419)532-3434, 20 miles N of Lima.
Holes: 18. **Yards:** 6,464/4,961. **Par:** 72/72. **Course Rating:** 69.9/67.9. **Slope:** 126/113. **Green Fee:** $17/$20. **Cart Fee:** $11/person. **Walking Policy:** Unrestricted walking. **Walkability:** 2. **Opened:** 1978. **Architect:** John Simmons. **Season:** March-Dec. **High:** June-Sept. **To obtain tee times:** Call 7 days in advance. **Miscellaneous:** Reduced fees (seniors, juniors), discount packages, range (grass), club rentals, credit cards (MC, V).
Reader Comments: Classy, friendly, No. 18-what a finisher! ... Under repair... Lots of outings ... Fair public course.

★★ COUNTRYSIDE GOLF COURSE
PU-1421 Struthers Coit Rd., Lowellville, 44436, Mahoning County, (330)755-0016, 5 miles S of Youngstown.
Holes: 18. **Yards:** 6,461/5,399. **Par:** 71/71. **Course Rating:** 70.5/70.1. **Slope:** N/A. **Green Fee:** $17/$19. **Cart Fee:** $16/cart. **Walking Policy:** Unrestricted walking. **Walkability:** 2. **Opened:** 1967. **Season:** March-Nov. **High:** May-Aug. **To obtain tee times:** Call. **Miscellaneous:** Reduced fees (weekdays, low season, seniors, juniors), credit cards (MC, V).

★★ CRANBERRY HILLS GOLF COURSE
PU-4891 Clovercrest Dr. N.W., Warren, 44483, Trumbull County, (330)847-2884, 1 miles E of Champion.
Holes: 9. **Yards:** 2,890/2,515. **Par:** 36/36. **Course Rating:** N/A. **Slope:** N/A. **Green Fee:** $8/$13. **Cart Fee:** $14/cart. **Walking Policy:** Unrestricted walking. **Walkability:** 2. **Opened:** 1930. **Season:** Year-round. **High:** April-Sept. **To obtain tee times:** Call golf shop. **Miscellaneous:** Reduced fees (weekdays, low season, seniors, juniors), metal spikes, club rentals, beginner friendly.
Special Notes: Formerly Champion Links Golf Club

★★★ CROOKED TREE GOLF CLUB
SP-3595 Mason Montgomery Rd., Mason, 45040, Warren County, (513)398-3933,.
Reader Comments: Leave the woods in the bag, or your bag will be in the woods. Good iron course ... Build new greens and it would be OK ... Rustic setting, requires variety of shots ... Short, tight greens hard to hold ... Greens need work, otherwise fine.
Special Notes: Call club for further information.

CRYSTAL SPRINGS GOLF CLUB
PU-745 N. Hopewell Rd., Hopewell, 43746, Muskingum County, (740)787-1114, (800)787-1705, 45 miles E of Columbus. **E-mail:** crystal@crystalspringsgolfclub.com. **Web:** www.crystalspringsgolfclub.com.
Holes: 18. **Yards:** 6,412/4,634. **Par:** 71/71. **Course Rating:** 70.1/66.2. **Slope:** 125/114. **Green Fee:** $16/$23. **Cart Fee:** $9/person. **Walking Policy:** Unrestricted walking. **Walkability:** 4. **Opened:** 1998. **Architect:** Ronald Cutlip. **Season:** Year round. **High:** May-Oct. **To obtain tee times:** Call (800)787-1705, or internet in 2000. **Miscellaneous:** Reduced fees (low season, twilight, seniors, juniors), club rentals, credit cards (MC, V).

★★★★ DARBY CREEK GOLF COURSE
PU-19300 Orchard Rd., Marysville, 43040, Union County, (937)349-7491, (800)343-2729, 18 miles NW of Dublin.
Holes: 18. **Yards:** 7,087/5,197. **Par:** 72/72. **Course Rating:** 73.1/68.9. **Slope:** 125/115. **Green Fee:** $18/$32. **Cart Fee:** $10/person. **Walking Policy:** Walking at certain times. **Walkability:** 3. **Opened:** 1993. **Architect:** Geoffrey S. Cornish/Brian Silva. **Season:** March-Dec. **High:** May-Oct. **To obtain tee times:** Call 7 days in advance. **Miscellaneous:** Reduced fees (weekdays, low season, twilight, seniors, juniors), range (grass), club rentals, credit cards (MC, V).
Reader Comments: Front 9 links, back 9 woodland ... Back 9 will eat you up! ... Contrasting 9s, well conditioned course ... Overall a little tight ... Nice small track, good value ... 12th hole great strategic par 4 ... 9 links plus 9 traditional equals unlimited joy.

★★★ DEER CREEK STATE PARK GOLF COURSE
R-20635 Waterloo Rd., Mount Sterling, 43143, Pickaway County, (740)869-3088, 45 miles SW of Columbus.
Holes: 18. **Yards:** 7,116/5,611. **Par:** 72/72. **Course Rating:** 73.7/71.7. **Slope:** 113/113. **Green Fee:** $17/$22. **Cart Fee:** $12/person. **Walking Policy:** Unrestricted walking. **Walkability:** 3. **Opened:** 1982. **Architect:** Jack Kidwell/Michael Hurdzan. **Season:** Year-round. **High:** May-Sept. **To obtain tee times:** Overnight park guests may call anytime for tee times. Others call Monday a.m. on week of play. **Miscellaneous:** Reduced fees (weekdays, low season, resort guests, twilight, seniors, juniors), discount packages, metal spikes, range (grass), club rentals, lodging, credit cards (MC, V, AE, D).
Reader Comments: Great lodge, average course ... Extremely well conditioned for public course ... Great greens.

★★ DEER LAKE GOLF CLUB
PU-6300 Lake Rd. W., Geneva, 44041, Ashtabula County, (440)466-8450, (800)468-8450.
Holes: 18. **Yards:** 6,104/5,839. **Par:** 72/74. **Course Rating:** 67.3/70.5. **Slope:** 110/110. **Green Fee:** $14/$16. **Cart Fee:** $10/person. **Walking Policy:** Unrestricted walking. **Walkability:** 1. **Opened:** 1967. **Architect:** Mr. Leoffler. **Season:** March-Nov. **High:** May-August. **To obtain tee times:** Call. **Miscellaneous:** Reduced fees (low season, seniors, juniors), metal spikes, club rentals, credit cards (MC, V), beginner friendly.

DEER RIDGE GOLF CLUB
PU-900 Comfort Plaza Dr., Bellville, 44813, Richland County, (419)886-7090, 45 miles N of Columbus. **Web:** www.bestcoursestoplay.com.

Holes: 18. **Yards:** 6,584/4,791. **Par:** 72/72. **Course Rating:** 71.8/67.6. **Slope:** 129/115. **Green Fee:** $27/$40. **Cart Fee:** Included in Green Fee. **Walking Policy:** Mandatory cart. **Walkability:** 5. **Opened:** 1999. **Architect:** Brian Huntley. **Season:** March-Nov. **High:** May-Sept. **To obtain tee times:** Call (419)886-7090. **Miscellaneous:** Reduced fees (twilight, seniors, juniors), range (grass/mats), credit cards (MC, V, D).

★★★ DEER TRACK GOLF CLUB
PU-9488 Leavitt Rd., Elyria, 44035, Lorain County, (216)986-5881, 30 miles W of Cleveland. **E-mail:** deertrack@centuryinter.net.com. **Web:** www.deertrack.webjump.com.
Holes: 18. **Yards:** 6,410/5,191. **Par:** 71/71. **Course Rating:** 70.3/68.7. **Slope:** 124/115. **Green Fee:** $17/$20. **Cart Fee:** $20/cart. **Walking Policy:** Unrestricted walking. **Walkability:** 1. **Opened:** 1989. **Architect:** Tony Dulio. **Season:** Year-round. **High:** April-Oct. **To obtain tee times:** Call golf shop. **Miscellaneous:** Reduced fees (low season, seniors), range (grass/mats), credit cards (MC, V).
Reader Comments: Not too hilly ... Fairways need work; strong par 3s ... Nice tight fairways ... Nice course, lots of water on back.

★★★ DETWILER GOLF COURSE
PU-4001 N. Summit St., Toledo, 43611, Lucas County, (419)726-9353, 3 miles N of Toledo.
Holes: 18. **Yards:** 6,497/5,137. **Par:** 71/71. **Course Rating:** 70.2/68.6. **Slope:** 114/108. **Green Fee:** $7/$26. **Cart Fee:** $12/person. **Walking Policy:** Unrestricted walking. **Walkability:** 2. **Opened:** 1971. **Architect:** Arthur Hills. **Season:** Year-round. **High:** April-Oct. **To obtain tee times:** Call up to 7 days in advance. **Miscellaneous:** Reduced fees (low season, twilight, seniors, juniors), metal spikes, range (grass/mats), club rentals, credit cards (MC, V, AE), beginner friendly.
Reader Comments: Solid course, not a great piece of land ... A very cheerful and accommodating staff ... Good city course ... Fun, fair, open, tough par 3s ... Very challenging.

★★½ DORLON GOLF CLUB
PU-18000 Station Rd., Columbia Station, 44028, Lorain County, (440)236-8234, 7 miles W of Strongsville. **E-mail:** dorlon@compuserve.com. **Web:** www.dorlon.com.
Holes: 18. **Yards:** 7,154/5,691. **Par:** 72/74. **Course Rating:** 74.0/67.4. **Slope:** 131/118. **Green Fee:** $14/$22. **Cart Fee:** $17/person. **Walking Policy:** Unrestricted walking. **Walkability:** 1. **Opened:** 1970. **Architect:** William Mitchell. **Season:** Year-round. **High:** May-Sept. **To obtain tee times:** Call (440)236-8234 or book on the web. **Miscellaneous:** Reduced fees (weekdays, low season, seniors, juniors), metal spikes, range (grass), club rentals, credit cards (MC, V).
Reader Comments: Needs upgrade ... Average course ... Very long, much water ... Long, straight.

EAGLE CREEK GOLF CLUB
PU-2406 New State Rd., Norwalk, 44857, Huron County, (419)668-8535, 1 miles S of Norwalk.
Holes: 18. **Yards:** 6,557/4,908. **Par:** 71/71. **Course Rating:** 70.7/68.6. **Slope:** 126/116. **Green Fee:** $20/$29. **Cart Fee:** $11/person. **Walking Policy:** Unrestricted walking. **Walkability:** 2. **Opened:** 1996. **Architect:** Brian Huntley. **Season:** March-Nov. **High:** May-Oct. **To obtain tee times:** Call up to 7 days in advance. Credit card guarantee needed for times 8 to 30 days in advance or for multiple tee times anytime. **Miscellaneous:** Reduced fees (weekdays, low season, seniors, juniors), range (grass), club rentals, credit cards (MC, V, AE, D).

★★ EAGLES NEST GOLF COURSE
PU-1540 St. Rte. No.28, Loveland, 45140, Clermont County, (513)722-1241, 15 miles E of Cincinnati.
Holes: 18. **Yards:** 6,145/4,868. **Par:** 71/71. **Course Rating:** 69.7/66.9. **Slope:** 120/108. **Green Fee:** $15/$18. **Cart Fee:** $11/person. **Walking Policy:** Unrestricted walking. **Walkability:** 1. **Architect:** Taylor Boyd. **Season:** Year-round. **High:** April-Sept. **To obtain tee times:** Call 7 days in advance. **Miscellaneous:** Reduced fees (seniors, juniors), metal spikes, range (grass/mats), club rentals, credit cards (MC, V, D).

★★★★½ EAGLESTICKS GOLF COURSE *Condition*
PU-2655 Maysville Pike, Zanesville, 43701, Muskingum County, (614)454-4900, (800)782-4493, 60 miles E of Columbus. **Web:** www.eaglesticksgolf.com.
Holes: 18. **Yards:** 6,508/4,137. **Par:** 70/70. **Course Rating:** 70.1/63.7. **Slope:** 120/96. **Green Fee:** $26/$31. **Cart Fee:** $10/person. **Walking Policy:** Unrestricted walking. **Walkability:** 4. **Opened:** 1990. **Architect:** Mike Hurdzan. **Season:** Year-round. **High:** June-Aug. **To obtain tee times:** Call pro shop up to one year in advance. **Miscellaneous:** Reduced fees (weekdays, low season, twilight, seniors, juniors), discount packages, range (grass), credit cards (MC, V, AE, D).
Notes: Ranked 20th in 1999 Best in State; Ranked 14th Americas Top 75 Affordable Courses.
Reader Comments: Best I've played ... Hilly, pretty ... Great routing, superb condition, too many short 4s ... Converted horse farm that's a thoroughbred ... Should be a 5, but 6-hour round ... Food, bar exceptional ... Worth the trip, plenty of well placed tee boxes for golfers of any level ... Fairways nice as other courses greens.

★★ THE ELMS COUNTRY CLUB

PU-1608 Manchester Rd. S.W., North Lawrence, 44666, Stark County, (330)833-2668, (800)600-3567, 45 miles S of Cleveland.
Holes: 27. **Yards:** 6,625/5,034. **Par:** 72/74. **Course Rating:** 70.0/67.2. **Slope:** 111/101. **Green Fee:** $20/$24. **Cart Fee:** $20/cart. **Walking Policy:** Unrestricted walking. **Walkability:** 2. **Opened:** 1932. **Architect:** Ed Rottman. **Season:** March-Dec. **High:** May-Sept. **To obtain tee times:** Call golf shop. **Miscellaneous:** Reduced fees (weekdays, low season, twilight, seniors, juniors), discount packages, range (grass/mats), club rentals, credit cards (MC, V).

EMERALD WOODS GOLF COURSE

PU-12501 N. Boone Rd., Columbia Station, 44028, Lorain County, (440)236-8940, 14 miles SW of Cleveland.
★★½ AUDREY'S/HEATHER STONE COURSE
Holes: 18. **Yards:** 6,673/5,295. **Par:** 70/71. **Course Rating:** 71.1/68.2. **Slope:** N/A. **Green Fee:** $18/$22. **Cart Fee:** $20/cart. **Walking Policy:** Unrestricted walking. **Walkability:** 3. **Opened:** 1967. **Architect:** Raymond McClain. **Season:** Year-round weather permitting. **High:** Summer. **To obtain tee times:** Call up to 7 days in advance for weekends and holidays. **Miscellaneous:** Reduced fees (weekdays, seniors), club rentals.
Reader Comments: Time to take this place to a new (higher) level ... Seems pricey for the course ... Not bad.
Special Notes: Also have a 9-hole course.
★★ SAINT ANDREWS/PINE VALLEY COURSE
Holes: 18. **Yards:** 6,629/5,080. **Par:** 72/73. **Course Rating:** 72.1/66.4. **Slope:** N/A. **Green Fee:** $20/$24. **Cart Fee:** $20/cart. **Walking Policy:** Unrestricted walking. **Walkability:** 3. **Opened:** 1967. **Architect:** Raymond McClain. **Season:** Year-round. **High:** June-August. **To obtain tee times:** Call up to 7 days for weekends and holidays, or further in advance with credit card. **Miscellaneous:** Reduced fees (weekdays, seniors), metal spikes, club rentals.

★★★ ERIE SHORES GOLF COURSE

PU-7298 Lake Rd. E., North Madison, 44057, Lake County, (216)428-3164, (800)225-3742, 40 miles E of Cleveland.
Holes: 18. **Yards:** 6,000/4,750. **Par:** 70/70. **Course Rating:** 68.2/67.0. **Slope:** 116/108. **Green Fee:** $12/$16. **Cart Fee:** $11/cart. **Walking Policy:** Unrestricted walking. **Walkability:** 1. **Opened:** 1957. **Architect:** Ben W. Zink. **Season:** Year-round. **High:** May-Sept. **To obtain tee times:** Call on Monday for upcoming weekend. **Miscellaneous:** Reduced fees (weekdays, low season, seniors, juniors), metal spikes, range (grass/mats), club rentals, credit cards (MC, V, D).
Reader Comments: Short, nice landscaping, always busy ... Good course for the money ... Good for women, some holes narrow with trees, accuracy needed, short ... Tight course, very well managed.

★½ ESTATE GOLF CLUB

PU-3871 Tschopp Rd., Lancaster, 43130, Fairfield County, (740)654-4444, (800)833-8463, 4 miles N of Lancaster.
Holes: 18. **Yards:** 6,405/5,680. **Par:** 71/72. **Course Rating:** 69.9/N/A. **Slope:** 113/N/A. **Green Fee:** $15/$18. **Cart Fee:** $22/cart. **Walking Policy:** Unrestricted walking. **Opened:** 1967. **Architect:** Donald Arledge. **Season:** Year-round. **High:** June-Sept. **To obtain tee times:** Call 7 days in advance. **Miscellaneous:** Reduced fees (weekdays, twilight, seniors, juniors), discount packages, metal spikes, range (grass), club rentals, credit cards (MC, V), beginner friendly.

★★★½ FAIRFIELD GOLF CLUB

PM-2200 John Gray Rd., Fairfield, 45014, Butler County, (513)867-5385, 2 miles N of Cincinnati.
Holes: 18. **Yards:** 6,250/4,900. **Par:** 70/70. **Course Rating:** 69.5/68.8. **Slope:** 123/113. **Green Fee:** $20/$22. **Cart Fee:** $11/person. **Walking Policy:** Unrestricted walking. **Walkability:** 3. **Opened:** 1968. **Architect:** Jack Kidwell/Michael Hurdzan. **Season:** March-Dec. **High:** June-Aug. **To obtain tee times:** Call 9 days in advance. **Miscellaneous:** Reduced fees (seniors, juniors), metal spikes, club rentals, credit cards (MC, V).
Reader Comments: The nicest public fairways I've seen ... Vastly improved ... Enjoyable ... Very nice course, short.

★★½ FAIRWAY PINES GOLF COURSE

PU-1777 Blaise-Nemeth Rd., Painesville, 44077, Lake County, (440)357-7800.
Reader Comments: Flat, open, needs TLC and more bunkers ... Very tough course when wind blows off Lake Erie ... Beautiful fairways and greens ... Nice fairways, greens.
Special Notes: Call club for further information.

★½ FALLEN TIMBERS FAIRWAYS

SP-7711 Timbers Blvd., Waterville, 43566, Lucas County, (419)878-4653, 12 miles S of Toledo.
Holes: 18. **Yards:** 6,054/4,969. **Par:** 70/70. **Course Rating:** 67.7/65.8. **Slope:** 109/105. **Green Fee:** $16/$25. **Cart Fee:** $12/person. **Walking Policy:** Unrestricted walking. **Walkability:** 1.

Opened: 1992. **Season:** Year-round. **High:** June-Aug. **To obtain tee times:** Call 7 days in advance. **Miscellaneous:** Reduced fees (weekdays, low season, twilight, seniors, juniors), metal spikes, range (grass/mats), club rentals, credit cards (MC, V, AE).

★★★ FLAGSTONE GOLF CLUB
PU-13683 St. Rte. 38, Marysville, 43040, Union County, (937)642-1816, (800)742-0899, 15 miles W of Columbus.
Holes: 18. **Yards:** 6,323/5,111. **Par:** 72/72. **Course Rating:** 69.6/68.9. **Slope:** 115/113. **Green Fee:** $14/$19. **Cart Fee:** $9/. **Walking Policy:** Unrestricted walking. **Walkability:** N/A. **Opened:** 1925. **Season:** Year-round. **High:** May-Sept. **To obtain tee times:** Call up to one week in advance. **Miscellaneous:** Reduced fees (weekdays, low season, twilight, seniors), metal spikes, club rentals, credit cards (MC, V).
Reader Comments: Affordable & family friendly ... Beautiful layout ... Tight, short challenge ... Nice course ... Good for a quick 9.

★★½ FOREST HILLS GOLF COURSE
PU-41971 Oberlin Rd., Elyria, 44035, Lorain County, (440)323-2632, 30 miles W of Cleveland.
Holes: 18. **Yards:** 6,161/5,125. **Par:** 70/71. **Course Rating:** 69.7/67.6. **Slope:** 117/105. **Green Fee:** $8/$14. **Cart Fee:** $10/person. **Walking Policy:** Unrestricted walking. **Walkability:** 2. **Architect:** Charlie Smith. **Season:** March-Dec. **High:** June-July-Aug. **To obtain tee times:** Call up to 7 days in advance for weekends and holidays. **Miscellaneous:** Reduced fees (weekdays, low season, seniors, juniors), metal spikes, range (grass/mats), club rentals, credit cards (MC, V), beginner friendly (junior clinics).
Reader Comments: Price is very reasonable ... A county-owned course ... Average golfer fun ... Busy, but a bargain ... Great value ... Long course, very good price.

★½ FOREST OAKS GOLF COURSE
PU-U.S. Rte. No.422 and St. Rte. No.305, Southington, 44470, Trumbull County, (330)898-2852.
Holes: 18. **Yards:** 6,122/5,867. **Par:** 72/72. **Course Rating:** N/A. **Slope:** N/A. **Green Fee:** $17/$18. **Cart Fee:** $16/cart. **Walking Policy:** Unrestricted walking. **Walkability:** 1. **Opened:** 1958. **Architect:** Myron Beechy. **Season:** March-Nov. **High:** May-Aug. **To obtain tee times:** Call golf shop. **Miscellaneous:** Reduced fees (weekdays, low season, seniors, juniors), metal spikes, range (grass/mats), club rentals, credit cards (MC, V, D).
Special Notes: Also has a 9-hole par 35.

FOWLER'S MILL GOLF COURSE
PU-13095 Rockhaven Rd., Chesterland, 44026, Geauga County, (440)729-7569, 30 miles E of Cleveland. **Web:** www.americangolf.com.
Holes: 27. **Green Fee:** $25/$58. **Cart Fee:** $3/person. **Walking Policy:** Unrestricted walking. **Opened:** 1972. **Architect:** Pete Dye. **Season:** March-Nov. **High:** June-Aug. **To obtain tee times:** Call up to 14 days in advance.

★★★★ LAKE/RIVER
Yards: 7,002/5,950. **Par:** 72/72. **Course Rating:** 74.7/73.9. **Slope:** 136/122. **Walkability:** 3.
Miscellaneous: Reduced fees (weekdays, low season, twilight, seniors, juniors), range (grass), club rentals, credit cards (MC, V, AE).
Notes: Ranked 20th in 1999 Best in State; 55th in 1996 America's Top 75 Affordable Courses.
Reader Comments: Lake and River nines great, Maple nine OK ... Hole No. 4 is the best hole in Cleveland ... Great early Pete Dye design ... Best in Ohio.
Special Notes: Formerly White/Blue

★★★★ MAPLE/LAKE
Yards: 6,595/5,913. **Par:** 72/72. **Course Rating:** 72.1/73.6. **Slope:** 128/123. **Walkability:** 3.
Miscellaneous: Reduced fees (weekdays, low season, twilight, seniors, juniors), range (grass), club rentals, credit cards (MC, V, AE).
Reader Comments: Wonderful course ... I was amazed to find a course this beautiful with such a good deals ... Overall awesome layout! A blast to play ... Excellent course. Very pricey ... Country club feel and price, decent course ... New clubhouse adds to quality ... Great design, run well, challenging, don't miss it.
Special Notes: Formerly Red/Blue

★★★★ RIVER/MAPLE
Yards: 6,385/5,797. **Par:** 72/72. **Course Rating:** 70.7/73.0. **Slope:** 125/123. **Walkability:** 2.
Miscellaneous: Reduced fees (weekdays, low season, twilight, seniors, juniors), metal spikes, range (grass), club rentals, credit cards (MC, V).
Reader Comments: Maple easy, fun 9 ... Beautiful, great value, scenic ... Great layout, will challenge anyone.
Special Notes: Formerly Red/White

★★★½ FOX DEN GOLF CLUB
PU-2770 Call Rd., Stow, 44224, Summit County, (330)673-3443, (888)231-4693, 8 miles N of Akron.

Holes: 18. **Yards:** 6,479/5,473. **Par:** 72/72. **Course Rating:** 70.4/69.0. **Slope:** 115/114. **Green Fee:** $16/$26. **Cart Fee:** $10/person. **Walking Policy:** Unrestricted walking. **Walkability:** 3. **Opened:** 1966. **Architect:** Frank Schmiedel. **Season:** March-Nov. **High:** May-Sept. **To obtain tee times:** Call ahead anytime. **Miscellaneous:** Reduced fees (weekdays, low season, seniors, juniors), range (grass/mats), credit cards (MC, V).
Reader Comments: Great for outings ... Short track, but fun ... Easy course, good condition ... Nice course, good value ... Not long, beautifully manicured, each hole uniquely designed.

THE FOX'S DEN GOLF COURSE
PU-1221 Irmscher St., Celina, 45822, Mercer County, (419)586-3102.
Holes: 18. **Yards:** 6,874/5,436. **Par:** 72/72. **Course Rating:** 72.4/70.4. **Slope:** 125/117. **Green Fee:** $22/$27. **Cart Fee:** $10/person. **Walking Policy:** Unrestricted walking. **Walkability:** 3. **Opened:** 1996. **Architect:** Jim Fazio. **Season:** Year-round. **High:** June-Aug. **To obtain tee times:** Call 1 week in advance. **Miscellaneous:** Reduced fees (weekdays, low season, twilight, seniors), range (grass), club rentals, credit cards (MC, V, D).

FOXFIRE GOLF CLUB
PU-10799 St. Rte. 104, Lockbourne, 43137, Pickaway County, (614)224-3694, 15 miles S of Columbus.
★★★ FOXFIRE COURSE
Holes: 18. **Yards:** 6,891/5,175. **Par:** 72/72. **Course Rating:** 72.7/69.1. **Slope:** 122/112. **Green Fee:** $18/$21. **Cart Fee:** $22/cart. **Walking Policy:** Unrestricted walking. **Walkability:** 3. **Opened:** 1974. **Architect:** Jack Kidwell. **Season:** Year-round. **High:** June-Sept. **To obtain tee times:** Call up to 14 days in advance. **Miscellaneous:** Reduced fees (low season, seniors, juniors), range (grass/mats), club rentals, credit cards (MC, V, AE).
Reader Comments: Deceptive, nice layout, par 5s long ... Long but fair. Have to hit them straight ... Always clean and neat ... Not bad, good value ... Nice clubhouse.
★★★★½ PLAYERS CLUB AT FOXFIRE
Holes: 18. **Yards:** 7,077/5,255. **Par:** 72/72. **Course Rating:** 74.2/70.3. **Slope:** 132/121. **Green Fee:** $25/$36. **Cart Fee:** $11/person. **Walking Policy:** Unrestricted walking. **Walkability:** 3. **Opened:** 1993. **Architect:** Jack Kidwell/Barry Serafin. **Season:** Year-round. **High:** June-Sept. **To obtain tee times:** Call up to 14 days in advance. **Miscellaneous:** Reduced fees (low season), range (grass/mats), club rentals, credit cards (MC, V, AE).
Reader Comments: Treelined fairways are absolutely beautiful ... Best public course in Central Ohio ... Terrific conditioning, private club quality ... Best in area, no easy holes ... Treated like royalty ... I've seen mountains with less slope than some at these greens ... Great challenge, nice layout ... So tough when wind blows.

★★½ GENEVA ON THE LAKE GOLF CLUB
PU-Golf Ave., Geneva On The Lake, 44041, Ashtabula County, (216)466-8797.
Yards: N/A. **Par:** N/A. **Course Rating:** N/A. **Slope:** N/A. **Green Fee:** N/A. **Walkability:** N/A. **Architect:** Stanley Thompson. **Miscellaneous:** Metal spikes.
Reader Comments: Work in progress, good for women ... Needs work, has potential ... With beautiful Lake Erie visible on many holes, it was hard to remember why I was there ... Good parkland course, fun and interesting.

★★★½ GLENEAGLES GOLF CLUB
PM-2615 Glenwood Dr., Twinsburg, 44087, Summit County, (216)425-3334, 20 miles SE of Cleveland.
Holes: 18. **Yards:** 6,545/5,147. **Par:** 72/72. **Course Rating:** 72.2/69.4. **Slope:** 121/115. **Green Fee:** $19/$22. **Cart Fee:** $10/person. **Walking Policy:** Unrestricted walking. **Walkability:** 2. **Opened:** 1990. **Architect:** Ted McAnlis. **Season:** April-Nov. **High:** June-Aug. **To obtain tee times:** Call up to 14 days in advance. **Miscellaneous:** Reduced fees (weekdays, twilight, seniors, juniors), metal spikes, range (grass), credit cards (MC, V).
Reader Comments: Challenging shorter course, maintained well, short par 5s, many doglegs left ... Course is blossoming under city ownership ... Good test ... Good layout. Gets better each year.

★★★ GLENVIEW GOLF COURSE
PU-10965 Springfield Pike, Cincinnati, 45246, Hamilton County, (513)771-1747.
Holes: 27. **Yards:** 7,036/5,142. **Par:** 72/72. **Course Rating:** 74.2/69.9. **Slope:** 137/121. **Green Fee:** $20/$26. **Cart Fee:** $12/person. **Walking Policy:** Unrestricted walking. **Walkability:** 3. **Opened:** 1974. **Architect:** Arthur Hills/Mike Hurdzan. **Season:** Year-round. **High:** May-Sept. **To obtain tee times:** Automated tee time service allows subscribers to call 9 days in advance. Non subscribers call 1 week in advance. Out of town players call golf shop. **Miscellaneous:** Reduced fees (weekdays, low season, twilight, seniors, juniors), metal spikes, range (grass/mats), club rentals, credit cards (MC, V).
Reader Comments: Brutal from the black tees ... Once outstanding, starting a comeback ... Good public course, challenging from the tips.

OHIO

THE GOLF CENTER AT KINGS ISLAND

PU-6042 Fairway Dr., Mason, 45040, Warren County, (513)398-7700, 25 miles N of Cincinnati.
Web: www.thegolfcenter.com.
Opened: 1971. **Architect:** Jack Nicklaus/D.Muirhead/Jay Morrist. **Season:** March-Dec. **High:** May-Sept.

★★★ BRUIN COURSE

Holes: 18. **Yards:** 3,394/3,394. **Par:** 60/60. **Course Rating:** N/A. **Slope:** N/A. **Green Fee:** $13/$14. **Cart Fee:** $12/person. **Walking Policy:** Unrestricted walking. **Walkability:** 3. **To obtain tee times:** Call up to 7 days in advance for weekends and holidays. **Miscellaneous:** Reduced fees (weekdays, seniors, juniors), metal spikes, range (grass/mats), club rentals, credit cards (MC, V, AE, D), beginner friendly.
Reader Comments: Great beginner course or short iron course ... Driveable par 4s make you feel like a gorilla, course beautifully maintained ... Good executive course ...Excellent condition ... Plenty of trouble if shots run astray.

★★★½ GRIZZLY COURSE (NORTH/SOUTH)

Holes: 27. **Yards:** 6,784/5,156. **Par:** 72/72. **Course Rating:** 72.5/69.4. **Slope:** 136/122. **Green Fee:** $26/$65. **Cart Fee:** $12/person. **Walking Policy:** Walking at certain times. **Walkability:** 3. **To obtain tee times:** Call up to 7 days in advance for weekends and holidays. Call up to 21 days in advance for Monday-Thursday. **Miscellaneous:** Reduced fees (weekdays, low season, twilight, seniors), metal spikes, range (grass/mats), club rentals, credit cards (MC, V, AE, D, Diners Club, Carte Blanche), beginner friendly (bruin par 3-4 mid-length course).
Reader Comments: Mix of old and new holes ... Expensive, well maintained ... Better hit 'em straight! ... Forget the rollercoasters; play this course ... Good shape, nice challenge ... Great condition year round ... The greens were like standing on carpet ... Too expensive... Very good layout, but expensive.

★★★½ GRIZZLY COURSE (NORTH/WEST)

Holes: 27. **Yards:** 6,795/5,210. **Par:** 72/72. **Course Rating:** 72.8/69.6. **Slope:** 136/125. **Green Fee:** N/A/$65. **Cart Fee:** $12/person. **Walking Policy:** Walking at certain times. **Walkability:** 3. **To obtain tee times:** Call up to 7 days in advance for weekends and holidays. Call up to 21 days in advance for Monday - Thursday. **Miscellaneous:** Reduced fees (weekdays, low season, twilight, seniors), metal spikes, range (grass/mats), club rentals, credit cards (MC, V, AE, D, Diners Club, Carte Blanche), beginner friendly (bruin course par 3 and 4 mid-length).

★★★½ GRIZZLY COURSE (SOUTH/WEST)

Holes: 27. **Yards:** 6,719/5,118. **Par:** 72/72. **Course Rating:** 72.4/69.6. **Slope:** 136/118. **Green Fee:** $26/$65. **Cart Fee:** $12/person. **Walking Policy:** Walking at certain times. **Walkability:** 3. **To obtain tee times:** Call up to 7 days in advance for weekends and holidays. Call up to 21 days in advance for Monday - Thursday. **Miscellaneous:** Reduced fees (weekdays, low season, twilight, seniors), metal spikes, range (grass/mats), club rentals, credit cards (MC, V, AE, D, Diners Club, Carte Blanche), beginner friendly (bruin course par 3 and 4 mid-length).
Notes: 1973-77 PGA Ohio Kings Island Open; 1978-1989 LPGA Championship; 1990-1999 Senior PGA Kroger Classic.
Special Notes: Formerly The Jack Nicklaus Sports Center.

★★★★ THE GOLF CLUB AT YANKEE TRACE *Service*

PM-10000 Yankee St., Centerville, 45458, Montgomery County, (937)438-4653, 15 miles S of Dayton.
Holes: 18. **Yards:** 7,139/5,204. **Par:** 72/72. **Course Rating:** 75.5/70.5. **Slope:** 140/124. **Green Fee:** $34/$37. **Cart Fee:** $12/person. **Walking Policy:** Unrestricted walking. **Walkability:** N/A. **Opened:** 1995. **Architect:** Gene Bates. **Season:** March-Dec. **High:** March-Oct. **To obtain tee times:** Call 7 days in advance. **Miscellaneous:** Reduced fees (twilight, juniors), range (grass), club rentals, credit cards (MC, V, AE, D).
Reader Comments: Excellent course ... 4 best finishing holes in area ... Good layout, pricey, some elevation on sheltered fairways ... Good layout, friendly, helpful ... Great practice facilities, nice new course ... Tough from tips ... Nice practice area ... Fast greens, great finishing holes ... Why can't they all be like this?

★★★ THE GOLF COURSES OF WINTON WOODS

PU-1515 W. Sharon Rd., Cincinnati, 45240, Hamilton County, (513)825-3770, 14 miles N of Cincinnati. **Web:** www.hamiltgoncountyparks.org.com.
Holes: 18. **Yards:** 6,376/4,554. **Par:** 72/72. **Course Rating:** 70.0/66.6. **Slope:** 120/108. **Green Fee:** $19/$19. **Cart Fee:** $11/person. **Walking Policy:** Unrestricted walking. **Walkability:** 3. **Opened:** 1993. **Architect:** Michael Hurdzan. **Season:** March-Dec. **High:** May-Sept. **To obtain tee times:** Call 5 days in advance beginning at 6 P.M. **Miscellaneous:** Reduced fees (seniors, juniors), metal spikes, range (grass/mats), club rentals, credit cards (MC, V).
Reader Comments: Always nice ... Well-kept country course, best practice range I have seen ... Improvements on front 9 really helped ... Playable and fun ... Pace of play sometimes slow, nice course ... Challenging and scenic.

★★½ GRANDVIEW GOLF CLUB
PU-13404 Old State Rd., Middlefield, 44062, Geauga County, (440)834-1824, 8 miles S of Chardon.
Holes: 18. **Yards:** 6,200/5,451. **Par:** 70/72. **Course Rating:** 70.4/70.2. **Slope:** 113/114. **Green Fee:** $11/$20. **Cart Fee:** $10/person. **Walking Policy:** Unrestricted walking. **Walkability:** 4. **Opened:** 1929. **Architect:** Richard W. LaConte/Ted McAnlis. **Season:** April-Nov. **High:** June-Aug. **To obtain tee times:** Call. **Miscellaneous:** Reduced fees (seniors, juniors), credit cards (MC, V). **Reader Comments:** Wooded, scenic, hilly, fast greens ... A fun little course, good value.

★★★★ GRANVILLE GOLF COURSE
PU-555 Newark Rd., Granville, 43023, Licking County, (740)587-4653, 30 miles E of Columbus.
Holes: 18. **Yards:** 6,559/5,197. **Par:** 71/71. **Course Rating:** 71.3/69.6. **Slope:** 128/123. **Green Fee:** $29/$34. **Cart Fee:** $12/person. **Walking Policy:** Walking at certain times. **Walkability:** 3. **Opened:** 1925. **Architect:** Donald Ross/Jack Kidwell. **Season:** Year-round. **High:** April-Nov. **To obtain tee times:** Call 7 days in advance with credit card to guarantee. **Miscellaneous:** Reduced fees (twilight), metal spikes, range (grass/mats), club rentals, credit cards (MC, V, AE, D). **Reader Comments:** Excellent design ... Greens are lightning & true ... Always a treat ... Great old track, easy access, good value ... A joy to play, great views ... Breathtaking beauty, devious greens ... Character galore ... Terrific course in quaint college town.

★★ GREAT TRAIL GOLF COURSE
PU-10154 Great Trail Dr., Minerva, 44657, Carroll County, (330)868-6770, 15 miles E of Canton.
Holes: 27. **Yards:** N/A. **Par:** N/A. **Course Rating:** N/A. **Slope:** N/A. **Green Fee:** $12/$14. **Cart Fee:** $14/cart. **Walking Policy:** Unrestricted walking. **Walkability:** 5. **Opened:** 1970. **Architect:** Romain Fry. **Season:** Year-round weather permitting. **High:** June-Sept. **To obtain tee times:** Call golf shop. **Miscellaneous:** Reduced fees (weekdays, resort guests), discount packages, lodging, credit cards (MC, V).

★★ GREEN CREST GOLF COURSE
PU-7813 Bethany Rte. 1, Middletown, 45042, Butler County, (513)777-2090.
Special Notes: Call club for further information.

★★★ GREEN HILLS GOLF CLUB
PU-1959 S. Main St., Clyde, 43410, Sandusky County, (419)547-7947, (800)234-4766, 50 miles E of Toledo. **Web:** www.greenhillsgolf.com.
Holes: 18. **Yards:** 6,239/5,437. **Par:** 71/74. **Course Rating:** 68.5/69.7. **Slope:** 102/100. **Green Fee:** $9/$20. **Cart Fee:** $20/cart. **Walking Policy:** Walking at certain times. **Walkability:** 3. **Opened:** 1958. **Architect:** T. Crockett/B. Crockett/M. Fritz. **Season:** March-Jan. **High:** June-Aug. **To obtain tee times:** Call up to 7 days in advance. **Miscellaneous:** Reduced fees (weekdays, low season), range (grass), club rentals, credit cards (MC, V, D), beginner friendly (executive 9-hole course). **Reader Comments:** Short but interesting, very nice owners! ... Fun track.

★★ GREEN VALLEY GOLF CLUB
SP-2673 Pleasant Valley Rd., N.E., New Philadelphia, 44663, Tuscarawas County, (330)364-2812, 20 miles S of Canton.
Holes: 18. **Yards:** 6,500/5,200. **Par:** 72/73. **Course Rating:** 71.7/67.8. **Slope:** 119/115. **Green Fee:** $14/$15. **Cart Fee:** $17/cart. **Walking Policy:** Unrestricted walking. **Walkability:** 4. **Opened:** 1961. **Season:** Year-round. **High:** May-Aug. **To obtain tee times:** Call 1 day in advance. **Miscellaneous:** Reduced fees (weekdays, low season, twilight, juniors), discount packages, range (grass/mats), club rentals, credit cards (MC, V, AE, D, Bank Debit Cards), beginner friendly (specials weekdays before 1:30).

GREENTREE GOLF CLUB
PU-5505 Greentree Road, Lebanon, 45036, Warren County, (513)727-1009, 25 miles N of Cincinnati.
Holes: 9. **Yards:** 3,148/2,499. **Par:** 36/36. **Course Rating:** 69.8/66.3. **Slope:** 116/113. **Green Fee:** $16/$31. **Cart Fee:** $22/person. **Walking Policy:** Walking at certain times. **Walkability:** 4. **Opened:** 1999. **Season:** Year-round. **High:** April-Nov. **To obtain tee times:** Call 7 days in advance for weekends only. **Miscellaneous:** Reduced fees (weekdays, seniors, juniors), metal spikes.

★★ GROVEBROOK GOLF CLUB
5525 Hoover Rd., Grove City, 43123, Franklin County, (614)875-2497.
Yards: 6,027/5,099. **Par:** 71/71. **Course Rating:** 67.8/67.7. **Slope:** 113/11. **Green Fee:** $13/$17. **Walkability:** N/A. **Miscellaneous:** Metal spikes.

★★★★½ HAWKS NEST GOLF CLUB *Value, Condition*
PU-2800 E. Pleasant Home Rd., Creston, 44691, Wayne County, (330)435-4611, 6 miles N of Wooster.

Holes: 18. **Yards:** 6,670/4,767. **Par:** 72/72. **Course Rating:** 71.5/67.9. **Slope:** 124/110. **Green Fee:** $22/$27. **Cart Fee:** $11/person. **Walking Policy:** Unrestricted walking. **Walkability:** 2. **Opened:** 1993. **Architect:** Steve Burns. **Season:** April-Dec. **High:** May-Oct. **To obtain tee times:** Call one year in advance. **Miscellaneous:** Reduced fees (weekdays, seniors, juniors), range (grass), club rentals, credit cards (MC, V), beginner friendly (junior and ladies groups). **Reader Comments:** Awesome layout in Amish country ... Well worth the trip, great layout ... Each hole makes you want to play the next ... A gem ... Greens better than any private club ... Great course, a little pricey ... Don't play on a windy day ... Great course, slow play ... Good clubhouse, nice course.

★★★★ HAWTHORNE HILLS GOLF CLUB
SP-1000 Fetter Rd., Lima, 45801, Allen County, (419)221-1891, 74 miles N of Dayton.
Holes: 27. **Yards:** 6,710/5,695. **Par:** 72/72. **Course Rating:** 71.6/71.9. **Slope:** 119/118. **Green Fee:** $17/$19. **Cart Fee:** $10/person. **Walkability:** N/A. **Opened:** 1963. **Architect:** Harold Paddock. **Season:** March-Nov. **High:** May-Sept. **To obtain tee times:** Call in advance. **Miscellaneous:** Reduced fees (weekdays), metal spikes, range (grass), club rentals. **Reader Comments:** Hilly layout in the flatlands ... Will test your skills ... Solid, mature, cheap, everyone's favorite ... Excellent ... Nice older course, longer than most ... Very busy ... A superior public course. Well maintained ... Always in great shape.

★★★★ HEATHERWOODE GOLF CLUB
PU-88 Heatherwoode Blvd., Springboro, 45066, Warren County, (513)748-3222, 15 miles S of Dayton.
Holes: 18. **Yards:** 6,730/5,069. **Par:** 71/71. **Course Rating:** 72.9/69.8. **Slope:** 138/127. **Green Fee:** $42/$52. **Cart Fee:** $3/person. **Walking Policy:** Unrestricted walking. **Walkability:** 4. **Opened:** 1991. **Architect:** Denis Griffiths. **Season:** Year-round. **High:** May-Aug. **To obtain tee times:** Call 7 days in advance. **Miscellaneous:** Reduced fees (weekdays, low season, twilight, seniors, juniors), range (grass/mats), club rentals, credit cards (MC, V, AE). **Reader Comments:** Good staff, play back tees ... When the wind blows, no one shoots 59 ... Heavily played, excellent rangers ... Fastest greens in area ... Great course, great shape ... Well preserved natural setting ... Good course, everyone should play.

★★★ HEMLOCK SPRINGS GOLF CLUB
PU-4654 Cold Springs Rd., Geneva, 44041, Ashtabula County, (216)466-4044, (800)HEMLOCK, 40 miles E of Cleveland.
Holes: 18. **Yards:** 6,812/5,453. **Par:** 72/72. **Course Rating:** 72.8/73.8. **Slope:** 123/115. **Green Fee:** $12/$25. **Cart Fee:** $10/person. **Walking Policy:** Unrestricted walking. **Walkability:** 3. **Opened:** 1961. **Architect:** Benjamin W. Zink. **Season:** April-Nov. **High:** June-Aug. **To obtain tee times:** Call 1-800-HEMLOCK anytime. **Miscellaneous:** Reduced fees (weekdays, low season, twilight, seniors, juniors), discount packages, range (grass/mats), club rentals, credit cards (MC, V, AE, D). **Reader Comments:** A relaxed course surrounded by vineyard ... Difficult, use every club in your bag ... Great variety of holes ... Good course ... No 2 holes alike ... Long, excellent condition ... Beautiful, challenging course, worth returning.

★★½ HIAWATHA GOLF COURSE
PU-901 Beech St., Mount Vernon, 43050, Knox County, (740)393-2886, 40 miles NE of Columbus.
Holes: 18. **Yards:** 6,721/5,100. **Par:** 72/74. **Course Rating:** 71.5/68.5. **Slope:** 121/116. **Green Fee:** $12/$14. **Cart Fee:** $11/person. **Walking Policy:** Unrestricted walking. **Walkability:** 2. **Opened:** 1962. **Architect:** Jack Kidwell. **Season:** March-Nov. **High:** July-Aug. **To obtain tee times:** Call. **Miscellaneous:** Reduced fees (weekdays, low season, twilight, seniors, juniors), discount packages, credit cards (MC, V). **Reader Comments:** Old course fun, wide assortment of tees ... Good golf for the money ... Fun to play! ... Great value, elevated greens, snack bar.

★★½ HICKORY FLAT GREENS
PU-54188 Township Rd. 155, West Lafayette, 43845, Coshocton County, (740)545-7796, 2 miles SW of West Lafayette.
Holes: 18. **Yards:** 6,600/5,124. **Par:** 72/72. **Course Rating:** 70.4/68.3. **Slope:** 109/105. **Green Fee:** $16/$16. **Cart Fee:** $11/person. **Walking Policy:** Unrestricted walking. **Walkability:** 2. **Opened:** 1970. **Architect:** Jack Kidwell. **Season:** Year-round. **High:** May-Sept. **To obtain tee times:** Call anytime. **Miscellaneous:** Reduced fees (weekdays, low season, twilight, seniors, juniors), discount packages, metal spikes, range (grass), club rentals, credit cards (MC, V). **Reader Comments:** Wide open level course continually improving ... Flat course, beautiful layout, wide fairways ... Easy to play ... Like the name says, a mostly flat course.

★★½ HICKORY GROVE GOLF CLUB
PU-6302 State Rte. 94, Harpster, 43323, Wyandot County, (614)496-2631, (800)833-6619, 15 miles N of Marion.

Holes: 18. **Yards:** 6,874/5,376. **Par:** 72/76. **Course Rating:** 71.0/69.1. **Slope:** 108/105. **Green Fee:** $15/$15. **Cart Fee:** $20/person. **Walking Policy:** Unrestricted walking. **Walkability:** 3. **Opened:** 1963. **Architect:** J. Craig Bowman. **Season:** March-Nov. **High:** June-Aug. **To obtain tee times:** Call. **Miscellaneous:** Reduced fees (weekdays, twilight), discount packages, metal spikes, range (grass), club rentals, credit cards (MC, V, D).

Reader Comments: Wide open, great greens, sometimes windy ... Nice layout ... Long course, nice greens.

★★ HICKORY GROVE GOLF COURSE

SP-1490 Fairway Dr., Jefferson, 44047, Ashtabula County, (440)576-3776, 55 miles E of Cleveland.
Holes: 18. **Yards:** 6,500/5,593. **Par:** 72/73. **Course Rating:** 70.9/71.5. **Slope:** N/A. **Green Fee:** $10/$17. **Cart Fee:** $18/cart. **Walking Policy:** Unrestricted walking. **Walkability:** 2. **Opened:** 1962. **Season:** April-Oct. **High:** June-Aug. **To obtain tee times:** Call up to 14 days in advance. **Miscellaneous:** Range (grass), club rentals, credit cards (MC, V).

★★ HICKORY NUT GOLF CLUB

PU-23601 Royalton Rd., Columbia Station, 44028, Lorain County, (440)236-8008, 1 miles W of Strongsville.
Holes: 18. **Yards:** 6,424/6,424. **Par:** 71/73. **Course Rating:** 69.5/N/A. **Slope:** 124/N/A. **Green Fee:** $16/$18. **Cart Fee:** $20/cart. **Walking Policy:** Unrestricted walking. **Walkability:** 1. **Opened:** 1968. **Season:** April-Oct. **To obtain tee times:** First come, first served. **Miscellaneous:** Reduced fees (seniors), metal spikes, club rentals.

★★★ HICKORY WOODS GOLF COURSE

PU-1240 Hickory Woods Dr., Loveland, 45140, Clermont County, (513)575-3900, 15 miles N of Cincinnati.
Holes: 18. **Yards:** 6,105/5,115. **Par:** 70/71. **Course Rating:** 70.1/69.4. **Slope:** 122/113. **Green Fee:** $18/$24. **Cart Fee:** $11/person. **Walking Policy:** Unrestricted walking. **Walkability:** 3. **Opened:** 1983. **Architect:** Dennis Acomb. **Season:** Year-round. **High:** April-Aug. **To obtain tee times:** Call 7 days in advance. **Miscellaneous:** Reduced fees (low season, seniors, juniors), metal spikes, club rentals, credit cards (MC, V, AE).

Reader Comments: Great layout, beautiful during fall, back 9 excellent ... Short, tight, heavily played but enjoyable ... Good iron course ... Back 9 very tight ... Good golf experience ... Nice all around course ... Interesting layout, great bar ... Pretty course ... Wooded, hilly, scenic.

★½ HIDDEN HILLS GOLF CLUB

PU-4886 County Rd. 16, Woodville, 43469, Sandusky County, (419)849-3693, (877)849-GOLF, 20 miles SE of Toledo.
Holes: 18. **Yards:** 5,686/4,724. **Par:** 72/72. **Course Rating:** N/A. **Slope:** N/A. **Green Fee:** $10/$17. **Cart Fee:** $18/cart. **Walking Policy:** Unrestricted walking. **Walkability:** 2. **Opened:** 1968. **Architect:** Elizabeth Pierce. **Season:** May-Nov. **High:** June-Aug. **To obtain tee times:** No tee times necessary unless in a group of 9 or more. **Miscellaneous:** Reduced fees (weekdays, low season, twilight, seniors, juniors), club rentals, credit cards (MC, V, AE, D), beginner friendly (junior, woman's, beginner programs).

★½ HIDDEN LAKE GOLF COURSE

PU-5370 E. State Rd. 571, Tipp City, 45371, Miami County, (937)667-8880, 12 miles N of Dayton.
Holes: 18. **Yards:** 6,562/5,357. **Par:** 72/72. **Course Rating:** 70.5/69.3. **Slope:** 114/111. **Green Fee:** $9/$18. **Cart Fee:** $9/. **Walking Policy:** Unrestricted walking. **Walkability:** N/A. **Opened:** 1988. **Architect:** Don Dick. **Season:** Year-round. **High:** March-Nov. **To obtain tee times:** Call 7 days in advance. **Miscellaneous:** Reduced fees (low season, seniors, juniors), metal spikes, club rentals, credit cards (MC, V, AE, D).

★★½ HIGHLAND PARK GOLF CLUB

PU-3550 Green Rd., Cleveland, 44122, Cuyahoga County, (216)348-7273.
Reader Comments: Long, new clubhouse ... Very inexpensive, great service, very polite people ... Nice new clubhouse ... Nice greens ... Former Cleveland Open course.
Special Notes: Call club for further information.

★★½ HILLCREST GOLF CLUB

800 W. Bigelow, Findlay, 45840, Hancock County, (419)423-7211.
Yards: 6,981/5,146. **Par:** 72/72. **Course Rating:** 71.7/67.8 **Slope:** 112/107. **Green Fee:** $20/$23. **Walkability:** N/A. **Architect:** Ed Rettig/Gene Cleary. **Miscellaneous:** Metal spikes.
Reader Comments: Always green, long ... Okay ... Hard to remember course. Fun bar.

★★★★ HILLIARD LAKES GOLF CLUB

PU-31665 Hilliard Rd., Westlake, 44145, Cuyahoga County, (440)871-9578, 15 miles W of Cleveland.

Holes: 18. **Yards:** 6,785/5,636. **Par:** 72/75. **Course Rating:** 70.0/74.0. **Slope:** 124/118. **Green Fee:** $18/$18. **Cart Fee:** $24/cart. **Walking Policy:** Unrestricted walking. **Walkability:** 1. **Opened:** 1968. **Architect:** Ms. Zaleski. **Season:** March-Nov. **High:** May-Sept. **To obtain tee times:** Call golf shop. **Miscellaneous:** Reduced fees (weekdays, seniors, juniors), metal spikes, range (grass/mats), credit cards (MC, V).

Reader Comments: Excellent course, great layout ... Keep it straight or course gets tough ... Beautiful course ... Exciting to play; requires all shots ... The best public golf course I have ever played ... Nice fairways.

★★★½ HINCKLEY HILLS GOLF COURSE
PU-300 State Rd., Hinckley, 44233, Medina County, (330)278-4861, 17 miles S of Cleveland.
Holes: 18. **Yards:** 6,846/5,478. **Par:** 73/72. **Course Rating:** 71.6/70.9. **Slope:** 125/118. **Green Fee:** $27/$27. **Cart Fee:** $24/cart. **Walking Policy:** Walking at certain times. **Walkability:** 4. **Opened:** 1964. **Architect:** Harold Paddock Sr. **Season:** April-Nov. **High:** May-Sept. **To obtain tee times:** Call golf shop. **Miscellaneous:** Discount packages, metal spikes, club rentals, credit cards (MC, V).

Reader Comments: Very tough course, need to take cart, need all your skill ... Be in shape before you mark this 18 ... Hilly, well-maintained, challenging ... Nice layout, burns out in late summer... Tough, honest layout.

★★ HOLLY HILLS GOLF CLUB
PU-4699 N. State Hwy. 42, Waynesville, 45068, Warren County, (513)897-4921, 20 miles SE of Dayton.
Holes: 18. **Yards:** 6,785/N/A. **Par:** 71/N/A. **Course Rating:** 72.3/N/A. **Slope:** N/A. **Green Fee:** $15/$18. **Cart Fee:** $19/person. **Walking Policy:** Unrestricted walking. **Walkability:** N/A. **Opened:** 1962. **Architect:** William Diddle. **Season:** March-Nov. **To obtain tee times:** Call up to 7 days advance. **Miscellaneous:** Reduced fees (weekdays, twilight, seniors, juniors), metal spikes, range (grass), credit cards (MC, V).

★★½ HOMESTEAD GOLF COURSE
PU-5327 Worley Rd., Tipp City, 45371, Miami County, (937)698-4876.
Yards: N/A. **Par:** N/A. **Course Rating:** N/A. **Slope:** N/A. **Green Fee:** $17/$20. **Walkability:** N/A. **Architect:** Bill Amick. **Miscellaneous:** Metal spikes.

Reader Comments: Nice little course ... Very flat, some good water holes ... Great course ... Best greens around, requires many placement shots ... A good place to play for a duffer (like me).

★★ HOMESTEAD SPRINGS GOLF COURSE
PU-5888 London Lancaster Rd., Groveport, 43125, Franklin County, (614)836-5872, 15 miles SE of Columbus.
Holes: 18. **Yards:** 6,463/4,907. **Par:** 72/72. **Course Rating:** 69.7/N/A. **Slope:** 111/N/A. **Green Fee:** $25/$27. **Cart Fee:** $10/person. **Walking Policy:** Unrestricted walking. **Walkability:** 2. **Opened:** 1972. **Architect:** Harlan (Bud) Rainier. **Season:** Year-round. **High:** April-Oct. **Miscellaneous:** Club rentals.

★★½ HUBBARD GOLF COURSE
PU-6233 W. Liberty St. S.E., Hubbard, 44425, Trumbull County, (330)534-9026.
Reader Comments: Best course, value and fun to play, great layout ... Best condition in years ... A challenge, fun.
Special Notes: Call club for further information.

★★★½ HUESTON WOODS GOLF COURSE
PU-6962 Brown Rd., Oxford, 45056, Butler County, (513)523-8081, (800)282-7275, 25 miles N of Cincinnati.
Holes: 18. **Yards:** 7,005/5,258. **Par:** 72/72. **Course Rating:** 73.1/69.1. **Slope:** 132/120. **Green Fee:** $18/$25. **Cart Fee:** $12/person. **Walking Policy:** Unrestricted walking. **Walkability:** 3. **Opened:** 1969. **Architect:** Jack Kidwell. **Season:** Year-round. **High:** June-Sept. **To obtain tee times:** Call 7 days in advance for weekdays. Call 7:30 a.m. Monday for upcoming weekend. Hotel guests may make tee times at any time with reservation number. **Miscellaneous:** Reduced fees (weekdays, low season, resort guests, twilight, seniors, juniors), discount packages, metal spikes, range (grass/mats), club rentals, lodging (97 rooms), credit cards (MC, V, AE, D).

Reader Comments: Long, wooded, lots of doglegs ... Worth the time, keep it in fairway ... A great, long, woodsy course ... Bring something to do between shots. Good test though ... Variety of shots ... Long, tight & cheap! ... Nice state park course ... First-class facility. Greens are good ... Yardage markers every where.

INDIAN SPRINGS GOLF CLUB
PU-11111 State Rte. 161, Mechanicsburg, 43044, Champaign County, (937)834-2111, (800)752-7846, 23 miles W of Dublin.
Holes: 27. **Green Fee:** $26/$35. **Cart Fee:** $10/person. **Walking Policy:** Unrestricted walking. **Walkability:** 4. **Opened:** 1990. **Architect:** Jack Kidwell. **Season:** March-Oct. **High:** June-Aug. **To**

obtain tee times: Call 7 days in advance. **Miscellaneous:** Reduced fees (weekdays, low season, twilight, seniors, juniors), range (grass), club rentals, credit cards (MC, V).

★★★★ **LAKES/WOODS**
Yards: 6,949/5,176. **Par:** 72/72. **Course Rating:** N/A. **Slope:** N/A.

★★★★ **RESERVE/LAKES**
Yards: 7,008/5,463. **Par:** 72/72. **Course Rating:** N/A. **Slope:** N/A.

★★★★ **RESERVE/WOODS**
Yards: 7,123/5,733. **Par:** 72/72. **Course Rating:** 73.8/72.6. **Slope:** 126/122.
Notes: Ranked 36th in 1996 America's Top 75 Affordable Courses.
Reader Comments: Busy course, treacherous greens ... Long, best value in Central Ohio ... Good golf experience ... Fine course, but slow ... Tough layout from tips ... Every hole is memorable ... New 9 needs growing time ... Very nice fairways ... Pro shop needs attitude adjustment, but great greens and fairways, great layout.

★★½ **IRISH HILLS GOLF COURSE**
PU-7020 Newark Rd., Mount Vernon, 43050, Knox County, (740)397-6252.
Holes: 18. **Yards:** 6,503/5,890. **Par:** 71/75. **Course Rating:** 69.9/72.9. **Slope:** 115/120. **Green Fee:** $10/$13. **Cart Fee:** $9/person. **Walking Policy:** Unrestricted walking. **Walkability:** 1. **Opened:** 1928. **Season:** March-Nov. **High:** June-Aug. **To obtain tee times:** Call golf shop. **Miscellaneous:** Credit cards (MC, V, AE).
Reader Comments: Beautiful front nine ... Good place for beginners ... Front 9 has some great holes ... Challenging course ... Front 9 a lot of pine trees, back 9 wide open.

★★★ **IRONWOOD GOLF CLUB**
SP-1015 W. Leggett, Wauseon, 43567, Fulton County, (419)335-0587, 30 miles W of Toledo.
Holes: 18. **Yards:** 6,965/5,306. **Par:** 72/74. **Course Rating:** 72.7/69.8. **Slope:** 118/111. **Green Fee:** $14/$22. **Cart Fee:** $11/person. **Walking Policy:** Unrestricted walking. **Walkability:** 1. **Opened:** 1971. **Architect:** Ben Hadden/Margaret Alan. **Season:** March-Nov. **High:** June-Aug. **To obtain tee times:** Call 7 days in advance. **Miscellaneous:** Reduced fees (weekdays), range (grass), club rentals.
Reader Comments: Country setting, beautiful, fun! ... Long, tough into the wind! ... Well-kept.

★★★½ **IRONWOOD GOLF COURSE**
PU-445 State Rd., Hinckley, 44233, Medina County, (330)278-7171.
Holes: 18. **Yards:** 6,360/5,785. **Par:** 71/74. **Course Rating:** 69.7/72.8. **Slope:** 118/124. **Green Fee:** $22/$25. **Cart Fee:** $22/cart. **Walking Policy:** Unrestricted walking. **Walkability:** 3. **Opened:** 1967. **Architect:** Harold Paddock. **Season:** April-Oct. **Miscellaneous:** Reduced fees (seniors), metal spikes, credit cards (MC, V).
Reader Comments: Tight fairways, hilly, challenging, need cart ... Nice place for all skill levels ... Hilly, well-maintained, some tough holes ... Long, challenging & fun to play.

★★★★ **J.E. GOOD PARK GOLF CLUB**
PM-530 Nome Ave., Akron, 44320, Summit County, (330)864-0020, 35 miles S of Cleveland.
Holes: 18. **Yards:** 6,663/4,926. **Par:** 71/71. **Course Rating:** 72.0/69.1. **Slope:** 123/115. **Green Fee:** $20/$22. **Cart Fee:** $10/person. **Walking Policy:** Unrestricted walking. **Walkability:** 1. **Opened:** 1926. **Architect:** Bertie Way. **Season:** March-Dec. **High:** May-Oct. **To obtain tee times:** Call 7 days in advance for weekends and holidays. **Miscellaneous:** Reduced fees (low season, seniors, juniors).
Reader Comments: Not bad for city owned, very tight ... Nice city golf course, reasonable prices ... Lots of doglegs, tough course ... Pleasing to the eye, fun to play, nice greens ... Outstanding public track ... A great city-run golf experience ... Narrow fairways treelined. Small, tight greens ... The toughest and best in our area.

★★★ **JAMAICA RUN GOLF CLUB**
PU-8781 Jamaica Rd., Germantown, 45327, Montgomery County, (937)866-4333, 15 miles SW of Dayton.
Holes: 18. **Yards:** 6,587/5,092. **Par:** 72/72. **Course Rating:** 70.8/68.6. **Slope:** 128/123. **Green Fee:** N/A/$22. **Cart Fee:** $11/person. **Walking Policy:** Unrestricted walking. **Walkability:** 2. **Opened:** 1989. **Architect:** Denny/Mays/Bowman. **Season:** Year-round. **High:** March-Oct. **To obtain tee times:** Call 7 days in advance. **Miscellaneous:** Reduced fees (low season, seniors, juniors), metal spikes, range (grass/mats), club rentals, credit cards (MC, V), beginner friendly (junior, women, beginner programs).
Reader Comments: Wide open, great value ... Some forced carries over water ... Staff is excellent. Layout is fun ... Greens are fair ... Nice 'plain' course ... Fun course to play, Great value.

★★½ **JAYCEE GOLF COURSE**
PU-12100 Pleasant Valley Rd., Chillicothe, 45601, Ross County, (614)775-7659, 60 miles S of Columbus.
Holes: 18. **Yards:** 6,893/5,181. **Par:** 72/74. **Course Rating:** 72.0/69.8. **Slope:** 124/117. **Green Fee:** $10/$12. **Cart Fee:** $10/person. **Walking Policy:** Unrestricted walking. **Walkability:** N/A.

Opened: 1957. **Architect:** Ted Cox/Jack Kidwell. **Season:** March-Dec. **High:** June-July. **To obtain tee times:** Call 7 days in advance. **Miscellaneous:** Reduced fees (weekdays, seniors, juniors), metal spikes, range (grass), club rentals, credit cards (MC, V).
Reader Comments: Very flat and wide open, fun to play ... Improving a good layout ... Easy course if your drives are straight.

★★★ JAYCEE PUBLIC GOLF COURSE
PU-2710 Jackson Rd., Zanesville, 43701, Muskingum County, (740)452-1860.
Holes: 18. **Yards:** 6,660/6,200. **Par:** 71/76. **Course Rating:** 67.8/72.3. **Slope:** 101/96. **Green Fee:** $13/$16. **Cart Fee:** $10/person. **Walking Policy:** Unrestricted walking. **Walkability:** 3.
Opened: 1949. **Architect:** Zanesville Jaycees. **Season:** Year-round. **High:** May-Sept. **To obtain tee times:** Call 7 days in advance for weekends only. **Miscellaneous:** Reduced fees (twilight, seniors, juniors), metal spikes, range (grass), club rentals, credit cards (MC, V), beginner friendly (junior clinics).
Reader Comments: Fairly open, some rolling hills, well kept ... Long but so enjoyable, tough for women ... Wonderful layout.

★★½ KINGS MILL GOLF COURSE
SP-2500 Berringer Rd., Waldo, 43356, Marion County, (740)726-2626, (877)218-8488, 35 miles N of Columbus.
Holes: 18. **Yards:** 6,099/5,318. **Par:** 70/74. **Course Rating:** 68.1/68.8. **Slope:** 106/109. **Green Fee:** $18/$19. **Cart Fee:** $20/cart. **Walking Policy:** Unrestricted walking. **Walkability:** 3.
Opened: 1966. **Architect:** Jack Kidwell. **Season:** March-Dec. **High:** May-Oct. **To obtain tee times:** Call 7 days in advance, or further in advance with a credit card. **Miscellaneous:** Reduced fees (low season, juniors), discount packages, metal spikes, club rentals, credit cards (MC, V, AE).
Reader Comments: Requires all levels of the game ... OK to play for a change of pace or place ... Hardest back 9 around.

★★ KINGSWOOD GOLF COURSE
PU-4188 Irwin Simpson Rd., Mason, 45040, Warren County, (513)398-5252, 14 miles N of Cincinnati.
Holes: 18. **Yards:** 6,305/5,462. **Par:** 71/74. **Course Rating:** 69.8/66.3. **Slope:** 116/113. **Green Fee:** $16/$31. **Cart Fee:** $22/person. **Walking Policy:** Walking at certain times. **Walkability:** 3.
Opened: 1970. **Season:** Year-round. **High:** April-Nov. **To obtain tee times:** Call 7 days in advance for weekends only. **Miscellaneous:** Reduced fees (weekdays, seniors, juniors), metal spikes.

KITTY HAWK GOLF CLUB
PM-3383 Chuck Wagner Lane, Dayton, 45414, Montgomery County, (937)237-5424.
★★½ EAGLE COURSE
Holes: 18. **Yards:** 7,115/5,887. **Par:** 72/75. **Course Rating:** 72.8/74.3. **Slope:** 120/123. **Green Fee:** $18/$20. **Cart Fee:** $22/cart. **Walking Policy:** Unrestricted walking. **Walkability:** 1.
Opened: 1962. **Architect:** Robert Bruce Harris. **Season:** Year-round. **High:** April-Oct. **To obtain tee times:** Call Tuesday at noon for upcoming weekend. **Miscellaneous:** Reduced fees (low season, seniors, juniors), range (grass), club rentals, credit cards (MC, V).
Reader Comments: Heavily played municipal, price is right for value, upgraded layout ... Very good, tough from the tips. Condition variable ... Good municipal course.
★★ HAWK COURSE
Holes: 18. **Yards:** 6,766/5,638. **Par:** 72/73. **Course Rating:** 71.1/73.3. **Slope:** 118/121. **Green Fee:** $18/$20. **Cart Fee:** $22/cart. **Walking Policy:** Unrestricted walking. **Walkability:** 1.
Opened: 1962. **Architect:** Robert Bruce Harris. **Season:** Year-round. **High:** April-Oct. **To obtain tee times:** Call Tuesday at noon for the upcoming weekend. **Miscellaneous:** Reduced fees (low season, seniors, juniors), range (grass), club rentals, credit cards (MC, V).
Special Notes: Also has 18-hole par-3 course called Kitty Course.

★★★ LAKESIDE GOLF COURSE
PU-PO Box 680, St. Rte. 60, Beverly, 45715, Washington County, (740)984-4265, 18 miles N of Marietta.
Holes: 18. **Yards:** 6,318/4,384. **Par:** 70/70. **Course Rating:** 71.4/67.0. **Slope:** 109/103. **Green Fee:** $27/$30. **Cart Fee:** Included in Green Fee. **Walking Policy:** Unrestricted walking. **Walkability:** 3. **Opened:** 1959. **Season:** Jan.-Dec. **High:** May-Sept. **To obtain tee times:** Call for weekends and holidays. **Miscellaneous:** Reduced fees (weekdays, twilight, seniors), metal spikes, range (grass), club rentals, lodging, credit cards (MC, V).
Reader Comments: Long front 9, tough. Short back 9 ... 9s play like two different courses ... Improvements being made ... Good course.

★★ LARCH TREE GOLF COURSE
PU-2765 N. Snyder Rd., Trotwood, 45426, Montgomery County, (937)854-1951, 6 miles NW of Dayton. **E-mail:** larchtree@erinet.com.

Holes: 18. Yards: 6,982/5,912. Par: 72/74. Course Rating: 71.5/72.7. Slope: 107/107. Green Fee: $15/$22. Cart Fee: $11/person. Walking Policy: Unrestricted walking. Walkability: 1. Opened: 1971. Architect: Jack Kidwell. Season: Year-round. High: May-Oct. To obtain tee times: Call up to 21 days in advance. Miscellaneous: Reduced fees (low season, seniors, juniors), range (grass), club rentals, credit cards (MC, V, AE, D).
Special Notes: Also has an executive course.

★★★★½ THE LEGENDS OF MASSILLON *Condition*
PM-2700 Augusta Dr., Massillon, 44646, Stark County, (330)830-4653, (888)830-7277, 60 miles S of Cleveland. Web: www.thelegends.com.
Holes: 18. Yards: 7,002/4,696. Par: 72/72. Course Rating: 73.7/67.0. Slope: 121/108. Green Fee: $22/$34. Cart Fee: $10/person. Walking Policy: Unrestricted walking. Walkability: 2. Opened: 1995. Architect: John Robinson. Season: April-Oct. High: June-Sept. To obtain tee times: Call. Miscellaneous: Reduced fees (weekdays, low season, twilight, seniors, juniors), range (grass), club rentals, credit cards (MC, V).
Reader Comments: Great layout, plenty of sand and water ... Great new course ... Good, fair course. Cheat sheet given, read it ... Well run ... Play in spring, it's tough when rough is up ... Best course and food in Cleveland area ... Great condition, has length ... Very well maintained, big greens, professional... What a layout!

★★★ LIBERTY HILLS GOLF CLUB
PU-665 Rd. 190 W., Bellefontaine, 43311, Logan County, (937)592-4653, (800)816-2255, 50 miles W of Columbus.
Holes: 18. Yards: 6,005/4,400. Par: 70/70. Course Rating: 68.0/64.0. Slope: 115/104. Green Fee: $17/$18. Cart Fee: $9/person. Walking Policy: Unrestricted walking. Walkability: 3. Opened: 1920. Architect: Barry Serafin. Season: Feb.-Dec. High: May-Oct. To obtain tee times: Call anytime. Miscellaneous: Reduced fees (weekdays, seniors, juniors), range (grass/mats), credit cards (MC, V), beginner friendly (adult beginning golf league).
Reader Comments: Delightful course ... Short par 4s, long par 3s ... Hilly & good greens ... Country club atmosphere at bargain rates.

★★½ LICKING SPRINGS TROUT & GOLF CLUB
PU-2250 Horns Hill Rd., Newark, 43055, Licking County, (614)366-2770, (800)204-3638, 35 miles E of Columbus.
Holes: 18. Yards: 6,400/5,035. Par: 71/71. Course Rating: 70.0/68.7. Slope: 116/107. Green Fee: $14/$15. Cart Fee: $10/person. Walking Policy: Unrestricted walking. Walkability: 4. Opened: 1960. Architect: Jack Kidwell. Season: Year-round. High: May-Sept. To obtain tee times: Call. Tee times required for weekends. Miscellaneous: Reduced fees (weekdays, low season, twilight, seniors, juniors), metal spikes, club rentals, credit cards (MC, V, AE).
Reader Comments: Trout streams come into play often ... Plan to play again ... Very scenic course ... Old fashioned, well-manicured course ... A must-play, very scenic.

★★★½ THE LINKS AT ECHO SPRINGS *Value*
PU-5940 Loudon St., Johnstown, 43031, Licking County, (740)587-1890, (800)597-3240, 30 miles E of Columbus. Web: www.echosprings1.com.
Holes: 18. Yards: 6,900/4,465. Par: 72/72. Course Rating: 72.4/65.0. Slope: 127/108. Green Fee: $20/$24. Cart Fee: $10/person. Walking Policy: Walking at certain times. Walkability: 3. Opened: 1996. Architect: Barry Serafin. Season: March-Dec. High: May-Oct. To obtain tee times: Call up to 7 days in advance. Miscellaneous: Reduced fees (weekdays), range (grass), club rentals, credit cards (MC, V, AE).
Reader Comments: Starts out tough first 5 holes ... Very good condition and layout ... Young & restless, developing nicely ... Better hit it straight on front nine ... Nice new course, needs a middle set of tees ... Fun course, lots of different shots ... New course that already seems mature. Loved it the first time I played it.

LOCUST HILLS GOLF CLUB
PU-5575 N. River Rd., Springfield, 45502, Clark County, (937)265-5152, (800)872-4918, 6 miles SE of Springfield.
GOLD 18
Holes: 36. Yards: 6,708/4,616. Par: 72/72. Course Rating: 70.9/65.7. Slope: 118/103. Green Fee: $12/$17. Cart Fee: $10/person. Walking Policy: Unrestricted walking. Walkability: 3. Opened: 1966. Architect: The Kitchens. Season: March-Dec. High: May-Sept. To obtain tee times: Call 7 days in advance. Miscellaneous: Reduced fees (low season, juniors), range (grass), club rentals, credit cards (MC, V).
★★½ RED 18
Holes: 36. Yards: 6,576/4,641. Par: 72/72. Course Rating: 68.3/63.7. Slope: 109/100. Green Fee: $12/$17. Cart Fee: $10/person. Walking Policy: Unrestricted walking. Walkability: 3. Opened: 1966. Architect: The Kitchens. Season: March-Dec. High: May-Sept. To obtain tee times: Call 7 days in advance. Miscellaneous: Reduced fees (low season, juniors), range (grass), club rentals, credit cards (MC, V).

Reader Comments: Flat and wide open ... Excellent value for family and juniors ... Very pretty. Good golf ... Country setting, some testy holes ... Good public course ... Always working to improve.

★★ LOST NATION GOLF COURSE
PM-38890 Hodgson Rd., Willoughby, 44094, Lake County, (440)953-4280, 25 miles E of Cleveland. **Holes:** 18. **Yards:** 6,400/5,700. **Par:** 72/73. **Course Rating:** 69.4/70.9. **Slope:** 113/112. **Green Fee:** $13/$19. **Cart Fee:** $11/person. **Walking Policy:** Unrestricted walking. **Walkability:** 2. **Opened:** 1928. **Architect:** H.S. Colt/C.H. Allison. **Season:** Year-round. **High:** May-Oct. **To obtain tee times:** Call 7 days in advance. **Miscellaneous:** Reduced fees (weekdays, low season, seniors, juniors), discount packages, metal spikes, range (grass/mats), club rentals, credit cards (MC, V, AE, D).

LOYAL OAK GOLF COURSE
PU-2909 S. Cleve-Mass Rd., Norton, 44203, Summit County, (330)825-2904, 10 miles W of Akron. **Holes:** 27. **Yards:** N/A. **Par:** N/A. **Course Rating:** N/A. **Slope:** N/A. **Green Fee:** $13/$17. **Cart Fee:** $17. **Walking Policy:** Unrestricted walking. **Walkability:** N/A. **Opened:** 1931. **Season:** March-Nov. **High:** May-Sept. **To obtain tee times:** Call anytime. **Miscellaneous:** Reduced fees (seniors, juniors), metal spikes, club rentals.
- ★★ FIRST/SECOND
- ★★ FIRST/THIRD
- ★★ SECOND/THIRD

★★ LYONS DEN GOLF
PU-Rte. 93 at 21, Canal Fulton, 44614, Stark County, (330)854-9910, (800)801-6007, 14 miles S of Akron. **E-mail:** lyonsgolf@aol.com.
Holes: 18. **Yards:** 5,520/4,519. **Par:** 69/69. **Course Rating:** 65.0/65.0. **Slope:** 97/102. **Green Fee:** $12/$20. **Cart Fee:** $18/cart. **Walking Policy:** Unrestricted walking. **Walkability:** 3. **Opened:** 1962. **Architect:** Bill Lyons. **Season:** Year-round. **High:** May-Sept. **To obtain tee times:** Call. **Miscellaneous:** Reduced fees (weekdays, low season, seniors, juniors), discount packages, metal spikes, range (grass/mats), club rentals, credit cards (MC, V) (lessons).

★½ MAHONING GOLF COURSE
PU-710 East Liberty St., Girard, 44420, Trumbull County, (330)545-2517, 45 miles E of Cleveland. **E-mail:** mahoningcc@prod.net.
Holes: 18. **Yards:** 6,276/5,810. **Par:** 70/73. **Course Rating:** N/A. **Slope:** N/A. **Green Fee:** $13/$18. **Cart Fee:** $16/cart. **Walking Policy:** Unrestricted walking. **Walkability:** 1. **Opened:** 1919. **Season:** Year-round weather permitting. **High:** May-Sept. **To obtain tee times:** Call up to 10 days in advance for weekends. **Miscellaneous:** Reduced fees (weekdays, low season, seniors, juniors), discount packages, metal spikes.

★★★½ MANAKIKI GOLF CLUB
PU-35501 Eddy Rd., Willoughby, 44094, Lake County, (440)942-2500, 18 miles E of Cleveland. **Holes:** 18. **Yards:** 6,625/5,390. **Par:** 72/72. **Course Rating:** 71.4/72.8. **Slope:** 128/121. **Green Fee:** $15/$25. **Cart Fee:** $10/person. **Walking Policy:** Unrestricted walking. **Walkability:** 4. **Opened:** 1929. **Architect:** Donald Ross. **Season:** March-Dec. **High:** May-Sept. **To obtain tee times:** Call 5 days in advance beginning at noon. **Miscellaneous:** Reduced fees (low season, seniors, juniors), metal spikes, club rentals, credit cards (MC, V).
Reader Comments: Wonderful restaurant in clubhouse, enjoyable 18 holes ... Very good track ... A grand old course ... Wow, what a nice course, difficult ... Slow at times ... Well maintained, tough, good greens ... Great holes from tips ... Nice additions, No. 8 now plays as a true No. 1 handicap par 4 ... Great strategic course.

★★★ MAPLE RIDGE GOLF COURSE
PU-Rte. 45, P.O. Box 17, Austinburg, 44010, Ashtabula County, (440)969-1368, (800)922-1368, 50 miles E of Cleveland.
Holes: 18. **Yards:** 6,001/5,400. **Par:** 70/70. **Course Rating:** 68.5/69.0. **Slope:** 113/115. **Green Fee:** $15/$17. **Cart Fee:** $22/cart. **Walking Policy:** Unrestricted walking. **Walkability:** 3. **Opened:** 1960. **Architect:** Lawrence Porter. **Season:** March-Nov. **High:** June-Aug. **To obtain tee times:** Call 14 days in advance. **Miscellaneous:** Reduced fees (seniors, juniors), metal spikes, club rentals, credit cards (MC, V).
Reader Comments: Fun course ... Good all-around course ... Back 9 too short ... Scenic, good value ... It's challenging, lots of trees. Narrow fairways ... Tight treelined course ... Easy walking.

★★★★ MAPLECREST GOLF COURSE
PU-219 Tallmadge Rd., Kent, 44240, Portage County, (330)673-2722.
Holes: 18. **Yards:** 6,412/5,285. **Par:** 71/72. **Course Rating:** 69.2/67.8. **Slope:** 108/113. **Green Fee:** $15/$22. **Cart Fee:** $18/. **Walking Policy:** Unrestricted walking. **Walkability:** N/A. **Opened:** 1926. **Architect:** Edward Ashton. **Season:** March-Oct. **High:** May-Aug. **To obtain tee times:** Call after preceding Sunday. **Miscellaneous:** Reduced fees (weekdays, seniors), metal spikes, range (grass).

Reader Comments: Beautiful landscaping makes it a pleasure ... Great track ... Nothing prettier, great rolling greens, outstanding ... Relatively short, absolutely beautiful course ... Toughest 3s around ... Real par 5s, tough par 3s. A shotmaker's course ... Always perfect condition.

★★★★ MAUMEE BAY RESORT GOLF COURSE
PU-1750 Park Rd. No.2, Oregon, 43618, Lucas County, (419)836-9009, 12 miles E of Toledo.
Holes: 18. **Yards:** 6,941/5,221. **Par:** 72/72. **Course Rating:** 73.3/70.5. **Slope:** 129/118. **Green Fee:** $21/$27. **Cart Fee:** $12/person. **Walking Policy:** Walking at certain times. **Walkability:** 2. **Opened:** 1991. **Architect:** Arthur Hills. **Season:** April-Oct. **High:** May-Aug. **To obtain tee times:** Call 7 days in advance for weekdays. Call on Wednesday at 8 a.m. for upcoming weekend or holiday. **Miscellaneous:** Reduced fees (weekdays, low season, twilight, seniors, juniors), discount packages, metal spikes, range (grass/mats), club rentals, lodging, credit cards (MC, V, AE, D, Diners Club), beginner friendly.
Reader Comments: Tough links course, hazards everywhere ... No trees, lots of wind, this is golf! ... A touch of Scotland in Ohio ... Developing into the finest course I have ever played ... Target golf to score well ... Long, long rough ... Can be tough when wind is up ... Service great.

MAYFAIR COUNTRY CLUB
SP-2229 Raber Rd., Uniontown, 44685, Summit County, (330)699-2209.
★★½ EAST COURSE
Holes: 18. **Yards:** 5,288/4,769. **Par:** 64/65. **Course Rating:** 99/100. **Slope:** 68/68. **Green Fee:** $21/$23. **Walkability:** N/A. **Architect:** Edmund B. Ault. **Miscellaneous:** Metal spikes.
Reader Comments: Good for beginners ... Nice course ... Short course but great value with breakfast bar ... Challenging course, well maintained ... Greens are in excellent condition ... Nice breakfast golf special.
★★★½ WEST COURSE
Holes: 18. **Yards:** 6,048/5,435. **Par:** 70/70. **Course Rating:** 68.5/69.6. **Slope:** 116/109. **Green Fee:** $27/$30. **Walkability:** N/A. **Architect:** Edmund B. Ault. **Miscellaneous:** Metal spikes.
Reader Comments: Challenging from back tees .... Well-bunkered greens ... New electric control system will help course condition ... Good and bad, but ok to play ... If you're on, you can score, big greens ... Fun course, some tough holes ... Call for the specials.

★★ MIAMI SHORES GOLF COURSE
PM-Rutherford Dr., Troy, 45373, Miami County, (937)335-4457, 15 miles N of Dayton. **Web:** www.troy-ohio-usa.com.
Holes: 18. **Yards:** 6,200/5,417. **Par:** 72/73. **Course Rating:** 67.6/68.5. **Slope:** 97/101. **Green Fee:** N/A/$20. **Cart Fee:** $11/person. **Walking Policy:** Unrestricted walking. **Walkability:** 1. **Opened:** 1949. **Architect:** Donald Ross. **Season:** March-Dec. **High:** June-Aug. **To obtain tee times:** Call up to 8 days in advance. **Miscellaneous:** Club rentals, credit cards (MC, V), beginner friendly (junior and beginner clinics).

★★★★ MIAMI WHITEWATER FOREST GOLF COURSE
PM-8801 Mount Hope Rd., Harrison, 45030, Hamilton County, (513)367-4627, 18 miles NW of Cincinnati.
Holes: 18. **Yards:** 6,780/5,093. **Par:** 72/72. **Course Rating:** 72.1/69.3. **Slope:** 125/110. **Green Fee:** $16/$19. **Cart Fee:** $12/person. **Walking Policy:** Unrestricted walking. **Walkability:** 2. **Opened:** 1959. **Architect:** Hamilton County Park District. **Season:** March-Dec. **High:** June-Aug. **To obtain tee times:** Call 5 days in advance starting at 6 p.m. **Miscellaneous:** Reduced fees (seniors, juniors), metal spikes, range (mats), club rentals, credit cards (MC, V).
Reader Comments: Excellent county course ... Best place to go ... Thick rough, real thick ... Tough holes No. 5, No. 7, No. 11, No. 18 ... Sits next to lake, big greens, friendly staff ... Old-style course.

★★★½ MILL CREEK GOLF CLUB *Service, Value*
SP-7259 Penn Rd., Ostrander, 43061, Delaware County, (740)666-7711, (800)695-5175, 10 miles N of Dublin.
Holes: 18. **Yards:** 6,300/5,100. **Par:** 72/72. **Course Rating:** 69.0/70.0. **Slope:** 111/111. **Green Fee:** $17/$22. **Cart Fee:** $10/person. **Walking Policy:** Unrestricted walking. **Walkability:** 1. **Opened:** 1973. **Architect:** Bill Black. **Season:** Feb.-Dec. **High:** June-Sept. **To obtain tee times:** Call up to 14 days in advance with credit card to guarantee. **Miscellaneous:** Reduced fees (weekdays, low season, seniors, juniors), discount packages, range (grass), credit cards (MC, V, AE, D).
Reader Comments: Some very good holes, not long ... A great value ... Family-owned, excellent service! ... Really women-friendly, challenging ... Not long, but some challenging holes ...Wide open good greens ... Enjoyable.

MILL CREEK PARK GOLF COURSE
PU-W. Golf Dr., Boardman, 44512, Mahoning County, (330)740-7112, 7 miles SW of Youngstown.
★★★½ NORTH COURSE
Holes: 18. **Yards:** 6,412/5,889. **Par:** 70/74. **Course Rating:** 71.9/74.4. **Slope:** 124/117. **Green Fee:** $17/$21. **Cart Fee:** $19/cart. **Walking Policy:** Unrestricted walking. **Walkability:** 1. **Opened:** 1928. **Architect:** Donald Ross. **Season:** April-Nov. **High:** June-Sept. **To obtain tee**

times: Call or come in Wednesday 6 a.m. for upcoming weekend. **Miscellaneous:** Reduced fees (low season, twilight, seniors, juniors), metal spikes, club rentals, credit cards (MC, V), beginner friendly.

Reader Comments: Very nice course; cut out of woods ... Great bunkering ... Greens most appealing part of course. Nice service ... If you're a little wild, you will see a lot of squirrels in the woods ... Winding holes, a lot of doglegs ... Busy at times ... A real treat to play.

★★★★ SOUTH COURSE

Holes: 18. **Yards:** 6,511/6,102. **Par:** 70/75. **Course Rating:** 71.8/74.9. **Slope:** 129/118. **Green Fee:** $17/$21. **Cart Fee:** $19/person. **Walking Policy:** Unrestricted walking. **Walkability:** 1. **Opened:** 1937. **Architect:** Donald Ross & Assoc. **Season:** April-Nov. **High:** June-Sept. **To obtain tee times:** Call or come in person Wednesday 6 a.m. for upcoming weekend or holiday. **Miscellaneous:** Reduced fees (low season, twilight, seniors, juniors), metal spikes, club rentals, credit cards (MC, V).

Reader Comments: Long & tough course, lots of trees ... Worth the price ... Nicer than North course ... Very narrow ... A design that demands accuracy ... Outstanding, my all-time favorite. **Special Notes:** Also have an 18-hole par-3 course.

★★ MINERVA LAKE GOLF CLUB

PU-2955 Minerva Lake Rd., Columbus, 43231, Franklin County, (614)882-9988, 10 miles N of Columbus.

Holes: 18. **Yards:** 5,638/N/A. **Par:** 69/N/A. **Course Rating:** 67.8/N/A. **Slope:** 103/N/A. **Green Fee:** $14/$16. **Cart Fee:** $18/cart. **Walking Policy:** Unrestricted walking. **Walkability:** 2. **Opened:** 1931. **Architect:** Woody Waugh. **Season:** March-Dec. **High:** May-July. **To obtain tee times:** Call 7 days in advance. **Miscellaneous:** Reduced fees (weekdays, low season, twilight, seniors), metal spikes, club rentals, credit cards (MC, V, D).

★★★★ MOHICAN HILLS GOLF CLUB *Value+*

PU-25 Ashland County Rd. 1950, Jeromesville, 44840, Ashland County, (419)368-3303, 10 miles W of Wooster.

Holes: 18. **Yards:** 6,536/4,976. **Par:** 72/72. **Course Rating:** 71.1/67.9. **Slope:** 122/112. **Green Fee:** $18/$20. **Cart Fee:** $10/person. **Walking Policy:** Unrestricted walking. **Walkability:** 2. **Opened:** 1972. **Architect:** Jack Kidwell. **Season:** March-Dec. **High:** June-Aug. **To obtain tee times:** Call 7 days in advance. **Miscellaneous:** Reduced fees (weekdays), range (grass), club rentals, credit cards (MC, V).

Reader Comments: Challenging, beautiful & affordable ... Great layout and condition ... Beautiful course, killer greens ... Friendly staff ... Scenic, rolling hills, nice people in clubhouse ... Picturesque, fast undulating greens ... Out of the way, great value! ... Outstanding for professionalism and presentation ...Can't be beat.

NEUMANN GOLF COURSE

PM-7215 Bridgetown Rd., Cincinnati, 45248, Hamilton County, (513)574-1320, 10 miles W of Cincinnati. **E-mail:** bterasksm@aol.com.

Holes: 27. **Green Fee:** $19/$19. **Cart Fee:** $11/person. **Walking Policy:** Unrestricted walking. **Walkability:** 4. **Opened:** 1965. **Architect:** William H. Diddel. **Season:** Year-round. **High:** March-Nov. **To obtain tee times:** Call 2 days in advance for weekends. **Miscellaneous:** Reduced fees (weekdays, low season, twilight, seniors, juniors), metal spikes, range (mats), club rentals, credit cards (MC, V), beginner friendly (beginner classes and youth camps).

★★ RED/BLUE

Yards: 6,069/4,288. **Par:** 70/72. **Course Rating:** 67.7/60.3. **Slope:** 105/90.

★★ RED/WHITE

Yards: 5,957/4,349. **Par:** 71/72. **Course Rating:** 67.7/60.9. **Slope:** 108/91.

★★ WHITE/BLUE

Yards: 6,200/4,279. **Par:** 71/72. **Course Rating:** 68.9/60.9. **Slope:** 111/90.

★★ NORTHMOOR GOLF CLUB

SP-8330 State Rte. 703 E., Celina, 45822, Mercer County, (419)394-4896, 30 miles SW of Lima.
Holes: 18. **Yards:** 5,802/5,086. **Par:** 70/70. **Course Rating:** 66.8/68.0. **Slope:** 102/102. **Green Fee:** $15/$18. **Cart Fee:** $8/person. **Walking Policy:** Unrestricted walking. **Walkability:** 1. **Opened:** 1923. **Architect:** Alex "Nipper" Campbell. **Season:** Year-round. **High:** April-Oct. **To obtain tee times:** Call up to 14 days in advance for weekends and holidays. **Miscellaneous:** Reduced fees (weekdays, low season), range (grass/mats), club rentals, credit cards (MC, V, AE, D).

★★½ OAK GROVE GOLF COURSE

PU-14901 German Church Rd., Atwater, 44201, Portage County, (330)823-8823, 4 miles N of Alliance. **Web:** www.angelfire.com/oh2/OakGrove.
Holes: 18. **Yards:** 6,570/5,550. **Par:** 71/75. **Course Rating:** 69.4/70.5. **Slope:** N/A. **Green Fee:** $13/$15. **Cart Fee:** $16/cart. **Walking Policy:** Unrestricted walking. **Walkability:** 1. **Opened:** 1928. **Season:** Year-round. **High:** June-Aug. **To obtain tee times:** Call golf shop. **Miscellaneous:** Reduced fees (weekdays), range (grass), club rentals.
Reader Comments: Nice course ... Not much of a challenge, good value.

OAK KNOLLS GOLF CLUB
PU-6700 State Rte. 43, Kent, 44240, Portage County, (330)673-6713, 10 miles NE of Akron.
★★★ EAST COURSE
Holes: 18. **Yards:** 6,882/5,508. **Par:** 72/73. **Course Rating:** 71.8/70.1. **Slope:** 118/111. **Green Fee:** $19/$24. **Cart Fee:** $20/cart. **Walking Policy:** Unrestricted walking. **Walkability:** 3. **Opened:** 1963. **Architect:** Howard Morrette. **Season:** March-Nov. **High:** May-Sept. **To obtain tee times:** Call anytime. **Miscellaneous:** Reduced fees (weekdays, low season, twilight, seniors, juniors), metal spikes, range (grass/mats), credit cards (MC, V, D).
Reader Comments: Rolling ... Best course in rain ... You won't regret it ... No. 13 kills me every time ... Average ... Good.
★★½ WEST COURSE
Holes: 18. **Yards:** 6,373/5,681. **Par:** 72/72. **Course Rating:** 69.0/71.3. **Slope:** 112/112. **Green Fee:** $19/$26. **Cart Fee:** $20/cart. **Walking Policy:** Unrestricted walking. **Walkability:** 3. **Opened:** 1970. **Architect:** Jon Wegenek. **Season:** April-Sept. **High:** May-Sept. **To obtain tee times:** Call anytime. **Miscellaneous:** Reduced fees (weekdays, low season, twilight, seniors, juniors), metal spikes, range (grass/mats), credit cards (MC, V, D).
Reader Comments: Long par 4s, true test ... Great place to spend a day of golf ... Tougher of the two 18s ... Predominantly open, though some holes offer challenge ... More hills than East Course.

★★★½ OAK SHADOWS GOLF CLUB
PU-1063 Oak Shadows Drive, New Philadelphia, 44663, Tuscarawas County, (330)343-2426, (888)802-7289, 30 miles S of Canton.
Holes: 18. **Yards:** 7,015/5,207. **Par:** 72/72. **Course Rating:** 73.0/73.6. **Slope:** 132/127. **Green Fee:** $15/$28. **Cart Fee:** $10/person. **Walking Policy:** Walking at certain times. **Walkability:** 4. **Opened:** 1996. **Architect:** John Robinson. **Season:** Year-round. **High:** May-Oct. **To obtain tee times:** Call beginning Nov. 1 of year for the following year. **Miscellaneous:** Reduced fees (weekdays, low season, twilight, seniors, juniors), metal spikes, range (grass), credit cards (MC, V, AE, D).
Reader Comments: Friendly service, some mean holes! ... Sensational, tough layout ... Fairways and greens very good ... Tough for casual player ... Great layout ... Front 9 new, back mature ... A young course, but a comer.

★★★★ ORCHARD HILLS GOLF & COUNTRY CLUB *Value*
SP-11414 Caves Rd., Chesterland, 44026, Geauga County, (440)729-1963, 20 miles E of Cleveland. **E-mail:** tpatter625@aol.com.
Holes: 18. **Yards:** 6,409/5,651. **Par:** 72/72. **Course Rating:** 71.1/72.6. **Slope:** 126/122. **Green Fee:** $21/$30. **Cart Fee:** $22/person. **Walking Policy:** Unrestricted walking. **Walkability:** 4. **Opened:** 1962. **Architect:** Gordon Alves. **Season:** April-Nov. **High:** May-Sept. **To obtain tee times:** Tee times for members only. **Miscellaneous:** Reduced fees (weekdays, seniors, juniors), club rentals, credit cards (MC, V, AE).
Reader Comments: Best public-access course in Ohio! Perfect condition, laid out around an apple orchard ... Scenic, long par 4s, hard fast greens ... Very challenging course, unique U-shaped par 5 ... Fun & challenging ... Watch for trees ... Beautiful autumn ... Fun course, tough greens, friendly staff.

ORCHARD HILLS GOLF CENTER & GOLF ACADEMY
9575 Brehm Road, Cincinnati, 45252, Hamilton County.
Special Notes: Call club for further information.

★★★ OTTAWA PARK GOLF COURSE
PU-13120 Anne Road, Toledo, 43606, Lucas County, (419)472-2059.
Holes: 18. **Yards:** 5,079/4,715. **Par:** 71/71. **Course Rating:** 64.2/67.2. **Slope:** 110/111. **Green Fee:** $13/$13. **Cart Fee:** $20/cart. **Walking Policy:** Unrestricted walking. **Walkability:** 4. **Opened:** 1899. **Architect:** Sylvanus Pierson Jermain/Arthur Hill. **Season:** Year-round weather permitting. **High:** June-August. **To obtain tee times:** Call Pro Shop. **Miscellaneous:** Reduced fees (low season, twilight, seniors, juniors), metal spikes, club rentals, credit cards (MC, V, AE, D).
Reader Comments: Short, huge old trees, well kept ... Much improved course. I like to play there, and price is right ... Tight fairways, old and traditional ... Good course, friendly atmosphere.

★★★ OXBOW GOLF & COUNTRY CLUB
PU-County Rd. 85, Belpre, 45714, Washington County, (740)423-6771, (800)423-0443, 120 miles SE of Columbus.
Holes: 18. **Yards:** 6,558/4,858. **Par:** 71/72. **Course Rating:** 70.9/68.8. **Slope:** 117/109. **Green Fee:** $15/$20. **Cart Fee:** $12/person. **Walking Policy:** Unrestricted walking. **Walkability:** 2. **Opened:** 1974. **Architect:** Jack Kidwell. **Season:** Year-round. **High:** May-July. **To obtain tee times:** Call golf shop. **Miscellaneous:** Reduced fees (seniors, juniors), discount packages, metal spikes, range (grass/mats), club rentals, credit cards (MC, V, D), beginner friendly (lessons, junior league).

Reader Comments: Everything was good ... Nice layout ... Great 18th hole ... Variety of holes ... Long, beautiful, tough ... Enjoyable test, out of the way.

★★★½ PEBBLE CREEK GOLF CLUB
PU-4300 Algire Rd., Lexington, 44904, Richland County, (419)884-3434, 4 miles S of Mansfield. **Holes:** 18. **Yards:** 6,554/5,195. **Par:** 72/72. **Course Rating:** 70.8/69.1. **Slope:** 117/113. **Green Fee:** $16/$19. **Cart Fee:** $11/person. **Walking Policy:** Unrestricted walking. **Walkability:** 3. **Opened:** 1971. **Architect:** Richard LaConte/Jack Kidwell. **Season:** March-Oct. **High:** June-Aug. **To obtain tee times:** Call in March, April, May for tee times for the year. **Miscellaneous:** Reduced fees (weekdays, low season, seniors, juniors), range (grass), club rentals, credit cards (MC, V, AE, D).
Reader Comments: Variety of shots needed. Quick, great greens! ... Perfect greens, hard course ... Nice course ... Superior public course, hard to find, but worth it ... Test of golf, variety of holes, need all shots ... Fair test at a reasonable fee.

PEBBLE CREEK GOLF COURSE
PU-9799 Prechtel Road, Cincinnati, 45252, Hamilton County, (513)385-4442. **Holes:** 18. **Yards:** 6,029/4,550. **Par:** 70/70. **Course Rating:** 70.0/67.3. **Slope:** 124/111. **Green Fee:** $17/$28. **Cart Fee:** $12/person. **Walking Policy:** Unrestricted walking. **Walkability:** 3. **Opened:** 1991. **Architect:** Mike Macke. **Season:** Year-round. **High:** April-Sept. **To obtain tee times:** May call 7 days in advance. **Miscellaneous:** Reduced fees (low season, twilight, seniors, juniors), club rentals, credit cards (MC, V, AE, D).

★½ PHEASANT RUN GOLF COURSE
PU-711 Pheasant Run Dr., La Grange, 44050, Lorain County, (440)355-5035, 35 miles SW of Cleveland. **Holes:** 18. **Yards:** 6,345/5,006. **Par:** 72/72. **Course Rating:** 69.3/67.5. **Slope:** 111/108. **Green Fee:** $13/$16. **Cart Fee:** $17/cart. **Walking Policy:** Unrestricted walking. **Walkability:** 1. **Opened:** 1964. **Season:** Year-round. **High:** March-Nov. **To obtain tee times:** Call or come in. **Miscellaneous:** Reduced fees (low season, seniors, juniors), club rentals, credit cards (MC, V).

★★ PINE BROOK GOLF COURSE
PU-11043 N. Durkee Rd., Grafton, 44044, Lorain County, (440)748-2939, (800)236-8689, 22 miles SW of Cleveland. **Holes:** 18. **Yards:** 6,062/5,225. **Par:** 70/70. **Course Rating:** 66.8/68.9. **Slope:** 113/109. **Green Fee:** $15/$19. **Cart Fee:** $18/cart. **Walking Policy:** Unrestricted walking. **Walkability:** 2. **Opened:** 1959. **Architect:** Pete Dye. **Season:** Year-round. **High:** June-Aug. **To obtain tee times:** Call anytime. **Miscellaneous:** Reduced fees (weekdays, seniors, juniors), discount packages, metal spikes, range (grass/mats), club rentals, credit cards (MC, V).

★★★ PINE HILL GOLF COURSE
SP-4382 Kauffman Rd., Carroll, 43112, Fairfield County, (614)837-3911, 18 miles SE of Columbus. **Holes:** 18. **Yards:** 6,673/4,927. **Par:** 72/72. **Course Rating:** 68.9/64.5. **Slope:** 112/102. **Green Fee:** $14/$15. **Cart Fee:** $10/person. **Walking Policy:** Unrestricted walking. **Walkability:** 3. **Opened:** 1965. **Architect:** Jack Kidwell. **Season:** Year-round. **High:** May-Aug. **To obtain tee times:** Call for weekend or holiday with credit card to guarantee. **Miscellaneous:** Metal spikes, credit cards (MC, V, D).
Reader Comments: Excellent place to play ... Rolling hills, good test ... Very scenic course! ... Must have good ball placement ... Nice people ... A very pleasant course.

★★★★ PINE HILLS GOLF CLUB
PU-433 W. 130th St., Hinckley, 44233, Medina County, (330)225-4477, 20 miles SW of Cleveland. **Holes:** 18. **Yards:** 6,482/5,685. **Par:** 72/73. **Course Rating:** 71.2/74.3. **Slope:** 124/126. **Green Fee:** $30/$30. **Cart Fee:** $10/person. **Walking Policy:** Unrestricted walking. **Walkability:** 5. **Opened:** 1957. **Architect:** Harold Paddock. **Season:** April-Dec. **High:** April-Nov. **To obtain tee times:** Call golf shop. **Miscellaneous:** Metal spikes, club rentals, credit cards (MC, V).
Reader Comments: Very challenging layout ... As close to a country club as it gets ... A rare gem ... Pride in ownership ... Hard to get tee time, but worth the effort ... Excellent condition, friendly staff ... Tough course ... No. 18 awesome finishing hole ... Good target golf ... Among finest public courses in Ohio. Great!

★★ PINE RIDGE COUNTRY CLUB
PU-30601 Ridge Rd., Wickliffe, 44092, Lake County, (216)943-0293, (800)254-7275, 15 miles NE of Cleveland. **Holes:** 18. **Yards:** 6,137/5,672. **Par:** 71/75. **Course Rating:** 69.6/73.0. **Slope:** 118/122. **Green Fee:** $13/$17. **Cart Fee:** $12/person. **Walking Policy:** Mandatory cart. **Walkability:** N/A. **Opened:** 1924. **Architect:** Harold Paddock. **Season:** Year-round. **High:** April-Oct. **To obtain tee times:** Call 7:00 a.m. Monday for upcoming weekend. Call 7 days in advance for Weekdays. **Miscellaneous:** Reduced fees (weekdays, low season, twilight, seniors), discount packages, metal spikes, caddies, club rentals, credit cards (MC, V).

★★½ PINE VALLEY GOLF CLUB
PU-469 Reimer Rd., Wadsworth, 44281, Medina County, (330)335-3375, 1 miles E of Wadsworth. **Holes:** 18. **Yards:** 6,097/5,268. **Par:** 72/74. **Course Rating:** 68.5/67.9. **Slope:** 109/107. **Green Fee:** $13/$17. **Cart Fee:** $18/person. **Walking Policy:** Unrestricted walking. **Walkability:** 2. **Opened:** 1962. **Architect:** Cliff Deming. **Season:** March-Nov. **High:** May-Oct. **To obtain tee times:** Call golf shop. **Miscellaneous:** Reduced fees (weekdays, seniors), metal spikes, range (grass), credit cards (MC, V).
Reader Comments: Fun course, fun staff, fun day ... Nice people ... Great bargain ... Owners bend over backward to please ... Not long, wide open on front, trees on back.

THE PINES GOLF CLUB
PU-1319 N. Millborne Rd., Orrville, 44667, Wayne County, (330)684-1414, (888)684-1020, 25 miles SW of Akron. **Holes:** 18. **Yards:** 6,525/5,181. **Par:** 71/72. **Course Rating:** 70.8/69.7. **Slope:** 119/114. **Green Fee:** $12/$18. **Cart Fee:** $8/person. **Walking Policy:** Unrestricted walking. **Walkability:** 3. **Opened:** 1963. **Season:** Year-round weather permitting. **High:** May-Sept. **To obtain tee times:** Call anytime. **Miscellaneous:** Reduced fees (weekdays, low season, seniors, juniors), range (grass/mats), club rentals, credit cards (MC, V).

★★★½ PIPESTONE GOLF CLUB
PU-4344 Benner Rd., Miamisburg, 45342, Montgomery County, (937)866-4653, 8 miles S of Dayton. **E-mail:** pstne@aol.com. **Holes:** 18. **Yards:** 6,939/5,207. **Par:** 72/72. **Course Rating:** 72.1/69.2. **Slope:** 137/121. **Green Fee:** $26/$34. **Cart Fee:** $12/person. **Walking Policy:** Unrestricted walking. **Walkability:** 4. **Opened:** 1992. **Architect:** Arthur Hills. **Season:** March-Dec. **High:** June-Aug. **To obtain tee times:** Call 7 days in advance. **Miscellaneous:** Reduced fees (low season, twilight, seniors, juniors), range (grass), club rentals, credit cards (MC, V).
Reader Comments: A country club for the public ... Solid, tough course ... Some blind holes ... Good fundamentals ... Great place to play ... Wide range of difficulty from the different tees ... Long, excellent staff ... Best food in county ... Challenging layout, good value.

★★★ PLEASANT HILL GOLF CLUB
PU-6487 Hankins Rd., Middletown, 45044, Butler County, (513)539-7220, 5 miles S of Cincinnati. **Holes:** 18. **Yards:** 6,586/4,723. **Par:** 71/71. **Course Rating:** 70.9/66.9. **Slope:** 117/107. **Green Fee:** $18/$21. **Cart Fee:** $11/person. **Walking Policy:** Unrestricted walking. **Walkability:** 2. **Opened:** 1969. **Architect:** Jack Kidwell. **Season:** Year-round. **High:** June-July. **To obtain tee times:** Call Monday for weekend; call anytime for weekday. **Miscellaneous:** Reduced fees (low season, seniors, juniors), range (grass), club rentals, credit cards (MC, V).
Reader Comments: Service was good ... Wide open, long par 3s ... Good greens, very reasonable ... No. 8 and No. 17 very good holes.

PLEASANT HILL GOLF COURSE
PU-13461 Aquilla Rd., Chardon, 44024, Geauga County, (440)285-2428, 30 miles E of Cleveland. **Holes:** 27. **Green Fee:** $10/$20. **Cart Fee:** $20/cart. **Walking Policy:** Unrestricted walking. **Walkability:** 2. **Opened:** 1965. **Architect:** Dalton Pfouts. **Season:** March-Nov. **High:** May-Nov. **To obtain tee times:** Call. **Miscellaneous:** Reduced fees (weekdays, low season, seniors), metal spikes, club rentals, credit cards (MC, V).
★★½ FRONT/BACK
Yards: 6,212/5,446. **Par:** 71/71. **Course Rating:** 67.5. **Slope:** 113.
★★½ FRONT/MIDDLE
Yards: 6,308/5,174. **Par:** 70/70. **Course Rating:** 67.5. **Slope:** 113.
★★½ MIDDLE/BACK
Yards: 6,351/5,276. **Par:** 71/71. **Course Rating:** 67.5. **Slope:** 113.
Reader Comments: Shorter than your scores reflect ... Rough a foot deep ... Good spring & fall course ... Several tough holes, good greens ... Enjoyed it, needs more challenges.

★★★½ PLEASANT VALLEY COUNTRY CLUB
PU-3830 Hamilton Rd., Medina, 44256, Medina County, (330)725-5770, 25 miles S of Cleveland. **Holes:** 18. **Yards:** 6,912/4,984. **Par:** 72/72. **Course Rating:** 73.4/68.9. **Slope:** 123/113. **Green Fee:** $23/$27. **Cart Fee:** $20/cart. **Walking Policy:** Unrestricted walking. **Walkability:** 2. **Opened:** 1970. **Architect:** Jack Kidwell. **Season:** April-Nov. **High:** June-Aug. **To obtain tee times:** Call up to 7 days in advance. **Miscellaneous:** Reduced fees (weekdays, juniors).
Reader Comments: Very difficult, challenging, long ... Nice course ... Front open, back tight and long ... Excellent condition ... Great 17th hole, nice imagination in layout ... Beautiful, challenging ... Good course.

★★½ POWDERHORN GOLF COURSE
PU-3991 Bates Rd., Madison, 44057, Lake County, (216)428-5951, (800)863-3742, 40 miles E of Cleveland.

Holes: 18. **Yards:** 6,004/4,881. **Par:** 70/70. **Course Rating:** 68.5/67.6. **Slope:** 117/113. **Green Fee:** $16/$18. **Cart Fee:** $12/person. **Walking Policy:** Unrestricted walking. **Walkability:** 4. **Opened:** 1981. **Architect:** Anderson & Lesniak. **Season:** Year-round. **High:** April-Oct. **To obtain tee times:** Call 7 days in advance. **Miscellaneous:** Reduced fees (weekdays, low season, seniors, juniors), discount packages, club rentals, credit cards (MC, V).

Reader Comments: Scenic, good shape, cheap, everything an Ohio course should be ... Fun, challenging and nerve wrecking! ... Some tough holes, some easy holes ... Course says 'Here I Am, Come and Get It.'

PRAIRIE VIEW GOLF COURSE

PU-SR 67 26820, Waynesfield, 45896, Auglaize County, (419)568-7888, 12 miles E of Wapakoneta. **E-mail:** p.v.golf@brightnet.com.

Holes: 18. **Yards:** 6,348/5,575. **Par:** 72/72. **Course Rating:** N/A. **Slope:** 115/113. **Green Fee:** $12/$16. **Cart Fee:** $10/person. **Walking Policy:** Unrestricted walking. **Walkability:** 2. **Opened:** 1991. **Architect:** Charles Buffenbarger. **Season:** March-Nov. **High:** May-Sept. **To obtain tee times:** Call 1 day in advance. **Miscellaneous:** Reduced fees (weekdays, seniors, juniors), metal spikes, range (grass/mats), club rentals.

★★★½ PUNDERSON STATE PARK GOLF COURSE

PU-11755 Kinsman Rd., Newbury, 44065, Geauga County, (440)564-5465, 25 miles E of Cleveland.

Holes: 18. **Yards:** 6,815/5,769. **Par:** 72/72. **Course Rating:** 72.9/72.3. **Slope:** 125/122. **Green Fee:** $20/$29. **Cart Fee:** $12/person. **Walking Policy:** Walking at certain times. **Walkability:** 3. **Opened:** 1969. **Architect:** Jack Kidwell. **Season:** March-Nov. **High:** June-Aug. **To obtain tee times:** Call at 7 a.m. on the Thursday prior to weekend. **Miscellaneous:** Reduced fees (weekdays, low season, twilight, seniors), metal spikes, club rentals, lodging, credit cards (MC, V, AE, D, Diners Club).

Reader Comments: Very tough course in a beautiful state park. Be ready to play, it could be a long round ... Ohio's state park courses are great! ... Scenic course, hole 8 toughest in state ... Tests every part of game ... No. 8 is spectacular ... Long and longer in the wind ... Basic course, friendly staff.

QUAIL HOLLOW RESORT & COUNTRY CLUB

11080 Concord-Hambden Rd., Painesville, 44077, Lake County, (440)350-3500, (800)792-0258, 30 miles E of Cleveland. **E-mail:** steveranney@ourclub.com.

★★★★ DEVLIN-VON HAGGE COURSE

Holes: 18. **Yards:** 6,712/4,389. **Par:** 72/72. **Course Rating:** 72.2/65.7. **Slope:** 130/107. **Green Fee:** $65/$90. **Cart Fee:** Included in Green Fee. **Walking Policy:** Walking at certain times. **Walkability:** 4. **Opened:** 1972. **Architect:** B. Devlin & von Hagge. **Season:** April-Nov. **High:** June-Aug. **To obtain tee times:** Overnight guests or member guests only may call.

Miscellaneous: Reduced fees (weekdays, low season, twilight, juniors), discount packages, range (grass/mats), club rentals, lodging (150 rooms), credit cards (MC, V, AE, D, All), beginner friendly (front tees).

Reader Comments: Great experience, excellent place for tournament ... Pro-style course ... Expensive, good service & greens ... Little pricey, well maintained even thought it gets a lot of play ... Wow, what fun that was! ... Challenging, excellent, resort golf at its best. Nike Tour needs to keep this one. Superb finishing holes.

★★★★ WEISKOPF-MORRISH COURSE *Condition+*

Holes: 18. **Yards:** 6,872/5,166. **Par:** 71/71. **Course Rating:** 73.9/70.0. **Slope:** 130/117. **Green Fee:** $50/$75. **Cart Fee:** $18/person. **Walking Policy:** Unrestricted walking. **Walkability:** 4. **Opened:** 1996. **Architect:** Tom Weiskopf/Jay Morrish. **Season:** March-Oct. **High:** June-Aug. **To obtain tee times:** Overnight guests or member guests only may call. **Miscellaneous:** Reduced fees (twilight), range (grass/mats), club rentals, lodging (150 rooms), credit cards (MC, V, AE, Diners Club), beginner friendly (front tees).

Notes: Ranked 19th in 1999 Best in State; 9th in 1996 Best New Upscale Courses.

Reader Comments: Fun course, but tight ... Great par 5s ... Mint shape, memorable holes, not for the hacker... Very challenging, but playable for most skill levels, provided you play the tees that best suit skill ... Local knowledge important ... The starter was very informative.

★★★½ RACCOON HILL GOLF CLUB

PU-485 Judson Rd., Kent, 44240, Portage County, (330)673-2111, 10 miles NE of Akron.

Holes: 18. **Yards:** 6,068/4,650. **Par:** 71/71. **Course Rating:** 69.2/67.0. **Slope:** 115/106. **Green Fee:** $15/$26. **Cart Fee:** $9/person. **Walking Policy:** Unrestricted walking. **Walkability:** N/A. **Opened:** 1989. **Architect:** Bill Snetsinger. **Season:** March-Nov. **High:** May-Sept. **To obtain tee times:** Call. **Miscellaneous:** Reduced fees (weekdays, low season, twilight, seniors, juniors), metal spikes.

Reader Comments: Tight back 9 is fun ... A lot of doglegs, improving every day ... New owner took over several years ago & it's developed into a very nice course ... Good challenging course, very long, nice broken dogleg on back 9.

OHIO

★★★ RACCOON INTERNATIONAL GOLF CLUB
PU-3275 Worthington Rd. S.W., Granville, 43023, Licking County, (740)587-0921, (888)692-7898, 15 miles E of Columbus, Oh. **Web:** www.raccooninternational.com.
Holes: 18. **Yards:** 6,586/6,094. **Par:** 72/72. **Course Rating:** N/A. **Slope:** 125/116. **Green Fee:** $15/$20. **Cart Fee:** $10/person. **Walking Policy:** Walking at certain times. **Walkability:** 3. **Opened:** 1973. **Season:** Year-round. **High:** March-Oct. **To obtain tee times:** Call golf shop. **Miscellaneous:** Reduced fees (weekdays, low season, resort guests, twilight, juniors), credit cards (MC, V), beginner friendly ($99 lesson series).
Reader Comments: Priced right ... Lies would improve if the raccoons left ... Some interesting holes, new owners have put money back into the course ... Good vacation spot ... Nice simple course ... New upgrades, long par 5s.

★★★★ RAINTREE COUNTRY CLUB
PU-4350 Mayfair Rd., Uniontown, 44685, Summit County, (330)699-3232, (800)371-0017, 5 miles S of Akron.
Holes: 18. **Yards:** 6,936/5,030. **Par:** 72/72. **Course Rating:** 73.0/68.5. **Slope:** 127/114. **Green Fee:** $15/$32. **Cart Fee:** $10/person. **Walking Policy:** Walking at certain times. **Walkability:** 3. **Opened:** 1992. **Architect:** Brian Huntley. **Season:** Year-round. **High:** April-Oct. **To obtain tee times:** Call or come in up to 1 year in advance. **Miscellaneous:** Reduced fees (weekdays, low season, resort guests, twilight, seniors, juniors), discount packages, range (grass/mats), club rentals, credit cards (MC, V).
Reader Comments: Extremely challenging course ... Ohio's little piece of Carolina ... Great closing hole ... Pricey, slow play, but worth the money ... Good par 4s ... Nicely laid out for average golfer... Great layout, should be in better shape ... Multiple tees makes it playable for all. No. 13 is brutal, No. 18 is great risk and reward.

★★½ RAYMOND MEMORIAL GOLF CLUB
PM-3860 Trabue Rd., Columbus, 43228, Franklin County, (614)645-8454, 5 miles W of Columbus.
Holes: 18. **Yards:** 7,000/5,800. **Par:** 72/72. **Course Rating:** 69.9/67.9. **Slope:** 113/113. **Green Fee:** $14/$18. **Cart Fee:** $21/cart. **Walking Policy:** Unrestricted walking. **Walkability:** 3. **Opened:** 1953. **Architect:** Robert Trent Jones. **Season:** Year-round. **High:** April-Sept. **To obtain tee times:** Call 7 days ahead. **Miscellaneous:** Reduced fees (weekdays, low season, twilight, seniors, juniors), metal spikes, club rentals, credit cards (MC, V).
Reader Comments: Good municipal course ... Super staff, wide open but challenging course ... Nice course, often too crowded ... Fairways wide, few trees, flat, little water.

★½ REEVES GOLF COURSE
PU-4747 Playfield Lane, Cincinnati, 45226, Hamilton County, (513)321-1433.
Holes: 18. **Yards:** 6,200/5,630. **Par:** 70/74. **Course Rating:** 68.4/70.2. **Slope:** 109/102. **Green Fee:** $17/$17. **Cart Fee:** $10/person. **Walking Policy:** Unrestricted walking. **Walkability:** 1. **Opened:** 1965. **Architect:** William H. Diddel. **Season:** Year-round. **High:** May-Sept. **To obtain tee times:** Xeta computer system or call 1 day in advance. **Miscellaneous:** Reduced fees (low season, seniors, juniors), metal spikes, range (grass/mats), club rentals.
Special Notes: Also has a 9-hole par-3 course.

REID PARK MEMORIAL GOLF COURSE
PU-1325 Bird Rd., Springfield, 45505, Clark County, (937)324-7725, 43 miles W of Columbus.
★★★ NORTH COURSE
Holes: 18. **Yards:** 6,760/5,035. **Par:** 72/72. **Course Rating:** 72.5/69.2. **Slope:** 130/118. **Green Fee:** $16/$16. **Cart Fee:** $20. **Walking Policy:** Unrestricted walking. **Walkability:** N/A. **Opened:** 1967. **Architect:** Jack Kidwell. **Season:** Jan.-Dec. **High:** May-Oct. **To obtain tee times:** Call 8 days in advance. **Miscellaneous:** Reduced fees (twilight), metal spikes.
Reader Comments: You will need all your clubs on this one ... Tough back 9, especially No. 15 ... Great public course, tough test ... Greenskeeper is working wonders ... Tough, entertaining course. Very tense first hole!.
★★½ SOUTH COURSE
Holes: 18. **Yards:** 6,500/4,895. **Par:** 72/72. **Course Rating:** 69.0/66.5. **Slope:** 110/102. **Green Fee:** $16/$16. **Cart Fee:** $20/. **Walking Policy:** Unrestricted walking. **Walkability:** N/A. **Opened:** 1967. **Architect:** Jack Kidwell. **Season:** Year-round. **High:** May-Oct. **To obtain tee times:** Call eight days in advance. **Miscellaneous:** Reduced fees (twilight), metal spikes, range (grass), club rentals.
Reader Comments: Pin placement determines your score ... No sand traps, flat, confidence builder ... Fun! ... Nice public course.

★★★½ THE RESERVE AT THUNDER HILL
PU-7050 Griswold Rd., Madison, 44057, Geauga County, (216)298-3474, 35 miles E of Cleveland.
Holes: 18. **Yards:** 7,223/5,524. **Par:** 72/72. **Course Rating:** 78.0. **Slope:** 151/127. **Green Fee:** $25/$30. **Cart Fee:** Included in Green Fee. **Walking Policy:** Mandatory cart. **Walkability:** N/A. **Opened:** 1976. **Architect:** Fred Slagle. **Season:** April-Dec. **High:** May-Sept. **To obtain tee

times: Call anytime. **Miscellaneous:** Reduced fees (low season, seniors, juniors), discount packages, metal spikes, credit cards (MC, V).
Reader Comments: Very challenging ... Difficult ... Toughest course I have ever played.

★★½ RICKENBACKER GOLF CLUB
PU-5600 Airbase Rd., Groveport, 43125, Franklin County, (614)491-5000, 15 miles SE of Columbus.
Holes: 18. **Yards:** 7,003/5,476. **Par:** 72/72. **Course Rating:** 72.6/71.2. **Slope:** 117/117. **Green Fee:** $21/$24. **Cart Fee:** Included in Green Fee. **Walking Policy:** Walking at certain times. **Walkability:** 1. **Opened:** 1959. **Architect:** Col. Frank Hager. **Season:** Year-round. **High:** May-Sept. **To obtain tee times:** Call up to 7 days in advance. **Miscellaneous:** Reduced fees (weekdays, low season), metal spikes, range (grass), club rentals, credit cards (MC, V, AE, D).
Reader Comments: Nice layout, remote ... Long and flat ... OK public course ... Long but very walkable ... Good for the average player.

★★★ RIDGE TOP GOLF COURSE
PU-7441 Tower Rd., Medina, 44256, Medina County, (330)725-5500, (800)679-9839, 20 miles S of Cleveland.
Holes: 18. **Yards:** 6,211/4,968. **Par:** 71/71. **Course Rating:** 70.0/67.9. **Slope:** 114/107. **Green Fee:** $18/$23. **Cart Fee:** $20/cart. **Walking Policy:** Unrestricted walking. **Walkability:** 3.
Opened: 1970. **Architect:** Robert Pennington. **Season:** March-Nov. **High:** June-Aug. **To obtain tee times:** Call golf shop. **Miscellaneous:** Reduced fees (weekdays, low season, seniors, juniors), credit cards (MC, V, D).
Reader Comments: Nice layout, open front nine, interesting back nine ... Small, undulating fast greens ... Excellent condition ... Wonderful people running course ... Bring your putter! ... No. 10 super ... If you can find this place located in farm country, play it!

★★ RIVER BEND GOLF COURSE
PU-5567 Upper River Rd., Miamisburg, 45342, Montgomery County, (937)859-8121, 5 miles S of Dayton.
Holes: 18. **Yards:** 7,000/5,980. **Par:** 72/75. **Course Rating:** 70.8/N/A. **Slope:** 112/N/A. **Green Fee:** $13/$20. **Cart Fee:** $10/person. **Walking Policy:** Unrestricted walking. **Walkability:** 1.
Opened: 1963. **Architect:** Robert Bruce Harris. **Season:** Year-round. **High:** June-Aug. **To obtain tee times:** Call 7 days in advance. **Miscellaneous:** Reduced fees (low season, seniors, juniors), club rentals.

★★★★½ RIVER GREENS GOLF COURSE *Value, Condition, Pace*
PU-22749 State Rte. 751, West Lafayette, 43845, Coshocton County, (740)545-7817, (888)584-4495, 25 miles SW of New Philadelphia. **E-mail:** rggolf@clover.net. **Web:** www.rivergreens.com.
Holes: 27. **Yards:** 6,561/5,248. **Par:** 72/73. **Course Rating:** 71.1/70.2. **Slope:** 120/115. **Green Fee:** $18/$21. **Cart Fee:** $11/person. **Walking Policy:** Unrestricted walking. **Walkability:** 1.
Opened: 1967. **Architect:** Jack Kidwell. **Season:** March-Dec. **High:** March-Sept. **To obtain tee times:** Call 7 day in advance. **Miscellaneous:** Reduced fees (seniors, juniors), discount packages, range (grass/mats), club rentals, credit cards (MC, V).
Reader Comments: Fairways and greens very good. Well maintained ... Lush fairways, great greens ... Truly a hidden gem. Best greens around ... Very challenging 27 holes. A lot of different play ... Always in good condition ... A real treat to play.

★★★½ RIVERBY HILLS GOLF CLUB
PU-16571 W. River Rd., Bowling Green, 43402, Wood County, (419)878-5941, 9 miles N of Bowling Green.
Holes: 18. **Yards:** 6,856/5,316. **Par:** 72/72. **Course Rating:** 72.1/69.4. **Slope:** 125/113. **Green Fee:** $22/$26. **Cart Fee:** $12/person. **Walking Policy:** Unrestricted walking. **Walkability:** 4.
Opened: 1926. **Architect:** Harold Paddock. **Season:** March-Nov. **High:** June-Aug. **To obtain tee times:** Call golf shop. **Miscellaneous:** Reduced fees (low season, seniors, juniors), range (grass), credit cards (MC, V).
Reader Comments: Basic golf ... Country setting. Good variety ... Decent course ... Great back 9; No. 12 dogleg left, water on left and in front of green ... Two different 9s. Front is open and long. Back is narrow and wooded ... Good course design.

★★ ROCKY FORK GOLF & TENNIS CENTER
9965 State Rte. 124, Hillsboro, 45133, Highland County, (937)393-9004.
Special Notes: Call club for further information.

★★ ROLLING ACRES GOLF COURSE
PU-63 State Rte. 511, Nova, 44859, Ashland County, (419)652-3160, 12 miles N of Ashland.
Holes: 18. **Yards:** 6,590/5,022. **Par:** 71/71. **Course Rating:** 70.2/68.6. **Slope:** 117/109. **Green Fee:** $10/$19. **Cart Fee:** $18/cart. **Walking Policy:** Unrestricted walking. **Walkability:** 3.
Opened: 1963. **Season:** March-Nov. **High:** June-Aug. **Miscellaneous:** Reduced fees (weekdays, low season, seniors, juniors), metal spikes, club rentals, credit cards (MC, V, AE).

★★½ ROLLING GREEN GOLF CLUB
PU-15900 Mayfield Rd., Huntsburg, 44046, Geauga County, (440)636-5171, (888)833-7442, 50 miles E of Cleveland.
Holes: 18. **Yards:** 6,551/5,512. **Par:** 71/71. **Course Rating:** 70.1/69.4. **Slope:** 120/111. **Green Fee:** $12/$20. **Cart Fee:** $20/cart. **Walking Policy:** Unrestricted walking. **Walkability:** 2. **Opened:** 1970. **Season:** April-Oct. **High:** June-Aug. **To obtain tee times:** Call golf shop. **Miscellaneous:** Reduced fees (weekdays, seniors, juniors), range (grass), credit cards (MC, V).
Reader Comments: Lush, good advice from starter, no waiting ... Great place to play for the dollars ... Pretty country course ... Very enjoyable ... Fairly easy, variety of holes ... Average course ... Nice course and landscaping ... Good walking course ... A fun course, easy to score on.

★½ ROLLING GREEN GOLF COURSE
7656 Lutz Ave. NW, Massillon, 44646, Stark County, (216)854-3800.
Special Notes: Call club for further information.

★★½ ROLLING MEADOWS GOLF CLUB
PU-11233 Industrial Pkwy., Marysville, 43040, Union County, (937)873-4567, 15 miles W of Columbus.
Holes: 18. **Yards:** 6,750/5,832. **Par:** 71/71. **Course Rating:** 71.1/72.0. **Slope:** 119/119. **Green Fee:** $17/$20. **Cart Fee:** $10/person. **Walking Policy:** Unrestricted walking. **Walkability:** 3. **Opened:** 1996. **Architect:** David Savic. **Season:** March-Dec. **High:** May-Sept. **To obtain tee times:** Call up to 7 days in advance. **Miscellaneous:** Reduced fees (weekdays, low season, seniors), metal spikes, club rentals, credit cards (MC, V, AE, D).
Reader Comments: Very wide, easy course, few trees ... Basic golf ... New course, improving each year... Wide open, maturing, getting better all the time.

ROSES RUN COUNTRY CLUB
PU-2636 N. River Rd., Stow, 44224, Summit County, (330)688-4653, 30 miles S of Cleveland.
Web: www.rosesrun.com.
Holes: 18. **Yards:** 6,859/4,964. **Par:** 72/72. **Course Rating:** 73.3/69.3. **Slope:** 128/116. **Green Fee:** $38/$44. **Cart Fee:** Included in Green Fee. **Walking Policy:** Mandatory cart. **Walkability:** 5. **Opened:** 1999. **Architect:** Brian Huntley. **Season:** April-Nov. **High:** June-Aug. **Miscellaneous:** Reduced fees (seniors), range (grass/mats), credit cards (MC, V, AE).

★★★½ ROYAL AMERICAN LINKS GOLF CLUB
PU-3300 Miller Paul Rd., Galena, 43021, Delaware County, (614)965-1215, 17 miles N of Columbus.
Holes: 18. **Yards:** 6,859/5,172. **Par:** 72/72. **Course Rating:** 72.5/69.2. **Slope:** 127/117. **Green Fee:** $20/$38. **Cart Fee:** $12/person. **Walking Policy:** Unrestricted walking. **Walkability:** 1. **Opened:** 1992. **Architect:** Michael Hurdzan. **Season:** Year-round. **High:** June-Sept. **To obtain tee times:** Call 7 days in advance. **Miscellaneous:** Reduced fees (weekdays, low season, twilight, seniors), range (grass), club rentals, credit cards (MC, V, D).
Reader Comments: Great track, but pricey ... Good layout, fast greens, expensive ... Wide open if wind not blowing ... No. 18 is a great finishing hole ... A great layout ... Excellent condition ... Slick greens, great links style ... Wind always a factor ... Good greens ... Attentive staff, great blind shots.

RUNNING FOX GOLF COURSE
PU-310 Sunset, Chillicothe, 45601, Ross County, (740)775-9955, 42 miles S of Columbus.
Holes: 27. **Green Fee:** $10/$12. **Cart Fee:** $19/person. **Walking Policy:** Unrestricted walking. **Walkability:** 2. **Opened:** 1974. **Architect:** Ted Cox. **Season:** Year-round. **High:** June-July. **To obtain tee times:** Call anytime. **Miscellaneous:** Reduced fees (weekdays, low season, seniors, juniors), discount packages, metal spikes, range (grass/mats), club rentals, credit cards (MC, V, AE, D).
★★ RED/BLUE
Yards: 6,549/5,645. **Par:** 72/72. **Course Rating:** 70.5/68.5. **Slope:** 113/108.
★★ RED/WHITE
Yards: 6,538/5,685. **Par:** 72/72. **Course Rating:** 70.5/68.5. **Slope:** 113/108.
★★ WHITE/BLUE
Yards: 6,568/6,220. **Par:** 72/72. **Course Rating:** 70.5/68.5. **Slope:** 113/108.

★★½ SAFARI GOLF CLUB
PU-P.O. Box 400, Powell, 43065, Delaware County, (614)645-3444, 15 miles N of Columbus.
Holes: 18. **Yards:** 6,507/4,827. **Par:** 72/72. **Course Rating:** N/A. **Slope:** 109/110. **Green Fee:** N/A. **Walking Policy:** Unrestricted walking. **Walkability:** 1. **Architect:** Jimmy Duros. **Season:** Year-round. **High:** May-Sept. **To obtain tee times:** Call on Monday for upcoming weekend. **Miscellaneous:** Reduced fees (weekdays, seniors, juniors), metal spikes, range (grass), club rentals, credit cards (MC, V, D).

OHIO

Reader Comments: Tight course, yell 'fore' and whole course ducks ... Good value, so-so course (lots of parallel fairways)... Easy track ... It's hard to find fault with this old course's design ... Staff enthusiastic and informative ... Nice short course, fairly flat, no surprises.

★★½ ST. ALBANS GOLF CLUB

PU-3833 Northridge Rd. N.W., Alexandria, 43001, Licking County, (740)924-8885, 25 miles E of Columbus.
Holes: 18. Yards: 6,732/5,513. Par: 71/71. Course Rating: 71.6/71.1. Slope: 112/112. Green Fee: N/A/$27. Cart Fee: $17/cart. Walking Policy: Unrestricted walking. Walkability: 3. Opened: 1988. Architect: Tony Price. Season: March-Dec. High: May-Aug. To obtain tee times: Call golf shop. Miscellaneous: Reduced fees (low season, seniors), metal spikes, credit cards (MC, V).
Reader Comments: Worth the drive ... Entertaining, harder than it looks ... Hidden jewel, good test for a low fee ... Good value.

★★★½ SAINT DENIS GOLF COURSE

PU-10660 Chardon Rd., Chardon, 44024, Geauga County, (440)285-2183, (800)843-5676, 25 miles NE of Cleveland.
Holes: 18. Yards: 6,600/5,900. Par: 72/72. Course Rating: 72.5/72.0. Slope: 115/117. Green Fee: $22/$26. Cart Fee: $10/person. Walking Policy: Unrestricted walking. Walkability: 3. Opened: 1967. Season: April-Oct. To obtain tee times: Call up to 7 days in advance. Miscellaneous: Reduced fees (weekdays, seniors), metal spikes, credit cards (MC, V).
Reader Comments: Nice course ... Parallel fairways ... Good course for the average golfer... Hidden treasure ... Lots of hills, good test of golf ... Inexpensive and challenging, but crowded.

★★★ SALEM HILLS GOLF & COUNTRY CLUB

SP-12688 Salem-Warren Rd., Salem, 44460, Mahoning County, (330)337-8033, 15 miles S of Youngstown.
Holes: 18. Yards: 7,146/5,597. Par: 72/72. Course Rating: 74.3/69.7. Slope: 126/114. Green Fee: N/A/$25. Cart Fee: $10/person. Walking Policy: Unrestricted walking. Walkability: 2. Opened: 1966. Season: April-Nov. High: June-Aug. To obtain tee times: Call (330)337-8033. Miscellaneous: Reduced fees (weekdays, seniors, juniors), range (grass/mats), credit cards (MC, V).
Reader Comments: Tough course ... Very professionally maintained. Big greens tough ... Course interesting ... Decent course ... Great old layout, No. 4 is brutal ... Nice.

★★★★ SALT FORK STATE PARK GOLF COURSE *Value*

PU-14755 Cadiz Rd., Lore City, 43755, Guernsey County, (614)432-7185, (800)282-7275, 6 miles E of Cambridge.
Holes: 18. Yards: 6,056/5,241. Par: 71/71. Course Rating: 68.3/69.7. Slope: 126/123. Green Fee: $14/$18. Cart Fee: $12/person. Walking Policy: Unrestricted walking. Walkability: 5. Opened: 1972. Architect: Jack Kidwell. Season: Year-round. High: May-Oct. To obtain tee times: Call golf shop as far in advance as you like. Miscellaneous: Reduced fees (weekdays, low season, resort guests, seniors, juniors), discount packages, metal spikes, range (grass/mats), club rentals, lodging (148 rooms), credit cards (MC, V, AE, D).
Reader Comments: Great greens ... Game & body must be in shape for this track ... Take your pack mule ... Very hilly, fast greens, awesome golf ... Best hills course in Ohio ... Better bring your short game ... Always superior condition ... Incredible views, immaculate condition ... Lots of fun.

★★★★ SAWMILL CREEK GOLF & RACQUET CLUB

R-300 Sawmill, Huron, 44839, Erie County, (419)433-3789, (800)SAWMILL, 60 miles W of Cleveland.
Holes: 18. Yards: 6,702/5,124. Par: 71/71. Course Rating: 72.3/69.4. Slope: 128/115. Green Fee: $54/$58. Cart Fee: $15/person. Walking Policy: Walking at certain times. Walkability: 2. Opened: 1974. Architect: George Fazio/Tom Fazio. Season: April-Oct. High: June-Sept. To obtain tee times: Call golf shop. Off season call Sawmill Creek Resort at 1-800-SAWMILL. Miscellaneous: Reduced fees (low season), discount packages, metal spikes, club rentals, lodging (245 rooms), credit cards (MC, V, AE, D).
Reader Comments: Heavy traffic, fairly flat, small greens, good scenery ... Do not miss these lightning fast greens ... Tremendous par 3s, tricky greens ... Very long.

SHAKER RUN GOLF CLUB *Service*

PU-4361 Greentree Rd., Lebanon, 45036, Warren County, (513)727-0007, 8 miles N of Lebanon.
Web: www.shakerrungolfclub.com.
Holes: 27. Green Fee: $40/$76. Cart Fee: Included in Green Fee. Walking Policy: Walking at certain times. Walkability: 4. Opened: 1979. Architect: Arthur Hills/Michael Hurdzan. Season: Year-round. High: May-Oct. To obtain tee times: Call 7 days in advance. Miscellaneous: Reduced fees (weekdays, low season, twilight, seniors, juniors), discount packages, range (grass), club rentals, credit cards (MC, V, AE).

OHIO

★★★★½ **LAKESIDE/MEADOWS**
Yards: 6,991/5,046. **Par:** 72/72. **Course Rating:** 73.7/68.4. **Slope:** 136/118.
★★★★½ **MEADOWS/WOODLANDS**
Yards: 7,092/5,161. **Par:** 72/72. **Course Rating:** 74.1/69.6. **Slope:** 134/119.
★★★★½ **WOODLANDS/LAKESIDE**
Yards: 6,963/5,075. **Par:** 72/72. **Course Rating:** 74.0/68.8. **Slope:** 138/121.
Notes: Ranked 21st in 1999 Best in State.
Reader Comments: Fantastic course, average shape, very pricey ... Hit long, move fast, have fun ... Good parkland course, nice conditions ... Heavy woods, much water, very challenging ... Bring A game ... Pricey but beautiful, challenging ... Best track in Ohio, tough, tough, tough ... Most bang for the buck in area.

★★½ **SHAMROCK GOLF CLUB**
PU-4436 Powell Rd., Powell, 43065, Delaware County, (614)792-6630, 12 miles N of Columbus.
Holes: 18. **Yards:** 6,300/5,400. **Par:** 71/71. **Course Rating:** 67.5/68.0. **Slope:** 115/110. **Green Fee:** $14/$19. **Cart Fee:** $11. **Walking Policy:** Walking at certain times. **Walkability:** N/A.
Opened: 1988. **Architect:** Jack Kidwell and Michael Hurdzan. **Season:** Year-round. **High:** May-Oct. **To obtain tee times:** Call 7 days in advance. **Miscellaneous:** Reduced fees (low season, twilight, seniors, juniors), metal spikes, range (grass), club rentals, credit cards (MC, V, D).
Reader Comments: Tight course ... An OK little course ... Great staff & practice range ... Fairways too close to each other.

★★★½ **SHARON WOODS GOLF COURSE**
PM-11355 Swing Road, Cincinnati, 45241, Hamilton County, (513)769-4325, 15 miles N of Cincinnati.
Holes: 18. **Yards:** 6,652/5,288. **Par:** 70/70. **Course Rating:** 72.0/68.3. **Slope:** 131/116. **Green Fee:** $19/$19. **Cart Fee:** $12/person. **Walking Policy:** Unrestricted walking. **Walkability:** 4.
Opened: 1938. **Architect:** William Diddel. **Season:** March-Dec. **High:** April-Sept. **To obtain tee times:** Call up to 5 days in advance starting at 6 p.m. **Miscellaneous:** Reduced fees (seniors, juniors), metal spikes, club rentals, credit cards (MC, V).
Reader Comments: Beautiful setting, Bobby Jones hit the first drive ... Great course, great bargain ... Outstanding, hard to get on, very challenging ... Bent fairways are nice ... Trees, hills and horizon combine as a scenic backdrop ... Great shape ... Hard par 4s ... Incredible for a public course ... Tough, long layout, beautiful.

★★★ **SHAWNEE HILLS GOLF COURSE**
PU-18753 Egbert Rd., Bedford, 44146, Cuyahoga County, (440)232-7184, 10 miles SE of Cleveland.
Holes: 18. **Yards:** 6,366/5,884. **Par:** 71/73. **Course Rating:** 69.9/72.5. **Slope:** 114/116. **Green Fee:** $12/$18. **Cart Fee:** $9/person. **Walking Policy:** Unrestricted walking. **Walkability:** 3.
Opened: 1957. **Architect:** Ben Zink. **Season:** March-Dec. **High:** May-Sept. **To obtain tee times:** Call up to 5 days in advance. **Miscellaneous:** Reduced fees (low season, seniors, juniors), discount packages, metal spikes, range (mats), club rentals, credit cards (MC, V), beginner friendly (driving range, lessons and additional short course).
Reader Comments: Great for beginners ... Open course, easy to score on ... Nice walk-on course ... Front 9 super, back a little more difficult ... Some memorable holes ... Interesting but not provocative.

★★ **SHAWNEE LOOKOUT GOLF CLUB**
PU-2030 Lawrencburg, North Bend, 45052, Hamilton County, (513)941-0120, 15 miles W of Downtown Cincinnati.
Holes: 18. **Yards:** 6,016/4,912. **Par:** 70/70. **Course Rating:** N/A. **Slope:** N/A. **Green Fee:** $7/$16. **Cart Fee:** $12/person. **Walking Policy:** Unrestricted walking. **Walkability:** 5. **Opened:** 1979. **Architect:** Jack Kidwell/Michael Hurdzan. **Season:** March-Oct. **High:** June-Aug.
Miscellaneous: Reduced fees (low season, seniors, juniors), metal spikes, club rentals, credit cards (MC, V).

★★★ **SHAWNEE STATE PARK GOLF COURSE**
P.O. Box 148, Friendship, 45630, Scioto County, (740)858-6681.
Yards: 6,837/5,748. **Par:** 72/72. **Course Rating:** 71.7/71.6. **Slope:** 117/117. **Green Fee:** $9/$17. **Walkability:** N/A. **Architect:** Jack Kidwell/Michael Hurdzan. **Miscellaneous:** Metal spikes.
Reader Comments: Challenging–subtle, nice greens ... Well-placed hazards counter the width and flat terrain ... Good facilities for state course ... Nice course ... Beautiful holes over water, nice bridge nearby.

SHELBY OAKS GOLF CLUB
PU-9900 Sidney Freyburg Rd., Sidney, 45365, Shelby County, (937)492-2883, 3 miles N of Sidney. **E-mail:** cowboylebright.net.
Holes: 27. **Green Fee:** $18/$21. **Cart Fee:** $11/person. **Walking Policy:** Unrestricted walking. **Walkability:** 3. **Opened:** 1964. **Architect:** Ken Killian/Dick Nugent. **Season:** March-Nov. **High:**

May-Oct. **To obtain tee times:** Call up to 7 days in advance. **Miscellaneous:** Reduced fees (twilight), metal spikes, range (grass/mats), credit cards (MC, V), beginner friendly.

★★½ SOUTH/NORTH
Yards: 6,561/5,465. **Par:** 72/72. **Course Rating:** 70.5/70.5. **Slope:** 115/111.
Reader Comments: Very good 27 hole course ... Big, fast greens ... Not difficult but fun ... Excellent practice area, nice test of golf ... Wide driving areas.

★★½ SOUTH/WEST
Yards: 6,100/5,700. **Par:** 72/72. **Course Rating:** 70.5/70.5. **Slope:** 113/111.
Reader Comments: Long course, tough par 4.

★★½ WEST/NORTH
Yards: 6,650/5,205. **Par:** 72/72. **Course Rating:** 70.9/70.9. **Slope:** 115/111.

★★ SKYLAND GOLF COURSE
PU-2085 Center Rd., Hinckley, 44233, Medina County, (330)225-5698, 20 miles S of Cleveland.
Holes: 18. **Yards:** 6,239/5,491. **Par:** 72/74. **Course Rating:** 68.9/70.7. **Slope:** 113/112. **Green Fee:** $18/$23. **Cart Fee:** $20/cart. **Walking Policy:** Unrestricted walking. **Walkability:** 3.
Opened: 1932. **Architect:** James O. Rhodes. **Season:** April-Oct. **High:** June-Sept. **To obtain tee times:** Call golf shop. **Miscellaneous:** Reduced fees (weekdays, seniors, juniors), range (grass), club rentals, credit cards (MC, V, AE).

★★½ SKYLAND PINES GOLF CLUB
PU-3550 Columbus Rd. N.E., Canton, 44705, Stark County, (330)454-5131, 5 miles E of Canton.
Holes: 18. **Yards:** 6,467/5,279. **Par:** 72/72. **Course Rating:** 69.6/69.6. **Slope:** 113/113. **Green Fee:** $15/$25. **Cart Fee:** $9/person. **Walking Policy:** Unrestricted walking. **Walkability:** 1.
Season: Feb.-Dec. **High:** April-Nov. **To obtain tee times:** Call golf shop in advance.
Miscellaneous: Reduced fees (low season), metal spikes, range (grass/mats), club rentals, credit cards (MC, V, D).
Reader Comments: Short, but tight ... Best public course greens I've ever played, can be very fast ... Even in August, hitting greens like throwing darts.

SLEEPY HOLLOW GOLF COURSE
PM-9445 Brecksville Rd., Brecksville, 44141, Cuyahoga County, (440)526-4285, 15 miles S of Cleveland.
Holes: 18. **Yards:** 6,630/5,715. **Par:** 71/73. **Course Rating:** 71.9/73.5. **Slope:** 124/128. **Green Fee:** $23/$26. **Cart Fee:** $10/person. **Walking Policy:** Unrestricted walking. **Walkability:** 4.
Opened: 1925. **Architect:** Stanley Thompson. **Season:** March-Dec. **High:** May-Sept. **To obtain tee times:** Call golf shop at noon 5 days in advance. **Miscellaneous:** Reduced fees (low season, seniors, juniors), discount packages, metal spikes, range (mats), club rentals, credit cards (MC, V).
Reader Comments: Best-designed course I have ever played ... Nice rolling course ... Beautiful layout, greens could be better ... Great old track ... Wide fairways, but tough, nice doglegs ... Nothing 'sleepy' here, lots of hills and blind shots.

★★★ SOUTH TOLEDO GOLF CLUB
PU-3915 Heatherdowns Blvd, Toledo, 43614, Lucas County, (419)385-4678.
Reader Comments: Looks good and plays well ... Fun to play, flat ... A fair challenge ... I especially enjoyed hole No. 7, the par-3 island green ... Keeps getting better ... Old-style country club-type course ... Good public layout.
Special Notes: Call club for further information.

SPLIT ROCK GOLF COURSE
PU-10210 Scioto Darby Rd., Orient , 43146, Pickaway County, (614)877-9755, 10 miles S of Columbus.
Holes: 18. **Yards:** 6,809/5,046. **Par:** 72/72. **Course Rating:** 72.0/68.1. **Slope:** 125/116. **Green Fee:** $15/$18. **Cart Fee:** $11/person. **Walking Policy:** Unrestricted walking. **Walkability:** 3.
Opened: 1998. **Architect:** Michael Hurdzan/Dana Fry. **Season:** March-Dec. **High:** June-Aug. **To obtain tee times:** Call up to 2 weeks in advance. **Miscellaneous:** Reduced fees (weekdays), range (grass), credit cards (MC, V).

★★ SPRING HILLS GOLF CLUB
PU-S Rte 43, Box 128, East Springfield, 43925, Jefferson County, (740)543-3270, 13 miles NW of Steubenville.
Holes: 18. **Yards:** 6,558/5,560. **Par:** 71/71. **Course Rating:** 70.9/67.0. **Slope:** 119/119. **Green Fee:** $14/$16. **Cart Fee:** $14/person. **Walking Policy:** Unrestricted walking. **Walkability:** 2.
Opened: 1970. **Season:** Feb.-Dec. **High:** March-Nov. **To obtain tee times:** Call golf shop.
Miscellaneous: Reduced fees (weekdays, low season, seniors, juniors), metal spikes, range (grass), club rentals, credit cards (MC, V).

★★★★½ STONEWATER GOLF CLUB *Service, Condition+, Pace*

SP-1 Club Dr., Highland Heights, 44143, Cuyahoga County, (440)461-4653, 16 miles E of Cleveland. **Web:** www.stonewatergolf.com.

Holes: 18. **Yards:** 7,100/5,067. **Par:** 72/72. **Course Rating:** 75.2/70.0. **Slope:** 139/124. **Green Fee:** $39/$75. **Cart Fee:** $19/person. **Walking Policy:** Walking at certain times. **Walkability:** 3. **Opened:** 1996. **Architect:** Hurdzan/Fry Golf Design. **Season:** March-Dec. **High:** May-Oct. **To obtain tee times:** Non-members may call up to 7 days in advance. A limited number of more advance times are available each day which may be reserved by paying a privilege fee. **Miscellaneous:** Reduced fees (weekdays, low season, twilight), range (grass), caddies, club rentals, credit cards (MC, V, AE).
Notes: Ranked 10th in 1999 Best in State.
Reader Comments: Pricey, but one of the best Ohio public courses ... Great mix of holes, great condition ... First class but you pay for it ... Great layout, close to airport ... Scenic wetlands, demanding layout, superb ... Outstanding, expensive ... Outstanding, worth repeating ... Lovely course, great design.

★★★½ SUGAR BUSH GOLF CLUB, INC.

PU-11186 North State Rte. 88, Garrettsville, 44231, Portage County, (330)527-4202, 33 miles SE of Cleveland.

Holes: 18. **Yards:** 6,571/4,727. **Par:** 72/72. **Course Rating:** 72.4/66.4. **Slope:** 121/106. **Green Fee:** $15/$30. **Cart Fee:** $19/cart. **Walking Policy:** Unrestricted walking. **Walkability:** 4. **Opened:** 1965. **Architect:** Harold Paddock. **Season:** March-Nov. **High:** June-Sept. **To obtain tee times:** Call (330)527-4202 w/credit card to secure times. **Miscellaneous:** Reduced fees (weekdays, low season, twilight, seniors, juniors), metal spikes, credit cards (MC, V).
Reader Comments: Best greens in Northern Ohio ... Nice variety of holes ... Gets better every year... Shh, let's keep it a secret ... Challenging for all golfers, nice fairways ... Every hole has a natural beauty ... Two contrasting nines, stay out of trees & watch out for maple syrup buckets ... Great sights, challenging and fair.

★★½ SUGAR CREEK GOLF COURSE

SP-950 Elmore E. Rd., Elmore, 43416, Ottwa County, (419)862-2551, 20 miles S of Toledo.
E-mail: srodawalt@aol.com.

Holes: 18. **Yards:** 6,331/5,092. **Par:** 71/71. **Course Rating:** 66.5/64.4. **Slope:** 102/98. **Green Fee:** $12/$14. **Cart Fee:** $18/cart. **Walking Policy:** Walking at certain times. **Walkability:** 3. **Opened:** 1963. **Architect:** Stan Neeb/Leon Neeb. **Season:** March-Dec. **High:** June-Sept. **To obtain tee times:** Call anytime. **Miscellaneous:** Reduced fees (weekdays, low season, twilight, seniors, juniors), discount packages, metal spikes, range (grass/mats), club rentals, credit cards (MC, V).
Reader Comments: Green on side of hill requires skill ... Fun course, some tricky holes ... Short course with some demanding holes ... You use all your clubs ... The creek holes are nice.

★★½ SUGAR ISLE GOLF COUNTRY

PU-2469 Dayt-Lakeview Rd., New Carlisle, 45344, Clark County, (937)845-8699, 15 miles N of Dayton.

Holes: 18. **Yards:** 6,754/5,636. **Par:** 72/72. **Course Rating:** 70.2/71.1. **Slope:** 107/110. **Green Fee:** $16/$20. **Cart Fee:** $10/person. **Walking Policy:** Unrestricted walking. **Walkability:** 2. **Opened:** 1974. **Architect:** Jack Kidwell/Michael Hurdzan. **Season:** Year-round. **High:** June-Sept. **To obtain tee times:** Call 7 days in advance. Groups of 20 or more may call further in advance with deposit. **Miscellaneous:** Reduced fees (weekdays, seniors), range (grass), club rentals, credit cards (MC, V).
Reader Comments: Very challenging course ... Enjoyable No. 18, a par 3 island green ... Nice course, two-tiered greens ... Tough course (narrow fairways), lots of trees and water.

★★ SUNNYHILL GOLF COURSE

PU-3734 Sunnybrook Rd., Kent, 44240, Portage County, (330)673-1785, 5 miles E of Akron.
E-mail: 27sunny@gateway.net.

Holes: 27. **Yards:** 6,289/5,083. **Par:** 71/72. **Course Rating:** 69.4/69.1. **Slope:** 119/113. **Green Fee:** $18/$25. **Cart Fee:** $10/person. **Walking Policy:** Unrestricted walking. **Walkability:** 3. **Opened:** 1921. **Architect:** Ferdinand Garbin. **Season:** March-Jan. **High:** May-Aug. **To obtain tee times:** Call ahead. **Miscellaneous:** Reduced fees (weekdays, low season, seniors, juniors), range (mats), club rentals, credit cards (MC, V, D), beginner friendly (lessons, middle 9 is good beginner course).
Special Notes: 9-hole par-34 Middle Course.

SWEETBRIAR GOLF & PRO SHOP

PU-750 Jaycox Rd., Avon Lake, 44012, Lorain County, (216)933-9001, 20 miles W of Cleveland.
Green Fee: $17/$22. **Cart Fee:** $20/cart. **Walking Policy:** Unrestricted walking. **Walkability:** N/A. **Opened:** 1966. **Architect:** Ron Palmer. **Season:** Year-round. **High:** May-Oct. **To obtain tee times:** Call on Wednesday morning for upcoming weekend. No tee times for weekdays.

Miscellaneous: Reduced fees (low season, twilight, seniors, juniors), metal spikes, range (mats), club rentals, credit cards (MC, V).

★★★ **FIRST/SECOND**
Yards: 6,491/5,521. **Par:** 72/74. **Course Rating:** 68.7/68.9. **Slope:** 106/105.
Reader Comments: Basic golf ... Very nicely maintained. Fairly priced ... 27 holes long and wide open, good value ... A beautiful course, 27 holes and a pro shop with everything a golfer could ask for.... Bit expensive (with cart) ... Always busy.

★★★ **FIRST/THIRD**
Yards: 6,075/5,414. **Par:** 70/73. **Course Rating:** 66.3/68.0. **Slope:** 100/105.

★★★ **SECOND/THIRD**
Yards: 6,292/5,411. **Par:** 72/73. **Course Rating:** 67.5/68.3. **Slope:** 104/104.

★★½ **SYCAMORE HILLS GOLF CLUB**
SP-3728 W. Hayes Ave. (U.S. Rte. 6), Fremont, 43420, Sandusky County, (419)332-5716, (800)336-5716, 3 miles W of Fremont.
Holes: 27. **Yards:** 6,221/5,076. **Par:** 70/72. **Course Rating:** 67.3/66.3. **Slope:** 110/107. **Green Fee:** $14/$16. **Cart Fee:** $10/person. **Walking Policy:** Unrestricted walking. **Walkability:** 2. **Opened:** 1964. **Architect:** Doug Michael. **Season:** March-Dec. **High:** April-Sept. **To obtain tee times:** Call in advance for weekends and holidays 1-(800)336-5716. **Miscellaneous:** Reduced fees (weekdays, low season, seniors, juniors), range (grass), club rentals, credit cards (MC, V, D), beginner friendly.
Reader Comments: 3 to choose, 3 to win or 3 to lose ... 27 good holes ... Getting better every year... 2 tough finishing holes, nice course ... Interesting, requires many different shots.

★★½ **TABLE ROCK GOLF CLUB**
PU-3005 Wilson Rd., Centerburg, 43011, Knox County, (740)625-6859, (800)688-6859, 20 miles N of Columbus. **Web:** www.tablerock.com.
Holes: 18. **Yards:** 6,729/5,303. **Par:** 72/72. **Course Rating:** 71.4/69.2. **Slope:** 119/115. **Green Fee:** $15/$20. **Cart Fee:** $11/person. **Walking Policy:** Unrestricted walking. **Walkability:** 1. **Opened:** 1973. **Architect:** Jack Kidwell. **Season:** Year-round. **High:** May-Sept. **To obtain tee times:** Call 14 days in advance. **Miscellaneous:** Reduced fees (weekdays, low season, twilight, seniors, juniors), range (grass), club rentals, credit cards (MC, V, AE, D).
Reader Comments: Good, cheap country course, outstanding back 9... Enjoyable course ... Jekyll & Hyde layout, score on front 9, back 9 gets tight ... Nice track at a reasonable fee ... Greens hard ... Good deal, very well kept.

TAM O'SHANTER GOLF COURSE
PU-5055 Hills and Dales Rd. N.W., Canton, 44708, Stark County, (330)477-5111, (800)462-9964, 50 miles S of Cleveland.
★★★★ **DALES COURSE**
Holes: 18. **Yards:** 6,509/5,317. **Par:** 70/74. **Course Rating:** 70.4/69.7. **Slope:** 110/109. **Green Fee:** $14/$27. **Cart Fee:** $10/person. **Walking Policy:** Unrestricted walking. **Walkability:** 3. **Opened:** 1928. **Architect:** Leonard Macomber. **Season:** March-Dec. **High:** April-Oct. **To obtain tee times:** Call up to a year in advance with credit card to guarantee. **Miscellaneous:** Reduced fees (weekdays, low season, seniors, juniors), range (grass), club rentals, credit cards (MC, V).
Reader Comments: Very challenging, thick rough, usually have a 'snowman' or two ... Good professional course, hard for high-handicap players ... Great for weekend getaway ... Championship course ... Good challenge.

★★★ **HILLS COURSE**
Holes: 18. **Yards:** 6,385/5,076. **Par:** 70/74. **Course Rating:** 69.1/67.4. **Slope:** 104/102. **Green Fee:** $14/$27. **Cart Fee:** $10/person. **Walking Policy:** Unrestricted walking. **Walkability:** 3. **Opened:** 1930. **Architect:** Merle Paul. **Season:** March-Dec. **High:** April-Oct. **To obtain tee times:** Call up to 1 year in advance with credit card to guarantee. **Miscellaneous:** Reduced fees (weekdays, low season, seniors, juniors), range (grass), club rentals, credit cards (MC, V).
Reader Comments: Outstanding! ... Less crowded ... Good not great ... Good layout.
Special Notes: Spikeless shoes encouraged.

★★ **TAMARAC GOLF CLUB**
PU-500 Stevick Rd., Lima, 45807, Allen County, (419)331-2951, 4 miles E of Lima.
Holes: 18. **Yards:** 6,109/5,029. **Par:** 72/72. **Course Rating:** 69.8/67.9. **Slope:** 112/108. **Green Fee:** $15/$20. **Cart Fee:** $18/person. **Walking Policy:** Unrestricted walking. **Walkability:** 2. **Opened:** 1950. **Architect:** Bob Holopeter. **Season:** March-Dec. **High:** April-Sept. **To obtain tee times:** Call anytime. **Miscellaneous:** Reduced fees (weekdays, low season, twilight, seniors), range (grass), club rentals, credit cards (MC, V, D), beginner friendly (par-3 course).
Special Notes: Also has 9-hole par-3 course.

★★★ **TAMER WIN GOLF & COUNTRY CLUB**
PU-2940 Niles Cortland Rd. N.E., Cortland, 44410, Trumbull County, (330)637-2881, 20 miles N of Youngstown. **E-mail:** twgolf2881@aol.com.

Holes: 18. **Yards:** 6,275/5,623. **Par:** 71/74. **Course Rating:** 70.0/71.6. **Slope:** 114/116. **Green Fee:** $18/$20. **Cart Fee:** $9/person. **Walking Policy:** Unrestricted walking. **Walkability:** 3. **Opened:** 1961. **Architect:** Charles E. Winch. **Season:** April-Dec. **High:** May-Sept. **To obtain tee times:** Call for weekends and holidays. Tee times are taken and available 7 days a week. **Miscellaneous:** Reduced fees (low season, seniors, juniors), metal spikes, credit cards (MC, V, AE, D). **Reader Comments:** Good course, but management could be better ... Excellent course, move quickly on holes ... Good mid-level venue ... Good basic golf ... Great back 9, friendly front 9 ... Lots of trees on back nine ... Good community course.

★★ TANGLEWOOD GOLF CLUB

PU-1086 Cheshire Rd., Delaware, 43015, Delaware County, (740)548-6715, 10 miles N of Columbus. **E-mail:** jscott@midohio.net. **Web:** www.midohio.net/tanglewood.
Holes: 18. **Yards:** 6,950/6,300. **Par:** 72/72. **Course Rating:** 69.0/69.0. **Slope:** 113/113. **Green Fee:** $20/$23. **Cart Fee:** $10/person. **Walking Policy:** Walking at certain times. **Walkability:** 1. **Opened:** 1967. **Architect:** Jack Kidwell. **Season:** March-Nov. **To obtain tee times:** Call up to 7 days in advance. **Miscellaneous:** Reduced fees (weekdays), metal spikes, range (grass), club rentals, credit cards (MC, V).

★★★½ TANNENHAUF GOLF CLUB

PU-11411 McCallum Ave., Alliance, 44601, Stark County, (330)823-4402, (800)533-5140, 10 miles E of Canton.
Holes: 18. **Yards:** 6,694/4,763. **Par:** 72/72. **Course Rating:** 71.3/66.1. **Slope:** 121/109. **Green Fee:** $18/$25. **Cart Fee:** $10/person. **Walking Policy:** Unrestricted walking. **Walkability:** 2. **Opened:** 1959. **Architect:** James G. Harrison/Fred Garvin. **Season:** Year-round weather permitting. **High:** June-Aug. **To obtain tee times:** Call. **Miscellaneous:** Reduced fees (weekdays, low season, twilight, seniors, juniors), discount packages, range (grass), club rentals, credit cards (MC, V, AE, D).
Reader Comments: Long par 5s ... Enjoyable and challenging ... Beautiful ... Very long, big greens. Use every club in bag ... A challenge for all handicaps ... Good specials. Play it twice.

★★½ THORN APPLE COUNTRY CLUB

SP-1051 Alton Darby Creek Rd., Galloway, 43119, Franklin County, (614)878-7703, 10 miles W of Columbus.
Holes: 18. **Yards:** 7,037/5,901. **Par:** 72/74. **Course Rating:** 72.6/71.7. **Slope:** 116/115. **Green Fee:** $16/$17. **Cart Fee:** $18/cart. **Walking Policy:** Unrestricted walking. **Walkability:** 2. **Opened:** 1966. **Architect:** Jack Kidwell. **Season:** Year-round. **High:** April-Oct. **To obtain tee times:** Call 7 days in advance for weekends and holidays. **Miscellaneous:** Reduced fees (twilight), metal spikes, club rentals, credit cards (MC, V).
Reader Comments: Some good challenging holes ... Hard for average golfer ... Length off the tee is required ... Flat but challenging, hard in wind ... Good rural course, long, wide fairways, good driving course ... Some great holes.

THUNDERBIRD HILLS GOLF CLUB

PU-1316 Mudbrook Rd., SR 13, Huron, 44839, Erie County, (419)433-4552, 40 miles W of Cleveland.
★★★½ NORTH COURSE
Holes: 18. **Yards:** 6,464/5,993. **Par:** 72/74. **Course Rating:** 70.3/74.0. **Slope:** 109/121. **Green Fee:** $19/$21. **Cart Fee:** $12/person. **Walking Policy:** Unrestricted walking. **Walkability:** 3. **Opened:** 1960. **Architect:** Bruce Palmer. **Season:** Year-round. **High:** April-Nov. **To obtain tee times:** Call. **Miscellaneous:** Reduced fees (weekdays, low season, seniors, juniors), metal spikes, range (mats), club rentals, credit cards (MC, V, D).
Reader Comments: Great public course, good values ... Classic golf, good layout ... A challenge ... Traditional course, very well-kept, fast greens ... Lots of water, blind shots, a course to talk about ... Nice greens, good value ... Interesting ... Older established course.
★★★½ SOUTH COURSE
Holes: 18. **Yards:** 6,235/4,660. **Par:** 72/72. **Course Rating:** 68.9/65.6. **Slope:** 114/103. **Green Fee:** $20/$23. **Cart Fee:** $12/person. **Walking Policy:** Walking at certain times. **Walkability:** 3. **Opened:** 1995. **Architect:** Bruce Palmer. **Season:** April-Oct. **To obtain tee times:** Call in advance. **Miscellaneous:** Reduced fees (weekdays, seniors, juniors), metal spikes, range (mats), club rentals, credit cards (MC, V, D).
Reader Comments: New course, long and fun to play ... Wide open, relatively new course, little trouble ... Not as good as North course, needs to mature ... Great course ... Nice greens, good value ... Matured quickly into an excellent course ... Still young, needs to mature ... Stop and play, best northern Ohio course for the money.

★★★½ TREE LINKS GOLF COURSE

PU-3482 C.R. 10, Bellefontaine, 43311, Logan County, (937)592-7888, (800)215-7888, 35 miles NW of Columbus.
Holes: 18. **Yards:** 6,421/4,727. **Par:** 73/73. **Course Rating:** 70.1/66.6. **Slope:** 121/115. **Green Fee:** $35/$35. **Cart Fee:** Included in Green Fee. **Walking Policy:** Unrestricted walking.

Walkability: 5. **Opened:** 1992. **Season:** Year-round. **High:** March-Oct. **To obtain tee times:** Call 1 day in advance. **Miscellaneous:** Reduced fees (weekdays, low season, seniors, juniors), discount packages, metal spikes, range (grass), club rentals, credit cards (MC, V).
Reader Comments: Many trees, difficult ... A true diamond in the rough, lots of trees, narrow, makes you hit tough shots, fast greens ... Great price & service, challenging course ... Interesting layout makes this course worth playing. Short but tough ... Great layout, lots of potential! ... Exceptional view in fall.

TURKEYFOOT LAKE GOLF LINKS

PU-294 W. Turkeyfoot Lake Rd., Akron, 44319, Summit County, (330)644-5971, (800)281-4484, 5 miles S of Akron.
Holes: 27. **Green Fee:** $15/$28. **Cart Fee:** $22/cart. **Walking Policy:** Unrestricted walking.
Walkability: 3. **Opened:** 1925. **Architect:** Harry Smith. **Season:** March-Dec. **High:** May-Sept. **To obtain tee times:** Call for weekend tee times. **Miscellaneous:** Reduced fees (weekdays, low season, seniors, juniors), metal spikes.
★★★★ **FIRST/SECOND**
Yards: 6,168/5,190. **Par:** 71/72. **Course Rating:** 70.0/68.4. **Slope:** 116/111.
Reader Comments: Fast greens, landscaped, 3 nines ... Great greens ... Great front 9 ... Old course has charisma & good par 5s ... Beautiful, quaint, picturesque with surrounding lakes.
★★★★ **FIRST/THIRD**
Yards: 5,452/4,678. **Par:** 71/72. **Course Rating:** 66.8/61.3. **Slope:** 116/111.
★★★★ **SECOND/THIRD**
Yards: 5,122/4,322. **Par:** 70/70. **Course Rating:** 65.0/65.1. **Slope:** 116/111.

★★★½ TURNBERRY GOLF COURSE

PM-1145 Clubhouse Rd., Pickerington, 43147, Fairfield County, (614)645-2582, 12 miles E of Columbus.
Holes: 18. **Yards:** 6,757/5,440. **Par:** 72/73. **Course Rating:** 71.1/68.8. **Slope:** 114/110. **Green Fee:** $17/$24. **Cart Fee:** $10/person. **Walking Policy:** Walking at certain times. **Walkability:** N/A. **Opened:** 1991. **Architect:** Arthur Hills. **Season:** Year-round. **High:** April-Oct. **To obtain tee times:** Call 7 days in advance. **Miscellaneous:** Reduced fees (weekdays, low season, twilight, seniors, juniors), discount packages, metal spikes, range (grass), club rentals, credit cards (MC, V).
Reader Comments: Great layout, a very fun place to play ... Tough to get up & down, elevated greens ... Open, well conditioned ... Good city course.

★★ TWIN LAKES GOLF COURSE

SP-2220 Marion Ave. Rd., Mansfield, 44903, Richland County, (419)529-3777, 2 miles SW of Mansfield.
Holes: 18. **Yards:** 6,343/5,843. **Par:** 71/75. **Course Rating:** 70.0/69.8. **Slope:** N/A. **Green Fee:** $14/$17. **Cart Fee:** $10/person. **Walking Policy:** Unrestricted walking. **Walkability:** 3. **Opened:** 1960. **Architect:** Jack Kidwell. **Season:** Year-round. **High:** June-July-Aug. **To obtain tee times:** Call Pro Shop. **Miscellaneous:** Reduced fees (weekdays, low season, twilight, seniors, juniors), discount packages, metal spikes, club rentals, credit cards (MC, V), beginner friendly (junior and adult clinics).

★★½ TWIN RUN GOLF COURSE

PU-2505 Eaton Rd., Hamilton, 45013, Butler County, (513)868-5833, 15 miles NW of Cincinnati.
Holes: 18. **Yards:** 6,551/5,391. **Par:** 72/74. **Course Rating:** 70.8/69.9. **Slope:** 123/112. **Green Fee:** $17/$17. **Cart Fee:** $10/person. **Walking Policy:** Unrestricted walking. **Walkability:** 3.
Opened: 1963. **Architect:** William Diddel. **Season:** March-Dec. **High:** March-Oct. **To obtain tee times:** Call on Monday for upcoming weekend. Tee times required on weekends; open golf on weekdays. **Miscellaneous:** Reduced fees (low season, seniors, juniors), metal spikes, range (grass/mats), club rentals.
Reader Comments: Solid weekend golf at affordable price ... Decent public course ... Best service and value for the dollar ... Worth the round! ... Very open, but still fun.

VALLEY VIEW GOLF CLUB

PU-1212 Cuyahoga St., Akron, 44313, Summit County, (330)928-9034.
Holes: 27. **Green Fee:** $14/$16. **Cart Fee:** $8/. **Walking Policy:** Unrestricted walking.
Walkability: N/A. **Opened:** 1956. **Architect:** Carl Springer. **Season:** March-Nov. **High:** May-Sept. **To obtain tee times:** Call 7 days in advance. **Miscellaneous:** Reduced fees (weekdays, seniors), metal spikes.
★★★½ **RIVER/LAKES**
Yards: 6,183/5,277. **Par:** 72/72. **Course Rating:** 68.2/68.7. **Slope:** 111/115.
Reader Comments: Crowded but fun ... Rather short but fun course ... Well-kept secret ... Lakes & River 9s better than the Valley 9. Good challenge.
★★★½ **VALLEY/LAKES**
Yards: 6,168/5,464. **Par:** 72/72. **Course Rating:** 68.2/69.3. **Slope:** 109/112.
★★★½ **VALLEY/RIVER**
Yards: 6,293/5,327. **Par:** 72/72. **Course Rating:** 68.7/69.2. **Slope:** 111/114.

★★½ VALLEY VIEW GOLF COURSE
PU-1401 George Rd, Lancaster, 43130, Fairfield County, (614)687-1112, (800)281-7305, 20 miles SE of Columbus.
Holes: 18. **Yards:** 6,400. **Par:** 71. **Course Rating:** 68.9. **Slope:** 117. **Green Fee:** $15/$17. **Cart Fee:** $18/cart. **Walkability:** 3. **Opened:** 1956. **Architect:** Bill George. **Season:** Year-round. **High:** June-Sept. **To obtain tee times:** Call. **Miscellaneous:** Metal spikes, credit cards (MC, V).
Reader Comments: Nice to play ... Back 9 is fun, lots of blind shots ... Tests all clubs ... Very hilly, some long canyons ... Hilly, small greens, short but challenging and unique ... Lots of rolling hills.

★★★½ VALLEYWOOD GOLF CLUB
SP-13502 Airport Hwy., Swanton, 43558, Lucas County, (419)826-3991, 15 miles W of Toledo.
Holes: 18. **Yards:** 6,364/5,588. **Par:** 71/73. **Course Rating:** 69.6/71.6. **Slope:** 115/121. **Green Fee:** $20/$24. **Cart Fee:** $11/person. **Walking Policy:** Unrestricted walking. **Walkability:** 3. **Opened:** 1929. **Architect:** Arthur Hill. **Season:** Feb.-Dec. **High:** April-Nov. **To obtain tee times:** Call 7 days in advance. **Miscellaneous:** Reduced fees (seniors), club rentals, credit cards (MC, V, D).
Reader Comments: Challenging layout! ... Solid test, long par 4s ... Fun, interesting ... Pure golf at its best ... Nice operation ... Tough first hole, tough finishing holes ... Nice layout ... Very fair.

★★★★ THE VINEYARD GOLF COURSE *Service*
PM-600 Nordyke Rd., Cincinnati, 45255, Hamilton County, (513)474-3007, 10 miles E of Cincinnati.
Holes: 18. **Yards:** 6,789/4,747. **Par:** 71/71. **Course Rating:** 72.8/65.7. **Slope:** 132/113. **Green Fee:** $22/$26. **Cart Fee:** $12/person. **Walking Policy:** Unrestricted walking. **Walkability:** 3. **Opened:** 1987. **Architect:** Jack Kidwell/Michael Hurdzan. **Season:** March-Nov. **High:** May-Sept. **To obtain tee times:** Call 5 days in advance of play at 6 p.m. **Miscellaneous:** Reduced fees (seniors, juniors), discount packages, metal spikes, club rentals, credit cards (MC, V), beginner friendly (beginner group lessons).
Reader Comments: I'd pay it every week if I could ... Service is icing on the course ... Fair and challenging ... Treat you like an honored guest ... Great course and service ... Great for walking ... Beautiful course, best value ... Very tight, very good greens, fairways like a carpet.

WEATHERWAX GOLF COURSE
PM-5401 Mosiman Rd., Middletown, 45042, Butler County, (513)425-7886, 35 miles N of Cincinnati.
★★★½ VALLEYVIEW/HIGHLANDS COURSE
Holes: 18. **Yards:** 6,799/5,253. **Par:** 72/72. **Course Rating:** 72.4/68.8. **Slope:** 125/113. **Green Fee:** N/A/$21. **Cart Fee:** $10/person. **Walking Policy:** Unrestricted walking. **Walkability:** 2. **Opened:** 1972. **Architect:** Arthur Hills. **Season:** Year-round. **High:** April-Nov. **To obtain tee times:** Call 7 days in advance after 10 A.M. **Miscellaneous:** Reduced fees (low season, seniors, juniors), discount packages, metal spikes, range (grass), club rentals, credit cards (MC, V).
Reader Comments: Hills, beauty, challenge, wow! ... Newly refurbished, bent-grass fairways ... Great value, good condition ... Lots of holes to test your game ... Greens are wonderful. Each hole is a challenge. Very reasonably priced ... Good test, a must play.
★★★½ WOODSIDE/MEADOWS COURSE
Holes: 18. **Yards:** 7,189/5,547. **Par:** 72/72. **Course Rating:** 73.8/71.3. **Slope:** 123/114. **Green Fee:** N/A/$21. **Cart Fee:** $10/person. **Walking Policy:** Unrestricted walking. **Walkability:** 2. **Opened:** 1972. **Architect:** Arthur Hills. **Season:** Year-round. **High:** April-Nov. **To obtain tee times:** Call up to 7 days in advance for weekends and holidays after 10 a.m. **Miscellaneous:** Reduced fees (low season, seniors, juniors), discount packages, metal spikes, range (grass), club rentals, credit cards (MC, V).
Reader Comments: Probably the best value of any course I've ever played, well maintained & challenging ... Best layout around, no tricks ... The renovation is a success ... Greens are wonderful. Each hole is a challenge ... Good for all skill levels ... Great public course in the middle of nowhere. What a pleasant surprise.

★★★½ WESTCHESTER GOLF COURSE
PU-6300 Bent Grass Blvd., Canal Winchester, 43110, Franklin County, (614)834-4653, 12 miles N of Columbus.
Holes: 18. **Yards:** 6,800/5,482. **Par:** 72/72. **Course Rating:** 71.5/70.4. **Slope:** 127/121. **Green Fee:** $29/$39. **Cart Fee:** $8/person. **Walking Policy:** Walking at certain times. **Walkability:** 4. **Opened:** 1998. **Architect:** Michael Hurdzan/Dana Fry/Bill Kerman. **Season:** Feb.-Dec. **High:** April-Sept. **To obtain tee times:** Call Pro Shop. **Miscellaneous:** Reduced fees (low season, twi light), range (grass), club rentals, credit cards (MC, V), beginner friendly (junior, ladies programs).
Reader Comments: Great new track ... Uniform quality, thoroughly enjoyable experience ... New course, flat, good condition ... Still new, great greens ... This will be a dandy ... Lots of trouble yet very fair ... Excellent service, everyone smiles!

★½ WESTERN RESERVE GOLF & COUNTRY CLUB
SP-1543 Fixler Rd., Sharon Center, 44274, Medina County, (330)239-2839, 10 miles S of Cleveland.

Holes: 18. Yards: 6,239/4,599. Par: 71/72. Course Rating: 73.6/72.5. Slope: 124/109. Green Fee: $14/$19. Cart Fee: $20/cart. Walking Policy: Unrestricted walking. Walkability: 2. Opened: 1964. Architect: Timmy Thompson. Season: Year-round. High: Aug.-Oct. To obtain tee times: Call. Miscellaneous: Reduced fees (weekdays, low season, twilight, seniors, juniors), discount packages, metal spikes, club rentals.

★½   WESTERN ROW GOLF COURSE
PU-7392 Mason-Montgomery Rd., Mason, 45040, Warren County, (513)398-8886, 19 miles N of Cincinnati.
Holes: 18. Yards: 6,746/5,701. Par: 72/72. Course Rating: 71.4/71.2. Slope: 121/120. Green Fee: n/A/$17. Cart Fee: $18/cart. Walking Policy: Unrestricted walking. Walkability: 1. Opened: 1963. Architect: William Diddel. Season: Year-round. High: April-Oct. To obtain tee times: First come, first served. Miscellaneous: Reduced fees (low season, twilight, seniors, juniors), metal spikes, club rentals, credit cards (MC, V, D).

★★★   WHETSTONE GOLF & SWIM CLUB
PU-5211 Marion Mt. Gilead Rd., Caledonia, 43314, Marion County, (740)389-4343, (800)272-3215, 6 miles NE of Marion.
Holes: 18. Yards: 6,674/5,023. Par: 72/72. Course Rating: 71.7/73.6. Slope: 120/111. Green Fee: $12/$15. Cart Fee: $21. Walking Policy: Unrestricted walking. Walkability: N/A. Opened: 1971. Architect: Dick LaConte. Season: April-Oct. To obtain tee times: Call 7 days in advance. Miscellaneous: Reduced fees (weekdays, seniors), metal spikes, range (grass), credit cards (MC, V, AE). Reader Comments: Greens are very good ... Wide open fairways ... Long course, flat ... Some tough holes ... Fun and challenging ... Some difficult holes, but you can score. An enjoyable round ... Better than average.

★★   WILLANDALE GOLF CLUB
PU-2870 Winklepleck Rd., Sugarcreek, 44681, Tuscarawas County, (330)852-4395, 8 miles W of New Philadelphia.
Holes: 18. Yards: 6,200/6,006. Par: 72/72. Course Rating: 67.4/66.4. Slope: 107/100. Green Fee: $13/$13. Cart Fee: $10/person. Walking Policy: Unrestricted walking. Walkability: 2. Opened: 1929. Season: Year-round. High: May-Oct. To obtain tee times: Call golf shop. Miscellaneous: Reduced fees (weekdays, low season, seniors), discount packages, range (grass/mats), club rentals, credit cards (MC, V, AE, Debit card.).
Special Notes: New Clubhouse, restaurant & golf shop opened June 1999.

★★   WILLOW CREEK GOLF CLUB
PU-15905 Darrow Rd., Vermilion, 44089, Erie County, (440)967-4101, 40 miles W of Cleveland.
Holes: 18. Yards: 6,356/5,419. Par: 72/76. Course Rating: 68.0/68.0. Slope: 108/111. Green Fee: $15/$18. Cart Fee: $9/person. Walking Policy: Unrestricted walking. Walkability: 1. Opened: 1948. Architect: Dick Palmer. Season: March-Dec. High: April-Sept. To obtain tee times: Call 7 days in advance for upcoming weekend. Miscellaneous: Reduced fees (weekdays, low season, seniors), discount packages, metal spikes, range (grass), club rentals. Notes: P.G.A. Player Ability Test held yearly.

★★½   WILLOW RUN GOLF COURSE
PU-State Rtes. 310 and 161, Pataskala, 43001, Licking County, (740)927-1932.
Special Notes: Call club for further information.

★★★★   WINDMILL LAKES GOLF CLUB   *Condition*
PU-6544 State Rte. 14, Ravenna, 44266, Portage County, (330)297-0440, 30 miles SE of Cleveland.
Holes: 18. Yards: 6,936/5,368. Par: 70/70. Course Rating: 73.8/70.4. Slope: 128/115. Green Fee: $23/$48. Cart Fee: $10/person. Walking Policy: Walking at certain times. Walkability: 1. Opened: 1971. Architect: Edward Ault Sr. Season: March-Nov. High: May-Sept. To obtain tee times: Call 2 days in advance, or up to 2 days in advance with credit card to guarantee. Miscellaneous: Reduced fees (low season, twilight, seniors, juniors), range (grass/mats), club rentals, credit cards (MC, V). Reader Comments: Great layout, very tough ... You'll need your long irons here ... Expensive, but worth it ... Bring your A game or you'll walk away with an F on your card ... True greens, long, worth playing ... Very tight fairways, average-size greens, very nice course ... Tee-to-green in excellent condition.

★★★½   WOODLAND GOLF CLUB
PU-4900 Swisher Rd., Cable, 43009, Champaign County, (937)653-8875, (888)395-2001, 36 miles NW of Columbus.
Holes: 18. Yards: 6,473/4,886. Par: 71/71. Course Rating: 70.3/67.7. Slope: 123/119. Green Fee: $19/$22. Cart Fee: $11/person. Walking Policy: Unrestricted walking. Walkability: 5. Opened: 1972. Architect: Jack Kidwell. Season: Year-round. High: April-Oct. To obtain tee

times: Call ahead anytime. **Miscellaneous:** Reduced fees (low season, seniors, juniors), range (grass), club rentals, credit cards (MC, V, D).
Reader Comments: Some short holes that detract ... True to its name ... Ride don't walk! Long! Real tester!.

★★★ THE WOODS GOLF CLUB

PU-12083 U.S. 127 S., Van Wert, 45891, Van Wert County, (419)238-0441, 40 miles E of Ft. Wayne.
Holes: 18. **Yards:** 6,775/5,025. **Par:** 72/72. **Course Rating:** 70.4/70.4. **Slope:** 118/116. **Green Fee:** $14/$16. **Cart Fee:** $9/person. **Walking Policy:** Unrestricted walking. **Walkability:** 1.
Opened: 1962. **Architect:** William Spear. **Season:** March-Dec. **High:** May-Sept. **To obtain tee times:** Call on Monday for upcoming weekend. **Miscellaneous:** Range (grass/mats), club rentals, credit cards (MC, V).
Reader Comments: Lots of play.

★★ WOOLDRIDGE WOODS GOLF AND SWIM CLUB

SP-1313 S. Main St., Mansfield, 44907, Richland County, (419)756-1026, 60 miles N of Columbus.
Holes: 18. **Yards:** 5,963/5,089. **Par:** 71/71. **Course Rating:** 67.2/68.4. **Slope:** 105/105. **Green Fee:** $14/$17. **Cart Fee:** $10/person. **Walking Policy:** Unrestricted walking. **Walkability:** 3.
Opened: 1924. **Season:** Year-round. **High:** June-July-Aug. **To obtain tee times:** Call Pro Shop.
Miscellaneous: Reduced fees (weekdays, low season, twilight, seniors, juniors), discount packages, metal spikes, range (grass/mats), club rentals, credit cards (MC, V), beginner friendly (junior and adult clinics).
Special Notes: Formerly Possum Run Golf Club; Woodridge Golf & Swim Club.

WOUSSICKETT GOLF COURSE

PU-6311 Mason Road, Sandusky, 44870, Erie County, (419)359-1141, (800)950-4766, 60 miles W of Cleveland. **Web:** www.greenhillsgolf.com.
Holes: 18. **Yards:** 5,992/4,916. **Par:** 70/71. **Course Rating:** 66.6/67.6. **Slope:** 98/101. **Green Fee:** $9/$20. **Cart Fee:** $20/cart. **Walking Policy:** Walking at certain times. **Walkability:** 3.
Opened: 1984. **Architect:** T.Crockett/B.Crockett. **Season:** March-Nov. **High:** June-Aug. **To obtain tee times:** Call up to 7 days in advance. **Miscellaneous:** Reduced fees (weekdays, low season), range (grass), club rentals, credit cards (MC, V, D), beginner friendly.

★★ WYANDOT GOLF COURSE

SP-3032 Columbus Rd., Centerburg, 43011, Knox County, (740)625-5370, (800)986-4653, 25 miles N of Columbus.
Holes: 18. **Yards:** 6,422/5,486. **Par:** 72/72. **Course Rating:** 68.4/70.3. **Slope:** 113/115. **Green Fee:** $14/$19. **Cart Fee:** $11/person. **Walking Policy:** Unrestricted walking. **Walkability:** 1.
Opened: 1978. **Architect:** Noah Salyers. **Season:** Year-round. **High:** April-Oct. **To obtain tee times:** Call golf shop. **Miscellaneous:** Reduced fees (weekdays, low season, seniors), metal spikes, club rentals, credit cards (MC, V, AE, D).

★★★★ YANKEE RUN GOLF COURSE

PU-7610 Warren Sharon Rd., Brookfield, 44403, Trumbull County, (330)448-8096, (800)446-5346, 60 miles NW of Pittsburgh, PA. **E-mail:** kmcmul3492.com. **Web:** www.yankeerun.com.
Holes: 18. **Yards:** 6,501/5,140. **Par:** 70/73. **Course Rating:** 70.7/69.0. **Slope:** 119/109. **Green Fee:** $22/$25. **Cart Fee:** $9/person. **Walking Policy:** Unrestricted walking. **Walkability:** 4.
Opened: 1931. **Architect:** Bill Jones/Jerry Mathews. **Season:** March-Nov. **High:** May-Sept. **To obtain tee times:** Call anytime in advance with credit card. **Miscellaneous:** Reduced fees (weekdays, low season, seniors, juniors), discount packages, club rentals, credit cards (MC, V, AE, D).
Reader Comments: Real value ... Longest 6,500 yards I ever played ... Fairways & greens are great ... Gorgeous views ... Best around ... Short but tough! ... Fast paced course up and down tees to greens ... Worth the trip ... Very strong par 3s. Tough pins can make course come alive ... Solid. Better than advertised.

★★★★ ZOAR VILLAGE GOLF CLUB

PU-P.O. Box 647, Zoar, 44697, Tuscarawas County, (330)874-4653, (888)874-4654, 1 miles S of Zoar.
Holes: 18. **Yards:** 6,535/5,235. **Par:** 72/72. **Course Rating:** 70.7/69.7. **Slope:** 117/115. **Green Fee:** $22/$24. **Cart Fee:** $20/cart. **Walking Policy:** Walking at certain times. **Walkability:** 2.
Opened: 1975. **Architect:** Geoffrey Cornish. **Season:** March-Dec. **High:** July-Aug. **To obtain tee times:** Call up to 10 months in advance. **Miscellaneous:** Reduced fees (weekdays, seniors), discount packages, range (grass), club rentals, credit cards (MC, V).
Reader Comments: A gem hidden away ... Undulating, well-kept greens ... Greens very fast ... Take good care of golfers ... Good value ... A good test ... Nice clubhouse. Very good service ... Always in good condition ... Course is getting tougher & I'm getting older ... Fair layout and price. Usually in good shape.

★★½ ADAMS MUNICIPAL GOLF COURSE
PM-5801 E. Tuxedo Blvd., Bartlesville, 74006, Washington County, (918)337-5313, 45 miles N of Tulsa.
Holes: 18. **Yards:** 6,819/5,655. **Par:** 72/74. **Course Rating:** 72.0/71.8. **Slope:** 119/117. **Green Fee:** $15/$15. **Cart Fee:** $16/cart. **Walking Policy:** Unrestricted walking. **Walkability:** N/A. **Opened:** 1963. **Architect:** Floyd Farley. **Season:** Year-round. **High:** March-Oct. **To obtain tee times:** Come in person one week in advance for weekdays. For weekend play call five days in advance. **Miscellaneous:** Reduced fees (weekdays, twilight, seniors, juniors), metal spikes, range (grass), club rentals.
Reader Comments: Nice clean ... Municipal course, well maintained, back 9 will surprise you. Tough! ... Good track bargain green fees.

ALVA GOLF & COUNTRY CLUB
SP-P O BOX 42, Alva, 73717, (580)327-2296, 85 miles W. of Ponca City.
Special Notes: Call club for further information.

★★★½ ARROWHEAD GOLF COURSE
PU-HC-67, Box 6, Canadian, 74425, Pittsburg County, (918)339-2769, 20 miles N of McAlester.
Holes: 18. **Yards:** 6,741/5,342. **Par:** 72/75. **Course Rating:** 71.4/N/A. **Slope:** 119/N/A. **Green Fee:** $9/$11. **Cart Fee:** $8/person. **Walking Policy:** Unrestricted walking. **Walkability:** N/A. **Opened:** 1965. **Architect:** Floyd Farley. **Season:** Year-round. **High:** April-Sept. **To obtain tee times:** Call one week in advance. **Miscellaneous:** Reduced fees (weekdays, low season, twilight, seniors, juniors), discount packages, metal spikes, range (grass), club rentals, lodging, credit cards (MC, V, D).
Reader Comments: Nice course ... Variety of holes ... Beautiful vistas, deer, etc ... Tight course, with deer and panoramic views ... Good doglegs, lots of trees, nice greens, I'd pay to play again ... This course even in the summer was very well watered. Also the golf pro was very helpful in getting lessons and buying equipment ... A beautiful course in the trees.

ATOKA TRAILS GOLF CLUB
PU-220 City Lake Road, Atoka, 74525, Atoka County, (405)889-7171, 2 miles W of Atoka. **E-mail:** dcochran@010.net.
Holes: 9. **Yards:** 6,233/2,479. **Par:** 72/72. **Course Rating:** 68.5/68.5. **Slope:** 109/109. **Green Fee:** $7/$14. **Cart Fee:** $14/cart. **Walking Policy:** Unrestricted walking. **Walkability:** 3. **Opened:** 1971. **Season:** Year-round. **High:** March-Sept. **To obtain tee times:** No tee times. **Miscellaneous:** Reduced fees (twilight), range (grass), club rentals, beginner friendly (clinics). **Special Notes:** Formerly Atoka Golf Course

★★★★ BAILEY RANCH GOLF CLUB
PU-10105 Larkin Bailey Blvd., Owasso, 74055, Tulsa County, (918)272-9339, 8 miles N of Tulsa.
Holes: 18. **Yards:** 6,753/4,898. **Par:** 72/72. **Course Rating:** 73.1/68.4. **Slope:** 132/115. **Green Fee:** $15/$23. **Cart Fee:** $10/person. **Walking Policy:** Walking at certain times. **Walkability:** 3. **Opened:** 1993. **Architect:** Bland Pittman. **Season:** Year-round. **High:** April-Oct. **To obtain tee times:** Call shop shop 8 days in advance beginning at 11:00 a.m. **Miscellaneous:** Reduced fees (weekdays, low season, twilight, seniors, juniors), range (grass), club rentals, credit cards (MC, V, AE, D), beginner friendly (beginner and junior clinics).
Reader Comments: Good course, worth the money ... Tough greens, a real challenge ... Good layout, risk and reward course ... Very challenging course to play ... Links-style course ... Best affordable golf in Oklahoma ... Excellent and difficult.

★★★½ BATTLE CREEK GOLF CLUB
PM-3200 N. Battle Creek Dr., Broken Arrow, 74012, Tulsa County, (918)259-8633, 5 miles E of Tulsa.
Holes: 18. **Yards:** 7,273/5,580. **Par:** 72/72. **Course Rating:** 76.4/69.8. **Slope:** 130/118. **Green Fee:** $17/$46. **Cart Fee:** $11/person. **Walking Policy:** Walking at certain times. **Walkability:** 5. **Opened:** 1997. **Architect:** Bland Pittman. **Season:** Year-round. **High:** May-Sept. **To obtain tee times:** Call golf shop. **Miscellaneous:** Reduced fees (weekdays, low season, resort guests, twilight, seniors, juniors), range (grass), credit cards (MC, V, AE, D).
Reader Comments: Tough course, great ... Computerized carts–awesome ... Staff super ... 94 sand traps ... Beautiful course to play. Great greens. Great layout ... Outstanding new course.

BLACKWELL GOLF COURSE
PU-Rte. 2, Blackwell, 74631, Kay County, (580)363-1228, 10 miles NW of Ponca City.
Special Notes: Call club for further information.

★★★½ BOILING SPRINGS GOLF CLUB
PU-R.R. 2 Box 204-1A, Woodward, 73801, Woodward County, (580)256-1206, 130 miles NW of Oklahoma City.
Holes: 18. **Yards:** 6,511/4,944. **Par:** 71/75. **Course Rating:** 71.3/68.6. **Slope:** 120/117. **Green Fee:** $12/$25. **Cart Fee:** $15/person. **Walking Policy:** Unrestricted walking. **Walkability:** 4.

OKLAHOMA

Opened: 1979. **Architect:** Don Sechrest. **Season:** Year-round. **High:** April-Oct. **To obtain tee times:** Tee times required. **Miscellaneous:** Reduced fees (weekdays, seniors, juniors), range (grass), club rentals, credit cards (MC, V, AE, D).
Reader Comments: Very challenging–trees, terrain, enjoyable layout ... Fun layout with good greens ... Interesting layout, really enjoyed. Neat elevation changes ... Beautiful, you wouldn't believe you're in western Oklahoma ... Augusta on the great plains .... A hidden masterpiece.

BRENT BRUEHL MEMORIAL GOLF COURSE
PU-1400 Airport Rd., Purcell, 73080, (405)527-5114, 30 miles S of Oklahoma City.
Holes: 18. **Yards:** 6,318/5,234. **Par:** 71/71. **Course Rating:** 70.1/69.8. **Slope:** 119/114. **Green Fee:** $10/$15. **Walkability:** 3.
Special Notes: Call club for further information.

BRISTOW COUNTRY CLUB
SP-Country Club Dr., Bristow, 74010, Creek County, (918)367-5156.
Holes: 9. **Yards:** 6,247/5,343. **Par:** 72/73. **Course Rating:** 68.6/70.8. **Slope:** 111/122. **Green Fee:** $10/$14. **Cart Fee:** $18/cart. **Walking Policy:** Unrestricted walking. **Walkability:** 3.
Season: Year-round. **High:** May-Sept. **To obtain tee times:** Call (918)367-5156.
Miscellaneous: Reduced fees (weekdays, twilight), range (grass), credit cards (MC, V, D).
Special Notes: Two sets of tees.

BROADMOORE GOLF COURSE
PU-500 Willow Pine Dr., Oklahoma City, 73160, (405)794-1529.
Special Notes: Call club for further information.

BROOKSIDE GOLF COURSE
PU-9016 S. Shields, Oklahoma City, 73160, (405)632-9666.
Special Notes: Call club for further information.

★★★★ CEDAR CREEK GOLF COURSE *Value*
R-P.O. Box 10, Broken Bow, 74728, McCurtain County, (580)494-6456, 60 miles NE of Paris, TX.
Holes: 18. **Yards:** 6,724/5,762. **Par:** 72/72. **Course Rating:** 72.1/N/A. **Slope:** 132/N/A. **Green Fee:** $15/$20. **Cart Fee:** $18/cart. **Walking Policy:** Unrestricted walking. **Walkability:** 5.
Opened: 1975. **Architect:** Floyd Farley/Art Proctor. **Season:** Year-round. **High:** April-Oct. **To obtain tee times:** Call at least 7 days in advance. **Miscellaneous:** Reduced fees (weekdays, low season, resort guests, twilight, seniors, juniors), discount packages, metal spikes, range (grass), club rentals, lodging, credit cards (MC, V, D), beginner friendly.
Reader Comments: Good layout, worth money ... A very well-kept secret–hidden in the mountains of SE Oklahoma, a gem ... Beautiful course–deer ran across the fairway ... Extremely tight; leave driver at home ... Course is the 'Augusta' of Oklahoma.... Beautiful setting–challenging holes abound... Scenic, hidden secret.

CEDAR LAKES GOLF COURSE
4746 Monrovia St., Fort Sill, 73503, (580)353-8569 .
Holes: 18. **Yards:** 6,725/5,477. **Par:** 72/72. **Course Rating:** 71.8/71/1. **Slope:** 123/123. **Green Fee:** $6.00/$18.00. **Walkability:** 4.

CEDAR VALLEY GOLF CLUB
PU-210 Par Ave., Guthrie, 73044, Logan County, (405)282-4800, 25 miles N of Oklahoma City.
★★★½ AUGUSTA COURSE
Holes: 18. **Yards:** 6,602/5,170. **Par:** 70/72. **Course Rating:** 70.3/69.1. **Slope:** 108/117. **Green Fee:** $13/$15. **Cart Fee:** $16/person. **Walking Policy:** Unrestricted walking. **Walkability:** 4.
Opened: 1975. **Architect:** Duffy Martin/Floyd Farley. **Season:** Year-round. **High:** May-Aug.-Sept. **To obtain tee times:** Call 1 day in advance for weekdays. Call 7 days in advance for weekends.
Miscellaneous: Reduced fees (weekdays, seniors, juniors), range (grass), club rentals, credit cards (MC, V, AE, D), beginner friendly (ladies, junior clinics).
Reader Comments: I have only been playing 3 years. This was one of the most enjoyable rounds. Very friendly people. Challenging course. Great day of golf ... Short, no traps, fun ... Very well laid out. Nice landscaping.
★★½ INTERNATIONAL COURSE
Holes: 18. **Yards:** 6,520/4,955. **Par:** 70/72. **Course Rating:** 71.1/68.4. **Slope:** 112/115. **Green Fee:** $13/$15. **Cart Fee:** $16/person. **Walking Policy:** Unrestricted walking. **Walkability:** 3.
Opened: 1974. **Architect:** Duffy Martin/Floyd Farley. **Season:** Year-round. **High:** May-Aug.-Sept. **To obtain tee times:** Call one day in advance for weekdays. Call seven days in advance for weekends. **Miscellaneous:** Reduced fees (weekdays, seniors, juniors), range (grass), club rentals, credit cards (MC, V, AE, D), beginner friendly (ladies, junior clinics).
Reader Comments: Good beginner course ... Wide open, good water holes ... Playable yet challenging.

CHANDLER GOLF COURSE
PU-Rte. 2, Box 231, Chandler, 74834, Lincoln County, (405)258-3068.

Holes: 9. **Yards:** 6,364/5,026. **Par:** 72/76. **Course Rating:** 69.7/69.7. **Slope:** 111/111. **Green Fee:** $10/$12. **Cart Fee:** $16/cart. **Walking Policy:** Unrestricted walking. **Walkability:** 5. **Opened:** 1972. **Season:** Year-round. **High:** May-Aug. **To obtain tee times:** Call golf shop. **Miscellaneous:** Reduced fees (weekdays, twilight, juniors), range (grass), club rentals, beginner friendly.

CHEROKEE GROVE GOLF CLUB
PU-519 Quail Run Rd., Grove, 74344, Delaware County, (918)786-9852, 45 miles S of Joplin, MO.
Holes: 9. **Yards:** 3,240/2,657. **Par:** 36/36. **Course Rating:** 70.7/69.2. **Slope:** 128/109. **Green Fee:** $18/$18. **Cart Fee:** $20/cart. **Walking Policy:** Unrestricted walking. **Walkability:** 4. **Opened:** 1979. **Architect:** Vince Bizik. **Season:** Year-round. **High:** April-Oct. **To obtain tee times:** First come, first served. No tee times required. **Miscellaneous:** Range (grass), club rentals, credit cards (MC, V).

CHEROKEE TRAILS GOLF COURSE
PU-S. Hwy. 62, Tahlequah, 74465, Cherokee County, (918)458-4294, 60 miles E of Tulsa.
Holes: 9. **Yards:** 6,460/5,300. **Par:** 72/72. **Course Rating:** 71.2/69.8. **Slope:** 121/117. **Green Fee:** $5/$10. **Cart Fee:** $15/cart. **Walking Policy:** Unrestricted walking. **Walkability:** 1. **Opened:** 1954. **Architect:** Amon Baker. **Season:** Year-round. **High:** June-Sept. **To obtain tee times:** First come, first served. **Miscellaneous:** Reduced fees (low season, twilight, seniors, juniors), discount packages, range (grass), club rentals, credit cards (MC, V), beginner friendly (clinics).
Special Notes: Formerly known as Sequoyah Golf Course

CHERRY SPRINGS GOLF COURSE
PU-700 E. Balentine Rd., Tahlequah, 74464, (918)456-5100, 55 miles SE of Tulsa.
Holes: 18. **Yards:** 6,814/4,950. **Par:** 72/72. **Course Rating:** 72.8/63.9. **Slope:** 127/99. **Green Fee:** $14.00/$16.00. **Walkability:** 4. **Architect:** Burl Berry.
Special Notes: Call club for further information.

CHOCTAW CREEK GOLF COURSE
PU-2200 N. Hiwassee Rd., Choctaw, 73020, Oklahoma County, (405)769-7166, 8 miles E of Oklahoma City.
Holes: 18. **Yards:** 6,400/5,200. **Par:** 71/74. **Course Rating:** 70.6/71.1. **Slope:** 122/123. **Green Fee:** $8/$14. **Cart Fee:** $17/cart. **Walking Policy:** Unrestricted walking. **Walkability:** 3. **Opened:** 1989. **Architect:** Tom Billings. **Season:** Year-round. **High:** April-Oct. **To obtain tee times:** For weekend tee times call 1 week in advance. For weekday tee times call 1 day in advance. **Miscellaneous:** Reduced fees (weekdays, twilight, seniors, juniors), range (grass/mats), club rentals, credit cards (MC, V, D).

CIMARRON NATIONAL GOLF CLUB
PU-500 Duffy's Way, Guthrie, 73044, Logan County, (405)282-7888, 20 miles N of Oklahoma City.
★★★ **AQUA CANYON COURSE**
Holes: 18. **Yards:** 6,415/5,339. **Par:** 70/71. **Course Rating:** 69.6/68.2. **Slope:** 114/110. **Green Fee:** $14/$16. **Cart Fee:** $18/cart. **Walking Policy:** Unrestricted walking. **Walkability:** 4. **Opened:** 1994. **Architect:** Floyd Farley. **Season:** Year-round. **High:** April-Sept. **To obtain tee times:** Call one day in advance for weekdays. Call one week in advance for weekends and holidays. **Miscellaneous:** Reduced fees (weekdays), range (grass), club rentals, credit cards (MC, V, AE, D).
Reader Comments: Fun course ... Excellent design ... These folks treat you right! All employees great! ... One of the best courses in Oklahoma ... Beautiful course, great golf atmosphere.

★★★ **CIMARRON COURSE**
Holes: 18. **Yards:** 6,653/5,559. **Par:** 70/70. **Course Rating:** 68.1/72.8. **Slope:** 120/132. **Green Fee:** $14/$16. **Cart Fee:** $18/cart. **Walking Policy:** Walking at certain times. **Walkability:** 5. **Opened:** 1992. **Architect:** Floyd Farley. **Season:** Year-round. **High:** May-Sept. **To obtain tee times:** Call one day in advance for weekdays. Call one week in advance for weekends and holidays. **Miscellaneous:** Reduced fees (weekdays), range (grass), club rentals, credit cards (MC, V, AE, D).
Reader Comments: Good all round course, no sand ... Best course under $35.00 in the area and also most challenging, bring 2 sleeves ... Lots of water ... I found it a fun course to play.

★★★★ **COFFEE CREEK GOLF COURSE**
PU-4000 N. Kelly, Edmond, 73003, Oklahoma County, (405)340-4653, 8 miles N of Oklahoma City.
Holes: 18. **Yards:** 6,700/5,200. **Par:** 70/70. **Course Rating:** 71.5/70.5. **Slope:** 129/122. **Green Fee:** $20/$25. **Cart Fee:** $12/person. **Walking Policy:** Unrestricted walking. **Walkability:** 3. **Opened:** 1991. **Season:** Year-round. **High:** May-Sept. **To obtain tee times:** Call seven days in advance for weekdays. Monday beginning at 7:15 A.M. for upcoming weekend. **Miscellaneous:** Reduced fees (weekdays, twilight, seniors, juniors), range (grass), club rentals, credit cards (MC, V, AE, D).
Reader Comments: Nice layout, great pace of play ... Enjoyable ... Very nice course, like a resort course ... Requires all shots, helpful staff ... Beautifully conditioned ... Excellent maintenance! ... Has some great holes for a muny ... Hands down the BEST public course in Oklahoma!

COMANCHE GOLF COURSE
PU-HC 64, Comanche, 73529, (770)439-8879.
Special Notes: Call club for further information.

CRIMSON CREEK GOLF CLUB
PU-800 Babcock Dr., El Reno, 73036, Canadian County, (405)422-4653, 25 miles W of Oklahoma City. **E-mail:** dormie1@aol.com. **Web:** www.crimsoncreek.com.
Holes: 18. **Yards:** 6,992/5,491. **Par:** 72/72. **Course Rating:** 74.2/73.5. **Slope:** 128/132. **Green Fee:** $16/$19. **Cart Fee:** $9/person. **Walking Policy:** Unrestricted walking. **Walkability:** 4. **Opened:** 1998. **Architect:** P.B. Dye. **Season:** Year-round. **High:** May-Sept. **To obtain tee times:** Call golf shop 3 days in advance at 7:00 A.M. **Miscellaneous:** Reduced fees (weekdays, twilight, seniors, juniors), range (grass), club rentals, credit cards (MC, V).
Special Notes: Formerly El Reno Golf & Country Club

CUSHING GOLF COURSE
SP-Cushing, 74023, (918)225-6734.
Holes: 18. **Yards:** 6,292/5,260. **Par:** 70/70. **Course Rating:** 69.5/68.9. **Slope:** 115/99. **Green Fee:** $21/$35. **Walkability:** 3. **Architect:** Perry Maxwell.
Special Notes: Call club for further information.

DIETRICH MEMORIAL GOLF COURSE
SP-South Country Club Rd., Andarko, 73005, (405)247-5075, 60 miles SW of Oklahoma City.
Special Notes: Call club for further information.

DOBY SPRINGS GOLF COURSE
PU-70 Doby Springs Rd., Buffalo, 73834, (580)735-2654.
Holes: 18. **Yards:** 3,068/2,465. **Par:** 36/37. **Course Rating:** N/A. **Slope:** 112/108. **Green Fee:** $6/$6. **Walkability:** 2.
Special Notes: Call club for further information.

DRUMRIGHT GOLF COURSE
PU-Hwy 33, Drumright, 74030, (918)352-9424.
Holes: 9. **Yards:** 6,280/5,248. **Par:** 72/72. **Course Rating:** 69.3. **Slope:** 109. **Green Fee:** $8/$10. **Walkability:** 3.
Special Notes: Call club for further information.

DUNCAN GOLF & COUNTRY CLUB
SP-1800 North 10, Duncan, 73533, Stephens County, (405)255-7706.
Holes: 18. **Yards:** 6,450/5,397. **Par:** 71/71. **Course Rating:** 71.6/71/8. **Slope:** 124/125. **Green Fee:** $20/$20. **Walkability:** N/A.
Special Notes: Call club for further information.

EAGLE CREST GOLF COURSE
PU-40th & Border, Muskogee, 74401, Muskogee County, (918)682-0866.
Holes: 18. **Yards:** 6,506/4,517. **Par:** 72/72. **Course Rating:** 69.7/66.8. **Slope:** 119/112. **Green Fee:** $15/$18. **Cart Fee:** $20/cart. **Walking Policy:** Unrestricted walking. **Walkability:** 3. **Opened:** 1987. **Season:** Year-round. **High:** April-Nov. **To obtain tee times:** Call for Tee Times weekends only. **Miscellaneous:** Reduced fees (weekdays, low season, twilight, seniors, juniors), range (grass), club rentals, credit cards (MC, V, AE, D), beginner friendly (9-hole Village Course).

EARLYWINE PARK GOLF COURSE
PM-11500 S. Portland Ave., Oklahoma City, 73170, Oklahoma County, (405)691-1727.
★★★★ **NORTH COURSE**
Holes: 18. **Yards:** 6,721/4,843. **Par:** 72/72. **Course Rating:** 71.9/70.4. **Slope:** 126/122. **Green Fee:** $14/$14. **Cart Fee:** $16/person. **Walking Policy:** Unrestricted walking. **Walkability:** 4. **Opened:** 1977. **Architect:** Randy Heckenkemper. **Season:** Year-round. **High:** March-Nov. **To obtain tee times:** Call one day in advance for weekdays and for weekends call the previous weekend. **Miscellaneous:** Reduced fees (weekdays, low season, twilight, seniors, juniors), range (grass), club rentals, credit cards (MC, V), beginner friendly.
Reader Comments: Excellent greens ... Great links-style layout along lake ... A real pleasure ... One of the best muny course designs in OKC ... Excellent public course ... Picturesque, fun.
★★½ **SOUTH COURSE**
Holes: 18. **Yards:** 6,728/5,388. **Par:** 71/71. **Course Rating:** 69.5/71.6. **Slope:** 107/117. **Green Fee:** $14/$14. **Cart Fee:** $16/person. **Walking Policy:** Unrestricted walking. **Walkability:** 2. **Opened:** 1976. **Architect:** Floyd Farley. **Season:** Year-round. **High:** March-Nov. **To obtain tee times:** Call one day in advance for weekdays and for weekends call the previous weekend. **Miscellaneous:** Reduced fees (weekdays, low season, twilight, seniors, juniors), range (grass), club rentals, credit cards (MC, V), beginner friendly.
Reader Comments: Older course ...Tough tight course ... Nice course ... Fun, challenging.

OKLAHOMA

EAST LAKE HILLS RESORT GOLF COURSE
R-Rte. 1, Vian, 74962, (918)773-8436.
Holes: 18. **Yards:** 6,455/5,538. **Par:** 72/74. **Course Rating:** 69.8/74. **Slope:** 117/120. **Green Fee:** N/A. **Walkability:** 3.
Special Notes: Call club for further information.

★★★ ELK CITY GOLF & COUNTRY CLUB
SP-108 Lakeridge Rd., Elk City, 73644, Beckham County, (405)225-3556, 1 miles S of Elk City.
Holes: 18. **Yards:** 6,208/4,678. **Par:** 71/71. **Course Rating:** 68.9/65.9. **Slope:** 106/98. **Green Fee:** $10/$18. **Cart Fee:** $18/cart. **Walking Policy:** Unrestricted walking. **Walkability:** 2.
Opened: 1954. **Architect:** Bob Dunning/Don Sechrest. **Season:** Year-round. **High:** May-Oct. **To obtain tee times:** Call golf shop. **Miscellaneous:** Reduced fees (weekdays, twilight), range (grass), club rentals, beginner friendly (lessons).
Reader Comments: Fun course ... Two nines completely different ... A variety of interesting holes.

FAIRVIEW LAKESIDE COUNTRY CLUB
SP-Longdale St., Longdale, 73755, (405)227-3225.
Holes: 18. **Yards:** 3,126/2,623. **Par:** 35/35. **Course Rating:** 67.0/67.7. **Slope:** N/A. **Green Fee:** N/A. **Walkability:** N/A.
Special Notes: Call club for further information.

★★½ FALCONHEAD RESORT & COUNTRY CLUB
SP-605 Falconhead Dr., Burneyville, 73430, Love County, (580)276-9284, 25 miles SW of Ardmore. **E-mail:** fpoa@brightok.net. **Web:** www.redriver.net/falconhead.
Holes: 18. **Yards:** 6,404/5,280. **Par:** 72/71. **Course Rating:** 70.2/70.3. **Slope:** 125/120. **Green Fee:** $25/$35. **Cart Fee:** Included in Green Fee. **Walking Policy:** Mandatory cart. **Walkability:** 3. **Opened:** 1960. **Architect:** Waco Turner. **Season:** Year-round. **High:** April-Oct. **To obtain tee times:** Call 1 day in advance. **Miscellaneous:** Reduced fees (resort guests, seniors, juniors), discount packages, range (grass), club rentals, lodging (16 rooms), credit cards (MC, V, AE, D).
Reader Comments: A challenge ... Home of the Waco Turner Open PGA tour... Great fast greens, flat front ... Beautiful design; tough long par 4s, clubhouse neat ... Good golf with great atmosphere, great people.

★★★½ FIRE LAKE GOLF COURSE
PU-1901 S. Gordon Cooper, Shawnee, 74801, Pottawatomie County, (405)275-4471, 30 miles E of Oklahoma City. **E-mail:** mwood@potawatomi.org. **Web:** support.potawatomi.org.
Holes: 18. **Yards:** 6,335/4,992. **Par:** 70/71. **Course Rating:** 69.6/N/A. **Slope:** 121/N/A. **Green Fee:** $8/$14. **Cart Fee:** $18/person. **Walking Policy:** Unrestricted walking. **Walkability:** 2.
Opened: 1982. **Architect:** Don Sechrest. **Season:** Year-round. **High:** March-Sept. **To obtain tee times:** Call 7 days in advance. **Miscellaneous:** Reduced fees (twilight, seniors, juniors), metal spikes, range (grass), club rentals, credit cards (MC, V, D).
Reader Comments: Lots of water but fun to play ... Great layout ... Original 9 holes are really good test ... Very pretty, lots of water ... Good use of land.

★★★★ FOREST RIDGE GOLF CLUB *Condition+*
SP-7501 E. Kenosha, Broken Arrow, 74014, Wagoner County, (918)357-2282, 12 miles SE of Tulsa. **E-mail:** marketing@forestridge.com. **Web:** www.forestridge.com.
Holes: 18. **Yards:** 7,069/5,341. **Par:** 71/72. **Course Rating:** 74.8/73.3. **Slope:** 137/132. **Green Fee:** $30/$75. **Cart Fee:** Included in Green Fee. **Walking Policy:** Unrestricted walking. **Walkability:** 3. **Opened:** 1989. **Architect:** Randy Heckenkemper. **Season:** Year-round. **High:** March-Oct. **To obtain tee times:** Call four days in advance. **Miscellaneous:** Reduced fees (weekdays, low season, twilight), range (grass), club rentals, credit cards (MC, V, AE, D).
Reader Comments: Best public in Tulsa, good people, good help ... Great course, take extra balls ... Very well kept, fairways tight ... Could be a country club ... The best in Tulsa ... Good small course, well maintained ... Faaaantastic fuuun! ... The best public golf in the state... A jewel. Favorite course in Tulsa ... Great value.

★★★ FORT COBB STATE PARK GOLF COURSE
R-P.O. Box 497, Fort Cobb, 73038, Caddo County, (405)643-2398, 6 miles N of Fort Cobb.
Holes: 18. **Yards:** 6,620/5,485. **Par:** 70/71. **Course Rating:** 69.8/74.4. **Slope:** 117/129. **Green Fee:** $14/$16. **Cart Fee:** $9/person. **Walking Policy:** Unrestricted walking. **Walkability:** 2.
Opened: 1960. **Architect:** Floyd Farley/Don Sechrest. **Season:** Year-round. **High:** May-Sept. **To obtain tee times:** Call 7 days in advance or day of. First come, first served. **Miscellaneous:** Reduced fees (weekdays, twilight, seniors, juniors), range (grass), club rentals, credit cards (MC, V, AE, D).
Reader Comments: Challenging ... Open front, tight back ... Lots of wildlife. Enjoyable.

FORT SILL GOLF CLUB
Bldg. 1275 Quinette Rd., Fort Sill, 73503, Comanche County, (580)353-0411.

Holes: 18. Yards: 6,505/5,197. Par: 72/72. Course Rating: 71.8/70.6. Slope: 128/124. Green Fee: $5/$12. Walkability: N/A.

★★½ FOUNTAINHEAD STATE GOLF COURSE

R-HC60 Box 1350, Checotah, 74426, McIntosh County, (918)689-3209, 60 miles S of Tulsa.
Holes: 18. Yards: 6,919/4,864. Par: 72/72. Course Rating: 71.3/67.3. Slope: 116/98. Green Fee: $8/$13. Cart Fee: $17/cart. Walking Policy: Unrestricted walking. Walkability: 3. Opened: 1964. Architect: Floyd Farley. Season: Year-round. High: March-Oct. To obtain tee times: Call seven days in advance. Miscellaneous: Reduced fees (weekdays, twilight, seniors, juniors), discount packages, metal spikes, range (grass), club rentals, lodging, credit cards (MC, V, AE, D).
Reader Comments: Tough, tough, with narrow fairways ... State course, great value, linoleum greens, super condition ... Beautiful views, hilly, rocky in some places, fun course ... Good course for a state park ... Great course for the beginning player.

GIL MORGAN MUNICIPAL GOLF COURSE

PU-800 E. 7th., Wewoka, 74884, Seminole County, (405)257-3292, 75 miles E of Oklahoma City.
Holes: 18. Yards: 6,555/5,400. Par: 72/72. Course Rating: 69.7/69.5. Slope: 112/110. Green Fee: $10/$12. Walkability: 5.
Special Notes: Call club for further information.

★★ GLEN EAGLES GOLF COURSE

PU-20239 E. 41st St., Broken Arrow, 74014, Wagoner County, (918)355-4422, 30 miles E of Tulsa.
Holes: 18. Yards: 6,909/5,257. Par: 72/72. Course Rating: 72.2/73.0. Slope: 115/116. Green Fee: $14/$16. Cart Fee: $18/person. Walking Policy: Unrestricted walking. Walkability: 2.
Opened: 1994. Season: Year-round. High: May-Sept. To obtain tee times: Call golf shop.
Miscellaneous: Reduced fees (seniors, juniors), range (grass/mats), club rentals, credit cards (MC, V, D).

★★★ THE GOLF CLUB AT CIMARRON TRAILS

PU-1400 Lovers Lane, Perkins, 74059, Payne County, (405)547-5701, 70 miles NE of Oklahoma City.
Holes: 18. Yards: 6,859/5,128. Par: 72/72. Course Rating: 74.0/65.8. Slope: 124/106. Green Fee: $12/$17. Cart Fee: $9/person. Walking Policy: Unrestricted walking. Walkability: 3.
Opened: 1994. Architect: Kevin Benedict. Season: Year-round. High: March-Aug. To obtain tee times: Call 7 days in advance. Miscellaneous: Reduced fees (weekdays, twilight, juniors), range (grass), club rentals, credit cards (MC, V, AE, D).
Reader Comments: Good golf ... Great course, well designed ... Hilly with good greens, challenging approach shots, fairly open ... Nice course, open, water, some trees.

GREENS GOLF COURSE

PU-Hwy. 44, Burns Flat, 73624, (580)562-4354 .
Holes: 18. Yards: 6,574/5,756. Par: 72/74. Course Rating: N/A. Slope: N/A. Green Fee: $8/$10. Walkability: 2.
Special Notes: Call club for further information.

HENRIETTA COUNTRY CLUB

SP-Country Club Rd., Henrietta, 74437, (918)652-8664.
Holes: 18. Yards: 6,006/5,250. Par: 72/73. Course Rating: 69.5. Slope: 111. Green Fee: $10/$13. Walkability: 5.
Special Notes: Call club for further information.

★★★ HERITAGE HILLS GOLF COURSE

PU-3140 Tee Dr., Claremore, 74017, Rogers County, (918)341-0055, 30 miles N of Tulsa.
E-mail: snaphk@aol.com.
Holes: 18. Yards: 6,760/5,324. Par: 71/72. Course Rating: 72.7/70.0. Slope: 129/117. Green Fee: $17/$17. Cart Fee: $20/cart. Walking Policy: Unrestricted walking. Walkability: 3.
Opened: 1977. Architect: Don Sechrest. Season: Year-round. High: April-Sept. To obtain tee times: For weekday tee time call 1 day in advance or come in 2 days in advance. For weekend and holidays call Wednesday prior at 7 a.m. by phone or in person. Miscellaneous: Reduced fees (weekdays, twilight, seniors, juniors), discount packages, range (grass), club rentals, credit cards (MC, V, AE).
Reader Comments: Great course ... Have to use every club in your bag ... Another very good course ... Challenging, but fair ... Very challenging, had to play controlled shots, undulating greens ... Outstanding golf course for the money ... Very pretty fun to play. Well kept.

IDABELL COUNTRY CLUB

SP-Lincoln Rd., Idabell, 74745, (580)286-7545, 200 miles S of Tulsa.
Holes: 18. Yards: N/A. Par: N/A. Course Rating: N/A. Slope: N/A. Green Fee: $15/$20. Cart Fee: $15/cart. Walking Policy: Unrestricted walking. Walkability: 1. Opened: 1945. Season: Year-round. High: March-Sept. To obtain tee times: First come, first served. Miscellaneous: Range (grass), beginner friendly (junior clinics).

★★★★ JIMMIE AUSTIN GOLF COURSE

PU-Seminole Municipal Park, Norman, 73019, Seminole County, (405)325-6716, 20 miles S of Oklahoma City.
Holes: 18. **Yards:** 6,542/5,336. **Par:** 71/72. **Course Rating:** 70.5/71.4. **Slope:** 116/112. **Green Fee:** $12/$12. **Cart Fee:** $16/cart. **Walking Policy:** Unrestricted walking. **Walkability:** 5.
Opened: 1951. **Architect:** Bob Cupp. **Season:** Year-round. **High:** June-Aug. **To obtain tee times:** Call Monday for following weekend. **Miscellaneous:** Reduced fees (twilight), club rentals, credit cards (MC, V).
Notes: Ranked 10th in 1999 Best in State.
Reader Comments: Nice new design, great course ... Nice course, good holes ... Lots of sand ... Probably one of the 3 or 4 best courses in Oklahoma since renovation ... Would love to play it once a week ... Fun yet challenging ... A fun course to play everyday, not too intimidating ... Great old course, reconditioned.

★★★ JOHN CONRAD REGIONAL GOLF COURSE

PU-711 S. Douglas Blvd., Midwest City, 73130, Oklahoma County, (405)732-2209, 1 miles E of Oklahoma City.
Holes: 18. **Yards:** 6,854/5,511. **Par:** 72/74. **Course Rating:** 72.0/70.8. **Slope:** 124/119. **Green Fee:** $15/$15. **Cart Fee:** $17/cart. **Walking Policy:** Unrestricted walking. **Walkability:** 2.
Opened: 1971. **Architect:** Floyd Farley. **Season:** Year-round. **High:** April-Oct. **To obtain tee times:** Call 24 hours in advance on weekdays. Call Saturday for next Saturday and Sunday.
Miscellaneous: Reduced fees (twilight, seniors, juniors), discount packages, metal spikes, range (grass/mats), club rentals, credit cards (MC, V).
Reader Comments: Good course for money ... An excellent experience ... One of the better courses ... Good municipal track.

KAH-WAH-C GOLF COURSE

PU-Rte. 2, Fairfax, 74637, Osage County, (918)642-5351, 3 miles E of Ponca City.
Holes: 9. **Yards:** 3,100/2,740. **Par:** 36/37. **Course Rating:** 69.5/69.8. **Slope:** 118/119. **Green Fee:** $8/$10. **Cart Fee:** $7/person. **Walking Policy:** Unrestricted walking. **Walkability:** 2.
Opened: 1922. **Season:** Year-round. **High:** April-Oct. **Miscellaneous:** Reduced fees (low season), metal spikes, club rentals, beginner friendly.
Special Notes: Formerly Kah Wah Country Club

★★★★½ KARSTEN CREEK GOLF CLUB *Service, Condition+, Pace+*

SP-1800 South Memorial Dr., Stillwater, 74074, Payne County, (405)743-1658, 5 miles W of Stillwater.
Holes: 18. **Yards:** 7,095/4,906. **Par:** 72/72. **Course Rating:** 74.8/70.1. **Slope:** 142/127. **Green Fee:** $125/$125. **Cart Fee:** Included in Green Fee. **Walking Policy:** Unrestricted walking.
Walkability: 4. **Opened:** 1994. **Architect:** Tom Fazio. **Season:** Year-round. **High:** April-Sept. **To obtain tee times:** Call three days in advance unless you are coming from out of state.
Miscellaneous: Range (grass), caddies, club rentals, credit cards (MC, V, AE).
Notes: Ranked 3rd in 1999 Best in State; 16th in 1996 America's Top 75 Upscale Courses.
Reader Comments: Would pay any price to play this gem ... Unbelievable. Forgot I was in Oklahoma ... Carved out of oak and mountain streams ... The best in Oklahoma ... Best public course I have ever played ... Great course ... Pure golf pleasure - what a gem ... I loved the layout, you can't see any other holes from the hole you are on! ... Best university course in the country. One of Fazio's best.

KEYSTONE GOLF COURSE

SP-South Airport Rd., P.O. Box 289, Cleveland, 74020, Pawnee County, (918)358-2277, 1 miles S of Cleveland.
Holes: 9. **Yards:** 3,078/2,968. **Par:** 36/37. **Course Rating:** 69.8/70.8. **Slope:** 109/108. **Green Fee:** N/A. **Cart Fee:** $15/cart. **Walking Policy:** Unrestricted walking. **Walkability:** 2. **Opened:** 1971. **Season:** Year-round. **High:** April-August. **To obtain tee times:** No tee times required.
Miscellaneous: Reduced fees (weekdays, juniors), club rentals, credit cards (MC, V, D), beginner friendly.

★★★½ KICKING BIRD GOLF COURSE

PU-1600 E. Danforth Rd., Edmond, 73034, Oklahoma County, (405)341-5350, 10 miles N of Oklahoma City.
Holes: 18. **Yards:** 6,722/5,051. **Par:** 70/70. **Course Rating:** 71.8/69.3. **Slope:** 123/112. **Green Fee:** $17/$22. **Cart Fee:** $10/cart. **Walking Policy:** Unrestricted walking. **Walkability:** 3.
Opened: 1971. **Architect:** Floyd Farley/Mark Hayes. **Season:** Year-round. **High:** May-Sept. **To obtain tee times:** Call one day in advance for weekdays and call one week in advance for weekends. **Miscellaneous:** Reduced fees (weekdays, twilight, seniors, juniors), range (grass/mats), club rentals, credit cards (MC, V, AE, D).
Reader Comments: Great shape ... Tough, home of many Oklahoma championships ... Some redesign, all new greens down to bases, 1 1/2 yrs., very good condition, good hole mix ... Well maintained ... Recently renovated. Great layout ... One of the better munies in the country.

★★★½ LAFORTUNE PARK GOLF COURSE
PM-5501 S. Yale Ave., Tulsa, 74135, Tulsa County, (918)596-8627.
Holes: 18. **Yards:** 6,970/5,780. **Par:** 72/73. **Course Rating:** 72.8/72.9. **Slope:** 123/122. **Green Fee:** $10/$17. **Cart Fee:** $10/person. **Walking Policy:** Unrestricted walking. **Walkability:** 2. **Opened:** 1960. **Architect:** Floyd Farley. **Season:** Year-round. **High:** March-Aug. **To obtain tee times:** Call golf shop for same day reservation. **Miscellaneous:** Reduced fees (twilight, seniors, juniors), range (grass/mats), club rentals, credit cards (MC, V).
Reader Comments: Great public course, good driving range.... Has only par-3 course in Tulsa as well as regular course. Usually allowed to play alone ... A pretty layout. One of the finest courses in Tulsa. Lots par 4s ... Long, challenging course ... Always friendly and course great.

LAKE HEFNER GOLF CLUB
PM-4491 S. Lake Hefner Dr., Oklahoma City, 73116, Oklahoma County, (405)843-1565.
★★★½ NORTH COURSE
Holes: 18. **Yards:** 6,970/5,169. **Par:** 72/72. **Course Rating:** 74.2/69.6. **Slope:** 128/117. **Green Fee:** $10/$15. **Cart Fee:** $19/cart. **Walking Policy:** Unrestricted walking. **Walkability:** 3. **Opened:** 1963. **Architect:** Randy Heckenkemper. **Season:** Year-round. **High:** March-Sept. **To obtain tee times:** Call 1 day in advance for weekdays. Call Saturday for following weekend and holidays. **Miscellaneous:** Reduced fees (twilight, seniors, juniors), range (grass), club rentals, credit cards (MC, V), beginner friendly (8 instructors, 3-hole academy).
Reader Comments: Good for the money ... Redone 1996 ... Good design, clubhouse, staff... Links-type course, beautiful views ... Tough ... Flat course with few trees. Nice view of Lake Hefner ... Clever and challenging.
★★★ SOUTH COURSE
Holes: 18. **Yards:** 6,305/5,393. **Par:** 70/73. **Course Rating:** 68.9/71.2. **Slope:** 111/115. **Green Fee:** $9/$14. **Cart Fee:** $17/cart. **Walking Policy:** Unrestricted walking. **Walkability:** 3. **Opened:** 1962. **Architect:** Floyd Farley. **Season:** Year-round. **High:** March-Sept. **To obtain tee times:** Call 1 day in advance for weekdays and 7 days in advance for weekends and holidays. **Miscellaneous:** Reduced fees (twilight, seniors, juniors), range (grass), club rentals, credit cards (MC, V).
Reader Comments: Not extremely difficult, but fun. Best driving range around ... Old course and I love it ... Well-laid out course ... Easier than North.
Special Notes: Also has 3-hole par-9 Academy Course.

★★½ LAKE MURRAY RESORT GOLF
R-3310 S. Lake Murray Dr., Ardmore, 73401, Carter County, (405)223-6613, 5 miles S of Dallas.
Holes: 18. **Yards:** 6,250/4,800. **Par:** 70/71. **Course Rating:** 69.2/70.8. **Slope:** 122/122. **Green Fee:** $14/$18. **Cart Fee:** $18/cart. **Walking Policy:** Unrestricted walking. **Walkability:** 2. **Opened:** 1960. **Architect:** Floyd Farley. **Season:** Year-round. **High:** May-Sept. **To obtain tee times:** Call up to 7 days in advance. **Miscellaneous:** Reduced fees (twilight, seniors, juniors), discount packages, range (grass), club rentals, lodging, credit cards (MC, V, AE, D), beginner friendly.
Reader Comments: Feel of resort, good test ... Tight course with some tough par 4s ... Good layout ... Fun course to play, several pretty holes.

★★★ LAKE TEXOMA GOLF RESORT
R-P.O. Box 279, Kingston, 73439, Marshall County, (580)564-3333, 65 miles N of Dallas, TX.
Holes: 18. **Yards:** 6,523/5,747. **Par:** 71/74. **Course Rating:** 71.4/68.7. **Slope:** 126/111. **Green Fee:** $14/$18. **Cart Fee:** $18/cart. **Walking Policy:** Unrestricted walking. **Walkability:** 3. **Opened:** 1958. **Architect:** Floyd Farley. **Season:** Year-round. **High:** April-Oct. **To obtain tee times:** Tee times taken 7 days in advance. **Miscellaneous:** Reduced fees (twilight, seniors, juniors), range (grass), club rentals, lodging, credit cards (MC, V, AE, D).
Reader Comments: Pretty with lake view ... Wide open.

LAKESIDE GOLF COURSE
PM-129 E. Colorado, Walters, 73572, Cotton County, (580)875-3829, 25 miles S of Lawton.
Holes: 18. **Yards:** 5,146/4,093. **Par:** 70/68. **Course Rating:** 63.9/63.9. **Slope:** 103/103. **Green Fee:** $7/$7. **Walkability:** 2.
Special Notes: Call club for further information.

★★ LAKESIDE MEMORIAL GOLF CLUB
PM-5201 N. Washington, Stillwater, 74075, Payne County, (405)372-3399, 60 miles N of Oklahoma City.
Holes: 18. **Yards:** 6,698/5,124. **Par:** 70/71. **Course Rating:** 73.0/71.5. **Slope:** 128/122. **Green Fee:** $12/$16. **Cart Fee:** $9/person. **Walking Policy:** Unrestricted walking. **Walkability:** 3. **Opened:** 1946. **Architect:** Labron Harris Sr. **Season:** Year-round. **High:** April-Sept. **To obtain tee times:** Call (405)372-3399 5 days in advance. **Miscellaneous:** Reduced fees (twilight, seniors), range (grass), club rentals, credit cards (MC, V), beginner friendly.

★★★ LAKEVIEW GOLF COURSE
PU-3905 N. Commerce, Ardmore, 73401, Carter County, (405)223-4260, 88 miles S of Oklahoma City.

Holes: 18. **Yards:** 6,881/5,032. **Par:** 71/72. **Course Rating:** 71.2/67.5. **Slope:** 114/113. **Green Fee:** $9/$11. **Cart Fee:** $18/cart. **Walking Policy:** Unrestricted walking. **Walkability:** 2. **Opened:** 1971. **Architect:** Fillmore Vaughn. **Season:** Year-round. **High:** April-Sept. **To obtain tee times:** Call Wednesday for upcoming weekend. **Miscellaneous:** Reduced fees (weekdays, twilight, seniors, juniors), range (grass), club rentals, credit cards (MC, V, AE, D).
Reader Comments: For the money—some of the best greens ... Best in area: Fast, large greens, wide open, great staff, food and range.

LAKEWOOD GOLF COURSE
PU-3101 Lakewood Dr., Ada, 74820, Pontotoc County, (580)332-5151, 80 miles SE of Oklahoma City.
Holes: 9. **Yards:** 5,990/5,390. **Par:** 71/71. **Course Rating:** 67.8/N/A. **Slope:** 112/N/A. **Green Fee:** $8/$10. **Cart Fee:** $17/cart. **Walking Policy:** Unrestricted walking. **Walkability:** 5. **Opened:** 1968. **Season:** Year-round. **High:** May-Aug. **Miscellaneous:** Reduced fees (weekdays, twilight, seniors, juniors), club rentals.

LAWTON MUNICIPAL GOLF COURSE
PM-Airport Rd., Lawton, 73502, Comanche County, (580)353-4493, 50 miles N of Wichitaw Falls, TX.
Holes: 18. **Yards:** 6,800/5,325. **Par:** 72/74. **Course Rating:** 72.9/N/A. **Slope:** 102/100. **Green Fee:** $10/$12. **Cart Fee:** $18/cart. **Walking Policy:** Unrestricted walking. **Walkability:** 1. **Architect:** Jack Greer. **Season:** Year-round. **High:** April-June. **Miscellaneous:** Reduced fees (juniors), club rentals, beginner friendly.
Special Notes: Formerly Lawton Public Golf Course

★★★ LEW WENTZ MEMORIAL GOLF COURSE
PM-2928 L.A. Cann Dr., Ponca City, 74604, Kay County, (405)767-0433, 80 miles NE of Tulsa.
Holes: 18. **Yards:** 6,400/5,450. **Par:** 71/70. **Course Rating:** 70.0/71.8. **Slope:** 125/123. **Green Fee:** $13/$14. **Cart Fee:** $17/cart. **Walking Policy:** Unrestricted walking. **Walkability:** 3. **Opened:** 1940. **Architect:** Floyd Farley. **Season:** Year-round. **High:** April-Oct. **To obtain tee times:** Call two days in advance. **Miscellaneous:** Reduced fees (weekdays, seniors, juniors), metal spikes, club rentals, credit cards (MC, V).
Reader Comments: Always fun—timeless layout ... One of the best munyies ... Beautiful course, especially the back nine along the lake.

LINCOLN PARK GOLF COURSE
PM-4001 N.E. Grand Blvd., Oklahoma City, 73111, Oklahoma County, (405)424-1421.
★★★ EAST COURSE
Holes: 18. **Yards:** 6,535/5,467. **Par:** 70/71. **Course Rating:** 70.0/66.2. **Slope:** 120/112. **Green Fee:** $9/$15. **Cart Fee:** $19/cart. **Walking Policy:** Unrestricted walking. **Walkability:** 4. **Opened:** 1925. **Architect:** Arthur Jackson. **Season:** Year-round. **High:** April-Sept. **To obtain tee times:** Call or come in one week in advance for weekends and call or come in one day in advance for weekdays. **Miscellaneous:** Reduced fees (twilight, seniors, juniors), range (grass), club rentals, credit cards (MC, V).
Reader Comments: Enjoyable city course ... Open course, tough on a windy day ... Easy, fun old parkland course.
★★½ WEST COURSE
Holes: 18. **Yards:** 6,600/5,587. **Par:** 71/71. **Course Rating:** 70.7/68.4. **Slope:** 121/115. **Green Fee:** $9/$15. **Cart Fee:** $19/cart. **Walking Policy:** Unrestricted walking. **Walkability:** 4. **Opened:** 1922. **Architect:** Arthur Jackson. **Season:** Year-round. **High:** April-Sept. **To obtain tee times:** Call one week in advance for weekends and one day in advance for weekdays. **Miscellaneous:** Reduced fees (twilight, seniors, juniors), range (grass), club rentals, credit cards (MC, V).
Reader Comments: Very good for the amount of play. You have to have shots ... Good muny golf ... Publinks the old fashioned way.

LINDSAY MUNICIPAL GOLF COURSE
PM-Hwy. 76 , Lindsay, 73052, McClain County, (405)756-3611, 3 miles N of Norman. **Web:** www.teedoffattelepath.com.
Holes: 9. **Yards:** 3,285/2,989. **Par:** 36/75. **Course Rating:** 70.0/73.4. **Slope:** 118/125. **Green Fee:** N/A. **Cart Fee:** $15/cart. **Walking Policy:** Unrestricted walking. **Walkability:** 2. **Opened:** 1962. **Season:** Year-round. **High:** May-Oct. **Miscellaneous:** Club rentals, beginner friendly.

MEADOWLAKE MUNICIPAL GOLF COURSE
PM-2000 West Rupe, Enid, 73703, Garfield County, (580)234-3080, 12 miles NW of Oklahoma City.
Holes: 18. **Yards:** 6,416/5,801. **Par:** 71/73. **Course Rating:** 71.3/74.2. **Slope:** 117/125. **Green Fee:** $12/$15. **Cart Fee:** $12/cart. **Walking Policy:** Unrestricted walking. **Walkability:** 2. **Opened:** 1950. **Architect:** Tripp Davis. **Season:** Year-round. **High:** April-July. **Miscellaneous:** Reduced fees (twilight, seniors, juniors), range (grass), club rentals, credit cards (MC, V), beginner friendly (beginner tees, clinics).

OKLAHOMA

Special Notes: Formerly Meadowlake Golf Course

MOHAWK PARK GOLF CLUB
PM-5223 E. 41st St. N., Tulsa, 74115, Tulsa County, (918)425-6871.

★★★ PECAN VALLEY COURSE
Holes: 18. **Yards:** 6,499/5,130. **Par:** 70/70. **Course Rating:** 71.6/69.6. **Slope:** 124/119. **Green Fee:** $8/$15. **Cart Fee:** $18/cart. **Walking Policy:** Unrestricted walking. **Walkability:** N/A. **Opened:** 1957. **Architect:** Floyd Farley. **Season:** Year-round. **High:** June-July. **To obtain tee times:** You can call seven days in advance if you are a member of Tee Time Service Computer. **Miscellaneous:** Reduced fees (twilight, seniors, juniors), metal spikes, club rentals.
Reader Comments: Good variety for public course ... A good fun course to play ... A nice course ... Good short challenge.

★★★½ WOODBINE COURSE
Holes: 18. **Yards:** 6,898/6,202. **Par:** 72/76. **Course Rating:** 71.0/73.9. **Slope:** 115/127. **Green Fee:** $8/$15. **Cart Fee:** $17/cart. **Walking Policy:** Unrestricted walking. **Walkability:** N/A. **Opened:** 1927. **Architect:** William H. Diddel. **Season:** Year-round. **High:** June-July. **To obtain tee times:** Must be a member of computer Tee Time Service. You can then call seven days in advance. **Miscellaneous:** Reduced fees (twilight, seniors, juniors), metal spikes, club rentals.
Reader Comments: A good fun course to play ... This is a nice course ... Good long open course, good for beginners ... Good public course.

OKEENE MUNICIPAL GOLF COURSE
PM-401 S. Phillips, Okeene, 73763, Blaine County, (405)822-3435, 3 miles S of Enid.
Holes: 9. **Yards:** 2,932/2,752. **Par:** 35/35. **Course Rating:** 69.0/69.0. **Slope:** N/A. **Green Fee:** $10/$13. **Cart Fee:** $13/cart. **Walking Policy:** Unrestricted walking. **Walkability:** 1. **Opened:** 1950. **Season:** Year-round. **High:** March-Sept. **Miscellaneous:** Reduced fees (weekdays, twilight, juniors), range (grass).

OSAGE CREEK GOLF CLUB
PU-Hwy. 28 - Will Rogers Tpke., Adair, 74330, Mayes County, (918)785-4166, 32 miles NE of Tulsa.
Holes: 18. **Yards:** 7,024/5,540. **Par:** 72/72. **Course Rating:** 73.8/74.8. **Slope:** 111/111. **Green Fee:** $5/$12. **Walkability:** 1. **Architect:** Charles Bland.
Special Notes: Call club for further information.

PAGE BELCHER GOLF COURSE
PM-6666 S. Union Ave., Tulsa, 74132, Tulsa County, (918)446-1529. **E-mail:** pagebgc@aol.com.

★★★½ OLD PAGE COURSE
Holes: 18. **Yards:** 6,826/5,532. **Par:** 71/71. **Course Rating:** 72.0/71.5. **Slope:** 123/118. **Green Fee:** $16/$19. **Cart Fee:** $18/cart. **Walking Policy:** Unrestricted walking. **Walkability:** 3. **Opened:** 1977. **Architect:** Leon Howard. **Season:** Year-round. **High:** April-Oct. **To obtain tee times:** Call (918)582-6000. **Miscellaneous:** Reduced fees (weekdays, twilight, seniors, juniors), range (grass), club rentals, credit cards (MC, V, AE, D).
Reader Comments: Old course, good value ... City course well kept ... Great classic course ... My favorite ... Nice muny, public course ... Good course, greens ... Very good and fun, course is always good ... Beautiful ... Enjoyable golf.

★★★★ STONE CREEK COURSE
Holes: 18. **Yards:** 6,539/5,144. **Par:** 71/71. **Course Rating:** 72.3/69.9. **Slope:** 132/127. **Green Fee:** $16/$19. **Cart Fee:** $18/cart. **Walking Policy:** Unrestricted walking. **Walkability:** 3. **Opened:** 1987. **Architect:** Don Sechrest. **Season:** Year-round. **High:** April-Oct. **To obtain tee times:** Call (918)582-6000. **Miscellaneous:** Reduced fees (weekdays, twilight, seniors, juniors), range (grass), club rentals, credit cards (MC, V, AE, D).
Notes: Ranked 7th in 1999 Best in State; 41st in 1996 America's Top 75 Affordable Courses.
Reader Comments: Great course, good value ... Placement a must. Tough greens ... The best of the city-owned ... Some beautiful holes ... Good course–love the zoysia fairways ... Good layout, lots of bunkers and water ... Fair tee boxes for women ... Best public course in Tulsa.

PAULS VALLEY MUNICIPAL GOLF COURSE
PM-South Airport Rd., Pauls Valley, 73075, Garvin County, (405)238-7462.
Holes: 9. **Yards:** 3,403/2,602. **Par:** 72/72. **Course Rating:** 70.2/70.1. **Slope:** 108/125. **Green Fee:** $9/$11. **Cart Fee:** $17/cart. **Walking Policy:** Walking at certain times. **Walkability:** 1. **Opened:** 1992. **Season:** Year-round. **High:** March-Oct. **Miscellaneous:** Range (grass), club rentals, beginner friendly.

PRYOR MUNICIPAL GOLF COURSE
PM-East Highway 69A, Pryor, 74361, Mayes County, (918)825-3056, 28 miles E of Tulsa.
Holes: 18. **Yards:** 6,549/5,649. **Par:** 72/72. **Course Rating:** 71.2/68.1. **Slope:** 124/109. **Green Fee:** $9/$14. **Cart Fee:** $18/cart. **Walking Policy:** Unrestricted walking. **Walkability:** 2. **Season:** Year-round. **High:** April-Oct. **To obtain tee times:** No tee times required. First come first served. **Miscellaneous:** Reduced fees (low season, twilight, seniors, juniors), club rentals.

OKLAHOMA

★★½ QUARTZ MOUNTAIN GOLF COURSE
R-Rte. 1, Box 35, Lone Wolf, 73655, Kiowa County, (405)563-2520, 17 miles N of Altus.
Holes: 18. **Yards:** 6,595/5,706. **Par:** 71/71. **Course Rating:** 70.8/73.4. **Slope:** 119/123. **Green Fee:** $11/$16. **Cart Fee:** $9/person. **Walking Policy:** Unrestricted walking. **Walkability:** 2. **Opened:** 1958. **Architect:** Floyd Farley/Art Proctor. **Season:** Year-round. **High:** May-Aug. **To obtain tee times:** Call 7 days in advance for tee times. **Miscellaneous:** Reduced fees (weekdays, twilight, seniors, juniors), discount packages, range (grass), club rentals, lodging, credit cards (MC, V, AE, D).
Reader Comments: Very picturesque ... Great setting for golf course ... Beautiful.

RIVERSIDE MUNICIPAL GOLF COURSE
PM-Rte. 1, Box 3625, Clinton, 73601, Custer County, (580)323-5958, 120 miles E of Oklahoma City.
Holes: 18. **Yards:** 6,880/4,921. **Par:** 70/70. **Course Rating:** 68.8/70.2. **Slope:** 113/119. **Green Fee:** $7/$14. **Cart Fee:** $16/cart. **Walking Policy:** Unrestricted walking. **Walkability:** 1. **Opened:** 1925. **Season:** Year-round. **High:** June-Aug. **To obtain tee times:** Call 3 days in advance. **Miscellaneous:** Reduced fees (weekdays, seniors, juniors), range (grass), club rentals, credit cards (MC, V), beginner friendly (junior golf program, ladies clinics, Tuesday night scramble).

ROCK CREEK GOLF COURSE
PU-Hwy. 69, Hugo, 74743, Choctaw County, (580)326-6130, 100 miles NE of Dallas.
Holes: 9. **Yards:** 5,995. **Par:** 72. **Course Rating:** 69. **Slope:** 106. **Green Fee:** $6/$10. **Walkability:** 2.
Special Notes: Call club for further information.

ROMAN NOSE GOLF COURSE
PU-St. Hwy. 8A, Watonga, 73772, Blaine County, (580)623-7989, 8 miles N of Watonga.
Holes: 18. **Yards:** 6,139/4,599. **Par:** 70/70. **Course Rating:** 70.5/N/A. **Slope:** 123/N/A. **Green Fee:** $15/$15. **Cart Fee:** $18/cart. **Walking Policy:** Unrestricted walking. **Walkability:** 5. **Opened:** 1957. **Architect:** Floyd Farley/Tripp Davis. **Season:** Year-round. **High:** April-Nov. **To obtain tee times:** Call golf shop. **Miscellaneous:** Reduced fees (twilight, seniors, juniors), discount packages, club rentals, lodging (57 rooms), credit cards (MC, V, AE, D).

★★ SAND SPRINGS MUNICIPAL GOLF COURSE
PU-1801 N. McKinley, Sand Springs, 74063, Tulsa County, (918)246-2606, 8 miles NW of Tulsa.
Holes: 18. **Yards:** 6,113/4,692. **Par:** 71/70. **Course Rating:** 69.5/68.4. **Slope:** 125/118. **Green Fee:** $7/$16. **Cart Fee:** $19/cart. **Walking Policy:** Unrestricted walking. **Walkability:** 4. **Opened:** 1956. **Architect:** Floyd Farley. **Season:** Year-round. **High:** April-Oct. **To obtain tee times:** Call golf shop. **Miscellaneous:** Reduced fees (weekdays, low season, twilight, seniors, juniors), discount packages, range (grass), club rentals, credit cards (MC, V).

★★ SAPULPA MUNICIPAL GOLF COURSE
PM-On Highway 66, Sapulpa, 74067, Creek County, (918)224-0237, 1 miles SW of Sapulpa.
Holes: 18. **Yards:** 6,675/5,087. **Par:** 71/70. **Course Rating:** 72.4/69.2. **Slope:** 128/112. **Green Fee:** $14/$16. **Cart Fee:** $19/cart. **Walking Policy:** Unrestricted walking. **Walkability:** 2. **Opened:** 1995. **Architect:** Jerry Slack/Mark Hayes. **Season:** Year-round. **High:** June-Aug. **To obtain tee times:** Call (918)224-0237 two days in advance. **Miscellaneous:** Reduced fees (weekdays, twilight, seniors, juniors), club rentals, credit cards (MC, V, D), beginner friendly.

SAYRE GOLF COURSE
PU-, Sayre, 73662, Beckham County, (405)928-9046, 110 miles W of Oklahoma City.
Holes: 9. **Yards:** 3,098/2,486. **Par:** 36/36. **Course Rating:** N/A. **Slope:** N/A. **Green Fee:** $8/$8.
Special Notes: Call club for further information.

★★½ SEQUOYAH STATE PARK GOLF CLUB
R-Rte. 1, Box 201, Hulbert, 74441, Cherokee County, (918)772-2297, 45 miles SE of Tulsa.
Holes: 18. **Yards:** 5,860/5,555. **Par:** 70/73. **Course Rating:** 66.7/69.9. **Slope:** 109/113. **Green Fee:** $14/$16. **Cart Fee:** $18/cart. **Walking Policy:** Unrestricted walking. **Walkability:** 4. **Opened:** 1954. **Architect:** Floyd Farley. **Season:** Year-round. **High:** June-Aug. **To obtain tee times:** Call seven days in advance. **Miscellaneous:** Reduced fees (weekdays, twilight, seniors, juniors), discount packages, range (grass), club rentals, lodging, credit cards (MC, V, AE, D).
Reader Comments: Very beautiful setting, several fairways run along Lake Fort Gibson ... Pleasantly scenic course, lots of hills.

SHANGRI-LA GOLF RESORT
R-R.R. No.3, Afton, 74331, Delaware County, (918)257-4204, (800)331-4060, 90 miles NE of Tulsa.
★★★★ BLUE COURSE
Holes: 18. **Yards:** 7,012/5,892. **Par:** 72/73. **Course Rating:** 73.7/74.8. **Slope:** 131/126. **Green Fee:** $75/$90. **Cart Fee:** Included in Green Fee. **Walking Policy:** Walking at certain times. **Walkability:** 3. **Opened:** 1970. **Architect:** Don Sechrest. **Season:** Year-round. **High:** April-Oct.

OKLAHOMA

To obtain tee times: Must be a member, guest of a member or a guest of the resort to play.
Miscellaneous: Reduced fees (low season, juniors), discount packages, range (grass), club rentals, lodging, credit cards (MC, V, AE, D).
Reader Comments: Good place to tee it up ... Great golf holes ... Tough ... Great course getting better ... Beautiful set up ... Good golf packages ... Challenging.

★★★★ **GOLD COURSE**
Holes: 18. **Yards:** 5,802/4,586. **Par:** 70/71. **Course Rating:** 67.9/66.8. **Slope:** 124/112. **Green Fee:** $75/$85. **Cart Fee:** Included in Green Fee. **Walking Policy:** Walking at certain times. **Walkability:** 4. **Opened:** 1980. **Architect:** Don Sechrest. **Season:** Year-round. **High:** April-Oct.
To obtain tee times: Must be a member, a guest of a member or a guest of the resort to play.
Miscellaneous: Reduced fees (low season, juniors), discount packages, metal spikes, range (grass), club rentals, lodging, credit cards (MC, V, AE, D).
Reader Comments: Great for the money ... Tough ... Great resort golf ... A lot of water and really fair to play ... Good course ... Loved the contrast between front and back nines ... Challenging par 3s. Short, fun course.

SHATTUCK GOLF & COUNTRY CLUB
PU-1 1/2 South Shattuck Hwy. 283, Shattuck, 73858, Ellis County, (580)938-2445, 25 miles SW of Woodward.
Holes: 9. **Yards:** 3,156/2,870. **Par:** 36/36. **Course Rating:** N/A. **Slope:** N/A. **Green Fee:** $8/$12. **Walkability:** 3. **Architect:** Ned Stuart.
Special Notes: Call club for further information.

★★★½ **SILVERHORN GOLF CLUB**
PU-11411 N. Kelley Ave., Oklahoma City, 73131, Oklahoma County, (405)752-1181, 10 miles N of Oklahoma City.
Holes: 18. **Yards:** 6,800/4,943. **Par:** 71/71. **Course Rating:** 73.4/71.0. **Slope:** 128/113. **Green Fee:** $24/$29. **Cart Fee:** $9/person. **Walking Policy:** Unrestricted walking. **Walkability:** 3. **Opened:** 1991. **Architect:** Randy Heckenkemper. **Season:** Year-round. **High:** April-Sept. **To obtain tee times:** Call five days in advance. **Miscellaneous:** Reduced fees (weekdays, low season, twilight, seniors, juniors), metal spikes, range (grass), club rentals, credit cards (MC, V, AE, D).
Reader Comments: Excellent fairways ... Very friendly staff ... Great bunker placement ... Nice people ... Super layout ... Spunky design and fun to play.

★★★ **SOUTH LAKES GOLF COURSE**
PU-9253 S. Elwood, Jenks, 74037, Tulsa County, (918)746-3760, 3 miles SW of Tulsa.
Holes: 18. **Yards:** 6,340/5,242. **Par:** 71/71. **Course Rating:** 68.6/70.4. **Slope:** 113/116. **Green Fee:** $18/$18. **Cart Fee:** $20/cart. **Walking Policy:** Unrestricted walking. **Walkability:** 2. **Opened:** 1989. **Architect:** Randy Heckenkemper. **Season:** Year-round. **High:** April-Sept. **To obtain tee times:** Call golf shop. **Miscellaneous:** Reduced fees (twilight, seniors, juniors), range (grass/mats), club rentals, credit cards (MC, V).
Reader Comments: Short course good for seniors ... Easy to walk. Seniors specials ... Excellent challenge for short yardage course ... Good practice facilities.

★★ **SPUNKY CREEK COUNTRY CLUB**
SP-1890 Country Club Dr., Catoosa, 74015, Rogers County, (918)266-2207, 3 miles E of Tulsa.
Holes: 18. **Yards:** 6,639/5,748. **Par:** 72/73. **Course Rating:** 71.5/72.9. **Slope:** 124/127. **Green Fee:** $14/$16. **Cart Fee:** $9/person. **Walking Policy:** Unrestricted walking. **Walkability:** N/A. **Opened:** 1921. **Architect:** Perry Maxwell. **Season:** Year-round. **High:** March-Oct. **To obtain tee times:** Call two days in advance beginning at 7 a.m. **Miscellaneous:** Reduced fees (weekdays, low season, twilight, seniors, juniors), metal spikes, club rentals, credit cards (MC, V).

STROUD MUNICIPAL GOLF COURSE
PM-Hwy. 99 North, Stroud, 74079, Lincoln County, (918)968-2105, 45 miles W of Tulsa.
Holes: 9. **Yards:** 6,300/5,426. **Par:** 70/70. **Course Rating:** 70.2/68.4. **Slope:** 118/113. **Green Fee:** 2. **Walkability:** N/A.
Special Notes: Call club for further information.

SULPHUR HILLS GOLF COURSE
PU-Country Club Dr., Sulphur, 73086, Murray County, (580)622-5057, 1 miles N of Sulphur.
Holes: 9. **Yards:** 6,450/5,760. **Par:** 72/78. **Course Rating:** 69.5/72.0. **Slope:** 107/107. **Green Fee:** $7/$10. **Cart Fee:** $16/cart. **Walking Policy:** Unrestricted walking. **Walkability:** 2. **Opened:** 1965. **Season:** Year-round. **High:** May-Sept. **Miscellaneous:** Reduced fees (twilight, juniors), club rentals.

★★★ **SUNSET HILLS GOLF COURSE**
PU-Sunset Lane, Guymon, 73942, Texas County, (580)338-7404, 120 miles N of Amarillo, TX.
Holes: 18. **Yards:** 6,732/5,780. **Par:** 71/74. **Course Rating:** 70.3/68.0. **Slope:** 108/112. **Green Fee:** $10/$13. **Cart Fee:** $16/cart. **Walking Policy:** Unrestricted walking. **Walkability:** 4. **Opened:** 1932. **Architect:** Bob Dunning. **Season:** Year-round. **High:** June-Aug. **To obtain tee

times: Call at 8:00 A.M. on Friday to reserve. **Miscellaneous:** Reduced fees (twilight), range (grass), club rentals, beginner friendly.
Reader Comments: Great for Oklahoma Panhandle ... Wind is always a factor.

SYCAMORE SPRINGS GOLF COURSE
SP-Rte 2, 2555 Golf Course Rd., Wilburton, 74578, Latimer County, (918)465-3161, 75 miles SW of Ft. Smith, Arizona.
Holes: 9. **Yards:** 5,895/5,355. **Par:** 70/70. **Course Rating:** N/A. **Slope:** N/A. **Green Fee:** $9/$11. **Walkability:** 2.
Special Notes: Call club for further information.

★★★ THUNDERCREEK GOLF COURSE
PM-2300 W Hwy. 270, Mc Alester, 74502, Pittsburg County, (918)423-5799, 90 miles N of Tulsa.
Holes: 18. **Yards:** 6,835/5,033. **Par:** 72/72. **Course Rating:** 69.5/72.0. **Slope:** 135/110. **Green Fee:** $12/$18. **Cart Fee:** $20/person. **Walking Policy:** Unrestricted walking. **Walkability:** 3.
Opened: 1994. **Season:** Year-round. **High:** March-June. **To obtain tee times:** Call Monday for weekend times. **Miscellaneous:** Reduced fees (twilight), range (grass), credit cards (MC, V, AE, D).
Reader Comments: Improving each year ... Lets you make a gambling decision on each hole ... A lot of different holes.

TISHOMINGO GOLF AND RECREATION
PU-St. Hwy. 99, Tishomingo, 73460, Johnston County, (580)371-2604, 35 miles E of Ardmore.
Holes: 9. **Yards:** 3,187/2,480. **Par:** 36/36. **Course Rating:** N/A. **Slope:** N/A. **Green Fee:** $10/$12. **Cart Fee:** $14/cart. **Walking Policy:** Walking at certain times. **Walkability:** 2. **Opened:** 1940. **Season:** Year-round. **High:** June-Aug. **Miscellaneous:** Range (grass).
Special Notes: Formerly Tishomingo Golf Course

TRADITION GOLF CLUB
PU-15200 Traditions Blvd., Edmond, 73013, Oklahoma County, (405)330-7989, 4 miles N of Oklahoma City.
Holes: 18. **Yards:** 5,000/3,642. **Par:** 60/60. **Course Rating:** 61.4/59.0. **Slope:** 97/90. **Green Fee:** $11/$17. **Cart Fee:** $8/person. **Walking Policy:** Unrestricted walking. **Walkability:** 3.
Opened: 1998. **Architect:** Raymond Hearn. **Season:** Year-round. **High:** April-Oct.
Miscellaneous: Reduced fees (weekdays, twilight, seniors, juniors), discount packages, range (grass/mats), club rentals, credit cards (MC, V, AE, D), beginner friendly.

★★★ TROSPER PARK GOLF COURSE
PU-2301 S.E. 29th, Oklahoma City, 73129, Oklahoma County, (405)677-8874.
Holes: 18. **Yards:** 6,631/5,067. **Par:** 71/71. **Course Rating:** 71.5/74.1. **Slope:** 125/114. **Green Fee:** $10/$15. **Cart Fee:** $19/cart. **Walking Policy:** Unrestricted walking. **Walkability:** 3.
Opened: 1960. **Architect:** Arthur Jackson. **Season:** Year-round. **High:** March-Sept. **To obtain tee times:** Call Saturday morning for following weekend; 1 day in advance for weekdays.
Miscellaneous: Reduced fees (twilight, seniors, juniors), range (grass), club rentals, credit cards (MC, V), beginner friendly (lessons available).
Reader Comments: One of the toughest finishing holes around ... Some water and creeks ... City owned ... Fun to play. No. 18 has everybody talking ... Interesting course, enjoyable to play.

TWIN OAKS GOLF COURSE
PU-Rte. 2, Duncan, 73533, Stephens County, (580)252-4714, 60 miles S of Oklahoma City.
Holes: 18. **Yards:** 6,312/4,323. **Par:** 71/71. **Course Rating:** N/A. **Slope:** N/A. **Green Fee:** $7/$9. **Walkability:** 3.
Special Notes: Call club for further information.

VINITA GOLF AND TENNIS CLUB
PU-South Fairgrounds Rd., Vinita, 74301, Craig County, (918)256-8100, 40 miles N of Tulsa.
Holes: 18. **Yards:** 6,200/5,048. **Par:** 70/70. **Course Rating:** 69.6/65.6. **Slope:** 112/102. **Green Fee:** $15/$21. **Cart Fee:** Included in Green Fee. **Walking Policy:** Unrestricted walking. **Walkability:** 3. **Opened:** 1922. **Season:** Year-round. **High:** April-Nov. **Miscellaneous:** Range (grass), club rentals, credit cards (MC, V), beginner friendly (individual and group lesson plan available).
Special Notes: Formerly Buffalo Ridge Country Club

WEATHERFORD GOLF COURSE
SP-Rader Park, Weatherford, 73096, Custer County, (580)772-3832.
Holes: 18. **Yards:** 6,543/4,979. **Par:** 71/73. **Course Rating:** 71.2/62.4. **Slope:** 125/93. **Green Fee:** $13/$16. **Cart Fee:** $18/cart. **Walking Policy:** Unrestricted walking. **Walkability:** 3.
Architect: Labron Harris. **Season:** Year-round. **High:** April-Oct. **To obtain tee times:** Tee times are required only on weekends and holidays. **Miscellaneous:** Reduced fees (twilight, seniors), range (grass), club rentals, credit cards (MC, V).

WESTBURY COUNTRY CLUB
SP-2101 Westbury Dr., Yukon, 73099, Canadian County, (405)324-0707, 10 miles W of Oklahoma City.
Holes: 18. **Yards:** 6,874/6,276. **Par:** 72/74. **Course Rating:** 72.3/71.6. **Slope:** 122/130. **Green Fee:** $15/$17. **Walkability:** 1.
Special Notes: Call club for further information.

★★ WESTWOOD PARK GOLF COURSE
PU-2400 Westport Dr., Norman, 73069, Cleveland County, (405)292-9700, 17 miles S of Oklahoma City.
Holes: 18. **Yards:** 6,015/5,525. **Par:** 70/74. **Course Rating:** 67.7/71.0. **Slope:** 108/120. **Green Fee:** $8/$16. **Cart Fee:** $20/cart. **Walking Policy:** Unrestricted walking. **Walkability:** 1. **Opened:** 1967. **Architect:** Floyd Farley. **Season:** Year-round. **High:** April-Sept. **To obtain tee times:** Weekend tee times only. Call as early as Saturday for following weekend. **Miscellaneous:** Reduced fees (weekdays, twilight, seniors, juniors), range (grass), rentals, credit cards (MC, V).

★★★½ WHITE HAWK GOLF CLUB
SP-14515 S. Yale Ave., Bixby, 74008, Tulsa County, (918)366-4653, 10 miles S of Tulsa.
Holes: 18. **Yards:** 6,982/5,148. **Par:** 72/72. **Course Rating:** 74.1/N/A. **Slope:** 134/N/A. **Green Fee:** $22/$27. **Cart Fee:** $10/person. **Walking Policy:** Unrestricted walking. **Walkability:** 3. **Opened:** 1994. **Architect:** Randy Heckenkemper. **Season:** Year-round. **High:** May-Oct. **To obtain tee times:** Nonmembers call 7 days in advance. **Miscellaneous:** Reduced fees (weekdays, low season, twilight, seniors, juniors), discount packages, range (grass), club rentals, credit cards (MC, V, AE, D).
Reader Comments: Very nice, great staff ... Very good course ... Nice variety of holes ... Overall great value.

WILDHORSE GOLF COURSE
PU-128 Wildhorse Dr., Velma, 73091, Stephens County, (580)444-3338, 16 miles E of Duncan.
Holes: 9. **Yards:** 3,003/3,003. **Par:** 70/70. **Course Rating:** 62.4. **Slope:** NA. **Green Fee:** $7/$10. **Walkability:** 3.

WOODWARD MUNICIPAL GOLF COURSE
PM-Crystal Beach Park, Woodward, 73802, Woodward County, (580)256-9028, 150 miles W of Oklahoma City.
Holes: 9. **Yards:** 3,163/2,983. **Par:** 35/38. **Course Rating:** 68.5/72.5. **Slope:** 95/110. **Green Fee:** N/A. **Cart Fee:** $16/cart. **Walking Policy:** Unrestricted walking. **Walkability:** 1. **Season:** Year-round. **High:** April-Sept. **Miscellaneous:** Reduced fees (twilight), range (grass), club rentals.

OREGON

BAKER CITY GOLF CLUB
PU-2801 Indiana Ave., Baker City, 97814, Baker County, (541)523-2358, 130 miles NW of Boise, Idaho.
Holes: 18. **Yards:** 6,340/5,750. **Par:** 70/72. **Course Rating:** 67.7/71.0. **Slope:** 118/120. **Green Fee:** $20/$20. **Cart Fee:** $20/cart. **Walking Policy:** Unrestricted walking. **Walkability:** 3.
Opened: 1934. **Season:** March-Oct. **High:** June-Aug. **To obtain tee times:** Call Pro Shop.
Miscellaneous: Reduced fees (juniors), club rentals, credit cards (MC, V).

BANDON DUNES RESORT
R-57744 Round Lake Dr., Bandon, 97411, Coos County, (541)347-4380, (888)345-6008, 16 miles S of CoosBay. **Web:** www.bandondunesgolf.com.
Holes: 18. **Yards:** 6,844/5,178. **Par:** 72/72. **Course Rating:** 74.2/72.1. **Slope:** 138/127. **Green Fee:** $35/$100. **Walking Policy:** Unrestricted walking. **Walkability:** 2. **Opened:** 1999. **Architect:** David McLay Kidd/James Kidd. **Season:** Year-round. **High:** May-Oct. **To obtain tee times:** Call reservations. **Miscellaneous:** Reduced fees (low season), range (grass), caddies, club rentals, lodging (69 rooms), credit cards (MC, V, AE, D).
Notes: Ranked 1st in 1999 Best New Upscale Public.
Special Notes: Formerly known as Bandon Dunes Golf Club.

BATTLE CREEK GOLF CLUB
PU-6161 Commercial St. SE, Salem, 97306, Marion County, (503)585-1402.
Holes: 18. **Yards:** 6,015/4,945. **Par:** 72/72. **Course Rating:** 117.0/113.0. **Slope:** 69/68. **Green Fee:** $23/$25. **Cart Fee:** $20/cart. **Walking Policy:** Unrestricted walking. **Walkability:** 2.
Opened: 1959. **Architect:** Bill Stevely. **Season:** Year-round. **High:** April-Oct. **To obtain tee times:** Call Pro Shop. **Miscellaneous:** Reduced fees (weekdays, juniors), metal spikes, club rentals, credit cards (MC, V), beginner friendly.

BLACK BUTTE RANCH
R-Hwy. 20, Black Butte Ranch, 97759, Deschutes County, (541)595-1500, (800)399-2322, 25 miles NE of Bend. **Web:** www.blackbutteranch.com.
★★★★ **BIG MEADOW COURSE**
Holes: 18. **Yards:** 6,850/5,678. **Par:** 72/72. **Course Rating:** 71.3/70.4. **Slope:** 125/124. **Green Fee:** $42/$58. **Cart Fee:** $28/cart. **Walking Policy:** Unrestricted walking. **Walkability:** 2.
Opened: 1971. **Architect:** Robert Muir Graves. **Season:** March-Nov. **To obtain tee times:** Guests may call 14 days in advance; non-guests 7 days. **Miscellaneous:** Reduced fees (weekdays, low season, twilight, juniors), range (grass), club rentals, lodging, credit cards (MC, V, AE, D), beginner friendly (seasonal weekly clinics).
Reader Comments: Like playing in an old-growth forest ... Most beautiful in central Oregon ... Beautiful wooded track you can walk ... One of our favorites ... Very accommodating ... The views of the Cascades are inspiring ... Can you say Nirvana?... Great people. Great service ... Designer missed the boat on this one ... Great course; best area in Oregon for weather... Very nice attitude ... Problems with reactivated water springs of '96 & '97 have all been corrected.
★★★★ **GLAZE MEADOW COURSE**
Holes: 18. **Yards:** 6,574/5,616. **Par:** 72/72. **Course Rating:** 71.5/72.1. **Slope:** 128/120. **Green Fee:** $42/$58. **Cart Fee:** $28/cart. **Walking Policy:** Unrestricted walking. **Walkability:** 3.
Opened: 1982. **Architect:** Gene "Bunny" Mason. **Season:** March-Nov. **High:** June-Sept. **To obtain tee times:** Guests may call up to 14 days in advance, nonguests 7 days. **Miscellaneous:** Reduced fees (weekdays, low season, twilight, juniors), discount packages, range (grass), club rentals, lodging, credit cards (MC, V, AE, D), beginner friendly (seasonal weekly clinics).
Notes: Ranked 12th in 1997 Best in State.
Reader Comments: Scenic, quality golf experience ... You will use every club in your bag ... Best course in central Oregon ... Green and nice ... Spectacular setting. Good value ... Perfect mountain course, beautiful ... Flood damage on a few holes ... Bring some balls–tight ... 'Woodsy feel,' the true Northwest ... Shorter and harder of two.

★★★ **BROADMOOR GOLF COURSE**
PU-3509 N.E. Columbia Blvd., Portland, 97211, Multnomah County, (503)281-1337, 4 miles NE of Portland.
Holes: 18. **Yards:** 6,467/5,388. **Par:** 72/74. **Course Rating:** 70.2/69.5. **Slope:** 122/111. **Green Fee:** $22/$26. **Cart Fee:** $24/cart. **Walking Policy:** Unrestricted walking. **Walkability:** 3.
Opened: 1931. **Architect:** George Junor. **Season:** Year-round. **High:** May-Sept. **To obtain tee times:** Call golf shop 7 days in advance. **Miscellaneous:** Reduced fees (weekdays, low season, juniors), metal spikes, club rentals, credit cards (MC, V).
Reader Comments: My home course; very challenging ... Very wet during winter months ... Just another public course ... Enough challenge to be fun ... Susceptible to pooling in rainy weather ... Inexpensive ... Nice course for a lot of traffic ... Straightforward ... Blend of interesting and exciting ... Cute, public 18 holes, challenging drives (long holes) ... Lots of water, trees, very hilly ... Good food and drink.

★★★ CEDAR LINKS GOLF CLUB
PU-3155 Cedar Links Dr., Medford, 97504, Jackson County, (541)773-4373, (800)853-2754.
Holes: 18. **Yards:** 6,215/5,145. **Par:** 70/71. **Course Rating:** 68.9/68.7. **Slope:** 114/112. **Green Fee:** $22/$24. **Cart Fee:** $9/person. **Walking Policy:** Unrestricted walking. **Walkability:** 2. **Opened:** 1972. **Architect:** Coverstone/Graves. **Season:** Year-round. **High:** April-Sept. **To obtain tee times:** Call golf shop up to 7 days in advance. **Miscellaneous:** Reduced fees (seniors, juniors), metal spikes, range (mats), club rentals, credit cards (MC, V, D), beginner friendly (clinics).
Reader Comments: Worth playing if in the area ... Good bar ... Excellent service ... A very nice course, improving, very fair ... Great course to sharpen your skills; very pretty ... Muddy when wet–slow play ... Damned good ... Muny-type course ... Minimum facilities. Small, but short course ... Good for a public course, no gimmies here ... Short–too much watering–okay course.

★★★ COLWOOD NATIONAL GOLF CLUB
PU-7313 N.E. Columbia Blvd., Portland, 97218, Multnomah County, (503)254-5515.
Holes: 18. **Yards:** 6,200/5,800. **Par:** 70/74. **Course Rating:** 69.1/71.0. **Slope:** 115/111. **Green Fee:** $26/$39. **Cart Fee:** $22/cart. **Walking Policy:** Unrestricted walking. **Walkability:** 1. **Opened:** 1930. **Architect:** A. Vernon Macan. **Season:** Year-round. **High:** April-Oct. **To obtain tee times:** Call seven days in advance. **Miscellaneous:** Reduced fees (juniors), metal spikes, club rentals, credit cards (MC, V), beginner friendly.
Reader Comments: Short but challenging ... Some really nice holes ... Duck the jets, noisy ... Straight and open course. Good to play at beginning of season ... Nice greens–real challenging holes ... Average course, not worth what they charge ... A good test of holes. Harder than it looks ... Nice course for much traffic.

EAGLE CREST RESORT
R-1522 Cline Falls Rd., Redmond, 97756, Deschutes County, (541)923-4653, 5 miles E of Redmond.
★★★½ RESORT COURSE
Holes: 18. **Yards:** 6,673/5,395. **Par:** 72/72. **Course Rating:** 71.5/69.8. **Slope:** 128/120. **Green Fee:** N/A/$45. **Cart Fee:** $25/cart. **Walking Policy:** Unrestricted walking. **Walkability:** 3. **Opened:** 1986. **Architect:** Gene "Bunny" Mason. **Season:** Year-round. **High:** July-Sept. **To obtain tee times:** Public may call 14 days in advance but must guarantee with a credit card. Owners 30 days in advance; tournaments 6 months in advance with credit card guarantee. **Miscellaneous:** Reduced fees (low season), range (grass), club rentals, lodging, credit cards (MC, V, AE, D).
Reader Comments: High desert. It's a challenge from start to finish ... Excellent resort course. Accommodations are outstanding ... In great shape for winter play ... Great layout & scenery ... Good resort facility with both easy & difficult holes ... Dynamite greens. Fast ... Beautiful course ... First-class condition. Good challenge ... Have played this several times; doesn't get as crowded as the Ridge course and people are really nice ... Both Eagle Crest courses are nice.
★★★★ RIDGE COURSE
Holes: 18. **Yards:** 6,927/4,792. **Par:** 72/72. **Course Rating:** 73.0/66.1. **Slope:** 131/115. **Green Fee:** N/A/$45. **Cart Fee:** $25/cart. **Walking Policy:** Unrestricted walking. **Walkability:** 2. **Opened:** 1990. **Architect:** John Thronson. **Season:** Year-round. **High:** July-Sept. **To obtain tee times:** Public may call 14 days in advance but must guarantee with a credit card. Owners 30 days in advance; tournaments 6 months in advance with credit card guarantee. **Miscellaneous:** Reduced fees (low season, juniors), range (grass), club rentals, lodging, credit cards (MC, V, AE, D), beginner friendly (junior program).
Reader Comments: Tough course to walk. I prefer not to use carts. Hard to do here ... Well kept–very scenic–easy to make par ... The beauty and scenery like links course ... Beautiful area, well-kept summer course ... Great fast greens. Package deals/room and golf ... Excellent greens; lush fairways ... Best resort in Oregon.
Special Notes: Formerly Eagle Crest course.

★★★★½ EAGLE POINT GOLF COURSE *Pace*
PU-100 Eagle Point Dr., Eagle Point, 97524, Jackson County, (541)826-8225, 9 miles NE of Medford.
Holes: 18. **Yards:** 7,099/5,071. **Par:** 72/72. **Course Rating:** 74.3/68.9. **Slope:** 131/113. **Green Fee:** $35/$40. **Cart Fee:** $20/cart. **Walking Policy:** Unrestricted walking. **Walkability:** 2. **Opened:** 1996. **Architect:** Robert Trent Jones Jr. **Season:** Year-round. **High:** May-Sept. **To obtain tee times:** Call up to 7 days in advance. Additional fees for bookings prior to 7 days. **Miscellaneous:** Reduced fees (weekdays, low season, twilight, juniors), metal spikes, range (grass), club rentals, credit cards (MC, V, AE).
Notes: Ranked 7th in 1999 Best in State.
Reader Comments: Best course in southern Oregon! ... As good as it gets ... Very fun design. Good test. Wonderful scenery ... Long course, beautiful setting.... Tough par 3s, great par 5s, play the course ... Great design. Needs maturity ... Best in the West ... Incredible value! Pristine condition ... Challenging but fair... Great find, always in excellent shape ... Great course, play even during wet weather. Price is good also.

★★★½ EASTMORELAND GOLF COURSE

PU-2425 S.E. Bybee Blvd., Portland, 97202, Multnomah County, (503)775-2900.
Holes: 18. **Yards:** 6,529/5,646. **Par:** 72/74. **Course Rating:** 71.7/71.4. **Slope:** 123/117. **Green Fee:** $21/$23. **Cart Fee:** $26/cart. **Walking Policy:** Unrestricted walking. **Walkability:** N/A.
Opened: 1921. **Architect:** H. Chandler Egan. **Season:** Year-round. **High:** June-Sept. **To obtain tee times:** Call six days in advance. **Miscellaneous:** Reduced fees (seniors, juniors), metal spikes, club rentals, credit cards (MC, V).
Notes: Ranked 15th in 1999 Best in State; 37th in 1996 America's Top 75 Affordable Courses. 1990 USGA Public Links.
Reader Comments: Because of publicity, this course has become too popular ... Over- used track, back nine memorable ... Some beautiful holes ... Nice way to spend a day ... Busy place, well run. Fine layout in great condition ... Older muny ... Wonderful, old growth trees; challenging course ... Watch for demented goose ... Easy on the wallet ... Drainage is a problem.

★★★★½ ELKHORN VALLEY GOLF COURSE *Value+*

PU-32295 N. Fork Rd., Lyons, 97358, Marion County, (503)897-3368, 36 miles E of Salem.
Holes: 9. **Yards:** 3,169/2,009. **Par:** 36/36. **Course Rating:** 71.4/63.8. **Slope:** 136/109. **Green Fee:** $27/$27. **Cart Fee:** $22/cart. **Walking Policy:** Unrestricted walking. **Walkability:** 1.
Opened: 1996. **Architect:** Don Cutler. **Season:** March-Oct. **High:** June-Sept. **To obtain tee times:** Call golf shop. **Miscellaneous:** Reduced fees (juniors), metal spikes, club rentals, credit cards (MC, V, D).
Reader Comments: The best nine-hole course anywhere ... Slow play ... Hidden jewel ... Good value ... Brings you back to nature ... The only drawback: The scenery ruins my game ... A diamond in the rough ... Very lush fairways ... Very well laid-out course in a stunning setting ... Stay in the fairways; no rough; 'jungle' ... Mountain beauty ... This is just a nine-hole course, but it has to be the most beautiful and challenging course I have ever played.

★★★½ EMERALD VALLEY GOLF CLUB

SP-83301 Dale Kuni Rd., Creswell, 97426, Lane County, (541)895-2174, 10 miles S of Eugene.
Holes: 18. **Yards:** 6,873/5,713. **Par:** 72/73. **Course Rating:** 73.0/70.8. **Slope:** 126/122. **Green Fee:** $28/$31. **Cart Fee:** $22/cart. **Walking Policy:** Unrestricted walking. **Walkability:** 2.
Opened: 1964. **Architect:** Bob Baldock. **Season:** Year-round. **High:** June-Sept. **To obtain tee times:** Call up to 7 days in advance. **Miscellaneous:** Reduced fees (weekdays, low season, twilight, seniors, juniors), range (grass/mats), club rentals, credit cards (MC, V, AE).
Notes: 1981 USGA Public Links Women's Championships.
Reader Comments: Price is right ... Best value in Eugene/Creswell ... Average course but fun ... Greens have gone from exceptional to average ... Fast, sloping greens, rough shape ... Established golf course–beautiful setting ... Course had a very interesting layout. Has potential to be a great golf course, but something drastic needs to be done as far as course upkeep ... Another good course for winter play. The course will sneak up on you.

★★★★ FOREST HILLS GOLF COURSE

SP-36260 S.W. Tongue Lane, Cornelius, 97113, Washington County, (503)357-3347, 25 miles W of Portland.
Holes: 18. **Yards:** 6,173/5,673. **Par:** 72/74. **Course Rating:** 69.7/72.1. **Slope:** 126/123. **Green Fee:** $32/$32. **Cart Fee:** $24/cart. **Walking Policy:** Unrestricted walking. **Walkability:** 2.
Opened: 1927. **Architect:** Don Bell. **Season:** Year-round. **High:** May-Sept. **To obtain tee times:** Call golf shop seven days in advance. Saturday, Sunday and holidays no 9-hole play or twosomes before 1 p.m. **Miscellaneous:** Reduced fees (juniors), range (grass/mats), club rentals, credit cards (MC, V, AE).
Reader Comments: Well maintained. Well laid out ... A gem in hiding ... Probably my favorite in Oregon ... Doesn't stand out–nice course with view of Mt. Hood ... Good value, good test ... Pretty rolling layout, lots of variety ... Many great holes. Too wet in summer.

★★★ GEARHART GOLF LINKS

PU-N. Marion St., Gearhart, 97138, Clatsop County, (503)738-3538, 90 miles NW of Portland.
Holes: 18. **Yards:** 6,089/5,882. **Par:** 72/74. **Course Rating:** 68.7/70.5. **Slope:** 114/112. **Green Fee:** $27/$27. **Cart Fee:** $25/cart. **Walking Policy:** Unrestricted walking. **Walkability:** 2.
Opened: 1892. **Season:** Year-round. **High:** April-Oct. **To obtain tee times:** Call anytime. **Miscellaneous:** Metal spikes, range (grass), club rentals, lodging (100 rooms), credit cards (MC, V).
Reader Comments: Best to play in summer or fall ... Great! One of oldest courses west of Mississippi ... 18th hole worth the price of admission ... Small greens, great old coast course ... Winds from ocean can be tough ... Course & greens in poor condition ... Finally, course improvements will make this a jewel ... Very windy–easy to lose ball.

GLENDOVEER GOLF COURSE

PU-14015 N.E. Glisan, Portland, 97230, Multnomah County, (503)253-7507.
★★★½ EAST COURSE

Holes: 18. **Yards:** 6,296/5,142. **Par:** 73/75. **Course Rating:** 69.3/73.5. **Slope:** 119/120. **Green Fee:** $20/$22. **Cart Fee:** $24/cart. **Walking Policy:** Unrestricted walking. **Walkability:** 4. **Opened:** 1926. **Architect:** John Junor. **Season:** Year-round. **High:** May-Sept. **To obtain tee times:** Call tee time number (292-8570) six days in advance. **Miscellaneous:** Reduced fees (seniors, juniors), metal spikes, range (mats), club rentals.

Reader Comments: Gets lots of play, but well maintained, lots of trees ... Glendoveer, both East and West are great courses for high handicappers and not cumbersome. A good walk for a summer afternoon ... A great course–superior for women, too! ... Good layout–beautiful setting ... Somewhat hilly, with lots of trees ... Classic old course–a favorite ... Just good, nothing more.

★★★ **WEST COURSE**

Holes: 18. **Yards:** 5,922/5,117. **Par:** 71/75. **Course Rating:** 67.5/70.8. **Slope:** 111/110. **Green Fee:** $20/$22. **Cart Fee:** $24/cart. **Walking Policy:** Unrestricted walking. **Walkability:** 2. **Opened:** 1926. **Architect:** Frank Stenzel. **Season:** Year-round. **High:** May-Sept. **To obtain tee times:** Call tee time number (292-8570) six days in advance. **Miscellaneous:** Reduced fees (seniors, juniors), metal spikes, range (mats), club rentals.

Reader Comments: Easy to walk ... Basic beginner course ... Gets lots of play, easier than East Course ... Dried out ... Easier for weaklings! ... A fine place, nothing spectacular ... A little easier than the East ... Nice old-growth trees. Flat.

★★½ **THE GOLF CLUB OF OREGON**

PU-905 NW Spring Hill Dr., Albany, 97321, Benton County, (541)928-8338, 20 miles S of Salem.
Holes: 18. **Yards:** 5,836/5,089. **Par:** 70/71. **Course Rating:** 67.8/68.9. **Slope:** 111/117. **Green Fee:** $22/$22. **Cart Fee:** $20/cart. **Walking Policy:** Unrestricted walking. **Walkability:** 2. **Opened:** 1930. **Season:** Year-round. **High:** May-Sept. **To obtain tee times:** Call up to 7 days in advance. **Miscellaneous:** Reduced fees (low season, seniors, juniors), metal spikes, range (mats), club rentals, beginner friendly.

Reader Comments: Beautiful fir trees ... You get what you pay for with this course. Fun to play ... Cheap but course reflects it ... Fair public course.

★★★ **GRANTS PASS GOLF CLUB**

SP-230 Espey Rd., Grants Pass, 97527, Josephine County, (541)476-0849.
Holes: 18. **Yards:** 6,425/5,300. **Par:** 72/73. **Course Rating:** 71.5/71.4. **Slope:** 131/121. **Green Fee:** $30/$30. **Cart Fee:** $20/cart. **Walking Policy:** Unrestricted walking. **Walkability:** 3. **Opened:** 1947. **Architect:** Bob Baldock/Robert L. Baldock. **Season:** Year-round. **High:** March-Oct. **To obtain tee times:** Call 48 hours in advance. **Miscellaneous:** Reduced fees (juniors), metal spikes, range (grass/mats), club rentals, credit cards (MC, V).

Reader Comments: Two distinct 9s ... Fun course, not too difficult, but a fun way to kill a day ... Slow play ... Good value–muny-type course ... Challenging! Back nine is up and down. A little rough for a country club.

★★½ **GRESHAM GOLF COURSE**

SP-2155 N.E. Division St., Gresham, 97030, Multnomah County, (503)665-3352, 15 miles E of Portland.
Holes: 18. **Yards:** 6,008/5,294. **Par:** 72/72. **Course Rating:** 68.1/69.6. **Slope:** 109/110. **Green Fee:** $19/$22. **Cart Fee:** $24/cart. **Walking Policy:** Walking at certain times. **Walkability:** 1. **Opened:** 1965. **Season:** Year-round. **High:** June-Sept. **Miscellaneous:** Metal spikes, range (grass/mats), club rentals, credit cards (MC, V).

Reader Comments: Not bad–very wet conditions ... Good for intermediates, too long for beginners ... Creative use of space ... Vanilla ... Course really holds water, it's better in summer.

★★½ **HARBOR LINKS GOLF COURSE**

PU-601 Harbor Isles Blvd., Klamath Falls, 97601, Klamath County, (541)882-0609. **E-mail:** harborl@cosnet.net.
Holes: 18. **Yards:** 6,272/5,709. **Par:** 72/72. **Course Rating:** 69.3/71.2. **Slope:** 117/119. **Green Fee:** $18/$30. **Cart Fee:** $20/cart. **Walking Policy:** Unrestricted walking. **Walkability:** 1. **Opened:** 1986. **Architect:** Ken Black. **Season:** Year-round. **High:** June-Sept. **To obtain tee times:** Call up to 7 days in advance. **Miscellaneous:** Reduced fees (weekdays, low season, twilight, seniors, juniors), range (mats), club rentals, credit cards (MC, V, AE), beginner friendly (ladies and mens clinics).

Reader Comments: Easy walk ... Well-groomed, fun course ... Fair test of golf. Nice friendly staff. Good food at reasonable prices ... Wide open with lots of water. Flat ... Good course–excellent condition ... Tranquil lakeside course. Beautiful fall evenings ... Lots of water but fun ... Play scenery and beat the wind ... Short muny-type course.

HERON LAKES GOLF COURSE

PU-3500 N. Victory Blvd., Portland, 97217, Multnomah County, (503)289-1818.
★★★★ **GREAT BLUE COURSE**
Holes: 18. **Yards:** 6,916/5,285. **Par:** 72/72. **Course Rating:** 73.6/69.8. **Slope:** 132/120. **Green Fee:** $31/$31. **Cart Fee:** $26/cart. **Walking Policy:** Unrestricted walking. **Walkability:** 1. **Opened:** 1971. **Architect:** Robert T. Jones Sr./Robert T. Jones Jr. **Season:** Year-round. **High:**

March-Oct. To obtain tee times: Call Tee Time Inc. at (503)292-8570. **Miscellaneous:** Reduced fees (weekdays, low season, seniors, juniors), metal spikes, range (grass/mats), club rentals, credit cards (MC, V, AE, D).

Reader Comments: Championship layout. Never dull ... Tough course, lots of bunkers ... Possibly the best public course in Portland ... A little too flat and open for my taste, not bad over all ... Beautiful course. Great value ... Tough finishing holes ... Lots of water/Great challenge/Even on a dry day ... Layout surpasses every public I have seen ... Crowded city course ... Good course for amount of traffic ... Noisy location by I-5 and Portland speedway.

★★★½ GREENBACK COURSE

Holes: 18. **Yards:** 6,608/5,240. **Par:** 72/72. **Course Rating:** 71.6/69.4. **Slope:** 123/113. **Green Fee:** $19/$21. **Cart Fee:** $26/cart. **Walking Policy:** Unrestricted walking. **Walkability:** 1. **Opened:** 1970. **Architect:** Robert Trent Jones Jr. **Season:** Year-round. **High:** March-Oct. **To obtain tee times:** Call Tee Time Inc. at (503)292-8570. **Miscellaneous:** Reduced fees (low season, seniors, juniors), metal spikes, range (grass/mats), club rentals, credit cards (MC, V, AE, D).

Reader Comments: Great course for price. Real challenge from Blues ... Nice course to play ... Good flat course. Some challenge ... Great for beginners ... Don't play when rainy ... Great links course ... Good value, slow play ... Fun city muny ... Gets a lot of play, nothing too outstanding ... A little easier than its sister course ... Slow play detracts from overall good course.

HIDDEN VALLEY GOLF COURSE

PU-775 N. River Rd., Cottage Grove, 97424, Lane County, (541)942-3046, 20 miles S of Eugene. **Holes:** 10. **Yards:** 2,771/2,355. **Par:** 35/35. **Course Rating:** 66.6/68.4. **Slope:** 108/114. **Green Fee:** $11/$16. **Cart Fee:** $16/cart. **Walking Policy:** Unrestricted walking. **Walkability:** 2. **Opened:** 1929. **Season:** Year-round. **High:** May-Sept. **To obtain tee times:** Call up to 2 weeks in advance. **Miscellaneous:** Reduced fees (weekdays, low season, seniors, juniors), club rentals, beginner friendly.

★★★★ INDIAN CREEK GOLF CLUB *Value*

PU-3605 Brookside Dr., Hood River, 97031, Hood River County, (541)386-7770, 60 miles E of Portland. **Holes:** 18. **Yards:** 6,118/4,547. **Par:** 72/72. **Course Rating:** 70.2/67.7. **Slope:** 124/116. **Green Fee:** $24/$32. **Cart Fee:** $25/cart. **Walking Policy:** Unrestricted walking. **Walkability:** 4. **Opened:** 1990. **Architect:** Carl Martin/Dave Martin. **Season:** Year-round. **High:** April-Oct. **To obtain tee times:** Call up to 7 days in advance. **Miscellaneous:** Reduced fees (low season, twilight, seniors, juniors), range (grass/mats), club rentals, credit cards (MC, V, D), beginner friendly (junior program, individual and group lessons).

Reader Comments: This is a neat course but very hilly ... Very, very nice course ... Two mountains for scenery–great greens ... Fantastic views/requires variety of shots ... Fun course ... Beautiful layout, creative hole design ... Just raised prices. Bring your wind ball ... Nice pleasant atmosphere ... Unfortunately, more people have discovered this fun course ... Water, mountains, sun and fun for all ability.

★★★½ JUNIPER GOLF CLUB

SP-139 S.E. Sisters Ave., Redmond, 97756, Deschutes County, (541)548-3121, (800)600-3121. **Holes:** 18. **Yards:** 6,525/5,598. **Par:** 72/72. **Course Rating:** 70.8/70.9. **Slope:** 127/119. **Green Fee:** $20/$32. **Cart Fee:** $22/cart. **Walking Policy:** Unrestricted walking. **Walkability:** 4. **Opened:** 1953. **Architect:** Tim Berg. **Season:** Year-round. **High:** May-Oct. **To obtain tee times:** Call one month in advance. **Miscellaneous:** Reduced fees (low season, juniors), metal spikes, range (grass/mats), club rentals, credit cards (MC, V).

Reader Comments: Nice course for friendly betting game! ... Staff needs to lighten up ... Watch the aircraft, on final, gear down ... Good test. Uneventful front 9, fun back ... Bargain compared to overpriced Bend courses ... Easy to play–fun course ... Hard to get tee times ... Ho hum, but improving ... This is a great course for its value and location.

★★★½ KAH-NEE-TA RESORT GOLF CLUB

R-P.O. Box K, Warm Springs, 97761, Wasco County, (541)553-1112, (800)831-0100, 115 miles SE of Portland. **E-mail:** kah-nee-taresort.com. **Holes:** 18. **Yards:** 6,352/5,195. **Par:** 72/73. **Course Rating:** 73.1/70.0. **Slope:** 123/116. **Green Fee:** $30/$35. **Cart Fee:** $26/cart. **Walking Policy:** Unrestricted walking. **Walkability:** 1. **Opened:** 1972. **Architect:** William Bell/Bunny Mason. **Season:** Year-round. **High:** March-Oct. **To obtain tee times:** Call up to 14 days in advance. **Miscellaneous:** Reduced fees (weekdays, low season, resort guests, seniors, juniors), discount packages, metal spikes, range (grass), club rentals, lodging (169 rooms), credit cards (MC, V, AE, D, Diners Club), beginner friendly (schools and clinics).

Reader Comments: Above average. Easy par 5s ... Jewel in the desert, 17th among toughest ... Great greens ... A nice resort course, some real challenging holes ... Wish the front side were more like the back ... Excellent highlands desert course ... Beautiful course. Very few players. No need for tee times ... Several very beautiful holes along the Warm Springs River.

★½ KENTUCK GOLF COURSE
PU-675 Golf Course Lane, North Bend, 97459, Coos County, (541)756-4464, 4 miles N of North Bend.
Holes: 18. **Yards:** 5,393/4,469. **Par:** 70/70. **Course Rating:** 65.5/69.8. **Slope:** 99/107. **Green Fee:** $16/$18. **Cart Fee:** $20/cart. **Walking Policy:** Unrestricted walking. **Walkability:** 2. **Opened:** 1962. **Season:** Year-round. **High:** May-Sept. **Miscellaneous:** Range (grass), club rentals, credit cards (MC, V, D), beginner friendly.

LAKERIDGE GOLF COURSE
PU-Klamath Hwy. 140, Lakeview, 97630, Lake County, (541)947-3855, 3 miles W of Lakeview. **E-mail:** lakeridge@transport.com.
Holes: 9. **Yards:** 3,323/2,965. **Par:** 36/37. **Course Rating:** 70.0/71.6. **Slope:** 119/121. **Green Fee:** $18/$18. **Cart Fee:** $15/cart. **Walking Policy:** Unrestricted walking. **Walkability:** 1. **Season:** Year-round. **High:** June-Aug. **To obtain tee times:** Call. **Miscellaneous:** Reduced fees (seniors, juniors), metal spikes, range (grass), club rentals, credit cards (MC, V), beginner friendly.
Special Notes: Formerly Lakeridge Golf Course.

★★ LAKESIDE GOLF & RACQUET CLUB
SP-3245 N.E. 50th Street, Lincoln City, 97367, Lincoln County, (541)994-8442, 50 miles W of Salem. **E-mail:** lakesidegolf@wcn.net.
Holes: 18. **Yards:** 5,007/4,318. **Par:** 66/71. **Course Rating:** 64.9/66.2. **Slope:** 109/104. **Green Fee:** $27/$35. **Cart Fee:** $25/cart. **Walking Policy:** Unrestricted walking. **Walkability:** 4. **Opened:** 1925. **Season:** Year-round. **High:** May-Sept. **To obtain tee times:** Call. **Miscellaneous:** Reduced fees (low season, resort guests, twilight, seniors, juniors), discount packages, metal spikes, club rentals, credit cards (MC, V, AE, D), beginner friendly.
Special Notes: Formerly Lakeside Golf Club

★★★½ LANGDON FARMS GOLF CLUB
PU-24377 N.E. Airport Rd., Aurora, 97002, Marion County, (503)678-4653, 15 miles S of Portland. **Web:** www.ob-sports.com.
Holes: 18. **Yards:** 6,950/5,249. **Par:** 71/71. **Course Rating:** 73.3/69.4. **Slope:** 125/114. **Green Fee:** $45/$75. **Cart Fee:** Included in Green Fee. **Walking Policy:** Unrestricted walking. **Walkability:** 3. **Opened:** 1995. **Architect:** John Fought/Robert Cupp. **Season:** Year-round. **High:** June-Sept. **To obtain tee times:** Call up to 60 days in advance. **Miscellaneous:** Reduced fees (weekdays, low season, twilight, juniors), discount packages, range (grass/mats), club rentals, credit cards (MC, V, AE, D), beginner friendly (three full time instructors).
Reader Comments: Fair course, good service. ... Fun to drive cart through the old barn ... Lousy location (freeway) but otherwise great ... Nice clubhouse ... Can't beat the location; right on I-5 ... Course, a bit slow ... Always slow, too much money for an OK layout ... Great layout and practice facility ... Best service in the state, but expensive ... Dunes-type course.

★★★★ LOST TRACKS GOLF CLUB
PU-60205 Sunset View Dr., Bend, 97702, Deschutes County, (541)385-1818.
Holes: 18. **Yards:** 7,003/5,287. **Par:** 72/73. **Course Rating:** 72.7/71.1. **Slope:** 131/128. **Green Fee:** $29/$48. **Cart Fee:** $25/person. **Walking Policy:** Unrestricted walking. **Walkability:** 2. **Opened:** 1996. **Architect:** Brian Whitcomb. **Season:** Year-round. **High:** June-Sept. **To obtain tee times:** Call 7 days in advance. Credit card guarantee required. 30 days for parties of 12 or more. **Miscellaneous:** Reduced fees (low season, resort guests, twilight, seniors, juniors), range (grass), club rentals, credit cards (MC, V), beginner friendly.
Reader Comments: Sagebrush close to fairway, A.K.A 'lost ball' ... Great staff, great value ... Walking through train car to par-3 water green a real trip! ... Best course in central Oregon, great value ... A fantastic setting & great course ... Had to quit because of extremely slow pace ... Very short and broken-up fairways ... Hidden gem. Don't miss it if in Bend ... Rain checks ... Deceptively long ... We had to go back twice. Best value in Bend.

★★★½ MCNARY GOLF CLUB
SP-155 McNary Estates Drive North , Keizer, 97303, Marion County, (503)393-4653, 45 miles S of Portland. **E-mail:** ghatmcnary@aol.com.
Holes: 18. **Yards:** 6,215/5,325. **Par:** 71/71. **Course Rating:** 69.2/70.4. **Slope:** 121/117. **Green Fee:** $30/$40. **Cart Fee:** $24/cart. **Walking Policy:** Unrestricted walking. **Walkability:** 2. **Opened:** 1962. **Season:** Year-round. **High:** April-Oct. **To obtain tee times:** Call golf club. **Miscellaneous:** Reduced fees (weekdays, low season, twilight, juniors), club rentals, credit cards (MC, V).
Reader Comments: My home course. A nice place to belong/play! ... Course condition good only in summer... Winds through housing development. It's a challenge ... Long walks between holes ... Solid course, very good greens. Well maintained ... Generally I like courses without houses so close, husband refuses to play without insurance card! ... Flat, no-frills course ... Good challenge to play.

OREGON

★★★★ MEADOW LAKES GOLF COURSE *Value+, Pace*
PU-300 Meadow Lakes Dr., Prineville, 97754, Crook County, (541)447-7113, (800)577-2797, 38
miles NE of Bend.
Holes: 18. **Yards:** 6,731/5,155. **Par:** 72/72. **Course Rating:** 71.7/69.0. **Slope:** 125/121. **Green
Fee:** $20/$31. **Cart Fee:** $11/person. **Walking Policy:** Unrestricted walking. **Walkability:** N/A.
Opened: 1993. **Architect:** William Robinson. **Season:** Year-round. **High:** June-Sept. **To obtain
tee times:** Call up to one year in advance guaranteed with credit card, otherwise six days without credit card. **Miscellaneous:** Reduced fees (low season), discount packages, metal spikes,
range (grass/mats), club rentals, credit cards (MC, V, D).
Notes: 1996 Golf Digest's Environmental Leaders in Golf Award.
Reader Comments: Nice, affordable muny with H20 on every hole ... Water on every hole. If you
hook or fade, you are in trouble ... Great value. Excellent condition, basically unknown ... Friendly
western atmosphere–outstanding! ... Superb smalltown gem ... Very flat ... Excellent layout for
the location ... A very good public course ... Good to play in the winter... Friendly people, great
clubhouse and fun course.

★★ MERIWETHER NATIONAL GOLF CLUB
PU-5200 S.W. Rood Bridge Rd., Hillsboro, 97123, Washington County, (503)648-4143, 25 miles
W of Portland.
Holes: 27. **Yards:** 6,719/5,766. **Par:** 72/73. **Course Rating:** 71.3/67.2. **Slope:** 121/112. **Green
Fee:** $24/$30. **Cart Fee:** $20/cart. **Walking Policy:** Walking at certain times. **Walkability:** 2.
Opened: 1960. **Architect:** Fred Federsfield. **Season:** Year-round. **High:** April-Oct. **To obtain tee
times:** Call up to 7 days in advance. **Miscellaneous:** Reduced fees (juniors), metal spikes,
range (grass), club rentals, credit cards (MC, V), beginner friendly.

★★★ MOUNTAIN HIGH GOLF COURSE
PU-60650 China Hat Rd., Bend, 97702, Deschutes County, (541)382-1111.
Holes: 18. **Yards:** 6,656/5,268. **Par:** 72/72. **Course Rating:** 72.0/69.2. **Slope:** 131/120. **Green
Fee:** $40/$48. **Cart Fee:** Included in Green Fee. **Walking Policy:** Unrestricted walking.
Walkability: 2. **Opened:** 1986. **Season:** Apr.-Nov. **High:** May-Oct. **To obtain tee times:** Call golf
shop. **Miscellaneous:** Reduced fees (low season), metal spikes, range (mats), club rentals,
credit cards (MC, V), beginner friendly.
Reader Comments: Never crowded, one nice 600-yard par 5 ... Narrow, long front 9 ... Tough
tees. Be humble, play the right tees ... Short, tight and enjoyable ... Good value ... Homes too
close to fairways ... Tight fairways but pleasant.

MOUNTAIN VIEW GOLF CLUB
PU-27195 S.E. Kelso Rd., Boring, 97009, Clackamas County, (503)663-4869, 15 miles SE of
Portland.
Holes: 18. **Yards:** 6,056/5,294. **Par:** 71/73. **Course Rating:** 69.2/69.2. **Slope:** 122/111. **Green
Fee:** $20/$24. **Cart Fee:** $25/cart. **Walking Policy:** Unrestricted walking. **Walkability:** 3.
Opened: 1963. **Architect:** Jack Waltmeyer. **Season:** Year-round. **High:** April-Oct. **To obtain tee
times:** Call golf shop. **Miscellaneous:** Reduced fees (weekdays, seniors, juniors), metal spikes,
range (mats), club rentals, credit cards (MC, V, D).

MYRTLE CREEK GOLF COURSE
PU-1316 Fairway Drive, Myrtle Creek, 97457, Douglas County, (541)863-4653, (888)869-7853,
220 miles S of Portland. **E-mail:** mcgc@rosenet.net. **Web:** www.cybergolf/myrtlecreekgolf.com.
Holes: 18. **Yards:** 6,637/4,868. **Par:** 72/72. **Course Rating:** 72.3/69.4. **Slope:** 135/124. **Green
Fee:** $23/$29. **Cart Fee:** $20/cart. **Walking Policy:** Unrestricted walking. **Walkability:** 4.
Opened: 1997. **Architect:** Graham Cooke. **Season:** Year-round. **High:** May-Oct. **To obtain tee
times:** Book up to 14 days in advance. **Miscellaneous:** Reduced fees (weekdays, low season,
resort guests, twilight, seniors, juniors), discount packages, metal spikes, range (grass), club
rentals, credit cards (MC, V).
Notes: 1998 Recognized by Golf Digest as the 7th Most Affordable New Course.

NINE PEAKS MADRAS GOLF & COUNTRY CLUB
1152 NW Golf Course Lane, Madras, 97741, Jefferson County, (541)475-3511.
Special Notes: Call club for further information.

OAK HILLS GOLF CLUB
PU-1919 Recreation Lane, Sutherlin, 97479, Douglas County, (541)459-4422, 12 miles N of
Roseburg. **Web:** www.golfoakhills.com.
Holes: 18. **Yards:** 6,811/5,388. **Par:** 72/72. **Course Rating:** 71.6/71.9. **Slope:** 129/122. **Green
Fee:** $22/$25. **Cart Fee:** $20/cart. **Walkability:** 3. **Opened:** 1971. **Season:** Year-round. **High:**
May-Oct. **To obtain tee times:** Seven day call in basis. **Miscellaneous:** Reduced fees (week-
days, low season, twilight, juniors), discount packages, range (grass/mats), club rentals, credit
cards (MC, V).
Special Notes: Formerly Sutherlin Knolls Golf Course

OREGON

★★★ OAK KNOLL GOLF COURSE
PU-6335 Hwy. 22, Independence, 97351, Polk County, (503)378-0344, 6 miles W of Salem.
Holes: 18. **Yards:** 6,208/5,239. **Par:** 72/72. **Course Rating:** 68.6/69.2. **Slope:** 113/113. **Green Fee:** $22/$25. **Cart Fee:** $20/cart. **Walking Policy:** Unrestricted walking. **Walkability:** 1.
Opened: 1926. **Architect:** Bill Ashby. **Season:** Year-round. **High:** May-Oct. **To obtain tee times:** Call golf shop. **Miscellaneous:** Reduced fees (weekdays, low season, seniors, juniors), discount packages, metal spikes, range (grass), club rentals, credit cards (MC, V), beginner friendly.
Reader Comments: Slow play is common. Good greens, but small ... An OK public course ... Nice inexpensive course ... Always a wait ... Solid, but simple. Price is a little high ... Drainage problems in the winter ... Family golf course, beginner's course ... Friendly ... Average course.

★★★½ OCEAN DUNES GOLF LINKS
PU-3345 Munsel Lake Rd., Florence, 97439, Lane County, (541)997-3232, (800)468-4833, 60 miles W of Eugene.
Holes: 18. **Yards:** 6,018/5,044. **Par:** 71/73. **Course Rating:** 70.0/73.8. **Slope:** 124/129. **Green Fee:** $28/$35. **Cart Fee:** $24/cart. **Walking Policy:** Unrestricted walking. **Walkability:** 3.
Opened: 1963. **Architect:** William G. Robinson. **Season:** Year-round. **High:** April-Nov. **To obtain tee times:** Call golf shop. **Miscellaneous:** Reduced fees (twilight, seniors, juniors), metal spikes, range (grass/mats), club rentals, credit cards (MC, V, D).
Reader Comments: Irons off the tee ... Tough course! Many blind shots ... Narrow fairways, biggest sand traps in world ... Undiscovered gem. Don't write about it ... Always fun to play, good value ... Tight fairways, use caution with drives ... If windy, forget it, don't even bother ... Another great course with links and hills ... Beautiful course ... 14 holes run through Oregon sand dunes.

OLALLA VALLEY GOLF COURSE
PU-1022 Olalla Rd., Toledo, 97391, Lincoln County, (541)336-2121, 7 miles E of Newport.
Holes: 18. **Yards:** 6,027/5,507. **Par:** 72/74. **Course Rating:** 69.2/72.7. **Slope:** 127/124. **Green Fee:** $22/$22. **Cart Fee:** $18/cart. **Walking Policy:** Unrestricted walking. **Walkability:** 4.
Season: Year-round. **High:** June-Oct. **To obtain tee times:** Please call. **Miscellaneous:** Reduced fees (juniors), range (grass), club rentals, credit cards (MC, V), beginner friendly.

★★★ OREGON CITY GOLF CLUB
PU-20124 S. Beavercreek Rd., Oregon City, 97045, Clackamas County, (503)656-2846, 15 miles S of Portland.
Holes: 18. **Yards:** 5,964/5,259. **Par:** 71/75. **Course Rating:** 67.9/69.4. **Slope:** 116/113. **Green Fee:** $18/$30. **Cart Fee:** $25/cart. **Walking Policy:** Unrestricted walking. **Walkability:** 2.
Opened: 1922. **Architect:** H. Beals/R. Seon/J. Herberger. **Season:** Year-round. **High:** April - Sept. **To obtain tee times:** Call up to 14 days in advance. **Miscellaneous:** Reduced fees (weekdays, low season, seniors, juniors), club rentals, credit cards (MC, V).
Reader Comments: Pretty good wet-weather course ... Getting better with age; short ... Good basic course ... Nice course, close to work, not too difficult ... Slowest round ever, had to walk off after 9 ... Overpriced but good golf ... Lots of new and good improvements.

★★★★ OREGON GOLF ASSN. MEMBERS COURSE AT TUKWILA
PU-2990 Boones Ferry Rd., Woodburn, 97071, Marion County, (503)981-6105.
Holes: 18. **Yards:** 6,650/5,498. **Par:** 72/72. **Course Rating:** 71.6/71.9. **Slope:** 126/127. **Green Fee:** $26/$45. **Cart Fee:** $22/cart. **Walking Policy:** Unrestricted walking. **Walkability:** 2.
Opened: 1996. **Architect:** Bill Robinson. **Season:** Year-round. **High:** May-Oct. **To obtain tee times:** Call up to 5 days in advance. **Miscellaneous:** Reduced fees (twilight, juniors), metal spikes, range (grass/mats), club rentals, credit cards (MC, V, D).
Notes: Ranked tied for 8th in 1996 Best New Affordable Courses.
Reader Comments: Beautiful greens. Perfect location ... Great layout, challenging but fair. Great value ... Fast, friendly & fun ... Can be a killer from the Blue tees ... Fair to all ... Great test of golf ... Older front 9 better than new back ... Very reasonable price ... Great stroll through the Hazel-nut Orchard ... Good facility, needs clubhouse ... Like playing a country club ... Trying to get tee times for weekends is a joke ... Even the forward tees have ball washers, benches, garbage cans, etc.

★★★★ PERSIMMON COUNTRY CLUB
SP-500 S.E. Butler Rd., Gresham, 97080, Multnomah County, (503)661-1800, 25 miles E of Portland. **E-mail:** www.persimmongolf.com.
Holes: 18. **Yards:** 6,678/4,852. **Par:** 72/72. **Course Rating:** 71.2/66.1. **Slope:** 125/112. **Green Fee:** $45/$75. **Cart Fee:** Included in Green Fee. **Walking Policy:** Unrestricted walking.
Walkability: 4. **Opened:** 1993. **Architect:** Gene "Bunny" Mason. **Season:** Year-round. **High:** May-Sept. **To obtain tee times:** Call up to 3 days in advance. **Miscellaneous:** Reduced fees (low season, twilight), metal spikes, range (grass/mats), club rentals, credit cards (MC, V, AE, D).
Reader Comments: Very nice ... Too expensive when compared to other Portland-area courses ... Rolling terrain; aim at Mount Hood ... 9th and 18th are breathtaking ... Snobbish attitude by some behind counter; course too high priced for value; very hilly ... Spectacular views–wonderful course, always a treat to play ... Tough course up and down hills ... An outstanding course in

every respect ... Beautiful views; challenging but fair course ... Too far between green & tee. Not walkable; overpriced.

★★½ PROGRESS DOWNS GOLF COURSE
PU-8200 S.W. Scholls Ferry Rd., Beaverton, 97005, Washington County, (503)646-5166, 4 miles S of Portland. **Web:** www.golf2eagle.com.
Holes: 18. **Yards:** 6,426/5,626. **Par:** 71/73. **Course Rating:** 69.8/71.7. **Slope:** 112/115. **Green Fee:** N/A. **Walking Policy:** Unrestricted walking. **Walkability:** 1. **Opened:** 1966. **Architect:** City of Portland. **Season:** Year-round. **High:** April-Oct. **To obtain tee times:** In person seven days in advance or phone in six days in advance. **Miscellaneous:** Reduced fees (weekdays, seniors, juniors), metal spikes, range (mats), caddies, club rentals, credit cards (MC, V, AE, D).
Reader Comments: Ordinarily in perfect condition, easier! ... Needs TLC ... Overall fun place, great range and golf shop ... Going through major needed repairs ... Overplayed, overcrowded muny, I only play it early morning in summer before work, still crowded.

★★★★½ PUMPKIN RIDGE GOLF CLUB GHOST CREEK
Service, Condition, Pace
PU-12930 Old Pumpkin Ridge Rd., North Plains, 97133, Washington County, (503)647-9977, (888)594-4653, 20 miles W of Portland. **E-mail:** info@pumpkinridge.com. **Web:** www.pumpkinridge.com.
Holes: 18. **Yards:** 6,839/5,206. **Par:** 71/71. **Course Rating:** 73.6/70.4. **Slope:** 135/125. **Green Fee:** $115/$115. **Cart Fee:** $15/person. **Walking Policy:** Unrestricted walking. **Walkability:** 2. **Opened:** 1992. **Architect:** Bob Cupp. **Season:** Year-round. **High:** May-Oct. **To obtain tee times:** Seven days advanced $4.00. Thirty days advanced $10.00 fee prepaid. Sixty days advanced $20.00 fee prepaid. **Miscellaneous:** Reduced fees (weekdays, low season, twilight, juniors), range (grass/mats), caddies, club rentals, credit cards (MC, V, AE), beginner friendly (golf schools, instructions, clinics).
Notes: Ranked 81st in 1997-98 America's 100 Greatest; 5th in 1999 Best in State. 1993-94; 96 USGA Amateur; 2000 U.S. Junior Amateur and U.S. Girls Junior.
Reader Comments: Best ever, great condition ... The way golf should be ... Always challenging–sometimes too wet ... Every hole a challenge, every club used ... Fantastic country club atmosphere ... A world-class course ... Best public course in Oregon ... Design good, poor walking course ... Excellent service ... Overrated, nothing special ... Greens are great ... Too expensive for the average golfer ... Had a reservation mixup and an executive of the course met me at the practice range with an apology and a gift with balls, tees and markers.

★★★★ QUAIL RUN GOLF COURSE
PU-16725 Northridge Dr., La Pine, 97739, Deschutes County, (541)536-1303, (800)895-4653, 10 miles S of Sunriver.
Holes: 9. **Yards:** 7,024/5,414. **Par:** 72/72. **Course Rating:** 73.4/71.0. **Slope:** 135/128. **Green Fee:** $32/$32. **Cart Fee:** $12/cart. **Walking Policy:** Unrestricted walking. **Walkability:** 2. **Opened:** 1991. **Architect:** Jim Ramey. **Season:** March-Nov. **High:** June-Sept. **To obtain tee times:** Call up to 30 days in advance. **Miscellaneous:** Reduced fees (low season, twilight, juniors), discount packages, metal spikes, range (grass), club rentals, credit cards (MC, V, D).
Reader Comments: Surprising course–9 holes but all very good ... In great shape ... Nice people ... Hidden gem in central Oregon ... Fun course for the money ... Great value: love this course ... Good greens & pace ... Best 9-holer I've played, used to be a secret but it's been discovered ... I have never played on fairways that looked like putting greens ... Wow are those greens slick.

★★★½ QUAIL VALLEY GOLF COURSE
PU-12565 N.W. Aerts Rd., Banks, 97106, Washington County, (503)324-4444, 20 miles W of Portland. **E-mail:** qvgc@teleport.com. **Web:** quailvalleygolf.com.
Holes: 18. **Yards:** 6,603/5,519. **Par:** 72/72. **Course Rating:** 71.1/71.1. **Slope:** 119/115. **Green Fee:** $30/$36. **Cart Fee:** $24/person. **Walking Policy:** Unrestricted walking. **Walkability:** 1. **Opened:** 1994. **Architect:** John Zoller Jr. **Season:** Year-round. **High:** June-Sept. **To obtain tee times:** Call up to 7 days in advance. **Miscellaneous:** Reduced fees (juniors), range (grass/mats), club rentals, credit cards (MC, V, AE).
Reader Comments: Good quality golf. Friendly staff ... Wide open, wind provides the challenge ... Boring off the tee. Approach is everything ... Fairly flat. No. 18 is tough finisher ... Wind, water, wow ... Excellent track for relatively new course ... Good course: a little pricey for basic public ... Enjoyable, playable, tough greens ... Perfect greens, friendly staff ... Best public greens in Oregon.

THE RESERVE VINEYARDS & GOLF CLUB   *Service+*
SP-4805 SW 229th Ave., Aloha, 97007, Washington County, (503)649-8191, 20 miles W of Portland. **Web:** www.reservegolf.com.
★★★½ CUPP COURSE
Holes: 18. **Yards:** 6,852/5,198. **Par:** 72/72. **Course Rating:** 72.6/69.6. **Slope:** 132/115. **Green Fee:** $70/$90. **Cart Fee:** Included in Green Fee. **Walking Policy:** Unrestricted walking. **Walkability:** 1. **Opened:** 1998. **Architect:** Bob Cupp. **Season:** Year-round. **High:** April-Oct. **To**

obtain tee times: Call up to 30 days in advance. **Miscellaneous:** Reduced fees (weekdays, low season, twilight, juniors), range (grass), club rentals, credit cards (MC, V, AE, D).
Reader Comments: The newer course, less challenging ... Ran out of land ... Bring your run-up shot ... Odd course. Quirky ... First-year course, needs maturing. Shared clubhouse is great! ... Good shape, good test ... Very new course, short and sporty ... Great PGA caliber links course, open fairways with tough-to-hit greens ... Too much sand ... Fun challenges, great value!.

★★★★½ FOUGHT COURSE *Condition*

Holes: 18. **Yards:** 7,172/5,189. **Par:** 72/72. **Course Rating:** 74.3/70.1. **Slope:** 134/121. **Green Fee:** $70/$90. **Cart Fee:** Included in Green Fee. **Walking Policy:** Unrestricted walking. **Walkability:** 1. **Opened:** 1997. **Architect:** John Fought. **Season:** Year-round. **High:** April-Oct. **To obtain tee times:** Call up to 30 days in advance. **Miscellaneous:** Reduced fees (weekdays, low season, twilight, juniors), range (grass), club rentals, credit cards (MC, V, AE, D).
Notes: Ranked 12th in 1999 Best in State. Fred Meyer Challenge.
Reader Comments: Can't see the greens for the bunkers ... First-class facility! ... Another great course to play ... Risk and reward courses, fun ... Super course, bring a couple of sand wedges and your sand game ... In three more years it will be 5-stars ... Great course with hole variety, spendy ... Country club feel ... If you've played one hole you've played them all ... Course is too good to pass up ... Very good shape for newer course.

RESORT AT THE MOUNTAIN

R-68010 E. Fairway Ave., Welches, 97067, Clackamas County, (503)622-3151, (800)669-4653, 45 miles E of Portland.
Holes: 27. **Green Fee:** $22/$44. **Cart Fee:** $27/cart. **Walking Policy:** Unrestricted walking.
Walkability: 2. **Opened:** 1928. **Season:** Year-round. **High:** May-Oct. **To obtain tee times:** Call up to 14 days in advance. **Miscellaneous:** Reduced fees (weekdays, low season, resort guests, twilight, juniors), discount packages, metal spikes, club rentals, lodging (170 rooms), credit cards (MC, V, AE, D, Diners Club), beginner friendly (twilight, junior fees)

★★★½ FOXGLOVE/PINECONE

Yards: 5,950/4,685. **Par:** 70/71. **Course Rating:** 68.0/70.0. **Slope:** 118/118.
Reader Comments: Too tough. No place for whiners. Challenging ... Friendly staff ... The two older 9s are not worth the trip ... Beautiful scenery, very different 9s ... Pleasant course, with some nice challenges ... Beautiful layout, secluded ... The ground was very moist ... Three 9 holes are styled very differently ... Superb setting.

★★★½ FOXGLOVE/THISTLE

Yards: 6,608/5,203. **Par:** 72/74. **Course Rating:** 70.0/74.0. **Slope:** 121/110.
Reader Comments: The longest two 9s ... Great layout, tight fairways ... Beautiful course. Scenic views. Good maintenance ... Nature and golf at their best.

★★★½ PINECONE/THISTLE

Yards: 6,302/4,826. **Par:** 70/71. **Course Rating:** 68.0/70.0. **Slope:** 114/102.
Reader Comments: Bring your camera. Short, but very narrow ... The original 18—Thistle is long and flat; Pinecone, short, tricky ... Great layout, tight fairways ... Breath-taking views ... Fine public course ... Gorgeous setting overall—some truly beautiful holes and some good challenges.

★★★½ RIVER'S EDGE GOLF RESORT

R-400 NW Pro Shop Dr., Bend, 97701, Deschutes County, (541)389-2828.
Holes: 18. **Yards:** 6,683/5,381. **Par:** 72/73. **Course Rating:** 72.6/71.8. **Slope:** 137/135. **Green Fee:** $18/$36. **Cart Fee:** $12/person. **Walking Policy:** Unrestricted walking. **Walkability:** N/A. **Opened:** 1988. **Architect:** Robert Muir Graves. **Season:** Year-round. **High:** May-Sept. **To obtain tee times:** Call. Credit card will hold reservation more than one week. **Miscellaneous:** Reduced fees (weekdays, low season, resort guests, twilight, juniors), discount packages, metal spikes, range (grass/mats), club rentals, lodging, credit cards (MC, V).
Reader Comments: Wow, Indiana Jones golf. What an adventure ... Kind of a weird course. Local knowledge a plus ... Tough course in downtown Bend ... Don't walk this one! ... Seems tricked up, not fair ... If you like elevation changes, you'll love it ... Best workout I've had in years ... Best value in central Oregon ... Long narrow fairways, up and down hills ... Has some great and different holes that give it a little value ... Tougher than it looks ... Very steep terrain.

★★½ RIVERIDGE GOLF COURSE

PU-3800 N. Delta Hwy., Eugene, 97408, Lane County, (541)345-9160.
Holes: 18. **Yards:** 6,256/5,146. **Par:** 71/71. **Course Rating:** 68.6/67.7. **Slope:** 116/112. **Green Fee:** $24/$30. **Cart Fee:** $20/cart. **Walking Policy:** Unrestricted walking. **Walkability:** 3. **Opened:** 1990. **Architect:** Ric Jeffries. **Season:** Year-round. **High:** May-Sept. **To obtain tee times:** Call seven days in advance. **Miscellaneous:** Reduced fees (weekdays, seniors, juniors), metal spikes, range (grass/mats), club rentals, credit cards (MC, V), beginner friendly (covered driving range, two full-time teachers).
Reader Comments: Enjoyable, worth the stop if travelling through area ... Good practice facilities ... Nice, short, well-maintained easy course ... Lookout for Nos. 11 and 12 ... Doesn't drain off well ... Very busy course ... Very clean course.

OREGON

★★★½ ROSE CITY MUNICIPAL GOLF CLUB
PU-2200 NE 71st, Portland, 97213, Multnomah County, (503)253-4744.
Holes: 18. **Yards:** 6,455/5,619. **Par:** 72/72. **Course Rating:** N/A. **Slope:** 118/117. **Green Fee:** $11/$22. **Cart Fee:** $25/cart. **Walking Policy:** Unrestricted walking. **Walkability:** 2. **Architect:** George Otten. **Season:** Year-round. **High:** June-Aug. **To obtain tee times:** Call up to 6 days in advance. **Miscellaneous:** Reduced fees (weekdays), metal spikes, club rentals, credit cards (MC, V, D).
Reader Comments: Great old type course. Fun ... Great course for all skill levels ... Play this course a lot in both winter and summer ... Keen competition, a little tough! ... Very nice, old, inner-city course ... Very busy on weekends ... Classic style with long, tree-lined fairways ... Underrated course ... Difficult, old, affordable ... Best old course in Portland.

★★★★½ RUNNING Y RANCH RESORT   *Value, Condition, Pace*
R-5790 Coopers Hawk Rd., Klamath Falls, 97601, Klamath County, (541)850-5580, (888)850-0275, 10 miles W of Klamath Falls. **E-mail:** runningy.com.
Holes: 18. **Yards:** 7,133/4,842. **Par:** 72/72. **Course Rating:** 73.0/66.3. **Slope:** 125/120. **Green Fee:** $34/$45. **Cart Fee:** $26/cart. **Walking Policy:** Unrestricted walking. **Walkability:** 2. **Opened:** 1997. **Architect:** Arnold Palmer/Ed Seay/Erik Larsen. **Season:** Year-round. **High:** June-Sept. **To obtain tee times:** Call Pro Shop at (999)850-0275 two weeks in advance. **Miscellaneous:** Reduced fees (low season, resort guests, juniors), discount packages, range (grass), club rentals, lodging (83 rooms), credit cards (MC, V, AE, D).
Notes: Ranked 4th in 1999 Best in State. 1998 Pacific Northwest Open.
Reader Comments: Good everyday course. Use all your clubs ... Too short ... Nice views–a fun course ... Always immaculate ... Not friendly, golf shop staff a bit rude ... Four tee-box locations, challenging ... See bald eagles on back 9, great views ... Great value ... Beautiful, challenging, greens are amazing ... Loved the course, good, tough, fair holes, two different 9s ... Excellent layout, way to go Arnie!.

★★★★ SALEM GOLF CLUB
SP-2025 Golf Course Rd., Salem, 97302, Marion County, (503)363-6652.
Holes: 18. **Yards:** 6,200/5,163. **Par:** 72/72. **Course Rating:** 69.6/70.0. **Slope:** 114/113. **Green Fee:** $35/$40. **Cart Fee:** $24/cart. **Walking Policy:** Unrestricted walking. **Walkability:** 1. **Opened:** 1928. **Architect:** Ercel Kay. **Season:** Year-round. **High:** July-Sept. **To obtain tee times:** Call two days in advance for weekdays or on Monday for the upcoming weekend. **Miscellaneous:** Reduced fees (low season, twilight, juniors), metal spikes, range (grass/mats), caddies, club rentals, credit cards (MC, V).
Reader Comments: Great old course. Stay out of the trees ... Good setting, can be a fine course ... Played it once, had a great time ... Narrow, tree-lined fairways and large greens of medium speed, beautiful course ... Over-priced ... Huge number of tourneys, many divots. Lovely old trees and a staff that can and does sell everything ... Large fir trees, old traditional course, lots of fun.

★½ SANDELIE GOLF COURSE
28333 SW Mountain Rd., West Linn, 97068, Clackamas County, (503)655-1461.
Special Notes: Call club for further information.

★★★★ SANDPINES GOLF LINKS   *Pace*
PU-1201 35th St., Florence, 97439, Lane County, (541)997-1940, (800)917-4653, 60 miles W of Eugene.
Holes: 18. **Yards:** 6,954/5,346. **Par:** 72/72. **Course Rating:** 74.3/65.8. **Slope:** 129/111. **Green Fee:** $35/$48. **Cart Fee:** $26/cart. **Walking Policy:** Unrestricted walking. **Walkability:** 2. **Opened:** 1993. **Architect:** Rees Jones. **Season:** Year-round. **High:** June-Oct. **To obtain tee times:** Call two weeks in advance or sign up for golf package (800)917-4653. **Miscellaneous:** Reduced fees (twilight), discount packages, metal spikes, range (grass/mats), club rentals, credit cards (MC, V, AE).
Notes: Ranked 9th in 1999 Best in State; 1st in 1996 America's Top 75 Affordable Courses.
Reader Comments: Best greens in Northwest, challenging. Had a blast ... Fantastic! Beautiful. Be prepared for wind ... Played 18 in the driving NW rain and it was the best. Course played excellent even though I didn't ... Pretty, fun, good test. Gets little play in the middle of nowhere ... If you can't play until afternoon, go fly a kite, wind.is unbelievable ... Wonderful test on the dunes ... You can see the ocean in a few spots on the back nine ... Awesome variety ... Breathtaking ... Play early, it blows later.

★★½ SANTIAM GOLF CLUB
PU-8724 Golf Club Rd. S.E., Aumsville, 97325, Marion County, (503)769-3485, 15 miles SE of Salem.
Holes: 18. **Yards:** 6,392/5,469. **Par:** 72/72. **Course Rating:** 69.9/70.7. **Slope:** 123/119. **Green Fee:** $20/$20. **Cart Fee:** $20/cart. **Walking Policy:** Unrestricted walking. **Walkability:** N/A. **Opened:** 1958. **Architect:** Fred Federspiel. **Season:** Year-round. **High:** July-Sept. **To obtain tee times:** Call one week in advance for Friday through Monday. **Miscellaneous:** Reduced fees (seniors, juniors), metal spikes, range (grass), club rentals.

Reader Comments: Pretty open, but many water hazards ... Steadily improving course ... A little rough ... Not much more to be recommended ... Making improvements, look for a better condition soon ... Lots and lots of tourneys. Not a challenging course ... A smile would be nice ... Many improvements to course in last few years ... Good public course.

SHADOW BUTTE GOLF CLUB

PM-1345 Golf Course Rd., Ontario, 97914, Malheur County, (541)889-9022, (888)303-4653, 60 miles NW of Boise.
Holes: 18. **Yards:** 6,795/5,742. **Par:** 72/74. **Course Rating:** 70.4/73.3. **Slope:** 116/120. **Green Fee:** $10/$12. **Cart Fee:** $16/cart. **Walking Policy:** Unrestricted walking. **Walkability:** 2.
Opened: 1968. **Season:** Feb.-Nov. **High:** March-June. **To obtain tee times:** Call golf shop up to 7 days in advance. **Miscellaneous:** Reduced fees (juniors), metal spikes, range (grass), club rentals, credit cards (MC, V).
Special Notes: Formerly known as Edisto-Butte Municipal Golf Course.

★★½ SHIELD CREST GOLF COURSE

SP-3151 Shield Crest Dr., Klamath Falls, 97603, Klamath County, (541)884-5305, 70 miles E of Medford. **E-mail:** byrdie@internetcds.com.
Holes: 18. **Yards:** 7,005/5,464. **Par:** 72/74. **Course Rating:** 71.8/68.2. **Slope:** 117/116. **Green Fee:** $21/$25. **Cart Fee:** $11/person. **Walking Policy:** Unrestricted walking. **Walkability:** 2.
Opened: 1989. **Season:** March-Nov. **High:** July-Sept. **To obtain tee times:** Call up to 3 days in advance. **Miscellaneous:** Reduced fees (weekdays, low season, seniors, juniors), range (grass), club rentals, credit cards (MC, V), beginner friendly.
Reader Comments: Great, let it rip, well kept ... Because of where this course is located, there are some turf issues ... Very long, big hitter's course ... Still a young course, fairly simple layout. Great greens ... Long, wide fairways, tight doglegs, good golf.

★★★★ STONERIDGE GOLF COURSE *Value*

PU-500 E. Antelope Rd., Eagle Point, 97524, Jackson County, (541)830-4653, 8 miles NE of Medford.
Holes: 18. **Yards:** 6,738/4,986. **Par:** 72/72. **Course Rating:** 72.6/72.6. **Slope:** 132/118. **Green Fee:** $22/$26. **Cart Fee:** $10/person. **Walking Policy:** Unrestricted walking. **Walkability:** 3.
Opened: 1995. **Architect:** James Cochran. **Season:** Year-round. **High:** March-Nov. **To obtain tee times:** Call up to 7 days in advance. **Miscellaneous:** Reduced fees (low season), metal spikes, range (grass/mats), club rentals, credit cards (MC, V).
Reader Comments: This is all you need in a course, has it all. Must play ... My brother and I discovered this course last summer, easily my favorite course in Oregon. Will definitely go back ... Hilly, beautiful, great value ... Muddy when wet, slow play ... Nice course, hilly, good ... Beautiful, challenging, greens are amazing ... Don't walk if you are out of shape.

SUNRIVER LODGE & RESORT *Service*
★★★★½ CROSSWATER CLUB *Condition, Pace*

R-P.O. Box 4818, Sunriver, 97707, Deschutes County, (541)593-6196, (800)547-3922, 12 miles S of Bend. **E-mail:** sunriver-resort.com.
Holes: 18. **Yards:** 7,683/5,359. **Par:** 72/72. **Course Rating:** 76.9/69.8. **Slope:** 150/125. **Green Fee:** $95/$135. **Cart Fee:** Included in Green Fee. **Walking Policy:** Unrestricted walking. **Walkability:** 2. **Opened:** 1995. **Architect:** Robert Cupp/John Fought. **Season:** April-Oct. **High:** June-Aug. **To obtain tee times:** Must be a Sunriver Lodge guest. Make tee times at time of lodge reservation. **Miscellaneous:** Reduced fees (low season, resort guests, twilight, juniors), discount packages, range (grass), club rentals, lodging (200 rooms), credit cards (MC, V, AE, D).
Notes: Golf Digest School site. Ranked 80th in 1999-2000 America's 100 Greatest; 1st in 1998 Best in State; 1st in 1995 Best New Resort Courses.
Reader Comments: Golf utopia, I want to die here ... Great place to eat! ... Wonderful design, a beautiful test. Great use of Tag River ... Great golf course, staff not friendly enough, still an A-... Worth the travel ... Best overall course in Oregon ... Too many long carries over water... What a wonderful course! Very scenic ... They don't call it cross-water for nothing ... You need to be a dart player to play this target course ... The best, unbelievable ... Expensive, very challenging ... I spent so much time there in the bulrushes.

★★★½ NORTH WOODLANDS COURSE

R-P.O. Box 3609, Sunriver, 97707, Deschutes County, (541)593-3703, 12 miles S of Bend. **Web:** www.sunriver_resort.com.
Holes: 18. **Yards:** 6,880/5,446. **Par:** 72/72. **Course Rating:** 73.0/70.3. **Slope:** 131/118. **Green Fee:** $30/$80. **Cart Fee:** $15/person. **Walking Policy:** Unrestricted walking. **Walkability:** 2.
Opened: 1981. **Architect:** Robert Trent Jones Jr. **Season:** April-Oct. **High:** June-Aug. **To obtain tee times:** Lodge guests may make tee times at time of reservation. **Miscellaneous:** Reduced fees (low season, resort guests, twilight, juniors), discount packages, range (grass), club rentals, lodging, credit cards (MC, V, AE, D).
Notes: Golf Digest School site. Ranked 6th in 1999 Best in State.
Reader Comments: Costs too much! ... Lots of geese, putting is interesting ... Overpriced, but nice.... Most accessible and playable of Sunriver courses ... Great staff, fun test of golf, wonder-

ful resort ... Crowded, a disappointment ... Too short from standard tees, play back tees ... Great holes in the pines ... I could play this course every day ... Scenic views, good condition ... At this price I expected more ... Fair for women ... A great course for amateurs. Walkable. Always fun.

★★★★ SOUTH MEADOWS COURSE
R-P.O. Box 3609, Sunriver, 97707, Deschutes County, (541)593-3750, 12 miles S of Bend. **Web:** www.sunriver-resort.com.
Holes: 18. **Yards:** 7,012/5,304. **Par:** 71/71. **Course Rating:** N/A. **Slope:** N/A. **Green Fee:** $45/$85. **Cart Fee:** $15/person. **Walking Policy:** Unrestricted walking. **Walkability:** 1. **Opened:** 1999. **Architect:** John Fought. **Season:** April-Oct. **High:** June-Aug. **To obtain tee times:** Lodge guest at time of reservation. **Miscellaneous:** Reduced fees (low season, resort guests, twilight, juniors), discount packages, range (grass), club rentals, lodging, credit cards (MC, V, AE, D).
Reader Comments: Great view of Mount Batchelor ... Very nice place to play ... Very nice feel to it ... More wide open than sister course ... A relatively forgiving course that still presents a challenge ... Need to lower p.m. rates ... Fun resort course ... Was in poor condition due to pending remodeling ... Totally redone for summer 1999.

★★★★ TOKATEE GOLF CLUB *Value*
PU-54947 McKenzie Hwy., Blue River, 97413, Lane County, (541)822-3220, (800)452-6376, 47 miles E of Eugene. **E-mail:** tokatee@pond.net. **Web:** www.tokatee.com.
Holes: 18. **Yards:** 6,842/5,651. **Par:** 72/72. **Course Rating:** 72.0/71.2. **Slope:** 126/115. **Green Fee:** $35/$35. **Cart Fee:** $26/cart. **Walking Policy:** Unrestricted walking. **Walkability:** 2. **Opened:** 1966. **Architect:** Ted Robinson. **Season:** Feb.-Nov. **High:** June-Sept. **To obtain tee times:** Call in advance. **Miscellaneous:** Reduced fees (juniors), metal spikes, range (grass), club rentals, credit cards (MC, V).
Notes: Ranked 10th in 1999 Best in State.
Reader Comments: One of the best in the state. Beautiful! ... Overrated; not that exciting ... Excellent, wide open, mountain course ... Great Cascade Mountain setting ... Watched elk on the hillside, fun ... Fairly open, definitely overrated ... Excellent value, great course tee to green ... A little gem, don't miss it ... Wonderful: great value ... Scenic valley and strong test ... God's golf course ... Good course, good maintenance ... Anyone playing in Oregon must play this one ... The best public course!

★½ TOP O SCOTT GOLF COURSE
PU-12000 S.E. Stevens Rd., Portland, 97266, Clackamas County, (503)654-5050, 6 miles SE of Portland.
Holes: 18. **Yards:** 4,826/3,670. **Par:** 67/67. **Course Rating:** 64.5/65.4. **Slope:** 100/101. **Green Fee:** $17/$19. **Cart Fee:** $22/cart. **Walking Policy:** Unrestricted walking. **Walkability:** 3. **Opened:** 1926. **Season:** Year-round. **High:** May-Oct. **To obtain tee times:** Call golf shop. **Miscellaneous:** Reduced fees (seniors, juniors), discount packages, metal spikes, range (mats), club rentals, credit cards (MC, V).

★★★½ TRYSTING TREE GOLF CLUB
PU-34028 Electric Rd., Corvallis, 97333, Benton County, (541)752-3332, 34 miles SW of Salem. **E-mail:** thetree@peak.org.
Holes: 18. **Yards:** 7,014/5,516. **Par:** 72/72. **Course Rating:** 73.9/71.3. **Slope:** 129/118. **Green Fee:** $28/$28. **Cart Fee:** $22/cart. **Walking Policy:** Unrestricted walking. **Walkability:** 1. **Opened:** 1988. **Architect:** Ted Robinson. **Season:** Year-round. **High:** May-Oct. **To obtain tee times:** Call 7 days in advance. **Miscellaneous:** Reduced fees (juniors), metal spikes, range (grass/mats), club rentals, credit cards (MC, V, D).
Reader Comments: College students rule ... Great greens, all year... Prefer courses without the too-close-to-the- other-fairway feel due to lack of trees ... Good test, diverse holes, back 9 tough ... Nice links-style course ... Well-drained course. Excellent back to back ... Wide open. Need to place shots ... Still a new course but getting better!

★½ UMATILLA GOLF COURSE
PU-705 Willamette, Umatilla, 97882, Umatilla County, (541)922-3006, 54 miles SW of Walla Walla.
Holes: 18. **Yards:** 6,000/5,700. **Par:** 70/72. **Course Rating:** 68.9/74.0. **Slope:** 119/113. **Green Fee:** $10/$16. **Cart Fee:** $24/. **Walking Policy:** Unrestricted walking. **Walkability:** N/A. **Opened:** 1968. **Season:** Year-round. **High:** March-Oct. **To obtain tee times:** Show up or call within half an hour. **Miscellaneous:** Reduced fees (low season, juniors), discount packages, metal spikes, range (grass), club rentals, lodging, credit cards (MC, V, D).

VERNONIA GOLF CLUB
PU-15961 Timber Rd. E, Vernonia, 97064, Columbia County, (503)429-6811, (800)644-6535, 35 miles NW of Portland.
Holes: 18. **Yards:** 5,750/5,116. **Par:** 70/73. **Course Rating:** 68.5/69.8. **Slope:** 111/114. **Green Fee:** $18/$25. **Cart Fee:** $24/cart. **Walking Policy:** Unrestricted walking. **Walkability:** 3. **Opened:** 1928. **Architect:** Fred R. Fulmer III. **Season:** Year-round. **High:** June-Sept. **To obtain tee times:** Call. 800 number only good from Washington & Oregon. **Miscellaneous:** Reduced

fees (weekdays, seniors, juniors), discount packages, metal spikes, range (grass), club rentals, credit cards (MC, V), beginner friendly.
Special Notes: New 9-hole course added 1999 for total of 18 holes.

★★★½ WESTIN SALISHAN LODGE & GOLF RESORT
R-Hwy. 101, Gleneden Beach, 97388, Lincoln County, (541)764-3632, (800)890-0387, 58 miles W of Salem.
Holes: 18. **Yards:** 6,453/5,389. **Par:** 72/72. **Course Rating:** 72.3/72.3. **Slope:** 132/128. **Green Fee:** $35/$65. **Cart Fee:** $30/cart. **Walking Policy:** Unrestricted walking. **Walkability:** 3.
Opened: 1965. **Architect:** Fred Federspiel. **Season:** Year-round. **High:** May-Oct. **To obtain tee times:** Call two weeks in advance. **Miscellaneous:** Reduced fees (low season, resort guests, juniors), discount packages, metal spikes, range (mats), club rentals, lodging (205 rooms), credit cards (MC, V, AE, D, Diners Club), beginner friendly (beginner private and group lessons).
Notes: Ranked 14th in 1997 Best in State; 68th in 1996 America's Top 75 Affordable Courses.
Reader Comments: It gives you a little bit of everything ... Front 9 has very poor drainage; overvalued ... Wet and windy, good layout, ocean course ... Ocean view ... The guest is king ... Good old Oregon coast course ... Greens very fast ... Overrated! ... Challenge, can be wet and very windy ... Overpriced 'resort' course ... Course conditions vary from hole to hole ... The challenge makes it worthwhile.

★★★★ WIDGI CREEK GOLF CLUB
SP-18707 SW Century Dr., Bend, 97702, Deschutes County, (541)382-4449, 160 miles S of Portland. **E-mail:** www.widgi.com. **Web:** www.widgi.com.
Holes: 18. **Yards:** 6,879/5,070. **Par:** 72/72. **Course Rating:** 72.2/68.8. **Slope:** 136/123. **Green Fee:** $29/$75. **Cart Fee:** $28/person. **Walking Policy:** Unrestricted walking. **Walkability:** 2.
Opened: 1991. **Architect:** Robert Muir Graves. **Season:** March-Nov. **High:** May-Sept. **To obtain tee times:** Call up to 30 days in advance; Only 7 days for twilight and any specials.
Miscellaneous: Reduced fees (weekdays, low season, twilight, juniors), discount packages, metal spikes, range (grass), club rentals, lodging (4 rooms), credit cards (MC, V).
Reader Comments: Beautiful! ... Great traditional layout in the woods ... Vacation time for families: bad time ... You will use every club and shot in your bag ... Hidden gem ... Good winter course. Nice variety of tees ... Very manicured ... Great driving range ... Narrow, takes your breath away, reasonable price ... Overrated, good shots find trouble ... Small undulating greens, must bring accurate game ... One of the top courses in the area ... Very pleasant.

WILDHORSE RESORT GOLF COURSE
PU-72787 Hwy. 331, Pendleton, 97801, Umatilla County, (541)276-5588, (800)654-WILD, 5 miles E of Pendleton. **Web:** www.wildhorseresort.com.
Holes: 18. **Yards:** 7,112/5,718. **Par:** 72/72. **Course Rating:** 73.8/72.1. **Slope:** 125/122. **Green Fee:** $20/$28. **Cart Fee:** $24/cart. **Walking Policy:** Unrestricted walking. **Walkability:** 2.
Opened: 1998. **Architect:** John Steidel. **Season:** Year-round. **High:** April-Sept. **To obtain tee times:** Call 7 days in advance. **Miscellaneous:** Reduced fees (weekdays, resort guests, twilight, juniors), discount packages, range (grass), club rentals, lodging (200 rooms), credit cards (MC, V, AE, D), beginner friendly (junior golf, lessons).
Notes: C.W.C. PGA Chapter Championship.

PENNSYLVANIA

★★ **ALLENTOWN MUNICIPAL GOLF COURSE**
PM-3400 Tilghman St., Allentown, 18104, Lehigh County, (610)395-9926, 65 miles S of Philadelphia.
Holes: 18. **Yards:** 6,763/4,917. **Par:** 72/72. **Course Rating:** 72.0/71.3. **Slope:** 127/123. **Green Fee:** $15/$20. **Cart Fee:** $22/cart. **Walking Policy:** Unrestricted walking. **Walkability:** 3.
Opened: 1952. **Architect:** A.L. Weisenberger Assoc. **Season:** Year-round. **High:** May-Sept. **To obtain tee times:** In person seven days in advance. **Miscellaneous:** Reduced fees (low season, twilight, seniors, juniors), range (grass).

★★ **APPLEWOOD GOLF COURSE**
PU-Mt. Zion Rd., Harding, 18643, Luzerne County, (570)388-2500, 15 miles NW of Wilkes-Barre.
E-mail: applewd@epix.net.
Holes: 9. **Yards:** 2,812/2,145. **Par:** 35/35. **Course Rating:** 33.2/32.0. **Slope:** 110/106. **Green Fee:** $13/$19. **Cart Fee:** $13/person. **Walking Policy:** Unrestricted walking. **Walkability:** 3.
Opened: 1995. **Architect:** Jim Blaukovitch & Associates. **Season:** April-Nov. **High:** May-Sept. **To obtain tee times:** Call up to 7 days in advance. Tee times required on weekdays/holidays.
Miscellaneous: Reduced fees (weekdays, low season, twilight), metal spikes, range (mats), club rentals, credit cards (MC, V), beginner friendly.

★★★½ **ARMITAGE GOLF COURSE**
PM-800 Orrs Bridge Rd., Mechanicsburg, 17055, Cumberland County, (717)737-5344, 5 miles W of Harrisburg. **E-mail:** Armitagecpaonline.com.
Holes: 18. **Yards:** 6,000/5,200. **Par:** 70/70. **Course Rating:** 67.2/67.6. **Slope:** 116/111. **Green Fee:** $15/$20. **Cart Fee:** $10/person. **Walking Policy:** Unrestricted walking. **Walkability:** 3.
Opened: 1962. **Architect:** Ed Ault. **Season:** March-Dec. **High:** May-Sept. **To obtain tee times:** Call up to 7 days in advance. **Miscellaneous:** Reduced fees (twilight, seniors, juniors), range (grass/mats), credit cards (MC, V).
Reader Comments: Excellent short-but-tough course ... A lot of sidehill lies, but interesting to play ... Did not hit it straight, but still love the place ... Heavily played. Short but tricky ... Busy, but fun local course; 17th is great ... Fantastic condition. Like U.S. Open fairways.

★★ **ARNOLD'S GOLF CLUB**
PU-R.D. No.2, Nescopeck, 18635, Luzerne County, (520)752-7022.
Special Notes: Call club for further information.

★★★ **ARROWHEAD GOLF COURSE**
PU-1539 Weavertown Rd., Douglassville, 19518, Berks County, (610)582-4258, 9 miles E of Reading.
Holes: 18. **Yards:** 6,002/6,002. **Par:** 71/71. **Course Rating:** 68.9/73.4. **Slope:** 116/124. **Green Fee:** $14/$17. **Cart Fee:** $17/cart. **Walking Policy:** Unrestricted walking. **Walkability:** N/A.
Opened: 1954. **Architect:** John McLean. **Season:** Year-round. **To obtain tee times:** Call or come in. **Miscellaneous:** Reduced fees (weekdays, low season, twilight), metal spikes, range (grass/mats), club rentals.
Reader Comments: Love the greens ... Nice test of golf ... Carts restricted to paths ... Well-kept public facility ... Good course, nice holes, good value ... Old fashioned... Standard fare, get what you pay for.

★★★★ **ASHBOURNE COUNTRY CLUB**
SP-Ashbourne & Oak Lane Rds., Cheltenham, 19012, Montgomery County, (215)635-3090, 5 miles NW of Philadelphia. **Web:** www.ashbourne.com.
Holes: 18. **Yards:** 6,037/5,263. **Par:** 70/72. **Course Rating:** 69.2/71.5. **Slope:** 121/125. **Green Fee:** $39/$75. **Cart Fee:** Included in Green Fee. **Walking Policy:** Walking at certain times. **Walkability:** 3. **Opened:** 1924. **Architect:** J. Franklyn Meehan. **Season:** All year round. **High:** May-Oct. **To obtain tee times:** Call 6 days in advance, with major credit card on weekends.
Miscellaneous: Reduced fees (weekdays, low season, twilight, juniors), club rentals, credit cards (MC, V, AE, D), beginner friendly (practice course Cedarbrook Hill).
Reader Comments: A little expensive, but a tough, tight demanding course .... Fine old course ... Close to Philly yet a country club feel ... Great shotmaker's course... Country club atmosphere, old, classic, short ... Best value in suburban Philadelphia ... Best fairways, better than private clubs ... Old-style.

★★★ **AUBREYS GOLF CLUB**
PU-Mercer Rd., Butler, 16001, Butler County, (412)287-4832.
Special Notes: Call club for further information.

★★★½ **BAVARIAN HILLS GOLF COURSE**
PU-Mulligan Rd., St. Mary's, 15857, Elk County, (814)834-3602, 135 miles N of Pittsburgh.
Holes: 18. **Yards:** 5,986/4,693. **Par:** 71/73. **Course Rating:** 68.8/67.2. **Slope:** 126/115. **Green Fee:** $20/$25. **Cart Fee:** $10/person. **Walking Policy:** Unrestricted walking. **Walkability:** 5.
Opened: 1990. **Architect:** Bill Love/Brian Ault. **Season:** April-Nov. **High:** June-Aug. **To obtain**

tee times: Call Monday for upcoming weekend. **Miscellaneous:** Reduced fees (weekdays), range (mats), club rentals, credit cards (MC, V).
Reader Comments: Short, scenic course ... Nice mountain course ... Fun to play.... Tricky greens ... Very hilly, good greens, fairly short ... Beautiful views ... A fair course for everyone.

★★★ BEDFORD SPRINGS GOLF COURSE
R-Business Rte. 220 S., Bedford, 15522, Bedford County, (814)623-8700, 80 miles E of Pittsburgh.
Holes: 18. **Yards:** 7,000/5,535. **Par:** 74/74. **Course Rating:** N/A. **Slope:** N/A. **Green Fee:** N/A.
Walking Policy: Mandatory cart. **Walkability:** 3. **Opened:** 1924. **Architect:** Donald Ross.
Season: May-Oct. **High:** June-Sept. **To obtain tee times:** Call up to 12 hours in advance.
Miscellaneous: Metal spikes, range (grass), club rentals, credit cards (MC, V, AE, D).
Reader Comments: Classic old course ... Good for all handicaps ... Great for longball hitters ... Scenic ...Nice greens.

★★★½ BETHLEHEM MUNICIPAL GOLF CLUB
PM-400 Illicks Mills Rd., Bethlehem, 18017, Northampton County, (610)691-9393.
Holes: 18. **Yards:** 7,017/5,119. **Par:** 71/71. **Course Rating:** 73.6/70.6. **Slope:** 127/113. **Green Fee:** $12/$25. **Cart Fee:** $11/person. **Walking Policy:** Unrestricted walking. **Walkability:** 3.
Opened: 1956. **Architect:** William Gordon/David Gordon. **Season:** Year-round. **High:** March-Oct. **To obtain tee times:** Residents sign up Thursday, others sign up Friday for $1 fee.
Miscellaneous: Reduced fees (weekdays, twilight, seniors, juniors), range (grass/mats), club rentals, credit cards (MC, V).
Reader Comments: Good muny course ... Excellent conditions, hit it long and straight ... Always in great condition-layout a little plain ... Every other course seems short after this.

BLACK HAWK GOLF COURSE
PU-644 Blackhawk Rd., Beaver Falls, 15010, Beaver County, (724)843-2542, 35 miles NW of Pittsburgh. **E-mail:** blckhawk@tristate.pgh.net.
★★★ FIRST COURSE
Holes: 18. **Yards:** 6,114/5,365. **Par:** 72/72. **Course Rating:** 67.7/68.6. **Slope:** 113/113. **Green Fee:** $13/$21. **Cart Fee:** $10/person. **Walking Policy:** Unrestricted walking. **Walkability:** 2.
Opened: 1927. **Architect:** Paul Frable. **Season:** Year-round. **High:** June-Aug. **To obtain tee times:** Call 7 days in advance for weekends and holidays only. **Miscellaneous:** Reduced fees (weekdays, low season, seniors), metal spikes, range (grass/mats), club rentals, credit cards (MC, V, AE, D), beginner friendly (golf clinics, junior programs, women's clinics).
Reader Comments: Economical and convenient ... Great fast greens, good public course ... Up and down challenges ... Old-style, small greens; short on hazards ... .Plenty of play.
★★½ SECOND COURSE
Holes: 18. **Yards:** 6,285/5,552. **Par:** 72/72. **Course Rating:** 67.7/68.6. **Slope:** 112/113. **Green Fee:** $13/$21. **Cart Fee:** $10/person. **Walking Policy:** Unrestricted walking. **Walkability:** 2.
Opened: 1927. **Architect:** Paul Frable. **Season:** Year-round. **High:** June-Aug. **To obtain tee times:** Call 7 days in advance. **Miscellaneous:** Reduced fees (weekdays, low season, seniors), metal spikes, range (grass/mats), club rentals, credit cards (MC, V, AE, D).
Reader Comments: Wide fairways, big greens, friendly assistant pro ... Hilly, gets a lot of play ... Long, challenging ... Blind shots, awkward lies.

★★★ BLACKWOOD GOLF COURSE
PU-510 Red Corner Rd., Douglassville, 19518, Berks County, (610)385-6200, 12 miles E of Reading.
Holes: 18. **Yards:** 6,403/4,826. **Par:** 70/70. **Course Rating:** 68.6/62.0. **Slope:** 115/95. **Green Fee:** $12/$28. **Cart Fee:** $22/cart. **Walking Policy:** Unrestricted walking. **Walk-ability:** 2.
Opened: 1970. **Architect:** William Gordon. **Season:** Year-round. **High:** May-Sept. **To obtain tee times:** Call 2 weeks in advance. **Miscellaneous:** Reduced fees (weekdays, low season, twilight, seniors), metal spikes, range (grass/mats), club rentals.
Reader Comments: Wide fairways and good shape ... Very scenic, enjoyable layout ... Solid public course, very open ... Great practice facility ... Nice little course ... Some holes a little long for seniors ... Friendly staff, wide open.

★★½ BLUE MOUNTAIN VIEW GOLF COURSE
PU-Blue Mt. Dr., R.D. 1, Box 106, Fredericksburg, 17026, Lebanon County, (717)865-4401, 23 miles E of Harrisburg.
Holes: 18. **Yards:** 6,010/4,520. **Par:** 71/73. **Course Rating:** 68.2/64.9. **Slope:** 110/101. **Green Fee:** $11/$20. **Cart Fee:** $9/person. **Walking Policy:** Unrestricted walking. **Walkability:** 3.
Opened: 1963. **Architect:** William and David Gordon. **Season:** Year-round. **High:** April-Sept. **To obtain tee times:** Call golf shop. **Miscellaneous:** Reduced fees (weekdays, low season, seniors, juniors), metal spikes.
Reader Comments: Good variety of holes ... Fast greens, hills ... Food is great at lunch room ... Pleasant mountain course ... Nice layout for average golfer.

PENNSYLVANIA

★★ BON-AIR GOLF CLUB
PU-505 McCormick Rd., Coraopolis, 15108, Allegheny County, (412)262-2992, 10 miles W of Pittsburgh.
Holes: 18. **Yards:** 5,821/4,809. **Par:** 71/73. **Course Rating:** 68.5/69.5. **Slope:** 117/120. **Green Fee:** $12/$18. **Cart Fee:** $12/person. **Walking Policy:** Unrestricted walking. **Walkability:** 4. **Opened:** 1932. **Season:** Year-round. **High:** April-Sept. **To obtain tee times:** Call 24 hours in advance. **Miscellaneous:** Reduced fees (weekdays, low season, seniors), discount packages, metal spikes, club rentals, credit cards (MC, V, AE).

BRIARWOOD GOLF CLUB
PM-4775 W. Market St., York, 17404, York County, (717)792-9776, (800)432-1555, 40 miles N of Baltimore, MD.

★★★ EAST COURSE
Holes: 18. **Yards:** 6,608/5,193. **Par:** 72/72. **Course Rating:** 69.7/67.8. **Slope:** 116/112. **Green Fee:** $21/$29. **Cart Fee:** $13/person. **Walking Policy:** Unrestricted walking. **Walkability:** 3. **Opened:** 1955. **Architect:** Charles Klingensmith. **Season:** Year-round. **High:** March-Oct. **To obtain tee times:** Call anytime in advance. **Miscellaneous:** Reduced fees (weekdays, low season, resort guests, twilight, seniors), discount packages, metal spikes, range (grass/mats), club rentals, credit cards (MC, V, MAC/Cirrus).
Reader Comments: Great greens...Good muny course, friendly staff, old course...Fairly flat, old course...Good but crowded...Wide open, can let it rip...Medium difficulty...Always well groomed...Good greens ... A good place to play ... Old course, wide open, big greens, okay conditions.... Nine hole leagues ... Old-fashioned fun ... Mature course, not too much trouble, lots of open space ... Couple tough holes.

★★★ WEST COURSE
Holes: 18. **Yards:** 6,400/4,820. **Par:** 70/70. **Course Rating:** 69.7/67.3. **Slope:** 119/112. **Green Fee:** $21/$29. **Cart Fee:** $13/person. **Walking Policy:** Unrestricted walking. **Walkability:** 3. **Opened:** 1990. **Architect:** Ault Clark Associates. **Season:** Year-round. **High:** March-Oct. **To obtain tee times:** Call anytime in advance. **Miscellaneous:** Reduced fees (weekdays, low season, resort guests, twilight, seniors), discount packages, metal spikes, club rentals, credit cards (MC, V, MAC/Cirrus).
Reader Comments: A good place to play ... Great layout, needs time to mature ... Scenic course, helpful people ... Short course ... Good finishing holes.

★★★★ THE BRIDGES GOLF CLUB
PU-6729 York Rd, Abbottstown, 17301, Adams County, (717)624-9551, 17 miles W of York.
Holes: 18. **Yards:** 6,713/5,104. **Par:** 72/72. **Course Rating:** 71.7/69.6. **Slope:** 132/113. **Green Fee:** $30/$43. **Cart Fee:** $12/person. **Walking Policy:** Unrestricted walking. **Walkability:** 3. **Opened:** 1995. **Architect:** Altland Brothers. **Season:** March-Dec. **High:** May-Oct. **To obtain tee times:** Call 14 days in advance. **Miscellaneous:** Reduced fees (weekdays, resort guests, seniors, juniors), discount packages, range (grass), club rentals, lodging (13 rooms), credit cards (MC, V, AE, D).
Reader Comments: One of the nicest public courses in the state ... Great use of wetlands ... First tee is a good distance from starter, no onlookers ... A must play ever year ... Keep carts on paths ... Keeps your interest, need to be a shotmaker ... Covered bridge on No. 2 ... Better be able to putt ... Breathtaking 15th hole ... Great variety of holes.... Quaint; bridges, birdhouses, lots of wildlife.

BUCK HILL GOLF CLUB
SP-Golf Dr., Buck Hill Falls, 18323, Monroe County, (570)595-7730, 50 miles N of Allentown.
Holes: 27. **Walking Policy:** Mandatory cart. **Opened:** 1901. **Architect:** Donald Ross. **Season:** April-Nov. **High:** June-Sept. **To obtain tee times:** Call 7 days in advance. Groups of 12 or more may call farther in advance.

★★★ RED/BLUE
Yards: 6,150/5,370. **Par:** 70/72. **Course Rating:** 69.8/70.2. **Slope:** 120/121. **Green Fee:** $30/$45. **Cart Fee:** $14/person. **Walkability:** 3. **Miscellaneous:** Reduced fees (twilight), metal spikes, range (grass), club rentals, credit cards (MC, V).
Reader Comments: Red course is a hidden gem. No houses ... Country club atmosphere, good condition ... Excellent pro, staff.

★★★ RED/WHITE
Yards: 6,300/5,620. **Par:** 70/72. **Course Rating:** 70.4/71.2. **Slope:** 122/124. **Green Fee:** $50/$75. **Cart Fee:** Included in Green Fee. **Walkability:** 4. **Miscellaneous:** Reduced fees (weekdays, twilight), metal spikes, range (grass), club rentals, credit cards (MC, V).
Reader Comments: All three nines are super, requires a long hitter to score well. Most greens are small...Great scenery...Good shape.

★★★ WHITE/BLUE
Yards: 6,450/5,550. **Par:** 72/72. **Course Rating:** 71.0/72.8. **Slope:** 126/126. **Green Fee:** $39/$75. **Cart Fee:** Included in Green Fee. **Walkability:** 3. **Miscellaneous:** Reduced fees (twilight), metal spikes, range (grass), club rentals, credit cards (MC, V), beginner friendly (clinics).

PENNSYLVANIA

Reader Comments: Very hilly. Not a level shot on this course ... Great to play in late Sept., early Oct. ... Wildlife galore ... Tight, everything small ... Good test. Plenty of uphill, downhill, sidehill lies.

★★★★ **BUCKNELL GOLF CLUB** *Pace*
SP-P.O. Box 297, Lewisburg, 17837, Union County, (570)523-8193, 60 miles N of Harrisburg.
Holes: 18. **Yards:** 6,253/4,851. **Par:** 70/71. **Course Rating:** 70.0/67.8. **Slope:** 132/122. **Green Fee:** $32/$37. **Cart Fee:** $13/person. **Walking Policy:** Unrestricted walking. **Walkability:** 3. **Opened:** 1930. **Architect:** Edmund B. Ault. **Season:** March-Nov. **High:** June-Aug. **To obtain tee times:** Call 7 days in advance. **Miscellaneous:** Reduced fees (weekdays), range (grass), club rentals, credit cards (MC, V).
Reader Comments: Very pretty, college crowd ... Beautiful, quiet and tight ... A great classic layout ... Terrific value; many interesting holes ... Very challenging, yet short course. The greens are very fast and sloping ... Have to be in the fairway and have great touch around the greens.

★★★½ **BUTLER'S GOLF COURSE**
PU-800 Rock Run Rd., Elizabeth, 15037, Allegheny County, (412)751-9121, (800)932-1001, 15 miles SE of Pittsburgh. **Web:** www.butlersgolf.com.
Holes: 18. **Yards:** 6,606/5,560. **Par:** 72/73. **Course Rating:** 68.9/70.8. **Slope:** 117/119. **Green Fee:** $21/$30. **Cart Fee:** $11/person. **Walking Policy:** Walking at certain times. **Walkability:** 2. **Opened:** 1928. **Architect:** John Butler. **Season:** Year-round. **High:** April-Oct. **To obtain tee times:** Call 7 days in advance for weekday. Call Tuesday 10 a.m. for weekend play.
Miscellaneous: Reduced fees (weekdays, low season, twilight, seniors, juniors), metal spikes, range (grass), club rentals, lodging (4 rooms), credit cards (MC, V, AE, D, Diners Club), beginner friendly (novice association wednesday evenings).
Reader Comments: Well maintained, greens are true ... Good pro shop ... A pleasant surprise; country club atmosphere ... One of the nicer public treks in western Pa. ... One of my favorite courses ... Good stretch of finishing holes.

★★½ **CABLE HOLLOW GOLF CLUB**
PU-RD #2, Norberg Rd, Russell, 16345, Warren County, (814)757-4765, 150 miles N of Pittsburgh.
Holes: 18. **Yards:** 6,300/5,200. **Par:** 72/73. **Course Rating:** 68.7/69.0. **Slope:** 108/109. **Green Fee:** $9/$17. **Cart Fee:** $18/cart. **Walking Policy:** Unrestricted walking. **Walkability:** 2. **Opened:** 1968. **Season:** March-Nov. **High:** June-Aug. **To obtain tee times:** Call anytime in advance. **Miscellaneous:** Reduced fees (weekdays, low season, twilight, seniors), metal spikes, club rentals, credit cards (MC, V, AE, D).
Reader Comments: Beautiful to play, especially in fall ... Great service, hometown country feel.

CARROLL VALLEY GOLF RESORT
★★★★ **CARROLL VALLEY COURSE**
R-121 Sanders Rd., Fairfield, 17320, Adams County, (717)642-8252, (800)548-8504, 10 miles W of Gettysburg.
Holes: 18. **Yards:** 6,633/5,005. **Par:** 71/72. **Course Rating:** 71.2/67.6. **Slope:** 120/114. **Green Fee:** $22/$29. **Cart Fee:** $12/person. **Walking Policy:** Walking at certain times. **Walkability:** 3. **Opened:** 1965. **Architect:** Ed Ault. **Season:** Year-round. **High:** April-Oct. **To obtain tee times:** Call Friday for following Monday-Sunday tee times. Groups and packages may call farther in advance. **Miscellaneous:** Reduced fees (weekdays, low season, resort guests, twilight, seniors), discount packages, metal spikes, club rentals, lodging, credit cards (MC, V, D).
Reader Comments: Scenic. Very challenging. A must play ... If golf goes bad, the trout in the stream are ready, No. 9 rates a 10 ... Long and windy ... All around great course and facility... Long par fours ... Great scenery in fall ... Breathtaking views, watch the glider planes ... Wandering creeks and ponds.

★★★★ **MOUNTAIN VIEW COURSE**
PU-Bullfrog Rd., Fairfield, 17320, Adams County, (717)642-5848, 8 miles W of Gettysburg.
Holes: 18. **Yards:** 6,343/5,024. **Par:** 71/70. **Course Rating:** 70.2/68.2. **Slope:** 122/113. **Green Fee:** $24/$30. **Cart Fee:** $13/person. **Walking Policy:** Unrestricted walking. **Walkability:** 2. **Opened:** 1979. **Architect:** Ault & Clark. **Season:** March-Nov. **High:** April-Oct. **To obtain tee times:** Call Friday the following Monday-Sunday tee times. Groups and golf packages may call any time. **Miscellaneous:** Reduced fees (weekdays, low season, resort guests, twilight, seniors), discount packages, range (grass/mats), club rentals, credit cards (MC, V, AE, D).
Reader Comments: Very good course, fair, challenging ... Beautiful course along the mountains.

★★★ **CASTLE HILLS GOLF COURSE**
PU-110 W. Oakwood Way, New Castle, 16105, Lawrence County, (724)652-8122, 40 miles N of Pittsburgh.
Holes: 18. **Yards:** 6,501/5,530. **Par:** 72/73. **Course Rating:** 69.7/73.3. **Slope:** 118/114. **Green Fee:** $16/$20. **Cart Fee:** $10/person. **Walking Policy:** Unrestricted walking. **Walkability:** 2. **Opened:** 1930. **Season:** March-Dec. **High:** May-Sept. **To obtain tee times:** Call. **Miscellaneous:** Reduced fees (weekdays, low season, seniors, juniors), discount packages, range (grass), club rentals, credit cards (MC, V, D).
Reader Comments: Tight fairways, great par threes ... Fun course, great chilli dogs.

PENNSYLVANIA

★★ CEDAR RIDGE GOLF COURSE
PU-1225 Barlow Two Taverns Rd., Gettysburg, 17325, Adams County, (717)359-4480, 5 miles SE of Gettysburg.
Holes: 18. **Yards:** 6,132/5,546. **Par:** 72/72. **Course Rating:** 69.5/69.3. **Slope:** 114/114. **Green Fee:** $13/$19. **Cart Fee:** $10/person. **Walking Policy:** Unrestricted walking. **Walkability:** 2. **Opened:** 1987. **Architect:** Roger Weaver. **Season:** Year-round. **High:** April-Nov. **To obtain tee times:** Call 3 weeks ahead. **Miscellaneous:** Reduced fees (weekdays, low season, twilight, seniors), metal spikes, club rentals, credit cards (V, AE, D).

CEDARBROOK GOLF COURSE
PU-215, Rte. 981, Belle Vernon, 15012, Westmoreland County, (724)929-8300, 25 miles S of Pittsburgh.
★★★½ GOLD COURSE
Holes: 18. **Yards:** 6,710/5,138. **Par:** 72/72. **Course Rating:** 72.4/70.2. **Slope:** 135/121. **Green Fee:** $20/$29. **Cart Fee:** $10/person. **Walking Policy:** Unrestricted walking. **Walkability:** 3. **Architect:** Michael Hurdzan. **Season:** Year-round. **High:** April-Sept. **To obtain tee times:** Call 7 days in advance. **Miscellaneous:** Reduced fees (low season, seniors, juniors), metal spikes, range (grass), club rentals, credit cards (MC, V, AE, D).
Reader Comments: Challenging and well-maintained ... Play it from the tips ... Excellent playing experience ... Tie your shoes tight in case you're overswinging; much too long and tough ...Flat and well maintained.
★★★ RED COURSE
Holes: 18. **Yards:** 6,154/4,577. **Par:** 71/71. **Course Rating:** 68.3/65.3. **Slope:** 120/111. **Green Fee:** $20/$29. **Cart Fee:** $10/person. **Walking Policy:** Unrestricted walking. **Walkability:** 3. **Architect:** Michael Hurdzan. **Season:** Year-round. **High:** April-Sept. **To obtain tee times:** Call 7 days in advance. **Miscellaneous:** Reduced fees (low season, seniors, juniors), metal spikes, range (grass/mats), club rentals, credit cards (MC, V, AE, D).
Reader Comments: Much easier than the Gold course ... Short but has good design; great value ... Would be better if longer... Short tricky holes, along with challenging lengthy holes.

★★★½ CENTER SQUARE GOLF CLUB
PU-Rte. 73 and Whitehall Rd., Center Square, 19422, Montgomery County, (610)584-5700, 25 miles W of Philadelphia.
Holes: 18. **Yards:** 6,296/5,598. **Par:** 71/73. **Course Rating:** 69.3/70.6. **Slope:** 119/114. **Green Fee:** $17/$26. **Cart Fee:** $36/cart. **Walking Policy:** Walking at certain times. **Walkability:** 4. **Opened:** 1963. **Architect:** Edward Ault. **Season:** Year-round. **High:** April-Oct. **To obtain tee times:** Call seven days in advance for weekdays. Call Wednesday a.m. for weekend. **Miscellaneous:** Reduced fees (twilight, seniors), range (grass), club rentals, credit cards (MC, V, AE).
Reader Comments: Great daily fee course ... Very scenic ... Never had a long round, great for the price ... No. 18 is very challenging for a par three ... Great greens ... Fun local course; friendly staff; conditions better since 1997 WAPL championship.

★★★★ CENTER VALLEY CLUB
PU-3300 Center Valley Pky., Center Valley, 18034, Lehigh County, (610)791-5580, 3 miles S of Allentown/Bethlehem.
Holes: 18. **Yards:** 6,916/4,932. **Par:** 72/72. **Course Rating:** 74.1/70.6. **Slope:** 135/123. **Green Fee:** $25/$61. **Cart Fee:** Included in Green Fee. **Walking Policy:** Walking at certain times. **Walkability:** 2. **Opened:** 1992. **Architect:** Geoffrey Cornish. **Season:** April-Dec. **High:** May-Oct. **To obtain tee times:** Call up to 7 days in advance with credit card. **Miscellaneous:** Reduced fees (twilight), range (grass/mats), club rentals, credit cards (MC, V, AE, D).
Reader Comments: Nicest fairways in area ... Nike Tour venue, challenging greens ... Myrtle Beach in Pennsylvania ... You'll use every club ... Two completely different nines. Great staff ... No.18 a card killer ... Blind shots ... Fair except for a couple of tricky holes ... Many mounds ... Links style front nine, complemented by a more traditional back nine ... Large, well-kept greens.

★★★★ CHAMPION LAKES GOLF COURSE
PU-R.D. 1, Box 285, Bolivar, 15923, Westmoreland County, (724)238-5440, 50 miles E of Pittsburgh. **Web:** www.pagolf.com.
Holes: 18. **Yards:** 6,608/5,556. **Par:** 71/74. **Course Rating:** 69.0/72.1. **Slope:** 128/127. **Green Fee:** $24/$29. **Cart Fee:** $10/person. **Walking Policy:** Unrestricted walking. **Walkability:** 3. **Opened:** 1968. **Architect:** Paul Erath. **Season:** April-Dec. **High:** May-Sept. **To obtain tee times:** Call as far in advance as you like. Tee times are required. **Miscellaneous:** Reduced fees (weekdays, low season), metal spikes, range (grass/mats), club rentals, lodging (9 rooms), credit cards (MC, V, AE).
Reader Comments: Score here and you can score anywhere ... First five holes will kill you ... Super view on a hard mountain course ... Among the best anywhere, out of the way, but tremendous challenge; great staff awaits ... Most holes tree lined ... Nice course with tough greens.

★★ CHEROKEE GOLF COURSE
PU-217 Elysburg Rd., Danville, 17821, Northumberland County, (520)275-2005, (888)843-1633, 3 miles E of Danville on Rte. 54.
Holes: 18. **Yards:** 6,037/4,524. **Par:** 72/72. **Course Rating:** 68.4/65.1. **Slope:** 114/102. **Green Fee:** $15/$19. **Cart Fee:** $10/person. **Walking Policy:** Unrestricted walking. **Walkability:** 1. **Opened:** 1973. **Architect:** Brouse Family. **Season:** Year-round. **High:** May-Aug. **To obtain tee times:** Call anytime. **Miscellaneous:** Reduced fees (weekdays), metal spikes, club rentals, credit cards (MC, V, AE, D).

CHERRY WOOD GOLF COURSE
PU-204 Truxall Rd., Apollo, 15613, Westmoreland County, (724)727-2546, 35 miles NE of Pittsburgh.
Holes: 9. **Yards:** 6,230/3,970. **Par:** 70/70. **Course Rating:** N/A. **Slope:** N/A. **Green Fee:** $16/$18. **Cart Fee:** $20/cart. **Walking Policy:** Unrestricted walking. **Walkability:** 3. **Opened:** 1997. **Architect:** John S. Chernega. **Season:** April-Oct. **High:** July. **To obtain tee times:** Call golf shop. **Miscellaneous:** Reduced fees (weekdays, seniors), metal spikes, range (grass), club rentals, credit cards (MC, V), beginner friendly (novice league, lessons).
Special Notes: Member Audubon Cooperative Sanctuary Program.

★★★★½ CHESTNUT RIDGE GOLF CLUB *Service, Value, Condition*
PU-1762 Old William Penn Highway, Blairsville, 15717, Indiana County, (724)459-7188, (800)770-0000, 35 miles E of Pittsburgh.
Holes: 18. **Yards:** 6,321/5,130. **Par:** 72/72. **Course Rating:** 70.7/70.2. **Slope:** 129/119. **Green Fee:** $25/$30. **Cart Fee:** $10/person. **Walking Policy:** Unrestricted walking. **Walkability:** 2. **Opened:** 1964. **Architect:** Harrison/Garbin. **Season:** April-Nov. **High:** May-Sept. **To obtain tee times:** Call 7 days in advance. **Miscellaneous:** Reduced fees (weekdays), discount packages, metal spikes, range (grass), credit cards (MC, V, AE).
Reader Comments: Classy place ... Short fun course, lots of challenging wedge shots ... Great restaurant ... Beautiful in September/October ... Wide open ... Level landing areas, good variety of holes ... Nice back nine especially 14, 15 and 16. Pleasing to the eye and different than the rest of course.

★★★★½ TOM'S RUN AT CHESTNUT RIDGE
Holes: 18. **Yards:** 6,812/5,363. **Par:** 72/72. **Course Rating:** 73.0/71.2. **Slope:** 134/126. **Green Fee:** $45/$50. **Cart Fee:** $10/person. **Walking Policy:** Unrestricted walking. **Walkability:** 3. **Opened:** 1993. **Architect:** Bill Love/Ault & Clark. **Season:** April-Nov. **High:** April-Nov. **To obtain tee times:** Call 7 days in advance. **Miscellaneous:** Reduced fees (weekdays, twilight), discount packages, metal spikes, range (grass), credit cards (MC, V, AE).
Reader Comments: Front nine placement golf, back nine open and longer ... Challenging, mountain views breathtaking ... Holes 3, 4 and 5 beautiful ... Easy to play for ladies. Pretty level ... Nos. 2-4 are a real test ... Excellent greens ... True test from the tips.

★★½ COBB'S CREEK GOLF CLUB
PM-72 Lansdowne Ave., Philadelphia, 19151, Philadelphia County, (215)877-8707.
Holes: 18. **Yards:** 6,660/6,130. **Par:** 71/71. **Course Rating:** 68.6/68.1. **Slope:** 117/114. **Green Fee:** $23/$28. **Cart Fee:** $25/cart. **Walking Policy:** Unrestricted walking. **Walkability:** 4. **Opened:** 1916. **Architect:** Hugh Wilson. **Season:** Year-round. **High:** April-Oct. **To obtain tee times:** Call 7 days in advance. **Miscellaneous:** Reduced fees (weekdays, twilight, seniors, juniors), metal spikes, range (grass/mats), club rentals, credit cards (MC, V).
Reader Comments: Another Bethpage Black, waiting for an angel ... Interesting challenge ... Good muny course that gets lots of play.

★★★½ CONLEY'S RESORT INN
R-740 Pittsburgh Rd., Rte. 8, Butler, 16002, Butler County, (724)586-7711, (800)344-7303, 7 miles N of Butler.
Holes: 18. **Yards:** 6,200/5,625. **Par:** 72/72. **Course Rating:** 69.0/69.0. **Slope:** 110/110. **Green Fee:** $22/$32. **Cart Fee:** $12/person. **Walking Policy:** Walking at certain times. **Walkability:** 3. **Opened:** 1963. **Architect:** Nicholas Innotti. **Season:** Year-round. **High:** April-Oct. **To obtain tee times:** Call up to one year in advance. **Miscellaneous:** Reduced fees (weekdays, low season, resort guests, twilight, seniors), discount packages, metal spikes, club rentals, lodging (56 rooms), credit cards (MC, V, AE, D).
Reader Comments: One testy hole ... Always in good playing condition ... Great finishing hole; very good restaurant ... Great scenery and challenge.

★★★ COOL CREEK COUNTRY CLUB
PU-Cool Creek Rd., Wrightsville, 17368, York County, (717)252-3691, (800)942-2444, 10 miles W of Lancaster.

Holes: 18. **Yards:** 6,521/5,703. **Par:** 71/70. **Course Rating:** 71.1/72.6. **Slope:** 118/118. **Green Fee:** $25/$33. **Cart Fee:** $14/person. **Walking Policy:** Unrestricted walking. **Walkability:** 3. **Opened:** 1948. **Architect:** Chester Ruby. **Season:** Year-round. **High:** April-Oct. **To obtain tee times:** Call. Credit cards required to reserve tee times during high season on weekends. **Miscellaneous:** Reduced fees (weekdays, low season, resort guests, twilight, seniors, juniors), discount packages, range (mats), club rentals, credit cards (MC, V, AE), beginner friendly (beginner lessons, beginner leagues).

Reader Comments: Friendly, open fairways ... Front nine gives you opportunity for low score. You will need it for the back 9 ... Comfortable country course.... Back nine is excellent.

★★½ COREY CREEK GOLF CLUB

SP-U.S. Rte. No.6 E., Mansfield, 16933, Tioga County, (570)662-3520, 35 miles SW of Elmira, NY. **E-mail:** goleepix.net. **Web:** www.coreycreekgolf.com.
Holes: 18. **Yards:** 6,571/4,920. **Par:** 72/72. **Course Rating:** 71.1/66.0. **Slope:** 120/110. **Green Fee:** $12/$27. **Cart Fee:** $12/person. **Walking Policy:** Walking at certain times. **Walkability:** 4. **Opened:** 1927. **Architect:** Herb Peterson/Jack Marsh. **Season:** April-Nov. **High:** May-Oct. **To obtain tee times:** Call anytime in advance. **Miscellaneous:** Reduced fees (weekdays, low season, twilight), discount packages, club rentals, credit cards (MC, V).

Reader Comments: Interesting ... Undulating greens the character of this course ... Creek/ ponds in play on 6 holes ... A hidden gem, great greens ... No. 12 a memorable downhill dogleg right.

★★★★ COUNTRY CLUB AT WOODLOCH SPRINGS

R-Woodloch Dr., Hawley, 18428, Wayne County, (717)685-2100, 7 miles E of Scranton. **E-mail:** woodgolf@woodloch.com. **Web:** www.woodloch.com.
Holes: 18. **Yards:** 6,579/4,973. **Par:** 72/72. **Course Rating:** 72.3/71.6. **Slope:** 143/130. **Green Fee:** $60/$75. **Cart Fee:** Included in Green Fee. **Walking Policy:** Walking at certain times. **Walkability:** 5. **Opened:** 1992. **Architect:** Rocky Roquemore. **Season:** May-Nov. **High:** June-Sept. **To obtain tee times:** Call 7 days in advance. Must be staying at the resort to secure tee times. **Miscellaneous:** Reduced fees (weekdays), range (grass/mats), club rentals, lodging, credit cards (MC, V, AE, D).

Reader Comments: Nice mountain course, many carries over wetlands, chasms ... Tricky par fives ... Good condition.... Better every year ... Beautiful place, great course ... Very hilly, difficult ... Requires target-golf shots ... Absolutely fantastic greens.

COUNTRY CLUB OF HERSHEY

R-1000 E. Derry Rd., Hershey, 17033, Dauphin County, (717)533-2464, (800)900-4653, 12 miles E of Harrisburg.

★★★★ EAST COURSE

Holes: 18. **Yards:** 7,061/5,645. **Par:** 71/71. **Course Rating:** 73.6/71.6. **Slope:** 128/127. **Green Fee:** $90/$90. **Cart Fee:** Included in Green Fee. **Walking Policy:** Mandatory cart. **Walkability:** 3. **Opened:** 1970. **Architect:** George Fazio. **Season:** Year-round. **High:** May-Oct. **To obtain tee times:** Call 60 days in advance without fee. Credit Card guarantee. 24 hour cancel. **Miscellaneous:** Reduced fees (weekdays, low season, twilight), discount packages, metal spikes, range (grass), club rentals, lodging, credit cards (MC, V, AE).

Reader Comments: A good challenge, especially from blues ... Every hole seems to be uphill ... Demands long tee shots ... Lots of sand ... Tight and fast... A great test ... Great finishing hole.... Back and forth but challenging ... Long par fours, greens were a challenge.

★★★½ SOUTH COURSE

PU-600 W Demy Rd, Hershey, 17033, Dauphin County, (717)534-3450.
Holes: 18. **Yards:** 6,204/4,856. **Par:** 71/72. **Course Rating:** 69.9/69.6. **Slope:** 121/107. **Green Fee:** $22/$52. **Cart Fee:** $8/person. **Walking Policy:** Walking at certain times. **Walkability:** 4. **Opened:** 1927. **Architect:** Maurice McCarthy. **Season:** Year-round. **High:** June-July-Aug.-Sept. **To obtain tee times:** Call one week in advance. May call earlier for a tee time reservation fee of $3.00 per person. **Miscellaneous:** Reduced fees (weekdays, low season, twilight, seniors), metal spikes, club rentals, credit cards (MC, V, AE), beginner friendly (clinics, lessons, leagues).

Reader Comments: Good condition, greens firm ... Shotmakers course .... Beautiful old course; Hogan, Snead played here ... Tough for average golfer... Greens always in good shape, not long but very challenging.

★★★★ WEST COURSE

Holes: 18. **Yards:** 6,860/5,908. **Par:** 73/76. **Course Rating:** 73.1/74.7. **Slope:** 131/127. **Green Fee:** $115/$115. **Cart Fee:** Included in Green Fee. **Walking Policy:** Mandatory cart. **Walkability:** 4. **Opened:** 1930. **Architect:** Maurice McCarthy. **Season:** Year-round. **High:** May-Oct. **To obtain tee times:** Call 60 days in advance without fee. Credit card guarantee. 24 hour cancel. **Miscellaneous:** Reduced fees (juniors), discount packages, metal spikes, range (grass), club rentals, lodging (18 rooms), credit cards (MC, V, AE).

Reader Comments: Very nice layout, lots of play ... A great old course ... Always a treat to play and smell the chocolate ... Much more of a placement course than East ... Heavily played. Easier then East, but more scenic .... This course has character.... Long par fives ... Not for wild hitters.

PENNSYLVANIA

CROSS CREEK RESORT
PU-Rd. 3 Box 152, Titusville, 16354, Venango County, (814)827-9611, (800)461-3173, 4 miles S of Erie. **E-mail:** ccresor@csonline.net. **Web:** www.crosscreekresort.com.

★★★ NORTH COURSE
Holes: 18. **Yards:** 6,467/5,226. **Par:** 70/72. **Course Rating:** 68.6/68.4. **Slope:** 112/108. **Green Fee:** $30/$36. **Cart Fee:** $14/person. **Walking Policy:** Walking at certain times. **Walkability:** 2. **Opened:** 1959. **Architect:** Wyn Treadway. **Season:** April-Oct. **High:** June-Aug. **To obtain tee times:** Call golf shop. **Miscellaneous:** Reduced fees (low season), discount packages, metal spikes, club rentals, lodging (94 rooms), credit cards (MC, V, AE, D).
Reader Comments: Well maintained and manicured ... Some of the hardest par threes, plus good distance holes ... Excellent food ... Interesting holes, especially par three third ... Tiny greens.

SOUTH COURSE
Holes: 9. **Yards:** 3,137/2,417. **Par:** 36/36. **Course Rating:** 34.0/33.1. **Slope:** N/A/108. **Green Fee:** $30/$36. **Cart Fee:** $14/person. **Walking Policy:** Walking at certain times. **Walkability:** 2. **Opened:** 1959. **Architect:** Ferdinand Garbin. **Season:** April-Oct. **High:** June-Aug. **To obtain tee times:** Call golf shop. **Miscellaneous:** Reduced fees (low season), discount packages, metal spikes, range (grass/mats), club rentals, lodging (94 rooms), credit cards (MC, V, AE, D).

★★★ CULBERTSON HILLS GOLF RESORT
R-Rte. 6N W., Edinboro, 16412, Erie County, (814)734-3114, (800)734-8191, 15 miles S of Erie. **E-mail:** chpro@velocity.net. **Web:** www.culbertsonhills.com.
Holes: 18. **Yards:** 6,813/5,514. **Par:** 72/72. **Course Rating:** 72.4/71.4. **Slope:** 128/124. **Green Fee:** $22/$25. **Cart Fee:** $12/person. **Walking Policy:** Walking at certain times. **Walkability:** 3. **Opened:** 1931. **Architect:** Thomas Bendelow. **Season:** April-Nov. **High:** June-Aug. **To obtain tee times:** Call golf shop. **Miscellaneous:** Reduced fees (weekdays, low season), discount packages, metal spikes, club rentals, lodging, credit cards (MC, V).
Reader Comments: Fun out and back course ... Good old style course with mature trees. L-o-n-g, bring your driver. No sand traps ... My favorite course; I'd rather break par here then at St Andrews! ... Drive it straight to score, but greens pretty open.

★★½ CUMBERLAND GOLF CLUB
SP-2395 Ritner Hwy., Carlisle, 17013, Cumberland County, (717)249-5538, 5 miles S of Carlisle. **Holes:** 18. **Yards:** 6,900/N/A. **Par:** 72/N/A. **Course Rating:** 70.4/N/A. **Slope:** 121/N/A. **Green Fee:** $13/$18. **Cart Fee:** $18/cart. **Walkability:** N/A. **Opened:** 1962. **Architect:** James Gilmore Harrison/Ferdinand Garbin. **Season:** March-Dec. **High:** April-Sept. **To obtain tee times:** Call in advance. **Miscellaneous:** Metal spikes, range (grass/mats), club rentals, credit cards (MC, V, AE, D).
Reader Comments: Great value, easy to walk, medium fast greens ... Mature trees, greens always in good shape ... Long and short par fours, straightaway par fives, long par threes ... Last two holes will wear you out and drive you to the clubhouse bar ... Nice length. Use all of your clubs ... Pure, solid golf.

★★★½ DAUPHIN HIGHLANDS GOLF COURSE
PU-650 S. Harrisburg St., Harrisburg, 17113, Dauphin County, (717)986-1984, 5 miles E of Harrisburg.
Holes: 18. **Yards:** 7,035/5,327. **Par:** 72/72. **Course Rating:** 73.4/70.1. **Slope:** 125/114. **Green Fee:** $20/$28. **Cart Fee:** $12/person. **Walking Policy:** Unrestricted walking. **Walkability:** 5. **Opened:** 1995. **Architect:** Bill Love. **Season:** Year-round. **High:** April-Oct. **To obtain tee times:** Call 6 days in advance. **Miscellaneous:** Reduced fees (weekdays, low season, twilight, seniors, juniors), range (grass/mats), club rentals, credit cards (MC, V).
Reader Comments: Beautiful views, great layout, hard to walk ... Nice course but slow, 5 1/2-6hrs. .... Open; Tough in the wind ... Every hole offers a different challenge ... One of the best public tracks in Harrisburg area ... Longball course ... Picturesque.

★★½ DEEP VALLEY GOLF COURSE
PU-169 Hartmann Rd., Harmony, 16037, Butler County, (724)452-8021, 25 miles NE of Pittsburgh. **Holes:** 18. **Yards:** 6,310/N/A. **Par:** 72/N/A. **Course Rating:** N/A. **Slope:** N/A. **Green Fee:** $12/$18. **Cart Fee:** $22/cart. **Walking Policy:** Unrestricted walking. **Walkability:** 2. **Opened:** 1958. **Season:** Year-round. **High:** March-Oct. **To obtain tee times:** First come, first served. **Miscellaneous:** Reduced fees (low season, seniors), metal spikes, club rentals.
Reader Comments: Narrow fairways. Many holes with lay-ups .... Nice challenging back nine ... Hard fairways ... Nice back nine.

★★★★ DEER RUN GOLF CLUB
SP-287 Monier Road, Gibsonia, 15044, Allegheny County, (724)265-4800, 3 miles E of Pittsburgh. **Holes:** 18. **Yards:** 7,018/5,238. **Par:** 72/73. **Course Rating:** 74.2/71.2. **Slope:** 134/128. **Green Fee:** $28/$36. **Cart Fee:** $14/person. **Walking Policy:** Walking at certain times. **Walkability:** 3. **Opened:** 1994. **Architect:** Ron Forse. **Season:** Year-round. **High:** May-Aug. **To obtain tee times:** Call 2 days in advance. **Miscellaneous:** Metal spikes, range (grass), club rentals, credit cards (MC, V).

Reader Comments: Hidden gem; great track ... Beautiful foliage, outstanding condition ... Four sets of tees. Anyone can play it ... Nice fairways, holes don't play on top of each other ... A little hilly ... Clubhouse very nice.

★★★ DONEGAL HIGHLANDS GOLF CLUB
PU-Rte. 31 and Clay Pike, Donegal, 15628, Westmoreland County, (724)423-7888, 35 miles SE of Pittsburgh.
Holes: 18. **Yards:** 6,130/4,520. **Par:** 72/72. **Course Rating:** 69.6/65.7. **Slope:** 121/113. **Green Fee:** $17/$27. **Cart Fee:** $12/person. **Walking Policy:** Unrestricted walking. **Walkability:** 2. **Opened:** 1991. **Architect:** James Gayton/Ron Forse. **Season:** March-Nov. **High:** June-Aug. **To obtain tee times:** Call 7 days in advance. **Miscellaneous:** Reduced fees (weekdays, low season, seniors, juniors), discount packages, range (grass), club rentals, credit cards (MC, V, D).
Reader Comments: Open front, back short but tough. Fun course ... The nines are like two different courses ... You need to be familiar with course ... Fun to play, staff aims to please ... Links and parkland. Great greens.

★★★ DOWN RIVER GOLF CLUB
PU-134 Rivers Bend Drive, Everett, 15537, Bedford County, (814)652-5193, 40 miles S of Altoona.
Holes: 18. **Yards:** 6,900/5,513. **Par:** 72/73. **Course Rating:** 70.6/70.7. **Slope:** 124/118. **Green Fee:** $18/$20. **Cart Fee:** $12/person. **Walking Policy:** Unrestricted walking. **Walkability:** 2. **Opened:** 1967. **Architect:** Xen Hassenplug. **Season:** April-Nov. **High:** June-Sept. **To obtain tee times:** Call up to one week in advance. **Miscellaneous:** Reduced fees (weekdays, low season, twilight, juniors), discount packages, metal spikes, range (grass), credit cards (MC, V, AE, D).
Reader Comments: Greens are very good, nice course to walk ... A good variety of holes. Beautiful in the fall, lots of choices to make ... Very different front and back nines. Nice course.

★★★ DOWNING GOLF COURSE
PU-Troupe Rd., Harborcreek, 16421, Erie County, (814)899-5827, 6 miles E of Erie.
Holes: 18. **Yards:** 7,175/6,259. **Par:** 72/74. **Course Rating:** 73.0/74.4. **Slope:** 114/115. **Green Fee:** $12/$15. **Cart Fee:** $15/person. **Walking Policy:** Unrestricted walking. **Walkability:** N/A. **Opened:** 1962. **Architect:** Garbin/Harrison. **Season:** Year-round. **High:** March-Nov. **To obtain tee times:** For Saturday call on Wednesday; call anytime for other days. **Miscellaneous:** Reduced fees (low season, twilight), metal spikes, range (grass).
Reader Comments: Very long, very fair, play is heavy ... Course in excellent shape, better than some country clubs ... A tough classy old lady.

★★★★ DOWNINGTOWN COUNTRY CLUB
PU-85 Country Club Drive, Downingtown, 19335, Chester County, (610)269-2000, 25 miles W of Philadelphia. **E-mail:** proshop@golfdowningtown.com.
Web: www.golfdowningtown.com.
Holes: 18. **Yards:** 6,619/5,092. **Par:** 72/72. **Course Rating:** 72.9/69.4. **Slope:** 132/119. **Green Fee:** $49/$59. **Cart Fee:** $20/person. **Walking Policy:** Unrestricted walking. **Walkability:** 2. **Opened:** 1966. **Architect:** George Fazio. **Season:** Year-round. **High:** May-Sept. **To obtain tee times:** Call up to 7 days in advance. **Miscellaneous:** Reduced fees (weekdays, low season, twilight, seniors), discount packages, metal spikes, club rentals, credit cards (MC, V, AE).
Reader Comments: Great renovation ... First time I've played there in three years-What a difference ... Nice clubhouse. Great deal ... Great old style course ... Nice 19th hole for watching first tee ... Classic shotmakers course ... Target greens ... Very fair, but challenging.

★★★ DUCK HOLLOW GOLF CLUB
PU-347 Duck Hollow Rd., Uniontown, 15401, Fayette County, (412)439-3150, 40 miles S of Pittsburgh.
Holes: 18. **Yards:** 6,538/6,112. **Par:** 72/74. **Course Rating:** 69.5/68.9. **Slope:** 120/115. **Green Fee:** $17/$22. **Cart Fee:** $11/person. **Walking Policy:** Walking at certain times. **Walkability:** 3. **Opened:** 1975. **Season:** Year-round. **High:** June-Aug. **To obtain tee times:** Call 7 days in advance. **Miscellaneous:** Reduced fees (weekdays, low season, seniors, juniors), discount packages, range (grass), club rentals, credit cards (MC, V).
Reader Comments: Nice course, make sure to lay up on 15th ... Bunkers makes it more challenging ... Many tricky holes.

★★★½ EDGEWOOD IN THE PINES GOLF COURSE
PU-R.R.1, Box 1601-A, Drums, 18222, Luzerne County, (570)788-1101, 5 miles N of Hazleton.
Holes: 18. **Yards:** 6,721/5,184. **Par:** 72/72. **Course Rating:** 71.9/69.9. **Slope:** 132/118. **Green Fee:** $13/$28. **Cart Fee:** $12/person. **Walking Policy:** Walking at certain times. **Walkability:** 3. **Opened:** 1980. **Architect:** David Gordon. **Season:** Year-round. **High:** May-Aug. **To obtain tee times:** Call 7 days in advance. **Miscellaneous:** Reduced fees (weekdays, low season, twilight), metal spikes, club rentals, credit cards (MC, V, AE).
Reader Comments: Course always in good condition ... Very nice; challenging ... Undiscovered jewel.... Tight, tends to be crowded ... Fun, relaxed place ... Played in the fall, full of leaves, beautiful.

PENNSYLVANIA

★★★½ EMPORIUM COUNTRY CLUB
SP-Cameron Rd., Star Rte., Emporium, 15834, Cameron County, (814)486-2241, 50 miles SE of Bradford.
Holes: 18. **Yards:** 6,032/5,233. **Par:** 72/72. **Course Rating:** 68.5/69.0. **Slope:** 118/115. **Green Fee:** $20/$25. **Cart Fee:** $11/person. **Walking Policy:** Mandatory cart. **Walk-ability:** 5. **Opened:** 1954. **Architect:** Members. **Season:** March-Nov. **High:** April-Sept. **To obtain tee times:** Call golf shop. **Miscellaneous:** Reduced fees (weekdays, juniors), discount packages, metal spikes, range (grass/mats), club rentals, credit cards (MC, V).
Reader Comments: Front nine wide open, back nine tight with trees ... Proof that 'if you build it, they will come'... Front nine lulls you to sleep. Back nine awakens you very rudely. Very interesting. Beautiful views ...A gem in the middle of nowhere.

★½ ERIE GOLF CLUB
PU-6050 Old Zuck Rd., Erie, 16506, Erie County, (814)866-0641.
Holes: 18. **Yards:** 5,682/4,977. **Par:** 69/72. **Course Rating:** 67.2/68.2. **Slope:** 111/109. **Green Fee:** $11/$14. **Cart Fee:** $15/person. **Walking Policy:** Unrestricted walking. **Walkability:** N/A. **Opened:** 1964. **Architect:** James Gilmore Harrison. **Season:** March-Nov. **High:** April-Oct. **To obtain tee times:** Call Wednesday for Saturday. **Miscellaneous:** Reduced fees (twilight, seniors, juniors), metal spikes, club rentals.

★½ EXETER GOLF CLUB
PU-811 Shelbourne Rd., Reading, 19606, Berks County, (610)779-1211.
Holes: 9. **Yards:** 3,000/2,555. **Par:** 35/35. **Course Rating:** N/A. **Slope:** N/A. **Green Fee:** $14/$18. **Cart Fee:** $20/cart. **Walking Policy:** Unrestricted walking. **Walkability:** 3. **Opened:** 1957. **Architect:** Enrico Filippini. **Season:** March-Dec. **High:** April-Nov. **To obtain tee times:** Call anytime, no restrictions. **Miscellaneous:** Reduced fees (weekdays, twilight), metal spikes, club rentals, credit cards (MC, V), beginner friendly.

★★★½ FAIRVIEW GOLF COURSE
PU-2399 Quentin Road, Lebanon, 17042, Lebanon County, (717)273-3411, (800)621-6557, 5 miles S of Lebanon. **E-mail:** info@distinctgolf.com. **Web:** www.distinctgolf.com.
Holes: 18. **Yards:** 6,227/5,221. **Par:** 71/73. **Course Rating:** 69.2/72.9. **Slope:** 106/115. **Green Fee:** $12/$25. **Cart Fee:** $12/person. **Walking Policy:** Unrestricted walking. **Walkability:** 2. **Opened:** 1959. **Architect:** Frank Murray/Russell Roberts. **Season:** Year-round. **High:** May-Sept. **To obtain tee times:** Call up to 14 days in advance. **Miscellaneous:** Reduced fees (weekdays, low season, twilight, seniors, juniors), metal spikes, range (mats), club rentals, credit cards (MC, V).
Reader Comments: Short, must place shots, well maintained ... Great shape with much play ... Excellent condition and experience ... Play about six times a year and always enjoy, good food in lunch room.

★★ FERNWOOD RESORT & COUNTRY CLUB
R-Rte. 209, Bushkill, 18324, Monroe County, (717)588-9500, (800)233-8103, 12 miles NE of Stroudsburg.
Holes: 18. **Yards:** 6,100/4,800. **Par:** 71/71. **Course Rating:** 68.8/63.3. **Slope:** 125/115. **Green Fee:** $32/$46. **Cart Fee:** Included in Green Fee. **Walking Policy:** Mandatory cart. **Walkability:** 3. **Opened:** 1968. **Architect:** Nicholas Psiahas. **Season:** April-Nov. **High:** July-Sept. **To obtain tee times:** Call anytime. **Miscellaneous:** Reduced fees (low season, resort guests, twilight), discount packages, metal spikes, range (grass/mats), club rentals, lodging (900 rooms), credit cards (MC, V, AE).

★★★½ FIVE PONDS GOLF CLUB
PU-1225 West Street Road, Warminster, 18974, Bucks County, (215)956-9727, 14 miles N of Philadelphia. **E-mail:** 5ponds@netaxs.com. **Web:** http://www.netaxs.com/5ponds.
Holes: 18. **Yards:** 6,681/5,365. **Par:** 71/71. **Course Rating:** 71.0/70.1. **Slope:** 121/117. **Green Fee:** $23/$27. **Cart Fee:** $12/person. **Walking Policy:** Walking at certain times. **Walkability:** 2. **Opened:** 1988. **Architect:** X.G. Hassenplug. **Season:** Year-round. **High:** April-Oct. **To obtain tee times:** Call 7 days in advance. **Miscellaneous:** Reduced fees (weekdays, low season, twilight, seniors), range (grass), club rentals, credit cards (MC, V, MAC).
Reader Comments: Lots of water ... A lot of hills ... Some tough holes, some easy holes ... Brutal 9th green. Gets heavy play ... Very good value, well maintained. Gotta play again.

★★ FLATBUSH GOLF COURSE
PU-940 Littletown Rd., Littletown, 17340, Adams County, (717)359-7125, (800)942-2444, 40 miles S of Harrisburg.
Holes: 18. **Yards:** 6,671/5,247. **Par:** 71/71. **Course Rating:** 71.6/69.6. **Slope:** 121/119. **Green Fee:** $17/$21. **Cart Fee:** $10/person. **Walking Policy:** Unrestricted walking. **Walkability:** 3. **Opened:** 1989. **Architect:** Ault & Clark. **Season:** Year-round. **High:** April-Oct. **To obtain tee times:** Call 7-10 days in advance, especially for weekends. **Miscellaneous:** Reduced fees (low season, twilight, seniors), metal spikes, range (grass), club rentals, credit cards (MC, V).

PENNSYLVANIA

★★★ FLYING HILLS GOLF COURSE
PU-10 Village Center Dr., Reading, 19607, Berks County, (610)775-4063, 5 miles S of Reading.
Holes: 18. **Yards:** 6,023/5,176. **Par:** 70/70. **Course Rating:** 68.2/68.8. **Slope:** 118/118. **Green Fee:** $19/$21. **Cart Fee:** $21/person. **Walking Policy:** Unrestricted walking. **Walkability:** 4. **Opened:** 1971. **Architect:** Mr. Rahenkamp. **Season:** Year-round. **High:** March-Sept. **To obtain tee times:** Call golf shop. **Miscellaneous:** Reduced fees (weekdays, low season), metal spikes, club rentals.
Reader Comments: Very good greens, tight course ... Tight fairways due to homes, good value ... Nice little secret, best 18th hole around ... Hilly. Good layout. Great and challenging greens ... Too tight for a driver–hit irons.

★★½ FOUR SEASONS GOLF CLUB
PU-750 Slocum Ave., Exeter, 18643-1030, Luzerne County, (570)655-8869, 6 miles N of Wilkes-Barre.
Holes: 18. **Yards:** 5,524/4,136. **Par:** 70/70. **Course Rating:** 64.5/62.0. **Slope:** 102/91. **Green Fee:** $13/$15. **Cart Fee:** $9/person. **Walking Policy:** Unrestricted walking. **Walkability:** 1. **Opened:** 1960. **Season:** Year-round. **High:** May-Sept. **To obtain tee times:** Call Monday for weekend or holiday. **Miscellaneous:** Reduced fees (weekdays, twilight), metal spikes, club rentals, credit cards (MC, V, AE, D), beginner friendly (golf schools and lessons).
Reader Comments: Nice open course. No frills, just golf ... They seem to be working to make it better ... Short, great par 3s ... Adequate; open all-year ... Great place, tries to accommodate everyone ... Easy flat layout.

★★★ FOX HOLLOW GOLF CLUB
PU-2020 Trumbauersville Rd., Quakertown, 18951, Bucks County, (215)538-1920.
Holes: 18. **Yards:** 6,613/4,984. **Par:** 71/71. **Course Rating:** 70.2/67.1. **Slope:** 123/120. **Green Fee:** N/A. **Walking Policy:** Walking at certain times. **Walkability:** 1. **Opened:** 1957. **Architect:** Dave Gordon. **Season:** Year-round. **High:** May-Sept. **To obtain tee times:** Call 10 days in advance. **Miscellaneous:** Reduced fees (weekdays, low season, twilight, seniors, juniors), range (grass), club rentals, credit cards (MC, V, AE), beginner friendly (junior, beginner clinics, PGA Pro).
Reader Comments: Excellent value, no trouble getting tee times ... Good winter course ... From the tips a test ... Short, fun... Very friendly professional staff. A course I'll never stop playing. Beautiful greens.

★★★ FOX RUN GOLF COURSE
PU-4240 River Road , Beaver Falls, 15010, Beaver County, (724)847-3568, 30 miles NW of Pittsburgh.
Holes: 18. **Yards:** 6,510/5,337. **Par:** 72/72. **Course Rating:** 69.6/72.2. **Slope:** 113/117. **Green Fee:** $13/$19. **Cart Fee:** $10/person. **Walking Policy:** Unrestricted walking. **Walkability:** 2. **Opened:** 1962. **Architect:** Max Mesing. **Season:** Year-round. **High:** May-Sept. **To obtain tee times:** Call (724)847-3568. **Miscellaneous:** Reduced fees (low season, seniors), metal spikes, range (grass/mats).
Reader Comments: Greens are small, fast and hard to hold ... Nice.... Greens are true, open .... Good place for our league ... It keeps getting better, good value ... Great staff, good course for women ... Needs to add some bunkers ... Some good challenging holes over water.

★★★★ FOXCHASE GOLF CLUB
PU-300 Stevens Rd., Stevens, 17578, Lancaster County, (717)336-3673, 50 miles NW of Philadelphia. **E-mail:** foxchasegc@desupernet.net. **Web:** www.foxchasegolf.com.
Holes: 18. **Yards:** 6,796/4,690. **Par:** 72/72. **Course Rating:** 72.7/66.9. **Slope:** 124/116. **Green Fee:** $20/$43. **Cart Fee:** Included in Green Fee. **Walking Policy:** Walking at certain times. **Walkability:** 3. **Opened:** 1991. **Architect:** John Thompson. **Season:** Year-round. **High:** April-Oct. **To obtain tee times:** Credit card numbers required for all weekend and holiday tee times. **Miscellaneous:** Reduced fees (weekdays, low season, twilight, seniors, juniors), range (grass/mats), club rentals, credit cards (MC, V, D).
Reader Comments: Good course, good shape, good service ... Nice range ... 14th is a bear ... Short but fun ... Ego builder ... Fast greens that really break ... Short, interesting links course. Need to putt well to score ... Scenic and wide open ... Wind always a factor. Best from black tees.

★ FRANKLIN D. ROOSEVELT GOLF CLUB
PM-20th & Pattison Ave., Philadelphia, 19145, Philadelphia County, (215)462-8997.
Holes: 18. **Yards:** 5,894/5,413. **Par:** 69/69. **Course Rating:** 68.7/68.7. **Slope:** 110/110. **Green Fee:** $19/$23. **Cart Fee:** $25/cart. **Walking Policy:** Unrestricted walking. **Walkability:** 1. **Opened:** 1933. **Season:** Year-round. **High:** April-Sept. **To obtain tee times:** Call 7 days in advance. **Miscellaneous:** Reduced fees (weekdays, twilight, seniors, juniors), metal spikes, range (grass), club rentals, credit cards (MC, V).

★★★½ GALEN HALL COUNTRY CLUB
PU-Galen Hall Rd., P.O. Box 129, Wernersville, 19565, Berks County, (610)678-9535, 10 miles W of Reading. **E-mail:** galenhallcc@netzero.net.

Holes: 18. **Yards:** 6,271/5,117. **Par:** 72/73. **Course Rating:** 70.2/68.8. **Slope:** 113/113. **Green Fee:** $10/$23. **Cart Fee:** $10/person. **Walking Policy:** Walking at certain times. **Walkability:** 4. **Opened:** 1917. **Architect:** Alex Findlay/A.W.Tillinghast. **Season:** Year-round. **High:** May-Oct. **To obtain tee times:** Call anytime for present year. **Miscellaneous:** Reduced fees (weekdays, low season, twilight, seniors, juniors), metal spikes, range (grass), club rentals, lodging, credit cards (MC, V, AE, D).

Reader Comments: Course and greens very good ... Blind shots on a few holes, but acceptable ... Mountain views, fastest greens in country ... Tough course, island par three ... Small greens, a lot of uneven lies.... Old, great par threes, tricky greens, lots of hills ... Superb greens, shotmaking course.

★★★ GENERAL WASHINGTON COUNTRY CLUB
PU-2750 Egypt Rd., Audubon, 19407, Montgomery County, (610)666-7602, 4 miles W of Philadelphia.
Holes: 18. **Yards:** 6,400/5,300. **Par:** 71/72. **Course Rating:** 70.3/70.5. **Slope:** 119/119. **Green Fee:** $14/$40. **Cart Fee:** $11/person. **Walking Policy:** Walking at certain times. **Walkability:** 3. **Opened:** 1945. **Architect:** William F. Mitchell. **Season:** Year-round. **High:** April-Oct. **To obtain tee times:** 7 days in advance for non-members, 14 days for members (AGPA). **Miscellaneous:** Reduced fees (low season, twilight, seniors, juniors), discount packages, metal spikes, range (mats), club rentals, credit cards (MC, V, AE).
Reader Comments: Simple course, but it challenges a pretty good variety of skills. Watch the bunkers ... Many doglegs.

★★★ GLEN BROOK GOLF CLUB
PU-Glenbrook Rd., Stroudsburg, 18360, Monroe County, (570)421-3680, 75 miles W of New York City.
Holes: 18. **Yards:** 6,536/5,234. **Par:** 72/72. **Course Rating:** 71.4/69.4. **Slope:** 123/117. **Green Fee:** $36/$43. **Cart Fee:** Included in Green Fee. **Walking Policy:** Walking at certain times. **Walkability:** 3. **Opened:** 1924. **Architect:** Robert White. **Season:** April-Nov. **High:** May-Oct. **To obtain tee times:** Call golf shop. **Miscellaneous:** Reduced fees (weekdays, low season, resort guests, twilight, seniors), discount packages, metal spikes, club rentals, lodging (12 rooms), credit cards (MC, V).
Reader Comments: Great mountain course. Lots of deer ... On the move, getting better each year.

★★ THE GOLF CLUB AT SHEPHERD HILLS
PU-1160 S. Krocks Rd., Wescosville, 18106, Lehigh County, (610)391-0644.
Holes: 18. **Yards:** 6,500/5,842. **Par:** 70/73. **Course Rating:** 69.5/70.8. **Slope:** 116/115. **Green Fee:** $25/$34. **Cart Fee:** $12/person. **Walking Policy:** Unrestricted walking. **Walkability:** 1. **Opened:** 1964. **Season:** Year-round. **High:** May-Sept. **To obtain tee times:** Call club. **Miscellaneous:** Reduced fees (weekdays, low season, seniors, juniors), club rentals, credit cards (MC, V).

★★★ GRAND VIEW GOLF CLUB
PU-1000 Clubhouse Dr., North Braddock, 15104, Allegheny County, (412)351-5390, 8 miles E of Pittsburgh. **E-mail:** gvga@pgh.net. **Web:** pittsburghgolf.com.
Holes: 18. **Yards:** 6,111/4,817. **Par:** 71/71. **Course Rating:** 71.9/69.4. **Slope:** 132/122. **Green Fee:** $33/$40. **Cart Fee:** Included in Green Fee. **Walking Policy:** Walking at certain times. **Walkability:** 5. **Opened:** 1996. **Architect:** Garbin. **Season:** Year-round. **High:** April-Sept. **To obtain tee times:** Call 7 days in advance. **Miscellaneous:** Reduced fees (low season, twilight, seniors, juniors), metal spikes, range (grass/mats), club rentals, credit cards (MC, V, AE).
Reader Comments: Position golf. Take plenty of old balls ... Very unique! ... Great views of city and river, target golf, fun ... Blind landing areas ... Leave driver in bag, tight.

★★½ GRANDVIEW GOLF CLUB
PU-2779 Carlisle Rd., York, 17404, York County, (717)764-2674, 4 miles N of York.
Holes: 18. **Yards:** 6,639/5,578. **Par:** 72/73. **Course Rating:** 71.0/71.0. **Slope:** 122/119. **Green Fee:** $20/$26. **Cart Fee:** $12/person. **Walking Policy:** Unrestricted walking. **Walkability:** 3. **Opened:** 1924. **Season:** Year-round. **High:** April-Oct. **To obtain tee times:** Call. **Miscellaneous:** Reduced fees (weekdays, low season, resort guests, twilight, seniors, juniors), discount packages, club rentals, credit cards (MC, V, D), beginner friendly.
Reader Comments: Sneaky long, especially par threes ... Quirky, fun course. Some holes are too close, so watch out.

★★½ GREEN ACRES GOLF CLUB
PU-RD No.4, Rte. 408, Titusville, 16354, Crawford County, (814)827-3589, 2 miles W of Hydentown.
Holes: 9. **Yards:** 3,200/3,000. **Par:** 36/36. **Course Rating:** N/A. **Slope:** N/A. **Green Fee:** N/A. **Walking Policy:** Unrestricted walking. **Walkability:** 2. **Opened:** 1974. **Architect:** A. Kalkbrenner/D. Kalkbrenner/R. Howe. **Season:** April-Oct. **High:** June-Aug. **To obtain tee times:** Call. **Miscellaneous:** Reduced fees (low season, seniors), metal spikes, range (grass), club rentals.

Reader Comments: Course is short, service is great ... Friendly staff always ... Beginners course. Wanna drive a green?

GREEN MEADOWS GOLF COURSE

PU-2451 N Brickyard Rd., North East, 16428, Erie County, (814)725-5009, 15 miles E of Erie.
Holes: 18. Yards: 5,988/5,144. Par: 72/71. Course Rating: 67.1/68.0. Slope: 102/102. Green Fee: $13/$16. Cart Fee: $18/cart. Walking Policy: Unrestricted walking. Walkability: 1. Opened: 1975. Architect: Bob Boyd. Season: April-Oct. High: June-Aug. To obtain tee times: First come, first served. Miscellaneous: Reduced fees (seniors), range (grass), credit cards (MC, V, D).

★★½ GREEN POND COUNTRY CLUB

PU-3604 Farmersville Rd., Bethlehem, 18017, Northampton County, (610)691-9453.
Holes: 18. Yards: 6,521/5,541. Par: 71/74. Course Rating: 69.4/69.7. Slope: 126/112. Green Fee: $20/$25. Cart Fee: $13/person. Walking Policy: Unrestricted walking. Walkability: 2. Opened: 1931. Architect: Alex Findley. Season: Year-round. High: April-Nov. To obtain tee times: Tee times only on weekends, call the Monday before. Miscellaneous: Reduced fees (seniors, juniors), range (grass), credit cards (MC, V, AE, D).
Reader Comments: Short, narrow, good walking course ... The friendliest golf pro and staff ever... Always crowded, lots of trees! ... Small greens.

★★★½ GREENCASTLE GREENS GOLF CLUB

SP-2000 Castlegreen Dr., Greencastle, 17225, Franklin County, (717)597-1188, (717)593-9192, 75 miles NW of Baltimore.
Holes: 18. Yards: 6,908/5,315. Par: 72/74. Course Rating: 72.6/70.3. Slope: 129/124. Green Fee: $17/$28. Cart Fee: $12/person. Walking Policy: Walking at certain times. Walkability: 5. Opened: 1991. Architect: Robert L. Elder. Season: Year-round. High: April-Oct. To obtain tee times: Call up to 7 days in advance. Miscellaneous: Reduced fees (weekdays, low season, twilight, seniors, juniors), discount packages, metal spikes, range (grass/mats), club rentals, credit cards (MC, V).
Reader Comments: Hilly keep it in the fairway ... Par threes are fun, filled with waterfalls and an island green par four ... Some memorable holes.

★★★ GROFF'S FARM GOLF CLUB

PU-650 Pinkerton Rd., Mount Joy, 17552, Lancaster County, (717)653-2048.
Holes: 18. Yards: 6,403/4,863. Par: 71/71. Course Rating: 70.6/67.3. Slope: 121/107. Green Fee: $17/$24. Cart Fee: $11/person. Walking Policy: Unrestricted walking. Walkability: 3. Opened: 1998. Architect: Ed Beidel. Season: Year-round. High: April-Sept. To obtain tee times: Call Golf shop. Miscellaneous: Reduced fees (weekdays, low season, twilight, seniors, juniors), range (grass/mats), club rentals, lodging (2 rooms), credit cards (MC, V, D), beginner friendly (beginner classes).
Reader Comments: Nos. 16 and 18 are truly unique ... First 15 holes are great, last three another story ... Interesting links course ... Scenes from Pa. farmland, beautiful greens are firm and hold ... Open, windy ... Three fantastic finishing holes (Charlie's Corner).

★★★½ HARRISBURG NORTH GOLF COURSE

PU-1724 Rte. 25, Millersburg, 17061, Dauphin County, (717)692-3664, 24 miles NE of Harrisburg.
Holes: 18. Yards: 6,960/6,600. Par: 71/71. Course Rating: 68.8/69.2. Slope: 115/117. Green Fee: $10/$17. Cart Fee: $27/person. Walking Policy: Unrestricted walking. Walkability: 3. Opened: 1963. Architect: Harlin Wills. Season: Year-round. High: June-Aug. To obtain tee times: Call anytime. Miscellaneous: Range (grass), credit cards (MC, V).
Reader Comments: Good variety, good service, great view ... Nice greens, No. 10 very difficult par three ... No. 10 is a long par three over water, over a tree ... Exceptional course in a busy area.

★★★★½ HARTEFELD NTL. GOLF CLUB *Service, Condition+*

PU-1 Hartefeld Dr., Avondale, 19311, Chester County, (610)268-8800, (800)240-7373, 35 miles S of Philadelphia. Web: www.hartefeld.com.
Holes: 18. Yards: 6,969/5,065. Par: 71/71. Course Rating: 73.2/69.8. Slope: 131/123. Green Fee: $55/$110. Cart Fee: Included in Green Fee. Walking Policy: Unrestricted walking. Walkability: 3. Opened: 1995. Architect: Tom Fazio. Season: Year-round. High: May-October. To obtain tee times: Call 14 days in advance. Miscellaneous: Reduced fees (low season, twilight), range (grass/mats), club rentals, credit cards (MC, V, AE, D).
Notes: Ranked 16th in 1999 Best in State; 6th in 1996 Best New Upscale Courses. 1998-1999 Bell Atlantic Classic Senior PGA Tour.
Reader Comments: Shotmaker's course, site of senior Bell Atlantic Classic ... Great conditions. Contoured beautifully with nature ... Stay out of the rough rough ... Excellent facility ... Must play ... Fast greens, great layout, food is awesome ... Great clubhouse ... Nice design, keep it in the fairway ... Fair but tough, could use more water holes.

PENNSYLVANIA

★★★½ HAWK VALLEY GOLF CLUB
PU-1319 Crestview Dr., Denver, 17517, Lancaster County, (717)445-5445, (800)522-4295, 5 miles NE of Denver.
Holes: 18. **Yards:** 6,628/5,661. **Par:** 72/72. **Course Rating:** 70.3/70.2. **Slope:** 132/119. **Green Fee:** $20/$28. **Cart Fee:** $12/person. **Walking Policy:** Walking at certain times. **Walkability:** 3. **Opened:** 1971. **Architect:** William Gordon. **Season:** Year-round. **High:** April-Nov. **To obtain tee times:** Weekday call 8 days in advance; weekend and holidays call anytime in advance.
Miscellaneous: Reduced fees (juniors), discount packages, metal spikes, club rentals, credit cards (MC, V, AE, D).
Reader Comments: Tough public course, nice people, great greens ... Nice greens, always improving course ... Very challenging greens ... A bit off the beaten path, but worth it ... Quick sloping greens ... Interesting course, good mix of sand, water and trees.

★★★½ HERITAGE HILLS GOLF RESORT & CONFERENCE CENTER
R-2700 Mt. Rose Ave., York, 17402, York County, (717)755-4653, (800)942-2444, 25 miles S of York. **E-mail:** golf@hhgr.com. **Web:** www.hhgr.com.
Holes: 18. **Yards:** 6,330/5,075. **Par:** 71/71. **Course Rating:** 70.8/68.9. **Slope:** 122/110. **Green Fee:** $29/$35. **Cart Fee:** $15/person. **Walking Policy:** Walking at certain times. **Walkability:** 3. **Opened:** 1989. **Architect:** Russell Roberts. **Season:** Year-round. **High:** April-Sept. **To obtain tee times:** Call golf shop. **Miscellaneous:** Reduced fees (weekdays, low season, twilight, seniors), discount packages, range (mats), club rentals, lodging (104 rooms), credit cards (MC, V, AE, D).
Reader Comments: Need every club in bag ... Fantastic, tough finishing hole. Beautiful resort course ... Nice layout, good for all caliber of play, interesting holes ... Very scenic and challenging ... Scenic with hills and good rolls.

★★★ HICKORY HEIGHTS GOLF CLUB
PU-116 Hickory Heights Dr., Bridgeville, 15017, Allegheny County, (412)257-0300, 12 miles SW of Pittsburgh.
Holes: 18. **Yards:** 6,531/5,002. **Par:** 72/72. **Course Rating:** 71.6/69.6. **Slope:** 131/125. **Green Fee:** $30/$48. **Cart Fee:** Included in Green Fee. **Walking Policy:** Walking at certain times. **Walkability:** 4. **Opened:** 1992. **Architect:** Michael Hurdzan. **Season:** Year-round. **High:** April-Oct. **To obtain tee times:** Call 7 days in advance. **Miscellaneous:** Reduced fees (weekdays, low season, twilight, seniors, juniors), metal spikes, range (grass), club rentals, credit cards (MC, V, AE).
Reader Comments: Tight fairways, small greens ... Hilly ... Challenging, fair... Interesting par 3s.

HICKORY VALLEY GOLF CLUB
PU-1921 Ludwig Rd., Gilbertsville, 19525, Montgomery County, (610)754-9862, 25 miles NW of Philadelphia.
★★★½ AMBASSADOR GOLF COURSE
Holes: 18. **Yards:** 6,442/5,058. **Par:** 72/72. **Course Rating:** 70.3/69.0. **Slope:** 116/116. **Green Fee:** $19/$38. **Cart Fee:** $12/person. **Walking Policy:** Walking at certain times. **Walkability:** 2. **Opened:** 1968. **Architect:** Ron Pritchard. **Season:** Year-round. **High:** April-Oct. **To obtain tee times:** Call golf shop. **Miscellaneous:** Reduced fees (low season, twilight, seniors, juniors), metal spikes, range (mats), club rentals, credit cards (MC, V, D).
Reader Comments: Hilly. Good layout. Great greens ... Two excellent nines. Many demanding holes with a good creek running through entire course, well maintained ... Always in good shape, back nine tougher ... A good walk, play back tees.
★★★★ PRESIDENTIAL GOLF COURSE
Holes: 18. **Yards:** 6,676/5,271. **Par:** 72/72. **Course Rating:** 72.8/71.2. **Slope:** 133/128. **Green Fee:** $28/$50. **Cart Fee:** $12/person. **Walking Policy:** Walking at certain times. **Walkability:** 1. **Opened:** 1968. **Architect:** Ron Pritchard. **Season:** Year-round. **High:** April-Oct. **To obtain tee times:** Call 7 days in advance. **Miscellaneous:** Reduced fees (low season, twilight, seniors), metal spikes, range (mats), club rentals, credit cards (MC, V, D).
Reader Comments: Scenic. Excellent layout. Great greens ... New nine worth the trip ... Intangibles are everything. I just like this place ... Tough course makes you play golf ... Great combination of holes ... Two nines (old and new) very different ... Promising, tight. Thinking course, pull the right club.

★★★½ HIDDEN VALLEY FOUR SEASONS RESORT
R-One Craighead Dr., Hidden Valley, 15502, Somerset County, (814)443-8444, (800)458-0175, 60 miles SE of Pittsburgh.
Holes: 18. **Yards:** 6,589/5,027. **Par:** 72/72. **Course Rating:** 73.5/69.2. **Slope:** 142/129. **Green Fee:** $32/$42. **Cart Fee:** $17/person. **Walking Policy:** Mandatory cart. **Walkability:** 5. **Opened:** 1987. **Architect:** Russell Roberts. **Season:** April-Nov. **High:** June-Aug. **To obtain tee times:** Call 800 number. Weekday tee times taken 14 days in advance. **Miscellaneous:** Reduced fees (weekdays, low season, resort guests, twilight), discount packages, metal spikes, range (grass/mats), club rentals, lodging, credit cards (MC, V, AE, D, Diners Club).
Reader Comments: Scenic mountain course ... Excellent greens, great scenery ... Good challenge for average golfer ... Very hilly but great course. Tight fairways! ... Woods and great vistas.

PENNSYLVANIA

★★★★ HIDEAWAY HILLS GOLF CLUB
PU-Carney Road, Kresgville, 18333, Monroe County, (610)681-6000, 30 miles N of Allentown.
Web: www.hideawaygolf.com.
Holes: 18. **Yards:** 6,933/5,047. **Par:** 72/72. **Course Rating:** 72.7/68.4. **Slope:** 127/116. **Green Fee:** $29/$42. **Cart Fee:** $15/person. **Walking Policy:** Mandatory cart. **Walkability:** 5. **Opened:** 1994. **Season:** March-Dec. **High:** April-Oct. **To obtain tee times:** Call golf shop.
Miscellaneous: Reduced fees (low season, resort guests, twilight), range (grass), club rentals, lodging (36 rooms), credit cards (MC, V, AE, D).
Reader Comments: Another one with great views. Elevated tees ... Many blind shots ... Great course, courteous ... A diamond in the rough! ... Elevation changes make the par threes spectacular ... Great diversity of holes ... Choices for all levels of play ... Scenic, island green, best kept secret in Poconos.

★★★½ HONEY RUN GOLF & COUNTRY CLUB
SP-3131 S. Salem Church Rd., York, 17404, York County, (717)792-9771, (800)475-4657, 3 miles W of York.
Holes: 18. **Yards:** 6,797/5,948. **Par:** 72/72. **Course Rating:** 72.4/74.0. **Slope:** 123/125. **Green Fee:** $20/$32. **Cart Fee:** $13/person. **Walking Policy:** Walking at certain times. **Walkability:** 4. **Opened:** 1971. **Architect:** Edmund B. Ault. **Season:** Year-round. **High:** May-Aug. **To obtain tee times:** Call golf shop as far in advance as needed. **Miscella-neous:** Reduced fees (weekdays, low season, resort guests, twilight, seniors, juniors), discount packages, metal spikes, range (grass), club rentals, credit cards (MC, V).
Reader Comments: Tough but fair, once hosted Nike Tour event ... Gets better on back nine ... A real gem, good variety of holes ... Use every club ... Longest par fives ... Best greens for public in the area ... You get more than what you pay for.

★★★½ HORSHAM VALLEY GOLF CLUB
PU-500 Babylon Rd., Ambler, 19002, Montgomery County, (215)646-4707, 15 miles NW of Philadelphia. **Web:** www.horshamvalleygolf.com.
Holes: 18. **Yards:** 5,115/4,430. **Par:** 66/66. **Course Rating:** 62.4/60.8. **Slope:** 102/96. **Green Fee:** $16/$28. **Cart Fee:** $24/cart. **Walking Policy:** Unrestricted walking. **Walkability:** 1. **Opened:** 1957. **Architect:** Jack Melville/Doug Melville. **Season:** Year-round. **High:** April-Oct. **To obtain tee times:** Weekdays 1 day in advance; weekends 7 days in advance. **Miscellaneous:** Reduced fees (weekdays, low season, twilight, seniors, juniors), discount packages, metal spikes, range (grass), club rentals, credit cards (MC, V, AE, D).
Reader Comments: Short and sweet ... Best hot dogs in Pa. ... Friendly staff, short course, but tricky ... Short course, tight. Severely sloping greens on par threes.

INDIAN RUN GOLF CLUB
PU-1975 Avella Road, Avella, 15312, Washington County, (724)587-0330, 50 miles W of Pittsburgh.
Holes: 18. **Yards:** 6,256/4,886. **Par:** 72/72. **Course Rating:** 70.7/69.3. **Slope:** 129/123. **Green Fee:** $25/$35. **Cart Fee:** Included in Green Fee. **Walking Policy:** Walking at certain times. **Walkability:** 4. **Opened:** 1998. **Architect:** David Black. **Season:** Year-round. **High:** May-Sept. **To obtain tee times:** Call golf shop. **Miscellaneous:** Reduced fees (weekdays, low season, seniors), credit cards (MC, V, AE, D).

★½ INDIAN RUN GOLF COURSE
RD No. 2, Mc Clure, 17841, Snyder County, (717)658-2080.
Special Notes: Call club for further information.

★½ INGLESIDE GOLF CLUB
PU-104 Horseshoe Drive, Thorndale, 19372, Chester County, (610)384-9128, 30 miles W of Philadelphia.
Holes: 18. **Yards:** 5,106/4,800. **Par:** 68/68. **Course Rating:** 64.2/62.9. **Slope:** 111/109. **Green Fee:** $19/$25. **Cart Fee:** $13/person. **Walking Policy:** Unrestricted walking. **Walkability:** 3. **Opened:** 1964. **Season:** Year-round. **High:** April-Oct. **To obtain tee times:** Call 7 days in advance. **Miscellaneous:** Reduced fees (twilight, seniors, juniors), range (grass/mats), club rentals, credit cards (MC, V).

★★★½ IRON MASTERS COUNTRY CLUB
SP-RD No. 1, Roaring Spring, 16673, Bedford County, (814)224-2915, 15 miles S of Altoona.
Holes: 18. **Yards:** 6,644/5,683. **Par:** 72/75. **Course Rating:** 72.2/73.6. **Slope:** 130/119. **Green Fee:** $31/$31. **Cart Fee:** $14/person. **Walking Policy:** Unrestricted walking. **Walkability:** N/A. **Opened:** 1962. **Architect:** Edmund B. Ault. **Season:** April-Dec. **High:** June-Aug. **To obtain tee times:** Call 14 days in advance. **Miscellaneous:** Reduced fees (weekdays), discount packages, metal spikes, club rentals, credit cards (MC, V).
Reader Comments: Blind tee shots, fast greens, interesting, hilly, wooded ... Great layout, fair but need to keep ball in play, nice people ... Good test. Much variety in holes.

JACKSON VALLEY GOLF COURSE
PU-1947 Jackson Run Road, Warren, 16365, Warren County, (814)489-7803, 50 miles SE of Erie. **Web:** www.jacksonvalley.com.
Holes: 18. **Yards:** 6,442/5,642. **Par:** 71/73. **Course Rating:** 69.3/71.4. **Slope:** 117/116. **Green Fee:** $18/$20. **Cart Fee:** $10/person. **Walking Policy:** Walking at certain times. **Walkability:** 4.
Opened: 1961. **Season:** March-Dec. **High:** May-Sept. **Miscellaneous:** Reduced fees (weekdays, low season, resort guests), discount packages, club rentals, lodging (12 rooms), credit cards (MC, V, D).

★½ JOHN F. BYRNE GOLF COURSE
PU-9500 Leon St., Philadelphia, 19114, Philadelphia County, (215)632-8666.
Holes: 18. **Yards:** 5,200/4,662. **Par:** 67/67. **Course Rating:** 65.0/61.4. **Slope:** 107/98. **Green Fee:** $16/$20. **Cart Fee:** $26/cart. **Walking Policy:** Unrestricted walking. **Walkability:** 4.
Season: Year-round. **High:** May-Oct. **To obtain tee times:** Call 7 days in advance.
Miscellaneous: Reduced fees (weekdays, low season, twilight, seniors, juniors), discount packages, metal spikes, club rentals, credit cards (MC, V, AE, D).

★★½ KIMBERTON GOLF CLUB
PU-Rte. 23, Kimberton, 19442, Chester County, (610)933-8836, 30 miles W of Philadelphia.
Holes: 18. **Yards:** 6,304/5,010. **Par:** 70/71. **Course Rating:** 69.4/67.4. **Slope:** 123/112. **Green Fee:** $15/$30. **Cart Fee:** $22/cart. **Walking Policy:** Unrestricted walking. **Walkability:** 1.
Opened: 1962. **Architect:** George Fazio. **Season:** Year-round. **High:** May-Sept. **To obtain tee times:** Call 7 days in advance. **Miscellaneous:** Reduced fees (weekdays, low season, twilight, seniors, juniors), metal spikes, club rentals, credit cards (MC, V).
Reader Comments: Tight, challenging, water-filled ... Many doglegs ... Greens offer a challenge ... Flat, easy-walking course.

★★★ LENAPE HEIGHTS GOLF COURSE
PU-950 Golf Course Rd., Ford City, 16226, Armstrong County, (724)763-2201, 40 miles NE of Pittsburgh.
Holes: 18. **Yards:** 6,145/4,869. **Par:** 71/71. **Course Rating:** 69.0/67.6. **Slope:** 119/114. **Green Fee:** $15/$20. **Cart Fee:** $10/person. **Walking Policy:** Unrestricted walking. **Walkability:** 3.
Opened: 1967. **Architect:** Ferdinand Garbin. **Season:** Year-round. **High:** March-Oct. **To obtain tee times:** Call Tuesday for upcoming weekend. **Miscellaneous:** Reduced fees (weekdays, low season), metal spikes, club rentals, credit cards (MC, V, AE, D).
Reader Comments: Hilly course ... Par five moat hole is great ... Keeps getting better ... Hilly, but very walkable ... You'll hit every club in the bag.

LIMEKILN GOLF CLUB
PU-1176 Limekiln Pike, Ambler, 19002, Montgomery County, (215)643-0643, 10 miles NW of Philadelphia.
Holes: 27. **Green Fee:** $24/$31. **Cart Fee:** $12/person. **Walking Policy:** Walking at certain times. **Walkability:** 2. **Opened:** 1966. **Architect:** Wrenn/Janis. **Season:** Year-round. **High:** April-Oct. **To obtain tee times:** Call Monday for upcoming weekend. Tee times required for weekends and holidays. **Miscellaneous:** Reduced fees (low season, twilight, seniors), metal spikes, range (grass/mats), club rentals, credit cards (MC, V).
★★★ BLUE/RED
Yards: 6,200/5,282. **Par:** 70/72. **Course Rating:** 67.5/67.5. **Slope:** 114/114.
Reader Comments: Nice. Some short holes. Greens a challenge ....Three nines speed up play, easy to walk ... Short and flat ... Holes range from easy to very difficult.
★★★ RED/WHITE
Yards: 6,240/5,227. **Par:** 70/71. **Course Rating:** 67.8/67.8. **Slope:** 114/114.
Reader Comments: Easiest of the three 18s ... White No. 9 tough finishing hole, but White is easiest of three nines.
★★★ WHITE/BLUE
Yards: 6,415/5,848. **Par:** 70/71. **Course Rating:** 68.7/68.7. **Slope:** 114/114.
Reader Comments: Toughest of the three 18s ... Good test of skills. Blue No. 9 great finishing hole ... Short driving range, great grill ... Course is always in good shape ... Challenging course for average golfers ... Nice course, no gimmicks.

★★★½ LINDEN HALL GOLF CLUB
R-R.D. No. 1, Dawson, 15428, Fayette County, (724)529-2366, (800)944-3238, 37 miles S of Pittsburgh. **Web:** www.lindenhallpa.com.
Holes: 18. **Yards:** 6,675/5,900. **Par:** 72/77. **Course Rating:** 71.2/73.6. **Slope:** 122/123. **Green Fee:** $18/$25. **Cart Fee:** $22/cart. **Walking Policy:** Unrestricted walking. **Walkability:** 2.
Opened: 1950. **Architect:** Pete Snead. **Season:** Year-round. **High:** March-Nov. **To obtain tee times:** Call one week in advance. **Miscellaneous:** Reduced fees (weekdays, low season, resort guests, seniors, juniors), discount packages, range (grass), club rentals, lodging (75 rooms), credit cards (MC, V, AE, D).

PENNSYLVANIA

Reader Comments: Good layout ... No. 18 a thrill ... Good length, walkable, No. 6 a great par 4 ... Some picturesque holes, front nine better than back ... No. 13 a beautiful par 5 ... From the back tees it will test you and your bag ... Beautiful mountain layout.

★★★½ LOCH NAIRN GOLF CLUB
PU-RR No. 1, 514 A McCue Rd., Avondale, 19311, Chester County, (610)268-2234.
Special Notes: Call club for further information.

★★★½ LOCUST VALLEY GOLF CLUB
PU-5525 Locust Valley Rd., Coopersburg, 18036, Lehigh County, (610)282-4711, 45 miles N of Philadelphia.
Holes: 18. **Yards:** 6,451/5,444. **Par:** 72/74. **Course Rating:** 71.0/71.3. **Slope:** 132/121. **Green Fee:** $19/$27. **Cart Fee:** $11/person. **Walking Policy:** Walking at certain times. **Walkability:** 2. **Opened:** 1954. **Architect:** William Gordon & Sons. **Season:** March-Dec. **High:** May-Sept. **To obtain tee times:** Call 7 days in advance. **Miscellaneous:** Reduced fees (weekdays, low season, twilight, seniors), metal spikes, club rentals, credit cards (MC, V).
Reader Comments: Tight course plenty of trees ... Tough despite little water... Will eat your lunch if you can't hit 'em straight ... Old course with lots of big pine trees, always in good condition ... Greens are fast ... Neat old course, great views.

★★★ LOST CREEK GOLF CLUB
SP-Rte. No. 35, Oakland Mills, 17076, Juniata County, (717)463-2450, 30 miles NE of Harrisburg.
Holes: 18. **Yards:** 6,579/5,318. **Par:** 71/71. **Course Rating:** 70.6/68.9. **Slope:** 116/113. **Green Fee:** $16/$24. **Cart Fee:** $14/person. **Walking Policy:** Unrestricted walking. **Walkability:** 3. **Opened:** 1965. **Season:** Year-round. **High:** June-August. **To obtain tee times:** Call 1 week in advance. **Miscellaneous:** Reduced fees (weekdays, seniors), range (mats).
Reader Comments: Nice course to play ... Nice people.

★★★ MACOBY RUN GOLF COURSE
PU-5275 McLeans Station Rd., Green Lane, 18054, Montgomery County, (215)541-0161, 20 miles SE of Allentown.
Holes: 18. **Yards:** 6,238/4,938. **Par:** 72/72. **Course Rating:** 69.7/67.9. **Slope:** 116/110. **Green Fee:** $13/$23. **Cart Fee:** $18/cart. **Walking Policy:** Unrestricted walking. **Walkability:** 5. **Opened:** 1991. **Architect:** David Horn, Architerra P.C. **Season:** Year-round. **High:** May-Sept. **To obtain tee times:** Call 7 days in advance. **Miscellaneous:** Reduced fees (low season, twilight, seniors, juniors), metal spikes, range (grass/mats), club rentals, credit cards (MC, V).
Reader Comments: Hilly, scenic. Front nine very good, back nine flat. Some short holes. Enjoyable rounds ... Enjoyable round, young course, nice staff ... Tough walking.

★★★ MAJESTIC RIDGE GOLF CLUB
PU-2437 Adin Lane, Chambersburg, 17201, Franklin County, (717)267-3444, (888)743-4346, 50 miles S of Harrisburg.
Holes: 18. **Yards:** 6,481/4,349. **Par:** 72/70. **Course Rating:** 72.3/64.4. **Slope:** 132/112. **Green Fee:** $11/$26. **Cart Fee:** $14/person. **Walking Policy:** Walking at certain times. **Walkability:** 5. **Opened:** 1992. **Season:** Year-round. **High:** May-Sept. **To obtain tee times:** Call golf shop. **Miscellaneous:** Reduced fees (weekdays, low season, twilight, seniors), discount packages, range (grass/mats), club rentals, credit cards (MC, V, AE).
Reader Comments: Quite hilly, variety of tees, placement golf ... Making improvements, short from white tees ... A lot of blind shots ... Great layout ... Very challenging. Lots of hidden hazards.

★★★½ MANADA GOLF CLUB
PU-609 Golf Lane, Grantville, 17028, Dauphin County, (717)469-2400, 15 miles N of Harrisburg.
Holes: 18. **Yards:** 6,705/5,276. **Par:** 72/72. **Course Rating:** 70.7/68.8. **Slope:** 117/111. **Green Fee:** $18/$25. **Cart Fee:** $12/person. **Walking Policy:** Unrestricted walking. **Walkability:** 2. **Opened:** 1963. **Architect:** William Gordon. **Season:** Year-round. **High:** April-Sept. **To obtain tee times:** Weekends phone early. **Miscellaneous:** Reduced fees (weekdays, low season, twilight, seniors, juniors), metal spikes, club rentals, credit cards (MC, V).
Reader Comments: Great greens, wide open ... Scorecards were very helpful ... Wide open ... No. 18 a good finishing hole.

★★★ MANOR GOLF CLUB
PU-R.D. 8, Bran Rd., Sinking Spring, 19608, Berks County, (610)678-9597, 75 miles W of Philadelphia.
Holes: 18. **Yards:** 5,425/4,660. **Par:** 70/70. **Course Rating:** 65.7/62.2. **Slope:** 108/101. **Green Fee:** $14/$21. **Cart Fee:** $10/person. **Walking Policy:** Unrestricted walking. **Walkability:** 4. **Opened:** 1923. **Architect:** Alex Findley. **Season:** Year-round. **High:** April-Oct. **To obtain tee times:** Call golf shop. **Miscellaneous:** Reduced fees (weekdays, low season, twilight, juniors), metal spikes, range (grass), club rentals.
Reader Comments: Up and down, fun. Variety, fair, good value ... Mountain climbing ... Lots of elevation change, eat your Wheaties if you walk.

★½ MANOR VALLEY GOLF CLUB
PU-2095 Denmark Manor Rd., Export, 15632, Westmoreland County, (724)744-4242, 28 miles E of Pittsburgh on Rte. 22.
Holes: 18. **Yards:** 6,327/6,327. **Par:** 72/79. **Course Rating:** 69.9/71.7. **Slope:** N/A. **Green Fee:** $17/$18. **Cart Fee:** $10/person. **Walking Policy:** Unrestricted walking. **Walkability:** 2. **Opened:** 1963. **Architect:** Frye Brothers. **Season:** March-Dec. **High:** April-Oct. **To obtain tee times:** Call anytime. **Miscellaneous:** Reduced fees (seniors), club rentals.

★★★ MAYAPPLE GOLF LINKS
PU-1 Mayapple Dr., Carlisle, 17013, Cumberland County, (717)258-4088, 1 miles SW of Carlisle.
Holes: 18. **Yards:** 6,541/5,595. **Par:** 71/72. **Course Rating:** 71.3/69.6. **Slope:** 116/114. **Green Fee:** $12/$19. **Cart Fee:** $11/person. **Walking Policy:** Walking at certain times. **Walkability:** 1. **Opened:** 1990. **Architect:** Ron Garl. **Season:** Year-round. **High:** May-Sept. **To obtain tee times:** Call up to one week in advance. **Miscellaneous:** Reduced fees (weekdays, low season, resort guests, twilight, seniors), metal spikes, range (grass), credit cards (MC, V, AE).
Reader Comments: Small greens ... Nice links layout ... The 17th is a tough hole, don't hit onto mounds ... Homes and condos a little too close on some holes of the back nine ... Always windy.

★★★ MAYFIELD GOLF CLUB
PU-I-80 Exit 9N Pa. Rte. 68, Clarion, 16214, Clarion County, (814)226-8888, 90 miles NE of Pittsburgh.
Holes: 18. **Yards:** 6,990/5,439. **Par:** 72/72. **Course Rating:** 73.0/71.0. **Slope:** 117/118. **Green Fee:** $12/$22. **Cart Fee:** $10/person. **Walking Policy:** Walking at certain times. **Walkability:** N/A. **Opened:** 1974. **Architect:** X.G. Hassenplug. **Season:** April-Oct. **High:** June-Aug. **To obtain tee times:** Call. **Miscellaneous:** Reduced fees (weekdays), discount packages, metal spikes, range (grass), lodging.
Reader Comments: Hilly course ... Greens were very sloped ... Great back nine.

★★★ MEADOWINK GOLF CLUB
PU-4076 Bulltown Rd., Murrysville, 15668, Westmoreland County, (724)327-8243, 20 miles E of Pittsburgh.
Holes: 18. **Yards:** 6,139/5,103. **Par:** 72/72. **Course Rating:** 68.2/66.9. **Slope:** 125/118. **Green Fee:** $18/$23. **Cart Fee:** $12/person. **Walking Policy:** Unrestricted walking. **Walkability:** 3. **Opened:** 1970. **Architect:** Ferdinand Garbin. **Season:** Year-round. **High:** April-Sept. **To obtain tee times:** Call 7 days in advance. One year in advance for group outings over 16 people. **Miscellaneous:** Reduced fees (weekdays, seniors), discount packages, metal spikes, club rentals, credit cards (MC, V).
Reader Comments: Lot of bang for buck, great local course ... Stunning par 3 11th ... A hilly challenge in the suburbs ... 18 is a par 5 that's really a 4½ ... Price right, open course ... 1st hole (par 5) uphill/downhill, you won't see your 1st and 2nd shot land. A lot of blind holes .... Hilly.

★★ MERCER PUBLIC GOLF COURSE
PU-281 Golf Rd., Mercer, 16137, Mercer County, (724)662-9951, 60 miles N of Pittsburgh.
Holes: 18. **Yards:** 6,194/5,366. **Par:** 72/72. **Course Rating:** 70.4/69.9. **Slope:** 111/111. **Green Fee:** $13/$16. **Cart Fee:** $10/person. **Walking Policy:** Walking at certain times. **Walkability:** 2. **Opened:** 1959. **Architect:** Mike Maneini. **Season:** Year-round. **High:** May-Sept. **To obtain tee times:** Call golf club. **Miscellaneous:** Reduced fees (low season, seniors), metal spikes, range (grass), club rentals, beginner friendly.

★★ MIDDLETOWN COUNTRY CLUB
PU-420 N. Bellevue Ave., Langhorne, 19047, Bucks County, (215)757-6953, 14 miles N of Philadelphia.
Holes: 18. **Yards:** 5,930/5,675. **Par:** 69/69. **Course Rating:** N/A. **Slope:** N/A. **Green Fee:** $16/$27. **Cart Fee:** $13/person. **Walking Policy:** Unrestricted walking. **Walkability:** N/A. **Opened:** 1918. **Season:** Year-round. **High:** May-Oct. **To obtain tee times:** Call 7 days in advance. **Miscellaneous:** Reduced fees (weekdays, low season, twilight, seniors, juniors), discount packages, metal spikes, club rentals, credit cards (MC, V, AE, D).

★★★½ MILL RACE GOLF COURSE
R-RR No. 2, Box 81-B, Benton, 17814, Columbia County, (570)925-2040, 35 miles SE of Wilkes-Barre.
Holes: 18. **Yards:** 6,096/4,791. **Par:** 70/71. **Course Rating:** 68.6/68.3. **Slope:** 126/122. **Green Fee:** $14/$18. **Cart Fee:** $10/person. **Walking Policy:** Walking at certain times. **Walkability:** 1. **Opened:** 1970. **Architect:** Geoffrey Cornish. **Season:** March-Nov. **High:** May-Aug. **To obtain tee times:** Call 7 days in advance. **Miscellaneous:** Reduced fees (weekdays, seniors, juniors), range (grass), club rentals, credit cards (MC, V).
Reader Comments: Still a solid round of golf ... Short, but tough ... Beautiful setting. Good holes ... Pretty setting, flat and easy to walk ... One of the nicest short courses in central Pa.

★★★ MOCCASIN RUN GOLF COURSE

PU-Box 402, Schoff Rd., Atglen, 19310, Chester County, (610)593-7322, 40 miles W of Philadelphia. **Holes:** 18. **Yards:** 6,400/5,275. **Par:** 72/72. **Course Rating:** 70.6/70.4. **Slope:** 119/120. **Green Fee:** $22/$32. **Cart Fee:** $12/person. **Walking Policy:** Unrestricted walking. **Walkability:** 3. **Opened:** 1988. **Architect:** John Thompson. **Season:** Year-round. **High:** April-Oct. **To obtain tee times:** Call 7 days in advance for weekdays and holidays. **Miscellaneous:** Reduced fees (weekdays, low season, twilight, seniors, juniors), discount packages, metal spikes, range (grass/mats), club rentals, credit cards (MC, V, All Debit Cards).
Reader Comments: Wide open course ... Good beginners course ... Not very hard ... Nice greens ... Family owned, nice people, nice shape ... Great condition ... Wide open. Super 18th hole.

★★½ MOHAWK TRAILS GOLF COURSE

PU-RD No. 7, Box 243, New Castle, 16102, Lawrence County, (724)667-8570, 50 miles N of Pittsburgh.
Holes: 18. **Yards:** 6,324/N/A. **Par:** 72/N/A. **Course Rating:** 70.3/N/A. **Slope:** 108/N/A. **Green Fee:** $15/$17. **Cart Fee:** $19/cart. **Walking Policy:** Unrestricted walking. **Walkability:** 3. **Opened:** 1965. **Architect:** Eichenlaub family. **Season:** March-Dec. **High:** May-Sept. **To obtain tee times:** Call 7 days in advance. Weekday tee times for 8 or more. **Miscellaneous:** Reduced fees (weekdays, low season, seniors), metal spikes, club rentals, credit cards.
Reader Comments: Fun to play, great people ... Nice little course. Friendly ... All right.

★★★ MONROE VALLEY GOLF CLUB

PU-23 Ironwood Lane, Jonestown, 17038, Lebanon County, (717)865-2375, 20 miles N of Harrisburg.
Holes: 18. **Yards:** 6,884/5,254. **Par:** 72/72. **Course Rating:** 71.9/65.0. **Slope:** 115/108. **Green Fee:** $15/$25. **Cart Fee:** $11/person. **Walking Policy:** Unrestricted walking. **Walkability:** 2. **Opened:** 1968. **Architect:** Edmund B. Ault. **Season:** Year-round. **High:** May-Sept. **To obtain tee times:** Call 7 days in advance. **Miscellaneous:** Reduced fees (weekdays, low season, twilight, seniors, juniors), range (grass/mats), club rentals, credit cards (MC, V).
Reader Comments: Great greens ... Quiet setting ... Inexpensive, usually crowded ... Lots of fun ... Wide open. Good course ... Long, but wide open; good test if you are good with fairway woods ... Straight, little trouble.

★★★½ MOUNT AIRY LODGE GOLF COURSE

R-42 Woodland Rd., Mount Pocono, 18344, Monroe County, (570)839-8811, (800)441-4410, 30 miles E of Scranton.
Holes: 18. **Yards:** 7,123/5,771. **Par:** 72/73. **Course Rating:** 74.3/73.3. **Slope:** 138/122. **Green Fee:** $40/$50. **Cart Fee:** $16/cart. **Walking Policy:** Mandatory cart. **Walkability:** 5. **Opened:** 1980. **Architect:** Hal Purdy. **Season:** April-Nov. **High:** May-Sept. **To obtain tee times:** Call any time of year, but at least 7 days in advance. **Miscellaneous:** Reduced fees (weekdays, resort guests, twilight), discount packages, club rentals, lodging, credit cards (MC, V, AE, D).
Reader Comments: Beauty. Challenging ... Fun 18 holes ... Challenging course, great views from Mountain Top ... Excellent greens, difficult ... Nice course, big greens.

★★ MOUNT ODIN PARK GOLF CLUB

PU-Mt. Odin Park Dr., Greensburg, 15601, Westmoreland County, (412)834-2640, 30 miles SE of Pittsburgh. **E-mail:** bernpga@sgi.net.
Holes: 18. **Yards:** 5,395/4,733. **Par:** 70/72. **Course Rating:** 65.0/68.0. **Slope:** 108/104. **Green Fee:** $15/$16. **Cart Fee:** $9/person. **Walking Policy:** Unrestricted walking. **Walkability:** 4. **Opened:** 1935. **Architect:** X.G. Hassenplug. **Season:** March-Dec. **High:** April-Sept. **To obtain tee times:** Come in person weekend prior or call on Monday for upcoming weekend. **Miscellaneous:** Discount packages, metal spikes, range (grass/mats), club rentals.

MOUNTAIN MANOR INN & GOLF CLUB

SP-Creek Rd., Marshall's Creek, 18335, Monroe County, (717)223-1290, 100 miles N of Philadelphia.

★★½ BLUE/YELLOW COURSE

Holes: 18. **Yards:** 6,233/5,079. **Par:** 71/71. **Course Rating:** 68.5/68.5. **Slope:** 115/115. **Green Fee:** $20/$30. **Cart Fee:** $30/cart. **Walking Policy:** Unrestricted walking. **Walkability:** 2. **Opened:** 1945. **Architect:** Russell Scott. **Season:** April-Nov. **High:** April-Oct. **To obtain tee times:** No tee times. **Miscellaneous:** Reduced fees (weekdays, low season, resort guests, twilight), discount packages, metal spikes, club rentals, lodging (100 rooms), beginner friendly (executive course).
Reader Comments: Fun, nice views, great value ... Flat ... Lots of beginners ... Nice holes ... Flat, wide open.

★★★½ ORANGE/SILVER COURSE

Holes: 18. **Yards:** 6,426/5,146. **Par:** 73/73. **Course Rating:** 71.0/71.5. **Slope:** 132/124. **Green Fee:** $20/$30. **Cart Fee:** $30/cart. **Walking Policy:** Unrestricted walking. **Walkability:** 5.

Opened: 1945. **Architect:** Russell Scott. **Season:** April-Nov. **High:** April-Oct. **To obtain tee times:** No tee times. **Miscellaneous:** Reduced fees (weekdays, low season, resort guests, twilight), discount packages, metal spikes, club rentals, lodging (100 rooms), beginner friendly (executive course).
Reader Comments: Great test of golf ... Difficult layout, challenging (especially par-six hole) ... Bring your hiking boots ... Fun, true test of shotmaking, nice views ... Very hilly.

MOUNTAIN VALLEY GOLF COURSE
PU-Burma and Brockton Roads., Mahanoy City, 17948, Schuylkill County, (570)467-2242, 9 miles N of Pottsville.
★★½ **MAPLE/PINE**
Holes: 18. **Yards:** 6,446/4,885. **Par:** 72/72. **Course Rating:** 70.5/70.5. **Slope:** 130/118. **Green Fee:** $13/$18. **Cart Fee:** $10/person. **Walking Policy:** Walking at certain times. **Walkability:** 4.
Opened: 1969. **Architect:** Ault, Clark and Assoc. **Season:** March-Nov. **High:** May-Sept.
Miscellaneous: Reduced fees (low season, twilight, seniors), range (grass/mats), club rentals, credit cards (MC, V).
★★½ **OAK/MAPLE**
Holes: 18. **Yards:** 6,515/5,003. **Par:** 72/72. **Course Rating:** 70.8/71.2. **Slope:** 129/121. **Green Fee:** $13/$18. **Cart Fee:** $10/person. **Walking Policy:** Walking at certain times. **Walkability:** 4.
Opened: 1969. **Architect:** Ault, Clark and Assoc. **Season:** March-Nov. **High:** May-Sept.
Miscellaneous: Reduced fees (low season, twilight, seniors), range (grass/mats), club rentals, credit cards (MC, V).
★★½ **PINE/OAK**
Holes: 18. **Yards:** 6,347/4,766. **Par:** 72/72. **Course Rating:** 70.1/69.5. **Slope:** 130/115. **Green Fee:** $13/$18. **Cart Fee:** $10/person. **Walking Policy:** Walking at certain times. **Walkability:** 4.
Opened: 1969. **Architect:** Ault, Clark and Assoc. **Season:** March-Nov. **High:** May-Sept.
Miscellaneous: Reduced fees (low season, twilight, seniors), range (grass/mats), club rentals, credit cards (MC, V).
Reader Comments: An up and comer ... New holes, great rates ... Wide fairways, but narrow par threes ... Beautiful conditioned course, beautiful holes, great value.

★★ MURRYSVILLE GOLF CLUB
PU-3804 Sardis Rd., Murrysville, 15668, Westmoreland County, (724)327-0726, 20 miles E of Pittsburgh.
Holes: 18. **Yards:** 5,575/5,250. **Par:** 70/74. **Course Rating:** 64.4/67.2. **Slope:** 99/107. **Green Fee:** $17/$19. **Cart Fee:** $10/person. **Walking Policy:** Walking at certain times. **Walkability:** 1.
Opened: 1938. **Architect:** James Noble & Son. **Season:** April-Nov. **High:** June-Aug. **To obtain tee times:** No tee times needed. **Miscellaneous:** Reduced fees (seniors), metal spikes, club rentals, credit cards (MC, V).

NEMACOLIN WOODLANDS RESORT & SPA *Service*
R-Rte. 40 E., Farmington, 15437, Fayette County, (724)329-6111, (800)422-2736, 65 miles SE of Pittsburgh. **Web:** www.nemacolin.com.
★★★★ **MYSTIC ROCK GOLF COURSE**
Holes: 18. **Yards:** 6,832/4,800. **Par:** 72/72. **Course Rating:** 75.0/68.8. **Slope:** 146/125. **Green Fee:** $125/$150. **Cart Fee:** Included in Green Fee. **Walking Policy:** Mandatory cart.
Walkability: 2. **Opened:** 1995. **Architect:** Pete Dye/Mike O'Conner. **Season:** April-Nov. **High:** May-Oct. **To obtain tee times:** Resort guests call 60 days in advance. Daily fee may call 7 days in advance. **Miscellaneous:** Reduced fees (low season, resort guests, twilight), discount packages, range (grass/mats), club rentals, lodging, credit cards (MC, V, AE).
Notes: Ranked 4th in 1995 Best New Resort Courses.
Reader Comments: Enjoyed the entire day from driving range to 18th ... Great, challenging course ... Pete Dye's best, resort is five star, course is better ... Slick greens. Target golf ... Pete Dye with a blank checkbook. What can be better? ... Pricey but fun ... Beautiful. Too bad I can't pay my mortgage now.
★★★½ **WOODLANDS LINKS GOLF CLUB**
Holes: 18. **Yards:** 6,814/4,825. **Par:** 71/71. **Course Rating:** 73.0/67.3. **Slope:** 131/115. **Green Fee:** $79/$79. **Cart Fee:** Included in Green Fee. **Walking Policy:** Mandatory cart. **Walkability:** N/A. **Opened:** 1976. **Architect:** Joe Hardy/Willard Rockwell. **Season:** April-Nov. **High:** May-Sept.
To obtain tee times: Resort guests call 60 days in advance. Daily fee call 7 days in advance.
Miscellaneous: Reduced fees (low season, twilight), range (grass), club rentals, lodging, credit cards (MC, V, AE).
Reader Comments: Expensive, worth it ... Fair test of golf skills. Beautiful facility ... Lots of sand ... Mature course, great views, playable ... Primo greens ... Nice scenery.... Very scenic particularly the back nine.

★★½ NORTH FORK COUNTRY CLUB
SP-120 Court Dr., Johnstown, 15905, Cambria County, (814)288-2822, 5 miles SE of Pittsburgh.

Holes: 18. **Yards:** 6,470/5,762. **Par:** 72/72. **Course Rating:** 71.2/72.0. **Slope:** 130/114. **Green Fee:** $20/$22. **Cart Fee:** $12/person. **Walking Policy:** Unrestricted walking. **Walkability:** 4. **Opened:** 1934. **Architect:** Fred Garbin. **Season:** April-Oct. **High:** June-Aug. **To obtain tee times:** Call up to 7 days in advance. Open to the public Monday and Wednesday. **Miscellaneous:** Reduced fees (juniors), discount packages, metal spikes, credit cards (MC, V, AE, D). **Reader Comments:** Excellent greens, hilly course ... Have to be a mountain goat to walk ... Good greens, half of course is on side of hill.

★★★½ NORTH HILLS GOLF COURSE
PU-1450 N. Center St., Corry, 16407, Erie County, (814)664-4477, 1 miles NE of Corry.
Holes: 18. **Yards:** 6,800/5,146. **Par:** 71/72. **Course Rating:** 71.0/71.4. **Slope:** 115/119. **Green Fee:** $11/$28. **Cart Fee:** $20/person. **Walking Policy:** Unrestricted walking. **Walkability:** 3. **Opened:** 1967. **Architect:** Edmond Ault. **Season:** April-Oct. **High:** July-Aug. **To obtain tee times:** First come, first served. **Miscellaneous:** Reduced fees (weekdays, low season, twilight), metal spikes, range (grass), club rentals, credit cards (MC, V). **Reader Comments:** Great public course, lots of play, cheap ... Great course in good condition ... Lots of hills ... Great condition, almost country club quality ... Hidden gem for the price, picturesque ... Picturesque holes, very well kept. Tight, narrow fairways.

★★½ NORTH PARK GOLF COURSE
PM-Kummer Rd., Allison Park, 15101, Allegheny County, (724)935-1967.
Holes: 18. **Yards:** 6,805/5,352. **Par:** 72/72. **Course Rating:** 71.0/69.9. **Slope:** 117/115. **Green Fee:** $14/$17. **Cart Fee:** $17/cart. **Walking Policy:** Unrestricted walking. **Walkability:** 4. **Opened:** 1934. **Architect:** X.G. Hassenplug. **Season:** Year-round. **High:** July-Sept. **To obtain tee times:** First come, first served. **Miscellaneous:** Reduced fees (seniors, juniors), metal spikes, club rentals. **Reader Comments:** Big long course ... Slow play on weekends ... No. 8 par four one of toughest in area ... Good value, nice condition, especially for county course.

★★½ NORTHAMPTON VALLEY COUNTRY CLUB
SP-Rte. 332, Richboro, 18954, Bucks County, (215)355-2234, 15 miles NE of Philadelphia. **Web:** www.nvgc.com.
Holes: 18. **Yards:** 6,377/5,586. **Par:** 70/70. **Course Rating:** 69.2/70.0. **Slope:** 123/118. **Green Fee:** $26/$34. **Cart Fee:** $14/person. **Walking Policy:** Walking at certain times. **Walkability:** 2. **Opened:** 1964. **Architect:** Ed Ault. **Season:** Year-round. **High:** April-Oct. **To obtain tee times:** Call Pro Shop. **Miscellaneous:** Reduced fees (weekdays, twilight, seniors, juniors), range (mats), club rentals, credit cards (MC, V, AE, D). **Reader Comments:** Short but a challenge. No. 18 is a sucker hole ... Tight course ... Friendly staff, dining on site, some challenge, a lot of play ... Short, big greens, a lot of play ... Leave the driver at home.

NORTHWIND GOLF LODGE
PU-700 S. Shore Trail, Indian Lake, 15926, Somerset County, (814)754-4653, 15 miles E of Johnstown.
Holes: 18. **Yards:** 6,199/5,244. **Par:** 72/72. **Course Rating:** 70.2/70.0. **Slope:** 128/124. **Green Fee:** $18/$20. **Cart Fee:** $12/person. **Walking Policy:** Unrestricted walking. **Walkability:** 2. **Architect:** Musser Engineering Inc. **Season:** March-Nov. **High:** June-Aug. **To obtain tee times:** Call. **Miscellaneous:** Reduced fees (weekdays, low season, resort guests, twilight), discount packages, metal spikes, range (grass/mats), club rentals, lodging, credit cards (MC, V, AE, D).

★★½ OAKBROOK GOLF COURSE
PU-251 Golf Course Rd, Stoystown, 15563, Somerset County, (814)629-5892, 3 miles E of Jennerstown on Rte. 30.
Holes: 18. **Yards:** 5,935/5,400. **Par:** 71/73. **Course Rating:** 66.6/69.4. **Slope:** 107/110. **Green Fee:** $20/$22. **Cart Fee:** $10/person. **Walking Policy:** Unrestricted walking. **Walkability:** 1. **Opened:** 1965. **Architect:** H.J. Hillegas. **Season:** April-Nov. **High:** June-Aug. **To obtain tee times:** Call Pro Shop one week in advance—Wednesday, Friday, weekends and holidays. Ball rack system. **Miscellaneous:** Range (grass/mats), club rentals, beginner friendly (juniors, groups and private lessons available). **Reader Comments:** Fun golf course ... Good medium course ... Nice course in mountain setting. Very easy to walk ... Great open course, beautiful in the fall ... Short, greens flat.

★★★★ OLDE HOMESTEAD GOLF CLUB
PU-6598 Rte. 309, New Tripoli, 18066, Lehigh County, (610)298-4653, 15 miles NW of Allentown.
Holes: 18. **Yards:** 6,900/5,013. **Par:** 72/72. **Course Rating:** 73.8/68.5. **Slope:** 132/115. **Green Fee:** $28/$38. **Cart Fee:** $10/person. **Walking Policy:** Walking at certain times. **Walkability:** 4. **Opened:** 1995. **Architect:** Jim Blaukovitch. **Season:** March-Dec. **High:** May-Oct. **To obtain tee times:** Call 7 days in advance. **Miscellaneous:** Reduced fees (weekdays, low season, twilight, seniors, juniors), range (grass/mats), club rentals, credit cards (MC, V, AE), beginner friendly (beginners league Wednesday 5 p.m).

Reader Comments: Par 5s make you think. Some tough par 4s. Stern test from back tees in wind ... Wide open ... Great practice facility ... Great views, excellent condition ... Hillsides and water, ball-swallowing rough, scenic ... Holes 9, 10 and 11 are the best consecutive in Lehigh Valley ... Challenging greens ... Bring your 'A' game. 1st hole very tough ... Front nine good, back nine incredible ... A quiet gem.

OLDE STONEWALL GOLF CLUB
PU-1495 Mercer Rd., Ellwood City, 16117, Lawrence County, (724)752-4653, 30 miles NW of Pittsburgh. **Web:** www.oldestonewall.com.
Holes: 18. **Yards:** 6,934/5,089. **Par:** 70/70. **Course Rating:** 74.9/70.6. **Slope:** 145/124. **Green Fee:** $75/$125. **Cart Fee:** Included in Green Fee. **Walking Policy:** Unrestricted walking. **Walkability:** 3. **Opened:** 1999. **Architect:** Michael Hurdzan/Dana Fry. **Season:** Year-round. **High:** May-Oct. **To obtain tee times:** Public call one week in advance secured with major credit card. 24 hour cancellation policy. **Miscellaneous:** Reduced fees (low season), range (grass), club rentals, credit cards (MC, V, AE).

★★½ OVERLOOK GOLF COURSE
PM-2040 Lititz Pike, Lancaster, 17601, Lancaster County, (717)569-9551, 60 miles W of Philadelphia.
Holes: 18. **Yards:** 6,100/4,962. **Par:** 70/71. **Course Rating:** 69.2/68.4. **Slope:** 110/113. **Green Fee:** $14/$25. **Cart Fee:** $11/person. **Walking Policy:** Unrestricted walking. **Walkability:** 3. **Opened:** 1928. **Architect:** Abe Domback. **Season:** Year-round. **High:** May-Aug. **To obtain tee times:** Call 14 days in advance for weekends only. **Miscellaneous:** Reduced fees (low season, seniors, juniors), club rentals, credit cards (MC, V), beginner friendly (junior discount).
Reader Comments: Standard muny, decent design, decent value ... Nice condition ... Small greens ... Best township-run course ... A very hilly course layout.

★★½ PANORAMA GOLF COURSE
PU-Rte. 1, Forest City, 18421, Susquehanna County, (570)222-3525, 2 miles W of Forest City.
Holes: 18. **Yards:** 7,256/5,345. **Par:** 72/74. **Course Rating:** 73.0/N/A. **Slope:** 122/112. **Green Fee:** N/A. **Walkability:** 2. **Opened:** 1964. **Season:** April-Nov. **High:** July-Aug. **To obtain tee times:** Call 7 days in advance. **Miscellaneous:** Reduced fees (weekdays, seniors), range (grass), club rentals, credit cards (MC, V).
Reader Comments: Nice greens, long holes ... Great facility in middle of nowhere. Play blues if you dare ... Fun layout.

★★ PARK GOLF COURSE
PU-13115 State Highway 618, Conneaut Lake, 16316, Crawford County, (814)382-9974, 10 miles E of Meadville. **E-mail:** parkgolf@toolcity.net. **Web:** www.parkgolf@toolcity.com.
Holes: 18. **Yards:** 6,000/4,778. **Par:** 71/71. **Course Rating:** 68.0/66.7. **Slope:** 113/109. **Green Fee:** $15/$20. **Cart Fee:** $10/person. **Walking Policy:** Unrestricted walking. **Walkability:** 1. **Opened:** 1945. **Season:** April-Oct. **High:** May-Sept. **To obtain tee times:** Call golf shop. **Miscellaneous:** Reduced fees (low season, seniors), metal spikes, club rentals.

★★★ PARK HILLS COUNTRY CLUB
SP-Highland Ave., Altoona, 16602, Blair County, (814)944-2631.
Holes: 18. **Yards:** 6,032/4,877. **Par:** 71/70. **Course Rating:** 69.4/68.3. **Slope:** 126/121. **Green Fee:** $44/$44. **Cart Fee:** Included in Green Fee. **Walking Policy:** Walking at certain times. **Walkability:** 4. **Opened:** 1966. **Architect:** James Gilmore Harrison. **Season:** April-Nov. **High:** July. **To obtain tee times:** Call up to 3 days in advance. **Miscellaneous:** Club rentals, credit cards (MC, V).
Reader Comments: Small greens, high rough ... Back nine will kill walkers ... Tight back nine, open front. Great course ... Tight, short, fast greens, hilly, challenging.

★★★ PAXON HOLLOW COUNTRY CLUB
PU-850 Paxon Hollow Rd., Media, 19063, Delaware County, (610)353-0220, 10 miles W of Philadelphia. **E-mail:** paxongolf@aol.com. **Web:** www.marple.net/paxongolf.
Holes: 18. **Yards:** 5,655/4,952. **Par:** 71/72. **Course Rating:** 67.6/69.8. **Slope:** 121/118. **Green Fee:** $15/$32. **Cart Fee:** $14/person. **Walking Policy:** Walking at certain times. **Walkability:** 5. **Opened:** 1927. **Architect:** James Blaukovitch. **Season:** Year-round. **High:** June-Aug. **To obtain tee times:** Call 610-353-0220. **Miscellaneous:** Reduced fees (weekdays, low season, twilight, seniors), range (grass), club rentals, credit cards (MC, V, AE, D).
Reader Comments: Grip it and rip it, then hit a mulligan ... Some exceptional holes ... Short, irons off most tees, well kept ... Hilly, short course; Nos. 1, 9, 18 great holes ... Nice layout ... Excellent for busy course. Greens putt true.

PENN NATIONAL GOLF CLUB & INN
PU-3720 Clubhouse Dr., Fayetteville, 17222, Franklin County, (717)352-3000, (800)221-7366, 39 miles SW of Harrisburg.

PENNSYLVANIA

★★★★ FOUNDERS COURSE
Holes: 18. **Yards:** 6,958/5,367. **Par:** 72/72. **Course Rating:** 73.2/70.1. **Slope:** 129/116. **Green Fee:** $19/$40. **Cart Fee:** $15/person. **Walking Policy:** Unrestricted walking. **Walkability:** 2. **Opened:** 1968. **Architect:** Ed Ault. **Season:** Year-round. **High:** April-Oct. **To obtain tee times:** Call golf club up to 30 days in advance. **Miscellaneous:** Reduced fees (weekdays, low season, twilight, seniors, juniors), discount packages, range (grass), club rentals, lodging, credit cards (MC, V, AE, D).
Reader Comments: Good walking course, great shape usually ... Tight but fair ... Has a beautiful view and demands ball placement ... If its a bad score is being made, it's me, not the course ... Great layout but difficult ... A gem in the middle of nowhere.

★★★★ IRON FORGE COURSE
Holes: 18. **Yards:** 7,009/5,246. **Par:** 72/72. **Course Rating:** 72.9/69.5. **Slope:** 123/114. **Green Fee:** $19/$40. **Cart Fee:** $15/person. **Walking Policy:** Unrestricted walking. **Walkability:** 2. **Opened:** 1996. **Architect:** William R. Love. **Season:** March-Nov. **High:** April-Oct. **To obtain tee times:** Call golf club up to 30 days in advance. **Miscellaneous:** Reduced fees (weekdays, low season, twilight, seniors, juniors), discount packages, range (grass), club rentals, lodging (36 rooms), credit cards (MC, V, AE, D).
Reader Comments: Good shape for new course, great risk-reward shots ... A neat links ... Excellent from start to finish ... One of the best courses in Central Pa. ... Out of sight. Great ... Nice compliment to Founders.

PENNSYLVANIA STATE UNIVERSITY GOLF COURSE
PU-1523 W. College Ave., State College, 16801, Centre County, (814)865-4653, 5 miles SE of State College. **Web:** www.psu.edu\dept\golfcourses.

★★★★ BLUE COURSE
Holes: 18. **Yards:** 6,525/5,128. **Par:** 72/72. **Course Rating:** 72.0/69.8. **Slope:** 128/118. **Green Fee:** $28/$28. **Cart Fee:** $14/person. **Walking Policy:** Unrestricted walking. **Walkability:** 2. **Opened:** 1970. **Architect:** Harrison and Garbin/Tom Clark. **Season:** March-Nov. **High:** June-Sept. **To obtain tee times:** Call up to 5 days in advance. **Miscellaneous:** Reduced fees (twilight), discount packages, range (mats), club rentals, lodging, credit cards (MC, V, AE, D), beginner friendly (Nittany Course [6-hole learning center]).
Reader Comments: Excellent redesign. Hard to get tee times however ... Good challenge, 'Happy Valley' a great place ... ... Nice doglegs, very inexpensive ... Well designed and maintained ... The new holes make all the difference.

★★½ WHITE COURSE
Holes: 18. **Yards:** 6,008/5,212. **Par:** 70/70. **Course Rating:** 68.2/69.4. **Slope:** 115/116. **Green Fee:** $21/$21. **Cart Fee:** $14/person. **Walking Policy:** Walking at certain times. **Walkability:** 3. **Opened:** 1994. **Architect:** Harrison and Garbin/Tom Clark. **Season:** Mar-Nov. **High:** Jun-Sept. **To obtain tee times:** Call up to 7 days in advance. **Miscellaneous:** Reduced fees (twilight), discount packages, metal spikes, range (mats), club rentals, lodging, credit cards (MC, V, AE, D), beginner friendly (nittany course (6-hole learning center)).
Reader Comments: Great family course ... Fun to play. PSU needs another 18, not bigger football stadium ... Great old school design holes, small greens, great bunkers.

★★ PERRY GOLF COURSE
PU-220 Zion's Church Rd., Shoemakersville, 19555, Berks County, (610)562-3510, 12 miles N of Reading.
Holes: 18. **Yards:** 6,000/4,686. **Par:** 70/70. **Course Rating:** 68.1/68.5. **Slope:** 112/116. **Green Fee:** $11/$16. **Walking Policy:** Unrestricted walking. **Walkability:** 1. **Opened:** 1964. **Season:** Year-round. **High:** May-Sept. **To obtain tee times:** Call golf shop. **Miscellaneous:** Reduced fees (twilight, seniors), metal spikes, club rentals.

★★★ PICKERING VALLEY GOLF CLUB
PU-450 S. White Horse Rd., Phoenixville, 19460, Chester County, (610)933-2223, 20 miles W of Philadelphia.
Holes: 18. **Yards:** 6,572/5,135. **Par:** 72/72. **Course Rating:** 71.0/65.5. **Slope:** 127/117. **Green Fee:** $22/$31. **Cart Fee:** $20/cart. **Walking Policy:** Walking at certain times. **Walkability:** 3. **Opened:** 1985. **Architect:** John Thompson. **Season:** Year-round. **High:** April-Oct. **To obtain tee times:** Call 7 days in advance on weekends. **Miscellaneous:** Reduced fees (weekdays, twilight, seniors), range (grass), club rentals.
Reader Comments: Open on the front nine ... Hilly, scenic, long. Some great short holes ... Just great golf ... Contrasting nines, first open, back tight, good track ... Three fairly long downhill par 3s make the course ... No. 18 is a tough par 4 ... Very scenic.

★★★★ PILGRIM'S OAK GOLF COURSE
PU-1107 Pilgrim's Pathway, Peach Bottom, 17563, Lancaster County, (717)548-3011, 24 miles S of Lancaster. **E-mail:** pilgrim@epix.net. **Web:** www.pilgrimsoak.com.
Holes: 18. **Yards:** 7,043/5,064. **Par:** 72/71. **Course Rating:** 73.4/70.7. **Slope:** 138/129. **Green Fee:** $20/$36. **Cart Fee:** $12/person. **Walking Policy:** Unrestricted walking. **Walkability:** 5.

PENNSYLVANIA

Opened: 1996. **Architect:** Michael Hurdzan. **Season:** Year-round. **High:** May-Oct. **To obtain tee times:** Call up to 14 days in advance. **Miscellaneous:** Reduced fees (weekdays, low season, twilight, seniors), range (grass), club rentals, credit cards (MC, V, Debit Card).
Reader Comments: Great, challenging, fun ... Some spectacular holes. Brutally tough ... Tour-quality, worth taking trouble to find it ... Small, undulating greens tricky ... Players track, smallish greens with undulations ... Blind shots ... Long and open, but can also be tight into some greens ... Neat par threes ... Big elevation changes.

★★★½ PINE ACRES COUNTRY CLUB
SP-1401 W. Warren Rd., Bradford, 16701, McKean County, (814)362-2005, 8 miles S of Bradford.
Holes: 18. **Yards:** 6,700/5,600. **Par:** 72/72. **Course Rating:** 70.3/72.3. **Slope:** 120/120. **Green Fee:** $22/$22. **Cart Fee:** $22/cart. **Walking Policy:** Unrestricted walking. **Walkability:** 2.
Opened: 1965. **Architect:** James G. Harrison. **Season:** April-Oct. **High:** June-Aug. **To obtain tee times:** Call 7 days in advance for weekends and holidays only. **Miscellaneous:** Range (grass), club rentals, credit cards (MC, V).
Reader Comments: Very challenging on some holes, easy to walk ... Contoured very nice throughout the mountainside ... Great time, people are so nice there.

★★★½ PINE CREST GOLF CLUB
PU-101 Country Club Dr., Lansdale, 19446, Montgomery County, (215)855-6112, 25 miles N of Philadelphia.
Holes: 18. **Yards:** 6,331/5,284. **Par:** 70/70. **Course Rating:** 69.3/68.1. **Slope:** 122/118. **Green Fee:** $21/$35. **Cart Fee:** $14/person. **Walking Policy:** Walking at certain times. **Walkability:** 2.
Opened: 1990. **Architect:** Ron Prichard. **Season:** Year-round. **High:** May-Oct. **To obtain tee times:** Call. **Miscellaneous:** Reduced fees (weekdays, low season, twilight, seniors, juniors), club rentals, credit cards (MC, V, AE, D).
Reader Comments: Well maintained; well defined fairways ... Outstanding greens ... Interesting mix of holes ... Short, tight course. Great clubhouse.

★★★★ PINE GROVE GOLF COURSE
PU-401 Diamond Rd., Grove City, 16127, Mercer County, (724)458-9942.
Yards: N/A. **Par:** N/A. **Course Rating:** N/A. **Slope:** N/A. **Green Fee:** N/A. **Walkability:** N/A.
Architect: John Deitrick. **Miscellaneous:** Metal spikes.
Reader Comments: Can almost see whole course in one look ... Just like a country club, great public course ... User-friendly course. Keeps pressure on. Good bang for your buck.

★★ PINE HILL GOLF COURSE
PU-263 Leech Rd., Greenville, 16125, Mercer County, (724)588-8053, 60 miles N of Pittsburgh.
Web: www.pinehillgc.com.
Holes: 18. **Yards:** 6,013/5,430. **Par:** 72/72. **Course Rating:** 67.1/66.9. **Slope:** 98/103. **Green Fee:** $12/$15. **Cart Fee:** $17/cart. **Walking Policy:** Unrestricted walking. **Walkability:** 1.
Opened: 1967. **Architect:** Charles Loreno. **Season:** April-Nov. **High:** June-Aug. **To obtain tee times:** Call. **Miscellaneous:** Reduced fees (weekdays), range (grass), club rentals, beginner friendly (junior golf clinic).

★½ PINE HILLS GOLF COURSE
PU-140 S Keyser Ave., Taylor, 18517, Lackawanna County, (570)562-0138, 3 miles SW of Scranton.
Holes: 18. **Yards:** 6,011/5,304. **Par:** 71/71. **Course Rating:** N/A. **Slope:** N/A. **Green Fee:** $9/$10. **Cart Fee:** $20/cart. **Walking Policy:** Unrestricted walking. **Walkability:** 3. **Opened:** 1967.
Architect: Andrew Evanish. **Season:** Year-round. **High:** May-Aug. **To obtain tee times:** Call Pro Shop. **Miscellaneous:** Reduced fees (weekdays, seniors), metal spikes, beginner friendly.

★★½ PITTSBURGH NORTH GOLF CLUB
PU-3800 Bakerstown Rd., Bakerstown, 15007, Allegheny County, (724)443-3800, 16 miles N of Pittsburgh.
Holes: 27. **Yards:** 7,021/5,075. **Par:** 72/73. **Course Rating:** 73.3/68.4. **Slope:** 134/114. **Green Fee:** $16/$23. **Cart Fee:** $20/person. **Walking Policy:** Walking at certain times. **Walkability:** N/A. **Opened:** 1950. **Architect:** O.J. Price. **Season:** Year-round. **High:** June-Aug. **To obtain tee times:** Call 7 days in advance. **Miscellaneous:** Reduced fees (low season, seniors, juniors), metal spikes, range (grass/mats), club rentals, credit cards (MC, V, D).
Reader Comments: Hard to walk, hilly, nice course ... Great value, tough layout ... Challenging, price right.

★★½ PLEASANT VALLEY GOLF CLUB
SP-, Stewartstown, 17363, York County, (717)993-2184, 5 miles N of Balto. MD.
Holes: 18. **Yards:** 6,497/5,462. **Par:** 72/74. **Course Rating:** 69.7/70.5. **Slope:** 116/117. **Green Fee:** $17/$20. **Cart Fee:** $11/person. **Walking Policy:** Unrestricted walking. **Walkability:** 2.
Opened: 1964. **Architect:** Charles Shirey. **Season:** Year-round. **High:** March-Oct. **To obtain tee times:** Call golf shop. **Miscellaneous:** Reduced fees (weekdays, low season, twilight, seniors,

juniors), discount packages, range (mats), club rentals, credit cards (MC, V, AE, D), beginner friendly (lessons and clinics available. late day playing times).
Reader Comments: Economical golf ... Great buy: golf, breakfast and lunch for $33.00 ... Greens hard ... Short, open course, hard greens and fairways.

★★ PLEASANT VALLEY GOLF COURSE

PU-R.R. No. 1, Box 58, Vintondale, 15961, Indiana County, (814)446-6244, 10 miles N of Johnstown.
Holes: 18. **Yards:** 6,498/5,361. **Par:** 71/72. **Course Rating:** 69.8/70.3. **Slope:** 124/115. **Green Fee:** $13/$15. **Cart Fee:** $11/person. **Walking Policy:** Walking at certain times. **Walkability:** N/A. **Opened:** 1966. **Architect:** Telford M. Dixon. **Season:** March-Dec. **High:** May-Oct. **To obtain tee times:** Call golf shop. **Miscellaneous:** Reduced fees (weekdays, low season, juniors), discount packages, metal spikes, range (grass), club rentals, credit cards (MC, V, D).

POCONO MANOR INN & GOLF CLUB

R-P.O. Box 7, Pocono Manor, 18349, Monroe County, (570)839-7111, (800)233-8150, 20 miles S of Scranton.
★★½ EAST COURSE
Holes: 18. **Yards:** 6,565/5,977. **Par:** 72/75. **Course Rating:** 69.0/74.0. **Slope:** 118/117. **Green Fee:** $23/$38. **Cart Fee:** $20/person. **Walking Policy:** Mandatory cart. **Walkability:** 4. **Opened:** 1919. **Architect:** Donald Ross. **Season:** April-Nov. **High:** May-Oct. **To obtain tee times:** Outside play may call one week in advance. **Miscellaneous:** Reduced fees (weekdays, resort guests, twilight), discount packages, range (grass), club rentals, lodging (250 rooms), credit cards (MC, V, AE).
Reader Comments: Straight, firm greens, no irrigation ... Nice mountain course ... Shotmaker's dream ... Enjoyed the funnel hole, need to play twice.
★★ WEST COURSE
Holes: 18. **Yards:** 7,013/5,236. **Par:** 72/72. **Course Rating:** 72.3/72.0. **Slope:** 117/114. **Opened:** 1960. **Architect:** George Fazio. **Season:** April-Nov. **High:** May-Oct. **To obtain tee times:** Call Pro Shop. **Miscellaneous:** Reduced fees (weekdays, resort guests, twilight), discount packages, range (grass), club rentals, lodging (250 rooms), credit cards (MC, V, AE), beginner friendly (private instruction).

★★★½ QUAIL VALLEY GOLF CLUB

SP-901 Teeter Rd., Littletown, 17340, Adams County, (717)359-8453, 45 miles NE of Baltimore.
Holes: 18. **Yards:** 7,042/5,218. **Par:** 72/72. **Course Rating:** 72.9/69.5. **Slope:** 123/113. **Green Fee:** $18/$29. **Cart Fee:** $11/person. **Walking Policy:** Unrestricted walking. **Walkability:** 2. **Opened:** 1993. **Architect:** Paul Hicks. **Season:** Year-round. **High:** March-Oct. **To obtain tee times:** Call 7 days in advance. **Miscellaneous:** Reduced fees (weekdays, low season, twilight, seniors, juniors), range (grass/mats), credit cards (MC, V).
Reader Comments: Great layout, hard greens ... Hard to find, but that's good. Friendly pro shop folks ... Great course, it has something for every golfer no matter what level you play at. Always enjoy the challenge whenever I play there.

★★★★ QUICKSILVER GOLF CLUB *Condition*

PU-2000 Quicksilver Rd., Midway, 15060, Washington County, (724)796-1811, 18 miles W of Pittsburgh.
Holes: 18. **Yards:** 7,120/5,067. **Par:** 72/74. **Course Rating:** 75.7/68.6. **Slope:** 145/115. **Green Fee:** $38/$55. **Cart Fee:** Included in Green Fee. **Walking Policy:** Walking at certain times. **Walkability:** 2. **Opened:** 1990. **Architect:** Don Nagode. **Season:** March-Dec. **High:** May-Sept. **To obtain tee times:** Call or come in 6 days in advance. **Miscellaneous:** Reduced fees (low season, twilight, seniors, juniors), metal spikes, range (grass/mats), club rentals, credit cards (MC, V, AE, D, Diners Club), beginner friendly (beginner clinics).
Reader Comments: Best greens you'll play ... I played terribly but had a great time doing so ... Very challenging and you have to hit it straight ... Use every club in bag, long but plays fair ... Toughest greens in Pittsburgh area ... Play in spring or fall for discount price.

★★½ RICH MAIDEN GOLF COURSE

PU-R.D. No. 2, Box 2099, Fleetwood, 19522, Berks County, (610)926-1606, (800)905-9555, 10 miles N of Reading.
Holes: 18. **Yards:** 5,635/5,145. **Par:** 69/70. **Course Rating:** 63.6/64.9. **Slope:** 97/99. **Green Fee:** $16/$21. **Cart Fee:** $20/cart. **Walking Policy:** Unrestricted walking. **Walkability:** 3. **Opened:** 1932. **Architect:** Jake Merkel. **Season:** Year-round. **High:** April-Sept. **To obtain tee times:** Call or come in. **Miscellaneous:** Reduced fees (weekdays, low season, twilight, seniors, juniors), discount packages, metal spikes, club rentals.
Reader Comments: Good short course, tough elevated greens ... Best food in America ... Many short holes ... Good length variations on holes ... Great par threes ... Granite cliff uphill par three.

★★ RIVER VALLEY COUNTRY CLUB

RD 4, Box 582, Westfield, 16950, Tioga County, (814)367-2202, 30 miles S of Corning.

Holes: 18. **Yards:** 6,258/5,625. **Par:** 72/72. **Course Rating:** 70.2/67.1. **Slope:** 116/111. **Green Fee:** $15/$18. **Cart Fee:** $24/person. **Walking Policy:** Unrestricted walking. **Walkability:** 5. **Opened:** 1964. **Architect:** Geoffrey Cornish. **Season:** April-Nov. **High:** June-Aug. **To obtain tee times:** Call in advance. **Miscellaneous:** Reduced fees (weekdays, low season), discount packages, credit cards (MC, V, AE, D).

★★★★ RIVERSIDE GOLF CLUB

PU-24527 Hwy. 19, Cambridge Springs, 16403, Crawford County, (814)398-4537, (877)228-5322, 18 miles S of Erie.
Holes: 18. **Yards:** 6,334/5,287. **Par:** 71/72. **Course Rating:** 69.7/69.5. **Slope:** 119/116. **Green Fee:** $17/$27. **Cart Fee:** $13/person. **Walking Policy:** Walking at certain times. **Walkability:** 1. **Opened:** 1915. **Season:** March-Nov. **High:** May-Sept. **To obtain tee times:** Call 30 days in advance for local and up to a year in advance for out-of-area travelers. **Miscellaneous:** Reduced fees (weekdays, low season, twilight, seniors, juniors), discount packages, range (grass), club rentals, credit cards (MC, V, AE, D), beginner friendly (junior academy ladies learning league).
Reader Comments: Very fair course, not long or tight ... Excellent condition ... Bring all your clubs ... A hidden treasure ... Very green even in drought, par 3s stack up ... Great shape, friendly ... Play this one with extra golf balls ... Short and wide open ... Most sand I've seen up north.

★½ ROLLING FIELDS GOLF COURSE

PU-Hankey Church Rd., Murraysville, 15668, Westmoreland County, (724)335-7522, 15 miles E of Pittsburgh.
Holes: 18. **Yards:** 6,085/5,025. **Par:** 70/72. **Course Rating:** 68.9/N/A. **Slope:** 105/110. **Green Fee:** $12/$16. **Cart Fee:** $19/cart. **Walking Policy:** Unrestricted walking. **Walkability:** 4. **Opened:** 1955. **Architect:** John Chernega. **Season:** Year-round. **High:** April-Oct. **To obtain tee times:** Call 7 days in advance. **Miscellaneous:** Reduced fees (weekdays, seniors, juniors), metal spikes, club rentals.

★★½ ROLLING GREEN GOLF CLUB

PU-Rte. 136, Eighty-four, 15301, Washington County, (724)222-9671, 20 miles S of Pittsburgh.
Holes: 18. **Yards:** 6,000/4,500. **Par:** 71/71. **Course Rating:** N/A. **Slope:** N/A. **Green Fee:** $18/$20. **Cart Fee:** $20/cart. **Walking Policy:** Walking at certain times. **Walk-ability:** 3. **Opened:** 1957. **Season:** March-Oct. **High:** May-July. **To obtain tee times:** Call up to 5 days in advance for weekends. **Miscellaneous:** Reduced fees (weekdays, low season, seniors, juniors), metal spikes, club rentals, credit cards (MC, V).
Reader Comments: They don't call it Rolling Green for nothing, hills and more hills ... Short course ... Very difficult greens and challenging course ... Plays very long ... Many marshy areas.

★★ ROLLING HILLS GOLF COURSE

PU-RD No. 1, Rte. 208, Pulaski, 16143, Lawrence County, (724)964-8201, 10 miles E of Youngstown.
Holes: 18. **Yards:** 6,000/5,552. **Par:** 71/76. **Course Rating:** N/A. **Slope:** N/A. **Green Fee:** $9/$14. **Cart Fee:** $9/person. **Walking Policy:** Unrestricted walking. **Walkability:** 3. **Opened:** 1967. **Architect:** Frank Kwolsek. **Season:** Year-round. **High:** June-Aug. **To obtain tee times:** Call in advance. Required on weekends. **Miscellaneous:** Reduced fees (weekdays, low season, seniors, juniors), discount packages, metal spikes, club rentals, credit cards (MC, V).

★★ ROLLING MEADOWS GOLF CLUB

PU-23 Rolling Meadows Rd., Ashland, 17921, Schuylkill County, (570)875-1204, 12 miles N of Pottsville. **Web:** www.rollingmeadowsgolf.com.
Holes: 18. **Yards:** 5,200/5,200. **Par:** 68/69. **Course Rating:** 70.0/72.0. **Slope:** N/A. **Green Fee:** $14/$16. **Cart Fee:** $14/cart. **Walking Policy:** Unrestricted walking. **Walkability:** 3. **Opened:** 1964. **Season:** Year-round. **High:** June-Aug. **To obtain tee times:** Tee times not necessary. **Miscellaneous:** Reduced fees (weekdays, low season, twilight, seniors), discount packages, club rentals, beginner friendly.

★★★★ ROYAL OAKS GOLF COURSE

PU-3350 W. Oak St., Lebanon, 17042, Lebanon County, (717)274-2212, 15 miles NE of Hershey.
Holes: 18. **Yards:** 6,486/4,695. **Par:** 71/71. **Course Rating:** 71.4/66.9. **Slope:** 121/109. **Green Fee:** $15/$32. **Cart Fee:** $8/person. **Walking Policy:** Unrestricted walking. **Walkability:** 2. **Opened:** 1992. **Architect:** Ron Forse. **Season:** Year-round. **High:** April-Nov. **To obtain tee times:** Available 7 days in advance unless credit card number or deposit is taken. Tee times required 7 days a week. **Miscellaneous:** Reduced fees (weekdays, low season, twilight, seniors, juniors), metal spikes, range (grass), club rentals, credit cards (MC, V, AE, D).
Reader Comments: Walkable, great layout, love this course ... Great fairways ... Makes you feel like you are playing in a tournament ... Super greens (lightning fast) ... Fairways are lush, challenging par threes ... These are the greens of our lives ... Very difficult ... Reminds me of Myrtle Beach, water, waste areas ... Variety at every hole.

PENNSYLVANIA

★★★ SAXON GOLF COURSE
PU-839 Ekastown Rd., Sarver, 16055, Butler County, (724)353-2130.
Holes: 18. **Yards:** 6,603/5,131. **Par:** 72/72. **Course Rating:** N/A. **Slope:** N/A. **Green Fee:** $16/$19. **Cart Fee:** $19/cart. **Walking Policy:** Unrestricted walking. **Walkability:** 1. **Opened:** 1960. **Architect:** Frank E. Ekas. **Season:** April-Nov. **High:** July-Aug. **To obtain tee times:** Call one week before. **Miscellaneous:** Metal spikes, range (grass), beginner friendly.
Reader Comments: Great walkng course, fun to play ... One of the most well kept in area ... Nice fairways, great greens ... Very walkable ... Only flat layout in Western Pa.

★★★ SCRANTON MUNICIPAL GOLF COURSE
PM-1099 Golf Club Road, Lake Ariel, 18436, Lackawanna County, (570)689-2686, 10 miles E of Scranton.
Holes: 18. **Yards:** 6,638/5,763. **Par:** 72/73. **Course Rating:** 69.9/70.6. **Slope:** 113/112. **Green Fee:** $15/$23. **Cart Fee:** $20/cart. **Walking Policy:** Unrestricted walking. **Walkability:** 4. **Opened:** 1960. **Season:** April-Nov. **High:** June-Aug. **To obtain tee times:** Call golf shop. **Miscellaneous:** Metal spikes, range (grass/mats), club rentals.
Reader Comments: Verdant rolling terrain and greens in great shape. Played fast ... Play it from the blues for a challenge ... Needs work and overpriced ... Best muny greens you have ever seen.

★★½ SEVEN SPRINGS COUNTRY CLUB
PU-357 Pineview Dr., Elizabeth, 15037, Allegheny County, (412)384-7730, 3 miles S of Elizabeth.
Holes: 18. **Yards:** 6,451/5,474. **Par:** 71/71. **Course Rating:** 68.7/68.2. **Slope:** 115/104. **Green Fee:** $16/$25. **Cart Fee:** $22/cart. **Walking Policy:** Walking at certain times. **Walkability:** 3. **Opened:** 1954. **Season:** Year-round. **High:** June-Sept. **To obtain tee times:** Call one week in advance. **Miscellaneous:** Reduced fees (weekdays, low season, twilight, seniors), metal spikes, range (grass), credit cards (MC, V, D), beginner friendly (par-3 course available).
Reader Comments: Beautiful mountain course ... Nice clubhouse ... Open fairways ... Good course for lazy Sunday, relaxing day ... Very hilly, dry, blind holes ... Cut out of woods, requires accurate drives.

★★★½ SEVEN SPRINGS MOUNTAIN RESORT GOLF COURSE
R-RD No. 1, Champion, 15622, Westmoreland County, (814)352-7777, (800)452-2223, 60 miles SE of Pittsburgh. **Web:** www.7springs.com.
Holes: 18. **Yards:** 6,404/4,934. **Par:** 71/72. **Course Rating:** 71.7/68.3. **Slope:** 132/111. **Green Fee:** $55/$65. **Cart Fee:** Included in Green Fee. **Walking Policy:** Walking at certain times. **Walkability:** 3. **Opened:** 1969. **Architect:** Xen Hassenplug. **Season:** April-Oct. **High:** July-Aug. **To obtain tee times:** Call 48 hours in advance unless a guest at the resort then tee times can be made same time as reservation. **Miscellaneous:** Reduced fees (weekdays, low season, resort guests, twilight), discount packages, range (grass), club rentals, lodging (500 rooms), credit cards (MC, V, D), beginner friendly (clinics for house guests).
Reader Comments: Scenery great as is course, fun course to play ... Challenging and fun mountain course ... Top of the mountain makes wind tough ... Scenic, tough 4th hole ... Long par fives, short everything else ... Cannot get home in two at No. 17 ... Two tough finishing holes.

★★★ SHADOW BROOK GOLF COURSE
PU-615 5R 6E, Tunkhannock, 18657, Wyoming County, (717)836-5417, (800)955-0295. **E-mail:** shadowb@epix.net. **Web:** www.shadowbrookresort.com.
Yards: 5,907/4,700. **Par:** 71/71. **Course Rating:** 68.1/66.3. **Slope:** 115/110. **Green Fee:** $16/$22. **Cart Fee:** $10/person. **Walking Policy:** Unrestricted walking. **Walkability:** 3. **Architect:** Karl Schmidt. **Season:** April-March. **High:** April-Oct. **Miscellaneous:** Reduced fees (low season, resort guests, twilight, seniors), discount packages, range (grass), club rentals, lodging (73 rooms), credit cards (MC, V, AE, D, Diners Club), beginner friendly (junior clinic month of July).
Reader Comments: Nice challenging course ... Normal front 9, short back 9 ... Back 9 very hilly, short, tight ... Good mix of holes, nice greens ... Must think carefully of where to put the ball.

SHAWNEE INN GOLF RESORT
R-River Rd., Shawnee-on-Delaware, 18356, Monroe County, (570)424-4050, (800)742-9633, 90 miles W of New York City. **E-mail:** golf@shawneeinn.com. **Web:** www.shawneeinn.com.
Holes: 27. **Green Fee:** $40/$80. **Cart Fee:** Included in Green Fee. **Walking Policy:** Mandatory cart. **Walkability:** 1. **Opened:** 1906. **Architect:** A.W. Tillinghast/William Diddel. **Season:** April-Nov. **High:** May-Aug. **To obtain tee times:** Confirm tee times with credit card. Cancellation policy is 24 hours. **Miscellaneous:** Reduced fees (weekdays, low season, resort guests, twilight, seniors), discount packages, range (grass/mats), club rentals, lodging, credit cards (MC, V, AE, D, Diners Club).
★★★½ RED/BLUE
Yards: 6,800/5,650. **Par:** 72/74. **Course Rating:** 72.2/71.4. **Slope:** 132/121.
Reader Comments: Flat open course ... Great Tillie layout.
★★★½ RED/WHITE
Yards: 6,589/5,424. **Par:** 72/74. **Course Rating:** 72.4/71.1. **Slope:** 131/121.
Reader Comments: Nice hotel, excellent layout.

PENNSYLVANIA

★★★½ WHITE/BLUE
Yards: 6,665/5,398. **Par:** 72/74. **Course Rating:** 72.8/72.5. **Slope:** 129/123.
Reader Comments: Good food, good course, value ... An old course that is coming back, should be very good.

★★ SILVER SPRINGS GOLF CLUB
PU-136 Sample Bridge Rd., Mechanicsburg, 17055, Cumberland County, (717)766-0462, (877)766-0462, 10 miles NW of Harrisburg.
Holes: 18. **Yards:** 6,000/5,500. **Par:** 70/70. **Course Rating:** 68.0/66.0. **Slope:** 114/109. **Green Fee:** $15/$20. **Cart Fee:** $20/cart. **Walking Policy:** Unrestricted walking. **Walkability:** 3. **Architect:** George Fazio. **Season:** Year-round. **High:** March-Nov. **To obtain tee times:** Call Pro Shop. **Miscellaneous:** Reduced fees (weekdays, low season, twilight), range (grass/mats), club rentals, credit cards (MC, V).

★★★ SINKING VALLEY COUNTRY CLUB
Cape Cod Rd., Altoona, 16601, Blair County, (814)684-0662.
Special Notes: Call club for further information.

★★ SKYLINE GOLF COURSE
PU-118 Petrilak Road, Greenfield Twp., 18407, Lackawanna County, (570)282-5993, 15 miles NW of Scranton. **E-mail:** skylnegolf@aol.com. **Web:** members.aol.com/skylnegolf.
Holes: 18. **Yards:** 4,719/3,866. **Par:** 66/66. **Course Rating:** N/A. **Slope:** N/A. **Green Fee:** $9/$11. **Cart Fee:** $10/person. **Walking Policy:** Unrestricted walking. **Walkability:** 2. **Opened:** 1959. **Architect:** Carl Weinschenk/Andrew Petrilak. **Season:** April-Nov. **High:** June-Aug. **To obtain tee times:** Call on weekends. **Miscellaneous:** Reduced fees (seniors), club rentals, beginner friendly.

★★★ SKYTOP LODGE
R-#1 Skytop, Rte. 390, Skytop, 18357, Monroe County, (570)595-8910, (800)345-7759, 35 miles SE of Scranton.
Holes: 18. **Yards:** 6,256/5,683. **Par:** 71/75. **Course Rating:** 70.2/72.8. **Slope:** 121/122. **Green Fee:** $25/$45. **Cart Fee:** $20/person. **Walking Policy:** Walking at certain times. **Walkability:** 1. **Opened:** 1928. **Architect:** Robert White. **Season:** April-Oct. **High:** June-Sept. **To obtain tee times:** Tee times required. Call golf shop. **Miscellaneous:** Discount packages, range (grass), club rentals, lodging (200 rooms), credit cards (MC, V, AE), beginner friendly (beginner ladies and junior golf clinics. Brian Boyle 2-day golf school).
Reader Comments: One of the best in Poconos, great resort ... Surprisingly tough ... Always in great shape, sporty course ... Good course, but good views ... Deer everywhere, very good greens.

SOUTH HILLS GOLF CLUB
PU-925 Westminster Ave., Hanover, 17331, York County, (717)637-7500, 35 miles N of Baltimore.
Holes: 27. **Green Fee:** $10/$25. **Cart Fee:** $11/person. **Walking Policy:** Walking at certain times. **Walkability:** N/A. **Opened:** 1959. **Architect:** William Gordon/David Gordon. **Season:** Year-round. **High:** May-Oct. **To obtain tee times:** Call golf shop. **Miscellaneous:** Reduced fees (weekdays, low season, seniors, juniors), metal spikes, range (grass), club rentals.
★★★½ NORTH/SOUTH
Yards: 6,575/5,704. **Par:** 71/71. **Course Rating:** N/A. **Slope:** N/A.
Reader Comments: Elevation changes make course tougher ... Fun to play ... Old course, mature trees, nice setting, great course ... Good greens.
★★★½ NORTH/WEST
Yards: 6,709/5,196. **Par:** 72/72. **Course Rating:** N/A. **Slope:** N/A.
Reader Comments: North and new West best combo ... Watch the tree on No. 2; it's claimed lots of shots. Need a long drive on No. 5 or you won't see the pond. No. 13 surrounded by bunkers at green.
★★★½ SOUTH/WEST
Yards: 6,478/5,076. **Par:** 71/71. **Course Rating:** 71.3/72.8. **Slope:** 125/121.
Reader Comments: Tough course.

★★ SOUTH PARK GOLF COURSE
PM-E. Park Dr., Library, 15129, Allegheny County, (412)835-3545, 8 miles S of Pittsburgh.
Holes: 27. **Yards:** 6,584/5,580. **Par:** 72/73. **Course Rating:** 70.9/70.6. **Slope:** 123/114. **Green Fee:** $14/$17. **Cart Fee:** $17/cart. **Walking Policy:** Unrestricted walking. **Walkability:** 4. **Opened:** 1928. **Season:** Year-round. **High:** June-Aug. **To obtain tee times:** No tee times. **Miscellaneous:** Reduced fees (seniors, juniors), metal spikes, club rentals.
Special Notes: Also has 9-hole course.

★★★ SOUTHMOORE GOLF COURSE
PU-235 Moorestown Dr., Bath, 18014, Northampton County, (610)837-7200, 15 miles E of Allentown.

Holes: 18. **Yards:** 6,183/4,955. **Par:** 71/71. **Course Rating:** 71.2/65.0. **Slope:** 126/112. **Green Fee:** $23/$49. **Cart Fee:** $13/person. **Walking Policy:** Unrestricted walking. **Walkability:** 3. **Opened:** 1994. **Architect:** Jim Blaukovich. **Season:** Year-round. **High:** May-Oct. **To obtain tee times:** Call 5 days in advance. **Miscellaneous:** Reduced fees (weekdays, low season, resort guests, twilight, seniors, juniors), metal spikes, range (grass), club rentals, credit cards (MC, V, AE), beginner friendly.

Reader Comments: Good conditions, plain design, good service ... Good test of golf makes you think all the way around... Nice test of skills ... Might not need driver ... Interesting par threes, long par fives ... Pretty course. Great view.

★★★ SPORTSMANS GOLF CLUB
SP-3800 Linglestown Rd., Harrisburg, 17110, Dauphin County, (717)545-0023.
Holes: 18. **Yards:** 6,541/5,334. **Par:** 71/73. **Course Rating:** 73.0/70.8. **Slope:** 130/125. **Green Fee:** $23/$23. **Cart Fee:** $12/person. **Walking Policy:** Unrestricted walking. **Walkability:** 2. **Opened:** 1965. **Architect:** James Gilmore Harrison/Ferdinand Garbin. **Season:** Year-round. **High:** April-Oct. **To obtain tee times:** Call up to one week in advance. **Miscellaneous:** Reduced fees (weekdays, low season, twilight, seniors), range (grass/mats), club rentals, credit cards (MC, V).
Reader Comments: Heavy play, good walk ... Golfer's course. Has everything ... Interesting.

★★ SPRING HOLLOW GOLF COURSE
PU-3350 Schulkill Rd., Spring City, 19475, Chester County, (610)948-5566, 20 miles E of Reading. **Web:** www.spring-hollow.com.
Holes: 18. **Yards:** 6,218/5,075. **Par:** 70/70. **Course Rating:** 69.1/67.7. **Slope:** 113/113. **Green Fee:** $15/$26. **Cart Fee:** $13/person. **Walking Policy:** Walking at certain times. **Walkability:** 4. **Opened:** 1994. **Architect:** John Thompson. **Season:** Year-round. **High:** April-Oct. **To obtain tee times:** Call up to 14 days in advance. **Miscellaneous:** Reduced fees (weekdays, low season, twilight, seniors, juniors), club rentals, credit cards (MC, V).

★★ SPRINGDALE GOLF CLUB
PU-65 Springdale Dr., Uniontown, 15401, Fayette County, (412)439-4400, 50 miles S of Pittsburgh.
Holes: 18. **Yards:** 5,850/4,951. **Par:** 70/71. **Course Rating:** 67.5/68.5. **Slope:** 115/115. **Green Fee:** $12/$15. **Cart Fee:** $20/person. **Walking Policy:** Unrestricted walking. **Walkability:** 2. **Season:** March-Nov. **High:** June-Aug. **To obtain tee times:** First come, first served. **Miscellaneous:** Reduced fees (weekdays, low season, seniors), metal spikes.

★★★★ SPRINGWOOD GOLF CLUB
PU-601 Chestnut Hill Rd., York, 17402, York County, (717)747-9663. **E-mail:** swoodgolf @aol.com.
Holes: 18. **Yards:** 6,826/5,075. **Par:** 72/72. **Course Rating:** 73.4/69.7. **Slope:** 131/113. **Green Fee:** $25/$60. **Cart Fee:** Included in Green Fee. **Walking Policy:** Mandatory cart. **Walkability:** 4. **Opened:** 1998. **Architect:** Tom Clark/Dan Schlegel. **Season:** Year-round. **High:** April-Oct. **To obtain tee times:** Call (717)747-9663. **Miscellaneous:** Reduced fees (low season, resort guests, twilight), range (grass/mats), club rentals, credit cards (MC, V, AE, D, Diners Club).
Reader Comments: Nice elevation changes, good condition ... Bent grass tee to green. Lots of interesting holes ... I hope no one else finds this place ... In immaculate condition. The people were extremely hospitable. You could see the whole course from the parking lot. It was like driving up to a ski mountain.

★★½ STANDING STONE GOLF CLUB
PU-Rte. 26 N., Huntingdon, 16652, Huntingdon County, (814)643-4800.
Holes: 18. **Yards:** 6,593/5,528. **Par:** 70/70. **Course Rating:** 71.4/71.1. **Slope:** 120/120. **Green Fee:** $20/$25. **Cart Fee:** Included in Green Fee. **Walking Policy:** Mandatory cart. **Walkability:** N/A. **Opened:** 1973. **Architect:** Geoffrey Cornish. **Season:** March-Nov. **High:** March-Sept. **To obtain tee times:** Call 7 days in advance. **Miscellaneous:** Reduced fees (twilight), metal spikes, range (grass), club rentals.
Reader Comments: Best kept secret in my area. Love it! ... Wide open and long ... Usually not crowded... Number 16 toughest and prettiest par four I ever played ... Lots of water.

★★★½ STATE COLLEGE ELKS COUNTRY CLUB
SP-Rte. 322 Box 8, Boalsburg, 16827, Centre County, (814)466-6451, 5 miles E of State College.
Holes: 18. **Yards:** 6,369/5,095. **Par:** 71/72. **Course Rating:** 70.9/70.2. **Slope:** 123/119. **Green Fee:** $32/$32. **Cart Fee:** $12/person. **Walking Policy:** Unrestricted walking. **Walkability:** 3. **Opened:** 1964. **Architect:** Erdman. **Season:** April-Nov. **High:** May-Sept. **To obtain tee times:** Call 3 days in advance. **Miscellaneous:** Range (grass), club rentals, credit cards (MC, V, AE, D).
Reader Comments: Some challenging holes. Great condition ... Mountain goat golf ... Putting a real challenge.... Challenging when windy, great clubhouse ... Pleasure to play ... Staff helpful ... Challenging, some water, some length, 18 fast greens ... Long par threes.

★★★★ STONE HEDGE COUNTRY CLUB
PU-R.D. No. 4, Tunkhannock, 18657, Wyoming County, (570)836-5108, (800)452-2582, 22 miles W of Scranton. **E-mail:** stonehedge@epix.net.

Holes: 18. **Yards:** 6,644/5,046. **Par:** 71/71. **Course Rating:** 71.9/69.7. **Slope:** 124/122. **Green Fee:** $25/$43. **Cart Fee:** Included in Green Fee. **Walking Policy:** Mandatory cart. **Walkability:** 4. **Opened:** 1991. **Architect:** Jim Blaukovitch. **Season:** April-Dec. **High:** May-Sept. **To obtain tee times:** Call three days in advance or earlier if out of town. **Miscellaneous:** Reduced fees (weekdays, low season, twilight, seniors), range (grass), credit cards (MC, V).

Reader Comments: Let it rip on the front, shotmaking ability on the back ... Tough, tough, tough ... Beautiful course, great layout, middle of nowhere ... Great natural setting ... Par three No. 4 is pretty ... Big greens, great holes ... Impossible second hole ... Back nine awesome, best in state.

★★★★ STOUGHTON ACRES GOLF CLUB *Service+, Value+*

PU-904 Sunset Dr., Butler, 16001, Butler County, (724)285-3633, 40 miles S of Pittsburgh.
Holes: 18. **Yards:** 6,100/5,012. **Par:** 71/72. **Course Rating:** 67.3/N.A. **Slope:** 114/N/A. **Green Fee:** N/A. **Walking Policy:** Unrestricted walking. **Walkability:** 3. **Architect:** Van Smith. **Season:** April-Dec. **High:** June-Aug. **To obtain tee times:** Call for weekends and holidays. **Miscellaneous:** Metal spikes.

Reader Comments: Has a little of everything ... Beautiful back nine, hilly, nice people ... Best value in Western Pa. ... Very nice family run golf course ... No. 11 one of best par fours around.

★★★½ SUGARLOAF GOLF CLUB

PU-RR 2, Box 508, Sugarloaf, 18249, Luzerne County, (570)384-4097, (888)342-5784, 6 miles W of Hazleton. **E-mail:** sugarloafgolfclub.com. **Web:** www.sugarloafgolfclub.com. **Holes:** 18. **Yards:** 6,845/5,620. **Par:** 72/72. **Course Rating:** 73.0/72.8. **Slope:** 122/120. **Green Fee:** $16/$24. **Cart Fee:** $26/cart. **Walking Policy:** Walking at certain times. **Walkability:** 3. **Opened:** 1967. **Architect:** Geoffrey Cornish. **Season:** March-Nov. **High:** July-Aug. **To obtain tee times:** Call. **Miscellaneous:** Reduced fees (weekdays, low season, twilight), metal spikes, range (grass), club rentals, credit cards (MC, V, AE, MAC).

Reader Comments: Beautiful scenery, location... Wide open front and wooded back ... Back nine much tougher ... Back tees can bring you to your knees ... Big greens, nice holes.

★★★½ SUNSET GOLF COURSE

PU-Geyer's Church Rd. & Sunset Dr., Middletown, 17057, Dauphin County, (717)944-5415, 12 miles E of Harrisburg.
Holes: 18. **Yards:** 6,328/5,255. **Par:** 70/71. **Course Rating:** 69.1/69.9. **Slope:** 113/113. **Green Fee:** $10/$20. **Cart Fee:** $11/cart. **Walking Policy:** Unrestricted walking. **Walkability:** 3. **Architect:** Air Force. **Season:** Year-round. **High:** May-Sept. **To obtain tee times:** Call golf shop. **Miscellaneous:** Reduced fees (low season, seniors, juniors), metal spikes, range (mats), club rentals, credit cards (MC, V).

Reader Comments: Some good holes, greens good. Good value ... Watch out for commercial jets in landing areas ... Great course for the price ... Front 9 a lot of fun, 2 reachable par 5s ... Good view of Three Mile Island ... No. 10 is gorgeous. Par 3s will make or break your score.

★★ SYLVAN HEIGHTS GOLF COURSE

PU-Rte. 65, Ellwood-New Castle Rd., New Castle, 16101, Lawrence County, (724)658-8021, 50 miles N of Pittsburgh.
Holes: 18. **Yards:** 6,081/6,781. **Par:** 71/71. **Course Rating:** 69.8/70.0. **Slope:** 128/118. **Green Fee:** $9/$13. **Cart Fee:** $15/person. **Walking Policy:** Unrestricted walking. **Walkability:** 2. **Season:** Year-round. **High:** April-Oct. **To obtain tee times:** Call anytime. **Miscellaneous:** Reduced fees (seniors), metal spikes.

★★★½ TAM O'SHANTER GOLF CLUB

PU-I-80 And Rte. 18 N., Hermitage, 16159, Mercer County, (724)981-3552.
Holes: 18. **Yards:** 6,537/5,385. **Par:** 72/76. **Course Rating:** 69.4/70.2. **Slope:** 121/113. **Green Fee:** $21/$25. **Cart Fee:** $10/person. **Walking Policy:** Walking at certain times. **Walkability:** 3. **Opened:** 1931. **Architect:** Emil Loeffler. **Season:** March-Nov. **High:** June-Sept. **To obtain tee times:** Call. Tee times available daily. **Miscellaneous:** Reduced fees (weekdays, low season, resort guests, seniors, juniors), discount packages, metal spikes, range (grass/mats), club rentals, lodging, credit cards (MC, V, D).

Reader Comments: Fun course for anyone ... Many short holes ... Worth the trip from Pittsburgh ... Old, beautiful, traditional golf course ... No. 3 is a great five, lovely first nine ... Fun to play with some exciting holes.

★★★ TAMIMENT RESORT & CONFERENCE CENTER GOLF CLUB

R-Bushkill Falls Rd., Tamiment, 18371, Pike County, (717)588-6652, (800)233-8105, 75 miles W of New York.
Holes: 18. **Yards:** 6,858/5,598. **Par:** 72/72. **Course Rating:** 72.7/71.9. **Slope:** 130/124. **Green Fee:** $15/$45. **Cart Fee:** $15/person. **Walking Policy:** Mandatory cart. **Walkability:** 3. **Opened:** 1951. **Architect:** Robert Trent Jones. **Season:** April-Nov. **High:** May-Sept. **To obtain tee times:** Hotel guests at time room reservations are made. Nonguests may call up to 10 days in advance. **Miscellaneous:** Reduced fees (weekdays, low season, resort guests, twilight, seniors, juniors), discount packages, range (mats), club rentals, lodging, credit cards (MC, V, AE, D).

Reader Comments: Great price for Poconos ... Fun, beautiful scenery ... Needs shorter ladies tees ... Long holes, short holes, rolling greens.

★★★½ TANGLEWOOD MANOR GOLF CLUB & LEARNING CENTER

PU-Scotland Rd., Quarryville, 17566, Lancaster County, (717)786-2220, 10 miles S of Lancaster. **Web:** www.twgolf.com.
Holes: 18. **Yards:** 6,457/5,321. **Par:** 72/74. **Course Rating:** 70.7/70.0. **Slope:** 118/118. **Green Fee:** $17/$24. **Cart Fee:** $12/person. **Walking Policy:** Walking at certain times. **Walkability:** 3. **Opened:** 1969. **Architect:** Chester Ruby. **Season:** March-Dec. **High:** May-Oct. **To obtain tee times:** Call golf shop up to 2 weeks in advance. **Miscellaneous:** Reduced fees (weekdays, low season, twilight, seniors, juniors), discount packages, range (grass/mats), club rentals, credit cards (MC, V).
Reader Comments: Good course, good renovation ... Good greens ... Look out for No. 18 ... Out of this world condition ... Very playable ... No. 18's a killer, par 5 uphill out of bounds all along right side of fairway, creek crosses fairway 235 yards from tee, 535 yards long ... Respectable.

★½ TIMBER RIDGE GOLF CLUB

PU-RD No. 6, Box 2057, Mount Pleasant, 15666, Westmoreland County, (412)547-1909, 17 miles SE of Pittsburgh.
Holes: 18. **Yards:** 6,600/5,277. **Par:** 72/72. **Course Rating:** 69.9/68.9. **Slope:** 126/112. **Green Fee:** $15/$20. **Cart Fee:** $12/person. **Walking Policy:** Unrestricted walking. **Walkability:** 4. **Opened:** 1983. **Architect:** Fred Garbin. **Season:** Year-round. **High:** April-Oct. **To obtain tee times:** First come, first served. Call 7 a.m.-9 a.m. **Miscellaneous:** Reduced fees (weekdays, low season, seniors, juniors), metal spikes, club rentals, credit cards (MC, V, D).

★★★★ TOFTREES RESORT

R-1 Country Club Lane, State College, 16803, Centre County, (814)238-7600, (800)252-3551, 90 miles NW of Harrisburg. **Web:** wwwtoftrees.com.
Holes: 18. **Yards:** 7,018/5,555. **Par:** 72/72. **Course Rating:** 74.3/72.2. **Slope:** 138/125. **Green Fee:** $34/$47. **Cart Fee:** $15/person. **Walking Policy:** Walking at certain times. **Walkability:** 3. **Opened:** 1968. **Architect:** Ed Ault. **Season:** April-Nov. **High:** May-Oct. **To obtain tee times:** Public, 14 days in advance; Resort guests, 60 days in advance. **Miscellaneous:** Reduced fees (weekdays, low season, twilight, seniors), discount packages, range (grass), club rentals, lodging (135 rooms), credit cards (MC, V, AE, D, Diners Club).
Reader Comments: Good condition, a scenic fun layout ... Beginners stay home! ... Happy Valley's best. Well laid out course ... Fast greens but true ... No flat lies anywhere ... Long and challenging ... Play back tees for great par threes and fives ... Good restaurant ... Great for women, too, but still can challenge.

★★★ TOWANDA COUNTRY CLUB

SP-RR 06, Box 6180, Towanda, 18848, Bradford County, (570)265-6939, 1 miles E of Towanda. **E-mail:** tcc@sosbbs.
Holes: 18. **Yards:** 5,958/5,127. **Par:** 71/76. **Course Rating:** 68.0/69.0. **Slope:** 112/102. **Green Fee:** $32/$40. **Cart Fee:** Included in Green Fee. **Walking Policy:** Mandatory cart. **Walkability:** 4. **Opened:** 1927. **Architect:** Bill Glenn/Warner Burger. **Season:** April-Dec. **High:** May-Sept. **To obtain tee times:** Call golf shop. **Miscellaneous:** Club rentals, credit cards (MC, V).
Reader Comments: Great little course. Small, fast greens; few blind shots ... Fun golf course ... Short and hilly. Friendly.

★★★½ TREASURE LAKE GOLF CLUB

R-13 Treasure Lake, Dubois, 15801, Clearfield County, (814)375-1807, 110 miles NE of Pittsburgh.
Holes: 18. **Yards:** 6,284/5,198. **Par:** 72/74. **Course Rating:** 71.4/71.4. **Slope:** 135/129. **Green Fee:** $34/$39. **Cart Fee:** $14/person. **Walking Policy:** Unrestricted walking. **Walkability:** 5. **Opened:** 1972. **Architect:** Dominic Palombo. **Season:** May-Oct. **High:** June-Aug. **To obtain tee times:** Call up to 14 days in advance. **Miscellaneous:** Reduced fees (twilight, juniors), club rentals, lodging, credit cards (MC, V, AE, D).
Reader Comments: Talk about tight ... Nice people, great course ... Target golf ... Not bad for mountain course ... Trying to hit down a tunnel on every shot ... Must have all golf shots.

★★½ TURBOT HILLS GOLF COURSE

PU-Rte. 405 North, Milton, 17847, Northumberland County, (570)742-7455, 1 miles N of Milton.
Holes: 18. **Yards:** 6,557/5,242. **Par:** 71/74. **Course Rating:** 71.5/69.2. **Slope:** 120/116. **Green Fee:** $15/$19. **Cart Fee:** $11/person. **Walking Policy:** Unrestricted walking. **Walkability:** 3. **Opened:** 1927. **Season:** Year-round. **High:** June-Sept. **To obtain tee times:** Call golf shop. **Miscellaneous:** Range (grass/mats), club rentals, credit cards (MC, V, AE).
Reader Comments: Challenging par 4s, par 3s ... Nice old layout, great bar ... Need all your clubs ... Nice holes, good condition, nice greens.

★★★★ TURTLE CREEK GOLF COURSE

PU-303 W. Ridge Pike, Limerick, 19468, Montgomery County, (610)489-5133, 15 miles W of King of Prussia. **Web:** www.turtlecreekgolf.com.

Holes: 18. **Yards:** 6,702/5,131. **Par:** 72/72. **Course Rating:** 72.1/68.6. **Slope:** 127/115. **Green Fee:** $25/$47. **Cart Fee:** Included in Green Fee. **Walking Policy:** Unrestricted walking. **Walk-ability:** 3. **Opened:** 1997. **Architect:** Ed Beidel. **Season:** March-Dec. **High:** June-Sept. **Miscellaneous:** Reduced fees (twilight, seniors), range (grass/mats), club rentals, credit cards (MC, V, D).
Reader Comments: Links style ... Greens excellent ... Great value, No. 18 will make you work ... Welcome addition to public golf scene ... Very new but already in great shape ... New course, superb layout. Greens are very fast.

★★★½ TWIN PONDS GOLF COURSE
PU-700 Gilbertsville Rd., Gilbertsville, 19525, Montgomery County, (610)369-1901.
Holes: 18. **Yards:** 5,588/4,747. **Par:** 70/70. **Course Rating:** 65.5/67.7. **Slope:** 111/119. **Green Fee:** N/A. **Cart Fee:** $20/person. **Walking Policy:** Walking at certain times. **Walkability:** 2.
Opened: 1963. **Season:** Year-round. **High:** March-Nov. **To obtain tee times:** Call. **Miscellaneous:** Reduced fees (weekdays, twilight, seniors), metal spikes, range (grass), club rentals.
Reader Comments: Short. Good condition ... Short course, small greens ... Fairly flat ... Don't get above the hole! ... Nice mix of short and long par threes, fours and fives. Great 19th hole.

★½ TWINING VALLEY GOLF CLUB
PU-1400 Twining Rd., Dresher, 19025, Montgomery County, (215)659-9917, 5 miles N of Philadelphia.
Holes: 18. **Yards:** 6,513/5,300. **Par:** 71/72. **Course Rating:** 65.9/N/A. **Slope:** 114/N/A. **Green Fee:** $20/$24. **Cart Fee:** $24/person. **Walking Policy:** Walking at certain times. **Walkability:** 3.
Opened: 1931. **Architect:** Jock Mellville. **Season:** Year-round. **High:** April-Oct. **To obtain tee times:** Call 7 days in advance. **Miscellaneous:** Metal spikes, range (grass/mats), club rentals, credit cards (MC, V, AE, D).

★★★★ TYOGA COUNTRY CLUB
SP-RR 6, Wellsboro, 16901, Tioga County, (570)724-1653, 50 miles S of Corning, NY.
Holes: 18. **Yards:** 6,335/5,227. **Par:** 71/73. **Course Rating:** 71.3/70.8. **Slope:** 135/128. **Green Fee:** $45/$49. **Cart Fee:** Included in Green Fee. **Walking Policy:** Mandatory cart. **Walkability:** 5. **Opened:** 1923. **Architect:** Edmund B. Ault. **Season:** April-Nov. **High:** June-Sept. **To obtain tee times:** Call golf shop. **Miscellaneous:** Discount packages, range (grass), club rentals, credit cards (MC, V).
Reader Comments: Great golf course and fun to play ... Beautiful mountain views and landscaping ... People were pleasant and helpful. Great fun! ... An absolute must for fall golf. Tough, hilly course, No. 1 sets the stage.

★★★★ UPPER PERK GOLF COURSE *Value*
PU-2324 Ott Road, Pennsburg, 18073, Montgomery County, (215)679-5594, 50 miles NE of Philadelphia.
Holes: 18. **Yards:** 6,381/5,249. **Par:** 71/71. **Course Rating:** 70.0/69.6. **Slope:** 117/113. **Green Fee:** $18/$30. **Cart Fee:** $20/cart. **Walking Policy:** Walking at certain times. **Walkability:** 2.
Opened: 1977. **Architect:** Bob Hendricks. **Season:** March-Dec. **High:** May-Sept. **To obtain tee times:** Call up to 10 days in advance. **Miscellaneous:** Reduced fees (weekdays, low season, twilight, seniors, juniors), credit cards (MC, V).
Reader Comments: Demanding layout ... Big greens and well maintained, forgiving yet very challenging ... Open course ... Best kept secret near Philadelphia.

★★½ VALLEY FORGE GOLF CLUB
PU-401 N. Gulf Rd., King Of Prussia, 19406, Montgomery County, (610)337-1776, 25 miles W of Philadelphia.
Holes: 18. **Yards:** 6,200/5,668. **Par:** 71/73. **Course Rating:** 68.1/70.0. **Slope:** 107/113. **Green Fee:** $12/$23. **Cart Fee:** $26/cart. **Walking Policy:** Unrestricted walking. **Walkability:** 3.
Opened: 1929. **Architect:** Alex Findlay. **Season:** Year-round. **High:** May-Sept. **To obtain tee times:** Call on Monday for weekend or holiday times. **Miscellaneous:** Reduced fees (weekdays, twilight), metal spikes.
Reader Comments: Flat course, few hazards ... No clubhouse ... OK place to work on your game ... Basic golf but cheap.

★★ VALLEY GREEN GOLF & COUNTRY CLUB
PU-RD No. 2, Box 449F, Greensburg, 15601, Westmoreland County, (724)837-6366, 40 miles SE of Pittsburgh.
Holes: 18. **Yards:** 6,345/5,450. **Par:** 72/72. **Course Rating:** 67.5/67.5. **Slope:** 104/104. **Green Fee:** $17/$20. **Cart Fee:** $18/cart. **Walking Policy:** Unrestricted walking. **Walkability:** 1.
Opened: 1965. **Architect:** X.G. Hassenplug. **Season:** Year-round. **High:** April-Sept. **To obtain tee times:** Call golf shop. **Miscellaneous:** Reduced fees (seniors), metal spikes, range (grass), club rentals.

★★½ VALLEY GREEN GOLF COURSE
PU-1227 Valley Green Rd., Etters, 17319, York County, (717)938-4200, 15 miles S of Harrisburg.

Holes: 18. **Yards:** 6,000/5,500. **Par:** 71/71. **Course Rating:** 67.0/67.0. **Slope:** 110/109. **Green Fee:** $15/$23. **Cart Fee:** $12/person. **Walking Policy:** Unrestricted walking. **Walkability:** 3. **Opened:** 1964. **Architect:** Short/Leggett. **Season:** March-Nov. **High:** April-Oct. **To obtain tee times:** Call golf shop 7 days in advance. **Miscellaneous:** Reduced fees (weekdays, low season, twilight, seniors, juniors), metal spikes, club rentals, credit cards (MC, V).
Reader Comments: Short but always in good condition ... Very difficult approaches to uphill greens from uneven lies, harder than it looks.... A great neighborhood course, good twilight deal ... Short par 4s, tough rolling greens ... No. 18 a plateau par three ... Fairly hilly with some tiny greens on front nine.

★★ VENANGO TRAIL GOLF COURSE
SP-970 Freeport Rd., Mars, 16046, Butler County, (412)776-4400, 18 miles N of Pittsburgh.
Holes: 18. **Yards:** 6,200/5,518. **Par:** 72/72. **Course Rating:** 69.9/74.0. **Slope:** 120/117. **Green Fee:** $11/$20. **Cart Fee:** $10/person. **Walking Policy:** Walking at certain times. **Walkability:** N/A. **Opened:** 1954. **Architect:** James Gilmore Harrison. **Season:** Year-round. **High:** April-Oct. **To obtain tee times:** Call 48 hours in advance. **Miscellaneous:** Reduced fees (weekdays, low season, seniors, juniors), discount packages, metal spikes, credit cards (MC, V, AE, D).

★★ VENANGO VALLEY INN & GOLF CLUB
PU-Rte. 19, Venango, 16440, Crawford County, (814)398-4330, 30 miles S of Erie.
Holes: 18. **Yards:** 6,202/4,769. **Par:** 71/71. **Course Rating:** 69.9/69.0. **Slope:** 101/101. **Green Fee:** $9/$16. **Cart Fee:** $9/person. **Walking Policy:** Unrestricted walking. **Walk-ability:** 2. **Opened:** 1972. **Architect:** Paul E. Erath. **Season:** Year-round. **High:** May-Sept. **To obtain tee times:** Call (814)398-4330. **Miscellaneous:** Reduced fees (weekdays, seniors), discount packages, metal spikes, club rentals, credit cards (MC, V).

★★★ WATER GAP COUNTRY CLUB
SP-Mountain Rd., Delaware Water Gap, 18327, Monroe County, (570)476-0300, 70 miles W of New York City. **E-mail:** wgcc1.@noln. **Web:** www.pocono.com.
Holes: 18. **Yards:** 6,237/5,199. **Par:** 72/74. **Course Rating:** 69.0/69.0. **Slope:** 125/114. **Green Fee:** $38/$45. **Cart Fee:** Included in Green Fee. **Walking Policy:** Walking at certain times. **Walkability:** 5. **Opened:** 1921. **Architect:** Robert White. **Season:** March-Nov. **High:** July-Sept. **To obtain tee times:** Call 5 days in advance. **Miscellaneous:** Reduced fees (weekdays, seniors), discount packages, metal spikes, club rentals, lodging (23 rooms), credit cards (MC, V, AE, D, Discover).
Reader Comments: Great old course ... King of the blind shot ... Time warp golf.

★★★ WEDGEWOOD GOLF CLUB
PU-4875 Limeport Pike, Coopersburg, 18036, Lehigh County, (610)797-4551, 4 miles S of Allentown.
Holes: 18. **Yards:** 6,162/5,622. **Par:** 71/72. **Course Rating:** 68.8/65.8. **Slope:** 122/108. **Green Fee:** $19/$39. **Cart Fee:** $22/cart. **Walking Policy:** Walking at certain times. **Walkability:** 2. **Opened:** 1963. **Architect:** William Gordon/David Gordon. **Season:** Year-round. **High:** April-Sept. **To obtain tee times:** Call golf shop. **Miscellaneous:** Reduced fees (weekdays, low season, twilight, seniors), metal spikes, range (grass), club rentals, credit cards (MC, V).
Reader Comments: Open, not many trees, good walking course ... Good for beginners and seniors ... Short ego course. Relatively open so shots from the rough usually playable. Course is full on weekends but usually moves along pretty well.

WHITE DEER PARK & GOLF COURSE
PU-352 Allenwood Camp Ln., Montgomery, 17752, Lycoming County, (570)547-2186, 8 miles S of Williamsport.
★★★½ CHALLENGE
Holes: 18. **Yards:** 6,605/4,742. **Par:** 72/72. **Course Rating:** 71.6/68.4. **Slope:** 133/125. **Green Fee:** $13/$22. **Cart Fee:** $13/person. **Walking Policy:** Unrestricted walking. **Walkability:** 4. **Opened:** 1989. **Architect:** Lindsay Ervin and Assoc. **Season:** Year-round. **High:** May-Sept. **To obtain tee times:** Call 28 days in advance. **Miscellaneous:** Reduced fees (weekdays, low season, twilight, seniors, juniors), metal spikes, range (grass), club rentals, credit cards (MC, V, D), beginner friendly (clinics, school, lessons, par-3 course).
Reader Comments: Need every club ... Very scenic, challenging, a good buy for the buck ... Tight, fun ... Nice holes, good value ... Well-maintained ... One of my favorites, lots of variety.
★★½ VINTAGE
Holes: 18. **Yards:** 6,405/4,843. **Par:** 72/72. **Course Rating:** 69.7/68.5. **Slope:** 122/120. **Green Fee:** $13/$22. **Cart Fee:** $13/person. **Walking Policy:** Unrestricted walking. **Walkability:** 3. **Opened:** 1965. **Architect:** Kenneth J. Polakowski. **Season:** Year-round. **High:** May-Sept. **To obtain tee times:** Call 28 days in advance. **Miscellaneous:** Reduced fees (weekdays, low season, twilight, seniors, juniors), metal spikes, range (grass), club rentals, credit cards (MC, V, D).
Reader Comments: Wide open but still challenging on some holes ... Nice big greens ... Well laid out and plays to all skill levels ... Conquer this one before attempting Challenge Course.

PENNSYLVANIA

★★★½ WHITETAIL GOLF CLUB
PU-2679 Klein Rd., Bath, 18014, Northampton County, (610)837-9626, 7 miles N of Allentown.
Web: www.whitetailgolfclub.com.
Holes: 18. **Yards:** 6,432/5,152. **Par:** 72/72. **Course Rating:** 70.6/65.3. **Slope:** 128/113. **Green Fee:** $22/$45. **Cart Fee:** Included in Green Fee. **Walking Policy:** Walking at certain times.
Walkability: 3. **Opened:** 1993. **Architect:** Jim Blaukovitch. **Season:** Year-round. **High:** May-Oct.
To obtain tee times: Call 7 days in advance, 7 days a week. **Miscellaneous:** Reduced fees (weekdays, low season, twilight, seniors, juniors), discount packages, range (grass), club rentals, credit cards (MC, V, AE).
Reader Comments: Great greens, rolling hills ... Fast greens always windy ... Some very long par fours ... There are a couple of real treacherous holes! ... Usually a fun time ... Big fast greens.

★★★★ WILKES-BARRE GOLF CLUB
PM-1001 Fairway Dr., Wilkes-Barre, 18702, Luzerne County, (570)472-3590, 10 miles N of Wilkes-Barre.
Holes: 18. **Yards:** 6,912/5,690. **Par:** 72/74. **Course Rating:** 72.8/73.2. **Slope:** 125/115. **Green Fee:** $18/$24. **Cart Fee:** $14/person. **Walking Policy:** Walking at certain times. **Walkability:** 3. **Opened:** 1968. **Architect:** Geoffrey Cornish. **Season:** April-Nov. **High:** June-Aug. **To obtain tee times:** Call one week in advance. **Miscellaneous:** Reduced fees (weekdays, low season, twilight, seniors, juniors), discount packages, metal spikes, range (grass/mats), club rentals, credit cards (MC, V, AE).
Reader Comments: A good course, long par 3s ... Watch for wildlife ... Long and sometimes tight ... Fast greens, busy ... Beautiful mountain course ... One of the best munies I have played.

★★★½ WILLOW HOLLOW GOLF COURSE
PU-619 Prison Road, Leesport, 19533, Berks County, (610)373-1505, 6 miles N of Reading.
Web: www.distinctgolf.com.
Holes: 18. **Yards:** 5,810/4,435. **Par:** 70/70. **Course Rating:** 67.1/64.1. **Slope:** 105/99. **Green Fee:** $11/$22. **Cart Fee:** $11/person. **Walking Policy:** Walking at certain times. **Walkability:** 3. **Opened:** 1959. **Architect:** Harvey Haupt. **Season:** Year-round. **High:** May-Sept. **To obtain tee times:** Call up to 30 days in advance for weekends. For weekdays call up to 14 days in advance. **Miscellaneous:** Reduced fees (weekdays, twilight, seniors), discount packages, metal spikes, club rentals, credit cards (MC, V), beginner friendly (berks county junior golf).
Reader Comments: Fast greens ... Interesting shots, don't overclub ... Excellent for average hitters ... Short, well kept course ... Short but can't just fire away. No. 17 is as tough as they come.

★★½ WOODLAND HILLS COUNTRY CLUB
SP-4166 Lower Saucon Road, Hellertown, 18055, Northampton County, (610)838-7192, 5 miles NE of Hellertown. **Web:** www.woodlandhillscountryclub.com.
Holes: 18. **Yards:** 6,761/5,965. **Par:** 72/72. **Course Rating:** 70.3/68.1. **Slope:** 121/110. **Green Fee:** $22/$27. **Cart Fee:** $13/person. **Walking Policy:** Walking at certain times. **Walkability:** 3. **Opened:** 1968. **Season:** Year-round. **High:** April-Sept. **To obtain tee times:** Call 10 days in advance. **Miscellaneous:** Reduced fees (weekdays, seniors, juniors), metal spikes, range (grass), club rentals, credit cards (MC, V).
Reader Comments: Nice layout, enjoyable ... Nos. 16, 17, 18 very tough finish ... Condition vastly improved in last five years ... Nice course; no surprises.

WOODLOCH SPRINGS COUNTRY CLUB
SP-RD #1, Hawley, 18428, 570)685-2100, (800)572-6658, 35 miles NE of Scranton.
Holes: 18. **Yards:** 6,127/4,973. **Par:** 72/72. **Course Rating:** 70.4/71.6. **Slope:** 133/130. **Green Fee:** $60/$75. **Cart Fee:** Included in Green Fee. **Walking Policy:** Walking at certain times.
Walkability: 5. **Opened:** 1992. **Architect:** Rocky Rogermore. **Season:** April-Nov. **High:** June-Oct. **To obtain tee times:** Guests of resort 10 days in advance. **Miscellaneous:** Range (mats), club rentals, lodging, credit cards (MC, V, AE, D).

★★★★ WYNCOTE GOLF CLUB
PU-50 Wyncote Dr., Oxford, 19363, Chester County, (610)932-8900, 50 miles SW of Philadelphia. **E-mail:** jimp@wyncote.com. **Web:** www.wyncote.com.
Holes: 18. **Yards:** 7,012/5,454. **Par:** 72/72. **Course Rating:** 74.0/71.6. **Slope:** 130/126. **Green Fee:** $30/$65. **Cart Fee:** $15/person. **Walking Policy:** Unrestricted walking. **Walkability:** 2. **Opened:** 1993. **Architect:** Brian Ault of Ault, Clark & Assoc. **Season:** Year-round. **High:** May-Oct. **To obtain tee times:** Call one week in advance. Credit card must be used to reserve weekend tee times. **Miscellaneous:** Reduced fees (weekdays, low season, twilight, seniors, juniors), discount packages, range (grass/mats), caddies, club rentals, credit cards (MC, V, AE, D), beginner friendly (group clinics with reduced rates).
Notes: Ranked 25th in 1999 Best in State.
Reader Comments: Scotland in Pennsylvania ... Course is turning into championship caliber ... Worth the trip. Superb greens ... Fairways like carpets, fast greens ... Scenic ... Few trees, but lots of challenge ... Spoil yourself once or twice a year ... Great front 9 ... Pure golf ... Great design, need local knowledge ... Great practice area ... Tough, but good.

RHODE ISLAND

BRISTOL GOLF CLUB
PU-95 Tupelo St., Bristol, 02809, (401)254-1282.
Special Notes: Call club for further information.

★★★ COUNTRY VIEW GOLF CLUB
PU-49 Club Lane, Harrisville, 02830, Providence County, (401)568-7157, 15 miles N of Providence. **E-mail:** rickcvgc@aol.com.
Holes: 18. **Yards:** 6,067/4,755. **Par:** 70/70. **Course Rating:** 69.2/67.0. **Slope:** 119/105. **Green Fee:** $16/$25. **Cart Fee:** $24/cart. **Walking Policy:** Unrestricted walking. **Walkability:** 2. **Opened:** 1965. **Architect:** Carl Dexter. **Season:** March-Nov. **High:** June-Sept. **To obtain tee times:** Call up to seven days in advance for weekdays. For weekends call Monday. **Miscellaneous:** Reduced fees (weekdays, low season, twilight, seniors), club rentals, credit cards (MC, V, D).
Reader Comments: Solid course ... Tiny greens ... Tough first 9, easy second 9 ... A fun little course ... Play it when you need a good score ... Tight front, open back ... Demanding par 3s.

★★★ CRANSTON COUNTRY CLUB
PU-69 Burlingame Rd., Cranston, 02921, Providence County, (401)826-1683, 7 miles S of Providence. **E-mail:** ejgolfpro@aol.com.
Holes: 18. **Yards:** 6,750/5,499. **Par:** 71/72. **Course Rating:** 71.4/71.9. **Slope:** 126/120. **Green Fee:** $27/$35. **Cart Fee:** $12/person. **Walking Policy:** Unrestricted walking. **Walkability:** 3. **Opened:** 1970. **Architect:** Geoffrey Cornish. **Season:** March-Dec. **High:** May-Sept. **To obtain tee times:** Call Tuesday for upcoming weekend. For weekdays call three days in advance. **Miscellaneous:** Reduced fees (weekdays, low season, twilight, seniors), range (grass/mats), club rentals, credit cards (MC, V, D).
Reader Comments: Nice layout, slow play ... Working to improve course ... Greens need work ... Could be top notch.

★★★½ EXETER COUNTRY CLUB
PU-320 Ten Rod Rd., Exeter, 02822, Washington County, (401)295-1178, 15 miles S of Warwick.
Holes: 18. **Yards:** 6,919/5,733. **Par:** 72/72. **Course Rating:** N/A. **Slope:** 123/115. **Green Fee:** N/A. **Walkability:** N/A. **Architect:** Geoffrey S. Cornish. **Season:** March-Nov. **High:** June-Sept. **Miscellaneous:** Reduced fees (low season, twilight), metal spikes, range (grass), lodging, credit cards (MC, V).
Reader Comments: Always in great shape ... Beautiful, slow greens—wicked slow! ... Tee times hard to get, course is a challenge ... Wide open, fun track ... Very nice course, slow play however ... Will play there again ... Several water holes ... Crowded ... Used every club.

★★½ FOSTER COUNTRY CLUB
SP-67 Johnson Rd., Foster, 02825, Providence County, (401)397-7750, 32 miles W of Providence.
Holes: 18. **Yards:** 6,200/5,500. **Par:** 72/74. **Course Rating:** 69.5/70.0. **Slope:** 114/112. **Green Fee:** $23/$27. **Cart Fee:** $22/cart. **Walking Policy:** Unrestricted walking. **Walkability:** 3. **Opened:** 1964. **Season:** April-Dec. **High:** May-Sept. **To obtain tee times:** Call 7 days in advance. **Miscellaneous:** Reduced fees (twilight), discount packages, metal spikes, club rentals, credit cards (MC, V).
Reader Comments: Not a bad course but too easy ... Ends with two Par 3s ... Funky back 9 ... Several water holes ... Several blind holes ... Hit the big dog.

★★★ FOXWOODS GOLF & COUNTRY CLUB AT BOULDER HILLS
PU-87 Kingston Rd., Richmond, 02898, Washington County, (401)539-4653.
Holes: 18. **Yards:** 6,004/4,881. **Par:** 70/70. **Course Rating:** 69.1/67.7. **Slope:** 131/126. **Green Fee:** $25/$52. **Cart Fee:** Included in Green Fee. **Walking Policy:** Mandatory cart. **Walkability:** 5. **Opened:** 1995. **Architect:** Tripp Davis III. **Season:** March-Dec. **High:** June-Sept. **To obtain tee times:** Call up to 5 days in advance. **Miscellaneous:** Range (grass/mats), club rentals, credit cards (MC, V, AE).
Reader Comments: Challenging, many blind shots ... Appropriately named ... Carts on paths only ... Mountain course, can't see some landing areas ... Played free on casino points! ... You'll figure out why they named it Boulder Hills ... Narrow, target golf ... Still rough around the edges ... Gets better every season ... Position is everything.

★★★½ GREEN VALLEY COUNTRY CLUB
SP-371 Union St., Portsmouth, 02871, Newport County, (401)849-2162, 5 miles N of Newport.
Holes: 18. **Yards:** 6,830/5,459. **Par:** 71/71. **Course Rating:** 72.0/69.5. **Slope:** 126/120. **Green Fee:** $30/$33. **Cart Fee:** $22/cart. **Walking Policy:** Walking at certain times. **Walkability:** 3. **Opened:** 1957. **Architect:** Manuel Raposa. **Season:** March-Dec. **High:** May-Oct. **To obtain tee times:** Call three days in advance. **Miscellaneous:** Reduced fees (weekdays, low season, twilight), metal spikes, range (grass), club rentals, credit cards (MC, V, AE, D).

RHODE ISLAND

Reader Comments: Old course, tiny greens; good pace of play ... Tee times hard to get ... Great pro shop ... Challenging ... Beautiful views of Narragansett Bay ... A real gem, always look forward to a chance to play here ... Difficult to walk, but worth it.

★★★ LAUREL LANE GOLF CLUB
SP-309 Laurel Lane, West Kingston, 02892, Washington County, (401)783-3844, 25 miles S of Providence.
Holes: 18. **Yards:** 6,031/5,381. **Par:** 71/70. **Course Rating:** 68.1/70.8. **Slope:** 113/115. **Green Fee:** $24/$28. **Cart Fee:** $20/cart. **Walking Policy:** Unrestricted walking. **Walkability:** 3. **Opened:** 1961. **Architect:** Richard Holly Sr./John Thoren/John Bota. **Season:** March-Dec. **High:** June-Sept. **To obtain tee times:** Call golf shop. **Miscellaneous:** Reduced fees (weekdays, low season, twilight, juniors), metal spikes, range (grass/mats), club rentals, credit cards (MC, V, D), beginner friendly.
Reader Comments: Short with some real quirky holes ... Don't let this one fool you, plays tough ... Slow play, very basic ... Front 9 is easy, back is very tight ... Strong back 9 ... Very challenging middle nine holes ... Short course, yet tough to score.

★½ MEADOW BROOK GOLF CLUB
PU-163 Kingstown Rd., Wyoming, 02898, Washington County, (401)539-8491, 32 miles S of Providence.
Holes: 18. **Yards:** 6,075/5,605. **Par:** 71/73. **Course Rating:** N/A. **Slope:** N/A. **Green Fee:** $12/$15. **Cart Fee:** $15/cart. **Walking Policy:** Unrestricted walking. **Walkability:** 2. **Opened:** 1929. **Architect:** Rob Roy Rawlings. **Season:** Apr-Feb. **High:** Jul-Aug. **To obtain tee times:** First come, first serve. **Miscellaneous:** Reduced fees (weekdays, low season, twilight), metal spikes, range (grass).

★★ MELODY HILL GOLF COURSE
PU-Off Saw Mill Rd., Harmony, 02829, Providence County, (401)949-9851, 15 miles S of Providence.
Holes: 18. **Yards:** 6,185/N/A. **Par:** 71. **Course Rating:** 69.0/N/A. **Slope:** 113. **Green Fee:** $19/$22. **Cart Fee:** $20/cart. **Walking Policy:** Unrestricted walking. **Walkability:** 3. **Opened:** 1967. **Architect:** Samuel Mitchell. **Season:** April-Nov. **High:** May-Aug. **To obtain tee times:** First come, first serve. **Miscellaneous:** Reduced fees (twilight, seniors), club rentals.

★★★★ MONTAUP COUNTRY CLUB
SP-500 Anthony Rd., Portsmouth, 02871, Newport County, (401)683-9107, 15 miles N of Newport.
Holes: 18. **Yards:** 6,429/5,430. **Par:** 71/73. **Course Rating:** 71.7/72.3. **Slope:** 126/120. **Green Fee:** $37/$42. **Cart Fee:** $28/cart. **Walking Policy:** Unrestricted walking. **Walkability:** 1. **Opened:** 1923. **Architect:** Geoffrey S. Cornish. **Season:** Year-round. **High:** May-Oct. **To obtain tee times:** Call golf shop. **Miscellaneous:** Club rentals, credit cards (MC, V).
Reader Comments: Great course, greens superb and fast, dry in winter ... Start on back nine if possible ... Good food ... Short but must be accurate ... Long iron play a plus ... Good walking course ... Toughest first hole anywhere.

★★★★ NORTH KINGSTOWN MUNICIPAL GOLF COURSE
PM-615 Callahan Road, North Kingstown, 02852, Washington County, (401)294-4051, 15 miles S of Providence.
Holes: 18. **Yards:** 6,161/5,227. **Par:** 70/70. **Course Rating:** 69.3/69.5. **Slope:** 123/115. **Green Fee:** $20/$31. **Cart Fee:** $24/cart. **Walking Policy:** Unrestricted walking. **Walkability:** 3. **Opened:** 1943. **Architect:** Unknown. **Season:** March-Dec. **High:** May-Oct. **To obtain tee times:** Call 2 days in advance beginning at 8 a.m. during regular season. **Miscellaneous:** Reduced fees (weekdays, low season, twilight, seniors, juniors), range (grass), club rentals.
Reader Comments: Tight fairways; nice greens ... Tough when wind blows ... Awesome challenge. Great clubhouse ... Nice Par 5's ... Runs on time ... Greens are best ... Straight is better than long here.

★★★½ RICHMOND COUNTRY CLUB
PU-74 Sandy Pond Rd., Richmond, 02832, Washington County, (401)364-9200, 30 miles S of Providence.
Holes: 18. **Yards:** 6,826/4,974. **Par:** 71/71. **Course Rating:** 72.1/70.4. **Slope:** 121/113. **Green Fee:** $25/$30. **Cart Fee:** $20/cart. **Walking Policy:** Unrestricted walking. **Walkability:** 1. **Opened:** 1993. **Architect:** Cornish & Silva. **Season:** April-Dec. **High:** June-Sept. **To obtain tee times:** Call one day in advance beginning at 7 a.m. **Miscellaneous:** Reduced fees (weekdays, twilight), club rentals, beginner friendly.
Reader Comments: Cape Cod style course ... Easy walking course ... Tee to green never a bad lie ... Pines evoke North Carolina ... Leave your woods at home ... Better markers needed ... Fairways like carpets ... Tough back 9 design ... Refreshing change of pace ... Make sure you stay for dinner ... Can score if you keep it straight.

RHODE ISLAND

★★★½ TRIGGS MEMORIAL GOLF COURSE
PU-1533 Chalkstone Ave., Providence, 02909, Providence County, (401)521-8460.
Holes: 18. **Yards:** 6,596/5,598. **Par:** 72/73. **Course Rating:** 71.9/N/A. **Slope:** 126/N/A. **Green Fee:** $29/$32. **Cart Fee:** $25/cart. **Walking Policy:** Unrestricted walking. **Walkability:** 2. **Opened:** 1933. **Architect:** Donald Ross. **Season:** Year-round. **High:** June-Aug. **To obtain tee times:** Call. **Miscellaneous:** Reduced fees (low season, seniors), metal spikes, club rentals, credit cards (MC, V).
Reader Comments: Fairways & greens were great ... Wide open, but long ... Shaggy on the edges, excellent greens ... Hidden Ross gem ... Good course layout ... Worth a look!

WASHINGTON VILLAGE GOLF COURSE
PU-2 Fairway Dr., Coventry, 02816, Kent County, (401)823-0010, 4 miles E of Warwick.
Holes: 9. **Yards:** 2,525/1,993. **Par:** 33/33. **Course Rating:** N/A. **Slope:** N/A. **Green Fee:** $18/$19. **Cart Fee:** $21/cart. **Walking Policy:** Unrestricted walking. **Walkability:** 2. **Opened:** 1970. **Architect:** Karl Augenstein. **Season:** Year-round. **High:** April-Sept. **Miscellaneous:** Reduced fees (weekdays, low season, seniors, juniors), metal spikes, club rentals, credit cards (MC, V), beginner friendly (school programs, lessons).

★★★½ WINNAPAUG COUNTRY CLUB
SP-184 Shore Rd., Westerly, 02891, Washington County, (401)596-1237, 30 miles S of Providence.
Holes: 18. **Yards:** 6,345/5,113. **Par:** 72/72. **Course Rating:** 70.6/69.1. **Slope:** 124/110. **Green Fee:** $30/$35. **Cart Fee:** $24/cart. **Walking Policy:** Unrestricted walking. **Walkability:** 3. **Opened:** 1922. **Architect:** Donald Ross. **Season:** Year-round. **High:** June-Sept. **To obtain tee times:** Call seven days in advance. **Miscellaneous:** Reduced fees (weekdays, resort guests, twilight, seniors, juniors), discount packages, metal spikes, range (grass), club rentals, lodging, credit cards (MC, V, AE).
Reader Comments: Decent course worth playing ... Improves every year ... Old Ross design grows on you ... Short but extremely tight ... Wind can be nasty, bump and run ... Great test ... I make it a point to play here at least once a year.

★½ THE AIKEN GOLF CLUB
SP-555 Highland Park Dr., Aiken, 29801, Aiken County, (803)649-6029, 20 miles N of Augusta, GA.
Holes: 18. **Yards:** 6,200/5,400. **Par:** 70/70. **Course Rating:** 68.0/N/A. **Slope:** 115/N/A. **Green Fee:** $9/$9. **Cart Fee:** $9/person. **Walking Policy:** Unrestricted walking. **Walkability:** 3. **Opened:** 1912. **Architect:** J.R. Inglis. **Season:** Year-round. **High:** Spring. **To obtain tee times:** Tee times are not required. **Miscellaneous:** Metal spikes.

★★★½ ARCADIAN SHORES GOLF CLUB
PU-701 Hilton Rd., Myrtle Beach, 29577, Horry County, (843)449-5217, (800)449-5217.
Holes: 18. **Yards:** 6,938/5,229. **Par:** 72/72. **Course Rating:** 73.2/69.9. **Slope:** 136/117. **Green Fee:** $39/$88. **Cart Fee:** Included in Green Fee. **Walking Policy:** Mandatory cart. **Walkability:** 3. **Opened:** 1974. **Architect:** Rees Jones. **Season:** Year-round. **High:** March-May/Oct. **To obtain tee times:** Call up to 1 year in advance or book a golf package through Wyndham Myrtle Beach Resort–1-800-248-9228. **Miscellaneous:** Reduced fees (low season, resort guests, juniors), discount packages, range (grass), club rentals, lodging (385 rooms), credit cards (MC, V, AE, D), beginner friendly (Arcadian classic golf school).
Reader Comments: Very plush ... Great variety of holes ... Beautiful old course ... Fun to play ... Friendly service; starter remembered us from 6 months ago ... Straight ahead golf ... Old-style course, very good test ... A must-play every time. Very fine ... A timeless, classic design, solid and joyful.

★★★★ ARROWHEAD COUNTRY CLUB
PU-1201 Burcal Rd., Myrtle Beach, 29577, Horry County, (843)236-3243, (800)236-3243, 3 miles W of Myrtle Beach.
Holes: 18. **Yards:** 6,666/4,812. **Par:** 72/72. **Course Rating:** 71.1/71.2. **Slope:** 130/116. **Green Fee:** $41/$90. **Cart Fee:** Included in Green Fee. **Walking Policy:** Mandatory cart. **Walkability:** 3. **Opened:** 1994. **Architect:** Tom Jackson/Ray Floyd. **Season:** Year-round. **High:** Spring/Fall. **To obtain tee times:** Book through accommodations host or call golf shop. **Miscellaneous:** Reduced fees (juniors), range (grass), club rentals, credit cards (MC, V, AE).
Reader Comments: Best-conditioned course I ever played ... Lots of water, always in good condition, tough but fair ... Loved it! ... Course and staff can get no better, must play ... Challenging, mature ... Good elevation changes ... Great condition, friendly, good value, great golf ... My pick of all Myrtle Beach courses.

★★★½ AZALEA SANDS GOLF CLUB
PU-2100 Hwy. 17 S., North Myrtle Beach, 29582, Horry County, (843)272-6191, (800)252-2312, 10 miles N of Myrtle Beach.
Holes: 18. **Yards:** 6,902/5,172. **Par:** 72/72. **Course Rating:** 72.5/70.2. **Slope:** 123/119. **Green Fee:** $26/$60. **Cart Fee:** Included in Green Fee. **Walking Policy:** Walking at certain times. **Walkability:** 1. **Opened:** 1972. **Architect:** Gene Hamm. **Season:** Year-round. **High:** Spring/Fall. **To obtain tee times:** Call golf shop. **Miscellaneous:** Reduced fees (low season, resort guests, twilight, juniors), discount packages, metal spikes, club rentals, credit cards (MC, V, AE, D).
Reader Comments: Relaxing, fair test of skills ... Fast, good conditions ... Fun to play, well maintained ... Very courteous staff ... Good, solid beach course, great greens ... Well established, well kept ... Distance computers on carts were great ... Nice track, very accommodating, old, enjoyable course.

BAY TREE GOLF PLANTATION
PU-P.O. Box 240, North Myrtle Beach, 29597, Horry County, (843)399-6166, (800)845-6191, 8 miles N of Myrtle Beach.
★★★½ GOLD COURSE
Holes: 18. **Yards:** 6,942/5,264. **Par:** 72/72. **Course Rating:** 72.0/69.7. **Slope:** 135/117. **Green Fee:** $19/$42. **Cart Fee:** $20/person. **Walking Policy:** Walking at certain times. **Walkability:** 2. **Opened:** 1972. **Architect:** George Fazio/Russell Breedon. **Season:** Year-round. **High:** March-April. **To obtain tee times:** Call anytime. **Miscellaneous:** Reduced fees (low season, juniors), discount packages, metal spikes, range (grass), club rentals, lodging (350 rooms), credit cards (MC, V).
Reader Comments: Sweet track, could spend the whole day! ... Large trees, nice landscape ... Fine test of golf, well maintained ... Test for average golfer ... Warm up and be ready ... Staff takes good care of you ... Enjoyable, fun course ... Unmatched customer service ... Good value. Fun to play.
Special Notes: 1977 LPGA Tour Championship
★★★½ GREEN COURSE
Holes: 18. **Yards:** 7,044/5,362. **Par:** 72/72. **Course Rating:** 72.5/69.0. **Slope:** 135/118. **Green Fee:** $19/$42. **Cart Fee:** $20/cart. **Walking Policy:** Walking at certain times. **Walkability:** 2. **Opened:** 1972. **Architect:** George Fazio/Russell Breedon. **Season:** Year-round. **High:** March-April. **To obtain tee times:** Call anytime. **Miscellaneous:** Reduced fees (low season, juniors), discount packages, metal spikes, range (grass), club rentals, lodging (350 rooms), credit cards (MC, V).

Reader Comments: Good layout, fun to play, long ... Stay away if you don't like water ... Nothing special but some good holes ... Challenging ... Pinehurst in Myrtle Beach ... Very well kept and playable ... Recently renovated. Excellent condition, superb service ... Very scenic, tight.

★★★½ **SILVER COURSE**

Holes: 18. **Yards:** 6,871/5,417. **Par:** 72/72. **Course Rating:** 70.5/69.0. **Slope:** 131/116. **Green Fee:** $19/$42. **Cart Fee:** $20/cart. **Walking Policy:** Walking at certain times. **Walkability:** 2. **Opened:** 1972. **Architect:** George Fazio/Russell Breedon. **Season:** Year-round. **High:** March-April. **To obtain tee times:** Call anytime. **Miscellaneous:** Reduced fees (low season, juniors), discount packages, metal spikes, range (grass), club rentals, lodging (350 rooms), credit cards (MC, V).

Reader Comments: Nice resort ... Good course ... Good 54-holes complex for average golfer ... Good course layout, great value ... Enjoyable, fun course ... Open, no trouble, good conditions ... Fair condition.

★★★½ **BEACHWOOD GOLF CLUB**

R-1520 Hwy. 17 South , North Myrtle Beach, 29582, Horry County, (803)272-6168, (800)526-4889, 12 miles N of Myrtle Beach. **E-mail:** info@beachwood.com. **Web:** www.beachwoodgolf.com. **Holes:** 18. **Yards:** 6,844/4,947. **Par:** 72/72. **Course Rating:** 71.4/67.6. **Slope:** 120/111. **Green Fee:** $18/$46. **Cart Fee:** $20/person. **Walking Policy:** Mandatory cart. **Walkability:** 1. **Opened:** 1968. **Architect:** Gene Hamm. **Season:** Year-round. **High:** March-April/Oct. **To obtain tee times:** Call or e-mail. **Miscellaneous:** Reduced fees (low season, twilight, seniors, juniors), discount packages, range (grass), club rentals, credit cards (MC, V, AE).

Reader Comments: You'll like putting the ball here ... Like playing on carpet ... Success hasn't spoiled this old standby; it's fun and close to town ... Very playable course ... Nice people ... Old but good ... The greens here are as good as it gets ... Excellent condition, excellent value ... Tough to beat value.

BELLE TERRE GOLF COURSE

R-4073 U.S. Hwy. 501, Myrtle Beach, 29579, Horry County, (843)236-8888, (800)340-0072, 3 miles NW of Myrtle Beach.

★★★½ **CHAMPIONSHIP COURSE**

Holes: 18. **Yards:** 7,013/5,049. **Par:** 72/72. **Course Rating:** 74.0/69.6. **Slope:** 134/126. **Green Fee:** $20/$70. **Cart Fee:** $18/person. **Walking Policy:** Mandatory cart. **Walkability:** 2. **Opened:** 1995. **Architect:** Rees Jones. **Season:** Year-round. **High:** Spring/Fall. **To obtain tee times:** Call or make arrangements with your accommodations golf director. **Miscellaneous:** Reduced fees (low season, resort guests, juniors), discount packages, range (grass), club rentals, credit cards (MC, V, AE, D).

Reader Comments: Very demanding for accuracy ... Where did they get all that water? ... Nice, but too expensive ... Beautiful ... Bring extra balls ... Very enjoyable ... Good shape, fast play, great layout! ... Mounds and bunkers everywhere ... A good solid course ... Very nice some tough holes, good value.

★★★½ **SKINS COURSE**

Holes: 18. **Yards:** 3,201/2,802. **Par:** 58/58. **Course Rating:** 57.8. **Slope:** 93. **Green Fee:** $15/$30. **Cart Fee:** $15/person. **Walking Policy:** Unrestricted walking. **Walkability:** 1. **Opened:** 1995. **Architect:** Rees Jones. **Season:** Year-round. **High:** Spring/Fall. **To obtain tee times:** Call. **Miscellaneous:** Reduced fees (low season, resort guests, juniors), discount packages, metal spikes, range (grass), club rentals, credit cards (MC, V, AE, D).

Reader Comments: Best service I've ever seen. ... Need to choose the right set of tees to play ... Close to awesome! ... Enjoyable ... Best executive course ever played ... Service was outstanding ... A trip to reality for hackers.

★★½ **BERKELEY COUNTRY CLUB**

SP-Old Hwy. 52, Moncks Corner, 29461, Berkeley County, (843)761-4880, 20 miles N of Charleston.

Holes: 18. **Yards:** 6,696/5,100. **Par:** 72/72. **Course Rating:** 71.2/67.9. **Slope:** 114/106. **Green Fee:** $15/$19. **Cart Fee:** $12/person. **Walking Policy:** Walking at certain times. **Walkability:** 1. **Opened:** 1959. **Architect:** George Cobb. **Season:** Year-round. **High:** April-Aug. **To obtain tee times:** Call 2 days in advance. **Miscellaneous:** Reduced fees (weekdays, low season, seniors, juniors), range (grass), club rentals, credit cards (MC, V).

Reader Comments: Nice course, nice setting, nice people ... Good scoring opportunities.

★★★★ **BLACKMOOR GOLF CLUB**

R-6100 Longwood Rd., Hwy. 707, Murrells Inlet, 29576, Harry County, (843)650-5555, (800)650-5555, 12 miles S of Myrtle Beach. **Holes:** 18. **Yards:** 6,614/4,807. **Par:** 72/72. **Course Rating:** 71.1/67.9. **Slope:** 126/115. **Green Fee:** $23/$70. **Cart Fee:** $18/person. **Walking Policy:** Mandatory cart. **Walkability:** 3. **Opened:** 1990. **Architect:** Gary Player. **Season:** Year-round. **High:** Spring/Fall. **To obtain tee times:** Call golf shop. **Miscellaneous:** Reduced fees (low season, resort guests, juniors), discount packages, metal spikes, range (grass), club rentals, credit cards (MC, V).

SOUTH CAROLINA

Reader Comments: Super but quirky layout ... Very nice, very costly ... Excellent course. Expensive ... Beautiful layout ... Great course, nice clubhouse ... Course winds, then woods, my favorite kind ... A must play ... Dogleg city ... Solid course, lots of water ... Great condition ... Very good service.

★★★½ BONNIE BRAE GOLF CLUB
SP-1116 Ashmore Bridge Road, Greenville, 29605, Greenville County, (864)277-9838, 3 miles W of Mauldin.
Holes: 18. **Yards:** 6,484/5,316. **Par:** 72/74. **Course Rating:** 70.7/69.6. **Slope:** 127/116. **Green Fee:** $15/$22. **Cart Fee:** $10/person. **Walking Policy:** Unrestricted walking. **Walkability:** 2. **Opened:** 1961. **Architect:** Charles Willimon. **Season:** Year-round. **High:** April-May-June. **To obtain tee times:** Tee times accepted 7 days in advance. Call golf shop. **Miscellaneous:** Range (grass), club rentals, credit cards (MC, V), beginner friendly.
Reader Comments: Wide open. Big greens ... Great course! ... Wide fairways, large firm greens ... A challenge ... Fun to walk ... Challenging playable layout ... Good walking course, open, well maintained ... Outstanding service.

★★½ BOSCOBEL GOLF CLUB
SP-Hwy. 76, Pendleton, 29670, Anderson County, (864)646-3991, 28 miles SW of Greenville.
Holes: 18. **Yards:** 6,400/5,023. **Par:** 71/72. **Course Rating:** 69.8/67.8. **Slope:** 115/114. **Green Fee:** $13/$19. **Cart Fee:** $18/cart. **Walking Policy:** Unrestricted walking. **Walkability:** 3. **Opened:** 1932. **Architect:** Fred Bolton. **Season:** Year-round. **High:** March-Aug. **To obtain tee times:** Call 1 day in advance. **Miscellaneous:** Reduced fees (twilight), discount packages, metal spikes, credit cards (MC, V).
Reader Comments: Good course for beginners & high handicappers ... Good older course. Condition great. Owners putting in $ ... Nice friendly staff, good test, good value ... Fun course.

BUCK CREEK GOLF CLUB
PU-701 Bucks Trail, Hwy. 9, Longs, 29568, Horry County, (843)399-2660, (800)344-0982, 6 miles NE of North Myrtle Beach.
Holes: 27. **Green Fee:** $22/$66. **Cart Fee:** $18/person. **Walking Policy:** Mandatory cart. **Walkability:** 3. **Opened:** 1990. **Architect:** Tom Jackson. **Season:** Year-round. **High:** Spring/Fall. **To obtain tee times:** Call.
★★★½ CYPRESS/TUPELO
Yards: 6,865/4,956. **Par:** 72/72. **Course Rating:** 72.4/68.4. **Slope:** 132/124. **Miscellaneous:** Reduced fees (low season, twilight, juniors), discount packages, metal spikes, range (grass), club rentals, credit cards (MC, V).
Reader Comments: Best greens in Myrtle, much improved condition ... Turned into a real gem ... Tough, challenging ... I'm in heaven, do we have to go home?... Great layout, excellent value ... Water everywhere ... Target golf, fun to play, lots of water ... Friendly staff, lots of challenges ... Ate my shorts. Too much water.
★★★½ MEADOW/CYPRESS
Yards: 6,751/4,972. **Par:** 72/72. **Course Rating:** 71.1/67.5. **Slope:** 126/117. **Miscellaneous:** Reduced fees (weekdays, low season, resort guests, twilight, seniors, juniors), discount packages, metal spikes, range (grass), club rentals, credit cards (MC, V).
Reader Comments: Nice course; challenging holes ... Good value, good course ... Tight, challenging, always enjoyable ... Three different nines ... Too much water ... Player-friendly golf from white tees ... Water everywhere ... The courses are fantastic.
★★★½ MEADOW/TUPELO
Yards: 6,729/4,972. **Par:** 72/72. **Course Rating:** 71.6/67.5. **Slope:** 126/117. **Miscellaneous:** Reduced fees (low season, twilight, juniors), discount packages, metal spikes, range (grass), club rentals, credit cards (MC, V).
Reader Comments: Lean & mean, must drive well ... Mixture of holes from very easy to difficult.

BURNING RIDGE GOLF CLUB
R-Hwy. 501 W., Conway, 29577, Horry County, (843)347-0538, (800)833-6337, 5 miles E of Myrtle Beach. **Web:** www.linksgroup.com.
★★★ EAST COURSE
Holes: 18. **Yards:** 6,780/4,524. **Par:** 72/72. **Course Rating:** 73.1/65.4. **Slope:** 132/111. **Green Fee:** $29/$65. **Cart Fee:** Included in Green Fee. **Walking Policy:** Mandatory cart. **Walkability:** 3. **Opened:** 1985. **Architect:** Gene Hamm. **Season:** Year-round. **High:** Fall/Spring. **To obtain tee times:** Call 2 days in advance. **Miscellaneous:** Reduced fees (weekdays, low season, twilight, juniors), discount packages, range (grass), club rentals, credit cards (MC, V, D).
Reader Comments: Well-protected greens add challenge ... Good course, accommodating ... Difficult course ... Good greens, great staff, fun course.
★★★½ WEST COURSE
Holes: 18. **Yards:** 6,714/4,831. **Par:** 72/72. **Course Rating:** 73.0/66.2. **Slope:** 128/112. **Green Fee:** $29/$65. **Cart Fee:** Included in Green Fee. **Walking Policy:** Mandatory cart. **Walkability:** 3. **Opened:** 1980. **Architect:** Gene Hamm. **Season:** Year-round. **High:** Spring/Fall. **To obtain**

tee times: Call 2 days in advance. **Miscellaneous:** Reduced fees (weekdays, low season, twilight, juniors), discount packages, range (grass), club rentals, credit cards (MC, V, D).
Reader Comments: Well-maintained with a very courteous staff ... Water, water everywhere, bring your floaters ... Average.

★★★★½ CALEDONIA GOLF & FISH CLUB *Service, Condition+*
PU-369 Caledonia Dr., Pawleys Island, 29585, Georgetown County, (843)237-3675, (800)483-6800, 1 miles S of Pawleys Island. **Web:** www.fishclub.com.
Holes: 18. **Yards:** 6,526/4,957. **Par:** 70/70. **Course Rating:** 70.9/68.2. **Slope:** 132/113. **Green Fee:** $75/$130. **Cart Fee:** Included in Green Fee. **Walking Policy:** Unrestricted walking.
Walkability: 3. **Opened:** 1994. **Architect:** Mike Strantz. **Season:** Year-round. **High:** Spring/Fall.
To obtain tee times: Call golf shop or hotel golf director for tee times. **Miscellaneous:** Discount packages, club rentals, credit cards (MC, V, AE, D), beginner friendly.
Notes: Ranked 13th in 1999 Best in State; 31st in 1996 America's Top 75 Upscale Courses.
Reader Comments: No. 1 course in Myrtle Beach ... Very nice layout, good condition ... One of the prettiest courses anywhere ... Great course, need all the shots ... Excellent, one of the best ... Challenge for all handicaps ... Gorgeous live oaks ... A must ... Hands down best in Myrtle Beach.

★★★ CALHOUN COUNTRY CLUB
SP-Rte. 3 Country Club Rd., St. Matthews, 29135, Calhoun County, (843)823-2465, (877)501-3177, 3 miles S of St. Matthews.
Holes: 18. **Yards:** 6,339/4,812. **Par:** 71/71. **Course Rating:** 70.9/66.4. **Slope:** 119/110. **Green Fee:** $10/$25. **Cart Fee:** $10/person. **Walking Policy:** Walking at certain times. **Walkability:** 4.
Opened: 1957. **Architect:** Ellis Maples. **Season:** Year-round. **High:** March-April. **To obtain tee times:** Call golf shop. **Miscellaneous:** Reduced fees (weekdays, twilight, seniors, juniors), metal spikes, range (grass), club rentals, credit cards (MC, V), beginner friendly (clinics and lessons).
Reader Comments: Definitely worth the drive ... Good course ... Outstanding hot dogs ... Too difficult from tips with any wind ... Many elevation changes. Pretty par 3s. A jewel in th middle of nowhere ... Nice, country golf course ... Good course with some tough holes in rural area ... A hidden treasure.

★½ CAROLINA DOWNS COUNTRY CLUB
PU-294 Shiloh Rd., York, 29745, York County, (803)684-5878, 18 miles S of Charlotte, NC.
Holes: 18. **Yards:** 6,335/4,624. **Par:** 72/72. **Course Rating:** 69.5/67.4. **Slope:** 141/123. **Green Fee:** $23/$28. **Cart Fee:** Included in Green Fee. **Walking Policy:** Walking at certain times.
Walkability: 2. **Opened:** 1984. **Architect:** Boony Harper. **Season:** Year-round. **High:** May-Oct.
To obtain tee times: No starting times. **Miscellaneous:** Reduced fees (weekdays, low season, seniors, juniors), discount packages, range (grass), credit cards (MC, V, AE, D), beginner friendly.

CAROLINA SPRINGS GOLF CLUB
SP-1680 Scuffletown Rd., Fountain Inn, 29644, Greenville County, (864)862-3551, 8 miles S of Greenville.
Holes: 27. **Green Fee:** $30/$42. **Cart Fee:** Included in Green Fee. **Walkability:** 2. **Opened:** 1968. **Architect:** Russel Breaden. **Season:** Year-round. **High:** April-Sept. **To obtain tee times:** Call up to 5 days in advance. **Miscellaneous:** Reduced fees (weekdays, low season, twilight, seniors, juniors), discount packages, range (grass/mats), club rentals, credit cards (MC, V, AE, D).
★★★ PINES/CEDAR
Yards: 6,676/5,084. **Par:** 72/72. **Course Rating:** 72.6/68.9. **Slope:** 132/116. **Walking Policy:** Walking at certain times.
Reader Comments: Three 9s that are divine with good facilities. Love it for the price ... Good value, mediocre layout ... 27 well-maintained holes.
★★★ WILLOWS/CEDAR
Yards: 6,643/5,135. **Par:** 72/72. **Course Rating:** 72.0/68.5. **Slope:** 126/113. **Walking Policy:** Unrestricted walking.
Reader Comments: Nice course ... Every hole is different.
★★★ WILLOWS/PINES
Yards: 6,815/5,223. **Par:** 72/72. **Course Rating:** 72.8/69.3. **Slope:** 130/119. **Walking Policy:** Walking at certain times.
Reader Comments: Willows and Pines OK ... Two mature 9, a fair test of accuracy ... Good public course, playable for all golfers.

★★★★ CEDAR CREEK GOLF CLUB
SP-2475 Club Dr., Aiken, 29803, Aiken County, (803)648-4206, 5 miles S of Aiken.
E-mail: cedarcr005@aol.com.
Holes: 18. **Yards:** 7,206/5,182. **Par:** 72/72. **Course Rating:** 74.1/68.6. **Slope:** 142/113. **Green Fee:** $36/$36. **Cart Fee:** Included in Green Fee. **Walking Policy:** Walking at certain times.
Walkability: 4. **Opened:** 1991. **Architect:** Arthur Hills. **Season:** Year-round. **High:** April-Sept. **To obtain tee times:** Call 7 days in advance. **Miscellaneous:** Reduced fees (weekdays, low season, twilight, seniors, juniors), discount packages, metal spikes, range (grass), club rentals, credit cards (MC, V, AE).

SOUTH CAROLINA

Reader Comments: Wildlife refuge, deer and turkeys, very nice ... Long, tough and fun! Great conditions, a real gem ... First class. Perfect greens. Beautiful clubhouse ... Excellent all around ... Many hillside holes ... Skills tester.

★★½ CHARLESTON MUNICIPAL GOLF COURSE
PM-2110 Maybank Hwy., Charleston, 29412, Charleston County, (803)795-6517.
Holes: 18. **Yards:** 6,411/5,202. **Par:** 72/72. **Course Rating:** 70.2/69.2. **Slope:** 112/114. **Green Fee:** $10/$15. **Cart Fee:** $20/cart. **Walking Policy:** Unrestricted walking. **Walkability:** 1. **Opened:** 1927. **Architect:** John E. Adams. **Season:** Year-round. **High:** Spring/Fall. **To obtain tee times:** Call or come in 7 days in advance for threesomes and foursomes. **Miscellaneous:** Reduced fees (twilight, seniors, juniors), metal spikes, range (grass/mats), club rentals, credit cards (MC, V).
Reader Comments: Has some interesting holes ... Heavy traffic, great shape ... Cheap, accessible ... Traditional design. Small greens ... Decent municipal course ... Very flat, nothing tricky ... Interesting layout, more difficult than appears.

★★★½ CHARLESTON NATIONAL COUNTRY CLUB
SP-1360 National Dr., Mount Pleasant, 29466, Charleston County, (843)884-7799, 10 miles E of Charleston. **E-mail:** bartwolfe@aol.com. **Web:** www.cngolfacademy.com.
Holes: 18. **Yards:** 6,975/5,103. **Par:** 72/72. **Course Rating:** 74.0/70.8. **Slope:** 140/126. **Green Fee:** $32/$75. **Cart Fee:** Included in Green Fee. **Walking Policy:** Mandatory cart. **Walkability:** 3. **Opened:** 1989. **Architect:** Rees Jones. **Season:** Year-round. **High:** Spring/Fall. **To obtain tee times:** Call. **Miscellaneous:** Reduced fees (weekdays, low season, resort guests, twilight, seniors, juniors), discount packages, metal spikes, range (grass/mats), club rentals, credit cards (MC, V, D), beginner friendly (beginner, junior, ladies, seniors).
Reader Comments: Best inland course in Charleston ... Wide fairways, narrow greens, great views ... Beautiful location, great course ... Friendly management ... Outstanding in every way, greens perfect. Fast! ... Tough venue, especially when wind is up ... Very nice, extremely challenging ... Could be best course in Charleston.

★★★★ CHERAW STATE PARK GOLF COURSE
PU-100 State Park Rd., Cheraw, 29520, Chesterfield County, (803)537-2215, (800)868-9630, 40 miles of Florence.
Holes: 18. **Yards:** 6,900/5,408. **Par:** 72/72. **Course Rating:** 73.4/70.8. **Slope:** 130/120. **Green Fee:** $13/$18. **Cart Fee:** $12/person. **Walkability:** N/A. **Architect:** Tom Jackson. **Season:** Year-round. **High:** March-June. **To obtain tee times:** Call. **Miscellaneous:** Reduced fees (weekdays), discount packages, metal spikes, range (grass/mats), lodging, credit cards (MC, V).
Reader Comments: Challenging layout, scenic ... Will test any golfer ... Very good value and some interesting holes ... Beautiful ... Good course, beautiful, easy on wallet ... Rolling, mountainous terrain, beautiful!

★★★ CHEROKEE VALLEY GOLF CLUB
SP-253 Chinquapin Rd., Tigerville, 29688, Greenville County, (864)895-7689, 15 miles N of Greenville.
Holes: 18. **Yards:** 6,713/4,545. **Par:** 72/72. **Course Rating:** 72.1/69.7. **Slope:** 135/119. **Green Fee:** $25/$39. **Cart Fee:** Included in Green Fee. **Walking Policy:** Mandatory cart. **Walkability:** 5. **Opened:** 1993. **Architect:** P.B. Dye. **Season:** Year-round. **High:** March-Oct. **To obtain tee times:** Call up to 5 days in advance. **Miscellaneous:** Reduced fees (weekdays, low season, twilight, seniors, juniors), discount packages, metal spikes, range (grass/mats), club rentals, credit cards (MC, V, AE).
Reader Comments: Very tough ... Good layout, poor greens ... Good course, challenging holes, had fun! ... Hard to find, harder to leave ... Great use of terrain in layout, just needs work ... Good range & putting green.

★★★ CHESTER GOLF CLUB
SP-770 Old Richburg Rd., Chester, 29706, Chester County, (803)581-5733, 45 miles S of Charlotte.
Holes: 18. **Yards:** 6,811/5,347. **Par:** 72/72. **Course Rating:** 72.0/70.1. **Slope:** 124/116. **Green Fee:** $20/$25. **Cart Fee:** $14/person. **Walking Policy:** Walking at certain times. **Walkability:** 2. **Opened:** 1971. **Architect:** Russell Breeden. **Season:** Year-round. **High:** April-Oct. **To obtain tee times:** Call. **Miscellaneous:** Range (grass), credit cards (MC, V).
Reader Comments: Tight landing areas off tee ... I'll go back ... Well kept, fun to play ... Good golf, seldom crowded ... Friendly folks, not very challenging ... Course OK, wide open.

★★ CHICKASAW POINT COUNTRY CLUB
500 Hogan Dr., Westminster, 29693, Oconee County, (864)972-9623.
Special Notes: Call club for further information.

THE CLUB AT SEABROOK ISLAND *Service*
R-1002 Landfall Way, Seabrook Island, 29455, Charleston County, (843)768-1000, 20 miles S of Charleston.

SOUTH CAROLINA

★★★★ **CROOKED OAKS COURSE**
Holes: 18. **Yards:** 6,832/5,250. **Par:** 72/72. **Course Rating:** 73.2/70.1. **Slope:** 126/119. **Green Fee:** $50/$120. **Cart Fee:** Included in Green Fee. **Walking Policy:** Mandatory cart. **Walkability:** 2. **Opened:** 1982. **Architect:** Robert T. Jones Sr. **Season:** Year-round. **High:** Feb.-Aug. **To obtain tee times:** Must be a resort guest to play. Tee times may be reserved with golf package. **Miscellaneous:** Discount packages, range (grass), club rentals, lodging, credit cards (MC, V, AE, D).
Reader Comments: Very pleasant, expensive ... Nice ... Course in fair condition ... Long and tough ... A real treat. Beautiful layout ... Left driver in bag most of the day ... Wonderful course will be better.

★★★★ **OCEAN WINDS COURSE**
Holes: 18. **Yards:** 6,805/5,524. **Par:** 72/72. **Course Rating:** 73.5/73.1. **Slope:** 130/127. **Green Fee:** $50/$120. **Cart Fee:** Included in Green Fee. **Walking Policy:** Mandatory cart. **Walkability:** N/A. **Opened:** 1976. **Architect:** Willard Byrd. **Season:** Year-round. **High:** Feb.-Aug. **To obtain tee times:** Must be a resort guest to play. Tee times may be reserved with golf packages. **Miscellaneous:** Discount packages, range (grass), club rentals, lodging, credit cards (MC, V, AE, D).
Reader Comments: Enjoyable ... Best of the two courses ... Great links holes ... Winds make it a great challenge ... Great service from check in ... Great experience, great people, houses don't intrude ... Target golf by the ocean, fun ... All-around nice greens. Friendly ... I love this course.

★★½ **COBB'S GLEN COUNTRY CLUB**
SP-2201 Cobb's Way, Anderson, 29621, Anderson County, (864)226-7688, (800)624-7688, 3 miles N of Anderson. **E-mail:** cobbsglen@carol.net. **Web:** www.cobbsglen.com.
Holes: 18. **Yards:** 7,002/5,312. **Par:** 72/72. **Course Rating:** 72.3/72.0. **Slope:** 129/121. **Green Fee:** $20/$25. **Cart Fee:** $10/. **Walking Policy:** Walking at certain times. **Walkability:** 3. **Opened:** 1975. **Architect:** George Cobb. **Season:** Year-round. **High:** April-Oct. **To obtain tee times:** Call 2 days in advance. **Miscellaneous:** Reduced fees (weekdays, seniors, juniors), discount packages, metal spikes, range (grass/mats), club rentals, lodging, credit cards (MC, V, AE), beginner friendly (get linked).
Reader Comments: Friendly staff ... Good layout ... Fun course when in shape ... Long course from back markers ... Challenging, you get use of all your clubs ... Good test of golf, fast greens ... Excellent big fast greens, tough from tips.

★½ **COLDSTREAM COUNTRY CLUB**
SP-Hwy. 60/Lake Murray Blvd., Irmo, 29063, Lexington County, (803)781-0114, 10 miles NW of Columbia. **E-mail:** golf@the isp.net.
Holes: 18. **Yards:** 6,155/5,097. **Par:** 71/71. **Course Rating:** 70.1/68.7. **Slope:** 122. **Green Fee:** $24/$35. **Cart Fee:** Included in Green Fee. **Walking Policy:** Mandatory cart. **Walkability:** 3. **Opened:** 1974. **Season:** Year-round. **High:** April-Oct. **To obtain tee times:** Call 48 hours in advance. Members have priority tee times on weekends. **Miscellaneous:** Reduced fees (weekdays, low season, resort guests, twilight, seniors, juniors), discount packages, club rentals, credit cards (MC, V, AE).

★★★½ **COLONIAL CHARTERS GOLF CLUB**
PU-301 Charter Dr., Longs, 29301, Horry County, (843)399-4653, (800)833-6337, 20 miles N of Myrtle Beach.
Holes: 18. **Yards:** 6,769/5,079. **Par:** 72/72. **Course Rating:** 73.0/70.2. **Slope:** 131/120. **Green Fee:** $29/$65. **Cart Fee:** Included in Green Fee. **Walking Policy:** Mandatory cart. **Walkability:** 3. **Opened:** 1988. **Architect:** John Simpson. **Season:** Year-round. **High:** Spring/Fall. **To obtain tee times:** Call golf shop. **Miscellaneous:** Reduced fees (low season, twilight, juniors), discount packages, range (grass), club rentals, lodging, credit cards (MC, V, D).
Reader Comments: Good layout ... One expects to find water at the beach; you do here ... Nice layout, fairways great condition ... Out a little but worth the ride ... Very user friendly.

★★★½ **COOPER'S CREEK GOLF CLUB**
SP-700 Wagener Hwy. #113, Pelion, 29123, Lexington County, (803)894-3666, (800)828-8463, 25 miles W of Columbia.
Holes: 18. **Yards:** 6,582/4,565. **Par:** 72/73. **Course Rating:** 70.6/63.6. **Slope:** 131/99. **Green Fee:** $8/$15. **Cart Fee:** $15/person. **Walking Policy:** Unrestricted walking. **Walkability:** 3. **Opened:** 1973. **Architect:** Red Chase. **Season:** Year-round. **High:** April-Oct. **To obtain tee times:** Call up to 3 days in advance. **Miscellaneous:** Range (grass), club rentals, credit cards (MC, V, AE).
Reader Comments: Very decent course, lots of water holes ... Lots of fun ... Good golf experience, though it is long & tight.

★★★½ **COOSAW CREEK COUNTRY CLUB**
SP-4210 Club Course Dr., North Charleston, 29420, Dorchester County, (843)767-9000, 10 miles NW of Charleston. **Web:** www.coosawcreek.com.
Holes: 18. **Yards:** 6,593/5,064. **Par:** 71/71. **Course Rating:** 71.3/69.1. **Slope:** 129/117. **Green Fee:** $18/$37. **Cart Fee:** $17/person. **Walking Policy:** Walking at certain times. **Walkability:** 3. **Opened:**

1993. **Architect:** Arthur Hills. **Season:** Year-round. **High:** Spring/Fall. **To obtain tee times:** Call no more than 7 days in advance. **Miscellaneous:** Reduced fees (weekdays, low season, juniors), discount packages, metal spikes, range (grass), club rentals, credit cards (MC, V, AE).
Reader Comments: Good course ... Nice greens ... Fair layout, great greens ... Good service, fun ... Always in great condition ... Nice greens, consistent ... Very enjoyable ... Fun course ... Nice course, friendly people ... A real test, nice greens. A lot of fun (and good golf).

★★★ COUNTRY CLUB OF BEAUFORT
SP-8 Barnwell Dr., Beaufort, 29902, Beaufort County, (843)522-1605, (800)869-1617, 40 miles N of Hilton Head.
Holes: 18. **Yards:** 6,506/4,764. **Par:** 72/72. **Course Rating:** 71.5/67.8. **Slope:** 130/120. **Green Fee:** $35/$60. **Cart Fee:** Included in Green Fee. **Walking Policy:** Walking at certain times. **Walkability:** 2. **Opened:** 1973. **Architect:** Russell Breedon. **Season:** Year-round. **High:** Spring/Fall. **To obtain tee times:** Call up to 7 days in advance. **Miscellaneous:** Reduced fees (twilight, juniors), discount packages, range (grass), club rentals, credit cards (MC, V, D).
Reader Comments: Nice layout, a lot of wildlife ... Truly enjoyable at reasonable cost ... Greens too long, pace excellent ... Good golf, Nos.17 & 18 great closers ... Fun course, good value ... Great pace of play & very low cost.

★★★★ COUNTRY CLUB OF HILTON HEAD
SP-70 Skull Creek Dr., Hilton Head Island, 29926, Beaufort County, (843)681-4653, 35 miles NE of Savannah, GA.
Holes: 18. **Yards:** 6,919/5,373. **Par:** 72/72. **Course Rating:** 73.6/71.3. **Slope:** 132/123. **Green Fee:** $52/$85. **Cart Fee:** Included in Green Fee. **Walking Policy:** Mandatory cart. **Walkability:** 2. **Opened:** 1987. **Architect:** Rees Jones. **Season:** Year-round. **High:** Spring/Fall. **To obtain tee times:** Call up to 90 days in advance. **Miscellaneous:** Reduced fees (low season, twilight), metal spikes, range (grass/mats), club rentals, credit cards (MC, V, AE, D, Diners Club).
Reader Comments: Nice course, enjoyable ... Great value ... Beautiful layout ... Great staff ... Staff and facilities wonderful ... Excellent course ... Short, but nice gem on Hilton Head ... Great course, always in excellent condition, great facilities ... Always a pleasure, even with alligators!

★★★★ CROWFIELD GOLF & COUNTRY CLUB
SP-300 Hamlet Circle, Goose Creek, 29445, Berkeley County, (803)764-4618, 20 miles NW of Charleston. **E-mail:** crowgolf@aol.com. **Web:** www.chrlstngolf.com.
Holes: 18. **Yards:** 7,003/5,682. **Par:** 72/72. **Course Rating:** 73.7/67.3. **Slope:** 134/121. **Green Fee:** $30/$69. **Cart Fee:** Included in Green Fee. **Walking Policy:** Walking at certain times. **Walkability:** 4. **Opened:** 1990. **Architect:** Bob Spence. **Season:** Year-round. **High:** Spring. **To obtain tee times:** Call anytime in advance with credit card to guarantee. **Miscellaneous:** Reduced fees (weekdays, low season, twilight), discount packages, range (grass), club rentals, credit cards (MC, V, AE, D).
Reader Comments: Challenges all skill levels ... Tough layout, rolling greens ... Excellent course ... Always gets the best of me ... Loved the back nine! ... Excellent greens, keep going back ... Testing but fair ... Excellent, can get pricey ... Don't plan on lowering your handicap here.

★★★ CYPRESS BAY GOLF CLUB
R-Hwy 17, North Myrtle Beach, 29566, Horry County, (803)249-1017, (800)833-5638, 7 miles N of Myrtle Beach.
Holes: 18. **Yards:** 6,502/4,920. **Par:** 72/72. **Course Rating:** 71.2/69.0. **Slope:** 122/113. **Green Fee:** $28/$59. **Cart Fee:** $19/person. **Walking Policy:** Walking at certain times. **Walkability:** 1. **Opened:** 1972. **Architect:** Russell Breedon. **Season:** Year-round. **High:** Spring/Fall. **To obtain tee times:** Call. **Miscellaneous:** Reduced fees (low season, twilight), metal spikes, club rentals.
Reader Comments: Short course w/strategic hazards, a target-type course ... Fast greens ... Tough course, but fair ... Open, great par 3s ... Very nice, try hard to please.

DAUFUSKIE ISLAND CLUB & RESORT *Service*
SP-P.O. Box 23285, Hilton Head Island, 29925, Beaufort County, (843)341-4810, (800)648-6778.
★★★★ BLOODY POINT *Pace+*
Holes: 18. **Yards:** 6,900/5,220. **Par:** 72/72. **Course Rating:** 73.2/69.7. **Slope:** 135/126. **Green Fee:** $80/$145. **Cart Fee:** Included in Green Fee. **Walking Policy:** Unrestricted walking. **Walkability:** 1. **Opened:** 1991. **Architect:** Tom Weiskopf/Jay Morrish. **Season:** Year-round. **High:** March-June/Sept.-Nov. **To obtain tee times:** Call golf club. **Miscellaneous:** Reduced fees (resort guests), metal spikes, range (grass), credit cards (MC, V, AE, D).
Reader Comments: Great course ... Relaxing, fun to play, great staff ... Beautiful course ... Enjoy the boat ride and great golf.
★★★★ MELROSE COURSE *Pace+*
Holes: 18. **Yards:** 7,081/5,575. **Par:** 72/72. **Course Rating:** 74.2/72.3. **Slope:** 138/126. **Green Fee:** $80/$145. **Cart Fee:** Included in Green Fee. **Walking Policy:** Unrestricted walking. **Walkability:** 1. **Opened:** 1987. **Architect:** Jack Nicklaus. **Season:** Year-round. **High:** March-June/Sept.-Nov. **To obtain tee times:** Call golf club. **Miscellaneous:** Reduced fees (resort guests), metal spikes, range (grass), lodging, credit cards (MC, V, AE, D).

Reader Comments: Typical Nicklaus, angled, shallow greens, designed for high long iron fades ... Last 3 holes are great! ... Can't say enough about it, 5 stars ... Nothing like it ... Accommodating staff, awesome finishing holes ... Last three holes are the poor man's Pebble Beach.

DEER TRACK GOLF RESORT
R-1705 Platt Blvd., Surfside Beach, 29575, Horry County, (843)650-2146, (800)548-9186, 2 miles S of Myrtle Beach.

★★★½ **SOUTH COURSE**

Holes: 18. **Yards:** 6,916/5,226. **Par:** 71/71. **Course Rating:** 72.9/70.6. **Slope:** 119/120. **Green Fee:** $8/$42. **Cart Fee:** $20/cart. **Walking Policy:** Walking at certain times. **Walkability:** 1. **Opened:** 1974. **Architect:** Bob Toski/Porter Gibson. **Season:** Year-round. **High:** Spring/Fall. **To obtain tee times:** Call golf shop. **Miscellaneous:** Reduced fees (weekdays, low season, resort guests, twilight, juniors), discount packages, metal spikes, range (grass/mats), club rentals, lodging, credit cards (MC, V).
Reader Comments: Very good, good service ... Lots of water... Tough course ... Good layout. Fair greens ... Casual and enjoyable ... Staff went out of their way to please ... Lots of play, can be slow ... Good value.

★★★½ **TOSKI LINKS**

Holes: 18. **Yards:** 7,203/5,353. **Par:** 72/72. **Course Rating:** 73.5/69.6. **Slope:** 121/119. **Green Fee:** $8/$42. **Cart Fee:** $20/cart. **Walking Policy:** Walking at certain times. **Walkability:** 1. **Opened:** 1974. **Architect:** Bob Toski/Porter Gibson. **Season:** Year-round. **High:** Spring/Fall. **To obtain tee times:** Call golf shop. **Miscellaneous:** Reduced fees (weekdays, low season, resort guests, twilight, juniors), discount packages, metal spikes, range (grass/mats), club rentals, lodging, credit cards (MC, V).
Reader Comments: Very good ... Redone bunkering gives it some character... Very enjoyable, wide fairways, challenging approaches ... Large trees, nice landscape ... Good course ... Tough course ... Long, long, longest! Yikes bring every club! ... Great greens... Enjoyable but not spectacular... Great course, challenge.

★★★★½ **THE DUNES GOLF & BEACH CLUB** *Condition*
SP-9000 N. Ocean Blvd., Myrtle Beach, 29572, Horry County, (843)449-5914.
Holes: 18. **Yards:** 7,165/5,390. **Par:** 72/72. **Course Rating:** 72.1/72.3. **Slope:** 141/132. **Green Fee:** $80/$133. **Cart Fee:** Included in Green Fee. **Walking Policy:** Unrestricted walking. **Walkability:** 2. **Opened:** 1948. **Architect:** Robert Trent Jones. **Season:** Year-round. **High:** Spring/Fall. **To obtain tee times:** Call. **Miscellaneous:** Reduced fees (low season), discount packages, range (grass), caddies, club rentals, credit cards (MC, V, AE).
Notes: Ranked 16th in 1999 Best in State. 1994-98 Senior Tour Championship; 1962 Women's U.S. Open.
Reader Comments: Best greens around ... Everything you want in a golf course ... Outstanding course, very special ... Staff was great ... Classic golf ... Very good course & beautiful ... Perfection except for cost ... Great design, great service ... Fine design. Too expensive ... Classic golf, need all shots, wonderful course.

★★★½ **THE DUNES WEST GOLF CLUB**
SP-3535 Wando Plantation Way, Mount Pleasant, 29464, Charleston County, (803)856-9000, 10 miles E of Charleston.
Holes: 18. **Yards:** 6,871/5,278. **Par:** 72/72. **Course Rating:** 73.4/69.2. **Slope:** 131/118. **Green Fee:** $30/$60. **Cart Fee:** Included in Green Fee. **Walking Policy:** Mandatory cart. **Walkability:** N/A. **Opened:** 1991. **Architect:** Arthur Hills. **Season:** Year-round. **High:** March-May/Oct. **To obtain tee times:** Credit card required for reserving more than 14 days in advance.
Miscellaneous: Reduced fees (weekdays, low season, resort guests, twilight, juniors), discount packages, metal spikes, range (grass), club rentals, credit cards (MC, V, AE).
Reader Comments: Beautiful course. Pure southern hospitality ... Excellent fairways & greens ... Great challenge but playable for amateur ... Fast pace of play. Excellent value ... Good value. Beautiful clubhouse. Good staff ... Outstanding value, smooth greens ... Above-average golf ... Bring your 'A' putting. Fun course.

★ **DUSTY HILLS COUNTRY CLUB**
SP-225 Country Club Rd., Marion, 29571, Marion County, (803)423-2721, 20 miles E of Florence.
Holes: 18. **Yards:** 6,120/4,995. **Par:** 72/74. **Course Rating:** 69.0/68.0. **Slope:** 114/101. **Green Fee:** $12/$12. **Cart Fee:** $12/person. **Walking Policy:** Unrestricted walking. **Walkability:** 2. **Opened:** 1928. **Season:** Year-round. **High:** March-May/Sept.-Nov. **To obtain tee times:** Call golf shop a day in advance. **Miscellaneous:** Reduced fees (resort guests, seniors), discount packages, range (grass), club rentals.

★★★½ **EAGLE NEST GOLF CLUB**
R-Hwy. 17 N., North Myrtle Beach, 29597, Horry County, (803)249-1449, (800)543-3113, 1 miles N of North Myrtle Beach.
Holes: 18. **Yards:** 6,901/5,105. **Par:** 72/72. **Course Rating:** 73.0/69.8. **Slope:** 120/116. **Green Fee:** $12/$43. **Cart Fee:** $18/person. **Walking Policy:** Walking at certain times. **Walkability:** 3.

Opened: 1971. **Architect:** Gene Hamm. **Season:** Year-round. **High:** March-April/Oct. **To obtain tee times:** Call up to 1 year in advance. **Miscellaneous:** Reduced fees (resort guests, twilight), discount packages, metal spikes, range (grass/mats), club rentals, credit cards (MC, V, AE).
Reader Comments: Cannot be beat for the price ... Toughest finishing holes in Myrtle Beach ... Nice layout. Always in good shape ... Loved the wildlife, loved the course ... Great back 9, very enjoyable, must work shots ... Great natural track, keep them straight.

EAGLE'S POINTE GOLF CLUB
PU-1 Eagle's Pointe Dr., Bluffton, 29910, Beaufort County, (843)686-4457, (888)325-1833, 7 miles W of Hilton Head. **Web:** www.eaglespointe.com.
Holes: 18. **Yards:** 6,738/5,210. **Par:** 71/71. **Course Rating:** 72.5/69.8. **Slope:** 130/119. **Green Fee:** $50/$79. **Cart Fee:** $18/person. **Walking Policy:** Walking at certain times. **Walkability:** 1. **Opened:** 1998. **Architect:** Davis Love III. **Season:** Year-round. **High:** March-Apr.-Oct. **To obtain tee times:** Call 1(888)325-1833. **Miscellaneous:** Reduced fees (weekdays, low season, twilight, juniors), range (grass), club rentals, credit cards (MC, V, AE, D), beginner friendly.

★★★ EASTPORT GOLF CLUB
PU-Hwy. 17, North Myrtle Beach, 29597, Horry County, (8043)249-3997, (800)334-9035, 2 miles N of N. Myrtle Beach.
Holes: 18. **Yards:** 6,202/4,698. **Par:** 70/70. **Course Rating:** 69.1/65.7. **Slope:** 116/114. **Green Fee:** $6/$33. **Cart Fee:** $16/cart. **Walking Policy:** Mandatory cart. **Walkability:** 3. **Opened:** 1988. **Architect:** Denis Griffiths & Assoc. **Season:** Year-round. **High:** March-May. **To obtain tee times:** Call 2 days in advance. **Miscellaneous:** Reduced fees (weekdays), metal spikes, club rentals, credit cards (MC, V).
Reader Comments: Fun to play, although short ... Underrated, tough course ... Neat little course, great greens ... Great finishing holes ... Very tight with houses & roads very close ... Rough made the play tough ... Short, but very nice ... Best greens I have seen in Myrtle Beach ... Challenging greens, excellent course.

★★★ EDISTO BEACH GOLF CLUB
R-24 Fairway Dr., Edisto Island, 29438, Colleton County, (843)869-1111, 45 miles S of Charleston.
Holes: 18. **Yards:** 6,212/5,306. **Par:** 71/72. **Course Rating:** 69.9/70.3. **Slope:** 127/120. **Green Fee:** $30/$44. **Cart Fee:** Included in Green Fee. **Walking Policy:** Walking at certain times. **Walkability:** 1. **Opened:** 1973. **Architect:** Tom Jackson. **Season:** Year-round. **High:** April-Nov. **To obtain tee times:** Call golf shop. **Miscellaneous:** Reduced fees (weekdays, low season, resort guests, juniors), discount packages, club rentals, lodging, credit cards (MC, V, D).
Reader Comments: Very challenging ... Greens excellent! Management friendly. Fun course! ... Short and fun. Tight fairways ... Beautiful golf course ... Water everywhere.

★★½ FALCON'S LAIR GOLF COURSE
SP-1308 Falcon's Dr., Walhalla, 29691, Oconee County, (864)638-0000, 40 miles SW of Greenville.
Holes: 18. **Yards:** 6,955/5,238. **Par:** 72/74. **Course Rating:** 73.2/70.6. **Slope:** 134/123. **Green Fee:** $18/$30. **Cart Fee:** $12/person. **Walking Policy:** Walking at certain times. **Walkability:** 5. **Opened:** 1991. **Architect:** Harry Bowers. **Season:** Year-round. **High:** March-Oct. **To obtain tee times:** First come, first served. **Miscellaneous:** Reduced fees (weekdays, low season, twilight, seniors, juniors), discount packages, range (grass/mats), club rentals, credit cards (MC, V).
Reader Comments: Offers some tough greens to hit ... Great mountain course ... Trouble if you aren't straight ... Inexpensive ... Not crowded, trouble around greens ... Tough mountainous course, small greens ... A real challenge. Greens hold ... Good course.

★★★ FORT MILL GOLF CLUB
SP-101 Country Club Dr., Fort Mill, 29716, York County, (803)547-2044, 15 miles S of Charlotte, NC.
Holes: 18. **Yards:** 6,826/5,427. **Par:** 72/72. **Course Rating:** 72.7/71.6. **Slope:** 123/125. **Green Fee:** $19/$25. **Cart Fee:** $14/person. **Walking Policy:** Walking at certain times. **Walkability:** 2. **Opened:** 1948. **Architect:** Donald Ross/George Cobb. **Season:** Year-round. **High:** April-Sept. **To obtain tee times:** Call on Wednesday for upcoming weekend. Weekdays call up to 2 days in advance. **Miscellaneous:** Credit cards (MC, V).
Reader Comments: Fun and rewarding ... Tougher than it looks ... Difficult ... Good course to walk, well kept.

★★★ FOX CREEK GOLF CLUB
SP-Hwy. 15 S., Lydia, 29079, Darlington County, (843)332-0613, 20 miles W of Florence.
Holes: 18. **Yards:** 6,903/5,271. **Par:** 72/72. **Course Rating:** 72.7/67.9. **Slope:** 128/106. **Green Fee:** $13/$18. **Cart Fee:** $10/person. **Walking Policy:** Walking at certain times. **Walkability:** 1. **Opened:** 1988. **Architect:** Ernest Wallace. **Season:** Year-round. **High:** Feb.-May/Sept.-Nov. **To obtain tee times:** Call golf shop. **Miscellaneous:** Reduced fees (weekdays, resort guests, seniors, juniors), discount packages, metal spikes, range (grass), club rentals, credit cards (MC, V).

SOUTH CAROLINA

Reader Comments: Good layout ... Great finishing par 5 ... Staff very friendly ... Great course for the money ... Slowly maturing ... Good small town course.

★★★ FOXBORO GOLF CLUB
R-1438 Wash Davis Rd., Summerton, 29148, Clarendon County, (803)478-7000, (800)468-7061, 75 miles NE of Charleston.
Holes: 18. **Yards:** 6,889/5,386. **Par:** 72/72. **Course Rating:** 71.9/68.4. **Slope:** 121/114. **Green Fee:** $15/$29. **Cart Fee:** Included in Green Fee. **Walking Policy:** Mandatory cart. **Walkability:** 1. **Opened:** 1988. **Architect:** Porter Gibson. **Season:** Year-round. **High:** Spring/Fall. **To obtain tee times:** Call golf shop. **Miscellaneous:** Reduced fees (low season, juniors), discount packages, metal spikes, club rentals, credit cards (MC, V, AE, D).
Reader Comments: A good course to play on any day ... Open links-style course ... Flat course, great greens ... Very accommodating ... Fun public course, easy play.

FRIPP ISLAND RESORT
★★★★ OCEAN CREEK *Service*
R-88 Ocean Creek Blvd., Fripp Island, 29920, Beaufort County, (843)838-1576, (800)845-4100, 19 miles SE of Beaufort. **Web:** www.frippislandresort.com.
Holes: 18. **Yards:** 6,643/4,884. **Par:** 71/71. **Course Rating:** 72.0/69.5. **Slope:** 132/121. **Green Fee:** $44/$69. **Cart Fee:** Included in Green Fee. **Walking Policy:** Unrestricted walking. **Walkability:** 3. **Opened:** 1995. **Architect:** Davis Love III. **Season:** Year-round. **High:** Sept.-Nov./March-May. **To obtain tee times:** Central tee time reservations (800)933-0050.
Miscellaneous: Reduced fees (weekdays, low season, resort guests, twilight, juniors), discount packages, range (grass), club rentals, lodging (300 rooms), credit cards (MC, V, AE, D), beginner friendly (clinics, wee links).
★★★★ OCEAN POINT GOLF LINKS *Value*
R-250 Ocean Point Drive, Fripp Island, 29920, Beaufort County, (843)838-1521, (800)845-4100, 19 miles SE of Beaufort. **Web:** www.frippislandresort.com.
Holes: 18. **Yards:** 6,556/4,908. **Par:** 72/72. **Course Rating:** 72.2/69.5. **Slope:** 132/113. **Green Fee:** $44/$69. **Cart Fee:** Included in Green Fee. **Walking Policy:** Unrestricted walking. **Walkability:** 2. **Opened:** 1962. **Architect:** George W. Cobb. **Season:** Year-round. **High:** Mar.-May/Sept.-Nov. **To obtain tee times:** Central tee time reservations (800)933-0050.
Miscellaneous: Reduced fees (weekdays, low season, resort guests, twilight, juniors), discount packages, range (grass), club rentals, lodging (300 rooms), credit cards (MC, V, AE, D), beginner friendly (clinics, wee links).
★★★★ SOUTH CAROLINA NATIONAL GOLF CLUB *Value, Pace*
PU-Eight Waveland Ave., Cat Island, 29902, (843)524-0300, (800)845-4100, 4 miles SE of Beaufort. **Web:** www.frippislandresort.com.
Holes: 18. **Yards:** 6,625/4,970. **Par:** 71/71. **Course Rating:** 72.0/67.4. **Slope:** 126/116. **Green Fee:** $35/$49. **Cart Fee:** Included in Green Fee. **Walking Policy:** Unrestricted walking. **Walkability:** 2. **Opened:** 1986. **Architect:** George W. Cobb. **Season:** Year-round. **High:** Sept-Nov./March-May. **To obtain tee times:** Central Tee Time Reservations (800)933-0050.
Miscellaneous: Reduced fees (weekdays, low season, resort guests, twilight, juniors), discount packages, range (grass), club rentals, credit cards (MC, V, AE, D), beginner friendly (clinics, junior golf school, wee links).

★★★★ GLEN DORNOCH WATERWAY GOLF LINKS
R-4840 Glen Dornoch Way, Little River, 29566, Horry County, (843)249-2541, (800)717-8784, 15 miles N of Myrtle Beach. **E-mail:** glen@sccoast.net. **Web:** www.glendornoch.com.
Holes: 18. **Yards:** 6,850/5,002. **Par:** 72/72. **Course Rating:** 73.2/69.8. **Slope:** 141/129. **Green Fee:** $48/$103. **Cart Fee:** $20/person. **Walking Policy:** Mandatory cart. **Walkability:** 3. **Opened:** 1996. **Architect:** Clyde Johnston. **Season:** Year-round. **High:** Spring/Fall. **To obtain tee times:** Call up to a year in advance. **Miscellaneous:** Reduced fees (low season), discount packages, range (grass), club rentals, credit cards (MC, V, AE).
Notes: Ranked 22nd in 1999 Best in State.
Reader Comments: Outstanding, a fantastic finish ... Beautiful scenery ... Good shape for a new course, holes along the water just beautiful ... Excellent layout, superb finishing holes ... Sensational layout ... A real test, can't say enough about the service ... Can't wait to return ... Every hole is a challenge ... Top grade.

★★★★ GOLDEN BEAR GOLF CLUB
SP-72 Golden Bear Way, Hilton Head, 29926, Beaufort County, (843)689-2200, 42 miles SE of Savannah. **Web:** www.goldenbeargolfclub.com.
Holes: 18. **Yards:** 7,014/4,974. **Par:** 72/72. **Course Rating:** 73.7/69.3. **Slope:** 132/120. **Green Fee:** $49/$74. **Cart Fee:** $21/person. **Walking Policy:** Walking at certain times. **Walkability:** 2. **Opened:** 1992. **Architect:** Bruce Burland. **Season:** Year-round. **High:** Spring/Fall. **To obtain tee times:** Call golf shop 6:30 a.m.-6:30 p.m. **Miscellaneous:** Reduced fees (low season, resort guests, twilight, juniors), discount packages, metal spikes, range (grass), club rentals, credit cards (MC, V, AE).

SOUTH CAROLINA

Reader Comments: Underrated, fair test of golf ... Good layout, average amenities ... Great greens ... Good condition, testing golf ... Water, water everywhere! Loved it ... Terrific, difficult but fair ... Great condition, great service ... A winner ... Great golf experience, wonderful service.

★★★ GOLDEN HILLS GOLF & COUNTRY CLUB
SP-100 Scotland Dr., Lexington, 29072, Lexington County, (803)957-3355, 15 miles W of Columbia.
Holes: 18. **Yards:** 6,561/4,951. **Par:** 71/71. **Course Rating:** 71.2/68.0. **Slope:** 134/113. **Green Fee:** $19/$38. **Cart Fee:** $10/person. **Walking Policy:** Unrestricted walking. **Walkability:** 2. **Opened:** 1988. **Architect:** Ron Garl. **Season:** Year-round. **High:** Spring. **To obtain tee times:** Call 2 days in advance. **Miscellaneous:** Reduced fees (weekdays, low season), metal spikes, club rentals, credit cards (MC, V).
Reader Comments: Fun, hilly course, several holes along small river.

★★★½ THE GOLF CLUB OF SOUTH CAROLINA AT CRICKENTREE
SP-1084 Langford Rd., Blythewood, 29016, Richland County, (803)754-8600, 12 miles NE of Columbia.
Holes: 18. **Yards:** 7,002/4,791. **Par:** 72/72. **Course Rating:** 74.2/71.3. **Slope:** 140/130. **Green Fee:** $29/$39. **Cart Fee:** Included in Green Fee. **Walking Policy:** Mandatory cart. **Walkability:** 4. **Opened:** 1987. **Architect:** Ken Killian. **Season:** Year-round. **High:** Spring/Fall. **To obtain tee times:** Call golf shop. **Miscellaneous:** Reduced fees (weekdays, twilight, seniors), metal spikes, range (grass), club rentals, credit cards (MC, V).
Reader Comments: Toughest course I have ever played ... Challenging layout .... Could play this course 1,000 times and not get bored ... The more you play it, the better you'll play it.

★★★★ HARBOUR TOWN GOLF LINKS
R-11 Lighthouse Lane, Hilton Head Island, 29928, Beaufort County, (843)363-4485, (800)955-8337, 45 miles N of Savannah, GA. **Web:** www.seapines.com.
Holes: 18. **Yards:** 6,916/5,019. **Par:** 71/71. **Course Rating:** 74.0/69.0. **Slope:** 136/117. **Green Fee:** $165/$215. **Cart Fee:** Included in Green Fee. **Walking Policy:** Unrestricted walking. **Walkability:** 1. **Opened:** 1969. **Architect:** Pete Dye. **Season:** Year-round. **High:** Spring/Fall. **To obtain tee times:** Call with credit card to guarantee. **Miscellaneous:** Reduced fees (low season, resort guests, juniors), discount packages, range (grass), club rentals, lodging, credit cards (MC, V, AE, D).
Notes: Ranked 71st in 1999-2000 America's 100 Greatest; 3rd in 1999 Best in State; 8th in 1996 America's Top 75 Upscale Courses. MCI Classic.
Reader Comments: AWESOME! ... Great par 3s make this course ... Each hole memorable ... Unbelievable layout. When in shape, greens must be awesome ... Proves that you don't need 7,000 yards to be great ... Pricey, good looking, playable ... Tight track, great design ... A little expensive, but worth every penny.

HEATHER GLEN GOLF LINKS
PU-Hwy. 17 N., Little River, 29566, Horry County, (843)249-9000, (800)868-4536, 12 miles N of Myrtle Beach. **E-mail:** glen@sccoast.net. **Web:** wwwheatherglen.com.
Holes: 27. **Cart Fee:** $20/person. **Walking Policy:** Mandatory cart. **Walkability:** 2. **Opened:** 1987. **Architect:** Willard Byrd/Clyde Johnston. **Season:** Year-round. **High:** Spring/Fall. **To obtain tee times:** Call anytime.
★★★★ RED/BLUE
Yards: 6,771/5,053. **Par:** 72/72. **Course Rating:** 72.4/69.3. **Slope:** 127/117. **Green Fee:** $25/$81. **Miscellaneous:** Reduced fees (juniors), range (grass), club rentals, credit cards (MC, V, AE).
Reader Comments: Good course, fun to play ... Could play every day ... Don't have to go to Scotland, it's here. Great test of golf ... Great challenge, must hit it straight ... Every hole is different ... Most hospitable rangers ... Great layout, some memorable holes ... Quality hole after hole.
★★★★ RED/WHITE
Yards: 6,783/5,101. **Par:** 72/72. **Course Rating:** 72.4/69.3. **Slope:** 130/117. **Green Fee:** $30/$81. **Miscellaneous:** Reduced fees (juniors), discount packages, range (grass), club rentals, credit cards (MC, V, AE).
Reader Comments: Need to play all 3 nines ... Everything is top notch ... Wonderful mature golf course. Diabolical traps ... Top 10 in Myrtle Beach area ... Enjoy wildlife as well as golf ... Railroad ties, nest bunkers, gimmicky ... Beautifully planned holes. A true gem! ... All 27 holes are different.
★★★★ WHITE/BLUE
Yards: 6,822/5,127. **Par:** 72/72. **Course Rating:** 72.4/69.3. **Slope:** 130/117. **Green Fee:** $30/$81. **Miscellaneous:** Reduced fees (juniors), discount packages, range (grass), club rentals, credit cards (MC, V, AE).
Reader Comments: Fair test, my game not up to it ... No two holes alike ... Very good course ... Lots of trouble, need every club ... Course management is a must, go with a good sand game ... Beautiful course, a pleasure to play ... Many memorable holes.

★★★★½ HERITAGE CLUB *Service*

PU-Hwy. 17 S., Pawleys Island, 29585, Georgetown County, (843)237-3424, (800)377-2315, 20 miles S of Myrtle Beach.
Holes: 18. **Yards:** 7,100/5,325. **Par:** 71/71. **Course Rating:** 74.2/71.0. **Slope:** 137/125. **Green Fee:** $30/$75. **Cart Fee:** $18/person. **Walking Policy:** Mandatory cart. **Walkability:** N/A.
Opened: 1986. **Architect:** Dan Maples. **Season:** Year-round. **High:** March/April/Oct. **To obtain tee times:** Call up to 9 months in advance. Deposit required during high season.
Miscellaneous: Reduced fees (low season, resort guests), discount packages, metal spikes, range (grass/mats), club rentals, credit cards (MC, V, AE).
Notes: Ranked 21st in 1999 Best in State.
Reader Comments: Nicest river course ... First class ... Elegant ... WOW! ... A great test ... Excellent clubhouse ... Beautiful course, ready to go back ... Like playing in a postcard, so beautiful ... Water, beautiful grounds, nice greens ... One of the best, tough, challenging, a player's course! ... Plantation golf at its best.

★★★½ HERON POINT GOLF CLUB

R-6980 Blue Heron Blvd., Myrtle Beach, 29575, Horry County, (843)650-6664, (800)786-1671, 60 miles N of Charleston.
Holes: 18. **Yards:** 6,477/4,734. **Par:** 72/72. **Course Rating:** 71.0/69.2. **Slope:** 120/121. **Green Fee:** $35/$49. **Cart Fee:** Included in Green Fee. **Walking Policy:** Walking at certain times.
Walkability: 2. **Opened:** 1989. **Architect:** Willard Byrd. **Season:** Year-round. **High:** Spring/Fall.
To obtain tee times: Call 7 days in advance. **Miscellaneous:** Reduced fees (weekdays, low season, resort guests, twilight, seniors, juniors), discount packages, metal spikes, range (grass), club rentals, credit cards (MC, V, D).
Reader Comments: Good value. Average beach course ... Friendly, playable, good course ... Nice course, friendly staff ... A hidden gem, generally underrated ... Fun course, score well, little trouble ... Watch for wild turkeys, fox & deer ... Helpful distance signs, have to place shots carefully, excellent starter.

★★★½ HICKORY KNOB GOLF CLUB

R-off Hwy. 378, McCormick, 29835, McCormick County, (864)391-2450, (800)491-1764, 8 miles N of McCormick.
Holes: 18. **Yards:** 6,560/4,905. **Par:** 72/72. **Course Rating:** 72.1/67.3. **Slope:** 119/120. **Green Fee:** $13/$18. **Cart Fee:** $12/person. **Walking Policy:** Unrestricted walking. **Walkability:** 3.
Architect: Tom Jackson. **Season:** Year-round. **High:** April-Oct. **To obtain tee times:** Call golf shop. **Miscellaneous:** Reduced fees (weekdays, twilight, seniors, juniors), discount packages, metal spikes, range (grass), club rentals, lodging (77 rooms), credit cards (MC, V, D).
Reader Comments: Good value, scenic course ... Best state park course ... Best course no one knows about ... Excellent course with very courteous staff.
Special Notes: Call club for further information.

★ HILLANDALE GOLF COURSE

PU-105 S. Parker Rd., Greenville, 29609, Greenville County, (864)250-1700.
Yards: 5,465/5,100. **Par:** 71/71. **Course Rating:** N/A. **Slope:** N/A. **Green Fee:** $15/$20.
Miscellaneous: Metal spikes.

★★½ HILLCREST GOLF CLUB

PU-1099 Old St. Matthews Rd., Orangeburg, 29116, Orangeburg County, (803)533-6030, 2 miles SE of Orangeburg.
Holes: 18. **Yards:** 6,722/5,208. **Par:** 72/72. **Course Rating:** 70.5/67.8. **Slope:** 119/107. **Green Fee:** $12/$14. **Cart Fee:** $9/person. **Walking Policy:** Unrestricted walking. **Walkability:** 1.
Opened: 1972. **Architect:** Russell Breeden. **Season:** Year-round. **High:** March-May. **To obtain tee times:** Call golf shop. **Miscellaneous:** Reduced fees (low season), discount packages, metal spikes, range (grass/mats), club rentals, credit cards (MC, V, AE, D).
Reader Comments: Very friendly and value was tremendous. ... Good back nine.

HILTON HEAD NATIONAL GOLF CLUB

PU-60 Hilton Head National Dr., Bluffton, 29910, Beaufort County, (843)842-5900, (888)955-1234, 1 miles W of Hilton Head Island. **E-mail:** hhngc@hargray.com. **Web:** www.scratch-golf.com.
Holes: 27. **Green Fee:** $40/$105. **Cart Fee:** Included in Green Fee. **Walking Policy:** Mandatory cart. **Walkability:** 1. **Opened:** 1989. **Architect:** Gary Player & Bobby Weed. **Season:** Year-round. **High:** Spring/Fall. **To obtain tee times:** Call golf shop. **Miscellaneous:** Reduced fees (weekdays, low season, resort guests, twilight, juniors), discount packages, metal spikes, range (grass), club rentals, credit cards (MC, V, AE), beginner friendly (lessons available).
★★★★ NATIONAL/PLAYER
Yards: 6,659/4,563. **Par:** 72/72. **Course Rating:** 72.0/66.2. **Slope:** 128/106.
Reader Comments: Great course, great staff! ... Lots of fun & variety ... Gary Player did good ... Links-style, no even lies, excellent course ... Superb greens, good finishing stretch ... A golfer's

dream, best I have ever played ... What a course, a fantastic value ... It gets better every time! ... Fair test, new 9 excellent.

★★★★ **PLAYER/WEED**
Yards: 6,718/4,682. **Par:** 72/72. **Course Rating:** 71.7/66.0. **Slope:** 132/111.
Reader Comments: Great course, great staff! ... Lots of fun & variety ... Gary player did good ... Links-style, no even lies, excellent course ... Superb greens, good finishing stretch ... A golfer's dream, best I have ever played ... What a course, a fantastic value ... It gets better every time! ... Fair test, new nine excellent.

★★★★ **WEED/NATIONAL**
Yards: 6,655/4,631. **Par:** 72/72. **Course Rating:** 71.5/66.0. **Slope:** 125/108.
Reader Comments: Great course, great staff! ... Lots of fun & variety ... Gary player did good ... Links-style, no even lies, excellent course ... Superb greens, good finishing stretch ... A golfer's dream, best I have ever played ... What a course, a fantastic value ... It gets better every time! ... Fair test, new nine excellent.

HUNTER'S CREEK GOLF & COUNTRY CLUB *Service*
SP-702 Hunter's Creek Blvd., Greenwood, 29649, Greenwood County, (864)223-9286, (888)763-6741, 47 miles SW of Greenville.
Holes: 27. **Green Fee:** $26/$39. **Cart Fee:** Included in Green Fee. **Walking Policy:** Unrestricted walking. **Walkability:** 4. **Opened:** 1994. **Architect:** Tom Jackson. **Season:** Year-round. **High:** April-June. **To obtain tee times:** Call 5 days in advance. **Miscellaneous:** Reduced fees (weekdays, low season, juniors), metal spikes, range (grass), credit cards (MC, V, AE, D).
★★★★ **MAPLE/WILLOW** *Value, Condition, Pace*
Yards: 6,999/4,977. **Par:** 72/72. **Course Rating:** 73.6/67.5. **Slope:** 133/119.
Reader Comments: Great, great new course. Good value ... 27 of the toughest ... Very enjoyable, good layout ... A gem in Emerald City ... A fun course, but not easy, uses every club.
★★★★ **OAK/MAPLE** *Value, Condition, Pace*
Yards: 6,920/5,000. **Par:** 72/72. **Course Rating:** 73.6/67.8. **Slope:** 133/122.
★★★★ **WILLOW/OAK** *Value, Condition, Pace*
Yards: 6,837/4,931. **Par:** 72/72. **Course Rating:** 73.6/67.8. **Slope:** 133/122.
Special Notes: Formerly Hunter's Creek Plantation Golf Club.

★★★½ INDIAN RIVER GOLF CLUB
SP-200 Congaree Hunt Dr., West Columbia, 29170, Lexington County, (803)955-0080, 15 miles W of Columbia.
Holes: 18. **Yards:** 6,507/4,643. **Par:** 71/71. **Course Rating:** 71.7/66.9. **Slope:** 133/113. **Green Fee:** N/A. **Cart Fee:** Included in Green Fee. **Walking Policy:** Walking at certain times. **Walkability:** 4. **Opened:** 1992. **Architect:** Lyndell Young. **Season:** Year-round. **High:** March-May. **To obtain tee times:** Call up to 14 days in advance. **Miscellaneous:** Reduced fees (weekdays, low season, resort guests, twilight, seniors, juniors), discount packages, metal spikes, range (grass), club rentals, credit cards (MC, V, AE).
Reader Comments: Nice greens ... Decent layout ... Use every shot you know on this one ... Needs some work ... Nice course.

★★★½ INDIAN WELLS GOLF CLUB
PU-100 Woodlake Dr., Garden City, 29576, Horry County, (843)651-1505, (800)833-6337, 10 miles S of Myrtle Beach.
Holes: 18. **Yards:** 6,624/4,872. **Par:** 72/72. **Course Rating:** 71.9/68.2. **Slope:** 125/118. **Green Fee:** $5/$40. **Cart Fee:** $18/person. **Walking Policy:** Walking at certain times. **Walkability:** 2. **Opened:** 1984. **Architect:** Gene Hamm. **Season:** Year-round. **High:** Spring/Fall. **To obtain tee times:** Call up to 1 year in advance. **Miscellaneous:** Reduced fees (low season, resort guests, twilight, juniors), discount packages, range (grass), club rentals, credit cards (MC, V, D).
Reader Comments: Nice brother, sister act across the street from each other ... Good value, lots of water ... Worth the drive ... Nice course, good value ... Water on 15 of 18 holes ... Good course, good test ... Bring extra balls, fun.

★★★ INDIGO CREEK GOLF PLANTATION
PU-P.O. Box 15437, Surfside Beach, 29587, Horry County, (803)650-0381, (800)833-6337, 10 miles S of Myrtle Beach.
Holes: 18. **Yards:** 6,750/4,921. **Par:** 72/72. **Course Rating:** 72.4/69.7. **Slope:** 134/126. **Green Fee:** $26/$60. **Cart Fee:** Included in Green Fee. **Walking Policy:** Mandatory cart. **Walkability:** N/A. **Opened:** 1990. **Architect:** Willard Byrd. **Season:** Year-round. **High:** Spring/Fall. **To obtain tee times:** Call 800 number 2 days in advance. **Miscellaneous:** Reduced fees (low season, twilight), discount packages, metal spikes, range (grass), club rentals, credit cards (MC, V, D).
Reader Comments: Nice course ... Very enjoyable, works all aspects of game ... Nice greens, tight play at times ... A tough, but fair course ... Condition was wet but very playable ... Difficult course to play, great challenge.

ISLAND GREEN GOLF CLUB
455 Sunehanna Dr., Unit STE-1, Myrtle Beach, 29575, Horry County, (803)650-2186.

Holes: 27. **Green Fee:** $25/$71. **Walkability:** N/A. **Architect:** William Mooney.

★★★ **DOGWOOD/HOLLY**

Yards: 6,200/4,610. **Par:** 72/72. **Course Rating:** 66.4/66.8. **Slope:** 115/116.
Reader Comments: Great course ... A fun course. Some houses are too close to the fairway. I found a couple ... Tough but still fun ... 3 short 9 hole courses. Good condition. Excellent value. Superior service.

★★★ **DOGWOOD/TALL OAKS**

Yards: 6,012/4,596. **Par:** 72/72. **Course Rating:** 66.4/66.8. **Slope:** 118/115.
Reader Comments: Tough track, water, sloping fairways ... Some narrow fairways, an island green ... Good for average golfer ... Nice course.

★★★ **HOLLY/TALL OAKS**

Yards: 6,243/4,704. **Par:** 72/72. **Course Rating:** 67.0/67.0. **Slope:** 115/115.
Reader Comments: Good course ... Beautiful, nice challenge ... Look out for gators ... Nice course, did not like playing among condos ... Good layout.

★★★½ **ISLAND WEST GOLF CLUB**

R-U.S. Hwy. 278, Bluffton, 29910, Beaufort County, (843)689-6660, 25 miles NE of Savannah.
Holes: 18. **Yards:** 6,803/4,938. **Par:** 72/72. **Course Rating:** 72.1/66.5. **Slope:** 129/116. **Green Fee:** $39/$65. **Cart Fee:** Included in Green Fee. **Walking Policy:** Walking at certain times. **Walkability:** 1. **Opened:** 1991. **Architect:** Fuzzy Zoeller/Clyde Johnston. **Season:** Year-round. **High:** Spring/Fall. **To obtain tee times:** Call up to a year in advance. Reservations for 8 or more players require credit card. **Miscellaneous:** Reduced fees (low season, resort guests, twilight, juniors), discount packages, metal spikes, range (grass), club rentals, credit cards (MC, V, AE).
Reader Comments: A pleasure ... Very nice layout ... Good value ... Very playable for all skill levels, very attractive ... Typical beach golf ... Great for all types of players ... Good layout! Watch for the gators!

★★★½ **KIAWAH ISLAND GOLF & TENNIS RESORT**

R-4255 Bohicket Rd., Johns Island, 29455, Charleston County, (843)768-7431, (800)854-2471, 20 miles S of Charleston.
Holes: 18. **Yards:** 6,759/4,671. **Par:** 72/72. **Course Rating:** 73.8/69.8. **Slope:** 146/121. **Green Fee:** $50/$80. **Cart Fee:** Included in Green Fee. **Walking Policy:** Walking at certain times. **Walkability:** 1. **Opened:** 1989. **Architect:** Clyde Johnston. **Season:** Year-round. **High:** April-Oct. **To obtain tee times:** Call anytime. **Miscellaneous:** Reduced fees (low season, resort guests, twilight, juniors), discount packages, metal spikes, range (grass), club rentals, lodging (600 rooms), credit cards (MC, V, AE, D, Diners Club).
Reader Comments: Interesting & fair ... Nice greens. Straightforward challenge ... Great, warm up at this before playing Kiawah ... Best value on island ... Challenging course ... Beautiful course, watch out for the gators.

KIAWAH ISLAND RESORT *Service*

R-12 Kiawah Beach Dr., Kiawah Island, 29455, Charleston County, (843)768-2121, (800)654-2924, 21 miles S of Charleston.

★★★★ **COUGAR POINT**

Holes: 18. **Yards:** 6,887/4,776. **Par:** 72/72. **Course Rating:** 73.0/66.3. **Slope:** 134/112. **Green Fee:** $110/$139. **Cart Fee:** Included in Green Fee. **Walking Policy:** Walking at certain times. **Walkability:** 2. **Opened:** 1976. **Architect:** Gary Player. **Season:** Year-round. **High:** Spring/Fall. **To obtain tee times:** Call up to 5 days in advance with credit card to guarantee. **Miscellaneous:** Reduced fees (low season, resort guests, twilight, juniors), discount packages, metal spikes, range (grass), caddies, club rentals, lodging, credit cards (MC, V, AE, D, Diners Club).
Reader Comments: Very good grouping of fine courses, each unique in its playability and diversity ... Enjoyable, good test of golf ... Fine facility and service ... Water, water, water... Smart move with the changes ... Intimidating, yet scoreable ... Excellent condition ... Very distinctive holes & fair ... Resort course at its finest.

★★★★★ **OCEAN COURSE** *Condition+, Pace*

R-1000 Ocean Course Dr., Kiawah Island, 29455, Charleston County, (843)768-2121, 21 miles S of Charleston.
Holes: 18. **Yards:** 7,371/5,327. **Par:** 72/72. **Course Rating:** 76.7/72.9. **Slope:** 145/133. **Green Fee:** $145/$195. **Cart Fee:** Included in Green Fee. **Walking Policy:** Walking at certain times. **Walkability:** 2. **Opened:** 1991. **Architect:** Pete Dye. **Season:** Year-round. **High:** Spring/Fall. **To obtain tee times:** Call up to 5 days in advance with credit card to guarantee. **Miscellaneous:** Reduced fees (low season, resort guests, juniors), discount packages, metal spikes, range (grass), caddies, club rentals, lodging, credit cards (MC, V, AE, D, Diners Club).
Notes: Ranked 62nd in 1999-2000 America's 100 Greatest; 2nd in 1999 Best in State; 7th in 1996 America's Top 75 Upscale Courses. 1997 World Cup; 1991 Ryder Cup.
Reader Comments: Great target golf. Great scenery ... Outstanding! ... Best public links course in U.S. ... Just play it ... Take the most difficult course you've played and multiply it by 2 ... Brutal,

but a must-play ... Unbelievable views, hard to concentrate ... One of a kind ... Humbling gourmet golf ... Trouble everywhere.

★★★★ OSPREY POINT
R-Governors Dr., Kiawah Island, 29455, Charleston County, (843)768-2121, 21 miles S of Charleston.
Holes: 18. **Yards:** 6,871/5,023. **Par:** 72/72. **Course Rating:** 72.9/69.6. **Slope:** 137/120. **Green Fee:** $110/$139. **Cart Fee:** Included in Green Fee. **Walking Policy:** Walking at certain times. **Walkability:** 2. **Opened:** 1988. **Architect:** Tom Fazio. **Season:** Year-round. **High:** Spring/Fall. **To obtain tee times:** Call up to 5 days in advance with credit card to guarantee. **Miscellaneous:** Reduced fees (low season, resort guests, twilight, juniors), discount packages, metal spikes, range (grass), club rentals, lodging, credit cards (MC, V, AE, D, Diners Club).
Reader Comments: Beautiful ... Expensive but worth it ... Beautiful fair layout ... Greens and fairways generous. Very playable to 30 handicapper or scratch golfer. Loads of fun ... Loved the water holes ... Gentler than Ocean ... Tops ... Outstanding clubhouse and facilities. Excellent service ... Immaculate condition. Fast pace.

★★★★ TURTLE POINT *Condition*
R-Turtle Point Lane, Kiawah Island, 29455, Charleston County, (843)768-2121, (800)845-2471, 21 miles S of Charleston.
Holes: 18. **Yards:** 6,925/5,205. **Par:** 72/72. **Course Rating:** 74.0/71.1. **Slope:** 142/126. **Green Fee:** $110/$139. **Cart Fee:** Included in Green Fee. **Walking Policy:** Walking at certain times. **Walkability:** 2. **Opened:** **Architect:** Jack Nicklaus. **Season:** Year-round. **High:** Spring/Fall. **To obtain tee times:** May call 5 days in advance with credit card to guarantee. **Miscellaneous:** Reduced fees (low season, resort guests, juniors), discount packages, metal spikes, range (grass), club rentals, lodging, credit cards (MC, V, AE, D, Diners Club).
Reader Comments: No trickery ... Incredible views ... Score here, you can score anywhere ... Nice resort course ... Holes along the ocean very exciting ... Loads of fun even in the pouring rain ... What a resort course should be ... Very fair driving areas ... Water holes are fantastic, great staff.

LADY'S ISLAND COUNTRY CLUB
SP-139 Frances Marion Circle, Beaufort, 29902, Beaufort County, (843)524-3635, 7 miles E of Beaufort. **Web:** www.liccgolf.com.
MARSH COURSE
Holes: 18. **Yards:** 6,000/5,192. **Par:** 72/72. **Course Rating:** 67.4/68.4. **Slope:** 104/107. **Green Fee:** $35/$39. **Cart Fee:** Included in Green Fee. **Walking Policy:** Walking at certain times. **Walkability:** 1. **Opened:** 1971. **Season:** Year-round. **High:** Spring/Fall. **To obtain tee times:** Call. **Miscellaneous:** Range (grass), club rentals, credit cards (MC, V, AE, D).
★½ PINES COURSE
Holes: 18. **Yards:** 7,003/5,357. **Par:** 72/72. **Course Rating:** 73.4/71.0. **Slope:** 124/126. **Green Fee:** $35/$39. **Cart Fee:** Included in Green Fee. **Walking Policy:** Walking at certain times. **Walkability:** 1. **Opened:** 1971. **Season:** Year-round. **High:** Spring/Fall. **To obtain tee times:** Call. **Miscellaneous:** Range (grass), club rentals, credit cards (MC, V, AE, D), beginner friendly.

★★★½ LAKE MARION GOLF CLUB
R-P.O. Box 160, Santee, 29142, Orangeburg County, (803)854-2554, (800)344-6534, 50 miles SE of Columbia.
Holes: 18. **Yards:** 6,670/5,254. **Par:** 72/72. **Course Rating:** 72.1/69.8. **Slope:** 121/112. **Green Fee:** $25/$48. **Cart Fee:** Included in Green Fee. **Walking Policy:** Mandatory cart. **Walkability:** 3. **Opened:** 1979. **Architect:** Eddie Riccoboni. **Season:** Year-round. **High:** March-May. **To obtain tee times:** Call golf shop. **Miscellaneous:** Reduced fees (juniors), discount packages, metal spikes, range (grass/mats), club rentals, credit cards (MC, V, AE).
Reader Comments: Very nice course, nice people ... A must ... Good winter-time course, to keep grooved ... One of the best ... Popular, lots of play ... Quite a challenge, good design ... Nice course, you're welcomed ... Great shape ... Beautiful old course, no Myrtle/Disney distractions here ... Scenic, enjoyable ... Solid track.

★★★½ LAKEWOOD LINKS GOLF CLUB
SP-3600 Greenview Pkwy., Sumter, 29150, Sumter County, (803)481-5700, 40 miles E of Columbia. **E-mail:** lakewoodlinks@yahoo.com. **Web:** http://www.geocities.com/augusta/fairway/7462.
Holes: 18. **Yards:** 6,857/5,042. **Par:** 72/72. **Course Rating:** 71.7/68.2. **Slope:** 123/116. **Green Fee:** $20/$35. **Cart Fee:** Included in Green Fee. **Walking Policy:** Mandatory cart. **Walkability:** 2. **Opened:** 1989. **Architect:** J. Porter Gibson. **Season:** Year-round. **High:** Feb.-April. **To obtain tee times:** Call in advance. **Miscellaneous:** Reduced fees (weekdays, low season, resort guests, twilight, seniors, juniors), discount packages, range (grass), club rentals, credit cards (MC, V).
Reader Comments: Pace of play excellent, wonderful atmosphere ... Water, water everywhere, very nice staff ... Bring lots of balls, plenty of water, favorite in SC ... Good course, greens just ok ... Neat little layout ... Excellent scramble course.

★★★½ LEGEND OAK'S PLANTATION GOLF CLUB

PU-118 Legend Oaks Way, Summerville, 29485, Dorchester County, (803)821-4077, 19 miles N of Charleston.
Holes: 18. **Yards:** 6,974/4,945. **Par:** 72/72. **Course Rating:** 72.3/69.4. **Slope:** 124/116. **Green Fee:** $38/$38. **Cart Fee:** $12. **Walking Policy:** Unrestricted walking. **Walkability:** 3. **Opened:** 1994. **Architect:** Scott Pool. **Season:** Year-round. **High:** March-Nov. **To obtain tee times:** Call 7 days in advance. **Miscellaneous:** Reduced fees (low season, twilight), discount packages, metal spikes, range (grass), club rentals, credit cards (MC, V).
Reader Comments: Nice layout ... Think course management ... Up-and-coming course ... Play at least once a year. Great value! ... Nice course, enjoyed it ... Wonderful layout ... Excellent layout, good par 4s ... You'll use every club in your bag ... Good, worth a return ... Excellent ... Name describes it, beautiful scenery.

THE LEGENDS *Service*

R-Hwy. 501, Myrtle Beach, 29577, Horry County, (843)236-5181, (800)377-2315, 5 miles W of Myrtle Beach.

★★★★ HEATHLAND COURSE

Holes: 18. **Yards:** 6,785/5,115. **Par:** 71/71. **Course Rating:** 72.3/71.0. **Slope:** 127/121. **Green Fee:** $30/$80. **Cart Fee:** $20/person. **Walking Policy:** Mandatory cart. **Walkability:** 3. **Opened:** 1990. **Architect:** Tom Doak. **Season:** Year-round. **High:** March-April/Oct. **To obtain tee times:** Call up to 9 months in advance. **Miscellaneous:** Reduced fees (low season, resort guests), discount packages, range (grass/mats), club rentals, lodging, credit cards (MC, V, AE).
Reader Comments: Great service ... True challenge, super shape, great holes ... An A+! ... Outstanding facility, great practice range ... Nice course, very good clubhouse ... Like playing in Scotland ... Best of the 3 Legends courses ... Can't miss, true links course ... Target golf, not for squeamish! ... Worth the price, a standout.

★★★½ MOORLAND COURSE

Holes: 18. **Yards:** 6,799/4,905. **Par:** 72/72. **Course Rating:** 72.8/72.8. **Slope:** 135/118. **Green Fee:** $30/$80. **Cart Fee:** $20/person. **Walking Policy:** Mandatory cart. **Walkability:** 4. **Opened:** 1990. **Architect:** P.B. Dye. **Season:** Year-round. **High:** March-April/Oct. **To obtain tee times:** Call up to 9 months in advance. **Miscellaneous:** Reduced fees (low season, resort guests), discount packages, range (grass/mats), club rentals, lodging, credit cards (MC, V, AE).
Notes: South Carolina Amateur, South Carolina Senior Amateur, Dupont World Amateur.
Reader Comments: Terrific value for top quality, hard courses ... Great links course that you could play every day for the rest of your life ... Tremendous place, very exciting ... Awesome ... Slow play ... First class in every way ... Fun, good value, great condition ... Pricey but worth it, a true Scottish flavor ... Like a postcard.

★★★★ PARKLAND COURSE

Holes: 18. **Yards:** 7,170/5,543. **Par:** 72/72. **Course Rating:** 74.9/71.0. **Slope:** 137/125. **Green Fee:** $30/$80. **Cart Fee:** $20/person. **Walking Policy:** Mandatory cart. **Walkability:** 2. **Opened:** 1992. **Architect:** Legends Group Design. **Season:** Year-round. **High:** March-April/Oct. **To obtain tee times:** Call for up to 9 months in advance. **Miscellaneous:** Reduced fees (low season, resort guests), discount packages, range (grass/mats), club rentals, lodging, credit cards (MC, V, AE).
Reader Comments: Nice complex, just overcrowded ... Great design, deep bunkers ... Factory with class, spectacular signature hole ... Fun to play ... Best of the 3, long and hard ... Great facilities all around ... Flat out good! ... Most 'American' of Legends courses.

★★★ THE LINKS AT CYPRESS BAY

PU-P.O. Box 680, Little River, 29566, Horry County, (803)249-1017, (800)833-6337, 25 miles N of Myrtle Beach.
Holes: 18. **Yards:** 6,502/5,004. **Par:** 72/72. **Course Rating:** 70.0/69.0. **Slope:** 118/113. **Green Fee:** $31/$54. **Cart Fee:** $16. **Walking Policy:** Walking at certain times. **Walkability:** N/A. **Opened:** 1970. **Architect:** Russell Breeden. **Season:** Year-round. **High:** March-June/Sept. **To obtain tee times:** Call 1 day in advance. **Miscellaneous:** Reduced fees (low season, resort guests, twilight, juniors), discount packages, metal spikes, club rentals, lodging, credit cards (MC, V, D).

★★★½ THE LINKS AT STONO FERRY

PU-5365 Forest Oaks Dr., Hollywood, 29449, Charleston County, (843)763-1817, 12 miles S of Charleston.
Holes: 18. **Yards:** 6,606/4,928. **Par:** 72/72. **Course Rating:** 70.9/69.2. **Slope:** 132/119. **Green Fee:** $25/$50. **Cart Fee:** Included in Green Fee. **Walking Policy:** Unrestricted walking. **Walkability:** 2. **Opened:** 1989. **Architect:** Ron Garl. **Season:** Year-round. **High:** March-May/Sept.-Oct. **To obtain tee times:** Call up to 30 days in advance as long as tee time is guaranteed with a credit card. **Miscellaneous:** Reduced fees (weekdays, low season, twilight, seniors, juniors), discount packages, range (grass), club rentals, credit cards (MC, V, AE, D).
Reader Comments: Fun, fun course ... Great location ... Never get tired of playing it (I love back 9) ... Great layout, great value ... Good mix of relatively easy and challenging holes ... Scenic

holes. Reasonably priced ... ... Very visual back 9 along waterway, unforgettable 14th ... Beautiful course, great improvements.

★★★★ LINKS O'TRYON
11250 Newcut Rd., Campobello, 29322, Spartanburg County, (864)468-4995, (888)525-4657, 20 miles N of Greenville.
Holes: 18. **Yards:** 7,100/5,011. **Par:** 72/72. **Course Rating:** 72.1/67.4. **Slope:** 130/113. **Green Fee:** $30/$55. **Cart Fee:** Included in Green Fee. **Walking Policy:** Walking at certain times. **Walkability:** 4. **Opened:** 1988. **Architect:** Tom Jackson. **Season:** Year-round. **High:** March-Nov. **To obtain tee times:** Call. **Miscellaneous:** Reduced fees (weekdays, twilight), metal spikes, range (grass), club rentals, credit cards (MC, V, AE, D).
Reader Comments: Great location to see mountains ... Good course, small fast greens ... Want to go back! ... Beautiful course, scenic views of mountains ... Tough entrances to every green ... Well kept, beautiful ... Hard par 3s ... Out of the way but worth the effort.

★★★ LINRICK GOLF COURSE
PM-356 Campground Rd., Columbia, 29203, Richland County, (803)754-6331, 7 miles N of Columbia.
Holes: 18. **Yards:** 6,919/5,243. **Par:** 73/73. **Course Rating:** 72.8/69.4. **Slope:** 125. **Green Fee:** $10/$12. **Cart Fee:** $8. **Walking Policy:** Unrestricted walking. **Walkability:** N/A. **Opened:** 1972. **Architect:** Russell Breeden. **Season:** Year-round. **High:** March-Sept. **To obtain tee times:** Tuesday through Friday available Monday morning after 9:00 a.m.; Saturday through Monday available on Thursday morning after 9:00 a.m. **Miscellaneous:** Reduced fees (seniors, juniors), metal spikes, range (grass), club rentals.
Reader Comments: Sweet upland air, gentle people ... A good setup for a public course ... Priced like a muny, plays like a monster ... Excellent course.

LITCHFIELD BEACH & GOLF RESORT
R-Hwy 17S, Pawleys Island, 29585, Georgetown County, (843)237-3411, (800)844-5590, 20 miles S of Myrtle Beach. **E-mail:** info@mbn.com. **Web:** www.mbn.com.
★★★½ LITCHFIELD COUNTRY CLUB
Holes: 18. **Yards:** 6,752/5,264. **Par:** 72/72. **Course Rating:** 72.6/69.9. **Slope:** 130/119. **Green Fee:** $35/$82. **Cart Fee:** $20/person. **Walking Policy:** Unrestricted walking. **Walkability:** 2. **Opened:** 1966. **Architect:** Willard Byrd. **Season:** Year-round. **High:** March-April/Oct.-Nov. **To obtain tee times:** Call golf shop. **Miscellaneous:** Reduced fees (low season, resort guests, juniors), discount packages, range (grass/mats), caddies, club rentals, lodging, credit cards (MC, V, AE, D).
Reader Comments: Excellent layout, good for all handicaps ... Par 5s reachable for good golfers, great course ... Old style layout with lots of trees ... Pleasant staff ... Always in great condition and easy to play ... Fun & fair.

★★★★ THE RIVER CLUB
Holes: 18. **Yards:** 6,677/5,084. **Par:** 72/72. **Course Rating:** 72.2/66.5. **Slope:** 125/110. **Green Fee:** $40/$82. **Cart Fee:** $20/person. **Walking Policy:** Unrestricted walking. **Walkability:** 2. **Opened:** 1986. **Architect:** Tom Jackson. **Season:** Year-round. **High:** March-April/Oct. **To obtain tee times:** Contact your hotel golf director or call up to 1 year in advance. **Miscellaneous:** Reduced fees (low season, resort guests, twilight, juniors), discount packages, range (grass/mats), caddies, club rentals, lodging, credit cards (MC, V, AE, D, Diners Club).
Reader Comments: Give me another shot at that tricky No. 18 ... Tougher than others at Litchfield ... Typical Myrtle Beach, very nice ... Excellent course for all levels of play ... Most difficult of the courses ... Beautiful, lots of lagoons ... Great shape, friendly ... New bent-grass greens to be installed in May 2000.

★★★★ WILLBROOK PLANTATION GOLF CLUB
Holes: 18. **Yards:** 6,704/4,963. **Par:** 72/72. **Course Rating:** 71.8/67.7. **Slope:** 125/118. **Green Fee:** $40/$82. **Cart Fee:** $20/person. **Walking Policy:** Unrestricted walking. **Walkability:** 2. **Opened:** 1988. **Architect:** Dan Maples. **Season:** Year-round. **High:** March-April/Oct.-Nov. **To obtain tee times:** Call golf shop. **Miscellaneous:** Reduced fees (low season, resort guests, juniors), discount packages, range (grass/mats), caddies, club rentals, lodging, credit cards (MC, V, AE, D).
Reader Comments: My favorite resort, this course is super... Open fairways ... Good plantation course ... Take an extra club, wet ... Hard course with nice greens ... Thoroughly enjoyable, very scenic ... Excellent greens, very fast & challenging layout ... Beautiful low country setting, giant oak trees.

★★★★ THE LONG BAY CLUB
R-350 Foxtail Dr., Longs, 29568, Horry County, (843)399-2222, (800)344-5590, 15 miles NW of North Myrtle Beach. **E-mail:** info@mbn.com. **Web:** www.mbn.com.
Holes: 18. **Yards:** 7,021/5,598. **Par:** 72/72. **Course Rating:** 74.3/72.1. **Slope:** 137/127. **Green Fee:** $46/$94. **Cart Fee:** $20/person. **Walking Policy:** Unrestricted walking. **Walkability:** 5. **Opened:** 1988. **Architect:** Jack Nicklaus. **Season:** Year-round. **High:** Spring/Fall. **To obtain tee times:** Contact your hotel golf director or Tee Time Central up to 1 year in advance.

Miscellaneous: Reduced fees (low season, resort guests, twilight, juniors), discount packages, range (grass/mats), club rentals, credit cards (MC, V, AE, D, Diners Club).
Reader Comments: Golden Bear at his best ... I love a challenge ... Once played, never forgotten, outstanding ... Nice design, long & tough ... Sand, sand, sand & more sand ... Fun to play, fast pace, a little pricey ... Challenging, fair, great mounding ... Hard for medium handicap ... Long with lots of moguls, sand, water.

★★★½ MAN O' WAR GOLF
R-5601 Leeshire Blvd., Myrtle Beach, 29579, Horry County, (843)236-8000, 5 miles W of Myrtle Beach.
Holes: 18. **Yards:** 6,967/4,965. **Par:** 72/72. **Course Rating:** 72.9/71.2. **Slope:** 133/121. **Green Fee:** $20/$75. **Cart Fee:** Included in Green Fee. **Walking Policy:** Mandatory cart. **Walkability:** 2. **Opened:** 1996. **Architect:** Dan Maples. **Season:** Year-round. **High:** March-April, Oct. **To obtain tee times:** Call up to 1 year in advance. **Miscellaneous:** Reduced fees (weekdays, twilight, juniors), metal spikes, range (grass), club rentals, credit cards (MC, V).
Reader Comments: Attractive course, a challenge for all levels ... Back to back island greens ... Target after target ... Nice bent-grass greens ... Lots of water, very nice greens ... Superb condition ... A hacker's delight ... Lots of sand & water, but a very fair test ... Excellent greens ... Playable & fun.

★★★½ MIDLAND VALLEY COUNTRY CLUB
SP-151 Midland Dr., Aiken, 29829, Aiken County, (803)663-7332, (800)486-0240, 10 miles N of Augusta, GA.
Holes: 18. **Yards:** 6,849/5,542. **Par:** 71/74. **Course Rating:** 72.1/71.8. **Slope:** 127/125. **Green Fee:** $29/$39. **Cart Fee:** Included in Green Fee. **Walking Policy:** Mandatory cart. **Walkability:** 3. **Opened:** 1961. **Architect:** Ellis Maples. **Season:** Year-round. **High:** March-June. **To obtain tee times:** Call 1-800-486-0240. **Miscellaneous:** Reduced fees (low season, seniors), range (grass), club rentals, credit cards (MC, V, AE, D).
Notes: 1997 U.S. Open Qualifier.
Reader Comments: Terrific fun, always in great shape ... Nice quiet setting ... Just love South and North Carolina golf ... Playable course, difficult holes.

★½ MILER COUNTRY CLUB
SP-400 Country Club Blvd., Summerville, 29483, Dorchester County, (803)873-2210, 20 miles W of Charleston.
Holes: 18. **Yards:** 6,001/5,400. **Par:** 71/71. **Course Rating:** 68.8/68.9. **Slope:** 114/110. **Green Fee:** $17/$32. **Cart Fee:** $12/person. **Walking Policy:** Unrestricted walking. **Walkability:** 1. **Opened:** 1925. **Architect:** Ricciboni/Kemp. **Season:** Year-round. **High:** Spring/Fall. **To obtain tee times:** Call. **Miscellaneous:** Reduced fees (weekdays, low season, twilight), metal spikes.

MYRTLE BEACH NATIONAL GOLF CLUB
R-4900 National Dr., Myrtle Beach, 29579, Horry County, (843)448-2308, (800)344-5590, 8 miles W of Myrtle Beach. **E-mail:** info@mbn.com. **Web:** www.mbn.com.
★★★★ KINGS NORTH
Holes: 18. **Yards:** 7,017/4,816. **Par:** 72/72. **Course Rating:** 72.6/67.0. **Slope:** 136/122. **Green Fee:** $100/$122. **Cart Fee:** $20/person. **Walking Policy:** Unrestricted walking. **Walkability:** 2. **Opened:** 1973. **Architect:** Arnold Palmer/Francis Duane. **Season:** Year-round. **High:** Spring/Fall. **To obtain tee times:** Contact your hotel golf director or call Tee Time Central up to 1 year in advance. **Miscellaneous:** Reduced fees (low season, resort guests, juniors), discount packages, range (grass/mats), club rentals, credit cards (MC, V, AE, D, Diners Club).
Notes: Ranked 18th in 1999 Best in State.
Reader Comments: Excellent mix of hole layouts ... Recently remodeled, excellent, was very welcomed ... What a course! ... Great holes, women-friendly ... Good track, well run ... Good layout, fun, challenging ... Lighting fast greens, great course ... Good but overpriced ... Dazzling, stuns the senses, a must play.
★★★½ SOUTHCREEK
Holes: 18. **Yards:** 6,416/4,723. **Par:** 72/72. **Course Rating:** 70.5/66.5. **Slope:** 123/109. **Green Fee:** $27/$62. **Cart Fee:** $20/person. **Walking Policy:** Unrestricted walking. **Walkability:** 2. **Opened:** 1975. **Architect:** Arnold Palmer/Francis Duane. **Season:** Year-round. **High:** Spring/Fall. **To obtain tee times:** Contact your hotel golf director or call Tee Time Central up to 1 year in advance. **Miscellaneous:** Reduced fees (weekdays, low season, resort guests, twilight, juniors), discount packages, range (grass/mats), club rentals, credit cards (MC, V, AE, D, Diners Club).
Reader Comments: Outstanding clubhouse ... Short, tight and tricky ... Very playable, slick greens and tighter than average ... Fun course with wide fairways ... Loved course ... Fun course to score on ... A fine piece of work ... Fun to play, great service.
★★★½ WEST COURSE
Holes: 18. **Yards:** 6,866/5,307. **Par:** 72/72. **Course Rating:** 73.0/69.0. **Slope:** 119/109. **Green Fee:** $27/$62. **Cart Fee:** $20/person. **Walking Policy:** Unrestricted walking. **Walkability:** 1. **Opened:** 1973. **Architect:** Arnold Palmer/Francis Duane. **Season:** Year-round. **High:** March-April/Oct. **To obtain tee times:** Contact your hotel golf director or call Tee Time Central up to 1

year in advance. **Miscellaneous:** Reduced fees (low season, resort guests, juniors), discount packages, range (grass/mats), club rentals, credit cards (MC, V, AE, D, Diners Club).
Reader Comments: Great fairways and greens ... Very enjoyable ... Fast greens, plush fairways ... Fits a wide range of golfers ... Good test ... Course is always in very good shape, play goes smoothly and service is great ... A very enjoyable and playable layout.

★★★½ MYRTLE WEST GOLF CLUB

PU-Hwy. 9 W., North Myrtle Beach, 29582, Horry County, (843)756-0550, (800)842-8390, 11 miles N of No. Myrtle Beach. **Web:** www.myrtlewest.com.
Holes: 18. **Yards:** 6,787/4,859. **Par:** 72/72. **Course Rating:** 72.7/67.9. **Slope:** 132/113. **Green Fee:** $33/$70. **Cart Fee:** Included in Green Fee. **Walking Policy:** Mandatory cart. **Walkability:** 2. **Opened:** 1989. **Architect:** Tom Jackson. **Season:** Year-round. **High:** Spring/Fall. **To obtain tee times:** Call up to 12 months in advance. Call up to 2 days in advance with golf card or coupon. **Miscellaneous:** Reduced fees (weekdays, low season, resort guests, twilight, seniors, juniors), discount packages, range (grass), club rentals, credit cards (MC, V, AE).
Reader Comments: Fun to play, not difficult, ego booster ... Good course, good value ... Greens could have been better, nice layout ... Plenty of water, quick greens ... Good track, great greens ... Good course, very enjoyable ... Enjoyable to play ... Short but with a lot of variety.

MYRTLEWOOD GOLF CLUB

SP-Hwy. 17 at 48th Ave. N., Myrtle Beach, 29577, Horry County, (843)449-5134, (800)283-3633. **Web:** www.myrtlebeachtrips.com.
★★★★ PALMETTO COURSE
Holes: 18. **Yards:** 6,953/5,176. **Par:** 72/72. **Course Rating:** 73.7/70.1. **Slope:** 135/117. **Green Fee:** $27/$64. **Cart Fee:** $20/person. **Walking Policy:** Mandatory cart. **Walkability:** 1. **Opened:** 1973. **Architect:** Edmund Ault. **Season:** Year-round. **High:** Spring/Fall. **To obtain tee times:** Call in advance. Deposit or credit card required in high season. Hotel guests contact golf director to reserve tee times. **Miscellaneous:** Reduced fees (low season, resort guests, juniors), discount packages, range (grass), club rentals, lodging (100 rooms), credit cards (MC, V, AE, D).
Reader Comments: Typical beach course ... Great to play, not tough, very fair ... Very good staff, good golf ... Good course, nice greens ... Typical Myrtle Beach course ... Solid golf, nice people, well run.
★★★★ PINEHILLS COURSE
Holes: 18. **Yards:** 6,640/4,906. **Par:** 72/72. **Course Rating:** 72.0/67.4. **Slope:** 125/113. **Green Fee:** $27/$64. **Cart Fee:** $20/person. **Walking Policy:** Mandatory cart. **Walkability:** 1. **Opened:** 1993. **Architect:** Arthur Hills. **Season:** Year-round. **High:** Spring/Fall. **To obtain tee times:** Call in advance. Deposit or credit card required in high season. Or, contact your hotel golf director to reserve times. **Miscellaneous:** Reduced fees (low season, resort guests, seniors), discount packages, range (grass), club rentals, credit cards (MC, V, AE, D).
Reader Comments: You'll want to play it again ... Fun older course ... Best service and value. These guys are good ... Very good fairways, greens, service ... Driving landing areas small, leave driver home ... Great course ... Pro shop is friendly ... Nice course, needs rangers ... Good course.

★★★½ NORTHWOODS GOLF CLUB

PU-201 Powell Rd., Columbia, 29203, Richland County, (803)786-9242, 4 miles S of Columbia.
Holes: 18. **Yards:** 6,800/5,000. **Par:** 72/72. **Course Rating:** 71.9/67.8. **Slope:** 122/116. **Green Fee:** $19/$28. **Cart Fee:** $11/person. **Walking Policy:** Walking at certain times. **Walkability:** 3. **Opened:** 1990. **Architect:** P.B. Dye. **Season:** Year-round. **High:** May-Oct. **To obtain tee times:** Call 7 days in advance. Out-of-state players may call up to 30 days in advance. **Miscellaneous:** Reduced fees (weekdays, low season, twilight, seniors, juniors), discount packages, metal spikes, range (grass/mats), club rentals, credit cards (MC, V, AE).
Reader Comments: A little expensive, good course ... Very relaxing place ... Unusual challenges of deep fairway bunkers hiding greens. Tees and practice excellent. Greens have some severe slopes. Course was wet because of rain, but no standing water. Will return ... Very good service, a sleeper.

★★★ OAK HILLS GOLF & COUNTRY CLUB

PU-7629 Fairfield Rd., Columbia, 29203, Richland County, (803)735-9830, (800)263-5218.
Holes: 18. **Yards:** 6,894/4,574. **Par:** 72/72. **Course Rating:** 72.4/65.8. **Slope:** 122/110. **Green Fee:** $23/$39. **Cart Fee:** Included in Green Fee. **Walking Policy:** Unrestricted walking. **Walkability:** 5. **Opened:** 1990. **Architect:** Steve Melnyk. **Season:** Year-round. **High:** Spring/Fall. **To obtain tee times:** Call up to 3 days in advance. **Miscellaneous:** Reduced fees (weekdays, low season, twilight, seniors, juniors), discount packages, range (grass/mats), club rentals, credit cards (MC, V, AE, D).
Reader Comments: Good layout ... Very nice track. Hilly and tricky ... Still too much rock, but better ... Nice track.

★★ OAKDALE COUNTRY CLUB

SP-3700 W. Lake Dr., Florence, 29501, Florence County, (843)662-0368, 5 miles W of Florence.

SOUTH CAROLINA

Holes: 18. **Yards:** 6,300/5,000. **Par:** 72/73. **Course Rating:** 70.3/68.8. **Slope:** 123/114. **Green Fee:** $15/$20. **Cart Fee:** $10/person. **Walking Policy:** Walking at certain times. **Walkability:** 1. **Opened:** 1964. **Architect:** Roland "Robby" Robertson. **Season:** Year-round. **High:** March-April. **To obtain tee times:** Call golf shop. **Miscellaneous:** Metal spikes, range (grass/mats), club rentals.

★★★★ OCEAN CREEK GOLF COURSE *Service*
R-90B Ocean Creek Blvd., Fripp Island, 29920, Beaufort County, (843)838-1576, (800)933-0050, 30 miles N of Hilton Head. **E-mail:** frippislandresort.com.
Holes: 18. **Yards:** 6,629/4,824. **Par:** 71/71. **Course Rating:** 72.0/69.5. **Slope:** 132/121. **Green Fee:** $49/$69. **Cart Fee:** Included in Green Fee. **Walking Policy:** Unrestricted walking. **Walkability:** 2. **Opened:** 1995. **Architect:** Davis Love III/Bob Spence. **Season:** Year-round. **High:** Spring/Fall. **To obtain tee times:** Call 800 number. **Miscellaneous:** Reduced fees (low season, resort guests, twilight, juniors), discount packages, range (grass), club rentals, lodging (370 rooms), credit cards (MC, V, AE, D), beginner friendly (Wee Links tees).
Reader Comments: Needs to mature a bit ... Short course, enjoyed ... Great service ... Excellent layout, great alligators ... Very good ocean holes ... Challenging, but fair.

★★★★ OCEAN POINT GOLF LINKS *Value*
R-250 Ocean Point Dr., Fripp Island, 29920, Beaufort County, (803)838-1521, (800)845-4100, 20 miles SE of Beaufort.
Holes: 18. **Yards:** 6,590/4,951. **Par:** 72/72. **Course Rating:** 72.2/69.5. **Slope:** 129/113. **Green Fee:** $44/$69. **Cart Fee:** Included in Green Fee. **Walking Policy:** Walking at certain times. **Walkability:** 1. **Opened:** 1964. **Architect:** George Cobb. **Season:** Year-round. **High:** Spring/Fall. **To obtain tee times:** Call golf shop or make reservation through resort. **Miscellaneous:** Reduced fees (weekdays, low season, resort guests, twilight, juniors), discount packages, range (grass/mats), club rentals, lodging, credit cards (MC, V, AE, D).
Reader Comments: Nice track ... Everything was great ... Can be very difficult if played in the wind ... Spend a week ... Views, wildlife, friendly staff ... Great service, beautiful, fun, ocean views ... Nice mix of ocean & woods; great views ... Excellent finishing holes both 9 or 18, a must play.

★★★½ OLD CAROLINA GOLF CLUB
PU-90 Buck Island Rd., Bluffton, 29910, Beaufort County, (843)785-6363, (888)785-7274, 6 miles W of Hilton Head Island.
Holes: 18. **Yards:** 6,805/4,475. **Par:** 72/71. **Course Rating:** 73.1/67.0. **Slope:** 142/121. **Green Fee:** $49/$83. **Cart Fee:** Included in Green Fee. **Walking Policy:** Unrestricted walking. **Walkability:** 3. **Opened:** 1996. **Architect:** Clyde Johnston. **Season:** Year-round. **High:** Spring/Fall. **To obtain tee times:** Call up to 4 months in advance. **Miscellaneous:** Reduced fees (low season, resort guests, twilight, juniors), discount packages, metal spikes, range (grass), club rentals, credit cards (MC, V, AE).
Reader Comments: Good assortment of holes ... A unique course, two different nines ... Great greens ... Turtles and gators and snakes, oh my! Marshland everywhere ... Plenty of water, back 9 winds through forest ... Favorite course in the low country ... New course. Fun to play ... Great new course, is maturing nicely.

★★★★ OLD SOUTH GOLF LINKS
PU-50 Buckingham Plantation Dr., Bluffton, 29910, Beaufort County, (843)785-5353, (800)257-8997, 1 miles W of Hilton Head Island.
Holes: 18. **Yards:** 6,772/4,776. **Par:** 72/71. **Course Rating:** 72.4/69.6. **Slope:** 129/123. **Green Fee:** $49/$83. **Cart Fee:** Included in Green Fee. **Walking Policy:** Unrestricted walking. **Walkability:** 2. **Opened:** 1991. **Architect:** Clyde Johnston. **Season:** Year-round. **High:** March-April. **To obtain tee times:** Call golf shop. **Miscellaneous:** Reduced fees (low season, resort guests, twilight, juniors), discount packages, metal spikes, range (grass), club rentals, credit cards (MC, V, AE).
Reader Comments: Short course, good scenery ... Challenging but fair ... A fun & scenic course ... Great course, great people, great value ... Tough back nine, great scenery! ... Good layout, can score well ... Home course away from home, great facility ... New course coming along ... Wide rolling fairways, island greens and fairways.

OLD TABBY LINKS SPRING ISLAND
P.O. Box 2419, Beaufort, 29901.
Holes: 18. **Yards:** 7,004/5,022. **Par:** 72/72. **Course Rating:** 73.9/69.2. **Slope:** 131/123. **Green Fee:** N/A. **Walkability:** N/A. **Architect:** Arnold Palmer/Ed Seay.

★★★½ OYSTER REEF GOLF CLUB
SP-155 High Bluff Rd., Hilton Head Island, 29925, Beaufort County, (843)681-7717, (800)728-6662, 35 miles NE of Savannah, GA. **E-mail:** orgc99@aol.com.
Holes: 18. **Yards:** 7,027/5,288. **Par:** 72/72. **Course Rating:** 73.7/69.8. **Slope:** 131/118. **Green Fee:** $48/$89. **Cart Fee:** Included in Green Fee. **Walking Policy:** Mandatory cart. **Walkability:**

2. **Opened:** 1982. **Architect:** Rees Jones. **Season:** Year-round. **High:** Spring/Fall. **To obtain tee times:** Call up to 90 days in advance. **Miscellaneous:** Reduced fees (low season, resort guests, juniors), discount packages, range (grass), club rentals, credit cards (MC, V, AE, D), beginner friendly (head teaching professional, group lessons).

Reader Comments: Excellent layout ... Very good value, superb condition ... Very well-placed bunkers. Par-3 No. 6 stunning ... Nice course ... Re-seeded greens are excellent ... Nice playable course, fair test ... A real pleasure. Put it on your list!

PALMETTO DUNES RESORT   *Service*

R-P.O. Box 5849, Hilton Head, 29938, Beaufort County, (800)827-3006, 50 miles NE of Savannah.

★★★★½ **ARTHUR HILLS COURSE**   *Pace*
(803)785-1140.

Holes: 18. **Yards:** 6,651/4,999. **Par:** 72/72. **Course Rating:** 71.4/68.5. **Slope:** 127/118. **Green Fee:** $75/$110. **Cart Fee:** Included in Green Fee. **Walking Policy:** Unrestricted walking. **Walkability:** 1. **Opened:** 1986. **Architect:** Arthur Hills. **Season:** Year-round. **High:** April/Oct. **To obtain tee times:** Resort guests call up to 90 in advance. Others call up to 60 days in advance. **Miscellaneous:** Reduced fees (resort guests), discount packages, range (grass), club rentals, lodging, credit cards (MC, V, AE).

Reader Comments: Excellent, fun to play ... Best on Hilton Head ... Nice layout, excellent service, well kept ... Great design and condition., thoroughly enjoyable ... Challenging, lush, wicked finish ... Worth every cent ... Magnificent condition and layout, a gem ... Mature beach course, lots of water, fair ... Super, super, super.

★★★★ **GEORGE FAZIO COURSE**
(803)785-1133.

Holes: 18. **Yards:** 6,875/5,273. **Par:** 70/70. **Course Rating:** 74.2/70.8. **Slope:** 132/127. **Green Fee:** $50/$81. **Cart Fee:** Included in Green Fee. **Walking Policy:** Walking at certain times. **Walkability:** 1. **Opened:** 1974. **Architect:** George Fazio. **Season:** Year-round. **High:** April/Oct. **To obtain tee times:** Resort guests call up to 90 days in advance. Others call up to 60 days in advance. **Miscellaneous:** Reduced fees (resort guests, juniors), discount packages, club rentals, lodging, credit cards (MC, V, AE).

Reader Comments: Tough par 4s ... A brutally difficult par 70 ... Everyone should play, outstanding ... Excellent service ... Nice layout, short ... Top-notch all around ... Well established immaculate course, a pleasure ... Sand, sand everywhere .. Good variety ... Tough track, requires good long iron play.

★★★½ **ROBERT TRENT JONES COURSE**
(803)785-1136.

Holes: 18. **Yards:** 6,710/5,425. **Par:** 72/72. **Course Rating:** 72.2/70.3. **Slope:** 123/123. **Green Fee:** $55/$81. **Cart Fee:** Included in Green Fee. **Walking Policy:** Unrestricted walking. **Walkability:** 1. **Opened:** 1969. **Architect:** Robert Trent Jones. **Season:** Year-round. **High:** April/Oct. **To obtain tee times:** Resort guests call 90 days in advance. Outside guests call 60 days in advance. **Miscellaneous:** Reduced fees (low season, resort guests, juniors), discount packages, range (grass/mats), club rentals, lodging, credit cards (MC, V, AE), beginner friendly.

Reader Comments: Superb conditions ... Great layout, perfect conditions ... Lots of wind, enjoyable ... Good resort course ... Love to play course, still too much money ... Memorable holes, good service ... Good, fair course ... Bring your best game ... Typical resort, wide open ... No. 10 tough with ocean wind.

PALMETTO HALL PLANTATION

R-108 Fort Howell Dr., Hilton Head Island, 29926, Beaufort County, (843)689-4100, (800)827-3006, 30 miles N of Savannah, GA.

★★★★ **ARTHUR HILLS COURSE**

Holes: 18. **Yards:** 6,918/4,956. **Par:** 72/72. **Course Rating:** 72.2/68.6. **Slope:** 132/119. **Green Fee:** $55/$90. **Cart Fee:** Included in Green Fee. **Walking Policy:** Mandatory cart. **Walkability:** 2. **Opened:** 1991. **Architect:** Arthur Hills. **Season:** Year-round. **High:** Spring/Fall. **To obtain tee times:** Call golf shop. **Miscellaneous:** Reduced fees (resort guests, juniors), discount packages, range (grass), club rentals, credit cards (MC, V, AE).

Reader Comments: Best hills course in southeast, not a bad hole on entire course ... Great experience ... Excellent, enjoyable ... Superb layout ... Unique layout, mounding & hazards (crowded) ... Lots of water, challenging, 18th great finish ... Front nine easy, back nine tougher ... Try to match it.

★★★★ **ROBERT CUPP COURSE**

Holes: 18. **Yards:** 7,079/5,220. **Par:** 72/72. **Course Rating:** 74.8/71.1. **Slope:** 141/126. **Green Fee:** $55/$90. **Cart Fee:** Included in Green Fee. **Walking Policy:** Unrestricted walking. **Walkability:** 2. **Opened:** 1993. **Architect:** Robert Cupp. **Season:** Year-round. **High:** Spring/Fall. **To obtain tee times:** Call golf shop. **Miscellaneous:** Reduced fees (resort guests, juniors), discount packages, range (grass), club rentals, credit cards (MC, V, AE).

Reader Comments: Great condition, enjoyable ... Unique design, geometric layout ... Awesome service, plush conditions, excellent ... Great resort course, not crowded ... Punishing but enjoyable, if you like geometric shapes ... Great demanding layout ... Unique layout ... One of my favorites.

★★★ PARKLAND GOLF CLUB
SP-295 E. Deadfall Rd., Greenwood, 29649, Greenwood County, (864)229-5086, 40 miles S of Greenville.
Holes: 18. **Yards:** 6,520/5,130. **Par:** 72/72. **Course Rating:** 70.8/68.3. **Slope:** 124/115. **Green Fee:** $13/$16. **Cart Fee:** $11/person. **Walking Policy:** Unrestricted walking. **Walkability:** 2. **Opened:** 1985. **Architect:** John Park. **Season:** Year-round. **High:** March-Nov. **To obtain tee times:** Call golf shop. **Miscellaneous:** Reduced fees (weekdays, low season, twilight, seniors, juniors), discount packages, metal spikes, range (grass), club rentals, credit cards (MC, V), beginner friendly.
Reader Comments: Good course ... Traditional golf ... A very tight public course, demands good shotmaking, some very challenging par 4s over water ... Excellent but difficult.

★★★ PATRIOTS POINT LINKS
PU-1 Patriots Point Rd., Mount Pleasant, 29464, Charleston County, (843)881-0042, (800)221-2424, 2 miles N of Charleston. **E-mail:** linkschad@aol.com. **Web:** www.charlestonharborresort.com.
Holes: 18. **Yards:** 6,838/5,562. **Par:** 72/72. **Course Rating:** 72.1/71.0. **Slope:** 118/115. **Green Fee:** $30/$75. **Cart Fee:** Included in Green Fee. **Walking Policy:** Walking at certain times. **Walkability:** 1. **Opened:** 1981. **Architect:** Willard Byrd. **Season:** Year-round. **High:** Spring/Fall. **To obtain tee times:** Call golf shop. **Miscellaneous:** Reduced fees (weekdays, low season, resort guests, twilight, juniors), discount packages, metal spikes, range (grass), club rentals, lodging (150 rooms), credit cards (MC, V, AE, D), beginner friendly (clinics and discounts).
Reader Comments: Easy, wide open, inexpensive ... Nice layout. Good price ... Simple, straight-forward design ... Great value ... Beautiful view of harbor on finishing holes ... Average course, stay away when windy ... Some pretty holes ... Flat course on windy point near harbor.

★★★★ PAWLEYS PLANTATION GOLF CLUB
R-Hwy. 17, Pawleys Island, 29585, Georgetown County, (843)237-6200, (800)367-9959, 30 miles S of Myrtle Beach.
Holes: 18. **Yards:** 7,026/4,979. **Par:** 72/72. **Course Rating:** 74.8/70.1. **Slope:** 140/126. **Green Fee:** $65/$120. **Cart Fee:** $20/person. **Walking Policy:** Mandatory cart. **Walkability:** 1. **Opened:** 1988. **Architect:** Jack Nicklaus. **Season:** Year-round. **High:** Spring/Fall. **To obtain tee times:** Call golf shop. **Miscellaneous:** Reduced fees (low season, resort guests), range (grass), club rentals, credit cards (MC, V, AE, D).
Notes: Ranked 23rd in 1999 Best in State.
Reader Comments: Tough par 3s with wind, nice layout ... Wonderful ... Tough, fun ... Unique holes on marsh ... Good challenge ... Loved it! ... One of the finest in Myrtle Beach ... Excellent. Typical Nicklaus ... Interesting holes, good condition ... Classic ... Rate this in my top 5 anywhere ... Phenomenal layout, a real beauty.

★★½ PAWPAW COUNTRY CLUB
SP-600 George St., Bamberg, 29003, Bamberg County, (803)245-4171, 50 miles S of Columbia.
Holes: 18. **Yards:** 6,733/5,010. **Par:** 72/72. **Course Rating:** 72.3/67.5. **Slope:** 133/114. **Green Fee:** $12/$17. **Cart Fee:** $9/person. **Walking Policy:** Unrestricted walking. **Walkability:** 1. **Architect:** Russell Breeden. **Season:** Year-round. **To obtain tee times:** Call golf shop. **Miscellaneous:** Reduced fees (weekdays, juniors), range (grass), club rentals, lodging, credit cards (MC, V).
Reader Comments: Good all over ... Getting better every day! ... Easy course ... Good course for rural area, good layout.

★★★½ PERSIMMON HILL GOLF CLUB
PU-Rte. 3, Box 364, Saluda, 29138, Saluda County, (803)275-3522, 35 miles NE of Augusta, GA.
Holes: 18. **Yards:** 6,925/5,449. **Par:** 72/73. **Course Rating:** 72.3/71.1. **Slope:** 122/121. **Green Fee:** $10/$18. **Cart Fee:** $12/person. **Walking Policy:** Walking at certain times. **Walkability:** 3. **Opened:** 1962. **Architect:** Russell Breedon. **Season:** Year-round. **High:** March-May. **To obtain tee times:** Call 7 days in advance. **Miscellaneous:** Reduced fees (weekdays, low season, twilight), discount packages, metal spikes, range (grass/mats), club rentals, credit cards (MC, V, AE).
Reader Comments: Hidden jewel ... Good fun! ... 600+ yard finishing hole. No. 11 would stump the pros ... Wide fairways, large greens and trees everywhere. The way I would build a course ... Small greens keep it interesting ... Great place to take a group ... Very playable and fair, impressive layout.

★★★½ PINE FOREST COUNTRY CLUB
SP-1000 Congressional Blvd., Summerville, 29483, Dorchester County, (803)851-1193, 3 miles W of Summerville.
Holes: 18. **Yards:** 6,905/5,007. **Par:** 72/72. **Course Rating:** 73.6/67.7. **Slope:** 140/120. **Green Fee:** $28/$52. **Cart Fee:** Included in Green Fee. **Walking Policy:** Walking at certain times. **Walkability:** 2. **Opened:** 1992. **Architect:** Bob Spence. **Season:** Year-round. **High:** March-May. **To obtain tee times:** Call golf shop. **Miscellaneous:** Reduced fees (weekdays, low season, twilight, juniors), discount packages, range (grass), club rentals, credit cards (MC, V).

SOUTH CAROLINA

Reader Comments: Very hard course ... Long track ... Hidden gem in Summerville ... Might be the toughest course in South Carolina ... Tight. Tough ... Tough layout, lots of water ... Ast yet unknown, but will be popular soon ... Long, difficult par 4s, fun to play ... Tough the first time you play it but loads of fun.

★★★★ PINE LAKES INTERNATIONAL COUNTRY CLUB *Service*
SP-5603 Woodside Ave., Myrtle Beach, 29577, Horry County, (843)449-6459, (800)446-6817. **Web:** www.pinelakes.com.
Holes: 18. **Yards:** 6,700/5,162. **Par:** 71/71. **Course Rating:** 72.0/70.5. **Slope:** 130/121. **Green Fee:** $45/$110. **Cart Fee:** Included in Green Fee. **Walking Policy:** Mandatory cart. **Walkability:** 1. **Opened:** 1927. **Architect:** Robert White. **Season:** Year-round. **High:** March-April. **To obtain tee times:** Call up to 1 year in advance with deposit. **Miscellaneous:** Reduced fees (resort guests, twilight), discount packages, range (grass/mats), club rentals, credit cards (MC, V, AE).
Reader Comments: Chowder a nice touch ... Service exceptional ... Straightforward, not tricked up ... A solid refuge from tricked up beach golf ... Excellent! A must play ... Good course and the best total golf experience on Myrtle Beach. You can't not have fun ... Like the Mimosa cocktails ... An extraordinary experience!

★★ PINETUCK GOLF CLUB
SP-2578 Tuckaway Rd., Rock Hill, 29730, York County, (803)327-1141, 20 miles S of Charlotte, NC.
Holes: 18. **Yards:** 6,567/4,870. **Par:** 71/74. **Course Rating:** 71.7/68.2. **Slope:** 127/111. **Green Fee:** $18/$24. **Cart Fee:** $14/person. **Walking Policy:** Walking at certain times. **Walkability:** 2. **Opened:** 1971. **Architect:** George Dunlap. **Season:** Year-round. **High:** March-Oct. **To obtain tee times:** Call anytime for weekends and holidays. **Miscellaneous:** Reduced fees (weekdays, twilight, seniors, juniors), discount packages, range (grass), credit cards (MC, V).

★★½ PINEVIEW GOLF CLUB
SP-7305 Myrtle Beach Hwy., Gable, 29051, Sumter County, (803)495-3514, 20 miles S of Florence.
Holes: 18. **Yards:** 7,000/5,344. **Par:** 72/72. **Course Rating:** 73.0/70.2. **Slope:** 127/119. **Green Fee:** $20/$38. **Cart Fee:** Included in Green Fee. **Walking Policy:** Mandatory cart. **Walkability:** 1. **Opened:** 1974. **Architect:** Russell Breeden. **Season:** Year-round. **High:** March-April. **To obtain tee times:** Call golf shop. **Miscellaneous:** Reduced fees (weekdays, low season, resort guests, twilight, seniors, juniors), discount packages, range (grass), club rentals, lodging, credit cards (MC, V).
Reader Comments: Nice layout ... New management making improvements ... Challenging course, greens OK ... Greens were perfect.

★½ POCALLA SPRINGS COUNTRY CLUB
SP-1700 Hwy. 15 S., Sumter, 29150, Sumter County, (803)481-8322.
Holes: 18. **Yards:** 6,350/5,500. **Par:** 71/71. **Course Rating:** 68.0/65.0. **Slope:** 115/111. **Green Fee:** $7/$10. **Cart Fee:** $8/. **Walking Policy:** Unrestricted walking. **Walkability:** N/A. **Opened:** 1920. **Architect:** Ed Riccoboni. **Season:** Year-round. **High:** April-Sept. **To obtain tee times:** Call golf shop. **Miscellaneous:** Reduced fees (weekdays, low season, resort guests, twilight, seniors, juniors), discount packages, metal spikes, range (grass), club rentals, credit cards (MC, V).

PORT ROYAL GOLF CLUB
R-10A Grasslawn Ave., Hilton Head, 29928, Beaufort County, (843)681-1760, (800)234-6318, 40 miles NE of Savannah, GA.
★★★½ BARONY COURSE
Holes: 18. **Yards:** 6,530/5,253. **Par:** 72/72. **Course Rating:** 71.6/70.1. **Slope:** 129/115. **Green Fee:** $49/$80. **Cart Fee:** Included in Green Fee. **Walking Policy:** Mandatory cart. **Walkability:** N/A. **Opened:** 1968. **Architect:** Willard Byrd. **Season:** Year-round. **High:** March-May/Sept. **To obtain tee times:** Call 800 number. **Miscellaneous:** Reduced fees (low season, resort guests, twilight, juniors), discount packages, metal spikes, range (grass/mats), club rentals, credit cards (MC, V, AE).
Reader Comments: Easy layout ... Fun course ... Very good service, fair golf ... Very pretty. Ocean views ... Nice, not too hard to play ... Basic course ... A bit pricey ... Lots of fun ... Pretty standard stuff ... Good enjoyable course.
★★★ PLANTER'S ROW COURSE
Holes: 18. **Yards:** 6,520/5,126. **Par:** 72/72. **Course Rating:** 71.7/68.9. **Slope:** 133/116. **Green Fee:** $49/$80. **Cart Fee:** Included in Green Fee. **Walking Policy:** Mandatory cart. **Walkability:** N/A. **Opened:** 1983. **Architect:** George Cobb/Willard Byrd. **Season:** Year-round. **High:** March-May. **To obtain tee times:** Call 800 number. **Miscellaneous:** Reduced fees (low season, resort guests, twilight, juniors), discount packages, metal spikes, range (grass/mats), club rentals, credit cards (MC, V, AE).
Reader Comments: Too expensive ... Very good service, fair golf ... Put the driver away ... Great value ... Tight fairways, good greens, great views ... Layout fair, pace of play slow ... Nice ... Good enjoyable course ... Very hard water holes ...Treelined fairways.

SOUTH CAROLINA

★★★ ROBBER'S ROW COURSE
Holes: 18. **Yards:** 6,642/5,000. **Par:** 72/72. **Course Rating:** 72.6/70.4. **Slope:** 134/115. **Green Fee:** $54/$80. **Cart Fee:** Included in Green Fee. **Walking Policy:** Mandatory cart. **Walkability:** N/A. **Opened:** 1968. **Architect:** Willard Byrd. **Season:** Year-round. **High:** March-May/Sept. **To obtain tee times:** Call 800 number. **Miscellaneous:** Reduced fees (low season, resort guests, twilight, juniors), discount packages, metal spikes, range (grass/mats), club rentals, credit cards (MC, V, AE).
Reader Comments: Enjoyable ... Very good service ... Most forgiving for women ... Good condition, bring your best sand wedge ... Nice clubhouse ... Fantastic greens ... Good design, some holes are on sites of the Civil War.

★★★½ POSSUM TROT GOLF CLUB
R-Possum Trot Rd., North Myrtle Beach, 29582, Horry County, (843)272-5341, (800)626-8768.
Holes: 18. **Yards:** 6,966/5,160. **Par:** 72/72. **Course Rating:** 73.0/69.6. **Slope:** 127/111. **Green Fee:** $32/$64. **Cart Fee:** Included in Green Fee. **Walking Policy:** Walking at certain times. **Walkability:** 3. **Opened:** 1968. **Architect:** Russell Breeden. **Season:** Year-round. **High:** Spring/Fall. **To obtain tee times:** Call anytime. **Miscellaneous:** Reduced fees (twilight, juniors), discount packages, range (grass/mats), club rentals, credit cards (MC, V, AE, D), beginner friendly.
Reader Comments: A must play ... Great course, great staff ... Nice mix of holes. Computerized carts are a help ... Well maintained, nice personnel ... Like an old friend ... Feel at home, relaxing, not easy, not tough ... Fun course for all levels ... Outstanding in every way ... Great old course, good Bermuda greens.

★★★½ QUAIL CREEK GOLF CLUB
PU-Hwy. 501 W., Myrtle Beach, 29578, Horry County, (843)347-0549, (800)833-6337.
Holes: 18. **Yards:** 6,812/5,287. **Par:** 72/72. **Course Rating:** 72.8/70.2. **Slope:** 119/112. **Green Fee:** $4/$41. **Cart Fee:** $19/person. **Walking Policy:** Walking at certain times. **Walkability:** 3. **Opened:** 1966. **Architect:** Gene Hamm. **Season:** Year-round. **High:** Spring/Fall. **To obtain tee times:** Call golf shop. **Miscellaneous:** Reduced fees (low season, twilight, juniors), range (grass), credit cards (MC, V, D).
Reader Comments: Lots of sand ... Beat course I've played ... Excellent layout ... Long and winding but very forgiving for the average golfer ... Fast pace, OK design, enjoyable ... Wide open & fun, good warm up ... Easy course, good course for intermediate players ... Generous fairways ... A great morale booster.

★★★ RACCOON RUN GOLF CLUB
PU-8950 Hwy. 707, Myrtle Beach, 29575, Horry County, (843)650-2644, 10 miles S of Myrtle Beach.
Holes: 18. **Yards:** 7,349/5,535. **Par:** 73/73. **Course Rating:** 74.0/69.5. **Slope:** 120/109. **Green Fee:** $18/$35. **Cart Fee:** $18/person. **Walking Policy:** Mandatory cart. **Walkability:** 1. **Opened:** 1977. **Architect:** Gene Hamm. **Season:** Year-round. **High:** Feb.-April. **To obtain tee times:** Call up to 6 months in advance. **Miscellaneous:** Reduced fees (low season, juniors), metal spikes, club rentals, credit cards (MC, V).
Reader Comments: Good greens ... OK for average golfer ... Long and rough, great fun ... Good course ... Not a high profile course, but good value for price.

★★★★ REGENT PARK GOLF CLUB
PU-6000 Regent Pkwy., Fort Mill, 29715, York County, (803)547-1300, 16 miles S of Charlotte, NC.
Holes: 18. **Yards:** 6,848/5,245. **Par:** 72/72. **Course Rating:** 72.6/69.5. **Slope:** 132/123. **Green Fee:** $43/$52. **Cart Fee:** Included in Green Fee. **Walking Policy:** Mandatory cart. **Walkability:** 4. **Opened:** 1994. **Architect:** Ron Garl. **Season:** Year-round. **High:** April-Oct. **To obtain tee times:** Call 3 days in advance starting at 8 a.m. **Miscellaneous:** Reduced fees (resort guests, twilight, seniors, juniors), metal spikes, range (grass/mats), club rentals, lodging, credit cards (MC, V, AE, D).
Reader Comments: Outstanding practice facility ... Great course, pricey though ... Good greens ... Well conditioned but too expensive ... Well-kept course, one of the nicest in the area ... Good staff, fun to play. Beautiful place, great course ... Great challenge, always in great shape.

★★★ RIVER CLUB ON THE ASHLEY
SP-222 Fairington Dr., Summerville, 29485, Dorchester County, (843)873-7110, (800)230-1639, 19 miles NW of Charleston.
Holes: 18. **Yards:** 6,712/5,025. **Par:** 72/72. **Course Rating:** 71.2/68.1. **Slope:** 117/114. **Green Fee:** $15/$30. **Cart Fee:** $15/cart. **Walking Policy:** Walking at certain times. **Walkability:** 1. **Opened:** 1971. **Architect:** Russell Breelan. **Season:** Year-round. **High:** April-May. **To obtain tee times:** Call golf shop. **Miscellaneous:** Reduced fees (weekdays, low season, twilight, juniors), metal spikes, range (grass), club rentals, credit cards (MC, V), beginner friendly.
Reader Comments: Nothing better ... Another must-play course, fast greens, plush fairways ... Great, but greens were rough ... Good pace of play.

SOUTH CAROLINA

★★★★ RIVER FALLS PLANTATION

SP-100 Player Blvd., Duncan, 29334, Spartanburg County, (864)433-9192, 10 miles N of Greenville. **Web:** www.riverfallsgolf.com.
Holes: 18. **Yards:** 6,734/4,928. **Par:** 72/72. **Course Rating:** 72.1/68.2. **Slope:** 127/125. **Green Fee:** $35/$45. **Cart Fee:** Included in Green Fee. **Walking Policy:** Walking at certain times. **Walkability:** 5. **Opened:** 1990. **Architect:** Gary Player. **Season:** Year-round. **High:** April-Aug. **To obtain tee times:** Call golf shop. **Miscellaneous:** Reduced fees (low season, resort guests, seniors, juniors), discount packages, range (grass), club rentals, credit cards (MC, V, AE, D).
Reader Comments: Forgiving ... Enjoyable ... Rough is tough! Keep it straight ... Greens great, service excellent, very slow play ... Excellent in every way ... Hilly ... An interesting, challenging course ... Always in great shape, fairways tight, learn to draw & fade ... Lots of hills.

THE RIVER GOLF CLUB

PU-307 Riverside Blvd., North Augusta, 29841, Aiken County, (803)202-0110, 1 miles N of Augusta. **E-mail:** riverclub@gabn.net. **Web:** www.rivergolfclub.com.
Holes: 18. **Yards:** 6,847/5,081. **Par:** 71/71. **Course Rating:** 72.2/68.4. **Slope:** 130/114. **Green Fee:** $15/$30. **Cart Fee:** $13/person. **Walking Policy:** Walking at certain times. **Walkability:** 1. **Opened:** 1998. **Architect:** Jim Fazio. **Season:** Year-round. **High:** March-May. **To obtain tee times:** Call (803)202-0110. **Miscellaneous:** Reduced fees (weekdays, twilight, seniors, juniors), range (grass), club rentals, credit cards (MC, V, AE), beginner friendly (beginner clinics).

★★★½ RIVER HILLS GOLF & COUNTRY CLUB

PU-3670 Ceder Creek Run, Little River, 29566, Horry County, (803)399-2100, (800)264-3810, 10 miles N of Myrtle Beach.
Holes: 18. **Yards:** 7,006/4,932. **Par:** 72/72. **Course Rating:** 73.3/67.7. **Slope:** 136/120. **Green Fee:** $15/$55. **Cart Fee:** $20/person. **Walking Policy:** Mandatory cart. **Walkability:** 3. **Opened:** 1989. **Architect:** Tom Jackson. **Season:** Year-round. **High:** Spring/Fall. **To obtain tee times:** Call up to 1 year in advance. **Miscellaneous:** Reduced fees (twilight, juniors), discount packages, metal spikes, range (grass), club rentals, credit cards (MC, V).
Reader Comments: Unknown delight ... Hidden gem ... Must hit ball long and hit targets, great shape ... Tight, tough to keep in bounds, nice course ... Great tournament course ... Great range, restaurant, much water, can't let it fly ... Nice layout ... Beach favorite.

RIVER OAKS GOLF PLANTATION

R-831 River Oaks Dr., Myrtle Beach, 29577, Horry County, (803)236-2222.
Holes: 27. **Green Fee:** $25/$60. **Cart Fee:** Included in Green Fee. **Walking Policy:** Mandatory cart. **Walkability:** N/A. **Opened:** 1987. **Architect:** Gene Hamm. **Season:** Year-round. **High:** Spring/Fall. **To obtain tee times:** Call golf shop or book through hotel. **Miscellaneous:** Reduced fees (low season, resort guests, twilight, juniors), discount packages, metal spikes, range (grass), club rentals, credit cards (MC, V, AE).

★★★½ BEAR/FOX

Yards: 6,778/5,133. **Par:** 72/72. **Course Rating:** 72.0/69.7. **Slope:** 126/116.
Reader Comments: Typical beach course ... Very nice & lush ... Great design. Excellent staff. Great condition ... Good blend of holes and hazards ... Beautiful oak trees ... Relaxed atmosphere... Hidden jewel. Too tough for high handicappers ... Nice layout ... Good plantation course ... Water everywhere.

★★★½ OTTER/BEAR

Yards: 6,877/5,188. **Par:** 72/72. **Course Rating:** 72.5/69.7. **Slope:** 125/118.
Reader Comments: Course is a sleeper in Myrtle, good layout and fun to play ... Bring plenty of golf balls, you'll need them ... Decent, but nothing fancy ... Don't slice ... The Bear (9 holes) is just that ... U.S. Open rough ... Well maintained, treelined but fair.

★★★½ OTTER/FOX

Yards: 6,791/5,043. **Par:** 72/72. **Course Rating:** 71.7/69.7. **Slope:** 125/118. .
Reader Comments: Beautiful course, hard play, trees galore ... I would play it again ... Lots of water ... Fun place to take the family ... Fox was great ... Three interesting and different nines ... Great warm-up ... Great layout, some water.

★★★½ ROBBERS ROOST GOLF COURSE

PU-Hwy. 17 N., North Myrtle Beach, 29597, Horry County, (843)249-1471, (800)352-2384.
Holes: 18. **Yards:** 7,148/5,387. **Par:** 70/72. **Course Rating:** 74.4/70.2. **Slope:** 137/116. **Green Fee:** $29/$56. **Cart Fee:** Included in Green Fee. **Walking Policy:** Mandatory cart. **Walkability:** 1. **Opened:** 1968. **Architect:** Russell Breeden. **Season:** Year-round. **High:** March-April. **To obtain tee times:** Call up to 1 year in advance. **Miscellaneous:** Reduced fees (low season, twilight, juniors), discount packages, metal spikes, range (grass), club rentals, credit cards (MC, V, AE, D).
Reader Comments: Typical beach course ... Easy to keep it in play; nice par-5s ... OK for average golfer ... Variety of shots ... Long par 4s, water, trees, super par 5s ... Very enjoyable beach course ... Good course, greens ... Nice track, plays long ... Excellent for middle handicap.

★★½   ROLLING HILLS GOLF CLUB
PU-1790 Hwy. 501, Galavants Ferry, 29544, Horry County, (803)358-4653, (800)633-2380, 20 miles W of Conway.
Holes: 18. **Yards:** 6,749/5,141. **Par:** 72/72. **Course Rating:** 72.6/68.3. **Slope:** 133/109. **Green Fee:** $2/$18. **Cart Fee:** $20/person. **Walking Policy:** Walking at certain times. **Walkability:** 3. **Opened:** 1988. **Architect:** Gene Hamm. **Season:** Year-round. **High:** Spring/Fall. **To obtain tee times:** Call (800)633-2480. **Miscellaneous:** Reduced fees (weekdays, low season, resort guests, twilight, seniors, juniors), discount packages, metal spikes, range (grass), club rentals, credit cards (MC, V, AE, D).
Reader Comments: Very enjoyable ... A little out of the way but worth the trip ... Beautiful course ... Wide open ... Basic golf course ... Good tune-up for the Beach ... Improving by leaps and bounds.

ROSE HILL COUNTRY CLUB
One Clubhouse Dr., Bluffton, 29910, Beaufort County, (843)757-2160.
Special Notes: Call club for further information.

★★½   SALUDA VALLEY COUNTRY CLUB
SP-598 Beaver Dam Rd., Williamston, 29697, Anderson County, (864)847-7102, 20 miles S of Greenville.
Holes: 18. **Yards:** 6,430/5,126. **Par:** 72/72. **Course Rating:** 70.8/69.4. **Slope:** 119/114. **Green Fee:** $15/$21. **Cart Fee:** $10/person. **Walking Policy:** Unrestricted walking. **Walkability:** 2. **Opened:** 1964. **Architect:** William B. Lewis. **Season:** Year-round. **High:** April-Sept. **To obtain tee times:** Call 3 days in advance. **Miscellaneous:** Reduced fees (weekdays), metal spikes, range (grass/mats), credit cards (MC, V).
Reader Comments: Good layout, improvements have been made ... Good layout & condition ... Short, open ... Plenty of trees ... Nice course, but short ... Nice old layout, super value ... Short course, good for all.

★★★½   SANTEE NATIONAL GOLF CLUB
R-Hwy. 6 W., Santee, 29142, Orangeburg County, (803)854-3531, (800)448-0152, 60 miles NW of Charleston.
Holes: 18. **Yards:** 6,858/4,748. **Par:** 72/72. **Course Rating:** 72.1/68.2. **Slope:** 120/116. **Green Fee:** $25/$47. **Cart Fee:** Included in Green Fee. **Walking Policy:** Mandatory cart. **Walkability:** 2. **Opened:** 1989. **Architect:** Porter Gibson. **Season:** Year-round. **High:** Spring/Fall. **To obtain tee times:** Call (800)488-0152 or call the Golf Santee Package office at 1-800-345-7888. **Miscellaneous:** Reduced fees (resort guests), discount packages, metal spikes, range (grass), club rentals, lodging (8 rooms), credit cards (MC, V, AE, D).
Reader Comments: You'll need very club in your bag ... Very nice course ... Good layout ... Nice place—nice people ... Very popular ... Some great holes, greens good , fairways OK ... Wide fairways. Good greens. Great price ... Excellent all the time ... Good layou ... A challenge.

★★★   SEA GULL GOLF CLUB
PU-P.O. Box 2607,Hwy. 17S, Pawleys Island, 29585, Georgetown County, (843)448-5931, (800)TEE-OFFS, 20 miles S of Myrtle Beach. **Web:** www.linksgroup.com.
Holes: 18. **Yards:** 6,910/5,250. **Par:** 72/72. **Course Rating:** 74.0/69.6. **Slope:** 134/120. **Green Fee:** $34/$70. **Cart Fee:** Included in Green Fee. **Walking Policy:** Walking at certain times. **Walkability:** 3. **Opened:** 1968. **Architect:** Gene Hamm. **Season:** Year-round. **High:** Spring/Fall. **To obtain tee times:** Call (800)TEE-OFFS. **Miscellaneous:** Reduced fees (low season, juniors), club rentals, lodging (100 rooms), credit cards (MC, V, D), beginner friendly.
Reader Comments: Old standard ... Nice greens, watch out for gators! ... Some great golf holes, and pretty ... Great value for your money ... Nice layout, can score well ... Wide fairways, fun course to play.

SEA PINES PLANTATION CLUB
R-100 N. Sea Pines Dr., Hilton Head Island, 29928, Beaufort County, (843)842-8484, (800)SEA-PINE, 30 miles E of Savannah, GA. **Web:** www.seapines.com.
★★★½   OCEAN COURSE
Holes: 18. **Yards:** 6,906/5,325. **Par:** 72/72. **Course Rating:** 72.8/71.1. **Slope:** 133/124. **Green Fee:** $79/$95. **Cart Fee:** Included in Green Fee. **Walking Policy:** Unrestricted walking. **Walkability:** 2. **Opened:** 1960. **Architect:** George Cobb, Mark McCumber. **Season:** Year-round. **High:** Spring/Fall. **To obtain tee times:** Call (800)SEA-PINE. **Miscellaneous:** Reduced fees (low season, resort guests, juniors), discount packages, range (grass), club rentals, lodging, credit cards (MC, V, AE, D).
Reader Comments: Friendly, good family course. Watch for alligators. Much improved ... Challenging course with great ocean holes and view ... If it's windy, bring an extra sleeve or two ... Everything vacation golf should be ... Great course, tough ... Nice track ... Tight fairways ... Good value for the pricey area.

SOUTH CAROLINA

★★★½ SEA MARSH COURSE
Holes: 18. **Yards:** 6,515/5,054. **Par:** 72/72. **Course Rating:** 70.0/69.8. **Slope:** 120/123. **Green Fee:** $69/$86. **Cart Fee:** Included in Green Fee. **Walking Policy:** Unrestricted walking. **Walkability:** 2. **Opened:** 1964. **Architect:** George Cobb. **Season:** Year-round. **High:** Spring/Fall. **To obtain tee times:** Call 800 number. **Miscellaneous:** Reduced fees (low season, resort guests, twilight, juniors), discount packages, range (grass), club rentals, lodging, credit cards (MC, V, AE, D).
Reader Comments: Vacation course, relaxing and not too difficult. Solid, no frills and fun to walk ... I love this place–felt like home! ... Enjoyable ... Not long, but challenging for all golfers ... Good basic course.

★★★ SHADOWMOSS PLANTATION GOLF CLUB
SP-20 Dunvegan Dr., Charleston, 29414, Charleston County, (843)556-8251, (800)338-4971.
Holes: 18. **Yards:** 6,700/5,200. **Par:** 72/72. **Course Rating:** 72.4/70.2. **Slope:** 123/120. **Green Fee:** $22/$45. **Cart Fee:** Included in Green Fee. **Walking Policy:** Walking at certain times. **Walkability:** 1. **Opened:** 1971. **Architect:** Russell Breeden. **Season:** Year-round. **High:** March-May. **To obtain tee times:** Call up to 6 months in advance. **Miscellaneous:** Reduced fees (weekdays, low season, resort guests, twilight, juniors), discount packages, metal spikes, range (grass), club rentals, credit cards (MC, V, AE, D), beginner friendly.
Reader Comments: Best golf value in Charleston is also most improved course, under 4 hours to play ... Tough par 3s on back 9 ... High value. Noticeable improvements ... Excellent course. Good people! ... Excellent greens.

SHIPYARD GOLF CLUB
R-P.O. Drawer 7229, Hilton Head Island, 29938, Beaufort County, (843)686-8802.
Holes: 27. **Green Fee:** $59/$88. **Cart Fee:** Included in Green Fee. **Walkability:** 2. **Architect:** George W. Cobb. **To obtain tee times:** Call.
★★★ BRIGANTINE/CLIPPER
Yards: 6,858/5,202. **Par:** 72/72. **Course Rating:** 73.0/70.5. **Slope:** 128/116. **Walking Policy:** Mandatory cart. **Season:** Year-round. **High:** Feb.-May. **Miscellaneous:** Reduced fees (twilight), range (grass/mats), club rentals, lodging, credit cards (MC, V, AE).
Reader Comments: Short resort course ... Good vacation course. Surrounded by homes ... A very pleasant experience ... Quick greens, a fair challenge ... Plenty of water, not a bad course ... Enjoyable long iron target course ... Staff was great ... Slow play ... Okay for an average player.
★★★ CLIPPER/GALLEON
Yards: 6,878/5,391. **Par:** 72/72. **Course Rating:** 73.0/70.5. **Slope:** 129/119. **Walking Policy:** Mandatory cart. **Season:** Year-round. **High:** Spring/ Fall. **Miscellaneous:** Reduced fees (twilight), discount packages, range (grass/mats), club rentals, lodging, credit cards (MC, V, AE).
Notes: 1983-1986 Hilton Senior P.G.A. Tour International.
Reader Comments: Nice water holes ... Fun course, very nice ... Golf course is OK, but not really interesting ... Hilton Head golf, alligators, water.
★★★ GALLEON/BRIGANTINE
Yards: 6,738/5,127. **Par:** 72/72. **Course Rating:** 72.6/68.8. **Slope:** 128/114. **Walking Policy:** Unrestricted walking. **Season:** Feb.-May. **Miscellaneous:** Reduced fees (twilight), range (grass/mats), caddies, club rentals, lodging, credit cards (MC, V, AE).
Reader Comments: Nice old Hilton Head course but the holes tend to look alike on the three nines ... Lots of water, good layout ... A most pleasurable experience. Gators let us play through ... Tough, tight, too much water!

★★★★ SOUTH CAROLINA NATIONAL GOLF CLUB *Value, Pace*
SP-8 Waveland Ave., Beaufort, 29902, Beaufort County, (843)524-0300, (800)221-9582, 1 miles E of Beaufort.
Holes: 18. **Yards:** 6,625/4,933. **Par:** 71/71. **Course Rating:** 71.0/67.4. **Slope:** 127/116. **Green Fee:** $35/$49. **Cart Fee:** Included in Green Fee. **Walking Policy:** Walking at certain times. **Walkability:** 1. **Opened:** 1985. **Architect:** George Cobb. **Season:** Year-round. **To obtain tee times:** Call up to a year in advance at 1-800-933-0050. **Miscellaneous:** Reduced fees (low season, resort guests, twilight, juniors), discount packages, metal spikes, range (grass), club rentals, credit cards (MC, V, AE, D), beginner friendly (wee links).
Reader Comments: A sleeper in the Hilton Head area ... Back-to-back par 3s across the marsh are the best I've seen ... Lots of improvement ... Short with lots of strategy ... Great service, 1st class ... Very pretty. Great value.

★★★ SPRING LAKE COUNTRY CLUB
SP-1375 Spring Lake Rd., York, 29745, York County, (803)684-4898, 20 miles SW of Charlotte, NC.
Holes: 18. **Yards:** 6,748/4,975. **Par:** 72/72. **Course Rating:** 72.8/67.3. **Slope:** 126/108. **Green Fee:** $16/$25. **Cart Fee:** $13/person. **Walking Policy:** Walking at certain times. **Walkability:** 3. **Opened:** 1960. **Architect:** Fred Bolton/Bob Renaud. **Season:** Year-round. **High:** May-Oct. **To obtain tee times:** Call for Fridays, weekends and holidays. **Miscellaneous:** Metal spikes, range (grass), club rentals, credit cards (MC, V), beginner friendly (golf lessons).

Reader Comments: Nice course, tough pin placements, tough greens ... Beautiful greens and plush fairways, always well kept.

★★★½ STONEY POINT GOLF CLUB
SP-709 Swing About Dr., Greenwood, 29648, Greenwood County, (864)942-0900, 35 miles S of Greenville.
Holes: 18. **Yards:** 6,760/5,060. **Par:** 72/72. **Course Rating:** 72.1/70.3. **Slope:** 125/120. **Green Fee:** $15/$22. **Cart Fee:** $13/person. **Walking Policy:** Walking at certain times. **Walkability:** 3. **Opened:** 1990. **Architect:** Tom Jackson. **Season:** Year-round. **High:** Spring/Fall. **To obtain tee times:** Call 7 days in advance. **Miscellaneous:** Reduced fees (twilight, seniors, juniors), range (grass), club rentals, credit cards (MC, V).
Reader Comments: Very enjoyable. Mix of hard and easy holes ... Hated to leave! ... Nice course ... You will need all your clubs and skill. A great challenge ... Great golf, great scenery ... Good for average golfer ... Love the challenge, tight.

★★½ SUMMERSETT GOLF CLUB
SP-111 Pilot Rd., Greenville, 29609, Greenville County, (864)834-4781, 5 miles N of Greenville.
Holes: 18. **Yards:** 6,025/4,910. **Par:** 72/72. **Course Rating:** 68.3/67.6. **Slope:** 114/119. **Green Fee:** $12/$19. **Cart Fee:** $11/person. **Walking Policy:** Walking at certain times. **Walkability:** 3. **Opened:** 1938. **Architect:** Tom Jackson. **Season:** Year-round. **High:** April-Aug. **To obtain tee times:** Call 7 days in advance. **Miscellaneous:** Reduced fees (seniors), discount packages, metal spikes, club rentals, credit cards (MC, V).
Reader Comments: Scenery will astound you ... Could be great just need some work ... Tight, lots of water ... Many hills.

★★★★ SURF GOLF & BEACH CLUB
SP-1701 Springland Lane, North Myrtle Beach, 29597, Horry County, (843)249-1524, (800)765-7873, 60 miles S of Wilmington.
Holes: 18. **Yards:** 6,842/5,178. **Par:** 72/72. **Course Rating:** 73.1/68.2. **Slope:** 131/109. **Green Fee:** $38/$75. **Cart Fee:** $18/person. **Walking Policy:** Mandatory cart. **Walkability:** 1. **Opened:** 1960. **Architect:** George Cobb. **Season:** Year-round. **High:** Spring/Fall. **To obtain tee times:** Contact golf shop or have hotel make tee times. **Miscellaneous:** Reduced fees (low season), discount packages, range (grass/mats), club rentals, credit cards (MC, V).
Reader Comments: Fantastic, a traditional gem ... Perfect greens ... Great and then some! Purists would love it! ... Must play! Bent greens are great! ... Outstanding ... Class operation ... Great old-style course, excellent condition ... New greens, great course, doglegs, water ... Mature, traditional course. Fine experience.

★★★★½ TIDEWATER GOLF CLUB & PLANTATION *Condition*
PU-4901 Little River Neck Rd., North Myrtle Beach, 29582, Horry County, (843)249-3829, (800)446-5363, 10 miles N of Myrtle Beach. **Web:** www.tide-water.com.
Holes: 18. **Yards:** 7,078/4,615. **Par:** 72/72. **Course Rating:** 74.8/67.1. **Slope:** 144/115. **Green Fee:** $90/$135. **Cart Fee:** Included in Green Fee. **Walking Policy:** Unrestricted walking. **Walkability:** 3. **Opened:** 1990. **Architect:** Ken Tomlinson. **Season:** Year-round. **High:** Feb.-May/Sept.-Nov. **To obtain tee times:** Call golf shop, deposit required. **Miscellaneous:** Reduced fees (juniors), range (grass), club rentals, lodging (100 rooms), credit cards (MC, V, AE).
Notes: Ranked 15th in 1999 Best in State; 29th in 1996 America's Top 75 Upscale Courses.
Reader Comments: Fairest test of all ... Incredibly beautiful ... Doesn't get much better than this ... Great greens, great layout ... Great par 3s, many memorable holes, great practice facility, good layout ... Outstanding facility, top-notch conditions ... Challenging holes, great variety ... Beautiful, expensive ... Toughest around.

★★★½ TIMBERLAKE PLANTATION GOLF CLUB
SP-284 Club Dr., Chapin, 29036, Lexington County, (803)345-9909, 30 miles NW of Columbia.
Holes: 18. **Yards:** 6,703/5,111. **Par:** 72/72. **Course Rating:** 73.2/69.8. **Slope:** 132/118. **Green Fee:** $16/$22. **Cart Fee:** $12/person. **Walking Policy:** Unrestricted walking. **Walkability:** 2. **Opened:** 1986. **Architect:** Willard Byrd. **Season:** Year-round. **High:** April-May/Aug.-Nov. **To obtain tee times:** Call 7 days in advance. **Miscellaneous:** Reduced fees (weekdays, low season, resort guests, seniors, juniors), discount packages, metal spikes, range (grass), club rentals, credit cards (MC, V, AE).
Reader Comments: Nice course, fun to play ... Great public golf! ... Excellent ... Tough layout but very playable. The more I play it, the smarter I get ... Get caught up in the beauty and score high! ... Fairways great, greens need work.

TOURNAMENT PLAYER'S CLUB OF MYRTLE BEACH
PU-1199 TPC Blvd., Myrtle Beach, 29576, Horry County, (843)357-3399, (888)742-8721, 90 miles N of Charleston, SC. **E-mail:** tpcmbbox@mail.pgatour.com. **Web:** www.tpc-mb.com.
Holes: 18. **Yards:** 6,950/5,118. **Par:** 72/72. **Course Rating:** 74.0/70.3. **Slope:** 145/125. **Green Fee:** $54/$153. **Cart Fee:** $22/person. **Walking Policy:** Walking at certain times. **Walkability:** 2. **Opened:** 1999. **Architect:** Tom Fazio/Lanny Wadkins. **Season:** Year-round. **High:** Feb.-May/

Sept.-Nov. **To obtain tee times:** Call golf shop at (888)742-8721. **Miscellaneous:** Reduced fees (twilight, juniors), range (grass), club rentals, credit cards (MC, V, AE), beginner friendly (5 tee box options).
Notes: Ranked 9th in 1999 Best New Upscale Public. Home of the Ingersoll-Rand Senior Tour Championship.

★★★★ TRADITION GOLF CLUB

PU-1027 Willbrook Blvd., Pawleys Island, 29585, Georgetown County, (843)237-5041, 20 miles S of Myrtle Beach. **Web:** www.tradition.com.
Holes: 18. **Yards:** 6,919/5,111. **Par:** 72/72. **Course Rating:** 73.0/68.4. **Slope:** 130/113. **Green Fee:** $42/$89. **Cart Fee:** $20/person. **Walking Policy:** Walking at certain times. **Walkability:** 4.
Opened: 1995. **Architect:** Ron Garl. **Season:** Year-round. **High:** Spring/Fall. **To obtain tee times:** Call with credit card to reserve. **Miscellaneous:** Reduced fees (low season, twilight), discount packages, metal spikes, range (grass), club rentals, credit cards (MC, V), beginner friendly (5 sets of tees).
Reader Comments: Well run, well maintained, enjoyable ... Just great .:. Very enjoyable layout, chipping & putting key ... Superior in every way ... Have not played a course in better condition ... Highly enjoyable ... Drive straight, many water hazards ... New, but great design ... Good 3s, reachable 5s, plateau landing areas.

★★★★ TRUE BLUE GOLF CLUB

PU-900 Blue Stem Dr., Pawleys Island, 29585, Georgetown County, (803)235-0900, (888)483-6800, 20 miles S of Myrtle Beach. **E-mail:** trueblue@s.c.coast.net. **Web:** www.truebluegolfl.com.
Holes: 18. **Yards:** 6,980/5,880. **Par:** 72/72. **Course Rating:** 74.3/71.4. **Slope:** 145/123. **Green Fee:** $50/$90. **Cart Fee:** $18/person. **Walking Policy:** Mandatory cart. **Walkability:** 2. **Opened:** 1998. **Architect:** Mike Strantz. **Season:** Year-round. **High:** Spring/Fall. **To obtain tee times:** Call toll-free number. **Miscellaneous:** Range (grass/mats), club rentals, credit cards (MC, V, AE, D).
Notes: Ranked 7th in 1999 Best in State.
Reader Comments: Every design concept in golf included in 18 holes ... Awesome ... Good layout, tricked-up a bit ... Lots of sand ... Tough approaches into greens, challenging ... Multiple tees, unique challenge ... New, will be great ... Solid. A come-backer ... Awesome layout. Needs time to mature ... New, beautiful, expensive.

★★★½ VERDAE GREENS GOLF CLUB

R-650 Verdae Blvd., Greenville, 29607, Greenville County, (864)676-1500, (800)849-7529, 90 miles SW of Charlotte, NC.
Holes: 18. **Yards:** 7,041/5,012. **Par:** 72/72. **Course Rating:** 74.2/68.1. **Slope:** 140/116. **Green Fee:** $38/$52. **Cart Fee:** Included in Green Fee. **Walking Policy:** Walking at certain times.
Walkability: 4. **Opened:** 1989. **Architect:** Willard Byrd. **Season:** Year-round. **High:** March-Nov.
To obtain tee times: Call 7 days in advance. **Miscellaneous:** Reduced fees (weekdays, low season, resort guests, twilight, seniors, juniors), discount
packages, range (grass/mats), club rentals, lodging (275 rooms), credit cards (MC, V, AE).
Reader Comments: Fun, pretty, challenging, perfect ... Great layout, very busy, but good pace ... A little pricey for area, hard, fast greens ... Great layout .:. Good layout with some demanding holes ... A must play.

★★★ VILLAGE GREEN GOLF CLUB

SP-Hwy. 176, Gramling, 29348, Spartanburg County, (864)472-2411, 14 miles NW of Spartanburg.
Holes: 18. **Yards:** 6,372/5,280. **Par:** 72/74. **Course Rating:** 71.0/70.0. **Slope:** 122/123. **Green Fee:** $14/$19. **Cart Fee:** $10/person. **Walking Policy:** Unrestricted walking. **Walkability:** 3.
Opened: 1969. **Architect:** Russell Breeden/Dan Breeden. **Season:** Year-round. **High:** April-Sept. **To obtain tee times:** Call on Thursday for upcoming weekend. **Miscellaneous:** Metal spikes, range (grass), club rentals.
Reader Comments: Great hiding place with great service ... Short course, good for beginners ... Short course in good shape and fair price.

★★★½ WACHESAW PLANTATION EAST

SP-911 Riverwood Dr., Murrells Inlet, 29576, Georgetown County, (843)357-2090, (888)922-0027, 90 miles N of Charleston.
Holes: 18. **Yards:** 6,993/4,995. **Par:** 72/72. **Course Rating:** 73.6/68.8. **Slope:** 135/117. **Green Fee:** $55/$107. **Cart Fee:** Included in Green Fee. **Walking Policy:** Walking at certain times. **Walkability:** 1. **Opened:** 1996. **Architect:** Clyde Johnston. **Season:** Year-round. **High:** Spring/Fall. **To obtain tee times:** Call golf shop or book through hotel. **Miscellaneous:** Reduced fees (low season, resort guests, juniors), discount packages, range (grass/mats), club rentals, credit cards (MC, V, AE).
Notes: 1997 LPGA Susan G. Komen International.
Reader Comments: Felt like the only person on the course, great design ... Best greens ... Great layout ... A real test ... A top-quality course ... Great playable course ... Everything you

want, this course has it ... Pleasant to play ... Very enjoyable ... Woman friendly, like GPS system ... A winner.

★★★½ THE WALKER COURSE AT CLEMSON UNIVERSITY

SP-110 Madren Center Dr., Clemson, 29634, Pickens County, (864)656-0236, 40 miles S of Greenville. **Web:** www.clemson.edu.

Holes: 18. **Yards:** 6,911/4,667. **Par:** 72/72. **Course Rating:** 72.8/65.7. **Slope:** 137/107. **Green Fee:** $26/$47. **Cart Fee:** Included in Green Fee. **Walking Policy:** Unrestricted walking. **Walkability:** 4. **Opened:** 1995. **Architect:** D.J. DeVictor. **Season:** Year-round. **High:** March-Oct. **To obtain tee times:** Call up to 3 days in advance. **Miscellaneous:** Reduced fees (weekdays, low season, twilight, seniors, juniors), range (grass/mats), club rentals, lodging (89 rooms), credit cards (MC, V, AE), beginner friendly.

Reader Comments: Beautiful layout, course condition improved ... Last four holes will bring you to your knees ... Superb university course ... Still maturing, great layout ... Every hole was memorable ... A highly playable, scenic course, challenging and fun ... New course, will be great in a few years ... Nice course ... Hilly!

WATERFORD GOLF CLUB

SP-1900 Clubhouse Rd., Rock Hill, 29730, (803)324-0300.
Special Notes: Call club for further information

WATERWAY HILLS GOLF CLUB

R-9731 Hwy. 17N, Restaurant Row, Myrtle Beach, 29578, Horry County, (843)449-6488, (800)344-5590. **E-mail:** info@mbn.com. **Web:** www.mbn.com.

Holes: 27. **Walkability:** 2. **Opened:** 1975. **Architect:** Robert Trent Jones/Rees Jones. **Season:** Year-round. **High:** Spring/Fall. **To obtain tee times:** Call your hotel golf director or Tee Time Central 800 number up to 1 year in advance

★★★½ LAKES/RAVINES

Yards: 6,339/4,825. **Par:** 72/72. **Course Rating:** 70.6/67.3. **Slope:** 123/110. **Green Fee:** $27/$62. **Cart Fee:** $20/person. **Walking Policy:** Unrestricted walking. . **Miscellaneous:** Reduced fees (low season, resort guests, twilight, juniors), discount packages, range (grass), club rentals, credit cards (MC, V, AE, D, Diners Club).

Reader Comments: Good course ... Confidence booster... Fun track ... Staff very friendly, course nice ... Nice layout, original ... Basic course, tight fairways ... Unique, fun, interesting course ... Average layout. Always in great condition ... Solid, terrific and worth the trip ... Love the Gondola ride from parking lot to 1st tee.

★★★½ OAKS/LAKES

Yards: 6,461/5,069. **Par:** 72/72. **Course Rating:** 71.0/68.7. **Slope:** 119/113. **Green Fee:** $27/$62. **Cart Fee:** $20/person. **Walking Policy:** Walking at certain times. **Miscellaneous:** Reduced fees (low season, resort guests, twilight, juniors), discount packages, range (grass/mats), club rentals, credit cards (MC, V, AE, D, Diners Club, Carte Blanche).

Reader Comments: Tight course, you will like it ... Trees add challenge ... Cable car ride over the waterway to golf course ... Very fair and straightforward ... Nice 3 nine-hole courses.

★★★½ RAVINES/OAKS

Holes: 27. **Yards:** 6,420/4,914. **Par:** 72/72. **Course Rating:** 70.8/67.6. **Slope:** 121/113. **Green Fee:** $23/$58. **Cart Fee:** $18/person. **Walking Policy:** Walking at certain times. **Miscellaneous:** Reduced fees (low season, resort guests, twilight, juniors), discount packages, range (grass/mats), club rentals, credit cards (MC, V, AE, D, Diners Club, Carte Blanche).

Reader Comments: All 3 courses are fun. Need extra golf balls ... Short course, driver not a necessity ... Ravine Course very difficult ... Nice courses to warm up on ... Tee off in real wilderness, what fun!

★★★ WEDGEFIELD PLANTATION GOLF CLUB

SP-Hwy 701 N., Georgetown, 29440, Georgetown County, (843)546-8587, 5 miles N of Georgetown.

Holes: 18. **Yards:** 6,299/5,249. **Par:** 72/73. **Course Rating:** 70.2/69.9. **Slope:** 124/119. **Green Fee:** $35/$55. **Cart Fee:** Included in Green Fee. **Walking Policy:** Mandatory cart. **Walkability:** 1. **Opened:** 1974. **Architect:** Porter Gibson. **Season:** Year-round. **High:** Spring/Fall. **To obtain tee times:** Call golf shop. **Miscellaneous:** Reduced fees (low season, twilight), discount packages, metal spikes, range (grass), club rentals, credit cards (MC, V).

Reader Comments: Will always be on my list in South Carolina ... Gators! Great old oaks! ... Excellent fun to play ... Needs some sparkle, has potential ... Quiet challenge, nice layout ... Challenging, choose your shots ... Excellent course, tight fairways, fast greens.

★★★½ THE WELLMAN CLUB

PU-Hwy. 41-51 S., 328 Country Club Dr., Johnsonville, 29555, Florence County, (803)386-2521, (800)258-2935, 42 miles W of Myrtle Beach. **E-mail:** wellmanclub@wellmanclub.com. **Web:** www.wellmanclub.com.

Holes: 18. **Yards:** 7,018/5,281. **Par:** 72/72. **Course Rating:** 73.9/69.5. **Slope:** 129/105. **Green Fee:** $16/$28. **Cart Fee:** $15/person. **Walking Policy:** Walking at certain times. **Walkability:** 2.

SOUTH CAROLINA

Opened: 1966. **Architect:** Ellis Maples/Ed Seay. **Season:** Year-round. **High:** March-April. **To obtain tee times:** Call at least 2 days in advance. **Miscellaneous:** Reduced fees (weekdays, low season, resort guests, seniors, juniors), discount packages, range (grass), club rentals, credit cards (MC, V, AE), beginner friendly.
Reader Comments: Challenging layout ... It's a bear from tips. Excellent value ... Very nice course, reasonable ... Course is generally in good shape ... Hidden treasure ... Good golf experience.

★½ WHITE PINES GOLF CLUB
PU-614 Mary Lane, Camden, 29020, Kershaw County, (803)432-7442, 5 miles NE of Camden.
Holes: 18. **Yards:** 6,373/4,806. **Par:** 72/72. **Course Rating:** 69.4/66.9. **Slope:** 115/112. **Green Fee:** $17/$24. **Cart Fee:** Included in Green Fee. **Walking Policy:** Mandatory cart. **Walkability:** 1. **Opened:** 1969. **Architect:** Griffen Fletcher. **Season:** Year-round. **High:** April-Oct. **To obtain tee times:** First come, first served. **Miscellaneous:** Reduced fees (weekdays, resort guests, seniors), discount packages, metal spikes, range (grass), club rentals.

★★★½ WICKED STICK GOLF LINKS
R-1051 Coventry Rd., Myrtle Beach, 29575, Horry County, (843)215-2500, (800)797-8425, 5 miles S of Myrtle Beach. **E-mail:** wkdstk@sccoast.net. **Web:** www.wickedstick.com.
Holes: 18. **Yards:** 7,001/4,911. **Par:** 72/72. **Course Rating:** 72.2/70.1. **Slope:** 129/123. **Green Fee:** $35/$57. **Cart Fee:** $20/person. **Walking Policy:** Walking at certain times. **Walkability:** 1. **Opened:** 1995. **Architect:** Clyde Johnston/John Daly. **Season:** Year-round. **High:** Feb.-April/Oct.-Nov. **To obtain tee times:** Call up to 13 months in advance. Advance tee times must be secured by credit card. **Miscellaneous:** Reduced fees (low season, resort guests, twilight, juniors), discount packages, metal spikes, range (grass/mats), club rentals, credit cards (MC, V), beginner friendly.
Reader Comments: Great course ... Windy! Enjoyed it ... A wide open, fun course ... Nice, tough with wind ... Enjoyable ... Good variety of holes, needs a little age ... Links course, nice shape ... Great links ... Tricky, hard to play, green's good ... Neat par 5s ... Wide open, I like it, different.

WILD DUNES RESORT
★★★½ HARBOR COURSE
R-5881 Palmetto Dr., Isle of Palms, 29451, Charleston County, (843)886-2301, (800)845-8880, 12 miles SW of Charleston.
Holes: 18. **Yards:** 6,446/4,774. **Par:** 70/70. **Course Rating:** 70.9/68.1. **Slope:** 124/117. **Green Fee:** $45/$100. **Cart Fee:** Included in Green Fee. **Walking Policy:** Mandatory cart. **Walkability:** 3. **Opened:** 1986. **Architect:** Tom Fazio. **Season:** Year-round. **High:** Spring/Fall. **To obtain tee times:** Call golf shop at (843)886-2164. **Miscellaneous:** Reduced fees (low season, resort guests, twilight, juniors), discount packages, club rentals, lodging, credit cards (MC, V, AE, D).
Reader Comments: Top 5 favorites ... Tight as hell ... Consistent greens. Great course ... Can't believe how much trouble you can get in on a short course ... Sun & water, what more could you want ... Great service, hit the ball straight or lose it ... Good water holes, views add joy ... Pricey, but a superb golf experience.

★★★★ LINKS COURSE
R-5757 Palm Blvd., Isle of Palms, 29451, Charleston County, (803)886-2180, (800)845-8880, 12 miles NE of Charleston.
Holes: 18. **Yards:** 6,722/4,849. **Par:** 72/72. **Course Rating:** 72.7/69.1. **Slope:** 131/121. **Green Fee:** $50/$145. **Cart Fee:** Included in Green Fee. **Walking Policy:** Unrestricted walking. **Walkability:** 2. **Opened:** 1980. **Architect:** Tom Fazio. **Season:** Year-round. **High:** Spring/Fall. **To obtain tee times:** Call golf shop. **Miscellaneous:** Reduced fees (low season, resort guests, juniors), discount packages, metal spikes, range (grass/mats), caddies, club rentals, lodging, credit cards (MC, V, AE, D, Diners Club).
Notes: Ranked 10th in 1999 Best in State; 26th in 1996 America's Top 75 Upscale Courses. 1985 U.S. Senior Amateur Championship.
Reader Comments: Tremendous challenge, good layout ... A treat ... One of the very best, a true test of golf, punishing when windy ... Good links course, lots of roll ... Resort course, resort cost, resort enjoyment ... Beautiful, challenging coastal track, memorable ... Tight, water, great 18th ... Spectacular course from 1-18.

WILD WING PLANTATION *Service*
★★★★ AVOCET COURSE *Condition*
R-1000 Wild Wing Blvd., Conway, 29526, Horry County, (843)347-9464, (800)736-9464, 7 miles N of Myrtle Beach. **E-mail:** wildwing@sccoast.net. **Web:** www.wildwing.com.
Holes: 18. **Yards:** 7,127/5,298. **Par:** 72/72. **Course Rating:** 74.4/70.4. **Slope:** 129/118. **Green Fee:** $30/$90. **Cart Fee:** $20/person. **Walking Policy:** Mandatory cart. **Walkability:** 2. **Opened:** 1993. **Architect:** Larry Nelson/Jeff Brauer. **Season:** Year-round. **High:** April/Oct. **To obtain tee times:** Call with credit to guarantee or book through hotel. **Miscellaneous:** Reduced fees (weekdays, low season, resort guests, twilight), discount packages, range (grass), club rentals, lodging (144 rooms), credit cards (MC, V, AE, D).
Notes: 1994 Top 10 Best New Course in America.

Reader Comments: Outstanding complex ... One of Myrtle's sleepers; well designed; memorable ... Leaves you breathless! ... Great design. Super condition. Interesting holes ... A true test! ... Best condition & greens in area. Great staff ... Excellent ... Good fun, good condition, fair test ... First-class complex, best layout.

★★★★ **FALCON COURSE** *Condition*

Holes: 18. **Yards:** 7,082/5,190. **Par:** 72/72. **Course Rating:** 74.4/70.4. **Slope:** 134/118. **Green Fee:** $30/$90. **Cart Fee:** $20/person. **Walking Policy:** Walking at certain times. **Walkability:** 3. **Opened:** 1994. **Architect:** Rees Jones. **Season:** Year-round. **High:** April/Oct. **To obtain tee times:** Call with credit to guarantee or book through hotel. **Miscellaneous:** Reduced fees (weekdays, low season, resort guests, twilight), discount packages, range (grass), club rentals, lodging (144 rooms), credit cards (MC, V, AE, D).

Reader Comments: Beautiful greens, nice staff ... Excellent facilities ... Immaculate, can eat off the fairway ... Demanding shotmaker's course ... Always in great shape ... Fun to play ... I have played every course at this facility. The conditions have always been excellent, the grounds are immaculate, and the staff very courteous.

★★★★ **HUMMINGBIRD COURSE** *Condition*

Holes: 18. **Yards:** 6,853/5,168. **Par:** 72/72. **Course Rating:** 73.6/69.5. **Slope:** 135/123. **Green Fee:** $24/$70. **Cart Fee:** $20/person. **Walking Policy:** Mandatory cart. **Walkability:** 2. **Opened:** 1992. **Architect:** Willard Byrd. **Season:** Year-round. **High:** April/Oct. **To obtain tee times:** Call with credit to guarantee or book through hotel. **Miscellaneous:** Reduced fees (weekdays, low season, resort guests, twilight), discount packages, range (grass), club rentals, credit cards (MC, V, AE, D).

Reader Comments: Excellent experience ... What a great group of courses ... Very nice, will play again ... Great greens. Yardage books very good ... Great condition, best greens ... Excellent condition. Great clubhouse. Friendly staff ... My personal favorite ... Challenging and fair. Pretty layout with interesting variety of holes.

★★★★½ **WOOD STORK COURSE** *Condition+, Pace*

Holes: 18. **Yards:** 7,044/5,409. **Par:** 72/72. **Course Rating:** 74.1/70.7. **Slope:** 130/121. **Green Fee:** $25/$84. **Cart Fee:** $20/person. **Walking Policy:** Mandatory cart. **Walkability:** 1. **Opened:** 1991. **Architect:** Willard Byrd. **Season:** Year-round. **High:** April/Oct. **To obtain tee times:** Call with credit to guarantee or book through hotel. **Miscellaneous:** Reduced fees (weekdays, low season, resort guests, twilight), discount packages, range (grass), club rentals, lodging (144 rooms), credit cards (MC, V, AE, D).

Reader Comments: Great course! Excellent greens! ... Outstanding ... Had a great time at this course ... Great fairways, tough rough ... Great condition, good layout, great golf ... Cannot beat ... Don't miss this one! ... Fun layout in great shape ... Very pretty, neat swales, unexpected hazards ... Lots of trees! Great clubhouse.

WINYAH BAY GOLF CLUB

PU-South Island Rd., Georgetown, 29440, Georgetown County, (843)527-7765, (877)527-7765. **Special Notes:** Call club for further information.

★★★★ **THE WITCH**

R-1900 Hwy. 544, Conway, 29526, Horry County, (843)448-1300, 8 miles N of Myrtle Beach. **Holes:** 18. **Yards:** 6,702/4,812. **Par:** 71/71. **Course Rating:** 71.2/69.0. **Slope:** 133/109. **Green Fee:** $44/$93. **Cart Fee:** Included in Green Fee. **Walking Policy:** Mandatory cart. **Walkability:** 4. **Opened:** 1989. **Architect:** Dan Maples. **Season:** Year-round. **High:** Feb.-May/Sept.-Nov. **To obtain tee times:** Call golf shop. Deposit required during peak season. **Miscellaneous:** Reduced fees (low season, juniors), discount packages, metal spikes, range (grass), club rentals, credit cards (MC, V).

Reader Comments: Amazing ... Scenic layout ... Great but hard, fair from whites ... Love it! Beautiful! ... More impressive each time I return ... Great design. Great people ... Unique, great layout, good golf ... Lovely and a true test for low handicap ... Lush fairways & greens ... Nice surprises, great layout, each nine different.

★★★★ **THE WIZARD GOLF COURSE**

PU-4601 Leeshore Blvd., Myrtle Beach, 29579, Horry County, (843)236-9393, 8 miles W of Myrtle Beach. **Web:** www.golflink.net/wizard. **Holes:** 18. **Yards:** 6,721/4,972. **Par:** 71/71. **Course Rating:** 71.9/70.2. **Slope:** 128/119. **Green Fee:** $26/$69. **Cart Fee:** $18/person. **Walking Policy:** Mandatory cart. **Walkability:** 3. **Opened:** 1996. **Architect:** Dan Maples. **Season:** Year-round. **High:** Feb.-May/Sept.-Nov. **To obtain tee times:** Call up to 1 year in advance. **Miscellaneous:** Reduced fees (weekdays, low season, twilight, juniors), discount packages, metal spikes, range (grass), club rentals, credit cards (MC, V).

Reader Comments: Well designed, wind a factor ... Good course, great greens ... Like its turf, great greens and unusual clubhouse. Best buy for the buck ... Open & nice greens ... What fun, a real challenge ... No. 18 requires 2 water carries ... Very good course made great by course condition and service ... Greens in great shape.

SOUTH DAKOTA

ABERDEEN COUNTRY CLUB
SP-NW 8th Ave., Aberdeen, 57401, (605)225-8135.
Special Notes: Call club for further information.

BELLE FOURCHE COUNTRY CLUB
PU-S. Hwy. 85, Belle Fourche, 57717, Butte County, (605)892-3472.
Holes: 9. **Yards:** 3,012/2,554. **Par:** 36/36. **Course Rating:** 68.9/68.0. **Slope:** 122/117. **Green Fee:** $22/$24. **Cart Fee:** $20/cart. **Walking Policy:** Unrestricted walking. **Walkability:** 3. **Opened:** 1927. **Season:** Year-round. **High:** April-Oct. **Miscellaneous:** Reduced fees (weekdays, low season), range (grass), club rentals, credit cards (MC, V, AE, D).

THE BLUFFS
PU-2021 E. Main St., Vermillion, 57069, Clay County, (605)677-7058, 60 miles S of Sioux Falls.
Holes: 18. **Yards:** 6,684/4,926. **Par:** 72/72. **Course Rating:** 72.4/63.9. **Slope:** 123/100. **Green Fee:** $14/$18. **Cart Fee:** $18/cart. **Walking Policy:** Unrestricted walking. **Walkability:** 3. **Opened:** 1996. **Architect:** Pat Wyss. **Season:** April-Oct. **High:** June-Aug. **To obtain tee times:** Call up to 7 days in advance. **Miscellaneous:** Range (grass), club rentals, credit cards (MC, V). **Notes:** Ranked 4th in 1999 Best in State.

BRANDON GOLF COURSE
PU-2100 E. Aspen Blvd., Brandon, 57005, Minnehaha County, (605)582-7100, 1 miles E of Brandon.
Holes: 18. **Yards:** 6,243/5,073. **Par:** 71/71. **Course Rating:** 73.2/69.7. **Slope:** 116/109. **Green Fee:** $14/$17. **Cart Fee:** $10/person. **Walking Policy:** Unrestricted walking. **Walkability:** 2. **Opened:** 1980. **Architect:** Wyss Assoc. **Season:** April-Nov. **High:** June-Aug. **To obtain tee times:** Call 7 days in advance. **Miscellaneous:** Range (grass), club rentals, credit cards (MC, V, D). **Special Notes:** Previously Brandon Valley Golf Course

BROADLAND CREEK NATIONAL GOLF CLUB
PU-N. Airport Rd., Huron, 57350, (605)352-1535.
Special Notes: Call club for further information.

★★½ CENTRAL VALLEY GOLF CLUB
SP-Highway 38, Hartford, 57033, Minnehaha County, (605)528-3971, 8 miles W of Sioux Falls.
Holes: 18. **Yards:** 6,326/5,115. **Par:** 72/72. **Course Rating:** 70.1/68.6. **Slope:** 121/110. **Green Fee:** $14/$17. **Cart Fee:** $20/cart. **Walking Policy:** Unrestricted walking. **Walkability:** 3. **Opened:** 1969. **Architect:** Mike Smith. **Season:** April-Oct. **High:** May-Sept. **To obtain tee times:** Call 7 days in advance. **Miscellaneous:** Reduced fees (weekdays, seniors, juniors), range (grass), club rentals, credit cards (MC, V, AE), beginner friendly (group golf lessons).
Reader Comments: Not a walker's course ... Too long from green to next tee box ... Great value ... Open course, some good holes ... Few hazards ... Reachable par 4s ... Best greens in the state ... Challenging ... Short course, but smooth and fast greens.

★★½ EDGEBROOK GOLF COURSE
PM-Rte. #1 Box 1A, Brookings, 57006, Brookings County, (605)692-6995, 1 miles S of Brookings.
Holes: 18. **Yards:** 6,078/5,041. **Par:** 70/70. **Course Rating:** N/A. **Slope:** 113/111. **Green Fee:** $13/$16. **Walkability:** 2. **Opened:** 1974. **Architect:** Patrick H. Wyss. **Season:** April-Oct. **High:** May-July. **To obtain tee times:** Call. **Miscellaneous:** Metal spikes, range (grass), club rentals.
Reader Comments: Fast, fast greens, not overly long ... Few hazards on back 9... Not the toughest course but you will use most clubs in your bag ... Get your putter working ... Flat, long course ... Going to be excellent with trees in future.

★★★ ELMWOOD GOLF COURSE
PU-2604 W. Russell, Sioux Falls, 57104, Minnehaha County, (605)367-7092.
Holes: 18. **Yards:** 6,850/5,750. **Par:** 72/72. **Course Rating:** 72.1/72.0. **Slope:** 129/125. **Green Fee:** $13/$15. **Cart Fee:** $10/person. **Walking Policy:** Unrestricted walking. **Walkability:** 1. **Opened:** 1923. **Architect:** Lawrence Packard. **Season:** April-Oct. **High:** May-Aug. **To obtain tee times:** Come in 7 days in advance or call 6 days in advance. **Miscellaneous:** Reduced fees (twilight), range (grass/mats), club rentals, credit cards (MC, V, D).
Reader Comments: Spectacular air show from military and commercial jets ... Nice old course ... Dry fairways ... Good track, but busy ... Great staff, excellent pros ... Okay for the price ... Where I learned the game.

★★★ FOX RUN GOLF COURSE
PU-600 W. 27th St., Yankton, 57078, Yankton County, (605)668-5205, 75 miles SW of Sioux Falls.
Holes: 18. **Yards:** 6,792/5,209. **Par:** 72/72. **Course Rating:** 70.8/68.6. **Slope:** 122/115. **Green Fee:** $16/$19. **Cart Fee:** $18/cart. **Walking Policy:** Unrestricted walking. **Walkability:** 2. **Opened:** 1993. **Architect:** Patrick Wyss. **Season:** March-Oct. **High:** May-Aug. **To obtain tee times:** Call golf shop 7 days in advance. **Miscellaneous:** Reduced fees (weekdays), range (grass/mats), club rentals, credit cards (MC, V).

SOUTH DAKOTA

Reader Comments: Excellent condition for young course ... Nos. 9 and 18 are great holes ... Prairie course, long and wide ... 18th hole is spectacular risk and reward hole ... Good design calls for good shotmaking, will improve with age ... New course, no shade, gonna be great!

★★★½ HART RANCH GOLF COURSE
PU-Spring Creek Rd., Rapid City, 57701, Pennington County, (605)341-5703, 8 miles S of Rapid City.
Holes: 18. **Yards:** 6,841/4,999. **Par:** 72/72. **Course Rating:** 72.5/70.1. **Slope:** 127/124. **Green Fee:** $17/$25. **Cart Fee:** $20/cart. **Walking Policy:** Unrestricted walking. **Walkability:** 4. **Opened:** 1985. **Architect:** Patrick Wyss. **Season:** April-Oct. **High:** June-Aug. **To obtain tee times:** Call up to 7 days in advance. **Miscellaneous:** Range (grass), club rentals, credit cards (MC, V, AE, D).
Reader Comments: Awesome scenery ... The 16th is like the Valley of Death ... Use the whole bag and a beautiful setting to boot ... Beautiful, tough back 9, altogether enjoyable ... No. 15 is too difficult for me ... Back 9 made this worth stopping for... Excellent course ... Rustic, but nice.

★★★★ HILLCREST GOLF & COUNTRY CLUB
SP-2206 Mulberry, Yankton, 57078, Yankton County, (605)665-4621, 6 miles SW of Sioux Falls.
Holes: 18. **Yards:** 6,874/5,726. **Par:** 72/73. **Course Rating:** 72.2/72.2. **Slope:** 130/126. **Green Fee:** $25/$35. **Cart Fee:** $18/cart. **Walking Policy:** Unrestricted walking. **Walkability:** 2. **Opened:** 1953. **Architect:** Chick Adams. **Season:** April-Nov. **High:** June-Aug. **To obtain tee times:** Call 7 days in advance. **Miscellaneous:** Reduced fees (weekdays), range (grass), club rentals, credit cards (MC, V).
Reader Comments: It's been nice for 20+ years ... Really tough championship course ... Half the greens are small derby hat greens ... Tough to stay on and tougher for short chip shots ... Very beautiful... Great golf course and maybe the best in S.D. ... Truest value in entire state ... Most courteous staff ... Small, speedy greens ... Friendly service ... Greens shed water well ... Short course, not much trouble.

★★ HILLSVIEW GOLF CLUB
PU-4201 SD Hwy. 34, Pierre, 57501, Hughes County, (605)224-6191, 180 miles NE of Rapid City.
Holes: 18. **Yards:** 6,828/5,470. **Par:** 72/73. **Course Rating:** 71.4/73.9. **Slope:** 122/119. **Green Fee:** $16/$16. **Cart Fee:** $18/cart. **Walking Policy:** Unrestricted walking. **Walkability:** 1. **Opened:** 1965. **Architect:** Charles Maddox. **Season:** April-Oct. **High:** June-Aug. **To obtain tee times:** Call golf shop. **Miscellaneous:** Reduced fees (juniors), metal spikes, range (grass/mats), club rentals, credit cards (MC, V).

KUEHN PARK GOLF COURSE
PU-2904 Kuehn Park Rd., Sioux Falls, 57106, Minnehaha County, (605)362-2811.
Holes: 9. **Yards:** 2,076/1,704. **Par:** 30/30. **Course Rating:** 72.1/72.0. **Slope:** 129/125. **Green Fee:** $12/$17. **Cart Fee:** $18/cart. **Walking Policy:** Unrestricted walking. **Walkability:** N/A. **Opened:** 1976. **Architect:** Don Herfort. **Season:** April-Oct. **High:** May-Aug. **To obtain tee times:** Come in up to 7 days in advance or call up to 6 days in advance. **Miscellaneous:** Reduced fees (weekdays, seniors, juniors), range (grass/mats), club rentals, credit cards (MC, V).

★★★½ LAKEVIEW GOLF COURSE
PM-3300 N. Ohlman, Mitchell, 57301, Davison County, (605)995-8460, 1 miles W of Mitchell.
E-mail: turfexp@aol.com.
Holes: 18. **Yards:** 6,670/5,808. **Par:** 72/73. **Course Rating:** 71.3/72.6. **Slope:** 124/125. **Green Fee:** $18/$18. **Cart Fee:** $10/person. **Walking Policy:** Unrestricted walking. **Walkability:** 2. **Opened:** 1978. **Architect:** Richard Watson. **Season:** April-Oct. **High:** June-Aug. **To obtain tee times:** Call or stop by anytime. **Miscellaneous:** Range (grass), club rentals, credit cards (MC, V), beginner friendly (free youth lessons, group discounts and lessons).
Reader Comments: Excellent course, challenging ... Older course, lots of trees ... Mix of old treelined holes with new holes with water ... Wonderful but difficult greens ... Good municipal... Good value.

★★ LEE PARK GOLF COURSE
PM-8th Ave. N.W., Aberdeen, 57401, Brown County, (605)626-7092, 200 miles NW of Sioux Falls.
Holes: 18. **Yards:** 6,346/5,138. **Par:** 72/72. **Course Rating:** 69.6/68.3. **Slope:** 128/122. **Green Fee:** $13/$15. **Cart Fee:** $15/cart. **Walking Policy:** Walking at certain times. **Walkability:** 1. **Opened:** 1933. **Season:** April-Nov. **High:** June-Aug. **To obtain tee times:** Call for weekend play. **Miscellaneous:** Reduced fees (weekdays, twilight), metal spikes, range (grass), club rentals, credit cards (MC, V, D).

MADISON COUNTRY CLUB
SP-W. Hwy. 34, Madison, 57042, Lake County, (605)256-3991, 3 miles W of Madison.
Holes: 18. **Yards:** 6,162/4,803. **Par:** 71/71. **Course Rating:** 69.9/68.2. **Slope:** 120/112. **Green Fee:** $16/$25. **Cart Fee:** $20/cart. **Walking Policy:** Unrestricted walking. **Walkability:** 3. **Opened:** 1946. **Season:** April-Oct. **High:** June-July-Aug. **To obtain tee times:** Call up to one week ahead. **Miscellaneous:** Range (grass), club rentals.

★★★★ MEADOWBROOK GOLF COURSE
PU-3625 Jackson Blvd., Rapid City, 57702, Pennington County, (605)394-4191.
Holes: 18. **Yards:** 7,054/5,603. **Par:** 72/72. **Course Rating:** 73.0/71.1. **Slope:** 138/130. **Green Fee:** $19/$26. **Cart Fee:** $18/cart. **Walking Policy:** Unrestricted walking. **Walkability:** 2. **Opened:** 1976. **Architect:** David Gill. **Season:** Year-round. **High:** April-Oct. **To obtain tee times:** Call up to 1 day in advance or through advance booking for an additional $4 per player. **Miscellaneous:** Reduced fees (weekdays, low season, seniors, juniors), range (grass/mats), club rentals.
Notes: Ranked 3rd in 1999 Best in State; 56th in 1996 America's Top 75 Affordable Courses. 1984 Women's Public Links.
Reader Comments: Many strategic holes ... Challenging ... Every hole gets better, slow on weekends ... Creek makes it interesting ... Best public in state or several states for that matter... Interesting par 5s make the course great ... A must play ... Better be long and straight ... Great layout ... A touch of heaven on this course! ... Lush fairways.

★★★½ PRAIRIE GREEN GOLF COURSE
PU-600 E. 69th St., Sioux Falls, 57108, Minnehaha County, (605)367-6076, (800)585-6076.
E-mail: prairiegreen@dakotagolf.com. **Web:** www.dakotagolf.com.
Holes: 18. **Yards:** 7,179/5,250. **Par:** 72/72. **Course Rating:** 74.2/70.2. **Slope:** 134/122. **Green Fee:** $20/$24. **Cart Fee:** $10/person. **Walking Policy:** Unrestricted walking. **Walkability:** 3. **Opened:** 1995. **Architect:** Dick Nugent. **Season:** April-Oct. **High:** May-Sept. **To obtain tee times:** Call 7 days in advance. **Miscellaneous:** Reduced fees (weekdays, twilight, seniors, juniors), discount packages, range (grass), club rentals, credit cards (MC, V, D).
Notes: Ranked 2nd in 1999 Best in State; 5th in 1996 Best New Affordable Courses.
Reader Comments: Wow! Scotland in South Dakota! Nice links course ... Water, water everywhere ... Too long between tees ... Walkers at a disadvantage ... Tough and long ... Bring the sand wedge ... Bring your driver and hit it well, otherwise you'll shoot big numbers ... Give this course some time to get better... True test of golf... Too much room between greens and tees ... Tight fairways.

RAPID CITY ELKS GOLF COURSE
SP-3333 E. 39th St., Rapid City, 57703, Pennington County, (605)393-0522, 3 miles SE of Rapid City.
Holes: 18. **Yards:** 6,126/4,932. **Par:** 72/72. **Course Rating:** 70.9/69.9. **Slope:** 131/131. **Green Fee:** $17/$21. **Cart Fee:** $20/cart. **Walking Policy:** Unrestricted walking. **Walkability:** 3. **Opened:** 1960. **Architect:** Pat Wyss. **Season:** April-Nov. **High:** June-Sept. **To obtain tee times:** Call 24 hours in advance of pay date. Elk members may call 48 hours in advance of play date. **Miscellaneous:** Range (grass), club rentals, credit cards (MC, V, D).

★★★★ SOUTHERN HILLS GOLF COURSE
PM-W Hwy. 18, Hot Springs, 57747, Fall River County, (605)745-6400, 45 miles S of Rapid City.
Holes: 9. **Yards:** 2,969/2,435. **Par:** 35/35. **Course Rating:** 35.1/34.7. **Slope:** 130/121. **Green Fee:** $20/$20. **Cart Fee:** $20/cart. **Walking Policy:** Unrestricted walking. **Walkability:** 5. **Opened:** 1979. **Architect:** Dick Phelps/Brad Benz. **Season:** March-Oct. **High:** June-Aug. **To obtain tee times:** Call Pro Shop. **Miscellaneous:** Range (grass), club rentals, credit cards (MC, V).
Reader Comments: Walking this course is like hiking in the Alps ... Only 9 holes but the best anywhere ... Lots of fairly extreme elevation changes and steeply graded greens ... Sidehill and downhill putts can be a real adventure ... Beautiful setting, well maintained, friendly staff. I wish it had 9 more holes.

SPEARFISH CANYON COUNTRY CLUB
SP-120 Spearfish Canyon Drive, Spearfish, 57783, Lawrence County, (605)642-7156. **E-mail:** sccc@vcn.com.
Holes: 18. **Yards:** 6,616/5,399. **Par:** 71/72. **Course Rating:** 71.0/70.3. **Slope:** 121/118. **Green Fee:** $15/$30. **Cart Fee:** $12/person. **Walking Policy:** Unrestricted walking. **Walkability:** 5. **Opened:** 1922. **Season:** Year-round. **High:** May-Sept. **To obtain tee times:** Call 7 days in advance. **Miscellaneous:** Reduced fees (weekdays, low season, juniors), discount packages, range (grass), club rentals, credit cards (MC, V), beginner friendly (junior and ladies group lessons).

★★½ TWO RIVERS GOLF CLUB
PU-150 S. Oak Tree Lane, Dakota Dunes, 57049, Union County, (605)232-3241, 6 miles N of Sioux City.
Holes: 18. **Yards:** 5,820/5,246. **Par:** 70/73. **Course Rating:** 69.0/71.0. **Slope:** 120/112. **Green Fee:** $14/$18. **Cart Fee:** $11/person. **Walking Policy:** Unrestricted walking. **Walkability:** 1. **Opened:** 1921. **Season:** April-Oct. **High:** June-Sept. **To obtain tee times:** May call 7 days in advance. **Miscellaneous:** Reduced fees (weekdays, low season), metal spikes, range (grass/mats), club rentals, credit cards (MC, V, AE, D).
Reader Comments: Greens are as good as Dakota Dunes ... Very little room for error... Country club course turned public, newer replacement holes need maturing ... Old course with lots of trees ... Pretty short ... Awesome course, very tough, one of my favorites.

SOUTH DAKOTA

★★★ **WATERTOWN MUNICIPAL GOLF COURSE**
PM-351 S. Lake Dr., Watertown, 57201, Codington County, (605)882-6262.
Holes: 18. **Yards:** 5,220/5,858. **Par:** 72/78. **Course Rating:** 67.4/71.3. **Slope:** 106/114. **Green Fee:** $15/$17. **Cart Fee:** $18/cart. **Walking Policy:** Unrestricted walking. **Walkability:** 1. **Architect:** Phil Wigton. **Season:** April-Oct. **High:** May-Sept. **To obtain tee times:** Call 7 days in advance for weekends. Call up to same day for weekday. **Miscellaneous:** Range (grass), club rentals.
Reader Comments: Good shape for a muny ... Good test of golf ... Fun course to play ... Too easy ... Well kept secret for S.D. ... A steal ... Fun for scoring.

★★★★ **WILLOW RUN GOLF COURSE**
PU-E. Hwy. 38/42, Sioux Falls, 57103, Minnehaha County, (605)335-5900.
Holes: 18. **Yards:** 6,505/4,855. **Par:** 71/71. **Course Rating:** 71.1/68.7. **Slope:** 127/119. **Green Fee:** $14/$17. **Cart Fee:** $9/. **Walking Policy:** Unrestricted walking. **Walkability:** N/A. **Opened:** 1988. **Architect:** Joel Goldstrand. **Season:** March-Nov. **High:** May-Oct. **To obtain tee times:** Call 7 days in advance. **Miscellaneous:** Reduced fees (weekdays, twilight, seniors, juniors), discount packages, metal spikes, range (grass), club rentals, credit cards (MC, V).
Reader Comments: Best in town ... Nice course layout ... The best public course in S.D.! ... One of the most fun courses! ... Good value ... Out in the country ... Fun to play ... Price is right ... The staff at this course always impresses me ... Tough rough.

TENNESSEE

ANDREW JOHNSON GOLF CLUB
PU-615 Lick Hollow Rd., Greeneville, 37744, Greene County, (423)636-1476, (800)421-2149, 1 miles SW of Greenville.
Holes: 18. **Yards:** 6,103/4,776. **Par:** 70/70. **Course Rating:** 68.1/66.6. **Slope:** 114/113. **Green Fee:** $12/$14. **Cart Fee:** $12/person. **Walking Policy:** Walking at certain times. **Walkability:** 2. **Opened:** 1989. **Architect:** Robert Walker. **Season:** Year-round. **High:** April-Aug. **To obtain tee times:** Call golf shop. **Miscellaneous:** Reduced fees (weekdays), metal spikes, range (grass), club rentals, credit cards (MC, V).

★½ AUDUBON PARK GOLF COURSE
PM-4160 Park Ave., Memphis, 38117, Shelby County, (901)683-6941. **E-mail:** cwhiteaud@aol.com.
Holes: 18. **Yards:** 6,347/5,615. **Par:** 70/71. **Course Rating:** 68.7/N/A. **Slope:** 114/N/A. **Green Fee:** $7/$18. **Cart Fee:** $20/cart. **Walking Policy:** Unrestricted walking. **Walkability:** 2. **Opened:** 1952. **Architect:** John Stevens. **Season:** Year-round. **High:** June-Sept. **To obtain tee times:** Call golf Shop. **Miscellaneous:** Reduced fees (weekdays, seniors, juniors), metal spikes, range (grass), club rentals, credit cards (MC, V).

★★★ BANEBERRY GOLF & RESORT
PU-704 Harrison Ferry Rd., Baneberry, 37890, Jefferson County, (423)674-2500, (800)951-4653, 35 miles E of Knoxville. **E-mail:** golfrest@baneberrygolf.com. **Web:** www.golfrest@baneberrygolf.com.
Holes: 18. **Yards:** 6,694/4,829. **Par:** 71/72. **Course Rating:** 72.6/68.5. **Slope:** 125/117. **Green Fee:** $14/$17. **Cart Fee:** $13/person. **Walking Policy:** Unrestricted walking. **Walkability:** 2. **Opened:** 1972. **Architect:** Bob Thompson. **Season:** Year-round. **High:** March-June/Sept.-Oct. **To obtain tee times:** Call golf shop. **Miscellaneous:** Discount packages, metal spikes, range (grass), club rentals, lodging (36 rooms), credit cards (MC, V, AE, D).
Reader Comments: Keep it in play & you can score ... Very enjoyable, demanding ... Mountain views ... Good views ... Lots of blind shots with irons ... Great staff, very accommodating.

BEAR TRACE AT CHICKASAW
PU-9555 State Rte. 100, Henderson, 38340, Cumberland County, (888)944-2327
Holes: 18. **Yards:** 7,118/5,375. **Par:** 72/72. **Course Rating:** N/A. **Slope:** N/A. **Green Fee:** N/A. **Walkability:** N/A. **Architect:** Jack Nicklaus.
Special Notes: Course still under construction. Information not available.

BEAR TRACE AT CUMBERLAND MOUNTAIN
PU-407 Wild Plum Lane, Crossville, 38555, Cumberland County, (931)707-1640, (888)800-BEAR, 5 miles S of Crossville. **Web:** www.beartrace.com.
Holes: 18. **Yards:** 6,900/5,066. **Par:** 72/72. **Course Rating:** 72.0/70.0. **Slope:** 130/120. **Green Fee:** $15/$40. **Cart Fee:** $16/. **Walking Policy:** Walking at certain times. **Walkability:** 4. **Opened:** 1998. **Architect:** Jack Nicklaus. **Season:** Year-round. **High:** April-Oct. **To obtain tee times:** Call toll free number. **Miscellaneous:** Reduced fees (weekdays, low season, twilight, seniors, juniors), discount packages, range (grass), club rentals, credit cards (MC, V, AE).

★★★½ BENT CREEK GOLF VILLAGE
R-3919 E. Pkwy., Gatlinburg, 37738, Sevier County, (423)436-3947, (800)251-9336, 12 miles SW of Gatlinburg. **E-mail:** bentcreek@earthlink.net. **Web:** www.sunterra.com.
Holes: 18. **Yards:** 6,182/5,111. **Par:** 72/73. **Course Rating:** 70.3/69.2. **Slope:** 127/117. **Green Fee:** $20/$35. **Cart Fee:** $16/person. **Walking Policy:** Walking at certain times. **Walkability:** 3. **Opened:** 1972. **Architect:** Gary Player. **Season:** Year-round. **High:** March-Nov. **To obtain tee times:** Tee times may be made up to a year in advance and must be guaranteed with a major credit card. **Miscellaneous:** Reduced fees (weekdays, low season, resort guests, twilight, seniors, juniors), discount packages, club rentals, lodging, credit cards (MC, V, AE).
Reader Comments: Front fairly open, back 9 in mountains ... Tricky back side! Better use yardage guide! ... Great layout, requires accuracy ... Excellent layout ... Hilly back, slow pace sometimes ... Nice bent greens. Back 9 very tight ... Real challenge ... Very hilly.

BENT TREE GOLF COURSE
PU-2993 Paul Coffman Dr., Jackson, 38301, (901)425-8620.
Holes: 18. **Yards:** N/A. **Par:** N/A. **Course Rating:** N/A. **Slope:** N/A. **Green Fee:** N/A. **Walkability:** N/A. **Opened:** 1997. **Architect:** Randy Wilson.
Special Notes: Call club for further information.

★★★½ BIG CREEK GOLF CLUB
SP-6195 Woodstock-Cuba Rd., Millington, 38053, Shelby County, (901)353-1654, 6 miles S of Millington.
Holes: 18. **Yards:** 7,052/5,086. **Par:** 72/72. **Course Rating:** 72.8/69.6. **Slope:** 121/111. **Green Fee:** $18/$32. **Cart Fee:** $10/person. **Walking Policy:** Unrestricted walking. **Walkability:** 2. **Opened:** 1977. **Architect:** G.S. Mitchell. **Season:** Year-round. **High:** April-Sept. **To obtain tee

times: Public may call 4 days in advance. **Miscellaneous:** Reduced fees (weekdays, low season, twilight, seniors, juniors), metal spikes, range (grass), club rentals, credit cards (MC, V, AE). **Reader Comments:** Fun course, greens are champion bermuda, a real challenge ... Many long holes, flat front nine, many doglegs, hilly back nine ... Pretty nice, lots of trouble to get into ... Long from back tees, with big greens.

BIG SOUTH FORK COUNTRY CLUB
PU-Rte. 2, Jamestown, 38556, (615)879-8197.
Special Notes: Call club for further information.

★★½ BRAINERD GOLF COURSE
PU-5203 Old Mission Rd., Chattanooga, 37411, Hamilton County, (423)855-2692. **Web:** www.chattanooga.gov/cpr/golf.
Holes: 18. **Yards:** 6,468/5,403. **Par:** 72/72. **Course Rating:** 69.8/69.9. **Slope:** 119/118. **Green Fee:** $10/$20. **Cart Fee:** $10/person. **Walking Policy:** Walking at certain times. **Walkability:** 2. **Opened:** 1926. **Architect:** Donald Ross. **Season:** Year-round. **High:** April-Sept. **To obtain tee times:** For advance tee times call (423)757-7274, for same day call golf shop. **Miscellaneous:** Reduced fees (weekdays, seniors, juniors), club rentals, credit cards (MC, V).
Reader Comments: Very good course, crowded ... Nice public course ...Great course ... Great for us wannabes ... Good tune-up course ... Beautiful, nice layout, shorter course, busy ... Rangers try to keep pace steady.

★★★½ BROWN ACRES GOLF COURSE
PU-406 Brown Rd., Chattanooga, 37421, Hamilton County, (423)855-2680, 5 miles N of Chattanooga.
Holes: 18. **Yards:** 6,774/4,923. **Par:** 71/71. **Course Rating:** 72.5/66.1. **Slope:** 122/110. **Green Fee:** $15/$20. **Cart Fee:** $10/person. **Walking Policy:** Walking at certain times. **Walkability:** 3. **Opened:** 1975. **Architect:** Grant Wencel. **Season:** Year-round. **High:** April-Oct. **To obtain tee times:** Call 2 days in advance. **Miscellaneous:** Reduced fees (seniors, juniors), range (grass/mats), club rentals, credit cards (MC, V).
Reader Comments: Large bent-grass greens ... Good course ... Well taken care of ... Good track, good price. Fair and challenging.

★★½ BUFFALO VALLEY GOLF COURSE
PU-190 Country Club Dr., Unicoi, 37692, Unicoi County, (423)928-1022, 3 miles SE of Johnson City.
Holes: 18. **Yards:** 6,624/4,968. **Par:** 71/72. **Course Rating:** 71.7/69.6. **Slope:** 119/111. **Green Fee:** $13/$17. **Cart Fee:** $11/person. **Walking Policy:** Unrestricted walking. **Walkability:** 3. **Season:** Year-round. **High:** April-Oct. **To obtain tee times:** Call 8 days in advance. **Miscellaneous:** Reduced fees (weekdays, low season, juniors), metal spikes, range (grass), club rentals, credit cards (MC, V).
Reader Comments: Nice mix of mountain and valley holes.

★½ CAMELOT GOLF COURSE
PU-908 Pressman's Home Rd., Rogersville, 37857, Hawkins County, (423)272-7499, (800)764-7499 , 10 miles N of Rogersville.
Holes: 18. **Yards:** 6,844/5,035. **Par:** 73/73. **Course Rating:** 72.3/68.2. **Slope:** 119/110. **Green Fee:** $11/$12. **Cart Fee:** $9/person. **Walking Policy:** Unrestricted walking. **Walkability:** 4. **Opened:** 1987. **Architect:** Robert Thomason. **Season:** Year-round. **High:** June-Aug. **To obtain tee times:** Call golf shop. **Miscellaneous:** Metal spikes.

★½ CARROLL LAKE GOLF CLUB
SP-1305 Carroll Lake Rd., McKenzie, 38201, Carroll County, (901)352-5998, (800)871-2128, 45 miles N of Jackson.
Holes: 18. **Yards:** 6,020/4,868. **Par:** 71/71. **Course Rating:** 68.0/68.0. **Slope:** 123/120. **Green Fee:** $10/$17. **Cart Fee:** $20/cart. **Walking Policy:** Unrestricted walking. **Walkability:** 3. **Opened:** 1961. **Architect:** R. Albert Anderson. **Season:** Year-round. **High:** April-Nov. **To obtain tee times:** Call golf shop. **Miscellaneous:** Reduced fees (weekdays, low season, seniors, juniors), metal spikes, club rentals, credit cards (MC, V, AE).

★★ CATTAILS AT MEADOW VIEW
PU-1901 Meadowview Parkway, Kingsport, 37660, Sullivan County, (423)578-6622.
Holes: 18. **Yards:** 6,704/4,452. **Par:** 71/71. **Course Rating:** 72.5/65.9. **Slope:** 130/116. **Green Fee:** N/A/$32. **Cart Fee:** $10/person. **Walking Policy:** Unrestricted walking. **Walkability:** 3. **Opened:** 1998. **Architect:** Denis Griffiths. **Season:** Year-round. **High:** April-Nov. **To obtain tee times:** Hotel guests may call 30 days in advance, all other tee times maximum 7 days in advance. **Miscellaneous:** Reduced fees (low season, seniors, juniors), discount packages, metal spikes, range (grass), club rentals, lodging (195 rooms), credit cards (MC, V, AE, D).
Special Notes: Formerly known as Meadowview Golf Club.

★★★½ CLINCHVIEW GOLF & COUNTRY CLUB

PU-Rte 3, Box 1425, Hwy. 11W., Bean Station, 37708, Grainger County, (423)993-2892, 50 miles E of Knoxville.

Holes: 18. **Yards:** 6,901/4,724. **Par:** 72/72. **Course Rating:** 72.3/66.3. **Slope:** 121/110. **Green Fee:** $15/$18. **Cart Fee:** $11/person. **Walking Policy:** Unrestricted walking. **Walkability:** 1. **Opened:** 1969. **Season:** Year-round. **High:** March-April-Oct. **To obtain tee times:** Call golf shop. **Miscellaneous:** Reduced fees (low season, twilight), range (grass), club rentals, credit cards (MC, V, AE, D).

Reader Comments: Very good atmosphere ... Always a pleasure to play ... Sand would make it better... Colorful tee boxes. Improves each year.

★★½ COUNTRY HILLS GOLF COURSE

PU-1501 Saundersville Rd., Hendersonville, 37075, Sumner County, (615)824-1100, 10 miles N of Nashville.

Holes: 18. **Yards:** 6,100/4,800. **Par:** 70/70. **Course Rating:** 71.2/67.8. **Slope:** 119/114. **Green Fee:** $13/$25. **Cart Fee:** $10/person. **Walking Policy:** Unrestricted walking. **Walkability:** 5. **Opened:** 1990. **Architect:** Leon Howard. **Season:** Year-round. **High:** March-Oct. **To obtain tee times:** Call 7 days in advance. **Miscellaneous:** Reduced fees (weekdays, low season, twilight, seniors, juniors), discount packages, metal spikes, range (grass), club rentals, credit cards (MC, V, AE).

Reader Comments: Very tight course demanding shots ... Very hilly ... Scenic hills.

★★★ THE CROSSINGS GOLF CLUB

SP-2585 Hwy.. 81 N., Jonesboro, 37659, Washington County, (423)348-8844, 75 miles N of Knoxville.

Holes: 18. **Yards:** 6,366/5,072. **Par:** 72/72. **Course Rating:** 70.1/68.2. **Slope:** 118/112. **Green Fee:** $25/$25. **Cart Fee:** $10/person. **Walking Policy:** Unrestricted walking. **Walkability:** 2. **Opened:** 1994. **Architect:** Gary Roger Baird. **Season:** Year-round. **High:** March-Oct. **To obtain tee times:** Call 5 days in advance. **Miscellaneous:** Metal spikes, range (grass), credit cards (MC, V, AE, D).

Reader Comments: Maturing ... Good service ... Extremely playable, yet very challenging ... Fun to play, a lot of potential ... Good greens. Fairways close together ... Short course–not in good shape yet ... Short, but fun to play.

★★★½ CUMBERLAND GARDENS RESORT

PU-Hwy.. 70 East, Crab Orchard, 37723, Cumberland County, (931)484-5285, 45 miles W of Knoxville. **E-mail:** cgardens@usit.net. **Web:** www.midtenn.net.

Holes: 18. **Yards:** 6,689/5,021. **Par:** 72/72. **Course Rating:** 74.2/70.9. **Slope:** 132/123. **Green Fee:** $25/$36. **Cart Fee:** Included in Green Fee. **Walking Policy:** Mandatory cart. **Walkability:** 5. **Opened:** 1988. **Architect:** Robert Renaud. **Season:** Year-round. **High:** April-Oct. **To obtain tee times:** Call weekdays at 8 a.m. and weekends at 7 a.m. **Miscellaneous:** Reduced fees (weekdays, low season, resort guests), discount packages, metal spikes, range (grass), club rentals, lodging (32 rooms), credit cards (MC, V, AE, D).

Reader Comments: Excellent mountain views, great elevated tees ... Great potential, beautiful ... Great view, lost 8 balls ... Tough hilly course, tight holes ... Best public course in 100 miles ... Knock your eyes out scenery ... Could really be a gem ... Needs work, but a fun course to play ... Like playing on top of the world.

★★ DAVY CROCKETT GOLF COURSE

PM-4380 Rangeline, Memphis, 38127, Shelby County, (901)358-3375.

Holes: 18. **Yards:** 6,200/5,900. **Par:** 72/72. **Course Rating:** 68.5/67.2. **Slope:** 118/114. **Green Fee:** $12/$13. **Cart Fee:** $20/cart. **Walking Policy:** Unrestricted walking. **Walkability:** 4. **Opened:** 1961. **Architect:** Harry Isabelle. **Season:** Year-round. **High:** April-Oct. **To obtain tee times:** Call golf shop. **Miscellaneous:** Reduced fees (weekdays, seniors, juniors), metal spikes, club rentals, credit cards (MC, V, D).

★★½ DEAD HORSE LAKE GOLF COURSE

PU-9700 Sherrill Lane, Knoxville, 37932, Knox County, (423)693-5270, 10 miles W of Knoxville.

Holes: 18. **Yards:** 6,225/5,132. **Par:** 71/73. **Course Rating:** 69.1/N/A. **Slope:** 116/N/A. **Green Fee:** $15/$20. **Cart Fee:** $10/person. **Walking Policy:** Unrestricted walking. **Walkability:** 2. **Opened:** 1973. **Architect:** Joe Parker/Pete Parker. **Season:** Year-round. **High:** Mar-Aug. **To obtain tee times:** Call 7 days in advance. **Miscellaneous:** Reduced fees (seniors), metal spikes, range (grass/mats), credit cards (MC, V).

Reader Comments: Short and easy ... Basic golf... Nice layout ... Nice bar ... I had fun ... Improving, but fairways need some work ... Lots of good holes ... Reworking some holes ... Getting better.

★★★★ DEER CREEK GOLF CLUB

SP-445 Deer Creek Dr., Crossville, 38558, Cumberland County, (931)456-0178, 60 miles W of Knoxville.

Holes: 18. **Yards:** 6,251/4,917. **Par:** 72/72. **Course Rating:** 69.6/67.2. **Slope:** 122/114. **Green Fee:** $15/$23. **Cart Fee:** $13/person. **Walking Policy:** Walking at certain times. **Walkability:** 3. **Opened:** 1989. **Architect:** Robert Renaud. **Season:** Year-round. **High:** April-Oct. **To obtain tee times:** Call 3 days in advance. **Miscellaneous:** Reduced fees (low season), discount packages, range (grass/mats), club rentals, credit cards (MC, V, D).

Reader Comments: Short course ... Very friendly ... Nice course ... Greens excellent, nice layout ... Very fair and good greens ... Beautiful course, very playable ... Always great shape ... Very playable and interesting ... Good greens ... Always fun. Wide landing areas ... Great greens, friendly people fun for all.

DEERFIELD RESORT

R-1001 The Clubhouse Drive, La Follette, 37766, Campbell County, (423)566-0040, (800)325-2PUTT. **E-mail:** brendan@ccdi.net. **Web:** www.greenatdeerfield.com.
Holes: 18. **Yards:** 6,716/4,776. **Par:** 71/71. **Course Rating:** 72.8/69.8. **Slope:** 131/125. **Green Fee:** $30/$35. **Cart Fee:** Included in Green Fee. **Walking Policy:** Mandatory cart. **Walkability:** 4. **Opened:** 1995. **Architect:** Bobby Clampett. **Season:** Year-round. **High:** May-Nov. **To obtain tee times:** Earliest tee times can be made 1 week in advance. **Miscellaneous:** Reduced fees (low season), metal spikes, range (grass), club rentals, lodging (200 rooms), credit cards (MC, V, D), beginner friendly.

★★½ DYERSBURG MUNICIPAL GOLF COURSE

PM-Golf Course Rd., Dyersburg, 38024, Dyer County, (901)286-7620.
Holes: 18. **Yards:** 3,180/2,637. **Par:** 71/71. **Course Rating:** 69.7/71.0. **Slope:** 117/118. **Green Fee:** $8/$8. **Cart Fee:** $14/cart. **Walking Policy:** Unrestricted walking. **Walkability:** 3. **Architect:** Scott Nall. **Season:** Year-round. **High:** May-Sept. **To obtain tee times:** Call. **Miscellaneous:** Metal spikes.

Reader Comments: Fun course to play ... Great course, fun to play, good shape ... Very affordable golf!

★★★★ EAGLE'S LANDING GOLF CLUB

PU-1556 Old Knox Hwy., Sevierville, 37876, Sevier County, (865)429-4223, 20 miles E of Knoxville.
Holes: 18. **Yards:** 6,919/4,591. **Par:** 72/72. **Course Rating:** 73.5/68.8. **Slope:** 134/120. **Green Fee:** $30/$46. **Cart Fee:** Included in Green Fee. **Walking Policy:** Mandatory cart. **Walkability:** 3. **Opened:** 1994. **Architect:** D.J. Devictor. **Season:** Year-round. **High:** May-Oct. **To obtain tee times:** Call up to 30 days in advance for tee times. **Miscellaneous:** Reduced fees (weekdays, low season, twilight, juniors), discount packages, metal spikes, range (grass), club rentals, credit cards (MC, V).

Reader Comments: Nice course ... Excellent course ... Great par 3s, excellent condition & greens ... Fairly tough for a public course ... Great course, affordable, good staff ... Expensive ... Very tough from tips ... Tough course from the back.

★★★½ EASTLAND GREEN GOLF COURSE

PU-550 Club House Lane, Clarksville, 37043, Montgomery County, (931)358-9051, 35 miles NW of Nashville.
Holes: 18. **Yards:** 6,437/4,790. **Par:** 72/72. **Course Rating:** 71.5/68.4. **Slope:** 123/116. **Green Fee:** $17/$22. **Cart Fee:** $16/cart. **Walking Policy:** Unrestricted walking. **Walkability:** 3. **Opened:** 1990. **Architect:** East Green Development Corp. **Season:** Year-round. **High:** April-Aug. **To obtain tee times:** Call 5 days in advance. **Miscellaneous:** Reduced fees (twilight, seniors, juniors), metal spikes, range (grass), club rentals, credit cards (MC, V, AE, D).

Reader Comments: Nice layout, good value ... Enjoyable, greens in good shape ... Favorite place in the fall, leaves turning ... Greens always run nice. Good solid course. Needs more length ... Nice, will be tougher when trees mature ... Best course in Montgomery county ... Very playable.

★★★★ EGWANI FARMS GOLF COURSE *Service*

PU-3920 Singleton Station Rd., Rockford, 37853, Blount County, (423)970-7132, 8 miles S of Knoxville.
Holes: 18. **Yards:** 6,708/4,680. **Par:** 72/72. **Course Rating:** 71.9/66.1. **Slope:** 126/113. **Green Fee:** $45/$50. **Cart Fee:** Included in Green Fee. **Walking Policy:** Mandatory cart. **Walkability:** N/A. **Opened:** 1991. **Architect:** D.J. DeVictor. **Season:** Year-round. **High:** April-Oct. **To obtain tee times:** Call 7 days in advance. **Miscellaneous:** Reduced fees (low season), metal spikes, range (grass), club rentals, credit cards (MC, V).

Reader Comments: Good course; great people! ... Great course, great everything ... Superb course, worth the money ... Pricey, links style ... Fantastic service ... Nice but expensive ... Treat for daily fee player ... Nice course, overpriced ... Tough, good condition ... Some very tough holes ... Immaculate condition.

★★½ ELIZABETHTON MUNICIPAL GOLF CLUB

PM-185 Buck Van Hess Drive, Elizabethton, 37643, Carter County, (423)542-8051, 9 miles W of Johnson City.

Holes: 18. **Yards:** 6,339/4,335. **Par:** 72/72. **Course Rating:** 71.2/67.7. **Slope:** 129/118. **Green Fee:** $14/$21. **Cart Fee:** $11/person. **Cart Fee:** Included in Green Fee. **Walking Policy:** Unrestricted walking. **Walkability:** 3. **Opened:** 1934. **Architect:** D.J. DeVictor. **Season:** Year-round. **High:** April-Sept. **To obtain tee times:** Call 7 days in advance. **Miscellaneous:** Reduced fees (low season), range (grass), club rentals, credit cards (MC, V).
Reader Comments: Best municipal course ever played.

★★★½ FALL CREEK FALLS STATE PARK GOLF COURSE
PU-Rte. 3, Pikeville, 37367, Bledsoe County, (423)881-5706, (800)250-8611, 20 miles N of Pikeville.
Holes: 18. **Yards:** 6,669/6,051. **Par:** 72/72. **Course Rating:** 71.6/74.8. **Slope:** 127/126. **Green Fee:** $19/$19. **Cart Fee:** $10/person. **Walking Policy:** Unrestricted walking. **Walkability:** 2. **Opened:** 1972. **Architect:** Joe Lee. **Season:** Year-round. **High:** May-Oct. **To obtain tee times:** Call at least two weeks in advance. **Miscellaneous:** Reduced fees (seniors, juniors), discount packages, range (grass), club rentals, lodging, credit cards (MC, V, AE, D), beginner friendly.
Reader Comments: One of the best state park courses anywhere ... It's great ... Excellent fast greens ... Tough but fair, be sure to tour the park! ... Nice layout, plenty of deer, great challenge, demanding ... Women-friendly.

FOREST HILL GOLF COURSE
PU-200 Kubo Rd., Drummonds, 38023-0157, Tipton County, (901)835-2152, 20 miles N of Memphis.
Holes: 18. **Yards:** 6,609/5,220. **Par:** 72/72. **Course Rating:** 71.5/69.8. **Slope:** 122/118. **Green Fee:** $15/$25. **Cart Fee:** $10/person. **Walking Policy:** Walking at certain times. **Walkability:** 3. **Opened:** 1993. **Architect:** Hiroshi Kubo. **Season:** Year-round. **High:** March-Oct. **To obtain tee times:** Call 7 days in advance. **Miscellaneous:** Reduced fees (weekdays, twilight, seniors), range (grass), credit cards (MC, V).

★★★½ FORREST CROSSING GOLF COURSE
PU-750 Riverview Dr., Franklin, 37064, Williamson County, (615)794-9400, 15 miles S of Nashville.
Holes: 18. **Yards:** 6,968/5,011. **Par:** 72/72. **Course Rating:** 73.6/69.1. **Slope:** 125/114. **Green Fee:** $23/$33. **Cart Fee:** $10/person. **Walking Policy:** Walking at certain times. **Walkability:** 1. **Opened:** 1988. **Architect:** Gary Roger Baird. **Season:** Year-round. **High:** April-Oct. **To obtain tee times:** Call 8 days in advance. **Miscellaneous:** Reduced fees (weekdays, low season, twilight, seniors), discount packages, metal spikes, range (grass/mats), club rentals, credit cards (MC, V, AE).
Reader Comments: Challenging course, thinking man's course, not just grip it and rip it...Great for shorter hitters ...Play it, you'll use a lot of your clubs ... No. 16 makes your blood flow ... Has some very challenging holes.

★★ FOX MEADOWS GOLF COURSE
PM-3064 Clarke Rd., Memphis, 38115, Shelby County, (901)362-0232.
Holes: 18. **Yards:** 6,545/5,095. **Par:** 71/72. **Course Rating:** 69.9/66.7. **Slope:** 108/102. **Green Fee:** $13/$15. **Cart Fee:** $20/cart. **Walking Policy:** Unrestricted walking. **Walkability:** 1. **Opened:** 1960. **Architect:** Chic Adams. **Season:** Year-round. **High:** May-Sept. **To obtain tee times:** Call anytime. **Miscellaneous:** Reduced fees (seniors, juniors), metal spikes, club rentals.

★½ GALLOWAY GOLF COURSE
PU-3815 Walnut Grove Rd., Memphis, 38111, Shelby County, (901)685-7805.
Holes: 18. **Yards:** 5,844/5,472. **Par:** 71/73. **Course Rating:** 67.4/71.3. **Slope:** 109/117. **Green Fee:** $13/$15. **Cart Fee:** $19/cart. **Walking Policy:** Unrestricted walking. **Walkability:** N/A. **Opened:** 1926. **Season:** Year-round. **High:** Apr.-Oct. **To obtain tee times:** Call 7 days in advance (computer system). **Miscellaneous:** Reduced fees (juniors), metal spikes, club rentals.

★★★½ GATLINBURG GOLF COURSE
PU-520 Dollywood Lane, Pigeon Forge, 37868, Sevier County, (423)453-3912, (800)231-4128, 5 miles SW of Pigeon Forge.
Holes: 18. **Yards:** 6,281/4,718. **Par:** 71/72. **Course Rating:** 72.3/68.9. **Slope:** 132/117. **Green Fee:** $25/$35. **Cart Fee:** $16/person. **Walking Policy:** Walking at certain times. **Walkability:** 5. **Opened:** 1955. **Architect:** William B. Langford/Bob Cupp. **Season:** Year-round. **High:** May-Oct. **To obtain tee times:** Call 7 days in advance. **Miscellaneous:** Reduced fees (low season, twilight, juniors), discount packages, metal spikes, club rentals, credit cards (MC, V).
Reader Comments: Best course in the Tennessee Smokies, front 9 open, back 9 in mountains. Beautiful holes! ... Tight fairways, good greens, little pricey ... My favorite course of all time ... Nos. 1 & 13 are fantastic ... Tight, hilly, No. 12 par 3 is beautiful, tee is about 200 feet above green ... All hilly lies, some great holes.

GRAYSBURG HILLS GOLF COURSE

PU-910 Graysburg Hills Rd., Chuckey, 37641, Greene County, (423)234-8061, 12 miles NE of Greenville.

Holes: 27. **Green Fee:** $20/$26. **Cart Fee:** $12/person. **Walking Policy:** Walking at certain times. **Walkability:** 3. **Opened:** 1978. **Season:** Year-round. **High:** April-Oct. **To obtain tee times:** Call up to 1 year in advance. **Miscellaneous:** Reduced fees (twilight), discount packages, metal spikes, range (grass), club rentals, credit cards (MC, V, AE, D).

★★★★½ **FODDERSTACK/CHIMNEYTOP** *Value+*

Yards: 6,875/5,362. **Par:** 72/72. **Course Rating:** 73.0/70.5. **Slope:** 134/123. **Architect:** Rees Jones/Larry Packard.

Reader Comments: Superb golf! Ready to play it again ... 27 holes, excellent condition, great layout ... Friendly staff, good test, good value ... Long, challenging, demanding ... Great course, great value, nice folks! ... Best overall golf experience. Bury me at Graysburg ... Enjoyable ... Good price, nice placement course, fun day.

★★★★½ **KNOBS/CHIMNEYTOP**

Yards: 6,743/5,474. **Par:** 72/72. **Course Rating:** 72.2/71.3. **Slope:** 133/125. **Architect:** Rees Jones/Larry Packard.

Reader Comments: Chimney Top very difficult, wooded ... Excellent layout, very challenging ... No matter how you play this course, it is great ... Best combo of golf, value, service. Playable, challenging, conditioned ... Service makes you want to go back ... Excellent golf ... Hidden Rees Jones layout, find it and love it.

★★★★½ **KNOBS/FODDERSTACK**

Yards: 6,834/5,562. **Par:** 72/72. **Course Rating:** 72.8/71.2. **Slope:** 128/122. **Architect:** Rees Jones.

Reader Comments: Best golf within 100 miles ... Great course in beautiful farm country! ... Beautiful views, a good challenge ... Super track, best in Tennessee ... Tough track, exceptional service ... 27 holes, the original 18 are a gem. Good greens ... Original 18 still great for walking.

★★★ THE GREENS AT DEERFIELD

R-1001 The Clubhouse Dr., LaFollette, 37766, Campbell County, (423)566-0040, (800)325-2788, 45 miles N of Knoxville.

Holes: 18. **Yards:** 6,716/4,776. **Par:** 71/71. **Course Rating:** 72.8/69.8. **Slope:** 131/125. **Green Fee:** $30/$35. **Cart Fee:** Included in Green Fee. **Walking Policy:** Mandatory cart. **Walkability:** 5. **Opened:** 1995. **Architect:** Bobby Clampett. **Season:** Year round. **High:** March-Oct. **To obtain tee times:** Call 7 days in advance. **Miscellaneous:** Reduced fees (low season), discount packages, metal spikes, range (grass), club rentals, lodging, credit cards (MC, V, D).

Reader Comments: You haven't seen hills till you've been here ... Brutish, some holes require a stiff upper lip ... Great greens, beautiful scenery ... Remote, but tee shot at No. 3 worth trip ... Tough course. Good condition, very tight ... Very quiet setting, great holes ... Accuracy required.

GREYSTONE GOLF CLUB

PU-2555 Hwy.. 70 E., Dickson, 37056, Dickson County, (615)446-0044, 25 miles W of Nashville.
E-mail: greystonegc.com. **Web:** www.greystonegc.com.

Holes: 18. **Yards:** 6,858/4,919. **Par:** 72/72. **Course Rating:** 73.1/69.0. **Slope:** 131/123. **Green Fee:** $30/$55. **Cart Fee:** Included in Green Fee. **Walking Policy:** Mandatory cart. **Walkability:** 4. **Opened:** 1998. **Architect:** Mark McCumber. **Season:** Year-round. **High:** May-Sept. **Miscellaneous:** Reduced fees (weekdays, low season, twilight, juniors), discount packages, range (grass), club rentals, credit cards (MC, V, AE, D).

★★★ HARPETH HILLS GOLF COURSE

PM-2424 Old Hickory Blvd., Nashville, 37221, Davidson County, (615)862-8493.

Holes: 18. **Yards:** 6,900/5,200. **Par:** 72/72. **Course Rating:** 73.1/71.2. **Slope:** 126/124. **Green Fee:** $14/$14. **Cart Fee:** $16/. **Walking Policy:** Unrestricted walking. **Walkability:** N/A. **Opened:** 1968. **Season:** Year-round. **High:** May-Sept. **To obtain tee times:** Call seven days in advance. **Miscellaneous:** Metal spikes, range (grass), club rentals.

Reader Comments: Friendly people, enjoyable round of golf ... Best in metro Nashville ... Good fair course ... Best city course in Nashville ... Difficult course for a muny ... Nice condition with fast greens. Easy course layout, which is great for beginners.

HEATHERHURST GOLF CLUB

R-P.O. Box 2000, Fairfield Glade, 38558, Cumberland County, (615)484-3799, 6 miles W of Crossfield.

Holes: 27. **Green Fee:** $16/$38. **Cart Fee:** $9. **Walking Policy:** Walking at certain times. **Walkability:** N/A. **Opened:** 1988. **Architect:** Gary Roger Baird. **Season:** Year-round. **High:** April-Oct. **To obtain tee times:** Call 5 days in advance. **Miscellaneous:** Discount packages, metal spikes, range (grass), club rentals, lodging, credit cards (MC, V, AE, D).

★★★★ **CREEK/MOUNTAIN**

Yards: 6,800/4,789. **Par:** 72/72. **Course Rating:** 70.2/66.9. **Slope:** 123/112.

Reader Comments: Excellent value, beautiful course ... Great 27 holes. Good layout ... Mountain 9 has magnificent starting hole ... Mountain No. 7 good par 5 with great view. Very scenic and fun ... Fun course ... Very playable, enjoy the flowers & scenery ... Nice clubhouse, tough but fair course, good practice facilities.

★★★★ PINE/CREEK
Yards: 6,700/4,630. **Par:** 72/72. **Course Rating:** 69.2/66.8. **Slope:** 119/111.
Reader Comments: Good course ... Excellent scenery. Saw deer on course with fog as a backdrop ... Nice combination ... I would play these combinations all the time ... Offers a challenge ... Excellent, maintained but crowded ... Short course for long hitters ... Good greens.

★★★★ PINE/MOUNTAIN
Yards: 6,650/4,637. **Par:** 72/72. **Course Rating:** 69.4/66.1. **Slope:** 120/110.
Reader Comments: Beautiful scenery, mountain golf ... Great for shorter hitters. Always in great condition! ... Fun eighteen ... Excellent, maintained but crowded ... Good greens.
Special Notes: Formerly known as Fairfield Glade Resort.

★★★½ HENRY HORTON STATE PARK GOLF COURSE
PU-4358 Nashville Hwy.., Chapel Hill, 37034, Marshall County, (615)364-2319, 30 miles S of Nashville.
Holes: 18. **Yards:** 7,060/5,625. **Par:** 72/73. **Course Rating:** 74.3/72.1. **Slope:** 128/117. **Green Fee:** $19/$19. **Cart Fee:** $20/person. **Walking Policy:** Unrestricted walking. **Walkability:** 3.
Opened: 1963. **Season:** Year-round. **High:** May-July. **To obtain tee times:** Call Tuesday for upcoming weekend or call 6 days in advance. **Miscellaneous:** Reduced fees (seniors, juniors), discount packages, range (grass), club rentals, lodging (72 rooms), credit cards (MC, V, AE).
Reader Comments: Huge greens, wide open ... Nice long course ... Big greens, best in TN. Fair layout ... Long, big greens, some wildlife ... Excellent golf ... A few great holes ... Excellent state park course. Huge greens ... Good state park course.

★★★★ HERMITAGE GOLF COURSE
PU-3939 Old Hickory Blvd., Old Hickory, 37138, Davidson County, (615)847-4001, 10 miles NE of Nashville. **Web:** www.hermitagegolf.com.
Holes: 18. **Yards:** 6,775/5,475. **Par:** 72/72. **Course Rating:** 71.9/70.8. **Slope:** 122/120. **Green Fee:** $27/$37. **Cart Fee:** $13/person. **Walking Policy:** Walking at certain times. **Walkability:** 2.
Opened: 1986. **Architect:** Gary Roger Baird. **Season:** Year-round. **High:** April-Oct. **To obtain tee times:** Call 5 days in advance. May make tee times up to one year in advance with credit card. **Miscellaneous:** Reduced fees (twilight), range (grass/mats), club rentals, credit cards (MC, V, AE, D).
Notes: LPGA Sara Lee Classic since 1988.
Reader Comments: Friendly staff, no trick holes, always in good condition ... Lots of sand ... Looks easy, but will eat your lunch! ... Good course, excellent staff, super value ... Love it! ... Great shape & fun to play ... Best overall golf experience in Nashville ... Beautiful course, pricey ... Good service. Scenic by the river.

HIDDEN VALLEY GOLF CLUB
PU-307 Henderson Rd., Jackson, 38305, (901)424-3146.
Special Notes: Call club for further information.

★½ HUNTERS POINT GOLF CLUB
PU-Highway 231 North, Lebanon, 37087, Wilson County, (615)444-7521, 25 miles E of Nashville.
Holes: 18. **Yards:** 6,573/5,600. **Par:** 72/73. **Course Rating:** 69.6/71.5. **Slope:** 108/111. **Green Fee:** $10/$15. **Cart Fee:** $10/. **Walking Policy:** Unrestricted walking. **Walkability:** 1. **Opened:** 1966. **Architect:** Robert Renaud. **Season:** Year-round. **High:** May-Oct. **To obtain tee times:** First come, first served. **Miscellaneous:** Reduced fees (weekdays, low season, seniors, juniors), discount packages, metal spikes, range (grass), club rentals, credit cards (MC, V, D).

★★★ INDIAN HILLS GOLF CLUB
PU-405 Calumet Trace, Murfreesboro, 37127, Rutherford County, (615)895-3642, 25 miles SE of Nashville. **E-mail:** dave@indianhillsgc.com. **Web:** www.indianhillsgc.com.
Holes: 18. **Yards:** 6,716/5,237. **Par:** 72/72. **Course Rating:** 72.9/70.3. **Slope:** 126/118. **Green Fee:** $10/$25. **Cart Fee:** $10/person. **Walking Policy:** Walking at certain times. **Walkability:** 2.
Opened: 1988. **Season:** Year-round. **High:** April-Oct. **To obtain tee times:** Call three days in advance. **Miscellaneous:** Reduced fees (weekdays, low season, twilight, seniors, juniors), discount packages, metal spikes, range (grass), club rentals, credit cards (MC, V, AE).
Reader Comments: Come on down ... Course in best shape. New excellent owners and pro ... Some holes have character, best practice range in town ... Nice course. Not in good shape ... Nice layout through nice homes.

★★ IRONWOOD GOLF COURSE
PU-3801 Ironwood Rd., Cookeville, 38501, Putnam County, (931)528-2331, 80 miles W of Nashville.
Holes: 18. **Yards:** 6,311/5,023. **Par:** 72/72. **Course Rating:** 70.7/68.5. **Slope:** 123/112. **Green Fee:** $11/$11. **Cart Fee:** $10/person. **Walking Policy:** Unrestricted walking. **Walkability:** 3.
Opened: 1971. **Architect:** Bobby Nichols. **Season:** Year-round. **High:** April-Sept. **To obtain tee

times: First come, first served. **Miscellaneous:** Reduced fees (weekdays, low season, seniors, juniors), range (grass), club rentals, credit cards (MC, V, D).

★★★ KNOXVILLE GOLF COURSE
PM-3925 Schaad Rd., Knoxville, 37912, Knox County, (865)687-4359.
Holes: 18. **Yards:** 6,528/5,325. **Par:** 72/72. **Course Rating:** 71.5/69.7. **Slope:** 119/110. **Green Fee:** $10/$14. **Cart Fee:** $10/. **Walking Policy:** Unrestricted walking. **Walkability:** N/A. **Opened:** 1984. **Architect:** D.J. DeVictor. **Season:** Year-round. **High:** April-Nov. **To obtain tee times:** Call one week in advance. **Miscellaneous:** Reduced fees (weekdays, twilight, seniors, juniors), metal spikes, club rentals, credit cards (MC, V).
Reader Comments: For all golfers ... friendly staff ... Home course slowly improving, good to walk ... Good challenge ... Wide treelined fairways, short par 3s ... Awesome greens; challenging layout ... Average course for an average day of golf.

LAMBERT ACRES GOLF CLUB
SP-3402 Tuckaleechee Park, Maryville, 37803, Blount County, (423)982-9838, 4 miles E of Maryville.
Holes: 27. **Green Fee:** $17/$17. **Cart Fee:** $8/person. **Walking Policy:** Unrestricted walking. **Walkability:** 3. **Opened:** 1965. **Architect:** Don Charles. **Season:** Year-round. **High:** May-Oct. **To obtain tee times:** First come, first served. **Miscellaneous:** Metal spikes, club rentals.

★★½ RED/orange
Yards: 6,282/4,753. **Par:** 72/72. **Course Rating:** 70.1/68.3. **Slope:** 121/105.
Reader Comments: Great public course, no tee times required! ... Good greens, rest of course needs work ... Walking allowed ... Variety of good holes, cheap good golf ... 27 holes in the foothills of the Smoky Mountains, beautiful!... Beautiful mountain views ... Forgiving and fun.

★★½ RED/WHITE
Yards: 6,480/4,511. **Par:** 72/72. **Course Rating:** 70.8/66.2. **Slope:** 118/102.
Reader Comments: The scenery is breathtaking. Mountains and more mountains ... Nice fairways in summer, but heavy play ... Easy layout, short, still no tee times, slow to get off.

★★½ WHITE/ORANGE
Yards: 6,292/4,704. **Par:** 72/72. **Course Rating:** 69.6/66.4. **Slope:** 119/105.
Reader Comments: Mountains provide beautiful backdrop, good variety ... This is easiest of the combos, White needs to be longer ... Nice fairways in summer, but heavy play ... Challenges, but not so much that you can get down on self.

★★★½ THE LEGACY GOLF CLUB
PU-100 Ray Floyd Dr., Springfield, 37172, Robertson County, (615)384-4653, 20 miles N of Nashville.
Holes: 18. **Yards:** 6,755/4,860. **Par:** 72/72. **Course Rating:** 73.3/68.2. **Slope:** 131/118. **Green Fee:** $15/$21. **Cart Fee:** $11/person. **Walking Policy:** Unrestricted walking. **Walkability:** 3. **Opened:** 1996. **Architect:** Ray Floyd/Augusta Golf, Inc. **Season:** Year-round. **High:** June-Sept. **To obtain tee times:** May call up to 5 days in advance. **Miscellaneous:** Reduced fees (low season, seniors, juniors), range (grass), club rentals, credit cards (MC, V, AE, D).
Reader Comments: Tight fairways: Leave driver in bag. Tricky greens ... Challenging course, demanding ... Must hit it straight ... Superb challenge from the tips ... Excellent routing with good variety ... Needs better maintenance ... Tough course, challenging but fun ... Good layout.

LEGENDS CLUB OF TENNESSEE
★★★½ ROPER'S KNOB COURSE *Condition*
SP-1500 Legends Club Lane, Franklin, 37068, Williamson County, (615)790-1300, 15 miles S of Nashville.
Holes: 18. **Yards:** 7,113/5,290. **Par:** 71/71. **Course Rating:** 74.7/71.4. **Slope:** 129/121. **Green Fee:** $55/$85. **Cart Fee:** Included in Green Fee. **Walking Policy:** Mandatory cart. **Walkability:** 2. **Opened:** 1992. **Architect:** Tom Kite/Bob Cupp. **Season:** Year-round. **High:** April-Oct. **To obtain tee times:** Call up to 30 days in advance. **Miscellaneous:** Reduced fees (weekdays, low season, twilight), discount packages, range (grass), club rentals, credit cards (MC, V, AE, D).
Reader Comments: Beautiful layout ... Nice layout but slow ... Price breaks my heart. Top notch staff and teaching school ... Long & tough. Excellent condition ... One of the most underrated courses in TN ... I love this course ... Great course but long!

★★ LONG HOLLOW GOLF COURSE
PU-1080 Long Hollow Pike, Gallatin, 37066, Sumner County, (615)451-3120, 25 miles E of Nashville.
Holes: 18. **Yards:** 6,000/4,952. **Par:** 70/70. **Course Rating:** 66.7/66.6. **Slope:** 109/101. **Green Fee:** $18/$20. **Cart Fee:** $20/person. **Walking Policy:** Unrestricted walking. **Walkability:** 1. **Opened:** 1983. **Architect:** Kevin Tucker. **Season:** Year-round. **High:** May-Sept. **To obtain tee times:** Call. **Miscellaneous:** Reduced fees (weekdays), range (grass/mats), club rentals, credit cards (MC, V).

★★★★ MARRIOTT'S GOLF CLUB AT SHILOH FALLS
SP-P.O. Box 11, Pickwick Dam, 38365, Hardin County, (901)689-5050, 100 miles E of Memphis.
Holes: 18. **Yards:** 6,713/5,156. **Par:** 72/72. **Course Rating:** 73.1/71.3. **Slope:** 136/128. **Green Fee:** $32/$49. **Cart Fee:** Included in Green Fee. **Walking Policy:** Walking at certain times.
Walkability: 5. **Opened:** 1993. **Architect:** Jerry Pate. **Season:** Year-round. **High:** April-Oct. **To obtain tee times:** Call up to 14 days in advance. **Miscellaneous:** Reduced fees (weekdays, low season, resort guests, juniors), discount packages, range (grass), club rentals, lodging, credit cards (MC, V, AE, D).
Reader Comments: An experience ... One of the best I've played. Tough, but very playable ... One unique hole, signature par 3 drops 100 yards to green, ride cable car down to putt ... Long par 3s, beautiful scenery ... Wonderful autumn experience! By far my all-time favorite course!

MCCABE FIELD GOLF COURSE
PU-46th Ave. & Murphy Rd., Nashville, 37209, Davidson County, (615)862-8491.
Holes: 27. **Green Fee:** $18/$18. **Cart Fee:** $18/cart. **Walking Policy:** Unrestricted walking.
Walkability: 1. **Opened:** 1939. **Season:** Year-round. **High:** April-Sept. **To obtain tee times:** Call 7 days in advance. **Miscellaneous:** Reduced fees (seniors, juniors), metal spikes, club rentals, credit cards (MC, V).
★★ MIDDLE/NORTH
Yards: 6,481/5,876. **Par:** 71/71. **Course Rating:** 69.6/69.6. **Slope:** 112/112.
★★ MIDDLE/SOUTH
Yards: 6,023/5,590. **Par:** 70/70. **Course Rating:** 68.6/68.6. **Slope:** 110/110.
★★ NORTH/SOUTH
Yards: 6,522/5,866. **Par:** 71/71. **Course Rating:** 69.7/69.7. **Slope:** 111/111.

★★★★ THE MEDALIST AT AVALON GOLF CLUB
SP-1299 Oak Chase Blvd., Lenoir City, 37772, Loudon County, (423)986-4653, (877)471-4653, 12 miles W of Knoxville. **Web:** www.avalongolf.com.
Holes: 18. **Yards:** 6,764/5,261. **Par:** 72/72. **Course Rating:** 72.2/70.0. **Slope:** 131/113. **Green Fee:** $38/$48. **Cart Fee:** Included in Green Fee. **Walking Policy:** Walking at certain times. **Walkability:** 5. **Opened:** 1997. **Architect:** Joe Lee/Rocky Roquemore. **Season:** Year-round. **High:** March-Oct. **To obtain tee times:** Tee times can be made by calling golf shop 7 days in advance.
Miscellaneous: Range (grass), club rentals, credit cards (MC, V, AE), beginner friendly.
Reader Comments: Awesome greens ... Good course, but not yet worth the price ... New course; maturing ... Wonderful finishing hole ... Too bad you can't walk it ... Super course ... New course. Expensive to play, needs to mature ... Helpful staff & true greens ... Very nice new course. Very pretty finishing hole.

★★½ MEMPHIS OAKS GOLF CLUB
SP-4143 E Holmes Rd, Memphis, 38118, Shelby County, (901)363-4744, 10 miles S of Memphis.
Holes: 18. **Yards:** 6,271/5,212. **Par:** 71/71. **Course Rating:** 70.8/N/A. **Slope:** 119/N/A. **Green Fee:** $18/$38. **Cart Fee:** $15/person. **Walking Policy:** Mandatory cart. **Walkability:** 1. **Opened:** 1963. **Architect:** John Frazier. **Season:** Year-round. **High:** June-Sept. **To obtain tee times:** Call up to 7 days in advance. **Miscellaneous:** Reduced fees (weekdays, low season, twilight), metal spikes, range (grass), club rentals, credit cards (MC, V).
Reader Comments: Good layout ... Watch for errant shots from parallel fairways ...Hit the ball straight ... Very tight course. Narrow. Doglegs left and right ... Good practice putting green ... Fun course, short, typically irons only, fun, tight ... Sneaky long, tight with lots of doglegs, sand and some water ... Well maintained.

★★ MOCCASIN BEND GOLF CLUB
PU-381 Moccasin Bend Rd., Chattanooga, 37405, Hamilton County, (423)267-3585, 3 miles N of Chattanooga. **E-mail:** wggolff@aol.com.
Holes: 18. **Yards:** 6,469/5,290. **Par:** 72/72. **Course Rating:** 69.6/69.0. **Slope:** 111/109. **Green Fee:** $14/$18. **Cart Fee:** $10/person. **Walking Policy:** Walking at certain times. **Walkability:** 2. **Opened:** 1966. **Architect:** Alex McKay. **Season:** Year-round. **High:** April-Oct. **To obtain tee times:** Call for weekends and holidays. **Miscellaneous:** Reduced fees (twilight, seniors, juniors), discount packages, range (grass), club rentals, credit cards (MC, V), beginner friendly (free tips at practice tee).

★★★ MONTGOMERY BELL STATE PARK GOLF COURSE
PU-800 Hotel Ave., Burns, 37029, Dickson County, (615)797-2578, (800)250-8613, 35 miles W of Nashville.
Holes: 18. **Yards:** 6,196/4,961. **Par:** 71/72. **Course Rating:** 69.3/68.8. **Slope:** 121/116. **Green Fee:** $20/$22. **Cart Fee:** $22/person. **Walking Policy:** Unrestricted walking. **Walkability:** 3. **Opened:** 1970. **Architect:** Gary Roger Baird. **Season:** Year-round. **High:** April-Nov. **To obtain tee times:** Call 6 days in advance. **Miscellaneous:** Reduced fees (seniors, juniors), discount packages, range (grass), lodging, credit cards (MC, V, AE, D), beginner friendly

TENNESSEE

Reader Comments: Nice state course, deer & turkey around. Fun to play ... Short, nice & pretty layout ... Good golf, low price, excellent grass ... State park, beautiful setting, good condition ... Beautiful scenery, deer watch you ... Very good state park course. Greens hold your shot.

MT AIRY GOLF & ATHLETIC CLUB
SP-100 Madison Drive, Dunlap, 37327, Sequatchie County, (423)949-6036, 40 miles N of Dunlop. **E-mail:** www.mtairygolf@bledsoe.net. **Web:** www.mtairygolf.com.
Holes: 18. **Yards:** 6,850/4,855. **Par:** 72/72. **Course Rating:** 72.3/N/A. **Slope:** 132/N/A. **Green Fee:** $15/$20. **Cart Fee:** $12/person. **Walking Policy:** Unrestricted walking. **Walkability:** 5. **Opened:** 1995. **Architect:** Dennis Mills. **Season:** Year-round. **High:** April-Oct. **To obtain tee times:** Call (423)949-6036. **Miscellaneous:** Reduced fees (weekdays, low season, twilight, seniors), range (grass), club rentals, credit cards (MC, V, D), beginner friendly (clinics).
Special Notes: Formerly Mount Airy Golf Club

★★★½ NASHBORO GOLF CLUB
PU-1101 Nashboro Blvd., Nashville, 37217, Davidson County, (615)367-2311.
Holes: 18. **Yards:** 6,887/5,485. **Par:** 72/75. **Course Rating:** 73.5/72.3. **Slope:** 134/121. **Green Fee:** $37/$45. **Cart Fee:** Included in Green Fee. **Walking Policy:** Walking at certain times. **Walkability:** 4. **Opened:** 1975. **Architect:** B.J. Wihry. **Season:** Year-round. **High:** April-Sept. **To obtain tee times:** Weekend tee times may be made beginning the Monday prior to the weekend. Weekday tee times amy be made up to 14 days in advance. **Miscellaneous:** Reduced fees (weekdays, low season, twilight), discount packages, range (grass), club rentals, credit cards (MC, V, AE, D), beginner friendly (clinics, lessons).
Reader Comments: Course condition greatly improved ... Used every club, enjoyed every hole ... Expensive good ... tight fairways ... Moderate rural course ... Good course for area.

OLD FORT GOLF CLUB
PM-1028 Golf Lane, Murfreesboro, 37129, Rutherford County, (615)896-2448.
E-mail: twilkinpga@aol.com.
Holes: 18. **Yards:** 6,859/4,971. **Par:** 72/72. **Course Rating:** 73.1/69.4. **Slope:** 127/114. **Green Fee:** $20/$24. **Cart Fee:** $9/person. **Walking Policy:** Unrestricted walking. **Walkability:** 2. **Opened:** 1985. **Architect:** Leon Howard. **Season:** Year-round. **High:** April-Oct. **To obtain tee times:** Call Golf Shop. **Miscellaneous:** Reduced fees (low season, seniors), range (grass), club rentals, credit cards (MC, V).

★★★ ORGILL PARK GOLF COURSE
PU-9080 Bethuel Rd., Millington, 38053, Shelby County, (901)872-3610, 10 miles N of Memphis.
E-mail: jesse@orgillpark.com. **Web:** www.orgillpark.com.
Holes: 18. **Yards:** 6,384/4,574. **Par:** 70/71. **Course Rating:** 68.6/68.3. **Slope:** 113/108. **Green Fee:** $14/$15. **Cart Fee:** $9/person. **Walking Policy:** Unrestricted walking. **Walkability:** 3. **Opened:** 1972. **Architect:** Press Little. **Season:** Year-round. **High:** April-Sept. **To obtain tee times:** Call 1 day in advance for weekdays and 2 days in advance for weekends.
Miscellaneous: Reduced fees (weekdays, low season, seniors, juniors), metal spikes, range (grass), club rentals, credit cards (MC, V, AE, D).
Reader Comments: Good course, water, no sand. It does make you think about shots ... Bermuda greens, pine trees, water, challenging but fair... Best municipal course in Memphis, fun and challenging ... Grip it and rip it course, fun, no bunkers ... Beautiful scenery.

★★½ PARIS LANDING GOLF COURSE
PU-16055 Hwy..79 N., Buchanan, 38222, Henry County, (901)644-1332, 40 miles S of Clarksville.
Holes: 18. **Yards:** 6,612/6,408. **Par:** 72/72. **Course Rating:** 72.9/72.9. **Slope:** 126/124. **Green Fee:** $19/$20. **Cart Fee:** $22/person. **Walking Policy:** Unrestricted walking. **Walkability:** 5. **Opened:** 1971. **Architect:** Benjamin Wihry. **Season:** Year-round. **High:** April-June/Sept.-Oct. **To obtain tee times:** Call (901)644-1332. **Miscellaneous:** Discount packages, range (grass), lodging (130 rooms), credit cards (MC, V, AE, D).
Reader Comments: Beautiful course on lake ... Excellent scenery ... Good test of golf skills, must drive it straight ... Par 3 to lake can be compared to anywhere. it is beautiful.

★★★★ PATRIOT HILLS GOLF CLUB
SP-735 Constitution Dr., Jefferson City, 37760, Jefferson County, (423)475-4466, 30 miles E of Knoxville. **Web:** www.dandridgegolf.com.
Holes: 18. **Yards:** 6,710/4,974. **Par:** 72/72. **Course Rating:** 72.4/67.1. **Slope:** 126/115. **Green Fee:** $16/$21. **Cart Fee:** $11/person. **Walking Policy:** Unrestricted walking. **Walkability:** 4. **Opened:** 1997. **Season:** Year-round. **High:** May-Oct. **To obtain tee times:** Call golf shop. **Miscellaneous:** Reduced fees (weekdays, twilight), range (grass), club rentals, credit cards (MC, V, D), beginner friendly (junior clinics, ladies clinics, individual lessons).
Reader Comments: Nice, short, challenging ... Maturing. Nice layout! ... Good greens, always a pleasure ... New course, excellent staff, very playable ... Very good greens ... An every-stick-in-the-bag layout ... Good course management. Well taken care of ... One of the best values in Tennessee.

TENNESSEE

★★★½ PICKWICK LANDING STATE PARK GOLF COURSE
PU-Hwy.. No.57 P.O. Box 15, Pickwick Dam, 38365, Hardin County, (901)689-3149, 120 miles E of Memphis.
Holes: 18. **Yards:** 6,478/5,229. **Par:** 72/72. **Course Rating:** 70.2/68.7. **Slope:** 118/115. **Green Fee:** $19/$19. **Cart Fee:** $20/cart. **Walking Policy:** Unrestricted walking. **Walkability:** 5.
Opened: 1973. **Architect:** Benjamin Whiry. **Season:** Year-round. **High:** March-Sept. **To obtain tee times:** Call Golf Shop. **Miscellaneous:** Reduced fees (weekdays, low season, juniors), discount packages, range (grass), club rentals, lodging (100 rooms), credit cards (MC, V, AE, D).
Reader Comments: Great public facility ... Blind holes; bring a lot of balls! ... Nice surprise, hilly, makes for interesting lies ... Harder than it looks ... Nice, not overly challenging ... Average course. Fun to play ... Always beautiful condition.

★★ PINE HILL GOLF COURSE
PM-1005 Alice Ave., Memphis, 38106, Shelby County, (901)775-9434.
Holes: 18. **Yards:** 5,908/5,014. **Par:** 72/73. **Course Rating:** 65.9/66.7. **Slope:** 114/116. **Green Fee:** $9/$11. **Walking Policy:** Unrestricted walking. **Walkability:** N/A. **Season:** Year-round. **High:** May-Sept. **To obtain tee times:** First come, first served. **Miscellaneous:** Reduced fees (seniors, juniors), metal spikes, range (grass), club rentals, credit cards (MC, V, AE).

PINE OAKS GOLF CLUB
PM-1709 Buffalo Road, Johnson City, 37604, Washington County, (423)434-6250.
Holes: 18. **Yards:** 6,271/4,905. **Par:** 71/73. **Course Rating:** 68.4/69.1. **Slope:** 109/114. **Green Fee:** $14/$18. **Cart Fee:** $12/person. **Walking Policy:** Unrestricted walking. **Walkability:** 3.
Opened: 1962. **Architect:** Alexander McKay. **Season:** Year-round. **High:** April-Aug. **To obtain tee times:** Call up to 8 days in advance. **Miscellaneous:** Reduced fees (weekdays, low season, juniors), metal spikes, club rentals, credit cards (MC, V).

★★★½ QUAIL RIDGE GOLF COURSE
PU-4055 Altruria Rd., Bartlett, 38135, Shelby County, (901)386-6951, 5 miles N of Memphis.
Holes: 18. **Yards:** 6,600/5,206. **Par:** 71/70. **Course Rating:** 71.8/70.8. **Slope:** 128/117. **Green Fee:** $22/$32. **Cart Fee:** $10/person. **Walking Policy:** Walking at certain times. **Walkability:** 3.
Opened: 1994. **Architect:** David Pfaff. **Season:** Year-round. **High:** April-Oct. **To obtain tee times:** Call 5 days in advance. **Miscellaneous:** Reduced fees (low season, twilight, seniors, juniors), range (grass/mats), club rentals, credit cards (MC, V, AE, D).
Reader Comments: A hidden gem in Memphis suburbs; accommodating staff ... Course is great ... Fast play ... Senior citizens friendly ... Very fine layout, good greens ... A real golf experience!

★★½ THE QUARRY GOLF CLUB
PU-1001 Reads Lake Rd., Chattanooga, 37415, Hamilton County, (423)875-8888, 6 miles N of Chattanooga.
Holes: 9. **Yards:** 2,890/N/A. **Par:** 34/N/A. **Course Rating:** N/A. **Slope:** N/A. **Green Fee:** $15/$18. **Cart Fee:** $10/person. **Walking Policy:** Unrestricted walking. **Walkability:** 2. **Opened:** 1972. **Architect:** Joe Lee. **Season:** Year-round. **High:** May-Aug. **To obtain tee times:** Call for tee times as early as 3 days in advance. **Miscellaneous:** Reduced fees (weekdays, seniors, juniors), club rentals, credit cards (MC, V, AE, D).
Reader Comments: Never crowded ... Clever layout, fairly maintained ... Unusual design. Too short. Fun to play.

THE RIDGES GOLF & COUNTRY CLUB
1501 Ridges Club Dr., Jonesborough, 37659.
Special Notes: Call club for further information.

RIDGEWOOD GOLF COURSE
PU-387 County Rd. 603, Athens, 37303, (423)263-5672.
Special Notes: Call club for further information.

★★★★ RIVER ISLANDS GOLF CLUB
PU-9610 Kodak Rd., Kodak, 37764, Knox County, (423)933-0100, (800)347-4837, 15 miles E of Knoxville. **Web:** www.riverislandsgolf.com.
Holes: 18. **Yards:** 7,001/4,973. **Par:** 72/72. **Course Rating:** 75.4/69.4. **Slope:** 133/118. **Green Fee:** $29/$49. **Cart Fee:** Included in Green Fee. **Walking Policy:** Mandatory cart. **Walkability:** 2. **Opened:** 1990. **Architect:** Arthur Hills. **Season:** Year-round. **High:** April-Oct. **To obtain tee times:** Call golf shop. **Miscellaneous:** Reduced fees (weekdays, low season, twilight), discount packages, metal spikes, range (grass), club rentals, credit cards (MC, V, AE, D).
Notes: Ranked 8th in 1999 Best in State.
Reader Comments: Beautiful layout on river, great condition ... Course is ALWAYS in perfect condition ... Very good course ... Nice condition, water everywhere ... Great, scenic, fun, great value ... Spectacular layout, expensive but good golf ... Great for any skill level ... This course is pure enjoyment ... Beautiful, immaculate.

★★★ RIVER RUN GOLF CLUB
PU-1701 Tennessee Ave., Crossville, 38555, Cumberland County, (931)456-4060, (800)465-3069, 60 miles E of Knoxville.
Holes: 18. **Yards:** 6,550/4,844. **Par:** 72/72. **Course Rating:** 71.9/70.0. **Slope:** 124/121. **Green Fee:** $16/$22. **Cart Fee:** Included in Green Fee. **Walking Policy:** Walking at certain times. **Walkability:** 5. **Opened:** 1983. **Architect:** Ron Garl, Bob Renau. **Season:** Year-round. **High:** April-Oct. **To obtain tee times:** Tee Times in advance with a credit card. Failure to cancel will result in credit card charge. **Miscellaneous:** Reduced fees (low season, resort guests, twilight, seniors), discount packages, range (grass), club rentals, lodging (45 rooms), credit cards (MC, V).
Reader Comments: Wonderful experience all around ... Unique layout, needs some work ... Mountain course, island green par 3... Excellent condition, fast greens, new ownership, better.

★★★½ ROAN VALLEY GOLF ESTATES
SP-Hwy. 421 S., Mountain City, 37683, Johnson County, (423)727-7931, 20 miles N of Boone, NC.
Holes: 18. **Yards:** 6,736/4,370. **Par:** 72/72. **Course Rating:** 71.8/68.9. **Slope:** 120/107. **Green Fee:** $32/$41. **Cart Fee:** Included in Green Fee. **Walking Policy:** Walking at certain times. **Walkability:** 5. **Opened:** 1982. **Architect:** Dan Maples. **Season:** April-Nov. **High:** May-Oct. **To obtain tee times:** Call anytime. **Miscellaneous:** Reduced fees (weekdays, low season, juniors), metal spikes, club rentals, lodging, credit cards (MC, V).
Reader Comments: Very scenic and hilly, good to play ... Great mountain course ... Interesting layout, some flat, some hilly ... Course always in good shape ... True mountain golf, scenic, enjoyable, remote ... Play in fall when leaves are changing, breathtaking.

★★★ SADDLE CREEK GOLF CLUB
PU-1480 Fayetteville Hwy.., Lewisburg, 37091, Marshall County, (931)270-7280, 50 miles S of Nashville. **E-mail:** scgolf@tnweb.com.
Holes: 18. **Yards:** 6,700/4,999. **Par:** 72/72. **Course Rating:** 71.9/67.9. **Slope:** 127/120. **Green Fee:** $19/$25. **Cart Fee:** $10/person. **Walking Policy:** Mandatory cart. **Walkability:** 3. **Opened:** 1995. **Architect:** Gene Bates. **Season:** Year-round. **High:** May-Oct. **To obtain tee times:** Call 5 days in advance. **Miscellaneous:** Reduced fees (weekdays, twilight, seniors, juniors), range (grass), club rentals, credit cards (MC, V, AE), beginner friendly (junior clinics, ladies clinics, golf school).
Reader Comments: Front nine tricky, back nine wide open & long ... Two different nines, one tight and one very open ... Front 9 is excellent, back getting better ... Good public course.

★★★½ SHILOH FALLS GOLF COURSE
SP-Old South Rd., Pickwick Dam, 38365, Hardin County, (901)689-5050.
Holes: 18. **Yards:** 6,724/5,156. **Par:** 72/72. **Course Rating:** 73.6/71.2. **Slope:** 131/122. **Green Fee:** $28/$49. **Cart Fee:** Included in Green Fee. **Walking Policy:** Mandatory cart. **Walkability:** 5. **Architect:** Jerry Pate/Fred Couples. **Season:** Year-round. **High:** May-Sept. **To obtain tee times:** Call up to 2 weeks in advance. **Miscellaneous:** Reduced fees (weekdays, low season, twilight, seniors, juniors), credit cards (MC, V, AE, D, Diners Club).
Reader Comments: Nice course! Will go back ... Great course when it's in shape ... Very nice ... For your money, best course in area ... This course offers a great day on the links.

SMYRNA MUNICIPAL GOLF COURSE
PM-101 Sam Ridley Pkwy., Smyrna, 37167, Rutherford County, (615)459-2666.
Holes: 18. **Yards:** 6,414/5,264. **Par:** 72/72. **Course Rating:** 70.4/71.1. **Slope:** 120/118. **Green Fee:** N/A/$18. **Cart Fee:** $9/person. **Walking Policy:** Unrestricted walking. **Walkability:** 3. **Opened:** 1976. **Architect:** Ed Connor. **Season:** Year-round. **High:** April-Aug. **To obtain tee times:** Call 3 days in advance. **Miscellaneous:** Reduced fees (low season, seniors, juniors), range (grass), club rentals, credit cards (MC, V).
Special Notes: Formerly Smyrna National Golf Course

★½ SOUTHWEST POINT GOLF COURSE
PU-Decatur Highway S., Kingston, 37763, Roane County, (423)376-5282, 40 miles W of Knoxville.
Holes: 18. **Yards:** 6,673/6,086. **Par:** 72/74. **Course Rating:** 70.3/70.0. **Slope:** N/A. **Green Fee:** $12/$22. **Cart Fee:** $10/person. **Walking Policy:** Unrestricted walking. **Walkability:** N/A. **Opened:** 1964. **Architect:** Alex McKay. **Season:** Year-round. **High:** Mar-Aug. **To obtain tee times:** Tee times not required. **Miscellaneous:** Reduced fees (weekdays, low season, twilight, seniors), metal spikes, club rentals, credit cards (MC, V).
Special Notes: Spikeless encouraged.

SPARTA GOLF & COUNTRY CLUB
SP-Rte. 3, Sparta, 38583, (423)738-5836, 100 miles E of Nashville.
Special Notes: Call club for further information.

★★★★ SPRINGHOUSE GOLF CLUB
R-18 Springhouse Lane, Nashville, 37214, Davidson County, (615)871-7759.
Holes: 18. **Yards:** 7,007/5,126. **Par:** 72/72. **Course Rating:** 74.0/70.2. **Slope:** 133/118. **Green Fee:** $60/$75. **Cart Fee:** Included in Green Fee. **Walking Policy:** Mandatory cart. **Walkability:**

TENNESSEE

3. **Opened:** 1990. **Architect:** Larry Nelson/Jeff Brauer. **Season:** Year-round. **High:** April-Oct. **To obtain tee times:** Tee times are required and are taken up to 7 days in advance. Opryland hotel guests call 30 days in advance. **Miscellaneous:** Reduced fees (weekdays, low season, seniors, juniors), range (grass), club rentals, lodging (2,900 rooms), credit cards (MC, V, AE, D). **Notes:** 1994-99 BellSouth Senior Classic.

Reader Comments: Very expensive but excellent–tough layout ... Great pro shop. Excellent course ... Great layout & the friendliest staff anywhere. Fast greens,18 holes built on very little land ... Love it, great moguls ... Beautiful resort course, hard, great greens, pricey ... Some great holes, some bland holes ... Greatest staff.

★★★ STONEBRIDGE GOLF COURSE

PU-3049 Davies Plantation Rd. South, Lakeland, 38002, Shelby County, (901)382-1886, 5 miles W of Memphis.

Holes: 18. **Yards:** 6,788/5,012. **Par:** 71/71. **Course Rating:** 73.3/66.8. **Slope:** 133/113. **Green Fee:** $20/$44. **Cart Fee:** $12/person. **Walking Policy:** Walking at certain times. **Walkability:** 3. **Opened:** 1972. **Architect:** George W. Cobb. **Season:** Year-round. **High:** April-Sept. **To obtain tee times:** Call 5 days in advance. **Miscellaneous:** Reduced fees (weekdays, low season), range (grass/mats), club rentals, credit cards (MC, V, AE, D).

Reader Comments: Nice course, long ... Narrow, not for average player... Good shape, got to think! ... Sweet! ... Good par 5s ... Long par 4s ... Double dogleg par 5 difficult but fun.

★★★★ STONEHENGE GOLF CLUB

PU-222 Fairfield Blvd., Fairfield Glade, 38558, Cumberland County, (615)484-3731, (800)GOLF-120, 60 miles W of Knoxville. **Web:** www.stonehengegolf.com.

Holes: 18. **Yards:** 6,549/5,043. **Par:** 72/72. **Course Rating:** 71.5/70.2. **Slope:** 131/124. **Green Fee:** N/A. **Cart Fee:** Included in Green Fee. **Walking Policy:** Mandatory cart. **Walkability:** 4. **Opened:** 1984. **Architect:** Joe Lee/Rocky Roquemore. **Season:** March-Nov. **High:** April-Oct. **To obtain tee times:** Call golf shop up to 30 days in advance to book tee times. **Miscellaneous:** Reduced fees (low season, resort guests, twilight, juniors), discount packages, range (grass), club rentals, lodging, credit cards (MC, V, AE, D).

Notes: Ranked 3rd in 1999 Best in State; 40th in 1996 America's Top 75 Affordable Courses.

Reader Comments: Great course, great views, worth any price ... Mountain course. Fairways and greens great ... One of the best in state, outstanding ... A real tough beauty with bent fairways ... Great practice greens ... Positively best ... Fairways like carpet, beautiful vistas.

★★★ SWAN LAKE GOLF COURSE

PM-581 Dunbar Cave Rd., Clarksville, 37043, Montgomery County, (931)648-0479, 40 miles NW of Nashville.

Holes: 18. **Yards:** 6,419/5,155. **Par:** 71/72. **Course Rating:** 70.5/69.0. **Slope:** 116/112. **Green Fee:** $14/$14. **Cart Fee:** $16/cart. **Walking Policy:** Unrestricted walking. **Walkability:** 3. **Architect:** Benjamin Wihry. **Season:** Year-round. **High:** March-Oct. **To obtain tee times:** Call Wednesday for Saturday tee times. Call Thursday for Sunday. **Miscellaneous:** Reduced fees (seniors), credit cards (MC, V).

Notes: Rated No. 11 in nation by Golf Digest Third Edition of Places to Play.

Reader Comments: Best value, tough course ... Good municipal course.

★★ T.O. FULLER GOLF COURSE

PM-1400 Pavillion Dr., Memphis, 38109, Shelby County, (901)543-7771.

Holes: 18. **Yards:** 6,000/5,656. **Par:** 72/73. **Course Rating:** 71.0/72.0. **Slope:** 117/110. **Green Fee:** $16/$18. **Cart Fee:** $11/person. **Walking Policy:** Unrestricted walking. **Walkability:** 4. **Opened:** 1956. **Architect:** City of Memphis. **Season:** Year-round. **High:** May-Dec. **To obtain tee times:** Call 5 days in advance. **Miscellaneous:** Reduced fees (weekdays, low season, seniors, juniors), metal spikes, club rentals, credit cards (MC, V, AE, D).

★★½ TED RHODES GOLF COURSE

PU-1901 Ed Temple Blvd., Nashville, 37208, Davidson County, (615)862-8463.

Holes: 18. **Yards:** 6,660/5,732. **Par:** 72/72. **Course Rating:** 71.8/68.3. **Slope:** 120/115. **Green Fee:** $8/$16. **Cart Fee:** $14/cart. **Walking Policy:** Unrestricted walking. **Walkability:** N/A. **Opened:** 1994. **Architect:** Gary Roger Baird. **Season:** Year-round. **High:** May-Sept. **To obtain tee times:** Call 7 days in advance. **Miscellaneous:** Reduced fees (seniors, juniors), metal spikes, range (grass), club rentals.

Reader Comments: Lots of water, not easily walked, small greens ... Excellent greens and plenty of hazards. Makes for an interesting round ... Excellent course for all players ... Excellent golf pro, good service ...Good reworking of old course ... Always happy to see you.

★★★½ THREE RIDGES GOLF COURSE

PU-6101 Wise Springs Rd., Knoxville, 37918, Knox County, (423)687-4797.

Holes: 18. **Yards:** 7,035/5,225. **Par:** 72/72. **Course Rating:** 73.2/70.7. **Slope:** 128/121. **Green Fee:** $10/$27. **Cart Fee:** $12/person. **Walking Policy:** Unrestricted walking. **Walkability:** N/A. **Opened:** 1991. **Architect:** Ault, Clark & Assoc. **Season:** Year-round. **High:** April-Oct. **To obtain**

TENNESSEE

tee times: Call 7 days in advance. **Miscellaneous:** Reduced fees (weekdays, twilight, seniors, juniors), metal spikes, range (grass), club rentals, credit cards (MC, V, AE, D, Diners Club).
Reader Comments: Great layout. Long walk. Best value ... Good challenge ... Long from back tees ... Good value, nice practice facilities ... Great course, can't walk back nine ... Toughest public course in area ... Good course, very fast greens ... Tough from tips. Good layout.

★★★ TWO RIVERS GOLF COURSE
PM-3140 McGavock Pike, Nashville, 37214, Davidson County, (615)889-2675, 10 miles E of Nashville.
Holes: 18. **Yards:** 6,595/5,336. **Par:** 72/72. **Course Rating:** 71.5/70.4. **Slope:** 120/116. **Green Fee:** $18/$18. **Cart Fee:** $18/cart. **Walking Policy:** Unrestricted walking. **Walkability:** 2.
Opened: 1968. **Architect:** Dave Bennett/Leon Howard. **Season:** Year-round. **High:** April-Sept.
To obtain tee times: Call up to seven days in advance, seven days a week. **Miscellaneous:** Club rentals, credit cards (MC, V).
Reader Comments: One of Nashville's best public courses ... Good public course, easy walk ... Tight little course, pace-conscious employees, quick golf.

★★½ WARRIOR'S PATH STATE PARK
PU-P.O. Box 5026, Kingsport, 37663, Sullivan County, (423)323-4990, 90 miles E of Knoxville.
Holes: 18. **Yards:** 6,601/5,328. **Par:** 72/72. **Course Rating:** 71.5/72.4. **Slope:** 123/117. **Green Fee:** $17/$20. **Cart Fee:** $11/person. **Walking Policy:** Unrestricted walking. **Walkability:** 4.
Opened: 1972. **Architect:** George Cobb. **Season:** Year-round. **High:** March-Aug. **To obtain tee times:** Call 7 days in advance. **Miscellaneous:** Reduced fees (weekdays, low season, seniors, juniors), discount packages, range (grass/mats), caddies, club rentals, lodging, credit cards (MC, V), beginner friendly.
Reader Comments: Not bad, walking allowed ... Very pretty, crowded on weekend ... Fairways and greens very nice ... Excellent staff, average layout ... Very hilly course ... Work is being done. Course is getting better... Nice State Park golf.

★★★ WHITTLE SPRINGS GOLF COURSE
PU-3113 Valley View Dr., Knoxville, 37917, Knox County, (423)525-1022, (800)527-1022.
Holes: 18. **Yards:** 6,000/4,884. **Par:** 70/70. **Course Rating:** 68.3/67.4. **Slope:** 106/111. **Green Fee:** $13/$15. **Cart Fee:** $11/person. **Walking Policy:** Mandatory cart. **Walkability:** 1. **Season:** Year-round. **High:** March-Sept. **To obtain tee times:** Call Golf Shop. **Miscellaneous:** Reduced fees (weekdays, seniors, juniors), metal spikes, range (grass), beginner friendly (golf lessons).
Reader Comments: Country club atmosphere on very good course ... Good walkable short course, good public course ... Very short, oldest course operated in city.

★★★★ WILLOW CREEK GOLF CLUB
PU-12003 Kingston Pike, Knoxville, 37922, Knox County, (423)675-0100, 12 miles W of Knoxville. **E-mail:** tinwhistl1@aol.com. **Web:** www.willowcreekgolf.com.
Holes: 18. **Yards:** 6,986/5,557. **Par:** 72/74. **Course Rating:** 73.5/71.9. **Slope:** 130/119. **Green Fee:** $25/$35. **Cart Fee:** $15/person. **Walking Policy:** Walking at certain times. **Walkability:** 2.
Opened: 1988. **Architect:** Bill Oliphant. **Season:** Year-round. **High:** April-Oct. **To obtain tee times:** Call 7 days in advance. **Miscellaneous:** Reduced fees (low season, twilight, juniors), range (grass), club rentals, credit cards (MC, V, AE).
Reader Comments: Great course ... A course that is already mature ... Golf with an attitude, expensive ride ... Very good condition, country club atmosphere ... Always keep in great shape ... Good design ... Best public golf conditions in Tennessee.

WILLOWBROOK GOLF CLUB
PU-6751 McMinnville Hwy.., Manchester, 37355, Coffee County, (931)728-8989, (931)728-8989, 5 miles N of Manchester.
Holes: 18. **Yards:** 6,689/5,304. **Par:** 72/72. **Course Rating:** 72.7/71.4. **Slope:** 128/122. **Green Fee:** $18/$30. **Cart Fee:** $9/person. **Walking Policy:** Walking at certain times. **Walkability:** 2.
Opened: 1995. **Architect:** Jerry Lemons. **Season:** Year-round. **High:** April-Oct. **To obtain tee times:** Call Golf Shop up to 4 days in advance. Outings can be booked with a deposit.
Miscellaneous: Reduced fees (weekdays, low season, resort guests, twilight, seniors, juniors), range (grass), club rentals, credit cards (MC, V, AE).

★★★ WINDTREE GOLF COURSE
PU-810 Nonaville Rd., Mount Juliet, 37122, Wilson County, (615)754-4653, 15 miles NE of Nashville.
Holes: 18. **Yards:** 6,557/5,126. **Par:** 72/72. **Course Rating:** 71.1/69.6. **Slope:** 124/117. **Green Fee:** $24/$33. **Cart Fee:** $10/cart. **Walking Policy:** Walking at certain times. **Walkability:** 3.
Opened: 1991. **Architect:** John LaFoy. **Season:** Year-round. **High:** April-Sept. **To obtain tee times:** Call Mondays for upcoming weekend. **Miscellaneous:** Reduced fees (twilight), range (grass), club rentals, credit cards (MC, V, AE).
Reader Comments: Nashville area's best-kept secret ... Some very tight holes, excellent service, good pro ... Super nice course ... Needs more trees. Good greens.

TEXAS

★★ ALICE MUNICIPAL GOLF COURSE
PM-Texas Blvd., Alice, 78332, Jim Wells County, (361)664-7033, 40 miles W of Corpus Christi.
Holes: 18. **Yards:** 6,099/5,066. **Par:** 71/72. **Course Rating:** 67.8/65.6. **Slope:** 108/100. **Green Fee:** $6/$7. **Cart Fee:** $15/cart. **Walking Policy:** Unrestricted walking. **Walkability:** 1. **Architect:** Ralph Plummer. **Season:** Year-round. **High:** April-Aug. **To obtain tee times:** Call Wednesday for upcoming weekend. **Miscellaneous:** Reduced fees (seniors), metal spikes, credit cards (MC, V).

★★ ALPINE GOLF COURSE
PU-2385 Smelley Rd., Longview, 75605, Gregg County, (903)753-4515, 45 miles W of Shreveport, LA. **E-mail:** alpgc@aol.com.
Holes: 18. **Yards:** 5,435/4,795. **Par:** 70/70. **Course Rating:** 67.4/67.4. **Slope:** 108/108. **Green Fee:** $19/$19. **Cart Fee:** $8/person. **Walking Policy:** Unrestricted walking. **Walkability:** 2. **Opened:** 1955. **Architect:** W.L. Benningfield. **Season:** Year-round. **High:** March-July. **To obtain tee times:** Call golf shop. **Miscellaneous:** Range (mats), club rentals, credit cards (MC, D).
Special Notes: Formerly Alpine Golf Club

★★★ ANDREWS COUNTY GOLF COURSE
PU-920 Golf Course Road, Andrews, 79714, Andrews County, (915)524-1462, 36 miles NW of Odessa.
Holes: 18. **Yards:** 6,300/5,331. **Par:** 70/72. **Course Rating:** 68.9/69.7. **Slope:** 116/110. **Green Fee:** $18/$25. **Cart Fee:** $18/cart. **Walking Policy:** Unrestricted walking. **Walkability:** 1. **Architect:** Warren Cantrell. **Season:** Year-round. **High:** May-Oct. **To obtain tee times:** Call golf shop. **Miscellaneous:** Range (grass/mats), credit cards (MC, V, AE, D).
Reader Comments: Neat course–great value ... Fast greens, has nasty par 3 on front ... Soft, grassy fairways ... Narrow fairways, greens are excellent.

★½ ASCARATE PARK GOLF COURSE
PU-6900 Delta Dr., El Paso, 79905, El Paso County, (915)772-7381.
Holes: 18. **Yards:** 6,505/5,650. **Par:** 71/72. **Course Rating:** 69.4/66.2. **Slope:** 114/107. **Green Fee:** $5/$10. **Cart Fee:** $16/cart. **Walking Policy:** Unrestricted walking. **Walkability:** N/A. **Opened:** 1958. **Architect:** George Hoffman. **Season:** Year-round. **High:** Year-round. **To obtain tee times:** Call one week in advance for weekends only. **Miscellaneous:** Reduced fees (weekdays, twilight, seniors, juniors), metal spikes, range (grass), club rentals.
Special Notes: Also has 9-hole course.

★★★½ THE BANDIT GOLF CLUB *Pace*
PU-6019 FM 725, New Braunfels, 78130, Guadalupe County, (830)609-4665, (888)923-7846, 5 miles E of New Braunfels.
Holes: 18. **Yards:** 6,928/5,253. **Par:** 71/71. **Course Rating:** 73.6/70.3. **Slope:** 133/126. **Green Fee:** $40/$56. **Cart Fee:** Included in Green Fee. **Walking Policy:** Unrestricted walking. **Walkability:** 4. **Opened:** 1997. **Architect:** Keith Foster. **Season:** Year-round. **High:** Feb.-May/Oct.-Dec. **To obtain tee times:** Call one week in advance. Earlier tee times for additional $10.00 charge. **Miscellaneous:** Metal spikes, range (grass), club rentals, credit cards (MC, V, AE, D), beginner friendly (complimentary golf clinics).
Reader Comments: Have to use all clubs from back tees ... Great find! ... Great par 3s ... Great layout–challenging holes ... Bring your 'A' game ... New course–needs maturing, long ... Course is well maintained, overpriced.

BARTON CREEK RESORT & COUNTRY CLUB *Service*
★★★½ CRENSHAW-COORE COURSE
R-8212 Barton Club Dr., Austin, 78735, Travis County, (512)329-4608, (800)336-6158, 12 miles W of Austin.
Holes: 18. **Yards:** 6,678/4,843. **Par:** 71/71. **Course Rating:** 71.0/67.2. **Slope:** 124/110. **Green Fee:** $95/$95. **Cart Fee:** Included in Green Fee. **Walking Policy:** Unrestricted walking. **Walkability:** 3. **Opened:** 1991. **Architect:** Ben Crenshaw/Bill Coore. **Season:** Year-round. **High:** Spring/Fall. **To obtain tee times:** Must be an overnight resort guest, club member or conference guest. **Miscellaneous:** Discount packages, metal spikes, range (grass/mats), club rentals, lodging, credit cards (MC, V, AE).
Notes: Ranked 24th in 1999 Best in State.
Reader Comments: Nice wide fairways ... Wonderful course–super people ... Resort is plush & friendly ... Great layout, beautiful scenery, huge greens ... Biggest greens in Texas ... Excellent layout–well kept–good service ... Too many blind shots ... All 3 are great courses ... Lady friendly, scenic hill country.
★★★★½ FAZIO COURSE *Condition*
R-8212 Barton Club Dr., Austin, 78735, Travis County, (512)329-4001, (800)336-6158, 12 miles W of Austin.
Holes: 18. **Yards:** 6,956/5,207. **Par:** 72/72. **Course Rating:** 74.0/69.4. **Slope:** 135/120. **Green Fee:** N/A/$135. **Cart Fee:** Included in Green Fee. **Walking Policy:** Unrestricted walking. **Walkability:** 4. **Opened:** 1986. **Architect:** Tom Fazio. **Season:** Year-round. **High:** Spring/Fall. **To**

obtain tee times: Must be an overnight resort guest, club member or conference guest.
Miscellaneous: Discount packages, metal spikes, range (grass/mats), club rentals, lodging, credit cards (MC, V, AE).
Notes: Ranked 2nd in 1999 Best in State; 21st in 1996 America's Top 75 Upscale Courses.
Reader Comments: The best there is! ... Beautiful–great layout ... Great golf, great experience ... Clubhouse and spa fantastic ... Rangers keep it moving, 4-hour round ... Great, challenging, must play every club ... Won't let you hunt balls in waterfalls.

★★★★ **PALMER-LAKESIDE COURSE** *Condition, Pace*
R-1800 Clubhouse Hill Dr., Spicewood, 78669, Travis County, (830)693-4589, (800)888-2257, 25 miles W of Austin.
Holes: 18. **Yards:** 6,657/5,067. **Par:** 71/71. **Course Rating:** 71.0/71.0. **Slope:** 124/124. **Green Fee:** $95/$95. **Cart Fee:** Included in Green Fee. **Walking Policy:** Unrestricted walking. **Walkability:** 4. **Opened:** 1986. **Architect:** Arnold Palmer/Ed Seay. **Season:** Year-round. **High:** Spring/Fall. **To obtain tee times:** Must be an overnight resort guest, club member or a conference guest.
Miscellaneous: Metal spikes, range (grass/mats), club rentals, lodging, credit cards (MC, V, AE).
Reader Comments: Mostly fun, challenging course ... Scenic and fun to play ... Awesome course ... Pristine condition–interesting holes ... Very good-professional staff ... Not safe to go in rough, stay straight ... Beautiful setting, excellent course.

★★½ **BATTLE LAKE GOLF COURSE**
PU-4443 Battle Lake Road, Mart, 76664, McLennan County, (254)876-2837, 15 miles SE of Waco. **Web:** www.battlelakegolf.com.
Holes: 18. **Yards:** 6,608/5,254. **Par:** 72/74. **Course Rating:** 70.7/69.3. **Slope:** 116/112. **Green Fee:** $6/$12. **Cart Fee:** $10/person. **Walking Policy:** Unrestricted walking. **Walkability:** 3. **Season:** Year-round. **High:** March-Oct. **To obtain tee times:** Call 7 days in advance for weekends and holidays. **Miscellaneous:** Reduced fees (weekdays, low season, twilight, seniors, juniors), metal spikes, range (grass/mats), club rentals, credit cards (MC, V, D).
Reader Comments: Wide open ... Modest parkland layout in rural Texas ... Back 9 is a neat layout, front 9 poor ... It will be a very good course in time.

★★★½ **THE BATTLEGROUND AT DEER PARK GOLF COURSE**
PU-1600 Georgia Ave., Deer Park, 77536, Harris County, (281)478-4653, 20 miles SE of Houston.
Holes: 18. **Yards:** 6,942/5,526. **Par:** 72/72. **Course Rating:** 73.6/73.1. **Slope:** 130/134. **Green Fee:** $24/$30. **Cart Fee:** $10/person. **Walking Policy:** Unrestricted walking. **Walkability:** 2. **Opened:** 1996. **Architect:** Tom Knickerbocker/Charlie Epps. **Season:** Year-round. **High:** March-May. **To obtain tee times:** Call up to 7 days in advance. **Miscellaneous:** Reduced fees (weekdays, twilight, seniors, juniors), metal spikes, range (grass/mats), club rentals, credit cards (MC, V, AE).
Reader Comments: Friendliest pro shop personnel in Texas ... Fairways make for good shots even for mid-handicaps ... Needs to grow up some more ... Nice job for dead-flat land ... Fairly new with a good start ... Lots of water and spacious well-kept greens.

★★★ **BAY FOREST GOLF COURSE**
PM-201 Bay Forest Dr., LaPorte, 77571, Harris County, (281)471-4653, 20 miles SE of Houston.
Holes: 18. **Yards:** 6,756/5,094. **Par:** 72/72. **Course Rating:** 72.4/69.0. **Slope:** 126/113. **Green Fee:** $13/$19. **Cart Fee:** $20/cart. **Walking Policy:** Unrestricted walking. **Walkability:** 1. **Opened:** 1988. **Architect:** Riviere/Marr. **Season:** Year-round. **High:** April-Oct. **To obtain tee times:** Call Monday for the following 7 days. **Miscellaneous:** Reduced fees (twilight, seniors), metal spikes, range (grass), club rentals, credit cards (MC, V, AE, D).
Reader Comments: A test for mid-handicapper ... Great course for a muny ... Lots of trees, small clubhouse ... A hidden value ... Great muny for the money.

BAYOU DIN GOLF CLUB
PU-8537 LaBelle Rd., Beaumont, 77705, Jefferson County, (409)796-1327, 85 miles E of Houston.
Holes: 27. **Green Fee:** $12/$17. **Cart Fee:** $8/person. **Walking Policy:** Unrestricted walking. **Architect:** Jimmy Whetcher. **Season:** Year-round. **High:** March-Aug. **To obtain tee times:** Call golf shop.
★★★ **BAYOU BACK/LINKS 9**
Yards: 6,495/5,233. **Par:** 71/71. **Course Rating:** 70.6/64.7. **Slope:** 118/105. **Walkability:** 2. **Opened:** 1959. **Miscellaneous:** Reduced fees (weekdays, twilight, seniors, juniors), metal spikes, range (grass/mats), club rentals, credit cards (MC, V).
Reader Comments: The new 9 (Links 9) is the best in Beaumont ... Good condition in spite of heavy play ... Friendly people ... 27 holes-the links 9 is very good ... Good value, nice people.
★★★ **BAYOU FRONT/BAYOU BACK**
Yards: 6,285/5,339. **Par:** 71/71. **Course Rating:** 68.5/64.4. **Slope:** 108/98. **Walkability:** 1. **Opened:** 1961. **Miscellaneous:** Reduced fees (twilight, seniors, juniors), metal spikes, range (grass/mats), club rentals, credit cards (MC, V).
Reader Comments: Fun course ... Long and flat, greens hold and roll true.
★★★ **BAYOU FRONT/LINKS 9**

Yards: 7,020/5,672. **Par:** 72/72. **Course Rating:** 72.1/66.1. **Slope:** 116/103. **Walkability:** 2. **Opened:** 1961. **Miscellaneous:** Reduced fees (weekdays, twilight, seniors, juniors), metal spikes, range (grass/mats), club rentals, credit cards (MC, V).
Reader Comments: Back 9 par 5 is great fun ... Very friendly to an 18 handicap.

★★½ BAYOU GOLF CLUB
PU-2800 Ted Dudley Dr., Texas City, 77590, Galveston County, (409)643-5850, 30 miles SE of Houston.
Holes: 18. **Yards:** 6,665/5,448. **Par:** 72/73. **Course Rating:** 71.0/73.0. **Slope:** 114/118. **Green Fee:** $10/$14. **Cart Fee:** $16/cart. **Walking Policy:** Unrestricted walking. **Walkability:** 1. **Opened:** 1974. **Architect:** Joe Finger. **Season:** Year-round. **To obtain tee times:** Call Wednesday for weekend times. Open play weekdays. **Miscellaneous:** Reduced fees (twilight, seniors, juniors), range (grass), club rentals.
Reader Comments: Good course, too many stairs to clubhouse ... The layout is fun, links-style course, lots of wind ... Flat course.

BEAR CREEK GOLF WORLD
PU-16001 Clay Rd., Houston, 77084, Harris County, (281)855-4720.
★★★ CHALLENGER COURSE
Holes: 18. **Yards:** 5,295/4,432. **Par:** 66/66. **Course Rating:** 64.2/64.7. **Slope:** 103/103. **Green Fee:** $17/$49. **Cart Fee:** $11/person. **Walking Policy:** Walking at certain times. **Walkability:** 1. **Opened:** 1968. **Architect:** Bruce Littell. **Season:** Year-round. **High:** April-Oct. **To obtain tee times:** Call 3 days in advance. Members may call 14 days in advance. **Miscellaneous:** Reduced fees (weekdays, low season, twilight, seniors, juniors), metal spikes, range (grass), club rentals, credit cards (MC, V, AE).
Reader Comments: 8 par 3's, nice little par 66 ... Worth playing ... Good condition for the high traffic ... Good course for beginners.
★★★½ MASTERS COURSE
Holes: 18. **Yards:** 7,131/5,544. **Par:** 72/72. **Course Rating:** 74.1/72.1. **Slope:** 133/125. **Green Fee:** $17/$56. **Cart Fee:** $11/person. **Walking Policy:** Walking at certain times. **Walkability:** 1. **Opened:** 1972. **Architect:** Jay Riviere. **Season:** Year-round. **High:** April-Oct. **To obtain tee times:** Call 3 days in advance. Members may call 14 days in advance. **Miscellaneous:** Reduced fees (weekdays, low season, twilight, seniors, juniors), metal spikes, range (grass), club rentals, credit cards (MC, V, AE).
Notes: Ranked 20th in 1999 Best in State.
Reader Comments: A very friendly course ... Can be demanding ... Good course to play ... Nice course, but not worth price ... When wind blows, course plays very tough.
★★★ PRESIDENTS COURSE
Holes: 18. **Yards:** 6,562/5,728. **Par:** 72/72. **Course Rating:** 69.1/70.6. **Slope:** 110/111. **Green Fee:** $17/$49. **Cart Fee:** $11/person. **Walking Policy:** Walking at certain times. **Walkability:** 1. **Opened:** 1968. **Architect:** Jay Riviere. **Season:** Year-round. **High:** April-Oct. **To obtain tee times:** Call 3 days in advance. Members may call up to 14 days in advance. **Miscellaneous:** Reduced fees (weekdays, low season, twilight, seniors, juniors), discount packages, metal spikes, range (grass), club rentals, credit cards (MC, V, AE).
Reader Comments: Big pine trees–keep it low ... Too expensive to play ... Good condition for the high traffic.

★★★ BLACKHAWK GOLF CLUB
PU-2714 Kelly Lane, Pflugerville, 78660, Travis County, (512)251-9000, 15 miles NE of Austin.
E-mail: bhgc@swbell.net. **Web:** www.ccsi.com.
Holes: 18. **Yards:** 7,103/5,538. **Par:** 72/72. **Course Rating:** 73.5/71.1. **Slope:** 123/121. **Green Fee:** $37/$48. **Cart Fee:** $11/person. **Walking Policy:** Walking at certain times. **Walkability:** 2. **Opened:** 1991. **Architect:** Hollis Stacy/Charles Howard. **Season:** Year-round. **High:** April-Sept. **To obtain tee times:** Call up to 5 days in advance. **Miscellaneous:** Reduced fees (weekdays, low season, twilight, seniors, juniors), metal spikes, range (grass/mats), club rentals, credit cards (MC, V, AE).
Reader Comments: Groundskeeping not on par with good layout ... Good personnel ... Long course ... Fair, fun & challenging ... Links-style course, good value for money.

★★★ BLUEBONNET COUNTRY GOLF COURSE
SP-Rte. 2, Box 3471, Navasota, 77868, Grimes County, (409)894-2207.
Holes: 18. **Yards:** 6,495/5,159. **Par:** 72/72. **Course Rating:** 71.0/70.4. **Slope:** 129/129. **Green Fee:** $6/$18. **Cart Fee:** $18/cart. **Walking Policy:** Walking at certain times. **Walkability:** 4. **Opened:** 1972. **Architect:** Jay Riviere. **Season:** Year-round. **High:** Spring/Fall. **To obtain tee times:** Call on Monday for upcoming weekend. Call up to 7 days in advance for holiday. **Miscellaneous:** Reduced fees (weekdays, twilight, seniors, juniors), metal spikes, credit cards (MC, V, AE, D).
Reader Comments: Very nice and fair course ... Improving course in recent times ... Nice layout–lots of trees and rough ... A surprise in the middle of nowhere ... Quiet, peaceful country course. Good value ... Beautiful setting.

TEXAS

★★★½ BLUEBONNET HILL GOLF CLUB
PU-9100 Decker Lane, Austin, 78724, Travis County, (512)272-4228.
Holes: 18. **Yards:** 6,503/5,241. **Par:** 72/72. **Course Rating:** 70.0/69.4. **Slope:** 113/115. **Green Fee:** $9/$24. **Cart Fee:** $18/cart. **Walking Policy:** Unrestricted walking. **Walkability:** 3. **Opened:** 1991. **Architect:** Jeff Brauer. **Season:** Year-round. **High:** March-Aug. **To obtain tee times:** Call 5 days in advance for weekdays. Call on Thursday at 7:30 a.m. for upcoming weekend.
Miscellaneous: Reduced fees (weekdays, twilight, seniors, juniors), metal spikes, range (grass), club rentals, credit cards (MC, V).
Reader Comments: Very tough with wind ... Good range with good targets and balls ... Great fast greens, Very friendly staff, fee too high ... Great greens–ego booster ... Rocks in rough ... Open, short, average golfer can play.

★★★ BRACKENRIDGE PARK MUNICIPAL GOLF COURSE
PU-2315 Ave. B, San Antonio, 78215, Bexar County, (210)226-5612, 2 miles N of San Antonio.
Holes: 18. **Yards:** 6,185/5,216. **Par:** 72/72. **Course Rating:** 70.1/69.2. **Slope:** 122/112. **Green Fee:** $11/$16. **Cart Fee:** $18/cart. **Walking Policy:** Unrestricted walking. **Walkability:** 1. **Opened:** 1916. **Architect:** Albert Warren Tillinghast. **Season:** Year-round. **High:** March-Nov. **To obtain tee times:** Call golf shop. **Miscellaneous:** Reduced fees (weekdays, low season, twilight, seniors, juniors), discount packages, metal spikes, club rentals, credit cards (MC, V), beginner friendly.
Reader Comments: Very affordable and fun course ... Old–but good! ... Short wide fairways make this course fun for all ... Overplayed but what a history ... Wonderful setting– short parallel fairways ... Best tacos in town at golf course ... Beautiful layout, running creek through golf course. Greens good shape. Lots of oak trees.

★★½ BRIARWOOD GOLF CLUB
SP-4511 Briarwood Dr., Tyler, 75709, Smith County, (903)593-7741. **E-mail:** briarwoodgolf@juno.com.
Holes: 18. **Yards:** 6,487/4,735. **Par:** 71/71. **Course Rating:** 70.6/66.1. **Slope:** 118/111. **Green Fee:** $15/$31. **Cart Fee:** $11/person. **Walking Policy:** Unrestricted walking. **Walkability:** 4. **Opened:** 1955. **Season:** Year-round. **High:** May-Oct. **To obtain tee times:** Call golf shop.
Miscellaneous: Reduced fees (weekdays, twilight, juniors), metal spikes, range (grass), club rentals, credit cards (MC, V), beginner friendly (beginner clinics, rules and etiquette seminars).
Reader Comments: Fun to play, a must if in Tyler ... Good course from back tees, others just average ... Interesting par 3s.

★★★½ BRIDLEWOOD GOLF CLUB
PU-4000 West Windsor, Flower Mound, 75028, Denton County, (972)355-4800, 20 miles NW of Dallas. **Web:** www.bridlewoodgolf.com.
Holes: 18. **Yards:** 7,036/5,278. **Par:** 72/72. **Course Rating:** 73.6/70.7. **Slope:** 130/120. **Green Fee:** $60/$79. **Cart Fee:** Included in Green Fee. **Walking Policy:** Unrestricted walking. **Walkability:** 3. **Opened:** 1997. **Architect:** D.A. Weibring/Maury Miller. **Season:** Year-round. **High:** March-Oct. **To obtain tee times:** Call up to 6 days in advance. **Miscellaneous:** Reduced fees (weekdays, low season, twilight, seniors, juniors), range (grass), club rentals, credit cards (MC, V, AE, D), beginner friendly.
Reader Comments: Well designed & tough ... Great layout, great management ... Beautiful, tough course ... Needs to grow two more years .... Fun course until the lightning storm ... Open, not much trouble unless the west Texas wind starts to howl ... A little pricey. Superfast greens.

★★ BROCK PARK GOLF COURSE
PM-8201 John Ralston Rd., Houston, 77044, Harris County, (281)458-1350.
Holes: 18. **Yards:** 6,487/5,650. **Par:** 72/74. **Course Rating:** 70.7/N/A. **Slope:** 114/N/A. **Green Fee:** $4/$12. **Cart Fee:** $17/cart. **Walking Policy:** Unrestricted walking. **Walkability:** 5. **Opened:** 1952. **Architect:** A.C. Ray. **Season:** Year-round. **To obtain tee times:** Call on Wednesday starting at 6:35 for upcoming weekend. First come, first served weekdays. **Miscellaneous:** Reduced fees (weekdays, twilight), metal spikes, range (grass), club rentals.

★★ BROWNSVILLE COUNTRY CLUB
PM-1800 W. San Marcelo, Brownsville, 78521, Cameron County, (956)541-2582.
Holes: 18. **Yards:** 6,066/4,846. **Par:** 70/70. **Course Rating:** 69.5/65.5. **Slope:** 107/113. **Green Fee:** $5/$9. **Cart Fee:** $8/person. **Walking Policy:** Unrestricted walking. **Walkability:** 1. **Opened:** 1972. **Architect:** Don Sechrest. **Season:** Year-round. **High:** Dec.-April. **To obtain tee times:** Call golf shop. **Miscellaneous:** Reduced fees (twilight), metal spikes, club rentals.

★½ BRYAN GOLF COURSE
PU-206 W. Villa Maria, Bryan, 77801, Brazos County, (409)823-0126, 84 miles NW of Houston.
Holes: 18. **Yards:** 6,243/5,857. **Par:** 70/70. **Course Rating:** 69.6/67.1. **Slope:** 110/106. **Green Fee:** $9/$16. **Cart Fee:** $8/person. **Walking Policy:** Unrestricted walking. **Walkability:** 2. **Opened:** 1925. **Architect:** Fred Marburry. **Season:** Year-round. **High:** April-Aug. **To obtain tee times:** Call golf shop. **Miscellaneous:** Reduced fees (weekdays, low season, twilight, seniors, juniors), metal spikes, club rentals, credit cards (MC, V, AE, D).

TEXAS

★★★★ BUFFALO CREEK GOLF CLUB
PU-624 Country Club Dr., Rockwall, 75087, Rockwall County, (972)771-4003, 15 miles E of Dallas.
Holes: 18. **Yards:** 7,012/5,209. **Par:** 71/71. **Course Rating:** 73.8/67.0. **Slope:** 135/113. **Green Fee:** $40/$75. **Cart Fee:** Included in Green Fee. **Walking Policy:** Unrestricted walking. **Walkability:** 3. **Opened:** 1992. **Architect:** Weiskopf/Morrish. **Season:** Year-round. **High:** April-Oct. **To obtain tee times:** Call 5 days in advance. **Miscellaneous:** Reduced fees (weekdays, low season, twilight, seniors, juniors), discount packages, range (grass), club rentals, credit cards (MC, V, AE).
Reader Comments: Excellent variety, good shape ... Helpful staff ...Try the tips if you dare ... Great par 5s ... Carts have pin positioning displays–exact yardages ... Super par-5 16th. ... Tough in the wind ... Greens in great condition. Smooth, fast and generally consistent from green to green ... Playable for any handicap.

★★½ CANYON LAKE GOLF CLUB
SP-405 Watts Lane, Canyon Lake, 78133, Comal County, (830)899-3372, 25 miles N of San Antonio.
Holes: 18. **Yards:** 6,528/4,726. **Par:** 72/72. **Course Rating:** 70.1/67.9. **Slope:** 126/114. **Green Fee:** $20/$30. **Cart Fee:** Included in Green Fee. **Walking Policy:** Unrestricted walking. **Walkability:** 4. **Opened:** 1980. **Season:** Year-round. **High:** Nov.-May. **To obtain tee times:** Call up to 7 days in advance. **Miscellaneous:** Reduced fees (weekdays, resort guests, twilight, seniors, juniors), range (grass), club rentals, credit cards (MC, V, AE, D).
Reader Comments: A pleasant golf experience ... Beautiful scenery, deer everywhere ... Short, but interesting.

★★★★ CANYON SPRINGS GOLF CLUB *Service*
PU-24400 Canyon Golf Rd., San Antonio, 78258, Bexar County, (210)497-1770, (888)800-1511, 3 miles N of San Antonio. **E-mail:** tolivarri@canyonsprings.com. **Web:** www.canyonsprings.com.
Holes: 18. **Yards:** 7,077/5,234. **Par:** 72/72. **Course Rating:** 72.8/70.0. **Slope:** 130/115. **Green Fee:** $60/$85. **Cart Fee:** Included in Green Fee. **Walking Policy:** Unrestricted walking. **Walkability:** 4. **Opened:** 1998. **Architect:** Tom Walker. **Season:** Year-round. **High:** March-June/Sept.-Nov. **To obtain tee times:** Call golf shop up to 30 days in advance. **Miscellaneous:** Reduced fees (weekdays, low season, twilight, seniors, juniors), discount packages, range (grass), club rentals, credit cards (MC, V, AE, D), beginner friendly.
Reader Comments: Great new course. Great layout, not cheap, but a must play ... Hilly, well-conditioned course ... Very scenic, especially the waterfalls ... Not walkable. Huge distances between some tees and greens ... Great service, great course ... Challenge from back tees ... Bring your 'A+++' game, great experience.

★★★½ CAPE ROYALE GOLF COURSE
SP-Lake Livingstone, Coldspring, 77331, San Jacinto County, (409)653-2388, (800)707-7022, 40 miles NE of Conroe. **E-mail:** phendrix@lcc.net.
Holes: 18. **Yards:** 6,088/4,941. **Par:** 70/70. **Course Rating:** 66.1/64.7. **Slope:** 113/103. **Green Fee:** $11/$23. **Cart Fee:** $10/person. **Walking Policy:** Walking at certain times. **Walkability:** 5. **Opened:** 1972. **Architect:** Bruce Littell. **Season:** Year-round. **High:** March-July. **Miscellaneous:** Reduced fees (weekdays, twilight, juniors), metal spikes, range (grass), credit cards (MC, V, AE, D).
Reader Comments: Sloping greens and fairways make it picturesque ... Wonderful views of lake ... Beautiful scenic course in deep woods ... Great place for a bunch of vacations ... Up, down, tricky, tight, local knowledge helpful.

★½ CASA BLANCA GOLF COURSE
PU-3900 Casa Blanca, Laredo, 78041, Webb County, (956)791-7262.
Holes: 18. **Yards:** 6,390/5,631. **Par:** 72/72. **Course Rating:** 71.0/68.9. **Slope:** 115/115. **Green Fee:** $8/$10. **Cart Fee:** $14/cart. **Walking Policy:** Unrestricted walking. **Walkability:** N/A. **Opened:** 1922. **Architect:** Carter Morrish/Roy Becthol. **Season:** Year-round. **High:** Feb.-Oct. **To obtain tee times:** Call on Wednesday for upcoming weekend. **Miscellaneous:** Reduced fees (weekdays, seniors, juniors), discount packages, metal spikes, range (grass), club rentals, credit cards (MC, V, AE, D).

★★★★ CEDAR CREEK GOLF COURSE
PM-8250 Vista Colina, San Antonio, 78255, Bexar County, (210)695-5050.
Holes: 18. **Yards:** 7,103/5,535. **Par:** 72/72. **Course Rating:** 73.4/70.8. **Slope:** 132/113. **Green Fee:** $30/$44. **Cart Fee:** Included in Green Fee. **Walking Policy:** Unrestricted walking. **Walkability:** 4. **Opened:** 1989. **Architect:** Finger/Dye/Spann. **Season:** Year-round. **High:** Year-round. **To obtain tee times:** Call golf shop. **Miscellaneous:** Reduced fees (weekdays, low season, twilight, seniors, juniors), metal spikes, range (grass/mats), club rentals, credit cards (MC, V, AE, D).
Reader Comments: Fun to play–great value ... Holes too similar... Good layout, but very hilly ... Hilly, beautiful greens, good shape, challenging. Year round play, come play! ... I love this course.

Poor man's La Cantera ... Fun layout in rolling hills ... Beautiful course. Slow play due to cart limitations & elevation challenges.

★★★ CEDAR CREST GOLF COURSE
PU-1800 Southerland, Dallas, 75223, Dallas County, (214)670-7615.
Holes: 18. **Yards:** 6,550/5,594. **Par:** 71/75. **Course Rating:** 71.0/76.0. **Slope:** 121/116. **Green Fee:** $11/$14. **Cart Fee:** $18/cart. **Walking Policy:** Unrestricted walking. **Walkability:** N/A. **Opened:** 1923. **Architect:** A.W. Tillinghast. **Season:** Year-round. **High:** April-Sept. **To obtain tee times:** Call two days in advance. **Miscellaneous:** Reduced fees (twilight, seniors, juniors), metal spikes, range (grass), caddies, club rentals, credit cards (MC, V, AE, D).
Reader Comments: Very pleasant surprise. Long Par 3s. Great round ... Solid city course–uphill 18 ... Good condition ... Great design, maintenance & upkeep could be improved ... The course was in great shape for a muny and very challenging, especially No. 1, a 635-yard par 5 downhill where I chipped in for birdie!

★★ THE CEDARS ON BERGSTROM
PU-10326 Golf Course Rd., Austin, 78719, Travis County, (512)385-4653, 10 miles SE of Austin.
E-mail: tgann26601@aol.com.
Holes: 18. **Yards:** 6,576/5,300. **Par:** 71/72. **Course Rating:** 69.5/70.5. **Slope:** 115/116. **Green Fee:** $10/$15. **Cart Fee:** $10/person. **Walking Policy:** Unrestricted walking. **Walkability:** 3.
Opened: 1954. **Architect:** Curly Tice/George Williams. **Season:** Year-round. **High:** May-Oct. **To obtain tee times:** Call up to 7 days in advance. **Miscellaneous:** Reduced fees (weekdays, twilight, seniors, juniors), metal spikes, range (grass), club rentals, credit cards (MC, V), beginner friendly (junior practice area).

★★½ CHAMBERS COUNTY GOLF COURSE
PU-1 Pinchback Dr., Anahuac, 77514, Chambers County, (409)267-8235, 43 miles W of Houston.
Holes: 18. **Yards:** 6,909/5,014. **Par:** 72/73. **Course Rating:** 71.5/67.5. **Slope:** 116/106. **Green Fee:** $10/$15. **Cart Fee:** $16/person. **Walking Policy:** Unrestricted walking. **Walkability:** 1.
Opened: 1975. **Architect:** Leon Howard/R.T. Pinch. **Season:** Year-round. **High:** June-Aug. **To obtain tee times:** Call golf shop Thursday 7 a.m. **Miscellaneous:** Reduced fees (weekdays, twilight), metal spikes, range (grass/mats), club rentals, credit cards (MC, V, AE, D).
Reader Comments: Blind water hazards on a couple of par 4's are costly ... Lots of trees, tight fairways ... Laid-back atmosphere.

★★★½ CHASE OAKS GOLF CLUB
PU-7201 Chase Oaks Blvd., Plano, 75025, Collin County, (972)517-7777, 14 miles N of Dallas.
E-mail: mailbox@chaseoaks.com. **Web:** www.chaseoaks.com.
Holes: 18. **Yards:** 6,762/5,105. **Par:** 72/72. **Course Rating:** 74.4/70.0. **Slope:** 139/128. **Green Fee:** $37/$57. **Cart Fee:** $12/person. **Walking Policy:** Walking at certain times. **Walkability:** 4.
Opened: 1986. **Architect:** Von Hagge/Devlin. **Season:** Year-round. **High:** April-Nov. **To obtain tee times:** Call 3 days in advance at 8 a.m. **Miscellaneous:** Reduced fees (weekdays, low season, twilight, seniors, juniors), range (grass/mats), club rentals, credit cards (MC, V, AE, D, Diners Club).
Reader Comments: Excellent course, beautiful, playable, and challenging ... Excellent food ... Unforgiving, high slope, blind shots ... Tough layout if the wind blows ... Inspired layout, I wish it wasn't so expensive.... Truly great finish ... Tough course ... Good greens ... Better hit it straight or bring extra balls.

★★★ CHESTER W. DITTO GOLF CLUB
PM-801 Brown Blvd., Arlington, 76011, Tarrant County, (817)275-5941, 20 miles SW of Dallas.
Holes: 18. **Yards:** 6,727/5,555. **Par:** 72/72. **Course Rating:** 70.8/71.2. **Slope:** 117/116. **Green Fee:** $10/$12. **Cart Fee:** $8/person. **Walking Policy:** Unrestricted walking. **Walkability:** N/A. **Opened:** 1982. **Architect:** Killian/Nugent. **Season:** Year-round. **High:** April-Sept. **To obtain tee times:** Call Tuesday at 6 a.m. for Wednesday through the next Tuesday. **Miscellaneous:** Reduced fees (weekdays, twilight, seniors, juniors), metal spikes, range (grass), club rentals, credit cards (MC, V, D).
Reader Comments: Lots of hills–don't walk ... Don't leave it in the bag, good course to try that new swing ... Plays long–good value ... Front 9 was bland. Great greens for a public course ... Narrow and hilly and always crowded ... Good muny–nice layout of holes.

★★★ CIELO VISTA GOLF COURSE
PU-1510 Hawkins, El Paso, 79925, El Paso County, (915)591-4927.
Holes: 18. **Yards:** 6,411/5,421. **Par:** 71/71. **Course Rating:** 69.4/69.4. **Slope:** 122/113. **Green Fee:** $14/$18. **Cart Fee:** $16/cart. **Walking Policy:** Unrestricted walking. **Walkability:** 1.
Opened: 1977. **Architect:** Marvin Ferguson. **Season:** Year-round. **High:** April-Oct. **To obtain tee times:** Call on Tuesday at 7 a.m. for upcoming weekend. **Miscellaneous:** Reduced fees (weekdays, twilight), range (grass), club rentals, credit cards (MC, V).
Reader Comments: Price-to-stroke ratio is good ... Most beautiful hole in Texas: No.15. Unusual combination of links-type front 9 with hilly and pine treelined back 9.

★★★½ CIRCLE C GOLF CLUB
PU-7401 Hwy. 45, Austin, 78739, Travis County, (512)288-4297.
Holes: 18. **Yards:** 6,859/5,236. **Par:** 72/72. **Course Rating:** 72.7/69.9. **Slope:** 122/120. **Green Fee:** $36/$51. **Cart Fee:** $14/cart. **Walking Policy:** Walking at certain times. **Walkability:** 4. **Opened:** 1992. **Architect:** Jay Morrish. **Season:** Year-round. **High:** Spring/Fall. **To obtain tee times:** Call 10 days in advance, or further in advance for groups of 12 or more. **Miscellaneous:** Reduced fees (weekdays, low season, twilight, juniors), discount packages, range (grass), club rentals, credit cards (MC, V, AE).
Reader Comments: Great layout ... Tough from the tips ... Need local knowledge ... Beautiful overseeded greens and fairways ... Excellent service, well run ... Good course for average golfer ... Challenging hill country layout.

★★½ CLEAR LAKE GOLF CLUB
PU-1202 Reseda Dr., Houston, 77062, Harris County, (281)488-0250, 15 miles S of Downtown Houston. **Web:** www.clearlakegolf.com.
Holes: 18. **Yards:** 6,757/5,924. **Par:** 72/72. **Course Rating:** 71.7/71.1. **Slope:** 113/111. **Green Fee:** $19/$37. **Cart Fee:** Included in Green Fee. **Walking Policy:** Walking at certain times. **Walkability:** 3. **Opened:** 1964. **Architect:** Jay Riviere. **Season:** Year-round. **High:** April-June-Oct. **To obtain tee times:** Call up to 7 days in advance. **Miscellaneous:** Reduced fees (low season, twilight, seniors, juniors), range (grass), club rentals, credit cards (MC, V, AE, D).
Reader Comments: Great value ... Nice course, well maintained ... Holes too far from each other ... Good length with small greens.

★★ CLEBURNE MUNY GOLF COURSE
Country Club Rd., Cleburne, 76031, Johnson County, (817)641-4501.
Special Notes: Call club for further information.

★★★★ THE CLIFFS RESORT *Pace*
R-Star Rte. Box 19, Graford, 76449, Palo Pinto County, (940)779-4040, (888)843-2543, 75 miles NW of Ft. Worth.
Holes: 18. **Yards:** 6,808/4,876. **Par:** 71/71. **Course Rating:** 73.9/68.4. **Slope:** 143/124. **Green Fee:** $36/$75. **Cart Fee:** Included in Green Fee. **Walking Policy:** Mandatory cart. **Walkability:** 5. **Opened:** 1988. **Architect:** Bruce Devlin/Robert von Hagge. **Season:** Year-round. **High:** April-Sept. **To obtain tee times:** Call 7 days in advance. **Miscellaneous:** Reduced fees (weekdays, low season, twilight, seniors, juniors), discount packages, range (grass), club rentals, lodging, credit cards (MC, V, AE, D).
Reader Comments: High over the lake, very hard in the wind ... Extreme challenge 'Straight hitters'... Beautiful, scenic, hard-but so pretty, who cares ... Very unique, challenging course ... Nothing else like it, breathtaking lake views ... Challenging, well kept, good service.

★★½ THE CLUB AT RUNAWAY BAY
SP-400 Half Moon Way, Runaway Bay, 76426, Wise County, (940)575-2228, 45 miles NW of Fort Worth.
Holes: 18. **Yards:** 7,032/5,446. **Par:** 72/72. **Course Rating:** 73.1/68.2. **Slope:** 124/108. **Green Fee:** $30/$50. **Cart Fee:** $10/person. **Walking Policy:** Walking at certain times. **Walkability:** 3. **Opened:** 1968. **Architect:** Leon Howard. **Season:** Year-round. **High:** April-June/Oct. **To obtain tee times:** Call up to seven days in advance. **Miscellaneous:** Reduced fees (low season, resort guests, twilight, juniors), discount packages, range (grass/mats), club rentals, lodging (4 rooms), credit cards (MC, V, AE, D).
Reader Comments: Outstanding clubhouse and service ... Greens & staff are great ... Excellent greens, fairways fair.

★★★ COLUMBIA LAKES
R-188 Freeman Blvd., West Columbia, 77486, Brazoria County, (409)345-5455, (800)231-1030, 50 miles SE of Houston.
Holes: 18. **Yards:** 6,967/5,280. **Par:** 72/72. **Course Rating:** 75.7/71.7. **Slope:** 131/122. **Green Fee:** $50/$65. **Cart Fee:** Included in Green Fee. **Walking Policy:** Unrestricted walking. **Walkability:** 2. **Opened:** 1972. **Architect:** Jack Miller/Tom Fazio. **Season:** Year-round. **High:** April-June/Sept.-Oct. **To obtain tee times:** Call golf shop. **Miscellaneous:** Reduced fees (weekdays, low season, resort guests), discount packages, metal spikes, range (grass/mats), club rentals, lodging (160 rooms), credit cards (MC, V, AE, D, Diners Club).
Reader Comments: The best in the Houston Area ... Great weekend getaway ... Good conference course ... Course a challenge; nice clubhouse ... Overall good value... Difficult. Fair facilities.

COMANCHE TRAIL GOLF CLUB
PM-4200 S. Grand, Amarillo, 79103, Randall County, (806)378-4281.
ARROWHEAD COURSE
Holes: 18. **Yards:** 6,940/5,279. **Par:** 72/72. **Course Rating:** 71.9/70.2. **Slope:** 121/118. **Green Fee:** $13/$17. **Cart Fee:** $20/cart. **Walking Policy:** Unrestricted walking. **Walkability:** 1. **Opened:** 1999. **Architect:** Bob Cupp. **Season:** Year-round. **High:** March-Sept. **To obtain tee**

times: Call on Thursday mornings at 7:00 a.m. for weekends. Call 1 day in advance for week-days. **Miscellaneous:** Reduced fees (twilight, seniors, juniors), range (grass), club rentals, credit cards (MC, V, D).

★★½ **TOMAHAWK COURSE**
Holes: 18. **Yards:** 7,180/5,524. **Par:** 72/72. **Course Rating:** 72.9/70.0. **Slope:** 117/108. **Green Fee:** $9/$13. **Cart Fee:** $20/cart. **Walking Policy:** Unrestricted walking. **Walkability:** 1. **Opened:** 1990. **Architect:** Charles Howard. **Season:** Year-round. **High:** March-Sept. **To obtain tee times:** Call on Thursday morning at 7:00 a.m. for upcoming weekend. Call 1 day in advance for week-days. **Miscellaneous:** Reduced fees (twilight, seniors, juniors), range (grass), club rentals, credit cards (MC, V, D).
Reader Comments: Wind blows constantly ... Excellent staff (friendly) ... Good layout ... Links-type course with landing zones for each shot. Match the tee box with your capability and shoot straight.

COMANCHE TRAIL GOLF COURSE
PM-800 Comanche Park Rd., Big Spring, 79720, Howard County, (915)264-2366, 37 miles E of Midland.
Holes: 18. **Yards:** 6,327/5,098. **Par:** 71/72. **Course Rating:** 68.9/66.1. **Slope:** 113/98. **Green Fee:** $9/$14. **Cart Fee:** $18/cart. **Walking Policy:** Unrestricted walking. **Walkability:** 3. **Opened:** 1934. **Architect:** William Cantrell. **Season:** Year-round. **High:** March-Nov. **To obtain tee times:** Call on Wednesday for upcoming weekend. Walk-ins welcome weekdays. **Miscellaneous:** Reduced fees (seniors, juniors), metal spikes, credit cards (MC, V, AE, D).

★★½ **CONNALLY GOLF COURSE**
PU-7900 Concord Rd., Waco, 76705, McLennan County, (254)799-6561, 5 miles NE of Waco.
Holes: 18. **Yards:** 6,975/5,950. **Par:** 72/73. **Course Rating:** 72.5/73.8. **Slope:** 116/120. **Green Fee:** $9/$12. **Cart Fee:** $10/person. **Walking Policy:** Unrestricted walking. **Walkability:** N/A. **Opened:** 1959. **Architect:** Ralph Plummer. **Season:** Year-round. **High:** April-Sept. **To obtain tee times:** Call 7 days in advance for weekends and holidays only. **Miscellaneous:** Reduced fees (twilight, seniors, juniors), metal spikes, range (grass/mats), club rentals, credit cards (MC, V).
Reader Comments: Long par 4s. Short par 5s. Great par 3s ... Back 9 has more character ... Greens are top notch.

★★★★ **COTTONWOOD CREEK GOLF COURSE**
PU-5200 Bagby Dr., Waco, 76711, McLennan County, (254)752-2474. **E-mail:** maxr@ci.waco.tx.us. **Web:** www.waco-texas.com.
Holes: 18. **Yards:** 7,140/5,716. **Par:** 72/72. **Course Rating:** 73.5/71.9. **Slope:** 129/N/A. **Green Fee:** $12/$15. **Cart Fee:** $11/person. **Walking Policy:** Unrestricted walking. **Walkability:** 3. **Opened:** 1985. **Architect:** Joe Finger. **Season:** Year-round. **High:** March-Oct. **To obtain tee times:** Call five days in advance. **Miscellaneous:** Reduced fees (weekdays, seniors, juniors), range (grass), club rentals, credit cards (MC, V), beginner friendly (city of waco junior golf program).
Reader Comments: Long, good shape, big improvement with new management ... Wide open ... Some blind shots ... Great layout, good test ... Weird routing ... Outstanding tough course ... Windy, awesome greens–fast.

★★★ **COUNTRY VIEW GOLF CLUB**
PU-240 W. Beltline Rd., Lancaster, 75146, Dallas County, (972)227-0995, 13 miles S of Dallas.
Holes: 18. **Yards:** 6,609/5,048. **Par:** 71/71. **Course Rating:** 71.0/68.2. **Slope:** 120/114. **Green Fee:** $12/$17. **Cart Fee:** $20/cart. **Walking Policy:** Unrestricted walking. **Walkability:** N/A. **Opened:** 1989. **Architect:** Ron Garl. **Season:** Year-round. **High:** April-Oct. **To obtain tee times:** Call three days prior to play. **Miscellaneous:** Reduced fees (low season, twilight, seniors, juniors), metal spikes, range (grass), club rentals, credit cards (MC, V, D).
Reader Comments: Great staff, good course ... Fairways a little sparse, greens good, adequate conditions ... Improved quality; friendly starter; oh, those elevated greens ... 17th one of toughest holes in area.

★★★½ **CREEKVIEW GOLF CLUB**
PU-1602 E. Hwy. 175, Crandall, 75114, Kaufman County, (972)427-3811, 20 miles SE of Dallas.
Holes: 18. **Yards:** 7,238/5,459. **Par:** 72/72. **Course Rating:** 74.1/71.2. **Slope:** 119/115. **Green Fee:** $31/$43. **Cart Fee:** Included in Green Fee. **Walking Policy:** Mandatory cart. **Walkability:** 2. **Opened:** 1995. **Architect:** Dick Phelps. **Season:** Year-round. **High:** Spring/Fall. **To obtain tee times:** Call up to 7 days in advance for weekdays. Call on Wednesday for upcoming weekend. **Miscellaneous:** Reduced fees (twilight, seniors, juniors), discount packages, range (grass/mats), club rentals, credit cards (MC, V, AE, D), beginner friendly.
Reader Comments: Long flat course susceptible to high winds ... Not bad for the money ... Excellent condition, bent grass greens–fast ... Great condition–open & windy.

★ **CROSS CREEK GOLF CLUB**
800 Bellwood Golf Rd., Tyler, 75709, Smith County, (903)597-4871.
Special Notes: Call club for further information.

TEXAS

★★★½ CROSS TIMBERS GOLF COURSE
PU-1181 S. Stewart, Azle, 76020, Polker County, (817)444-4940, 14 miles NW of Fort Worth.
Holes: 18. **Yards:** 6,734/5,051. **Par:** 72/72. **Course Rating:** 71.5/68.2. **Slope:** 128/113. **Green Fee:** $18/$22. **Cart Fee:** $10/person. **Walking Policy:** Unrestricted walking. **Walkability:** 5.
Opened: 1995. **Architect:** Jeff Brauer. **Season:** Year-round. **High:** March-Oct. **To obtain tee times:** Call 3 days prior to play. **Miscellaneous:** Reduced fees (weekdays, twilight, seniors, juniors), metal spikes, range (grass), club rentals, credit cards (MC, V, AE).
Reader Comments: Good challenge ... Needs more variation on back 9 ... Good fair test. Greens hold great ... Fun course–changes in elevation ... Off the beaten track but worth the drive .... Very hilly and wind is a problem ... Cross Timbers–best club sandwiches ever ... Tough course to walk, beware the Cross Timbers bounce.

★★½ CRYSTAL FALLS GOLF COURSE
PU-3400 Crystal Falls Pkwy., Leander, 78641, Travis County, (512)259-5855, 14 miles N of Austin.
Holes: 18. **Yards:** 6,654/5,194. **Par:** 72/72. **Course Rating:** 72.3/70.0. **Slope:** 126/123. **Green Fee:** $18/$27. **Cart Fee:** $10/person. **Walking Policy:** Unrestricted walking. **Walkability:** 5.
Opened: 1990. **Architect:** Charles Howard/Jack Miller. **Season:** Year-round. **High:** April-Oct. **To obtain tee times:** Call three days in advance. **Miscellaneous:** Reduced fees (weekdays, low season, twilight, seniors, juniors), discount packages, range (grass), club rentals, credit cards (MC, V).
Reader Comments: Stay on fairway, target golf ... Many blind shots ... Great little ole course in a small town ... Great setting; extremely challenging ... Tight fairways, not a level lie on the course.

CYPRESSWOOD GOLF CLUB
PU-21602 Cypresswood Dr., Spring, 77373, Harris County, (281)821-6300, 16 miles N of Houston. **Web:** www.cypresswood.com.
★★★½ CREEK COURSE
Holes: 18. **Yards:** 6,937/5,549. **Par:** 72/72. **Course Rating:** 72.0/69.1. **Slope:** 124/113. **Green Fee:** $31/$38. **Cart Fee:** $24/person. **Walking Policy:** Unrestricted walking. **Walkability:** 3.
Opened: 1988. **Architect:** Rick Forester. **Season:** Year-round. **High:** March-Oct. **To obtain tee times:** Call up to 3 days in advance. **Miscellaneous:** Reduced fees (weekdays, twilight, seniors, juniors), metal spikes, range (grass/mats), club rentals, credit cards (MC, V, AE).
Reader Comments: Good public layout, challenging enough from tips ... Great place to play ... Courses were being reconditioned after flooding ... Best views and setting of all Houston courses. Very quiet & peaceful.
★★★½ CYPRESS COURSE
Holes: 18. **Yards:** 6,906/5,599. **Par:** 72/72. **Course Rating:** 71.8/67.6. **Slope:** 123/111. **Green Fee:** $31/$38. **Cart Fee:** $24/person. **Walking Policy:** Unrestricted walking. **Walkability:** 1.
Opened: 1987. **Architect:** Rick Forester. **Season:** Year-round. **High:** March-Oct. **To obtain tee times:** Call up to 3 days in advance. **Miscellaneous:** Reduced fees (weekdays, twilight, seniors, juniors), metal spikes, range (grass), club rentals, credit cards (MC, V, AE).
Reader Comments: Great place to play ... Courses were being reconditioned after flooding ... Tough course. Fun to play. 3-4 really tough holes ... Great condition.
★★★★ TRADITION COURSE
Holes: 18. **Yards:** 7,220/5,255. **Par:** 72/72. **Course Rating:** 74.4/68.9. **Slope:** 134/122. **Green Fee:** $65/$75. **Cart Fee:** Included in Green Fee. **Walking Policy:** Unrestricted walking. **Walkability:** 4. **Opened:** 1998. **Architect:** Keith Foster. **Season:** Year-round. **High:** March-Oct. **To obtain tee times:** Call up to 3 days in advance. **Miscellaneous:** Reduced fees (twilight), metal spikes, range (grass), club rentals, credit cards (MC, V, AE).
Reader Comments: Terrific layout–will use all your clubs ... Nice length, good layout ... One of best public courses in Houston. Hard & long ... Excellent and fun ... Beautiful atmosphere, especially in the morning.

★★★½ DEL LAGO GOLF RESORT
R-600 La Costa Blvd., Montgomery, 77356-5349, Montgomery County, (409)582-6100, (800)335-2446, 50 miles N of Houston.
Holes: 18. **Yards:** 7,007/5,854. **Par:** 72/72. **Course Rating:** 72.6/71.7. **Slope:** 131/122. **Green Fee:** $50/$65. **Cart Fee:** Included in Green Fee. **Walking Policy:** Walking at certain times. **Walkability:** 2. **Opened:** 1985. **Architect:** Dave Marr/Jay Riviere. **Season:** Year-round. **High:** May-Oct. **To obtain tee times:** Call. **Miscellaneous:** Reduced fees (weekdays, resort guests, twilight, seniors, juniors), discount packages, metal spikes, range (grass/mats), club rentals, lodging, credit cards (MC, V, AE, D).
Reader Comments: Friendly atmosphere ... Generally good experience ... Hard hill country, beautiful views ... Very scenic, good challenge ... Good resort getaway.

★★★½ DELAWARE SPRINGS GOLF COURSE
PM-Hwy. 281 S., Burnet, 78611, Burnet County, (512)756-8951, 50 miles NW of Austin.
Holes: 18. **Yards:** 6,819/5,770. **Par:** 72/71. **Course Rating:** 72.0/66.5. **Slope:** 121/107. **Green Fee:** $16/$26. **Cart Fee:** $9/person. **Walking Policy:** Walking at certain times. **Walkability:** 3.
Opened: 1992. **Architect:** Dave Axland/Don Proctor. **Season:** Year-round. **High:** March-Sept. **To**

obtain tee times: Call up to 14 days in advance. **Miscellaneous:** Reduced fees (twilight, seniors, juniors), metal spikes, range (grass/mats), club rentals, credit cards (MC, V, AE, D).
Reader Comments: Unique–Great Staff! ... Good shape, played when very hot, nice people ... Great value ... Real gem... Watch out for rattlesnakes in summer ... Short course for women, fun to play ... Too long from greens to tees to walk ... Tough rough. Busy place....Pricey for a muny, blind fairways, keep in play.

★★½ DEVINE GOLF COURSE
PU-116 Malone Dr., Devine, 78016, Medina County, (830)665-9943, 30 miles S of San Antonio.
Holes: 18. **Yards:** 6,600/5,100. **Par:** 72/72. **Course Rating:** 70.4/67.5. **Slope:** 121/105. **Green Fee:** $12/$18. **Cart Fee:** $16/cart. **Walking Policy:** Unrestricted walking. **Walkability:** 3.
Opened: 1968. **Architect:** Built by members, Steve Mrak. **Season:** Year-round. **High:** May-July.
To obtain tee times: Call one week in advance. **Miscellaneous:** Reduced fees (twilight, seniors, juniors), credit cards (MC, V, AE, D).
Reader Comments: Two different 9s, fun course ... Some holes are laid out funny ... Like playing two different courses.

EAGLE'S BLUFF COUNTRY CLUB
SP-99 Eagle's Bluff Blvd., Bullard, 75757, Cherokee County, (903)825-2999, (877)972-GOLF, 90 miles E of Dallas.
Holes: 18. **Yards:** 6,421/4,967. **Par:** 71/71. **Course Rating:** 71.1/69.0. **Slope:** 133/126. **Green Fee:** $33/$40. **Cart Fee:** $12/person. **Walking Policy:** Unrestricted walking. **Walkability:** 3.
Opened: 1999. **Architect:** Carlton Gipson. **Season:** Year-round. **High:** Year-round. **To obtain tee times:** Call 5 days in advance. **Miscellaneous:** Reduced fees (twilight, seniors), range (grass), club rentals, credit cards (MC, V, AE, D), beginner friendly.
Special Notes: Formerly Eagle's Bluff Golf Club.

★★½ ECHO CREEK COUNTRY CLUB
SP-FM 317, Athens, 75778, Henderson County, (903)852-7094, 10 miles E of Tyler.
Holes: 18. **Yards:** 6,200/5,000. **Par:** 71/73. **Course Rating:** 69.2/69.2. **Slope:** 120/118. **Green Fee:** $12/$18. **Cart Fee:** $18/cart. **Walking Policy:** Unrestricted walking. **Walkability:** 3.
Opened: 1989. **Architect:** Rusty Lambert. **Season:** Year-round. **High:** March-Aug. **To obtain tee times:** Call golf shop. **Miscellaneous:** Reduced fees (resort guests, seniors), metal spikes, range (grass), club rentals.
Reader Comments: Good course way out in sticks ... Very good par 5s, water, elevated greens ... Nice challenge.

★½ ELM GROVE GOLF COURSE
PU-3202 Milwaukee, Lubbock, 79407, Lubbock County, 806-799-7801.
Holes: 18. **Yards:** 6,401/5,480. **Par:** 71/72. **Course Rating:** N/A. **Slope:** N/A. **Green Fee:** $8/$13. **Cart Fee:** $9/person. **Walking Policy:** Unrestricted walking. **Walkability:** 2. **Season:** Year-round.
To obtain tee times: Call up to 3 days in advance. **Miscellaneous:** Reduced fees (twilight, seniors, juniors), metal spikes, range (grass/mats), club rentals, credit cards (MC, V, AE, D).
Special Notes: Spikeless shoes preferred.

★★★★ EVERGREEN POINT GOLF CLUB
PU-1530 Evergreen Point Rd., Baytown, 77520, Harris County, (281)837-9000, 20 miles SE of Houston.
Holes: 18. **Yards:** 7,000/5,298. **Par:** 72/72. **Course Rating:** 73.0/72.2. **Slope:** 129/130. **Green Fee:** $22/$30. **Cart Fee:** $18/cart. **Walking Policy:** Unrestricted walking. **Walkability:** 3.
Opened: 1996. **Architect:** Jay Riviere/Dave Marr. **Season:** Year-round. **High:** June-Nov. **To obtain tee times:** Call up to 7 days in advance. **Miscellaneous:** Reduced fees (twilight, seniors, juniors), range (grass), club rentals, credit cards (MC, V, AE, D).
Reader Comments: Nice course. It gets better every year ... Great bargain, good layout ... Surprisingly good course, All holes are different ... Great layout, take mosquito spray ... Flat with subtle trouble ... Young and great potential ... Good change of elevation ... Beautiful landscaping, lots of mature trees.

★★★★ THE FALLS RESORT & COUNTRY CLUB *Pace*
SP-1001 N. Falls Dr., New Ulm, 78950, Colorado County, (409)992-3123, (800)992-3930, 60 miles W of Houston.
Holes: 18. **Yards:** 6,757/5,326. **Par:** 72/73. **Course Rating:** 72.3/70.0. **Slope:** 135/125. **Green Fee:** $47/$62. **Cart Fee:** Included in Green Fee. **Walking Policy:** Walking at certain times. **Walkability:** 3. **Opened:** 1985. **Architect:** Jay Riviere/Dave Marr. **Season:** Year-round. **High:** March-Aug. **To obtain tee times:** Call 4 days in advance. **Miscellaneous:** Reduced fees (weekdays, resort guests), metal spikes, range (grass/mats), club rentals, lodging (19 rooms), credit cards (MC, V, AE).
Reader Comments: Tough course ... A long drive from Houston but worth it ... Great golf. Tough from back tees for a 6 handicapper ... The best fairways in Texas ... Lots of pine trees ... One of

my favorites; twilight is the best time to play ... Great layout, not crowded ... Wild life galore–deer, birds, golfers!.

FIREWHEEL GOLF PARK
PM-600 W. Blackburn Rd., Garland, 75044, Dallas County, (972)205-2795, 10 miles N of Dallas.

★★★½ LAKES COURSE
Holes: 18. **Yards:** 6,625/5,215. **Par:** 71/71. **Course Rating:** 72.0/69.1. **Slope:** 126/110. **Green Fee:** $18/$26. **Cart Fee:** $20/cart. **Walking Policy:** Unrestricted walking. **Walkability:** 3. **Opened:** 1987. **Architect:** Dick Phelps. **Season:** Year-round. **High:** April-Sept. **To obtain tee times:** Call on Thursday at 8:00 a.m. for Friday through Thursday. **Miscellaneous:** Reduced fees (twilight, seniors), metal spikes, range (grass/mats), club rentals, credit cards (MC, V, AE).
Reader Comments: Excellent course, very tight ... Excellent public course, good pace ... Good course, lots of water ... Like playing on a snake with trees ... Nice greens, nice fairways, elevation changes ... Hidden but delightful challenge ... Tee shot a premium.

★★★½ OLD COURSE
Holes: 18. **Yards:** 7,054/5,692. **Par:** 72/72. **Course Rating:** 74.1/71.7. **Slope:** 129/117. **Green Fee:** $18/$26. **Cart Fee:** $20/person. **Walking Policy:** Unrestricted walking. **Walkability:** 2. **Opened:** 1983. **Architect:** Dick Phelps. **Season:** Year-round. **High:** April-Sept. **To obtain tee times:** Call on Thursday at 8:00 a.m. for Friday through Thursday. **Miscellaneous:** Reduced fees (twilight, seniors), metal spikes, range (grass/mats), club rentals, credit cards (MC, V, AE).
Reader Comments: Great value, tough layout ... Good course usually in great shape ... Well-seasoned course ... Another good Texas public course ... Challenging ... Fun and demanding ... Classic old-style course ... Still one of the best munies around.

★★★ FLYING L RANCH GOLF COURSE
R-P.O. Box 1959, Bandera, 78003, Bandera County, (830)796-8466, (800)646-5407, 40 miles NW of San Antonio. **Web:** www.flyingl.com.
Holes: 18. **Yards:** 6,646/5,442. **Par:** 72/72. **Course Rating:** 71.0/69.9. **Slope:** 123/109. **Green Fee:** $17/$20. **Cart Fee:** $10/person. **Walking Policy:** Unrestricted walking. **Walkability:** 2. **Opened:** 1975. **Season:** Year-round. **High:** April-Sept. **To obtain tee times:** Call 14 days in advance. **Miscellaneous:** Reduced fees (weekdays, resort guests, twilight, seniors, juniors), discount packages, metal spikes, range (grass), club rentals, lodging, credit cards (MC, V, AE, D).
Reader Comments: Use every club in bag.... Nice setting–fun course ... Scenic views and impressive design ... Take your family. Great dude ranch ... Fun little country track with nicest staff you could wish for ... Nice layout ... Very enjoyable golf ... Relaxed ... Back 9's greens are super.

★★★★ FOREST CREEK GOLF CLUB
PU-99 Twin Ridge Pkwy., Round Rock, 78664, Williamson County, (512)388-2874, 10 miles N of Austin. **Web:** www.forestcreek.com.
Holes: 18. **Yards:** 7,084/5,601. **Par:** 72/72. **Course Rating:** 72.8/71.9. **Slope:** 130/124. **Green Fee:** $43/$55. **Cart Fee:** Included in Green Fee. **Walking Policy:** Walking at certain times. **Walkability:** 4. **Opened:** 1989. **Architect:** Dick Phelps. **Season:** Year-round. **High:** March-Oct. **To obtain tee times:** Call 7 days in advance. **Miscellaneous:** Reduced fees (weekdays, low season, twilight, seniors, juniors), metal spikes, range (grass/mats), club rentals, credit cards (MC, V, AE, D), beginner friendly.
Reader Comments: On-cart GPS displays distances & hole features ... Narrow & challenging–long from tips ... A great test, but fair to all handicaps ... A challenging course! ... Course demands management of game ... You will use every club in your bag. Fun and creative round of golf ... Great variety of holes.

★★ FORT BROWN MEMORIAL GOLF COURSE
PM-300 River Levee Rd., Brownsville, 78520, Cameron County, (956)541-0394, (956)685-7202.
Holes: 18. **Yards:** 6,172/4,803. **Par:** 72/72. **Course Rating:** 67.0/67.0. **Slope:** 108/108. **Green Fee:** $7/$8. **Cart Fee:** $8/person. **Walking Policy:** Unrestricted walking. **Walkability:** 1. **Opened:** 1958. **Season:** Year-round. **High:** Jan.-March. **To obtain tee times:** Call up to 1 day in advance. **Miscellaneous:** Reduced fees (twilight, juniors), range (grass), club rentals, credit cards (MC, V, AE).
Special Notes: Was Fort Brown Municipal Golf Course

FOUR SEASONS RESORT & CLUB *Service*
4150 N. MacArthur Blvd., Irving, 75038, Dallas County, (972)717-2530, (800)332-3442, 10 miles NW of Dallas.

★★★★ COTTONWOOD VALLEY COURSE
SP-**Holes:** 18. **Yards:** 6,862/5,320. **Par:** 71/72. **Course Rating:** 73.4/70.6. **Slope:** 133/116. **Green Fee:** $135/$150. **Cart Fee:** Included in Green Fee. **Walking Policy:** Mandatory cart. **Walkability:** 3. **Opened:** 1983. **Architect:** Robert Trent Jones/Jay Morrish. **Season:** Year-round. **High:** Feb.-Oct. **To obtain tee times:** Open to resort guests one day a week when TPC course is closed. **Miscellaneous:** Reduced fees (low season, resort guests, twilight), discount packages, range (grass), club rentals, lodging, credit cards (MC, V, AE, Diners Club).
Reader Comments: Outstanding course condition ... Better than the TPC next door ... Equal to TPC–wind a bit more in play ... Beautiful course, well staffed, excellent condition ... Greens were

OK. Pace of play OK, restaurant very good ... Good course, but too expensive ... Both courses are different.

★★★★ TPC COURSE
R-Holes: 18. **Yards:** 6,899/5,340. **Par:** 70/70. **Course Rating:** 73.5/70.6. **Slope:** 135/116. **Green Fee:** $150/$170. **Cart Fee:** Included in Green Fee. **Walking Policy:** Mandatory cart. **Walkability:** 3. **Opened:** 1986. **Architect:** Jay Morrish/Byron Nelson/Ben Crenshaw. **Season:** Year-round. **High:** Feb.-Oct. **To obtain tee times:** Resort guests may call up to 45 days in advance. **Miscellaneous:** Reduced fees (low season, resort guests, twilight), discount packages, range (grass), club rentals, lodging, credit cards (MC, V, AE, Diners Club). **Notes:** 1983-99 GTE Byron Nelson Classic.
Reader Comments: Too long for a mid-handicapper ... Outstanding, tough ... Condition/service excellent, course not hard ... Well conditioned, super staff, tough but playable ... Very challenging–very fast greens ... Expensive but a thrill to play. A true PGA test ... Cold towels from beverage cart in summer!

★½ FOX CREEK GOLF COURSE
PU-Rte. 3, Hempstead, 77445, Waller County, (409)826-2131, 40 miles NW of Houston.
Holes: 18. **Yards:** 6,180/4,680. **Par:** 71/71. **Course Rating:** 69.4/N/A. **Slope:** 114/N/A. **Green Fee:** $10/$16. **Cart Fee:** $9/person. **Walking Policy:** Unrestricted walking. **Walkability:** 2. **Season:** Year-round. **High:** March-Sept. **Miscellaneous:** Reduced fees (weekdays, seniors, juniors), metal spikes, range (mats), credit cards (MC, V).

FREEPORT GOLF COURSE
PM-830 Slaughter Rd., Freeport, 77541, Brazoria County, (409)233-8311.
Holes: 18. **Yards:** 6,169/5,787. **Par:** 71/71. **Course Rating:** 69.0/71.2. **Slope:** 113/112. **Green Fee:** $10/$13. **Cart Fee:** $17/cart. **Walking Policy:** Unrestricted walking. **Walkability:** 2. **Season:** Year-round. **High:** April-Sept. **Miscellaneous:** Metal spikes, range (grass), club rentals, beginner friendly (ladies, seniors, juniors).

★★★ GABE LOZANO SR. GOLF CENTER
PM-4401 Old Brownsville Rd., Corpus Christi, 78405, Nueces County, (361)883-3696, 3 miles W of Corpus Christi.
Holes: 27. **Yards:** 6,953/5,149. **Par:** 72/72. **Course Rating:** 72.6/68.8. **Slope:** 128/112. **Green Fee:** $12/$15. **Cart Fee:** $8/person. **Walking Policy:** Unrestricted walking. **Walkability:** 2. **Opened:** 1962. **Architect:** Leon Howard. **Season:** Year-round. **High:** Feb.-April. **To obtain tee times:** Call 24 hours in advance (all days). **Miscellaneous:** Reduced fees (weekdays, twilight, seniors, juniors), discount packages, metal spikes, range (grass), club rentals, credit cards (MC, V), beginner friendly.
Reader Comments: Acceptable for the amount of traffic it gets. Crowded ... Excellent shape, considering all the snow birds ... 256-yard par 3 ... Plenty of water ... Needs some tender care.

★½ GAINESVILLE MUNICIPAL GOLF CLUB
PM-200 S. Rusk, Gainesville, 76240, Cooke County, (940)668-4560.
Special Notes: Call club for further information.

★★★ GALVESTON ISLAND MUNICIPAL GOLF COURSE
PM-1700 Sydnor Lane, Galveston, 77554, Galveston County, (409)744-2366, 50 miles SE of Houston.
Holes: 18. **Yards:** 6,969/5,407. **Par:** 72/73. **Course Rating:** 73.0/71.4. **Slope:** 131/121. **Green Fee:** $13/$25. **Cart Fee:** $10/person. **Walking Policy:** Unrestricted walking. **Walkability:** N/A. **Opened:** 1989. **Architect:** Carlton Gipson. **Season:** Year-round. **High:** April-Oct. **To obtain tee times:** Call Tuesday at 8 a.m. Call 4 days in advance for holiday. **Miscellaneous:** Reduced fees (weekdays, resort guests, twilight, seniors, juniors), discount packages, metal spikes, range (grass/mats), club rentals, credit cards (MC, V, AE, D).
Reader Comments: Tough course, very windy ... Even when the wind doesn't blow, it's still windy ... Excellent muny–lots of water ... Very tough back 9 ... A little maintenance would make it a great experience.

GARDEN VALLEY GOLF RESORT
R-22049 FM 1995, Lindale, 75771, Smith County, (903)882-6107, (800)443-8577, 80 miles E of Dallas.
★★★★ DOGWOOD COURSE
Holes: 18. **Yards:** 6,754/5,532. **Par:** 72/72. **Course Rating:** 72.4/72.5. **Slope:** 132/130. **Green Fee:** $45/$64. **Cart Fee:** Included in Green Fee. **Walking Policy:** Mandatory cart. **Walkability:** 5. **Opened:** 1992. **Architect:** John Sanford. **Season:** Year-round. **High:** April-Oct. **To obtain tee times:** Call (800)443-8577 x 221. Locals call golf shop. Call 7 days in advance. **Miscellaneous:** Reduced fees (weekdays, low season, resort guests, twilight, seniors, juniors), discount packages, range (grass), club rentals, credit cards (MC, V, AE).
Reader Comments: Beautiful layout, piney woods ... Challenging, hilly ... Great clubhouse ... Beautiful in the spring. Dogwood trees in bloom ... Course is a little unbalanced from front 9 to

back 9. Back is the most beautiful I've played ... Most challenging course in Texas ... Gorgeous in spring when azaleas are blooming.

★★½ HUMMINGBIRD COURSE

Holes: 18. **Yards:** 6,446/5,131. **Par:** 71/71. **Course Rating:** 71.0/69.0. **Slope:** 128/125. **Green Fee:** $8/$21. **Cart Fee:** $12/person. **Walking Policy:** Unrestricted walking. **Walkability:** 4. **Architect:** Leon Howard. **Season:** Year-round. **High:** April-Oct. **To obtain tee times:** Call (800)443-8577 x 221. Locals call golf shop. Call 7 days in advance. **Miscellaneous:** Reduced fees (weekdays, low season, twilight, seniors), discount packages, range (grass), club rentals, credit cards (MC, V, AE).

Reader Comments: Great par-3 15th all over water ... Great clubhouse ... Real nice track some great holes ... Beautiful–user friendly ... Challenging course, keeps you guessing.

★★½ GLENBROOK GOLF COURSE

PU-8205 N. Bayou Dr., Houston, 77017, Harris County, (713)649-8089, 15 miles S of Houston. **Holes:** 18. **Yards:** 6,427/5,258. **Par:** 71/71. **Course Rating:** 70.7/70.7. **Slope:** 120/117. **Green Fee:** $11/$14. **Cart Fee:** $9/person. **Walking Policy:** Unrestricted walking. **Walkability:** 3. **Opened:** 1924. **Architect:** Robert McKinney. **Season:** Year-round. **High:** April-Oct. **To obtain tee times:** Call or stop by anytime after 7 a.m. Thursday. **Miscellaneous:** Reduced fees (weekdays, low season, twilight, seniors, juniors), discount packages, metal spikes, club rentals, credit cards (MC, V).

Reader Comments: I like the layout. Beware of the bayou ... Lots of long shots over bayous ... Fun course, but always busy ... Coming along well after revamp ... No driving range ... Good test of shot making.

★★★½ THE GOLF CLUB AT CINCO RANCH

PU-23030 Cinco Ranch Blvd., Katy, 77450, Fort Bend County, (281)395-4653, 20 miles W of Houston. **Holes:** 18. **Yards:** 7,044/5,263. **Par:** 72/72. **Course Rating:** 73.7/70.3. **Slope:** 132/118. **Green Fee:** $40/$50. **Cart Fee:** Included in Green Fee. **Walking Policy:** Mandatory cart. **Walkability:** 2. **Opened:** 1994. **Architect:** Carlton Gipson. **Season:** Year-round. **High:** April-June. **To obtain tee times:** Nonresidents may call up to 7 days in advance. Residents may call up to 9 days in advance. **Miscellaneous:** Reduced fees (weekdays, twilight, seniors, juniors), metal spikes, range (grass), club rentals, credit cards (MC, V, AE, D).

Reader Comments: Strategic delight ... Great practice range. Wind always blows ... Very enjoyable day. ... Fairly new course with small trees–will only get better as it ages.

★★★½ THE GOLF CLUB AT FOSSIL CREEK

PU-3401 Clubgate Dr., Fort Worth, 76137, Tarrant County, (817)847-1900. **Holes:** 18. **Yards:** 6,865/5,066. **Par:** 72/72. **Course Rating:** 73.6/68.5. **Slope:** 131/111. **Green Fee:** $60/$75. **Cart Fee:** Included in Green Fee. **Walking Policy:** Mandatory cart. **Walkability:** 5. **Opened:** 1987. **Architect:** Arnold Palmer/Ed Seay. **Season:** Year-round. **High:** March-June/Sept. **To obtain tee times:** Call 5 days in advance. **Miscellaneous:** Reduced fees (weekdays, twilight), range (grass), club rentals, credit cards (MC, V, AE).

Reader Comments: Great breakfast ... Always windy, carts have distance info ... Worth every penny ... Greens are like trying to putt on a high/low shag carpet ... Beautiful course, but pricey ... An excellent facility ... Try watering fairways! ... Great views around the course.

GRAND PRAIRIE MUNICIPAL GOLF COURSE

PM-3202 S.E. 14th St., Grand Prairie, 75052, Dallas County, (972)263-0661, 5 miles S of Dallas. **Holes:** 27.**Green Fee:** $16/$18. **Cart Fee:** $21/cart. **Walking Policy:** Unrestricted walking. **Walkability:** 1. **Opened:** 1964. **Architect:** Ralph Plummer. **Season:** Year-round. **High:** May-Sept. **To obtain tee times:** 7 a.m. in person or 8 a.m. by phone on Thursdays for weekends and holidays only.

★★★ RED/BLUE

Yards: 6,500/5,465. **Par:** 72/72. **Course Rating:** 71.0/65.3. **Slope:** 118/102. **Miscellaneous:** Reduced fees (twilight, seniors, juniors), range (grass), club rentals, credit cards (MC, V).

Reader Comments: Three 9s, very enjoyable play ... Fun muny for less experienced golfers ... Tough to walk ... Fairly easy muny ... Open fairways but lined with water everywhere.

★★★ RED/WHITE

Yards: 6,219/5,176. **Par:** 71/71. **Course Rating:** 69.5/64.2. **Slope:** 94/98. **Miscellaneous:** Reduced fees (twilight, seniors, juniors), metal spikes, range (grass), club rentals, credit cards (MC, V).

Reader Comments: Fairly short par 4s and 5s, long par 3s.

★★★ WHITE/BLUE

Yards: 6,309/5,275. **Par:** 71/71. **Course Rating:** 69.5/64.3. **Slope:** 112/98. **Miscellaneous:** Reduced fees (twilight, seniors, juniors), range (grass), club rentals, credit cards (MC, V).

Reader Comments: Toughest par 3s in Dallas from back tees.

★★★ GRAPEVINE GOLF COURSE

PU-3800 Fairway Dr., Grapevine, 76051, Tarrant County, (817)410-3377, 15 miles NW of Dallas.

Holes: 18. **Yards:** 6,953/5,786. **Par:** 72/72. **Course Rating:** 72.0/72.8. **Slope:** 113/117. **Green Fee:** $17/$20. **Cart Fee:** $20/cart. **Walking Policy:** Unrestricted walking. **Walkability:** 3. **Opened:** 1979. **Architect:** Joe Finger/Byron Nelson. **Season:** Year-round. **High:** April-Sept. **To obtain tee times:** Call 3 days in advance, 7 a.m. in person or 1 p.m. by phone. **Miscellaneous:** Reduced fees (twilight, seniors, juniors), range (grass/mats), club rentals, credit cards (MC, V, AE).
Reader Comments: Great public course ... Impossible to get weekend tee time ... Should be outstanding with planned changes ... No-nonsense marshals keep things moving ... An improving value, good for walkers ... Good open design ... Long—airplane noise, good layout.

★½ GRAYSON COUNTY COLLEGE GOLF COURSE
PU-56 Golf Drive, Denison, 75020, Grayson County, (903)786-9719, 70 miles N of Dallas.
Holes: 18. **Yards:** 6,633/4,876. **Par:** 72/72. **Course Rating:** 70.0/67.7. **Slope:** 114/108. **Green Fee:** $9/$13. **Cart Fee:** $18/cart. **Walking Policy:** Unrestricted walking. **Walkability:** 3. **Opened:** 1961. **Architect:** Joe Finger. **Season:** Year-round. **High:** May-June. **To obtain tee times:** Call by noon Wednesday for upcoming weekend. **Miscellaneous:** Reduced fees (weekdays, twilight), metal spikes, range (grass), club rentals, credit cards (MC, V).

★★★★ GREATWOOD GOLF CLUB
PU-6767 Greatwood Pkwy., Sugar Land, 77479, Fort Bend County, (281)343-9999, (888)343-4001, 4 miles SW of Sugar Land.
Holes: 18. **Yards:** 6,836/5,220. **Par:** 72/72. **Course Rating:** 72.6/70.0. **Slope:** 130/125. **Green Fee:** $48/$65. **Cart Fee:** Included in Green Fee. **Walking Policy:** Mandatory cart. **Walkability:** 3. **Opened:** 1990. **Architect:** Carlton Gipson. **Season:** Year-round. **High:** March-Oct. **To obtain tee times:** Call 7 days in advance of the day you wish to play, starting at 8 a.m. **Miscellaneous:** Reduced fees (twilight, seniors, juniors), metal spikes, range (grass/mats), club rentals, credit cards (MC, V, AE, Diners Club).
Reader Comments: Tough holes sneak up & run up your score ... Testing, undulating greens ... Really great facility ... Short par 4s, long par 3s ... Great layout, enjoyable ... Great condition & great views. Challenging ... Good public layout ... Don't try to walk. Greens to tees—miles.

★★ GREEN MEADOWS GOLF CLUB
PU-6138 Franz Rd., Katy, 77493, Harris County, (281)391-3670, 8 miles W of Houston.
Holes: 18. **Yards:** 5,440/4,949. **Par:** 70/70. **Course Rating:** 66.3/70.5. **Slope:** 104/110. **Green Fee:** $10/$21. **Cart Fee:** $10/person. **Walking Policy:** Unrestricted walking. **Walkability:** 1. **Opened:** 1965. **Architect:** Jay Riviere. **Season:** Year-round. **High:** Jan.-Aug. **To obtain tee times:** Foursomes call on Thursday starting at 8 a.m. for weekends. **Miscellaneous:** Reduced fees (twilight, seniors), metal spikes, club rentals, credit cards (MC, V, AE, D).

★★★ GROVER C. KEATON GOLF COURSE
PM-2323 Jim Miller Rd., Dallas, 75227, Dallas County, (214)670-8784.
Holes: 18. **Yards:** 6,511/5,054. **Par:** 72/72. **Course Rating:** 70.6/68.1. **Slope:** 113/113. **Green Fee:** $11/$14. **Cart Fee:** $17/cart. **Walking Policy:** Unrestricted walking. **Walkability:** N/A. **Opened:** 1978. **Architect:** Dave Bennett. **Season:** Year-round. **High:** March-Aug. **To obtain tee times:** Call two days in advance. **Miscellaneous:** Reduced fees (weekdays, low season, twilight, seniors, juniors), metal spikes, range (grass), club rentals, credit cards (MC, V, AE).
Reader Comments: Best-kept secret in Dallas ... Very narrow ... First 5 holes the toughest ... Good place to play a quick round.

★★ GUS WORTHAM PARK GOLF COURSE
PU-7000 Capitol, Houston, 77011, Harris County, (713)921-3227.
Holes: 18. **Yards:** 6,400/6,000. **Par:** 72/74. **Course Rating:** 69.5/74.2. **Slope:** 113/118. **Green Fee:** $10/$14. **Cart Fee:** $18/cart. **Walking Policy:** Unrestricted walking. **Walkability:** N/A. **Season:** Year-round. **High:** April-May. **To obtain tee times:** Call one day in advance. **Miscellaneous:** Reduced fees (weekdays, twilight, seniors, juniors), metal spikes, range (grass), club rentals, credit cards (MC, V, AE).

★★ HEATHER RUN GOLF & FISH CLUB
SP-1600 Western Oaks Dr., Waco, 76712, McLennan County, (254)772-8100.
Holes: 18. **Yards:** 6,400/5,040. **Par:** 70/70. **Course Rating:** 70.7/68.7. **Slope:** 127/120. **Green Fee:** $10/$13. **Cart Fee:** $9/person. **Walking Policy:** Unrestricted walking. **Walkability:** 3. **Opened:** 1969. **Architect:** Greg Juster. **Season:** Year-round. **High:** April-Nov. **To obtain tee times:** Call up to 7 days in advance. Call up to 60 days in advance for large groups. **Miscellaneous:** Reduced fees (weekdays, low season, resort guests, twilight, seniors, juniors), discount packages, metal spikes, range (grass), club rentals, credit cards (MC, V, AE, D).

★★½ HENRY HOMBERG MUNICIPAL GOLF COURSE
PU-5940 Babe Zaharias Dr., Beaumont, 77705, Jefferson County, (409)842-3220, 75 miles E of Houston.
Holes: 18. **Yards:** 6,786/5,660. **Par:** 72/73. **Course Rating:** 71.2/70.0. **Slope:** 116/116. **Green Fee:**

TEXAS

$8/$9. **Cart Fee:** $15/cart. **Walking Policy:** Unrestricted walking. **Walkability:** 1. **Opened:** 1930. **Architect:** Ralph Plummer. **Season:** Year-round. **High:** March-June. **To obtain tee times:** Call 2 days in advance for weekends or holidays at 9 a.m. **Miscellaneous:** Reduced fees (weekdays, twilight, seniors, juniors), metal spikes, range (grass/mats), club rentals, credit cards (MC, V, AE). **Reader Comments:** Get there early to beat the crowd ... Fun to walk ... Back 9 really good ... Heavily wooded.

★★ HERMANN PARK GOLF COURSE
PU-2215 N. MacGregor, Houston, 77030, Harris County, (713)526-0077. **E-mail:** pstark@bslgolf.com. **Web:** www.houston.sidewalk.msn.com/bslgolf. **Holes:** 18. **Yards:** 6,014/4,724. **Par:** 70/70. **Course Rating:** 67.9/63.7. **Slope:** 117/99. **Green Fee:** $19/$27. **Cart Fee:** $10/person. **Walking Policy:** Walking at certain times. **Walkability:** 2. **Opened:** 1922. **Architect:** John Bredemus/Carlton Gipson. **Season:** Year-round. **High:** March-Oct. **To obtain tee times:** First come, first served, or call up to one week in advance. **Miscellaneous:** Reduced fees (twilight, seniors, juniors), range (grass/mats), club rentals, credit cards (MC, V, AE).

★★★½ HIDDEN CREEK GOLF CLUB
PU-700 S. Burleson Ave., Burleson, 76028, Tarrant County, (817)447-4444, 14 miles S of Fort Worth. **Holes:** 18. **Yards:** 6,753/4,968. **Par:** 71/71. **Course Rating:** 73.8/N/A. **Slope:** 139/N/A. **Green Fee:** $28/$49. **Cart Fee:** $13/person. **Walking Policy:** Unrestricted walking. **Walkability:** 4. **Opened:** 1997. **Architect:** Steve Plumer. **Season:** Year-round. **High:** March-Nov. **To obtain tee times:** Please call five days in advance. **Miscellaneous:** Reduced fees (low season, twilight, seniors, juniors), range (grass), club rentals, credit cards (MC, V, AE, D), beginner friendly. **Reader Comments:** Outstanding greens for public course ... Nice design ... Good course, needs to mature... Beautiful new course, very interesting design, beautiful greens, lovely clubhouse, great value ... Last 3 holes are brutal–true test ... Refreshing, tough 1st time, let's go again.

★★★ HIDDEN HILLS PUBLIC GOLF COURSE
PU-N. Hwy. 70, Pampa, 79066, Gray County, (806)669-5866, 56 miles NE of Amarillo. **Holes:** 18. **Yards:** 6,463/5,196. **Par:** 71/71. **Course Rating:** 69.4/68.0. **Slope:** 122/116. **Green Fee:** $7/$12. **Cart Fee:** $17/cart. **Walking Policy:** Unrestricted walking. **Walkability:** 5. **Opened:** 1990. **Architect:** Ray Hardy. **Season:** Year-round. **High:** May-Sept. **To obtain tee times:** Call for tee times on Saturday, Sunday, and holidays. **Miscellaneous:** Reduced fees (weekdays, twilight, seniors, juniors), range (grass), club rentals, credit cards (MC, V). **Reader Comments:** Great place to play ... The course name is very fitting. Never a flat lie. Perfectly-maintained grass. Always windy. The facilities are new and very nice. Play it if you get a chance ... Hilly, good challenge ... Keep it in fairway.

★★★★ HILL COUNTRY GOLF CLUB *Service*
R-9800 Hyatt Resort Dr., San Antonio, 78251, Bexar County, (210)520-4040, (888)901-4653, 15 miles W of San Antonio. **Holes:** 18. **Yards:** 6,913/4,781. **Par:** 72/72. **Course Rating:** 73.9/67.8. **Slope:** 136/114. **Green Fee:** $60/$110. **Cart Fee:** Included in Green Fee. **Walking Policy:** Unrestricted walking. **Walkability:** 3. **Opened:** 1993. **Architect:** Arthur Hills. **Season:** Year-round. **High:** Spring/Fall. **To obtain tee times:** Hotel guests can make tee times with room reservations. Others call 7 days in advance. **Miscellaneous:** Reduced fees (weekdays, low season, twilight, juniors), discount packages, metal spikes, range (grass/mats), club rentals, lodging, credit cards (MC, V, AE, D, Diners Club). **Reader Comments:** Excellent course & service ... Innovative course–good use of technology ... Very severe greens, not an easy 2-putt anywhere ... Demands good tee shots ... Super par-5 8th ... Love the cacti with golf balls! ... Treelined, challenging, resort course, best from back tees ... Easy for women from red tees.

★★★½ HOGAN PARK GOLF COURSE
PM-3600 N. Fairground Rd., Midland, 79705, Midland County, (915)685-7360. **Holes:** 36. **Yards:** 6,615/5,775. **Par:** 70/72. **Course Rating:** 68.5/69.0. **Slope:** 110/103. **Green Fee:** $9/$17. **Cart Fee:** $17/cart. **Walking Policy:** Unrestricted walking. **Walkability:** 2. **Opened:** 1959. **Architect:** Charles Campbell/Jimmy Gamewell. **Season:** Year-round. **High:** May-Oct. **To obtain tee times:** Call golf shop. **Miscellaneous:** Reduced fees (weekdays, low season, twilight, seniors, juniors), metal spikes, range (grass), club rentals, credit cards (MC, V). **Reader Comments:** A very good course to spend Sunday afternoon ... Harder than its slope rating ... Can reach all par 5s in 2 ... Wide open fairways.

HORSESHOE BAY RESORT
★★★★ APPLEROCK COURSE
R-Bay W. Blvd., Horseshoe Bay, 78657, Burnet County, (830)598-6561, 45 miles W of Austin. **Web:** www.horseshoe-bay-resort.com.

Holes: 18. **Yards:** 6,999/5,509. **Par:** 72/72. **Course Rating:** 73.9/71.6. **Slope:** 134/117. **Green Fee:** $70/$121. **Cart Fee:** Included in Green Fee. **Walking Policy:** Mandatory cart. **Walkability:** 4. **Opened:** 1986. **Architect:** Robert Trent Jones. **Season:** Year-round. **High:** March-Nov. **To obtain tee times:** Call seven days in advance. **Miscellaneous:** Reduced fees (weekdays, low season, resort guests, juniors), discount packages, metal spikes, range (grass), club rentals, lodging, credit cards (MC, V, AE, D).
Reader Comments: Beautiful Texas golf ... New Bermuda-grass greens will be its salvation ... Scenic hill country layout, very playable ... Great views, great layout ... Love Nos. 10, 11 and 12 ... Beautiful, wildlife good.

★★★★ RAM ROCK COURSE
R-Bay W. Blvd., Horseshoe Bay, 78657, Burnet County, (830)598-6561, 45 miles W of Austin. **Web:** www.horseshoe-bay-resort.com.
Holes: 18. **Yards:** 6,946/5,306. **Par:** 71/71. **Course Rating:** 73.9/71.4. **Slope:** 137/121. **Green Fee:** $70/$121. **Cart Fee:** Included in Green Fee. **Walking Policy:** Mandatory cart. **Walkability:** 5. **Opened:** 1981. **Architect:** Robert Trent Jones. **Season:** Year-round. **High:** March-Nov. **To obtain tee times:** Call seven days in advance. **Miscellaneous:** Reduced fees (weekdays, low season, resort guests, juniors), discount packages, metal spikes, range (grass), club rentals, lodging, credit cards (MC, V, AE, D).
Notes: Ranked 11th in 1999 Best in State.
Reader Comments: A lot of elevation changes ... Nice hard layout ... The toughest 18 in Texas, bring your 'A' game ... Low handicaps only, long–no bailouts ... Very difficult course, long, tight ... Play back tees and be humbled ... Finest golf in the hill country ... Tough course.

★★★★ SLICK ROCK
R-Rte. Big Spur, Horseshoe Bay, 78657, Burnet County, (830)598-2561, 45 miles W of Austin. **Web:** www.horseshoe-bay-resort.com.
Holes: 18. **Yards:** 6,834/5,832. **Par:** 72/72. **Course Rating:** 72.6/70.2. **Slope:** 125/115. **Green Fee:** $70/$121. **Cart Fee:** Included in Green Fee. **Walking Policy:** Mandatory cart. **Walkability:** 2. **Opened:** 1972. **Architect:** Robert Trent Jones. **Season:** Year-round. **High:** March-Nov. **To obtain tee times:** Call seven days in advance. **Miscellaneous:** Reduced fees (weekdays, low season, resort guests, juniors), discount packages, metal spikes, range (grass), club rentals, lodging, credit cards (MC, V, AE, D).
Reader Comments: Easiest of 3 ... As relaxing as a hot bath ... Low handicaps only ... Beautiful, scenic course. Good service ... Tough par 3s. Very scenic ... Excellent resort course ... Fun to play ... Let rough grow and increase rating ... Pricey, club built to score well on ... Wildlife abounds.

★★★ HOUSTON OAKS
PU-22602 Hegar Rd., Hockley, 77447, Harris County, (713)757-5465, (800)865-4657, 30 miles NW of Houston.
Holes: 18. **Yards:** 6,880/5,238. **Par:** 72/73. **Course Rating:** 70.8/68.3. **Slope:** 120/109. **Green Fee:** $10/$25. **Cart Fee:** $9/person. **Walking Policy:** Walking at certain times. **Walkability:** N/A. **Opened:** 1993. **Architect:** Tom Fazio. **Season:** Year-round. **High:** Spring/Fall. **To obtain tee times:** Call 1 days in advance for weekdays and Thursday at 9 a.m. for upcoming weekend. **Miscellaneous:** Reduced fees (weekdays, twilight, seniors, juniors), discount packages, metal spikes, range (grass), club rentals, credit cards (MC, V, AE).
Reader Comment: Long distance between 9 & 10 ... Two different 9s ... Super tight front 9, open back but hard to figure out first time ... No. 17 fun short par 4 (256 yds.) that just kills me ... 19th hole cheeseburgers worth 18 holes to get ... Better since new owners.

HYATT BEAR CREEK GOLF & RACQUET CLUB
PU-3500 Bear Creek Court, DFW Airport, 75261, Dallas County, (972)615-6800.
★★★★ EAST COURSE
Holes: 18. **Yards:** 6,670/5,620. **Par:** 72/72. **Course Rating:** 72.5/72.4. **Slope:** 127/124. **Green Fee:** $48/$88. **Cart Fee:** Included in Green Fee. **Walking Policy:** Walking at certain times. **Walkability:** 3. **Opened:** 1981. **Architect:** Ted Robinson. **Season:** Year-round. **High:** April-Nov. **To obtain tee times:** Call 5 days in advance. **Miscellaneous:** Reduced fees (weekdays, low season, twilight, seniors, juniors), discount packages, range (grass), club rentals, credit cards (MC, V, AE, D).
Reader Comments: Great resort course ... East tougher of 2 ... Good condition, mind stopping for airplane shadows? ... Both courses are heavily used ... Hit a lot of low punch shots to keep the ball under the airplanes ... Fairly tight, but not as tight as the West ... Noisy. Good layout. Lots of fun. Good test.

★★★★ WEST COURSE
Holes: 18. **Yards:** 6,675/5,570. **Par:** 72/72. **Course Rating:** 72.7/72.5. **Slope:** 130/122. **Green Fee:** $48/$88. **Cart Fee:** Included in Green Fee. **Walking Policy:** Walking at certain times. **Walkability:** 3. **Opened:** 1981. **Architect:** Ted Robinson. **Season:** Year-round. **High:** April-Nov. **To obtain tee times:** Call 5 days in advance. **Miscellaneous:** Reduced fees (weekdays, low season, twilight, seniors, juniors), discount packages, range (grass), club rentals, credit cards (MC, V, AE, D).

Reader Comments: Expensive, but a pretty and challenging course ... Very busy, challenging, good greens, little expensive ... Even airplanes cannot spoil this golf ... Very difficult when windy; crowded on weekends ... Play both course for a really good value ... Tee ball in play a must.

INDIAN CREEK GOLF CLUB
PM-1650 W. Frankford, Carrollton, 75007, Denton County, (972)492-3620, (800)369-4137, 10 miles N of Dallas.

★★★ CREEKS COURSE
Holes: 18. Yards: 7,218/4,967. Par: 72/72. Course Rating: 74.7/68.2. Slope: 136/114. Green Fee: $22/$28. Cart Fee: $10/person. Walking Policy: Unrestricted walking. Walkability: 1. Opened: 1984. Architect: Dick Phelps. Season: Year-round. High: March-Oct. To obtain tee times: Call 3 days in advance. Miscellaneous: Reduced fees (weekdays, twilight, seniors, juniors), range (grass/mats), club rentals, credit cards (MC, V).
Reader Comments: Tight course-semi tough ... Very good value ... Tougher layout of 2 ... Trees, trees, trees. Keep it in the fairway or else ... Fairways outstanding, smooth Bermuda greens, but hard ... Good challenge. Lots of irons from the tee.

★★★ LAKES COURSE
Holes: 18. Yards: 7,060/5,367. Par: 72/72. Course Rating: 72.9/69.9. Slope: 135/114. Green Fee: $22/$28. Cart Fee: $10/person. Walking Policy: Unrestricted walking. Walkability: 1. Opened: 1987. Architect: Dick Phelps. Season: Year-round. High: March-Oct. To obtain tee times: Call 3 days in advance. Miscellaneous: Reduced fees (weekdays, twilight, seniors, juniors), range (grass/mats), club rentals, credit cards (MC, V).
Reader Comments: Lots of water but still open ...Lakes has bent greens, Creeks has Bermuda ... Great bent grass greens, fairways could be better.... Flat, lots of traps and water ... Good bent greens–good value for fees.

★★★½ IRON HORSE GOLF COURSE
PU-6200 Skylark Circle, North Richland Hill, 76180, Tarrant County, (817)485-6666, 10 miles NE of Fort Worth. Web: www.golfinthe southwest.com.
Holes: 18. Yards: 6,580/5,083. Par: 70/70. Course Rating: 71.8/69.6. Slope: 130/119. Green Fee: $30/$40. Cart Fee: $12/person. Walking Policy: Unrestricted walking. Walkability: 4. Opened: 1990. Architect: Dick Phelps. Season: Year-round. High: March-Oct. To obtain tee times: Call 3 days in advance. Miscellaneous: Reduced fees (weekdays, twilight, seniors, juniors), metal spikes, range (grass/mats), club rentals, credit cards (MC, V, AE, Diners CLub), beginner friendly (lessons available).
Reader Comments: Easy start, tough in the finish ... Great condition, interesting design ... Good value, friendly staff, do not walk ... Tight but interesting ... Fun layout, makes you hit you irons well ... Beautifully conditioned–tough but fair course ... The course is always in an excellent condition ... Requires all shots.

★★★ J.F. SAMMONS PARK GOLF COURSE
PM-2727 W. Adams Ave., Temple, 76504, Bell County, (254)778-8282, 50 miles N of Austin.
Holes: 18. Yards: 6,100/4,450. Par: 70/70. Course Rating: 69.8/65.8. Slope: 129/110. Green Fee: $6/$13. Cart Fee: $10/person. Walking Policy: Unrestricted walking. Walkability: 2. Opened: 1987. Season: Year-round. High: Spring/Fall. To obtain tee times: Call 7 days in advance. Deposit required for groups of 16 or more. Miscellaneous: Reduced fees (weekdays, low season, twilight, seniors, juniors), metal spikes, range (grass), club rentals, credit cards (MC, V, AE), beginner friendly.
Reader Comments: Tricky short course with water in play on 7 of front 9 ... Must have long irons ready ... Short and nice. Accurate iron shots needed.

JERSEY MEADOW GOLF COURSE
PU-8502 Rio Grande, Houston, 77040, Harris County, (713)896-0900.
★★★ BLANCO
Holes: 18. Yards: 6,583/5,383. Par: 72/72. Course Rating: 70.5/69.9. Slope: 120/103. Green Fee: $27/$36. Cart Fee: Included in Green Fee. Walking Policy: Walking at certain times. Walkability: 1. Opened: 1956. Architect: Carlton Gibson. Season: Year-round. High: April-Oct. To obtain tee times: Call one week in advance for weekdays and weekends. Miscellaneous: Reduced fees (weekdays, low season, twilight, seniors, juniors), range (grass), club rentals, credit cards (MC, V, AE).
Reader Comments: Long Bermuda rough puts premium on accurate drives and approaches ... Course OK, greens fair, but they are improving ... Some holes are challenging.
★★★ BRAZOS
Holes: 18. Yards: 6,383/5,215. Par: 72/72. Course Rating: 70.4/65.8. Slope: 118/108. Green Fee: $27/$36. Cart Fee: Included in Green Fee. Walking Policy: Walking at certain times. Walkability: 1. Opened: 1956. Architect: Carlton Gibson. Season: Year-round. High: April-Oct. To obtain tee times: Call one week in advance for weekdays and weekends. Miscellaneous: Reduced fees (weekdays, low season, twilight, seniors, juniors), range (grass), club rentals, credit cards (MC, V, AE).
Reader Comments: Nice greens.

★★★ RIO GRANDE
Holes: 18. **Yards:** 6,400/5,098. **Par:** 72/72. **Course Rating:** 68.9/64.2. **Slope:** 118/107. **Green Fee:** $27/$36. **Cart Fee:** Included in Green Fee. **Walking Policy:** Walking at certain times. **Walkability:** 1. **Opened:** 1956. **Architect:** Carlton Gibson. **Season:** Year-round. **High:** April-Oct. **To obtain tee times:** Call one week in advance for weekdays and weekends. **Miscellaneous:** Reduced fees (weekdays, low season, twilight, seniors, juniors), range (grass), club rentals, credit cards (MC, V, AE).
Reader Comments: Very good greens ... In better shape than it use to be ... Gets lots of play ... I had a great time at this course. The course was very nice and very well maintained even with the drought that hit that area last year. The people, as nice as you can find. I'd love to go back ... Immaculate greens.

★★★ JIMMY CLAY GOLF COURSE
PM-5400 Jimmy Clay Dr., Austin, 78744, Travis County, (512)444-0999.
Holes: 18. **Yards:** 6,857/5,036. **Par:** 72/72. **Course Rating:** 72.4/68.5. **Slope:** 124/110. **Green Fee:** $12/$14. **Cart Fee:** $8/person. **Walking Policy:** Unrestricted walking. **Walkability:** N/A. **Opened:** 1974. **Architect:** Joseph Finger. **Season:** Year-round. **High:** Aug. **To obtain tee times:** Call 1 day in advance. Call on Friday for weekend. **Miscellaneous:** Reduced fees (weekdays, twilight, seniors, juniors), metal spikes, range (grass), club rentals.
Reader Comments: Will be great when current maintenance projects are finished ... Good test, long with plenty of hazards ... Challenging ... Every hole is a challenge ... Good course... Long, wide open ... Great value—okay course.

★★½ JOHN PITMAN MUNICIPAL GOLF COURSE
PM-S. Main St., Hereford, 79045, Deaf Smith County, (806)363-7139.
Holes: 18. **Yards:** 6,545/4,870. **Par:** 71/71. **Course Rating:** 69.6/66.2. **Slope:** 113/113. **Green Fee:** $9/$12. **Cart Fee:** $18/cart. **Walking Policy:** Unrestricted walking. **Walkability:** 4. **Opened:** 1972. **Season:** Year-round. **High:** March-Sept. **To obtain tee times:** Call Wednesday. **Miscellaneous:** Reduced fees (weekdays, seniors, juniors), range (grass), club rentals, credit cards (MC, V).
Reader Comments: 2 sides different, good greens ... Simple, short but has a couple of challenging holes ... Well laid out ... Some tough holes on windy days.

★★½ KILLEEN MUNICIPAL GOLF COURSE
PM-406 Roy Reynolds Dr., Killeen, 76543, Bell County, (254)699-6034, 50 miles N of Austin.
Holes: 18. **Yards:** 6,700/5,109. **Par:** 72/72. **Course Rating:** 69.5/68.3. **Slope:** 107/109. **Green Fee:** $9/$13. **Cart Fee:** $16/cart. **Walking Policy:** Unrestricted walking. **Walkability:** 3. **Opened:** 1969. **Architect:** Jay Riviere. **Season:** Year-round. **High:** March-Oct. **To obtain tee times:** Call Wednesday for upcoming weekend. **Miscellaneous:** Reduced fees (twilight, seniors, juniors), metal spikes, range (grass), club rentals, credit cards (MC, V).
Reader Comments: Not a tough challenge, but a good change of pace ... Back 9 most enjoyable and challenging water holes ... Very good value ... Good value for dollar, fun track.

★★★ KINGWOOD COVE GOLF CLUB
PU-805 Hamblen Rd., Kingwood, 77339, Harris County, (281)358-1155, 20 miles N of Houston.
Holes: 18. **Yards:** 6,722/5,601. **Par:** 71/71. **Course Rating:** 71.9/73.2. **Slope:** 118/114. **Green Fee:** $28/$40. **Cart Fee:** $12/person. **Walking Policy:** Unrestricted walking. **Walkability:** 3. **Opened:** 1967. **Season:** Year-round. **High:** Spring/Fall. **To obtain tee times:** Call up to 7 days in advance. **Miscellaneous:** Reduced fees (weekdays, low season, twilight, seniors, juniors), discount packages, metal spikes, range (grass/mats), club rentals, credit cards (MC, V, AE, D, Diners Club).
Reader Comments: Fair layout–1 tough par 3 ... Nice, quiet trek in the woods ... Nicest place in Texas ... Play in summer, no drainage ... Lots of hills and water, needs some sand to make more interesting.

★★★ L.B. HOUSTON PARK GOLF COURSE
PM-11223 Luna Rd., Dallas, 75229, Dallas County, (214)670-6322.
Holes: 18. **Yards:** 6,705/5,596. **Par:** 72/73. **Course Rating:** 70.8/72.8. **Slope:** 126/113. **Green Fee:** $7/$17. **Cart Fee:** $18/cart. **Walking Policy:** Unrestricted walking. **Walkability:** 1. **Opened:** 1967. **Architect:** Dave Bennett/Leon Howard. **Season:** Year-round. **To obtain tee times:** Weekdays call two days in advance. Weekends call at 12 noon or come in person 6 a.m. to 12 noon Thursday. **Miscellaneous:** Reduced fees (weekdays, twilight, seniors, juniors), metal spikes, range (grass), club rentals, credit cards (MC, V, AE, D).
Reader Comments: Good value ... Good public course–holds water when it rains ... Consistently good greens ... Confidence builder... Another muny, fast play early mornings ... Could be nice with less play & better conditioning ... Tight course ... Treelined, requires a straight tee shot.

★½ L.E. RAMEY GOLF COURSE
PU-FM 3320, Kingsville, 78363, Kleberg County, (512)592-1101, 30 miles S of Corpus Christi.

Holes: 18. **Yards:** 6,995/5,540. **Par:** 72/72. **Course Rating:** 72.5/71.3. **Slope:** 128/107. **Green Fee:** $8/$10. **Cart Fee:** $15/cart. **Walking Policy:** Unrestricted walking. **Walkability:** 1. **Opened:** 1974. **Season:** Year-round. **High:** March-June. **Miscellaneous:** Reduced fees (weekdays, twilight), metal spikes, range (grass), club rentals, credit cards (MC, V, AE, D).

★★★★½ LA CANTERA GOLF CLUB *Service+, Condition*
R-16641 La Cantera Pkwy., San Antonio, 78256, Bexar County, (210)558-4653, (800)446-5387.
E-mail: info@lacanteragolf.com. **Web:** www.lacanteragolf.com.
Holes: 18. **Yards:** 7,001/4,953. **Par:** 72/72. **Course Rating:** 72.5/67.1. **Slope:** 134/108. **Green Fee:** $60/$125. **Cart Fee:** Included in Green Fee. **Walking Policy:** Walking at certain times. **Walkability:** 4. **Opened:** 1994. **Architect:** Weiskopf/Morrish. **Season:** Year-round. **High:** March-Oct. **To obtain tee times:** Call up to 6 days in advance. Call 7-30 days in advance with an additional $10 per person charge. Resort guests call 60 days in advance. **Miscellaneous:** Reduced fees (weekdays, low season, twilight, juniors), discount packages, metal spikes, range (grass), club rentals, lodging (508 rooms), credit cards (MC, V, AE, D).
Notes: Ranked 14th in 1999 Best in State; 1st in 1995 Best New Public Courses. .
Reader Comments: Close to Heaven, fun, use all 14 clubs; your putting must be on! ... Excellent–aim for the rollercoaster... Beautiful course layout, challenging, lots of elevation changes ... Spectacular quarry course. 1st hole longer than most air flights ... Impossible to walk! ... Easy for women from red tees.

★★★★ LADY BIRD JOHNSON MUNICIPAL GOLF COURSE *Value*
PM-Hwy. 16 S., Fredericksburg, 78624, Gillespie County, (830)997-4010, (800)950-8147, 70 miles N of San Antonio.
Holes: 18. **Yards:** 6,432/5,092. **Par:** 72/72. **Course Rating:** 70.3/68.0. **Slope:** 125/112. **Green Fee:** $11/$18. **Cart Fee:** $18/person. **Walking Policy:** Unrestricted walking. **Walkability:** 3. **Opened:** 1969. **Architect:** Jeffrey Brauer. **Season:** Year-round. **High:** March-Nov. **To obtain tee times:** Call golf shop. **Miscellaneous:** Reduced fees (weekdays), metal spikes, range (grass/mats), club rentals, credit cards (MC, V).
Reader Comments: Great course, scenic ... New clubhouse, best condition in Southwest Texas ... Fun–clean & well run! ... Best value in Texas. Excellent shape ... Fun & scenic.... 2 distinct sides-both fun.... Blood pressure drops 10 ... Short, fun course ... Watch out for rough.

★★★ LAKE ARLINGTON GOLF COURSE
PU-1516 Green Oaks Blvd. W., Arlington, 76013, Tarrant County, (817)451-6101, 25 miles W of Dallas.
Holes: 18. **Yards:** 6,637/5,485. **Par:** 71/71. **Course Rating:** 70.7/71.0. **Slope:** 117/114. **Green Fee:** $10/$12. **Cart Fee:** $8/. **Walking Policy:** Unrestricted walking. **Walkability:** N/A. **Opened:** 1963. **Architect:** Ralph Plummer. **Season:** Year-round. **High:** April-Aug. **To obtain tee times:** Call on Tuesday starting 6 a.m. for Wednesday through next Tuesday. **Miscellaneous:** Reduced fees (twilight, seniors, juniors), metal spikes, range (grass), club rentals, credit cards (MC, V, D).
Reader Comments: Two fine holes ... Good, inexpensive ... Fun little track, not 1 sand trap ... Back 9 better ... Nice, challenging, short ... Back-to-back par 5s on the back 9.

★★★ LAKE HOUSTON GOLF CLUB
PU-27350 Afton Way, Huffman, 77336, Harris County, (281)324-1841, 20 miles NE of Houston.
Holes: 18. **Yards:** 6,940/5,553. **Par:** 72/72. **Course Rating:** 74.2/73.3. **Slope:** 131/130. **Green Fee:** $23/$36. **Cart Fee:** Included in Green Fee. **Walking Policy:** Walking at certain times. **Walkability:** 4. **Opened:** 1971. **Architect:** Jay Riviere. **Season:** Year-round. **High:** Spring/Fall. **To obtain tee times:** Call up to 7 days in advance. **Miscellaneous:** Reduced fees (weekdays, twilight, seniors, juniors), discount packages, metal spikes, range (grass), club rentals, credit cards (MC, V, AE), beginner friendly (junior and beginner golf clinics).
Reader Comments: Great old course ... Nice fair course ... Quiet, treelined course ... Remember the mosquito repellant ... Worth a visit ... A tough course at a reasonable price.

★★½ LAKE PARK GOLF COURSE
PU-6 Lake Park Rd., Lewisville, 75067, Denton County, (972)436-5332, 15 miles N of Dallas.
E-mail: lpgolf@gte.net. **Web:** metroplexweb.com.
Holes: 18. **Yards:** 6,135/4,960. **Par:** 70/70. **Course Rating:** 68.3/N/A. **Slope:** 108/N/A. **Green Fee:** $10/$24. **Cart Fee:** $11/person. **Walking Policy:** Unrestricted walking. **Walkability:** 1. **Opened:** 1996. **Architect:** Richard Watson/Jeffrey Brauer. **Season:** Year-round. **High:** April-Oct. **To obtain tee times:** Call up to 3 days in advance. Call on Wednesday at 8 a.m. for upcoming weekend. **Miscellaneous:** Reduced fees (weekdays, twilight, seniors, juniors), metal spikes, range (grass), club rentals, credit cards (MC, V, AE, Diners Club), beginner friendly.
Reader Comments: Good place to work on your game ... Windy and a little short ... Nice, solid, little course... Short, easy–good place to build ego.

★★ LAKE WHITNEY COUNTRY CLUB
SP-Rte. 1, Box 2075, Whitney, 76692, Hill County, (254)694-2313, 55 miles S of Ft. Worth.
E-mail: lwcc@whitneytx.net.

Holes: 18. **Yards:** 6,296/5,020. **Par:** 70/71. **Course Rating:** 67.6/69.8. **Slope:** 113/113. **Green Fee:** $11/$15. **Cart Fee:** $11/person. **Walking Policy:** Unrestricted walking. **Walkability:** 3. **Opened:** 1968. **Architect:** Leon Howard. **Season:** Year-round. **High:** March-Nov. **To obtain tee times:** Call golf shop. **Miscellaneous:** Reduced fees (weekdays, low season, resort guests, twilight, seniors, juniors), discount packages, metal spikes, range (grass/mats), club rentals.

LAKEWAY RESORT
R-602 Lakeway Dr., Austin, 78734, Travis County, (512)261-7173, 12 miles SW of Austin.
★★★½ **LIVE OAK COURSE**
Holes: 18. **Yards:** 6,643/5,472. **Par:** 72/72. **Course Rating:** N/A. **Slope:** 121/122. **Green Fee:** $38/$46. **Cart Fee:** $12/person. **Walking Policy:** Unrestricted walking. **Walkability:** 1. **Architect:** Leon Howard. **Season:** Year-round. **High:** Spring/Fall. **To obtain tee times:** Call. **Miscellaneous:** Reduced fees (weekdays), discount packages, metal spikes, range (grass/mats), lodging, credit cards (MC, V, AE).
Reader Comments: Lots of deer ... Original 18, very nice, well maintained ... Fun course ... Tight fairways ... OK, but not great golf, beautiful scenery ... Be accurate.
★★★½ **YAUPON COURSE**
Holes: 18. **Yards:** 6,565/5,032. **Par:** 72/72. **Course Rating:** N/A. **Slope:** 123/119. **Green Fee:** $38/$46. **Cart Fee:** $12/person. **Walking Policy:** Unrestricted walking. **Walkability:** 5. **Architect:** Leon Howard. **Season:** Year-round. **High:** Spring/Fall. **To obtain tee times:** Call. **Miscellaneous:** Reduced fees (weekdays), discount packages, metal spikes, range (grass/mats), lodging, credit cards (MC, V, AE).
Reader Comments: Don't forget to yell fore at the deer ... Beautiful course, great views ... Hills & canyons, blind shots, well maintained ... Fun ... Great hill country layout ... Killer uphill, long par 5 into the wind.

★★½ LANDA PARK MUNICIPAL GOLF COURSE
PM-310 Golf Course Dr., New Braunfels, 78130, Comal County, (210)608-2174, 30 miles N of San Antonio.
Holes: 18. **Yards:** 6,103/4,919. **Par:** 72/72. **Course Rating:** 68.9/67.4. **Slope:** 112/106. **Green Fee:** $15/$15. **Cart Fee:** $18/person. **Walking Policy:** Unrestricted walking. **Walkability:** 2. **Opened:** 1932. **Architect:** David Bennett/Leon Howard. **Season:** Year-round. **High:** Jan.-Aug. **To obtain tee times:** Call up to 2 days in advance. Call at 9 a.m. on Thursday for upcoming weekend. **Miscellaneous:** Metal spikes, club rentals.
Reader Comments: Not a difficult course, but good course. Inexpensive and fun to walk ... Pleasant experience for little money ... Varied holes–enjoyable ... Fun, lots of water.

★★ LEON VALLEY GOLF COURSE
PU-709 E. 24th Ave., Belton, 76513, Bell County, (254)939-5271. **E-mail:** beltongolf@aol.com. **Web:** www.leonvalley.com.
Holes: 18. **Yards:** 6,652/5,370. **Par:** 72/73. **Course Rating:** 70.1/69.7. **Slope:** 117/114. **Green Fee:** $11/$14. **Cart Fee:** $9/person. **Walking Policy:** Unrestricted walking. **Walkability:** 1. **Opened:** 1959. **Architect:** Dick Normand. **Season:** Year-round. **High:** April-Sept. **To obtain tee times:** Tee times accepted year round. **Miscellaneous:** Reduced fees (twilight, seniors, juniors), range (grass/mats), club rentals, credit cards (MC, V, D), beginner friendly (lessons and clinics).

★★★ LIONS MUNICIPAL GOLF COURSE
PM-2901 Enfield Rd., Austin, 78703, Travis County, (512)477-6963.
Holes: 18. **Yards:** 6,001/4,931. **Par:** 71/71. **Course Rating:** N/A. **Slope:** 118/N/A. **Green Fee:** N/A. **Walkability:** N/A. **Architect:** Leon Howard. **Season:** Year-round. **High:** June-Aug. **Miscellaneous:** Reduced fees (twilight), metal spikes.
Reader Comments: Hogan once took a 14 on the 16th ... Pretty, short, tight, but tough ... A classic; good for every golfer... Too slow ... Short–fun course with a bite ... Could use more maintenance ... Would be a great muny if they watered the fairways. Some holes have character.... Excellent tight/short municipal course.

LONGWOOD GOLF CLUB
PU-13300 Longwood Trace, Cypress, 77429, Harris County, (281)373-4100, 10 miles NW of Houston.
Holes: 27. **Green Fee:** $55/$65. **Cart Fee:** Included in Green Fee. **Walking Policy:** Mandatory cart. **Walkability:** 3. **Opened:** 1995. **Architect:** Keith Fergus/Harry Yewens. **Season:** Year-round. **High:** Spring/Fall. **To obtain tee times:** Call up to 5 days in advance.
★★★½ **PALMETTO/POST OAK**
Yards: 6,647/4,872. **Par:** 72/72. **Course Rating:** 72.2/72.2. **Slope:** 133/133. **Miscellaneous:** Reduced fees (weekdays, twilight, seniors, juniors), range (grass), credit cards (MC, V, AE).
Reader Comments: Good layout ... Outstanding, but overpriced ... Great snack bar. Excellent burgers ... It can be walked-it's a real course ... Great public course with personality behind the counter ... Maturing nicely ... Good challenge.

★★★½ PINE/PALMETTO
Yards: 6,758/4,860. **Par:** 72/72. **Course Rating:** 72.8/68.9. **Slope:** 136/123. **Miscellaneous:**
Reduced fees (weekdays, twilight, seniors, juniors), range (grass), credit cards (MC, V, AE).
★★★½ POST OAK/PINE
Yards: 6,925/5,094. **Par:** 72/70. **Course Rating:** 73.6/69.9. **Slope:** 139/124. **Miscellaneous:**
Reduced fees (weekdays, twilight, seniors, juniors), metal spikes, range (grass), credit cards
(MC, V, AE).
Reader Comments: Great layout, good shotmaker's course ... Have to hit long to play well ...
New course that will soon be very nice ... Challenging yet fair, rolling terrain ... Aptly named, big-
time length and timber ... Looks like Carolina not Texas ... No 2 holes alike ... Great 27 holes ...
Bring long irons.

LOST VALLEY GOLF SHOP
R-P.O. Box 2170, Bandera, 78003, Bandera County, (830)460-7958, (800)378-8681, 30 miles N
of San Antonio.
Holes: 18. **Yards:** 6,210/N/A. **Par:** 72/N/A. **Course Rating:** 69.2/N/A. **Slope:** 116/N/A. **Green
Fee:** $10/$15. **Cart Fee:** $10/person. **Walking Policy:** Walking at certain times. **Walkability:**
N/A. **Opened:** 1955. **Season:** Year-round. **High:** Apr-Aug. **To obtain tee times:** Call.
Miscellaneous: Reduced fees (resort guests, twilight, seniors, juniors), discount packages,
metal spikes, club rentals, lodging, credit cards (MC, V, AE).

★★ MAXWELL GOLF CLUB
PM-1002 S. 32nd St., Abilene, 79602, Taylor County, (915)692-2737, 160 miles W of Dallas.
Holes: 18. **Yards:** 6,125/5,031. **Par:** 71/71. **Course Rating:** 68.1/66.5. **Slope:** 111/105. **Green
Fee:** $12/$17. **Cart Fee:** $17/cart. **Walking Policy:** Unrestricted walking. **Walkability:** 3.
Opened: 1930. **Season:** Year-round. **High:** July-Aug. **To obtain tee times:** Call 7 days in
advance. **Miscellaneous:** Reduced fees (twilight, seniors, juniors), metal spikes, range (grass),
club rentals, credit cards (MC, V, AE).

★★★ MEADOWBROOK GOLF COURSE
PM-1815 Jenson Rd., Fort Worth, 76112, Tarrant County, (817)457-4616, 5 miles E of Ft. Worth.
Holes: 18. **Yards:** 6,363/5,000. **Par:** 71/71. **Course Rating:** 70.2/68.4. **Slope:** 126/116. **Green
Fee:** $6/$20. **Cart Fee:** $18/cart. **Walking Policy:** Unrestricted walking. **Walkability:** 3. **Opened:**
1924. **Season:** Year-round. **High:** April-Oct. **To obtain tee times:** Call up to 7 days in advance.
Miscellaneous: Reduced fees (twilight, seniors, juniors), metal spikes, club rentals, credit cards
(MC, V, AE, D).
Reader Comments: Hilly, tight and tough ... Good mix of tough and average—nice old course ...
Fine design-needs work... Good par 5s; hilly.... No. 5 the meanest par 4 you ever saw ... Course
is on every hill in Fort Worth ... Pretty for late summer conditions ... Older established course,
nicely done ... Much improved.

MEADOWBROOK MUNICIPAL GOLF COMPLEX
PU-601 Municipal Dr., Lubbock, 79403, Lubbock County, (806)765-6679.
★★★ CANYON
Holes: 18. **Yards:** 6,450/5,511. **Par:** 72/72. **Course Rating:** 71.6/74.3. **Slope:** 120/117. **Green
Fee:** $15/$19. **Cart Fee:** $9/person. **Walking Policy:** Unrestricted walking. **Walkability:** 3.
Opened: 1934. **Architect:** Warren Cantrell/Baxter Spann. **Season:** Year-round. **High:** April-Sept.
To obtain tee times: Call 7 days in advance. **Miscellaneous:** Reduced fees (weekdays, twilight,
seniors, juniors), range (grass/mats), club rentals, credit cards (MC, V, D).
Reader Comments: A scenic surprise. Enjoy the walk ... Best layout in town. Some greens are
in rough shape ... Good layout. New staff is making improvements....Helpful staff, tricky
course–have to set up shots off the tee ... Watch out for prairie dogs on 18.
★★ CREEK
Holes: 18. **Yards:** 6,276/5,011. **Par:** 70/70. **Course Rating:** 69.0/70.5. **Slope:** 117/113. **Green
Fee:** $15/$19. **Cart Fee:** $9/person. **Walking Policy:** Unrestricted walking. **Walkability:** 2.
Opened: 1934. **Architect:** Warren Cantrell. **Season:** Year-round. **High:** June-Oct. **To obtain tee
times:** Call 7 days in advance. **Miscellaneous:** Reduced fees (weekdays, twilight, seniors,
juniors), range (grass/mats), club rentals, credit cards (MC, V, D).

★★★½ MEMORIAL PARK GOLF COURSE
PU-1001 Memorial Loop Park E., Houston, 77007, Harris County, (713)862-4033.
Holes: 18. **Yards:** 7,164/5,459. **Par:** 72/72. **Course Rating:** 73.0/67.7. **Slope:** 122/114. **Green
Fee:** $23/$32. **Cart Fee:** $10/person. **Walking Policy:** Unrestricted walking. **Walkability:** 1.
Opened: 1936. **Architect:** John Bredemus/Baxter Spann. **Season:** Year-round. **High:** April-Aug.
To obtain tee times: Call up to 3 days in advance. **Miscellaneous:** Reduced fees (weekdays,
twilight), metal spikes, range (grass/mats), club rentals, credit cards (MC, V, AE, D).
Reader Comments: Texas hospitality at its best ... One of the best in Houston ... Must play it if
in Houston! ... Terrific rebuilding ... Excellent renovation, very good challenge from the tips ...
One of the few courses you can walk; great, long old style ... Wide fairways keep most tee
shots playable.

★½ MESQUITE GOLF COURSE
PU-825 N. Hwy. 67, Mesquite, 75150, Dallas County, (972)270-7457, 15 miles E of Dallas.
Holes: 18. **Yards:** 6,280/5,028. **Par:** 71/72. **Course Rating:** 69.1/70.2. **Slope:** 116/113. **Green Fee:** $5/$16. **Walking Policy:** Unrestricted walking. **Walkability:** N/A. **Opened:** 1963. **Architect:** Marvin Ferguson. **Season:** Year-round. **High:** March-Oct. **To obtain tee times:** Call Thursday for Saturday, Sunday and holidays. Weekdays call two days in advance. **Miscellaneous:** Reduced fees (weekdays, low season, twilight, seniors, juniors), metal spikes, range (grass), club rentals, credit cards (MC, V).

★★★½ MILL CREEK GOLF & COUNTRY CLUB
R-1610 Club Circle, Salado, 76571, Bell County, (254)947-5698, (800)736-3441, 50 miles N of Austin. **Web:** www.millcreekgolfresort.com.
Holes: 18. **Yards:** 6,486/5,250. **Par:** 71/73. **Course Rating:** 72.1/69.6. **Slope:** 128/114. **Green Fee:** $52/$62. **Cart Fee:** Included in Green Fee. **Walking Policy:** Mandatory cart. **Walkability:** 3. **Opened:** 1981. **Architect:** Robert Trent Jones Jr. **Season:** Year-round. **High:** March-Oct. **To obtain tee times:** Call up to 1 day in advance. **Miscellaneous:** Reduced fees (weekdays, resort guests), discount packages, range (grass), club rentals, lodging (23 rooms), credit cards (MC, V).
Reader Comments: Very testy ball eater ... Long water carries, little expensive, pretty course ... Quiet, peaceful course ... Short but fun ... Rolling layout–club selection crucial.... Short but interesting ... Tough little course ... Hilly, bumpy, thick rough ... Interesting layout. Some real tough holes for long hitters.

★★★★ MISSION DEL LAGO GOLF COURSE   *Value*
PM-1250 Mission Grande, San Antonio, 78214, Bexar County, (210)627-2522, 2 miles S of San Antonio.
Holes: 18. **Yards:** 7,200/5,601. **Par:** 72/72. **Course Rating:** 73.6/70.2. **Slope:** 130/121. **Green Fee:** $21/$40. **Cart Fee:** Included in Green Fee. **Walking Policy:** Unrestricted walking. **Walkability:** 5. **Opened:** 1989. **Architect:** Denis Griffiths. **Season:** Year-round. **High:** Spring/Fall. **To obtain tee times:** Call up to 90 days in advance. **Miscellaneous:** Reduced fees (weekdays, low season, resort guests, twilight, seniors, juniors), discount packages, metal spikes, range (grass), club rentals, credit cards (MC, V, AE, D).
Reader Comments: A good, solid test of your 'A' game ... Challenging, well-bunkered and lots of variety in shots ... Open fairways. Very good facilities ... Plays like a links course ... Better than average muny.

★★½ MORRIS WILLIAMS GOLF CLUB
PM-4305 Manor Rd., Austin, 78723, Travis County, (512)926-1298.
Holes: 18. **Yards:** 6,636/5,273. **Par:** 72/72. **Course Rating:** 71.5/70.4. **Slope:** 121/117. **Green Fee:** $14/$15. **Cart Fee:** $20/cart. **Walking Policy:** Unrestricted walking. **Walkability:** 3. **Opened:** 1964. **Architect:** Leon Howard. **Season:** Year-round. **High:** March-Nov. **To obtain tee times:** Call 1 day in advance for weekdays and Friday a.m. for weekends and holidays. **Miscellaneous:** Reduced fees (weekdays, twilight, seniors, juniors), discount packages, metal spikes, range (grass), club rentals, credit cards (MC, V, D).
Reader Comments: Getting better ... Good winter course ... Long, open, short rough ... It's getting better and still is a challenge ... Tough course, must work the ball ... Good elevation changes.

★★ NOCONA HILLS GOLF COURSE
SP-179 Country Club Dr., Nocona, 76255, Montague County, (940)825-3444, 58 miles E of Wichita Falls.
Holes: 18. **Yards:** 6,155/4,971. **Par:** 72/72. **Course Rating:** 71.3/64.1. **Slope:** 111/103. **Green Fee:** $13/$18. **Cart Fee:** $17/cart. **Walking Policy:** Walking at certain times. **Walkability:** 5. **Opened:** 1973. **Architect:** Leon Howard/Charles Howard. **Season:** Year-round. **High:** April-Nov. **To obtain tee times:** Call up to 7 days in advance. **Miscellaneous:** Reduced fees (seniors, juniors), range (grass), club rentals, lodging (28 rooms), credit cards (MC, V, D).

OLD ORCHARD GOLF CLUB
PU-13134 FM 1464, Richmond, 77469, Fort Bend County, (281)277-3300, 15 miles SW of Houston.
Holes: 27. **Green Fee:** $35/$65. **Cart Fee:** Included in Green Fee. **Walking Policy:** Unrestricted walking. **Walkability:** 2. **Opened:** 1990. **Architect:** C. Gibson/H. Yewens/K. Fergus. **Season:** Year-round. **High:** Spring/Fall. **To obtain tee times:** Call or come in up to 6 days in advance. **Miscellaneous:** Reduced fees (twilight, seniors, juniors), metal spikes, range (grass/mats), club rentals, credit cards (MC, V, AE).
★★★★ BARN/RANGE
Yards: 6,927/5,166. **Par:** 72/72. **Course Rating:** 73.6/69.4. **Slope:** 127/114.
Reader Comments: 27 fine holes–fabulous service ... Nice design–requires accurate iron play–small greens ... Hidden gem. Tough but fair. A must play in Houston ... Hilly, nice course. Good scenery ... Always in great shape, tough and tight ... Excellent and fun ... Great greens and a good challenge.

TEXAS

★★★★ STABLES/BARN
Yards: 6,888/5,035. **Par:** 72/72. **Course Rating:** 73.5/69.0. **Slope:** 130/113.
Reader Comments: Get BBQ at turn ... Lots of old pecan trees ... Tricky greens ... One of the best in Texas.

★★★★ STABLES/RANGE
Yards: 6,687/5,010. **Par:** 72/72. **Course Rating:** 71.7/68.1. **Slope:** 124/111.
Reader Comments: Difficult, tight fairways, well maintained ... Great course ... Excellent greens, nice fairways, scenic layout ... Range course in wind is tough.

★★½ OLMOS BASIN GOLF CLUB
PM-7022 N. McCullough, San Antonio, 78216, Bexar County, (210)826-4041.
Yards: N/A. **Par:** N/A. **Course Rating:** N/A. **Slope:** N/A. **Green Fee:** N/A. **Walkability:** N/A.
Architect: George Hoffman. **Miscellaneous:** Metal spikes.
Reader Comments: Ball carries well ... Fun course. Good shape for a muny. Good golf value ... Good test for all players ... Good food, nice greens ... Centrally located, no range on site, honest test ... Open course, good for beginners.

★★★ OSO BEACH MUNICIPAL GOLF COURSE
PU-5601 S. Alameda, Corpus Christi, 78412, Nueces County, (361)991-5351.
Holes: 18. **Yards:** 6,223/4,994. **Par:** 70/70. **Course Rating:** 69.9/68.8. **Slope:** 119/118. **Green Fee:** $12/$15. **Cart Fee:** $16/cart. **Walking Policy:** Walking at certain times. **Walkability:** 1.
Opened: 1938. **Architect:** John Bredemus. **Season:** Year-round. **High:** Jan.-April. **To obtain tee times:** Call two days in advance. **Miscellaneous:** Reduced fees (twilight, seniors, juniors), metal spikes, club rentals, credit cards (MC, V).
Reader Comments: One of the toughest munies in Texas (water, windy) ... Beginner's course. Flat and straight. Confidence builder ... Good greens ... Need to be a straight ball hitter ... Best fairways for a municipal course with lots of rounds ... Very nice, no tricks.

★★★★½ PAINTED DUNES DESERT GOLF COURSE *Service+, Value+, Condition, Pace*
PU-12000 McCombs, El Paso, 79934, El Paso County, (915)821-2122. **E-mail:** pdgolf@gte.net.
Holes: 18. **Yards:** 6,925/5,717. **Par:** 72/72. **Course Rating:** 74.0/74.5. **Slope:** 137/123. **Green Fee:** $19/$23. **Cart Fee:** $18/cart. **Walking Policy:** Unrestricted walking. **Walkability:** 3.
Opened: 1991. **Architect:** Ken Dye. **Season:** Year-round. **High:** April-May/Sept.-Oct. **To obtain tee times:** Call 7 days in advance for weekdays. Call Monday starting at 7 a.m. for upcoming weekend. **Miscellaneous:** Reduced fees (twilight, seniors, juniors), range (grass/mats), club rentals, credit cards (MC, V, AE).
Notes: Ranked 10th in 1999 Best in State; 1994, 1995, 1996 Second Stage P.G.A. Tour Qualifying; 1997 Western C.P.C.; 1997 Western C.P.C.; 1995 Southwest Amateur.
Reader Comments: Congenial staff ... If you get off the fairway expect to beat up your irons! ... Excellent value for the modest green fee ... Best kept secret in golf! ... Challenging desert course. Great course ... Winter time conditions very nice ... Lots of trouble–drive straight or use another club.

★★ PALACIO REAL COUNTRY CLUB
PU-Monte Cristo Rd., Edinburg, 78539, Hidalgo County, (956)381-0964.
Holes: 18. **Yards:** 6,204/4,550. **Par:** 71/70. **Course Rating:** 70.4/68.6. **Slope:** 115/113. **Green Fee:** $12/$14. **Cart Fee:** $14/cart. **Walking Policy:** Walking at certain times. **Walkability:** 1.
Opened: 1974. **Season:** Year-round. **High:** Oct.-March. **To obtain tee times:** Call 24 hours in advance. **Miscellaneous:** Reduced fees (low season, twilight), discount packages, range (grass), club rentals, lodging (6 rooms), credit cards (MC, V, AE, D), beginner friendly (individual lessons).

★★★ PALO DURO CREEK GOLF CLUB
SP-50 Country Club Dr., Canyon, 79015, Randall County, (806)655-1106, 12 miles S of Amarillo.
Holes: 18. **Yards:** 6,865/5,120. **Par:** 72/74. **Course Rating:** 72.1/69.9. **Slope:** 117/105. **Green Fee:** $10/$15. **Cart Fee:** $16/cart. **Walking Policy:** Unrestricted walking. **Walkability:** 2.
Architect: Henry Hughes. **Season:** Year-round. **High:** April-Sept. **To obtain tee times:** Call golf shop. **Miscellaneous:** Reduced fees (twilight, seniors, juniors), range (grass), club rentals, credit cards (MC, V).
Reader Comments: Greens show panhandle weather–will bite ... Challenging, good value ... A hidden gem. Hope its not discovered! ... Short course ... Good layout-rapidly improving.

★★½ PASADENA MUNICIPAL GOLF COURSE
PM-1000 Duffer, Houston, 77034, Harris County, (281)481-0834.
Holes: 18. **Yards:** 6,750/4,910. **Par:** 72/72. **Course Rating:** 72.2/67.9. **Slope:** 118/108. **Green Fee:** $9/$13. **Cart Fee:** $19/cart. **Walking Policy:** Unrestricted walking. **Walkability:** 4. **Opened:** 1978. **Architect:** Jay Riviere. **Season:** Year-round. **High:** March-Aug. **To obtain tee times:** Call on Wednesday 7:30 a.m. for weekend/holiday tee times. **Miscellaneous:** Reduced fees (weekdays, twilight, seniors, juniors), metal spikes, range (grass), club rentals, credit cards (MC, V, AE, D, Diners Club).

TEXAS

Reader Comments: Good folks, fun for beginners ... Wide open course, very easy when no wind, always busy ... Very long from green to tee ... Everything you'd expect from a budget muny ... Wonderful ... Don't walk if over 50.

PEACH TREE GOLF CLUB
SP-6212 CR 152 W., Bullard, 75757, Smith County, (903)894-7079, 9 miles S of Tyler.
★★★★ OAKHURST COURSE
Holes: 18. **Yards:** 6,813/5,086. **Par:** 72/72. **Course Rating:** 72.3/69.0. **Slope:** 126/118. **Green Fee:** $19/$29. **Cart Fee:** $11/person. **Walking Policy:** Unrestricted walking. **Walkability:** 3. **Opened:** 1993. **Architect:** Carlton Gibson. **Season:** Year-round. **High:** April-Sept. **To obtain tee times:** Call 6 days in advance. **Miscellaneous:** Reduced fees (twilight, seniors), metal spikes, range (grass), club rentals, credit cards (MC, V, AE, D).
Reader Comments: Course has matured in the past years ... 3 tough finishing holes, always into the wind ... Tough in the summer ... Nice design & layout-lots of trees-fun to play tee to green ... Best in area ... Good course for average golfer. Nice greens.
★½ PEACH TREE COURSE
Holes: 18. **Yards:** 5,556/4,467. **Par:** 70/71. **Course Rating:** 65.7/65.5. **Slope:** 109/111. **Green Fee:** $13/$19. **Cart Fee:** $11/person. **Walking Policy:** Unrestricted walking. **Walkability:** 1. **Opened:** 1986. **Architect:** Dan Hurst. **Season:** Year-round. **High:** April-Sept. **To obtain tee times:** First come, first served. **Miscellaneous:** Reduced fees (weekdays, twilight, seniors, juniors), metal spikes, range (grass), club rentals, credit cards (MC, V, AE, D), beginner friendly.

★★★½ PECAN VALLEY GOLF CLUB
PU-4700 Pecan Valley Dr., San Antonio, 78223, Bexar County, (210)333-9018, (800)336-3418, 6 miles S of San Antonio.
Holes: 18. **Yards:** 7,010/5,335. **Par:** 71/71. **Course Rating:** 73.9/65.7. **Slope:** 131/118. **Green Fee:** $75/$95. **Cart Fee:** Included in Green Fee. **Walking Policy:** Unrestricted walking. **Walkability:** 2. **Opened:** 1963. **Architect:** J. Press Maxwell. **Season:** Year-round. **High:** Spring/Fall. **To obtain tee times:** Call 14 days in advance with credit card. **Miscellaneous:** Reduced fees (weekdays, low season, twilight, seniors, juniors), metal spikes, range (grass), club rentals, credit cards (MC, V, AE).
Reader Comments: Great course, old, but excellent shape ... Has some great holes ... Friendly people ... Watch out for tree branches, seem to be ball magnets ... Tight—need to hit it straight ... Be in fairway—stray you pay ... Greatest staff in Texas ... Strong history—good value for fee.

PECAN VALLEY GOLF COURSE
6400 Pecan Dr., Fort Worth, 76126, Tarrant County, (817)249-1845, 2 miles SW of Dallas.
★★½ HILLS COURSE
PM-**Holes:** 18. **Yards:** 6,577/5,275. **Par:** 72/72. **Course Rating:** 71.4/69.7. **Slope:** 128/115. **Green Fee:** $12/$15. **Cart Fee:** $16/cart. **Walking Policy:** Unrestricted walking. **Walkability:** 2. **Architect:** Ralph Plummer/Bland Pittman. **Season:** Year-round. **High:** April-Nov. **To obtain tee times:** Call up to 5 days in advance. **Miscellaneous:** Reduced fees (weekdays, low season, twilight, seniors, juniors), discount packages, range (grass), club rentals, credit cards (MC, V, AE, D).
Reader Comments: Very good place to work on your game ... Always open no matter the weather ... Good course-getting better ... Old layout, parking area long way from club ... More character than River Course but not as well tended ... Stay in the fairway or else! ... Good value, needs more trees.
★★★ RIVER COURSE
PU-**Holes:** 18. **Yards:** 6,562/5,419. **Par:** 71/72. **Course Rating:** 71.3/69.6. **Slope:** 124/109. **Green Fee:** $15/$20. **Cart Fee:** $18/cart. **Walking Policy:** Unrestricted walking. **Walkability:** 1. **Architect:** Ralph Plummer/Bland Pittman. **Season:** Year-round. **High:** April-Nov. **To obtain tee times:** Call Monday at noon for that week. **Miscellaneous:** Reduced fees (weekdays, low season, twilight, seniors, juniors), range (grass), club rentals, credit cards (MC, V, AE, D).
Reader Comments: Good condition after no rain ... Demanding layout, accuracy a must ... Preferred over the Hills Course by locals ... Good layout & quality for the $. Great finishing hole! ... Enjoyable course, better than Hills ... Old course with history .... Well maintained for the price, not very challenging.

PERRYTON MUNICIPAL GOLF COURSE
402 SE 24th. St., Perryton, 79070, Ochiltree County, (806)435-5381.
Special Notes: Call club for further information.

★★★ PHEASANT TRAILS GOLF COURSE
PM-Hwy. 119, Dumas, 79029, Moore County, (806)935-7375, 45 miles N of Amarillo.
Holes: 18. **Yards:** 6,481/5,292. **Par:** 71/71. **Course Rating:** 69.5/70.5. **Slope:** 111/117. **Green Fee:** $10/$13. **Cart Fee:** $18/cart. **Walking Policy:** Unrestricted walking. **Walkability:** 3. **Opened:** 1945. **Season:** Year-round. **High:** March-Nov. **To obtain tee times:** Call Friday for weekend. **Miscellaneous:** Reduced fees (twilight, seniors, juniors), metal spikes, range (grass), club rentals, credit cards (MC, V).

Reader Comments: For a little town I think they do a great job ... 2 different 9s, new 9 longer and challenging, old 9 fun ... Best fairways on a municipal course in Texas panhandle ... Can play ball down all year.

★★½ PHILLIPS COUNTRY CLUB
Sterling Rd., Borger, 79007, Hutchinson County, (806)274-6812.
Special Notes: Call club for further information.

★★★½ PINE FOREST GOLF CLUB
SP-2509 Riverside Dr., Bastrop, 78602, Bastrop County, (512)321-1181, 30 miles E of Austin.
E-mail: golfer@bluebon.net. **Web:** www.golfclubsusa.com/fore.
Holes: 18. **Yards:** 6,700/5,000. **Par:** 72/72. **Course Rating:** 71.5/69.0. **Slope:** 126/114. **Green Fee:** $25/$35. **Cart Fee:** Included in Green Fee. **Walking Policy:** Mandatory cart. **Walkability:** 5. **Opened:** 1979. **Architect:** Don January. **Season:** Year-round. **High:** Mar.-May/Sept.-Nov.
Miscellaneous: Metal spikes, range (grass), club rentals, credit cards (MC, V, AE, D).
Reader Comments: Can't get used to all the blind shots ... Great course for money ... Great par 3s ... Fun course to play–interesting tricky holes set in hills on Colorado River ... Early morning is the best tee time. Not for beginners ... Hidden value–varied holes.

PINE RIDGE GOLF COURSE
PU-5615 Pine Mill Road, Paris, 75462, Lamar County, (903)785-8076, 2 miles NE of Paris.
Holes: 18. **Yards:** 5,855/4,462. **Par:** 72/72. **Course Rating:** 67.1/N/A. **Slope:** 106/N/A. **Green Fee:** $10/$12. **Cart Fee:** $18/cart. **Walking Policy:** Unrestricted walking. **Walkability:** 2. **Opened:** 1987. **Architect:** Raney/Exum. **Season:** Year-round. **High:** April-Oct. **To obtain tee times:** Call for weekends. **Miscellaneous:** Reduced fees (weekdays), metal spikes, range (grass), club rentals, credit cards (MC, V, D), beginner friendly (lessons available).

★★★½ PINNACLE COUNTRY CLUB
SP-200 Pinnacle Club Dr., Mabank, 75147, Henderson County, (903)451-9797, 60 miles SE of Dallas.
Holes: 18. **Yards:** 6,641/5,222. **Par:** 71/71. **Course Rating:** 72.9/70.8. **Slope:** 135/129. **Green Fee:** $16/$29. **Cart Fee:** $9/person. **Walking Policy:** Walking at certain times. **Walkability:** 4. **Opened:** 1988. **Architect:** Don January. **Season:** Year-round. **High:** March-Aug. **To obtain tee times:** Call 3 days in advance. **Miscellaneous:** Reduced fees (weekdays, twilight, seniors), discount packages, metal spikes, range (grass/mats), club rentals, credit cards (MC, V, AE).
Reader Comments: Believe this is the tightest course I've played ... Tight shotmaker's course ... Hidden away. Hard to find, but worthwhile experience ... Beautiful trip through the woods, have to hit the fairway.

★★½ PLANO MUNICIPAL GOLF COURSE
4501 E. 14th St., Plano, 75074, Collin County, (972)423-5444.
Special Notes: Call club for further information.

★★★ PLANTATION GOLF CLUB
PU-4701 Plantation Lane, Frisco, 75035, Collin County, (972)335-4653, 20 miles N of Dallas.
E-mail: perry.arthur@clubcorp.com.
Holes: 18. **Yards:** 6,382/5,945. **Par:** 72/72. **Course Rating:** 70.9/70.4. **Slope:** 122/113. **Green Fee:** $39/$58. **Cart Fee:** Included in Green Fee. **Walking Policy:** Mandatory cart. **Walkability:** 1. **Opened:** 1988. **Architect:** Richard Ellis. **Season:** Year-round. **High:** Year-round. **To obtain tee times:** Call up to 7 days in advance. **Miscellaneous:** Reduced fees (weekdays, low season, twilight, seniors, juniors), discount packages, range (grass), club rentals, credit cards (MC, V, AE, D).
Reader Comments: Nice course–front & back complete opposites ... Put No. 1 tee back where it was ... Not much distance OK to play ... Lot of irons off the tees ... Did anyone see a bunker? I didn't. ... Tight but fun.

★★½ QUAIL CREEK COUNTRY CLUB
Bastrop Highway, San Marcos, 78666, Hays County, (512)353-1665.
Special Notes: Call club for further information.

★★★★ THE QUARRY GOLF CLUB *Condition*
PU-444 E. Basse Rd., San Antonio, 78209, Bexar County, (210)824-4500, (800)347-7759.
E-mail: proshop@quarrygolf.com. **Web:** www.quarrygolf.com.
Holes: 18. **Yards:** 6,740/4,897. **Par:** 71/71. **Course Rating:** 72.4/67.4. **Slope:** 128/115. **Green Fee:** $80/$95. **Cart Fee:** Included in Green Fee. **Walking Policy:** Unrestricted walking. **Walkability:** 3. **Opened:** 1993. **Architect:** Keith Foster. **Season:** Year-round. **High:** March-Nov. **To obtain tee times:** Call 30 days in advance with credit card. **Miscellaneous:** Reduced fees (twilight, juniors), metal spikes, range (grass), club rentals, credit cards (MC, V, AE, D).
Notes: Ranked 6th in 1999 Best in State; 28th in 1996 America's Top 75 Upscale Courses.
Reader Comments: Outstanding back 9 makes up for front 9 ... 2 courses–front links–back traditional. ... Fun course ... Outstanding use of natural resources ... Quarry setting was great, very

unique layout ... Lots of rocks ... Long back 9 ... Need to play a lot to learn the right shots.... Breathtaking views, good service.

QUICKSAND GOLF COURSE
PU-2305 Pulliam St., San Angelo, 76905, Tom Green County, (915)482-8337, (877)520-4653.
E-mail: quicksandgc.com. **Web:** www.quicksandgc.com.
Holes: 18. **Yards:** 7,171/5,023. **Par:** 72/72. **Course Rating:** 75.0/69.5. **Slope:** 140/121. **Green Fee:** $17/$32. **Cart Fee:** $9/person. **Walking Policy:** Walking at certain times. **Walkability:** 2.
Opened: 1997. **Architect:** Michael Hurdzan/Dana Fry. **Season:** Year-round. **High:** March-Oct. **To obtain tee times:** Call 1 week in advance. **Miscellaneous:** Reduced fees (twilight, juniors), metal spikes, range (grass), club rentals, credit cards (MC, V, AE, D).
Special Notes: Previously Quicksand Golf Club

★★½ RABBIT RUN GOLF CLUB
,Beaumont, , Jefferson County, (409)866-7545.
Special Notes: Call club for further information.

RANCHO VIEJO RESORT & COUNTRY CLUB
R-No.1 Rancho Viejo Dr., Rancho Viejo, 78575, Cameron County, (956)350-4000, (800)531-7400, 3 miles N of Brownsville.
★★★ EL ANGEL COURSE
Holes: 18. **Yards:** 6,318/5,087. **Par:** 71/72. **Course Rating:** 71.5/67.6. **Slope:** 120/113. **Green Fee:** $35/$40. **Cart Fee:** $12/person. **Walking Policy:** Walking at certain times. **Walkability:** 1.
Opened: 1971. **Architect:** Dennis W. Arp. **Season:** Year-round. **High:** Oct.-May. **To obtain tee times:** Hotel guests 30 days in advance. **Miscellaneous:** Reduced fees (low season, resort guests, juniors), discount packages, metal spikes, range (grass), club rentals, lodging (63 rooms), credit cards (MC, V, AE).
Reader Comments: Had a great time ... Front and back 9s entirely different, back 9 in quarry is a good experience ... Easier than the Diablo course.
★★★ EL DIABLO COURSE
Holes: 18. **Yards:** 6,847/5,556. **Par:** 70/73. **Course Rating:** 73.7/70.7. **Slope:** 129/122. **Green Fee:** $35/$40. **Cart Fee:** $12/person. **Walking Policy:** Walking at certain times. **Walkability:** 1.
Opened: 1971. **Architect:** Dennis W. Arp. **Season:** Year-round. **High:** Oct.-May. **To obtain tee times:** Hotel guests 30 days in advance. **Miscellaneous:** Reduced fees (low season, resort guests, juniors), discount packages, metal spikes, range (grass), club rentals, lodging, credit cards (MC, V, AE).
Reader Comments: Beautiful greens ... Overpriced–not very challenging. Resort hotel setting ... Devil–good challenge ... A real test when the wind blows.

★★½ RATLIFF RANCH GOLF LINKS
PU-7500 N. Grandview, Odessa, 79768, Ector County, (915)550-8181, 3 miles N of Odessa.
Holes: 18. **Yards:** 6,800/4,900. **Par:** 72/72. **Course Rating:** 73.0/68.9. **Slope:** 122/110. **Green Fee:** $12/$17. **Cart Fee:** $10/person. **Walking Policy:** Unrestricted walking. **Walkability:** 2.
Opened: 1988. **Architect:** Jeff Brauer. **Season:** Year-round. **High:** March-Sept. **To obtain tee times:** Call Thursday for upcoming weekend or holiday. **Miscellaneous:** Reduced fees (weekdays, twilight, seniors, juniors), range (grass/mats), club rentals, credit cards (MC, V, D), beginner friendly (beginner clinics, junior programs).
Reader Comments: There is no rough only rocks ... Very hard. Nicely-contoured greens, challenging water holes ... 12th hole is the best par 3 in W. Texas ... Links style.

RAYBURN COUNTRY CLUB & RESORT
R-1000 Wingate Blvd., Sam Rayburn, 75951, Jasper County, (409)698-2271, (800)882-1442, 3 miles N of Sam Rayburn.
Holes: 27. **Green Fee:** $28/$35. **Cart Fee:** $20/cart. **Walking Policy:** Walking at certain times. **Walkability:** 5. **Opened:** 1967. **Architect:** Riviere/Von Hagge/Devlin/R.Trent Jones. **Season:** Year-round. **High:** Spring/Fall. **To obtain tee times:** Call golf shop. **Miscellaneous:** Reduced fees (twilight, juniors), range (grass/mats), club rentals, lodging, credit cards (MC, V, AE, D).
★★★½ BLUE/GOLD
Yards: 6,731/5,824. **Par:** 72/72. **Course Rating:** 71.3/72.2. **Slope:** 116/126.
Reader Comments: Great golf resort ... Nice hideaway, excellent restaurants close ... Challenging course, beautiful scenery ... Favorite resort, excellent food & lodging. When I die my ashes are to be placed on hole No. 4.
★★★½ BLUE/GREEN
Yards: 6,719/5,237. **Par:** 72/72. **Course Rating:** 72.5/71.0. **Slope:** 129/123.
Reader Comments: Green 9 hilly and tight, almost unplayable.
★★★½ GOLD/GREEN
Yards: 6,728/5,301. **Par:** 72/72. **Course Rating:** 72.2/71.0. **Slope:** 124/118.
Reader Comments: Excellent resort community, good all around ... Hill Country golf in East Texas, great layout.

TEXAS

★★★★ RIDGEVIEW RANCH GOLF CLUB
PU-2501 Ridgeview Dr., Plano, 75025, Collin County, (972)390-1039.
Holes: 18. **Yards:** 7,025/5,335. **Par:** 72/72. **Course Rating:** 74.1/70.4. **Slope:** 130/117. **Green Fee:** $30/$53. **Cart Fee:** $13/person. **Walking Policy:** Walking at certain times. **Walkability:** 3. **Architect:** Jeff Braurer. **Season:** Year-round. **High:** April-Aug. **Miscellaneous:** Reduced fees (twilight, seniors, juniors), discount packages, metal spikes, range (grass/mats), club rentals, credit cards (MC, V, AE), beginner friendly (junior clinics).
Reader Comments: User friendly, no forced carries ... My favorite, I love the changes in elevation ... Challenging but fun on each hole ... Good value for seniors ... Placement shots a must off tee with irons ... Great walking course, suited for all levels ... Tough in the wind ... Some great par 3s across a rocky creek.

★★★½ RIO COLORADO GOLF COURSE
PU-FM 2668 and Riverside Park, Bay City, 77414, Matagorda County, (409)244-2955, 80 miles S of Houston.
Holes: 18. **Yards:** 6,824/5,020. **Par:** 72/72. **Course Rating:** 73.1/69.1. **Slope:** 127/116. **Green Fee:** $13/$20. **Cart Fee:** $11/person. **Walking Policy:** Unrestricted walking. **Walkability:** 2. **Opened:** 1993. **Architect:** Gary Player Design Company. **Season:** Year-round. **High:** April-Oct. **To obtain tee times:** Call 2 days in advance at 8 a.m. for weekends and holidays. **Miscellaneous:** Reduced fees (twilight, seniors, juniors), discount packages, metal spikes, range (grass), club rentals, credit cards (MC, V, AE).
Reader Comments: Open front, tight back ... Flat, long par 5s, plenty of bunkers, nice course.

★★★½ RIVER BEND RESORT
R-Rte. 8, Box 649, Brownsville, 78520, Cameron County, (956)548-0192, 3 miles W of Brownsville.
Holes: 18. **Yards:** 6,828/5,126. **Par:** 72/72. **Course Rating:** 72.6/71.7. **Slope:** 119/119. **Green Fee:** $14/$19. **Cart Fee:** $9/person. **Walking Policy:** Unrestricted walking. **Walkability:** 1. **Opened:** 1985. **Architect:** Mike Ingram. **Season:** Year-round. **High:** Nov.-March. **To obtain tee times:** Call up to 3 days in advance. **Miscellaneous:** Reduced fees (weekdays, twilight), discount packages, range (grass), club rentals, lodging, credit cards (MC, V).
Reader Comments: You get what you pay for ... Acceptable ... Very windy. Water everywhere. Nice course ... Very outstanding greens, challenge in 40mph winds ... Good condition in spite of drought. Don't use driver on every Par 4.

★★ RIVER CREEK PARK GOLF COURSE
PU-1177 Farmarket Rd., Burkburnett, 76354, Wichita County, (940)855-3361, 10 miles N of Wichita Falls.
Holes: 18. **Yards:** 6,800/5,100. **Par:** 71/73. **Course Rating:** 69.0/69.1. **Slope:** 104/104. **Green Fee:** $7/$8. **Cart Fee:** $10/person. **Walking Policy:** Unrestricted walking. **Walkability:** N/A. **Architect:** Buddy Pierson/Richard Boyd. **Season:** Year-round. **High:** May-July. **To obtain tee times:** Call up to one week in advance. **Miscellaneous:** Reduced fees (twilight, seniors, juniors), metal spikes, range (grass), club rentals, credit cards (MC, V).

RIVER RIDGE GOLF CLUB
PU-3133 Brazos Oak Lane, Sealy, 77474, Austin County, (409)885-3333, (800)553-7517, 35 miles W of Houston. **E-mail:** BBBBlackie@wolrdnet.att.net.
Holes: 27. **Green Fee:** $55/$65. **Cart Fee:** Included in Green Fee. **Walking Policy:** Unrestricted walking. **Walkability:** 4. **Opened:** 1998. **Architect:** Jay Riviere. **Season:** Year-round. **High:** March-May/Sept.-Nov. **To obtain tee times:** Call 7 days in advance. **Miscellaneous:** Reduced fees (weekdays, twilight, seniors, juniors), discount packages, range (grass), club rentals, credit cards (MC, V, AE), beginner friendly (lessons & clinics).
PARKLAND/RIDGE
Yards: 7,201/5,486. **Par:** 72/72. **Course Rating:** 73.6/71.3. **Slope:** 133/122.
RIVER/PARKLAND
Yards: 6,946/5,344. **Par:** 71/71. **Course Rating:** 71.5/70.8. **Slope:** 129/121.
RIVER/RIDGE
Yards: 6,925/5,228. **Par:** 71/71. **Course Rating:** 72.1/70.1. **Slope:** 125/119.

RIVER TERRACE
PU-16777 Wallisville Rd., Channelview, 77530, Harris County .
Special Notes: Call club for further information.

★★★ RIVERCHASE GOLF CLUB
PU-700 Riverchase Dr., Coppell, 75019, Dallas County, (972)462-8281, 5 miles NW of Dallas.
Holes: 18. **Yards:** 6,593/6,041. **Par:** 71/71. **Course Rating:** 72.0/70.5. **Slope:** 124/119. **Green Fee:** $25/$65. **Cart Fee:** Included in Green Fee. **Walking Policy:** Walking at certain times. **Walkability:** 2. **Opened:** 1988. **Architect:** George Fazio. **Season:** Year-round. **High:** April-Oct. **To obtain tee times:** Call up to 7 days in advance. **Miscellaneous:** Reduced fees (weekdays, low season, twilight, seniors, juniors), discount packages, range (grass/mats), club rentals, credit cards (MC, V, AE).

Reader Comments: Nice course–very open & long ... Can always get on, nice staff, bent greens ... Excellent layout, condition and value! ... Difficult in wind ... Keep it in the fairway ... Pricey daily fee course, close to Cowboys training center.

RIVERSIDE GOLF CLUB

PU-3000 Riverside Pkwy., Grand Prairie, 75050, Dallas County, (817)640-7800, 20 miles SW of Dallas.
Holes: 18. **Yards:** 7,025/5,175. **Par:** 72/72. **Course Rating:** 74.4/69.5. **Slope:** 132/113. **Green Fee:** $48/$58. **Cart Fee:** Included in Green Fee. **Walking Policy:** Walking at certain times. **Walkability:** 3. **Opened:** 1984. **Architect:** Roger Packard. **Season:** Year-round. **High:** Spring/Fall. **To obtain tee times:** Call 5 days in advance. Credit card required for weekend reservation. Times are available farther out with prepayment of full amount. **Miscellaneous:** Reduced fees (weekdays, twilight, seniors, juniors), discount packages, metal spikes, range (grass), club rentals, credit cards (MC, V, AE, D).
Reader Comments: Good public course ... Some fun holes, lots of water, good golf ... No. 18 very tough finish ... Tests your mettle ... Open course for great scoring ... Avoid playing if windy ... Hilly, & lots of blind shots.

RIVERSIDE GOLF CLUB

PU-3001 Riverside Club Dr., San Angelo, 76903, (915)653-6130.
Holes: 18. **Yards:** 6,499/5,397. **Par:** 72/72. **Course Rating:** 70.5/69.8. **Slope:** 113/105. **Green Fee:** $11/$16. **Cart Fee:** $8/person. **Walking Policy:** Unrestricted walking. **Walkability:** 1. **Opened:** 1965. **Architect:** John Dublin. **Season:** Year-round. **To obtain tee times:** Call 1 week in advance for weekdays; Thursday at 7 a.m. for weekends. **Miscellaneous:** Reduced fees (juniors), metal spikes, range (grass/mats), club rentals, credit cards (MC, V, D).

RIVERSIDE GOLF COURSE

PU-302 McWright Rd., Victoria, 77901, Victoria County, (512)573-4521, 94 miles SE of San Antonio.
Holes: 27.**Green Fee:** $10/$12. **Cart Fee:** $12/cart. **Walking Policy:** Unrestricted walking. **Walkability:** 1. **Opened:** 1953. **Architect:** Ralph Plummer/Jay Riviere. **Season:** Year-round. **High:** May-Sept. **To obtain tee times:** First come, first served. **Miscellaneous:** Reduced fees (weekdays, juniors), metal spikes.
★★★ **RED/BLUE**
Yards: 6,488/5,121. **Par:** 72/72. **Course Rating:** 71.4/70.4. **Slope:** 122/117.
Reader Comments: Worth the effort. Good value ... Wonderful experience ... Huge pecan trees line fairways. Good test ... Always in excellent shape.
★★★ **RED/WHITE**
Yards: 6,606/5,497. **Par:** 72/72. **Course Rating:** 71.4/70.4. **Slope:** 122/117.
Reader Comments: Great golf for modest green fee ... You can play a different combination for a week.
★★★ **WHITE/BLUE**
Yards: 6,430/5,150. **Par:** 72/72. **Course Rating:** 70.8/70.4. **Slope:** 121/117.
Reader Comments: Limited facilities but a real fun place to play ... Good value ... A challenge, makes you think about your iron shots.

★★★ **RIVERSIDE MUNICIPAL GOLF COURSE**
PM-203 McDonald, San Antonio, 78210, Bexar County, (210)533-8371.
Holes: 18. **Yards:** 6,729/5,730. **Par:** 72/72. **Course Rating:** 72.0/72.0. **Slope:** 128/121. **Green Fee:** $6/$16. **Cart Fee:** $15/cart. **Walking Policy:** Unrestricted walking. **Walkability:** N/A. **Opened:** 1929. **Architect:** Vern Schmidt. **Season:** Year-round. **High:** April-Sept. **To obtain tee times:** May call up to a week in advance. **Miscellaneous:** Reduced fees (weekdays, low season, resort guests, twilight, seniors, juniors), discount packages, metal spikes, club rentals, credit cards (MC, V, AE, D).
Reader Comments: Good par 3s ... Tough par 5s ... Flat river layout but challenging ... City course. Price is right ... Old course with heavy use ... Long course ... Back 9 is better than front.

RIVERWOOD GOLF COURSE

Highway 105, Vidor, 77662, Orange County, (409)768-1710.
Special Notes: Call club for further information.

ROCKWOOD GOLF COURSE

PM-1851 Jacksboro Hwy., Fort Worth, 76114, Tarrant County, (817)624-1771, 2 miles W of Fort Worth.
★★ **RED/WHITE**
Holes: 18. **Yards:** 6,340/5,556. **Par:** 71/73. **Course Rating:** 72.0/N/A. **Slope:** 115/N/A. **Green Fee:** $12/$16. **Cart Fee:** $19/cart. **Walking Policy:** Unrestricted walking. **Walkability:** 2. **Opened:** 1940. **Architect:** John Bredemus. **Season:** Year-round. **High:** March-Oct. **To obtain tee times:** Call golf shop 5 days in advance or register in golf shop 7 days prior. **Miscellaneous:**

Reduced fees (weekdays, twilight, seniors, juniors), range (grass), club rentals, credit cards (MC, V, AE, D), beginner friendly (junior clinics, lessons available).
Special Notes: Formerly South/North Course.

★★ RIVER
Holes: 9. **Yards:** 6,994/5,778. **Par:** 72/76. **Course Rating:** 67.5/69.5. **Slope:** 115/115. **Green Fee:** $12/$16. **Cart Fee:** $19/cart. **Walking Policy:** Unrestricted walking. **Walkability:** 3. **Opened:** 1940. **Architect:** John Bredemus. **Season:** Year-round. **High:** March-Oct. **To obtain tee times:** Call 7 days in advance. **Miscellaneous:** Reduced fees (weekdays, twilight, seniors, juniors), metal spikes, club rentals, credit cards (MC, V, AE, D).
Special Notes: Play twice for 18 holes.

★★½ ROLLING HILLS GOLF CLUB
R-P.O. Box 1242, Hilltop Lakes, 77871, Leon County, (409)855-2100, 38 miles NE of Bryan-College Station.
Holes: 18. **Yards:** 6,330/5,635. **Par:** 72/73. **Course Rating:** 70.1/71.5. **Slope:** 111/117. **Green Fee:** $14/$17. **Cart Fee:** $16/cart. **Walking Policy:** Unrestricted walking. **Walkability:** N/A. **Opened:** 1958. **Architect:** C.M. Mimms. **Season:** Year-round. **High:** May-Aug. **To obtain tee times:** Call golf shop. **Miscellaneous:** Metal spikes, range (grass), club rentals, lodging, credit cards (MC, V, AE).
Reader Comments: Isolated but worth the trip ... Long course, very little traffic.

ROSS ROGERS GOLF CLUB
PM-722 N.W. 24th St., Amarillo, 79107, Potter County, (806)378-3086.
★★½ EAST COURSE
Holes: 18. **Yards:** 6,858/5,575. **Par:** 72/72. **Course Rating:** 70.8/69.5. **Slope:** 112/111. **Green Fee:** $9/$13. **Cart Fee:** $18/cart. **Walking Policy:** Unrestricted walking. **Walkability:** 2. **Opened:** 1977. **Architect:** James Rettenberry. **Season:** Year-round. **High:** May-Oct. **To obtain tee times:** Call or come in. **Miscellaneous:** Reduced fees (weekdays, seniors, juniors), range (grass/mats), club rentals, credit cards (MC, V, D).
Reader Comments: Play 150+ rounds per year–greens excellent in spite of freezing weather. ... Nice, well taken care of ... Good 36-hole public course ... Wind, wind, wind ... You need long irons and fairway woods here.
★★★ WEST COURSE
Holes: 18. **Yards:** 6,602/5,392. **Par:** 72/72. **Course Rating:** 69.2/68.2. **Slope:** 110/108. **Green Fee:** $9/$13. **Cart Fee:** $18/cart. **Walking Policy:** Unrestricted walking. **Walkability:** 1. **Opened:** 1940. **Architect:** James Rettenberry. **Season:** Year-round. **High:** May-Oct. **To obtain tee times:** Call or walk in. **Miscellaneous:** Reduced fees (weekdays, seniors, juniors), range (grass/mats), club rentals, credit cards (MC, V, D).
Reader Comments: Greens are improving ... Pretty good layout. Challenging ... Shorter than East Course ... Long with southwest wind ... A little easier than the East, but not much.

★★★★ ROY KIZER GOLF COURSE
PU-5400 Jimmy Clay Dr., Austin, 78744, Travis County, (512)444-0999.
Holes: 18. **Yards:** 6,749/5,018. **Par:** 71/71. **Course Rating:** 71.6/N/A. **Slope:** 125/N/A. **Green Fee:** $17/$23. **Cart Fee:** $8/person. **Walking Policy:** Unrestricted walking. **Walkability:** N/A. **Opened:** 1994. **Architect:** Randolph Russell. **Season:** Year-round. **To obtain tee times:** Call Tuesday for Friday, Saturday and Sunday. Call 3 days in advance for weekdays. **Miscellaneous:** Reduced fees (weekdays, twilight, seniors, juniors), metal spikes, range (grass), club rentals, credit cards (MC, V, AE, D).
Reader Comments: Wonderful links-style course–very tough if windy ... Good test from tips ... Good links course, wind is challenge ... Wide open ... Easy, no trees ... Walkable–good layout ... An excellent links style course. County-club conditions for the most part.

★★★ SAN SABA MUNICIPAL GOLF COURSE
PM-Golf Course Rd., San Saba, 76877, San Saba County, (915)372-3212, 90 miles NW of Austin.
Holes: 18. **Yards:** 6,904/5,246. **Par:** 72/72. **Course Rating:** 72.5/69.0. **Slope:** 119/113. **Green Fee:** $9/$13. **Cart Fee:** $9/person. **Walking Policy:** Unrestricted walking. **Walkability:** 1. **Opened:** 1972. **Architect:** Sorrell Smith. **Season:** Year-round. **High:** March-Oct. **To obtain tee times:** First come, first served. **Miscellaneous:** Metal spikes, range (grass), club rentals, credit cards (MC, V, AE).
Reader Comments: Must see & play to appreciate ... Back 9 is pretty, lots of trees ... From tree-lined to wide open–interesting course ... Fun course to play. Pecan tree puts on the squeeze ... Great variety, tough & quirky but pretty course ... Very difficult (tight) back 9.

★½' SCOTT SCHREINER KERRVILLE MUNICIPAL GOLF COURSE
PM-1 Country Club Dr., Kerrville, 78028, Kerr County, (830)257-4982, 60 miles NW of San Antonio.
Holes: 18. **Yards:** 6,453/4,826. **Par:** 70/70. **Course Rating:** N/A. **Slope:** N/A. **Green Fee:** $12/$18. **Cart Fee:** $18/cart. **Walking Policy:** Unrestricted walking. **Walkability:** 2. **Opened:** 1921. **Architect:** John Bredemus/R.D. Kaiser/Joe Finger. **Season:** Year-round. **High:** April-Oct.

TEXAS

To obtain tee times: Call 3 days in advance. **Miscellaneous:** Reduced fees (twilight, juniors), range (grass), club rentals.

★★½ SEVEN OAKS RESORT & COUNTRY CLUB
SP-1300 Circle Dr., Mission, 78572, Hidalgo County, (956)581-6267, 7 miles W of McAllen.
E-mail: seven_oaks_resort@yahoo.com. **Web:** www.7oaksresort.com.
Holes: 18. **Yards:** 6,089/4,867. **Par:** 70/70. **Course Rating:** 69.3/69.0. **Slope:** 113/111. **Green Fee:** N/A/$14. **Cart Fee:** $17/cart. **Walking Policy:** Unrestricted walking. **Walkability:** 1.
Opened: 1983. **Season:** Year-round. **High:** Nov.-March. **To obtain tee times:** Call 1 day in advance. **Miscellaneous:** Reduced fees (low season, juniors), range (grass/mats), club rentals, credit cards (MC, V, AE, D).
Reader Comments: Could be outstanding course if better maintained ... Some holes were short for par 4s ... Hard fairways and greens, bump and run it ... Front 9 is tight, back longer, more open.

★★½ SHADOW HILLS GOLF COURSE
PU-6002 3rd St., Lubbock, 79499, Lubbock County, (806)793-9700. **E-mail:** shgc@door.net.
Holes: 18. **Yards:** 6,777/5,594. **Par:** 72/72. **Course Rating:** 71.2/71.2. **Slope:** 118/118. **Green Fee:** $10/$19. **Cart Fee:** $9/person. **Walking Policy:** Unrestricted walking. **Walkability:** 3.
Opened: 1982. **Season:** Year-round. **High:** June-August. **To obtain tee times:** Weekday play no tee times required. Tee times are required for weekend and holiday play. You can call to book a time starting Monday for the upcoming weekend or holiday at 1(806)793-9700. **Miscellaneous:** Reduced fees (weekdays, twilight, seniors, juniors), metal spikes, range (grass), club rentals, credit cards (MC, V, D).
Reader Comments: Flat but fun ... When newly-planted trees age it will be challenging ... Unique layout, very tough at times.

★★ SHARPSTOWN MUNICIPAL GOLF COURSE
PM-6600 Harbor Town Dr., Houston, 77036, Harris County, (713)988-2099.
Holes: 18. **Yards:** 6,660/5,883. **Par:** 70/72. **Course Rating:** 69.7/72.0. **Slope:** 113/113. **Green Fee:** $5/$14. **Cart Fee:** $16/cart. **Walking Policy:** Unrestricted walking. **Walkability:** 1. **Opened:** 1957. **Architect:** Ralph Plummer. **Season:** Year-round. **To obtain tee times:** Call up to 3 days in advance for weekends and holidays. **Miscellaneous:** Reduced fees (weekdays, twilight, seniors, juniors), metal spikes, club rentals, credit cards (MC, V).

★★½ SHARY MUNICIPAL GOLF COURSE
PM-2201 Mayberry, Mission, 78572, Hidalgo County, (956)580-8770, 6 miles W of McAllen.
Holes: 27. **Yards:** 6,025/4,893. **Par:** 71/71. **Course Rating:** 68.9/68.8. **Slope:** 105/105. **Green Fee:** $9/$10. **Cart Fee:** $8/person. **Walking Policy:** Unrestricted walking. **Walkability:** N/A.
Opened: 1929. **Architect:** George Williams. **Season:** Year-round. **High:** Jan.-March. **To obtain tee times:** Call one day in advance. **Miscellaneous:** Reduced fees (juniors), metal spikes, range (grass), club rentals.
Reader Comments: Very good muny ... A fair test of golf ... Good condition ... Wide open only a few trees, with 27 holes there was no wait ... Good for straight short hitters.

SHERRILL PARK GOLF COURSE
PM-2001 E. Lookout Dr., Richardson, 75082, Collin County, (972)234-1416, 10 miles N of Dallas.
★★★ COURSE NO.1
Holes: 18. **Yards:** 6,900/5,182. **Par:** 72/72. **Course Rating:** 72.4/70.0. **Slope:** 124/120. **Green Fee:** $22/$30. **Cart Fee:** $10/person. **Walking Policy:** Unrestricted walking. **Walkability:** 3.
Opened: 1971. **Architect:** D.A. Weibring and Golf Resources. **Season:** Year-round. **High:** May-Nov. **To obtain tee times:** Weekend times taken on Friday by phone. Weekdays, first come, first served. **Miscellaneous:** Reduced fees (weekdays, twilight, seniors, juniors), discount packages, metal spikes, range (grass), club rentals, credit cards (MC, V).
Reader Comments: Much improved after redesign ... Good muny ... Don't need a driver ... Enjoyable place to play & not overpriced ... Drive on 18 is pure & testy ... Lovely treelined golf course ... Hot, dry summer! But fun.
★★ COURSE NO.2
Holes: 18. **Yards:** 6,083/5,476. **Par:** 70/70. **Course Rating:** 66.0/68.0. **Slope:** 113/113. **Green Fee:** $14/$17. **Cart Fee:** $10/person. **Walking Policy:** Unrestricted walking. **Walkability:** 3.
Opened: 1971. **Architect:** Leon Howard. **Season:** Year-round. **High:** May-Nov. **To obtain tee times:** Weekdays call one week in advance. Weekends call the Friday before. **Miscellaneous:** Reduced fees (weekdays, twilight, seniors, juniors), discount packages, metal spikes, range (grass), club rentals, credit cards (MC, V).

★★★½ SILVERHORN GOLF CLUB OF TEXAS
PU-1100 W. Bitters Rd., San Antonio, 78216, Bexar County, (210)545-5300, 12 miles NW of San Antonio.
Holes: 18. **Yards:** 6,922/5,271. **Par:** 72/72. **Course Rating:** 73.1/66.4. **Slope:** 129/109. **Green Fee:** $75/$80. **Cart Fee:** Included in Green Fee. **Walking Policy:** Unrestricted walking. **Walkability:** 2. **Opened:** 1995. **Architect:** Randy Heckenkemper. **Season:** Year-round. **High:** Feb.-May/

Sept.-Nov. **To obtain tee times:** Call up to 7 days in advance. Call up to 30 days in advance for additional $10 per person. **Miscellaneous:** Reduced fees (low season, twilight, seniors, juniors), discount packages, metal spikes, range (grass), club rentals, credit cards (MC, V, AE, D).
Reader Comments: Some interesting blind shots on back 9 ... Great new course. Super greens and layout. Great service ... Friendly staff, good marshalls ... Hard to beat ... Had flooding problems but recovering usually outstanding condition ... Hilly, scenic, breathtaking.

★★½ SINTON MUNICIPAL GOLF COURSE
Special Notes: Call club for further information.

★★½ SLEEPY HOLLOW GOLF & COUNTRY CLUB
SP-4747 S. Loop 12, Dallas, 75216, Dallas County, (214)371-3433, 7 miles S of Dallas.
Holes: 18. **Yards:** 7,031/5,878. **Par:** 71/71. **Course Rating:** 73.4/74.1. **Slope:** 125/123. **Green Fee:** $20/$30. **Cart Fee:** $11/person. **Walking Policy:** Unrestricted walking. **Walkability:** 2.
Opened: 1961. **Architect:** Press Maxwell. **Season:** Year-round. **High:** March-Oct. **To obtain tee times:** Call after 8 a.m. on Tuesdays for the following week. **Miscellaneous:** Reduced fees (twilight), metal spikes, range (grass), club rentals, credit cards (MC, V, AE, D).
Reader Comments: Tons of H20–don't slice ... Lots of seniors ... 600-yard par 5 is a killer ... Long, use every club ... 18th is a neat hole ... Best-kept secret in Dallas.

★★★½ SOUTH PADRE ISLAND GOLF CLUB
R-1 Golf House Dr., Laguna Vista, 78578, Cameron County, (956)943-5678, 7 miles W of South Padre Island. **E-mail:** spigc@ies.net. **Web:** www.southpadreislandgolf.com.
Holes: 18. **Yards:** 6,931/5,406. **Par:** 72/72. **Course Rating:** 73.1/68.0. **Slope:** 130/116. **Green Fee:** $25/$55. **Cart Fee:** $10/person. **Walking Policy:** Unrestricted walking. **Walkability:** 3.
Opened: 1997. **Architect:** Chris Cole/Steve Caplinger. **Season:** Year-round. **High:** Jan.-Mar/May-Aug. **To obtain tee times:** Call up to 7 days in advance. **Miscellaneous:** Reduced fees (weekdays, low season, resort guests, twilight, seniors, juniors), discount packages, metal spikes, range (grass), club rentals, credit cards (MC, V, AE, D).
Reader Comments: Wind blew so hard a high drive might end up in the next county. Turf hard but greens OK. Need trees to break the constant wind ... Great course ... Links feeling, flat, winds from all directions, good greens ... Tough course. Needs to mature.

SOUTHERN OAKS GOLF CLUB
PU-13765 Southern Oaks Dr., Fort Worth, 76028, Tarrant County, (817)426-2400.
Holes: 18. **Yards:** 7,302/5,369. **Par:** 71/71. **Course Rating:** 75.0/71.6. **Slope:** 132/120. **Green Fee:** $50/$65. **Cart Fee:** Included in Green Fee. **Walking Policy:** Unrestricted walking.
Walkability: 3. **Opened:** 1999. **Architect:** Mark Brooks. **Season:** Year-round. **High:** March-Nov.
To obtain tee times: Phone starting 5 days in advance. **Miscellaneous:** Reduced fees (weekdays, twilight, seniors, juniors), discount packages, metal spikes, range (grass), club rentals, credit cards (MC, V, AE, D), beginner friendly.

★ SOUTHWEST GOLF CENTER
PU-Hollywood & Coulter, Amarillo, 79119, Potter County, (806)355-7161, 1 miles SW of Amarillo.
Holes: 18. **Yards:** 7,018/5,700. **Par:** 72/74. **Course Rating:** 69.7/73.0. **Slope:** 100/104. **Green Fee:** $8/$12. **Cart Fee:** $18/cart. **Walking Policy:** Unrestricted walking. **Walkability:** 2. **Opened:** 1967. **Architect:** Bobby Westfall. **Season:** Year-round. **High:** Apr-Oct. **To obtain tee times:** Call up to 10 days in advance. **Miscellaneous:** Reduced fees (weekdays, low season, seniors, juniors), discount packages, metal spikes, range (grass), club rentals, credit cards (MC, V, D).

★★★½ SOUTHWYCK GOLF CLUB
PU-2901 Clubhouse Dr., Pearland, 77584, Brazoria County, (713)436-9999, 10 miles S of Houston.
Holes: 18. **Yards:** 7,015/5,211. **Par:** 72/72. **Course Rating:** 72.9/68.9. **Slope:** 123/112. **Green Fee:** $25/$45. **Cart Fee:** Included in Green Fee. **Walking Policy:** Walking at certain times.
Walkability: 3. **Opened:** 1988. **Architect:** Ken Kavanaugh. **Season:** Year-round. **High:** Spring/Fall. **Miscellaneous:** Reduced fees (weekdays, low season, twilight, seniors, juniors), discount packages, range (grass), club rentals, credit cards (MC, V, AE, D).
Reader Comments: Too long to walk ... Solid links course that always is in excellent shape; Challenging but fair; friendly staff ... Some challenging holes when the wind blows ... Nice layout ... Links style, tough course.... Would play each week if I won the lottery ... Some good par 4s, don't have to hit driver all day.

★★★★ SQUAW VALLEY GOLF COURSE
PU-HCR 51-45B Hwy. 67, Glen Rose, 76043, Somervell County, (254)897-7956, (800)831-8259, 60 miles SW of Fort Worth.
Holes: 18. **Yards:** 7,062/5,014. **Par:** 72/72. **Course Rating:** 73.6/70.0. **Slope:** 130/117. **Green Fee:** $22/$30. **Cart Fee:** $10/person. **Walking Policy:** Walking at certain times. **Walkability:** 4.
Opened: 1992. **Architect:** Jeff Brauer. **Season:** Year-round. **High:** April-Oct. **To obtain tee times:** Call or come in 5 days in advance. **Miscellaneous:** Reduced fees (weekdays, twilight, seniors), metal spikes, range (grass/mats), club rentals, credit cards (MC, V, D).

Reader Comments: Great value, super layout ... Wide open course. Not much trouble ... Well worth the trip. Lots of fun ... Immaculate condition ... Front 9 links style, back 9 river crossing. Greens excellent–fairways generous–good test ... Best-kept secret in the area ... Back 9 more interesting than front.

★★½ STEPHEN F. AUSTIN GOLF COURSE
SP-Park Rd. 38, San Felipe, 77473, Austin County, (409)885-2811, 40 miles W of Houston.
Holes: 18. **Yards:** 5,813/5,137. **Par:** 70/70. **Course Rating:** 67.3/69.7. **Slope:** 120/111. **Green Fee:** $15/$23. **Cart Fee:** $10/person. **Walking Policy:** Walking at certain times. **Walkability:** 3. **Opened:** 1953. **Season:** Year-round. **High:** May-June-July. **To obtain tee times:** Call on Thursday at 8 a.m. for upcoming weekend. **Miscellaneous:** Reduced fees (seniors), metal spikes, club rentals, credit cards (MC, V, AE).
Reader Comments: Beautiful oak trees and rolling hills ... Walking allowed, very enjoyable course ... Very good ... Easy short course, great beginners course ... Fun.

★★★½ STEVENS PARK GOLF COURSE
PM-1005 N. Montclair, Dallas, 75208, Dallas County, (214)670-7506.
Holes: 18. **Yards:** 6,005/5,000. **Par:** 71/71. **Course Rating:** 69.2/68.0. **Slope:** 120/118. **Green Fee:** $14/$17. **Cart Fee:** $18/cart. **Walking Policy:** Mandatory cart. **Walkability:** 4. **Opened:** 1922. **Architect:** Arthur Davis. **Season:** Year-round. **High:** April-Dec. **To obtain tee times:** Call 2 days in advance for weekdays. Come in Thursday at 6 a.m. or call by noon. **Miscellaneous:** Reduced fees (weekdays, twilight, seniors, juniors), club rentals, credit cards (MC, V, D).
Reader Comments: One of my favorite 'old style' courses ... Good old course–hills & giant oaks ... Some interesting short par 4s. Nos. 5 & 6 are best on course ... Great greens ... Some interesting and challenging hole layouts. I love hole No.15–at the green, you turn around and downtown Dallas is framed on top of the fairway!

★★★★ SUGARTREE GOLF CLUB *Value*
SP-Hwy. 1189, P.O. Box 98, Dennis, 76439, Parker County, (817)596-4991, 35 miles W of Fort Worth.
Holes: 18. **Yards:** 6,775/5,254. **Par:** 71/71. **Course Rating:** 72.8/71.0. **Slope:** 138/126. **Green Fee:** $23/$36. **Cart Fee:** $10/person. **Walking Policy:** Unrestricted walking. **Walkability:** 3. **Opened:** 1987. **Architect:** Phil Lumsden. **Season:** Year-round. **High:** March-Oct. **To obtain tee times:** Call up to 7 days in advance. **Miscellaneous:** Reduced fees (weekdays, low season, twilight, seniors, juniors), range (grass), club rentals, credit cards (MC, V, AE, D).
Reader Comments: A hidden gem in the middle of nowhere ... I loved this course, scenery was great... Very tight course, need properly-placed tee shots ... Lots of doglegs, good character ... Very scenic, fun to play ... 1st par 3 impossible ... Tricky and extremely great value ... Distances, difficult or impossible to find.

★★★★ SWEETWATER COUNTRY CLUB *Pace*
SP-1900 Country Club Lane, Sweetwater, 79556, Nolan County, (915)235-8093, 45 miles E of Abilene.
Holes: 18. **Yards:** 6,362/5,316. **Par:** 71/72. **Course Rating:** 70.0/N.A. **Slope:** 118/N.A. **Green Fee:** $15/$20. **Cart Fee:** $13/cart. **Walking Policy:** Unrestricted walking. **Walkability:** N/A. **Opened:** 1957. **Architect:** M.C. Alston. **Season:** Year-round. **High:** April-Aug. **To obtain tee times:** Call. **Miscellaneous:** Metal spikes, range (grass/mats), club rentals.
Reader Comments: Very challenging, lots of OB ... Nice course. Pretty course ... Excellent greens ... Narrow treelined fairways.

★★★★ TANGLERIDGE GOLF CLUB
PU-818 TangleRidge Dr., Grand Prairie, 75052, Dallas County, (972)299-6837, 30 miles SW of Dallas.
Holes: 18. **Yards:** 6,835/5,187. **Par:** 72/72. **Course Rating:** 72.2/70.2. **Slope:** 129/117. **Green Fee:** $39/$49. **Cart Fee:** $11/person. **Walking Policy:** Unrestricted walking. **Walkability:** 4. **Opened:** 1995. **Architect:** Jeff Brauer. **Season:** Year-round. **High:** May-Sept. **To obtain tee times:** Call up to 3 days in advance at 8 a.m. **Miscellaneous:** Reduced fees (twilight, seniors, juniors), range (grass), club rentals, credit cards (MC, V, AE, D).
Reader Comments: Best management in area ... Blind holes, up and down (sidehill lies) ... Great pro staff-great course ... Good driving course, long from back ... Challenging tight par 4s that make or break you ... Hard, long, be accurate ... Challenging layout ... Hard fairways, great greens ... Good course design. Tough but fair.

★★★★ TANGLEWOOD RESORT
R-Hwy. 120 N., Pottsboro, 75076, Grayson County, (903)786-4140, (800)833-6569, 68 miles N of Dallas.
Holes: 18. **Yards:** 6,993/4,925. **Par:** 72/72. **Course Rating:** 73.7/67.5. **Slope:** 128/104. **Green Fee:** $27/$38. **Cart Fee:** $12/person. **Walking Policy:** Walking at certain times. **Walkability:** 3. **Opened:** 1971. **Architect:** Ralph Plummer/Arnold Palmer. **Season:** Year-round. **High:** Spring/Fall. **To obtain tee times:** Call golf shop up to 30 days in advance. **Miscellaneous:**

Reduced fees (twilight, juniors), discount packages, metal spikes, range (grass), club rentals, lodging, credit cards (MC, V, AE, D).
Reader Comments: A good challenge from back tees ... Well-maintained course ... Excellent! Best course in northern Texas ... Good value for the money-nice course ... Good resort ... Lovely area, especially the wildlife.

TAPATIO SPRINGS RESORT & CONFERENCE CENTER
R-W. Johns Rd., Boerne, 78006, Kendall County, (830)537-4197, (800)999-3299, 25 miles NW of San Antonio.
Holes: 27. **Green Fee:** $80/$95. **Cart Fee:** Included in Green Fee. **Walking Policy:** Mandatory cart. **Walkability:** 4. **Opened:** 1980. **Architect:** Billy Johnston. **Season:** Year-round. **High:** Spring/Fall. **To obtain tee times:** Call 7 days in advance. Resort guest 30 days in advance with hotel confirmation. **Miscellaneous:** Reduced fees (weekdays, resort guests, twilight, juniors), discount packages, range (grass/mats), club rentals, lodging (123 rooms), credit cards (MC, V, AE, D).
★★★½ **LAKES/VALLEY**
Yards: 6,504/5,185. **Par:** 72/72. **Course Rating:** 71.4/70.4. **Slope:** 133/127.
★★★½ **RIDGE/LAKES**
Yards: 6,265/4,757. **Par:** 70/70. **Course Rating:** 70.5/67.9. **Slope:** 130/118.
★★★½ **VALLEY/RIDGE**
Yards: 6,513/5,122. **Par:** 72/72. **Course Rating:** 71.7/70.2. **Slope:** 133/126.
Reader Comments: Something for every player ... Good resort. Plenty of deer ... Awesome course—beautiful layout in hill country—a must play ... Wonderful scenery, tricky canyon holes ... Fun course with some interesting holes ... Wildlife abounds in this Texas hill country location ... Fair course, even for a high handicapper.

TENISON PARK GOLF COURSE
PM-3501 Samuell, Dallas, 75223, Dallas County, (214)670-1402, 3 miles E of Dallas.
★★★½ **EAST COURSE**
Holes: 18. **Yards:** 6,772/5,392. **Par:** 72/75. **Course Rating:** 72.0/70.2. **Slope:** 123/113. **Green Fee:** $14/$17. **Cart Fee:** $17/cart. **Walking Policy:** Unrestricted walking. **Walkability:** 2. **Opened:** 1927. **Architect:** Ralph Plummer. **Season:** Year-round. **High:** April-Oct. **To obtain tee times:** For weekend times come in person on Thursday at 6 a.m. or phone in at noon. **Miscellaneous:** Reduced fees (weekdays, twilight, seniors, juniors), metal spikes, range (mats), club rentals, credit cards (MC, V, AE), beginner friendly (first swing classes, group lessons).
Reader Comments: Good challenge ... Two great courses ... Trevino's Ghost lives here, tough ... Love it—solid city course ... Very popular course ... A real fun, but tough muny ... Well maintained for price ... Good course at a very good price.
★★★ **WEST COURSE**
Holes: 18. **Yards:** 6,822/5,648. **Par:** 72/75. **Course Rating:** 72.0/72.2. **Slope:** 121/118. **Green Fee:** $14/$17. **Cart Fee:** $17/cart. **Walking Policy:** Unrestricted walking. **Walkability:** 4. **Opened:** 1927. **Architect:** Ralph Plummer. **Season:** Year-round. **High:** April-Oct. **To obtain tee times:** For weekend times come in person on Thursday at 6 a.m. or phone in at noon. **Miscellaneous:** Reduced fees (weekdays, twilight, seniors, juniors), metal spikes, range (mats), club rentals, credit cards (MC, V, AE), beginner friendly (first swing classes, group lessons).
Reader Comments: Excellent big city course ... A hilly site for the middle of Dallas ... Hills are tough to walk ... Very fast greens ... Club pro is great. I met him when I was on the putting green & he came and gave me a free lesson! Talk about service!

★★ TEXAS A&M UNIVERSITY GOLF COURSE
PU-Bizzell St., College Station, 77843, Brazos County, (409)845-1723, 100 miles NW of Houston. **E-mail:** jandrews@rec.tamu.edu. **Web:** www.recsports.tamu.edu.com.
Holes: 18. **Yards:** 6,361/4,711. **Par:** 70/70. **Course Rating:** 70.2/71.4. **Slope:** 122/111. **Green Fee:** $17/$20. **Cart Fee:** $18/cart. **Walking Policy:** Unrestricted walking. **Walkability:** 4. **Opened:** 1951. **Architect:** Ralph Plummer, Jackie Burke, Jr. **Season:** Year-round. **High:** April-Oct. **To obtain tee times:** Only one week in advance available on Friday, Saturday, Sunday. **Miscellaneous:** Reduced fees (weekdays, twilight), range (grass), club rentals, credit cards (MC, V, AE, D), beginner friendly (saturday instruction).

★★★★ TEXAS STAR GOLF COURSE
PU-1400 Texas Star Pkwy., Euless, 76040, Tarrant County, (817)685-7888, (888)TEX-STAR. **Web:** www.texasstargolf.com.
Holes: 18. **Yards:** 6,936/4,962. **Par:** 71/71. **Course Rating:** 73.6/69.7. **Slope:** 135/124. **Green Fee:** $37/$53. **Cart Fee:** $12/person. **Walking Policy:** Unrestricted walking. **Walkability:** 4. **Opened:** 1997. **Architect:** Keith Foster. **Season:** Year-round. **High:** April-June/Sept-Nov. **To obtain tee times:** Call 5 days in advance and secure with a credit card. **Miscellaneous:** Reduced fees (twilight, seniors, juniors), range (grass/mats), club rentals, credit cards (MC, V, AE, D).
Reader Comments: Beautiful, challenging, highly recommended ... Slick greens ... Newer course—will hopefully improve with age ... Wear your thinking cap ... Marshals everywhere ... Course design & layout is unique ... Great diversity of holes on this golf course ... Tight wooded fairways, uphill, downhill, and open links-style holes.

★★★★ TIERRA SANTA GOLF CLUB

PU-1901 Club de Amistad, Weslaco, 78596, Hidalgo County, (956)973-1811, (800)838-5769, 4 miles S of Weslaco. **E-mail:** carl_baker@msn.com. **Web:** www.tierrasanta.com@msn.com. **Holes:** 18. **Yards:** 7,101/5,283. **Par:** 72/72. **Course Rating:** 74.5/72.5. **Slope:** 140/125. **Green Fee:** $26/$29. **Cart Fee:** $10/person. **Walking Policy:** Unrestricted walking. **Walkability:** 3. **Opened:** 1997. **Architect:** Jeff Brauer. **Season:** Year-round. **High:** Nov.-March. **To obtain tee times:** Call up to 2 days in advance. **Miscellaneous:** Reduced fees (weekdays, low season, resort guests, twilight, seniors, juniors), discount packages, metal spikes, range (grass), club rentals, credit cards (MC, V, AE, D), beginner friendly.
Reader Comments: New, but a good deal for south Texas ... Great course ... New course. It should improve ... A challenge ... Made you feel at home! ... Course was very dry, & greens were extremely fast.

★★★½ TIMARRON GOLF & COUNTRY CLUB

PU-14000 Byron Nelson Pkwy., Southlake, 76092, Tarrant County, (817)481-7529, 20 miles E of Fort Worth.
Holes: 18. **Yards:** 7,100/5,330. **Par:** 72/72. **Course Rating:** 74.2/71.3. **Slope:** 137/120. **Green Fee:** $45/$60. **Cart Fee:** Included in Green Fee. **Walking Policy:** Mandatory cart. **Walkability:** N/A. **Opened:** 1994. **Architect:** Byron Nelson /Baxter Spann. **Season:** Year-round. **High:** March-April. **To obtain tee times:** Call three days in advance. **Miscellaneous:** Reduced fees (weekdays), metal spikes, range (grass), club rentals, credit cards (MC, V, AE).
Notes: Ranked 9th in 1999 Best in State; 7th in 1995 Best New Public Courses.
Reader Comments: Interesting finishing hole ... Beautiful design, fun to play ... Modern layout with some great holes and blind shots ... Carts tell exact yardage to pin and/or water ... Great par-5 18th with island green ... Too many multi-level fairways! ... Wow! Beautiful course. Challenging and rewarding.

★ TIMBER-VIEW GOLF COURSE

PU-4508 E. Enon, Fort Worth, 76140, Tarrant County, (817)478-3601, 10 miles S of Fort Worth.
Holes: 18. **Yards:** 6,486/5,406. **Par:** 72/72. **Course Rating:** 70.4/70.0. **Slope:** N/A. **Green Fee:** $12/$18. **Cart Fee:** $20/cart. **Walking Policy:** Unrestricted walking. **Walkability:** 1. **Opened:** 1963. **Architect:** Thomas Fouts. **Season:** Year-round. **High:** March-Sept. **To obtain tee times:** First come, first served 7 days a week. **Miscellaneous:** Reduced fees (weekdays, seniors), discount packages, metal spikes, club rentals, credit cards (MC, V).

★★½ TONY BUTLER GOLF COURSE

PU-2640 S. M St., Harlingen, 78550, Cameron County, (956)430-6685, 120 miles S of Corpus Christi.
Holes: 27. **Yards:** 6,320/5,680. **Par:** 71/71. **Course Rating:** 69.1/69.1. **Slope:** 113/112. **Green Fee:** $10/$10. **Cart Fee:** $9/person. **Walking Policy:** Unrestricted walking. **Walkability:** N/A. **Opened:** 1927. **Architect:** Dennis W. Arp. **Season:** Year-round. **High:** Oct.-March. **To obtain tee times:** Call one day in advance starting at 6:30 a.m. Tee times required every day during Oct./March. **Miscellaneous:** Reduced fees (juniors), metal spikes, range (grass), club rentals, credit cards (MC, V).
Reader Comments: Good course, not easy for a high handicapper ... Needs water and it would be a good course ... Old course, lots of play, but well kept, fun to play ... Contoured greens, can be tough if windy ... Always come back once a year to play.

★★★★ TOUR 18

PU-3102 FM 1960 E., Humble, 77338, Harris County, (281)540-1818, (800)856-8687, 22 miles NE of Houston. **Web:** www.tour18.com.
Holes: 18. **Yards:** 6,782/5,380. **Par:** 72/72. **Course Rating:** 72.2/66.6. **Slope:** 126/113. **Green Fee:** $70/$85. **Cart Fee:** Included in Green Fee. **Walking Policy:** Mandatory cart. **Walkability:** 3. **Opened:** 1992. **Architect:** Dennis Wilkerson. **Season:** Year-round. **High:** April-May/Sept.-Nov. **To obtain tee times:** Call 30 days in advance beginning at 8:00 a.m. Call 60 days in advance for foursomes prepaying. **Miscellaneous:** Reduced fees (low season, twilight, juniors), range (grass/mats), club rentals, credit cards (MC, V, AE).
Reader Comments: Very good, flows well ... One of the top 10 courses in Texas—without a doubt ... Neat concept ... Wonderful experience but expensive ... I parred Amen Corner, what more can I say ... All imitated courses should be proud ... Wonderful experience. Must play at least once in lifetime ... Fun, Challenging.

★★★½ TOUR 18 GOLF CLUB

PU-8718 Amen Corner, Flower Mound, 75022, Tarrant County, (817)430-2000, (800)946-5310, 10 miles NW of DFW Airport. **Web:** www.tour18.com.
Holes: 18. **Yards:** 7,033/5,493. **Par:** 72/72. **Course Rating:** 74.3/66.3. **Slope:** 138/119. **Green Fee:** $75/$120. **Cart Fee:** Included in Green Fee. **Walking Policy:** Mandatory cart. **Walkability:** 4. **Opened:** 1995. **Architect:** D. Wilkerson/B. Jacobsen/J. Williams. **Season:** Year-round. **High:** Spring/Fall. **To obtain tee times:** Call up to 7 days in advance with credit card; up to 90 days

prepaid non-refundable. **Miscellaneous:** Reduced fees (low season, twilight), metal spikes, range (grass/mats), caddies, club rentals, credit cards (MC, V, AE).

Reader Comments: Overpriced but fun to play ... Neat experience, play once for the novelty ... Only play early in season, greens are in bad shape in summer ... If you can't play the real deal, this is the next best thing ... Bring all of your ability ... Incredible, but needs to mature.

★★ TREELINE GOLF CLUB
SP-17505 N. Eldridge Pkwy., Tomball, 77375, Harris County, (281)376-1542, (888)800-5199, 12 miles NW of Houston. **E-mail:** rampy@treelinegolf.com. **Web:** www.treelinegolf.com.
Holes: 18. **Yards:** 6,010/4,752. **Par:** 70/70. **Course Rating:** 68.4/62.3. **Slope:** 117/99. **Green Fee:** $14/$30. **Cart Fee:** $10/person. **Walking Policy:** Unrestricted walking. **Walkability:** 2. **Opened:** 1953. **Architect:** Jay Riviere. **Season:** Year-round. **High:** April-Oct. **To obtain tee times:** Call on Wednesday for weekend. 6 days in advance for Monday-Friday. **Miscellaneous:** Reduced fees (weekdays, low season, twilight, seniors, juniors), range (grass), club rentals, credit cards (MC, V, AE, D), beginner friendly.

★★★½ TURTLE HILL GOLF COURSE
PU-Rte. 373 N., P.O. Box 660, Muenster, 76252, Cooke County, (940)759-4896, (877)759-4896, 18 miles NW of Gainesville. **E-mail:** theturtle@nortexinfo.net. **Web:** www.theturtle.com.
Holes: 18. **Yards:** 6,510/4,821. **Par:** 72/73. **Course Rating:** 72.2/69.5. **Slope:** 123/116. **Green Fee:** $22/$34. **Cart Fee:** Included in Green Fee. **Walking Policy:** Unrestricted walking. **Walkability:** 5. **Opened:** 1993. **Architect:** Dick Murphy. **Season:** Year-round. **High:** April-Sept. **To obtain tee times:** Call 7 days in advance. **Miscellaneous:** Reduced fees (weekdays, low season, twilight, seniors, juniors), discount packages, metal spikes, range (grass/mats), club rentals, credit cards (MC, V, D).

Reader Comments: Once you get there, grip it and rip it, good for the ego and scoring average ... Fun, beautiful holes, not easy to get to ... Very scenic on tees ... 100-foot elevated tee box on par 3 ... Back 9 is awesome, especially No. 11 ... Excellent layout ... Very challenging for high handicapper.

★★★½ TWIN CREEKS GOLF CLUB
PU-501 Twin Creeks Dr., Allen, 75013, Collin County, (972)390-8888, 30 miles N of Dallas.
Holes: 18. **Yards:** 6,924/4,790. **Par:** 72/72. **Course Rating:** N/A. **Slope:** N/A. **Green Fee:** $38/$65. **Cart Fee:** Included in Green Fee. **Walking Policy:** Unrestricted walking. **Walkability:** 2. **Opened:** 1995. **Architect:** Palmer Course Design Co. **Season:** Year-round. **High:** April-Oct. **To obtain tee times:** Call 5 days in advance. **Miscellaneous:** Reduced fees (weekdays, twilight, juniors), range (grass/mats), club rentals, credit cards (MC, V, AE).

Reader Comments: Very tough–precision shots necessary ... Monitors in cart-tough greens ... Great winter conditions, overseeded well, slow though ... Nice course, too expensive ... Great greens ... Deceptive, looks quiet–is not ... Good basic golf ... A bit pricey.

★★★ TWIN WELLS GOLF COURSE
PU-2000 E. Shady Grove Rd., Irving, 75060, Dallas County, (972)438-4340, 2 miles S of Texas Stadium.
Holes: 18. **Yards:** 6,636/6,239. **Par:** 72/72. **Course Rating:** 70.9/69.3. **Slope:** 117/113. **Green Fee:** $18/$28. **Cart Fee:** $22/cart. **Walking Policy:** Unrestricted walking. **Walkability:** 2. **Opened:** 1988. **Architect:** Brian Ault/Bill Love. **Season:** Year-round. **High:** March-Dec. **To obtain tee times:** Call up to 3 days in advance. **Miscellaneous:** Reduced fees (weekdays, low season, twilight, seniors, juniors), discount packages, range (grass/mats), club rentals, credit cards (MC, V, AE).

Reader Comments: Very nice city course ... Very nice short course ... Wide open ... Good course and fun to play ... Decent mix of short and long holes, deceptive bunkering.

UNDERWOOD GOLF COMPLEX
SUNRISE COURSE
M-3200 Coe Ave., El Paso, 79904, El Paso County, (915)562-2066.
SUNRISE COURSE
Holes: 18. **Yards:** 6,942/5,498. **Par:** 72/72. **Course Rating:** 73.1/71.1. **Slope:** 126/124. **Green Fee:** $8/$18. **Cart Fee:** $16/cart. **Walking Policy:** Unrestricted walking. **Walkability:** 3. **Opened:** 1993. **Architect:** Finger-Dye-Spann. **Season:** Year-round. **High:** April-Nov. **To obtain tee times:** Call for weekday tee times only. Lottery system for weekends. **Miscellaneous:** Reduced fees (weekdays, twilight, juniors), range (grass), credit cards (MC, V, D), beginner friendly.
★★★★ SUNSET COURSE
SP-3200 Coe Ave., El Paso, 79904, El Paso County, (915)562-2066.
Holes: 18. **Yards:** 6,629/5,531. **Par:** 72/72. **Course Rating:** 70.4/70.4. **Slope:** 120/109. **Green Fee:** $8/$18. **Cart Fee:** $16/cart. **Walking Policy:** Unrestricted walking. **Walkability:** 1. **Opened:** 1945. **Season:** Year-round. **High:** April-Nov. **To obtain tee times:** Call for weekday tee times only. Lottery system for weekends. **Miscellaneous:** Reduced fees (weekdays, twilight, juniors), range (grass), club rentals, credit cards (MC, V, D), beginner friendly.

TEXAS

Reader Comments: Grass on greens kept very well ... Flat ... Narrow fairways with lots of rough ... This is an army course, well kept.

★★½ VALLEY INN & COUNTRY CLUB
SP-FM Rd. 802 and Central Blvd., Brownsville, 78520, Cameron County, (956)548-9199.
Holes: 18. **Yards:** 6,538/4,924. **Par:** 70/71. **Course Rating:** 72.3/69.7. **Slope:** 125/116. **Green Fee:** $15/$17. **Cart Fee:** $18/cart. **Walking Policy:** Walking at certain times. **Walkability:** 2. **Opened:** 1917. **Season:** Year-round. **High:** Jan.-April. **Miscellaneous:** Reduced fees (twilight), club rentals, credit cards (MC, V, AE, D).
Reader Comments: Could be great ... Good test of golf, course needs work.

★★★★ WATERWOOD NATIONAL RESORT & COUNTRY CLUB
R-One Waterwood, Huntsville, 77340, San Jacinto County, (409)891-5050, (800)441-5211, 75 miles N of Houston.
Holes: 18. **Yards:** 6,872/5,029. **Par:** 71/73. **Course Rating:** 73.7/68.0. **Slope:** 142/117. **Green Fee:** $30/$50. **Cart Fee:** $20/cart. **Walking Policy:** Unrestricted walking. **Walkability:** 3. **Opened:** 1975. **Architect:** Roy Dye. **Season:** Year-round. **High:** April-June. **To obtain tee times:** Call up to 7 days in advance. **Miscellaneous:** Reduced fees (low season, twilight, seniors, juniors), discount packages, metal spikes, range (grass), club rentals, lodging, credit cards (MC, V, AE, D, Diners Club).
Notes: Ranked 5th in 1999 Best in State.
Reader Comments: Unbelievably difficult. Best par 3 in Texas ... Good experience, restaurant ... Nice course, a little out of the way ... Tough affordable championship golf ... Course favors long tee shots. I am able to hit the long ball, so the course sets up well for me giving me more options.

★★★½ WEDGEWOOD GOLF CLUB
PU-5454 Hwy. 105 W., Conroe, 77304, Montgomery County, (409)441-4653, 50 miles N of Houston. **E-mail:** wdgewood@icc.net. **Web:** http://houstonsidewalk.com/bslgolf.
Holes: 18. **Yards:** 6,817/5,071. **Par:** 72/72. **Course Rating:** 73.7/69.6. **Slope:** 134/128. **Green Fee:** $20/$40. **Cart Fee:** $10/person. **Walking Policy:** Unrestricted walking. **Walkability:** 3. **Opened:** 1988. **Architect:** Ron Prichard. **Season:** Year-round. **High:** Spring/Fall. **To obtain tee times:** Call 7 days in advance for weekdays. Call on Wednesday for upcoming weekend. **Miscellaneous:** Reduced fees (weekdays, twilight, seniors, juniors), range (grass/mats), club rentals, credit cards (MC, V, AE).
Reader Comments: Very tight ... Difficult course, but fair ... Lots of ups & downs, hilly ... Great par-3, excellent staff ... Fun—good holes out there ... A challenge & variety of holes.

★★ WEEKS PARK MUNICIPAL GOLF COURSE
PM-4400 Lake Park Dr., Wichita Falls, 76302, Wichita County, (940)767-6107.
Holes: 18. **Yards:** 6,470/4,915. **Par:** 72/73. **Course Rating:** 70.0/67.8. **Slope:** 117/109. **Green Fee:** $11/$14. **Cart Fee:** $9/person. **Walking Policy:** Unrestricted walking. **Walkability:** 1. **Architect:** Jeff Brauer. **Season:** Year-round. **High:** April-Oct. **To obtain tee times:** Call golf shop. **Miscellaneous:** Reduced fees (weekdays, twilight, seniors, juniors), club rentals, credit cards (MC, V), beginner friendly (beginner lessons year round).

★★★★ WHITE BLUFFS GOLF CLUB   *Pace*
SP-Golf Dr. 1, Whitney, 76692, Hill County, (254)694-4000, (888)944-8325, 40 miles NW of Waco.
Holes: 18. **Yards:** 6,845/5,292. **Par:** 72/72. **Course Rating:** 73.3/72.4. **Slope:** 132/128. **Green Fee:** $38/$62. **Cart Fee:** Included in Green Fee. **Walking Policy:** Unrestricted walking. **Walkability:** 3. **Opened:** 1992. **Architect:** Bruce Lietzke/Lee Singletary. **Season:** Year-round. **High:** April-Oct. **To obtain tee times:** Call up to 7 days in advance. **Miscellaneous:** Reduced fees (resort guests, twilight, juniors), range (grass), club rentals, lodging, credit cards (MC, V, AE, D).
Reader Comments: Enjoyed every hole ... Unrecognized beauty ... Two great courses ... Nice—not as pretty as Cliffs ... Difficult greens ... Old course wide open, new course tight as flossing teeth ... Nice view of Lake Whitney ... Tight, excellent greens, tougher than it looks... Great condition, great accommodations.

★★★½ WILLOW SPRINGS GOLF CLUB
PM-202 Coliseum Rd., San Antonio, 78219, Bexar County, (210)226-6721.
Holes: 18. **Yards:** 7,221/5,631. **Par:** 72/72. **Course Rating:** 73.9/72.5. **Slope:** 134/120. **Green Fee:** $14/$17. **Cart Fee:** $18/cart. **Walking Policy:** Unrestricted walking. **Walkability:** 2. **Opened:** 1923. **Architect:** Emil Loeffler/John McGlynn. **Season:** Year-round. **High:** Nov.-Aug. **To obtain tee times:** Call in advance. **Miscellaneous:** Reduced fees (weekdays, twilight, seniors, juniors), metal spikes, club rentals, credit cards (MC, V, AE, D).
Reader Comments: Muny course, major challenge ... Needs some TLC, but good challenge of golf ... My home course, challenging risks & rewards for long hitters ... Needs driving range to warm up ... Fun, good test.

WINDROSE GOLF COURSE
PU-6235 Pinelakes Blvd., Spring, 77379, Harris County, (281)370-8900, 20 miles NW of Houston. **E-mail:** windrosegolfclub@pdq.net.

Holes: 18. **Yards:** 7,203/5,355. **Par:** 72/72. **Course Rating:** 73.0/N/A. **Slope:** 128/N/A. **Green Fee:** $50/$60. **Cart Fee:** Included in Green Fee. **Walking Policy:** Mandatory cart. **Walkability:** 2. **Opened:** 1998. **Architect:** Rick Forester. **Season:** Year-round. **High:** April-June/Sept.-Nov. **To obtain tee times:** Call 3 days in advance. **Miscellaneous:** Reduced fees (weekdays, twilight, seniors, juniors), range (grass), club rentals, credit cards (MC, V, AE), beginner friendly.

★★★ WOODLAKE COUNTRY CLUB

SP-6500 Woodlake Pkwy, San Antonio, 78244, Bexar County, (210)661-6124.
Special Notes: Call club for further information..

★★½ WOODLAND HILLS GOLF COURSE

PU-319 Woodland Hills Dr., Nacogdoches, 75961, Nacogdoches County, (409)564-2762, 120 miles NE of Houston.
Holes: 18. **Yards:** 6,620/5,069. **Par:** 72/73. **Course Rating:** 72.6/72.9. **Slope:** 133/123. **Green Fee:** $10/$19. **Cart Fee:** $10/person. **Walking Policy:** Unrestricted walking. **Walkability:** 5.
Opened: 1972. **Architect:** Don January/Bill Martindale. **Season:** Year-round. **High:** April-Aug.
Miscellaneous: Reduced fees (weekdays, twilight, seniors, juniors), metal spikes, range (grass), club rentals, credit cards (MC, V), beginner friendly.
Reader Comments: Interesting variety of holes ... Tight fairways, requires all your clubs ... Too many blind shots to ravines! ... Getting better ... Great layout, trees, trees, trees ... Long and open–lots of slope changes.

THE WOODLANDS RESORT & COUNTRY CLUB

★★★★ NORTH COURSE

R-2301 N. Millbend Dr., The Woodlands, 77380, Montgomery County, (281)367-1100, 22 miles N of Houston.
Holes: 18. **Yards:** 6,881/5,245. **Par:** 72/72. **Course Rating:** 72.2/72.1. **Slope:** 126/120. **Green Fee:** $55/$75. **Cart Fee:** $14/person. **Walking Policy:** Unrestricted walking. **Walkability:** 3.
Opened: 1976. **Architect:** Joe Lee. **Season:** Year-round. **High:** Spring/Fall. **To obtain tee times:** Call. **Miscellaneous:** Reduced fees (weekdays, low season, twilight, juniors), discount packages, metal spikes, range (grass/mats), club rentals, lodging (400 rooms), credit cards (MC, V, AE, D).
Reader Comments: Nice resort course, great meeting facility.... Lots of trees, hit 'em straight.... Nice but expensive. Too many bunkers ... Good shape. Greens like glass (slick) ... The course is always ready for a tournament ... Worth the time.... Excellent merchandise in shop.

★★★★ TPC AT THE WOODLANDS

PU-1730 S. Millbend Dr., The Woodlands, 77380, Montgomery County, (281)367-7285, 25 miles N of Houston.
Holes: 18. **Yards:** 7,018/5,326. **Par:** 72/72. **Course Rating:** 73.7/72.1. **Slope:** 136/128. **Green Fee:** $90/$130. **Cart Fee:** Included in Green Fee. **Walking Policy:** Unrestricted walking.
Walkability: 2. **Opened:** 1985. **Architect:** von Hagge/Devlin. **Season:** Year-round. **High:** April-Oct. **To obtain tee times:** Call up to 7 days in advance. **Miscellaneous:** Reduced fees (weekdays, twilight, juniors), discount packages, metal spikes, range (grass/mats), club rentals, lodging, credit cards (MC, V, AE, D).
Notes: Ranked 22nd in 1999 Best in State. Shell Houston Open site.
Reader Comments: Fun to play–a real treat ... A little pricey ... Beautiful facility-good service ... Very well maintained, exciting course ... Lots of good golf shots to make ... It's a championship course for everyone ... Nos.17 and 18 are 2 of the most challenging par 4s ... Nice staff, long, difficult course.

★★ WORLD HOUSTON GOLF CLUB

PU-4000 Greens Rd., Houston, 77032, Harris County, (281)449-8384.
Holes: 18. **Yards:** 6,642/5,204. **Par:** 72/72. **Course Rating:** 71.2/71.4. **Slope:** 119/123. **Green Fee:** $19/$29. **Cart Fee:** Included in Green Fee. **Walking Policy:** Unrestricted walking.
Walkability: 1. **Architect:** Garrett Gill/George B. Williams. **Season:** Year-round. **High:** March-Oct. **To obtain tee times:** Call golf shop. **Miscellaneous:** Reduced fees (low season, twilight, seniors, juniors), discount packages, metal spikes, club rentals, credit cards (MC, V, AE).

★★½ Z BOAZ GOLF COURSE

PM-3240 Lackland Rd., Fort Worth, 76116, Tarrant County, (817)738-6287.
Holes: 18. **Yards:** 6,033/4,782. **Par:** 70/70. **Course Rating:** 69.6/68.0. **Slope:** 124/107. **Green Fee:** $11/$13. **Cart Fee:** $19/cart. **Walking Policy:** Unrestricted walking. **Walkability:** 3.
Opened: 1937. **Architect:** Ralph Plummer. **Season:** Year-round. **High:** April-Aug. **To obtain tee times:** Call Mondays after noon for the following week. Computer (817)926-4653.
Miscellaneous: Reduced fees (weekdays, low season, twilight, seniors, juniors), discount packages, club rentals, credit cards (MC, V, D).
Reader Comments: Short, average public course, heavily used ... A course that was neglected–getting better ... Good short course, convenient ... Much improved recently ... Course was recently taken back by the city. It is improving daily, it may soon be a good place to play.

THE BARN GOLF COURSE
PU-305 W. Pleasant View, Ogden, 84404, (801)782-7320.
Holes: 18. **Yards:** N/A. **Par:** N/A. **Course Rating:** N/A. **Slope:** N/A. **Green Fee:** N/A.
Walkability: N/A. **Architect:** Keith Downs.
Special Notes: Call club for further information.

★★ **BEN LOMOND GOLF COURSE**
PU-1800 N. Hwy. #89, Ogden, 84404, Weber County, (801)782-7754, 5 miles N of Ogden.
Holes: 18. **Yards:** 6,176/5,445. **Par:** 72/72. **Course Rating:** 67.2/68.6. **Slope:** 104/107. **Green Fee:** $14/$18. **Cart Fee:** $18/cart. **Walking Policy:** Unrestricted walking. **Walkability:** 1.
Opened: 1956. **Season:** March-Dec. **High:** May-Sept. **To obtain tee times:** Call Thursday for weekends and holidays. For weekdays call 1 day in advance. **Miscellaneous:** Reduced fees (seniors, juniors), club rentals, credit cards (MC, V).

★★★★ **BIRCH CREEK GOLF CLUB** *Value+, Pace+*
PU-550 East 100 North, Smithfield, 84335, Cache County, (435)563-6825, 7 miles N of Logan.
Holes: 18. **Yards:** 6,770/5,734. **Par:** 72/72. **Course Rating:** 71.6/70.7. **Slope:** 122/117. **Green Fee:** $18/N/A. **Cart Fee:** $18/cart. **Walking Policy:** Unrestricted walking. **Walkability:** 4.
Opened: 1953. **Architect:** Dale Schvaneveldt/Joseph B. Williams. **Season:** March-Nov. **High:** May-Sept. **To obtain tee times:** Call Monday for Tuesday/Wednesday, Wednesday for Thursday/Friday, Thursday for weekend and Monday. **Miscellaneous:** Reduced fees (seniors, juniors), range (grass/mats), club rentals, credit cards (MC, V, D).
Reader Comments: Greens are tough ... Grass is excellent ... Plenty of trees, gullies, and water... Very good for a rural area ... Beautiful setting ... Worth the 1-hour drive ... Keep it in play and you can score well ... Best kept secret in Utah ... Good layout with great par 3s ... Excellent value ... Solid golf course.

★★★½ **BONNEVILLE GOLF COURSE**
PU-954 Connor St., Salt Lake City, 84108, Salt Lake County, (801)583-9513, 4 miles SE of Saltlake.
Holes: 18. **Yards:** 6,824/5,860. **Par:** 72/74. **Course Rating:** 71.0/71.6. **Slope:** 120/119. **Green Fee:** $20/$20. **Cart Fee:** $20/cart. **Walking Policy:** Unrestricted walking. **Walkability:** 4.
Opened: 1929. **Architect:** William F. Bell. **Season:** March-Nov. **High:** April-Sept. **To obtain tee times:** Call tee-time number 7 days in advance or course 48 hours prior to day of play. **Miscellaneous:** Reduced fees (seniors, juniors), range (grass/mats), club rentals, credit cards (MC, V).
Reader Comments: Good variety of holes ... Beautiful scenery ... Hasn't changed in 30 years ... Excellent test of golf... Fun to play ... Outstanding view... Favorite to play in SLC ... Always in good shape ... Older course, but a great challenge ... Best in Salt Lake City.

★★★★ **BOUNTIFUL RIDGE GOLF COURSE** *Value+*
PU-2430 S. Bountiful Blvd., Bountiful, 84010, Davis County, (801)298-6040, 5 miles N of Salt Lake City.
Holes: 18. **Yards:** 6,523/5,098. **Par:** 71/72. **Course Rating:** 70.2/67.6. **Slope:** 122/116. **Green Fee:** $19/$21. **Cart Fee:** $10/person. **Walking Policy:** Unrestricted walking. **Walkability:** 4.
Opened: 1975. **Architect:** William H. Neff. **Season:** March-Nov. **High:** May-Aug. **To obtain tee times:** For weekdays call 6 days prior. Call Monday prior for Weekends/Holidays. Special fee book for out of state. **Miscellaneous:** Reduced fees (seniors, juniors), discount packages, club rentals, credit cards (MC, V).
Reader Comments: Many improvements ... Best bunkers in Utah ... Incredible view of the valley ... Mountainside golf, views of great Salt Lake ... Everything breaks to the lake ... Better keep it straight, especially off the tee ... Best muny around ... Don't miss this one ... Gorgeous views ... Perfect golf.

★★½ **CEDAR RIDGE GOLF COURSE**
PU-200 East 900 North, Cedar City, 84720, Iron County, (435)586-2970, 170 miles N of Las Vegas.
Holes: 18. **Yards:** 6,635/5,076. **Par:** 71/71. **Course Rating:** 69.7/68.5. **Slope:** 118/113. **Green Fee:** $20/$20. **Cart Fee:** $8/person. **Walking Policy:** Unrestricted walking. **Walkability:** 2.
Opened: 1962. **Season:** Feb.-Dec. **High:** May-Sept. **To obtain tee times:** Does not take them. **Miscellaneous:** Reduced fees (seniors), range (grass), club rentals, credit cards (MC, V).
Notes: Reader Comments: Great mountain course ... Always good condition ... Fast greens, great location, good challenge ... Excellent layout ... Short course with a few neat holes ... Bombs away on the wide open back 9 ... Great scenery.

★★★ **DAVIS PARK GOLF COURSE**
PU-1074 E. Nicholls Rd., Fruit Heights, 84037, Davis County, (801)546-4154, 17 miles N of Salt Lake City.
Holes: 18. **Yards:** 6,481/5,295. **Par:** 71/71. **Course Rating:** 69.3/68.7. **Slope:** 117/114. **Green Fee:** $17/$18. **Cart Fee:** $9/. **Walking Policy:** Unrestricted walking. **Walkability:** 2. **Opened:** 1964. **Architect:** Pierre Hualde/Ernie Schnieter. **Season:** March-Nov. **High:** May-Aug. **To obtain tee times:** Call 1 day in advance for weekdays and Thursday for upcoming weekend.

Miscellaneous: Reduced fees (weekdays, seniors, juniors), range (grass), club rentals, credit cards (MC, V).
Reader Comments: Good variety of shots required ... Great views, better walking course ... In great shape despite heavy play ... Able to score well ... Looks easier then it really is ... A hidden treasure ... Busy but a fun course.

DINALAND GOLF COURSE

PU-675 S. 2000 East, Vernal, 84078, (435)781-1428, 180 miles E of Salt Lake City.
Holes: 18. **Yards:** 6,773/5,094. **Par:** 72/72. **Course Rating:** 71.5/67.7. **Slope:** 129/116. **Green Fee:** $16/$18. **Cart Fee:** $17/cart. **Walking Policy:** Unrestricted walking. **Walkability:** 3.
Architect: Jim McPhiliomy. **Season:** March-Nov. **High:** June-Aug. **To obtain tee times:** Call 7 days in advance. Groups of 20 or more call 6 months in advance. **Miscellaneous:** Reduced fees (seniors, juniors), range (grass), club rentals, credit cards (MC, V), beginner friendly.

★★★ DIXIE RED HILLS GOLF CLUB

PU-645 West 1250 North, St. George, 84770, Washington County, (435)634-5852, 100 miles N of Las Vegas.
Holes: 9. **Yards:** 2,564/N/A. **Par:** 34/N/A. **Course Rating:** 65.9/N/A. **Slope:** 119/N/A. **Green Fee:** $25/$25. **Cart Fee:** $20/cart. **Walking Policy:** Unrestricted walking. **Walkability:** 1.
Opened: 1965. **Season:** Year-round. **High:** Oct.-May. **To obtain tee times:** Call. **Miscellaneous:** Reduced fees (low season), range (grass/mats), club rentals, credit cards (MC, V).
Reader Comments: Fun course ... Nice nine holes ... Love the Red Rocks ... Tougher than it looks ... Beautiful ... Best keep secret in Utah ... Nice holes at foot of mountains ... Scenic course; not long, but fun.

★★★ EAGLE MOUNTAIN GOLF COURSE

PU-960 E. 700 S., Brigham City, 84302, Box Elder County, (435)723-3212, 45 miles N of Salt Lake City.
Holes: 18. **Yards:** 6,769/4,767. **Par:** 71/71. **Course Rating:** 71.4/65.4. **Slope:** 119/101. **Green Fee:** $17/$18. **Cart Fee:** $9/person. **Walking Policy:** Unrestricted walking. **Walkability:** 4.
Opened: 1989. **Architect:** Bill Neff. **Season:** March-Nov. **High:** April-Sept. **To obtain tee times:** Call one day in advance for weekdays and two days in advance for weekends and holidays.
Miscellaneous: Range (grass), club rentals, credit cards (MC, V).
Reader Comments: Local course, well kept, hilly, lots of trouble ... Good service ... Front 9 is a challenging walk ... Pro shop is one of the best stocked ... Extremely popular course ... Back 9 interesting ... Carry your bag and be in shape .... Every hole is a new challenge—wind, hills.

★★★½ EAGLEWOOD GOLF COURSE

PU-1110 E. Eaglewood Dr., North Salt Lake City, 84054, Davis County, (801)299-0088, 10 miles N of Salt Lake City.
Holes: 18. **Yards:** 6,800/5,200. **Par:** 71/71. **Course Rating:** 71.1/68.8. **Slope:** 121/112. **Green Fee:** $20/$20. **Cart Fee:** $10/person. **Walking Policy:** Unrestricted walking. **Walkability:** 4.
Opened: 1994. **Architect:** Keith Foster. **Season:** March-Nov. **High:** June-Aug. **To obtain tee times:** Call two days in advance. **Miscellaneous:** Reduced fees (weekdays, low season, juniors), discount packages, metal spikes, range (grass), club rentals, credit cards (MC, V).
Reader Comments: Fun mountain course ... Beautiful setting ... Lots of water and hazards ... Lies high above Salt Lake Flats ... Interesting layout ... Hard to walk ... Nice clubhouse ... Tough course from back tees ... Houses too close ... Too many blind shots ... Hard to believe quality and challenges for the cost.

★★★★½ ENTRADA AT SNOW CANYON *Pace*

R-2511 W. Entrada Trail, St. George, 84770, Washington County, (435)674-7500, 325 miles S of Salt Lake City. **E-mail:** steveshapgolfentrada.com. **Web:** www.golfentrada.com.
Holes: 18. **Yards:** 7,262/5,454. **Par:** 72/72. **Course Rating:** 74.4/70.8. **Slope:** 127/121. **Green Fee:** $25/$75. **Cart Fee:** Included in Green Fee. **Walking Policy:** Mandatory cart. **Walkability:** 3. **Opened:** 1996. **Architect:** Johnny Miller/Fred Bliss. **Season:** Year-round. **High:** Oct.-May. **To obtain tee times:** Call 30 days in advance. **Miscellaneous:** Reduced fees (low season, twilight), discount packages, range (grass), club rentals, credit cards (MC, V, AE).
Notes: Ranked 2nd in 1999 Best in State.
Reader Comments: A tough but beautiful course ... Exceptional beauty ... Lava rock rough is too tough ... Good value, I'll be back ... Bring your A+ game .... The front is idyllic, the back 9 a volcanic nightmare ... Test of your skills ... My favorite; great rewards for great risks ... Hawaii, Cabo, Troon and Pebble all in one! ... Golf in the wild west set near red cliffs.

★★★ GLADSTAN GOLF CLUB

PU-One Gladstan Dr., Payson, 84651, Utah County, (801)465-2549, (800)634-3009, 20 miles S of Provo.
Holes: 18. **Yards:** 6,509/4,782. **Par:** 71/71. **Course Rating:** 70.7/67.4. **Slope:** 121/111. **Green Fee:** $16/$17. **Cart Fee:** $15/. **Walking Policy:** Unrestricted walking. **Walkability:** 5. **Opened:** 1988. **Architect:** William Howard Neff. **Season:** March-Nov. **High:** May-Aug. **To obtain tee**

times: Call Monday for the following week. **Miscellaneous:** Reduced fees (seniors, juniors), discount packages, metal spikes, range (grass/mats), club rentals, credit cards (MC, V, AE, D).
Reader Comments: Two completely different 9s ... Memorable holes ... Fine mountain course ... Beautiful mountain setting ... Never crowded ... Exciting back 9 ... Lots of scrub oak! Bring extra balls! ... Good staff ... Short, tight ... Elevation changes ... Not boring.

★★ GLENDALE GOLF COURSE
PU-1630 W. 2100 S., Salt Lake City, 84119, Salt Lake County, (801)974-2403
Holes: 18. **Yards:** 6,908/5,815. **Par:** 72/73. **Course Rating:** 70.9/72.5. **Slope:** 117/120. **Green Fee:** $18/$18. **Cart Fee:** $20/cart. **Walking Policy:** Unrestricted walking. **Walkability:** 1.
Opened: 1973. **Architect:** William F. Bell. **Season:** March-Nov. **High:** May-Aug. **To obtain tee times:** Call tee-time number 7 days in advance or golf shop 1 day in advance. **Miscellaneous:** Reduced fees (weekdays, seniors, juniors), metal spikes, range (grass), club rentals, credit cards (MC, V, D).

★★ GLENMOOR GOLF & COUNTRY CLUB
PU-9800 S. 4800 W., South Jordan, 84095, Salt Lake County, (801)280-1742, 12 miles SW of Salt Lake City.
Holes: 18. **Yards:** 6,900/5,800. **Par:** 72/72. **Course Rating:** 71.3/71.5. **Slope:** 121/121. **Green Fee:** $20/$20. **Cart Fee:** $20/cart. **Walking Policy:** Unrestricted walking. **Walkability:** 3.
Opened: 1965. **Architect:** William H. Neff. **Season:** Year-round. **High:** May-Sept. **To obtain tee times:** Call 7 days in advance. Call Monday for Tuesday-Thursday. Call Thursday for Sat., Sunday and Monday. **Miscellaneous:** Reduced fees (low season, seniors), range (grass), club rentals, credit cards (MC, V).

★★★★ THE GOLF CLUB AT THANKSGIVING POINT *Service*
PU-10650 Northwest Frontage Rd., Lehi, 84043, (801)768-7400
Holes: 18. **Yards:** N/A. **Par:** N/A. **Course Rating:** N/A. **Slope:** N/A. **Green Fee:** N/A.
Walkability: N/A. **Opened:** 1997. **Architect:** Johnny Miller/Fred Bliss.
Notes: Ranked 1st in 1999 Best in State.
Reader Comments: Great course ... Incredible layout ... The greatest course in the intermountain area ... If I could justify it financially I'd play it every time ... Bring your 'A' game ... Outstanding, new course ... Tough in the wind ... Many many recently planted trees ... Needs to mature.

★★★½ GREEN SPRING GOLF COURSE
PU-588 N. Green Spring Dr., Washington, 84780, Washington County, (435)673-7888, 2 miles N of St. George.
Holes: 18. **Yards:** 6,562/4,887. **Par:** 71/71. **Course Rating:** 71.9/68.9. **Slope:** 130/118. **Green Fee:** $20/$32. **Cart Fee:** $10/person. **Walking Policy:** Unrestricted walking. **Walkability:** 4.
Opened: 1989. **Architect:** Gene Bates. **Season:** Year-round. **High:** Oct.-May. **To obtain tee times:** Call 30 to 60 days in advance. 1st day of month for next month. Example: May 1st for June. **Miscellaneous:** Reduced fees (weekdays, low season, twilight, juniors), discount packages, range (grass/mats), club rentals, credit cards (MC, V).
Notes: Ranked 9th in 1999 Best in State.
Reader Comments: One of the best in Utah ... Fun to play ... Some memorable holes ... Good layout ... Great natural features ... Tough to walk, but worth it ... Natural desert golf, not 'tricked up'... Excellent bargain—a must in in St. George ... Wonderful vistas ... Great service ... Houses going up like weeds, still fun though ... Canyon holes great ... Like hitting over Grand Canyon.

HILL AFB GOLF COURSE
Bldg. 720, Hill AFB, 84056, (801)777-1108
Holes: 18.
Special Notes: Call club for further information.

★★★★½ HOBBLE CREEK GOLF CLUB *Value+*
PU-E. Hobble Creek Canyon Rd., Springville, 84663, Utah County, (801)489-6297, 15 miles S of Provo.
Holes: 18. **Yards:** 6,315/5,435. **Par:** 71/73. **Course Rating:** 69.4/69.5. **Slope:** 120/117. **Green Fee:** $9/$18. **Cart Fee:** $20/person. **Walking Policy:** Unrestricted walking. **Walkability:** 3.
Opened: 1966. **Architect:** William F. Bell. **Season:** March-Nov. **High:** July-Sept. **To obtain tee times:** Call Monday for Tuesday through the following Monday. **Miscellaneous:** Reduced fees (seniors, juniors), metal spikes, range (grass), club rentals, credit cards (MC, V).
Reader Comments: Best in the state ... Worth the drive ... Mountain golf with hint of Augusta! ... Great day of golf ... Great Canyon course ... Beautiful mountain setting ... Spectacular fall colors ... Peaceful setting... Fun course design ... Friendly staff.

★★★½ HOMESTEAD GOLF CLUB
R-700 N. Homestead Dr., Midway, 84049, Wasatch County, (435)654-5588, (800)327-7220, SE of Salt Lake City. **E-mail:** homesteadresort.com. **Web:** www.homesteadresort.com.
Holes: 18. **Yards:** 7,017/5,091. **Par:** 72/72. **Course Rating:** 73.0/68.8. **Slope:** 135/118. **Green Fee:** $25/$45. **Cart Fee:** $10/person. **Walking Policy:** Unrestricted walking. **Walkability:** 3.

Opened: 1990. **Architect:** Bruce Summerhays. **Season:** April-Oct. **High:** June-Sept. **To obtain tee times:** Hotel guests call 30 days in advance, others call one week in advance. **Miscellaneous:** Reduced fees (weekdays, low season, resort guests, twilight, seniors), discount packages, range (grass), club rentals, lodging (155 rooms), credit cards (MC, V, AE, D, Diners Club). **Reader Comments:** Beautiful mountain course ... Upper 9 is great new course ... Lots of fun! ... Rather long ... Personnel very accommodating ... Resort course, lots of rental bags.

★★½ LAKESIDE GOLF COURSE
PU-1201 N. 1100 W., West Bountiful, 84087, Davis County, (801)295-1019, 10 miles N of Salt Lake City.
Holes: 18. **Yards:** 6,030/4,895. **Par:** 71/71. **Course Rating:** 67.2/66.5. **Slope:** 113/115. **Green Fee:** $17/$18. **Cart Fee:** $9/person. **Walking Policy:** Unrestricted walking. **Walkability:** 1. **Opened:** 1966. **Architect:** William H. Neff. **Season:** March-Oct. **High:** June-Aug. **To obtain tee times:** Call Mondays for Tuesday-Friday. Call Thursday for Saturday, Sunday and Monday. **Miscellaneous:** Reduced fees (seniors, juniors), range (grass/mats), club rentals, credit cards (MC, V, D).
Reader Comments: Wide open ... Short, easy holes ... Nice course, great for practice rounds ... Lots of diverse shots ...Family oriented.

LOGAN GOLF & COUNTRY CLUB
SP-710 N. 15th E, Logan, 84321, (801)753-6050
Holes: 18.
Special Notes: Call club for further information.

★★★½ LOGAN RIVER GOLF COURSE
PU-550 W. 1000 S., Logan, 84321, Cache County, (435)750-0123, (888)750-0123, 80 miles N of Salt Lake City.
Holes: 18. **Yards:** 6,502/5,048. **Par:** 71/71. **Course Rating:** 70.5/78.9. **Slope:** 124/117. **Green Fee:** $17/$17. **Cart Fee:** $9/. **Walking Policy:** Unrestricted walking. **Walkability:** 2. **Opened:** 1993. **Architect:** Robert Muir Graves. **Season:** March-Oct. **High:** June-Sept. **To obtain tee times:** Call 7 days in advance. **Miscellaneous:** Reduced fees (seniors, juniors), range (grass), club rentals, credit cards (MC, V).
Reader Comments: Tightest course I've ever played ... Need to hit it straight.. Humbling design ... Hard! In spectacular condition ... Tough course! Accuracy is critical.

★★ MEADOW BROOK GOLF COURSE
PU-4197 S. 1300 W., Taylorsville, 84123, Salt Lake County, (801)266-0971, 4 miles S of Salt Lake City.
Holes: 18. **Yards:** 6,800/5,605. **Par:** 72/72. **Course Rating:** 70.0/67.9. **Slope:** 110/104. **Green Fee:** $17/$18. **Cart Fee:** $17/. **Walking Policy:** Unrestricted walking. **Walkability:** 1. **Opened:** 1953. **Architect:** Mick Riley. **Season:** March-Dec. **High:** May-Oct. **To obtain tee times:** Call golf shop. **Miscellaneous:** Reduced fees (weekdays, seniors, juniors), metal spikes, range (grass), caddies, club rentals.
Notes: 1955 Utah Open.

MILLSITE GOLF COURSE
PU-Canyon Rd., Ferron, 84523, (801)384-2887.
Holes: 18. **Architect:** Scott Truman.
Special Notes: Call club for further information.

★★★★ MOAB GOLF CLUB *Value+*
PU-2705 S.E. Bench Rd., Moab, 84532, Grand County, (435)259-6488, 220 miles E of Salt Lake City.
Holes: 18. **Yards:** 6,819/4,725. **Par:** 72/72. **Course Rating:** 72.2/69.6. **Slope:** 125/110. **Green Fee:** $20/$20. **Cart Fee:** $10/person. **Walking Policy:** Unrestricted walking. **Walkability:** 3. **Opened:** 1960. **Season:** Year-round. **High:** Spring/Fall. **To obtain tee times:** Call 30 days in advance with credit card. **Miscellaneous:** Reduced fees (juniors), discount packages, range (grass), club rentals, credit cards (MC, V).
Reader Comments: Beautiful layout in the Red Rock hills ... Back 9 great ... Great course, great views, great people ... Blend of old and new 9s ... Red Rocks and green grass, most beautiful course in the state.

★★★ MOUNT OGDEN GOLF COURSE
PU-1787 Constitution Way, Ogden, 84403, Weber County, (801)629-8700
Holes: 18. **Yards:** 6,300/4,980. **Par:** 71/72. **Course Rating:** 70.5/69.5. **Slope:** 121/111. **Green Fee:** $18/$18. **Cart Fee:** $10/person. **Walking Policy:** Unrestricted walking. **Walkability:** 5. **Opened:** 1985. **Architect:** Bill Neff. **Season:** March-Nov. **High:** April-Oct. **To obtain tee times:** Call on Wednesday for weekend tee times. Weekdays, call one day in advance. **Miscellaneous:** Reduced fees (seniors, juniors), range (grass), club rentals, credit cards (MC, V).
Reader Comments: Spectacular views and challenging course ... Must take two extra sleeves .... Challenging for long drives, pay attention! ... Great views ... Narrow course.

MOUNTAIN DELL GOLF CLUB

PU-Parleys Canyon, Salt Lake City, 84109, Salt Lake County, (801)582-3812, 6 miles E of Salt Lake City.

★★★½ CANYON COURSE

Holes: 18. **Yards:** 6,787/5,447. **Par:** 72/73. **Course Rating:** 71.3/71.1. **Slope:** 126/112. **Green Fee:** $20/$20. **Cart Fee:** $10/person. **Walking Policy:** Unrestricted walking. **Walkability:** 5. **Opened:** 1962. **Architect:** William H. Neff. **Season:** April-Nov. **High:** June-Aug. **To obtain tee times:** Call tee-time system. **Miscellaneous:** Reduced fees (weekdays, twilight, seniors, juniors), range (grass), club rentals, credit cards (MC, V).

Reader Comments: Mix of old and new holes ... Challenge for low handicappers ... Canyon makes putting tough ... Well maintained ... Ball carries a long way in high altitude ... Seldom hot ... Mountain setting ... My favorite two courses ... Easier course than the Lake Course ... Back 9 fun ... Good value.

★★★½ LAKE COURSE

Holes: 18. **Yards:** 6,709/5,066. **Par:** 71/71. **Course Rating:** 72.2/67.6. **Slope:** 129/109. **Green Fee:** $20/$20. **Cart Fee:** $10/person. **Walking Policy:** Unrestricted walking. **Walkability:** 5. **Opened:** 1991. **Architect:** William H. Neff. **Season:** April-Nov. **High:** June-Aug. **To obtain tee times:** Call tee-time number. **Miscellaneous:** Reduced fees (weekdays, twilight, seniors, juniors), range (grass), club rentals, credit cards (MC, V).

Reader Comments: Almost as tough as the Canyon Course ... Little room for mistakes ... Must be able to hit long drives over canyons ... Beautiful setting, excellent public course ... Great price.

★★ MOUNTAIN VIEW GOLF CLUB

PU-2400 W. 8660 S., West Jordan, 84084, Salt Lake County, (801)255-9211, 10 miles S of Salt Lake City.

Holes: 18. **Yards:** 6,764/5,827. **Par:** 72/72. **Course Rating:** 70.2/69.9. **Slope:** 112/118. **Green Fee:** $10/$20. **Cart Fee:** $20/cart. **Walking Policy:** Unrestricted walking. **Walkability:** 1. **Opened:** 1968. **Architect:** William H. Neff. **Season:** Feb.-Dec. **High:** May-Sept. **To obtain tee times:** Call Monday for Tuesday, Wednesday, Thursday, Friday. Call Thursday for Saturday, Sunday and Monday. **Miscellaneous:** Reduced fees (seniors, juniors), range (grass), club rentals, credit cards (MC, V), beginner friendly.

★★½ MURRAY PARKWAY GOLF CLUB

PU-6345 S. Murray Pkwy. Ave., Murray, 84123, Salt Lake County, (801)262-4653, 8 miles S of Salt Lake City.

Holes: 18. **Yards:** 6,800/5,800. **Par:** 72/72. **Course Rating:** 71.3/71.0. **Slope:** 120/118. **Green Fee:** $19/$19. **Cart Fee:** $10/person. **Walking Policy:** Unrestricted walking. **Walkability:** 1. **Opened:** 1986. **Architect:** Robert Muir Graves. **Season:** March-Nov. **High:** June-Aug. **To obtain tee times:** Call Monday for Tuesday-Friday tee times. Call Thursday for Saturday, Sunday and Monday. We start accepting calls 7:00 a.m. Monday and Thursday. **Miscellaneous:** Reduced fees (juniors), range (grass), club rentals, credit cards (MC, V, D).

Reader Comments: Hard to get on ... Short yardage, fun and popular, nice hilly contours ... Bumps and mounds impart character... Great view of surrounding mountains. Great pullcarts ... Always a fun experience in the wind ... Don't let flat fool you; it bites ... Open course, next to a busy highway.

OLD MILL GOLF CLUB

PU-6080 S. Wasatch Blvd., Salt Lake City, 84121, Salt Lake County County, (801)424-1302, 10 miles S of Salt Lake City.

Holes: 18. **Yards:** 6,769/5,618. **Par:** 71/71. **Course Rating:** 69.9/68.3. **Slope:** 125/115. **Green Fee:** $24/$24. **Cart Fee:** $11/person. **Walking Policy:** Unrestricted walking. **Walkability:** 4. **Opened:** 1998. **Architect:** Gene Bates. **Season:** March-Nov. **High:** May-Aug. **To obtain tee times:** Call 7 days in advance. **Miscellaneous:** Range (grass/mats), club rentals, credit cards (MC, V, AE).

★★★ PARK CITY GOLF COURSE

PU-Lower Park Ave., Park City, 84060, Summit County, (801)615-5800, 25 miles SE of Salt Lake City.

Holes: 18. **Yards:** 6,754/5,600. **Par:** 72/72. **Course Rating:** 71.7/71.4. **Slope:** 127/123. **Green Fee:** $20/$33. **Cart Fee:** $12/person. **Walking Policy:** Unrestricted walking. **Walkability:** 3. **Opened:** 1963. **Architect:** Bill Neff. **Season:** April-Oct. **High:** May-Sept. **To obtain tee times:** Call seven days in advance. Two or more tee times require a credit card. **Miscellaneous:** Reduced fees (low season), range (mats), club rentals, credit cards (MC, V, AE, D).

Reader Comments: Look out for moose ... Park City's best course; scenery great ... Played golf and skied the same day ... Ball goes long way ... Tricky breaks on greens ... What a great way to spend the day.

★★½ THE RESERVE AT EAST BAY

PU-1860 S. E. Bay Blvd., Provo, 84601, Utah County, (801)373-6262, 49 miles S of Salt Lake City.

Holes: 27. Yards: 6,932/5,125. Par: 72/72. Course Rating: 72.1/66.6. Slope: 123/106. Green Fee: $20/$22. Cart Fee: $20/cart. Walking Policy: Unrestricted walking. Walkability: 2. Opened: 1986. Architect: William H. Neff. Season: March-Nov. High: May-Sept. To obtain tee times: Call 1 day in advance. May call Thursday for weekend reservations. Miscellaneous: Reduced fees (twilight), range (grass), club rentals, credit cards (MC, V, AE, D).
Reader Comments: Recent improvements make course more playable ... The water hazards!! ... Need marshals and better maintenance ... Greens are challenging ... Lots of water.

★★★ RIVERBEND GOLF COURSE
PU-12800 S. 1040 W., Riverton, 84065, Salt Lake County, (801)253-3673, 15 miles S of Salt Lake City.
Holes: 18. Yards: 6,876/5,081. Par: 72/72. Course Rating: 69.9/68.7. Slope: 118/111. Green Fee: $18/$22. Cart Fee: $10/person. Walking Policy: Unrestricted walking. Walkability: 5. Opened: 1995. Architect: Gene Bates. Season: Year-round. High: April-Oct. To obtain tee times: Call Thursday for upcoming weekend. Miscellaneous: Reduced fees (seniors, juniors), range (grass), club rentals, credit cards (MC, V).
Reader Comments: Makes me feel as if I'm playing the PGA ... Many elevation changes ... Great setting ... Use all your clubs ... Great cheeseburger! ... Excellent course, fair greens ... Two distinct 9s ... Good personnel... Course has character... Good variety of holes ... Neat layout with a lot of sand ... Wind a constant companion ... Unique back 9.

ROOSEVELT GOLF COURSE
PU-1155 Clubhouse Dr., Roosevelt, 84066, (801)722-9644
Holes: 18.
Special Notes: Call club for further information.

★★ ROSE PARK GOLF CLUB
PU-1386 N. Redwood Rd., Salt Lake City, 84116, Salt Lake County, (801)596-5030, 5 miles NW of Salt Lake City.
Holes: 18. Yards: 6,696/5,816. Par: 72/75. Course Rating: 69.6/70.8. Slope: 109/112. Green Fee: $17/$18. Cart Fee: $10/person. Walking Policy: Unrestricted walking. Walkability: 2. Opened: 1960. Architect: Mick Riley/William F. Bell. Season: Feb.-Dec. High: May-Sept. To obtain tee times: Call 7 days in advance. Miscellaneous: Reduced fees (seniors, juniors), range (grass), club rentals, credit cards (MC, V).

★★½ ROUND VALLEY COUNTRY CLUB
PU-1875 E Round Valley Rd., Morgan, 84050, Morgan County, (801)829-3796, 3 miles E of Morgan. E-mail: rdvlygolf@aol.com.
Holes: 18. Yards: 6,732/5,153. Par: 72/72. Course Rating: 71.5/69.0. Slope: 122/114. Green Fee: $18/N/A. Walking Policy: Unrestricted walking. Walkability: 3. Season: Year-round. High: June-Oct. Miscellaneous: Reduced fees (weekdays, seniors, juniors), range (grass), club rentals, credit cards (MC, V, AE, D).
Reader Comments: Nice country course ... Water in play on nearly every hole ... Good views ... Has on-course campground ... Several tight holes along Weber River, new back 9 ... Lots of water on front 9.

★★½ ST. GEORGE GOLF CLUB
PU-2190 S. 1400 E., St. George, 84790, Washington County, (435)634-5854, 110 miles NE of Las Vegas.
Holes: 18. Yards: 7,213/5,197. Par: 73/73. Course Rating: 71.7/68.9. Slope: 123/114. Green Fee: $35/$35. Cart Fee: $20/person. Walking Policy: Unrestricted walking. Walkability: 3. Opened: 1975. Architect: David Bingaman. Season: Year-round. High: Oct.-May. To obtain tee times: Call 14 days in advance. Miscellaneous: Reduced fees (low season), club rentals, credit cards (MC, V).
Reader Comments: Accuracy a must ... Great for seniors ... Much improved over past years ... Excellent greens ... Great winter getaway ... Great walking course ... Basic golf ... Best golf for price in St. George ... More great views ... Nice clubhouse ... Good staff ... Good golf experience.

★★★ SCHNEITER'S BLUFF AT WEST POINT
PU-300 N. 3500 W., West Point, 84015, Davis County, (801)773-0731, 20 miles N of Salt Lake City.
Holes: 18. Yards: 6,833/5,419. Par: 72/72. Course Rating: 70.2/67.3. Slope: 115/113. Green Fee: $18/$18. Cart Fee: $18/cart. Walking Policy: Unrestricted walking. Walkability: 2. Opened: 1995. Architect: E. Schneiter/B. Schneiter/J. Schneiter. Season: Feb.-Nov. High: June-Sept. To obtain tee times: Call Thursday for upcoming weekend. Call 1 day in advance for weekday. Miscellaneous: Reduced fees (seniors, juniors), discount packages, range (grass), club rentals, credit cards (MC, V, D).
Reader Comments: Great winter golf ... Well maintained ... Fun course ... Good staff ... Flat course, wide fairways, few bunkers ... Short but difficult layout ... Swing away, good winter course in Utah.

★½ SCHNEITER'S PEBBLE BROOK LINKS

PU-8968 South 1300 E., Sandy, 84094, Salt Lake County, (801)566-2181, 7 miles SE of Salt Lake City.

Holes: 18. **Yards:** 4,469/4,121. **Par:** 68/68. **Course Rating:** 63.6/66.8. **Slope:** 100/106. **Green Fee:** $16/$18. **Cart Fee:** $18/cart. **Walking Policy:** Unrestricted walking. **Walkability:** 4. **Opened:** 1974. **Architect:** Schneiter Golf. **Season:** Year-round. **High:** April-Oct. **To obtain tee times:** Call tee-time number. **Miscellaneous:** Reduced fees (seniors, juniors), metal spikes, range (grass/mats), club rentals, credit cards (MC, V, AE, D), beginner friendly (junior golf programs).

★★★ SCHNEITER'S RIVERSIDE GOLF COURSE

PU-5460 S. Weber Dr., Ogden, 84405, Weber County, (801)399-4636, 30 miles N of Salt Lake City.

Holes: 18. **Yards:** 6,177/5,217. **Par:** 71/71. **Course Rating:** 68.4/68.5. **Slope:** 114/113. **Green Fee:** $18/$18. **Cart Fee:** $18/cart. **Walking Policy:** Walking at certain times. **Walkability:** 2. **Opened:** 1961. **Architect:** Ernie Schneiter . **Season:** March-Nov. **High:** May-Sept. **To obtain tee times:** Call Thursday for upcoming weekend. For weekday call one day in advance. **Miscellaneous:** Reduced fees (seniors, juniors), range (grass/mats), club rentals, credit cards (MC, V, AE, D), beginner friendly.

Reader Comments: Excellent, mature public course ... Course is always in excellent shape ... Fun place to play, but crowded ... Making great improvements ... Short; tight; treelined; friendly staff.

★★½ SHERWOOD HILLS RESORT GOLF COURSE

R-Highway 89-91, Wellsville, 84339, Cache County, (435)245-6055, 6 miles S of Logan.

Holes: 9. **Yards:** 3,315/2,830. **Par:** 36/37. **Course Rating:** 69.8/70.5. **Slope:** 109/111. **Green Fee:** $18/$19. **Cart Fee:** $20/cart. **Walking Policy:** Unrestricted walking. **Walkability:** 3. **Opened:** 1973. **Architect:** Mark Dixon Ballif. **Season:** April-Nov. **High:** June-Aug. **To obtain tee times:** Call anytime in advance. **Miscellaneous:** Reduced fees (weekdays, resort guests, seniors), discount packages, range (grass), club rentals, lodging (85 rooms), credit cards (MC, V).

Reader Comments: Short par 5s, great view in the fall ... A great walking course ... Comfy little course, seldom crowded ... some narrow holes ... Deer and other wildlife ... Great service.

★★★½ SKY MOUNTAIN GOLF COURSE

PU-1030 N 2600 W, Hurricane, 84737, Washington County, (435)635-7888.

Holes: 18. **Yards:** 6,312/5,044. **Par:** 72/72. **Course Rating:** 69.9/66.4. **Slope:** 115/107. **Green Fee:** $16/$27. **Cart Fee:** $9/person. **Walking Policy:** Unrestricted walking. **Walkability:** 4. **Opened:** 1994. **Architect:** Jeff Hardin. **Season:** Year-round. **High:** Oct.-May. **To obtain tee times:** Call Monday beginning at 7:00 a.m. for following Monday-Sunday. **Miscellaneous:** Range (grass), club rentals, credit cards (MC, V, AE, D).

Reader Comments: Great setting, but windy ... Beautiful course with beautiful views ... In Phoenix would be $150 ... Like playing in the sky ... Friendly staff... Play it twice, the scenery alone makes it worth it ... Loved this course so much played it twice.

SOUTH MOUNTAIN GOLF CLUB

PU-1247 E. Rambling Rd., Draper, 84020, Salt Lake County, (801)495-0500. **E-mail:** southmountaingolf@juno.com. **Web:** www.southmountaingolf.com.

Holes: 18. **Yards:** 7,080/5,165. **Par:** 72/72. **Course Rating:** 73.4/69.8. **Slope:** 130/118. **Green Fee:** $45/$80. **Cart Fee:** Included in Green Fee. **Walking Policy:** Mandatory cart. **Walkability:** N/A. **Opened:** 1998. **Architect:** David Graham/Gary Panks. **Season:** Year-round. **High:** April-Oct. **To obtain tee times:** Call 7 days in advance. **Miscellaneous:** Reduced fees (weekdays, low season, twilight, juniors), club rentals, credit cards (MC, V, AE, D).

Notes: Ranked 3rd in 1999 Best in State.

★★½ SOUTHGATE GOLF CLUB

PM-1975 S. Tonaquint Dr., St. George, 84770, Washington County, (435)628-0000, 120 miles N of Las Vegas.

Holes: 18. **Yards:** 6,138/5,504. **Par:** 70/70. **Course Rating:** 70.3/66.8. **Slope:** 121/112. **Green Fee:** $25/$25. **Cart Fee:** $20/cart. **Walking Policy:** Unrestricted walking. **Walkability:** 3. **Opened:** 1984. **Architect:** William Neff. **Season:** Year-round. **High:** Oct.-May. **To obtain tee times:** Call 14 days weeks in advance. **Miscellaneous:** Reduced fees (low season, juniors), range (grass/mats), club rentals, credit cards (MC, V).

Reader Comments: Front nine needs work ... Tough course, well laid out ... Very accommodating ... Back 9 best part of course ... Super golf pro instructor ... Fairly flat, open fairways.

★★½ SPANISH OAKS GOLF CLUB

PU-2300 E. Powerhouse Rd., Spanish Fork, 84660, Utah County, (801)798-9816, 7 miles N of Provo.

Holes: 18. **Yards:** 6,358/5,319. **Par:** 72/73. **Course Rating:** 68.7/68.9. **Slope:** 116/113. **Green Fee:** $15/$15. **Cart Fee:** $15/cart. **Walking Policy:** Unrestricted walking. **Walkability:** N/A. **Opened:** 1983. **Architect:** Billy Casper/Gary Darling. **Season:** March-Oct. **High:** May-Sept. **To obtain tee times:** Call one week in advance. **Miscellaneous:** Reduced fees (twilight, seniors, juniors), metal spikes, range (grass), club rentals, credit cards (MC, V, AE, D).

Reader Comments: Short and open ... Good greens ... Always windy ... Short back 9 ... Super challenge for high handicapper ... Wide fairways ... Plays longer than yardage ... Fun course, mountain views ... One or two especially challenging par 4s and a picturesque setting make the back 9 a treat.

★★½ STANSBURY PARK GOLF CLUB

PU-#1 Country Club Dr., Tooele, 84074, Tooele County, (801)328-1483, 25 miles SE of Salt Lake City.
Holes: 18. **Yards:** 6,831/5,722. **Par:** 72/72. **Course Rating:** 71.6/71.5. **Slope:** 125/121. **Green Fee:** $13/$15. **Cart Fee:** $7/person. **Walking Policy:** Unrestricted walking. **Walkability:** N/A. **Opened:** 1972. **Architect:** Bill Neff. **Season:** Feb.-Nov. **High:** June-Aug. **To obtain tee times:** Call Thursday for weekends. Call Saturday or Sunday for following weekdays. **Miscellaneous:** Reduced fees (weekdays, low season), metal spikes, range (grass), club rentals.
Reader Comments: Water on 16 holes ... Beautiful terrain ... A challenge for all ... Good price.

SUNBROOK GOLF CLUB

PU-2366 West Sunbrook Drive, St. George, 84770, Washington County, (435)634-5866, 120 miles N of Las Vegas.
Holes: 27. **Green Fee:** $22/$38. **Cart Fee:** $10/person. **Walking Policy:** Unrestricted walking. **Walkability:** 3. **Opened:** 1990. **Architect:** Ted G. Robinson/John Harbottle. **Season:** Year-round. **High:** Oct.-May. **To obtain tee times:** Call golf shop 14 days prior or computer system 15 days. **Miscellaneous:** Reduced fees (low season), range (grass/mats), club rentals, credit cards (MC, V).
★★★★ POINTE/BLACKROCK
Yards: 6,758/5,155. **Par:** 72/72. **Course Rating:** 73.8/71.4. **Slope:** 133/125.
Reader Comments: Excellent test of golf ... 27 holes with a good variety ... Great natural features ... Tough to walk but worth it ... Excellent value ... You don't get to be the most popular in St. George by mistake ... Blackrock is maturing nicely ... Best course in St. George area! ... Friendly folks ... Best public ever played.
★★★★ POINTE/WOODBRIDGE
Yards: 6,818/5,286. **Par:** 72/72. **Course Rating:** 73.0/71.1. **Slope:** 129/121.
Notes: Ranked 5th in 1999 Best in State.
Reader Comments: One of the best courses in Utah ... Tough but fair, worth playing again and again ... Hands down the best in Southern Utah! ... Good Ted Robinson design, excellent shape ... Bring your 'A' putting game ... Target golf ... The best public course in the state! ... Sporty, fair golf course...Course management key to scoring here ... Beautiful and exciting ... Great view.
★★★★ WOODBRIDGE/BLACKROCK
Yards: 6,828/5,233. **Par:** 72/72. **Course Rating:** 74.0/74.1. **Slope:** 134/126.

★★★ TRI-CITY GOLF COURSE

PU-1400 N. 200 E., American Fork, 84003, Utah County, (801)756-3594, 30 miles S of Salt Lake City.
Holes: 18. **Yards:** 7,077/6,304. **Par:** 72/73. **Course Rating:** 73.0/73.0. **Slope:** 125/124. **Green Fee:** $18/$18. **Cart Fee:** $16/cart. **Walking Policy:** Unrestricted walking. **Walkability:** 2. **Opened:** 1972. **Architect:** Joe Williams. **Season:** March-Oct. **High:** May-Aug. **To obtain tee times:** Call up to 10 days in advance. **Miscellaneous:** Reduced fees (seniors, juniors), range (grass), club rentals, credit cards (MC, V).
Reader Comments: Long, narrow, tough, old course ... Elevation is 5,000 feet ... Golf in a heavy forest ... Gnarly old trees everywhere ... Tight driving holes ... Nice greens ... Long track with a couple of unfair holes.

★★★★ VALLEY VIEW GOLF COURSE

PU-2501 E. Gentile, Layton, 84040, Davis County, (801)546-1630, 15 miles N of Salt Lake City.
Holes: 18. **Yards:** 6,652/5,755. **Par:** 72/74. **Course Rating:** 71.0/73.2. **Slope:** 123/125. **Green Fee:** $19/$19. **Cart Fee:** $18/cart. **Walking Policy:** Unrestricted walking. **Walkability:** 5. **Opened:** 1974. **Architect:** William Hull. **Season:** March-Nov. **High:** May-Sept. **To obtain tee times:** Call Thursday 7 a.m. for Friday, Saturday, Sunday and Monday holidays. One day in advance for weekdays. **Miscellaneous:** Reduced fees (juniors), range (grass), club rentals, credit cards (MC, V, D).
Notes: Ranked 8th in 1999 Best in State.
Reader Comments: Long, good test of golf ... Large greens tough to putt ... One of the best that nobody knows about ... Great value ... Very good public course ... Beautiful golf course in excellent condition ... Greens can be wicked ... The views are wonderful as the course is to play ... A must.

WASATCH STATE PARK GOLF CLUB

PU-P.O. Box 10, Midway, 84049, Wasatch County, (435)654-0532, 35 miles E of Salt Lake City.
★★★★ LAKE *Value+*
Holes: 18. **Yards:** 6,942/5,573. **Par:** 72/72. **Course Rating:** 72.0/71.5. **Slope:** 128/123. **Green Fee:** $18/$20. **Cart Fee:** $20/cart. **Walking Policy:** Unrestricted walking. **Walkability:** 2.

Architect: Bill Neff. **Season:** April-Nov. **High:** July-Aug. **To obtain tee times:** Call 7 a.m. Monday for weekends. Call 7 a.m. Thursday for following weekdays. **Miscellaneous:** Reduced fees (seniors, juniors), range (grass/mats), club rentals, credit cards (MC, V).
Reader Comments: 36 enjoyable and playable holes ... Scenic, worth the drive ... Memorable experience ... State park,... Great pros ... Great price ... Nice in the fall.

★★★½ **MOUNTAIN**

Holes: 18. **Yards:** 6,459/5,009. **Par:** 71/71. **Course Rating:** 70.4/67.4. **Slope:** 125/119. **Green Fee:** $28/$30. **Cart Fee:** Included in Green Fee. **Walking Policy:** Mandatory cart. **Walkability:** 3. **Opened:** 1998. **Architect:** Bill Neff, Sr. **Season:** April-Nov. **High:** July-Aug. **To obtain tee times:** Call 7 a.m. Monday for weekends. Call 7 a.m. Thursday for following weekdays. **Miscellaneous:** Reduced fees (seniors, juniors), range (grass/mats), club rentals, credit cards (MC, V).
Reader Comments: Great burgers ... Mother Nature at her finest ... Great family courses.

★★½ **WEST RIDGE GOLF COURSE**

PU-5055 S. W. Ridge Blvd., West Valley City, 84118, Salt Lake County, (801)966-4653, 10 miles SW of Salt Lake City.
Holes: 18. **Yards:** 6,734/5,027. **Par:** 71/71. **Course Rating:** 72.2/68.1. **Slope:** 125/118. **Green Fee:** $16/$18. **Cart Fee:** $9/person. **Walking Policy:** Unrestricted walking. **Walkability:** 4. **Opened:** 1991. **Architect:** William Howard Neff. **Season:** March-Nov. **High:** April-Aug. **To obtain tee times:** Call 7 days in advance. **Miscellaneous:** Reduced fees (weekdays, low season, seniors, juniors), discount packages, range (grass), club rentals, credit cards (MC, V, AE, D).
Reader Comments: Short but tight ... Greens very undulating ... Usually windy ... Wonderfully laid -out course for area ... Hilly ... Harder than it looks ... Great views ... Excellent upkeep ... Greens in fine shape and fast ... Good value ... Nice people on staff.

★★★★ **WINGPOINTE GOLF COURSE**

PU-3602 W. 100 N., Salt Lake City, 84122, Salt Lake County, (801)575-2345,
Holes: 18. **Yards:** 7,101/5,228. **Par:** 72/72. **Course Rating:** 73.3/72.0. **Slope:** 131/125. **Green Fee:** N/A/$20. **Cart Fee:** $20/cart. **Walking Policy:** Walking at certain times. **Walkability:** 3. **Opened:** 1990. **Architect:** Arthur Hills. **Season:** Year-round. **High:** May-Oct. **To obtain tee times:** Call tee-time number up to 7 days in advance. **Miscellaneous:** Reduced fees (weekdays, low season, seniors, juniors), range (grass), club rentals, credit cards (MC, V).
Notes: Ranked 10th in 1997 Best in State.
Reader Comments: Great links course located next to the Salt Lake City airport ... Lots of variety from different tee boxes ... Great test, especially from the tips ... Arthur Hills created a gem out of salt marsh ... Great pro ... Windy, windy, windy ... Jets over your head always ... Could be in Scotland ... Unique layout! ...Lots of 'trouble'.... The best course I've played and cheap.

★★★½ **WOLF CREEK GOLF RESORT** *Value*

SP-3900 N. Wolf Creek Dr., Eden, 84310, Weber County, (801)745-3365
Holes: 18. **Yards:** 6,845/5,332. **Par:** 72/72. **Course Rating:** 73.4/71.0. **Slope:** 134/127. **Green Fee:** $20/$25. **Cart Fee:** $10/person. **Walking Policy:** Unrestricted walking. **Walkability:** 5. **Architect:** Mark Dixon Ballif. **Season:** March-Nov. **High:** May-Sept. **To obtain tee times:** Call 1 week in advance. **Miscellaneous:** Reduced fees (weekdays, low season, resort guests, twilight, seniors, juniors), discount packages, range (grass/mats), club rentals, credit cards (MC, V, AE).
Reader Comments: Fine mountain course with great scenery...My favorite course in Utah!...Greens are like putting on ice...Fantastic mountain scenery...Two distinct 9s ... Can't beat the scenery ... Unbelievable greens ... Back 9 is older, more mature ... Hope they keep up condition ... Mountain setting ... Beautiful track.

★★ ALBURG COUNTRY CLUB
SP-230 Rte.129, South Alburg, 05440, Grand Isle County, (802)796-3586, 40 miles N of Burlington. **E-mail:** golf@alburg.com. **Web:** www.alburg.com.
Holes: 18. **Yards:** 6,434/5,536. **Par:** 72/75. **Course Rating:** 70.2/71.2. **Slope:** 119/120. **Green Fee:** $12/$25. **Cart Fee:** $20/cart. **Walking Policy:** Unrestricted walking. **Walkability:** 3.
Opened: 1967. **Architect:** Dick Ellison. **Season:** May-Oct. **High:** July-Aug. **To obtain tee times:** Call on Wednesday for upcoming weekend. **Miscellaneous:** Reduced fees (weekdays, low season, twilight, juniors), discount packages, metal spikes, range (grass/mats), club rentals.

BARTON GOLF CLUB
PU-Telfer Hill, Barton, 05822, Orleans County, (802)525-1126.
Holes: 18. **Yards:** 5,800/5,200. **Par:** 70/72. **Course Rating:** 68.0/68.0. **Slope:** 115/115. **Green Fee:** $15/$15. **Cart Fee:** $10/person. **Walking Policy:** Unrestricted walking. **Walkability:** 2.
Opened: 1990. **Architect:** Brian King. **Season:** May-Oct. **High:** July-Aug. **To obtain tee times:** Call Golf Shop. **Miscellaneous:** Reduced fees (twilight), credit cards (MC, V).

★★★★½ BASIN HARBOR CLUB *Service*
R-Basin Harbor Rd., Vergennes, 05491, Addison County, (802)475-2309, 30 miles S of Burlington.
Holes: 18. **Yards:** 6,511/5,700. **Par:** 72/72. **Course Rating:** 70.7/67.1. **Slope:** 120/113. **Green Fee:** $37/$42. **Cart Fee:** $30/cart. **Walking Policy:** Unrestricted walking. **Walkability:** 2.
Opened: 1927. **Architect:** A. Campbell/R. Mitchell/G. Cornish. **Season:** May-Oct. **High:** July-Aug. **To obtain tee times:** Public may call 2 days in advance. Resort guests may call anytime in advance. **Miscellaneous:** Reduced fees (low season, resort guests, twilight, juniors), discount packages, range (grass), club rentals, lodging, credit cards (MC, V), beginner friendly.
Reader Comments: Very weather dependent, but a gem ... Lushest fairways in Vermont ... Beautiful setting ... Classic setting; charming ... Plush ... Can be windy on the lake holes ... Scenic views of Lake Champlain ... Fast greens, great vacation spot.

BRATTLEBORO COUNTRY CLUB
SP-Upper Dummerston Rd., Brattleboro, 05301, Windham County, (802)257-7380.
Holes: 18. **Yards:** 6,500/5,300. **Par:** 71/71. **Course Rating:** N/A. **Slope:** N/A. **Green Fee:** $30/N/A. **Cart Fee:** $14/person. **Walking Policy:** Unrestricted walking. **Walkability:** 4. **Opened:** 1914. **Architect:** Tom MacNamara/Steve Durkee. **Season:** Mid April-Mid Nov. **High:** June-Aug. **To obtain tee times:** Call 2 days in advance. **Miscellaneous:** Reduced fees (juniors), discount packages, range (grass), club rentals, credit cards (MC, V).

CEDAR KNOLL COUNTRY CLUB
PU-Highway VT #116, Hinesburg, 05461, Chittenden County, (802)482-3186, 15 miles SE of Burlington.
Holes: 27. **Green Fee:** $22/$22. **Cart Fee:** $23/cart. **Walking Policy:** Unrestricted walking. **Walkability:** 3. **Opened:** 1994. **Architect:** Raymond Ayer. **Season:** April-Oct. **High:** July-Aug. **To obtain tee times:** Call ahead. **Miscellaneous:** Reduced fees (twilight, seniors), range (grass/mats), club rentals, credit cards (MC, V, AE, D).
NORTH/SOUTH
Yards: 5,863/4,646. **Par:** 71/70. **Course Rating:** 68.5/68.0. **Slope:** 119/108.
NORTH/WEST
Yards: 6,541/5,360. **Par:** 72/72. **Course Rating:** 70.8/69.5. **Slope:** 124/112.
SOUTH/WEST
Yards: 6,072/4,924. **Par:** 71/70. **Course Rating:** 67.7/67.1. **Slope:** 117/109.
Special Notes: 9 holes after 5:00 p.m. Formerly Cedar Knolls Golf Club.

★★½ CHAMPLAIN COUNTRY CLUB
SP-Rte. 7 North, Swanton, 05488, Franklin County, (802)527-1187, 3 miles N of St. Albans.
Holes: 18. **Yards:** 6,237/5,266. **Par:** 70/70. **Course Rating:** 69.9/70.4. **Slope:** 123/117. **Green Fee:** $25/$28. **Cart Fee:** $26/cart. **Walking Policy:** Unrestricted walking. **Walkability:** 1.
Opened: 1915. **Architect:** Duer Irving Sewall/Graham Cook. **Season:** April-Nov. **High:** July-Aug. **To obtain tee times:** June-Oct. call 3 days in advance for weekends and holidays.
Miscellaneous: Reduced fees (weekdays, low season, twilight), discount packages, range (grass), caddies, club rentals, credit cards (MC, V, D), beginner friendly (ladies, junior clinics).
Reader Comments: Challenging small greens ... Good layout ... Very average course, but always fun ... A fair test of golf.

★★★½ COUNTRY CLUB OF BARRE
SP-Plainfield Rd., Barre, 05641, Washington County, (802)476-7658, 4 miles E of Barre.
Holes: 18. **Yards:** 6,218/5,407. **Par:** 71/71. **Course Rating:** 70.2/71.7. **Slope:** 123/124. **Green Fee:** $35/$35. **Cart Fee:** $15/person. **Walking Policy:** Unrestricted walking. **Walkability:** 4.
Opened: 1924. **Architect:** Wayne Stiles. **Season:** April-Oct. **High:** June-Aug. **To obtain tee times:** Call up to 7 days in advance. **Miscellaneous:** Range (grass/mats), credit cards (MC, V).
Reader Comments: Challenging course in the middle of nowhere ... Several blind holes, tough but nice ... Very scenic ... Demanding layout ... Tight and fairly long ... Hilly.

★★★½ CROWN POINT COUNTRY CLUB

SP-Weathersfield Center Rd., Springfield, 05156, Windsor County, (802)885-1010, 100 miles N of Hartford, CT.
Holes: 18. **Yards:** 6,602/5,542. **Par:** 72/72. **Course Rating:** 71.2/71.3. **Slope:** 123/117. **Green Fee:** $40/$50. **Cart Fee:** $28/person. **Walking Policy:** Unrestricted walking. **Walkability:** 3.
Opened: 1953. **Architect:** William Mitchell. **Season:** April-Oct. **High:** July-Aug. **To obtain tee times:** Call up to 3 days in advance. **Miscellaneous:** Reduced fees (weekdays, twilight, juniors), range (grass/mats), club rentals, credit cards (MC, V).
Reader Comments: Good value especially compared to other area courses ... Sloping fairways make it tough to position drives ... Good clubhouse and food. Great views ... Fast greens, beautiful scenery, great par 3s ... A real test of skill. Key as usual is keeping ball in the fairway.

ENOSBURG FALLS COUNTRY CLUB

PU-11 Elm St., Enosburg Falls, 05450, Franklin County, (802)933-2296.
Holes: 18. **Yards:** 5,897/4,869. **Par:** 72/72. **Course Rating:** 67.4/67.1. **Slope:** 116/110. **Green Fee:** $20/$23. **Cart Fee:** $20/cart. **Walking Policy:** Unrestricted walking. **Walkability:** 3.
Opened: 1962. **Season:** May-Oct. **High:** June-Aug. **To obtain tee times:** Not mandatory. **Miscellaneous:** Credit cards (MC, V).

★½ ESSEX COUNTRY CLUB

PU-332 Old Stage Rd., Essex Junction, 05452, Chittenden County, (802)879-3232, 10 miles NE of Burlington.
Holes: 18. **Yards:** 6,500/5,700. **Par:** 72/72. **Course Rating:** 70.4/69.0. **Slope:** 117/112. **Green Fee:** $21/$23. **Cart Fee:** $20/cart. **Walking Policy:** Unrestricted walking. **Walkability:** 2.
Opened: 1988. **Architect:** Graham Cooke. **Season:** April-Nov. **High:** June-Sept. **To obtain tee times:** Call golf shop. **Miscellaneous:** Reduced fees (twilight), range (grass/mats), club rentals, credit cards (MC, V).

★★★★ GLENEAGLES GOLF COURSE AT THE EQUINOX

R-Historic Rte. 7-A., Manchester Village, 05254, Bennington County, (802)362-3223, 70 miles NE of Albany, NY.
Holes: 18. **Yards:** 6,423/5,082. **Par:** 71/71. **Course Rating:** 71.3/65.2. **Slope:** 129/117. **Green Fee:** $85/$95. **Cart Fee:** $18/person. **Walking Policy:** Walking at certain times. **Walkability:** 3.
Opened: 1926. **Architect:** Rees Jones/Walter Travis. **Season:** May-Nov. **High:** May-Sept. **To obtain tee times:** Call up to 7 days in advance. **Miscellaneous:** Reduced fees (resort guests, twilight), discount packages, club rentals, lodging (183 rooms), credit cards (MC, V, AE, D), beginner friendly (lessons).
Reader Comments: Worth the trip ... Long course, never lets up on you ... A little heaven here on earth ... Old New England beauty ... Elegant ... Great views, watch the 18th finish from the clubhouse ... Beautiful in fall ... One goofy hole across a road, some blind holes.

★★★★½ GREEN MOUNTAIN NATIONAL GOLF COURSE

PM-Rte. 100, Barrows Town Rd., Killington, 05751, Rutland County, (802)422-4653, 15 miles E of Rutland. **Web:** www.gmngc.com.
Holes: 18. **Yards:** 6,589/4,740. **Par:** 71/71. **Course Rating:** 72.6/68.0. **Slope:** 139/118. **Green Fee:** $48/$52. **Cart Fee:** $17/person. **Walking Policy:** Walking at certain times. **Walkability:** 3.
Opened: 1996. **Architect:** Gene Bates. **Season:** May-Nov. **High:** June-Oct. **To obtain tee times:** Call up to 7 days in advance. **Miscellaneous:** Reduced fees (low season, twilight, juniors), discount packages, range (grass/mats), club rentals, credit cards (MC, V, AE).
Notes: Ranked 2nd in 1999 Best in State; 5th in 1997 Best New Upscale Public Courses.
Reader Comments: The setting is classic ... Awesome ... You need a sherpa to get to the 10th tee ... Bring lots of balls ... Whites play tougher than most blues ... Beyond beautiful in Fall ... Incredible elevation changes ... The rugged beauty of this course is amazing ... Every hole could have been a picture postcard ... Challenging without being severe.

★★★ HAYSTACK GOLF CLUB

PU-70 Spyglass Drive, Wilmington, 05363, Windham County, (802)464-8301, 3 miles N of Wilmington. **E-mail:** golfinfo@haystackgolf.com. **Web:** www.haystackgolf.com.
Holes: 18. **Yards:** 6,549/5,396. **Par:** 72/74. **Course Rating:** 71.5/71.4. **Slope:** 128/122. **Green Fee:** $40/$49. **Cart Fee:** $16/person. **Walking Policy:** Walking at certain times. **Walkability:** 3.
Opened: 1972. **Architect:** Desmond Muirhead. **Season:** May-Nov. **High:** July-Aug. **To obtain tee times:** Call in advance. Groups welcome. **Miscellaneous:** Reduced fees (weekdays, low season, resort guests, twilight, juniors), discount packages, range (grass/mats), club rentals, credit cards (MC, V, AE, D), beginner friendly.
Reader Comments: Fun to play ... The crummiest practice balls around ... Some very good holes ... A must–play mountain course–watch the weather ... Pat Bradley's brother is the pro ... Challenging course, close fairways can be dangerous ... Very tough greens ... Great views.

JOHN P. LARKIN COUNTRY CLUB

SP-N. Main St., Windsor, 05089, Windsor County, (802)674-6491, 7 miles N of Windsor.

Holes: 9. **Yards:** 5,382/4,924. **Par:** 68/72. **Course Rating:** 65.1/68.2. **Slope:** 105/109. **Green Fee:** $20/$25. **Cart Fee:** $22/cart. **Walking Policy:** Unrestricted walking. **Walkability:** 5. **Opened:** 1923. **Architect:** MIT Students. **Season:** April-Oct. **High:** June-July-Aug. **To obtain tee times:** In person or by phone. **Miscellaneous:** Club rentals, credit cards (MC, V). **Special Notes:** Was Windsor Country Club

★★★★ KILLINGTON GOLF RESORT
R-Killington Rd., Killington, 05751, Rutland County, (802)422-6700, 16 miles E of Rutland. **E-mail:** dpfannenstein@killington.com. **Web:** www.killington.com.
Holes: 18. **Yards:** 6,326/5,108. **Par:** 72/72. **Course Rating:** 70.6/71.2. **Slope:** 126/123. **Green Fee:** $50/$50. **Cart Fee:** $15/person. **Walking Policy:** Unrestricted walking. **Walkability:** 4. **Opened:** 1984. **Architect:** Geoffrey Cornish. **Season:** May-Oct. **High:** July-Aug.-Sept. **To obtain tee times:** Call up to 7 days in advance. Golf packages may be reserved when hotel reservations are made. **Miscellaneous:** Reduced fees (low season, twilight, juniors), discount packages, metal spikes, range (mats), club rentals, lodging (1,000 rooms), credit cards (MC, V, AE, D).
Reader Comments: The scenery was breathtaking ... Lots of blind shots, lots of up & down terrain ... A very good mountain course ... Unparalleled views ... Very wet early spring ... Great vacation course ... Tough course. Good challenges. Walking is tiring ... A typical ski resort golf course ... Like playing a roller coaster...Target golf, some wild elevation changes.

★★★ KWINIASKA GOLF CLUB
SP-5531 Spear St., Shelburne, 05482, Chittenden County, (802)985-3672, 7 miles S of Burlington. **Web:** www.kwiniaska.com.
Holes: 18. **Yards:** 7,048/5,627. **Par:** 72/72. **Course Rating:** 72.5/72.6. **Slope:** 128/119. **Green Fee:** $27/$27. **Cart Fee:** $22/cart. **Walking Policy:** Unrestricted walking. **Walkability:** 3. **Opened:** 1964. **Architect:** Bradford Caldwell. **Season:** April-Nov. **High:** June-Aug. **To obtain tee times:** Call 1 day in advance for weekends and holidays. Open play during the week. **Miscellaneous:** Reduced fees (twilight), metal spikes, range (grass), club rentals, credit cards (MC, V).
Reader Comments: Long, wide open course ... Great greens ... Long when wind is blowing ... The course looks easy, but the layout is more than bargained for ... Tough to gauge yardages ... I'd return ... A definite must in Vermont.

★★★ LAKE MOREY COUNTRY CLUB
R-Lake Morey Rd., Fairlee, 05045, Orange County, (802)333-4800, (800)423-1227, 167 miles N of Boston, MA.
Holes: 18. **Yards:** 6,024/4,942. **Par:** 70/70. **Course Rating:** 68.4/68.0. **Slope:** 118/116. **Green Fee:** $28/$35. **Cart Fee:** $28/cart. **Walking Policy:** Walking at certain times. **Walkability:** 3. **Opened:** 1910. **Architect:** Geoffrey Cornish. **Season:** April-Nov. **High:** July-Aug. **To obtain tee times:** Public may call up to 4 days in advance. Members may call up to 7 days in advance. Resort guests may book when room reservation is made. **Miscellaneous:** Reduced fees (low season, resort guests, twilight, seniors), discount packages, range (grass/mats), club rentals, lodging (160 rooms), credit cards (MC, V).
Reader Comments: Good course complements excellent inn & surroundings ... Some lovely holes ... Nice course, beautiful colors, tough ravines! ... Back nine tougher than front ... Crowded ... Too easy from whites ... Tougher than it looks ... You could get lost finding next tee!

★★ LAKE ST. CATHERINE COUNTRY CLUB
SP-Rte. 30 Lake Rd., Poultney, 05764, Rutland County, (802)287-9341, 3 miles S of Rutland.
Holes: 18. **Yards:** 6,293/4,940. **Par:** 72/72. **Course Rating:** 70.9/68.2. **Slope:** 127/116. **Green Fee:** $20/$27. **Cart Fee:** $27/cart. **Walking Policy:** Unrestricted walking. **Walkability:** 5. **Opened:** 1986. **Season:** April-Oct. **High:** July-Aug. **To obtain tee times:** Call up to 7 days in advance. **Miscellaneous:** Reduced fees (low season), discount packages, metal spikes, club rentals, credit cards (MC, V), beginner friendly (toons new england school of golf).

★★½ MONTAGUE GOLF CLUB
SP-2 Golf Lane, Randolph, 05060, Orange County, (802)728-3806, 20 miles S of Montpelier.
Holes: 18. **Yards:** 5,910/5,064. **Par:** 70/71. **Course Rating:** 68.6/68.7. **Slope:** 115/117. **Green Fee:** $23/$28. **Cart Fee:** $25/cart. **Walking Policy:** Unrestricted walking. **Walkability:** 1. **Opened:** 1925. **Season:** April-Oct. **High:** June-Aug. **To obtain tee times:** Call 2 days in advance. **Miscellaneous:** Reduced fees (weekdays, low season, twilight), discount packages, range (grass), club rentals, credit cards (MC, V), beginner friendly (beginner golf clinics).
Reader Comments: Easy course, walkable ... Very interesting holes on 1st 9 ... Beautiful views, great test of skills ... Uncrowded ... Not much challenge ... Bring your lob wedge for No. 17.

★★ MOUNT ANTHONY GOLF & TENNIS CENTER
PU-943 Bank St., Bennington, 05201, Bennington County, (802)447-7079, 30 miles E of Albany.
Holes: 18. **Yards:** 6,146/4,942. **Par:** 71/71. **Course Rating:** 70.5/67.7. **Slope:** 125/106. **Green Fee:** $25/$30. **Cart Fee:** $11/person. **Walking Policy:** Unrestricted walking. **Walkability:** 4. **Opened:** 1897. **Architect:** Jay Jerome. **Season:** April-Oct. **High:** July-Sept. **To obtain tee times:** Call up to 7 days in advance. **Miscellaneous:** Metal spikes.

VERMONT

★★★½ MOUNT SNOW GOLF CLUB
R-Country Club Rd., West Dover, 05356, Windham County, (802)464-5642, (800)451-4211, 26 miles W of Brattleboro.
Holes: 18. **Yards:** 6,894/5,436. **Par:** 72/72. **Course Rating:** 72.4/72.8. **Slope:** 130/121. **Green Fee:** N/A/$49. **Cart Fee:** $16/person. **Walking Policy:** Unrestricted walking. **Walkability:** 5. **Opened:** 1964. **Architect:** Geoffrey Cornish. **Season:** May-Oct. **High:** July-Aug. **To obtain tee times:** Call Pro Shop. **Miscellaneous:** Reduced fees (weekdays, low season, resort guests, twilight, juniors), discount packages, metal spikes, range (grass/mats), club rentals, lodging, credit cards (MC, V, AE, D), beginner friendly (golf school, large practice facility).
Reader Comments: Difficult but fun ... Worth the drive ... Not a flat stance on course, great layout and scenery ... Some holes very tight ... Go for the serenity ... Too many blind holes ... Wow! ... I saw a bear on 17 & 18 once ... Need to play the course twice.

★★★½ NESHOBE GOLF CLUB
SP-Town Farm Rd., Brandon, 05733, Rutland County, (802)247-3611, 2 miles NE of Rutland.
E-mail: neshgolf@together.net. **Web:** neshobe.com.
Holes: 18. **Yards:** 6,362/5,042. **Par:** 72/71. **Course Rating:** 71.6/64.9. **Slope:** 125/115. **Green Fee:** $34/$36. **Cart Fee:** $28/cart. **Walking Policy:** Unrestricted walking. **Walkability:** 3. **Opened:** 1959. **Architect:** Steve Durkee. **Season:** April-Oct. **High:** June-Aug. **To obtain tee times:** Call or come in up to 5 days in advance. **Miscellaneous:** Reduced fees (twilight, juniors), range (grass), club rentals, credit cards (MC, V).
Reader Comments: Another hidden gem, but not for long ... Great new holes added ... Great layout ... Pristine fairways and greens ... New '9' wonderful.

★★★ NEWPORT COUNTRY CLUB
SP-Pine Hill Rd., Newport, 05855, Orleans County, (802)334-2391, 80 miles NE of Burlington.
Holes: 18. **Yards:** 6,453/5,312. **Par:** 72/72. **Course Rating:** 69.4/69.5. **Slope:** 109/110. **Green Fee:** $23/$23. **Cart Fee:** $22/cart. **Walking Policy:** Unrestricted walking. **Walkability:** 2. **Architect:** Ralph Barton. **Season:** April-Oct. **High:** July-Aug. **To obtain tee times:** Call up to 2 days in advance. **Miscellaneous:** Reduced fees (twilight), range (grass), club rentals, credit cards (MC, V).
Reader Comments: Challenging course ... Wide fairways ... Unbelievable views, interesting layout, good golf ... Very scenic finishing hole ... New clubhouse ... Restaurant great.

★★★ ORLEANS COUNTRY CLUB
SP-Rte. 58, P.O. Box 217, Orleans, 05860, Orleans County, (802)754-2333.
Holes: 18. **Yards:** 6,200/5,595. **Par:** 72/72. **Course Rating:** 69.3/71.8. **Slope:** 121/124. **Green Fee:** $24/$24. **Cart Fee:** $22/cart. **Walking Policy:** Unrestricted walking. **Walkability:** 1. **Opened:** 1929. **Architect:** Alex Reid. **Season:** April-Oct. **High:** June-Sept. **To obtain tee times:** Call up to 1 day in advance after 9 a.m. **Miscellaneous:** Discount packages, metal spikes, range (grass), credit cards (MC, V).
Reader Comments: Flat. Very walkable. Great food ... Fun little course ... Friendly atmosphere ... Best banana cream pie anywhere ... Seems quite popular.

★★★ PROCTOR-PITTSFORD COUNTRY CLUB
PU-Corn Hill Rd., Proctor, 05763, Rutland County, (802)483-9379, 3 miles N of Rutland.
Holes: 18. **Yards:** 6,052/5,446. **Par:** 70/72. **Course Rating:** 69.4/66.1. **Slope:** 121/115. **Green Fee:** $30/$30. **Cart Fee:** $13/person. **Walking Policy:** Unrestricted walking. **Walkability:** 3. **Opened:** 1927. **Architect:** Henry Collin/Ray Keyser. **Season:** April-Nov. **High:** July-Aug. **To obtain tee times:** Call 2 days in advance. **Miscellaneous:** Reduced fees (twilight), range (grass), club rentals, credit cards (MC, V).
Reader Comments: Beautiful marble clubhouse ... New meets old, new wins ... A slice on No. 10 requires a pail and shovel ... Scenic, fun, challenging ... Tight fairways, excellent greens ... Old time golfer's course ... Fantastic views ... Nine new holes wonderful.

★★½ RALPH MYHRE COUNTRY CLUB OF MIDDLEBURY COLLEGE
SP-Rte. 1, Middlebury, 05753, Addison County, (802)443-5125, 1 miles S of Middlebury.
Holes: 18. **Yards:** 6,379/5,337. **Par:** 71/72. **Course Rating:** 71.3/66.9. **Slope:** 129/120. **Green Fee:** $18/$30. **Cart Fee:** $24/cart. **Walking Policy:** Unrestricted walking. **Walkability:** 3. **Opened:** 1927. **Architect:** Ralph Myhre. **Season:** April-Oct. **High:** July-Aug. **To obtain tee times:** Call Pro Shop. **Miscellaneous:** Reduced fees (twilight, juniors), range (grass/mats), club rentals, credit cards (MC, V).
Reader Comments: Very challenging par 3s ... Wide fairways. Tough but fair ... College course ... Beautiful scenery, average golf ... Lots of bunkers ... Nice place to play ... Quiet.

★★½ ROCKY RIDGE GOLF CLUB
SP-7470 Rte. 116, St. George, 05495, Chittenden County, (802)482-2191, 12 miles S of Burlington.
Holes: 18. **Yards:** 6,000/5,230. **Par:** 72/72. **Course Rating:** 69.1/68.7. **Slope:** 124/110. **Green Fee:** $22/$22. **Cart Fee:** $22/cart. **Walking Policy:** Unrestricted walking. **Walkability:** 3.

VERMONT

Opened: 1963. **Architect:** Ernest Farrington. **Season:** April-Nov. **High:** July-Aug. **To obtain tee times:** Call Thursday at 7 a.m. for upcoming weekend. **Miscellaneous:** Reduced fees (twilight), metal spikes, range (grass), club rentals, credit cards (MC, V, AE).
Reader Comments: A great course. A thorough challenge for all ... Good assortment of holes ... Course needs work ... Relatively short, but some tight holes ... A couple of holes the devil designed ... Challenging walk, 13th an uphill nightmare.

★★★★½ RUTLAND COUNTRY CLUB *Condition*
SP-N. Grove St., Rutland, 05701, Rutland County, (802)773-3254. **E-mail:** golfrcc@together.net.
Holes: 18. **Yards:** 6,134/5,368. **Par:** 70/71. **Course Rating:** 69.7/71.6. **Slope:** 125/125. **Green Fee:** N/A/$75. **Cart Fee:** $27/. **Cart Fee:** Included in Green Fee. **Walking Policy:** Mandatory cart. **Walkability:** 3. **Opened:** 1902. **Architect:** George Low. **Season:** April-Oct. **High:** June-Aug. **To obtain tee times:** Call one day in advance. Tee times available 48 hours in advance.
Miscellaneous: Club rentals, credit cards (MC, V).
Notes: Ranked 4th in 1997 Best in State.
Reader Comments: Hilly back nine. Slick greens. Good food ... Some beautiful holes and scenery ... On the short side, but a real test of golf ... Putting can test your pride and your score ... Aged to perfection.

★★★★ ST. JOHNSBURY COUNTRY CLUB *Value*
SP-Rte. 5 Memorial Dr., St. Johnsbury, 05819, Caledonia County, (802)748-9894, (800)748-8899, 5 miles N of Boston.
Holes: 18. **Yards:** 6,323/4,685. **Par:** 70/70. **Course Rating:** 70.4/65.8. **Slope:** 129/104. **Green Fee:** $33/$38. **Cart Fee:** $13/person. **Walking Policy:** Unrestricted walking. **Walkability:** 4.
Opened: 1923. **Architect:** Willie Park/Mungo Park-Cornish/J.Havers. **Season:** April-Oct. **High:** July-Aug. **To obtain tee times:** Call up to 3 days in advance. **Miscellaneous:** Reduced fees (resort guests, twilight), metal spikes, range (grass/mats), club rentals, credit cards (MC, V).
Reader Comments: Fabulous back 9, worth the trip ... Tough greens, good variety of holes ... Classic Vermont elevations and rocks ... A real roller-coaster ... One cannot say all the good things about this course ... Very lush greens, ruff is tough.

★★★½ STOWE COUNTRY CLUB
R-Cape Cod Rd., Stowe, 05672, Lamoille County, (802)253-4893, (800)253-4754, 37 miles E of Burlington.
Holes: 18. **Yards:** 6,206/5,346. **Par:** 72/74. **Course Rating:** 70.4/66.5. **Slope:** 122/115. **Green Fee:** $35/$65. **Cart Fee:** $16/person. **Walking Policy:** Unrestricted walking. **Walkability:** 3.
Opened: 1950. **Architect:** Walter Barcomb. **Season:** May-Oct. **High:** July-Sept. **To obtain tee times:** Call one month in advance. Credit card required to reserve weekends and holidays.
Miscellaneous: Reduced fees (weekdays, low season, resort guests, twilight), discount packages, range (grass/mats), club rentals, credit cards (MC, V, AE, D, Diners Club).
Reader Comments: Nice course on difficult terrain ... Lovely ... Watch out for black flies ... Many blind shots ... A great work out if you walk the course ... Careful or you will not want to play anywhere else.

STRATTON MOUNTAIN COUNTRY CLUB
R-R.R. 1 Box 145, Stratton Mountain, 05155, Windham County, (802)297-4114, (800)787-2886, 40 miles S of Rutland. **Web:** www.stratton.com.
Holes: 27. **Green Fee:** $59/$75. **Cart Fee:** $17/person. **Walking Policy:** Walking at certain times. **Walkability:** 4. **Opened:** 1965. **Architect:** Geoffrey Cornish. **Season:** May-Oct. **High:** July-Aug. **To obtain tee times:** Call up to 14 days in advance. **Miscellaneous:** Reduced fees (weekdays, low season, resort guests, twilight, juniors), discount packages, metal spikes, range (grass/mats), club rentals, lodging, credit cards (MC, V, AE, D), beginner friendly (Stratton Golf School).

★★★½ LAKE/FOREST
Yards: 6,526/5,153. **Par:** 72/74. **Course Rating:** 71.2/69.8. **Slope:** 125/123.
Reader Comments: Great variation in elevation ... Challenging course makes you use good iron selection ... Beautiful setting; relaxing day of golf ... Fun layout. Mountain golf at its best! ... Slow play, but worth the wait ... Wonderful getaway of golf.

★★★½ LAKE/MOUNTAIN
Yards: 6,602/5,410. **Par:** 72/74. **Course Rating:** 72.0/71.1. **Slope:** 125/124.

★★★½ MOUNTAIN/FOREST
Yards: 6,478/5,163. **Par:** 72/74. **Course Rating:** 71.2/69.9. **Slope:** 126/123.
Notes: 1990-1995 Hosted McCall's L.P.G.A. Golf Classic.

★★★★ SUGARBUSH GOLF COURSE *Pace*
R-Golf Course Rd., Warren, 05674, Washington County, (802)583-6725, (800)537-8427, 45 miles SE of Burlington.
Holes: 18. **Yards:** 6,524/5,187. **Par:** 72/72. **Course Rating:** 71.7/70.4. **Slope:** 128/119. **Green Fee:** $38/$49. **Cart Fee:** $17/person. **Walking Policy:** Walking at certain times. **Walkability:** 5.
Opened: 1962. **Architect:** Robert Trent Jones Sr. **Season:** May-Oct. **High:** July-Oct. **To obtain**

tee times: Public may call 6 days in advance; preferred tee times can be made through golf packages. **Miscellaneous:** Reduced fees (weekdays, low season, resort guests, twilight, juniors), discount packages, metal spikes, range (grass/mats), club rentals, lodging (150 rooms), credit cards (MC, V, AE, D).
Reader Comments: Great views, fall colors with snow ... Great golf ... Lots of fun, nice greens ... Very good test ... Bring balls ... Good stay & play package ... Owned the course on a fall day.

★★★½ TATER HILL COUNTRY CLUB
SP-Popple Dungeon Rd., Windham, 05143, Windsor County, (802)875-2517, 6 miles W of Manchester. **E-mail:** tathill@sover.net. **Web:** www.taterhill.com.
Holes: 18. **Yards:** 6,801/4,979. **Par:** 72/72. **Course Rating:** 72.3/64.7. **Slope:** 129/113. **Green Fee:** $55/$72. **Cart Fee:** Included in Green Fee. **Walking Policy:** Unrestricted walking.
Walkability: 5. **Opened:** 1964. **Architect:** Don Warner. **Season:** May-Oct. **High:** July-Aug. **To obtain tee times:** Call up to 7 days in advance. **Miscellaneous:** Reduced fees (weekdays, low season, twilight, juniors), discount packages, range (grass), club rentals, credit cards (MC, V, AE), beginner friendly.
Reader Comments: Long walk between holes, fun layout ... Great shape with bizarre greens ... Keep this course a secret ... Jekyll & Hyde 9s ... A gem hidden in Vermont's interior ... Old and new 9s make a beautiful mix ... Very enjoyable.

★★½ WEST BOLTON GOLF CLUB
PU-RD 1 Box 305, W. Bolton Rd., Jericho, 05465, Chittenden County, (802)434-4321, 20 miles NE of Burlington.
Holes: 18. **Yards:** 5,880/5,094. **Par:** 70/71. **Course Rating:** 66.3/65.7. **Slope:** 109/103. **Green Fee:** $15/$20. **Cart Fee:** $18/cart. **Walking Policy:** Unrestricted walking. **Walkability:** 3.
Opened: 1983. **Architect:** Xen Wheeler. **Season:** May-Oct. **High:** June-Aug. **To obtain tee times:** Call 7 days in advance. **Miscellaneous:** Reduced fees (twilight, seniors, juniors), club rentals, credit cards (MC, V, D).
Reader Comments: Friendly one with nature setting ... Very much improved ... Tiny greens, nice views ... Great fall colors...A gem of a golf course in a beautiful spot.

★★★ WILLISTON GOLF CLUB
PU-P.O. Box 541, Williston, 05495, Chittenden County, (802)878-3747, 7 miles E of Burlington.
Holes: 18. **Yards:** 5,685/4,753. **Par:** 69/72. **Course Rating:** 68.0/64.1. **Slope:** 118/106. **Green Fee:** $22/$22. **Cart Fee:** $21/cart. **Walking Policy:** Unrestricted walking. **Walkability:** 1.
Opened: 1926. **Architect:** Ben Murray. **Season:** May-Nov. **High:** July-Aug. **To obtain tee times:** Call Thursday at 7 a.m. for upcoming weekend. Come in and register for weekdays.
Miscellaneous: Reduced fees (twilight), metal spikes, club rentals, credit cards (MC, V).
Reader Comments: Short but tough little course ... Beautiful in the fall, well worth the money ... A gem ... Tests short game ... Beautiful flowers. Easy to score well ... Every hole was something different...Deceiving.

★★★★ WOODSTOCK COUNTRY CLUB
R-Fourteen The Green, Woodstock, 05091, Windsor County, (802)457-6674, 30 miles E of Rutland.
Holes: 18. **Yards:** 6,001/4,924. **Par:** 69/71. **Course Rating:** 69.0/67.0. **Slope:** 121/113. **Green Fee:** $58/$75. **Cart Fee:** $18/person. **Walking Policy:** Unrestricted walking. **Walkability:** 1.
Opened: 1895. **Architect:** Robert T. Jones Sr. **Season:** May-Nov. **High:** July-Aug. **To obtain tee times:** Call day of play. **Miscellaneous:** Reduced fees (weekdays, low season, resort guests, twilight), discount packages, range (grass), club rentals, lodging (144 rooms), credit cards (MC, V, AE), beginner friendly.
Reader Comments: Very busy resort course ... Short but enjoyable ... Fantastic layout, naturally beautiful ... One stream that can drive you crazy ... Tough par 3s ... (20 ft. wide brook with current ... Leave your driver in the trunk, it's all shotmaking.

VIRGINIA

★★★ ALGONKIAN REGIONAL PARK GOLF COURSE
PU-47001 Fairway Dr., Sterling, 20165, Loudoun County, (703)450-4655, 20 miles W of Washington DC.
Holes: 18. **Yards:** 7,015/5,795. **Par:** 72/72. **Course Rating:** 73.5/74.0. **Slope:** 125/113. **Green Fee:** $23/$34. **Cart Fee:** $26/cart. **Walking Policy:** Unrestricted walking. **Walkability:** 1. **Opened:** 1972. **Architect:** Ed Ault. **Season:** Year-round. **High:** May-Dec. **To obtain tee times:** Call or come in Tuesdays at 6:30 a.m. for upcoming weekend or holiday. **Miscellaneous:** Reduced fees (weekdays, resort guests, seniors, juniors), range (mats), club rentals, lodging, credit cards (MC, V, ATM Debit), beginner friendly (junior golf program, lessons).
Reader Comments: Longer than it looks ... Great place to practice driving ... Some long par 4s and 5s ... Wet, long roughs, lot of deer ... Great course, but far out ... Wears fairway woods out.

★★★★ AUGUSTINE GOLF CLUB *Condition*
PU-76 Monument Dr., Stafford, 22554, Stafford County, (540)720-7374, 30 miles S of Washington, DC. **Web:** www.washington.sidewalk.com.
Holes: 18. **Yards:** 6,850/4,838. **Par:** 71/71. **Course Rating:** 71.9/68.2. **Slope:** 130/119. **Green Fee:** $55/$75. **Cart Fee:** Included in Green Fee. **Walking Policy:** Walking at certain times. **Walkability:** 3. **Opened:** 1995. **Architect:** Rick Jacobson. **Season:** Year-round. **High:** April-Nov. **To obtain tee times:** Call up to 7 days in advance. **Miscellaneous:** Reduced fees (low season, twilight, seniors), range (grass/mats), club rentals, credit cards (MC, V, AE, D).
Notes: Ranked 10th in 1999 Best in State; 5th in 1996 Best New Upscale Courses.
Reader Comments: Superb, beautiful setting, bring your A game ... Awesome ... Worth the drive ... Best bloody Marys ... Picture postcard holes ... No easy holes ... May be one of the top 5 in Virginia ... Intimidating first 2 holes ... The course is very fair. No. 2 is a tough 460-yard par 4 ... Greens absolutely true ... Don't publicize this course so when I go back I can have it to myself.

★★★ BELMONT GOLF COURSE
PM-1600 Hilliard Rd., Richmond, 23228, Henrico County, (804)501-4653, 5 miles N of Richmond. **Web:** www.co.henrico.va.us.com.
Holes: 18. **Yards:** 6,350/5,418. **Par:** 71/73. **Course Rating:** 70.6/72.6. **Slope:** 126/130. **Green Fee:** $17/$20. **Cart Fee:** $11/person. **Walking Policy:** Unrestricted walking. **Walkability:** 2. **Opened:** 1903. **Architect:** A.W. Tillinghast. **Season:** Year-round. **High:** April-Oct. **To obtain tee times:** Call up to 7 days in advance for Weekdays. Call Monday morning for upcoming weekend. **Miscellaneous:** Reduced fees (seniors, juniors), metal spikes, club rentals.
Notes: 1949 PGA Championship.
Reader Comments: Traditional design; toughest opening hole in public golf ... Decent course, some holes sadistic from the whites ... Pretty course, need for accuracy ... Good public course, used to be a country club ... Well-maintained muny ... Great old course, easy to walk.

★½ BIDE-A-WEE GOLF CLUB
PU-1 Bide-A-Wee Drive, Portsmouth, 23701, Portsmouth County, (757)393-8600, 5 miles S of Portsmouth.
Holes: 18. **Yards:** 7,069/5,518. **Par:** 72/74. **Course Rating:** 72.2/66.4. **Slope:** 121/113. **Green Fee:** $25/$30. **Cart Fee:** $10/person. **Walking Policy:** Walking at certain times. **Walkability:** 1. **Opened:** 1955. **Architect:** Curtis Strange/Tom Clark. **Season:** Year-round. **High:** April-Sept. **To obtain tee times:** Call 1 week in advance. **Miscellaneous:** Reduced fees (weekdays, juniors), range (grass/mats), club rentals, credit cards (MC, V, D).

★★★½ BIRDWOOD GOLF COURSE
PU-410 Golf Course Drive, Charlottesville, 22903, Albemarle County, (804)293-4653, 1 miles W of Charlottesville. **E-mail:** bird5126@mindspring.com.
Holes: 18. **Yards:** 6,820/5,041. **Par:** 72/72. **Course Rating:** 72.8/65.2. **Slope:** 132/116. **Green Fee:** $18/$55. **Cart Fee:** $15/person. **Walking Policy:** Walking at certain times. **Walkability:** 4. **Opened:** 1984. **Architect:** Lindsey Ervin. **Season:** Year-round. **High:** April-Oct. **To obtain tee times:** Call up to 7 days in advance. **Miscellaneous:** Reduced fees (weekdays, low season, resort guests, twilight, juniors), discount packages, range (grass/mats), club rentals, lodging, credit cards (MC, V, AE).
Notes: U.S. Women's Public Links.
Reader Comments: Beautiful course, great views ... Downhill par 3s were fun, great setting ... Back nine par 3s give you vertigo. Great value ... Super layout ... Play in summer, uncrowded, lots of water ... Challenging course, and beautiful surroundings.

★★★½ BIRKDALE GOLF & COUNTRY CLUB
SP-8511 Royal Birkdale Dr., Chesterfield, 23832, Chesterfield County, (804)739-8800, 15 miles SW of Richmond.
Holes: 18. **Yards:** 6,544/4,459. **Par:** 71/71. **Course Rating:** 71.1/N/A. **Slope:** 122/N/A. **Green Fee:** $32/$38. **Cart Fee:** Included in Green Fee. **Walking Policy:** Mandatory cart. **Walkability:** 3. **Opened:** 1990. **Architect:** Dan Maples. **Season:** Year-round. **High:** May-Oct. **To obtain tee times:** Call 7 days in advance. **Miscellaneous:** Reduced fees (weekdays, low season, resort

guests, twilight, seniors, juniors), discount packages, range (grass/mats), club rentals, credit cards (MC, V, AE).

Reader Comments: Fun, for a change ... Playable, fun, friendly ... Good greens. Service good to excellent ...Good test of golf. Very nice greens.

★★ BOW CREEK GOLF COURSE

PM-3425 Clubhouse Rd., Virginia Beach, 23452, Virginia Beach City County, (757)431-3763, 10 miles W of Norfolk.
Holes: 18. **Yards:** 5,917/5,181. **Par:** 70/70. **Course Rating:** 70.4/68.4. **Slope:** 114/104. **Green Fee:** $17/N/A. **Cart Fee:** $10/person. **Walking Policy:** Unrestricted walking. **Walkability:** 1. **Opened:** 1960. **Architect:** John Aragona/Fred Sappenfield. **Season:** Year-round. **High:** April-Sept. **To obtain tee times:** Call after 8 a.m. on Wednesday for weekend. First come, first served on weekdays. **Miscellaneous:** Reduced fees (low season, twilight, seniors, juniors), range (grass), club rentals, lodging, credit cards (MC, V).

★★★½ BRISTOW MANOR GOLF CLUB

PU-11507 Valley View Dr., Bristow, 20136, Prince William County, (703)368-3558, 25 miles SW of Washington D.C.
Holes: 18. **Yards:** 7,102/5,527. **Par:** 72/74. **Course Rating:** 72.9/73.4. **Slope:** 129/128. **Green Fee:** $15/$52. **Cart Fee:** $13/person. **Walking Policy:** Walking at certain times. **Walkability:** 2. **Opened:** 1993. **Architect:** Ken Killian. **Season:** Year-round. **High:** March-Nov. **To obtain tee times:** Call anytime in advance. **Miscellaneous:** Reduced fees (weekdays, low season, twilight, seniors, juniors), range (grass), club rentals, credit cards (MC, V, AE).

Reader Comments: One of the best in the D.C. area ... Challenging excellent fairways ... Stay in the fairway ... Looks very easy driving up the lane, forget about it ... Links style in peaceful, isolated setting ... Tough to find, but worth the search ... A beautiful layout, great bunkering, learn the explosion shot ... Computerized carts give you yardages.

★★½ THE BROOKWOODS GOLF CLUB

PU-7325 Club Dr., Quinton, 23141, New Kent County, (804)932-3737, 15 miles E of Richmond.
Holes: 18. **Yards:** 6,498/5,057. **Par:** 72/72. **Course Rating:** 71.2/69.5. **Slope:** 123/119. **Green Fee:** $15/$21. **Cart Fee:** $11/person. **Walking Policy:** Walking at certain times. **Walkability:** 3. **Opened:** 1974. **Architect:** Algie Pulley. **Season:** Year-round. **High:** April-Oct. **To obtain tee times:** Call anytime in advance. **Miscellaneous:** Reduced fees (twilight, seniors, juniors), range (grass/mats), club rentals, credit cards (MC, V).

Reader Comments: Continuous improvements to course ... Well designed. Tight. Pretty holes. Great value ... Every hole is different.

★★★ BRYCE RESORT GOLF COURSE

R-P.O. Box 3, Basye, 22810, Shenandoah County, (540)856-2124, (800)821-1444, 100 miles SW of Washington, D.C. **E-mail:** golfinfo@bryceresort.com. **Web:** www.bryceresort.com.
Holes: 18. **Yards:** 6,261/5,240. **Par:** 71/71. **Course Rating:** 68.8/70.1. **Slope:** 122/120. **Green Fee:** $24/$45. **Cart Fee:** Included in Green Fee. **Walking Policy:** Mandatory cart. **To obtain tee times:** Up to four days in advance for nonmembers. **Miscellaneous:** Reduced fees (weekdays, low season, twilight), discount packages, range (grass), club rentals, lodging, credit cards (MC, V, AE, D).

Reader Comments: Good for the money, a good test ... Good front nine, back hilly and 18's a par 3 ... Uncrowded, mountain views, pretty ... Tricky lies. Fun to play ... Worth a trip from Washington, D.C.

BULL RUN COUNTRY CLUB

PU-3520 James Madison Hwy., Haymarket, 20169, Prince William County, (703)753-7777, (877)753-7770, 12 miles W of Manassas. **E-mail:** bullruncc@aol.com. **Web:** www.bullruncountryclub.com.
Holes: 18. **Yards:** 6,961/5,069. **Par:** 72/72. **Course Rating:** 73.1/68.3. **Slope:** 134/110. **Green Fee:** $45/$85. **Cart Fee:** Included in Green Fee. **Walking Policy:** Walking at certain times. **Walkability:** 3. **Opened:** 1999. **Architect:** Rick Jacobson. **Season:** Year-round. **High:** April-Oct. **To obtain tee times:** Phone up to 5 days in advance. **Miscellaneous:** Reduced fees (weekdays, low season, twilight, seniors, juniors), range (grass), club rentals, credit cards (MC, V, AE, D, Diners Club), beginner friendly (clinics).

★★½ CARPER'S VALLEY GOLF CLUB

PU-1400 Millwood Pike, Winchester, 22602, Frederick County, (540)662-4319, 65 miles NW of Washington, D.C.
Holes: 18. **Yards:** 6,125/4,930. **Par:** 70/71. **Course Rating:** 69.5/67.5. **Slope:** 118/107. **Green Fee:** $10/$23. **Cart Fee:** $13/person. **Walking Policy:** Walking at certain times. **Walkability:** 2. **Opened:** 1962. **Architect:** Ed Ault. **Season:** Year-round. **High:** April-Oct. **To obtain tee times:** Call or come in up to 5 days in advance. **Miscellaneous:** Reduced fees (weekdays, low season, twilight, juniors), discount packages, metal spikes, range (grass), club rentals, credit cards (MC, V), beginner friendly (clinics).

VIRGINIA

Reader Comments: Long course, worth the trip ... A 'good ol boys' course, rough around edges ... Great course, friendly clubhouse.

★★★ CAVERNS COUNTRY CLUB RESORT
R-910 T.C. Northcott Bv., Luray, 22835, Page County, (540)743-7111, 80 miles W of Washington, D.C. **E-mail:** luraycaverns@rica.net. **Web:** www.luraycaverns.com.
Holes: 18. **Yards:** 6,499/5,499. **Par:** 72/72. **Course Rating:** 71.2/72.4. **Slope:** 117/120. **Green Fee:** $22/$33. **Cart Fee:** $12/person. **Walking Policy:** Unrestricted walking. **Walkability:** 3. **Opened:** 1976. **Architect:** Mal Purdy. **Season:** Year-round. **High:** April-June/Sept.-Oct. **To obtain tee times:** Call up to 7 days in advance. **Miscellaneous:** Reduced fees (weekdays, low season), discount packages, metal spikes, credit cards (MC, V, AE, D).
Reader Comments: Magnificent setting. Course seems irrelevant compared to surroundings. Course condition has its ups and downs ... Demanding 1st hole ... I would recommend this course to anyone ... Nice views for holes on back nine ... Fun layout, good course.... Great views, open fairways.

CEDAR HILLS COUNTRY CLUB
SP-RR No. 1 Box 598, Jonesville, 24263, Lee County, (540)346-1535, 85 miles N of Knoxville, TN.
Holes: 18. **Yards:** 6,466/5,057. **Par:** 71/71. **Course Rating:** 69.3/65.2. **Slope:** 111/101. **Green Fee:** $10/$15. **Cart Fee:** $10/person. **Walking Policy:** Unrestricted walking. **Walkability:** 2. **Opened:** 1967. **Architect:** Horace Smith. **Season:** Year-round. **High:** Apr-Oct. **To obtain tee times:** Call anytime. **Miscellaneous:** Reduced fees (weekdays, juniors), metal spikes, range (grass/mats), club rentals, credit cards (MC, V).

CLEAR CREEK GOLF CLUB
PU-19732 Harleywood Rd., Bristol, 24202, (540)466-4833.
Holes: 18. **Yards:** N/A. **Par:** N/A. **Course Rating:** N/A. **Slope:** N/A. **Green Fee:** N/A. **Walkability:** N/A. **Opened:** 1997. **Architect:** Jack Sykes/Chris Chrisman.

★★★ THE COLONIAL GOLF COURSE
PU-8285 Diascund Rd ., Williamsburg, 23089, James City County County, (757)566-1600, 12 miles W of Williamsburg. **E-mail:** golf@golfcolonial.com. **Web:** www.golfcolonial.com.
Holes: 18. **Yards:** 6,809/4,568. **Par:** 72/72. **Course Rating:** 73.1/66.3. **Slope:** 132/109. **Green Fee:** $80/$80. **Cart Fee:** Included in Green Fee. **Walking Policy:** Unrestricted walking. **Walkability:** 3. **Opened:** 1995. **Architect:** Lester George. **Season:** Year-round. **High:** April-Oct. **To obtain tee times:** Call anytime. **Miscellaneous:** Reduced fees (low season, twilight, seniors, juniors), discount packages, range (grass/mats), club rentals, credit cards (MC, V, AE, D), beginner friendly (3-hole practice course on site).
Reader Comments: Beautiful layout ... Great staff ... Excellent test of golf, tight fairways ... Fast greens ...Very hilly.

★★★½ THE CROSSINGS GOLF CLUB
PU-800 Virginia Center Pkwy., Glen Allen, 23060, Henrico County, (804)261-0000, 9 miles N of Richmond. **Web:** www.thecrossingsgolf.com.
Holes: 18. **Yards:** 6,619/5,625. **Par:** 72/72. **Course Rating:** 70.7/73.2. **Slope:** 126/128. **Green Fee:** $27/$45. **Cart Fee:** Included in Green Fee. **Walking Policy:** Walking at certain times. **Walkability:** 3. **Opened:** 1979. **Architect:** Joe Lee. **Season:** Year-round. **High:** March-Nov. **To obtain tee times:** Call 7 days in advance. **Miscellaneous:** Reduced fees (weekdays, low season, twilight, juniors), range (grass), club rentals, credit cards (MC, V, AE, D).
Reader Comments: Public course, where Jeb Stuart fell ... Best public layout in Richmond ... Great stop on the way to Myrtle Beach ... Good course ... Big greens, back very tough, 18 a solid finisher ... Watch the water on the back nine.

CYPRESS CREEK GOLFERS' CLUB
SP-600 Cypress Creek Pkwy., Smithfield, 23430, Isle of White County, (757)365-4774, 14 miles S of Newport News. **Web:** www.golfsouth.com.
Holes: 18. **Yards:** 7,159/5,136. **Par:** 72/72. **Course Rating:** 74.1/68.8. **Slope:** 130/113. **Green Fee:** $35/$55. **Cart Fee:** Included in Green Fee. **Walking Policy:** Unrestricted walking. **Walkability:** 3. **Opened:** 1998. **Architect:** Tom Clark/Curtis Strange. **Season:** Year-round. **High:** April-Oct. **To obtain tee times:** Call 7 days in advance. **Miscellaneous:** Reduced fees (weekdays, twilight, juniors), range (grass/mats), club rentals, credit cards (MC, V, AE).

★★★½ CYPRESS POINT COUNTRY CLUB
SP-5340 Club Head Rd., Virginia Beach, 23455, Virginia Beach City County, (757)490-8822.
Holes: 18. **Yards:** 6,680/5,440. **Par:** 72/72. **Course Rating:** 71.5/70.8. **Slope:** 124/114. **Green Fee:** $33/$39. **Cart Fee:** Included in Green Fee. **Walking Policy:** Mandatory cart. **Walkability:** 2. **Opened:** 1987. **Architect:** Tom Clark/Brian Ault. **Season:** Year-round. **High:** April-Oct. **To obtain tee times:** Call up to 7 days in advance for weekdays. Call on Wednesday for upcoming weekend. **Miscellaneous:** Range (grass), club rentals, credit cards (MC, V, AE).
Reader Comments: Fair condition, lower price ... Surrounded by housing ... 17th is beautiful. Very playable. Great set of par threes ... Big, wide open, long, fun.

VIRGINIA

★★★★½ **DRAPER VALLEY GOLF CLUB** *Service+, Value+, Condition, Pace+*
PU-2800 Big Valley Drive, Draper, 24324, Pulaski County, (540)980-4653, 60 miles S of Roanoke.
E-mail: dvgcfz@usit.net.
Holes: 18. **Yards:** 7,046/4,793. **Par:** 72/72. **Course Rating:** 73.3/65.6. **Slope:** 125/113. **Green Fee:** $16/$28. **Cart Fee:** $10/person. **Walking Policy:** Walking at certain times. **Walkability:** 3.
Opened: 1992. **Architect:** Harold Louthen. **Season:** Year-round. **High:** March-Nov. **To obtain tee times:** Call 7 days in advance. **Miscellaneous:** Reduced fees (weekdays, low season, twilight, seniors), discount packages, range (grass), club rentals, credit cards (MC, V).
Reader Comments: Excellent course, friendly staff, must play ... Back nine is a pleasure. Very tranquil ... Some unusual holes, mostly wide open ... Great young course ... Wide open, let 'em fly.

★★ **FAMILY GOLF CENTER AT OWL'S CREEK**
PU-411 S. Birdneck Rd., Virginia Beach, 23451, Virginia Beach City County, (757)428-2800, 15 miles E of Norfolk.
Holes: 18. **Yards:** 3,779/2,575. **Par:** 62/62. **Course Rating:** 59.2/59.9. **Slope:** 77/86. **Green Fee:** $10/$16. **Cart Fee:** $8/person. **Walking Policy:** Walking at certain times. **Walkability:** 1.
Opened: 1988. **Season:** Year-round. **High:** May-Oct. **To obtain tee times:** Call. **Miscellaneous:** Reduced fees (low season, twilight, seniors, juniors), metal spikes, range (grass/mats), club rentals, credit cards (MC, V, AE).

FORD'S COLONY COUNTRY CLUB *Service+*
R-240 Ford's Colony Dr., Williamsburg, 23188, James City County, (757)258-4130, 5 miles NW of Williamsburg. **Web:** www.fordscolony.com.
BLACKHEATH COURSE
Holes: 18. **Yards:** 6,621/5,390. **Par:** 71/71. **Course Rating:** 71.8/70.5. **Slope:** 133/119. **Green Fee:** $40/$90. **Cart Fee:** Included in Green Fee. **Walking Policy:** Mandatory cart. **Walkability:** 3. **Opened:** 1999. **Architect:** Dan Maples. **Season:** Year-round. **High:** April-Oct. **To obtain tee times:** Call up to 7 days in advance. **Miscellaneous:** Reduced fees (weekdays, low season, resort guests, twilight, juniors), discount packages, range (grass/mats), club rentals, lodging, credit cards (MC, V, AE).
Special Notes: Formerly Gold Course plus 9 new holes.
★★★★ **COMMONWEALTH COURSE**
Holes: 18. **Yards:** 6,769/5,424. **Par:** 71/71. **Course Rating:** 72.3/N/A. **Slope:** 124/109. **Green Fee:** $40/$90. **Cart Fee:** Included in Green Fee. **Walking Policy:** Mandatory cart. **Walkability:** 3. **Opened:** 1987. **Architect:** Dan Maples. **Season:** Year-round. **High:** April-Oct. **To obtain tee times:** Call up to 7 days in advance. **Miscellaneous:** Reduced fees (weekdays, low season, resort guests, twilight), discount packages, metal spikes, range (grass/mats), club rentals, lodging, credit cards (MC, V, AE).
Reader Comments: Challenging ... Magnificent ... Always a good time ... Every tee box on back wows you ... Beautiful course, wide fairways ... GPS system on the cart is fantastic, super pro, great staff ... Requires good course management ... One of the best in Virginia ... Lots of risk-reward oppurtunities for all skill levels.
Special Notes: Course re-opening Spring 2000. Formerly Blue/Gold course.
★★★★½ **MARSH HAWK COURSE** *Value, Pace*
Holes: 18. **Yards:** 6,738/5,579. **Par:** 72/72. **Course Rating:** 72.3/72.3. **Slope:** 124/124. **Green Fee:** $40/$90. **Cart Fee:** Included in Green Fee. **Walking Policy:** Mandatory cart. **Walkability:** 3. **Opened:** 1985. **Architect:** Dan Maples. **Season:** Year-round. **High:** April-Oct. **To obtain tee times:** Call up to 7 days in advance. **Miscellaneous:** Reduced fees (weekdays, low season, resort guests, twilight), discount packages, range (grass/mats), club rentals, lodging, credit cards (MC, V, AE).
Reader Comments: Good setup, typical resort track ... These are a beautiful set of courses, looking forward to the new 18 ... Perfect greens. No trick holes ... Challenging design. Tough for short hitters ... Great GPS system ... Host of state open ... Excellent variety; some cavernous bunkers.... Good test. Watch the water.
Special Notes: Formerly Red/White Course

★★★ **FOREST GREENS GOLF CLUB**
PU-4500 Poa Annua Lane, Triangle, 22172, Prince William County, (703)221-0123, 32 miles S of Washington, DC.
Holes: 18. **Yards:** 6,839/5,007. **Par:** 72/72. **Course Rating:** 71.8/68.7. **Slope:** 129/119. **Green Fee:** $20/$38. **Cart Fee:** $11/person. **Walking Policy:** Walking at certain times. **Walkability:** 4.
Opened: 1996. **Architect:** Clyde Johnston. **Season:** Year-round. **High:** April-Oct. **To obtain tee times:** Call up to 3 days in advance. **Miscellaneous:** Reduced fees (weekdays, low season, twilight, seniors, juniors), metal spikes, range (grass), credit cards (MC, V).
Reader Comments: Fairly new, good test of golf ... Tight, short course. You need all the shots ... Great layout, very hilly, lots of trees, a ball eater, great condition.

★★★½ THE GAUNTLET GOLF CLUB AT CURTIS PARK

SP-18 Fairway Dr., Fredericksburg, 22406, Stafford County, (540)752-0963, (888)755-7888, 10 miles N of Fredericksburg.

Holes: 18. **Yards:** 6,857/4,955. **Par:** 72/72. **Course Rating:** 72.8/69.8. **Slope:** 137/126. **Green Fee:** $39/$59. **Cart Fee:** Included in Green Fee. **Walking Policy:** Walking at certain times. **Walkability:** 3. **Opened:** 1995. **Architect:** P.B. Dye. **Season:** Year-round weather permitting. **High:** March-Oct. **To obtain tee times:** Call up to 7 days in advance. Credit card required to reserve weekends and holidays. **Miscellaneous:** Reduced fees (weekdays, low season, twilight, seniors), discount packages, metal spikes, range (grass/mats), club rentals, credit cards (MC, V). **Notes:** Ranked 10th in 1996 Best New Affordable Courses.

Reader Comments: Cruel greens and bunkers, know your yardage ... Excellent value, unique holes, attractive ... Requires straight accurate shots ... Early holes are beautiful but treacherous ... Truly a 'gauntlet' ... Many interesting holes and hills ... Blind tee shots, course circles a lake, very beautiful.

★★½ GLENWOOD GOLF CLUB

PU-3100 Creighton Rd., Richmond, 23223, Henrico County, (804)226-1793, 3 miles E of Richmond.

Holes: 18. **Yards:** 6,464/5,197. **Par:** 71/75. **Course Rating:** 70.0/72.1. **Slope:** 114/120. **Green Fee:** $12/$22. **Cart Fee:** $12/person. **Walking Policy:** Walking at certain times. **Walkability:** 3. **Opened:** 1927. **Architect:** Fred Findlay. **Season:** Year-round. **High:** May-Oct. **To obtain tee times:** Call up to 7 days in advance. **Miscellaneous:** Reduced fees (weekdays, twilight, seniors, juniors), metal spikes, club rentals, credit cards (MC, V), beginner friendly.

Reader Comments: Open course. Well kept greens ... Very forgiving, wide fairways ... A fair, straightforward old course ... Long, good for beginner and long hitter ... Very flat ... Greens small.

GOLDEN HORSESHOE GOLF CLUB *Service*

R-401 S. England St., Williamsburg, 23185, Williamsburg City County, (757)220-7696, (800)447-8679, 45 miles SE of Richmond.

★★★★½ GOLD COURSE *Condition*

Holes: 18. **Yards:** 6,817/5,168. **Par:** 71/71. **Course Rating:** 73.6/70.6. **Slope:** 138/127. **Green Fee:** $55/$125. **Cart Fee:** Included in Green Fee. **Walking Policy:** Unrestricted walking. **Walkability:** 3. **Opened:** 1963. **Architect:** Robert Trent Jones. **Season:** Year-round. **High:** April-Oct. **To obtain tee times:** Public may call up to 14 days in advance. Guests may reserve tee times with hotel reservations at any time. **Miscellaneous:** Reduced fees (low season, resort guests, twilight), metal spikes, range (grass/mats), club rentals, lodging, credit cards (MC, V, AE, D, Diners Club).

Notes: Golf Digest School site. Ranked 6th in 1999 Best in State.

Reader Comments: Must play, don't miss it ... Beautiful, but difficult ... Best par 3s in state ... Narrow course ... Renovation is fantastic! ... A dynamite setting ... Large greens, narrow fairways. Rewarded for a good drive. Have to be crafty when in trouble. Greens rolled true.

★★★★ GREEN COURSE *Pace*

Holes: 18. **Yards:** 7,120/5,348. **Par:** 72/72. **Course Rating:** 74.3/70.8. **Slope:** 132/124. **Green Fee:** $45/$115. **Cart Fee:** Included in Green Fee. **Walking Policy:** Unrestricted walking. **Walkability:** 3. **Opened:** 1991. **Architect:** Rees Jones. **Season:** Year-round. **High:** April-Oct. **To obtain tee times:** Public may call up to 14 days in advance. Guests may book tee times with room reservation at any time. **Miscellaneous:** Reduced fees (low season, resort guests, twilight, juniors), metal spikes, range (grass/mats), club rentals, lodging, credit cards (MC, V, AE, D, Diners Club).

Notes: Golf Digest School site. Ranked 8th in 1997 Best in State. 1998 USGA Senior Women's Amateur Championship.

Reader Comments: Worth the trip ... Very enjoyable, nice mix of holes ... Narrow and occasionally nasty ... Beautiful golf town ... Interesting rolling terrain ... More forgiving than sister course ... Back nine is better than front ... Tough course. Good finishing hole.

Special Notes: Also 9-hole executive course.

★★½ GOOSE CREEK GOLF CLUB

SP-43001 Golf Club Rd., Leesburg, 22075, Loudoun County, (703)729-2500, 35 miles W of Washington, D.C.

Holes: 18. **Yards:** 6,400/5,235. **Par:** 72/72. **Course Rating:** 70.3/71.3. **Slope:** 121/120. **Green Fee:** $22/$42. **Cart Fee:** Included in Green Fee. **Walking Policy:** Mandatory cart. **Walkability:** 4. **Opened:** 1952. **Architect:** Bill Gordon. **Season:** Year-round. **High:** April-Sept. **To obtain tee times:** Call up to 4 days in advance. **Miscellaneous:** Reduced fees (weekdays, low season, twilight, seniors, juniors), metal spikes, club rentals, credit cards (MC, V, AE).

Reader Comments: Good design ... Hilly, small greens ... Okay for an afternoon off work ... Course is very tight ... Blind shots.

GORDEN TRENT GOLF COURSE

PU-Rd. No. 632, Stuart, 24171, Patrick County, (540)694-3805.
Special Notes: Call club for further information.

VIRGINIA

GREEN'S FOLLY GOLF COURSE
PU-1085 Green's Folly Rd., South Boston, 24592, Halifax County, (804)572-4998, 60 miles N of Raleigh.
Holes: 18. **Yards:** 6,800/5,600. **Par:** 71/75. **Course Rating:** 72.0/68.0. **Slope:** 121/120. **Green Fee:** $9/$13. **Cart Fee:** $8/person. **Walking Policy:** Unrestricted walking. **Walkability:** 3. **Architect:** Fred Findlay. **Season:** Year-round. **High:** April-Sept. **To obtain tee times:** Call. **Miscellaneous:** Reduced fees (weekdays, low season, twilight, seniors, juniors), metal spikes, range (grass/mats), club rentals, beginner friendly (junior schools, beginner ladies clinics).

THE HAMPTONS GOLF COURSE
PU-320 Butler Farm Rd., Hampton, 23666, Hampton City County, (757)766-9148. **E-mail:** mlmiller@city.hampton.va.us.
Holes: 27. **Green Fee:** $16/$19. **Cart Fee:** $9/person. **Walking Policy:** Walking at certain times. **Walkability:** 1. **Opened:** 1989. **Architect:** Michael Hurdzan. **Season:** Year-round. **High:** March-Oct. **To obtain tee times:** Call 48 hours in advance. **Miscellaneous:** Reduced fees (low season, seniors, juniors), range (grass), club rentals, credit cards (MC, V, AE).

★★½ **LAKES/LINKS**
Yards: 6,283/4,965. **Par:** 71/71. **Course Rating:** 69.4/67.2. **Slope:** 110/103.
Reader Comments: Overall the course was a good outing at a great price. Don't come here hungry. ... Always a pleasure ... Typical public course, not taken care of by players.

★★½ **WOODS/LAKES**
Yards: 6,401/5,398. **Par:** 71/71. **Course Rating:** 70.9/65.7. **Slope:** 118/107.
Reader Comments: Not as easy as it looks, well maintained...Enjoyable layout, requires accurate tee shots.

★★½ **WOODS/LINKS**
Yards: 5,940/4,857. **Par:** 70/70. **Course Rating:** 66.8/60.4. **Slope:** 106/88.
Reader Comments: Stay in fairway on Links ... Great public course ... Woods and Links is a good combination ... Nice playable course, people were friendly and helpful ... British style links.

★★★½ HANGING ROCK GOLF CLUB
PU-1500 Red Lane, Salem, 24135, Salem City County, (540)389-7275, (800)277-7497, 9 miles W of Roanoke.
Holes: 18. **Yards:** 6,828/4,463. **Par:** 73/72. **Course Rating:** 72.3/62.6. **Slope:** 125/106. **Green Fee:** $22/$30. **Cart Fee:** $12/person. **Walking Policy:** Walking at certain times. **Walkability:** 3. **Opened:** 1991. **Architect:** Russell Breeden. **Season:** Year-round. **High:** April-Oct. **To obtain tee times:** Call 1 day in advance for weekday. Call Wednesday at 9 a.m. for upcoming weekend or holiday. **Miscellaneous:** Reduced fees (weekdays, low season, resort guests, twilight, seniors, juniors), discount packages, metal spikes, range (grass/mats), club rentals, credit cards (MC, V). **Reader Comments:** Very pleasant experience ... Nice mountain course ... Beautiful vistas, challenging topography ... Fantastic course great value ... Best golf for price.

★★★★ HELL'S POINT GOLF COURSE
PU-2700 Atwoodtown Rd., Virginia Beach, 23456, Virginia Beach City County, (757)721-3400, (888)821-3401, 15 miles E of Norfolk.
Holes: 18. **Yards:** 6,966/5,003. **Par:** 72/72. **Course Rating:** 73.3/71.2. **Slope:** 130/116. **Green Fee:** $30/$60. **Cart Fee:** Included in Green Fee. **Walking Policy:** Unrestricted walking. **Walkability:** 1. **Opened:** 1982. **Architect:** Rees Jones. **Season:** Year-round. **High:** April-Oct. **To obtain tee times:** Call up to 7 days in advance or book through hotel golf package up to 1 year in advance. **Miscellaneous:** Reduced fees (weekdays, low season, resort guests, twilight), discount packages, range (grass/mats), club rentals, credit cards (MC, V, AE, D). **Reader Comments:** Golfer's dream, keep it straight! ... Nice course, great greens ... Course is one of the most interesting. Service is very, very good. Best course in this area. Outstanding design ... Tough course from back tees ... Tight, water-laden and tree-lined ... Have to hit all golf shots, tough course.

★★★ HERNDON CENTENNIAL GOLF CLUB
PU-909 Ferndale Ave., Herndon, 20170, Fairfax County, (703)471-5769, 30 miles NW of Washington, D.C.
Holes: 18. **Yards:** 6,445/5,025. **Par:** 71/71. **Course Rating:** 68.7/68.4. **Slope:** 116/114. **Green Fee:** $26/$32. **Cart Fee:** $13/person. **Walking Policy:** Unrestricted walking. **Walkability:** 2. **Opened:** 1979. **Architect:** Edmond Ault. **Season:** Year-round. **High:** May-Sept. **To obtain tee times:** Call 7 days in advance for weekdays. Come in up to 7 days in advance for weekends or call Monday prior for remaining times. **Miscellaneous:** Reduced fees (weekdays, low season, twilight, seniors, juniors), range (grass), club rentals, credit cards (MC, V, D). **Notes:** 1996-1999 Men's U.S. Amateur Public Links Sectional Qualifier, 1996-1998 Women's U.S.Amateur Public Links Sectional Qualifier. **Reader Comments:** Good muny course ... Great value, good shape ... Short. Good upkeep, especially greens ... Trees planted 15 years ago have now grown up.

VIRGINIA

HERON RIDGE GOLF CLUB
PU-2973 Heron Ridge Drive, Virginia Beach, 23456, Virginia Beach County, (757)426-3800.
Holes: 18. **Yards:** 7,017/5,011. **Par:** 72/72. **Course Rating:** 73.9/68.5. **Slope:** 131/111. **Green Fee:** $33/$57. **Cart Fee:** Included in Green Fee. **Walking Policy:** Mandatory cart. **Walkability:** 2. **Opened:** 1999. **Architect:** Fred Couples/Gene Bates. **Season:** Year-round. **High:** March-Nov. **To obtain tee times:** Advanced tee times require major credit card to hold tee times.
Miscellaneous: Reduced fees (weekdays, low season, twilight, seniors, juniors), range (grass), club rentals, credit cards (MC, V, AE).

★★★ HIDDEN CREEK GOLF CLUB
SP-11599 N. Shore Dr., Reston, 22090, Fairfax County, (703)437-4222.
Yards: N/A. **Par:** N/A. **Course Rating:** N/A. **Slope:** N/A. **Green Fee:** N/A. **Walkability:** N/A. **Architect:** Edmund B. Ault. **Miscellaneous:** Metal spikes.
Reader Comments: Excellent, challenging ... Long and tight ... Rolling hills, tough from back tees, good shape.
Special Notes: Call club for further information.

★★★½ HIGHLANDS GOLFERS' CLUB
PU-8135 Highland Glen Dr., Chesterfield, 23838, Chesterfield County, (804)796-4800, 15 miles S of Richmond.
Holes: 18. **Yards:** 6,711/5,019. **Par:** 72/72. **Course Rating:** 72.1/68.7. **Slope:** 133/120. **Green Fee:** N/A/$55. **Cart Fee:** Included in Green Fee. **Walking Policy:** Mandatory cart. **Walkability:** 4. **Opened:** 1995. **Architect:** Barton Tuck. **Season:** Year-round. **High:** April-Oct. **To obtain tee times:** Call golf shop. **Miscellaneous:** Reduced fees (low season, twilight, juniors), range (grass), club rentals, credit cards (MC, V, AE).
Reader Comments: Friendly staff. Nice place to play ... Fastest greens I have ever played. Hidden gem ...Felt like a country club, good variety of holes ... A hard test of iron shots.

HOLLOWS GOLF COURSE
SP-14501 Greenwood Church Rd., Montpelier, 23192, Hanover County, (804)798-2949, 10 miles NW of Richmond.
Holes: 27. **Green Fee:** $19/$25. **Cart Fee:** $11/person. **Walking Policy:** Unrestricted walking. **Walkability:** 3. **Opened:** 1984. **Architect:** Brian Ault/Tom Clark. **Season:** Year-round. **High:** April-Oct. **To obtain tee times:** Call 7 days in advance. **Miscellaneous:** Reduced fees (weekdays, low season, twilight, seniors, juniors), metal spikes, club rentals, credit cards (MC, V).
★★½ COTTAGE/ROAD
Yards: 5,969/4,642. **Par:** 70/70. **Course Rating:** 67.9/63.3. **Slope:** 112/103.
Reader Comments: Great price ... Fun course, great for seniors.
★★½ LAKE/COTTAGE
Yards: 5,829/4,662. **Par:** 70/70. **Course Rating:** 67.7/63.6. **Slope:** 115/106.
★★½ LAKE/ROAD
Yards: 5,966/4,750. **Par:** 70/70. **Course Rating:** 68.0/67.1. **Slope:** 112/109.
Reader Comments: Level course, good greens ... Average to good layout, acceptable condition ... A friendly, fun course for middle-handicap golfers ... Forgiving course. ... Green is built up and hard to hit.

HOLSTON HILLS COUNTRY CLUB
SP-1000 Country Club Rd., Marion, 24354, Smyth County, (540)783-7484, 40 miles NE of Bristol.
Holes: 18. **Yards:** 6,536/5,171. **Par:** 72/75. **Course Rating:** 70.8/70.6. **Slope:** 126/119. **Green Fee:** $22/$28. **Cart Fee:** $10/person. **Walking Policy:** Unrestricted walking. **Walkability:** 4. **Opened:** 1946. **Architect:** Edmund B. Ault. **Season:** Year-round. **High:** June-Aug. **To obtain tee times:** Tee times not required. **Miscellaneous:** Reduced fees (weekdays).

THE HOMESTEAD RESORT *Service*
R-P.O. Box 2000, Hot Springs, 24445, Bath County, (800)838-1766, 65 miles NW of Roanoke.
Web: www.thehomestead.com.
★★★★½ CASCADES COURSE *Condition*
(540)839-7994.
Holes: 18. **Yards:** 6,566/5,448. **Par:** 70/71. **Course Rating:** 72.9/72.9. **Slope:** 136/137. **Green Fee:** $75/$150. **Cart Fee:** $20/person. **Walking Policy:** Unrestricted walking. **Walkability:** 3. **Opened:** 1923. **Architect:** William Flynn. **Season:** April-Oct. **High:** April-Oct. **To obtain tee times:** Call golf shop. **Miscellaneous:** Reduced fees (low season, resort guests, twilight, juniors), discount packages, metal spikes, range (grass), caddies, club rentals, lodging (500 rooms), credit cards (MC, V, AE, D, Diners Club).
Notes: Ranked 53rd in 1999-2000 America's 100 Greatest; 1st in 1999 Best in State; USGA Championship host; site of 2000 U.S. Mid-Amateur; site of 2000 NCAA Mens Golf Championship.
Reader Comments: The greatest! ... One of the best experience in my short golf life ... Tough ... A golf monument has gotten even better through course upgrade ... Some tough blind holes, but

trust the directional flags ... Back-to-back par fives at 16 and 17 are a blast ... Outstanding mountain course, tests every club ... Tough, unrelenting, fast greens ... Lived up to its reputation.

★★★½ LOWER CASCADES COURSE
(540)839-7995.
Holes: 18. **Yards:** 6,619/4,726. **Par:** 72/70. **Course Rating:** 72.2/65.5. **Slope:** 127/116. **Green Fee:** $45/$95. **Cart Fee:** $20/person. **Walking Policy:** Unrestricted walking. **Walkability:** 4. **Opened:** 1962. **Architect:** Robert Trent Jones. **Season:** April-Oct. **High:** April-Oct. **To obtain tee times:** Call Pro Shop. **Miscellaneous:** Reduced fees (low season, resort guests, twilight, juniors), discount packages, metal spikes, range (grass/mats), caddies, club rentals, lodging (500 rooms), credit cards (MC, V, AE, D, Diners Club).
Reader Comments: An above average layout in a fabulous mountain valley ... Wide open picturesque ... Played three times, saw Sam Snead there each time ... Open layout ... Should get more and better recognition ... Excellent service.

★★★★ THE OLD COURSE
(540)839-7739.
Holes: 18. **Yards:** 6,200/5,150. **Par:** 71/72. **Course Rating:** 70.1/70.0. **Slope:** 121/117. **Green Fee:** $45/$90. **Cart Fee:** $20/person. **Walking Policy:** Unrestricted walking. **Walkability:** 3. **Opened:** 1892. **Architect:** Donald Ross. **Season:** April-Oct. **High:** April-Oct. **To obtain tee times:** Call golf shop. **Miscellaneous:** Reduced fees (low season, resort guests, twilight, juniors), discount packages, metal spikes, range (grass/mats), caddies, club rentals, lodging (500 rooms), credit cards (MC, V, AE, D, Diners Club).
Reader Comments: Course for all ages ... Wonderful old layout, beautiful setting, great views of the old hotel ... A great walking course ... Super improvements ... New tees, traps, rerouting, plus excellent new practice area ... Good old course. Great shape ... Friendly, helpful staff ... A wonderful surprise. Excellent course ... Difficulty is all in the small fast greens ... Never crowded, underrated.

★★★½ HONEY BEE GOLF CLUB
PU-5016 S Independence Blvd., Virginia Beach, 23456, Virginia Beach County, (757)471-2768.
Holes: 18. **Yards:** 6,075/4,929. **Par:** 70/70. **Course Rating:** 69.6/67.0. **Slope:** 123/104. **Green Fee:** $27/$44. **Cart Fee:** Included in Green Fee. **Walking Policy:** Unrestricted walking. **Walkability:** 1. **Opened:** 1988. **Architect:** Rees Jones. **Season:** Year-round. **High:** March-Oct. **To obtain tee times:** Call Wednesday for upcoming weekend. Otherwise call 7 days in advance. **Miscellaneous:** Reduced fees (weekdays, low season, twilight, seniors, juniors), discount packages, range (grass), club rentals, credit cards (MC, V, AE).
Reader Comments: Short course, but great service and condition ... Enjoyable ... Another great public course ... Fast greens ... Not too long but plenty of trouble.

★★★ IVY HILL GOLF CLUB
SP-1327 Ivy Hill Drive, Forrest, 24551, Bedford County, (804)525-2680.
Holes: 18. **Yards:** 7,047/4,893. **Par:** 72/72. **Course Rating:** 74.2/67.8. **Slope:** 130/110. **Green Fee:** $15/$20. **Cart Fee:** $13/person. **Walking Policy:** Walking at certain times. **Walkability:** 5. **Architect:** J. Porter Gibson. **Season:** Year-round. **High:** April-Oct. **To obtain tee times:** Call or come in and make tee times in advance. **Miscellaneous:** Reduced fees (weekdays, low season, seniors), metal spikes, range (grass/mats), club rentals, credit cards (MC, V), beginner friendly (clinics, junior clinics and lessons).
Reader Comments: Continues improvement ... Tough, but fair ... Hilly ... Front nine in relaxing rural setting. Back nine in beautiful residential area.

★★ JORDAN POINT GOLF CLUB
SP-Jordan Point Rd., Hopewell, 23860, Prince George County, (804)458-0141, 80 miles SE of Richmond.
Holes: 18. **Yards:** 6,585/4,944. **Par:** 72/72. **Course Rating:** 70.7/68.6. **Slope:** 129/113. **Green Fee:** $19/$24. **Cart Fee:** $11/person. **Walking Policy:** Walking at certain times. **Walkability:** 3. **Opened:** 1955. **Architect:** Russell Breeden. **Season:** Year-round. **High:** April-Oct. **To obtain tee times:** Call up to 7 days in advance. **Miscellaneous:** Reduced fees (seniors), club rentals, credit cards (MC, V, AE, D).

KASTLE GREENS GOLF CLUB
PU-11446 Rogues Rd., Midland, 22728, Fauquier County, (540)788-4410, (877)283-4653, 18 miles S of Manassas. **E-mail:** kggolf@erols.com. **Web:** www.kastlegreens.com.
Holes: 18. **Yards:** 6,732/5,331. **Par:** 72/72. **Course Rating:** 73.8/70.5. **Slope:** 132/122. **Green Fee:** $20/$32. **Cart Fee:** $13/person. **Walking Policy:** Walking at certain times. **Walkability:** 1. **Opened:** 1998. **Architect:** Gary Cordova. **Season:** Year-round. **High:** April-Oct. **To obtain tee times:** Call (800)883-5674. **Miscellaneous:** Reduced fees (weekdays, low season, twilight, seniors), range (grass/mats), club rentals, credit cards (MC, V), beginner friendly.

★★ KEMPSVILLE GREENS GOLF CLUB
PU-4840 Princess Anne Rd., Virginia Beach, 23462, Virginia Beach City County, (757)474-8441.

Holes: 18. **Yards:** 5,849/4,538. **Par:** 70/70. **Course Rating:** 67.8/63.8. **Slope:** 114/94. **Green Fee:** $12/$20. **Cart Fee:** $9/person. **Walking Policy:** Unrestricted walking. **Walkability:** 1. **Opened:** 1954. **Architect:** Ellis Maples. **Season:** Year-round. **High:** June-Aug. **To obtain tee times:** Call Friday after 8 a.m. for upcoming weekend and holiday. Open play during the week. **Miscellaneous:** Reduced fees (weekdays, twilight, seniors, juniors), metal spikes, range (grass/mats), club rentals, credit cards (MC, V). **Special Notes:** Follow up on question 7, 8, 9.

★★★½ KILN CREEK GOLF & COUNTRY CLUB

SP-1003 Brick Kiln Blvd., Newport News, 23602, Newport News City County, (757)988-3220, 30 miles W of Norfolk.
Holes: 27. **Yards:** 6,889/5,313. **Par:** 72/72. **Course Rating:** 73.4/69.5. **Slope:** 130/119. **Green Fee:** $35/$60. **Cart Fee:** Included in Green Fee. **Walking Policy:** Mandatory cart. **Walkability:** 3. **Opened:** 1989. **Architect:** Tom Clark. **Season:** Year-round. **High:** April-Oct. **To obtain tee times:** Call one week in advance. **Miscellaneous:** Reduced fees (weekdays, low season), range (grass/mats), club rentals, lodging, credit cards (MC, V, AE).
Reader Comments: Super course for a public course. Reasonable ... Some of those sand traps made you feel like Lawrence of Arabia ... Back tees are monsters. Very tough par threes. 460-yard par four finish.

KINGSMILL RESORT & CLUB

R-1010 Kingsmill Rd., Williamsburg, 23185, James City County, (757)253-3906, (800)832-5665, 50 miles E of Richmond. **Web:** www.kingsmill.com.

★★★½ PLANTATION COURSE

Holes: 18. **Yards:** 6,543/4,880. **Par:** 72/72. **Course Rating:** 71.3/67.9. **Slope:** 119/116. **Green Fee:** $55/$80. **Cart Fee:** Included in Green Fee. **Walking Policy:** Mandatory cart. **Walkability:** 3. **Opened:** 1986. **Architect:** Arnold Palmer/Ed Seay. **Season:** Year-round. **High:** April-Oct. **To obtain tee times:** Resort guests may make tee times with room reservation. Others may call 1 day in advance. **Miscellaneous:** Reduced fees (low season, resort guests, twilight), discounts, metal spikes, range (grass/mats), club rentals, lodging (400 rooms), credit cards (MC, V, AE, D).
Reader Comments: Much easier than River course ... Some great holes, fun ... Any course here is great ... Great greens.

★★★★ RIVER COURSE

Holes: 18. **Yards:** 6,837/4,646. **Par:** 71/71. **Course Rating:** 73.3/65.3. **Slope:** 137/116. **Green Fee:** $65/$125. **Cart Fee:** Included in Green Fee. **Walking Policy:** Mandatory cart. **Walkability:** 4. **Opened:** 1975. **Architect:** Pete Dye. **Season:** Year-round. **High:** April-Oct. **To obtain tee times:** Resort guests may make tee times with room reservation. Others may call 1 day in advance. **Miscellaneous:** Reduced fees (low season, resort guests, twilight), discount packages, metal spikes, range (grass/mats), club rentals, lodging (400 rooms), credit cards (MC, V, AE, D). **Notes:** Ranked 12th in 1997 Best in State. PGA Tour's Annual Michelob Championship at Kingsmill.
Reader Comments: A fine resort with friendly people ... Plays longer than it reads ... Tight demanding course. River's beautiful ... 16-17-18 as good as any finishing stretch anywhere. Very benign for Dye ... Scenic vistas, pro quality ... One of the tough tracks on the East coast ... Miss a good shot by just a little bit and it's very penalizing.
Special Notes: Also 9-hole par 3 Bray Links.

★★★★ WOODS COURSE

Holes: 18. **Yards:** 6,784/5,140. **Par:** 72/72. **Course Rating:** 72.7/68.7. **Slope:** 131/120. **Green Fee:** $60/$100. **Cart Fee:** Included in Green Fee. **Walking Policy:** Mandatory cart. **Walkability:** 3. **Opened:** 1995. **Architect:** Tom Clark/Curtis Strange. **Season:** Year-round. **High:** April-Oct. **To obtain tee times:** Resort guests may make tee times with room reservation. Others may call 1 day in advance. **Miscellaneous:** Reduced fees (low season, resort guests, twilight), discount packages, metal spikes, range (grass/mats), club rentals, lodging, credit cards (MC, V, AE, D). **Notes:** Ranked 13th in 1997 Best in State.
Reader Comments: One fun course to play ... Even better than the River course ... Fun layout, some short holes; very picturesque ... A jewel in the quiet corner of the resort ... .Gorgeous, but difficult ... Best of the Kingsmill courses ... Must hit it straight ... Curtis, you did good ... Slick greens.
Special Notes: Also 9-hole par 3 Bray Links course.

★★★★ KISKIACK GOLF CLUB

R-8104 Club Dr., Williamsburg, 23188, (757)566-2200, (800)989-4728, 45 miles E of Richmond.
Holes: 18. **Yards:** 6,775/4,902. **Par:** 72/71. **Course Rating:** 72.7/67.8. **Slope:** 128/112. **Green Fee:** N/A. **Cart Fee:** Included in Green Fee. **Walking Policy:** Mandatory cart. **Walkability:** 3. **Opened:** 1997. **Architect:** John LaFoy/Vinny Giles. **Season:** Year-round. **High:** Apr-May/Sept-Nov. **Miscellaneous:** Reduced fees (low season, twilight, juniors), range (grass/mats), club rentals, credit cards (MC, V, AE, D).
Reader Comments: Wonderful new course in Williamsburg. Layout is eye appealing and challenging ... Easy to play, does not overwhelm you ... Great greens ... A steal, OK for high handicaps ... Very good new links style course ... Short but tight, challenging ... Some great holes ...

Exciting new layout. Staff very pleasant. Delightful ... Some scenic & interesting holes; needs to mature a bit.

★★★ LAKE WRIGHT GOLF COURSE
PM-6282 N. Hampton Blvd., Norfolk, 23502, Norfolk City County, (757)459-2255.
Holes: 18. **Yards:** 6,174/5,297. **Par:** 70/70. **Course Rating:** 68.8/68.2. **Slope:** 116/105. **Green Fee:** $18/$20. **Cart Fee:** $20/person. **Walking Policy:** Walking at certain times. **Walkability:** 2. **Opened:** 1969. **Architect:** Al Jamison. **Season:** Year-round. **High:** April-Nov. **To obtain tee times:** Call 3 day in advance for weekends only. **Miscellaneous:** Reduced fees (weekdays, low season, seniors, juniors), range (grass/mats), club rentals, lodging.
Reader Comments: Open course with few hazards. Great greens ... Fun layout, usually OK shape ... Killer par 3s.

LAKEVIEW GOLF COURSE
SP-4101 Shen Lake Drive, Harrisonburg, 22801, Rockingham County, (540)434-8937, 2 miles E of Harrisonburg.
Holes: 27. **Green Fee:** $21/$24. **Cart Fee:** $22/cart. **Walking Policy:** Unrestricted walking. **Walkability:** 3. **Opened:** 1962. **Architect:** Edmund Ault. **Season:** Year-round. **High:** April-Oct. **To obtain tee times:** Call up to 7 days in advance. **Miscellaneous:** Reduced fees (twilight), range (mats), club rentals, credit cards (MC, V).
★★★ LAKE/PEAK
Yards: 6,517/5,637. **Par:** 72/72. **Course Rating:** 71.0/71.8. **Slope:** 119/113.
Reader Comments: A broad variety of hills, valleys, water and woods ... Busy course, enjoyable for all handicaps ... Lake 9th hole is challenging par 4, requiring a long blind drive and a long iron to a green guarded in front by a pond ... A nice walkable layout in central Va.
★★★ LAKE/SPRING
Yards: 6,303/5,383. **Par:** 72/72. **Course Rating:** 70.9/70.1. **Slope:** 120/115.
Reader Comments: Challenging ... Another course with great views. Solid par 4s ... Best public course in area ... Spring nine is OK, Lake nine is eye-appealing, reasonable cost ... Par 5s reachable in two; several wide fairways.
★★★ PEAK/SPRING
Yards: 6,640/5,410. **Par:** 72/72. **Course Rating:** 71.3/70.1. **Slope:** 121/116. .
Reader Comments: A nice walkable layout ... Challenging ... Nice scenery. Course has character ... Excellent views ... Good greens, good layout.

★★★★ LANSDOWNE GOLF CLUB *Condition*
R-44050 Woodridge Pkwy., Lansdowne, 20176, Loudoun County, (703)729-4071, (800)541-4801, 35 miles W of Washington, D.C.
Holes: 18. **Yards:** 7,057/5,213. **Par:** 72/72. **Course Rating:** 74.6/70.6. **Slope:** 139/124. **Green Fee:** $85/$95. **Cart Fee:** Included in Green Fee. **Walking Policy:** Mandatory cart. **Walkability:** 5. **Opened:** 1991. **Architect:** Robert Trent Jones Jr. **Season:** Year-round. **High:** April-Nov. **To obtain tee times:** Monday-Thursday call 5 days in advance. Friday-Sunday call 2 days in advance. **Miscellaneous:** Reduced fees (low season, resort guests, twilight), discount packages, range (grass/mats), club rentals, lodging, credit cards (MC, V, AE).
Reader Comments: Worth the buck once a year ... Near Dulles ... Zoysia grass. Great lies ... Super course conditions and practice area, great hotel ... Deer at dusk on the beautiful back nine ... Back harder than front ... Super course all around, great service .... 16, 17 and 18 very tough ... Demands accuracy and thought or you will be playing from the beautiful surroundings.

★★ LEE PARK GOLF COURSE
PU-3108 Homestead Dr., Petersburg, 23805, Petersburg City County, (804)733-5667, 25 miles S of Richmond.
Holes: 18. **Yards:** 6,037/4,946. **Par:** 70/70. **Course Rating:** 68.0/62.2. **Slope:** 108/96. **Green Fee:** $17/$20. **Cart Fee:** $10/person. **Walking Policy:** Unrestricted walking. **Walkability:** 1. **Opened:** 1945. **Architect:** Fred Findley. **Season:** Year-round. **High:** June-Aug. **To obtain tee times:** None taken. **Miscellaneous:** Reduced fees (weekdays, twilight, seniors, juniors), range (grass/mats), club rentals, credit cards (MC, V).

★★★½ LEE'S HILL GOLFERS' CLUB
SP-10200 Old Dominion Pkwy., Fredericksburg, 22408, Spotsylvania County, (540)891-0111, (800)930-3636, 50 miles N of Richmond. **Web:** www.golfsouth.com.
Holes: 18. **Yards:** 6,805/5,064. **Par:** 72/72. **Course Rating:** 72.4/69.2. **Slope:** 128/115. **Green Fee:** $41/$66. **Cart Fee:** Included in Green Fee. **Walking Policy:** Mandatory cart. **Walkability:** 1. **Opened:** 1993. **Architect:** Bill Love. **Season:** Year-round. **High:** April-Oct. **To obtain tee times:** Call 1 week in advance. **Miscellaneous:** Reduced fees (resort guests, twilight), discount packages, range (grass/mats), club rentals, credit cards (MC, V, AE).
Reader Comments: Great greens. Tough rough ... Links style ... Good par 3s ... Very enjoyable to play. Basic golf ... Service and shape of course gives special experience ... Nice, fair, enjoyable, must play.

★★★★ THE LEGENDS AT STONEHOUSE
PU-9540 Old Stage Rd., Toano, 23168, James City County, (757)566-1138, (888)825-3436, 10 miles W of Williamsburg.
Holes: 18. **Yards:** 6,963/5,085. **Par:** 71/71. **Course Rating:** 75.0/69.1. **Slope:** 140/121. **Green Fee:** $40/$85. **Cart Fee:** $20/person. **Walking Policy:** Unrestricted walking. **Walkability:** 4. **Opened:** 1996. **Architect:** Mike Stranz. **Season:** Year-round. **High:** March-Nov. **To obtain tee times:** Call up to 1 year in advance. **Miscellaneous:** Discount packages, range (grass), club rentals, credit cards (MC, V, AE).
Notes: Ranked 1st in 1996 Best New Upscale Courses; 4th in 1999 Best in State.
Reader Comments: The best, unreal ... Each hole could be signature hole elsewhere ... Some novelty, tricky, blind holes ... As good as it gets. They even had grazing sheep ... Championship course, tough but fair, great shape ... Some holes impossible for ladies ... Great layout with huge, fast, undulating greens ... Deserves accolades it has received ... Absolutely breathtaking.

★★★ MANASSAS PARK PUBLIC GOLF COURSE
PU-9701 Manassas Dr., Manassas Park, 20111, Price William County, (703)335-0777, 20 miles SW of Washington, DC.
Holes: 18. **Yards:** 6,651/4,747. **Par:** 72/72. **Course Rating:** 72.5/68.1. **Slope:** 133/118. **Green Fee:** $15/$30. **Cart Fee:** $12/person. **Walking Policy:** Walking at certain times. **Walkability:** 5. **Opened:** 1996. **Architect:** Jerry Slack. **Season:** Year-round. **High:** April-Oct. **To obtain tee times:** Call up to 3 days in advance. **Miscellaneous:** Reduced fees (weekdays, low season, twilight, seniors, juniors), metal spikes, range (grass), club rentals, credit cards (MC, V).
Reader Comments: Physically exhausting. Mentally stimulating ... Too many blind shots, strange holes ... Target golf ... Tough, hills ... Wow! what a roller coaster ride! ... Too tight for average play ... The perfect game for this course is long and straight, otherwise bring a bag full of balls.

★★½ MARINERS LANDING GOLF & COUNTRY CLUB
SP-Rte. 1, Box 119, Huddleston, 24104, Bedford County, (540)297-7888, 35 miles SE of Roanoke.
Holes: 18. **Yards:** 7,155/5,640. **Par:** 72/72. **Course Rating:** 74.5/68.1. **Slope:** 130/113. **Green Fee:** $25/$38. **Cart Fee:** Included in Green Fee. **Walking Policy:** Walking at certain times. **Walkability:** 4. **Opened:** 1994. **Architect:** Robert Trent Jones. **Season:** Year-round. **High:** April-Sept. **To obtain tee times:** Call golf shop. **Miscellaneous:** Reduced fees (weekdays, low season, twilight, juniors), range (grass), club rentals, credit cards (MC, V).
Reader Comments: Greatly improved ... Huge greens on par 3s ... Excellent greens ... New clubhouse, beautiful scenery.

★★½ MASSANUTTEN RESORT GOLF COURSE
R-P.O. Box 1227, Harrisonburg, 22801, Rockingham County, (540)289-4941, 100 miles S of Washington DC.
Holes: 18. **Yards:** 6,408/5,117. **Par:** 72/73. **Course Rating:** 70.5/69.8. **Slope:** 123/128. **Green Fee:** $40/$50. **Cart Fee:** Included in Green Fee. **Walking Policy:** Unrestricted walking. **Walkability:** 5. **Opened:** 1975. **Architect:** Frank Duane/Richard Watson. **Season:** Year-round weather permitting. **High:** April-Oct. **To obtain tee times:** Call up to 14 days in advance. **Miscellaneous:** Reduced fees (resort guests, juniors), metal spikes, range (mats), club rentals, lodging, credit cards (MC, V, AE, D).
Reader Comments: Tight fairways on most holes ... Beautiful mountain course ... Course layout difficult, blind holes, hilly, sloping greens ... Chiseled into a mountain. Golf on a ski slope ... Pace excellent. 3½ hours per round.

★★½ MEADOWCREEK GOLF COURSE
PM-1400 Pen Park Rd., Charlottesville, 22901, Albemarle County, (804)977-0615.
Holes: 18. **Yards:** 6,051/4,568. **Par:** 70/70. **Course Rating:** 68.5/62.0. **Slope:** 118/105. **Green Fee:** $21/$23. **Cart Fee:** $12/person. **Walking Policy:** Unrestricted walking. **Walkability:** 3. **Opened:** 1973. **Architect:** Buddy Loving/Bill Love. **Season:** Year-round. **High:** April-Sept. **To obtain tee times:** Call 2 days in advance. **Miscellaneous:** Reduced fees (weekdays, twilight, seniors, juniors), range (grass/mats), club rentals, credit cards (MC, V).
Reader Comments: Very good for muny. Greens very slow... Downhill 1st hole ... Service makes up for other items.... Intricate public course ... Well-placed traps, bring your wedge ... Nice mix of open fairways, rolling hills, mountain views.

MEADOWS FARMS GOLF COURSE
PU-4300 Flat Run Rd., Locust Grove, 22508, Orange County, (540)854-9890, 16 miles W of Fredericksburg. **E-mail:** blewis@nsgemlink.com. **Web:** www.meadowsfarms.com.
Holes: 27. **Green Fee:** $19/$39. **Cart Fee:** Included in Green Fee. **Walking Policy:** Walking at certain times. **Walkability:** 4. **Opened:** 1993. **Architect:** Bill Ward. **Season:** Year-round. **High:** April-Oct. **To obtain tee times:** Call at least 7 days in advance.
★★★½ ISLAND GREEN/LONGEST HOLE
Yards: 7,005/4,541. **Par:** 72/72. **Course Rating:** 73.2/65.3. **Slope:** 129/109. **Miscellaneous:** Reduced fees (weekdays, low season, twilight, seniors, juniors), range (grass), club rentals, lodging (3 rooms), credit cards (MC, V), beginner friendly.

VIRGINIA

Reader Comments: Par six! 841 yards! ... Great course, great shape ... Always a good time ... Huge greens, challenging course ... A must see. Baseball hole a treat ... 19 holes, really, 1st is a warm-up hole ... Great value, good change of pace.

★★★½ **ISLAND GREEN/WATERFALL**
Yards: 6,058/4,075. **Par:** 70/70. **Course Rating:** 68.9/62.8. **Slope:** 123/100. **Miscellaneous:** Reduced fees (weekdays, low season, twilight, seniors, juniors), range (grass/mats), club rentals, credit cards (MC, V).

★★★½ **LONGEST HOLE/WATERFALL**
Yards: 6,871/4,424. **Par:** 72/72. **Course Rating:** 72.7/65.1. **Slope:** 123/105. **Miscellaneous:** Reduced fees (weekdays, low season, twilight, seniors, juniors), range (grass/mats), club rentals, lodging (3 rooms), credit cards (MC, V).

★★★ **MILL QUARTER PLANTATION GOLF COURSE**
SP-1525 Mill Quarter Dr., Powhatan, 23139, Powhatan County, (804)598-4221, (804)598-4221, 22 miles W of Richmond. **E-mail:** ddaniels@millquarter.com. **Web:** www.millquarter.com.
Holes: 18. **Yards:** 6,943/4,936. **Par:** 72/72. **Course Rating:** 72.2/73.6. **Slope:** 118/123. **Green Fee:** $16/$28. **Cart Fee:** $28/cart. **Walking Policy:** Walking at certain times. **Walkability:** 1.
Opened: 1973. **Architect:** Ed Ault. **Season:** Year-round. **High:** April-Sept. **To obtain tee times:** Call 7 days in advance. **Miscellaneous:** Reduced fees (weekdays, low season, resort guests, twilight, seniors), discount packages, range (grass), club rentals, credit cards (MC, V, AE).
Reader Comments: Vastly improved in last few years ... Very public, lots of new golfers ... Good walking course.... Long from whites ... Small greens.

NEWPORT NEWS GOLF CLUB AT DEER RUN
PU-901 Clubhouse Way, Newport News, 23608, Newport News City County, (757)886-7925, 10 miles E of Williamsburg.

★★★½ **CARDINAL COURSE**
Holes: 18. **Yards:** 6,624/4,789. **Par:** 72/72. **Course Rating:** 70.9/62.8. **Slope:** 118/102. **Green Fee:** $27/$27. **Cart Fee:** $18/cart. **Walking Policy:** Unrestricted walking. **Walkability:** 2. **Opened:** 1966. **Architect:** Ed Ault. **Season:** Year-round. **High:** April-Nov. **To obtain tee times:** Call 7 days in advance for weekdays. Call Thursday beginning at 7 a.m. for weekends and holidays. **Miscellaneous:** Reduced fees (low season), range (grass/mats), club rentals, credit cards (MC, V).
Reader Comments: Excellent value, real nice people ... Lots of trees, tough course.... Great course for cheap rates. Can't beat the value ... Nice track for a comfortable, if long, day.

★★★½ **DEER RUN COURSE**
Holes: 18. **Yards:** 7,209/5,295. **Par:** 72/72. **Course Rating:** 73.7/70.0. **Slope:** 133/113. **Green Fee:** $36/$36. **Cart Fee:** Included in Green Fee. **Walking Policy:** Mandatory cart. **Walkability:** 2. **Opened:** 1966. **Architect:** Ed Ault. **Season:** Year-round. **High:** April-Nov. **To obtain tee times:** Call 7 days in advance for weekdays. Call Thursday beginning 7 a.m. for weekends and holidays. **Miscellaneous:** Range (grass/mats), club rentals, credit cards (MC, V).
Notes: 1999 U.S.G.A. Women's State Team Matches; 1997 U.S.G.A. Four-Ball Championship.
Reader Comments: Some trees, tougher course ... Great 17th hole ... Absolute cannon required from back tees. Generous fairways and big greens. Deer everywhere ... Long finishing holes ... Great value, tough ... Championship course is a great test.

★★ **OCEAN VIEW GOLF COURSE**
PU-9610 Norfolk Ave., Norfolk, 23503, Norfolk City County, (757)480-2094.
Holes: 18. **Yards:** 6,200/5,642. **Par:** 70/70. **Course Rating:** 69.5/69.0. **Slope:** 117/116. **Green Fee:** $15/$15. **Cart Fee:** Included in Green Fee. **Walking Policy:** Walking at certain times. **Walkability:** N/A. **Opened:** 1929. **Season:** Year-round. **High:** April-Oct. **To obtain tee times:** Call one week in advance. **Miscellaneous:** Reduced fees (weekdays, low season, twilight, seniors, juniors), discount packages, metal spikes, club rentals, credit cards (MC, V).

★★★★ **OLDE MILL GOLF RESORT**
R-Rte. 1, Box 84, Laurel Fork, 24352, Carroll County, (540)398-2211, (800)753-5005, 55 miles N of Winston-Salem, NC. **E-mail:** oldemill@tcia.net. **Web:** www.oldemill.net.
Holes: 18. **Yards:** 6,833/4,876. **Par:** 72/72. **Course Rating:** 72.7/70.4. **Slope:** 127/134. **Green Fee:** $29/$42. **Cart Fee:** $13/person. **Walking Policy:** Walking at certain times. **Walkability:** 4.
Opened: 1973. **Architect:** Ellis Maples. **Season:** Year-round. **High:** April-Oct. **To obtain tee times:** Call between 8 a.m. and 6 p.m. anytime. **Miscellaneous:** Reduced fees (weekdays, low season, resort guests, twilight, seniors), discount packages, metal spikes, range (grass), club rentals, lodging, credit cards (MC, V, AE, D).
Reader Comments: Hidden jewel, difficult for high handicappers ... Beautiful views ... View from 10th tee great ... Tough. Bring lots of balls ... Water on 10 holes.

★★ **OLE MONTEREY GOLF CLUB**
PU-1112 Tinker Creek Lane, Roanoke, 24019, Roanoke City County, (540)563-0400.
Holes: 18. **Yards:** 6,712/6,287. **Par:** 71/71. **Course Rating:** N/A. **Slope:** 116/112. **Green Fee:** N/A. **Walkability:** N/A. **Architect:** Fred Findlay. **Season:** Year-round. **High:** April-Oct. **Miscellaneous:** Reduced fees (weekdays), metal spikes.

★★½ PENDERBROOK GOLF CLUB
SP-3700 Golf Trail Lane, Fairfax, 22033, Fairfax County, (703)385-3700, 14 miles W of Washington, DC.
Holes: 18. **Yards:** 6,152/5,042. **Par:** 71/72. **Course Rating:** 71.2/69.1. **Slope:** 130/121. **Green Fee:** $27/$35. **Cart Fee:** $13/person. **Walking Policy:** Unrestricted walking. **Walkability:** N/A. **Opened:** 1979. **Architect:** Edmund B. Ault. **Season:** Year-round. **High:** March-Oct. **To obtain tee times:** Call 3 days in advance starting at 8 a.m. **Miscellaneous:** Reduced fees (weekdays, low season, seniors, juniors), metal spikes, club rentals, credit cards (MC, V).
Reader Comments: Under new management, looking up ... Place is clean, well maintained ... Holes 9-12 test your courage ... No. 8 is best on course ... Some challenging water ... Short, tight, but often a long round.

★★★ PIANKATANK RIVER GOLF CLUB
SP-P.O. Box 424, Rte. 708, Hartfield, 23071, Middlesex County, (804)776-6516, (800)303-3384, 60 miles E of Richmond.
Holes: 18. **Yards:** 6,751/4,894. **Par:** 72/72. **Course Rating:** 73.6/70.0. **Slope:** 130/113. **Green Fee:** $22/$40. **Cart Fee:** Included in Green Fee. **Walking Policy:** Walking at certain times. **Walkability:** 4. **Opened:** 1996. **Architect:** Algie Pulley. **Season:** Year-round. **High:** April-Nov. **To obtain tee times:** Call up to 7 days in advance. **Miscellaneous:** Reduced fees (weekdays, low season, resort guests, twilight, seniors, juniors), discount packages, range (grass), club rentals, credit cards (MC, V).
Reader Comments: Tremendous value, great experience ... Front challenging ... Scenic and fun ... This course is always in great shape. The front nine is hilly but the back nine is more open.

PLEASANT VALLEY GOLFERS' CLUB
SP-4715 Pleasant Valley Rd., Chantilly, 20151, Fairfax County, (703)631-7902, 20 miles W of Washington, D.C. **Web:** www.golfmid.com.
Holes: 18. **Yards:** 6,915/5,106. **Par:** 72/72. **Course Rating:** 135.0/118.0. **Slope:** 73/69. **Green Fee:** $60/$85. **Cart Fee:** $21/person. **Walking Policy:** Unrestricted walking. **Walkability:** 2. **Opened:** 1998. **Architect:** Tom Clark. **Season:** Year-round. **High:** May-Sept. **To obtain tee times:** Call reservation line at (703)222-7900 or online booking at www.foreteetimes.com. **Miscellaneous:** Reduced fees (twilight), range (grass/mats), club rentals, credit cards (MC, V, AE), beginner friendly (lessons available).
Special Notes: Beginner schools in June 2000.

★★★½ POHICK BAY REGIONAL GOLF COURSE
PU-10301 Gunston Rd., Lorton, 22079, Fairfax County, (703)339-8585, 15 miles from Washington, DC.
Holes: 18. **Yards:** 6,405/4,948. **Par:** 72/72. **Course Rating:** 71.7/68.9. **Slope:** 131/121. **Green Fee:** $25/$34. **Cart Fee:** $25/cart. **Walking Policy:** Unrestricted walking. **Walkability:** 5. **Opened:** 1982. **Architect:** George W. Cobb/John LaFoy. **Season:** Year-round. **High:** April-Nov. **To obtain tee times:** Call or come in starting at 6:30 p.m. on Tuesday for upcoming Friday through following Thursday. **Miscellaneous:** Reduced fees (weekdays, low season, twilight, seniors, juniors), range (mats), club rentals, credit cards (MC, V), beginner friendly.
Reader Comments: Great challenge, leave driver at home ... Tough course. Keep it straight off the tee ... Great variety of non-gimmicky holes ... Needs better conditioning to be higher rated.

★★½ PRINCE WILLIAM GOLF COURSE
PU-14631 Vint Hill Rd, Nokesville, 20181, Prince William County, (703)754-7111, (800)218-8463, 8 miles SW of Manassas.
Holes: 18. **Yards:** 6,606/5,455. **Par:** 70/72. **Course Rating:** 70.1/71.6. **Slope:** 119/119. **Green Fee:** $23/$38. **Walking Policy:** Walking at certain times. **Walkability:** 2. **Season:** Year-round. **High:** April-Oct. **To obtain tee times:** Call up to 7 days in advance. **Miscellaneous:** Reduced fees (twilight, seniors), metal spikes, range (mats), club rentals, credit cards (MC, V, AE).
Reader Comments: Difficult design ... Lots of potential, could be great ... Stop on the way home for practice ... Open fairways ... Fairly wide open track with several interesting decisions.

★★★★ RASPBERRY FALLS GOLF & HUNT CLUB *Service*
PU-41601 Raspberry Dr., Leesburg, 20176, Loudoun County, (703)779-2555. **E-mail:** jdevine@raspberryfalls.com. **Web:** www.raspberryfalls.com.
Holes: 18. **Yards:** 7,191/4,854. **Par:** 72/72. **Course Rating:** 75.6/67.8. **Slope:** 140/113. **Green Fee:** $65/$80. **Cart Fee:** Included in Green Fee. **Walking Policy:** Unrestricted walking. **Walkability:** 4. **Opened:** 1996. **Architect:** Gary Player. **Season:** Year-round. **High:** April-Oct. **To obtain tee times:** Call up to 8 days in advance. Up to 45 days in advance on golf packages. Packages start at $95.00. **Miscellaneous:** Reduced fees (weekdays, low season, twilight), range (grass), club rentals, credit cards (MC, V, AE, D).
Notes: Ranked 7th in 1999 Best in State.

VIRGINIA

Reader Comments: Fun to play ... Excellent links-type course ... Wonderful range of geography ... Good par 3s ... Fun but different, great views ... All players treated like VIPs ... Visually striking but playable ... Penal bunkering ... If the wind blows watch out.

★★★ RED WING LAKE GOLF COURSE
PU-1080 Prosperity Rd., Virginia Beach, 23451, Virginia Beach City County, (757)437-4845.
Holes: 18. **Yards:** 7,080/5,285. **Par:** 72/72. **Course Rating:** 73.7/68.1. **Slope:** 125/102. **Green Fee:** $18/$25. **Cart Fee:** $9/person. **Walking Policy:** Walking at certain times. **Walkability:** N/A. **Opened:** 1971. **Architect:** George Cobb. **Season:** Year-round. **High:** April-Oct. **To obtain tee times:** Call 1 day in advance. **Miscellaneous:** Reduced fees (twilight, seniors, juniors), discount packages, metal spikes, range (grass), club rentals, credit cards (MC, V).
Reader Comments: Wide fairways ... A very good public course ... Beautiful in spring.... Good price for locals.

★★★ RESTON NATIONAL GOLF COURSE
PU-11875 Sunrise Valley Dr., Reston, 22091, Fairfax County, (703)620-9333, 25 miles W of Washington, DC.
Holes: 18. **Yards:** 6,871/5,936. **Par:** 71/72. **Course Rating:** 72.9/74.3. **Slope:** 126/132. **Green Fee:** $40/$72. **Cart Fee:** Included in Green Fee. **Walking Policy:** Walking at certain times. **Walkability:** 2. **Opened:** 1967. **Architect:** Edmund Ault. **Season:** Year-round. **High:** April-Oct. **To obtain tee times:** Call Monday at 8 a.m. for weekdays. Call Wednesday at 8 a.m. for upcoming weekend. **Miscellaneous:** Reduced fees (weekdays, low season, twilight, seniors, juniors), discount packages, metal spikes, caddies, club rentals, credit cards (MC, V, AE), beginner friendly.
Reader Comments: First class operation ... Hilly ... Very accessible, good shot values, well placed traps ... Hidden gem, very playable ... Pricey ... Heavily played, good track, well managed.

★★ RINGGOLD GOLF CLUB
PU-1493 Ringgold Rd., Ringgold, 24586, Pittsylvania County, (804)822-8728, 5 miles E of Danville.
Holes: 18. **Yards:** 6,588/4,816. **Par:** 72/72. **Course Rating:** 72.3/64.2. **Slope:** 124/107. **Green Fee:** $17/$20. **Cart Fee:** $8/person. **Walking Policy:** Unrestricted walking. **Walkability:** N/A. **Opened:** 1962. **Architect:** Gene Hamm. **Season:** Year-round. **High:** April-Sept. **To obtain tee times:** Call after Wednesday for threesomes and foursomes. Less than three on Blue only. **Miscellaneous:** Reduced fees (weekdays, low season, seniors), metal spikes, club rentals, credit cards (MC, V).

★★★ RIVER'S BEND GOLF CLUB
PU-11700 Hogans Alley, Chester, 23836, Chesterfield County, (804)530-1000, (800)354-2363, 10 miles S of Richmond. **E-mail:** riversbend@aol.com. **Web:** www.riversbendgolf.com.
Holes: 18. **Yards:** 6,671/4,932. **Par:** 71/71. **Course Rating:** 71.9/67.8. **Slope:** 132/117. **Green Fee:** $20/$39. **Cart Fee:** $13/person. **Walking Policy:** Walking at certain times. **Walkability:** 4. **Opened:** 1990. **Architect:** Steve Smyers. **Season:** Year-round. **High:** April-Oct. **To obtain tee times:** Call 7 days in advance. **Miscellaneous:** Reduced fees (weekdays, low season, twilight, seniors, juniors), discount packages, range (grass), club rentals, credit cards (MC, V, AE).
Reader Comments: You must trust your clubs ... Nice course, good layout, good condition ... Great par 3s. Couple of contrived holes ... Fun layout ... Overall value good. Shows improvement ... Some very difficult holes, especially 18th.

RIVERFRONT GOLF CLUB
PU-5200 River Club Drive , Suffolk, 23435, Suffolk County, (757)484-2200, 10 miles W of Norfolk. **Web:** www.riverfrontgolf.com.
Holes: 18. **Yards:** 6,735/5,259. **Par:** 72/72. **Course Rating:** 72.5/69.7. **Slope:** 129/117. **Green Fee:** $39/$79. **Cart Fee:** $15/person. **Walking Policy:** Unrestricted walking. **Walkability:** 1. **Opened:** 1999. **Architect:** Tom Doak. **Season:** Year-round. **High:** May-Nov. **To obtain tee times:** Call (757)484-2200 24 hours a day. **Miscellaneous:** Reduced fees (weekdays, low season, resort guests, twilight), discount packages, range (grass), club rentals, credit cards (MC, V, AE, D), beginner friendly (teaching center).
Special Notes: Formerly known as Harbour View Golf Club.

★★★★ ROYAL NEW KENT GOLF CLUB
PU-5300 Bailey Road, Williamsburg, 23160, Providence Forge County, (804)966-7023, (888)253-4363, 20 miles E of Williamsburg. **Web:** www.legendsgolf.com.
Holes: 18. **Yards:** 7,291/5,231. **Par:** 72/72. **Course Rating:** 76.5/72.0. **Slope:** 147/130. **Green Fee:** $40/$85. **Cart Fee:** $20/person. **Walking Policy:** Unrestricted walking. **Walkability:** 4. **Opened:** 1996. **Architect:** Mike Strantz. **Season:** Year-round. **High:** March-Nov. **To obtain tee times:** Call up to 9 months in advance. **Miscellaneous:** Discount packages, range (grass), club rentals, credit cards (MC, V, AE).
Notes: Ranked 84th in 1999-2000 America's 100 Greatest; 2nd in 1999 Best in State; 1st in 1997 Best New Upscale Courses.
Reader Comments: A links masterpiece. Very fair off the tee. Toughest approach shots any-

where ... Absolutely sensational ... Fantastic finishing holes ... Good attempt at an Irish links but a bit contrived, pricey ... Unforgiving for errant shots ... Nine cars in the lot on Saturday morning ... If you score well, here join the tour ...Toughest bunkers this side of Scotland ... Breathtaking views.

★★★ ROYAL VIRGINIA GOLF CLUB
PU-3181 Dukes Rd., Hadensville, 23067, Goochland County, (804)457-2041, 31 miles SE of Charlottesville.
Holes: 18. **Yards:** 7,106/N/A. **Par:** 72/N/A. **Course Rating:** 73.4/N/A. **Slope:** 131/N/A. **Green Fee:** $15/$24. **Cart Fee:** $12/. **Walking Policy:** Walking at certain times. **Walkability:** N/A. **Opened:** 1993. **Architect:** Algie Pulley. **Season:** Year-round. **High:** Dec.-Feb. **To obtain tee times:** Call seven days in advance. **Miscellaneous:** Reduced fees (weekdays, low season, twilight, seniors), metal spikes, credit cards (MC, V).
Reader Comments: Very difficult course, long from Whites ... Tough but fair course ... Plays long. Lots of change in elevation ... Good potential ... Beautiful wooded, picturesque, fantastic greens.

★★★ SHENANDOAH CROSSING RESORT & COUNTRY CLUB
R-1944 Shenandoah Crossing Dr., Gordonsville, 22942, Louisa County, (540)832-9544, 30 miles NW of Charlottesville.
Holes: 18. **Yards:** 6,192/4,713. **Par:** 72/72. **Course Rating:** 69.8/66.5. **Slope:** 119/111. **Green Fee:** $30/$35. **Cart Fee:** Included in Green Fee. **Walking Policy:** Walking at certain times. **Walkability:** 4. **Opened:** 1991. **Architect:** Buddy Loving. **Season:** Year-round. **High:** April-Oct. **To obtain tee times:** Call up to 7 days in advance. **Miscellaneous:** Reduced fees (weekdays, low season, twilight, seniors, juniors), discount packages, range (grass), club rentals, lodging (60 rooms), credit cards (MC, V).
Reader Comments: Working to improve ... Good price for nice course ... Unknown, unspoiled but excellent value ... Good value great scenery.

SHENANDOAH VALLEY GOLF CLUB
SP-134 Golf Club Circle, Front Royal, 22630, Warren County, (540)636-4653, 15 miles S of Winchester.
Holes: 27.**Green Fee:** $10/$31. **Cart Fee:** $13/person. **Walking Policy:** Unrestricted walking. **Walkability:** N/A. **Opened:** 1966. **Architect:** Buddy Loving. **Season:** Year-round. **High:** March-Oct. **To obtain tee times:** Weekly tee sheets come out Monday morning. **Miscellaneous:** Reduced fees (weekdays, low season, twilight, juniors), discount packages, metal spikes, range (grass/mats), club rentals, lodging, credit cards (MC, V, AE, D).
★★★★ BLUE/RED *Value*
Yards: 6,399/5,000. **Par:** 72/73. **Course Rating:** 71.1/67.8. **Slope:** 126/116.
Reader Comments: Great staff, good value and nice golf ... Good small course, interesting holes, need all shots ... Long drive from D.C., but fun to play ... Mountain beauty.
★★★★ RED/WHITE *Value*
Yards: 6,121/4,700. **Par:** 71/71. **Course Rating:** 69.6/66.3. **Slope:** 122/114.
Reader Comments: Tight fairways ... Great for mid-level players.at for mid-level players.
★★★★ WHITE/BLUE *Value*
Yards: 6,330/4,900. **Par:** 71/71. **Course Rating:** 70.7/66.2. **Slope:** 122/113.

SHENVALEE GOLF CLUB
R-P.O. Box 930, New Market, 22844, Shenandoah County, (540)740-9930, 95 miles W of Washington, DC.
Holes: 27. **Green Fee:** $24/$27. **Cart Fee:** $13/person. **Walkability:** 3. **Opened:** 1924. **Architect:** Edmund B. Ault. **Season:** Year-round. **High:** April-Oct. **To obtain tee times:** Call golf shop.
★★★★ CREEK/MILLER
Yards: 6,595/4,757. **Par:** 71/71. **Course Rating:** 71.1/65.0. **Slope:** 120/102. **Walking Policy:** Mandatory cart. **Miscellaneous:** Reduced fees (weekdays, low season, resort guests, twilight), discount packages, range (grass/mats), club rentals, lodging (42 rooms), credit cards (MC, V, AE, D).
Reader Comments: Excellent value—short, but interesting 27 holes have attracted our group for 20 years ... Down home and great! ... The view from No. 3 on the creek course of the mountains and Shenandoah valley is second to none ... I have visited Shenvalee for 32 years and they just keep improving.
★★★★ OLDE/CREEK
Yards: 6,358/4,821. **Par:** 71/72. **Course Rating:** 70.1/65.2. **Slope:** 117/103. **Green Walking Policy:** Walking at certain times. **Miscellaneous:** Reduced fees (weekdays, low season, resort guests, twilight), discount packages, range (grass/mats), club rentals, lodging (42 rooms), credit cards (MC, V, AE, D).
Reader Comments: Good hospitality, everything you need at your finger tips ... The course to play when you want to shoot a low score ... Lots of water but easily avoided, scenic and fun ... Old course, fairly short, small hard greens.
★★★★ OLDE/MILLER
Yards: 6,297/4,738. **Par:** 71/71. **Course Rating:** 70.1/65.1. **Slope:** 119/104. **Walking Policy:** Walking at certain times. **Miscellaneous:** Reduced fees (low season, resort guests, twilight),

discount packages, range (grass/mats), club rentals, lodging (42 rooms), credit cards (MC, V, AE, D).

Reader Comments: Excellent, staff most accommodating ... Short course, good conditions ... Valley course fairly easy ... Much fun to play with great hospitality and food.

★★ SKYLAND LAKES GOLF COURSE

PU-Mile Post 202.2 Blue Ridge Parkway, Fancy Gap, 24328, Carroll County, (540)728-4923, 50 miles NW of Winston-Salem.

Holes: 18. **Yards:** 6,500/5,955. **Par:** 71/71. **Course Rating:** 70.0/69.0. **Slope:** 119/118. **Green Fee:** $18/$25. **Cart Fee:** Included in Green Fee. **Walking Policy:** Mandatory cart. **Walkability:** 3. **Opened:** 1990. **Architect:** Welch DeBoard. **Season:** Year-round. **High:** April-Sept. **To obtain tee times:** Call in advance. **Miscellaneous:** Reduced fees (weekdays, low season, twilight, seniors), metal spikes, club rentals, credit cards (MC, V), beginner friendly.

★★★ SLEEPY HOLE GOLF COURSE

PU-4700 Sleepy Hole Rd., Suffolk, 23435, Suffolk City County, (757)538-4100, 12 miles SW of Norfolk.

Holes: 18. **Yards:** 6,813/5,121. **Par:** 72/72. **Course Rating:** 72.6/64.8. **Slope:** 124/108. **Green Fee:** $24/$36. **Cart Fee:** Included in Green Fee. **Walking Policy:** Unrestricted walking. **Walkability:** 2. **Opened:** 1972. **Architect:** Russell Breeden. **Season:** Year-round. **High:** April-Oct. **To obtain tee times:** Call up to 7 days in advance. **Miscellaneous:** Reduced fees (weekdays, low season, twilight, seniors, juniors), range (grass/mats), club rentals, credit cards (MC, V, AE), beginner friendly (free instruction, reduced fee for off peak, loaner equipment).

Notes: 1978-1986 LPGACrestar Classic.

Reader Comments: Many good improvements ... Plays longer than yardage ... Established, long, comfortable, scenic ... Greens tend to be bare.... Some of the most difficult holes in the Tidewater area ... 18th is a beauty.

SOMERSET GOLF CLUB

PU-35448 Somerset Ridge Rd., Locust Grove, 22508, Orange County, (540)423-1500, 16 miles W of Fredericksburg. **E-mail:** somersetgac@hotmail.com.

Holes: 19. **Yards:** 6,832/5,262. **Par:** 72/72. **Course Rating:** 73.6/71.1. **Slope:** 136/131. **Green Fee:** $35/$45. **Cart Fee:** $14/person. **Walking Policy:** Unrestricted walking. **Walkability:** 4. **Opened:** 1997. **Architect:** Jerry Slack. **Season:** Year-round. **High:** March-Oct. **To obtain tee times:** Call up to 7 days in advance. **Miscellaneous:** Reduced fees (weekdays, low season, twilight, seniors, juniors), range (grass/mats), club rentals, credit cards (MC, V, AE, D).

★★★½ SOUTH RIDING GOLFERS' CLUB

SP-43237 Golf View Dr., South Riding, 20152, Loudoun County, (703)327-6660, 25 miles SW of Washington, D.C. **E-mail:** srgolfclub@aol.com. **Web:** www.golfsouth.com.

Holes: 18. **Yards:** 7,147/5,004. **Par:** 72/72. **Course Rating:** 74.5/68.9. **Slope:** 133/116. **Green Fee:** $40/$85. **Cart Fee:** Included in Green Fee. **Walking Policy:** Mandatory cart. **Walkability:** 2. **Opened:** 1997. **Architect:** Dan Maples. **Season:** Year-round. **High:** April-Oct. **To obtain tee times:** Call 7 days in advance. **Miscellaneous:** Reduced fees (weekdays, twilight), range (grass/mats), club rentals, credit cards (MC, V, AE), beginner friendly (golf clinics).

Reader Comments: Nothing tricky, straightforward good golf ... Challenging for us mid-handicaps ... Good hole variety ... Bring your putting game, fun and challenging ... A great course, too bad houses are in play.

★★½ SOUTH WALES GOLF COURSE

SP-18363 Golf Lane, Jeffersonton, 22724, Culpeper County, (540)937-3250, 50 miles W of Washington, DC.

Holes: 18. **Yards:** 7,077/5,020. **Par:** 71/73. **Course Rating:** 73.2/68.5. **Slope:** 123/104. **Green Fee:** $12/$31. **Cart Fee:** $22/cart. **Walking Policy:** Unrestricted walking. **Walkability:** 3. **Opened:** 1960. **Architect:** Edmund B. Ault. **Season:** Year-round. **High:** April-Oct. **To obtain tee times:** Call up to 14 days in advance. **Miscellaneous:** Reduced fees (weekdays, low season, twilight, seniors, juniors), metal spikes, range (mats), club rentals, credit cards (MC, V, D).

Reader Comments: A change of pace, not bad.... Magnificent track from tips. Elegant design compensates for any shortcomings ... Good value.

★★★★ STONEHOUSE GOLF CLUB *Service, Condition*

P.O. Box 3508, Williamsburg, 23188, Williamsburg City County, (757)253-6992.

Reader Comments: Best four par 3s ever ... Great golfing experience, mammoth greens ... Many blind holes, too tough for most players ... 17 great holes, but No. 14 crosses the line between creative and silly. Don't expect to get around in under 5 hours ... Breathtaking hole designs. Monstrous from the tips. Huge greens, elevation changes, blind shots, a thinking course ... Everything's so BIG.

Special Notes: Call club for further information.

★★★½ STONELEIGH GOLF CLUB
SP-35271 Prestwick Court, Round Hill, 20141, Loudoun County, (703)589-1402, 40 miles W of Washington, DC. **E-mail:** stoneleigh@erols.com. **Web:** www.stoneleighgolf.com.
Holes: 18. **Yards:** 6,709/4,837. **Par:** 72/72. **Course Rating:** 73.1/69.1. **Slope:** 141/121. **Green Fee:** $48/$58. **Cart Fee:** Included in Green Fee. **Walking Policy:** Walking at certain times.
Walkability: 4. **Opened:** 1992. **Architect:** Lisa Maki. **Season:** Year-round. **High:** March-Nov. **To obtain tee times:** Call 3 days in advance. **Miscellaneous:** Reduced fees (low season), discount packages, range (grass/mats), caddies, club rentals, credit cards (MC, V), beginner friendly.
Reader Comments: Plays like a mountain course, very scenic and tough ... ...Great view on No. 2 ... Holes 2 and 3 are killers ... You usually play better the second time ... Beautiful vistas, some very strange holes ... Outstanding course.

★★½ STUMPY LAKE GOLF CLUB
PU-4797 E. Indian River Rd., Virginia Beach, 23456, Virginia Beach City County, (757)467-6119.
Holes: 18. **Yards:** 6,800/5,200. **Par:** 72/72. **Course Rating:** 72.2/67.1. **Slope:** 119/97. **Green Fee:** $19/$21. **Cart Fee:** $10/person. **Walking Policy:** Walking at certain times. **Walkability:** N/A. **Opened:** 1944. **Architect:** Robert Trent Jones. **Season:** Year-round. **High:** April-Oct. **To obtain tee times:** Call on Wednesday at noon for upcoming weekend. First come, first served on weekdays. **Miscellaneous:** Reduced fees (weekdays, low season, twilight, seniors, juniors), range (grass/mats), club rentals, credit cards (MC, V, AE).
Reader Comments: Better than its name ... Outstanding layout. Very interesting. Beautiful all year, no houses. Great, great course, needs better service ... Challenging doglegs. Wide fairways.

★★★ SUFFOLK GOLF COURSE
PU-1227 Holland Rd., Suffolk, 23434, Suffolk City County, (757)539-6298, 2 miles W of Suffolk.
Holes: 18. **Yards:** 6,340/5,561. **Par:** 72/72. **Course Rating:** 70.3/71.1. **Slope:** 121/112. **Green Fee:** $12/$17. **Cart Fee:** $8/person. **Walking Policy:** Walking at certain times. **Walkability:** 2.
Opened: 1950. **Architect:** Dick Wilson. **Season:** Year-round. **High:** May-Sept. **To obtain tee times:** Call up to 7 days in advance. Call at 8 a.m. Wednesday for upcoming weekend. **Miscellaneous:** Reduced fees (weekdays, seniors, juniors), range (mats), club rentals.
Reader Comments: Great doglegs on back nine ... Might not use a driver from 11-17, good closing par five ... I have never met a golfer that did not like this facility/course. Every golfer wants to play it over and over again. Super public course. Staff great, too.

SUMMIT GOLF CLUB
PU-140 Country Club Dr., Cross Junction, 22625, Frederick County, (540)888-4188.
Special Notes: Call club for further information.

★★★ SYCAMORE CREEK GOLF COURSE
PU-1991 Manakin Rd., Manakin Sabot, 23103, Goochland County, (804)784-3544, 15 miles W of Richmond.
Holes: 18. **Yards:** 6,256/4,431. **Par:** 70/70. **Course Rating:** 70.6/64.6. **Slope:** 126/111. **Green Fee:** $33/$42. **Cart Fee:** Included in Green Fee. **Walking Policy:** Mandatory cart. **Walkability:** 4. **Opened:** 1992. **Architect:** Mike Hurzdan. **Season:** Year-round. **High:** April-Oct. **To obtain tee times:** Call 3 days in advance. Call on Wednesday for upcoming weekend or holiday.
Miscellaneous: Reduced fees (weekdays, low season, twilight, seniors, juniors), range (grass), club rentals, credit cards (MC, V, AE, D).
Reader Comments: Perfect for the tight budget, nice layout and conditions at fair price ... Good par threes, otherwise short ... Some great short par 4s, short but fun layout.

★★★★½ THE TIDES INN *Pace*
R-Golden Eagle Dr., Irvington, 22480, Lancaster County, (804)438-5501, (800)843-3746, 70 miles E of Richmond.
Holes: 18. **Yards:** 6,963/5,384. **Par:** 72/72. **Course Rating:** 74.3/70.9. **Slope:** 134/126. **Green Fee:** $40/$70. **Cart Fee:** $15/person. **Walking Policy:** Walking at certain times. **Walkability:** 3.
Opened: 1976. **Architect:** George Cobb. **Season:** March-Dec. **High:** April-Oct. **To obtain tee times:** Call golf shop. Hotel guests may reserve tee times anytime in advance. **Miscellaneous:** Reduced fees (weekdays, low season, resort guests), discount packages, metal spikes, range (grass/mats), club rentals, lodging, credit cards (MC, V, AE).
Notes: Ranked 14th in 1997 Best in State.
Reader Comments: Best value in the state ... Several super holes ... Steady as ever... Pleasant ... Wonderful staff ... A gem ... Risk-reward adventure ... Nice family resort, comfortable ... Great course, good service ... Wonderful course, No. 9, 18 feature major water, can be intimidating.

★★★½ TIDES LODGE
R-1 St. Andrews Lane, Irvington, 22480, Lancaster County, (804)438-6200, (800)248-4337, 65 miles E of Richmond.
Holes: 18. **Yards:** 6,586/5,121. **Par:** 72/72. **Course Rating:** 71.5/69.2. **Slope:** 124/116. **Green Fee:** $25/$53. **Cart Fee:** $15/. **Walking Policy:** Unrestricted walking. **Walkability:** N/A. **Opened:** 1959. **Architect:** Sir Guy Campbell/George Cobb. **Season:** March-Dec. **High:** May-Oct. **To**

VIRGINIA

obtain tee times: Call at least one week in advance to get desired time. **Miscellaneous:** Reduced fees (weekdays, low season, resort guests, twilight), discount packages, metal spikes, range (grass), caddies, club rentals, lodging, credit cards (MC, V, AE).
Reader Comments: Fun to play, difficult but fair ... Beautiful, especially in the fall. Excellent five-star resort ... Nice track, very pretty in spring with all the flowers in bloom ... User friendly ... Underrated.

TWIN LAKES GOLF COURSE
PU-6201 Union Mill Rd., Clifton, 20124, Fairfax County, (703)631-9099, 20 miles W of Washington DC.
★★★ LAKES COURSE
Holes: 18. **Yards:** 6,788/5,627. **Par:** 73/73. **Course Rating:** 73.0/72.6. **Slope:** 132/119. **Green Fee:** $24/$34. **Cart Fee:** $24/person. **Walking Policy:** Unrestricted walking. **Walkability:** 3. **Opened:** 1967. **Architect:** Charles Schalestock. **Season:** Year-round. **High:** May-Sept. **To obtain tee times:** Call (703)758-1800 for advance times, golf shop for day of play/walk-on times (if available). Tee time strongly recommended. **Miscellaneous:** Reduced fees (weekdays, seniors, juniors), range (grass), club rentals, credit cards (MC, V).
Reader Comments: Beautiful scenery ... Fair ... Open, rolling ... Extensive remodeling, 2nd 18 under way, looking forward to going back ... Hilly but walkable ... Full 36 will have two distinct feels and challenges.
OAKS COURSE
Holes: 18. **Yards:** 6,710/4,686. **Par:** 71/71. **Course Rating:** 73.0/65.7. **Slope:** 139/109. **Green Fee:** $28/$34. **Cart Fee:** $23/cart. **Walking Policy:** Unrestricted walking. **Walkability:** 3. **Opened:** 1998. **Architect:** Denis Griffiths. **Season:** Year-round. **To obtain tee times:** Call (703)758-1800 for advance times, golf shop for day of play/walk-on times (if available). Tee time strongly recommended. **Miscellaneous:** Reduced fees (weekdays, seniors, juniors), metal spikes, range (grass/mats), club rentals, credit cards (MC, V).

★★★½ VIRGINIA OAKS GOLF CLUB
SP-7950 Virginia Oaks Dr., Gainesville, 20155, Prince William County, (703)754-4200, 1 mile W of Gainsville.
Holes: 18. **Yards:** 6,928/4,852. **Par:** 72/71. **Course Rating:** 73.5/72.0. **Slope:** 133/115. **Green Fee:** $35/$69. **Cart Fee:** Included in Green Fee. **Walking Policy:** Unrestricted walking. **Walkability:** 2. **Opened:** 1995. **Architect:** P.B. Dye. **Season:** Year-round. **High:** April-Oct. **To obtain tee times:** Call up to 7 days in advance. **Miscellaneous:** Reduced fees (weekdays, low season, twilight, seniors, juniors), range (grass/mats), club rentals, credit cards (MC, V, AE).
Reader Comments: You must play this course, it's great! ... A great golfing experience, some very tough holes...Good test of all shots ... Beautiful setting on Lake Manassas ... Blind shots, fast greens, but immaculate ... One of northern Virginia's better courses ... Great conditions, very helpful staff ... Enjoyed layout and views ... Beautiful setting ... Very strategic greens ... Tricky hazards ... Tough greens.

WESTFIELDS GOLF CLUB
PU-13940 Balmoral Greens Ave., Clifton, 20124, Fairfax County, (703)631-3300, 20 miles W of Washington, D.C.
Holes: 18. **Yards:** 6,897/4,597. **Par:** 71/71. **Course Rating:** 73.1/65.9. **Slope:** 136/114. **Green Fee:** $50/$89. **Cart Fee:** Included in Green Fee. **Walking Policy:** Unrestricted walking. **Walkability:** 3. **Opened:** 1998. **Architect:** Fred Couples/Gene Bates. **Season:** Year-round. **High:** May-Sept.-Oct. **Miscellaneous:** Reduced fees (weekdays, low season, twilight), range (grass/mats), club rentals, lodging (400 rooms), credit cards (MC, V, AE, D), beginner friendly.

★★½ WESTLAKE GOLF & COUNTRY CLUB
SP-360 Chestnut Creek Dr., Hardy, 24101, Franklin County, (540)721-4214, (800)296-7277, 20 miles SE of Roanoke.
Holes: 18. **Yards:** 6,540/4,582. **Par:** 72/72. **Course Rating:** 71.7/65.6. **Slope:** 128/114. **Green Fee:** $19/$24. **Cart Fee:** $10/person. **Walking Policy:** Walking at certain times. **Walkability:** N/A. **Opened:** 1989. **Architect:** Russell Breeden. **Season:** Year-round. **High:** May-Sept. **To obtain tee times:** Call up to 3 days in advance. **Miscellaneous:** Reduced fees (twilight, juniors), metal spikes, range (grass), club rentals, credit cards (MC, V).
Reader Comments: Surprisingly tough ... Steady improvement. Never great but good ... A little gimmicky, tight, can play tough ... Up and down, all around. Blind holes ... Beautiful old clubhouse, some beautiful scenery.

★★★ WESTPARK GOLF CLUB
SP-59 Clubhouse Dr. S.W., Leesburg, 20175, Loudoun County, (703)777-7023, 20 miles W of Fairfax. **E-mail:** eliaspga@aol.com.
Holes: 18. **Yards:** 6,521/5,027. **Par:** 71/71. **Course Rating:** 71.1/69.0. **Slope:** 121/111. **Green Fee:** $22/$30. **Cart Fee:** $15/person. **Walking Policy:** Walking at certain times. **Walkability:** 3. **Opened:** 1968. **Architect:** Edward Ault. **Season:** Year-round weather permitting. **High:** April-Oct. **To obtain tee times:** Call on Tuesday for upcoming weekend. **Miscellaneous:** Reduced fees

VIRGINIA

(weekdays, low season, twilight, seniors), metal spikes, range (mats), club rentals, credit cards (MC, V, AE, Diners CLub).

Reader Comments: The sleeper of the bunch ... Across-the-board solid golf course ... Great variety of traditional holes, all fair. No. 13 is one of the toughest, holes I play all year ... Good practice chipping, putting green ... A reasonable price and conditioned public course.

★★★½ **WILLIAMSBURG NATIONAL GOLF CLUB**
PU-3700 Centerville Rd., Williamsburg, 23188, Williamsburg City County, (757)258-9642, (800)826-5732, 40 miles E of Richmond. **Web:** www.wngc.com.
Holes: 18. **Yards:** 6,950/5,200. **Par:** 72/72. **Course Rating:** 72.9/69.7. **Slope:** 130/127. **Green Fee:** $33/$53. **Cart Fee:** $16/person. **Walking Policy:** Walking at certain times. **Walkability:** 3.
Opened: 1995. **Architect:** Jim Lipe. **Season:** Year-round. **High:** April-May-Oct. **To obtain tee times:** Call anytime in advance with credit card to reserve. **Miscellaneous:** Reduced fees (weekdays, low season, resort guests), metal spikes, range (grass), club rentals, credit cards (MC, V, AE).
Reader Comments: Take a camera ... Nice layout, very good service ... Great layout, great people, played it in the fall, off season the pace of play was great and so was the condition ... 9th and 18th holes are a test, good endings ... Very, very nice course. Lots of trouble ... Great back nine, superlative service.

WINTERGREEN RESORT
R-P.O. Box 706, Wintergreen, 22958, Nelson County, (804)325-8250, (800)266-2444, 43 miles W of Charlottesville. **E-mail:** wintergreenresort.com. **Web:** www.wintergreenresort.com.
★★★★ **DEVIL'S KNOB GOLF CLUB**
Holes: 18. **Yards:** 6,576/5,101. **Par:** 70/70. **Course Rating:** 72.4/68.6. **Slope:** 126/118. **Green Fee:** $37/$80. **Cart Fee:** $17/person. **Walking Policy:** Unrestricted walking. **Walkability:** 5.
Opened: 1976. **Architect:** Ellis Maples. **Season:** April-Oct. **High:** May-Oct. **To obtain tee times:** Call up to one year in advance. **Miscellaneous:** Reduced fees (weekdays, low season, resort guests), discount packages, range (grass/mats), club rentals, lodging (350 rooms), credit cards (MC, V, AE, D).
Reader Comments: Great mountain course; very tight ... Greens are murder... Tough course for left-to-right player ... ... Beautiful resort, unbelievable views, great facilities ... Unique property. Could be classic mountainside course ... Many short dog legs ... Narrow, short, but great shape ... Awesome elevations.
★★★★ **STONEY CREEK AT WINTERGREEN**
Holes: 27. **Yards:** 7,003/5,500. **Par:** 72/72. **Course Rating:** 74.0/71.0. **Slope:** 132/125. **Green Fee:** $37/$80. **Cart Fee:** $16/person. **Walking Policy:** Unrestricted walking. **Walkability:** 3.
Opened: 1988. **Architect:** Rees Jones. **Season:** Year-round. **High:** May-Oct. **To obtain tee times:** Call pro shop up to 90 days in advance. **Miscellaneous:** Reduced fees (weekdays, low season, resort guests), discount packages, range (grass), club rentals, lodging, credit cards (MC, V, AE).
Notes: Ranked 6th in 1997 Best in State.
Reader Comments: Picturesque, memorable, must play ... Beautiful mountains, wonderful layout ... Outstanding, do not miss this one ... Some beautiful holes ... If putting is not the best, forget about score and enjoy the view ... Good mountain course, out of the way.

★★ **WOLF CREEK GOLF & COUNTRY CLUB**
SP-Rte. 1 Box 421, Bastian, 24314, Bland County, (540)688-4610, 20 miles NW of Wytheville.
Holes: 18. **Yards:** 6,380/4,788. **Par:** 71/71. **Course Rating:** 71.3/71.0. **Slope:** 122/128. **Green Fee:** $15/$20. **Cart Fee:** $10/person. **Walking Policy:** Walking at certain times. **Walkability:** 4.
Opened: 1982. **Architect:** Maurice Brackett. **Season:** Year-round. **High:** April-Oct. **To obtain tee times:** Call 7 days in advance for weekends; 2 days in advance for weekdays. **Miscellaneous:** Reduced fees (weekdays, low season, seniors, juniors), discount packages, range (grass), club rentals, credit cards (MC, V, AE), beginner friendly (monday special).

★★½ **WOODLANDS GOLF COURSE**
PU-9 Woodland Rd., Hampton, 23663, Hampton City County, (757)727-1195.
Holes: 18. **Yards:** 5,391/4,154. **Par:** 69/69. **Course Rating:** 65.6/62.9. **Slope:** 113/106. **Green Fee:** $12/$16. **Cart Fee:** $16/cart. **Walking Policy:** Unrestricted walking. **Walkability:** 1.
Opened: 1927. **Architect:** Donald Ross. **Season:** Year-round. **High:** April-Sept. **To obtain tee times:** Call 3 days in advance after noon. **Miscellaneous:** Reduced fees (weekdays, seniors, juniors), club rentals, credit cards (MC, V).
Reader Comments: Short, very good greens.

WASHINGTON

★★★½ ALDERBROOK GOLF & YACHT CLUB
R-300 Country Club Drive, Union, 98592, Mason County, (360)898-2560, (888)898-2560, 35 miles NW of Olympia. **Web:** www.alderbrookgolf.com.
Holes: 18. **Yards:** 6,326/5,500. **Par:** 72/73. **Course Rating:** 70.9/72.2. **Slope:** 122/125. **Green Fee:** $27/$33. **Cart Fee:** $24/cart. **Walking Policy:** Unrestricted walking. **Walkability:** 2. **Opened:** 1966. **Architect:** Ray Coleman. **Season:** Year-round. **High:** April-Oct. **To obtain tee times:** Call Monday prior to weekend or holiday. **Miscellaneous:** Reduced fees (weekdays, low season, resort guests, twilight, seniors, juniors), discount packages, metal spikes, range (grass), club rentals, lodging, credit cards (MC, V).
Reader Comments: A jewel off the beaten path ... Beautiful mountain views ... Tight course ... Good conditions ... Trees and more trees ... Good course to walk ... Best to play in July/August ... Good contrast between narrow front 9 and wide open back 9 ... Surrounding forest is a nice background.

★★★★ APPLE TREE GOLF COURSE *Pace*
PU-8804 Occidental Ave., Yakima, 98908, Yakima County, (509)966-5877, 200 miles E of Seattle. **Web:** www.appletreegolf.com.
Holes: 18. **Yards:** 6,892/5,428. **Par:** 72/72. **Course Rating:** 73.3/72.0. **Slope:** 129/124. **Green Fee:** $25/$50. **Cart Fee:** $25/cart. **Walking Policy:** Unrestricted walking. **Walkability:** 3. **Opened:** 1992. **Architect:** John Steidel/Apple Tree Partnership. **Season:** Year-round. **High:** March-Oct. **To obtain tee times:** Call up to 30 days in advance when calling from outside the Yakima area. Call 7 days in advance in the Yakima area. Groups of 16 or more may book up to 1 year in advance. **Miscellaneous:** Reduced fees (weekdays, low season, twilight, seniors, juniors), range (grass), club rentals, credit cards (MC, V).
Notes: Ranked 9th in 1999 Best in State.
Reader Comments: Well-named course routed through apple orchards ... Lushest lawn east of the mountains ... Great island green ... Great condition .... Price is good, but difficult to get on ... Good food ... Nice people ... Best course in Washington ... Keeps getting better as course matures ... Great front 9 ... Enjoy the apple blossoms in spring, apples in fall.

★★★ AUBURN GOLF COURSE
PU-29630 Green River Rd., Auburn, 98002, King County, (253)833-2350.
Holes: 18. **Yards:** 6,350/6,004. **Par:** 71/71. **Course Rating:** 69.5/68.4. **Slope:** 116/109. **Green Fee:** $19/$21. **Cart Fee:** $10/cart. **Walking Policy:** Unrestricted walking. **Walkability:** 3. **Opened:** 1969. **Architect:** Milton Bauman/Glenn Proctor. **Season:** Year-round. **High:** June-Sept. **To obtain tee times:** Call up to 7 days in advance. **Miscellaneous:** Metal spikes.
Reader Comments: Recent improvements ... Wet in winter... More upgrades each year... Short course, some nice holes ... Good for seniors ... Great staff, friendly members ... Nice layout.

AVALON GOLF CLUB
PU-19345 Kelleher Rd., Burlington, 98233, Skagit County, (360)757-1900, (800)624-0202, 55 miles N of Seattle. **E-mail:** bkruhlak@avalonlinks.com. **Web:** www.avalonlinks.com.
Holes: 27. **Green Fee:** $22/$39. **Cart Fee:** $25/cart. **Walking Policy:** Unrestricted walking. **Walkability:** 1. **Opened:** 1991. **Architect:** Robert Muir Graves. **Season:** Year-round. **High:** May-Sept. **To obtain tee times:** Call up to 7 days in advance, or 14 days on internet or up to one year prepaid. **Miscellaneous:** Reduced fees (weekdays, low season, twilight, seniors, juniors), discount packages, range (grass), caddies, club rentals, credit cards (MC, V), beginner friendly (free ladies clinics).
★★★½ NORTH/SOUTH
Yards: 6,803/5,534. **Par:** 72/72. **Course Rating:** 73.3/72.7. **Slope:** 132/127.
Reader Comments: Tough test ... Great practice facilities ... Great view of valley below ... Caddies available ... My home course, like an old pal ... Course lined with incredible blackberries ... Use all 14 clubs ... 27 holes of pure golf, gets better each year... Wet in off season.
★★★½ NORTH/WEST
Yards: 6,629/5,236. **Par:** 72/72. **Course Rating:** 72.3/71.6. **Slope:** 125/122.
Reader Comments: Hidden gem, bunkering adds character ... Play free on your birthday ... Wonderful staff ... Great doglegs ... Could use better water drainage ... Good value ... Great setting ... Woods, water and O.B. make this course challenging ... Good walking ... Three distinct 9s. You'd better hit the fairway!.
★★★½ WEST/SOUTH
Yards: 6,576/5,318. **Par:** 72/72. **Course Rating:** 71.3/72.2. **Slope:** 129/122.
Reader Comments: A beautiful course, not particularly long, but challenging ... Been back many times ... Leave driver in the bag ... Emphasis on accuracy! ... Needs better drainage.

★★★ BATTLE CREEK GOLF COURSE
PU-6006 Meridian Ave. N., Marysville, 98271, Snohomish County, (360)659-7931, (800)655-7931, 30 miles N of Seattle.
Holes: 18. **Yards:** 6,575/5,391. **Par:** 73/73. **Course Rating:** 71.4/70.9. **Slope:** 125/124. **Green Fee:** $20/$25. **Cart Fee:** $21/cart. **Walking Policy:** Unrestricted walking. **Walkability:** 3.

Opened: 1990. **Architect:** Fred Jacobson. **Season:** Year-round. **High:** May-Aug. **To obtain tee times:** Call up to 7 days in advance. **Miscellaneous:** Reduced fees (weekdays, low season, twilight, seniors, juniors), discount packages, metal spikes, range (grass), club rentals, credit cards (MC, V).

Reader Comments: Long hitters have decisions to make ... Potential, potential, potential ... Tight, fun layout ... Great views! ... Treelined holes ... Greens improving ... Nice track, needs some work.

★★½ BELLEVUE MUNICIPAL GOLF COURSE

PM-5500 140th N.E., Bellevue, 98005, King County, (425)451-7250.
Holes: 18. **Yards:** 5,800/5,100. **Par:** 71/71. **Course Rating:** 66.5/68.6. **Slope:** 110/111. **Green Fee:** $20/$20. **Cart Fee:** $23/cart. **Walking Policy:** Unrestricted walking. **Walkability:** 1.
Opened: 1969. **Season:** Year-round. **High:** May-Aug. **To obtain tee times:** Call Monday after 9 a.m. for the following 7 days. **Miscellaneous:** Reduced fees (low season, twilight, seniors, juniors), metal spikes, range (mats), club rentals.
Reader Comments: Good muny course ... Super bang for your buck ... Nice setting ... Water, water... Always crowded ... Friendly staff, eager to please ... Good layout ... Has country club potential.

★★★ BROOKDALE GOLF COURSE

PU-1802 Brookdale Rd. E., Tacoma, 98445, Pierce County, (253)537-4400, (800)281-2428.
Holes: 18. **Yards:** 6,435/5,835. **Par:** 71/74. **Course Rating:** 70.3/73.1. **Slope:** 119/113. **Green Fee:** $10/$20. **Cart Fee:** $20/cart. **Walking Policy:** Unrestricted walking. **Walkability:** 1.
Opened: 1931. **Architect:** Al Smith. **Season:** Year-round. **High:** April-Oct. **To obtain tee times:** Call or stop by up to 30 days in advance. **Miscellaneous:** Reduced fees (weekdays, low season, twilight, seniors, juniors), metal spikes, club rentals, credit cards (MC, V).
Reader Comments: Good course to play year-round ... Old course, easy test ... Good course in rain ... Wide open, nice greens, inexpensive ... My kids play Brookdale at every opportunity ... Great prices for seniors ... Excellent management ... Condition, condition, condition.

★★½ CAMALOCH GOLF COURSE

PU-326 N. E. Camano Dr., Camano Island, 98292, Island County, (360)387-3084, (800)628-0469, 45 miles N of Seattle.
Holes: 18. **Yards:** 6,171/5,192. **Par:** 71/71. **Course Rating:** 70.0/70.9. **Slope:** 125/122. **Green Fee:** $15/$25. **Cart Fee:** $20/cart. **Walking Policy:** Unrestricted walking. **Walkability:** 2.
Opened: 1990. **Architect:** Bill Overdorf. **Season:** Year-round. **High:** May-Sept. **To obtain tee times:** Call in advance. Walk-ons welcome. **Miscellaneous:** Reduced fees (weekdays, low season, twilight, seniors, juniors), metal spikes, range (grass), club rentals, credit cards (MC, V, D), beginner friendly.
Reader Comments: A nice, semi-residential course ... Good afternoon overall ... Getting better each year... Fun to play ... Challenging with great greens ... Great little course to take the wife ... Short and pretty.

★★★½ CANYON LAKES GOLF COURSE

PU-3700 Canyon Lakes Dr., Kennewick, 99337, Benton County, (509)582-3736. **E-mail:** canyon3736@aol.com. **Web:** www.cybergolf.com/canyonlakes.
Holes: 18. **Yards:** 6,973/5,543. **Par:** 72/72. **Course Rating:** 73.4/72.0. **Slope:** 127/124. **Green Fee:** $20/$30. **Cart Fee:** $12/person. **Walking Policy:** Unrestricted walking. **Walkability:** 3.
Opened: 1981. **Architect:** John Steidel. **Season:** Year-round. **High:** March-Nov. **To obtain tee times:** Call 7 days in advance. Groups of 8 or more any time. **Miscellaneous:** Reduced fees (weekdays, resort guests, twilight, juniors), discount packages, range (grass), club rentals, lodging (87 rooms), credit cards (MC, V, AE), beginner friendly (18-hole putting course).
Reader Comments: Fastest greens in eastern Washington! ... One of my favorite places to play ... Excellent service in pro shop ... Local knowledge helps ... Good fun ... While visiting the in-laws, course made my week ... Don't play when the wind blows ... Great practice facility ... Liked barber poles at 150 yards ... Super value, great service. We felt welcome.

★★★½ CAPITOL CITY GOLF CLUB

PU-5225 Yelm Hwy. S.E., Olympia, 98513, Thurston County, (360)491-5111, (800)994-2582.
Holes: 18. **Yards:** 6,536/5,510. **Par:** 72/72. **Course Rating:** 70.9/71.7. **Slope:** 123/122. **Green Fee:** $17/$22. **Cart Fee:** $13/. **Walking Policy:** Unrestricted walking. **Walkability:** N/A. **Opened:** 1961. **Architect:** Norman Woods. **Season:** Year-round. **High:** June-Aug. **To obtain tee times:** Call seven days ahead. **Miscellaneous:** Reduced fees (weekdays, low season, twilight, seniors, juniors), metal spikes, range (grass), club rentals, credit cards (MC, V).
Reader Comments: Great winter course ... Great greens at a great price ... Fun and challenging ... One of my favorites ... Easy to walk ... Good drainage ... Good test ... Friendly, helpful staff.

★½ CARNATION GOLF COURSE

PU-1810 W Snoqualmie River Rd. N.E., Carnation, 98014, King County, (206)583-0314, 10 miles E of Redmond. **E-mail:** cgc@accessone.com. **Web:** www.carnationgolf.com.

Holes: 18. **Yards:** 6,011/4,599. **Par:** 72/72. **Course Rating:** 67.7/65.0. **Slope:** 111/102. **Green Fee:** $22/$25. **Cart Fee:** $24/cart. **Walking Policy:** Unrestricted walking. **Walkability:** 1. **Opened:** 1967. **Architect:** Bob Tachell. **Season:** Year-round. **High:** May-Oct. **To obtain tee times:** Call up to 14 days in advance. **Miscellaneous:** Reduced fees (weekdays, low season, twilight, seniors, juniors), metal spikes, range (grass/mats), club rentals, credit cards (MC, V).

★★★ CEDARCREST GOLF CLUB

PU-6810 84th St. N.E., Marysville, 98270, Snohomish County, (360)659-3566, 35 miles N of Seattle.

Holes: 18. **Yards:** 5,811/4,846. **Par:** 70/70. **Course Rating:** 67.0/66.6. **Slope:** 114/112. **Green Fee:** N/A/$21. **Cart Fee:** $20/cart. **Walking Policy:** Unrestricted walking. **Walkability:** 3. **Opened:** 1927. **Architect:** John Steidel. **Season:** Year-round. **High:** June-Aug. **To obtain tee times:** Call 7 days in advance. Call Saturday for next Saturday and Sunday. **Miscellaneous:** Reduced fees (seniors, juniors), metal spikes, club rentals, credit cards (MC, V, D).

Reader Comments: Lots of sand and water... Great year-round golf ... What great improvements.

★★★½ CEDARS GOLF CLUB

PU-15001 N.E. 181st St., Brush Prairie, 98606, Clark County, (360)687-4233, 20 miles N of Portland, OR.

Holes: 18. **Yards:** 6,423/5,216. **Par:** 72/73. **Course Rating:** 71.2/71.1. **Slope:** 129/117. **Green Fee:** $24/$26. **Cart Fee:** $22/cart. **Walking Policy:** Walking at certain times. **Walkability:** 3. **Opened:** 1975. **Architect:** Jerry James. **Season:** Year-round. **High:** May-Oct. **To obtain tee times:** Call up to 7 days in advance. **Miscellaneous:** Reduced fees (juniors), metal spikes, range (grass), club rentals, credit cards (MC, V).

Reader Comments: Target golf ... Fine when not wet ... Tight course ... Big trees ... Fun to play ... Shotmaking course ..... Lots of water hazards ... Great service ... Target golf at its best ... Nice clubhouse and pro shop ... Great view ... Beautiful, woodsy, hilly course.

★★★ CHEWELAH GOLF & COUNTRY CLUB

SP-2537 Sand Canyon Rd., Chewelah, 99109, Stevens County, (509)935-6807, 40 miles N of Spokane.

Holes: 18. **Yards:** 6,531/5,672. **Par:** 72/74. **Course Rating:** 70.9/72.2. **Slope:** 125/124. **Green Fee:** $8/$18. **Cart Fee:** $23/cart. **Walking Policy:** Unrestricted walking. **Walkability:** 2. **Opened:** 1976. **Architect:** Keith Hellstrom. **Season:** April-Oct. **High:** May-Sept. **To obtain tee times:** Call 30 days in advance.
. **Miscellaneous:** Reduced fees (weekdays, seniors, juniors), range (mats), club rentals, lodging, credit cards (MC, V).

Reader Comments: Tight, narrow and challenging ... Fun and reasonably priced ... Set in trees, demanding course ... Nice small town course ... Rattle the pines ... Affordable golf.

★★★★ CLASSIC COUNTRY CLUB

PU-4908 208th St. E., Spanaway, 98387, Pierce County, (253)847-4440, (800)924-9557, 60 miles S of Seattle.

Holes: 18. **Yards:** 6,793/5,580. **Par:** 72/72. **Course Rating:** 73.6/73.3. **Slope:** 133/128. **Green Fee:** $20/$45. **Cart Fee:** $23/cart. **Walking Policy:** Unrestricted walking. **Walkability:** N/A. **Opened:** 1991. **Architect:** Bill Overdorf. **Season:** Year-round. **High:** May-Oct. **To obtain tee times:** Call or come in up to 7 days in advance. **Miscellaneous:** Reduced fees (weekdays, low season, twilight, seniors, juniors), discount packages, metal spikes, range (grass/mats), club rentals, credit cards (MC, V, AE, JCB).

Reader Comments: One of the best in Washington ... Great course with interesting holes ... Undulating, fast greens ... Views of Mt. Rainier... Great greens, super-dry in winter... Best in Tacoma area .... Good wet weather course ... The greens will eat you alive ... Lots of trees, stray off fairway and bring your foxhound ... Continuing to grow into a good course ... Walkable, fun.

★ CLOVER VALLEY GOLF COURSE

PU-5180 Country Club Way SE, Port Orchard, 98366, Kitsap County, (360)871-2236.
Holes: 18. **Yards:** 5,370/4,799. **Par:** 69/70. **Course Rating:** 65.0/67.0. **Slope:** 102/107. **Green Fee:** $6/$16. **Cart Fee:** $18/cart. **Walkability:** N/A. **Opened:** 1966. **Season:** Year-round. **High:** May-Sept. **To obtain tee times:** Call. **Miscellaneous:** Metal spikes.

★★★½ COLUMBIA POINT GOLF COURSE

PM-225 Columbia Point Dr., Richland, 99352, Benton County, (509)946-0710. **Web:** www.cybergolf.com/columbiapoint.
Holes: 18. **Yards:** 6,555/4,651. **Par:** 72/72. **Course Rating:** 70.0/65.9. **Slope:** 121/107. **Green Fee:** $15/$30. **Cart Fee:** $12/person. **Walking Policy:** Unrestricted walking. **Walkability:** 3. **Opened:** 1997. **Architect:** Jim Engh. **Season:** Year-round. **High:** April-Oct. **To obtain tee times:** Call up to 7 days in advance. **Miscellaneous:** Reduced fees (weekdays, low season, twilight, seniors, juniors), discount packages, range (grass), club rentals, credit cards (MC, V, AE).

Reader Comments: Great new course, what a surprise ... Easy course to walk ... Great job on renovation ... Great golf for the $ ... Easy to walk.

★★★★ THE CREEK AT QUALCHAN GOLF COURSE

PU-301 E. Meadowlane Rd., Spokane, 99204, Spokane County, (509)448-9317.
Holes: 18. **Yards:** 6,599/5,538. **Par:** 72/72. **Course Rating:** 71.6/72.3. **Slope:** 127/126. **Green Fee:** $16/$22. **Cart Fee:** $22/cart. **Walking Policy:** Unrestricted walking. **Walkability:** N/A.
Opened: 1993. **Architect:** William Robinson. **Season:** March-Oct. **High:** May-Sept. **To obtain tee times:** Nonresidents may call anytime with credit card to guarantee. **Miscellaneous:** Reduced fees (juniors), discount packages, metal spikes, range (grass), club rentals, credit cards (MC, V).
Reader Comments: Good public course ... Excellent value ... Friendly people ... In mountain range along creek ... Tough from the tips ... Drive it straight ... Lots of variety, loads of fun to play ... One of many great unique Spokane courses.

★★½ DESERT AIRE GOLF COURSE

SP-505 Club House Way W., Desert Aire, 99349, Grant County, (509)932-4439, 60 miles NE of Yakima.
Holes: 18. **Yards:** 6,501/5,786. **Par:** 72/73. **Course Rating:** 70.5/72.6. **Slope:** 115/120. **Green Fee:** $16/$18. **Cart Fee:** $15/person. **Walking Policy:** Unrestricted walking. **Walkability:** N/A.
Opened: 1975. **Architect:** Jim Krause. **Season:** Year-round. **High:** June-Oct. **To obtain tee times:** Call one week in advance. **Miscellaneous:** Discount packages, metal spikes, range (grass), club rentals, lodging, credit cards (MC, V).
Reader Comments: Well maintained, nice greens, good views ... Fun but somewhat tricky ... Scenic along Columbia River... Liked the front 9 not the back ... Good course, very dry, good value ... Wind, wind, windy ... Very fair and a good test of golf.

★★★★½ DESERT CANYON GOLF RESORT   *Service, Condition+*

R-1201 Desert Canyon Blvd., Orondo, 98843, Douglas County, (509)784-1111, (509)258-4173, 25 miles N of Wenatchee. **E-mail:** desertcanyon@desertcanyon.com. **Web:** www.desertcanyon.com.
Holes: 18. **Yards:** 7,293/4,899. **Par:** 72/72. **Course Rating:** 74.0/67.5. **Slope:** 127/104. **Green Fee:** $42/$75. **Cart Fee:** Included in Green Fee. **Walking Policy:** Mandatory cart. **Walkability:** N/A. **Opened:** 1993. **Architect:** Jack Frei. **Season:** March-Nov. **High:** June-Sept. **To obtain tee times:** Call 7 days in advance, or pre-pay up to 30 days in advance. **Miscellaneous:** Reduced fees (weekdays, low season, twilight, seniors, juniors), discounts, range (grass), club rentals, lodging, credit cards (MC, V, AE).
Notes: Ranked 2nd in 1999 Best in State; 35th in 1996 America's Top 75 Upscale Courses.
Reader Comments: Best course in Washington ... Target golf ... Great greens ... Majestic panoramic vistas ... A bear from blues ... Shotmaking a must ... Great test ... 18 signature holes ... Fairways are like carpet ... Great clubhouse ... Great views of Columbia River... An oasis in the middle of nowhere ... Washington's best desert course ...18-hole putting course is a MUST DO!

★★★½ DOWNRIVER GOLF CLUB

PU-N. 3225 Columbia Circle, Spokane, 99205, Spokane County, (509)327-5269.
Holes: 18. **Yards:** 6,130/5,592. **Par:** 71/73. **Course Rating:** 68.8/70.9. **Slope:** 115/114. **Green Fee:** $19/$19. **Cart Fee:** $23/cart. **Walking Policy:** Unrestricted walking. **Walkability:** 2.
Opened: 1927. **Architect:** Local Citizens Committee. **Season:** Feb.-.Nov. **High:** May-Sept. **To obtain tee times:** Call anytime. **Miscellaneous:** Metal spikes, club rentals, credit cards (MC, V).
Reader Comments: Beautiful old pines, gorgeous on a summer morning ... Old and still good ... Traditional layout that keeps you coming back ... Scenic, treelined course ... Great people ... Nice layout ... Outstanding day of golf ... Tight and narrow, small greens ... Good service, condition and price, my favorite course.

★★★½ DRUIDS GLEN GOLF CLUB

PU-29925 207th Ave. S.E., Kent, 98042, King County, (253)638-1200, 25 miles SE of Seattle. **E-mail:** druidsglengolf.com.
Holes: 18. **Yards:** 7,146/5,354. **Par:** 72/72. **Course Rating:** 74.8/70.6. **Slope:** 137/121. **Green Fee:** $29/$53. **Cart Fee:** $28/cart. **Walking Policy:** Unrestricted walking. **Walkability:** 3.
Opened: 1997. **Architect:** Keith Foster. **Season:** Year-round. **High:** March-Oct. **To obtain tee times:** Call up to 7 days in advance. **Miscellaneous:** Reduced fees (weekdays, low season, twilight, seniors, juniors), metal spikes, range (grass), caddies, club rentals, credit cards (MC, V).
Reader Comments: Fun, new course ... Still developing ... Challenge on every hole, tight and narrow ... My favorite in Washington! Great par 3s ... Great views of Mt. Rainier! ... Needs some work, but getting there ... New and good ... Lots of potential, needs TLC ... Best new course in Seattle area.

★★★½ DUNGENESS GOLF & COUNTRY CLUB

SP-1965 Woodcock Rd., Sequim, 98382, Clallam County, (360)683-6344, (800)447-6826, 105 miles NW of Seattle. **Web:** www.dungenessgcc.com.
Holes: 18. **Yards:** 6,372/5,344. **Par:** 72/72. **Course Rating:** 70.4/70.1. **Slope:** 123/119. **Green Fee:** $22/$26. **Cart Fee:** $22/cart. **Walking Policy:** Unrestricted walking. **Walkability:** 2.
Opened: 1970. **Architect:** Ray Coleman. **Season:** Year-round. **High:** March-Oct. **To obtain tee times:** Call 60 days in advance. **Miscellaneous:** Reduced fees (weekdays, twilight, juniors), dis-

count packages, metal spikes, range (grass), club rentals, credit cards (MC, V), beginner friendly (group lessons).

Reader Comments: Great winter course ... Tight fairways ... Worth the drive ... Fun ... Wind can make it tough ... Easy to walk ... Dry in March ... Good value, usually great weather... A top 20 for the state.

★★★★ EAGLEMONT GOLF CLUB
SP-4127 Eaglemont Dr., Mount Vernon, 98274, Skagit County, (360)424-0800, (800)368-8876, 23 miles S of Bellingham.
Holes: 18. **Yards:** 7,006/5,307. **Par:** 72/72. **Course Rating:** 73.4/70.7. **Slope:** 134/124. **Green Fee:** $37/$47. **Cart Fee:** Included in Green Fee. **Walking Policy:** Mandatory cart. **Walkability:** 5. **Opened:** 1994. **Architect:** John Steidel. **Season:** Year-round. **High:** June-Aug. **To obtain tee times:** Call 7 days in advance. **Miscellaneous:** Reduced fees (weekdays, low season, twilight, seniors, juniors), metal spikes, range (grass), club rentals, credit cards (MC, V, AE).
Reader Comments: An undiscovered jewel ... Tough from the blues ... Penal target course ... Good test for better players ... Most gorgeous course in Northwest ... Bring plenty of balls ... 18 unique holes... Elevation changes ... A fun ride. Seriously, don't try to walk this one ... Great weekday prices ... Nice and friendly.

★★★ ECHO FALLS PUBLIC COUNTRY CLUB
PU-20414 121 First Ave. S.E., Snohomish, 98296, Snohomish County, (360)668-3030, 10 miles NE of Bellevue.
Holes: 18. **Yards:** 6,123/4,357. **Par:** 70/71. **Course Rating:** 69.4/64.6. **Slope:** 132/115. **Green Fee:** $27/$47. **Cart Fee:** $13/person. **Walking Policy:** Unrestricted walking. **Walkability:** 3. **Opened:** 1992. **Architect:** Jack Frei. **Season:** Year-round. **High:** April-Sept. **To obtain tee times:** Call 5 days in advance. **Miscellaneous:** Reduced fees (weekdays, low season, resort guests, twilight, seniors, juniors), discount packages, metal spikes, range (mats), club rentals, credit cards (MC, V, AE).
Reader Comments: Nos. 17 and 18 great finishing holes ... Good restaurant ... Beautiful course and clubhouse ...Tough to walk ... Short course but fun ... Island green at 18 ... One of the best ... Fine track ... Decent shorter course ... Several challenging holes with water.

★★★½ ELK RUN GOLF CLUB
PU-22500 S.E. 275th Place, Maple Valley, 98038, King County, (425)432-8800, (800)244-8631, 35 miles S of Seattle.
Holes: 18. **Yards:** 5,847/5,400. **Par:** 71/71. **Course Rating:** 68.7/70.4. **Slope:** 117/115. **Green Fee:** $22/$30. **Cart Fee:** $22/cart. **Walking Policy:** Unrestricted walking. **Walkability:** 3. **Opened:** 1989. **Architect:** Pete Peterson. **Season:** Year-round. **High:** May-Aug. **To obtain tee times:** Call up to 5 days in advance. **Miscellaneous:** Reduced fees (weekdays, low season, seniors, juniors), discount packages, metal spikes, range (mats), club rentals, credit cards (MC, V), beginner friendly.
Reader Comments: Wide open spaces ... Greens great ... Tough course ... New holes are impressive ... Great front 9 ... Good year-round ... Nice course, great condition, good value.

★★ ENUMCLAW GOLF CLUB
PM-45220 288 Ave. S.E., Enumclaw, 98022, King County, (360)825-2827, 40 miles SE of Seattle.
Holes: 18. **Yards:** 5,561/5,211. **Par:** 70/71. **Course Rating:** 66.0/68.8. **Slope:** 106/110. **Green Fee:** $19/$19. **Cart Fee:** $22/cart. **Walking Policy:** Unrestricted walking. **Walkability:** 3. **Season:** Year-round. **High:** July-Aug. **To obtain tee times:** Call up to 10 days in advance. **Miscellaneous:** Reduced fees (seniors, juniors), metal spikes, club rentals, credit cards (MC, V).

★★★½ ESMERALDA GOLF COURSE
PM-3933 E. Courtland, Spokane, 99207, Spokane County, (509)487-6291.
Holes: 18. **Yards:** 6,249/5,594. **Par:** 70/72. **Course Rating:** 68.7/72.7. **Slope:** 108/116. **Green Fee:** $15/$19. **Cart Fee:** $22/cart. **Walking Policy:** Unrestricted walking. **Walkability:** 1. **Opened:** 1956. **Architect:** Francis James. **Season:** Feb.Nov. **High:** May-Aug. **To obtain tee times:** Call 1 day in advance for weekdays or 7 days in advance for weekends. **Miscellaneous:** Reduced fees (twilight, seniors), metal spikes, range (grass/mats), club rentals, credit cards (MC, V).
Reader Comments: Fairly easy but in good shape ... Treed municipal with small greens, little rough ... Old, short course, reasonable rates ... Workingman's muny ... Best course to start the season on ... Always green in summer... Friendly pro shop ... Plays fast ... My home course.

★★ THE FAIRWAYS AT WEST TERRACE
PU-9810 W. Melville Rd, Cheney, 99004, Spokane County, (509)747-8418, 8 miles W of Spokane.
Holes: 18. **Yards:** 6,459/5,152. **Par:** 72/72. **Course Rating:** 69.0/68.9. **Slope:** 117/120. **Green Fee:** $13/$20. **Cart Fee:** $22/cart. **Walking Policy:** Unrestricted walking. **Walkability:** 1. **Opened:** 1987. **Season:** Year-round. **High:** June-Sept. **To obtain tee times:** Call golf shop. Tee times open Saturday for the following week. **Miscellaneous:** Reduced fees (weekdays, low season, twilight, seniors, juniors), metal spikes, range (grass), club rentals, credit cards (MC, V, D).

★★★ FOSTER GOLF LINKS
PM-13500 Interuban Ave. S., Tukwila, 98168, King County, (206)242-4221, 6 miles S of Seattle.
Holes: 18. **Yards:** 4,930/4,695. **Par:** 69/70. **Course Rating:** 62.3/65.1. **Slope:** 94/98. **Green Fee:** $21/$23. **Cart Fee:** $20/cart. **Walking Policy:** Unrestricted walking. **Walkability:** 1. **Opened:** 1925. **Architect:** George Eddie. **Season:** Year-round. **High:** May-Sept. **To obtain tee times:** Call 7 days in advance. **Miscellaneous:** Reduced fees (weekdays, low season, twilight, seniors, juniors), metal spikes, club rentals, credit cards (MC, V).
Reader Comments: Good course for beginners ... A family outing ... Easy walking flat track ... A good public course ... Nice little city course, a river runs through it ... Great course for the weekend warrior ... Nice short course, becoming more popular.

★★½ GALLERY GOLF COURSE
PU-3065 N. Cowpens Rd., Whidbey Island, Oak Harbor, 98278, Island County, (360)257-2178, 60 miles N of Seattle. **E-mail:** mwzgallery@aol.com.
Holes: 18. **Yards:** 6,351/5,454. **Par:** 72/74. **Course Rating:** 76.1/66.0. **Slope:** 128/113. **Green Fee:** $20/$22. **Cart Fee:** $14/cart. **Walking Policy:** Unrestricted walking. **Walkability:** 3. **Opened:** 1948. **Architect:** U.S. Navy. **Season:** Year-round. **High:** June-Sept. **To obtain tee times:** Call (360)257-2178. **Miscellaneous:** Reduced fees (low season, twilight, juniors), metal spikes, range (grass), club rentals, credit cards (MC, V, AE, D).
Reader Comments: Got caught in rain but still enjoyed the round ... Good in wet weather... Terrific views of Puget Sound ... Great fees ... Nicely-designed holes on back 9 ... Good winter course.

★★★ GLENEAGLES GOLF COURSE
PU-7619 Country Club Dr., Arlington, 98223, Snohomish County, (360)435-6713, (888)232-4653, 42 miles NE of Seattle.
Holes: 18. **Yards:** 6,002/4,937. **Par:** 70/70. **Course Rating:** 69.8/69.9. **Slope:** 129/125. **Green Fee:** $23/$29. **Cart Fee:** $10/person. **Walking Policy:** Unrestricted walking. **Walkability:** 3. **Opened:** 1995. **Architect:** William Teufel. **Season:** Year-round. **High:** April-Sept. **To obtain tee times:** Call 7 days in advance. **Miscellaneous:** Reduced fees (weekdays, low season, twilight, seniors, juniors), metal spikes, range (grass), club rentals, credit cards (MC, V, AE), beginner friendly (couples, beginner twilight leagues).
Reader Comments: Short but don't let that fool you ... Enjoyable from regular tees ... Practice your irons! ... Stay out of the woods ... A new stop for me and I will definitely go back ... Short, tight course ... Nice clubhouse ... Service was outstanding.

GOLD MOUNTAIN GOLF COMPLEX
PU-7263 W. Belfair Valley Rd., Bremerton, 98312, Kitsap County, (360)415-5432, 25 miles SW of Seattle.

★★★★ CASCADE COURSE   *Value*
Holes: 18. **Yards:** 6,707/5,306. **Par:** 71/74. **Course Rating:** 71.3/69.9. **Slope:** 120/116. **Green Fee:** $22/$26. **Cart Fee:** $24/cart. **Walking Policy:** Unrestricted walking. **Walkability:** 3. **Opened:** 1970. **Architect:** Jack Reimer. **Season:** Year-round. **High:** April-Sept. **To obtain tee times:** Call 7 days in advance at 11 a.m. Groups of 12-27 may book 30 days in advance, and groups of 28 or more may book up to 1 year in advance. **Miscellaneous:** Reduced fees (weekdays, low season, twilight, seniors, juniors), range (grass), club rentals, credit cards (MC, V).
Reader Comments: Mountain course in excellent condition ... Great elevation changes ... Best value on peninsula ... First-class facilities ... I've still got a soft spot for the original 18 ... Always good condition, great greens! ... Classic golf layout, perfect! ... Quality course for the price.

★★★★½ OLYMPIC COURSE   *Value, Condition*
Holes: 18. **Yards:** 7,003/5,220. **Par:** 72/72. **Course Rating:** 73.5/70.0. **Slope:** 131/116. **Green Fee:** $32/$36. **Cart Fee:** $24/cart. **Walking Policy:** Unrestricted walking. **Walkability:** 3. **Opened:** 1996. **Architect:** John Harbottle. **Season:** Year-round. **High:** April-Sept. **To obtain tee times:** Call 7 days in advance at 11 a.m. Groups of 12-27 may book 30 days in advance, and groups of 28 or more may book up to 1 year in advance. **Miscellaneous:** Reduced fees (weekdays, low season, twilight, seniors, juniors), range (grass), club rentals, credit cards (MC, V).
Notes: Ranked 3rd in 1999 Best in State.
Reader Comments: Gorgeous layout and brilliant greens .... Finest newer 18 in the area–love it ... A driver's dream ... Lots of cool looking holes ... Great strategic layout, fun for all levels of play ... Unbeatable value ... As good a course as any in the Northwest ... Gorgeous fairways ... Nice personnel.

★★ GRANDVIEW GOLF COURSE
PU-7738 Portal Way, Custer, 98240, Whatcom County, (360)366-3947, (877)644-GOLF.
Holes: 18. **Yards:** 6,514/5,673. **Par:** 72/72. **Course Rating:** 70.8/71.2. **Slope:** 118/120. **Green Fee:** $18/$24. **Cart Fee:** $22/cart. **Walking Policy:** Unrestricted walking. **Walkability:** 1. **Season:** Year-round. **High:** May-Sept. **To obtain tee times:** Call golf shop. **Miscellaneous:** Reduced fees (weekdays, low season, twilight, seniors, juniors), metal spikes, club rentals, credit cards (MC, V, D, ATM), beginner friendly.

WASHINGTON

★★★½ HANGMAN VALLEY GOLF COURSE *Value*
PU-E. 2210 Hangman Valley Rd., Spokane, 99223, Spokane County, (509)448-1212.
Holes: 18. **Yards:** 6,906/5,699. **Par:** 72/71. **Course Rating:** 71.9/71.6. **Slope:** 126/118. **Green Fee:** $16/$22. **Cart Fee:** $22/cart. **Walking Policy:** Unrestricted walking. **Walkability:** 3.
Opened: 1969. **Architect:** Bob Baldock. **Season:** March-Oct. **High:** May-Sept. **To obtain tee times:** Call Tuesday at 7 a.m. for the next 7 days. **Miscellaneous:** Reduced fees (seniors, juniors), metal spikes, club rentals, credit cards (MC, V, D).
Reader Comments: Outstanding public course, always in great shape ... Beautiful setting ... Great experience ... A perfect mixture of tough but fair.

★★★★ HARBOUR POINTE GOLF CLUB
PU-11817 Harbour Pointe Blvd., Mukilteo, 98275, Snohomish County, (425)355-6060, (800)233-3128, 15 miles N of Seattle. **E-mail:** harbourpointe@msn.com.
Holes: 18. **Yards:** 6,862/4,842. **Par:** 72/72. **Course Rating:** 72.8/68.8. **Slope:** 135/117. **Green Fee:** $35/$59. **Cart Fee:** $14/person. **Walking Policy:** Unrestricted walking. **Walkability:** 3.
Opened: 1990. **Architect:** Arthur Hills. **Season:** Year-round. **High:** May-Oct. **To obtain tee times:** Call 7 days in advance. **Miscellaneous:** Reduced fees (weekdays, low season, twilight, juniors), metal spikes, range (grass/mats), club rentals, credit cards (MC, V, AE).
Notes: Ranked 58th in 1996 America's Top 75 Affordable Courses.
Reader Comments: Good course ... Great challenge from the tips ... Beautiful course ... What happened here? ... Too many houses ... What a view on No. 11. Pace of play is excellent, especially for Puget Sound ... Course getting better.

★★★½ HIGH CEDARS GOLF CLUB
PU-14604 149th St. Court E., Orting, 98360, Pierce County, (360)893-3171, 14 miles SE of Tacoma.
Holes: 27. **Yards:** 6,303/5,409. **Par:** 71/71. **Course Rating:** 69.7/70.7. **Slope:** 114/115. **Green Fee:** $22/$30. **Cart Fee:** $22/cart. **Walking Policy:** Unrestricted walking. **Walkability:** 1.
Opened: 1971. **Season:** Year-round. **High:** April-Nov. **To obtain tee times:** Call 7 days in advance. **Miscellaneous:** Reduced fees (weekdays, twilight, seniors, juniors), discount packages, metal spikes, range (mats), club rentals, credit cards (MC, V).
Reader Comments: Good layout ... Best Mt. Rainier view ... Excellent service ... Daffodils in spring ... Great greens, fun to play, a fair test of skill ... Nice little course ... Nice putting course.

★★★★ HOMESTEAD GOLF & COUNTRY CLUB
R-115 E. Homestead Blvd., Lynden, 98264, Whatcom County, (360)354-1196, (800)354-1196, 15 miles N of Bellingham. **Web:** www.cybergolf.com/homestead.
Holes: 18. **Yards:** 6,927/5,570. **Par:** 72/72. **Course Rating:** 73.2/72.0. **Slope:** 129/124. **Green Fee:** $30/$40. **Cart Fee:** $10/person. **Walking Policy:** Unrestricted walking. **Walkability:** 2.
Opened: 1995. **Architect:** Bill Overdorf. **Season:** Year-round. **High:** April-Oct. **To obtain tee times:** Call 7 days in advance. **Miscellaneous:** Reduced fees (weekdays, low season, resort guests, twilight, seniors, juniors), discount packages, range (grass), club rentals, lodging (20 rooms), credit cards (MC, V, AE, D).
Reader Comments: Hidden gem; good layout ... Gilligan's Island at the 18th ... The course just keeps getting better and better... Great shape always a good experience ...The most friendly and helpful pro shop ... Lots of whoop-de-do's.

★★★★ HORSESHOE LAKE GOLF CLUB
PU-1250 S.W. Clubhouse Ct., Port Orchard, 98367, Kitsap County, (253)857-3326, (800)843-1564, 10 miles W of Tacoma.
Holes: 18. **Yards:** 6,105/5,115. **Par:** 71/71. **Course Rating:** 68.0/68.0. **Slope:** 116/112. **Green Fee:** $21/$31. **Cart Fee:** Included in Green Fee. **Walking Policy:** Mandatory cart. **Walkability:** 3. **Opened:** 1992. **Architect:** Jim Richardson. **Season:** Year-round. **To obtain tee times:** Call up to 7 days in advance. **Miscellaneous:** Reduced fees (weekdays, low season, twilight, seniors, juniors), discount packages, metal spikes, range (grass), credit cards (MC, V, AE, D).
Reader Comments: Short but neat ... Good value ... Short course ... Didn't like mandatory cart rule on back 9. I'm a walker... Best-kept secret in Washington.

HOT SPRINGS GOLF COURSE
PU-One St. Martin Rd., Carson, 98610, Skamania County, (509)427-5150, (800)607-3678, 45 miles E of Portland, OR.
Holes: 18. **Yards:** 6,407/5,244. **Par:** 72/72. **Course Rating:** 69.8/73.3. **Slope:** 113/119. **Green Fee:** $20/$25. **Cart Fee:** $20/cart. **Walking Policy:** Unrestricted walking. **Walkability:** 1.
Opened: 1991. **Season:** Year-round. **High:** May-Sept. **To obtain tee times:** Call golf shop. **Miscellaneous:** Reduced fees (low season, seniors), discount packages, metal spikes, range (grass), club rentals, lodging (22 rooms), credit cards (MC, V).

★★★★ INDIAN CANYON GOLF COURSE *Value*
PU-W. 4304 W. Dr., Spokane, 99204, Spokane County, (509)747-5353.

Holes: 18. **Yards:** 6,255/5,943. **Par:** 72/72. **Course Rating:** 70.7/65.9. **Slope:** 126/115. **Green Fee:** $23/$23. **Cart Fee:** $23/cart. **Walking Policy:** Unrestricted walking. **Walkability:** 4. **Opened:** 1935. **Architect:** H. Chandler Egan. **Season:** March-Oct. **High:** May-Sept. **To obtain tee times:** Call anytime in advance. Reserve with credit card. **Miscellaneous:** Reduced fees (twilight, juniors), metal spikes, range (grass/mats), club rentals, credit cards (MC, V).
Notes: Ranked 5th in 1999 Best in State; 6th in 1996 America's Top 75 Affordable Courses.
Reader Comments: Gorgeous, hilly, lined with ponderosa pines ...Exceptionally courteous service ... Holds your interest ... The best in eastern Washington ... Great value ... I've played this NW gem of a muny for nearly 20 years and it's always a challenge ... If you walk, be prepared for a cardiac workout ... My favorite course on the planet!

★★★ JACKSON PARK GOLF COURSE
PM-1000 NE 135th St., Seattle, 98125, King County, (206)363-4747.
Holes: 27. **Yards:** 6,186/5,540. **Par:** 71/74. **Course Rating:** 68.2/70.2. **Slope:** 115/117. **Green Fee:** $18/$22. **Walking Policy:** Unrestricted walking. **Walkability:** 3. **Opened:** 1928. **Architect:** Henry Tucker, Frank James. **Season:** Year-round. **High:** March-Sept. **Miscellaneous:** Reduced fees (low season, twilight, seniors, juniors), metal spikes, range (mats), club rentals, credit cards (MC, V), beginner friendly (junior, adult, executive ladies programs).
Reader Comments: Stays busy ... Great public course, bit rough ... Hilly ... I can always score ... Treelined, narrow fairways ... Good value for the money.

★★★ JEFFERSON PARK GOLF COURSE
PM-4101 Beacon Ave., Seattle, 98108, King County, (206)762-4513.
Holes: 18. **Yards:** 6,182/5,449. **Par:** 70/72. **Course Rating:** 68.3/70.2. **Slope:** 112/116. **Green Fee:** $22/$22. **Cart Fee:** $20/cart. **Walking Policy:** Unrestricted walking. **Walkability:** 3. **Opened:** 1917. **Architect:** Robert Johnstone/Jim Barnes. **Season:** Year-round. **High:** March-Oct. **To obtain tee times:** Call or in person up to 7 days in advance. **Miscellaneous:** Reduced fees (weekdays, low season, twilight, seniors, juniors), metal spikes, range (mats), club rentals, credit cards (MC, V).
Reader Comments: Scenic course ... Fred Couple's home ... Fair test ... Narrow treelined fairways ... The trees keep getting taller (100'+)... Good city course but needs work ... Crowded.

★★★★ KAYAK POINT GOLF COURSE
PU-15711 Marine Dr., Stanwood, 98292, Snohomish County, (360)652-9676, (800)562-3094, 45 miles N of Seattle. **Web:** www.kayakgolf.com.
Holes: 18. **Yards:** 6,719/5,332. **Par:** 72/72. **Course Rating:** 72.9/71.1. **Slope:** 138/125. **Green Fee:** $20/$30. **Cart Fee:** $27/cart. **Walking Policy:** Unrestricted walking. **Walkability:** 4. **Opened:** 1977. **Architect:** Ron Fream. **Season:** Year-round. **High:** May-Sept. **To obtain tee times:** Call 7 days in advance for weekdays. Call Monday a.m. for upcoming weekend. Call anytime in advance with credit card guarantee. **Miscellaneous:** Reduced fees (weekdays, low season, twilight, seniors, juniors), metal spikes, range (grass/mats), club rentals, credit cards (MC, V, AE).
Notes: Ranked 39th in 1996 America's Top 75 Affordable Courses.
Reader Comments: Beautiful course ... Tight and challenging ... Pretty walks through tunnels of trees ... A Pebble wannabe ... Best putting course ... Bring the straight sticks, all of them ... Long from the tips.

★½ KENWANDA GOLF COURSE
PU-14030 Kenwanda Dr., Snohomish, 98290, Snohomish County, (360)668-1166, 15 miles NE of Everett.
Holes: 18. **Yards:** 5,336/5,336. **Par:** 69/72. **Course Rating:** 65.3/70.4. **Slope:** 119/126. **Green Fee:** $20/$20. **Walking Policy:** Unrestricted walking. **Walkability:** 3. **Opened:** 1962. **Architect:** Dr. Roy Goss. **Season:** Year-round. **High:** June-Aug. **To obtain tee times:** Call up to 7 days in advance. **Miscellaneous:** Metal spikes, club rentals, credit cards (MC, V).

★★★½ LAKE CHELAN GOLF COURSE
PM-1501 Golf Course Dr., Chelan, 98816, Chelan County, (509)682-8026, (800)246-5361, 45 miles N of Wenatchee.
Holes: 18. **Yards:** 6,440/5,501. **Par:** 72/72. **Course Rating:** 70.3/70.9. **Slope:** 119/113. **Green Fee:** $21/$27. **Cart Fee:** $23/cart. **Walking Policy:** Unrestricted walking. **Walkability:** 3. **Opened:** 1971. **Architect:** Ron Sloan. **Season:** March-Nov. **High:** June-Aug. **To obtain tee times:** Call up to 7 days in advance. **Miscellaneous:** Reduced fees (twilight, seniors, juniors), discount packages, metal spikes, range (grass), club rentals, credit cards (MC, V).
Reader Comments: Outstanding municipal course ... Elevated greens make it excellent test ... My home course ... Great view of lake, outside holes best ... Excellent unknown course.

★★★½ LAKE PADDEN GOLF COURSE *Value*
PU-4882 Samish Way, Bellingham, 98226, Whatcom County, (360)738-7400, 80 miles N of Seattle.
Holes: 18. **Yards:** 6,675/5,496. **Par:** 72/72. **Course Rating:** 72.0/71.9. **Slope:** 124/122. **Green Fee:** $17/$22. **Cart Fee:** $22/cart. **Walking Policy:** Unrestricted walking. **Walkability:** 2. **Opened:** 1970. **Architect:** Proctor & Goss. **Season:** Year-round. **High:** May-Sept. **To obtain tee

times: Call 7 days in advance. **Miscellaneous:** Reduced fees (low season, seniors, juniors), range (grass/mats), club rentals, credit cards (MC, V, AE).

Reader Comments: Heavy seasonal traffic ... A real test ... Lots of potential ... A diamond still waiting to be polished ... Great bang for your buck ... Big, undulating greens ... A very nice layout.

★★★½ LAKE SPANAWAY GOLF COURSE

PM-15602 Pacific Ave., Tacoma, 98444, Pierce County, (253)531-3660, 30 miles S of Seattle. **Holes:** 18. **Yards:** 6,938/5,459. **Par:** 71/74. **Course Rating:** 73.0/71.3. **Slope:** 125/118. **Green Fee:** $16/$22. **Cart Fee:** $20/cart. **Walking Policy:** Unrestricted walking. **Walkability:** 2. **Opened:** 1967. **Architect:** A.V. Macan. **Season:** Year-round. **High:** May-Oct. **To obtain tee times:** Call 5 days in advance. **Miscellaneous:** Reduced fees (weekdays, seniors, juniors), metal spikes, range (grass/mats), club rentals, credit cards (MC, V, D).

Reader Comments: Nice winter course, good people ... Good municipal course ... Nice course for the money ... Consistent–always good ... Bring your best game, lots of doglegs ... Best golf value in Tacoma area.

★★★ LAKE WILDERNESS GOLF COURSE

PU-25400 Witte Rd. S.E., Maple Valley, 98038, King County, (425)432-9405, 30 miles SE of Seattle. **Holes:** 18. **Yards:** 5,218/4,544. **Par:** 70/70. **Course Rating:** 66.1/66.6. **Slope:** 118/117. **Green Fee:** $5/$22. **Cart Fee:** $20/cart. **Walking Policy:** Unrestricted walking. **Walkability:** 3. **Architect:** Ray Coleman. **Season:** Year-round. **High:** June-Aug. **To obtain tee times:** Call or come in up to 14 days in advance. **Miscellaneous:** Reduced fees (weekdays, low season, twilight, seniors, juniors), discount packages, metal spikes, club rentals, credit cards (MC, V, AE).

Reader Comments: Tight fairways ... Fun to play ... Good course ... Highly underrated ... Short ... Lots of houses.

LAKELAND VILLAGE GOLF COURSE

SP-Old Ranch Rd., Allyn, 98524, Mason County, (360)275-6100, 40 miles W of Olympia. **Web:** www.lakelandliving.com. **Holes:** 27. **Cart Fee:** $24/cart. **Walking Policy:** Unrestricted walking. **Walkability:** 3. **Opened:** 1972. **Architect:** Bunny Mason. **Season:** Year-round. **High:** Summer. **To obtain tee times:** Call up to 7 days in advance. **Miscellaneous:** Reduced fees (weekdays, low season, twilight, seniors, juniors), metal spikes, range (grass), club rentals, credit cards (MC, V).

★★★ GENERATION 1/GENERATION 2

Yards: 5,724/4,925. **Par:** 71/72. **Course Rating:** 68.8/69.2. **Slope:** 117/119. **Green Fee:** $25/$25.

Reader Comments: Great golf community ... Great summer golf fun ... Wet, but fun course ... 27 Holes with lots of water.

★★★ GENERATION 2/GENERATION 3

Yards: 6,471/5,334. **Par:** 72/72. **Course Rating:** 71.5/71.0. **Slope:** 122/121.

★★★ GENERATION 3/GENERATION 1

Yards: 5,915/5,081. **Par:** 72/72. **Course Rating:** 68.5/69.6. **Slope:** 114/117.

★★★½ LEAVENWORTH GOLF CLUB

SP-9101 Icicle Rd., Leavenworth, 98826, Chelan County, (509)548-7267, 110 miles E of Seattle. **Web:** www.leavenworthgolf.com. **Holes:** 18. **Yards:** 5,711/5,343. **Par:** 71/71. **Course Rating:** 67.0/69.6. **Slope:** 110/112. **Green Fee:** $22/$25. **Cart Fee:** $22/cart. **Walking Policy:** Unrestricted walking. **Walkability:** 2. **Opened:** 1927. **Season:** April-Nov. **High:** April-Oct. **To obtain tee times:** Call on Monday prior to play. **Miscellaneous:** Metal spikes, club rentals, credit cards (MC, V, AE, D).

Reader Comments: Beautiful course in the mountains ... Fun course next to river ... May be distracted by running salmon ... Short, tight course ... Premium on iron play ... Short but challenging ... Nice setting in mountain valley ... Good food ... Beautifully kept ... Black bear sitings.

★★★★ LEGION MEMORIAL GOLF COURSE   *Pace*

PM-144 W Marine View Dr., Everett, 98201, Snohomish County, (425)259-4653. **Holes:** 18. **Yards:** 6,900/4,805. **Par:** 72/72. **Course Rating:** 71.2/65.9. **Slope:** 116/100. **Green Fee:** $22/$30. **Cart Fee:** $21/cart. **Walking Policy:** Unrestricted walking. **Walkability:** 2. **Opened:** 1934. **Architect:** Steve Burns. **Season:** Year-round. **High:** May-Sept. **To obtain tee times:** Call up to 7 days in advance for weekdays. Call on Monday for upcoming weekend. **Miscellaneous:** Reduced fees (seniors, juniors), club rentals, credit cards (MC, V), beginner friendly (junior golf camps, junior club).

Reader Comments: Marvelous improvement with rebuilding ... Good job ... Dry course in winter golf ... What tremendous improvements with the remodel ... Outstanding ... New layout with water and sand, views ... Dry, very dry!

★★★★ LEWIS RIVER GOLF COURSE

PU-3209 Lewis River Rd., Woodland, 98674, Cowlitz County, (360)225-8254, (800)341-9426, 30 miles N of Portland.

Holes: 18. **Yards:** 6,352/5,260. **Par:** 72/73. **Course Rating:** 69.5/68.9. **Slope:** 124/118. **Green Fee:** $25/$31. **Cart Fee:** $24/cart. **Walking Policy:** Unrestricted walking. **Walkability:** 2. **Opened:** 1968. **Season:** Year-round. **High:** June-Sept. **To obtain tee times:** Call up to 7 days in advance. **Miscellaneous:** Reduced fees (twilight, seniors, juniors), metal spikes, range (grass), club rentals, credit cards (MC, V).
Reader Comments: Best 18 holes in southern Washington ... Constantly improving ... Beautiful course ... Lots of water ... Great shape ... Great back 9–for long hitters.

★★★½ LIBERTY LAKE GOLF CLUB

PU-E. 24403 Sprague, Liberty Lake, 99019, Spokane County, (509)255-6233, 20 miles E of Spokane.
Holes: 18. **Yards:** 6,373/5,801. **Par:** 70/74. **Course Rating:** 69.8/75.7. **Slope:** 121/134. **Green Fee:** $16/$22. **Cart Fee:** $23/cart. **Walking Policy:** Unrestricted walking. **Walkability:** 3.
Opened: 1959. **Architect:** Curly Houston. **Season:** Year-round. **High:** June-Sept. **To obtain tee times:** Call on Tuesday for following week. **Miscellaneous:** Reduced fees (low season, twilight, seniors, juniors), metal spikes, range (grass/mats), club rentals, credit cards (MC, V, D).
Reader Comments: Continue to improve course ... Best $ value in Spokane ... Small greens ... Good practice green ... Deceptively hard ... Longtime favorite ... Great views ... Good muny.

LIPOMA FIRS GOLF COURSE

PU-18615 110th Ave. E., Puyallup, 98374, Pierce County, (253)841-4396, (800)649-4396, 10 miles SE of Tacoma.
Holes: 27. **Green Fee:** $17/$22. **Cart Fee:** $20/cart. **Walking Policy:** Unrestricted walking. **Walkability:** N/A. **Opened:** 1989. **Architect:** Bill Stowe. **Season:** Year-round. **High:** April-Oct. **To obtain tee times:** Call up to 7 days in advance. **Miscellaneous:** Reduced fees (weekdays, low season, twilight, seniors, juniors), metal spikes, range (grass/mats), club rentals.

★★★ GOLD/BLUE

Yards: 6,805/5,517. **Par:** 72/72. **Course Rating:** 72.2/70.8. **Slope:** 122/116.
Reader Comments: Great winter course, drains well ... Maturing into a good course ... Excellent clubhouse and restaurant ... Good summer evening course ... Can do 18 holes in 4 hours ... Good layout, but rocky soil ... 27 holes with excellent views of Mt. Rainier... Tight challenging course ... Good greens.

★★★ GREEN/BLUE

Yards: 6,687/5,473. **Par:** 72/72. **Course Rating:** 70.0/70.6. **Slope:** 122/117. .
Reader Comments: Outstanding facility ... Fairways need some topsoil ... Much improved, friendly staff, excellent place for seniors and all who can hit ball straight ... Fairly flat course.

★★★ GREEN/GOLD

Yards: 6,722/5,476. **Par:** 72/72. **Course Rating:** 72.1/70.4. **Slope:** 122/117. .
Reader Comments: Very accommodating ... Excellent clubhouse and restaurant ... Lots of rocks in rough ... No waiting ... Good condition, easy layout, very enjoyable.

★★½ MADRONA LINKS GOLF COURSE

PU-3604 22nd Ave. N.W., Gig Harbor, 98335, Pierce County, (253)851-5193, 2 miles NW of Tacoma.
Holes: 18. **Yards:** 5,602/4,737. **Par:** 71/73. **Course Rating:** 65.5/65.6. **Slope:** 110/110. **Green Fee:** $20/$22. **Cart Fee:** $20/cart. **Walking Policy:** Unrestricted walking. **Walkability:** N/A.
Opened: 1978. **Architect:** Ken Tyson. **Season:** Year-round. **High:** March-Oct. **To obtain tee times:** Call or come in 7 days in advance. **Miscellaneous:** Reduced fees (twilight, seniors, juniors), metal spikes, range (grass/mats), club rentals, credit cards (MC, V).
Reader Comments: Nice local course ... Great restaurant ... An excellent short 18-hole course ... Some of the best greens in area ... Sweet and short, but don't hit a Madrona tree ... Links? Hills and valleys more like it ... Leave your driver at home.

★★★ MAPLEWOOD GOLF COURSE

PU-4050 Maple Valley Hwy., Renton, 98055, King County, (425)277-4444, 2 miles SE of Renton.
Holes: 18. **Yards:** 6,005/5,400. **Par:** 72/72. **Course Rating:** 67.8/68.7. **Slope:** 112/114. **Green Fee:** $15/$25. **Cart Fee:** $20/cart. **Walking Policy:** Unrestricted walking. **Walkability:** 2.
Opened: 1928. **Architect:** Al Smith. **Season:** Year-round. **High:** March-Nov. **To obtain tee times:** Call 7 days in advance for weekdays. Call Monday for upcoming weekend.
Miscellaneous: Reduced fees (seniors, juniors), metal spikes, range (mats), club rentals, credit cards (MC, V).
Reader Comments: Three putting greens ... A great mix of styles, tough track ...Great teaching staff and facility ... Good food ... New changes are right on ... Crowded.

★★★★½ MCCORMICK WOODS GOLF COURSE *Service, Condition*

PU-5155 McCormick Woods Dr. S.W., Port Orchard, 98367, Kitsap County, (360)895-0130, (800)373-0130, 2 miles SW of Port Orchard. **Web:** www.mccormickwoodsgolf.com.
Holes: 18. **Yards:** 7,040/5,758. **Par:** 72/72. **Course Rating:** 74.6/73.6. **Slope:** 136/131. **Green Fee:** $25/$55. **Cart Fee:** $13/person. **Walking Policy:** Unrestricted walking. **Walkability:** 3.
Opened: 1988. **Architect:** Jack Frei. **Season:** Year-round. **High:** June-Sept. **To obtain tee

times: From out of state, call 30 days in advance. State residents call 5 days in advance after 9 a.m. Weekends and holidays require credit card to reserve. **Miscellaneous:** Reduced fees (weekdays, low season, twilight, seniors), metal spikes, range (grass/mats), club rentals, credit cards (MC, V, AE, D), beginner friendly (5 sets of tees, practice facilities).
Notes: Ranked 7th in 1999 Best in State.
Reader Comments: Closest thing to a country club ... Fairways and greens are immaculate ... Outstanding view of Mt. Rainier... Difficult, beautiful layout ... Best public course in Washington ...Great pro shop ... The one course to play in the peninsula ... 5-star restaurant ... We were treated like royalty! ... Great course, good food!

★★★ MEADOW PARK GOLF COURSE
PM-7108 Lakewood Dr. W., Tacoma, 98467, Pierce County, (253)473-3033, 27 miles S of Seattle.
Holes: 18. **Yards:** 6,093/5,262. **Par:** 71/73. **Course Rating:** 68.9/70.2. **Slope:** 116/115. **Green Fee:** $16/$24. **Cart Fee:** $18/cart. **Walking Policy:** Unrestricted walking. **Walkability:** 3.
Opened: 1917. **Architect:** John Steidel. **Season:** Year-round. **High:** May-Sept. **To obtain tee times:** Call 7 days in advance. **Miscellaneous:** Reduced fees (weekdays, low season, twilight, seniors, juniors), discount packages, metal spikes, range (mats), club rentals, credit cards (MC, V).
Reader Comments: Super muny ... Outstanding clubhouse ... Friendly people ... Never know it's in the middle of Tacoma ... Flat front 9, hilly back 9 ... A challenge to play ... Can be wet ... Fun course, lots of variety.

★★★★ MEADOWWOOD GOLF COURSE *Value*
PU-E. 24501 Valley Way, Liberty Lake, 99019, Spokane County, (509)255-9539, 12 miles E of Spokane.
Holes: 18. **Yards:** 6,846/5,880. **Par:** 72/72. **Course Rating:** 72.1/73.5. **Slope:** 126/131. **Green Fee:** $12/$22. **Cart Fee:** $23/cart. **Walking Policy:** Walking at certain times. **Walkability:** 3.
Opened: 1988. **Architect:** Robert Muir Graves. **Season:** March-Nov. **High:** May-Aug. **To obtain tee times:** Nonresidents may call anytime in advance. **Miscellaneous:** Reduced fees (twilight, seniors, juniors), metal spikes, range (mats), club rentals, credit cards (MC, V, D).
Reader Comments: Long, well-groomed layout with water... Trio of amazing finishing holes ... Windy ... Outstanding value ... Deep rough, keep it on the fairway! ... Probably the best bargain in golf! ... Favorite course in Spokane.

★★★★ MERIWOOD GOLF COURSE
PU-4550 Meriwood Dr., Lacey, 98516, Thurston County, (360)412-0495, (800)558-3348, 10 miles S of Olympia.
Holes: 18. **Yards:** 7,170/5,600. **Par:** 72/72. **Course Rating:** 74.6/72.8. **Slope:** 128/123. **Green Fee:** $30/$49. **Cart Fee:** Included in Green Fee. **Walking Policy:** Walking at certain times. **Walkability:** 4. **Opened:** 1995. **Architect:** Bill Overdorf. **Season:** Year-round. **High:** April-Sept. **To obtain tee times:** Call 7 days in advance. **Miscellaneous:** Reduced fees (weekdays, low season, twilight, seniors, juniors), discount packages, metal spikes, range (grass), club rentals, credit cards (MC, V, AE).
Notes: Ranked 64th in 1996 America's Top 75 Affordable Courses.
Reader Comments: Real test of golf ... Gorgeous course ... Nice people ... Excellent layout— quite difficult ... Doesn't get better... Classic Northwest golf ... Need to be in command of your game ... Target golf ... Give it a few years, it will be excellent ... Putting course is a 'don't miss.'

★★★ MINT VALLEY GOLF CLUB
PU-4002 Pennsylvania St., Longview, 98632, Cowlitz County, (360)577-3395, (800)928-8929, 38 miles N of Portland.
Holes: 18. **Yards:** 6,379/5,231. **Par:** 71/71. **Course Rating:** 69.4/69.0. **Slope:** 114/109. **Green Fee:** $10/$22. **Cart Fee:** $24/cart. **Walking Policy:** Unrestricted walking. **Walkability:** 1.
Opened: 1976. **Architect:** Ronald Fream. **Season:** Year-round. **High:** May-Sept. **To obtain tee times:** Call up to 7 days in advance. **Miscellaneous:** Reduced fees (weekdays, low season, twilight, seniors, juniors), metal spikes, range (grass/mats), club rentals, credit cards (MC, V).
Reader Comments: Prettiest course in Washington from June to September ... Inexpensive golf for a well laid -out course ... Back 9 is harder than front ... Over hill and dale. Demands shot shaping ... Wet in winter.

★★½ MOUNT ADAMS COUNTRY CLUB
SP-1250 Rockyford, Toppenish, 98448, Yakima County, (509)865-4440, 2 miles S of Toppenish.
Holes: 18. **Yards:** 6,261/5,707. **Par:** 72/73. **Course Rating:** 70.1/72.8. **Slope:** 123/127. **Green Fee:** $21/$21. **Cart Fee:** $22/cart. **Walking Policy:** Unrestricted walking. **Walkability:** 1.
Architect: Designed by members. **Season:** Year-round. **High:** May-Aug. **To obtain tee times:** Members call 1 week in advance. All others Thursday prior to weekend. **Miscellaneous:** Range (grass/mats), club rentals, credit cards (MC, V).
Reader Comments: Long, straight, tough in wind, interesting greens ... Great people! ... Friendly course ... Great price ... Flat ... Risky drivable par 4s ... Lightning fast greens ... Good test.

★★★ MOUNT SI GOLF COURSE

PU-9010 Boalch Ave. S.E., Snoqualmie, 98065, King County, (425)888-1541, 27 miles SE of Seattle.
Holes: 18. **Yards:** 6,304/5,439. **Par:** 72/72. **Course Rating:** 68.5/68.8. **Slope:** 116/108. **Green Fee:** $23/$28. **Cart Fee:** $22/cart. **Walking Policy:** Unrestricted walking. **Walkability:** 2. **Opened:** 1927. **Architect:** Gary Barter. **Season:** Year-round. **High:** April-Sept. **To obtain tee times:** Call anytime. **Miscellaneous:** Reduced fees (low season, twilight, seniors, juniors), metal spikes, range (grass), club rentals, credit cards (MC, V).
Reader Comments: Pretty course, a little odd but fun ... Nice scenery ... Fairly easy track, nice area ... Good exercise ... Best restaurant in area ... Mountain views.

NEWAUKUM VALLEY GOLF COURSE

PU-153 Newaukum Golf Dr., Chehalis, 98532, Lewis County, (360)748-0461, 85 miles S of Seattle.
Holes: 27. **Green Fee:** $12/$23. **Cart Fee:** $20/cart. **Walking Policy:** Unrestricted walking. **Walkability:** 3. **Opened:** 1979. **Architect:** H.M. Date/J.H. Date. **Season:** Year-round. **High:** May-Sept. **To obtain tee times:** Call anytime. **Miscellaneous:** Reduced fees (weekdays, low season, twilight, seniors, juniors), discount packages, metal spikes, club rentals, credit cards (MC, V).
★★ EAST/WEST
Yards: 6,213/5,287. **Par:** 72/72. **Course Rating:** 68.4/68.9. **Slope:** 109/110.
★★ SOUTH/EAST
Yards: 6,168/5,102. **Par:** 72/72. **Course Rating:** 68.5/68.3. **Slope:** 109/108.
★★ SOUTH/WEST
Yards: 6,491/5,519. **Par:** 72/72. **Course Rating:** 69.9/70.6. **Slope:** 113/112.

★★ NILE GOLF CLUB

SP-6601 244th S.W., Mountlake Terrace, 98043, Snohomish County, (425)776-5154, 5 miles N of Seattle.
Holes: 18. **Yards:** 5,000/4,617. **Par:** 68/69. **Course Rating:** 64.5/66.0. **Slope:** 105/106. **Green Fee:** $25/$25. **Cart Fee:** $21/cart. **Walking Policy:** Unrestricted walking. **Walkability:** 3. **Opened:** 1969. **Architect:** Norman Woods. **Season:** Year-round. **High:** June-Aug. **To obtain tee times:** Call. **Miscellaneous:** Reduced fees (juniors), metal spikes, club rentals, credit cards (MC, V).

★★ NISQUALLY VALLEY GOLF CLUB

15425 Mosman St. NE, Yelm, 98597, Thurston County, (360)458-3332.
Special Notes: Call club for further information.

★★★★ NORTH BELLINGHAM GOLF COURSE *Pace*

PU-205 W. Smith Rd., Bellingham, 98226, Whatcom County, (360)398-8300, (888)322-6242.
Holes: 18. **Yards:** 6,816/5,160. **Par:** 72/72. **Course Rating:** 72.5/68.9. **Slope:** 125/112. **Green Fee:** $19/$32. **Cart Fee:** $11/person. **Walking Policy:** Unrestricted walking. **Walkability:** 2. **Opened:** 1995. **Architect:** Ted Locke. **Season:** Year-round. **High:** May-Sept. **To obtain tee times:** Call up to 7 days in advance. **Miscellaneous:** Reduced fees (weekdays, low season, twilight, seniors, juniors), discount packages, range (grass/mats), club rentals, credit cards (MC, V, AE, D, JCB).
Reader Comments: A bit of old Scotland transformed ... Good winter course ... Drains well... Greens greased lightning ... Good condition, enjoyable course with reasonable prices ... Minimalist links through fields ... Windy track ... Bring your 'A' game ... Keep it straight.

★★★ NORTH SHORE GOLF & COUNTRY CLUB

PU-4101 N. Shore Blvd. N.E., Tacoma, 98422, Pierce County, (253)927-1375, (800)447-1375.
Holes: 18. **Yards:** 6,305/5,442. **Par:** 71/73. **Course Rating:** 69.9/70.7. **Slope:** 120/119. **Green Fee:** $18/$28. **Cart Fee:** $20/cart. **Walking Policy:** Unrestricted walking. **Walkability:** N/A. **Opened:** 1961. **Architect:** Glen Proctor/Roy Goss. **Season:** Year-round. **High:** May-Sept. **To obtain tee times:** Call 7 days in advance. **Miscellaneous:** Reduced fees (weekdays, low season, twilight, juniors), metal spikes, range (grass/mats), club rentals, credit cards (MC, V, AE).
Reader Comments: Excellent design ... Nice, fast greens ... Narrow in spots ... A few great holes ... Friendly staff ... Great pro shop ... Fun course, must be on your toes ... Nice staff .... Challenge to play ... Good year-round course.

★★ OAKSRIDGE GOLF COURSE

PU-1052 Monte-Elma Rd., Elma, 98541, Grays Harbor County, (360)482-3511, 80 miles SW of Seattle.
Holes: 18. **Yards:** 5,643/5,423. **Par:** 70/72. **Course Rating:** 65.3/68.9. **Slope:** 100/108. **Green Fee:** $12/$15. **Cart Fee:** $17/cart. **Walking Policy:** Unrestricted walking. **Walkability:** 1. **Opened:** 1935. **Season:** Year-round. **High:** June-Sept. **To obtain tee times:** Call up to 1 day in advance. **Miscellaneous:** Reduced fees (low season, seniors, juniors), metal spikes, range (mats), club rentals, credit cards (MC, V).

WASHINGTON

★★ OCEAN SHORES GOLF COURSE
R-500 Canal Dr. N.E., Ocean Shores, 98569, Grays Harbor County, (360)289-3357, 130 miles SW of Seattle.
Holes: 18. **Yards:** 6,252/5,173. **Par:** 71/72. **Course Rating:** 70.2/69.6. **Slope:** 115/115. **Green Fee:** $15/$25. **Cart Fee:** $22/cart. **Walking Policy:** Unrestricted walking. **Walkability:** 2.
Opened: 1965. **Architect:** Ray Coleman. **Season:** Year-round. **High:** May-Sept. **To obtain tee times:** Call up to 1 year in advance; at least 7 days in advance. **Miscellaneous:** Reduced fees (low season, seniors, juniors), discount packages, metal spikes, club rentals, credit cards (MC, V).

PORT LUDLOW GOLF COURSE
R-751 Highland Dr., Port Ludlow, 98365, Jefferson County, (360)437-0272, (800)732-1239, 20 miles NW of Seattle. **E-mail:** golfteetimes@orminc.com. **Web:** visitportludlow.com.
Holes: 27. **Green Fee:** $29/$55. **Cart Fee:** $14/person. **Walking Policy:** Unrestricted walking.
Opened: 1975. **Architect:** Robert Muir Graves. **Season:** Year-round. **High:** May-Sept. **To obtain tee times:** Resort guests may make tee times up to 6 months in advance. Public may call up to 7 days in advance.

★★★★ TIDE/TIMBER
Yards: 6,787/5,598. **Par:** 72/72. **Course Rating:** 72.7/72.9. **Slope:** 131/126. **Walkability:** 3. **Miscellaneous:** Reduced fees (weekdays, low season, resort guests, twilight), discount packages, metal spikes, range (grass/mats), club rentals, lodging (225 rooms), credit cards (MC, V, AE).
Reader Comments: Fast greens ... Great area and natural settings ... I love the new 9 but boy it is tough ... Absolutely fine greens for winter... Beautiful! Supreme conditions ... No bail out areas ... One of Washington's best ... Play all weekend ... Best winter value ... Outstanding work by greenkeepers.

★★★★ TIMBER/TRAIL
Yards: 6,746/5,112. **Par:** 72/72. **Course Rating:** 73.6/70.8. **Slope:** 138/124. **Walkability:** 5.
Miscellaneous: Reduced fees (low season, resort guests, twilight), discount packages, metal spikes, range (grass/mats), club rentals, credit cards (MC, V, AE).
Reader Comments: Trail 9 has fantastic views ... Difficult, narrow fairways in canyons of firs ... Trail 9 the best ... Beautiful but too expensive ... Home course. I love it ... Target golf at its best ... Special ... Plan a trip around it ... Hard but fun ... Before you go, practice, then bring a lot of balls ... Best in state.

★★★★ TRAIL/TIDE
Yards: 6,683/5,192. **Par:** 72/72. **Course Rating:** 73.1/71.3. **Slope:** 138/124. **Walkability:** 3.
Miscellaneous: Reduced fees (low season, resort guests, twilight), discount packages, metal spikes, range (grass/mats), club rentals, credit cards (MC, V, AE).
Reader Comments: Hit it straight ... Don't miss playing Trail 9 ... One of my favorites ... Great service ... Joy to play ... Tough, tough, tough ... A tribute to the Pacific Northwest ... Good condition ... One of the most beautiful courses ... A great nature walk ... Nice people–great day.

★★★ QUAIL RIDGE GOLF COURSE
PU-3600 Swallows Nest Dr., Clarkston, 99403, Asotin County, (509)758-8501, 100 miles S of Spokane.
Holes: 18. **Yards:** 5,861/4,675. **Par:** 71/71. **Course Rating:** 68.1/66.2. **Slope:** 114/107. **Green Fee:** $17/$19. **Cart Fee:** $21/cart. **Walking Policy:** Unrestricted walking. **Walkability:** 4.
Opened: 1966. **Architect:** Mark Poe. **Season:** Year-round. **High:** April-Sept. **To obtain tee times:** Call 7 days in advance. **Miscellaneous:** Reduced fees (seniors, juniors), range (mats), club rentals, credit cards (MC, V).
Reader Comments: Course has some fun holes ... Very nice since the addition of the new 9 ... Get a cart, all holes on a hill... Great layout, accuracy and length needed to score ... Rolling terrain, busy but fun course ... Nice pro shop and clubhouse ... Great service staff ... Best drainage in area ... Short, but fair.

★★★½ RIVERBEND GOLF COMPLEX
PU-2019 W. Meeker St., Kent, 98032, King County, (253)854-3673, 18 miles S of Seattle.
Holes: 18. **Yards:** 6,633/5,538. **Par:** 72/72. **Course Rating:** 70.1/70.1. **Slope:** 119/114. **Green Fee:** $19/$23. **Cart Fee:** $20/cart. **Walking Policy:** Unrestricted walking. **Walkability:** 2.
Opened: 1989. **Architect:** John Steidel. **Season:** Year-round. **High:** April-Sept. **To obtain tee times:** Call. **Miscellaneous:** Reduced fees (weekdays, low season, twilight, seniors, juniors), metal spikes, range (mats), caddies, club rentals, lodging, credit cards (MC, V).
Reader Comments: Links style ... Plays long, lots of water and sand ... Fair shotmaking course ... Good course to play on summer evenings ... Popular local public course, well managed ... Challenge if the rough is set up for tournament ... Good value ... Flat, but well designed holes ... Gets better as the trees grow... Good tournament layout.

★★★ RIVERSIDE COUNTRY CLUB
PU-1451 N.W. Airport Rd., Chehalis, 98532, Lewis County, (360)748-8182, (800)242-9486, 27 miles S of Olympia. **E-mail:** riversidecc@localaccess.com.

Holes: 18. **Yards:** 6,155/5,456. **Par:** 71/72. **Course Rating:** 69.3/71.2. **Slope:** 118/116. **Green Fee:** $13/$23. **Cart Fee:** $20/cart. **Walking Policy:** Unrestricted walking. **Walkability:** 1. **Opened:** 1927. **Architect:** Roy Goss/Glenn Proctor. **Season:** Year-round. **High:** April-Sept. **To obtain tee times:** Call up to 7 days in advance. **Miscellaneous:** Reduced fees (weekdays, low season, twilight, seniors, juniors), metal spikes, range (grass/mats), club rentals, credit cards (MC, V, D).
Reader Comments: Nice rural course ... Quiet in the countryside ... Never crowded ... Worth a stop ... Nice ... Go for broke or play safe ... Short but fun, good value... Pro shop good ... Big beautiful trees, lining narrow fairways.

★★ ROLLING HILLS GOLF COURSE
PU-2485 N.E. McWilliams Rd., Bremerton, 98311, Kitsap County, (360)479-1212.
Holes: 18. **Yards:** 5,910/5,465. **Par:** 70/70. **Course Rating:** 67.9/71.0. **Slope:** 115/117. **Green Fee:** $20/$22. **Cart Fee:** $20/cart. **Walking Policy:** Unrestricted walking. **Walkability:** 3. **Opened:** 1972. **Architect:** Don Hogan. **Season:** Year-round. **High:** April-Sept. **To obtain tee times:** Call up to 7 days in advance. **Miscellaneous:** Reduced fees (low season, seniors, juniors), metal spikes, club rentals, credit cards (MC, V, AE, D).

★★½ SAGE HILLS GOLF CLUB
PU-10400 Sagehill Rd. SE, Warden, 98857, Grant County, (509)349-2603, 2 miles S of Warden.
Holes: 18. **Yards:** 6,591/5,128. **Par:** 71/73. **Course Rating:** 71.4/69.0. **Slope:** 122/114. **Green Fee:** $17/$22. **Cart Fee:** $11/person. **Walking Policy:** Unrestricted walking. **Walkability:** 3. **Opened:** 1967. **Season:** March-Nov. **High:** May-Aug. **To obtain tee times:** Call 1 week in advance. **Miscellaneous:** Reduced fees (weekdays, low season, resort guests, seniors, juniors), discount packages, range (mats), club rentals, credit cards (MC, V).
Reader Comments: Interesting, some different blind, flat holes ... Long, uphill finishing hole ... True and consistent greens ... Overall design is fair... Pretty good course in the country.

★★★★ SEMIAHMOO GOLF & COUNTRY CLUB *Service, Pace*
SP-8720 Semiahmoo Pkwy., Blaine, 98230, Whatcom County, (360)371-7005, (800)231-4425, 40 miles S of Vancouver. **Web:** www.semi-ah-moo.com.
Holes: 18. **Yards:** 7,005/5,288. **Par:** 72/72. **Course Rating:** 74.5/71.6. **Slope:** 130/126. **Green Fee:** $39/$65. **Cart Fee:** $17/person. **Walking Policy:** Unrestricted walking. **Walkability:** 1. **Opened:** 1986. **Architect:** Arnold Palmer/Ed Seay. **Season:** Year-round. **High:** May-Sept. **To obtain tee times:** Call 3 days in advance for weekdays; 1 day in advance for Saturday and 2 days in advance for Sunday. Hotel guests may book up to 90 days in advance. **Miscellaneous:** Reduced fees (weekdays, low season, resort guests, twilight), discount packages, range (grass/mats), club rentals, lodging (200 rooms), credit cards (MC, V, AE).
Notes: Ranked 10th in 1999 Best in State; 69th in 1996 America's Top 75 Upscale Courses.
Reader Comments: Course continues to improve ... Nice Palmer design ... Generous fairways with Palmer's tricky greens ... Excellent staff... Loved the layout, service and condition ... The perfect vacation ... Great day of golf ... Great couples course! ... Great location! ... Play this one a lot ... One of my favorites.

★★★★ SHUKSAN GOLF CLUB
PU-1500 E. Axton Rd., Bellingham, 98226, Whatcom County, (360)398-8888, (800)801-8897, 5 miles NE of Bellingham.
Holes: 18. **Yards:** 6,706/5,253. **Par:** 72/72. **Course Rating:** 70.3/68.5. **Slope:** 128/118. **Green Fee:** $20/$37. **Cart Fee:** $11/person. **Walking Policy:** Unrestricted walking. **Walkability:** 4. **Opened:** 1994. **Architect:** Rick Dvorak. **Season:** Year-round. **High:** April-Oct. **To obtain tee times:** Call 7 days in advance. **Miscellaneous:** Reduced fees (weekdays, low season, twilight, seniors, juniors), discount packages, range (grass/mats), club rentals, credit cards (MC, V, D).
Reader Comments: Tough, challenging, exciting ... Water on almost every hole ... Worth the trip ... Great condition ... Beautiful in the fall–the oranges, yellows, browns and greens ... Nice clubhouse ... Fun and forgiving ...Must keep it in play ... View from white tees outstanding. Ladies get short changed if playing reds.

★★ SIMILK BEACH GOLF COURSE
PU-12518 Christiansen Rd., Anacortes, 98221, Skagit County, (360)293-3444, 5 miles E of Anacortes.
Holes: 18. **Yards:** 6,177/5,788. **Par:** 72/74. **Course Rating:** 68.4/72.3. **Slope:** 110/112. **Green Fee:** $19/$22. **Cart Fee:** $22/cart. **Walking Policy:** Unrestricted walking. **Walkability:** 2. **Opened:** 1955. **Architect:** Jim Turner. **Season:** Year-round. **High:** May-Sept. **To obtain tee times:** Call 14 days in advance. **Miscellaneous:** Reduced fees (weekdays, low season, juniors), metal spikes, range (mats), club rentals, credit cards (MC, V).

★★★★ SKAMANIA LODGE GOLF COURSE *Service*
R-1131 Skamania Lodge Way, Stevenson, 98671, Skamania County, (509)427-2541, (800)293-0418, 45 miles E of Portland.

Holes: 18. **Yards:** 5,776/4,362. **Par:** 70/69. **Course Rating:** 68.9/65.2. **Slope:** 127/115. **Green Fee:** $20/$40. **Cart Fee:** $26/cart. **Walking Policy:** Unrestricted walking. **Walkability:** 3. **Opened:** 1993. **Architect:** Bunny Mason. **Season:** Year-round. **High:** June-Oct. **To obtain tee times:** Lodge guests may call upon confirmation of reservations. Others call up to 14 days in advance. **Miscellaneous:** Reduced fees (low season, resort guests, twilight, juniors), discount packages, metal spikes, range (grass/mats), club rentals, lodging (195 rooms), credit cards (MC, V, AE, D, Diners Club).

Reader Comments: Nice layout and lodge...Leave your driver home...Great views ... Impeccable maintenance ... Tight, tight, tight ... Beautiful setting ... Narrow, shotmaker's course ... Extremely beautiful mountain setting with lush vegetation, ponds, and hilly terrain ... Not for the fainthearted!

★★★½ SNOHOMISH GOLF COURSE
PU-7806 147th Ave. S.E., Snohomish, 98290, Snohomish County, (360)568-2676, 20 miles NE of Seattle.

Holes: 18. **Yards:** 6,858/5,980. **Par:** 72/74. **Course Rating:** 72.7/74.1. **Slope:** 126/129. **Green Fee:** $20/$25. **Cart Fee:** $21/cart. **Walking Policy:** Unrestricted walking. **Walkability:** 3. **Opened:** 1967. **Architect:** Roy Goss. **Season:** Year-round. **High:** May-Sept. **To obtain tee times:** Call 7 days in advance. **Miscellaneous:** Reduced fees (weekdays, twilight, seniors, juniors), discount packages, metal spikes, range (grass/mats), club rentals, credit cards (MC, V).

Reader Comments: Great course with good value ... Great course all year... Treelined, fun, use all clubs ... Can be wet in winter ... Large greens are nice targets ... Great long-iron course ... A granddaddy of a course.

★★★ SNOQUALMIE FALLS GOLF COURSE
PU-35109 Fish Hatchery Rd. SE, Fall City, 98024, King County, (425)222-5244, 25 miles E of Seattle.

Holes: 18. **Yards:** 5,452/5,224. **Par:** 71/71. **Course Rating:** 64.9/69.6. **Slope:** 102/114. **Green Fee:** $20/$27. **Cart Fee:** $22/cart. **Walking Policy:** Unrestricted walking. **Walkability:** 1. **Opened:** 1963. **Season:** Year-round. **High:** May-Sept. **To obtain tee times:** Call up to 6 days in advance. **Miscellaneous:** Reduced fees (weekdays, low season, seniors, juniors), metal spikes, range (grass), club rentals, credit cards (MC, V).

Reader Comments: Short course, ego builder ... Great greens ... Good basic golf ... Good course to walk ... Lowland course next to river... Worth a stop ... Intermediate course ... Good public course ... Family fun.

★★★★ SUDDEN VALLEY GOLF & COUNTRY CLUB
SP-2145 Lake Whatcom Blvd., Bellingham, 98226, Whatcom County, (360)734-6435, (360)734-6435, 8 miles E of Bellingham.

Holes: 18. **Yards:** 6,553/5,627. **Par:** 72/72. **Course Rating:** 71.8/72.8. **Slope:** 126/124. **Green Fee:** $22/$37. **Cart Fee:** $23/cart. **Walking Policy:** Unrestricted walking. **Walkability:** 3. **Opened:** 1970. **Architect:** Ted Robinson. **Season:** Year-round. **High:** July-Sept. **To obtain tee times:** Call up to 7 days in advance. **Miscellaneous:** Reduced fees (weekdays, low season, twilight, juniors), discount packages, metal spikes, range (grass/mats), club rentals, credit cards (MC, V, AE).

Reader Comments: Flat front on lake, hilly back ... Pretty back 9, hilly and narrow .... A real gem–rivals Capilano for scenery .... Favorite summer course ... Back 9 tough ... Undiscovered, laid back atmosphere ... Drainage getting better... Long from the tips ...Beautiful, mountainous, lakefront golf.

★★★½ SUMNER MEADOWS GOLF LINKS
PM-14802 8th St. E., Sumner, 98390, Pierce County, (253)863-8198, (888)258-3348, 5 miles N of Sumner. **Web:** www.cybergolf.com.

Holes: 18. **Yards:** 6,801/5,295. **Par:** 72/72. **Course Rating:** 72.3/69.8. **Slope:** 124/115. **Green Fee:** $17/$28. **Cart Fee:** $21/cart. **Walking Policy:** Unrestricted walking. **Walkability:** 1. **Opened:** 1995. **Architect:** Lynn William Horn. **Season:** Year-round. **High:** April-Sept. **To obtain tee times:** Call up to 2 weeks in advance. **Miscellaneous:** Reduced fees (weekdays, low season, twilight, seniors, juniors), metal spikes, range (grass/mats), club rentals, credit cards (MC, V, AE).

Reader Comments: Best links-style course in Washington ... Nice staff ... Short, but water and wind can make challenging ... Great for the $ ... Tight course packed with goodies ... You'll enjoy it! ... Unique for western Washington because of the lack of trees ... Water, water, hit em straight.

★★ SUN DANCE GOLF COURSE
PU-9725 N. 9 Mile Rd., Nine Mile Falls, 99026, Spokane County, (509)466-4040, 9 miles NW of Spokane. **E-mail:** sundance@sundance.com. **Web:** www.sundance.com.

Holes: 18. **Yards:** 6,208/5,452. **Par:** 70/72. **Course Rating:** 68.0/72.6. **Slope:** 112/119. **Green Fee:** $9/$17. **Cart Fee:** $22/cart. **Walking Policy:** Unrestricted walking. **Walkability:** 1. **Opened:** 1963. **Architect:** Dale Knott. **Season:** March-Nov. **High:** July-August. **To obtain tee times:** Call up to 7 days in advance. **Miscellaneous:** Reduced fees (weekdays, seniors, juniors), range (mats), club rentals, credit cards (MC, V, D).

WASHINGTON

★★★ SUN WILLOWS GOLF CLUB
PU-2035 N. 20th St., Pasco, 99301, Franklin County, (509)545-3440, 110 miles S of Spokane. **Web:** www.sunwillows.xtcom.com.
Holes: 18. **Yards:** 6,800/5,600. **Par:** 72/72. **Course Rating:** 70.1/68.2. **Slope:** 119/119. **Green Fee:** $18/$18. **Cart Fee:** $24/cart. **Walking Policy:** Unrestricted walking. **Walkability:** 2. **Opened:** 1959. **Architect:** Robert Muir Graves. **Season:** Year-round. **High:** March-Sept. **To obtain tee times:** Call up to 7 days in advance. **Miscellaneous:** Reduced fees (twilight, juniors), metal spikes, range (grass), club rentals, credit cards (MC, V).
Reader Comments: I like it ... Good flat course ... Nice public course, good shape, wind will be a factor ... Open and tight holes reward good course management ... Helpful congenial pros ... A good summer course after a long day on the road ... A great city course if you can get on it ... Fast greens ... Good value.

★★★ SUNLAND GOLF & COUNTRY CLUB
SP-109 Hilltop Dr., Sequim, 98382, Clallam County, (360)683-8365, 100 miles NE of Seattle.
Holes: 18. **Yards:** 6,319/5,557. **Par:** 72/73. **Course Rating:** 70.4/71.5. **Slope:** 120/120. **Green Fee:** $28/$33. **Cart Fee:** $22/cart. **Walking Policy:** Unrestricted walking. **Walkability:** N/A. **Opened:** 1971. **Architect:** A. Vernon Macan. **Season:** Year-round. **High:** April-Sept. **To obtain tee times:** Call seven days in advance. **Miscellaneous:** Reduced fees (juniors), metal spikes, range (grass), club rentals, credit cards (MC, V).
Reader Comments: Plays well in winter ... Narrow fairways, fast greens, pleasant ... Tight holes through subdivision ... Best value in NW, wish I lived there ... Curves to right, slicer's delight.

★★½ SUNTIDES GOLF COURSE
PU-231 Pence Rd., Yakima, 98908, Yakima County, (509)966-9065, 2 miles NW of Yakima.
Holes: 18. **Yards:** 6,015/5,509. **Par:** 70/71. **Course Rating:** 66.4/70.6. **Slope:** 110/116. **Green Fee:** $20/$20. **Cart Fee:** $20/cart. **Walking Policy:** Unrestricted walking. **Walkability:** 1. **Opened:** 1963. **Architect:** Joe Grier. **Season:** Feb.-Nov. **High:** May-June. **To obtain tee times:** Call 3 days in advance. **Miscellaneous:** Reduced fees (juniors), range (mats), club rentals, credit cards (MC, V).
Reader Comments: Good short public course ... Crowded ... Pleasant course, fast greens ... Pro remembers names ... Nice old course, great people and great value ... Wide open, condition improving ... Good track ... Kept in fine shape.

★★ TALL CHIEF GOLF COURSE
PU-1313 Snoqualmie River Rd. S.E., Fall City, 98024, King County, (425)222-5911, 21 miles SE of Seattle.
Holes: 18. **Yards:** 5,422/4,867. **Par:** 70/71. **Course Rating:** 66.0/66.5. **Slope:** 119/117. **Green Fee:** $20/$24. **Cart Fee:** $22/cart. **Walking Policy:** Unrestricted walking. **Walkability:** 3. **Opened:** 1965. **Architect:** Frank Avant. **Season:** Year-round. **High:** June-Sept. **To obtain tee times:** Call 6 days in advance. **Miscellaneous:** Reduced fees (weekdays, low season, twilight, seniors, juniors), discount packages, metal spikes, club rentals, credit cards (MC, V), beginner friendly (group lessons).

★★½ THREE LAKES GOLF CLUB
2695 Golf Dr., Malaga, 98828, Chelan County, (509)663-5448.
Special Notes: Call club for further information.

★★★½ THREE RIVERS GOLF COURSE
PU-2222 S. River Rd., Kelso, 98626, Cowlitz County, (360)423-4653, (800)286-7765, 40 miles N of Portland.
Holes: 18. **Yards:** 6,846/5,455. **Par:** 72/72. **Course Rating:** 72.1/68.5. **Slope:** 127/120. **Green Fee:** $14/$21. **Cart Fee:** $23/cart. **Walking Policy:** Unrestricted walking. **Walkability:** 3. **Opened:** 1982. **Architect:** Robert Muir Graves. **Season:** Year-round. **High:** May-Sept. **To obtain tee times:** Call up to 7 days in advance. **Miscellaneous:** Reduced fees (low season, twilight, seniors, juniors), metal spikes, range (grass/mats), club rentals, credit cards (MC, V), beginner friendly.
Reader Comments: Great for beginners, flat, wide open ... Outstanding winter course in both condition and price ... Most enjoyable ... Nice course even during rainy season .... Built on St. Helens' ash ... Dry, good value, playable.

★★★ TRI-CITY COUNTRY CLUB
SP-314 N. Underwood, Kennewick, 99336, Benton County, (509)783-6014, 120 miles SW of Spokane.
Holes: 18. **Yards:** 4,855/4,300. **Par:** 65/65. **Course Rating:** 62.5/65.2. **Slope:** 112/115. **Green Fee:** $22/$30. **Cart Fee:** $24/cart. **Walking Policy:** Unrestricted walking. **Walkability:** 3. **Opened:** 1938. **Architect:** Bert Lesley. **Season:** Year-round. **High:** May-Sept. **To obtain tee times:** Non-members may call 2 days in advance. **Miscellaneous:** Reduced fees (juniors), club rentals.
Reader Comments: Great short course ... Deceptively tight ... Good for short game ... Old golf course but well-kept ... Accuracy a must ... Made to feel welcome ... Small, but tight, with big course features.

★★★½ TRI-MOUNTAIN GOLF COURSE

PU-1701 N.W. 299th St., Ridgefield, 98642, Clark County, (360)887-3004, (888)874-6686, 15 miles N of Portland. **Web:** www.cybergolf.com.
Holes: 18. **Yards:** 6,580/5,284. **Par:** 72/72. **Course Rating:** 71.1/69.8. **Slope:** 120/117. **Green Fee:** $16/$31. **Cart Fee:** $24/cart. **Walking Policy:** Unrestricted walking. **Walkability:** 2.
Opened: 1994. **Architect:** Bill Robinson. **Season:** Year-round. **High:** April-Oct. **To obtain tee times:** Call 7 days in advance at 7 a.m. **Miscellaneous:** Reduced fees (weekdays, low season, twilight, seniors, juniors), discount packages, range (mats), club rentals, credit cards (MC, V).
Reader Comments: Windy, best public greens in the northwest ... Lots of sand and water... Makes me think ... Fun to play ... Great new clubhouse ... Excellent design ... Great greens ... Good morning course, British open winds in afternoon ... Getting better... Will drive extra miles to play here.

★★★½ TUMWATER VALLEY GOLF CLUB

PM-4611 Tumwater Valley Dr., Tumwater, 98501, Thurston County, (360)943-9500, (888)943-9500, 60 miles S of Seattle.
Holes: 18. **Yards:** 7,154/5,504. **Par:** 72/72. **Course Rating:** 73.1/70.4. **Slope:** 120/114. **Green Fee:** $19/$26. **Cart Fee:** $22/cart. **Walking Policy:** Unrestricted walking. **Walkability:** 2.
Opened: 1970. **Architect:** John Graham. **Season:** Year-round. **High:** May-Oct. **To obtain tee times:** Call up to eight days in advance. **Miscellaneous:** Reduced fees (weekdays, low season, twilight, seniors, juniors), metal spikes, range (grass), club rentals, credit cards (MC, V), beginner friendly (junior program, lessons, beginner women's league).
Reader Comments: Wide fairways most holes, nice walking course ... Good summer course ... Good muny ... Long from tips ... Good test of golf ... Flat, wide-open, often soggy ... An old 'experienced' course. What you see is what you get ... Course next to beer brewery.

★½ TYEE VALLEY GOLF COURSE

PU-2401 S. 192nd, Seattle, 98188, King County, (206)878-3540.
Special Notes: Call club for further information.

★★½ VETERANS MEMORIAL GOLF COURSE

PU-201 E. Rees, Walla Walla, 99362, Walla Walla County, (509)527-4507.
Holes: 18. **Yards:** 6,646/5,732. **Par:** 72/72. **Course Rating:** N/A. **Slope:** 114/121. **Green Fee:** $16/$16. **Cart Fee:** $24/cart. **Walking Policy:** Unrestricted walking. **Walkability:** 2. **Architect:** Frank James. **Season:** Year-round. **High:** April-Sept. **To obtain tee times:** Call golf shop.
Miscellaneous: Reduced fees (seniors, juniors), metal spikes, range (grass/mats), club rentals, credit cards (MC, V), beginner friendly (group lessons).
Reader Comments: Mature course. Takes advantage of terrain ... Friendly pro and staff ... Good course ... Well groomed and a variety of holes...Nice layout lined with trees ... The more you play this course the more you like it ... Greens are incredibly true and awesome ... A real jewel... Parklike setting.

VICWOOD GOLF LINKS

PU-8383 Vicwood Lane, Lacey, 98516, Thurston County, (360)455-8383, (800)558-3348, 10 miles N of Olympia.
Holes: 18. **Yards:** 6,887/5,202. **Par:** 72/72. **Course Rating:** 72.8/64.9. **Slope:** 123/105. **Green Fee:** $23/$38. **Cart Fee:** $12/person. **Walking Policy:** Unrestricted walking. **Walkability:** 4.
Opened: 1999. **Architect:** Peter L. H. Thompson. **Season:** Year-round. **High:** April-Sept. **To obtain tee times:** Call. **Miscellaneous:** Reduced fees (weekdays, low season, twilight, seniors, juniors), credit cards (MC, V, AE).
Notes: Ranked 10th in 1999 Best New Affordable Public.

★★★½ WALTER E. HALL MEMORIAL GOLF COURSE

PM-1226 W. Casino Rd., Everett, 98204, Snohomish County, (425)353-4653, 25 miles N of Seattle.
Holes: 18. **Yards:** 6,450/5,657. **Par:** 72/73. **Course Rating:** 69.6/71.6. **Slope:** 117/118. **Green Fee:** $16/$22. **Cart Fee:** $21/cart. **Walking Policy:** Unrestricted walking. **Walkability:** 1.
Opened: 1972. **Architect:** John Steidel. **Season:** Year-round. **High:** April-Oct. **To obtain tee times:** Call 7 days in advance for weekdays. Call on Monday at 9 a.m. for upcoming weekend.
Miscellaneous: Reduced fees (seniors, juniors), metal spikes, club rentals, credit cards (MC, V).
Reader Comments: A fun old course in pretty good condition ... Back 9 rolling hills ... Great for beginners ... Good to walk, continuing improvements ... Helpful pro shop ... Learned to play the game here ... Flat, easily accessible muny ... Huge greens ... A few punishing holes.

★★½ WANDERMERE GOLF COURSE

PU-N. 13700 Wandermere Road, Spokane, 99208, Spokane County, (509)466-8023, 10 miles N of Spokane. **E-mail:** wandgolf@aol.com.
Holes: 18. **Yards:** 6,115/5,420. **Par:** 70/71. **Course Rating:** 68.9/70.7. **Slope:** 109/111. **Green Fee:** $18/$20. **Cart Fee:** $22/cart. **Walking Policy:** Unrestricted walking. **Walkability:** 3.
Opened: 1929. **Architect:** Lee Wayne Ross. **Season:** March-Nov. **High:** June-Sept. **To obtain**

tee times: Call up to 1 day in advance for weekdays; up to 7 days in advance for weekends beginning at 6:30 a.m. **Miscellaneous:** Reduced fees (seniors, juniors), range (grass/mats), club rentals, credit cards (MC, V).
Reader Comments: It's fun ... Wide open ... You play up the hill and down the valley ... Well run ... Good older course, new changes are great ... Great setting ... The pro will find you a game ... Nice place to spend an afternoon ... Great for ladies and seniors.

★½ WEST RICHLAND MUNICIPAL GOLF COURSE

PM-4000 Fallon Dr., West Richland, 99352, Benton County, (509)967-2165, 200 miles E of Seattle.
Holes: 18. **Yards:** 6,103/5,516. **Par:** 70/70. **Course Rating:** 67.7/70.3. **Slope:** 114/114. **Green Fee:** $13/$13. **Cart Fee:** $20/cart. **Walking Policy:** Unrestricted walking. **Walkability:** 1.
Opened: 1950. **Season:** Year-round. **High:** March-Oct. **To obtain tee times:** Call.
Miscellaneous: Metal spikes, range (grass), club rentals.

★★★ WEST SEATTLE GOLF COURSE

PM-4470 35th Ave. S.W., Seattle, 98126, King County, (206)935-5187, 5 miles S of Seattle.
Holes: 18. **Yards:** 6,600/5,700. **Par:** 72/72. **Course Rating:** 70.9/72.6. **Slope:** 119/123. **Green Fee:** $18/$22. **Cart Fee:** $20/cart. **Walking Policy:** Unrestricted walking. **Walkability:** 3.
Opened: 1939. **Architect:** H.C. Egan. **Season:** Year-round. **High:** May-Sept. **To obtain tee times:** Call up to 7 days in advance. **Miscellaneous:** Reduced fees (low season, twilight, seniors, juniors), metal spikes, club rentals, credit cards (MC, V).
Reader Comments: Great value, getting better... Sweeping views of Seattle ... Staff is the best ... A bread-and-butter municipal course ... Lots of play ... My home course. I love it, warts and all ... Best of the three Seattle municipals ... Long for a municipal course.

★★★½ WILLOWS RUN GOLF CLUB

PU-10402 Willows Rd. N.E., Redmond, 98052, King County, (425)883-1200, 10 miles E of Seattle. **Web:** www.willowsrun.com.
Holes: 18. **Yards:** 6,806/5,633. **Par:** 72/72. **Course Rating:** 71.6/71.4. **Slope:** 119/121. **Green Fee:** $24/$49. **Cart Fee:** $24/cart. **Walking Policy:** Unrestricted walking. **Walkability:** 1.
Opened: 1994. **Architect:** Lisa Maki. **Season:** Year-round. **High:** March-Oct. **To obtain tee times:** Call 7 days in advance. **Miscellaneous:** Reduced fees (weekdays, low season, twilight, seniors, juniors), discount packages, metal spikes, range (grass/mats), caddies, club rentals, credit cards (MC, V).
Reader Comments: Super golf course ... Links course, good test ... Good staff ... Exceptional greens, you get what you pay for... Flat, good walking course ... New course within wetlands, no trees ... Good links-type course ... Nice meadow course ... Usually great shape.

ALPINE LAKE RESORT

R-700 West Alpine Drive , Terra Alta, 26764, Preston County, (304)789-2481, (800)752-7179, 30 miles SE of Morgantown. **Web:** www.alpinelake.com.
Holes: 18. **Yards:** 6,069/4,902. **Par:** 72/73. **Course Rating:** 69.1/68.8. **Slope:** 122/111. **Green Fee:** $15/$27. **Cart Fee:** $12/person. **Walking Policy:** Walking at certain times. **Walkability:** 4.
Opened: 1968. **Architect:** Brian Farse. **Season:** April-Oct. **High:** May-Sept. **Miscellaneous:** Reduced fees (twilight, seniors), discount packages, range (grass/mats), lodging (35 rooms), credit cards (MC, V, AE, D).
Special Notes: Formerly known as Alpine Lakes Resort

BARBOUR COUNTRY CLUB

SP-US Rte. 119, Philippi, 26416, (304)457-2156.
Special Notes: Call club for further information.

BEAVER CREEK GOLF CLUB

SP-800 Country Club Drive, Beaver, 25813, Raleigh County, (304)763-9116, (800)842-5604, 3 miles S of Beckley.
Holes: 18. **Yards:** 5,040/3,865. **Par:** 70/70. **Course Rating:** 71.2/68.5. **Slope:** 133/129. **Green Fee:** $11/$13. **Cart Fee:** $10/person. **Walking Policy:** Unrestricted walking. **Walkability:** 4.
Opened: 1986. **Season:** Year-round. **High:** April-Aug. **To obtain tee times:** Call 1-800-842-5604 anytime. **Miscellaneous:** Metal spikes, range (grass), club rentals, credit cards (MC, V, AE, D).
Special Notes: Formerly Beaver Creek Golf & Country Club.

★★½ BEL MEADOW COUNTRY CLUB

SP-Rte. 1 Box 450, Mount Clare, 26408, Harrison County, (304)623-3701, 5 miles S of Clarksburg. **Web:** www.belmeadow.com.
Holes: 18. **Yards:** 6,938/5,517. **Par:** 72/72. **Course Rating:** 73.0/71.5. **Slope:** 126/122. **Green Fee:** $19/$22. **Cart Fee:** $11/person. **Walking Policy:** Walking at certain times. **Walkability:** 1.
Opened: 1965. **Architect:** Robert Trent Jones. **Season:** Year-round. **High:** May-Sept. **To obtain tee times:** Call 7 days in advance during season (April-Oct.) for weekends and holidays.
Miscellaneous: Reduced fees (weekdays, low season, twilight, seniors, juniors), metal spikes, range (grass/mats), club rentals, credit cards (MC, V, AE, D), beginner friendly (beginner clinic, junior rates, after-hour specials).
Reader Comments: Nice layout ... Present owners making improvements ... Conditions improved ... New range ... Challenging and very fun ... Nice folks making a commitment to restore ... Good, basic golf ... Well-designed ... Easier front and a more difficult back.

★★ BIG BEND GOLF CLUB

PU-P.O. Box 329, Riverview Drive, Tornado, 25202, Kanawha County, (304)722-0400, 15 miles SW of Charleston.
Holes: 18. **Yards:** 6,327/5,762. **Par:** 71/72. **Course Rating:** 69.6/N/A. **Slope:** 116/N/A. **Green Fee:** $12/$15. **Cart Fee:** $10/person. **Walking Policy:** Unrestricted walking. **Walkability:** 1.
Opened: 1964. **Architect:** Evans Family. **Season:** Year-round. **High:** May-Oct. **To obtain tee times:** Call up to 7 days in advance. **Miscellaneous:** Reduced fees (low season, twilight), metal spikes, range (grass), club rentals, credit cards (MC, V).

★★★★ CACAPON RESORT

R-Rte. 1, Box 230, Berkeley Springs, 25411, Morgan County, (304)258-1022, (800)225-5982, 10 miles S of Berkeley Springs.
Holes: 18. **Yards:** 6,940/5,510. **Par:** 72/72. **Course Rating:** 72.3/70.6. **Slope:** 126/118. **Green Fee:** $22/$26. **Cart Fee:** $20/cart. **Walking Policy:** Unrestricted walking. **Walkability:** 2.
Opened: 1974. **Architect:** Robert Trent Jones, Sr. **Season:** Year-round weather permitting.
High: April-Oct. **To obtain tee times:** Resort guests with lodging deposit; all others call 7 days in advance. **Miscellaneous:** Reduced fees (low season, seniors), discount packages, metal spikes, range (grass), club rentals, lodging (48 rooms), credit cards (MC, V, AE, Diners Club).
Reader Comments: Beautiful layout and a great price ... Almost heaven ... Great value ... Worth the drive ... My favorite ... Beautiful and challenging ... Beautiful setting ... My all-time favorite: Price, course, everything ... A jewel ... Bring bug spray in summer ... Outstanding, outstanding, outstanding.

★★★ CANAAN VALLEY RESORT GOLF COURSE

R-Rte. 1, Box 330, Davis, 26260, Tucker County, (304)866-4121x2632, (800)622-4121, 80 miles W of Harrisonburg, VA.
Holes: 18. **Yards:** 6,982/5,820. **Par:** 72/72. **Course Rating:** 73.4/71.8. **Slope:** 125/115. **Green Fee:** $30/$33. **Cart Fee:** $30/cart. **Walking Policy:** Unrestricted walking. **Walkability:** 2.
Opened: 1968. **Architect:** Geoffrey Cornish. **Season:** April-Nov. **High:** June-Aug. **To obtain tee times:** Resort guests may book tee times with room reservations. Others may call golf shop.
Miscellaneous: Reduced fees (weekdays, low season, twilight, seniors), discount packages, metal spikes, range (grass/mats), club rentals, lodging (300 rooms), credit cards (MC, V, AE, D, Diners Club).

Reader Comments: Beautiful scenery ... Good challenge ... Wide open ... Bring wind gear ... Bring your driver.

CLEARFORD VALLEY GOLF COURSE
PU-Rte. 971, Oceana, 24870, (304)682-6209.
Special Notes: Call club for further information.

DEERFIELD GOLF CLUB
SP-New Jackson Mill Rd., Weston, 26452, (304)269-1139.
Special Notes: Call club for further information.

★★★ ESQUIRE GOLF COURSE
PU-Esquire Dr., Barboursville, 25504, Cabell County, (304)736-1476, 10 miles S of Huntington.
Holes: 18. **Yards:** 6,905/5,250. **Par:** 72/72. **Course Rating:** 72.2/69.2. **Slope:** 116/104. **Green Fee:** $28/$30. **Cart Fee:** Included in Green Fee. **Walking Policy:** Walking at certain times. **Walkability:** 2. **Opened:** 1975. **Architect:** X.G. Hassenplug. **Season:** Year-round. **High:** April-Oct. **To obtain tee times:** Call up to 7 days in advance. **Miscellaneous:** Range (grass), club rentals, credit cards (MC, V, AE).
Reader Comments: Too many houses along fairways ... Best conditions in spring ... Fairways were burned out in the summer ... Challenging ... Decent public course.

★★★★ GLADE SPRINGS RESORT *Service, Pace*
R-200 Lake Dr., Daniels, 25832, Raleigh County, (304)763-2050, (800)634-5233, 8 miles S of Beckley. **Web:** www.gladesprings.com.
Holes: 18. **Yards:** 6,941/4,884. **Par:** 72/72. **Course Rating:** 73.5/67.6. **Slope:** 135/118. **Green Fee:** $80/$80. **Cart Fee:** Included in Green Fee. **Walking Policy:** Unrestricted walking. **Walkability:** 3. **Opened:** 1973. **Architect:** George Cobb. **Season:** Year-round. **High:** May-Oct. **To obtain tee times:** Resort guests may book tee times with confirmed room reservation. Public may call 7 days in advance. **Miscellaneous:** Reduced fees (low season, resort guests, juniors), range (grass), club rentals, lodging (88 rooms), credit cards (MC, V, AE, D).
Notes: Ranked 5th in 1997 Best in State.
Reader Comments: Challenging, but fair ... Wonderful ... Beautiful resort ... Great experience ... Saw a lot of deer ... Nice practice area ... Very playable ... A high price for me, but fair for the facility ... Great service.

GLENVILLE GOLF CLUB
PU-Sycamore Road, Glenville, 26351, Gilmer County, (304)462-5907, 55 miles SW of Clarksburg.
Holes: 9. **Yards:** 2,840/2,312. **Par:** 35/37. **Course Rating:** 65.4/N/A. **Slope:** 111/N/A. **Green Fee:** $14/$14. **Cart Fee:** $16/cart. **Walking Policy:** Unrestricted walking. **Walkability:** 3. **Opened:** 1948. **Season:** March-Oct. **High:** May-Aug. **To obtain tee times:** Call 48 hours in advance for Memorial Day weekend to Labor Day weekend, weekends and holidays. **Miscellaneous:** Reduced fees (low season), club rentals, credit cards (MC, V).

★★½ GOLF CLUB OF WEST VIRGINIA
PU-Box 199, Rte. 1, Waverly, 26184, Wood County, (304)464-4420, 10 miles NE of Parkersburg.
Holes: 18. **Yards:** 6,018/5,011. **Par:** 70/71. **Course Rating:** 68.9/67.9. **Slope:** 116/109. **Green Fee:** $20/$30. **Cart Fee:** Included in Green Fee. **Walking Policy:** Unrestricted walking. **Walkability:** 4. **Opened:** 1950. **Architect:** Lauren Parish. **Season:** Year-round. **High:** April-Sept. **To obtain tee times:** Call anytime. **Miscellaneous:** Reduced fees (weekdays, low season, twilight, seniors, juniors), discount packages, metal spikes, club rentals, credit cards (MC, V, D).
Reader Comments: Very hilly ... Take a cart ... Fun ... Good for high-handicapper ... Lovely fall scenery ... Blind shots.

★★★ GRANDVIEW COUNTRY CLUB
PU-1500 Scottridge Dr., Beaver, 25813, Raleigh County, (304)763-2520, 8 miles S of Beckley.
Holes: 18. **Yards:** 6,834/4,910. **Par:** 72/72. **Course Rating:** 70.2/67.3. **Slope:** 112/107. **Green Fee:** $14/$18. **Cart Fee:** $18/cart. **Walking Policy:** Walking at certain times. **Walkability:** N/A. **Opened:** 1973. **Architect:** Randy Scott/Glenn Scott. **Season:** May-Nov. **High:** June-Aug. **To obtain tee times:** Call. **Miscellaneous:** Metal spikes, range (grass).
Reader Comments: Short and wide open ... Bring a driver and money for the local sharks ... Easy, fun ... Some beautiful holes with overlooks ... Can be demanding ... Great for all levels ... Very affordable.

THE GREENBRIER *Service+*
R-300 W. Main St., White Sulphur Springs, 24986, Greenbrier County, (304)536-1110, (800)624-6070, 250 miles SW of Washington, DC. **E-mail:** joanna_honaker@greenbrier.com. **Web:** www.greenbrier.com.
★★★★ GREENBRIER COURSE *Condition*
Holes: 18. **Yards:** 6,675/5,095. **Par:** 72/72. **Course Rating:** 73.1/69.8. **Slope:** 135/118. **Green Fee:** $72/$225. **Cart Fee:** Included in Green Fee. **Walking Policy:** Walking at certain times. **Walkability:** 2. **Opened:** 1924. **Architect:** Seth Raynor/Jack Nicklaus. **Season:** April-Nov. **High:**

April-Oct. **To obtain tee times:** Resort guests call up to 6 months in advance. Public may call up to 3 days in advance. **Miscellaneous:** Reduced fees (resort guests, juniors), discount packages, range (grass/mats), caddies, club rentals, lodging, credit cards (MC, V, AE, D).
Notes: Ranked 2nd in 1999 Best in State. 1994 Solheim Cup; 1979 Ryder Cup.
Reader Comments: Great challenge ... Beautiful ... Great diversity ... Expensive, but worth the splurge ... The ultimate experience. Real class ... Tough ... Absolutely great ... Wonderful golf, service and food, and if you're lucky you'll get to see Sam Snead ... All you want in a course ... A gem ... My favorite ... There's no place like it.

★★★ MEADOWS COURSE
Holes: 18. **Yards:** 6,807/5,001. **Par:** 71/71. **Course Rating:** 72.4/68.5. **Slope:** 132/115. **Green Fee:** $72/$225. **Cart Fee:** Included in Green Fee. **Walking Policy:** Walking at certain times. **Walkability:** 2. **Opened:** 1963. **Architect:** Bob Cupp. **Season:** Year-round. **High:** April-Oct. **To obtain tee times:** Resort guests may reserve up to 6 months in advance. **Miscellaneous:** Reduced fees (low season, juniors), discount packages, range (grass/mats), caddies, club rentals, lodging (650 rooms), credit cards (MC, V, AE, D, Diners Club), beginner friendly (golf schools, clinics).
Reader Comments: New holes are a great improvement ... Most open of the three courses ... You need to be accurate ... My third choice, but it's still The Greenbrier ... Super facilities ... Beautiful.
Special Notes: Formerly Lakeside Course.

★★★★ OLD WHITE COURSE
Holes: 18. **Yards:** 6,652/5,179. **Par:** 70/70. **Course Rating:** 72.2/69.7. **Slope:** 131/119. **Green Fee:** $72/$225. **Cart Fee:** Included in Green Fee. **Walking Policy:** Walking at certain times. **Walkability:** 3. **Opened:** 1913. **Architect:** C.B. Macdonald/S.J. Raynor. **Season:** Year-round. **High:** April-Oct. **To obtain tee times:** Resort guests call up to 6 months in advance. Public may call up to 3 days in advance. **Miscellaneous:** Reduced fees (low season, juniors), discount packages, range (grass/mats), caddies, club rentals, lodging, credit cards (MC, V, AE, D), beginner friendly (golf schools, clinics).
Notes: Ranked 3rd in 1999 Best in State.
Reader Comments: Best resort golf anywhere. A true gem ... Tradition, history and Sam Snead ... A little pricey ... Beautiful ... Rugged beauty ... Great service ... Walkable ... My husband's favorite; No. 2 on my list ... Sneaky tough ... The best course at the best resort in the land.

★★★ GREENHILLS COUNTRY CLUB
SP-Rte. 56, Ravenswood, 26164, Jackson County, (304)273-3396, 38 miles N of Charleston.
Holes: 18. **Yards:** 6,252/5,192. **Par:** 72/74. **Course Rating:** 68.6/69.0. **Slope:** 119/108. **Green Fee:** $19/$24. **Cart Fee:** $13/person. **Walking Policy:** Unrestricted walking. **Walkability:** 3. **Opened:** 1959. **Architect:** Paul Lemon. **Season:** Year-round. **High:** April-Oct. **To obtain tee times:** Call up to 6 days in advance. **Miscellaneous:** Reduced fees (weekdays, low season, resort guests), discount packages, metal spikes, range (grass/mats), lodging, credit cards (MC, V, AE, D).
Reader Comments: Well worth the money ... Great pace ... Some tight holes ... Plenty of rolling hills ... Excellent.

★★½ HIGHLAND SPRINGS GOLF COURSE
PU-1600 Washington Pike, Wellsburg, 26070, Brooke County, (304)737-2201.
Holes: 18. **Yards:** 6,853/5,739. **Par:** 72/75. **Course Rating:** 72.4/72.1. **Slope:** 118/113. **Green Fee:** $7/$18. **Walking Policy:** Unrestricted walking. **Walkability:** 4. **Opened:** 1963. **Architect:** James Gilmore Harrison. **Season:** March-Dec. **High:** June-Aug. **To obtain tee times:** Call in advance for weekends and holidays. **Miscellaneous:** Reduced fees (weekdays, seniors, juniors), metal spikes, credit cards (MC, V).
Reader Comments: Basic ... Open ... Clubhouse adequate ... No-frills golf.

LAKEVIEW RESORT & CONFERENCE CENTER
R-Rte. 6 Box 88A, Morgantown, 26505, Monongalia County, (304)594-2011, (800)624-8300, 10 miles S of Morgantown.
★★★★ LAKEVIEW COURSE
Holes: 18. **Yards:** 6,800/5,432. **Par:** 72/72. **Course Rating:** 72.8/71.8. **Slope:** 130/118. **Green Fee:** $25/$45. **Cart Fee:** $15/person. **Walking Policy:** Mandatory cart. **Walkability:** 3. **Opened:** 1954. **Architect:** Jim Harrison. **Season:** Year-round. **High:** June-Sept. **To obtain tee times:** Hotel guests may call up to 30 days in advance. Public may call 10 days in advance. **Miscellaneous:** Reduced fees (weekdays, low season, resort guests, juniors), discount packages, club rentals, lodging (187 rooms), credit cards (MC, V, AE, D, Diners Club).
Notes: Ranked 5th in 1999 Best in State.
Reader Comments: A true test ... Nice layout ... Difficult ... Thumbs up ... Good test with lake and mountain views ... Love the scenery ... Good for meetings ... Great restaurant ... Always a treat ... Lovely trees ... Don't bring a slice, but bring your camera.

★★★½ MOUNTAINVIEW COURSE
Holes: 18. **Yards:** 6,447/5,242. **Par:** 72/72. **Course Rating:** 71.9/70.2. **Slope:** 126/124. **Green Fee:** $22/$27. **Cart Fee:** $15/person. **Walking Policy:** Walking at certain times. **Walkability:** 4.

WEST VIRGINIA

Opened: 1984. **Architect:** Brian Ault. **Season:** April-Oct. **High:** June-Sept. **To obtain tee times:** Hotel guests may call up to 30 days in advance. Public may call 10 days in advance.
Miscellaneous: Reduced fees (weekdays, low season, resort guests, juniors), discount packages, club rentals, lodging (187 rooms), credit cards (MC, V, AE, D, Diners Club).
Reader Comments: A lot of blind shots ... Very hilly ... Big elevation changes ... OK if you're a mountain goat ... Eighteen holes on a 15-hole area ... Nice course ... Getting better every year ... Magnificent views.

★★★ LAVELETTE GOLF CLUB
PU-Lynn Oak Dr., Lavelette, 25535, Wayne County, (304)525-7405, 5 miles S of Huntington.
Holes: 18. **Yards:** 6,262/5,257. **Par:** 71/71. **Course Rating:** 69.5/72.6. **Slope:** 118/120. **Green Fee:** $15/$17. **Cart Fee:** $11/person. **Walking Policy:** Unrestricted walking. **Walkability:** N/A.
Opened: 1991. **Architect:** Bill Ward Jr. **Season:** Year-round. **High:** May-Sept. **To obtain tee times:** Call 6 days in advance. **Miscellaneous:** Reduced fees (weekdays), metal spikes, range (grass/mats), club rentals, credit cards (MC, V, AE, D).
Reader Comments: Open ... Very hilly ... Has a par 6 ... Fair price ... Short.

★★½ LEWISBURG ELKS COUNTRY CLUB
SP-Rte. 219 N., Lewisburg, 24901, Greenbrier County, (304)645-3660, 2 miles N of Lewisburg.
Holes: 18. **Yards:** 5,609/4,314. **Par:** 70/70. **Course Rating:** 66.8/64.5. **Slope:** 111/114. **Green Fee:** $17/$20. **Cart Fee:** $10/person. **Walking Policy:** Unrestricted walking. **Walkability:** 3.
Opened: 1940. **Architect:** Ray Vaughan. **Season:** Year-round. **High:** May-Oct. **To obtain tee times:** Call golf shop at (304)645-3660 or (304)645-5718. **Miscellaneous:** Reduced fees (low season), discount packages, club rentals, credit cards (MC, V).
Reader Comments: Fun ... Short and tight ... Can leave the driver home ... Great little course.

★★★★ LOCUST HILL GOLF COURSE   *Value*
SP-1 St. Andrews Dr., Charles Town, 25414, Jefferson County, (304)728-7300, 2 miles W of Charles Town.
Holes: 18. **Yards:** 7,005/5,112. **Par:** 72/72. **Course Rating:** 73.5/72.0. **Slope:** 128/120. **Green Fee:** $16/$29. **Cart Fee:** $15/person. **Walking Policy:** Walking at certain times. **Walkability:** 3.
Opened: 1991. **Architect:** Edward Ault/Guy Rando. **Season:** Year-round. **High:** May-Oct. **To obtain tee times:** Call Monday after 7 a.m. for upcoming weekend. Call up to 7 days in advance for weekdays. **Miscellaneous:** Reduced fees (weekdays, low season, resort guests, twilight, seniors), discount packages, range (grass), club rentals, credit cards (MC, V).
Reader Comments: Good test; variety of holes; nice setting ... Very good layout ... Difficult from the tips ... Shining example of what golf is ... Some really fun holes ... Very playable ... Pace of play could be better ... Several risk/reward decisions can make or break a round ... A bargain.

MEADOW PONDS GOLF COURSE
PU-Rte. 7 W., Cassville, 26527, Monongalia County, (304)328-5570, 60 miles S of Pittsburg.
Holes: 18. **Yards:** 5,328/5,026. **Par:** 69/69. **Course Rating:** 64.9/63.9. **Slope:** 102/100. **Green Fee:** $10/$12. **Walking Policy:** Unrestricted walking. **Walkability:** N/A. **Opened:** 1963.
Architect: Bob Holt. **Season:** Year-round. **To obtain tee times:** Call Mondays. **Miscellaneous:** Reduced fees (weekdays), metal spikes, range (grass), club rentals, credit cards (MC, V, AE, D).

MILL CREEK GOLF COURSE
SP-Rte 1, Keyser, 26726, (304)289-3160.
Special Notes: Call club for further information.

MOUNTAINEER GOLF & COUNTRY CLUB
SP-Rte. 19, Pursglove, 26546, (304)328-5520.
Special Notes: Call club for further information.

MOUNTAINEERS WOODVIEW GOLF COURSE
PU-Ballentine Rd., New Cumberland, 26047, Hancock County, (304)564-5765, 6 miles N of Weirton, W.V.
Holes: 18. **Yards:** 6,077/5,295. **Par:** 71/72. **Course Rating:** 65.9/71.0. **Slope:** 118/109. **Green Fee:** $15/$19. **Cart Fee:** $10/person. **Walking Policy:** Walking at certain times. **Walkability:** 4.
Opened: 1958. **Architect:** Robert Hillis. **Season:** March-Nov. **High:** April-Nov. **Miscellaneous:** Reduced fees (low season, seniors, juniors), discount packages, range (grass), club rentals, credit cards (MC, V).
Special Notes: Formerly Woodview Golf Course.

OAKHURST LINKS
PU-1 Montague Drive, P.O. Box 639, White Sulphur Springs, 24986, Greenbrier County, (304)536-1884, 3 miles N of White Sulphur Springs. **E-mail:** oakhurst@metone.net. **Web:** www.oakhurstlinks.com.
Holes: 9. **Yards:** 2,235/N/A. **Par:** N/A. **Course Rating:** N/A. **Slope:** N/A. **Green Fee:** $80/$80.
Walking Policy: Unrestricted walking. **Walkability:** 4. **Opened:** 1884. **Architect:** Russell

Montague/Bob Cupp. **Season:** April-Oct. **To obtain tee times:** Call anytime in advance, or use internet. **Miscellaneous:** Credit cards (MC, V, AE).
Special Notes: Unique antique course. Equipment included with green fees. Formerly Oakhurst Links

OGLEBAY RESORT & CONFERENCE CENTER
PU-Oglebay Park, Rte. 88N., Wheeling, 26003, Ohio County, (304)243-4050, 55 miles SW of Pittsburgh, PA. **E-mail:** speidel@hgo.net. **Web:** www.oglebay-resort.com.
ARNOLD PALMER DESIGN
(800)752-9436.
Holes: 18. **Yards:** 6,717/5,125. **Par:** 71/72. **Course Rating:** N/A. **Slope:** N/A. **Green Fee:** N/A/$65. **Cart Fee:** Included in Green Fee. **Walking Policy:** Mandatory cart. **Walkability:** 3.
Opened: 2000. **Architect:** Arnold Palmer. **Season:** April-Nov. **High:** May-Sept. **Miscellaneous:** Reduced fees (twilight), discount packages, range (grass), club rentals, lodging (202 rooms), credit cards (MC, V, AE, D), beginner friendly.
Special Notes: New course opening spring 2000.
★★ CRISPIN COURSE
(800)624-6988.
Holes: 18. **Yards:** 5,627/5,100. **Par:** 71/71. **Course Rating:** 66.6/68.4. **Slope:** 109/103. **Green Fee:** $19/$19. **Cart Fee:** $12/person. **Walking Policy:** Unrestricted walking. **Walkability:** 4.
Opened: 1933. **Architect:** Robert Biery. **Season:** March-Nov. **High:** Jan.-Dec. **To obtain tee times:** Resort guests may call up to 1 year in advance with reservation. Public may call up to 60 days in advance. **Miscellaneous:** Discount packages, metal spikes, range (mats), caddies, club rentals, lodging, credit cards (MC, V, AE, D), beginner friendly (new forward tees).
★★★½ SPEIDEL GOLF CLUB
800)624-6988.
Holes: 18. **Yards:** 7,000/5,241. **Par:** 71/71. **Course Rating:** 73.5/69.7. **Slope:** 137/120. **Green Fee:** $55/$55. **Cart Fee:** Included in Green Fee. **Walking Policy:** Unrestricted walking.
Walkability: 3. **Opened:** 1971. **Architect:** Robert Trent Jones. **Season:** March-Nov. **High:** May-Sept. **To obtain tee times:** Resort guests may call up to 1 year in advance with reservation. Public may call up to 60 days in advance. **Miscellaneous:** Reduced fees (weekdays, resort guests), discount packages, metal spikes, range (grass) caddies, club rentals, lodging (244 rooms), credit cards (MC, V, AE, D).
Notes: Ranked 69th in 1996 America's Top 75 Affordable Courses.
Reader Comments: Great to play ... Hilly ... Beautiful views ... Nice rolling hills and scenery ... A little expensive, but good mountain golf ... Great place for a family to play ... Nice. Would go back again ... Very challenging ... Be ready for sidehill lies.

★★★½ PIPESTEM GOLF CLUB
PU-Pipestem State Park, Pipestem, 25979, Summers County, (304)466-1800, (800)225-5982.
Holes: 18. **Yards:** 6,884/5,623. **Par:** 72/72. **Course Rating:** 72.4/72.0. **Slope:** 124/117. **Green Fee:** $17/$26. **Cart Fee:** $20/cart. **Walking Policy:** Unrestricted walking. **Walkability:** 3.
Opened: 1970. **Architect:** Geoffrey Cornish. **Season:** Year-round. **High:** May-Sept. **To obtain tee times:** Guests may book tee times with room reservation. Public may call 7 days in advance.
Miscellaneous: Reduced fees (weekdays, low season, seniors), discount packages, metal spikes, range (grass), club rentals, lodging, credit cards (MC, V, AE).
Reader Comments: Beautiful mountain course ... Great layout ... Lots of fun ... Pleasant ... Lots of wildlife ... Can be real foggy early in the morning ... Very nice ... Excellent track.

PRESTON COUNTRY CLUB
SP-Rte. 7, Kingwood, 26537, Preston County, (304)329-2100, 2 miles E of Morgantown.
Holes: 18. **Yards:** 7,001/5,398. **Par:** 72/72. **Course Rating:** 73.2/70.2. **Slope:** 130/115. **Green Fee:** $20/$24. **Cart Fee:** $14/person. **Walking Policy:** Walking at certain times. **Walkability:** 3.
Season: Feb.-Nov. **High:** June-Aug. **To obtain tee times:** Call after Tuesday for weekends or holidays. **Miscellaneous:** Metal spikes, credit cards (MC, V).
Special Notes: Formerly Preston County Country Club

★★½ RIVERSIDE GOLF CLUB
PU-Rte. 1, Mason, 25260, Mason County, (304)773-5354, (800)261-3031, 1 miles SE of Charleston.
Holes: 18. **Yards:** 6,198/4,842. **Par:** 70/72. **Course Rating:** 69.2/72.0. **Slope:** 118/117. **Green Fee:** $15/$18. **Cart Fee:** $10/person. **Walking Policy:** Unrestricted walking. **Walkability:** 1.
Opened: 1975. **Architect:** Kidwell/Hurdzan. **Season:** Year-round. **High:** April-Sept. **To obtain tee times:** Call golf shop. **Miscellaneous:** Reduced fees (weekdays), club rentals, credit cards (MC, V).
Reader Comments: Can get tight in places ... Flat; easy to walk.

RIVERVIEW COUNTRY CLUB
SP-Rte. 17, Madison, 25130, Boone County, (304)369-9835, 6 miles S of Madison.

Holes: 18. **Yards:** 6,069/5,069. **Par:** 70/70. **Course Rating:** 67.8/69.3. **Slope:** 114/116. **Green Fee:** $15/$20. **Cart Fee:** $10/person. **Walking Policy:** Unrestricted walking. **Walkability:** 4. **Opened:** 1964. **Season:** Year-round. **High:** April-Oct. **To obtain tee times:** Call 24 hours in advance. **Miscellaneous:** Reduced fees (weekdays), range (grass), club rentals, credit cards (MC, V, AE, D), beginner friendly.
Special Notes: Formerly Stonebridge Golf Club

RIVIERA COUNTRY CLUB
SP-Rte. 1, Lesage, 25537, Cabell County, (304)736-7778, 5 miles N of Huntington.
Holes: 18. **Yards:** 6,200/5,400. **Par:** 70/69. **Course Rating:** 66.9/66.6. **Slope:** 108/104. **Green Fee:** $16/$19. **Cart Fee:** $10/person. **Walking Policy:** Unrestricted walking. **Walkability:** 1. **Architect:** Patsy Jefferson. **Season:** Year-round. **High:** April-Nov. **To obtain tee times:** For weekday, weekends and holidays call up to 7 days in advance. Call at least 3 days in advance for week and start time. **Miscellaneous:** Credit cards (MC, V, AE).

ROANE COUNTRY CLUB
SP-Rte. 1, Spencer, 25276, (304)927-2899.
Special Notes: Call club for further information.

★★ SANDY BRAE GOLF COURSE
PU-19 Osborne Mills Rd., Clendenin, 25045, Kanawha County, (304)341-8004, 25 miles N of Charleston.
Holes: 18. **Yards:** 5,648/5,312. **Par:** 69/74. **Course Rating:** 66.7/N/A. **Slope:** 101/98. **Green Fee:** $11/$14. **Cart Fee:** $8/person. **Walking Policy:** Unrestricted walking. **Walkability:** N/A. **Opened:** 1965. **Architect:** Edmund B. Ault. **Season:** Year-round. **High:** April-Oct. **To obtain tee times:** Call 7 days in advance. **Miscellaneous:** Reduced fees (weekdays, low season, twilight, seniors), metal spikes, club rentals, credit cards (MC, V).

★★½ SCARLET OAKS COUNTRY CLUB
SP-2 Dairy Rd., Poca, 25159, Putnam County, (304)755-8079, 15 miles NW of Charleston.
Holes: 18. **Yards:** 6,700/5,036. **Par:** 72/72. **Course Rating:** 72.3/69.3. **Slope:** 129/109. **Green Fee:** $27/$30. **Cart Fee:** Included in Green Fee. **Walking Policy:** Mandatory cart. **Walkability:** 4. **Opened:** 1980. **Architect:** McDavid family. **Season:** March-Dec. **High:** June-July. **To obtain tee times:** Call 7 days in advance. **Miscellaneous:** Metal spikes, range (grass), club rentals, credit cards (MC, V, AE, D, Diners Club).
Reader Comments: Greens are better than the fairways ... Take extra balls ... Challenging ... Tough ... Very scenic.

SHAWNEE GOLF COURSE
PU-Rte. 25, Institute, 25112, Kanawha County, (304)341-8030, 4 miles W of Charleston.
Holes: 9. **Yards:** 2,978/N/A. **Par:** 36/N/A. **Course Rating:** 67.3/N/A. **Slope:** 106/N/A. **Green Fee:** N/A. **Cart Fee:** $10/person. **Walking Policy:** Unrestricted walking. **Walkability:** 1. **Architect:** Gary Player. **Season:** Year-round. **High:** April-Oct. **Miscellaneous:** Reduced fees (low season, seniors), club rentals, credit cards (MC, V).

★½ SLEEPY HOLLOW GOLF & COUNTRY CLUB
SP-Golf Course Rd., Charles Town, 25414, Jefferson County, (304)725-5210.
Holes: 18. **Yards:** 6,600/5,766. **Par:** 72/72. **Course Rating:** 70.6/72.3. **Slope:** 115/104. **Green Fee:** $10/$17. **Cart Fee:** $12/person. **Walking Policy:** Unrestricted walking. **Walkability:** 3. **Opened:** 1962. **Architect:** L.L. Love. **Season:** Year-round. **High:** May-Aug. **To obtain tee times:** Call anytime. **Miscellaneous:** Reduced fees (weekdays, low season, twilight, seniors), discount packages, metal spikes, range (grass).

★★★★½ SNOWSHOE MOUNTAIN *Value, Condition+*
R-10 Snowshoe Dr., Snowshoe, 26209, Pocahontas County, (304)572-6500, 30 miles S of Elkins. **E-mail:** chierlihy@snowshoemtn.com.. **Web:** www.snowshoemtn.com.
Holes: 18. **Yards:** 7,045/4,363. **Par:** 72/72. **Course Rating:** 75.5/65.3. **Slope:** 142/120. **Green Fee:** $59/$90. **Cart Fee:** Included in Green Fee. **Walking Policy:** Unrestricted walking. **Walkability:** 5. **Opened:** 1993. **Architect:** Gary Player. **Season:** April-Nov. **High:** June-Oct. **To obtain tee times:** Call golf shop. **Miscellaneous:** Reduced fees (weekdays, low season, resort guests, twilight), discount packages, metal spikes, range (grass), club rentals, lodging (900 rooms), credit cards (MC, V, AE), beginner friendly (beginner cardinal school of golf).
Notes: Ranked 4th in 1999 Best in State.
Reader Comments: Well worth the drive ... Beautiful mountain course ... Lots of elevation changes ... Terrific ... My favorite ... Spectacular ... Don't miss this one ... Beyond scenic ... Well-manicured ... One of my top 10 ... Truly world-class mountain golf ... Wonderful ... Nirvana.

★★ SOUTH HILLS GOLF CLUB
PU-1253 Gihon Rd., Parkersburg, 26101, Wood County, (304)422-8381, 70 miles N of Charleston.
Holes: 18. **Yards:** 6,467/4,842. **Par:** 71/71. **Course Rating:** 71.2/70.3. **Slope:** 129/115. **Green Fee:** $13/$15. **Cart Fee:** $9/person. **Walking Policy:** Unrestricted walking. **Walkability:** N/A.

Opened: 1953. Architect: Gary Grandstaff. Season: Year-round. High: May-Sept. To obtain tee times: Call. Miscellaneous: Reduced fees (low season), discount packages, metal spikes, range (grass), club rentals, credit cards (MC, V, AE, D).

★★½ STONEBRIDGE GOLF CLUB

SP-Burke St. Ext., Rte. 5, Martinsburg, 25401, Berkeley County, (304)263-4653, 1 miles W of Martinsburg.
Holes: 18. Yards: 6,253/5,056. Par: 72/72. Course Rating: 69.7/67.9. Slope: 119/108. Green Fee: $18/$28. Cart Fee: $12/person. Walking Policy: Walking at certain times. Walkability: 4. Opened: 1922. Architect: Bob Elder. Season: Year-round weather permitting. High: May-Sept. To obtain tee times: Call 7 days in advance. Miscellaneous: Reduced fees (weekdays, low season, resort guests, twilight), discount packages, range (grass/mats), club rentals, credit cards (MC, V, AE, D).
Reader Comments: Tight front; new back is wide open ... Memorable ... Improving ... Hilly ... Fun.

★★ SUGARWOOD GOLF CLUB

PU-Sugarwood Rd., Lavelette, 25535, Wayne County, (304)523-6500, 6 miles S of Huntington.
Holes: 18. Yards: 6,000/N/A. Par: 69/N/A. Course Rating: 66.7/N/A. Slope: 102/N/A. Green Fee: $15/$18. Cart Fee: $10/person. Walking Policy: Unrestricted walking. Walkability: 1. Opened: 1965. Architect: Dave Whechel. Season: Year-round. High: May-Sept. To obtain tee times: Call. Miscellaneous: Metal spikes, range (grass), club rentals, credit cards (MC, V).

★★★ TWIN FALLS STATE PARK GOLF COURSE

PU-P.O. Box 1023, Mullens, 25882, Wyoming County, (304)294-4044, (800)225-5982, 23 miles SW of Beckley.
Holes: 18. Yards: 6,382/5,202. Par: 71/71. Course Rating: 70.1/69.5. Slope: 122/112. Green Fee: $19/$22. Cart Fee: $19/cart. Walking Policy: Unrestricted walking. Walkability: 3. Opened: 1968. Architect: Geoffrey Cornish/George Cobb. Season: Year-round. High: June-Oct. To obtain tee times: Call (304)294-4044 or 1-800-CALL WVA. Miscellaneous: Reduced fees (weekdays, low season, seniors), discount packages, metal spikes, club rentals, lodging, credit cards (MC, V, AE, Diners Club).
Reader Comments: Back nine is fun ... Nice ... Easy ... Good clubhouse ... Challenging, but fair ... Can't wait to go back.

★★★ TYGART LAKE COUNTRY CLUB

PU-Rte.1 Knottsville Rd., Grafton, 26354, Taylor County, (304)265-3100, 4 miles E of Grafton.
Holes: 18. Yards: 6,257/5,420. Par: 72/75. Course Rating: 70.0/71.0. Slope: 115/113. Green Fee: $13/$18. Cart Fee: $12/person. Walking Policy: Unrestricted walking. Walkability: 2. Opened: 1969. Architect: James Gilmore Harrison/Ferdinand Garbin. Season: March-Oct. High: June-Aug. To obtain tee times: Call up to 14 days in advance. Miscellaneous: Metal spikes, range (grass/mats), club rentals.
Reader Comments: Very nice par 3s ... Beautiful ... Outstanding variety ... Very good value ... Wide open.

★★½ VALLEY VIEW GOLF COURSE

PU-Rte. #220 South, Moorefield, 26836, Hardy County, (304)538-6564, 145 miles W of Washington, DC.
Holes: 18. Yards: 6,129/4,928. Par: 71/72. Course Rating: 68.0/65.4. Slope: 108/110. Green Fee: $16/$19. Cart Fee: $15/cart. Walking Policy: Unrestricted walking. Walkability: 3. Opened: 1969. Architect: Russell Roberts. Season: Year-round. High: May-Aug. To obtain tee times: First come, first served. Miscellaneous: Reduced fees (twilight), metal spikes, range (grass), club rentals.
Reader Comments: A great, informal course.

WHITE OAK COUNTRY CLUB

SP-Summerly Rd., Oak Hill, 25901, (304)465-5639.
Special Notes: Call club for further information.

★★★½ WOODRIDGE PLANTATION GOLF CLUB

R-301 Woodridge Dr., Mineral Wells, 26150, Wood County, (304)489-1800, (800)869-1001, 1 miles S of Mineral Wells.
Holes: 18. Yards: 6,830/5,031. Par: 71/71. Course Rating: 72.7/70.5. Slope: 128/116. Green Fee: $18/$35. Cart Fee: Included in Green Fee. Walking Policy: Mandatory cart. Walkability: 2. Opened: 1993. Architect: John Salyers. Season: Year-round. High: March-Nov. To obtain tee times: Call golf shop. Miscellaneous: Range (grass), club rentals, credit cards (MC, V, AE).
Reader Comments: Very enjoyable ... Best in its area ... I like this course a lot ... Very nice; very challenging ... Mounding reminded me of some Myrtle Beach courses ... We held a semi-annual scramble there. Everyone was pleased with the course and the facility.

WEST VIRGINIA

THE WOODS RESORT

R-Mountain Lake Rd., Hedgesville, 25427, Berkeley County, (304)754-7222, (800)248-2222, 90 miles W of Washington DC.

Holes: 27.**Cart Fee:** $11/person. **Walking Policy:** Walking at certain times. **Walkability:** 3. **Opened:** 1989. **Architect:** Ray Johnston. **Season:** Year-round. **High:** April-Sept. **To obtain tee times:** Call 5 days in advance.

★★★½ **MOUNTAIN VIEW BACK/STONY LICK** *Pace*
Yards: 6,423/5,077. **Par:** 72/72. **Course Rating:** 68.9/69.1. **Slope:** 116/118. **Green Fee:** $24/$35. **Miscellaneous:** Reduced fees (weekdays, low season, twilight, seniors, juniors), discount packages, range (grass/mats), club rentals, lodging (100 rooms), credit cards (MC, V, AE), beginner friendly (golf clinics).
Reader Comments: Awesome front nine ... Enjoyable ... Pretty scenery ... Good variety.

★★★½ **MOUNTAIN VIEW FRONT/STONY LICK**
Yards: 6,517/5,095. **Par:** 72/72. **Course Rating:** 68.9/69.1. **Slope:** 116/118. **Green Fee:** $24/$35. **Miscellaneous:** Reduced fees (weekdays, low season, twilight, seniors, juniors), discount packages, range (grass/mats), club rentals, lodging, credit cards (MC, V, AE).

★★★½ **MOUNTAIN VIEW GOLF COURSE**
Yards: 6,608/4,900. **Par:** 72/71. **Course Rating:** 71.8/68.3. **Slope:** 126/114. **Green Fee:** $22/$32. **Miscellaneous:** Reduced fees (weekdays, low season, twilight, seniors, juniors), discount packages, range (grass/mats), club rentals, lodging, credit cards (MC, V, AE).
Reader Comments: Improves each year ... A bargain ... Fun ... I'll return ... Challenging ... Tough to select proper club ... Stays open in cold weather.

WORTHINGTON GOLF CLUB

PU-3414 Roseland Ave, Parkersburg, 26104, (304)428-4297.

Holes: 18. **Yards:** 6,106/4,967. **Par:** 71/71. **Course Rating:** 68.0/67.1. **Slope:** 108/107. **Green Fee:** $14/$16. **Cart Fee:** $11/person. **Walking Policy:** Unrestricted walking. **Walkability:** 2. **Opened:** 1941. **Architect:** A.P. Taylor. **Season:** March-Nov. **High:** May-Aug. **To obtain tee times:** Call golf shop. 18-hole threesomes or foursomes Saturday and Sunday. **Miscellaneous:** Reduced fees (seniors), rentals, credit cards (MC, V, D).

★★★★ ABBEY SPRINGS GOLF COURSE
R-Country Club Dr., P.O. Box 587, Fontana on Geneva Lake, 53125, Walworth County, (414)275-6111, 50 miles SW of Milwaukee. **E-mail:** golfpro@elknet.net. **Web:** www.abbeysprings.com. **Holes:** 18. **Yards:** 6,466/5,439. **Par:** 72/72. **Course Rating:** 71.4/72.4. **Slope:** 133/129. **Green Fee:** $70/$75. **Cart Fee:** Included in Green Fee. **Walking Policy:** Walking at certain times. **Walkability:** 5. **Opened:** 1971. **Architect:** Ken Killian/Dick Nugent. **Season:** April-Nov. **High:** June-Sept. **To obtain tee times:** Call up to 30 days in advance. **Miscellaneous:** Reduced fees (weekdays, low season, juniors), discount packages, range (grass), club rentals, credit cards (MC, V, AE, D).
Reader Comments: Wonderful setting in hilly terrain ... Hilly and challenging ... Beautiful views ... Hilly, resort type course but tight fairways, fun ... Views of Lake Geneva ... Straight tee shots required ... Super scenic ... Too hilly ... Not nice for slicers ... No better on a fall afternoon.

ALPINE RESORT GOLF COURSE
R-P.O. Box 200, Egg Harbor, 54209, Door County, (920)868-3232, 60 miles NE of Green Bay. **E-mail:** alpine@mail.wiscnet.net. **Web:** www.alpineresort.com.
Holes: 27. **Green Fee:** $22/$26. **Cart Fee:** $24/cart. **Walking Policy:** Unrestricted walking. **Walkability:** 4. **Opened:** 1926. **Architect:** Francis H. Schaller. **Season:** May-Oct. **High:** July-Aug. **To obtain tee times:** Call (920)868-3232. **Miscellaneous:** Reduced fees (weekdays, resort guests, twilight), discount packages, metal spikes, club rentals, lodging (40 rooms), credit cards (MC, V, AE).
★★★ RED/BLUE
Yards: 5,858/5,440. **Par:** 71/70. **Course Rating:** 67.6/70.5. **Slope:** 114/117.
Reader Comments: Scenery uplifting ... Lots of fun ... No. 9 on Blue Course the county's finest hole ... Resort course ... 3-4 scenic holes ... Crowded ... A few picturesque holes overlooking bay, good value ... Bluff through area is neat, interesting.
★★★ RED/WHITE
Yards: 6,047/5,879. **Par:** 70/73. **Course Rating:** 67.9/72.4. **Slope:** 109/118.
★★★ WHITE/BLUE
Yards: 6,207/5,837. **Par:** 71/73. **Course Rating:** 69.4/72.8. **Slope:** 117/122.

★★★★ ANTIGO BASS LAKE COUNTRY CLUB
P.O. Box 268, Antigo, 54409, Langlade County, (715)623-6196.
Special Notes: Call club for further information.

★★½ BARABOO COUNTRY CLUB
SP-1010 Lake St., Hwy.123 So., Baraboo, 53913, Sauk County, (608)356-8195, (800)657-4981, 35 miles N of Madison. **E-mail:** info@baraboocountryclub.com. **Web:** www.baraboocountryclub.com.
Holes: 18. **Yards:** 6,570/5,681. **Par:** 72/72. **Course Rating:** 71.3/72.5. **Slope:** 124/122. **Green Fee:** $29/$35. **Cart Fee:** $14/person. **Walking Policy:** Unrestricted walking. **Walkability:** 3. **Opened:** 1962. **Architect:** Edward Lawrence Packard. **Season:** April-Oct. **High:** June-Aug. **To obtain tee times:** Call or come in up to 7 days in advance. **Miscellaneous:** Reduced fees (weekdays, low season, twilight), discount packages, range (grass), club rentals, credit cards (MC, V).
Reader Comments: Fast play ... Old club, kept well ... Nothing memorable, but back 9 very scenic ... Underrated ... Steep hills.

★★½ BEAVER DAM COUNTRY CLUB
PU-Highway 33 NW-W8884 Sunset Dr., Beaver Dam, 53916, Dodge County, (920)885-4106, 2 miles N of Beaver Dam.
Holes: 18. **Yards:** 5,976/5,219. **Par:** 72/70. **Course Rating:** 67.6/73.0. **Slope:** 111/121. **Green Fee:** $20/$24. **Cart Fee:** $20/cart. **Walking Policy:** Walking at certain times. **Walkability:** 3. **Opened:** 1969. **Season:** April-Oct. **High:** June-July. **To obtain tee times:** Call golf shop. **Miscellaneous:** Reduced fees (twilight), club rentals, credit cards (MC, V, AE).
Reader Comments: Good course ... Several risk/reward decisions on short holes ... Wide open, tough in the wind ... Tough course.

★★ BIG OAKS GOLF COURSE
6117 123rd St., Kenosha, 53140, Kenosha County, (414)694-4200.
Special Notes: Call club for further information.

BLACKWOLF RUN GOLF CLUB *Service+*
R-1111 W. Riverside Dr., Kohler, 53044, Sheboygan County, (920)457-4446, (800)618-5535, 55 miles N of Milwaukee. **Web:** www.blackwolfrun.com.
★★★★★ MEADOW VALLEYS COURSE *Condition+, Pace*
Holes: 18. **Yards:** 7,142/5,065. **Par:** 72/72. **Course Rating:** 74.7/69.5. **Slope:** 143/125. **Green Fee:** $105/$105. **Cart Fee:** $17/person. **Walking Policy:** Unrestricted walking. **Walkability:** 4. **Opened:** 1988. **Architect:** Pete Dye. **Season:** April-Oct. **High:** June-Sept. **To obtain tee times:** Call up to 14 days in advance. Guests may book anytime in advance with confirmed hotel reser-

vation. **Miscellaneous:** Reduced fees (low season, twilight), range (grass/mats), caddies, club rentals, lodging, credit cards (MC, V, AE, D).
Notes: Ranked 6th in 1999 Best in State. 1998 U.S. Women's Open; 1995-97 Andersen Consulting World Championship.
Reader Comments: Expensive, but a lot of fun ... Best course I ever played ... Outstanding, tough, beautiful ... More golfer-friendly than River Course ... Some holes not for your average 12 handicapper ... Pleasant rustic quality ... Plays long, even longer in wind ... Great views and challenging golf ... Awesome back nine ... Treated like a king ... Not for the faint of heart! ... Best bathrooms on a golf course.

★★★★★ **RIVER COURSE** *Condition+, Pace*
Holes: 18. **Yards:** 6,991/5,115. **Par:** 72/72. **Course Rating:** 74.9/70.7. **Slope:** 151/128. **Green Fee:** $136/$136. **Cart Fee:** $17/person. **Walking Policy:** Unrestricted walking. **Walkability:** 4. **Opened:** 1988. **Architect:** Pete Dye. **Season:** April-Oct. **High:** June-Sept. **To obtain tee times:** Call up to 14 days in advance. Guests may book anytime in advance with confirmed hotel reservation. **Miscellaneous:** Reduced fees (low season, twilight), range (grass/mats), caddies, club rentals, lodging, credit cards (MC, V, AE, D).
Notes: Ranked 55th in 1999-2000 America's 100 Greatest; 1st in 1999 Best in State; 12th in 1996 America's Top 75 Upscale Courses. 1998 U.S. Women's Open; 1995-97 Andersen Consulting World Championship.
Reader Comments: Best in Midwest ... Fairways like greens ... What a layout! Tough but fair... Exceptional! Deer everywhere ... Play the U.S. Open here ... The 13th is unequalled ... Visually intimidating ... Very small room for error; greens are treacherous ... Scenic, many interesting holes ... God intended this to be a golf course ... Holes 5-13 carved out of nature ... Bring lots of ammo ... Log clubhouse is outstanding ... Golf heaven! ... Mecca, all golfers must go.

★★★★½ **THE BOG** *Service, Condition*
PU-3121 County Hwy. I, Saukville, 53080, Ozaukee County, (414)284-7075, (800)484-3264, 28 miles N of Milwaukee.
Holes: 18. **Yards:** 7,110/5,110. **Par:** 72/72. **Course Rating:** 74.9/70.3. **Slope:** 142/124. **Green Fee:** $59/$118. **Cart Fee:** Included in Green Fee. **Walking Policy:** Unrestricted walking. **Walkability:** 2. **Opened:** 1995. **Architect:** Arnold Palmer/Ed Seay. **Season:** April-Nov. **High:** June-Oct. **To obtain tee times:** Call golf shop. **Miscellaneous:** Reduced fees (weekdays, low season, twilight), range (grass), club rentals, credit cards (MC, V, AE).
Reader Comments: Target golf at its finest ... 12th hole unique, excellent ... Too expensive for common folks ... Too many blind shots and gimmicks ... Great secret ... Beautiful scenery! ... Excellent design ... Great facilities and services, a bit too pricey ... Arnold Palmer should be proud. Excellent use of land contours ... Have to play at least 3 times ... Very hard for women.

THE BRIDGES GOLF COURSE
PU-2702 Shopko Drive, Madison, 53704, Dane County, (608)244-1822. **Web:** www.golfthebridges.com.
Holes: 18. **Yards:** 6,725/5,228. **Par:** 72/72. **Course Rating:** 72.0/N/A. **Slope:** 132/N/A. **Green Fee:** $26/$29. **Cart Fee:** $13/person. **Walking Policy:** Unrestricted walking. **Walkability:** 3. **Opened:** 2000. **Architect:** Graves Feick Design. **Season:** March-Nov. **High:** June-Aug. **To obtain tee times:** Call one week in advance, or via website. **Miscellaneous:** Reduced fees (low season, twilight), range (grass/mats), club rentals, credit cards (MC, V).

★½ **BRIDGEWOOD GOLF COURSE**
PU-1040 Bridgewood Dr., Neenah, 54956, Winnebago County, (920)722-9819.
Holes: 18. **Yards:** 6,030/5,907. **Par:** 71/71. **Course Rating:** 65.1/N/A. **Slope:** N/A. **Green Fee:** $16/$17. **Cart Fee:** $15/cart. **Walking Policy:** Unrestricted walking. **Walkability:** 2. **Opened:** 1949. **Architect:** Jack Taylor. **Season:** April-Nov. **High:** May-Aug. **To obtain tee times:** No tee times given. **Miscellaneous:** Reduced fees (weekdays, seniors, juniors), metal spikes, club rentals, beginner friendly (pro lessons).

BRIGHTON DALE GOLF CLUB
PU-830-248th Ave., Kansasville, 53139, Kenosha County, (414)878-1440, 21 miles SW of Kenosha.
★★★½ **BLUE SPRUCE COURSE** *Value*
Holes: 18. **Yards:** 6,687/5,988. **Par:** 72/72. **Course Rating:** 72.0/72.1. **Slope:** 129/125. **Green Fee:** $20/$24. **Cart Fee:** $22/cart. **Walking Policy:** Unrestricted walking. **Walkability:** 3. **Opened:** 1992. **Architect:** David Gill. **Season:** April-Nov. **High:** May-Sept. **To obtain tee times:** Call 12 days in advance. **Miscellaneous:** Reduced fees (weekdays, low season), metal spikes, range (mats), club rentals, credit cards (MC, V).
Reader Comments: Great value, fun to play ... Good public course ... Better be straight! ... Very challenging, long par 3s ... Middle of nowhere, but a very nice complex ... Over played ... Best value ... Narrow, treelined ... Still a bargain ... Front 9 the best.
Special Notes: Also has a 9-hole course.
★★★½ **WHITE BIRCH COURSE**
Holes: 18. **Yards:** 6,977/6,206. **Par:** 72/72. **Course Rating:** 73.3/73.2. **Slope:** 130/126. **Green Fee:** $20/$24. **Cart Fee:** $24/cart. **Walking Policy:** Unrestricted walking. **Walkability:** 3.

Opened: 1992. Architect: David Gill. Season: April-Nov. High: May-Sept. To obtain tee times: Call 12 days in advance. Miscellaneous: Reduced fees (weekdays, low season), metal spikes, range (mats), club rentals, credit cards (MC, V).

Reader Comments: First-class layout ... Wider than Blue Course, but longer ... Challenging course if you don't mind the wait! ... Very nice ... Great variety, gets better with time.

★★★★ BRISTLECONE PINES GOLF CLUB *Pace*

SP-1500 E. Arlene Dr., Hartland, 53029, Waukesha County, (414)367-7880, 20 miles W of Milwaukee.

Holes: 18. Yards: 7,005/5,033. Par: 71/71. Course Rating: 74.1/69.4. Slope: 138/120. Green Fee: $75/$75. Cart Fee: Included in Green Fee. Walking Policy: Unrestricted walking. Walkability: 3. Opened: 1996. Architect: Scott Miller. Season: April-Nov. High: June-Aug. To obtain tee times: Call up to 2 days in advance. Miscellaneous: Reduced fees (weekdays, low season), range (grass), caddies, club rentals, credit cards (MC, V, AE).

Reader Comments: Expensive, but first class ... Very playable for all levels ... 16th tempting risk/reward ... Outstanding new course. Will only improve ... Pleasantly surprising ... Solid, fun course, through back 9 is short ... A couple of holes are bizarre.

★★★ BRISTOL OAKS COUNTRY CLUB

SP-16801-75th St., Bristol, 53104, Kenosha County, (414)857-2302, 25 miles W of Milwaukee.
E-mail: info@bristoloaks.com. Web: www.bristoloaks.com.
Holes: 18. Yards: 6,319/5,437. Par: 72/72. Course Rating: 70.1/70.9. Slope: 120/116. Green Fee: $18/$24. Cart Fee: $25/cart. Walking Policy: Walking at certain times. Walkability: 2. Opened: 1964. Architect: Edward Lockie. Season: Year-round. High: May-Oct. To obtain tee times: Call golf shop at (414)857-2302. Miscellaneous: Reduced fees (weekdays, low season, twilight, seniors), discount packages, range (grass/mats), club rentals, credit cards (MC, V, AE).

Reader Comments: Average public course ... Nice course, friendly, fair priced ... Getting better ... Standard public course ... Challenging, with country beauty ... Ego booster ... Excellent course, very pretty ... Making improvements.

★★★★ BROWN COUNTY GOLF COURSE *Value*

PU-897 Riverdale Dr., Oneida, 54155, Brown County, (920)497-1731, 7 miles W of Green Bay.
Holes: 18. Yards: 6,729/5,801. Par: 72/73. Course Rating: 72.1/72.7. Slope: 133/127. Green Fee: $22/$32. Cart Fee: $25/cart. Walking Policy: Unrestricted walking. Walkability: 3. Opened: 1957. Architect: Edward Lawrence Packard. Season: April-Oct. High: June-Aug. To obtain tee times: Call 1 day in advance for weekdays. Call Monday at 6 p.m. for upcoming weekend or holiday. Call up to 1 week in advance at 6:00 P.M. Miscellaneous: Reduced fees (seniors, juniors), range (grass/mats), club rentals, credit cards (MC, V).

Reader Comments: Good course for any golfer ... Best bang for the buck, great layout ... Great course ... Beautiful wooded course, great deal ... Slow on weekends, otherwise great ... Pleasant, challenging course ... Pack a lunch ... Nice mature course ... Too long for most women ... Very pretty in late fall ... An absolute steal for the money!

★★★★ BROWN DEER PARK GOLF COURSE

PU-7835 N. Green Bay Rd., Milwaukee, 53209, Milwaukee County, (414)352-8080, 10 miles N of Milwaukee.
Holes: 18. Yards: 6,716/5,927. Par: 71/71. Course Rating: 72.6/68.7. Slope: 132/125. Green Fee: $25/$61. Cart Fee: $24/cart. Walking Policy: Unrestricted walking. Walkability: 3. Opened: 1929. Architect: George Hansen/Roger Packard/Andy North. Season: April-Oct. High: June-Sept. To obtain tee times: Call or come in. Call (414)643-GOLF. Miscellaneous: Reduced fees (weekdays, low season, seniors, juniors), range (grass/mats), club rentals, credit cards (MC, V). Notes: Ranked 8th in 1997 Best in State.

Reader Comments: Rough is too deep for most amateurs ... OK before and after Greater Milwaukee Open ... Bentgrass fairways are fantastic ... A test of golf ... Championship course, many trees, fast greens ... Wonderful traditional course ... Crowded but challenging ... Very long for women ... Old park with enormous trees ... Stay out of the rough!

★★½ BROWNS LAKE GOLF COURSE

PU-3110 S. Browns Lake Dr., Burlington, 53105, Racine County, (414)878-3714, 25 miles SW of Milwaukee.
Holes: 18. Yards: 6,449/5,706. Par: 72/73. Course Rating: 70.2/70.4. Slope: 122/121. Green Fee: $20/$20. Cart Fee: $24/cart. Walking Policy: Unrestricted walking. Walkability: 3. Opened: 1923. Architect: David Gill. Season: April-Oct. High: June-Sept. To obtain tee times: Call 7 days in advance for a $4 charge. Miscellaneous: Reduced fees (seniors, juniors), metal spikes, range (grass), club rentals.

Reader Comments: Can use all the clubs ... Mature trees ... Nice variety of holes, good greens ... A fun, sporty course, some long par 4s.

BUTTERNUT HILLS GOLF COURSE

PU-Gay Rd. & County Rd. B, Sarona, 54870, Washburn County, (715)635-8563.

WISCONSIN

Special Notes: Call club for further information.

★★ CASTLE ROCK GOLF COURSE
PU-W. 6285 Welch Prairie Rd., Mauston, 53948, Junea County, (608)847-4658, (800)851-4853, 2 miles NW of Wisconsin Dells. **E-mail:** crgc@mwt.net. **Web:** www.mwt.net/crgc.
Holes: 18. **Yards:** 6,160/5,318. **Par:** 72/71. **Course Rating:** 70.1/70.6. **Slope:** 126/122. **Green Fee:** $22/$25. **Cart Fee:** $23/cart. **Walking Policy:** Unrestricted walking. **Walkability:** 3.
Opened: 1991. **Architect:** Art Johnson/Jim Van Pee/Gary Van Pee. **Season:** April-Oct. **High:** June-Aug. **To obtain tee times:** Call golf shop. **Miscellaneous:** Reduced fees (weekdays, twilight, seniors, juniors), discount packages, range (grass), club rentals, credit cards (MC, V).

★★★½ CHASKA GOLF COURSE
PU-Wisconsin Ave. Exit 138 West, Appleton, 54912, Outagamie County, (920)757-5757, 90 miles N of Milwaukee.
Holes: 18. **Yards:** 6,912/5,864. **Par:** 72/72. **Course Rating:** 72.8/73.2. **Slope:** 129/126. **Green Fee:** $20/$25. **Cart Fee:** $24/cart. **Walking Policy:** Unrestricted walking. **Walkability:** 2.
Opened: 1975. **Architect:** Lawrence Packard. **Season:** April-Nov. **High:** May-Aug. **To obtain tee times:** Call 5 days in advance. **Miscellaneous:** Reduced fees (twilight, seniors, juniors), range (grass), club rentals, credit cards (MC, V).
Reader Comments: Wide open with lots of bunkers ... Great course tee-to-green ... You'll hit all clubs ... So much sand you need a camel ... Generally open, but strategic water adds lots of interest and challenge.

★★★½ CHERRY HILLS LODGE & GOLF COURSE
R-5905 Dunn Rd., Sturgeon Bay, 54235, Door County, (920)743-3240, (800)545-2307, 40 miles NE of Green Bay.
Holes: 18. **Yards:** 6,163/5,432. **Par:** 72/72. **Course Rating:** 69.2/71.0. **Slope:** 121/122. **Green Fee:** $20/$30. **Cart Fee:** $13/person. **Walking Policy:** Unrestricted walking. **Walkability:** 4.
Opened: 1977. **Season:** April-Oct. **High:** June-Aug. **To obtain tee times:** Call anytime.
Miscellaneous: Reduced fees (weekdays, low season, twilight, seniors, juniors), discount packages, metal spikes, range (grass), club rentals, lodging (31 rooms), credit cards (MC, V, AE, D).
Reader Comments: Everything breaks toward Lake Michigan ... Great restaurant ... Interesting layout, course experience helps scoring ... Several unusual holes, interesting ... Good place for romantic weekend! ... Solid country golf ... Great facilities ... Open front, hilly back ... Lots of hills.

★★★ CHRISTMAS MOUNTAIN VILLAGE GOLF CLUB
R-S. 944 Christmas Mountain Rd., Wisconsin Dells, 53965, Sauk County, (608)254-3971, 40 miles NW of Madison.
Holes: 18. **Yards:** 6,589/5,479. **Par:** 71/71. **Course Rating:** 72.1/72.1. **Slope:** 129/126. **Green Fee:** $40/$44. **Cart Fee:** Included in Green Fee. **Walking Policy:** Walking at certain times.
Walkability: 3. **Opened:** 1970. **Architect:** Art Johnson. **Season:** March-Nov. **High:** May-Sept. **To obtain tee times:** Call up to 14 days in advance or book a golf package anytime.
Miscellaneous: Reduced fees (low season, twilight, seniors), discount packages, metal spikes, range (grass), club rentals, lodging, credit cards (MC, V, AE, D).
Reader Comments: Enjoyable and fun course for men and women ... Friendly, fast moving, sporty ... New 9 on the way looks enticing! ... Too many short par 4s ... Mature pines, very good layout ... Typical resort golf.

★★★★ CLIFTON HIGHLANDS GOLF COURSE *Service, Value*
PU-Cty. Rds. MM & F, Prescott, 54021, Pierce County, (715)262-5141, (800)657-6845, 30 miles E of St. Paul. **E-mail:** bjohnson@pressenter.com. **Web:** www.pressenter.com/clifton.
Holes: 18. **Yards:** 6,632/5,235. **Par:** 72/72. **Course Rating:** 71.8/69.8. **Slope:** 127/119. **Green Fee:** $22/$28. **Cart Fee:** $24/cart. **Walking Policy:** Unrestricted walking. **Walkability:** 3.
Opened: 1974. **Architect:** Dr. Gordon Emerson. **Season:** April-Oct. **High:** June-July-Aug.-Sept.
To obtain tee times: Call 7 days in advance. **Miscellaneous:** Reduced fees (low season, twilight, seniors, juniors), discount packages, range (grass/mats), club rentals, credit cards (MC, V, D).
Reader Comments: Good course, well maintained ... Out in the country, pretty good value ... Fun course ... Huge breaking putts ... Pretty course ... Variety of shots needed, never a straight putt ... Great all around course ... Always in nice condition.

★★★ CLIFTON HOLLOW GOLF CLUB
PU-12166 W. 820th. Ave., River Falls, 54022, Pierce County, (715)425-9781, (800)487-8879, 30 miles E of St. Paul.
Holes: 18. **Yards:** 6,381/5,117. **Par:** 71/72. **Course Rating:** 69.6/68.6. **Slope:** 118/114. **Green Fee:** $22/$28. **Cart Fee:** $24/cart. **Walking Policy:** Unrestricted walking. **Walkability:** 2.
Opened: 1973. **Architect:** Gordon Emerson. **Season:** April-Nov. **High:** June-Aug. **To obtain tee times:** Call 7 days in advance. **Miscellaneous:** Reduced fees (weekdays, seniors, juniors), range (grass), club rentals, credit cards (MC, V).

WISCONSIN

Reader Comments: Sandy soil, playable anytime ... I am a member here: I love it! ... Good value, not well known ... A llama would help a lot ... Too many short tricky holes ... Open and forgiving for duffers like me. Yet enough challenge to avoid boredom ... Enjoyable, pleasant round.

COACHMAN'S GOLF RESORT
984 County Hwy. A, Edgerton, 53534, Dane County, (608)884-8484. **Holes:** 27
★★★ **RED/BLUE**
★★★ **RED/WHITE**
★★★ **WHITE/BLUE**
Special Notes: Call club for further information.

★★★★ COUNTRY CLUB OF WISCONSIN
PU-2241 Highway. W., Grafton, 53024, Ozaukee County, (414)375-2444, 20 miles N of Milwaukee.
Holes: 18. **Yards:** 7,049/5,499. **Par:** 72/72. **Course Rating:** 74.5/67.3. **Slope:** 136/119. **Green Fee:** $28/$56. **Cart Fee:** $13/person. **Walking Policy:** Walking at certain times. **Walkability:** 4.
Opened: 1994. **Architect:** Mattingly/Kuehn. **Season:** April-Nov. **High:** May-Sept. **To obtain tee times:** Call 7 days in advance with credit card to reserve a time. **Miscellaneous:** Reduced fees (weekdays, low season, twilight, juniors), discount packages, range (grass), club rentals, credit cards (MC, V, AE).
Reader Comments: Nice country course, flat, wide fairways, lots of trees ... Tough tee shots, local knowledge is a must ... One of best in Milwaukee area, challenging ... Some tricky holes ... Not yet matured ... Great test from black tees, 5th very difficult approach ... Tough course for average golfer ... Watch out for the water ... Fun unique design, lots of wildlife ... Some gimmicky holes.

★★ COUNTRYSIDE GOLF CLUB
PU-W. 726 Weiler Rd., Kaukauna, 54130, Outagamie County, (920)766-2219, 2 miles E of Kaukauna.
Holes: 18. **Yards:** 6,183/5,187. **Par:** 71/71. **Course Rating:** 69.1/69.0. **Slope:** 115/111. **Green Fee:** $17/$19. **Cart Fee:** $22/cart. **Walking Policy:** Unrestricted walking. **Walkability:** 2.
Opened: 1964. **Season:** April-Oct. **High:** June-Aug. **To obtain tee times:** Call in advance. **Miscellaneous:** Reduced fees (weekdays, low season, seniors, juniors), range (grass), club rentals.

★★★ CRYSTAL SPRINGS GOLF CLUB
PU-N. 8055 French Rd., Seymour, 54165, Outagamie County, (920)833-6348, (800)686-2984, 17 miles W of Green Bay.
Holes: 18. **Yards:** 6,596/5,497. **Par:** 72/73. **Course Rating:** 70.7/74.5. **Slope:** 120/124. **Green Fee:** $18/$21. **Cart Fee:** $24/cart. **Walking Policy:** Unrestricted walking. **Walkability:** N/A.
Opened: 1967. **Architect:** Edward Lockie. **Season:** April-Nov. **High:** June-Aug. **To obtain tee times:** Call golf shop. **Miscellaneous:** Reduced fees (twilight, seniors, juniors), range (grass/mats), club rentals, credit cards (MC, V).
Reader Comments: Hills make average course interesting ... Friendly ... Several difficult, hilly doglegs; short par 4s on back nine; unusual layout ... Long front 9 ... Bring bug spray ... Harder than it looks.

★★★ CUMBERLAND GOLF CLUB
PM-2400 5th St., Cumberland, 54829, Barron County, (715)822-4333, 2 miles W of Cumberland.
Holes: 18. **Yards:** 6,272/5,004. **Par:** 72/71. **Course Rating:** 70.7/70.1. **Slope:** 129/116. **Green Fee:** $23/$26. **Cart Fee:** $24/cart. **Walking Policy:** Unrestricted walking. **Walkability:** 4.
Opened: 1991. **Architect:** Don Herfort. **Season:** April-Oct. **High:** June-Aug. **To obtain tee times:** Call up to 5 days in advance. **Miscellaneous:** Reduced fees (weekdays, low season), range (grass), club rentals, credit cards (MC, V), beginner friendly (junior golf).
Reader Comments: Challenging, with lots of water and very scenic ... Clubhouse is nice ... Pretty land, rolling hills ... Friendly, nice small-town course.

★★½ CURRIE PARK GOLF COURSE
PM-3535 North Mayfair Rd., Milwaukee, 53222, Milwaukee County, (414)453-7030, 11 miles NW of Milwaukee. **Web:** www.countryparks.com.
Holes: 18. **Yards:** 6,420/5,811. **Par:** 71/72. **Course Rating:** 68.6/72.4. **Slope:** 115/120. **Green Fee:** $11/$22. **Cart Fee:** $24/cart. **Walking Policy:** Unrestricted walking. **Walkability:** 3.
Architect: George Hansen. **Season:** April-Nov. **High:** June-Aug. **To obtain tee times:** Call (414)643-4653 up to 7 days in advance. Call golf course directly on day of play. **Miscellaneous:** Reduced fees (twilight, seniors, juniors), club rentals, credit cards (MC, V).
Reader Comments: It's a fun course to play. Could be a very nice one ... Crowded ... What you would expect from a county course ... This is the epitome of a muny course ... Great for seniors and kids ... Short, easy to walk ... Good value ... Nice course, small greens ... Ego booster.

★★★½ DEERTRAK GOLF COURSE
PU-W. 930 Hwy. O, Oconomowoc, 53066, Dodge County, (920)474-4444, 25 miles NW of Milwaukee.

Holes: 18. **Yards:** 6,313/5,114. **Par:** 72/72. **Course Rating:** 70.2/69.2. **Slope:** 120/116. **Green Fee:** N/A. **Walking Policy:** Unrestricted walking. **Walkability:** 4. **Opened:** 1986. **Architect:** Don Chapman. **Season:** March-Nov. **To obtain tee times:** Call. **Miscellaneous:** Reduced fees (seniors), credit cards (MC, V).

Reader Comments: One of southwestern Wisconsin's finest courses ... Pretty design ... A little too short ... Lots of variation ... Beautiful, scenic, fun ... Scenic par 3s ... Good test, requires all the clubs ... Enjoyable, well kept ... A short but interesting layout.

★★★½ DELBROOK GOLF COURSE

PM-700 S. 2nd St., Delavan, 53115, Walworth County, (414)728-3966, 45 miles SW of Milwaukee.
Holes: 18. **Yards:** 6,519/5,599. **Par:** 72/72. **Course Rating:** 70.8/71.3. **Slope:** 123/121. **Green Fee:** $11/$24. **Cart Fee:** $10/person. **Walking Policy:** Unrestricted walking. **Walkability:** 2. **Opened:** 1928. **Architect:** James Foulis. **Season:** March-Nov. **High:** June-Aug. **To obtain tee times:** Call up to 7 days in advance. **Miscellaneous:** Reduced fees (weekdays, low season, twilight), range (grass), credit cards (MC, V, AE, D).

Reader Comments: The greens are very undulating ... OK ... My home course ... Easy looking, yet you need your brain ... A nice round of golf ... Not too tough a muny course, a good walk.

★★★ DEVIL'S HEAD RESORT & CONVENTION CENTER

R-S. 6330 Bluff Rd., Merrimac, 53561, Sauk County, (608)493-2251, (800)472-6670, 35 miles N of Madison. **E-mail:** info@www.devils-head.com. **Web:** www.devils-head.com.
Holes: 18. **Yards:** 6,861/5,141. **Par:** 73/73. **Course Rating:** 72.4/64.4. **Slope:** 129/113. **Green Fee:** $26/$59. **Cart Fee:** Included in Green Fee. **Walking Policy:** Walking at certain times. **Walkability:** 5. **Opened:** 1973. **Architect:** Art Johnson. **Season:** April-Oct. **High:** June-Aug. **To obtain tee times:** Nonguests call 14 days in advance for weekdays or 2 days in advance for weekends. **Miscellaneous:** Reduced fees (weekdays, low season, twilight), discount packages, club rentals, lodging, credit cards (MC, V, AE, D).

Reader Comments: Great layout ... Great resort golf ... Fairly short course, need to be straight ... Could be in top 5 of beautiful courses in Wis. ... Challenging, great views ... Peaceful walk through nature.

★★★½ DOOR CREEK GOLF COURSE

PU-4321 Vilas, Cottage Grove, 53527, Dane County, (608)839-5656, 3 miles E of Madison.
Holes: 27. **Yards:** 6,475/5,189. **Par:** 71/71. **Course Rating:** 70.5/69.7. **Slope:** 119/111. **Green Fee:** $22/$24. **Cart Fee:** $10/person. **Walking Policy:** Unrestricted walking. **Walkability:** 3. **Opened:** 1990. **Architect:** Bradt family. **Season:** Year-round. **High:** May-Sept. **To obtain tee times:** Call up to 7 days in advance. **Miscellaneous:** Reduced fees (weekdays, low season, seniors, juniors), metal spikes, range (grass/mats), club rentals, credit cards (MC, V, D).

Reader Comments: Always a favorite to play ... Short but sweet layout ... Good local course ... It is developing nicely ... Wonderful, well managed ... Nice course at a great price!

★★★ DRETZKA PARK GOLF COURSE

PU-12020 W. Bradley Rd., Milwaukee, 53224, Milwaukee County, (414)354-7300.
Holes: 18. **Yards:** 6,832/5,680. **Par:** 72/72. **Course Rating:** 70.8/74.6. **Slope:** 124/123. **Green Fee:** $23/$27. **Cart Fee:** $24/cart. **Walking Policy:** Unrestricted walking. **Walkability:** 5. **Opened:** 1967. **Architect:** Evert Kincaid. **Season:** March-Nov. **High:** May-Sept. **To obtain tee times:** Call (414)643-GOLF. **Miscellaneous:** Reduced fees (twilight, seniors, juniors), range (grass/mats), club rentals, credit cards (MC, V).

Reader Comments: Long and challenging ... Long, tough county course near Milwaukee ... Good par 4s, long par 3s ... Could be really nice ... Excellent value for the money, beautiful landscape ... Good test ... Steep climbs on 9 and 18 holes ... An effort to walk.

★★★½ DRUGAN'S CASTLE MOUND

PU-W 7665 Sylvester Rd., Holmen, 54636, La Crosse County, (608)526-3225, 12 miles N of LaCrosse. **E-mail:** drugansgolfdine@centuryinter.net. **Web:** www.drugans.com.
Holes: 18. **Yards:** 6,583/4,852. **Par:** 72/72. **Course Rating:** 70.7/67.5. **Slope:** 120/110. **Green Fee:** $20/$23. **Cart Fee:** $23/cart. **Walking Policy:** Unrestricted walking. **Walkability:** 3. **Opened:** 1970. **Season:** April-Nov. **High:** June-Aug. **To obtain tee times:** Call or come in up to 14 days in advance. **Miscellaneous:** Reduced fees (juniors), club rentals, credit cards (MC, V, AE, D).

Reader Comments: Many strategically-placed bunkers, long hitter's course ... Lovely, rolling test with very reasonable green fees ... Excellent test of all clubs ... One of nicest public courses around ... Great country course ... Beautiful.

EAGLE BLUFF GOLF COURSE

PU-Rte. 1 County Trunk D, Hurley, 54534, Iron County, (715)561-3552, 3 miles W of Hurley.
Holes: 18. **Yards:** 5,870/5,327. **Par:** 70/68. **Course Rating:** 67.9/73.1. **Slope:** 122/126. **Green Fee:** $18/$18. **Cart Fee:** $18/cart. **Walking Policy:** Unrestricted walking. **Walkability:** 4. **Opened:** 1967. **Architect:** Homer Fieldhouse. **Season:** May-Oct. **High:** July-Aug. **To obtain tee times:** Call golf shop. **Miscellaneous:** Club rentals, credit cards (MC, V, AE).

WISCONSIN

★★★★ EAGLE RIVER GOLF COURSE *Value*
PU-527 McKinley Blvd., Eagle River, 54521, Vilas County, (715)479-8111, 70 miles N of Wausau.
Holes: 18. **Yards:** 6,103/5,167. **Par:** 71/72. **Course Rating:** 69.3/67.8. **Slope:** 121/119. **Green Fee:** $24/$30. **Cart Fee:** $13/person. **Walking Policy:** Unrestricted walking. **Walkability:** 3.
Opened: 1923. **Architect:** Don Herfort. **Season:** May-Oct. **High:** July-Aug. **To obtain tee times:** Threesomes and foursomes call 7 days in advance. Twosomes and singles call 2 days in advance. **Miscellaneous:** Reduced fees (low season, resort guests, twilight, juniors), discount packages, range (grass), club rentals, credit cards (MC, V, D).
Reader Comments: Variety of holes ... Nice course, price is right ... Hidden treasure of Wisconsin ... Great scenic beauty, excellent ... Nothing fancy; solid golf course ... Very challenging.

EDGEWOOD GOLF COURSE
SP-W240, S10050 Castle Rd., Big Bend, 53103, Waukesha County, (414)662-3110, 20 miles SW of Milwaukee.
★★★ OAKS
Holes: 18. **Yards:** 6,783/5,411. **Par:** 72/72. **Course Rating:** 72.3/70.8. **Slope:** 134/126. **Green Fee:** $35/$45. **Cart Fee:** Included in Green Fee. **Walking Policy:** Mandatory cart. **Walkability:** 3. **Opened:** 1969. **Architect:** Fred Millies. **Season:** April-Oct. **High:** June-Aug. **To obtain tee times:** Call up to 7 days in advance. **Miscellaneous:** Reduced fees (low season, seniors, juniors), range (grass), club rentals, credit cards (MC, V, AE, D).
Special Notes: Formerly Red/White Course. Spikeless shoes encouraged.
★★★ PINES
Holes: 18. **Yards:** 6,551/5,386. **Par:** 72/72. **Course Rating:** 70.7/69.9. **Slope:** 122/117. **Green Fee:** $23/$33. **Cart Fee:** $12/person. **Walking Policy:** Unrestricted walking. **Walkability:** 3.
Opened: 1969. **Architect:** Fred Millies. **Season:** April-Oct. **High:** June-Aug. **To obtain tee times:** Call up to 7 days in advance. **Miscellaneous:** Reduced fees (low season, seniors, juniors), range (grass), club rentals, credit cards (MC, V, AE, D).
Special Notes: Formerly White/Gold course.

★★★½ EVANSVILLE COUNTRY CLUB
PU-8501 Cemetery Rd., Evansville, 53536, Rock County, (608)882-6524, 30 miles S of Madison.
Holes: 18. **Yards:** 6,559/5,366. **Par:** 72/72. **Course Rating:** 71.0/70.3. **Slope:** 127/122. **Green Fee:** $20/$22. **Cart Fee:** $20/cart. **Walking Policy:** Unrestricted walking. **Walkability:** 3.
Opened: 1964. **Architect:** Built by members. **Season:** April-Oct. **High:** June-Aug. **To obtain tee times:** Call up to 7 days in advance. **Miscellaneous:** Reduced fees (low season, juniors), metal spikes, range (grass), club rentals, credit cards (MC, V).
Reader Comments: Always a favorite, well maintained ... Very nice. Back nine wide open ... Gets better every year ... Front and back 9 two styles of courses ... A hidden gem ... Hilly, lots of trees.

EVERGREEN GOLF CLUB
PU-Hwys. No.12 and 67N., Elkhorn, 53121, Walworth County, (414)723-5722, (800)868-8618, 3 miles N of Elkhorn. **Web:** www.evergreengolf.com.
Holes: 27. **Green Fee:** $25/$32. **Cart Fee:** $13/person. **Walking Policy:** Walking at certain times. **Walkability:** 2. **Opened:** 1973. **Architect:** Dick Nugent/Gary Welsh. **Season:** Year-round.
High: May-Sept. **To obtain tee times:** Call in advance. 2 day cancellation required.
Miscellaneous: Reduced fees (weekdays, low season), discount packages, range (grass), club rentals, credit cards (MC, V, D).
★★★½ EAST/SOUTH
Yards: 6,537/5,284. **Par:** 72/72. **Course Rating:** 71.9/70.6. **Slope:** 127/120.
Reader Comments: Great conditions and service ... Demands accurate approaches. Small greens ... Nice course ... Open year round, a treat in Wisconsin ... New 9 maturing nicely ... Three really good 9s ... Some par 5s are too short ... Best course in area ... Ego booster... Holes 9 to 11 are three great holes.
★★★½ NORTH/EAST
Yards: 6,306/5,343. **Par:** 72/72. **Course Rating:** 70.9/71.3. **Slope:** 125/121.
★★★½ NORTH/SOUTH
Yards: 6,541/5,435. **Par:** 72/72. **Course Rating:** 71.8/71.5. **Slope:** 128/123.

★½ FAR VU GOLF COURSE
PU-4985 State Rd. 175, Oshkosh, 54901, Winnebago County, (920)231-2631, 6 miles N of Fond Du Lac.
Holes: 18. **Yards:** 6,192/5,381. **Par:** 72/74. **Course Rating:** 69.3/71.1. **Slope:** N/A. **Green Fee:** $16/$18. **Cart Fee:** $24/cart. **Walking Policy:** Unrestricted walking. **Walkability:** 1. **Opened:** 1964. **Architect:** Norman Pfeiffer. **Season:** April-Oct. **High:** June-Aug. **To obtain tee times:** Call 7 days in advance. **Miscellaneous:** Reduced fees (seniors, juniors), club rentals, credit cards (MC, V).

★★★ FOREST HILLS PUBLIC GOLF COURSE
PU-600 Losey Blvd. N., La Crosse, 54601, La Crosse County, (608)784-0567. **E-mail:** holtzer@execac.com. **Web:** www.forest-hills.net.

Holes: 18. **Yards:** 6,063/5,275. **Par:** 71/72. **Course Rating:** 69.5/70.4. **Slope:** 123/119. **Green Fee:** $22/$24. **Cart Fee:** $21/cart. **Walking Policy:** Unrestricted walking. **Walkability:** 3. **Opened:** 1901. **Season:** April-Dec. **High:** May-Sept. **To obtain tee times:** Call up to 5 days in advance. **Miscellaneous:** Reduced fees (weekdays, low season), range (grass), club rentals, credit cards (MC, V, D, Diners Club).
Reader Comments: Lots of trees. Beautiful setting ... Leave driver at home. Tight fairways. Fairway and greens excellent ... Too tight for a public course.... Very tight front 9.

FOX HILLS RESORT
R-250 W. Church St., Mishicot, 54228, Manitowoc County, (920)755-2831, (800)950-7615, 30 miles SE of Green Bay. **E-mail:** foxhills@dct.com. **Web:** www.fox-hills.com.
Holes: 27. **Green Fee:** $15/$24. **Cart Fee:** $12/cart. **Walking Policy:** Unrestricted walking. **Walkability:** 2. **Opened:** 1961. **Architect:** Edward Lockie. **Season:** April-Nov. **High:** June-Aug. **To obtain tee times:** Call, no requirements.

★★★ FOX CREEK BLUE NINE
Yards: 2,929/2,648. **Par:** 35/36. **Course Rating:** N/A. **Slope:** N/A. **Miscellaneous:** Reduced fees (weekdays, low season, resort guests, twilight, seniors, juniors), discount packages, range (grass), club rentals, lodging, credit cards (MC, V, AE, D).
Reader Comments: Nice layout, invites you back ... Take beginners here to learn the swing ... Blue and White course very pretty and challenging ... Crowded ... Expensive for the course condition ... Excellent course.

★★★ FOX CREEK RED NINE
Yards: 3,291/2,950. **Par:** 36/37. **Course Rating:** N/A. **Slope:** N/A. **Miscellaneous:** Reduced fees (weekdays, low season, twilight, seniors), discount packages, range (grass), club rentals, lodging, credit cards (MC, V, AE, D).
Special Notes: Formerly Classic Course-Front/Back

★★★ FOX CREEK WHITE NINE
Miscellaneous: Reduced fees (weekdays, low season, twilight, seniors), discount packages, range (grass), club rentals, lodging, credit cards (MC, V, AE, D).
Special Notes: Formerly Classic Course-Front/Blue

★★★½ FOX HILLS NATIONAL GOLF CLUB
Holes: 18. **Yards:** 7,017/5,366. **Par:** 72/72. **Course Rating:** 73.8/71.0. **Slope:** 136/124. **Green Fee:** $30/$46. **Cart Fee:** $25/cart. **Walking Policy:** Unrestricted walking. **Walkability:** 2. **Opened:** 1988. **Architect:** Bob Lohmann. **Season:** April-Nov. **High:** June-Aug. **To obtain tee times:** No restrictions, just call. **Miscellaneous:** Reduced fees (weekdays, low season, resort guests, twilight, seniors, juniors), discount packages, range (grass), club rentals, lodging (335 rooms), credit cards (MC, V, AE, D).
Reader Comments: Long, wide open, windy ... Great, challenging links ... Could really be nice ... Friendly, tough with a wind blowing ... Interesting links course ... Real challenge when wind comes up ... A lot of mounds ... Dunes, dunes and more dunes ... Tough course to score on.

★★★★ FOXFIRE GOLF CLUB *Service*
PU-Hwy. 54 & Hwy. 10, Waupaca, 54981, Waupaca County, (715)256-1700, 60 miles SW of Green Bay. **E-mail:** firefox@execpc.com. **Web:** www.foxfiregc.com.
Holes: 18. **Yards:** 6,528/5,022. **Par:** 70/70. **Course Rating:** 70.9/69.4. **Slope:** 124/115. **Green Fee:** $22/$31. **Cart Fee:** $12/person. **Walking Policy:** Unrestricted walking. **Walkability:** 1. **Opened:** 1996. **Architect:** David Truttman & Assoc. **Season:** April-Nov. **High:** June-Sept. **To obtain tee times:** Call up to 10 days in advance or anytime in advance with credit card to guarantee. **Miscellaneous:** Reduced fees (weekdays, low season, twilight, seniors, juniors), range (grass), club rentals, lodging (80 rooms), credit cards (MC, V, D), beginner friendly (adult group golf lessons, junior golf academy).
Reader Comments: Play this gem before the word gets out ... Nicest people ... Fun course with tight fairways ... Can score well if you keep it out of the water ... Great new links ... Facilities are great, the first hole is spooky, too much water. Long par 3s ... Short but challenging ... Fun course with true variety.

GENEVA NATIONAL GOLF CLUB *Service*
★★★★ PALMER COURSE *Condition*
R-1221 Geneva National Ave. S., Lake Geneva, 53147, Walworth County, (414)245-7000, 45 miles SW of Milwaukee. **E-mail:** palomagolf@aol.com. **Web:** www.genevanationalresort.com.
Holes: 18. **Yards:** 7,177/4,904. **Par:** 72/72. **Course Rating:** 74.7/68.5. **Slope:** 140/122. **Green Fee:** $95/$105. **Cart Fee:** Included in Green Fee. **Walking Policy:** Mandatory cart. **Walkability:** 4. **Opened:** 1991. **Architect:** Arnold Palmer/Ed Seay. **Season:** March-Oct. **High:** June-Sept. **To obtain tee times:** Call 30 days in advance. **Miscellaneous:** Reduced fees (weekdays, low season, resort guests, twilight), discount packages, range (grass), club rentals, lodging, credit cards (MC, V, AE, D).
Notes: Ranked 10th in 1997 Best in State.
Reader Comments: A lot of fun ... Spectacular holes ... Nice resort, soothing on eyes ... Top notch country club with all the amenities ... Weather permitting, a great fall golf getaway ... All 45 holes

are great ... 17th along the lake is wonderful ... 17th is like Pebble Beach's 18th ... Great complex, expensive but worth it ... Finishing holes are spectacular ... You will be doglegged to death.

★★★★ TREVINO COURSE *Condition*

R-1221 Geneva National Ave. S., Lake Geneva, 53147, Walworth County, (414)245-7000, 50 miles SW of Milwaukee. **E-mail:** palomagolf@aol.com. **Web:** www.genevanationalresort.com. **Holes:** 18. **Yards:** 7,120/5,193. **Par:** 72/72. **Course Rating:** 74.5/70.1. **Slope:** 137/124. **Green Fee:** $95/$105. **Cart Fee:** Included in Green Fee. **Walking Policy:** Mandatory cart. **Walkability:** 4. **Opened:** 1991. **Architect:** Lee Trevino/Wm. Graves Design Co. **Season:** March-Oct. **High:** May-Oct. **To obtain tee times:** Call 30 days in advance. **Miscellaneous:** Reduced fees (weekdays, low season, resort guests, twilight), discount packages, range (grass), club rentals, lodging, credit cards (MC, V, AE, D).

Reader Comments: Every hole is unique, thoroughly enjoyable ... Not quite as scenic as either Palmer 18 or Player 9 but probably plays toughest ... Cut out of woods ... Look out for those trees! ... Beautiful layout ... Nice but vanilla course ... Difficult ... Beautiful setting ... There are some pretty tough holes for women ... Hilly, lets you fade like Trevino.

Special Notes: Also has 9-hole Player Course.

★½ GEORGE WILLIAMS COLLEGE GOLF COURSE

PU-350 N. Lake Shore, Williams Bay, 53191, Walworth County, (414)245-9507, 40 miles SW of Milwaukee. **Web:** www.augeowms.org.
Holes: 18. **Yards:** 5,066/4,721. **Par:** 67/68. **Course Rating:** 63.4/65.5. **Slope:** 102/106. **Green Fee:** $10/$21. **Cart Fee:** $20/cart. **Walking Policy:** Unrestricted walking. **Walkability:** 2. **Opened:** 1906. **Architect:** James Naismith. **Season:** April-Nov. **High:** July-Aug. **To obtain tee times:** Call golf shop. **Miscellaneous:** Reduced fees (weekdays, twilight, seniors, juniors), club rentals, lodging (80 rooms), credit cards (MC, V), beginner friendly (youth and senior programs).
Special Notes: Formerly known as George Williams College Golf Club

★★ GOLDEN SANDS GOLF COMMUNITY

SP-300 Naber Rd., Cecil, 54111, Shawano County, (715)745-2189, 35 miles NW of Green Bay. **Holes:** 18. **Yards:** 6,122/4,888. **Par:** 71/72. **Course Rating:** 69.2/68.5. **Slope:** 117/113. **Green Fee:** $20/$25. **Cart Fee:** $24/cart. **Walking Policy:** Unrestricted walking. **Walkability:** 3. **Opened:** 1970. **Season:** May-Oct. **High:** June-Aug. **To obtain tee times:** Call up to two weeks in advance. **Miscellaneous:** Reduced fees (twilight), discount packages, range (grass), club rentals, credit cards (MC, V, AE, D).

★★★ THE GOLF CLUB AT CAMELOT

PU-W. 192 Highway 67, Lomira, 53048, Dodge County, (920)269-4949, (800)510-4949, 30 miles N of Milwaukee.
Holes: 18. **Yards:** 6,121/5,338. **Par:** 70/72. **Course Rating:** 68.8/70.2. **Slope:** 124/123. **Green Fee:** $20/$23. **Cart Fee:** $24/cart. **Walking Policy:** Unrestricted walking. **Walkability:** 4. **Opened:** 1966. **Architect:** Homer Fieldhouse. **Season:** March-Nov. **High:** July-Aug. **To obtain tee times:** Call up to 7 days in advance. **Miscellaneous:** Reduced fees (weekdays, low season, resort guests, twilight, seniors, juniors), discount packages, range (grass/mats), club rentals, credit cards (MC, V).

Reader Comments: Short course ... Nice course to play, great holes ... Fun course. Working hard to get better ... Nice little track.

THE GOLF COURSES OF LAWSONIA

R-W2615 S. Valley View Dr., Green Lake, 54941, Green Lake County, (920)294-3320, (800)529-4453, 35 miles SW of Oshkosh.

★★★★ LINKS COURSE *Pace*

Holes: 18. **Yards:** 6,764/5,078. **Par:** 72/71. **Course Rating:** 72.8/68.9. **Slope:** 130/114. **Green Fee:** $44/$54. **Cart Fee:** $16/person. **Cart Fee:** Included in Green Fee. **Walking Policy:** Walking at certain times. **Walkability:** 5. **Opened:** 1930. **Architect:** William Langford. **Season:** April-Nov. **High:** June-Sept. **To obtain tee times:** Call anytime 8 months in advance. **Miscellaneous:** Reduced fees (weekdays, low season, resort guests, twilight), discount packages, range (grass/mats), club rentals, lodging (100 rooms), credit cards (MC, V, AE, D).
Notes: Ranked 60th in 1996 America's Top 75 Affordable Courses.

Reader Comments: One of the truest links layouts in Wisconsin ... Closest thing to Scotland in Wisconsin ... Old, unique, fun, bring your short game ... A must play for all serious golfers ... 7th a risky par 3 ... Memorable holes ... One of the best secrets in the state, don't tell! ... Don't play either course with a hangover ... A great old links course ... Great, natural Wisconsin setting ... Deep bunkers.

★★★★ WOODLANDS COURSE

Holes: 18. **Yards:** 6,618/5,106. **Par:** 72/72. **Course Rating:** 71.5/69.1. **Slope:** 129/120. **Green Fee:** $44/$70. **Cart Fee:** Included in Green Fee. **Walking Policy:** Walking at certain times. **Walkability:** 3. **Opened:** 1982. **Architect:** Rocky Roquemore. **Season:** April-Nov. **High:** June-Sept. **To obtain tee times:** Call anytime up to 8 months in advance. **Miscellaneous:** Reduced fees (weekdays, low season, resort guests, twilight), discount packages, metal spikes, range (grass/mats), club rentals, lodging (150 rooms), credit cards (V, AE, D).

WISCONSIN

Notes: Ranked 10th in 1999 Best in State.
Reader Comments: Lots of trees! ... Narrow, leave the driver in the trunk ... Great contrast to Links Course ... Pure serenity every hole, leaves you breathless ... More scenic and scoreable than Links. Quarry 2nd hole and par 3 3rd are memorable ... Many unique holes, gorgeous and demanding ... 16th great par 3 ... Beautiful modern wooded course ... The yin to the Links' yang ... Very scenic.

GRAND GENEVA RESORT & SPA *Service*
★★★★ **BRUTE COURSE**
R-7036 Grand Geneva Way, Lake Geneva, 53147, Walworth County, (414)248-2556, (800)558-3417, 40 miles SW of Milwaukee. **Web:** www.grandgeneva.com.
Holes: 18. **Yards:** 6,997/5,244. **Par:** 72/72. **Course Rating:** 73.8/70.0. **Slope:** 136/129. **Green Fee:** $65/$115. **Cart Fee:** Included in Green Fee. **Walking Policy:** Mandatory cart. **Walkability:** 5. **Opened:** 1969. **Architect:** Robert Bruce Harris. **Season:** April-Nov. **High:** May-Sept. **To obtain tee times:** Guests may call 60 days in advance. Public may call up to 14 days with credit card to reserve. **Miscellaneous:** Reduced fees (weekdays, low season, resort guests, twilight), discount packages, range (grass/mats), club rentals, lodging (355 rooms), credit cards (MC, V, AE, D, Diners Club).
Reader Comments: Wonderful, though tough and pricey ... Lives up to its name ... Big greens ... Tough but fair ... Southern European taste ... Great resort course ... Very challenging, not much room for error ... Large sand traps.

★★★★ **HIGHLANDS COURSE**
R-7036 Grand Way, Lake Geneva, 53147, Walworth County, (414)248-2556, (800)558-3417, 40 miles SW of Milwaukee. **Web:** www.grandgeneva.com.
Holes: 18. **Yards:** 6,633/5,038. **Par:** 71/71. **Course Rating:** 71.5/68.3. **Slope:** 125/115. **Green Fee:** $65/$100. **Cart Fee:** Included in Green Fee. **Walking Policy:** Mandatory cart. **Walkability:** 5. **Opened:** 1969. **Architect:** Pete Dye/Jack Nicklaus/Bob Cupp. **Season:** April-Nov. **High:** May-Sept. **To obtain tee times:** Guests may call 60 days in advance. Public may call up to 14 days with credit card to reserve. **Miscellaneous:** Reduced fees (weekdays, low season, twilight), discount packages, range (grass/mats), club rentals, lodging (355 rooms), credit cards (MC, V, AE, D, Diners Club).
Reader Comments: Good contrast between short and long par 4s ... Much improved last two years ... Magical display of environment ... Was redesigned into vanilla resort course ... Very nice time ... Work greatly improved course ... Changes made it more playable.

★★½ GRANT PARK GOLF COURSE
PU-100 Hawthorne Ave., South Milwaukee, 53172, Milwaukee County, (414)762-4646, 12 miles S of Milwaukee.
Holes: 18. **Yards:** 5,174/5,147. **Par:** 67/71. **Course Rating:** 64.1/68.4. **Slope:** 110/103. **Green Fee:** $8/$18. **Cart Fee:** $24/cart. **Walking Policy:** Unrestricted walking. **Walkability:** 2. **Opened:** 1920. **Architect:** George Hansen. **Season:** Year-round. **High:** June-Aug. **To obtain tee times:** Walk-ons accepted. Members of automated system may call up to 7 days in advance.
Miscellaneous: Reduced fees (weekdays, low season, twilight, seniors, juniors), metal spikes, club rentals, credit cards (MC, V).
Reader Comments: Lots of trees, big rolling greens, fun ... 80-year-old course ... Still has three tough par 3s ... Great place to go with your better half ... Overlooking Lake Michigan. Beautiful views.

★★ GREENFIELD PARK GOLF COURSE
PM-12100 W. Greenfield Ave., West Allis, 53214, Milwaukee County, (414)453-1750, 10 miles SW of Milwaukee. **Web:** www.countyparks.com.
Holes: 18. **Yards:** 6,026/5,572. **Par:** 69/71. **Course Rating:** 66.7/68.4. **Slope:** 113/120. **Green Fee:** $11/$22. **Cart Fee:** $24/cart. **Walking Policy:** Unrestricted walking. **Walkability:** 3. **Architect:** George Hansen. **Season:** April-Nov. **High:** June-Aug. **To obtain tee times:** Call reservation line (414)643-4653 up to 7 days in advance. Call golf course directly on the day of play. **Miscellaneous:** Reduced fees (twilight, seniors, juniors), credit cards (MC, V).

★★ HALLIE GOLF CLUB
2196 110th Street, Chippewa Falls, 54729, Chippewa County, (715)723-8524, (800)830-3007, 1 miles N of Eau Claire. **E-mail:** edsgolf@discovernet.net. **Web:** www.halliegolf.com.
Holes: 18. **Yards:** 5,787/4,822. **Par:** 70/70. **Course Rating:** 67.5/63.1. **Slope:** 120/112. **Green Fee:** $20/$25. **Cart Fee:** $12/person. **Walking Policy:** Unrestricted walking. **Walkability:** 2. **Opened:** 1928. **Architect:** Art Tungen. **Season:** April-Oct. **High:** June-July. **To obtain tee times:** Call no more than 6 days in advance. Internet booking available. **Miscellaneous:** Reduced fees (weekdays, low season, seniors, juniors), discount packages, range (grass/mats), club rentals, credit cards (MC, V, AE), beginner friendly.

HANSEN PARK GOLF COURSE
PM-9800 W. Underwood Creek Pkwy., Wauwatosa, 53226, Milwaukee County, (414)453-4454, 8 miles NW of Milwaukee. **Web:** www.countyparks.com.

Holes: 18. **Yards:** 2,217/2,217. **Par:** 55/55. **Course Rating:** N/A. **Slope:** N/A. **Green Fee:** $6/$10. **Cart Fee:** $15/cart. **Walking Policy:** Unrestricted walking. **Walkability:** 2. **Season:** April-Nov. **High:** June-Aug. **To obtain tee times:** Call golf course directly up to 7 days in advance. **Miscellaneous:** Reduced fees (seniors, juniors), club rentals, beginner friendly.

★★½ HARTFORD GOLF CLUB
SP-7072 Lee Rd., Hartford, 53027, Washington County, (414)673-2710, 30 miles NW of Milwaukee.
Holes: 18. **Yards:** 6,406/5,850. **Par:** 72/74. **Course Rating:** 69.8/72.3. **Slope:** 114/119. **Green Fee:** $24/$28. **Cart Fee:** $24/person. **Walking Policy:** Unrestricted walking. **Walkability:** 3. **Opened:** 1933. **Architect:** Killian/Nugent. **Season:** April-Dec. **High:** May-Sept. **To obtain tee times:** Call 7 days in advance. **Miscellaneous:** Reduced fees (twilight), range (grass), caddies, club rentals, credit cards (MC, V).
Reader Comments: Beautiful greens. Fun to play ... Wide open course. Can be a bit windy at times, making play tough. Otherwise, a solid course ... Two very different nines ... Very fast greens. Nice overall.

★★★ HAWTHORNE HILLS GOLF CLUB
PM-4720 County Hwy. I, Saukville, 53080, Ozaukee County, (262)692-2151, 25 miles N of Milwaukee.
Holes: 18. **Yards:** 6,657/5,352. **Par:** 72/72. **Course Rating:** 70.8/69.4. **Slope:** 119/114. **Green Fee:** $14/$22. **Cart Fee:** $24/cart. **Walking Policy:** Unrestricted walking. **Walkability:** 3. **Opened:** 1965. **Architect:** Bob Lohmann. **Season:** April-Oct. **High:** April-Oct. **To obtain tee times:** Residents up to 7 days in advance. Nonresidents up to 3 days in advance. **Miscellaneous:** Reduced fees (weekdays, low season, seniors, juniors), club rentals, credit cards (MC, V).
Reader Comments: Pretty country course ... Great value, nice greens ... Very scenic. Nice greens ... Very hilly throughout ... Nice little track ... Nice muny layout ... Great deal for county residents.

★★★★ HAYWARD GOLF & TENNIS CENTER *Value*
PU-16005 Wittwer St., Hayward, 54843, Sawyer County, (715)634-2760.
Holes: 18. **Yards:** 6,685/5,200. **Par:** 72/72. **Course Rating:** 71.8/70.0. **Slope:** 125/119. **Green Fee:** $28/$28. **Cart Fee:** $24/cart. **Walking Policy:** Unrestricted walking. **Walkability:** 2. **Architect:** Ken Killian. **Season:** April-Oct. **High:** June-Sept. **Miscellaneous:** Reduced fees (twilight, juniors), range (grass), club rentals, credit cards (MC, V).
Reader Comments: Beautiful fairways and greens ... Bring warm clothes ... Great vacation spot ... Nice public course, fun ... Flat course, but really improved ... Very accommodating and friendly.

★★½ HICKORY HILLS COUNTRY CLUB
PU-W 3095 Hickory Hills Rd., Chilton, 53014, Calumet County, (920)849-2912, (888)849-2912, 25 miles SE of Appleton.
Holes: 18. **Yards:** 6,130/5,916. **Par:** 71/72. **Course Rating:** N/A. **Slope:** 121/117. **Green Fee:** $12/$13. **Walking Policy:** Unrestricted walking. **Walkability:** 2. **Season:** May-Nov. **High:** June-Aug. **To obtain tee times:** Call. **Miscellaneous:** Reduced fees (weekdays), discount packages, metal spikes, range (mats), club rentals, credit cards (MC).
Reader Comments: Short, but interesting layout ... Nice course, not difficult ... Friendly staff. Easy accessibility. A fun place to play every day ... Weekends are slow ... Course needs work.

★★★½ HIGH CLIFF GOLF COURSE
PU-W. 5055 Golf Course Rd., Sherwood, 54169, Calumet County, (920)734-1162, 2 miles E of Sherwood.
Holes: 18. **Yards:** 6,106/4,932. **Par:** 71/71. **Course Rating:** 67.1/62.7. **Slope:** 113/104. **Green Fee:** $16/$22. **Cart Fee:** $22/cart. **Walking Policy:** Unrestricted walking. **Walkability:** 3. **Opened:** 1968. **Architect:** Homer Fieldhouse. **Season:** April-Oct. **To obtain tee times:** Call 7 days in advance. **Miscellaneous:** Reduced fees (seniors, juniors), range (grass), lodging, credit cards (MC, V, D).
Reader Comments: My favorite course ... Interesting holes, front 9 especially ... Front much tougher than back, not bad ... Challenging course, small greens, needs work ... Front 9 very good.

★★★ HILLMOOR GOLF CLUB
SP-333 E.Main Street, Lake Geneva, 53147, Walworth County, (414)248-4570, 70 miles N of Chicago.
Holes: 18. **Yards:** 6,350/5,360. **Par:** 72/72. **Course Rating:** 70.1/65.3. **Slope:** 123/113. **Green Fee:** $24/$38. **Cart Fee:** $15/person. **Walking Policy:** Walking at certain times. **Walkability:** 3. **Opened:** 1924. **Architect:** James Foulis. **Season:** March-Dec. **High:** May-Oct. **To obtain tee times:** Call in advance. **Miscellaneous:** Reduced fees (weekdays, low season, twilight, seniors, juniors), discount packages, range (grass/mats), club rentals, lodging, credit cards (MC, V).
Reader Comments: Good value for Lake Geneva area ... Challenging, tricky greens, beautiful scenery ... Interesting layout, good staff ... Different, challenging ... Busy during the summer ... Some interesting holes ... Fun course to play.

HON-E-KOR COUNTRY CLUB

SP-1141 Riverview Dr., Box 439, Kewaskum, 53040, Washington County, (414)626-2520, 5 miles N of West Bend.
Holes: 27. **Green Fee:** $25/$30. **Cart Fee:** $25/cart. **Walking Policy:** Unrestricted walking. **Opened:** 1962. **Architect:** Jim Korth. **Season:** April-Nov. **High:** May-Sept. **To obtain tee times:** Call 2 days in advance. **Miscellaneous:** Reduced fees (weekdays, low season, seniors, juniors), range (grass/mats), club rentals, credit cards (MC, V).
★★½ **RED/BLUE**
Yards: 6,011/5,164. **Par:** 70/71. **Course Rating:** 68.7/70.3. **Slope:** 118/122. **Walkability:** 3.
Reader Comments: Several great holes, most not memorable ... Good iron practice ... Very short, great greens ... Good course.
★★½ **RED/WHITE**
Yards: 5,959/5,145. **Par:** 70/71. **Course Rating:** 66.0/70.3. **Slope:** 116/122. **Walkability:** 4.
★★½ **WHITE/BLUE**
Yards: 6,033/5,161. **Par:** 70/70. **Course Rating:** 67.6/70.3. **Slope:** 120/122. **Walkability:** 5.

★★★½ HUDSON GOLF CLUB

378 Frontage Rd., Hudson, 54016, St. Croix County, (715)386-6515.
Special Notes: Call club for further information.

★★★★ IDLEWILD GOLF COURSE

PU-4146 Golf Valley Dr., Sturgeon Bay, 54235, Door County, (920)743-3334, 40 miles NE of Green Bay.
Holes: 18. **Yards:** 6,889/5,886. **Par:** 72/73. **Course Rating:** 72.7/73.4. **Slope:** 130/128. **Green Fee:** $18/$24. **Cart Fee:** $12/person. **Walking Policy:** Unrestricted walking. **Walkability:** 2. **Opened:** 1978. **Season:** April-Oct. **High:** June-Sept. **To obtain tee times:** Call anytime in advance during season. **Miscellaneous:** Reduced fees (weekdays, low season, resort guests, twilight, seniors, juniors), discount packages, range (grass), club rentals, credit cards (MC, V).
Reader Comments: Need to stay in the fairway! ... Tough, trouble will find you, great greens ... Scenic, lots of wildlife on course ... Nice place to play ... No. 9 is a par 5 with island green. Best greens in Door County.

★★ INSHALLA COUNTRY CLUB

R-N 11060 Clear Lake Rd., Tomahawk, 54487, Lincoln County, (715)453-3130, 3 miles N of Tomahawk.
Holes: 18. **Yards:** 5,659/5,269. **Par:** 70/70. **Course Rating:** 66.6/65.5. **Slope:** 109/104. **Green Fee:** $20/$24. **Cart Fee:** $26/cart. **Walking Policy:** Unrestricted walking. **Walkability:** 2. **Opened:** 1964. **Architect:** John Hein/John F. Hein. **Season:** April-Nov. **High:** June-Aug. **To obtain tee times:** Call up to 7 days in advance. **Miscellaneous:** Reduced fees (low season, twilight, juniors), metal spikes, club rentals, credit cards (MC, V, AE, D).

IVES GROVE GOLF LINKS

PU-14101 Washington Ave., Sturtevant, 53177, Racine County, (414)878-3714, 6 miles SW of Racine.
Holes: 27. **Green Fee:** $18/$20. **Cart Fee:** $23/person. **Walking Policy:** Unrestricted walking. **Walkability:** N/A. **Opened:** 1971. **Architect:** David Gill. **Season:** March-Nov. **High:** May-Sept. **To obtain tee times:** Call 7 days in advance. **Miscellaneous:** Reduced fees (seniors, juniors), metal spikes, range (grass/mats).
★★★ **BLUE/RED**
Yards: 7,000/5,370. **Par:** 72/72. **Course Rating:** 73.0/N/A. **Slope:** 131/N/A.
Reader Comments: Fairly wide open, nicely maintained ... Decent course, good price ... Often crowded ... Has potential ... Well run, great condition ... Sand to the left, sand to the right ... Too open.
★★★ **RED/WHITE**
Yards: 6,965/5,440. **Par:** 72/72. **Course Rating:** 72.8/N/A. **Slope:** 130/N/A.
Reader Comments: Nicely kept. Good service ... Always windy ... Few trees, take out the driver ... Wide open but fun ... Kept in excellent shape ... Windiest layout in Wisconsin, but worth it ... Nice public facility.
★★★ **WHITE/BLUE**
Yards: 6,985/5,380. **Par:** 72/72. **Course Rating:** 73.0/N/A. **Slope:** 131/N/A.

★★★ JOHNSON PARK GOLF COURSE

PM-6200 Northwestern Ave., Racine, 53406, Racine County, (414)637-2840, 20 miles S of Milwaukee.
Holes: 18. **Yards:** 6,683/5,732. **Par:** 72/74. **Course Rating:** 70.8/73.0. **Slope:** 117/120. **Green Fee:** $15/$22. **Cart Fee:** $22/cart. **Walking Policy:** Unrestricted walking. **Walkability:** 4. **Opened:** 1931. **Architect:** Todd Sloan. **Season:** April-Dec. **High:** June-Aug. **To obtain tee times:** Call 7 days in advance with credit card to guarantee. **Miscellaneous:** Reduced fees

WISCONSIN

(weekdays, low season, seniors, juniors), metal spikes, range (grass/mats), club rentals, credit cards (MC, V, D).

Reader Comments: Busy city course ... Old, tired, needs work ... Very busy muny layout, but challenging ... Solid course design ... Old established muny course. Nice ... Marshals very helpful and effective ... Good muny, fast play, nice design, woods.

KETTLE HILLS GOLF COURSE

PU-3375 State Hwy. 167 W., Richfield, 53076, Washington County, (414)255-2200, 20 miles NW of Milwaukee.

★★★½ PONDS/WOODS COURSE

Holes: 18. **Yards:** 6,787/5,171. **Par:** 72/72. **Course Rating:** 72.5/69.6. **Slope:** 128/123. **Green Fee:** $23/$27. **Cart Fee:** $11/person. **Walking Policy:** Unrestricted walking. **Walkability:** 4. **Opened:** 1987. **Architect:** Don Zimmermann. **Season:** April-Nov. **High:** May-Sept. **To obtain tee times:** Call up to 9 days in advance. **Miscellaneous:** Reduced fees (weekdays, low season, twilight, juniors), range (grass/mats), club rentals, credit cards (MC, V).

Reader Comments: Reasonably-priced golf, nice layout ... Great potential ... A couple of holes aren't too fair for a high handicap ... Gimmicks ... Great course, good challenge ... Lots of trees and elevation changes, fun ... No. 18 a trick hole, should be par 6 ... Nice and friendly. Mom and pop-ish ... Don't play No. 18 in the dark!

★★★½ VALLEY COURSE

Holes: 18. **Yards:** 6,455/5,088. **Par:** 72/72. **Course Rating:** 70.9/69.2. **Slope:** 122/116. **Green Fee:** $20/$27. **Cart Fee:** $11/person. **Walking Policy:** Unrestricted walking. **Walkability:** 3. **Opened:** 1990. **Architect:** Don Zimmermann. **Season:** April-Nov. **High:** May-Sept. **To obtain tee times:** Call up to 9 days in advance. **Miscellaneous:** Reduced fees (weekdays, low season, twilight, seniors, juniors), range (grass/mats), club rentals, credit cards (MC, V).

Reader Comments: Getting better ... Not as good as other course ... Funky layout, gets better as you get familiar with it ... The last two holes are odd ... Beautiful and fun ... Young course with quirky holes ... Great par 5s, beautiful views ... Course layout not conventional but good ... Interesting track ... Very scenic ... More wide open than the Ponds/Woods Course.

★★★½ KETTLE MORAINE GOLF CLUB

PU-4299 Highway 67, Dousman, 53118, Waukesha County, (414)965-6200, 4 miles S of Dousman. **Holes:** 18. **Yards:** 6,406/5,203. **Par:** 72/72. **Course Rating:** 70.3/69.5. **Slope:** 118/116. **Green Fee:** $27/$30. **Cart Fee:** $12/person. **Walking Policy:** Unrestricted walking. **Walkability:** 3. **Opened:** 1969. **Architect:** Dwayne Dewey Laak. **Season:** April-Nov. **High:** June-Sept. **To obtain tee times:** Call up to 21 days in advance. **Miscellaneous:** Reduced fees (low season, twilight), range (grass), club rentals, credit cards (MC, V).

Reader Comments: Fun course with variety ... Beautiful scenery ... Some nice holes, plenty of nature ... Nice course for the money ... Always open late in the year ... Mix of hills and flat holes ... Nice course.

★★ KILLARNEY HILLS GOLF COURSE

PU-163 Radio Rd, River Falls, 54022, Pierce County, (715)425-8501, (800)466-7999, 23 miles E of St. Paul, MN. **Holes:** 18. **Yards:** 6,434/5,055. **Par:** 72/73. **Course Rating:** 70.8/64.4. **Slope:** 120/107. **Green Fee:** $15/$19. **Cart Fee:** $18/cart. **Walking Policy:** Unrestricted walking. **Walkability:** 3. **Opened:** 1994. **Architect:** Gordon Emerson. **Season:** April-Nov. **High:** May-Aug. **To obtain tee times:** Call. **Miscellaneous:** Reduced fees (twilight, seniors, juniors), metal spikes, range (grass), club rentals, credit cards (MC, V).

★★★ KOSHKONONG MOUNDS COUNTRY CLUB

SP-W 7670 Koshkonong Mounds Rd., Fort Atkinson, 53538, Jefferson County, (920)563-2823, 40 miles S of Madison. **Holes:** 18. **Yards:** 6,432/5,813. **Par:** 71/72. **Course Rating:** 70.0/72.1. **Slope:** 121/121. **Green Fee:** $20/$23. **Cart Fee:** $22/person. **Walking Policy:** Walking at certain times. **Walkability:** N/A. **Opened:** 1944. **Architect:** Art Johnson. **Season:** April-Oct. **High:** May-Aug. **To obtain tee times:** Call 2 days in advance. **Miscellaneous:** Credit cards (MC, V).

Reader Comments: Out of the way and unique ... My home course, wish it were private ... A sporty course.

★★½ KRUEGER-HASKELL GOLF COURSE

PM-1611 Hackett St., Beloit, 53511, Rock County, (608)362-6503, 90 miles NW of Chicago. **Holes:** 18. **Yards:** 6,103/5,550. **Par:** 70/71. **Course Rating:** 69.0/71.5. **Slope:** 121/N/A. **Green Fee:** $15/$23. **Cart Fee:** $22/cart. **Walking Policy:** Unrestricted walking. **Walkability:** 3. **Opened:** 1917. **Architect:** Stanley Pelchar. **Season:** March-Nov. **High:** May-Aug. **To obtain tee times:** Call golf shop. **Miscellaneous:** Reduced fees (twilight, seniors, juniors), beginner friendly (group clinics). **Special Notes:** Formerly Krueger Municipal Golf Club

LAKE ARROWHEAD GOLF COURSE

PU-1195 Apache Lane, Nekoosa, 54457, Adams County, (715)325-2929, 13 miles S of Wisconsin Rapids. **E-mail:** lakearro@wctc.net. **Web:** www.wctc.net/lake.arrowhead.

LAKES COURSE

Holes: 18. **Yards:** 7,105/5,272. **Par:** 72/72. **Course Rating:** 74.8/71.0. **Slope:** 140/124. **Green Fee:** $32/$47. **Cart Fee:** $13/person. **Walking Policy:** Mandatory cart. **Walkability:** 2. **Opened:** 1983. **Architect:** Ken Killian. **Season:** April-Oct. **High:** May-Sept. **To obtain tee times:** Call up to 30 days in advance. Groups of 16 call more anytime in advance. **Miscellaneous:** Reduced fees (low season, twilight), discount packages, range (grass), club rentals, lodging, credit cards (MC, V, D).

★★★★ **PINES COURSE** *Condition*

Holes: 18. **Yards:** 6,624/5,213. **Par:** 72/72. **Course Rating:** 72.3/70.2. **Slope:** 135/125. **Green Fee:** $32/$47. **Cart Fee:** $13/person. **Walking Policy:** Unrestricted walking. **Walkability:** 2. **Opened:** 1983. **Architect:** Killian/Nugent. **Season:** April-Oct. **High:** May-Sept. **To obtain tee times:** Call up to 30 days in advance. Groups of 16 call more anytime in advance.

Miscellaneous: Reduced fees (low season, twilight), discount packages, range (grass), club rentals, lodging, credit cards (MC, V, D).

Reader Comments: Favors the left-to-right fade hitter ... One of best in central Wisconsin, heavy bunkering, fun while being challenging ... A course you want to tell all your friends about ... Good Bloody Marys ... Monster sand traps, solid golf ... Best kept secret in Wisconsin ... Excellent course in the middle of nowhere.

★½ **LAKE BEULAH COUNTRY CLUB**

SP-N9430 E. Shore Drive, Mukwonago, 53149, Walworth County, (414)363-8147, 20 miles W of Milwaukee.

Holes: 18. **Yards:** 5,715/4,891. **Par:** 68/69. **Course Rating:** 66.7/69.8. **Slope:** 108/113. **Green Fee:** $18/$22. **Cart Fee:** $22/cart. **Walking Policy:** Unrestricted walking. **Walkability:** 2. **Architect:** Roy & James Jacobs. **Season:** April-Nov. **High:** July-Aug. **To obtain tee times:** Call up to 7 days in advance. **Miscellaneous:** Reduced fees (low season, seniors, juniors), metal spikes, club rentals, credit cards (MC, V).

Special Notes: Also have a 9-hole course.

★★★½ **LAKE BREEZE GOLF CLUB** *Value*

PU-6333 Highway 110, Winneconne, 54986, Winnebago County, (920)582-7585, (800)330-9189, 10 miles NW of Oshkosh.

Holes: 18. **Yards:** 6,896/5,748. **Par:** 72/72. **Course Rating:** 72.2/71.9. **Slope:** 121/118. **Green Fee:** $14/$21. **Cart Fee:** $11/person. **Walking Policy:** Unrestricted walking. **Walkability:** 2. **Opened:** 1991. **Architect:** Homer Fieldhouse. **Season:** April-Oct. **High:** June-Aug. **To obtain tee times:** Call 1 day in advance. **Miscellaneous:** Reduced fees (low season, twilight, seniors, juniors), discount packages, range (grass), club rentals, credit cards (MC, V).

Reader Comments: Very nice for a young course ... As the name suggests, play the wind ... A fun day ... Nice facility ... Good local public course, cheap ... Some interesting holes ... Back nine better.

★★★½ **LAKE LAWN RESORT GOLF COURSE**

R-Highway 50 E., Delavan, 53115, Walworth County, (414)728-7900, (800)338-5253, 45 miles SW of Milwaukee.

Holes: 18. **Yards:** 6,418/5,215. **Par:** 70/70. **Course Rating:** 69.2/64.1. **Slope:** 120/107. **Green Fee:** $55/$65. **Cart Fee:** Included in Green Fee. **Walking Policy:** Walking at certain times. **Walkability:** 3. **Opened:** 1928. **Architect:** Dick Nugent. **Season:** April-Oct. **High:** June-Sept. **To obtain tee times:** Resort guests may book anytime in advance with room reservation. Public may call 2 weeks in advance. **Miscellaneous:** Reduced fees (weekdays, low season, resort guests, twilight), discount packages, range (grass), club rentals, lodging (284 rooms), credit cards (MC, V, AE, D, Diners Club).

Reader Comments: Fast and challenging greens and traps ... Not long, but fun ... A nice track. Closing holes weak ... 3rd hole runs along lake ... Easy course if you keep it straight. Small greens. Good conditioning. Nice resort ... Pretty nice lake view throughout.

LAKE PARK GOLF COURSE

PU-N. 112 W. 17300 Mequon Rd., Germantown, 53022, Washington County, (414)255-4200, 15 miles N of Milwaukee.

Holes: 27. **Green Fee:** $9/$23. **Cart Fee:** $11/person. **Walking Policy:** Unrestricted walking. **Walkability:** 2. **Opened:** 1974. **Architect:** Lloyd B. Robinson. **Season:** April-Oct. **High:** May-Sept. **To obtain tee times:** Call golf shop. **Miscellaneous:** Reduced fees (weekdays, low season, twilight, seniors), metal spikes, credit cards (MC, V).

★★ **RED/BLUE**

Yards: 6,642/5,875. **Par:** 72/73. **Course Rating:** 71.9/76.0. **Slope:** 126/129.

★★ **RED/WHITE**

Yards: 7,010/6,069. **Par:** 72/75. **Course Rating:** 73.6/77.2. **Slope:** 131/134.

★★ **WHITE/BLUE**
Yards: 6,812/6,068. **Par:** 72/76. **Course Rating:** 72.9/77.0. **Slope:** 126/131.

★★ **LAKE SHORE GOLF COURSE**
PU-2175 Punhoqua St., Oshkosh, 54901, Winnebago County, (920)235-6200, 85 miles N of Milwaukee.
Holes: 18. **Yards:** 6,030/5,162. **Par:** 70/71. **Course Rating:** 68.2/69.4. **Slope:** 120/119. **Green Fee:** $17/$18. **Cart Fee:** $18/cart. **Walking Policy:** Unrestricted walking. **Walkability:** 1. **Opened:** 1920. **Season:** April-Nov. **High:** June-Aug. **To obtain tee times:** Call 7 days in advance for weekdays, weekends and holidays. **Miscellaneous:** Reduced fees (twilight, seniors, juniors), range (grass/mats), club rentals, credit cards (MC, V), beginner friendly (junior program).

LAKE WINDSOR GOLF CLUB
PU-4628 Golf Rd., Windsor, 53598, Dane County, (608)255-6100, 5 miles N of Madison.
Holes: 27. **Green Fee:** $10/$20. **Cart Fee:** $9/person. **Walking Policy:** Unrestricted walking. **Walkability:** N/A. **Opened:** 1963. **Season:** March-Nov. **High:** June-Aug. **To obtain tee times:** Call one week in advance. **Miscellaneous:** Reduced fees (weekdays, low season, twilight, seniors, juniors), metal spikes, club rentals, credit cards (MC, V).
★★★ **RED/BLUE**
Yards: 5,983/5,143. **Par:** 71/71. **Course Rating:** 68.0/72.0. **Slope:** 115/122.
Reader Comments: Nice layout, very playable ... Overrated and overpriced ... I love the frequent water hole challenges ... Wet and sloppy at times ... 27 holes of pleasure golf ... It's hard to lose your ball ... First to open, last to close in area ... Freeway noise ... Good course to inflate ego.
★★★ **RED/WHITE**
Yards: 6,228/5,348. **Par:** 72/72. **Course Rating:** 69.2/73.0. **Slope:** 118/127.
★★★ **WHITE/BLUE**
Yards: 6,157/5,215. **Par:** 71/71. **Course Rating:** 68.5/73.0. **Slope:** 118/127.

★★½ **LAKE WISCONSIN COUNTRY CLUB**
SP-N1076 Golf Rd., Prairie Du Sac, 53578, Columbia County, (608)643-2405, 2 miles E of Prairie Du Sac.
Holes: 18. **Yards:** 5,860/5,147. **Par:** 70/71. **Course Rating:** 68.2/69.3. **Slope:** 116/115. **Green Fee:** $33/$38. **Cart Fee:** $25/cart. **Walking Policy:** Unrestricted walking. **Walkability:** 2. **Opened:** 1925. **Season:** April-Oct. **High:** June-Aug. **To obtain tee times:** Tee times taken 1 week in advance. **Miscellaneous:** Reduced fees (low season), range (grass), club rentals, credit cards (MC, V).
Reader Comments: Accurate second shots needed, good par 5s ... Pretty small-town course on river, well run ... Challenging greens, back 9 too many par 3s ... Two totally different 9s, front and back ... Good vacation golf ... Front 9 challenging, back 9 no problem.

★★★ **LAKEWOODS FOREST RIDGES GOLF COURSE**
R-H.C. 73, Cable, 54821, Bayfield County, (715)794-2698, (800)255-5937, 80 miles SE of Duluth.
Holes: 18. **Yards:** 6,270/4,442. **Par:** 71/71. **Course Rating:** 70.9/66.9. **Slope:** 137/123. **Green Fee:** $45/$45. **Cart Fee:** Included in Green Fee. **Walking Policy:** Mandatory cart. **Walkability:** N/A. **Opened:** 1995. **Architect:** Joel Goldstrand. **Season:** May-Oct. **High:** June-Sept. **To obtain tee times:** Call 7 days in advance. **Miscellaneous:** Reduced fees (low season, resort guests, twilight), discount packages, metal spikes, range (grass/mats), club rentals, lodging, credit cards (MC, V, D).
Reader Comments: Very interesting, pleasure to play ... Accuracy a must ... Great layout.

LINCOLN PARK GOLF COURSE
PM-1000 West Hampton Avenue, Milwaukee, 53209, Milwaukee County, (414)962-2400, 5 miles N of Milwaukee. **Web:** www.countyparks.com.
Holes: 9. **Yards:** 2,538/2,538. **Par:** 33/33. **Course Rating:** N/A. **Slope:** N/A. **Green Fee:** $11/$22. **Cart Fee:** $24/cart. **Walking Policy:** Unrestricted walking. **Walkability:** 2. **Season:** April-Nov. **High:** June-Aug. **To obtain tee times:** Call reservation line (414)643-4653 up to 7 days in advance. Call golf course directly on the day of play. **Miscellaneous:** Reduced fees (twilight, seniors, juniors), club rentals, credit cards (MC, V).

★★ **LITTLE RIVER COUNTRY CLUB**
SP-N2235 Shore Dr., Marinette, 54143, Marinette County, (715)732-2221, 2 miles S of Marinette.
Holes: 18. **Yards:** 5,749/5,083. **Par:** 70/71. **Course Rating:** 65.7/68.0. **Slope:** 108/111. **Green Fee:** $19/$21. **Walking Policy:** Unrestricted walking. **Walkability:** 1. **Opened:** 1927. **Season:** April-Oct. **To obtain tee times:** Call up to 7 days in advance. **Miscellaneous:** Reduced fees (weekdays), range (grass), club rentals, credit cards (MC, V).

★★★ **LUCK GOLF COURSE**
PM-1520 S. Shore Dr., Luck, 54853, Polk County, (715)472-2939, 65 miles NE of St. Paul, MN.
Holes: 18. **Yards:** 6,122/5,198. **Par:** 71/72. **Course Rating:** 70.0/70.4. **Slope:** 122/119. **Green Fee:** N/A/$25. **Cart Fee:** $11/person. **Walking Policy:** Unrestricted walking. **Walkability:** 3.

WISCONSIN

Opened: 1938. Season: April-Nov. High: June-Aug. To obtain tee times: Call up to 4 days in advance. Miscellaneous: Reduced fees (weekdays, juniors), metal spikes, range (grass), club rentals, credit cards (MC, V).
Reader Comments: Will improve, tight ... Hilly course, good value ... Lot of trouble, unique ... Esthetically beautiful ... Fun to play. Tough undulating greens ... Nice small-town layout ... Beautiful, mature course.

★★★½ MADELINE ISLAND GOLF CLUB
SP-P.O. Box 83, La Pointe, 54850, Ashland County, (715)747-3212, 25 miles N of Ashland.
Holes: 18. Yards: 6,366/5,506. Par: 71/72. Course Rating: 71.0/71.7. Slope: 131/127. Green Fee: $36/$47. Cart Fee: $26/cart. Walking Policy: Unrestricted walking. Walkability: 3. Opened: 1966. Architect: Robert Trent Jones Sr. Season: May-Oct. High: June-Sept. To obtain tee times: Call anytime. Miscellaneous: Reduced fees (low season, twilight, juniors), range (grass), club rentals, credit cards (MC, V).
Reader Comments: Could be great ... Great vacation course ... Nice course, worth the ferry trip ... Excellent golf course, but the highlight is the island.

★★★ MAPLECREST COUNTRY CLUB
PU-9401 18th St., Kenosha, 53144, Kenosha County, (414)859-2887, 25 miles S of Milwaukee.
Holes: 18. Yards: 6,396/5,056. Par: 71/71. Course Rating: 70.9/71.0. Slope: 121/124. Green Fee: $16/$23. Cart Fee: $24/cart. Walking Policy: Unrestricted walking. Walkability: 2. Opened: 1929. Architect: Leonard Macomber. Season: March-Nov. High: May-Sept. To obtain tee times: Call 7 days in advance. Miscellaneous: Reduced fees (low season, twilight, seniors), metal spikes, range (grass), club rentals, credit cards (MC, V).
Reader Comments: Inexpensive; fast, undulating awesome greens ... A nice layout, doesn't drain well ... Best-kept secret in SE Wisconsin ... Great potential ... Lots of character, fun yet challenging ... Old and rustic ... Challenging par 3s, I like this course.

★★½ MAPLE GROVE COUNTRY CLUB
SP-W. 4142 County B, West Salem, 54669, La Crosse County, (608)786-0340, 10 miles NW of LaCrosse.
Holes: 18. Yards: 6,485/5,578. Par: 71/71. Course Rating: 70.1/70.9. Slope: 122/121. Green Fee: $20/$22. Cart Fee: $22/cart. Walking Policy: Unrestricted walking. Walkability: 3. Opened: 1929. Architect: Leland Thompson. Season: April-Nov. High: June-Aug. To obtain tee times: Call 7 days in advance. Groups of 30 or more call anytime. Miscellaneous: Reduced fees (weekdays, low season, twilight, seniors), discount packages, metal spikes, range (grass/mats), club rentals, credit cards (MC, V).
Reader Comments: Lots of potential ... Long back ... Nice hilly course ... Beautiful layout.

★½ MARSHFIELD COUNTRY CLUB
PU-11426 Wren Rd., Marshfield, 54449, Wood County, (715)384-4409, (800)690-4409, 1 miles W of Marshfield.
Holes: 18. Yards: 6,004/5,376. Par: 70/70. Course Rating: N/A. Slope: 115/111. Green Fee: $17/$18. Cart Fee: $20/cart. Walking Policy: Unrestricted walking. Walkability: N/A. Season: April-Nov. High: May-Sept. To obtain tee times: Call. Miscellaneous: Reduced fees (weekdays, low season, twilight, seniors, juniors), metal spikes, range (grass/mats), club rentals, credit cards (MC, V, AE, D).

★★★★ MASCOUTIN GOLF CLUB
PU-W1635 County Trunk A, Berlin, 54923, Green Lake County, (920)361-2360, 20 miles W of Oshkosh.
Holes: 18. Yards: 6,821/5,133. Par: 72/73. Course Rating: 72.8/69.9. Slope: 130/122. Green Fee: $24/$40. Cart Fee: $14/person. Walking Policy: Walking at certain times. Walkability: 2. Opened: 1975. Architect: Larry Packard, Rick Jacobs. Season: April-Oct. High: May-Sept. To obtain tee times: Call anytime. Miscellaneous: Reduced fees (weekdays, low season, twilight, juniors), discount packages, range (grass), club rentals, credit cards (MC, V).
Reader Comments: Always in nice condition ... Tougher than it looks ... Need to hit every club in your bag ... Long course, open, good elevation changes ... Fairly flat fairways with big greens. Some memorable holes ... Sporty and scenic ... Much underrated; this is a tough track ... Bring extra ammo.

★★ MAXWELTON BRAES GOLF RESORT
7200 Hwy. 57, Baileys Harbor, 54202, Door County, (920)839-2321.
Special Notes: Call club for further information.

★★ MAYVILLE GOLF CLUB
PU-325 S. German St., Mayville, 53050, Dodge County, (920)387-2999, 25 miles S of Fond du Lac.
Holes: 18. Yards: 6,173/5,235. Par: 71/72. Course Rating: 69.5/70.0. Slope: 119/115. Green Fee: $18/$26. Cart Fee: $13/person. Walking Policy: Unrestricted walking. Walkability: 4. Opened: 1931. Architect: Bob Lohmann. Season: April-Oct. High: June-Aug. To obtain tee

WISCONSIN

times: Call 7 days in advance. **Miscellaneous:** Reduced fees (weekdays, low season, twilight, seniors, juniors), club rentals, credit cards (MC, V).

★★★ MCGAUSLIN BROOK GOLF & COUNTRY CLUB
SP-17067 Clubhouse Lane, Lakewood, 54138, Oconto County, (715)276-7623, 75 miles NW of Green Bay.
Holes: 18. **Yards:** 5,926/4,886. **Par:** 70/70. **Course Rating:** 67.1/62.5. **Slope:** 115/105. **Green Fee:** $19/$23. **Cart Fee:** $18/cart. **Walking Policy:** Unrestricted walking. **Walkability:** 2.
Opened: 1965. **Season:** April-Oct. **High:** July-Aug. **To obtain tee times:** Call up to 1-3 days prior. **Miscellaneous:** Reduced fees (weekdays, low season), metal spikes, club rentals, credit cards (MC, V, D).
Reader Comments: Fun course to play, interesting layout ... Excellent northern Wisconsin course, tight back 9 ... Crowded ... Two different 9s ... Best in 50-mile radius.

★★ MEADOW LINKS GOLF COURSE
PU-1540 Johnston Dr., Manitowoc, 54220, Manitowoc County, (920)682-6842, 35 miles SE of Green Bay.
Holes: 18. **Yards:** 5,934/5,254. **Par:** 72/72. **Course Rating:** 67.8/69.2. **Slope:** 114/114. **Green Fee:** $12/$18. **Cart Fee:** $20/cart. **Walking Policy:** Unrestricted walking. **Walkability:** 3.
Opened: 1929. **Season:** April-Oct. **High:** June-Aug. **To obtain tee times:** Call golf shop.
Miscellaneous: Reduced fees (seniors, juniors), metal spikes, club rentals, credit cards (MC, V).

★★ MEEK-KWON PARK GOLF COURSE
PM-6333 W. Bonniwell Rd 136nth, Mequon, 53092, Ozaukee County, (414)242-1310, 25 miles N of Milwaukee.
Holes: 18. **Yards:** 6,465/5,472. **Par:** 70/70. **Course Rating:** 70.5/70.8. **Slope:** 120/118. **Green Fee:** $11/$22. **Cart Fee:** $22/cart. **Walking Policy:** Unrestricted walking. **Walkability:** 4.
Opened: 1974. **Season:** April-Oct. **High:** June-Aug. **To obtain tee times:** Call 3 days in advance. **Miscellaneous:** Reduced fees (seniors), credit cards (MC, V).

★★½ MERRILL GOLF CLUB
PU-1604 O'Day St., Merrill, 54452, Lincoln County, (715)536-2529, 20 miles N of Wausau.
Holes: 18. **Yards:** 6,456/5,432. **Par:** 72/72. **Course Rating:** 70.2/70.0. **Slope:** 120/111. **Green Fee:** $12/$21. **Cart Fee:** $21/cart. **Walking Policy:** Unrestricted walking. **Walkability:** 3.
Opened: 1932. **Architect:** Tom Vardon. **Season:** April-Oct. **High:** June-Aug. **To obtain tee times:** Call 7 days in advance. **Miscellaneous:** Reduced fees (weekdays, low season, twilight, seniors, juniors), range (mats), club rentals, credit cards (MC, V, AE, D).
Reader Comments: Several blind second shots ... Easy ... Sleeper, pleasant surprise. Interesting and challenging ... Nice course, tough greens.

MID-VALLEE GOLF COURSE
PU-3134 Apple Creek Rd., De Pere, 54115, Brown County, (920)532-6674, 10 miles S of Green Bay.
Holes: 27. **Green Fee:** $18/$24. **Cart Fee:** $22/cart. **Walking Policy:** Unrestricted walking. **Walkability:** 3. **Opened:** 1963. **Architect:** Edward Lockie. **Season:** April-Oct. **High:** June-Aug.
To obtain tee times: Call up to 7 days in advance. **Miscellaneous:** Reduced fees (weekdays, twilight, seniors, juniors), discount packages, range (grass/mats), club rentals, credit cards (MC, V).
★★★ BLUE/WHITE
Yards: 6,134/5,025. **Par:** 70/70. **Course Rating:** 69.1/N/A. **Slope:** 122/119.
★★★ RED/BLUE
Yards: 6,024/4,952. **Par:** 70/70. **Course Rating:** 69.1/N/A. **Slope:** 122/120.
★★★ RED/WHITE
Yards: 6,078/5,193. **Par:** 70/70. **Course Rating:** 69.1/68.3. **Slope:** 122/118.
Reader Comments: Just had an overhaul ... Added a third 9 ... Friendly staff; plays longer and more difficult then it looks ... Course redesign was beneficial ... Nice course for mid-range handicappers ... Has a couple of great par 3s.

MILL RUN GOLF CLUB
PU-3905 Kane Rd., Eau Claire, 54703, Eau Claire County, (715)834-1766, (800)241-1766, 65 miles E of Minneapolis/St. Paul. **Web:** www.millrungolf.com.
★★★ HIDDEN CREEK AT MILL RUN
Holes: 18. **Yards:** 6,078/4,744. **Par:** 70/71. **Course Rating:** 68.7/66.6. **Slope:** 116/109. **Green Fee:** $22/$24. **Cart Fee:** $12/person. **Walking Policy:** Unrestricted walking. **Walkability:** 2.
Opened: 1981. **Architect:** Gordon Emerson. **Season:** April-Oct. **High:** April-Oct. **To obtain tee times:** Call 7 days in advance. **Miscellaneous:** Reduced fees (weekdays, seniors, juniors), discount packages, range (grass), club rentals, credit cards (MC, V, AE, D).
Reader Comments: Nice course, wish it was closer ... Great value, country club feel ... Usually pleasing course, wind always a factor ... Short, wide open ... Short, nice course, well maintained ... Open but challenging ... Outstanding landscaping.

WILD RIDGE AT MILL RUN
Holes: 18. **Yards:** 7,034/5,252. **Par:** 72/72. **Course Rating:** N/A. **Slope:** N/A. **Green Fee:** $35/$50. **Cart Fee:** Included in Green Fee. **Walking Policy:** Walking at certain times. **Walkability:** 3. **Opened:** 1999. **Architect:** Greg Martin. **Season:** April-Oct. **High:** May-Sept. **To obtain tee times:** Call 7 days in advance with credit card. **Miscellaneous:** Reduced fees (twilight), range (mats), club rentals, credit cards (MC, V, AE, D).

★★½   **MUSKEGO LAKES COUNTRY CLUB**
SP-S. 100 W. 14020 Loomis Rd., Muskego, 53150, Waukesha County, (414)425-6500, 13 miles SW of Franklin.
Holes: 18. **Yards:** 6,498/5,493. **Par:** 71/72. **Course Rating:** 71.5/71.7. **Slope:** 126/123. **Green Fee:** $21/$30. **Cart Fee:** $13/person. **Walking Policy:** Unrestricted walking. **Walkability:** 2. **Opened:** 1969. **Architect:** Larry Packard. **Season:** April-Nov. **High:** May-Sept. **To obtain tee times:** Call up to 7 days in advance. Discount for a foursome with carts on weekends. **Miscellaneous:** Reduced fees (weekdays, low season, twilight, seniors, juniors), range (grass/mats), club rentals, credit cards (MC, V, AE, D).
Reader Comments: Nice course, fairly long, some very challenging holes. Very hilly ... Bring your bug spray and your ball retriever ... Good layout ... New par 5 unfair ... Good greens ... Resort type course.

★★★½   **MYSTERY HILLS GOLF CLUB**
PU-3149 Dickinson Rd., De Pere, 54115, Brown County, (920)336-6077, 2 miles SE of Green Bay.
Holes: 18. **Yards:** 6,254/5,569. **Par:** 72/72. **Course Rating:** 70.1/72.2. **Slope:** 120/120. **Green Fee:** $18/$20. **Cart Fee:** $24/cart. **Walking Policy:** Unrestricted walking. **Walkability:** 4. **Opened:** 1963. **Season:** Year-round. **High:** May-Aug. **To obtain tee times:** Call up to 6 months in advance. **Miscellaneous:** Reduced fees (weekdays, low season, seniors, juniors), range (grass/mats), club rentals, credit cards (MC, V, D).
Reader Comments: Nice views ... Has improved immensely in last 3 years ... Requires many different shots; some interesting risk-reward holes ... Greens very hard to read ... Always open for play unless there is snow on ground ... No. 17 is a quirky hole ... Very interesting course ... Good variety.

★★★★   **NAGA-WAUKEE GOLF COURSE**   *Value*
PU-1897 Maple Ave., Pewaukee, 53072, Waukesha County, (414)367-2153, 20 miles W of Milwaukee.
Holes: 18. **Yards:** 6,780/5,796. **Par:** 72/72. **Course Rating:** 71.8/72.6. **Slope:** 125/125. **Green Fee:** $20/$35. **Cart Fee:** $12/person. **Walking Policy:** Unrestricted walking. **Walkability:** 3. **Opened:** 1966. **Architect:** Lawrence Packard. **Season:** April-Dec. **High:** May-Sept. **To obtain tee times:** Call 4 days in advance. **Miscellaneous:** Reduced fees (weekdays, low season, twilight, seniors, juniors), metal spikes, range (grass/mats), club rentals, credit cards (MC, V).
Reader Comments: Excellent greens ... I would play it again ... As challenging and manicured as any ... Bring your climbing boots if you walk ... Hilly, good layout. 16th has great view ... Hard to get on ... Most popular course in all of Cheeseland. Very accommodating staff. Outstanding design ... Outstanding views in fall ... Great vistas.

NEMADJI GOLF COURSE   *Service+*
PU-5 N. 58th St. E., Superior, 54880, Douglas County, (715)394-9022. **E-mail:** suppro@aol.com. **Web:** www.downsdd\nemadji.htmp.
★★★★   **EAST/WEST COURSE**   *Value*
Holes: 18. **Yards:** 6,701/5,252. **Par:** 72/72. **Course Rating:** 72.7/70.7. **Slope:** 133/124. **Green Fee:** $12/$20. **Cart Fee:** $20/cart. **Walking Policy:** Unrestricted walking. **Walkability:** 3. **Opened:** 1981. **Architect:** D.W. Herfort. **Season:** April-Oct. **High:** June-Aug. **To obtain tee times:** Call up to 14 days in advance. **Miscellaneous:** Reduced fees (low season, twilight, juniors), range (grass/mats), caddies, club rentals, credit cards (MC, V, AE, D).
Reader Comments: Good people ... Good course. Fairly flat ... Always very busy. Excellent practice area. Friendly people ... Good value, well run ... An excellent course for service ... Great condition, fast greens, excellent fairways ... Pleasant layout, well managed and well maintained.
★★★½   **NORTH/SOUTH COURSE**
Holes: 18. **Yards:** 6,362/4,983. **Par:** 71/71. **Course Rating:** 69.7/67.8. **Slope:** 120/114. **Green Fee:** $12/$20. **Cart Fee:** $20/cart. **Walking Policy:** Unrestricted walking. **Walkability:** 1. **Opened:** 1932. **Architect:** Stanley Pelchar. **Season:** April-Oct. **High:** June-Aug. **To obtain tee times:** Call up to 14 days in advance. **Miscellaneous:** Reduced fees (low season, twilight, juniors), range (grass/mats), caddies, club rentals, credit cards (MC, V, AE, D).
Reader Comments: Challenging ... The weather can change very quickly because of the winds over Lake Superior ... Always a challenge! ... Looks easy, but has its challenging holes. Great value! ... Very easy when dry ... Pleasant layout, well managed and well maintained ... In remarkable condition for all the play it gets.

WISCONSIN

★★★ NEW BERLIN HILLS GOLF COURSE
PM-13175 W. Graham St., New Berlin, 53151, Waukesha County, (414)780-5200, 9 miles W of Milwaukee.
Holes: 18. **Yards:** 6,517/5,346. **Par:** 71/71. **Course Rating:** 71.7/70.8. **Slope:** 127/123. **Green Fee:** $18/$31. **Cart Fee:** $13/person. **Walking Policy:** Unrestricted walking. **Walkability:** 3.
Opened: 1908. **Season:** April-Nov. **High:** May-Sept. **To obtain tee times:** Call up to 7 days in advance. **Miscellaneous:** Reduced fees (seniors, juniors), club rentals, credit cards (MC, V).
Reader Comments: Greens are tough to putt; looks easy but isn't ... No challenge ... Lots of good changes ... Slowly getting better ... Old; tiny, fast greens ... Challenging greens. A nice area secret.

★★★★ NEW RICHMOND GOLF CLUB
SP-1226 180th Ave., New Richmond, 54017, St. Croix County, (715)246-6724, 30 miles NE of St. Paul, MN.
Holes: 18. **Yards:** 6,716/5,547. **Par:** 72/73. **Course Rating:** 72.5/71.7. **Slope:** 136/129. **Green Fee:** $27/$32. **Cart Fee:** $12/person. **Walking Policy:** Unrestricted walking. **Walkability:** 3.
Opened: 1923. **Architect:** Bill Kidd Sr./Don Herfort. **Season:** April-Oct. **High:** June-Aug. **To obtain tee times:** Call 2 days in advance. **Miscellaneous:** Reduced fees (low season, seniors, juniors), range (grass/mats), club rentals, credit cards (MC, V).
Reader Comments: Down to earth service and wonderful layout ... Beautiful course. Challenging yet fun to play ... Two very different 9s, both good ... A real sleeper, great facility ... Very hard to beat for public course ... A wonderful course, good greens, requires shotmaking ... Excellent small-town course ... A well-kept jewel in the woods.

★★½ NICOLET COUNTRY CLUB
PU-Hwy. 8, Laona, 54541, Forest County, (715)674-4780, 1 miles W of Laona. **E-mail:** nccgolf@newnorth.net.
Holes: 18. **Yards:** 4,713/4,093. **Par:** 67/67. **Course Rating:** 62.2/62.3. **Slope:** 104/100. **Green Fee:** $19/$23. **Cart Fee:** $19/cart. **Walkability:** 2. **Opened:** 1960. **Season:** April-Oct. **High:** June-Sept. **To obtain tee times:** Call up to 7 days in advance. **Miscellaneous:** Range (grass), club rentals, credit cards (MC, V).
Reader Comments: Short but difficult, excellent condition ... Short, woody, leave driver in bag ... Very enjoyable course ... Interesting little course, back 9 is a lot of fun but short ... Hilly.

★★★ NIPPERSINK COUNTRY CLUB
PU-N1055 Tombeau Rd., Genoa City, 53128, Walworth County, (262)279-6311, (888)744-6944, 50 miles NW of Chicago. **E-mail:** nippergolf@aol.com.
Holes: 18. **Yards:** 6,600/6,299. **Par:** 71/75. **Course Rating:** 69.4/67.3. **Slope:** 119/114. **Green Fee:** $14/$19. **Cart Fee:** $26/cart. **Walking Policy:** Walking at certain times. **Walkability:** 3.
Opened: 1922. **Architect:** James Foulis, Jr. **Season:** March-Nov. **High:** July-Aug. **To obtain tee times:** Call golf shop 7 days in advance. **Miscellaneous:** Reduced fees (weekdays, low season, resort guests, twilight, seniors, juniors), discount packages, club rentals, lodging (44 rooms), credit cards (MC, V, D), beginner friendly (golf academy).
Reader Comments: Fun for your kids ... Good value, acceptable service and condition ... A couple of holes need to be reworked... Beautiful course. Good traps.

★★★★ NORTHBROOK COUNTRY CLUB *Value*
SP-407 NorthBrook Dr., Luxemburg, 54217, Kewaunee County, (920)845-2383, 15 miles NE of Green Bay.
Holes: 18. **Yards:** 6,223/5,495. **Par:** 71/72. **Course Rating:** 69.2/70.9. **Slope:** 121/116. **Green Fee:** $13/$23. **Cart Fee:** $23/cart. **Walking Policy:** Unrestricted walking. **Walkability:** 3.
Opened: 1971. **Architect:** Ed Langert. **Season:** April-Oct. **High:** June-Aug. **To obtain tee times:** Call 7 days in advance. **Miscellaneous:** Reduced fees (weekdays, low season, seniors, juniors), range (grass), caddies, club rentals, credit cards (MC, V).
Reader Comments: Short game and putting skills a must ... Well kept, greens are hard and fast ... Small, quick greens ... Variety of play, wooded and water, nice course ... No. 10 is tough and intimidating ... A pure gem ... One of the best courses in area ... Tight fairways, elevation changes.

★★★★ NORTHWOOD GOLF COURSE
PU-6301 Hwy. 8 W., Rhinelander, 54501, Oneida County, (715)282-6565, 2 miles W of Rhinelander.
Holes: 18. **Yards:** 6,724/5,338. **Par:** 72/72. **Course Rating:** 73.1/71.3. **Slope:** 140/129. **Green Fee:** $31/$31. **Cart Fee:** $24/cart. **Walking Policy:** Unrestricted walking. **Walkability:** 4.
Opened: 1989. **Architect:** Don Herfort. **Season:** April-Oct. **High:** June-Sept. **To obtain tee times:** Call up to 14 days in advance. **Miscellaneous:** Reduced fees (juniors), discount packages, range (grass), club rentals, credit cards (MC, V).
Reader Comments: Leave your driver in your bag! ... A great test of golf ... Tight, beautiful fairways and vistas ... Water holes are killers ... As beautiful in fall as it is tough all year... One great course ... Bring plenty of balls ... Don't miss, will challenge the best! ... Well-kept secret ... Tighter

than Scrooge ... Excellent course, beautiful, challenging, wilderness ... Beautiful course in the woods.

OAK RIDGE GOLF COURSE
SP-Bowers Lake Rd., Milton, 53563, Rock County, (608)868-4353, 4 miles N of Janesville.
Holes: 27. **Yards:** 5,949/5,519. **Par:** 71/72. **Course Rating:** 69.9/69.5. **Slope:** 117/111. **Green Fee:** $20/$23. **Cart Fee:** $20/cart. **Walking Policy:** Unrestricted walking. **Walkability:** 2.
Opened: 1975. **Season:** March-Nov. **High:** June-Aug. **To obtain tee times:** Call golf shop.
Miscellaneous: Reduced fees (low season, seniors, juniors), range (grass), club rentals, credit cards (MC, V, D).

★★★★ OAKWOOD PARK GOLF COURSE
PM-3600 W. Oakwood Rd., Franklin, 53132, Milwaukee County, (414)281-6700, 8 miles S of Milwaukee.
Holes: 18. **Yards:** 7,008/6,179. **Par:** 72/72. **Course Rating:** 72.5/74.4. **Slope:** 121/123. **Green Fee:** $10/$23. **Cart Fee:** $24/cart. **Walking Policy:** Walking at certain times. **Walkability:** 2.
Opened: 1971. **Architect:** Edward Lawrence Packard. **Season:** April-Oct. **High:** June-Aug. **To obtain tee times:** Call reservation automated tee time system at (414)643-GOLF.
Miscellaneous: Reduced fees (weekdays, seniors, juniors), range (grass/mats), club rentals, credit cards (MC, V).
Reader Comments: An excellent layout for an inexpensive public course ... Tough par 4s ... Long and open ... Solid course ... Deceiving, tough ... Municipal course, inexpensive, nicest staff in the country! ... Outstanding muny, you won't be disappointed.

★★★½ OLD HICKORY COUNTRY CLUB
SP-Hwy. 33 E., W7596, Beaver Dam, 53916, Dodge County, (920)887-7577, 30 miles NE of Madison. **Web:** www.oldhickorycc.com.
Holes: 18. **Yards:** 6,721/5,372. **Par:** 72/73. **Course Rating:** 72.5/72.8. **Slope:** 129/127. **Green Fee:** $40/$50. **Cart Fee:** $12/person. **Walking Policy:** Unrestricted walking. **Walkability:** 4.
Opened: 1920. **Architect:** Tom Bendelow. **Season:** April-Oct. **High:** June-Aug. **To obtain tee times:** Call 7 days in advance. **Miscellaneous:** Reduced fees (low season), range (grass/mats), club rentals, credit cards (MC, V).
Reader Comments: Too may blind holes! ... Nice course in the middle of nowhere ... A fine test of golf ... Nicely-wooded, older, remodeled course. A few blind holes; that's how they used to build them ... Outstanding old-style golf ... Love the oaks and hickorys ... Mature trees, well maintained greens, nice layout.

★★★ OLDE HIGHLANDER GOLF CLUB AT OLYMPIA RESORT
R-1350 Royale Mile Rd., Oconomowoc, 53066, Waukesha County, (414)567-6048, 30 miles W of Milwaukee.
Holes: 18. **Yards:** 6,458/5,688. **Par:** 72/71. **Course Rating:** 70.5/72.4. **Slope:** 118/119. **Green Fee:** $24/$28. **Cart Fee:** $12/person. **Walking Policy:** Walking at certain times. **Walkability:** 2.
Opened: 1971. **Architect:** Randy Warobick. **Season:** April-Nov. **High:** June-Sept. **To obtain tee times:** Call. **Miscellaneous:** Reduced fees (weekdays, low season, twilight, seniors, juniors), discount packages, metal spikes, range (grass), club rentals, lodging, credit cards (MC, V, AE, D).
Reader Comments: Overpriced ... Not always in great condition ... Big improvements ... Fun to play ... Good course, great potential ... Condition better than past years ... Wide variety of holes.

★½ PAGANICA GOLF COURSE
PU-3850 Silverlake, Oconomowoc, 53066, Waukesha County, (262)567-0171, 29 miles W of Milwaukee.
Holes: 18. **Yards:** 6,576/5,663. **Par:** 72/74. **Course Rating:** 70.7/71.5. **Slope:** 116/116. **Green Fee:** $24/$26. **Cart Fee:** $11/person. **Walking Policy:** Unrestricted walking. **Walkability:** 2.
Opened: 1965. **Architect:** Luke Frye. **Season:** March-Dec. **High:** June-Aug. **To obtain tee times:** Call 7 days in advance. **Miscellaneous:** Reduced fees (low season, seniors), range (grass/mats), club rentals.

★★½ PECKS WILDWOOD GOLF COURSE
PU-10080 Highway 70 W., Minocqua, 54548, Oneida County, (715)356-3477, 70 miles N of Wausau.
Holes: 18. **Yards:** 5,869/5,483. **Par:** 71/71. **Course Rating:** 68.6/71.0. **Slope:** 115/118. **Green Fee:** $25/$25. **Cart Fee:** $20/cart. **Walking Policy:** Unrestricted walking. **Walkability:** N/A.
Opened: 1983. **Season:** April-Oct. **To obtain tee times:** Call. **Miscellaneous:** Reduced fees (low season), discount packages, range (mats), club rentals, credit cards (MC, V).
Reader Comments: Great vacation golf with kids along, nice people ... Several very challenging holes ... OK all around ... Very tight course, fun to play ... Good place to play with your wife.

★★★★ PENINSULA STATE PARK GOLF COURSE
PU-Hwy. 42, Ephraim, 54211, Door County, (920)854-5791, 70 miles NE of Green Bay.
Holes: 18. **Yards:** 6,266/5,428. **Par:** 71/72. **Course Rating:** 69.6/70.6. **Slope:** 123/121. **Green Fee:** $22/$26. **Cart Fee:** $22/cart. **Walking Policy:** Unrestricted walking. **Walkability:** 4.

WISCONSIN

Opened: 1921. **Architect:** Edward Lawrence Packard. **Season:** May-Oct. **High:** June-Sept. **To obtain tee times:** Call up to 14 days in advance, or come in during season. **Miscellaneous:** Reduced fees (twilight, juniors), metal spikes, range (grass), club rentals.

Reader Comments: Great vistas ... Bring your camera, play in fall colors ... Very steep hills, a good walk for flat bellies ... Crowded but enjoyable ... Wonderful layout, improving each year ... Pretty, pretty pretty ... Hard to get tee times ... Breathtaking views on many holes.

★★★ PETRIFYING SPRINGS GOLF COURSE
PU-4909 7th St., Kenosha, 53144, Kenosha County, (414)552-9052, 1 miles N of Kenosha. **Holes:** 18. **Yards:** 5,979/5,588. **Par:** 71/72. **Course Rating:** 67.8/70.9. **Slope:** 119/122. **Green Fee:** $20/$24. **Cart Fee:** $22/cart. **Walking Policy:** Unrestricted walking. **Walkability:** 3. **Opened:** 1936. **Architect:** Joseph A. Roseman. **Season:** April-Nov. **High:** June-Aug. **To obtain tee times:** Call 12 days in advance for a fee of $4. **Miscellaneous:** Club rentals, credit cards (MC, V).

Reader Comments: Short, but great terrain and fun to play ... Nice layout! ... Nice, but too short ... Tough terrain, good test for your game ... Front 9 plain and simple. The last 3 holes are a challenge ... Great course, busy all the time ... Slow.

★★ PINEWOOD COUNTRY CLUB
PM-4660 Lakewood Rd., Harshaw, 54529, Oneida County, (715)282-5500, (800)674-6396, 13 miles S of Minocqua. **E-mail:** cbgolf1@newnorth.net. **Web:** www.minocqua.org/pinewood. **Holes:** 18. **Yards:** 6,245/4,854. **Par:** 70/70. **Course Rating:** 69.8/67.7. **Slope:** 123/115. **Green Fee:** $22/$24. **Cart Fee:** $28/person. **Walking Policy:** Unrestricted walking. **Walkability:** 5. **Opened:** 1962. **Architect:** Al Broman Jr. **Season:** April-Oct. **High:** June-Aug. **To obtain tee times:** Call golf shop. **Miscellaneous:** Reduced fees (low season, twilight, juniors), range (grass/mats), club rentals, lodging, credit cards (MC, V, D).

★★★ PLEASANT VIEW GOLF CLUB
PM-1322 Pleasant View Dr., Middleton, 53562, Dane County, (608)831-6666, 1 miles N of Madison. **Holes:** 18. **Yards:** 6,436/5,514. **Par:** 72/72. **Course Rating:** 70.0/67.5. **Slope:** 122/116. **Green Fee:** $25/$29. **Cart Fee:** $28/cart. **Walking Policy:** Unrestricted walking. **Walkability:** 5. **Opened:** 1957. **Architect:** Art Johnson. **Season:** April-Oct. **High:** June-Aug. **To obtain tee times:** Call golf shop. **Miscellaneous:** Reduced fees (weekdays, low season, twilight, seniors, juniors), discount packages, range (grass/mats), club rentals, credit cards (MC, V).

Reader Comments: Always windy, bring climbing boots ... Offers several pleasant views of Wisconsin's capitol, several miles away ... Hilly ... Nicest public course in Madison area ... Stay away on weekends ... Beautiful setting, excellent public course.

★★★ PORTAGE COUNTRY CLUB
SP-E. Hwy. No. 33, Portage, 53901, Columbia County, (608)742-5121, 6 miles E of Portage. **Holes:** 18. **Yards:** 6,356/4,946. **Par:** 72/74. **Course Rating:** 70.4/68.0. **Slope:** 127/119. **Green Fee:** $28/$34. **Cart Fee:** $14/person. **Walking Policy:** Unrestricted walking. **Walkability:** 4. **Architect:** Art Johnson. **Season:** April-Nov. **High:** May-Aug. **To obtain tee times:** Call up to 7 days in advance. **Miscellaneous:** Reduced fees (weekdays), range (grass), club rentals, credit cards (MC, V).

Reader Comments: Nice local country club ... Not very interesting ... Needs TLC ... Fastest greens ever ... Difficult greens. A little tricked up.

★★★½ QUIT-QUI-OC GOLF CLUB
PU-500 Quit-Qui-Oc Lane, Elkhart Lake, 53020, Sheboygan County, (920)876-2833, 50 miles N of Milwaukee. **Holes:** 18. **Yards:** 6,178/5,134. **Par:** 70/71. **Course Rating:** 69.6/64.9. **Slope:** 119/109. **Green Fee:** $21/$27. **Cart Fee:** $13/person. **Walking Policy:** Unrestricted walking. **Walkability:** 4. **Opened:** 1925. **Architect:** Bendelow/Wiese. **Season:** April-Nov. **High:** May-Sept. **To obtain tee times:** Call 4 days in advance. **Miscellaneous:** Reduced fees (weekdays, low season, resort guests, twilight, seniors, juniors), range (grass/mats), club rentals, credit cards (MC, V).

Reader Comments: Lots of fun holes, enjoyable ... Good variety ... Scenic ... Beautiful Wisconsin parkland course ... Short fun course. Scenic ... Rolling, variable terrain, good food in clubhouse ... Challenging lots of long par 3s ... Needs work ... Wonderful course!

★★★½ RAINBOW SPRINGS GOLF CLUB
PU-S103 W33599 Hwy. 99, Mukwonago, 53149, Waukesha County, (414)363-4550, (800)465-3631, 30 miles SW of Milwaukee. **Holes:** 18. **Yards:** 6,914/5,135. **Par:** 72/72. **Course Rating:** 73.4/69.8. **Slope:** 132/120. **Green Fee:** $22/$26. **Cart Fee:** $13/person. **Walking Policy:** Walking at certain times. **Walkability:** N/A. **Opened:** 1964. **Architect:** Francis Schroedel. **Season:** April-Nov. **High:** June-Sept. **To obtain tee times:** Call up to 14 days in advance with credit card to guarantee. 48-hour cancellation policy. **Miscellaneous:** Reduced fees (weekdays, low season, twilight, seniors, juniors), discount packages, metal spikes, range (grass), club rentals, credit cards (MC, V).

Reader Comments: Magnificent ... Water, no sand, tough rough ... Very desolate place, course is flat ... Needs sand traps ... A long hard course with water everywhere ... Flat but tough ... Kind of tight ... Plays long ... New lost ball record.

★★★½ REEDSBURG COUNTRY CLUB
SP-Hwy. 33, Reedsburg, 53959, Sauk County, (608)524-6000, 14 miles SW of Wisconsin Dells.
Holes: 18. **Yards:** 6,300/5,324. **Par:** 72/73. **Course Rating:** 70.5/70.3. **Slope:** 129/124. **Green Fee:** N/A/$38. **Cart Fee:** $14/person. **Walking Policy:** Walking at certain times. **Walkability:** 4.
Opened: 1924. **Architect:** Ken Killian/Dick Nugent. **Season:** March-Nov. **High:** June-Aug. **To obtain tee times:** Call up to 30 days in advance. **Miscellaneous:** Reduced fees (weekdays, low season, twilight), range (grass), club rentals, credit cards (MC, V).
Reader Comments: Nicely wooded older course. Some holes memorable. Some blind greens ... Great older course, sneaky tough fast greens ... Short but a lotta fun ... Very good! ... Beautiful scenery, the greens were small and very hard to putt ... Nice average course, good variety.

★★★½ REID GOLF COURSE
PM-1100 E. Fremont, Appleton, 54915, Outagamie County, (920)832-5926.
Holes: 18. **Yards:** 5,968/5,296. **Par:** 71/72. **Course Rating:** 67.6/69.1. **Slope:** 114/115. **Green Fee:** $16/$19. **Cart Fee:** $19/cart. **Walking Policy:** Unrestricted walking. **Walkability:** 3.
Opened: 1941. **Architect:** Miller Cohenen. **Season:** April-Oct. **High:** June-Aug. **To obtain tee times:** Call 3 days in advance. **Miscellaneous:** Reduced fees (twilight, seniors, juniors), metal spikes, range (grass), club rentals.
Reader Comments: Easy course, crowded ... Some great holes and views on the bluffs ... Middle of the road muny ... OK muny course, slow play ... Nice muny course, good condition ... Lots of trees, must be very accurate.

★★★ THE RIDGES GOLF COURSE
SP-2311 Griffith Ave., Wisconsin Rapids, 54494, Wood County, (715)424-3204, 90 miles N of Madison. **E-mail:** ridges@wctc.net. **Web:** www.ridgesgolfcourse.com.
Holes: 18. **Yards:** 6,289/5,018. **Par:** 72/72. **Course Rating:** 71.3/69.9. **Slope:** 129/122. **Green Fee:** $42/$42. **Cart Fee:** $24/person. **Walking Policy:** Unrestricted walking. **Walkability:** 3.
Opened: 1963. **Season:** April-Oct. **High:** June-Aug. **To obtain tee times:** Call anytime.
Miscellaneous: Reduced fees (low season), discount packages, range (grass/mats), club rentals, credit cards (MC, V, AE).
Reader Comments: Fun back nine ... Wooded, sporty course, greens are big and greatly improved. Some good holes, some boring ... Back nine great scenery ... Very friendly, interesting layout of holes ... One of the tougher back 9s I've played. Kind of tricked up ... Overpriced ... Too many tricked-up holes.

★★★½ RIVER FALLS GOLF CLUB
SP-1011 E. Division St., River Falls, 54022, Pierce County, (715)425-0032, (800)688-1511, 3 miles E of River Falls. **E-mail:** rfgc2@pressenter.com.
Holes: 18. **Yards:** 6,596/5,142. **Par:** 72/72. **Course Rating:** 72.0/69.9. **Slope:** 126/118. **Green Fee:** $21/$29. **Cart Fee:** $24/cart. **Walking Policy:** Unrestricted walking. **Walkability:** 3. **Opened:** 1929. **Season:** April-Oct. **High:** May-Sept. **To obtain tee times:** Call 3 days in advance. **Miscellaneous:** Reduced fees (seniors, juniors), range (grass), credit cards (MC, V, AE).
Reader Comments: Mature course, hidden greens, excellent ... Does not get better with age ... Good layout, some tight holes ... Beautiful layout, many interesting holes ... What a great little course, nothing super, just an enjoyable day ... Fun course, lots of blind shots ... OK.

★★½ RIVERDALE COUNTRY CLUB
PU-5008 South 12th St., Sheboygan, 53081, Sheboygan County, (920)458-2561, 50 miles N of Milwaukee.
Holes: 18. **Yards:** 5,875/5,651. **Par:** 70/72. **Course Rating:** 67.4/71.3. **Slope:** 109/116. **Green Fee:** $13/$21. **Cart Fee:** $22/cart. **Walking Policy:** Unrestricted walking. **Walkability:** 2.
Opened: 1929. **Season:** April-Oct. **High:** June-Aug. **To obtain tee times:** Call on Wednesday for upcoming weekend. **Miscellaneous:** Range (grass), club rentals, credit cards (MC, V).
Reader Comments: Very friendly people ... Average course, but worth playing ... Old course, rolling fairways increase challenge ... Nice back nine ... Short, very sloped greens ... Old, interesting course ... Course has lots of potential.

★★★½ RIVERMOOR COUNTRY CLUB
SP-30802 Waterford Dr., Waterford, 53185, Racine County, (414)534-2500, 20 miles SW of Milwaukee.
Holes: 18. **Yards:** 6,256/5,839. **Par:** 70/72. **Course Rating:** 68.7/72.7. **Slope:** 121/125. **Green Fee:** $22/$28. **Cart Fee:** $12/person. **Walking Policy:** Unrestricted walking. **Walkability:** 2.
Opened: 1929. **Architect:** Billy Sixty Jr. **Season:** March-Nov. **High:** June-Aug. **To obtain tee times:** Call 7 days in advance. **Miscellaneous:** Reduced fees (low season, twilight, seniors), metal spikes, club rentals, credit cards (MC, V, D).

WISCONSIN

Reader Comments: Classic old course ... Short, tight, sporty golf course ... Very nice greens ... Down-home friendly Wisconsin, one beer at the bar and you are old friends ... Tiny target greens ... Excellent course, beautiful, challenging ... Tough course. Very congested with narrow fairways ... Tight course, old, mature and interesting.

★★★½ RIVERSIDE GOLF COURSE
PM-2100 Golf Course Rd., Janesville, 53545, Rock County, (608)757-3080, 35 miles S of Madison. E-mail: julgolf@aol.com.
Holes: 18. Yards: 6,508/5,147. Par: 72/72. Course Rating: 70.7/68.9. Slope: 123/116. Green Fee: $22/$25. Cart Fee: $12/person. Walking Policy: Unrestricted walking. Walkability: 3. Opened: 1924. Architect: Robert Bruce Harris. Season: April-Nov. High: June-Aug. To obtain tee times: Call up to 10 days in advance. Miscellaneous: Reduced fees (weekdays, seniors, juniors), range (grass), club rentals, credit cards (MC, V).
Reader Comments: Great public course ... Best muny in state ... Real challenging, very good course ... Older course means lots of old trees ... Old, beautiful course ... Always fun to play. A good variety of holes ... All putts break toward the river.

★★★½ ROCK RIVER HILLS GOLF COURSE
SP-Main St. Rd., Horicon, 53032, Dodge County, (920)485-4990, 45 miles NW of Milwaukee.
Holes: 18. Yards: 6,243/5,160. Par: 70/70. Course Rating: 70.5/70.0. Slope: 127/121. Green Fee: $21/$28. Cart Fee: $24/cart. Walking Policy: Unrestricted walking. Walkability: 2. Opened: 1969. Architect: Homer Fieldhouse/Bob Lohmann. Season: April-Nov. High: June-Aug. To obtain tee times: Call up to 7 days in advance. Miscellaneous: Reduced fees (low season, twilight, seniors, juniors), range (grass), club rentals, credit cards (MC, V).
Reader Comments: Not a long course ... Shhh, don't let Milwaukee hear about this hidden gem ... Best-kept secret in SE Wisconsin ... Meticulously groomed ... Watch out for loons, beavers and muskrats.

★★★½ ROLLING MEADOWS GOLF COURSE
PM-560 W. Rolling Meadows Dr., Fond Du Lac, 54937, Fond Du Lac County, (920)929-3735, 55 miles N of Milwaukee. E-mail: jobb@powercom.net.
Holes: 27. Yards: 7,000/5,100. Par: 72/72. Course Rating: 73.5/69.5. Slope: 131/121. Green Fee: $25/$28. Cart Fee: $25/cart. Walking Policy: Unrestricted walking. Walkability: 2. Opened: 1973. Architect: Nugent & Associates. Season: April-First Snow. High: May-Aug. To obtain tee times: Call Mondays for following Sat., Sun. and Monday. For rest of the week call a week in advance. Miscellaneous: Reduced fees (seniors, juniors), range (grass/mats), club rentals, lodging (300 rooms), credit cards (MC, V), beginner friendly (free junior lesson program).
Reader Comments: Better layout since redesigned the course ... Many different looks, nice and challenging layout ... People very friendly and accommodating ... Good muny, not great ... Best muny in the Midwest.

★★★ ROYAL SCOT GOLF COURSE & SUPPER CLUB
PU-4831 Church Rd., New Franken, 54229, Brown County, (920)866-2356, 5 miles N of Green Bay.
Holes: 18. Yards: 6,572/5,474. Par: 72/72. Course Rating: 70.7/70.7. Slope: 122/118. Green Fee: $20/$23. Cart Fee: $24/cart. Walking Policy: Unrestricted walking. Walkability: 2. Opened: 1971. Architect: Don Herfort. Season: April-Oct. High: June-Aug. To obtain tee times: Call up to 7 days in advance. Miscellaneous: Reduced fees (seniors, juniors), metal spikes, range (grass), club rentals, credit cards (MC, V, D).
Reader Comments: Great greens ... Beautiful older course. Everything good ... Fun course, friendly staff ... Tough par 3s. Wide open. Easy walk ... Older course, back 9 can be wet at times ... Basic golf.

★★★½ ST. CROIX NATIONAL GOLF CLUB
PU-1603 County Rd. V, Somerset, 54025, (715)247-4200, 2 miles S of Somerset. Web: www.saintcroixnational.com.
Holes: 18. Yards: 6,909/5,251. Par: 72/72. Course Rating: 73.9/66.3. Slope: 138/119. Green Fee: $36/$46. Cart Fee: $26/cart. Walking Policy: Unrestricted walking. Walkability: 5. Opened: 1996. Architect: Joel Goldstrand. Season: April-Oct. High: June-Aug. To obtain tee times: Call up to 7 days in advance. Miscellaneous: Reduced fees (twilight), range (grass), club rentals, credit cards (MC, V, AE, D).
Reader Comments: Beautiful location, difficult ... Great Stevie Wonder course: all blind shots ... Hit 'em straight or lose 'em ... Very scenic, former ski area ... Very hilly, great course ... Up and down through hills and swales, got tiring ... Memorable holes.

★★★★ ST. GERMAIN MUNICIPAL GOLF CLUB   *Value*
PU-9041 Hwy. 70 W., P.O. 385, St. Germain, 54558, Vilas County, (715)542-2614, 3 miles W of St. Germain.
Holes: 18. Yards: 6,651/5,233. Par: 72/72. Course Rating: 72.2/70.3. Slope: 130/121. Green Fee: $25/$33. Cart Fee: $12/person. Walking Policy: Unrestricted walking. Walkability: 3.

WISCONSIN

Opened: 1993. **Architect:** Don Stepanik, Jr. **Season:** April-Oct. **High:** June-Sept. **To obtain tee times:** Call up to 14 days in advance. **Miscellaneous:** Reduced fees (low season, twilight), discount packages, range (grass), club rentals, lodging, credit cards (MC, V, AE, D), beginner friendly.
Reader Comments: Narrow. Lots of deer and eagles, beautiful layout. Kept in great condition ... Fun new course ... Best course in North Central Wisconsin ... Great vacation course in Northwoods ... Scenic. Large pine trees.

★★ SCENIC VIEW COUNTRY CLUB
PU-4415 Club Dr., Slinger, 53086, Washington County, (414)644-5661, (800)472-6411, 20 miles NW of Milwaukee. **Web:** www.svgolf.com.
Holes: 18. **Yards:** 6,296/5,358. **Par:** 72/71. **Course Rating:** 68.6/70.1. **Slope:** 115/115. **Green Fee:** $20/$26. **Cart Fee:** $26/person. **Walking Policy:** Unrestricted walking. **Walkability:** 4.
Opened: 1961. **Architect:** Robert Raasch. **Season:** March-Nov. **High:** June-Aug. **To obtain tee times:** Call up to seven days in advance. **Miscellaneous:** Reduced fees (weekdays, low season, seniors), range (grass), club rentals, credit cards (MC, V, AE), beginner friendly (golf lessons).

★★★★ SENTRYWORLD GOLF COURSE *Condition*
PU-601 N. Michigan Ave., Stevens Point, 54481, Portage County, (715)345-1600, 90 miles N of Madison.
Holes: 18. **Yards:** 6,951/5,108. **Par:** 72/72. **Course Rating:** 74.4/71.0. **Slope:** 142/126. **Green Fee:** $40/$70. **Cart Fee:** Included in Green Fee. **Walking Policy:** Unrestricted walking. **Walkability:** 3. **Opened:** 1981. **Architect:** Robert Trent Jones Jr. **Season:** April-Oct. **High:** June-Aug. **To obtain tee times:** Call golf shop. **Miscellaneous:** Reduced fees (weekdays, low season, twilight), discount packages, range (grass), club rentals, credit cards (MC, V, AE).
Notes: Ranked 4th in 1999 Best in State; 18th in 1996 America's Top 75 Upscale Courses.
Reader Comments: Beautiful course ... Impeccable, beautiful, the tops! ... Tough, tough, course. The flower hole rocks ... A championship course outlined with flowers galore ... Excellent course but pricey ... Overrated big time ... A great place to play at least once ... Rough is nicer than some courses' fairways ... Can't beat the flower hole, No. 16 ... Great scenery. Friendly, challenging, great conditions.

★★½ SHAWANO LAKE GOLF CLUB
PU-W5714 Lake Drive, Shawano, 54166, Shawano County, (715)524-4890, 25 miles NW of Green Bay. **E-mail:** tknorr@mail.wisc.net.
Holes: 18. **Yards:** 6,231/5,496. **Par:** 71/71. **Course Rating:** 72.9/70.4. **Slope:** 124/124. **Green Fee:** $17/$22. **Cart Fee:** $11/person. **Walking Policy:** Unrestricted walking. **Walkability:** 4.
Opened: 1922. **Architect:** Marty Garrity. **Season:** April-Nov. **High:** June-Sept. **To obtain tee times:** Call up to 14 days in advance. **Miscellaneous:** Reduced fees (weekdays, low season, resort guests, twilight, seniors, juniors), discount packages, range (grass), club rentals, credit cards (MC, V).
Reader Comments: Could be one of the best, needs watering; old course ... Tree lined, blind shots, small greens. Good mix of difficult and easy holes ... Improving.

★★½ SHEBOYGAN TOWN & COUNTRY CLUB
PU-W1945 County J, Sheboygan, 53083, Sheboygan County, (920)467-2509, 5 miles W of Sheboygan.
Holes: 27. **Yards:** 5,990/4,974. **Par:** 71/71. **Course Rating:** 68.1/67.9. **Slope:** 117/112. **Green Fee:** $20/$23. **Cart Fee:** $21/cart. **Walking Policy:** Unrestricted walking. **Walkability:** 3.
Opened: 1962. **Architect:** Homer Fieldhouse. **Season:** April-Nov. **High:** July. **To obtain tee times:** Call 5 days in advance. Call 12 days in advance or more for larger groups.
Miscellaneous: Reduced fees (weekdays, twilight, seniors, juniors), range (grass), club rentals, credit cards (MC, V, D), beginner friendly (group lessons).
Reader Comments: A great course ... Great pro shop, very accommodating ... Continued improvement in the quality each year... Good bang for the buck.

SILVER SPRING GOLF COURSE
PU-N.56 W.21318 Silver Spring Rd., Menomonee Falls, 53051, Waukesha County, (414)252-4666, 7 miles E of Menomonee Falls.
FALLS COURSE
Holes: 18. **Yards:** 5,564/5,160. **Par:** 70/72. **Course Rating:** 71.8/70.5. **Slope:** 123/120. **Green Fee:** $26/$26. **Cart Fee:** $13/person. **Walking Policy:** Walking at certain times. **Walkability:** 3.
Season: Year-round. **High:** June-Aug. **To obtain tee times:** Call 7 days in advance over the phone. **Miscellaneous:** Reduced fees (weekdays, low season, twilight), range (grass/mats), club rentals, credit cards (MC, V, AE).
★★★½ ISLAND COURSE
Holes: 18. **Yards:** 6,744/5,616. **Par:** 72/70. **Course Rating:** 72.4/67.9. **Slope:** 134/124. **Green Fee:** $32/$32. **Cart Fee:** $13/person. **Walking Policy:** Walking at certain times. **Walkability:** 3.
Season: Year-round. **High:** June-Aug. **To obtain tee times:** Call 7 days in advance over the

WISCONSIN

phone. **Miscellaneous:** Reduced fees (weekdays, low season, twilight), range (grass/mats), club rentals, credit cards (MC, V, AE).
Reader Comments: Some very challenging holes ... Enjoyable, a challenging layout, beautiful ... Island hole still fun ... Always trying to improve all services ... Great facilities ... Had a nice time.

★★★½ SKYLINE GOLF CLUB
SP-11th and Golf Rd., Black River Falls, 54615, Jackson County, (715)284-2613, 125 miles NW of Madison.
Holes: 18. **Yards:** 6,371/5,122. **Par:** 72/72. **Course Rating:** 70.6/69.4. **Slope:** 123/112. **Green Fee:** $21/$23. **Cart Fee:** $21/cart. **Walking Policy:** Unrestricted walking. **Walkability:** 5.
Opened: 1957. **Architect:** Edward L. Packard/Brent Wadsworth. **Season:** April-Nov. **High:** May-Aug. **To obtain tee times:** Call golf shop. **Miscellaneous:** Reduced fees (low season, resort guests, twilight), range (grass), club rentals, credit cards (MC, V).
Reader Comments: Short course and hilly ... A beautiful clubhouse and a nice lush green course ... Best golf value in this part of Wisconsin ... Nice small-town course ... Nicely done ... Beautiful course and scenery, the fairways were too hilly for me.

★★½ SONGBIRD HILLS GOLF CLUB
PU-W259 N8700 Hwy. J, Hartland, 53029, Waukesha County, (414)246-7050, 15 miles W of Milwaukee.
Holes: 18. **Yards:** 5,556/5,074. **Par:** 70/70. **Course Rating:** 66.2/64.0. **Slope:** 110/105. **Green Fee:** $20/$24. **Cart Fee:** $22/cart. **Walking Policy:** Unrestricted walking. **Walkability:** 4.
Opened: 1992. **Architect:** Harold E. Hoffman. **Season:** April-Nov. **High:** June-Aug. **To obtain tee times:** Call. **Miscellaneous:** Reduced fees (weekdays, low season, twilight, seniors, juniors), metal spikes, range (grass), club rentals, credit cards (MC, V).
Reader Comments: Nice short track ... Very short course, although I like feeling like Tiger when I play wedge second shots into par 4s ... Hackers' paradise ... Very tight, gimmicky course ... Strange layout, fun to play ... Very short, but nice.

★★½ SOUTH HILLS COUNTRY CLUB
PU-3047 Hwy 41, Franksville, 53126, Racine County, (414)835-4441, (800)736-4766, 15 miles S of Milwaukee.
Holes: 18. **Yards:** 6,403/6,107. **Par:** 72/76. **Course Rating:** 69.4/75.0. **Slope:** 118/125. **Green Fee:** $18/$22. **Cart Fee:** $24/cart. **Walking Policy:** Unrestricted walking. **Walkability:** 2.
Opened: 1927. **Season:** Year-round weather permitting. **High:** May-Oct. **To obtain tee times:** Call 7 days in advance. **Miscellaneous:** Reduced fees (weekdays, low season), discount packages, metal spikes, range (grass/mats), club rentals, credit cards (MC, V, AE).
Reader Comments: Good place if you are not in a hurry ... They need water, great potential ... Low price ... Too open ... Some back and forth, and pretty wide open ... Kind of boring ... Large grass range, nice banquet facility.

★★★½ SPARTA MUNICIPAL GOLF COURSE
PM-1210 E Montgomery St., Sparta, 54656, Monroe County, (608)269-3022, 25 miles E of La Crosse.
Holes: 18. **Yards:** 6,544/5,648. **Par:** 72/72. **Course Rating:** 70.8/71.6. **Slope:** 127/125. **Green Fee:** $20/$23. **Cart Fee:** $23/cart. **Walking Policy:** Unrestricted walking. **Walkability:** 1.
Opened: 1984. **Architect:** Art Johnson. **Season:** April-Oct. **High:** May-July. **To obtain tee times:** Call up to 2 days in advance. **Miscellaneous:** Reduced fees (low season, seniors, juniors), range (grass), club rentals, credit cards (MC, V), beginner friendly.
Reader Comments: Very inexpensive. Nice layout ... Nice muny course, reasonable ... Best in area. Greens challenging to putt ... Great deal.

★★★★ SPOONER GOLF CLUB
SP-County Trunk H N., Spooner, 54801, Washburn County, (715)635-3580, 85 miles N of Eau Claire.
Holes: 18. **Yards:** 6,417/5,084. **Par:** 71/72. **Course Rating:** 70.9/68.8. **Slope:** 128/117. **Green Fee:** $24/$27. **Cart Fee:** $25/cart. **Walking Policy:** Unrestricted walking. **Walkability:** 3.
Opened: 1930. **Architect:** Tom Vardon/G. Emerson. **Season:** April-Oct. **High:** June-Aug. **To obtain tee times:** Call 30 days in advance starting on the 25th of the preceding month. **Miscellaneous:** Reduced fees (weekdays, twilight), range (grass), club rentals, credit cards (MC, V).
Reader Comments: No. 18 is one of the best! ... Will go back ... Well-groomed and fun to play ... Don't pass it up ... Worth playing, good shape and layout ... Fun vacation course, great No. 18 ... A sleeper, terrific value ... One of Wisconsin's finest ... Very enjoyable.

★★½ SPRING VALLEY COUNTRY CLUB
PU-23913 Wilmot Rd., Salem, 53168, Kenosha County, (414)862-2626, 8 miles W of Kenosha.
Holes: 18. **Yards:** 6,354/5,968. **Par:** 70/70. **Course Rating:** 70.1/68.9. **Slope:** 119/113. **Green Fee:** N/A/$21. **Cart Fee:** $12/person. **Walking Policy:** Unrestricted walking. **Walkability:** 3.
Opened: 1924. **Architect:** William B. Langford/Theodore J. Moreau. **Season:** Year-round. **High:**

April-Nov. **To obtain tee times:** Call anytime. **Miscellaneous:** Reduced fees (weekdays, low season, twilight, seniors), range (grass), credit cards (MC, V).
Reader Comments: Lots of woods, boo! ... Slow ... Good husband and wife course ... Nice rolling hills ... Offers some very interesting holes ... Hilly, fun course, nothing fancy.

★★½ SPRING VALLEY GOLF COURSE

PU-400 Van Buren Rd., Spring Valley, 54767, Pierce County, (715)778-5513, (800)236-0009, 40 miles E of Minneapolis/St. Paul.
Holes: 18. **Yards:** 6,114/4,735. **Par:** 71/72. **Course Rating:** 70.0/68.0. **Slope:** 124/116. **Green Fee:** $16/$19. **Cart Fee:** $10/person. **Walking Policy:** Unrestricted walking. **Walkability:** 5. **Opened:** 1974. **Architect:** Gordy Emerson. **Season:** April-Oct. **High:** May-Sept. **To obtain tee times:** Call up to 1 week in advance. **Miscellaneous:** Reduced fees (weekdays, low season, twilight, seniors, juniors), discount packages, club rentals, credit cards (MC, V, AE, D).
Reader Comments: Narrow fairways but beautiful! Uncrowded. A good test of your game ... Don't tell too many about this course. It's my summer get away ... Breathtaking back 9 ... 8-13 are carved out of the woods.

THE SPRINGS GOLF CLUB RESORT

R-400 Springs Dr., Spring Green, 53588, Sauk County, (608)588-7707, (800)822-7774, 35 miles NW of Madison.
Holes: 27. **Green Fee:** $55/$65. **Cart Fee:** Included in Green Fee. **Walking Policy:** Unrestricted walking. **Walkability:** 3. **Opened:** 1969. **Season:** Year-round. **High:** April-Oct. **To obtain tee times:** Resort guests and members call 7 days in advance. Public call 6 days in advance.

★★★★ BACK/NORTH *Pace*

Yards: 6,534/5,285. **Par:** 72/72. **Course Rating:** 71.9/70.6. **Slope:** 134/125. **Architect:** R. Jones Sr./R. Packard/A. North. **Miscellaneous:** Reduced fees (low season, twilight), discount packages, range (grass), club rentals, lodging (80 rooms), credit cards (MC, V, AE, D).
Reader Comments: Very nice resort, 45 minutes from Madison ... New 9 by Packard and North is gorgeous. All 27 are fun. Resort offers good service ... Great course, overpriced ... Unrecognized gem ... Fantastic layout and breathtaking fall foliage ... Excellent condition, challenging, really keeps you on your game ... Original 18 one of the best in state ... North 9 super! Good family resort courses.

★★★★ FRONT/BACK *Pace*

Yards: 6,562/5,334. **Par:** 72/72. **Course Rating:** 71.5/70.3. **Slope:** 132/123. **Architect:** Robert T. Jones Sr. **Miscellaneous:** Reduced fees (low season, twilight), discount packages, range (grass), club rentals, lodging (80 rooms), credit cards (MC, V, AE, D).

★★★★ FRONT/NORTH *Pace*

Yards: 6,544/5,673. **Par:** 72/72. **Course Rating:** 71.6/70.7. **Slope:** 130/124. **Architect:** Robert T. Jones Sr. **Miscellaneous:** Reduced fees (low season, twilight), discount packages, metal spikes, range (grass), club rentals, lodging, credit cards (MC, V, AE, D).

★★½ SQUIRES COUNTRY CLUB

PU-4970 Country Club Rd., Port Washington, 53074, Ozaukee County, (262)285-3402, 3 miles W of Milwaukee. **Web:** www.squirescc.com.
Holes: 18. **Yards:** 5,800/5,067. **Par:** 70/70. **Course Rating:** 67.3/68.2. **Slope:** 112/112. **Green Fee:** N/A/$24. **Cart Fee:** $12/person. **Walking Policy:** Unrestricted walking. **Walkability:** 3. **Opened:** 1927. **Architect:** Milton Karrels. **Season:** April-Oct. **High:** June-Aug. **To obtain tee times:** Call 7 days in advance. **Miscellaneous:** Reduced fees (weekdays, twilight, seniors, juniors), range (grass), club rentals, credit cards (MC, V, D).
Reader Comments: Short course, but some challenging holes ... Great course right on Lake Michigan. Offers chance to create shots and use your whole bag ... Ho hum, decent value ... Short and fun ... Sporty and fun ... Some day I'll hit No. 6 in two.

★★ SUN PRAIRIE GOLF COURSE

PU-Happy Valley Rd., Sun Prairie, 53590, Dane County, (608)837-6211, 2 miles N of Sun Prairie.
Holes: 18. **Yards:** 6,658/5,289. **Par:** 72/73. **Course Rating:** 71.3/65.0. **Slope:** 117/102. **Green Fee:** $22/$24. **Cart Fee:** $22/cart. **Walking Policy:** Unrestricted walking. **Walkability:** 3. **Opened:** 1961. **Season:** April-Nov. **High:** June-Aug. **Miscellaneous:** Range (grass), club rentals, credit cards (MC, V).

TEAL WING GOLF CLUB

R-12425 N. Ross Road, Hayward, 54843, Sawyer County, (715)462-9051, 20 miles NE of Hayward. **Web:** www.tealwing.com.
Holes: 18. **Yards:** 6,379/5,218. **Par:** 72/72. **Course Rating:** 72.1/71.2. **Slope:** 139/127. **Green Fee:** $30/$48. **Cart Fee:** $12/person. **Walking Policy:** Unrestricted walking. **Walkability:** 3. **Opened:** 1995. **Season:** May-Oct. **High:** July-Aug. **To obtain tee times:** Call golf shop. **Miscellaneous:** Reduced fees (low season, resort guests, twilight), metal spikes, range (grass), club rentals, lodging (25 rooms), credit cards (MC, V), beginner friendly.
Special Notes: Spikeless shoes encouraged.

WISCONSIN

★★★ TELEMARK GOLF CLUB
R-Telemark Rd., Cable, 54821, Bayfield County, (715)798-3104, 100 miles NE of Eau Claire.
E-mail: slgr@win.bright.net. **Web:** www.cable4fun.com/golf27.htm.
Holes: 18. **Yards:** 6,403/5,691. **Par:** 72/72. **Course Rating:** 70.6/67.0. **Slope:** 128/119. **Green Fee:** $28/$28. **Cart Fee:** $12/person. **Walking Policy:** Walking at certain times. **Walkability:** 4.
Opened: 1970. **Season:** May-Oct. **High:** June-Sept. **To obtain tee times:** Call anytime in advance. **Miscellaneous:** Reduced fees (low season, twilight), discount packages, range (grass), club rentals, lodging (8 rooms), credit cards (MC, V).
Reader Comments: Cut amongst the beautiful hills and woods ... Tight, narrow holes ... Great back 9 ... Miss the fairway, lose your ball ... A gem with a few rough edges.

★★ THAL ACRES LINKS & LANES
PU-N6109 CTHM, Westfield, 53964, Marquette County, (608)296-2850, 50 miles N of Madison.
Holes: 18. **Yards:** 5,672/5,211. **Par:** 70/72. **Course Rating:** 66.5/69.3. **Slope:** 114/118. **Green Fee:** $20/$24. **Cart Fee:** $24/cart. **Walking Policy:** Unrestricted walking. **Walkability:** 2.
Opened: 1963. **Season:** April-Oct. **High:** June-Aug. **To obtain tee times:** Call anytime.
Miscellaneous: Reduced fees (weekdays, low season, seniors), metal spikes, range (grass), club rentals, credit cards (MC, V).

★★½ TRAPP RIVER GOLF CLUB
PU-Hwy. WW, Wausau, 54403, Marathon County, (715)675-3044, 8 miles NE of Wausau.
E-mail: welsgof@aol.com.
Holes: 18. **Yards:** 6,335/4,935. **Par:** 72/72. **Course Rating:** 69.3/67.3. **Slope:** 116/109. **Green Fee:** $15/$21. **Cart Fee:** $11/person. **Walking Policy:** Unrestricted walking. **Walkability:** 2.
Opened: 1963. **Architect:** Sloan. **Season:** April-Nov. **High:** June-Aug. **To obtain tee times:** Call up to 1 month in advance. **Miscellaneous:** Reduced fees (low season, twilight, seniors, juniors), range (grass/mats), club rentals, credit cards (MC, V, AE, D), beginner friendly.
Reader Comments: Beautiful back 9 ... Few good holes ... Lots of fun and good service ... Much improved over previous years.

★★★★ TRAPPERS TURN GOLF CLUB
PU-652 Trappers Turn Dr., Wisconsin Dells, 53965, Sauk County, (608)253-7000, (800)221-8876, 50 miles N of Madison. **E-mail:** trappers@midplains.net. **Web:** www.trappersturn.com.
Holes: 18. **Yards:** 6,773/5,017. **Par:** 72/72. **Course Rating:** 72.0/69.5. **Slope:** 133/122. **Green Fee:** $45/$68. **Cart Fee:** Included in Green Fee. **Walking Policy:** Walking at certain times.
Walkability: 5. **Opened:** 1991. **Architect:** Andy North/Roger Packard. **Season:** April-Oct. **High:** July-Aug. **To obtain tee times:** Call up to 30 days in advance. Resort guests and outings call anytime in advance. **Miscellaneous:** Reduced fees (weekdays, low season, resort guests, twilight), discount packages, range (grass), club rentals, lodging, credit cards (MC, V, AE, D).
Reader Comments: Very nice but overrated, overpriced ... Best course I've played. Once a year a must ... A couple of blah holes but the rest compensate ... A beautiful course in great shape ... Some of the best holes in Wisconsin, especially the 'fan' par 3 ... Everything is great ... A beauty, Nos. 9 and 18 unbelievable holes ... I drive 3 hours one way twice a year to play this course.

★★★ TREE ACRES GOLF COURSE
PU-5254 Pleasant Dr, Plover, 54467, Portage County, (715)341-4530.
Holes: 18. **Yards:** 6,159/4,775. **Par:** 72/72. **Course Rating:** 69.2/67.3. **Slope:** 114/107. **Green Fee:** $19/$22. **Cart Fee:** $10/person. **Walking Policy:** Unrestricted walking. **Walkability:** 1.
Opened: 1991. **Architect:** Don Stepanik. **Season:** April-Oct. **High:** May-Aug. **To obtain tee times:** Call golf shop. **Miscellaneous:** Reduced fees (weekdays, low season, seniors, juniors), range (grass), club rentals, credit cards (MC, V), beginner friendly (golf school program).
Reader Comments: Great place to golf with your kids, wide open fairways with few hazards ... Well taken care of ... Takes all sorts of shots, from a 130-yard par 3 to a 565-yard par 5 ... Very busy ... Short par 4s.

★★★½ TROUT LAKE GOLF & COUNTRY CLUB
PU-3800 Hwy. 51 N., Arbor Vitae, 54568, Vilas County, (715)385-2189, 80 miles N of Wausau.
Holes: 18. **Yards:** 6,175/5,263. **Par:** 72/71. **Course Rating:** 69.9/70.3. **Slope:** 124/122. **Green Fee:** $27/$33. **Cart Fee:** $12/person. **Walking Policy:** Unrestricted walking. **Walkability:** 2.
Opened: 1926. **Architect:** Charles Maddox/Frank P. MacDonald. **Season:** April-Oct. **High:** June-Sept. **To obtain tee times:** Call 14 days in advance. **Miscellaneous:** Reduced fees (low season), metal spikes, club rentals, credit cards (MC, V).
Reader Comments: Nice and secluded ... Surprisingly fun, trim, and enjoyable ... Not a bad course, would play again ... Nice country course ... Course is excellent.

★★★★½ TURTLEBACK GOLF & CONFERENCE CENTER
Value+, Condition, Pace
PU-W. Allen Rd., Rice Lake, 54868, Barron County, (715)234-7641, 1 miles W of Rice Lake.
Holes: 18. **Yards:** 6,604/5,291. **Par:** 71/71. **Course Rating:** 72.0/70.6. **Slope:** 129/120. **Green Fee:** $25/$32. **Cart Fee:** $22/cart. **Walking Policy:** Unrestricted walking. **Walkability:** 3.

Opened: 1982. **Architect:** Todd Severud. **Season:** April-Oct. **High:** June-Aug. **To obtain tee times:** Call up to 14 days in advance. **Miscellaneous:** Reduced fees (weekdays, low season), range (grass), club rentals, credit cards (MC, V).
Reader Comments: Great greens, good layout ... Bring your Crenshaw touch for these greens ... When I die, bury me here. This is golfers' heaven ... Challenging course, improved in past years ... Tough, but fair! ... Best course in Northern Wisconsin ... Great course, needs some maturing.

★★★ TUSCUMBIA GOLF CLUB

SP-Illinois Ave., Green Lake, 54941, Green Lake County, (920)294-3240, (800)294-3381, 65 miles N of Milwaukee.
Holes: 18. **Yards:** 6,301/5,619. **Par:** 71/71. **Course Rating:** 70.1/73.2. **Slope:** 122/123. **Green Fee:** $26/$41. **Cart Fee:** $12/person. **Walking Policy:** Unrestricted walking. **Walkability:** 2.
Opened: 1896. **Architect:** Tom Bendelow. **Season:** April-Oct. **High:** June-Sept. **To obtain tee times:** Call. **Miscellaneous:** Reduced fees (low season, twilight, seniors, juniors), discount packages, metal spikes, range (grass/mats), club rentals, credit cards (MC, V, D).
Reader Comments: Interesting to play 100-year-old course ... What a nice course ... Wonderfully challenging, oldest course in state ... Basic golf on old course ... Nice course, nice people, could use some work ... Back and forth holes ... Nice old course.

★½ TWIN LAKES COUNTRY CLUB

SP-1230 Legion Dr., Twin Lakes, 53181, Kenosha County, (414)877-2500, 50 miles SW of Milwaukee.
Holes: 18. **Yards:** 5,930/4,946. **Par:** 70/71. **Course Rating:** 67.2/67.3. **Slope:** 115/113. **Green Fee:** $19/$25. **Cart Fee:** $12/person. **Walking Policy:** Unrestricted walking. **Walkability:** 4.
Opened: 1912. **Architect:** Leonard Macomber. **Season:** March-Nov. **High:** June-Aug. **To obtain tee times:** Call 7 days in advance. **Miscellaneous:** Reduced fees (weekdays, twilight, seniors), range (grass/mats), club rentals, credit cards (MC, V), beginner friendly (golf schools).

★★½ TWIN OAKS GOLF COURSE

PU-4871 County Hwy. R, Denmark, 54208, Brown County, (920)863-2716, 5 miles S of Green Bay.
Holes: 18. **Yards:** 6,468/5,214. **Par:** 72/72. **Course Rating:** 69.6/68.3. **Slope:** 116/103. **Green Fee:** $16/$20. **Cart Fee:** $11/person. **Walking Policy:** Unrestricted walking. **Walkability:** 2.
Opened: 1968. **Season:** March-Nov. **High:** June-Aug. **To obtain tee times:** Call up to 7 days in advance. **Miscellaneous:** Reduced fees (weekdays, seniors, juniors), metal spikes, range (grass), club rentals, credit cards (MC, V, D).
Reader Comments: Course being upgraded ... Friendly staff, could use a little upkeep ... Conditions improved ... One nice hole, others nothing special ... Basic golf.

★★★½ TWO OAKS NORTH GOLF CLUB

PU-Cty. Hwy. F, Wautoma, 54982, Waushara County, (920)787-7132, (800)236-6257, 35 miles W of Oshkosh.
Holes: 18. **Yards:** 6,552/5,034. **Par:** 72/72. **Course Rating:** 70.7/68.3. **Slope:** 120/111. **Green Fee:** $14/$28. **Cart Fee:** $24/cart. **Walking Policy:** Unrestricted walking. **Walkability:** 3.
Opened: 1995. **Architect:** Robert Lohmann/John Houdek. **Season:** April-Oct. **High:** June-Aug. **To obtain tee times:** Call up to 10 days in advance. **Miscellaneous:** Reduced fees (weekdays, low season, resort guests, twilight, seniors, juniors), discount packages, range (grass/mats), club rentals, credit cards (MC, V, AE, D).
Reader Comments: Front 9 is back and forth but back 9 has interesting, sporty holes ... Flat, some trees, good beginners' place ... Nice shorter course, need to be good with all of your short irons ... Course is maturing well ... Fun to play ... Nice layout, back tees make it ... Very good, friendly people.

★★★★½ UNIVERSITY RIDGE GOLF COURSE *Service, Value, Condition+*

PU-7120 County Trunk PD, Verona, 53593, Dane County, (608)845-7700, (800)897-4343, 8 miles SW of Madison. **Web:** www.wisc.edu/ath/.com.
Holes: 18. **Yards:** 6,888/5,005. **Par:** 72/72. **Course Rating:** 73.2/68.9. **Slope:** 142/121. **Green Fee:** $34/$51. **Cart Fee:** $15/person. **Walking Policy:** Unrestricted walking. **Walkability:** 3.
Opened: 1991. **Architect:** Robert Trent Jones Jr. **Season:** April-Oct. **High:** May-Sept. **To obtain tee times:** Call up to 6 days in advance. Groups of 8 or more may book anytime in advance.
Miscellaneous: Reduced fees (low season, twilight, juniors), metal spikes, range (grass/mats), club rentals, credit cards (MC, V, AE).
Reader Comments: Beautiful, rolling layout, woodsy ... Fun, challenging, playable ... One of the best in Wisconsin ... Overrated, underchallenged, expensive ... Very diverse. Incredible conditions ... Superb in every regard ... Love it, hate it, I can't get enough of this course! ... Two separate 9s, two wonderful adventures ... Surprisingly snobby for a university course ... Be ready for a great day.

WISCONSIN

★★½ UTICA HILLS GOLF COURSE
PU-3350 Knott Rd., Oshkosh, 54903, Winnebago County, (920)233-4446, 5 miles W of Fond Du Lac.
Holes: 18. **Yards:** 6,185/5,368. **Par:** 72/72. **Course Rating:** 68.8/69.9. **Slope:** 117/117. **Green Fee:** $19/$21. **Cart Fee:** $22/cart. **Walking Policy:** Unrestricted walking. **Walkability:** 2. **Opened:** 1974. **Architect:** Robert Petzel. **Season:** April-Dec. **High:** June-Aug. **To obtain tee times:** Call up to 7 days in advance. **Miscellaneous:** Reduced fees (seniors, juniors), range (grass), club rentals, credit cards (MC, V).
Reader Comments: Miss fairway and still make par, wide open ... Always windy but good for beginners ... Nice little 'hidden' course.

★★★½ VOYAGER VILLAGE COUNTRY CLUB
SP-28851 Kilkare Rd., Danbury, 54830, Burnett County, (715)259-3911, (800)782-0329, 15 miles E of Webster.
Holes: 18. **Yards:** 6,638/5,711. **Par:** 72/72. **Course Rating:** 71.6/72.4. **Slope:** 123/122. **Green Fee:** $21/$25. **Cart Fee:** $24/cart. **Walking Policy:** Unrestricted walking. **Walkability:** 3. **Opened:** 1970. **Architect:** William James Spear. **Season:** April-Oct. **High:** June-Aug. **To obtain tee times:** Call 5 days in advance. **Miscellaneous:** Reduced fees (weekdays), discount packages, range (grass), club rentals, credit cards (MC, V).
Reader Comments: Wow, I love it ... Good track, out of the way, but worth it ... Saw a black bear, red fox and whitetail deer ... Tough, tiring ... Scenic, every hole different, very good food ... Interesting, winds through the woods, I always see wild animals.

★★★ WANAKI GOLF COURSE
PM-20830 W. Libson Rd., Menomonee Falls, 53051, Waukesha County, (414)252-3480.
Holes: 18. **Yards:** 6,569/5,012. **Par:** 71/70. **Course Rating:** 71.4/69.2. **Slope:** 127/117. **Green Fee:** $25/$29. **Walking Policy:** Unrestricted walking. **Walkability:** 1. **Opened:** 1968. **Architect:** Billy Sixty, Jr. **Season:** April-Nov. **High:** May-Aug. **Miscellaneous:** Reduced fees (twilight, seniors, juniors), metal spikes, club rentals, credit cards (MC, V).
Reader Comments: Some goofy holes, some very nice holes, nice course ... Nice public course ... Could be a great layout ... Looks easy till you play... Long layout through the woods ... Long and wooded. Nice par 5s.

WARNIMONT PARK GOLF COURSE
PM-5400 South Lake Drive, Cudahy, 53110, Milwaukee County, (414)481-1400, 8 miles S of Milwaukee. **Web:** www.countyparks.com.
Holes: 18. **Yards:** 2,717/2,717. **Par:** 54/54. **Course Rating:** N/A. **Slope:** N/A. **Green Fee:** $6/$10. **Cart Fee:** $15/cart. **Walking Policy:** Unrestricted walking. **Walkability:** 2. **Season:** April-Nov. **High:** June-Aug. **To obtain tee times:** Call golf course directly up to 7 days in advance. **Miscellaneous:** Reduced fees (seniors, juniors), club rentals, beginner friendly.

★★★★½ WASHINGTON COUNTY GOLF COURSE *Value, Pace*
PM-6439 Clover Rd., Hartford, 53027, Washington County, (414)670-6616, (888)383-GOLF. **Web:** www.golfwcgc.com.
Holes: 18. **Yards:** 7,007/5,200. **Par:** 72/72. **Course Rating:** 73.1/69.5. **Slope:** 130/118. **Green Fee:** $16/$48. **Cart Fee:** $13/cart. **Walking Policy:** Unrestricted walking. **Walkability:** 3. **Opened:** 1997. **Architect:** Arthur Hills/Brian Yoder. **Season:** April-Nov. **High:** May-June-July-Aug. **Miscellaneous:** Reduced fees (low season, twilight, seniors, juniors), discount packages, range (grass), club rentals, credit cards (MC, V, AE), beginner friendly (3-hole practice course).
Reader Comments: Good layout for a county course, tough! ... Wide open ... A bit pricey, but what a great course ... British links-type county course. Great potential ... Fantastic course, rarely crowded ... Relatively unknown, as wonderful a course as you can imagine ... Great design, generous greens ... Super ... Excellent new public course.

★★★ WESTERN LAKES GOLF CLUB
SP-W287 N1963 Oakton Rd., Pewaukee, 53072, Waukesha County, (414)691-1181, 20 miles W of Milwaukee. **E-mail:** wlgc1@juno.com.
Holes: 18. **Yards:** 6,587/5,618. **Par:** 72/72. **Course Rating:** 71.2/71.8. **Slope:** 124/123. **Green Fee:** $24/$34. **Cart Fee:** $26/cart. **Walking Policy:** Unrestricted walking. **Walkability:** 3. **Opened:** 1963. **Architect:** Lawrence Packard. **Season:** April-Nov. **High:** June-Sept. **To obtain tee times:** Call up to 7 days in advance. **Miscellaneous:** Reduced fees (weekdays, low season, twilight), discount packages, range (grass/mats), club rentals, credit cards (MC, V, AE).
Reader Comments: Low and wet in the spring, nothing fancy, OK course ... Average course, no memorable holes ... Has improved ... A fair test, not remarkable ... Good all around ... Good local course but a lot of traffic ... Nice layout, had a nice time ... Fun.

★★ WESTHAVEN GOLF CLUB
PU-1400 Westhaven St., Oshkosh, 54904, Winnebago County, (920)233-4640.
Holes: 18. **Yards:** 5,877/5,175. **Par:** 70/70. **Course Rating:** 67.6/71.6. **Slope:** 115/118. **Green Fee:** $20/$22. **Cart Fee:** $22/cart. **Walking Policy:** Unrestricted walking. **Walkability:** 2.

Opened: 1969. **Architect:** Homer Fieldhouse. **Season:** April-Nov. **High:** April-Sept. **To obtain tee times:** Call. **Miscellaneous:** Reduced fees (twilight, seniors, juniors), metal spikes, range (grass), club rentals, credit cards (MC, V, AE, D).

★★★★ WHISPERING SPRINGS GOLF CLUB *Value*
PU-380 Whispering Springs Rd., Fond du Lac, 54935, Fond du Lac County, (920)921-8053, 4 miles E of Fond du Lac.
Holes: 18. **Yards:** 6,961/5,207. **Par:** 72/72. **Course Rating:** 73.9/70.3. **Slope:** 134/122. **Green Fee:** $31/$38. **Cart Fee:** $13/person. **Walking Policy:** Unrestricted walking. **Walkability:** 1. **Opened:** 1997. **Architect:** Bob Lohmann/Michael Benkusky. **Season:** March-Nov. **High:** June-Sept. **Miscellaneous:** Reduced fees (weekdays, low season, twilight, seniors, juniors), range (grass), club rentals, credit cards (MC, V, D).
Reader Comments: Excellent new course with several great holes ... Top notch course ... Still new and not well known yet ... Great new course in Central Wisconsin, not a bad hole on course ... Excellent design, fun to play yet challenging, good value ... Too many sand traps, nice rocks ... Shhh, keep this place to yourself ... Great views ... Interesting holes.

WHISTLING STRAITS GOLF CLUB
PU-S 8501 County LS, Haven, 53083, Mosel County, (920)457-5653, 5 miles S of Cheboygan.
Holes: 18. **Yards:** 7,288/5,381. **Par:** 72/72. **Course Rating:** 151.0/132.0. **Slope:** 77/72. **Green Fee:** $104/$166. **Walking Policy:** Unrestricted walking. **Walkability:** 4. **Opened:** 1998. **Architect:** Pete Dye. **Season:** April-Oct. **High:** June-Aug. **To obtain tee times:** Hotel guests can book as far in advance as they would like. Public can book within two weeks. **Miscellaneous:** Reduced fees (low season, twilight), range (grass), caddies, club rentals, lodging (357 rooms), credit cards (MC, V, AE, D).
Notes: Ranked 3rd in 1999 Best in State; 2nd in 1999 Best New Upscale Public.

★★★ WHITNALL PARK GOLF CLUB
PU-5879 S. 92nd St., Hales Corners, 53130, Milwaukee County, (414)425-7931, 5 miles SW of Milwaukee.
Holes: 18. **Yards:** 6,335/5,879. **Par:** 71/74. **Course Rating:** 69.6/72.6. **Slope:** 118/120. **Green Fee:** $12/$27. **Cart Fee:** $24/cart. **Walking Policy:** Unrestricted walking. **Walkability:** 4. **Opened:** 1932. **Architect:** George Hansen. **Season:** April-Nov. **High:** June-Sept. **To obtain tee times:** 5 day advance tee times using automated system. Call same day only. **Miscellaneous:** Reduced fees (low season, twilight, seniors, juniors), club rentals, credit cards (MC, V).
Reader Comments: Nice course, lots of trees, not very forgiving, very mature course ... My home course, always a challenge ... Views from some holes outstanding ... Pleasant park setting, fun layout.

★★ WILDERNESS RESORT & GOLF COURSE
R-511 E. Adams St., P.O. Box 830, Wisconsin Dells, 53965, Sauk County, (608)253-4653, (800)867-9453, 35 miles NW of Madison. **Web:** www.golfwildernesswoods.com.
Holes: 18. **Yards:** 6,700/5,489. **Par:** 71/71. **Course Rating:** 70.8/68.9. **Slope:** 131/122. **Green Fee:** $55/$65. **Cart Fee:** $20/cart. **Walking Policy:** Mandatory cart. **Walkability:** 4. **Opened:** 1997. **Architect:** Art Johnson. **Season:** April-Oct. **High:** June-Aug. **To obtain tee times:** Call up to 30 days in advance. **Miscellaneous:** Reduced fees (weekdays, low season, resort guests, twilight), discount packages, range (grass/mats), club rentals, lodging (380 rooms), credit cards (MC, V, AE, D), beginner friendly (little links).

★★★ WILLOW RUN GOLF CLUB
SP-N12 W26506 Golf Rd., Pewaukee, 53072, Waukesha County, (414)544-8585, 15 miles W of Milwaukee.
Holes: 18. **Yards:** 6,384/5,183. **Par:** 71/71. **Course Rating:** 71.0/70.0. **Slope:** 119/114. **Green Fee:** $27/$31. **Cart Fee:** $26/cart. **Walking Policy:** Walking at certain times. **Walkability:** 2. **Opened:** 1966. **Architect:** Dewey Slocum. **Season:** March-Dec. **High:** June-Sept. **To obtain tee times:** Call up to 7 days in advance. **Miscellaneous:** Reduced fees (weekdays, low season, twilight, seniors, juniors), discount packages, range (grass/mats), club rentals, credit cards (MC, V).
Reader Comments: Not very challenging ... Fun both for women and men ... Wonderful course, good value, nice folks ... Too much traffic ... Open, less challenging, great for outings.

★★ WINAGAMIE GOLF COURSE
SP-3501 Winagamie Dr., Neenah, 54956, Winnebago County, (920)757-5453, 6 miles W of Appleton.
Holes: 18. **Yards:** 6,355/5,422. **Par:** 73/73. **Course Rating:** 69.5/69.9. **Slope:** 115/115. **Green Fee:** $16/$18. **Cart Fee:** $20/cart. **Walking Policy:** Unrestricted walking. **Walkability:** 2. **Opened:** 1963. **Architect:** Julius Jacobson. **Season:** April-Nov. **High:** May-Aug. **To obtain tee times:** Call. **Miscellaneous:** Reduced fees (weekdays, low season, twilight, seniors, juniors), discount packages, range (grass), club rentals, credit cards (MC, V).

WISCONSIN

★★★ WISCONSIN RIVER GOLF CLUB
PU-705 W. River Dr., Stevens Point, 54481, Portage County, (715)344-9152, 100 miles N of Madison.
Holes: 18. **Yards:** 6,695/4,924. **Par:** 72/72. **Course Rating:** 71.9/68.5. **Slope:** 126/118. **Green Fee:** $20/$23. **Cart Fee:** $10/person. **Walking Policy:** Unrestricted walking. **Walkability:** 2. **Opened:** 1961. **Architect:** Larry Roberts. **Season:** April-Nov. **High:** June-Aug. **To obtain tee times:** Call anytime. **Miscellaneous:** Reduced fees (low season, seniors, juniors), metal spikes, range (grass), club rentals, credit cards (MC, V, D).
Reader Comments: Great scenery playing along the Wisconsin River, nice course for your dollars ... Good golf at great prices ... Sweet 18, need to have a good 3- and 5-wood ... Course greatly improved over the years ... Bring the bug spray!

★★½ WOODSIDE COUNTRY CLUB
PU-530 Erie Rd., Green Bay, 54311, Brown County, (920)468-5729.
Holes: 18. **Yards:** 5,817/5,291. **Par:** 71/71. **Course Rating:** 67.6/69.8. **Slope:** 115/115. **Green Fee:** $17/$19. **Cart Fee:** $20/cart. **Walking Policy:** Unrestricted walking. **Walkability:** 3. **Season:** April-Oct. **High:** June-Aug. **To obtain tee times:** Call up to 7 days in advance. **Miscellaneous:** Reduced fees (weekdays, seniors, juniors), metal spikes, club rentals, credit cards (MC, V).
Reader Comments: OK course at a good price ... Front 9 is a lot of fun, could use a little TLC ... Front 9 short, but unusual holes ... Holes No. 4 and No. 8 are great ... Several blind shots.

YAHARA HILLS GOLF COURSE
PM-6701 E. Broadway, Madison, 53718, Dane County, (608)838-3126.
★★★ EAST COURSE
Holes: 18. **Yards:** 7,200/6,115. **Par:** 72/72. **Course Rating:** 71.9/73.4. **Slope:** 116/118. **Green Fee:** $18/$22. **Cart Fee:** $24/cart. **Walking Policy:** Unrestricted walking. **Walkability:** 3. **Opened:** 1967. **Architect:** Art Johnson. **Season:** April-Nov. **High:** April-Aug. **To obtain tee times:** Call 7 days in advance. **Miscellaneous:** Reduced fees (low season, seniors, juniors), metal spikes, range (grass), club rentals, credit cards (MC, V).
Reader Comments: Good for muny course ... Both courses long, wide open, huge greens ... Excellent muny golf. Good test. Outstanding value ... Not interesting ... Fun muny, cheap, pretty easy ... Wide open, usually windy, fair deal ... It all looks the same.
★★½ WEST COURSE
Holes: 18. **Yards:** 7,000/5,705. **Par:** 72/73. **Course Rating:** 71.6/71.4. **Slope:** 118/116. **Green Fee:** $18/$22. **Cart Fee:** $24/cart. **Walking Policy:** Unrestricted walking. **Walkability:** 3. **Opened:** 1967. **Architect:** Art Johnson. **Season:** April-Nov. **High:** April-Aug. **To obtain tee times:** Call 7 days in advance. **Miscellaneous:** Reduced fees (low season, seniors, juniors), metal spikes, range (grass), club rentals, credit cards (MC, V).
Reader Comments: Good low-budget course. More fun than East ... Very nice muny ... Great for my kids ... Nice course, nothing spectacular ... Lots of traffic ... Let it rip ... God's country.

★★½ AIRPORT GOLF CLUB

PU-4801 Central, Cheyenne, 82009, Laramie County, (307)637-6418, 100 miles N of Denver, CO. **E-mail:** mikelepore@msn.com.
Holes: 18. **Yards:** 6,121/5,661. **Par:** 70/74. **Course Rating:** 67.1/69.5. **Slope:** 99/112. **Green Fee:** $14/$14. **Cart Fee:** $18/cart. **Walking Policy:** Unrestricted walking. **Walkability:** 2.
Opened: 1927. **Season:** Year-round. **High:** May-Oct. **To obtain tee times:** Call on Friday for upcoming weekend. **Miscellaneous:** Reduced fees (twilight), range (grass), club rentals, credit cards (MC, V, D).
Reader Comments: One nine with trees and water, the other is flat and open ... Picturesque ... Good, practical course.

★★★ BELL NOB GOLF CLUB

PU-4600 Overdale Dr., Gillette, 82718, Campbell County, (307)686-7069, 140 miles W of Rapid City, SD.
Holes: 18. **Yards:** 7,024/5,555. **Par:** 72/72. **Course Rating:** 70.8/70.6. **Slope:** 119/116. **Green Fee:** $18/$18. **Cart Fee:** $9/person. **Walking Policy:** Unrestricted walking. **Walkability:** 4.
Opened: 1981. **Architect:** Frank Hummel. **Season:** April-Oct. **High:** May-Aug. **To obtain tee times:** Call up to 7 days in advance. **Miscellaneous:** Range (grass), club rentals, credit cards (MC, V).
Reader Comments: Nice ... Lots of wildlife ... Wide open ... Wind can make it a challenge.

★★★★ BUFFALO GOLF CLUB *Value+, Pace+*

PU-P.O. Box 759, Buffalo, 82834, Johnson County, (307)684-5266, 110 miles N of Casper.
Holes: 18. **Yards:** 6,556/5,512. **Par:** 71/72. **Course Rating:** 69.9/70.6. **Slope:** 116/115. **Green Fee:** $20/$20. **Cart Fee:** $19/cart. **Walking Policy:** Unrestricted walking. **Walkability:** 4.
Opened: 1928. **Architect:** Bill Poirot. **Season:** March-Nov. **High:** May-Sept. **To obtain tee times:** Call anytime. **Miscellaneous:** Range (grass/mats), club rentals, credit cards (MC, V).
Reader Comments: Short, but fun ... Good elevation changes ... Mountain view, beautiful old cottonwood trees ...Not much trouble ... Need to update clubhouse ... Lots of wildlife.

CASPER MUNICIPAL GOLF COURSE

PM-2120 Allendale, Casper, 82601, Natrona County, (307)234-2405, 300 miles N of Denver.
Holes: 27. **Green Fee:** $15/$15. **Cart Fee:** $8/person. **Walking Policy:** Unrestricted walking.
Walkability: 3. **Opened:** 1929. **Architect:** Robert Muir Graves. **Season:** March-Oct. **High:** May-Aug. **To obtain tee times:** Call 1 day in advance beginning at 7 a.m. **Miscellaneous:** Metal spikes, range (grass/mats), club rentals.

★★★ HIGHLANDS/LINKS

Yards: 6,562/5,500. **Par:** 71/73. **Course Rating:** 69.7/69.7. **Slope:** 113/118.
Reader Comments: Short, but fun ... Busy ... Good holes ... Challenging.

★★★ HIGHLANDS/PARK

Yards: 6,253/5,492. **Par:** 70/72. **Course Rating:** 68.1/69.3. **Slope:** 108/113.
Reader Comments: Fair and forgiving ... Nice ... Some rough areas ...Will always be my favorite.

★★★ PARK/LINKS

Yards: 6,317/5,384. **Par:** 71/71. **Course Rating:** 68.4/68.8. **Slope:** 108/112.

CHEYENNE COUNTRY CLUB

SP-800 Stinner Rd., Cheyenne, 82001, Laramie County, (307)637-2230, 120 miles N of Denver, Colorado.
Holes: 18. **Yards:** 6,619/5,320. **Par:** 72/73. **Course Rating:** 69.2/70.2. **Slope:** 114/113. **Green Fee:** $24/$50. **Cart Fee:** $19/cart. **Walking Policy:** Unrestricted walking. **Walkability:** 2.
Opened: 1912. **Architect:** Dick Phelps. **Season:** March-Dec. **High:** June-Aug. **To obtain tee times:** Call. **Miscellaneous:** Range (grass/mats), club rentals, credit cards (MC, V).

COTTONWOOD COUNTRY CLUB

PU-West 15th St., Torrington, 82240, Goshen County, (307)532-3868, 198 miles N of Denver.
Holes: 18. **Yards:** 6,298/5,344. **Par:** 72/73. **Course Rating:** 69.9/70.5. **Slope:** 126/127. **Green Fee:** $15/$16. **Cart Fee:** $14/cart. **Walking Policy:** Unrestricted walking. **Walkability:** 1.
Season: Year-round. **High:** May-Aug. **To obtain tee times:** Not needed. **Miscellaneous:** Range (grass), club rentals, credit cards (MC, V), beginner friendly).

★★★ DOUGLAS COMMUNITY CLUB

PU-64 Golf Course Rd., Douglas, 82633, Converse County, (307)358-5099, 50 miles E of Casper.
Holes: 18. **Yards:** 6,253/5,323. **Par:** 71/72. **Course Rating:** 68.4/68.5. **Slope:** 107/103. **Green Fee:** $15/$18. **Cart Fee:** $9/person. **Walking Policy:** Unrestricted walking. **Walkability:** 3.
Opened: 1974. **Architect:** Vern Knisley. **Season:** April-Oct. **High:** June-Aug. **To obtain tee times:** Call Pro Shop. **Miscellaneous:** Reduced fees (weekdays), range (grass/mats), club rentals, credit cards (MC, V), beginner friendly.
Reader Comments: Pretty, wide open ... Short, but a bargain ... Variety ... Beautiful ... Soft greens ... A nice surprise in the middle of nowhere.

WYOMING

★★★ FRANCIS E. WARREN AFB GOLF COURSE
PU-7103 Randall Ave., F.E. Warren AFB, 82005, Laramie County, (307)773-3556, 1 miles NW of Cheyenne.
Holes: 18. **Yards:** 6,652/5,036. **Par:** 72/73. **Course Rating:** 69.6/67.0. **Slope:** 112/111. **Green Fee:** $9/$16. **Cart Fee:** $16/cart. **Walking Policy:** Unrestricted walking. **Walkability:** 1. **Opened:** 1949. **Architect:** U.S. Government. **Season:** Year-round. **High:** April-Oct. **To obtain tee times:** Call 2 days in advance. **Miscellaneous:** Reduced fees (twilight), discount packages, range (grass), club rentals, lodging, credit cards (MC, V).
Reader Comments: Few hazards ... Open fairways ... No. 18 a good challenge ... Lots of antelope on the course.

★★★ GREEN HILLS MUNICIPAL GOLF COURSE
PM-1455 Airport Rd., Worland, 82401, Washakie County, (307)347-8972, 180 miles S of Billings, MT.
Holes: 18. **Yards:** 6,444/5,104. **Par:** 72/72. **Course Rating:** 69.3/68.0. **Slope:** 113/113. **Green Fee:** $16/$18. **Cart Fee:** $16/cart. **Walking Policy:** Unrestricted walking. **Walkability:** 3. **Opened:** 1954. **Architect:** Dennis Smith/Dennis Bower. **Season:** April-Oct. **High:** June-Aug. **To obtain tee times:** Call anytime. **Miscellaneous:** Reduced fees (juniors), range (grass), club rentals, beginner friendly (beginner golf class through local college).
Reader Comments: I played about eight times in a three-week period in July. I arrived fairly early on weekday mornings, without a reserved tee time, and always got a game within 20 minutes ... Old, established and fun ... Easy to score.

★★★★ JACKSON HOLE GOLF & TENNIS CLUB *Service, Pace*
R-5000 Spring Gulch Rd., Jackson, 83001, Teton County, (307)733-3111, 8 miles N of Jackson.
Holes: 18. **Yards:** 7,168/6,036. **Par:** 72/73. **Course Rating:** 72.3/73.2. **Slope:** 133/125. **Green Fee:** $85/$125. **Cart Fee:** Included in Green Fee. **Walking Policy:** Walking at certain times. **Walkability:** 1. **Opened:** 1963. **Architect:** Robert Trent Jones, Jr. **Season:** April-Oct. **High:** June-Aug. **To obtain tee times:** Call anytime with credit card. **Miscellaneous:** Reduced fees (low season, twilight), range (grass), club rentals, credit cards (MC, V, AE).
Notes: Ranked 1st in 1999 Best in State; 40th in 1996 America's Top 75 Upscale Courses.
Reader Comments: Beautiful ... Views, views, views! ... If you visit, play here. Trust me ... Difficult for high-handicappers ... Postcard quality ... Relatively flat ... Tight, but fair ... Perfect setting ... Teton Mountains are breathtaking.

★★½ JACOBY GOLF COURSE
PU-University of Wyoming, Laramie, 82071, Albany County, (307)745-3111, 140 miles N of Denver, CO. **Web:** www.uwyo.edu/jacobygc.
Holes: 18. **Yards:** 6,590/5,480. **Par:** 70/72. **Course Rating:** 69.3/69.3. **Slope:** 114/121. **Green Fee:** $13/$19. **Cart Fee:** $18/cart. **Walking Policy:** Unrestricted walking. **Walkability:** 2. **Opened:** 1932. **Season:** March-Oct. **High:** June-Aug. **To obtain tee times:** Call 1 day in advance. Call on Thursday for all weekend. **Miscellaneous:** Reduced fees (juniors), range (grass), club rentals, credit cards (MC, V), beginner friendly (junior golf, group lessons).
Notes: Rocky Mountain Intercollegiate.
Reader Comments: Wide open ... A little tight ... Nice ... A bargain on I-80.

★★ KENDRICK GOLF COURSE
PU-Big Goose Rd., Sheridan, 82801, Sheridan County, (307)674-8148, 125 miles SE of Billings, MT.
Holes: 18. **Yards:** 6,800/5,549. **Par:** 72/73. **Course Rating:** 71.3/70.8. **Slope:** 116/113. **Green Fee:** $19/$19. **Cart Fee:** $19/cart. **Walking Policy:** Unrestricted walking. **Walkability:** 3. **Opened:** 1940. **Architect:** Edward A. Hunnicutt/Frank Hummel. **Season:** April-Oct. **High:** May-July. **To obtain tee times:** Call one week in advance. **Miscellaneous:** Reduced fees (juniors), range (grass), club rentals, credit cards (MC, V).

LANDER GOLF & COUNTRY CLUB
PU-1 Golf Course Dr., Lander, 82520, (307)332-4653.
Special Notes: Call club for further information.

NEW CASTLE COUNTRY CLUB
SP-2302 W. Main, New Castle, 82701, (307)746-2639.
Special Notes: Call club for further information.

★★★½ OLIVE GLENN GOLF & COUNTRY CLUB
SP-802 Meadow Lane, Cody, 82414, Park County, (307)587-5551, 102 miles S of Billings, MT.
Holes: 18. **Yards:** 6,880/5,654. **Par:** 72/72. **Course Rating:** 71.6/71.2. **Slope:** 124/120. **Green Fee:** $28/$35. **Cart Fee:** $10/person. **Walking Policy:** Unrestricted walking. **Walkability:** 2. **Opened:** 1970. **Architect:** Bob Baldock. **Season:** April-Oct. **High:** June-Aug. **To obtain tee times:** Call up to 7 days in advance. **Miscellaneous:** Reduced fees (juniors), discount packages, range (grass/mats), club rentals, credit cards (MC, V).

WYOMING

Notes: Ranked 5th in 1999 Best in State.
Reader Comments: Enjoyable ... Scenic ... Friendly, unpretentious, challenging ... Beautiful course ... Good value ... Nice scenery ... Windy.

★★★ POWELL COUNTRY CLUB
PU-600 Highway 114, Powell, 82435, Park County, (307)754-7259, 7 miles E of Powell.
Holes: 18. **Yards:** 6,473/5,088. **Par:** 72/72. **Course Rating:** 69.4/67.3. **Slope:** 117/113. **Green Fee:** $14/$18. **Cart Fee:** $18/cart. **Walking Policy:** Unrestricted walking. **Walkability:** 3.
Opened: 1949. **Season:** April-Oct. **High:** June-Sept. **Miscellaneous:** Reduced fees (weekdays, juniors), range (grass), club rentals, credit cards (MC, V).
Reader Comments: Very good ... Two very distinct sides: back nine is hard and front nine is narrow ... Will improve as it matures ... Fun for all.

PURPLE SAGE GOLF CLUB
SP-P.O. Box 755, Evanston, 82930, Uinta County, (307)789-2383, 75 miles E of Salt Lake City, UT.
Holes: 9. **Yards:** 2,960/2,684. **Par:** 36/36. **Course Rating:** 67.5/68.9. **Slope:** 110/119. **Green Fee:** $18/$18. **Cart Fee:** $16/cart. **Walking Policy:** Unrestricted walking. **Walkability:** 3.
Season: April-Oct. **High:** June-Aug. **To obtain tee times:** Call golf shop. **Miscellaneous:** Range (grass/mats), club rentals, credit cards (MC, V).

★★★ RENDEZVOUS MEADOWS GOLF CLUB
PU-55 Clubhouse Rd., Pinedale, 82941, Sublette County, (307)367-4252, 1 miles N of Pinedale.
E-mail: mlauger@wyoming.com.
Holes: 9. **Yards:** 3,255/2,760. **Par:** 36/36. **Course Rating:** 69.8/70.3. **Slope:** 118/118. **Green Fee:** $14/$18. **Cart Fee:** $15/cart. **Walking Policy:** Unrestricted walking. **Walkability:** 2.
Opened: 1985. **Architect:** William Hull. **Season:** April-Oct. **High:** July-Aug. **To obtain tee times:** Call in advance for weekends. Tee times recommended during the week but not mandatory.
Miscellaneous: Reduced fees (weekdays), range (grass), club rentals, credit cards (MC, V), beginner friendly.
Reader Comments: A wonderful 9-hole course worth getting off the beaten trail ... Very good course for beginners ... Great views of mountains ... Very enjoyable.

★★★½ RIVERTON COUNTRY CLUB
SP-4275 Country Club Dr., Riverton, 82501, Fremont County, (307)856-4779, 117 miles W of Casper.
Holes: 18. **Yards:** 7,064/5,549. **Par:** 72/72. **Course Rating:** 72.2/71.0. **Slope:** 128/119. **Green Fee:** $20/$30. **Cart Fee:** $10/person. **Walking Policy:** Unrestricted walking. **Walkability:** 2.
Opened: 1970. **Architect:** Richard Watson. **Season:** March-Oct. **High:** June-Aug. **To obtain tee times:** Call up to 7 days in advance. **Miscellaneous:** Range (grass), club rentals, credit cards (MC, V).
Reader Comments: Fun ... Long and challenging from the tips ... Canal system really comes into play. Lots and lots of water ... Good value.

★★½ SARATOGA INN RESORT
R-P.O. Box 869, 601 East Pic Pike Road, Saratoga, 82331, Carbon County, (307)326-5261, 80 miles W of Laramie.
Holes: 9. **Yards:** 3,425/2,943. **Par:** 36/36. **Course Rating:** 69.7/71.4. **Slope:** 112/113. **Green Fee:** $59/$59. **Cart Fee:** $20/cart. **Walking Policy:** Unrestricted walking. **Walkability:** 1.
Season: May-Oct. **High:** July-Aug. **To obtain tee times:** Tee times are normally required Saturday and Sunday mornings only. **Miscellaneous:** Reduced fees (resort guests), club rentals, lodging (50 rooms), credit cards (MC, V, AE, D), beginner friendly (driving net, putting green).
Reader Comments: Interesting ... A lot of fun ... Climate makes it tough on the course.

SHERIDAN COUNTRY CLUB
SP-1992 West 5th, Sheridan, 82801, (307)674-8135.
Special Notes: Call club for further information.

SINCLAIR GOLF CLUB
SP-Golf Course Road, Sinclair, 82334, Carson County, (307)324-7767, 7 miles E of Rawlins, Wyoming.
Holes: 18. **Yards:** 5,865/5,405. **Par:** 71/72. **Course Rating:** 69.5/68.3. **Slope:** 113/113. **Green Fee:** $16/$18. **Walking Policy:** Unrestricted walking. **Walkability:** 1. **Opened:** 1947. **Season:** April-Oct. **High:** June-Aug. **To obtain tee times:** Call golf shop. **Miscellaneous:** Reduced fees (weekdays), discount packages, range (mats), club rentals, credit cards (MC, V), beginner friendly.

★★★ STAR VALLEY RANCH COUNTRY CLUB
SP-P.O. Box 159, Thayne, 83127, Lincoln County, (307)883-2230, 50 miles S of Jackson, WY.
E-mail: ebuchler@juno.com. **Web:** www.starvalleywy.com/sura/golf.htm.
Holes: 27. **Yards:** 6,446/5,950. **Par:** 73/73. **Course Rating:** 68.7/71.0. **Slope:** 113/121. **Green Fee:** $16/$37. **Cart Fee:** $17/cart. **Walking Policy:** Unrestricted walking. **Walkability:** 3.
Opened: 1970. **Season:** April-Oct. **High:** June-Aug. **To obtain tee times:** Call or come in 4 days

in advance. **Miscellaneous:** Reduced fees (weekdays, twilight), range (grass), club rentals, credit cards (MC, V).
Reader Comments: Beautiful setting ... Lots of neat holes ... Houses too close to fairways ... Took 5 1/2 hours on a weekday.

★★★★ TETON PINES RESORT & COUNTRY CLUB *Service, Pace*
R-3450 Clubhouse Dr., Jackson, 83001, Teton County, (307)733-1733, (800)238-2223, 5 miles W of Jackson. **E-mail:** info@tetonpines.com. **Web:** www.tetonpines.com.
Holes: 18. **Yards:** 7,412/5,486. **Par:** 72/72. **Course Rating:** 74.8/70.1. **Slope:** 137/124. **Green Fee:** $55/$155. **Cart Fee:** Included in Green Fee. **Walking Policy:** Mandatory cart. **Walkability:** 2. **Opened:** 1987. **Architect:** Arnold Palmer/Ed Seay. **Season:** May-Oct. **High:** June-Sept. **To obtain tee times:** Call anytime. **Miscellaneous:** Reduced fees (low season, resort guests, juniors), discount packages, range (grass/mats), caddies, club rentals, lodging (18 rooms), credit cards (MC, V, AE, Diners Club).
Notes: Ranked 4th in 1999 Best in State.
Reader Comments: Beautiful, but expensive ... Great views of Tetons ... Lots of tricky holes with water ... Need a lot of water balls ... Tough for seniors. It's long ... Nice challenge.

★★★ TORRINGTON MUNICIPAL GOLF COURSE
PM-W. 15th. St., Torrington, 82240, Goshen County, (307)532-3868.
Holes: 18. **Yards:** 6,298/5,344. **Par:** 72/73. **Course Rating:** 69.9/70.5. **Slope:** 126/127. **Green Fee:** $15/$16. **Cart Fee:** $14/cart. **Walking Policy:** Unrestricted walking. **Walkability:** 2.
Season: Year-round. **High:** June-Aug. **To obtain tee times:** Call in advance for weekends only.
Miscellaneous: Reduced fees (weekdays), range (grass), club rentals, credit cards (MC, V).
Reader Comments: Very good back nine ... Open front and a tighter back ... Good golf shop.

WHEATLAND GOLF CLUB
PU-1253 E. Coal Rd., Wheatland, 82201, (307)322-3675.
Special Notes: Call club for further information.

★★★ WHITE MOUNTAIN GOLF COURSE
PU-1501 Clubhouse Dr., Rock Springs, 82901, Sweetwater County, (307)352-1415.
Holes: 18. **Yards:** 7,000/5,666. **Par:** 72/73. **Course Rating:** 72.4/73.1. **Slope:** 122/115. **Green Fee:** $15/$15. **Cart Fee:** $15/person. **Walking Policy:** Unrestricted walking. **Walkability:** N/A. **Opened:** 1979. **Architect:** Dick Phelps/Donald G. Brauer. **Season:** April-Oct. **High:** June-Sept. **To obtain tee times:** Call one week in advance. **Miscellaneous:** Reduced fees (juniors), range (grass/mats), club rentals.
Reader Comments: At this altitude, the ball flies ... Good summer weather; friendly players ... Nice course ... Very windy ... I hope not many find it.

Part II

Canada

ALBERTA

BANFF SPRINGS GOLF COURSE
★★★½ **STANLEY THOMPSON 18**
R-One Golf Course Rd., Banff, T0L 0C0, (403)762-6833, 70 miles NW of Calgary. **E-mail:** dwood@bsh.cphotels.ca. **Web:** banffspringsgolf.com.
Holes: 18. **Yards:** 7,072/5,607. **Par:** 71/71. **Course Rating:** 74.4/72.5. **Slope:** 142/139. **Green Fee:** $70/$150. **Cart Fee:** Included in Green Fee. **Walking Policy:** Unrestricted walking. **Walkability:** 3. **Opened:** 1928. **Architect:** Stanley Thompson. **Season:** May-Oct. **High:** July-Sept. **To obtain tee times:** Call or fax with a credit card to guarantee. **Miscellaneous:** Reduced fees (low season, resort guests, juniors), discount packages, range (mats), club rentals, lodging (780 rooms), credit cards (MC, V, AE, D, Diners Club, JCB).
Reader Comments: Incredible views; chipping over elk to the green (a natural hazard)... Let's be honest: Too many elk ... Beautiful rocky mountain course ... Great old course, camera a must.

★★★½ **TUNNEL 9**
R-One Golf Course Rd., Banff, T0L 0C0, (403)762-6833, 70 miles NW of Calgary. **E-mail:** dwood@bsh.cphotels.ca. **Web:** banffspringsgolf.com.
Holes: 9. **Yards:** 3,325/2,806. **Par:** 36/36. **Course Rating:** 73.8/67.0. **Slope:** 134/121. **Green Fee:** N/A. **Cart Fee:** $18/person. **Walking Policy:** Unrestricted walking. **Walkability:** 3. **Opened:** 1989. **Architect:** Bill Robinson. **Season:** May-Oct. **High:** July-Aug.-Sept. **To obtain tee times:** Call or fax with a credit card to guarantee. **Miscellaneous:** Reduced fees (low season), discount packages, range (mats), club rentals, lodging, credit cards (MC, V, AE, D, Diners Club, JCB), beginner friendly (beginner swing classes).
Reader Comments: Terrific course and atmosphere.

★★★½ **BARRHEAD GOLF CLUB**
PU-P.O. Box 4090, Barrhead, T7N 1A1, (780)674-3053, (888)674-3053, 60 miles NW of Edmonton.
Holes: 18. **Yards:** 6,593/5,351. **Par:** 72/72. **Course Rating:** 72.0/71.0. **Slope:** 127/120. **Green Fee:** $15/$25. **Cart Fee:** $24/person. **Walking Policy:** Unrestricted walking. **Walkability:** 3. **Opened:** 1991. **Architect:** Les Furber. **Season:** April-Oct. **High:** June-Aug. **To obtain tee times:** Call 7 days in advance. **Miscellaneous:** Reduced fees (low season, twilight), discount packages, metal spikes, range (grass/mats), club rentals, credit cards (MC, V, AE).
Reader Comments: Jewel of Northern Alberta! ... Good greens.

★★ **BROADMOOR PUBLIC GOLF COURSE**
PU-2025 Oak St., Sherwood Park, T8A 0W9, (403)467-7373, 10 miles E of Edmonton.
Holes: 18. **Yards:** 6,345/5,517. **Par:** 71/71. **Course Rating:** 69.5/70.4. **Slope:** 122/120. **Green Fee:** $23/$25. **Cart Fee:** $24/cart. **Walking Policy:** Unrestricted walking. **Walkability:** 2. **Opened:** 1960. **Architect:** Norman H. Woods. **Season:** April-Oct. **High:** May-June. **To obtain tee times:** Call 3 days in advance. **Miscellaneous:** Reduced fees (weekdays, twilight, seniors, juniors), metal spikes, range (grass/mats), club rentals, credit cards (MC, V, AE).

★★★½ **CANMORE GOLF & CURLING CLUB**
SP-2000 8th Ave., Canmore, T1W 1A2, Canada County, (403)678-4785, 55 miles W of Calgary. **E-mail:** canpro@telusplanet.net.
Holes: 18. **Yards:** 6,309/5,258. **Par:** 71/72. **Course Rating:** 69.1/68.7. **Slope:** 122/119. **Green Fee:** $45/$45. **Cart Fee:** $17/cart. **Walking Policy:** Unrestricted walking. **Walkability:** 3. **Opened:** 1961. **Architect:** Bill Newis. **Season:** April-Oct. **High:** June-Aug. **To obtain tee times:** Resort guests and golf packages book starting April 1st. Public call 3 days in advance. **Miscellaneous:** Reduced fees (low season, resort guests, juniors), range (mats), club rentals, credit cards (MC, V, AE).
Reader Comments: Underrated mountain course ... Old cabin for a pro shop has real charm ... Nice mountain course ... Unsung gem ... Enjoyable day–good value ... Greens awesome ... A nice country course ... Scenery is otherworldly. Tough to bring eyes back to fairway ... Great small-town course in mountain setting ... Very scenic and reasonably priced.

★★★★ **COLONIALE GOLF & COUNTRY CLUB**
SP-10 Country Club Dr., Beaumont, T4X 1M1, (780)929-4653, 2 miles S of Edmonton. **E-mail:** cgcc@telusplanet.net.
Holes: 18. **Yards:** 7,020/5,344. **Par:** 72/72. **Course Rating:** 73.8/72.1. **Slope:** 145/126. **Green Fee:** $30/$48. **Cart Fee:** Included in Green Fee. **Walking Policy:** Mandatory cart. **Walkability:** 3. **Opened:** 1993. **Architect:** Bill Newis. **Season:** April-Oct. **High:** May-Sept. **To obtain tee times:** Call 4 days in advance with credit card to guarantee and 24-hour cancellation. **Miscellaneous:** Reduced fees (weekdays, low season, twilight, seniors, juniors), discount packages, range (grass/mats), club rentals, credit cards (MC, V).

Reader Comments: Real test of golf. You will use every club and all of your wits to score well ... Very nice layout ... Best public access course in Edmonton area ... Gets better every year ... Nice layout and the best tee boxes ... Great variety, great people ... Bring your 'A' game ... Interesting and challenging. Great value ... Strategic locations of hazards, tough and beautiful.

★★★ CONNAUGHT GOLF CLUB

SP-2802 13th Ave. S.E., Medicine Hat, T1A 3P9, (403)526-0737, 185 miles E of Calgary.
Holes: 18. **Yards:** 6,993/5,800. **Par:** 72/73. **Course Rating:** 74.0/73.5. **Slope:** 128/126. **Green Fee:** $32/$32. **Cart Fee:** $25/cart. **Walking Policy:** Unrestricted walking. **Walkability:** 2. **Architect:** A.L. (Ron) Ehlert. **Season:** April-Oct. **High:** June-Aug. **To obtain tee times:** Nonmembers may call 1 day in advance for weekdays, and Thursdays for upcoming weekend. **Miscellaneous:** Reduced fees (low season, juniors), range (mats), club rentals, credit cards (MC, V, AE), beginner friendly (beginner swing, junior program).
Reader Comments: Nice course ... This course is one of the best in southern Alberta .... It offers the best for all levels of golfers ... It is not too hard and not too easy ... On a beautiful day, the course is impeccable. On a windy day, it is impossible ... The pro shop and pros are amazing ... The best junior program south of Calgary.

★★★½ COTTONWOOD GOLF & COUNTRY CLUB

SP-Box 28, Site 2, RR #1, DeWinton, TOL OXO, (403)938-7200, 10 miles SE of Calgary.
Holes: 18. **Yards:** 6,747/5,054. **Par:** 72/72. **Course Rating:** 72.5/67.5. **Slope:** 129/118. **Green Fee:** N/A/$50. **Cart Fee:** $25/person. **Walking Policy:** Unrestricted walking. **Walkability:** 2. **Opened:** 1990. **Architect:** Bill Newis. **Season:** April-Oct. **High:** June-July. **To obtain tee times:** Call 4 days in advance starting at noon. **Miscellaneous:** Reduced fees (twilight, juniors), range (grass/mats), club rentals, credit cards (MC, V, AE).
Reader Comments: Nice family course ... Great layout, great practice area ... Island green ... Service is good.

COUNTRYSIDE GOLF COURSE

PU-51466 Range Rd. 232, Sherwood Park, T8B 1L1, (780)467-9254, 6 miles SE of Edmonton.
E-mail: golf@apexmail.com.
Holes: 27. **Green Fee:** $24/$29. **Cart Fee:** $24/cart. **Walking Policy:** Unrestricted walking. **Walkability:** 2. **Opened:** 1986. **Architect:** Solomon. **Season:** April-Oct. **High:** May-Oct. **To obtain tee times:** Call up to 5 days in advance for weekdays. Call on Monday for upcoming weekend or holiday. **Miscellaneous:** Reduced fees (weekdays, seniors, juniors), discount packages, range (grass/mats), club rentals, credit cards (MC, V, AE).
MEADOWS/PRAIRIES
Yards: 6,980/5,874. **Par:** 73/72. **Course Rating:** 69.5/N/A. **Slope:** 113/N/A.
MEADOWS/WOODLANDS
Yards: 6,221/5,328. **Par:** 72/72. **Course Rating:** N/A. **Slope:** N/A.
WOODLAND/PRAIRIES
Yards: 6,447/5,520. **Par:** 73/72. **Course Rating:** N/A. **Slope:** N/A.

★★★★ D'ARCY RANCH GOLF CLUB

PU-Hwy. 29 and Milligan Dr., Okotoks, TOL 1T0, (403)938-4455, (800)803-8810, 14 miles S of Calgary.
Holes: 18. **Yards:** 6,919/5,529. **Par:** 72/73. **Course Rating:** 72.3/71.3. **Slope:** 126/122. **Green Fee:** $50/$50. **Cart Fee:** $26/cart. **Walking Policy:** Unrestricted walking. **Walkability:** 4. **Opened:** 1991. **Architect:** Finger/Dye/Spann. **Season:** April-Oct. **High:** May-Sept. **To obtain tee times:** Outside of province, call 7 days in advance. Local, call 2 days in advance. Call Thursday at 7 a.m. for weekends and holidays. **Miscellaneous:** Reduced fees (twilight), range (grass/mats), club rentals, credit cards (MC, V, AE).
Reader Comments: Tough when windy. Nice staff ... One of my favorite local clubs ... An excellent setup ... Challenging public course ... Great course ... Really enjoyed this course ... Good value ... Really like the layout, it's always in good shape.

★★★ DINOSAUR TRAIL GOLF & COUNTRY CLUB

PU-P.O. Box 1511, Drumheller, T0J 0Y0, (403)823-5622, 110 miles NE of Calgary.
Holes: 18. **Yards:** 6,401/5,093. **Par:** 72/73. **Course Rating:** 71.2/68.4. **Slope:** 135/110. **Green Fee:** $32/$32. **Cart Fee:** $25/cart. **Walking Policy:** Unrestricted walking. **Walkability:** 5. **Opened:** 1995. **Architect:** Sid Puddicombe. **Season:** May-Oct. **High:** June-Aug. **To obtain tee times:** Call up to 14 days in advance. Credit card required for 3 or more players. **Miscellaneous:** Reduced fees (seniors, juniors), range (grass/mats), club rentals, credit cards (MC, V).
Reader Comments: Back 9 is 'world's toughest hole' a calendar come to life ... Very unique layout in the Canadian badlands. Small town service and charm. A real joy.... Two different 9s ... Back nine is worth the drive ... Alberta's Arizona ... The back nine is difficult but most memorable. A must play for back hills ... Courteous staff, a very enjoyable course.

CANADA

★★★ THE DUNES GOLF & WINTER CLUB
PU-RR #1, Site 4, Box 1, Grande Prairie, T8V 5N3, (403)538-4333, (888)224-2252. **E-mail:** dunes@telusplanet.net.
Holes: 18. **Yards:** 6,418/5,274. **Par:** 71/72. **Course Rating:** 69.3/70.1. **Slope:** 124/123. **Green Fee:** $20/$28. **Cart Fee:** $24/cart. **Walking Policy:** Unrestricted walking. **Walkability:** 3.
Opened: 1992. **Architect:** Mel Watchhorn. **Season:** March-Oct. **High:** April-Sept. **To obtain tee times:** Call up to 14 days in advance with credit card. Call 1 day in advance for weekdays. Call Friday for upcoming weekend or holiday. **Miscellaneous:** Reduced fees (low season, seniors), discount packages, range (grass/mats), club rentals, credit cards (MC, V, AE).
Reader Comments: Maturing nicely ... Great layout ... The clubhouse is big and spacious with a very friendly staff and the prices are reasonable.

★½ EAGLE ROCK GOLF COURSE
PU-TWP 510, RR 234, South Edmonton, T6H 4N6, (780)464-4653, 5 miles SE of Edmonton.
Holes: 18. **Yards:** 6,660/5,644. **Par:** 71/71. **Course Rating:** 72.0/71.4. **Slope:** 123/121. **Green Fee:** $19/$30. **Cart Fee:** $24/cart. **Walking Policy:** Unrestricted walking. **Walkability:** 3.
Opened: 1990. **Architect:** Sid Puddicome. **Season:** April-Nov. **High:** June-Aug. **To obtain tee times:** Call 7 days in advance. **Miscellaneous:** Reduced fees (weekdays, twilight, seniors, juniors), range (grass), club rentals, credit cards (MC, V), beginner friendly (4 sets of tees).

★★★½ GOOSE HUMMOCK GOLF RESORT
PU-P.O. Box 1221, Gibbons, T0A 1N0, Canada County, (780)921-2444, 10 miles N of Edmonton.
E-mail: goosehum@telusplanet.net. **Web:** www.golfthegoose.com.
Holes: 18. **Yards:** 6,604/5,408. **Par:** 71/71. **Course Rating:** 72.5/71.5. **Slope:** 135/121. **Green Fee:** $27/$34. **Cart Fee:** $24/cart. **Walking Policy:** Unrestricted walking. **Walkability:** 2.
Opened: 1989. **Architect:** Bill Robinson. **Season:** April-Oct. **High:** June-Aug. **To obtain tee times:** Call 14 days in advance with credit card, or 2 days in advance without credit card. **Miscellaneous:** Reduced fees (twilight, seniors, juniors), metal spikes, range (grass/mats), club rentals, credit cards (MC, V, AE), beginner friendly (private and corporate lesson packages).
Reader Comments: Very challenging ... Beautiful in September! ... Most difficult course in area. Interesting holes ... Used eight clubs on tee shots, course management a must.

★★½ HENDERSON LAKE GOLF CLUB
PU-S. Parkside Dr., Lethbridge, T1J 4A2, (403)329-6767, 120 miles S of Calgary.
Holes: 18. **Yards:** 6,512/5,976. **Par:** 70/75. **Course Rating:** 70.5/73.1. **Slope:** 120/123. **Green Fee:** $30/$30. **Cart Fee:** $24/cart. **Walking Policy:** Unrestricted walking. **Walkability:** 1.
Opened: 1917. **Architect:** Norman H. Woods. **Season:** April-Oct. **High:** May-Aug. **To obtain tee times:** Call two days in advance. **Miscellaneous:** Reduced fees (low season, twilight, juniors), discount packages, metal spikes, club rentals, credit cards (MC, V).
Reader Comments: Well taken care of. Fall golf can be challenging due to leaves ... Good old track ... Flat track ... Good condition.

HERITAGE POINTE GOLF & COUNTRY CLUB
R-R.R. No.1, Heritage Pointe Dr., De Winton, T0L 0X0, (403)256-2002, 6 miles S of Calgary.
E-mail: inform@heritagepointe.com. **Web:** www.heritagepointe.com.
Holes: 27. **Green Fee:** N/A/$75. **Cart Fee:** Included in Green Fee. **Walking Policy:** Unrestricted walking. **Walkability:** 5. **Opened:** 1992. **Architect:** Ron Garl. **Season:** April-Oct. **High:** June-Aug. **To obtain tee times:** Call 7 days in advance with credit card. **Miscellaneous:** Reduced fees (twilight, seniors, juniors), discount packages, range (grass), club rentals, credit cards (MC, V, AE, Diners Club), beginner friendly (3-hole practice facility).
★★★★ DESERT/HERITAGE
Yards: 7,044/4,967. **Par:** 72/73. **Course Rating:** 74.0/68.0. **Slope:** 128/129.
Reader Comments: Excellent service ... With 3 9s it offers a terrific test, some tough greens when the wind blows ... A great links course ... Outstanding service, gorgeous views, tough holes ... Best first tee I have ever played ... Scenery from forest to prairie foothills is nice ... Terrific greens, great views from Heritage and Pointe courses.
★★★★ POINTE/DESERT
Yards: 6,936/4,944. **Par:** 72/72. **Course Rating:** 73.0/67.0. **Slope:** 131/125.
Reader Comments: A must play when in Calgary ... Desert 9 brutal in wind ... Service is good ... Best golf course in Western Canada ... Very challenging.
★★★★ POINTE/HERITAGE
Yards: 6,904/4,773. **Par:** 72/73. **Course Rating:** 73.0/66.0. **Slope:** 137/128.
Reader Comments: Great shape, a little pricey ... Pointe/Heritage best combo ... Target golf at its best ... Picturesque ... Local knowledge a big help...Spectacular.

HINTON GOLF CLUB
PU-Hwy. 16 W., Hinton, T7V 1Y2, (403)865-2904, 175 miles W of Edmonton.
Holes: 18. **Yards:** 6,729/5,700. **Par:** 72/72. **Course Rating:** 72.0/70.0. **Slope:** 125/N/A. **Green Fee:** $27/$27. **Cart Fee:** $24/cart. **Walking Policy:** Unrestricted walking. **Walkability:** 3.

Opened: 1964. Architect: N/A. Season: April-Oct. High: May-Aug. To obtain tee times: Call anytime. Miscellaneous: Reduced fees (twilight, juniors), discount packages, metal spikes, range (grass/mats), club rentals, credit cards (MC, V, AE).

★★½ INDIAN LAKES GOLF CLUB
PU-Hwy 60 South of Hwy 16, Enoch, T7X 3Y3, (780)470-4653, 6 miles N of Edmonton. Web: www.indianlakes.ab.ca.com.
Holes: 18. Yards: 6,650/5,600. Par: 71/71. Course Rating: 69.5/67.0. Slope: 128/128. Green Fee: $23/$26. Cart Fee: $24/cart. Walking Policy: Unrestricted walking. Walkability: 2. Opened: 1989. Architect: William G. Robinson. Season: April-Oct. High: June-Aug. To obtain tee times: Call 2 days in advance. Miscellaneous: Reduced fees (seniors, juniors), range (grass), club rentals, credit cards (MC, V, AE, Debit or Interac).
Reader Comments: Very natural layout, great variety ... Good layout, could use more care, great potential.

★★★ IRONHEAD GOLF & COUNTRY CLUB
PU-P.O. Box 69, Wabamun, T0E 2K0, (780)892-4653, 30 miles W of Edmonton, Alberta.
Holes: 18. Yards: 6,805/5,442. Par: 72/72. Course Rating: 72.0/70.4. Slope: 132/124. Green Fee: $20/$25. Cart Fee: $22/cart. Walking Policy: Unrestricted walking. Walkability: 4. Opened: 1987. Architect: Les Furber. Season: April-Oct. High: June-Aug. Miscellaneous: Reduced fees (weekdays, juniors), discount packages, metal spikes, range (grass), club rentals, credit cards (MC, V, AE).
Reader Comments: Great layout, condition of course improving ... Beautiful course ... Tee boxes are so good, they could be the greens on some courses! Fantastic.

★★★★½ JASPER PARK LODGE GOLF COURSE *Value*
R-Box 40, Jasper, T0E 1E0, (780)852-6089, 210 miles W of Edmonton. E-mail: pcooper@jpl.cphotels.ca.
Holes: 18. Yards: 6,663/5,935. Par: 71/75. Course Rating: 70.5/73.5. Slope: 121/122. Green Fee: $40/$69. Cart Fee: $16/person. Walking Policy: Unrestricted walking. Walkability: 3. Opened: 1925. Architect: Stanley Thompson. Season: April-Oct. High: June-Sept. To obtain tee times: Call anytime. Miscellaneous: Reduced fees (low season, twilight, juniors), discount packages, metal spikes, range (grass/mats), club rentals, lodging, credit cards (MC, V, AE, D, Diners Club, JCB).
Reader Comments: A must in Canada ... Played in Oct. still in Aug. shape ... Great value, tough but fair ... Beautiful setting, elk & geese have right of way ... Bears too! ... Beautiful scenery, great resort in mountains... Beautiful spot, nice lodge, nature at its best.

KANANASKIS COUNTRY GOLF CLUB *Service*
R-P.O. Box 1710, Kananaskis Village, T0L 2H0, (403)591-7070, 50 miles SW of Calgary.
★★★★½ MT. KIDD COURSE *Value*
Holes: 18. Yards: 7,083/5,539. Par: 72/72. Course Rating: 72.8/71.5. Slope: 134/127. Green Fee: $40/$60. Cart Fee: $14/person. Walking Policy: Unrestricted walking. Walkability: 3. Opened: 1983. Architect: Robert Trent Jones Sr. Season: May-Oct. High: June-Sept. To obtain tee times: Call up to 60 days in advance with credit card. Miscellaneous: Reduced fees (twilight, seniors, juniors), metal spikes, range (grass/mats), club rentals, lodging, credit cards (MC, V, AE).
Reader Comments: Golf heaven ... A jewel! ... Even better than my 1985 Pebble Beach round. Located in the Canadian Rockies ... What a view; unbeatable on a clear day; a bit of a walk between tees and greens ... Great mountain course ... Well bunkered ... Spectacular mountain view ... Great place, but windy ... Stay in the fairway or pay.
★★★★½ MT. LORETTE COURSE *Value+*
Holes: 18. Yards: 7,102/5,429. Par: 72/72. Course Rating: 74.1/69.8. Slope: 137/123. Green Fee: $40/$60. Cart Fee: $14/person. Walking Policy: Unrestricted walking. Walkability: 2. Opened: 1983. Architect: Robert Trent Jones Sr. Season: May-Oct. High: June-Sept. To obtain tee times: Call up to 60 days in advance with credit card. Miscellaneous: Reduced fees (twilight, seniors, juniors), metal spikes, range (grass/mats), club rentals, lodging, credit cards (MC, V, AE).
Reader Comments: Don't miss it! ... Courses/staff/condition/location A+++ ... Flatter than Kidd but no less challenging; lots of water in play ... Best in Western Canada ... Intimidating ... Better of two courses, more water, better target golf ... The ultimate in majestic Rockies!

★★★ LAKESIDE GREENS GOLF & COUNTRY CLUB
SP-555 Lakeside Greens Dr., Chestermere, T1X 1O5, (403)569-9111, 4 miles E of Calgary.
Holes: 18. Yards: 6,804/5,063. Par: 71/71. Course Rating: 72.5/68.8. Slope: 134/118. Green Fee: $30/$37. Cart Fee: $24/cart. Walkability: 1. Opened: 1992. Architect: Bill Newis. Season: April-Oct. High: June-Aug. To obtain tee times: Call 5 days in advance for weekdays. Call on Thursday at 7 a.m. for upcoming weekend. Miscellaneous: Reduced fees (weekdays, twilight, seniors, juniors), metal spikes, range (mats), credit cards (MC, V, AE, Debit Card).
Reader Comments: A fun course to play; houses a little close on a few holes ... Variety, tough, plenty of water on back nine.

★★½ LAND-O-LAKES GOLF CLUB
SP-102 Fairway Dr., Coaldale, T1M 1H1, (403)345-2582, 6 miles E of Lethbridge.
Holes: 18. **Yards:** 6,459/5,634. **Par:** 71/72. **Course Rating:** 72.0/73.0. **Slope:** 119/126. **Green Fee:** $24/$28. **Cart Fee:** $20/person. **Walking Policy:** Unrestricted walking. **Walkability:** 3. **Opened:** 1987. **Architect:** Les Furber. **Season:** April-Oct. **High:** May-Sept. **To obtain tee times:** Call 2 days in advance. **Miscellaneous:** Reduced fees (weekdays, juniors), discount packages, range (grass/mats), club rentals, credit cards (MC, V, Interac).
Reader Comments: Well maintained, many water hazards. Make sure you have extra balls and a ball retriever. Too many houses ... Well–treated, beautiful course ... Good muny type course.

★★★ THE LINKS AT SPRUCE GROVE
PU-Calahoo Rd., Spruce Grove, T7X 3B4, (780)962-4653, 10 miles W of Edmonton.
Holes: 18. **Yards:** 6,767/5,748. **Par:** 72/72. **Course Rating:** 71.0/72.0. **Slope:** 125/126. **Green Fee:** $28/$33. **Cart Fee:** $26/cart. **Walking Policy:** Unrestricted walking. **Walkability:** 3. **Opened:** 1983. **Architect:** Bill Robinson. **Season:** April-Oct. **High:** June-Aug. **To obtain tee times:** Call 2 days in advance. **Miscellaneous:** Reduced fees (weekdays, low season, twilight, seniors, juniors), metal spikes, range (grass/mats), club rentals, credit cards (MC, V).
Reader Comments: Very nice layout and friendly staff ... Long and tough ... Very good prairie course ... Helpful pro shop.

THE LINKS OF GLENEAGLES
PU-100 GlenEagles Dr., Cochrane, T0L 0W1, (403)932-1086, 9 miles W of Calgary. **Web:** www.golfcanada.com.
Holes: 18. **Yards:** 7,019/5,222. **Par:** 72/72. **Course Rating:** 73.1/70.5. **Slope:** 136/124. **Green Fee:** $40/$60. **Cart Fee:** $26/cart. **Walking Policy:** Unrestricted walking. **Walkability:** 4. **Opened:** 1998. **Architect:** Les Furber. **Season:** April-Oct. **High:** May-Oct. **To obtain tee times:** Bookings available 60 days in advance by phone. **Miscellaneous:** Reduced fees (low season, twilight, juniors), range (grass), club rentals, credit cards (MC, V, AE, Debit).

★★★ MAPLE RIDGE GOLF COURSE
1240 Mapleglade Dr. S.E., Calgary, (403)974-1825
Yards: N/A. **Par:** N/A. **Course Rating:** N/A. **Slope:** N/A. **Green Fee:** N/A. **Walkability:** N/A. **Miscellaneous:** Metal spikes.
Reader Comments: A good, in-demand public course ... Very good public course. Good value ... Pleasant and reasonable ... Challenging for lower handicaps yet easy enough for a beginner to enjoy ... Nice mixture of water, trees.

★★ MCCALL LAKE GOLF COURSE
PU-1600 32nd Ave. N.E., Calgary, T2P 2M5, (403)291-3596.
Holes: 18. **Yards:** 6,788/5,568. **Par:** 71/71. **Course Rating:** 71.3/71.7. **Slope:** 121/127. **Green Fee:** $26/$26. **Cart Fee:** $25/cart. **Walking Policy:** Unrestricted walking. **Walkability:** 2. **Opened:** 1982. **Architect:** Bill Newis. **Season:** April-Oct. **High:** April-Sept. **Miscellaneous:** Reduced fees (twilight), metal spikes, range (mats), credit cards (MC, V, Debit), beginner friendly. **Special Notes:** Also has 9-hole par 3.

★★★½ MCKENZIE MEADOWS GOLF CLUB
PU-17215 McKenzie Meadows Dr. SE, Calgary, T2H 0J9, (403)257-2255.
Holes: 18. **Yards:** 6,508/5,132. **Par:** 72/72. **Course Rating:** 70.5/67.8. **Slope:** 124/116. **Green Fee:** $37/$39. **Cart Fee:** $25/cart. **Walking Policy:** Unrestricted walking. **Walkability:** 3. **Opened:** 1996. **Architect:** Gary Browning & Associates. **Season:** April-Oct. **High:** June-Sept. **To obtain tee times:** Call up to 3 days in advance. **Miscellaneous:** Reduced fees (weekdays, twilight), range (grass), club rentals, credit cards (MC, V, AE).
Reader Comments: Shot my best round ever ... A very short course; takes the driver out of play ... Lots of dogleg holes. Plenty of water and sand. This course can make you feel and play like a real pro ... Great new course, play often, best round ever here ... A very good public course for the average golfer.

★★½ MEDICINE HAT GOLF & COUNTRY CLUB
SP-P.O. Box 232, Medicine Hat, T1A 7E9, (403)527-8086, 180 miles SW of Calgary.
Holes: 18. **Yards:** 6,612/5,606. **Par:** 72/72. **Course Rating:** 72.5/72.5. **Slope:** 131/123. **Green Fee:** $30/$30. **Cart Fee:** $25/cart. **Walking Policy:** Unrestricted walking. **Walkability:** 2. **Opened:** 1933. **Architect:** Tom Bendelow. **Season:** April-Oct. **To obtain tee times:** Call 2 days in advance. **Miscellaneous:** Reduced fees (low season, twilight), range (mats), club rentals, credit cards (MC, V, AE, D).
Reader Comments: Great course ... Very scenic ... Beautiful course, well cared for ... Treelined fairways and large greens ... Can't get into a lot of trouble.

★★ OLDS GOLF CLUB
PU-R.R. #1, Site 2, Box 13, Olds, T4H 1P2, (403)556-8008, (800)310-9297, 45 miles N of Calgary.

Holes: 18. Yards: 6,662/5,886. Par: 72/73. Course Rating: 70.4/72.5. Slope: 121/121. Green Fee: $24/$28. Cart Fee: $25/cart. Walking Policy: Unrestricted walking. Walkability: 3. Opened: 1982. Season: May-Oct. High: June-Aug. To obtain tee times: Call on Wednesday for upcoming weekend or holiday. Call on Friday for following week. Miscellaneous: Reduced fees (weekdays, juniors), metal spikes, range (grass), club rentals, credit cards (MC, V, Debit Cards).

★★★★ PARADISE CANYON GOLF & RESORT
R-185 Canyon Blvd., Lethbridge, T1K 6V1, (403)381-7500, (877)707-GOLF, 120 miles S of Calgary.
Holes: 18. Yards: 6,810/5,282. Par: 71/71. Course Rating: 73.1/70.6. Slope: 132/127. Green Fee: $25/$45. Cart Fee: $30/cart. Walking Policy: Unrestricted walking. Walkability: 4. Opened: 1992. Architect: Bill Newis. Season: March-Nov. High: June-Sept. To obtain tee times: Call 3 days in advance. Miscellaneous: Reduced fees (weekdays, low season, twilight), range (grass/mats), club rentals, lodging (50 rooms), credit cards (MC, V, AE).
Reader Comments: Shotmaker's dream. Nice people ... Very nice course, great practice facility ... Narrow fairways. Tough lies ... Very challenging, stay out of the moguls, scenic views throughout the entire course ... Good course ... Excellent, take your choice of difficulty ... Beautiful greens, tee boxes, fairways, views!

★★★ PHEASANTBACK GOLF & COUNTRY CLUB
PU-P.O. Box 1625, Stettler, T0C 2L0, (403)742-4653, 5 miles N of Stettler.
Holes: 18. Yards: 6,104/4,631. Par: 71/71. Course Rating: 70.0/67.5. Slope: 127/113. Green Fee: $25/$30. Cart Fee: $25/cart. Walking Policy: Unrestricted walking. Walkability: 5. Opened: 1995. Architect: Bill Robinson. Season: April-Oct. High: June-Aug. To obtain tee times: Call 1 week in advance. Miscellaneous: Reduced fees (low season, resort guests, twilight, seniors, juniors), discount packages, metal spikes, range (grass), club rentals, credit cards (MC, V).
Reader Comments: A fun course ... Hidden jewel ... A course that should be played at least 2 times to best figure out both the layout and the trouble spots ... Lots of water but fair ... A great course.

★★½ PICTURE BUTTE GOLF & WINTER CLUB
SP-P.O. Box 359, Picture Butte, T0K 1V0, (403)732-4157, 20 miles N of Lethbridge.
Holes: 18. Yards: 6,390/5,127. Par: 72/73. Course Rating: 70.5/71.5. Slope: 116/122. Green Fee: $13/$25. Cart Fee: $25/cart. Walking Policy: Unrestricted walking. Walkability: 2. Opened: 1963. Architect: Les Furber/Jim Eremko. Season: March-Oct. High: May-Sept. To obtain tee times: Call 1 day in advance for weekday play, 5 days in advance for weekend play. Miscellaneous: Reduced fees (weekdays, low season, twilight, seniors, juniors), metal spikes, range (grass), club rentals, credit cards (MC, V, Intac).
Reader Comments: Ash hole is our favorite ... Beautiful course ... Course in great shape ... Short course ... Very enjoyable.

★★★ PONOKA COMMUNITY GOLF COURSE
PU-P.O. Box 4145, Ponoka, T4J 1R5, (403)783-4626, 60 miles S of Edmonton.
Holes: 18. Yards: 6,500/5,800. Par: 72/72. Course Rating: 69.9/72.4. Slope: 121/131. Green Fee: $23/$27. Cart Fee: $25/cart. Walking Policy: Unrestricted walking. Walkability: 3. Opened: 1987. Architect: William G. Robinson. Season: April-Oct. High: June-Aug. To obtain tee times: Call 2 days in advance for weekdays. Call Thursday for upcoming weekend. Call anytime in advance with credit card. Miscellaneous: Metal spikes, credit cards (MC, V, AE).
Reader Comments: Great golf, back nine fantastic ... Hard course, have to have a good short game ... Liked this course, return at least once a year ... A very nice natural course with changes in elevation ... Worth a stop.

★★★½ THE RANCH GOLF & COUNTRY CLUB
SP-52516 Range Rd. 262, Spruce Grove, T7Y 1A5, (780)470-4700, 3 miles W of Edmonton.
Holes: 18. Yards: 6,526/5,082. Par: 71/71. Course Rating: 70.4/70.7. Slope: 129/124. Green Fee: $29/$37. Cart Fee: $26/cart. Walking Policy: Unrestricted walking. Walkability: 3. Opened: 1989. Architect: Western Golf. Season: April-Oct. High: May-Sept. To obtain tee times: Call 2 days in advance. Miscellaneous: Reduced fees (weekdays, low season, twilight, juniors), range (mats), club rentals, credit cards (MC, V, AE).
Reader Comments: Enjoyable short course ... A great track, three great finishing holes ... Variety of holes, challenging for everyone.

★★★★ REDWOOD MEADOWS GOLF & COUNTRY CLUB   Pace
SP-Box 1 Site 7 R.R.No.1, Calgary, T2P 2G4, (403)949-3663.
Holes: 18. Yards: 7,000/6,108. Par: 72/73. Course Rating: 72.7/74.0. Slope: 129/134. Green Fee: $50/$50. Cart Fee: $28/cart. Walking Policy: Unrestricted walking. Walkability: 2. Opened: 1976. Architect: Stan Leonard. Season: April-Oct. High: May-Sept. To obtain tee times: Call three days in advance for weekdays only. Miscellaneous: Reduced fees (juniors), range (grass), club rentals, credit cards (MC, V, AE, Debit).

CANADA

Reader Comments: Rustic country setting–hard course ... Great natural beauty ... My favorite course in the Calgary area; long from the tips with lots of woods ... Very imaginative design ... Free range balls ... Beautiful foothills course, well kept, challenging.

★★★ RIVER BEND GOLF & RECREATION AREA
PU-P.O. Box 157, Red Deer, T4N 5E8, Red Deer County, (403)343-8311, 4 miles N of Red Deer.
E-mail: riverbend@reddeer.net. **Web:** www.riverbend.reddeer.net.
Holes: 18. **Yards:** 6,700/5,514. **Par:** 72/72. **Course Rating:** 71.9/70.4. **Slope:** 129/119. **Green Fee:** $29/$31. **Cart Fee:** $26/cart. **Walking Policy:** Unrestricted walking. **Walkability:** 1. **Opened:** 1986. **Architect:** Bill Robinson. **Season:** April-Oct. **High:** June-Aug. **To obtain tee times:** Booking 6 days in advance. **Miscellaneous:** Reduced fees (juniors), range (grass/mats), club rentals, credit cards (MC, V, Debit), beginner friendly (9-hole mini-links, range and practice area).
Reader Comments: An excellent course–good greens ... Good variety of golf holes ...Wide fairways, large greens, several water holes ... A challenging, interesting course in a pretty setting.

★★½ RIVERSIDE GOLF COURSE
PU-8630 Rowland Rd., Edmonton, T6A 3X1, (780)496-8702.
Holes: 18. **Yards:** 6,306/5,984. **Par:** 71/75. **Course Rating:** 71.0/74.0. **Slope:** 114/N/A. **Green Fee:** $24/$27. **Cart Fee:** $20/cart. **Walking Policy:** Unrestricted walking. **Walkability:** N/A. **Opened:** 1951. **Season:** April-Oct. **High:** May-Aug. **To obtain tee times:** Call two days in advance. **Miscellaneous:** Reduced fees (low season), metal spikes, club rentals, credit cards (MC, V).
Reader Comments: Best public course in area ... Caters to average golfer ... New tee boxes last season, Very popular course ... Old-style golf, very mature, well treed ... Strong finish.

★★ SHAGANAPPI POINT GOLF COURSE
PM-1200-26 St. S.W., Calgary, T2P 2M5, (403)974-1810, 2 miles W of Downtown Calgary.
Holes: 27. **Yards:** 5,195/N/A. **Par:** 68/N/A. **Course Rating:** 66.1/N/A. **Slope:** 112/N/A. **Green Fee:** N/A. **Cart Fee:** $26/cart. **Walking Policy:** Unrestricted walking. **Walkability:** 3. **Opened:** 1917. **Season:** April-Oct. **High:** May-July. **To obtain tee times:** Call 4 days in advance. **Miscellaneous:** Reduced fees (twilight, seniors, juniors), metal spikes, range (mats), club rentals, credit cards (MC, V, Debit Card).

★★½ SHAW-NEE SLOPES GOLF COURSE
SP-820 James McKevitt Rd. S.W., Calgary, T2Y2E7, (403)256-1444.
Holes: 18. **Yards:** 6,478/5,691. **Par:** 72/72. **Course Rating:** 70.5/71.0. **Slope:** 122/123. **Green Fee:** $35/$38. **Cart Fee:** $26/cart. **Walking Policy:** Unrestricted walking. **Walkability:** 3. **Opened:** 1965. **Architect:** R.F.Moote & Assoc. Ltd. **Season:** April-Nov. **High:** June-Aug. **To obtain tee times:** Call up to 4 days in advance. **Miscellaneous:** Reduced fees (weekdays, twilight, seniors), range (mats), club rentals, credit cards (MC, V).
Reader Comments: Whenever I come to this course I say to myself, 'Damn, I love golf!' ... Tight, houses, good staff ... This course will excite you.

★½ SHERWOOD PARK GOLF COURSE
PU-52321 Range Rd. 233, Sherwood Park, T8B 1C8, (780)467-5060, 1 miles S of Sherwood Park.
Holes: 18. **Yards:** 6,045/5,859. **Par:** 70/72. **Course Rating:** 67.3/73.3. **Slope:** 112/129. **Green Fee:** $23/$25. **Cart Fee:** $24/cart. **Walking Policy:** Unrestricted walking. **Walkability:** 3. **Opened:** 1960. **Architect:** William Brinkworth. **Season:** April-Oct. **High:** May-Sept. **To obtain tee times:** Call Wednesday for upcoming weekend. Call 2 days in advance for weekdays. **Miscellaneous:** Reduced fees (weekdays, low season, twilight), range (grass/mats), club rentals, credit cards (MC, V).

SILVERTIP GOLF COURSE
PU-1000 SilverTip Trail, Canmore, T1W 2V1, (403)678-1600, (877)877-5444, 45 miles W of Calgary. **E-mail:** gandrew@silvertipresort.com. **Web:** silvertipresort.com.
Holes: 18. **Yards:** 7,200/5,131. **Par:** 72/72. **Course Rating:** 74.1/69.0. **Slope:** 153/131. **Green Fee:** $75/$125. **Cart Fee:** Included in Green Fee. **Walking Policy:** Mandatory cart. **Walkability:** 5. **Opened:** 1998. **Architect:** Les Furber. **Season:** May-Oct. **High:** June-Sept. **To obtain tee times:** Book groups 1 year in advance. General public foursomes after March 1. **Miscellaneous:** Reduced fees (low season, twilight), range (grass/mats), club rentals, credit cards (MC, V, AE), beginner friendly (instructor available).
Notes: Ranked 2nd in 1999 Best New Canadian.

SPRUCE MEADOWS GOLF & COUNTRY CLUB
PU-P.O. Box 548, Sexsmith, TOH 3C0, (780)568-4653, 12 miles N of Grande Prairie. **E-mail:** smeadows@telusplanet.net. **Web:** www.smeadow@telusplanet.net.
Holes: 18. **Yards:** 6,527/5,909. **Par:** 71/72. **Course Rating:** 73.0/73.0. **Slope:** 117/N/A. **Green Fee:** $20/$20. **Cart Fee:** $20/cart. **Walking Policy:** Unrestricted walking. **Walkability:** 2. **Opened:** 1982. **Architect:** Ed Sodergren. **Season:** April-Oct. **To obtain tee times:** Call anytime. **Miscellaneous:** Reduced fees (weekdays, low season, resort guests, seniors, juniors), discount

packages, range (grass/mats), club rentals, credit cards (MC, V, Debit Cards), beginner friendly (free junior lessons).

★★ VICTORIA GOLF COURSE
PU-12130 River Rd., Edmonton, T5N 0E0, (780)496-4710
Holes: 18. **Yards:** 6,081/6,081. **Par:** 71/73. **Course Rating:** 66.8/72.1. **Slope:** 99/112. **Green Fee:** $24/$27. **Cart Fee:** $20/cart. **Walking Policy:** Unrestricted walking. **Walkability:** 2. **Opened:** 1907. **Architect:** City of Edmonton. **Season:** April-Oct. **High:** June-Sept. **To obtain tee times:** Call up to 2 days in advance. **Miscellaneous:** Reduced fees (weekdays, low season), discount packages, metal spikes, range (mats), club rentals, credit cards (MC, V), beginner friendly (lessons).

★★★ WINTERGREEN GOLF & COUNTRY CLUB
SP-P.O. Bag No. 2, Bragg Creek, T0L 0K0, Canada County, (403)949-3333, 3 miles SW of Calgary. **E-mail:** bsmythe@skiwintergreen.com. **Web:** www.skiwintergreen.com.
Holes: 18. **Yards:** 6,595/5,047. **Par:** 71/71. **Course Rating:** 72.0/69.9. **Slope:** 137/128. **Green Fee:** $42/$45. **Cart Fee:** $27/cart. **Walking Policy:** Unrestricted walking. **Walkability:** 4. **Opened:** 1991. **Architect:** Bill Newis. **Season:** April-Oct. **High:** June-Sept. **To obtain tee times:** Call 4 days in advance. **Miscellaneous:** Reduced fees (weekdays, low season, twilight, seniors, juniors), range (grass/mats), club rentals, credit cards (MC, V, AE, Debit Card).

Reader Comments: A gem in the foothills ... Reminded me of Muirfield Village ... I fell in love with mountain courses because of Wintergreen. The views are outstanding ... Tough track, lots of hills ... At peak, this course plays like Banff & Kananaskis. Know your clubs!

WOLF CREEK GOLF RESORT
R-R-R. No.3 Site 10, Ponoka, T4J 1R3, (403)783-6050, 70 miles S of Edmonton. **E-mail:** wlfcreek@telusplanet.net. **Web:** www.wolfcreekgolf.com.
Holes: 27. **Green Fee:** $50/$50. **Cart Fee:** $25/cart. **Walking Policy:** Unrestricted walking. **Walkability:** 3. **Opened:** 1984. **Architect:** Rod Whitman. **Season:** April-Oct. **High:** June-Sept. **To obtain tee times:** Call anytime with credit card.

★★★★½ EAST/SOUTH
Yards: 6,818/5,144. **Par:** 70/70. **Course Rating:** 74.2/69.0. **Slope:** 135/117. **Miscellaneous:** Reduced fees (twilight, seniors, juniors), discount packages, metal spikes, range (grass), caddies, club rentals, credit cards (MC, V, AE, Diners Club).

Reader Comments: Be careful, this wolf will bite ... Home of the Alberta Open; a test for all; must be straight ... Great course, very narrow in spots ... The toughest test of golf in Alberta ... Great links course ... Excellent, challenging, different... Championship challenge, not for a beginner ... Small but quite fair greens.

★★★★½ SOUTH/WEST
Yards: 6,730/4,990. **Par:** 70/70. **Course Rating:** 74.5/69.0. **Slope:** 135/117. **Miscellaneous:** Reduced fees (seniors, juniors), discount packages, metal spikes, range (grass), caddies, club rentals, credit cards (MC, V, AE).

Reader Comments: Rugged, unforgiving terrain ... Links style, flat, South nine longer ... Tough with wind ... West nine great, South nine long even for pros ... Great test ... Best sub-400 yard par 4 I've played (No. 4 on the West 9).

★★★★½ WEST/EAST
Yards: 6,516/4,880. **Par:** 70/70. **Course Rating:** 72.3/69.0. **Slope:** 138/117. **Miscellaneous:** Reduced fees (twilight, seniors, juniors), discount packages, metal spikes, range (grass/mats), caddies, club rentals, credit cards (MC, V, AE, Diners Club).

Reader Comments: Not for the fainthearted, accuracy a must ... Very difficult for average golfer ... Links style, very challenging, scenic, if the wind blows, watch out ... Very unusual and interesting.

BRITISH COLUMBIA

★★½ ARBUTUS RIDGE GOLF & COUNTRY CLUB
SP-3515 Telegraph Rd., Cobble Hill, V0R 1L0, (250)743-5000, 18 miles N of Victoria. **E-mail:** golfarbutus@islandnet.com. **Web:** www.sunnygolf.com.
Holes: 18. **Yards:** 6,168/5,113. **Par:** 70/71. **Course Rating:** 69.9/64.8. **Slope:** 123/109. **Green Fee:** $35/$45. **Cart Fee:** $30/cart. **Walking Policy:** Unrestricted walking. **Opened:** 1988. **Architect:** William/Robinson. **Season:** Year-round. **High:** May-Sept. **To obtain tee times:** Call 4 days in advance. **Miscellaneous:** Reduced fees (weekdays, low season, twilight, juniors), range (grass/mats), club rentals, credit cards (MC, V, AE).

Reader Comments: Great views of ocean ... Hilly, good condition, can walk ... Nice clubhouse ... Distance from green to tee far... Very good.

★★ BELMONT GOLF COURSE
SP-22555 Telegraph Trail, Langley, V1M 354, (604)888-9898, (888)456-4224, 10 miles NE of Langley.
Holes: 18. **Yards:** 6,416/4,951. **Par:** 70/70. **Course Rating:** 70.5/68.1. **Slope:** 122/114. **Green Fee:** $25/$44. **Cart Fee:** $26/cart. **Walking Policy:** Unrestricted walking. **Walkability:** 3. **Opened:** 1993. **Architect:** Les Furber. **Season:** Year-round. **High:** June–Sept. **To obtain tee times:** Call five days in advance at 9 a.m. **Miscellaneous:** Reduced fees (weekdays, low season, twilight, seniors, juniors), metal spikes, club rentals, credit cards (MC, V, AE).

★★★★ BIG SKY GOLF & COUNTRY CLUB
R-1690 Airport Rd., Pemberton, V0N 2L0, (604)894-6106, (800)668-7900, 85 miles N of Vancouver. **E-mail:** bigsky@bigskygolf.com. **Web:** www.bigskygolf.com.
Holes: 18. **Yards:** 7,001/5,208. **Par:** 72/72. **Course Rating:** 73.5/70.0. **Slope:** 133/114. **Green Fee:** $60/$125. **Cart Fee:** $30/cart. **Walking Policy:** Unrestricted walking. **Walkability:** 1. **Opened:** 1994. **Architect:** Bob Cupp. **Season:** April-Oct. **High:** June-Sept. **To obtain tee times:** Call golf shop. **Miscellaneous:** Reduced fees (weekdays, low season, twilight, juniors), discount packages, range (grass/mats), caddies, club rentals, credit cards (MC, V, AE), beginner friendly (golf academy).
Reader Comments: Very scenic, a good challenge ... Unbelievable scenery ... Difficult greens, fast, steep ... Course great, rough impossible ... Great golf academy ... The most breathtaking scenery of any course I've played.

★★ BURNABY MOUNTAIN GOLF COURSE
PU-7600 Halifax St., Burnaby, V5A 4M8, (604)280-7355, 10 miles E of Vancouver.
Holes: 18. **Yards:** 6,301/5,830. **Par:** 71/72. **Course Rating:** N/A. **Slope:** N/A. **Green Fee:** $31/$31. **Cart Fee:** $26/cart. **Walking Policy:** Unrestricted walking. **Walkability:** 3. **Opened:** 1969. **Season:** Year-round. **High:** April–Sept. **To obtain tee times:** Call 2 days in advance at noon. **Miscellaneous:** Reduced fees (twilight, seniors, juniors), metal spikes, range (mats), club rentals, credit cards (MC, V).

★★★★ CASTLEGAR GOLF CLUB
PU-P.O. Box 3430, Castlegar, V1N 3N8, (250)365-5006, (800)666-0324, 180 miles N of Spokane. **Holes:** 18. **Yards:** 6,677/6,178. **Par:** 72/76. **Course Rating:** 72.6/75.9. **Slope:** 127/133. **Green Fee:** $24/$27. **Cart Fee:** $27/cart. **Walking Policy:** Unrestricted walking. **Walkability:** 3. **Opened:** 1958. **Architect:** Designed by members. **Season:** April-Oct. **High:** June-Sept. **To obtain tee times:** Outside 60 miles may call anytime within reason. **Miscellaneous:** Reduced fees (twilight), discount packages, metal spikes, club rentals, credit cards (MC, V, Bank Debit Card).
Reader Comments: Great variety, casual atmosphere ... Excellent greens ... Nice scenery; good variety of holes ... Looong! But fair ... Natural beauty and variety ... Scenic, good course. Saw a bear! Good greens ... Peaceful with deer and bear sightings, nice layout ... A jewel in a mountain setting ... Mountainous, rocky, no hooks or slices, beautiful!! ... Very friendly staff, excellent course.

★★★★ CHATEAU WHISTLER GOLF CLUB *Service*
R-4612 Blackcomb Way, Whistler, V0N 1B4, Canada County, (604)938-2095, 75 miles N of Vancouver. **Web:** www.chateauwhistlerresort.com.
Holes: 18. **Yards:** 6,635/5,157. **Par:** 72/72. **Course Rating:** 73.0/70.0. **Slope:** 142/124. **Green Fee:** $110/$175. **Cart Fee:** Included in Green Fee. **Walking Policy:** Mandatory cart. **Walkability:** 4. **Opened:** 1993. **Architect:** Robert Trent Jones Jr. **Season:** May-Oct. **High:** June-Sept. **To obtain tee times:** Call 7 days a week. Resort guests may book within same calendar year. **Miscellaneous:** Reduced fees (low season, resort guests, twilight, juniors), discount packages, club rentals, lodging (558 rooms), credit cards (MC, V, AE, D, Diners Club).
Reader Comments: The most beautiful I've played, great challenge.... The best Whistler has to offer! ... This is golf nirvana. A must play ... Great holes. Fantastic views ... Every hole was a signature hole—great! ... Dramatic, fabulous elevation changes ... Great scenery, tough first 3 holes ... Spectacular course—can't wait to return ... Absolutely beautiful! ... Mountain golf can be addicting!

★★★ CHRISTINA LAKE GOLF CLUB
SP-339 2nd Ave., Christina Lake, V0H 1H0 (250)447-9313, 12 miles E of Grand Forks. **E-mail:** ddevito@sunshinecable.com. **Web:** www.christinalakegolfclub.com.
Holes: 18. **Yards:** 6,615/5,725. **Par:** 72/73. **Course Rating:** 71.5/71.3. **Slope:** 125/123. **Green Fee:** $24/$37. **Cart Fee:** $27/cart. **Walking Policy:** Unrestricted walking. **Walkability:** 2. **Opened:** 1963. **Architect:** Les Furber. **Season:** April-Oct. **High:** July-Sept. **To obtain tee times:** Out of town may book tee times in advance. E-mail ddevito@sunshinecable.com. **Miscellaneous:** Reduced fees (twilight, juniors), discount packages, metal spikes, range (grass), club rentals, credit cards (MC, V, Direct Debit).
Reader Comments: Great, straightforward round of golf ... Very scenic ... Very friendly ... Very good value, a thinking man's course ... Best fairways I played all year, firm ... Very good layout.

★★★½ CORDOVA BAY GOLF COURSE
PU-5333 Cordova Bay Rd., Victoria, V8Y 2L3, (250)658-4075, 15 miles N of Downtown Victoria.

Holes: 18. **Yards:** 6,642/5,269. **Par:** 72/72. **Course Rating:** 72.0/72.0. **Slope:** 122/119. **Green Fee:** $42/$45. **Cart Fee:** $27/cart. **Walking Policy:** Unrestricted walking. **Walkability:** 1. **Opened:** 1991. **Architect:** Bill Robinson. **Season:** Year-round. **High:** May-Sept. **To obtain tee times:** Prepay up to 1 year in advance. **Miscellaneous:** Reduced fees (weekdays, low season, twilight, juniors), metal spikes, range (mats), club rentals, credit cards (MC, V, AE). **Reader Comments:** Solid 3+ rating ... Friendly service and course condition ... Nice practice range and restaurant. Good winter play ... Staff was very accommodating ... Good placement of moguls to increase difficulty ... Nice array of holes ... Flat, good walk and nice view ... Greens are true ... Good value and fun.

★★★★ CROWN ISLE RESORT & GOLF COMMUNITY
R-399 Clubhouse Dr., Courtenay, V9N 9G3, (250)703-5050, (888)338-8439, 100 miles NW of Victoria. **E-mail:** golf@crownisle.com.
Holes: 18. **Yards:** 7,024/5,169. **Par:** 72/72. **Course Rating:** 74.2/68.5. **Slope:** 133/114. **Green Fee:** $35/$60. **Cart Fee:** $28/cart. **Walking Policy:** Unrestricted walking. **Walkability:** 2. **Opened:** 1993. **Architect:** Graham Cooke & Assoc. **Season:** Year-round. **High:** April-Oct. **To obtain tee times:** Call Golf Shop. **Miscellaneous:** Reduced fees (weekdays, low season, twilight, juniors), discount packages, range (grass/mats), club rentals, lodging (25 rooms), credit cards (MC, V, AE, Interact), beginner friendly (golf school).
Reader Comments: Best course on Vancouver Island ... Excellent test of golf with great variety of holes ... Great course—fabulous clubhouse ... Challenging layout—one of top new courses ... Best practice facility I have ever seen ... Outstanding condition ... The best ... Scenic area. Beautifully maintained. Lots of tee choices. Great clubhouse ... Good driving course ... Huge clubhouse ... Fun course to play.

★★ DUNCAN MEADOWS GOLF COURSE
SP-Highway 18 & North Rd., Duncan, V9L 6K9, (250)746-8993, 35 miles N of Victoria.
Holes: 18. **Yards:** 6,616/5,356. **Par:** 72/72. **Course Rating:** 72.6/66.6. **Slope:** 128/114. **Green Fee:** $25/$35. **Cart Fee:** $26/cart. **Walking Policy:** Unrestricted walking. **Walkability:** 3. **Opened:** 1993. **Architect:** Claude Muret. **Season:** Year-round. **High:** June-Aug. **To obtain tee times:** Call up to 4 days in advance. **Miscellaneous:** Reduced fees (low season, twilight, seniors, juniors), range (grass/mats), club rentals, credit cards (MC, V, Debit Card).

DUNES AT KAMLOOPS
SP-652 Dunes Dr., Kamloops, V2B 8M8, (250)579-3300, (888)881-4653, 7 miles N of Downtown Kamloops. **E-mail:** dunes@kamloops.net. **Web:** www.dunes.kamloops.com.
Holes: 18. **Yards:** 7,120/5,405. **Par:** 72/72. **Course Rating:** 73.8/70.6. **Slope:** 125/113. **Green Fee:** $38/$52. **Cart Fee:** $24/cart. **Walking Policy:** Unrestricted walking. **Walkability:** 2. **Opened:** 1996. **Architect:** Graham Cooke. **Season:** March-Oct. **High:** April-Sept. **To obtain tee times:** Call up to 4 days in advance. **Miscellaneous:** Reduced fees (low season, twilight), metal spikes, range (grass), club rentals, credit cards (MC, V, AE).

★★★ EAGLE POINT GOLF & COUNTRY CLUB
PU-8888 Barnhartvale Rd., Kamloops, V2C 6W1, (250)573-2453, (888)863-2453, 225 miles NE of Vancouver.
Holes: 18. **Yards:** 6,762/5,315. **Par:** 72/72. **Course Rating:** 73.4/70.6. **Slope:** 135/126. **Green Fee:** $39/$45. **Cart Fee:** $28/cart. **Walking Policy:** Unrestricted walking. **Walkability:** 4. **Opened:** 1991. **Architect:** Robert Heaslip. **Season:** March-Oct. **High:** April-Sept. **To obtain tee times:** Call golf shop. **Miscellaneous:** Reduced fees (weekdays, low season, resort guests, twilight, juniors), discount packages, range (grass/mats), club rentals, credit cards (MC, V, AE), beginner friendly.
Reader Comments: Quite hilly, must be accurate ... A beautiful course in a beautiful setting ... Great men's night on Tuesdays ... Hilly demanding layout—a lot of fun.

★★ EAGLECREST GOLF CLUB
SP-2035 Island Hwy. W., Qualicum Beach, V9K 1G1, (250)752-6311, (800)567-1320, 25 miles N of Nanaimo.
Holes: 18. **Yards:** 6,013/5,430. **Par:** 71/71. **Course Rating:** 70.6/71.0. **Slope:** 126/123. **Green Fee:** $25/$40. **Cart Fee:** $27/cart. **Walking Policy:** Unrestricted walking. **Walkability:** 3. **Opened:** 1971. **Architect:** Warren Radomski. **Season:** Year-round. **High:** May-Oct. **To obtain tee times:** Call 1-800-567-1320. Call anytime or book through hotel with credit card to guarantee. Call 2 days prior for group bookings. For 12 or more call 6 months in advance. **Miscellaneous:** Reduced fees (weekdays, low season, resort guests, twilight, juniors), discount packages, metal spikes, range (mats), club rentals, credit cards (MC, V, AE).

★★★½ FAIRMONT HOT SPRINGS RESORT
R-P.O. Box 10, Fairmont Hot Springs, V0B 1L0, (250)345-6514, (800)663-4979, 200 miles SW of Calgary.
Holes: 18. **Yards:** 6,522/5,488. **Par:** 72/72. **Course Rating:** 71.8/71.4. **Slope:** 126/125. **Green Fee:** $40/$50. **Cart Fee:** $23/cart. **Walking Policy:** Unrestricted walking. **Walkability:** 3.

Opened: 1963. **Architect:** Lloyd Wilder. **Season:** April-Oct. **High:** May-Sept. **To obtain tee times:** Call. **Miscellaneous:** Reduced fees (weekdays, low season, resort guests, twilight, juniors), discount packages, metal spikes, club rentals, lodging, credit cards (MC, V, AE, D).

Reader Comments: Beautiful scenery, always a pleasure to play...Always a treat, tough but fair, great shape...Good mountain golf...Good restaurant ... Great view. Friendly & helpful.... Beautiful valley views! ... Great value- tough greens... Outstanding views (catch your breath) ... Great little course. Worth a stop to play it.... Nice improvements to course.

★★★½ FAIRMONT RIVERSIDE GOLF RESORT

SP-5099 Riverview Dr., Fairmont Hot Springs, V0B 1L0, (250)345-6346, (800)665-2112, 180 miles W of Calgary.

Holes: 18. **Yards:** 6,507/5,488. **Par:** 71/71. **Course Rating:** 71.8/71.4. **Slope:** 128/125. **Green Fee:** $35/$55. **Cart Fee:** $24/cart. **Walking Policy:** Unrestricted walking. **Walkability:** 1. **Opened:** 1988. **Architect:** Bill Newis. **Season:** March-Nov. **High:** June-Sept. **To obtain tee times:** Call in advance, credit card required. **Miscellaneous:** Reduced fees (weekdays, resort guests, twilight, juniors), discount packages, range (grass/mats), club rentals, credit cards (MC, V), beginner friendly (CPGA pro-training facility).

Reader Comments: One of the best ... Enjoy the scenery ... Was able to be aggressive there ... Scenic, great value ... Great course with great scenery. Excellent layout, very scenic... Challenging, narrow, long carries ... A nice resort-style course ... This course has grown on me—some very long and difficult holes.

★★★½ FAIRVIEW MOUNTAIN GOLF CLUB

SP-Old Golf Course Rd., Oliver, V0H 1T0, (250)498-3521, (888)95-LINKS, 70 miles S of Kelowna. **E-mail:** fvgolf@otvcablelan.net. **Web:** www.fairviewmountain.com.

Holes: 18. **Yards:** 6,557/5,382. **Par:** 72/73. **Course Rating:** 71.5/73.5. **Slope:** 129/127. **Green Fee:** $42/$45. **Cart Fee:** $14/person. **Walking Policy:** Unrestricted walking. **Walkability:** 4. **Opened:** 1991. **Architect:** Les Furber. **Season:** March-Oct. **High:** June-Sept. **To obtain tee times:** Call 5 days in advance. **Miscellaneous:** Reduced fees (low season, twilight, juniors), discount packages, metal spikes, range (mats), club rentals, credit cards (MC, V, AE).

Reader Comments: Nice course—good use of terrain! ... Best kept secret in the interior... A hidden gem. A must play ... This was the surprise of the year! ... Outstanding golf. Outstanding views ... Golf and nature at its best ... This course was a real find!

★★★½ FAIRWINDS GOLF & COUNTRY CLUB

R-3730 Fairwinds Dr., Nanoose Bay, V9P 9S6, (250)468-7666, (888)781-2777, 6 miles N of Nanaimo. **E-mail:** info@fairwinds.bc.ca.

Holes: 18. **Yards:** 6,151/5,173. **Par:** 71/71. **Course Rating:** 70.6/70.7. **Slope:** 123/129. **Green Fee:** $32/$45. **Cart Fee:** $26/cart. **Walking Policy:** Unrestricted walking. **Walkability:** 4. **Opened:** 1988. **Architect:** Les Furber/Jim Eremko. **Season:** Year-round. **High:** May-Oct. **To obtain tee times:** Resort guests may book anytime with confirmed room reservation. Public may call 5 days in advance. **Miscellaneous:** Reduced fees (weekdays, low season, twilight, seniors, juniors), discount packages, metal spikes, range (grass/mats), club rentals, lodging, credit cards (MC, V, AE).

Reader Comments: Short but pretty. I'll forever remember seeing bald eagles' nest ... Good to very good ... Just excellent ... Good, tight, short course ... Beautiful scenery, target golf at its best ... Great food ... Very good facilities. Tight fairways, good greens ... Tougher than yardage indicates.

★★★½ THE FALLS GOLF & COUNTRY CLUB

SP-8341 Nixon Rd., Rosedale, V0X 1X0, Canada County, (604)794-3380, (800)862-3168, 60 miles E of Vancouver. **Web:** www.thefalls.ca.com.

Holes: 18. **Yards:** 6,426/N/A. **Par:** 71/N/A. **Course Rating:** 70.6/N/A. **Slope:** 130/N/A. **Green Fee:** $30/$69. **Cart Fee:** Included in Green Fee. **Walking Policy:** Mandatory cart. **Walkability:** 5. **Opened:** 1996. **Architect:** Ted Locke. **Season:** Feb.-Nov. **High:** June-Sept. **To obtain tee times:** Call up to 7 days in advance. **Miscellaneous:** Reduced fees (weekdays, low season, resort guests, twilight, seniors, juniors), range (grass), club rentals, credit cards (MC, V).

Reader Comments: A very dramatic course with incredible virtue ... A real challenge—hilly and tight ... Spectacular views. Best new course in British Columbia ... Spectacular elevation, well maintained.

★½ FORT LANGLEY GOLF COURSE

SP-9782 McKinnon Crescent, Fort Langley, V1M 2R5, (604)888-5911, 14 miles NW of Langley.

Holes: 18. **Yards:** 6,428/5,681. **Par:** 70/75. **Course Rating:** 70.0/71.5. **Slope:** 115/126. **Green Fee:** $30/$35. **Cart Fee:** $26/cart. **Walking Policy:** Unrestricted walking. **Walkability:** 3. **Opened:** 1968. **Architect:** James Bryce / Tony Turney. **Season:** Year-round. **High:** May-Sept. **To obtain tee times:** Call 7 days in advance for weekdays. Call Thursday at 7 a.m. for weekends. **Miscellaneous:** Reduced fees (weekdays, low season, twilight, seniors, juniors), discount packages, metal spikes, range (grass), club rentals, credit cards (MC, V, AE, Diners Club).

★★ FRASERVIEW GOLF COURSE

PM-7800 Vivian St., Vancouver, V5S 2V8, (604)257-6923

Holes: 18. Yards: 6,700/5,890. Par: 72/72. **Course Rating:** 71.4/72.6. **Slope:** 121/116. **Green Fee:** $34/$37. **Cart Fee:** $25/cart. **Walking Policy:** Unrestricted walking. **Walkability:** 3. **Opened:** 1934. **Architect:** Howard Norman/Tom McBroom. **Season:** Year-round. **High:** April-Oct. **To obtain tee times:** Call 5 days in advance at 7 P.M. for tee times. **Miscellaneous:** Reduced fees (low season, twilight, seniors, juniors), club rentals, credit cards (MC, V), beginner friendly (learning academy, junior program).

★★★½ FURRY CREEK GOLF & COUNTRY CLUB
PU-150 Country Club Road, P.O. Box 1000, Lions Bay, V0N 2E0, Furry Creek County, (604)896-2216, (888)922-9461, 12 miles N of Lions Bay. **E-mail:** info@furrycreekgolf.com. **Web:** www.furrycreek.com.
Holes: 18. Yards: 6,001/4,730. Par: 72/71. **Course Rating:** 71.5/68.7. **Slope:** 132/118. **Green Fee:** $55/$90. **Cart Fee:** Included in Green Fee. **Walking Policy:** Mandatory cart. **Walkability:** 5. **Opened:** 1993. **Architect:** Robert Muir Graves. **Season:** March-Nov. **High:** July-Sept. **To obtain tee times:** Call up to 10 days in advance. **Miscellaneous:** Reduced fees (weekdays, low season, twilight, seniors, juniors), discount packages, metal spikes, range (grass), club rentals, credit cards (MC, V, AE).
Reader Comments: Punishing mountain course ... Target golf with spectacular views ... One of the most scenic golf courses in the world. Beautiful vistas from every tee, fairway and green ... Views rival Hawaii ... Great setting, tough course. Not for everyone ... Superb service and the14th hole is one of the best anywhere ... You cannot beat the value.

★★★★ GALLAGHER'S CANYON GOLF & COUNTRY CLUB
SP-4320 Gallagher's Dr. W., Kelowna, V1W 3Z9, (250)861-4240, 2 miles NE of Kelowna.
Holes: 18. Yards: 6,890/5,505. Par: 72/73. **Course Rating:** 73.5/73.8. **Slope:** 136/131. **Green Fee:** $35/$80. **Cart Fee:** $30/cart. **Walking Policy:** Unrestricted walking. **Walkability:** 3. **Opened:** 1980. **Architect:** Bill Robinson / Les Furber. **Season:** April-Oct. **High:** May-Sept. **To obtain tee times:** Call anytime within same calendar year. **Miscellaneous:** Reduced fees (low season, twilight, juniors), discount packages, metal spikes, range (grass), caddies, club rentals, credit cards (MC, V, AE).
Reader Comments: Wow! Take a camera ... Hilly course, great variety and views ... Tough par 4 on 1st hole ... Spectacular views. Tough but forgiving ... Scenery, course and golf beautiful. Staff positive ... Bring your best game ... One of BC's best ... Great golf and reasonably priced ... Hidden treasure ... Loved the place ... Great practice facility, friendly staff, loved it.

★★★★ GOLDEN GOLF & COUNTRY CLUB   *Value, Pace*
SP-576 Dogtooth Rd., Golden, V0A 1H0, (250)344-2700, 150 miles W of Calgary.
Holes: 18. Yards: 6,818/5,380. Par: 72/72. **Course Rating:** 72.8/66.3. **Slope:** 134/121. **Green Fee:** $25/$42. **Cart Fee:** $27/cart. **Walking Policy:** Unrestricted walking. **Walkability:** 4. **Opened:** 1985. **Architect:** Les Furber. **Season:** April-Oct. **High:** June-Sept. **To obtain tee times:** Call anytime. **Miscellaneous:** Reduced fees (twilight, seniors, juniors), discount packages, range (grass), club rentals, credit cards (MC, V, AE, Debit Cards), beginner friendly (CPGA lessons available).
Reader Comments: The golf is excellent ... Great new back nine, great fairways and greens ... A treasure in the Rockies! Breathtaking scenery and good holes ... Not to miss! Outstanding peaceful setting, views ... Quiet, unpretentious gem! Back 9 spectacular holes ... A hidden jewel.... Snow-capped mountain view at end of each fairway ... Fantastic scenery, wonderful layout, staff excellent.

★★★ GORGE VALE GOLF CLUB
SP-1005 Craigflower Rd., Victoria, V9A 2X9, (250)386-3401, 2 miles W of Victoria. **E-mail:** gorgevalegolf_club@bc.sympatico.ca. **Web:** www.gorgevalegolf.com.
Holes: 18. Yards: 6,452/5,836. Par: 72/74. **Course Rating:** 71.3/74.4. **Slope:** 131/137. **Green Fee:** $45/$60. **Cart Fee:** $30/cart. **Walking Policy:** Unrestricted walking. **Walkability:** 4. **Opened:** 1930. **Architect:** A.V. Macan. **Season:** Year-round. **High:** March–Oct. **To obtain tee times:** Call 2 days in advance. **Miscellaneous:** Reduced fees (juniors), metal spikes, range (grass), club rentals, credit cards (MC, V).
Reader Comments: Lots of interesting holes ... A fun course for all levels ... Very good layout for hilly terrain ... Great men's night ... Well established and maintained.

GREYWOLF GOLF COURSE
R-1860 Greywolf Dr., Panorama, V0A 1T0, (250)342-6941, (800)663-2929, 80 miles SW of Calgary. **Web:** www.panoramaresort.com.
Holes: 18. Yards: 7,140/5,400. Par: 72/72. **Course Rating:** 73.5/69.6. **Slope:** 137/122. **Green Fee:** $65/$95. **Cart Fee:** Included in Green Fee. **Walking Policy:** Mandatory cart. **Walkability:** 5. **Opened:** 1999. **Architect:** Doug Carrick. **Season:** May-Oct. **High:** May-Oct. **To obtain tee times:** Call. **Miscellaneous:** Reduced fees (twilight), discount packages, club rentals, lodging (500 rooms), credit cards (MC, V, AE).
Notes: Ranked 1st in 1999 Best New Canadian.

★★★★ **HARVEST GOLF CLUB** *Service, Condition*
R-2725 Klo Rd., Kelowna, V1W 4S1, (250)862-3103, (800)257-8577, 200 miles NE of Vancouver. **E-mail:** proshop@harvestgolf.com. **Web:** www.harvestgolf.com.
Holes: 18. **Yards:** 7,104/5,454. **Par:** 72/72. **Course Rating:** 73.0/61.1. **Slope:** 128/119. **Green Fee:** $44/$75. **Cart Fee:** $30/cart. **Walking Policy:** Unrestricted walking. **Walkability:** 3.
Opened: 1994. **Architect:** Graham Cooke. **Season:** March-Oct. **High:** May-Sept. **To obtain tee times:** Call from November 1 for entire following season. **Miscellaneous:** Reduced fees (low season, twilight, juniors), discount packages, range (grass/mats), club rentals, credit cards (MC, V, AE, En Route).
Reader Comments: Great course, wonderful stuff ... Beautifully manicured and wide open, great views ... Superb course that winds its way through orchards ... What a pleasant, relaxing course to play ... Very forgiving ... Very well groomed course ... Excellent facility ... Apples and sunshine along with golf super! ... Delicious apples and great golf–what more could you ask for?

★★★½ **KELOWNA SPRINGS GOLF CLUB**
SP-480 Penno Rd., Kelowna, V1X 6S3, Canada County, (250)765-4653. **E-mail:** golf@kelonasprings.com. **Web:** www.kelonasprings.com.
Holes: 18. **Yards:** 6,156/5,225. **Par:** 71/71. **Course Rating:** 69.6/70.0. **Slope:** 117/118. **Green Fee:** $28/$40. **Cart Fee:** $26/cart. **Walking Policy:** Unrestricted walking. **Walkability:** 1.
Opened: 1990. **Architect:** Les Furber. **Season:** March-Nov. **High:** April-Oct. **To obtain tee times:** Call golf shop. **Miscellaneous:** Reduced fees (low season, twilight, juniors), discount packages, club rentals, credit cards (MC, V, AE, Debit Cards).
Reader Comments: Short but tough course ... Short course, put the ball in the right place to see your next target or all of the green; easy walk ... Getting better as it matures.

★★★★ **KOKANEE SPRINGS GOLF RESORT**
R-Box 96, Crawford Bay, V0B 1E0, (250)227-9362, (800)979-7999, 120 miles N of Spokane, WA.
Holes: 18. **Yards:** 6,537/5,747. **Par:** 71/74. **Course Rating:** 72.0/68.4. **Slope:** 135/128. **Green Fee:** $41/$46. **Cart Fee:** $12/person. **Walking Policy:** Unrestricted walking. **Walkability:** 5.
Opened: 1967. **Architect:** Norman Woods. **Season:** April-Oct. **High:** July-Sept. **To obtain tee times:** Call 800 number. **Miscellaneous:** Reduced fees (resort guests, twilight, juniors), discount packages, metal spikes, range (grass/mats), club rentals, lodging (26 rooms), credit cards (MC, V, AE).
Reader Comments: An unknown gem! One of the best in Canada ... Forest/mountain course ... Beautiful course in spring ... Challenging but fair ... Classic mountain course, top 10 in BC ... Fantastic scenery, great tough challenge. Wildlife.

THE LONE WOLF GOLF CLUB
PU-P.O. Box 300, Taylor, V0C 2K0, (250)789-3711, 12 miles S of Fort St. John.
Holes: 18. **Yards:** 6,817/5,968. **Par:** 72/73. **Course Rating:** 72.5/68.5. **Slope:** 128/118. **Green Fee:** $22/$25. **Cart Fee:** $25/cart. **Walking Policy:** Unrestricted walking. **Walkability:** 2.
Opened: 1995. **Architect:** Albers Bros. **Season:** April-Oct. **High:** June-Aug. **To obtain tee times:** Call 1 day in advance. Advance booking for groups available. **Miscellaneous:** Reduced fees (weekdays, seniors, juniors), discount packages, metal spikes, range (grass/mats), club rentals, credit cards (MC, V, AE, Debit Card).
Special Notes: Formerly Taylor Golf and Country Club.

★★★ **MAYFAIR LAKES GOLF & COUNTRY CLUB**
SP-5460 North 7 Rd., Richmond, V6V 1R7, Canada County, (604)276-0505, 7 miles S of Vancouver. **Web:** www.mayfairlakes.com.
Holes: 18. **Yards:** 6,641/5,277. **Par:** 71/72. **Course Rating:** 71.3/71.3. **Slope:** 123/126. **Green Fee:** $45/$65. **Cart Fee:** $30/cart. **Walking Policy:** Unrestricted walking. **Walkability:** 1.
Opened: 1989. **Architect:** Les Furber. **Season:** Year-round. **High:** May-Oct. **To obtain tee times:** Call 2 days in advance at 9 a.m. for weekdays and Friday 9 a.m. for weekends.
Miscellaneous: Reduced fees (weekdays, low season, twilight, seniors, juniors), metal spikes, range (grass/mats), club rentals, credit cards (MC, V, AE).
Reader Comments: Nice facility, well maintained, good food ... Bring your ball retriever (13 holes with water)... Greens are like putting on glass ... Grooming is immaculate ... Lots of water–tight ... Good drainage—well designed course.

★★★ **MCCLEERY GOLF COURSE**
PM-7188 MacDonald St., Vancouver, V6N 1G2, (604)257-8191.
Holes: 18. **Yards:** 6,265/5,010. **Par:** 71/71. **Course Rating:** 69.6/67.1. **Slope:** 126/110. **Green Fee:** $34/$37. **Cart Fee:** $26/cart. **Walking Policy:** Unrestricted walking. **Walkability:** 2.
Opened: 1959. **Architect:** Ted Baker & Associates. **Season:** Year-round. **High:** April-Oct. **To obtain tee times:** Call (604)280-1818 up to 5 days in advance. **Miscellaneous:** Reduced fees (low season, twilight, seniors, juniors), range (mats), club rentals, credit cards (MC, V), beginner friendly (golf academy).
Reader Comments: Majestic back 9 ... Recently reconstructed–nicely varied layout ... Very solid muny. Nos.10-12 especially tough ... Good public course ... Good value ... Beautiful!

CANADA

★★★½ MEADOW GARDENS GOLF COURSE
SP-19675 Meadow Gardens Way, Pitt Meadows, V3Y 1Z2, (604)465-5474, (800)667-6758, 12 miles E of Vancouver.
Holes: 18. **Yards:** 7,041/5,519. **Par:** 72/72. **Course Rating:** 74.7/72.8. **Slope:** 134/130. **Green Fee:** $35/$55. **Cart Fee:** $25/cart. **Walking Policy:** Unrestricted walking. **Walkability:** 2. **Opened:** 1994. **Architect:** Les Furber/Jim Eremko. **Season:** Year-round. **High:** April-Oct. **To obtain tee times:** Call 7 days in advance. **Miscellaneous:** Reduced fees (weekdays, low season, twilight, seniors, juniors), metal spikes, range (grass/mats), caddies, club rentals, credit cards (MC, V, AE, Diners Club).
Reader Comments: Good greens ... Great 18th hole ... No weak holes, lots of water and trouble ... Interesting water hazards ... Tough greens ... Tricky but fun ... Nicely conditioned, easy to walk.

★★★½ MORNINGSTAR GOLF CLUB
PU-525 Lowry's Rd., Parksville, V9P 2R8, (250)248-8161, 30 miles N of Nanaimo.
Holes: 18. **Yards:** 7,018/5,313. **Par:** 72/72. **Course Rating:** 74.5/71.2. **Slope:** 139/135. **Green Fee:** $25/$55. **Cart Fee:** $30/cart. **Walking Policy:** Unrestricted walking. **Walkability:** 1. **Opened:** 1991. **Architect:** Les Furber/Jim Eremko. **Season:** Year-round. **High:** March-Nov. **To obtain tee times:** Call 7 days in advance. **Miscellaneous:** Reduced fees (weekdays, low season, resort guests, twilight, juniors), discount packages, metal spikes, range (grass), club rentals, credit cards (MC, V, AE).
Reader Comments: Very tough layout ... Great design ... Very nice course, good day out ... The hazards are perfectly placed ... Good challenge, nice area.

★★★ NANAIMO GOLF CLUB
SP-2800 Highland Blvd., Nanaimo, V95 3N8, Canada County, (250)758-6332, 70 miles N of Victoria. **E-mail:** admin@nangolf.nisa.com. **Web:** www.nangolf.nisa.com.
Holes: 18. **Yards:** 6,667/5,648. **Par:** 72/72. **Course Rating:** 73.2/68.5. **Slope:** 129/119. **Green Fee:** $34/$45. **Cart Fee:** $26/cart. **Walking Policy:** Unrestricted walking. **Walkability:** 2. **Opened:** 1962. **Architect:** A.V. McCann. **Season:** Year-round. **High:** April-Sept. **To obtain tee times:** Call 2 days in advance. **Miscellaneous:** Reduced fees (low season), metal spikes, range (mats), club rentals, credit cards (MC, V, Interac).
Reader Comments: Conditioning getting better all the time ... Beautiful scenery, everything slopes to water ... Established course. Nice greens. Can get windy ... Classic, long, challenging course, great views.

★★★★ NICKLAUS NORTH GOLF COURSE
R-8080 Nicklaus North Blvd., Whistler, V0N 1B0, (604)938-9898, (800)386-9898, 90 miles N of Vancouver. **E-mail:** info@nicklausnorth.com. **Web:** www.nicklausnorth.com.
Holes: 18. **Yards:** 6,908/4,730. **Par:** 71/71. **Course Rating:** 73.8/66.3. **Slope:** 138/113. **Green Fee:** $60/$125. **Cart Fee:** Included in Green Fee. **Walking Policy:** Unrestricted walking. **Walkability:** 1. **Opened:** 1995. **Architect:** Jack Nicklaus. **Season:** May-Oct. **High:** June-Sept. **To obtain tee times:** Call anytime within season. Groups may book up to 2 years in advance. **Miscellaneous:** Reduced fees (low season, twilight, juniors), discount packages, range (grass), club rentals, lodging (24 rooms), credit cards (MC, V, AE).
Reader Comments: I could play No. 12 and the last four holes all day long here ... Easy walking ... Still the best in Canada ... Excellent service from start to finish ... A couple thrilling par threes, and a testing stretch of finishing holes ... Lots of tough holes ... Bring your 'A' game, good challenges ... Amazing condition.

NORTHLANDS GOLF COURSE
PU-3400 Anne MacDonald Way, North Vancouver, V7G 2S7, (604)924-2950
Holes: 18. **Yards:** 6,504/5,135. **Par:** 71/71. **Course Rating:** 71.5/70.1. **Slope:** 132/123. **Green Fee:** $35/$47. **Cart Fee:** $26/cart. **Walking Policy:** Unrestricted walking. **Walkability:** 4. **Opened:** 1997. **Architect:** Les Furber. **Season:** Feb.-Dec. **High:** May-Sept. **To obtain tee times:** Phone 3 days in advance beginning at 9:00 A.M. **Miscellaneous:** Reduced fees (weekdays, low season, twilight, seniors, juniors), metal spikes, club rentals, credit cards (MC, V).

NORTHVIEW GOLF & COUNTRY CLUB
PU-6857 168th St., Surrey, V3S 8E7, (604)576-4653, (888)574-2211, 18 miles SE of Vancouver.
E-mail: golf@northviewgolf.com. **Web:** www.northviewgolf.com.
★★★★ CANAL COURSE
Holes: 18. **Yards:** 7,101/5,314. **Par:** 72/72. **Course Rating:** 74.4/70.1. **Slope:** 137/108. **Green Fee:** $40/$60. **Cart Fee:** $30/cart. **Walking Policy:** Unrestricted walking. **Walkability:** 1. **Opened:** 1995. **Architect:** Arnold Palmer. **Season:** Year-round. **High:** April-Sept. **To obtain tee times:** Call 7 days in advance at 9 a.m. **Miscellaneous:** Reduced fees (weekdays, low season, twilight, seniors, juniors), metal spikes, range (grass/mats), club rentals, credit cards (MC, V, AE, Diners Club).
Reader Comments: About 7,100 yards from the tips, a wide-open swingfest ... The best value around ... Wide open, good conditions, good facilities ... Great clubhouse ... Challenging.

CANADA

★★★½ RIDGE COURSE
Holes: 18. **Yards:** 6,900/5,231. **Par:** 72/72. **Course Rating:** 72.8/70.1. **Slope:** 135/123. **Green Fee:** $50/$80. **Cart Fee:** $30/cart. **Walking Policy:** Unrestricted walking. **Walkability:** 3. **Opened:** 1994. **Architect:** Arnold Palmer. **Season:** Year-round. **High:** April-Sept. **To obtain tee times:** Call 7 days in advance at 9 a.m. **Miscellaneous:** Reduced fees (weekdays, low season, twilight, seniors, juniors), metal spikes, range (grass/mats), club rentals, credit cards (MC, V, AE, Diners Club).
Reader Comments: Toughest 3 starting holes you'll find anywhere ... WOW! ... A great walking course ... Good variety of holes ... A very satisfying course to play.

★★★★ OLYMPIC VIEW GOLF CLUB
PU-643 Latoria Rd., Victoria, V9C 3A3, (250)474-3671
Holes: 18. **Yards:** 6,530/5,308. **Par:** 72/73. **Course Rating:** 72.0/70.7. **Slope:** 133/125. **Green Fee:** $35/$55. **Cart Fee:** $30/cart. **Walking Policy:** Unrestricted walking. **Walkability:** 3. **Opened:** 1990. **Architect:** Bill Robinson. **Season:** Year-round. **High:** April-Oct. **To obtain tee times:** Call 3 days in advance or up to 90 days in advance with a credit card. **Miscellaneous:** Reduced fees (weekdays, low season, twilight, juniors), discount packages, metal spikes, range (mats), club rentals, credit cards (MC, V, AE).
Reader Comments: Top notch golf course ... Beautiful and challenging ... Tough course, picturesque, much water ... Very scenic ... Price was very good ... Great views from every hole, keep it straight ... Wonderful design, hilly, tough! ... View is beautiful! Outstanding in every aspect! ... Spectacular B.C. golf ... Nature at its best.

OSOYOOS GOLF & COUNTRY CLUB
SP-12300 Golf Course Drive, Osoyoos, V0H 1V0, (250)495-7003, 81 miles S of Kelowna. **E-mail:** mail@golfosoyoos.com. **Web:** www.golfosoyoos.com.
Holes: 27. **Green Fee:** $35/$41. **Cart Fee:** $28/cart. **Walking Policy:** Unrestricted walking. **Walkability:** 3. **Opened:** 1971. **Architect:** Boyd Barr. **Season:** March-Dec. **High:** July-Aug. **To obtain tee times:** Call. **Miscellaneous:** Reduced fees (low season, twilight, juniors), discount packages, metal spikes, range (grass/mats), club rentals, credit cards (MC, V, AE, Debit Card)

★★★ DESERT/MEADOWS
Yards: 6,318/5,303. **Par:** 72/72. **Course Rating:** 69.8/71.8. **Slope:** 118/123. .
Reader Comments: Great 27-hole facility with friendly and courteous staff (they're always approachable and accommodating) ... 3 nines—take your pick, they're all great ... A good course for walking ... A desert course in Canada ... Good course for all handicap levels.

★★★ PARK/DESERT
Yards: 6,223/5,109. **Par:** 72/72. **Course Rating:** 69.8/71.8. **Slope:** 118/123.
Reader Comments: All around great experience ... Good layout. Good for all handicaps ... Unbelievable variety at one course.

★★★ PARK/MEADOWS
Yards: 6,323/5,214. **Par:** 72/72. **Course Rating:** 69.7/71.7. **Slope:** 116/121.
Reader Comments: Great view of bay and hillside ... Good layout. Good for all handicaps.

★★★ PEACE PORTAL GOLF COURSE
SP-16900 4th Ave., South Surrey, V4A 9N3, Canada County, (604)538-4818, (800)354-7544, 30 miles S of Vancouver. **E-mail:** info@peaceportalgolf.com. **Web:** www.peaceportalgolf.com.
Holes: 18. **Yards:** 6,363/5,621. **Par:** 72/73. **Course Rating:** 70.9/73.5. **Slope:** 130/133. **Green Fee:** $45/$49. **Cart Fee:** $29/cart. **Walking Policy:** Unrestricted walking. **Walkability:** 4. **Opened:** 1928. **Architect:** Francis L. James. **Season:** Year-round. **High:** April-Sept. **To obtain tee times:** Call 7 days in advance at 8 a.m. for weekdays. Call Thursday at 8 a.m. for upcoming weekend. **Miscellaneous:** Reduced fees (low season, twilight, juniors), metal spikes, range (grass/mats), club rentals, credit cards (MC, V, AE).
Reader Comments: Great old-style, treed course that you just can't build anymore ... Beautiful old established course ... A great course—well maintained ... Very hilly, flat lies are rare ... Has character ... Grand old course.

★★½ PENTICTON GOLF & COUNTRY CLUB
SP-Eckhardt Ave. W., Penticton, V2A 6K3, (250)492-8727, 27 miles S of Kelowna. **E-mail:** pentictongolf@img.net.
Holes: 18. **Yards:** 6,131/5,609. **Par:** 70/72. **Course Rating:** 70.0/73.0. **Slope:** 127/130. **Green Fee:** $40/$40. **Cart Fee:** $23/cart. **Walking Policy:** Unrestricted walking. **Walkability:** 1. **Opened:** 1920. **Architect:** Les Furber. **Season:** Feb.-Nov. **High:** April-Oct. **To obtain tee times:** Call 1 day in advance. **Miscellaneous:** Reduced fees (low season, resort guests, twilight, juniors), discount packages, metal spikes, club rentals, credit cards (MC, V).
Reader Comments: Easy to walk—short but tough course ... Lots of trees/water/bunkers ... A great pro shop staff ... Our winter course, stays open the longest in autumn ... Walking delight ... Great course for beginners ... Very friendly staff.

CANADA

★★★ PITT MEADOWS GOLF CLUB
SP-13615 Harris Rd., Pitt Meadows, V3Y 2R8, (604)465-4711, 20 miles E of Vancouver. **Web:** www.pittmeadowsgolf.com.
Holes: 18. **Yards:** 6,516/5,927. **Par:** 72/74. **Course Rating:** 71.8/73.3. **Slope:** 125/123. **Green Fee:** $35/$45. **Cart Fee:** $28/cart. **Walking Policy:** Unrestricted walking. **Walkability:** 1.
Opened: 1963. **Architect:** Built by members. **Season:** Year-round. **High:** May-Oct. **To obtain tee times:** Call 2 days in advance. **Miscellaneous:** Reduced fees (low season, juniors), metal spikes, range (grass/mats), club rentals, credit cards (MC, V, Interact).
Reader Comments: Good challenge ... Great staff ... Nicely re-shaped flattish course.

PREDATOR RIDGE GOLF RESORT
R-360 Commonage Rd., Vernon, V1T 6M8, (250)542-3436, 36 miles N of Kelowna.
Holes: 27. **Green Fee:** $58/$75. **Cart Fee:** $30/cart. **Walking Policy:** Unrestricted walking.
Walkability: 4. **Opened:** 1991. **Architect:** Les Furber. **Season:** April-Oct. **High:** June-Sept. **To obtain tee times:** Call up to 1 year in advance with credit card. **Miscellaneous:** Reduced fees (low season, resort guests, twilight, juniors), discount packages, metal spikes, range (grass), club rentals, lodging, credit cards (MC, V, AE).
★★★★ OSPREY/PEREGRINE
Yards: 7,087/5,514. **Par:** 71/71. **Course Rating:** 76.0/72.9. **Slope:** 131/131.
Reader Comments: Wow! ... Challenging ... Great value ... One of the interiors' best ... What a layout. Exceptionally memorable ... My favorite in North America! ... Great setting for golf ... Probably the best in valley, fast greens ... 5-Star, best I've played, worth every dollar ... Must play if in central B.C.... What a course! Worth the trip alone!
★★★★ RED TAIL/OSPREY
Yards: 7,099/5,373. **Par:** 71/71. **Course Rating:** 76.0/72.9. **Slope:** 131/131.
Reader Comments: Wow! ... Challenging ... Best course in the Okanagan. Great value ... One of the interiors' best ... What a layout. Exceptionally memorable ... My favorite in North America! ... Great setting for golf ... Probably the best in valley, fast greens ... 5-Star, best I've played, worth every dollar ... Must play if in central B.C.... What a course! Worth the trip alone!
★★★★ RED TAIL/PEREGRINE
Yards: 7,144/5,513. **Par:** 72/72. **Course Rating:** 76.0/72.9. **Slope:** 131/131.
Reader Comments: Wow! ... Challenging ... Best course in the Okanagan. Great value ... One of the interiors' best ... What a layout. Exceptionally memorable ... My favorite in North America! ... Great setting for golf ... Probably the best in valley, fast greens ... 5-Star, best I've played, worth every dollar ... Must play if in central B.C.... What a course! Worth the trip alone!

★★★½ THE REDWOODS
PU-22011 88th Ave., Langley, V1M 2M3, (604)882-5132, 25 miles E of Vancouver. **E-mail:** info@redwoods-golf.com. **Web:** www.redwoods-golf.com.
Holes: 18. **Yards:** 6,516/5,452. **Par:** 71/71. **Course Rating:** 72.3/71.3. **Slope:** 131/123. **Green Fee:** $15/$58. **Cart Fee:** $28/cart. **Walking Policy:** Unrestricted walking. **Walkability:** 3.
Opened: 1994. **Architect:** Ted Locke. **Season:** Year-round. **High:** April-Oct. **To obtain tee times:** Call 2 days in advance from 9 a.m. **Miscellaneous:** Reduced fees (weekdays, low season, twilight, seniors, juniors), metal spikes, range (mats), club rentals, credit cards (MC, V, AE), beginner friendly (extensive lesson program).
Reader Comments: Excellent layout ... Good test of all the clubs in the bag ... Tall trees line narrow fairways–leave driver in bag ... A little gem, variety, strategy, scenery, it's all here ... Interesting rolling layout with fabulous scenery ... Quality course in natural setting ... Great for all levels.

★★★½ RIVERSHORE GOLF LINKS
SP-330 Rivershore Drive , Kamloops, V2H I5I, (250)573-4622, 10 miles E of Kamloops. **E-mail:** rivershore_golf@bc.sympatico.ca. **Web:** rivershoregolflinks.com.
Holes: 18. **Yards:** 7,007/5,445. **Par:** 72/72. **Course Rating:** 74.8/71.3. **Slope:** 135/122. **Green Fee:** $35/$52. **Cart Fee:** $28/cart. **Walking Policy:** Unrestricted walking. **Walkability:** 1.
Opened: 1982. **Architect:** Robert Trent Jones Sr. **Season:** March-Oct. **High:** April-Sept. **To obtain tee times:** Call golf shop. **Miscellaneous:** Reduced fees (weekdays, low season, resort guests, twilight, juniors), discount packages, metal spikes, range (grass/mats), club rentals, lodging, credit cards (MC, V, AE).
Reader Comments: Feels like Scotland ... Great tee areas. Great layout. Links-style course ... Great links course ... A good challenge, some long walks between holes ... Good condition, good service, good price ... Nice to walk, with risk and reward holes ... Links style, very tough when wind blows.

★★½ RIVERSIDE GOLF RESORT
SP-P.O. Box 993, Fairmont Hot Springs, V0B 1L0, (250)345-6346, (800)665-2112, 15 miles of Invermere. **E-mail:** info@golfriverside.com. **Web:** www.golfriverside.com.
Holes: 18. **Yards:** 6,507/6,102. **Par:** 71/71. **Course Rating:** 71.1/70.3. **Slope:** 129/119. **Green Fee:** $39/$59. **Cart Fee:** $25/cart. **Walking Policy:** Unrestricted walking. **Walkability:** 1.
Opened: 1987. **Season:** March-Nov. **High:** June-Sept. **To obtain tee times:** Call anytime in

advance for upcoming season after Jan. 15. **Miscellaneous:** Reduced fees (weekdays, resort guests, twilight, juniors), discount packages, range (grass/mats), caddies, club rentals, credit cards (MC, V), beginner friendly (CPGA pro lessons).

Reader Comments: All handicap levels will enjoy ... Wide fairways—fair greens ... Beautiful scenery—enjoy.

★★★½ RIVERWAY PUBLIC GOLF COURSE
PM-9001 Riverway Place, Burnaby, V5J 5J3, (604)280-4653, 2 miles E of Vancouver.
Holes: 18. **Yards:** 7,004/5,437. **Par:** 72/72. **Course Rating:** 73.4/72.0. **Slope:** 132/125. **Green Fee:** $39/$39. **Cart Fee:** $26/cart. **Walking Policy:** Unrestricted walking. **Walkability:** 2.
Opened: 1995. **Architect:** Les Furber. **Season:** Year-round. **High:** June-Aug. **To obtain tee times:** Call 2 days in advance at noon. **Miscellaneous:** Reduced fees (low season, twilight, seniors, juniors), metal spikes, range (mats), club rentals, credit cards (MC, V).

Reader Comments: Best public course in British Columbia ... Scotland comes to B.C., a real links-style course ... Links style. Very few trees or shrubbery ... Great fairways and greens.

★★½ ROSSLAND TRAIL COUNTRY CLUB
SP-P.O. Box 250, Trail, V1R 4L5, Canada County, (250)693-2255, 10 miles N of Trail. **E-mail:** golfrtee@wkpowerlink.com.
Holes: 18. **Yards:** 6,489/5,786. **Par:** 72/72. **Course Rating:** 70.1/73.1. **Slope:** 121/129. **Green Fee:** $37/$37. **Cart Fee:** $26/cart. **Walking Policy:** Unrestricted walking. **Walkability:** 2.
Opened: 1963. **Architect:** Reg Stone/Roy Stone. **Season:** March-Oct. **High:** June-Aug. **To obtain tee times:** Call golf shop or book through hotel. **Miscellaneous:** Reduced fees (twilight, juniors), discount packages, metal spikes, range (grass), club rentals, credit cards (MC, V, Bank), beginner friendly (group clinics).

Reader Comments: Love this course- good greens—if I was limited to only 1 course for my life it would be here ... Well groomed.

★★½ SHADOW RIDGE GOLF CLUB
SP-3770 Bulman, Kelowna, V1Y 7P7, (250)765-7777, **E-mail:** shadow_ridge@the sun.net. **Web:** golfokanagan.com.
Holes: 18. **Yards:** 6,475/5,777. **Par:** 71/72. **Course Rating:** 70.3/74.0. **Slope:** 123/130. **Green Fee:** $28/$35. **Cart Fee:** $26/cart. **Walking Policy:** Unrestricted walking. **Walkability:** 1.
Opened: 1988. **Season:** March-Nov. **High:** April-Sept. **To obtain tee times:** Call anytime. **Miscellaneous:** Reduced fees (weekdays, resort guests, twilight, juniors), discount packages, metal spikes, range (mats), club rentals, credit cards (MC, V, AE).

Reader Comments: Fun lower-cost course ... Lots of play, good value ... Great service in pro shop ... Very nice, good price, loved the treelined fairways ... Not too tough for juniors/ladies, tough enough for all levels.

★★½ SHANNON LAKE GOLF COURSE
PU-2649 Shannon Lake Rd., Westbank, V4T 1V6, Canada County, (250)768-4577, 5 miles S of Kelowna. **E-mail:** shannonlk@home.com.
Holes: 18. **Yards:** 6,316/5,494. **Par:** 71/72. **Course Rating:** 70.9/70.9. **Slope:** 125/116. **Green Fee:** $30/$39. **Cart Fee:** $26/cart. **Walking Policy:** Unrestricted walking. **Walkability:** 2.
Opened: 1985. **Architect:** Bob Kains. **Season:** March-Nov. **High:** June-Aug. **To obtain tee times:** Call Golf Shop at (250)768-4577. **Miscellaneous:** Reduced fees (weekdays, low season, resort guests, twilight, juniors), discount packages, metal spikes, range (grass), club rentals, credit cards (MC, V).
Notes: 1999 Zone II BCGA Seniors Tournament.

Reader Comments: Needed improvements being made ... Nice course ... In the Ponderosas.

★★★ SPALLUMCHEEN GOLF & COUNTRY CLUB
PU-P.O. Box 218, 9701, Hwy. 97 N., Vernon, V1T 6M2, (250)545-5824, 8 miles N of Vernon.
Holes: 18. **Yards:** 6,423/5,294. **Par:** 71/71. **Course Rating:** 70.2/74.6. **Slope:** 118/129. **Green Fee:** $40/$42. **Cart Fee:** $26/cart. **Walking Policy:** Unrestricted walking. **Walkability:** 2.
Opened: 1972. **Architect:** Bill Simms/Cyril Foster. **Season:** April-Oct. **High:** June-Aug. **To obtain tee times:** Call up to 2 days in advance. **Miscellaneous:** Reduced fees (twilight), discount packages, metal spikes, range (grass/mats), club rentals, credit cards (MC, V, AE), beginner friendly (9-hole, par-35 executive course).

Reader Comments: Fun course ... Long course, well laid out ... Good greens, easy walk ... Pro shop staff outstanding.

★★★★ SPRINGS AT RADIUM GOLF RESORT
R-Stanley St. and Columbia Ave., Radium Hot Springs, V0A 1M0, Canada County, (250)347-6200, (800)667-6444, 90 miles W of Banff. **Web:** www.springsresort.bc.ca.com.
Holes: 18. **Yards:** 6,767/5,163. **Par:** 72/72. **Course Rating:** 72.3/70.3. **Slope:** 129/126. **Green Fee:** $49/$55. **Cart Fee:** $27/cart. **Walking Policy:** Unrestricted walking. **Walkability:** 3.
Opened: 1988. **Architect:** Les Furber. **Season:** March-Oct. **High:** June-Sept. **To obtain tee times:** Call from January 9th for the upcoming year with credit card to reserve. **Miscellaneous:**

Reduced fees (weekdays, twilight, juniors), discount packages, range (grass), club rentals, credit cards (MC, V, AE).

Reader Comments: Unique track ... Outstanding. Staff 1st rate, food outstanding. Sets the standard! A home course away from home ... Always a pleasure to play ... A very playable course; good views in the valley ... Awesome view, very friendly ... Spectacular views ... Course condition excellent every year... Awesome; if you can live through the first two holes, you can relax.

★★★ SQUAMISH VALLEY GOLF & COUNTRY CLUB

SP-2458 Mamquam Rd., Squamish, V0N 3G0, (604)898-9691, (888)349-3688, 50 miles N of Vancouver. **E-mail:** svgcc@mountain-inter.net. **Web:** www.sunnygolf@bcgolf.guide.com. **Holes:** 18. **Yards:** 6,495/5,148. **Par:** 72/72. **Course Rating:** 71.8/69.9. **Slope:** 132/113. **Green Fee:** $35/$45. **Cart Fee:** $30/cart. **Walking Policy:** Unrestricted walking. **Walkability:** 1. **Opened:** 1970. **Architect:** Gordon McKay/Robert Muir Graves. **Season:** March-Nov. **High:** May-Sept. **To obtain tee times:** Call up to 7 days in advance. **Miscellaneous:** Reduced fees (low season, twilight, seniors, juniors), metal spikes, range (grass/mats), club rentals, credit cards (MC, V).
Reader Comments: Underrated, the best value of any course in the Whistler corridor ... Nice mountain views and good combination of hazards.

★★★★ STOREY CREEK GOLF CLUB

SP-McGimpsey Rd., Campbell River, V9W 6J3, (250)923-3673, 7 miles S of Campbell River. **E-mail:** storeycreek@connected.bc.ca. **Web:** www.crcn.net/storeycreek.com. **Holes:** 18. **Yards:** 6,657/5,434. **Par:** 72/72. **Course Rating:** 73.1/72.0. **Slope:** 138/129. **Green Fee:** $31/$43. **Cart Fee:** $28/cart. **Walking Policy:** Unrestricted walking. **Walkability:** 1. **Opened:** 1989. **Architect:** Les Furber. **Season:** Year-round. **High:** April-Oct. **To obtain tee times:** Call 2 days in advance or more than 2 days with full prepayment. **Miscellaneous:** Reduced fees (low season, resort guests, twilight, juniors), discount packages, range (grass/mats), club rentals, credit cards (MC, V).
Reader Comments: Beautiful treelined course ... Beautiful setting. Watch out for deer ... Superb championship layout ... Solid driving is the key ... Good walking ... Carved out of rain forest. Very challenging ... Wooded course, fairly new with old-style flavor.

★★ SUMMERLAND GOLF & COUNTRY CLUB

SP-2405 Mountain Ave., Summerland, V0H 1Z0, (250)494-9554, 3 miles S of Summerland. **Holes:** 18. **Yards:** 6,535/5,655. **Par:** 72/72. **Course Rating:** 70.7/73.4. **Slope:** 121/128. **Green Fee:** $30/$38. **Cart Fee:** $25/cart. **Walking Policy:** Unrestricted walking. **Walkability:** 2. **Opened:** 1980. **Architect:** Jim McIntyre. **Season:** March-Oct. **High:** June-Sept. **To obtain tee times:** Call up to 4 days in advance. **Miscellaneous:** Reduced fees (low season, resort guests, twilight, juniors), discount packages, metal spikes, range (grass), club rentals, credit cards (MC, V).

★★★ SUNSET RANCH GOLF & COUNTRY CLUB

SP-4001 Anderson Rd., Kelowna, V1X 7V8, (250)765-7700, . **E-mail:** sunset@silk.net. **Web:** sunsetranchbc.com. **Holes:** 18. **Yards:** 6,558/5,752. **Par:** 72/72. **Course Rating:** 71.2/73.3. **Slope:** 128/125. **Green Fee:** $29/$49. **Cart Fee:** $25/cart. **Walking Policy:** Unrestricted walking. **Walkability:** 3. **Opened:** 1991. **Architect:** J. Bruce Carr. **Season:** March-Oct. **High:** June-Sept. **To obtain tee times:** Call Golf Shop. **Miscellaneous:** Reduced fees (low season, resort guests, twilight, juniors), metal spikes, range (grass), club rentals, credit cards (MC, V, AE).
Reader Comments: Tough course for higher handicappers ... Unforgiving course if off the fairway ... Nice setting, nice view of airport ... Good par threes.

★★★½ SWAN-E-SET BAY RESORT & COUNTRY CLUB

SP-16651 Rannie Rd., Pitt Meadows, V3Y 1Z1, (604)465-3888, (800)235-8188, 27 miles E of Vancouver. **E-mail:** swaneset@axionet.com. **Web:** www.swaneset.com. **Holes:** 36. **Yards:** 7,000/5,632. **Par:** 72/72. **Course Rating:** 73.8/71.5. **Slope:** 130/120. **Green Fee:** $30/$62. **Cart Fee:** $25/cart. **Walking Policy:** Unrestricted walking. **Walkability:** 2. **Opened:** 1993. **Architect:** Lee Trevino. **Season:** Year-round. **High:** April-Oct. **To obtain tee times:** Call 7 days in advance. **Miscellaneous:** Reduced fees (weekdays, low season, twilight, juniors), metal spikes, range (grass/mats), club rentals, credit cards (MC, V, AE, Diners Club).
Reader Comments: Links style ... Magnificent clubhouse ... Best around ... Good challenging holes ... Was a fun day ... Huge beautiful clubhouse.

★★★★½ TRICKLE CREEK GOLF RESORT

R-500 Gerry Sorensen Way, Kimberley, Canada County, (250)427-3389, (888)874-2553, **E-mail:** trickle@rockies.net. **Web:** www.tricklecreek.com. **Holes:** 18. **Yards:** 6,896/5,082. **Par:** 72/72. **Course Rating:** 72.9/64.6. **Slope:** 133/117. **Green Fee:** $44/$49. **Cart Fee:** $24/cart. **Walking Policy:** Unrestricted walking. **Walkability:** 5. **Opened:** 1993. **Architect:** Les Furber. **Season:** May-Oct. **High:** May-Sept. **To obtain tee times:** Call anytime starting January 1st for the upcoming year. **Miscellaneous:** Reduced fees (weekdays, twilight), discount packages, metal spikes, range (grass), club rentals, lodging (80 rooms), credit cards (MC, V, AE).

CANADA

Reader Comments: Each hole a picture, best in the area ... One of finest in B.C. ... One of the most challenging courses I've played ... Scenic locale ... Great shape with friendly helpful staff ... Best kept secret. Interesting! ... Breathtaking location in charming town; Nos. 11-13 awesome. Could play here forever ... Incredible, but never a level stance.

★★★½ UNIVERSITY GOLF CLUB
PU-5185 University Blvd., Vancouver, V6T 1X5, Canada County, (604)224-1818
Holes: 18. **Yards:** 6,584/5,653. **Par:** 72/72. **Course Rating:** 71.5/71.9. **Slope:** 122/122. **Green Fee:** $32/$50. **Cart Fee:** $32/cart. **Walking Policy:** Unrestricted walking. **Walkability:** 3. **Opened:** 1929. **Architect:** Davey Black. **Season:** Year-round. **High:** April-Oct. **To obtain tee times:** Call 7 days in advance with credit card. **Miscellaneous:** Reduced fees (low season, twilight), metal spikes, range (mats), club rentals, credit cards (MC, V, AE).
Reader Comments: A hidden gem ... Old-fashioned course, tougher than you think ... Par 3s short ... Hilly ... Good course, great setting.

★★★½ VERNON GOLF & COUNTRY CLUB
SP-800 Kalamalka Lake Rd., Vernon, V1T 6V2, Canada County, (250)542-9126, 2 miles S of Vernon. **E-mail:** pro@vernongolf.com. **Web:** www3.bc.sympatico.ca/vernongolf.com.
Holes: 18. **Yards:** 6,597/5,666. **Par:** 72/74. **Course Rating:** 71.1/71.4. **Slope:** 123/118. **Green Fee:** $25/$45. **Cart Fee:** $27/cart. **Walking Policy:** Unrestricted walking. **Walkability:** 3. **Opened:** 1913. **Architect:** Ernie Brown/Graham Cooke. **Season:** March-Oct. **High:** May-Aug. **To obtain tee times:** Call Thurs. after 2 p.m. for play on Sat., Sun. and Mon. Call Sun. after 2 p.m. for Tues.-Fri. **Miscellaneous:** Reduced fees (low season, twilight), discount packages, range (mats), club rentals, credit cards (MC, V), beginner friendly.
Reader Comments: Good retirement course; no one in a hurry ... Harder than it looks. Great friendly staff ... Good course, always enjoyable playing ... Excellent greens ... Hilly.

★★★★ WESTWOOD PLATEAU GOLF & COUNTRY CLUB
Service+, Condition
PU-3251 Plateau Blvd., Coquitlam, V3E 3B8, Canada County, (604)552-0777, (800)580-0785, 12 miles E of Vancouver. **E-mail:** jmclaughlin@westwood/plateau.bc.ca.com. **Web:** www.westwoodplateaugolf.bc.ca.com.
Holes: 18. **Yards:** 6,770/5,014. **Par:** 72/72. **Course Rating:** 71.9/68.2. **Slope:** 136/123. **Green Fee:** $90/$125. **Cart Fee:** Included in Green Fee. **Walking Policy:** Mandatory cart. **Walkability:** 4. **Opened:** 1995. **Architect:** Michael Hurdzan. **Season:** April-Oct. **High:** June-Sept. **To obtain tee times:** More than a week in advance requires $25 reservation fee per foursome. **Miscellaneous:** Reduced fees (weekdays, low season, twilight, juniors), range (grass/mats), club rentals, lodging, credit cards (MC, V, AE, Diners Club).
Reader Comments: Spectacular scenery ... First-class mountain golf ...No. 15's the best par 4 in B.C.; excellent yardage book ... Used every club in the bag ... Wow, elegant, artful, thrilling ... Excellent service ... Trees and views, challenging ... Exceptional views and natural setting... Hilly, fun, good view of city.

★★★★ WHISTLER GOLF CLUB
R-4001 Whistler Way, Whistler, V0N 1B4, Canada County, (604)932-3280, (800)376-1777, 80 miles N of Vancouver. **Web:** www.whistlergolf.com.
Holes: 18. **Yards:** 6,400/5,434. **Par:** 72/72. **Course Rating:** 71.3/70.5. **Slope:** 132/120. **Green Fee:** $80/$125. **Cart Fee:** $30/cart. **Walking Policy:** Unrestricted walking. **Walkability:** 2. **Opened:** 1982. **Architect:** Arnold Palmer. **Season:** May-Oct. **High:** June-Sept. **To obtain tee times:** Call within 30 days of play. Hotel guests call anytime. **Miscellaneous:** Reduced fees (low season, twilight), discount packages, metal spikes, range (grass/mats), club rentals, lodging, credit cards (MC, V, AE).
Reader Comments: Beautiful surroundings, very playable course ... Don't miss this one. Not too long, but tricky, target golf ... Nice views, tight course ... Soak up the views.

MANITOBA

★★★½ CLEAR LAKE GOLF COURSE
PU-Box 328, Onanole, R0J 1N0, (204)848-4653, 150 miles NW of Winnipeg.
Holes: 18. **Yards:** 6,070/6,070. **Par:** 72/72. **Course Rating:** 69.3/72.7. **Slope:** 120/130. **Green Fee:** $24/$28. **Cart Fee:** $13/person. **Walking Policy:** Unrestricted walking. **Walkability:** 4. **Opened:** 1933. **Architect:** Stanley Thompson. **Season:** May-Oct. **High:** June-Aug. **To obtain tee times:** Call up to 7 days in advance. **Miscellaneous:** Reduced fees (low season, twilight, juniors), metal spikes, club rentals, credit cards (MC, V).
Reader Comments: Excellent location and course ... Beautiful forest scenery, great game ... Fine old course ... Beautiful setting, located in hilly area of mostly flat Manitoba ... Good service,

course friendly to all levels of play ... Most beautiful course in Manitoba ... Scenic, hilly even on the prairies.

★★★★ FALCON LAKE GOLF COURSE

PU-South Shore Rd. & Green, Falcon Lake, R0E 0N0, (204)349-2554, 85 miles E of Winnipeg.
Holes: 18. **Yards:** 6,937/5,978. **Par:** 72/73. **Course Rating:** 72.6/72.0. **Slope:** 121/115. **Green Fee:** $26/$30. **Cart Fee:** $23/cart. **Walking Policy:** Unrestricted walking. **Walkability:** 2.
Opened: 1958. **Architect:** Norman Woods. **Season:** April-Oct. **High:** July-Aug. **To obtain tee times:** Call up to 14 days in advance beginning at 7 p.m. **Miscellaneous:** Reduced fees (weekdays, twilight, seniors, juniors), metal spikes, range (grass/mats), club rentals, lodging, credit cards (MC, V, AE).
Reader Comments: Great fall colors, immaculate fairways and greens, still the golf is excellent ... Plays long, very scenic, quite flat ... Best course in Manitoba ... Lovely parkland setting ... Challenging wilderness layout ... Beautiful greens ... Very enjoyable, excellent condition ... Very long, scenic. Good mixture of holes, wide, treelined fairways a fair test from any tee box.

★★★★ HECLA GOLF COURSE AT GULL HARBOR RESORT *Condition*

R-P.O. Box 1000, Riverton, R0C 2R0, (204)279-2072, (800)267-6700, 110 miles N of Winnipeg.
Holes: 18. **Yards:** 6,678/5,535. **Par:** 72/72. **Course Rating:** 71.7/70.7. **Slope:** 122/118. **Green Fee:** $23/$27. **Cart Fee:** $23/cart. **Walking Policy:** Unrestricted walking. **Walkability:** 2.
Opened: 1975. **Architect:** Jack Thompson. **Season:** May-Oct. **High:** June-Aug. **To obtain tee times:** Public may call 14 days in advance. Resort guests may call anytime. **Miscellaneous:** Reduced fees (twilight, seniors, juniors), discount packages, metal spikes, range (grass), club rentals, lodging, credit cards (MC, V, AE).
Reader Comments: Manitoba's Pebble Beach, ... A scenic test of golf ... Worth the trip and then some ... Stunning, a great golf experience ... Wide, forgiving fairways with challenging par 3s and water views to die for; bunkers are well groomed ... Beautiful views of Lake Winnipeg ... The grass was lush, green and just so nice to play. The scenery is beautiful.

★★½ JOHN BLUMBERG GOLF COURSE

PU-4540 Portage Ave., Headingley, R4H IC8, (204)986-3490, 1 miles W of Winnipeg.
Holes: 27. **Yards:** 6,343/5,844. **Par:** 71/71. **Course Rating:** 70.2/68.0. **Slope:** 116/111. **Green Fee:** $18/$18. **Cart Fee:** $22/cart. **Walking Policy:** Unrestricted walking. **Walkability:** 5.
Opened: 1969. **Architect:** Robbie Robinson. **Season:** April-Nov. **High:** May-Sept. **To obtain tee times:** Call 3 days in advance. **Miscellaneous:** Reduced fees (twilight, seniors, juniors), metal spikes, range (grass/mats), club rentals, credit cards (MC, V, AE), beginner friendly.
Reader Comments: Easily best muny ... Busy. River holes are tough ... Difficult ... Course needs more work, especially fairways ... Flat, caters to the masses.

★★★ LARTERS AT ST. ANDREWS GOLF & COUNTRY CLUB

SP-30 River Rd., St. Andrews, R1A 2V1, (204)334-2107, 5 miles N of Winnipeg.
Holes: 18. **Yards:** 6,226/5,274. **Par:** 70/70. **Course Rating:** 70.0/69.7. **Slope:** 120/113. **Green Fee:** $27/$30. **Cart Fee:** $27/cart. **Walking Policy:** Unrestricted walking. **Walkability:** 1.
Opened: 1990. **Architect:** David Wagner. **Season:** April-Oct. **High:** May-Sept. **To obtain tee times:** Non-members call 7 days in advance. **Miscellaneous:** Reduced fees (twilight, juniors), discount packages, range (grass/mats), club rentals, credit cards (MC, V, AE, Diners Club).
Reader Comments: Well groomed and challenging, lots of variety ... Great staff ... Crowded, great greens.

THE LINKS AT QUARRY OAKS *Service*

PU-Box 3629, Hwy. 311 E., Steinbach, R0A 2A0, (204)326-4653, 35 miles SE of Winnipeg.
E-mail: quarryo@ccco.net. **Web:** www.ccco.net/quarry_oaks.
Holes: 27. **Green Fee:** $32/$54. **Cart Fee:** Included in Green Fee. **Walking Policy:** Unrestricted walking. **Walkability:** 3. **Opened:** 1992. **Architect:** Les Furber. **Season:** April-Oct. **High:** June-Aug. **To obtain tee times:** Call 14 days in advance with credit card. **Miscellaneous:** Reduced fees (weekdays, low season, twilight, seniors, juniors), discount packages, range (grass), club rentals, credit cards (MC, V, AE), beginner friendly (green tees cut yardage in half).
★★★★ DESERT/OAK
Yards: 6,808/5,136. **Par:** 72/72. **Course Rating:** 72.1/65.5. **Slope:** 136/110.
★★★★ OAK/QUARRY
Yards: 7,000/5,407. **Par:** 72/72. **Course Rating:** 73.7/66.9. **Slope:** 140/119.
★★★★ QUARRY/DESERT
Yards: 7,100/5,405. **Par:** 72/72. **Course Rating:** 74.2/67.2. **Slope:** 139/118.
Reader Comments: Great service, variety, pace, free range, and ice on board carts ... Grass in fairways and greens too long ... Excellent service, bring your A-game ... Easily #1 in province ... Wow! Variety, challenge, everything ... VIP treatment, public course with private club treatment and atmosphere.

★★½ SELKIRK GOLF & COUNTRY CLUB

SP-100 Sutherland Ave., Selkirk, R1A 2B1, (204)482-2050, 20 miles N of Winnipeg.

CANADA

Holes: 9. **Yards:** 6,433/5,862. **Par:** 71/72. **Course Rating:** 69.4/72.2. **Slope:** 117/117. **Green Fee:** $13/$25. **Cart Fee:** $24/cart. **Walking Policy:** Unrestricted walking. **Walkability:** 1. **Opened:** 1931. **Architect:** Jack Thompson. **Season:** April-Oct. **High:** June-Aug. **To obtain tee times:** Call 3 days in advance. **Miscellaneous:** Reduced fees (low season, twilight), range (mats), club rentals, credit cards (MC, V, Debit Card).

Reader Comments: Nice rural course ... Took only 3 1/2 hours for 18 holes ... Good variety of holes, challenging, inexpensive ... Good all around.

★★★½ STEINBACH FLY-IN GOLF COURSE
SP-P.O. Box 3716, Steinbach, R0A 2A0, Canada County, (204)326-6813.
Holes: 18. **Yards:** 6,544/5,445. **Par:** 72/73. **Course Rating:** 72.3/70.2. **Slope:** 125/115. **Green Fee:** $14/$26. **Cart Fee:** $26/cart. **Walking Policy:** Unrestricted walking. **Walkability:** 1. **Opened:** 1970. **Architect:** Robbie Robinson. **Season:** April-Oct. **High:** May-Sept. **To obtain tee times:** Call 2 days in advance. **Miscellaneous:** Reduced fees (weekdays, low season, twilight, seniors, juniors), discount packages, range (grass), club rentals, credit cards (MC, V), beginner friendly.

Reader Comments: Solid value ... Lots of flowers, water and hills ... Big improvement with recent upgrades ... Fair is first word that comes to mind.

★★★★ TEULON GOLF & COUNTRY CLUB *Value*
SP-Hwy. 7 N., Teulon, R0C 3B0, (204)886-4653, 30 miles N of Winnipeg.
Holes: 18. **Yards:** 6,426/5,256. **Par:** 72/71. **Course Rating:** 71.0/69.0. **Slope:** 115/111. **Green Fee:** $15/$27. **Cart Fee:** $24/cart. **Walking Policy:** Unrestricted walking. **Walkability:** 2. **Opened:** 1961. **Architect:** Robert Heaslip. **Season:** April-Oct. **High:** June-Aug. **To obtain tee times:** Call 2 days in advance. Walk-ons welcome in off-peak season. **Miscellaneous:** Reduced fees (weekdays, low season, twilight, seniors, juniors), discount packages, range (grass/mats), club rentals, credit cards (MC, V, AE).

Reader Comments: Flat and windy ... This course has matured, ... Beautiful country course ... Very nice course ... Small town food and service, great value.

NEW BRUNSWICK

★★★½ THE ALGONQUIN AT ST. ANDREWS BY-THE-SEA
R-151 Reed Ave., St. Andrews, E0G 2X0, (506)529-7142, 60 miles SW of Saint John.
Holes: 18. **Yards:** N/A. **Par:** N/A. **Course Rating:** N/A. **Slope:** N/A. **Green Fee:** $25/$50. **Cart Fee:** $32/cart. **Walking Policy:** Unrestricted walking. **Walkability:** 4. **Opened:** 1894. **Architect:** Donald Ross. **Season:** April-Nov. **High:** June-Sept. **To obtain tee times:** Call anytime throughout season. During off season tee times can be obtained when booking accommodation (506)529-8823. **Miscellaneous:** Reduced fees (low season, twilight), discount packages, range (grass), club rentals, lodging (238 rooms), credit cards (MC, V, AE, D, Diners Club, En Route).

Reader Comments: In the process of redesigning ... Beautiful location ... Very picturesque ... Tough course but fair ... Friendly course ... Great views ... Fun to play... Sea views are memorable, classic design.

★★★ AROOSTOOK VALLEY COUNTRY CLUB
SP-, Four Falls, E0J 1V0, Victoria County, (207)476-8083, 3 miles NE of Fort Fairfield, ME.
Holes: 18. **Yards:** 6,304/5,397. **Par:** 72/72. **Course Rating:** 69.9/70.0. **Slope:** 117/119. **Green Fee:** $22/$22. **Cart Fee:** $22/cart. **Walking Policy:** Unrestricted walking. **Walkability:** 4. **Opened:** 1927. **Architect:** Howard Watson. **Season:** April-Oct. **High:** June-Aug. **Miscellaneous:** Reduced fees (low season), metal spikes, range (grass), club rentals, credit cards (MC, V).

Reader Comments: Tough walk., various lakes ... Different ... Dramatic par fives, fast greens, great variety.

★½ COUNTRY MEADOWS GOLF CLUB
SP-149 Catamount Rd., Indian Mountain, E1G 3A7, Westmerland County, (506)858-8909, 8 miles N of Moncton.
Holes: 18. **Yards:** 6,314/5,363. **Par:** 72/72. **Course Rating:** 69.1/71.1. **Slope:** 116/119. **Green Fee:** $20/$23. **Cart Fee:** $23/cart. **Walking Policy:** Unrestricted walking. **Walkability:** 2. **Opened:** 1973. **Architect:** Doug Sullivan. **Season:** April-Oct. **High:** May-Sept. **To obtain tee times:** Call ahead, 2 days maximum. **Miscellaneous:** Reduced fees (weekdays, low season), metal spikes, range (grass), club rentals, credit cards (MC, V, AE), beginner friendly.

★★★ COVERED BRIDGE GOLF & COUNTRY CLUB
PU-190 Golf Club Road, Hartland, E7P3K4, Carleton County, (506)375-1112, (888)346-5777, 65 miles N of Fredericton.
Holes: 18. **Yards:** 6,609/5,412. **Par:** 72/72. **Course Rating:** 71.3/N/A. **Slope:** 132/111. **Green Fee:** $30/$30. **Cart Fee:** $24/cart. **Walking Policy:** Unrestricted walking. **Walkability:** 3. **Opened:** 1992. **Architect:** John Robinson. **Season:** May-Oct. **High:** June-Aug. **To obtain tee

times: Call 4 days in advance. **Miscellaneous:** Reduced fees (resort guests), discount packages, range (grass), club rentals, lodging (12 rooms), credit cards (MC, V, AE, Diners Club), beginner friendly (Little Swingers program for 10 and under).

Reader Comments: Great target course, not crowded, challenging ... Fun, wind can be a factor ... Will be a great course when trees grow more ... Very picturesque ... New course—will be super when trees grow in more ... Excellent ... Young course, good potential, scenic ... Excellent condition ... A good test of golf.

★★★★ EDMUNDSTON GOLF CLUB

PU-570 Victoria St., C.P. 263, Edmundston, E3V 3K9, Madawaska County, (506)735-3086, 200 miles E of Quebec City.

Holes: 18. **Yards:** 6,694/5,342. **Par:** 73/73. **Course Rating:** 71.6/69.5. **Slope:** 124/119. **Green Fee:** $25/$35. **Cart Fee:** $28/cart. **Walking Policy:** Unrestricted walking. **Walkability:** 3.
Opened: 1926. **Season:** May-Oct. **High:** June-Aug. **To obtain tee times:** Call (506) 735-4831.
Miscellaneous: Reduced fees (low season, twilight), discount packages, metal spikes, range (grass), caddies, credit cards (MC, V).

Reader Comments: It's an outstanding course ... Lots of tight fairways, ... Bring all your clubs–You'll be hitting them all ... My favorite course, I give it 4 stars ... Majestic trees. Breathtaking peacefulness ... Likely the best course in New Brunswick–excellent facilities, good architecture ... Exceptional, golf at it's best ... Difficult, fun at every turn.

★★½ FREDERICTON GOLF & CURLING CLUB

SP-331 Golf Club Rd., Fredericton, E3B 429, Canada County, (506)458-1003. **E-mail:** hgcogolf@nbnet.nb.ca. **Web:** hgcogolf.hypermart.net.

Holes: 18. **Yards:** 6,285/5,450. **Par:** 70/72. **Course Rating:** 67.7/72.0. **Slope:** 120/122. **Green Fee:** $35/$45. **Cart Fee:** $30/cart. **Walking Policy:** Unrestricted walking. **Walkability:** 3.
Opened: 1917. **Architect:** C. Robinson/G. Cornish/W. Robinson. **Season:** April-Nov. **High:** July-Sept. **To obtain tee times:** Walk-ons welcome. **Miscellaneous:** Range (grass), club rentals, credit cards (MC, V), beginner friendly (cpga group clinics).

Reader Comments: Best greens in province ... Easy to get to, scenic, nice golf course ... Short course but challenging.

GAGE GOLF & CURLING ASSOCIATION

13 Waterville Rd. R.R. 3, Oromocto, E2V 2G3, (506)357-9343.
Special Notes: Call club for further information.

GOLF BOUCTOUCHE

PU-Case Postale 568, Bouctouche, E0A 1G0, Canada County, (506)743-5251, 30 miles N of Moncton.

Holes: 18. **Yards:** 6,182/5,301. **Par:** 72/72. **Course Rating:** 68.0/69.0. **Slope:** 114/113. **Green Fee:** $22/$25. **Cart Fee:** $26/cart. **Walking Policy:** Unrestricted walking. **Walkability:** 1.
Opened: 1982. **Season:** May-Oct. **High:** July-August. **To obtain tee times:** Call 2 days in advance. **Miscellaneous:** Reduced fees (weekdays, low season), range (grass), caddies, club rentals, credit cards (MC, V).

GOWAN BRAE GOLF & COUNTRY CLUB

SP-150 Youghall Dr., Bathurst, E2A 3Z1, Gloucester County, (506)546-2707
Holes: 18. **Yards:** 6,577/5,979. **Par:** 72/74. **Course Rating:** 71.3/73.0. **Slope:** 129/125. **Green Fee:** $36/$36. **Cart Fee:** $30/cart. **Walking Policy:** Unrestricted walking. **Walkability:** 3.
Opened: 1958. **Architect:** Robbie Robinson. **Season:** May-Nov. **High:** July-Aug. **To obtain tee times:** Call 2 days in advance. **Miscellaneous:** Reduced fees (twilight), range (grass/mats), club rentals, credit cards (MC, V, Inter-Act).

GRAND FALLS GOLF CLUB

SP-803 Main St., Grand-Sault, E3Y 1A7, (506)475-6008, 120 miles N of Fredericton. **Web:** www.sn2000.nb.ca.

Holes: 18. **Yards:** 6,632/5,122. **Par:** 72/72. **Course Rating:** 70.6/68.6. **Slope:** 122/111. **Green Fee:** $25/$30. **Cart Fee:** $30/cart. **Walking Policy:** Unrestricted walking. **Walkability:** 4.
Opened: 1990. **Architect:** Bob Moote. **Season:** May-Oct. **High:** June-Sept. **To obtain tee times:** Call golf shop. **Miscellaneous:** Reduced fees (low season, juniors), discount packages, range (grass), club rentals, credit cards (MC, V).
Notes: 1998 Host of NB Junior Championship.

★★★ HAMPTON COUNTRY CLUB

PU-William Bell Dr., Rte. 100, Hampton, E0G 1Z0, Kings County, (506)832-3411, 18 miles E of Saint John.

Holes: 18. **Yards:** 6,291/5,430. **Par:** 72/73. **Course Rating:** 69.9/72.0. **Slope:** 118/132. **Green Fee:** $32/$35. **Cart Fee:** $25/cart. **Walking Policy:** Unrestricted walking. **Walkability:** 3.
Opened: 1972. **Architect:** Cecil Manuge. **Season:** May-Oct. **High:** June-Aug. **To obtain tee times:** Call 2 days in advance. **Miscellaneous:** Reduced fees (low season, twilight), discount packages, range (grass), club rentals, credit cards (MC, V).

Reader Comments: Million dollar view! 666-yard par 6. Interesting for all 18 holes ... Wow! Top-notch, well-kept secret, fun to play ...Course almost always in good shape. Service very good ... Hilly in spots ... Par-6 hole is fun. Local knowledge essential to score.

★★ LAKESIDE GOLF CLUB

SP-1896 Rte. 134, Lakeville, E1H 1A7, Westmorland County, (506)861-9441, 3 miles E of Moncton.
Holes: 18. **Yards:** 5,880/5,612. **Par:** 70/71. **Course Rating:** 67.3/68.3. **Slope:** 110/117. **Green Fee:** $25/$25. **Cart Fee:** $25/cart. **Walking Policy:** Unrestricted walking. **Walkability:** 1.
Opened: 1926. **Season:** May-Nov. **High:** July-Aug. **To obtain tee times:** Call 20 days in advance. **Miscellaneous:** Metal spikes, range (grass/mats), club rentals, credit cards (MC, V).

LE CLUB DE GOLF DE ST. IGNACE

SP-R.R. H1, Site 1, Box 11, St. Ignace, E0A 2Z0, Kent County, (506)876-3737, 55 miles N of Moncton.
Holes: 18. **Yards:** 6,325/5,694. **Par:** 72/72. **Course Rating:** 70.2/73.0. **Slope:** 125/131. **Green Fee:** $20/$25. **Cart Fee:** $25/cart. **Walking Policy:** Unrestricted walking. **Walkability:** 4.
Opened: 1984. **Architect:** Geoffrey Cornish. **Season:** May-Oct. **High:** July-Aug. **To obtain tee times:** Call Golf Shop. **Miscellaneous:** Reduced fees (weekdays), discount packages, metal spikes, range (grass/mats), club rentals, credit cards (MC, V, AE).

★★★★ MACTAQUAC PROVINCIAL PARK GOLF CLUB

PU-1256 Rte. 105, Mactaquac, E6L 1B5, (506)363-4925, 15 miles N of Fredericton.
Holes: 18. **Yards:** 7,030/5,756. **Par:** 72/72. **Course Rating:** 74.0/71.0. **Slope:** 131/117. **Green Fee:** $30/$35. **Cart Fee:** $24/cart. **Walking Policy:** Unrestricted walking. **Walkability:** 2.
Opened: 1970. **Architect:** William Mitchell. **Season:** May-Oct. **High:** May-Oct. **To obtain tee times:** Call 2 days in advance for locals, anytime for nonresidents. **Miscellaneous:** Reduced fees (low season, twilight), range (grass), club rentals, credit cards (MC, V).
Reader Comments: Long, big greens and fairways, 14th is a great risk/reward hole ... Pretty ... Best in New Brunswick, outstanding golf ... Beautiful, immaculate ... Best-kept secret ... Great value, $30 Canadian green fees for entire day. Course very well kept. Resulted in many skipped classes last semester ... Excellent greens and fairways, very challenging, good practice area.

★★½ MAGNETIC HILL GOLF & COUNTRY CLUB

PU-1 Tee Time Dr., Moncton, E1G 3T7, Westmorland County, (506)858-1611, **E-mail:** maghill@auracom.com. **Web:** www.maghillgolf.com.
Holes: 18. **Yards:** 5,692/5,292. **Par:** 70/70. **Course Rating:** 66.4/69.2. **Slope:** 112/115. **Green Fee:** $29/$29. **Cart Fee:** $27/cart. **Walking Policy:** Unrestricted walking. **Walkability:** 3.
Opened: 1967. **Season:** May-Oct. **High:** June-Aug. **To obtain tee times:** Call Golf Shop.
Miscellaneous: Range (grass/mats), club rentals, credit cards (MC, V), beginner friendly.
Reader Comments: Very good ... Short par 4s ... Good condition ... Well-maintained ... Hilly, enjoy playing there ... Challenging short course, interesting blend of holes, staff friendly.

MAPLEWOOD GOLF & COUNTRY CLUB

PU-2572 Rte. 115, Irishtown, E1H 2L8, (506)858-7840, (506)858-7840, 6 miles N of Moncton.
Holes: 18. **Yards:** 6,301/5,081. **Par:** 71/71. **Course Rating:** 69.3/67.2. **Slope:** 118/111. **Green Fee:** $25/$25. **Cart Fee:** $25/cart. **Walking Policy:** Unrestricted walking. **Walkability:** 2. **Opened:** 1983. **Architect:** Dale Rasmussen. **Season:** May-Oct. **High:** July-Aug. **To obtain tee times:** Tee times required until 2 p.m. everyday. Call 2 days in advance. Call Thursday or after for Saturday and Sunday tee times. **Miscellaneous:** Metal spikes, club rentals, credit cards (MC, V, AE).

MIRAMICHI GOLF & COUNTRY CLUB

SP-930 Water St., Miramichi, E1V 3M5, Northhumberland County, (506)622-2068 **Web:** http://www.compuwer.nb.ca.mgcc.com.
Holes: 18. **Yards:** 6,212/5,371. **Par:** 71/71. **Course Rating:** 69.3/73.0. **Slope:** 116/127. **Green Fee:** $30/$30. **Cart Fee:** $24/cart. **Walking Policy:** Unrestricted walking. **Walkability:** 1.
Opened: 1925. **Architect:** John Robinson. **Season:** May-Oct. **High:** June-Sept. **To obtain tee times:** Call golf shop 2 days in advance. **Miscellaneous:** Discount packages, metal spikes, range (grass), caddies, club rentals, credit cards (MC, V), beginner friendly (junior program).

★★★ MONCTON GOLF AND COUNTRY CLUB

SP-212 Coverdale Rd., Riverview, E1B 4T9, Westmorland County, (506)387-3855, 1 miles N of Moncton.
Holes: 18. **Yards:** 6,263/5,654. **Par:** 70/72. **Course Rating:** 69.0/71.4. **Slope:** 123/119. **Green Fee:** $40/$40. **Cart Fee:** $30/cart. **Walking Policy:** Unrestricted walking. **Walkability:** 1.
Opened: 1929. **Architect:** Stanley Thompson. **Season:** May-Oct. **High:** June-Sept. **To obtain tee times:** Call up to 2 days in advance. **Miscellaneous:** Range (grass), caddies, club rentals, credit cards (MC, V, AE).
Reader Comments: Wonderful short course. Par 3s will keep your score above par ... Well wooded; challenging; good test.

CANADA

★★½ PETITCODIAC VALLEY GOLF & COUNTRY CLUB
SP-Golf Course Rd., Petitcodiac, E0A 2H0, (506)756-8129, 25 miles W of Moncton.
Holes: 18. **Yards:** 5,932/5,581. **Par:** 71/71. **Course Rating:** 66.7/71.1. **Slope:** 114/119. **Green Fee:** $24/$24. **Cart Fee:** $20/cart. **Walking Policy:** Unrestricted walking. **Walkability:** 3.
Opened: 1960. **Season:** April-Oct. **High:** July-Sept. **To obtain tee times:** Call Golf Shop.
Miscellaneous: Reduced fees (resort guests, seniors, juniors), discount packages, range (grass), club rentals, credit cards (MC, V).
Reader Comments: Best-kept secret in New Brunswick ... Family course, with many blind shots. Local knowledge needed ... Expansion is maturing nicely. Good pricing.

PINE NEEDLES GOLF & COUNTRY CLUB
PU-R.R. No.1, P.O. Box 1, Shediac, E0A 3G0, (506)532-4634, 20 miles NE of Moncton. **E-mail:** pineneed@fundy.net.
Holes: 27. **Cart Fee:** $24/cart. **Walking Policy:** Unrestricted walking. **Season:** May-Oct. **High:** July-Aug. **To obtain tee times:** Call 2 days in advance for weekends and holidays.
Miscellaneous: Reduced fees (twilight), club rentals, credit cards (MC, V).
★★★½ ORCHARD/RIVER
Yards: 6,091/5,354. **Par:** 72/73. **Course Rating:** 67.6/69.8. **Slope:** 112/123. **Green Fee:** $24/$24. **Walkability:** 3. **Opened:** 1990.
Reader Comments: Beautiful course ... Friendly staff ... Well-marked and nicely-maintained 27 holes, with some interesting challenges ... Interesting layout. 3 different tests and surroundings.
★★★½ PINE/ORCHARD
Yards: 5,919/5,280. **Par:** 71/72. **Course Rating:** 66.2/69.4. **Slope:** 106/119. **Green Fee:** $25/$25. **Walkability:** 1. **Opened:** 1973.
★★★½ RIVER/PINE
Yards: 6,430/5,338. **Par:** 73/73. **Course Rating:** 69.7/71.4. **Slope:** 119/127. **Green Fee:** $25/$25. **Walkability:** 1. **Opened:** 1990.

RESTIGOUCHE GOLF & COUNTRY CLUB
PU-Box 8 Site 11 R.R. 2, Campbellton, E3N 3E8, (506)789-7628
Holes: 18. **Yards:** 5,652/4,989. **Par:** 70/73. **Course Rating:** 69.1/69.0. **Slope:** 126/119. **Green Fee:** $20/$27. **Cart Fee:** $22/cart. **Walking Policy:** Unrestricted walking. **Walkability:** 5.
Opened: 1923. **Season:** May-Oct. **High:** July-Aug. **To obtain tee times:** Call 1 day in advance.
Miscellaneous: Reduced fees (low season), metal spikes, club rentals, credit cards (MC, V).

★★½ RIVERBEND GOLF & FISHING CLUB
PU-541 Rte. 628 Durham Bridge, Fredericton, E3A 9C1, York County, (506)452-7277, 15 miles N of Fredericton.
Holes: 18. **Yards:** 6,436/5,466. **Par:** 72/72. **Course Rating:** 71.0/71.1. **Slope:** 121/114. **Green Fee:** $21/$24. **Cart Fee:** $22/cart. **Walking Policy:** Unrestricted walking. **Walkability:** 1.
Opened: 1992. **Architect:** Graham Cooke. **Season:** April-Oct. **High:** May-Sept. **To obtain tee times:** Call 24 hours in advance. **Miscellaneous:** Reduced fees (weekdays), discount packages, range (grass), club rentals, credit cards (MC, V).
Reader Comments: An excellent test ... Great greens ... Some very interesting holes ... Challenging, well-kept greens, long walk ... Very tough, friendly staff and owners, country setting.

★★★ ROCKWOOD PARK GOLF COURSE
PM-1255 Sandy Point Road, St. John, E2L 4B3, St. John County, (506)634-0090.
Holes: 18. **Yards:** 6,017/5,023. **Par:** 70/69. **Course Rating:** 68.0/69.0. **Slope:** 117/113. **Green Fee:** $21/$26. **Cart Fee:** $26/cart. **Walking Policy:** Unrestricted walking. **Walkability:** 4.
Opened: 1973. **Season:** May-Oct. **High:** June-Sept. **To obtain tee times:** Call 1 day in advance.
Miscellaneous: Reduced fees (weekdays, low season, twilight, seniors, juniors), metal spikes, range (mats), club rentals, credit cards (MC, V, AE).
Reader Comments: One great municipal course–huge tough greens ... Hidden gem, accuracy essential, No. 17 worth the trip ... Excellent muny course, big greens ... Challenging and exceptionally picturesque muny course. Excellent value ... Well-kept course, great greens and fairways.

ST. STEPHEN GOLF CLUB
PU-Old Bay Rd., P.O. Box 272, St. Stephen, E3L 2X2, Charlotte County, (506)466-5336, 60 miles W of St. John, New Brunswick.
Holes: 18. **Yards:** 6,075/6,075. **Par:** 71/71. **Course Rating:** 69.1/74.0. **Slope:** 122/124. **Green Fee:** $24/$24. **Cart Fee:** $23/cart. **Walking Policy:** Unrestricted walking. **Walkability:** 2.
Opened: 1982. **Architect:** Clayton Van Tassel. **Season:** May-Oct. **High:** July-Aug. **To obtain tee times:** Tee times not required. **Miscellaneous:** Reduced fees (twilight), metal spikes, range (grass/mats), club rentals, credit cards (V).

★★½ SUSSEX GOLF & CURLING CLUB
SP-148 Piccadilly Rd., Sussex, E0E 1P0, (506)433-9040, 40 miles E of St. John.
Holes: 18. **Yards:** 6,287/5,752. **Par:** 72/73. **Course Rating:** 69.7/72.0. **Slope:** 117/119. **Green Fee:** $25/$30. **Cart Fee:** $25/cart. **Walking Policy:** Unrestricted walking. **Walkability:** 4.

CANADA

Opened: 1973. **Season:** May-Oct. **High:** July-Sept. **To obtain tee times:** Call 2 days in advance. **Miscellaneous:** Reduced fees (low season), discount packages, range (grass), club rentals, credit cards (MC, V, AE).
Reader Comments: Good layout, requires every club ... Well-kept secret, charming ... Just getting better. Some great long holes ... A few 'monster holes', especially in the wind ... Nos. 17 & 18 toughest finish in east. Beautiful in fall.

★★½ WESTFIELD GOLF & COUNTRY CLUB
SP-8 Golf Club Rd., Westfield, E0G 3J0, (506)757-2907, 20 miles N of St. John.
Holes: 18. **Yards:** 5,799/5,710. **Par:** 69/72. **Course Rating:** 66.8/70.0. **Slope:** 113/114. **Green Fee:** $35/$35. **Cart Fee:** $25/cart. **Walking Policy:** Unrestricted walking. **Walkability:** 4.
Opened: 1917. **Season:** May-Oct. **High:** July-Aug. **To obtain tee times:** Call 2 days in advance.
Miscellaneous: Metal spikes, club rentals, credit cards (V).
Reader Comments: Short, old course ... Nice views. Good mix of holes ... Blind tee shots ... Well wooded and challenging; good test.

NEWFOUNDLAND

★★½ BLOMIDON GOLF & COUNTRY CLUB
SP-Wess Valley Rd., Corner Brook, A2H 6J3, (709)634-5550.
Holes: 18. **Yards:** 5,500/5,400. **Par:** 69/72. **Course Rating:** 67.0/70.0. **Slope:** 116/121. **Green Fee:** $30/N/A. **Cart Fee:** $25/cart. **Walking Policy:** Unrestricted walking. **Walkability:** 5.
Opened: 1952. **Architect:** Alfred H. Tull. **Season:** May-Oct. **High:** June-Aug. **To obtain tee times:** Call or come in up to 3 days in advance. **Miscellaneous:** Discount packages, metal spikes, range (grass), club rentals, credit cards (MC, V, Debit Cards).

★★★★ TERRA NOVA PARK LODGE & GOLF COURSE
R-General Delivery, Port Blandford, A0C 2G0, (709)543-2626, 140 miles W of St. John's.
Holes: 18. **Yards:** 6,546/5,433. **Par:** 71/71. **Course Rating:** 71.9/72.5. **Slope:** 128/129. **Green Fee:** $35/$43. **Cart Fee:** $28/cart. **Walking Policy:** Unrestricted walking. **Walkability:** 3.
Opened: 1984. **Architect:** Robbie Robinson/Doug Carrick. **Season:** May-Oct. **High:** July-Sept.
To obtain tee times: Call anytime during the season with credit card to guarantee.
Miscellaneous: Reduced fees (weekdays, low season, resort guests, twilight, juniors), discount packages, range (grass/mats), caddies, club rentals, lodging, credit cards (MC, V, AE, D, En Route), beginner friendly (golf school, junior camps).
Reader Comments: Unbelievable scenery ... An excellent course with great views! ... Absolutely beautiful, tight and challenging ... Fabulous scenery, great vacation spot.

NOVA SCOTIA

★★★ ABERCROMBIE GOLF CLUB
SP-P.O. Box 516, New Glasgow, B2H 5E7, (902)752-6249, 90 miles W of Halifax.
Holes: 18. **Yards:** 6,300/N/A. **Par:** 72/N/A. **Course Rating:** 71.0/N/A. **Slope:** 124/N/A. **Green Fee:** $35/$35. **Cart Fee:** $18/person. **Walking Policy:** Unrestricted walking. **Walkability:** 3.
Opened: 1918. **Architect:** Clinton E. Robinson. **Season:** May-Sept. **High:** July-Aug. **To obtain tee times:** Call 10 days in advance. **Miscellaneous:** Reduced fees (twilight), metal spikes, range (grass/mats), club rentals, credit cards (V).
Reader Comments: A good value ... Good, fair test of golf ... Excellent fairways, greens, clubhouse.

★★★ AMHERST GOLF CLUB
SP-P.O. Box 26, Amherst, B4H 3Z6, (902)667-8730, 2 miles W of Amherst.
Holes: 18. **Yards:** 6,367/5,439. **Par:** 71/71. **Course Rating:** 71.0/71.0. **Slope:** 122/115. **Green Fee:** $35/$35. **Cart Fee:** $27/cart. **Walking Policy:** Unrestricted walking. **Walkability:** 3.
Opened: 1906. **Architect:** Clinton E. Robinson. **Season:** May-Oct. **High:** July-Aug. **To obtain tee times:** Call. **Miscellaneous:** Reduced fees (weekdays, twilight), metal spikes, range (grass), club rentals, credit cards (V).
Reader Comments: Solid golf course, scenic. Windier than House of Commons ... Old course with character ... Slick greens ... Always in good condition. Delightful to play ... Great finishing hole.

★★½ ANTIGONISH GOLF & COUNTRY CLUB
SP-P.O. Box 1341, Antigonish, B2G 2L7, (902)863-4797.
Holes: 18. **Yards:** 6,605/5,109. **Par:** 72/72. **Course Rating:** 73.0/69.0. **Slope:** 130/118. **Green Fee:** $25/$40. **Cart Fee:** $27/cart. **Walking Policy:** Unrestricted walking. **Walkability:** 3.
Opened: 1926. **Architect:** Bob Moote. **Season:** May-Oct. **High:** July-Aug. **To obtain tee times:**

Call. **Miscellaneous:** Reduced fees (twilight), discount packages, range (grass), club rentals, credit cards (MC, V, AE), beginner friendly (clinics).
Reader Comments: Par 3s exciting, valleys and hillsides ... Oceanside, great.

★★★★½ BELL BAY GOLF CLUB *Service, Value+, Condition+, Pace+*

PU-P.O. Box 641, Baddeck, B0E 1B0, (902)295-1333, (800)565-3077. **E-mail:** bellbay@auracom.com. **Web:** www.bellbaygolfclub.com.
Holes: 18. **Yards:** 7,037/5,185. **Par:** 72/72. **Course Rating:** 74.7/70.0. **Slope:** 137/120. **Green Fee:** $59/$59. **Cart Fee:** $30/cart. **Walking Policy:** Unrestricted walking. **Walkability:** 3. **Opened:** 1997. **Architect:** Thomas McBroom. **Season:** May-Oct. **High:** July-Aug.-Sept. **To obtain tee times:** Call golf shop. **Miscellaneous:** Reduced fees (low season, juniors), discount packages, range (grass), club rentals, credit cards (MC, V, AE), beginner friendly (golf schools available).
Reader Comments: New, immaculate. Tiny 17th with large teeth. World class ... Interesting design, wonderful setting ... Only 18 months old. Are your sure? An outstanding countryside facility with a bright future ... Fits in with CB Highlands ... Best four finishing holes ever.

★★½ BRIGHTWOOD GOLF & COUNTRY CLUB

SP-227 School St., Dartmouth, B3A 2Y5, (902)469-7879.
Holes: 18. **Yards:** 5,579/5,276. **Par:** 68/71. **Course Rating:** 66.6/70.6. **Slope:** 116/122. **Green Fee:** N/A. **Walking Policy:** Unrestricted walking. **Walkability:** 5. **Opened:** 1914. **Architect:** W. Parks Jr./D. Ross/Robert Moote. **Season:** April-Oct. **To obtain tee times:** Call 1 day in advance. **Miscellaneous:** Metal spikes, credit cards (V, AE).
Reader Comments: A good test of golf ... Scenic vistas of Halifax Harbour, well-wooded, hilly ...Tough.

★★★ DUNDEE RESORT GOLF COURSE

R-R.R. 2, West Bay, B0E 3K0, Richmond County, (902)345-0420, (800)565-1774, 7 miles E of West Bay. **E-mail:** proshop@auracom.com. **Web:** www.chatsubo.com/dundee.
Holes: 18. **Yards:** 6,475/5,236. **Par:** 72/72. **Course Rating:** 71.9/71.7. **Slope:** 135/131. **Green Fee:** $38/$45. **Cart Fee:** $31/cart. **Walking Policy:** Unrestricted walking. **Walkability:** 4. **Opened:** 1977. **Architect:** Bob Moote. **Season:** May-Oct. **High:** June-Sept. **To obtain tee times:** Call with a credit card confirmation. 48-hour cancellation policy. **Miscellaneous:** Reduced fees (weekdays, resort guests, twilight), discount packages, club rentals, lodging, credit cards (MC, V, AE, D, Diners Club).
Reader Comments: Fantastic highlands golf ... Very hilly ... Magnificent views ... Panoramic views of the lake, some tricky hillside greens and bring your climbing boots if you don't book a cart, there's a lot of up and down.

GRANDVIEW GOLF & COUNTRY CLUB

SP-431 Crane Hill Road, Westphal, B2Z 1J5, Halifax County County, (902)435-3278, 6 miles E of Dartmouth. **E-mail:** grandvu@istar.ca.
Holes: 18. **Yards:** 6,475/5,571. **Par:** 72/73. **Course Rating:** 71.5/71.4. **Slope:** 128/127. **Green Fee:** $45/$48. **Cart Fee:** $26/cart. **Walking Policy:** Unrestricted walking. **Walkability:** 1. **Architect:** Cornish Robinson. **Season:** May-Oct. **High:** July-Aug. **To obtain tee times:** Guests may book tee times 2 days in advance—Saturday and Sunday A.M. Members only. **Miscellaneous:** Reduced fees (twilight), range (grass), club rentals, credit cards (MC, V, AE, Diners Club).

★★★★★ HIGHLANDS LINKS GOLF COURSE *Service, Value+, Pace+*

PU-Cape Breton Highlands Nat'l Pk., Ingonish Beach, B0C 1L0, Canada County, (902)285-2600, (800)441-1118, 70 miles W of Sydney. **E-mail:** gordie_callan@pch.gc.ca. **Web:** www.golfnet.com.
Holes: 18. **Yards:** 6,596/5,243. **Par:** 72/72. **Course Rating:** 73.9/73.3. **Slope:** 141/131. **Green Fee:** $38/$58. **Cart Fee:** $31/cart. **Walking Policy:** Unrestricted walking. **Walkability:** 4. **Opened:** 1941. **Architect:** Stanley Thompson/Graham Cooke. **Season:** May-Oct. **High:** June-Oct. **To obtain tee times:** Call anytime; exceptions made for lodge guests. **Miscellaneous:** Reduced fees (twilight, juniors), discount packages, caddies, club rentals, credit cards (MC, V, AE).
Reader Comments: A splendid walk through marvelous scenery ... Stanley Thompson classic ... Wow! ... Outstanding golf course in the middle of nowhere ... A hidden gem; golf as it should be! Worth going out of your way for! ... Very scenic and challenging ... Fun course in great condition ... You have to play it to understand. Wow ... This is as good as it gets!

★★★ KEN-WO COUNTRY CLUB

SP-9514 Commercial St., New Minas, B4N 3E9, Kings County, (902)681-5388, 60 miles NW of Halifax. **E-mail:** kenwo@glinx.com.
Holes: 18. **Yards:** 6,308/5,958. **Par:** 70/72. **Course Rating:** 69.9/71.6. **Slope:** 122/118. **Green Fee:** $29/$37. **Cart Fee:** $26/person. **Walking Policy:** Unrestricted walking. **Walkability:** 3. **Opened:** 1921. **Season:** April-Nov. **High:** June-Aug. **To obtain tee times:** Call 3 days in advance. **Miscellaneous:** Reduced fees (twilight), discount packages, range (grass), club rentals, credit cards (MC, V, AE).

CANADA

Reader Comments: Good test of golf ... Nice course, solid back nine, excellent conditioning ... Nice place, mix of farmland & woods, good challenge ... Very pretty course. Great staff at club ... My home course for 50 years, I'm a lucky man!

LINGAN COUNTRY CLUB

SP-P.O. Box 1252, 1225 Grand Lake Rd., Sydney, B1P 6J9, (902)562-1112, 260 miles N of Halifax. **Holes:** 18. **Yards:** 6,620/5,834. **Par:** 72/74. **Course Rating:** 71.4/73.5. **Slope:** 125/129. **Green Fee:** $24/$42. **Cart Fee:** $29/cart. **Walking Policy:** Unrestricted walking. **Walkability:** 2. **Opened:** 1908. **Architect:** Stanley Thompson. **Season:** May-Oct. **High:** July-Aug. **To obtain tee times:** Call (902)562-1112. **Miscellaneous:** Metal spikes, range (grass), club rentals, credit cards (MC, V, AE).

OSPREY RIDGE GOLF CLUB

PU-270 Harold Whynot Road, Bridgewater, B4V 2W6, Lanenburg County, (902)543-6666, 60 miles SW of Halifax. **E-mail:** tom@ospreyridge.ns.ca. **Web:** www.ospreyridge.ns.ca. **Holes:** 18. **Yards:** 6,575/5,098. **Par:** 72/72. **Course Rating:** 72.3/70.9. **Slope:** 137/126. **Green Fee:** $30/$40. **Cart Fee:** $25/cart. **Walking Policy:** Unrestricted walking. **Walkability:** 4. **Opened:** 1998. **Architect:** Graham Cooke. **Season:** April-Oct. **High:** May-Sept. **To obtain tee times:** Call (902)543-6666. Out of province patrons have one year advance bookings available. **Miscellaneous:** Reduced fees (low season, twilight), discount packages, range (grass), club rentals, credit cards (MC, V, AE, Diners Club).

★★★ PARAGON GOLF & COUNTRY CLUB

SP-368 Brookside Dr., Kingston, B0P 1R0, (902)765-2554, 100 miles NW of Halifax. **Holes:** 18. **Yards:** 6,245/5,580. **Par:** 72/72. **Course Rating:** 69.6/72.7. **Slope:** 120/124. **Green Fee:** $35/$35. **Cart Fee:** $25/cart. **Walking Policy:** Unrestricted walking. **Walkability:** 3. **Opened:** 1964. **Architect:** Gordie Shaw. **Season:** April-Oct. **High:** May-Aug. **To obtain tee times:** Nonmembers call 1 day in advance. **Miscellaneous:** Reduced fees (twilight), club rentals, credit cards (V). **Reader Comments:** Very well laid out. Particularly pretty in spring ... Excellent test of golf, excellent condition ... The course is always in good shape!

★★★½ THE PINES RESORT HOTEL GOLF COURSE

R-P.O. Box 70, Digby, B0V 1A0, (902)245-7709, (800)667-4637, 150 miles SW of Halifax. **Holes:** 18. **Yards:** 6,222/5,865. **Par:** 71/75. **Course Rating:** 70.0/73.0. **Slope:** 121/131. **Green Fee:** $38/$40. **Cart Fee:** $30/cart. **Walking Policy:** Unrestricted walking. **Walkability:** 3. **Opened:** 1932. **Architect:** Stanley Thompson. **Season:** May-Oct. **High:** July-Sept. **To obtain tee times:** Call. No restrictions. **Miscellaneous:** Discount packages, club rentals, lodging, credit cards (MC, V, AE, D, Diners Club). **Reader Comments:** A top-notch pleasure all around ... People very warm and helpful, a good course ... Digby is a charming fishing village ... Course is fair to all skill levels, nicely maintained ... Superb inn ... Very interesting holes.

★★★ THE TRURO GOLF CLUB

SP-86 Golf St., Truro, B2N 5C7, (902)893-4650, 50 miles NW of Halifax. **E-mail:** rick.morley@ns.sympatico.ca. **Holes:** 18. **Yards:** 6,500/5,636. **Par:** 71/72. **Course Rating:** 70.9/72.4. **Slope:** 123/125. **Green Fee:** $20/$40. **Cart Fee:** $26/cart. **Walking Policy:** Unrestricted walking. **Walkability:** 1. **Opened:** 1903. **Architect:** Robbie Robinson/Stanley Thompson. **Season:** April-Nov. **High:** May-Sept. **To obtain tee times:** Call 1 day in advance. **Miscellaneous:** Reduced fees (low season, twilight), metal spikes, range (grass), club rentals, credit cards (MC, V, AE). **Reader Comments:** Nice track ... Farmland; can be very windswept; well maintained, good test ... Tidy course and very enjoyable.

ONTARIO

AGUASABON GOLF COURSE

PU-Beach Rd., Terrace Bay, P0T 2W0, (807)825-3844, 130 miles E of Thunder Bay. **Holes:** 9. **Yards:** 3,200/2,900. **Par:** 36/37. **Course Rating:** N/A. **Slope:** N/A. **Green Fee:** N/A. **Cart Fee:** $20/cart. **Walkability:** 2. **Opened:** 1964. **Season:** May-Oct. **High:** June-Aug. **To obtain tee times:** First come, first served. **Miscellaneous:** Reduced fees (low season, twilight, seniors, juniors), metal spikes, range (grass), club rentals, credit cards (MC, V).

★★★★½ ANGUS GLEN GOLF CLUB *Condition+*

PU-10080 Kennedy Rd., Markham, L6C 1N9, (905)887-5157, 25 miles N of Toronto. **Web:** www.angusglen.com. **Holes:** 18. **Yards:** 7,400/5,721. **Par:** 72/72. **Course Rating:** 76.0/73.3. **Slope:** 143/129. **Green Fee:** $85/$110. **Cart Fee:** Included in Green Fee. **Walking Policy:** Mandatory cart. **Walkability:**

3. **Opened:** 1994. **Architect:** Doug Carrick. **Season:** April-Nov. **High:** May-Oct. **To obtain tee times:** Call 60 days in advance. **Miscellaneous:** Reduced fees (low season), range (grass/mats), club rentals, credit cards (MC, V, AE, Enroute, Diners Club).
Reader Comments: Great course ... Bring your 'A' game, and your wallet ... Target golf ... Beautiful layout. Immaculate condition ... Tough! Terrific in all respects ... Very tough on a windy day ... Par 3's with long carry.

★★★ BAY OF QUINTE COUNTRY CLUB
SP-R.R. No.2 Trent Rd., Belleville, K8N 4Z9, (613)968-7063, 115 miles E of Toronto.
Holes: 18. **Yards:** 6,840/5,701. **Par:** 72/73. **Course Rating:** 72.4/71.4. **Slope:** 125/113. **Green Fee:** $27/$38. **Cart Fee:** $30/cart. **Walking Policy:** Unrestricted walking. **Walkability:** 2.
Opened: 1921. **Architect:** Howard Watson. **Season:** April-Nov. **High:** May-Sept. **To obtain tee times:** Call 5 days in advance for weekdays. Call Thursday at noon for upcoming weekend or holiday. **Miscellaneous:** Reduced fees (low season, twilight, juniors), range (grass/mats), club rentals, credit cards (MC, V).
Notes: 1996 Ontario Amateur.
Reader Comments: Not overly challenging. A recreational course ... Long walks, green to tee and parking lot to course ... Long par 4's ... Relatively flat.

★★★½ BEECHWOOD GOLF & COUNTRY CLUB
SP-4680 Thorold Townline Rd., Niagara Falls, L2E 6S4, (905)680-4653.
Holes: 18. **Yards:** 6,700/5,400. **Par:** 72/72. **Course Rating:** 73.0/69.8. **Slope:** 127/116. **Green Fee:** $35/$40. **Cart Fee:** $30/cart. **Walking Policy:** Unrestricted walking. **Walkability:** 3.
Opened: 1960. **Architect:** R. Moote/B. Antonsen. **Season:** April-Nov. **High:** April-Sept. **To obtain tee times:** Local non-members call 4 days in advance. Visitors may reserve in advance without restrictions. **Miscellaneous:** Reduced fees (weekdays, low season, twilight), discount packages, metal spikes, club rentals, credit cards (MC, V, AE).
Reader Comments: Slick greens, fun course, not overbearing ... No pushover ... Improves each year ... Sporty layout, excellent greens ... Fast greens.

★★★ BROCKVILLE COUNTRY CLUB
SP-P.O. Box 42, Brockville, K6V 5T7, (613)342-3023, 1 miles W of Brockville.
Holes: 18. **Yards:** 6,343/5,288. **Par:** 72/72. **Course Rating:** 70.4/72.2. **Slope:** 126/129. **Green Fee:** N/A/$48. **Walking Policy:** Unrestricted walking. **Walkability:** 5. **Opened:** 1914. **Architect:** Stanley Thompson/Clinton Robinson. **Season:** May-Oct. **High:** July-Aug. **To obtain tee times:** 24-hour advance bookings. **Miscellaneous:** Reduced fees (twilight, juniors), range (grass/mats), club rentals, credit cards (MC, V, Intevac).
Reader Comments: Challenging ... Interesting par 3s, many elevation changes ... Excellent layout.

★★★ BROOKLEA GOLF & COUNTRY CLUB
SP-Highway 93 , Midland, L4R 2E1, Simoe County, (705)526-7532, (800)257-0428, 90 miles N of Toronto. **E-mail:** clubhouse@brookleagolf.com. **Web:** www.brookleagolf.com.
Holes: 18. **Yards:** 6,645/5,585. **Par:** 72/72. **Course Rating:** 71.2/71.4. **Slope:** 126/126. **Green Fee:** $40/$45. **Cart Fee:** $15/person. **Walking Policy:** Unrestricted walking. **Walkability:** 3.
Opened: 1959. **Architect:** Rene Muylaert. **Season:** April-Nov. **High:** June-Sept. **To obtain tee times:** Call up to 4 days in advance. **Miscellaneous:** Reduced fees (weekdays, resort guests, twilight), discount packages, range (grass), club rentals, credit cards (MC, V, AE), beginner friendly (West Nine Executive Course).
Reader Comments: Part links, part park, nice experience ... Great course, good value, friendly staff, fair to all golfers ... Well groomed, easy access ... Excellent 19th hole.

★★ CALABOGIE HIGHLANDS RESORT & GOLF CLUB
PU-981 Barryvale Rd., Calabogie, K0J 1H0, Renfrew County, (613)752-2171, 55 miles SW of Ottawa. **E-mail:** info@calabogiehighlandsgolf.com. **Web:** www.calabogiehighlandsgolf.com.
Holes: 18. **Yards:** 6,735/5,632. **Par:** 72/72. **Course Rating:** 71.4/72.0. **Slope:** 126/129. **Green Fee:** $19/$28. **Cart Fee:** $25/cart. **Walking Policy:** Unrestricted walking. **Walkability:** 3.
Opened: 1983. **Architect:** Dolgos & Assoc. **Season:** April-Nov. **High:** June-Aug. **To obtain tee times:** Call up to 7 days in advance. **Miscellaneous:** Reduced fees (weekdays, low season, resort guests, twilight, juniors), discount packages, metal spikes, range (grass/mats), club rentals, lodging (8 rooms), credit cards (MC, V, AE, Interac), beginner friendly.
Special Notes: Also has 9-hole, par-35 course.

★★½ CALEDON COUNTRY CLUB
PU-2121 Old Baseline Rd., R.R. No.1, Inglewood, L0N 1K0, Peel County, (905)838-0121, 10 miles N of Toronto. **Web:** www.golfcaledon.com.
Holes: 18. **Yards:** 6,140/5,414. **Par:** 71/73. **Course Rating:** 71.5/70.5. **Slope:** 132/121. **Green Fee:** $35/$55. **Cart Fee:** $30/cart. **Walking Policy:** Unrestricted walking. **Walkability:** 5.
Opened: 1961. **Architect:** Rene Muylaert. **Season:** April-Nov. **High:** June-Aug. **To obtain tee times:** Call up to 7 days in advance. **Miscellaneous:** Reduced fees (weekdays, low season, twi-

light, seniors, juniors), metal spikes, range (grass/mats), club rentals, credit cards (MC, V, AE, En Route).

Reader Comments: Rustic and pleasant ... Fantastic in October ... Very hilly ... Interesting elevation changes ... Short, scenic and enjoyable golf.

★★ CARDINAL GOLF CLUB

PU-2740 Hwy. 9, R.R. No.1, Kettleby, L0G 1J0, (905)841-2195, 20 miles N of Toronto. **Web:** www.golfcoursecanada.com/cardinal.

Holes: 18. **Yards:** 6,450/5,750. **Par:** 72/72. **Course Rating:** 71.5/64.9. **Slope:** 114/104. **Green Fee:** $25/$45. **Cart Fee:** $14/person. **Walking Policy:** Unrestricted walking. **Walkability:** 2. **Opened:** 1989. **Architect:** Dan Lavis. **Season:** April-Nov. **High:** June-Aug. **To obtain tee times:** Call up to 14 days in advance. **Miscellaneous:** Reduced fees (weekdays, low season, twilight, seniors, juniors), metal spikes, range (grass/mats), club rentals, credit cards (MC, V, AE).
Special Notes: Also has 18-hole par-58 short course; Kettle Creek executive course.

★★★½ CARLISLE GOLF & COUNTRY CLUB

PU-523 Carlisle Rd., Carlisle, L0R 1H0, (905)689-8820, (800)661-4343, 10 miles N of Burlington.
Holes: 27. **Yards:** 6,557/5,232. **Par:** 72/72. **Course Rating:** 70.6/72.9. **Slope:** 119/105. **Green Fee:** $45/$50. **Cart Fee:** $32/cart. **Walking Policy:** Unrestricted walking. **Walkability:** 2.
Opened: 1991. **Architect:** Ted Baker. **Season:** April-Nov. **High:** June-Aug. **To obtain tee times:** Call up to 7 days in advance. **Miscellaneous:** Reduced fees (weekdays, low season, twilight, seniors, juniors), discount packages, range (grass/mats), club rentals, credit cards (MC, V, AE).
Reader Comments: Nice fast greens ... Great practice facilities ... Beautifully maintained ... Great value ... Good tournament facility ... Course conditions excellent.

CENTENNIAL GOLF COURSE

PU-R.R. 11 320 Thompson Rd., Thunder Bay, (807)767-4600.
Holes: 9. **Yards:** 3,316/2,962. **Par:** 36/36. **Course Rating:** 35.8/35.8. **Slope:** 123/107. **Green Fee:** $20/N/A. **Cart Fee:** $22/cart. **Walking Policy:** Unrestricted walking. **Walkability:** 1.
Opened: 1985. **Season:** May-Sept. **High:** June-July. **To obtain tee times:** Call 4 days in advance. **Miscellaneous:** Reduced fees (twilight), metal spikes, range (grass), club rentals, credit cards (MC, V, AE), beginner friendly (golf programs, instruction).

★★½ CHAPPLES GOLF COURSE

PU-530 Chapples Dr., Thunder Bay, (807)625-2582.
Holes: 18. **Yards:** 6,184/5,555. **Par:** 71/71. **Course Rating:** 69.5/70.6. **Slope:** 108/111. **Green Fee:** $21/$21. **Cart Fee:** $22/cart. **Walking Policy:** Unrestricted walking. **Walkability:** 1.
Season: April-Oct. **High:** June-Aug. **To obtain tee times:** Call 2 days prior. Every second time is reserved. **Miscellaneous:** Reduced fees (juniors), discount packages, metal spikes, range (grass), club rentals, credit cards (MC, V).
Reader Comments: Central location. Good shape ... Very special in the fall.

★★★½ CHESTNUT HILL GOLF & COUNTRY CLUB

SP-13300 Leslie St., Richmond Hill, L4E 1A2,, (416)213-7456, 20 miles N of Toronto.
Holes: 18. **Yards:** 7,087/5,492. **Par:** 72/73. **Course Rating:** 74.5/70.5. **Slope:** N/A. **Green Fee:** $60/$75. **Cart Fee:** $20/. **Walking Policy:** Unrestricted walking. **Walkability:** N/A. **Opened:** 1994. **Architect:** Rene Muyleart. **Season:** April-Oct. **High:** June-Aug. **To obtain tee times:** Call 3 days in advance. **Miscellaneous:** Reduced fees (weekdays, juniors), metal spikes, range (grass), caddies, club rentals, credit cards (MC, V, AE).
Reader Comments: Short but fun; reachable par 5s and good greens ... A good layout ... Short, different kind of course, with different lies ... Nice course, some very challenging holes ... Tough ... Excellent condition ... Very playable.

★★½ CHIPPEWA GOLF AND COUNTRY CLUB

SP-400 Rankin St. Highway 21 North, Southampton, N0H 2L0, Grey County, (519)797-3684, 20 miles W of Owen Sound. **E-mail:** chippewag@bmts.com. **Web:** www.brucecountygolf.com.
Holes: 18. **Yards:** 6,420/5,392. **Par:** 72/72. **Course Rating:** 69.5/70.0. **Slope:** 116/109. **Green Fee:** $22/$28. **Cart Fee:** $25/cart. **Walking Policy:** Unrestricted walking. **Walkability:** 2.
Opened: 1964. **Architect:** S. Thompson. **Season:** April-Nov. **High:** May-Sept. **To obtain tee times:** Call Sunday for the upcoming week. **Miscellaneous:** Reduced fees (low season, twilight), discount packages, range (grass), club rentals, credit cards (MC, V, AE).
Reader Comments: Country course is short and flat but fairly tight fairways ... The greens are fast, consistent and true.

★★½ DEER RUN GOLF CLUB

PU-Bloomfield Rd. No.1, Blenheim, N0P 1A0, Kent County, (519)676-1566, 11 miles S of Chothom.
Holes: 18. **Yards:** 6,548/5,567. **Par:** 72/72. **Course Rating:** 72.9/71.9. **Slope:** 136/122. **Green Fee:** $11/$27. **Cart Fee:** $12/person. **Walking Policy:** Unrestricted walking. **Walkability:** 3.
Opened: 1993. **Architect:** Bill Dickie Assoc. **Season:** April-Nov. **High:** June-July/Sept.-Nov. **To obtain tee times:** Call golf shop. **Miscellaneous:** Reduced fees (weekdays, low season, twi-

light), discount packages, metal spikes, range (grass), club rentals, credit cards (MC, V, AE), beginner friendly (twilight).

Reader Comments: Nice layout, course usually very well kept ... Real surprise. Play it. No. 16 is a killer... Nice course to play with wife ... Great value before May 15 and after Sept 15. Course in very good shape all year... Nice challenge.

DEERHURST RESORT
★★★★½ **DEERHURST HIGHLANDS GOLF COURSE** *Condition*
R-R.R. No. 4, Huntsville, P0A 1K0, (705)789-2381, (800)461-4393, 120 miles N of Toronto. **Web:** www.deerhurst.on.ca.
Holes: 18. **Yards:** 7,011/5,393. **Par:** 72/73. **Course Rating:** 74.5/71.2. **Slope:** 140/125. **Green Fee:** $79/$120. **Cart Fee:** Included in Green Fee. **Walking Policy:** Mandatory cart. **Walkability:** 5. **Opened:** 1990. **Architect:** Robert Cupp/T. McBroom. **Season:** May-Oct. **High:** June-Aug. **To obtain tee times:** Call 7 days in advance. **Miscellaneous:** Reduced fees (weekdays, low season, resort guests, twilight), discount packages, metal spikes, range (grass/mats), club rentals, lodging, credit cards (MC, V, AE).
Reader Comments: A must play ... Outstanding ... Peaceful, gorgeous scenery, play it in the fall ... Fall round with early colors was best ever ... Great elevation changes, mixed links and parkland, excellent value ... Great views ... Many beautiful and strong holes ... Best public course in Canada! Tough! ... Arguably the best public course in Ontario ... Great resort, wonderful facilities.

★★★ **DEERHURST LAKESIDE GOLF COURSE**
R-1235 Deerhurst Dr., Huntsville, P1H 2E8, (705)789-7878, (800)461-4393, 120 miles N of Toronto. **Web:** www.deerhurst.on.ca.
Holes: 18. **Yards:** 4,700/3,800. **Par:** 65/65. **Course Rating:** 62.4/63.0. **Slope:** 101/104. **Green Fee:** $26/$50. **Cart Fee:** Included in Green Fee. **Walking Policy:** Walking at certain times. **Walkability:** 3. **Opened:** 1972. **Architect:** C.E. Robinson/T.McBroom. **Season:** April-Oct. **High:** July-Sept. **To obtain tee times:** Call. **Miscellaneous:** Reduced fees (low season, resort guests, twilight, juniors), discount packages, metal spikes, range (grass/mats), club rentals, lodging, credit cards (MC, V, AE, D).
Reader Comments: Well maintained ... Very scenic vacationland ... Great executive course ... Beautifully sculpted from Ontario wilderness into a clean, scenic and challenging course ... Everyone very accommodating.

DELHI GOLF & COUNTRY CLUB
SP-905 James St., Delhi, N4B 2E2, (519)582-1621, 40 miles SE of London.
Holes: 18. **Yards:** 6,400/5,200. **Par:** 71/72. **Course Rating:** 71.3/69.4. **Slope:** 114/121. **Green Fee:** $24/$28. **Cart Fee:** $27/cart. **Walking Policy:** Unrestricted walking. **Walkability:** 3. **Opened:** 1960. **Architect:** George Coreno. **Season:** March-Dec. **High:** May-Sept. **To obtain tee times:** Call golf shop. **Miscellaneous:** Reduced fees (weekdays, twilight, seniors, juniors), discount packages, range (grass), club rentals, credit cards (MC, V, AE, Debit).

★★★ DON VALLEY GOLF COURSE
PM-4200 Yonge St., Toronto, M2P 1N9, (416)392-2465.
Holes: 18. **Yards:** 6,109/5,048. **Par:** 71/73. **Course Rating:** 70.0/69.0. **Slope:** 124/120. **Green Fee:** $35/$40. **Cart Fee:** $28/cart. **Walking Policy:** Unrestricted walking. **Walkability:** 4. **Opened:** 1956. **Architect:** Howard Watson/David Moote. **Season:** April-Nov. **High:** July-Aug. **To obtain tee times:** Call up to 5 days in advance. **Miscellaneous:** Reduced fees (twilight, seniors, juniors), caddies, club rentals, credit cards (MC, V, AE).
Reader Comments: Must play in the fall. Best deal in town for seniors ... Muny course– good value right in city ... Great layout ... Good course for the price ... Fun public course in the city.

★★★ DOON VALLEY GOLF CLUB
PU-500 Doon Valley Dr., Kitchener, N2P 1B4, (519)741-2939, 60 miles W of Toronto.
Holes: 18. **Yards:** 6,193/5,507. **Par:** 72/73. **Course Rating:** 68.1/N/A. **Slope:** 115/106. **Green Fee:** $26/$30. **Cart Fee:** $25/cart. **Walking Policy:** Unrestricted walking. **Walkability:** 2. **Opened:** 1955. **Architect:** Clinton E. Robinson. **Season:** April-Nov. **High:** May-Oct. **To obtain tee times:** Call Saturday a.m. for following weekend. Call up to 7 days in advance at 7 p.m. for weekdays. **Miscellaneous:** Reduced fees (weekdays, twilight, juniors), discount packages, range (grass), club rentals, credit cards (MC, V, AE).
Reader Comments: A bargain ... Very enjoyable–good facilities ... Very nice layout. Nice course. Moves well ... Always in good condition, have to be able to hit draws.

★★★★ EAGLE CREEK GOLF COURSE
PU-109 Royal Troon Lane, Ottawa, K0A 1T0, (613)832-0728, 18 miles W of Ottawa.
Holes: 18. **Yards:** 7,067/5,413. **Par:** 72/72. **Course Rating:** 74.3/71.5. **Slope:** 134/125. **Green Fee:** $60/$70. **Cart Fee:** $30/cart. **Walking Policy:** Unrestricted walking. **Walkability:** 3. **Opened:** 1991. **Architect:** Ken Venturi/Ken Skodacek. **Season:** April-Oct. **High:** June-Aug. **To obtain tee times:** Call 7 days in advance. Reservations with credit card. Foursome anytime. **Miscellaneous:** Metal spikes, range (grass), club rentals, credit cards (MC, V, AE, Diners Club).

CANADA

EMERALD GREENS GOLF COURSE

PU-R.R. 12 2370 Dawson Rd., Thunder Bay, P7B 5E3, (807)767-4511, 4 miles N of Thunder Bay.

Holes: 9. **Yards:** 2,600/2,400. **Par:** 35/35. **Course Rating:** 66.0/65.8. **Slope:** 102/102. **Green Fee:** $19/$22. **Cart Fee:** $20/cart. **Walking Policy:** Unrestricted walking. **Walkability:** 3. **Opened:** 1977. **Season:** May-Oct. **High:** July-Aug. **To obtain tee times:** Call 2 days in advance. **Miscellaneous:** Reduced fees (weekdays, juniors), metal spikes, range (grass/mats), club rentals.

★★ FANSHAWE GOLF CLUB

SP-2835 Sunningdale Rd. East, London, N5X 3Y7, (519)455-2770.

Holes: 36. **Yards:** 6,233/6,425. **Par:** 70/70. **Course Rating:** 69.0/71.2. **Slope:** 108/121. **Green Fee:** $24/$24. **Cart Fee:** $26/cart. **Walking Policy:** Unrestricted walking. **Walkability:** 3. **Opened:** 1958. **Architect:** John Moffatt Sr. **Season:** April-Nov. **High:** May-Sept. **To obtain tee times:** Call 2 days in advance. **Miscellaneous:** Reduced fees (twilight), metal spikes, range (grass), club rentals, credit cards (MC, V, Debit Card).

FIRE FIGHTERS GORMLEY GREEN GOLF CLUB

PU-P.O. Box 278, Gormley, L0H 1G0, (905)888-1219, 12 miles N of Toronto.

★★ CIRCLE COURSE

Holes: 18. **Yards:** 6,618/5,658. **Par:** 70/70. **Course Rating:** 72.0/N/A. **Slope:** 115/N/A. **Green Fee:** $30/$44. **Cart Fee:** $25/cart. **Walking Policy:** Unrestricted walking. **Walkability:** N/A. **Opened:** 1978. **Architect:** Rene Muylaert/Charles Muylaert. **Season:** April-Nov. **High:** June-Sept. **To obtain tee times:** Call. **Miscellaneous:** Reduced fees (weekdays, twilight, seniors), metal spikes, range (grass/mats), club rentals, credit cards (V, AE).

★★★ CREEK COURSE

Holes: 18. **Yards:** 6,948/5,958. **Par:** 72/72. **Course Rating:** 73.1/N/A. **Slope:** 128/N/A. **Green Fee:** $30/$44. **Cart Fee:** $25/cart. **Walking Policy:** Unrestricted walking. **Walkability:** 4. **Architect:** Rene Muylaert. **Season:** April-Nov. **High:** June-Sept. **To obtain tee times:** Call. **Miscellaneous:** Reduced fees (weekdays, twilight, seniors), metal spikes, range (grass/mats), club rentals, credit cards (V, AE).

FIRE FIGHTERS ROLLING HILLS GOLF CLUB

PU-P.O. Box 519, Gormley, LOH 1G0, (905)888-1955, 12 miles N of Toronto.

★★ BLUE

Holes: 18. **Yards:** 6,340/5,664. **Par:** 72/75. **Course Rating:** 68.5/N/A. **Slope:** 112/N/A. **Green Fee:** $26/$44. **Cart Fee:** $25/cart. **Walking Policy:** Unrestricted walking. **Walkability:** 3. **Season:** April-Nov. **High:** June-Sept. **To obtain tee times:** Call. **Miscellaneous:** Reduced fees (weekdays, twilight, seniors), metal spikes, club rentals, credit cards (MC, V, AE).

★★ GOLD

Holes: 18. **Yards:** 4,010/3,681. **Par:** 62/62. **Course Rating:** N/A. **Slope:** N/A. **Green Fee:** $18/$30. **Cart Fee:** $25/cart. **Walking Policy:** Unrestricted walking. **Walkability:** 2. **Season:** April-Nov. **High:** June-Sept. **To obtain tee times:** Call. **Miscellaneous:** Reduced fees (weekdays, twilight, seniors), metal spikes, club rentals, credit cards (MC, V, AE).

★★½ RED

Holes: 18. **Yards:** 4,894/N/A. **Par:** 70/N/A. **Course Rating:** 61.3/N/A. **Slope:** 95/N/A. **Green Fee:** $22/$34. **Cart Fee:** $25/cart. **Walking Policy:** Unrestricted walking. **Walkability:** 1. **Season:** April-Nov. **High:** June-Sept. **To obtain tee times:** Call. **Miscellaneous:** Reduced fees (weekdays, twilight, seniors), metal spikes, club rentals, credit cards (MC, V, AE).

FLAMBOROUGH HILLS GOLF CLUB

SP-P.O. Box 9, Copetown, L0R 1J0, (905)627-1743, 15 miles W of Hamilton. **E-mail:** flamhill@skyline.net. **Web:** www.flamborohills-golf.com.

Holes: 27. **Green Fee:** $30/$40. **Cart Fee:** $32/cart. **Walking Policy:** Unrestricted walking. **Walkability:** 3. **Opened:** 1960. **Season:** March-Oct. **High:** June-Sept. **To obtain tee times:** Call 10 days in advance for weekdays. Call on Tuesday for upcoming weekend. **Miscellaneous:** Reduced fees (weekdays, seniors), club rentals, credit cards (MC, V, Interac).

★★½ HILLS/LAKES

Yards: 6,580/5,280. **Par:** 73/73. **Course Rating:** 69.5/69.2. **Slope:** 114/118.

CANADA

★★½ **HILLS/WOODS**
Yards: 6,331/5,458. **Par:** 73/73. **Course Rating:** 68.5/70.9. **Slope:** 116/121.
★★½ **WOODS/LAKES**
Yards: 6,259/5,292. **Par:** 72/72. **Course Rating:** 69.0/70.0. **Slope:** 114/117.

★★★★ **FOREST CITY NATIONAL GOLF CLUB**
PU-16540 Robin's Hill Rd., London, N6A 4C1, (519)451-0994.
Holes: 18. **Yards:** 6,850/5,119. **Par:** 72/72. **Course Rating:** 73.6/69.4. **Slope:** 132/116. **Green Fee:** $50/$60. **Cart Fee:** Included in Green Fee. **Walking Policy:** Unrestricted walking.
Walkability: 3. **Opened:** 1993. **Architect:** Craig Schreiner. **Season:** April-Nov. **High:** June-Aug.
To obtain tee times: Call up to 7 days in advance. **Miscellaneous:** Reduced fees (weekdays, low season, twilight), range (grass/mats), club rentals, credit cards (MC, V, Debit Card).
Reader Comments: Hidden gem ... A true classic ... One of the nicest courses around in all ways ... Great golf course feels like you're the only group playing ... Staff excellent–course a must-play ... Outstanding staff and facility ... Recent host to 2 Ontario Opens. Great layout ... Best bang for your bucks ... Visionary course design ... Great value.

FORT WILLIAM COUNTRY CLUB
SP-R.R. 4, 1350 Mountain Rd., Thunder Bay, P7J 1C2, (807)475-4721.
Holes: 18. **Yards:** 6,700/5,795. **Par:** 72/74. **Course Rating:** 71.0/73.0. **Slope:** 131/123. **Green Fee:** $45/$45. **Cart Fee:** $26/cart. **Walking Policy:** Unrestricted walking. **Walkability:** 3. **Opened:** 1923. **Architect:** Stanley Trumbull. **Season:** April-Oct. **High:** May-Sept. **To obtain tee times:** Call.
Miscellaneous: Reduced fees (juniors), range (grass), club rentals, credit cards (MC, V).

★★★★ **GLEN ABBEY GOLF CLUB**
PU-1333 Dorval Dr., Oakville, L6J 4Z3, Canada County, (905)844-1811, 20 miles W of Toronto.
Web: www.clublink.com.
Holes: 18. **Yards:** 7,112/5,520. **Par:** 73/74. **Course Rating:** 75.5/71.4. **Slope:** 140/117. **Green Fee:** $115/$225. **Cart Fee:** Included in Green Fee. **Walking Policy:** Mandatory cart.
Walkability: 4. **Opened:** 1977. **Architect:** Jack Nicklaus. **Season:** April-Oct. **High:** May-Oct. **To obtain tee times:** Call from March 1 for upcoming season with credit card. No changes or cancellations accepted within two weeks of tee time. **Miscellaneous:** Reduced fees (low season), range (grass), club rentals, credit cards (MC, V, AE, Diners Club, Enroute).
Reader Comments: Worth the dough ... Great course. Beautiful condition. Excellent clubhouse ... Great course. ... Just after open, Wow... Don't miss a stop here–heavenly ... Course is immaculate–first rate service ... A special place–just superb! ... First class service & good golf ... Good test of golf. Excellent ... Play just before Canadian Open.

HAWK RIDGE GOLF CLUB
PU-P.O. Box 874, Orillia, L3V 6K8, (705)329-4653, 60 miles N of Toronto. **E-mail:**
hrgweb@hawkridgegolf.com. **Web:** www.hawkridgegolf.com.
★★★½ **MEADOW'S NEST**
Holes: 18. **Yards:** 6,933/5,994. **Par:** 72/72. **Course Rating:** 72.0/72.0. **Slope:** 120/120. **Green Fee:** $35/$45. **Cart Fee:** $30/cart. **Walking Policy:** Unrestricted walking. **Walkability:** 2. **Opened:** 1991. **Architect:** Rene Muylaert/Bruce Dodson. **Season:** April-Nov. **High:** June-Sept. **To obtain tee times:** Call golf shop. **Miscellaneous:** Reduced fees (low season, resort guests, twilight, seniors, juniors), discount packages, range (grass/mats), club rentals, credit cards (MC, V, AE).
Reader Comments: 36 holes of great golf ... Linksy, a joy to play ... Long course, don't bring Grandma ... Great course ... Meadow nine long ... Best public course in the area. Very strong winds most of the time ... Good value and usually easy to get tee times ... A good outing ... Great course, getting even better.
TIMBER RIDGE
Holes: 18. **Yards:** 6,584/5,739. **Par:** 71/71. **Course Rating:** N/A. **Slope:** N/A. **Green Fee:** $35/$45. **Cart Fee:** $30/cart. **Walking Policy:** Unrestricted walking. **Walkability:** 2. **Opened:** 1999. **Architect:** Bruce Dodson. **Season:** April-Nov. **High:** June-Sept. **To obtain tee times:** Call golf shop. **Miscellaneous:** Reduced fees (low season, resort guests, twilight, seniors, juniors), discount packages, range (grass/mats), club rentals, credit cards (MC, V, AE), beginner friendly (junior clinics, lessons, golf packages).

HIDDEN LAKE GOLF & COUNTRY CLUB
SP-1137 #1 Side Rd., Burlington, L7R 3X4, Halton County, (905)336-3660, 35 miles W of Toronto. **Web:** www.hiddenlakegolf.com.
OLD COURSE
Holes: 18. **Yards:** 6,622/5,331. **Par:** 71/70. **Course Rating:** 71.1/69.7. **Slope:** 122/112. **Green Fee:** $25/$59. **Cart Fee:** $32/cart. **Walking Policy:** Unrestricted walking. **Walkability:** 3.
Opened: 1963. **Architect:** Dick Kirkpatrick. **Season:** March-Nov. **High:** May-Sept. **To obtain tee times:** Call up to 6 days in advance. Call anytime if out of province. **Miscellaneous:** Reduced fees (weekdays, low season, twilight, seniors, juniors), range (grass), club rentals, credit cards (MC, V, AE).

CANADA

HIDDEN LAKE GOLF CLUB
SP-1137 #1 Side Rd., Burlington, L7R 3X4, Halton County, (905)336-3660, 35 miles W of Toronto. **Web:** www.hiddenlakegolf.com.
★★★ **NEW COURSE**
Holes: 18. **Yards:** 6,645/5,017. **Par:** 72/71. **Course Rating:** 72.1/68.9. **Slope:** 124/117. **Green Fee:** $25/$59. **Cart Fee:** $32/cart. **Walking Policy:** Unrestricted walking. **Walkability:** 3. **Opened:** 1984. **Architect:** Dick Kirkpatrick. **Season:** March-Nov. **High:** May-Sept. **To obtain tee times:** Call up to 6 days in advance. Call anytime if out of province. **Miscellaneous:** Reduced fees (weekdays, low season, twilight, seniors, juniors), range (grass), club rentals, credit cards (MC, V, AE).
Reader Comments: Marvelous ... Wide fairways, good variety ... Good condition.
Special Notes: Formerly Hidden Lake Golf & Country Club

★★★½ **HOCKLEY VALLEY RESORT**
R-R.R. No.1, Orangeville, L9W 2Y8, (519)942-0754, 30 miles NW of Toronto.
Holes: 18. **Yards:** 6,403/4,646. **Par:** 70/70. **Course Rating:** 71.0/71.0. **Slope:** 130/126. **Green Fee:** $45/$95. **Cart Fee:** Included in Green Fee. **Walking Policy:** Mandatory cart. **Walkability:** 5. **Opened:** 1989. **Architect:** Thomas McBroom. **Season:** April-Nov. **High:** June-Sept. **To obtain tee times:** Hotel guests can book anytime. Others call 7 days in advance. **Miscellaneous:** Reduced fees (weekdays, low season, resort guests, twilight), discount packages, range (grass/mats), club rentals, lodging (104 rooms), credit cards (MC, V, AE, D).
Reader Comments: Magnificent vistas ... McBroom with a paintbrush. Play it in September, fabulous colors ... Wonderful vistas. Plays longer than yardage suggests, links with lots of elevation changes ... Beautiful setting, good golf ... Super people, beautiful in fall. Score takes a beating ... Fun to play ... Very scenic. An autumn beauty.

★★ **HORNBY GLEN GOLF COURSE INC.**
PU-8286 Hornby Rd., Hornby, L0P 1E0, (905)878-3421. **E-mail:** hornbygolf@globalserv.net.
Holes: 18. **Yards:** 6,740/5,698. **Par:** 72/73. **Course Rating:** 70.5/69.5. **Slope:** 110/108. **Green Fee:** $30/$38. **Cart Fee:** $30/cart. **Walking Policy:** Unrestricted walking. **Walkability:** 1. **Opened:** 1964. **Architect:** Robert Moote/David S. Moote. **Season:** April-Nov. **High:** June-Sept. **Miscellaneous:** Reduced fees (weekdays, twilight, seniors, juniors), range (grass), club rentals, credit cards (MC, V, Interact), beginner friendly.
Special Notes: Formerly Hornby Tower Golf Course

HORSESHOE VALLEY RESORT
R-R.R. No.1, Barrie, L4M 4Y8, (705)835-2790, 60 miles N of Toronto. **Web:** www.horseshoeresort.com.
HIGHLANDS COURSE
Holes: 9. **Yards:** 3,358/2,913. **Par:** 36/36. **Course Rating:** 35.7/36.9. **Slope:** 124/129. **Green Fee:** $40/$45. **Cart Fee:** $32/cart. **Walking Policy:** Unrestricted walking. **Walkability:** 3. **Opened:** 1974. **Architect:** Rene Muylaert. **Season:** April-Oct. **High:** June-Sept. **To obtain tee times:** Resort guests may book with room reservation 60 days out. Others call 7 days in advance. A valid credit card number is required to reserve a tee-time. **Miscellaneous:** Reduced fees (weekdays, low season, twilight), range (grass), club rentals, lodging (102 rooms), credit cards (MC, V, AE, Diners Club).
★★★½ **VALLEY COURSE**
Holes: 18. **Yards:** 6,202/5,232. **Par:** 72/72. **Course Rating:** 69.7/70.9. **Slope:** 131/129. **Green Fee:** $75/$85. **Cart Fee:** Included in Green Fee. **Walking Policy:** Walking at certain times. **Walkability:** 4. **Opened:** 1974. **Architect:** Rene Muylaert. **Season:** April-Oct. **High:** June-Sept. **To obtain tee times:** Resort guests may book with room reservation 60 days out. Others call 7 days in advance. A valid credit card number is required to reserve a tee-time. **Miscellaneous:** Reduced fees (weekdays, low season, twilight), range (grass/mats), club rentals, lodging (102 rooms), credit cards (MC, V, AE, Diners Club).
Reader Comments: Nice old course ... Take your 'A' game ... A good resort course ... I love this course ... Tough track, plenty of variety ... Great terrain ... Great course with lots of spectacular scenery.... Fall golf at its best, very scenic ... Good variety of holes ... Pleasure to play.

★★½ **HUMBER VALLEY GOLF COURSE**
40 Beattie Ave., Toronto, M9W 2M3, (416)392-2488.
Reader Comments: Enjoyable and relaxing ... Good condition ... Great shape ... Nice layout.
Special Notes: Call club for further information.

HUNTSVILLE DOWNS GOLF LIMITED
PU-182 Golf Course Rd., Huntsville, P1H 1N7, (705)789-4512, 140 miles N of Toronto. **E-mail:** hdgc@surenet.net. **Web:** www.golfcoursecanada.com.
Holes: 18. **Yards:** 6,270/5,217. **Par:** 72/72. **Course Rating:** 70.4/65.6. **Slope:** 129/122. **Green Fee:** $45/$50. **Cart Fee:** $30/cart. **Walking Policy:** Unrestricted walking. **Walkability:** 4. **Opened:** 1998. **Architect:** John Robinson. **Season:** April-Oct. **High:** April-Oct. **To obtain tee**

times: Call up to 1 week in advance. **Miscellaneous:** Reduced fees (low season, twilight, juniors), discount packages, range (grass), club rentals, credit cards (MC, V, AE), beginner friendly (junior, mens and ladies).
Special Notes: Formerly Huntsville Downs Golf & Country Club.

★★ INDIAN CREEK GOLF & COUNTRY CLUB
SP-120 Indian Creek Rd. W., Chatham, N7M 5L6, Kent County, (519)354-7666.
Holes: 18. **Yards:** 6,200/5,471. **Par:** 71/73. **Course Rating:** 68.6/71.4. **Slope:** 113/119. **Green Fee:** $15/$18. **Cart Fee:** $22/cart. **Walking Policy:** Unrestricted walking. **Walkability:** 2.
Opened: 1956. **Architect:** Paul Sironen. **Season:** March-Dec. **High:** May-Oct. **To obtain tee times:** Call up to 7 days in advance. **Miscellaneous:** Reduced fees (low season, twilight, seniors, juniors), discount packages, metal spikes, club rentals, credit cards (MC, V).

KENOGAMISIS GOLF COURSE
SP-P.O. Box 729, Geraldton, P0T 1M0, (807)854-1029, 180 miles NE of Thunder Bay.
Holes: 9. **Yards:** 6,558/5,982. **Par:** 72/74. **Course Rating:** 69.4/72.6. **Slope:** 114/116. **Green Fee:** $22/$22. **Cart Fee:** $20/cart. **Walking Policy:** Unrestricted walking. **Walkability:** 3.
Opened: 1937. **Architect:** Stanley Thompson. **Season:** May-Sept. **High:** July-Aug. **To obtain tee times:** Not required. **Miscellaneous:** Reduced fees (weekdays, juniors), metal spikes, club rentals, credit cards (V).

KINGSVILLE GOLF AND COUNTRY CLUB
SP-640 C. Rd. 20 West, Kingsville, N9Y 2E9, Essex County, (519)733-6585, 35 miles SE of Windsor. **E-mail:** kinggolf@mnsi.net.
Holes: 27. **Green Fee:** N/A/$45. **Cart Fee:** $15/person. **Walking Policy:** Unrestricted walking.
Opened: 1925. **Architect:** R.Moote and Associates. **Season:** March-Nov. **High:** June-Aug. **To obtain tee times:** Call 2 days in advance.
★★★½ RED/WHITE
Yards: 6,364/5,808. **Par:** 72/73. **Course Rating:** 70.9/72.7. **Slope:** 126/120. **Walkability:** 2.
Miscellaneous: Reduced fees (low season, twilight, juniors), metal spikes, range (grass), credit cards (MC, V).
Reader Comments: Red/White the easiest of the three ... Big trees, very flat ... Good par 3s.
★★★½ WHITE/GOLD
S **Yards:** 6,394/5,288. **Par:** 72/72. **Course Rating:** 71.1/70.0. **Slope:** 132/119. **Walkability:** 4.
Miscellaneous: Reduced fees (low season, twilight, juniors), metal spikes, range (grass), credit cards (MC, V).
Reader Comments: Overrated, medium course.
★★★½ RED/GOLD
Yards: 6,622/5,545. **Par:** 27/73. **Course Rating:** 72.9/71.3. **Slope:** 134/120. **Walkability:** 4.
Miscellaneous: Reduced fees (low season, twilight, juniors), range (grass), credit cards (MC, V).
Reader Comments: Good course ... Worth a drive.

LAKE JOSEPH CLUB
R-RR 2, Port Carling, P0B 1J0, (705)765-2020, (800)291-9899, 120 miles N of Toronto.
Holes: 18. **Yards:** 6,985/5,081. **Par:** 72/72. **Course Rating:** 71.9/69.8. **Slope:** 132/123. **Green Fee:** $70/$160. **Cart Fee:** $18/person. **Walking Policy:** Unrestricted walking. **Walkability:** 5.
Opened: 1996. **Architect:** Thomas McBroom. **Season:** May-Oct. **High:** July-Aug. **To obtain tee times:** Clublink Resort Guests or Clublink Members call (705)765-2000. **Miscellaneous:** Reduced fees (low season, twilight, juniors), range (grass), club rentals, lodging (42 rooms), credit cards (MC, V, AE, Diners Club).
Special Notes: Also has 9 hole academy course.

★★½ THE LINKS OF ROCKWAY GLEN
SP-3290 9th St. Louth, St. Catharines, L2R 6P7, (905)641-4536, 5 miles W of St. Catharines.
E-mail: rockway@niagra.com.
Holes: 18. **Yards:** 6,914/5,033. **Par:** 72/72. **Course Rating:** 72.0/68.9. **Slope:** 124/118. **Green Fee:** $37/$42. **Cart Fee:** $32/cart. **Walking Policy:** Unrestricted walking. **Walkability:** 2.
Opened: 1991. **Architect:** Robert Moote. **Season:** April-Oct. **High:** May-Sept. **To obtain tee times:** Call golf shop. **Miscellaneous:** Reduced fees (weekdays, low season), range (grass), club rentals, credit cards (MC, V).
Reader Comments: Improving and not played a lot; hunt for it and be rewarded ... On an old grapevine property, interesting ... Will be even better as it matures ... Good course for high and low handicaps ... A good new semi-private course.

LIONHEAD GOLF & COUNTRY CLUB *Service*
PU-8525 Mississauga Rd., Brampton, L6V 3N2, Peel Region County, (905)455-4900, 10 miles W of Brampton. **Web:** www.golflionhead.com.
★★★★ LEGENDS COURSE
Holes: 18. **Yards:** 7,198/5,730. **Par:** 72/72. **Course Rating:** 77.0/74.0. **Slope:** 153/138. **Green Fee:** $75/$120. **Cart Fee:** $15/person. **Walking Policy:** Mandatory cart. **Walkability:** 5. **Opened:**

1991. **Architect:** Ted Baker. **Season:** April-Nov. **High:** May-Oct. **To obtain tee times:** Book 2 weeks in advance. Book with credit card one to 60 days in advance. 24-hour cancellation policy. **Miscellaneous:** Reduced fees (low season, twilight), range (grass/mats), club rentals, credit cards (MC, V, Diners Club), beginner friendly (mens and womens lessons through academy). **Notes:** Export A Skins, Altamira (Michael Jordan Celebrity).
Reader Comments: Outstanding course! Tough! Great! ... Slope 153, wow!... Interesting ... Excellent customer service ... Great golf course ... One of the best public courses in Ontario ... One of best I've ever seen and played ... Long and tough-golf as it should be! ... Service outstanding ... Plush greens ... Enjoyed it so much I didn't care about my score. You're treated like royalty.

★★★★ **MASTERS COURSE**
Holes: 18. **Yards:** 7,035/5,553. **Par:** 72/72. **Course Rating:** 75.0/72.0. **Slope:** 146/131. **Green Fee:** $75/$110. **Cart Fee:** $15/person. **Cart Fee:** Included in Green Fee. **Walking Policy:** Mandatory cart. **Walkability:** 4. **Opened:** 1991. **Architect:** Ted Baker. **Season:** April-Nov. **High:** May-Oct. **To obtain tee times:** Book with credit card one to 60 days in advance. Call 2 weeks in advance. 24-hour cancellation policy. **Miscellaneous:** Reduced fees (low season, twilight), range (grass/mats), club rentals, credit cards (MC, V, Diners Club), beginner friendly.
Reader Comments: Fun to play ... Keeps coming at you with no let up ... Often underrated, but exceptional in its own way ... Great condition ... First class service ... Very good, great practice facility ... Easier than Legend, still a good test ... Excellent! ... Fast greens, nice course layout, well maintained ... A true test of your ability.

★★★★ **LOCH MARCH GOLF & COUNTRY CLUB** *Service*
PU-1755 Old Carp Rd., Kanata, K2K 1X7, Canada County, (613)839-5885, 28 miles W of Ottawa. **Web:** www.lochmarch.com.
Holes: 18. **Yards:** 6,750/5,178. **Par:** 72/72. **Course Rating:** 71.6/64.6. **Slope:** 129/113. **Green Fee:** $42/N/A. **Cart Fee:** $26/cart. **Walking Policy:** Unrestricted walking. **Walkability:** 3. **Opened:** 1987. **Architect:** Mark Fuller. **Season:** May-Nov. **High:** June-Aug. **To obtain tee times:** Call 2 days in advance. **Miscellaneous:** Discount packages, metal spikes, range (grass/mats), club rentals, credit cards (MC, V, AE, Interac).
Reader Comments: Very scenic, great test of golf ... Great clubhouse and service ... Strong opening hole ... Good all-around course ... Cut through virgin forest and wetlands ... Top calibre course at low dollars ... A gem! ... Excellent practice facilities, great greens ... Very challenging, good layout ... Every hole a choice/challenge. Great hamburgers! ... Excellent shape. Playable. One of my favorites.

LOMBARD GLEN GOLF CLUB
SP-R.R. No.1, Lombardy, K0G 1L0, (613)283-5318, 5 miles SW of Smith Falls.
Holes: 18. **Yards:** 6,061/4,890. **Par:** 70/71. **Course Rating:** 68.1/67.0. **Slope:** 113/111. **Green Fee:** $26/$27. **Cart Fee:** $26/cart. **Walking Policy:** Unrestricted walking. **Walkability:** 1. **Opened:** 1967. **Architect:** David Moote. **Season:** April-Nov. **High:** June-Sept. **To obtain tee times:** Call up to 7 days in advance. **Miscellaneous:** Reduced fees (twilight), metal spikes, range (grass), club rentals, credit cards (MC, V, AE), beginner friendly.

★★ **MANDERLEY ON THE GREEN**
SP-R.R. No.3, North Gower, K0A 2T0, (613)489-2066, 6 miles S of Ottawa.
Holes: 18. **Yards:** 6,414/5,668. **Par:** 71/71. **Course Rating:** 70.0/72.0. **Slope:** 123/126. **Green Fee:** $15/$32. **Cart Fee:** $14/person. **Walking Policy:** Unrestricted walking. **Walkability:** 2. **Opened:** 1964. **Architect:** Howard Watson. **Season:** April-Oct. **High:** June-Sept. **To obtain tee times:** Call 2 days in advance. **Miscellaneous:** Reduced fees (weekdays, low season, twilight), discount packages, metal spikes, range (grass/mats), club rentals, credit cards (MC, V, AE).

MANITOUWADGE GOLF COURSE
PU-P.O. Box 3097, Manitouwadge, P0T 2C0, (807)826-4265, 250 miles E of Thunder Bay.
Holes: 9. **Yards:** 3,250/N/A. **Par:** 36/N/A. **Course Rating:** 72.2/N/A. **Slope:** 129/N/A. **Green Fee:** N/A. **Cart Fee:** $24/cart. **Walking Policy:** Unrestricted walking. **Walkability:** 4. **Opened:** 1971. **Season:** May-Sept. **High:** July-Aug. **To obtain tee times:** Not required. **Miscellaneous:** Reduced fees (twilight, seniors, juniors), discount packages, club rentals, credit cards (MC, V, AE), beginner friendly (junior programs).

★★ **MAPLES OF BALLANTRAE LODGE & GOLF CLUB**
R-R.R. No.4, Stouffville, L4A 7X5, (905)640-6077, 30 miles NE of Toronto.
Holes: 18. **Yards:** 6,715/5,250. **Par:** 72/73. **Course Rating:** 70.0/69.5. **Slope:** 126/116. **Green Fee:** $20/$46. **Cart Fee:** $28/cart. **Walking Policy:** Unrestricted walking. **Walkability:** 3. **Opened:** 1982. **Architect:** R.F. Moote & Assoc. **Season:** April-Nov. **High:** June-Aug. **To obtain tee times:** Call 1 day in advance for weekdays. Call Thursday at 8 a.m. for upcoming weekend or holiday. **Miscellaneous:** Reduced fees (weekdays, low season, resort guests, twilight, seniors, juniors), discount packages, metal spikes, range (grass), club rentals, lodging (20 rooms), credit cards (MC, V, AE).
Special Notes: Also 9 hole executive course.

CANADA

★★★ MARKHAM GREEN GOLF CLUB
SP-120 Rouge Bank Drive, Markham, L3S 4B7, (905)294-6156, 15 miles NE of Toronto.
Holes: 9. **Yards:** 2,873/2,662. **Par:** 35/35. **Course Rating:** 33.6/35.6. **Slope:** 128/122. **Green Fee:** $35/$39. **Cart Fee:** $25/cart. **Walking Policy:** Unrestricted walking. **Walkability:** 3. **Opened:** 1954. **Architect:** Jim Johnson. **Season:** April-Nov. **High:** May-Sept. **To obtain tee times:** Call up to five days in advance. **Miscellaneous:** Reduced fees (low season, twilight, juniors), range (grass), club rentals, credit cards (MC, V, AE).
Reader Comments: Great tune-up 9 ... Pretty.

★★½ MILL RUN GOLF & COUNTRY CLUB
SP-269 Durham Rd. #8, Uxbridge, L9P 1R1, (905)852-6212, (800)465-8633, 7 miles W of Toronto.
Holes: 18. **Yards:** 6,800/5,385. **Par:** 72/72. **Course Rating:** 72.8/70.5. **Slope:** 131/117. **Green Fee:** $24/$37. **Cart Fee:** $25/cart. **Walking Policy:** Unrestricted walking. **Walkability:** 2. **Opened:** 1985. **Architect:** Rene Muylaert. **Season:** April-Oct. **High:** June-Aug. **To obtain tee times:** Call up to 5 days in advance. **Miscellaneous:** Reduced fees (weekdays, low season, twilight, seniors, juniors), discount packages, metal spikes, range (grass), club rentals, credit cards (MC, V, AE, Interact).
Reader Comments: Worth the 80-minute drive, staff is super ... Great service, good value for the price ... Great value. Tough 10th, 11th, 17th and 18th.

★★★★ MONTERRA GOLF COURSE
R-R.R. No.3, Collingwood, L9Y 3Z2, Canada County, (705)445-0231x6531, 75 miles N of Toronto. **E-mail:** mail@bluemountain.ca. **Web:** www.bluemountain.ca.
Holes: 18. **Yards:** 6,581/5,139. **Par:** 72/72. **Course Rating:** 71.8/69.5. **Slope:** 129/116. **Green Fee:** $29/$64. **Cart Fee:** $15/person. **Walking Policy:** Unrestricted walking. **Walkability:** 4. **Opened:** 1989. **Architect:** Thomas McBroom. **Season:** May-Nov. **High:** May-Oct. **To obtain tee times:** Resort guests call when confirming reservation. General public call 10 days in advance. **Miscellaneous:** Reduced fees (low season, resort guests, twilight), discount packages, range (grass/mats), club rentals, lodging, credit cards (MC, V, AE).
Reader Comments: Very nice value. Lots of ups and downs ... 18 unique holes. New challenge on every tee. Love it! ... Fair tee positions for women, a rarity ... Fast greens ... Read the yardage book to score well ... Another McBroom gem, a thinker's course ... Very challenging.

MUNICIPAL GOLF COURSE
PU-R.R. 2 Twin City Crossroads, Thunder Bay, (807)939-1331.
Holes: 9. **Yards:** 2,862/2,832. **Par:** 36/36. **Course Rating:** 64.6/66.2. **Slope:** 95/101. **Green Fee:** $21/$21. **Cart Fee:** $22/cart. **Walking Policy:** Unrestricted walking. **Walkability:** 1. **Season:** April-Oct. **High:** June-July-Aug. **To obtain tee times:** Call two days prior. Every second time is a reserved time. **Miscellaneous:** Reduced fees (low season, juniors), discount packages, metal spikes, club rentals, credit cards (MC, V).

★★★½ NOBLETON LAKES GOLF CLUB
PU-125 Nobleton Lakes Dr., Nobelton, L0G 1N0, (905)859-4070, 20 miles N of Toronto. **Web:** www.nobletonlakesgolf.com.
Holes: 18. **Yards:** 7,089/5,819. **Par:** 72/72. **Course Rating:** 75.3/72.8. **Slope:** 145/N/A. **Green Fee:** $74/$80. **Cart Fee:** Included in Green Fee. **Walking Policy:** Mandatory cart. **Walkability:** 5. **Opened:** 1975. **Architect:** Rene & Charlie Muylaert. **Season:** April-Nov. **High:** May-Oct. **To obtain tee times:** Call 5 days in advance. **Miscellaneous:** Reduced fees (low season, twilight), range (grass), club rentals, credit cards (MC, V, AE).
Reader Comments: Superb layout ... Good condition, challenging layout ... Hidden gem, great fall golf ... Fast, tricky greens, wildlife ... A terrific course.

NORTH SHORE GOLF COURSE
PU-P.O. Box 95, Red Rock, P0T 2P0, (807)887-2006, 70 miles W of Thunder Bay.
Holes: 9. **Yards:** 6,500/6,048. **Par:** 72/N/A. **Course Rating:** 71.8/69.9. **Slope:** 131/121. **Green Fee:** $17/$19. **Cart Fee:** $20/cart. **Walking Policy:** Unrestricted walking. **Walkability:** 3. **Opened:** 1960. **Season:** May-Oct. **High:** June-July. **Miscellaneous:** Reduced fees (weekdays, seniors, juniors), range (grass), club rentals, credit cards (MC, V, Interac).

★★ NORTHRIDGE PUBLIC GOLF COURSE
PM-320 Balmoral Dr., Brantford, N3R 7S2, (519)753-6112, 15 miles W of Hamilton.
Holes: 18. **Yards:** 6,300/5,830. **Par:** 72/74. **Course Rating:** 68.5/72.1. **Slope:** 110/114. **Green Fee:** $24/$24. **Cart Fee:** $24/cart. **Walking Policy:** Unrestricted walking. **Walkability:** 2. **Opened:** 1957. **Season:** April-Nov. **High:** June-Sept. **To obtain tee times:** Call up to 7 days in advance. **Miscellaneous:** Reduced fees (twilight), discount packages, range (grass), club rentals, credit cards (MC, V, AE).

★★★½ THE OAKS OF ST. GEORGE GOLF CLUB
SP-269 German School Rd., R.R. No.1, Paris, N3L 3E1, (519)448-3673, 2 miles NW of Brantford.

Holes: 18. **Yards:** 6,338/5,628. **Par:** 72/72. **Course Rating:** 71.1/69.8. **Slope:** 123/118. **Green Fee:** $30/$35. **Cart Fee:** $26/cart. **Walking Policy:** Unrestricted walking. **Walkability:** 3. **Opened:** 1992. **Architect:** David Moote/R.F. Moote. **Season:** May-Oct. **High:** June-Sept. **To obtain tee times:** Call golf shop to book tee times. **Miscellaneous:** Reduced fees (twilight, seniors, juniors), discount packages, range (grass/mats), club rentals, credit cards (MC, V). **Reader Comments:** Real gem, short but fair with excellent layout ... Tight layout ... Price is right ... Challenging course ... I like it! ... Think your way around this one ... Beware the foxes, they might steal your golf balls ... Great variety from hole to hole and greens were in great shape, 10th hole is beautiful.

OLIVER'S NEST GOLF & COUNTRY CLUB

PU-P.O. Box 75, Lindsay, K9V 4R8, Victoria County, (705)953-2093, (888)953-6378, 3 miles W of Lindsay. **E-mail:** admin@oliversnest.com. **Web:** www.oliversnest.com.
Holes: 18. **Yards:** 6,625/5,185. **Par:** 71/72. **Course Rating:** 72.2/65.2. **Slope:** 127/111. **Green Fee:** $32/$45. **Cart Fee:** $26/cart. **Walking Policy:** Unrestricted walking. **Walkability:** 3. **Opened:** 1997. **Architect:** Graham Cooke. **Season:** April-Nov. **High:** June-Aug. **To obtain tee times:** Call 888-953-6378. **Miscellaneous:** Reduced fees (weekdays, low season, twilight, seniors, juniors), discount packages, range (grass), club rentals, credit cards (MC, V, Debit cards).

★★★★ OSPREY VALLEY RESORTS

PU-R.R. No.2, Alton, L0N 1A0, (519)927-9034, (800)833-1561, 20 miles NW of Toronto.
Holes: 18. **Yards:** 6,810/5,248. **Par:** 71/71. **Course Rating:** 72.6/69.0. **Slope:** 128/118. **Green Fee:** $65/$76. **Cart Fee:** $30/cart. **Walking Policy:** Unrestricted walking. **Walkability:** 2. **Opened:** 1992. **Architect:** Douglas Carrick. **Season:** April-Dec. **High:** May-Sept. **To obtain tee times:** Call with credit card to reserve. **Miscellaneous:** Reduced fees (twilight, seniors), metal spikes, club rentals, credit cards (MC, V, AE).
Reader Comments: Scotland/Ireland with North America conditions ... Links-style—a little bit of Scotland, fabulous track! ... Great links style, peaceful ... Worth the drive ... Twilight rate is a steal, great design ... Hidden gem ... Best public course in Ontario ... Brutal in the wind ... Great fairways, great greens, great rough, great sand, great wind ... Ontario's best-kept secret.

★★ PAKENHAM HIGHLANDS GOLF CLUB

PU-Hwy. 15 at McWatty Rd., Pakenham, K0A 2X0, Canada County, (613)624-5550, 25 miles W of Ottawa. **E-mail:** pak@calabogiehighlandsgolf.com. **Web:** www.calabogiehighlandsgolf.com.
Holes: 18. **Yards:** 6,561/5,360. **Par:** 72/72. **Course Rating:** 70.2/70.0. **Slope:** 122/113. **Green Fee:** $25/$28. **Cart Fee:** $25/cart. **Walking Policy:** Unrestricted walking. **Walkability:** 3. **Opened:** 1994. **Architect:** Rick Fleming. **Season:** April-Oct. **High:** June-Aug. **To obtain tee times:** Call 5 days in advance. **Miscellaneous:** Reduced fees (weekdays, twilight), discount packages, metal spikes, club rentals, credit cards (MC, V, AE, Interac).
Special Notes: New 9 opening spring 2000.

PENINSULA GOLF CLUB

PM-P.O. Bag TM Peninsula Rd, Marathon, P0T 2E0, (807)229-1392, 180 miles NE of Thunder Bay.
Holes: 9. **Yards:** 6,032/5,352. **Par:** 72/71. **Course Rating:** 68.0/69.0. **Slope:** 128/111. **Green Fee:** $13/$20. **Cart Fee:** $20/cart. **Walking Policy:** Unrestricted walking. **Walkability:** 4. **Opened:** 1948. **Architect:** Stanley Thomson. **Season:** May-Sept. **High:** July-Aug. **To obtain tee times:** Call in advance. **Miscellaneous:** Reduced fees (seniors, juniors), metal spikes, range (mats), club rentals, credit cards (V, Interact).

★★★★ PENINSULA LAKES GOLF CLUB *Condition+*

SP-569 Hwy. 20 W., Fenwick, L0S 1C0, (905)892-8844, 15 miles W of Niagra Falls Ontario.
Holes: 18. **Yards:** 6,500/5,523. **Par:** 72/73. **Course Rating:** 72.5/71.3. **Slope:** 131/121. **Green Fee:** $28/$55. **Cart Fee:** $30/cart. **Walking Policy:** Unrestricted walking. **Walkability:** 3. **Opened:** 1980. **Architect:** Rene Muylaert. **Season:** April-Nov. **High:** June-Aug. **To obtain tee times:** Call 5 days in advance for foursome. No restrictions for 12 people or more. **Miscellaneous:** Range (grass/mats), credit cards (MC, V).
Reader Comments: Extraordinary ... Beautiful, fast greens ... Hidden gem ... Slick greens, happy staff, immaculate condition ... Wonderful design ... One the nicest between Buffalo and Toronto ... Beautiful course, new clubhouse ... Great course, fierce greens, and bunkering.

PHEASANT RUN GOLF CLUB

SP-18033 Warden Avenue, Sharon, L0G 1V0, (905)898-3917, 35 miles N of Toronto. **E-mail:** proshop@pheasantrungolf.com. **Web:** www.pheasantrungolf.com.
Holes: 27. **Green Fee:** $40/$65. **Cart Fee:** $16/person. **Walking Policy:** Unrestricted walking. **Opened:** 1980. **Architect:** Rene Muylaert/Charles Muylaert. **Season:** April-Nov. **To obtain tee times:** Book anytime.
★★★ MIDLANDS/HIGHLANDS
Yards: 6,460/5,205. **Par:** 73/73. **Course Rating:** 72.8/67.0. **Slope:** 136/127. **Walkability:** 5. **Miscellaneous:** Reduced fees (weekdays, low season, twilight, juniors), range (grass), club rentals, credit cards (MC, V, AE), beginner friendly (Uplands 9).

Reader Comments: Fun course ... Reduced rates in fall–excellent value ... 3 unique nines: 2 tough, 1 flat and shorter. All fun ... You will use every club in your bag.

★★★ **SOUTHERN UPLAND/HIGHLANDS**
Yards: 6,254/5,041. **Par:** 72/72. **Course Rating:** 71.0/65.3. **Slope:** 135/124. **Walkability:** 3.
Miscellaneous: Reduced fees (weekdays, low season, twilight, juniors), metal spikes, range (grass), club rentals, credit cards (MC, V, AE), beginner friendly (junior program).
Reader Comments: Great course to walk ... Good golf.

★★★ **SOUTHERN UPLAND/MIDLANDS**
Yards: 6,058/4,880. **Par:** 71/71. **Course Rating:** 70.9/65.0. **Slope:** 33/120.
Walkability: 3. **Miscellaneous:** Reduced fees (weekdays, low season, twilight, juniors), metal spikes, range (grass/mats), club rentals, credit cards (MC, V, AE), beginner friendly (junior program).

★★½ **PINE KNOT GOLF & COUNTRY CLUB**
SP-5421 Hamilton Rd., Dorchester, N0L 1G6, (519)268-3352, (800)414-3270, 7 miles E of London.
Holes: 18. **Yards:** 6,500/5,003. **Par:** 71/71. **Course Rating:** 71.7/69.0. **Slope:** 127/115. **Green Fee:** $32/$38. **Cart Fee:** $28/cart. **Walking Policy:** Unrestricted walking. **Walkability:** 2.
Opened: 1992. **Architect:** John Robinson. **Season:** April-Dec. **High:** June-Aug.-Sept. **To obtain tee times:** 5 Day advance booking. **Miscellaneous:** Reduced fees (low season, twilight), discount packages, club rentals, credit cards (MC, V, AE).
Reader Comments: Score early, the last 4 holes are tough ... Friendly people, good service ... Wide open, but enjoyable course.

PINES OF GEORGINA GOLF CLUB
SP-P.O. Box 44, Hwy. 48, Pefferlaw, L0E 1N0, (705)437-1669, 50 miles NE of Toronto.
Holes: 18. **Yards:** 6,012/5,457. **Par:** 70/70. **Course Rating:** 67.8/65.7. **Slope:** 112/107. **Green Fee:** $25/$32. **Cart Fee:** $14/person. **Walking Policy:** Unrestricted walking. **Walkability:** 2.
Opened: 1992. **Architect:** R.F. (Bob) Moote & Assoc. **Season:** April-Nov. **High:** June-Aug. **To obtain tee times:** Call 7 days in advance. **Miscellaneous:** Reduced fees (weekdays, low season, twilight), discount packages, metal spikes, club rentals, credit cards (MC, V, Debit Bank Cards).

★★★ **PINESTONE GOLF & CONFERENCE CENTER**
SP-P.O. Box 809, Haliburton, K0M 1S0, (705)457-3444, (800)461-0357, 120 miles NE of Toronto.
E-mail: pinestone@sympatico.ca. **Web:** www.pinestone.on.ca.
Holes: 18. **Yards:** 6,024/5,448. **Par:** 71/73. **Course Rating:** 70.4/72.6. **Slope:** 141/137. **Green Fee:** $40/$55. **Cart Fee:** $30/cart. **Walking Policy:** Unrestricted walking. **Walkability:** 4.
Opened: 1976. **Architect:** J. Elstone/J. Davidson. **Season:** May-Oct. **High:** July-Sept. **To obtain tee times:** Call 6 a.m. to 6 p.m. daily. **Miscellaneous:** Reduced fees (weekdays, low season, resort guests), discount packages, range (grass), club rentals, lodging (103 rooms), credit cards (MC, V, AE).
Reader Comments: Tough course, staff could not be more accommodating ... Great landscape ... Picturesque ... Good midweek dinner deals.

★★★½ **RENFREW GOLF CLUB**
SP-1108 Golf Course Road, Renfrew, K7V 4A4, (613)432-7729, (888)805-3739. **E-mail:** renfrew.golf.club@renfrew.net. **Web:** www.ottawagolf.com/renfrew.
Holes: 18. **Yards:** 6,440/5,650. **Par:** 71/74. **Course Rating:** 71.1/72.7. **Slope:** 127/125. **Green Fee:** $27/$29. **Cart Fee:** $25/cart. **Walking Policy:** Unrestricted walking. **Walkability:** 4.
Opened: 1929. **Architect:** George Cumming. **Season:** May-Oct. **High:** June-Sept. **To obtain tee times:** Call 5 days in advance. **Miscellaneous:** Reduced fees (low season, juniors), metal spikes, range (grass), club rentals, credit cards (MC, V, AE).
Reader Comments: Very scenic, hilly, and challenging ... Best course in Ottawa Valley ... The best value for your $$s—a must play! ... Great value, very challenging, nice long layout ... Excellent value ... Hidden masterpiece.

★★★ **RICHMOND HILL GOLF CLUB**
PU-8755 Bathurst St., Richmond Hill, L4C 0H4, (905)889-4653, 5 miles N of Toronto. **E-mail:** winstonerhgolf.com. **Web:** www.rhgolf.com.
Holes: 18. **Yards:** 6,004/4,935. **Par:** 70/70. **Course Rating:** 67.8/64.0. **Slope:** 120/N/A. **Green Fee:** $25/$58. **Cart Fee:** $30/cart. **Walking Policy:** Unrestricted walking. **Walkability:** 3.
Opened: 1992. **Architect:** Rene Muyleart. **Season:** April-Nov. **High:** June-Aug. **To obtain tee times:** Call 2 days in advance with credit card. Purchase a green fee package for 4 day advance booking. **Miscellaneous:** Reduced fees (weekdays, low season, twilight, seniors), discount packages, metal spikes, range (mats), club rentals, credit cards (MC, V, AE, Interac).
Reader Comments: The best 18th hole of this list. Very well-maintained course. Good clubhouse. Challenging course ... Wonderful layout ... Excellent food ... Great finishing hole.

★★ **RICHVIEW GOLF & COUNTRY CLUB**
SP-2204 Bronty Rd., Oakville, L6L 6M9, (905)827-1211.
Holes: 18. **Yards:** 6,100/5,200. **Par:** 71/71. **Course Rating:** 69.3/65.0. **Slope:** 115/107. **Green Fee:** $43/$52. **Cart Fee:** $30/cart. **Walking Policy:** Unrestricted walking. **Walkability:** 3.

CANADA

Opened: 1965. **Architect:** Clinton E. Robinson. **Season:** Year-round. **High:** April-Oct. **To obtain tee times:** Please Call 10 days in advance. **Miscellaneous:** Reduced fees (low season, twilight, seniors), discount packages, club rentals, credit cards (MC, V, AE).

RIVENDELL GOLF CLUB
SP-R.R. No.1, Verona, K0H 2W0, (613)374-3404, 18 miles N of Kingston. **E-mail:** info@rivendellgolf.on.ca. **Web:** www.rivendellgolf.on.ca.
Holes: 18. **Yards:** 6,218/5,173. **Par:** 71/71. **Course Rating:** 68.5/68.9. **Slope:** 116/116. **Green Fee:** $23/$27. **Cart Fee:** $25/cart. **Walking Policy:** Unrestricted walking. **Walkability:** 3.
Opened: 1979. **Architect:** Robert Heaslip. **Season:** May-Oct. **High:** June-Sept. **To obtain tee times:** Call golf shop 48 hours in advance. **Miscellaneous:** Reduced fees (low season, resort guests, twilight), club rentals, credit cards (MC, V, AE, Interac).

★★½ RIVER ROAD GOLF COURSE
PM-2115 River Rd., London, N6A 4C3, (519)452-1822, 100 miles SW of Toronto.
Holes: 18. **Yards:** 6,480/5,386. **Par:** 72/72. **Course Rating:** 72.6/70.0. **Slope:** 130/126. **Green Fee:** $24/$24. **Cart Fee:** $26/cart. **Walking Policy:** Unrestricted walking. **Walkability:** 3.
Opened: 1992. **Architect:** Bill Fox Sr. **Season:** March-Dec. **High:** June-Aug. **To obtain tee times:** Call 2 days in advance. **Miscellaneous:** Reduced fees (twilight), discount packages, metal spikes, club rentals, credit cards (MC, V).
Reader Comments: Very good for city-run course ... Very nice, especially for a city course ... Great layout. Great value ... Very tight and a tough test ... You better hit a straight ball ... Best greens in London area.

★★★ ROSELAND GOLF & CURLING CLUB
PM-455 Kennedy Dr. W., Windsor, N9G 1S8, (519)969-3810, 5 miles S of Detroit.
Holes: 18. **Yards:** 6,588/5,914. **Par:** 72/74. **Course Rating:** 70.6/73.1. **Slope:** 119/123. **Green Fee:** $24/$30. **Cart Fee:** $28/cart. **Walking Policy:** Unrestricted walking. **Walkability:** 1.
Opened: 1928. **Architect:** Donald Ross. **Season:** April-Oct. **High:** June-Aug. **To obtain tee times:** Call Wednesday 9 a.m. for Saturday and Thursday 9 a.m. for Sunday and Monday holidays. **Miscellaneous:** Reduced fees (weekdays, low season, twilight, seniors), club rentals, credit cards (MC, V).
Reader Comments: Very good for city-owned course ... Classic layout. Conditioning improving yearly ... Lots of play, busy, challenging ... My favorite walk in the park ... Bring all your clubs

★★★½ ROYAL WOODBINE GOLF CLUB
SP-195 Galaxy Blvd., Toronto, M9W 6R7, (416)674-4653, 1 miles W of Toronto.
Holes: 18. **Yards:** 6,446/5,102. **Par:** 71/71. **Course Rating:** 72.3/71.2. **Slope:** 139/120. **Green Fee:** $120/$120. **Cart Fee:** Included in Green Fee. **Walking Policy:** Walking at certain times.
Walkability: 3. **Opened:** 1992. **Architect:** Michael Hurdzan. **Season:** April-Nov. **High:** May-Sept. **To obtain tee times:** Call with credit card. **Miscellaneous:** Reduced fees (low season, twilight), range (grass/mats), club rentals, credit cards (MC, V, AE, Enroute), beginner friendly (lessons, clinics, camps).
Reader Comments: Great staff ... True business person course ... An inner-city treat ... Good course given its location near airport ... City golf at its best ... A hoot to play ... Premium on accuracy ... Great use of available land.

★★★★ ST. ANDREWS VALLEY GOLF CLUB
PU-368 St. John Sideroad E., Aurora, L4G 3G8, (905)727-7888, 20 miles N of Toronto. **E-mail:** st.andrewsgc@ani.on.ca. **Web:** www.standrewsvalley.com.
Holes: 18. **Yards:** 7,304/5,536. **Par:** 72/72. **Course Rating:** 77.4/68.5. **Slope:** 143/123. **Green Fee:** $29/$75. **Cart Fee:** $15/person. **Walking Policy:** Unrestricted walking. **Walkability:** 4.
Opened: 1993. **Architect:** Rene Muylaert. **Season:** April-Nov. **High:** June-Aug. **To obtain tee times:** Call up to 14 days in advance. **Miscellaneous:** Reduced fees (weekdays, twilight), discount packages, metal spikes, range (grass/mats), club rentals, credit cards (MC, V, AE, Diners Club).
Reader Comments: Great shape. Friendly staff ... Deceptively difficult ... Multiple hazards, punishing rough, roller coaster greens ... Don't challenge the 9th hole ... Excellent driving range ... True test from any tee box ... Play safe or pay big time ... Great all-around experience, well-bunkered with mix of water.

★★★ ST. CLAIR PARKWAY GOLF COURSE
PU-132 Moore Line, Mooretown, N0N 1M0, (519)867-2810, (877)362-3344, 12 miles S of Sarnia. **E-mail:** pkwygolf@ebtech.net. **Web:** www.sarnia.com/parkway.
Holes: 18. **Yards:** 6,720/5,731. **Par:** 71/72. **Course Rating:** 70.5/71.0. **Slope:** 118/122. **Green Fee:** $20/$30. **Cart Fee:** $27/cart. **Walking Policy:** Unrestricted walking. **Walkability:** 2.
Opened: 1971. **Architect:** William Aimers. **Season:** April-Nov. **High:** July-Aug. **To obtain tee times:** Call up to 7 days in advance. **Miscellaneous:** Reduced fees (low season, twilight, seniors), club rentals, credit cards (MC, V).
Reader Comments: Good rough, mostly trees, very effective.

★★★½ SAUGEEN GOLF CLUB
PU-R.R. #2, Port Elgin, N0H 2C6, (519)389-4031, 25 miles SW of Owen Sound.
Holes: 27. **Yards:** 6,453/N/A. **Par:** 72/N/A. **Course Rating:** 70.2/N/A. **Slope:** 123/N/A. **Green Fee:** $35/N/A. **Cart Fee:** $27/cart. **Walking Policy:** Unrestricted walking. **Walkability:** 3. **Opened:** 1925. **Architect:** Stanley Thompson, David Moote. **Season:** April-Oct. **High:** July-Aug. **To obtain tee times:** Call 3 days in advance after 1 p.m. **Miscellaneous:** Reduced fees (weekdays, resort guests), range (grass), club rentals, credit cards (MC, V).
Reader Comments: Hidden gem ... Good layout ... Pleasant surprise ... Very well maintained. Excellent practice area ... Beautiful course ... New 9 fantastic–now 27 holes ... Have incorporated new with old ... Playable for all golfers ... Excellent.

★★★★ SILVER LAKES GOLF & COUNTRY CLUB *Condition*
SP-21114 Yonge St., R.R. No.1, Newmarket, L3Y 4V8, (905)836-8070, 5 miles N of Newmarket.
Holes: 18. **Yards:** 7,029/5,210. **Par:** 72/74. **Course Rating:** 73.0/72.9. **Slope:** 131/130. **Green Fee:** $55/$65. **Cart Fee:** $30/cart. **Walking Policy:** Unrestricted walking. **Walkability:** 1. **Opened:** 1994. **Architect:** David Moote. **Season:** April-Nov. **High:** June-Aug. **To obtain tee times:** Call 5 days in advance. **Miscellaneous:** Reduced fees (weekdays, low season, twilight, seniors, juniors), range (grass), club rentals, credit cards (MC, V, AE, Diners Club), beginner friendly (junior and ladies clinics available).
Reader Comments: Best-kept secret in Ontario ... Myrtle Beach North ... Well groomed ... Lots of water, lots of trees and very quiet ... Very pretty in late spring ... Great layout, looking forward to return ... Tight course, a real test! ... Have to plan each shot.

★★★ STRATHCONA GOLF COURSE
PU-500 Hodder Ave., Thunder Bay, (807)683-8251.
Holes: 18. **Yards:** 6,507/5,852. **Par:** 72/73. **Course Rating:** 73.4/72.9. **Slope:** 130/115. **Green Fee:** $21/$21. **Cart Fee:** $22/cart. **Walking Policy:** Unrestricted walking. **Walkability:** 3. **Season:** April-Oct. **High:** July-Aug. **To obtain tee times:** Call 2 days prior. Every second time is reserved. **Miscellaneous:** Reduced fees (low season, juniors), discount packages, metal spikes, club rentals, credit cards (MC, V).
Reader Comments: Difficult, challenges competitive golfer ... Loads of fun.

SUMMERHEIGHTS GOLF LINKS
PU-1160 S. Branch Rd., Cornwall, K6H 5R6, Stormont County, (613)938-8009, 70 miles S of Ottawa.
SOUTH/NORTH
Holes: 18. **Yards:** 6,345/5,372. **Par:** 72/72. **Course Rating:** 69.8/71.1. **Slope:** 120/123. **Green Fee:** $27/$32. **Cart Fee:** $30/cart. **Walking Policy:** Unrestricted walking. **Walkability:** 2. **Opened:** 1962. **Architect:** Robert Heaslip. **Season:** April-Oct. **High:** June-Aug. **To obtain tee times:** Call 2 days in advance. **Miscellaneous:** Reduced fees (low season, twilight), range (grass), club rentals, credit cards (MC, V, AE), beginner friendly (junior programs).
WEST
Holes: 18. **Yards:** 6,236/5,301. **Par:** 72/72. **Course Rating:** 69.5/70.0. **Slope:** 118/113. **Green Fee:** $27/$32. **Cart Fee:** $30/cart. **Walking Policy:** Unrestricted walking. **Walkability:** 2. **Opened:** 1966. **Architect:** Robert Heaslip. **Season:** April-Oct. **High:** June-Aug. **To obtain tee times:** Call 2 days in advance. **Miscellaneous:** Range (grass), club rentals, credit cards (MC, V, AE), beginner friendly (junior programs).
Special Notes: Formerly West/North course.

★★½ SUTTON CREEK GOLF & COUNTRY CLUB
SP-R.R. No.2, Walker and Guesto, Essex, N8M 2X6, (519)726-6179, 10 miles S of Windsor.
Holes: 18. **Yards:** 6,856/5,286. **Par:** 72/73. **Course Rating:** 72.5/70.5. **Slope:** 132/118. **Green Fee:** $30/$40. **Cart Fee:** $15/person. **Walking Policy:** Unrestricted walking. **Walkability:** 2. **Opened:** 1988. **Architect:** Robert Heaslip. **Season:** April-Nov. **High:** June-Sept. **To obtain tee times:** Call golf shop. **Miscellaneous:** Reduced fees (weekdays, seniors, juniors), range (grass), credit cards (MC, V).
Reader Comments: Has matured well. Tough 1st hole ... Very good course and facilities.

★★ TAM O'SHANTER GOLF COURSE
PU-2481 Birchmount Rd., Toronto, M1T 2M6, (416)392-2547.
Holes: 18. **Yards:** 6,043/4,958. **Par:** 71/70. **Course Rating:** 68.4/67.2. **Slope:** 120/109. **Green Fee:** $17/$30. **Cart Fee:** $29/cart. **Walking Policy:** Unrestricted walking. **Walkability:** 2. **Season:** April-Dec. **High:** June-Sept. **To obtain tee times:** Call up to 5 days in advance. **Miscellaneous:** Caddies, club rentals, credit cards (MC, V, AE), beginner friendly (lesson programs).

★★ THAMES VALLEY GOLF COURSE
PU-850 Sunninghill Ave., London, N6H 3L9, (519)471-5750.
Holes: 27. **Yards:** 6,314/5,759. **Par:** 71/75. **Course Rating:** 70.5/72.9. **Slope:** 122/126. **Green**

CANADA

Fee: N/A/$24. Cart Fee: $26/cart. **Walking Policy:** Unrestricted walking. **Walkability:** 2. **Opened:** 1924. **Architect:** John Innes. **Season:** April-Nov. **High:** May-Sept. **To obtain tee times:** Call up to 2 days in advance. **Miscellaneous:** Metal spikes, club rentals, credit cards (MC, V).

THUNDER BAY COUNTRY CLUB
SP-R.R. 17 1055 Oliver Rd., Thunder Bay, P7B 6C2, (807)344-8141.
Holes: 9. **Yards:** 5,981/5,203. **Par:** 72/72. **Course Rating:** 69.1/69.0. **Slope:** 126/120. **Green Fee:** $32/$40. **Cart Fee:** $20/cart. **Walking Policy:** Unrestricted walking. **Walkability:** 5. **Opened:** 1912. **Architect:** Stanley Thompson. **Season:** April-Oct. **High:** June-July-Aug. **To obtain tee times:** Members book up to 48 hours in advance. Nonmembers, walk-ons, out-of-towners phone golf shop. **Miscellaneous:** Reduced fees (low season, seniors, juniors), range (grass), club rentals, credit cards (MC, V).

★★★½ THUNDERBIRD GOLF & COUNTRY CLUB
PU-995 Myrtle Rd. W., Ashburn, L0B 1A0, Canada County, (905)686-1121, 18 miles NE of Whitby. **E-mail:** tbgc@inforamp.com. **Web:** www.thunderbirdgolfclub.com.
Holes: 18. **Yards:** 7,019/5,828. **Par:** 72/72. **Course Rating:** 72.9/71.0. **Slope:** 127/N/A. **Green Fee:** $45/$55. **Cart Fee:** $28/cart. **Walking Policy:** Unrestricted walking. **Walkability:** 2. **Opened:** 1961. **Architect:** Wilson Paterson. **Season:** April-Nov. **High:** June-Aug. **To obtain tee times:** Call 7 days in advance with credit card to reserve. **Miscellaneous:** Reduced fees (week-days, low season, twilight), discount packages, range (grass/mats), club rentals, credit cards (MC, V, AE), beginner friendly (golf clinics).
Reader Comments: A good, fun little course ... Home of CPGA Qualifying School ... Busy, crowded ... Lots of golf to be had here ... Good value ... Classic old course; gimmicky 3rd hole ... A solid, straight-forward test.

★★★★ UPPER CANADA GOLF COURSE *Value+*
PU-R.R. No.1, Morrisburg, K0C 1X0, (613)543-2003, (800)437-2233, 50 miles S of Ottawa.
Holes: 18. **Yards:** 6,900/6,008. **Par:** 72/73. **Course Rating:** 71.8/74.2. **Slope:** 121/130. **Green Fee:** $34/$39. **Cart Fee:** $30/cart. **Walking Policy:** Unrestricted walking. **Walkability:** 1. **Opened:** 1966. **Architect:** Robbie Robinson. **Season:** April-Nov. **High:** June-Aug. **To obtain tee times:** Call 14 days in advance. **Miscellaneous:** Reduced fees (low season, twilight, seniors, juniors), discount packages, range (grass), club rentals, credit cards (MC, V, AE, Intrerac).
Reader Comments: Very challenging. Lots of wildlife ... Huge greens, beautiful ... More interesting the more I play it ... Very busy ... Excellent condition ... Scenery excellent ... Back nine very long ... Quality at low cost ... Tough course from back tees, great back tees, great walk, great back nine.

★★★★ WHIRLPOOL GOLF COURSE
PU-3351 Niagara Parkway, Niagara Falls, L2E 6T2, (905)356-1140, 4 miles N of Niagra Falls. **Web:** www.niagarapark.com.
Holes: 18. **Yards:** 7,122/6,011. **Par:** 72/72. **Course Rating:** 71.8/75.4. **Slope:** 119/128. **Green Fee:** $49/$49. **Cart Fee:** $30/cart. **Walking Policy:** Unrestricted walking. **Walkability:** 2. **Opened:** 1951. **Architect:** Stanley Thompson/David Moote. **Season:** March-Nov. **High:** June-Sept. **To obtain tee times:** Call anytime in advance with credit card. **Miscellaneous:** Reduced fees (low season, twilight), discount packages, club rentals, credit cards (MC, V, AE), beginner friendly (new forward tees).
Reader Comments: Great layout! ... Long par three, 240 yds. A course you could play again and again ... Nice fairways, very pretty course ... Best public course in South Ontario ... Very long and beautiful course ... Long traditional course, what you see is what you get ... Always booked in advance, beautiful layout.

★★★ WILLO-DELL COUNTRY CLUB LTD.
SP-10325 Willodell Rd., Port Robinson, L0S 1K0, (905)295-8181, (800)790-0912, 6 miles S of Niagara Falls.
Holes: 18. **Yards:** 6,407/5,752. **Par:** 72/73. **Course Rating:** 70.0/71.0. **Slope:** 123/144. **Green Fee:** $32/$40. **Cart Fee:** $32/cart. **Walking Policy:** Unrestricted walking. **Walkability:** 3. **Opened:** 1964. **Architect:** Nicol Thompson. **Season:** April-Oct. **High:** June-Aug. **To obtain tee times:** Members call 7 days in advance. Nonmembers call 3 days in advance. **Miscellaneous:** Reduced fees (low season, twilight), discount packages, metal spikes, range (grass), club rentals, credit cards (MC, V).
Reader Comments: Reworked and still more work being done on course. Will be fantastic when it is completed ... Most trouble on right ... Well maintained. Uncommon value ... A good change of pace.... Great, friendly people and area.

PRINCE EDWARD ISLAND

★★½ BELVEDERE GOLF CLUB
SP-P.O. Box 253, Charlottetown, C1A 7K4, (902)368-7104.

952

Holes: 18. **Yards:** 6,425/5,380. **Par:** 72/74. **Course Rating:** 69.8/73.2. **Slope:** 121/123. **Green Fee:** $50/$65. **Cart Fee:** $25/cart. **Walking Policy:** Unrestricted walking. **Walkability:** 1. **Opened:** 1906. **Season:** May-Oct. **High:** June-Aug. **To obtain tee times:** Call (902)892-7383 in summer; (902)566-5542 in winter. **Miscellaneous:** Club rentals, credit cards (MC, V).
Reader Comments: Great greens ... Good value ... Will be much improved ... All new greens and tees. It was good before, now it's super... Old course renovated—excellent.

BRUDENELL RIVER RESORT
★★★★ **BRUDENELL RIVER GOLF COURSE** *Value*
R-Roseneath, C0A 1R0, (902)652-2332, (800)377-8336, 30 miles SE of Charlottetown.
Holes: 18. **Yards:** 6,542/5,052. **Par:** 72/69. **Course Rating:** 72.0/70.5. **Slope:** 131/129. **Green Fee:** $37/$46. **Cart Fee:** $29/cart. **Walking Policy:** Unrestricted walking. **Walkability:** 2. **Opened:** 1969. **Architect:** Robbie Robinson. **Season:** May-Oct. **High:** June-Sept. **To obtain tee times:** Call or Fax in advance. Confirmation provided with credit card reference. **Miscellaneous:** Reduced fees (low season, seniors), discount packages, range (grass), caddies, club rentals, lodging, credit cards (MC, V, AE).
Reader Comments: Very scenic ... Once is never enough ... Beautiful old course ... Some very good holes ... One of the best ... Looks challenging ... Wonderful resort course ... Lovely, friendly course ... I'd play this the rest of my life.... Great layout—pretty setting and good value.

DUNDARAVE GOLF COURSE *Value*
R-, Roseneath, C0A 1R0, (902)652-8965, (800)377-8336, 30 miles SE of Charlottetown.
Holes: 18. **Yards:** 7,284/4,997. **Par:** 72/72. **Course Rating:** 76.2/64.9. **Slope:** 139/112. **Green Fee:** $48/$60. **Cart Fee:** $29/cart. **Walking Policy:** Unrestricted walking. **Walkability:** 3. **Opened:** 1999. **Architect:** Robbie Robinson. **Season:** May-Oct. **High:** June-Sept. **To obtain tee times:** Call or Fax in advance. Confirmation provided with credit card reference. **Miscellaneous:** Reduced fees (low season, seniors), discount packages, range (grass), caddies, club rentals, lodging, credit cards (MC, V, AE).

★½ **GLEN AFTON GOLF CLUB**
PU-Nine Mile Creek R.R. 2, Cornwall, C0A 1H0, (902)675-3000, 15 miles SW of Charlottetown.
Holes: 18. **Yards:** 5,736/5,490. **Par:** 70/70. **Course Rating:** 67.5/70.1. **Slope:** 111/115. **Green Fee:** $20/$25. **Cart Fee:** $22/cart. **Walking Policy:** Unrestricted walking. **Walkability:** 1. **Opened:** 1973. **Architect:** William Robinson. **Season:** May-Nov. **High:** July-Sept. **To obtain tee times:** Call golf shop. **Miscellaneous:** Reduced fees (low season), metal spikes, club rentals, credit cards (MC, V).

★★★½ **GREEN GABLES GOLF COURSE**
PU-Rte. No.6, Cavendish, C0A 1N0, (902)963-2488, 25 miles NW of Charlottetown.
Holes: 18. **Yards:** 6,459/5,589. **Par:** 72/74. **Course Rating:** 71.5/72.0. **Slope:** 122/124. **Green Fee:** $18/$38. **Cart Fee:** $26/cart. **Walking Policy:** Unrestricted walking. **Walkability:** 4. **Opened:** 1939. **Architect:** Stanley Thompson. **Season:** May-Oct. **High:** June-Sept. **To obtain tee times:** Call golf shop. **Miscellaneous:** Reduced fees (weekdays, low season, twilight), range (grass), club rentals, credit cards (MC, V).
Reader Comments: Historical site ... Good old-fashioned Stanley Thompson course ... A beautiful, scenic fine golf course ... Very pretty scenery ... Some great holes ... Great views of ocean ... Wide fairways, enjoyable course ... Like the layout ... Play around Anne's house and Cavenish beach ... Beautiful course, with many water holes.

★★★★★ **THE LINKS AT CROWBUSH COVE** *Value+, Condition+*
PU-P.O. Box 204, Morell, C0A 1S0, Kings County, (902)961-73000, (800)377-8337, 25 miles E of Charlottetown. **E-mail:** crowbush@gov.pe.ca. **Web:** www.gov.pe.ca/golf.
Holes: 18. **Yards:** 6,936/5,490. **Par:** 72/72. **Course Rating:** 74.9/68.1. **Slope:** 148/120. **Green Fee:** $48/$60. **Cart Fee:** $29/cart. **Walking Policy:** Unrestricted walking. **Walkability:** 3. **Opened:** 1993. **Architect:** Thomas McBroom. **Season:** May-Oct. **High:** June-Sept. **To obtain tee times:** Call ten days in advance with credit card number. **Miscellaneous:** Reduced fees (low season, resort guests, seniors), discount packages, range (grass), club rentals, credit cards (MC, V, AE).
Reader Comments: Pebble Beach of Canada ... Best ever, my favorite ... Tops in Maritimes, Eastern Canada ... Very windy-on ocean, loved it ... Superb ... Excellent seaside course. Real bargain ... A must!! ... Best course I've ever played ... Best public course in Canada ... Wonderful McBroom course ... Drove 25 hours to play it and would do it again ... World class, great service, a must play!

★★★★ **MILL RIVER GOLF COURSE** *Value*
R-O'Leary RR#3, O'Leary, C0B 1V0, Prince County, (902)859-8873, (800)377-8339, 35 miles NW of Summerside. **E-mail:** rmark99@hotmail.com.
Holes: 18. **Yards:** 6,827/5,983. **Par:** 72/72. **Course Rating:** 75.0/70.5. **Slope:** 132/127. **Green Fee:** $33/$41. **Cart Fee:** $29/cart. **Walking Policy:** Unrestricted walking. **Walkability:** 3. **Opened:**

CANADA

1971. **Architect:** C.E. (Robbie) Robinson. **Season:** May-Oct. **High:** June-Sept. **To obtain tee times:** Call up to 10 days in advance. **Miscellaneous:** Reduced fees (low season, seniors), discount packages, range (grass), club rentals, lodging (90 rooms), credit cards (MC, V, AE).
Reader Comments: Lot of shots needed ... Old course, some great holes, demands accuracy ... Many doglegs but a fun course ... Thinking and positioning required ... Challenging and pretty ... The seafood and scenery are spectacular.

★½ RUSTICO RESORT GOLF & COUNTRY CLUB
R-R.R. No.3, South Rustico, C0A 1N0, (902)963-2357, (800)465-3734, 12 miles N of Charlottetown. **E-mail:** rustico@auracom.com. **Web:** www.rusticoresort.com.
Holes: 18. **Yards:** 6,675/5,550. **Par:** 73/73. **Course Rating:** N/A/71.8. **Slope:** N/A/118. **Green Fee:** $23/$29. **Cart Fee:** $27/cart. **Walking Policy:** Unrestricted walking. **Walkability:** 1. **Opened:** 1980. **Architect:** John Langdale. **Season:** April-Oct. **High:** July-Aug. **To obtain tee times:** Call. **Miscellaneous:** Reduced fees (weekdays, low season, resort guests, twilight, seniors, juniors), discount packages, metal spikes, range (grass), club rentals, lodging (35 rooms), credit cards (MC, V, Diners Club), beginner friendly.

★★★ STANHOPE GOLF & COUNTRY CLUB
PU-York R.R. No.1, Stanhope, C0A 1P0, (902)672-2842, 15 miles N of Charlottetown.
Holes: 18. **Yards:** 6,600/5,785. **Par:** 72/74. **Course Rating:** 73.3/72.8. **Slope:** 131/120. **Green Fee:** $20/$37. **Cart Fee:** $29/cart. **Walking Policy:** Unrestricted walking. **Walkability:** 2. **Opened:** 1970. **Architect:** Robbie Robinson. **Season:** May-Oct. **High:** July-Aug. **To obtain tee times:** Call 1 day ahead. **Miscellaneous:** Reduced fees (weekdays, low season, resort guests), discount packages, metal spikes, range (grass), caddies, club rentals, credit cards (MC, V, AE, Interact).
Reader Comments: Fun, wide open, inexpensive ... Good for ego ... Great views along ocean ... Don't fight the wind! Scenic ... Windswept! ... Wind and water. Back nine worth the wait.

★★★ SUMMERSIDE GOLF CLUB
PU-Bayview Dr., Summerside, C1N 1A9, (902)436-2505, (877)505-2505, 30 miles SE of Charlottetown.
Holes: 18. **Yards:** 6,428/5,773. **Par:** 72/72. **Course Rating:** N/A. **Slope:** 125/119. **Green Fee:** $31/$37. **Cart Fee:** $26/cart. **Walking Policy:** Unrestricted walking. **Walkability:** 1. **Opened:** 1926. **Architect:** John Watson. **Season:** May-Oct. **High:** July-Aug. **To obtain tee times:** Call 1(877)505-2505. **Miscellaneous:** Reduced fees (low season, twilight), discount packages, range (grass/mats), club rentals, credit cards (MC, V, AE).
Reader Comments: Picturesque, and wide open ... Very good, grounds well kept.

QUEBEC

★★ BAIE MISSISQOI GOLF CLUB
PU-321 Ave. Venise W., Venise-en-Quebec, J0J 2K0, (450)244-5932, 40 miles SE of Montreal.
Holes: 18. **Yards:** 6,357/5,664. **Par:** 72/73. **Course Rating:** 69.0/69.9. **Slope:** 114/113. **Green Fee:** $15/$30. **Cart Fee:** $24/cart. **Walking Policy:** Unrestricted walking. **Walkability:** 3. **Opened:** 1962. **Architect:** Gerry Huot. **Season:** April-Oct. **High:** June-Aug. **To obtain tee times:** Call 3 days in advance. **Miscellaneous:** Reduced fees (weekdays, low season, twilight, juniors), metal spikes, range (grass/mats), club rentals, lodging, credit cards (MC, V), beginner friendly.

CLUB DE GOLF METROPOLITAIN
PU-9555 Blvd. du Golf, Anjou, H1J 2Y2, (514)356-2666, 10 miles E of Montreal.
Holes: 18. **Yards:** 7,005/5,830. **Par:** 72/72. **Course Rating:** 73.0/73.6. **Slope:** 130/131. **Green Fee:** $25/$45. **Cart Fee:** $25/cart. **Walking Policy:** Unrestricted walking. **Walkability:** 1. **Opened:** 1998. **Architect:** Graham Cooke. **Season:** April-Nov. **High:** May-Aug. **Miscellaneous:** Reduced fees (weekdays, low season), range (mats), club rentals, credit cards (MC, V, AE, Diners Club). **Special Notes:** Also 18 hole Par 3 (2989 yards).

★★½ GOLF DORVAL
PM-2000 Ave. Revechon, Dorval, H9P 2S7, (514)631-6624, 5 miles W of Montreal.
Holes: 36. **Yards:** 6,743/5,232. **Par:** 72/70. **Course Rating:** 71.9/69.5. **Slope:** 123/110. **Green Fee:** $19/$33. **Cart Fee:** $26/cart. **Walking Policy:** Unrestricted walking. **Walkability:** 2. **Opened:** 1982. **Architect:** Graham Cooke. **Season:** April-October. **High:** June-JAug. **To obtain tee times:** First come first served. **Miscellaneous:** Reduced fees (weekdays, low season, twilight, seniors), range (mats), club rentals, credit cards (MC, V).
Reader Comments: Easy access from major highways ... Very busy muny with good greens ... Great golf course, good shape, good service.

GRAY ROCKS GOLF CLUB
SP-525 Rue Principale, Mont Tremblant, J0T 1Z0, (819)425-2771x7604, (800)567-6744, 78 miles NW of Montreal. **E-mail:** info@grayrocks.com. **Web:** www.grayrocks.com.

CANADA

★★★ LA BELLE COURSE
Holes: 18. **Yards:** 6,330/5,623. **Par:** 72/72. **Course Rating:** 70.0/72.0. **Slope:** 119/118. **Green Fee:** $30/$42. **Cart Fee:** $32/cart. **Walking Policy:** Unrestricted walking. **Walkability:** 3. **Season:** May-Oct. **High:** July-Aug. **Miscellaneous:** Reduced fees (weekdays, low season, resort guests, twilight), discount packages, range (mats), club rentals, lodging (150 rooms), credit cards (MC, V, AE), beginner friendly (clinics, children's clinics, lessons).

★★★ LA BETE COURSE
Holes: 18. **Yards:** 6,825/5,150. **Par:** 72/72. **Course Rating:** 73.0/69.8. **Slope:** 131/119. **Green Fee:** $50/$100. **Cart Fee:** Included in Green Fee. **Walking Policy:** Mandatory cart. **Walkability:** 4. **Opened:** 1998. **Architect:** Graham Cooke and Associates. **Season:** May-Oct. **High:** July-Aug. **To obtain tee times:** Available any time. **Miscellaneous:** Reduced fees (weekdays, low season, resort guests, twilight), discount packages, club rentals, lodging (150 rooms), credit cards (MC, V, AE).
Reader Comments: La Bete, the new 18 holes, is spectacular ... Course well groomed ... Nice scenic views ... Good challenge and the service is excellent.

★★★★ LE CHATEAU MONTEBELLO
R-392 Rue Notre Dame, Montebello, J0V 1L0, (819)423-4653, 60 miles W of Montreal. **E-mail:** mkucynia@lcm.cphotels.ca. **Web:** www.chateaumontebello.com.
Holes: 18. **Yards:** 6,235/4,998. **Par:** 70/72. **Course Rating:** 70.0/72.0. **Slope:** 129/128. **Green Fee:** $46/$65. **Cart Fee:** Included in Green Fee. **Walking Policy:** Walking at certain times. **Walkability:** 4. **Opened:** 1929. **Architect:** Stanley Thompson. **Season:** May-Oct. **High:** June-Sept. **To obtain tee times:** Call 7 days in advance. Hotel guests may book times when making reservations. **Miscellaneous:** Reduced fees (weekdays, low season, twilight), discount packages, range (grass/mats), club rentals, lodging, credit cards (MC, V, AE, D, Diners Club).
Reader Comments: Very hilly fun to play ... Fun layout with old-style challenges ... Don't expect a flat lie ... Scenic ... Good course where you'll use every club in the bag ... Fast greens, well-groomed fairways ... A must play ... Excellent short course with panoramic views ... I'll play it again ... Foliage in the fall is amazing.

★★★½ LE CLUB DE GOLF CARLING LAKE
R-Rte. 327 N., Pine Hill, J0V 1A0, (514)337-1212, 60 miles N of Montreal.
Holes: 18. **Yards:** 6,691/5,421. **Par:** 72/73. **Course Rating:** 71.5/71.5. **Slope:** 126/123. **Green Fee:** $41/$43. **Cart Fee:** $12/person. **Walking Policy:** Mandatory cart. **Walkability:** 5. **Opened:** 1961. **Architect:** Howard Watson. **Season:** May-Oct. **High:** June-Sept. **To obtain tee times:** Call with credit card number to reserve. **Miscellaneous:** Reduced fees (weekdays, low season, twilight), metal spikes, club rentals, lodging (100 rooms), credit cards (MC, V, AE).
Reader Comments: Play in the fall–colors are outstanding ... Scenic layout ... Maybe the best in Quebec ... Great design ... The best course, close to home ... Conditions, quality, price at its best ... Hidden jewel, very seldom busy ... Super views in the fall.

★★½ LE GOLF CHANTECLER
PU-2520, chemin Du Club, Ste. Adele, J8B 3C3, (450)229-3742, (800)363-2587, 30 miles N of Montreal.
Holes: 18. **Yards:** 6,215/6,090. **Par:** 70/74. **Course Rating:** N/A. **Slope:** N/A. **Green Fee:** $44/$50. **Cart Fee:** Included in Green Fee. **Walking Policy:** Walking at certain times. **Walkability:** 4. **Season:** May-Oct. **High:** June-Sept. **To obtain tee times:** Call 3 days in advance. **Miscellaneous:** Reduced fees (weekdays, low season, resort guests), discount packages, metal spikes, club rentals, lodging, credit cards (MC, V, AE).
Reader Comments: Undulating greens ... Many elevated tees ... Fun to play, great night life.

LE MANOIR RICHELIEU
R-19 Ran Terrebonne, P.O. Box 338, Point-au-Pic, G0T 1M0, (418)665-2526, (800)665-8082, 75 miles E of Quebec City.
Holes: 18. **Yards:** 6,300/5,205. **Par:** 71/72. **Course Rating:** 70.0/72.0. **Slope:** 131/115. **Green Fee:** $56/$80. **Cart Fee:** Included in Green Fee. **Walking Policy:** Mandatory cart. **Walkability:** 5. **Opened:** 1921. **Architect:** Herbert Strong. **Season:** May-Oct. **High:** June-Sept. **To obtain tee times:** Call up to 7 days in advance. **Miscellaneous:** Reduced fees (weekdays, low season, resort guests), discount packages, club rentals, lodging (400 rooms), credit cards (MC, V, AE).
Special Notes: Formerly Manoir Richelieu

★★★ LE ROYAL BROMONT GOLF CLUB
SP-400 Chemin Compton, Bromont, J2L 1E9, (450)534-5582, (888)281-0017, 45 miles SE of Montreal. **Web:** www.mediaweb.ca/royalbromont.
Holes: 18. **Yards:** 6,611/5,181. **Par:** 72/72. **Course Rating:** 72.2/70.3. **Slope:** 127/123. **Green Fee:** $35/$55. **Cart Fee:** Included in Green Fee. **Walking Policy:** Unrestricted walking. **Walkability:** 2. **Opened:** 1993. **Architect:** Graham Cooke. **Season:** April-Nov. **High:** June-Sept. **To obtain tee times:** Call up to 7 days in advance. **Miscellaneous:** Reduced fees (low season, twilight), discount packages, range (mats), club rentals, credit cards (MC, V, AE, Interact).

CANADA

Reader Comments: Greens were fast and true ... Great clubhouse ... Summer condition in May ... Good course ... One of the best in Quebec ... Nice, clean ... Front nine in a field, back nine in woods, very nice ... Great course conditions.

MONTREAL MUNICIPAL GOLF COURSE
PM-4235 Viau St., Montreal, H2A 1M1, (514)872-4653.
Holes: 9. **Yards:** 1,800/1,400. **Par:** N/A. **Course Rating:** N/A. **Slope:** N/A. **Green Fee:** N/A. **Walkability:** N/A. **Opened:** 1923. **Architect:** Albert Murray. **Season:** April-Oct. **High:** June-July. **To obtain tee times:** Call 1 day in advance. **Miscellaneous:** Metal spikes, range (grass), club rentals.

★★★½ OWL'S HEAD
R-181 Chemin Owl's Head, Mansonville, J0E 1X0, (450)292-3666, (800)363-3342, 75 miles SE of Montreal. **E-mail:** info@owlshead.com. **Web:** www.owlshead.com.
Holes: 18. **Yards:** 6,671/5,210. **Par:** 72/72. **Course Rating:** 72.0/69.0. **Slope:** 126/119. **Green Fee:** $35/$42. **Cart Fee:** $27/cart. **Walking Policy:** Unrestricted walking. **Walkability:** 2. **Opened:** 1992. **Architect:** Graham Cooke. **Season:** May-Oct. **High:** June-Aug. **To obtain tee times:** Hotel guests can reserve anytime. Public may call up to 5 days in advance. **Miscellaneous:** Reduced fees (weekdays, low season, twilight), discount packages, range (grass/mats), club rentals, lodging (45 rooms), credit cards (MC, V, AE).
Reader Comments: Great layout ... Better than expected. Worth the trip ... Some great vistas from elevated tees ... Good place to bring your wife ... Great scenery ... Beautiful and playable ... Marvelous views, and great value for the US dollar ... Wonderful country setting ... The most scenic course in Eastern Canada.

TREMBLANT GOLF RESORT
R-3005 Chemin Principal, Mont Tremblant, J0T 1Z0, (819)681-4653, 88-TREMBLANT, 90 miles N of Mont Tremblant.
★★★★ LE DIABLE (THE DEVIL)
Holes: 18. **Yards:** 7,056/4,651. **Par:** 71/71. **Course Rating:** 73.0/131.0. **Slope:** 69/122. **Green Fee:** $40/$100. **Cart Fee:** Included in Green Fee. **Walking Policy:** Mandatory cart. **Walkability:** 4. **Opened:** 1998. **Architect:** Michael Hurdzan, Dana Fry. **Season:** May-Oct. **High:** June-Sept. **To obtain tee times:** Resort guests may book with room reservation. Public may call up to 7 days in advance. **Miscellaneous:** Reduced fees (weekdays, low season, resort guests, twilight), discount packages, range (grass), club rentals, lodging (1,400 rooms), credit cards (MC, V, AE).
★★★★ LE GEANT (THE GIANT)
Holes: 18. **Yards:** 6,826/5,115. **Par:** 72/72. **Course Rating:** 73.0/68.2. **Slope:** 131/113. **Green Fee:** $40/$100. **Cart Fee:** Included in Green Fee. **Walking Policy:** Mandatory cart. **Walkability:** 4. **Opened:** 1998. **Architect:** Michael Hurdzan, Dana Fry. **Season:** May-Oct. **High:** June-Sept. **To obtain tee times:** Resort guests may book with room reservation. Public may call up to 7 days in advance. **Miscellaneous:** Reduced fees (weekdays, low season, resort guests, twilight), discount packages, range (grass), club rentals, lodging (1,400 rooms), credit cards (MC, V, AE).
Reader Comments: First class ... Could also be 6-stars ... Fantastic scenery ... Spectacular holes ... One of nicest courses I've played ... High-end value ... Outstanding views ... Pro layout ... Excellent condition, fair layout ... Best course in Quebec ... Great mountain course ... Play the course in June ... Bring a dozen balls, a narrow, demanding course—Beautiful!

SASKATCHEWAN

★★★ COOKE MUNICIPAL GOLF COURSE
PU-900 22nd St. E., Prince Albert, S6V 1P1, Canada County, (306)763-2502, 90 miles NE of Saskatoon.
Holes: 18. **Yards:** 6,319/5,719. **Par:** 71/72. **Course Rating:** 69.4/72.6. **Slope:** 118/112. **Green Fee:** $19/$26. **Cart Fee:** $24/cart. **Walking Policy:** Unrestricted walking. **Walkability:** 3. **Opened:** 1935. **Architect:** Hubert Cooke/Danny Jutras. **Season:** April-Oct. **High:** June-Aug. **To obtain tee times:** Call one day in advance at 8 a.m. Call Friday a.m. for Saturday and Sunday and holidays. **Miscellaneous:** Reduced fees (low season, twilight, juniors), discount packages, metal spikes, range (grass/mats), club rentals, credit cards (MC, V, AE, Debit), beginner friendly (junior lessons).
Reader Comments: Beautiful grounds, small clubhouse, neat ... Best muny in Saskatchewan ... Long and straight, very few doglegs ... Good bang for your buck.

★★★ ELMWOOD GOLF & COUNTRY CLUB
SP-P.O. Box 373, Swift Current, S9H 3V8, Canada County, (306)773-2722.
Holes: 18. **Yards:** 6,380/5,610. **Par:** 71/74. **Course Rating:** 70.2/72.0. **Slope:** 120/119. **Green Fee:** $13/$24. **Cart Fee:** $25/person. **Walking Policy:** Unrestricted walking. **Walkability:** 3. **Opened:** 1924. **Architect:** William Brinkworth. **Season:** April-Oct. **High:** May-Sept. **To obtain**

tee times: Reservations one day in advance. **Miscellaneous:** Metal spikes, range (grass), club rentals, credit cards (MC, V, Interac), beginner friendly (clinics, lessons).
Reader Comments: Challenging, nice layout ... Best-kept secret ... Excellent course-very well groomed ... Best value I've ever played ... Great track.

★★★ ESTEVAN WOODLAWN GOLF CLUB
PU-P.O. Box 203, Estevan, S4A 2A3, (306)634-2017, 2 miles SE of Estevan.
Holes: 18. **Yards:** 6,320/5,409. **Par:** 71/72. **Course Rating:** 70.0/73.0. **Slope:** 123/118. **Green Fee:** $24/$24. **Cart Fee:** $24/cart. **Walking Policy:** Unrestricted walking. **Walkability:** 1.
Opened: 1945. **Architect:** Les Furber. **Season:** May-Oct. **High:** June-Aug. **To obtain tee times:** Call 24 hours in advance. **Miscellaneous:** Reduced fees (juniors), range (grass), club rentals, credit cards (MC, V, AE, Interact).
Reader Comments: Easy to get on and well priced ... Great condition, a bit flat ... Mature condition of course for early season visit ... Forgiving front, water on back.

★★★ MAINPRIZE REGIONAL PARK & GOLF COURSE
PU-Box 488, Midale, S0C 1S0, (306)458-2452.
Holes: 18. **Yards:** 7,022/5,672. **Par:** 72/72. **Course Rating:** 74.7/72.2. **Slope:** 128/118. **Green Fee:** $16/$20. **Cart Fee:** $23/cart. **Walking Policy:** Unrestricted walking. **Walkability:** 5.
Opened: 1994. **Architect:** John Robinson. **Season:** May-Oct. **High:** June-Aug. **To obtain tee times:** Call golf shop seven days in advance. **Miscellaneous:** Reduced fees (weekdays, juniors), discount packages, range (grass), club rentals, lodging (5 rooms), credit cards (MC, V, Interact), beginner friendly (practice facility).
Reader Comments: A gem of a links-type course ... Tough on a windy day ... Rarely see other golfers ... Easy to get on during the week ... Classic links course with long par 4s.

★★★½ NORTH BATTLEFORD GOLF & COUNTRY CLUB
SP-No. 1 Riverside Drive , North Battleford, S9A 2Y3, (306)937-5659, 60 miles E of Saskatoon.
E-mail: golf@battlefords.com. **Web:** http://battlefords.com/golf.
Holes: 18. **Yards:** 6,638/5,609. **Par:** 72/74. **Course Rating:** 71.6/66.4. **Slope:** 119/112. **Green Fee:** $15/$26. **Cart Fee:** $24/cart. **Walking Policy:** Unrestricted walking. **Walkability:** 3.
Opened: 1969. **Architect:** Ray Buffel. **Season:** April-Oct. **High:** June-Aug. **To obtain tee times:** Call golf shop. **Miscellaneous:** Reduced fees (twilight, seniors, juniors), discount packages, range (grass), club rentals, credit cards (MC, V).
Reader Comments: The par 5s were the best ... Has good version of Amen Corner... Very good course and facilities ... Set along the Saskatchewan River.

★★★★ WASKESIU GOLF COURSE
PU-P.O. Box 234, Waskesiu Lake, S0J 2Y0, (306)663-5302, 50 miles N of Prince Albert.
Holes: 18. **Yards:** 6,051/5,710. **Par:** 70/71. **Course Rating:** 67.5/71.0. **Slope:** 111/111. **Green Fee:** $20/$26. **Cart Fee:** $25/cart. **Walking Policy:** Unrestricted walking. **Walkability:** 4.
Opened: 1936. **Architect:** Stanley Thompson. **Season:** May-Sept. **High:** Jul-Aug. **To obtain tee times:** Call one day in advance at 9 a.m. or when the golf shop opens. Call in advance with credit card confirmation at (306)663-5300. **Miscellaneous:** Reduced fees (twilight, juniors), metal spikes, range (mats), club rentals, credit cards (MC, V, AE).
Reader Comments: A solid challenge ... Short, scenic and well maintained ... A walker's delight ... It is pristine, mature—the type of course you want to play in your bare feet. Gorgeous!

THE WILLOWS GOLF & COUNTRY CLUB
PU-382 Cartwright Street, Saskatoon, S7T 1B1, (306)956-4653. **E-mail:** wgcc@sk.sympatico.ca.
★★½ BRIDGES/XENA COURSE
Holes: 18. **Yards:** 7,070/5,564. **Par:** 72/72. **Course Rating:** 73.1/71.8. **Slope:** 130/128. **Green Fee:** $31/$38. **Cart Fee:** $11/person. **Walking Policy:** Unrestricted walking. **Walkability:** 2.
Opened: 1991. **Architect:** Bill Newis. **Season:** April-Oct. **High:** May-Aug. **To obtain tee times:** Call 7 days in advance. **Miscellaneous:** Reduced fees (weekdays, low season, twilight, seniors, juniors), range (grass/mats), club rentals, credit cards (MC, V, AE), beginner friendly (kids sport program).
Reader Comments: Superb clubhouse ... Well-kept course ... Both courses offer a links-style treat ... Effective challenges and interesting play.
★★½ LAKES/ISLAND COURSE
Holes: 18. **Yards:** 6,839/5,137. **Par:** 71/71. **Course Rating:** 72.5/69.4. **Slope:** 125/121. **Green Fee:** $31/$38. **Cart Fee:** $11/person. **Walking Policy:** Unrestricted walking. **Walkability:** 2.
Opened: 1991. **Architect:** Bill Newis. **Season:** April-Oct. **High:** May-Aug. **To obtain tee times:** Call 7 days in advance. **Miscellaneous:** Reduced fees (weekdays, low season, twilight, seniors, juniors), range (grass/mats), club rentals, credit cards (MC, V, AE), beginner friendly (kids sport program).
Reader Comments: Love the greens here, especially the island ... Typical prairie course, well-bunkered greens ... Huge mounds along fairways very enjoyable, massive clubhouse ... A very reasonable course to play with some tough holes.

Part III

Mexico

BAJA NORTE

BAJAMAR OCEAN FRONT GOLF RESORT
R-KM 77.5 Carrectora Esenica Tijuana, Ensenada (011)-52-615-50161, (800)225-2418, 20 miles S of Ensenada.
★★★★ **LAGOS/VISTA** *Value*
Holes: 27. **Yards:** 6,967/4,696. **Par:** 71/71. **Course Rating:** 74.0/66.6. **Slope:** 137/113. **Green Fee:** $60/$85. **Cart Fee:** Included in Green Fee. **Walking Policy:** Mandatory cart. **Walkability:** 2. **Opened:** 1975. **Architect:** Percy Clifford/David Fleming. **Season:** Year-round. **High:** May-Sept. **To obtain tee times:** Call golf shop (011)52-615-50161. **Miscellaneous:** Reduced fees (weekdays, low season, resort guests, twilight, seniors), discount packages, range (grass), club rentals, lodging (82 rooms), credit cards (MC, V, AE).
Reader Comments: Ocean nine has great views ... Working man's Pebble Beach ... Million $ views ... Watch for whales! ... Absolutely spectacular.
★★★★ **OCEANO/LAGOS**
Holes: 27. **Yards:** 6,903/5,103. **Par:** 71/71. **Course Rating:** 73.6/70.8. **Slope:** 135/116. **Green Fee:** $60/$85. **Cart Fee:** Included in Green Fee. **Walking Policy:** Mandatory cart. **Walkability:** 2. **Opened:** 1975. **Architect:** Percy Clifford/David Fleming. **Season:** Year-round. **High:** May-Sept. **To obtain tee times:** Call golf shop 011-52-615-50161. **Miscellaneous:** Reduced fees (weekdays, low season, resort guests, twilight, seniors), discount packages, range (grass), club rentals, lodging (82 rooms), credit cards (MC, V, AE).
★★★★ **VISTA/OCEANO**
Holes: 27. **Yards:** 7,145/5,175. **Par:** 72/72. **Course Rating:** 74.7/71.1. **Slope:** 138/119. **Green Fee:** $60/$85. **Cart Fee:** Included in Green Fee. **Walking Policy:** Mandatory cart. **Walkability:** 2. **Opened:** 1975. **Architect:** Percy Clifford/David Fleming. **Season:** Year-round. **High:** May-Sept. **To obtain tee times:** Call golf shop 011-52-615-50161. **Miscellaneous:** Reduced fees (weekdays, low season, resort guests, twilight, seniors), discount packages, range (grass), club rentals, lodging (82 rooms), credit cards (MC, V, AE).

★★★★ **REAL DEL MAR GOLF CLUB** *Value*
R-19 1/2 KM Ensenada, Toll Rd., Tijuana, Baja, (663)134-06, (800)803-6038, 16 miles S of San Diego, CA.
Holes: 18. **Yards:** 6,403/5,033. **Par:** 72/72. **Course Rating:** 70.5/68.5. **Slope:** 131/119. **Green Fee:** $59/$69. **Cart Fee:** Included in Green Fee. **Walking Policy:** Mandatory cart. **Walkability:** 3. **Opened:** 1993. **Architect:** Pedro Guerreca. **Season:** Year-round. **High:** June-Sept. **To obtain tee times:** Call 7 days in advance. **Miscellaneous:** Reduced fees (weekdays, low season, resort guests, twilight, seniors, juniors), discount packages, range (grass/mats), caddies, club rentals, lodging (76 rooms), credit cards (MC, V).
Reader Comments: Always pristine condition ... Lots of water, bushes and no adjoining fairways ... Great restaurant ... 17th hole is my favorite ... Small landing areas ... Great restaurant ... Double dogleg par 5 onto an island green with a bunker in front—that's golf! ... Target golf—can be windy.

★★★ **TIJUANA COUNTRY CLUB**
SP-Blvd. Agua Caliente No. 11311, Col. Avia, Tijuana (668)178-55, 20 miles S of San Diego, CA.
Holes: 18. **Yards:** 6,869/5,517. **Par:** 72/72. **Course Rating:** 73.0/72.0. **Slope:** 129/127. **Green Fee:** $22/$27. **Cart Fee:** $20/person. **Walking Policy:** Unrestricted walking. **Walkability:** N/A. **Opened:** 1927. **Architect:** William P. Bell. **Season:** Year-round. **To obtain tee times:** Call up to 30 days in advance. **Miscellaneous:** Reduced fees (twilight, seniors, juniors), discount packages, metal spikes, range (grass), caddies, club rentals, credit cards (MC, V).
Reader Comments: Tacos were great ... Greens are fantastic. My caddy spoke English ... A nice traditional course.

BAJA SUR

★★ **BAJA COUNTRY CLUB**
SP-Canon San Carlos, KM. 15.25 S/N, Ensenada, B.C. Mexico, Ensenada, (619)424-6977, (888)8GOLF19, 8 miles S of Ensenada.
Holes: 18. **Yards:** 6,859/5,203. **Par:** 72/72. **Course Rating:** 73.1/69.5. **Slope:** 131/117. **Green Fee:** $35/$45. **Cart Fee:** Included in Green Fee. **Walking Policy:** Mandatory cart. **Walkability:** 1. **Opened:** 1991. **Architect:** Enrique Valenzuela. **Season:** Year-round. **High:** Jan-Oct. **To obtain tee times:** Call anytime. **Miscellaneous:** Reduced fees (weekdays, twilight), discount packages, metal spikes, range (grass/mats), club rentals, credit cards (MC, V, AE).

MEXICO

★★★★ CABO REAL GOLF CLUB *Condition*
KM 19.5 Carreterra, Transpeninsular, San Jose Del Cabo, 23410 (114)400-40, (800)227-1212.
Yards: N/A. **Par:** N/A. **Course Rating:** N/A. **Slope:** N/A. **Green Fee:** $110/$165. **Cart Fee:** Included in Green Fee. **Walking Policy:** Mandatory cart. **Walkability:** N/A. **Miscellaneous:** Metal spikes.
Reader Comments: The ocean holes are spectacular ... Great photo ops ... Too hot in summer, but super course ... Double check all distances ... Will go back ... Beautiful and challenging—but a bit pricey ... Several challenging holes ... Breathtaking ... Stunning design.
Special Notes: Call club for further information.

★★★ CABO SAN LUCAS COUNTRY CLUB *Pace*
SP-Carretera Transpeninsular KM 3.6, Cabo San Lucas, 23410, (114)346-53, (888)328-8501. E-mail: golfcabo@cabonet.mx.com. **Web:** www.allaboutcabosanlucas.
Holes: 18. **Yards:** 7,220/5,302. **Par:** 72/72. **Course Rating:** 75.4/70.9. **Slope:** 137/122. **Green Fee:** $55/$143. **Cart Fee:** Included in Green Fee. **Walking Policy:** Mandatory cart. **Walkability:** 2. **Opened:** 1994. **Architect:** Roy Dye. **Season:** Year-round. **High:** Nov.-May. **To obtain tee times:** Call golf shop from U.S. and Canada at (888)328-8501 or 01152-114-346-53.
Miscellaneous: Reduced fees (low season, resort guests, twilight, juniors), discount packages, metal spikes, range (grass/mats), club rentals, lodging (62 rooms), credit cards (MC, V, AE), beginner friendly (golf academy).
Reader Comments: Excellent course for average golfer ... Boring, flat, repetitive, all the holes began to look the same ... No clubhouse.

★★½ CAMPO DE GOLF SAN JOSE
PU-Paseo Finisterra #1, San Jose del Cabo, 23400 (114)209-05, 150 miles S of La Paz. **E-mail:** cgolf@bcsi.telmex.nen.mx.
Holes: 9. **Yards:** 3,111/2,443. **Par:** 35/35. **Course Rating:** 68.0/70.0. **Slope:** N/A. **Green Fee:** $55/$55. **Cart Fee:** $50/person. **Walking Policy:** Walking at certain times. **Walkability:** 3. **Opened:** 1988. **Architect:** Mario Schjtanan/Joe Finger. **Season:** Year-round. **High:** Nov.-Feb. **To obtain tee times:** Call (114) 209-05. **Miscellaneous:** Club rentals, credit cards (MC, V, AE).
Reader Comments: Lots of red tile roofs to hit if you slice ... Good nine-hole warm-up on way to Cabo area ... The views of the Sea of Cortez was great ... Best bargain golf in the area.

★★★★½ THE OCEAN COURSE AT CABO DEL SOL *Condition, Pace*
R-103 Carraterra Transpeninsular Hwy., Los Cabos, 23410, (114)582-00, (800)386-2465, 4 miles NE of Cabo San Lucas.
Holes: 18. **Yards:** 7,037/4,696. **Par:** 72/72. **Course Rating:** 74.1/67.1. **Slope:** 137/111. **Green Fee:** $125/$220. **Cart Fee:** Included in Green Fee. **Walking Policy:** Walking at certain times. **Walkability:** 4. **Opened:** 1994. **Architect:** Jack Nicklaus. **Season:** Year-round. **High:** Oct.-June. **To obtain tee times:** Call 800 No. for prepaid advance tee times. Locally call up to 7 days in advance. **Miscellaneous:** Reduced fees (weekdays, low season, resort guests), discount packages, metal spikes, range (grass), club rentals, lodging (750 rooms), credit cards (MC, V, AE).
Reader Comments: Great layout, better views ... Target course ... A combination of Troon North and Pebble Beach and better than both of them ... Challenging but fair ... Too expensive ... No. 17 from championship tee worth the green fee ... Golf heaven!

PALMILLA GOLF CLUB
SP-Carretera Transpeninsular KM 27, San Jose del Cabo (114)452-50, (800)386-2465, 27 miles N of San Jose del Cabo.
Holes: 27. **Cart Fee:** Included in Green Fee. **Walking Policy:** Mandatory cart. **Walkability:** N/A. **Opened:** 1992. **Architect:** Jack Nicklaus. **Season:** Year-round. **High:** Oct.-May. **To obtain tee times:** Hotel Palmilla guests may call up to 1 year in advance. Public may call 7 days in advance. **Miscellaneous:** Reduced fees (weekdays, low season, resort guests), discount packages, metal spikes, range (grass), club rentals, lodging, credit cards (MC, V, AE).
★★★★ ARROYO/OCEAN *Condition, Pace*
Yards: 6,849/5,029. **Par:** 72/72. **Course Rating:** 73.4/62.8. **Slope:** 136/106. **Green Fee:** $75/$180.
Reader Comments: Real target golf ... Another great Baja course, big arroyos ... Facilities excellent, but overpriced ... Some great risk-reward shots ... Great layout ... A must play ... I played 36 holes alone, in one day—wow ... Stay in bounds, lots of snakes ... Desert golf the way it was meant to be.
★★★★ MOUNTAIN/ARROYO *Condition, Pace*
Yards: 6,939/5,858. **Par:** 72/72. **Course Rating:** 74.3/67.1. **Slope:** 144/109. **Green Fee:** $75/$165.
★★★★ MOUNTAIN/OCEAN *Condition, Pace*
Yards: 7,114/5,219. **Par:** 72/72. **Course Rating:** 74.9/68.8. **Slope:** 139/109. **Green Fee:** $75/$165.

COLIMA

★★ CAMINO REAL LAS HADAS RESORT
R-, Manzanillo, (333)400-00. **E-mail:** zlo@caminoreal.com. **Web:** www.caminoreal.com.
Holes: 18. **Yards:** 6,435/4,773. **Par:** 71/71. **Course Rating:** 71.3/67.9. **Slope:** 139/117. **Green Fee:** N/A/$50. **Cart Fee:** $36/cart. **Walking Policy:** Unrestricted walking. **Walkability:** 1. **Opened:** 1974. **Architect:** Roy Dye. **Season:** Year-round. **High:** Year-round. **To obtain tee times:** Call or fax your tee times. **Miscellaneous:** Reduced fees (resort guests), discount packages, metal spikes, range (grass), caddies, club rentals, lodging (250 rooms), credit cards (MC, V, AE).
Special Notes: Cart or Caddie mandatory. Formerly known as Las Hadas Resort.

★★★★ ISLA NAVIDAD GOLF CLUB
R-, Manzanillo (335)555-56.
Yards: N/A. **Par:** N/A. **Course Rating:** N/A. **Slope:** N/A. **Green Fee:** $80/$80. **Cart Fee:** Included in Green Fee. **Walkability:** N/A. **Miscellaneous:** Metal spikes, caddies.
Reader Comments: Spectacular ... Exquisite course. Perfect condition ... Play golf and then go to Poncho's in Barra and watch the sunset ... Oasis in the middle of nowhere!
Special Notes: Call club for further information.

GUERRERO

★★★ ACAPULCO PRINCESS CLUB DE GOLF
R-A.P. 1351, Acapulco, 39300 (746)910-00, 7 miles E of Acapulco.
Holes: 18. **Yards:** 6,355/5,400. **Par:** 72/72. **Course Rating:** 69.4/69.6. **Slope:** 117/115. **Green Fee:** $70/$95. **Cart Fee:** Included in Green Fee. **Walking Policy:** Mandatory cart. **Walkability:** 1. **Opened:** 1971. **Architect:** Ted Robinson. **Season:** Year-round. **High:** Nov.-April. **To obtain tee times:** Guests of hotel may call up to 2 days in advance. Non-guests call 1 day in advance.
Miscellaneous: Reduced fees (resort guests, juniors), discount packages, metal spikes, range (grass), club rentals, lodging (1,021 rooms), credit cards (MC, V, AE, Diners Club), beginner friendly (private lessons, clinics available).
Reader Comments: Fabulous golf resort, great food ... Beautiful. Fair for all levels ... Back nine more fun ... Decent golf.

★★★ CAMPO DE GOLF IXTAPA GOLF COURSE
PU-Blvd. Ixtapa S/N, Ixtapa, (755)311-63, 3 miles S of Zihuantanejo.
Holes: 18. **Yards:** 6,868/5,801. **Par:** 72/72. **Course Rating:** 70.0/N/A. **Slope:** N/A. **Green Fee:** $50/$50. **Cart Fee:** $25/cart. **Walking Policy:** Unrestricted walking. **Walkability:** 2. **Opened:** 1975. **Architect:** Robert Trent Jones Jr. **Season:** Year-round. **High:** Nov.-April. **To obtain tee times:** First come, first served. **Miscellaneous:** Reduced fees (twilight, seniors, juniors), metal spikes, range (grass/mats), caddies, club rentals, credit cards (MC, V, AE).
Reader Comments: Old traditional course. 2 or 3 blind shots ... Watch out for alligators! Great greens ... Picturesque holes ... A fun course in a fun location! You can drive through a coconut harvest, chip over a crocodile-filled lake, and putt right next to the beach!

★★★ MARINA IXTAPA CLUB DE GOLF
R-Calle De La Darsena s/n Lote 8 Final de, Ixtapa, 40880, (755)314-10, 130 miles of Acapulco.
Holes: 18. **Yards:** 6,800/5,197. **Par:** 72/72. **Course Rating:** 74.1/73.2. **Slope:** 138/128. **Green Fee:** $65/$85. **Cart Fee:** Included in Green Fee. **Walking Policy:** Mandatory cart. **Walkability:** 3. **Opened:** 1994. **Architect:** Robert von Hagge. **Season:** Year-round. **High:** Dec.-April. **To obtain tee times:** Call golf shop. **Miscellaneous:** Reduced fees (weekdays, low season, resort guests, twilight, seniors, juniors), discount packages, metal spikes, range (grass/mats), caddies, club rentals, lodging, credit cards (MC, V, AE).
Reader Comments: The most difficult course I've ever played ... Great setup, friendly, challenging ... Location idyllic ... Water on 14 holes!

★★★½ PIERRE MARQUES GOLF CLUB
R-Playa Revolcadero, Acapulco, 39300, (746)610-00, 7 miles E of Acapulco.
Holes: 18. **Yards:** 6,557/5,197. **Par:** 72/73. **Course Rating:** 71.5/69.8. **Slope:** 127/116. **Green Fee:** $70/$95. **Cart Fee:** Included in Green Fee. **Walking Policy:** Mandatory cart. **Walkability:** 1. **Opened:** 1967. **Architect:** Percy Clifford. **Season:** Year-round. **High:** Nov.-March. **To obtain tee times:** Guests may call up to 2 days in advance. Non-guests may call up to 1 day in advance. **Miscellaneous:** Reduced fees (resort guests, juniors), discount packages, metal spikes, range (grass), club rentals, lodging (320 rooms), credit cards (MC, V, AE, Diners Club).
Reader Comments: Good value ... Fun golf.

MEXICO

JALISCO

EL TAMARINDO CHAMPIONSHIP ECOLOGICAL RESORT
R-El Tamarindo KM 7.5 Carretera Melaque-Pu, Manzanillo, 48970, Cihuatlan County, (335)1-50-32, 30 miles N of Manzanillo. **E-mail:** bdo@bay.net.mx.
Holes: 18. **Yards:** 6,682/4,907. **Par:** 72/72. **Course Rating:** 72.9/67.8. **Slope:** 132/117. **Green Fee:** $55/$110. **Cart Fee:** Included in Green Fee. **Walking Policy:** Mandatory cart. **Walkability:** 4. **Opened:** 1997. **Architect:** David Fleming. **Season:** Year-round. **High:** Dec.-April. **Miscellaneous:** Reduced fees (resort guests), discount packages, metal spikes, range (grass), caddies, club rentals, lodging (30 rooms), credit cards (MC, V, AE).
Special Notes: Formerly El Tamarino Golf Course

FOUR SEASONS RESORT
R-Bahia De Banderas, Punta De Mita-Nayarit, 63734, 011-52-329-16037, (800)332-3442, 25 miles N of Puerto Vallarta. **E-mail:** sam.logan@fourseasons.com. **Web:** www.fshr.com.
Holes: 18. **Yards:** 7,014/5,037. **Par:** 72/72. **Course Rating:** 72.9/68.4. **Slope:** 131/116. **Green Fee:** $125/$125. **Cart Fee:** Included in Green Fee. **Walking Policy:** Mandatory cart. **Walkability:** 4. **Opened:** 1999. **Architect:** Jack Nicklaus. **Season:** Year-round. **High:** Dec.-April. **To obtain tee times:** Call 011-52-329-16037. **Miscellaneous:** Discount packages, range (grass), club rentals, lodging (140 rooms), credit cards (MC, V, AE, D, Diners Club).
Special Notes: Formerly Punta Mita

★★★½ MARINA VALLARTA CLUB DE GOLF
PU-Puerto Vallarta, (322)105-45
Reader Comments: Best resort in Puerto Vallarta ... Great design, caddies are wonderful .... Nearby airport distracting ... Ocean views great—course overpriced ... Great practice facility ... Alligators in the water hazards.
Special Notes: Call club for further information.

MORELOS

COUNTRY CLUB COCOYOC
R-Circuito Del Hombre S/N, Cocoyoc, 62738, (735)611-88, 65 miles S of Mexico City.
Holes: 18. **Yards:** 6,287/5,250. **Par:** 72/72. **Course Rating:** 69.7/68.1. **Slope:** 127/116. **Green Fee:** $65/$65. **Cart Fee:** $15/cart. **Walking Policy:** Unrestricted walking. **Walkability:** 3. **Opened:** 1977. **Architect:** Mario Schjetnan. **Season:** Year-round. **Miscellaneous:** Reduced fees (weekdays, resort guests), discount packages, metal spikes, range (grass), caddies, club rentals, lodging, credit cards (MC, V, AE).

OAXACA

TANGOLUNDA GOLF COURSE
SP-Conocido Huatulco, Huatulco, 70989, (958)100-37, 150 miles W of Oaxaca.
Holes: 18. **Yards:** 6,870/5,605. **Par:** 72/72. **Course Rating:** 74.6/73.8. **Slope:** 131/126. **Green Fee:** $40/$50. **Cart Fee:** $33/cart. **Walkability:** 5. **Opened:** 1991. **Architect:** Mario Schjetnandantan. **Season:** Year-round. **High:** Dec.-April. **To obtain tee times:** Call. **Miscellaneous:** Reduced fees (juniors), discount packages, metal spikes, range (grass), caddies, club rentals, lodging, credit cards (MC, V, AE).

QUITANA ROO

★★★ POK-TA-POK CLUB DE GOLF CANCUN
R-KM 7.5 Blvd. Kukulcan, Hotel Zone, Cancun, (988)312-30, (988)312-77
Holes: 18. **Yards:** 6,602/5,244. **Par:** 72/72. **Course Rating:** 71.9/71.0. **Slope:** 121/120. **Green Fee:** $80/$100. **Cart Fee:** Included in Green Fee. **Walking Policy:** Walking at certain times. **Walkability:** 2. **Architect:** Robert Trent Jones Jr. **Season:** Year-round. **High:** Dec.-April. **To**

obtain tee times: Call. **Miscellaneous:** Reduced fees (low season, resort guests, twilight), metal spikes, range (grass), caddies, club rentals, credit cards (MC, V, AE).
Reader Comments: Long Bermuda grass greens hard to putt ... Gusty gulf winds make club selection hard ... Not too exciting ... No waiting.

SINALOA

EL CID GOLF & COUNTRY CLUB
R-Av. Camaron Sabalo S/N, Mazatlan, 82110, 011-526-913-5611, (888)521-6011. **E-mail:** mazatlan@elcid.com. **Web:** www.elcid.com.
Holes: 27. **Green Fee:** $45/$80. **Cart Fee:** Included in Green Fee. **Walking Policy:** Walking at certain times. **Walkability:** 1. **Opened:** 1973. **Architect:** Lee Trevino. **Season:** Nov.-April. **High:** Feb.-March. **To obtain tee times:** Phone direct, e-mail or by fax. **Miscellaneous:** Reduced fees (low season, resort guests, seniors, juniors), range (grass), caddies, club rentals, lodging (1,300 rooms), credit cards (MC, V, AE), beginner friendly
★★★ **EL MORO/CASTILLA**
Yards: 6,623/5,417. **Par:** 72/72. **Course Rating:** 71.8/71.1. **Slope:** 131/127. .
Special Notes: Caddies mandatory if walking.
★★★ **MARINA/CASTILLA**
R-Av. Camaron Sabalo S/N, Mazatlan, 82110, 011-526-913-5611, (888)521-6011. **E-Yards:** 6,657/5,220. **Par:** 72/72. **Course Rating:** 71.4/68.8. **Slope:** 124/122.
Special Notes: Caddies mandatory if walking.
★★★ **MARINA/EL MORO**
Yards: 6,880/5,329. **Par:** 72/72. **Course Rating:** 72.7/70.7. **Slope:** 126/124.
Reader Comments: Only time I washed my golf ball was in someone's pool! ... Great caddies ... Fun place, will go often ... Narrow fairways. Greens difficult to read.
Special Notes: Caddies mandatory if walking.

ESTRELLA DEL MAR GOLF AND BEACH RESORT COMM.
R-Camino Isla De la piedra KM10, Mazatlan, 82110, 011-52-69-82-33-00, (888)587-0609.
Holes: 18. **Yards:** 7,002/5,442. **Par:** 72/72. **Course Rating:** 73.4/68.9. **Slope:** 125/113. **Green Fee:** $55/$85. **Cart Fee:** Included in Green Fee. **Walking Policy:** Mandatory cart. **Walkability:** 3. **Opened:** 1996. **Architect:** Robert Trent Jones Jr. **Season:** Year-round. **High:** Nov-April. **To obtain tee times:** Call up to 7 days in advance. **Miscellaneous:** Reduced fees (low season, resort guests), metal spikes, range (grass), club rentals, lodging (30 rooms), credit cards (MC, V).

SONORA

★★★½ **MARINA SAN CARLOS CAMPO DE GOLF**
SP-Int.Campo deGolf ent.LomaBonita ySolimar, San Carlos, 85506, (622)6-11-02, 12 miles N of Guaymas, Sonora. **E-mail:** golfmsccsidek.com.mx.
Holes: 18. **Yards:** 6,542/5,072. **Par:** 72/73. **Course Rating:** 71.0/63.9. **Slope:** 118/104. **Green Fee:** $35/$50. **Cart Fee:** Included in Green Fee. **Walking Policy:** Mandatory cart. **Walkability:** 1. **Opened:** 1977. **Architect:** Roy Dye. **Season:** Year-round. **High:** Oct.-April. **To obtain tee times:** Call golf shop. **Miscellaneous:** Reduced fees (low season, twilight, juniors), discount packages, metal spikes, range (grass), club rentals, lodging, credit cards (MC, V).
Reader Comments: Good layout ... Beautiful ocean views ... Very nice clubhouse. Course exceeded expectations.

Part IV

The Islands

THE ISLANDS

ABACO

★★★★ TREASURE CAY GOLF CLUB
R-P.O. Box AB 22183, Treasure Cay, Bahamas County, (242)365-8045, (800)327-1584. **E-mail:** info@treasurecay.com. **Web:** www.treasurecay.com.
Holes: 18. **Yards:** 6,985/5,690. **Par:** 72/73. **Course Rating:** N/A. **Slope:** N/A. **Green Fee:** $50/$60. **Cart Fee:** $25/person. **Walking Policy:** Walking at certain times. **Walkability:** 1. **Opened:** 1965. **Architect:** Dick Wilson. **Season:** Year-round. **High:** Nov.-April. **To obtain tee times:** Not required. **Miscellaneous:** Reduced fees (resort guests), discount packages, metal spikes, range (grass), club rentals, lodging (96 rooms), credit cards (MC, V, AE).
Reader Comments: Play this for unhurried tranquility ... Desert-type course, windy ... Generally very tight ... Very little play.

ARUBA

★★★★½ TIERRA DEL SOL COUNTRY CLUB *Condition, Pace*
R-Malmokweg 2/N, (297)860-978, 10 miles N of Oranjestad. **Web:** tdsteetime@setarnet.aw.
Holes: 18. **Yards:** 6,811/5,002. **Par:** 71/71. **Course Rating:** 74.2/70.6. **Slope:** 132/121. **Green Fee:** $85/$120. **Cart Fee:** Included in Green Fee. **Walking Policy:** Mandatory cart. **Walkability:** 4. **Opened:** 1995. **Architect:** Robert Trent Jones Jr. **Season:** Year-round. **High:** Nov.-April. **To obtain tee times:** Call or book through hotel. **Miscellaneous:** Reduced fees (low season, resort guests, twilight, juniors), discount packages, range (grass), club rentals, lodging, credit cards (MC, V, AE, D).
Reader Comments: Wind-wind-wind! A golfing oasis! ... Bring a chin strap for your golf cap ... Beauty—must see to believe ... Good afternoon special ... A great challenge. Fast and grainy greens ... Views were fantastic ... Windy, rocky and full of goats ... Arizona by the beach ... Nice clubhouse ... Talk about wind ... Ah! Aruba.

BARBADOS

★★★★½ ROYAL WESTMORELAND BARBADOS
R-, St. James, (246)422-3916, 5 miles N of Bridgeton.
Holes: 18. **Yards:** 6,870/5,333. **Par:** 72/72. **Course Rating:** 74.4/72.5. **Slope:** 130/124. **Green Fee:** N/A. **Cart Fee:** Included in Green Fee. **Walking Policy:** Mandatory cart. **Walkability:** 4. **Opened:** 1994. **Architect:** Robert Trent Jones Jr. **Season:** Year-round. **High:** Dec.-April. **To obtain tee times:** Must be resident at Royal Westmoreland. **Miscellaneous:** Reduced fees (low season, resort guests), discount packages, range (grass), caddies, club rentals, lodging, credit cards (MC, V, AE), beginner friendly.
Notes: 2000 European Seniors Tour Event; 1996-1999 Barbados Open; 1997 Shell Wonderful World of Golf Match.
Reader Comments: Incredible experience ... Greens young ... Great views ... Putts break to ocean!.

★★ SANDY LANE GOLF CLUB
R-Sandy Lane, St. James, (246)432-1311.
Holes: 18. **Yards:** 6,553/5,520. **Par:** 72/72. **Course Rating:** 70.2/70.8. **Slope:** 122/120. **Green Fee:** $55/$85. **Walking Policy:** Unrestricted walking. **Walkability:** N/A. **Opened:** 1961. **Architect:** Robertson Ward. **Season:** Year-round. **High:** Dec.-April. **To obtain tee times:** Call 48 hours in advance. Resort guests may book tee times at time of room reservation.
Miscellaneous: Reduced fees (low season, resort guests, twilight), metal spikes, range (grass), caddies, club rentals, lodging, credit cards (MC, V, AE).

BERMUDA

★★★ BELMONT GOLF & COUNTRY CLUB
R-P.O. Box WK 251, Warwick, WKBX, (441)236-6400, 5 miles W of Hamilton.
Holes: 18. **Yards:** 5,800/4,900. **Par:** 70/72. **Course Rating:** 68.6/67.7. **Slope:** 128/116. **Green Fee:** $65/$65. **Cart Fee:** $21/person. **Walking Policy:** Walking at certain times. **Walkability:** 2. **Opened:** 1928. **Architect:** Deveraux Emmits. **Season:** Year-round. **High:** Oct.-May. **To obtain tee times:** Resort Guests may call up to 60 days in advance. Others may call 2 days in advance.

Miscellaneous: Reduced fees (resort guests, twilight, juniors), metal spikes, range (mats), club rentals, lodging, credit cards (MC, V, AE).
Reader Comments: Short course, wind makes holes difficult ... Somewhat quirky ... Easy to play, no frills ... Great views, beautiful condition ... Blind holes, elevated greens. Very challenging for the average duffer.

★★★★ CASTLE HARBOUR GOLF CLUB
R-6 Paynters Rd., Hamilton Parish, (441)293-2040x6670, 5 miles E of Hamilton.
Holes: 18. **Yards:** 6,440/4,995. **Par:** 71/71. **Course Rating:** 71.3/69.2. **Slope:** 128/116. **Green Fee:** $70/$125. **Cart Fee:** $24/person. **Walking Policy:** Mandatory cart. **Walkability:** 5. **Opened:** 1930. **Architect:** Charles H. Banks. **Season:** Year-round. **High:** April-June/Sept.-Nov. **To obtain tee times:** Resort guests may call 30 days in advance. Others may call 2 days in advance.
Miscellaneous: Reduced fees (low season, resort guests, twilight, juniors), discount packages, metal spikes, club rentals, lodging (400 rooms), credit cards (MC, V, AE, Bermuda).
Reader Comments: Fantastic opening hole ... Great views ... Need map to get from tee to greens ... First hole view is breathtaking ... Don't slice on 18 ... Downhill lies to uphill greens.

★★★★½ THE MID OCEAN CLUB *Service, Pace*
SP-1 Mid Ocean Club Dr., St. George's, GE 02, (441)293-0330, 7 miles E of Hamilton.
Holes: 18. **Yards:** 6,512/5,042. **Par:** 71/71. **Course Rating:** 72.0/69.5. **Slope:** 138/121. **Green Fee:** $140/$140. **Cart Fee:** $40/cart. **Walking Policy:** Unrestricted walking. **Walkability:** 5. **Opened:** 1922. **Architect:** Charles Blair McDonald. **Season:** Year-round. **High:** Oct.-June. **To obtain tee times:** Local resort guests may play Monday, Wednesday and Friday only. Book through hotel. **Miscellaneous:** Metal spikes, range (grass/mats), caddies, club rentals, lodging, credit cards (MC, V, AE).
Reader Comments: Vacation golf at a golf shrine ... Caddies & clubhouse are great ... Rolling fairways, uphill climbs ... If there is a heaven, I hope it is like Mid Ocean ... The layout is legendary ... Unbelievable beauty ... Best in Bermuda by long shot ... Worth the money.

★★★★ OCEAN VIEW GOLF COURSE *Pace*
PU-2 Barkers Hill Rd, Devonshire, DV05, (441)295-9077, 3 miles E of Hamilton.
Holes: 9. **Yards:** 2,940/2,450. **Par:** 35/36. **Course Rating:** 67.3/67.3. **Slope:** 122/119. **Green Fee:** $33/$33. **Cart Fee:** $18/person. **Walking Policy:** Walking at certain times. **Walkability:** 3. **Season:** Year-round. **High:** Sept.-May. **To obtain tee times:** Call (441)295-6500.
Miscellaneous: Reduced fees (twilight, juniors), range (grass/mats), club rentals, credit cards (MC, V, AE).
Reader Comments: Bring lots of balls ... Scenic, tricky, nice people ... Good challenge.

★★★★ PORT ROYAL GOLF COURSE
PU-Middle Rd., Southampton, SNBX, (441)234-0972.
Holes: 18. **Yards:** 6,561/5,577. **Par:** 71/72. **Course Rating:** 72.0/72.5. **Slope:** 134/127. **Green Fee:** $72/$82. **Cart Fee:** $50/person. **Walking Policy:** Walking at certain times. **Walkability:** 3. **Opened:** 1970. **Architect:** Robert Trent Jones. **Season:** Year-round. **High:** April-Dec. **To obtain tee times:** Call (441)295-6500 up to 4 days in advance. **Miscellaneous:** Reduced fees (twilight, seniors, juniors), range (grass/mats), club rentals, credit cards (MC, V, AE).
Reader Comments: Best course on the island ... Windy ... Bring a camera ... Challenging but fair ... 16th great par 3 ... Nice views and good test ... A must play with a world class par 3 that will scare you and thrill you with it's beauty ... Nice to walk ... Adjust putting stroke for sandy greens.

RIDDELL'S BAY GOLF & COUNTRY CLUB
SP-Riddell's Bay Rd., Warwick, WK 236 (WK BX), (441)238-1060.
Holes: 18. **Yards:** 5,668/5,324. **Par:** 70/72. **Course Rating:** 66.6/69.7. **Slope:** 118/114. **Green Fee:** $60/$80. **Cart Fee:** $40/cart. **Walking Policy:** Unrestricted walking. **Walkability:** 2. **Opened:** 1922. **Architect:** Devereaux Emmett. **Season:** Year-round. **To obtain tee times:** Must be staying at a local hotel to play. Call up to 1 day in advance. **Miscellaneous:** Reduced fees (weekdays), discount packages, club rentals, credit cards (MC, V, AE).

★★★½ ST. GEORGE'S GOLF COURSE
PU-1 Park Rd., St. George's, GE 03, (441)297-8067. **E-mail:** stgeorgesgc@northrock.bm.
Holes: 18. **Yards:** 4,043/3,344. **Par:** 62/62. **Course Rating:** 62.8/62.8. **Slope:** 103/100. **Green Fee:** $44/$44. **Cart Fee:** $18/person. **Walking Policy:** Walking at certain times. **Walkability:** 3. **Opened:** 1985. **Architect:** Robert Trent Jones, Sr. **Season:** Year-round. **High:** April-Oct. **To obtain tee times:** Call up to 30 days in advance, or fax up to 6 months in advance. **Miscellaneous:** Reduced fees (twilight), club rentals, credit cards (MC, V, AE).
Reader Comments: Outstanding ocean view on first ... Some of the par 4s could be par 3s ... Short fun course ... Very tight layout ... Hidden gem.

★★★★ SOUTHAMPTON PRINCESS GOLF COURSE
R-101 South Shore Rd., Southampton, SN 02, (441)239-6952.

Holes: 18. **Yards:** 2,737/2,229. **Par:** 54/54. **Course Rating:** 53.7/53.2. **Slope:** 81/77. **Green Fee:** $52/$57. **Cart Fee:** Included in Green Fee. **Walking Policy:** Walking at certain times. **Walkability:** 4. **Opened:** 1971. **Architect:** Theodore G. Robinson. **Season:** Year-round. **High:** April-Nov. **To obtain tee times:** Call or fax in advance. **Miscellaneous:** Reduced fees (resort guests, twilight, juniors), discount packages, club rentals, lodging, credit cards (MC, V, AE).
Reader Comments: Great irons test ... Best par-3 course in the world ... Great views ... What else would you expect in Bermuda.

CAYMAN ISLAND

★★★★ **THE LINKS AT SAFE HAVEN**
SP-, Grand Cayman, (345)949-5988. **Web:** www.safehavenlimited.com.
Holes: 18. **Yards:** 6,606/4,765. **Par:** 71/71. **Course Rating:** 75.1/71.2. **Slope:** 139/128. **Green Fee:** $120/$120. **Cart Fee:** Included in Green Fee. **Walking Policy:** Walking at certain times. **Walkability:** 1. **Opened:** 1994. **Architect:** Roy Case. **Season:** Year-round. **High:** Dec.-May. **To obtain tee times:** Non-members call one day in advance. **Miscellaneous:** Reduced fees (low season, twilight), discount packages, metal spikes, range (grass), club rentals, credit cards (MC, V, AE).
Reader Comments: Great layout! ... Plenty of water, on the ocean, windy ... No greenside bunkers ... Missed the course record by only 20 strokes because of the wind. Warm and beautiful ... Practice range with floating balls!

DOMINICAN REPUBLIC

BAVARO RESORT GOLF COURSE
R-Bavaro Punta Cana, Augueg, (809)686-5797.
Holes: 18. **Yards:** 6,710/5,608. **Par:** 72/72. **Course Rating:** 73.5/74.0. **Slope:** 145/137. **Green Fee:** $37/$63. **Walking Policy:** Walking at certain times. **Walkability:** 1. **Season:** Year-round. **High:** Nov.-April. **Miscellaneous:** Range (grass), club rentals, credit cards (MC, V).

CARIBBEAN VILLAGE PLAYA GRANDE GOLF COURSE
R-, Rio San Juan, (809)248-5314, 48 miles of Puerto Plata Airport.
Holes: 18. **Yards:** 7,046/4,488. **Par:** 72/72. **Course Rating:** 74.9/66.7. **Slope:** 126/111. **Green Fee:** $59/$59. **Cart Fee:** $24/cart. **Walking Policy:** Unrestricted walking. **Walkability:** 4. **Opened:** 1997. **Architect:** Robert Trent Jones. **Season:** Year round. **High:** All. **To obtain tee times:** Call. **Miscellaneous:** Reduced fees (resort guests), caddies, club rentals, lodging (300 rooms) (lessons available).
Special Notes: Also rent shoes.

CASA DE CAMPO RESORT & COUNTRY CLUB *Service*
R-, La Romana, (809)523-2332x3158, (888)212-5073, 45 miles NW of Santo Domingo.
★★★★ **LINKS COURSE** *Pace*
Holes: 18. **Yards:** 6,602/4,410. **Par:** 71/71. **Course Rating:** 70.0/65.7. **Slope:** 124/113. **Green Fee:** $90/$100. **Cart Fee:** Included in Green Fee. **Walking Policy:** Mandatory cart. **Walkability:** 2. **Opened:** 1976. **Architect:** Pete Dye. **Season:** Year-round. **High:** Dec.-April. **To obtain tee times:** Fax golf shops at (809)523-8800. **Miscellaneous:** Reduced fees (resort guests, twilight, juniors), discount packages, metal spikes, range (grass), caddies, club rentals, lodging (285 rooms), credit cards (MC, V, AE).
Reader Comments: Play over a runway on 18 ... Fun course ... Going back next year ... Holes 12-16 as good as is gets ... No holes along the ocean, but thumbs up for Dye! ... Not as spectacular as the Teeth ... Challenging for good player but well designed so amateur can enjoy them too.
★★★★★ **TEETH OF THE DOG** *Value, Pace+*
Holes: 18. **Yards:** 6,989/4,779. **Par:** 72/72. **Course Rating:** 74.1/72.9. **Slope:** 140/130. **Green Fee:** $90/$150. **Cart Fee:** Included in Green Fee. **Walking Policy:** Mandatory cart. **Walkability:** 3. **Opened:** 1970. **Architect:** Pete Dye. **Season:** Year-round. **High:** Dec.-April. **To obtain tee times:** Fax Golf Office at (809)523-8800. **Miscellaneous:** Reduced fees (resort guests, twilight, juniors), discount packages, metal spikes, range (grass), caddies, club rentals, lodging (285 rooms), credit cards (MC, V, AE).
Notes: Shell Wonderful World of Golf—Hoerman Cup (Caribbean Championship).
Reader Comments: For me it's Pebble Beach of the Caribbean! ... I loved No. 18 ... Ocean holes breathtaking ... Watch out for low flying airplanes ... Fabulous par 3's ... Go to the juice bar ... Stunning gem ... Caddies very informative and know the course like the back of their hands ... Paradise! Could we live here?.

THE ISLANDS

CAYACOA COUNTRY CLUB
PU-Autopista Duarte Kilometer 20, Santo Domingo, (809)561-7288.
Holes: 18. **Yards:** 6,726/5,307. **Par:** 72/72. **Course Rating:** 73.5/71.9. **Slope:** 139/130. **Green Fee:** $30/$55. **Cart Fee:** Included in Green Fee. **Walking Policy:** Walking at certain times. **Walkability:** 1. **Season:** Year-round. **High:** Nov.-April. **Miscellaneous:** Reduced fees (twilight, juniors), range (grass), caddies, club rentals, credit cards (MC, V, AE).

ISABEL VILLAS GOLF CLUB
PU-, Santo Domingo, (809)562-1555.
Holes: 9. **Yards:** N/A. **Par:** N/A. **Course Rating:** N/A. **Slope:** N/A. **Green Fee:** $10/$17.
Walking Policy: Unrestricted walking. **Walkability:** N/A.

METRO COUNTRY CLUB
R-Juan Dolio, San Pedro De Macoris, (809)526-3515, 30 miles E of Sante Domingo. **E-mail:** mcountry@codetel.net.do. **Web:** www.atlanticametro.com.
Holes: 18. **Yards:** 6,398/5,262. **Par:** 72/72. **Course Rating:** 70.5/69.9. **Slope:** 123/115. **Green Fee:** $55/$55. **Cart Fee:** $25/cart. **Walking Policy:** Walking at certain times. **Walkability:** 2. **Opened:** 1995. **Architect:** Charles Ankrom. **Season:** Year-round. **High:** Jan.-May. **To obtain tee times:** Call. **Miscellaneous:** Reduced fees (twilight), discount packages, range (grass), caddies, club rentals, lodging, credit cards (MC, V, AE).

PLAYA DORADO GOLF COURSE
PU-, Puerto Plata, (809)320-3344, 5 miles N of Puerto Plata.
Holes: 18. **Yards:** 6,730/5,361. **Par:** 72/72. **Course Rating:** 71.5/69.9. **Slope:** 124/N/A. **Green Fee:** $30/$34. **Cart Fee:** $23/cart. **Walking Policy:** Unrestricted walking. **Walkability:** 1. **Opened:** 1974. **Season:** Year-round. **High:** Sept.-May. **To obtain tee times:** Fax or call 2-3 weeks in advance. **Miscellaneous:** Reduced fees (resort guests, juniors), range (grass), caddies, club rentals, lodging, credit cards (MC, V, AE), beginner friendly (lessons available).
Special Notes: Caddies mandatory, extra charge. Several resorts surround the course. 9 holes played only in afternoons.

★★★ RADISSON PUERTO PLATA GOLF RESORT
Playa Dorado Dr., Puerto Plata, (809)586-5360.
Reader Comments: Beautiful ocean holes ... Nice layout. Interesting holes ... Flat course, tough when wind blows, lots of water.
Special Notes: Call club for further information.

GRAND BAHAMA ISLAND

BAHAMAS PRINCESS RESORT & CASINO *Service*
★★★★ EMERALD COURSE
R-P.O. Box F-40207, Freeport, 242)352-6721, 52 miles SE of Palm Beach, FL.
Holes: 18. **Yards:** 6,679/5,722. **Par:** 72/75. **Course Rating:** 72.3/73.1. **Slope:** 121/121. **Green Fee:** $51/$72. **Cart Fee:** Included in Green Fee. **Walking Policy:** Mandatory cart. **Walkability:** 1. **Opened:** 1964. **Architect:** Dick Wilson. **Season:** Year-round. **High:** Nov.-April. **To obtain tee times:** Call. Tee times required Nov.-April. **Miscellaneous:** Reduced fees (low season, resort guests, juniors), discount packages, range (grass), club rentals, lodging (965 rooms), credit cards (MC, V, AE, D).
Reader Comments: Tough rough. Makes you play in the middle ... Bring a lot of balls ... Expect more in the Bahamas ... Very courteous and accoMmodating staff ... Typical tourist course.
★★★ RUBY COURSE
R-P.O. Box F 207, Freeport, (242)352-6721, 52 miles SE of Palm Beach, FL.
Holes: 18. **Yards:** 6,750/5,622. **Par:** 72/74. **Course Rating:** 72.4/72.4. **Slope:** 122/120. **Green Fee:** $51/$72. **Cart Fee:** Included in Green Fee. **Walking Policy:** Mandatory cart. **Walkability:** 1. **Opened:** 1964. **Architect:** Joe Lee. **Season:** Year-round. **High:** Nov.-April. **To obtain tee times:** Call. Tee times are required Nov.-April. **Miscellaneous:** Reduced fees (low season, resort guests, juniors), discount packages, range (grass), club rentals, lodging (965 rooms), credit cards (MC, V, AE, D).
Reader Comments: Also a great course!...Few memorable holes...Both courses are comparable and a challenge...Pretty course...Small greens offer challenge for second shots...Excellent layout, great climate, worth the money ... Pleasant surprise.

FORTUNE HILLS GOLF & COUNTRY CLUB
R-P.O. Box 5-42619, Freeport, (242)373-4500.
Holes: 9. **Yards:** 6,916/6,164. **Par:** 72/74. **Course Rating:** 71.5/75.6. **Slope:** 116/125. **Green Fee:** $34/$34. **Cart Fee:** $34/cart. **Walking Policy:** Walking at certain times. **Walkability:** 2. **Opened:** 1971. **Architect:** Joe Lee. **Season:** Year-round. **High:** Nov.-April. **To obtain tee times:**

THE ISLANDS

Call (242)373-4500 or (242)373-2222. **Miscellaneous:** Metal spikes, range (mats), club rentals, lodging (24 rooms), credit cards (MC, V, D).

★★★½ THE LUCAYAN RESORT
R-P.O. Box F42500, Freeport, (242)373-1066, (800)LUCAYAN, 2 miles E of Freeport. **E-mail:** golfslatters@hotmail.com.
Holes: 18. **Yards:** 6,824/5,978. **Par:** 72/75. **Course Rating:** 72.1/74.5. **Slope:** 128/129. **Green Fee:** $60/$86. **Cart Fee:** Included in Green Fee. **Walking Policy:** Walking at certain times. **Walkability:** 2. **Opened:** 1962. **Architect:** Dick Wilson. **Season:** Year-round. **High:** Oct.-March. **To obtain tee times:** Call one day in advance. **Miscellaneous:** Reduced fees (low season, resort guests, juniors), discount packages, range (grass), caddies, club rentals, lodging (600 rooms), credit cards (MC, V, AE, D), beginner friendly (free clinics, guides).
Reader Comments: Nice resort course, green on No. 17 is huge ... Best in Bahamas ... Tough but fair, friendly folks ... A beautiful surprise.

JAMAICA

CAYMANAS GOLF COURSE
SP-Spanish Town, St. Catherine, (876)922-3388, 10 miles E of Kingston.
Holes: 18. **Yards:** 6,570/6,130. **Par:** 72/72. **Course Rating:** 71.0/70.0. **Slope:** 70/72. **Green Fee:** $35/$50. **Cart Fee:** $20/cart. **Walking Policy:** Unrestricted walking. **Walkability:** 2. **Opened:** 1958. **Architect:** Howard Watson. **Season:** Year-round. **High:** May-Sept. **To obtain tee times:** Call. **Miscellaneous:** Reduced fees (resort guests, juniors), metal spikes, range (grass), caddies, club rentals, credit cards (MC, V, AE).
Special Notes: Packages through The Jamaica Pegasus Hotel.

★★★★ HALF MOON GOLF, TENNIS & BEACH CLUB   *Pace*
R-Rose Hall, Montego Bay, (876)953-2560, (800)626-0592, 7 miles E of Montego Bay.
Holes: 18. **Yards:** 7,119/5,148. **Par:** 72/72. **Course Rating:** 73.7/68.9. **Slope:** 127/115. **Green Fee:** $130/$130. **Cart Fee:** $30/person. **Walking Policy:** Unrestricted walking. **Walkability:** 1. **Opened:** 1961. **Architect:** Robert Trent Jones. **Season:** Year-round. **High:** Dec.-April. **To obtain tee times:** Call or come in. **Miscellaneous:** Reduced fees (resort guests), discount packages, metal spikes, range (grass), caddies, club rentals, lodging (425 rooms), credit cards (MC, V, AE).
Notes: 1989-90 Jamaica Open.
Reader Comments: Great caddies ... No ocean holes but luxurious ... Food good, service everywhere ... You would swear they trimmed the greens and fairways with scissors ... Wind adds to difficulty ... Super, a pleasure to play.

★★½ IRONSHORE GOLF & COUNTRY CLUB
R-P.O. Box 531, Montego Bay No.2, St. James, (876)953-2800.
Holes: 18. **Yards:** 6,600/5,400. **Par:** 72/73. **Course Rating:** 72.0/73.0. **Slope:** N/A. **Green Fee:** $34/$45. **Cart Fee:** $29/. **Walking Policy:** Unrestricted walking. **Walkability:** N/A. **Opened:** 1971. **Architect:** Robert Moote. **Season:** Year-round. **High:** Dec.-April. **To obtain tee times:** Call. **Miscellaneous:** Reduced fees (low season, resort guests, juniors), discount packages, metal spikes, range (grass), caddies, club rentals, credit cards (MC, V, AE).
Reader Comments: Kinda rough, but it's Jamaica, who cares ... Chatty caddies ... Makes use of water and jungle ... Big greens ... The people are wonderful.

★★★ NEGRIL HILLS GOLF CLUB
PU-Negril P.O., Westmoreland, (876)957-4638.
Holes: 9. **Yards:** 6,333/5,036. **Par:** 72/72. **Course Rating:** N/A. **Slope:** N/A. **Green Fee:** $58/N/A. **Cart Fee:** $34/cart. **Walking Policy:** Unrestricted walking. **Walkability:** 5. **Opened:** 1994. **Architect:** Robert Simmonds. **Season:** Year-round. **High:** Dec.-April. **To obtain tee times:** Call ahead of times. **Miscellaneous:** Reduced fees (resort guests), discount packages, metal spikes, range (grass), caddies, club rentals, credit cards (MC, V).
Reader Comments: Best caddie I've ever had ... The perfect complement to a full service beach resort, friendly staff, knowledgeable caddies ... Warm and inviting, incredible experience ... Beautiful course in the Jamaican mountains. Very tough.

★★★★ SANDALS GOLF & COUNTRY CLUB   *Service, Pace+*
SP-Upton, Ocho Rios, (876)975-0119, (800)726-3257. **E-mail:** sgcgolf@cwjamaica.com. **Web:** www.sandals.com.
Holes: 18. **Yards:** 6,311/4,961. **Par:** 71/72. **Course Rating:** 128.0/120.0. **Slope:** 71/69. **Green Fee:** $70/$70. **Cart Fee:** $30/cart. **Walking Policy:** Unrestricted walking. **Walkability:** 3. **Opened:** 1954. **Architect:** P.K. Saunders. **Season:** Year-round. **High:** Dec.-March. **To obtain tee times:** No tee times. **Miscellaneous:** Reduced fees (resort guests), discount packages, metal spikes, range (grass/mats), caddies, club rentals, credit cards (MC, V, AE, D), beginner friendly (lessons available).

THE ISLANDS

Reader Comments: Excellent caddies, beautiful setting ... Open, not a lot of trouble ... Good views, rolling terrain, wet in December ... Foliage outstanding ... Golfing in paradise.

★★★½ **SUPER CLUBS GOLF CLUB AT RUNAWAY BAY** *Pace*
R-Runaway Bay P.O. Box 58, St. Ann, (876)973-7319, 15 miles W of Ocho Rios.
Holes: 18. **Yards:** 6,871/5,389. **Par:** 72/72. **Course Rating:** 72.4/70.3. **Slope:** 124/117. **Green Fee:** $50/$80. **Cart Fee:** $35/cart. **Walking Policy:** Unrestricted walking. **Walkability:** 2. **Opened:** 1960. **Architect:** James Harris. **Season:** Year-round. **High:** Jan.-March. **To obtain tee times:** First come, first served. **Miscellaneous:** Reduced fees (low season, resort guests), discount packages, metal spikes, range (grass/mats), caddies, club rentals, lodging (236 rooms), credit cards (MC, V, AE).
Reader Comments: Great par 4's ... The caddies are a lot of fun ... Wide open and long ... Wiry rough ... Greens are like a billiard table ... Good if you like wind ... Decent course, bring your driver and listen to the caddies.

★★★★ **THE TRYALL CLUB, RESORT & VILLAS**
R-Sandy Bay Main Rd., Hanover, (876)956-5681, 15 miles W of Montego Bay. **E-mail:** tryallclub@cwjamaica.com . **Web:** www.thetryallclub.co.uk.
Holes: 18. **Yards:** 6,772/5,669. **Par:** 71/73. **Course Rating:** 72.5/72.5. **Slope:** 133/122. **Green Fee:** $150/$150. **Cart Fee:** $27/cart. **Walking Policy:** Unrestricted walking. **Walkability:** 3. **Opened:** 1959. **Architect:** Ralph Plummer. **Season:** Year-round. **High:** Dec.-April. **To obtain tee times:** Call 1 day in advance. **Miscellaneous:** Reduced fees (low season, resort guests), discount packages, metal spikes, range (grass), caddies, club rentals, lodging, credit cards (MC, V, AE, Diners Club).
Reader Comments: Still by far, 'the best in Jamaica, mon' ... Expensive, but play if once for the experience ... Fast greens ... What more can be said! Best vacation I have ever had ... Beautiful scenery ... Outstanding course ... Wind can be interesting.

★★★½ **WYNDHAM ROSE HALL RESORT AND COUNTRY CLUB**
R-Box 999, Montego Bay, W.I., , St. James County, (876)953-2650x89, 10 miles NE of Montego Bay.
Holes: 18. **Yards:** 6,617/5,309. **Par:** 72/73. **Course Rating:** 71.8/73.5. **Slope:** 130/118. **Green Fee:** $70/$80. **Cart Fee:** $40/cart. **Walking Policy:** Mandatory cart. **Walkability:** 5. **Opened:** 1973. **Architect:** Hank Smedley. **Season:** Year-round. **High:** Nov.-May. **To obtain tee times:** Contact golf shop (ext. 89) in advance. **Miscellaneous:** Reduced fees (low season, resort guests, twilight), discount packages, metal spikes, range (grass), caddies, club rentals, lodging (488 rooms), credit cards (MC, V, AE, Diners Club, Key card).
Reader Comments: Play early, it gets to hot in afternoon ... Caddies were very helpful, course winds through mountains and nice scenery ... Front 9 OK, back in hills very good ... Beautiful views ... Still having dreams about Rose Hall ... Some outstanding holes ... What a mix, very humbling.

NEVIS

★★★★ **FOUR SEASONS RESORT NEVIS** *Service+, Pace*
R-Pinney's Beach, (869)469-1111.
Holes: 18. **Yards:** 6,766/5,153. **Par:** 71/71. **Course Rating:** 73.6/71.5. **Slope:** 132/128. **Green Fee:** $125/$125. **Cart Fee:** Included in Green Fee. **Walking Policy:** Mandatory cart. **Walkability:** 5. **Opened:** 1991. **Architect:** Robert Trent Jones Jr. **Season:** Year-round. **High:** Dec.-April. **To obtain tee times:** Call in advance with resort reservations or make them daily. **Miscellaneous:** Range (grass), club rentals, lodging (198 rooms), credit cards (MC, V, AE, D).
Reader Comments: Spectacular ocean views ... Tough mountain terrain ... 600 yard, par 5 down the mountain ... Enjoyed this track immensely ... Oh Boy! Watch out for the goats! ... Unbelievable setting, golf in never, never land ... 15th is a roller coaster.

NEW PROVIDENCE

★★½ **CABLE BEACH GOLF CLUB**
R-W. Bay St., Nassau, Bahamas County, (242)327-6000x6746, (800)432-0221.
Holes: 18. **Yards:** 7,040/6,114. **Par:** 72/72. **Course Rating:** 72.0/72.0. **Slope:** N/A. **Green Fee:** $50/$75. **Cart Fee:** $60/cart. **Walking Policy:** Walking at certain times. **Walkability:** 1. **Opened:** 1929. **Architect:** Deveraux Emmet. **Season:** Year-round. **High:** Dec.-April. **To obtain tee times:** Call club. **Miscellaneous:** Reduced fees (low season, resort guests, juniors), discount packages, metal spikes, range (grass/mats), club rentals, lodging, credit cards (MC, V, AE).
Reader Comments: Better hit it straight, lots of water ... Some challenging holes.

THE ISLANDS

★★★ PARADISE ISLAND GOLF CLUB
R-P.O. Box N-4777, Nassau, (242)363-3925.
Holes: 18. **Yards:** 6,770/6,003. **Par:** 72/73. **Course Rating:** 71.6/71.4. **Slope:** 114/124. **Green Fee:** $60/$155. **Cart Fee:** Included in Green Fee. **Walking Policy:** Mandatory cart. **Walkability:** 2. **Opened:** 1961. **Architect:** Dick Wilson. **Season:** Year-round. **High:** Nov.-April. **To obtain tee times:** Call in advance. **Miscellaneous:** Reduced fees (weekdays, low season, resort guests, juniors), discount packages, metal spikes, range (grass/mats), club rentals, lodging, credit cards (MC, V, AE, D).
Reader Comments: If you can get on, bring lots of $ ... Another great vacation course, very pretty ocean holes ... Nice par 3 along ocean.

★★ SOUTH OCEAN GOLF & BEACH RESORT
R-S. Ocean Dr., Nassau, Bahamas County, (242)362-4391x23. **E-mail:** clarion@batelnet.bs. **Web:** www.clarionnassau.com.
Holes: 18. **Yards:** 6,707/5,908. **Par:** 72/72. **Course Rating:** 72.5/75.0. **Slope:** 128/130. **Green Fee:** $70/$80. **Cart Fee:** $60/cart. **Walking Policy:** Mandatory cart. **Walkability:** 4. **Opened:** 1972. **Architect:** Joe Lee. **Season:** Year-round. **High:** Nov.-April. **To obtain tee times:** Call 24 hours in advance. **Miscellaneous:** Reduced fees (low season, resort guests, juniors), discount packages, metal spikes, range (grass), club rentals, lodging (259 rooms), credit cards (MC, V, AE, D, Diners Club).

PUERTO RICO

★★★½ BAHIA BEACH PLANTATION
PU-Rte. 187 Km. 4.2, Rio Grande, 00745, (787)256-5600, 16 miles E of San Juan.
Holes: 18. **Yards:** 6,695/5,648. **Par:** 72/72. **Course Rating:** 71.5/72.5. **Slope:** 124/124. **Green Fee:** $30/$75. **Cart Fee:** Included in Green Fee. **Walking Policy:** Mandatory cart. **Walkability:** 1. **Opened:** 1991. **Architect:** J.B. Gold. **Season:** Year-round. **High:** Nov.-April. **To obtain tee times:** Call 7 days in advance or reserve through e-mail www.golfbahia.com. **Miscellaneous:** Reduced fees (weekdays, low season, twilight, seniors, juniors), metal spikes, range (grass/mats), club rentals, credit cards (MC, V, AE, Diners Club).
Reader Comments: Nice layout ... Good variety ... Tight fairways, a challenge to club selection ... Watch out if it's windy! ... Not plush but has a raw beauty ... Last three holes finish along the beach, spectacular ... Most difficult layout in Puerto Rico ... Iguanas abound.

★★½ BERWIND COUNTRY CLUB
SP-Rte. 187 KM 4.7, Rio Grande, 00745, (787)876-3056, 15 miles E of San Juan. **E-mail:** bcc@isppr.com.
Holes: 18. **Yards:** 7,011/5,772. **Par:** 72/72. **Course Rating:** 72.6/72.1. **Slope:** 127/123. **Green Fee:** $50/$50. **Cart Fee:** Included in Green Fee. **Walking Policy:** Mandatory cart. **Walkability:** 1. **Opened:** 1962. **Architect:** Tillingham. **Season:** Year-round. **High:** Oct.-April. **To obtain tee times:** Call before you come. Club is open to non-members weekdays before 11:00 a.m only. **Miscellaneous:** Reduced fees (juniors), range (grass/mats), club rentals, credit cards (MC, V, AE, A.T.M.).
Reader Comments: Small greens, plays long...Improving considerably ... Very nice course, good service.

★★½ DORADO DEL MAR COUNTRY CLUB
SP-200 Dorado del Mar, Dorado, 00646, (787)796-3065, 25 miles W of San Juan.
Holes: 18. **Yards:** 6,937/5,283. **Par:** 72/72. **Course Rating:** 75.2/71.9. **Slope:** 138/125. **Green Fee:** $60/$95. **Cart Fee:** Included in Green Fee. **Walking Policy:** Mandatory cart. **Walkability:** 3. **Opened:** 1998. **Architect:** Chi Chi Rodriguez. **Season:** Year-round. **High:** Dec.-April. **Miscellaneous:** Reduced fees (weekdays, twilight, juniors), range (grass), club rentals, credit cards (MC, V, AE).
Reader Comments: One of the top courses in PR, beautiful ocean holes ... Very challenging golf course ... Remodeled course, a bit expensive ... Ocean breezes, tough course.

HYATT DORADO BEACH RESORT
R-Carr. 693, Dorado, 00646, (787)796-8961, 22 miles W of San Juan.
★★★★ EAST COURSE
Holes: 18. **Yards:** 6,985/5,883. **Par:** 72/72. **Course Rating:** 72.5/74.2. **Slope:** 132/126. **Green Fee:** $70/$125. **Cart Fee:** $40/person. **Walking Policy:** Mandatory cart. **Walkability:** 3. **Opened:** 1958. **Architect:** Robert Trent Jones. **Season:** Year-round. **High:** Dec.-March. **To obtain tee times:** Resort guests call in advance. Others call same day. **Miscellaneous:** Reduced fees (resort guests, twilight, juniors), discount packages, range (grass), club rentals, lodging, credit cards (MC, V, AE, D).

THE ISLANDS

★★★★ **WEST COURSE**

Holes: 18. **Yards:** 6,913/5,883. **Par:** 72/74. **Course Rating:** 74.5/75.2. **Slope:** 132/132. **Green Fee:** $70/$125. **Cart Fee:** $40/person. **Walking Policy:** Mandatory cart. **Walkability:** 3. **Opened:** 1958. **Architect:** Robert Trent Jones. **Season:** Year-round. **High:** Dec.-March. **To obtain tee times:** Resort guests call in advance. Others call day of play. **Miscellaneous:** Reduced fees (weekdays, low season, resort guests, twilight, juniors), discount packages, range (grass), club rentals, lodging, credit cards (MC, V, AE, D).

HYATT REGENCY CERROMAR BEACH

R-Rte. 693, Dorado, 00646, (787)796-8915x3213, 26 miles W of San Juan.

★★★½ **NORTH COURSE**

Holes: 18. **Yards:** 6,841/5,547. **Par:** 72/72. **Course Rating:** 72.2/71.1. **Slope:** 125/121. **Green Fee:** $30/$105. **Cart Fee:** $20/person. **Walking Policy:** Mandatory cart. **Walkability:** 2. **Opened:** 1971. **Architect:** Robert Trent Jones. **Season:** Year-round. **High:** Dec.-March. **To obtain tee times:** Resort guests may call anytime during stay. Non-guests call day of play. **Miscellaneous:** Reduced fees (weekdays, low season, resort guests, twilight, seniors, juniors), discount packages, range (grass), club rentals, lodging (506 rooms), credit cards (MC, V, AE, D, Diners Club).

★★★½ **SOUTH COURSE**

Holes: 18. **Yards:** 7,047/5,486. **Par:** 72/72. **Course Rating:** 73.1/70.8. **Slope:** 127/120. **Green Fee:** $30/$100. **Cart Fee:** $20/person. **Walking Policy:** Mandatory cart. **Walkability:** 2. **Opened:** 1971. **Architect:** Robert Trent Jones. **Season:** Year-round. **High:** Dec.-March. **To obtain tee times:** Resort guests may call anytime during stay. Non-guests call day of play. **Miscellaneous:** Reduced fees (weekdays, low season, resort guests, twilight, juniors), discount packages, range (grass), club rentals, lodging (506 rooms), credit cards (MC, V, AE, D, Diners Club).

PALMAS DEL MAR COUNTRY CLUB

R-1 Country Club Drive, Humacao, 00792, (787)285-2255, 1 miles S of Humacao.

FLAMBOYAN COURSE

Holes: 18. **Yards:** 7,117/5,434. **Par:** 72/72. **Course Rating:** 75.2/71.3. **Slope:** 136/125. **Green Fee:** $106/$165. **Cart Fee:** Included in Green Fee. **Walking Policy:** Mandatory cart. **Walkability:** 4. **Opened:** 1998. **Architect:** Rees Jones. **Season:** Year-round. **High:** Dec.-April. **To obtain tee times:** Resort guests with golf package may call upon confirmation. Guests without package call 3 days in advance. Others call same day. **Miscellaneous:** Reduced fees (weekdays, low season, resort guests, twilight), discount packages, range (grass), club rentals, lodging (250 rooms), credit cards (MC, V, AE, D, Diners Club).

★★★½ **PALM COURSE**

Holes: 18. **Yards:** 6,610/5,248. **Par:** 71/72. **Course Rating:** 73.1/71.3. **Slope:** 131/125. **Green Fee:** $94/$145. **Cart Fee:** Included in Green Fee. **Walking Policy:** Mandatory cart. **Walkability:** 4. **Opened:** 1974. **Architect:** Gary Player. **Season:** Year-round. **High:** Dec.-April. **To obtain tee times:** Resort guests with golf package may call upon confirmation. Guests w/o package call 3 days in advance. Others call same day. **Miscellaneous:** Reduced fees (weekdays, low season, resort guests, twilight), discount packages, range (grass), club rentals, lodging (250 rooms), credit cards (MC, V, AE, D, Diners Club).

Notes: 1995 Shell's Wonderful World of Golf.

★★ PUNTA BORINQUEN GOLF CLUB

PU-Golf St., Ramey, Aguadilla, 00604, (787)890-2987, 25 miles NE of Mayaguez.

Holes: 18. **Yards:** 6,869/4,908. **Par:** 72/71. **Course Rating:** 71.5/71.0. **Slope:** 130/119. **Green Fee:** $18/$20. **Cart Fee:** $24/cart. **Walking Policy:** Walking at certain times. **Walkability:** 3. **Opened:** 1948. **Architect:** P. Dye. **Season:** Year-round. **High:** Nov.-March. **To obtain tee times:** Call after 7 a.m. on Thursday for upcoming weekend. **Miscellaneous:** Reduced fees (weekdays, twilight, juniors), range (grass), caddies, club rentals, credit cards (MC, V, AE, Debit Cards), beginner friendly (pro clinics, junior golf team and clinics).

Notes: 1998 Puerto Rico Amateur Championship.

THE ISLANDS

RIO MAR COUNTRY CLUB *Service*

R-Call Box 2888, Palmer, 00721, Rio Grande County, (787)888-8811, 25 miles E of San Juan.

★★★★ **OCEAN COURSE**
Holes: 18. **Yards:** 6,845/5,510. **Par:** 72/72. **Course Rating:** 70.7/69.0. **Slope:** 126/124. **Green Fee:** $75/$125. **Cart Fee:** Included in Green Fee. **Walking Policy:** Mandatory cart. **Walkability:** 3. **Opened:** 1975. **Architect:** George Fazio/Tom Fazio. **Season:** Year-round. **High:** Dec.-May. **To obtain tee times:** Call. **Miscellaneous:** Reduced fees (low season, resort guests, twilight, juniors), metal spikes, range (grass), club rentals, lodging, credit cards (MC, V, AE).
Reader Comments: Scenic 17th ... Great course, sea wind, water and lizards ... No roll ... Easy layout, 16th very tough ... Features iguanas ... Plugged balls ... Beautiful course, and pretty tough & great combo!

★★★½ **RIVER COURSE**
Holes: 18. **Yards:** 6,945/5,119. **Par:** 72/72. **Course Rating:** 74.5/69.8. **Slope:** 135/120. **Green Fee:** $75/$125. **Cart Fee:** Included in Green Fee. **Walking Policy:** Mandatory cart. **Walkability:** 3. **Opened:** 1975. **Architect:** Greg Norman. **Season:** Year-round. **High:** Dec.-May. **To obtain tee times:** Call. **Miscellaneous:** Reduced fees (low season, resort guests, twilight, juniors), metal spikes, range (grass), club rentals, lodging, credit cards (MC, V, AE).
Reader Comments: A treat! ... Better than its twin ... Greens large ... Converted me to a Greg Norman design fan ... Give it another year, then wow! ... Narrow fairways. Well bunkered ... Some trees needed.

★★★½ **WYNDHAM EL CONQUISTADOR RESORT AND COUNTRY CLUB**
R-Rd. 987, K.M. 3.4, Las Croabas, 00738, (787)863-6784, 31 miles E of San Juan.
Holes: 18. **Yards:** 6,662/5,131. **Par:** 72/72. **Course Rating:** 72.5/70.9. **Slope:** 131/130. **Green Fee:** $80/$165. **Cart Fee:** Included in Green Fee. **Walking Policy:** Mandatory cart. **Walkability:** 5. **Opened:** 1992. **Architect:** Arthur Hills. **Season:** Year-round. **High:** Dec.-May. **To obtain tee times:** Call golf shop. **Miscellaneous:** Reduced fees (low season, twilight, juniors), discount packages, metal spikes, range (grass), club rentals, lodging (918 rooms), credit cards (MC, V, AE).
Reader Comments: Very hilly & interesting holes ... Blue Caribbean on right, rain forest left ... Tricky layout ... Lousy first hole but excellent fun next 17 ... Awesome vistas ... Only course where I reach par 4s in one ... Putting a real challenge.

ST. CROIX

★★½ **BUCCANEER HOTEL GOLF COURSE**
R-P.O. Box 218, Christiansted, 00820, (340)773-2100, (800)255-3881, 3 miles E of Christiansted. **E-mail:** jljtcj@viaccess.net. **Web:** www.the buccaneer.com.
Holes: 18. **Yards:** 5,736/4,505. **Par:** 70/70. **Course Rating:** 67.3/64.3. **Slope:** 116/108. **Green Fee:** $30/$55. **Cart Fee:** $15/person. **Walking Policy:** Unrestricted walking. **Walkability:** 4. **Opened:** 1973. **Architect:** Robert Joyce. **Season:** Year-round. **High:** Dec.-April. **To obtain tee times:** Call golf shop. **Miscellaneous:** Reduced fees (low season, resort guests, juniors), discount packages, club rentals, lodging (150 rooms), credit cards (MC, V, AE, Diners Club).
Reader Comments: The golf shop staff was terrific ... Great tropical scenery ... World class water view ... Short—really short!

★★★★ **CARAMBOLA GOLF CLUB**
R-72 Estate River, Kingshill, 00851, (340)778-5638. **E-mail:** cgcgolf@viaccess.net. **Web:** www.golfvi.com.
Holes: 18. **Yards:** 6,843/5,424. **Par:** 72/73. **Course Rating:** 72.7/71.0. **Slope:** 131/123. **Green Fee:** $36/$76. **Cart Fee:** $14/person. **Walking Policy:** Walking at certain times. **Walkability:** 3. **Opened:** 1966. **Architect:** Robert Trent Jones, Sr. **Season:** Year-round. **High:** Dec.-April. **To obtain tee times:** Resort guests by mail or phone up to 30 days in advance. Nonguests call 24 hours in advance. **Miscellaneous:** Reduced fees (low season, resort guests, twilight), discount packages, metal spikes, range (grass), club rentals, lodging, credit cards (MC, V, AE).
Reader Comments: Friendly members gave pointers ... On-course service was terrific ... Last four holes close to beach ... Good restaurant and bar ... Hilly terrain, breezy.

ST. KITTS

★★½ **ROYAL ST. KITTS GOLF CLUB**
PU-P.O. Box 315, Frigate Bay, (869)465-8339, 2 miles N of Basseterre.
Holes: 18. **Yards:** 6,918/5,349. **Par:** 72/72. **Course Rating:** 73.0/69.0. **Slope:** 125/N/A. **Green Fee:** $31/$35. **Cart Fee:** $40/cart. **Walking Policy:** Mandatory cart. **Walkability:** N/A. **Opened:**

THE ISLANDS

1976. **Architect:** Harris/Thompson/Wolveridge/Fream. **Season:** Year-round. **High:** Dec-May. **To obtain tee times:** Call. **Miscellaneous:** Reduced fees (resort guests, seniors, juniors), discount packages, metal spikes, range (grass), club rentals, credit cards (MC, V, AE, D).
Reader Comments: A difficult course, you have to play the wind ... A challenge ... Lots of monkeys ... Constant breeze off the Atlantic.

ST. MAARTEN

★★½ **MULLET BAY GOLF CLUB**
P.O. Box 309, Phillipsburg, (599)552-801 1, 10 miles of Phillipsburg.
Holes: 18. **Yards:** 6,300/5,700. **Par:** 70/71. **Course Rating:** 69.0/68.0. **Slope:** 115/111. **Green Fee:** $65/$125. **Cart Fee:** Included in Green Fee. **Walking Policy:** Mandatory cart. **Walkability:** N/A. **Opened:** 1971. **Architect:** Joe Lee. **Season:** Year-round. **High:** Nov.-May. **To obtain tee times:** Call golf professional. **Miscellaneous:** Reduced fees (resort guests), discount packages, metal spikes, range (grass), club rentals, lodging, credit cards (MC, V, AE).
Reader Comments: Fun-windy! ... Interesting layout.

ST. THOMAS

★★★½ **MAHOGANY RUN GOLF COURSE**
PU-No.1 Mahogany Run Rd. N., 00801, (340)777-6006, (800)253-7103. **Web:** www.st_thomas.com/mahogany.
Holes: 18. **Yards:** 6,022/4,873. **Par:** 70/70. **Course Rating:** 70.1/72.6. **Slope:** 123/111. **Green Fee:** $85/$85. **Cart Fee:** $15/person. **Walking Policy:** Mandatory cart. **Walkability:** 4. **Opened:** 1980. **Architect:** George Fazio/Tom Fazio. **Season:** Year-round. **High:** Oct.-April. **To obtain tee times:** Call up to 3 days in advance with golf package. Others call 2 days in advance. **Miscellaneous:** Reduced fees (twilight), discount packages, metal spikes, range (grass/mats), club rentals, credit cards (MC, V, AE, D).
Reader Comments: Very tight and windy, club selection tough ... Challenge the Triangle, bring extra balls! ... Different type of course ... The Devil's Triangle was heavenly ... Sandy greens ... WOW! Play at least once ... Facilities need a face lift ... Too many blind and layup shots.

TOBAGO

MOUNT IRVINE BAY GOLF CLUB
R-Mt. Irvine P.O. Box 222, Scarborough, W.I., Trinidad County, (868)639-8871. **E-mail:** mtirvine@tstt.net.tt. **Web:** www.mtirvine.com.
Holes: 18. **Yards:** 6,793/5,558. **Par:** 72/74. **Course Rating:** 72.1/71.6. **Slope:** N/A. **Green Fee:** $48/$48. **Cart Fee:** $36/cart. **Walking Policy:** Unrestricted walking. **Walkability:** 3. **Opened:** 1968. **Architect:** Commander John D. Harris. **Season:** Year-round. **High:** Dec-March. **To obtain tee times:** Call golf shop. Attendant will confirm tee time. **Miscellaneous:** Reduced fees (resort guests), discount packages, metal spikes, range (grass), caddies, club rentals, lodging (105 rooms), credit cards (MC, V, AE, Diners Club).

TURKS & CAICOS

★★★★ **PROVO GOLF CLUB** *PACE+*
R-Grace Bay Rd., Providenciales, Turks and Caicos Islands County, (649)946-5991. **E-mail:** provgolf@tciway.com. **Web:** www.provogolfclub.com.
Holes: 18. **Yards:** 6,642/4,979. **Par:** 72/72. **Course Rating:** 71.2/68.5. **Slope:** 124/116. **Green Fee:** $95/$120. **Cart Fee:** Included in Green Fee. **Walking Policy:** Mandatory cart. **Walkability:** 1. **Opened:** 1992. **Architect:** Karl Litten. **Season:** Year-round. **High:** Dec.-April. **To obtain tee times:** Call golf shop, E-mail or fax. **Miscellaneous:** Reduced fees (resort guests), discount packages, range (grass/mats), club rentals, credit cards (MC, V, AE).
Reader Comments: World class No. 12, par 5 into trade winds ... Almost too beautiful to be real ... Windy as hell but a lot of fun ... Makes you feel great to be alive and golfing! ... Flamingos are native to the course ... Bring lots of balls.

Geographical Directory by Town/City

A

Abbottstown, PA, The Bridges G.C., *694*
Aberdeen, MD
Beechtree G.C., *348*
Ruggles G.Cse., *358*
Aberdeen, NC, Legacy G. Links, *602*
Aberdeen, SD
Aberdeen C.C., *761*
Lee Park G.Cse., *762*
Abilene, KS, Chisholm Trail G.Cse., *314*
Abilene, TX, Maxwell G.C., *799*
Abita Springs, LA, Abita Springs G.& C.C., *334*
Absecon, NJ, Marriott's Seaview Resort, *537*
Acapulco, Guerrero, Acapulco Princess Club De Golf, *961*
Acapulco, Guerrero
Pierre Marques G.C., *961*
Accokeek, MD, Potomac Ridge G. Links, *356*
Accord, NY, Rondout C.C., *578*
Ackworth, IA, Shady Oaks G.Cse., *310*
Acme, MI, Grand Traverse Resort, *402*
Acushnet, MA, Acushnet River Valley G.Cse., *361*
Acworth, GA
Centennial G.C., *202*
Cobblestone G.Cse., *204*
Ada, OK
Lakewood G.Cse., *672*
Osage G.C., *673*
Adams, MN, Cedar River C.C., *453*
Addison, IL, Oak Meadows G.Cse., *266*
Adel, IA, River Valley G.Cse., *309*
Adrian, MI
Center View G.Cse., *388*
Woodlawn G.C., *449*
Advance, NC, Oak Valley G.C., *606*
Afton, NY, Afton G.C., *552*
Afton, OK, Shangri-La Golf Resort, *674*
Aguadilla, Puerto Rico, Punta Borinquen G.C., *972*
Aiea, HI, Pearl C.C., *229*
Aiken, SC
The Aiken G.C., *729*
Cedar Creek G.C., *732*
Midland Valley C.C., *746*
Akron, NY
Dande Farms C.C., *562*
Rothland G.Cse., *578*
Akron, OH
J.E. Good Park G.C., *641*
Turkeyfoot Lake G. Links, *660*
Valley View G.C., *660*
Alachua, FL, Heritage Links C.C. at Turkey Creek, *160*
Alameda, CA, Chuck Corica Golf Complex, *54*
Alamogordo, NM, Desert Lakes G.Cse., *546*
Alamosa, CO, Cattails G.C., *108*
Albany, MN, Albany G.Cse., *450*
Albany, NY, The New Course at Albany, *574*
Albany, OR, The G.C. of Oregon, *681*
Albert Lea, MN, Green Lea G.Cse., *459*
Albion, MI, Tomac Woods G.Cse., *441*
Albion, NY, Ricci Meadows G.Cse., *577*

Albuquerque, NM
Arroyo Del Oso Mun. G.Cse., *546*
Isleta Eagle G.Cse., *547*
Ladera G.Cse., *547*
Los Altos G.Cse., *548*
Paradise Hills G.C., *549*
Tijeras Arroyo G.Cse., *551*
University of New Mexico G.Cse., *551*
Aledo, IL, Hawthorn Ridge G.C., *256*
Alexandria, KY, A.J. Jolly G.Cse., *321*
Alexandria, MN, Alexandria G.C., *450*
Alexandria, OH, St. Albans G.C., *654*
Algonquin, IL, Golf Club of Illinois, *254*
Alhambra, CA, Alhambra Mun. G.Cse., *47*
Alice, TX, Alice Mun. G.Cse., *779*
Aliso Viejo, CA, Aliso Viejo G.C., *47*
Allegan, MI, Cheshire Hills G.Cse., *389*
Allen, TX, Twin Creeks G.C., *813*
Allendale, MI, The Meadows G.C., *419*
Allentown, PA, Allentown Mun. G.Cse., *692*
Alliance, NE, Skyview G.Cse., *509*
Alliance, OH, Tannenhauf G.C., *659*
Allison Park, PA, North Park G.Cse., *712*
Alloway, NJ, Holly Hills G.C., *536*
Allyn, WA, Lakeland Village G.Cse., *858*
Alma, AR, Eagle Crest G.Cse., *42*
Aloha, OR, The Reserve Vineyards & G.C., *686*
Alpena, MI, Alpena G.C., *380*
Alpharetta, GA
Crooked Creek G.C., *204*
Riverpines G.C., *216*
The Champions Club of Atlanta, *203*
White Columns G.C., *220*
Alpine, AL, Alpine Bay G. & C.C., *2*
Alto, MI
Saskatoon G.C., *434*
Tyler Creek Recreation Area, *443*
Alton, IL
Cloverleaf G.Cse., *247*
Spencer T. Olin Community G.Cse., *276*
Alton, Ontario, Osprey Valley Resorts, *948*
Altoona, IA
Terrace Hills G.Cse., *310*
Park Hills C.C., *713*
Sinking Valley C.C., *719*
Alva, OK, Alva G. & C.C., *664*
Amana, IA, Amana Colonies G.Cse., *302*
Amarillo, TX
Comanche Trail G.C., *785*
Ross Rogers G.C., *807*
Southwest G.Ctr., *809*
Ambler, PA
Horsham Valley G.C., *706*
Limekiln G.C., *707*
Amelia Island, FL
Amelia Island Plantation, *137*
The G.C. at Amelia Island, *157*
Amenia, NY, Island Green C.C., *569*
American Fork, UT, Tri-City G.Cse., *823*
Americus, GA, Brickyard Plantation G.C., *201*
Ames, IA, Veenker Memorial G.Cse.-Iowa State Univ., *311*
Amesbury, MA, Amesbury G. & C.C., *361*
Amherst, MA

Amherst G.C., *361*
Hickory Ridge C.C., *368*
Amherst, NH
Amherst C.C., *521*
Ponemah Green Family G.Ctr., *526*
Souhegan Woods G.C., *527*
Amherst, Nova Scotia, Amherst G.C., *936*
Amherst, NY, Grover Cleveland G.Cse., *567*
Amsterdam, NY, City of Amsterdam Mun.
    G.Cse., *560*
Anaconda, MT
Fairmont Hot Springs Resort, *500*
Old Works G.Cse., *501*
Anacortes, WA, Similk Beach G.Cse., *863*
Anaheim, CA
Anaheim Hills G.Cse., *47*
Dad Miller G.Cse., *57*
Anahuac, TX, Chambers County G.Cse., *784*
Anchorage, AK, Anchorage G.Cse., *16*
Anchorage, KY, Long Run G.C., *328*
Andarko, OK, Dietrich Memorial G.Cse., *667*
Anderson, AL, Anderson Creek G.C., *2*
Anderson, SC, Cobb's Glen C.C., *734*
Andover, KS, Terradyne Resort Hotel & C.C.,
    319
Andrews AFB, MD, Andrews AFB G.Cse.,
    347
Andrews, IN, Etna Acres G.Cse., *286*
Andrews, TX, Andrews County G.Cse., *779*
Angel Fire, NM, Angel Fire C.C., *546*
Angels Camp, CA, Greenhorn Creek G.C.,
    65
Angola, IN
Lake James G.C., *290*
Zollner G.Cse. at Tri-State Univ., *301*
Anjou, Quebec, Club De Golf Metropolitain,
    954
Ankeny, IA
Briarwood G.Cse., *303*
Otter Creek G.C., *308*
Ann Arbor, MI
Huron Hills G.Cse., *409*
Leslie Park G.Cse., *414*
Stonebridge G.C., *437*
University of Michigan G.Cse., *444*
Annadale, MN, Albion Ridges G.Cse., *450*
Annapolis, MD, Annapolis G.C., *347*
Anniston, AL
Indian Oaks G.C., *8*
Pine Hill C.C., *12*
Anoka, MN
Greenhaven C.C., *459*
Rum River Hills G.C., *470*
Anthony, NM
Anthony C.C., *546*
Dos Lagos G.C., *546*
Antigo, WI, Antigo Bass Lake C.C., *876*
Antigonish, Nova Scotia, Antigonish G. &
    C.C., *936*
Antioch, IL, Antioch G.C., *241*
Apache Junction, AZ, Apache Creek G.C.,
    18
Apalachin, NY
Apalachin G.Cse., *552*
The Links at Hiawatha Landing, *571*
Apollo Beach, FL, Apollo Beach G. & Sea
    Club, *137*
Apollo, PA, Cherry Wood G.Cse. *697*
Apple Valley, MN, Valleywood G.Cse., *473*
Appleton, WI
Chaska G.Cse., *879*
Reid G.Cse., *897*

Aptos, CA, Aptos Seascape G.Cse., *48*
Arab, AL, Twin Lakes G.Cse., *15*
Arbor Vitae, WI, Trout Lake G. & C.C., *902*
Arcadia, CA, Santa Anita G.Cse., *93*
Arcadia, FL, Sunnybreeze G.Cse., *189*
Ardmore, OK
Lake Murray Resort Golf, *671*
Lakeview G.Cse., *671*
Arlington, TX
Chester W. Ditto G.C., *784*
Lake Arlington G.Cse., *797*
Arlington, WA, Gleneagles G.Cse., *855*
Arnold, MD, Bay Hills G.C., *347*
Arnolds Park, IA, Emerald Hills G.C., *305*
Arundel, ME, Dutch Elm G.C., *341*
Arvada, CO
Indian Tree G.C., *115*
Lake Arbor G.Cse., *116*
West Woods G.C., *124*
Arvin, CA, Sycamore Canyon G.C., *100*
Ashburn, Ontario, Thunderbird G. & C.C.,
    952
Asheville, NC
Buncombe County Mun. G.C., *591*
Great Smokies Resort G.C., *599*
The Grove Park Inn Resort, *599*
Ashland, NE
Ashland C.C., *504*
Quarry Oaks G.C., *509*
Ashland, NH, White Mtn. C.C., *528*
Ashland, PA, Rolling Meadows G.C., *717*
Ashtabula, OH, Chapel Hills G.Cse., *629*
Ashville, OH, Cooks Creek G.C., *630*
Aspen, CO, Aspen G.Cse., *106*
Atascadero, CA, Chalk Mtn. G.C., *53*
Atglen, PA, Moccasin Run G.Cse., *710*
Athens, AL, Chriswood G.C., *3*
Athens, GA, University of Georgia G.C., *219*
Athens, TN, Ridgewood G.Cse., *775*
Athens, TX, Echo Creek C.C., *788*
Athol, MA, Elinwood C.C., *365*
Atlanta, GA
Bobby Jones G.C., *200*
Browns Mill G.Cse., *201*
Lakeside C.C., *210*
North Fulton G.Cse., *213*
Atlanta, MI, Elk Ridge G.C., *394*
Atlantis, FL, Atlantis C.C. & Inn, *138*
Atoka, OK, Atoka Trails G.C., *664*
Attala, AL, Wills Creek C C, *15*
Attica, IN, Harrison Hills G. & C.C., *288*
Attleboro, MA, Stone Lea G.Cse., *376*
Atwater, CA, Rancho Del Ray G.C., *86*
Atwater, OH, Oak Grove G.Cse., *646*
Atwood, MI, Antrim Dells G.C., *380*
Au Gres, MI, Huron Breeze G. & C.C., *409*
Auburn, AL
Auburn Links at Mill Creek, *2*
Indian Pines G.C., *8*
Pin Oaks G.C., *12*
Auburn, CA, The Ridge G.Cse., *88*
Auburn, IL, Edgewood G.Cse., *250*
Auburn, ME, Prospect Hill G.Cse., *344*
Auburn, NY, Auburn G. & C.C., *553*
Auburn, WA, Auburn G.Cse., *850*
Audubon, PA, General Washington C.C., *703*
Augueg, Dominican Republic, Bavaro
    Resort G.Cse., *967*
Augusta, AR, Cypress Creek C.C., *42*
Augusta, GA
Forest Hills G.C., *206*
Goshen Plantation C.C., *207*

Brampton, Ontario, Lionhead G. & C.C., 945
Brandenburg, KY, Doe Valley G.C., 323
Brandon, MS
Bay Pointe Resort & G.C., 476
Willow Creek G.C., 484
Brandon, SD, Brandon G.Cse., 761
Brandon, VT, Neshobe G.C., 828
Brandywine, MD, Robin Dale G.C., 357
Branson, MO
Holiday Hills G.Cse., 489Pointe Royale G.C., 494
Thousand Hills G.C., 498
Brantford, Ontario, Northridge Public G.Cse., 947
Brantingham, NY, Brantingham G.C., 556
Braselton, GA, Chateau Elan Resort, 203
Brattleboro, VT, Brattleboro C.C., 825
Brazil, IN, Forest Park G.Cse., 286
Breckenridge, CO, Breckenridge G.C., 107
Brecksville, OH, Sleepy Hollow G.Cse., 656
Breeze Pt. Twshp, Grand View Lodge Resort, 458
Breezy Point, MN, Breezy Point Resort, 452
Bremen, GA, Maple Creek G.Cse., 212
Bremerton, WA
Gold Mtn. Golf Complex, 855
Rolling Hills G.Cse., 863
Brentwood, NY, Brentwood C.C., 556
Bretton Woods, NH, Mount Washington Hotel & Resort, 524
Brevard, NC, Glen Cannon C.C., 598
Brewster, MA
Captains G.Cse., 363
Ocean Edge G.C., 372
Bridgeport, MI, Green Acres G.Cse., 403
Bridgeport, NY, Rogue's Roost G.C., 577
Bridgeville, PA, Hickory Heights G.C., 705
Bridgewater, MA, Olde Scotland Links at Bridgewater, 372
Bridgewater, NJ, Green Knoll G.Cse., 535
Bridgewater, Nova Scotia, Osprey Ridge G.C., 938
Bridgman, MI, Pebblewood C.C., 425
Bridgton, ME, Bridgton Highlands C.C., 341
Brigantine, NJ, Brigantine G. Links, 530
Brigham City, UT, Eagle Mtn. G.Cse., 817
Brighton, CO, Riverdale G.C., 120
Brighton, MI
Huron Meadows G.Cse., 409
Oak Pointe, 422
Bristol, IL, Blackberry Oaks G.Cse., 243
Bristol, IN, Raber G.Cse., 295
Bristol, RI, Bristol G.C., 726
Bristol, VA, Clear Creek G.C., 833
Bristol, WI, Bristol Oaks C.C., 878
Bristow, OK, Bristow C.C., 665
Bristow, VA, Bristow Manor G.C., 832
Broadview Heights, OH, Briarwood G.Cse., 627
Brockport, NY
Brockport C.C., 556
Deerfield C.C., 562
Brockton, MA, D.W. Field G.C., 365
Brockville, Ontario, Brockville C.C., 939
Broken Arrow, OK
Battle Creek G.C., 66
Forest Ridge G.C., 668
Glen Eagles G.Cse., 669
Broken Bow, OK, Cedar Creek G.Cse., 665
Bromont, Quebec, Le Royal Bromont G.C., 955
Bronston, KY, Woodson Bend Resort, 333

Bronx, NY
Mosholu G.Cse., 574
Pelham-Split Rock G.Cse., 575
Van Cortlandt Park G.C., 585
Brookfield, OH, Yankee Run G.Cse., 663
Brookings, SD, Edgebrook G.Cse., 761
Brookland, AR, Beverly Hills G.Cse., 41
Brookline, MA, Putterham G.C., 374
Brooklyn Park, MN, Edinburgh USA G.C., 456
Brooklyn, MI
Clark Lake G.C., 389
Greenbrier G.Cse., 404
Hills Heart of The Lakes G.C., 408
Brooklyn, NY
Dyker Beach G.Cse., 563
Marine Park G.C., 572
Brooksville, FL
Sherman Hills G.C., 187Silverthorn C.C., 188
The Dunes G.C. at Seville, 152
World Woods G.C., 199
Brookville, IN, Brook Hill G.C., 283
Broomfield, CO, Eagle G.C., 110
Brown Summit, NC, Bryan Park & G.C., 591
Brownsburg, IN, Westchase G.C., 300
Brownsville, TX
Brownsville C.C., 782
Fort Brown Memorial G.Cse., 789
River Bend Resort, 805
Valley Inn & C.C., 814
Brunswick, GA, Oak Grove Island G.C., 213
Brunswick, ME
Brunswick G.C., 341
Nas Brunswick G.Cse., 343
Brush Prairie, WA, Cedars G.C., 852
Brusly, LA, Westside G.C., 339
Brutus, MI
Hidden River G. & Casting Club, 407
Maple River Club, 417
Bryan, TX, Bryan G.Cse., 782
Bryant, AL, Hidden Valley G.C., 7
Buchanan, TN, Paris Landing G.Cse., 774
Buck Hill Falls, PA, Buck Hill G.C., 694
Buena, NJ, Buena Vista C.C., 531
Buffalo Grove, IL
Arboretum G.C., 241
Buffalo Grove G.C., 244
Buffalo, OK, Doby Springs G.Cse., 667
Buffalo, WY, Buffalo G.C., 907
Buford, GA, Emerald Pointe G.C. at Lake Lanier Islands, 205
Buhl, ID, Clear Lake C.C., 236
Buies Creek, NC, Keith Hills C.C., 601
Bull Shoals, AR, Rivercliff G.C., 45
Bullard, TX
Eagle's Bluff C.C., 788
Peach Tree G.C., 802
Burbank, CA, Debell G.C., 57
Burkburnett, TX, River Creek Park G.Cse., 805
Burleson, TX, Hidden Creek G.C., 793
Burley, ID, Burley City Municipal, 235
Burlingame, CA, Crystal Springs G.C., 56
Burlington, IA, Flint Hills Mun. G.C., 305
Burlington, MI, Turtle Creek G.C., 442
Burlington, NC
Indian Valley G.Cse., 600
Shamrock G.C., 615
Burlington, Ontario
Hidden Lake G. & C.C., 943
Hidden Lake G.C., 944
Burlington, WA, Avalon G.C., 850

991

Kansas City, KS
Dread G.C., *314*
Dub's Dread G.C., *314*
Painted Hills G.Cse., *317*
Kansas City, MO
Hodge Park G.Cse., *489*
Longview Lake G.Cse., *491*
Minor Park G.C., *492*
Royal Meadows G.Cse., *496*
Swope Memorial G.Cse., *497*
Tiffany Greens G.C., *498*
Kansasville, WI, Brighton Dale G.C., *877*
Kapalua, HI
Kapalua G.C., *224*
Kapolei, HI
Kapolei G.Cse., *225*
Ko Olina G.C., *226*
Katy, TX
Green Meadows G.C., *792*
The G.C. at Cinco Ranch, *791*
Kaukauna, WI, Countryside G.C., *880*
Kearney, NE, Meadowlark Hills G.Cse., *508*
Keene, NH
Bretwood G.Cse., *521*
Keene C.C., *524*
Keesler AFB, MS, Bay Breeze G.Cse., *476*
Keithville, LA
Alpine Meadows G.C., *334*
Meadowlake C.C., *337*
Keizer, OR, McNary G.C., *683*
Kellogg, ID, Shoshone G. & Tennis Club, *239*
Kelowna, British Columbia
Gallagher's Canyon G. & C.C., *923*
Harvest G.C., *924*
Kelowna Springs G.C., *924*
Shadow Ridge G.C., *928*
Sunset Ranch G. & C.C., *929*
Kelso, WA, Three Rivers G.Cse., *865*
Kenai, AK, Kenai G.Cse., *16*
Kendallville, IN, Cobblestone G.Cse., *284*
Kennebunkport, ME, Cape Arundel G.C., *341*
Kennett, MO, Kennett C.C., *490*
Kennewick, WA
Canyon Lakes G.Cse., *851*
Tri-City C.C., *865*
Kenosha, WI
Big Oaks G.Cse., *876*
Maplecrest C.C., *891*
Petrifying Springs G.Cse., *896*
Kensington, CT, Timberlin G.C., *133*
Kent, OH
Maplecrest G.Cse., *644*
Oak Knolls G.C., *647*
Raccoon Hill G.C., *650*
Sunnyhill G.Cse., *657*
Kent, WA
Druids Glen G.C., *853*
Riverbend Golf Complex, *862*
Kerhonkson, NY, Hudson Valley Resort & Spa, *568*
Kerman, CA, Fresno West G. & C.C., *62*
Kernersville, NC
Pine Knolls G.C., *608*
Pine Tree G.C., *608*
Kerrville, TX, Scott Schreiner Kerrville Mun. G.Cse., *807*
Ketchum/Sun Valley, ID, Bigwood G.Cse., *235*
Kettleby, Ontario, Cardinal G.C., *940*
Kewadin, MI, A-Ga-Ming G.C., *380*
Kewaskum, WI, Hon-E-Kor C.C., *887*

Key Biscayne, FL, Crandon Golf at Key Biscayne, *148*
Key West, FL, Key West G.C., *163*
Keyser, WV, Mill Creek G.Cse., *871*
Keystone, CO, Keystone Ranch G.Cse., *116*
Kiamesha Lake, NY, Concord Resort Hotel, *560*
Kiawah Island, SC, Kiawah Island Resort, *742*
Kihei, HI
Makena Resort G.Cse., *227*
Silversword G.C., *231*
Killeen, TX, Killeen Mun. G.Cse., *796*
Killington, VT
Green Mtn. National G.Cse., *826*
Killington Golf Resort, *827*
Kimberley, British Columbia, Trickle Creek Golf Resort, *929*
Kimberton, PA, Kimberton G.C., *707*
Kincheloe, MI, Kincheloe Memorial G.Cse., *411*
King of Prussia, PA, Valley Forge G.C., *723*
Kingman, AZ, Valle Vista C.C., *39*
Kings Mountain, NC, Woodbridge G. Links, *619*
Kings Park, NY, Sunken Meadow State Park G.C., *582*
Kingshill, USVI, Carambola G.C., *973*
Kingsport, TN
Cattails at Meadow View, *766*
Warrior's Path State Park, *778*
Kingston, NH, Kingston Fairways G.C., *524*
Kingston, Nova Scotia, Paragon G. & C.C., *938*
Kingston, OK, Lake Texoma Golf Resort, *671*
Kingston, TN, Southwest Point G.Cse., *776*
Kingsville, Ontario, Kingsville G. & C.C., *945*
Kingsville, TX, L.E. Ramey G.Cse., *796*
Kingwood, TX, Kingwood Cove G.C., *796*
Kingwood, WV, Preston C.C., *872*
Kirksville, MO, Kirksville C.C., *490*
Kissimmee, FL
Falcon's Fire G.C., *154*
Kissimmee Bay C.C., *164*
Kissimmee G.C., *164*
Orange Lake C.C., *173*
Poinciana G. & Racquet Resort, *178*
Remington G.C., *180*
Kitchener, Ontario, Doon Valley G.C., *941*
Kitty Hawk, NC
Duck Woods C.C., *596*
Sea Scape G. Links, *614*
Klamath Falls, OR
Harbor Links G.Cse., *681*
Running Y Ranch Resort, *688*
Shield Crest G.Cse., *689*
Knightstown, IN, Royal Hylands G.C., *295*
Knoxville, IL, Laurel Greens Public Golfers Club, *261*
Knoxville, TN
Dead Horse Lake G.Cse., *767*
Knoxville G.Cse., *772*
Three Ridges G.Cse., *777*
Whittle Springs G.Cse., *778*
Willow Creek G.C., *778*
Kodak, TN, River Islands G.C., *775*
Kohala Coast, HI, Mauna Lani Resort, *228*
Kohler, WI, Blackwolf Run G.C., *876*
Kokomo, IN, Green Acres G.C., *288*
Koloa, HI, Poipu Bay Resort G.C., *229*
Kresgville, PA, Hideaway Hills G.C., *706*

L

La Belle, FL, Oxbow G.C., *174*
La Center, KY, Ballard County C.C., *321*
La Crosse, WI, Forest Hills Public G.Cse., *882*
La Follette, TN, Deerfield Resort, *768*
La Grange, CA, Hidden Hills Resort & G.C., *67*
La Grange, IL, Timber Trails C.C., *277*
La Grange, KY
La Grange Woods C.C., *326*
Oldham County C.C., *329*
La Grange, OH, Pheasant Run G.Cse., *648*
La Jolla, CA, Torrey Pines G.Cse., *102*
La Mirada, CA, La Mirada G.C., *69*
La Pine, OR, Quail Run G.Cse., *686*
La Place, LA, Belle Terre C.C., *335*
La Pointe, WI, Madeline Island G.C., *891*
La Porte, IN, Briar Leaf G.C., *283*
La Quinta, CA
Indian Springs C.C., *68*
La Quinta Resort & Club, *70*
PGA West Resort, *82*
La Romana, Dominican Republic, Casa De Campo Resort & C.C., *967*
La Salle, IL, Senica Oak Ridge G.Cse., *274*
La Veta, CO, Grandote Peaks G.C., *113*
Lacey, WA
Meriwood G.Cse., *860*
Vicwood G. Links, *866*
Laconia, NH, Laconia C.C., *524*
Lady Lake, FL
Orange Blossom Hills G. & C.C., *172*
Tierra Del Sol G.C., *191*
Lafayette, CO, Indian Peaks G.C., *115*
Lafayette, IN, Lafayette G.C., *290*
Lafayette, LA, City Park G.Cse., *335*
Lafayette, NJ, Farmstead G. & C.C., *533*
LaFayette, NY, Orchard Valley G.C., *575*
LaFollette, TN, The Greens at Deerfield, *770*
LaGrange, GA, The Fields G.C., *205*
Laguna Vista, TX, South Padre Island G.C., *809*
Lahaina, HI, Kaanapali G.Cses., *223*
Lake Ann, MI, Mistwood G.Cse., *420*
Lake Ariel, PA, Scranton Mun. G.Cse., *718*
Lake Bluff, IL, Lake Bluff G.C., *260*
Lake Buena Vista, FL, Walt Disney World Resort, *195*
Lake Charles, LA
Mallard Cove G.Cse., *337*
Pine Shadows G.Ctr., *338*
Lake City, FL, Quail Heights C.C., *179*
Lake City, MI, Missaukee G.C., *420*
Lake Forest, IL, Deerpath Park G.Cse., *249*
Lake Geneva, WI
Geneva National G.C., *883*
Grand Geneva Resort & Spa, *885*
Hillmoor G.C., *886*
Lake Havasu City, AZ, London Bridge G.C. *28*
Lake Lanier Islands, GA, Renaissance Pineisle Resort, *215*
Lake Lure, NC, Lake Lure G. & Beach Resort, *601*
Lake Mary, FL, Timacuan G. & C.C., *191*
Lake Mills, IA, Rice Lake G. & C.C., *309*
Lake Milton, OH, Lakeside G.Cse.*42*
Lake Orion, MI, Bald Mtn. G.Cse., *380*
Lake Ozark, MO
Osage National G.C., *493*

The Lodge of Four Seasons, *491*
Lake Park, GA, Francis Lake G.C., *206*
Lake Placid, NY
Craig Wood G.Cse., *561*
Lake Placid Resort, *570*
Whiteface Club On Lake Placid, *586*
Lake St. Louis, MO, Hawk Ridge G.C., *489*
Lake Village, AR, Lake Village C.C., *44*
Lake Worth, FL
Doug Ford's Lacuna G.C., *152*
Lake Worth G.C., *164*
The Club at Winston Trails, *146*
Lakeland, FL
Big Cypress G. & C.C., *139*
Bramble Ridge G.Cse., *142*
Cleveland Heights G.Cse., *145*
Huntington Hills G. & C.C., *161*
Sandpiper G.C., *185*
Schalamar Creek G. & C.C., *186*
The Club at Eaglebrooke, *142*
Wedgewood G. & C.C., *196*
Lakeland, TN, Stonebridge G.Cse., *777*
Lakeview, OR, Lakeridge G.Cse., *683*
Lakeville, MA
Lakeville C.C., *369*
Poquoy Brook G.C., *374*
Lakeville, New Brunswick, Lakeside G.C., *934*
Lakewood, CA, Lakewood C.C., *71*
Lakewood, CO, Fox Hollow at Lakewood G.Cse., *113*
Lakewood, IL
Redtail G.C., *272*
Lakewood, NJ
Lakewood C.C., *537*
Woodlake C.C., *545*
Lakewood, WI, McGauslin Brook G. & C.C., *892*
Lakin, KS, Lakin Mun. G.Cse., *316*
Lambertville, MI, Maple Grove G.Cse., *416*
Lanai City, HI
The Challenge at Manele, *221*
The Experience at Koele, *221*
Lancaster, KY, The Peninsula Golf Resort, *329*
Lancaster, OH
Estate G.C., *633*
Valley View G.Cse., *661*
Lancaster, PA, Overlook G.Cse., *713*
Lancaster, TX, Country View G.C., *786*
Lander, WY, Lander G. & C.C., *908*
Langhorne, PA, Middletown C.C., *709*
Langley, British Columbia
Belmont G.Cse., *920*
The Redwoods, *927*
Lansdale, PA, Pine Crest G.C., *715*
Lansdowne, VA, Lansdowne G.C., *840*
Lansford, ND, Lansford C.C., *621*
Lansing, MI
Chisholm Hills C.C., *389*
Groesbeck Mun. G.Cse., *404*
Royal Scot G.Cse., *433*
Laona, WI, Nicolet C.C., *894*
Lapeer, MI
Lapeer C.C., *414*
Rolling Hills G.C., *432*
LaPorte, TX, Bay Forest G.Cse., *780*
Laramie, WY, Jacoby G.Cse., *908*
Laredo, TX, Casa Blanca G.Cse., *783*
Largo, FL
Bardmoor North G.C., *138*
East Bay G.C., *153*

Marion, SC, Dusty Hills C.C., *736*
Marion, VA, Holston Hills C.C., *837*
Markham, Ontario
Angus Glen G.C., *938*
Markham Green G.C., *947*
Marne, MI, Western Greens G.Cse., *446*
Marquette, MI
Chocolay Downs G.Cse., *389*
Marquette G. & C.C., *417*
Marriottsville, MD, Waverly Woods G.C., *360*
Mars, PA, Venango Trail G.Cse., *724*
Marseilles, IL, The Bourne G.C., *244*
Marshall's Creek, PA, Mountain Manor Inn & G.C., *710*
Marshall, MI, The Medalist G.C., *419*
Marshall, MN, Marshall G.C., *464*
Marshalltown, IA, American Legion Memorial G.Cse., *302*
Marshfield, MA, Green Harbor G.C., *367*
Marshfield, WI, Marshfield C.C., *891*
Marshville, NC, Eagle Chase G.C., *596*
Marstons Mills, MA, Olde Barnstable Fairgrounds G.Cse., *372*
Mart, TX, Battle Lake G.Cse., *780*
Martinsburg, WV, Stonebridge G.C., *874*
Marysville, CA, Plumas Lake G. & C.C., *83*
Marysville, MI, Marysville G.Cse., *418*
Marysville, OH
Darby Creek G.Cse., *631*
Flagstone G.C., *634*
Rolling Meadows G.C., *653*
Marysville, WA
Battle Creek G.Cse., *850*
Cedarcrest G.C., *852*
Maryville, MO, Mozingo Lake G.Cse., *493*
Maryville, TN, Lambert Acres G.C., *772*
Mashpee, MA
New Seabury C.C., *371*
Quashnet Valley C.C., *374*
Mason City, IA, Highland Park G.Cse., *306*
Mason, MI
Branson Bay G.Cse., *385*
El Dorado G.Cse., *394*
Mason Hills G.Cse., *418*
Mason, OH
Crooked Tree G.C., *631*
Kingswood G.Cse., *642*
The G.Ctr. at Kings Island, *636*
Western Row G.Cse., *662*
Mason, WV, Riverside G.C., *872*
Massena, NY, Massena C.C., *573*
Massillon, OH
Rolling Green G.Cse., *653*
The Legends of Massillon, *643*
Mather, CA, Mather G.Cse., *74*
Matthews, NC, The Divide, *595*
Mattoon, IL, Meadowview G.Cse., *264*
Mattydale, NY, Brooklawn G.Cse., *557*
Maunaloa, HI, Kaluakoi Hotel & G.C., *224*
Mauston, WI, Castle Rock G.Cse., *879*
Mays Landing, NJ, Mays Landing C.C., *538*
Mayville, MI, Greenbriar G.C., *404*
Mayville, WI, Mayville G.C., *891*
Mazatlan, Sinaloa
El Cid G. & C.C., *963*
Estrella Del Mar G. & Beach Resort Comm., *963*
McAfee, NJ, Great Gorge C.C., *534*
McAlester, OK, Thundercreek G.Cse., *676*
McCall, ID, McCall Mun. G.Cse., *237*
McCalla, AL, Tannehill National G.Cse., *14*
McClure, PA, Indian Run G.Cse., *706*

McComb, MS, Quail Hollow G.Cse., *482*
McConnell AFB, KS, Twin Lakes G.Cse., *320*
McCook, NE, Heritage Hills G.Cse., *505*
McCormick, SC, Hickory Knob G.C., *740*
McDonough, GA, Georgia National G.C., *206*
McHenry, IL
Boone Creek G.C., *244*
Chapel Hill C.C., *246*
McHenry, MD, The G.C. at Wisp, *352*
McKenzie, TN, Carroll Lake G.C., *766*
McKinleyville, CA, Beau Pre G.C., *49*
McNabb, IL, Edgewood Park G.Cse., *251*
McPherson, KS, Turkey Creek G.Cse., *320*
McRae, GA, Wallace Adams G.Cse., *220*
Mebane, NC, Mill Creek G.C., *604*
Mechanicsburg, OH, Indian Springs G.C., *640*
Mechanicsburg, PA
Armitage G.Cse., *692*
Silver Springs G.C., *719*
Medford, NJ, Golden Pheasant G.C., *534*
Medford, OR, Cedar Links G.C., *679*
Media, PA, Paxon Hollow C.C., *713*
Medicine Hat, Alberta
Connaught G.Cse., *913*
Medicine Hat G. & C.C., *916*
Medina, MN, Baker National G.Cse., *450*
Medina, OH
Bunker Hill G.Cse., *628*
Pleasant Valley C.C., *649*
Ridge Top G.Cse., *652*
Melbourne, FL, Baytree National G. Links, *139*
Memphis, MI, Belle River G. & C.C., *381*
Memphis, TN
Audubon Park G.Cse., *765*
Davy Crockett G.Cse., *767*
Fox Meadows G.Cse., *769*
Galloway G.Cse., *769*
Memphis Oaks G.C., *773*
Pine Hill G.Cse., *775*
T.O. Fuller G.Cse., *777*
Mena, AR, Ouachita G.Cse., *44*
Menahga, MN, Blueberry Pines G.C., *451*
Menifee, CA, Menifee Lakes C.C., *75*
Menominee, MI, North Shore G.C., *421*
Menomonee Falls, WI
Silver Spring G.Cse., *899*
Wanaki G.Cse., *904*
Mequon, WI, Meek-Kwon Park G.Cse., *892*
Merced, CA, Merced Hills G.C., *75*
Mercer, PA, Mercer Public G.Cse., *709*
Meriden, CT, Hunter G.C., *128*
Meriden, KS, Village Greens G.C., *320*
Meridianville, AL, Colonial G.C., *4*
Merrill, WI, Merrill G.C., *892*
Merrillville, IN
Broadmoor C.C., *283*
Turkey Creek C.C., *298*
Merrimac, WI, Devil's Head Resort & Convention Ctr., *881*
Merritt Island, FL, Savannahs at Sykes Creek G.C., *185*
Mesa, AZ
Dobson Ranch G.C., *21*
Las Sendas G.C., *27*
Longbow G.C., *28*
Painted Mtn. G.C., *31*
Superstition Springs G.C., *36*
The Arizona Golf Resort & Conf. Ctr., *18*
Mescalero, NM, Inn of The Mtn. Gods G.Cse., *547*

Mesick, MI, Briar Downs G.Cse., *385*
Mesquite, NV
Oasis Resort Hotel Casino, *516*
Peppermill Palms G.Cse., *517*
Mesquite, TX, Mesquite G.Cse., *800*
Methuen, MA
Hickory Hills G.C., *368*
Merrimack G.C., *370*
Mexico, MO, Arthur Hills G.C., *485*
Miami Beach, FL
Bayshore G.Cse., *139*
Normandy Shores G.Cse., *171*
Miami Lakes, FL, Don Shula's G.C., *151*
Miami Shores, FL, Miami Shores C.C., *170*
Miami, FL
Costa Del Sol G. & C.C., *147*
Country Club of Miami, *147*
Doral Golf Resort & Spa, *151*
Fontainebleau G.Cse., *155*
Int'l Links Miami Melreese G.Cse., *163*
Miami National G.C., *169*
Palmetto G.Cse., *175*
University C.C., *193*
Miamisburg, OH
Pipestone G.C., *649*
River Bend G.Cse., *652*
Michigan City, IN, Michigan City Municipal
    Course, *292*
Midale, Saskatchewan, Mainprize Regional
    Park & G.Cse., *957*
Middle Island, NY
Middle Island C.C., *573*
Spring Lake G.C., *581*
Middleburg, FL, Ravines G. & C.C., *180*
Middlebury, VT, Ralph Myhre C.C. of
    Middlebury College, *828*
Middlefield, CT, Lyman Orchards G.C., *129*
Middlefield, OH, Grandview G.C., *637*
Middleport, NY, Niagara Orleans C.C., *575*
Middleton, WI, Pleasant View G.C., *896*
Middletown, CA, Hidden Valley Lake G. &
    C.C., *67*
Middletown, DE, Back Creek G.C., *135*
Middletown, IN
Tri County G.C., *298*
Valley View G.Cse., *299*
Middletown, NY, Town of Wallkill G.C., *584*
Middletown, OH
Green Crest G.Cse., *637*
Pleasant Hill G.C., *649*
Weatherwax G.Cse., *661*
Middletown, PA, Sunset G.Cse., *721*
Midland, GA, Bull Creek G.Cse., *201*
Midland, MI
Currie Mun. G.Cse., *392*
Sandy Ridge G.Cse., *434*
Midland, Ontario, Brooklea G. & C.C., *939*
Midland, TX, Hogan Park G.Cse., *793*
Midland, VA, Kastle Greens G.C., *838*
Midway, PA, Quicksilver G.C., *716*
Midway, UT
Homestead G.C., *818*
Wasatch State Park G.C., *823*
Midwest City, OK, John Conrad Regional
    G.Cse., *670*
Milan, IL, Indian Bluff G.Cse., *258*
Milan, NM, Zuni Mtn. G.Cse., *551*
Milford, KS, Rolling Meadows G.Cse., *318*
Milford, MI
Kensington Metro Park G.Cse., *411*
Mystic Creek G.C., *421*
Mililani, HI, Mililani G.C., *229*

Milledgeville, GA, Little Fishing Creek G.C.,
    212
Millersburg, PA, Harrisburg North G.Cse.,
    704
Milliken, CO, Mad Russian G.Cse., *117*
Millington, TN
Big Creek G.C., *765*
Orgill Park G.Cse., *774*
Millis, MA, Glen Ellen C.C., *367*
Millstadt, IL, Triple Lakes G.Cse., *278*
Milpitas, CA
Spring Valley G.C., *97*
Summit Pointe G.C., *98*
Milton, FL
Tanglewood G. & C.C., *190*
The Moors G.C., *171*
Milton, KS, Suppesville G.Cse., *319*
Milton, NJ, Bowling Green G.C., *530*
Milton, PA, Turbot Hills G.Cse., *722*
Milton, WI, Oak Ridge G.Cse., *895*
Milwaukee, WI
Brown Deer Park G.Cse., *878*
Currie Park G.Cse., *880*
Dretzka Park G.Cse., *881*
Lincoln Park G.Cse., *890*
Mineral Wells, WV, Woodridge Plantation
    G.C., *874*
Minerva, OH, Great Trail G.Cse., *637*
Minneapolis, MN
Columbia G.Cse., *454*
Francis A. Gross G.Cse., *457*
Hiawatha G.Cse., *459*
Minocqua, WI, Pecks Wildwood G.Cse., *895*
Minot, ND
Minot C.C., *621*
Souris Valley G.C., *622*
Miramichi, New Brunswick, Miramichi G. &
    C.C., *934*
Mishicot, WI, Fox Hills Resort, *883*
Mission, TX,
Seven Oaks Resort & C.C., *808*
Shary Mun. G.Cse., *808*
Missoula, MT
Highlands G.C., *500*
Larchmont G.Cse., *500*
Mitchell, IN, Saddle Brook C.C., *296*
Mitchell, SD, Lakeview G.Cse., *762*
Mitchellville, MD
Enterprise G.Cse., *351*
Lake Arbor C.C., *353*
Moab, UT, Moab G.C., *819*
Moberly, MO, Timber Lake G.Cse., *498*
Mobile, AL, Azalea City G.Cse., *2*
Mobile, AL, The Linksman G.C., *10*
Modesto, CA
Creekside G.Cse., *56*
Dryden Park G.Cse., *59*
Momence, IL, South Shore G.Cse., *275*
Moncks Corner, SC, Berkeley C.C., *730*
Moncton, New Brunswick, Magnetic Hill G. &
    C.C., *934*
Monmouth, IL, Gibson Woods G.Cse., *253*
Monroe, CT, Whitney Farms G.Cse., *134*
Monroe, LA, Chennault Park G.Cse., *335*
Monroe, MI
Green Meadows G.Cse., *403*
Raisin River C.C., *429*
Monroe, NC
Monroe C.C., *604*
Stonebridge G.C., *616*
Mont Tremblant, Quebec
Gray Rocks G.C., *954*

Tremblant Golf Resort, 956
Montague, MI
Hickory Knoll G.Cse., 407
Montague, MI, Old Channel Trail G.C., 423
Montague, NJ, High Point C.C., 535
Montauk, NY, Montauk Downs State Park
G.Cse., 574
Montebello, CA, Montebello C.C., 76
Montebello, Quebec, Le Chateau
Montebello, 955
Montego Bay, Jamaica
Half Moon Golf, Tennis & Beach Club, 969
Wyndham Rose Hall Resort And C.C., 970
Monterey, CA
Laguna Seca G.C., 70
Old Del Monte G.Cse., 80
Montevallo, AL
Montevallo G.C., 11
Lagoon Park G.Cse., 9
River Run G.Cse., 13
Montgomery, NY, Stony Ford G.Cse., 582
Montgomery, PA, White Deer Park & G.Cse.,
724
Montgomery, TX, Del Lago Golf Resort, 787
Monticello, MN
Monticello C.C., 465
Silver Springs G.Cse., 471
Monticello, NY, Kutsher's C.C., 570
Montpelier, VA, Hollows G.Cse., 837
Montreal, Quebec, Montreal Mun. G.Cse.,
956
Montrose, CO, Montrose G.Cse., 117
Moodus, CT, Banner Resort & C.C., 125
Moorefield, WV, Valley View G.Cse., 874
Moorestown, NJ, Willow Brook C.C., 545
Mooresville, IN, Eagle Pines G.C., 285
Mooresville, NC
Mallard Head C.C., 603
Town of Mooresville G.Cse., 617
Mooretown, Ontario, St. Clair Parkway
G.Cse., 950
Moorhead, MN, The Meadows G.Cse., 464
Morehead City, NC
Brandywine Bay G. & C.C., 590
Morehead City C.C., 604
Morehead, KY, Eagle Trace G.Cse., 323
Morell, Prince Edward Is., The Links at
Crowbush Cove, 953
Morenci, MI, De Mor Hills G.Cse., 392
Moreno Valley, CA
Moreno Valley Ranch G.C., 76
Moreno Valley, CA, Quail Ranch G.C., 85
Morgan, UT, Round Valley C.C., 821
Morganton, NC, Quaker Meadows G.C., 611
Morgantown, KY, Hidden Valley G.Cse., 325
Morgantown, WV, Lakeview Resort & Conf.
Ctr., 870
Morrill, NE, Rolling Green G.C., 509
Morris, IL, Nettle Creek C.C., 265
Morrisburg, Ontario, Upper Canada G.Cse.,
952
Morro Bay, CA, Morro Bay G.Cse., 77
Morton Grove, IL, Chick Evans G.Cse., 246
Mosca, CO, Great Sand Dunes G.Cse. at
Zapata Ranch, 114
Moscow, ID, University of Idaho G.Cse., 240
Mott, ND, Mott C.C., 621
Moulton, AL, Deer Run G.Cse., 5
Moultonborough, NH, Ridgewood C.C., 526
Mound, MN, Lakeview Golf of Orono, 461
Mount Airy, MD, The Links at Challedon, 353
Mount Clare, WV, Bel Meadow C.C., 868

Mount Dora, FL
Country Club of Mount Dora, 148
Mount Dora G.C., 171
Mount Joy, PA, Groff's Farm G.C., 704
Mount Juliet, TN, Windtree G.Cse., 778
Mount Pleasant, PA, Timber Ridge G.C., 722
Mount Pleasant, SC
Charleston National C.C., 733
Patriots Point Links, 750
The Dunes West G.C., 736
Mount Pocono, PA, Mount Airy Lodge
G.Cse., 710
Mount Sterling, OH, Deer Creek State Park
G.Cse., 631
Mount Vernon, OH
Chapel Hill G.Cse., 629
Hiawatha G.Cse., 638
Irish Hills G.Cse., 641
Mount Vernon, WA, Eaglemont G.C., 854
Mountain City, TN, Roan Valley Golf Estates,
776
Mountain Home, AR, Twin Lakes G.C., 46
Mountain View, CA, Shoreline G. Links at
Mtn. View, 95
Mountain View, MO, Mountain View G.Cse.,
493
Mountlake Terrace, WA, Nile G.C., 861
Mt. Carmel, IL, Mount Carmel Mun. G.C., 264
Mt. Clemens, MI, Cracklewood G.C., 391
Mt. Laurel, NJ, Ramblewood C.C., 541
Mt. Pleasant, MI
Pleasant Hills G.C., 427
Pohlcat G.Cse., 428
Riverwood Resort, 431
Mt. Plymouth, FL, Mount Plymouth G.C., 171
Mt. Prospect, IL
Mount Prospect G.C., 264
Old Orchard C.C., 267
Mt. Vernon, IL, Indian Hills G.Cse., 258
Muenster, TX, Turtle Hill G.Cse., 813
Mukilteo, WA, Harbour Pointe G.C., 856
Mukwonago, WI
Lake Beulah C.C., 889
Rainbow Springs G.C., 896
Mullens, WV
Sugarwood G.C., 874
Twin Falls State Park G.Cse., 874
Muncie, IN, Maplewood G.C., 292
Mundelein, IL
Countryside G.Cse., 248
Four Winds G.C., 252
Indian Valley C.C., 259
Pine Meadow G.C., 269
Steeple Chase G.C., 276
Village Green C.C., 278
Murfreesboro, TN
Indian Hills G.C., 771
Old Fort G.C., 774
Murphy, NC, Cherokee Hills G. & C.C., 593
Murray, KY, Frances E. Miller G.Cse., 324
Murray, UT, Murray Parkway G.C., 820
Murraysville, PA, Rolling Fields G.Cse., 717
Murrells Inlet, SC
Blackmoor G.C., 730
Wachesaw Plantation East, 757
Murrieta, CA, The SCGA Members' Club at
Rancho California, 93
Murrysville, PA
Meadowink G.C., 709
Murrysville G.C., 711
Muscatine, IA, Muscatine Mun. G.Cse., 307

Muscle Shoals, AL, Cypress Lakes G. &
 C.C., *5*
Muskego, WI, Muskego Lakes C.C., *893*
Muskegon, MI
Chase Hammond G.Cse., *388*
Fruitport G.C., *398*
Lincoln G.C., *415*
Oak Ridge G.C., *422*
Muskogee, OK, Eagle Crest G.Cse., *667*
Myrtle Beach, SC
Arcadian Shores G.C., *729*
Arrowhead C.C., *729*
Belle Terre G.Cse., *730*
Heron Point G.C., *740*
Island Green G.C., *741*
Man O' War Golf, *746*
Myrtle Beach National G.C., *746*
Myrtlewood G.C., *747*
Pine Lakes Int'l C.C., *751*
Quail Creek G.C., *752*
Raccoon Run G.C., *752*
River Oaks Golf Plantation, *753*
The Dunes G. & Beach Club, *736*
The Legends, *744*
The Wizard G.Cse., *760*
Tournament Player's Club of Myrtle Beach,
 756
Waterway Hills G.C., *758*
Wicked Stick G. Links, *759*
Myrtle Creek, OR, Myrtle Creek G.Cse., *684*

N

N. Aurora, IL, Fox Valley G.C., *252*
Nacogdoches, TX, Woodland Hills G.Cse.,
 815
Nags Head, NC, Nags Head G. Links, *605*
Nampa, ID, Centennial G.C., *235*
Nampa, ID, Ridgecrest G.C., *238*
Nanaimo, British Columbia, Nanaimo G.C.,
 925
Nanoose Bay, British Columbia, Fairwinds
 G. & C.C., *922*
Nantucket, MA, Miacomet G.C., *370*
Napa, CA
Chimney Rock G.Cse., *54*
Napa Mun. G.C., *78*
Silverado C.C. & Resort, *95*
The Chardonnay G.C., *53*
Naperville, IL
Country Lakes G.C., *248*
Naperville, IL, Springbrook G.Cse., *276*
Naperville, IL, Tamarack G.C., *277*
Naples, FL
Lely Resort G. & C.C., *165*
Marco Shores C.C., *167*
Marriott's G.C. at Marco, *168*
Naples Beach Hotel & G.C., *171*
Palm River C.C., *175*
Quality Inn & Suites Golf Resort, *179*
Tiburon G.C., *190*
Valencia G.Cse. at Orangetree, *194*
Nashville, IN, Salt Creek G.C., *296*
Nashville, MI, Mulberry Fore G.Cse., *420*
Nashville, TN
Harpeth Hills G.Cse., *770*
McCabe Field G.Cse., *773*
Nashboro G.C., *774*
Springhouse G.C., *776*
Ted Rhodes G.Cse., *777*
Two Rivers G.Cse., *778*
Nassau, New Providence

Cable Beach G.C., *970*
Paradise Island G.C., *971*
South Ocean G. & Beach Resort, *971*
Natchez, MS
Duncan Park G.Cse., *478*
Naugatuck, CT, Hop Brook G.Cse., *128*
Navarre, FL, The Club at Hidden Creek, *146*
Navasota, TX, Bluebonnet Country G.Cse.,
 781
Nebraska City, NE, Wildwood G.Cse., *510*
Needles, CA, Needles Mun. G.Cse., *78*
Neenah, WI
Bridgewood G.Cse., *877*
Winagamie G.Cse., *905*
Nekoosa, WI, Lake Arrowhead G.Cse., *889*
Nellis AFB, NV
Nellis AFB G.Cse., *516*
Sunrise Vista G.C., *519*
Neosho, MO, Neosho Mun. G.Cse., *493*
Neptune, NJ
Jumping Brook C.C., *536*
Shark River G.Cse., *543*
Nescopeck, PA, Arnold's G.C., *692*
Neshanic, NJ, Hillsborough C.C., *536*
Nevada, MO, Frank E. Peters Mun. G.Cse.,
 488
New Baltimore, MI
Cedar Glen G.C., *388*
Salt River C.C., *434*
New Bedford, MA, New Bedford Mun.
 G.Cse., *371*
New Berlin, WI, New Berlin Hills G.Cse., *894*
New Bern, NC
Carolina Pines G. & C.C., *592*
Fairfield Harbour C.C., *597*
The Emerald G.C., *597*
New Boston, MI, Willow Metropark G.Cse.,
 448
New Braunfels, TX
Landa Park Mun. G.Cse., *798*
The Bandit G.C., *779*
New Britain, CT, Stanley G.C., *132*
New Buffalo, MI, Whittaker Woods G.C., *447*
New Carlisle, OH, Sugar Isle Golf Country,
 657
New Castle, KY, Henry County C.C., *325*
New Castle, PA
Castle Hills G.Cse., *695*
Mohawk Trails G.Cse., *710*
Sylvan Heights G.Cse., *721*
New Castle, WY, New Castle C.C., *908*
New Cumberland, WV, Mountaineers
 Woodview G.Cse., *871*
New Era, MI, Grand View G.Cse., *403*
New Franken, WI, Royal Scot G.Cse. &
 Supper Club, *898*
New Glasgow, Nova Scotia, Abercrombie
 G.C., *936*
New Haven, CT
Alling Memorial G.Cse., *125*
Yale G.Cse., *134*
New Haven, MI, Oak Ridge G.C., *422*
New Hempstead, NY, New York C.C., *574*
New Hudson, MI, Coyote G.C., *390*
New Iberia, LA, Sugar Oaks G. & C.C., *339*
New Lenox, IL, The Sanctuary G.Cse., *273*
New Market, VA, Shenvalee G.C., *845*
New Melle, MO, New Melle Lakes G.C., *493*
New Milford, CT, Candlewood Valley C.C.,
 126
New Minas, Nova Scotia, Ken-Wo C.C., *937*
New Orleans, LA

North Sutton, NH, Country Club of New Hampshire, *522*
North Tonawanda, NY, Deerwood G.Cse., *562*
North Truro, MA, Highland G. Links, *368*
North Vancouver, British Columbia, Northlands G.Cse., *925*
Northampton, MA, Pine Grove G.Cse., *373*
Northborough, MA, Juniper Hill G.Cse., *369*
Northbrook, IL, Sportsman's C.C., *276*
Northfield, MN
Northfield G.C., *466*
Willinger's G.C., *474*
Northport, MI, Matheson Greens G.Cse., *418*
Northport, NY, Crab Meadow G.C., *561*
Northville, MI, Salem Hills G.C., *433*
Norton, MA, Norton C.C., *371*
Norton, OH, Loyal Oak G.Cse., *644*
Norwalk, CT, Oak Hills G.C., *130*
Norwalk, OH, Eagle Creek G.C., *632*
Norway, MI, Oak Crest G.Cse., *422*
Norwich, CT, Norwich G.Cse., *129*
Norwich, NY, Canasawacta C.C., *557*
Norwood, MA, Norwood C.C., *371*
Nova, OH, Rolling Acres G.Cse., *652*
Novato, CA, Indian Valley G.C., *68*
Novi, MI
The Links of Novi, *415*
Westbrooke G.Cse., *446*

O

O'Fallon, IL, Tamarack C.C., *277*
O'Fallon, MO, The Falls G.C., *488*
O'Leary, Prince Edward Is., Mill River G.Cse., *953*
Oak Bluffs, MA, Farm Neck G.C., *366*
Oak Brook, IL
Oak Brook G.Cse., *265*
Oak Brook Hills Hotel & Resort, *266*
George W. Dunne National G.Cse., *253*
Oak Grove, MO, Bent Oak G.C., *485*
Oak Harbor, WA, Gallery G.Cse., *855*
Oak Hill, WV, White Oak C.C., *874*
Oak Island, NC, Oak Island G. & C.C., *606*
Oakes, ND, Oakes G.C., *621*
Oakland Mills, PA, Lost Creek G.C., *708*
Oakland Township, MI, Beaver Creek Golf Links, *381*
Oakland, CA, Lake Chabot G.Cse., *70*
Oakland, MD, Oakland G.Cse., *355*
Oakland, ME, Waterville C.C., *346*
Oakland, MI, Twin Lakes G.C., *443*
Oakland, NE, Oakland G.Cse., *508*
Oakville, Ontario
Glen Abbey G.C., *943*
Richview G. & C.C., *949*
Ocala, FL
Golden Ocala G. & C.C., *157*
The C.C. at Silver Springs Shores, *147*
Ocean Isle Beach, NC
Brick Landing Plantation G. & C.C., *590*
Ocean Isle Beach G.Cse., *606*
Ocean Shores, WA, Ocean Shores G.Cse., *862*
Ocean Springs, MS
Gulf Hills G.C., *479*
Pine Island G.C., *481*
St. Andrews G.C., *482*
Oceana, WV, Clearford Valley G.Cse., *869*
Oceanside, CA
Emerald Isle, *61*

Oceanside Mun. G.Cse., *79*
Ocho Rios, Jamaica, Sandals G. & C.C., *969*
Ocoee, FL, Forest Lake G.C. of Ocoee, *155*
Oconomowoc, WI
Deertrak G.Cse., *880*
Olde Highlander G.C. at Olympia Resort, *895*
Paganica G.Cse., *895*
Odessa, FL, The Eagles G.C., *153*
Odessa, TX, Ratliff Ranch G. Links, *804*
Ogden, UT
Ben Lomond G.Cse., *816*
Mount Ogden G.Cse., *819*
Schneiter's Riverside G.Cse., *822*
The Barn G.Cse., *816*
Ojai, CA
Ojai Valley Inn & Spa, *80*
Soule Park G.Cse., *97*
Okeene, OK, Okeene Mun. G.Cse., *673*
Oklahoma City, OK
Broadmoore G.Cse., *665*
Brookside G.Cse., *665*
Earlywine Park G.Cse., *667*
Lake Hefner G.C., *671*
Lincoln Park G.Cse., *672*
Silverhorn G.C., *675*
Trosper Park G.Cse., *676*
Okoboji, IA, Brooks G.C., *303*
Okolona, MS, Okolona C.C., *481*
Okotoks, Alberta, D'Arcy Ranch G.C., *913*
Olathe, KS, Heritage Park G.Cse., *315*
Olathe, KS, Lakeside Hills G.Cse., *316*
Old Hickory, TN, Hermitage G.Cse., *771*
Old Orchard Beach, ME, Dunegrass G.C., *341*
Olds, Alberta, Olds G.C., *916*
Olive Branch, MS
Cherokee Valley G.C., *477*
Links of Whispering Woods, *479*
Plantation G.C., *481*
Wedgewood G.Cse., *483*
Oliver, British Columbia, Fairview Mtn. G.C., *922*
Olney, MD, Trotters Glen G.Cse., *359*
Olympia, WA, Capitol City G.C., *851*
Olympic Valley, CA, Resort at Squaw Creek, *88*
Omaha, NE
Applewood G.Cse., *504*
Benson Park G.Cse., *504*
Elmwood Park G.Cse., *505*
Miracle Hill G. & Tennis Ctr., *508*
The Knolls G.Cse., *507*
Tiburon G.C., *509*
Onamia, MN, Izatys G. & Yacht Club, *460*
Onanole, Manitoba, Clear Lake G.Cse., *930*
Oneida, WI, Brown County G.Cse., *878*
Onekama, MI, The Heathlands of Onekama, *406*
Oneonta, AL, Limestone Springs G.C., *9*
Onset, MA, Bay Pointe C.C., *362*
Ontario, CA, Whispering Lakes G.Cse., *104*
Ontario, OR, Shadow Butte G.C., *689*
Opelika, AL, Grand National G.C., *6*
Orange City, FL, The Pines G.C., *177*
Orange City, IA, Landsmeer G.C., *307*
Orange Park, FL, Eagle Harbor G.C., *152*
Orange, CT
Grassy Hill C.C., *127*
Orange Hills C.C., *130*
Orangeburg, SC, Hillcrest G.C., *740*
Orangeville, Ontario, Hockley Valley Resort, *944*

1010

Rancho Murieta, CA, Rancho Murieta C.C., *86*

Rancho Palos Verdes, CA, Los Verdes G.Cse., *73*

Rancho Santa Fe, CA, Morgan Run Resort & Club, *76*

Rancho Santa Margarita, CA, Tijeras Creek G.C., *101*

Rancho Viejo, TX, Rancho Viejo Resort & C.C., *804*

Randolph, NY, Cardinal Hills G.Cse., *557*

Randolph, VT, Montague G.C., *827*

Rangeley, ME, Mingo Springs G.Cse., *343*

Rantoul, IL, Willow Pond G.Cse., *280*

Rapid City, SD
Hart Ranch G.Cse., *762*
Meadowbrook G.Cse., *763*
Rapid City Elks G.Cse., *763*

Ratcliff, AR, Little Creek Recreational Club, *44*

Rathdrum, ID, Twin Lakes Village G.Cse., *240*

Ravenna, MI, Ravenna G.Cse., *430*

Ravenna, OH, Windmill Lakes G.C., *662*

Ravenswood, WV, Greenhills C.C., *870*

Rawlings, MD, The Mtn. Club at Rawlings, *354*

Ray Township, MI, Northbrook G.C., *421*

Ray, MI, Pine Valley G.C., *426*

Ray, ND, The Links of North Dakota at Red Mike Resort, *621*

Raymond, MS, Eagle Ridge G.Cse., *478*

Reading, PA
Exeter G.C., *701*
Flying Hills G.Cse., *702*

Red Deer, Alberta, River Bend G. & Recreation Area, *918*

Red Lodge, MT, Red Lodge Mtn. Resort G.Cse., *502*

Red Rock, Ontario, North Shore G.Cse., *947*

Red Wing, MN, Mississippi National G. Links, *465*

Redding, CA, Gold Hills G.C., *63*

Redford, MI, Glenhurst G.Cse., *400*

Redmond, OR
Eagle Crest Resort, *679*
Juniper G.C., *682*

Redmond, WA, Willows Run G.C., *867*

Reedsburg, WI, Reedsburg C.C., *897*

Rehoboth Beach, DE, Old Landing G.C., *135*

Rehoboth, MA
Hillside C.C., *368*
Rehoboth C.C., *374*
Sun Valley G.Cse., *377*

Renfrew, Ontario, Renfrew G.C., *949*

Reno, NV
Arrowcreek G.C., *511*
Lake Ridge G.Cse., *515*
Northgate G.Cse., *516*
Rosewood Lakes G.Cse., *518*
Sierra Sage G.Cse., *518*
Washoe County G.C., *519*
Wolf Run G.C., *520*

Rensselaer, IN, Curtis Creek C.C., *285*

Renton, WA, Maplewood G.Cse., *859*

Republic, MO, Eagle Crest G. & C.C., *487*

Reston, VA
Hidden Creek G.C., *837*
Reston National G.Cse., *844*

Rexburg, ID, Teton Lakes G.Cse., *240*

Rexford, NY, Riverview C.C., *577*

Reynoldsburg, OH, Blacklick Woods G.Cse., *625*

Rhinelander, WI, Northwood G.Cse., *894*

Rialto, CA, El Rancho Verde G.Cse., *60*

Rice Lake, WI, Turtleback G. & Conf. Ctr., *902*

Richardson, TX, Sherrill Park G.Cse., *808*

Richboro, PA, Northampton Valley C.C., *712*

Richfield, MN, Rich Acres G.Cse., *469*

Richfield, WI, Kettle Hills G.Cse., *888*

Richland, WA, Columbia Point G.Cse., *852*

Richmond Hill, Ontario
Chestnut Hill G. & C.C., *940*
Richmond Hill G.C., *949*

Richmond, British Columbia, Mayfair Lakes G. & C.C., *924*

Richmond, IL, Hunter C.C., *258*

Richmond, KY, Gibson Bay G.Cse., *324*

Richmond, MO, Shirkey G.C., *497*

Richmond, OH, Blackmoor G.C., *626*

Richmond, RI
Foxwoods G. & C.C. at Boulder Hills, *726*
Richmond C.C., *727*

Richmond, TX, Old Orchard G.C., *800*

Richmond, VA
Belmont G.Cse., *831*
Glenwood G.C., *835*

Richton Park, IL, Urban Hills C.C., *278*

Ridge Manor, FL, Whispering Oaks C.C., *198*

Ridgefield, CT, Ridgefield G.Cse., *131*

Ridgefield, WA, Tri-Mountain G.Cse., *866*

Ridgway, CO, Fairway Pines G.C., *112*

Rifle, CO, Rifle Creek G.Cse., *120*

Rincon, GA, Lost Plantation, *212*

Ringgold, GA, Windstone G.C., *220*

Ringgold, VA, Ringgold G.C., *844*

Rio Grande, Puerto Rico
Bahia Beach Plantation, *971*
Berwind C.C., *971*

Rio Rico, AZ, Rio Rico Resort & C.C., *34*

Rio San Juan, Dominican Republic, Caribbean Village Playa Grande G.Cse., *967*

Rio Verde, AZ, Tonto Verde G.C., *37*

Rio Vista, CA, Rio Vista G.C., *89*

Ripon, CA, Jack Tone Golf, *68*

Rising Sun, MD, Chantilly Manor C.C., *349*

River Falls, WI
Clifton Hollow G.C., *879*
Killarney Hills G.Cse., *888*
River Falls G.C., *897*

River Vale, NJ
Pascack Brook G. & C.C., *540*
River Vale C.C., *542*

Riverdale, IL, Joe Louis The Champ G.C., *259*

Riverhead, NY, Indian Island C.C., *569*

Riverside, CA
El Rivino C.C., *61*
Indian Hills G.C., *68*
Jurupa Hills C.C., *69*
Van Buren G.Ctr., *103*

Riverton, Manitoba, Hecla G.Cse. at Gull Harbor Resort, *931*

Riverton, UT, Riverbend G.Cse., *821*

Riverton, WY, Riverton C.C., *909*

Riverview, FL, Summerfield G.C., *189*

Riverview, MI, Riverview Highlands G.Cse., *431*

Riverview, New Brunswick, Moncton G. & C.C., *934*

Riverwoods, IL, Deerfield Park G.C., *249*

Roanoke, VA, Ole Monterey G.C., *842*

Talking Stick G.C., 37
The Phoenician G.C., 32
Tournament Players Club of Scottsdale, 38
Troon North G.C., 38
Scottsville, NY
Chili C.C., 559
Cragie Brae G.C., 561
Seabrook Island, SC, The Club at Seabrook Island, 733
Sealy, TX, River Ridge G.C., 805
Seaside, CA, Bayonet/Black Horse G.Cse., 49
Seattle, WA
Jackson Park G.Cse., 857
Jefferson Park G.Cse., 857
Tyee Valley G.Cse., 866
West Seattle G.Cse., 867
Sebastian, FL, Sebastian Mun. G.Cse., 186
Sebring, FL
Country Club of Sebring, 148
Golf Hammock C.C., 158
Harder Hall C.C., 160
Spring Lake G. & Tennis Resort, 188
Secor, IL, Fairlakes G.Cse., 251
Sedona, AZ
Oakcreek C.C., 30
Sedona Golf Resort, 35
Selkirk, Manitoba, Selkirk G. & C.C., 931
Sellersburg, IN
Covered Bridge G.C., 285
Hidden Creek G.C., 289
Selma, CA, Selma Valley G.Cse., 94
Semmes, AL, Magnolia Grove G.C., 10
Seneca, KS, Seneca G.C., 319
Sequim, WA
Dungeness G. & C.C., 853
Sunland G. & C.C., 865
Sevierville, TN, Eagle's Landing G.C., 768
Sewell, NJ, Maple Ridge G.C., 537
Sexsmith, Alberta, Spruce Meadows G. & C.C., 918
Seymour, IN, Shadowood G.Cse., 296
Seymour, WI, Crystal Springs G.C., 880
Shakopee, MN
Lone Pines C.C., 462
Stonebrooke G.C., 471
Shalimar, FL, Shalimar Pointe G. & C.C., 187
Shallotte, NC, Brierwood G.C., 590
Sharon Center, OH, Western Reserve G. & C.C., 661
Sharon, Ontario, Pheasant Run G.C., 948
Shattuck, OK, Shattuck G. & C.C., 675
Shawano, WI, Shawano Lake G.C., 899
Shawnee, KS, Tomahawk Hills G.C., 319
Shawnee, OK, Fire Lake G.Cse., 668
Shawnee-on-Delaware, PA, Shawnee Inn Golf Resort, 718
Sheboygan, WI
Riverdale C.C., 897
Sheboygan Town & C.C., 899
Shediac, New Brunswick, Pine Needles G. & C.C., 935
Shelburne, VT, Kwiniaska G.C., 827
Shelby, MI, Oceana G.C., 423
Shelby, MT, Marias Valley G. & C.C., 501
Shelby Township, MI
Cherry Creek G.C., 388
Stony Creek G.Cse., 438
Shelby, NC
Pine Grove G.C., 608
River Bend G.C., 612
Shelbyville, KY

Shelbyville C.C., 331
Weissinger Hills G.Cse., 332
Shelbyville, MI, Orchard Hills G.Cse., 423
Shenandoah, IA, American Legion C.C., 302
Shepherd, MI, Winding Brook G.C., 448
Shepherdsville, KY, Maplehurst G.Cse., 328
Sheridan, WY
Kendrick G.Cse., 908
Sheridan C.C., 909
Sherwood Park, Alberta
Broadmoor Public G.Cse., 912
Countryside G.Cse., 913
Sherwood Park G.Cse., 918
Sherwood, WI, High Cliff G.Cse., 886
Shoemakersville, PA, Perry G.Cse., 714
Short Hills, NJ, East Orange G.Cse., 532
Shortsville, NY, Winged Pheasant G. Links, 587
Show Low, AZ, Silver Creek G.C., 36
Shreveport, LA
Huntington Park G.Cse., 336
Northwood G. & C.C., 337
Querbes Park G.Cse., 338
Sicklerville, NJ, Freeway G.Cse., 534
Sidney, NE, Hillside G.Cse., 506
Sidney, OH, Shelby Oaks G.C., 655
Sierra Vista, AZ, Pueblo Del Sol C.C., 33
Sikeston, MO
Bootheel G.C., 485
Sikeston C.C., 497
Siloam Springs, AR, Dawn Hill G. & Racquet Club, 42
Silver City, NM, Silver City G.C., 550
Silverthorne, CO, Eagles Nest G.C., 111
Simi Valley, CA, Simi Hills G.C., 96
Sinclair, WY, Sinclair G.C., 909
Sinking Spring, PA, Manor G.C., 708
Sinton, TX, Sinton Mun. G.Cse., 809
Sioux City, IA, Green Valley G.Cse., 306
Sioux Falls, SD
Elmwood G.Cse., 761
Kuehn Park G.Cse., 762
Prairie Green G.Cse., 763
Willow Run G.Cse., 764
Skaneateles, NY, Skaneateles Greens C.C., 580
Sky Valley, GA, Sky Valley G. & Ski Resort, 217
Skytop, PA, Skytop Lodge, 719
Slidell, LA
Oak Harbor G.C., 337
Pinewood C.C., 338
Royal G.C., 338
Slinger, WI, Scenic View C.C., 899
Smithfield, UT, Birch Creek G.C., 816
Smithfield, VA, Cypress Creek Golfers' Club, 833
Smithtown, NY, Smithtown Landing G.C., 580
Smithville, MO, Paradise Pointe G.C., 494
Smyrna, DE, Garrisons Lake C.C., 135
Smyrna, GA, Fox Creek G.C., 206
Smyrna, TN, Smyrna Mun. G.Cse., 776
Sneads Ferry, NC, North Shore C.C., 605
Snellville, GA, Trophy Club of Gwinnett, 219
Snohomish, WA
Echo Falls Public C.C., 854
Kenwanda G.Cse., 857
Snohomish G.Cse., 864
Snoqualmie, WA, Mount Si G.Cse., 861
Snow Camp, NC, Sourwood Forest G.Cse., 615

Springville, UT, Hobble Creek G.C., 818
Spruce Grove, Alberta
The Links at Spruce Grove, 916
The Ranch G. & C.C., 917
Squamish, British Columbia, Squamish
Valley G. & C.C., 929
Stacy, MN, Falcon Ridge G.Cse., 456
Stafford, VA, Augustine G.C., 831
Stamford, CT
E. Gaynor Brennan Mun. G.Cse., 127
Sterling Farms G.C., 132
Standish, MI, Pine River G.C., 426
Stanhope, Prince Edward Is., Stanhope G. &
C.C., 954
Stanton, NE, Elkhorn Acres G.Cse., 505
Stanwood, MI, St. Ives G.C., 433
Stanwood, WA, Kayak Point G.Cse., 857
Star City, IN, Pond View G.Cse., 294
Starkville, MS, Mississippi State Univ.
G.Cse., 480
State Center, IA, Lincoln Valley G.C., 307
State College, PA
Pennsylvania State Univ. G.Cse., 714
Toftrees Resort, 722
Stateline, NV, Edgewood Tahoe G.Cse., 513
Staten Island, NY
La Tourette G.C., 570
Silver Lake G.Cse., 580
South Shore G.Cse., 581
Statesboro, GA, Eagle Creek G.C., 205
Statesville, NC
Broken Arrow G. Links, 590
Twin Oaks G.Cse., 617
Ste. Adele, Quebec, Le Golf Chantecler, 955
Steamboat Springs, CO
Haymaker G.Cse., 114
Sheraton Steamboat Resort & G.C., 121
Steinbach, Manitoba
Steinbach Fly-In G.Cse., 932
The Links at Quarry Oaks, 931
Sterling Heights, MI
Maple Lane G.Cse., 417
Plum Brook G.C., 427
Rammler G.C., 429
Sunnybrook G.C., 438
Sterling, IL
Emerald Hill G. & Learning Ctr., 251
Lake View C.C., 261
Sterling, VA, Algonkian Regional Park
G.Cse., 831
Stettler, Alberta, Pheasantback G. & C.C.,
917
Stevens Point, WI
Sentryworld G.Cse., 899
Wisconsin River G.C., 906
Stevens, PA, Foxchase G.C., 702
Stevenson, WA, Skamania Lodge G.Cse.,
863
Stevinson, CA, Stevinson Ranch G.C., 98
Stewartstown, PA, Pleasant Valley G.C., 715
Stillwater, MN, Oak Glen G.C., 466
Stillwater, OK
Karsten Creek G.C., 670
Lakeside Memorial G.C., 671
Stockbridge, GA, Southerness G.C., 218
Stockton, CA
Swenson Park G.C., 99
The Reserve at Spanos Creek, 88
Van Buskirk Park G.Cse., 103
Stone Mountain, GA, Stone Mtn. Park G.C.,
218
Stoney Creek, NC, Stoney Creek G.C., 616

Stonington, CT, Pequot G.C., 130
Stouffville, Ontario, Maples of Ballantrae
Lodge & G.C., 946
Stow, MA
Butternut Farm G.C., 363
Stow Acres C.C., 376
Stow, OH
Fox Den G.C., 634
Roses Run C.C., 653
Stowe, VT, Stowe C.C., 829
Stoystown, PA, Oakbrook G.Cse., 712
Stratton Mountain, VT, Stratton Mtn. C.C.,
829
Street, MD, Geneva Farm G.C., 351
Stroud, OK, Stroud Mun. G.Cse., 675
Stroudsburg, PA, Glen Brook G.C., 703
Stuart, FL
Martin County G. & C.C., 169
The Champions Club at Summerfield, 144
Stuart, VA, Gorden Trent G.Cse., 835
Sturgeon Bay, WI
Cherry Hills Lodge & G.Cse., 879
Idlewild G.Cse., 887
Sturgis, MI
Green Valley G.C., 404
Saint Joe Valley G.C., 433
Sturtevant, WI, Ives Grove G. Links, 887
Suffern, NY, Spook Rock G.Cse., 581
Suffolk, VA
Riverfront G.C., 844
Sleepy Hole G.Cse., 846
Suffolk G.Cse., 847
Sugar Grove, IL, Prestbury C.C., 271
Sugar Hill, GA, Sugar Hill G.C., 219
Sugar Land, TX, Greatwood G.C., 792
Sugarcreek, OH, Willandale G.C., 662
Sugarloaf, PA, Sugarloaf G.C., 721
Sulphur, OK, Sulphur Hills G.Cse., 675
Summerfield, FL, Eagle Ridge G.C. at Del
Webb Spruce Creek, 153
Summerfield, NC, Greensboro National G.C.,
599
Summerland, British Columbia,
Summerland G. & C.C., 929
Summerside, Prince Edward Is.,
Summerside G.C., 954
Summerton, SC, Foxboro G.C., 738
Summerville, SC
Legend Oak's Plantation G.C., 744
Miler C.C., 746
Pine Forest C.C., 750
River Club on the Ashley, 752
Sumner, WA, Sumner Meadows G. Links,
864
Sumter, SC
Lakewood Links G.C., 743
Pocalla Springs C.C., 751
Sun City West, AZ, Hillcrest G.C., 26
Sun Prairie, WI, Sun Prairie G.Cse., 901
Sun Valley, ID
Elkhorn Resort, 236
Sun Valley Resort G.Cse., 239
Sunbury, OH, Bent Tree G.C., 625
Sunfield, MI, Centennial Acres G.Cse., 388
Sunnyvale, CA, Sunnyvale G.Cse., 99
Sunol, CA, Sunol Valley G.Cse., 99
Sunrise, FL, Sunrise C.C., 190
Sunriver, OR, Sunriver Lodge & Resort, 689
Sunset Beach, NC
Angel's Trace G. Links, 588
Ocean Ridge Plantation, 606
Oyster Bay G. Links, 607

Z

Alphabetical Directory by Course

Belle Terre G.Cse., *730*
Belleview Biltmore Resort & G.C., *139*
Bellevue Mun. G.Cse., *851*
Bello Woods G.C., *381*
Bellport C.C., *554*
Bellwood Oaks G.Cse., *450*
Belmont G. & C.C., *965*
Belmont G.Cse. (Langley, British Columbia), *920*
Belmont G.Cse. (Richmond, VA), *831*
Belvedere C.C., *41*
Belvedere G.C. (Charlevoix, MI), *382*
Belvedere G.C. (Charlottetown, PRINCE EDWARD ISLAND), *952*
Belvedere Plantation G. & C.C., *589*
Bemidji Town & C.C., *451*
Ben Geren Regional Park G.Cse., *41*
Ben Hawes State Park Golf, *321*
Ben Lomond G.Cse., *816*
Bennett Valley G.Cse., *49*
Benson Park G.Cse., *504*
Bent Brook G.Cse., *2*
Bent Creek G.Cse., *485*
Bent Creek Golf Village, *765*
Bent Oak G.C. (Oak Grove, MO), *485*
Bent Oak G.C. (Titusville, FL), *139*
Bent Pine G.C., *382*
Bent Tree G.C., *625*
Bent Tree G.Cse., *765*
Bergen Point C.C., *554*
Berkeley C.C., *730*
Berkshire G.C., *313*
Berwind C.C., *971*
The Bethel Inn & C.C., *340*
Bethel Island G.Cse., *49*
Bethlehem C.C., *521*
Bethlehem Mun. G.C., *693*
Bethpage State Park G.Cses., *554*
Beulah Mun. G.Cse., *620*
Beverly G. & Tennis Club, *362*
Beverly Hills G.Cse., *41*
Bey Lea G.C., *529*
Biddeford Saco C.C., *340*
Bide-A-Wee G.C., *831*
Bidwell Park G.Cse., *50*
Big Beaver Creek G.Cse., *625*
Big Bend G.C., *868*
Big Creek G.C., *765*
Big Cypress G. & C.C., *139*
Big Hickory G.Cse., *321*
Big Met G.C., *625*
Big Oaks C.C., *476*
Big Oaks G.Cse., *876*
Big Run G.C., *242*
Big Sky G. & C.C., *920*
Big Sky G.C., *499*
Big South Fork C.C., *766*
Bigwood G.Cse., *235*
Bill & Payne Stewart G.Cse., *485*
Bill Roberts Mun. G.Cse., *499*
The Biltmore G.Cse., *139*
Binder Park G.Cse., *382*
Bing Maloney G.Cse., *50*
Binks Forest G.Cse., *140*
Birch Creek G.C., *816*
Birch Ridge G.C., *16*
Birck Boilermaker Golf Complex, *282*
Birdwood G.Cse., *831*
Birkdale G. & C.C., *831*
Birkdale G.C., *589*
Bittersweet G.C., *242*
Black Bear G. & C.C., *530*

Black Bear G.C., *140*
Black Bear Golf Resort, *382*
Black Butte Ranch, *678*
Black Creek G.C., *200*
Black Forest & Wilderness Valley Golf Resort, *382*
Black Hawk G.Cse., *693*
Black Lake Golf Resort, *50*
Black Mtn. G. & C.C., *511*
Black Mtn. G.Cse., *589*
Black Rock G.Cse., *348*
Black Squirrel G.C., *282*
Blackberry Oaks G.Cse., *243*
Blackberry Patch G.Cse., *383*
Blackfoot Mun. G.Cse., *235*
Blackhawk G.C. (Galena, OH), *625*
Blackhawk G.C. (Pflugerville, TX), *781*
Blackhawk G.C. (St. Charles, IL), *243*
Blackheath G.C., *383*
Blackjack Bay G. Links, *476*
Blackledge C.C., *125*
Blacklick Woods G.Cse., *625*
Blackmoor G.C. (Murrells Inlet, SC), *730*
Blackmoor G.C. (Richmond, OH), *626*
Blackthorn G.C., *283*
Blackwell G.Cse., *664*
Blackwolf Run G.C., *876*
Blackwood G.Cse., *693*
Blair Park G.C., *589*
Blissful Meadows G.C., *362*
Blomidon G. & C.C., *936*
Bloomingdale G.C., *243*
Bloomingdale Golfer's Club, *140*
Blossom Trails G.Cse., *383*
Blue Ash G.Cse., *626*
Blue Cypress G.C., *140*
Blue Fox Run G.C., *125*
Blue Heron Pines G.C., *530*
Blue Hill G.C., *555*
Blue Mtn. View G.Cse., *693*
Blue Ridge C.C., *589*
Blue Rock G.Cse., *362*
Blue Skies C.C., *50*
Blue Stone G.C., *555*
Blueberry Pines G.C., *451*
Bluebonnet Country G.Cse., *781*
Bluebonnet Hill G.C., *782*
Bluewater Bay Resort, *140*
Bluff Creek G.Cse., *451*
Bluff Point G. & C.C., *555*
The Bluffs, *761*
Bluffton G.C., *626*
Blythe Mun. G.C., *50*
Bob O'Link G.Cse., *626*
Bob-O-Link G.Cse., *626*
Bob-O-Link Golf Enterprises, *321*
Bobby Jones G.C., *200*
Bobby Jones Golf Complex, *141*
Bobcat Trail G. & C.C., *141*
Boca Raton Resort & Club, *141*
Bodega Harbour G. Links, *50*
The Bog , *877*
Bogie Busters G.C., *321*
Bogie Lake G.C., *383*
Bogue Banks C.C., *589*
Boiling Springs G.C., *664*
Bois De Sioux G.C., *620*
Bolton Field G.Cse., *627*
Bon Vivant C.C., *243*
Bon-Air G.C., *694*
Bonaventure C.C., *141*
Bonita Springs G.C., *142*

Buccaneer Hotel G.Cse., *973*
Buck Creek G.C., *731*
Buck Hill G.C., *694*
Buckeye Hills C.C., *627*
Bucknell G.C., *695*
Buena Vista C.C., *531*
Buffalo Creek G.C., *783*
Buffalo Dunes G.Cse., *313*
Buffalo G.C., *907*
Buffalo Grove G.C., *244*
Buffalo Hill G.Cse., *499*
Buffalo Run G.Cse., *108*
Buffalo Valley G.Cse., *766*
Bull Creek G.Cse., *201*
Bull Run C.C., *832*
Bulle Rock , *348*
Buncombe County Mun. G.C., *591*
Bunker Hill G.Cse. (Dubuque, IA), *303*
Bunker Hill G.Cse. (Medina, OH), *628*
Bunker Hill G.Cse. (Princeton, NJ), *531*
Bunker Hills G.Cse., *452*
Bunker Links Mun. G.Cse., *244*
Bunn G.Cse., *245*
Burley City Municipal, *235*
Burnaby Mtn. G.Cse., *920*
Burning Ridge G.C., *731*
Burns Park G.Cse., *41*
Burr Oak G.C., *386*
Butler's G.Cse., *695*
Butternut Farm G.C., *363*
Butternut Hills G.Cse., *878*
Byrncliff G.C., *557*
Byron Hills G.C., *386*
Byron Hills G.Cse., *245*
C-Way G.C., *557*
Caberfae Peaks Ski & Golf Resort, *386*
Cabin Brook G.C., *322*
Cable Beach G.C., *970*
Cable Hollow G.C., *695*
Cabo Real G.C., *960*
Cabo San Lucas C.C., *960*
Cacapon Resort, *868*
Cahaba Valley G. & C.C., *3*
Cain's Burning Oak C.C., *387*
Calabash G. Links, *591*
Calabogie Highlands Resort & G.C., *939*
Caledon C.C., *939*
Caledonia G. & Fish Club, *732*
Calhoun C.C., *732*
California Club, *143*
California G.Cse., *628*
Calimesa C.C., *51*
Callaway Gardens Resort, *202*
Calusa Lakes G.Cse., *143*
Calvada Valley G. & C.C., *512*
Calvert City G. & C.C., *322*
Camaloch G.Cse., *851*
Camarillo Springs G.Cse., *52*
Cambell House C.C., *232*
Cambrian Ridge G.C., *3*
Cambridge C.C., *349*
Camelot G.Cse., *766*
Camillus C.C., *557*
Camino Real Las Hadas Resort, *961*
Campbell's Scottish Highlands G.Cse., *522*
Campo De Golf Ixtapa G.Cse., *961*
Campo De Golf San Jose, *960*
Canaan Valley Resort G.Cse., *868*
Canajoharie C.C., *557*
Canasawacta C.C., *557*
Candia Woods G. Links, *522*
Candlestone G.C., *387*

Candlewood Valley C.C., *126*
Canebrake G.C., *476*
Canmore G. & Curling Club, *912*
Cannon AFB G.Cse. – Whispering Winds, *546*
Cannon G.C., *453*
Canoa Hills G.Cse., *19*
Canterberry G.Cse., *108*
Cantigny Golf, *245*
Canton Public G.C., *126*
Canyon Lake G.C., *783*
Canyon Lakes C.C., *52*
Canyon Lakes G.Cse., *851*
Canyon South G.Cse., *52*
Canyon Springs G.C., *783*
Canyon Springs G.Cse., *235*
Cape Arundel G.C., *341*
Cape Cod C.C., *363*
Cape Coral G. & Tennis Resort, *143*
Cape G. & Racquet Club, *592*
Cape Jaycee Mun. G.Cse., *486*
Cape May National G.C., *531*
Cape Royale G.Cse., *783*
Capitol City G.C. (Jackson, MS), *477*
Capitol City G.C. (Olympia, WA), *851*
Capri Isles G.C., *143*
Captains G.Cse., *363*
Carambola G.C., *973*
Cardinal Creek G.Cse., *245*
Cardinal G.C., *940*
Cardinal G.Cse., *245*
Cardinal Hills G.Cse., *557*
Carey Park G.C., *313*
Caribbean Village Playa Grande G.Cse., *967*
Caribou C.C., *341*
Carillon G.C., *245*
Carleton Glen G.C., *387*
Carlisle G. & C.C., *940*
Carlton Oaks C.C., *52*
Carmel Mtn. Ranch C.C., *52*
Carmel Valley Ranch G.C., *52*
Carnation G.Cse., *851*
Carolina Downs C.C., *732*
Carolina Lakes G.C., *592*
Carolina National G.C., *592*
Carolina Pines G. & C.C., *592*
Carolina Shores G. & C.C., *593*
Carolina Springs G.C., *732*
The Carolina, *592*
Caroline G.C., *477*
Carper's Valley G.C., *832*
Carriage Greens C.C., *245*
Carriage Hills C.C., *453*
Carrington G.C., *620*
Carroll Lake G.C., *766*
Carroll Meadows G.Cse., *628*
Carroll Mun. G.Cse., *304*
Carroll Park G.Cse., *349*
Carroll Valley Golf Resort, *695*
Carthage Mun. G.Cse., *486*
Cary C.C., *246*
Casa Blanca G.Cse., *783*
Casa De Campo Resort & C.C., *967*
Casa Grande Mun. G.Cse., *19*
Cascades G.Cse., *387*
Casolwood G.Cse., *558*
Casper Mun. G.Cse., *907*
Casperkill C.C., *558*
Cassel Hills G.Cse., *628*
Cassville G.C., *486*
Castine G.C., *341*
Castle Creek C.C., *53*
Castle Harbour G.C., *966*

1032

Grovebrook G.Cse., 637
Grover C. Keaton G.Cse., 792
Grover Cleveland G.Cse., 567
Gulf Harbour G. & C.C., 160
Gulf Hills G.C., 479
Gulf Shores G.C., 6
Gulf State Park G.Cse., 7
Gull Lake View G.C., 404
Gunpowder G.C., 353
Gunter's Landing G.Cse., 7
Gus Wortham Park G.Cse., 792
Gustin G.C., 489
H. Smith Richardson G.Cse., 128
Habitat G.Cse., 160
Haggin Oaks G.Cse., 65
Haile Plantation G. & C.C., 160
Half Moon Bay G.C., 66
Half Moon Golf, Tennis & Beach Club, 969
Halifax Plantation G.C., 160
Hall of Fame G.Cse., 160
Hallie G.C., 885
Hamilton G.C., 500
Hamilton Mill G.Cse., 207
Hamlet Wind Watch G.C., 567
Hampden C.C., 367
Hampshire C.C., 405
Hampton C.C., 933
Hampton Club, 208
Hampton Cove G.C., 7
Hampton Hills G.Cse., 459
The Hamptons G.Cse., 836
Hanah Country Inn & Golf Resort, 568
Hanging Rock G.C., 836
Hanging Tree G.C., 288
Hangman Valley G.Cse., 856
Hanover C.C. (Hanover, NH), 523
Hanover C.C. (Wrightstown, NJ), 535
Hansen Dam G.Cse., 66
Hansen Park G.Cse., 885
Happy Trails Resort, 25
Hapuna G.Cse., 222
Harbor Club, 208
Harbor Links G.Cse. (Klamath Falls, OR), 681
Harbor Links G.Cse. (Port Washington, NY), 568
Harbor Pines G.C., 535
Harbor Point G.Cse., 405
Harborside Int'l G.Ctr., 255
Harbour Pointe C.C., 568
Harbour Pointe G.C., 856
Harbour Ridge G.C., 128
Harbour Town G. Links, 739
Harbourtowne Golf Resort & C.C., 353
Hard Labor Creek State Park G.Cse., 208
Harder Hall C.C., 160
Harding Park G.C., 66
Harpeth Hills G.Cse., 770
Harrisburg North G.Cse., 704
Harrison C.C., 43
Harrison Hills G. & C.C., 288
Harrison Park G.Cse., 256
Hart Ranch G.Cse., 762
Hartefeld National G.C., 704
Hartford G.C., 886
Hartland Glen G. & C.C., 405
Hartland Mun. G.Cse., 325
Harvest G.C., 924
Hastings C.C., 405
Haven G.C., 25
Hawaii Kai G.Cse., 222
Hawaii Prince G.C., 222
Hawk Hollow G.C., 406

Hawk Ridge G.C. (Lake St. Louis, MO), 489
Hawk Ridge G.C. (Orillia, Ontario), 943
Hawk Valley G.C., 705
Hawks Nest G.C., 637
Hawkshead G. Links, 406
Hawksnest G. & Ski Resort, 599
Hawley G. & C.C., 459
Haworth G.C., 535
Hawthorn Ridge G.C., 256
Hawthorn Suites at Midlane Golf Resort, 256
Hawthorne Hills G.C. (Lima, OH), 638
Hawthorne Hills G.C. (Saukville, WI), 886
Haymaker G.Cse., 114
Haystack G.C., 826
Hayward G. & Tennis Ctr., 886
Headwaters C.C., 459
Heart River Mun. G.Cse., 620
Heather Glen G. Links, 739
Heather Highlands G.C., 406
Heather Hill C.C., 367
Heather Hills G.Cse., 406
Heather Run G. & Fish Club, 792
Heatherhurst G.C., 770
Heatherwoode G.C., 638
The Heathlands of Onekama, 406
Hecla G.Cse. at Gull Harbor Resort, 931
Hedingham G.C., 599
Helfrich G.Cse., 289
Hell's Point G.Cse., 836
Hemlock Springs G.C., 638
Henderson G.C., 208
Henderson Lake G.C., 914
Hendricks Field G.Cse., 535
Henrietta C.C., 669
Henry County C.C., 325
Henry Homberg Mun. G.Cse., 792
Henry Horton State Park G.Cse., 771
Heritage Bluffs G.C., 256
Heritage C.C., 367
Heritage Club, 740
The Heritage G.C., 208
Heritage Glen G.C., 406
Heritage Highlands G. & C.C., 26
Heritage Hills G.Cse. (Claremore, OK), 669
Heritage Hills G.Cse. (McCook, NE), 505
Heritage Hills Golf Resort & Conf. Ctr., 705
Heritage Links C.C. at Turkey Creek, 160
Heritage Palms G.C., 66
Heritage Park G.Cse., 315
Heritage Pointe G. & C.C., 914
Hermann Park G.Cse., 793
Hermitage G.Cse., 771
Hermon Meadow G.C., 342
Herndon Centennial G.C., 836
Heron Lakes G.Cse., 681
Heron Point G.C., 740
Heron Ridge G.C., 837
Hesperia G. & C.C., 66
Hessel Ridge G.Cse., 407
Hesston Municipal Golf Park, 316
Hiawatha G.Cse. (Minneapolis, MN), 459
Hiawatha G.Cse. (Mount Vernon, OH), 638
Hickam G.Cse., 223
Hickory Flat Greens, 638
Hickory Grove G.C., 638
Hickory Grove G.Cse., 639
Hickory Heights G.C., 705
Hickory Hills C.C. (Chilton, WI), 886
Hickory Hills C.C. (Hickory Hills, IL), 256
Hickory Hills G.C. (Jackson, MI), 407
Hickory Hills G.C. (Methuen, MA), 368
Hickory Hollow G.Cse., 407

Hickory Knob G.C., *740*
Hickory Knoll G.Cse., *407*
Hickory Nut G.C., *639*
Hickory Point G.C., *256*
Hickory Ridge C.C., *368*
Hickory Ridge G.Ctr., *256*
Hickory Valley G.C., *705*
Hickory Woods G.Cse., *639*
Hidden Creek G.C. (Burleson, TX), *793*
Hidden Creek G.C. (Reston, VA), *837*
Hidden Creek G.C. (Sellersburg, IN), *289*
Hidden Greens G.C., *460*
Hidden Hills G.C., *639*
Hidden Hills G.Cse., *306*
Hidden Hills Public G.Cse., *793*
Hidden Hills Resort & G.C., *67*
Hidden Lake G. & C.C., *943*
Hidden Lake G.C., *944*
Hidden Lake G.Cse., *639*
Hidden Lakes G.Cse., *316*
Hidden Lakes Golf Resort, *237*
Hidden Oaks G.Cse., *336*
Hidden River G. & Casting Club, *407*
Hidden Trails C.C., *489*
Hidden Valley C.C., *547*
Hidden Valley Collection of Great Golf, *407*
Hidden Valley Four Seasons Resort, *705*
Hidden Valley G.C. (Bryant, AL), *7*
Hidden Valley G.C. (Jackson, TN), *771*
Hidden Valley G.C. (Norco, CA), *67*
Hidden Valley G.Cse. (Cottage Grove, OR), *682*
Hidden Valley G.Cse. (Lawson, MO), *489*
Hidden Valley G.Cse. (Lincoln, NE), *505*
Hidden Valley G.Cse. (Morgantown, KY), *325*
Hidden Valley G. Links, *489*
Hidden Valley Lake G. & C.C., *67*
Hideaway Hills G.C., *706*
High Cedars G.C., *856*
High Cliff G.Cse., *886*
High Hampton Inn & C.C., *599*
High Mtn. G.C., *535*
High Point C.C., *535*
High Point G.C., *7*
High Pointe G.C., *408*
Highland Creek G.C., *600*
Highland Falls G.C., *514*
Highland Falls G.Cse.-Palm Valley, *514*
Highland G.C. (Conyers, GA), *209*
Highland G.C. (Escanaba, MI), *408*
Highland G.Cse., *237*
Highland G. Links, *368*
Highland Hills G.Cse. (De Witt, MI), *408*
Highland Hills G.Cse. (Greeley, CO), *114*
Highland Oaks G.C., *8*
Highland Oaks G.Cse., *8*
Highland Park C.C. (Highland Park, IL), *257*
Highland Park G.C., *639*
Highland Park G.Cse. (Bloomington, IL), *257*
Highland Park G.Cse. (Mason City, IA), *306*
Highland Park G.Cse. (St. Paul, MN), *460*
Highland Park Golf, *8*
Highland Springs G.C., *257*
Highland Springs G.Cse., *870*
Highland Woods G.Cse., *257*
The Highlands G. & C.C., *237*
Highlands G.C., *500*
Highlands G.Cse., *506*
Highlands Golfers' Club, *837*
Highlands Links G.Cse., *937*
Highlands Ranch G.C., *114*
Highlands Reserve G.C., *161*

Highpoint G.Cse., *325*
Hilaman Park Mun. G.Cse., *161*
Hiland G.C., *568*
Hill AFB G.Cse., *818*
Hill Country G.C., *793*
Hillandale C.C., *479*
Hillandale G.Cse., *740*
Hillcrest C.C., *368*
Hillcrest G. & C.C., *762*
Hillcrest G.C. (Durango, CO), *114*
Hillcrest G.C. (Findlay, OH), *639*
Hillcrest G.C. (Orangeburg, SC), *740*
Hillcrest G.C. (Sun City West, AZ), *26*
Hillcrest G.C. (Winston-Salem, NC), *600*
Hilldale G.C., *257*
Hillendale G.Cse., *568*
Hilliard Lakes G.C., *639*
Hillmoor G.C., *886*
Hills Heart of The Lakes G.C., *408*
Hillsborough C.C., *536*
Hillside C.C., *368*
Hillside G.Cse., *506*
Hillsview G.C., *762*
Hilltop G.Cse., *408*
Hilo Mun. G.C., *223*
Hilton Head National G.C., *740*
Himark G.Cse., *506*
Hinckley Hills G.Cse., *640*
Hindman Park G.Cse., *43*
Hinton G.C., *914*
Hobble Creek G.C., *818*
Hockley Valley Resort, *944*
Hodge Park G.Cse., *489*
Hog Neck G.Cse., *353*
Hogan Park G.Cse., *793*
Holden Hills C.C., *368*
Holiday Hills G.Cse., *489*
Holiday Island C.C., *43*
Holiday Valley Resort, *568*
Hollows G.Cse., *837*
Holly Hills G.C. (Alloway, NJ), *536*
Holly Hills G.C. (Waynesville, OH), *640*
Holly Ridge G.C., *368*
Hollydale G.Cse., *460*
Hollydot G.Cse., *114*
Holmes Park G.Cse., *506*
Holston Hills C.C., *837*
Holyoke C.C., *368*
Hombre G.C., *161*
Homestead G. & C.C., *856*
Homestead G.C., *818*
Homestead G.Cse., *640*
The Homestead Resort, *837*
Homestead Springs G.Cse., *640*
Hominy Hill G.Cse., *536*
Hon-E-Kor C.C., *887*
Honey Bee G.C., *838*
Honey Creek G.C., *489*
Honey Run G. & C.C., *706*
Honeywell G.Cse., *289*
Hooper G.C., *523*
Hop Brook G.Cse., *128*
Hope Dale C.C., *369*
Hornby Glen G.Cse. Inc., *944*
Horse Thief C.C., *67*
Horseshoe Bay Resort, *793*
Horseshoe Lake G.C., *856*
Horseshoe Valley Resort, *944*
Horsham Valley G.C., *706*
Horton Smith G.Cse., *490*
Hot Springs C.C., *43*
Hot Springs G.Cse., *856*

Hound Ears Club, *600*
Houston Lake C.C., *209*
Houston Oaks (Hockley, TX), *794*
Houston Oaks G.Cse., *325*
Howard D. Kellogg G.Cse., *257*
Howell Park G.Cse. (Baton Rouge, LA), *336*
Howell Park G.Cse. (Farmingdale, NJ), *536*
Hualalai G.C., *223*
Hubbard G.Cse., *640*
Hubbard Trail G. & C.C., *257*
Hudson G.C., *887*
Hudson Mills Metro Park G.Cse., *409*
Hudson Valley Resort & Spa, *568*
Hueston Woods G.Cse., *640*
Hughes Creek G.C., *258*
Hulman Links G.Cse., *289*
Humber Valley G.Cse., *944*
Hunter C.C., *258*
Hunter G.C., *128*
Hunter Ranch G.Cse., *67*
Hunter's Creek G.C., *161*
Hunter's Creek Plantation G.C., *741*
Hunter's Ridge G.C. (Howell, MI), *409*
Hunter's Ridge G.C. (Marion, IA), *306*
Hunters Point G.C., *771*
Huntington Hills G. & C.C., *161*
Huntington Park G.Cse., *336*
Huntsville Downs Golf Limited, *944*
Huntsville Mun. G.Cse., *8*
Huron Breeze G. & C.C., *409*
Huron Hills G.Cse., *409*
Huron Meadows G.Cse., *409*
Hyannis G.C. at Iyanough Hills, *369*
Hyatt Bear Creek G. & Racquet Club, *794*
Hyatt Dorado Beach Resort, *971*
Hyatt Regency Cerromar Beach, *972*
Hyde Park G.C., *161*
Hyde Park G.Cse., *569*
Hyland Hills G.C., *600*
Hyland Hills G.Cse., *115*
Idabell C.C., *669*
Idle Wyld G.C., *409*
Idlewild G.Cse., *887*
Illinois State Univ. G.Cse., *258*
Imperial Lakewoods G.C., *162*
Incline Village Golf Resort, *514*
Indian Bayou G. & C.C., *162*
Indian Bluff G.Cse., *258*
Indian Boundary G.Cse., *258*
Indian Canyon G.Cse., *856*
Indian Creek G. & C.C., *945*
Indian Creek G.C. (Carrollton, TX), *795*
Indian Creek G.C. (Hood River, OR), *682*
Indian Creek G.Cse., *506*
Indian Hills G.C. (Murfreesboro, TN), *771*
Indian Hills G.C. (Riverside, CA), *68*
Indian Hills G.Cse., *258*
Indian Island C.C., *569*
Indian Lake Estates G. & C.C., *162*
Indian Lake Hills G.Cse., *410*
Indian Lakes G.C., *915*
Indian Lakes Resort, *258*
Indian Meadows G.Cse., *506*
Indian Mound G.C., *523*
Indian Oaks G.C., *8*
Indian Peaks G.C., *115*
Indian Pines G.C., *8*
Indian River G.C. (Indian River, MI), *410*
Indian River G.C. (West Columbia, SC), *741*
Indian Run G.C. (Avella, PA), *706*
Indian Run G.C. (Scotts, MI), *410*
Indian Run G.Cse., *706*

Indian Springs C.C., *68*
Indian Springs G.C. (Louisville, KY), *326*
Indian Springs G.C. (Mechanicsburg, OH), *640*
Indian Springs Metro Park G.Cse., *410*
Indian Trails C.C., *507*
Indian Trails G.Cse., *410*
Indian Tree G.C., *115*
Indian Valley C.C., *259*
Indian Valley G.C., *68*
Indian Valley G.Cse., *600*
Indian Wells G.C., *741*
Indiana Univ. G.C., *289*
Indianhead G.C., *507*
Indigo Creek Golf Plantation, *741*
Indigo Lakes G.C., *162*
Industry Hills Sheraton Resort & Conf. Ctr., *68*
Ingersoll Memorial G.C., *259*
Ingleside G.C., *706*
Inkster Valley G.Cse., *410*
Inn of The Mtn. Gods G.Cse., *547*
Innsbrook Resort & Conference Ctr., *490*
Innsbruck Resort & G.C., *209*
Inshalla C.C., *887*
Int'l City Mun. G.Cse., *209*
Int'l G.C., *162*
Int'l Links Miami Melreese G.Cse., *163*
Interlochen G. & C.C., *411*
Inver Wood G.Cse., *460*
Inverness Hotel & G.C., *115*
Inwood G.Cse., *259*
Irish Hills G.Cse., *641*
Iron Eagle Mun. G.Cse., *507*
Iron Horse G.Cse., *795*
Iron Masters C.C., *706*
Ironhead G. & C.C., *915*
Ironhorse G.C. (Leawood, KS), *316*
Ironhorse G.C. (Logansport, IN), *289*
Ironhorse G.Cse., *259*
Ironshore G. & C.C., *969*
Ironwood G.C. (Fishers, IN), *290*
Ironwood G.C. (Howell, MI), *411*
Ironwood G.C. (Wauseon, OH), *641*
Ironwood G.Cse. (Byron Center, MI), *411*
Ironwood G.Cse. (Cookeville, TN), *771*
Ironwood G.Cse. (Gainesville, FL), *163*
Ironwood G.Cse. (Hinckley, OH), *641*
Ironwood G.Cse. (Normal, IL), *259*
Iroquois G.C., *326*
Irv Warren memorial G. Cse. *306*
Isabel Villas G.C., *968*
Isla Navidad G.C., *961*
Island Green C.C., *569*
Island Green G.C., *741*
Island Oaks G.C., *569*
Island View G.Cse., *460*
Island West G.C., *742*
Island's End G. & C.C., *569*
Isle Dauphine G.C., *8*
Isleta Eagle G.Cse., *547*
Ives Grove G. Links, *887*
Ivy Hill G.C., *838*
Izatys G. & Yacht Club, *460*
J.E. Good Park G.C., *641*
J.F. Sammons Park G.Cse., *795*
Jacaranda G.C., *163*
Jack O'Lantern Resort, *523*
Jack Tone Golf, *68*
Jackpot G.C., *514*
Jackson Hole G. & Tennis Club, *908*
Jackson Park G.Cse. (Chicago, IL), *259*
Jackson Park G.Cse. (Seattle, WA), *857*

La Quinta Resort & Club, *70*
La Tourette G.C., *570*
Lacoma G.Cse., *260*
Laconia C.C., *524*
Ladera G.Cse., *547*
Lady Bird Johnson Mun. G.Cse., *797*
Lady's Island C.C., *743*
Lafayette G.C., *290*
Lafayette G.Cse., *326*
Lafortune Park G.Cse., *671*
Lagoon Park G.Cse., *9*
Laguna Seca G.C., *70*
Lake Arbor C.C., *353*
Lake Arbor G.Cse., *116*
Lake Arlington G.Cse., *797*
Lake Arrowhead C.C., *210*
Lake Arrowhead G.Cse., *889*
Lake Barkley State Park, *327*
Lake Beulah C.C., *889*
Lake Blackshear G. & C.C., *210*
Lake Bluff G.C., *260*
Lake Breeze G.C., *889*
Lake Carlsbad G.Cse., *547*
Lake Chabot G.Cse., *70*
Lake Chelan G.Cse., *857*
Lake Cora Hills G.Cse., *412*
Lake Doster G.C., *412*
Lake Guntersville G.C., *9*
Lake Hefner G.C., *671*
Lake Hills G.C., *290*
Lake Hills G.Cse., *500*
Lake Houston G.C., *797*
Lake James G.C., *290*
Lake Joseph Club, *945*
Lake Las Vegas Resort, *515*
Lake Lawn Resort G.Cse., *889*
Lake Lure G. & Beach Resort, *601*
Lake Maloney G.Cse., *507*
Lake Marion G.C., *743*
Lake Michigan Hills G.C., *412*
Lake Morey C.C., *827*
Lake Murray Resort Golf, *671*
Lake of The Woods G.C., *261*
Lake of The Woods G.Cse., *490*
Lake Orlando G.C., *164*
Lake Padden G.Cse., *857*
Lake Panorama National G.Cse., *306*
Lake Park G.Cse. (Germantown, WI), *889*
Lake Park G.Cse. (Lewisville, TX), *797*
Lake Placid Resort, *570*
Lake Powell National G.C., *27*
Lake Ridge G.Cse., *515*
Lake Shastina Golf Resort, *71*
Lake Shawnee G.Cse., *316*
Lake Shore C.C., *571*
Lake Shore G.Cse. (Oshkosh, WI), *890*
Lake Shore G.Cse. (Taylorville, IL), *261*
Lake Spanaway G.Cse., *858*
Lake St. Catherine C.C., *827*
Lake Tahoe G.Cse., *71*
Lake Texoma Golf Resort, *671*
Lake Valley G. & C.C., *490*
Lake Valley G.C., *116*
Lake View C.C., *261*
Lake Village C.C., *44*
Lake Whitney C.C., *797*
Lake Wilderness G.Cse., *858*
Lake Windsor G.C., *890*
Lake Wisconsin C.C., *890*
Lake Worth G.C., *164*
Lake Wright G.Cse., *840*
Lakeland Hills G.Cse., *413*

Lakeland Village G.Cse., *858*
Lakepoint Resort G.Cse., *9*
Lakeridge G.Cse., *683*
Lakes of Taylor G.C., *413*
Lakes of The North Deer Run, *413*
Lakeside C.C. (Atlanta, GA), *210*
Lakeside C.C. (Elwood, NE), *507*
Lakeside G. & Racquet Club, *683*
Lakeside G.C. (Lakeville, NEW BRUNSWICK), *934*
Lakeside G.C. (Lexington, KY), *327*
Lakeside G.C. (Waseca, MN), *461*
Lakeside G.Cse. (Beverly, OH), *642*
Lakeside G.Cse. (Walters, OK), *671*
Lakeside G.Cse. (West Bountiful, UT), *819*
Lakeside Greens G. & C.C., *915*
Lakeside Hills G.Cse., *316*
Lakeside Links, *413*
Lakeside Memorial G.C., *671*
Lakeside Mun. G.Cse., *307*
Lakeview C.C., *307*
Lakeview G.C., *211*
Lakeview G.Cse. (Ardmore, OK), *671*
Lakeview G.Cse. (Harrisonburg, VA), *840*
Lakeview G.Cse. (Mitchell, SD), *762*
Lakeview Golf of Orono, *461*
Lakeview Hills C.C. & Resort, *413*
Lakeview National G.Cse., *461*
Lakeview Resort & Conf. Ctr., *870*
Lakeville C.C., *369*
Lakeway Resort, *798*
Lakewood C.C. (Lakewood, CA), *71*
Lakewood C.C. (Lakewood, NJ), *537*
Lakewood G.Cse. (Ada, OK), *672*
Lakewood G.Cse. (Madison, ME), *343*
Lakewood Links G.C., *743*
Lakewood Shores Resort, *414*
Lakewoods Forest Ridges G.Cse., *890*
Lakin Mun. G.Cse., *316*
Lambert Acres G.C., *772*
Land-O-Lakes G.C., *916*
Landa Park Mun. G.Cse., *798*
Lander G. & C.C., *908*
Landings G.C., *211*
Landsmeer G.C., *307*
Lane Creek G.C., *211*
Lane Tree G.C., *601*
Langdon Farms G.C., *683*
Langston G.Cse., *136*
Lansbrook G.Cse., *165*
Lansdowne G.C., *840*
Lansford C.C., *621*
Lapeer C.C., *414*
Larch Tree G.Cse., *642*
Larchmont G.Cse., *500*
Larry Gannon G.C., *369*
Larters at St. Andrews G. & C.C., *931*
Larue County C.C., *327*
Las Cruces C.C., *547*
Las Positas G.Cse., *71*
Las Sendas G.C., *27*
Las Vegas G.C., *515*
Las Vegas National G.C., *515*
Las Vegas Paiute Resort, *515*
Lassing Pointe G.Cse., *327*
Laura Walker G.Cse., *211*
Laurel Greens Public Golfers Club, *261*
Laurel Lakes G.C., *291*
Laurel Lane G.C., *727*
Laurel Springs G.C., *211*
Laurel View G.Cse., *128*
Lavelette G.C., *871*

1044

1048

Raintree Golf Resort, *180*
Raisin River C.C., *429*
Raisin Valley G.C., *429*
Ralph Myhre C.C. of Middlebury College, *828*
Ramblewood C.C., *541*
Rammler G.C., *429*
Rams Hill C.C., *85*
Ramsey G.C., *469*
The Ranch G. & C.C., *917*
Rancho Bernardo Inn, *85*
Rancho Canada G.C., *86*
Rancho Carlsbad C.C., *86*
Rancho Del Ray G.C., *86*
Rancho Manana G.C., *33*
Rancho Maria G.C., *86*
Rancho Murieta C.C., *86*
Rancho Park G.Cse., *87*
Rancho San Diego G.C., *87*
Rancho San Joaquin G.C., *87*
Rancho San Marcos G.C., *87*
Rancho Solano G.Cse., *87*
Rancho Viejo Resort & C.C., *804*
Rancocas G.C., *541*
Randall Oaks G.C., *272*
Randolph Park G.Cse., *33*
Rapid City Elks G.Cse., *763*
Raspberry Falls G. & Hunt Club, *843*
Ratliff Ranch G. Links, *804*
Rattle Run G.Cse., *430*
The Raven G.C. at Sabino Springs, *33*
The Raven G.C. at South Mtn., *34*
Ravenna G.Cse., *430*
Ravines G. & C.C., *180*
Rayburn C.C. & Resort, *804*
Raymond Memorial G.C., *651*
Razorback Park G.Cse., *45*
Real Del Mar G.C., *959*
Rebsamen Park G.Cse., *45*
Recreation Park G.Cse., *88*
The Red Apple Inn & C.C., *45*
Red Arrow G.C., *430*
Red Carpet G.C., *309*
Red Hawk C.C., *272*
Red Hawk Ridge G.C., *119*
Red Lodge Mtn. Resort G.Cse., *502*
Red River G.C., *45*
Red Wing Lake G.Cse., *844*
Reddeman Farms G.C., *430*
Redgate Mun. G.Cse., *357*
Redhawk G.C. (Sparks, NV), *517*
Redhawk G.C. (Temecula, CA), *88*
Redland G. & C.C., *180*
Redtail G.C., *272*
Redwood Meadows G. & C.C., *917*
The Redwoods, *927*
Reedsburg C.C., *897*
Reedy Creek G.Cse., *611*
Reems Creek G.C., *611*
Reeves G.Cse., *651*
Reflection Bay G.C., *517*
Regatta Bay G. & C.C., *180*
Regent Park G.C., *752*
Rehoboth C.C., *374*
Reid G.Cse., *897*
Reid Park Memorial G.Cse., *651*
Remington G.C., *180*
Renaissance Pineisle Resort, *215*
Renaissance Vinoy Resort, *181*
Rend Lake G.Cse., *272*
Rendezvous Meadows G.C., *909*
Renfrew G.C., *949*
Renwood C.C., *272*

The Reserve at East Bay, *820*
The Reserve at Spanos Creek, *88*
The Reserve at Thunder Hill, *651*
The Reserve Vineyards & G.C., *686*
Resort at Squaw Creek, *88*
Resort at The Mtn., *687*
Restigouche G. & C.C., *935*
Reston National G.Cse., *844*
The Revere at Anthem, *517*
Reynolds Park G.C., *612*
Reynolds Plantation (Eatonton, GA), *215*
Reynolds Plantation (Greensboro, GA), *215*
Rhodes Ranch C.C., *517*
Ricci Meadows G.Cse., *577*
Rice Lake G. & C.C., *309*
Rich Acres G.Cse., *469*
Rich Maiden G.Cse., *716*
Rich Spring G.C., *469*
Rich Valley G.C., *469*
Richmond C.C., *727*
Richmond Forest G.C., *430*
Richmond Hill G.C., *949*
Richmond Pines C.C., *612*
Richter Park G.C., *131*
Richview G. & C.C., *949*
Rickenbacker G.C., *652*
Riddell's Bay G. & C.C. *966*
Ridder G.C., *374*
The Ridge at Castle Pines North, *119*
The Ridge G.Cse., *88*
Ridge Top G.Cse., *652*
Ridgecrest G.C., *238*
Ridgefield G.Cse., *131*
Ridgemark G. & C.C., *89*
The Ridges G. & C.C., *775*
The Ridges G.Cse., *897*
Ridgeview G.Cse., *430*
Ridgeview Ranch G.C., *805*
Ridgewood C.C., *526*
Ridgewood G.Cse. (Athens, TN), *775*
Ridgewood G.Cse. (Longville, MN), *469*
Ridgewood Lakes G.C., *181*
Rifle Creek G.Cse., *120*
Ringgold G.C., *844*
Rio Colorado G.Cse., *805*
Rio Hondo G.C., *89*
Rio Mar C.C., *973*
Rio Mimbres C.C., *550*
Rio Rico Resort & C.C., *34*
Rio Secco G.C., *518*
Rio Vista G.C., *89*
Rivendell G.C., *950*
River Bend G. & Recreation Area, *918*
River Bend G.C. (Ormond Beach, FL), *181*
River Bend G.C. (Shelby, NC), *612*
River Bend G.Cse. (Hastings, MI), *430*
River Bend G.Cse. (Miamisburg, OH), *652*
River Bend Resort, *805*
River Club on the Ashley, *752*
The River Club, *181*
River Course at The Alisal, *89*
River Creek Park G.Cse., *805*
River Downs Golfers' Club, *357*
River Falls G.C., *897*
River Falls Plantation, *753*
The River G.C., *753*
River Greens G.Cse., *652*
River Hills C.C., *181*
River Hills G. & C.C., *753*
River Islands G.C., *775*
River Meadow G.C., *344*
River Oaks G.C., *495*

Rothland G.Cse., *578*
Rotonda G. & C.C. (Rotonda, FL), *182*
Rouge Park G.C., *432*
Round Hill C.C., *374*
Round Valley C.C., *821*
Rowley C.C., *375*
Roy Kizer G.Cse., *807*
Royal American Links G.C., *653*
Royal G.C., *338*
Royal Hylands G.C., *295*
Royal Lakes G. & C.C., *216*
Royal Links G.C., *518*
Royal Meadows G.Cse., *496*
Royal New Kent G.C., *844*
Royal Oak G.C., *183*
Royal Oaks G.C. (Cartersville, GA), *216*
Royal Oaks G.C. (Troy, MO), *496*
Royal Oaks G.Cse. (Lebanon, PA), *717*
Royal Oaks G.Cse. (Whiteman AFB, MO), *496*
Royal Scot G.Cse. & Supper Club, *898*
Royal Scot G.Cse., *433*
Royal St. Kitts G.C., *973*
Royal Tee C.C., *183*
Royal Virginia G.C., *845*
Royal Westmoreland Barbados, *965*
Royal Woodbine G.C., *950*
Royce Brook G.C., *542*
Ruby View G.Cse., *518*
Ruffled Feathers G.C., *273*
Rugby C.C., *622*
Ruggles G.Cse., *358*
Rum Pointe Seaside G. Links, *358*
Rum River Hills G.C., *470*
Running Fox G.Cse., *653*
Running Y Ranch Resort, *688*
Rush Creek G.C., *470*
Rush Lake Hills G.C., *433*
Russell C.C., *318*
Rustico Resort G. & C.C., *954*
Rutgers Univ. G.Cse., *542*
Rutland C.C., *829*
Ruttger's Bay Lake Lodge, *470*
Sable Oaks G.C., *345*
Saddle Brook C.C., *296*
Saddle Creek G.C. (Copperopolis, CA), *90*
Saddle Creek G.C. (Lewisburg, TN), *776*
Saddle Hill C.C., *375*
Saddle Rock G.Cse., *120*
Saddlebrook G.C., *296*
Saddlebrook Resort, *183*
Safari G.C., *653*
The Sagamore G.C., *578*
Sagamore Spring G.C., *375*
Sagamore-Hampton G.C., *527*
Sage Hills G.C., *863*
Sage Lakes Municipal Golf, *238*
Sage Meadows G.C., *45*
St. Albans G.C., *654*
St. Andrew's G.Cse., *318*
St. Andrews G. & C.C., *273*
St. Andrews G.C. (Cedar Rapids, IA), *309*
St. Andrews G.C. (Ocean Springs, MS), *482*
St. Andrews G.Cse., *496*
St. Andrews Valley G.C., *950*
St. Anne C.C., *375*
St. Augustine Shores G.C., *184*
St. Charles G.C., *470*
St. Clair Parkway G.Cse., *950*
St. Clair Shores C.C., *433*
St. Croix C.C., *345*
St. Croix National G.C., *898*
St. Denis G.Cse., *654*

St. George G.C., *821*
St. George's G.Cse., *966*
St. Germain Mun. G.C., *898*
St. Ives G.C., *433*
St. James Plantation, *613*
St. Joe Valley G.C., *433*
St. John's G.C., *433*
St. Johns County G.C., *184*
St. Johnsbury C.C., *829*
St. Lawrence Univ. G.& C.C., *578*
St. Lucie West C.C., *184*
St. Marlo C.C., *216*
St. Simons Island Club, *216*
St. Stephen G.C., *935*
Salem G.C., *688*
Salem Glen C.C., *613*
Salem Hills G. & C.C., *654*
Salem Hills G.C., *433*
Salina Mun. G.C., *318*
Salinas Fairways G.Cse., *91*
Saline County G. & C.C., *273*
Salmon Creek C.C., *579*
Salmon Falls C.C., *345*
Salt Creek G.C., *296*
Salt Fork State Park G.Cse., *654*
Salt River C.C., *434*
Saluda Valley C.C., *754*
Samoset Resort G.C., *345*
San Bernardino G.C., *91*
San Clemente Mun. G.C., *91*
San Dimas Canyon G.C., *91*
San Geronimo G.Cse., *91*
San Ignacio G.C., *34*
San Jose Mun. G.Cse., *91*
San Juan Hills C.C., *92*
San Juan Oaks G.C., *92*
San Luis Rey Downs Golf Resort, *92*
San Ramon Royal Vista G.C., *92*
San Saba Mun. G.Cse., *807*
San Vicente Inn & G.C., *92*
Sanborn G. & C.C., *309*
Sanctuary C.C., *579*
The Sanctuary G.Cse., *273*
Sand Barrens G.C., *542*
Sand Creek G.C., *238*
Sand Point Elks G.Cse., *239*
Sand Springs Mun. G.Cse., *674*
Sandals G. & C.C., *969*
Sandalwood G.Cse., *231*
Sandelie G.Cse., *688*
Sandestin Resort, *184*
Sandpines G. Links, *688*
Sandpiper Bay G. & C.C., *613*
Sandpiper G.C., *185*
Sandpiper G.Cse., *92*
Sandridge G.C., *185*
Sandy Brae G.Cse., *873*
Sandy Burr C.C., *375*
Sandy Hollow G.Cse., *274*
Sandy Lane G.C., *965*
Sandy Pines G.Cse., *296*
Sandy Ridge G.Cse. (Colfax, NC), *613*
Sandy Ridge G.Cse. (Midland, MI), *434*
Santa Ana G.C., *550*
Santa Anita G.Cse., *93*
Santa Barbara G.C., *93*
Santa Clara G. & Tennis Club, *93*
Santa Fe C.C., *550*
Santa Maria G.Cse., *338*
Santa Rita G.C., *34*
Santa Rosa G. & Beach Club, *185*
Santa Teresa G.C., *93*

Tiara Rado G.Cse., *123*
Tiburon G.C. (Naples, FL), *190*
Tiburon G.C. (Omaha, NE), *509*
The Tides Inn, *847*
Tides Lodge, *847*
Tidewater G.C. & Plantation, *756*
Tierra Del Sol C.C. (Aruba), *965*
Tierra Del Sol G.C. (California City, CA), *101*
Tierra Del Sol G.C. (Lady Lake, FL), *191*
Tierra Del Sol G.Cse. (Belen, NM), *551*
Tierra Santa G.C., *812*
Tiffany Greens G.C., *498*
Tiger Point G. & C.C., *191*
Tijeras Arroyo G.Cse., *551*
Tijeras Creek G.C., *101*
Tijuana C.C., *959*
Tilden Park G.Cse., *101*
Timacuan G. & C.C., *191*
Timarron G. & C.C., *812*
Timber Creek G.Cse., *472*
Timber Lake G.Cse., *498*
Timber Point G.Cse., *584*
Timber Ridge G.C. (Mount Pleasant, PA), *722*
Timber Ridge G.C. (Talladega, AL), *14*
Timber Ridge G.C., *441*
Timber Trace G.C., *441*
Timber Trails C.C., *278*
Timber-View G.Cse., *812*
Timbercreek G.C., *14*
Timberlake Plantation G.C., *756*
Timberlin G.C., *133*
Timberline G.Cse., *311*
Timberon G.C., *551*
The Timbers G.C., *441*
The Timbers of Troy, *358*
Timberstone G.Cse., *441*
Timberton G.C., *483*
Tioga C.C., *584*
Tipsinah Mounds G.Cse., *473*
Tipton Mun. G.Cse., *298*
Tishomingo G. & Recreation, *676*
Toad Valley Public G.Cse. & Drvg.Rge., *311*
Toana Vista G.Cse., *519*
Tobacco Road G.C., *617*
Toftrees Resort, *722*
Tokatee G.C., *690*
Tom O'Leary G.Cse., *623*
Tomac Woods G.C., *441*
Tomahawk Hills G.C., *319*
Tomasso's Chemung G.Cse., *584*
Tomoka Oaks G. & C.C., *191*
Tonto Verde G.C., *37*
Tony Butler G.Cse., *812*
Tony Lema G.Cse., *102*
Top O Scott G.Cse., *690*
Topeka Public G.C., *319*
Torres Blancas G.C., *38*
Torrey Pines G.Cse., *102*
Torrington Mun. G.Cse., *910*
Tory Pines G.C., *527*
Touisset C.C., *377*
Tour 18 G.C., *812*
Tour 18, *812*
Tournament Player's Club of Myrtle Beach, *756*
Tournament Players Club at Heron Bay, *191*
Tournament Players Club at Sawgrass, *192*
Tournament Players Club at The Canyons, *519*
Tournament Players Club of Scottsdale, *38*
Tournament Players Club of Tampa Bay, *192*
Towanda C.C., *722*

Town of Mooresville G.Cse., *617*
Town of Wallkill G.C., *584*
Towne Lake Hills G.C., *219*
Tracy G. & C.C., *102*
Tradition G.C. (Edmond, OK), *676*
Tradition G.C. (Pawleys Island, SC), *757*
The Tradition, *617*
Tramark G.Cse., *483*
Trapp River G.C., *902*
Trappers Turn G.C., *902*
Treasure Cay C.C., *965*
Treasure Lake G.C., *722*
Tree Acres G.Cse., *902*
Tree Links G.Cse., *659*
Treeline G.C., *813*
Treetops Sylvan Resort, *442*
Tregaron G.Cse., *509*
Tremblant Golf Resort, *956*
Tri County C.C., *584*
Tri County G.C., *298*
Tri-City C.C., *865*
Tri-City G.Cse., *823*
Tri-Mountain G.Cse., *866*
Tri-Way G.C., *298*
Trickle Creek Golf Resort, *929*
Triggs Memorial G.Cse., *728*
Trillium Links, *617*
Trini Alvarez El Rio Mun. G.Cse., *38*
Triple Lakes G.Cse., *278*
Troon North G.C., *38*
The Trophy Club of Apalachee, *219*
Trophy Club of Gwinnett, *219*
The Trophy Club of Orlando, *192*
The Trophy Club, *298*
Trosper Park G.Cse., *676*
Trotters Glen G.Cse., *359*
Trout Lake G. & C.C., *902*
True Blue G.C., *757*
Trull Brook G.Cse., *378*
The Truro G.C., *938*
Truth Or Consequences Mun. G.Cse., *551*
The Tryall Club, Resort & Villas, *970*
Trysting Tree G.C., *690*
Tubac Golf Resort, *39*
Tuckaway G.Cse., *278*
Tucumcari Mun. G.Cse., *551*
Tumwater Valley G.C., *866*
Tunxis Plantation C.C., *133*
Turbot Hills G.Cse., *722*
Turf Valley Resort, *359*
Turkey Creek C.C., *298*
Turkey Creek G.Cse., *320*
Turkey Mtn. G.Cse., *46*
Turkey Run G.Cse., *299*
Turkeyfoot Lake G. Links, *660*
Turnberry G.Cse., *660*
Turnberry Isle Resort & Club, *192*
Turnbull Bay G.Cse., *193*
Turtle Bay Resort, *231*
Turtle Creek G.C. (Burlington, MI), *442*
Turtle Creek G.C. (Rockledge, FL), *193*
Turtle Creek G.Cse., *722*
Turtle Hill G.Cse., *813*
Turtleback G. & Conf. Ctr., *902*
Tuscumbia G.C., *903*
Tustin Ranch G.C., *102*
Twelve Bridges G.C., *102*
Twin Birch G.Cse., *443*
Twin Bridges G.C., *299*
Twin Brook G.Cse., *443*
Twin Brooks G.C., *443*
Twin Creeks G.C., *813*

White Pines G.C. (Camden, SC), *759*
White Plains Regional Park G.C., *360*
Whiteface Club on Lake Placid, *586*
Whitefish G.C., *474*
Whitefish Lake G.C., *502*
Whiteford Valley G.C., *447*
Whitepath G.C., *220*
Whitetail G.C., *725*
Whitewater C.C., *220*
Whitnall Park G.C., *905*
Whitney Farms G.Cse., *134*
Whittaker Woods G.C., *447*
Whittier Narrows G.Cse., *104*
Whittle Springs G.Cse., *778*
Wicked Stick G. Links, *759*
Wicker Memorial Park G.Cse., *300*
Wicomico Shores Mun. G.Cse., *360*
Widgi Creek G.C., *691*
Widow's Walk G.Cse., *379*
The Wigwam G. & C.C., *40*
Wild Dunes Resort, *759*
Wild Horse G.C. (Gothenburg, NE), *510*
Wild Horse G.C. (Henderson, NV), *520*
Wild Oaks G.C., *544*
Wild Wing Plantation, *759*
Wild Wood C.C., *587*
Wildcreek G.Cse., *520*
Wilderness Resort & G.Cse., *905*
Wildfire at Desert Ridge G.C., *40*
Wildflower at Fair Hills, *474*
Wildhawk G.C., *105*
Wildhorse G.Cse., *677*
Wildhorse Resort G.Cse., *691*
The Wilds G.C., *474*
Wildwood G.Cse., *510*
Wilkes-Barre G.C., *725*
Willandale G.C., *662*
William J. Devine G.Cse., *379*
William S. Rea G.Cse., *300*
William Sahm G.Cse., *300*
Williamsburg National G.C., *849*
Willimantic C.C., *134*
Willinger's G.C., *474*
Willis Case G.Cse., *124*
Williston G.C., *830*
Williston Mun. G.Cse., *623*
Willo-Dell C.C. Ltd., *952*
Willow Brook C.C., *545*
Willow Brook G.Cse., *198*
Willow Brook Public G.C., *448*
Willow Creek G.C. (Brandon, MS), *484*
Willow Creek G.C. (Knoxville, TN), *778*
Willow Creek G.C. (Rochester, MN), *475*
Willow Creek G.C. (Vermilion, OH), *662*
Willow Creek G.Cse., *312*
Willow Hollow G.Cse., *725*
Willow Lakes G.Cse., *510*
Willow Metropark G.Cse., *448*
Willow Oaks G.C., *15*
Willow Park G.C., *105*
Willow Pond G.Cse., *280*
Willow Run G.C., *905*
Willow Run G.Cse. (Pataskala, OH), *662*
Willow Run G.Cse. (Sioux Falls, SD), *764*
Willow Springs G.C., *814*
Willow Tree G.Cse., *320*
Willowbrook C.C., *587*
Willowbrook G.C., *778*
Willowdale G.C. (Luling, LA), *339*
Willowdale G.C. (Scarborough, ME), *346*
The Willows G. & C.C., *957*
Willows Run G.C., *867*

Wills Creek C C, *15*
Wilmette G.Cse., *280*
Winagamie G.Cse., *905*
Winchendon C.C., *379*
Winchester G.C., *300*
Windance C.C., *484*
Windbrook C.C., *498*
Windham C.C., *587*
Windham G. & C.C., *528*
Winding Brook G.C., *448*
Winding Creek G.Cse. (Holland, MI), *448*
Windmill Lakes G.C., *662*
Windrose G.Cse., *814*
Windsor G.C., *105*
Windsor Parke G.C., *198*
Windstone G.C., *220*
Windtree G.Cse., *778*
Winged Pheasant G. Links, *587*
Wingpointe G.Cse., *824*
Winnapaug C.C., *728*
Winnetka G.C., *280*
Winona C.C., *484*
Wintergreen G. & C.C., *919*
Wintergreen Resort, *849*
Winyah Bay G.C., *760*
Wisconsin River G.C., *906*
The Witch, *760*
The Wizard G.Cse., *760*
Wolf Creek G. & C.C., *849*
Wolf Creek G.C., *280*
Wolf Creek Golf Resort, *919*
Wolf Creek Resort Resort, *824*
Wolf Run G.C., *520*
Wolverine G.C., *448*
Woodbine G.Cse., *280*
Woodbridge G. Links, *619*
Woodcreek G.C., *105*
Wooded View G.C., *301*
Woodfield G. & C.C., *449*
Woodford Hills C.C., *333*
Woodhaven C.C., *134*
Woodlake C.C. (Lakewood, NJ), *545*
Woodlake C.C. (San Antonio, TX), *815*
Woodlake C.C. (Vass, NC), *619*
Woodland G.C., *662*
Woodland Hills , *312*
Woodland Hills C.C., *725*
Woodland Hills G.C., *449*
Woodland Hills G.Cse. (Eagle, NE), *510*
Woodland Hills G.Cse. (Nacogdoches, TX), *815*
Woodland Park Fujiki G. & C.C., *124*
The Woodlands G.Cse., *360*
Woodlands G.Cse., *849*
The Woodlands Resort & C.C., *815*
Woodlawn G.C., *449*
Woodlawn Springs G.C., *333*
Woodley Lakes G.C., *105*
Woodloch Springs C.C., *725*
Woodridge Plantation G.C., *874*
Woodrow W. Dumas G.Cse., *339*
Woodruff G.Cse., *281*
Woods Fort C.C., *498*
The Woods G.C., *663*
The Woods Resort, *875*
Woodside C.C., *906*
Woodson Bend Resort, *333*
Woodstock C.C., *830*
Woodward Mun. G.Cse., *677*
Wooldridge Woods G. & Swim Club, *663*
World Golf Village, *199*
World Houston G.C., *815*

NOTES

NOTES

NOTES

NOTES

NOTES

NOTES

NOTES

NOTES

NOTES